D1681226

mate.
global men's culture 2.0
WINTER 2012
TEL AVIV'S UNMISTAKABLE UPTURN
MANHATTAN OF THE MIDDLE EAST
50 YEARS OF JAMES BOND
SIMPLY FIND YOUR ADONIS ON
FACE BOOK
LITERARY SUPERSTAR
DAVID SEDARIS CONQUERED THE WORLD
FROM TRAILER TRASH TO TRAILER FLASH
ACROSS RUSSIA
A NEW ERA FOR ARABIA
PARADISE FOUND
mate.
global queer culture 2.0
ISTANBOOM!
RAMBLING REPUBLICANS
BOOT CAMP TRAINING
GLOBALISATION
GAY
RESPECT MY AUTHORITY
20 POOFS IN POWER
4 COOL CITIES
WINTER 2010
JAY BRANNAN
BOUNCE BACK BEIRUT
JIM CARREY & EWAN McGREGOR FALLING IN LOVE
GET A KID
2009
ROBOT LOVE
ROYAL DECAY
ALL SEXED OUT & WRECKED BY COKE
CUTE BOYS
GOLD RUSH
(UN)SAVOURY SEX TALK AROUND THE WORLD
MOSCOW WHERE BILLIONAIRES BINGE ON GUILTLESS VODKA
I ♥ BKLN
COMPANY PRIDE
GAY CHATTER AT THE WATER COOLER
TOP 10 ARCHITECTS
LOCKUP TIME
SUMMER 2010
Trans gression
DON'T ASK DON'T TELL
ARGENTINA
FALL 2011
Available on the App Store
Available on Android
Available on PC & Mac
mate.
FACE BOOK

edge
MEDIA NETWORK
STAY CONNECTED
ANYTIME, ANYWHERE
EDGE mobile apps for iPhone, Android and now iPad deliver the very latest in LGBT news, entertainment, nightlife and more - right to your fingertips - free!
GAY IN AMERICA
AN INTIMATE LOOK AT GAY LIFE IN THE US
THE GIRL WITH THE DRAGON TATTOO
PUTTING TOGETHER THE HOTTEST MOVIE OF THE YEAR
REX REED
SEXY, SASSY & STILL CALLING THE SHOTS
Android Tablet capabilities coming in Spring 2012!
Visit edgeonthenet.com/mobile

2012/2013

41st EDITION

BRUNO GMÜNDER

Imprint

PUBLISHER	BRUNO GMÜNDER VERLAG GMBH Kleiststraße 23-26 · D-10787 · Berlin · GERMANY Tel +49 / (0)30 / 615 00 30 · Fax +49 / (0)30 / 615 00 320 E-mail: info@spartacus.de www.brunogmuender.com
EDITOR IN CHIEF	Briand Bedford
EDITORIAL TEAM	Robert J. Gieseler · Dirk Zielke · Björn Vieth ·
ADVERTISING SALES & EDITORIAL ASSISTANCE	Oliver Ambach · Dirk Baumgartl · Felipe Frozza · Robert J. Gieseler · Kristin Hansen · Shintaro Koizumi · Jérôme Martres · Ferenc Rakiás · Chawangsak Saranopakun · Paul Sofianos
TRANSLATION	Briand Bedford · Rafael Cruz · Volker Eichler · Julien Hella · Chris Klar · Davide Miraglia
COVER PHOTOGRAPH	Photo © Richard Gerst (www.richardgerst.com) / istockphoto.com Models: Rodiney Santiago (www.rodineysantiago.com) & Josey Greenwell (www.facebook.com/joseygreenwell)
COVER DESIGN	Steffen Kawelke · Henning Wossidlo
LAYOUT	Enrico Dreher · Henning Wossidlo
MAPS	Orchidea de Santis · Henning Wossidlo
PRINTING	GGP Media GmbH, Pößneck, GERMANY
SPECIAL THANKS FOR ASSISTANCE GO TO	Tami Bibring, Rudy Bodner, Erwan Bothorel, Viachaslau (Slava) Bortnik, Roberto Brito, Christian Bräu,Thorsten Colling, Hans Danielkewitz, Fabian Fuentes, Francisco Guayasamin, Tron Hirsti, Christian Högl, Sebastian Kaim, Shintaro Koizumi, Oliver Leleux, Bertho Makso, Edgar Neidhardt, José Orjuela, David Verdún Padrón, Stzeve Polyak, Ferenc Rakias, Mike Ryan,Marc Sahli, Oliver Stevanovic, Jean Jacques Soukup, Tim Stallard, Joachim Stein, Bert Svallebolle, Tomasz Szypula, Henrik Thierlein, Sergey Tumanoff, Enrico Vetter, Juan Fernando Villafuerte, Gaby Wanzke, David Yeung and many more …

ISBN 978-3-86787-360-4

Please note that spartacus® published by BRUNO GMÜNDER VERLAG GMBH has no connection with any other business with the name of »SPARTACUS«, even if advertised in this book.

Please note that the inclusion of any establishment, business or organisation in this book or the appearance on the cover or on advertisements in spartacus® does not necessarily reflect the sexual orientation of owners, staff or models.

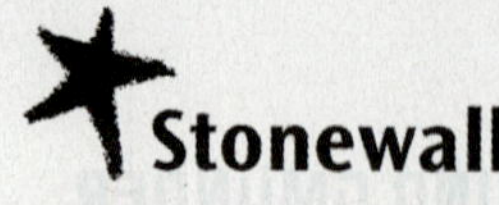

Worldwide Distribution

■ BRUNO GMÜNDER Verlag GmbH · Distribution
Kleiststraße 23-26 · D-10787 · Berlin · GERMANY
Tel +49 / (0)30 / 615 00 350
Fax +49 / (0)30 / 615 00 353
Email: distribution@brunogmuender.com
www.brunogmuender.com/distribution

Australia/New Zealand

■ BULLDOG BOOKS
Unit 41 566 • Gardeners Road • Alexandria, NSW2015
Ph. +61 (02) 9700-8860
Fax. +61 (02) 9700-8667
sales@bigpond.com.au
bulldogbooks@bigpond.com.au

Italy

■ BOOKS INTERNATIONAL
Via Battiferro 12/2 CD • 40129 Bologna
Ph. +39 051 6313025
Fax +39 051 4154993
booksint@unmondodi.com
www.booksinternational.it

Mexico / Latin America

■ EDICIONES FELOU SA
C/. Amsterdam 124, dept. 403 • Colonia Condesa
Deleg. Cuauhtemoc • CP 06170, Mexico DF
Ph. +55 52 560 651
Ventas@felou.com
sabermas@felou.com

Russia

■ TROYKA PRESS LTD.
Pervaya Yamskaya 8 • 127018 Moscow
Ph. +7 (095) 689 13 13
Fax. +7 (095) 689 92 87
troyka-press@mtu-net.ru

Spain

■ M.G. TRIANGULO DISTRIBUCIONES S.L.
Calle Hortaleza 64 • 28004 Madrid
Ph. +34 91 522 55 99
Fax. +34 91 523 12 79
triangulo@triangulodistribuciones.com
www.libreriaberkana.com

Switzerland

■ KAKTUS VERLAGSAUSLIEFERUNG
Langfeldstr. 54 • 8500 Frauenfeld
Ph. +41 (52) 722 31 90
Fax. +41 (52) 722 17 82
kaktus@solnet.ch

UK / Ireland

■ TURNAROUND
Unit 3, Olympia Trading Estate
Coburg Road • London N22 6TZ
Ph. +44 (020) 8829-3000
Fax. +44 (020) 8881-5088
orders@turnaround.uk.com
www.turnaround-uk.com

USA / CANADA

■ BOOKAZINE COMPANY, INC.
75 Hook Road • Bayonne, NJ 07002
Ph. +1 201 33 97 777
Fax. +1 201 33 97 778
tsmith@bookazine.com
www.bookazine.com

Single copies and our free mail order brochure may be ordered by mail from: **BRUNO GMÜNDER · Mail Order**
Zeughofstrasse 1 · 10997 Berlin · GERMANY
info@brunos.de · www.brunos.de

A cooperative action of GMFA , BZgA Bundeszentrale für gesundheitliche Aufklärung and BRUNO GMÜNDER VERLAG GMBH

Welcome

Dear Readers,

You are holding the 41st issue of the world's biggest gay guide in your hands. This cannot be taken for granted – then in these fast-moving times many people find a book is no longer up to date. We think that one should not close ones mind to technological achievements. However, proven media should also continue to be used. For this reason, an important and appropriate advancement was the development of our Spartacus application for iPhones, which was finally approved at the end of 2011 and went on sale. In addition to this we have our new website for accommodation. At **www.spartacusworld.com** you can see and book gay and gay-friendly accommodation worldwide.

Some of the gay highlights for 2012 include Mr. Gay World Competition in Johannesburg in April, EuroGames in Budapest at the end of June and the World Pride in London at the beginning of July.

Another top event for many gay Europeans is the Eurovision Song Contest, which will be held this year on the 26th May in Baku, Azerbaijan. After extensive research we discovered that this country is not only hostile to gay men but we received a warning about the police there. Avoid handing over your passport or drivers permit. It will cost a lot to get these out of their hands! Despite this Baku is said to be great! Who knows – maybe the contest will change the city and its inhabitants.

For an extensive list of all the major gay events worldwide, see our calendar at the back of this guide or on our website **www.spartacusworld.com**. Our gay calendar is constantly being updated and added to.

Not that much happened in 2011 on the political scene for the LGBT community. When the economic situation becomes difficult, the situation for minority groups generally worsens. This is happening in Hungary, Russia and several eastern European countries, where a revival of nationalism is taking place.

We think that everybody will find their preferred medium in our broad range on offer and make the most of it. Whether it is something to read on a beach or on holiday, or with our iPhone or laptop at home or on the road – there is a lot to discover. The situation remains exciting. Stay curious and enjoy your travels in 2012 with help from our printed guide and our new iPhone application.

Briand Bedford
CHIEF EDITOR

Listing of countries

SPARTACUS is divided into countries which are listed alphabetically in English. An exception to this rule is the Caribbean where all islands and countries in the Caribbean are listed under "C". Each country is broken down into cities and towns which are in the local language and also alphabetically listed. For the countries Australia, Canada & USA the state, territory or province has been listed alphabetically and divided into cities or towns. Should you have problems, refer to our index on page 1106, where all states, countries, cities and towns are alphabetically listed in all five SPARTACUS languages: English, German, French, Spanish and Italian.
Each country listed has specific information on the legal and social situation for gay men, including the legal age of consent. Furthermore information on gay festivals and special events are included.
Before this introduction for each country, you will find the following information:

	Example
Name: The name in the local language as well as in the 5 SPARTACUS languages	**Name:** Suid-Afrika • Südafrika • Afrique du Sud • Sudáfrica • Sud Africa
Location: geographical location	**Location:** Southern Africa
Initials: appropriate country abbreviation	**Initials:** ZA
Time: refers to the time zone in which the country is	**Time:** GMT +2
International Country Code: indicates the telephone code used to call this country	**International Country Code:** ☏ 27 (omit 0 of phone number)
International Access Code: refers to the dialling code used when in this country to call internationally	**International Access Code:** ☏ 09 or 091
Language: refers to the most common language/s spoken here	**Language:** English, Afrikaans, African languages
Area: refers to the size of a country	**Area:** 1,219,080 km² / 471,442 sq mi.
Currency: is the official money accepted here	**Currency:** 1 Rand (ZAR) = 100 Cents
Population: the number of inhabitants	**Population:** 43,240,000
Capital: the capital city	**Capital:** Cape Town (legislative capital); Pretoria (administrative capital)
Religions: the most common religions practised here	**Religions:** 78% Christians
Climate: a brief outline of the weather that can be expected throughout the year	**Climate:** Ranging from hot and dry in summer to cold and wet in winter. Sub-tropical to Mediterranean climates.
Important Gay Cities: cities which are of interest to the gay visitor	**Important gay cities:** Cape Town, Johannesburg

Information in an address entry

Each listing is made up of the name ❶, the corresponding SPARTACUS codes ❷, the opening hours ❸, the address ❹, the telephone number ❺, e-mail address ❻, & website address ❼.

Meaning of the different symbols
- ✉ address
- ☏ telephone number
- 💻 e-mail address, website address
- ☞ hint

■ A red square infront of a listing indicates that there is an advert for this listing either in our guide, on the app or website.

How to use SPARTACUS

Listing of categories

Within the different countries and cities the individual addresses are sorted into categories as follows:

National Gay Info
National Publications
National Publishers
National Companies
National Groups
National Helplines
Country Cruising
▼
Gay Info
Publications
Culture
Tourist Info
▼
Bars
Men's Clubs
Cafés
Danceclubs
Restaurants
Shows
Cinema
▼
Sex Shops/Blue Movies
Cinemas
Escorts & Studios
House of Boys
▼
Saunas/Baths
Fitness Studios
Massage
▼
Shopping/Services
▼
Hotels
Guest Houses
Apartments
Private Accommodation
▼
Groups
▼
Swimming
Cruising

Please use our freepost information card to be found at the back of this guidebook to inform us of any changes you might have come across while travelling. Please try to give us as much information as possible. We would be delighted to receive any information you may have which does not appear in this edition of SPARTACUS:

Bruno Gmünder Verlag GmbH • SPARTACUS-Redaktion
Kleiststrasse 23-26 • 10787 Berlin • GERMANY
info@spartacus.de

Code description

SPARTACUS codes mean the following (Codes in small letters mean a limitation):

!	A must
AC	Air conditioning
AK	St. Andrew's Cross
AYOR	At your own risk. Danger of personal attack or police activity
B	Bar with full range of alcoholic beverages
BF	Full breakfast
CC	All major credit cards accepted
D	Dancing / Discotheque
DM	Daily menu
DR	Darkroom
DU	Showers
F	Fetish (leather, latex or uniform)
FC	Free condoms
FH	Free extra towels
G	Gay. Exclusively or almost exclusively gay men
GH	Glory holes
GLM	Gay and lesbian mixed crowd
H	Hotel or other accommodation welcoming gay men
I	Internet access
LAB	Maze / Labyrinth
LM	Live music
M	Meals. Extensive menu available
MA	Mixed ages
MC	Middle-aged crowd (30 - 50 years old)
MSG	Massage on offer
NG	Not gay, but possibly of interest to gay men
NR	Non-smoking area
NU	Nudist area
OC	Mostly older gay men (50 or older)
OS	Outdoor seating, terrace or garden
P	Private club or strict door control
p	You must ring to enter
PA	Pets allowed
PI	Swimming pool
PK	Parking available
PP	Plunge pool
R	Frequented by hustlers
RES	Reservation advisable
RR	Relax room
RWB	Guestrooms with Balcony
RWS	Guestrooms with private bath/shower
RWT	Guestrooms with television
S	Shows or other events
SA	Dry sauna
SB	Steam bath
SH	Shop
SL	Sling
SNU	Strip shows
SOL	Solarium
ST	Drag shows
T	Transvestites and/or transsexual clientele
VA	Overnight guests allowed
VEG	Vegetarian meals on the menu
VR	Video room
VS	Video shows
W	Barrier-free for wheelchairs
WE	More popular at the weekend
WH	Whirlpool / Jacuzzi / Hot tub
WI	Free WiFi
WL	Extensive wine list
WO	Work-out equipment available
YC	Younger crowd (18-28 years old)

This codes are available as practical bookmark at the back of this guide!

1. Introduction

Gay men are known as world-class travellers, whether for business or leisure. When travelling abroad, it's vital to observe and respect countries' customs, but also be sure to avoid unknown places and health risks. On top of useful guidelines used at home, when travelling it's important to make extra rules, whether HIV positive or negative. Other sexually transmitted diseases (STDs) are often forgotten because of the greater threat of HIV. Accordingly, the late 1990s have seen dramatic increases in these infections in the Western world. Gay men, rightly choosing to live and express their sexuality free of religious and moral constraints, must also accept responsibility, both for their and their sexual partner's health.

In past years HIV infection has changed from a potentially deadly illness to a manageable, chronic, although incurable condition, thanks to the speed with which medicine has moved forward. Patients who previously struggled just to survive are now generally doing well, and can now take holidays abroad, almost without danger to themselves.

2. Travel

In most industrialized countries we get medical services at no extra cost. Be aware that when abroad you do not automatically have insurance cover. Generally medical costs are paid yourself up front, then recovered on your return home, either in full or part, from your social security, travel insurance or private healthcare (often it's covered by your credit card company – find out what is currently on offer). When travelling as citizen of the European Union to another country within the Union you are covered for all emergency situations provided that you have a European insurance card, (available from your health insurance company or in all cases to be found on the back of your social security card).

Vaccinations (e.g. against hepatitis A and B) and Prophylaxis (e.g. against malaria) offer high levels of protection against many infections. Some travel vaccinations, apart from those recommended in your own country, are also recommended or even mandatory. Your doctor can tell you about these.

HIV positive people can have all vaccinations made of dead pathogens without worry, where the toxins have been washed out, known as dead vaccines. If the immune system is weakened (less than 200 CD4 count) vaccinations may not offer sufficient immunity. Vaccinations where weakened living pathogens are injected, (e.g vaccination for Yellow Fever, mandatory in many countries), are normally OK for HIV positive people with a CD4 count of 400 or more.

Hygiene standards are not as high in all destinations as at home. Basically the same goes for the Third World as in European countries: Don't drink the tap water! Only drink boiled, filtered water, or mineral water from sealed bottles. Ice cubes in cocktails can also be problematic. With food, the simple rule is: cook, boil, peel or leave it! Anything else is risky (e.g. salads, dressings, creamy desserts, egg dishes). Contact a travel pharmacist.

For more information try www.cdc.gov/travel. This should tell you the medication you need, from diarrhoea to dressings. If doubtful, speak to a knowledgeable physician.

If taking regular medication, take several more days supply than you need, should your return journey be unexpectedly delayed, or in case you lose pills. In your hand luggage, take the medicines in original packing, including information sheets, showing drugs' chemical composition (some medications have other names elsewhere), a copy of prescriptions, and syringes and needles you need. Remember time differences, and plan medication accordingly.

Expert's tip: When entering some countries, doctors' letters are required, with name and short description of your medication (for example tablet or capsule). Diagnoses need not be provided.

International laws and regulations can be very different. When travelling abroad get information about current customs and entry requirements. Do this by phone or online from your foreign ministry, or the embassy or consulate of your destination country. Also remember some medications need to be kept refrigerated, and all should be kept dry, at room temperature or cooler, so no warmer than 30 degrees. In many third world countries, sterile dressings are not always available for wounds or injections, so when travelling there, particularly for longer stays, bring these yourself.

Always take sun lotions with high protection factors. Exposure to full sun, between midday and 3pm in hot countries, without sun protection, should be avoided, as you risk skin cancer and short-term immune system damage, resulting in a drop in the CD4 count for the HIV positive.

N.B. Good quality condoms and lube are not always available throughout the world.

3. HIV-Infection

HIV can only be transmitted if HIV virus is present in the human body. This occurs when there is contact between infected fluids, for example sperm, vaginal fluids or blood, and broken mucus membranes (anus, rectum, vagina, mouth, eyelids) or newly broken skin (cuts, stick wounds, abrasions).

Risk of infection occurs in:

- Unprotected anal sex, for both active and passive partners.
- Unprotected vaginal sex, for both women and men.
- Unprotected oral sex, for active partners (giving blow jobs) if cum gets in your mouth.
- Fisting (several fingers or a fist pushed into the rectum), if you don't wear rubber gloves and there is bleeding in the rectum of the one being fisted, or cuts on the hand of the one fisting.

Expert's tip: Many HIV experts believe, that the precum, secreted by many men before actual orgasm, coming into contact with the mucus membranes in the mouth during unprotected oral sex, constitutes a real risk in certain circumstances (where there is already another STD with discharge from the urethra, and high concentrations of HIV).

There is no known HIV risk with:

- Contact with saliva, tears, sweat, stools or urine.
- All normal contact like shaking hands, shared use of drinking glasses and crockery, toilets, swimming pools and saunas are completely risk-free.
- Infection from breath, from sneezing or coughing, an insect bite or sting- current evidence excludes these.

To reduce the risk of HIV infection you should always practice safer sex, and

- For anal and vaginal sex (fucking) always use condoms and plenty of water-based lube. Oil-based products damage condoms. If you are having sex with several partners at the same time, always use a new condom for each partner. Condoms also reduce the risk of catching other STDs.
- With oral sex (blow jobs) never come in the mouth of your partner. But this won't protect you from other STDs (gonorrhoea, syphilis and hepatitis). Use condoms for oral sex to minimise the obviously small risk associated with precum and HIV transmission by this route.
- With fisting always wear rubber gloves.

- If you're using intravenous drugs always use clean needles, syringes and water.

Expert's tip: Tip from the experts : it has been proven, that with an existing HIV infection a new infection with resistant HIV vruses is possible. This may interrupt a well-managed antiviral therapy, making it ineffective and impeding the start of forthcoming treatment. HIV positive people should not ignore safer sex!

If you have put yourself at risk of infection, you can reduce your likelihood of infection by immediately washing the contact area (skin wounds or mucus membrane) with soap and water, or if available disinfectant (washing the rectum is not advisable). Within a few weeks, a PEP or post-exposure prophylaxis, prescribed by a doctor, should be taken quickly. This can only reduce the risk, not stop it, and should never replace safer sex. To get precise information, contact an HIV treatment centre.

Of recent a small number of people has repeatedly recommended the application of HIV medication "as a precaution" against a possible risk of infection. Virtually all HIV experts are advising against this so-called pre-exposure prophylaxis (PreP). Not only that the financing is completely unclear (the costs would run to over 1000 Euros a month), but the safety of this measure is also more than questionable and completely out of proportion to conventional protective measures. The application of pre-exposure prohpylaxis (PreP) can only be meaningful in a very small number of exceptional cases.

Many patients, several weeks after exposure to HIV infection, develop a flu-like illness lasting several weeks. Symptoms often include fever, tiredness, skin rashes, joint and muscle pain, and swelling of the lymph nodes. If you are experiencing these symptoms following possible exposure, get to an HIV specialist to begin further treatment. After this phase the virus can spread throughout the body and start breaking down the immune system.

If the infection is left untreated for long it will destroy the immune system, allowing bacterial, viral and fungal infections to create life-threatening illnesses. This is the point where it's called AIDS or Acquired Immuno Deficiency Syndrome. Happily AIDS is becoming rarer in the West, due to the great success of HIV anti-viral therapies. But don't forget in the third world treatment is not sufficiently available, so AIDS is the number one cause of death amongst young adults in this part of the world

For HIV infection to be treated optimally, it's vital to get a quick diagnosis. You will need to take an HIV test, which detects special proteins, so-called antibodies, produced following exposure to HIV. The formation of these antibodies takes some weeks, so it's sensible to take the test 12 weeks after the exposure at the earliest. More recently another proof of diagnosis has become available, which detects HIV directly through the PCR method. This test can prove positive only 14 days after exposure to the virus, but is much more expensive than the antibody test, so is only used in certain situations.

A so-called "rapid test" has been licensed in a number of countries for quite a while already. This test detects antibodies to HIV – with the same certainty as the classic HIV antibody test – and is hence only meaningful 12 weeks after the infection risk at the earliest. A reactive test result must also be verified like with the classical HIV-antibody test by means of a confirmation test (western Blot test). The advantage of the quick tests is that no lab is necessary and the result is available after 15 to 20 minutes. Despite of the easy use, this HIV-test procedure also needs to be carried out by an expert.

Additional info: nowadays it is accepted that an optimally working HIV therapy with which the virus load is under the detection level can drastically lower the HIV-infection risk. Along with other reasons, that's why the HIV therapy nowadays starts earlier in some treatment centres. In combination with safer sex one can further reduce the spreading of HIV. To avoid infections with other sexually transmittable diseases, on no account forget to use condoms.

4. STDs- Sexually Transmitted Diseases

are infections caused by at least 20 separate pathogens (bacteria, viruses, fungal infections, parasites and amoeba), and are primarily transmitted by sexual contact, but can be passed on by simple bodily contact. Symptoms tend to show in the genital area, although not always. Recent years there have seen dramatic rises in these diseases. As well as by vaccination (hepatitis A and B), other infections are treated by medication – antibiotics for bacterial infections, antifungals, and antivirals – others are treated surgically (anal warts).

If you have any of the following symptoms or complaints you should consult a doctor:

- Discharge from penis or anus
- Red patches or white coating in mouth, genital or anal area.
- Sores (breaks in skin or mucus membranes), nodules or blisters in the mouth, genital or anal area.
- Extreme itching in genital or anal area.
- Painful and/or swollen lymph nodes
- Yellowing of skin and eyes.

What follows is a list describing most of the common STDs, with details of prevention of infection and quick diagnosis of the symptoms.

Syphillis

The likelihood of catching this has grown recently, especially within the gay scene. Its pathogens are bacteria, and are carried in infected bodily fluids (secretions), coming into contact with broken skin (lips, shaft of the penis) or mucus membrane (mouth, penis, vagina). Vaginal, oral or anal sex, and even kissing, have a risk of infection. Incubation time (the time between infection and illness) is about 2-4 weeks. The first signs are painless sores on the skin or mucus membranes, and swelling of the lymph nodes in the surrounding area, which will get better spontaneously after several weeks. Blood tests are needed to confirm syphilis. Treatment requires antibiotics.

Expert's tip: If there has been no treatment, after several more weeks, the second stage is reached, bringing swelling of lymph nodes, skin rashes, changes in mucus membranes, or patches of hair loss. The third stage is reached after some years, and includes attacks on skin, bones and brain, and ultimately death.

Gonorrhoea

Gonorrhoea is the most common STD, and is increasing hugely on the gay scene. Like syphilis, the pathogens are bacteria, and transmission occurs when there is contact between purulent secretions (sperm, vaginal or anal) and mucus membranes (penis, mouth, rectum, vagina) of your partner. Oral, (blow jobs), anal and vaginal sex are all risky. After an incubation period of 2-5 days, there is a pus discharge and burning when urinating. If the infection occurs in the rectum you get discharge, and frequently dull pain in the lower abdomen.Treatment is by antibiotics.

Expert's tip: The most common route of infection for those on the gay scene is by oral sex, from gonorrhoea in the throat (which is generally pain-free) into your partner's urethra.

Herpes

The herpes virus is transmitted by kissing (French kissing), oral, anal or vaginal sex, (Herpes genitalis), and mostly infects through tears in the mucus membrane of your partner. The infection can be triggered by agents which damage your immune system, for example fever, UV rays or stress, producing painful itchy blisters in the affected areas – lips, nose, genitals, or anus. Antiviral drugs are used to treat herpes outbreaks, either as local ointments or tablets.

Hepatitis

Hepatitis A and B viruses are found worldwide. The hepatitis A virus is passed through the bowel, so infected water and food, as well as anal sex, are risk factors. The hepatitis B virus is carried in the blood and via almost all types of sex – anal, oral and vaginal – and kissing, which safer sex doesn't protect you against! The first signs of infection are jaundice (yellowing of skin and eyes) and fatigue. A number of larger cities (in Europe: Berlin, Amsterdam and London) have recently been registering an increase in the number of hepatitis C infections in the gay scene. The reason for this increase has unfortunately not been established with absolute certainty yet. The most likely causes include an exchange of blood or body fluids when fisting, in S&M practices and with fresh piercings.
The therapeutic options available for hepatitis B and C have meanwhile become relatively good, but they are drawn-out and have many side effects. Inoculation against hepatitis A and B is therefore urgently recommended for all people with an active sex life. In the absence of a vaccine, infection with hepatitis C is unfortunately only preventable by not coming into contact with the partner's blood or bodily fluids.

Scabies

The scabies mite is a 0.2mm-sized parasite, found worldwide, living in the skin. It's transmitted by simple bodily contact, and is indicated by extremely severe itching in the affected skin area. Treatment involves the application of anti-parasitical lotion.

Public lice (crabs)

The pubic louse is a 1mm-sized flightless insect, transmitted by simple bodily contact. After several days or weeks there are small red itchy dots in the pubic hair. Scabies is treated with anti-parasitic lotions.

Anal warts

The wart virus is extremely common within the gay scene (50%), and is transmitted through sex, and also by infections carried on fingers and dildos. Ignoring it for long periods can lead to growth of small »cauliflower-like« warts on genitals or anus. Treatment is protracted, and is achieved by using chemical (burning or immune system-strengthening) products, or surgically.
Expert's tip: If ignored for a long time, particularly for the HIV positive, worst case scenario can be anal tumours (cancer). Obviously regular checking is vital!

Chlamydia

Chlamydia is transmitted in the same way as gonorrhoea. Therefore oral (blow jobs), anal and vaginal sex are a risk.
Also the symptoms are similar to those with gonorrhoea: however, the secretion from the urethra is mostly only glazed and not suppurating, and the burning of the urethra is substantially less painfully.
Infections of the pharynx and the rectum are mostly completely free of pain and are only discovered by a smear test. For the treatment of Chlamydia antibiotics are used.

Despite possible health risks when travelling long distance, I wish you happy action-packed trips. Thorough planning and some common sense will get you home safe and sound.

Dr. Horst Schalk
Doctor of General Medicine, Vienna.

★ Willkommen

Liebe Spartacus-Leser,

Ihr haltet die 41. Ausgabe des weltweit größten schwulen Reiseführers in Euren Händen. Dies ist keine Selbstverständlichkeit - denn in unserer heutigen schnelllebigen Zeit ist ein Buch für viele nicht mehr zeitgemäß. Wir denken, dass man sich den Errungenschaften der Technik nicht verschließen, gleichermaßen aber auch bewährte Medien nicht ungenutzt lassen sollte. Deswegen war eine wichtige und richtige Weiterentwicklung bei uns die Spartacus-Applikation für iPhones, die Ende des Jahres 2011 endlich zugelassen und zum Verkauf freigegeben wurde. Darüber hinaus bieten wir auch eine neue Webseite für Übernachtungsmöglichkeiten. Unter **www.spartacusworld.com** könnt Ihr somit fortan weltweit schwule oder schwulenfreundliche Unterkünfte finden und buchen.

Zu den schwulen Highlights für 2012 zählen u.a. die Mr. Gay World-Wahl im April in Johannesburg, die EuroGames in Budapest Ende Juni und der World Pride in London im Juli.

Ein weiteres Top-Ereignis für viele schwule Europäer ist der Eurovision Song Contest, der dieses Jahr am 26. Mai in Baku, Aserbaidschan stattfindet. Unsere intensiven Recherchen haben ergeben, dass es sich hierbei nicht nur um ein schwulenfeindliches Land handelt, sondern auch dringend vor den örtlichen Polizisten gewarnt werden muss. Vermeidet das Aushändigen von Pass oder Führerschein, es könnte Euch ein Vermögen kosten, diesen wieder zurück zu erhalten! Trotz alledem gilt Baku als eine tolle Stadt! Bleibt zu hoffen, dass der Wettbewerb die Situation für alle LGBT zum Besseren verändert.

Eine ausführliche Liste der wichtigsten schwulen Events in aller Welt ist wie immer im Kalender auf den letzten Seiten dieses Reiseführers und auf unserer Website unter **www.spartacusworld.com** zu finden. Dieser Veranstaltungskalender wird übrigens fortlaufend aktualisiert und erweitert.

Im Jahr 2011 hat sich politisch recht wenig für die LGBT-Community verändert. Sobald sich die Wirtschaftslage eintrübt, verschlechtert sich meistens auch die Situation von Minderheiten. Dies geschieht momentan in Ungarn, Russland und mehreren anderen osteuropäischen Ländern, in denen ein Wiedererwachen des Nationalismus zu beobachten ist.

Wir denken, dass jeder sein Medium bei uns finden wird und sinnvoll zu nutzen weiß. Ob als Strand- oder Reiselektüre mit dem bewährten Buch, oder mit dem iPhone bzw. Laptop zuhause oder unterwegs - es gibt viel zu entdecken. Die Lage bleibt auf jeden Fall spannend. Bewahrt Euch auch im kommenden Jahr eure Neugier und Freude am Reisen.

Briand Bedford
CHEFREDAKTEUR

Wie man SPARTACUS benutzt 

Sortierung der Länder

Der SPARTACUS ist in alphabetischer Reihenfolge nach den englischen Bezeichnungen der jeweiligen Länder aufgeteilt. Eine Ausnahme bildet die Karibik mit den jeweiligen Inseln und Ländern, die man unter dem Buchstaben »C« findet. Innerhalb der Länder erfolgt die Sortierung ebenfalls alphabetisch, jedoch sind die Namen der Städte in der jeweiligen Landessprache aufgelistet. Australien, Kanada und die USA sind jeweils noch in Bundesstaaten/Territorien/Provinzen eingeteilt und erst innerhalb dieser Listung werden die jeweiligen Städte alphabetisch aufgeführt. Sollten Sie dennoch Probleme haben, schlagen Sie einfach in unserem Inhaltsverzeichnis auf Seite 1106 nach. Dort sind alle Staaten, Länder und Städte in allen fünf SPARTACUS-Sprachen, also Englisch, Deutsch, Französisch, Spanisch und Italienisch, aufgeführt.
Für jedes Land haben wir spezifische Informationen über die rechtliche und soziale Situation von Gays zusammengetragen, dazu gehört auch das Schutzalter sowie Informationen zu Gay-Festivals und besonderen Events.
Vor der Einführung über jedes Land, finden Sie nachstehende Informationen:

Name: Der Name in der Landessprache sowie in den fünf SPARTACUS-Sprachen	➤	**Name:** Suid-Afrika • Südafrika • Afrique du Sud • Sudáfrica • Sud Africa
Location: geographische Lage	➤	**Location:** Southern Africa
Initials: übliche Landesabkürzung	➤	**Initials:** ZA
Time: bezieht sich auf die Zeitzone, in der ein Land liegt	➤	**Time:** GMT +2
International Country Code: gibt die internationale Vorwahlnummer des Landes für Anrufe aus dem Ausland an	➤	**International Country Code:** ☏ 27 (omit 0 of phone number)
International Access Code: ist die Vorwahlnummer des jeweiligen Landes, um von dort ins Ausland zu telefonieren	➤	**International Access Code:** ☏ 09 or 091
Language: bezieht sich auf die meistgesprochene(n) Sprache(n) im Land	➤	**Language:** English, Afrikaans, African languages
Area: Fläche des Landes	➤	**Area:** 1,219,080 km² / 471,442 sq mi.
Currency: ist die offizielle Landeswährung	➤	**Currency:** 1 Rand (ZAR) = 100 Cents
Population: Einwohnerzahl	➤	**Population:** 43,240,000
Capital: Hauptstadt	➤	**Capital:** Cape Town (legislative capital); Pretoria (administrative capital)
Religions: sind die im Land verbreiteten Religionen	➤	**Religions:** 78% Christians
Climate: Hier finden Sie eine kurze Übersicht über das Klima	➤	**Climate:** Ranging from hot and dry in summer to cold and wet in winter. Sub-tropical to Mediterranean climates.
Important Gay Cities: Städte, die für den schwulen Touristen von Interesse sind	➤	**Important gay cities:** Cape Town, Johannesburg

Gliederung der Adresseinträge

Der einzelne Eintrag enthält: den Namen ❶, die entsprechenden SPARTACUS Codes ❷, die Öffnungszeiten ❸, die Adresse ❹, die Telefonnummer ❺,die E-mail Adresse ❻ und schließlich die Web- Adresse ❼.

Die einzelnen Symbole bedeuten:

- ✉ Adresse
- ☏ Telefonnummer
- 💻 E-Mail Adresse, Website
- ☞ Hinweis

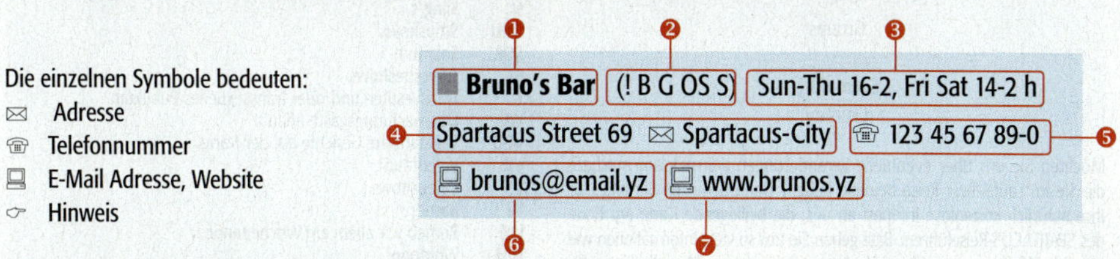

■ Ein rotes Quadrad zu Beginn des Adresseintrags verweist auf eine Kundenwerbung im Guide, bzw. auf die App oder Webseite.

★ Wie man SPARTACUS benutzt

Sortierung der Rubriken

Innerhalb der Länder und Städte sind die einzelnen Adresseinträge folgendermaßen sortiert:

National Gay Info
National Publications
National Publishers
National Companies
National Groups
National Helplines
Country Cruising
▼
Gay Info
Publications
Culture
Tourist Info
▼
Bars
Men's Clubs
Cafés
Danceclubs
Restaurants
Shows
Cinema
▼
Sex Shops/Blue Movies
Cinemas
Escorts & Studios
House of Boys
▼
Saunas/Baths
Fitness Studios
Massage
▼
Shopping/Services
▼
Hotels
Guest Houses
Apartments
Private Accommodation
▼
Groups
▼
Swimming
Cruising

Möchten Sie uns über eventuelle Veränderungen aufmerksam machen, die Sie im Laufe Ihrer Reise bemerkt haben? Dann benutzen Sie bitte, für Ihre natürlich kostenlose Infopost an uns, die beiliegende Karte am Ende des SPARTACUS-Reiseführers. Bitte geben Sie uns so viele Informationen wie möglich. Wir freuen uns über jede Art von Information, über die Sie verfügen, die aber noch nicht im SPARTACUS steht. Ihre Infos senden Sie bitte an:

Bruno Gmünder Verlag GmbH • SPARTACUS-Redaktion
Kleiststraße 23-26 • 10787 Berlin • GERMANY
info@spartacus.de

Beschreibung der Codes

Die Spartacus Codes bedeuten (Codes in Kleinbuchstaben bedeuten im Allgemeinen eine Einschränkung):-

!	Besonders empfehlenswert, ein Muss
AC	Klimaanlage
AK	Andreaskreuz
AYOR	Auf eigenes Risiko, möglicherweise gefährlich oder häufige Polizeikontrollen
B	Bar mit breitem Angebot alkoholischer Getränke
BF	umfangreiches Frühstück
CC	Alle gängigen Kreditkarten akzeptiert
D	Tanzmöglichkeit/Diskothek
DM	Täglich wechselnde Menüs
DR	Darkroom
DU	Dusche
F	Fetisch (Leder, Latex oder Uniform)
FC	Kondome gratis
FH	Extra Handtuch gratis
G	ausschließlich oder überwiegend schwules Publikum
GH	Glory Holes
GLM	Ausschließlich oder überwiegend schwul-lesbisches Publikum
H	schwulenfreundliche Unterkunft
I	Internetzugang
LAB	Labyrinth
LM	Live Musik
M	umfangreiches Speisenangebot
MA	gemischte Altersklassen
MC	Gäste mittleren Alters (30-50 Jahre)
MSG	Massage möglich
NG	Nicht schwul, aber interessant
NR	Nicht-Raucher Bereich
NU	FKK/Nacktbademöglichkeit
OC	Eher ältere Gäste (ab 50 Jahre)
OS	Terrasse oder Garten
P	Privatclub oder strenge Einlasskontrolle
p	Sie müssen klingeln
PA	Haustiere akzeptiert
PI	Swimmingpool
PK	Parkplätze vorhanden
PP	Tauchbecken
R	Regelmäßig Stricher
RES	Reservierung notwendig
RR	Ruheraum
RWB	Gästezimmer mit Balkon
RWS	Gästezimmer mit eigenem Bad/ eigener Dusche
RWT	Gästezimmer mit Fernseher
S	Shows/Veranstaltungen
SA	Trockensauna
SB	Dampfsauna
SH	Shop
SL	Sling/s
SNU	Stripshows
SOL	Solarium
ST	Travestieshows
T	Transvestiten und/oder transsexuelles Publikum
VA	Übernachtungsgäste erlaubt
VEG	Vegetarische Gerichte auf der Karte
VR	Videoraum
VS	Videoshows
W	Barrierefrei
WE	Betrieb vor allem am Wochenende
WH	Whirlpool
WI	kostenloses WiFi
WL	Ausführliche Weinkarte
WO	Bodybuilding möglich
YC	Junge Schwule (18 - 28)

Diese Codes gibt es als heraustrennbares Lesezeichen am Ende des Buches!

1. Einleitung

Schwule Männer sind vermutlich »Weltmeister« im Reisen – sowohl bei privaten Urlaubsreisen, als auch bei beruflichen. Wenn man sich in fremde Länder begibt, sollte man natürlich nicht nur die Landessitten beachten und respektieren, sondern auch berücksichtigen, dass die ungewohnte Umgebung auch gesundheitliche Risiken bergen kann. Zusätzlich zu den bereits zu Hause geltenden Regeln sollte man gerade unterwegs – egal ob HIV-negativ oder HIV-positiv – zusätzliche Verhaltensmaßregeln beachten.

Im Schatten der drohenden HIV-Infektion wurde den anderen sexuell übertragbaren Erkrankungen (STD – sexually transmitted deseases) unglücklicherweise kaum Beachtung geschenkt. Aus diesem Grund kam es in der zweiten Hälfte der 90er Jahre zu einem dramatischen Anstieg dieser Infektionskrankheiten auch in der westlichen Welt. Schwule Männer, die sich berechtigterweise die Freiheit nehmen, ihre Sexualität frei und ohne religiöse und moralische Zwänge auszuleben, übernehmen aber auch Verantwortung – Verantwortung für ihre eigene, aber auch für die Gesundheit ihres jeweiligen Sexual-Partners!

Die HIV-Infektion konnte in den vergangenen Jahren durch den rasanten Fortschritt der Medizin von einer meist schicksalhaft tödlichen in eine chronische und gut behandelbare, allerdings nicht heilbare Erkrankung verwandelt werden. Patienten, die früher ums nackte Überleben kämpften, geht es nun meistens gut, sie sind nun erfreulicherweise wieder in der Lage, beinahe gefahrlos ihren Urlaub auch im fernen Ausland zu verbringen.

2. Reisen

In den meisten Industrieländern sind wir gewohnt, medizinische Leistungen mehr oder weniger »kostenlos« in Anspruch zu nehmen. Bitte beachten Sie, dass Sie im Ausland nicht automatisch einen Versicherungsschutz genießen, das heißt, Sie müssen die ärztliche Leistung meist vorerst bezahlen und bekommen erst nach Ihrer Rückkehr die Kosten vollkommen oder teilweise von Ihrer Sozial-, Privat- oder Reiseversicherung (sehr oft ein Service der Kreditkartenfirma – erkundigen Sie sich aber bitte nach den jeweiligen Bedingungen) zurückerstattet. Wenn Sie als Bürger der Europäischen Union in ein anderes Land der Union reisen, genießen Sie gegen Vorlage der europäischen Krankenversicherungskarte (welche sie beim zuständigen Krankenversicherungsträger bekommen oder sich ohnehin auf der Rückseite Ihrer Sozialversicherungskarte befindet) in allen Staaten der Union und in der Schweiz einen Versicherungsschutz für Akutleistungen.

Impfungen (z.B. gegen Hepatitis A und B) und Prophylaxen (z.B. gegen Malaria) bieten einen sehr hohen Schutz gegen viele Infektionskrankheiten. Neben den in Ihrem Heimatland empfohlenen Impfungen sind in vielen Ländern weitere, sogenannte Reiseimpfungen empfohlen oder sogar vorgeschrieben. Ihr Arzt informiert Sie darüber gerne.

HIV-Positive können alle Impfungen, die mit abgetöteten Erregern, deren Teilen oder abgeschwächten Toxinen (Giftstoffen) durchgeführt werden, man spricht dann von sogenannten Totimpfstoffen, bedenkenlos erhalten. Lediglich wenn dass Immunsystem deutlich eingeschränkt ist (CD4-Zellen unter 200/ml), kann es zu einem verringerten Ansprechen und damit zu einem nur unzureichenden Impfschutz kommen. Impfungen, bei denen lebende abgeschwächte Krankheitserreger injiziert werden (zum Beispiel die in manchen Ländern vorgeschriebene Gelbfieberimpfung), sind bei HIV-Positiven nur unter strenger Abwägung des Risikos und im Regelfall nur bei einer sehr guten Abwehrlage (CD4-Zellen über 400/ml) möglich.

Hygiene ist nicht in allen Reiseländern so selbstverständlich wie bei uns. Grundsätzlich gilt in den meisten Ländern der 3. Welt aber möglicherweise auch in einigen europäischen Ländern: kein Wasser aus der Wasserleitung trinken! Entweder nur abgekochtes und gefiltertes Wasser oder solches aus originalverschlossenen Mineralwasserflaschen trinken. Eiswürfel in Cocktailgetränken können theoretisch bereits problematisch sein. Für die Ernährung gilt die einfache Regel: »cook it, boil it, peal it or leave it« – zu Deutsch: nur gut Gebratenes, Gekochtes und nur zu schälendes Obst (z.B. Bananen, Apfelsinen, Ananas unter hygienischen Bedingungen selbst geschält!) essen! Alles andere birgt Gefahren (z.B. Salate, Salatdressings, Cremes, Eierspreisen etc.) und sollte weggelassen werden.

Für alle Fälle denken Sie an eine Reiseapotheke (Infos z.B. unter www.Reiseapotheke.de oder www.m-ww.de/reisemedizin/reiseapotheke.html), in der die notwendigen Medikamente z.B. für mögliche Durchfallerkrankungen und Verbandsmaterial enthalten sein sollten. Im Zweifelsfall gilt: die Hilfe eines kompetenten Arztes aufsuchen.

Wenn Sie regelmäßig Medikamente einnehmen müssen, nehmen Sie auf jeden Fall für einige Tage mehr an Medikamenten mit als nötig, für den Fall, dass sich die Rückreise aus unerwarteten Gründen verschiebt oder dass Sie einige Tabletten verlieren. Nehmen Sie unbedingt die Medikamente in der Originalverpackung mit dem Beipacktext (darin steht auch die chemische Bezeichnung der Substanz, die meisten Medikamente haben in verschiedenen Ländern unterschiedliche Namen), sowie eventuell eine Kopie der Rezepte oder eventuell benötigte Spritzen und Kanülen im Handgepäck mit. Denken Sie an mögliche Zeitverschiebungen und planen Sie die Medikamenteneinnahme entsprechend.

Expertentipp: Bei der Einreise in einige Länder empfiehlt es sich, ein ärztliches Attest mitzuführen, in dem der Name und eine kurze Beschreibung der Medikamente (ob es sich zum Beispiel um Tabletten oder Kapseln handelt) angeführt ist (Musterformular www.homed.at unter »downloads«). Eine Diagnose muss übrigens nicht angegeben werden.

Internationale Gesetze und Vorschriften können sehr unterschiedlich sein. Wenn Sie ins Ausland reisen, erkundigen Sie sich bitte über die jeweiligen Zoll- und Einreisebestimmungen. Informationen erhalten Sie telefonisch oder im Internet bei Ihrem Außenministerium oder bei der Botschaft oder beim Konsulat des jeweiligen Landes.

Bitte bedenken Sie auch, dass einige Substanzen im Kühlschrank, alle anderen zumindest bei Zimmertemperatur, das heißt, nicht über 30°C, und trocken gelagert werden müssen. In vielen Ländern der 3.Welt ist es leider auch heute noch nicht selbstverständlich, dass bei der Versorgung von Wunden oder bei der Verabreichung von Injektionen frisches und steriles Material verwendet wird. Bei der Einreise in diese Länder empfiehlt es sich, vor allem bei längeren Aufenthalten, dieses selbst mitzubringen.

Auf keinen Fall sollten Sie ausreichend Sonnenschutzcremes mit hohem Schutzfaktor vergessen. Ein Aufenthalt in der prallen Sonne ist in südlichen Ländern zwischen 12.00 Uhr und 15.00 Uhr ohne Schutz wegen der Gefahr von Entstehung von Hauttumoren und der vorübergehenden Schädigung des Abwehrsystems (möglicher Abfall der CD4-Zellen bei HIV-Infizierten) nicht zu empfehlen.

Übrigens: Auch Kondome und Gleitgel sind nicht überall in der uns gewohnten Qualität erhältlich.

3. HIV-Infektion

Die HIV-Infektion kann nur dann Übertragen werden, wenn HI-Viren in den menschlichen Körper gelangen. Dies erfolgt, wenn infektiöse Flüssigkeiten wie zum Beispiel Sperma, Vaginalflüssigkeit oder Blut auf die intakte oder verletzte Schleimhaut (Anal, Mastdarm, Vaginal- oder Mundschleimhaut oder die Bindehaut des Auges) oder die frisch verletzte Haut (Schnitt-, Stich- oder Schürfwunden) gelangen.

Ein Infektionsrisiko besteht daher bei

- ungeschütztem Analverkehr, sowohl für den aktiven, als auch für den passiven Partner
- ungeschütztem Vaginalverkehr, sowohl für die Frau, als auch für den Mann
- ungeschütztem Oralverkehr, für den aktiven Partner (»den, der bläst«), wenn es zum Samenerguss im Mund kommt

- beim Fisten (Einführen mehrerer Finger oder der Faust in den Mastdarm) ohne Gummihandschuhe, wenn es zu Blutungen im Darmbereich des Gefisteten oder im Handbereich beim Fister kommt.

Expertentipp: Zahlreiche HIV-Experten sind der Ansicht, dass der Lusttropfen, den viele Männer vor dem eigentlichen Orgasmus absondern, und der beim ungeschützten Oralverkehr auf die Mundschleimhaut gelangen kann, eventuell unter ganz bestimmten Umständen (Vorhandensein einer anderen sexuell übertragbaren Erkrankung, die mit Ausfluss aus der Harnröhre einhergeht und einer gleichzeitig bestehenden hohen HI- Viruskonzentration) ein geringes Restrisiko bergen könnte.

Kein bekanntes HIV-Risiko besteht bei

- Kontakt mit Speichel, Tränenflüssigkeit, Schweiß, Harn oder Stuhl
- damit sind alle nur denkbaren Sozialkontakte wie Händeschütteln, gemeinsame Benutzung von Gläsern und Essbesteck, Toiletten, sowie der Besuch von Schwimmbädern oder Saunas absolut gefahrlos.
- auch eine Infektion durch Atemluft, durch Anniesen oder Anhusten oder Insektenstiche oder -bisse ist aufgrund der vorhandenen Datenlage eher ausgeschlossen!

Um das Risiko einer HIV-Infektion zu reduzieren, sollten Sie unbedingt Safer-Sex praktizieren und

- bei Anal- und Vaginalverkehr unbedingt Kondome und ausreichend (wasserlösliches) Gleitgel benutzen. Fetthaltige Cremes können das Kondom beschädigen. Bei gleichzeitigem Kontakt mit mehreren Partnern ist das Kondom beim Wechsel der Partner unbedingt zu wechseln. Kondome können auch das Risiko, andere sexuell übertragbare Krankheiten zu übertragen, reduzieren.
- beim Oralverkehr (»Blasen«) auf keinen Fall im Mund des Partners ejakulieren (abspritzen). Diese Maßnahme reicht allerdings nicht aus, um andere sexuell übertragbare Erkrankungen (wie zum Beispiel Tripper, Syphilis oder Hepatitis) zu verhindern. Wer auch die Übertragung dieser, beziehungsweise auch das oben erwähnte minimale Restrisiko des Lusttropfens bezüglich HIV verhindern will, sollte auch beim Oralverkehr ein Kondom benutzen.
- beim Fisten (»Faustfick«) immer Gummihandschuhe benutzen.
- sollten Sie intravenöse Drogen konsumieren, ist darauf zu achten, dass jeder seine eigenen Spritzutensilien (Spritze, Nadel, Spülflüssigkeit) benutzt.

Expertentipp: Inzwischen ist es bewiesen, dass es auch bei bereits HIV-Infizierten zu einer neuerlichen Infektion mit möglicherweise auch resistenten HI-Viren kommen kann. Dies kann eine gut laufende HIV-Therapie stören, sogar unwirksam machen oder den zukünftigen Therapiebeginn extrem erschweren. Daher sollten auch HIV-Positive auf Safer-Sex nicht verzichten!

Im Falle eines Infektionsrisikos besteht die Möglichkeit, die Übertragungswahrscheinlichkeit durch das sofortige Reinigen der Kontaktstelle (Hautwunde oder Schleimhaut) mit Wasser und Seife oder – wenn verfügbar mit Desinfektionsmitteln (ein Auswaschen des Mastdarmes ist nicht sinnvoll) – sowie die rasche (innerhalb weniger Stunden) vorsorgliche Einnahme einer HIV-Therapie (Postexpositionsprophylaxe=PEP) zu reduzieren. Diese Maßnahme kann das Infektionsrisiko nur reduzieren und nicht verhindern, kann also Safer-Sex nicht ersetzen! Genaue Information erhalten Sie in einem HIV-Behandlungszentrum.

Seit einiger Zeit gibt es immer wieder von einigen wenigen Stellen die Empfehlung eine HIV-Therapie „vorsorglich" vor einem möglichen Infektionsrisiko einzunehmen. Praktisch alle HIV-Experten raten von der Einnahme dieser so genannte Präexpostitionsprophylaxe (PreP) ab. Nicht nur, dass die Finanzierung (die Kosten würden sich für ein Monat auf mehr als € 1000 belaufen) vollkommen ungeklärt ist, ist die Sicherheit dieser Massnahme mehr als fragwürdig und steht in keinem Vergleich zu den herkömmlichen Schutzmassnahmen. Der Einsatz der Präexpostitionsprophylaxe (PreP) kann nur in ganz wenigen Ausnahmefällen sinnvoll sein.

Bei vielen Patienten tritt wenige Wochen nach einer erfolgten HIV-Infektion für 10-14 Tage oft ein grippeähnliches Krankheitsbild auf. Dabei kann es unter anderem zu Fieber, Müdigkeit, Hautausschlag, Gelenks- und Muskelschmerzen, sowie zu Lymphknotenschwellungen kommen. Sollten nach einem möglichen Infektionsrisiko diese Beschwerden auftreten, sollten Sie unbedingt einen HIV-Spezialisten aufsuchen, damit er weitere Maßnahmen einleiten kann.

Nach dieser Phase können sich die Viren im gesamten Körper ausbreiten und im Besonderen das Immunsystem schädigen. Bei jahrelangem unbehandeltem Fortschreiten der HIV-Infektion kommt es zu dessen Zerstörung und andere Krankheitserreger wie Bakterien, Viren oder Pilze können lebensbedrohliche Infektionen auslösen – dann erst spricht man von AIDS (Acquired Immuno Deficiency Syndrome = erworbenes Immunmangel Syndrom). Heute ist AIDS in der westlichen Welt auf Grund des großen Erfolges der HIV-Therapie glücklicherweise seltener geworden. Man sollte aber keinesfalls vergessen, dass in den meisten Ländern der 3.Welt diese Therapie nicht oder nur unzureichend zur Verfügung steht, und damit AIDS immer noch die Todesursache Nummer Eins bei jungen Erwachsenen darstellt.

Um die HIV-Infektion optimal behandeln zu können, muss diese allerdings auch rechtzeitig diagnostiziert werden. Dies erfolgt in der Regel mittels HIV-Test. Dieser weist spezielle Proteine, die sogenannten Antikörper, die der Mensch auf den Kontakt mit HIV bildet, nach. Die Bildung dieser Antikörper dauert einige Wochen, so dass dieser Test frühestens 12 Wochen nach einem Infektionsrisiko sinnvoll ist. Seit einiger Zeit steht allerdings ein weiteres Nachweisverfahren zur Verfügung: Dieses weist HI-Viren direkt mittels der sogenannten PCR-Methode nach. Dieser Infektionsnachweis ist meist bereits 14 Tage nach dem potentiellen Risiko aussagekräftig, allerdings auch wesentlich teurer als der Antikörpertest und wird daher nur bei besonderen Fragestellungen eingesetzt.

In vielen Ländern ist bereits seit einiger Zeit ein so genannter „Schnelltest" zugelassen. Dieser weist – mit der gleichen Sicherheit wie der klassische HIV-Antikörper-Test – Antikörper gegen HIV nach und ist daher frühestens 12 Wochen nach dem Infektionsrisiko aussagekräftig. Ein reaktives Testergebnis muss auch wie beim klassischen HIV-Antikörpertest mittels eines Bestätigungstests (Western-Blot-Test) verifiziert werden. Der Vorteil der Schnelltests ist, dass zur Durchführung kein Labor erforderlich ist, und das Ergebnis bereits nach 15 bis 20 Minuten vorliegt. Trotz der einfachen Handhabung gehört auch dieses HIV-Testverfahren in die Hand eines Fachmannes.

Zusatzinfo: Inzwischen gilt auch als gesichert, dass eine optimal wirkende HIV-Therapie, bei der sich die Viruslast unter der Nachweisgrenze befindet, das HIV-Infektionsrisiko drastisch senken kann. Unter anderem aus diesem Grund wird von manchen Behandlungszentren die HIV-Therapie bereits früher als bisher gestartet. In Kombination mit Safersex kann man auf diesem Weg die Weiterverbreitung von HIV zusätzlich reduzieren. Schon um eine Infektion mit anderen sexuell übertragbarer Erkrankungen zu vermeiden, sollte auf die Verwendung von Kondomen trotzdem keinesfalls verzichtet werden.

4. STD – Sexuell Übertragbare Erkrankungen

STD's (engl. sexually transmitted diseases) sind Infektionskrankheiten, die durch mindestens 20 verschiedene Erreger (Bakterien, Viren, Pilze, Einzeller und Parasiten) verursacht werden und in erster Linie durch Geschlechtsverkehr, aber auch in einigen Fällen durch engen körperlichen Kontakt übertragen werden können. Die Krankheitssymptome treten vor allem, aber nicht ausschließlich in der Genitalregion auf. In den vergangenen Jahren kam es zu einem dramatischen Anstieg dieser Infektionskrankheiten. Gegen einige existieren Schutzimpfungen (Hepatitis

A + B), andere werden medikamentös behandelt (Antibiotika bei bakteriellen-, Antimykotika bei Pilz- und antivirale Substanzen bei Virusinfektionen) andere wiederum chirurgisch (Feigwarzen).

Bei folgenden Symptomen (Beschwerden) sollte man unbedingt einen Arzt aufsuchen:

- Ausfluss aus der Harnröhre oder dem Anus
- Rötung oder weiße Beläge im Mund-, Genital- oder Analbereich
- Geschwüre (Substanzdefekte der Haut- oder Schleimhaut), Knötchen oder Bläschen im Mund-, Genital- oder Analbereich
- starker Juckreiz im Genital- oder Analbereich
- schmerzhafte und/oder geschwollene Lymphknoten
- Gelbfärbung von Haut und Augen

Im Folgenden werden die am häufigsten vorkommenden sexuell übertragbaren Infektionskrankheiten berücksichtigt. Besonders wird auf die Infektionswege (Prävention) und auf die Symptome (rasche Diagnosestellung) eingegangen.

Syphilis = Lues

Die Wahrscheinlichkeit, sich zu infizieren, steigt – gerade in der Szene – in letzter Zeit deutlich an! Die Erreger sind Bakterien und werden durch infektiöse Körperflüssigkeiten (Sekrete), die auf (meist defekte) Haut (Lippen, Penisschaft) oder Schleimhaut (Mund, Penis, Vagina) gelangen, übertragen. Sowohl Vaginal-, Oral-, oder Analverkehr, aber auch Küssen stellen ein Infektionsrisiko dar. Die Inkubationszeit (Zeit, die zwischen Infektion und Erkrankung verstreicht) beträgt 2-4 Wochen. Dann treten im sogenannten Primärstadium schmerzlose Geschwüre (Substanzdefekt von Haut- oder Schleimhaut) und Schwellung der regionären (benachbarten) Lymphknoten auf, die nach einigen Wochen spontan abheilen.
Der Nachweis einer Syphilis erfolgt mittels einer Blutuntersuchung, die Therapie besteht in der Gabe eines Antibiotikums.

Expertentipp: Wenn keine Behandlung erfolgt, kommt es nach einigen Wochen zum Sekundärstadium mit Lymphknotenschwellung, Hautausschlag, Schleimhautveränderungen oder fleckförmigen Haarausfall. Im darauffolgenden Tertiärstadium kann es nach Jahren zu einem Befall von Haut, Knochen, sowie Gehirn und damit zum Tod kommen.

Tripper = Gonorrhoe = GO

Der Tripper ist die häufigste Geschlechtskrankheit und nimmt in der schwulen Szene massiv zu.
Wie bei der Syphilis sind die Erreger Bakterien, die Übertragung erfolgt durch ein eitriges Sekret (Sperma, Vaginal- oder Analsekret), welches auf die Schleimhaut (Penis, Mund, Mastdarm, Vagina) des Partners gelangt. Somit stellt Oral- (Blasen), Anal-, Vaginalverkehr ein Risiko dar. Nach einer Inkubationszeit von 2-5 Tagen tritt ein eitriger Ausfluss sowie Brennen beim Harnlassen auf. Wenn die Infektion im Mastdarm erfolgte, kommt es zu einem eitrigen Ausfluss oft aber nur zu unspezifischen dumpfen Unterbauchschmerzen. Die Therapie besteht in der Gabe eines Antibiotikums.

Expertentipp: Häufigster Infektionsweg in der schwulen Szene: Ein Rachentripper (der meist beschwerdefrei verläuft) wird beim Oralverkehr auf die Harnröhre des Partners übertagen.

Herpes

Durch Küssen (Fieberblasen), Oral-, Anal- oder Vaginalverkehr (Herpes genitalis) gelangen die Herpesviren meist über einen Schleimhautdefekt in den Körper des Partners. Ist die Infektion erst erfolgt, kann es, vor allem ausgelöst durch immunsystemschädigende Einflüsse wie zum Beispiel Fieber, UV-Strahlen oder Stress, zu juckenden, schmerzenden Bläschen im betroffenen Gebiet (Lippen, Nasen-, Genital- oder Analbereich) kommen. Zur Behandlung der Herpesinfektion stehen antivirale Substanzen, welche lokal aufgetragen oder in Form von Tabletten geschluckt werden, zur Verfügung.

Hepatitis

Die Hepatitis A+B-Viren kommen weltweit vor. Die Heptatitis-A-Viren werden über den Darm ausgeschieden, somit stellen infiziertes Wasser und Nahrungsmittel sowie anale Sexualpraktiken ein Infektionsrisiko dar! Die Hepatitis-B-Viren werden über Blut und bei fast allen Sexual-Praktiken (Anal-, Oral-, Vaginalverkehr) sowie durch Küssen übertragen (Safer Sex schützt nicht!) Ist es erst zu einer Infektion gekommen tritt meist eine Gelbsucht (Gelbfärbung von Haut und Augen) sowie Müdigkeit auf.
In letzter Zeit verzeichnen einige Großstädte (in Europa: Berlin, Amsterdam und London) ein erhöhtes Auftreten der Hepatitis C in der schwulen Szene. Die Ursache dieses Anstieges ist leider noch nicht restlos geklärt. Vermutlich ist ein Austausch von Blut oder Körpersekreten beim Fisten, bei SM-Praktiken und bei frischen Piercings dafür verantwortlich.
Inzwischen gibt es relativ gute Therapiemöglichkeiten für die Hepatitis B und C, diese sind aber langwierig und nebenwirkungsreich. Aus diesem Grund ist eine Impfung gegen die Hepatitis A und B für alle sexuell aktive Menschen dringend zu empfehlen. Vor einer Hepatitis C schützt leider, mangels einer Impfung, nur das Vermeiden des Kontaktes mit Blut und anderen Körpersekreten des Partners..

Skabies = Krätze

Die Skabiesmilbe ist ein 0,2mm großer weltweit verbreiteter in der Haut lebender Parasit, der bei engem Körperkontakt übertragen wird und einen starken oft unerträglichen Juckreiz im Bereich der befallenen Hautregionen verursacht. Die Therapie besteht im Auftragen einer antiparasitären Lotion.

Filzläuse

Die Filzlaus ist ein ungefähr 1mm großes flügelloses Insekt und wird durch engen Körperkontakt übertragen. Nach einigen Tagen oder Wochen treten kleine rote juckende Punkte im Schamhaarbereich auf. Wie bei der Skabies verabreicht man antiparasitäre Lotionen.

Condylome = Feigwarzen

Die in der Szene extrem häufig vorkommenden (mehr als 50%) Condylomviren werden durch Geschlechtsverkehr, aber auch über Schmierinfektion (Finger, Dildo) übertragen. Nach monate- bis jahrelangem Verlauf kann es zur Ausbildung von kleinen »blumenkohlartigen« Wärzchen im Genital- und Analbereich kommen. Die Therapie ist langwierig und erfolgt mittels chemischer (ätzende oder Immunsystem stärkende) Substanzen oder chirurgisch.
Expertentipp: Bei unbehandeltem jahrelangem Verlauf kann im schlimmsten Fall und vor allem bei HIV-Positiven ein Analkarzinom (Krebs) entstehen! Daher sollte eine regelmäßige Kontrolle durchgeführt werden!

Chlamydien

Chlamydien werden auf die gleiche Weise übertragen wie Tripper. Somit stellt auch hier Oral- (Blasen), Anal- und Vaginalverkehr ein Risiko dar. Auch die Symptome sind ähnlich denen der bei Tripper: der Ausfluss aus der Harnröhre ist allerdings meist nur glasig und nicht eitrig, das Brennen der Harnröhre wesentlich weniger schmerzhaft. Infektionen des Rachenraumes und des Mastdarmes sind meist vollkommen beschwerdefrei und werde nur durch einen Abstrich der entsprechenden Region entdeckt. Auch zur Behandlung von Chlamydien werden Antibiotika eingesetzt.

Trotz der möglichen gesundheitlichen Risiken, die bei Reisen in ferne Länder eine Bedrohung für Ihre Gesundheit darstellen könnten, wünsche ich Ihnen eine erlebnisreiche und schöne Reise. Gute Planung und das richtige Maß an Vernunft lässt Sie gesund und munter wieder nach Hause zurückkehren.

Dr. Horst Schalk
Arzt für Allgemeinmedizin, Wien
www.horstschalk.at • www.homed.at

Chers lecteurs,

vous avez entre les mains la 41ème édition du plus grand guide de voyage gay. Ce n'est pas une évidence – car dans notre monde moderne, pour beaucoup de personnes les livres ne sont plus actuels. Nous pensons qu'il ne faut pas refuser les progrès de la technique mais aussi qu'il ne faut pas abandonner les médias qui ont fait leurs preuves. C'est pour cette raison que l'application Spartacus pour l'iPhone, autorisée et mise en vente fin 2011, a été un développement important et judicieux. De plus nous avons aussi un nouveau site web pour les hébergements. À l'adresse **www.spartacusworld.com** vous pouvez dorénavant chercher et trouver des hébergements gays et gay-friendly dans le monde entier.

Parmi les évènements-phare de 2012, on compte entre autres l'élection du Mr. Gay World en avril à Johannesbourg, les EuroGames à Budapest fin juin et la World Pride à Londres début juillet.

Un autre moment majeur de l'année pour beaucoup de gays européens : l'Eurovision Song Contest qui se déroule cette année le 26 mai à Bakou, Azerbaïdjan. Après des recherches intensives, nous sommes arrivés à la conclusion que ce pays est non seulement homophobe mais qu'il faut aussi se méfier de la police locale. Ne donnez pas vos papiers ou votre permis de conduire, il pourrait vous en coûter une fortune pour les récupérer. Reste que Bakou est une ville formidable ! En espérant que le concours apportera des améliorations à la situation de la communauté LBGT.

Une liste complète des évènements gays les plus importants dans le monde entier est disponible comme toujours à la fin de ce guide et sur notre site interne **www.spartacusworld.com**. Ce calendrier des évènements est d'ailleurs mis à jour et complété en continu.

En 2011 la situation politique pour la communauté LBGT a très peu changé. Dès que la situation économique s'obscurcit, la condition des minorités se dégrade aussi en général. Cela se produit en Hongrie, Russie et dans plusieurs pays d'Europe de l'Est dans lesquels une renaissance du nationalisme se produit.

Nous pensons que chacun trouvera son compte parmi les médias que nous proposons. Que ce soit à la plage ou en voyage avec le livre qui a déjà fait ses preuves, ou avec l'iPhone ou le notebook à la maison et en déplacement - il reste beaucoup à découvrir. Dans tous les cas, les voyages restent captivants : conservez cette année encore votre curiosité et votre plaisir pour les voyages.

Briand Bedford
EDITEUR EN CHEF

Comment utiliser votre SPARTACUS 

Classement des pays

SPARTACUS est classé par pays. Les pays sont ordonnés alphabétiquement sous leur nom en anglais, à l'exception des pays des caraïbes qui sont classés alphabétiquement sous Caribbean. Pour chaque pays, on trouve les noms des villes et villages classés alphabétiquement dans la langue nationale ou locale. Une exception a été faite pour l'Australie, le Canada et les Etats-Unis qui sont divisés par province ou état puis par ville ou village. Si vous avez des difficultés à trouver un lieu, veuillez vous référer à l'index en page 1106 qui recense alphabétiquement tous les noms de pays, villes et villages dans les cinq langues de SPARTACUS: anglais, allemand, français, espagnol et italien.

Pour chaque pays vous trouverez des informations concernant la situation légale et sociale des gais, y compris l'âge de la majorité sexuelle. Des informations supplémentaires sont fournies sur les festivals et autres manifestations qui ont lieu au cours de l'année.

Avant cette introduction pour chaque pays, vous trouverez les informations suivantes :

Name: indique le nom du pays dans la langue régionale et dans les cinq langues de SPARTACUS	➔	**Name:** Suid-Afrika • Südafrika • Afrique du Sud • Sudáfrica • Sud Africa
Location: indique la situation géographique du pays	➔	**Location:** Southern Africa
Initials: indique à l'abréviation générale du pays	➔	**Initials:** ZA
Time: indique le fuseau horaire du pays	➔	**Time:** GMT +2
International Country Code: indique l'indicatif à composer pour joindre le pays depuis l'étranger	➔	**International Country Code:** ☎ 27 (omit 0 of phone number)
International Access Code: indique l'indicatif à composer pour joindre le réseau téléphonique international depuis le pays	➔	**International Access Code:** ☎ 09 or 091
Language: indique les principales langues parlées dans le pays	➔	**Language:** English, Afrikaans, African languages
Area: indique la superficie du pays	➔	**Area:** 1,219,080 km² / 471,442 sq mi.
Currency: indique la monnaie en cours dans le pays	➔	**Currency:** 1 Rand (ZAR) = 100 Cents
Population: indique le nombre d'habitants du pays	➔	**Population:** 43,240,000
Capital: indique la capitale du pays	➔	**Capital:** Cape Town (legislative capital); Pretoria (administrative capital)
Religions: indique les religions pratiquées dans le pays	➔	**Religions:** 78% Christians
Climate: indique les caractéristiques climatiques du pays	➔	**Climate:** Ranging from hot and dry in summer to cold and wet in winter. Sub-tropical to Mediterranean climates.
Important Gay Cities: indique les principales villes gaies	➔	**Important gay cities:** Cape Town, Johannesburg

Classement des adresses

Chaque entrée comprend le nom de l'établissement ❶, les codes SPARTACUS ❷, les heures d'ouverture ❸, l'adresse ❹, le numéro de téléphone ❺, l'adresse du courrier électronique ❻, et du site Internet ❼.

Les codes ont la signification suivante:

- ✉ adresse
- ☎ numéro de téléphone
- 💻 l'adresse du courrier électronique et du site Internet
- ☞ voir aussi

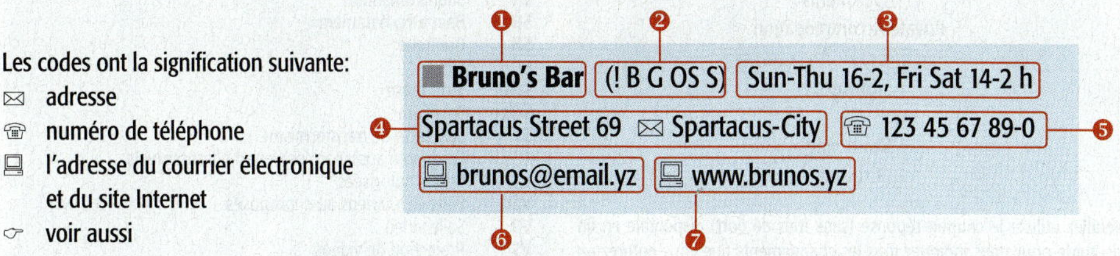

■ Un Une carré rouge en début d'adresse indique une annonce-client dans le guide, l'App ou sur le site web.

✱ Comment utiliser votre SPARTACUS

Classement des rubriques

Pour chaque pays et ville, vous trouverez les adresses classées sous les rubriques dans l'ordre suivant :

National Gay Info
National Publications
National Publishers
National Companies
National Groups
National Helplines
Country Cruising
▼
Gay Info
Publications
Culture
Tourist Info
▼
Bars
Men's Clubs
Cafés
Danceclubs
Restaurants
Shows
Cinema
▼
Sex Shops/Blue Movies
Cinemas
Escorts & Studios
House of Boys
▼
Saunas/Baths
Fitness Studios
Massage
▼
Shopping/Services
▼
Hotels
Guest Houses
Apartments
Private Accommodation
▼
Groups
▼
Swimming
Cruising

Veuillez utiliser le coupon-réponse (sans frais de port) disponible en fin de guide pour nous indiquer tous les changements que vous noterez au cours de vos voyages. Essayez d'être le plus complet possible dans vos indications. Nous seronts ravis de recevoir toute information qui n'apparaît pas dans cette édition de SPARTACUS :

Bruno Gmünder Verlag GmbH • SPARTACUS-Redaktion
Kleiststrasse 23-26 • 10787 Berlin • GERMANY
info@spartacus.de

Signification des codes

Les codes SPARTACUS signifient (les codes en minuscule impliquent une limitation) :

!	Un must
AC	Climatisation
AK	Croix de saint andré
AYOR	À vos risques et périls dangereux ou contrôles fréquents de la police
B	Bar avec boissons alcoolisées
BF	Petit déjeuner complet
CC	Principales cartes de crédit acceptées
D	Discothèque
DM	Plats du jour
DR	Darkroom
DU	Douche
F	Fétichiste (cuir, latex ou uniformes)
FC	Preservatifs gratuits
FH	2ieme serviette gratuite
G	Clientèle majoritairement gaie
GH	Glory holes
GLM	Clientèle majoritairement gaie et lesbienne
H	Hôtel / lieu d'hébergement où les gais sont bienvenus
I	Internet
LAB	Labyrinthe
LM	Musique live
M	Restauration / repas servis
MA	Tous âges
MC	Gais d'âge moyen (30 – 50 ans)
MSG	Massage possible
NG	Pas forcément gai mais intéressant
NR	Coin non-fumer
NU	Nudisme possible
OC	Gais plutôt âgés (+ 50 ans)
OS	Plein air, terrasse ou jardin
P	Club privé ou contrôle strict à l'entrée
p	Il faut sonner
PA	Animaux domestiques bienvenus
PI	Piscine
PK	Parking
PP	Bassin refroidissement
R	Fréquenté aussi par des gigolos
RES	Réservation nécessaire
RR	Salle repos
RWB	Tout les chambres ont balcon
RWS	Tout les chambres avec salle de bain/douche
RWT	Tout les chambres ont télévision
S	Spectacle ou autre manifestation
SA	Sauna finlandais
SB	Bain turc, hammam
SH	Boutique
SL	Sling
SNU	Strip-tease
SOL	Solarium
ST	Spectacle de transformisme
T	Fréquenté aussi par des travestis/transsexuels
VA	Visites autorisées
VEG	Plats végétariens aussi proposés
VR	Salle video
VS	Projection de vidéos
W	Accès handicapés
WE	fréquenté plutôt le week-end
WH	jacuzzi / bain à tourbillons
WI	WiFi gratuite
WL	carte des vins
WO	musculation possible
YC	clientèle jeune (18-28 ans)

Cette codes sont disponibles sous la forme d'un signet détachable en fin de livre.

1. Introduction

Les gays sont vraisemblablement les champions du voyage – pour les vacances ou pour les affaires. Quand on se rend dans un pays étranger, il faut bien entendu respecter les traditions du pays, mais aussi faire attention à d'éventuels risques concernant sa santé. Les règles valables à la maison sont à suivre aussi à l'étranger, mais elles doivent parfois être renforcées et ce, que l'on soit séropositif ou séronégatif. Avec la menace d'une infection par le VIH, les autres maladies sexuellement transmissibles (MST) ont été reléguées au second plan voire même ignorées. C'est la raison pour laquelle le nombre d'infections a fortement augmenté dans la seconde moitié des années 90. Les gays jouissent désormais d'une grande liberté sexuelle, mais ne doivent pas oublier qu'ils sont responsables non seulement de leur santé mais également de celle de leurs partenaires. Grâce aux rapides progrès de la médecine, une infection au VIH n'est plus automatiquement synonyme de mort et elle est devenue une maladie chronique soignable bien que toujours incurable. Les patients qui autrefois se battaient encore pour leur survie vont aujourd'hui bien et peuvent presque sans soucis partir en vacances à l'étranger.

2. Les voyages

Dans la plupart des pays industrialisés, nous sommes habitués à recevoir des soins médicaux presque gratuits. A l'étranger, il se peut que vous deviez les payer avant d'être remboursé, en totalité ou partiellement, dans votre pays d'origine par votre sécurité sociale, mutuelle ou assurance voyages (souvent couverte par votre agence de carte de crédit). Si vous êtes ressortissant de l'Union Européenne et que vous voyagez dans un autre pays de l'Union ou en Suisse, vous jouissez en cas de problème inopiné de la couverture sociale locale en présentant votre carte d'assuré social européenne (qui se trouve au dos de votre carte d'assuré social ou que vous pouvez retirer auprès de votre assurance).

Les vaccinations (par exemple contre l'hépatite A et B) et les traitements prophylactiques (par exemple contre la malaria) permettent de se protéger contre nombre de maladies infectieuses. Outre les vaccinations d'usage dans votre pays d'origine, certaines peuvent s'y ajouter avant le départ et d'autres sont même obligatoires. Renseignez-vous auprès de votre médecin.

Pour les séropositifs, les vaccins antigènes tués ou inactivés peuvent être utilisés sans problème, mis à part pour les patients avec un taux de CD4 est inférieur à 200/ml où la réaction peut être insuffisante. Les vaccins vivants atténués conseillés dans certains pays, comme celui contre la fièvre jaune, ne peuvent être faits qu'après un examen attentif du risque éventuel et ne sont en général possibles que dans le cas d'un taux de CD4 supérieur à 400/ml.

L'hygiène n'est pas aussi évidente à l'étranger que dans votre pays d'origine. Dans la plupart des pays du tiers-monde, mais éventuellement dans certains pays européens, il ne faut pas boire d'eau du robinet ! Seule l'eau bouillie ou filtrée et l'eau en bouteille avec sa capsule d'origine peuvent être consommées. Même un glaçon dans un cocktail peut être un problème. Pour la nourriture, on ne doit consommer que ce qui est bien cuit et les fruits à peler hygiéniquement (comme les bananes, les oranges, etc.). Le reste (comme les salades, le sauces, les crèmes, les plats d'œufs, etc.) est potentiellement dangereux. N'oubliez pas d'emporter une pharmacie de voyage contenant les médicaments, pansements et bandages nécessaires, si possible en nombre suffisant voire en plus grand nombre, au cas où vous perdriez quelques pilules (pour toute information consultez le site http://www.pharnet.com/public/pharmacie/pharma_voyage.htm ou votre médecin). Emportez également le mode d'emploi qui contient la liste des différents agents actifs (le nom d'un médicament varie parfois d'un pays à l'autre) ainsi qu'une photocopie de l'ordonnance de votre médecin et éventuellement des seringues et des canules. Pensez au décalage horaire pour la prise de vos médicaments.

Le conseil de l'expert : dans certains pays, il est recommandé d'emporter une attestation médicale contenant le nom et la description des médicaments, mais un diagnostic n'est pas absolument nécessaire.

La législation peut différer d'un pays à l'autre. Renseignez-vous avant de partir sur les formalités douanières et d'entrée auprès de votre ministère des affaires étrangères, de l'ambassade ou du consulat du pays correspondant.

N'oubliez pas également que certaines substances doivent être conservées dans le réfrigérateur, d'autres en dessous de 30°C et au sec. Dans de nombreux pays du tiers-monde, il n'est toujours pas évident de soigner les plaies avec du matériel stérile ou de pratiquer un injection avec du matériel jetable, il vaut donc mieux l'emporter soi-même si le séjour est long.

Il faut absolument utiliser une crème solaire à indice élevé et renoncer au bain de soleil dans les pays du sud entre midi et 15 heures sans protection pour éviter tout risque de cancer de la peau et d'affaiblissement temporaire du système immunitaire (chute possible du taux de CD4 pour les séropositifs).

Les préservatifs et le lubrifiant ne sont pas toujours de bonne qualité, prenez donc les vôtres !

3. Transmission du VIH

Le VIH se transmet par contact de liquide corporel infecté (par exemple sperme, sang, sécrétions vaginales) avec les muqueuses (anales, vaginales, buccales ou conjonctives) ou une plaie externe (piqûre, coupure ou éraflure).

Un risque d'infection est présent en cas de :

- rapport anal non protégé pour le partenaire actif et pour le partenaire passif
- rapport vaginal non protégé pour l'homme et la femme
- rapport oral non protégé avec éjaculation dans la bouche du partenaire actif
- fist fucking (introduction dans l'anus d'un ou plusieurs doigts ou du poing) sans gant en caoutchouc, en cas de saignement de la main ou d'hémorragie intestinale

Le conseil de l'expert : de nombreux spécialistes du sida pensent que le liquide pré-éjaculatoire peut être pour le partenaire pratiquant la fellation un risque de contamination dans des cas bien précis (une autre MST dont le germe est présent dans l'urètre ainsi qu'une concentration virale importante).

Il n'existe pas de risque de transmission connue en cas de :

- **contact avec la salive, les larmes, la transpiration,** l'urine ou les excréments
- contact social comme serrer la main, utiliser les mêmes verres, couverts, toilettes, à la piscine et au sauna
- contact aérien comme la respiration, l'éternuement, la toux
- piqûre ou morsure d'insecte.

Pour réduire le risque d'infection au VIH, il faut absolument pratiquer le safer sex (sexe sûr) et :

- utiliser lors du rapport vaginal et anal des préservatifs et suffisamment de lubrifiant à base d'eau, les crèmes grasses pouvant détériorer le préservatif. S'il y a rapport sexuel avec plusieurs partenaires, il faut utiliser un nouveau préservatif à chaque changement de partenaire. Les préservatifs peuvent limiter le risque de transmission d'autres MST.

- Pour la fellation, il ne faut en aucun cas éjaculer dans la bouche du partenaire. Cette mesure ne protège en revanche pas des autres MST comme la blennorragie, la syphilis ou l'hépatite. Contre les MST et le VIH (risque mineur en cas de contact avec le liquide pré-éjaculatoire) il faut utiliser un préservatif.
- Pour le fist-fucking, il faut obligatoirement utiliser des gants en caoutchouc.
- Si vous utilisez des drogues intraveineuses, chaque utilisateur doit avoir son matériel personnel (seringue, aiguille, liquide de nettoyage)

Le conseil de l'expert : il a été entre-temps démontré que les personnes déjà séropositives peuvent être réinfectées par des virus éventuellement résistents. C'est pourquoi les séropositifs ne devraient pas renoncer au safer sex !

En cas de risque d'infection, il est possible de laver la zone de contact (plaie ou muqueuse) avec de l'eau et du savon ou un désinfectant (un lavement étant à éviter) ainsi qu'une thérapie prophylactique (prophylaxie post-exposition = PPE) dans les heures qui suivent l'exposition au virus. Ces mesures ne peuvent que réduire et non empêcher le risque d'infection et ne sauraient remplacer le safer sex ! Pour plus d'informations, consultez un centre de traitement du VIH.
Depuis quelques temps certaines personnes recommandent une thérapie contre le VIH « à titre préventif » avant un possible risque d'infection. Pratiquement tous les experts déconseillent ces prophylaxies pré-exposition. Non seulement parce que le financement est tout à fait incertain (les coûts s'élèveraient à plus de 1000 € par mois) mais aussi parce que la certitude de telles mesures reste douteuse et incomparable aux mesures de préventions traditionnelles. La prophylaxie pré-exposition n'est judicieuse que dans un nombre restreint de cas.
Chez de nombreux patients, une infection de type grippal apparaît quelques semaines après la contamination au VIH (accompagnée éventuellement de fièvre, fatigue, réaction cutanée, douleurs articulaires et musculaires, inflammation des ganglions lymphatiques). Si ces signes apparaissent, contactez absolument un spécialiste qui pourra prendre les mesures nécessaires.

Après cette phase, les virus peuvent se répandre dans tout le corps et affaiblir le système immunitaire jusqu'à sa complète destruction après plusieurs années sans traitement ; des maladies bactériennes, virales ou des mycoses viennent alors s'y ajouter. On parle alors de sida (syndrome de l'immunodéficience acquise). Grâce aux grands progrès des thérapies, le sida est, dans les pays occidentaux, heureusement devenu rare, mais ceci ne devrait pas faire oublier qu'il n'y a pas ou pas suffisamment de traitement dans les pays du tiers-monde et que le sida reste la cause de mortalité numéro 1 chez les jeunes adultes.
Pour traiter au mieux une infection au VIH, il faut être dépisté assez tôt grâce à des tests qui mettent en évidence les anti-corps que le corps produit après un contact au VIH. La production d'anti-corps dure quelque semaines et un test est ainsi fiable après 12 semaines au moins après le risque d'infection. Depuis quelques années, il existe aussi un test détectant directement le virus à l'aide de la méthode PCR. Ce dépistage est possible 14 jours après le risque potentiel, mais il est plus cher que le premier et n'est donc utilisé que dans des cas précis.

Dans beaucoup de pays, le « test rapide » est déjà autorisé. Celui-ci dépiste les anticorps contre le VIH, avec la même certitude que le test classique aux anticorps VIH, et n'est pertinent de ce fait qu'au moins 12 semaines après une exposition à risque.
Un test positif doit être vérifié comme le test classique au moyen d'un test de confirmation (Test Western Blot). L'avantage du test rapide est qu'un laboratoire n'est pas nécessaire et que le résultat est disponible dans les 15-20 minutes. Malgré une manipulation facile, ce test VIH doit être réalisé par du personnel compétent.
Information supplémentaire: Il est désormais prouvé qu'une thérapie contre le VIH efficace qui maintenient la charge virale en-dessous du seuil de détection permet de limiter fortement le risque d'infection. Pour cette raison entre autres, la thérapie anti-virale débute plus tôt dans certains centres de traitement. En combinaison du safer-sex, on peut ainsi diminuer la propagation du VIH. Aussi pour éviter d'autres infections sexuellement transmissibles, l'utilisation du préservatif reste indispensable.

4. MST – maladies sexuellement transmissibles

Les MST sont des maladies infectieuses provoquées par plus de 20 agents pathologiques différents (bactéries, virus, champignons, protozoaires et parasites) en premier lieu lors d'un rapport sexuel mais dans certains cas lors d'un contact corporel étroit. Les symptômes sont localisés essentiellement, mais pas uniquement, sur les parties génitales. Ces dernières années, ces maladies infectieuses ont augmenté de façon sensible. Il existe des vaccins contre certaines d'entre elles (hépatite A et B), d'autres sont traitées par voie médicamenteuse (substances antibiotiques, antimycosiques et antivirales) d'autres enfin par voie chirurgicale (condylomes).

En cas de symptômes suivants, il faut absolument consulter un médecin :

- liquide purulent s'échappant de l'urètre ou de l'anus
- rougeur ou dépôt blanc dans les parties buccale, génitale ou anale
- ulcères sur la peau ou les muqueuses, vésicules dans les parties buccale, génitale ou anale
- forte démangeaison dans les parties génitale ou anale
- ganglions enflés et/ou douloureux
- jaunissement des yeux et de la peau

Nous allons maintenant nous pencher sur quelques maladies sexuellement transmissibles les plus fréquentes en insistant particulièrement sur la prévention et les symptômes.

La scabiose (gale)

Le sarcopte est un parasite mesurant 0,2 mm se transmettant par contact de la peau et qui provoque une démangeaison souvent insoutenable dans les régions touchées. La thérapie consiste en l'application d'une lotion antiparasitaire.

La syphilis (vérole)

La probabilité de se contaminer a fortement augmenté ces derniers temps !
Les bactéries responsables de l'infection se transmettent par contact de sécrétions infectées avec la peau (lèvres, pénis) ou les muqueuses (buccales, vaginales, péniennes). Le rapport sexuel oral, vaginal et anal ainsi que les baisers représentent ainsi un risque d'infection. La phase d'incubation s'élève à 2-4 semaines après laquelle apparaissent des plaies indolores sur la peau ou la muqueuse et une inflammation des

ganglions environnants dans le stade primaire qui disparaissent d'elles-mêmes après quelques semaines. Le dépistage de la syphilis s'effectue à l'aide d'un test sanguin et la thérapie consiste en l'administration d'un antibiotique.

Le conseil de l'expert : si aucun traitement n'est entrepris, le stade secondaire intervient quelques semaines plus tard (inflammation des ganglions, éruption cutanée, altération des muqueuses ou pertes de cheveux. Dans le stade tertiaire, la maladie peut entraîner une lésion de la peau, des os et du cerveau et ainsi, la mort.

La blennorragie (chaude pisse)

La blennorragie est la MST la plus fréquente et est en forte augmentation dans le milieu gay. Les bactéries responsables de l'infection se transmettent par contact de liquide purulent (sécrétion vaginale, séminale ou anale) avec les muqueuses péniennes, buccales, vaginales ou anales du partenaire. Les contacts oraux, vaginaux et anaux sont ainsi à risque. Après une phase d'incubation de 2 à 5 semaines, un liquide purulent s'échappe de l'urètre, accompagné d'une sensation de brûlure. En cas d'infection anale, le liquide s'échappe de l'anus, mais le patient peut ne ressent que des douleurs pelviennes. Le traitement est antibiotique.

Le conseil de l'expert : dans le milieu gay, l'infection touche le plus souvent la gorge après une fellation et passe souvent inaperçue.

L'herpès

Les virus de l'herpès se répandent par voie orale (boutons de fièvre), anale ou vaginale (herpès génital) par contact avec les muqueuses. L'infection est provoquée essentiellement par un affaiblissement du système immunitaire (par exemple une exposition aux UV ou le stress) et se manifeste par des démangeaisons, des vésicules douloureuses sur les lèvres, le nez ou les parties vaginales ou anales. Le traitement antiviral est local ou sous forme de pilules.

Hépatite

Les hépatites A et B sont rares. Les virus de type A sont présents dans les selles et contaminent ainsi l'eau et la nourriture et peuvent se répandre lors de contacts anaux. Les virus de type B sont présents dans le sang et les liquides corporels rendant une infection possible lors de baisers ou de contacts sexuels non protégés. Après contamination, une jaunisse apparaît fréquemment (jaunissement des yeux et de la peau) ainsi qu'une grande fatigue. Ces derniers temps on enregistre dans certaines grandes villes (en Europe: Berlin, Amsterdam et Londres) une augmentation des cas d'hépatite C dans la scène gay. La cause n'est malheureusement pas encore tout à fait résolue. Probablement le contact avec du sang ou des sécrétions corporelles pendant le fisting ou des pratiques SM ou encore des piercings récemment percés pourraient être responsables.

Il existe désormais des possibilités de traitements relativement efficaces contre les hépatites B et C, ceux-ci sont cependant longs et ont de nombreux effets secondaires. Pour cette raison la vaccination contre les hépatites A et B est fortement recommandée pour les personnes sexuellement actives. En l'absence d'un vaccin contre l'hépatite C, les contacts avec le sang et autres sécrétions corporelles du partenaire sont à éviter.

Les morpions

Le morpion est un insecte aptère mesurant 1 mm qui se transmet par contact corporel rapproché. Après quelques jours ou semaines, de petites rougeurs urticantes apparaissent dans la région pubienne et nécessite l'application d'une lotion antiparasitaire.

Le condylome (verrue génitale)

Les virus responsables des condylomes sont extrêmement fréquents dans le milieu gay (plus de 50%) et sont transmis par voie sexuelle mais aussi par contact indirect de la verrue avec la peau ou la muqueuse (doigt, godemiché). Après plusieurs mois ou années, de petites verrues apparaissent dans les parties anales et génitales. La longue thérapie consiste en l'application locale de substances chimiques, le renforcement du système immunitaire ou par voie chirurgicale.

Le conseil de l'expert : après plusieurs années sans traitement et chez les patients séropositifs, des carcinomes (cancer) peuvent se développer ! Il convient donc de se faire contrôler régulièrement !

Chlamydiose

La chlamydiose est transmise de la même façon que la gonorrhée (blennorragie): les relations sexuelles orales, anales ou vaginales présentent un risque. Les symptômes sont également similaires à ceux de la gonorrhée: l'écoulement de l'urètre est cependant plutôt vitreux et non pas purulent, et la sensation de brûlure de l'urètre est moins douloureuse.

Les infections de la gorge et du rectum restent souvent asymptomatiques et ne sont découvertes que par prélèvement sur la zone correspondante. Des antibiotiques sont aussi utilisées dans le traitement de la chlamydiose.

Malgré les risques médicaux qui peuvent survenir lors de voyage à l'étranger, une bonne préparation et un comportement raisonnable per mettent de passer un séjour agréable et de rentrer sain et reposé à la maison. Nous vous souhaitons un agréable voyage !

Dr Horst Schalk
Médecin généraliste, Vienne

Bienvenidos

Querido lector de Spartacus:

Está recibiendo en sus manos la edición número 41 de la guía de viajes gay más completa del mundo. Esto no es algo implícito, ya que en los tiempos que corren un libro ya no es algo moderno. Pensamos que, aunque no cuente con los adelantos de la técnica, a su vez, no se debe dejar de aprovechar las oportunidades que ofrece este tipo de medio. Es por esto que, a finales de 2011, decidimos desarrollar una aplicación de nuestra Spartacus para iPhone y ponerla a la venta. Además, también ofrecemos un nuevo sitio web con oportunidades de alojamiento. De ahora en adelante, usted puede buscar y reservar, en **www.spartacusworld.com**, alojamiento gay o gay friendly a nivel mundial.

Entre los eventos destacados para 2012 se distinguen, entre otros, la elección de Mr. Gay World en Johannesburgo, en el mes de abril, los EuroGames en Busdapest, a finales de junio, y el World Pride en Londres, a principios de julio.

Otro de los eventos destacados para muchos gays europeos es el Festival de la Canción de Eurovisión, que este año se celebrará en Bakú, Azerbaiyán, el 26 mayo. A través de nuestras intensivas investigaciones hemos concluido que no sólo se trata de un país hostil para los homosexuales, sino que también hay que advertir de manera urgente sobre la policía local. Evite entregar el pasaporte o el carnet de conducir, ya que podría costarle una fortuna recuperarlo. A pesar de todo esto, Bakú se presenta como una ciudad llena de encantos. Tan sólo nos queda esperar que este concurso mejore de alguna forma la situación del colectivo LGBT en este país.

Como siempre, puede encontrar una lista detallada con todos los eventos gays más relevantes a nivel mundial en nuestro calendario de eventos al final de nuestra guía de viajes y también en nuestro sitio web **www.spartacusworld.com**. Este calendario de eventos se actualiza y amplia continuamente.

En lo que a política se refiere, el pasado año 2011 cambió relativamente poco para la comunidad LGBT. El deterioro de la situación económica mundial ha traído consigo, a su vez, el deterioro de la situación para las minorías. Mientras lee estas líneas, esto está sucediendo en países como Hungría, Rusia y otros países de Europa del este, en donde el resurgimiento del nacionalismo es un hecho que no debe perderse de vista.

Con Spartacus, creemos que todo el mundo podrá encontrar su propio medio y que sabrá usarlo de la mejor manera. Ya sea como material de lectura en la playa o durante un viaje, contenido en el libro, en el iPhone o el portátil, en casa o mientras se desplaza; hay mucho que descubrir. En cualquier caso, la situación será siempre emocionante y esperamos que, para el próximo año, mantenga su curiosidad y sus ganas de viajar.

Briand Bedford
REDACTOR JEFE

Cómo usar el SPARTACUS 

Orden de los países

SPARTACUS se ha dividido por países enlistados alfabéticamente (siguiendo los nombres en inglés). Las islas y países del Caribe constituyen una excepción y se encuentran bajo la letra »C«. Todos los países están subdivididos por ciudades, indicadas en la lengua local e igualmente enlistadas alfabéticamente. En los casos de Australia, Canadá y Estados Unidos de América, los diferentes Estados o provincias figuran por alfabeto y están, a su vez, subdivididos por ciudades. En caso de no encontrar algo, puede consultarse el índice en la página 1106, donde los países y las ciudades se indican por orden alfabético en las cinco lenguas empleadas en la guía SPARTACUS: alemán, español, francés, inglés e italiano.
Como información específica sobre todos los países incluidos en la guía se explica, por ejemplo, la situación legal y social de los hombres gays, así como la edad de consentimiento para las relaciones sexuales. Además, ofrecemos información sobre festivales gays, acontecimientos especiales, etc.
Antes de la introducción a cada país, el lector encontrará la siguiente información:

Name: El nombre en la lengua local así como en las cinco lenguas empleadas en la guía SPARTACUS	➤	**Name:** Suid-Afrika • Südafrika • Afrique du Sud • Sudáfrica • Sud Africa
Location: ubicación geográfica	➤	**Location:** Southern Africa
Initials: indican la abreviatura usual del país	➤	**Initials:** ZA
Time: hace referencia al huso horario en que se encuentra el país	➤	**Time:** GMT +2
International Country Code: indica el prefijo telefónico empleado para llamar al país	➤	**International Country Code:** ☎ 27 (omit 0 of phone number)
International Access Code: indica el prefijo telefónico empleado para realizar llamadas internacionales desde el país	➤	**International Access Code:** ☎ 09 or 091
Language: indica la(s) lengua(s) más comunes habladas en el país	➤	**Language:** English, Afrikaans, African languages
Area: indica la superficie del país	➤	**Area:** 1,219,080 km² / 471,442 sq mi.
Currency: indica la moneda oficial aceptada en el país	➤	**Currency:** 1 Rand (ZAR) = 100 Cents
Population: el número de habitantes	➤	**Population:** 43,240,000
Capital: la ciudad capital del país	➤	**Capital:** Cape Town (legislative capital); Pretoria (administrative capital)
Religions: las religiones más importantes practicadas en el país	➤	**Religions:** 78% Christians
Climate: breve descripción del clima que se puede esperar a lo largo del año	➤	**Climate:** Ranging from hot and dry in summer to cold and wet in winter. Sub-tropical to Mediterranean climates.
Important Gay Cities: ciudades de especial interés para visitantes gays	➤	**Important gay cities:** Cape Town, Johannesburg

Orden de la información en los encabezados

Cada lista está constituida por el nombre ❶, los códigos SPARTACUS correspondientes ❷, los horarios de apertura ❸, la dirección ❹, el número de teléfono ❺, la dirección de correo electrónico ❻ y la dirección en internet ❼.

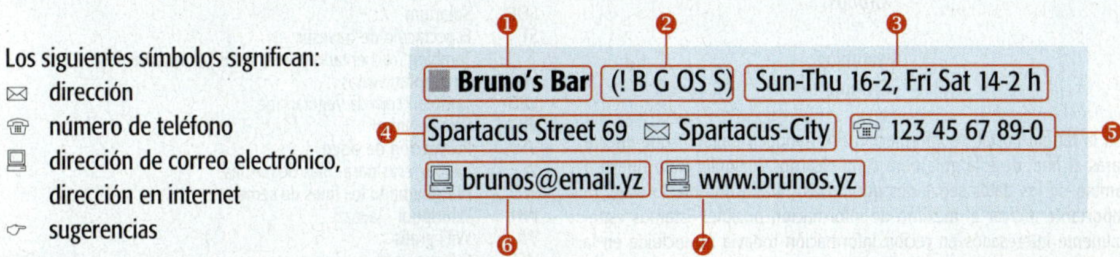

Los siguientes símbolos significan:

- ✉ dirección
- ☎ número de teléfono
- 💻 dirección de correo electrónico, dirección en internet
- ☞ sugerencias

■ Un cuadrado rojo al principio de la entrada de la dirección indica la publicidad de un cliente en la guía, en la aplicación o en el sitio web.

Cómo usar el SPARTACUS

Orden de los apartados

Bajo los encabezados de los países y de las ciudades, los títulos de las diferentes direcciones están ordenados de la siguiente manera:

National Gay Info
National Publications
National Publishers
National Companies
National Groups
National Helplines
Country Cruising
▼
Gay Info
Publications
Culture
Tourist Info
▼
Bars
Men's Clubs
Cafés
Danceclubs
Restaurants
Shows
Cinema
▼
Sex Shops/Blue Movies
Cinemas
Escorts & Studios
House of Boys
▼
Saunas/Baths
Fitness Studios
Massage
▼
Shopping/Services
▼
Hotels
Guest Houses
Apartments
Private Accommodation
▼
Groups
▼
Swimming
Cruising

Usa la tarjeta postal de información (de franqueo pagado) que encontrarás al final de esta guía para comunicarnos cualquier dato nuevo o cambio de los datos señalados que hayas notado durante tu viaje. Es importante indicar el máximo de información posible. Estamos especialmente interesados en recibir información todavía no incluida en la presente edición de la guía SPARTACUS.

Bruno Gmünder Verlag GmbH · SPARTACUS-Redaktion
Kleiststrasse 23-26 · 10787 Berlin · GERMANY
info@spartacus.de

Descripción de los códigos

Los códigos de SPARTACUS significan lo siguiente (Los códigos en letras minúsculas suelen implicar una restricción):

!	Especialmente recomendable
AC	Aire acondicionado
AK	Cruz San Andrés
AYOR	A su propio riesgo. Peligro de ser atacado o de actividades de la policía
B	Bar con oferta amplia de bedibas
BF	Desayuno tipo buffet
CC	Se acepta la mayoria de las tarjetas de crédito
D	Bailar / discoteca
DM	Menú de día
DR	Cuarto oscuro / sala oscura
DU	Ducha
F	Fetichismo (cuero, látex, uniformes)
FC	Preservativos gratuitos
FH	2a toalla gratis
G	Exclusivamente o casi exclusivamente público gay
GH	Glory Holes
GLM	Público gay y lesbiano mezclado
H	Hotel o tipo parecido de alojamiento donde se recibe bien a los gays
I	Internet
LAB	Labirinto
LM	Música en directo
M	Comida. Disponibilidad de menús completos
MA	Edades mixtas
MC	Clientes de edades medias (de 30 a 50 años)
MSG	Masajes
NG	No es gay pero posiblemente de interés para gays
NR	Zona para no fumadores
NU	Nudismo
OC	Clientes más bien mayores (+ 50 años)
OS	Terraza o jardín
P	Club privado o control estricto de acceso
p	Hay que tocar el timbre para entrar
PA	Se aceptan animales
PI	Piscina
PK	Plazas de parking
PP	Piscina para sumergirse
R	Bastante frecuentado por personas que ejercen la prostitución
RES	Se necesita reserva
RR	Sala de descanso
RWB	Habitación con balcón
RWS	Baño / ducha en la habitación
RWT	Habitación con televisión
S	Espectáculo / programa
SA	Sauna finlandesa
SB	Baño de vapor
SH	Tienda
SL	Sling
SNU	Espectáculos de striptease
SOL	Solarium
ST	Espectáculo de travestis
T	También frecuentado por travestis / transsexuales
VA	Se aceptan visitas
VEG	También comida vegetariana
VR	Sala de video
VS	Proyección de video
W	Sin barreras para sillas de ruedas
WE	Más animado los fines de semana
WH	Whirlpool / jacuzzi
WI	WiFi gratis
WL	Extensa carta de vinos
WO	Fisioculturismo / gimnasio
YC	Clientes jóvenes (18 a 29 años)

Los códigos de SPARTACUS también se encuentran impresos en el práctico separador que se encuentra al final del libro

1. Introducción

Los hombres gays son supuestamente los »campeones del mundo« en viajar, tanto si se trata de vacaciones como por motivos profesionales. Cuando se viaja a otros países, se deberían respetar no sólo las costumbres del país sino también tener en cuenta que un ambiente desconocido puede suponer riesgos para la salud. Además de las normas que se observarían en nuestro país, estando fuera deberían respetarse precisamente normas de comportamiento complementarias, independientemente de si uno es seropositivo o no.
A la sombra de las amenazantes infecciones del VIH, no se ha prestado demasiada atención a otras enfermedades de transmisión sexual (ETS). Por este motivo, se produjo en la segunda mitad de los años 90 un dramático aumento de estas enfermedades infecciosas en los países occidentales. Los gays que, con todo derecho, se toman la libertad de vivir su sexualidad de forma libre y sin prejuicios religiosos o morales, también tienen una responsabilidad, tanto hacia ellos mismos como hacia la salud de sus respectivos compañeros.
Las infecciones del VIH en los últimos años, gracias al rápido avance en la medicina, han pasado de ser una enfermedad mortal a una enfermedad crónica con un buen tratamiento, pero en ningún caso con curación. Aquellos pacientes que antes luchaban para sobrevivir, ahora les va en general mejor y algunos, afortunadamente, cuentan incluso con la posibilidad de pasar sus vacaciones en el extranjero casi sin riesgo.

2. Viajar

En la mayoría de los países desarrollados estamos acostumbrados a recibir prestaciones médicas más o menos a »bajo costo«. Por favor, tenga en cuenta que en el extranjero no dispone automáticamente de un seguro médico, lo que significa que normalmente primero debe abonarse dicha prestación médica y posteriormente, a la vuelta, le será reembolsado total o parcialmente por su seguro social, privado o asistencia en viaje (a menudo figura como servicio adjunto a su tarjeta de crédito, infórmese antes de las prestaciones) . Si viaja como ciudadano de la Unión Europea a otro país de la Unión, disfrutará, mediante presentación de su tarjeta de la seguridad social, en todos los estados de la Unión y en Suiza de cobertura médica para prestaciones de urgencia (aquéllas que recibiría como portador de la tarjeta de la seguridad social o bien aquéllas que se encuentran indicadas al dorso de su tarjeta de la seguridad social).
Las vacunaciones (por ejemplo contra la hepatitis A y B) y otros profilácticos (como contra la malaria) le ofrecen una alta protección contra muchas de las enfermedades infecciosas. Además de las vacunaciones recomendadas por su país, en muchos otros países se recomiendan o incluso están prescritas las llamadas vacunas de viaje. Su médico le informará de ello.
Los seropositivos pueden recibir todas aquellas vacunas que se realicen con virus muertos causantes de la enfermedad cuyas partes contengan débiles toxinas; aquí hablaríamos de las llamadas dosis de vacunación muerta. Cuando el sistema inmunológico se encuentra muy debilitado (células CD4 por debajo de 200/ml), se puede llegar sólo a un nivel insuficiente de protección con vacunas. Las vacunaciones que suponen una inyección en baja cantidad de virus vivos inactivos causantes de la enfermedad (como por ejemplo la vacunación contra la fiebre amarilla, obligatoria en algunos países) sólo son posibles, en los seropositivos, bajo una estricta valoración del riesgo-beneficio y en general sólo con un buen estado de defensas (células CD4 por encima de 400/ml).

La higiene no se percibe en todos los países de la misma manera como puede ser en su país. Generalmente, en la mayoría de países del Tercer Mundo y también en algunos países europeos, rige el principio: ¡no beber agua del grifo! Sólo beber agua hervida y filtrada o bien agua mineral correctamente embotellada. Los cubitos de hielo en los cócteles pueden ser teóricamente problemáticos. Para las comidas rige el fácil principio: "cook it, boil it, peal it or leave it«, en español: comer sólo lo cocinado, hervido o fruta que se pele (por ejemplo, plátanos, naranjas o piña que pele usted mismo) Todo lo demás puede conllevar peligro (por ejemplo, ensaladas, salsas, cremas, etc.) y debe evitarse.
En cualquier caso piense en un botiquín de viaje, en el que debería poner los medicamentos necesarios, como aquellos para posibles diarreas y vendajes. En caso de duda, consulte a un médico.
Si toma medicación regularmente, llévese en cualquier caso medicamentos para algunos días de más para eventualidades de que se pudiera retrasar la vuelta por motivos inesperados o que perdiera algunas pastillas. Llévese los medicamentos con su envoltura original junto con el prospecto (dentro está la composición química del medicamento, pues en muchos países los medicamentos tienen nombres diferentes), así como eventualmente también una copia de la receta o las inyecciones o aplicadores necesarios. Tenga en cuenta la posible diferencia de horario y planifique la toma de la medicación.

Consejo de experto: para los viajes a algunos países se recomienda llevar un informe médico en el que figure el nombre y una breve descripción del medicamento (si se trata, por ejemplo, de pastillas o cápsulas). El diagnóstico no debe especificarse.
Las legislaciones y reglamentos internacionales pueden ser muy diferentes. Si viaja al extranjero, infórmese por favor de las normas de entrada y aduana. Estas informaciones pueden adquirirse telefónicamente o en la página web de su Ministerio de Exteriores o de la embajada o consulado del país que corresponda.

Por favor tenga en cuenta que algunas sustancias deben mantenerse en el frigorífico y otras al menos a una temperatura de ambiente seco, pero nunca a más de 30°C. En muchos países del Tercer Mundo, hoy en día desgraciadamente no se utiliza todavía material nuevo y esterilizado para la cura de heridas o en las inyecciones. En los viajes a estos países se recomienda llevarlo uno mismo consigo, especialmente en estancias largas.
En ningún caso debe olvidarse la suficiente crema solar con un alto factor de protección. En los países tropicales, no se recomienda una exposición a pleno sol sin protección entre las 12h. y las 15h. debido al peligro de aparición de tumores en la piel y al grave perjuicio al sistema de defensas (posible pérdida de células CD4 en los seropositivos).
Por cierto: los preservativos y el lubricante no son de la misma calidad a la que estamos acostumbrados.

3. Infección del VIH

La infección del VIH sólo puede ser transmitida cuando los virus de VIH llegan al cuerpo humano. Esto se produce cuando flujos infectados como por ejemplo esperma, flujo vaginal o sangre llegan a las mucosas intactas o heridas (mucosa anal, rectal, vaginal o bucal o en la conjuntiva de los ojos) o en la piel recién lesionada (cortes, heridas punzantes o profundas).

Existe riesgo de infección en caso de:

- sexo anal sin protección, tanto para la parte activa como pasiva
- sexo vaginal sin protección, tanto para la mujer como para el hombre
- sexo oral sin protección para la parte activa (»el que chupa«) si el semen llega a la boca
- introducción de dedos o puño en el recto (»fisting«) sin un guante de plástico, cuando se produjeran heridas en la parte rectal o en las manos.

Consejo de experto: muchos expertos del VIH opinan que el líquido preseminal que sueltan muchos hombres antes del orgasmo y que en el sexo oral puede alcanzar la mucosa bucal, en algunas circunstancias determinadas, puede representar un riesgo reducido de infección (existencia anterior de otra enfermedad de transmisión sexual procedente de la uretra que pueda contener a su vez un alto concentrado del VIH).

No supone ningún riesgo de infección del VIH en caso de:

- contacto con la saliva, lágrimas, sudor, orina o defecaciones.
- todos los contactos sociales imaginables como darse la mano, el uso común de vasos, cubiertos, aseos, piscinas o saunas no representan ningún peligro
- también, gracias a los datos actuales, se excluye cualquier infección por la respiración, estornudos, toses o picaduras de insectos!

Para poder reducir el riesgo de infección del VIH, debe practicarse siempre el sexo seguro y

- en el sexo anal y vaginal utilizar preservativos y suficiente lubricante (hidrosoluble o de base acuosa). Las cremas con grasas dañan el preservativo. En el sexo con más de una persona a la vez, se debe cambiar también el preservativo. Los preservativos también pueden reducir el riesgo de transmitir otras enfermedades sexuales.
- en el sexo oral nunca eyacular en la boca de la otra persona. Esta medida no es suficiente para evitar otras enfermedades de transmisión sexual (como la gonorrea, la sífilis o la hepatitis). Quien quiera evitar la transmisión de estas enfermedades o también el mencionado riesgo mínimo de transmisión del VIH en el líquido preseminal, debería utilizar un preservativo para el sexo oral.
- en la introducción de dedos o puño (»fisting«) utilizar siempre un guante de plástico.
- si consume drogas por vía intravenosa, cada uno debe utilizar sus propios utensilios (jeringuilla, aguja, líquido de lavado).

Consejo de experto: entretanto, se conoce que entre los infectados por el VIH puede llegarse a una nueva infección con virus VIH más resistentes. Esto puede perjudicar el buen curso de una terapia anti-VIH, incluso inutilizarla o bien dificultar extremadamente un futuro comienzo de una terapia. Por ello, ¡los seropositivos no deben renunciar tampoco al sexo seguro!

En caso de riesgo de infección, existe la posibilidad de reducir la probabilidad de transmisión a través de un inmediato lavado de las partes en contacto (heridas cutáneas o mucosas) con agua y jabón o, si se encuentra disponible, con desinfectante (una limpieza de la zona rectal no tiene sentido) así como a través de la rápida toma preventiva de la terapia anti-VIH (en pocas horas), basada en profilácticos post-exposición. Esta medida sólo puede reducir el riesgo de infección pero nunca evitarlo y por tanto ¡no sustituye al sexo seguro! Para una información más detallada, puede dirigirse a un centro de información del VIH.
Desde hace algún tiempo, surge de manera reiterada, por parte de pocas fuentes, la recomendación de comenzar una terapia "preventiva" contra el VIH en caso de una posible infección. Prácticamente todos los expertos en VIH desaconsejan esta conocida como profilaxis preexposición (PPrE). No sólo se desconoce completamente la forma de financiación (se estima que los costes mensuales ascienden a más de 1000 €), sino que la seguridad de esta medida es más que cuestionable, además, no es comparable, en ningún caso, con las medidas de protección tradicionales. El uso de la profilaxis preexposición (PPrE) sólo puede aplicarse en muy pocos casos excepcionales.
En muchos pacientes, al cabo de pocas semanas de una infección del VIH aparece a menudo una enfermedad similar a la gripe en 10 o 14 días. Entre otras, puede ocasionar fiebre, fatiga, erupciones cutáneas, dolores musculares así como inflamación de los ganglios linfáticos. Si aparecieran estas circunstancias tras un posible riesgo de infección, debe consultar sin falta un especialista en VIH para que pueda tomar las medidas pertinentes. Después de esta fase, los virus se pueden extender por todo el cuerpo y dañar especialmente el sistema inmunológico. En casos de largas infecciones sin tratamiento se puede producir la destrucción del sistema imunólogico y dar lugar a otros causantes de enfermedades como bacterias, virus u hongos que pueden ocasionar infecciones mortales, entonces hablamos claramente del SIDA (Síndrome de Inmuno Deficiencia Adquirida = Acquired Immuno Deficiency Syndrome). Actualmente, el SIDA en los países occidentales aparece afortunadamente en menos casos debido al gran éxito de las terapias anti-VIH. Sin embargo no debe olvidarse nunca que en la mayoría de países del Tercer Mundo estas terapias no existen o sólo están disponibles de manera muy insuficiente y, por ello, el SIDA continúa siendo la causa de muerte número uno entre los jóvenes.

Para poder tratar mejor la infección del VIH, debe ser diagnosticada a tiempo. Esto se realiza en general a través del test VIH. Éste muestra proteínas especiales, los llamados anticuerpos, que el ser humano fabrica cuando entra en contacto con el VIH. La formación de estos anticuerpos tarda algunas semanas, de tal modo que el test debe realizarse como mínimo 12 semanas después del riesgo de infección. Desde hace algún tiempo, existe sin embargo otro procedimiento de análisis: éste comprueba directamente la existencia del VIH a través del llamado método PCR. Esta prueba de la infección es normalmente válida al cabo de 14 días después del riesgo potencial de infección, no obstante, es principalmente mucho más caro que el test de los anticuerpos y por ello se utiliza sólo en casos especiales.

En muchos países ya está aprobada desde hace algún tiempo la conocida como "prueba rápida". Esta comprueba – con la misma eficacia y seguridad que la prueba clásica de anticuerpos del VIH - la existencia de anticuerpos contra el VIH y es por lo tanto de valor informativo 12 semanas después de un riesgo significativo de infección. Un resultado positivo de esta prueba, al igual que pasa con la prueba clásica de anticuerpos del VIH, debe ser verificada por una prueba confirmatoria (test de Western Blot). La ventaja de las pruebas rápidas es que no se necesitan trabajos de laboratorio y es por esto que los resultados están listos en 15 o 20 minutos. A pesar de la facilidad de uso que ofrece este tipo prueba del VIH esta debe ser realizada por un experto.

Información adicional: mientras, tanto se considera también que un tratamiento óptimo contra el VIH, en el que la carga viral se encuentre por debajo del límite de detección, puede reducir el riesgo de infección por VIH de forma radical. Es en parte por este motivo que algunos centros de tratamiento comienzan la terapia contra el VIH antes de lo que se hacía anteriormente. En combinación con prácticas de sexo seguro se puede reducir también de esta manera la propagación del VIH. También para evitar el contagio de otras enfermedades de transmisión sexual debe mantenerse el uso de preservativos como un acto al que no se debe renunciar bajo ninguna circunstancia.

4. ETS – Enfermedades de Transmisión Sexual

Las ETS son enfermedades infecciosas causadas por al menos 20 elementos diferentes (bacterias, virus, hongos, microbios y parásitos) que pueden transmitirse en primer lugar a través de las relaciones sexuales pero también, en algunos casos, por un estrecho contacto corporal. Los síntomas de la enfermedad aparecen principalmente en los genitales pero no exclusivamente. En los últimos años, se produjo un dramático aumento de estas enfermedades infecciosas. Para algunas existen vacunaciones (hepatitis A y B), otras se tratan con medicamentos (antibióticos para las infecciones bacteriológicas, antimicóticos para infecciones fungosas y sustancias retrovirales para infecciones víricas) y otras con cirugía (condilomas).

En los siguientes síntomas (dolores) debe consultarse a un médico:

- secreciones de la uretra o del ano
- irritaciones o una capa blanca en la boca, genitales o ano

- úlceras (infecciones en la piel o las mucosas), vesículas en la boca, ganglios, en los genitales o el ano.
- fuerte escozor en la zona genital o anal
- dolores o inflamaciones de los ganglios linfáticos
- color amarillento en la piel y los ojos

A continuación hablaremos de las enfermedades de transmisión sexual más comunes. Se van a considerar especialmente las vías de infección (prevención) y sus síntomas (rápido diagnóstico).

Sarna

La sarna es un parásito vivo de unos 0,2 mm extendido por todo el mundo, que vive en la piel, puede transmitirse mediante el contacto corporal y ocasiona una fuerte e insoportable comezón en la zona de piel afectada. La terapia se basa en la aplicación de una loción antiparasitaria

Ladillas

La ladilla es un insecto sin alas de 1 mm aproximadamente y se transmite por el contacto corporal. Después de unos días o semanas, aparecen en la zona del pubis unas pequeñas manchas rojas que pican. Como en la sarna, se aplicará una loción antiparasitaria.

Sífilis

La posibilidad de infectarse ha aumentado bastante últimamente, isobre todo en el ambiente gay!

Los causantes son unas bacterias y se transmiten mediante flujos corporales infectados (secreciones) que entran en contacto con la piel mayoritariamente dañada (labios o prepucio) o con la mucosa (boca, pene, vagina). Tanto las prácticas de sexo vaginal, oral o anal como también los besos representan un riesgo de infección. El tiempo de incubación (tiempo que media entre la infección y la enfermedad) es de unas 2-4 semanas. Entonces aparecen, en un llamado estado primario, úlceras poco dolorosas (infecciones de la piel o las mucosas) y inflamaciones de los ganglios linfáticos regionales (contiguos), que después de algunas semanas pueden cicatrizar espontáneamente.

La confirmación de la sífilis se consigue a través de un análisis de sangre, la terapia se basa en la toma de antibióticos.

Consejo de experto: Si no se procede a un tratamiento, en un estado secundario, aparecen en unas semanas inflamaciones de los ganglios linfáticos, erupciones cutáneas, cambio de las mucosas o caída del cabello. En un estado terciario posterior, puede llegar al cabo de unos años a afectar la piel, los huesos así como el cerebro y suponer la muerte.

Gonorrea

La gonorrea es la enfermedad venérea más común y aumenta de forma masiva en el ambiente homosexual.

Como en la sífilis, los causantes son bacterias que se transmiten a través de secreciones purulentas (secreciones seminales, vaginales o anales), que entran en contacto con la mucosa de la otra persona (pene, boca, recto, vagina). Por ello, el sexo oral, anal y vaginal suponen un riesgo. Después de un tiempo de incubación de unos 2-5 días, aparecen supuraciones y escozores al orinar. Cuando la infección se produce en el ano, conlleva supuraciones pero a menudo sólo dolores intestinales indeterminados. La terapia se basa en la toma de antibióticos.

Consejo de experto: La vía de infección más común en el ambiente gay es la gonorrea en la garganta, que frecuentemente aparece sin dolor, y se transmite durante el sexo oral a la uretra del otro.

Herpes

Los virus del herpes se propagan mediante infecciones de las mucosas en el cuerpo de la otra parte a través de los besos, el sexo oral, anal o vaginal (herpes genital). Si se produce la infección, pueden comportar la formación de vesículas dolorosas y escozores en la zona afectada (labios, nariz, genitales o ano), principalmente a causa de situaciones que debiliten el sistema inmunológico como por ejemplo fiebre, rayos ultravioleta o estrés. Para el tratamiento de los herpes, existen sustancias antivirales que se aplican localmente o bien por la vía oral.

Hepatitis

Los virus de la hepatitis A y B se presentan en todo el mundo. El virus de la hepatitis A se transmite por vía fecal-oral, por lo que tanto el agua o la comida infectada como las prácticas de sexo anal suponen un riesgo de infección. El virus de la hepatitis B se transmiten a través de la sangre y en casi todas las prácticas sexuales (anal, oral y vaginal) así como a través de los besos (iel sexo seguro no protege!). Si se produce la infección, aparece mayoritariamente una ictericia (color amarillento de la piel y los ojos) así como cansancio.

Últimamente algunas grandes ciudades (en Europa: Berlín, Ámsterdam y Londres) han registrado un aumento en los casos de Hepatitis C dentro del ambiente gay. Lamentablemente, la causa de este aumento aún no ha sido determinada. Esto probablemente se deba a los intercambios de sangre o fluidos corporales que tienen lugar al hacer fisting, durante prácticas masoquistas o al hacer piercings.

Entretanto, existen opciones de tratamiento relativamente buenas para la hepatitis B y C, pero estas son molestas y con muchos efectos secundarios. Por esta razón se recomienda la vacunación contra la hepatitis A y B para todas las personas sexualmente activas. Desafortunadamente, no existe una vacuna contra la Hepatitis C, por ello, la única forma de protección es evitar el contacto con la sangre y otros fluidos corporales de la pareja.

Condiloma

Los virus del papiloma humano o condiloma, que aparecen muy frecuentemente en el ambiente homosexual (más del 50%), se transmiten mediante prácticas sexuales pero también a través de objetos externos infectados (dedos o consoladores). Después de unos meses o años, pueden conllevar la formación de pequeñas verrugas en forma de coliflor en la zona genital o anal.

La terapia es complicada y se realiza mediante sustancias químicas (ácidos o fuertes activadores del sistema inmunológico) o con cirugía.

Consejo de experto: en caso de no realizarse tratamiento, después de unos años puede acarrear, en el peor de los casos, especialmente en seropositivos, un carcinoma anal (cáncer). Por ello, se deben realizar controles regularmente.

Clamidia

La clamidia puede transmitirse de la misma forma que la gonorrea, es por esto que tanto el sexo oral (felación), como la penetración anal y/o vaginal representan aquí prácticas de riesgo. Los síntomas de la clamidia son también similares a los de la gonorrea, como la secreción por la uretra, la cual es, sin embargo, sobre todo transparente y no purulenta; la sensación de escozor en la uretra es mucho menos dolorosa. Las infecciones de garganta y recto son, por lo general, completamente asintomáticos y tan slo se detectan mediante un frotis de la región correspondiente. También para el tratamiento de la clamidia se utilizan antibióticos.

A pesar de los posibles riesgos para la salud que implica un viaje al exterior, la prevención y el comportamiento razonable permiten pasar una estancia agradable y regresar sano y salvo a casa iLes deseamos un viaje placentero!

Dr Horst Schalk
Médico de Medicina General, Viena

Benvenuti

Cari lettori di Spartacus:

state sfogliando la quarantunesima edizione della guida turistica gay più voluminosa del mondo. Non è certo un'ovvietà visto che al giorno d'oggi i libri cartacei sono considerati obsoleti. Personalmente riteniamo che non bisogna tagliarsi fuori dalle nuove possibilità che la tecnologia ci offre, allo stesso tempo però non bisogna trascurare i mezzi di comunicazione tradizionali. Per questo pensiamo che sia stata la decisione giusta l'aver sviluppato la nuova applicazione Spartacus per l'iPhone, lanciata sul mercato alla fine del 2011. Inoltre abbiamo creato un nuovo sito che vi aiuterà a trovare alloggio ovunque vi troviate. Infatti all'indirizzo **www.spartacusworld.com** potrete trovare e prenotare tantissime possibilità di pernottamento presso alloggi gay o gay-friendly.

Tra gli appuntamenti gay più importanti del 2012 è bene ricordare il Mr. Gay World che si svolgerà ad aprile a Johannesburg, gli EuroGames di Budapest a fine giugno e il World Pride di Londra a inizio luglio.

Un altro appuntamento di rilievo per molti gay europei è l'Eurovision Song Contest, che quest'anno si svolgerà il 26 maggio nella capitale dell'Azerbaigian, Baku. Svolgendo delle ricerche abbiamo rilevato che l'Azerbaigian non è solo un paese omofobo, ma anche un paese nel quale ci si deve ben guardare anche dalla polizia. Evitate di consegnare il vostro passaporto o la vostra patente poiché riaverli potrebbe costarvi una fortuna. Nonostante tutto Baku è considerata una bellissima città. Speriamo solo che l'Eurovision Song Contest darà un contributo per il miglioramento della situazione per la comunità LGBT.

Una lista più dettagliata degli appuntamenti gay in tutto il mondo la troverete come sempre nel calendario consultabile alle ultime pagine di questa guida o sul nostro sito **www.spartacusworld.com**. È bene ricordare che il suddetto calendario degli appuntamenti viene regolarmente e costantemente aggiornato.

Per quanto riguarda la comunità LGBT il 2011 non ha visto molti cambiamenti sul fronte politico. Infatti, non appena la situazione economica si appanna, peggiora, di solito, anche la situazione per le minoranze. Questo è proprio quello che sta accadendo in Ungheria, in Russia e in altri paesi dell'Europa dell'est, che stanno infatti vedendo risvegliare rigurgiti nazionalistici.

Siamo sicuri che ognuno di voi troverà da noi il mezzo di comunicazione più adatto alle proprie esigenze. Potrete infatti sceglierete di usare la nostra guida come lettura da spiaggia o da viaggio nella sua forma più tradizionale, il libro, o in forma digitale sul vostro portatile da consultare in casa o in giro. Qualsiasi scelta voi facciate, la nostra guida vi offrirà, come sempre, un amplissimo repertorio tutto da scoprire. Non ci rimane altro che augurarvi, anche per l'anno a venire, di poter continuare a coltivare la vostra passione per i viaggi.

Briand Bedford
CAPO REDATTORE

Classificazione dei paesi

Lo SPARTACUS è diviso in paesi che sono elencati in inglese secondo l'ordine alfabetico. Fanno eccezione i Caraibi con i loro rispettivi stati e le isole che si trovano sotto la voce "C" come Carribian/Caraibi. I paesi stessi poi, sono elencati secondo l'ordine alfabetico, ma i nomi delle città sono nella lingua nazionale del rispettivo paese. Per quanto riguarda l'Australia, il Canada e gli USA le città o province sono elencate in ordine alfabetico e sono divise in metropoli e città. Per ulteriori chiarimenti si raccommanda di andare a vedere l'indice su pagina 1106, dove tutti i paesi, metropoli e città sono elencati in ordine alfabetico e nelle cinque lingue dello SPARTACUS e cioè in inglese, tedesco, francese e spagnolo.

Per ogni paese abbiamo collezionato informazioni specifiche sulla situazione sociale e legale dei gay, incluso l'eta legale per avere rapporti sessuali. Ne fanno naturalmente anche parte le informazioni su eventuali festival gay e su eventi particolari.

Prima dell'introduzione su ogni paese si trovano le seguenti informazioni:

Name: il nome nella lingua locale e in tutte le 5 lingue dello SPARTACUS	➤ **Name:** Suid-Afrika • Südafrika • Afrique du Sud • Sudáfrica • Sud Africa
Location: posizione geografica	➤ **Location:** Southern Africa
Initials: indica l'abbreviazione commune des nome del paese	➤ **Initials:** ZA
Time: indica il fuso orario	➤ **Time:** GMT +2
International Country Code: indica il prefisso internazionale del paese per telefonare dall'estero in questo paese	➤ **International Country Code:** ☎ 27 (omit 0 of phone number)
International Access Code: indica il prefisso del respettivo paese che viene utilizzato per chiamare da questo paese all'estero	➤ **International Access Code:** ☎ 09 or 091
Language: si riferisce alla/e lingua/e più parlata/e	➤ **Language:** English, Afrikaans, African languages
Area: è l'estensione territoriale del paese	➤ **Area:** 1,219,080 km² / 471,442 sq mi.
Currency: è la moneta ufficiale del paese	➤ **Currency:** 1 Rand (ZAR) = 100 Cents
Population: numero degli abitanti	➤ **Population:** 43,240,000
Capital: capitale	➤ **Capital:** Cape Town (legislative capital); Pretoria (administrative capital)
Religions: sono le religioni più diffuse nel paese	➤ **Religions:** 78% Christians
Climate: qui si trovano informazioni sul probabile clima	➤ **Climate:** Ranging from hot and dry in summer to cold and wet in winter. Sub-tropical to Mediterranean climates.
Important Gay Cities: città che sono interessanti per turisti gay	➤ **Important gay cities:** Cape Town, Johannesburg

Strutturazione degli indirizzi

Ogni singolo elenco contiene il nome ❶, i rispettivi codici SPARTACUS ❷, gli orari d'apertura ❸, l'indirizzo ❹, il numero di telefono ❺, l'indirizzo e-mail ❻ e l'indirizzo del website ❼.

I singoli simboli significano:

- ✉ indirizzo
- ☎ numero di telefono
- 💻 indirizzo e-mail, indirizzo del website
- ☞ indicazione

■ Un quadratino rosso all'inizio dell'inserzione (listing) rimanda alla pubblicità sulla guida, sull'applicazione o sul sito.

Come utilizzare lo SPARTACUS

Classificazione delle rubriche

Per ogni paese e città troverete gli indirizzi classificati sotto le rubriche nell'ordine seguente:

National Gay Info
National Publications
National Publishers
National Companies
National Groups
National Helplines
Country Cruising

▼

Gay Info
Publications
Culture
Tourist Info

▼

Bars
Men's Clubs
Cafés
Danceclubs
Restaurants
Shows
Cinema

▼

Sex Shops/Blue Movies
Cinemas
Escorts & Studios
House of Boys

▼

Saunas/Baths
Fitness Studios
Massage

▼

Shopping/Services

▼

Hotels
Guest Houses
Apartments
Private Accommodation

▼

Groups

▼

Swimming
Cruising

Vuole informarci su eventuali cambiamenti che ha scoperto durante il Suo viaggio? In questo caso La preghiamo di utilizzare per la sua informazione la »Users information card« che si trova alla fine di questa edizione dello SPARTACUS. Naturalmente le spese di spedizione vanno a carico del destinatario. Quante informazioni ci dà meglio è. Le siamo grati di ogni tipo di informazione di cui Lei forse già dispone e che non si trova ancora in questa edizione dello SPARTACUS.

Bruno Gmünder Verlag GmbH · SPARTACUS-Redaktion
Kleiststrasse 23-26 · 10787 Berlin · GERMANY
info@spartacus.de

Significato dei codici

I codici dello SPARTACUS significano (I codici in lettere minuscole significano in generale una restrizione):

!	Da racommandare particolarmente
AC	Aria condizionata
AK	Croci a X
AYOR	A proprio rischio, forse si tratta di un luogo pericoloso o con molti controlli di polizia.
B	Bar con un' ampia offerta di bevande
BF	Prima colalazione in forma di buffet
CC	Tutte le carte di credito accettate
D	Discoteca
DM	Menù del giorno
DR	Darkroom
DU	Doccia
F	Feticismo (cuoio, latex, divisa)
FC	Preservativi gratuiti
FH	2° asciugamano gratuito
G	Sobratutto o esclusivamente gay
GH	Glory holes
GLM	Sobratutto o esclusivamente pubblico gay o lesbiche
H	Allogio dove i gay sono benvenuti
I	Internet
LAB	Labirinto
LM	Musica dal vivo
M	Vasta offerta di piatti
MA	Età mista
MC	Ospiti di età media (30 – 50 anni)
MSG	Massaggi possibile
NG	Non gay, ma interessante
NR	Area non fumatori
NU	Zona nudismo
OC	Piuttosto ospiti non giovani (+ 50 anni)
OS	Terazza o giardino
P	Club privato o controlli severi all' entrata
P	Si deve suonare alla porta
PA	Animali ammessi
PI	Piscina
PK	Parcheggio
PP	Vasca
R	Regolarmente marchettari
RES	Prenotazione necessaria
RR	Sala relax
RWB	Camera con balcone
RWS	Camera con bagno doccia
RWT	Camera con TV
S	Shows/eventi
SA	Sauna finnica
SB	Bagno di vapore
SH	Negozio
SL	Sling
SNU	Spogliarello maschile
SOL	Solario
ST	Show di travestiti
T	Anche travestiti/transsessuali
VA	Visite consentiti
VEG	Anche piatti vegetariani
VR	Sala video
VS	Videos shows
W	Senza barriere per i disabili
WE	Attività sopratutto il fine settimana
WH	Whirlpool
WI	WiFi gratis
WL	Ampia lista dei vini
WO	Possibile allenamento fitness
YC	Ospiti giovani (18 – 28 anni)

I codici SPARTACUS sono anche disponibili sotto la forma di un segnalibro strappabile alla fine della guida SPARTACUS.

1. Introduzione

I gay sono campioni dei viaggi, sia che si tratti di viaggi di diletto che di viaggi di lavoro. Qualora ci si rechi in paesi stranieri non si devono naturalmente rispettare e osservare le sole usanze nazionali, bensì occorre anche considerare il fatto che l'ambiente sconosciuto può nascondere dei rischi per la salute. In aggiunta alle regole già in uso nei luoghi in cui viviamo, si dovrebbero proprio cammin facendo e a prescindere dal fatto che si sia HIV positivi osservare alcune regole di comportamento supplementari.

All'ombra della minaccia dell'HIV, si presta sfortunatamente una ridotta attenzione alle malattie a trasmissione sessuale (STD – sexually transmitted deseases). Per questa ragione si è assistito nella seconda metà degli anni Novanta ad un aumento drammatico di queste malattie infettive pur anche nel mondo occidentale. Gli omosessuali che si prendono a ragione la libertà di sfogare liberamente e senza vincoli religiosi e moralistici la propria sessualità, se ne assumono anche la responsabilità – la responsabilità non solo della propria, ma anche della salute del proprio rispettivo partner sessuale!

L'infezione da HIV poté essere trasformata negli anni passati attraverso il progresso veloce della medicina da fatale malattia mortale a malattia cronica e ben curabile, seppur sempre non totalmente guaribile. I malati che prima combattevano per la pura sopravvivenza sono adesso nella condizione, per fortuna, di poter trascorrere le proprie vacanze, anche all'estero, quasi senza pericolo.

2. Viaggiare

Nella maggior parte dei paesi industrializzati siamo abituati a ricorrere a prestazioni mediche più o meno gratuitamente. Vi preghiamo di considerare il fatto che all'estero non godrete automaticamente di una copertura assicurativa, cioè dovrete generalmente pagare anticipatamente le cure mediche e solo al vostro rientro potrete ricevere il rimborso in parte o nella sua interezza dei costi sostenuti dalla propria assicurazione sociale, privata o di viaggio (molto spesso si tratta di un servizio della carta di credito – chiedete comunque informazioni circa le regole vigenti). Se, da cittadino dell'Unione Europea, ci si sposta in un altro paese dell'Unione, dietro presentazione del tesserino dell'assicurazione sanitaria europea (che si trova sul retro della propria tessera di previdenza sociale o da ritirarsi nella ASL di appartenenza) si ha diritto alla copertura sanitaria per trattamenti che riguardano malattie acute in tutti i paesi membri dell'Unione e in Svizzera.

Le vaccinazioni (per esempio contro l'epatite A e B) e la profilassi (per esempio contro la malaria) offrono alta protezione da malattie infettive. Accanto alle vaccinazioni che sono raccomandate nel proprio Paese, ci sono in altri stati delle vaccinazioni che vengono consigliate o addirittura prescritte. Il vostro medico vi informerà più dettagliatamente in proposito.

I sieroposotivi possono ricevere senza esitazione tutti i vaccini che vengono eseguiti con agenti patogeni neutralizzati, le cui parti o tossine indebolite (sostanze tossiche, si parla allora dei cosiddetti »sieri della morte«. Solo se il sistema immunitario risulta chiaramente indebolito (cellule CD4 sotto 200/ml), può arrivare ad una reazione ridotta e con ciò ad una profilassi vaccinica inadeguata. I vaccini nei quali vengono iniettati ridotti agenti patogeni vivi (per esempio il vaccino contro la febbre gialla prescritto in molti Paesi) sono possibili nel caso dei sieropositivi solo ponderando seriamente i rischi e di solito solo in una buon stato di difesa (cellule CD4 sopra 400/ml).

L'igiene non è un fenomeno così scontato in tutte le destinazioni come da noi. In linea di massima è di regola nella maggior parte dei Paesi del terzo mondo, ma possibilmente anche in altri Paesi d'Europa: non bere acqua corrente dal rubinetto! O solo acqua sterilizzata e filtrata o quella proveniente dalle bottiglie di acqua minerale, imbottigliata alla fonte. I cubetti di ghiaccio nei cocktail possono essere teoricamente problematici. Per il cibo vale la semplice regola: »cook it, boil it, peal it or leave it«- in italiano: mangiare solo frutta arrosto, bollita e con la buccia (per esempio banane, pere, ananas sbucciate esse stesse in condizioni igieniche)! Tutto il resto nasconde pericoli (per esempio le insalate, condimenti per insalate, creme, cibi con uova, ecc.) e bisognerebbe rinunciarvi. In ogni caso munitevi di una cosiddetta »farmacia da viaggio« che deve contenere i farmaci essenziali, come ad esempio quelli per possibili diarree o materiale di medicazione. Nel dubbio vale la regola: cercare l'aiuto di un medico competente.

Qualora doveste assumere regolarmente dei farmaci, portatevi in ogni caso più farmaci del dovuto, nel caso il viaggio del ritorno dovesse essere posticipato per motivi inaspettati o nel caso doveste smarrire alcune pillole. Portatevi assolutamente nel bagaglio a mano i farmaci nella loro confezione originale, insieme al foglietto illustrativo (sul quale è scritta la denominazione chimica della sostanza, visto che la maggior parte dei medicinali ha nei vari Paesi un nome diverso), così come pure eventualmente una copia della prescrizione medica o nel caso servissero le necessarie siringhe, aghi. Considerate il possibile fuso orario in determinati paesi e organizzatevi con rispettive assunzioni dei farmaci.

Consiglio di esperti: in viaggio verso alcuni Paesi si consiglia di portare con sé un certificato medico in cui sia indicato il nome e una breve descrizione del farmaco (se si tratta per esempio di compresse o di capsule). Non è necessario che sia indicata la diagnosi.

Leggi e norme internazionali possono differenziarsi notevolmente. Quando vi recate all'estero informatevi sulle norme doganali e su quelle relative all'entrata in un territorio straniero. Le informazioni potete riceverle telefonicamente o tramite internet presso il proprio Ministero degli Esteri o presso l'ambasciata o presso il consolato del rispettivo Paese.

Vi preghiamo di ricordarvi che alcune sostanze devono essere conservate in frigo, il resto almeno a temperatura ambiente, cioè non sopra i trenta gradi e all'asciutto. In molti Paesi del terzo mondo purtroppo, ancora oggi, la cura di ferite o l'uso di materiale nuovo o sterile durante un'iniezione non è una cosa scontata. Il viaggio in questi Paesi richiede, soprattutto nel caso in cui si tratti di un soggiorno lungo, che tale materiale venga portato con sé.

Non dovete mai dimenticare la crema solare con un alto fattore protettivo. Una permanenza in pieno sole nei Paesi del sud tra le 12.00 e le 15.00 senza protezione è sconsigliabile poiché c'è il rischio della comparsa di tumore alla pelle e del temporaneo danneggiamento del sistema immunitario (possibile diminuzione delle cellule CD4 nei soggetti affetti da HIV).

Inoltre: profilattici e lubrificante nella qualità in cui siamo abituati a reperirli solitamente non è facile dappertutto.

3. HIV

L'HIV può essere trasmessa solo quando i virus HI giungono nel corpo umano. Ciò ha luogo quando alcuni liquidi infetti come ad esempio sperma, liquidi vaginali o sangue raggiungono la mucosa intatta o ferita (anale, dell'intestino retto, della mucosa vaginale o della cavità orale o della congiuntiva dell'occhio) o della pelle ferita di fresco (taglio, puntura o scalfittura).

Un rischio di infezione si presenta:

- durante un rapporto anale non protetto, sia se si consideri il ruolo attivo che passivo della coppia;
- durante il rapporto vaginale non protetto, sia che si tratti dell'uomo che della donna;
- nel rapporto orale non protetto, qualora l'eiaculazione avvenga in bocca;
- durante l'introduzione di dita o del pugno nel retto senza che vi sia l'uso di guanti di plastica, quando si giunga all'insanguinamento della zona rettale di chi subisce il fisting o nella mano di chi esercita il ruolo attivo.

Consiglio di esperti : numerosi esperti dell'HIV sono dell'idea che gli umori che molti uomini secernono prima del vero e proprio orgasmo o durante il rapporto orale non protetto possano giungere alla mucosa della cavità orale ed eventualmente in particolari circostanze (presenza di un'altra malattia trasmessa sessualmente e che procede dalla secrezione dall'uretra o da una contemporanea alta concentrazione di virus HI) potrebbe nascondere un rischio ridotto.

Non sussiste nessun rischio di assunzione dell'HIV:

- al contatto con saliva, lacrime, sudore, urina o feci;
- in seguito a possibili contatti sociali come lo stringere le mani, l'utilizzo comune di bicchieri e posate, bagni, così come pure la frequentazione di piscine e saune è assolutamnete inoffensivo;
- nel caso di un'infezione attraverso l'aria, perché si è starnutito o tossito o in ragione di punture di insetti o di morsi e sulla base dei dati di cui disponiamo risulta piuttosto impossibile.

Per ridurre il rischio di un'infezione HIV bisognerebbe praticare assolutamente »sesso sicuro e protetto« (safer sex) e

- nei rapporti vaginali e anali usare assolutamente profilattici e sufficiente lubrificante idrosolubile. Le creme grasse potrebbero danneggiare il profilattico. Durante il rapporto promiscuo il profilattico deve essere cambiato sempre per ogni partner. I profilattici possono anche ridurre il rischio di trasmettere altre malattie a trasmissione sessuale.
- durante il rapporto orale non si deve in nessun caso eiaculare in bocca al partner. Questa misura non serve tuttavia ad evitare la trasmissione di altre malattie a trasmissione sessuale (come ad esempio gonorrea, sifilide o epatite). Chi vuole evitare la trasmissione di ciò e del sopra menzionato rischio minimo riguardante l'umore che precede l'orgasmo dovrebbe usare il profilattico anche durante il rapporto orale.
- durante il fisting bisogna usare assolutamente il guanto di plastica;
- nel caso di consumo di droghe endovenose bisogna ricordare che ognuno deve usare la sua propria siringa e il suo proprio ago.

Consiglio di esperti: ormai è dimostrato ed accertato che anche soggetti già infetti da HIV possono essere ricontaggiati da un'infezione caratterizzata possibilmente da virus HI più resistenti. Questo può essere di disturbo ad una terapia HIV che procede bene, e possono perfino renderla inefficace rendendo più difficile l'inizio futuro della terapia. Quindi i sieroposivi dovrebbero non rinunziare al »sesso sicuro e protetto«

Nel caso di un rischio infettivo vi è la possibilità di ridurre la probabilità di trasmissione attraverso la repentina pulizia del posto del contatto (ferita cutanea o mucosa) con acqua e sapone o se disponibile con un disinfettante (una pulizia del retto non è sensata) – così come la veloce (entro poche ore) e accorta assunzione di una terapia HIV (profilassi di postesposizione al rischio). Questa misura può non solo ridurre, ma anche ostacolare il rischio di infezione, ma non può sostituire il »sesso sicuro e protetto«! Per informazioni più dettagliate rivolgetevi ad un centro di trattamento HIV.
Da un tempo a questa parte qualcuno si ostina a consigliare di sottoporsi a una terapia antiretrovirale "preventiva" contro l'HIV prima di un eventuale contatto a rischio. Praticamente quasi tutti gli esperti di HIV sconsigliano questa cosiddetta profilassi pre-esposizione (PrEP) e non solo per una questione – ancora tutta aperta - di copertura dei costi (che per una terapia di un mese ammonterebbero a più di 1000 Euro), ma anche per la discutibilità della sua efficacia e sicurezza. In più, la suddetta profilassi non è lontanamente paragonabile, per efficacia, alle tradizionali misure di prevenzione fin'ora in uso. Il ricorso ad una profilassi pre-esposizione (PrEP) è plausibile solo in pochissimi casi eccezionali.

In molti pazienti compare spesso poche settimane dopo l'infezione HIV, per 10-14 giorni, un quadro clinico caratterizzato da influenza. Inoltre può tra l'altro trasformarsi in febbre, stanchezza, esantema, dolori muscolari e alle articolazioni, così come ingrossamento dei linfonodi. Nel caso dovessero comparire questi disturbi dopo un rischio di infezione, si deve assolutamente contattare uno specialista HIV, affinché si possano adottare ulteriori misure.
Dopo questa fase i virus possono espandersi in tutto il corpo e in particolare possono danneggiare il sistema immunitario. L'avanzamento di una trascurata infezione da HIV negli anni può arrivare a distruggere il virus stesso e altri agenti patogeni come batteri, virus e funghi possono causare infezioni fatali – solo dopo si parla di AIDS (Acquired Immuno Deficiency Syndrome =sindrome di immuno deficienza acquisita). Oggi l'AIDS nel mondo occidentale, sulla base del grande successo della terapia HIV, è diventata una malattia più rara. Ma non si dovrebbe in ogni caso dimenticare che nella maggior parte dei paesi del terzo mondo questa terapia non è a disposizione o lo è inadeguatamente e con ciò l'AIDS rappresenta pur sempre la causa di morte numero uno fra i giovani adulti.

Per poter trattare in modo ottimale l'infezione HIV, questa deve tuttavia anche venire diagnosticata in tempo. Questo ha luogo, di norma, attraverso il test HIV. Esso danneggia speciali proteine, i cosiddetti anticorpi che l'uomo forma a contatto con l'HIV. Il formarsi di questi anticorpi dura alcune settimane, cosicché questo test ha senso se viene fatto almeno 12 settimane dopo il rischio di infezione. Da un po' di tempo è presente tuttavia un ulteriore metodo di determinazione: questo indica i virus HI direttamente per mezzo del cosiddetto metodo PCR. La diagnosi può essere indicata per lo più già quattordici giorni dopo il rischio potenziale, tuttavia è anche molto più caro del test degli anticorpi e viene con ciò impiegato in particolari casi.

Già da un po' di tempo, in molti paesi è disponibile un "quick test" che ha lo stesso profilo di affidabilità di un normale test HIV. Il test rileva la presenza degli anticorpi contro l'HIV e i risultati del test cominciano ad essere affidabili al più presto dodici settimane dopo il contatto a rischio. Un risultato reattivo (quindi positivo), com per il caso dei test classici, deve essere verificato con un test di conferma (Western-Blot-Test). Il vantaggio del test veloce è che non sono necessari esami di laboratorio e il risultato è pronto già dopo 15-20 minuti. Nonostante la semplicità di questo test è comunque necessario che venga eseguito da mani esperte.

Informazioni aggiuntive: Ormai è accertato che un'efficace terapia contro l'HIV che fa abbassare la carica virale al di sotto del limite di rilevazione riduce notevolmente il rischio di contagio. Questo è anche uno dei motivi per il quale molti centri prescrivono la terapia antiretrovirale con più anticipo rispetto a come si è fatto fin'ora. Ciò, insieme al sesso protetto, può ridurre ulteriormente la diffusione dell'HIV. L'uso del preservativo è davvero irrinunciabile... già per il solo fatto di scongiurare il pericolo di contagio di altre malattie sessualmente trasmissibili.

4. Malattie a trasmissione sessuale (STD)

Le STD (dall'inglese: sexually transmitted diseases) sono malattie infettive che vengono causate da almeno 20 agenti patogeni (batteri, virus, funghi, organismi unicellulari e parassiti) e in prima linea attraverso rapporti sessuali, ma anche in alcuni casi possono essere trasmessi attraverso uno stretto contatto corporale. I sintomi delle malattie compaiono soprattutto, ma non esclusivamente, nella regione genitale. Negli anni passati si ebbe un drammatico aumento di queste malattie infettive. Alcune di esse (epatite A e B) sono evitabili attraverso dei vaccini preventivi, altre vengono curate con farmaci (antibiotici e sostanze antivirali) altre invece chirurgicamente (condiloma).

Alla comparsa dei seguenti sintomi si dovrebbe assolutamente consultare un medico:

- secrezione dal retto o dall'ano;
- arrossamento o comparsa di una patina biancastra nella zona orale, genitale e anale;
- ulcere (danneggiamento della pelle o della mucosa), noduli o vescichette nella zona orale, genitale o anale;
- forte prurito nella zona anale e genitale;
- dolorosi e/o gonfi linfonodi;
- ingiallimento di occhi e pelle.

Di seguito tratteremo le malattie infettive a trasmissione sessuale che si presentano più spesso. In particolare parleremo delle vie infettive (prevenzione) e dei sintomi (veloce formulazione della diagnosi).

Sifilide

Negli ultimi tempi l'infezione cresce significativamente – specialmente nella »scena«. Gli agenti patogeni sono batteri e vengono trasmessi attraverso umori corporali (secrezioni) che giungono su pelle di solito danneggiata (labbra, pene) o mucosa (bocca, pene, vagina). Sia il rapporto vaginale, orale e anale che i baci, rappresentano un rischio infettivo. Il tempo di incubazione (tempo che intercorre tra l'infezione e la malattia) corrisponde a 2-4 settimane. Poi compaiono nel cosiddetto primo periodo delle ulcere indolore (danneggiamento di pelle e di mucosa) e rigonfiamento dei linfonodi regionali (adiacenti), che dopo alcune settimane si rimarginano spontaneamente.
La diagnosi della sifilide ha luogo per mezzo di un esame del sangue, la terapia consiste nella somministrazione di un antibiotico.

Consiglio di esperti: se non si esegue una cura, si giunge dopo alcune settimane al secondo stadio caratterizzato da rigonfiamento dei linfonodi, eruzione cutanea, mutamento della mucosa o alopecia a chiazze. Nel seguente terzo stadio si giunge dopo anni all'infestazione di pelle, ossa, così come cervello e con ciò alla morte.

Gonorrea

La gonorrea è la malattia sessuale più frequente e cresce nella scena gay in maniera massiccia. Così come per la sifilide, i batteri sono gli agenti patogeni, la trasmissione ha luogo attraverso una secrezione purulenta (sperma, secrezioni anali e vaginali), la quale giunge alla mucosa (pene, bocca, retto, vagina) del partner. Per cui il rapporto orale, quello anale e il rapporto vaginale rappresentano un rischio. Dopo un periodo di incubazione di 2-5 giorni compare una secrezione purulenta così come del bruciore durante la minzione. Quando l'infezione ha luogo nel retto, la purulenta secrezione diventa spesso solo un dolore sordo del basso ventre. La terapia consiste nella somministrazione di un antibiotico.

Consiglio di esperti: la via più frequente dell'infezione nella scena gay è una gonorrea faringea (che per lo più passa senza problemi) che viene trasmessa durante il rapporto orale sull'uretra del partner.

Herpes

I virus dell'herpes giungono per lo più su una mucosa danneggiata del corpo del partner attraverso i baci, i rapporti orali, anali, vaginali (herpes genitalis). Dopo l'infezione può arrivare, soprattutto in seguito a un sistema immunitario cagionevole, come ad esempio febbre, raggi UV o stress, delle vescichette pruriginose e dolorose nella zona colpita (labbra, naso, genitali, zona anale). Per la cura dell'herpes sono presenti della sostanze antivirali, le quali possono essere applicate localmente o possono presentarsi nella forma di compresse.

Scabbia

L'acaro della scabbia è un parassita grande 0,2 mm, diffuso in tutto il mondo e che vive nella pelle e che si trasmette a stretto contatto corporale e provoca spesso un forte e insopportabile prurito in seno alla regione della regione colpita. La terapia consiste nell'applicazione di una lozione antiparassitaria.

Epatite

I virus delle epatiti A e B si presentano in tutto il mondo. I virus dell'epatite A vengono secreti dall'intestino, per cui l'acqua infetta e i prodotti alimentari così come le pratiche sessuali anali rappresentano un rischio infettivo. I virus dell'epatite B vengono trasmessi attraverso il sangue e attraverso le pratiche sessuali più disparate (anali, orali e vaginali) così come attraverso i baci (»il sesso sicuro« non protegge!). Una volta comparsa l'infezione, compare generalmente un'itterizia (ingiallimento della pelle e degli occhi) così come pure stanchezza.
Negli ultimi tempi, in alcune metropoli (in Europa: Berlino, Amsterdam e Londra) aumentano sempre più i casi di nuove infezioni da epatite C all'interno della scena gay. La causa di questo proliferarsi di casi non è ancora del tutto chiaro. Si pensa che ciò possa derivare dall'esposizione con sangue o escrementi altrui durante la pratica del fisting, di pratiche sadomaso o magari mentre si hanno piercing ancora freschi.
Oggi giorno ci sono farmaci relativamente efficaci contro l'epatite B e C, tuttavia sono delle cure piuttosto lunghe, complicate e con molti effetti collaterali. Proprio per questo, per i soggetti che abbiano un'intensa attività sessuale, è consigliabile farsi vaccinare contro le epatiti A e B. Mentre contro l'epatite C – a causa della mancanza di uno specifico vaccino – l'unica prevenzione possibile è evitare il contatto col sangue e gli escrementi del partner sessuale.

Piattole

La piattola è un insetto della grandezza di circa 1 mm e senza ali e si trasmette attraverso contatto corporale. Dopo alcuni giorni o settimane compaiono piccoli punti rossi e pruriginosi nella zona coperta dai peli del pube. Così come per la scabbia si somministrano delle lozioni antiparassitarie..

Condiloma

I virus del condiloma che si presentano nella scena frequentemente (più del 50%), vengono trasmessi attraverso i rapporti sessuali, ma anche tramite le infezioni da lubrificanti (dita, vibratori). Dopo mesi fino ad anni possono comparire formazioni di verruchette simili a cavolfiori sia nella zona genitale che in quella anale. La terapia è lunga è complicata e ha luogo per mezzo di sostanze chimiche (corrosive o corroboranti per il sistema immunitario) o chirurgicamente.

Consiglio di esperti: durante il decorso annuale e se non curato può, nel peggiore dei casi e soprattutto nei sieropositivi, nascere un carcinoma anale (cancro)! Di conseguenza dovrebbe essere eseguito un controllo regolare!

Clamidia

La clamidia può essere trasmessa nello stesso modo della gonorrea. Quindi anche in questo caso il sesso orale, anale e vaginale rappresentano un rischio. Anche i sintomi sono simili a quelli della gonorrea, tuttavia le secrezioni uretrali sono per lo più trasparenti piuttosto che biancastre, e il bruciore dell'uretra è molto meno doloroso. L'infezione della gola e del retto rimangono in genere completamente asintomatiche e quindi rilevabili solo attraverso uno striscio della zona corrispondente. Anche per il trattamento della clamidia vengono utilizzati gli antibiotici.

Nonostante i rischi possibili riguardanti la salute e capaci di rappresentare nei viaggi verso luoghi lontani una minaccia per la vostra salute, vi auguro di trascorrere un bel viaggio ricco di esperienze. E che una giusta misura di ragionevolezza possa consentirvi di ritornare a casa sani e pieni di buona salute.

Dr Horst Schalk
Medico di Medicina Generale, Vienna

International

Al-Fatiha Foundation
PO Box 33015 ✉ DC 20033 Washington, USA 💻 www.al-fatiha.org
Dedicated to lesbian, gay, bisexual, transexual, transgender and intersex (LGBTI) Muslims. Al-Fatiha promotes the progressive Islamic notions of peace, equality and justice. Founded in 1998, Al-Fatiha Foundation is a registered US-based non-profit, non-governmental organization.

Asociacion internacional de Familias por la Diversidad Sexual
💻 www.familiasporladiversidad.org
The FDS is a family organization that recognizes, values and promotes diversity as paradigm of the contemporary society. Website in Spanish.

Federation of Gay Games
584 Castro Street, Suite 343 ✉ CA 94114 San Francisco, USA
☎ +1 (415) 695-0222 💻 www.gaygames.org
As a non-profit organization, the foundation of the Federation of Gay Games is provided by individuals, local teams, sports organizations and corporate sponsors.

Forefront Migration Ltd
45 Sheppard Avenue East, Suite 900, Toronto, Ontario, Canada
✉ M2N 5W9 ☎ (1) 416 226 9889 💻 www.ForefrontMigration.ca
Forefront Migration assists those seeking to migrate to Canada. The firm is headed by a gay Canadian and U.S lawyer.

Gay Naturists International Mon-Fri 18-22h
5175 W Ajo Hwy #A-14 ✉ AZ 85735-9723 Tucson, USA
☎ +1 (954) 567-2700 💻 www.gaynaturists.org
Nudist organisation hosts the largest, all-nude, all-male gathering.

GLAAD
248 West 35th Street, 8th Floor ✉ NY 10001 New York, USA
☎ + 1 (212) 629-3322 💻 www.glaad.org
The Gay & Lesbian Alliance Against Defamation (GLAAD) is dedicated to promoting and ensuring fair, accurate and inclusive representation of people and events in the media as a means of eliminating homophobia and discrimination based on gender identity and sexual orientation.

Hirschfeld-Eddy-Stiftung
Chausseestraße 29 ✉ 10115 Berlin ☎ +49 (30) 78 95 47 78
💻 www.hirschfeld-eddy-stiftung.de
Hirschfeld-Eddy Foundation for the Human Rights of Lesbians, Gays, Bisexuals and Transgender People was founded in Berlin in June 2007.

Human Rights Watch
350 Fifth Avenue, 34th floor ✉ NY 10118-3299 New York, USA
☎ +1 (212) 290-4700 💻 www.hrw.org
Human Rights Watch is dedicated to protecting the human rights of people around the world. They nvestigate and expose human rights violations, they challenge governments and those who hold power to end abusive practices and respect international human rights law.

IGLHRC
350 Fifth Avenue, 34th Floor ✉ NY 10118 New York, USA
☎ +1 (212) 216-1814 💻 www.iglhrc.org
The mission of the International Gay and Lesbian Human Rights Commission (IGLHRC) is to secure the full enjoyment of the human rights of all people and communities subject to discrimination or abuse on the basis of sexual orientation or expression, gender identity or expression, and/or HIV status.

IGLTA (GLM T)
1201 NE 26th Street, Ste. 103, Ft. Lauderdale, USA
☎ (954) 954 630-1637 💻 www.lgbt.travel
International Gay and Lesbian Travel Association is an international network of travel industry business and professionals dedicated to the support of its members who have joined together to encourage gay travel throughout the world. IGLTA is committed to the welfare of gay and lesbian travelers, and to »shrinking the gay globe«. Spartacus is a proud member of IGLTA.

ILGA – International Lesbian, Gay, Bisexual, Trans and Intersex Association
17 rue de la Charité, Bruxelles Belgium ☎ 02 502 24 71 💻 www.ilga.org
ILGA's aim is to work for the equality of lesbian, gay, bisexual, trans and intersex people and their liberation from all forms of discrimination.

International Gay and Lesbian Chamber of Commerce (IGLCC)
465 Saint-Jean Street, Suite 102 ✉ QC H2Y 2R6 Montreal, Canada
☎ +1 (514) 287-2888 💻 www.iglcc.org
The IGLCC is the world's leading international LGBT business network. Our membership is made up of organizations that span 3 continents, represented by 15 chambers of commerce and business organizations in 13 countries.

LAMBDA GLBT Community Services
216 South Ochoa Street ✉ TX 79901 El Paso, USA
☎ +1 (206) 350-4283 💻 www.lambda.org
LAMBDA is a non-profit, gay, lesbian, bisexual, transgender organisation aiming to reducing homophobia, inequality, hate crimes, and discrimination by encouraging self-acceptance, cooperation and non-violence.

Lesbian and Gay Hospitality Exchange International (L/GHEI)
c/o J. Wiley, Smetana Str. 28 ✉ 13088 Berlin, Germany
☎ +49 (30) 691 9537 💻 www.lghei.org
Lesbian & Gay Hospitality Exchange International is a growing network of lesbians and gay men from around the world who offer their hospitality to other members at no charge. These hosts, in turn, are received when they travel. There are currently more than 500 listings in over 30 countries.

UNAIDS
20 Avenue Appia ✉ CH-1211 Genève/ Geneva 27, Switzerland
☎ +41 (22) 791 36 66 💻 www.unaids.org
As the main advocate for global action on HIV/AIDS, UNAIDS leads, strengthens and supports an expanded response aimed at preventing the transmission of HIV, providing care and support, reducing the vulnerability of individuals and communities to HIV/AIDS, and alleviating the impact of the epidemic.

World Congress of GLBT Jews – Keshet Ga'avah
P.O. Box 23379 ✉ DC 20026-3379 Washington - USA
☎ +1 (202) 452-7424 💻 glbtjews.org
The World Congress of Gay, Lesbian, Bisexual, and Transgender Jews: Keshet Ga'avah consists of more than 65 member organizations worldwide and holds conferences and workshops representing the interests of GLBT Jews around the world.

Albania

Name: Shqipëria · Albanien · Albanie
Location: Southeast Europe
Initials: AL
Time: GMT +1
International Country Code: ☏ 355 (omit 0 from area code)
International Access Code: ☏ 00
Language: Albanian, Greek
Area: 28,748 km² / 11,100 sq mi.
Currency: 1 Lek = 100 Qindarka
Population: 3,130,000
Capital: Tiranë
Religions: 70% Muslim, 30% Christians
Climate: Mild and moderate. Winters are cool, cloudy and wet, summers hot, clear and dry. The interior is cooler and wetter.

The age of sexual consent is 18 for homosexual men and 14 for lesbians and heterosexuals. The countryís anti-discrimination law was amended in 2010 to also include homosexuality, as part of the countryís efforts to join the EU. A gay partnership bill announced by the Albanian government in 2009 has foundered on the massive opposition of Muslim, Orthodox and Christian religious groups.
Even though the Albanian society has undergone some major changes in the last couple of years, the public attitude towards gays is still thoroughly determined by the homophobic propaganda spread under the Stalinist dictatorship of Enver Hoxha. Due to this outdated homophobia there is no gay scene in this country and the venues listed in this guide aren't gay, but are popular with the local gays. Being gay still is a taboo and most gay men don't dare to out themselves. We recommend to be discreet and not to hold hands or kiss in public, as people may be offended.
Nevertheless, homosexual acts are legal thanks to the work of the „The Association Gay Albania" group and also the ILGA in Brussels.
Tirana offers some venues of Western standard and there is a relatively reliable system of public transport. At night however, it is safer to take a taxi, because crime rates remain high despite the action undertaken by the government. The country itself has a lot to offer: beautiful landscapes and beaches, ancient historical sites and of course the mild Mediterranean climate.

Schwule Männer dürfen mit 18 Jahren sexuelle Kontakte haben, Lesben und Heterosexuelle mit 14. Im Zuge der Bemühungen um den EU-Beitritt wurde 2010 das Diskriminierungsverbot erweitert, das nunmehr die sexuelle Orientierung mit einschließt. Die Ankündigung der albanischen Regierung im Jahr 2009, einen Gesetzesentwurf auf den Weg zu bringen, der die eingetragene Partnerschaft für Homosexuelle zum Ziel hatte, scheiterte durch den massiven Widerstand religiöser Gruppierungen von Muslimen, Orthodoxen und Katholiken.
Zwar hat es in der albanischen Gesellschaft während der letzten Jahre einige bedeutsame Veränderungen gegeben, aber trotzdem ist die öffentliche Haltung gegenüber Schwulen immer noch stark durch die schwulenfeindliche Propaganda geprägt, welche unter der stalinistischen Diktatur von Enver Hoxha verbreitet wurde. Aufgrund dieser überholten Schwulenfeindlichkeit gibt es in Albanien keine echte Schwulenszene, und die Treffpunkte, die in diesem Guide aufgeführt sind, sind auch nicht explizit schwul, aber bei den ansässigen Homos sehr beliebt. Schwulsein ist immer noch ein Tabu, so dass die meisten homosexuellen Männer vor ihrem Coming Out zurückschrecken. Deshalb empfehlen wir, sich diskret zu verhalten. Das Händchenhalten oder Küssen in der Öffentlichkeit sollte man unterlassen, da manche Leute daran Anstoß nehmen könnten.
Doch dank der Verdienste der „The Association Gay Albania" und der ILGA in Brüssel sind öffentliche homosexuelle Kontakte legal.
In Tirana findet man einige Treffpunkte von westlichem Standard. Die öffentlichen Verkehrsmittel sind recht zuverlässig. Allerdings empfiehlt es sich nachts, ein Taxi zu nehmen, da die Kriminalität trotz der Bemühungen der Regierung weiterhin hoch ist. Neben dem milden Mittelmeerklima hat das Land eine Menge zu bieten: wunderschöne Landschaften, Strände und historische Sehenswürdigkeiten.

La majorité sexuelle est ainsi de 18 ans pour les rapports sexuels entre hommes et de 14 ans pour les lesbiennes et les hétérosexuels. Dans le cadre des efforts pour rejoindre l'UE, l'interdiction des discriminations a été élargie en 2010 et comprend désormais l'orientation sexuelle. L'annonce par le gouvernement albanais en 2009 de proposer une loi de partenariat enregistré pour les homosexuels a échoué en raison de résistances massives de la part de groupes musulmans, orthodoxes et catholiques.
Malgré les améliorations sensibles au sein de la société albanaise observées ces dernières années, la politique homophobe propagée par la dictature stalinienne de Enver Hoxha continue de marquer l'opinion publique.
En raison de cette homophobie dépassée, il n'existe pas de véritable milieu gay et les lieux de rencontres mentionnés dans ce guide ne sont pas explicitement gay mais très appréciés des homos locaux. Être homosexuel est encore un tabou, ce qui gêne la plupart des homosexuels dans leur coming out. C'est la raison pour laquelle nous vous conseillons de rester discret. Ainsi, il vaut mieux éviter de se tenir par la main ou de s'embrasser en public car cela pourrait choquer certaines personnes.
Pourtant, grâce au travail de „The Association Gay Albania" et de l'ILGA de Bruxelles, les relations homosexuelles sont devenues légales.
À Tirana, on trouve quelques lieux de rencontre à l'occidentale. Les transports en communs sont dignes de confiance, mais il est conseillé de prendre un taxi la nuit car la criminalité reste élevée, malgré les efforts du gouvernement. Outre son climat méditerranéen très doux, le pays a beaucoup à offrir : de magnifiques paysages, des plages ainsi que des curiosités historiques.

La edad de consentimiento para las relaciones sexuales es de 18 años para los hombres homosexuales y de 14 años para lesbianas y heterosexuales. Como parte de los esfuerzos para unirse a la UE, en 2010 se amplió la prohibición de la discriminación, la cual ahora también incluye a la orientación sexual. En 2009 el Gobierno albanés presentó un proyecto de ley que tenía como objetivo el registro de uniones civiles para homosexuales, pero este fracasó debido a

las objeciones masivas de grupos religiosos musulmanes, ortodoxos y católicos.
A pesar de que la sociedad albanesa ha experimentado importantes cambios en los últimos años, la actitud pública hacia los gays está todavía determinada por la propaganda homofóbica extendida por la dictadura stalinista de Enver Hoxha. Debido a esta homofobia no hay un ambiente gay en este país, de modo que las direcciones que aparecen en nuestro listado no son gay, pero son populares entre la población gay. Ser gay es un tabú y la mayoría de los gays no se atreven a hacer pública su realidad como tales. Recomendamos discreción y evitar tomarse de la mano o besarse en público, ya que la gente puede sentirse ofendida.
De cualquier manera, las actividades homosexuales son legales gracias a la labor del grupo „The Association Gay Albania" y de la ILGA en Bruselas.
Tirana ofrece algunas direcciones con estándares occidentales y cuenta con un sistema de transporte público relativamente confiable. De noche, sin embargo, es más seguro tomar un taxi ya que los índices de criminalidad aún son elevados a pesar de las medidas adoptadas por el gobierno. El país en sí mismo ofrece mucho: paisajes y playas de gran belleza, lugares históricos muy antiguos y por supuesto el clima agradable del Mediterráneo.

✖ Uomini omosessuali possono avere rapporti sessuali all'età di 18 anni mentre lesbiche ed eterosessuali all'età di 14 anni.

Contestualmente agli impegni per l'ingresso nell'Unione Europea, nel 2010 è stato ampliato il divieto di discriminazione, che adesso include anche l'orientamento sessuale. L'annuncio nel 2009 da parte del Governo albanese, di voler portare avanti un progetto di legge che aveva come scopo le unioni civili tra omosessuali, è fallito clamorosamente a causa di fortissimi resistenze da parte di gruppi religiosi mussulmani, ortodossi e cattolici.
Sebbene negli ultimi anni in Albania ci sono stati significativi cambiamenti, l'opinione pubblica nei confronti dei gay è ancora impregnata di propaganda antiomosessuale (diffusa già sotto la dittatura stalinista di Enver Hoxha). A causa di questa obsoleta omofobia, in Albania non esiste una vera e propria scena gay e i punti di incontro che sono elencati in questa guida non sono espressamente gay ma nonostante ciò sono molto frequentati dai gay del posto. Essere gay è ancora un tabu e perciò ben poche persone riescono a fare il coming out. Consigliamo, quindi, di mantenere un comportamento discreto; tenersi per mano o baciarsi in pubblico potrebbe comportare problemi.
Grazie comunque agli sforzi dell'associazione „The Association Gay Albania" e della ILGA a Bruxelles i contatti omosessuali sono legali.
A Tirana ci sono dei luoghi d'incontro di stile occidentale. I mezzi pubblici sono pittosto sicuri, tuttavia poichè la criminalità, nonostante gli sforzi del governo, è ancora alta, di notte vi consigliamo di prendere un taxi. Oltre al mite clima mediterraneo l'Albania ha tanto altro da offrire come per esempio bellissimi paesaggi, spiagge e monumenti.

NATIONAL GAY INFO

■ **Shoquata Gay Albania (SGA)**
PO Box 104 ✉ Tiranë
💻 www.angelfire.com/wizard/albaniagay/home.htm
The aims of the SGA are to support the interests of Albanian homosexuals (male and female) and to fight for full equality and integration into society. To spread positive and more objective information about the homosexual community and to fight prejudice, fanaticism, ignorance and hatred and to support the fight against the spread of AIDS.

Tiranë ☎ 042

BARS

■ **Canon Pub** (B MA NG)
Rr. Ismail Qemali
A popular pub in town, classical decor and pop music.

HOTELS

■ **Mondial** (AC B BF H M MA NG OS PI) All year
Rr. Muhamet Gjollesha *Next to police station, 2 km from city centre*
☎ (042) 323 72 💻 www.hotelmondial.com.al
Four-star hotel with two restaurants, one bar, 26 rooms and 6 suites with phone, sat-TV, balcony, safe and mini-bar. Laundry and room service available.

CRUISING

-Tranzit: Small park between the seat of the Socialist Party and the Ministry of Defence that connects Scanderbeg Square to the Deshmoret e Shkurtit Street (AYOR)
-Park Rinia
-Park across from Hotel Dajiti (ayor) (best evenings)
-Street the main bridge close to the pyramide and ends up to the street called Rruga e Elbasanit (especially small bridge between the two big bridges Deshmoret e Kombit Blvd. bridge and the Rruga e Elbasanit bridge)
-Park behind the Parliament building (after 20h).

Argentina

Name: Argentinien · Argentine
Location: South America
Initials: RA
Time: GMT -3
International Country Code: ☏ 54 (omit first 0 from area code)
International Access Code: ☏ 00
Language: Spanish
Area: 2,780,400 km² / 1,068,298 sq mi.
Currency: 1 Peso (Arg$) = 100 Centavos
Population: 41,343,201
Capital: Buenos Aires
Religions: 91 % Roman Catholic
Climate: Mostly moderate climate. The southeast is very dry, the southwest cold and wet. Summer is Dec-Mar. Winter is Jun-Sept.
Important gay cities: Buenos Aires

Homosexuality in Argentina is not a criminal offence. The Constitution includes a paragraph that bans some anti-gay discrimination. The age of consent is 16 years. During the last years the Argentinean society has become more tolerant towards homosexuality. Ever since August 2011, Argentine is the only South American country where homosexuals are allowed to marry. President Cristina Kirchner ultimately passed the law, which had only come about with the help of the opposition and a 15-hour senate debate, despite massive protests from Catholics.
The name Argentina means „silver". The country has a wide range of climate zones and landscapes: the Iguazú waterfall, the end of the earth at Ushuaia, the „tren de las nubes" (train on the clouds), the glaciers in Patagonia (Perito Moreno the most amazing one) and the recently opened gay Calu Beach in Mar del Plata.
Argentina is becoming an international gay centre. Many gays tourists from all over the world are choosing to visit Argentina. The favourable dollar exchange rate, the cultural life as well as the nightlife, are some of the reasons why they decide to visit this wonderful country. The annual Lesbian, Gay, Transvestite, Transsexual and Bisexual Pride Parade in Buenos Aires takes place each year in November with several thousand participants.

In Argentinien ist Homosexualität keine Straftat. Die Verfassung enthält einen Paragraphen, der Diskriminierung von Schwulen verbietet. Das sexuelle Schutzalter liegt bei 16 Jahren. Während der letzten Jahre ist die argentinische Bevölkerung Homosexuellen gegenüber immer toleranter geworden. Seit August 2010 ist Argentinien das einzige Land Südamerikas, das die Ehe für Homosexuelle geöffnet hat. Trotz massiver Proteste von katholischer Seite hat Präsidentin Cristina Kirchner das Gesetz unterzeichnet, das 15 Stunden lang im Senat debattiert wurde und nur mit Hilfe der Opposition zustande kam.
Übersetzt bedeutet Argentinien „Silber". Das Land hat viele unterschiedliche Klimazonen und Landschaften: den Iguazú-Wasserfall, das sogenannte Ende der Welt bei Ushuaia, den „tren de las nubes" (den „Zug auf den Wolken"), die Gletscher in Patagonien mit dem eindrucksvollen Perito Moreno und den kürzlich eröffneten Schwulenstrand Calu in Mar del Plata. Argentinien wird allmählich zu einer schwulen Hochburg. Viele schwule Touristen aus der ganzen Welt wählen Argentinien als Reiseziel. Gründe dafür sind unter anderem der günstige Dollarkurs sowie das Kultur- und Nachtleben. Jedes Jahr im November finden sich in Buenos Aires einige tausend Menschen zur großen Pride Parade für Lesben, Schwule, Transvestiten, Trans- und Bisexuelle ein.

L'homosexualité est légale en Argentine. La constitution contient un paragraphe qui interdit la discrimination des gays. La majorité sexuelle est fixée à 16 ans. Depuis quelques années, la société argentine se montre de plus en plus tolérante envers les homosexuels. Depuis août 2010, l'Argentine est le seul pays d'Amérique du Sud à reconnaître le mariage pour les homosexuels. Malgré des contestations massives du côté catholique, la présidente Cristina Kirchner a promulgué la loi qui fut débattue pendant 15 heures au Sénat et qui n'a pu aboutir que grâce aux efforts de l'opposition.
Argentine vient du mot „argent". Le pays s'étend sur plusieurs zones climatiques et offre des paysages très variés : la cascade de Iguazú, la „fin du monde" à Ushuaia, le „tren de las nubes" („train sur les nuages"), les glaciers de Patagonie avec le très impressionnant Perito Moreno et la plage homo de Calu, récemment ouverte à Mar del Plata.
L'Argentine est en train de devenir un véritable haut-lieu gay. Ainsi, de nombreux touristes gays du monde entier choisissent l'Argentine pour y passer leurs vacances, entre autres en raison du cours du dollar assez avantageux et de la richesse de la vie culturelle et nocturne. Chaque année, des milliers de personnes se retrouvent à Buenos Aires en novembre pour la grande Pride Parade des lesbiennes, gays, travestis, transsexuels et bisexuels.

La Homosexualidad no es un delito en Argentina. La Constitución contiene un artículo que prohibe la discriminación contra homosexuales, entre otras. La edad de consentimiento para tener relaciones sexuales es de 16 años. Durante los últimos años la sociedad argentina se ha vuelto más tolerante hacia la homosexualidad. Desde agosto de 2010, Argentina se ha convertido en el único país de América del Sur en legalizar el matrimonio para homosexuales. A pesar de las protestas masivas por parte del sector católico, la presidenta Cristina Kirchner firmó el proyecto de ley que fue debatido en el Senado durante 15 horas y que solo fue aprobado gracias a la ayuda de la oposición.
El nombre Argentina significa „ plata „. El país ofrece una amplia gama de climas y paisajes: las cataratas de Iguazú, el final de la tierra en Ushuaia, el „Tren de las Nubes", los glaciares de Patagonia (el más impresionante es el de Perito Moreno) y la recientemente inaugurada playa gay de Calu Beach en Mar del Plata.
Argentina poco a poco se convierte en un centro internacional gay. Muchos turistas gay de todo el mundo escogen a Argentina como destino turístico. La tasa de cambio favorable del dólar, la vida cultural así como la vida nocturna son algunas de las razones por las cuales prefieren visitar este país maravilloso. La marcha anual del Orgullo Lésbico, Gay, Trasveti, Transexual y Bisexual de Buenos Aires tiene lugar en noviembre con miles de participantes.

In Argentina l'omosessualità non è reato. La costituzione contiene un paragrafo che vieta discriminazioni contro i gay. L'età legale per rapporti sessuali è di 16 anni. Negli ultimi anni gli argentini sono diventati sempre più tolleranti nei confronti dell'omosessualità. Da agosto del 2010 l'Argentina è l'unico Paese dell'America del Sud ad aver aperto l'istituto del matrimonio agli omosessuali. Nonostante accese proteste da parte dei cattolici, il Presidente Cristina Kirchner ha firmato la legge, che è stata dibattuta per ben quindici ore al Senato e che è riuscita a passare solo grazie all'aiuto dell'opposizione.

Il Paese ha differenti climi e paesaggi: le cascate Iguazú, la cosiddetta fine del mondo presso Ushuaia, il „tren de las nubes", i ghiacciai in Patagonia con l'impressionante Perito Moreno e la nuova spiaggia gay Calu in Mar del Plata.

L'Argentina sta diventando una vera e propria roccaforte gay: turisti da tutto il mondo la scelgono per le loro vacanze. A motivare la vacanza sono il favorevole cambio del dollaro, la vita culturale e notturna. Migliaia di persone ogni anno partecipano alla Pride Parade che ha luogo a Buenos Aires a novembre.

NATIONAL GAY INFO

argentina 100x100 gay (GLM MA)
www.argentina100x100gay.com.ar

Che Argentinogay (GLM MA)
www.cheargentinogay.com.ar

Sentido G
Buenos Aires (011) 4942-8875 www.sentidog.com.ar
One of the most complete websites in spanish about gay news from Argentina and the world. Constantly updated.

NATIONAL PUBLICATIONS

Aji PiCante (G)
www.ajirevista.blogspot.com
Gay magazine for Ushuaia with information on films, radio and more.

Imperio G (G)
Uriburu 1076, Piso 8, Office 56 1114 Buenos Aires
(011) 4823-6914 www.revista-imperio.com
Bi-monthly magazine for Argentina.

Otra Guía. La (GLM)
Defensa 1120 1065 Buenos Aires (011) 4794-3177
www.laotraguiaweb.com.ar

NATIONAL COMPANIES

American Top Argentina Video Productions
Av. Cabildo 2230, 1°, G, Galeria Las Vegas C1428AAR Buenos Aires
M° Juramento 4781-5343 www.americantop.tv
Producer of gay porn films.

BUEGay Argentina (GLM) 10-18h
2032 Pueyrredón Ave, Floor 1 C1119ACQ Buenos Aires *Recoleta, Buenos Aires* (011) 4805 1401 www.buegay.com.ar
BUEGay Argentina, an IGLTA proud member, was founded in 2001, provides taylor-made tourism services for gay and lesbian in Argentina and in Latin America.

NATIONAL GROUPS

Bilioteca Crisálida Thu-Sat 16-20h
C/. Rivadavia 435 S.M. de Tucumán San Miguel de Tucumán
381 5980051 (mobile) www.crisalida.org.ar

Comunidad Homosexual Argentina (CHA) (GLM)
Tomás Liberti 1080 1165 Buenos Aires (011) 4361-6382
www.cha.org.ar

GENERAL GROUPS

GNetwork360 (GLM)
911 6094 4214 (mobile) www.gnetwork360.com

Bahía Blanca ☎ 0291

DANCECLUBS

Adonis (B D G SNU ST) Thu-Sat 23-?h
Belgrano 165 www.facebook.com/adonis.bahiablanca

Buenos Aires ☎ 011

Buenos Aires is considered nowadays as one of the most popular gay capital cities South America. It is a city with a typical European feel: wide green avenues with sumptuous public buildings and gardens. The Plaza de Mayo is an excellent example, surrounded by the cathedral, the Mayor's house and the „Manzana de las Luces" (Block of Lights).
The Avenida 9 de Julio is the most important avenue, crowned by the Obelisk - a symbol of the city. In the Corrientes Avenue you will find the main theatres and entertainment venues.
The gay scene is concentrated in the districts of Palermo, San Telmo, Recoleta and Barrio Norte. The CSD is celebrated the first Saturday of November (see: www.marchadelorgullo.org.ar), which is incidentally also the date when the first homosexual group was created in Argentina.

Heutzutage gilt Buenos Aires als eine der beliebtesten schwulen Hauptstädte Südamerikas. Es ist eine Stadt mit typisch europäischem Flair. Sie hat große grüne Alleen mit prächtigen öffentlichen Häusern und Gärten, wie z. B. der Plaza de Mayo mit seiner Kathedrale, und der „Manzana de las Luces" (das Haus des Lichtes).
Die Avenida de 9 Julio ist die interessanteste Strasse und wird durch einen Obelisken geschmückt, dem typischen Symbol für die Stadt. Kinos, Theater und weitere vergnügliche Treffpunkte findet man in der Avenida Corrientes.
Die Schwulenszene konzentriert sich auf die Bezirke von Palermo, San Telmo, Recoleta und Barrio Norte. Der CSD wird im November gefeiert (Näheres unter: www.marchadelorgullo.org.ar).

Aujourd'hui, Buenos Aires a la réputation de capitale sudaméricaine préférée des homos. La ville est typiquement européenne, avec ses grandes avenues bordées d'arbres et encadrées de splendides maisons et jardins comme par exemple le Plaza de Mayo avec sa cathédrale, la „Manzana de las Luces" (maison des lumières).
L'Avenida 9 de Julio est la plus intéressante et est ornée d'un obélisque, devenu le symbole de la ville. On trouve dans l'Avenida Corrientes des cinémas, des théâtres et d'autres lieux de divertissement .
Le milieu gay est situé dans les arrondissements de Palermo, San Telmo, Recoleta et Barrio Norte. La Gay Pride se déroule le premier samedi du mois de novembre (pour de plus amples informations, consulter le site www.marchadelorgullo.org.ar), date à laquelle la première association homosexuelle argentine a vu le jour.

Buenos Aires está considerada actualmente como una de las capitales gay más populares de Sudamérica. Es una ciudad con un aire típico europeo: amplias avenidas arboladas con suntuosos edificios públicos y jardines. La Plaza de Mayo es un excelente ejemplo, rodeada por la catedral, el Cabildo y la Manzana de las Luces.
La avenida de 9 Julio es la calle más interesante y está jalonada por un obelisco, el típico símbolo de la ciudad. En la avenida Corrientes se encuentran los cines, teatros y otros puntos de ocio.
La escena gay se concentra en los barrios de Palermo, San Telmo, Recoleta y Barrio Norte. La Marcha del Orgullo Gay se celebra el primer sábado de noviembre (ver: www.marchadelorgullo.org.ar), que coincide con la fecha en que se creó el primer grupo homosexual en Argentina.

Buenos Aires è diventata una delle capitali sudamericane più amate dai gay. È una città con un tipico flair europeo. Ci sono grandi viali con lussuosi palazzi e giardini com p.e. Plaza de Mayo con la sua cattedrale e la Manzana de las Luces.
Avenida 9 de Julio è il viale più interessante dove si trova tra l'altro un obelisco che rappresenta il simbolo della città. Nel'Avenida Corrientes invece si trovano numerosi cinema, teatri e altri punti d'incontro.
La scena gay si concentra nelle zone di Palermo, San Telmo, Recoleta e Barrio Norte. Il gay pride ha luogo il primo sabato di novembre (www.

marchadelorgullo.org.ar), data in cui venne fondata la prima organizzazione gay argentina.

NATIONAL PUBLICATIONS

GMAPS 360 (GLM)
C/. Franklin 1463, Florida Oeste ☎ (011) 5012 6161 ☎ 4760 4100 (fax)
www.Gmaps360.com
One of the most complete websites in Spanish including gay guides of Argentina.

NATIONAL COMPANIES

Esthetic Center International by Claudia Vaz (AC CC)
Tue,Thu-Sat 10.30-20.30h
A. Pueyrredón 1426, Barrio Norte *M° Pueyrredon Linea D* ☎ 4821-4964
www.claudiavaz.com.ar
Cosmetic treatment and plastic surgery. English spoken.

NATIONAL GROUPS

Federación Argentina LGBT (GLM)
☎ 4383-7413 ☎ 6370-1200 www.lgbt.org.ar

GAY INFO

Enrique Mitjans 10-20h
Sanchez de Bustamante 2584, 1° ☎ (011) 4803-0953
www.enriquemitjans.com.ar
Legal advice, as well as advice on the purchase of real estate and art in Argentina. Enrique is extremely friendly and helpful.

TOURIST INFO

Comisaría del Turista
☎ (011) 4346-5748
Tourist police station. English, Italian, French, Portugues and Ukranian spoken.

Oficina Central de Información Turística
Av. Santa Fe, 883 ☎ (011) 4312-2232 www.turismo.gov.ar

BARS

Bach Bar (B GLM MA S T) Wed-Sun 23-6h
José A. Cabrera 4390 *Palermo* ☎ (15) 5184-0137 (mobile)
www.bach-bar.com.ar
Wed & Thurs - Strippers and Draq Queens, Karaoke Sunday nights.

Cosmo Bar by Axel (! AC B CC G MA OS S WE)
Sun-Wed 12-24, Thu-Sat 12-1h
c/o Axel Hotel Buenos Aires, Venezuela, 649 *San Telmo*
☎ (011) 4136-9393 www.axelhotels.com
Design, music, sandwiches, cocktails, trends, see and be seen. There is much to discover at Cosmo Bar. Day or night, enjoy a coffee on a terrace or a drink at the bar. Share the most cosmopolitan atmosphere with your friends, savor each detail and let yourself be surprised. Cosmo Bar by Axel, it won't leave you indifferent.

Ego by Club V. (AC B G MA) Fri 23-?h
Bonpland 1690 ☎ 4771-4281

Flux (AC B G MA OS) Mon-Sat 19-?h
Marcelo T. de Alvear 980 *Corner with 9 de Julio, M° San Martín*
☎ (011) 5252-0258 www.fluxbar.com.ar
Happy Hour until 22h. DJs.

G Point (B D g S) Shows on Tue 22h
Av. 2a Rivadavia 14751, Ramos Mejia ☎ (011) 4654-2273
www.gpointpinar.com.ar

Olmo. El (B g m MC) from 6-3h
Av. Santa Fe 2502 *M° Pueyrredon, corner Av. Pueyrredon*
☎ (011) 4821-5828
Cruising area.

Oviedo (B g MC) 24hrs
Av. Santa Fe y Pueyrredon *M° Pueyrredon*

Search (AC B d G MA S SNU T) 23-?, show 0.30h
Azcuénaga 1007 *One block from Santa Fe Avenue* ☎ (011) 4824-0932

Sitges (! B d GLM MA S) Wed-Sun 22.30-4h
Av. Córdoba 4119 *Corner with Rawson* ☎ (011) 4861-3763
www.sitgesonline.com.ar

Sky Bar by Axel (B G MC S) Mon-Sun 12-2h (Oct.-Apr.)
c/o Axel Hotel Buenos Aires, Venezuela, 649 ☎ (011) 4136-9393
www.axelhotels.com/buenosaires
A glamorous garden bar & bistro that lights up with the swimming pool's reflection. Axel Sky Bar is ideal for a night-time cocktail or a delicious meal in the sun. Visible from different points of the hotel, the swimming pool invites you to cool down, to see and be seen. The chill out music relaxes the body in the solarium, the breeze enchants the most chic and cosmopolitan scene of Buenos Aires.

MEN'S CLUBS

Anchorena SW Gay (AC B CC DR G m MA MSG NU OS P r)
Mon 21-5h
Anchorena 1121 5° Piso *5th floor, between C7. Paraguay & C/. Mansilla, M° Pueyrredón and Agüero or just six block walk from M° Carlos Gardel, line B*
☎ (15) 5513 2916 (mobile)

Kadu (AC b DR f G MA NU P S VS) Wed 20, Fri 21, Sat 22-4, Sun 20-4h
C/. Sánchez de Bustamente, 1633 *Barrio de Palermo, M°-Agüero AV. Santa Fe Av. 3000* www.kadu.com.ar
Leather, sex and nude bar for men from 18-37 year old. With invitation only. Dress code applies.

Tom's (AC B DR G MA P VS) Daily 24 hrs.
C/. Viamonte 638, Subsuelo ☎ (011) 4322-4404
www.tomsbuenosaires.com
Cruising bar with DVD-cabines, glory holes and dark maze.

Zoom Buenos Aires (AC B DR G MA P VS) 24hrs
Uriburu 1018 *Between Av. Sante Fé & M.T. de Alvear, M° Facultad de Medicina* ☎ (011) 4827-4828 www.zoombuenosaires.com
Cruising bar with DVD-cabins, glory holes and dark labyrinth.

CAFES

Pride Café (AC B bf G I M MA S) 9-21h
C/. Balcarce, 869 *Corner Pasaje Giuffra* ☎ (011) 4300-6435
Homemade cakes, pastries and sandwiches.

Pride Hollywood (AC B BF G I MA S) 10-21h
C/. Humboldt 1897 *Corner Costa Rica* ☎ (011) 4776 6197
www.pridehollywood.com.ar
Homemade cakes, pastries and sandwiches.

DANCECLUBS

Amerika (! AC cc D DR G MA S VS) Thu-Sun 1-6h
Gascon 1040 ☎ (011) 4865-4416 www.ameri-k.com.ar
Two dance floors, one of the best discos in BA. The darkroom is always very busy.

Angel's (B D DR G MA r SNU T) Thu-Sat 0.30-7h
C/. Viamonte 2168 ☎ (011) 4331-3231 www.discoangels.com.ar

Bahrein Club (B cc D glm S)
C/. Lavalle 345 *Wed & Fri Gaynight* www.bahreinba.com

Club 69 (B D GLM S) Thu 0.30-?h
Niceto Vega 5510 ☎ (011) 4779-9396 www.club69.com.ar

Contramano (! AC B D G MA VS)
Fri & Sat 24-6, Sun 22-5, Summer 23-5h
Rodríguez Peña 1882 *Near Av. Santa Fé* ☎ (011) 4811-0494
www.contramano.com
One of the best places in town for over 25 years now. As popular as ever.

Glam (B D DR G S YC) Thu-Sat 1-7h
Cabrera 3046 ☎ (011) 4963-2521 www.glambsas.com.ar
Best on Thu & Sat night. Sun: Bear Night at 20h.

Human Club (! B D G WE YC) Sat 1.30-7h
Av. Costanera Norte Y Av. Sarmiento *Mandalay Complex*
www.humanclub.com.ar
„The" club of Buenos Aires gay nightlife.They usually do 2 parties a month.

Km Zero (B D GLM) Mon-Sun 23.30-?h Thu closed
Av. Santa Fe 2168 ☎ (011) 4822-7530 www.kmzero.com.ar

Marshall. La (D G MC S) Wed 22-3h
Maipú 444 ☎ (011) 4300 3487 www.lamarshall.com.ar
Also Works on Sat: from 22hs in Rivadavia 1392. From 22 to 23.30 tango classes and then milonga until 3.30hs. Programs may vary (with or without shows)

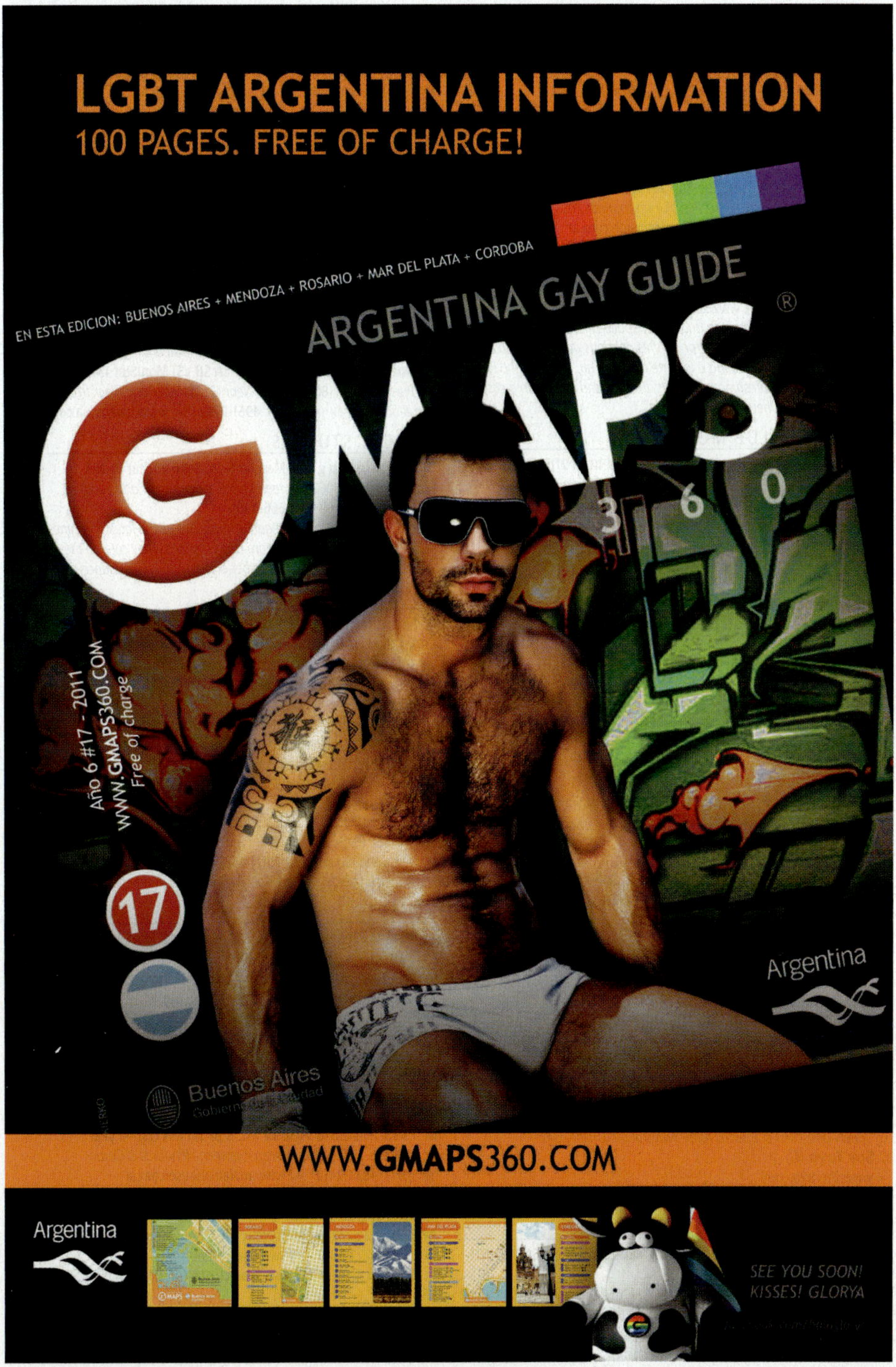

Argentina

Palacio (AC B D G MA S) 2nd Fri/Month 23-?h
Adolfo Alsina 940 www.palacioalsina.com
Famous gayparty once a month. Check website for details.

Rheo by Crobar (B D G) Fri 24-7h
Libertador 3886 *Paseo de la Infanta* www.rheo.com.ar

Sub. The (B D G YC) Fri & Sat 2-?h
Av. Cordoba 543 *Downtown* www.thesub.com.ar

RESTAURANTS

Inside (G M MC S SNU) Tue-Sun 20-?h
Bartolomé Mitre 1571 *M° Sáenz Peña/Uruguay, near Pasaje la Piedad*
(011) 4372-5439 www.restaurantinside.com.ar
Food not fantastic but good shows. (Tue & Wed Promo Pastas 2x1)

Kitchen By Axel (G M MA)
c/o Axel Hotel Buenos Aires, Venezuela, 649 *San Telmo*
(011) 4136-9393 www.axelhotels.com/buenosaires
Kitchen, an urban, cosmopolitan and trendy space where your tastes come first. Discover the excellent quality/price of its delicious gastronomic proposals and choose between dining à la carte or set menu, day or night. Enjoy its direct flavors and refreshing breakfasts, lunches and dinners in a casual and personal atmosphere.

SEX SHOPS/BLUE MOVIES

American Top Video (AC CC g) Mon-Sat 10.30-21h
Av. Cabildo 2230 / 1° J, Galería Las Vegas *M° Juramento, line D*
(011) 4781-5343 www.americantop.tv

SEX CINEMAS

ABC (G VS) 10-4, Sat & Sun 14-4h
Esmeralda 506
Four cinemas. Mon gay leather night 24-6h.

Apolo (G VS) Mon-Fri 10-1h
Rodriguez Peña 411

Box Cinema (G VS) 14-6, Sun 16-4h
Laprida 1423 *Near Av. Santa Fé -*
2 Cinemas.

Edén (G VS) 24hrs
Av. Santa Fé 1833 *Galería Bozzini*
2 cinemas.

Equix (G VS) 8-2, Fri & Sat -6, Sun 12-2h
Hipólito Yrigoyen 945

Flores (G VS)
Av. Rivadavia 7366 www.tigrenero.tk
Monthly leather night.

Ideal (G MA S VS) Mon-Fri 9-24, Sat 13-3, Sun 13-23.30h
Suipacha 378 *Near Av. Corrientes* (011) 4326-3300
5 cinemas.

Multicine (G VS) 24hrs
Lavalle 750, Galería *Between Maipú & Esmeralda, Sala Oscar Wilde*

Nuevo Victoria (b G MA VS) 8-1h
Hipólito Yrigoyen 965 *M° 9 de Julio* (011) 4331-4686

Once Plus (G VS) 10-6, Sun 14-2h
Av. Ecuador 54

ESCORTS & STUDIOS

Ratones On Line (G)
www.ratonesonline.com
Big variety of escorts in Buenos Aires, www.ratonesonline.com

Soy Tuyo (G)
www.soytuyo.com
Big variety of escorts in Buenos Aires

SAUNAS/BATHS

A Full (AC B BF DR DU FH G I m MA MSG PP RR SA SB SOL VS WH WO) 12-3, Fri 12-Sun 3h (non-stop)
C/. Viamonte 1770 *M° Callao* (011) 4371-7263 www.afullspa.com.ar
One of the largest saunas in Argentina serving the somewhat shy South American gay scene. Free internet access for visitors. There has been complains about unfriendly staff and lack of cleanliness.

Energy Spa for Men
(B DU FH G M MA MSG PP RR SA SB SOL VS WH WO) Daily 11.30-23.30h
Bravard, 1105 *Corner Av. Angel Gallard, near Parque Centenario, M° Angel Gallardo* (011) 4854-5625 www.energy-spa.com.ar
Energy Spa is a traditional sauna, which has been renovated in an Asian style. They also offer Wellness services such as oriental, medical or erotic massages. Simply ask for the key when you wish to use a cubical.

Homo Sapiens
(AC B DR DU FC FH G GH LAB m MA MSG OS RR SA SB VS) 12-24h
C/. Gascón, 956 *Near Av. Córdoba, 1 block from disco Amerika*
(011) 4862-6519
Sauna on 1200 m². Big cinema with large screen, rooftop terrace and maze. now with special amazingly relaxing massage beds! unique in BsAs!

Nagasaki (AC B DR DU FC FH G m MSG OC SA SB SL VS WH)
Daily 13-24h
Agüero 427 *M° Carlos Gardel, 70 m from Shopping Abasto*
(011) 4866-6335 www.nagasakispa.com
The biggest sauna in town. Small sauna and steam room.

Unikus (B DR G m MA MSG r SA SB VS) Mon-Sun 13-22h
Av. Pueyrredón 1180, Recoleta *Near C/. Mansilla, one block from Puerredón & Santa Fe Av* (011) 4961-7792 www.unikusspa.com.ar

FITNESS STUDIOS

Megatlón (b g MC) Mon-Fri 6-24, Sat 8-20 Sun 10-18h
Rodriguez Peña 1062 *Between Marcelo T de Alvear and Santa Fe*
(011) 4816-7009 6666-496
Slick, clean and busy, the Megatlón chain has all the latest machines and and a wide range of classes from pilates to step. They cater to the expat and wealthy crowd, with a large number of gay men in attendance.

BOOK SHOPS

Fedro (AC G) Mon-Sat 12-21h
Carlos Calvo 578, San Telmo *M° Independencia/San Juan*
(011) 4300-7551 www.fedrosantelmo.com.ar
Gay owned, selling books, DVDs, music. Workshops on Argentinian history in English and French.

Otras Letras (b CC GLM MC) Mon-Sun 12-20h
Soler 4796 *M° Lima, Avenida de Mayo* (011) 4831-5129
www.libreriaotrasletras.com
The first gay bookshop in South America for the LGBT community.

TRAVEL AND TRANSPORT

Mister Papi (G)
address upon request (011) 4372-4578 www.misterpapi.com.ar
Personal tour guide. City advisor. Walking tours in Buenos Aires.

HOTELS

Axel Hotel Buenos Aires (AC B BF CC glm I M MC PI RWB RWS RWT SA SB SOL VA WH WO) 24hrs
C/. Venezuela, 649-651 *San Telmo* (011) 4136-9393
www.axelhotels.com
Axel Hotel Buenos Aires is the first gay hotel in Latin America. There are forty-eight guestrooms (including superior rooms and a suite), restaurant, gym, sauna, Jacuzzi and pool. In the heart of the gay area. Ideal for cosmopolitan gay travellers and businessmen.

GUEST HOUSES

1555 Malabia House (AC B BF H I MA OS) All year
C/. Malabia 1555 *Palermo Viejo, between Honduras & Gorriti*
(011) 4833-2410 www.malabiahouse.com.ar
15 double rooms, private bathrooms. Personalized service. All rooms have TV.

Bayres (AC GLM OS)
Av. Córdoba 5842 *In old Palermo, M° Dorrego, line B*
(011) 4772-3877 www.bayresbnb.com

Calden Guest House Boutique (AC BF G I MA RWS RWT VA)
All year
Reconquista 755, 1°8 *M° Florida, behind Galerias Pacifico*
(011) 4893-1060 www.caldenargentina.com
Four double rooms, one triple. Gay owned. Tastefully decorated.

■ **Favela** (BF G OS VS WO) Sat-Tue, all year
Zonas de Tres Bocas, Delta del Tigre *Access only by boat*
☎ (011) 4954-0892 🖳 www.favela-delta.com.ar
Gay venue at the Delta del Tigre area. Facilities for water sports.

■ **Hostal Costa Rica** (BF cc g MC)
C/. Costa Rica 4137/39, Palermo ☎ (011) 4864-7390
🖳 www.hotelcostarica.com.ar
A great location and has numerous rooms for different budgets.

■ **Lugar Gay B&B**
(AC B BF G I MA MSG NU OS P RWB RWS RWT SOL WH) All year
Defensa 1120 *San Telmo* ☎ (011) 4300-4747 🖳 www.lugargay.com.ar
Seven double rooms, two single rooms and dormitory. Nice rooftop terrace with showers. Lugar Gay B&B was the first gay bed & breakfast in Buenos Aires.

■ **Palermo Viejo B&B** (AC BF G I MA OS RWS RWT) All year, 9-21h
Cnel. Niceto Vega 4629 ☎ (011) 4773-6012 🖳 www.palermoviejobb.com
Features 6 rustic and nice rooms.

APARTMENTS

■ **Landinargentina** (CC H)
Villarroel 1346 ☎ (011) 3535-7170 🖳 www.landinargentina.com
landinargentina is a team fully devoted to provide hosting assistance to persons who wish to temporarily live in Argentina. With efficiency and quality of service, they provide an effortless search for properties as well as the rent of all kinds of properties all along the country.

■ **BA4U Apartments** (CC GLM RWS RWT VA) Mon-Fri 9-19h
Santa Fé 2630, 7E ☎ (011) 4827-5293
🖳 www.ba4uapartments.com.ar
Personalized service and operated by gay owners. Wonderful apartments. Lots of facilities.

■ **BAires Rental** (AC bf cc GLM) 24hrs
Av. Santa Fé 2069 4° B ☎ (011) 4711-6303
🖳 www.bairesgayrental.com.ar
Privacy and comfort in the centre of Buenos Aires. Gay owned and operated.

■ **Best in BA** (AC G I MA RWS RWT VA) Office: Mon-Fri 9-19h
Pte. J. E. Uriburu 1689 2nd floor ☎ (011) 4803-5533
☎ 911-5114-2894 (mobile) 🖳 www.bestinba.com
Apartments located in all the best areas, convenient for gay travellers. F ree gay info.

■ **Friendly Apartments**
(AC CC glm I PI RWB RWS RWT SA VA WH WO) Reception 8-22, Sat 8-16h
Av. Callao 1234, Recoleta *M° Callao, Linea D* ☎ (011) 4816-9056
🖳 www.friendlyapartments.com
Fantastic, upmarket apartments. Some with whirlpool and sauna.

GENERAL GROUPS

■ **Centro de Documentación Gay-lesbico** (G)
Pasaje del Progreso, 949 ☎ (011) 4922-3351 🖳 www.sigla.org.ar
Gay-lesbian archives.

■ **Grupo NEXO**
Av. Callao, 339 6to B ☎ (011) 4374-4484 🖳 www.nexo.org

■ **Mariano Garcés Tango** (GLM MA) Mon-Sun 9-21h (booking in advance required)
Beauchef 973 - Apt."C" ☎ (15) 5654-1658 (mobile)
Gay tango classes (groups and indivivual), gay „milongas".

■ **SIGLA (Sociedad de Integración Gay-Lésbica Argentina)** (GLM)
Pasaje del Progreso, 949 ☎ (011) 4922-3351 🖳 www.sigla.org.ar
Political and social GLM group.

FETISH GROUPS

■ **Club de Osos de Buenos Aires** (G)
Humberto 1° 1662/4 ☎ (011) 4304-2443 🖳 www.ososbue.com
Bears group.

■ **Grupo los Fiesteros** (AC B DR F G MA NU P SNU VS)
5-6 parties per month from 20-24h
🖳 www.grupolosfiesteros.com.ar
Sex and nudist parties for all age groups.

SPORT GROUPS

■ **SAFG – Seleccion Argentina Futbolistas Gay**
🖳 www.safgay.com.ar
The Argentinian Gay Soccer National Team's (S.A.F.G.)

CRUISING

-Parke Rosedal after 23:00h
-Avenida Santa Fé (at Avenida Pueyrredón, best 1h)
-Avenida Santa Fé (at Avenida Callao)
-Avenida Cabildo (between Virrey del Pino and Avenida Monroe)
-Plaza Las Heras (Avenida Las Heras and Coronel Días) WE
-Ciudad Universitaria: Behind Universities in Nuñez by the river, in the bushes on the left hand side on the road (Sat, Sun afternoon, Bus 37, 45, 160)
-Reserva Ecológica (Avenida Belgrano, Viamonte and Avenida Costanera)
-Plaza Dorrego (San Telmo) flea-market (Sun)
-Estación de trenes Constitución (bathrooms) AYOR
-Estación de trenes Retiro (bathrooms) AYOR.

Córdoba ☎ 0351

BARS

■ **Agosto** (B GLM) Wed-Fri 22-4, Sat 22.30-4h
Libertad 187

■ **Beep Pub** (B DR GLM YC) Thu-Sun 24-10h
Sucre 173 *Between Av. Colón & Av. 9 de Julio* ☎ (0351) 425-6521
🖳 www.hangar18.fanspace.com
It's more an after hour bar.

■ **Ojo Bizarro. El** (B G) Thu-Sun 24-10h
Igualdad 176
An after hour bar.

■ **Somos Planta** (AYOR B G MC R T) Fri-Sun 24-?h
San Martín 666

DANCECLUBS

■ **Gloss** (B D GLM)
www.glossdisco.ucoz.com
■ **Ibiza** (B D GLM) Sun 0.30-5h
Chacabuco 544 ☎ ((15)) 357514 www.ibizadanceclub.ucoz.com
■ **Piaf** (B D GLM MA ST t WE) Sat, Sun and on public holidays 1-6h
Obispo Ceballos 45 *San Martín* ☎ (0351) 471-7914
■ **Zen** (AC B cc D G H M MA S ST T VS) Thu 22-?, Fri & Sat 24-6h
Av. Julio Roca 730 ☎ (15) 9608-8928 (mobile) ☎ 0351 1561-3432 (fax)
www.zendisco.com.ar
Bar, restaurant and disco at the weekend.

SEX CINEMAS

■ **30 Hot Cinema** (AC g VS) 14-3h
Humberto 1° 819 ☎ (0351) 429-041
■ **Tao Sex** (g SNU t VS WE) Mon-Thu 10-4, Fri & Sat -5, Sun 14-4h
Rivadavia 219 ☎ (0351) 423-2865
2 cinemas. Private cabines avaialble.
■ **Vips Cinema** (AC g VS) Mon-Sat 10-3, Sun 14-3h
Santa Rosa 212
2 cinemas, the smaller one has gay videos available.

SAUNAS/BATHS

■ **Club 466** (B DU G OS RR SA SB SOL VS WO) Mon-Sun 15-24h
Tucuman 466
■ **Estambul** (B DU G OS RR SA SB VS WO)
La Rioja 936 5000 www.estambulsauna.com

CRUISING

-Plaza San Martín
-Plaza Vélez-Sarsfield
-Avenida Argentina to Plaza Centenario onto Parque Sarmiento
-Río Primero (along the bank)
-Calle Buenos Aires (between Boulevard Illia and 27 de Abril)
-Calle Rivadavia (between 27 de Abril and 25 de Mayo)
-25 de Mayo (between Alvear and San Martín)
-9 de Julio (between San Martín and La Cañada)
-Dean Funes (between General Paz and San Martín)
-Santa Rosa (between Maipú and General Paz)
-Rosario de Santa Fé (between San Martín and Alvear)
-Galería San Martín (San Martín 50)
-Paseo de las Artes (this is a handcrafts market at the WE)
-Avenida Hipólito Yrigoyen (around the area of Teatro San Martín).

Corrientes ☎ 03783

DANCECLUBS

■ **Clinica. La** (B D G)
Uruguay 147
■ **Contramarcha** (B D G)
Piambre 2280 *At Cazadores Correntinos*

La Plata ☎ 0221

BARS

■ **Open** (B G) Fri & Sat 24-?h
C/. 10 entre 45 y 46

DANCECLUBS

■ **Juana** (B D G S SNU) Fri & Sat 24.30-6.30h
Av 44 nro 775 entre 10 y 11 ☎ (0221) 1555-76807
www.juanadisco.com.ar

Mar del Plata ☎ 0223

BARS

■ **Pin Up** (B D GLM S ST WE)
Santiago del Estero 2265 www.pinupweb.com

DANCECLUBS

■ **eXtasis** (B D glm MA)
Corrientes 2044 www.extasisdisco.com.ar

SEX CINEMAS

■ **Cine A** (g VS) 12-6h
San Martin / Av. Corrientes *At Corrientes, Galeria Florida*
■ **Cine Cristal** (DR G VS) 12-4h
Entre Rios 1789
■ **Cine Sex** (g VS) 12-4h
Belgrano 2331

GUEST HOUSES

■ **Hostería San Valentín** (B BF CC H OC) von Dec-1°Apr and Easter
Mitre 1168 *A 50 metros del mar* ☎ (0223) 495-4891

CRUISING

-Rambla Hotel Provincial
-Peatonal San Martín
-Playa Chica
-Playa Escondida (! NU), it's outside the city, but is full of nude gay people in the summer. Beautiful beach with wonderful guys. Cruising in the bushes
-Plaza Rocha.

Mendoza ☎ 0261

BARS

■ **Reserva. La** (B G m MC P S ST)
Av. Rivadavia 32 *Just off the main thoroughfare of Av. San Martin, in the city center* ☎ (0261) 420-3531
A small bar with inexpensive beer, wine, cocktails, and snacks. Live entertainment and drag shows. Busy place at the weekend.

DANCECLUBS

■ **Queen** (B D G MA S)
C/. 25 de Mayo, 318, Guaymallén www.queendisco.com
■ **Reserva. La** (B G MA S t)
Rivadavia 32 ☎ 4203-531

SEX CINEMAS

■ **Adam** (G VS) 12-4h
Av. San Martín 1672 ☎ 420-3837
■ **Porky's** (G VS) 10-3h
Lavalle 34

SAUNAS/BATHS

■ **Alternative Spa** (B cc DU G MA MSG SA VS WH)
Mon-Fri 14-23, Sat 14-Sun 10h (non-stop)
Av. José F. Moreno 1348 ☎ (0261) 420-0118
www.spaalternative-mza.com.ar
Sauna for 6 men, hydromassage for 6 men. Sat, Tue & Thu 50% off after 17.30h

CRUISING

-Avenida San Martín (between Rivadavia and Las Heras)
-Avenida Las Heras (between Av. San Martín and Av. Mitre)
-Avenida Mitre (between Av. Las Heras and Espejo)
-Calle Espejo (between Av. San Martín and Chile)
-Calle Chile (between C/. Espejo and Av. Las Heras)
-Calle Gutiérrez (between Calle Chile and Av. San Martín)
-Calle 25 de Mayo (between Las Heras and Calle Gutiérrez)
-Plaza Chile and Plaza Italia
-Plaza Independencia
-Calle Necochea (between San Martín and 25 de Mayo)
-Plaza San Martín
-Plazoleta O'Higgins
-Plazoleta Barraquero
-Parque General San Martín

Posadas ☎ 0355

DANCECLUBS

■ **Troyano** (B D G S) Fri & Sat 22-?h
Santa Fe 1655

CRUISING

-Plaza San Martin.

Rosario ☎ 0341

PUBLICATIONS

■ **AGmagazine** (GLM)
💻 www.agmagazine.info
A complete website in Spanish, about LGBT news from Argentina.
■ **Vox** Mon-Fri 10-20h
C./ Entre Ríos ☎ (0341) 448-5713 💻 www.voxargentina.org
LGBT monthly magazine for Rosario City, sponsored by the VOX Civic Association for the sexual minorities. For free in gay venues. Also gay group.

BARS

■ **Beso. El** (B D G MA)
Güemes 2631
Post dance pub, open until 8h.
■ **Del Mar** (B G MA) Mon-Sun 21-6h
Tucumàn & Balcarce ☎ 15541-2555
Very gay-friendly bar & restaurant. Excellent music.
■ **Inicio Pub** (B G MA) Mon-Sun 24-?h
Mitre 1880

DANCECLUBS

■ **Gotika City Club** (! B D GLM MA S) Fri & Sat 24-?h
Mitre 1539 ☎ (15) 519-2329 (mobile)
💻 www.gotikacityclub.com.ar
Amazing historic building turned to a huge gay disco in Rosario.
■ **Mistika** (B D G MA S ST) Thu-Sat 24-?h
San Martin 1443
■ **Refugio. El** (B D G MA ST) Fri-Sun
Laprida 845 ☎ (0341) 411-9201 💻 www.elrefugio.com.ar
A new location with the biggest dico in the city. Great atmosphere. The former Refugio Club still exists at Laprida 845, with excellent drag shows.

SEX CINEMAS

■ **Microcine de la Cortada** (G VS) 10-24.30h
Cortada Ricardone 44
Gay porn movies on Thu.

SAUNAS/BATHS

■ **Aqua Men** (B DR DU MSG SA SB WH)
Mon-Sat 12-24, Sun 16-24h
Maipú 1282 ☎ (0341) 447-6989 💻 www.aquamen.com.ar
The sauna offers a variety of packs such as wellness services, emergency unit and lockers. Bar service will be charged upon departure.

GENERAL GROUPS

■ **VOX Asociación Civil** Mon-Fri 10-14, 18-20h
Entre Ríos 1087, Planta alta ☎ (0341) 448-5713
💻 www.voxargentina.org
Civil association for Rosario and argentinian gay and lesbian rights.

HEALTH GROUPS

■ **Fundación SIviDA**
Zeballos 1416 ☎ (15) 507-5307 (mobile)

CRUISING

-Peatonal Córdoba (at night)
-Peatonal San Martín (at night)
-San Luis y Corrientes streets intersection (escorts zone).

Salta ☎ 0387

BARS

■ **Estación Tequila** (B G MA) 22-3, Fri & Sat -8h
San Luis 348

CRUISING

-Peatonal Alberti (G) (at night)
-Parque San Martín (t) (at night).

San Juan ☎ 0264

DANCECLUBS

■ **Rapsodia** (B D G MA) Sat & Sun 1-?h
Av. de Circunvalación 489 oeste

San Miguel de Tucumán ☎ 0381

BARS

■ **Divas** (B G MA)
Rivadavia 1322 esq Chile
💻 Divasdiscotucuma.blogspot.com
■ **Gel** (B g MA SNU)
San Juan 1101
This bar is not gay but has some strip shows sometimes.

DANCECLUBS

■ **Club Mix** (B D DR G MA S) Sat & Sun 1-4h
Libano 1020
■ **Margarito** (B D G MA) Wed-Sun 24-?h
Corrientes 1902

CRUISING

-Plaza Independencia
-Plaza Belgrano
-Parque 9 de Julio
-Parque Avellaneda
-Around Government Palace.

Santa Fé ☎ 0342

BARS

■ **Edén. El** (B G MA)
Mitre 2680, Santo Tomé
■ **Geo Pub** (B g MC) Tue-Sun 23-?h
Marcial Candoti 3137

DANCECLUBS

■ **Tudor Taberna** (B D G MA) Sat
Javier de la Rosa 325 *Barrio de Guadalupe*

CRUISING

-Plaza Mayo
-Plaza San Martín.

Suipacha ☎ 02324

DANCECLUBS

■ **Zona X** (! B D DR G MA OS) Thu-Sat 0:30-6h
Ruta 5 Km 128 ☎ (15) 6598 3483 (mobile)
💻 www.xzonax.com.ar
Very famous because „argentinian gauchos" go there.

Armenia

Name: Hayastan, Armeniya, Armenien, Arménie
Location: South Caucasus
Initials: ARM
Time: GMT +3
International Country Code: ☎ 374 (omit 0 from area code)
International Access Code: ☎ 00
Language: Armenian, Russian
Area: 29,800 km² / 11506 sq mi.
Currency: 1 Dram (ARD) = 100 Luma
Population: 3,026,000
Capital: Yerevan (Eriwan)
Religions: Armenian Apostolic 94%, other Christian 4%, Yezidi 2%
Climate: Highland continental, hot summers, cold winters. The best time to visit is May-July or Sept-Oct.

In December 2002 Armenia adopted a new Criminal Code and abolished the anti-gay article 116 that dated back to 1936. Since then, homosexuality is no longer punishable. At the same time a „gay scene" started to emerge in the capital Yerevan.
To this date, there is no gay rights movement in Armenia and society remains extremely homophobic. Despite the little progress Armenian society remains homophobic and therefore we strictly advise not to hold hands or kiss in public. Even if some venues listed in this guide are frequented by gays and lesbians that doesn't mean they can be compared to western gay bars and discos.
Nevertheless, Armenia has much to offer: as one of the cradles of Christian civilisation, it has over 40.000 churches and the capital alone has over 20 museums. The month of July is rich in events. In the beginning of the month, Yerevan hosts the Golden Apricot Film Festival followed by more and more popular Yerevan Jazz Festival. Outside the capital there is a sometimes stunningly beautiful countryside. Apart from the widespread homophobia, Armenians are said to be tempered, but friendly and welcoming people.

Im Dezember 2002 nahm Armenien ein neues Strafgesetzbuch an und schaffte gleichzeitig den Artikel 116 aus dem Jahre 1936 ab, der gegen Schwule und Lesben gerichtet war. Seitdem gilt Homosexualität nicht länger als Straftat. Gleichzeitig begann die Entwicklung einer kleinen Schwulenszene in der Hauptstadt Yerevan.
In Armenien gibt es bis heute keine Emanzipationsbewegung für Homosexuelle und die Gesellschaft bleibt nach wie vor extrem schwulenfeindlich. Trotz dieser kleinen Fortschritte ist die armenische Gesellschaft weiterhin von Homophobie geprägt. Aus diesem Grund raten wir allen Besuchern dringend davon ab, in der Öffentlichkeit Küsse oder andere körperliche Zeichen der Zuneigung auszutauschen. Obwohl einige der in diesem Reiseführer aufgeführten Veranstaltungsorte von Schwulen und Lesben besucht werden, sind sie nicht mit westlichen Schwulenbars und -discos vergleichbar.
Davon abgesehen hat Armenien viel zu bieten: als Wiege der christlichen Zivilisation verfügt das Land über mehr als 40.000 Kirchen und die Hauptstadt alleine hat über 20 Museen. Besonders viele Events finden im Juli statt, so das Eriwan das Golden Apricot Film Festival, gefolgt vom „Yerewan Jazz Festival', das sich einer von Jahr zu Jahr wachsenden Beliebtheit erfreut.
Den Besucher erwartet außerhalb der Stadt eine wunderschöne Landschaft. Abgesehen von der weit verbreiteten Schwulenfeindlichkeit gelten Armenier als etwas launige, aber nette und gastfreundliche Menschen.

En décembre 2002, l'Arménie a adopté un nouveau code pénal où ne figure plus l'article 116, datant de liannée 1936 et qui était dirigé contre les gays et les lesbiennes. Depuis, l'homosexualité níest plus illégale et on voit naître un milieu gay dans la capitale Erevan.
En Arménie, il níexiste jusquià aujourdíhui aucun mouvement díémancipation homosexuel et la société est extrêmement homophobe. Malgré ces quelques progrès, la société arménienne reste globalement homophobe et il est recommandé de ne pas échanger de signes díaffections ou de baisers en public. Bien que certains des lieux mentionnés dans ce guide soient fréquentés par des gays et des lesbiennes, ils ne peuvent en aucun cas être comparés aux bars et boîtes gays occidentaux.
LíArménie a cependant beaucoup à offrir : berceau de la civilisation chrétienne, le pays dispose de plus de 40 000 églises et la capitale compte, à elle seule, plus de 20 musées. Cíest en juillet quíont lieu la majorité des attractions : au début du mois se déroule le « Golden Apricot Film Festival », suivi du « Yerewan Jazz Festival » qui jouit díune popularité croissante díannée en année.
Le visiteur y trouvera également une magnifique nature hors des villes et une population certes généralement homophobe mais hospitalière et sympathique.

En diciembre de 2002, Armenia adoptó un nuevo código penal y con ello derogó el artículo 116 del año 1936, que iba dirigido en contra de gays y lesbianas. Desde entonces la homosexualidad no es más un acto criminal. A la vez empezó a desarrollarse un pequeño ambiente homosexual en la capital, Yerevan.
En Armenia, hasta hoy, todavía no existe un movimiento de emancipación para los homosexuales y la sociedad sigue siendo extremadamente intolerante. A pesar de estos pequeños avances, la sociedad armenia continúa siendo homófoba. Por este motivo, aconsejamos a todos los visitantes que no intercambien en público besos ni cualquier otra muestra de afecto. Aunque algunos de los lugares indicados en esta guía son frecuentados por gays y lesbianas, no son nunca comparables con los bares y discotecas gays occidentales.
Exceptuando esto, Armenia tiene mucho que ofrecer: como cuna de la civilización cristiana, el país posee más de 40.000 iglesias y la capital por sí sola tiene más de 20 museos. Especialmente, muchos de los eventos tienen lugar en julio. A principios de mes se celebra en Ereván el „Golden Apricot Film Festival", seguido del Festival de Jazz, que está ganando año tras año más popularidad.
Solamente en la capital hay más de 20 museos. Fuera de la ciudad, al visitante le espera un paisaje maravilloso. Independientemente de la tan extendida homofobia, los armenios están considerados como personas un poco caprichosas pero simpáticas y hospitalarias.

Dal dicembre del 2002 in Armenia vige un nuovo codice penale che tra l'altro ha omesso l'omofobo articolo 116 risalente al

1936. Da allora l'omosessualità non è più considerata reato. Contemporaneamente all'adozione del nuovo codice, nella capitale Yerevan, si è andata sviluppando una piccola scena gay.
Ancora in Armenia non esiste un vero e proprio movimento per l'emancipazione omosessuale e la società rimane estremamente omofoba. Nonostante questi piccoli passi avanti, la società armena rimane comunque molto omofoba. Quindi vi consigliamo massima discrezione in pubblico: evitate di baciarvi e di scambiarvi effusioni in luoghi pubblici. Anche se segnaliamo in questa guida alcuni bar e discoteche frequentabili da gay e lesbiche, bisogna comunque tener presente che non sono da paragonare a quelli occidentali. Per il resto l'Armenia ha davvero tanto da offrire: essendo la culla della civilizzazione cristiana, qui vi si trovano 40.000 chiese. La capitale, da sola, possiede oltre 20 musei. Nel mese di luglio hanno luogo molte manifestazioni culturali. All'inizio del mese ad Eriwan si svolge il festival del cinema Golden Apricot, seguito dal Yerewan Jazz Festival, che di anno in anno gode sempre più di una crescente attenzione.
Solo la capitale offre più di 20 musei. Fuori dalla città i turisti possono ammirare un paesaggio sbalorditivo. A parte per la diffusa omofobia, gli Armeni si distinguono per la loro simpatia e ospitalità.

NATIONAL GAY INFO

Gayarmenia.com (GLM)
www.gayarmenia.com
GayArmenia.com is a meeting place for LGBT Armenians around the world. It is a place where they can find new friends, travel info on Armenia and read the latest news on gay life. With personal adds and in Russian, English and French.

Pink Armenia
41/1 Nalbandyan, apt. 1a, Yerevan ✉ Yerevan ☎ (10) 561 396
www.pinkarmenia.org
iPINK Information, Education, Communicationî center. PINK Armenia started in 2007 and promotes the ideas of equality and acceptance of vulnerable groups.

Yerevan (Eriwan) ☎ 010

CAFES

Artbridge (B BF M MA NG)
Abovyan Street, 20 ☎ (010) 521 239
Great food and nice social place, a very American „Barnes & Noble Café"-type atmosphere. New and second hand books, souvenirs, and handcraft works are available here. Offers original coffee, a light European cuisine, daily breakfast and very good pasta.

RESTAURANTS

Square One (M MA NG) Daily 9-24h
Abovyan Street, 1/3 ☎ (094) 53 04 14 www.squareone.am
Eatery offering American dishes in a comfortable, friendly atmosphere from 9-2h. It has very gay-friendly staff and many mostly young GL people come here to taste the best burgers.

TRAVEL AND TRANSPORT

Hyur Service
50 Nalbandyan Street *Going up from Sakharov Square to Tumanyan intersection, on the right* ☎ 54 60 40 www.hyurservice.com
Furnished apartments for short or long term rentals in the capital. The company has offices in Los Angeles and in Paris.

HOTELS

Ararat (AC B BF H M MA NG OS PI PK RWB RWS RWT SA VS WO) All year
7 Grigor Lusavorich Street ☎ (010) 510 000 www.ararathotel.am
52 rooms and 5 suites with sat-TV, mini-bar, phone, internet access, WC/bath with floor heating and king size beds. Non-smoking rooms available.

CRUISING

-Opera Place (AYOR: discretion recommended, only a place for picking up people)
-Kom-aygui (also called Pleshka) - close to the Yerevan City Hall and the French Embassy - best place to pick up at night but beware of police raids.

Australia

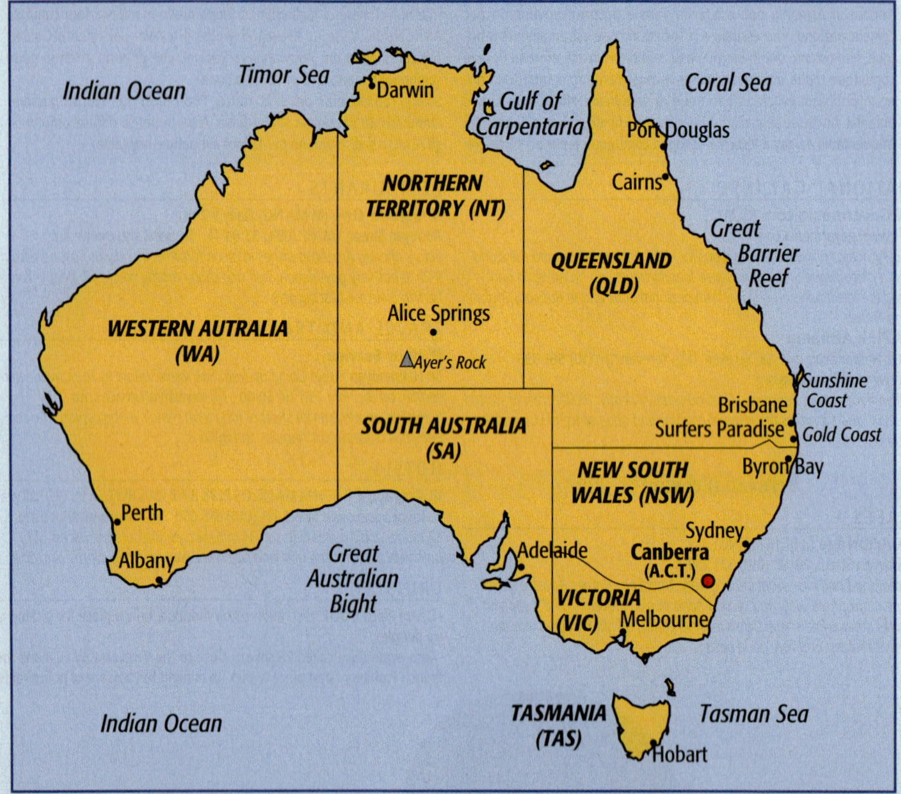

Name: Australien · Australie · Austrália
Location: Oceania
Initials: AUS
Time: GMT +8/+9.5/+10
International Country Code: ☎ 61 (omit first 0 from area code)
International Access Code: ☎ 0011
Language: English
Area: 7,692,030 km² / 2,969,932 sq mi.
Currency: 1 Australian Dollar (A$) = 100 Cents
Population: 20,111,000
Capital: Canberra
Religions: 68% Christians
Climate: The north is a tropical and the south a temperate zone. Temperate regions have 4 seasons and tropical areas only summer (wet) and winter (dry).
Important gay cities: Sydney, Melbourne, Brisbane, Cairns & Perth

The 2004 Marriage Amendment Act excludes complete equalization with heterosexual unions on a federal level, but efforts to change it are underway. On the 20th May 2008 the Civil Partnerships Act came into effect. However the government's policy on marriage, under Prime Minister Julia Gillard (Labour Party), apparently reflects the „traditional" view held in the community, that marriage should be between a man and a woman. The Government of Australia supports a state-based nationally consistent scheme for the registration of committed adult relationships that are not marriages. Under the Civil Partnership Act couples pension laws as well as visitation rights in hospitals have been amended.A Marriage Equality bill, introduced by the local Green Party to parliament in June 2009, was rejected in November 2009. The Greens thereupon announced a second attempt in the following legislative period.

A third of Australia's eight states and territories have varying laws regarding same-sex couples, but the ACT (Australian Capital Territory) law is considered the strongest. Tasmania is the first Australian federal state to have decided in favour of recognizing overseas same-sex marriages.

Australia is a federation of six states and two territories. For exact details please refer to the corresponding heading for each state or territory.

Australia, an island continent the size of Europe, offers an incredibly diverse gay travel experience: wonderful beaches, amazing rainforests, modern cities, ski areas in winter and the Red Centre with open space as far as the eye can see and wonderful never-ending blue skies. You will find the Australians friendly and hospitable, always pleased to show you their country.

Eine völlige Gleichstellung zur heterosexuellen Ehe schließt der Marriage Act von 2004 auf Bundesebene aus, doch es gibt Bestrebungen, dieses Gesetz zu modifizieren. Das Gesetz zur

Anerkennung eingetragener Partnerschaften ist am 20. Mai 2008 in Kraft getreten. Doch die Einstellung der damaligen Regierung unter der Premierministerin Julia Gillard (Labour-Partei) scheint eher den Ansichten der „traditionellen" Wählergruppen zu entsprechen, dass eine Eheschließung nur zwischen Mann und Frau möglich sein sollte. Die australische Regierung unterstützt ein staatliches, landesweit einheitliches System zur Eintragung fester Partnerbeziehungen, die dann jedoch nicht der Ehe gleichgestellt wären. Im Rahmen des neuen Partnerschaftsgesetzes sind die Regelungen für Rentenansprüche und Rechte bei Besuchen im Krankenhaus angeglichen worden. Eine im Juni 2009 von den hiesigen Grünen eingebrachte Gesetzesvorlage zur Gleichstellung der Homo-Ehe wurde im November 2009 abgelehnt. Die Grünen kündigten daraufhin einen zweiten Anlauf in der darauffolgenden Legislaturperiode an.

In einem Drittel von Australiens acht Bundesstaaten und Territorien gelten unterschiedliche Regelungen für gleichgeschlechtliche Paare, doch die Gesetzgebung in der Hauptstadtregion Australian Capital Territory wird als maßgeblich betrachtet. Als erster australischer Bundesstaat beschloss Tasmanien die Anerkennung gleichgeschlechtlicher Ehen, die im Ausland geschlossen wurden.

Australien ist eine Föderation aus sechs Bundesstaaten und zwei „Territorien". Die australischen Bundesstaaten und Territorien haben jeweils eigene Regelungen zu Homosexualität, Mindestalter und Anti-Diskriminierungsbemühungen. Genauere Einzelheiten sind im Einführungstext des betreffenden Bundesstaates oder Territoriums zu finden.

Australien ist ein Inselkontintent von der Größe Europas und kann schwulen Urlaubern eine unglaubliche Vielfalt an Reiseerfahrungen bieten: fantastische Strände, wunderbare Regenwälder, moderne Großstädte, Skipisten im Winter und das „Rote Zentrum" mit unverbauten Landschaften bis zum Horizont und wundervollem, schier endlosem blauem Himmel. Sie werden entdecken, dass die Australier ein äußerst freundliches und gastfreundliches Volk sind, immer hoch erfreut, Besuchern ihr Land zeigen zu dürfen.

Le Marriage Act de 2004 exclut les homosexuels de l'égalité totale devant le mariage au niveau fédéral mais des voix se lèvent pour modifier cette loi. La loi de reconnaissance des couples est entrée en vigueur le 20 mai 2008. Cependant l'attitude du gouvernement actuel et de son nouveau premier ministre Julia Gillard (Parti Travailliste) semble adopter les vues des groupes d'électeurs „traditionalistes" pour qui le mariage doit être réservé aux relations hommes-femmes. Le gouvernement australien soutient un système étatique, unique pour tout le pays, pour l'enregistrement des relations partenariales stables mais qui ne serait pas équivalent au mariage. Dans le cadre de cette loi de reconnaissance des couples, les droits à la retraite et les droits de visite à l'hôpital ont été alignés.

En juin 2009 une proposition de loi déposée par les Verts pour l'égalité au droit au mariage fut refusée au mois de novembre suivant. Les Verts ont sur ce annoncé une tentative pour la prochaine législature.

Dans un tiers des huit états fédéraux et territoires australiens, des règles différentes sont appliquées pour les couples de même sexe mais la législation de la région de la capitale Australian Capital Territory est considérée comme déterminante. La Tasmanie est le premier Etat australien à avoir reconnu le mariage gay conclu à l'étranger.

L'Australie est Etat fédéral composé de six États et de deux „ territoires „. Les droits des homoexuel(le)s diffèrent d'Etat en Etat : chacun dispose d'une législation propre concernant l'homosexualité, la majorité sexuelle et la discrimination et vous trouverez plus de détails dans les textes se rapportant à chacun d'eux.

L'Australie est à la fois une île et un continent de la taille de l'Europe et offre aux touristes tout ce qu'ils peuvent espérer : des plages fantastiques, des forêts vierges magnifiques, des villes modernes, des pistes de ski en hiver et le „ centre rouge „ avec ses paysages libres de toute construction et son ciel infiniment bleu. Les Australiens sont des gens très sympathiques et hospitaliers, toujours enchantés de pouvoir faire découvrir leur pays aux touristes.

La Ley del Matrimonio de 2004 excluyó la plena igualdad con el matrimonio heterosexual a nivel federal, pero se están llevando a cabo esfuerzos para modificar dicha ley.

La ley para el reconocimiento del registro de parejas entró en vigor el 20 de mayo de 2008. La posición del actual gobierno, con el nuevo primer ministro Julia Gillard (partido laboralista), parece que se corresponda más a las opiniones de los grupos de electores „tradicionales", que creen que el matrimonio sólo es posible entre hombre y mujer. El gobierno australiano apoya un sistema estatal y unitario para todo el país de registro de relaciones estables de pareja, que sin embargo no pueden ser equiparadas al matrimonio. En el marco de esta nueva legislación de parejas, las disposiciones sobre el derecho a renta y derechos de visita en el hospital han sido equiparadas. El proyecto de ley en materia de igualdad para matrimonios homosexuales presentado por los Verdes locales en junio de 2009 fue rechazado el mes de noviembre siguiente. Los Verdes han anunciado un segundo intento con respecto a dicha ley para el próximo período legislativo.

En una tercera parte de Australia, ocho estados federados y territorios, rigen diferentes regulaciones para las parejas del mismo sexo, pero la legislación de la región de la capital (Australian Capital Territory) se la considera como modelo. Tasmania ha pasado a ser el primer estado australiano en reconocer los matrimonios del mismo sexo contraídos en el extranjero.

Australia es una federación de 6 estados federados y dos territorios. Los estados y territorios australianos tienen respectivamente sus propias leyes sobre la homosexualidad, la edad de consentimiento y medidas anti-discriminación. Los datos más concretos se encontrarán en los textos de introducción de cada uno de los estados o territorios.

Australia es una isla-continente tan grande como Europa y ofrece a los turistas homosexuales una increíble variedad de experiencias por descubrir: fantásticas playas, maravillosas selvas, modernas ciudades, pistas de esquí en invierno y el llamado „centro rojo" con unos paisajes interminables hasta el mismo horizonte y espléndidos cielos azules.

Il Marriage Act del 2004 esclude a livello federale una piena equiparazione al matrimonio eterosessuale, tuttavia ci sono delle iniziative di modifica della legge. La legge sulle unioni civili è entrata in vigore il 20 maggio del 2008. Tuttavia l'attitudine del governo, sotto la guida del primo ministro Julia Gillard (Partito Laburista), risponde all'impostazione tradizionalista dei suoi elettori, ovvero l'impostazione secondo la quale il matrimonio deve essere contratto solo tra un uomo e una donna. Il governo australiano supporta un sistema unico per la registrazione civile delle coppie di fatto che tuttavia non può essere messo allo stesso piano di un matrimonio. La nuova legge sulle unioni civili parifica i regolamenti sulla previdenza sociale e il diritto di visita negli ospedali da parte del partner. A giugno del 2009 i verdi australiani hanno presentato un progetto di legge che tende a parificare il matrimonio omosessuale a quello eterosessuale, tuttavia il progetto è stato bocciato a novembre dello stesso anno. I Verdi hanno annunciato un ulteriore tentativo nel corso della prossima legislatura.

In un terzo degli otto Stati federali e Territori vigono diversi regolamenti per le coppie dello stesso sesso, anche se la legislazione della regione della capitale, ovvero di Australian Capital Territory, viene considerata la legislazione di riferimento. La Tasmania ha deciso di riconoscere i matrimoni omosessuali contratti all'estero, essendo così, il primo Stato federale australiano ad andare in questa direzione.

L'Australia è una federazione che comprende sei Stati Federali e due „Territori". Gli Stati Federali e i Territori australiani hanno regole differenti per quello che riguarda l'omosessualità, l'età del consenso e le leggi antidiscriminatorie. Per informazioni più dettagliate potete consultare il testo introduttivo dello Stato Federale o del Territorio che vi interessa.

L'Australia è un'isola continentale grande circa quanto l'Europa ed offre infinite attrazioni turistiche: fantastiche spiagge, meravigliose foreste pluviali, moderne metropoli, e sconfinati cieli azzurri. Scoprirete anche che gli australiani sono un popolo molto cordiale e ospitale che è molto lieto di mostrare il suo Paese ai visitatori.

NATIONAL GAY INFO

Fellow Traveller 21-5h
Level 3, 140 William Street ✉ NSW 2010 East Sydney
☎ (02) 9360 8934 💻 www.fellowtraveller.com.au
Gay & lesbian travel directory. Printed directory and online site with lots of information about hotels and other touristic operations in Australia. Associated with SX publications in NSW.

Gay and Lesbian Tourism Australia (GALTA)
PO Box 1522 ✉ QLD 4005 New Farm 💻 www.galta.com.au
National network of accredited tourism operators providing services to the G&L traveller. Wherever you travel in Australia, look for a GALTA member.

NATIONAL PUBLICATIONS

AXN
Level 3, 140 William Street ✉ NSW 2010 Sydney ☎ (02) 9360 8934
💻 www.axnational.com
Monthly free magazine.

DNA
PO Box 127 ✉ NSW 1825 Lidcombe ☎ (02) 9764 0200
💻 www.dnamagazine.com.au
Monthly national gay men's lifestyle magazine. Available at news agencies.

Gay Traveller (GLM) 9-17h
PO Box 6272 ✉ QLD 4870 Cairns ☎ (07) 4051 6667
💻 www.pinkguide.com
Gay travel guides for Australia and New Zealand.

Pink Directory. The
PO Box 153, 3 Holtermann Street ✉ NSW 2065 Crows Nest
☎ (02) 9437 4033 💻 www.thepinkdirectory.com.au
Directory of Australian gay businesses, services and accommodations.

NATIONAL COMPANIES

Rainbow Tourism
PO Box 20891 ✉ NSW 2002 World Square ☎ (02) 9016 4642
💻 www.rainbowtourism.com
Online booking service for gay travel in Australia, New Zealand and beyond.

NATIONAL GROUPS

Gay & Lesbian Rights Lobby
PO Box 304 ✉ NSW 2037 Glebe ☎ (02) 9571 5501
💻 www.glrl.org.au
Non-profit, community based advocacy and lobbying organization. Staffed only part-time.

Australian Capital Territory

Location: Southeast Australia
Initials: ACT
Time: GMT +10
Area: 2,330km² / 926 sq mi.
Population: 311,000
Capital: Canberra
Important gay cities: Canberra

Canberra ☎ 02

BARS

Tilley's (B glm M OS s) 8-?h
1/94 Wattle Street, Corner Brigalow Street, Lyneham *4 km from city centre, near youth hostel* ☎ (02) 6249 1543 💻 www.tilleys.com.au
Mixed bar and restaurant.

DANCECLUBS

Cube (AC B D GLM MA s) Thu 20.30-5, Fri 21-5, Sat 22-5, Sun -?h
33 Petrie Plaza *Beneath Antigo's restaurant* ☎ (02) 6257 1110
💻 www.cubenightclub.com.au
Canberra's gay and lesbian club. Different events Thu-Sun. Located between the merry-go-round and London Circuit on City Walk.

SEX SHOPS/BLUE MOVIES

Mustang Ranch (AC CC DR G MA VS) 9-24, Fri & Sat 24hrs
Unit 14, Molonglo Mall, Fyshwick ☎ (02) 6280 6969
Sex shop, back room, cinema.

HOTELS

Diamant Hotel Canberra
(AC B bf glm H I M MA PK RWS RWT SA WO) All year
15 Edinburgh Avenue *By Lake Burley Griffin at the intersection of Marcus Clarke St & Edinburgh Ave* ☎ (02) 9332 2011 💻 www.diamant.com.au

APARTMENTS

Forrest Hotel & Apartments
(AC b BF CC glm H I m PK RWS RWT VA) All year
30 National Circuit, Forrest *Next to Parliament House*
☎ (02) 6295 3433 💻 www.forresthotel.com

New South Wales

Location: South East AUS
Initials: NSW
Time: GMT +10
Area: 801,600 km² / 309,498 sq mi.
Population: 6,640,000
Capital: Sydney
Important gay cities: Sydney

Blue Mountains ☎ 02

APARTMENTS

Bygone Beautys Cottages (bf CC glm m OS PA PK RWS RWT) 10-17.30h
20-22 Grose Street, Leura ☎ (02) 4784 3117
💻 www.bygonebeautys.com.au
8 fully self-contained cottages.

Byron Bay ☎ 02

GUEST HOUSES

Amber Gardens (AC B BF CC GLM I MA OS PI PK RWB RWS RWT VA WH) All year. Check-in 12-18h
66 Plantation Drive, Ewingsdale *Northern Rivers* ☎ (02) 6684 8215
💻 www.ambergardens.net
Five guestrooms, all en-suite. Gay owned property.

Azabu (b bf CC glm I m MA MSG OS PI RWB RWS RWT) All year
317 Skinners Shoot Road *3km from the centre of Byron Bay*
☎ (02) 6680 9102 💻 www.azabu.com.au
Five luxury suites.

Coolamon Gaystay (G I MA OS PI RWS RWT)
600 Coolamon Scenic Drive *12mins drive from Byron Bay* ☎ (02) 66 847 096 ☎ (0403) 748 370 (mobile)
💻 www.coolamongaystay.com.au
Free pick-up service offered from local bus station. Shuttle service available from local airports (charge). Gay-owned and operated guesthouse.

Revelwood Rainforest Retreat (BF G I MSG PI PK RWB RWS RWT WH) All year, check in 14-22h
1029 Friday Hut Road, Binna Burra *Northern Rivers region*
☎ (02) 6687 2614 💻 www.revelwoodretreat.com.au
20 mins from Byron Bay and popular nude gay beach, with subtropical rainforest and creek.

Coffs Harbour ☎ 02

GUEST HOUSES

Santa Fe Luxury Bed & Breakfast
(BF CC glm m OS PI PK RWB RWS RWT) All year
235 The Mountain Way (off Gaudrons Rd) *10 km north of Coffs Harbour*
☎ (02) 6653 7700 💻 www.santafe.net.au

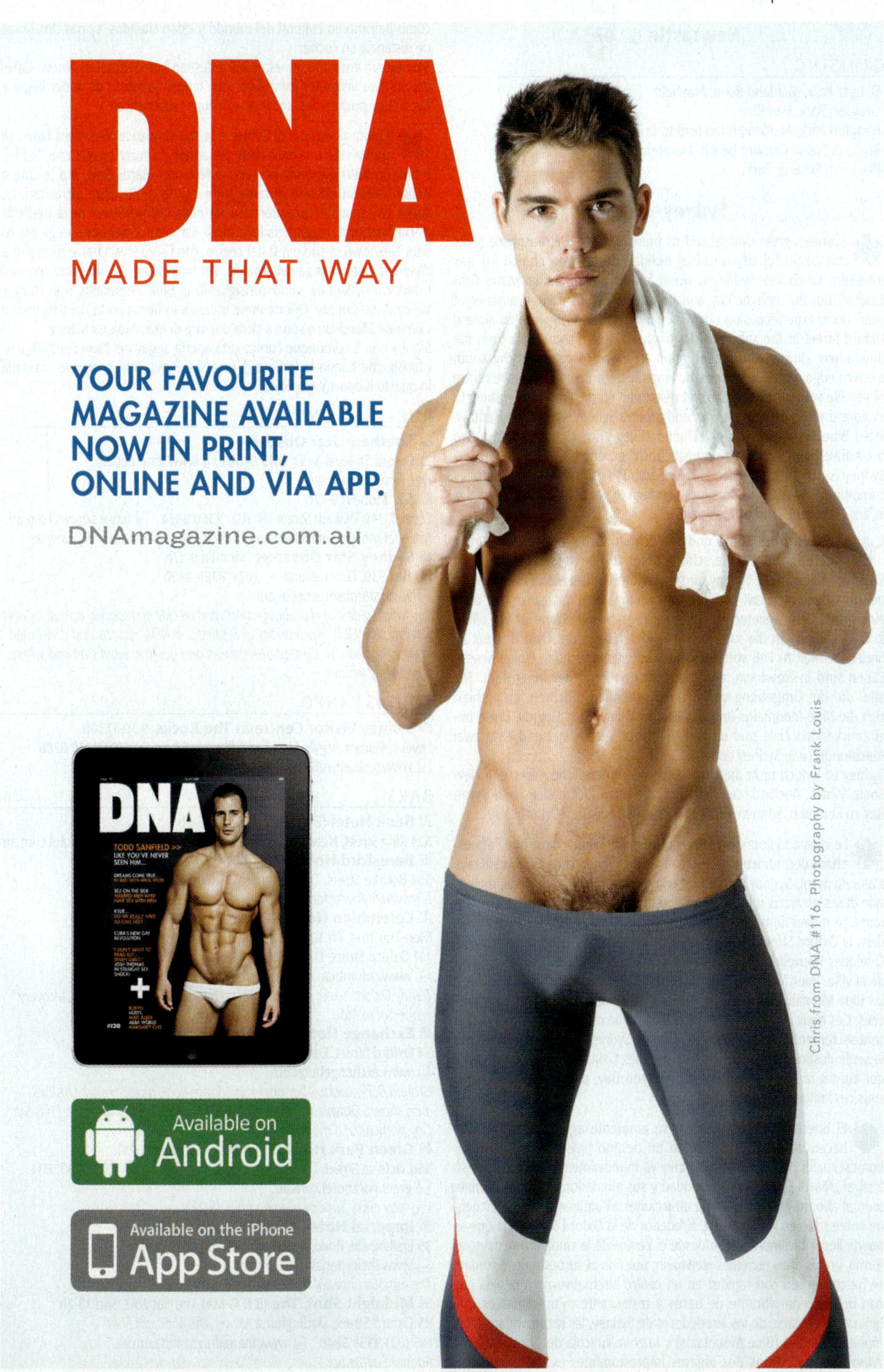

YOUR FAVOURITE MAGAZINE AVAILABLE NOW IN PRINT, ONLINE AND VIA APP.

DNAmagazine.com.au

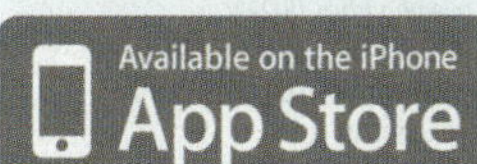

Chris from DNA #116, Photography by Frank Louis

Newcastle ☏ 02

CRUISING

-Dangar Park, Maitland Road, Mayfield
-Gregson Park, Hamilton
-Islington Park, Maitland Road (exit to Criterion Hotel)
-Rocks at Susan Gilmore Beach, Memorial Drive
-Blackbutt Reserve Park.

Sydney ☏ 02

Sydney's great climate and its friendly, relaxed atmosphere make this beautiful city an ideal holiday destination choice for gay travellers. Of course, Sydney is world famous for its annual Mardi Gras Festival, but this eclectic city and its surrounds has a large number of year-round experiences on offer. The gay scene is mostly located around Oxford Street in the suburb of Darlinghurst, just a short walk from the downtown. However in recent years Newtown, located on the south western edge of the downtown, has rapidly become an alternative centre of gay life with its vibrant bar and restaurant scene. For those wishing to explore the countryside close to and around Sydney, the World Heritage listed Blue Mountains and the Hunter Valley Wine Country, both a two hour drive from Sydney, are a great „bush" experience.
Sydney is not the only place in New South Wales that welcomes the gay community. Overseas visitors lucky enough to get to Byron Bay can relax in this „laid back" sub-tropical village.

Sydneys tolles Klima und seine freundliche, entspannte Atmosphäre machen diese schöne Stadt zu einem idealen schwulen Reiseziel. Natürlich ist Sydney für sein weltberühmtes Mardi Gras Festival bekannt, doch die Stadt und ihre Umgebung bieten das ganze Jahr über eine große Zahl weiterer Attraktionen. Die schwule Szene ist vor allem in Darlinghurst um die sogenannte Golden Mile in der Oxford Street zu finden- schnell zu Fuß von der Innenstadt aus erreichbar. Einige neuere Läden sind in Newtown, am südwestlichen Rand der Innenstadt. Für alle, die die Umgebung von Sydney erkunden möchten, empfehlen sich die Blue Mountains und das Hunter Valley Wine County. Diese beeindruckenden Ziele sind im Weltkulturerbe verzeichnet und etwa zwei Autostunden von Sydney entfernt.
Sydney ist jedoch nicht die einzige schwulenfreundliche Adresse in New South Wales. Ausländische Besucher, die das Glück haben nach Byron Bay zu kommen, können sich in diesem subtropischen Ort erholen.

Le climat toujours agréable qui règne à Sydney ainsi que l'atmosphère décontractée de la ville font de Sydney la destination idéale. Naturellement, Sydney est surtout connue pour son Mardi Gras, mais la ville et ses environs offrent grand nombre d'attractions toute l'année durant. Le milieu homo est situé à Darlinghurst aussi appelé Golden Mile dans la Oxford Street, quartier facile d'accès à pied depuis le centre-ville. Quelques nouvelles enseignes sont désormais à Newton, au Sud-Ouest de la ville. Pour tous ceux qui désirent découvrir les environs de Sydney, les Blue Montains ainsi que le Hunter Valley Wine County sont tous proches. Ces deux destinations de rêve font partie du Patrimoine mondial et sont seulement à deux heures de route de Sydney. Mais Sydney n'est pas la seule destination conseillée en Nouvelles Galles du Sud. Les touristes qui auront la chance de parvenir à Byron Bay, pourront se régénérer sous ces latitudes subtropicales.

El buen clima de Sydney y su ambiente agradable y relajado hacen de esta bonita ciudad un destino turístico ideal para los homosexuales. Naturalmente, Sydney es mundialmente conocida por su festival „Mardi Gras", pero la ciudad y sus alrededores ofrecen durante todo el año un gran número de atracciones. El ambiente gay se encuentra sobre todo en Darlinghurst, alrededor de la Oxford Street, a la que se puede llegar fácilmente a pie desde el centro de la ciudad. De cualquier forma, en los años recientes Newtown, ubicado al suroeste de la ciudad, se ha convertido con rapidez en un centro alternativo para la vida gay con una escena vibrante de bares y restaurantes. Para aquellos que quieran informarse de los alrededores de Sydney, les recomendamos las montañas azules (Blue Mountains) y la zona vinícola del „Hunter Valley Wine Country". Estos dos lugares impresionantes están catalogados como patrimonio cultural del mundo y están situados a unas dos horas de distancia en coche.
Sydney, sin embargo, no es el único destino homosexual en Nueva Gales del Sur. Los visitantes extranjeros que tengan la suerte de poder llegar a Byron Bay podrán descansar en este lugar subtropical.

Il fantastico clima di Sidney e la sua simpatica atmosfera fanno di questa città una delle mete più amate dal turista gay. Certo, Sidney è nota in tutto il mondo per la sua festa del Mardi Gras, ma la città e i suoi dintorni offrono durante tutto l'anno molte altre attrazioni. La scena gay si svolge prevalentemente nella Oxford Street nella periferia di Darlinghurst, raggiungibile a piedi dal centro. Sebbene negli ultimi anni Newtown, a sud ovest del centro, con i suoi vivaci bar e ristoranti è diventata una meta gay alternativa. Per tutti coloro che vogliano scoprire i dintorni di Sidney, sono consigliabili le Blue Mountains e la Hunter Valley Wine County. Queste mete mozzafiato fanno parte del Patrimonio Culturale Mondiale e sono a circa due ore di macchina da Sidney.
Sidney non è comunque l'unica città aperta ai gay nel New South Wales. I turisti, che hanno la fortuna di recarsi a Byron Bay, potranno rilassarsi in questo luogo subtropicale.

PUBLICATIONS

Southern Star Observer
21 Oxford St, level 3 ☏ 9015 6800 💻 www.sstar.net.au
Free weekly newspaper.

SX Mon-Fri 9-17h
Level 3, 140 William Street ☏ (02) 9360 8934 💻 www.sxnews.com.au
National monthly magazine and Sydney (local) gay weekly newspaper.

Sydney Star Observer Mon-Fri 9-17h
PO Box 939, Darlinghurst ☏ (02) 8265 0500
💻 www.starobserver.com.au
Australia's oldest and probably most read weekly newspaper, owned by and servicing the GLBTI community of Sydney and NSW regions and distributed in every capital city. Current news, views and guide to what's on and where. Free at gay venues.

TOURIST INFO

Sydney Visitor Centre at The Rocks 9.30-17.30h
Level 1, Corner Argyle Street and Playfair Street ☏ (02) 9240 8788
💻 www.sydneyvisitorcentre.com.au

BARS

Bank Hotel (B glm M MA OS s) 16-1h
324 King Street, Newtown ☏ (02) 8568 1900 💻 www.bankhotel.com.au

Beresford Hotel. The (B glm M MA OS)
354 Bourke Street, Darlinghurst ☏ (02) 9357 1111
💻 www.theberesford.com.au

Colombian Hotel (AC B GLM m MA S t)
Mon-Thu 10-4, Fri 10-6, Sat 11-6, Sun 11-4h
117 Oxford Street, Darlinghurst ☏ (02) 9360 2151
💻 www.colombian.com.au
Trendy Oxford Street pub with second floor cocktail bar. Popular „recovery" venue Sat to Mon.

Exchange Hotel (B D glm MA S) 10-4, Sat & Sun 9-6h
34 Oxford Street, Darlinghurst ☏ (02) 9331 1936
💻 www.exchangehotel.biz
Ground floor: cocktail bar and small dance floor, mixed crowd. Upstairs: drag shows. Downstairs: Phoenix Bar. Changing theme parties on Fri & Sat. Gay party once a month.

Green Park Hotel (B glm MA) 10-2, Sun 12-24h
360 Victoria Street, Darlinghurst *Cnr. Liverpool St* ☏ (02) 9380 5311
💻 greenparkhotel.com.au
Very gay every Sunday evening from 18-22h.

Imperial Hotel. The (B D GLM MA S ST)
35 Erskineville Road, Newtown ☏ (02) 9519 9899
💻 www.theimperialhotel.com.au
The famous Imperial Hotel reopened in 2010.

Midnight Shift, The (B D G MA) Thu-Sat 20-?, Sun 18-2h
85 Oxford Street, Darlinghurst *Above „The Midnight Shift"*
☏ (02) 9358 3848 💻 www.themidnightshift.com.au
Former Saddle bar

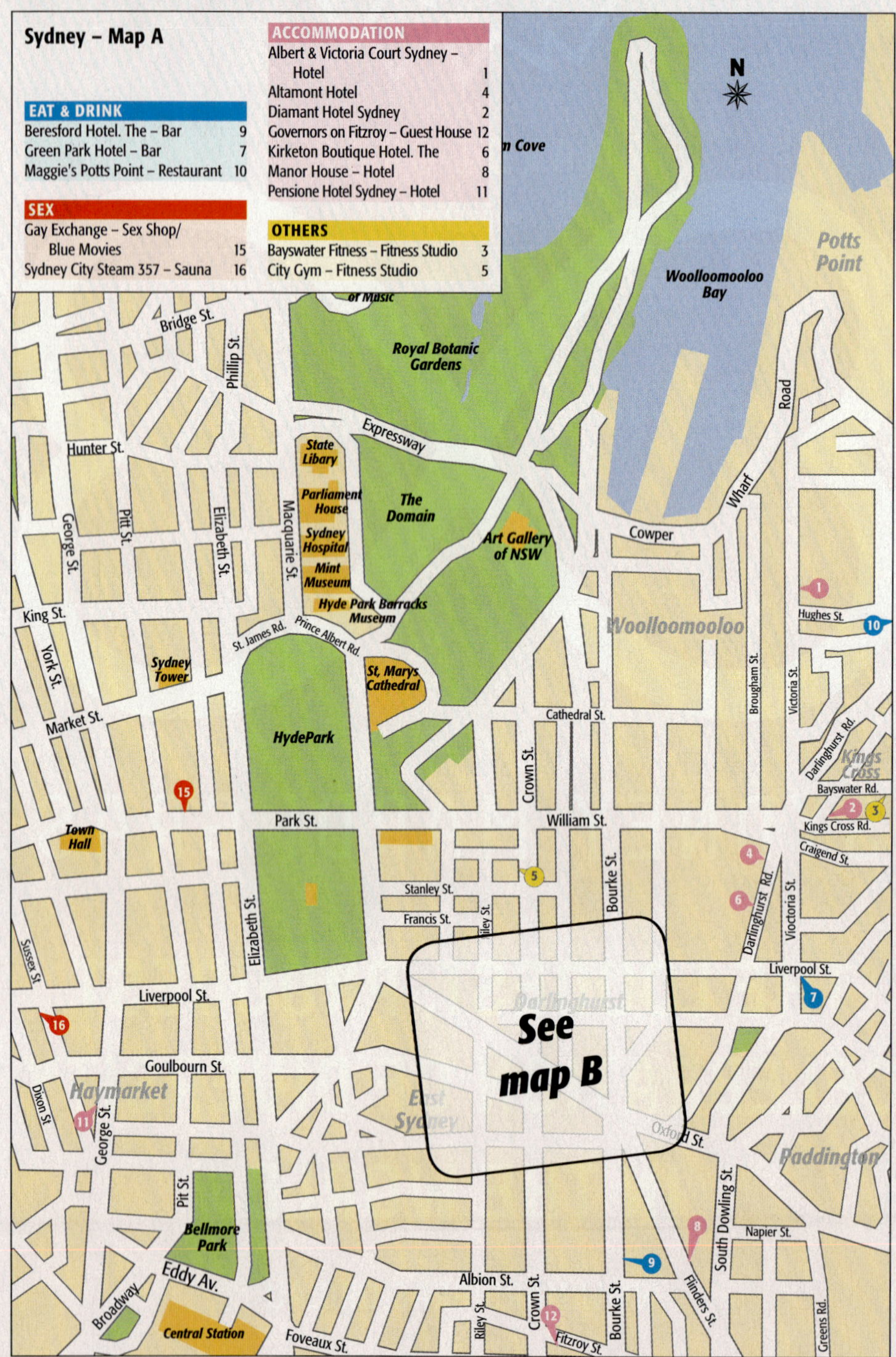
Sydney – Map A
EAT & DRINK
Beresford Hotel. The – Bar 9
Green Park Hotel – Bar 7
Maggie's Potts Point – Restaurant 10
SEX
Gay Exchange – Sex Shop/ Blue Movies 15
Sydney City Steam 357 – Sauna 16
ACCOMMODATION
Albert & Victoria Court Sydney – Hotel 1
Altamont Hotel 4
Diamant Hotel Sydney 2
Governors on Fitzroy – Guest House 12
Kirketon Boutique Hotel. The 6
Manor House – Hotel 8
Pensione Hotel Sydney – Hotel 11
OTHERS
Bayswater Fitness – Fitness Studio 3
City Gym – Fitness Studio 5
N
Woolloomooloo Bay
Potts Point
Royal Botanic Gardens
Bridge St.
Phillip St.
Expressway
Hunter St.
State Libary
Parliament House
The Domain
Sydney Hospital
Mint Museum
Art Gallery of NSW
Hyde Park Barracks Museum
Cowper
Wharf
Road
George St.
Pitt St.
Elizabeth St.
Macquarie St.
King St.
York St.
St. James Rd.
Prince Albert Rd.
Sydney Tower
St. Marys Cathedral
Woolloomooloo
Hughes St.
Brougham St.
Victoria St.
Cathedral St.
Darlinghurst Rd.
Kings Cross
Bayswater Rd.
Kings Cross Rd.
Craigend St.
Market St.
HydePark
Crown St.
Park St.
William St.
Town Hall
Stanley St.
Francis St.
Riley St.
Bourke St.
Darlinghurst Rd.
Vioctoria St.
Sussex St.
Elizabeth St.
Liverpool St.
Liverpool St.
See map B
Goulbourn St.
Haymarket
Dixon St
George St.
East Sydney
Oxford St.
Paddington
Pit St.
Bellmore Park
South Dowling St.
Napier St.
Eddy Av.
Broadway
Central Station
Foveaux St.
Albion St.
Riley St.
Crown St.
Fitzroy St.
Bourke St.
Flinders St.
Greens Rd.

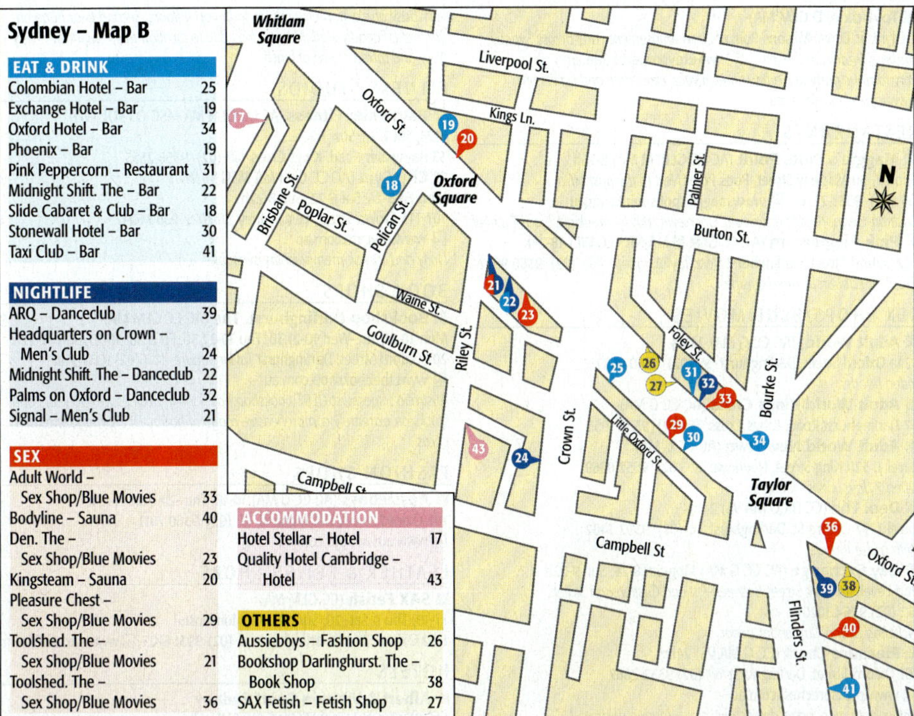

■ **Mr. Mary's** (AC B GLM m MA S ST T WE) 10-?h
106-110 George Street, Redfern *Cnr. Redfern Street* ☎ (02) 9690 0610
Open weekdays for lunch and nightly for dinner. Sunday roast from 18h. Shows Friday 21, 23 and 0.30h and Saturdays 22.30, 23.30 and 0.30h.

■ **Oxford Hotel** (AC B CC D F FC GLM LM m MA NR OS S T VEG W WL) 24hrs
134 Oxford Street, Darlinghurst *Taylor Square* ☎ (02) 9331 3467
🖳 www.theoxfordhotel.com.au
Home of the Sydney Harbour City Bears & Sydney Leather Pride. 4 bars, Polo Lounge, VIP lounge and The Underground bar. Outside deck area with 3 smoking areas.

■ **Slide Cabaret & Club** (AC B CC D glm M MA S) Tue-Sat 19-3, Sun 20-4h
41 Oxford Street, Darlinghurst ☎ (02) 8915 1899 🖳 www.slide.com.au
Stylish cocktail bar, restaurant, danceclub/lounge in state of art design. Restaurant till 21.30h. Live performers such as cabaret singers and jazz musicians.

■ **Sly Fox Hotel** (B glm MA S)
199 Enmore Road, Enmore *Cnr. Cambridge Street* ☎ (02) 9557 1016

■ **Stonewall Hotel** (! AC B D G m MA S SNU ST t) 11-6h
175 Oxford Street, Darlinghurst *Close to Taylor Square*
☎ (02) 9360 1963 🖳 www.stonewallhotel.com
Bar on 3 floors. Karaoke, drag shows and male dancers. Very popular especially with young men. Famous for it's underwear competitions and malebox pick up nights every Wednesday.

■ **Taxi Club** (B D glm M P S ST t)
Mon & Tue 12-2, Wed & Thu -4, Fri -6, Sat 14-6, Sun -4h
40-42 Flinders Street, Darlinghurst ☎ (02) 9331 4256 🖳 www.thetaxi.com.au
Also karaoke. Membership required or be guest of a member.

MEN'S CLUBS

■ **BBO – Bad Boys Orgies** (G MA NU P)
☎ (61) (0)414 722 800 🖳 www.orgyorgyorgy.com
Monthly naked sex parties.

■ **Headquarters on Crown** (! AC b CC DR F G m MA NU S VS)
Daily, 24hrs
273 Crown Street, Darlinghurst *100 m from Oxford Street*
☎ (02) 9331 6217 🖳 www.headquarters.com.au
See website for the latest details on parties such as „piss" and „naked sex" parties. Excellent men's cruise club.

■ **Signal** (AC DR f G m MA s VS WE)
Mon-Thu 11-3, Fri 11-Mon 3h (non-stop)
Corner Riley Street & Arnold Place, Darlinghurst *Above Toolshed in 81 Oxford St take elevator to 2nd floor* ☎ (02) 9331 8830
🖳 www.signalhouse.com.au

DANCECLUBS

■ **ARQ** (AC B D GLM MA S ST T WE) Thu-Sun 21-?h
16 Flinders Street, Darlinghurst *Taylor Square* ☎ (02) 9380 8700
🖳 www.arqsydney.com.au
Two level high energy dance venue with live entertainment. Different theme parties.

■ **Midnight Shift. The** (AC B CC D G MA S VS) Bar downstairs: Mon-Sun 12-6, nightclub upstairs: Fri & Sat 22-7h
85 Oxford Street, Darlinghurst *Between Crown & Riley*
☎ (02) 9360 4319 🖳 www.themidnightshift.com
Upstairs: Midnight Shift Nightclub, downstairs: The Shift Video Bar.

■ **Palms on Oxford** (AC B D GLM MA WE)
Thu & Sun 20-0, Fri & Sat -3h
124 Oxford Street, Darlinghurst ☎ (02) 9357 4166
🖳 www.facebook.com/pages/Palms-On-Oxford/214357675247446
Small dance club downstairs, popular dance music mainly 80's also including 90's through to todays Top40.

■ **Rising @ Phoenix** (B D G MA P) Sat & Sun 4-?h
34 Oxford Street, Darlinghurst *Downstairs at Exchange Hotel*
☎ (02) 9331 1936 🖳 risingdayclub.com.au

■ **Toybox** (B D GLM MA)
1 Olympic Drive, Milsons Poin *At Luna Amusement Park, across Sydney Harbour Bridge on the left* 🖳 www.toyboxparty.com.au
Very famous party just a few times a year. Exact date and tickets on www.toyboxparty.com.au

RESTAURANTS

■ **Maggie's Potts Point** (AC CC GLM M MA) 8-23h
Shop 7, 50 Macleay Street, Potts Point *Next to the post office*
☎ (02) 9331 2226 🖳 www.maggiespottspoint.com.au
Austrian-German café/restaurant. Open every day for breakfast, lunch & dinner.

■ **Pink Peppercorn** (AC CC GLM M MA NR VEG WL) 18-24h
122 Oxford Street, Darlinghurst *Near Taylor Square* ☎ (02) 9360 9922
Excellent Laotian inspired cuisine.

SEX SHOPS/BLUE MOVIES

■ **Adult World** (AC CC G MA) 24hrs
124a Oxford Street, Darlinghurst ☎ (02) 9360 8527
Video booths.

■ **Adult World Kings Cross** (AC CC G MA)
37 Darlinghurst Road, Kings Cross ☎ (02) 9358 1955

■ **Adult World Newtown** (AC CC G MA)
Level 1, 320 King Street, Newtown ☎ (02) 9557 0069
Open 7 days. Cruise lounge.

■ **Den. The** (CC DR G MA VS) 24hrs
Level 1, 97 Oxford St, Darlinghurst ☎ (02) 9332 3402
With cruise lounge.

■ **Gay Exchange** (AC CC G MA) Mon-Sat 8-24, Sun 9-22h
2nd Level, 44 Park Street *Between Pitt and Castlereagh Streets*
☎ (02) 9264 1020
Including Bruno Gmuender depot.

■ **Pleasure Chest** (CC G MA VS) 24hrs
161 Oxford Street, Darlinghurst ☎ (02) 9332 2667
🖳 www.pleasurechest.com.au
Cabins with glory holes downstairs, cruise lounge upstairs.

■ **Toolshed. The** (CC G MA)
10-1, Mon -24, Fri & Sat -4, Sun 10.30-24h
191 Oxford Street, Darlinghurst *Downstairs* ☎ (02) 9360 1100
🖳 www.toolshed.com.au

■ **Toolshed. The** (CC G MA)
81 Oxford Street, Darlinghurst *Level 1* ☎ (02) 9332 2792
🖳 www.toolshed.com.au

SAUNAS/BATHS

■ **Aarows** (AC b DR DU FC G GH m MA MSG SA SB SL t VS WH WO)
Daily, 24hrs
17 Bridge Street, Rydalmere *Western Suburbs - close to Parramatta*
☎ (02) 9638 0553 🖳 www.aarows.com.au
Sauna in the western suburbs. Mostly gay but open to all genders and sexual preferences.

■ **Bodyline** (AC B CC DR DU FC FH G I LAB M MA OS P PP RR SA SB SOL VS WH WO) Mon-Thu 12-7, Fri 12-Mon 7h (non-stop)
10 Taylor Street, Darlinghurst *Just off Oxford Street at Taylor Square*
☎ (02) 9360 1006 🖳 www.bodylinesydney.com.au
Four floors.

■ **Ken's at Kensington** (AC AK CC DR DU FC G GH I M MA MSG PI SA SB SH SL VR WH WO) Daily 11-5h
83 Anzac Parade, Kensington *4 km from Taylor Square*
☎ (02) 9662 1359 🖳 www.kensatkensington.com.au

■ **Kingsteam** (b DR DU FC FH G I m MC P RR SA SB SH VS WH WO)
Mon 10-24, Tue-Thu -6, Fri 10-Mon 6h (non-stop)
38-42 Oxford Street, Darlinghurst *Next to Exchange Hotel, 1st floor*
☎ (02) 9360 3431 🖳 www.kingsteam.com.au

■ **Sydney City Steam 357** (! AC B CC DR DU FC FH G GH I LAB M MA MSG NR RR RWT S SA SB SH SL VR VS W WH)
Mon-Thu 10-6, Fri 10-Mon 6h (non-stop)
357 Sussex Street *Close to Town Hall station* ☎ (02) 9267 6766
🖳 www.sydneycitysteam.com.au
Very busy and extremely popular sauna on 4 floors. Second floor nude on Sat night. Friendly staff. Many Asians due to location near Chinatown. Very busy and mixed crowd at lunch

FITNESS STUDIOS

■ **Bayswater Fitness** (AC CC GLM MA MSG OS SOL WO)
6-24, Sat 7-22, Sun 7-21h
33 Bayswater Road, Kings Cross ☎ (02) 9356 2555

■ **City Gym** (AC CC GLM MA MSG SB WO)
Mon-Fri 5-24, Sat 6-22, Sun 8-22h
107-113 Crown Street, East Sydney ☎ (02) 9360 6247
🖳 www.citygym.com.au
Daily and 10-visit memberships available.

BOOK SHOPS

■ **Bookshop Darlinghurst. The** (AC CC GLM MA)
Mon 10-21, Tue-Wed 10-21.30, Thu 10-22.30, Fri & Sat 10-23, Sun 11-22h
207 Oxford Street, Darlinghurst *Taylor Square* ☎ (02) 9331 1103
🖳 www.thebookshop.com.au
Australia's specialist GLBT bookshop has been in business for 30 years and stocks an extremely comprehensive range of books, DVDs, magazines and cards.

FASHION SHOPS

■ **Aussieboys** (AC CC G MA) 10-18, Thu -20, Sun 11-17h
102 Oxford Street, Darlinghurst ☎ (02) 9360 7011
🖳 www.aussieboys.com.au

LEATHER & FETISH SHOPS

■ **SAX Fetish** (CC GLM MA)
11-19, Thu & Sat -20, Sun 12-18h, Mon closed
110a Oxford Street, Darlinghurst ☎ (02) 9931 6105 🖳 www.saxfetish.com

HOTELS

■ **Albert & Victoria Court Sydney**
(AC BF CC GLM PK RWB RWS RWT VA) All year
122 Victoria Street, Potts Point ☎ (02) 9357 3200 🖳 www.AlbertVictoria.com
Albert & Victoria Court is a small, historic boutique hotel with 25 guestrooms and is centrally located in quiet Potts Point, the heart of Sydney's gastronomic precinct. It is within minutes of the Opera House, the Central Business District, the harbour and Oxford Street. All rooms with bath/WC, TV and phone.

■ **Altamont Boutique Hotel** (AC b BF CC glm H I PA PK RWS RWT WO) All year, reception: 8-20h
207 Darlinghurst Road, Darlinghurst *200 m from Kings Cross train station*
☎ (02) 9360 6000 🖳 www.altamont.com.au
All rooms with a queen or king size bed, en-suite bathrooms, cable TV, air-conditioning, tea/coffee facilities and continental breakfast.

■ **Arts Hotel** (BF CC g MC)
21 Oxford Street, Paddington *Near Greens Road* ☎ (02) 9361 0211
🖳 www.artshotel.com.au

■ **Diamant Hotel Sydney** (AC B BF CC glm H I M PK RWS RWT WO) All year
14 Kings Cross Road, Potts Point *200 m from Kings Cross Station*
☎ (02) 9332 2011 🖳 www.diamant.com.au
A premier luxury boutique hotel located in the heart of Sydney's most vibrant quarter. With 76 rooms elegantly designed.

■ **Hotel Stellar** (AC B bf CC glm H I M PK RWS RWT) All year, 24hrs
4 Wentworth Avenue *Off Oxford Street* ☎ (02) 9264 9754
🖳 www.hotelstellar.com
All the studios are stylishly designed and decorated. Each room also has its own kitchenette, complete with mini refrigerator, microwave, iron & ironing board, toaster, tea/coffee making facilities and utensils, in house movies and broadband internet.

■ **Kirketon Boutique Hotel. The**
(AC B CC glm H M MSG RWS RWT VA WO) All year
229 Darlinghurst Road, Darlinghurst *300 m from Kings Cross railway station* ☎ (02) 9332 2011 🖳 www.kirketon.com.au
One of the best boutique hotels in the world, positioned on the doorstep of Sydney's cafe, restaurant, bar and nightclub district.

Manor House Boutique Hotel Sydney
(AC BF CC glm I RWS RWT) All year
86 Flinders Street, Darlinghurst ☎ (02) 9380 6633
🖳 www.manorhouse.com.au
Small, historic boutique hotel with 18 guestrooms and is centrally located near Taylor Square/Oxford Street. All rooms with bath/WC, TV and phone.

Pensione Hotel Sydney (AC bf CC glm H RWS RWT) All year
631-635 George Street *Near Central Station* ☎ (02) 9265 8888
🖳 www.pensione.com.au
Located in the heart of Sydney's entertainment and theatre district.

Quality Hotel Cambridge (AC CC glm PI) All year
212 Riley Street ☎ (02) 9212 1111 🖳 www.cambridgehotel.com.au

GUEST HOUSES

Chelsea. The (BF CC glm OS RWB RWS RWT VA WO) All year, 8-19h
49 Womerah Avenue, Darlinghurst *5 mins to Oxford Street / Kings Cross*
☎ (02) 9380 5994 🖳 www.chelseaguesthouse.com
13 guestrooms with 4 singles with shared bathroom, 3 queen rooms, 3 queen deluxe rooms, one king room and two king suites with en-suite bathrooms.

Governors on Fitzroy (BF CC G I OS VA WH) All year
64 Fitzroy Street, Surry Hills ☎ (02) 9331 4652 🖳 www.governors.com.au
Shared bathrooms. Secluded spa in the garden.

GENERAL GROUPS

New Mardi Gras (GLM) Mon-Fri 10-17h
Suite 6, 94 Oxford Street, Darlinghurst ☎ (02) 9568 8600
🖳 www.mardigras.org.au
New Mardi Gras is the non-for-profit company that organises events such as the Sydney Gay & Lesbian Mardi Gras Parade, Party, Fair Day and Sleaze Ball.

FETISH GROUPS

Harbour City Bears Inc. (G)
PO Box 1532, Darlinghurst ☎ (02) 8572 9913 🖳 www.hcbears.com
Check the website for social events.

HEALTH GROUPS

ACON Mon-Fri 10-18h
9 Commonwealth Street, Surry Hills ☎ (02) 9206 2000 🖳 www.acon.org.au
Office for Community Support Network (CSN) and Bobby Goldsmith Foundation (BGF).

Taylor Square Clinic Mon-Fri 8-18, Sat 10-12h
393 Bourke Street, Darlinghurst ☎ (02) 9331 6151
Excellent gay men's health clinic.

SPECIAL INTEREST GROUPS

Queer Screen Limited (GLM) Mon-Fri 10-18h
PO Box 1081, Darlinghurst ☎ (02) 9332 4938
🖳 www.queerscreen.com.au
Organizers of the Sydney International Mardi Gras Film Festival.

SWIMMING

-Andrew Boy Charlton Pool at Woolloomooloo Bay (near the city and gay scene, here you will find the muscle boys)
-Cook & Phillip Pool at Hyde Park (heated indoor pool near the city and gay scene)
-Lady Jane Beach (g NU) near South Head. Official nude beach. Lady Jane is very small and picturesque and is reached by taking the bush walk from Camp Cove (take ferry or bus to Watsons Bay) Cruising on the cliff behind the beach until below the lighthouse (AYOR)
-Tamarama Beach
-Bondi Beach (northern end near headland), popular area
-Obelisk Beach (g NU) at Mosman, opposite side of the Harbour, from Lady Jane Bay, and next to Naval base
-Redleaf Pool Harbour Beach, near Woollahra Council Chambers on New South Head Road at Double Bay
-La Perouse Little Congwong Bay Beach (g), take the walk way to the second beach (on the side of the golf course)(AYOR). Cruising in the surrounding bushes.

CRUISING

-Rocks at Balmoral (daytime)
-Centennial Park (Oxford St. to park and then 500m further to middle entrance, AYOR)
-Rushcutters Bay Park (AYOR at night) (all day long)
-Lady Bay Beach (amongst the rocks, but be discreet)
-Grant's Park (south side of Coogee Beach from Surf Club to Sunstrip Pool; 11-2h)
-Cremorne Wharf (north side of harbor; 10-1h)
-Obelisk Beach, Mosman
-Rifle Range at Maroubra
-Red Leaf Pool (Woollahra on harbor)
-Rocks between Bondi Beach and Tamarama
All AYOR
-Darlinghurst wall (Darlinghurst Road from Oxford Street to Green Park, R)
-Opposite Clifford Park (Market Street, Parramatta)
-South side of Cooks River Bridge at Tempe
-Circular Quay
-Town Hall Station
-Belmore Park (Isabella Street, Parramatta)
-Fivedock, toilet behind Commonwealth Bank
-Werrong Beach, Otford
-Toilets at Crows Nest Community Centre (ground floor).

Tilba Tilba ☎ 02

GUEST HOUSES

■ **Green Gables** (BF CC GLM I OS PK RWB RWS RWT) All year
269 Corkhill Drive *Coastal route between Narooma & Bermagui*
☎ (02) 4473 7435 💻 www.greengables.com.au
An ideal location to break the journey between Sydney and Melbourne.

Northern Territory

Location: Northern Australia
Initials: NT
Time: GMT +9.5
Area: 1,346,200 km² / 519,768 sq mi.
Population: 196,000
Capital: Darwin
Important gay cities: Darwin

Darwin ☎ 08

DANCECLUBS

■ **Throb** (AC B D GLM MA S WE) Fri & Sat 23-4h
1st floor, 64 Smith Street ☎ (08) 8942 3435
💻 www.throbnightclub.com.au
Darwin's only gay nightclub. Drag show and entertainment Fri & Sat night. Show time is 1.30h.

HEALTH GROUPS

■ **Northern Territory AIDS Council Inc.** Mon-Fri 8.30-17h
46 Woods Street ☎ (08) 8941 1711 💻 www.ntahc.org.au

CRUISING

-Vesty's Beach (between Sailing Club and Ski Club showers, good at night; fairly safe, take insect repellent)
-Mindil Beach (either side of the casino)
-Along Esplanade at sunset
-Lameroo Beach (NU) (access from Esplanade)
-Casarina Free Beach (NU) (turn right towards the gun turret).

Queensland

Location: North East Australia
Initials: QLD
Time: GMT +10
Area: 1,727,200 km² / 666,872 sq mi.
Population: 3,707,000
Capital: Brisbane
Important gay cities: Brisbane, Cairns, Noosa, Port Douglas, Surfers Paradise

Airlie Beach ☎ 07

HOTELS

■ **Coral Sea Resort** (AC B bf CC DM glm I LM M MC OS PI PK RWB RWS RWT S VEG WL) All year
25 Oceanview Avenue *On Whitsunday Islands* ☎ (07) 4964 1300
☎ 1-800 075 061 (toll free) 💻 www.coralsearesort.com
A great selection of hotel rooms including deluxe suites and 1-3 bedroom apartments, penthouses and beach houses.

■ **Marina Shores** (AC BF H I RWB RWS RWT) All year
159 Shingley Drive ☎ (07) 49641500 💻 www.marinashores.com.au

■ **Waterfront Whitsunday**
(AC BF H I MSG OS PI PK RWB RWS RWT) All year
438 Shute Harbour Road ☎ (07) 4948 6500
💻 www.waterfrontwhitsunday.com.au

■ **Waters Edge** (AC H M OS PI PK RWB RWS RWT) All year
4 Golden Orchid Drive ☎ (07) 4948 4300
💻 www.watersedgewhitsundays.com.au

■ **Whitsunday Vista** (AC H I PK RWB RWS RWT)
1 Hermitage Drive ☎ (07) 4948 4000 💻 www.whitsundayvista.com.au

Brisbane ☎ 07

PUBLICATIONS

■ **Pride**
2/83 Alfred Street, Fortitude Valley ☎ 3216 0860
💻 www.queenslandpride.com.au
Free monthly magazine.

■ **Q News**
PO Box 605, Paddington ☎ 3852 5933 💻 www.qnews.com.au

BARS

■ **Beat. The** (AC B D glm m MA s SNU ST) 20-5h
677 Ann Street, Fortitude Valley *Brunswick train station, in Mall*
☎ (07) 3252 2543
4 dancefloors popular with the younger mixed gay & lesbian crowd.

■ **Wickham. The** (AC B CC D GLM M MA OS S ST T VS) Mon 9-24, Tue-Thu 9-?, Fri 9-5, Sat 10-5, Sun -24h
308 Wickham Street, Fortitude Valley ☎ (07) 3852 1301
💻 www.thewickham.com.au
Three bars: a DJ party bar, a lounge for relaxing with cocktails and a games room for those who like to gamble. Drag shows and guest DJs.

MEN'S CLUBS

■ **Den. The** (AC B CC DR F G VS) Sun-Thu 10-1, Fri & Sat -3h
187 Brunswick Street, Fortitude Valley *Fortitude Valley, corner of Brunswick St. & Barry Parade* ☎ (07) 3854 1981
Gay men's club and bookshop. Large range of toys, books and leather.

■ **Klub Kruise**
(AC B CC DR DU FC FH G I M MA MSG OS RR SH SOL VS WH) 11-?h
29 Mc Lachlan Street, Fortitude Valley ☎ (07) 3852 1161
💻 www.klubkruise.com

Three levels with theme rooms (car, motorbike, horse saddle etc), coffee facilities, free Internet, 2 suckatoriums, sling room, smoking area.

DANCECLUBS

■ **Family Nightclub** (AC B CC D GLM MA S VS) Fri, Sat & Sun 21-5h
8 McLachlan Street, Fortitude Valley ☎ (07) 3852 5000
🖳 www.thefamily.com.au
Large and modern entertainment venue on 4 levels, 2 dance floors, 4 bars. 3 genres of music and high standard in service. Gay & lesbian friendly. Gay on Sun.

SAUNAS/BATHS

■ **Bodyline Spa & Sauna** (DR DU FC FH G GH I LAB m MA MSG P SA SB SL VS WH) 11-1, Fri & Sat -5h
45 Peel Street, South Brisbane *Near South Bank* ☎ (07) 3846 4633
🖳 www.bodylineqld.com.au
Buddy night on Mon. Naked night on Wed, very popular. No membership fees.

■ **Wet Spa & Sauna** (AC CC DR DU FC FH G I LAB M MA P PI RR SA SB SL VS WH) 11-24, Fri & Sat -2h
22 Jeays Street, Bowen Hills *5 mins walk from Bowen Hills railways station*
☎ (07) 3854 1383 🖳 www.wet.com.au
Modern sauna with many facilities. Busy on Sun for the so-called „Wet Day". 2 movie lounges and a heated pool.

BOOK SHOPS

■ **Den Bookshop. The** (g) 9-24h
187 Brunswick Street, Fortitude Valley ☎ (07) 3252 7191

HOTELS

■ **George Williams** (AC B CC glm M OS WO) All year
317-325 George Street ☎ (07) 3308 0700 🖳 www.hgw.com.au

■ **M on Mary** (AC CC H M MA PI WO) All year
70 Mary Street ☎ 3503 8000 🖳 www.monmary.com.au
Aparthotel right in the city center.

FETISH GROUPS

■ **Bris Bears Social Club Inc.** 3rd & 5th Sat 19-2h
PO Box 6, Nundah ☎ (0468) 863 616 🖳 www.brisbears.org.au
Social club for men who like hairy men. Meets every 3rd & 5th Sat/month in the Mineshaft at Sportsman Hotel, downstairs bar.

HEALTH GROUPS

■ **Gay & Lesbian Welfare Association** Helpline 19-22h
PO Box 1078, Fortitude Valley ☎ (07) 3017 1717 🖳 www.glwa.org.au
Gay & lesbian telephone counselling & information service.

■ **Queensland Association for Healthy Communities**
Mon-Fri 9-17h
30 Helen Street, Newstead ☎ (07) 3017 1777 🖳 www.qahc.org.au
Promotes the health of the GLBT community in Queensland.

Cairns ☎ 07

Cairns is only a two hour and thirty minute flight from Sydney and is in the heart of tropical north Queensland. Its international airport and proximity to one of Australia's greatest tourist attractions, the Great Barrier Reef, makes Cairns a busy tourist destination. The best time to visit is from May through to October: as the tropical climate means a wet season from November to April. Cairns is recognized as Australia's leading gay travel destination and the perfect location from which to pursue leisure activities including sailing to the Great Barrier Reef, taking a tour to the Daintree Rainforest, or just relaxing around your hotel swimming pool. Cairns is a safe destination, gay tourists make this journey to tropical paradise year after year. Just one hour north of Cairns is Port Douglas, a true resort village beside the sea. With dazzling blue skies and long white beaches it has become an international holiday Mecca with budget to five star accommodation, shops, galleries, and enticing restaurants. It maintains an air of casual affluence, attracting a happy mix of backpackers, gay and lesbian travelers and „laid-back" travellers.

Zweieinhalb Flugstunden von Sydney entfernt, liegt Cairns im Herzen des tropischen North Queensland. Sein internationaler Flughafen und die Nähe zu einer der größten australischen Touristenattraktionen, dem Great Barrier Reef, machen es zu einem belebten Touristenziel. Die beste Reisezeit ist von Mai bis Oktober, da das tropische Klima von November bis Mai erhebliche Niederschläge bringt. Cairns ist anerkanntermaßen Australiens führendes schwules Reiseziel und hat eine perfekte Lage, um von dort Freizeitaktivitäten -wie Segeln zum Great Barrier Reef oder eine Tour durch den Daintree Regenwald zu starten- oder sich einfach am Hotelpool zu erholen. Da Cairns als ein sicheres Reiseziel gilt, kehren schwule Touristen Jahr für Jahr in dieses tropische Paradies zurück. Nur eine Stunde nördlich befindet sich Port Douglas, ein richtiger Urlaubsort am Meer. Mit strahlend blauem Himmel und langen weißen Stränden ist er zu einem internationalen Urlaubsmekka geworden. Hier findet man alles: von der einfachsten Unterkunft zum Fünf-Sterne-Hotel, Geschäfte und einladende Restaurants. Port Douglas hat sich die Atmosphäre unaufdringlichen Wohlstandes bewahrt und zieht so eine gute Mischung aus Rucksacktouristen, Schwulen und Lesben und „lockeren" Reisenden an.

Cairns est à deux heures de vol de Sydney, son aéroport international et la grande attraction du de la region, la Grande Barrière de Corail font de la ville du Nord du Queensland une ville ouverte. La meilleure période reste de mai à octobre, le climat tropical est ici synonyme de dépression, de mai à novembre la pluie est au rendez-vous. Cairns est la ville préférée des homos, point de départ pour des traversées en voilier ou des tours dans la forêt tropicale de Daintree. Parce que Cairns est une ville où l'on se sent en sécurité les homos y retournent d'année en année. Une heure au Nord se trouve Port Douglas, lieu de vacances en bord de mer: ciel bleu et plages de sable blanc infinies. En matière d'hébergement on y a l'embarras du choix: de l'hôtel une au cinq étoiles. Port Douglas est un lieu unique, mélange de baroudeurs avec leur sacs à dos et de vacanciers détendus.

A dos horas y media en avión desde Sydney está Cairns, en el corazón del tropical norte de Queensland. Su aeropuerto internacional y la proximidad a una de las atracciones turísticas más visitadas de Australia, la Gran Barrera de Coral, la convierten en un destino turístico animado. El mejor tiempo para ir es de mayo a octubre, puesto que el clima tropical conlleva muchas precipitaciones de noviembre a mayo. Cairns es reconocida como el destino gay más solicitado de Australia y tiene una perfecta situación para poder realizar todo tipo de actividades al aire libre, como navegar por la Gran Barrera de Coral o un tour por la selva de Diantree o, simplemente, relajarse en la piscina del hotel. Como Cairns está considerado como un destino seguro, cada año vuelven los turistas homosexuales a este paraíso tropical. A sólo una hora al norte se encuentra Port Douglas, un típico lugar de vacaciones al lado del mar. Con un cielo azul radiante y largas y blancas playas, se ha convertido en la meca internacional de las vacaciones. Aquí encuentra uno de todo: desde el alojamiento más sencillo hasta el hotel de cinco estrellas, tiendas, apetitosos restaurantes y bares. Port Douglas ha sabido conservar el ambiente de bienestar tranquilo y atrae a una buena mezcla de excursionistas con mochila, gays y lesbianas y viajeros alternativos.

A due ore e mezza di volo da Sidney, nel cuore del tropicale North Queensland, si trova Cairns. Il suo aereoporto internazionale e la vicinanza ad una delle più importanti attrazioni australiane, il Great Barrier Reef, ne fanno una delle più animate mete turistiche. Il periodo migliore per visitarla è da maggio ad ottobre, in quanto il clima tropicale tra novembre e maggio porta con se considerevoli precipitazioni. Cairns è la prima meta turistica australiana gay ed ha una posizione geografica ideale per praticare attività nel tempo libero, come fare vela sino al Great Barrier Reef o un'escursione nella foresta tropicale Daintree, oppure rilassarsi sul bordo della piscina dell'albergo. Un'ora piú a nord c'è Port Douglas, un vero e proprio luogo per vacanze sul mare. Grazie al suo splendente cielo blu ed alle sue spiagge bianche è una Mecca turistica internazionale. Qui si trova di tutto: dalla pensione familiare sino agli alberghi a cinque stelle, negozi e ristoranti invitanti. Port Douglas ha mantenuto un'atmosfera di benessere ed attira così un pubblico variopinto di turisti: da quelli con lo zaino in spalla, a gay e lesbiche, sino ai più comodi viaggiatori.

RESTAURANTS

■ **Red Ochre Grill** (AC B CC glm M)
Mon-Sat: lunch & dinner, Sat & Sun: dinner only
43 Shields Street ☏ (07) 4051 0100 🖳 www.redochregrill.com.au
Seafood and Australian specialities with outside dining on Sun.

SEX SHOPS/BLUE MOVIES

■ **Erotica Adult Shop** (CC f g MA t VS) 10-22h
10a Shields Street *City centre* ☏ (07) 4041 4069

HOTELS

■ **Skinny Dips Resort and Spa** (AC B BF CC G I M MA NU OS PI PK RWS RWT SA VA WH WO) Reception 8-17, bar/restaurant 11-22h
18 James Street *Close to airport, walking distance to city centre and gay night life* ☏ (07) 4051 4644 🖳 www.skinnydips.com.au
All rooms with en-suite, TV, radio, phone, refrigerator, tea/coffee. Poolside café, day guests welcome. Check out the website for details of Holiday Packages and Discount Offers.

■ **Turtle Cove Beach Resort** (! AC B BF CC G I M MA MSG NU OS PI PK RWB RWS RWT VA VS WH WO) All year
100 Captain Cook Highway, Wangetti Beach *On absolute private gay beach, 40 mins north of Cairns airport* ☏ (07) 4059 1800
🖳 www.turtlecove.com
Thirty modern en-suite rooms, most with ocean views. Poolside resturant, gymnasium and massage services available, day visitors welcome. Cairns Airport pick-up by arrangement.

SWIMMING

-Bucchans Point/Ellis Beach (25 km north of Cairns. Take bus 2XX or 1A from city. Unofficial nude beach)
-Yorkey's Knob (5 km north of Cairns).

CRUISING

-Cairns Esplanada (from city north to hospital)
-Buchan Point on Captain Cook Highway, approx. 25 km from centre of Cairns **P** righthand side, after sharp lefthand curve
-The Lagoon (Large open air swimming pool with artificial beach at the end of the Esplanade, close of the harbour, toilets and showers day and night, be discret).

Gold Coast ☏ 07

BARS

■ **Escape** (AC B D GLM MA S SNU ST t WE) Wed-Sat 21-5, Sun 15-?h
Level 1, 2 Cavill Avenue, Surfers Paradise *Opp. Surfers Paradises Beach*
☏ (04) 3871 1299 🖳 www.escapebar.com.au
Events are constantly changing.

■ **MP** (AC B CC D GLM MA S SNU ST t) Tue-Sun 22-5h
26 Orchid Avenue, Surfers Paradise *In the Forum Arcade*
☏ (07) 5526 2337 🖳 www.mpnightclub.com
Bar and dance club with drag shows, strippers and dance parties.

MEN'S CLUBS

■ **Den. The** (AC b DR G MA VS) 10-24h
2557 Gold Coast Highway, Mermaid Beach ☏ (07) 5575 4054
Adult shop and gay/bi male cruise club.

SEX SHOPS/BLUE MOVIES

■ **Club R** (CC DR G MA P VS) 16-24h
1/3 Alison Street, Surfers Paradise *In basement car park at Parkrise building, look for big number ONE on front door* ☏ (07) 5539 0955

HOTELS

■ **Sleeping Inn Surfers Backpackers Resort** (CC glm PI WH) 8-22h
26 Peninsular Drive, Surfer's Paradise *5 mins to gay beach & venues*
☏ (07) 5592 4455 🖳 www.sleepinginn.com.au
Eight double, 8 single rooms, 5 apartments, also shared rooms and dorms backpacker style.

GUEST HOUSES

Bush House B&B (AC BF CC FH G I MA MSG NU OS PA PI PK RES RWS RWT VA W WH) All year
52 Nancol Drive, Tallebudgera Valley *8.5 kms from M1 Motorway & beach*
☎ 0418 881 534 (mobile) 💻 www.bushhouse.net
A romantic getaway or a quiet retreat, exclusively for gay couples or singles.

SWIMMING

-Broadbeach (AYOR) (opposite Broadbeach International Hotel & Oasis Shopping Complex. Be a little bit more discreet, as it is usually mixed and touristy)
-Southport Spit (AYOR) (opposite Seaworld Dolphin and Whale Arena, very popular on Sat and Sun).

CRUISING

-The Spit (dunes opposite Sea World - AYOR police patrol here)
-Southport swimming pool (opposite Southport's Australia Fair Complex, best at night)
-Broadbeach Surf Life Saving Club (on the beach, best at night).

Hervey Bay ☎ 07

DANCECLUBS

Diversity @ Club Wharf (B D GLM MA S) 3rd Sat/month 20-3h
98 Wharf Street, Maryborough 💻 www.frasergays.com
See www.frasergays.com for details.

GUEST HOUSES

Kingfisher Bay Resort & Village (AC B GLM MA) All year
PMB 1 Urangan ☎ (07) 4120 3333 💻 www.kingfisherbay.com
A 4 star, international standard, fully integrated resort development. 152 hotel rooms overlooking lakes and bush land and 110 two and three bedroom self-contained villas with bush and sea views.

Port Douglas ☎ 07

GUEST HOUSES

Mai Tai Resort (AC BF CC GLM I MA NU OS PA PI PK RWB RWS RWT) All year
Lot 78, Mossman Mt. Molloy Road, Cassowary *10 mins by car from centre of Port Douglas* ☎ (07) 4098 4956 💻 www.maitai-resort.com.au
Pink Flamingo Resort (AC B CC glm MA MSG PI PK RWS RWT)
115 Davidson Street ☎ (07) 4099 6622 💻 www.pinkflamingo.com.au
Unique tropical sensuality, exuberant fun and bright stylish décor. Gay owned.

Sunshine Coast ☎ 07

RESTAURANTS

Berardo's (AC B GLM M MA OS) 18-?h
50 Hastings Street, Noosa Heads ☎ (07) 5447 5666
💻 www.berardos.com.au
Constantly voted one of Australia's leading restaurants.

GUEST HOUSES

Lake Weyba Cottages (AC BF cc glm MA MSG OS PI) All year
79 Clarendon Road, Peregian *90 mins south of Brisbane, 15 mins south of Noosa and 5 mins to Peregian Beach* ☎ (07) 5448 2285
💻 www.lakeweybacottages.com
Luxurious private cottages with spa, only 5 mins to gay beach.

APARTMENTS

Costa Nova Apartments (AC CC H MA MSG PI WH)
Mon-Fri 8.30-17, Sat -14.30, Sun -10h
1-3 Belmore Terrace, Noosa, Sunshine Beach ☎ (07) 5447 2709
💻 www.costanova.com.au
Self-contained apartments and penthouses, near Alexandria Bay, Noosa's premier gay, clothing optional beach.

Hideaway Men's Resort
(AC B bf cc G I M MSG OS PI PK RWB RWS RWT VA VS WH WO) All year
386 David Low Way, Peregian Beach *20 km north of the airport*
☎ (07) 5448 1006 💻 www.hideawaymensresort.net
Four doubles and 4 single apartments with own shower/WC, fax, TV, radio, kitchen, hair dryer and own key. Also the men's club David.
Horizons at Peregian (AC CC GLM I MA NU OS PA PI PK RWB RWS RWT VA WH) All year 7-22h
45 Lorikeet Drive, Noosa *80 mins north of Brisbane, 15 mins to Sunshine Coast airport, opposite to gay beach* ☎ (07) 5448 3444
💻 www.horizons-peregian.com
One of the most popular gay managed beach resorts in Australia. 18 large holiday apartments on 3 levels. Accommodate 4-6 persons. Heated outdoor saltwater swimming pool, hydrospa, BBQ, entertaining area and massage facilities. 100 metres to Ocean Surf beach.
Noosa Cove (BF CC G I MA NU OS PI PK RWB RWS RWT VA) All year
82 Upper Hastings Street, Noosa Heads *Close Alexandria Bay*
☎ (07) 5449 2668 💻 www.noosacove.com.au
One poolside studio and three, spacious, fully self contained, large apartments.

SWIMMING

All beaches are in the Noosa area:
-Alexandria Beach (45 minutes through National Park from Noosa Heads. (G, NU)
-The Spit (end of Hastings street)
-Noosa Woods (mouth of Noosa River).

Townsville ☎ 07

BARS

Sovereign Hotel (B D GLM M MA S) Thu-Sun 17-till late
807 Flinders Street *Ingham Road end* ☎ (07) 4771 2909
💻 www.sovereignhotel.com.au

SWIMMING

-Balding Bay/Rocky Bay (AYOR) (on Magnetic Island. Popular with gays who tend to congregate at the far end)
-Beyond Pallaranda (g NU).

CRUISING

-Flinders Mall (in centre of city, daytime on week days)
-P between Rower's Bay and Pallaranda
-Strand and Queen Parks.

Wongawallan ☎ 07

GUEST HOUSES

Tambaridge B&B (AC BF GLM MA) All year
1718 Tamborine-Oxenford Road *Gold Coast Mountains overlooking National Park* ☎ (07) 5545 4643 💻 www.tambaridge.com
Unique Guesthouse with tree-house like architecture. Gay owned and operated.

South Australia

Location: South Australia
Initials: SA
Time: GMT +9.5
Area: 984,000 km² / 379,922 sq mi.
Population: 1,520,000
Capital: Adelaide
Important gay cities: Adelaide

Adelaide ☎ 08

PUBLICATIONS

Blaze 9-17.30h
c/o Evolution Publishing, 231A Hutt Street ☎ (08) 8223 7255
💻 blaze.gaynewsnetwork.com.au
South Australia's LGBT newspaper.

BARS

■ **Flagstaff on Franklin** (B g MA)
233 Franklin Street *City*
Meeting place of Bear Men of Adelaide 3rd Fri/month 19h.

■ **Hampshire Hotel** (B GLM H M MA OS) 8-?, Sat & Sun 10-?h
110 Grote Street ☎ 8410 0722 🖳 www.thehampshire.com.au
Two bars, also restaurant.

DANCECLUBS

■ **Mars Bar** (B D GLM MA OS S ST) Wed-Sat 21-?h
120 Gouger Street *City* ☎ (08) 8231 9639 🖳 www.themarsbar.com.au
Shows Fri & Sat at 2h.

SEX SHOPS/BLUE MOVIES

■ **ClubX Ram Lounge** (AC b G MA VS) 10-24, Fri & Sat 10-1, Sun 12-20h
346 King William Street *Above „La Trattoria" restaurant*
☎ (08) 8212 3134 🖳 www.clubx.com.au

SAUNAS/BATHS

■ **Pulteney 431** (AC b DR DU FC FH G GH LAB m MA OS PI RR SA SB SL VS WH) Sun-Thu 12-1, Fri & Sat -3h
431 Pulteney Street *Next to Astor Hotel* ☎ (08) 8223 7506

BOOK SHOPS

■ **Imprints Booksellers** (CC glm)
Mon & Tue 9-18, Wed-Fri -21, Sat -18, Sun 11-18h
107 Hindley Street ☎ (08) 8231 4454 🖳 www.imprints.com.au
Adelaide's leading independent bookshop offers a range of quality books.

HEALTH GROUPS

■ **AIDS Council of South Australia** Mon-Fri 9-17h
64 Fullarton Road, Norwood ☎ (08) 8334 1611 🖳 www.acsa.org.au
Education, information & support programs.

■ **Clinic 275** Mon, Thu, Fri 10-16.30; Tue & Wed 11.30-18.30h
275 North Terrace *1st floor* ☎ (08) 8222 5075 🖳 www.stdservices.on.net
HIV-testing.

SPORT GROUPS

■ **Team Adelaide** (G)
PO Box 8205, Station Arcade 🖳 www.teamadelaide.org.au
Tennis, indoor bowling, and other sports.

SWIMMING

-The Broadway (South from Glenelg near kiosk and toilet block)
-Maslin's Beach (Legal nude beach, about 50 mins drive from Adelaide. Or take train from North Terrace, Adelaide to Noarlunga Centre and transfer to bus bus 741, 741A or 741G to Maslins Beach terminus, Gulf Parade, stop 97. Walk 1.8 km south to unclad section.)
-Tennyson Beach (On Grenfell or Currie Street take bus 139 or 139F (direction West Lakes Shopping Centre) to stop 32A on Military Road, walk about 80 m north along road to west side carpark and over sand dunes.)

CRUISING

All cruising areas are AYOR!
-Unley Road Park (between Greenhill Road and South Terrace, days only, access by car possible)
-Glen Osmond Road (AYOR) (night and day)
-Creswell Gardens (near Adelaide oval)
-Rundle Road, Parklands.

Kangaroo Island ☎ 08

APARTMENTS

■ **Lookout. The** (AC bf cc glm OS) All year
Willoughby Road *Cnr. Willoughby & Ian Roads* ☎ (08) 8553 1048
🖳 www.the-lookout.com.au
Private apartment on a bed & breakfast, self catering or full board basis for up to 4 people.

Kurralta Park ☎ 08

APARTMENTS

■ **Midway Apartments** (AC cc glm H PK RWB RWS RWT VA)
2a Warwick Avenue *Close to city, airport and beach* ☎ (08) 8293 7102
🖳 www.midwayapartments.com.au
Fully furnished 1 bedroom apartments, fully furnished, Kitchen, TV, DVD, air conditioned, close to city.

Tasmania

Location: Island off southern Australia
Initials: TAS
Time: GMT +10
Area: 67,800 km² / 26,177 sq mi.
Population: 473,000
Capital: Hobart
Important gay cities: Hobart

Hobart ☎ 03

BARS

■ **Flamingo's Dance Bar** (B D GLM MA) Fri & Sat 22-?h
201 Liverpool Street ☎ (03) 6294 6173 🖳 www.flamingosbar.com

■ **LaLaland** (B D glm m MA) Wed-Sat 18-?h
Corner Macquarie & Barracks Streets *Upstairs at Bakers Hotel*
☎ (03) 6224 9531

CAFES

■ **Kaos Cafe** (AC glm M) 12-24, Sat 10-24, Sun -22h
237 Elizabeth Street ☎ (03) 6231 5699
Possible to bring your own wine.

HOTELS

■ **Huon Bush Retreats** (BF CC GLM MA MSG PK RWB RWS VA)
Reception 8-20h, daily
300 Browns Road, Ranelagh, Huon Valley *50 mins south from Hobart*
☎ (03) 6264 2233 🖳 www.huonbushretreats.com
Self contained cabins, tipees and camp ground in a private nature reserve. Gay owned and operated.
This is a place to connect with nature.

GUEST HOUSES

■ **Elms of Hobart** (BF glm)
452 Elizabeth Street ☎ (03) 6231 3277 🖳 www.theelmsofhobart.com

APARTMENTS

■ **Corinda's Cottages** (BF CC GLM MA OS PK RWS RWT)
All year, 24hrs
17 Glebe Street *100 m from Aquatic Centre, opp. Queens Domain & tennis centre* ☎ (03) 6234 1590
🖳 www.corindascottages.com.au, www.2on2.com.au
Gay owned,5 fully self-contained cottages, 10% off for Spartacus readers.

Victoria

Location: South East Australia
Initials: VIC
Time: GMT +10
Area: 227,600 km² / 87,876 sq mi.
Population: 4,873,000
Capital: Melbourne
Important gay cities: Melbourne

Daylesford ☎ 03

GUEST HOUSES

■ **Balconies Daylesford** (AC BF CC DU FH GLM m MA NR OS PI PK RES RWB RWS RWT VEG WH WI) 24hrs

35 Perrins Street *2 mins from town centre* ☏ (03) 5348 1322
www.balconiesdaylesford.com.au
Luxury bed & breakfast with 9 en-suite rooms.

■ **Holyrood House** (BF CC glm I MA MSG OS PK RWB RWS VA) All year
51 Stanbridge Street *5 mins walk from Lake Daylesford and town centre*
☏ (03) 5348 4818 holyrood-house.com.au

Echuca ☏ 03

GUEST HOUSES

■ **Echuca Gardens** (AC BF CC GLM MA MSG NU OS PA RWB RWS RWT SA VA WH) All year
103 Mitchell Street *90 mins drive from Melbourne* ☏ (03) 5480 6522
www.echucagardens.com

Geelong ☏ 03

SWIMMING

-Point Impossible (take beach road out of Torquay to Breamlea)
-Point Addis (situated off the Geelong road to Angleseo, turn off 2km past Bell's Beach, popular).

CRUISING

-King's Park, King's Wharf
-Behind Newton Library.

Melbourne ☏ 03

Melbourne, with its trams, wide tree-lined streets, boutique hotels and Victorian architecture is Australia's „most European city". It also has a great reputation for its cultural events, café society and fine dining. Melbourne's climate is mild and variable with cool, wet winters and warm, dry summers. It has a beautiful hinterland ranging from mountains to ocean scenery to rainforest to rolling farmlands. Well-known destinations include Philip Island, the Great Ocean Road and the Yarra Valley wineries.
There's a large gay and lesbian community in Melbourne, supporting more than twenty bars and clubs, mostly located in Prahran, South Yarra, St Kilda and Collingwood.

Melbourne ist mit seinen Straßenbahnen, baumgesäumten Boulevards, seinen Hotels und beeindruckender viktorianischer Architektur die europäischste Stadt von Australien. Die Stadt ist berühmt für ihre Kulturveranstaltungen, Restaurants und Cafés. Melbournes Klima ist mild und wechselhaft; kühl und nass im Winter und warm und trocken im Sommer. Das reizvolle Hinterland ist sehr vielfältig: Berge, Meer, Regenwald und hügelige Felder. Bekannte Ausflugsziele sind Philip Island, Great Ocean Road und die Yarra Valley Weingüter.
Die bedeutende schwul-lesbische Gemeinschaft Melbournes unterstützt mehr als zwanzig Bars und Clubs, besonders in Prahran, South Yarra, St Kilda und Collingwood.

Melbourne avec ses trams, ses rues larges, ses hôtels particuliers et son architecture Victorienne est la ville la plus européenne en Australie. La ville est également réputée pour ses événements culturels et ses cafés et restaurants. A Melbourne le climat est tempéré et variable : froid et humide en hiver, chaud et sec en été. L'arrière pays est lui aussi multiple et attirant : Montagnes, forêt tropicale, et champs vallonnés. Philip Island, la Great Ocean Road ainsi que les vignobles de la Yarra Valley sont des endroits à visiter dans les environs de Melbourne.
Au total la communauté homo de la ville soutient une vingtaine de bars et clubs surtout dans les quartiers Prahran, South Yarra, St Kilda et Collingwood.

Melbourne con sus tranvías, amplias calles arboladas, boutiques, hoteles y arquitectura victoriana, es la ciudad „más europea" de Australia. También goza de una gran reputación por sus eventos culturales, la vida de los cafés y la gastronomía refinada. El clima de Melbourne es suave y variable; fresco y húmedo en invierno, caluroso y seco en verano. Sus magníficos alrededores son muy diversos: montes, mar, selva y campos con colinas. Las excursiones más conocidas son la isla Philip, Great Ocean Road y el valle vinícola de Yarra Valley.
Hay una nutrida comunidad de gays y lesbianas en Melbourne que da impulso a más de veinte bares y clubs localizados principalmente en Prahran, South Yarra, St. Kilda y Collingwood.

Con i suoi tram, le sue larghe strade a tre corsie, negozi, hotel, la sua architettura vittoriana, Melbourne è la città più europea dell'Australia. Inoltre la città é molto rinomata per i suoi eventi culturali, i suoi bar e i suoi ristoranti. Il clima di Melbourne è mite e mutevole: freddo ed umido d'inverno; caldo e secco d'estate. L'eccitante entroterra è vario: montagne, mare, foresta tropicale e terreni collinosi. Mete molto conosciute sono: Philip Island, Great Ocean Road e i vigneti della Yarra Valley. La comunità gay e lesbica di Melbourne é piuttosto grande. La scena conta più di venti bar e clubs, per lo più situati a Prahran, South Yarra a Collingwood.

NATIONAL PUBLICATIONS

■ **Q Magazine**
PO Box 7479, St. Kilda Road ☏ 422 632 690 www.qmagazine.com.au
A5 free to street glossy monthly gay lifestyle magazine. Australia wide publication.

Melbourne – Map A

EAT & DRINK

DT's Hotel – Bar	1
Greyhound – Bar	2

Melbourne – Map B

EAT & DRINK

Ezard – Restaurant	14
Laird Hotel. The – Bar	5

NIGHTLIFE

Club 80 – Men's Club	11
Peel Hotel. The – Danceclub	9
Sircuit – Men's Club	12

SEX

Subway Sauna	15
Wet on Wellington – Sauna	8

ACCOMMODATION

Adelphi – Hotel	14
Gatehouse. The – Guest House	10

OTHERS

Mannhaus – Leather & Fetish Shop	4
Eagle Leather – Fetish Shop	6

Melbourne – Map C

EAT & DRINK

Grevilles. The – Bar	25
Heaven @ 151 – Café	19
Priscilla's @ 153 – Bar	20

NIGHTLIFE

Heaven's Door – Danceclub	18
Ten Plus – Men's Club	22

SEX

55 Porter Street – Sauna	24

OTHERS

Beat Bookshop	21
Inya – Book Shop	26

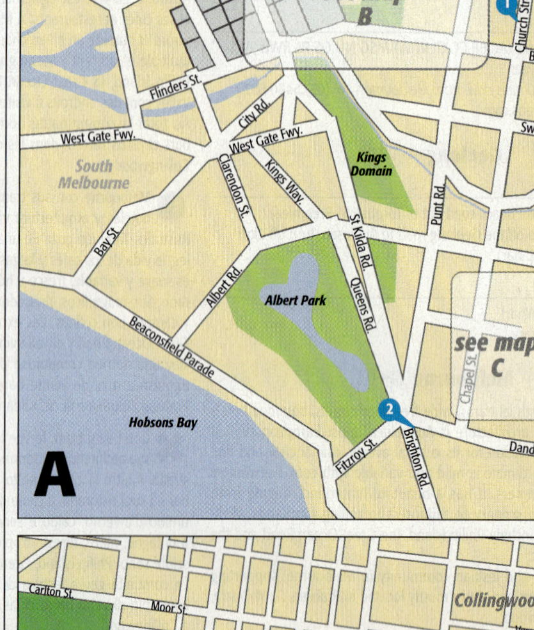

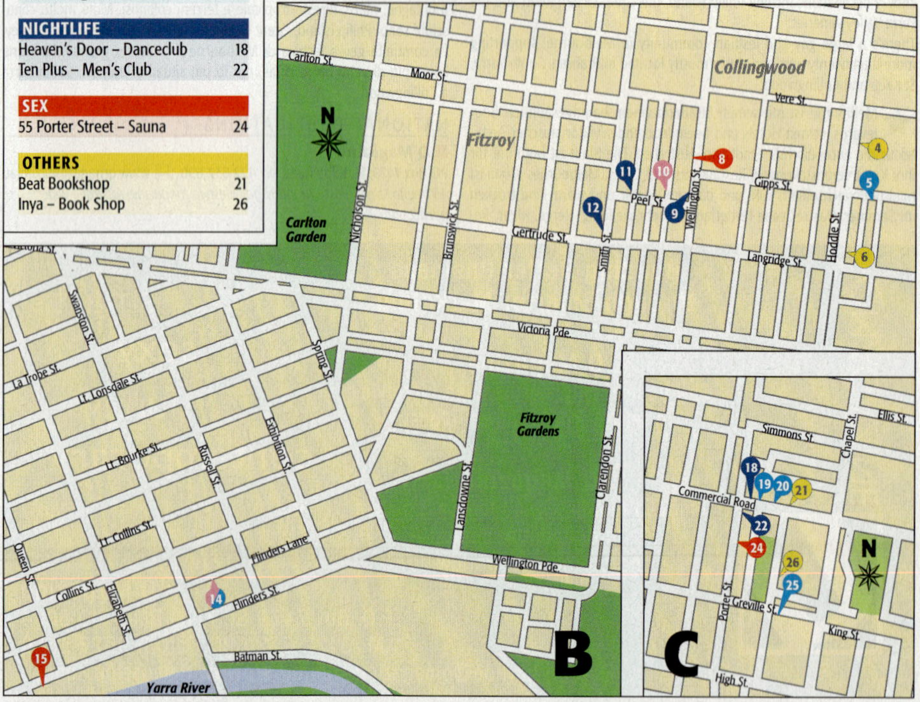

A
N
Yarra Bend N.P.
Yarra
Spencer St.
Victoria St
Hoodle Rd
see map B
Church Street
Bridge Rd.
Flinders St.
City Rd.
West Gate Fwy.
Swan St.
Kings Domain
South Melbourne
Clarendon St.
Kings Way.
Alexandra Av.
Punt Rd.
Bay St.
St Kilda Rd.
Toorak Rd.
Albert Rd.
Albert Park
Queens Rd.
Beaconsfield Parade
see map C
Chapel St.
Hobsons Bay
Fitzroy St.
Brighton Rd.
Dandenong Rd.

B
C
N
Carlton St.
Moor St.
Collingwood
Vere St.
Fitzroy
Carlton Garden
Nicholson St.
Brunswick St.
Peel St.
Wellington St.
Gipps St.
Gertrude St.
Smith St.
Langridge St.
Hoddle St.
Swanston St.
Victoria Pde.
La Trobe St.
Spring St.
Lt. Lonsdale St.
Exhibition St.
Lt. Bourke St.
Russell St.
Fitzroy Gardens
Lansdowne St.
Clarendon St.
Lt. Collins St.
Flinders Lane
Queen St.
Collins St.
Elizabeth St.
Flinders St.
Wellington Pde.
Batman St.
Yarra River
Ellis St.
Simmons St.
Chapel St.
Commercial Road
Porter St.
Greville St.
King St.
High St.

GAY INFO

JOY 94.9 (GLM) Daily 9-18h
Level 9, 225 Bourke Street ☎ (03) 9699 2949
🖳 www.joy.org.au
Australia's first and Melbourne's only dedicated gay and lesbian radio station.

PUBLICATIONS

MCV - Melbourne Community Voice
Suite 704, 365 Little Collins Street ☎ (03) 9602 2333
🖳 www.eevolution.com.au
Free weekly gay, lesbian, bi & transgender magazine.

BARS

The Greville (B D glm M MA S) 10-?h
162 Greville Street, Prahan *Near cnr. St. Edmonds Road*
☎ (03) 9529 6566 🖳 www.candybar.com.au
Former Candy Bar.

Priscilla's @ 153 (B D GLM M S ST) Wed-Sat 21-3h
153 Commercial Road, South Yarra ☎ (03) 9827 1669
🖳 www.facebook.com/pages/Priscillas-153/26257353523
Former Diva Bar!

DT's Hotel (AC B CC GLM M MA S ST VS)
Tue-Thu 16-?, Fri & Sat -1, Sun 14-23h
164 Church Street, Richmond ☎ (03) 9428 5724
🖳 www.dtshotel.com.au

Greyhound (B glm MA ST)
Thu & Fri 16-?, Sat & Sun 14-?h, closed Mon-Wed
1 Brighton Road, St Kilda ☎ (03) 9534 4189
🖳 www.greyhoundhotel.com.au
Great drag shows with top local drag stars on Sat.

Laird Hotel. The (! AC B F G H OS s) 17-?, Wed 20-?h
149 Gipps Street, Abbotsford ☎ (03) 9417 2832
🖳 www.lairdhotel.com
Home of Melbourne's leather/bear scene. TV lounge area, beer garden, 3 bars, pool table and games area. Also accommodation. Men only.

MEN'S CLUBS

Club 80 (! AC B DR F G I M MA p VS) 12-6, Fri & Sat -8h
10 Peel Street, Collingwood *2 km NE of Melbourne city centre. 300 m from tram stop „Smith St/Peel St"* ☎ (03) 9417 2182
🖳 www.club80.net
Amazing men's club on three floors of cruising, video lounge with the latest movies, cyber lounge with internet access, a coffee bar, private rooms and a pool table.

Sircuit (AC b DR F G MA VS WE)
Wed-Sat 17-4 (men only), Sun 15-4h (GLM)
103 Smith Street, Fitzroy *Tram 86-Smith Street* ☎ (03) 9416 3960
🖳 www.sircuit.com.au
Pool tables, 1st floor lounge (men only), 2 movie lounges (men only), live bands Sun.

Ten Plus (AC CC DR G I M MA OS VS)
Mon-Fri 12-6, Sat 12-Mon 6h
59 Porter Street, Prahran ☎ (03) 9525 0469
🖳 www.tenplus.com.au
Adult products, male cruise club, internet kiosk. Glory holes and army barracks area & outdoor garden beat. Closest sex venue to Commercial Rd.

CAFES

Heaven @ 151 (AC B BF CC GLM M MA OS WE)
Tue-Fri 11-23, Sat 10-24, Sun -22h
151 Commercial Road, South Yarra ☎ (03) 9827 9151
🖳 www.heavensdoor.com.au
Friendly and affordable café for full meals or coffee and drinks with outside courtyard and upstairs function room in the middle of the gay strip.

Ice (b CC G m MA)
30 Cato Street, Prahran *Close to Prahran Train Station*
☎ (03) 9510 8788 🖳 www.icecafe.com.au

DANCECLUBS

Heaven's Door (AC B CC D GLM MA OS S VS)
Wed & Fri 20-3, Thu 16-3, Sat 20-3, Sun 16-1h
147 Commercial Road ☎ (03) 9827 9147
🖳 www.myspace.com/heavensdoorbar
Stylish nightclub with 3 bars including semi-enclosed courtyard in the middle of the gay strip. Different music styles and shows every night. Wed Asian night with silky smooth RnB and latest video hits, Thu remixed 80s & 90s, Fri Twisted Disco uplifting vocal house, Sat full on & funky RnB, Sun chill out to classic video hits and late brunch in the courtyard.

Peel Hotel. The (! AC B D DR f G MA OS s SNU VS) Thu-Sat 21-?h
113 Wellington Street, Collingwood ☎ (03) 9419 4762
🖳 www.thepeel.com.au
Mainly gay male clientele. Free entry with 2 dance floors every Friday and Saturday. Retro high camp in the front bar with progressive dance floor anthems on the back dancefloor.

Trough Faggot (B D G MA)
🖳 www.troughfaggotparty.com
Rotating city venues. Check out www.troughfaggotparty.com for exact date and location.

RESTAURANTS

Ezard (AC CC glm M MA NR RES VEG WL)
Mon-Fri 12-14.30 & 18-22.30, Sat 18-22.30h
187 Flinders Lane, Melbourne City ☎ (03) 9639 6811
🖳 www.ezard.com.au
Award winning restaurant in The Adelphi Hotel. Australian „freestyle" cuisine.

SAUNAS/BATHS

55 Porter Street (AC b CC DR DU FC FH G GH LAB m MA MSG P RR SA SB SOL VS WH WO) 18-7, Sat 14-Mon 7h (non-stop)
55 Porter Street, Prahran *Close to Prahran Railway station*
☎ (03) 9529 5166
On two levels with large cruising maze and four glory holes cubicles.

Bay City Sauna Elsternwick
(b DR DU g m MA MSG RR SA SB VS) 12-1, Fri & Sat -3h
482d Glenhuntly Road, Elsternwick *Near Elsternwick station*
☎ (03) 9528 2381
Clean and friendly sauna in the suburbs of Melbourne with limited facilities. A sauna for men and women.

Spa Guy (B DR FC G m OC RR SA SB VS WH)
17-1, Fri & Sat 17-3, Sun 16-3h
553 Victoria Street, Abbotsford ☎ (03) 9428 5494

Subway Sauna (! AC B CC DR DU FC FH G GH I LAB M MA MSG OS RR SA SB SH SL VS WH) 24hrs
Vault 13, Banana Alley Vaults, 363 Flinders St, Melbourne City
Corner Flinders & Queensbridge Street ☎ (03) 9620 7766
🖳 www.subwaysauna.com.au
Recently renovated, with all new steam room, sauna, spa and shower area. Melbournes best gay mens sauna. Featuring all new rooms and cruising areas. A friendly atmosphere and a great place to meet!

Wet on Wellington (! AC B CC DR F FC G I m MA MSG OS P PI SA SB SL VS WE WH) Mon-Wed 12-3, Thu 12-Mon 2h (non-stop)
162 Wellington Street, Collingwood *At the corner of Wellington Street and Victoria Parade* ☎ (03) 9419 2210
🖳 www.wetonwellington.com.au
Also 25m-lap pool, video lounge and cruise areas. Probably the best sauna in town. Great facilities and modern, very popular.

BOOK SHOPS

Beat Bookshop (! CC F GLM MA T VS)
Mon-Thu 10-24, Fri & Sat -2, Sun 12-24h
159 Commercial Road, South Yarra *Commercial Road precinct*
☎ (03) 9827 8748
Melbourne's best & oldest gay adult bookshop serving the gay community for over 30 years. Great selection of gay movies, leather goods, magazines, adult toys, lubes, condoms, erection assists, pipes & bongs. Also a great

place to get all information about gay events and HIV related literature. Movie/Cruise lounge.

Hares & Hyenas (CC GLM)
Mon-Wed 9-18, Thu-Sat 9-18.30, Sun 11.30-18h
63 Johnston Street, Fitzroy ☎ (03) 9495 6589
www.hares-hyenas.com.au
Melbourne's queer bookshop, cafe and performance venue, with a very large range of GLBT books, DVDs, gifts and magazines. Free Wi-Fi. Best source for free information on events and queer life in Melbourne.

Inya (CC G I) Mon-Wed 10-21, Thu-Sat 10-24, Sun 10-21h
59 Izett Street, Prahran *Accross from Prahran markets* ☎ (03) 9510 3408
www.inya.com.au
Videos, books, lube and a great range of gay and lesbian merchandise on 2 floors.

LEATHER & FETISH SHOPS

Eagle Leather (AC CC F GLM)
Sun-Wed 11-19,Thu, Fri & Sat -21h & by appointment
80 Hoddle Street, Abbotsford *300 m south of Collingwood Town Hall*
☎ (03) 9417 2100 www.eagleleather.com.au
Australia' s largest retail store for mainly gay men into leather and rubber. Also conducts workshops, sponsors leather events and provides information for overseas visitors.

Lucrezia & de Sade (CC GLM MA) 11-19h
441 Brunswick Street, Fitzroy ☎ (03) 9416 3826
www.lucreziadesade.com.au

Mannhaus (F G) Tue & Sun 10-19, Wed-Sat -22h, closed Mon
130 Hoddle Street, Abbotsford ☎ (03) 9416 4800
www.mannhaus.com.au
Leatherwear, accessories, toys, etc.

HOTELS

Adelphi (AC B BF CC glm I M MC OS PI PK RWS RWT SB VA WO)
All year, 24hrs
187 Flinders Lane, Melbourne City *City centre* ☎ (03) 9650 7555
www.adelphi.com.au
Located in the heart of Melbourne. The mood is intimate, more like a club than a hotel. 34 rooms with 24h room service, amazing restaurants, cable TV and famous roof top pool.

Cosmopolitan Hotel (AC B BF glm H M RWS RWT) All year
2-8 Carlisle Street, St. Kilda *St Kilda on the doorstep of Luna Park*
☎ (03) 9534 0781 www.cosmopolitanhotel.com.au
Located in the heart of trendy St Kilda.

Pensione Melbourne (AC B BF CC glm H M RWS RWT) All year
16 Spencer Street *Situated in the heart of Melbourne* ☎ (03) 9621 3333
www.pensione.com.au
Located in the heart of Melbourne's CBD, a stone throw from many of Melbourne's major tourist attractions.

Prince. The (AC B BF glm I M PI PK RWS RWT VA) All year
2 Acland Street, St. Kilda *Close to Commercial Road* ☎ (03) 9536 1111
www.theprince.com.au
Trendy boutique hotel in the heart of St Kilda's restaurant district and two minutes from the beach.

GUEST HOUSES

169 Drummond Street (AC BF CC GLM I M PK RWB RWS RWT)
All year, 24hrs
169 Drummond Street, Carlton *20 mins to city centre* ☎ (03) 9663 3081
www.169drummond.com.au
Gay run guesthouse. 4 guestrooms. Great value for money. One of the best places to stay on a budget. All rooms with ensuite bathrooms.

Gatehouse. The (AC BF CC F G MA PK VA) All year
97 Cambridge Street, Collingwood *Check-in at Club 80*
☎ (03) 9417 2182 (Club 80) www.club80.net
Private 4-room guesthouse for gay & bisexual men into the leather scene.

GENERAL GROUPS

ALSO Foundation Mon-Fri 10-18h
Level 8, 225 Bourke Street, City ☎ (03) 9660 3900 www.also.org.au
Supports all manner of lesbian and gay community initiatives. Guide to gay & lesbian Melbourne produced annually (available for free online).

Gay and Lesbian Organisation of Business and Enterprise (GLOBE) (GLM)
164 Waverley Road, Malvern East ☎ (1300) 788 223
www.gaybusiness.com.au/globe
Social and business networking group within the GLBT community.

Midsumma Festival Inc (GLM)
Room C.1.20, The Convent, 1 St Heliers St, Abbotsford ☎ (03) 9415 9819
www.midsumma.org.au
Three weeks and four weekends of jam packed leading edge queer performance, music, art, spoken word, sports and parties.

HEALTH GROUPS

Carlton Clinic (CC GLM) Mon-Fri 8.30-19, Sat 9.30-12.30h
88 Rathdowne Street, Carlton *Cnr. Elgin Street, bus 200, 203, 205*
☎ (03) 9347 9422 www.carltonclinic.com.au
Gay and lesbian clinic.

Positive Living Centre
Tue & Wed 10-18, Thu -21, Fri -16h, Sat-Mon closed
31-51 Commercial Road, Prahran ☎ (03) 9863 0444
www.vicaids.asn.au
PLC provides a range of health related services for people living with HIV/AIDS.

VAC - GMHC Mon-Thu 9-21, Fri -17h
6 Claremont Street, South Yarra ☎ (03) 9865 6700
www.vicaids.asn.au
Victorian AIDS Council - Gay Men's Health Centre. The most important AIDS body in the state of Victoria which operates several STD clinics and self esteem groups.

SWIMMING

Most city and inner suburb swimming pools are cruisy especially Fitzroy, Collingwood and Prahran Pools. The Melbourne City Baths (Swanston St) are cruisy but as with all pools exercise caution as patrols are made of the facilities by management
-Beaconsfield Parade/Victoria Avenue (good for watching the muscle boys and rollerbladers)
-Middle Park/South Melbourne Beach (known as „Screech Beach") Situated at the end towards the Port Melbourne Lifesaving Club. (Used to be the most popular gay beach in Melbourne)
-Somers Beach (NU) (Two-hour drive from Melbourne on the Mornington Peninsula)
-St. Kilda Beach (on the lawn between Donovans restaurant and St Kilda Pier)
-Prahran swimming pool. 41 Essex Street, Prahran, (Open Oct-May. Outdoors heated public swimming. Popular with gays.)
- Sandridge Beach (The hot spot for gay action. Easily reached by taking the tram from the city to Port Melbourne / Station Pier and when you come off the tram walk west along the beach for about 20 mins until you reach the Dockyards and then look for the action in the low dunes and bushes).

CRUISING

Victorian police have regular plain clothes surveillance, so all areas are AYOR. Most beats around the city are busy (be guided by the graffiti) as are those on Bayside beaches and the Yarra River bank for 4-5 km out of the city up the river. In the suburbs most shopping complexes are busy but patrolled by in house security) :
-Princes Park
-Beaconsfield Parade (from Fitzroy Street, St. Kilda along beach front to Port Melbourne)
All the following are AYOR - be careful of gay bashers:
-Footscray Park near Paisley St and Pickett St, best times 12-15 and 20 to midnight.
-Point Ormond Beach (end of Glenhuntly Rd)
-Alma Park, between Alma Rd and Dandenong Rd, St Kilda East

-North Rd / East Boundary Rd, Ormond (police patrols) toilet block and night time action in bushes
-Hughesdale off Poath Rd near railway station (police patrols)
-Flinders Street station (several facilities including entrance from Elizabeth Street and at nearby Princes Bridge)
-Spencer Street station (on platforms 11 and 12, very busy)
-Queens Park Sunshine
-Elwood at major intersection Glenhuntly Rd/Barkly St/Marine Parade
-Near boatsheds on Yarra River (regular police raids).

Seaford ☎ 03

SAUNAS/BATHS

■ **Shed 16** (b DR DU FC G I LAB m MA MSG OS SA SB VS WO) 12-3h
16 Cumberland Drive *36 km southeast of Melbourne* ☎ (03) 9776 9279
🖳 www.shed16.com.au
Former Bay City Sauna Seaford

Western Australia

Location: West Australia
Initials: WA
Time: GMT +8
Area: 2,525,500 km² / 975,096 sq mi.
Population: 1,927,000
Capital: Perth
Important gay cities: Perth

Perth ☎ 08

GAY INFO

■ **Gay and Lesbian Community Services** (GLM MA)
Mon-Fri 19-22h
City West Lotteries House, 2 Delhi Street ☎ (08) 9420 7201 (counselling)
🖳 www.glcs.org.au
Information on the gay and lesbian scene. Also telephone counselling.

PUBLICATIONS

■ **Out in Perth**
PO Box 372, Bayswater ☎ 9371 9877 🖳 www.outinperth.com

BARS

■ **Court Hotel. The** (B GLM H OS S YC) Sun-Thu 12-24, Fri & Sat -2h
50 Beaufort Street, Northbridge *Cnr. James St* ☎ (08) 9328 5292
🖳 www.thecourt.com.au
Great mix of people. Very crowded on Fri & Sat nights. This is Perth's only full time gay bar.

■ **Luxe** (B glm H M S) Wed-Sat 18-2, Sun 17-22h
446 Beaufort Street, Mount Lawley ☎ (08) 9228 9680
Great mix of younger people.

DANCECLUBS

■ **Connections Night Club** (AC B D GLM MA S SNU ST) Tue-Sun 21-6h
81 James Street, Northbridge *Above Plaka Café* ☎ (08) 9328 1870
First hour every night - free entry and „nice price" drinks. Gay owned and managed.

SEX SHOPS/BLUE MOVIES

■ **Ram Lounge and Video** (DR G VS) 9-24h
114 Barrack Street *Via Club X* ☎ (08) 9325 3815
🖳 www.clubx.com.au
Cruisy backroom with sling etc.

■ **Vibrations Adult Shop** (AC CC G MA SNU T VS) Daily
354 A Charles Street, North Perth *Opp. McDonald's* ☎ (08) 9242 4501

SAUNAS/BATHS

■ **Perth Steam Works** (AC B CC DR FC FH G LAB m MA PI RR SA SB SL VS WH) Sun-Thu 12-1, Fri & Sat -3h
369 William Street, Northbridge *Entry Forbes Road, 10 mins walk from Perth Station* ☎ (08) 9328 2930 🖳 www.perthsteamworks.com.au
Sauna with mirror room, bondage and maze frequented by a mixed age group, younger in the evenings. Now with licensed bar.

HOTELS

■ **Criterion Hotel** (AC B BF CC glm M MA OS PK RWB RWS RWT) All year
560 Hay Street, Perth City ☎ (08) 9325 5155
🖳 www.criterion-hotel-perth.com.au
Rooms with bath or shower/WC, telephone, TV, radio, minibar, room service, own key.

GUEST HOUSES

■ **Abaca Palms** (AC BF CC FH G I m MA NR NU OS PK SA VA WH WI WO) All year
34 Whatley Crescent, Mount Lawley *Opp Mount Lawley Railway Staion*
☎ (08) 9271 2117 🖳 www.abacapalms.com
Guest house close to city and venues. 6 guestrooms with shared bath/WC, telephone, TV/video, radio, own key.

■ **Pension of Perth** (AC BF CC glm MA OS PI PK RWB RWS RWT VA WO) All year
3 Throssell Street *Opp. Hyde Park* ☎ (08) 9228 9049
🖳 www.pensionperth.com.au
4-star B&B. Great breakfasts and charming atmosphere.

■ **Richard's of Northbridge** (AC BF G I OS PK RWS RWT VA WH) 24hrs
165 Brisbane Street, Northbridge *1 km from city centre*
☎ (08) 9227 8303 🖳 members.iinet.net.au/~richbb/index.html
B&B with 2 double and 1 single room en-suite with own key, TV and phone. Discounts for Spartacus bookings.

■ **Swanbourne** (AC b BF CC glm I MA NU OS PI PK RWB RWS RWT VA WO) All year
5 Myera Street, Swanbourne *Between Perth and Port of Fremantle*
☎ (08) 9383 1981 🖳 www.swanbourneguesthouse.com.au
Two double rooms and one twin room, all en suite.

GENERAL GROUPS

■ **Freedom Centre** Wed 17-20, Fri 16-20, 2nd & 4th Sat/month 11-17h
1/471 William Street, Northbridge *Near cnr. Ruth St* ☎ (08) 9228 0354
🖳 www.freedom.org.au
Freedom Centre provides a safe and friendly space, information, support and referral for gay, lesbian, bisexual, queer, transgender and questioning youth. Check website for details.

■ **Pride Western Australia** (GLM MA) Mon-Fri 9-17h
PO Box 8463, Perth Business Centre ☎ (08) 9427 0828
🖳 www.pridewa.asn.au
Organizers of local gay pride. See their website for details.

HEALTH GROUPS

■ **WA AIDS Council** 8.30-17h, closed Sat & Sun
664 Murray Street, West Perth ☎ (08) 9482 0000 🖳 www.waaids.com
Peer support, information, education and sexual health testing for men with same sex attractions. Dealing directly with sexuality, HIV and other STI's.

SWIMMING

-Floriat Beach (AYOR) (not a nude beach but attract quite a few gay people, particularly at the northern end)
-South City Beach/Swanbourne (AYOR) (nude beaches. Gays congregate at the southern end of South City Beach and North Swanbourne)
-Warnbro Beach (Rockingham)
-Whitford's Beach.

CRUISING

All AYOR
-Fremantle (under bridges)
-Swanbourne Beach (at night, but helicopter surveillance).
-Fawkner Park (South Perth)
-Mosman Park (south end of Mosman Bay)
-Kings Park (near barbecue area; entrance from Thomas Street).

Austria

Name: Österreich · Autriche
Location: Central Europe
Initials: A
Time: GMT +1
International Country Code: ☏ 43 (omit from area code)
International Access Code: ☏ 00
Language: German
Area: 83,871 km² / 32,382 sq mi.
Currency: 1 Euro (€) = 100 Cents
Population: 8,115,000
Capital: Wien
Religions: 74% Catholic
Climate: Alpine climate with hot summers and cold, snowy winters.
Important gay cities: Wien

Austria is no longer bringing up the rear in Europe where lesbian and gay rights are concerned. Various developments have been set in motion ever since the country joined the EU – not least of all owing to the latterís pressure. Discriminatory legal provisions have been done away with and been replaced by a new age of consent (16) for everyone. An anti-discrimination law has been passed. And ever since 1.1.2010, gays and lesbians have also been able to register their partnerships in Austria. Gay initiatives like the lesbian organization "RosaLila PantherInnen" intend to fight for complete equalization.
The federal capital is also no longer alone in having a gay pride event (even if the Rainbow Parade does enjoy one of the most magnificent routes in the world, along Ringstrasse), having been joined by Innsbruck and Linz. And Kärnten hosts the annual Pink Lake Festival – a European gay community event. But Austriaës towns and cities also provide congenial subcultural options besides these events. In fact, everything a gay touristís heart desires can be found.
Austria is first and foremost a country that makes visitors feel welcome and has a lot to offer them in cultural and scenic terms, with something for every taste. Most of all the Austrian cuisine and coffee houses are not to be missed.

Österreich ist nicht länger eines der Schlusslichter in Europa, wenn es um die Rechte von Schwulen und Lesben geht. Viele Entwicklungen – nicht zuletzt auf Druck der EU – sind in Bewegung geraten, seitdem Österreich Mitglied der EU geworden ist. Diskriminierende strafrechtliche Bestimmungen wurden abgeschafft und durch ein neues Mündigkeitsalter (16) für alle ersetzt. Ein Antidiskriminierungsgesetz wurde etabliert. Und seit dem 1.1.2010 können Schwule und Lesben in Österreich ihre Partnerschaft eintragen lassen. Homosexuelle Initiativen, bzw. RosaLila PantherInnen wollen für eine vollkommene Gleichstellung kämpfen.
Inzwischen hat nicht nur die Bundeshauptstadt eine CSD-Veranstaltung (wenn auch die Regenbogenparade mit der Ringstraße über die wohl prächtigste Route weltweit verfügt) – sondern auch Innsbruck und Linz. In Kärnten findet alljährlich das Pink Lake-Festival statt – ein europäisches Event der Gay Community. Aber auch zwischen den Events haben Österreichs Städte ein sympathisches subkulturelles Angebot. Alles, was das Herz eines schwulen Touristen begehrt, kann man finden.
Vor allem ist Österreich ein gastliches Land, das landschaftlich und kulturell seinen Gästen viel und für jeden Geschmack etwas zu bieten hat. Vor allem die österreichische Küche und die Kaffeehäuser sollte man sich nicht entgehen lassen.

l'Autriche n'est plus la lanterne rouge en Europe en ce qui concerne les droits des gays et lesbiennes. De nombreuses évolutions – en grande partie sous la pression de l'Union Européenne – se sont faites depuis son adhésion à l'UE. Des lois discriminatoires furent abrogées et la majorité sexuelle fixée à 16 ans pour tous. Une loi contre les discriminations fut votée. Et depuis le 1er janvier 2010, les gays et lesbiennes peuvent conclure un partenariat enregistré. Des associations homosexuelles comme RosaLila PantherInnen se battent pour une égalité totale.
Désormais la capitale fédérale n'est plus la seule à proposer une Gay Pride (bien que l'itinéraire de la Regenbogenparade le long de la Ringstraße est un des plus beaux au monde) – mais aussi Innsbruck et Linz. En Carinthie, le Pink Lake Festival se tient tous les ans, un événement gay à l'échelle européenne. Outre ces grands événements, les villes autrichiennes ont bien plus à offrir, pour le plaisir des touristes gays. L'Autriche est avant tout un pays accueillant, culturellement riche et doté de beaux paysages, offrant à ses visiteurs beaucoup de choses, pour tous les goûts. A ne pas manquer, sa cuisine et ses fameux cafés.

Austria ya no es uno de los más rezagados en Europa en cuanto a los derechos de gays y lesbianas. Se han llevado a cabo muchos avances – no solo bajo presión por parte de la UE – desde que Austria se convirtiera en miembro de la UE. Se abolieron normativas penales discriminatorias, se introdujo una nueva edad de consentimiento (16) aplicable para todos y se estableció una ley contra la discriminación. Desde el 01.01.2010 los gays y lesbianas austriacos pueden legalizar sus uniones en un registro civil de parejas. Las iniciativas homosexuales, por ejemplo, Rosa Lila PantherInnen, quieren luchar por una futura igualdad completa.
Mientras tanto, no sólo la Capital Federal cuenta con un evento para la Marcha del Orgullo Gay (aunque el Regenbogenparade (Desfile de Arco Iris) cuente, gracias a la circunvalación conocida como la Ringstraße, con la ruta más bella del mundo), sino también Innsbruck y Linz. En Carintia, se celebra anualmente el Pink Lake-Festival (Festival del Lago Rosa), un evento europeo de la comunidad gay. Pero incluso en las temporadas entre eventos, las ciudades austriacas cuentan con una simpática oferta subcultural. Se puede encontrar todo lo que el corazón de un turista gay esta buscando.
Por encima de todo, Austria es un país hospitalario cuya oferta natural y cultural puede satisfacer a sus huéspedes en cantidad para todos los gustos. Especialmente no debería perderse la cocina austriaca y sus cafeterías.

Già da tempo l'Austria non è più fanalino di coda in Europa in tema di diritti omosessuali. Molti passi avanti sono stati fatti proprio da quando l'Austria è entrata a far parte dell'UE e molti anche a causa di pressioni di quest'ultima. Molte disposizioni penali discriminatorie sono state abolite e sostituite, per esempio, con l'in-

MORE THAN JUST ANOTHER GAY FRIENDLY HOTEL

DISCOVER YOURSELF

we support small & big scene institutions such as the "Life Ball" - europe´s biggest aids charity event or vienna´s christopher street day to local clubs of vienna

stay where the stars are & where international djs give a spontaneous gig troduzione di un'età del consenso di 16 anni valida per tutti. Inoltre è stata introdotta una legge antidiscriminatoria e dall'1 gennaio del 2010 è possibile, per le coppie omosessuali, far registrare la propria unione civile. Alcune associazioni omosessuali, come per esempio la RosaLila PantherInnen, lottano per una completa equiparazione. Ormai il Christopher Street Day non si svolge solo nella capitale (anche se la Regebogenparade ha, con la Ringstraße, uno dei più imponenti percorsi al mondo) bensì anche ad Innsbruck e a Linz. In Carinzia ogni anno ha luogo il Pink Lake Festival, una manifestazione culturale di respiro europeo. Ma oltre a questi eventi le città austriache offrono una vita subculturale abbastanza interessante. L'Austria è un paese molto ospitale che ha un'offerta paesaggistica e culturale che fa un po' per tutti i suoi visitatori. Da non perdere assolutamente sono la sua cucina e i suoi caffè.

NATIONAL GAY INFO

City Gay Guide (G)
c/o Pink Marketing GmbH, Zieglergasse 3/1 ✉ 1070 Wien
☎ (01) 789 1000-20 💻 www.gaynet.at
Gay guide for Graz, Linz, Salzburg and Innsbruck; for free at gay venues or by mailorder.

gaynet.at
c/o Pink Marketing GmbH, Zieglergasse 3/1 ✉ 1070 Wien
☎ (01) 789 1000-20 ☎ 0930 33 66 006
💻 www.gaynet.at
Austrian gay platform with information for tourists. Printed citymaps for Vienna, Graz, Linz, Salzburg and Innsbruck and austrian gayguide brochure.

NATIONAL PUBLICATIONS

LAMBDA-Nachrichten
c/o HOSI Wien, Novaragasse 40 ✉ 1020 Wien *Near Nestroyplatz*
☎ (01) 216 66 04 💻 www.hosiwien.at
News magazine for gays and lesbians with an emphasis on gay rights. Published 6x/year by HOSI Vienna and with a section on Vienna.

XTRA!
PO Box 77 ✉ 1043 Wien ☎ (0676) 530 30 00
💻 www.xtra-news.at
Free monthly gay magazine, available at gay venues. Austria's main magazine, especially popular in Vienna.

Vangardist (GLM)
Mariahilferstraße 101/23 ☎ 94 29 139
💻 www.vangardist.com
New and stylish gay onlinemag.

NATIONAL COMPANIES

Gay-Center.com (CC G)
💻 www.gay-center.com
Online-shop with a large selection of DVDs.

gayboy.at (GLM MA)
💻 www.gayboy.at
Austria`s largest online-community for gays and friends. Dating, event-tips, news, pictures, profiles.

Gayshop.at (CC G)
Quergasse 1 ✉ 8020 Graz ☎ (0676) 325 28 66 (mobile)
💻 www.gayshop.at
Online-shop with a large selection of videos, DVDs, toys and lubes.

queercard (GLM MA)
Operngasse 30/18, 1040 Wien 💻 www.queercard.info
Discounts on various shops and venues.

rainbow.at (GLM)
💻 www.rainbow.at
Austria`s largest queer-chat – for more than 13 years. Online community for gays and lesbians. Chat, video-chat, guide, event-tips.

NATIONAL GROUPS

1. Lesben- und Schwulenverband Österreichs – Homosexuelle Initiative (HOSI) Wien
Novaragasse 40 ✉ 1020 Wien *U-Praterstern/Nestoyplatz*
☎ (01) 216 66 04 (helpline) 💻 www.hosiwien.at
The most important, longest running and leading gay organisation in Austria. See HOSI-Zentrum in Vienna for more information regarding the gay centre and the activities there.

Aids-Hilfen Österreichs Mon-Fri 8.30-16.30h
Aids Hilfe Haus - Mariahilfer Gürtel 4 ✉ 1060 Wien ☎ (01) 599 37
💻 www.aidshilfen.at
Headquarters of the austrian aids support groups. Aidshilfen.at is the website of all austrian aids support groups providing information and contacts to many aids groups all over Austria.

COUNTRY CRUISING

-A2 (Südautobahn) P«P14», last P → Wien, behind km 13,5, from sunset
-A7 P Linz, Franzosenhausweg 22-?h.
-A 12 (Inntalautobahn) PKramsach, PZirl, PTelfs (all both directions)

Achenkirch ☎ 05246

APARTMENTS

Pension Montana
(B BF GLM H M MA OS PA PK RES RWB RWS RWT SL) All year
Achenkirch 118 *Tirol* ☎ (0664) 2378940 💻 www.winterbear.at
Three apartments for 2 to 5 persons and 2 rooms all with shower/WC. Café with sun terrace and cellar bar. Popular with „bears & otters" and their fans, next to ski lift and winter ski slopes.

Bad Gastein ☎ 06434

BARS

Regina Skibar (B GLM M MA)
Open daily from 10-16h (sunny days only)
Sportgastein *Between Bergstation and Mittelstation*
The bar is just on sunny days open.It has a gigantic terrace and sun loungers and laid-back music. Champagne, sandwiches, drinks amid high-alpine scenery.

CAFES

Regina's Coffee (b GLM MA)
Bahnhofsplatz
Espressobar.

Regina's Grand Caffé @ Hotel Weismayr (b GLM MA)
Kaiser Franz Josef Str. 6
Wiener Caféhaus.

DANCECLUBS

Regina Club @ Hotel Weismayr (D GLM MA)
Kaiser Franz Josef Str. 6

HOTELS

Das Regina
(B BF CC D GLM M MA MSG PA PK RWS RWT SA SB WH) All year
Karl-Heinrich-Waggerl-Straße 5 *Near Stubnerkogelbahn*
☎ (06434) 2161 - 0 💻 www.dasregina.com
The hotel has a relaxed atmosphere and a great wellness-area! Italian flair combined with new ideas and modern design. Great à la carte Restaurant and Bar with DJs spinning their records every night.

Miramonte (AC B BF CC glm H I M MA MSG OS PA PK RWB RWS RWT SA SB WH) All year
Reitlpromenade 3 *Close to the airports of Salzburg, Klagenfurt and Munich*
☎ (06434) 2577 💻 www.hotelmiramonte.com
The Miramonte Hotel is located in a turn of the 19th century building, completely renovated recently, to meet the needs of the modern wellness-seeking guest.

Finkenberg ☏ 05285

HOTELS

Sporthotel Stock
(BF H I MSG OS PI PK RWB RWS RWT SA SB WH WI WO) 7-23h
Dorf 142 *Next train station Mayrhofen* ☏ (05285) 6775 410
www.sporthotel-stock.com
Extravagant health spa paradise. Hotel combines wellness, fun and sports in beautiful panoramic mountain surrounding. Offers a wide range of leisure and sports activities.

Freistadt ☏ 0732

GENERAL GROUPS

Mühl4tel Andersrum (GLM MA) Last Fri/month 20-?h
Salzgasse 25 @ *LOCAL, in the cinema* ☏ (0732) 609 89 84
www.hosilinz.at
local regular and open group-meeting.

Fügen-Zillertal ☏ 05288

HOTELS

Apart-Hotel-Alpenhof
(BF glm I MA MSG OS PK RWB RWS RWT SA SB SOL VA WO) All year
Sängerweg 22 *Tirol* ☏ (05288) 620 50 www.alpenhof.cc
Apartments for 2-10 people with bath/shower, balcony, phone, TV, safe, heating, own key.

Graz ☏ 0316

GAY INFO

Schwulen- und Lesbenzentrum „feel free" (GLM)
Tue 15-18, Wed 11-12.Fri 10-midnight
Annenstraße 26 ☏ (0316) 36 66 01 (counselling) www.homo.at
Information and counselling, also library and café.

BARS

Elenor's (B BF GLM M MA) Mon-Sat 7-24, Sun 9-24h
Kaiserfeldgasse 19 ☏ (0664) 39 24 729
Bar with mediterranean flair.

Loft (B D GLM m MA) 16-3h, Fri & Sat - open end, closed Sun
Griesgasse 25 ☏ (0316) 91 29 226 www.loftgraz.at
On Wed & Thu 2-4-1 Longdrinks. See website for specials.

Mens Room (B D DR F G MA VS) 20-?h
Keesgasse 3 ☏ (0664) 392 47 29 www.stargayte.at

Murnockerl (AC B G M MA S VS) Mon-Sat 21-3h
Schönaugasse 22 ☏ (0664) 140 45 89 www.murnockerl.com

Pepis Club Beisl (B G MC) Daily 18-?h
Griesplatz 36 ☏ (0316) 719 277 www.gaypepi.com
Men only

Stargayte (B D DR f GLM MA T VS)
Mon-Thu & Sun 21-4, Fri & Sat and before public holidays 20h-open end
Keesgasse 3 *near Jakominiplatz* ☏ (0664) 392 47 29 www.stargayte.at
#1 Gay-Lesbian Club in Town, Thu women's night. No cover charge!

DANCECLUBS

Rosy @ Postgarage (D GLM MA) 22-6h
Dreihackengasse 42 *Near Griesplatz* ☏ (0699) 17 67 97 62 www.rosy.at
Biggest gay and lesbian party on two 2 floors. Takes place up to 5 times a year.

SEX SHOPS/BLUE MOVIES

1A Gaykino (DR G GH MA VS) Mon-Fri 10-19, Sat-17h
Bindergasse 8 *Near Stempfergasse* ☏ 813 190

Sexworld, Gay-Kino & Gayshop.at (AC CC G I MA VS) Mon-Fri 11-12 & 16-19h, Sat & Sun closed
Quergasse 1 *Near main station* ☏ (0676) 325 28 66 www.gayshop.at
DVDs, magazines, toys and movies.

SAUNAS/BATHS

■ **Babylon** (AK B DR FC FH G m MA RR SA SB SOL VS)
16-2h, Fri 16-Sun 24h (non-stop)
Feuerbachgasse 9 ☎ (0316) 30 82 44 💻 www.babylongraz.at

Innsbruck ☎ 0512

BARS

■ **Bacchus / Easy** (B CC D FC GLM MA NR P S T WE WI)
Bacchus: Fri, Sat & before public holidays 22-7;
Café Easy: Mon-Thu 10-2, Fri -3, Sat 19-4h
Salurnerstraße 18 *Opposite from the Casino, 300m from the train station*
☎ (0512) 94 02 10 💻 www.bacchus-tirol.at
Register on www.bacchus-tirol.at to get admittance. Smoking allowed.

■ **Dom Café** (B CC glm m MA OS) 17-1h
Pfarrgasse 3 ☎ (0512) 23 85 51

■ **Le Scorpion** (B GLM MA)
Maria-Theresien-Str. 49
mixed crowd and nice staff.

■ **M+M Bar** (B CC GLM) Tue-Sat 19-3h
Innstraße 45 ☎ (0699) 15 22 01 39 💻 www.mm-bar.at
Cocktail bar.

■ **Treffpunkt Arcad** (B BF F G M MA OS S)
Mon-Thu 10-1, Fri & Sat 12-1h, Sun & public holidays closed
Innstraße 2 *Near Metropol cinema* ☎ (0512) 0664 3940466
💻 www.treffpunkt-arcad.com
Mixed crowd, leather and jeans welcome.

GUEST HOUSES

■ **Haus Romeo**
☞ *Scheffau am Wilden Kaiser.*

APARTMENTS

■ **Haus Thomas** (glm I MA OS PA PI PK RWT VA) All year
Dandlweg 18, Telfs *22 km west of Innsbruck* ☎ (0664) 131 11 14
💻 www.hausthomas.at
4 star apartment (70 m²) situated in a private house, terrace to the garden, completely equipped.

GENERAL GROUPS

■ **HOSI-Tirol** (GLM MA T)
Thu 20.30-23.30h, Transgender each 1st Sat 20-23h
Meinhardstraße 16 *In the Kreidpassage* ☎ (0512) 587 586 💻 www.hositirol.at
The agency for LGBT-interests in Tyrol and the organizer of Queerattack! - the gay/lesbian/transgender festival in Tyrol.

SWIMMING

-Kranebitter Au (G MA NU) (Leave motorway A 12 Innsbruck to Bregenz at Innsbruck-Kranebitten, take road 171 to Zirl. P at „Standschützenkaserne" and get to the left bank of the river Inn. In summer only)

CRUISING

-Hofgarten (after sunset at Rennweg)

Klagenfurt ☎ 0463

BARS

■ **Palim-Palim** (B GLM H m MA t)
Mon-Fri 14-4, Sat, Sun & public holidays 19-4h
St. Veiter Straße 3 *Heuplatz, opposite shopping mall* ☎ (0463) 59 99 99
💻 www.palim-palim-bar.at
Former „Absolut" Bar.

■ **Stadtkrämer** (B GLM MA) Wed-Sat 19-2
Spitalgasse 11 💻 www.stadtkraemer.com

■ **Strass** (B GLM MA p) Wed-Sat 19-4h
Theatergasse 4 *entrance in Purtscherstrasse* ☎ (660) 344 51 26
💻 www.strass-bar.net

SEX CINEMAS

■ **Erotiklabyrinth** (b DR g m MA t) Mon-Sat 12-24h
Florian-Gröger-Straße 1 *Near fairground* ☎ (0650) 666 06 05
💻 www.erotiklabyrinth.com

HEALTH GROUPS

■ **AIDS Hilfe Kärnten** (MA)
Counselling: Mon, Tue, Thu 17-19; HIV-, Hep B & C-Test: Tue 17-19h
Bahnhofstrasse 22 *1st floor* ☎ (0463) 55 128 💻 www.hiv.at
Free anonymous counseling and blood-tests!

SWIMMING

-Keutschacher See - camping(NU)
-Forstsee.

CRUISING

-Schubert Park (behind theatre, evenings)
-Heiliger Geist Platz (in front of Quelle store, late evenings)
-Between Bahnhofstraße & bus station (evenings).

Kolbnitz ☎ 04783

GUEST HOUSES

■ **Gasthof Herkuleshof**
(B BF glm H I M OS PA PK RWB RWS RWT VA) 8-24h
Am Danielsberg ☎ (04783) 22 88 💻 www.herkuleshof.com
In a nature reserve area.

Lieboch ☎ 03136

BARS

■ **Du & Ich** (B bf CC g m MA OS)
Mon-Thu 16-24, Fri & Sat 7-2, Sun -24h
Packer Straße 75 *Near train station* ☎ (03136) 614 19 💻 duundich.at

www.xtra-news.at
XTRA!
ÖSTERREICHS GRÖSSTES GAYMAGAZIN
05/2011
www.xtra-news.at
XTRA!
ÖSTERREICHS GRÖSSTES GAYMAGAZIN
07/2011
www.xtra-news.at
PROUD TO LOVE HIM
PROUD TO LOVE HIM
XTRA!
ÖSTERREICHS GRÖSSTES GAYMAGAZIN
10. November 2011 – 16. Dezember 2011
11/2011
www.xtra-news.at
XTRA!
P.O.Box 77, A-1043 Vienna, Austria, Europe
www.xtra-news.at, office@xtra-news.at

Linz ☎ 0732

NATIONAL PUBLICATIONS

■ **PRIDE – Das lesbisch/schwule Österreichmagazin** (GLM MA)
Gerstnerstraße 13 ☎ (0732) 70 04 742 💻 www.pride.at
Gay magazine for the Austrian regions, popular outside Vienna. Published 6x/year since 1991.

BARS

■ **Julius** (b bf cc GLM M MA OS S t)
Fabrikstraße 18 *Tram 1/2/3-Hauptplatz* ☎ (0732) 609 898-8
💻 www.hosilinz.at/julius
Different weekly menu. Extensive breakfast menu.

■ **Lexx** (B d GLM OS t YC) Tue - Sat 19-2h
Baumbachstraße 9 *close to Neuer Dom* ☎ (0732) 77 06 54
Happy Hour Wed-Sat 20-22h.

■ **Stonewall** (B CC D gLm m MA S) Tue-Thu, Sun 20-4, Fri & Sat 22-4h (disco from 23h)
Rainerstraße 22 *Near station & Volksgarten* ☎ (0732) 60 04 38
💻 www.stonewall.at

CAFES

■ **Gösser Stub'n** (B glm I M MA) 11-1, Sat & Sun 18-1h
Starhembergstraße 11 *Neustadtviertel, Bus 21* ☎ (0732) 79 70 95

■ **Musikcafé Sax** (AC B GLM I m MA OS) Daily 15-4h
Klammstraße 6 ☎ (0732) 78 12 13
Thursdays Spaghetti for only € 1 from 20-22h

DANCECLUBS

■ **Blue Heaven** (AC B D DR GLM I m s VS WE YC)
Daily 21-4, Fri & Sat -4h, closed Sun
Starhembergstraße 11 *Neustadtviertel, Bus 21* ☎ (0664) 3420 582
💻 www.blueheaven.at

HOTELS

■ **Courtyard by Marriott Linz**
(AC B BF CC glm H I M MA MSG PA PK RWS RWT SA SB WO)
All year, 24hrs
Europaplatz 2 *Next to Design Center* ☎ (0732) 69 59-0
💻 www.courtyardlinz.com

■ **Landgraf Hotel & Loft** (B BF CC H M OS PA PK RWT WI)
Hauptstrasse 12 *next to Ars Electronica Center* ☎ (0732) 700 712
💻 www.hotellandgraf.com
Boutique Hotel with all amenities, 32 rooms and 3 suites.

■ **Park Inn by Radisson Linz**
(AC B H I M MA PK RWB RWS RWT W WO)
Hessenplatz 16-18 *Very close to Landstrasse, the main shopping street, 100m to Tram, 15mins walk to main station* ☎ (0732) 777 100 0
💻 www.parkinn.com/hotel-linz
The hotel features 175 rooms and Junior Suites, with modern facilities and decorated in colorful design. Surrounded by green parks.

■ **Pixel Hotel** (CC glm PK RWS RWT)
All year. Reservations via Hotel Kolping Linz
c/o Hotel Kolping Linz, Gesellenhausstraße 5 *5 different locations*
☎ (0650) 743 79 53 💻 www.pixelhotel.at
Extraordinary hotel-project with 5 unique rooms available in the city.

HEALTH GROUPS

■ **Aidshilfe Oberösterreich** Mon-Fri 9-13h
Blütenstraße 15/2 ☎ (0732) 21 70 💻 www.aidshilfe-ooe.at
Thu 16-17.30h: gay Phone 21 70-25; counselling & testing: Mon 14-18h, Wed 16-20h, Fri 10-14h.

■ **Dr. Georg Pfau** Mon, Tue, Thu 9-14, Wed 14-18, Fri 9-11h
Franckstraße 23 ☎ (0732) 60 38 31
💻 www.gaymed.at
Webpage that caters to gay men and their medical issues. Also doctor's surgery.

HELP WITH PROBLEMS

HOSI - Homosexuelle Initiative Linz (B FC GLM MA OS s WI)
Mon 20-22, Thu 18.30-22h
Fabrikstraße 18/1 *Tram 1/2/3 Hauptplatz; Bus 27: Lederergasse*
☎ (0732) 6098984 www.hosilinz.at
Workshops, events, performances - special offers for women, youth a.s.o. - counselling (personal counselling possible) - restaurant/bar (open Thu-Sat & Mon from 16h, Sun from 10h).

SWIMMING

-Weikerlsee (NU YC) (south of Linz in Pichling)
-Pleschingersee (G NU YC) (Linz-Urfahr, southeastern side of lake)

CRUISING

-Volksgarten (after sunset at »Volksgartenstraße«).

Pöllau ☎ (0316)

HOTELS

Chalet Masenberg (AC B BF glm MSG OS PK RWS SA SB VS)
All year
Oberneuberg 25 *12 km from Hartberg / Pöllau* ☎ (0316) 827 470
www.chalet-masenberg.at
The Chalet Masenberg is an elegant hide-away in the enchanting mountain world of the Oststeiermark. At 1.000 m above sea level, the views are fantastic. Excursions to Vienna or Graz possible. Thermal baths nearby. No TV-sets - to protect the atmosphere of the chalet!

Salzburg ☎ 0662

GAY INFO

Homosexuelle Initiative Salzburg (HOSI) (GLM MA T)
Tue 9-13 & 14-17, Wed 13-17 & 19-24, Fri & Sat 20-1, brunch 3rd Sun/month 11-?h
Gabelsbergerstrasse 26 *Bus 2, Bus Stop Stelzhamerstraße or Bayerhamerstraße* ☎ (0662) 43 59 27 www.hosi.or.at
Non-govenmental, non-profit group of volunteers, information center and consulting, library.

BARS

2-Stein (B CC d DR GLM I m MA S VS) 18-4, Thu-Sat -5h
Giselakai 9 *Near Staatsbrücke* ☎ (0662) 87 71 79
www.zweistein.at
Wed, Thu & Sat 22h men only on the 1st floor.

Mexxx Gaybar (AC B D G MA)
Sun-Thu 20.30-4, Fri & Sat -5h
Schallmooser Hauptstraße 20 ☎ (0699) 17 10 19 02
www.mexxxgaybar.at
Men-only bar!

Princess Bar (B CC d GLM MA S SNU ST t)
Sun-Thu 20-4, Fri & Sat -5h, closed Mon
Priesterhausgasse 22 ☎ (0699) 1900 9804
www.princess-salzburg.at
Funny Bar with motto parties, local crowd.

CAFES

Konditorei Rainberg (AC B bf CC g m MA OS WE)
8-20, Sun 9-19 (summer -22h), closed Mon (Oct.-June)
Hildmannplatz 5 *Near Neutor* ☎ 254 050
www.konditorei-rainberg.at
Pastry shop and coffee house.

Viva (B glm I m MA) Mon-Sat 7-22h
Schrannengasse 4

SEX SHOPS/BLUE MOVIES

Cruisingline (AC DR G MA NR T VS)
14-21h, closed Sun and public holidays
Mertensstraße 13 *Near main railway station - between Elisabethstraße and Plainstraße* www.cruisingline.at
Indoor-cruising with hardcore movies. DVDs for sale.

HOTELS

Hotel & Villa Auersperg
(B BF CC glm H I OS PA PK RWB RWS RWT SA SB VA) All year
Auerspergstraße 61 *Bus 2 Stelzhamerstraße* ☎ (0662) 88944 0
www.auersperg.at
Perfectly situated in the city centre of Salzburg, within walking distance of restaurants, shops and the historical old town. Sauna and steam bath on the rooftop terrace.

Mercure Salzburg Kapuzinerberg
(AC B H M MA MSG OS PA PK RWS RWT W WI WL) All year
Sterneckstrasse 20 *15 mins walk to Mirabellgarten or the old city of Salzburg, bus 2 Bayerhamer Str.* ☎ (0662) 8820310
www.mercure.com/5354
The 2011 renovated hotel with its 139 rooms including suites is the ideal spot for your trip to Salzburg.

HEALTH GROUPS

AIDS-Hilfe Salzburg Mon-Fri 10-12, Mon, Wed-Thu 17-19h
Linzer Bundesstraße 10, 2nd Floor ☎ (0662) 88 14 88
www.aidshilfen.at
Ask for further services and individual counselling.

CRUISING

-Mirabellgarten (after sunset around the »Rosenhügel«) AYOR.

Scheffau am Wilden Kaiser ☏ 05358

GUEST HOUSES

■ **Haus Romeo** (B BF CC G I PA PK RWB RWS RWT SA SB VA WO)
All year
Blaiken 71 *Between Kufstein and Kitzbühel. Airport shuttle services from Salzburg 60 mins or Munich 90 mins* ☏ (05358) 431 310
www.houseromeo.com
This exclusively gay guesthouse is located directly at the cableway of Scheffau, the starting point for the ski area "Skiwelt Wilder Kaiser / Brixental" with over 280 km of ski slopes, also ideal for snowboarding. A wellness area with steam room, sauna and fitness area is also available. All rooms have a DVD player and sat-TV. Your hosts Tom and Manfred offer refreshments at the bar. Summer activities include hiking, mountain biking, golf or mountain climbing as well as excursions to nearby Innsbruck, Salzburg ("The Sound of Music") and Munich.

St. Johann in Tirol ☏ 05352

HOTELS

■ **Landhaus Pöll** (B bf CC glm H M MA OS PA PI RWS RWT)
May-Oct & Dec-Mar, front desk: 7.30-24h
Speckbacherstraße 71 *Near Kitzbühel, 5 mins from train station*
☏ (05352) 671 33 www.poell.com
Friendly atmosphere and situated right on the ski slopes.

St. Pölten ☏ 02742

CRUISING

-Behind the bank at Domplatz
-End of Julius-Raab-Promenade (YC).

Velden am Wörther See

SWIMMING

-Forstsee (NU) (between Velden and Pörtschach).

Villach ☏ 04242

BARS

■ **Gentlemen's Club & Ladies also** (B D f glm H m MA S) Summer: Tue-Sun 19-2; winter: Tue-Sat 17-2, Sun 15-2h
Widnanngasse 6 www.gentlemensclubbar.com
■ **Soho** (B d glm m MA S WE) 19-2h
Freihausgasse 13 ☏ (04242) 24 755 www.barsoho.com
Every second Sat after hours 4-?h. During the week also live concerts.

SWIMMING

-Erlebnistherme Warmbad (g sa) (11-20 h)

Vöcklabruck ☏ 0732

GENERAL GROUPS

■ **Regenbogenstammtisch** (GLM MA) Thu 20-?h
Vorstadt 18 @ *Restaurant/Café Zur Brücke* ☏ 609 89 84
www.hosilinz.at
local open group-meeting.

Wels

CRUISING

-Volksgarten (near exhibition centre, summer)

Wien ☏ 01

On his way back from a crusade, King Richard the Lionheart fell into the hands of his Babenberg opponentís bailiffs in Vienna and was imprisoned in Dürnstein Castle. His lover Blondel discovered his whereabouts with the help of a love song they had written together – the ransom could be paid, and Viennaës city fortifications financed with it. Vienna hence owes her very existence as a city to a gay love story. The Austrian capital also has a lot to offer today: the Rainbow Parade is distinguished by one of the most impressive routes imaginable for any gay pride event. The Rainbow Ball and Life Ball favour Vienna with two society events that have come to outrank the legendary Opera Ball and are basking in international fame. But the metropolis by the Danube also has plenty of recreational value to offer all year round, not least of all the 21 km long river island traversing it near the city centre with several official nudist beaches – meaning that gay bathing and cruising is not only confined to the area known as "Toter Grund" at kilometre 6.

König Richard Löwenherz fiel auf dem Heimweg vom Kreuzzug in Wien den Häschern seines babenbergischen Gegenspielers in die Hände und wurde auf Burg Dürnstein eingesperrt. Sein Liebhaber Blondel entdeckte ihn mithilfe des gemeinsam gedichteten Liebesliedes – das Lösegeld konnte gezahlt und damit die Stadtbefestigung Wiens finanziert werden. Dass Wien also eine Stadt ist, verdankt es einer schwulen Liebesgeschichte. Und auch heute hat die Hauptstadt Österreichs vieles zu bieten: die Regenbogenparade zeichnet sich durch eine der imposantesten Routen aus, die man sich für eine CSD-Veranstaltung nur vorstellen kann. Mit Regenbogenball und Life Ball besitzt Wien zwei gesellschaftliche Events, die dem legendären Opernball inzwischen den Rang ablaufen und internationalen Ruf genießen. Aber auch das ganze Jahr über ist der Freizeitwert der Donaumetropole hoch: allein schon, dass sich eine 21 km lange Insel in Citynähe durch die Stadt zieht und im Sommer an ausgewiesenen Stellen zum FKK einlädt – nicht nur bei Kilometer 6, am Toten Grund, ist schwules Baden und Cruisen angesagt.

A son retour de croisade, le roi Richard Cœur de Lion fut capturé à Vienne par ses adversaires les Babenberg et emprisonné au château de Dürnstein. Blondel son amant le découvrit grâce à la chanson

vektorama.

d'amour composée ensemble – la rançon fut payée et finança la fortification de la ville de Vienne. Que Vienne soit devenue une ville est ainsi redevable à une histoire d'amour homosexuelle. Et de nos jours aussi Vienne a beaucoup à offrir. La Regenbogenparade (parade arc-en-ciel) est caractérisée par un des itinéraires les plus imposants, imaginable seulement pour une Gay Pride. Avec le Regenbogenball (Bal arc-en-ciel) et le Life Ball, Vienne organise deux événements qui détrônent désormais le légendaire bal de l'opéra et jouissent d'une réputation internationale. Les possibilités de sorties dans la métropole en bord du Danube sont importantes pendant toute l'année aussi : déjà grâce à une île qui s'étend sur 21 km située à proximité de la ville et qui est ouverte au naturisme en été à certains endroits – le cruising et les baignades entre gays ne se limitent pas seulement au kilomètre 6 sur le lieu-dit «Am toten Grund.»

De camino a casa desde las cruzadas, el rey Ricardo Corazón de León cayó en Viena en manos de sus contrincantes de Babenberg y fue encarcelado en Dürnstein. Su amante, el trovador Blondel, lo descubrió usando la historia de amor que compusieron juntos - se pudo así pagar el rescate y con él financiar las fortificaciones de Viena. Viena es una ciudad gracias a una historia de amor homosexual. Y también hoy en día la capital de Austria tiene mucho que ofrecer: el Regenbogenparade (Desfile del Arco Iris) se caracteriza por contar con una de las rutas más impresionantes que se puedan imaginar para una Marcha del Orgullo Gay. Con el Regenbogenball (Baile del Arco Iris) y el Life Ball (Baile de la Vida), Viena cuenta con dos eventos sociales que pueden competir con el Opernball (Baile de la Ópera) y que cuentan con renombre a nivel internacional. Pero también durante todo el año se puede disfrutar de una gran libertad en la metrópolis del Danubio: una isla cercana al centro de la ciudad, con 21 kilómetros de extensión que transcurren a lo largo de esta, ofrece durante el verano lugares designados para naturistas (FKK en alemán). No solo en los 6 kilómetros de Toten Grund están de moda las zonas de baño y cruising para homosexuales.

Il Re Riccardo Cuor di Leone, al suo ritorno dalla crociata a Vienna, è stato catturato dai suoi rivali Babenberg e rinchiuso nel castello Dürnstein. Il suo amante, Blondel, lo ha ritrovato sentendolo cantare una canzone d'amore che avevano composto insieme, sporto dalla finestra della sua cella. Il riscatto ha, così, reso possibile il finanziamento della fortificazione di Vienna. Che Vienna sia quindi potuta divenire una metropoli lo si deve appunto ad una storia d'amore gay. La città di Vienna ha davvero molto da offrire: la parata arcobaleno (Regenbogenparade), per esempio, si contraddistingue per il suo imponente percorso che ci si potrebbe aspettare solo per una parata nell'ambito del Christopher Street Day. Il Regenbogeball e il Life Ball sono due eventi culturali di fama internazionale così importanti che possono ormai essere considerati alla stregua del leggendario Opernball. Ma anche durante il resto dell'anno la metropoli sul Danubio offre molte attività per il tempo libero: in prossimità della città si estende un'isola di 21 chilometri che attira molta gente e che in certi punti offre molte possibilità per gli amanti del nudismo. La balneazione gay e il cruising non si limitano alla sola area del sesto chilometro - il cosiddetto Toter Grund.

GAY INFO

■ **HOSI-Zentrum** (GLM MA)
Heumühlgasse 14 *U Kettenbrückengasse* ☎ (01) 216 66 04
www.hosiwien.at
Gay-lesbian switchboard, organiser of www.regenbogenball.at and www.regenbogenparade.at (CSD). Youngster-Group Thu 17.30-24h. Lesbians Wed from 19h, mixed evening Tue from 19h, for special events see websites

■ **Trans*SchwulenQueer-Beratung Türkis Rosa Tippp**
(GLM MA) Mon, Wed, Fri 17-20 (Fri 19h YC)
Linke Wienzeile 102 *U4-Pilgramgasse* ☎ (01) 586 43 43 (G)
www.villa.at
Gay-lesbian switchboard located in the „Pink Violet Villa": counselling, information, GLB-groups, library. See website for events.

CULTURE

ART by SEPP of VIENNA Open by booking
Waaggasse 5/16 *Close to Karlsplatz and Opera House* ☎ (01) 587 36 30 🖳 www.sepp-of-vienna.at
Sepp Engelmaier works with photography and as independent graphic designer and artist.

TOURIST INFO

Wien Tourismus 9-19h
Albertinaplatz *Cnr. Maysedergasse* ☎ (01) 24 555 🖳 www.wien.info/gay

BARS

Alte Lampe (AC B G m MC S SNU ST)
17-1, Fri & Sat -3, summer from 20h
Heumühlgasse 13 *U4-Kettenbrückengasse* ☎ (01) 587 34 54 🖳 www.altelampe.at
Popular meeting place for middle aged and elderly men. Can be great fun!

Café X Bar (AC B CC G MA) 16-2, Sun 18-24h
Mariahilfer Straße 45 *Raimundhofpassage, U-Neubaugasse* 🖳 x-bar.at
American style bar, best in the evenings.

Cheri (B GLM m MA) Mon-Sat 18-4h
Franzensgasse 2 ☎ (0664) 116 23 38 🖳 www.cafe-cheri.at
Cosy little lounge-bar, reasonable prices.

Club Date (AC B f G m MA p R SNU T) Mon-Sun 20-4h
Schikanedergasse 12 *U-Kettenbrückengasse* ☎ (01) 581 21 84 🖳 www.clubdate.at
Cruising-bar and rent boys.

Felixx Café-Bar (! AC B GLM MA S)
Sun-Thu 18-3, Fri & Sat 18-4h
Gumpendorferstraße 5 *U-Museumsquartier/Mariahilferstraße* ☎ (01) 0650 3900 300; (0664) 27 23 010 (mobile) 🖳 www.felixx-bar.at
Exclusively furnished bar-café.

Goldener Spiegel (AC B CC DM G M MA NR p R)
Sun-Thu 17-1, Fri & Sat -2h
Linke Wienzeile 46 *U-Kettenbrückengasse, entrance Stiegengasse* ☎ (01) 586 66 08 🖳 www.goldenerspiegel.com
An institution. Plush and loaded with old pictures and photos. An exceptional combination: one side is an excellent restaurant with Austrian cuisine, the other one a rent bar. Also 3 separés for rent with shower and TV.

Mango (AC B G MA S) Daily 21-4h
Laimgrubengasse 3 *U-Kettenbrückengasse* ☎ (01) 920 47 14 🖳 www.mangobar.at

Merandy Lounge Club (B GLM MA)
Mon-Thu 19-2, Fri&Sat 20-6h
Mollardgasse 17 ☎ (0699) 110 71 974
de-de.facebook.com/people/Merandy-LoungeClub/100001544367084
New bar.

Peter's Operncafé Hartauer (AC B glm m MA S)
Tue-Sat 18-2h
Riemergasse 9 *U-Stubentor* ☎ (01) 512 89 81
www.petersoperncafe.at
Bar and café in it's 29th year, with lots of opera themed images on the walls. Art Nouveau ambiance and classical background music. Strong atmosphere! Check www.petersoperncafe.at for more infos.

Red Carpet (B d GLM M MA S)
Magdalenenstraße 2 *near Naschmarkt* ☎ (676) 7822966
www.redcarpet.co.at
New and trendy Cafe-Bar with gay events! Former „Otherside"

Schik (AC CC G I M MA WI)
Sun-Thu 19-2, Fri & Sat -4, Jul & Aug from 20h
Schikanedergasse 5 *U-Karlsplatz* ☎ (676) 743 63 78 (mobile)
www.schikbar.at
Cosy coffee-bar with internet access in the heart of Vienna's gay area, just across the street to the well-priced Carlton Opera Hotel.

Supercafé (B CC d glm M MA OS s VS) Tue-Sat 19.00-?h
Mariahilfer Straße 146 ☎ (0699) 81146339 www.supercafe.at
Latest gayfriendly bar with large selection of cocktails and food at reasonable prices.

Versteck. Das (B glm MA) Mon-Fri 18-24, Sat 19-24h
Grünangergasse 10 *Stairs down to Nikolaigasse, follow sign*
☎ (01) 513 40 53

Village (AC B G VS YC) 20-3h
Stiegengasse 8 *U-Kettenbrückengasse, near Naschmarkt*
☎ (676) 38 48 977 mobile www.village-bar.at

MEN'S CLUBS

Club Losch (b DR F G MA p WE) Fri & Sat 22-?h
Fünfhausgasse 1 *U6-Gumpendorfer Straße* ☎ (01) 895 99 79
www.club-losch.at
Fetish & Cruising Club, occasional parties on Sundays, see website for details. Clublocation of MLF Austria.

Eagle Vienna (! AC B DR F G MA p VS) Fri&Sat 18-4, Sun-Thu -2h
Blümelgasse 1 *U-Neubaugasse* ☎ (01) 587 26 61
www.eagle-vienna.com
One of the most famous leather bars in Vienna with a popular large darkroom with sling and cabins. Multi-lingual staff and integrated sex-shop.

HardOn (B DR F G MA P SH) Thu 20-2, Fri & Sat 22-5h
Hamburgerstraße 4 *near Naschmarkt* ☎ (01) 895 99 79
www.lmc-vienna.at
Home of the LMC Vienna. Dresscode. Fri: All fetish gear and masculine guys in jeans and sneakers, Sat: Special fetish/SM events. Sun: motto and irregular parties. free condoms. See website for details.

Sling Cruising Bar (! AC B BF DR F G I MA p VS) 15-4h
Kettenbrückengasse 4 *U-Kettenbrückengasse* ☎ (01) 586 23 62
www.sling.at
Modern, popular & cruisy. Sun: naked and mask parties 15-21h.

Stiefelknecht (B DR F FC G MA p SL VS) Thu-Sat 22-10h
Wimmergasse 20 *bus, entrance Stolberggasse*
☎ (676) 492 74 79 mobile club-stiefelknecht.at
A bit off the beaten track, but worth a visit for leather fans. One of Vienna's oldest gay bars – leather & denim. Dresscode on Sat & Sun.

CAFES

BaKul (B BF GLM MA OS S) Mon-Sun 9-2h
Margaretenstraße 58 *near Naschmarkt, U-Kettenbrückengasse*
www.bakul.at
Nice café, in the evenings bar and good music

... sex in the city!
SLING

■ **Boulevard** (B CC g M OS) 6.30-20h
Opernring 13-15 *in the Meridien Hotel* ☏ (01) 588 900
Gay friendly Cafe-Bar with french flair in the noble Le Meridien Hotel. Breakfast all day long

■ **Café Berg** (B BF GLM I M MA) 10-1h
Berggasse 8 *Near University, U-Schottentor* ☏ (01) 319 57 20
www.cafe-berg.at
Next to Löwenherz bookshop. Many students. Sexy staff.

■ **Gugg** (GLM m MA WI) Tue 18-22, Fri & Sat 16-1, Sun -22h
Heumühlgasse 14 *U4 Kettenbrückengasse* ☏ (01) 216 66 04
www.hosiwien.at
New Gay & Lesbian switchboard. Delicious cakes. Tourist information and free WLAN.

■ **Rifugio** (B G MA) 10-22h
Schönbrunner Straße 10 *Near U4-Kettenbrückengasse*
☏ (0699) 109 77 891 www.cafe-rifugio.at
Daily happy hour 15-20h.

■ **Café Savoy** (AC B GLM I M MA t) 12-2h
Linke Wienzeile 36 *U-Kettenbrückengasse* www.savoy.at
Traditional café with a beautiful interior.

■ **Testa Rossa** (B g m MA OS) Mon-Sat 7.30-23.30, Sun 10.30-20h
Ringstraßengalerie, Mahlerstraße 4 *Next to opera and famous shopping street „Kärtner Straße"* www.testarossawien.at

DANCECLUBS

■ **BallCanCan** (B D GLM MA S) 1st Sat/month 22h-?
Schwarzenbergplatz 10/1 *@ Ostklub* www.ballcancan.com
Queer Balkan-Clubbing with turkish and greek dance-music. .

■ **Drama!** (B D GLM MA S)
Ottakringerstraße 91 *Ottakringer Brewery, entrance Feßtgasse*
www.dramaclub.at
Irregular gay parties. Check www.dramaclub.at for details.

■ **FSK @ Pratersauna** (B D GLM MA)
Waldsteingartenstraße 135 www.pratersauna.tv
See website for details.

■ **Heaven Vienna** (! AC B CC D F GLM S ST T YC) 22-6h
www.heaven.at
„The" gay house club with national & international DJs, 2 dancefloors, shows, bars at various locations. For information check: www.heaven.at

■ **Homoriental** (B D GLM) 22-5h
Währingerstraße 59 *tram 37, 38, 40, 42, 42; metro U6, @ wuk-Foyer*
www.homoriental.wordpress.com
Gay-lesbian-trans-queer-party with oriental-Balkans-Turkish beats and tunes, friends welcome.

■ **MeatMarket** (B D GLM MA OS S) on irregular dates
www.myspace.com/clubmeatmarket
Special gay party on changing locations like „Badeschiff" or „Pratersauna". Watch out for flyers!

■ **Pitbull** (B D DR f G MA) 4th Fri/month 23-?h
Zieglergasse 26 *U3-Zieglergasse, @ Club Pi* www.pitbull-clubbing.at
Vienna's new fetish-event for bears and butch. See website for details.

■ **Queer:beat** (B D glm YC) 2nd and 4th Sat, 22-4h
Landstraßer Hauptstraße 38 *U3-Rochusgasse, @ Viperroom*
www.queerbeat.at
Very popular mixed party with alternative music, house and charts.

■ **UP!** (B D GLM MA S WE) 1st and 3rd Fri/month, 22-4h
Mariahilfer Straße 3 *U2-Museumsquartier, @ Lutz-Club*
www.upclub.at
Very popular events in the Lutz Club. See website for dates and details.

■ **Why Not** (! AC B D G S WE YC)
Fri, Sat & before public holidays 22-6h
Tiefer Graben 22 *U-Schwedenplatz* www.why-not.at
Vienna's longest running disco. Very popular! On 2 floors with 3 bars.

■ **Wiener Freiheit** (B D GLM m MA p s WE) Fri & Sat 21-4h
Schönbrunner Straße 25 *U-Kettenbrückengasse* ☏ (01) 913 91 11
www.wienerfreiheit.at
Popular amongst locals. Danceclub on WE and before public holidays only.

RESTAURANTS

■ **Aux Gazelles** (AC B BF CC DM glm M MC VEG WL)
Mon-Sat from 11h
Rahlgasse 5 *Near U- Museumsquartier/Mariahilferstraße*
☎ (01) 585 6645 🖳 www.auxgazelles.at

■ **Café Willendorf** (! B BF cc DM GLM I M MA OS PA RES t VEG WL)
18-2, meals -24h
Linke Wienzeile 102 *U-Pilgramgasse, near city centre* ☎ (01) 587 17 89
🖳 www.cafe-willendorf.at
Many vegetarian dishes, located in the „Rosa Lila Villa". Friendly staff, delicious food, good value for money and great atmosphere. Sunday-Brunch 10-15h

■ **Halle Cafe** (AC B CC DM glm LM M MA NR OS PA PK RES VEG) 10-2h
Museumsquartier 1 *U3-Volkstheater* ☎ (01) 523 70 01
🖳 www.diehalle.at

■ **Kunsthallencafe am Karlsplatz**
(B CC DM LM M MA NG NR OS PA RES VEG) 10-24h
Treitlstraße 2 *U1/U2/U4-Am Karlsplatz* ☎ (01) 587 00 73
🖳 www.kunsthallencafe.at

■ **Motto am Fluss** (AC B CC DM LM M MA NG NR OS PA RES VEG WL) 11.30-14, 18-2; bar: 18-4; cafe: 8-2h
Between Marien- und Schwedenbrücke *U1/U4-Schwedenplatz*
☎ (01) 252 55 10 🖳 www.mottoamfluss.at
The new hot-spot in Vienna, feel good and enjoy, recover and disengage. Conciously eat and drink healthy and celebrate parties. The incomparable design, the interior - in the style of Venice of the ,50's and the ambience in Motto on the river set new standards.

■ **Motto Bar-Restaurant** (AC B glm M MA OS PA RES S VEG WL)
18-2, Fri & Sat -4h
Schönbrunner Straße 30 *U-Pilgramgasse, entrance Rüdigergasse*
☎ (01) 587 06 72 🖳 www.motto.at
Chic and trendy restaurant & bar. Reservation recommended.

■ **Santo Spirito** (B glm M MA PA WL) daily 18-2, kitchen open -23h
Kumpfgasse 7 ☎ 512 99 98 🖳 www.santospirito.at
Café, Restaurant and Bar.

■ **schon schön** (AC B CC glm M MA)
Tue-Sat 11-23, kitchen open 12-14.30+19-22.30h
Lindengasse 53 *Cnr Andreasgasse* ☎ 06991 53 777 01
🖳 www.schon-schoen.at
Stylish restaurant, cocktailbar open Tue-Sat 19-2h.

■ **Sly & Arny** (B glm I M MA) Sun-Thu 18-1, Fri+Sat -2h
Lackierergasse 5 ☎ 405 0458 🖳 www.sly-arny.at
Stylish restaurant with bar, reasonable prices, many pizzas.

■ **Zum Stöger** (AC B CC G M MA OS WL)
Mon 17-24, Tue-Sat 11-24h, Sun closed
Ramperstorffergasse 63 *U4-Pilgramgasse, Bus 59a, 13a, 14a*
☎ (01) 544 75 96 🖳 www.zumstoeger.at
Excellent Viennese cuisine in a cosy atmosphere.

■ **Zum Roten Elefanten** (B glm M MA)
Mon-Fri 11.30-14, Tue-Sat 18-24h
Gumpendorferstraße 3 ☎ 966 80 08 🖳 www.zumrotenelefanten.at
Gayfriendly Café-Restaurant.

SEX SHOPS/BLUE MOVIES

■ **Kino Labyrinth** (B DR G MA t VS) Wed & Fri 13-1h
Favoritenstraße 164 *U-Reumannplatz* ☎ (01) 920 40 88
Far from the centre or the gay scene. Local crowd.

■ **Man for Man** (AC CC DR G GH MA VS) Mon-Sat 11-23, Sun & public holidays 14-23h
Hamburgerstraße 8 *U-Kettenbrückengasse* ☎ (01) 585 20 64
🖳 www.manforman.biz
Cabins, gay cinema, toys, books and DVDs.

■ **Sexworld** (! AC b CC DR F G MA VS)
Mon-Sat 10-20h, closed Sun & public holidays
Mariahilfer Straße 49 *U-Neubaugasse* ☎ (01) 587 66 56
🖳 www.sexworld.at
Gay section on 500 m², further 500 m² of cruising area. On 2 floors. Home of Spartacus XXL Store.

■ **Wiscot Center** (CC DR f G r VS)
Mon-Wed, Fri 10-24, Thu & Sat -3, Sun & public holidays 12-24h
Lerchenfelder Gürtel 45 *U-Thaliastrasse* ☎ (01) 0664 311 05 77
www.gayerotix.at
3 cinema rooms, cruisingarea on 500m², shop

SEX CINEMAS

■ **Sexworld Cinema** (AC b CC DR F G MA VS)
Mon-Sat 10-20h, closed Sun & public holidays
Mariahilfer Straße 49 *U-Neubaugasse* ☎ (01) 587 66 56
www.sexworld.at

ESCORTS & STUDIOS

■ **Boys & Men – First Class Escort Service**
(CC G MA MSG) 14-0.30h
Mariahilferstraße 123, ☎ (01) 99 88 99
www.gayescort.at
Well known gay escort service, established 1993. Nationwide home and hotel visits, strippers, international travel escorts.

SAUNAS/BATHS

■ **Apollo**
(B cc DR DU FC FH G m MC MSG OS p PI PK SA SB SOL VS) 14-2h
Wimbergergasse 34 *U-Burggasse* ☎ (699) 811 65 200 (mobile)
www.apollosauna.at
Sauna on 2 floors with terrace. Own parking. Partners' day on Mon, bears day on Tue.

■ **Frisco**
(B CC DR DU FC FH G I M MA MSG p RR S SA SB SOL VS WH)
15-24h, Tue closed
Schönbrunnerstraße 28 *Entrance Rüdigergasse* ☎ (01) 920 24 88
www.sauna-frisco.at
Fully renovated. Intimate sauna on 400 m² with whirlpool and bio-sauna.

■ **Kaiserbründl** (! AC B CC DR FC G GH LAB M MA MSG OS PI RR S SA SB SOL VS WO) Sun-Thu 14-24, Fri & Sat 14-2h
Weihburggasse 18 *U1/U3-Stephansplatz, 3 mins walk* ☏ (01) 513 32 93
🖳 www.kaiserbruendl.at
Beautiful and very exceptional interior: built in 1887 in Moorish style. 1200 m², 3 floors, 2 bars, darkroom-maze, video, cinema. New cruising steam bath. Mon & Wed: discount entrance fee for those under 25 years, Tue & Thu: „Partner Day", Fri & Sat various events. Wonderful new „chill-out" area.

■ **Sport Sauna** (AC B bf DR DU FC G m MA p RR SA SB SOL VS)
15-1, Fri 15- Sun 24h (non-stop)
Lange Gasse 10 *U-Volkstheater, Bus 13A-Piaristengasse* ☏ (01) 406 71 56
🖳 www.sportsauna.at
Intimate, very clean and modern sauna. Thu „Youngster day"

BOOK SHOPS

■ **Löwenherz** (! CC GLM MA W) Mon-Thu 10-19, Fri -20, Sat -18h
Berggasse 8 (Entrance: Wasagasse) *Near university, U-Schottentor, entrance Wasagasse, next to Café Berg* ☏ (01) 317 29 82
🖳 www.loewenherz.at
Vienna's gay and lesbian bookshop. www.loewenherz.at

LEATHER & FETISH SHOPS

■ **Spartacus XXL Store** (! AC b CC DR F g MA VS)
Mon-Sat 10-20h, closed Sun & public holidays
Mariahilfer Straße 49 *U3-Neubaugasse, at Sexworld* ☏ (01) 587 66 56
🖳 www.spartacus.at
Enormous sex warehouse on 2 floors. Own leather creations and every imaginable kind of toy.

■ **Tiberius** (CC F GLM MA S SH)
Mon-Fri 12-19, Sat 11-18h & by appointment
Lindengasse 2 *U-Neubaugasse* ☏ (01) 522 04 74 🖳 www.tiberius.at
Beautifuly designed shop, own leather & rubber collection, also lubes.

HOTELS

■ **Art Hotel Vienna. The** (B BF CC glm I MA PA) All year, 24hrs
Brandmayergasse 7-9 *Centrally located, near Naschmarkt, tram 14A/59A-Arbeitergasse* ☎ (01) 544 51 08 www.thearthotelvienna.at
W-LAN for free.

■ **Best Western Premier Kaiserhof Wien**
(AC B BF GLM H I PA PK RWS RWT SA SB VA WO) All year
Frankenberggasse 10 *U-Karlsplatz, Badener Bahn* ☎ (01) 505 17 01
www.hotel-kaiserhof.at
Traditional 4-star hotel in the historical heart of Vienna. Has been awarded as the best „Best Western Hotel in Central Europe" with the „Austrian Quality Award".

■ **Hotel Pension Wild**
(B BF cc DU G I MSG PA PK RR RWS RWT SA SB VA) All year
Lange Gasse 10 *U-Volkstheater* ☎ (01) 406 51 74 www.pension-wild.at
Vienna's traditional gay hotel. The Sport Sauna is on the premises, half price for hotelguests.

■ **Le Meridien** (AC B BF CC H M MA MSG PA PK RWB RWS RWT S SA SB VEG W WI WL WO) All year, 24hrs
Opernring 13-15 *U1+U2 Karlsplatz* ☎ (01) 588 90 0
www.lemeridienvienna.com
Gay-friendly luxury hotel in the very heart of Vienna. Minibar included. Sponsor of the famous Life-Ball.

■ **Roomz Vienna** (AC B BF H M PA PK RWS RWT VA VEG W WL WO) All year
Paragonstrasse 1 *U3 is next to the hotel, only 10 mins by underground to Stephansdome* ☎ (01) 7431 777 🖳 www.roomz-vienna.com
Experience the most exciting side of Vienna, surrounded by chic design and modern cosmopolites. A few minutes from downtown.

■ **Tyrol. Das** (AC B BF CC glm H I MA PK RWB RWS RWT SA SB SOL) All year
Mariahilfer Straße 15 *Museumsquartier, U-Neubaugasse*
☎ (01) 587 54 15 🖳 www.das-tyrol.at
All 30 rooms in this 4-star design hotel are decorated in the typical „Vienna Style" with original contemporary artwork. The hotel is situated in the art and cultural area of Vienna.

■ **Hotel Urania** (b BF CC glm M MA PA RWS RWT VA) All year
Obere Weißgerberstraße 7 *U-Schwedenplatz, U-Landstraße*
☎ (01) 713 17 11 🖳 www.hotel-urania.at/gay
36 rooms, each individually designed with historical decor, WC/shower, cable-TV & phone.

APARTMENTS

■ **Danobis Vienna Apartment** (GLM H I MA) All year
Rüdigergasse *M° Kettenbrückengasse* ☎ 660 52 44 596 💻 www.danobis.at
In the heart of gay Vienna near the underground and 10 mins walk to the historical centre. Affordable accommodation in perfectly central location, gay owned.

■ **Sling City Apartment** (b CC G H m MA NR PK RWS RWT WI) all year, check-in possible from 9-4h
Lambrechtgasse 16 *U4 Kettenbrückengasse, near Naschmarkt*
☎ (0664) 3358 8083 💻 www.sling.at/appartement
Check-In at Sling Club.

FETISH GROUPS

■ **LMC Vienna** (AC d DR F G MA VS)
Thu 17-open end (winter), Fri-Sat 22-open end
Hamburgerstraße 4 *Near U-Kettenbrückengasse*
☎ (0681) 108 55 105 (mobile) 💻 www.lmc-vienna.at
Leather & Motorbike Community of Vienna. At new location „HardOn".

HEALTH GROUPS

■ **AIDS Hilfe Wien** Mon-Fri 8.30-19h
Mariahilfer Gürtel 4 *U-Gumpendorfer Straße* ☎ (01) 599 37
💻 www.aids.at
Free HIV-tests: counselling Mon, Wed 16-20, Thu 9-13, Fri 14-18h.

SWIMMING

-Dechantlacke in the Lobau (NU) (take bus 91 A from Vienna International Center to restaurant Roter Hiasl, then 10mins walk)
-Donauinsel (NU) (take bus 33 B from Franz-Jonas-Platz to Überfuhrstraße, cross the »Jedleseer Bridge«, then 500m to the right)
-Wienerberg 1010 (Tram 65 → „Raxstraße", go to Sickingengasse via Raxstraße. There's a small lake, gay in the nudist area).

CRUISING

-Wertheimsteinpark (between Döblinger Hauptstraße & Heiligenstädter Straße, station S 45)
-Donauinsel »Toter Grund« (! NU) (take bus 91 A to Raffineriestraße/ Steinspornbrücke. After crossing the bridge 500m to the left. Very popular day&night in summer, beware of moskitos!)
-Florianigasse/Langegasse
-Beginning of Prater Hauptallee (ayor)
-Venediger Au (near big wheel in Prater)
-Türkenschanzpark (Hasenauerstraße / Litrowgasse & Hasenauerstraße / Gregor-Mendel-Straße, mainly at night)
-Rathauspark (!) (after sunset till dawn, very popular)
-Schweizer Garten (AYOR r) (next to Südbahnhof; Turks, Arabs)
-Nepomuk Berger Platz (cruising in the toilets).
-🅿Lobau, Finsterbuschstraße, very popular in summer and after sunset, cruising area between the small forest and the Neue Donau and at the toilet
-toilet U Keplerplatz, south exit, mainly afternoon and early evening, more older and hustlers, often police checks
-toilet U Neubaugasse, east exit Stiftgasse, very crowded from 10-20h, mixed age, often police checks
-toilet U Stephansplatz, exit Stephansdom, best time after 20h because there is no cleaner present
-toilet U Stubentor, exit Dr.-Karl-Lueger-Platz mainly older crowd, sometimes police checks
-toilet U Zieglergasse, west exit Schottenfeldgasse, very crowded from 10-22h, mixed age,often police checks

Bahrain

Name: Bahrain
Location: Middle East
Initials: BRN
Time: GMT +3
Language: Arabic, Persian, English
Area: 707 sq km
Population: 716,000
Capital: Al-Mahamah
Religions: Shi'a Muslim (70%), Sunni Muslim (15%), other

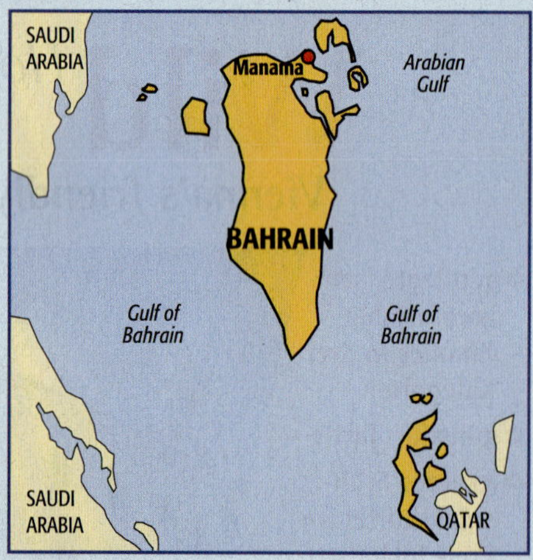

Bahrain's reputation as a relatively liberal and modern Persian Gulf state has made it a favourite with travellers in the region and an excellent introduction to the Gulf. It was once the seat of one of the great trading empires of the ancient world, and is redolent of the past. We have no information on the legal situation for homosexuals.

Bahrain genießt den Ruf eines relativ liberalen und modernen Golfstaats und konnte sich deshalb zu einem der beliebtesten Reiseziele am Persischen Golf entwickeln. Zudem bietet das Land einen idealen Einstieg in die Region. Früher war Bahrain Sitz einer der größten Handelsmächte der Antike und noch heute ist die Vergangenheit allgegenwärtig. Über die rechtliche Situation Homosexueller liegen uns keine Informationen vor.

Bahreïn a la réputation d'être un pays du Golfe relativement libéral et moderne et pourrait devenir pour cette raison une des destinations de voyage préférées dans le Golfe Persique. Le pays est en outre une porte d'entrée idéale pour la région. Bahreïn fut jadis le siège d'une des plus grandes puissances commerciales de l'Antiquité, et ce passé est encore omniprésent aujourd'hui. Nous ne disposons d'aucune information sur la situation légale des homosexuels.

Bahrain tiene una reputación de estado del Golfo relativamente liberal y moderno y por eso podría convertirse en el destino turístico preferido del Golfo Pérsico. Además, el país es una plataforma ideal para descubrir la región. En el pasado Bahrain fue la sede de una de las potencias comerciales más grandes de la Antigüedad y hoy en día todavía este pasado sigue estando presente. No disponemos de información sobre la situación jurídica de los homosexuales.

Bahrain gode della fama di una moderna e aperta città sul golfo. La sua modernità l'ha resa una meta turistica molto amata del Golfo Persico. Il Paese si presta ad ideale meta per iniziare a visitare quest'area geografica. Prima Bahrain era sede di una delle più grandi potenze commerciali dell'antichità e tutt'oggi il suo passato è ancora molto attuale. Non disponiamo di informazioni circa la situazione legale dell'omosessualità.

Al-Manamah

BARS

Sherlok Holmes (AC AYOR B G MC)
A meeting place for aircrews.

CAFES

Wendy's (AC AYOR B m MC NG)
Salah Al Deen Al Youbi Avenue *In Gulf Gate Hotel*
Cruising during weekend, mainly Thursday night.

DANCECLUBS

Barcode (AC AYOR D MC NG)
Gold City, level 2, Government Avenue *In the City Center Hotel*
Not a gay place but some gay guys can be found here.

CRUISING

(All are AYOR)
-Sheraton Hotel Health Club, 6 Palace Avenue
-Manama Park - Right by Gulafshan Restaurant, King Faisal Hwy street.
-Costa cafe at the City Center hotel

Belarus

Name: Weißrussland · Biélorussie · Bielorrussia · Russia Bianca
Location: Eastern Europe
Initials: BY
Time: GMT +2
International Country Code: ☎ 375
International Access Code: ☎ 8 (wait for tone) 10
Language: Belarusian, Russian
Area: 207,595 km² / 80,154 sq mi.
Currency: 1 Belarusian Ruble (BYR) = 100 Kopecks
Population: 9.776.000
Capital: Minsk
Religions: 60% Russian Orthodox, 8% Roman Catholic
Climate: Summer is warm but wet, while winter is grey and very cold.

Homophobic attitude, suspicions and prejudices are very strong in Belarus, although homosexuality was decriminalised in 1994. According to the study of the Belarusian Institute for Strategic Studies, conducted in the beginning of 2010, 62% of Belarusians believe that homosexuals should be criminally persecuted.
In general, few LGBT persons openly declare their sexual orientation. While it is easier to openly live in the capital and largest city, Minsk, LGBT people living in other places, especially in small towns and in rural areas, can face discrimination by the local population.
Negative statements about homosexuals by President Lukashenka in 2004, 2010 and 2011 also demonstrate that homophobic attitudes exist at the highest levels of government. In December 2010, addressing the All-Belarusian Peoples Assembly in Minsk, Lukashenka proclaimed that there are no sexual minorities in Belarus. On February 19, 2011, Lukashenka told the media that he "condemned 'faggotism'".
From 2004 through 2006 three foreign diplomats had been expelled from the country on the pretext of their sexual orientation.
The currently effective legislation provides no protection to victims in cases of discrimination on the basis of sexual orientation. Police refuse to register cases of brutality committed against representatives of sexual minorities and do not conduct investigations in cases of crimes motivated by homophobic prejudice. The police also conduct unprovoked actions in bars and cruising areas frequented by homosexuals.
Belarusian LGBT organizations have never been registered by the state and operate illegally. Their members have been targeted as hate crime victims many times. The vague wording of the recent amendments of the Criminal Code (December 2005) provides wide discretionary powers to the authorities allowing them to label activities of LGBT groups as illegal attempts to discredit or harm the Belarusian state.

Trotz Legalisierung der Homosexualität im Jahr 1994 grassieren in Weißrussland Schwulenfeindlichkeit, Verdächtigungen und Vorurteile.Eine vom Institut für strategischen Studien veröffentlichte Studie Anfang 2010 ergab, dass 62 % der Weißrussen glauben, dass Homosexuelle strafrechtlich verfolgt werden sollen.
Nur wenige haben den Mut zu ihrer sexuellen Orientierung öffentlich zu stehen. Während es in der Hauptstadt Minsk einfacher ist, sich zu outen, leiden Schwule und Lesben in kleinen Städten und ländlichen Gegenden besonders unter der Diskriminierung durch die Bevölkerung. Schwulenfeindliche Äußerungen von Präsident Lukaschenkos 2004, 2010 und 2011 zeigen deutlich, dass diese Einstellung bis in die höchsten Regierungskreise reicht. Im Dezember 2010 erklärt Lukaschenko bei einem öffentlichen Auftritt, dass es keine sexuellen Minderheiten in Weißrussland gebe. Am 19. Februar 2011 spricht gegenüber den Medien davon, dass er Homosexualität verachte. Zwischen Oktober 2004 und August 2006 sind drei ausländische Diplomaten unter dem Vorwand ihrer sexuellen Orientierung des Landes verwiesen worden.
Die aktuelle Gesetzeslage bietet Menschen, die wegen ihrer sexuellen Orientierung diskriminiert werden, keinen Schutz. Die Polizei weigert sich, gewalttätige Übergriffe auf Angehörige sexueller Minderheiten zu registrieren und nimmt bei von Schwulenfeindlichkeit motivierten Verbrechen keine Ermittlungen auf. Sie führt außerdem ohne jeden Anlass Einsätze in von Schwulen frequentierten Bars und Gegenden durch.
Da die weißrussischen LGBT-Organisationen nie staatlich anerkannt worden sind, ist ihre Arbeit ungesetzlich. Ihre Mitglieder werden häufig zur Zielscheibe von Hassverbrechen. Die schwammige Formulierung der jüngsten Änderungen des Strafgesetzbuches (Dezember 2005) gibt den Obrigkeiten weit reichende Ermessensbefugnisse, die Aktivitäten von Schwulenorganisationen als gesetzeswidrige Versuche der Schädigung oder Diskreditierung des weißrussischen Staates zu brandmarken.

Bien que l'homosexualité soit légale depuis 1994, l'homophobie, la suspicion et les préjugés courent les rues en Biélorussie. Une étude publiée par l'Institut pour des Etudes Stratégiques démontra début 2010 que 62% des Biélorusses pensent que les homosexuels devraient être poursuivis pénalement.
Peu d'entre eux ont le courage d'être ouvertement homosexuels. Alors que la «coming-out» est plus facile dans la capitale Minsk, les gays et lesbiennes souffrent particulièrement de la discrimination de la population dans les petites villes et dans les campagnes. Les diatribes du président Lukaschenko contre les gays en 2004, 2010 et 2011 montrent clairement que cette attitude touche aussi les plus hauts étages du pouvoir. En décembre 2010, Lukaschenko a déclaré dans une apparition publique qu'il n'y a pas de minorité homosexuelle en Biélorussie. Le 19 février 2011 il affirme dans les médias qu'il méprise l'homosexualité.
Entre octobre 2004 et août 2006, trois diplomates étrangers ont dû quitter le pays sous prétexte de leur orientation sexuelle.
Actuellement, la législation n'offre aucune protection aux victimes de discrimination motivée par l'orientation sexuelle. La police refuse de poursuivre les auteurs díagression envers les représentants de minorités sexuelles et nienquête même pas sur les crimes homophobes. En outre, elle improvise des razzias dans les bars gays et lieux de drague.
Les organisations LGBT biélorusses ne sont pas reconnues par l'Etat et sont ainsi illégales. Leurs membres sont la cible régulière de crimes haineux. La formulation floue des récentes modifications du code pénal (décembre 2005) donne aux autorités de larges marges de décision leur permettant de les considérer comme tentatives illégales de diffamation et de discrédit de l'Etat biélorusse.

Aunque la homosexualidad fue despenalizada en 1994, en Bielorrusia crecen la intolerancia, las sospechas y prejuicios hacia los homosexuales. Un estudio publicado por el Instituto para Estudios Estratégicos de principios de 2010, señaló que el 62% de los bielorrusos cree que la homosexualidad debería ser penalizada. Pocos son los que tienen la Valentía de demostrar en público su orientación sexual. Mientras que en la capital, Minsk, resulta fácil salir del armario, los gays y lesbianas de las pequeñas ciudades y zonas rurales sufren a causa de la discriminación ejercida por la población. Las declaraciones homófobas hechas públicas por el presidente Lukaschenko en 2004, 2010 y 2011, muestran con claridad que este tipo de mentalidad impregna hasta las altas esferas gubernamentales. En diciembre de 2010, Lukaschenko declaró durante un evento público que no existe una minoría homosexual en Bielorrusia. El 19 de febrero de 2011 afirmó frente a los medios de comunicación que él no menosprecia la homosexualidad. Entre octubre de 2004 y agosto de 2006 fueron expulsados del país tres diplomáticos extranjeros por acusaciones respecto a su orientación sexual. La situación jurídica actualmente no ofrece ninguna protección a las víctimas de discriminación por razón de su orientación sexual. La policía se niega a perseguir cualquier ataque violento contra los representantes de las minorías sexuales y no investiga ninguno de los delitos causados por la intolerancia hacia los homosexuales. Además, la policía realiza registros sin motivo aparente en bares y zonas de encuentro frecuentadas por los homosexuales.
Las organizaciones bielorrusas de gays, lesbianas y transexuales no están reconocidas por el Estado y operan en la clandestinidad. Sus representantes a menudo son el blanco de los delitos provocados por el odio. Las vagas formulaciones de la reciente reforma del código penal (diciembre de 2005) conceden a las autoridades potestades más amplias para calificar las actividades de las organizaciones homosexuales de intentos ilegales de dañar o desacreditar el estado bielorruso.

Anche se l'omosessualità non costituisce più reato dal 1994, l'omofobia e i pregiudizi regnano sovrani. Uno studio pubblicato all'inizio del 2010 da un istituto di studi strategici rileva che il 62% dei bielorussi pensa che l'omosessualità debba essere perseguitata penalmente. In Bielorussia sono in pochi ad avere il coraggio di dichiarare pubblicamente il proprio orientamento sessuale. Mentre nella capitale, Minsk, è più facile dichiararsi omosessuale, nella piccole città e nelle zone rurali gli omosessuali sono ancora vittime di forti discriminazioni. Le esternazioni omofobe del Presidente Lukaschenko nel 2004, nel 2010 e nel 2011 dimostrano chiaramente che l'omofobia è diffusa anche tra le sfere più alte del potere. Nel dicembre del 2010 Lukaschenko ha dichiarato che in Bielorussia non esistono minoranze sessuali. Il 19 febbraio 2011 ammette pubblicamente di disprezzare l'omosessualità.
Tra ottobre del 2004 ed agosto del 2006 tre diplomati stranieri sono stati espulsi dal paese con il pretesto del loro dubbio orientamento sessuale.
L'attuale situazione legislativa non offre alcuna tutela nei confronti delle discriminazioni che hanno origine nell'orientamento sessuale degli individui. La polizia si rifiuta di perseguire le aggressioni a rappresentanti di minoranze sessuali e inoltre non indaga sui crimini motivati da omofobia. Come se non bastasse non sono rari raid da parte della polizia in bar e cruising areas frequentati da gay.
Le organizzazioni LGBT bielorusse non sono riconosciute statalmente e operano nell'illegalità. I suoi membri sono spesso oggetto di crimini che hanno rigine nell'odio. La vaga formulazione nella recente modifica del codice penale (dicembre 2005) consente ampio potere discrezionale nel definire l'attività di un'organizzazione omosessuale come illegale infamia e discredito dello Stato bielorusso.

NATIONAL GAY INFO

Gaybelarus.by (GLM)
www.gaybelarus.by
News about gay life in Belarus.

GAYBY.NET
www.gayby.net
The best resource of gay news in Belarus (Russian, partly English). Daily updated.

NATIONAL GROUPS

Amnesty International Lesbian, Gay, Bisexual and Transgender Network – Belarus (AILGBT-Belarus)
PO Box 18 ✉ 246050 Gomel ☏ (029) 7380993
Founded in 1999. Activities: LGBT rights research and advocacy, consulting, human rights education, social activities. Received in 2004 the „Grizzly Bear Award" from ILGCN.

GayBelarus LGBT Human Rights Project
✉ Minsk ☏ (029) 8630000 gaybelarus.by
A civic association for LGBT people from all over the country. Local chapters in all regions. Minsk Pride organizer.

Gomel ☏ 232

DANCECLUBS

NEMO Club (D g MA r S SNU ST) 22-4, cafe: 12-4h
2 Naberezhnaya *Trolleybus stop „Z.I.P"* ☏ 70 17 00
Gay management and many gay visitors.

RESTAURANTS

Il Patio (B glm M MA) 12-3h
6 Kommunarov *Trolleybus stop „Lenin Square"*
Gay administration, partly gay waiters, many gay visitors. Italian restaurant.

HEALTH GROUPS

Vstrecha-Gomel Mon, Wed & Fri
ul. 2 Revolyutsionnaya, 8-5 ☏ (232) 57-83-97 mamba.ru/goomel
HIV/AIDS prevention group for gay and bi men.

CRUISING

- Railway station (MA) (area near the WC)
- „Gromiko" (YC) (park on Sovetskaya str., benches to the left of the monument to A. A. Gromiko)
- Cyber Café (YC) (Main Post Office on the Lenin Square)

- Gay beach (MA) (left bank of river Sozh, near Yakubobka village).
- WCs on the left bank of river Sozh.

Grodno ☎ 152

BARS

■ **Flint** (B D GLM M MA S) 23-6h
Ulitsa Gornovykh, 17 *Near fire station* ☎ (152) 54 19 26
🖳 www.clubflint.com
Gay-friendly management and many gay visitors.

HEALTH GROUPS

■ **Vstrecha-Grodno** Mon, Wed & Fri
ul. Ozheshko, 25-3-216 ☎ (029) 781-28-44
🖳 mamba.ru/VSTRECHA-GRODNO
HIV/AIDS prevention group for gay and bi men.

Minsk ☎ 17

CAFES

■ **Cafe Latte** (b g MC) 10-22h
Ulitsa Platonova, 10 *Bus 37, tram 3/6/7/8*

DANCECLUBS

■ **Casta Diva** (B DR G MA PK S ST WE) Daily 20-6h
Kropotkina st. 91a *Same building as Polish Embassy* ☎ 29 3775693
🖳 vk.com/castadivaclub
A great danceclub.

■ **6 A** (B D glm MC) Fri-Sun 23-5.30h
Ave Guerrilla, 6 „A" , Partizanskij District *M° Proletarian. Near railway station* ☎ (29) 860-24-89 🖳 www.cr6a.com
Former Lutik.Nice interior. Two dance floors and a bar. Friendly atmosphere.

SAUNAS/BATHS

■ **Banya #1** (NG SA SB YC)
Ulitsa Khmel'nitskogo, 24 ☎ (17) 232 40 04
Many students from nearby dormitories.

■ **Banya #6** (NG SA)
5 Marjevskaja Ulitsa ☎ (17) 236 01 73

■ **Banya #7** (NG OC SA SB)
Ulitsa Moskovskaya, 7a ☎ (17) 220 67 11
Attracts a more mature crowd. Discretion recommended.

GENERAL GROUPS

■ **Labrys**
🖳 labrys.by
Capital area lesbian group.

HEALTH GROUPS

■ **Vstrecha („Meeting")**
ul. Trostenetskaya, 3-13 ☎ (029) 405 04 11 🖳 www.vstrecha.by
The oldest gay group in Belarus, founded in early 90s. Prevention of HIV/AIDS; HIV+ support group and ILGA member

SWIMMING

-Nude beach on the banks of Minskoye Morye (Minsk lake)

CRUISING

-"Panikovka" (MA) or Central Square (on the benches around the fountain representing a boy and a swan and farther in the park, near the President's residence)
-Gorky Park (AYOR) (pathways near the central WC)
-Park Tchelyuskintsev: WC (AYOR, OC)
-Pobedy Park (Prospekt Pobeditelei, near the Komsomolskoye lake; mostly in the summer)
-"Soyuz On-Line" Cyber Café (YG) (Metro Oktyabryaskaya).

Vitebsk ☎ 21

CRUISING

- Victory Square (near the monument „3 Shtika")

Belgium

Name: Belgique/België · Belgien · Bélgica · Belgio
Location: Western Europe
Initials: BE
Time: GMT +1
International Country Code: ☎ 32
International Access Code: ☎ 00
Language: French, Dutch, also German in one province
Area: 32 545 km² / 11,780 sq mi.
Currency: 1 Euro (€) = 100 Cents
Population: 10,479,000
Capital: Bruxelles/Brussel
Religions: 80% Roman Catholic
Climate: Moderate climate with mild winters and cool summers.
Important gay cities: Bruxelles/Brussel, Antwerpen, Gent

Belgium is a very open-minded and liberal country. The general attitude towards homosexuality is very open-minded in Belgium. Actually the perception of homosexuality has dramatically changed in Belgium in the last decade or so. It does not mean that one does not encounter occasional negative reactions anymore. The Bill enabling the marriage among persons of the same sex was passed in 2003. Gay adoption came into force at the end of 2006. The age of consent for sexual intercourse is 16.

Belgium is actually divided in 3 language based communities: the Flemish-speaking community in the North and in Brussels with roughly 6 millions people, the French-speaking community in the South, the East and in Brussels with about 4,4 million people and the tiny German-speaking community along Germany's border with more or less 70,000 people. Each community has indeed its own Parliament and Executive body. They are responsible for matters such as language, culture, education, medical care. In addition to the communities are the regions: these are territory-based and include Flanders in the north, Wallonia in the southern and the eastern parts of the country and the region of Brussels-Capital right in the middle of Belgium. Each Region also has a parliament and executive body, responsible for economic development and several other related topics. The Federal Government in Brussels is responsible for public finances, budget, foreign affairs, defence, home affairs, police, justice, social affairs and pensions.

Ever since the early new elections in June 2010, Belgium has been trying to form a new government, which is turning out to be very difficult because of the great regional differences. A six-party coalition led by Elio di Rupo appeared to take shape in October 2011. But recurrent disputes within this coalition about budget plans prevented his election in parliament. Di Rupio then offered his resignation to King Albert II, but the king refused and called upon the parties to resume their talks - successfully. After 589 days of Belgium being governed by a provisional administration, di Rupoo has finally been elected prime minister on December 6 and is hence the world's first openly gay head of government.

Belgien ist ein ausgesprochen aufgeschlossenes und liberales Land. Auch die Einstellung zur Homosexualität ist in Belgien generell sehr tolerant. Tatsächlich hat sich die Einstellung zur Homosexualität hier besonders im letzten Jahrzehnt drastisch verändert. Was jedoch nicht heißt, dass man überhaupt nicht mehr auf gelegentlich negative Reaktionen stößt. Das Gesetz zur Anerkennung gleichgeschlechtlicher Ehen wurde schon im Jahr 2003 verabschiedet. Ende 2006 trat dann das Adoptionsrecht für homosexuelle Paare in Kraft. Das Schutzalter für Geschlechtsverkehr liegt bei 16 Jahren.

Belgien ist in drei sprachbasierte Gemeinschaften unterteilt: eine flämischsprachige Bevölkerungsgruppe von ungefähr 6 Millionen Menschen im Norden und in Brüssel, eine französischsprachige Gemeinschaft im Süden, Osten und in Brüssel mit rund 4,4 Millionen Einwohnern sowie die winzige deutschsprachige Gruppe entlang der deutschen Grenze mit etwa 70.000 Staatsbürgern. Dabei verfügt jede dieser Sprachgemeinschaften über ihr eigenes Parlament und ihre eigene Regierung, die unter anderem für die Pflege der Sprache, die Kulturpolitik, das Bildungswesen und die Gesundheitsversorgung zuständig ist. Neben diesen Gemeinschaften gibt es dann noch die Regionen: diese sind territorial definiert und umfassen Flandern im Norden, Wallonien im Südosten des Landes und die Region Brüssel-Hauptstadt genau in der Mitte von Belgien. Diese Regionen haben ebenfalls ihre eigenen Parlamente und Regierungen, die unter anderem für die Wirtschaftspolitik verantwortlich sind. Die Bundesregierung in Brüssel kümmert sich dabei um die öffentlichen Finanzen, den Staatshaushalt, Auslandsbeziehungen, die Verteidigung, innenpolitische Fragen, die Polizei, Justiz und sozialen Sicherungssysteme.

Seit den vorgezogenen Neuwahlen im Juni 2010 versucht Belgien eine neue Regierung zu bilden, das auf Grund der großen regionalen Differenzen große Schwierigkeiten bereitet. Im Oktober 2011 zeichnete sich zunächst eine Koalition von sechs Parteien ab, die von Elio di Rupo angeführt werden sollte. Doch zu seiner Wahl im Parlament kam es zunächst nicht, nachdem es wiederholt zu Auseinandersetzungen über den geplanten Haushalt innerhalb der gewünschten Koalition kam. Daraufhin reichte er bei König Albert II. sein Entlassungsgesuch ein, der die Zustimmung aber verweigerte und die Parteien aufrief, sich noch einmal zusammen zu setzen – mit Erfolg. Nachdem Belgien 589 Tage nur von einer kommissarischen Regierung geführt wurde, ist di Rupo am 06.12. zum Premierminister gewählt worden und ist damit der erste offen schwule Regierungschef weltweit.

La Belgique est un pays véritablement ouvert et libéral. De même l'attitude envers l'homosexualité est en général très tolérante. Dans les faits, l'attitude envers l'homosexualité a profondément changé en particulier ces dix dernières années. Ce qui ne veut pas dire que l'on ne soit pas confronté de temps à autres à des réactions négatives. La loi de reconnaissance du mariage de même sexe a déjà été adoptée en 2003. Fin 2006 le droit à l'adoption pour les couples homosexuels est ensuite entré en vigueur. L'âge légal pour les relations sexuelles est de 16 ans.

La Belgique est composée de trois communautés linguistiques: une communauté flamande de 6 millions de personnes dans le Nord et à Bruxelles, une communauté francophone de 4,4 millions d'habitants dans le Sud, dans l'Est et à Bruxelles ainsi qu'une très petite communauté germanophone de 70.000 personnes le long de la frontière avec l'Allemagne. Chacune de ces communautés dispose de son propre

Tels Quels
association des gays
et des lesbiennes

parlement et de son propre gouvernement compétent en matière de politique linguistique et culturelle, enseignement et services de santé. Outre ces communautés, il existe aussi les régions: celles-ci sont définies géographiquement et regroupent la Flandre dans le Nord, la Wallonie dans le Sud et la région Bruxelles-Capitale exactement dans le centre de la Belgique. Ces régions ont elles-même leurs propres parlements et gouvernements qui sont entre autres responsables de la politique économique. Le gouvernement fédéral à Bruxelles est en charge des finances publiques, du budget de l'Etat, des relations internationales, de la défense, des questions de politique intérieure, de la police, justice et systémes de sécurité sociale.
Depuis les élections avancées de juin 2010, la Belgique essaie avec de grosses difficultés de former un nouveau gouvernement en raison de forts différents régionaux. En octobre 2011, une coalition s'annonçait avec 6 partis sous la direction d'Elio di Rupo. Cependant il ne fut pas tout de suite élu au Parlement en raison de divergences sur le budget au sein de la coalition souhaitée. Suite à cela, il donna sa démission auprès du Roi Albert II qui la refusa et qui enjoignit les partis à trouver un terrain d'accord – avec succès. Après les 589 jours du gouvernement d'intérim belge, di Rupo a été élu premier ministre le 6 décembre et est devenu ainsi le premier chef de gouvernement ouvertement gay au monde.

Bélgica es un país esencialmente abierto y liberal. También la posición ante la homosexualidad en Bélgica es por lo general muy tolerante. En efecto, la postura ante la homosexualidad ha cambiado especialmente en la última década. Esto no quiere decir que uno ya no se pueda encontrar con reacciones negativas. La ley para el reconocimiento de las parejas del mismo sexo fue aprobada ya en el año 2003. A finales de 2006 entró en vigor el derecho de adopción para las parejas homosexuales. La edad de consentimiento para las relaciones sexuales queda fijada en los 16 años.
Bélgica está dividida en tres comunidades lingüísticas: un grupo de población de habla flamenca, con unos 6 millones de habitantes en el norte y en Bruselas, un grupo de habla francesa en el sur, el este y en Bruselas, con unos 4,4 millones de habitantes, así como un pequeño grupo de habla alemana a lo largo de la frontera alemana, con unos 70.000 habitantes. Cada una de estas comunidades lingüísticas dispone de un Parlamento propio y de su propio gobierno, que es competente para el mantenimiento de la lengua, la política cultural, la formación y la sanidad, entre otras materias. Junto a esas comunidades, están todavía las regiones: éstas están definidas territorialmente y comprenden Flandes, en el norte, Valonia, en el sureste del país, y la región de Bruselas-Capital, justo en el centro de Bélgica. Estas regiones disponen a su vez de sus propios Parlamentos y gobiernos, que son responsables de la política económica, entre otras. El gobierno federal en Bruselas se ocupa por tanto de las finanzas públicas, del presupuesto estatal, las relaciones exteriores, la defensa, cuestiones internas, policía, justícia y del sistema de seguridad social.
Desde las elecciones anticipadas en junio de 2010, Bélgica ha estado tratando de formar un nuevo gobierno, lo que debido a las grandes diferencias regionales resultaba un gran problema. En octubre de 2011 se firmaría una coalición de seis partidos liderada por Elio Rupo. Sin embargo, su elección en el Parlamento no tuvo lugar, después de repetidos altercados en relación a su forma de gobierno dentro de dicha coalición. A raíz de ello, presentó su solicitud de dimisión al Rey Alberto II, el cual denegó su autorización y convocó a los partidos para reunirse una vez más, esta vez con éxito. Tras 589 días de gobierno provisional en Bélgica, di Rupo, elegido Primer Ministro el 06/12/2011, se convierte en el primer Jefe de Gobierno abiertamente gay del mundo.

Il Belgio è un Paese particolarmente aperto e liberale. Anche l'atteggiamento nei confronti dell'omosessualità è generalmente molto tollerante. Il modo di vedere l'omosessualità in Belgio si è evoluto particolarmente nell'ultimo decennio. Tuttavia ciò non significa che non si possa incorrere ad occasionali reazioni negative. La legge per il riconoscimento delle coppie omosessuali è stata approvata già nel 2003. Alla fine del 2006 è entrata in vigore la legge sul diritto di adozione da parte di coppie omosessuali. L'età del consenso per i rapporti sessuali è di 16 anni.
Il Belgio è suddiviso in tre comunità linguistiche: al nord e a Bruxelles la comunità linguistica fiamminga di circa 6 milioni di persone, al sud, all'est e a Bruxelles la comunità linguistica francese che conta circa 4,4 milioni di persone e all'est, lungo il confine tedesco, il minuscolo gruppo linguistico tedesco di circa 70.000 persone. Ognuna di queste comunità linguistiche ha il suo proprio parlamento e il suo proprio governo, che tra gli altri compiti, ha anche la tutela della lingua, la politica culturale, l'istruzione e la sanità. Oltre a queste comunità ci sono anche le regioni che sono definite territorialmente: le Fiandre al nord, la Vallonia al sud-est del Paese e la regione di Bruxelles-Capitale esattamente al centro del Belgio. Anche queste regioni hanno il loro parlamento e il loro governo, che tra le tante responsabiltà hanno anche quella della politica economica. Il governo federale con sede a Bruxelles si occupa di finanza, di bilancio pubblico, di rapporti esteri, di difesa, di questioni interne, di polizia, di giustizia e di stato sociale. È già dalle elezioni anticipate del 2010 che il Belgio cerca di formare un nuovo governo; tuttavia a causa delle forti differenze regionali ciò continua a essere molto difficile, tanto che il Belgio si ritrovi ancora. Ad ottobre del 2011 si è profilata, in un primo momento, una coalizione di sei partiti che sarebbe dovuta essere guidata da Elio di Rupo. Tuttavia, dopo tutta una serie di scontri sulla legge finanziaria tutti interni alla coalizione, Elio di Rupo non è stato più eletto. In seguito a ciò, di Rupo ha presentato le dimissioni a Re Alberto II, che però non le ha accettate invitando, invece, i partiti a risedersi insieme ad un tavolo. Dopo che per 589 giorni il Belgio è stato guidato da un governo in carica per le procedure correnti, il 6 dicembre di Rupo è diventato primo ministro del paese e primo capo del governo al mondo dichiaratamente gay.

NATIONAL PUBLICATIONS

Tels Quels Magazine
81, rue Marché au Charbon ✉ 1000 Bruxelles ☎ 02 512 45 87
www.telsquels.be
Monthly magazine for the gay & lesbian French speaking community.

ZIZO-magazine (GLM)
Kammerstraat 22 ✉ 9000 Gent ☎ 09 223 69 29
www.zizo-magazine.be
Gay and lesbian bi-monthly magazine.

NATIONAL COMPANIES

Holidaypride
53, Rue du Midi ✉ 1000 Bruxelles ☎ 2 502 73 77
www.holidaypride.be
Holidaypride is a Belgian travel agency that offers a high quality travel advice, both online and in their travel agency in the heart of Brussels, two steps away from the Grand Place.

Visit Brussels (G)
www.visitbrussels.be/gay

NATIONAL GROUPS

Belgian Lesbian & Gay Pride (BLGP) (GLM)
42, Rue Marché au Charbon ✉ 1000 Brussel/Bruxelles ☎ 02 502 75 00
www.blgp.be
Organizers of the Belgian Lesbian & Gay Pride in Brussels which takes place each year in May.

COUNTRY CRUISING

-A3 (E40) Bruxelles → Liège P past Exit »Sterrebeek« (both sides)
-A7 (E19) Bruxelles → Paris P km 22.5
-A7 (E19) Bruxelles → Paris P km 39
-A7 (E19) Bruxelles → Paris P Hall (both sides)
-A8 (E19) Tournai → Lille P Froynnes (both sides)
-A13 (E313) Liège → Antwerpen P km 42.8/ Exit 24 (Wooded picnic

area at the right. Day and night)
-A13 (E313) Liège → Antwerpen P km 62.6 (Parking area and wooded area on both sides)
-A14 (E17) Antwerpen ⇆ Gent Exit km 79.0 (Leave motorway. P beside the forest. Cruising in forest and parked cars. Day and night)
Exit Linkeroever, cruising in P and in wooded area
-A15 (E42) Charleroi ⇆ Namur P between Fleurus and Gosselies
-A16 (E42) Mons ⇆ Tournai P Antoing (afternoon and evening)
-E40 Brussels - Liège Exit „Crisnée" (both sides).

Antwerpen

Antwerp is the most important harbour city in Belgium and is recognized as the world's most important trading centre for diamonds. Many famous artists came from this city, including Rubens, van Dyck and Bruegel. Antwerp is famous for its distinctive lifestyle. The unique ambience of Antwerp has attracted many talented artists and fashion designers to the city in the last few years. Famous sights include the market place (Grote Markt), the boulevard (Cogels-Osylei), the central station (Centraal Station), a ship museum (Stehen) and the Jewish quarter. Gay life is situated in the old city centre, between Stadspark, the main train station and Plantin- and Van Dijckkaai. Worth a mention are the numerous bars and leather clubs around the Van Aerdtstraat with their impressionable darkrooms. Leather scene tourist flood the city at the weekends.

Antwerpen ist die wichtigste Hafenstadt in Belgien und gilt als wichtigster Diamantenhandelsplatz der Welt. Daneben hat die Stadt viele bekannte Künstler hervorgebracht, darunter Rubens, van Dyck und Bruegel. Antwerpen ist für seine Lebenskunst bekannt. Das einzigartige Ambiente von Antwerpen hat dafür gesorgt, dass sich hier in den letzten Jahren viele talentierte Künstler und Modedesigner niedergelassen haben. Sehenswürdigkeiten sind der Marktplatz (Grote Markt), Prachtstraße (Cogels-Osylei), Bahnhof (Centraal Station), Schifffartsmuseum (Stehen) und das Judenviertel. Das schwule Leben spielt in der gesamten Altstadt zwischen Stadspark, Hauptbahnhof und Plantin- und Van Dijckkaai ab. Nicht zu vergessen die unzähligen Bars und Lederclubs rund um die Van Aerdtstraat mit ihren weitläufigen Darkrooms. An den Wochenenden ist ein regelrechter „Ledertourismus" aus dem benachbarten Ausland zu beobachten.

Anvers est le port le plus important de Belgique et est la plus grande place marchande de diamants du monde. En outre, la ville a développé une vie artistique riche dont Rubens, van Dyck et Bruegel ne sont que les personnalités les plus connues et qui continue d'exercer sa fascination auprès de jeunes artistes talentueux et autres stylistes de mode. Les curiosités sont la „Grote Markt" (place du marché), la rue „Cogels-Osylei" à l'architecture spectaculaire, la gare centrale, le „Schiffartsmuseum" et le quartier juif. Le milieu gay se situe dans la vieille ville entre le parc, la gare centrale et les quais „Plantinkaai" et „Van Dijckkaai", sans oublier les nombreux bars et clubs cuir autour de la rue „Van Aerdtstraat" avec leurs backrooms impressionnantes. Les week-ends, on assiste à un véritable „tourisme cuir" en provenance des pays avoisinants.

Amberes es la ciudad portuaria más importante de Bélgica y está considerada la sede más importante del mundo en comercio de diamantes. Además, la ciudad ha visto nacer a muchos artistas conocidos, entre ellos Rubens, Van Dyck y Bruegel. Amberes es conocida también por su estilo de vida. El ambiente genuino de Amberes ha contribuido a que muchos artistas y diseñadores de moda con talento se hayan instalado en los últimos años en la ciudad. Los atractivos principales son la plaza del mercado (Grote Markt), la calle Cogels-Osylei, la estación (Centraal Station), el museo de navegación (Stehen) y el barrio judío. La vida gay se concentra en toda la parte antigua, entre el parque, la estación central y los muelles Plantin y Van Dijck. No deben olvidarse tampoco los incontables bares y clubs de cuero alrededor de la Van Aerdtstraat con sus impresionantes cuartos oscuros. Los fines de semana se observa un cierto „turismo del cuero" de los países colindantes.

Anversa è la città anseatica più importante del Belgio ed è considerata uno dei più rilevanti centri del commercio di diamanti. Inoltre la città ha dato i natali a molti famosi artisti come per esempio Rubens, Van Dyck e Bruegel. Anversa è famosa per la sua vena artistica: la sua particolarissima atmosfera ha fatto sì che negli ultimi anni si trasferissero molti artisti e stilisti. Le attrazioni turistiche sono la Grote Markt, l'elegante viale Cogels-Osylei, la stazione centrale (Centraal Station), il Museo Nazionale della Navigazione (Stehen) e il quartiere ebraico. La scena gay si concentra un po ,in tutto il centro storico tra lo Stadspark, la stazione centrale e il Dijckaai. Nei pressi di Van Aerdtstraat si concentrano numerosi bar e club leather con notevoli darkroom. Al finesettimana la città si riempe di „turisti leather" provenienti dai Paesi confinanti.

GAY INFO

Roze Huis. Het – Antwerpse Regenboogkoepel
(B GLM MA OS) Tue-Wed 15-24, Thu 15-1, Fri 15-2, Sat 12-2, Sun 12-24, closed Mon, summer: from 12h, closed Mon
Draakplaats 1 *Zurenborg, tram 11* ☎ 03 288 00 84 (11-17h)
www.hetrozehuis.be
Antwerp's splendid gay and lesbian community house and information centre. On the ground floor café, called ,Den Draak' (The Dragon). The infrastructure on the 1st & 2nd floor is used by various gay and lesbian initiatives. Also GLBT library (Tue 18-20, Sat 15-17h). Free magazine ,De Magneet'.

PUBLICATIONS

Magneet. De
Draakplaats 1 www.hetrozehuis.be
Free brochure of GLBT organizations in Antwerp.

TOURIST INFO

Tourism Antwerp Mon-Sat 9-17.45, Sun 9-16.45h
Grote Markt 13 *City centre* ☎ 03 232 01 03 www.visitantwerpen.be

BARS

Body Boys (B G MA) 16-2, Fri & Sat -5, Sun -3h, closed Mon & Tue
Van Schoonhovenstraat 42 *Near Central station*
☎ 04 85 97 92 21 (mobile) www.body-boys.be
Happy hour Fri-Sun 23-24h.

Bonaparte (B glm MA s) 20-?h, closed Mon
Grote Markt 21 ☎ 03 231 96 26 www.bonaparte.be

Café Strange (B G MA OS VS) 21-?, Sun 17-?h
Dambruggestraat 161 ☎ 03 226 00 72
Antwerp's oldest gay bar.

Hessenhuis (B D GLM M MA OS) Sat & Sun:15-?h
Falconrui 59 *Near the trendy new harbour area „eilandje" and MAS Antwerp City museum* ☎ 03 231 13 56 www.hessenhuis.com
Brasserie, DJ evenings en Show evenings: bar/dance café.

Oink Oink (B F GLM M MA OS) 11-?, Sat 14-?h
Van Schoonbekeplein 3 www.oinkoinkbar.be
Sundays and public holidays only open with specail events.

Rox (AC B DR f G MA VS)
22-4, Fri -6, Sat -8, Sun -6h, closed Mon & Tue
Geulincxstraat 28 ☎ 04 95 75 50 11

MEN'S CLUBS

Boots. The (! AC B CC DR F G MA P VS WE) Fri & Sun 22.30-5h
Van Aerdtstraat 22 *Near Sint Jansplein* ☎ 04 76 49 79 31
www.the-boots.com
Lots of play areas. Strict door policy: you have to take a weekend membership and registration. If you come back you won't then need to fill any more forms.

Kinky's. The (AC CC DR G MA P VS)
Mon & Wed 19-?Tue & Thu 14-? Fri 20-?h
Lange Beeldekensstraat 10 *Near central station* ☎ 03 295 06 40
www.kinkys.be
Obligatory dress code: Mon, Tue,Wed Thu, Fri naked, slip or jockstrap. Included in the entrance fee are a locker, showers and towels.

Oink Club (B d DR F G MA p) 21-3, Fri & Sat -?h
Van Schoonbekeplein 3 www.oinkclub.be
3 floors.

Antwerpen

EAT & DRINK

Café DeLux – Café 16
Café Strange – Bar 18
Café-Restaurant Bourla – Restaurant 2
Garde Ville – Café 21
Hessenhuis – Bar 14
In de Schaduw van de Kathedraal – Restaurant 8
Monkey King – Restaurant 29
Oink Oink – Bar 13
Padi Asianfood Gallery – Restaurant 30
Popi Café – Café 4
Que Pasa – Café 28

NIGHTLIFE

Boots. The – Men's Club 15
Kinky's. The – Men's Club 23
Oink Club – Men's Club 13
Red & Blue – Danceclub 12

SEX

Badhuis. t' – Sauna 27
Erotheek Gay-Ron – Sex Shop/Blue Movies 22
Libidos-erotheek – Sex Shop/Blue Movies 31

ACCOMMODATION

Colombus – Hotel 20
Emperors 48 – Guest House 19
Guesthouse 26 – Guest House 6
Katshuis Bed & Coffee. 't – Guest House 7
Villa T. B&B – Guest House 17

OTHERS

Gay Planet Holidays – Travel & Transport 1
Tourism Antwerp – Tourist Info 9
Toys 4 Boys – Leather & Fetish Shop 11
Verschil. 't – Book Shop 10

CAFES

Cafe DeLux (b GLM m MA) 11-?h
Melkmarkt 18 ☎ 03 232 17 66 🖳 www.cafedelux.be

Draak. Den (B GLM m MA OS)
15-?, during summer 12-?h, closed on Mon
Draakplaats 1 *Zurenborg, tram 11* ☎ 03 290 53 04 🖳 www.dendraak.be
Place where you can find a lot of information about the gay life in Antwerp. Large terrace in summer (open from 12h).

Garde Ville (B GLM m MA) 12-22h
Nationalestraat 41 *Near Groenplaats* ☎ 04 77 88 17 45 (mobile)
🖳 www.gardeville.be

Nieuwe Kastaar. De (B GLM M MA)
10.30-?, Sat 17-?, Sun 11.30-?h, closed Mon
Londenstraat 26 ☎ 03 226 20 13 🖳 www.denieuwekastaar.be

Popi Café (! B GLM M MA OS S) Daily 14-1h
Plantinkaai 12 ☎ 03 231 61 31 🖳 www.popi.be

Que Pasa (B d GLM MA ST t)
Tue-Fri 20-2, Sat & Sun 18-?h, closed on Mon
Lange Koepoortstraat 1 *Cnr. Minderbroedersrui*
🖳 www.cafe-que-pasa.be

DANCECLUBS

D-Club (AC B cc D GLM MA S WE) Fri & Sat 22-?h
Damplein 27 ☎ 03 233 71 60 🖳 www.d-club.be
Club for openminded party people.

Red & Blue (AC B CC D DR G MA P SNU) Sat 23-7h
Lange Schipperskapelstraat 11-13 *Near the red-light-district*
☎ 03 213 05 55 🖳 www.redandblue.be

Dance floor and three bars. Entry fee applies. Also organizes large gay events. Sat night = men only! On first Sun/month „Studio 54" disco evenings.

RESTAURANTS

■ **Café-Restaurant Bourla** (B CC GLM M MA NR OS WI)
Mon-Fri 11-1, Sat 10-2h, closed Sun
Graanmarkt 7 *Near the Bourla* ☎ 03 232 16 32 🖳 www.bourla.be
Traditional cuisine at reasonable prices. Loyal local crowd

■ **In de Schaduw van de Kathedraal** (B DM glm M OS PA WL)
11-23h
Handschoenmarkt 17-19-21 *Near cathedral* ☎ 03 232 40 14
🖳 www.IndeSchaduwvandeKathedraal.be
As the name implies: in the shadow of the Cathedral.

■ **Mask'ara** (AC B CC D glm LM MA RES S SNU ST WE)
Please call and reserve in advance
Josef Reusenslei 17 *Borsbeek, near Antwerpen airport* ☎ 03 297 07 47
🖳 www.maskara.be
Voted the best spectacle-restaurant in Belgium 2008!

■ **Monkey King** (AC CC glm M MA NR OS VEG WE)
11.30-14 & 17-23, Tue-Sat 17-23h
Lange Dijkstraat 12 ☎ 03 226 38 11 🖳 www.monkeyking.be
Chinese restaurant.

■ **Padi Asianfood Gallery** (B cc glm M MA NR OS VEG WL)
Daily 18-23h
Koolkaai 9A *Opposite of Noorderterras, close to Red & Blue Disco*
☎ 03 225 14 46 🖳 www.padi-asianfood.be
Indonesian fusion restaurant.

SEX SHOPS/BLUE MOVIES

■ **Erotheek Gay-Ron** (CC DR G I MA VS) Mon-Fri 12-23, Sat 14-22h
Van Wesenbekestraat 54 *Near central station* ☎ 03 234 04 43
🖳 www.gayron.be
Films to watch, buy or hire. Cinema and private viewing booths. Toys, lubes, condoms.

■ **Erotische verbeelding** (gLm MA) 11-18h, closed on Sun
Kloosterstraat 165 ☎ 03 226 89 50 🖳 www.erotischeverbeelding.com
Erotic clothing for women.

■ **Libidos-erotheek** (g MA) 12-22h, Sun closed
Gemeentestraat 11 ☎ 03 233 10 01 🖳 www.libidos.be
Films to buy or hire and private viewing booths.

SAUNAS/BATHS

■ **Badhuis. 't** (AC B DR DU G M MA MSG p PI RR SA SB VS WH)
12-24, Fri & Sat -3h
Florisstraat 10 *Next to city park* ☎ 03 288 53 71
🖳 www.badhuisantwerpen.be
Cosy and hygienic gay sauna. Friendly staff.

■ **Gay sauna 't Herenhuis** (! B CC D DR DU f FH G M MA NU p PI RR SA SB SOL VS WH) 12-1, Fri & Sat -2h
De Lescluzestraat 63, Berchem *15 mins walk from Berchem station*
☎ 03 239 51 95 🖳 www.gaysaunaherenhuis.be
Large modern sauna. Meet hot men in a relaxed ambiance and enjoy the interesting atmosphere.

■ **Kouros** (! AC B CC DR DU FC G GH I LAB M MA MSG NR OS P PI PK PP RR SA SB SH SL SOL VEG VR VS WH WI) 12-24h
Botermelkbaan 50, Schoten *In Schoten, 15 km from Antwerp, Bus 610*
☎ 03 658 09 37 🖳 www.kouros.be
Sauna and garden on 3000 m². In- and outdoor swimming pool. Friendly atmosphere. Frequented mainly by Dutch, Belgian and German men.

BOOK SHOPS

■ **Verschil, 't** (AC B CC GLM MA OS) 11-18, Sun 13-18h
Minderbroedersrui 33 *Tram 4/7/11* ☎ 03 226 08 04 🖳 www.verschil.be
Gay and lesbian DVD, book and coffee shop. Also offers underwear and swimwear for men and toys for boys and girls.

LEATHER & FETISH SHOPS

■ **Philippe Moda Pelle** (CC F GLM) Mon-Fri 8-16.30, Sat 11.30-17h
Bovenrij 32 *15 mins from Antwerp by car* ☎ 014 21 91 03
🖳 www.pmp-leathershop.be
Specialist for leather clothing made by measure. Also repairs and changes.

■ **Toys 4 Boys** (CC F G MA)
Thu-Sat 11-20, Sun 14-17h and by appointment
Nosestraat 6 *Between Veemarkt & Sint Paulus Plaats* ☎ 03 232 08 27
🖳 www.toys4boysleather.com
Erotic Leather Clothes and Toys, Rubber, SM equipment, body piercing by appointment.

TRAVEL AND TRANSPORT

■ **Gay Planet Holidays** (CC GLM MA)
Mon-Fri 9.30-13 & 14-18h, Sat by appointment
Arme Duivelstraat 11 *Theatre district* ☎ 03 231 15 55
🖳 www.gayplanetholidays.com
Tour operator / travel agency with one of the largest choices on worldwide destinations in gay and gay-friendly hotels and B&Bs.

HOTELS

■ **Colombus** (B BF CC GLM I M MA PI PK RWS RWT WO) All year
Frankrijklei 4 *City centre* ☎ 03 233 03 90 🖳 colombushotel.com
3-star hotel, 28 rooms.

■ **Hotel Industrie** (BF CC glm H I MA PK RWS RWT) 24hrs
Emiel Banningstraat 52 ☎ 03 232 38 66 00 🖳 www.hotelindustrie.be

GUEST HOUSES

■ **Emperors 48** (cc glm I MA WO) All year
Keizerstraat 48 ☎ 04 86 03 33 97 (mobile) 🖳 www.emperors48.com
Hetero-friendly accommodation. 2 rooms or one apartment.

■ **Guesthouse 26** (B BF cc g MA)
Pelgrimsstraat 26 ☎ 03 289 39 95 🖳 www.guesthouse26.com

■ **Guesthouse G8** (BF F G I) Check-in from 17h
Trapstraat 20 *In the city centre of Antwerpen* ☎ 04 77 62 62 81 (mobile)
🖳 www.G8.be
For gay men only. The Belgium way of gay, fetish life. Exclusively gay B&B for those with a budget. Common room for up to 4 men and a double room.

■ **Guesthouse Leman** (BF g I OS RWS RWT) All year
Generaal Lemanstraat 16 *10 minutes from city centre* ☎ 03 294 04 41
🖳 www.leman16.be

■ **Katshuis Bed & Coffee. 't** (CC glm MA OS RWS RWT)
16-?, Mon & Thu 20-?h
Grote Pieter Potstraat 18-19 *In the historic centre near town hall & cathedral* ☎ 04 76 20 69 47 (mobile) 🖳 www.katshuis.be

■ **Villa T B&B** (b bf G MA) All year
Verversrui 17/19 ☎ 03 231 23 00 🖳 www.villat.be
3 rooms, all with own bathroom.

PRIVATE ACCOMMODATION

■ **Antwerp Mabuhay Lodgings** (BF glm I MA RWT VA) All year
Draakstraat 32 *Near Berchem train station, Zurenborg area*
☎ 0495 842 953 🖳 www.mabuhay.be
This property is very near the rainbow house of Antwerp and is owned by a gay couple.

HEALTH GROUPS

■ **Sensoa** Mon-Fri 9-17h
Kipdorpvest 48a *City centre, near Meir* ☎ 03 238 68 68
🖳 www.sensoa.be
Centre for sexual health and HIV.

HELP WITH PROBLEMS

■ **Veilig Vrijen lijn** Mon-Fri 14-22, Sat -17h
☎ 078 15 15 15 🖳 www.sensoa.be
Flemish helpline for HIV and STD.

CRUISING

-Stadspark (AYOR)
-Wolvenberg (wooded area between Berchem station and Grote Steenweg)
-Het Rot (left bank, drive through Waaslandtunnel, ca 1 km wooded area on left-hand side; M° 2/3/15 direction Zwijndrecht stop ‚Afrit 17').

Arlon

CRUISING

-Le Belvédère (Opp. St. Donant church, in summer, evenings).

Assenede

GUEST HOUSES

■ **Staaksken. ,t** (! BF DU FH GLM H I MA NR p PK RES RWB RWS RWT VA WE WI) All year
Staakstraat 138A *Between Antwerp, Gent, Bruges and North Sea coast*
☎ 09 344 09 54 🖳 www.staaksken.be
*A non-smoking 4**** romantic cottage which accommodates five guests in one single and two double rooms. The friendly B&B is surrounded by a large garden with a pond.*

Blankenberge

CRUISING

-Dunes direction Zeebrugge.

Bouillon

HOTELS

■ **Cosy** (B BF cc glm H I M MA OS PA PK RWS RWT) All year
23, rue Au-dessus de la Ville *500 m from town centre* ☎ 061 46 04 62
🖳 www.hotelcosy.be
Hotel with restaurant offering a daily changing menu, an extensive wine list and eleven cosy guestrooms.

Brugge

BARS

■ **B-In** (B glm M MC) Restaurant: 12-14.30 & 18.30-22h, closed Sun & Mon
Zonnekemeers *Oud-St Jan complex* ☎ 050 31 13 00 🖳 www.b-in.be

RESTAURANTS

■ **De Spieghel** (CC g M MA OS) 11-23h
Jacob van Maerlantstraat 1 *Historical village 5 km from Brugge*
☎ 050 37 11 30 🖳 www.despieghel.be

■ **Medici. De** (AC CC glm MA NR OS PA VEG) Daily 9-18h
Geldmuntstraat 9 ☎ 050 33 93 41
Located in a classified Art Deco house, the De Medici serves wonderful breakfast with a variety of coffees and teas from around the world, snacks and lunch with pasta and salads. All the dishes are freshly prepaired and have an exotic touch. Personal and friendly service in a cosy and relaxed atmosphere.

■ **Vlaamsche Pot. De** (B CC glm H M MA NR OS PA RES WL) 12-22h, closed Thu
Helmstraat 3 *Centre* ☎ 050 34 00 86 🖳 www.devlaamschepot.be
De Vlaamsche Pot can seat up to 200 people. The menu consists of various local dishes. Enjoy the waffles and pancakes in the afternoon or a variety of famous Belgian beers. All this in a super cosy and typical Bruggian atmosphere. When making a reservation, quote „Rainbow" and receive a glass of champagne per person for free.

HOTELS

■ **Hotel Fevery** (b BF cc glm H I MA PK RWS RWT)
Check-in 13-18, reception 7.30-22h
Collaert Mansionstraat 3 *10 mins walk to Grand Place, bus 4/14 from rail station to Gouden Handstraat* ☎ 050 331 269 🖳 www.hotelfevery.be

■ **Prinsenhof** (AC B BF GLM H I MC PA PK RWS RWT) All year
Ontvangersstraat 9 ☎ 050 34 26 90 🖳 www.prinsenhof.com
A superb small, family run hotel, with a warm ambience. All rooms have their own bathroom, AC, TV, CD & DVD-player, clock-radio, telephone with data port, mini-bar, trouser press,

GUEST HOUSES

■ **B.I.G. Guesthouse** (BF G I M MA NU OS PK RWT VA) All year, 24hrs
Kanunnik Duclosstraat 33 *7 mins from the centre, 20 mins from the nude beach* ☎ 0477 42 42 85 (mobile) 🖳 www.big-guesthouse.be
Moderate rates, 5 rooms with TV, internet and mini-bar. For gay men only.

Guesthouse The Eden Rose (BF GLM I OS PK RWS RWT VA)
All year
Prins Karellaan 25 *5 mins by car from city centre* ☎ 050 67 54 85
www.edenrose.be

SPECIAL INTEREST GROUPS

Jong & HiB (B D GLM S YC)
Koningin Elisabethlaan 92 *Bus stop Biekorf parking* ☎ 050 33 69 70
www.j-h.be
Group of young (-30 years) gays, lesbians, bisexuals, transgender and straights.

CRUISING

-Minnewaterpark - bridge at Bargeweg. After 22h
-Brugse Roeiclub / Waggelwaterbos (near to St John Hospital)
-Achterkant Station.

Brussel/Bruxelles

It becomes quickly obvious that Brussels has more to offer than justz the „Maneken Pis", the famous fountain figures of pissing young men or the „Atomium" when one takes a wonder around this city. Also it's reputation of being a grey and drab EC civil servant city rapidly loses its substance as soon as one enters one of the many bars, cafés or discos in the city. In Brussels over 30% of the population are foreigners, making it very multicultural and cosmopolitan. Even during the week many celebrations carry on to the early hours of the morning, when the buses and trams start running at 5am.
The gay scene is in the centre of the city at the „Grand Place". Here are also a multitude of gourmet locations near the Rue de Bouchers. For gay men and their friends many so-called „Soirrées" are organized. There is an annual gay film festival in Febuary and May and Gay Pride is in May.

Dass Brüssel mehr zu bieten hat als das „Maneken Pis", der bekannten Brunnenfigur eines pinkelnden Jünglings, und dem „Atomium", merkt man schnell. Auch das Trugbild als graue Beamtenstadt wegen des Sitzes der EU-Organisationen löst sich schnell auf, sobald man in eine der zahlreichen Bars, Cafés und Discotheken geht. Brüssel hat einen Ausländeranteil von fast 30%. Dementsprechend multikulturell und kosmopolitisch zeigt sich auch das Nachtleben. Es wird auch unter der Woche gerne bis in die Morgenstunden gefeiert, da Busse und Trams erst wieder ab 5 Uhr ihren Betrieb aufnehmen. Die schwule Szene befindet sich im Zentrum der Altstadt rund um den „Grand-Place". Hier liegen auch die zahlreichen Feinschmeckerlokale unweit der Rue de Bouchers. Alljährliches schwules Filmfestival ist im Febuar und Mai und der „Gay Pride" ist im Mai.

Bruxelles a bien plus à offrir que son „Manneken Pis", „l'Atomium" ou encore le quotidien gris des fonctionnaires européens. Il suffit d'entrer dans un des nombreux bars, cafés ou boîtes de nuit de la ville pour s'en persuader. Les étrangers représentent 30% de la population bruxelloise et la vie nocturne en est d'autant plus cosmopolite et multiculturelle. Même en semaine, on peut faire la fête jusqu'au matin et personne ne semble pressé puisque les transports en commun ne reprennent leur service qu'à 5 heures du matin. Le milieu gay se situe dans le centre de la vieille ville autour de la Grand-Place où se trouvent également nombre de restaurants fins. Le festival du cinéma et en février et en mai et la Gay Pride en mai.

Bruselas ofrece mucho más que el „Maneken Pis", la conocida figura de un niño haciendo pis, y el Atomium. También la típica imagen de una ciudad gris de funcionarios debido a ser la sede de las instituciones de la Unión Europea desaparece cuando uno va a sus muchos bares, cafés o discotecas. Bruselas tiene casi un 30% de extranjeros. En consecuencia, su vida nocturna es multicultural y cosmopolita. Entre semana se puede ir de fiesta hasta altas horas de la madrugada pues los buses y tranvías empiezan a funcionar de nuevo a partir de las 5. El ambiente gay se concentra en el centro de la parte antigua, alrededor de la „Grand Place". Aquí también están situados los mejores locales, cerca de la Rue de Bouchers. Para los gays y sus amigos se organizan diversas fiestas. El festival anual de cine gay está en febrero y en mayo y el día del Orgullo Gay en mayo.

Bruxelles ha molto più da offrire oltre alla famosa scultura del giovane che fa la pipì in una fontana „ il cosiddetto Maneken Pis" e l'Atomium. Vi ricrederete anche sulla brutta fama di Bruxelles come città grigia piena di impiegati che lavorano per le varie istituzioni europee: al più tardi vi ricrederete quando andrete in uno degli innumerevoli bar, cafè, e discoteche. Bruxelles ha una percentuale di stranieri di quasi 30%. Questo si riflette anche sulla multiculturalità della vita notturna. Anche durante la settimana si sta in giro fino al mattino, poiché i mezzi di trasporto pubblici riprendono il loro servizio alle 5 del mattino. La scena gay si concentra nella città vecchia, nei pressi della Grand Place. Nella zona di Rue de Bouchers ci sono anche molti negozi di specialità gastronomiche. Da ricordare sono anche l'annuale festival del cinema a febbraio e a maggio e il Gay Pride a maggio.

INTERNATIONAL ORGANISATIONS

ILGA – International Lesbian, Gay, Bisexual, Trans and Intersex Association
17 rue de la Charité ☎ 02 502 24 71 www.ilga.org
ILGA's aim is to work for the equality of lesbian, gay, bisexual, trans and intersex people and their liberation from all forms of discrimination.

GAY INFO

Rainbow House (b GLM MA) Wed-Sat 18.30-22.30h
42, rue Marché au Charbon *Near Grand Place, Ancienne Belgique & Bourse* ☎ 02 503 59 90 www.rainbowhouse.be
French & Dutch speaking gay & lesbian meeting and information point. Publishes the magazine „Rainbow Times".

Tels Quels Mon-Fri 9-17h (office) Bar -2h (Fri & Sat -4h)
81, Rue du Marché au Charbon ☎ 02 512 45 87 www.telsquels.be
Social service, bar, library, magazine, choir, young group, lesbian group, Brussels gay & lesbian film festival. Monthly magazine for the French speaking gay community. Also groups : Arlon, ☎ 063 41 34 10; Dinant ☎ 02 502 79 38; Mons ☎ 065 36 35 40; Namur ☎ 02 514 49 74; Tournai ☎ 02 502 79 38 and Verviers ☎ 087 30 13 58.

CULTURE

Pink Art Gallery @ Haute Antiques (CC) Daily 10-18h
207 Rue Haute *Next to the flea market, bus 48/27* ☎ 02 548 94 80
www.pinkart.be
Art gallery male homo-oriented in the centre of Bussels. The purpose is to offer a panorama of the art of the 19th and 20th century but also to exhibit contemporary artists. A book corner also presents the most importants books on the topic.

BARS

Baroque. Le (AC B F G MA S WE) Wed-Sun 17-5h
44, Rue Marché au Charbon www.barlebaroque.be
Bear and leather bar.

Belgica. Le (B GLM MA) Thu-Sat 22-3, Sun 20-3h
32, Rue Marché au Charbon *Near Grand Place* www.lebelgica.be
International DJs. Check www.lebelgica.be for parties.

Boys Boudoir (B CC GLM M YC) 18-5h
25, Rue Marché au Charbon *Center gay village* ☎ 02 614 58 38
www.leboysboudoir.be
The most elegant disco club in Brussels. DJs every WE.

Cancan, Le (B G S WE) Tue-Sun 4-4h
Rue des Pierres 55
Shows on Thursday at 10pm, Karaoke on Friday.

Chez Maman (AC B glm m MA ST T) Thu-Sat 24-?h
7, Rue des Grands Carmes www.chezmaman.be
Drag shows.

Christobar (B d GLM MA p) 17-?h
12, rue de la Fourche *Near Grand-Place* ☎ 04 841 411 65
www.christobar.be

Club (B GLM MA) Tue & Wed 20-?, Fri-Sun 16-?h, closed Mon
45 Rue des Pierres *M° Bourse* www.barclub.eu
Cosmopolitan gay-friendly bar in the center of Brussels.

Dolores (B GLM M MA) 15-?h
40, Rue Marché au Charbon *Close to Grand-Place* ☎ 04 77 66 12 15 (mobile)

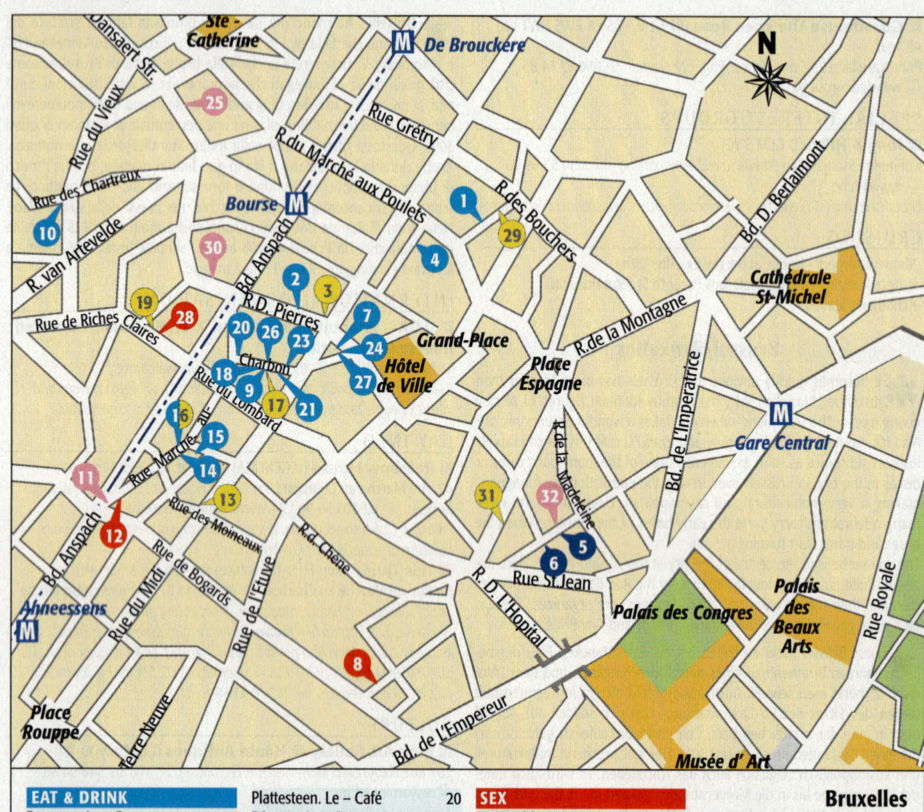

Bruxelles

EAT & DRINK

Baroque. Le – Bar	18
Belgica. Le – Bar	21
Boys Boudoir – Bar	23
Chez Maman – Bar	15
Christobar – Bar	1
Club – Bar	22
Dolores – Bar	9
Fontainas. Le – Café	14
H^2O – Restaurant	26
Homo Erectus Classicus. L' – Bar	24
Pintxo – Bar	7
Plattesteen. Le – Café	20
Réserve. La – Bar	4
Tels Quels – Café	16
Thai Talks – Restaurant	27
U 96 – Bar	2

NIGHTLIFE

Duquesnoy – Men's Club	5
Gay Tea Dance @ You – Danceclub	6
One X. The @ Steel Gate – Danceclub	10

SEX

Argos Video – Sex Shop/Blue Movies	28
Griffe. La – Sauna	8
Macho – Sauna	12

ACCOMMODATION

Downtown BXL – Private Accommodation	11
Hotel Café Pacific – Hotel	25
Hotel François – Hotel	30
Royal Windsor – Hotel	32

OTHERS

Boris Boy – Fashion Shop	13
Boutique Minuit – Leather & Fetish Shop	29
Darakan – Book Shop	3
Leatherneck – Leather & Fashion Shop	31
Rainbow House – Gay Info	17
RoB – Man to Man – Leather & Fetish Shop	19
Tels Quels – Gay Info	16

■ **Homo Erectus Classicus. L'** (AC B G MC) 15-3h
5, rue du Marché au Charbon *M° Bourse* ☎ 0475 83 11 07
💻 www.lhomoerectus.be
Lounge, bar, exposition. Cozy atmosphere.

■ **Homo Erectus. L'** (B G MA S SNU ST T) 12-3h
57, rue des Pierres *M° Bourse* ☎ 04 75 83 11 07
💻 www.lhomoerectus.be
Bar in a 17th century house with a lively atmosphere.

■ **Pintxo** (AC B d G m MA S ST) 16-?h, closed Mon
53, rue des Pierres *Near Grand-Place* ☎ 02 512 84 80

■ **Réserve. La** (AC B D G MC)
Mon, Thu & Fri 11-24; Wed 16-22; Sat & Sun 15-24h
2a, Petite rue au Beurre *M° Bourse* ☎ 02 511 66 06
The oldest established bar.

■ **U-96** (AC B F G MA p WE) Wed-Sun 17-2h
28, rue des Pierres *Near Grand-Place*

■ **Windsurf, Le** (B G)
14, rue Des Pierres ☎ 02 414 24 00

MEN'S CLUBS

■ **Duquesnoy** (AC B DR f G MA NU P VS)
Mon-Thu 21-3, Fri & Sat -5, Sun 15-19 & 21-3h
12, rue Duquesnoy *M° Gare Centrale* ☎ 02 502 38 83
💻 www.duquesnoy.com
Theme parties: 3rd Sun/month Spanking Club (from 15h), 1st Fri/month Suit & Tie (17h). Friendly staff.

CAFES

■ **Fontainas. Le** (B glm m OS) 11-24, Fri & Sat -2h
91, rue Marché au Charbon ☎ 02 503 31 12

■ **Plattesteen. Le** (B glm m OS) 11-24h
41, Rue Marché au Charbon ☎ 02 512 82 03
Cruisy terrace.

VISITBRUSSELS
SIZED FOR YOU
2012
brusselicious
brusselicious.be
PRIDE4EVERY 1
Visible Citizens
I want to be! Do you?
thepride.be
10th PINK SCREENS
filmfestival
www.pinkscreens.org
pinkscreens.org
LA DEMENCE
lademence.com

■ **Tels Quels** (B GLM m MA) 14-2, Fri & Sat -4h
81, rue Marché au Charbon ☎ 02 512 45 87 🖳 www.telsquels.be

DANCECLUBS

■ **Box, Le** (B D G)
7, rue des Riches Claires ☎ (0475) 70 79 00 (mobile) 🖳 www.boxclub.be
Three dancefloors.

■ **Gay Tea Dance @ You** (AC B CC D GLM MA) Sun 21-3h
18 rue Duquesnoy *Central city two steps away from Grand Place*
☎ 04 76 43 41 80 (mobile) 🖳 www.leyou.be

■ **La Demence** (! B CC D DR G MA S) 22-12h, irregular parties
208, Rue Blaes *Near Gare du Midi-Zuidstation; métro Porte de Hal*
☎ 02 511 97 89 🖳 www.lademence.com
Big parties 12 times/year. 5 floors, 4 bars, 3 dancefloors.

■ **The One X @ Steel Gate** (B D DR F G MC p S SNU VS)
Eight times per year, 23-10h
52, rue des Chartreux ☎ 0497 40 70 52 (mobile) 🖳 www.steelgate.be
Parties are held 8 times a year (about once every 6 weeks). Check the website www.theonex.net for details and www.steelgate.be for location details. Porn Superstar Jean Franko pres

RESTAURANTS

■ **Bla Bla and Gallery** (AC B CC g M MA OS S)
55, Rue des Capucins *Near antique market and flea market, bus stop Jeu d'balle* ☎ 02 503 59 18 🖳 www2.resto.be/blablaandgallery
Live music on Fri & Sat; Sun brunch.

■ **Fils de Jules. Le** (CC glm M MC)
Tue-Fri 12-14.30 & 19-23, Sat & Sun 19-24h
35, Rue du Page *Cnr. rue Américaine* ☎ 02 534 00 57
🖳 www.filsdejules.be

■ **H²O** (AC B CC glm M MA NR OS VEG WL) Daily 18-23h
27, Rue Marché au Charbon ☎ 02 512 38 43 🖳 www.restoh2o.be
Pasta, salads, menus and cocktails.

■ **Thai Talks** (b GLM M MA) 11-23h
51, rue des Pierres *Near Grand-Place* ☎ 04 862 492 60
🖳 www.thaitalks.be
Thai cuisine.

SEX SHOPS/BLUE MOVIES

■ **Argos Video** (CC F G) 12-22, Sun 15-20h
13, rue des Riches Claires ☎ 02 502 92 49 🖳 www.argosvideo.be

■ **Erot' X Stars** (G VS)
Mon-Sat 11-14 & 15-20, Sun & public holidays 12-18h
36, rue de Malines *Near Place Rogier* ☎ 02 217 77 37
Big choice of gay DVDs.

SAUNAS/BATHS

■ **Club 3000** (! B CC DR FC FH G GH I LAB M MA MSG OS RR SB SH SOL VS WH WO) 9-2, Fri -6, Sat 10-6, Sun 10-2h
9, boulevard Jamar *Near Gare du Midi* ☎ 02 522 10 50
🖳 www.club3000.net
Large sauna on 600 m² with 3 cinemas. Brunch on Sat & Sun.

■ **Griffe. La** (B CC DR FH G M MA RR SA SB VS WH)
Mon-Fri 11.30-23, Sat & Sun 13-23h
41-43, rue de Dinant *Close to Grand Place & Central Station*
☎ 02 512 62 51 🖳 www.saunalagriffe.eu
Sauna on 3 floors. Part of the scene since 1972.

■ **Macho** (! AC AK B DR DU F FC FH G GH LAB M MA MSG NU OS P PI RR SA SB SH SL SOL VS WH WO) 12-24h
106, rue Marché au Charbon *M° Fontainas / Annessens, near Grand-Place*
☎ 02 513 56 67 🖳 www.saunamacho.com
One of the largest and most popular sauna in Belgium. Frequented by a young and trendy crowd.

■ **Oasis. L'** (B DR FC FH G M MA MSG PI PP RR SA SB SOL VS WH WO) 11.30-24h
10, rue van Orley *M° Botanic/Madou* ☎ 02 218 08 00
🖳 www.oasis-sauna.be
Very big and luxurious bath house. Popular with bears.

■ **Spades 4** (! AC B CC D DR FC FH G M MA MSG NU OS p PI PP RR SA SB SH SOL VS WH WO) 12-24h
23-25, rue Bodeghem *M° Anneessens, 5 mins from Gare Midi*
☎ 02 502 07 72 🖳 www.saunaspades4.be
Under new management. One of the biggest saunas in Belgium on 1400 m². Nude sunbathing on the terrace in summer. Also Spades 4 in Ghent.

BOOK SHOPS

■ **Darakan** (GLM) Mon-Sat 11-18.30h
9, Rue du Midi ☎ 02 512 20 76 🖳 www.darakan.net

CONDOM SHOPS

■ **Ex Aequo** (g) Mon-Fri 9.30-17h
41, Rue Locquenghien ☎ 02 736 28 61 🖳 www.exaequo.be
Gay association for the prevention of AIDS and other sexually transmitted diseases. Also shop selling condoms & lubricants.

LEATHER & FETISH SHOPS

■ **Boris Boy** (CC F G MA) Mon-Sat 12-19, Sun 14-18h
95, rue du Midi *100 m from famous „Manneken Pis"* ☎ 02 502 66 26
🖳 www.borisboy.com
Clothes, leather, latex, toys & fun, DVD and mail order.

■ **Boutique Minuit** (CC glm T) 10.30-18.30h
60 Galerie du Centre ☎ 02 223 09 14 🖳 www.boutiqueminuit.com
Sexy underwear, rubber, latex, shoes and accessories for transvestites.

■ **Leatherneck** (CC glm MC) Daily 10-19h
48 rue des Epeuronniers *Near Grande Place* ☎ 02 511 54 34
🖳 www.leatherneck.be
Military, police and more.

■ **RoB - Man to Man** (F G MA) 10-18.30h, closed Sun & Mon
11, rue des Riches Claires ☎ 02 514 02 96 🖳 www.rob-brussel.be
Leather, rubber, twisted gear. Also hairdresser.

TRAVEL AND TRANSPORT

■ **Holidaypride** (GLM) Mon-Fri 10-19, Sat 12-18h
53, Rue du Midi ☎ 02 502 73 77 🖳 www.holidaypride.be
Agency specialised in travel services for gays, lesbians and their friends.

HOTELS

■ **Ecrins. Les** (AC B BF CC GLM MA NR RWS RWT) All year
15, rue du Rouleau *Centre, 12 km to Zaventem Airport, M° Sainte Catherine*
☎ 02 219 36 57 🖳 www.lesecrins.com
16 rooms. Some rooms with shower/WC on the corridor.

■ **Hotel Cafe Pacific** (AC B bf CC glm I m MA RWS RWT VA) All year
57, rue Antoine Dansaert *M° Saint Catherine* ☎ 02 213 00 80
🖳 www.hotelcafepacific.com
A wonderful boutique hotel. Small but ´very tastefully decorated. Close to the gay scene. Free WiFi throughout the hotel.

■ **Hotel François** (bf g) All year, 24hrs
Rue Borgval 15 *M° Bourse* ☎ 02 511 15 16 🖳 www.hotel-francois.be
Located at Place St. Gery and near Grand Place, in the heart of the gay area. Fully equipped rooms at reasonable prices.

■ **Royal Windsor Hotel Grand Place**
(AC B BF CC D glm H MA MSG SA WO) All year
5 rue Duquesnoy *Central station only 50m away* ☎ 02 505 5555
🖳 www.royalwindsorbrussels.com
Elegant and sophisticated, the 5 star Royal Windsor Hotel Grand Place Brussels boasts the best location in Brussels. Just off the world-famous Grand Place, the hotel is also in the heart of the Brussels' gay area and within walking distance from Brussels' Central Station, the Antique Market on the Sablon, the Royal Covered Galleries and Brussels' Royal Palace Gardens.

GUEST HOUSES

■ **B&B Welcome to my place** (bf glm H I MSG) All year
Place Quetelet 1 *M° Botanique* ☎ 0477 697842
🖳 www.welcometomyplace.be

■ **bed & breakfast 76** (BF G I MC NR RWT) All year
Avenue Seghers 76 ☎ (04) 75 63 62 35 🖳 www.76.be
The romantic, spacious and luxurious suite (65 m²/700 square feet) is on

the top floor of our Maison de Maître and has a king-size double bed. The appartment is decorated with original art deco antiques, other antiques furniture, design, paintings and prints.

■ **Bruxellesmabelle** (AC BF GLM MA p PK RWS RWT VS) All year
Address upon request *Quartier Louise* ☎ 04 96 93 92 52 (mobile)
🖳 www.bruxellesmabelle.com
The first LGT guesthouse since 1999 in Bruxelles. Low price, p.p./night. Big breakfast included. 4 charming standing rooms : egyptian-chinese-satin-side court. Personal welcome.

■ **Heart of Brussels B&B** (bf glm H I RWS RWT) All year
32, rue de l'Epargne *M° Rogier, close to Gare du Nord*
☎ 04 96 222 778 (mobile) 🖳 www.heartofbrussels.be

■ **Maison Noble** (AC BF CC glm I MA OS RWS RWT SB VA) All year
10, rue Marcq *M° Sainte-Catherine* ☎ 02 219 23 39 ☎ 0496 85 43 63
🖳 www.maison-noble.eu
Centrally located guest house with 3 cosy rooms. 10 mins walking distance to the gay area.

PRIVATE ACCOMMODATION

■ **B&B La CambreMidi** (bf GLM I OS PK RWS RWT)
Daily 7-10 & 14-23h
Boulevard du Midi, 41/2 *M° Midi, 5 mins walk* ☎ 04 955 05 650
🖳 www.lacambrebedandbreakfast.be
Gay owned B&B with one guestroom. Near gay area of Brussels. Motobikes very welcome, private parking free.

■ **Downtown BXL** (bf GLM I RWS RWT VA) 24hrs
118-120, Rue du Marché au Charbon *M° Anneessens*
☎ 04 75 29 07 21 (mobile) 🖳 www.downtownbxl.com
3 rooms with private bathroom & TV.

GENERAL GROUPS

■ **Petit Marais. Le** (G)
HE Concept, sprl, Rue des Pierres, 57 🖳 www.lepetitmarais.eu
This group, created in 2005 consists of owners of gay bars in Brussels and represents the gay buiseness in the capital.

FETISH GROUPS

■ **MSC Belgium** (F G MA)
Postbus 699 ☎ 02 203 08 48 🖳 www.mscbelgium.be
National fetish group. Member of ECMC.

SPECIAL INTEREST GROUPS

■ **Basta Brussel** (GLM YC)
Postbus 1696 🖳 www.bastaweb.be
Flemish gay group for youngsters.

CRUISING

-Bois de la Cambre „drève de Lorraine" (near Chaussée de La Hulpe, from noon till sunset) (AYOR, police harassment reported)
-Parc du Cinquantenaire (when you come from Shuman, enter the park and turn to the right) (AYOR)
-Place Fontainas/Rue des Bogards/Rue de la Gouttière (AYOR R)
-Parc Royal (Parc de Bruxelles), between Parliament and Palais Royal (M° Parc)
-Galeries de la Monnaie (underground toilets).

Charleroi

BARS

■ **Bad Boys. Le** (B g MA ST)
20, place de la Digue ☎ 07 142 12 58
🖳 badboyscharleroi.skyrock.com
Drag shows.

■ **Bahamas. Le** (B GLM MA) 21-?h
13, Rue Vauban ☎ 071 32 63 15

■ **Bar Mat'. Le** (B DR f G MA)
9, Rue de France ☎ 04 76 34 01 24
Cruising bar.

■ **Chez Nina** (B glm MA ST)
3, Avenue de l'Europe ☎ 071 366 308
🖳 www.nina-show-transformiste.be
Drag shows.

■ **Chicos. Los** (B g) 10-?h
69, Rue de la Régence ☎ 04 86 49 78 35 (mobile)

■ **Entre-Deux. L'** (B g m MA)
61, Boulevard Jacques Bertrand ☎ 07 130 03 35

■ **Pickles** (B GLM MA)
17-?, Fri 15-?, Sat 17-?, Sun 15-?h, closed Mon & Tue
6, rue du Moulin 🖳 www.pickles-bar.be

SEX SHOPS/BLUE MOVIES

■ **Cine Turenne** (DR g VS) 12-20h
35, Rue Turenne ☎ 07 132 55 97

■ **Fantasme** (g VS)
45, Rue Turenne ☎ 07 130 23 29

CRUISING

-Park near Palais de Justice (AYOR) (near lion statues).

De Panne

CRUISING

-Monument Léopold Ier (Esplanade, evenings)
-Leffrinckouke (1h walk, near factory hall, very popular).

Dilbeek

GENERAL GROUPS

■ **Sacha** (GLM) Mon-Thu 19-22h
Secretariaat O.C. Westrand, Kamerijklaan z/n ☏ 02 520 77 30
🖳 www.sacha-holebi.be

Gent

GAY INFO

■ **Casa Rosa** (B GLM m MA) 15-3h
Kammerstraat 22 *Next to town hall* ☏ 09 269 28 12
🖳 www.casarosa.be
Gay and lesbian information point. Organizes cultural events and parties as well.

■ **Holebifoon** (GLM) Mon & Thu 18.30-21.30, Wed 15.30-21.30h, closed on holidays
☏ (0800) 99 533 (toll free)
Gay and lesbian information switchboard. Chat on Wed 18-22h.

CULTURE

■ **Fonds Suzan Daniel** (GLM)
Postbus 569 ☏ 09 223 58 79 🖳 www.fondssuzandaniel.be
Gay-lesbian archives and documentation centre.

BARS

■ **King Street** (B G MA) 22-7h
Kammerstraat 49 ☏ 09 223 90 61
Well-established gay dance-café with a warm 70's interior.

■ **Por Que No** (B GLM MC OS WE) Fri-Tue 21-?h
Sint Denijslaan 155 *Situated back of railwaystation St-Pieters Ghent*
☏ 04 98 70 20 25 (mobile) 🖳 www.porqueno-gent.be
Lovely gay bar with a retro jukebox for young and old.

MEN'S CLUBS

■ **Adonis** (AC B cc DR f G MA VS WE)
14-?, Fri & Sat 20-?h, closed Mon & Wed (special parties)
Deinsesteenweg 14 ☏ 09 253 12 01 🖳 www.adonisgent.com
Trendy gay erotic bar with cruising area. Dress code on Fri: underwear, sexy fashion.

■ **Planète Plaisir** (B DR f G MC p VS) 21-5h, closed Mon
Sint-Pietersaalststraat 92 *Near station Gent-Sint-pieters*
☏ 04 77 473 960 (mobile) 🖳 www.planeteplaisir.be
Sex parties with dresscode on Fri & Sun. Well known for it's cruising parties.

CAFES

■ **barrazza** (! B D GLM I LM MA NR S WE WI) 12-4h
Hoefslagstraat 6 *Side alley of Langemunt, between Korenmarkt and Vrijdagmarkt* ☏ 473 769 522 🖳 www.barrazza.be
barrazza is a charming gay bar located in the heart of Ghent, in a side street of Long Mint in a 16th century building with a terrace near the water.

■ **Dixie. The** (B G m MA) 10-2, Sun 18-2h, closed Sat
Koningin Maria Hendrikaplein 37 ☏ 09 324 48 84
🖳 www.the-dixie.be

■ **Out. The** (B G I m OS YC) 14-4, Sat -5h
Hoogpoort 53 *M° Dampoort, located in front of the city hall*
☏ 09 330 45 90 🖳 www.the-out.com
Busy after 22h. Modern and colourful interior.

DANCECLUBS

■ **Atlantis** (B D GLM MA) 2nd Fri/month 23-?h
The Temple, Solariumdreef 7F, Destelbergen 🖳 www.atlantisnights.be

RESTAURANTS

■ **Allegro Moderato** (B CC glm M MA OS)
11.45-15 & 18-22h, Sun & Mon closed
Korenlei 7 *Centre, old harbour* ☏ 09 233 23 32 🖳 www.restoallegro.com

■ **Dinelli's Restaurant** (AC g M MA) 18-24h
Scheldestraat 66 ☏ 04 75 43 87 65

■ **L'odieux** (B g M MA) 12-14, 19-22h; closed Wed & Thu
Vlaanderenstraat 22 ☏ 04 75 82 39 18 (mobile) 🖳 www.lodieux.be

SAUNAS/BATHS

■ **Spades 4** (AC B DR DU FC FH G m MSG OS P PI RR SA SB SOL VS WH WO YC) 12-24, Sat & Sun 13-24h
Koning Albertlaan 172 *Near St. Pieters station* ☏ 09 338 86 50
🖳 www.saunaspades4our.be
Popular bath house. Same management as Spades 4 in Brussels.

BOOK SHOPS

■ **Gay-shop Hephaestion** (b cc GLM)
10-19, Fri & Sat 14-22, Sun 14-19h, closed Wed
Kammerstraat 29 ☏ 04 748 219 91 🖳 www.hephaestion.be
Books, movies, rainbow stuff, condoms and sexy toys.

HOTELS

■ **Chambres D'hotes Hotel Verhaegen** (BF CC glm I RWS RWT)
All year
Oude Houtlei 110 ☏ 09 265 07 60 🖳 www.hotelverhaegen.be

■ **Hotel Erasmus** (b BF CC glm H I OS RWS RWT VA) Reception 7-23h, closed from Dec 24th till Jan 11th
Poel 25 *City centre, Tram-Korenmarkt* ☏ 09 224 21 95
🖳 www.erasmushotel.be
All 12 rooms with own bath, telephone and TV. 10% discount for Spartacus-readers.

GUEST HOUSES

■ **Cuberdon B&B** (BF glm I MA SA) All year
Wolterslaan 76 ☏ 09 324 49 78 🖳 www.cuberdon.be

■ **Faja Lobi B&B** (B BF glm M MA OS PK RWB RWS) All year
Tarbotstraat 31 *10 mins walk from historical centre* ☏ 09 223 55 33
🖳 www.fajalobi.be

GENERAL GROUPS

■ **Verkeerd Geparkeerd** (GLM YC) Café Mon 20-23h
Kammerstraat 22 🖳 www.verkeerdgeparkeerd.be
Association for young G&L up to 25 years. For activities see website

CRUISING

-Blaarmeersen (Watersportbaan, at foot of hill)
-Citadelpark (Leopold II laan): down the hill it used to be cruising zone for gay pimps, has decreased a lot last years, due to police infiltrations, since most of those guys were illegals. However, there is still non-paid action (and thus more spontanaos and more pleasant) to be found on the alley up on the ‚hill' lining the leopold II laan, in the toilet between that hill and King Boudewijn's statue (direction of the station) and on the bush-alleys between the parking lot of the SMAK museum and the ‚hill'. Last years, due to outing of some police officers, repression of gay activities in the bushes by police has decreased. Nevertheless be carefull. Police nowadays mainly checks the park, in order to avoid every-now-and-then gay bashing by muslim immigrants. Usually safe.

Hasselt

BARS

■ **Silvergate** (B GLM MA) 22-?h, closed Tue & Wed
Zuivelmarkt 60 ☏ 04 76 669 432 🖳 www.silvergate.be

■ **Starlight Lounge** (AC B CC d GLM H OS S ST T WE YC)
20-?, Fri & Sat 22-?h
Maastrichterstraat 48 *Next to TT-center, opposite the post office*
☏ 01 122 55 85
Disco on Saturdays.

GENERAL GROUPS

■ **Limburgs Actiecentrum Homofilie - LACH** (GLM MA)
Kuringersteenweg 179 ☎ 01 125 22 94 🖳 www.lachvzw.be
Gay support group with monthly meetings for special interest groups (young gays, religion, married gays, bi-sexual etc.) Also café „Het Nieuwe Huis" Sat 21-2 & Sun 15-18 and 2nd & 4th Fri/month 20-2h (women only).

Kerkhove-Avelgem

SAUNAS/BATHS

■ **Sauna Nautilus** (B cc DR DU FC FH G I m MA MSG OS P PI RR SA SB SOL VS WH) 11-23h, Wed closed
Oudenaardsesteenweg 392 *Bus 92, 85* ☎ 56 32 04 04
🖳 www.saunanautilus.be
Heated pool in sunny garden, 2 saunas, steambath, sling, maze, cabins, glory holes showers, whirlpool, cosy bar, fireplace, internet, friendly-priced home-made snacks.

Knokke-Heist

BARS

■ **Apero. L'** (AC B CC GLM H MA OS s) 18-6h
Zoutelaan 3 *Near Lippenslaan, 100 m from beach* ☎ 05 062 75 40
🖳 www.lapero-bar.be

HOTELS

■ **Gresham** (B BF cc H MC) All year
Elisabethlaan 185 *50 m from the beach and the casino* ☎ 05 063 10 10
🖳 www.hotelgresham.be
The hotel has 9 comfortable rooms with TV, telephone and luxurious bathroom with toilet.

Kortrijk

BARS

■ **Boys. The** (B DR G MA VS) 21-?h, closed Mon
Papenstraat 9 ☎ 0484 73 20 29 🖳 www.theboyskortrijk.net

■ **Crisco** (AC B DR F G MA p VS) 21-3, Fri-Sun -?h
Oude Kasteelstraat 3 *5mins from railway station Kortrijk*
☎ 04 95 47 26 04 (mobile) 🖳 www.crisco.be
Safe sex party every 2nd Sun/month, entry 15-16h.

■ **Diferencia** (B GLM MA) 17-24h
Kasteelkaai 6

DANCECLUBS

■ **Mammisch.d** (B D GLM MA) Fri & Sat 22-?h
Papenstraat 34 ☎ 04 95 47 26 04

SEX SHOPS/BLUE MOVIES

■ **Erogaycinema Nr1** (DR f G MA VS) 13.30-21h, closed Sun
Papenstraat 34 ☎ 0475 52 77 82 (mobile)
🖳 www.gaycinemakortrijk.be
Slings, cabins, SM-room.

SAUNAS/BATHS

■ **Gay Sauna Max** (B DU G m MA OS RR SA SB VS WH)
Sun-Fri 13-?h, closed Sat
Stadelaan 21 *Near corner with Kortrijksestraat* ☎ (0474) 96 79 70
🖳 www.max21.be

■ **Kouros** (AK B DR DU G GH LAB MA OS SA SB SL VS WH)
Daily 13-22h
Mister Liebaertlaan 59 ☎ 056 21 64 89 🖳 www.sauna-kouros.be

CRUISING

-Kasteelkaai-Rooseveltplein

Leuven

BARS

■ **Key West** (B CC GLM MA) 21-?h, closed Sun & Mon
Dirk Boutslaan 12 ☎ 01 658 49 49 🖳 www.keywest.be

CAFES

■ **Rocco** (B GLM OS YC) 19-1h, closed Tue
Diestsesteenweg 24 *Corner behind railway station* 🖳 www.caferocco.be
Lively bar and headquarter of the local gay groups. Many students.

DANCECLUBS

■ **Showroom** (B D glm MA) 1st Fri/month 22-?h
Mechelsesteenweg 709, Herent *Between Leuven-Mechelen*
☎ 01 622 00 69 🖳 www.danceroom.be

SEX SHOPS/BLUE MOVIES

■ **Extase. L'** (g) 12.30-22, Sun 15-19h
Tiensevest 6 ☎ 01 620 25 12

GUEST HOUSES

■ **Lodging at 8** (BF GLM MA RWS RWT) 8-23h
Weldadigheidsstraat 8 *15 mins from train station* ☎ 04 75 93 72 21
🖳 www.lodgingat8.be
Lodging at 8 is gay-owned and run and combines a cosy atmosphere with everyday comfort. The three guestrooms have been completely renovated, paying special attention to old and new details.

GENERAL GROUPS

■ **Driekant** (b d GLM MA)
Diestsesteenweg 24, Kessel-Lo *Near train station of Leuven*
☎ 04 75 92 85 67 (mobile) 🖳 www.driekant.be

Liège

BARS

■ **Mama Roma. La** (AC B D GLM MA S ST T VS WE) Fri-Sun 22-?h
16, Rue des Célestines ☎ 04 223 47 69
Shows on Fri & Sun.

■ **Moustache Club Liège** (AC B d G H MA P S ST) 22-?h
31, Rue de la Casquette ☎ 04 795 242 82

■ **New Relax Café** (B CC d GLM MA OS S ST T)
8-2, Fri -3, Sat 10-3, Sun 12-2h
22, Rue Pont d'Avroy *Opp. „Palace" cinema, next to cathedral*
☎ 04 223 54 01 🖳 www.lerelaxcafe.be

■ **Open Bar** (B d GLM MA) Tue-Sat 22-?h
19, Rue des Mineurs ☎ 047 540 22 66 🖳 www.openbar.be
Popular.

■ **Petit Paris. Le** (B d GLM MA) Tue-Sun 11-?h
31 Place du Marché 🖳 www.le-petit-paris.be

MEN'S CLUBS

■ **Chap's. The** (B DR F G MA p VS) Fri & Sat 22.30-4.30, Sun 20-1h
68, Rue Bonne Femme 🖳 www.thechaps.info
Dresscode! Leather, rubber, uniforms, and jeans. Cage, golden shower cabine, St. Andrew's Cross, changing room, showers and videos.

■ **Spartacus** (AC B CC d DR F G MA P VS WE) 16-6, Sat & Sun 22-6h
12, Rue Saint-Jean en Isle *Centre* ☎ 04 223 12 59

SAUNAS/BATHS

■ **Aquari-Hom. L'** (AC B DR FC FH G M MA OS P RR SA SB SL VS WH) Mon, Thu, Fri 13-22, Tue 18-2, Wed 14-22, Sat 13-24, Sun 14 -22h
20, Rue d'Harscamp *In the borough of Longdoz* ☎ 04 222 47 41
🖳 www.aquarihom.be

GENERAL GROUPS

■ **Alliàge** (GLM) Meetings Fri 19-22h
7, Hors-Château ☎ 04 223 65 89 🖳 www.alliage.be
Regional group for the LGBT community.

CRUISING

-Canal Albert, Ile-de-Monsin (near Albert I Monument)
-Parc d'Avroy
-Place de la Cathédrale
-Place de la République Française (AYOR).

Maldegem

GUEST HOUSES

■ **Bed & Breakfast De Boshoeve**
(BF DU GLM I MA NR p PK RES VA WE WI) All year
Groot Burkeldreef 4 www.amivac.com/boshoeve9990
Country bed & breakfast near the historcal towns of Bruges and Damme. 2 double guestrooms.

Mechelen

GENERAL GROUPS

■ **HLWM (Homo- en Lesbiennewerking Mechelen)**
(B GLM MA NR) Fri 21-2h
Hanswijkstraat 74 ☎ 04 86 14 17 87 www.hlwm.be
Regular activities: sports, parties, trips, exhibitions.

CRUISING

-In front of bus station (AYOR) (next to post office, on afternoons)
-E19 Walem (near Mechelen).

Middelkerke

GUEST HOUSES

■ **Landgoed de Kastanjeboom**
(bf glm H M PK RWS RWT VA WH) All year
Lekestraat 10 *10 km from sea and Oostende* ☎ 05 155 59 17
www.landgoeddekastanjeboom.be
Manor house in the countryside.

Mol

CAFES

■ **Cher** (AC B glm MA) Tue & Sun 7-14, Wed-Sat 18-3h, closed Mon
St-Pieterstraat 5 *Near station* ☎ 01 432 32 42
www.cafecher.be

Mons

BARS

■ **New Half & Half** (B GLM MA) Wed-Sun 22-?h
2, rue de la Poterie ☎ 04 96 07 45 54 www.newhalfandhalf.be
■ **Question de Genres** (B GLM MA)
79, rue d' Havré www.questiondegenres.com

CRUISING

-Around church gardens
-P Heppignies near Fleurus (highway from Mons to Namur, 10 km from Charleroi; both sides, day and night).

Namur

BARS

■ **Baby Boy** (B GLM MA)
Rue des Brasseurs 112 www.babyboybar.be

HOTELS

■ **New Hôtel de Lives**
(AC B BF CC glm M MA OS PA PK RWS RWT VA) All year
Chaussée de Liege 1178 *6 km from centre of Namur, Bus 12 / bus stop in front of the hotel* ☎ 08 158 05 13 www.newhoteldelives.com
With 20 rooms in antique style.

CRUISING

-Parc Louise Marie (MA R WE) (evenings).

Oostende

BARS

■ **Bad Boys** (B DR G MA) Thu-Sun 21-?h
Ooststraat 55
■ **Valentino Club** (B G MA p) 23-?h, closed Thu
Kaaistraat 21 ☎ 059 80 54 11
www.club-valentino.be

CAFES

■ **Escape** (B CC g m MA) 11-24h, closed Tue
Visserskaai 13 *Near train station* ☎ 470 33 91 71
www.escapecafe.be

RESTAURANTS

■ **Beluga** (AC B CC DM glm MA NR OS PA VEG WL) 11-24h
Kemmelbergstraat 33 ☎ 05 951 15 88
www.belugaoostende.be
Seaside restaurant. Fine Dining. Upmarked.

SAUNAS/BATHS

■ **Aquarius** (B DR DU FH G GH I m MA RR SA SB SL SOL VS WH)
14-24, Jul-Aug 15-24h
Peter Benoitstraat 77 *10 mins from station* ☎ 0496 810 813
www.erosaunaoostende.com
Located in a beautiful town house.

GUEST HOUSES

■ **Villa Victor** (BF g MC) All year
Duinenstraat 239, Bredene *800 m from beach, 500 m from center 1500 m nude beach 4km from Oostende gay bars & gay disco*
☎ 04 756 727 03 www.villavictor.be
The only gay B&B on the beach in Belgium.

CRUISING

-Bredene (at the beginning of the dunes near the Military Hospital on the Blankenberghe side of Oostende in afternoons)
-Beach opposite Digue de Mer
-Lido Beach (afternoons)
-Maria-Hendrika Park.

Turnhout

GENERAL GROUPS

■ **Werkgroep Homofilie Kempen** (B GLM MA) 10-2h
De Merodelei 40 ☎ 04 86 88 22 37 (mobile)
www.whk.be

CRUISING

-P between Exit 24 and 25 (E 34).

Wachtebeke

PRIVATE ACCOMMODATION

■ **Villa Bed & Breakfast Annie Cousaert** (! BF DM DU FH GLM H I M MA NR OS p PK RES RWB RWT VA VEG WE WI) All year
Dahlialaan 17 *Between Antwerp, Gent & Holland* ☎ 09 344 09 54
www.amivac.com/bandbannie
Romantic villa B & B between Ghent - Bruges - Antwerp and Dutch North sea coast

Belize

Name: Belice
Location: Central America
Initials: BH
Time: GMT -6
International Country Code: ☎ 501 (omit 0 from area code)
International Access Code: ☎ 00
Language: English (official language), Spanish
Area: 22,965 km² / 8,867 sq mi.
Currency: 1 Belize Dollar (Bz$) = 100 Cents
Population: 283,000
Capital: Belmopan
Religions: 58% Roman Catholic, 28% Protestant
Climate: The dry season is from Nov-May. Summer (Jul-Nov) is hurricane season.

In Belize homosexual acts are not subject to any specific rule of law. The age of consent according to the information we have is 16. You should however be aware that, while it's not homophobic, public tolerance towards homosexuality only goes so far. In 1998 there was an outcry against a cruise ship with 900 gay men on board. Even though in reality there are few cases of open violence against gay men, the gay community is completely hidden. In Belize there is no gay rights movement working towards an improvement in gay rights.

Die Legalität der Ausübung homosexueller Handlungen ist in Belize nicht geregelt. Die Schutzaltersgrenze liegt nach unseren Informationen bei 16 Jahren. Allerdings sollte man beachten, dass sich die Toleranz der Bevölkerung gegenüber Schwulen in Grenzen hält bzw. schon fast homophob ist. So gab es 1998 großes Geschrei um ein Kreuzfahrtschiff mit 900 Gays an Bord. Es gibt zwar nur wenige Fälle offenkundiger Gewalt gegen Schwule, dennoch bewegt sich die Community völlig im Verborgenen. Es gibt in Belize keine Schwulenbewegung, die sich für eine Verbesserung der Rechte einsetzt.

Il n'existe pas de législation concernant l'homosexualité à Bélize. Selon nos informations, la majorité sexuelle est fixée à 16 ans, mais la population est plutôt homophobe et s'il y a peu de cas de violence physique, la communauté gay et lesbienne reste discrète. Un bateau de croisière transportant 900 gays a récemment provoqué l'indignation de la population bélizienne. Il n'existe pas non plus de mouvement d'émancipation défendant les droits des gays.

La legalidad de la práctica de actos homosexuales no está reglada en Belize. La edad de consentimiento está fijada, según nuestras informaciones, en los 16 años. Sin embargo, debe tenerse en cuenta que la actitud de la población hacia los homosexuales no es muy tolerante o es más bien casi homófoba. Así, en 1998 hubo una gran polémica por un crucero con 900 gays a bordo. Existen sólo pocos casos de violencia pública contra los homosexuales pero, de todos modos, la comunidad gay se mueve en un ambiente de clandestinidad. No hay en Belize ninguna asociación de homosexuales que promueva la defensa y mejora de derechos.

Il tema dell'omosessualità in Belize non è regolato dalla legge. L'età del consenso, secondo le nostre informazioni, è di 16 anni. Tuttavia bisogna tener presente che la tolleranza della popolazione nei confronti degli omosessuali è molto esigua: si potrebbe quasi parlare di omofobia. Nel 1998, per esempio, una crociera con 900 gay a bordo ha destato molto scalpore. Ci sono pochi casi di aperta violenza nei confronti di gay, tuttavia la comunità gay si muove piuttosto „sotterraneamente". In Belize non esiste nessun movimento o organizzazione gay che si impegna ad ottenere più diritti.

Belize City ☎ 02

SWIMMING

-Punta Gorda (G MA) (Beach at the mouth of the Moho River, can only be reached by boat, boat reservations at Tourism Centre in Punta Gorda, 11 Front Street.

CRUISING

-Lindsbergs Landing (from Ramad to Pub Amnesia, Thu-Sat ca. 23-2h).

Creek District ☎ 05

GUEST HOUSES

■ **Parrot Cove Lodge** (B BF glm M MA OS PI RWS)
False Sittee Point *Hopkins Bay* ☎ (05) 237 225
💻 www.ParrotCoveLodge.com

Placencia ☎ 05

HOTELS

■ **Singing Sands Inn** (AC b bf H MA MSG PI) All year
714 Maya Beach Way *Maya Beach* ☎ (05) 208 022
💻 www.singingsands.com
Six thatched cabanas, built from local hardwoods, primarily mahogany. The rooms are simply decorated, with local artwork and Guatemalan needlecraft. Each cabana has either a double or queen bed and a second single bed, separate bathroom with hot shower, and refrigerator.

San Pedro – Ambergris Caye ☎ 02

HOTELS

■ **Mata Rocks Resort** (AC b bf H m MA OS PI)
P.O. Box 47 ☎ (02) 26 23 36 💻 www.matarocks.com
■ **Paradise Villas** (AC b cc H m MA OS PI)
Belize Beach Resort Condos 💻 www.belizevilla.com
Gay owned.

SWIMMING

-Beach near Ramons Village (g YC).

Bermuda

Location: Western Atlantic Ocean
Initials: BMU
Time: GMT -4
International Country Code: ☎ 441 (no area codes)
International Access Code: ☎ 011
Language: English, Portuguese
Area: 21 km² / 8.11 sq mi.
Currency: Bermudian Dollar
Population: 62,997
Capital: Hamilton
Religions: Christian (28% Anglican, 15% Roman Catholic)
Climate: Apr-Oct for best weather and warmest water, ideal for diving.

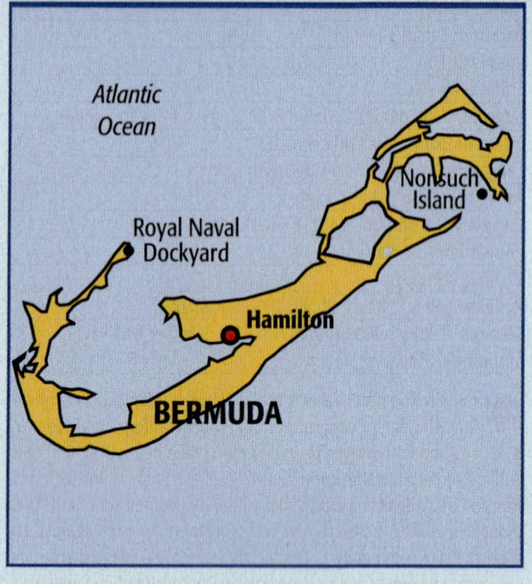

Regrettably we have not had any reply from the Attorney General in Bermuda to confirm our information, but according to our research Section 175 of the Penal Code in Bermuda used to prohibit homosexual activity between men with a penalty of up to 10 years' imprisonment and was revoked in March 1999.

In 1994 Bermuda's House of Assembly voted to legalize sex between men over age 18. It seems that this legislation was also passed by the Senate - a written reply to a Parliamentary Question dated 22 March 1999 does not include Bermuda amongst the British „dependent territories" where homosexuality is still illegal.

At a local press conference in February 2004 with the theme „International Year of the Family" the topic of Gay Unions in Bermuda were dismissed. This topic is not on any agenda. The Family Services Minister, Mrs. Patrice Minors, appears to have a moral problem accepting homosexuality and stated clearly that gay lobby groups can not count on her support. Gay rights will have to be patient in Bermuda, hardly surprising considering that interracial marriage was only legalized in the 1960's.

Bermuda is not in the Caribbean. The island is situated in the western Atlantic Ocean, nearly 600 nautical miles off the coast of North Carolina, USA.

Leider haben wir vom Generalstaatsanwalt der Bermuda-Inseln noch keine Antwort erhalten, die unsere Informationen bestätigen könnte, aber unseren Nachforschungen zufolge sieht Paragraph 175 des Strafgesetzbuches der Bermudas für gleichgeschlechtliche Handlungen zwischen Männern zwar Haftstrafen von bis zu 10 Jahren vor. Diese Reglung wurde jedoch im März 1999 aufgehoben.

Die gesetzgebende Körperschaft der Bermuda-Inseln hatte schon im Jahr 1994 beschlossen, Sex zwischen Männern ab 18 zu legalisieren. Allem Anschein nach wurde diese Gesetzesänderung auch vom Senat angenommen - eine schriftliche Antwort auf eine parlamentarische Anfrage vom 22. März 1999 zählt die Bermudas jedenfalls nicht mehr zu den britischen „Schutzgebieten", in denen die Homosexualität noch verboten ist.

Bei einer lokalen Pressekonferenz im Februar 2004 unter dem Motto „Internationales Jahr der Familie" wurde das Thema „Schwule Partnerschaften auf den Bermudas" jedoch abgewiesen. Dieses Thema ist auch sonst auf keiner Tagesordnung zu finden. Die Familienministerin, Frau Patrice Minors, hat anscheinend ein moralisches Problem damit, Homosexualität zu akzeptieren, und bezog deutlich die Stellung, dass schwule Lobbygruppen nicht auf ihre Unterstützung rechnen können. Die schwule Gleichberechtigung wird auf den Bermudas wohl noch etwas länger auf sich warten lassen, was kaum überrascht, wenn man bedenkt, dass gemischtrassige Ehen hier erst in den 1960er-Jahren legalisiert wurden.

Die Bermuda-Inseln befinden sich nicht in der Karibik. Sie liegen im Westatlantik, fast 600 nautische Meilen vor der Küste von North Carolina, USA.

Malheureusement, le procureur général des Bermudes n'a pas donné de réponse à notre demande quant à la situation des gays et lesbiennes de son pays. Néanmoins, nos investigations personnelles semblent indiquer que le paragraphe 175 du code pénal punissant les rapports homosexuels entre hommes de peines de prison pouvant aller jusqu'à 10 ans a été aboli en mars 1999. La législation bermudienne avait déjà décidé en 1994 de légaliser les rapports sexuels entre hommes de plus de 18 ans et cette modification de la loi semble avoir été ratifiée par le sénat. En réponse à une demande parlementaire, un texte du 22 mars 1999 ne compte plus les Bermudes parmi les protectorats britanniques dans lesquels l'homosexualité est interdite. Lors d'une conférence de presse locale sur „l'année internationale de la famille", le thème des „relations homosexuelles aux Bermudes" a été refusé et ne figure jamais à l'ordre du jour depuis. La ministre de la famille, Patrice Minors, semble avoir un problème moral quant à l'homosexualité et a rappelé que les lobbies homosexuels ne peuvent pas compter sur son soutien. La reconnaissance des droits des homosexuels risque donc de se faire attendre, ce qui n'étonnera personne quand on pense que la mixité raciale pour les couples n'a été acceptée que dans les années 60. Les Bermudes ne font pas parties des Caraïbes mais sont situées à près de 600 miles nautiques des côtes de la Caroline du Sud.

Desgraciadamente todavía no hemos recibido ninguna respuesta del fiscal general del Estado de las Islas Bermudas que pueda confirmarnos nuestra información pero, según nuestras investigaciones, el artículo 175 del código penal de las Bermudas prevé para las relaciones entre hombres penas de prisión de hasta 10 años, aunque sin embargo en marzo de 1999 fuera derogado.

El cuerpo legislativo de las islas Bermudas ya había decidido en el año 1994 que el sexo entre hombres debía legalizarse a partir de los 18 años. Al parecer, esta modificación legislativa también fue aceptada por el Senado; según una respuesta escrita a una demanda parlamentaria del 22 de marzo de 1999, las Bermudas no forman parte ya de los „protectorados" británicos en los que todavía está prohibida la homosexualidad.

En una rueda de prensa local de febrero del 2004 con el lema „Año Internacional de la Familia" fue rechazado el tema „Parejas homosexuales en las Bermudas". Este tema todavía no aparece en ninguna orden del día. La ministra de Familia, la Sra. Patrice Minors, probablemente tenga un problema moral para aceptar la homosexualidad y manifiesta así de forma clara que los grupos de presión gays no deben contar

con su apoyo. La equiparación de derechos en las Bermudas se hará esperar todavía un tiempo, lo que tampoco debería sorprendernos si tenemos en cuenta que aquí los matrimonios interraciales no fueron legalizados hasta los años 60.
Las islas Bermudas no se encuentran en el Caribe. Están en el Atlántico Occidental, a casi 600 millas náuticas de la costa de Carolina del Norte, en Estados Unidos.

Purtroppo ancora non abbiamo ricevuto alcuna risposta dalla magistratura che possa confermare le nostre informazioni. Secondo le nostre ricerche, il paragrafo 175 del codice penale delle Bermuda prevede fino a 10 anni di reclusione per atti sessuali tra 2 uomini. Tuttavia questo paragrafo è stato cancellato nel 1999.
L'organo legislativo delle Bermuda ha deciso già nel 1994 di legalizzare il sesso tra uomini dai 18 anni in su. Apparentemente questa modifica è stata recepita anche dal Senato. Una risposta per iscritto alla richiesta parlamentare del 22 marzo 1999 non considera più le Bermuda come „arie protette" britanniche, nelle quali l'omosessualità era vietata.
In una conferenza stampa locale in febbraio del 2004 dal nome „anno internazionale della famiglia" ci si è rifiutati di voler trattare il tema „coppie gay nelle Bermuda". Questo tema non si trova in nessun ordine del giorno. Il ministro della famiglia, Patrice Minors, ha, a quanto pare, un problema morale ad accettare l'omosessualità e ha reso ben chiaro che le lobby gay facciano bene a non contare sul sostegno del ministero. La parità omosessuale tarderà ad attuarsi nelle Bermuda, e ciò non dovrebbe stupire se si pensa che i matrimoni tra coppie di razza diversa vennero legalizzate solo negli anni sessanta.
Le isole delle Bermuda non fanno parte dei Caraibi. Si trovano a 600 miglia nautici dalla costa del North Carolina (USA).

Chaplain Bay

SWIMMING

-Intimate and pretty beach, around 200 yards (0.18 km) east of the famous Horseshoe Bay which is frequented by gay men.

Hamilton

BARS

Casey's Lounge (B NG) Mon-Sat 10-22h
25 Queen Street ☎ 292 99 94

Jasmine (B MA NG) 11-1h
101 South Shore Road ☎ 238-8000
www.fairmont.com/southampton/GuestServices/Restaurants/Jasmine.htm
Reservations are recommended for Afternoon Tea during the Summer season.

CAFES

Rock Island Coffee (BF m NG) Mon-Sat 7-18h
48 Reid Street www.rockisland.bm

DANCECLUBS

Splash (B D MA NG)
Bermudiana Road *At Portofino Restaurant* ☎ 296-3849

RESTAURANTS

Little Venice (B M MA NG) Mon-Fri 12-?, Sat 18.30-?h
Bermudian Road ☎ (441) 295-3503 www.littlevenice.bm
With a wine bar.

St George

GUEST HOUSES

Aunt Nea's Inn at Hillcrest (AC BF H MA WH)
1 Nea's Alley www.auntneas.com
A charming old Bermuda house with wonderful views of St. Georges harbour, the original capital of Bermuda. 15 units all with private bathrooms.

Bolivia

Name: Bolivien · Bolivie
Location: South America
Initials: BOL
Time: GMT -4
International Country Code: ☎ 591 (omit 0 from area code)
International Access Code: ☎ 00
Language: Spanish
Area: 1,098,581 km² / 424,162 sq mi.
Currency: 1 Boliviano (Bs) = 100 Centavos
Population: 9,182,000
Capital: La Paz
Religions: 95% Roman Catholic, 5% Protestant
Climate: Generally wet in summer (Nov-Apr) and dry in winter (May-Oct).

The Bolivian penal code does not mention homosexuality. The age of consent is 17 years old. Contravention of this law can lead to imprisonment of up to 5 years. Gay men are certainly not exempt from the illegal police checks, which are intended to ensure that „proper" restraint is maintained by intimidating people. Bolivia is a typical Latin American country full of macho guys with deeply-held prejudices. The gay scene is quite small, so gay tourists should not have high expectations!

Das bolivianische Strafgesetzbuch erwähnt Homosexualität nicht. Die Schutzaltersgrenze liegt bei 17 Jahren. Auf Zuwiderhandlung stehen ein bis fünf Jahre Gefängnis. Schwule werden hier aber nicht von illegalen Polizeikontrollen verschont, die nur dem Zweck dienen, „ordnungsgemäßes" Verhalten zu überwachen und Menschen einzuschüchtern. Bolivien ist ein typisch lateinamerikanisches Land voller Machos mit einer tief verankerten Voreingenommenheit. Es gibt eine ziemlich kleine Gay-Szene, Touristen sollten allerdings kaum Erwartungen haben.

Le code pénal bolivien ne mentionne pas l'homosexualité. La majorité sexuelle est fixée à 17 ans. Les contrevenants s'exposent à des peines allant d'une à cinq années de prison. Les gays ne sont pas non plus épargnés par les contrôles intempestifs de la police, soucieuse de faire respecter les règles de comportement social et en profite pour intimider la population gay. La Bolivie est un pays latino-américain où la mentalité macho et les préjugés traditionalistes ont toujours cours. Le milieu gay est plutôt petit et assez décevant pour les touristes.

El código penal boliviano no menciona la homosexualidad. La edad de consentimiento está fijada en los 17 años. Por su infracción se preven penas de cárcel de uno a cinco años. Los homosexuales no se libran tampoco aqui de los controles policiales ilegales, cuyo único objetivo es garantizar un „comportamiento ordenado" e intimidar a las personas. Bolivia es un típico país latino-americano lleno de machos con profundos y enraizados prejuicios. Existe un ambiente gay bastante pequeño, por lo que los turistas no deberían tener muchas esperanzas.

L'omosessualità non è citata dal codice penale boliviano. L'età del consenso per avere rapporti sessuali è di 17 anni. In caso si contravvenga all'età del consenso, la pena prevista va da uno a cinque anni di reclusione. Gli omosessuali non vengono risparmiati dai controlli polizieschi che hanno il solo scopo di sorvegliare su un comportamento consono all'ordine e di intimidire le persone. La Bolivia è un tipico paese latinoamericano pieno di macho e con radicati pregiudizi. Esiste una piccola scena gay ma non abbiate grandi aspettative in riguardo.

NATIONAL GROUPS

■ **Adesproc Libertad GLBT**
Avenida Héroes del Pacifico 1330 ✉ La Paz *Zona Miraflores*
☎ (02) 22 26 210 💻 www.libertadglbt.org

Cochabamba ☎ 042

BARS

■ **Bronx** (B G MA)
Pasaje Andres Muñoz N° 2, Sopacachi *Parque del Montículo*

CRUISING

-La Plaza de 14 septiembre (Thu-Sat 0-3h) - wear a cap to be recognized as an interested partner
-El Prado (AYOR at night).
-Plaza Colon (Thu-Sat 24-3h) – wear a cap or a red ribbon on a right knee

La Paz ☎ 02

BARS

■ **Café Cultural VOX** (B GLM YC) Daily 15-22h
Avenida Héroes del Pacifico 1330 *Zona Miraflores* ☎ (02) 222 62 10
■ **El Chamaco Pub** (B G)
Calle Gosalvez *Between 6 de Agosto y Av. Arce* ☎ 243 26 60
■ **Holiday** (B d glm MA)
Avenida Montes
■ **Mongo's** (! B GLM) Thu 22-3h
Hermanos Manchego 2444 ☎ 244 07 14
Gay Thursday's night

CAFES

■ **Vox** (b GLM MA) Mon-Sat
Avenida Héroes del Pacífico 1330, Miraflores *Thu-lesbian*

DANCECLUBS

■ **Punto G** (B D GLM MA)
Avenida Capitán Ravelo *Between Puente de las Américas and Belisario Salinas*
■ **Taurus** (B D GLM MA S)
Avenida Busch 1010 *Opp. „Sucre Tennis La Paz"* ☎ (70) 67 62 27
💻 www.geocities.com/taurusdiscobar
Special events and theme nights take place here on a regular basis.

TRAVEL AND TRANSPORT

■ **Turisbus**
Avenida Illampu 704 ☎ (02) 245 13 41 💻 www.travelperubolivia.com

HOTELS

■ **Panamericano** (B H M NG)
Avenida Manco Copac 454 ☎ (02) 34 08 10
Downtown location. 7 km from the airport. All rooms with telephone, private bath.
■ **Residencial Rosario** (BF CC H M) All year
Avenida Illampu 704, Casilla Centro ☎ (02) 245 16 58
💻 www.hotelrosario.com
There are 42 rooms in the colonial Hotel Rosario. The décor features many motifs from the Aymara and Quechua cultures.
One block of rooms is in the restored area of the original colonial building. The other blocks are new but follow the design and decoration of the colonial section. The last renovation was done in 2006.

CRUISING

-Plaza Avora (Avenida 20 de Octubre / Calle Belisario Salinas) - wear a cap to be recognized as an interested partner, only Tue after 22h
-Plaza P. Velasco (Avenida Montes / Calle Comercio) - Tue-Sun 0-4h
-Plaza Avenida 20 de Octubre cnr. Rosendo Gutierrez (Sopocachi) - transvestites, Wed-Sun 0-?h
-Calle 25 - Ingreso a Cota-Cota (Calacoto) - Fri-Sun 23-4h
-El Prado/Plaza del Estudiante (Avenida 16 de Julio / Av. Landaeta) - Wed-Sun 23-2h, AYOR
-Plaza Venezuela (Avenida 16 de Julio / Calle Loayza) - Sat/Sun 18-23h.

Santa Cruz ☎ 03

BARS

■ **Brujas. Las** (AYOR B g R) -6h
Avenida Cañoto/ Avenida Landivar
■ **Closet** (B GLM) 19-4h
Between Av. Virgen de Cotoca y Canal de Cotoca 2do anillo *Two blocks walk from Av. Virgen de Cotoca to Canal Cotoca, turn right and then walk one more block. The bar is right at the corner*
■ **Line** (B D g r) 19-?h
Avenida 26 de Febrero, 1005
■ **Tarantula** (B GLM) 18ñ1h
1er Anillo *In front of city park*

DANCECLUBS

■ **Alejandro** (B D GLM) Sat 23ñ6h
Calle Warnes *Between Cochabamba y La Paz*
■ **Fusion** (B D GLM) Thu-Sun 22ñ6h

RESTAURANTS

■ **Lorca** (AC B CC M MA NG OS S WE) Mon-Sat 9-3, Sun 18-23.30h
C/. Sucre, 8 *Cnr. René Moreno* ☎ (03) 334 05 62
💻 www.lorcasantacruz.org
French-Arabian food and a good wine list. Also concerts and art exhibitions. Very gay-friendly.

CRUISING

-Plaza 24 de Septiembre
-Parque del Arenal (AYOR)
-Avenida Coñoto
-El Cristo.

Sucre ☎ 064

CRUISING

-La Plaza (at night).

Bosnia-Hercegovina

Name: Bosna i Hercegovina · Bosnien-Herzegowina · Bosnie-Herzégovine · Bosnia-Erzegovina
Location: Southeast Europe
Initials: BIH
Time: GMT +1
International Country Code: ☏ 387
International Access Code: ☏ 00
Language: Bosnian, Serbian, Croatian
Area: 51,129 km² / 19,741 sq mi.
Currency: Convertible Mark (KM)
Population: 3,907,000
Capital: Sarajevo
Religions: 40% Muslim 31% Serbian-Orthodox 15% Catholics
Climate: A mix of Mediterranean and Central European climate and is more or less agreeable year round.

According to our information, homosexual acts between men in Bosnia and Hercegovina are not illegal (in Federation BiH since 1996 and in the Republika Srpska since 1998). The age of sexual consent is 16 for all. In addition, a Gender Equality Law was adopted in 2003. It stipulates that discrimination based on sexual orientation is prohibited by law.
Bosnia held its first LGBT Pride festival „Queer Sarajevo" in September 2008. At least eight people were injurred, six of them suffered head injuries. Iggy Pop cancelled his concert in Sarajevo. Before the event posters calling for death to gays appeared around the city and were removed by the police. Ever since the 1992-95 Bosnian war the multicultural city Sarajevo has become predominantly Muslim. Two prominent imams publicly condemned the festival, although they refrained from endorsing violence.

Nach unseren Informationen sind homosexuelle Handlungen zwischen Männern in Bosnien-Herzegowina nicht illegal. Allgemein gilt die Schutzaltergrenze von 16 Jahren. Zusätzlich wurde ein Gesetz zur Gleichstellung der Geschlechter Anfang 2003 verabschiedet. Es legt fest, dass Diskriminierungen aufgrund sexueller Orientierung verboten sind.
In Bosnien fand im September 2008 die erste CSD-Veranstaltung unter dem Titel „Queer Sarajevo" statt. Dabei wurden mindestens acht Menschen verletzt, sechs davon im Kopfbereich. Iggy Pop sagte sein Konzert in Sarajevo ab. Vor der Veranstaltung tauchten überall in der Stadt Plakate mit der Aufschrift „Tod den Schwulen" auf, die dann von der Polizei entfernt wurden. Seit dem Bosnien-Krieg von 1992-1995 leben im vormals multikulturellen Sarajevo vorwiegend Muslime. Zwei bekannte Imame hatten das Festival zwar öffentlich verurteilt, dabei jedoch nicht zu gewalttätigen Übergriffen aufgerufen.

Selon nos informations, les relations homosexuelles entre hommes ne sont pas illégales en Bosnie-Herzégovine (depuis 1996 dans la fédération de Bosnie-Herzégovine et depuis 1998 en République Srpska). La majorité sexuelle de 16 ans est valable pour tous. De plus une loi sur l'égalité des sexes a été votée en début d'année 2003. Elle affirme que les discriminations en raison de l'orientation sexuelle sont légalement interdites.
La première Gay Pride de Bosnie s'est déroulée en septembre 2008 sous la devise: „Queer Sarajevo". On a dû déplorer au moins huit personnes blessées, dont six au niveau de la tête. Iggy Pop a annulé son concert à Sarajevo. Avant la manifestation, des affiches avec la mention „Mort aux Pédés" sont apparues partout dans la ville et on été retirées par la police. Depuis la guerre de Bosnie de 1992 à 1995, une majorité de Musulmans vivent à Sarajevo, ville auparavant multiculturelle. Deux imams connus ont condamné certes publiquement le festival mais sans appeler pour autant à des actes de violence.

De acuerdo a nuestra información, las relaciones entre homosexuales no son ilegales en Bosnia-Herzegovina (desde 1996 en la Federación de Bosnia-Herzegovina y desde 1998 en la República de Srpska o ex República Yugoslava de Macedonia). La edad de consentimiento es de 16 años para todos. A inicios de 2003 se adoptó una ley que contempla la igualdad de todos los sexos. En ella se establece que toda forma de discriminación por motivos de orientación sexual queda prohibida.
In Bosnia se celebró en septiembre de 2008 la primera Marcha del Orgullo gay bajo el título de „Queer Sarajevo". Durante la celebración resultaron 8 personas heridas, 6 de ellos en la cabeza. Iggy Pop canceló su concierto en Sarajevo. Antes del evento habían aparecido por toda la ciudad carteles con el lema „Muerte a los homosexuales", que fueron sacados por la policía. Desde la guerra de Bosnia de 1992-1995 en la anteriormente multicultural Sarajevo viven mayoritariamente musulmanes. Dos conocidos imans habían condenado el festival públicamente, aunque no habían hecho llamado a que se produjeran ataques violentos.

Per quanto ne sappiamo, in Bosnia-Herzegowina i rapporti omosessuali tra uomini non sono illegali (nella federazione BiH dal 1996 e nella Repubblica Srpska dal 1998). L'età legale per rapporti sessuali è di 16 anni sia per eterosessuali sia per omosessuali. Inoltre all'inizio dell'anno 2003 è stata approvata una legge per la parificazione dei sessi. Questa legge vieta qualsiasi discriminazione che viene fatta in base all'orientamento sessuale delle persone.

Nel settembre del 2008 si è svolta in Bosnia il primo CSD con lo slogan „Queer Sarajevo". Durante la suddetta manifestazione ci sono stati almeno otto feriti, sei dei quali hanno riportato lesioni in testa. Iggy Pop ha disdetto il suo concerto a Sarajevo. Prima della manifestazione continuavano ad apparire per tutta la città cartelloni con su scritto „a morte gli omosessuali" che la polizia ha poi, a poco a poco, rimosso. Dalla guerra in Bosnia (1992-1995) vivono nella Sarajevo multiculturale di una volta per lo più mussulmani. Due noti imam avevano condannato la manifestazione senza tuttavia essersi richiamati ad atti di violenza contro di essa.

NATIONAL GROUPS

■ **Organization Q** (GLM)
✉ 71000 Sarajevo 💻 www.queer.ba
First LGBTIQ organization in the country with the aim of promotion of cultures, identities and human rights of Queer persons.

Sarajevo ☎ 033

BARS

■ **Bar. The** (B m MA NG)
Titiva 7 (Marsala Tita Street) ☎ (033) 061 237 059 (mobile)
There are no gay bars or clubs in Sarajevo. The ones listed are gay friendly or where people gather by default. More gays on Fri & Sat 11-2h.

DANCECLUBS

■ **Fis KULTURA** (B D glm MA p s) 22-3h
Musala Street ☎ (0)62 526 930 (mobile)
Irregular gay parties. Entrance reservation and info in advance at gayzurke@gmail.com

BOOK SHOPS

■ **Buybook** (CC)
Radićeva 4 ☎ 552 745 💻 www.buybook.ba
International bookstore. Some gay books possible.

CRUISING

All are AYOR:
-Park close to the presidency building and „The Bar" (see bars)
-Beside the Zeljeznica River in Ilidza
-Near President Hall in Veliki Park (after 24h).

Brazil

Name: Brasil · Brasilien · Brésil · Brasile
Location: Central & northeastern South America
Initials: BR
Time: GMT -3/-4
International Country Code: ☎ 55
International Access Code: ☎ 00
Language: Portuguese
Area: 8,547,404 km² / 3,285,632 sq mi.
Currency: 1 Real (R$) = 100 Centavos
Population: 186,405,000
Capital: Brasilia
Religions: 74% Roman Catholic, 15% Protestant
Climate: Mostly tropical climate. The south is unbearably sticky in summer (Dec-Feb) and rains non-stop in winter (Jun-Aug).
Important gay cities: Rio de Janeiro, São Paulo, Salvador

The age of consent in Brazil is 18. Minors are protected by the law from those over 18. "Seduction of minor" is a punishable offence. Gay marriages are not allowed, but stable unions have been frequently recognized by judicial courts for inheritance and social security purposes. Proposals have been forwarded by the Parliamentary Front to register same-sex couples as civil union and to recognize their rights. 2011 saw the highest court of appeal urging the equalization of civil partnerships with heterosexual marriage in a number of judgements, owed to the constitution expressly prohibiting discrimination. In the court's opinion, the protection provided by marriage and the family may not be limited to heterosexuals alone. These far-reaching decisions have put the politicians under pressure. But while political figures on the left have started several initiatives Rousseff, the head of government, has remained inactive, not wishing to scare off her Catholic voters over this issue.

Anti-discrimination laws have been approved in cities and states but with limited effectiveness. There is not yet a federal law which protects gays against discrimination, considering it a criminal offense. It is illegal for a business to refuse employment based on sexual orientation. The major cities like Rio and São Paulo have police hotlines for gay and lesbian communities.

In Brazil, the most courts in the state of Rio Grande do Sul recognize same-sex civil unions. The cities of Belo Horizonte (Minas Gerais), Natal (Rio Grande do Norte), Pelotas (RGS), Recife (Pernambuco), Porto Alegre (RS), Rio de Janeiro (Rio de Janeiro) and Sao Paulo (SP) grant equality for same-sex partners of state employees. There is no legal control measures in place to prevent or punish moral offenses against gays and lesbians.

A word of warning about the safety in Brazil: It is recommended to keep about US$30 in local currency on hand in case of an attack. Muggers often respond violently if you're only carrying small change.

Nevertheless Brazil remains extremely popular with gay tourists. The world famous Carnival in Rio in February as well as the world's largest Gay Pride in São Paulo in June are just two examples of the attractions Brazil has to offer.

Brasilien hat im Jahr 2010 erstmals eine Frau ins Präsidentenamt gewählt. Die Regierungskandidatin Dilma Rousseff hat in einer Stichwahl den Oppositionskandidaten José Serra geschlagen.

In Brasilien liegt das Schutzalter bei 18 Jahren. Das Gesetz schützt Minderjährige vor Kontakten mit über 18-jährigen. Die „Verführung

Minderjähriger" ist strafbar. Obwohl die Homo-Ehe nicht erlaubt ist, sind erklärt stabile Partnerschaften mehrmals per Gerichtsentscheid erbrechtlich und zum Zweck der sozialen Absicherung anerkannt worden. Von einer Parlamentarischen Front sind Gesetzesinitiativen auf den Weg gebracht worden, die gleichgeschlechtliche Partnerschaften als eheähnliche Verhältnisse „registrieren" und deren Rechte „anerkennen" würden. 2011 hat das Oberste Berufungsgericht in mehreren Urteilen die Angleichung der eingetragenen Partnerschaft an die heterosexuelle Ehe angemahnt, da die Verfassung ausdrücklich Diskriminierung verbiete. Der Schutz, den die Ehe und Familie gewährleiste, dürfe nicht auf Heterosexuelle allein beschränkt sein. Diese weit reichenden Entscheidungen setzt die Politik unter Druck. Während linke Politiker mehrere Initiativen starteten, will die Regierungschefin Rousseff in dieser Angelegenheit ihre katholischen Wähler nicht verschrecken und bleibt untätig.

In einigen Städten und Bundesstaaten sind Antidiskriminierungsgesetze erlassen worden, allerdings mit schwankendem Erfolg. Noch gibt es keine landesweit einheitliche Regelung, die diskriminierendes Verhalten zum Strafdelikt machen würde. Es ist für Arbeitgeber allerdings illegal, Bewerber wegen ihrer sexuellen Neigung abzulehnen. In Großstädten wie São Paulo und Rio hat die Polizei telefonische Notdienste für Schwule und Lesben eingerichtet. Im brasilianischen Bundesstaat Rio Grande do Sul werden gleichgeschlechtliche Partnerschaften von den meisten Gerichten anerkannt. Außerdem sind gleichgeschlechtliche Partner von Staatsbeamten in den Städten Belo Horizonte (Minas Gerais), Natal (Rio Grande do Norte), Pelotas (RGS), Recife (Pernambuco), Porto Alegre (RS), Rio de Janeiro (Rio de Janeiro) und Sao Paulo (SP) heterosexuellen Partnern gleichgestellt. Es besteht jedoch keine Medienkontrollinstanz, die moralische Verstöße gegen Schwule und Lesben verhindern oder unter Strafe stellen könnte. Dabei leben Schwule in Brasilien wahrhaftig nicht im Schlaraffenland: Im größten katholischen Land der Welt ist Homosexualität zwar nicht verboten, allerdings gelten Schwule und Lesben in der Machokultur oft nicht als gleichwertige Menschen. Eine Warnung hinsichtlich der persönlichen Sicherheit in Brasilien: Im Falle eines Überfalls ist es empfehlenswert, ungefähr 30 US-Dollar in der Landeswährung bei sich zu haben. Straßenräuber reagieren oft gewalttätig, wenn sie nur Kleingeld finden. Nichtsdestotrotz ist Brasilien bei schwulen Touristen nach wie vor äußerst beliebt. Der weltberühmte Karneval in Rio im Februar sowie die weltgrößte Gay Pride-Veranstaltung in São Paulo im Juni sind nur zwei Beispiele der vielen Attraktionen, die Brasilien zu bieten hat.

Au Brésil, la majorité sexuelle est fixée à 18 ans et la législation punit le détournement de mineurs. Bien que le mariage homosexuel ne soit pas légalement reconnu, les relations stables le sont en ce qui concerne la succession et la sécurité sociale. Un front parlementaire a présenté plusieurs projets permettant la reconnaissance des couples de même sexe et leur „enregistrement „.

En 2011, la Haute Cour d'Appel a réclamé dans plusieurs décisions d'harmoniser le partenariat enregistré avec le mariage hétérosexuel car la Constituion interdit explicitement la discrimination. La protection que permet le mariage ne doit pas être uniquement réservée aux hétérosexuels. Ces décisions importantes mettent les politiques sous pression. Alors que des politiciens de gauche ont débuté plusieurs initiatives, le chef de gouvernement, Mme Roussef, ne souhaite pas faire peur à ses électeurs catholiques et est restée inactive.

Des lois anti-discriminatoires ont également été adoptées dans plusieurs Etats mais leur efficacité varie beaucoup et il n'existe aucune loi anti-discriminatoire au niveau national. Il est toutefois interdit pour les employeurs de refuser un candidat pour sa seule orientation sexuelle. Dans les grandes villes comme São Paulo et Rio, la police a instauré un service téléphonique d'aide d'urgence pour les gays et lesbiennes.

Dans l'Etat de Rio Grande do Sul, les couples de même sexe sont reconnus devant la plupart des tribunaux. En outre, ils jouissent des mêmes droits que leurs concitoyens hétérosexuels dans les villes de Belo Horizonte, Natal, Pelotas, Recife, Porto Alegre, Rio de Janeiro et São Paulo, mais il n'y a aucune instance de contrôle qui punisse les infractions morales à l'encontre des gays et des lesbiennes. En cas d'agression, il est recommandé d'avoir toujours sur soi l'équivalent d'environ 30 dollars US car les brigands réagissent souvent de violemment quand ils ne trouvent que de la petite monnaie. Néanmoins, le Brésil est un pays très apprécié des touristes gays : le carnaval de Rio, célèbre dans le monde entier, mais également la plus grande Gay Pride du monde à São Paulo en juin sont deux exemples des nombreuses attractions que le Brésil a à offrir.

En Brasil, la edad de consentimiento está en los 18 años. La ley protege a los menores de los contactos con mayores de 18 años. La seducción de menores está considerada un delito penal. Aunque el matrimonio homosexual no está legalizado, varias decisiones judiciales han reconocido la situación de parejas estables para beneficios hereditarios o para la seguridad social. Un frente parlamentario de partidos presentó propuestas para que las parejas del mismo sexo puedan registrarse como tales y para que se les reconozcan sus derechos. En 2011, el Tribunal Supremo de Apelación ha instando en varios casos a la equiparación de las uniones civiles registradas al matrimonio heterosexual, ya que la Constitución prohíbe explícitamente la discriminación. La protección que se garantiza tanto al matrimonio como a la familia no debe limitarse únicamente a los heterosexuales. Estas decisiones de largo alcance ponen a la política bajo presión. Mientras los políticos de izquierdas ponen en marcha varias iniciativas en esta materia, la Presidenta Dilma Rousseff no quiere espantar a sus votantes católicos y esto la ha llevado a la inacción.

En algunas ciudades y estados federados, se han aprobado leyes en contra de la discriminación, pero todavía con poco éxito. No existe todavía ninguna normativa de ámbito estatal que penalice los comportamientos discriminatorios. Además, ningún trabajador puede ser rechazado por su orientación sexual. En grandes ciudades como São Paulo o Rio, la policía ha creado un servicio telefónico de urgencia para gays y lesbianas.

En el estado federado brasileño de Rio Grande do Sul, la mayoría de tribunales reconoce las parejas del mismo sexo. Además, en ciudades como Belo Horizonte (Minas Gerais), Natal (Rio Grande do Norte), Pelotas (RGS), Recife (Pernambuco), Porto Alegre (RGS), Rio de Janeiro (Rio de Janeiro) y Sao Paulo (SP), las autoridades municipales equiparan las parejas del mismo sexo con las parejas heterosexuales. No existe, sin embargo, ninguna instancia de control de los medios de comunicación que prohíba los ataques morales hacia gays y lesbianas o que penalice tales actuaciones.

Una advertencia para su seguridad personal en Brasil: en caso de robo o asalto, se recomienda llevar siempre consigo una cantidad de unos 30 dólares americanos en moneda nacional pues los ladrones callejeros reaccionan de un modo muy violento si sólo encuentran pocas monedas o dinero suelto.

A pesar de todo esto, Brasil sigue siendo un destino preferido para los turistas gays. El famoso Carnaval de Rio en febrero así como el Día del Orgullo Gay más grande del mundo de São Paulo en junio son sólo dos ejemplos de los muchos atractivos que ofrece Brasil.

In Brasile l'età del consenso è di 18 anni. La legge tutela i minorenni da rapporti con maggiorenni. Sedurre minorenni è un reato. Anche se le unioni tra gay non sono riconosciute, viene garantito alle coppie stabili il diritto ereditario e una copertura sociale. Da una frazione parlamentare è venuta la proposta di poter registrare le unioni tra gay come „familiari" ai fini dell'assicurazione sanitaria. Nel 2011 la Suprema Corte d'Appelo, in diverse sentenze, ha evocato l'urgenza di un'equiparazione delle unioni civili omosessuali al matrimonio eterosessuale, poiché la Costituzione vieta espressamente ogni forma di discriminazione. La tutela che si garantisce al matrimonio e alla famiglia non deve essere limitata agli eterosessuali. Queste sostanziali e importanti decisioni hanno messo la politica sotto pressione. Mentre i politici di sinistra hanno intrapreso molte iniziative in questo senso, il capo del governo Rousseff, in questa materia, si guarda bene dallo spaventare i suoi elettori cattolici.

Sono inoltre in vigore leggi antidiscriminatorie secondo le quali nessun datore di lavoro può dare lavoro in base all'orientamento sessuale. In grandi città come San Paolo, la polizia ha istituito delle linee telefoniche di emergenza per gay e lesbiche.
Nella regione Rio Grande do Sul le unioni registrate tra le coppie dello sesso sono riconosciute. Nelle città Belo Horizonte (Minas Gerais), Natal (Rio Grande do Norte), Pelotas (RGS), Recife (Pernambuco), Porto Alegre (RGS), Rio de Janeiro (Rio de Janeiro) e Sao Paulo (SP) le coppie dello stesso sesso godono degli stessi diritti di cui godono anche le coppie eterosessuali. Un consiglio per la vostra sicurezza in Brasile: nel caso in cui si venga rapinati, è meglio avere nel portafoglio almeno il corrispettivo di 30 dollari americani in valuta locale, poiché i rapinatori reagiscono spesso in maniera violenta quando trovano solo degli spiccioli.
Il Brasile rimane una meta molto amata dal turismo gay. Il celebre carnevale che si svolge a Rio in febbraio ed il più grande Christopher Street Day del mondo a São Paulo sono solo 2 esempi di tutte le attrazioni che offre il Brasile.

NATIONAL GAY INFO

Abalo.com.br
Rua Frei Caneca, 135 ✉ 01307-001 São Paulo ☎ (011) 3259 4938
💻 www.abalo.com.br
The latest gay news for Brazil and more.

Brazilian National Federation of Gay, Lesbian & Transgender Associations (GLM)
💻 www.abglt.org.br
No permanent office, since the Federation has a rotative presidency that takes care of the administration. See the web for further information.

Mixbrasil
Pça Americo Jacomino 81 ✉ 05437-010 São Paulo ☎ (011) 35622100
💻 www.mixbrasil.com.br

NATIONAL PUBLICATIONS

G Magazine
Fractal Edições Ltda. Rua São João Brito, 31 ✉ 04566-070 São Paulo ☎ (011) 5049 2140 💻 www.gonline.com.br

Junior
Praça Américo Jacomino, 81 - Sumaré, São Paulo ✉ São Paulo
💻 www.revistajunior.com.br
Monthly, glossy magazine.

ViaG
☎ (11) 3255-4956 💻 www.revistaviag.com.br
The first and only gay travel magazine in Brazil.

NATIONAL COMPANIES

Ipacom Travel (CC g H MA) Mon-Fri 10-18h
Rua Visconde de Piraja, 318/ sl. 26 ✉ 22410-000 Rio de Janeiro ☎ (021) 2521-0673 💻 www.riogayguide.com
IGLTA member. Services offered in English, German, French and Spanish.

Rio G Travel (CC G MA)
Rua Teixeira de Melo, 25-A, Ipanema ✉ 22410-010 Rio de Janeiro - RJ ☎ (021) 3813-0003 💻 www.riogtravel.com
For organisation and planning of your next trip to Brazil - these are the experts.

NATIONAL GROUPS

Associação Brasileira Interdisciplinar de AIDS
Rua da Candelária, 79/10° andar - Centro ✉ CEP 20091-020 Rio de Janeiro - RJ *Centro* ☎ (021) 2223-1040 💻 www.abiaids.org.br
Organisation fighting AIDS in Brazil.

Gai - Grupo Arco Íris
Rua Mundo Novo 62 ✉ 20031-010 Rio de Janeiro - RJ *Botafogo* ☎ (021) 2552 5995 💻 www.arco-iris.org.br
With local offices throughout Brazil.

Mix Festival of Sexual Diversity
Pça Americo Jacomino 81 ✉ 05437-010 São Paulo ☎ (011) 3562-2100
💻 www.mixbrasil.org.br
Every year in November there is this very important international film festival for gays and lesbians, with directors from all over the world.

Americana - São Paulo ☎ 019

BARS

Believin' (B G)
Rua Rui Barbosa 615 - Centro ☎ (019) 8111-3349

Aracajú - Sergipe ☎ 079

BARS

Coqueiral (B GLM MA s)
Av. Santos Dumont *Bairro Santo Antônio*

GENERAL GROUPS

Grupo Dialogay de Sergipe
Caixa Postal 298

CRUISING

-O Calçadão (Rua João Pessôa; 18-24h)
-Rua 24 horas (praia de Atalaia).

Araraquara - São Paulo ☎ 016

BARS

Paradiso (B glm MA S) Fri & Sat 23-?h
Avenida da Saudade 53, Centro ☎ (016) 3333-2572
💻 www.paradisocafe2005.zip.net
Three floors: dance floor, American bar and outdoor area.

Assis - São Paulo ☎ 018

BARS

Dama de Paus Club (B GLM S)
Rua José Nogueira Marmontel 927 - Centro
Show dance club.

Balneario Camboriu - Santa Catarina ☎ 047

DANCECLUBS

London Night Club (B D GLM ST)
Av. dos Estados, 1008 ☎ (047) 360-6125

Barretos - São Paulo ☎ 017

BARS

Seven (B GLM S)
Avenida Eng. Necker C. Camargos 2616 - Bairro: América ☎ (017) 3323-8642

Bauru - São Paulo ☎ 014

DANCECLUBS

Comossomos (B D DR GLM MA S ST) 23-?h
Rua Virgílio Malta 870 - Centro ☎ (014) 3227-9509
💻 www.comossomos.com.br
Drag shows and gogo boys. Reduced entrance fee before midnight.

SEX SHOPS/BLUE MOVIES

Cine Shopping Roma (g)
Rua Gustavo Maciel 6/54 ☎ (014) 212-2771

Belem - Parà ☎ 091

BARS

Clube Aconchego Entre Amigos (B GLM MA R) Sun 11-24h
Avenida Celestino Rocha 1000 - Coqueiro ☎ (091) 235-5783

■ **Go** (B DR G MA S) Fri & Sat 11.30-?h
Trav. Piedade 587 - Reduto ☎ (091) 223-7874
■ **NN 45** (B glm MC) Daily 9-2h
Avenida Conselheiro Furtado 2485 - São Braz *At 9 de Janeiro* ☎ (091) 9986-6856

DANCECLUBS

■ **Guetto** (AC B D G SNU ST) Fri-Sat 23-?h
Municipalidade 383 ☎ (091) 223-6323 🖳 www.gueto.com.br
■ **Reduto** (B D DR GLM OS S) Wed, Fri & Sat 23-?h
Travessa Rui Barbosa, 336 *At 28 de Setembro* ☎ (091) 225-3058

SEX SHOPS/BLUE MOVIES

■ **Susex** (g) Mon-Fri 9-19, Sat -1h
Rua Ó de Almeida 491 - Loja 12 - Campina ☎ (091) 224-6222

CRUISING

-Bar do Parque
-Bosque de Rodrigues
-Praça da Republica (YC) (Rua St. Antonio and J. Alfredo)
-Pierside and Market (during the day and early evening).

Belo Horizonte – Minas Gerais ☎ 031

BARS

■ **Estaçao 2000** (B D GLM MA S) Wed-Sun 20-?h
Avenida Barbacena 823 *Barro Preto* ☎ (031) 3337-3976
■ **Mineiro Bill** (B G MA) Thu-Sun 20-?h
Av. Pedro II 4001 *In front of Banco Real.* ☎ (031) 3471-3813

MEN'S CLUBS

■ **Spice Men** (b DR G m MA VS)
Tue-Fri 17-24, Sat & Sun 14-24h, Mon closed
Rua Juiz de Fora, 558 *Cnr. Rua Barbacena* ☎ (031) 3243-3610
🖳 www.spicemen.com.br

DANCECLUBS

■ **A Obra** (B D MA NG S)
R Rio Grande do Norte, 1168 Savassi ☎ (031) 3215-8077
🖳 www.aobra.com.br
■ **Andaluz Casa** (AC B CC D GLM MA WE) Wed-Sat 21-?h
Rua Congonhas 487- Santo Antônio ☎ (031) 3296-5942
🖳 www.andaluzbarcasa.com.br/site
■ **Eros Mix Club** (B D DR G r ST t) Wed-Sun 22-5h
Rua Aimorés 1840 *Lourdes* ☎ (031) 3222-4002
■ **Josefine** (! AC B D G SNU ST YC) Fri 21-5, Sat 23-6h
Rua Antônio de Albuquerque, 729 *Savassi* ☎ (031) 3225-2307
🖳 www.josefine.com.br
■ **UP!** (AC B CC D GLM WE) Fri & Sat midnight-?h
Av. Getúlio Vargas 1423

RESTAURANTS

■ **Cafe do Museu** (AC CC M NG) Wed-Sun 11h-midnight
Av. Prudente de Morais 202

SEX SHOPS/BLUE MOVIES

■ **Cine Regina** (G MA) Daily
Rua Bahia 484
■ **Video Boy Club** (G) 9-20h
Rua Paraiba, 330 Sala 1008, Savassi *Central Shopping Centre* ☎ (031) 3274-6282
Videos & DVDs.

SAUNAS/BATHS

■ **Sauna 24hrs** (B CC DR DU G MA NU p PI SA SB WH) 24hrs
Rua Timbiras, 2523 - Santo Agostinho *Lourdes* ☎ (031) 3275-2001
Diverse possibilities to get there by bus.
■ **Specific** (B DU FC FH G m MSG R RR SA SB VS) 14-23h
Avenida Álvares Cabral 950, Lourdes ☎ (031) 3337-5787
■ **Très Chic** (! B CC DR DU G GH MA P SA SB VS) Daily 14-22h
Rua Timbiras, 2040, Centro ☎ (031) 3226 7896
By far the best and most recently renovated sauna in Belo Horizonte. Cool bar, hot and clean steam bath with overlooking the bar. No go-go boys, rare in Belo Horizonte. Sundays very busy especially for the low prices. Very clean and large room upstairs.

GENERAL GROUPS

■ **Clube Rainbow** (G) Tue-Fri 14-18, Sat -20h
Av. Francisco Sá 830, SL-Prado
Publisher of the local monthly newspaper „Jornal Rainbow", free in gay venues.

CRUISING

-Avenida Alfonso Pena (from Rodoviaria to the town hall)
-Rua Goitacazes
-Parque Municipal (afternoon)
-Igreja de Lourdes (at night, R)
-Praçao da Liberdade (Funcionários)
- Shoppings Cidade (Rua Tupis, 337 - Centro), Diamond Mall (Avenida Olegário Maciel, 1600 - Lourdes) (Sat afternoon)
-'Little'/ ,Ferrorama' (Centro): Quarteirão, ruas Espírito Santo, Guajajaras, Rio de Janeiro e Tupis (Block made up by these streets at night) (R).

Blumenau – Santa Catarina ☎ 47

SAUNAS/BATHS

■ **Bruno** (B DU G MSG RR SA SB) Fri & Sat 16-23, Sun and days before public holiday 16-22h
Rua Presidente Vargas - 173 *Centro* ☎ (47) 3322-8054
🖳 www.brunosauna.com.br

Brasilia – Distrito Federal ☎ 061

BARS

■ **Barulho** (B G MA)
Quiosque nº 2, atrás da pista Carrera Kart
■ **Beirute** (B G MA)
109 Sul - Bloco A - Loja 2 / 4

CAFES

■ **Savana** (B glm M MA OS) 19-1h, closed Sun
SCLN 116 Bloco A Loja 4 ☎ (061) 347-9403

DANCECLUBS

■ **Garagem** (B D GLM WE) Fri-Sat 23-?h
SOF/Sul Quadra 16 - Cj. A - Lote 5/6 ☎ (061) 9970-7184

SAUNAS/BATHS

■ **Soho** (B cc DR DU FH G m MSG P r RR SA SB VS) 16-23h
SCS, Quadra 5, Bloco A, Subsolo 34 *Nicolas Caminha Building, close to Banco de Brasilia* ☎ (061) 3323-7799
Very friendly sauna with a high standard of hygiene.

CRUISING

-Parque Agua Mineral (swimming pools with warm mineral water; anywhere near the pool or the waterfall. Avoid toilets: military police!)
-Conjunto Nacional Shopping Mall, Commercial Sector South. Cruisy toilets: downstairs near middle of mall; upstairs on exterior terrace. Constant action. Located opp. main bus terminal
-Patio Brasil Shopping Center (YC toilets cruisy).

Brejoes – Bahia ☎ 075

HOTELS

■ **Cafe Club Brasil** (B GLM I M MA OS PI) All year
Cafe Club Hotel Facienda, CX005 *8 km to the city of Brejoes, 180 km to Intern. Airport Salvador* ☎ (075) 3654-2235 🖳 www.cafeclubbrasil.com
The first Gay-Resort in Brazil. For all who like the countryside with tropical nature, healthy food, exotic drinks at the pool. Portuguese, Spanish, English, German, Italian spoken

Búzios – Rio de Janeiro ☏ 22

RESTAURANTS

■ **Sawasdee** (B CC G M MA OS)
Av. José Bento Ribeiro Dantas 422, Orla Bardot ☏ (22) 2623-4644
www.sawasdee.com.br
A fantastic Thai restaurant with excellent cuisine and a wonderful seaside location. The staff is very gay-friendly and helpful and the dishes are of a very high quality.

GUEST HOUSES

■ **Our House** (AC b BF cc GLM PI PK RWB RWS RWT) All year
Ferradura *10 mins walk to the beach or the town centre*
☏ (22) 2623-1913 www.ourhousebrazil.com
■ **Pedrera. La** (AC B GLM I M MA OS PI PK RWB RWS RWT SA WH) All year
Rua 4, Cuadra C, Joao Fernandes ☏ (22) 2623-4753
www.lapedrerabuzios.com.br

Cabo Frio – Rio de Janeiro ☏ 022

DANCECLUBS

■ **Elite** (B D glm MA) Fri & Sat
Rua Henrique Terra 83

Campinas – São Paulo ☏ 019

BARS

■ **Oásis Video Bar** (B GLM MA) Wed-Sun 21-?h
Rua Antonio Alvares Lobo, 507 *Borough Botafogo* ☏ (019) 3232-4644
■ **Subway** (B glm MA) Thu-Sun 20-?h
Rua Maria Monteiro 30 *Borough Cambuí* ☏ (019) 3251-8781
www.clubsubway.com.br

DANCECLUBS

■ **Double Face** (B D g S ST) Fri-Sun
Rua Barão de Jaguara, 358 - Centro ☏ (019) 3236-7361
www.doubleface.com.br

SAUNAS/BATHS

■ **Atlântida** (B CC DU G M MA MSG PI SA SB VS WE WO) 14.30-23h
Rua Duque de Caxias, 536 - Centro *Near Largo do Pará*
☏ (019) 3232-0228 www.thermasatlantida.com.br
For those who don't want to use the sauna facilities there is a minimum consumption fee of R$ 15.-. Every 2nd Sunday/month special events including a dinner.

Campo Grande – Mato Grosso do Sul ☏ 067

SAUNAS/BATHS

■ **Thermas Ibiza Sauna** (B cc DR DU f G I m MSG RR SA SB SNU VS) 16-22, Sat 15-22, Sun -21h
Rua 14 de Julho 1212, Centro *Near to Av. Fernando Correa da Costa*
☏ (067) 3325-7035 www.thermasibiza.com
Discreet ambiance.

Canoa Quebrada – Ceará ☏ 088

HOTELS

■ **Pousada N. Horizonte** (G OS) All year
Rua Broadway ☏ (088) 342 17 305
Three double bedrooms, each with private bathroom and WC as well as a large terrace. Pousada in Brazilian style in the centre of Canoa Quebrada.

Chapecó – Santa Catarina ☏ 049

BARS

■ **Panacéia** (B glm)
Rua Porto Alegre 151 D - Centro ☏ (049) 9997-6782

Cuiabá – Mato Grosso ☏ 65

SAUNAS/BATHS

■ **Fifty Seven Club** (B DR DU FC FH G m MA MSG OS RR SA SB VS) Mon-Sat 16-22, Sun & public holidays 15-20h
Rua Jessé Pinto Freire 57 - Centro *Centre of town* ☏ (65) 3027-1577
www.saunaclub57.com.br

Curitiba – Paraná ☏ 041

BARS

■ **Side Caffe Bar** (B CC F GLM M MA S) Tue-Sun evenings
Alameda Cabral, 613, Centro ☏ (041) 3222-71511

CAFES

■ **Café do Teatro** (B CC F MA NG) Open every evening
Rua Amintas de Barros, 154, Centro ☏ (041) 3233-3920

DANCECLUBS

■ **Cats Club** (! AC B CC D DR GLM MA S SNU ST VS) Thu-Sat nights
Alameda Dr. Muricy, 949, Centro ☏ (041) 3224-5912
www.catsnightclub.com.br
■ **New SPM** (B D DR GLM MA S ST T) Fri & Sat nights
Rua Fernando Moreira, 185, Centro ☏ (041) 3225-1053
Former Acya.
■ **Skip Cat's** (B D GLM MA) Sat & Sun nights
Rua Saldanha Marinho, 206 ☏ (041) 3224-5912
■ **Studio 1001** (B CC D DR GLM MA S SNU ST T) Tue-Sat nights
Alameda Dr. Muricy, 1001 - Centro ☏ (041) 3018-1662

SEX CINEMAS

■ **Cine Morgenau** (G MA T VS)
Rua Conselheiro Laurindo, 1008, Centro ☏ (041) 232-5943
■ **Dragon Vídeo Box** (b G MC VS) Daily 22-?h
Rua Voluntários da Pátria, 475 ☏ (041) 3225-1496
www.dragoncwb.com.br

SAUNAS/BATHS

■ **Caracala** (B DR DU F FC FH G MA P RR SA SB VS) Daily 16-23h
Rua Alferes Poli 1039, Rebouças ☏ (041) 3333-6766
Sauna and bar. Guest in the bar can watch the boys shower.
■ **Opinião** (AC B CC DR DU F FH G m MA MSG P R RR S SA SB SNU VS WH WO) 16-24h
Rua Amintas de Barros 749, Alto da Rua XV *Near Hospital Osualdo Cruz*
☏ (041) 3262-1982
■ **Sauna 520** (AC B CC DR DU FC FH G m MSG R RR SA SB VS WH) 16-23, Fri & Sat -24h
Avenida Souza Naves 520, Cristo Rei *800 m from the station*
☏ (041) 3262-4582 www.sauna520.com.br
■ **Sauna Batel** (B DU G MSG P SA VS WE) Mon-Sat 16-23h
Teixeira Coelho, 35, Batel *Between Av. Batel and R. Dom Pedro II*
☏ (041) 3244-4251 www.saunabatel.com.br
Not a special and big sauna but reasonable clean. Actually is known as a hetero sauna, but everything goes there. There are some Rest cabins where even gang bangs happen!

CRUISING

-Rua XV de Novembre (square at the end of Rua das Flores)
-Park (Bosque do Papa - Bosque João Paulo II) in city centre - AYOR
-Botanical gardens Francisca Maria Garfunkel Rischbieter - AYOR
-Park Barigui, near station Viário do Campina de Siqueira - AYOR
-Park São Lourenço, Avenida Mateus Leme - AYOR.

Florianópolis – Santa Catarina ☏ 048

BARS

■ **Bar do Deca** (B GLM MA)
Praia Mole *Last bar to the left side of the beach*

Opens Dec-April, occasionally at weekends during the year. Beach bar on famous Praia Mole, the favorite LGBT spot during summer.

■ **Barbarella Lounge Bar** (B G MC) Wed-Sat 10-?h
Rua Saldanha Marinho, 351 *Corner with Anita Garibaldi – Downtown*
☎ (048) 3207-5666
Brand new lounge bar, another option for pre-clubbing downtown. Popular with a gay-friendly mixed crowd.

■ **Caravana** (B gLm MA)
Avenida das Rendeiras, 1672 - Lagoa da Conceição ☎ (048) 9154-6530
Fusion food and trailer – daily in summer, Wed-Sunday all year around. Call for opening times. The only openly lesbian bar in Floripa. Live music most days and a good mixed crowd. A great option for a happy hour on the way back from Praia Mole.

■ **Jivago Lounge** (B d GLM MA)
Rua Leoberto Leal, 04 *Downtown* ☎ (048) 3028-0788
🖳 www.jivagolounge.com
From Thursday to Sundays. Bar and a small dance floor. Favored by a more upmarket G&L crowd as a pre-club option.

■ **Rancho do Maneca** (B d GLM MA)
Rodovia SC 405 km1 ☎ (048) 3234-9295
The only alternative to the electronic scene, a traditional bar for country-loving boys of all ages that has karaoke nights, a pool table and live music. Mainly for men, but occasionally has women-only parties. Call for opening times.

CAFES

■ **Café das Artes** (AC BF CC H MA)
Mon-Fri 11.30-23, Sat & Sun 16-23h
Rua Esteves Junior, 734 *Centro* ☎ (048) 3223-0690

■ **GF** (b glm m MA)
Rua Afonso Delambert Neto - Lagoa da Conceição ☎ (048) 3232-6683

DANCECLUBS

■ **Concorde Club** (B D glm MA) Sat 23-?h
Av Rio Branco, 729 Centro ☎ (048) 3222-1981
🖳 www.concordeclub.com.br

■ **Mix Café Club** (AC B D DR GLM m MA S SNU ST)
Fri & Sun 23-?h & before public holidays and carnival
Rua Menino Deus, 47 ☎ (048) 3324-0102 🖳 www.mixcafe.com.br

RESTAURANTS

■ **Bistro and Guesthouse Isadora Duncan** (B glm H M)
Mon-Sat 19-1h
Rod. Jornalista Manuel de Menezes, 2658 ☎ (048) 3232 7210
🖳 www.bistroisadoraduncan.com.br
Intimate beachside restaurant, there are only five tables and a veranda, very cozy environment. They have a few lovely rooms too.

■ **It's Italian - (Tratoria do Guto)** (b g M MC)
Avenida Hercílio Luz, 1169 *Centro* ☎ (048) 3224-0974
🖳 www.itsitalian.com.br

SEX SHOPS/BLUE MOVIES

■ **Hunter Video Club** (cc DR g MC) Mon-Fri 11-22, Sat & Sun 15-22h
Rua Padre Roma, 431, Centro *3rd floor* ☎ (048) 3228-5868
Cinema with porn films. Private cubicles and more.

SEX CINEMAS

■ **Magia Video Club** (AC B DR G H MA SNU VS)
Mon-Fri 12-23, Sat & Sun 15-23h
Rua Hoepck, 76 ☎ (048) 3025-6039

SAUNAS/BATHS

■ **Hangar** (B cc DR DU G MSG PI R S SA SB ST VS) 15-23h
Rua Henrique Valgas, 112 *Centro* ☎ (048) 3225-5858
In a large, re-designed storage hall. Everything is in good order and is clean.

■ **Oceano** (B DR DU FH G m MC MSG RR SA SB VS WO) 15-23h
Rua Luiz Delfino, 231 *Near to Shopping Centre Beiramar*
☎ (048) 3222-4547 🖳 thermasoceanoflorianopolis.blogspot.com
A small sauna with all the necessary equipment with a middle aged clientele. No rent boys.

TRAVEL AND TRANSPORT

■ **Brazil Ecojourneys** (GLM)
Estrada Rozalia Paulina Ferreira 1132 ☎ (48) 33895619
🖳 www.brazilecojourneys.com

HOTELS

■ **Pousada Pau de Canela** (AC b BF CC H m MA MSG NU OS p WH) 24hrs
Rua Pau de Canela 606, Rio Tavares *Close to the beachs and near the Rio Tavares shopping center* ☎ (048) 3233-4989
🖳 www.pousadapaudecanela.com.br
A small luxury hotel only minutes from the most spectacular gay beaches and nightlife in Lagoa da Conceição.

GUEST HOUSES

■ **Pousada Natur Campeche** (BF CC glm H MC MSG OS PI SA WH) All year
Servidão Família Nunes, 59, Campeche ☎ (048) 3237-4011
🖳 www.naturcampeche.com.br

SWIMMING

-Praia Mole (left corner in front of Bar do Deca)
-Praia Galheta, 500 m north of Praia Mole (g NU)

Fortaleza – Ceará ☎ 085

BARS

■ **Barraca do Joca** (! B GLM m) 18-2h
Avenida Beira Mar, 3101, barraca 25-a *Praia do Nautico, opp. Hotel Beira-Mar* ☎ (085) 9969-2740

DANCECLUBS

■ **Divine** (! B D DR G m MA OS S SNU ST t VS) Wed-Thu 19-24, Fri-Sat 22.30-5, Sun 17.30-1h
Rua General Sampaio 1374, Centro ☎ (085) 3221-6435
The only place that is open and busy on a Sunday.

SAUNAS/BATHS

■ **California Club** (B CC DR DU FC FH G m MSG R RR S SA SB VS WO) 15-23h
Rua Barbara de Alencar 424, Centro ☎ (085) 3226-6556
🖳 www.californiathermas.com.br
Nice animated environment. One of the busiest but not the best sauna in Fortaleza working with many escorts. Special events from Wed-Sun.

■ **Dragon Health Club** (! B CC DR DU FC FH G I LM M MC MSG OS PI RR SA SB SH SOL VS WI) Daily 16-23h
Rua Almirante Jaceguai, 239, Praia de Iracema *Continuation of Av. dom Manuel* ☎ (085) 3219-1052 🖳 www.dragonclubfortaleza.com.br
A fantastic place, also beauty center and foot care. Sun with live music. Pool and solarium with bar service.

■ **Termas 2000** (! B cc DU FC FH G I m MSG RR SA SB VS) 14-23h
Rua Rocha Lima 1186, corner C./ Br. de Aracatí *Near the Ginásio Paulo Sarasate* ☎ (085) 3261-5077 🖳 www.termas2000.com.br
Happy hour until 18h.

■ **Via Centro** (b cc DR DU G SA SB SOL VS WO) 15-23h
Rua Tristão Gonçalves 744 ☎ (085) 3454-1499
🖳 www.viacentrothermas.com.br

HOTELS

■ **Sunflower Pousada-Hotel**
(AC BF CC glm H I MA OS p PK RWS VA) All year
Rua Silva Paulet, 300 *200 m from Avenida Beira Mar*
☎ (085) 3248-2427 🖳 www.sunflower-hotel.com
Wireless LAN Internet available. Friendly smart hotel with 18 suites.

APARTMENTS

■ **Residence Tabosa** (G OS PK RWB RWS RWT VA) All year
Ria Antonio Sugusto, 483, Apt , 1801, Praia de Iracema
☎ (085) 3248-7506

SWIMMING

-Praia de Iracema
-Praia Canoa Quebrada (NU) (several hours from the city)
-Praia do Cumbuco (nu) (in the dunes at the far western end, 1 hour from the city, near Icarai)
-Praia Jericoacoara (several hours to the west of the city)
-Praia do Futuro, Barraca Cabumba (WE) in the middle of the long beach next to the wind-cone.

CRUISING

-New Stone Jetty between Iracema and Meireles at the beginning of the Avenida Beira Mar de Meireles (after sunset)
-Southwest corner of the Praça do Ferreira
-Praça do Carmo (behind the church)
-Along the downtown section of Duque de Caixas Avenue
-Downtown cinemas (by the entrances and in the toilets).

Goiânia – Goiás ☎ 062

DANCECLUBS

■ **Disel Lounge** (AC B g YC)
Rua 5, 1155 *Setor Oeste* ☎ (062) 3215-2307
🖳 www.diselbrasil.com.br

Guarujá – São Paulo ☎ 013

CRUISING

-Seashore promenade around the facilities in city centre
-Beach 30 km west of the city.

Itacoatiara – Amazonas ☎ 092

GUEST HOUSES

■ **Amazonclub** (b BF g I M MA) All year
Vila de Lindoia, AM010 KM 183 from Manaus *Located 183 km from Manaus at a little lake of river Urubu* ☎ (092) 529-1040
🖳 www.amazonclub.net
Small, luxurious hotel in the rain forest. Swiss management. Internet connection via satelite. Jungle tours and boat rides available.

João Pessoa – Paraíba ☎ 083

SAUNAS/BATHS

■ **Thermas Parahyba** (AC b CC DU G I m MA MSG P SA SB SOL VS)
Tue-Sun 16-23h
Rua Duque de Caxias, 8 *Centro historico* ☎ (083) 3242-3726
🖳 www.thpb.com.br
New sauna. Steam room, lounge, WIFI, video room, relaxation room. Private parking, smoking area outside.

SWIMMING

-Praia da Tambaba (first „official" nude beach in the northeast; about 48km south of the town).

Joinville – Santa Catarina ☎ 047

DANCECLUBS

■ **Ivyx Club Mix** (D GLM)
Av. Procópio Gomes, 602

SAUNAS/BATHS

■ **Joinville** (B CC DU G MA MSG RR SA SB SOL VS WE) 15-22h
Rua Independencia, 721, Bairro Anita Garibaldi *Behind the bus station*
☎ (047) 3455-4681

Juiz de Fora – Minas Gerais ☎ 032

BARS

■ **Muzik** (B g MA)
Rua Espírito Santo, 1.081, Centro *Centro* ☎ (032) 3213-9796
🖳 www.muzik.com.br

GENERAL GROUPS

■ **MGM – Movimento Gay de Minas**
Rua São Sebastião, 345/2°andar *Centro* 🖳 www.mgm.org.br

Macapá – Amapá ☎ 096

CRUISING

-The jetty (activity on promenade)
-Zoological gardens and steps to the cathedral on a small hill, downtown
-Avenida Ribeiros.

Maceió – Alagoas ☎ 082

SAUNAS/BATHS

■ **Eros** (B DU FC FH G m MSG RR S SA SB VS) 17-23h
Rua Silvério Jorge, 563 - Praça Sinimbú *Near the Museu Theo Brandão*
☎ (082) 3221-4601 🖳 www.erosthermas.com.br

HOTELS

■ **Pousada Cavalo Marinho** (B BF glm OS RWS RWT VA WO) 24hrs
Rua da Praia, 55, Riacho Doce *Waterfront of Riacho Doce beach*
☎ (082) 3355-1247 🖳 www.pousadacavalomarinho.com
Gay owned. Owner speaks English, German and French. Canoes and bicycles available.

SWIMMING

-Praia de Ponta Verde (YC) (popular)
-Jatiúca (in front of Praia Verde Hotel)
-Ilha do Croa (NU) (across the river at Barra de Santo Antonio).

CRUISING

-Praça Sinimbú (Avenida Duque de Caxias, evenings)
-The following Praias: de Jatiúca, do Francês, de Pajuçara, da Avenida, de Sacarecica and Praia do Sabral.

Manaus – Amazonas ☎ 092

DANCECLUBS

■ **Boate dos Ingleses / Turbo Seven**
(AC B D DR glm MA S ST T VS WE) Sat & Sun 23-7h
Boulevard Vivaldo, 33 *Near Museu do Porto* ☎ (092) 3232-6793
■ **Club A2** (AC B CC D DR GLM MA OS SNU ST T) Fri & Sat 23-7h
Saldanha Marinho 780, Centro *By the Alex bar on Getulio Vargas Ave*
☎ (092) 3294-7373
Sunday special opening at 20h. Male strippers. A great place. For more details see: www.a2manaus.com

SAUNAS/BATHS

■ **H2O** (AC B cc DR DU FC G m MSG PI R RR SB SOL VS YC) 15-23h
Rua José Paranaguá, 657 *Near Chaminé Theatre* ☎ (092) 3234-6099
Many locals, best in the afternoon.

TRAVEL AND TRANSPORT

■ **Amazon Mystery Tours** (GLM)
Avenida Djalma Batista, 385, sala 303-A, N.S. das Graças
☎ (092) 3633-7844 🖳 www.amazon-outdoor.com
Organizes tours, books hotels for gays & lesbians all over Brazil. Booking only in advance. A receptive travel agency and tour operator.

HEALTH GROUPS

■ **Coordenação estadual DST-AIDS** (glm) 8-12 & 14-17h
c/o Hospital Tropical, Avenida Pedro Teixeira, 25, Dom Pedro
☎ (092) 3238-8375

CRUISING

-Ponta Negra beach (afternoons only)
-At the end of the beach by the „Coco gelado" stands (downstairs)
-300 m after „Coco gelado" in the direction of downtown (AYOR)
-Downtown (harbour area and bus terminal, AYOR)
-In the Amazonas Shopping Centre (in the toilets of the cinema on 2nd floor & in the toilets of post office „correios"). Security guards check sometimes.

Marília – São Paulo ☎ 014

BARS

■ **Ópera Club** (B G MC S ST) Sat & holidays 23.30-?h
Rua Bahia, 501 ☎ (014) 3432-2766 🖳 www.operaclub.com.br
For those over 18 with ID.

Natal – Rio Grande do Norte ☎ 084

DANCECLUBS

■ **Vogue** (B CC D G S SNU WE) Fri & Sat 22-?h
Rua Presidente Bandeira 385, Alecrim ☎ (084) 213-2853
🖳 www.voguenatal.com.br

SAUNAS/BATHS

■ **Eunápius Club** (B DR DU FH G M PI PP RR SA SB VS WO) 17-23h
Rua dos Tororós 2535, Lagoa Nova *Near CEASA, 10 mins from Natal Shopping and near bus terminal* ☎ (084) 234-8246
Modern and nice garden, out-door swimming pool, bar, clean, recommended. Monday reduced entrance fee.

■ **Rio Branco** (B DR DU G m MA OS p PI RR SB SH VS) 16-22, Fri-Sun 15-6h
Avenida Rio Branco, 821 ☎ (084) 201-2086
In city center, basic facilities, rather run down place.

■ **Termas Sol Natal** (b DR DU FC FH G I M MA MSG OS R RR SA SB SOL VS) 16-22h, Mon closed
Rua Coronel Flamínio, 42 - Santos Reis ☎ (084) 3202-9701
🖳 www.termassol.com.br
With a modern interior on three floors. Special events like bingo or live music on offer. Many escorts work here.

CRUISING

-Beach behind Morro de Careca, 15 mins on cruisy footpath starting at the big dune at Southern end of Ponte Negra Beach (afternoon, AYOR)
-on the beach between the Pestana Hotel and the Searhs Hotel around 16-23h.

Niterói – Rio de Janeiro ☎ 021

SWIMMING

-Itaipu
-Recanto de Itaipuaçu.

CRUISING

-São Francisco Beach and Ica Beach (from ferry take bus »Canto de Rio«).

Olinda – Pernambuco ☎ 081

HOTELS

■ **Pousada D'Olinda**
(AC b BF CC glm M MA PI PK RWB RWS RWT SOL VA) All year
Rua Prudente de Morais, 178, Praca Joao Alfredo Carmo
Opp. San Pedro church, bus exit Carmo ☎ (081) 3494 2559
🖳 www.pousadadolinda.com.br

SWIMMING

-Janga (behind the bridge over Rio Doce direction Janga)
-Pau Amarelo
-Itamaraca Island (beach) (a few miles from Olinda, easily accessible by bus, action possible at far end of the beach).

CRUISING

-Beach at Praia da Enseada (from afternoon, opposite Rio Doce).

Porto Alegre – Rio Grande Do Sul ☎ 051

BARS

■ **Neo** (B G S) Fri & Sat 23-?h
Av. Plínio Brasil Milano, 427 *Auxiliadora*

■ **Sunga** (B D DR G S)
Av. Cristovão Colombo 772, Floresta ☎ (051) 3286-2408
🖳 www.sungabar.com.br
Also at the beach in Tramandaí, Rua 15 de Novembro N°289 ☎ 684-3981.

■ **Venezianos** (AC B GLM M MA OS S) Tue-Sun 18-2h
Rua Joaquim Nabuco, 397 - Cidade Baixa ☎ (051) 3221-9275
🖳 www.venezianos.com.br
Tue: karaoke, Thu: show, live music

MEN'S CLUBS

■ **Eroticos Videos** (B d DR G MA SA SB SNU VS)
Mon-Fri 11-22, Sat & Sun 14-22h
Avenida Júlio de Castilhos, 648 ☎ (051) 3286-2479
Bar & blue movies with cabins upstairs. Mon, Wed & Fri show at 19h. Tea dance on Sun from 14h. Entrance for those over 18 only!

DANCECLUBS

■ **Cabaret Indiscretus** (AC B D DR G MA R SNU ST)
Tue-Sun 23.30-?h
Avenida Brasil, 1393 *São Geraldo* ☎ (051) 3222-3856

■ **Cine-Theatro Ypiranga** (B D glm MA S)
Av Cristóvão Colombo, 772 ☎ (051) 3286-2408
🖳 www.cinetheatro.com.br
Over 800 square meters, two bars, mezzanine, offering besides parties: cultural shows, plays, exhibitions, check website for current events.

■ **Ocidente** (AC B D G m MA S WE)
Avenida Osvaldo Aranha, 960,1

■ **Refugiu's Mega Danceteria** (! B cc D DR G I OS S)
Fri & Sat 23-?h
Rua Marcilio Dias, 290 - Menino Deus *Menino Deus* ☎ (051) 3231-3158
🖳 www.refugiusmegadanceteria.com.br
Two dancefloors on more than 700 m². Gogo boys, 3 bars, outdoor terrace and garden as well as regular shows.

■ **Vitraux Club** (B CC D G M MA SNU ST WE)
Tue-Thu 18-2, Fri & Sat 23-6h
Rua Conceição, 496 ☎ (051) 3221-7799 🖳 www.vitraux.com.br
Also café & bar with shows and 2 dance floors.

SAUNAS/BATHS

■ **Arpoador** (AC B DR DU FC FH G m MA RR SA SB VS) 15-23h
Rua Prof. Ivo Corseuil, 210, Petrópolis *Next to Jardim Botanico*
☎ (051) 3338-4306 🖳 www.saunaarpoador.com.br
Condoms and lube for free.

■ **Convés Sauna Clube** (AC DR DU FC FH G MA RR SB VS)
12-22, Sat -20, Sun 13-21h
Avenida Mauá 1897, Centro *Downtown, near central bus station*
☎ (051) 3286-7820 🖳 www.convessaunaclube.com
Condoms and lube for free.

■ **Plataforma**
(B DR DU FC FH G m MA MSG PP R RR S SA SB VS WH) 15-24h
Avenida Pernambuco, 2765, Bairro São Geraldo ☎ (051) 3395-1633

■ **Point Sul** (AC B CC DU FC FH G I MA MSG OS RR SA SB SOL VS)
13.30-22.30h
Rua Cabral 468, Bairro Rio Branco ☎ (051) 3331-6324
🖳 www.thermaspointsul.com.br

■ **Sauna Floresta** (b DU G I MA MSG SA SB WO) 15-22h
Rua Dr. Valle 88, Bairro Floresta *Near cnr. Av. Christovão Colombo*
☎ (051) 3312-6248 🖳 www.saunafloresta.com
Friendly and clean sauna that attracts bears and their admirers.

GENERAL GROUPS

■ **NUANCES - Grupo pela Livre Expressão Sexual**
Tue & Wed 19-21.30h
Praça Rui Barbosa, 220 - sala 52 ☎ (051) 3286-3325

■ **Somos**
Rua Jacinto Gomes, 378 ☎ (051) 3233-8423 🖳 www.somos.org.br
LGBT forum for Porto Alegre. Organizes the Gay Pride which takes place in June each year.

CRUISING

-Praça Da Alfandega (toilets)
-Rua dos Andradas
-Avenida Borges de Medeiros
-Rua Salgado Filho
-Avenida Independencia
-Ipanema Bathing Resort (close to town)
-Belem Novo Bathing Resort
-Avenida Jose Bonifácio (opp. Parque Farroupilha, car necessary)
-Parque Marinha do Brasil-Avenida Beida Rio (a car is useful to get here)
-Parque da Redenção
-Parque Farroupilha (park is dangerous at night)
-Rua da Praia Shopping.

Recife – Pernambuco ☎ 081

CINEMA

■ **Cine Boa Vista** (B GLM MA S t VS) Fri-Sun 21h
Rua Corredor do Bispo, 131, Boa Vista ☎ (081) 3222-9008
🖳 www.cineboavista.com

DANCECLUBS

■ **Métropole** (AC B CC D GLM MA S SNU WE) Fri & Sat 22-?h
Rua das Ninfas 125 *Boa Vista* ☎ (081) 3423-0123
🖳 www.metropoledance.com.br
Flashy disco on 3 floors, upper class.

■ **MKB (Meu Kaso Bar)** (B D DR GLM OS S WE) Thu-Sun 21-6h
Rua Oliveira Lima 778 *Boa Vista* ☎ (081) 3223-0921
🖳 www.meukasobar.com.br
2 dancefloors, terrace with Brazilian music, very relaxed and friendly place.

SEX CINEMAS

■ **Cine Mix** (B DR G MA OS r s VS) Daily 9-24h
Rua da Soledade 352, Boa Vista ☎ (081) 3231-7047

■ **Imperador** (g VS) Daily 9-24h
Rua do Imperador s/n, San Antonio

SAUNAS/BATHS

■ **Blue Thermas** (B DR DU FH G I m MSG R RR s SA SB VS)
15-23, Fri & Sat -24h
Rua José Domingues da Silva 147, Boa Viagem *In south Recife, at the Boa Viagem Beach* ☎ (081) 3462-3707 🖳 www.bluethermas.com.br
Free internet access for clients.

■ **Termas 111** (B cc DR DU MSG PI R RR SA SB VS) 15-23h
Rua Corredor do Bispo 111, Boa Vista ☎ (081) 3223-5883
🖳 www.pousadapeter.com.br/index_gaythermas.htm
Wed (20h) „Boy-Bingo"; live sex show Sun (20h) with dancing and drag. Not particularly clean but a fun place.

■ **Termas Boa Vista** (B CC DR DU I LAB M MSG R RR SA SB SOL VS)
15-23, Fri & Sat 15-6h
Rua Don Manoel Pereira 63, Boa Vista *Near CELPE* ☎ (081) 3423-3404
🖳 www.termasboavista.com.br
Big and popular sauna. Friendly staff. Free internet access.

GUEST HOUSES

■ **Banana Country** (B BF CC GLM I M OS PA PI PK RWB RWS RWT SA VA WH) All year
Estrada de Itapuama s/n, Cabo de Santo Agostinho *22km from Recife Airport* ☎ (081) 3522-9183 🖳 www.bananacountryclub.com
Beautiful place in the middle of the jungle and few metres from wonderful beaches. Gay owned & operated. 6 languages spoken.

SWIMMING

- ☞ Olinda
-Gaibu Beach , southern end, especially rocks towards Calhetas (1 hour south of Recife by bus from in front of the airport, change in Cabo de Santo Agostinho), at night
-Praia de Candeias
-Praia de Itamaraca
-Praia de Boa Viagem, in front of Hotel Savaroni near volleyball courts north of Praça Boa Viagem.

CRUISING

-Avenida Conde de Boa Vista (AYOR r) (day and night)
-Avenida Boa Viagem north of Praça Boa Viagem, afternoon and night (AYOR, R)
-Praça de Casa Forte (AYOR, at night)
-Shopping Center Recife (near C&A, ground floor)
-Parque 13 de maio (in the evening)
-Cais de Santa Rita (AYOR, at night)
-Patio de Sao Pedro (meeting point on Tuesday).

Rio de Janeiro ☎ 021

Rio is one of the most exciting cities in the world. The fantastic beaches and mountains provide a perfect setting - the city is aptly named „The Wonderful City". With over 6 million people, Rio is big by any standards. It's also very cosmopolitan, with a rich cultural life and history. Gay attractions are mostly concentrated in the beach neighbourhoods of Copacabana and Ipanema, making the city very easy to master. Copacabana is where most hotels are concentrated. You will also find here nightclubs, bars, baths and more. Ipanema is a smaller and more sophisticated version, with world-class shopping, restaurants and cafes. Sunday at the gay beach in Ipanema is a must!
Carnival is Rio's main event, with almost a week of non-stop partying. New Year's Eve in Copacabana is also very big. A good safety tip is never taking strangers back to your hotel room - go to one of the many sex hotels instead.

Rio gehört zu den aufregendsten Weltstädten und gilt als Tor zu Brasilien. Die prachtvollen Strände und Berge schaffen ein malerisches Panorama. Deshalb wird Rio auch „Die wunderbare Stadt" genannt und ist mit über sechs Millionen Einwohnern eine echte Metropole.
Mit ihrem breiten Kulturangebot und ihrer Geschichte ist sie eine weltoffene Stadt. Da die meisten schwulen Treffpunkte an der Copacabana und Ipanema sind, finden sich Besucher in Rio sehr gut zurecht. An der Copacabana gibt es die meisten Hotels. Hier gibt es auch Nachtclubs, Bars, Saunen und öffentliche Einrichtungen.
Ipanema dagegen ist kleiner und feiner und hat viele erstklassige Möglichkeiten zum Shoppen, Restaurants und Cafés. Der Sonntag am Schwulenstrand Ipanema ist ein Muss! Beim „Strandtest" tummeln sich viele gutgebaute Cariocas, also: Sonnenbrille auf, um beim Hinstieren nicht aufzufallen. Der Karneval in Rio ist natürlich das Hauptereignis, denn hier wird quasi eine Woche lang non-stop durchgefeiert. Auch der Silvesterabend an der Copacabana ist immer ein Erlebnis.
Allerdings ist davon abzuraten, fremde Bekanntschaften mit auf das Hotelzimmer zu nehmen. Es empfiehlt sich eher, auf eines der zahlreichen Sexhotels auszuweichen.

Rio fait partie des villes du monde les plus intéressantes et figure de porte sur le Brésil. Ses splendides plages forment un panorama pittoresque et ses 6 millions d'habitants font d'elle une vraie métropole. C'est à juste titre qu'on la nomme „ la ville formidable „.
De par sa culture et son histoire, Rio est une ville ouverte sur le monde. La plupart des lieux gays sont situés à Copacabana et Ipanema, les visiteurs se trouvent ainsi à bonne adresse, puisque c'est à Copacabana que se trouvent presque tous les hôtels. On y trouve également des boîtes, des bars, des saunas et une multitude de monuments.
Ipanema est par contre plus petit et plus chic et offre la possibilité de faire les boutiques, de manger dans les très bons restaurants ou encore

de s'installer à un café. Le dimanche sur la plage homo d'Ipanema est un must à ne pas manquer !

Les nombreux cariocas aux corps de rêve qui viennent faire la fête sur la plage sont un régal pour les yeux, n'oubliez pas vos lunettes de soleil pour ne pas vous faire trop remarquer ! Le carnaval de Rio est bien sûr l'événement de l'année car on le fête presque une semaine entière sans interruption. Le réveillon de la Saint-Sylvestre à Copacabana est également à ne pas manquer.

Malgré toutes ces remarques positives, il est préférable de ne pas emmener quelqu'un dans son hôtel mais d'aller dans un des nombreux hôtels de la ville réservés à cet usage .

Río está entre las ciudades del mundo más excitantes y está considerada la puerta de Brasil. Las magníficas playas y montañas conforman un panorama muy pintoresco. Por ello, a Río también se le llama „la ciudad maravillosa" y es, con más de 6 millones de habitantes, una auténtica metrópolis.

Con su amplia oferta cultural y su historia, es una ciudad abierta al mundo. Como la mayoría de puntos de encuentro gay están en Copacabana y en Ipanema, los turistas quedan muy cerca. En Copacabana se encuentra la mayoría de los hoteles. Aquí están también los clubes nocturnos, bares, saunas y otros edificios públicos, todo lo que el corazón desee. Ipanema, al contrario, es más pequeño y elegante, tiene muchas tiendas

de primera clase para ir de compras, restaurantes y cafés. Un domingo en la playa gay de Ipanema es de obligada visita! En la playa se mezclan muchos cariocas corpulentos, por tanto, póngase unas gafas de sol y cuidado con no caerse mientras mira. El Carnaval de Río es naturalmente el acontecimiento principal, pues aquí se festeja casi durante toda la semana sin parar. También la noche de Fin de Año en Copacabana es siempre una bonita experiencia.

Sin embargo, no aconsejamos subir a gente desconocida a la habitación del hotel. Se recomienda que mejor se vaya a cualquiera de los „hoteles de sexo".

✖ Rio è una delle città più eccitanti del mondo e rappresenta la cosiddetta porta del Brasile. Le bellissime spiagge e le montagne costituiscono un panorama pittoresco; per questo Rio viene anche chiamata „la meravigliosa città". Con i suoi sei milioni di abitanti è a tutti gli effetti una vera e propria metropoli. Con la sua vasta offerta culturale e la sua storia è una città aperta al mondo. Poiché la maggior parte dei posti gay si trova a Copacabana e a Ipanema, i turisti che soggiornano a Rio hanno una vasta scelta. La maggior parte degli alberghi sono a Capocabana. Qui vi si trovano anche locali notturni, bar, saune e luoghi pubblici.

Ipanema invece è più piccola e anche più sofisticata: qui ci sono ristoranti e bar di prima classe come anche molte occasioni per lo shopping di lusso. Un appuntamento da non perdere è la domenica alla spiaggia gay di Ipanema.Alla „festa di spiaggia" ci sono tanti Cariocas con corpi piuttosto scolpiti: mettere gli occhiali da sole e cercare di passare inosservati mentre li si osserva! Il carnevale di Rio è naturalmente l'evento principale in quanto si festeggia per una settimana non-stop. Anche la notte di San Silvestro a Copacabana non la si dimentica facilmente. Vi sconsigliamo di portare sconosciuti nella stanza d'albergo; si consiglia invece di scegliere uno dei numerosi hotel del sesso.

SHOWS

■ **Teatro Brigitte Blair I** (B g ST t)
Senador Dantas ☏ (021) 2220-5033

■ **Teatro Brigitte Blair II** (B g ST t)
Rua Miguel Lemos 51 H, Centro ☏ (021) 2220-5033

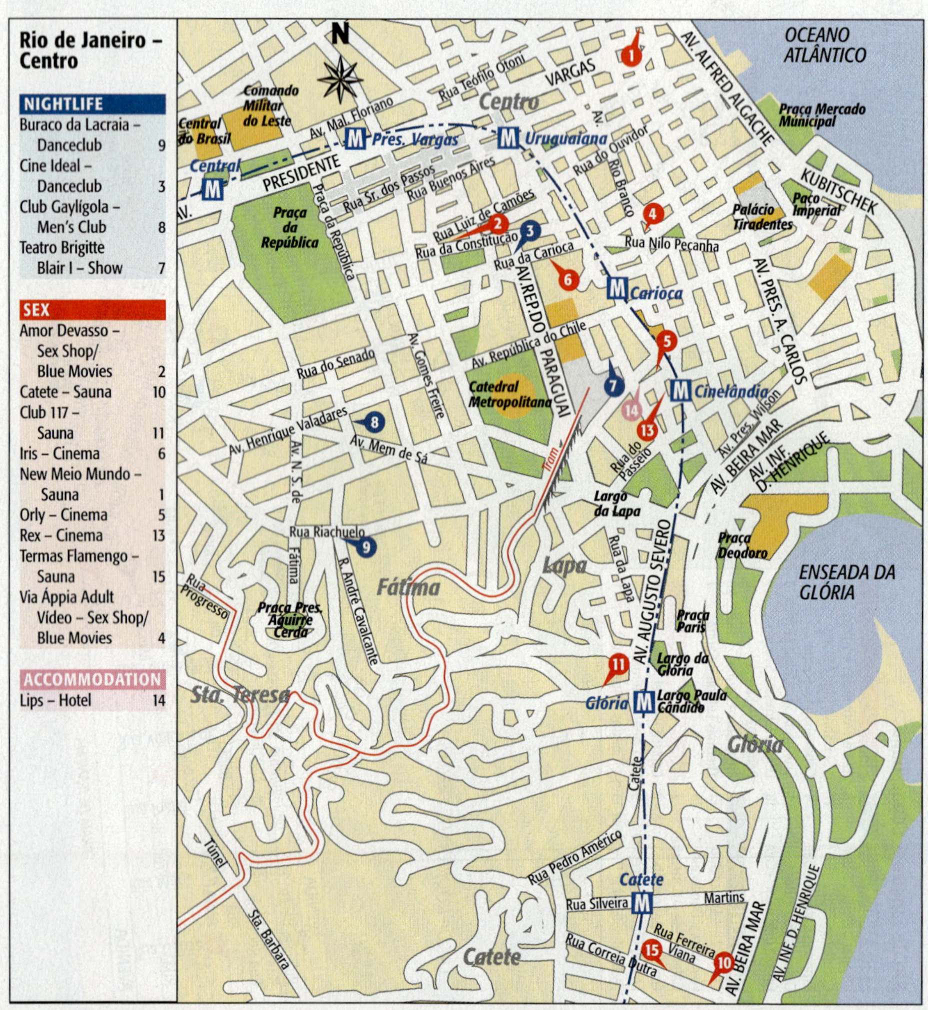

BARS

Boy bar by Gilles (AC B CC G MA r S)
Rua Raul Pompéia, 102 - Copacabana *Entrance via Galeria*
☎ (021) 2315-4993 💻 www.leboy.com.br
Belongs to the Club Le boy, Monday karaoke, drag shows on Sun from 1.30h. Entrance fee applies on Sundays.

Corujinha (AYOR B G OC R) Tue-Sun 12h-very late
Praça Serzedelo Correia, 9 , Copacabana *Small square off Av. Copacabana, next door to Club Incontru* ☎ (021) 2511-3305
The street in front of bar restaurant in the evening and night is the busiest hang out for R in Zona Sul of Rio except for saunas.

Expresso Carioca (B GLM MA) 9-3, Fri & Sat -4h
Rua Farme de Amoedo, 76, Ipanema ☎ (021) 2267-8604
Right along Rio's gayest street, this is a nice spot to enjoy a pina colada as you watch the boys from Ipanema go by, trance and house music.

Guimo's Pub (AC B MA NG S) 18-2h
Av Nossa Senhora de Copacabana, 1077, Copacabana *Situated at the back of the first floor*
Pub at the Copacabana with space for artistic performances. The place is not really gay but gayfriendly.

To Nem Ai (B G MA OS) 12-3h
Rua Farme de Amoedo 57 ☎ (021) 2247 8403
After beach bar on Ipanema's gayest street.

Up Turn Bar (B CC g s)
Av. das Américas, 2000 *Centro Comercial Freeway, Barra da Tijuca*
☎ (021) 3387-7957
Mixture of bar, kiosk and club, with electronic/house music.

MEN'S CLUBS

Club Gayligola (B DR G SNU)
Rua Ubaldino do Amaral, 50, Cruz Vermelha
💻 www.gayligola.com.br

CAFES

Caroline Cafe (AC B G MA)
Rua J J Seabra, 10, Jardim Botânico ☎ (021) 2540-0705
A modern stylish bar, rather relaxed place.

Lindóia Café e Bar (B glm M MC) Mon-Sat 8-24, Sun 8-20h
Av. N. Sra. Copacabana, 198-B *Copacabana* ☎ (021) 2244-7720
Happy hour 18-24h. Bar and restaurant with typical Brazilian dishes such as excellent Feijoada (Fri-Sun).

DANCECLUBS

00 (Zero Zero) (AC B CC D g YC)
Rua Padre Leonel Franca, 240 - Gávea *In old planetarium*
☎ (021) 2540-8041 💻 www.00site.com.br
Mostly gay on Sun, best night, great music (mostly Funk and House). Entrance fee on Thu from 22h, and Sun from 20h.

Boite 1140 (AC B D G MA S ST) Thu & Fri 23-5, Sat -6, Sun 22-5h
Rua Captião Menezes, 1140 *Praça Seca* ☎ (021) 3017-1792
💻 www.boite1140.com.br
This club is a classic, over 20 years old and still crowded every night. Three dancefloors, see their website for events: www.boite1140.com.br

Buraco da Lacraia (B D GLM MA S SNU) Fri & Sat 23-?h
Rua André Cavalcante, 58, Centro ☎ (021) 2242-0446
💻 www.buracodalacraia.com
Sometimes a pretty wild place, Fri they offer a free drink and nude waiters. Flyers available at: www.buracodalacraia.com

Casagrande (B D G MA)
Rua Cel. Tamarindo 2520 - Bangu ☎ (021) 3331-2171

Cine Ideal (B D G MA OS r WE) Fri & Sat 23.30-?h
Rua da Carioca, 64 *Centro* ☎ (021) 2221-1984 💻 cineideal.com.br

Cueva. La (B D G MA R) 23-?h, closed Mon
Rua Miguel Lemos, 51 *Copacabana* ☎ (021) 2237-6757
💻 www.boatelacueva.com

Dama de Ferro (B D G MC)
Rua Vinicius de Moraes 288, Ipanema www.damadeferro.com.br
Eletronic music, very gay crowd Fridays and Saturdays (after hours).

Fosfobox (B D g MA) 23-?h
Rua Siqueira Campos, 140 / 22a subsolo *Copacabana* (021) 2548-7498
Cool and intimate dance club in Copacabana's red light district. Discounted entrance fee applies with the flyer.

Galeria Cafe (AC B CC D GLM MC) Wed-Sun 22-?h
Rua Teixeira de Melo, 31, Lojas E-F. Ipanema *Gal Osório Square*
(021) 2523-8250 www.galeriacafe.com.br
Very small but packed on Thursdays! a small club.

Girl. La (B D gLm MA)
Rua Raul Pompéia, 102 / Galeria, Copacabana (021) 2247-8342
www.lagirl.com.br
Popular lesbian club.

Le Boy Club (AC B D DR f G MA S SNU ST) Tue-Sun 23-6h
Rua Raul Pompeia 102, Copacabana (021) 2513-4993
www.leboy.com.br
Show 1.30h. Popular on Tue, Sat and Sun. At the same address: Boy Bar & Restaurant (Wed-Mon 20-3h), La Girl Club Prive (Wed-Mon 21-3h), LeBoy Fitness (Tue-Sun 15-?h).

PaPa G (B D GLM MC S) Wed-Sun 22-?h
Travessa Almerinda Freitas, nº 42, Madureira (021) 2450-1253
www.papag.com.br
Flyer for discount entrance fee available at: www.papag.com.br/agenda.asp

Week. The (B D GLM MA) Fri & Sat 24-?h
Rua Sacadura Cabral, 154 (021) 2253-1020
This is the sister of Sao Paulos famous Week club, large dancefloor, popular with tourists, too.

SEX SHOPS/BLUE MOVIES

A2 Conveniências Eróticas (AC g) Mon-Sun 10-24h
Rua Visconde de Pirajá 177 - Ipanema (021) 2522-8827
www.a2rio.com.br

Amor Devasso (g VS) Mon-Fri 11-20, Sat 13-19h
Pca. Tiradentes 60/ sl. 302, Centro *M° Presidente Vargas*
(021) 2232-1758 www.amordevasso.com.br

Cox (AC CC G) Mon-Sat 11-19h, Sun closed
Rua Visconde de Pirajá, 281 loja 302, Ipanema *3rd floor*
(021) 3795-6698 www.mrcox.com.br
The only gay shop in Rio. swimsuits, accesorries, dildos, bags, gay books and more.

Erótic Arts Vídeo (GLM)
Rua Senador Dantas, 117/327 *Centro*

Sexy Rose (AC b CC G VS) Mon-Fri 9-22.30, Sat -20h
Rua Álvaro Alvim, 37 - Lj 6 *M° Cinelândia* (021) 2532-6262
Cruisy cabins with glory holes.

Via Áppia Adult Vídeo (AC cc G MA) Mon-Fri 10-20h
Av. Rio Branco 185 - sala 218 *Centro, near Carioca Subway station*
(021) 2524-5832
Adult gay videos only. Sale & rental.

SEX CINEMAS

Astor (G VS)
Avenida Ministro Edgar Romeiro, 236 *Madureira*

Iris (g)
Rua da Carioca, 49/51 *Centro, M° Carioca*
One of the oldest theatre-builidings of Rio. Very cruisy but no place to have sex.

Orly (G r T)
Rua Alcindo Guanabara, 17 *M° Cinelândia*
Very busy in afternoon. In small, not signposted side street Rua Alcindo Guanabara, 17/21 (side street off Restaurant Amarelinho).

Rex (g)
Rua Alvaro Alwim 36, Centro *M° Cinelandia*

SAUNAS/BATHS

Bonsucesso (b DR DU G MC MSG OS RR SA SB SOL VS)
13-22, Fri & Sat -23h
Rua Bonsucesso, 252 (021) 2260-9385
www.netgay.com.br/saunas/bonsucesso.htm

Boy Fitness. Le (B DR DU G m MA MSG SA SB VS WO)
Tue-Sun 15-5h
Rua Raul Pompéia, 102 - Copacabana *Entrance via Galeria*
(021) 2522-9175 www.leboy.com.br
This sauna is part of the „Le Boy"-complex with a big disco, a fashion-shop. Specials on Saturday (Bingo Boy) and Sunday (go-go's).

Catete (B DR DU FC FH G MA MSG RR SA SB VS) 13.30-24.30, Fri & Sat -6, Sun 15-0.30h
Rua Correia Dutra, 34, Catete *M° Catete* (021) 2265-5478
Sauna on 4 floors. Friendly staff and visitors. No „working boys". Busy on weekends.

Club 117 (! AC B BF CC DU G MA MSG p R RR S SA SB SH SNU ST VS WH) Tue-Sun 15-1h
Rua Cândido Mendes 117, Glória *M° Glória* (021) 2252-0160
www.club117.com.br
Spacious (680 m²) and popular on three floors. Previously it was a hotel that charged by the hour which explains the unusually large „cabins" (self-contained suites). It is one of the biggest and best saunas with „working boys" in Rio. Special events, like video-karaoke nights, strip shows and big dick contests! Don't be astonished if there are women at the counter; they're the owners.

Club 29 (b cc DR DU FH G I MA MSG RR SA SB VS) 13-4, Sun 15-24h
Rua Prof. Alfredo Gomes 29, Botafogo (021) 2286-6380
www.club29.com.br
Very small, cruisy atmosphere.

Copacabana
(AC B CC DR DU G m MA MSG PI RR SA SB SOL VS WH) 10-6h
Rua Dias da Rocha 83, Copacabana *Cnr. Rua Cinco de Julho*
(021) 2552-2330
Pay once and go in and out as often as you like.

Kabalk (B DU G m RR SA SB SOL VS WO) 15-24h
Rua Santa Luiza, 459, Maracanã *Near Praça Varnhagem*
(021) 2572-6210
Reading room and snack bar.

Mansão da Eva (AC B DR G OS S SA SB)
Rua Beneditinos 29 *Centro* (021) 2233-5644
www.netgay.com.br/boates/mansaodaeva.htm
New sauna.

New Meio Mundo (B DU G R SA SB SNU VS)
Mon-Sat 15-24h, closed Sun
Rua Theophilo Otoni, 18, Centro *Near Candelária, M° Uruguaiana, exit „Presidente Vargas"* (021) 2233-0930
newmeiomundo.blogspot.com
Sauna with young men awaiting the generosity of gentlemen.

Point 202 (B CC DU G MA MSG R RR S SA SB SNU VS WO)
Sun-Thu 15-1, Fri & Sat 15-3h
Rua Siqueira Campos 202, Copacabana *M° Siqueira Campos*
(021) 3816-1757 www.netgay.com.br/saunas/point.htm
Here you can expect many rent boys that can be quite pushy. Lots of action in the movie room. There are also suites with AC, TV and own bath with shower. Shows on Sat at 21h.

Projeto SB (AC B DR FC G I m MA MSG NU RR SA SB VS WH)
15-24, Fri & Sat -?h
Rua Dezenove de Fevereiro 162, Botafogo *M° Botafogo*
(021) 2244-4263 www.projetosb.com.br
Stylish and clean gay sauna recently opened in Botafogo for both members and guests. No rent boys.

Rio G Spa (b DR DU G I MA MSG RR SA SB VS) 15-24h
Rua Teixeira de Melo, 16, Ipanema *Near the General Osorio Pl. & General Osorio station* (021) 2523-5092 www.riogspa.com.br
Also offering different kinds of massage, facial and body treatments, hairdressing and depilation.

Spa 73 (B DU G MSG s SA SB VS WH) 15-24h
Rua Pereira de Almeida, 73 - Praça da Bandeira *Located at the begining of Rua do Matoso* (021) 2213-6480
www.netgay.com.br/saunas/spa73preco.htm

Spazio (B CC DR DU FC FH G GH M MSG OS PP R RR S SA SB SH SL SOL VS WO) Mon-Sat 15-1h, closed Sun
Rua Santo Amaro, 18, Glória *M° Glória* (021) 2221-4631
www.spazio18.com.br

■ **Termas Flamengo** (b DR G MA SA SB)
Rua Correia Dutra, 68A Flamengo ☎ (021) 2285-0197

■ **Thermas Leblon** (AC B cc DR DU F G m MA MSG RR SA SB VS WE) 12-6h
Rua Barão da Torre, 522, Ipanema *Off Rua Garcia d'Avila*
☎ (021) 2247-9169 🖳 www.termasleblon.com.br
Sauna with beauty salon. Mostly mature customers.

HOTELS

■ **Caprice Hotel** (G)
Avenida Nossa Sra. de Copacabana, 1079a ☎ (021) 2287-5841
Rooms by the hour.

■ **Lips** (AC B d glm)
Rua Senador Dantas, 46 *Centro* ☎ (021) 2210-3235
All rooms with TV and minibar. Rooms by the hour.

GUEST HOUSES

■ **Ananab** (AC b bf cc g MA PI WO) 24hrs
Rua Alice 681 *Laranjeiras* ☎ (021) 2557-6789 🖳 www.ananab.com
Gay owned.

■ **Maison. La** (BF CC glm MA PI)
Rua Sérgio Porto 58, Gávea ☎ (021) 3205-3585 🖳 www.lamaisonario.com

APARTMENTS

■ **Rio Copa/Ipanema Condos** (AC cc glm MA PI) 9-18h
Rua Joaquim Nabunco 11, Ap. 505, Copacabana *Near to hotel Sofitel*
☎ (021) 2227-5658 🖳 www.globecondos.com
Renovated apartments hosted by gay owners.

GENERAL GROUPS

■ **Grupo Arco-Iris** (GLM) Mon-Fri 11-17h
Rua do Senado, 230 - Cobertura ☎ (021) 2222-7286 🖳 arco-iris.org.br

SWIMMING

-The beach at the end of the Rua Farme de Amoedo in Ipanema is popular with gays (on the left side, mainly on WE)
-Recreio Beach. Nude sun bathing and cruisy woods. Great gay beach, discreet nudity, lots of action in the woods across the highway. Located several km outside of the city. A car is best but the bus is possible (553); head past Barra de Tijuca but keep going to Recreio (before Grumari Beach) until the view of the beach is obstructed by tall grass. Park on the right side of the highway and hop over the wire fence to the beach.

CRUISING

-Ipanema Beach (in front of Rua Farme de Amoedo)
-Copacabana Beach (just above Copacabana Palace Hotel known as »Stock Market« / bolsa de Copacabana)
-Botafogo Beach (AYOR) (weekdays until midnight and on Saturdays until 2h, very dangerous)
-Avenida Atlantica-Av. Copacabana
-Avenida Rio Branco in Cinelandia
-Praça Floriano (R) (there are small hotels in this area called »Somente Cavalheiros«, which means »men only«; you will have no problem bringing someone home with you whenever you want)
-Quinta da Boa Vista (AYOR) (closes at night)
-Parque do Flamengo (AYOR) (between Hotel Gloria and Botafogo, day and night)
-Praia do Arpoador (open air workout parcours).

Salvador – Bahia ☎ 071

✱ With over 3 million inhabitants, Salvador is Brazil's third major city and has grown in the last few years at an amazing pace. Salvador, also known as the black city of Brazil, is the capital of Bahia, in Northeast Brazil on the Atlantic coast.
The centre of the gay life is in the Rua Carlos Gomes and in this neighbourhood, where many bars, saunas and discos are to be found. The annual gay carnival takes place here in February on the ‚Praça Castro Alves'. Near „Teatro Castro Á lves" (in the „Campo Grande") in the small lane „Cerqueira Lima" or „Beco is the Artistas" are a number of gay/lesbian bars and discos(open from 19h, closed on Mondays).

★ Salvador hat sich in den letzten Jahren erstaunlich vergrößert und ist mit mittlerweile 3 Millionen Einwohnern Brasiliens drittgrößte Stadt. Salvador wird auch „Brasiliens schwarze Stadt" genannt und ist die Hauptstadt von Bahia im Nordosten Brasiliens an der Atlantikküste.
Das Zentrum des schwulen Lebens liegt an der Rua Carlos Gomes und in ihrer Nachbarschaft, wo viele Bars, Saunen und Diskotheken zu finden sind. Der jährliche schwule Karneval findet hier im Februar auf der „Praça Castro Alves" statt. In der Nähe des „Teatro Castro Álves" (am „Campo Grande") befindet sich die kleine Gasse „Cerqueira Lima" oder „Beco das Artistas", an der sich eine ganze Anzahl schwul/lesbischer Bars und Discos befinden (jeweils ab 19 Uhr, montags geschlossen).

✱ La population de Salvador a étonnamment augmenté ces dernières années et est passée à 3 millions d'habitants. Elle est ainsi la troisième plus grande ville du Brésil. Salvador est également appelée la „ville noire du Brésil" et c'est la capitale de Bahia, au nord-est du pays.Le centre de la vie gay se trouve dans la Rua Carlos Gomes et dans ses environs, où se trouvent beaucoup de bars, saunas et discothèques. Le carnaval annuel gay se déroule en février sur la „Praça Castro Alves". Dans les environs du „Teatro Castro Álves" (sur le „Campo Grande") se trouve la ruelle „Cerqueira Lima" ou „Beco das Artistas" où beaucoup de bars gays et lesbiens et boîtes se trouvent (ouverts dès 19h, fermés le lundi).

⬢ Salvador ha crecido de manera sorprendente en los últimos años y es ya con 3 millones de habitantes la tercera ciudad de Brasil. Salvador está considerada la „ciudad negra de Brasil" y es la capital de Bahia, en el noreste de Brasil, en la costa atlántica. El epicentro de la vida gay se sitúa en la Rua Carlos Gomes y en su vecindario, donde se encuentran infinidad de bares, saunas y discotecas. El carnaval anual gay tiene lugar cada Febrero en la „Praça Castro Alves". En las cercanías del „Teatro Castro Álves" (en „Campo Grande") se encuentra la pequeña callejuela „Cerqueira Lima" o „Beco das Artistas", en la que hay un gran número de bares y discotecas de gays y lesbianas (cerradas los lunes a partir de las 19 horas).

Negli ultimi anni Salvador è andata ingrandendosi sempre di più. Con i suoi 3 milioni di abitanti è la terza città più grande del Brasile. Salvador è chiamata anche „la città nera del Brasile" ed è il capoluogo di Bahia nel nord est del Brasile sulla costa Atlantica.
Il centro della vita gay è la ‚Rua Carlos Gomez' e i suoi dintorni: qui troverete molti bar, saune e discoteche. L'annuale carnevale gay ha luogo a febbraio nella ‚Praça Castro Alves'. Nei pressi del ‚teatro Castro Álves' (a ‚Campo Grande') si trova il piccolo vicolo ‚Avenida Cerqueira Lima' detto anche ‚Beco das Artistas': qui troverete moltissimi bar e discoteche gay (dalle 19:00 in poi - il lunedì chiusi).

BARS

Bahia Café (B M MA NG S) Mon-Fri open for lunch 11:30-15h
Lgo. dos Aflitos, s/nº Mirante dos Aflitos ☎ (071) 3341-7872
www.bahiacafe.com.br
Bar and restaurant, life music in the evening, call for current program.

Bar A2 Cultural (! B GLM m s YC) Tue-Sun 18-24h, closed Mon
Cerqueira Lima/Beco dos Artistas - Garcia *Directly opp. Camarim*
☎ (071) 3328-3273
Live music on Fri & Sat, half gay, half lesbian visitors. The small street between Camarim and Bar Cultural is fill of people at the WE. Also popular is the Bar G2 next door.

CAFES

Franco Cafe Lounge Bar (AC B GLM MC) Wed-Sun 18-4h
Rua da Paciência 295, Rio Vermelho ☎ (071) 3330 1755
☎ 9984-2433 (mobile) francocafe.com.br

MEN'S CLUBS

Cine Cabine 155 (AC DR G MA p VS) 17-24h
Rua Euricles de Matos, 155, Rio Vermelho ☎ (071) 313-2149
www.cinecabine155.com.br

DANCECLUBS

Off Club (B CC D GLM m S SNU WE)
Fri, Sat & before public holidays 24-6h
Rua Dias D'avila 33, Barra *Near Farol da Barra* ☎ (071) 3267-6215
☎ 9984-2433 www.offclub.com.br
The busiest gay disco of Salvador, middle-class clientele.

San Sebastian
Rua da Paciência, 227, Rio Vermelho ☎ (071) 3012.5013
www.sansebastiansalvador.com.br

RESTAURANTS

Maria Mata Mouro (AC CC glm M NR OS RES WL) 12-?h
Rua Inácio Acioli, 08, Pelourinho ☎ (071) 3321-3929
www.mariamatamouro.com.br

Pelô Bistrô at Casa do Amarelindo (B CC glm M MC OS PI)
Restaurant 11.30-22.30h, Panoramic Bar 16-23h
Rua das Portas do Carmo, nº 6 *Close the ancient Medicine University in Pelourinho district, at Casa Amarelindo* ☎ (071) 3266 8550
www.casadoamarelindo.com
Restaurant is situated within a tropical garden in the patio. Panoramic bar on 4th floor is an open terrace.

SEX SHOPS/BLUE MOVIES

Dreams. The (g)
Avenida Oceanica *Inside the Ondina Apart Hotel, ground floor*
www.thedreams.com.br

SAUNAS/BATHS

Casarão 25 (AC B cc DR G MA MSG SA SB SNU SOL VS WE WO) 15-22h
Rua Dom Marcos Teixeira, 25, Barra ☎ (071) 3264-1050
www.casarao25.com.br

Fox (B DU G MA MSG R RR SA SB VS) 15-22, Fri & Sat -23h
Rua das Rosas 682, Pituba ☎ (071) 3354-0047 www.saunafox.com.br
Comfortable sauna, to get there better take a cab.

■ **Olympus** (DU G MA MSG SA SB)
Rua Tuiuti 183, Carlos Gomes ☎ (071) 3329-0060
■ **Paradise** (B DR DU G MA MSG r SA SB WH)
Rua Leoni Ramos 59, Barra ☎ (071) 3237-7332
Sauna on 2 floors. Clean, crowdy but not really cruisy.
■ **Planetario 11** (B DU G I M MSG RR SB VS) Daily 15-23h
Rua José Duarte 11, Tororó ☎ (071) 3321-4511 🖳 www.planetario11.com.br
Situated in it centre of Salvador/Bahia, Planetario 11 is easy to reach. Well equipped sauna on three floors with various weekly programmes and thematic festivals throughout the year catering for gay male visitors.
■ **Rio's** (! B DR DU FC FH G I MA MSG PI PP R RR SA SB VS WH) 13-22, Fri-Sun 15-23h
Rua Almeida Sande, 8, Barris *Near „Conselho de Contabilidade" and „Edifícil Amapá"* ☎ (071) 3328-3275 🖳 www.saunarios.com.br
Clean and well equipped sauna. Really good place.
■ **Sauna Persona** (B DR G GH MA VR)
R. Cnso. Junqueira Ayres 230 ☎ (071) 329-1273
■ **Thermas Esgrima** (B DR G VR)
Ladeira de Santa Tereza, 2 ☎ (071) 3322-3813

TRAVEL AND TRANSPORT

■ **Rainbow Cruising Tour** (G) 8-20h
☎ (071) 8861-6381
Tour guide service. Check website for further information. English, Spanish, French & Italian spoken.

HOTELS

■ **Casa do Amarelindo** (AC B BF CC glm I M MC OS PA PI RWB RWS RWT SOL VA VS WH WO) All year
Rua das Portas do Carmo, N° 6 *Pelourinho* ☎ (071) 3266 8550
🖳 www.casadoamarelindo.com
Nestled in a fully restored 19th. century building, in the heart of the historical district. Near the gay places and the route for the carnival and gay parade.
■ **Catussaba** (AC BF CC H M MA OS PI) All year
Guarita's Beach Lane, 101, Alameda da Praia *Itapuã Beach*
☎ (071) 3374-8000 🖳 www.catussaba.com.br

GUEST HOUSES

■ **Pousada Estrela do Mar** (AC GLM H I MA RWS RWT VA)
Closed in June
Rua Afonso Celso 119 *100m from Off Club & lighthouse*
☎ (071) 3022-4882 🖳 www.estreladomarsalvador.com
Gay owned and managed.
■ **Pousada Papaya Verde** (AC BF glm MA MSG OS p PK RWB RWS VA) All year
Rua Engenheiro Milton Oliveira 177, Barra ☎ (071) 3267-1008
🖳 www.pousadapapayaverde.com
A pleasant 15 room hotel just a 5 mins walk to the main gay area and a 10 mins walk to the gay beach.

GENERAL GROUPS

■ **Grupo Gay da Bahia - GGB** Mon-Fri 10-20h
Rua Frei Vicente, 24, Pelourinho ☎ (071) 3321-1848 🖳 www.ggb.org.br
Publications: Boletim do GGB „Homo Sapiens", „Caderno De Textos Do GGB" „AIDS E Candomblé" „Guia Gay da Cidade do Salvador" „O Que Todo Munde Deve Saber Sobre A Homossexualidade". Politically & socially active group, addressing many issues, information about gay scene.

SWIMMING

-Porto da Barra (main gay beach, WE)
-Praia dos Artistas only near Bar Aruba (dirty water due to the river, take any bus that passes by Boca do Rio, big rainbow flag at beach, three gay beach bars, party on Sunday afternoon, until night)
-Stella Maris: gay only at beach bar „Barraca do Gaúcho", take bus to Praia do Flamengo.

CRUISING

-Jardim de Alá (ayor, at night)
-Campo Grande
-Shopping Barra (cruisy near food stores)
-Shopping Iguatemi
-Shopping Lapa
-Shopping Piedad
-Aero Clube Plaza Show
-Farol da Barra (rocks behind light house tower) AYOR
-Water front at Porto da Barra (especially in front of the Hotel Marazul, R)
-Avenida Oceanica (at the statue of Christ) AYOR and police.
-Avenida Oceanica/Rua Dr Artur Neiva

São José – Santa Catarina ☎ 48

DANCECLUBS

■ **Bartyra Night Club** (B D GLM MA S ST)
Margens da BR 101 - Km 202 - nº 2002 Barreiros ☎ (48) 8424-0491
🖳 www.fervo.com.br/empresas/bartyra/
Shows with Drag Queens, Strippers and Gogo Boys, call for info on days/times

São Leopoldo – Rio Grande do Sul ☎ 051

DANCECLUBS

■ **Danceteria Studio 54** (B D DR GLM MC S) Fri & Sat 23-?h
Rua Visconde de Pelotas, 87, Centro ☎ (051) 8402-1260

São Paulo – São Paulo ☎ 011

On the 8th of June, 2007 around one million evangelic Christians protested against homosexuality. A few days later 3.5 million visitors took part in the world's biggest Pride Parade! Along with the mayor, several ministers of the government took part. In 1997 the first Pride Parade had only about 2000 participants.
There are many other attractions in this city with over 10 million inhabitants. Dance clubs as well as the saunas are extremely popular. Enjoy this wonderful city but do pay attention to your own safety.

Am 8. Juni 2007 protestierten eine geschätzte Million evangelikale Christen gegen Homosexualität. Darauf antworteten einige Tage später 3.5. Millionen begeisterte Besucher des weltweit größten CSD! Neben dem Bürgermeister, nahmen auch mehrere Minister der Regierung teil. 1997 beim ersten CSD nahmen nur ungefähr 2000 Menschen teil.
Die 10-Millionen-Metropole birgt auch viele andere Attraktionen. Diskotheken und Saunen erfreuen sich großer Beliebtheit. Bei allen Vergnügungen in dieser wundervollen Stadt sollten Sie jedoch immer auch auf ihre persönliche Sicherheit achten. Brasilien liegt weltweit an vorderster Stelle, was Gewalt an Homosexuellen betrifft. Seit 1980 wurden c.a. 3000 Menschen wegen ihrer sexuellen Orientierung ermordet.

Le 8 juin 2007 ce sont environ un million de chrétiens évangélistes qui ont protesté contre l'homosexualité. Trois jours plus tard la réplique fut donnée par les 3,5 millions de participants à la CSD, la plus importante du monde ! Aux côté du maire plusieurs ministres du gouvernement étaient présents. En comparaison, la CSD de 1997 n'avait vu qu'à peu près 2000 participants. La métropole de 10 millions d'habitants a bien d'autres animations à offrir : les boîtes de nuit et les saunas deviennent de plus en plus populaires. Restez néanmoins prudents : faites attention à vos affaires personnelles et à vos objets de valeur.

El 8 de junio de 2007 protestaron aproximadamente un millón de cristianos evangélicos contra la homosexualidad. A ello respondieron tres días después 3,5 millones de personas en la marcha gay más grande del mundo! Junto al alcalde, también participaron varios ministros del gobierno. En 1997, durante la primera marcha gay, sólo participaron unas 2000 personas. Esta metrópolis de 10 millones de habitantes esconde sin embargo muchos otros atractivos. Los preferidos son las discotecas y las saunas. No obstante, en todas ellas debe tener en cuenta siempre su seguridad personal.

L'8 giugno del 2007 circa un milione di cristiani evangelisti hanno protestato contro l'omosessualità. Un paio di giorni più tardi, 3 milioni e mezzo di persone rispondevano allíoffensiva con il Christopher Street Day più frequentato del mondo. Oltre al sindaco vi hanno partecipato molti ministri della Repubblica. Nel 1997, al primo Christopher Street Day, cíerano solo 2000 persone circa. In questa metropoli di 10 milioni di abitanti ci sono naturalmente molte altre attrazioni. Discoteche e saune sono particolarmente amate. Nel divertirvi in questa fantastica città cercate di non trascurare la vostra sicurezza personale.

BARS

■ **Audio Delicatessen** (B GLM MA) Tue-Sun
R Mourato Coelho, 651 ☎ (011) 3097-0880
Modern bar/lounge.

■ **Bar da Fran** (B glm MA)
R dos Pinheiros, 735 ☎ (011) 3081-1643 💻 www.bardafran.com.br

■ **Boa Noite Rainha** (AC B glm)
R Vieira de Carvalho, 63 ☎ (011) 3333-6190

■ **Boteco Ouzar** (AC B gLm) Wed-Fri 17-?, Sat & Sun 16-?h
R Xavier de Almeida, 622 ☎ (011) 8303-3881
This place is very popular with lesbians.

■ **Caneca de Prata** (B G OC) 19-4h
Avenida Vieira de Carvalho, 55 *M° Republica* ☎ (011) 3222-5848
Popular with bears and gentlemen.

■ **Caverna do Dragão** (AC B glm)
R Vitória, 810
A place for the end of the night, a little rundown but charming.

■ **Farol Madalena** (B gLm M S) 18-4h
Rua Jericó 179, Vila Madalena ☎ 3032-6470 💻 www.farolmadalena.com.br

■ **Habeas Copus** (B D M MA) Daily 18-?h
Avenida Vieira de Carvalho, 94, Centro ☎ (011) 3222-7080

■ **O Gato Drinks & Arts** (AC B glm MA S) Thu-Sun 20-?h, Wed: cultural programmes, call for current shows
R Frei Caneca, 462 *Near Frei Caneca shopping mall also called the queer shopping mall.* ☎ (011) 3256-3656
With the feeling of an English pub.

■ **Queen** (AC B GLM M MA S ST) 18-22h
Rua Vitória, 826 *M° República* ☎ (011) 3333-78034
Restaurant, café and bar. Good drag shows.

■ **Ritz Bar e Restaurante** (AC B glm M)
Al Franca, 1088 ☎ (011) 3088-6808
It is popular with a lot of gays, journalists, modern and fashion people. It said

LABIRINTTU'S CLUB
Dry Steam
Steam
Spa
TV Room
Porn TV Room
Individual Relaxing
Reading Room
American Bar
Dark-Room
Price R$ 40,00
Every Day 24 Hours
LABIRINTTU'S CLUB

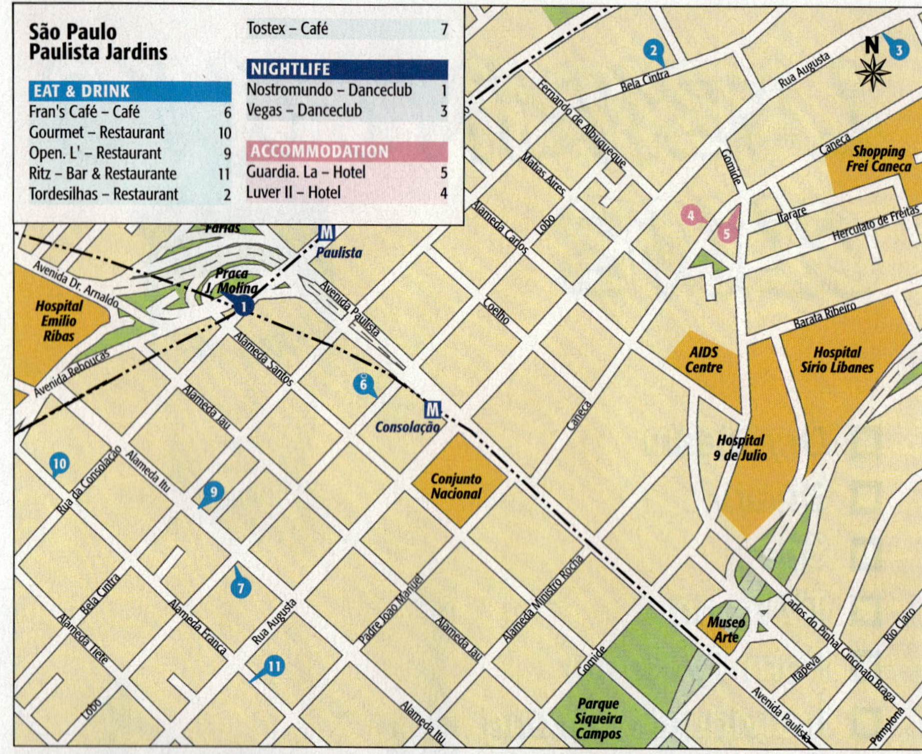

they have the best rice cookies of the city, impossible to go and not to eat one. In the weekends it gets crowdy and you might have to queue (the place is small). It has a branch office in the Olímpia Village, but gay place is here.

Vermont Itaim (AC B cc D GLM M MC OS S)
Tue-Thu 18-2, Fri & Sat 20-4, Sun 16-2h
Rua Pedroso Alvarenga 1192, Itaim Bibi ☎ (011) 3707 7721
www.vermontitaim.com.br
Every day live music. Fri & Sat also electronic music. Bar & restaurant.

Volt
www.barvolt.com.br
A very cool, new gay bar, all in neon.

MEN'S CLUBS

Blackout Sex Club (B CC DR F G MA NU p S VS)
Mon-Thu 16-24, Fri & Sat -5h
Largo do Arouche, 205, República *Vila Buarque, M° República*
☎ (011) 3337-3888 www.blackoutclub.com.br
Also known as Noescuro. Call first to confirm they are open. Sex club with huge DR. No cubicals. Clean and safe.

Gladiators (B cc DR G MA p) Daily 16-23h
Rua Dr. Penaforte Mendes 259 - Consolação ☎ (011) 3258-9340
www.gladiatorsbar.com
Sex club with glory holes and more.

RG (B CC DR G MA NU P SL) 18-24, Sat 20-4h, closed Mon & Tue
Rua Rio Grande, 33 - Vila Mariana ☎ (011) 5084-4534 www.rgbar.com.br

Station (B DR G MA p VS) 21-3, Fri & Sat 22-5h
Rua dos Pinheiros 352, Pinheiros ☎ (011) 3898-1293
www.stationvideobar.com.br

CAFES

Casa Café e Teatro (AC B glm MA S) Coffeeshop, bar and theater, call them for current shows.
R Treze de Maio, 176 ☎ (011) 3159-0546

Fran's Café (B BF glm MC) 24hrs
Rua Haddock Lobo, 586 ☎ (011) 4196-8680 www.franscafe.com.br

Tostex (B GLM MA) Mon-Sun 17-2h
Rua Haddock Lobo, 949, Cerqueira César ☎ (011) 3898-1265
www.tostexpraia.com.br

Vermont (AC B bf CC GLM M MA S WE) 6.30-1, Fri -3, Sat 7-3, Sun 10-1h
Av. Vieira de Carvalho, 10 *M° República* ☎ (011) 3222-5848
Typical gay bar, the place is frequented by older people during the week. On weekends the crowd is well mixed. Shows of drag queens and boys on Saturdays.

DANCECLUBS

A Lôca (B D GLM MA) Tue 24-6, Thu 24-7, Fri & Sat 24-10, Sun 19.30-7h
Rua Frei Caneca, 916, Consolação ☎ (011) 3159-8889 www.aloca.com.br
Tue: „Tapa na Pantera" (POP and electronic music), Thu: „Locuras" (Flash Back, Flash House, Disco Music, 80's, Dance Music, Fri & Sat: "Another Level" (techno and hard techno), Sun: „Grind" (rock, electro, 80's).

ABC Bailão (B cc D G m MA WE) Fri & Sat 22-5, Sun 19-1h
Rua Marquês de Itu, 182, Centro *M° República* ☎ (011) 3333-3537
www.abcbailao.com.br
Specially interesting for lovers of traditional Brazilian music.

Blue Space (B D DR G SNU ST) Fri & Sat 23-?h
Rua Brigadeiro Galvão, 723, Barra Funda ☎ (011) 3666-1616
www.bluespace.com.br
Popular Sunday T-Dance. 2 dancefloors, gogo dancers and other shows. Running for 10 years now.

BuBu (B D G MC S) Fri 23.59-?, Sat 23-?, Sun 19-?h
Rua dos Pinheiros 791 - Pinheiros ☎ (011) 3081-9659
www.bubulounge.com.br
A huge club.

Cantho (AC B D glm) Fri & Sat 23-?h
Largo do Arouche, 32
A sort of old fashioned club, still popular for the lovers of music of the 70s, 80s and 90s.

Clash Club (AC B D glm MA OS) Fri-Sun
Rua Barra Funda, 969 ☎ (011) 3661-1500 🖳 www.clashclub.com.br
Club featuring mainly rock and electronic music. On Sun it has a matinê with rock musicians, call for current programme.

D-Edge (B D glm MA) Wed-Sat 23-5h
Alameda Olga, 168, Barra Funda ☎ (011) 3667-8334
🖳 www.d-edge.com.br
Trendy dance club, good music.

Danger (AC B CC DR GLM MA S t VS) Wed-Sun 23-6h
Rua Rego Freitas, 470, Centro ☎ (011) 3211-0371
🖳 www.dangerdanceclub.net
Drag shows and gogo boys.

Flex
Av. Marquês de São Vicente, 1767 *Barra Funda* 🖳 www.flexclub.com.br
Brand new club

Freedom Club (B cc D DR G MA S) Fri & Sat 23-5, Sun 15-22.30h
Largo do Arouche, 6, Centro *M° República* ☎ (011) 3362-2325
🖳 www.freedomclub.com.br

Glória (B D glm MA) Fri-Sun
R 13 de Maio, 830 Bixiga ☎ (011) 3287-3700 🖳 www.clubegloria.com.br
Dance club, used to be a church, good on Fridays.

Megga
Rua Achilles Orlando Curtoto, 646 *Barra Funda* ☎ (011) 3063-5519
🖳 www.meggaclub.com.br

Nostromundo (B D f G MA SNU ST) Fri 23.30-4, Sat 23-4, Sun 18-1h
Rua da Consolação, 2554, Consolação *M° Consolação*
☎ (011) 3259-2945 🖳 www.nostromondo.com.br
Probably the oldest gay disco in town. Drags and go-go boys (T-dance on Sun at 18h).

Planet G (B D DR G MA SNU ST VS) Fri-Sun 23-?h
Rua Rego Freitas, 56, Centro ☎ (011) 3228-0014
Downtown club with 3 dance floors, go go boys, darkroom, videos and shows.

Trash 80's (AC B D g MA) Tue-Sat
R Álvaro de Carvalho, 40 Centro ☎ (011) 3262-4881
🖳 www.trash80s.com.br
Music of the 80s, gay on Thursdays and Saturdays.

Tunnel (AC B D GLM m MA S) Fri & Sat 23-6, Sun 19-24h
Rua dos Ingleses, 355, Bela Vista *M° Brigadeiro* ☎ (011) 3285-0246
🖳 www.tunnel.com.br
Established in 1992 ! Two dancefloors, different atmospheres. On Fri live shows with Brazilian music!

Ultra Diesel (AC B cc D glm YC) Fri-Sun
Rua Marquês de Itu, 284 - Vila Buarque - Centro ☎ (011) 3338-2493
🖳 www.ultradiesel.com.br

Vegas (B D g MA) Tue-Sat
R Augusta, 765 Centro ☎ (011) 323-3705 🖳 www.vegasclub.com.br
Gay on Friday and Saturday after hours

Week. The (B CC D GLM M MA OS s) Thu & Fri 20-?, Sat & Sun 14-?h
Rua Guaicurus, 324, Lapa ☎ (011) 3801-4346 🖳 www.theweek.com.br
Located in a tastefully decorated old house in Lapa. Spacious terraces. Live music at WE in open air as well as a restaurant. Try the Feijoada on Sat!

RESTAURANTS

Gourmet (B GLM M) Tue-Sun 21-3, 12-15h for lunch
Al Franca 1552, Jardins ☎ (011) 3064-7958

Open. L' (CC G M OS) Tue-Sun 19-1h
Alameda Itu 1466, Jardins *M° Consolaçao* ☎ (011) 3060-9013
Italian-Brazilian cuisine in a restaurant which seats 120 people.

Tordesilhas (AC B CC glm M OS RES)
12-15, 19-23h, Mon & Sun evening closed
Rua Bela Cintra, 465 *M° Consolação* ☎ (011) 3107-7444
🖳 www.tordesilhas.com
A small house, in a quiet street. Mara, the chief of the Tordesilhas welcomes you in this Brazilian, gay-friendly restaurant on two floors. Reservation in advance is recommended.

SEX SHOPS/BLUE MOVIES

Other Side Video (G VS) Tue-Fri 13-22, Sat 14-21h
Rua Peixoto Gomide, 69 Jardins *Near the shopping complex Frei Caneca*
☎ (011) 3120-7071 🖳 www.othersidevideos.com.br

R&R Amigos (AC G MA VS) Thu-Sat 13-22h
Rua Sena Madureira 755, Vila Mariana *Close to M° Vila Mariana*
☎ (011) 5571-1614 🖳 www.rramigos.com.br

SEX CINEMAS

Cine Arouche (g R) 9.30-22h
Largo do Arouche, 426 ☎ (011) 3105-4345

Cine Saci (g) 24hrs
Avenida São João, 285 *Centro* ☎ (011) 223-9191

Ponto Zen Cine (B DR G) 11-1, Fri & Sat -4h
Avenida São João, 1119 - Centro ☎ (011) 3337-2373

Republica (B DR G) 24hrs
Avenida Ipiranga, 752, Centro ☎ (011) 3222-7336
One of the most popular cinemas in the city.

SAUNAS/BATHS

Amazonas (B DR DU FC FH G m MSG OS PP RR SA SB SOL VS)
Mon 11-23, Tue-Fri 13-23, Sat 10-22, Sun 10-20h
Rua do Gasômetro, 641 - Brás ☎ (011) 3229-0047

Fragata (B DR DU G M MA MSG R RR SA SB SNU VS) 14-24h
Rua Francisco Leitão, 71 - Pinheiros *No subway yet, take a cab*
☎ (011) 3061-3653 🖳 www.termasfragata.com.br

Labirinttu's Club 24h (! AC B DR DU G I LAB MA MSG RR SA SB SH SOL VS WE WH) Daily, 24hrs
Rua Frei Caneca, 328, Consolação *M°Anhangabaú / M° Consolação*
☎ (011) 3237 1337 🖳 www.labirinttusclub.com.br
A popular 24 hour sauna that's clean and well equipped with many tourists. The only 24/7 sauna in the city. Popular especially with tourists. No rent boys. Large and very dark labyrinth. Lots of action in the steam room. Three floors with a large whirlpool and interesting showers.

Oásis (AC B CC DR DU FH G GH I LAB m MSG RR SA SB VS) 14-23.30h
Rua Dr. Cândido Espinheira 758, Perdizes *10 mins from M° Barra Funda*
☎ (011) 3873-2254 🖳 www.termasoasis.com.br
Due to its style full decoration this sauna has a very pleasant atmosphere. There is a large labyrinth and American bar.

Rouge 80. Le (B CC DR DU FC FH G m MA PI PP R RR SA SB VS WH) 14-1, Fri & Sat -5h
Rua Arruda Alvim, 175, Pinheiros *M° Clinicas, Trav. Teodoro Sampaio*
☎ (011) 3062-3043 🖳 www.thermaslerouge80.com.br
Popular and cruisy sauna on 750 m² with plenty of action. Only a few young men who like older men go to this bear venue. Busy with students from the nearby university during „happy hours" (call for exact times).

Termas for Friends (AC B CC DR DU FC FH G LAB m MA OS p PI RR SA SB SOL VS WH) 14-23h
Rua Morgado Matheus 365, Vila Mariana *M° Ana Rosa, near Ibirapuera's Park* ☎ (011) 5579-1887 🖳 www.termasforfriends.com.br
Big clean sauna on 700 m² with a great atmosphere and a winter garden.

Thermas Lagoa (AC B CC DR DU FH G M MA MSG OS R RR SA SB SH SNU VS WH WO) 14-24, Fri -2, Sat -1h
Rua Borges Lagoa 287, Vila Clementino *300 m from M° Santa Cruz*
☎ (5511) 5573-9689 🖳 www.thermaslagoa.com.br
Very popular and clean sauna which attracts a mixed crowd. Many good-looking rent boys. The facilities are very good and the atmosphere is relaxed. Daily events. Valet parking

Wild Thermas Club
(B CC DR DU FC FH G GH LAB m MSG OS PP SA SB SL VS WH) 14-24h
Rua Dr. Veiga Filho, 802 - Higienópolis *M° Marechal Deodoro, bus 8107 from downtown* ☎ (011) 3666-4908 🖳 www.wildthermasclub.com.br

HOTELS

155 Hotel (AC BF cc glm I MC RWS RWT VA) All year
Rua Martinho Prado, 173, Consolação ☎ (011) 315 015 55
🖳 www.155hotel.com.br
The rooms have a LCD TV with satellite service, free wireless Internet, intelligent air conditioning, digital coffee maker, and smoke detectors. All of the rooms are smoke-free with anti-allergenic beds. A 15 minute walk to the action in the Boubron area. Gay-friendly accommodation.

■ **Bourbon São Paulo** (AC B BF CC glm I M RWB RWS RWT WO) All year
Avenida Dr. Vieira de Carvalho, 99 *M° República* ☎ (011) 333 720 00
🖳 www.bourbon.com.br

■ **Guardia. La** (AC BF CC GLM M) All year
Rua Peixoto Gomide, 154, Jardins ☎ 3125-2300 🖳 www.laguardia.com.br
All modern conveniences including 24 hours room service and security service. Full Brazilian breakfast included in the room rate.

■ **Luver II** (g)
Rua Frei Caneca, 963 *Consolação* ☎ (011) 3287-7040
Rooms by the hour.

■ **Republica Park Hotel** (AC bf CC glm MA) All year
Av. Vieira de Carvalho 32, Centro *Vila Buarque* ☎ (011) 3226-5000
🖳 www.republicaparkhotel.com.br
Fully equipped suites, with telephone, mini-bar, TV, air conditioning, individual safe, and bathroom with jacuzzi. In the same group as the hotel La Guardia.

HEALTH GROUPS

■ **C.O.A. Centro de Orientação e Aconselhamento em AIDS e Doeças Sexualmente Transmissíveis** Mon-Fri 8-14h
Galeria Prestes Maia, Terreo *Centro* ☎ (011) 3241-2224
Information on AIDS and free HIV-tests.

CRUISING

-Rua Vieira de Carvalho in ‚Centro'- easy pickup point. In Brazil even the gay crusing areas are divided into classes!
-Avenida Ipiranga (AYOR R) (intersection of São João and São Luiz and São Luiz and Praça Roosevelt)(t)
-Avenida República de Libano (T) (area between Parque do Ibarapuera and the residential district of Avenida Sto. Amaro)
-Parque do Ibirpuera (WE) (Try the cycle paths or go by car at night)
-Praça Roosevelt (at night and at the weekend)
-Rua Rui Barbosa (from Zaccaro Theatre to Village Station Cabaret)
-Rua Santo Antonio (area leading from Major Quedinho á Treze de Maio)
-"Autorama"-area in Ibirapera park (between Detran & Bienal. Where the cars park. At night)
-Republica Square.

São Vicente – São Paulo ☎ 013

SAUNAS/BATHS

■ **Thermas Senador** (B DR G R SA SB VS) 15-23h
Rua Jacob Emerich 1.87 *At the end of the street to shopping centre Do S. Vicente* ☎ (013) 3466-1995 🖳 www.thermas-senador.com.br
Many escort boys.

SWIMMING

-Praia Itararé (near Ilha Porchat).

Sorocaba – São Paulo ☎ 015

SAUNAS/BATHS

■ **Studio L** (B SA SB VS) Thu-Sun 14-20h
Rua Padre Luiz 709 ☎ (015) 9118-0861 🖳 www.saunastudiol.com.br

Vitória – Espirito Santo ☎ 027

DANCECLUBS

■ **Move Music** (B cc D GLM MC S) Sat 23-?h
Av. Adalberto Simão Nader, 387, República ☎ (027) 3314-5968
🖳 www.movemusic.com.br

CRUISING

-Jardin de Penha Gamburi
-Praia Compridor
-Praia de Camburi
-Praia de Guarapari (Castanheiras Beach)
-Parque Moscoso
-Promenade Embarcadouro
-In front of Sao Luis Theatre (Rua 23 de Maio)
-Plaza Costa Pereira (R).

Bulgaria

Name: Bâlgarija · Bulgarien · Bulgarie
Location: Southeastern Europe
Initials: BG
Time: GMT +2
International Country Code: ☎ 359 (omit 0 from area code)
International Access Code: ☎ 00
Language: Bulgarian
Area: 110,910 km² / 42,822 sq mi.
Currency: 1 Lew (BGN) = 100 Stótinki
Population: 7,740,000
Capital: Sofia
Religions: 86% Orthodox Christian, 13% Muslim
Climate: Temperate climate, with cold damp winters and hot dry summers. Spring (Apr-Jun) is a good time to visit.

✱ In Bulgaria the age of consent is set at 14 for both homosexuals and heterosexuals. In certain cases, sex between men under the age of 18 is illegal. Registered partnership does not exist.
Bulgaria's recent inclusion into the EU has promoted some improvements, such as the introduction of new regulations against sexual orientation discrimination in the workplace. Since the 1st January 2004 a new anti-discrimination paragraph exists, which aims to protect gay men and lesbians from homophobic attacks, although until now no improvement can be mentioned. Even in the capital, Sofia, homophobia is wide spread in several social groups. A gay scene has yet to develop. A conservative basis exists and only the younger generation is more tolerant. Politicians are not prepared to address this problem.
Seldom does anyone come „out" in public. In the press the subject homosexuality is dismissed as pedophile behavior.
Extremists throwing rocks, bottles and gasoline bombs attacked the Bulgarian capital's first gay pride parade event which took place on the 28th June 2008. Around 150 participants were protected by the police

during the march. Bulgaria is famous for its coastline along the Black Sea; for its mountain landscape and forests; incredible ancient culture. The reasonable prices tend to attract a special type of visitor.

In Bulgarien liegt das einheitliche Mindestalter für alle sexuellen Orientierungen bei 14 Jahren. Unter gewissen Umständen könnte allerdings Sex unter Männern, die jünger als 18 sind, bestraft werden, von daher raten wir zu Vorsicht. Eingetragene Partnerschaften gibt es nicht.
Die kürzlich erfolgte Aufnahme Bulgariens in die EU hat einige Verbesserungen gebracht wie beispielsweise die Verabschiedung neuer Bestimmungen, die eine auf der sexuellen Orientierung basierende Diskriminierung am Arbeitsplatz verhindern sollen. Seit dem 1.1.2004 existiert ein Antidiskriminierungsartikel, welcher die Schwulen und Lesben vor Homophobie schützen soll. Aber bisher sollen keine Verbesserungen eingetreten sein.
Selbst in der Hauptstadt Sofia ist Homophobie unter einigen Bevölkerungsschichten verbreitet. Ein Szeneviertel hat sich bisher nicht entwickelt, genauso wenig offizielle Freizeitangebote.
Eine konservative Grundeinstellung ist vorherrschend, nur die jüngere Generation ist etwas toleranter. Die Politiker haben zusätzlich keinerlei Programme zum „heißen Eisen" Homosexualität bereit. Es gibt kaum Outings von Betroffenen und selbst in den Medien wird Homosexualität durch Themen wie Pädophilie angegriffen.
Berühmt ist Bulgarien durch seine Schwarzmeerküste, einer schönen Gebirgslandschaft und Wäldern; auch die günstigen Preise locken eine gewisse Besucherklientel.

La majorité est fixée à 14 ans pour tous mais le rapport sexuel entre mineurs peut éventuellement être puni et il est donc recommandé d'user de prudence. L'intégration de Bulgarie à l'Union Européenne a apporté quelques améliorations comme par exemple un texte empêchant la discrimination fondée sur l'orientation sexuelle sur le lieu de travail. Les partenariats entre couples de même sexe ne sont pas reconnus mais il existe depuis le premier janvier 2004 un article anti-discriminatoire protégeant les gays et lesbienne de l'homophobie. Depuis, aucun amélioration n'a été apportée à ce texte. Même à Sofia, la capitale, l'homophobie semble être répandue parmi certaines couches de la population et aucun milieu gay ne s'y est établi. La tendance est au conservatisme et seuls les jeunes sont un peu plus ouverts. Les politiciens ne semblent pas prêts non plus à s'aventurer sur ce terrain brûlant que représente l'homosexualité, Il n'existe que peu de coming out, et même la presse fustige l'homosexualité au même titre que la pédophilie.
La Bulgarie est célèbre pour sa côte bordant la Mer noire, un paysage montagneux et forestier splendide et des prix modérés attirent chaque année de nombreux touristes.

En Bulgaria, la edad de consentimiento para todas las orientaciones sexuales está fijada en los 14 años. Bajo determinadas circunstancias, no obstante, el sexo entre hombres menores de 18 años puede ser penalizado, por lo que recomendamos cuidado. No existe un registro de parejas.
La reciente incorporación de Bulgaria a la Unión Europea ha supuesto algunas mejoras como, por ejemplo, la aprobación de nuevas disposiciones que deberán evitar cualquier discriminación en los puestos de trabajo basada en la orientación sexual. Desde el 1.1.2004, hay un artículo en contra de la discriminación que deberá proteger a gays y lesbianas de la homofobia. Sin embargo, por ahora no están previstas otras mejoras.
En la misma capital, Sofia, la homofobia está muy extendida entre algunas capas de la población. De momento no se ha desarrollado ningún barrio de ambiente gay así como tampoco otras ofertas públicas de ocio.
Predomina en general una postura conservadora, sólo las generaciones más jóvenes son más tolerantes. Los políticos, además, tampoco han preparado ningún programa sobre el tema candente de la homosexualidad. Los afectados apenas salen del armario y en los medios de comunicación se ataca a la homosexualidad con temas como la pedofilia.
Bulgaria es famosa por su costa del Mar Negro, sus bellas montañas y bosques pero también los bajos precios atraen a una determinada clientela.

In Bulgaria l'età del consenso è di 14 anni per tutti gli orientamenti sessuali. In alcune circostanze tuttavia il sesso con ragazzi sotto i 18 anni potrebbe essere legalmente perseguibile, quindi raccomandiamo molta cautela. Le unioni registrate non sono ancora vigenti. Il recente ingresso di Bulgaria nell'Unione Europea ha portato alcuni miglioramenti come per esempio la ratifica di alcuni accordi che tutelano le discriminazioni (riguardanti gli orientamenti sessuali) sul posto di lavoro. Dall'1 gennaio del 2004 è entrato in vigore un articolo antidiscriminatorio che tutela gay e lesbiche dall'omofobia. Ma fino ad adesso non è stato percepito nessun miglioramento concreto.
Persino nella capitale Sofia è diffusa, in certi strati della popolazione, una certa omofobia. Non esiste un quartiere gay ne quantomeno offerte per il tempo libero. Qui regna suprema un'attitudine fondamentalmente conservatrice. Solo la nuova generazione è un po' più tollerante. I politici non hanno alcun programma circa lo scottante tema dell'omosessualità. Non ci sono casi di outing; e persino nei mass media, l'omosessualità viene attaccata con accuse come per esempio quello della pedofilia. La Bulgaria è famosa per la sua costa sul Mar Nero, per il suo paesaggio roccioso e per le sue valli. I prezzi, anch'essi sono piuttosto invitanti.

NATIONAL GAY INFO

Bulgayria
www.gay.bg
Online information about gay life in Bulgaria. Photo profiles of gay men.

Gemini - Bulgarian Gay Organisation (GLM MA)
Mon-Fri 10-18h
3 Vassil Levski Blvd. App. 7, 1st floor ✉ 1142 Sofia *Near National Place of Culture - NDK* ☎ (02) 987 68 72
LGBT rights, information centre & counselling. On Fridays at 18h everyone is invited to join an open meeting. At the office Gemini is the only library for LGBT and gender issues in Bulgaria.

Burgas ☎ 056

SEX SHOPS/BLUE MOVIES

3W-group (NG)
Morska str. 40

Hermes Sex Shop (NG)
Kiril and Metodii Street, 37 ☎ (056) 82 07 10

CRUISING

-At the main railway station and in the city park (AYOR)
-Nudist beach north of Burgas after the Burgas Hotel direction Nessebur (New Town) near the saltpan of Burgas. Bushes behind the dunes.
-Sunny Beach Resort. The resort is situated 42 km of Burgas. Walk along the beach south towards Nessebar, after the Burgas Hotel and the beach of the Council of Ministers you will find a nice and calm beach. Bushes behind the dunes.

Dobrich ☎ 058

SEX SHOPS/BLUE MOVIES

Cupidon (g) 10.30-19.30h
2 Svoboda Street www.sexshop.bg

Pleven ☎ 064

SEX SHOPS/BLUE MOVIES

Eros (g MA) 10-22h
Pirot Street 11 *Above History museum* ☎ 08 87 86 56 93

Plovdiv ☎ 032

BARS

■ **Caligula** (AC B D G MA S) 23-8h
30 Alexander Batenberg Street *Near McDonald's* ☎ (032) 626 86 7

■ **Make Up** (g MC) 17-1h
29 Petko Slaveykov Street *In the old town, next to Seven Hills Hotel* ☎ 088 7766199

SEX SHOPS/BLUE MOVIES

■ **Venera Amur** (g MA VS)
46 Avksentii Veleshki Street

SAUNAS/BATHS

■ **Monic Spa Club** (glm MC MSG SA SB) Daily 10-21h
16 Altseko Street *Kapana* ☎ 625 913 ☎ (0)88 9595761 (mobile)

CRUISING

-Alyosha hill (near the monument of a Russian soldier)
-Clock tower hill.

Rousse ☎ 082

SEX SHOPS/BLUE MOVIES

■ **Cupidon** (g) 10.30-20h
2 Baba Tonka Str. 🖳 www.sexshop.bg

■ **Eros 2000** (G) 10-22h
Slavqnska street, 3 *Near the Pinko Chinese restaurant* ☎ 08 89 60 40 25

Sliven ☎ 044

SEX SHOPS/BLUE MOVIES

■ **Eros 2000** (g) 10-19h
Slivnitsa street 8 *Near Dobri Jelyazkov shop* ☎ 0887 86 56 93

Sofia ☎ 02

NATIONAL GAY INFO

■ **GayGuide.net Sofia** (GLM)
🖳 sofia.gayguide.net
Permanently updated gay guide including reviews of all listed places. Information on gay-owned accommodation & gay-operated guided tours.

BARS

■ **Club Mystic** (B G MA)
71 Hritso Botev Blvd ☎ 088 7756362

■ **Essense** (B gLm MC) Wed-Sat 21-?h
29, Alexander Stamboliysky Blvd. *Opposite to KFC* ☎ (02) 089 999 86 66
Club popular with lesbians.

■ **Lips** (AC B D DR G MA P) Tue-Sat 20-8h
12 Bratya Miladinovi Street *Between Alexander Stamboliyski Blvd and Todor Alexandrov Blvd* ☎ 87 880 41 38 🖳 http://clublips.wordpress.com
Discrete, elegant and pleasant atmosphere in the centre of Sofia, quality service, private parties.

■ **Why Not** (B d G MA p R S) Daily 22-4h
31 Stamboliysky Boulevard *Below Pizzeria Capri, opposite KFC* ☎ (09) 866 630
Next to Pizzeria Capri, on the left side of the building (outside) you will find stairs leading to the cellar. Here is an iron door and you need to ring the bell. Certainly a crowded place on Friday and Saturday nights. A bar, several tables and sofas; a very small dance floor. No minimum consumption.

DANCECLUBS

■ **ID Club** (! AC B D DR G MA P S) Tue-Sat 21-5h
19 B Karnigradska Street *Cnr. Vitosha Boulevard* ☎ 0898 200 000 🖳 www.idclub.bg
Currently the place to be in Sofia.

SEX SHOPS/BLUE MOVIES

■ **Cupidon** (g) 10.30-21h
46 Boulevard Vasil Levski ☎ (02) 8966 22-726 🖳 www.sexshop.bg

■ **Erotic Center No 1** (g MA VS) 13-2h
Students Town, near Fantastico Shop, behind Germanos Shop, close to Hristo Botev Sports Hall ☎ (878) 429 739
Videos, underwear, toys, tools, lubes, condoms.

■ **Flamingo Center** (B DR g VS) 9-22, bar: Mon-Sat 15-3, Sun 14-24h
208 Tsar Simeon Street *M° stop Opaltehenska; tram 1/5/10* ☎ (02) 831 71 85 🖳 www.ero-market.com
Entrance fee. Also video rental. Two shops at 200 and 208 in the same street. Gay bar in the first floor. Be careful when you leave the place at night.

SAUNAS/BATHS

■ **Pancharevo Bath House** (NG SA SB WH) Sun 7-19h
Pancharevo suburb *15 km from the city centre*
Not a gay place but interesting on Sundays only.

■ **Taragon Steam** (AC G MA p SB) Thu-Sun 15-22h
10 Bratovan Street, Reduta District ☎ 0885703894 🖳 Sofiagaysauna.eu
Gay venue. Very private, discrete location.

HOTELS

■ **Scotty's Boutique Hotel** (CC GLM I NR RWS RWT) All year
11, Ekzarh Jossif Str. *Opposite the Sofia's Synagogue; side street of Old Market Hall Halite* ☎ 983 67 77 ☎ (0)88 9836777 (mobile) 🖳 www.scottyshotel.info
Gay-friendly accommodation in the city centre.

SPORT GROUPS

■ **Fat Cats Sports Club** (G)
☎ (089) 9921298 🖳 www.fat-cats.org
Gay sports club. Volleyball every Thu and 2nd Tue. Swimming and badminton. Please call for info on venues.

■ **Tangra Gay Sports Club** (G MA)
🖳 www.tangra-sport.org

CRUISING

-Yavorov boulevard from Tsarigradsko chausee in the summer, 17-21h at WE
-Park near the Main Railway Station Hristo Botev boulevard, south after the bus and tram, during sunset, 17-21h
-Toilet in the underpass in front of the National Palace of Culture
-Park near the school for priests at the end of Prewiter Kuzma street, 18-21h at WE.

Sozopol ☎ 0550

SWIMMING

-Famous nudist beach towards the south of „Harmanite" beach (towards Duni resort)
-After Harmanite beach go along the rocks until you reach Heaven's Bay.

Stara Zagora ☎ 042

SEX SHOPS/BLUE MOVIES

■ **Eros 2000** (g MA) 10-22h
Otets Paisii Street 42 ☎ 088 96 04 02 5

SAUNAS/BATHS

■ **Public Bath Pavel Banya** (AYOR MC NG PI SA SB)
ul. Knyaz Pavel 1, Pavel Banya *Pavel Banya is a small town close to the city of Stara Zagora* ☎ 088 5059331

Sunny Beach ☎ 0554

BARS

■ **Habibi** (B GLM MC S) Daily 16-4h
Royal Beach Barcelo Hotel, on the northern side of the hotel ☎ (0554) 888 140 133

The best gay and lesbian bar on the Bulgarian seaside. House and pop music every evening. Music requests from the DJ are available. The interior is beautiful orient/arabic style. Cosy atmosphere, attractive prices, variety of alcoholic and non-alcoholic drinks and cocktails. In the afternoon 2-4-1 happy hour for some of the cocktails.

SEX SHOPS/BLUE MOVIES

■ **Erotic Center No 1** (g MA VS) 10-17h
Near Svezhest Hotel and bus station traffic lights ☏ (878) 429 739
Videos, underwear, toys, tools, lubes, condoms.

SWIMMING

-The beach towards Nessebar, after the Bourgas Hotel. Many single gay men. Action possible in bushes. Watch out for theaves.

Varna ☏ 052

BARS

■ **ID Club** (AC B cc D DR GLM MA P r S SNU ST VS)
Tue-Sat 23-?, summer daily 23-?h
33 Slivnitsa Blvd *Part of the Cherno More Hotel in the Kaskada Complex*
☏ 0897 300 400 www.idclub.bg

DANCECLUBS

■ **Momo Exterior Club** (B D glm MA) Jun-Sep
Sea Garden
Open-air gay friendly disco.

SEX SHOPS/BLUE MOVIES

■ **Cupidon** (G) 10.30-20h
4 Radko Dimitrive Str. www.sexshop.bg

HOTELS

■ **Kamchia Park Hotel** (AC B BF CC D H M MA MSG NR NU OS PI PK RWB RWS RWT S VEG WI WL) 24hrs
Kamchia Resort *25 km south from Varna. Bus twice a day from Varna main bus station* ☏ (05) 144 8329 ☏ 144 8320 www.kamchia.net
Unique combination of dense forest, Kamchia river and widest Black Sea beach. Popular gay summer destination. For those looking for calm and silent place for relax.

SWIMMING

-Albena Resort (situated 32 km north from Varna. Walk along the beach south to Kranevo village, after Gergana Hotel there is a big, beautiful nudist beach; almost all single males are gay; action possible in the bushes beyond the dunes)
-Golden Sands Resort. The resort is situsted 15 km north of Varna
-The nudist beach, after the yacht port in front of Glarus Hotel.

Veliko Tarnovo ☏ 062

SEX SHOPS/BLUE MOVIES

■ **Eros 2000** (g MA) 10-22h
Mednikarska Street 2 *Above former Hali shop parking* ☏ 0889 60 40 25

CRUISING

-Garden Park famous as 7 hills.

Yambol ☏ 046

SEX SHOPS/BLUE MOVIES

■ **Sexshop** (NG)
Snec bar Biliana, Graf Ignatiev 251 ☏ 0887 616 239

Cambodia

Name: Kâmpuchéa · Kambodscha · Cambodge · Camboya · Cambogia
Location: Southeast Asia
Initials: KH
Time: GMT +7
International Country Code: ☏ 855 (omit 0 from area code)
International Access Code: ☏ 00
Language: Khmer, English, French
Area: 181,035 km² / 69,898 sq mi.
Currency: 1 Riel (CR) = 100 Sen
Population: 14,701,000
Capital: Phnom Penh
Religions: 88% Buddhism
Climate: Tropical climate. The rainy monsoon season is from May-Nov, the dry season from Dec-Apr. There's little seasonal temperature variation.

Homosexuality in Cambodia is legal. The age of consent is equal for heterosexuals and homosexuals and is set at the age of 18. Prostitution involving minors is a legal offence until completion of the 18th year of age. It is recommended to check the age on the ID card of anyone you may consider taking back to your hotel, to avoid trouble with under-aged guys.
Thanks to Cambodia's predominantly tolerant Buddhist culture, homosexuality is well accepted in the country. In February 2004, the former King Norodom Sihanouk published on his website that he was impressed by the possibility for same-sex couples to marry in San Francisco, and should his people wish to do the same, he would approve this because God loved a "wide range of tastes". Despite this royal declaration, the legislation has not changed, even if some cases of lesbian marriages have been reported by local newspapers.
In the last few years, the gay scene has grown rapidly. It is now common to meet kteuy (lady boys) in the streets of Phnom Penh or Siem Reap, some of whom appear in drag shows at the popular gay venues. Every year the number of gay bars, hotels or saunas grows. In Cambodia some local gay-themed movies have been successful.
Since 2004, the annual meeting point for the community is the Gay Pride Week which takes place in May in Phnom Penh. The mythical Angkor Temples or the gorgeous beaches in the south are just two reasons to visit Cambodia.

In Kambodscha ist Homosexualität legal. Für Hetero- und Homosexuelle gilt das gleiche Mindestalter von 15 Jahren. Prostitution mit Minderjährigen bis zur Vollendung des 18. Lebensjahres ist strafbar. Es ist ratsam, sich das Alter von Personen, die man mit ins Hotel nehmen möchte, anhand des Personalausweises bestätigen zu lassen, damit man sich keine Schwierigkeiten wegen Sex mit Minderjährigen einhandelt.
Dank der vorwiegend buddhistisch geprägten und somit toleranten Kultur Kambodschas stößt die gleichgeschlechtliche Liebe hier auf breite Akzeptanz. Im Februar 2004 hatte der ehemalige König Norodom Sihanouk auf seiner Website sogar verlauten lassen, er sei beeindruckt davon , dass gleichgeschlechtliche Paare in Kalifornien die Möglichkeit haben, sich trauen zu lassen, und falls sein Volk dies auch wünsche, würde er zustimmen, denn Gott liebe „eine große Vielfalt von Geschmäckern". Die Gesetzeslage blieb allerdings ungeachtet dieser königlichen Erklärung unverändert, selbst wenn die Landespresse von einigen lesbischen Heiraten berichtet hat.
Die Schwulenszene hat sich in den letzten Jahren rapide entwickelt. Auf den Straßen von Phnom Pen oder Siem Reap ist es mittlerweile keine Seltenheit mehr, so genannte Kteuy (bzw. Ladyboys) zu sehen, die oft auch in den Travestieshows der beliebten Schwulenbars auftreten. Die Zahl der schwulen Lokale, Hotels und Saunen wächst von Jahr zu Jahr. In Kambodscha sind auch schon einheimische Spielfilme mit schwuler Thematik erfolgreich produziert worden.
Seit 2004 trifft sich die schwule Community jährlich zur Gay Pride Week, die im Mai in Phnom Pen stattfindet. Die fantastischen Tempel von Angkor und herrlichen Strände im Süden sind also nur zwei gute Gründe für einen Kambodschabesuch.

Au Cambodge, l'homosexualité est légale. La majorité sexuelle hétéro et homosexuelle est de 15 ans. La prostitution sur mineurs de moins de 18 ans fait l'objet de poursuites pénales. Il est recommandé de vérifier sur la carte d'identité l'âge des personnes que l'on amène à l'hôtel afin d'éviter des poursuites pour relations sexuelles avec mineur. Le Cambodge, empreint de mansuétude bouddhiste, accorde une large tolérance pour les amours de même sexe. En février 2004, l'ancien roi Norodom Sihanouk faisait même part sur son site web de son enthousiasme que les couples gays puissent se marier en Californie et qu'il l'accepterait aussi si son peuple le souhaitait car Dieu aime « la diversité des goûts ». La situation juridique est toutefois restée inchangée malgré cette déclaration du roi, bien que la presse ait eu lieu de quelques mariages lesbiens.
La scène gay s'est développée rapidement ces dernières années. Dans les rues de Phnom Pen ou de Siem Reap, il n'est plus rare de croiser des « Kteuy » (Ladyboys) qui se produisent dans des shows de transformisme dans les meilleurs bars gays. Le nombre de bars, hôtels et saunas croît continuellement. Au Cambodge, des films avec pour sujet l'homosexualité ont rencontré un succès.
Depuis 2004, la communauté gay fête la Gay Pride Week en mai à Phnom Pen. Les fantastiques temples d'Angkor et les magnifiques plages au sud sont deux raisons parmi de nombreuses de visiter le pays.

En Camboya, la homosexualidad es legal y la edad mínima (también para heterosexuales) es de 15 años, la mayoría de edad. La prostitución con menores hasta alcanzar los 18 años de edad es penada por la ley. Aconsejamos comprobar el DNI de quien quiera llevar al hotel para evitar problemas con menores de edad.
La cultura budista y tolerante de Camboya brinda gran aceptación a parejas del mismo sexo. En febrero de 2004 el entonces Rey Norodom Sihanouk anunció lo impresionado que estaba con el matrimonio gay en California y, si su pueblo así lo deseaba, estaría conforme, porque Dios ama „una gran variedad de gustosî. Pero la legislación no ha cambiado a pesar de las declaraciones reales, aun cuando informes de prensa nacionales atestiguan algunos matrimonios de lesbianas.
El ambiente gay se ha desarrollado rápidamente en los últimos años. En las calles de Phnom Penh y Siem Riep ya no extraña la presencia de los ladyboys, que actúan frecuentemente en shows para transformistas de los locales gays más populares. El número de bares, saunas y hoteles gays crece sin cesar, incluso se han rodado con éxito películas de temática homosexual.
Cada mayo desde 2004 la comunidad gay se reúne para celebrar en Phnom Pen la Semana del Orgullo Gay. Los magníficos templos de Angkor y las hermosas playas en el sur son sólo dos buenas razones para visitar Camboya.

In Cambogia l'omosessualità è legale e l'età del consenso è di 15 anni sia per eterosessuali che per omosessuali. Il favoreggiamento della prostituzione di minori che non abbiano ancora compiuto il diciottesimo anno di età è considerato un reato penale. Per evitare di essere accusati di praticare sesso con minorenni, si consiglia di accertarsi, tramite carta d'identità, dell'età delle persone che ci si vuol portare in albergo. Grazie alla cultura di influenza prevalentemente buddista e quindi tollerante, l'omosessualità in Cambogia è abbastanza accettata. Nel febbraio 2004 l'ex re Norodom Sihanouk ha annunciato, sul suo sito, di essere colpito dal fatto che in California le coppie dello stesso sesso avessero l'opportunità di sposarsi, aggiungendo che, qualora il suo popolo lo volesse, sarebbe disposto ad accettare una situazione simile, poiché Dio ama la diversità. Tuttavia, nonostante queste dichiarazioni, la situazione legislativa è rimasta la stessa. Negli ultimi anni la scena gay si è evoluta rapidamente. Sulle strade di Phnom Penh e Siem Reap non è più raro vedere i cosiddetti Kteuy (o ladyboys). Il numero di locali, saune e hotel gay cresce di anno in anno. In Cambogia sono già stati girati diversi film televisivi locali a tematica gay, che hanno avuto discreto successo. Dal 2004, la comunità gay festeggia il Gay Pride Week, che si tiene ogni anno a maggio a Phnom Pen. I magnifici templi di Angkor e le belle spiagge del sud sono solo due dei buoni motivi per visitare la Cambogia.

NATIONAL COMPANIES

Tropical & Travellers Medical Clinic
No. 88, St. 108 (Wat Phnom Quarter) ✉ Phnom Penh
☎ (023) 336 802 🖳 www.travellersmedicalclinic.com
Established in 1997 by British doctor Dr. Gavin Scott and is dedicated to the diagnosis and treatment of the diseases that tourists and travellers are likely to encounter in a tropical country.

HEALTH GROUPS

Khmer HIV/AIDS NGO Alliance (KHANA)
#33, Street 71, Tonle Basac ✉ Phnom Penh 3 ☎ (023) 306 802
🖳 khana.org.kh

Phnom Penh ☎ 023

BARS

Blue Chilli Bar (B D G m MA r ST) 18-?h
36 Street 178 *Next to National museum* ☎ (012) 566 353
🖳 www.bluechillibar.com
Gay bar with DJ and dancing late into the night, also with intimate blue room.

Empire. The (AC b M MA NG) 16-24h
#34, Street 130, Daun Pehn, Phsaa Kandal 1 ☎ (077) 851 230
🖳 www.the-empire.org
Gay owned and managed.

Fly Lounge (B GLM MA PI S) 17-?h
21 Street 148 (riverside) ☎ (089) 509 007

Rainbow Bar (B G OS S) 16-?h
Shop No 73, Street 172 *Near National museum and Wat Ounalom* ☎ (097) 741 4187
🖳 www.facebook.com/profile.php?id=100002014097142

Tonle Sap (B glm H M MA t)
N°4 & 6 Eo, Street 104 *Riversite, near Wat Phnom* ☎ (023) 986 722
🖳 www.tonlesapguesthouse.com
Traditional Cambodian music, local men and transgenders. Dark and cruisy.

■ **Touk** (B glm m MA)
Corner of 178 Street and Sisowath Quay ☎ (012) 248 694
Gay night on Fri.

DANCECLUBS

■ **Gloryhole @ Pontoon Club** (B D glm MA s t) Thu 21-?h
No 80 Street 172 ☎ (016) 779 966 🖳 www.pontoonclub.com
Gay every Thu.

■ **Heart of Darkness** (B D glm MA r) Fri & Sat 19-?h
26 Street 51 Pasteur
Popular fun place with both straight and gay crowd.

■ **QG** (B D GLM MA P S) 22-4h
#28 Street 172 ☎ (023) 630 2691 🖳 www.qgphnompenh.com

RESTAURANTS

■ **Empire. The** (AC b M MA NG) 16-24h
#34, Street 130, Daun Pehn, Phsaa Kandal 1 ☎ (077) 851 230
🖳 www.the-empire.org
Khmer food aimed at Western tastes. Gay-owned and managed.

SAUNAS/BATHS

■ **Amam Café and Spa** (B DR DU FC G I M MA SA SB VS WH) 16.30-22h, closed Mon
20A Street 390, Bong Keng Kong 3 *Between Genocide Museum and Mao Tse Tung Blvd* ☎ (012) 950 916 🖳 www.amam-cambodia.com
Amam was the first gay sauna to open in Cambodia.

■ **Galaxy Khmer** (b DR DU G MA OS RR SB VS WH WO) Daily 12-24h
18 Street 246, Sangkat Chaktamok *Behind the old parliament, near the palace and the Himawari Hotel* ☎ (016) 686 789
🖳 www.galaxykhmer.com

■ **Romantic** (B DR DU G M MA MSG RR SA SB VS WH WO) 14-24h
59 Street 350, Sang Kat Boeung Keng Kang 3, Kan Chamkar Morn
☎ (011) 377 666 🖳 www.romanticcambodia.com
Probably the biggest gay sauna in Phnom Penh and definitely the most popular.

MASSAGE

■ **Hatha Khmer** (AC B G MSG) 13-24h
32B Street 368, Boeung Keng Kang III, Khan Chamkarmorn
☎ (077) 643 232 🖳 www.hathakhmerspa.com

HOTELS

■ **Bougainvillier** (AC B BF cc H I M MA OS) All year
277C Sisowath Quay *3 minutes from National Museum and Royal Palace*
☎ (023) 220 528 🖳 bougainvillierhotel.com
All rooms with air-conditioner, cable-TV, private safe, mini bar, internet ADSL access. Also restaurant.

■ **Pavilion** (AC B CC GLM I M OS PI PK RWB RWS RWT)
All year, 24hrs
227 Street 19, Khan Daun Penh *Next to the Royal Palace*
☎ (023) 22 22 80 🖳 www.thepavilion.asia
Boutique hotel with 20 double rooms and one suite. Some rooms whith private pools. Gay-friendly accommodation. No sex tourists / no joiners allowed.

GUEST HOUSES

■ **Manor House** (AC b bf glm I m MA MSG PI RWS VA) All year
21 Street 262, Daun Penh *Close to Independence Monument*
☎ (023) 992 566 🖳 www.manorhousecambodia.com
Gay owned and managed. Attractive gay staff.

GENERAL GROUPS

■ **Phom Penh Pride**
🖳 phnompenhpride.blogspot.com
Organisers of the Phom Penh Pride held in May. facebook.com/cambodiapride

HEALTH GROUPS

■ **Tropical & Travellers Medical Clinic**
Mon-Fri 8.30-12, 14-17; Sat 8.30-12h
88 Street 108 *Near Wat Phnom, between railway station & the river*
☎ (023) 306 802 🖳 www.travellersmedicalclinic.com
General practice for tropical medicine,skin disease, fevers, sexual diseases and HIV-tests.Blood tests and vaccinations. British doctor with 20 years of experience in Cambodia.

CRUISING

-Olympic stadium (inside)
-Park near Independence Monument (ayor)
-Along the corniche on the riverfront (Quai Sisowath) 20-23h; at night (AYOR)
-Le Cercle Sportif 96th Street (PI)
-Phnom Penh pagoda (ayor r)
-National Stadium near Central Market or Psar Thmaey
-Tonle Sap River front area along Sisowath Quay (R, junkies, some police! Very AYOR!)
-Royal Palace surroundings.

Siem Reap ☎ 063

BARS

■ **Linga** (B cc d g m MA MSG r) 11-late, spa 14-23h or by appointment
On the passage 20 m from the Old Market *Across from John McDermott Gallery Annex, The One Hotel and Hotel Be Angkor*
☎ (012) 246 912 (mobile) 🖳 www.lingabar.com
Tourists pay tourist prices for US/European decor, with fewer guys worth chatting up, and a scattering of insistent ladyboys offering you massages.

■ **Miss Wong** (B g MA)
On The Lane, parallel to Pub Street ☎ (092) 428 332

■ **Station Bar, The** (B G S)
7 street *close to Pub Street and The Lane*
🖳 thestationwinebarsiemreap.com
Drag shows and main emphasis on wine variety.

RESTAURANTS

Viroth's (B g M MA)
242 Wat Bo St. ☎ (016) 951 800
www.viroth-hotel.com/restaurant.php
Gay owned restaurant serving refined cambodian cuisine. Moderately priced food and drinks.

SAUNAS/BATHS

Blue Hatha Spa (G MSG SA SB WH WO) 12-24h
Stoeung thmey road *Old Market Area, on the way to Artisans d'Angkor*
☎ (063) 355 5801 bluehatha.webs.com

Men's Resort & Spa (AC B BF CC DU FC FH G I LAB M MA MSG NR OS PI PK RR RWB RWS RWT SA SB SOL VA VEG WH WI WO) Hotel 24hrs, swimming pool & gym: 7h-23h, sauna: 17.30-23h
Wat Bo Street *Wat Po Lanka district, tell the taxi driver to call for direction*
☎ (063) 963 503 www.mens-resort.com
MEN's Resort & Spa is the only „gay exclusive" venue in Siem Reap. The resort includes a boutique hotel with 10 rooms, a large swimming pool, and a Sauna open to outside guests.

MASSAGE

Hatha Khmer (G MSG)
No 92 Street 22, Wat Bo Village ☎ (077) 585 756
www.hathakhmerspa.com

TRAVEL AND TRANSPORT

Lolei Travel (GLM)
0432 Watdamnak Village Salakomreuk Commune ☎ 063 964 732
www.loleitravel.com/gay-travel

HOTELS

Golden Banana Boutique Resort (AC B BF glm I M MA MSG PI RWB RWS RWT VA) All year
Wat Damnak Area, Phum Wat Damnak, Kum Sala Komreuk, Krom 10
Close to Angkor Wat ☎ (012) 654 638 www.goldenbanana.info
Resort that has been designed with 16 villas and suites in the traditional Khmer (Cambodian) pagoda style with modern Asian interiors. Gay owned and managed.

Hotel Be Angkor (AC bf cc g MSG) All year, 24hrs
On the Passage, between the Old Maket and Bar Street *Old Market area*
☎ (063) 965 321 www.hotelbeangkor.com
A design hotel offering three artist inspired rooms by Cambodian based artists in the heart of the vibrant Old Market area near boutiques, restaurants, bars, day spas and much more. Opposite Linga Bar and Linga Spa, same gay owner.

Men's Resort & Spa (AC B BF CC DU FC FH G I LAB M MA MSG NR OS PI PK RR RWB RWS RWT SA SB SOL VA VEG WH WI WO) Hotel 24hrs, swimming pool & gym: 7h-23h, sauna: 17.30-23h
Wat Bo Street *Wat Po Lanka district, tell the taxi driver to call for direction*
☎ (063) 963 503 www.mens-resort.com
MEN's Resort & Spa is the only „gay exclusive" venue in Siem Reap. The resort includes a boutique hotel with 10 rooms, a large swimming pool, and a Sauna open to outside guests.

Shinta Mani (BF H I M MA MSG PI SB) All year
Junction of Oum Khum and 14th Street *In the old French Quarter*
☎ (063) 761 998 www.shintamani.com
Closed due to renovation until spring 2012. Gay-friendly hotel. Rooms with in-room safe, hair-dryer, telephone, cable-TV, wireless internet, tea & coffee making facilities, refrigerator.

Viroth's Hotel (AC B bf CC glm H I M MSG PI RWB RWS RWT SOL WH) All year
0658 Wat Bo Village, Street 23 *City centre* ☎ (063) 761 720
www.viroth-hotel.com
This gay-friendly hotel is located in the heart of Siem Reap, adjacent to the river, walking distance to restaurants and shopping areas.

GUEST HOUSES

Auberge Mont Royal (AC cc H M MA MSG) All year
497 Taphul *Near Old Market* ☎ (012) 630 131 (mobile)
www.auberge-mont-royal.com
Gay-friendly guest house with 11 private ensuite rooms.

Ei8ht Rooms Guesthouse (AC glm H I MA RWS RWT VA WI) 24/7
138/ 139 Stheoung Thmey Village, Svaydangkum Commune *20 mins from the airport and a short stroll from the Old Market and Pub St.*
☎ (063) 969 788 www.ei8htrooms.com
Small and discreet gay-friendly guest house, located in the heart of Siem Reap.

Golden Banana B&B (AC B BF CC GLM I M MA MSG OS PI RWS VA) All year
Phum Wat Damnak, Kum Sala Komreuk, Krom 10 *Near Martini Pub*
☎ 012 885 366 (mobile) www.golden-banana.com
Reasonably priced guesthouse. Simple but beautiful furnishings. Gay owned & run. Good looking and friendly staff. A massage is a must here.

APARTMENTS

One Hotel Angkor. The (AC cc H M MA MSG WH) All year, 24hrs
On the passage, 20 m from the Old Market *Old Market area*
☎ (012) 755 311 www.theonehotelangkor.com
A charming luxury one suite hotel in the heart of the vibrant Old Market area near boutiques, restaurants, bars, day spas and much more. Opposite Linga Bar and Linga Spa, same gay owner.

CRUISING

-Around the old market along the river.

Sihanoukville ☎ 034

DANCECLUBS

Blue Storm (AC B D glm m MA) 20-1h
Ekareach Street
Mixed and lively disco with modern decor. Cute staff and helpful management, that is eager to give information about the local gay scene.

HOTELS

Cheers Boutique Hotel (AC B bf cc D GLM M MA S) All year
129 Borey Kamakor Street, Sangkat 3 ☎ (034) 934 585
www.cheers-cambodia.com
The first 100% gay boutique hotel, restaurant & bar in Sihanoukville.

GUEST HOUSES

Sihanoukville Villa Hotel (AC B BF CC GLM H M RWT) All year
14 Mithona Street, Phum 4, Sangat 4, Khan Mitapheap *5 mins walk from Serindipity & Ochheuteal Beaches* ☎ (012) 1600 374 (mobile)
www.sihanoukville.info/sihanoukville-villa-hotel/
Handsome and accomodating staff. Sihanoukvilles first gay-friendly guest house.

Canada

Name: Kanada · Canadá

Location: North America

Initials: CDN

Time: GMT -4/ -5/ -6/ -7/ -8

International Country Code: ☏ 1

International Access Code: ☏ 011

Language: English, French

Area: 9,984,670 km² / 3,844,910 sq mi.

Currency: 1 Canadian Dollar (Can$) = 100 Cents

Population: 31,974,000

Capital: Ottawa

Religions: 43,6% Catholic, 29,2% Protestant

Climate: Summer (Jul & Aug) are best, when many of the country's festivals take place. The peak tourist season is between Jun-Sep.

Important gay cities: Montréal, Toronto, Vancouver

Canada is a very liberal country and has a very colourful gay scene. Canada's age of sexual consent has been bumped up two years to 16 on the 1st May 2008. There is however an exception concerning anal intercourse, prostitution and exploitation of dependant relationships where the age of consent is set at 18 years. Protection against discrimination on the grounds of homosexuality is protected by law. Legislation in Canada is extremely advanced: since 2005 same-sex partnerships are recognized for both homosexual and heterosexual couples, with the same rights as marriage, including adoption rights. The Conservative party won the recent elections, although only 59 per cent of the population voted, the lowest in federal election history.

A group from Rev. Fred Phelps' Westboro Baptist Church in Kansas (USA) was denyed enterance into Canada at a border crossing south of Winnipeg. Phelps runs the „God Hates Fags" website. Canadian hate laws give the government the power to deny entry to people likely to violate the law. The so-called church was listed as a hate group under the law following previous protests. For the gay tourist the three metropolises Toronto, Vancouver and Montréal are of particular interest. Canada is unspoiled nature with large, bustling cities. This variable country stretches across 6 time zones, is surrounded by three different oceans and is the second largest country in the world. In contrast to its image that Canada is a frost and cold country high up there in the north, the Canadians remain unchallenged when comparing their „joie du vivre „, and culture with that of the Europeans.

Kanada ist ein sehr liberales Land und hat eine sehr bunte schwullesbische Szene. Beim Schutzalter wird nicht zwischen homo- oder heterosexuellen Handlungen unterschieden: es liegt für alle bei 16 Jahren - allerdings mit den Einschränkungen, dass für Analverkehr, Prostitution und Sex mit Abhängigen generell die Altersgrenze bei 18 Jahren liegt. Der Schutz vor Diskriminierung aufgrund von Homosexu-

alität ist gesetzlich verankert. Die kanadische Rechtsprechung ist äußerst fortschrittlich: gleichgeschlechtliche Partnerschaften sind seit 2005 möglich und genießen die gleichen Rechte wie die Ehe - inklusive Adoption. Die konservative Partei ging aus den jüngsten Wahlen als Sieger hervor, allerdings haben auch nur 59 Prozent der Wahlberechtigten gewählt, was auf Bundesebene die niedrigste Wahlbeteiligung aller Zeiten darstellt. An einem Grenzübergang südlich von Winnipeg wurde einer Gruppe der Westboro-Baptistengemeinde des Pastors Fred Phelps aus Kansas (USA) die Einreise nach Kanada verweigert. Phelps ist Betreiber der Website „God Hates Fags". Die kanadische Gesetzgebung für Hassdelikte räumt der Regierung das Recht ein, die Einreise von Personen zu verhindern, die wahrscheinlich gegen das Gesetz verstoßen werden. Die so genannte „Kirchengemeinde" war zuvor nach Protesten in eine ebenfalls diesem Gesetz zufolge geführte Liste von Hass verbreitenden Gruppierungen aufgenommen worden.

Für die schwulen und lesbischen Reisenden sind besonders die drei Metropolen Toronto, Vancouver und Montréal von Interesse.

Kanada - das ist unberührte Natur und mittendrin quirlige Großstädte auf einer riesigen Fläche: dieses abwechslungsreiche Land erstreckt sich über 6 Zeitzonen, wird von drei Weltmeeren umgeben und ist damit das zweitgrößte Land der Welt. Entgegen dem Vorurteil, dass Kanada ein frostiges Land hoch im Norden ist, stehen die Kanadier den Europäern in punkto Lebenslust, Feierfreude und Kultur in nichts nach.

Le Canada est un pays très libéral et son milieu gay est haut en couleur. La majorité sexuelle est fixée à 16 ans pour tous sauf pour la pénétration anale, la prostitution et le rapport sexuel avec des personnes en situation d'autorité ou de confiance pour lesquels l'âge minimal reste fixé à 18 ans. La discrimination des homosexuel(le)s est également interdite par la loi. La juridiction canadienne est extrêmement progressiste: depuis 2005 les relations entre personnes de même sexe sont reconnues pour les homos comme pour les hétéros et garanti les mêmes droits que le mariage, y compris l'adoption.

Le Parti Conservateur est sorti vainqueur des dernières élections, cependant la participation ne s'est élevée qu'à 59%, ce qui représente la plus faible participation de tous les temps.

A un poste frontière au sud de Winnipeg, un groupe de la Westboro Baptist Church du pasteur Fred Phelps du Kansas (USA) s'est vu refuser l'entrée au Canada. Phelps exploite le site web „God Hates Fags" (Dieu déteste les pédés). La législation canadienne en matière d'incitation à la haine accorde le droit au gouvernement d'empêcher l'entrée aux personnes succesptibles d'enfreindre cette loi. Après des protestations, cette soi-disant „paroisse" a été enregistrée sur une liste des groupements incitant à la haine, liste elle-même issue de cette loi.

Pour les touristes gays et lesbiens, les trois métropoles Toronto, Vancouver et Montréal sont particulièrement intéressantes.

Le Canada, deuxième plus grand pays du monde, s'étale sur 6 fuseaux horaires et est entouré de trois océans. Ses villes animées trônent au milieu d'une nature préservée. Contrairement au préjugé représentant le Canada comme un pays du nord très froid, les canadiens n'ont rien à envier aux Européens en ce qui concerne la joie de vivre, le sens de la fête et la culture en général.

Canadá es un país muy liberal y tiene un ambiente gay-lésbico muy variado. En cuanto a la edad de consentimiento, no se diferencia entre homosexuales y heterosexuales: está fijada para todos en los 16 años; sin embargo existen limitaciones para el sexo anal, prostitución y para el sexo con menores, supuestos en los que generalmente la edad de consentimiento está en los 18 años. La protección en contra de la discriminación por razón de la homosexualidad está reglada por ley. La jurisprudencia canadiense es muy avanzada: desde 2005 las parejas del mismo sexo están reconocidas Aquí rige el principio de que las parejas de hecho registradas, tanto homosexuales como heterosexuales, son legales y gozan de los mismos derechos que un matrimonio, incluso la adopción.

El partido conservador salió ganador de las recientes elecciones, no obstante tan sólo votaron un 59% de los electores, lo que representa el nivel más bajo de participación electoral en el ámbito federal.

En un puesto fronterizo al sur de Winnipeg se denegó el permiso de entrada a Canadá a un grupo de la „comunidad de baptistas de Westboro" del pastor Fred Phelps de Kansas (EUA). Phelps es el divulgador de la página web llamada „Gob Hates Fags". La legislación canadiense para estos delitos confiere al gobierno el derecho de impedir la entrada de personas que presumiblemente vayan a infringir la ley. Esta tal llamada „comunidad religiosa" había sido inscrita anteriormente, debido a las protestas y según esta legislación, en la lista de asociaciones que fomentan el odio. Para los turistas gays y lesbianas, las tres metrópolis Toronto, Vancouver y Montreal son de gran interés.
Canadá significa naturaleza casi virgen y dinámicas ciudades en una extensión enorme de tierra: este país tan diverso se extiende por más de 6 husos horarios, está rodeado por 3 océanos y es el segundo país más grande del mundo. En contra del prejuicio que dice que Canadá es un país frío, los canadienses, por sus ganas de vivir, de fiesta y su cultura, no tienen nada que envidiar a los europeos.

Il Canada è un paese molto liberale che ha una scena gay molto variopinta. L'età del consenso è di 16 anni e non viene fatta differenza alcuna tra omosessuali ed eterosessuali; tuttavia ci sono restrizioni per quanto riguarda il sesso anale, la prostituzione e i rapporti di dipendenza: in questo caso l'età del consenso è di 18 anni. La tutela contro discriminazioni nei riguardi di omosessuali è un fondamento legislativo. La legge canadese è molto progressista: dal 2005 le unioni tra partner dello stesso sesso sono riconosciute dalla legge. Le convivenze registrate valgono sia per omosessuali che per eterosessuali con tutti i diritti che sono riconosciuti al matrimonio incluso il diritto di adozione.
Il partito conservatore è uscito vincente dalle ultime elezioni, anche se è da tener presente che solo il 59% degli aventi diritto si è recato alle urne, facendo registrare il minimo storico di affluenza alle urne.
Ad una dogana a sud di Winnipeg è stato vietato l'ingresso in Canada ad un gruppo di seguaci della chiesa battista di Westboro del pastore Fred Phelps proveniente dal Kansas. Fred Phelps è il responsabile del sito „God Hates Fags" (Dio odia i froci). La legislazione canadese per i delitti di odio riserva al governo il diritto di impedire l'ingresso nel Paese a persone che potrebbero eventualmente infrangere le leggi canadesi. La cosiddetta comunità ecclesiastica, dopo delle proteste, era già stata accolta da delle associazioni che erano già state inserite, per disposizione della legge sovramenzionata, nella cosiddetta lista dell'odio. Le 3 città più importanti dal punto di vista gay sono le metropoli di Toronto, Vancouver e Montreal: offrono una scena molto vivace. Il Canada offre una natura incontaminata. Questo Paese si contraddistingue per la sua varietà: il Canada è il secondo Paese al mondo per estensione, è attraversato da 6 fusi orari e viene circondato da 3 oceani. Per gioia di vivere, voglia di divertimento e cultura, i canadesi non hanno niente da invidiare agli europei.

NATIONAL GAY INFO

Canadian Lesbian & Gay Archives. The (GLM MA)
Tue-Thu 19.30-22h (and by appointment); closed in Aug
34 Isabella Street ✉ Toronto ☎ (416) 777-2755 🖳 www.clga.ca
Archives, library and research centre. Large collection of periodicals.

Guidemag.com (GLM MA)
2 Carlton Street, suite 1600, Toronto ✉ M5B 1J3 Toronto
☎ (416) 925-6665 🖳 www.guidemag.com
Gay travel website

NATIONAL PUBLICATIONS

Outlooks Mon-Fri 9-17h
1B, 1230A 17th Avenue SW ✉ AB T2T 0B8 Calgary ☎ (403) 228-1157
🖳 www.outlooks.ca
Monthly magazine distributed throughout Canada.

NATIONAL COMPANIES

Footprints (GLM)
19 Madison Street, Ste 300 ✉ ON M5R 2S2 Toronto ☎ (416) 962-8111
🖳 www.footprintstravel.com
Private, custom-designed luxury and experiential travel to destinations around the world.

Immigration Link Mon-Fri 9.30-17h, preferably by appointment
1 Gloucester Street, Suite 114B ✉ ON M4Y 1L8 Toronto *At Yonge Street*
☎ (416) 922-9495 🖳 www.gayimmigration.ca
Specialist in Canadian immigration for gays and lesbians, couples and singles.

SQUIRT (GLM MA)
491 Church Street, Toronto 🖳 www.squirt.org
A fantastic site, very unique and ideal for crusing world-wide. Join for free. Squirt has some great features to check out: www.squirt.org.

Wega Video (CC G)
930 Rue Sainte-Catherine Est ✉ QC H2L 2E7 Montréal *M° Beaudry*
☎ (514) 987-5993 🖳 www.wegavideo.ca
One of Canada's largest online adult gay video stores.

Alberta

Location: Southwest CDN
Initials: AB
Time: GMT -7
Area: 661,000 km² / 255,212 sq mi.
Population: 2,847,000
Capital: Edmonton
Important gay cities: Calgary and Edmonton

Calgary ☎ 403

GAY INFO

Calgary Outlink 19-22h
1528 16th Avenue SW ☎ (403) 234-8973 🖳 www.calgaryoutlink.ca
Peer support, information, library and drop-in centre.

PUBLICATIONS

GayCalgary and Edmonton Magazine
2136, 17th Avenue SW ☎ (403) 543-6960
🖳 www.gaycalgary.com
GayCalgary Online and GayCalgary and Edmonton Magazine are the resources for business, tourism, events, bars and entertainment for the GLBT community in Calgary and Edmonton.

BARS

Backlot. The (B CC GLM MA OS VS) 16-2h
209 10th Avenue SW *Access is down a small alley* ☎ (403) 265-5211
Not very large. Lounge with gas fireplace making it cozy in the winter. Friendly owner.

Calgary Eagle. The (B F G M MA)
17-24h, Fri & Sat -2, Sun 15-24h, closed Mon & Tue
424a 8th Avenue SE *Behind City Hall* ☎ (403) 263-5847
🖳 www.calgaryeagle.com
Gay leather bar with pool tables and restaurant.

Club Paradiso (B glm m MA S)
1413 9th Avenue SE *Upstairs* ☎ (403) 265-5739
🖳 www.villagecantina.ca
Entertainment on Fri & Sat.

Fab (B CC GLM M MA OS)
16-24, Fri -2, Sat 11-2, Sun -22h, closed Mon
1742 10th Avenue South West ☎ (403) 263-7411
🖳 www.fab-bar.com
Bar with restaurant.

Texas Lounge (B G MA) 11-2h
308B 17th Avenue SW *Behind Victoria's Restaurant* ☎ (403) 229-0911
🖳 www.goliaths.ca

DANCECLUBS

Club Sapien (B D GLM M MA) 17-?, Mon -23h
1140 10 Avenue SW *Near cnr. 11th Street SW* ☎ (403) 457-4464
🖳 www.clubsapien.ca
Dance club with bar & restaurant.

■ **Twisted Element** (AC B D GLM I MA S SNU)
Wed & Fri 20-3, Thu & Sat 21-3, Sun 19-3h
1006 11th Avenue SW ☏ (403) 802-0230 💻 www.twistedelement.ca
Featuring a lounge downstairs with karaoke and dragshows on wednesday nights when the dancefloor upstairs remains closed.

SEX SHOPS/BLUE MOVIES

■ **Priape** (F G) 12-20, Sun -18h
1322, 17th Avenue SW ☏ (403) 215-1800 💻 www.priape.com
Gay leather clothes & video store.

SAUNAS/BATHS

■ **Goliath's** (b DU FC G m MA P RR SB VS WH) 24hrs
308B 17th Avenue South West *Opp. Texas Lounge* ☏ (403) 229-0911
💻 www.goliaths.ca
For members only. Membership cards are valid for 6 months.

GUEST HOUSES

■ **11th Street Lodging** (bf CC glm H I OS PK RWB RWS RWT VA)
Check-in: 14-19h
1307 11th Street South West *Downtown* ☏ (403) 209-1800
💻 www.11street.com
Five doubles, 1 single with shared bath, 1 studio & 1 apartment with private bath. Rooms with balcony, radio, internet access and TV/VCR.

■ **Calgary Westways Guesthouse** (AC BF CC GLM I MSG PA PK RWB RWS RWT VA WH) All year
216 25th Avenue South West *Downtown* ☏ (403) 229-1758
💻 www.gaywestways.com
All 5 rooms with private baths, Hi-Def TV, DVD, free wireless.

CRUISING

-East end of Prince Island
-University of Calgary (Education Building, men's restroom, 2nd floor)
-13th Avenue South West (r) (between 6th & 7th Street South West)
-Washrooms at Glenmore Park, Calgary Zoo car park, Lindsay Park and Devonian Gardens.

Edmonton ☏ 780

GAY INFO

■ **Pride Centre of Edmonton** (AC GLM MA T)
Tue-Fri 13-22, Sat 14-18.30h, closed Sun & Mon
10608 - 105 Ave ☏ (780) 488-3234 (Infoline)
💻 www.pridecentreofedmonton.org

BARS

■ **Junction Bar & Eatery** (B CC D GLM M MA)
16-2, kitchen -20h, closed Sun
10242 106th Street *Cnr. 103rd Avenue* ☏ (780) 756-5667
💻 www.junctionedmonton.com
Former Boots ,n' Saddles. Now bar with restaurant and danceclub.

■ **Woody's** (AC B cc GLM M MA S) 12-24, WE -3h
11723 Jasper Avenue *Upstairs, bus 5* ☏ (780) 488-6636
Friendly pub with huge windows overlooking the street. No loud music. Also restaurant.

DANCECLUBS

■ **Buddy's** (AC B D f GLM MA S SNU) 21-3h
11725 Jasper Avenue *Downstairs, bus 5* ☏ (780) 488-6636
💻 www.buddysedmonton.com
Dance club with shows/events every night of the week.

■ **Flash** (B d glm MA)
10018 105 Street ☏ (780) 938-2941
Bar with a small dancefloor.

SAUNAS/BATHS

■ **Steamworks** (DR DU FC G GH I LAB M MA p SA SB SL VS WI)
Daily, 24hrs
11745 Jasper Ave *Back entrance next door to Buddys/Woodys building, bus 5* ☏ (780) 451-5554 💻 www.steamworksedmonton.com
2 floors with huge dry sauna on one floor and big maze.

BOOK SHOPS

■ **Audrey's Books** (GLM SH) 9-21, Sat 9.30-17.30, Sun 12-17h
10702 Jasper Avenue ☏ (780) 423-3487 ☏ 800-661-3649 (toll free)
💻 www.audreys.ca

CRUISING

It is illegal to be in any of the public parks after 22h and fines are imposed for those caught.

British Columbia

Location: Southwest CDN
Initials: BC
Time: GMT -8
Area: 949,000 km² / 366,409 sq mi
Population: 3,933,000
Capital: Victoria

Kamloops ☏ 250

GENERAL GROUPS

■ **Kamloops Gay and Lesbian Association** (GLM MA)
PO Box 2071 Stn A ☏ (250) 376-7311 💻 www.gaykamloops.ca

Kelowna ☏ 250

GUEST HOUSES

■ **Eagle's Nest B&B** (AC BF CC GLM I MA MSG PI PK RWB RWS RWT SA VA WH) All year
15620 Commonage Road *On Okanagan Lake* ☏ (866) 766-9350
💻 www.theeaglesnestbandb.com

Nanaimo ☏ 250

BARS

■ **70 Below** (B CC D GLM MA) 20-2, Fri & Sat 17-2h
70 Church Street *Under the Dorchester Hotel* ☏ (250) 716-0505
💻 www.70below.bravehost.com
Bar with karaoke shows on Wed.

Vancouver

✱ Vancouver, Canada's gateway to the Pacific, is the country's third largest and most beautiful city. With strong British and European roots, the city's growing ethnic groups include Southeast Asian, Iranian and an increasing number of Latin Americans who now call Vancouver home.
Vancouver has the mildest winters in the country. The average January temperature is 0°C, while in summer temperatures average around 20°C to 24°C from May to September. Vancouver can be a rainy city, but is never the less a year-round gay-friendly destination.
Several first class ski resorts (Whistler for example) are within the metropolitan area. Whistler hosts a Gay Ski Week each February and attracts hundreds of gay skiers from around the world.
Vancouver's „gay village" in the West End is concentrated along Davie Street. Attractions include the annual fireworks display on the English Bay and the Pride Parade at the end of July with gay events taking place a week long.
Vancouver is one of the cleanest cities in North America. The city has a good public transport system on land and on the water. Vancouver - a natural destination for the gay visitor.

★ Vancouver, Kanadas Tor zum Pazifik, ist die drittgrößte und schönste Stadt des Landes. Mit starken britischen und europäischen Wurzeln, zählen Menschen aus Südostasien, dem Iran und eine wachsende Zahl Lateinamerikaner zu den immer zahlreicher werdenden multikulturellen Bewohnern der Stadt, für die Vancouver zu einer neuen Heimat wurde.

Vancouver hat den mildesten Winter des Landes. Die durchschnittliche Temperatur im Januar beträgt 0°C, während im Sommer, von Mai bis September, die Durchschnittswerte zwischen 20 und 24°C liegen. In der Stadt kann es regnerisch sein, aber sie ist dennoch das ganze Jahr über ein schwulenfreundliches Reiseziel.
Im Einzugsgebiet der Stadt befinden sich einige erstklassige Skigebiete, wie beispielsweise Whistler. Dort findet jeden Februar eine schwule Skiwoche mit Hunderten schwuler Skifreunde aus aller Welt statt.
Vancouvers „schwules Viertel" im West End konzentriert sich um die Davie Street. Zu den Attraktionen gehört das jährliche Feuerwerk in der English Bay und die Pride Parade Ende Juli, die von einer Woche schwuler Veranstaltungen begleitet wird.
Vancouver ist eine der saubersten Städte Nordamerikas und verfügt zu Lande und auf dem Wasser über ein gutes öffentliches Nahverkehrsnetz. Ein Reiseziel für den schwulen Besucher!

Vancouver, la porte du Pacifique est la troisième plus grande ville du Canada et certainement la plus belle. A son origine, elle a été fortement imoregnée de culture anglaise et européene. Par la suite, des influences asiatiques et iraniennes se sont faites sentir. Aujourd'hui l'arrivée des Latino-américains vient encore plus renforcer le caractere cosmopolite de cette nouvelle patrie que Vancouver est devenue pour tant de personnes. Vancouver est la ville ayant le climat le plus doux de tout les pays. En janvier la température moyenne est de 0 degrés, alors que de mai à septembre elle oscille entre 20 et 24 degrés. Le temps est certes souvent pluvieux, ce n'est toutefois pas une raison suffisante pour ne pas être une destination préférée des gays. Dans les environs de la ville se trouve Whistler, station de ski très prisée. Il s'y tient les ans, au mois de février une semaine de ski réservée au gays où se retrouvent des skieurs de la terre entière. Le quartier homo de la ville: le West End se concentré sur la rue Davie Street. Parmi les attractions de la ville, on notera le feu d'artifice d'English Bay fin juin ainsi que la Pride Parade à la fin de juillet, une semaine composée d'évènements pour les gays. Vancouver, ville entre terre et eaux, fait partie des villes les plus propres d'Amérique du Nord ; de plus, son réseau de transports en commun performant, en fait véritablement une destination privilégiée pour le touriste gay.

Vancouver, la puerta de Canadá al Pacífico, es la tercera ciudad y la más bella del país. Con profundas raíces en la cultura británica y europea, la ciudad cuenta con una población cada vez más multicultural, entre cuyos habitantes aparecen también gentes del Sureste asiático, de Irán y un creciente número de latinoamericanos, para los que Vancouver se ha convertido en su nuevo hogar.
Vancouver tiene el invierno más suave del país. La temperatura media en enero llega a los 0°C, mientras que en verano, de mayo a septiembre, los valores oscilan entre los 20 y 24°C. La ciudad puede llegar a ser lluviosa, pero todo el año es un destino turístico tolerante con los homosexuales.
En los alrededores de la ciudad se encuentran algunas zonas de esquí de primer orden, como Whistler. Allí se celebra cada febrero una semana gay de esquí, con cientos de aficionados de todo el mundo.
El „barrio gay" de Vancouver en West End es concentrado por la calle Davie Street. Entre sus atracciones destacan los fuegos artificiales anuales en la English Bay, a finales de julio, y la Marcha del Orgullo Gay, al fin de julio, que viene acompañada de una semana repleta de actividades.

Vancouver, porta del Canada sul Pacifico, è la terza città del paese e, sicuramente, la più bella. Le radici sono britanniche ed europee, ma vi si trovano molti abitanti originari del Sud-Est Asiatico, dell'Iran, e sempre più latino-americani che formano una città decisamente multiculturale.
Vancouver ha l'inverno più mite del paese. La temperatura media in gennaio si aggira intorno a 0°C, mentre in estate, da maggio a settembre, è tra i 20 e i 24°C. Puó essere una città piovosa, ma ciò nonostante rimane, durante tutto l'anno, una delle mete turistiche preferite dai gay.
Nella regione di Vancouver si trovano alcune tra le migliori stazioni sciistiche, come ad esempio Whistler. Qui, ogni febbraio, ha luogo la settimana bianca gay con centinaia di ragazzi omosessuali, appassionati di sci, provenienti da tutto il mondo.

Il quartiere gay di Vancouver in West End è concentrato lungo la Davie Street. Tra le maggiori attrazioni vanno ricordati gli annuali fuochi d'artificio nella English Bay, alla fine di luglio, e il Gay Pride alla fine di luglio, accompagnato per un'intera settimana da manifestazioni di segno marcatamente gay.

GAY INFO

Qmunity (GLM MA) Mon-Fri 9-17h
1170 Bute Street, (Upstairs) *Cnr. Davie St., 2nd floor* ☎ 604-684-5307
www.qmunity.ca
Community centre serving and supporting LGBT people and their allies. Featuring „Out On The Shelves" Canada's largest gay & lesbian lending library for gay books, magazines and videos. Visitors welcome.

gayvancouver.net (GLM MA)
www.gayvancouver.net
Gay info-website for Vancouver.

Living Out Vancouver (GLM MA)
www.LOVmag.com
Bimonthly magazine on the local gay scene.

PUBLICATIONS

Lov
www.lovmag.com
Quarterly gay lifestyle magazine.

XTRA West Mon-Fri 9-17h
1033 Davie Street, Suite 501 ☎ 604-684-9696 www.xtra.ca
Vancouver's free gay and lesbian bi-weekly newspaper distributed throughout the Metro Vancouver area.

TOURIST INFO

Tourism Vancouver
200 Burrard Street ☎ 604-682-2222 www.tourismvancouver.com
Tourism centre.

BARS

1181 (B GLM MA) 17-2h
1181 Davie Street ☎ 604-787-7130 www.1181.ca
Stylish cocktail lounge.

LOV
boys of summer!
PRIDE
OUTGAMES
OUR STORIES, OURSELVES
7
TALES OF PRIDE
ISSUE 12
living out vancouver
SUMMER JUL-SEP 2011 . FREE
http://tjnphotography.tumblr.com

■ **Cruisey T** (B D GLM M MA S WE)
1 North Foot of Denman Street *At Harbour Cruises* ☎ 604-551-2628
💻 www.CruiseyT.com
Vancouver's fabulous „floating T-dance" with 4 hour harbour cruises onboard M/V Britannia. Each year from spring through fall. Ship sails from Harbour Cruises at the foot of Denman Street. DJs and special theme cruises. See www.CruiseyT.com for exact dates and times.

■ **Fountainhead Pub. The** (B cc GLM m MA OS) 11-24, Fri & Sat -1h
1025 Davie Street ☎ 604-687-2222 💻 www.thefountainheadpub.com
Has one of the best people-watching patios in the village.

■ **J Lounge** (AC B CC glm MA)
1216 Bute Street *Cnr. Davie St* ☎ 604-609-6665

■ **Oasis Ultra Lounge** (AC B cc GLM M MA OS s VS)
15.30-24, Fri & Sat -1h
1240 Thurlow Street *Upstairs, at Davie* ☎ 604-685-1724
💻http://www.facebook.com/pages/Oasis-Ultra-Lounge/147492995293680
Vancouver's only gay piano bar with guest pianists. Tapas style menu. Outdoor heated patio. No cover charge.

■ **PumpJack Pub. The** (B cc f G MA) 13-1, Fri & Sat -2h
1167 Davie Street ☎ 604-685-3417 💻 www.pumpjackpub.com
Jeans and leather bar, popular with bears but also frequented by drags and twinks. Lineups on weekend. No cover charge.

■ **Score on Davie** (AC B cc glm M MA OS S VS) 10-?h
1262 Davie Street ☎ 604-632-1646 💻 www.scoreondavie.com
Video sports restaurant and bar with 3 big screen TVs. Covered and heated patio on Davie Street. Margaritas and Martinis, brunch on WE.

DANCECLUBS

■ **Celebrities** (AC B D GLM MA S SNU ST) Tue-Sat 21-3h
1022 Davie Street *At Burrard St* ☎ 604-681-6180
💻 www.celebritiesnightclub.com
The cities's largest danceclub on various levels with special themed nights. Check www.celebritiesnightclub.com for details.

■ **Numbers** (AC B D G MA S SNU VS)
21-2, Fri & Sat -4, Sun 20-2h, Mon closed
1042 Davie Street ☎ 604-685-4077 💻 www.numbers.ca
Popular multi-level bar and dance club with 3 bars, dart boards, pool table. Weekly events include strip contests, live and lip-sync drag shows. Cash bar only. Cover charge Fri-Sat after 22.30h.

RESTAURANTS

■ **Hamburger Mary's** (B glm M MA OS s) 8-3, Fri & Sat -4, Sun -2h
1202 Davie Street *Cnr. Bute St* ☎ 604-687-1293 💻 www.hamburgermarys.ca
An institution in Vancouver.

SEX SHOPS/BLUE MOVIES

■ **Priape** (CC F G MA) 10-22, Sun 12-21h
1148 Davie Street ☎ 604-630 2330 💻 www.priape.com

SAUNAS/BATHS

■ **F212° Steam**
(AC CC DR DU FC G GH I LAB m MA RR SB VS WH WO) 24hrs
1048 Davie Street *Between Burrard & Thurlow, Davie Bus stops nearby*
☎ 604-689-9719 💻 www.f212.com
Very clean and well-equipped sauna on 6,500 sq ft. Membership has benefits. Premises completely renovated May 2010.

■ **M2M Vancouver** (AK DR DU F FC G MA p RR SB SL VS) 24hrs
1210 Granville Street *Near cnr. of Davie St* ☎ 604-684-6011
💻 www.m2mvancouver.com
Well-equipped play space, private and public rooms. Large maze, slings, group showers, deluxe steam room and videos. Membership at F212 will be accepted at M2M.

■ **Steam 1** (B CC DR DU G GH I M SB VS WO) 24hrs
430 Columbia Street, New Westminster *Opp. Columbia SkyTrain station*
☎ (604) 540-2117 💻 www.steam1.com
Rentals for both rooms and lockers are for 8 hours; thereafter a low overtime charge is applied. „Buddy Nite" on Mon & Wed. „Gym Nite" on Tue (18-2h) - discount with valid fitness club card. Under 28 year olds discount on Thu.

■ **Steamworks** (AC CC DR DU F FC FH G I LAB m MA SA SB SL VS WH WO) Daily, 24hrs
123 West Pender Street *One block north of Stadium skytrain station*
☎ 604-974-0602 💻 www.steamworks.ca
This sauna belongs to a group which has properties in Chicago, Seattle and Berkeley, USA as well as Toronto and Vancouver in Canada. Membership applies to all 5 bath houses.

GIFT & PRIDE SHOPS

■ **Little Sisters Book and Art Emporium**
(AC CC GLM MA PK T W) 10-23h
1238 Davie Street *Centre of Gay Davie Village* ☎ (604) 669-1753
💻 www.littlesisters.ca
Also information and ticket centre for numerous gay community events. Free maps of gay Vancouver available.

HOTELS

■ **Opus Vancouver** (AC B glm I M MC MSG PA PK RWS RWT VA WO) All year
322 Davie Street, Yaletown *Walking distance to Davie Village*
☎ 604- 642 6787 💻 www.opushotel.com

■ **Rosellen Suites at Stanley Park. The** (CC glm I PA PK RWS RWT VA) Office: Mon-Fri 9-17.30, Sat & Sun 9-15h
2030 Barclay Street *At Stanley Park, close to downtown attractions*
☎ 604 689-4807 💻 www.rosellensuites.com
Located in a quiet residential neighbourhood near Stanley Park, the 1 and 2-bedroom suites are among the largest in the city.

GUEST HOUSES

■ **Nelson House B&B** (BF CC GLM I PK RWB RWS RWT VA)
Closed 24, 25, 31 Dec; 1 Jan
977 Broughton Street *West End near downtown* ☎ 604-684-9793
💻 www.downtownbandb.com
Short walk to downtown & gay village. One suite with Jacuzzi, 3 rooms with private bath, 2 rooms share a hall-bath.

■ **West End Guest House** (BF GLM I MA PK RWS RWT WI)
8-20h
1362 Haro Street *West End* ☎ 604-681-2889
💻 www.westendguesthouse.com
Victorian style house. Rooms decorated with antiques. Feather beds and microfibre sheets. Sundeck for summer afternoons. Bikes for lending. Wi-fi complimentary and more.

HEALTH GROUPS

■ **AIDS Vancouver** 9-16h
1107 Seymour Street *Downtown - Seymour at Helmcken*
☎ 604-893-2201 💻 www.aidsvancouver.org
Gay Men's Health provides guys a range of health promotion, education, and support services regarding issues of sexual health. Houses AIDS Research Centre.

CRUISING

-Homer Street, downtown Vancouver between Davie and Drake streets (R)
-Stanley Park near the bridge west of Lost Lagoon
-Pacific Center Mall - 3rd floor washroom near atrium
-Wreck Beach - See swimming
-Kitsilano Park (at the pool)
-Central Park- Burnaby - washrooms and trails near Northern duck pond and horseshoe pitch. Enter off Boundary Road-
-Brunette River Park (New Westminster).

Victoria ☎ 250

BARS

■ **Paparazzi Nightclub** (AC B CC d GLM m MA ST VS) 13-2, Sun -24h
642 Johnson Street *Corner of Broad and Johnson Street*
☎ (250) 388-0505 💻 www.paparazzinightclub.com

DANCECLUBS

■ **Hush** (B D glm MA) Wed-Sun 21-2h
1325 Government Street ☎ (250) 385-0566 💻 hushnightclub.ca
Various parties. Call for exact info.

SAUNAS/BATHS

■ **Steamworks** (b DR DU FC G GH I m MA p RR SA SL VS)
18-8, Mon & Tue -2h
582 Johnson Street *Near Government St. in a side alley*
☎ (250) 383-6623 💻 www.steamworksvictoria.com

Manitoba

Location: Central CDN
Initials: MB
Time: GMT -6
Area: 650,000 km² / 250,965 sq mi.
Population: 1,145,000
Capital: Winnipeg

Winnipeg ☎ 204

PUBLICATIONS

■ **Outwords**
63 Albert Street, Suite 201 *2nd floor* ☎ (204) 942-4599
💻 www.outwords.ca
A free monthly newsmagazine for the LGBT communities of Winnipeg and Manitoba.

BARS

■ **Gio's** (AC B D GLM I MA OS P SNU ST) 16-2h
155 Smith Street *At York Ave* ☎ (204) 786-1236 💻 www.gios.ca

DANCECLUBS

■ **Club 200** (AC B CC D GLM M MA ST WE) 16-2, Sun 18-24h
190 Garry Street ☎ (204) 943-6045 💻 www.club200.ca
■ **Fame** (B D GLM MA)
279 Garry Street

SAUNAS/BATHS

■ **Aquarius Bath** (DR DU FC FH G RR SA SB VS WO) 24hrs
457 Notre Dame Avenue *Downtown* ☎ (204) 947-1763
💻 www.aquariusbath.ca
Two levels, lounge, gym and glory-holes in basement. This is not a men-only sauna as Tue, Thu and Sun are mixed days.

GENERAL GROUPS

■ **Rainbow Resource Centre** (AC GLM MA)
16-19, Fri 13-17h, closed Sat & Sun
170 Scott Street ☎ (204) 474-0212 💻 www.rainbowresourcecentre.org

CRUISING

-Bonnycastle Park (ayor) (at night)
-Assiniboine Park (AYOR) (washrooms & parking lot, 250 m west of Pavilion weekday afternoons)
-P Assiniboine Avenue (between Main and Fort Street)
-TD Centre concourse (AYOR) (washrooms near the food courts)
-Riverbank west of Granite Curling Club - nights (AYOR).

New Brunswick

Location: East CDN
Initials: NB
Time: GMT -4, -5
Area: 73,000 km² / 28,185 sq mi.
Population: 762,000
Capital: Fredericton

Fredericton ☎ 506

DANCECLUBS

■ **boom!** (AC B CC D GLM MA S ST T WE)
Thu-Sat 20-2, Sun 16-19, 22-2h
474 Queen Street *Downtown, next to Cora's restaurant*
☎ (506) 463-2666 💻 www.boomnightclub.ca
Sexy dance club, hot staff, excellent audio/video, lounge room upstairs.

CAMPING

■ **River's Edge Campground** (GLM I MA PA PI)
19 Cottage Lane, Durham Bridge *20 mins north of Fredericton on the Nashwaak River* ☎ (506) 459-8675
💻 www.riversedgecamp.ca

CRUISING

-Riverside park (AYOR) (located between the Lord Beaverbrook Hotel and the railway bridge)
-YMCA swimming bath.

Moncton ☎ 506

BARS

■ **Club Soho** (B GLM MA)
151 Mountain Road 💻 www.clubsohomoncton.com
■ **Triangles** (B D GLM MA ST) 20-2h, closed Mon
234 St George Street *At Archibald* ☎ (506) 857-8779
💻 www.trianglesbar.com
Bar & bistro.

Saint John ☎ 506

BARS

■ **Impulse** (B D GLM MA OS) Wed & Thu 21-1, Fri & Sat -2h
14-16 Charlotte Street

CRUISING

-Carlton Street (r) (near Old Stone Church)
-Princess Street (near Union)
-Rockwood Park (beach and trails).

St. Andrews ☎ 506

HOTELS

■ **Kingsbrae Arms Relais & Châteaux**
(AC B BF CC glm H M PI PK RWS RWT WO) May-Oct
219 King Street *Eastern Canada on the Atlantic Ocean, not far from Bar Harbor, Maine* ☎ (506) 529-1897 💻 www.kingsbrae.com
Luxury seaside resort.

Newfoundland

Location: East CDN
Initials: NF
Time: GMT -4
Area: 405,000 km² / 156,370 sq mi.
Population: 564,000
Capital: St. John's

Saint John's ☏ 709

BARS

■ **Zone 216** (B D f GLM MA) Fri & Sat 22-?h
216 Water Street ☏ (709) 754-2492

GUEST HOUSES

■ **Abba Inn** (AC BF CC glm I m PA PK RWB RWT VA WH) All year
36 Queen's Road *Near City Hall* ☏ (709) 754-0047
www.abbainn.com

Nova Scotia

Location: East CDN
Initials: NS
Time: GMT -4
Area: 56,000 km² / 21,612 sq mi.
Population: 948,000
Capital: Halifax

Halifax ☏ 902

PUBLICATIONS

■ **Wayves**
www.wayves.ca
For over 20 years, the monthly magazine for the LGBT community in Atlantic Canada.

BARS

■ **Company House. The** (B GLM MA s)
Mon & Tue 16-24, Wed-Fri 14-2, Sat 16-2h, closed Sun
2202 Gottingen Street *North End* ☏ (902) 404-3050
www.thecompanyhouse.ca
Events include: „Cheap Wine Thursdays"

■ **Menz Bar** (B BF CC D F G I M MC OS VS) 15-2h
2182 Gottingen Street *Level 2* ☏ (902) 446-6969 www.menzbar.ca
Gay Bar in Halifax catering to the over 30's crowd. Various theme nights and bar specials.

■ **Mollyz Diner & Bar** (B BF CC GLM I M MA OS)
11-21, Fri -2, Sat & Sun 8-22h
2182 Gottingen Street ☏ (902) 405-3376 www.mollyzdiner.ca
An edgy, upscale diner with great food and service.

■ **Reflections** (B D GLM MA S ST) 13-4, Sun 16-4h
5184 Sackville Street ☏ (902) 422-2957
www.reflectionscabaret.com

SAUNAS/BATHS

■ **SeaDog's Sauna & Spa** (B DR FC G GH I LAB m MA OS RR SA SB SH SL VS WH) Mon-Thu 16-24, Fri 16-Sun 24h (non-stop)
2199 Gottingen Street *Corner of Gottingen & Cunard. Look for 3 Black Anchors on the front door* ☏ (902) 444-3647 www.seadogs.ca

Smiths Cove ☏ 902

GUEST HOUSES

■ **Harbourview Inn. The** (AC B BF glm I MA OS PA PI PK RWS RWT VA) Opened 15/6 - 15/9 from 8-22.30h
25 Harbourview Road *Highway 101, exit 24 or 25* ☏ (902) 245-5686
www.theharbourviewinn.com

Sydney ☏ 902

BARS

■ **Club 418** (B D glm MA s) Wed-Sun 21-2h
418 George Street ☏ 562-2211 club418.webstarts.com

Ontario

Location: Central-West CDN
Initials: ON
Time: GMT -5
Area: 1,067,000 km² / 411,969 sq mi.
Population: 11,408,000
Capital: Toronto

Fort Erie ☏ 905

SAUNAS/BATHS

■ **Erie Sauna** (b DR DU FC FH G MA OS RR SB VS) 8-19, Fri & Sat -23h
216 Jarvis Street *The building is shared with a laundromat*
☏ (905) 994-8675

Guelph

CRUISING

-Royal City Park (along Wellington Street)
-Exhibition Park (parking lots at night).

Hamilton ☏ 905

BARS

■ **Embassy Club. The** (B D GLM MA s ST) 12-3h
54 King Street ☏ (905) 522-1100 embassy-nightclub.com

■ **Gravity Club** (B D GLM MA) 16-2h
121 Hughson Street ☏ (289) 389-8568 www.gravity-club.ca

SAUNAS/BATHS

■ **Central Spa** (AC DU G I LAB m SA SB SH SL VS WH)
Mon-Thu 10-2, Fri 10-Mon 2h (non-stop)
401 Main Street West *Right off highway 403* ☏ (905) 523-7636
www.centralspa.com

■ **Karel's Steambath** (b DR DU FC G GH MA MSG RR SB VS)
12-22, Fri & Sat -24, Sun 12-18h
12 Holton Avenue North ☏ (905) 549-9666
www.karelssteambaths.com

CAMPING

■ **Cedars Campground** (d GLM PI s)
1039 Concession 5 West, Millgrove ☏ (905) 659-3655
www.cedarscampground.com

Kitchener ☏ 519

BARS

■ **Club Renaissance** (AC B CC D GLM M MA S WE) Wed-Sat 21-3h
24 Charles Street West *Opp. Downtown Transit Center* ☏ (519) 570-2406
www.clubrenaissance.com
Upscale nightclub with friendly atmosphere.

CRUISING

-Victoria Park (AYOR) (parking lots at night)
-King Street (between Frederick and Victoria Streets late at night)
-Waterloo Park (in summer).

London ☏ 519

BARS

■ **Buck Wild** (B GLM MA) Thu & Sat 21-2, Fri -1h
722 York Street ☏ 268-2766

Free pool, dart boards, music, relaxed atmosphere, special drink prices, theme nights.

■ **Seven Night Club** (B D GLM MA OS)
347 Clarence Street ☎ 660-6755

SAUNAS/BATHS

■ **Central Spa** (AC B BF CC DR DU f FC FH G m MA P RR SA SB SH SL SOL VS WH WO) Mon-Wed 10-2, Thu 10-Mon 2h (non-stop)
722 York Street *Rear entrance* ☎ (519) 438-2625 💻 www.centralspa.com
Big sauna on 3 floors.

Maynooth ☎ 613

PRIVATE ACCOMMODATION

■ **Wildewood Guest House** (AC BF CC GLM M MA OS PK RWB WH) Reservations 9-22h
970 Madawaska Road, Box 121 *30 mins from Algonquin Park, 3hrs from Toronto or Ottawa* ☎ (613) 338-3134 💻 www.wildewood.net
Two guest rooms. Rates include full breakfast and 3 course dinner. Mastercard accepted.

Niagara Falls ☎ 905

GUEST HOUSES

■ **Absolute Elegance B&B**
(AC BF GLM OS PK RWB RWS RWT VA WH) 8-21h
6023 Culp Street *12 mins walk to the Falls* ☎ (905) 353-8522
☎ (877) 353-8522 (toll free) 💻 www.aebedandbreakfast.com
Victorian house. Both rooms with a king size bed, Jacuzzi and fireplace.

Oshawa ☎ 905

BARS

■ **Club 717** (B D GLM MA s T) Thu 21-2, Fri & Sat -3, Sun -24h
717 Wilson Road South ☎ (905) 434-4297 💻 www.club717.ca

Ottawa ☎ 613

PUBLICATIONS

■ **Capital XTRA!** (GLM) Mon-Fri 9-17h
503-251 Bank Street *In the heart of Ottawa's Rainbow Village*
☎ (613) 237-7133 💻 www.xtra.ca
Ottawa's free gay and lesbian paper. Published every 3rd week.

BARS

■ **Cell Block** (AC B d F G MA) Thu-Sun 21-2h
340 Somerset Street West *Between Bank & O'Connor St, in Centretown Pub*
☎ (613) 594-0233
Leather bar.

■ **Centretown Pub** (AC B CC D f GLM MA OS VS)
Wed-Sat 21-2, Sun 18-2h
340 Somerset Street West/Bank *Between Bank & O'Connor Street*
☎ (613) 594-0233
Bar with pool tables, pinball and games.

■ **Lookout Bar and Bistro. The** (B GLM M MA s) 12-2h
41 York Street *2nd floor* ☎ (613) 789-1624
💻 www.thelookoutbar.com
Popular and friendly place to start the evening.

■ **Swizzles** (B D GLM MA S VS) Mon-Fri 11-2, Sat 19-2, Sun 13-1h
246b Queen Street ☎ (613) 232-4200 💻 www.swizzles.ca
Karaoke bar.

DANCECLUBS

■ **Edge** (B D GLM OS ST YC) Fri & Sat 22-?h
212 Sparks Street *Cnr. Bank St*
3 bars, large dancefloor, rooftop patio overlooking downtown.

■ **Flamingo** (D GLM)
380 Elgin Street ☎ (613) 288-9243 💻 www.theflamingo.ca

SEX SHOPS/BLUE MOVIES

■ **One In Ten** (G MA VS) 12-22h, Sun closed
216 Bank Street *At Nepean* ☎ (613) 563 0110
Sex Shop featuring videos, toys and gloryholes in the back.

■ **Venus Envy Ottawa** (CC GLM MC) Mon & Tue 11-18; Wed, Thu & Sat 11-19; Fri 11-20; Sun 12-17h
320 Lisgar Street *One block East of Bank Street* ☎ (613) 789-4646
💻 www.venusenvy.ca
An education-oriented sex shop located in downtown Ottawa. A second store is in Halifax, NS.

SAUNAS/BATHS

■ **Club Ottawa** (AC B cc DR FC FH G m MA RR SA SB SH SOL VS WH) 24hrs
1069 Wellington Street *At Merton Street* ☎ (613) 722 8978

■ **Steamworks** (AC B cc DR FC FH G GH m RR SA SB SH VS WH) 24hrs
487 Lewis Street *Between O'Connor & Bank Streets* ☎ (613) 230 8431

GIFT & PRIDE SHOPS

■ **Wilde's** (CC G MA) Mon-Sat 11-21, Sun 12-18h
367 Bank Street *Cnr. Gilmour* ☎ (613) 234-5512 💻 www.wildes.ca
Large product range including magazines, DVDs and videos, which one can either rent or purchase.

GUEST HOUSES

■ **Inn on Somerset** (AC BF CC glm MA PK RWS SA WO) All year
282 Somerset Street West *Centre* ☎ (613) 236-9309
💻 www.innonsomerset.com
Friendly staff and atmosphere. Twelve rooms, 5 with private bath.

■ **Rideau Inn** (BF glm M MA OS RWS RWT) All year
177 Frank Street *Near Jack Purcell Park* ☎ (613) 688-2753
💻 www.rideauinn.ca
A charming Edwardian Bed & Breakfast, gay owned and operated, just a short walk to gay bars, saunas, bookstores and restaurants. A really comfortable and peaceful guesthouse.The bathrooms (mostly shared) are large. The beakfast is complete, a large choice of food and self-service coffee.

GENERAL GROUPS

■ **Pink Triangle Services (PTS Centre)** (AC GLM T) Mon-Fri 9-21h
251 Bank Street, Suite 301 *Near Bank & Cooper* ☎ (613) 563-4818
💻 www.pinktriangle.org
2nd largest GLBTQ library in N. America. Communitiy & resource centre.

CRUISING

-Rockcliff Park (daytime; close to parking lots)
-Major's Hill Park (very AYOR)
-Nepean Point (very AYOR)
-Mackenzie Street (AYOR G R).

Stratford ☎ 519

GUEST HOUSES

■ **Hundred Church Street. A** (AC BF CC GLM I MA PK WH) 8-20h
100 Church Street *150km southwest of Toronto* ☎ (519) 272-8845
💻 www.ahundredchurchst.ca
1902 home has been renovated to accommodate the visitors' needs. 4 rooms (some en-suite). Full breakfast provided. On-site parking. Gay owned.

Toronto ☎ 416

✱ Toronto, situated on the northern side of Lake Ontario, is the largest city in Canada, with 4.2 million inhabitants. It is an ultra-modern business and financial centre. Its name comes from the Huron Indian language, meaning „meeting place", and it's still a meeting place for one hundred different cultures. Despite being so cosmopolitan, the city has held onto its British roots and values, and is clean, reliable and safe. Toronto has a unique stunning skyline, dominated by the CN Tower,

which with its 553.33 metres is the world's tallest free standing tower. On a clear day you can see the spray from Niagara Falls one hundred kilometres away.
For lesbian and gay travellers there's loads on offer in the gay village, running from the intersection of Church and Isabella Streets up to Yonge Street, right in the heart of the attractive pedestrian-friendly city centre. Toronto has lots to offer, and is a fun, good-value destination, whether you're into culture, nightlife or the great annual Gay Pride festival taking place at the end of June/beginning of July.

Toronto, am Nordufer des Lake Ontario gelegen, ist mit 4,2 Mio. Einwohnern die größte Metropole Kanadas und gleichzeitig hypermodernes Wirtschafts- und Finanzzentrum. Der Name stammt aus der Sprache ihrer Ureinwohner, der Huron-Indianer, und bedeutet „Treffpunkt". Tatsächlich ist die Stadt noch immer ein Treffpunkt für über 100 verschiedene Kulturen. Doch trotz aller Internationalität hat sich die Stadt ihre britischen Wurzeln bewahrt und gilt als sicher, sauber und seriös. Durch den mit 553.33 m Höhe welthöchsten freistehenden Turm, den CN-Tower, erhält Toronto eine eindrucksvolle und unverwechselbare Skyline. An klaren Tagen soll man von hier sogar die Gischtwolke der etwa 100 km entfernten Niagara-Fälle sehen können.
Für schwul-lesbische Reisende gibt es ein riesiges Angebot im Gay Village, das sich von der Ecke Church Street/Isabella Street bis hinein in die Yonge Street erstreckt und somit genau im Herzen des schönen, fußgängerfreundlichen Zentrums liegt. Toronto bietet viel, ist günstig und ein spannendes Reiseziel, egal ob man wegen der Kultur, des Nachtlebens oder des tollen Pride-Festivals Ende Juni/Anfang Juli kommt.

La plus grande métropole du Canada, Toronto, est située sur la rive nord du lac Ontario. Son nom signifierait „lieu de rencontre" en huron. Cette ville est aujourd'hui encore un lieu de rencontre pour plus de cent cultures différentes. Malgré tout ce brassage culturel, la ville est restée attachée à ses racines britanniques et a la réputation d'être sûre, propre et sérieuse. Du haut des 553,33 m de la CN-Tower - la plus grande tour du monde -, on jouit d'une vue imprenable de Toronto. Par temps clair, on peut même distinguer le nuage de vapeur émanant des chutes du Niagara distantes de 100 km.
Les gays et lesbiennes trouveront dans cette ville un immense choix d'activités dans le Gay Village qui s'étend de l'angle Church Street/Isabella Street à la Yonge Street et est ainsi situé en plein centre du beau centre-ville piéton. Toronto est une destination bon marché qui a beaucoup à offrir, que ce soit sa culture, sa vie nocturne ou encore son Pride-Festival a la fin de juin/début de juillet.

Toronto está situada en la orilla norte del lago Ontario y es, con sus 4,2 millones de habitantes, la ciudad más grande de Canadá y, a su vez, un moderno centro económico y financiero. La palabra Toronto proviene del idioma aborigen hablado por la tribu india de los Urones y significa „punto de encuentro". De hecho, la ciudad sigue siendo a día de hoy el punto de encuentro de más de 100 culturas diferentes.
A pesar de toda esta internacionalidad, la ciudad ha mantenido sus raíces británicas con su carácter serio, limpio y seguro.
La torre CN es, con sus 553.33 metros de altitud, una de las estructuras no sostenidas por cables en tierra firme más alta del mundo y aporta a la ciudad un perfil impactante e inconfundible. Desde lo alto de esta, en días despejados, puede incluso divisarse las masas de agua que en forma de nubes emanan de las cataratas del Niagara a casi 100 Km de distancia.
La oferta de ocio gay en esta ciudad es, sin lugar a dudas, extensa. El Gay village, que se extiende desde la esquina de Church Street/ Isabella Street hasta bien entrada la Yonge Street, es el centro vital de esta oferta situada en una vistosa zona peatonal del centro la ciudad. Toronto tiene mucho que ofrecer, es un destino económico y emocionante, ya sea por su oferta cultural, su vida nocturna o sus increíbles festivales del Orgullo Gay al fin de junio/al principio de julio.

Toronto è situata sulla riva nord del lago Ontario e con i suoi 4,2 milioni di abitanti è la metropoli più grande del Canada e allo stesso tempo un modernissimo centro finanziario ed economico. Nonostante l'internazionalità di questa città, Toronto è riuscita a preservare le sue radici britanniche ed è considerata una città sicura, pulita ed efficiente. Lo skyline di Toronto è inconfondibile: lo si riconosce subito attraverso la sua torre televisiva, la CN-Tower, che è la costruzione più alta del mondo (553.33 metri). Quando il cielo è limpido, dalla CN-Tower, si riesce a vedere addirittura la nuvola di vapore delle cascate del Niagara.
Per il turismo gay e lesbico Toronto offre un'infinità di possibilità. Il Gay Villane si estende dall'angolo tra la Church Street/Isabelle Street fino alla Yonge Street, quindi nel bellissimo centro città, ed è facilmente percorribile a piedi. Toronto offre davvero tanto: è molto economica ed è un luogo turistico molto eccitante, indipendentemente dal tipo di vacanza che si decide di fare: viaggio culturale, vita notturna o in occasione del gay pride alla fine di giugno/principio luglio.

GAY INFO

519 Church Street Community Centre (GLM MA)
9-22, Sat -17, Sun 10-17h
519 Church Street ☎ (416) 392-6874 www.the519.org
Home of many GL groups and location for numerous gay events.

Guidemag.com (GLM MA)
2 Carlton Street, suite 1600 ☎ (416) 925-6665
www.guidemag.com
Gay travel website

Proud FM (GLM MA) 24hrs
65 Wellesley Street East, Suite 201 ☎ (416) 922-1039
www.proudfm.com
Commercial gay radio at 103.9 FM.

PUBLICATIONS

Fab Magazine Mon-Fri 9-18h
2 Carlton Street, Suite 1600 ☎ (416) 925-6665
www.fabmagazine.com
Free bi-weekly glossy gay men's magazine for Toronto.

Xtra! Mon-Fri 9-18h
2 Carlton Street, Suite 1600 ☎ (416) 925-6665 www.xtra.ca
Free bi-weekly magazine about the Toronto gay scene.

CULTURE

Buddies in Bad Times Theatre (GLM MA S)
12 Alexander Street *Cnr. Yonge Street, M° College* ☎ (416) 975-8555
www.buddiesinbadtimes.com
Queer theatre and a gathering place for the local community.

BARS

Black Eagle (B DR F G MA OS) 14-2h
457 Church Street *2nd floor* ☎ (416) 413-1219
www.blackeagletoronto.com
Toronto's foremost leather/denim/SM club with a strict dresscode.

Churchmouse & Firkin (B GLM M MA OS) 11-2h
475 Church Street *Cnr. Maitland Street* ☎ (416) 927-1735
http://churchmouse.firkinpubs.com
English pub.

College Street Bar (B CC d glm M MA S) 17-2h
574 College Street ☎ (416) 533-2417 www.collegestreetbar.com
Restaurant lounge with italian cuisine and live music.

Convento Rico. El (B D glm MA S ST T WE) Thu-Sun 19-3.30h
750 College Street *Next to Blockbuster Video, in the basement*
☎ (416) 588-7800 www.elconventorico.com
Latin nightclub.

Crews & Tango (B CC D GLM MA ST) 12-2, shows Wed-Sun at 23h
508-510 Church Street ☎ (416) 972-1662
www.crewsandtangos.com
Gay bar in old Victorian house, nice place to have some fun like dancing and talking.

Flash (B G MA S) Thu-Sat 16-2h
463 Church Street ☎ 925 8363 www.flashonchurch.com
New bar on Church!

George's Play (B GLM MA S ST t) 11-2h
504 Church Street *Cnr. Maitland Street* ☎ (416) 963-8251
www.playonchurch.com

■ **Gladaman's Den** (AC B CC GLM MA OS S WI) 13-2h
502A Yonge Street *2 blocks south of Wellesley Street* ☎ (416) 961-5808
💻 www.gladamansden.com
Neighbourhood pub by day. Concerts, drag shows & latin parties at night.

■ **Hair of the Dog** (B CC GLM M MA OS) 11.30-24, Thu-Sat -2h
425 Church Street ☎ (416) 964-2708 💻 www.hairofthedogpub.ca
Neighbourhood pub & restaurant. Great food served by very friendly staff.

■ **Lo'la** (B G MA OS) Wed-Sat 17-2, Sun 16-24h
7 Maitland Street *At Yonge Street* ☎ (416) 920-0946
💻 www.lolamartinis.com
Small, stylish lounge with patio.

■ **Pegasus on Church** (AC B CC GLM MA) 12-2h
489B Church Street *2nd floor* ☎ (416) 927-8832
💻 www.pegasusonchurch.com
Pool table and video games.

■ **Pinocchio** (AC B CC G MA OS p S VS) 11-2h
502-A Yonge Street *At Alexander* ☎ (416) 961-5808

■ **Remington's** (! AC B CC G m MA P SNU) 17-2h
379 Yonge Street ☎ (416) 977-2160 💻 www.remingtons.com
Great strippers. Second floor open on weekends, lots of girls who watch the male strippers, bottom floor male only. Cover charge applies.

■ **Slack's** (B gLm M MA) 16-2h, closed Mon
562 Church Street *Cnr. Wellesley* ☎ (416) 928-2151 💻 www.slacks.ca

■ **Woody's & Sailor** (AC B CC d G m MA S ST VS) 13-2h
465-467 Church Street *Between Maitland & Alexander, M° Wellesly*
☎ (416) 972-0887 💻 www.woodystoronto.com
Five bars. Regular theme parties and 17 monitors showing non-stop sexy videos, not to mention the hunky waiters. One of the most popular places in town.

■ **Zipperz & Cell Block** (AC B CC D GLM MA S WE) 12-2h
72 Carlton Street *Near Church Street* ☎ (416) 921-0066
💻 www.zipperzcellblock.com
Popular dance bar with shows.

CAFES

■ **Timothy's** (b GLM m MA)
500 Church Street *Cnr. Alexander Street* ☎ (416) 925-8550
💻 www.timothys.com

DANCECLUBS

■ **AX (AsianXpress)** (B D GLM MA)
☎ (416) 318-8950 💻 www.aznxp.com
For Asians and their friends. See www.aznxp.com for exact dates and location.

■ **Barn. The** (B D F GLM MA p) Wed-Sat 22-?h
418 Church Street *At the south end of Toronto's Gay Village*
☎ (416) 593-9696 💻 www.thebarnnightclub.com
One of the newer locations on 3 floors with pool tables and a fetish area.

■ **Fly** (AC B CC D GLM MA S T) Fri & Sat 22-6h
8 Gloucester Street ☎ (416) 410-5426 (info-line)
💻 www.flynightclub.com
Gay/Mixed crowd 19-36, local & international DJs. Fly is the original Babylon from the TV series „Queer as Folk". Cover charge applies.

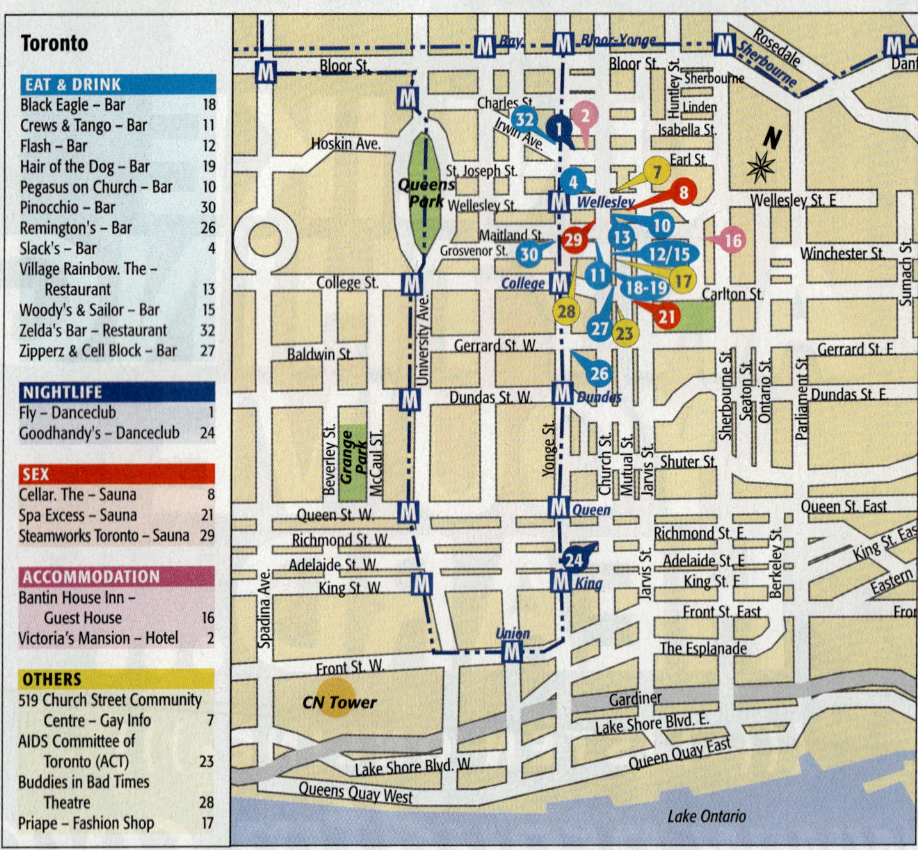

■ **Goodhandy's** (AC B CC D DR f GLM MA S T VS)
Mon 16-2, Tue 22-2, Wed 20-2, Thu 16-2, Fri & Sat 21-4h
120 Church St, 2nd floor *Cnr. Richmond, M° Queen Station*
www.goodhandys.com
Pansexual club. Transsexual on Mon-Thu.

■ **Guvernment** (B D glm MA) Fri & Sat 22-?h
132 Queens Quay East ☎ (416) 869-0045 www.theguvernment.com

■ **Pitbull** (B D F G MA S) 2nd Sat/month 22-3h
580 Church Street @ *Fuzion Lounge* ☎ 944 9888
www.fuzionexperience.com
Crowd Bear, Tattoos, Beef. Star DJs and GoGos.

■ **Snakepit @ Henhouse** (B D GLM MA) Wed 22-?h
1532 Dundas Street *Near cnr. Sheridan Avenue* ☎ (416) 534-5939
www.henhousetoronto.com
Weekly queer dance party.

RESTAURANTS

■ **Byzantium** (AC B CC D GLM M MA)
499 Church Street *M° Wellesley* ☎ (416) 922-3859 www.byz.ca
Restaurant and martini bar. DJs every Fri & Sat after 23h.

■ **Fire on the East Side** (B glm M MA OS) 11.30-1, Sat & Sun 10-1h
6 Gloucester Street ☎ (416) 960-3473 www.fireontheeastside.ca

■ **Village Rainbow. The** (AC B BF CC G M OS WE) 11-23h
477 Church Street ☎ (416) 961-0616
Bar & restaurant. Good breakfasts.

■ **Zelda's** (B CC DM GLM LM M MA OS s ST VEG WE WL)
Mon-Thu 12-23, Fri -1, Sat 11-1, Sun -23h
692 Yonge Street *M° Wellesley, cnr. Isabella Streets* ☎ (416) 922-2526
www.zeldas.ca
Extravagant, trashy or just plain weird; whatever it is, Zelda is a great place to have a bite. New location on Yonge Street on two levels with two patios, large stage for drag shows upstairs.

SEX SHOPS/BLUE MOVIES

■ **Priape** (CC F G) 10-21, Sun 12-18h
465 Church Street *2nd floor* ☎ (416) 586-9914 www.priape.com
Everything for leather fans.

SAUNAS/BATHS

■ **Cellar. The** (b DR DU f G GH RR SA SB SL VS) 24hrs
78 Wellesley Street East *Black door, no sign* ☎ (416) 975-1799
A night during the weekend it can be quite busy.

■ **Central Spa** (b DU G GH I m MA SA SB VS) 11-24, Fri & Sat -1h
1610 Dundas Street West *2nd floor* ☎ (416) 588-6191
www.centralspa.com

■ **Spa Excess** (! AC AK B CC DR FC FH G GH M MA OS RR S SA SB SH SL SOL VS WH WO) 24hrs
105 Carlton Street *Near corner of Carlton & Jarvis Streets*
☎ (416) 260-2363 www.spaexcess.com
One of the biggest saunas in Canada on 4 floors, with a sun-deck. Three large playrooms with glory hole cubicles, an open sling room, toys, 8 channels of video porn, lots of hall cruising and a large, comfortable, licensed lounge where you can drink alcohol.

■ **Steamworks Toronto**
(AC CC DR DU F FC G M MA P RR SA SB SOL VS WH WO) 24hrs
540 Church Street, level 2 *2nd floor* ☎ (416) 925-1571
www.steamworks.ca
Big facility on 11.800 sq. ft with full gym and a huge hot tub. The sauna belongs to a group which has properties in Chicago, Seattle and Berkeley, as well as Toronto and Vancouver.

BOOK SHOPS

■ **Glad Day** (AC CC GLM)
Mon-Wed 10-18.30, Thu -19, Fri -21, Sat -19, Sun 12-18h
598A Yonge Street *Half a block north of Wellesley St., 2nd floor*
☎ (416) 961-4161 www.gladdaybookshop.com
Established in 1970. It's the world's second LGBT bookshop, stocking over 15.000 titles in books, DVDs & magazines.

■ **This Ain't the Rosedale Library** (GLM)
10-22, Fri & Sat -23, Sun 13-21h
86 Nassau Street ☎ (416) 929-9912

TRAVEL AND TRANSPORT

■ **Out Adventures** (CC G MA) Mon-Fri 10-18h
523 Bloor Street W *M° Bathurst* ☎ (416) 531 8795
🖳 www.out-adventures.com
Guided gay-tours around the world.

HOTELS

■ **Victoria's Mansion** (AC CC glm I MA OS RWS RWT) All year
68 Gloucester Street *In the Church Street village* ☎ (416) 921 4625
🖳 www.victoriasmansion.com
Ten double rooms, 9 single and 2 studios. Victoria's Mansion steps to Bloor and Yonge, where shopping, dining, museums and trend-setting happens. This renovated historic mansion offers en suite bathrooms, television, coffee makers, microwaves and wireless internet.

GUEST HOUSES

■ **Banting House Inn** (GLM MA)
73 Homewood Ave ☎ 924 1548 🖳 www.bantinghouse.com
Nice B&B in a victorian style villa close to the gay scene in a quiet street.
■ **House on McGill** (AC BF CC GLM I MA OS RWB RWT VA)
All year, 8-20h
110 McGill Street *Yonge and College Streets* ☎ (416) 351-1503
🖳 www.mcgillbb.ca
Small B&B. 5 rooms with shared bath, 1 with private bath; all with balcony, radio, TV/VCR.

GENERAL GROUPS

■ **Queer West Arts and Culture Centre** (GLM) 9-21h
Box 204, Station C *West Village* ☎ (416) 551-1709 🖳 www.queerwest.org
Serving the bisexual, gay, lesbian, trans and queer community in west Toronto since 2001.

HEALTH GROUPS

■ **AIDS Committee of Toronto (ACT)** Mon-Thu 10-21, Fri -17h
399 Church Street *4th floor* ☎ (416) 340-2437 🖳 www.actoronto.org
HIV/AIDS-related resource library, counselling, support groups and practical help for those living with HIV/AIDS. HIV prevention, education and outreach programmes.

SWIMMING

-Hanlans Point Beach (g NU) (Toronto Island; take ferry from Harbour Castle Westin Hotel)
-Scarborough Beach (East of Warden Avenue; mostly gay, mostly nude, but occasional police hassle if nude)
-Cherry Beach (at the end of Cherry Street)
-Kew Beach (at the end of Woodbine Avenue).

CRUISING

-Balfour Park (AYOR) (St. Clair Avenue east of Yonge Street)
-Backyard (between Alexander and Maitland Streets, near Church Street)
-Church Street (between Carlton and Isabella Streets)
-Grosvenor/Bay and Yonge Streets (AYOR R)
-High Park (AYOR at night) (south end near Colbourne Lodge, very busy summer days too)
-Cawthra Park (behind 519 Community Centre).

Windsor ☎ 519

BARS

■ **Club 783** (B GLM MA OS) 17-2h
783 Wyandotte Street E *Near cnr. Marentette St* ☎ (519) 973-4916
🖳 club783.com

DANCECLUBS

■ **Wellington. The** (AC B CC D GLM MA S ST WE) Fri & Sat 21-2h
800 Wellington Ave ☎ (519) 971-0428

SAUNAS/BATHS

■ **Vesuvio** (b DU G m MA SA SB VS) 24hrs
563 Brant Street ☎ (519) 977-8578
We have received reports that this place is dirty, smells bad and the whole place had a general look of being in total disrepair.

Prince Edward Island

Location: In the Gulf of St. Lawrence
Initials: PE
Time: GMT -4
Area: 5,683.91 km² / 2,194.57 sq mi
Population: 141,000
Capital: Charlottetown

Vernon Bridge

GUEST HOUSES

■ **Rainbow Lodge** (BF cc G MC PK RWS) All year
7521 Trans Canada Highway *15 mins east of Charlottetown and 20 mins west of Wood Islands Ferry* ☎ (902) 651-2202 🖳 www.gaypei.com
Try their legendary Evening Lobster Suppers. Enjoy the garden or relax in the Great Room of the Lodge after a fun day of sightseeing, or cozy up in your suite and watch the setting sun. You will find either the Walnut Suite or Ash Suite to be a perfect ending to your day.

Québec

Location: West CDN
Initials: QC
Time: GMT -5
Area: 1,541,000 km² / 594,980 sq mi.
Population: 7,419,000
Capital: Québec
Important gay cities: Montréal and Québec

Drummondville ☎ 819

BARS

■ **Xcentrik** (AC B CC GLM MA S ST)
330 Lindsay ☎ (819) 474-5587

Montréal ☎ 514

Montreal is an exciting mix of French and English influences, with a historical place as one of the first North American settlements, set on an island in the estuary of the St Lawrence River. This mix of old and new lends the city, the largest French-speaking city after Paris, a European flair, and the generally friendly, open inhabitants do their best to make visitors immediately feel at home. Montreal is Canada's cultural heart, and the arts scene is vibrant and multi-faceted. Gay Pride at the end of July, the oldest film festival in Canada „Image and Nation" and the Black and Blue festival, both held in October are just a few examples of this city's numerous festivals.
The centre of the gay village, which is now a pedestrian zone, is located on Rue St. Catherine, between Av. Papineau and Rue St. Hubert. Here you will find many bars, dance and strip clubs, restaurants open 24/7, saunas and numerous cafes, where you can meet up with others experience the „joie de vivre" of this vibrant city.

Montréal ist ein spannender Mix aus englischen und französischen Einflüssen und hat auf einer Insel in der Mündung des St.-Lorenz-Stroms eine geschichtsträchtige Lage als eine der ersten nordamerikanischen Siedlungen. Die Mischung aus Alt und Neu gibt der Stadt, die immerhin die größte französischsprachige Stadt nach Paris ist, ein europäisches Flair, und die überaus freundlichen und offenen Einwohner tun ihr übriges, dass sich der Reisende hier sofort wohl fühlt. Montréal ist Kanadas kulturelles Zentrum und die Kunstszene ist sehr vielfältig.

Der Gay Pride (Ende Juli), das älteste schwullesbische Filmfestival Kanadas „Image & Nation" und das „Black & Blue" Festival (beide im Oktober) sind nur wenige Beispiele für die vielen Ereignisse der Stadt, die einer der Magneten für schwule Touristen in Nordamerika sind. Im Zentrum des Gay-Villages, jetzt eine Fußgängerzone auf der Rue St. Catherine (zwischen Av. Papineau und Rue St Hubert) gibt es unzählige Gay-Bars, Tanz- und Striplokale, nonstop geöffnete Restaurants, Saunen und jede Menge Cafés, in denen man ausgiebig flirten und das pulsierende Leben, den „joie de vivre" dieser quirligen Stadt genießen kann.

Montréal est un mélange étonnant d'influences françaises et anglaises, historiquement la première colonie nord-américaine à l'embouchure du St-Laurent. Modernité et histoire donnent un flair européen à la deuxième plus grande ville francophone au monde après Paris. Ses habitants sympathiques et ouverts savent accueillir les voyageurs. Montréal est le centre culturel du Canada et la scène artistique y est florissante.
La Gay Pride (fin juillet), le plus vieux festival cinématographie gay du Canada „ Image & Nation „ et le festival „ Black & Blue „ (tous deux en octobre) font partie des nombreuses animations de la ville, attirant les touristes en Amérique du Nord. Au centre du Village gay, une zone piétonne dans la Rue Ste-Catherine (entre Av. Papineau et Rue St-Hubert) foisonne de bars, clubs gays, boites de striptease, restaurants, saunas, cafés - où le flirt et la joie de vivre sont de rigueur.

Montreal, situada sobre la Isla de Montreal en la confluencia del Río San Lorenzo y del Río Ottawa, cuenta con una apasionante mezcla de influencias británicas y francesas que le aportan una posición histórica y geográfica única como uno de los primeros asentamientos en América del Norte.
La mezcla entre lo antiguo y lo moderno da a la ciudad un toque europeo y es que, al fin y al cabo, Montreal es la mayor ciudad francófona después de París. La amabilidad y el carácter abierto de sus gentes hacen que los visitantes se sientan de inmediato como en casa. Montreal es el centro cultural de Canadá y cuenta con una variada oferta artística.
El Orgullo Gay (a finales de julio), „Image & Nation", el festival de cine gay-lésbico más antiguo de Canadá, o el festival „Black & Blue" (ambos en octubre) son sólo algunos ejemplos de los muchos acontecimientos que ofrece esta ciudad; un autentico imán para turistas gays en América del Norte.
En el centro de la „Gay-Village", una zona peatonal de la calle Santa Catalina (entre la Av. Papineau y la Rue St Hubert), hay un sinnúmero de bares de ambiente, salas de baile, clubes de strip-tease, restaurantes abiertos las 24 horas, saunas y un montón de cafés donde poder ligar y disfrutar de la vida alborotada, la „joie de vivre", de esta animada ciudad.

Montreal è un mix molto interessante di influenze inglesi e francesi. La città è sita in un'isola alla foce del fiume San Lorenzo. Montreal è la più grande città francofona dopo Parigi. Il coesistere di vecchio e nuovo conferisce alla città un fascino molto europeo. L'apertura e la cordialità dei suoi abitanti fanno in modo che il turista si senta a suo agio. Montreal è il centro culturale del Canada e la scena artistica è molto variegata. Il Gay Pride (alla fine di luglio), il più antico festival cinematografico gay del Canada „Image & Nation" e il festival „Black & Blue" (entrambi ad ottobre) sono solo alcuni esempi dei tantissimi eventi cittadini che attirano turismo gay verso il Nordamerica. Al centro del Gay-Village, adesso divenuta un'sola pedonale sulla Rue St. Catherine (tra Av. Papineau e Rue St. Hubert), ci sono tantissimi bar gay, discoteche, locali striptease, ristoranti aperti 24 ore su 24, saune e caffè nei quali si può flirtare abbondantemente e godersi la vita, la „joie de vivre", di questa dinamica città.

GAY INFO

BBCM Foundation
94 Rue Sainte Catherine Est, Suite 5 ☎ (514) 875-7026
www.bbcm.org
Organizers of the 5 annual gay party events in Montreal, Festival: Black & Blue, Twist/Gay Pride, Red, Hot & Dry and Bal des Boys.

Centre Communautaire des Gais et Lesbiennes de Montréal (CCGLM) (GLM MA) Mon-Fri 10-12, 13-17h
2075, rue Plessis *Between Rue Ontario and Rue Sherbrooke*
☎ (514) 528-8424 www.ccglm.org
Also library.

Chambre de Commerce Gaie du Québec. La (GLM) Mon-Fri 10-17h
249, rue Saint-Jacques, Suite 302 ☎ (514) 522-1885 www.ccgq.ca

PUBLICATIONS

2B Mon-Fri 8-18h
1611, rue Amherst ☎ (514) 598-8188 www.2bmag.com
The only English-speaking GLBT magazine throughout Québec, covering Montréal and Ottawa areas. Events calendar and centerfold maps for visitors.

Être Mon-Fri 8-18h
1611, rue Amherst ☎ (514) 521-3873 www.etremag.com
Monthly French-speaking GLBT magazine covering Montréal, Québec and Ottawa/Gatineau areas.

Fugues
c/o Editions Nitram, 1276 rue Amherst ☎ (514) 848-1854
www.fugues.com
Free monthly publication for the French-speaking community with an agenda for Montréal.

Guide gai du Québec. Le 9-18h
1611, rue Amherst ☎ (514) 523-9463 www.guidegaiduquebec.com
Gay guide covering all regions of Québec and Ottawa.

RG Mon-Fri 8-18h
1611, rue Amherst ☎ (514) 523-9463 www.rgmag.com
Monthly French-speaking gay magazine. Event calendar & centerfold map for visitors.

CULTURE

Archives Gaies Du Québec. Les (G) Thu 19.30-21.30h
4067 Boulevard St.Laurent, #202 ☎ (514) 287-9987 www.agq.qc.ca

Image & Nation, Montreal international LGBT Film Festival
4067 Boulevard Saint-Laurent, Bureau 404 ☎ (514) 285-4467
www.image-nation.org
Montréal International Gay & Lesbian Film Festival.

BARS

Aigle Noir (! AC B F G MA VS) 8-3h
1315 Rue Sainte Catherine Est *M° Beaudry* ☎ (514) 529-0040
www.aiglenoir.com
Popular leather bar.

Apollon (AC B CC d G MA NR WE)
1450 Rue Sainte Catherine Est www.apollonmtl.com
New jeans/leather bar.

Cabaret Mado (AC B D GLM MA ST T) 16-3h
1115 rue Sainte-Catherine Est *M° Beaudry/Berri* ☎ (514) 525-7566
www.mado.qc.ca
Different events every day. Showtime 22.30h.

Citibar (AC B glm MA t) 10-3h
1603, Rue Ontario est ☎ (514) 525-4251
Neighbourhood bar with karaoke every night.

Club Date (AC B G OS s) 8-3h
1218 Rue Sainte-Catherine Est *M° Beaudry* ☎ (514) 521-1242
Piano bar with karaoke every night. Cosy & relaxed atmosphere.

Cocktail (B GLM MA S ST) 11-3h
1669 Rue Sainte-Catherine Est ☎ (514) 597-0814
Piano bar.

Drugstore. Le (! AC B D GLM m MA OS) 8-3h
1366 Rue Sainte-Catherine Est *M° Beaudry/Papineau* ☎ (514) 524-1960
Complex of many bars. Food, drink and large terraces with a stunning view over the village. Pool hall in the basement.

Gotha. Le (AC B GLM MA OS S) 16-3h
1641 Rue Amherst *M° Beaudry* ☎ (514) 526 1270
www.aubergell.com/en/gotha
Bar, lounge with a cosy fireplace. Directly under Aubergell B&B.

■ **JP** (AC B G MA R SNU) Wed-Sun 15-3h
1681 Rue Sainte Catherine Est *Cnr. Papineau and Sainte Catherine*
☎ (514) 521-1355
Formerly Adonis. After 21h mixed. rent-bar. Ladies also welcome.

■ **Relaxe** (B GLM MA) 12-3h
1309 Rue Sainte Catherine Est ☎ (514) 523-0578

■ **Rocky** (B G OC VS) Mon & Tue 10-2, Wed-Sun 10-3h
1673 Rue Sainte Catherine Est *M° Papineau* ☎ (514) 521-7865
Popular.

■ **Sky** (! AC CC D GLM MA OS PI S ST WH) 14-3h
1478 Rue Sainte Catherine Est *M° Beaudry/Papineau* ☎ (514) 529-6969
🖳 www.complexesky.com
Large complex on 3 levels with a pub on the 1st floor, especially popular after work. 2nd floor Sky Cabaret and 3rd floor sky club open on weekends. Large summer roof-top terrace with pools in summer. Nice place.

■ **Stock Bar** (B G MA R SNU) 20-3h
1171 Rue Sainte Catherine Est *M° Beaudry* ☎ (514) 842-1336
🖳 www.stockbar.ca
Stripper bar well worth a visit!

■ **Stud. Le** (AC B D F G MA VS) 10-3h
1812 rue Sainte Catherine Est *M° Papineau* ☎ (514) 598-8243
🖳 www.studbar.com
Attracts bears and leather guys. Sunday „disco" is popular. 2 bars.

■ **Taboo** (B G OC R SNU) 19-3h
1950 Boulevard de Maisonneuve Est *M° Papineau cnr. Rue Dorion*
☎(514)597-0010 🖳www.facebook.com/pages/Bar-Taboo/167340873325491
Young-looking strippers. This place should be taboo as only sleazy boys and pay-to-play men go here.

■ **Taverne Normandie** (AC B CC G MC OS VS)
Mon & Tue 10-2, Wed-Sun -3h
1295 Rue Amherst *M° Beaudry* ☎ (514) 522-2766
One of the oldest gay bars in town with XXX films. Popular at happy hour, 17-19h. Heated patio 8 months/year.

■ **Woof** (B G MA S) 9-3 summer, 15-3h winter
1661 Rue Sainte-Catherine Est *M° Papineau*
www.woof-montreal.com
Bear bar. Karaoke on Wed & Thu.

MEN'S CLUBS

■ **Campus. Le** (AC B G MA R SNU VS)
15-3, Sat & Sun 13-3h, Sun ladies night
1111 Rue Sainte Catherine Est *M° Beaudry, Berri Uqam*
☎ (514) 526-3616 www.campusmtl.com
The oldest and among the most famous stripper clubs in town. Regular muscular hotties with some twinks. Friendly atmosphere.

CAFES

■ **Kilo** (CC glm I M MA) Sun-Thu 11-23, Fri & Sat -24h
1495 rue Sainte-Catherine est ☎ (514) 596-3933
Friendly coffee shop with great cakes in the heart of the Village.

■ **La Mie Matinale** (glm m MA) Tue-Sat 8:30-19, Sun 8:30-17h
1371 rue Sainte-Catherine est ☎ 529 5656 www.lamiematinale.ca
Coffe and bakery with great croissants, muffins and coffee

■ **Second Cup du Village** (AC CC GLM I MA) 24hrs
1351 rue Sainte-Catherine est ☎ (514) 598 7727
www.secondcup.com
Coffee shop. A meeting place in the heart of the Village.

■ **Tinto** (glm m MA OS s)
1417 rue Amherst *between Berri-UQAM and Beaudry M°* ☎ 903-4100
www.cafetintomontreal.com
A paradise for coffee lovers. Art-exhibitions.

DANCECLUBS

■ **Circus Afterhours** (AC B D glm MA S) Thu-Sun 22-10h
917 Rue Ste-Catherine est *M°Berry UQAM* ☎ 844-3626
www.circusafterhours.com
Local and International DJs, two rooms, mostly straight but good and long parties.

■ **Club Bolo** (B D GLM MA) Fri 19.30-0.30h
2093, rue de la Visitation ☎ (514) 849-4777 www.clubbolo.com
Country line & two-step dancing club.

■ **Mec plus Ultra @ Belmont** (AC B CC D G NR) 10-late
4483 Saint Laurent Boulevard ☎ (514) 845-8443
www.lebelmont.com
Most popular monthly dance party for an alternative gay crowd.

■ **Red Lite** (B D glm YC) Sat & Sun 2-11h
1755 Rue Lierre *Vimont, Laval* ☎ (514) 967-3057 www.red-lite.com
House, Hip Hop.

■ **Sky** (! AC CC D GLM MA OS PI S ST WH) 14-3h
1478 Rue Sainte Catherine Est *M° Beaudry/Papineau* ☎ (514) 529-6969
www.complexesky.com
Large complex on 3 levels with a pub on the 1st floor, especially popular after work. 2nd floor Sky Cabaret and 3rd floor sky club open on weekends. Large summer roof-top terrace with pools in summer. Nice place.

■ **Stéréo** (AC B D GLM MA) Fri & Sat 22-?h
856, Rue Sainte-Catherine est ☎ (514) 658-2646
www.stereo-nightclub.com
Especially popular on Sunday morning when afterhours clubs close.

■ **Tools Club** (B D f G MC) Fri-Sun 22-3h
1592 Rue Sainte-Catherine Est ☎ (514) 523-4679
www.tools-club.com
Dark and cruisy, attracts a more mature crowd.

■ **Unity** (AC B D GLM OS S YC) Fri & Sat 22-3h
1171 Rue Sainte Catherine Est *M° Beaudry* ☎ (514) 523-2777
www.clubunitymontreal.com
Discotheque on 3 floors, international DJs & terrace on the roof top.

RESTAURANTS

■ **Dsens** (AC B GLM M MA OS) Tue-Thu 11.30-14 & 17-22, Fri 11.30-14 & 17-23, Sat 9.30-14 & 17-23, Sun 9.30-14 & 17-22h
1334 rue Sainte-Catherine Est *M° Beaudry* ☎ (514) 227-5556
www.dsens.ca
French cuisine.

■ **Ella Grill** (AC B CC GLM M MA) Mon-Wed 17.30-23, Thu-Sat -24h
1237 Rue Amherst ☎ (514) 523-5553
www.facebook.com/group.php?gid=2257853907
Great Mediterranean food in a trendy décor.

■ **Infidèles. Les** (AC CC glm M MA RWB WO) 18-23h
771, Rue Rachel Est *Plateau Mont-Royal* ☎ (514) 528-8555
www.lesinfideles.ca
French cuisine, bring your own wine. Non-smoking restaurant.

■ **La Paryse** (AC CC glm) Tue-Sat 11-23h
302 Rue Ontario Est ☎ (514) 842-2040 www.laparyse.com
Popular place for burgers and vegetarian food.

■ **O'Thym** (AC CC GLM M MA RWB WO) Tue-Fri 11.30-14, Tue-Sun18-22h
1112 Boul. de Maisonneuve Est ☎ (514) 525-3443 www.othym.com
French cuisine, bring your own wine. Non-smoking restaurant. Reservation recommended.

■ **Planète. Le** (AC B CC GLM M MA)
Mon-Fri 11.30-14.30, all week 17-23, Sun brunch 11-14.30h
1451 rue Sainte-Catherine est ☎ (514) 528-6953

■ **Resto du Village. Le** (AC B BF CC GLM M MA OS WE) 24hrs
1310 Rue Wolfe *M° Beaudry* ☎ (514) 524-5404
Popular diner late at night, after the bars close. Busy weekends.

■ **Saloon** (AC B BF CC GLM M MA)
Mon 11-23, Tue-Fri 11.30-24, Sat & Sun 10-24h
1333, Rue Sainte-Catherine est ☎ (514) 522-1333 www.lesaloon.ca
A trendy resto-bar with a hip crowd. A Village classic.

■ **Steak Frite St. Paul, Le** (B glm M MA)
1302 Rue Ste-Catherine Est *M° Beaudry* ☎ 439-1376 www.steakfrites.ca
For the meat lovers, bring your own wine.

SEX SHOPS/BLUE MOVIES

■ **Priape** (CC F G MA) Mon-Sat 10-21, Sun 12-21h
1311, Rue Sainte-Catherine Est ☎ (514) 521-8451 www.priape.com
Magazines, leather, jeans, rubber and toys etc.

■ **Wega Video** (DR G MA VS) 10-24h
930 Rue Sainte-Catherine Est ☎ (514) 987-5993 www.wegavideo.ca
Videos, DVDs, toys, lubes, leather & latex. 26 cabins in a maze.

SAUNAS/BATHS

■ **1286. Le** (B CC DR DU FC FH G GH m MA SA SB VS WH) 24hrs
1286 Chemin Chambly, Longueuil *10 mins from Pont Jacques-Cartier, bus 8 / 88* ☎ (450) 677-1286 www.1286.ca
Full of south shore residents. Student rates half-price.

■ **226. Le** (AC DR DU FC FH G MC RR SA SB SOL VS)
11-24, Thu 11-Sat 24h (non-stop)
243 Boulevard des Laurentides, Laval *M° Henry Bourassa*
☎ (450) 975-4556
Sauna busy from noon until evening. Dirty but busy.

■ **3481. Le**
(AC CC DR DU FC G GH H I M MSG NU P RR SA SB SH VS WH) 24hrs
3481 Montée Saint-Hubert *On Montreal's south shore* ☎ (450) 462-3481
www.sauna3481.ca
On 4.000 m². B&B available.

■ **5018. Le** (AC cc DR DU FC FH G m MA MSG OS RR SA SB VS WH) 24hrs
5018 Boulevard St-Laurent *M° Laurier, cnr. Rue St-Joseph*
☎ (514) 277-3555 www.le5018.com
Big sauna on four floors with roof top.

■ **Bain Colonial** (AC CC FC FH G m MSG RR SA SB SOL VS WH WO) 13-6h
3963 Avenue Colonial *At the corner of Napoleon* ☎ (514) 285-0132
www.baincolonial.com
Garden deck, old world charm, Turkish bath style.

■ **GI Joe** (AC B DR DU f G LAB m MA OS SA SB VS WH) 24hrs
1166 Rue Sainte Catherine Est *M° Beaudry* ☎ (514) 528-3326
Sauna on four floors.

■ **Oasis. L'** (AC B CC DR DU FC FH G GH M NR NU RR SA SB SL VR VS W WH WI YC) Daily, 24hrs
1390 rue Sainte Catherine Est *M° Beaudry / Papineau* ☎ (514) 521-0785
💻 www.saunaoasis.net
Always busy. Younger crowd after the bars close.

■ **Saint-Hubert** (AC B DR DU f FC FH G LAB m MSG RR SA SL VS)
Mon-Thu 10.30-3, Fri 10.30-Mon 3h (non-stop)
6527 rue Saint-Hubert *Near Plaza Saint-Hubert* ☎ (514) 277-0176
💻 www.saunasthubert.com
Discreet sauna where it is not unusual to meet married men.

■ **Sauna Centre-Ville**
(AC B CC DR DU G I M MA NU RR SA SB VS WH WI) 24hrs
1465 rue Sainte Catherine Est *M° Beaudry or Papineau*
☎ (514) 524-3486 💻 www.saunacentreville.com
Established. In 1990, one of The mots popolar bath bouse in Montreal.

■ **Club Sauna Spa, Le**
(AC b cc DR DU f FC FH G LAB m MA OS SA SB VS WH) 24hrs
961 Rue Rachel Est *Near Parc Lafontaine* ☎ (514) 528-1679
💻 www.saunaduplateau.com
Sauna on 4 floors with summer terrace. Former Sauna du Plateau.

FITNESS STUDIOS

■ **Energie Cardio** (glm MA) Mon-Fri 6-22, Sat 9-19, Sun -17h
845 rue Ste-Catherine Est, suite M52Z ☎ 288 7057

■ **Nautilus** (AC GLM MA SA WO) 6-22, Sun 9-20h
1431 rue St-André ☎ (514) 905-9999
Day pass available $15.

BOOK SHOPS

■ **Ménage A Trois** (cc GLM MA)
1672 Rue Sainte-Catherine Est *M° Papineau* ☎ (514) 656-5451
Small bookshop, upstairs with small gay section. Used porn movies on VHS and DVDs, old porn magazines and used books for sale in the basement. Cruise upstairs. Washroom in the basement.

LEATHER & FETISH SHOPS

■ **Cuir Mont-Royal** (CC F GLM)
826-A Mont Royal Est ☎ (514) 527-0238
💻 www.cuirmontroyal.com

■ **Fétiche Armada** (CC G)
Sun 12-20, Mon & Tue 10.30-18, Wed -21, Thu-Sa -22ht
1201 Sainte Catherine Est ☎ (514) 419-1089
💻 www.fetichearmada.com
New fetish shop with MisterB in-store and own line.

TRAVEL AND TRANSPORT

■ **Voyages Terre des Hommes/Voyages Express** (G)
Mon-Fri 9-18, Sat 11-16h
1201 Rue Sainte Catherine Est ☎ (514) 522-2225
💻 www.voyagesterredeshommes.com

HOTELS

■ **Gouverneur PlaceDupuis** (AC B glm H I MA RWS RWT)
All year, 24hrs
1415, Rue St. Hubert *M° Berri-UQAM* ☎ 842 4881
💻 www.gouverneur.com
4 stars, 132 rooms.

■ **Loft Hotel** (AC glm I MA RWS RWT) all year
334 Terrasse St Denis ☎ 439.1818 💻 www.lofthotel.ca
New and upscale hotel with luxury loft-suites.

■ **Opus Montréal**
(AC B BF CC glm I M MA OS PA RWS RWT SA VEG W WH) all year, 24hrs
10 Sherbrooke Ouest ☎ (514) 843 6000
💻 www.opusmontreal.com
This hotel provides the service and amenities of a luxury hotel within a stylish and intimate environment.

■ **Roberval, Le** (AC B glm H I MA RWS RWT) All year, 24hrs
505, boul. René-Lévesque Est ☎ 286 5215
💻 www.leroberval.com
In the heart of Montreal, rooms, studios and suites.

GUEST HOUSES

■ **Alexandre Logan (1870) B&B** (AC BF CC GLM I MA OS RWB RWS RWT) All year, reception 8-20h
1631, Alexandre De Sève *M° Beaudry/Papineau* ☎ (514) 598-0555
🖳 www.alexandrelogan.com

■ **Aubergell.com** (AC B BF CC glm I MA OS WO) All year
1641 rue Amherst *M° Berri/UQAM, in the gay village* ☎ (514) 597-0878
🖳 www.aubergell.com
Aubergell's 4 rooms and one suite offer modern design and lots of features. Owner Yvon can help you find your way in the gayest town in Canada.

■ **B&B Le Cartier** (AC BF CC GLM I MA OS PK RWB RWS RWT VA) All year, 24hrs
1219 rue Cartier *M° Papineau. One minute from Ste-Catherine street and subway station* ☎ (514) 917-1829 ☎ 1-877-5240495 (toll free)
🖳 www.bblecartier.com
Gay owned and operated, located in Montreal's downtown / gay village. Charming rooms/suites with beautiful backyard. Private apartment is also available.

■ **Bed & Breakfast du Village - BBV** (AC BF CC DU FC FH GLM I MA MSG NR OS PK RR RWS RWT VA WI) All year
1279 rue Montcalm *M° Berry/Uqam & Beaudry, near rue Ste-Catherine*
☎ (514) 522-4771 ☎ 1-888- 228-8455 (toll free) 🖳 www.bbv.qc.ca
A friendly and hospitable Bed & Breakfast situated in the heart of Montréal's gay village.

■ **Chasseur. Le** (AC bf CC glm I MA OS PA RWS RWT VA) All year, reception 10-22h
1567 Rue Saint-André *M° Berri-Uqam/Beaudry* ☎ (514) 521-2238
🖳 www.lechasseur.com

■ **Conciergerie. La** (AC BF CC G I MA MSG NU OS RWS WH WI WO) All year
1019 Rue Saint-Hubert *M° Berri-UQAM/Champ de Mars*
☎ (514) 289-9297 🖳 www.laconciergerie.ca
This beautiful and friendly Victorian home offers a total of 17 rooms (shared/private bath). All of the rooms are furnished with comfortable queen-size beds.

■ **Escogriffe B&B** (AC BF GLM I MA OS PK RWT VA) 8-20h
1264 Wolfe ☎ (514) 523-4800 🖳 www.lescogriffe.com
Centrally located and close to all main attractions. 5 rooms.

■ **Loggia Art B&B. A La** (AC BF CC FH GLM I MA MSG NR OS PK RWB RWS RWT SOL WI WO) 7-23h
1637 rue Amherst *M° Beaudry / Berry-UQAM* ☎ (514) 524-2493
🖳 www.laloggia.ca
Art & sleeping at a friend's place.

■ **Maison des Anges. La** (BF G OS)
1640 Alexandre de Seve *M° Beaudry/Papineau* ☎ (514) 527-9890
🖳 lamaisondesanges.info
Two rooms with queen beds.

■ **NU Zone** (AC BF G I MA NR NU OS RES RWS RWT SA WI) all year
1729 rue St-Hubert *M° Berri/UQAM* ☎ (514) 524-5292
🖳 www.nuzone.ca
Naturist environment for men only.

■ **Ruta Bagage B&B** (AC CC G MC MSG NU OS RWT VA) All year
1345 rue Sainte Rose *At Panet St* ☎ (514) 598-1586
🖳 www.rutabagage.qc.ca
Four rooms in the gay village.

■ **Saint-Christophe. Le** (AC BF CC G NU OS RWS RWT SOL VA WH) All year
1597 Rue Saint-Christophe *M° Berri* ☎ (514) 527-7836
🖳 www.stchristophe.com

■ **Sir Montcalm** (AC BF CC glm I MA OS PI PK RWB RWS RWT VA WH) All year
1453 rue Montcalm *M° Berri-UQAM/Beaudry* ☎ (514) 522-7747
🖳 www.sirmontcalm.com
Five guestrooms and a tourist-residence in the village with private entrance, full kitchen, shower/WC, floor heating, TV with DVD and stereo set. Wonderful sundeck and kitchen facilities.

■ **Turquoise B&B** (BF GLM NU OS PK VA) All year
1576 Rue Alexandre-DeSève *Near rue St. Catherine, between M° Beaudry & Papineau* ☎ (514) 523-9943 🖳 www.turquoisebb.com
Friendly, centrally located B&B.

APARTMENTS

■ **Aux Studios Montcalm** (AC glm I MA PA RWB RWS RWT) 8-24h
1279 de Montcalm *M° Beaudry, near rue Ste-Catherine*
☎ (514) 815-6195 🖳 www.auxstudiosmontcalm.com
Close to all main attractions.

■ **Studios du Centre-Ville** (AC GLM MA) 9-21h
1495 & 1497 rue Amherst ☎ (514) 574-0747 🖳 www.montrealstudios.ca
Non-smoker, no pets.

■ **Suites Labelle** (B glm H I MA RWS RWT) All year, 24hrs
1205, rue Labelle ☎ 514 840 1151 🖳 www.hotellabelle.com
Junior and executive suites downtown.

■ **Terrasses Saint-Urbain, Les** (glm H I MA RWB RWS RWT) all year
2115, rue St-Urbain ☎ 935 6499 🖳 www.aparthotelmontreal.com
Luxury Condominiums.

CAMPING

■ **Domaine de la Fierté** (B G M MA NU PI SA SOL WH) All year
2905, Montée Hamilton *In Sainte-Julienne/Rawdon ca. 50 km north of Montréal* ☎ (450) 834-2888 🖳 www.campingdelafierte.com

HEALTH GROUPS

■ **Rézo** (G MA) Mon-Fri 9-12, 13-17h
2075, rue Plessis, local 207 ☎ (514) 521 7778 🖳 www.rezosante.org
(former Séro Zéro)

HELP WITH PROBLEMS

■ **Gay Line** 19-23h
☎ (514) 866-5090 (from Montréal) 🖳 www.gayline.qc.ca
English speaking helpline for GLBT people.

CRUISING

-Rue Sainte-Catherine Est (Saint-Hubert Street to Champlain/Wolfe Street, after 21h)
-In front, in the little park west of Church Marie-Reine-du-Monde

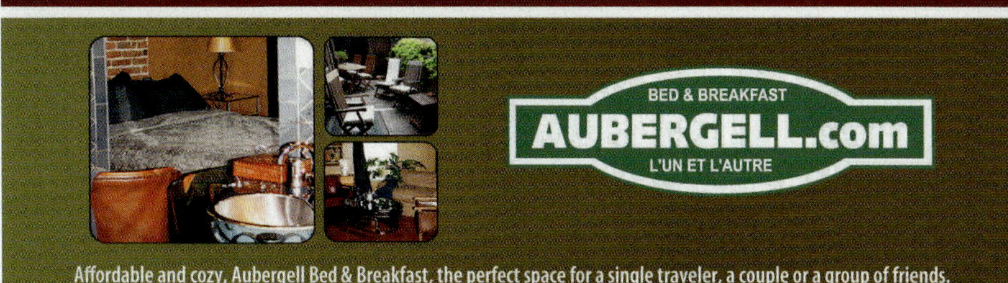

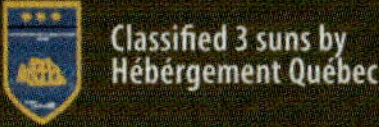

-Parc Baldwin (M° Papineau)
-Rue Champlain (R) (between Sainte Catherine Est and Boulevard René-Lévesque Est).

Québec ☏ 418

Quebec, named after its province, lies on Cap Diamant overlooking the St Lawrence River, and is the oldest city in Canada (404 years in 2012!). This historic part of Quebec is the birthplace of French-speaking settlements in North America, and its narrow winding lanes were declared a world heritage site by UNESCO.
The amazing parliament building is particularly worth visiting. The annual Summer Festival brings together artists from all over the world to gather in the streets; despite often freezing temperatures the famous Carnival brings a flavour of Rio to Quebec in February. Magnificent parades and traditional competitions like canoe races make for crazy unforgettable events. The majority of the gay community is centred around St Jean Street in the Old Town, where in close proximity you can find everything the gay heart could wish for, as well as meet the locals.

Die Hauptstadt der gleichnamigen Provinz Québec liegt auf dem Cap Diamant mit Blick auf den St.-Lorenz-Strom und ist die älteste Stadt des Landes (404 Jahre im Jahr 2012). Der historische Teil von Québec City ist die Wiege der frankophonen Besiedlung Nordamerikas und seine engen, gewundenen Gassen wurden von der UNESCO zum Weltkulturerbe erklärt. Besonders die wunderschönen Parlamentsgebäude sind einen Besuch wert. Beim jährlichen „Sommer-Festival" im Juli sorgen Künstler aus aller Welt für eine einzigartige Stimmung in den Straßen der Stadt und trotz oft niedriger Temperaturen weht jedes Jahr im Februar während des berühmten Karnevals ein Hauch von Rio durch Québec City. Prächtige Paraden und traditionelle Wettkämpfe wie das Kanurennen sorgen für ein unvergessliches närrisches Treiben. Die überschaubare Gay-Community trifft sich rund um die St. Jean Street nahe der Altstadt, wo sich auf kleinem Raum fast alles findet, was das schwul-lesbische Herz begehrt und es ein Leichtes ist, mit den Einheimischen in Kontakt zu kommen.

Québec, capitale de la province du même nom, située sur le Cap Diamant et offrant ainsi une vue imprenable sur le fleuve Saint-Laurent, est la plus vieille ville du pays (404 ans en 2012!). Sa partie historique est le berceau de la colonisation francophone en Amérique du nord et ses ruelles étroites et tortueuses figurent sur la liste du patrimoine culturel mondial de l'UNESCO. Les bâtiments parlementaires sont particulièrement intéressants. Lors du „Festival d'été", des artistes du monde entier donnent chaque année aux rues de la ville une ambiance unique. Malgré les températures souvent très basses, le célèbre festival de février donne à la ville un petit air de Rio: des défilés hauts en couleurs s'allient aux traditionnelles compétitions telles que la course en canoë pour une ambiance des plus folles. Le petit milieu gay se concentre autour de la rue Saint-Jean près de la vieille ville et offre à peu près tout ce que les gays et lesbiennes peuvent désirer. De plus, il est relativement facile d'entrer en contact avec la population locale!

La capital de la provincia del mismo nombre, Québec, está situada en el Cap Diamant con vistas al río San Lorenzo y es la ciudad más antigua del país (2012 de 404 años!). La parte histórica de la ciudad de Québec es el fuerte de la población francófona de Norteamérica y sus estrechas y curvadas calles fueron declaradas patrimonio de la humanidad por la UNESCO. Vale la pena visitar sobre todo el fantástico edificio del Parlamento. Durante el festival anual de verano en julio, artistas de todo el mundo dan un toque único a la ciudad y, a pesar de las bajas temperaturas del invierno, cada año se celebra en febrero el famoso carnaval a través de la ciudad. Grandes carrozas y las tradicionales competiciones de canoa recrean un ambiente inolvidable. La comunidad gay es pequeña y se reúne en la calle St. Jean, cerca de la zona antigua, donde en un reducido espacio se concentra casi todo lo que gays y lesbianas desean y es más fácil entrar en contacto con sus habitantes.

Il capoluogo dell'omonima Regione Quebec è situato sul Cap Diamant con vista sul fiume San Lorenzo ed è la città più antica del Paese (2012 di 404 anni!). La parte storica di Quebec City è la culla dell'insediamento francofono del Nord America e le sue strette stradine sono state dichiarate patrimonio culturale dall'UNESCO. Vale la pena venire a Quebec City già solo per visitare i meravigliosi edifici del parlamento.
Per l'annuale festival estivo che si svolge in luglio molti artisti da tutto il mondo ravvivano l'atmosfera delle strade. Nonostante le basse temperature, per il noto carnevale in febbraio, in città regna un'atmosfera simile a quella di Rio: per strada si possono ammirare gli sfarzosi cortei e le competizioni di lotta tradizionale come per esempio la gara delle canoe. La comunità gay, che è relativamente piccola si concentra nei pressi della St. Jean Street vicino alla città vecchia, dove su uno spazio piuttosto modesto, si concentra tutto quello che la comunità gay e lesbica può desiderare e dove è molto facile entrare in contatto con la gente del luogo.

BARS

■ **321** (AC B g m MA) 12-3h
321, Rue de la Couronne ☏ (418) 525-5107
Neighbourhood tavern.

■ **ForHom** (B G I MA OS P VS) 17-3h
221 rue Saint-Jean ☏ (418) 522-4918 🖳 www.forhom.ca
A cosy lounge bar on the first floor of a gay complex including sauna & sex shop.

■ **Bar 889** (AC B glm MA) 11-3h
889 Cote St. Genevieve ☏ (418) 524 5000
former St-Matthew.

DANCECLUBS

■ **Drague. Le** (! AC B D F GLM MA OS S ST) Thu-Sat from 23h
815 rue St. Augustin ☏ (418) 649-7212 🖳 www.ledrague.com
Complex with a pub (zone 1) with drag shows, a modern bar (zone 2) and a cruising bar (zone 3) especially for fetish fans. Disco nights Thu-Sat 23-3h in the basement of the Drague.

RESTAURANTS

■ **Oeuforie, L'** (AC BF CC glm M MA OS) Mon-Fri 7-22, Sat & Sun 8-22h
810 Honoré-Mercier ☏ (418) 521-4044 🖳 www.oeuforie.com
Great breakfasts & fresh pastas.

■ **Orsay, D'** (B CC glm M MA WL) Mon-Fri 7-, Sat+Sun 8-22h
65, rue De Buade *Place de l'Hôtel de Ville* ☎ 694-1582
www.restaurantbardorsay.com
European pub & restaurant.

■ **Postino** (AC B BF CC glm M MA OS) Mon-Fri 11.30-21, Sat & Sun 9-21h
296 Saint-Joseph ☎ (418) 647-0000 www.lepostino.com
Great Italian gastronomy on trendy Saint-Joseph Street in downtown Québec City.

SAUNAS/BATHS

■ **Backboys**
(AC CC DR DU FC FH G GH LAB m OC RR SA SB SH SL SOL VS WH) 24hrs
264 Rue de la Couronne *Near Boulevard Charest* ☎ (418) 521-6686
Sauna with mirrors rooms, glory holes, sling and TV lounge.

■ **Bloc 225** (AC B DR DU FC FH G GH LAB m MA RR SA SB SH VS WH) 24hrs
225 Rue St. Jean *Bus 7/800/801* ☎ (418) 523-2562
www.gayquebec.net/sauna.html
With a labyrinth and with black light.

■ **Hippocampe**
(AC CC DR FC FH G H I m MA RR SA SB SH SOL VS WH) 24hrs
31 rue McMahon ☎ (418) 692-1521 www.saunahippocampe.com
Sauna with 12 comfortable hotel rooms and free coffee in the morning.

HOTELS

■ **Hotel Hippocampe** (AC CC DR G M MA SA SB SOL VS WH) All year
31, rue McMahon ☎ (888) 388 1521 (mobile) www.hotelhippocampe.com
12 comfortable hotel rooms and free coffee in the morning. Sauna Hippocampe is in the same building.

GUEST HOUSES

■ **727 Guest House** (AC bf CC GLM I OS PK RWB RWS RWT) All year
727 Rue d'Aiguillon ☎ (418) 523-7705 www.727daiguillon.com
European-style guest house located in the old town. 9 rooms with private or shared bath and colour TV.

■ **Château du Faubourg. Le** (AC BF CC glm MA OS RWS) All year
429 Rue Saint Jean *City centre* ☎ (418) 524-2902
www.lechateaudufaubourg.com
High standard accommodation in a private château, reservation required.

CAMPING

■ **Domaine de l'Arc-en-Ciel** (B BF CC D G I M MA NU OS PI) May-Sep
1878 Rang 5 ☎ (418) 728-5522 www.dom-aec.com
Camping for men only. The only gay campground in Québec City area. Exit 266 of Highway 20. Half an hour out of Québec City by car on the South Shore of Saint-Laurent River.

CRUISING

-Lac Vert
-Rue St.Denis
-Rue St. Jean (north of Place d'Youville)
-Plains of Abraham (path along the cliffs, evenings)
-Terrace Dufferin.

Rouyn-Noranda ☎ 819

BARS

■ **Station D** (B D GLM MA OS) 14-?h, closed Mon & Tue
63 Perreault Ouest ☎ (819) 797-8696
Bar-disco with a terrace in summer.

Saint François-Du-Lac ☎ 450

CAMPING

■ **Domaine Emeraude** (B BF DU G I M MA MSG NU OS P PA PI PK RR S VA VS WE WH WI) May 1st-Sep 15th
261 Grande Terre ☎ 450-568-3634 www.domaine-emeraude.com
Camping and leisure center for gay naturist men. Lushly green and naturally beautiful locale. Ideal place to soak up the summer sun, relax and make new friends.

Sainte Marthe ☎ 450

CAMPING

■ **Camping Plein Bois** (B CC D G I MC NU OS PI) May-Sep
550 Chemin St-Henri *45 mins from Montreal, 90 mins from Ottawa*
☎ (450) 459-4646 www.campingpleinbois.com

Sept-Iles ☎ 418

CAFES

■ **Café du Port** (AC b CC glm m MA) 8-24h
495 Avenue Brochu ☎ (418) 962-9311

Sherbrooke ☎ 819

BARS

■ **Complexe 13-17** (AC B cc D G H m MA SA SNU VS WH)
Sauna 24hrs, bar 11-3, disco Fri 21-3h
13-17, Rue Bowen Sud *Cnr. rue King* ☎ (819) 562-2628
Entertainment complex on different floors with a bar with nude dancers, a sauna, a disco and a pub.

■ **Otre Zone. L'** (B D GLM MA OS S)
Tue & Wed 16-24; Thu, Fri & Sun -3; Sat 20-3h
252 Rue Dufferin *90 mins south of Montréal* ☎ (819) 565-5333
www.lotrezone.ca
Regular shows and theme nights, popular during the happy hour.

SAUNAS/BATHS

■ **Equus** (AC cc DU FC FH G m MC RR SA VS WH) 24hrs
13-17 Rue Bowen Sud ☎ (819) 569-5580
Located in a gay complex, the 13-17, which also offers a pub, a bar and a discotheque.

Trois Rivières ☎ 819

BARS

■ **Look resto-pub** (AC B CC D GLM M MA S) Tue-Sun 17-3h
210-st-Georges *Downtown* ☎ (819) 374-6650
DJ and karaoke.

Victoriaville ☎ 819

BARS

■ **QG** (B GLM MA S) Wed-Sun 16-3h
415 Boulevard Bois-Francs Sud ☎ (819) 758-0649

Saskatchewan

Location: Central CDN
Initials: SK
Time: GMT -6
Area: 652,000 km² / 251,737 sq mi.
Population: 1,024,000
Capital: Regina

Saskatoon ☎ 306

PUBLICATIONS

■ **Perceptions**
PO Box 8581 ☎ (306) 244-1930
Gay/lesbian news magazine published 8x/year.

BARS

■ **302 Lounge and Discothèque** (B D GLM MA) Wed-Sat 19-?h
302 Pacific Avenue ☎ (306) 665-6863 www.302lounge.com

■ **Diva's** (B GLM MA P) 20-3h, closed Mon & Tue
110-220 3rd Avenue South *Side alley entrance* ☎ (306) 665-0100
www.divasclub.ca

Cape Verde

Name: Kapverde Cap-Vert Cabo Verde Capo Verde
Location: Atlantic Ocean
Initials: RCV
Time: GMT -1
International Country Code: ☎ 238
Language: Portuguese (official)
Area: 4,036 km² / 1,556 sq miles
Currency: Escudo Caboverdiano (CVEsc)
Population: 507,000
Capital: Praia
Religions: 93% Roman Catholic
Climate: The best time to visit is between Feb and Jun.

The Embassy of Cap Verde in Germany refused to comment on the legal situation for homosexuals on the island. According to ILGA the Portuguese Penal Code of 1866, which stayed in force after independence, de facto criminalizes homosexual behaviour. Sections 390 and 391 prohibit „acts against nature", and „assaults on public or personal decency". Sections 405 and 406 prohibit „prostitution", and „the corruption of minors". Repeat offenders can be imprisoned.
This former Portuguese Island on Africa's western tip was a convenient base for ships transporting slaves to Europe and the Americas. In 1975, Cape Verde finally gained independence from Portugal.

Die kapverdische Botschaft in Deutschland hat jeglichen Kommentar zur Rechtslage von Homosexuellen auf der Inselgruppe verweigert. Laut ILGA kriminalisiert das portugiesische Strafgesetzbuch von 1866, das nach Erreichen der Unabhängigkeit in Kraft blieb, homosexuelle Lebensweisen. Die Paragrafen 390 und 391 untersagen „widernatürliche Handlungen" und „Verletzungen der öffentlichen oder persönlichen Sittlichkeit". In ähnlicher Manier verbieten die Paragrafen 405 und 406 die „Prostitution" und die „Verführung Minderjähriger". Wiederholungstäter können mit Freiheitsentzug bestraft werden.
Die ehemalige portugiesische Kolonie vor Afrikas Westküste stellte für den Sklavenhandel nach Europa sowie Nord- und Südamerika einen ideal gelegenen Stützpunkt dar. Kap Verde hat erst 1975 die Unabhängigkeit von Portugal erreicht.

L'ambassade capverdienne en Allemagne s'est refusée à tout commentaire sur la situation juridique des homosexuels dans l'archipel. Selon l'ILGA, le code pénal portugais de 1866 qui resta en vigueur après l'accession à l'indépendance criminalise le mode de vie homosexuel. Les paragraphes 390 et 391 interdisent les « actes contre-nature » et « les violations de la morale publique ou privée ». Les paragraphes 390 et 406 interdisent de la même façon la « prostitution » et le « détournement de mineur ». Les récidivistes peuvent se voir punir de prison.
L'ancienne colonie portugaise située juste en face des côtes d'Afrique de l'ouest présentait pour le trafic d'esclaves vers l'Europe et le continent américain une base idéale du point de vue géographique. L'accession à l'indépendance du Portugal n'a eu lieu qu'en 1975.

La embajada de Cabo Verde en Alemania nos negó cualquier tipo de comentario sobre la situación de los homosexuales en el archipiélago. Según la Asociación Internacional para Gays y Lesbianas (ILGA), el código penal portugués de 1866, que después de la independencia del país todavía permanece en vigor, criminaliza la homosexualidad. Los artículos 390 y 391 prohíben los „actos contra natura" y „las lesiones a la moralidad pública y personal". Del mismo modo, los artículos 405 y 406 prohíben la „prostitución" y la „corrupción de menores". Los reincidentes pueden ser penalizados con la pena privativa de libertad.
La antigua colonia portuguesa de la costa occidental africana era un punto ideal para el comercio de esclavos entre Europa y América. Cabo Verde logró la independencia de Portugal en el 1975.

L'ambasciata di Capo Verde in Germania ha rifiutato di dare qualsiasi commento sulla situazione legislativa dell'omosessualità sull'arcipelago. Secondo l'ILGA il codice penale portoghese del 1866, che è in vigore dall'indipendenza di Capo Verde dal Portogallo, criminalizza l'omosessualità. I paragrafi 390 e 391 proibiscono gli „atti contro-natura" e i „reati contro la morale pubblica ed il buon costume". Alla stessa maniera i paragrafi 405 e 406 vietano la prostituzione e la seduzione di minorenni. I recidivi possono essere puniti con una pena detentiva. L'ex colonia portoghese situata di fronte alla costa occidentale africana rappresentava la base strategica per la tratta di schiavi con l'Europa e con l'America del nord e del sud. Capo Verde ha ottenuto l'indipendenza dal Portogallo solo nel 1975.

Santa Maria, Sal

HOTELS

Porta do Vento (B H M MC OS)
☎ 242 21 21 💻 www.portadovento.com
Gay-friendly hotel with 15 rooms. Also open-space bar and restaurant.

Caribbean

Aruba

Location: Caribbean
Initials: ARU (NL)
Time: GMT -4
International Country Code: ☎ 297 (no area codes)
International Access Code: ☎ 00
Language: Dutch, Papiamento, English, Spanish, Castilian
Area: 193 km² / 75 sq mi.
Currency: 1 Aruba-Florin (Afl) = 100 Cents
Population: 99,000
Capital: Oranjestad
Religions: 80% Roman Catholic
Climate: Tropical marine climate with little seasonal temperature variation. The main tourist season is from Dec-Apr.

Aruba is an autonomous territory of the Netherlands with special status. Gay men lead a relatively untroubled and safe life here. The age of consent is 16 and sex between men is legal. According to the Dutch government Aruba belongs to the Dutch kingdom must recognize same-sex marriages against which, however, the local government in Aruba is fighting as well as against a court decision in favour of the Dutch government.

★ Aruba ist autonomer Teil der Niederlande mit Sonderstatus. Schwule Männer können auf Aruba relativ unbehelligt und sicher leben. Das Schutzalter liegt bei 16 Jahren und einvernehmlicher Sex zwischen Männern ist legal.
Nach Auffassung der Niederländischen Regierung muss das zum Niederländischen Königreich gehörende Aruba gleichgeschlechtliche Ehen anerkennen, wogegen sich aber die Regierung in Aruba stellt. Gegen eine Gerichtsentscheidung zugunsten der Niederländischen Regierung hat Aruba Rechtsmittel eingelegt.

Aruba est une île autonome des Pays-Bas jouissant d'un statut particulier. Pour les gais, la vie y est relativement sûre et calme. La majorité sexuelle est fixée à16 ans et les relations entre hommes sont légales si elles sont placées sous le signe du consentement mutuel. Daprès l'opinion du gouvernement néerlandais, Aruba faisant partie du royaume des Pays-Bas devrait reconnaître l'union de personnes de même sexe, ce que refuse le gouvernement arubais. Celui-ci a dailleurs même formé un recours contre une décision de justice en faveur du gouvernement néerlandais.

Aruba es una parte autónoma de los Países Bajos que posee un status especial. Homosexuales pueden vivir en la isla relativamente seguros y tranquilos. La edad de protección es de 16 años, y el sexo por acuerdo entre hombres es legal. Según la opinión del gobierno neerlandés, Aruba, que pertenece al reino de los Países Bajos, debería reconocer a los matrimonios del mismo sexo pero el gobierno en Aruba se opone a ello. Aruba ha interpuesto un recurso contra una decisión judicial a favor del gobierno neerlandés.

Aruba è una parte autonoma dei Paesi Bassi con statuto speciale. Qui i gay possono vivere senza essere importunati. L'età legale per rapporti sessuali è di 16 anni, ed i rapporti tra uomini sono legali purchè biconsensuali. Secondo il governo dei Paesi Bassi, Aruba, da Paese facente capo alla Corona olandese, dovrebbe riconoscere i matrimoni tra persone dello stesso sesso. Tuttavia il governo di Aruba rifiuta la direttiva facendo ricorso contro la decisione della Corte di giustizia olandese.

Oranjestad

BARS

■ **Jimmy's Place** (B D GLM M MA)
Tue-Thu 17-2, Fri & Sat 17-4, Sun 20-2h, Mon closed
Windstraat 32 *Cnr. Zandstraat* ☎ 58 22 550
www.jimmysaruba.com
In a new location is also known as „Buitenhofje". Happy hour daily from 17-18h. DJs on Thu, Fri & Sat.

■ **Paddock. The** (B cc g M MA) 10-2h, kitchen open 9-23h
Smith Blvd. 13 ☎ 58 32 334 www.paddock-aruba.com
Bar and restaurant. Happy hour daily.

GUEST HOUSES

■ **Little David** (AC BF glm I MA NU OS PA PI PK RWB RWS RWT)
All year
Seroe Blanco 56L, Regentspark *5 mins drive from the beach*
☎ 58 38 288 www.littledavidaruba.com
The only gay-friendly guesthouse in Aruba. Five guest rooms.

CRUISING

-Eagle Beach from 16-sunset (between La Quinta Resort and Dutch Village Hotel)
-Malmok 14-18h (by the beach).

Bahamas

Location: Caribbean
Initials: BS
Time: GMT -5
International Country Code: ☎ 1 242 (no area codes)
International Access Code: ☎ 011
Language: English, Creole
Area: 13 939 km² / 5,381 sq mi.
Currency: 1 Bahama Dollar (B$) = 100 Cents
Population: 323,000
Capital: Nassau
Religions: 31 % Baptist, 16% Anglican, 16% Catholic & 5% Methodist
Climate: Subtropical climate. Tropical storms in autumn (May-Nov)

Homosexuality is not illegal in the Bahamas. Only gay sex acts in public are deemed an offense, punishable with up to twenty years in prison.
The age of consent for heterosexuals is 16 and 18 for gays and lesbians. Residents and visitors alike are asked to comply with the laws relating to public decency. One cannot say that the general attitude here is hostile.

★ Homosexualität ist auf den Bahamas nicht illegal. Sexuelle Handlungen zwischen Schwulen werden jedoch als Vergehen erachtet, das mit bis zu zwanzig Jahren Gefängnis bestraft werden kann. Das Schutzalter für Heterosexuelle liegt bei 16 Jahren und für Homosexuelle bei 18 Jahren. Ortsansässige und Besucher sind in gleichem Maße angehalten, nicht gegen die Gesetze bezüglich des öffentlichen Anstands zu verstoßen. Man kann nicht sagen, dass die allgemeine Haltung gegenüber Homosexuellen feindlich wäre.

L'homosexualité n'est pas illégale aux Bahamas. Seuls les rapports sexuels entre gais en public sont considérés comme une offense punissable par une peine d'emprisonnement allant jusqu'à 20 ans.
La majorité sexuelle est fixée à 16 ans pour les hétérosexuels et à 18 pour les homosexuels. Les habitants tout autant que les touristes sont tenus à respecter les lois de décence publique. On ne peut pour autant pas dire que l'attitude générale est homophobe.

La homosexualidad no es ilegal en las Bahamas. Sin embargo, actos sexuales (homosexuales) en público se consideran un delito y son penalizados con hasta veinte años de prisión.
La edad de consentimiento es de 16 años para heterosexuales y de 18 años para gays y lesbianas. Se espera tanto de los residentes de las islas como de los turistas que cumplan con las leyes relacionadas con la „decencia en público" . No se puede decir que la actitud general hacia los gays sea hostil.

L´omosessualità alle Bahamas non è illegale. Tuttavia le relazioni sessuali tra gay sono considerate reato, punibile con carcere fino a venti anni. L´età minima per eterosessuali é di 16 anni e 18 per gay e lesbiche. Residenti e visitatori sono tenuti in egual misura a rispettare le leggi che si riferiscono al pubblico decoro. Non si può dire che l´opinione generale sia ostica nei confronti degli omosessuali.

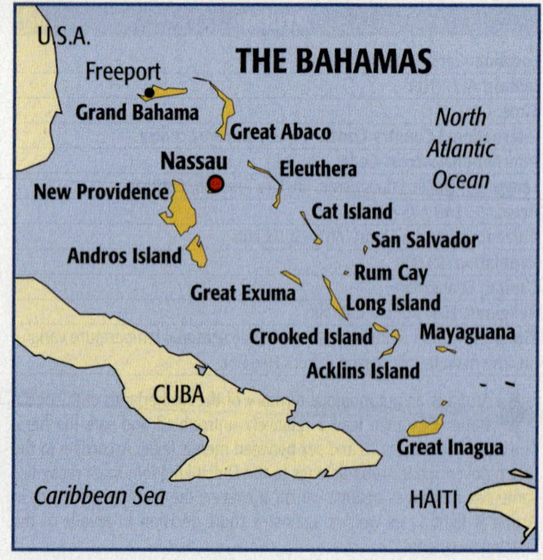

Nassau

BARS

Club Waterloo (B cc D g M MA s) Daily 20-4h
East Bay Street *1 km east of the Paradise Island Bridge* ☎ 393 7324
www.clubwaterloo.com
The front room and bar play rock and roll. There's a larger dance floor and an outside area.

Drop-Off Pub & Restaurant (B d M NG) Daily 11-6h
Bay Street *East of Rawston Square* ☎ 322 6284
Draws a huge crowd of cruise ship employees, club kids, cross-dressers and confused tourists. You can get a full meal here all night long. The menu features several cuisines, including Italian, British and of course, Bahamian. 14 types of beer on tap.

RESTAURANTS

Circa 1890 Fine Dining (AC B CC glm M MA WE) 12-15 & 18-24h
Shirely Street & Buen Retiro Road ☎ 356 5445
www.circa1890restaurant.com

SWIMMING

-Paradise Island
-Westend Esplanade, near the El Greco hotel (cruising at night)
-Cable Beach.

CRUISING

-Paradise Beach on Paradise Island.

Barbados

Name: Barbade
Location: Caribbean
Initials: BDS
Time: GMT -4
International Country Code: ☎ 1 246 (no area codes)
International Access Code: ☎ 011
Language: English
Area: 430 km² / 166 sq mi.
Currency: 1 Barbados Dollar (BDS$) = 100 Cents
Population: 270,000
Capital: Bridgetown
Religions: 55% Protestant, 5% Roman Catholic
Climate: Tropical climate. Best during the cooler, drier months (Feb-May). The rainy season is from Jun-Oct.

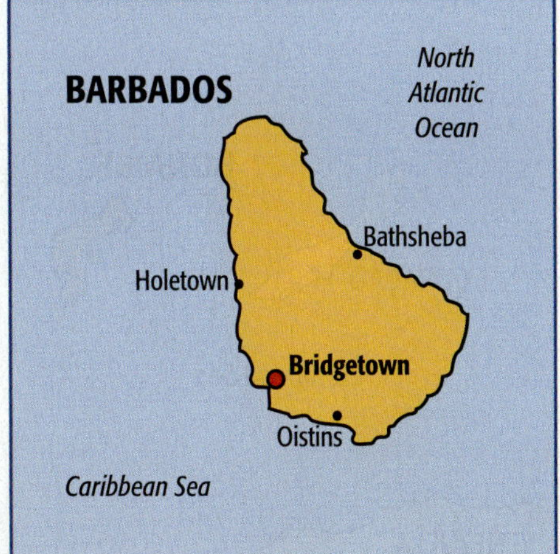

Homosexuality is illegal in Barbados. According to reports however, gays are not bothered by the police. Nonetheless, the gay scene is rather hidden from the public eye. Gay life takes place mostly on the southern coast (St. Michael, Christ Church) as well as on the west coast (St. James- Batts Rock). Cruising takes place on the beach and from cars. Especially worth mentioning is the „Thanksgiving Festival" that takes place in July and the Arts Festival in November.
The majority of gays on the island are more conservative or maintain a conservative facade. So keep this in mind when approaching men on the island. But the guys are friendly especially towards visitors so you should make friends easily. There are gay parties throughout the year with changing locations. It is all very discreet and the venue can change without much notice to maintain discretion.

Homosexualität ist auf Barbados illegal. Allerdings werden Schwule nicht von der Polizei verfolgt. Trotzdem ist die einheimische Schwulenszene von der Öffentlichkeit abgeschirmt. Das schwule Leben spielt sich vor allem an der Südküste (St. Michael, Christ Church) sowie an der Westküste (St. James - Batts Rock) ab. Man cruist am Strand oder per Auto-Blickkontakt. Erwähnenswert sind vor allem das im Juli stattfindende „Erntedank-Festival" und das sogenannte „Künstlerfest" im November.
Die schwulen Inselbewohner sind mehrheitlich konservativer oder bemühen sich, eine konservative Fassade aufrecht zu erhalten. Daran sollte man sich erinnern, wenn man hier mit ihnen ins Gespräch kommt. Ansonsten sind die Insulaner sehr freundlich, besonders zu Touristen, und Kontakte zu knüpfen dürfte nicht schwer sein. Schwule Parties finden das ganze Jahr über an verschiedenen Orten statt. Auch diesbezüglich herrscht große Diskretion, zu deren Wahrung sich die Veranstaltungsorte kurzfristig ändern können.

A la Barbade, l'homosexualité est un délit. D'après ce que nous savons, la police laisse les gais en paix. Pourtant, les gais s'y font très discrets. Les principaux lieux gais se trouvent surtout sur la côte sud (St. Michael, Christ Church) et sur la côte ouest (St. James - Batts Rock). On drague à la plage et en voiture. A voir: la grande fête de la Grâce (pour la récolte, en juin) et la fête des Artistes (en novembre).
Les habitants de l'île sont en majorité conservateurs ou essaient tout du moins de garder une apparence conservatrice. Il est important de s'en rappeler lorsque l'on s'entretient avec eux. Les insulaires sont aussi très amicaux, en particulier avec les touristes, et il est aisé de nouer des contacts. Des soirées gays ont lieu toute l'année à différents endroits. A ce propos aussi, une grande discrétion règne et les lieux sont susceptibles d'être changés à la dernière minute pour la maintenir.

La homosexualidad es ilegal en Barbados. De acuerdo a los informes, los gays no son perseguidos por la policía. A pesar de todo, el ambiente gay de los nativos se mantiene en cubierto, la vida gay se da sobre todo en la costa sur (St. Michael, Christ Church) así como también en la costa Occidental (St. James - Batts Rock). El „cruising" se practica en la playa o viajando en coche con contactos a primera vista. Digno de mención es el Festival de la Cosecha (en julio de cada año), así como la llamada Fiesta de los Artistas (noviembre).
Los habitantes gays de la isla son en su mayoría conservadores o tratan de mantener una fachada conservadora de cara al público. Esto es algo que vale la pena recordar aquí a la hora de entablar una conversación con desconocidos. Por otro lado, encontrará que los isleños son muy amables, sobre todo con los turistas y no le debería resultar difícil establecer contacto con ellos.
Se celebran fiestas gays durante todo el año en diversos lugares. En este sentido podrá observar también una gran discreción y es por esto que, para su protección, los lugares de evento pueden cambiar a corto plazo.

L'omosessualità è illegale nelle Barbados. Secondo i nostri dati però i gay non vengono disturbati dalla polizia. Stranamente però la vita gay è piuttosto nascosta e ha luogo soprattutto sulla costa meridionale (St. Michael, Christ Church) e su quella occidentale (St. James - Batts Rock). Ci si incontra sulla spiaggia e nelle macchine. Qui hanno luogo in luglio il grande Cropover Festival e in novembre l'Art Festival: due ragioni in più per evitare l'alta stagione e godersi le Barbados senza grandi folle.

I gay dell'isola sono per lo più conservatori o quanto meno si sforzano di sembrarlo. Questo è bene tenerlo presente quando ci si intrattiene con le persone del posto. Per il resto gli abitanti dell'isola sono molto cordiali, in particolar modo con i turisti. Allacciare contatti non dovrebbe essere così difficile. Tutto l'anno hanno luogo feste gay in diversi locali dell'isola. Ma anche qui c'è molta discrezione, infatti può capitare che la location possa essere cambiata poco prima del party.

SWIMMING

-Beaches north and south of Holetown on west coast
-Rockley beach, Dover beach on south coast.

Bridgetown

CAFES

■ **Waterfront Café** (B BF CC d M MA NG OS S) Mon-Sat 10-24h
Cavans Lane *On the Bridgetown Marina* ☏ 427-0093
🖳 www.waterfrontcafe.com.bb
Perfect views of the historic Barbados parliament building and clock tower. Situated on the Careenage (marina), offering a combination of Caribbean, American and seafood cuisine and includes many Bajan specialities. Jazz played 5 nights a week.

Christ Church

BARS

■ **Carib Beach Bar** (B MC NG) 11-?h
Worthing Beach ☏ 435-8540
A great gay-friendly spot to meet locals and visitors alike. Sunday evenings are said to be when the local gays come to hang out.

■ **McBride's Pub & Cookhouse** (B cc M MC NG)
St. Lawrence Gap ☏ 435-6352
Tuesday Night Karaoke has become the local gay hang out spot in Barbados. Cute boys and a pretty social atmosphere makes this a must do while in Barbados.

CRUISING

-Long Bay Beach (near the airport, also called „Chancery Lane Beach" usually quiet, lots of bushes, discreet nude bathing, take no valuables with you!)
-Rockley Beach (also called „Accra Beach", crowded on weekends and evenings. Easy to make contact)
-Saint Lawrence Gap (AYOR R) (after dark).

Speightstown

BARS

■ **Fisherman's Pub & Beach Bar** (B MA NG)
Queen Street ☏ 246 422 2703

St. James

BARS

■ **Lexy Piano Bar** (AC B cc MC NG) 21-?h
Second Street, Holetown *West aka Platinum Coast of Barbados*
☏ 432-5399 🖳 www.lexypianobar.com
Live music, good atmosphere, good drinks and gay-friendly atmosphere.

GUEST HOUSES

■ **Winchelsea Guest House** (AC H MA NG) All year
4th Ave, 72 West Terrace Gardens ☏ 438-2341
🖳 www.winchelseaguesthouse.com
Near the beach and easily accessible to the city.

APARTMENTS

■ **Barbados 4 U** (AC H PI)
Golden Haven, Sunset Crest, Holetown ☏ (0161) 428 04 48 (mobile)
🖳 www.barbados4u.co.uk
Twin bedroom with fitted wardrobes, bathroom, fully fitted kitchen, sat-TV, video, DVD, washing machine.

SWIMMING

-The west coast is the safest for swimming being the Caribbean side. The east coast is the Atlantic Side and not safe for swimming.
-Batts Rock Beach which is very popular amongst gay men and one of the best cruising areas on the island.

St. Joseph

SWIMMING

-Cattlewash Beach (along East Coast Road, best part is between holiday houses and Barclays Park, discreet NU possible)
-Batts Rock Beach (popular, with bushes and cliffs. On the west coast).

St. Michael

CRUISING

-Baxter's Road (AYOR R WE) (off Broad Street, at night).

Bonaire

Initials: BON (NL)
International Country Code: ☏ 599
International Access Code: ☏ 00
Language: Dutch, Papiamento, English, Spanish
Area: 280 km² / 90 sq mi.
Currency: 1 Netherland Antilles Guilder (ANG) = 100 Cents
Population: 10,185
Capital: Kralendijk
Religions: 80% Roman Catholics
Climate: Tropical climate that is moderated by north east trade winds

Under Article 255 of the penal code, homosexual acts are legal between adult males, and the age of consent is set at 16. The attitude of the general public towards homosexuality, however, is somewhat less tolerant than that of the Dutch mother country. Same-sexual marriages are recognized as a part of the Netherlands, however, cannot be entered into in the Antilles.

Homosexuelle Handlungen werden in Artikel 255 des Strafgesetzbuches abgehandelt. Zwischen erwachsenen Männern sind sie legal, und das Schutzalter liegt bei 16 Jahren. Allerdings ist die öffentliche Meinung Homosexuellen gegenüber hierzulande etwas weniger tolerant

als im niederländischen »Mutterland«. Als Teil der Niederlande werden gleichgeschlechtliche Ehen anerkannt, können aber in den Antillen nicht eingetragen werden.

Selon l'article 255 du code pénal l'homosexualité n'est pas considérée comme un délit. La majorité sexuelle est fixée à 16 ans. Notons toutefois que l'attitude de la population vis-à-vis des gais n'est pas aussi tolérante qu'aux les Pays-Bas. Faisant partie des Pays-Bas, les mariages homosexuels sont reconnus aux Antilles, mais ne peuvent y être enregistrés.

El artículo 255 del Código Penal dictamina sobre las actividades homosexuales. Estas son declaradas legales entre hombres adultos y la edad mínima de consentimiento queda establecida a los 16 años. La opinión pública de este país es menos tolerante con los gays que la de la madre patria, Holanda. Como parte de los Países Bajos, se reconocen los matrimonios entre personas del mismo sexo pero no pueden registrarse como tal en las Antillas.

Gli atti omosessuali vengono trattati nel paragrafo 255 del codice penale. Sono legali tra uomini adulti, l'età del consenso è di 16 anni. Comunque, l'opinione pubblica verso l'omosessualità è meno tollerante rispetto a quella della „madrepatria" olandese. Essendo, le Antille Olandesi, una dipendenza del Regno dei Paesi Bassi, le unioni tra coppie dello stesso sesso vengono pienamente riconosciute; tuttavia le unioni stesse non possono essere registrate nelle Antille.

APARTMENTS

Coco Palm Garden & Casa Oleander
(AC cc glm H I M MA OS PA PI RWS) All year
Kaya van Eps 9 (office) ✉ Bonaire ☎ 717-2108 ☎ 798 2108 (mobile)
cocopalmgarden.org
Eight studios and 15 apartments (self-catering). Various locations.

Ocean View Villas
(AC cc glm I MSG NU OS PK RWB RWS RWT VA) All year
Kaya Statius van Eps 6 ✉ Bonaire *Opp. Bachelor's Beach* ☎ 717-6105
www.oceanviewvillas.com
Three apartments with shower/WC, terrace, TV, kitchen, own key.

Sorobon ☎ 07

BARS

Karels Beach Bar (B NG)
12 Kaya J. N. E. Craane *Opp. Zeezicht Bar*
Live music on Sat evening.

APARTMENTS

Sorobon Beach Resort (AC B BF CC H M NG OS)
PO Box 14 *Situated directly at the Lagoon at Sorobon* ☎ (07) 717-8080
www.sorobonbeachresort.com
On a private beach, perfect for the active vacationer who wants to go diving, windsurfing, kayaking, kite surfing or snorkeling.

Cuba

Name: Kuba
Location: Caribbean
Initials: C
Time: GMT -5
International Country Code: ☎ 53
International Access Code: ☎ 119
Language: Spanish
Area: 110,860 km² / 42,803 sq mi.
Currency: 1 Cuban Peso (Cub$) = 100 Centavos
Population: 11,269,000
Capital: La Habana
Religions: 55% Roman Catholic
Climate: The hot, rainy season is from May-Oct. Winter (Dec-Apr) is the island's peak tourist season.

The Cuban penal code does not mention any age of consent. The Article 303 of the penal code states however, that the display of homosexuality in public is illegal. For this reason, we suggest you exhibit caution in public when you are with locals, especially on the streets of Havana and the beach Santa Maria where you find police patrols.
The police seem mainly interested in controlling locals who are seen with tourists, instead of combating local criminality against tourists, which has sadly increased. However, Mariela Castro, head of the National Center for Sex Education and the daughter of Raúl, aims to propose a bill to legalize same-sex unions to parliament. The above-mentioned centre also achieved a resolution by the public health ministry in June 2008, where the Cuban authorities passed a bill authorizing free sex-change operations for qualifying persons.
Local Cubans are extremely friendly and sexual contacts can easily be made, although a financial interest on the part of the locals is often a motivating factor.
Although the UN general assembly recently urged the US government to lift the financial, economic, and commercial blockade against Cuba, President Obama has extended the 18-year-old blockade one more year.
There are two currencies in Cuba: the Peso Convertible (CUC) for all tourists and the Cuban Peso for the locals. Avoid travelling with US Dollars, as these are not worth much when converted in Cuba and high fees are charged.

Das kubanische Strafgesetzbuch erwähnt keine Mindestalter. Artikel 303 des Strafgesetzbuches stellt jedoch fest, dass die öffentliche Zurschaustellung von Homosexualität strafbar ist. Deshalb schlagen wir vor, in der Öffentlichkeit Zurückhaltung zu üben, wenn Sie mit Ortsansässigen unterwegs sind. Dies besonders auf den Straßen Havannas und am Santa Maria Strand, wo die Polizeipatrouillen verstärkt präsent sind.
Die Polizei kontrolliert verstärkt Kubaner die mit Touristen gesehen werden, anstatt lokale Kriminalität gegen Touristen zu bekämpfen, die traurigerweise zugenommen hat.
Immerhin setzt sich Mariela Castro, die Leiterin vom Nationalen Zentrum für Sexualkunde und Tochter von Raúl, für eine Legalisierung gleichgeschlechtlicher Partnerschaften ein. Das oben erwähnte Zentrum erreichte im Juni 2008 gemeinsam mit dem Gesundheitsministerium eine Gesetzesänderung, die berechtigten Personen kostenlose Geschlechtsumwandlungsoperationen ermöglicht.
Kubaner sind äußerst freundlich und sexuelle Kontakte können leicht geknüpft werden. Dabei sind finanzielle oder wirtschaftliche Interessen jedoch nicht selten ein motivierender Faktor.
Obwohl die Generalversammlung der Vereinten Nationen kürzlich der US-Regierung nahegelegt hatte, die 18-jährige kommerzielle und

wirtschaftliche Blockade gegen Kuba aufzuheben, wurde diese durch Präsident Obama um ein Jahr verlängert.
Es gibt zwei Währungen in Kuba: den Peso „Konvertierbar" (CUC) für alle Touristen und den kubanischen Peso, für die Einheimischen. Vermeiden Sie, US-Dollars zu tauschen. Sie erhalten dafür einen schlechten Wechselkurs und müssen hohe Gebühren zahlen.

Le code pénal cubain ne mentionne pas de majorité sexuelle, cependant l'article 303 du code interdit l'ostentation de l'homosexualité. Pour cela nous recommandons une grande retenue sur les lieux publiques si vous êtes en compagnie de Cubains, en particulier à La Havane et sur la plage de Santa Maria où les patrouilles policières sont renforcées.
La police redouble les contrôles contre les Cubains vus avec des touristes au lieu de s'attaquer à la criminalité contre les touristes qui a malheureusement augmenté. Toutefois, la chef du Centre national sur la Sexualité et fille de Raúl, Mariela Castro, s'engage pour la légalisation des partenariats de même sexe. Ce centre a obtenu en juin avec le ministère de la santé la prise en charge gratuite des opérations de changement de sexe.
Les Cubains sont particulièrement sympathiques et les contacts sexuels sont faciles… des intérêts financiers ou économiques sont cependant fréquemment un facteur de motivation.
Bien que l'Assemblée générale des Nations Unies ait récemment suggéré au gouvernement US de lever les barrières commerciales et économiques, celles-ci furent prorogées d'un an par le président Obama.
Il existe deux monnaies cubaines : le Peso „ convertible „ (CUC) pour tous les touristes et le Peso cubain pour les autochtones. Evitez de changer vos dollars US afin d'éviter un mauvais taux de change et des frais élevés.

El Código Penal cubano no hace referencia a una edad mínima para mantener relaciones sexuales. Sin embargo, el artículo 303 del Código Penal señala que la manifestación pública de la homosexualidad es punible por la ley. Por esto le aconsejamos actuar con cautela en público o ante residentes, especialmente en La Habana y en la playa de Santa María, donde las patrullas tienen mayor presencia.
La policía controla a los cubanos que son vistos con turistas en lugar de combatir la delincuencia local contra los estos últimos, que desgraciadamente ha aumentado. Aún así, Mariela Castro, directora del Centro Nacional para la Educación Sexual e hija de Raúl, apostó por la legalización de las asociaciones del mismo sexo. En junio de 2008 el Centro previamente mencionado alcanzó conjuntamente con el Ministerio de Salud un cambio legislativo que permitirá a personas autorizadas llevar a cabo de manera gratuita la cirugía de reasignación de sexo.
Los cubanos son sumamente amigables y los contactos sexuales no son complicados, pero cabe mencionar que los intereses financieros o económicos son, a menudo, un factor de motivación.
Aunque la Asamblea General de las Naciones Unidas sugirió recientemente al gobierno de EE.UU. derogar el bloqueo comercial y económico que sufre Cuba desde hace 18 años, el Presidente Obama lo ha prorrogado por un año más.
Hay dos monedas en Cuba: el peso „convertible" (CUC), para turistas, y el peso cubano, para residentes. Evite cambiar dólares americanos ya que recibirá un cambio a la baja y tendrá que pagar tarifas más altas.

Il codice penale cubano non fa alcun riferimento all'età del consenso, tuttavia l'articolo 303 afferma che l'ostentazione pubblica dell'omosessualità è perseguibile penalmente. Vi consigliamo di essere molto discreti in pubblico, specialmente nelle strade de L'Havana e sulla spiaggia di Santa Maria, dove la polizia è abbastanza numerosa.
La polizia, invece di combattere la crescente criminalità locale che tra l'altro terrorizza anche i turisti, continua ad inasprire i controlli per i cubani che vengono visti con i turisti. Per fortuna c'è anche gente come Mariela Castro, sorella di Raúl, che dirige il Centro Nazionale per l'Educazione Sessuale e si batte per le unioni tra persone dello stesso sesso. A giugno del 2008 il suddetto centro, insieme al ministero per la salute, ha contribuito alla modifica di una legge che permette il trattamento gratuito per il cambio di sesso. I cubani sono molto amichevoli ed è abbastanza facile trovare rapporti di tipo sessuale, tuttavia spesso alla base c'è un interesse di tipo economico. Sebbene recentemente l'Assemblea Generale delle Nazioni Unite abbia suggerito di porre fine all'embargo commerciale ed economico che da 18 anni vige contro Cuba, il Presidente Obama lo ha prolungato ancora di un anno. A Cuba ci sono due monete: il Peso Cubano Convertibile (CUC), la valuta utilizzata dai turisti, e il Peso Cubano che è utilizzato principalmente dai cubani. Evitate di scambiare i dollari americani poiché il cambio è sfavorevole e le tasse da pagare molto alte.

NATIONAL COMPANIES

■ **Viazul**
Ave. 26 y Zoológico, Nuevo Vedado ✉ Cuidad de la Habana
☎ (07) 81 14 13 🖳 www.viazul.com
The best way to get around Cuba is in the air conditioned buses from this company.

NATIONAL GROUPS

■ **Centro Nacional de Educación Sexual (CENESEX)**
Calle 10 # 460, esq. 21, Vedado ✉ La Habana *Plaza de la Revolución*
☎ 55-2528 🖳 www.cenesex.sld.cu
This convention center in Havana's Vedado district may have been the largest gathering of openly gay activists ever on the communist-run island as they met for a one-day conference for the International Day Against Homophobia in May 2007. President Raul Castro's daughter Mariela, who has promoted the rights of sexual minorities, presided.

Cienfuegos ☎ 43

GUEST HOUSES

■ **Bella Perla Marina** (BF H OS) All year
C/.39 N° 5818 *On corner with 60 Ave. 100m from the Principal Ave*
☎ 518 991 🖳 www.flickr.com/photos/bellaperlamarina
Terrace and a big garden with a great view to the city and the bay. Two guestrooms, each with own bath. Garage.

La Habana ☎ 7

TRANSVESTITE / SHOWS

■ **Cabaret Las Vegas** (GLM S) Thu from 23h
Calzada de Infanta 25. Vedado *Between 25th and 27th Street, close to Hotel Nacional* ☎ 707939
Dragshows with disco.

BARS

■ **23 y P** (B g MC R)
C/. 23 y P *Near Hotel Nacional*
This is not a gay place. It is the nearest thing to a gay bar in Havana. It is simply a place where gay men meet and have a drink. Beware of the police outside this place, should you leave with a local.

■ **Bim-Bom** (g)
at end of C/. 23 *La Rampa, close to Hotel Nacional*
At daytime ice bar with snacks, at night bar and hot spot for gays and transvestites.

■ **Piano Bar Habaneciendo** (B glm MC) Mon & Tue from 23h
C/. Neptuno esquina Galiano *City centre*

RESTAURANTS

■ **Club Canarias** (B F MC NG)
C/. Zulueta /Agramonte *2nd floor, Opp. Bacardi House*
This small restaurant inside the Club Canarias offers basic but delicious dishes, including Crayfish and local specialities. Inexpensive and highly recommended.

■ **Fashion Habana** (B GLM M MA ST) Wed-Sun 18-3h
C/ Kessel 52 e/1ª y 2ª, Arroyo Naranjo ☎ 644 28 94
🖳 www.facebook.com/pages/Fashion-Bar-Habana/217535191600980
Private gay restaurant with transvestite shows.

■ **Fontana. La** (B M MA NG) 12-24h
C/. 3ra A y 46 miramar ☎ (07) 20 28 337

■ **Guarida. La** (B M MA NG)

Concordia 418 / Gervasio y Escobar ☏ (07) 866 90 47
🖳 www.laguarida.com

GUEST HOUSES

■ **Artedel Guest House** (AC b bf g M MA)
C/. 25 N° 2605 *Between 26 y 30 Miramar* ☏ (07) 20 24 612
🖳 www.cubaguesthouse.com
Private house in the residential area of Miramar.

■ **Elio Gay-Friendly Guesthouse** (AC glm MA) All year
C/. San Francisco 305 *Between San Rafael & San Miguel* ☏ 870 90 66

■ **Gay Friendly Hostal** (AC GLM MA) Daily, 24hrs
San José 875 *Between Oquendo y Soledad* ☏ 787 90789 ☏ 529 51543
🖳 www.bojirooms.com
Accommodations for everyone but especially gays and lesbians. 15 minutes walk from the biggest cruising spot of Habana. The owners speak English too.

■ **Rayís Casa Particular** (AC G MC RWB VA) All year
C/. Aguila, 309, secundo piso *Between C/. Neptuno & C/. Concordia*
☏ (07) 86 35 107
Ray is no longer running this guesthouse and since then we have received bad reports.

SWIMMING

-Santa Maria Beach/Mi Cayito (G) (east of Havana from Mar Azul Hotel to Itabo Hotel). Take a taxi from Havana (locals should accompany you) or take the bus opposite the Hotel Inglaterra. Be careful as the police patrol this beach and arrest locals who accompany you
-El Chivo (AYOR g) (east of Havana)
-El Malecón (g) near Miramar end. Here you will find many people meeting late at night. Watch out for police patrols.

CRUISING

Cruising in Havana is a part of life. There are specific cruising areas which are visited at night (AYOR) but otherwise the entire city is very cruisy. Be careful as many locals ask for money. Ask the locals where the „discos" and nightspots are, as these change all the time.
All cruising areas are AYOR. Be careful of police who do not allow locals to mix with tourists.
-Calle 23 in Vedado, from Calle L (cinema Yara) to the Malecòn: before midnight mainly between Calles L and M. After midnight the action moves to Malecón and Calle 23, and goes on till 3-4h
-In front of the Capitolio, from the cinema Payret to calle Reina (at night)
-Along Calle Obispo, in Habana Vieja (any time)
-Mi Cayito Beach, about 1 km before arriving at Guanabo, during the day in summer
-Fraternidad Park
-Central Park
-Feria de la Juventud
-Teatro Nacional outside
-Heladería Copelia (WE)
-El Chivito Beach (east of La Habana).

Trinidad ☏ 419

GUEST HOUSES

■ **Hostal Arcángel** (AC BF glm) All year
C/. Amargura 1 *Between Santa Ana & Alameda* ☏ (52) 68 26 15

CRUISING

-Céspedes Park, evening during WE.

Viñales ☏ 5

GUEST HOUSES

■ **Casa Marisol** (AC H OS) All year
Km1, Carreterra al Cementerio, Casa N°. 8 *Near the petrol station*
☏ 223 87 69 🖳 www.casavinales.com
Guesthouse in Viñales with hot water and meals. Beautiful mountain views. Gay travellers welcome. Dinner also available.

Dominican Republic

Name: Dominikanische Republik · République Dominicaine · República Dominicana · Repubblica Dominicana
Location: Caribbean
Initials: DOM
Time: GMT -4
International Country Code: ☏ 1 809 (no area codes)
International Access Code: ☏ 011
Language: Spanish, English
Area: 48,422 km² / 18,696 sq mi.
Currency: 1 Dom. Peso (Dom$) = 100 Centavos
Population: 8,895,000
Capital: Santo Domingo
Religions: 89% Roman Catholic
Climate: Tropical climate. There are 2 rainy seasons (Oct-May) along the northern coast (May-Oct) in the south.
Important gay cities: Santo Domingo

✱ The laws in the Dominican Republic make no distinction between homosexual and straight relations between adults (over 18 years). However, Article 330 of the penal code punishes „every violation of decorum and good behaviour on public streets" with a penalty of up to two years in prison, so it is advisable not to display too much affection in public, although this law is rarely applied. Other discrimination on the basis of sexual orientation does not appear prevalent.
As in many Spanish-speaking Catholic countries a discrimination and segregation applies between different economic groups. A large percentage of the male population appears to be bisexual. Many gay men lead double lives, due to family restraints and general attitudes towards homosexuality.
Santo Domingo is developing a small, but interesting gay scene, with a couple of nightspots and is well worth a visit. The gay movement is slow, although the first (and last) Pride parade took place in 2001. The media has a refreshingly gay-friendly attitude.

★ Die Gesetzgebung der Dominikanischen Republik trifft keinen Unterschied zwischen homo- und heterosexuellen Handlungen unter Volljährigen (über 18-Jährigen). Artikel 330 des Strafgesetzbuches sieht jedoch für „jegliche Zuwiderhandlung gegen Anstand und sittliches Verhalten auf öffentlichen Straßen" eine Strafe von bis zu zwei Jahren Freiheitsentzug vor. Es ist also nicht ratsam, in der Öffentlichkeit allzu große Zuneigung zu zeigen, selbst wenn dieses Gesetz nur selten zur Anwendung kommt. Andere Formen der Diskriminierung aufgrund der sexuellen Orientierung scheinen nicht besonders weit verbreitet zu sein.

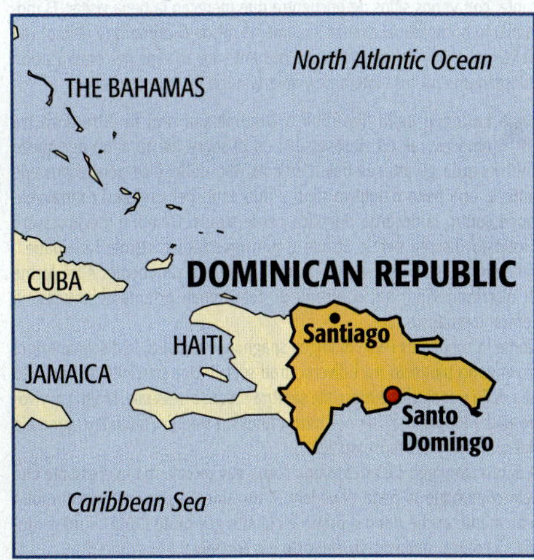

Wie in vielen spanischsprachigen, katholischen Ländern findet ein Großteil der Diskriminierung und Ausgrenzung stattdessen zwischen unterschiedlichen sozialen Schichten statt. Ein großer Prozentsatz der männlichen Bevölkerung scheint bisexuell zu sein. Viele schwule Männer leben ein Doppelleben, einerseits aus Rücksicht auf ihre Familien und andererseits wegen der allgemeinen Einstellung zur Homosexualität.
In Santo Domingo hat sich mittlerweile eine kleine, aber nichtsdestotrotz interessante Schwulenszene entwickelt, mit mehreren Veranstaltungsorten, deren Besuch sich lohnt. Die Schwulenbewegung kommt nur langsam voran, auch nach der ersten (und letzten) Pride Parade im Jahr 2001. Die Medien legen hingegen eine erfrischend schwulenfreundliche Einstellung an den Tag.

La législation de la République Dominicaine ne se prononce pas sur les relations sexuelles entre majeurs (de plus de 18 ans). L'article 330 du code pénal prévoit néanmoins une peine de prison pouvant aller jusqu'à deux ans pour „toute infraction aux bonnes mœurs sur la voie publique". Il est donc recommandé d'être discret en public même si cette loi n'est appliquée que rarement. D'autres formes de discrimination en raison de l'orientation sexuelle ne semblent pas très répandues.
Comme dans de nombreux pays hispanophones catholiques, la discrimination et l'exclusion se trouvent essentiellement entre les différentes couches sociales. Une grande partie de la population masculine semble être bisexuelle. Beaucoup de gays vivent leur homosexualité en secret par respect pour leur famille et en raison du peu de tolérance de la société.
A Saint-Domingue, un petit milieu gay s'est installé avec plusieurs lieux dignes d'intérêt. Les associations gays ne progressent que peu malgré la tenue de la première Gay Pride en 2001, mais les médias sont très ouverts envers les homosexuels.

La legislación de la República Dominicana no observa diferencias entre relaciones homosexuales y heterosexuales con mayores de 18 años. El artículo 330 del código penal prevé sin embargo una pena privativa de libertad de hasta 2 años para „actos contrarios a la razón y las buenas costumbres en las calles públicas". No es recomendable mostrar públicamente un gran amaneramiento, aunque esta ley se aplique poco. Otras formas de discriminación por motivo de la orientación sexual no parecen estar muy extendidas.
Como sucede en muchos países católicos de habla española, la mayoría de discriminaciones ocurren entre diferentes capas sociales. Un gran porcentaje de la población masculina parece bisexual. Muchos homosexuales viven una doble vida por respeto a sus familias y por la actitud general ante la homosexualidad.
En Santo Domingo se ha desarrollado un pequeño ambiente gay interesante, con varios sitios de encuentro que merecen la pena visitar. El movimiento homosexual avanza lentamente desde el primero (y último) Día del Orgullo Gay del año 2001. No obstante, los medios de comunicación adoptan una postura tolerante y abierta hacia los homosexuales.

La legge della Repubblica Dominicana non fa differenza tra omosessuali ed eterosessuali (al di sopra dei 18 anni) per quello che riguarda gli atti sessuali. L'articolo 330 del codice penale prevede tuttavia una pena detentiva (fino a due anni) per qualsiasi contravvenzione contro la decenza pubblica per le strade. Quindi è meglio essere piuttosto discreti per le strade e non mostrare particolari simpatie... sebbene questa legge viene applicata piuttosto raramente. Altre forme di discriminazioni nei confronti di determinati orientamenti sessuali semrano piuttosto rare.
Come in molti altri Paesi di lingua spagnola e cattolici, le discriminazioni avvengono piuttosto tra i diversi strati sociali. Una percentuale piuttosto alta della popolazione maschile sembra essere bisessuale. Molti gay vivono una „doppia vita" sia per motivi familiari sia per l'attitudine generale nei confronti dell'omosessualità.
A Santo Domingo c'è adesso una scena gay piccola ma interessante che vale comunque la pena di vedere. Il movimento gay si fa avanti molto lentamente anche dopo il primo e l'ultimo gay pride (2001). I mass media, di contro, si mostrano piuttosto gay friendly.

Las Terrenas

APARTMENTS

■ **Villa Pasion Tropical** (AC GLM H PI RWS RWT SOL) All year
C/. Maricó, Playa Ballenas *45 mins from Las Terrenas, 300 m from Las Ballenas beach* ☎ (+34) 690 343 975 (Spain)
🖳 www.pasion-tropical.com
Two apartments with large living room area and one bedroom studio available for rent seperately or together, accommodating a maximum of eight people. Two kitchens, a large terrace with an outdoor living and dining room. There is cable TV throughout. There is also a security guard at night.

Santiago

CRUISING

-Park at Calle El Sol (after 18h)
-Plaza de Dolores.

Santo Domingo

BARS

■ **Amazonia** (B gLm MA) Fri-Sun 20-2h
C/. Dr. Delgado 71, Gazcue ☎ 412-7629
■ **Click** (D G MA SNU) Thu - Sun
C/. Atarazana 11, Plaza Espana *Colonial Zone, Santo Domingo*
■ **ESEDEKU** (AC B GLM M MA WE)
Wed-Thu & Sun 20-1, Fri & Sat -3, Mon closed
341 Las Mercedes y Santome, Zona Colonial *Parallel to Conde Street*
☎ 869-6322 🖳 www.esedeku.com
Gay bar in Santo Domingo ideal for people interested in meeting local gay men.
■ **JD's** (B glm MA SNU ST) Wed-Sun, closed Mon & Tue
10 Jose Reyes, Zona Colonial ☎ 333-5905
Local gay bar/club frequented by mostly Dominicans. Fri & Sat nights are best and it can get very crowded. Usually a drag show and stripper at WE. The cover entitles you to a ticket that gets you Rum & Coke (Cubalibre) or Presidente beer.
■ **Punto** (AC B d GLM MA OS R S SNU ST)
19-2h, later on Fri & Sat
C/. de las Mercedes, 313 *Zona Colonial* ☎ 689-4163
🖳 www.grupoarena.com
Gallery & bar. Chill-out music. Large terrace & gardens.

DANCECLUBS

■ **Arena** (AC B CC D GLM H OS S YC)
Fri & Sat and before public holidays 16-?h
C/. des las Mercedes 313, Zona Colonial *Downtown between Santome and José Reyes Street* ☎ 689-4163 🖳 www.aireclub.com
The upstairs area is called Arena, which features the latest music and the downstairs area is called Punto, which has a more sophisticated lounge feel. The open-air courtyard is covered, but the stunning design remains.
■ **CHA** (B D GLM MA S T) Fri-Sun
Avenida George Washington 165 *Malecon, between Maximo Gomez & Lincoln*
Next to the restaurant Vesuvio. This disco is run by the famous Dominican TV drag queen Chachita Rubio.
■ **Gacela Club** (B D glm SNU)
Avenida Bolivar 72 *near the corner of Dr. Delgado*

SEX CINEMAS

■ **Lido** (AYOR g r) 18.30-22.30h
342 Avenida Mella *one block from the Mercado Modelo* ☎ 682-8082
Cruising in the toilets.

SAUNAS/BATHS

■ **Aqua** (b CC DR G MA MSG RR SA SB SOL WH)
Mon-Thu 15-2, Fri 15-Sun 2h (non-stop)
C/. Santiago Rodríguez, 68bis, Ciudad Colonial *Opp. Las Mercedes Church*

☎ 333-5607 🖳 www.grupoarena.com
Also beauty treatment and massage available.

HOTELS

■ **Caribe Colonial Hotel** (AC B BF g I M MA OS RWS RWT)
C/. Isabel Catolica 159, Zona Colonial ☎ 688-7799
🖳 www.hodelpa.com/caribe_colonial.php
Great location within walking distance to several restaurants, bars, and tourist attractions. Gay-friendly.

■ **Foreigners Club Hotel** (AC bf CC G I MA PA RWB RWS RWT VA) All year
102 Calle Canela, corner of Estrelleta Cuidad Nueva *2 blocks from El Conde, 4 blocks from Malecon* ☎ 689-3017
🖳 www.foreignersclubhotel.com

HEALTH GROUPS

■ **AIDS Hotline** Mon-Fri 8-18h
Apartado Postal 2484 ☎ 541-4400

SWIMMING

-Boca Chica Beach (50 km from the city)
-Embassy Beach (About 65 km from the city. Take Avenida Las Americas, highway to San Pedro de Macoris. Beach on the right with many coconut palms).

CRUISING

-Plaza Central (top floor)
-Calle Conde (all day)
-Plaza Independencia (r)
-Parque Colón (r)
-Playa Guibia (r) (Avenida Washington, El Malecon)
-Parque Mirador Sur (evenings)
-Plaza de la Catedral (at the end of Conde St. on the square in front the cathedral)
-Plaza de España (near Columbus house. WE 18-23h).

Sosúa

RESTAURANTS

■ **Linia 9** (b bf M MA NG) 9-23h
C/. Julio Arzenio ☎ 594 14 14 🖳 www.linia9.tk
Italian food.

HOTELS

■ **Tropix** (AC BF cc glm I m MA MSG OS PI RWB RWS WO) All year
C/. Libre 7, Puerto Plata *5 mins walk from the nearest beach, markets and clubs* ☎ (809) 571-2291 🖳 tropixhotel.com

GUEST HOUSES

■ **Casa Serena** (AC BF glm OS RES RWB RWS) All year
La Mulata Uno, Casa Blanca Grande *Approximately 1 km from Sosua*
☎ 571 3885 ☎ 3172544 (mobile)
🖳 www.casaserena-dr.com
Three standard rooms and one self catering studio. All have A/C and queen size beds. A safe and centrally located place to stay.

Grenada

Name: Grenade
Location: Caribbean
Initials: WG
Time: GMT -4
International Country Code: ☎ 1 473
International Access Code: ☎ 011
Language: English
Area: 344 km² / 133 sq mi.
Currency: 1 East Caribbean Dollar (EC$) = 100 Cents
Population: 107,000
Capital: Saint George's

Caribbean Sea
Petit Martinique
Hillsborough
Carriacou
GRENADA
Ronde Island
Grenville
North Atlantic Ocean
St. George's
Grenada

Religions: 55% Catholic, 30% Protestant
Climate: Average year-round temperature of 27°C (80°F). Rainy season is from Jun-Nov.

According to our knowledge, homosexuality is illegal in Grenada and the neighbouring island of Carriacou to the North. The tourist industry is developing steadily and is concentrated around St. George to the South. There is no gay scene as such. The following listed places should only be used as starting points.

Unseres Wissens nach ist Homosexualität auf Grenada illegal, wie auch auf der nördlich gelegenen Nachbarinsel Carriacou. Die Tourismusindustrie hat sich in den letzten Jahren stark weiterentwickelt, ist aber vor allem um die Stadt St. George's im Süden konzentriert. Es gibt keine Schwulenszene; die folgenden Adressen sollten nur als Ausgangspunkte dienen.

D'après ce que nous savons, l'homosexualité est un délit à Grenade et sur l'île voisine de Carriacou (au nord). L'industrie touristique est en plein essor, tout particulièrement à St George, dans le sud. Pas de vie gaie à proprement parler. Les établissements mentionnés ci-dessous ne sont cités qu'à titre d'information.

Por lo que sabemos la homosexualidad es ilegal en Grenada y en Carriacou, la isla vecina que queda al norte. La industria del turismo se está desarrollando y estableciendo casi exclusivamente en St. George, en el sur del país. No existe un ambiente gay propiamente dicho; las siguientes direcciones sirven sólo como punto de partida.

Per quanto ne sappiamo, l'omosessualitá è illegale a Grenada e a Carriacou, l'isola vicina situata al nord. L'industria del turismo si sta sviluppando quasi esclusivamente nel territorio di St. George al sud. Non c'è una vita gay vera e propria; i seguenti luoghi dovrebbero essere usati solo come punti di riferimento e di base.

St. George's

BARS

■ **Fantasia 2001** (AC B D g s) 20.30-?h
Morne Rouge ☎ 444 42 24

■ **St. James Hotel Bar** (B g)
Grand Etang Road *Downtown* ☎ 440 20 41

SWIMMING

-Grand Anse Beach (a wonderful beach with more than 5,5 km of white sand).

Guadeloupe

Name: Guadalupe
Location: Caribbean
Initials: GUA (F)
Time: GMT -4
International Country Code: ☏ 590 (no area codes)
International Access Code: ☏ 00
Language: French, Créole
Area: 1,780 km² / 687 sq mi.
Currency: 1 Euro (€) = 100 Cents
Population: 440,200
Capital: Basse-Terre
Religions: 90% Roman Catholic
Climate: Warm weather year-round. The evenings are coolest in winter (Dec-Feb). Wettest months are Jul-Nov which is also hurricane season.

Guadeloupe belongs to France and with it to the European Union. The legal situation corresponds to that in ☞ France. The island lying in the Caribbean exists geologically of two parts linked by Mangrove forests: the flat, white sandy area Grande-Terre with the economic center and international airport Pointe-à-Pitre (several times daily there are direct connections to Paris) and the tropical, overgrown Basse-Terre with its black sands from the active volcano.
The offshore islands Marie Gallant (still very originally) and Les Saintes (very touristic, but with Honeymoon lodgings, bays and beaches) invite investigation, as do the volcano, big and small waterfalls, the diving paradise of Jacques Cousteau, colourful markets. The standard of living , levels of medical care and the infrastructure are high thanks to France and the EU.
For favourable accommodation: see Gîtes de France.

Guadeloupe gehört zu Frankreich und damit zur europäischen Union. Die gesetzliche Situation entspricht der in ☞ Frankreich. Die in der Karibik liegende Insel besteht geologisch aus zwei durch Mangrovenwälder zu einem verbundenen Teil: dem flachen, weißsandigem Grande-Terre, mit dem Wirtschaftzentrum und internationalem Flughafen Pointe-à-Pitre (mehrmals täglich Direktverbindungen nach Paris) und dem durch den aktiven Vulkan schwarzsandigen und tropisch überwucherten Basse-Terre. Die vorgelagerten Inseln Marie-Galante (noch sehr ursprünglich) und Les Saintes (sehr touristisch, aber Honeymoon Unterkünfte, Buchten und Strände) laden zur Erkundung ein, ebenso wie der Vulkan, große und kleine Wasserfälle, das Tauchreservat Jacques Cousteau, bunte Märkte, Destillerien und koloniale Zeitzeugen.

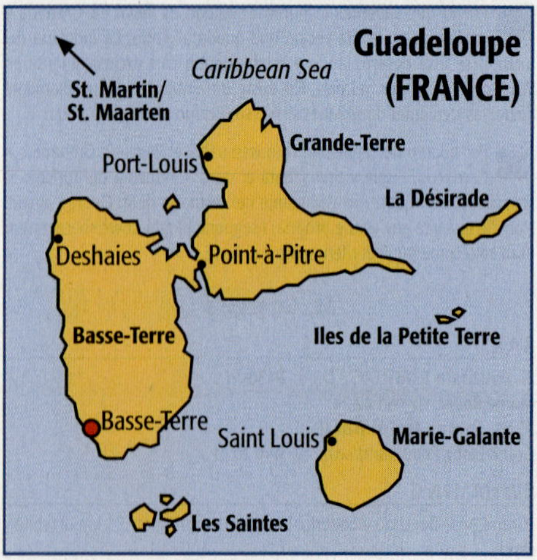

Der Lebensstandard und die Infrastruktur sind dank des Mutterlandes und der EU hoch, ebenso die medizinische Versorgung. Günstiges Unterkunftssystem: Gîtes de France.

La Guadeloupe fait partie intégrante de la ☞ France et donc de l'Union Européenne. La situation légale équivaut à celle du reste de la France. L'île des Antilles est constituée géographiquement de deux parties reliées entre elles par des forêts de mangroves : Grande-Terre, plate, au sable blanc, où se situe le centre économique ainsi que l'aéroport international de Pointe-à-Pitre (plusieurs vols quotidiens avec Paris) ; et Basse-Terre, avec sa végétation tropicale et son sable noir dû au volcan encore actif . Les îles voisines de Marie-Galante (encore très préservée) et Les Saintes (très touristique, hébergements « lune de miel », baies et plages) invitent à l'exploration, de même que le volcan, des cascades petites et grandes, la réserve sous-marine Jacques Cousteau, des marchés colorés, des distilleries et autres bâtiments de l'époque coloniale. Le niveau de vie et les infra-structures sont, grâce à la métropole et à l'UE, de bonne qualité, de même que l'assistance médicale. Un très bon moyen d'hébergement : les Gîtes de France.

Guadalupe pertenece a ☞ Francia y por tanto está en la Unión Europea. La situación jurídica es la misma que en Francia. Esta isla del Caribe está formada geológicamente de dos partes unidas por bosques tropicales: la llana y de arena blanca de Grande-Terre, con el centro económico y el aeropuerto internacional de Pointe-à-Pitre (con conexiones directas a París varias veces al día) y la zona volcánica con arenas negras y bosques tropicales de Basse-Terre. Las islas ribereñas de Marie-Galante (aún muy primitiva) y Les Saintes (muy turística, pero con alojamientos para lunas de miel, calas y playas) esperan a ser descubiertas, al igual que el volcán, los grandes y pequeños saltos de agua, la reserva de buceo Jacques Cousteau, los coloridos mercados, destilerías y otros vestigios coloniales. El nivel de vida y las infraestructuras son altos gracias a la metrópolis y a la UE, al igual que la cobertura médica.
Alojamiento recomendado: Gîtes de France.

Il Guadalupa è un dipartimento ☞ francese d'oltremare che appartiene quindi all'Unione Europea. La legge in vigore, quindi, è quella francese. Guadalupa è un'isola situata nei Caraibi formata da due isole separate da uno stretto canale. L'isola orientale si chiama Grande-Terre, è pianeggiante ed è formata da sabbia chiara; è il centro economico del Paese ed ospita l'aereoporto internazionale Pointe-à-Pitre che ha collegamneti giornalieri con Parigi. L'isola occidentale si chiama Basse-Terre ed è un ammasso vulcanico regno incontrastato della foresta tropicale. Da esplorare sono le antistanti isolette Marie-Galante (ancora molto intatta) e Les Saintes (molto turistica, con possibilità di pernottamento, con molte baie e spiagge), il vulcano, piccole e grandi cascate, la riserva marina Jacques Cousteau, variopinti mercati, distillerie e reperti coloniali. Grazie alla madreterra e all'UE lo standard di vita è piuttosto alto, le infrastrutture sono buone e la sanità efficiente.
Possibilità di alloggio economico: Gîtes de France.

Basse-Terre

RESTAURANTS

■ **Orangerie. L'** (b M NG)
Résidence Desmarais ☏ 81 13 17

Les Saintes

HOTELS

■ **Petits Saints aux Anacardiers. Les** (AC B g M MA PI SA)
La Savane - Terre-de-Haut *On a hill in front of the bay* ☏ 99 50 99
🖳 www.petitssaints.com
An ideal island get-away. Take boat or plane from Guadeloupe.

SWIMMING

-Crawen Beach (nudism suspended but practised). Breathtaking views.

Pointe-à-Pitre

HEALTH GROUPS

Centre Hospitalier de Pointe-à-Pitre
Route de Chauvel *North tower, 1st floor* ☎ 89 10 79
www.chu-guadeloupe.fr

CRUISING

-Rue Duplessis (along La Darse, the old port)
-Rue de Nozieres
-Rue Frebault
-Rue René Boisneuf.

Saint François

RESTAURANTS

Iguane Café (b M MA NG OS) Closed Tue
Route de la Pointe des Chateaux *chemin rural La Coulèe* ☎ 88 61 37
www.iguane-cafe.com
A must on the way back from the gay beach at Pointe Tarare.

HOTELS

Amaudo (B BF H M MA OS PI)
Anse à la Barque *Cocolo Beach* ☎ 88 87 00
www.im-caraibes.com/cocolo

SWIMMING

-Pointe Tarare (small, but very beautiful, only legal nudist beach of the island; many local and international gays; big cruising area, busy during the day; entrance not easy to find: direction Point des Chateaux - watch out for a sign „Restaurant Chez Ma Michel" (excellent lunch) and follow it to the parking of the restaurant, walk down hill).

Sainte Anne

BARS

Chez Elles (B M NG) Wed-Sun 19-?h
Les Galbas *Opp. Village artisanal* ☎ 88 92 36

SWIMMING

-Plage de la Caravelle (NU suspended). Beach is part of Club Med. Therefore access for non-hotel guests is only permitted from the side entrance at the beachfront. Beautiful but lots of hotel guests and their security guards.

Jamaica

Name: Jamaika · Jamaique · Giamaica
Location: Caribbean
Initials: JA
Time: GMT -5
International Country Code: ☎ 1 876
International Access Code: ☎ 011
Language: English
Area: 10,991 km² / 4,243 sq mi.
Currency: 1 Jamaican Dollar (J$) = 100 Cents
Population: 2,655,000
Capital: Kingston
Religions: 56% Protestant, 5% Catholic
Climate: Tropical climate, hot and humid. The interior is more moderate. Peak tourist season is from Dec-Apr.

The Jamaica Forum for Lesbians, All-sexuals and Gays (J-FLAG) has been campaigning since 1998 to overturn Jamaica's harsh sodomy laws, which outlaw homosexuality, which is punishable with up to 10 years hard labour. According to paragraphs 76-79 of the Jamaican penal code homosexuality is prohibited. Violence against lesbians and gays is commonplace and is given free reign by the government's refusal to tackle this situation. Queer-bashing is also fuelled by Jamaican popular music which glorifies the murder of gays. In September 2009 the British Honorary Consul, John Terry was murdered. A homophobic motive for this murder has been denied by the local police officials.
Jamaica continues to be the worlds most homophobic country in the western Hemisphere!

Die Organisation Jamaica Forum for Lesbians, All-sexuals and Gays (J-FLAG) kämpft seit 1998 gegen Jamaikas harte Sodomie-Gesetze, die Homosexualität verbieten und hart bestrafen z.B. mit bis zu 10 Jahren Arbeitslager. Gemäß Paragraphen 76-79 des jamaikanischen Strafgesetzbuches ist Homosexualität verboten.
Gewalt gegen Lesben und Schwule ist alltäglich und wird durch die Verweigerung der Regierung diese Situation anzupacken, nicht bekämpft. Das Zusammenschlagen von Schwulen wird obendrein durch die jamaikanische volkstümliche Musik angetrieben, die den Mord an Homosexuellen verherrlicht.
Im September 2009 wurde der britische Ehrenkonsul, John Terry ermordet. Ein homophobes Verbrechen wird vom örtlichen Polizeibehörden bestritten. Jamaika ist und bleibt das homophobste Land der westlichen Hemisphäre!

L'organisation Jamaica Forum for Lesbians, All-sexuals and Gays (J-FLAG) se bât depuis 1998 contre les lois draconiennes contre la sodomie qui interdisent l'homosexualité et la punissent lourdement, par exemple jusqu'à 10 ans de camp de travail. L'homosexualité est interdite selon les articles 76-79 du code pénal jamaïcain.
La violence contre les gays et lesbiennes est courante et n'est pas combattue, le gouvernement se refusant à intervenir. Cette violence est renforcée encore par la musique jamaïcaine populaire qui exalte les assassinats d'homosexuels.
En septembre 2009, le consul honoraire britannique Johny Terry fut assassiné. La police locale réfute le crime homophobe. La Jamaïque reste le pays le plus homophobe de l'hémisphère nord !

La Organización Foro Jamaicano para Lesbianas, Bisexuales y Gays (J-FLAG, por sus siglas en inglés) lucha desde 1998 contra las duras leyes antisodomía que castigan la homosexualidad en Jamaica con hasta 10 años de trabajos forzados. La homosexualidad aquí está prohibida conforme al artículo 76-79 del Código Penal jamaicano.
La violencia contra gays y lesbianas es muy común y el rechazo existente por parte del gobierno a la hora de hacer frente a esta situación supone un freno para combatir la homofobia. Las palizas a gays son promovidas por la música popular jamaicana, la cual glorifica el asesinato de homosexuales.
John Ferry, el cónsul honorario británico, fue asesinado en septiembre de 2009. Los crímenes homófobos como este suelen ser impugnados

por las autoridades policiales locales. ¡Jamaica sigue siendo el país más homofóbico del hemisferio occidental!

L'organizzazione Jamaica Forum for Lesbians, All-sexuals and Gays (J-FLAG) si batte già dal 1998 contro le severe leggi sulla sodomia che vietano e puniscono in maniera esemplare l'omosessualità (per esempio con un massimo di 10 anni di lavori forzati). Secondo i paragrafi 76-79 del codice penale giamaicano l'omosessualità è espressamente vietata. I casi di violenza contro lesbiche e gay sono giornalieri e il governo si rifiuta di prendere delle misure appropriate. La violenza nei confronti degli omosessuali viene incitata anche dalla musica popolare giamaicana, che per esempio esalta l'uccisione degli omosessuali. A settembre del 2009 è stato ucciso il console onorario britannico John Terry e la polizia nega che si sia trattato di un omicidio a sfondo omofobo. La Giamaica è uno dei paesi più omofobi dell'emisfero occidentale della terra.

NATIONAL GROUPS

Jamaica Forum for Lesbians All-Sexuals and Gays – J-FLAG
PO Box 1152 ✉ Kingston 8 ☎ 754-8704 🖳 www.jflag.org
J-FLAG has just celebrated ten years of existance, under very difficult local conditions.

Black River

GUEST HOUSES

Villa Hikaru (H OS PI W) All year
Treasure Beach ☎ (876) 965-0442 ☎ 860-713-9960 (toll free)
🖳 www.villahikaru.com
A four-bedroom villa in an unspoiled fishing village. Cook-housekeeper will shop, prepare and serve all meals.

Kingston

SWIMMING

-Wyndham Rosehall Resort Beach (next to cruise ship terminal).

Port Antonio

HOTELS

Mocking Bird Hill (BF cc H M OS) All year
P.O. Box 254 ☎ 993-7267 ☎ 993 7134
🖳 www.hotelmockingbirdhill.com
A luxury, eco-chic, boutique hotel with 10 rooms and a fantastic restaurant.

Martinique

Name: Martinica
Location: Caribbean
Initials: MAR
Time: GMT -4
International Country Code: ☎ 596 (no area code)
International Access Code: ☎ 00
Language: French, Créole
Area: 1,106 km² / 425 sq mi.
Currency: 1 Euro (€) = 100 Cents
Population: 387,000
Capital: Fort-de-France
Religions: 88% Roman Catholic
Climate: The best time to go to Martinique is the slightly cooler, drier season December - May.

Martinique is a French „Departement d'Outre-Mer/D.O.M." - one of France's overseas territories. The inhabitants and visitors are therefore subject to the same laws as in ☞ France. Martinique has become a very popular vacation island for Europeans, combining exotic tropical beauty with European and French comforts. This makes a holiday here particularly uncomplicated and enjoyable.

Martinique ist ein französisches Übersee-Département „D.O.M." und gilt damit als Teil des französischen Mutterlandes. Es gelten für die Bewohner (und Besucher) dieselben gesetzlichen Rechte und Pflichten wie in ☞ Frankreich. Martinique ist ein beliebtes Touristenziel für Europäer geworden, verbinden sich doch auf dieser Insel tropische Schönheit und Exotik mit europäischem und französischem Komfort. Das macht den Urlaub hier natürlich besonders einfach und angenehm.

La Martinique est un département d'outre-mer français et fait donc partie intégrante de la France. Les habitants et les touristes ont les mêmes droits et les mêmes obligations qu'en ☞ France métropolitaine. C'est un lieu de villégiature apprécié des Européens. La douceur tropicale, l'exotisme et le confort à la française rendront votre séjour particulièrement agréable.

Martinica es un „Dèpartement d'Outre-Mer/D.O.M" francés, y como tal es también considerada parte de la Madre Patria: Francia. Tanto para visitantes como para sus habitantes son valederas ☞ las leyes francesas. Martinica es hoy en dia una atracción turística para europeos, donde se conjugan a la perfección las bellezas exóticas de una isla tropical con el confort europeo. Por esta razón el turista puede disfrutar aqui unas vacaciones agradables sin complicaciones.

La Martinica è un „département d'outre mer/D.O.M." francese, quindi una parte della ☞ Francia. Legalmente i suoi abitanti ed i suoi visitatori sono soggetti agli stessi obblighi e doveri dei francesi. La Martinica è diventata un'amata meta turistica per gli europei che trovano su quest'isola una buona fusione di bellezza esotica e confort francese, un fatto che vi permette di passare delle vacanze piacevoli senza complicazioni.

Fort-de-France

BARS

Bar le Terminal (B glm MC)
104 rue Ernest Deproge
Gay-friendly bar.

Les Trois Islets

GUEST HOUSES

Carbet. Le (AC bf G I MA NU OS PA RWB RWT) All year
18 Rue des Alamandas, Anse Mitan *20 mins from the airport*
☎ 0596 66 03 31 🖳 www.lecarbet-gaybandb.com
Near the beach. Three rooms with loggia and kitchenette. Reservations required.

Rivière-Pilote

APARTMENTS

■ **Résidence Madikéra** (glm H MA OS PI PK RWS RWT VA) All year
La Renée ☎ 62 63 44 🖳 www.madikera.com
Six tourist apartments for rent.

Sainte Anne

SWIMMING

No nudism allowed but possible:
-Petite anse des salines/La Pointe Pie (about an hour from Fort-de-France). Turn right at the entrance of Les Salines and drive to the far end of the dirt road. At the parking lot a path leads through the bushes to „Plage des petites Salines" a sunny beach with occasionally naked gay men settle on the further part of the beach. Avoid WE or holidays. Please keep your shorts handy
-Anse Trabaud: At the turnaround before Sainte-Anne take the direction Les Salines then immediately turn left on the dirt road to Anse Trabaud. The 3 km long of rough dirt road is worth the ride. After a toll (you have to cross a private property) you reach paradise. Better to go on the right side of the beach (consider your right while looking toward the ocean) where nude sunbathers settle. Avoid WE and holidays
-No beach is classified as nude beach.

Puerto Rico

Name: Porto Rico
Location: Caribbean
Initials: PR
Time: GMT -4
International Country Code: ☎ 1 787 or 939
International Access Code: ☎ 011
Language: Spanish, English
Area: 8,959 km² / 3,435 sq mi.
Currency: 1 US Dollar (US$) = 100 Cents
Population: 3,927,776
Capital: San Juan
Religions: 72% Catholic
Climate: Tropical marine climate that is mild. Hurricane season (May-Nov). Tourist season Dec-Apr.
Important gay cities: San Juan

Puerto Rico is neither a state of the US, nor independent, but ‚freely associated' with the US. The Puertoricans are US-citizens but they are not entitled to vote in US-elections. This political position ‚in between' and considerable customs privileges ensure economical prosperity for this Caribbean island. We do not have any information concerning the penal code, but we assume that homosexuality is open to prosecution. Still Puerto Rico is the most liberal island in the whole of the Caribbean Sea. Gay activities take place only in the capital, San Juan.

Puerto Rico ist weder ein US-Staat, noch selbständig, sondern „frei assoziiert" mit den USA. Die Puertoricaner sind zwar Bürger der USA, besitzen aber kein Stimmrecht bei US-Wahlen. Diese politische Mittelstellung und erhebliche Zollvergünstigungen sichern dieser Karibikinsel wirtschaftliches Wohlergehen. Zwar liegen uns keine juristischen Informationen vor, aber wir vermuten, dass Homosexualität strafbar ist. Trotzdem ist Puerto Rico die liberalste Insel in der gesamten Karibik. Schwule Aktivitäten konzentrieren sich ganz und gar auf die Hauptstadt San Juan.

Porto Rico ne fait pas partie de la Confédération américaine et n'est pas non plus indépendante. L'île est „associée" aux Etats-Unis. Les gens y ont la citoyenneté américaine, mais ne disposent pas du droit de vote. Grâce à son statut mixte et à une liberté en matière de douanes, l'île jouit d'une certaine prospérité. Nous ne disposons d'aucune information concernant la situation des gais face à la loi. Il semblerait cependant que l'homosexualité soit condamnable. Il n'empêche que Porto Rico est une des îles les plus tolérantes des Caraïbes. La capitale gaie de l'île est San Juan.

Puerto Rico no es ni independiente ni un estado norteamericano, sino un estado libre asociado a los Estados Unidos. Los puertorriqueños son ciudadanos norteamericanos sin tener el derecho al voto en las elecciones norteamericanas. Esta situación política asi como las suntuosas ventajas aduaneras y migratorias, le brindan gran auge económico a esta isla caribeña. No poseemos información jurídica respecto al trato de la homosexualidad en la isla, pero suponemos que es penada. A pesar de ello, Puerto Rico es una de las islas caribeñas más liberales. Las actividades homosexuales se concentran por completo en la capital San Juan.

Porto Rico non è nè indipendente nè uno stato degli USA, ma „liberamente associato"agli USA. I portoricani sono cittadini degli USA, però non hanno diritto di voto nelle elezioni parlamentari degli USA. Questo compromesso politico e le agevolazioni doganali assicurano il benessere economico di quest'isola caraibica. Non abbiamo informazioni concrete ma presumiamo che qui l'omosessualità sia illegale. Nonostante ciò Porto Rico è l'isola più liberale dei Caraibi. Le attività gay sono concentrate nella capitale di San Juan.

NATIONAL GROUPS

■ **Sabana Litigation and AIDS Civil Rights Project**
1056 Muñoz Rivera, Suite 1004 ✉ PR 00927 Rio Piedras ☎ 759 8832

Carolina

GUEST HOUSES

■ **Caribe Mountain Villas** (AC b glm I MA MSG NU PA PI PK RWB RWS RWT S SNU VA WO) 8.30-22h
Carr. 857 K.m. 6.0 *20 mins from San Juan airport* ☎ 769 0860
The „Spartacus guests' kitchen" is stocked with a continental breakfast (juice, coffee/tea, pastry) the night before. Spartacus readers must mention Spartacus in order to receive this. All male resort, clothing optional.

San Juan

For the Caribbean, San Juan, with its highways and highrise buildings in the tourist quarter »Condado« may seem to have a very American feel to it. In this quarter (with its most beautiful bathing beach) and in Ocean View right next to it are most of the gay accommodations, venues and clubs. Approximately one kilometre from the old town of

San Juan, »Viejo San Juan«, which is so remarkable that it is included in the World Heritage List of UNESCO. This is the right place to go shopping and there are many nightclubs and bars.

Für karibische Verhältnisse wirkt das von Highways durchzogene San Juan mit den Hochhäusern im Urlauberviertel »Condado« sehr amerikanisch. In diesem Viertel (mit wunderschönem Badestrand) und nebenan in Ocean View liegen auch die meisten schwulen Unterkünfte und Ausgehmöglichkeiten. Etwa einen Kilometer entfernt liegt die Altstadt San Juans, »Viejo San Juan«, die so sehenswert ist, dass die UNESCO sie in ihrer Welterbeliste verzeichnet. Alt-San-Juan ist auch die richtige Gegend zum Shoppen und Bummeln.

Les autoroutes urbaines traversent San Juan, les tours se dressent dans le quartier résidentiel de »Condado«: on a l'impression d'être aux Etats-Unis. C'est à Condado (plages merveilleuses) et à Ocean View que vous trouverez la plupart des pensions gais, des bars et des boîtes. A un kilomètre de là, vous avez la vieille ville de San Juan. Elle fait partie du patrimoine de l'UNESCO. Viejo San Juan est le lieu idéal pour faire du shopping et sortir le soir.

San Juan, con sus Highways y sus rascacielos en la región vacacional »Condado«, se caracteriza por su apariencia norteamericana. En Condado, con sus maravillosas playas, y en el sector Ocean View se encuentran la mayoría de locales, pensiones y lugares de diversión gay. A 1 km. de distancia se encuentra la ciudad vieja San Juan, que por su belleza e importancia histórica, fue incluída dentro de la lista Patrimonio Cultural Mundial de la UNESCO. San Juan Viejo es el lugar ideal para ir de compras y disfrutar de la vida nocturna.

San Juan ha un aspetto molto americano: è attraversata da autostrade, il suo orizzonte è disegnato dai grattacieli del quartiere turistico di »Condado«. In questo quartiere (con una spiaggia favolosa) e nell' »Ocean View« si concentrano gli alberghi ed i locali gay. Ad un chilometro di distanza si trova il centro di San Juan, »viejo San Juan «, che per la sua bellezza è stato messo sotto protezione artistica dall'Unesco. Questa zona è la migliore per fare un giro dei negozi e per uscire di sera.

BARS

Atlantic Beach Hotel (B GLM M MA OS)
1 Calle Vendig ☎ 721 6900 🖳 www.atlanticbeachhotel.net
Great location at San Juan's most popular gay beach.

Circo (B D G MA S) 21-5h
650 C/. Condado *Walking distance from Condado area* ☎ 725 9676
🖳 www.CircoBar.com
Small dance floor.

Cups (B D gLm MA) Wed-Sat 19-4h
1708 C/. San Mateo ☎ 787 268 3570
San Juan's only lesbian bar.

Juniors (B D G P SNU) 8-4, Fri & Sa 9-6, Sun 4-4h
613 C/. Condado ☎ 723 94 77

Metro Lounge (B D GLM MA SNU)
Avenida Roosevelt 1367 ☎ 447-5253
Good alternative to clubs. Thu go-go boys, Fri girls night. Tribal sounds on Sun.

Tia Maria's (B GLM MC) Mon-Thu 11-24, Fri & Sat -2, Sun -24h
326 Avenida de Diego *Near the corner of Av. Ponce de León, Santurce, Bus B1* ☎ 724 40 11
Crowded venue. 2 pool tables.

MEN'S CLUBS

Male Depot Private Club (B DR G P R SNU VS)
Thu-Mon 22h-open end
#1527 Ponce de León, Local 101, Sector El Cinco ☎ 767 4118
🖳 www.maledepotpr.com
Cruise club.

DANCECLUBS

Kenny's (AC B CC D GLM MA OS p S SNU WE) Sat & Sun
Carretera 1 to Caguas *Road 1, Km. 23.6*
Ask a taxi driver to take you there, as it's located in the countryside. The entrance fee covers open bar the whole night for all drinks!

Krash (B D g MA S) Wed-Sun 22-4h, Mon & Tue special events
1257 Avenida Ponce de Leon *Santurce, near M° Cinema* ☎ 722 1131
🖳 krashpr.com
Now not as popular as it used to be.

Starz (AC B CC D GLM MA OS p S SNU WE) Sat
365 Avenida de Diego ☎ 593 3645
Across from Tia Maria's, Starz is only open on Saturday nights and has a younger crowd with a busy dance floor and multiple bars.

RESTAURANTS

Café Berlin (AC B BF CC g M MA OS) 11-23, Sat 9-23, Sun 10-22h
C/. San Francisco, 407, Plaza Colon *Old San Juan* ☎ 722 5205
Restaurant, bakery, delicatessen. Mostly vegetarian cuisine.

Pamela's Caribbean Cuisine (AC B glm M MA OS VEG) 12-15 (lunch), 15-19 (Tapas) & 19-22.30h (dinner)
C/. Santa Ana 1, Ocean Park *At Numero Uno Guest House* ☎ 726 5010
🖳 www.numero1guesthouse.com/pamelas.html
A handful of tables overlooking the beach are part of the superb Pamela's Caribbean Cuisine.

HOTELS

Atlantic Beach (AC B BF CC glm M MA OS RWS RWT S ST) All year
1 C/. Vendig, Condado *On Condado Beach* ☎ 721 6900
🖳 www.atlanticbeachhotel.net
Central location on beach with 37 rooms all with direct dial phone, cable-TV, priv. bath and WC. With restaurant and sundeck with bar.

Hostería del Mar (AC BF CC glm H M RWS RWT) All year
Tapia Street, N° 1, Ocean Park *On Ocean Park beach* ☎ 727 3302
🖳 www.hosteriadelmarpr.com
The ocean-front rooms have a fantastic view. Several rooms have a kitchenette and all rooms have private bathrooms. This hosteleria is located only 10 minutes from the airport and shopping areas. Gay-friendly accommodation.

Numero Uno on the Beach (AC B glm M PI RWS) All year
1 C/. Santa Ana Street, Ocean Park ☎ 726 5010
🖳 www.numero1guesthouse.com
14 rooms in total. Small, intimate and a casually elegant style. One of the premier small guest houses in San Juan!

GUEST HOUSES

Andalucia Guest House & Vacation Rentals (AC CC glm I M MA MSG OS PK RWS RWT WH) All year
2011 McLeary Street, Ocean Park *San Juan Metro Area* ☎ 309 3373
🖳 www.andalucia-puertorico.com
Relaxed casual and charming, near gay-friendly beach area, not far away from San Juan.

Coqui del Mar (AC CC glm H I MA MSG OS PA PK RWS RWT VA) All year, 24hrs
2218 C/. General del Valle *Bus C-52 and bus A-5* ☎ 787 220-4204
🖳 www.CoquiDelMar.com
Gay owned. Full apartment style units at less than hotel prices. 1/2 block from the gay friendly beaches of Ocean Park.

SWIMMING

-Beach between La Concha Hotel and Dupont Plaza Hotel (R) (especially next to Atlantic Beach Hotel, more tourists than locals)
-Ocean Park (more locals, busy on Sun).

CRUISING

-Plaza Río Piedras (near University, Hato Rey)
-Calle San Francisco, Old San Juan (R)
-Plaza de Armas, Old San Juan
-Plaza de las Américas
-Plaza Colón (bus stop).

Saint Kitts & Nevis

Location: Caribbean
Initials: KN
Time: GMT -4
International Country Code: ☎ 1 869
International Access Code: ☎ 011
Language: English
Area: 269 km² / 101 sq mi.
Currency: 1 East Caribbean Dollar (EC$) = 100 Cents
Population: 48,000
Capital: Basseterre
Religions: 87% Christian
Climate: Subtropical climate, that is tempered by constant sea breezes. Tourist season (Dec-Feb). Best time is summer (Jun-Aug).

The legal age of consent for sexual activity is 16 years. We have no further information about Saint Kitts and Nevis except that gay life is extremely hidden. Nevertheless a wonderful place to recover from the stress of everyday urban life.

Das Schultzalter liegt bei 16 Jahren. Über Saint Kitts und Nevis stehen uns keine Informationen zur Verfügung; wir wissen nur, dass das Leben der Homosexuellen sehr diskret verläuft. Dennoch kann man sich auf diesen wunderschönen Inseln vom städtischen Alltagsstress erholen.

La majorité sexuelle est fixée à 16 ans. Nous ne possédons aucune information sur Saint Kitts and Nevis si ce n'est que les gais n'affichent pas leur homosexualité publiquement. L'archipel reste cependant un lieu idyllique pour se reposer du stress quotidien de la ville.

La edad mínima de consentimiento está establecida a los 16 años. No tenemos informaciones sobre San Cristóbal y Nevis. Sólo sabemos que los gays llevan una vida extremadamente discreta. No obstante, estas islas maravillosas son ideales para olvidarse del estrés de la vida ajetreada en la ciudad.

L'età del consenso è di 16 anni. Non disponiamo di informazioni per quanto riguarda Saint Kitts e Nevis. Sappiamo soltanto che la vita gay è estremamente nascosta. Nonostante ciò questa meravigliosa isola è il posto ideale per riprendersi dallo stress quotidiano della vita urbana.

Basseterre

CRUISING

-Frigate Beach (WE)
-Along seafront (dock area and particularly where local buses depart)

Dieppe Bay

HOTELS

Golden Lemon Inn (AC cc H M MC OS PI) All year
☎ 465-7260 💻 www.goldenlemon.com
26 rooms and suites. Dinner by candlelight by the pool. The menus offer a fusion of Caribbean, Continental and Amerian cuisine.

St. Maarten

Initials: STM (NL)
International Country Code: ☎ 599
International Access Code: ☎ 00
Language: Dutch, Papiamento, English, Spanish
Area: 34 km² / 11 sq mi.
Currency: 1 Netherland Antilles Guilder (ANG) = 100 Cents
Population: 33,119
Capital: Philipsburg
Religions: 80% Roman Catholic
Climate: Tropical climate that is moderated by north east trade winds

Under Article 255 of the penal code, homosexual acts are legal between adult males, and the age of consent is set at 16. The attitude of the general public towards homosexuality, however, is somewhat less tolerant than that of the Dutch mother country. Same-sexual marriages are recognized as a part of the Netherlands, however, cannot be entered into in the Antilles.
Dutch law requires the kingdom's three parts - the Netherlands, Aruba and the Dutch Antilles - to recognize each other's legal documents, including marriage certificates. Recently a court in the Antilles capital of Willenstad upheld the requirement that the government must recognized marriages performed in the Netherlands.
The Antilles government's appeal to The Hague is unlikely to succeed, legal observers say, pointing to the failure of a similar case in 2005 that had been brought by the government of Aruba.

Homosexuelle Handlungen werden in Artikel 255 des Strafgesetzbuches abgehandelt. Zwischen erwachsenen Männern sind sie legal, und das Schutzalter liegt bei 16 Jahren. Allerdings ist die öffentliche Meinung Homosexuellen gegenüber hierzulande etwas weniger tolerant als im niederländischen „Mutterland". Als Teil der Niederlande werden gleichgeschlechtliche Ehen anerkannt, können aber selbst nicht in den Antillen eingetragen werden.
Die holländische Rechtsprechung zwingt alle drei Teile des Königsreichs – die Niederlande, Aruba und die Niederländischen Antillen – zur ge-

genseitigen Anerkennung rechtswirksamer Urkunden, einschließlich von Trauscheinen. Ein Gerichtshof in Willenstad, der Hauptstadt der Antillen, hat kürzlich ein Urteil bestätigt, dem zufolge die hiesige Regierung in den Niederlanden geschlossene Ehen anerkennen muss.
Die von der Regierung der Antillen in Den Haag eingelegte Berufung sei wenig aussichtsreich, meinen Rechtsbeobachter, und berufen sich dabei auf das Scheitern einer ähnlichen Klage, die im Jahr 2005 von der Regierung Arubas angestrengt worden war.

Selon l'article 255 du code pénal l'homosexualité n'est pas considérée comme un délit. La majorité sexuelle est fixée à 16 ans. Notons toutefois que l'attitude de la population vis-à-vis des gais n'est pas aussi tolérante qu'aux les Pays-Bas. Faisant partie des Pays-Bas, les mariages homosexuels sont reconnus aux Antilles, mais ne peuvent y être enregistrés.
La jurisprudence néerlandaise oblige les trois composants du Royaume - les Pays-Bas, Aruba et les Antilles néerlandaises - à la reconnaissance réciproque des documents juridiques, dont les actes de mariage. Une cour de justice de Willenstad, la capitale des Antilles, a confirmé récemment un jugement qui oblige le gouvernement local à accepter les mariages conclus aux Pays-Bas.
Des observateurs juridiques jugent que le recours intenté par le gouvernement des Antilles n'a que peu de chances d'aboutir en invoquant l'échec d'une plainte similaire intentée par le gouvernement d'Aruba en 2005.

El artículo 255 del Código Penal dictamina sobre las actividades homosexuales. Estas son declaradas legales entre hombres adultos y la edad mínima de consentimiento queda establecida a los 16 años. La opinión pública de este país es menos tolerante con los gays que la de la madre patria, Holanda. Como parte de los Países Bajos, se reconocen los matrimonios entre personas del mismo sexo pero no pueden registrarse como tal en las Antillas.
La jurisprudencia holandesa obliga a las tres partes del reino (los Países Bajos, Aruba y las Antillas Holandesas) al reconocimiento recíproco de documentos jurídicos, incluídos los certificados de matrimonio.
Un tribunal de Willenstad, la capital de las Antillas, confirmó recientemente una sentencia, en virtud de la cual el gobierno local debe reconocer todos los matrimonios celebrados en los Países Bajos.
El recurso de revisión interpuesto por el gobierno de las Antillas en la Haya parece que tendrá poco éxito, opinan algunos analistas jurídicos remitiéndose al fracaso de otro recurso similar que el gobierno de Aruba presentó en el año 2005.

Gli atti omosessuali vengono trattati nel paragrafo 255 del codice penale. Sono legali tra uomini adulti, l'età del consenso è di 16 anni. Comunque, l'opinione pubblica verso l'omosessualità è meno tollerante rispetto a quella della „madrepatria" olandese. Essendo, le Antille Olandesi, una dipendenza del Regno dei Paesi Bassi, le unioni tra coppie dello stesso vengono pienamente riconosciute; tuttavia le unioni stesse non possono essere registrate nelle Antille.
La giurisdizione olandese obbliga tutti e tre le parti del Regno - Paesi Bassi, Arube e Antille olandesi - al reciproco riconoscimento dei rispettivi certificati aventi effettività giuridica, compresi i certificati di morte.
Un tribunale di Willenstad, la capitale delle Antille, ha da poco confermato una sentenza secondo la quale il governo delle Antille deve riconoscere i matrimoni contratti nei Paesi Bassi. Secondo alcuni osservatori giuridici il ricorso da parte del governo delle Antille presentato a Den Haag ha poche chance. A questo proposito gli stessi osservatori ricordano infatti una causa simile presentata nel 2005 dal governo di Arubas.

St. Maarten ☏ 599

St Martin falls under the jurisdiction of Guadaloupe and thus belongs to France's overseas territories. The northern part of the island is French, the south is Dutch. The island of St Martin is the perfect place for a relaxing holiday has wonderful beaches (also with nude sunbathing). St Martin is along with Puerto Rico, the most liberal and gay-friendly island in the Caribbean. Daily flights are available with Air France from Paris to St. Martin (SXM).

St. Martin wird vom Regionalparlament des entfernten Guadeloupe regiert und ist damit Teil des französischen Überseedepartements. Der Nordteil der Insel ist französisch, der Süden niederländisch.
St. Martin ist eine herrliche Insel für Urlaub und Erholung mit wundervollen Stränden (FKK ist möglich). St. Martin ist neben Puerto Rico die liberalste und schwulenfreundlichste Insel der Karbik. Man kann täglich von Paris mit der Air France nach St. Martin (SXM) fliegen.

St Martin est administrée par la lointaine Guadeloupe et fait ainsi partie de l'Union Européenne. Le nord de l'île est français, le sud est hollandais. On passe d'agréables et reposantes vacances à St Martin. On y trouve de merveilleuses plages, accessibles également aux naturistes. St Martin, située près de Porto-Rico est des Caraïbes de loin l'île la plus libérale et la plus gay-friendly. St Martin (SXM) est quotidiennement reliée par Air-France depuis Paris.

A pesar de que St. Martin queda bastante lejos de Guadalupe, está bajo su jurisdicción y forma parte de la colonia francesa. No obstante la isla está dividida en la parte francesa del norte y la parte holandesa del sur.
St. Martin es una hermosa isla para las vacaciones y el descanso, con playas maravillosas (también para amantes del nudismo). St. Martin es, junto con Puerto Rico, la isla del Caribe más liberal y tolerante con los homosexuales. Además se puede volar diariamente con Air France a St. Martin (SXM) desde París.

St. Martin viene governato dal parlamento regionale della lontana Guadalupa e insieme a quest'ultima fa parte dei territori d'oltre mare francesi. La parte settentrionale dell'isola è francese, quella meridionale olandese. Quest'isola meravigliosa con le sue splendide spiaggie (anche per nudisti) è un posto ottimo per passare le vacanze e per rilassarsi. St. Martin è, accanto a Puerto Rico, l'isola dei Caraibi più liberale e tollerante nei confronti dell'omosessualità. È possibile andare a St. Martin (SXM) da Parigi ogni giorno con la Air France.

DANCECLUBS

Club Eros (B D GLM s ST t) Sat 23-?h
Rue Victor Maurasse, Marigot *Behind Arawhak restaurant, 1st floor*
☏ (590) 0690 32 58 64 www.erosclub-saintmartin.com
Bistro and dancing. Busy on Saturdays.

RESTAURANTS

Gauchos. Los (AC B glm M MA NR OS PK RES S VEG WL) 11.30-22.30h
Pelican Resort *At Pelican Resort, Simpson Bay* ☏ (599) 544 4084
The best Argentinian restaurant on the island! The owner Lisa is one of the most charming Sint Maarteners. Food and service are very good and while dining 2 tango dancers perform original Argentinian tango.

HOTELS

Royal Turtle Inn (AC BF CC g M OS PI) All year
Airport Road 114 ☏ (599) 452563 www.theroyalturtle.net
8 guestrooms all with TV, fridge and coffeemaker.

GUEST HOUSES

Villa Rainbow (AC bf G I MA MSG NU PI RWS RWT) Oct-May
Pic Paradis *French part of the island, between Cupecoy, Marigot, Grand Case, and the famous Orient Bay* ☏ (059) 069 076 62 35
www.villarainbow.fr
Small,luxury guesthouse welcoming gay guests.

SWIMMING

-Cupecoy Beach (g NU) (take bus from Philipsberg to Mullet Bay, then walk 20 mins following the road across the golf course and over the hill, then turn left onto the beach) near Delfina Hotel on the Dutch side of the island. Also cruising in bushes and caves, busy
-Bay Rouge (g NU) on the French side of the island on the way to Marigot. Also cruising in the bushes ca. 600 m from the entrance on the left.
-Baie Orientale (NU) (Cruising area is between Boo Boo Sam and Coco Beach restaurants and in the far south of the beach just after the Club Orient).

Virgin Islands (British)

Name: Les îles Vierges britanniques
Location: Caribbean
Initials: BVI
Time: GMT -4
International Country Code: ☎ 284
Language: English
Area: 153 km² / 59 sq mi.
Currency: US$ 1= 100 Cents
Population: 21,689
Capital: Roadtown
Religions: 45% Methodist, 21% Anglican
Climate: The peak tourist season is Dec-May. Better weather and clearer water between Apr & Aug.

The British Virgin Islands, consisting of 36 islands, is a British dependency in the Caribbean. In January 2001 the British government repealed local laws against homosexuality.
Discrimination on grounds of sexuality is prohibited under the 2007 Constitution.
British Virgin Islands lags far behind not only international standards for the care of persons suffering with HIV/AIDS, but far behind prevailing local standards.

Die British Virgin Islands bestehen aus 36 Inseln und sind ein britisches Protektorat in der Karibik. Im Januar 2001 hat die britische Regierung die örtlichen Verbote der Homosexualität aufgehoben.
In der neuen Verfassung von 2007 ist Diskriminierung aufgrund sexueller Orientierung verboten.
Die British Virgin Islands sind nicht nur im Vergleich mit internationalen Standards hinsichtlich der Pflege von Menschen mit HIV/AIDS äußerst rückständig, sondern auch im Vergleich mit den meisten ihrer Nachbarstaaten.

Les îles Vierges britanniques sont constituées de 36 îles sous protectorat britannique situées dans les Caraïbes. En janvier 2001, le gouvernement britannique a levé l'interdiction de l'homosexualité, en vigueur jusque là dans l'archipel.
La discrimination pour cause d'orientation sexuelle est interdite dans la nouvelle Constitution de 2007.
Les îles Vierges britanniques sont en retard en ce qui concerne les soins pour les personnes séropositives ou atteintes du sida et ce, non seulement par rapport au reste du monde mais même en comparaison à la plupart de leurs voisins géographiques.

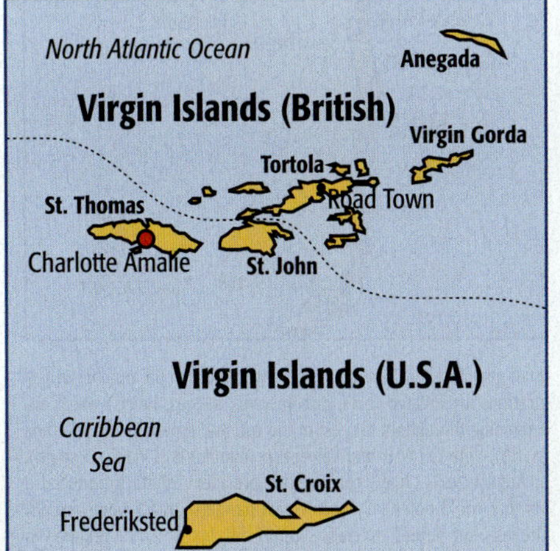

Las islas Vírgenes Británicas comprenden 36 islas y son un protectorado británico en el Caribe. En enero del 2001, el gobierno británico derogó la prohibición local contra la homosexualidad.
Según la nueva Constitución de 2007 se prohíbe la discriminación por motivo de la orientación sexual.
Las islas Vírgenes Británicas están todavía muy atrasadas en cuanto al cuidado de las personas con el SIDA, no sólo en comparación con los estándares internacionales sino también en comparación con la mayoría de sus países vecinos.

Le Isole Vergini Britanniche (British Virgin Islands) sono composte da 36 isole situate nei Carabi e sono una colonia britannica con autonomia interna. A gennaio del 2001 il governo britannico ha abolito i divieti concernenti l'omosessualità.
La nuova Costituzione del 2007 vieta espressamete le discriminazioni fondate sullíorientamento sessuale.
Per quello che riguarda l'assistenza di persone con HIV/AIDS, le Isole Vergini Britanniche sono molto arretrate non solo in confronto agli standard internazionali ma anche in confronto agli standard della maggior parte dei paesi vicini.

Tortola

HOTELS

Fort Recovery Villa Beach Resort
(AC bf CC g M MA MSG OS PI) All year
Road Town ☎ 495-4467 fortrecoverytortola.com
Great guest house on beach with private beachfront villas, on side of historic fort built by Dutch in 17th century. Run and owned by women.

Tamarind Club.The (B BF glm M PI)
East End *In Josiah's Bay* ☎ 495 2477 www.tamarindclub.com
An intimate hotel with a restaurant, bar/lounge and pool with swim up bar.

GUEST HOUSES

North Shore Cottages (cc H NG) All year
Long Bay Hill, Long Bay ☎ 495 4430
www.vacationaccommodationbvi.com
Five cottages. Gay-friendly accommodation.

SWIMMING

-Cane Garden Bay
-Apple Bay
-Josiah's Bay.

Virgin Islands of the USA

Name: Jungferninseln · Iles Vierges · Islas Virgenes · Isole Vergini
Location: Caribbean
Initials: VI
Time: GMT -4
International Country Code: ☎ 1 340
International Access Code: ☎ 011
Language: English
Area: 347 km² / 133 sq mi.
Currency: 1 US Dollar (US$) = 100 Cents
Population: 113,200
Capital: Charlotte Amalie (on St. Thomas)
Religions: mostly Christian
Climate: Subtropical climate, that is tempered by constant sea breezes. The rainy season is from May-Nov.

The Virgin Islands are the nearest neighbours to Puerto Rico. For the average tourist these islands are mainly a station on their Caribbean cruise to buy duty free goods. Next to that there are gay hotels and the fundamental gay entertainment amenities in Frederiksted on St. Croix. And more is not needed. You don't take a gay holiday on a Caribbean island. You go here to lounge on a beautiful beach in a lovely tropical climate, to recreate and play in a sparkling ocean.

Die Jungferninseln liegen in unmittelbarer Nachbarschaft zu Puerto Rico. Der Durchschnittstourist besucht diese Inseln vor allem als Station einer Karibik-Kreuzfahrt und um hier günstig zollfrei einzukaufen. Daneben gibt es auf »St. Croix« in Frederiksted und auf »St. Thomas« schwule Hotels und eine Grundausstattung an schwulen Unterhaltungsmöglichkeiten. Mehr ist auch nicht nötig, denn auf einer Karibikinsel macht man keinen schwulen Urlaub. Hierher fährt man, um sich im angenehmen tropischen Klima an einem wunderschönen Strand im herrlichen Meer zu tummeln und zu erholen.

Les Iles Vierges sont voisines de Porto Rico. En général, on y vient pour faire des achats en duty free. A Frederiksted sur Sainte Croix et sur Saint Thomas, il y a plusieurs hôtels et établissments gais. Cela suffit largement, car on ne vient pas aux Caraïbes pour passer des vacances 100% gaies. On y vient pour la douceur du climat et pour les plages enchanteresses.

Las Islas Vírgenes se localizan en las cercanías de Puerto Rico. La mayoría de los turistas que hacen un crucero por el Caribe hacen aquí una parada para aprovechar los interesantes precios de esta zona libre de impuestos. Pero en »St. Thomas« y en St. Croix existen también unas cuantas pensiones y locales de diversión gay. Mucho más tampoco hace falta, ya que el objetivo de la mayoría de los turistas gay es disfrutar del excelente clima, las bella playas y el mar azul, por lo que no se echa de menos una infraestructura homosexual.

Le Isole Vergini sono situate nelle immediate vicinanze di Porto Rico. Normalmente i turisti si fermano solo per fare scalo durante una crociera e per fare acquisti senza pagare tasse doganali. A Frederiksted, a »St. Croix« e a St. Thomas vi sono alcuni hotel e locali per gay. Non c'é molto di più, dato che ai Caraibi non si viene per il sesso, ma per godersi il clima e le spiaggie.

Saint Croix

HOTELS

Palms at Pelican Cove. The (AC B BF g M MSG OS PI RWB RWS RWT VA WO) All year
4126 La Grande Princesse *3 miles west of Christiansted* ☎ 778 8920
www.palmspelicancove.com
Gay owned business.

Sand Castle on the Beach (AC B cc GLM I M MA MSG NR NU OS PA PI PK RES RWB RWS RWT VEG WL WO) All year
127 Estate Smithfield ☎ 772 1205 www.sandcastleonthebeach.com
Beautiful beachfront hotel. Reservation requested. Six different room types to choose from. Gay owned and operated.

GUEST HOUSES

Villa Greenleaf on St. Croix (AC BF CC GLM I RWS RWT W) All year
11 Estate Montpellier, Christiansted ☎ 719-1958
☎ 1 888 282-1001 (toll free) www.villagreenleaf.com
Gay-owned guesthouse with 5 rooms, gourmet breakfast, cocktails & hors d'oeuvres at sunset.

Saint Thomas

HOTELS

Secret Harbour Beach Resort (AC B CC glm H M MA MSG OS PI PK RWB RWS RWT VA WO) All year, office hours 8-23h
6280 Estate Nazareth ☎ 775 6550 www.secretharbourvi.com
One of the first class addresses on the island. This modern, gay-friendly hotel has all the amenities you require and a wonderful beach location and a typical Caribbean atmosphere top it all. Great pool and even a tennis court.

SWIMMING

-Little Magen's Bay (g NU) (right side of Magen's Bay Beach).

Chile

Name: Chili · Cile
Location: South America
Initials: RCH
Time: GMT -4
International Country Code: ☎ 56 (omit 0 from area codes)
International Access Code: ☎ 00
Language: Spanish
Area: 756,006 km² / 291,930 sq mi.
Currency: 1 Chilean Peso (Chil$) = 100 Centavos
Population: 16,295,000
Capital: Santiago de Chile
Religions: 77% Roman Catholic
Climate: Santiago and central Chile are best in spring (Sep-Nov) or autumn (Feb-Apr). Parque Nacional del Paine and the lakes region are best in summer (Dec-Mar).
Important gay cities: Santiago de Chile

Same-sex relations are legal in Chile and have been so since 1998. The age of consent is 18. Sexual relations may only be practiced in the private sphere, otherwise they will be considered as an offence to the „moral and decent behaviour", and could be punished. Since 1997 homophobia has notably diminished in Chile. It remains one of the most serious forms of discrimination, according to studies from the University of Chile.

Since 2001 this country experienced a transition that allowed gay men to have an important presence in the media. Discrimination and segregation remain repudiated on the public sphere. An important example of this situation is that the Congress of Chile is considering a law for the civic union of homosexual couples. Thanks to the outings of famous personalities in the media, there is a increasing acceptability of gay lifestyles. This has lead to an increase in the number of gay locations in Santiago (bars, discothèques, saunas, hotels) which are expanding throughout the rest of the country, especially in La Serena (north), Viña del Mar and Valparaíso (middle) and Valdivia (south). In August 2011, Chile's conservative president Piñera introduced a bill that could potentially enable civil partnerships for homosexuals. The left-wing parties generally support this, but would be required to

negotiate with the unpopular president to do so. Whether the bill will pass through congress successfully was still uncertain at the time of going to press.
In addition, there are many tourist attractions of general interest such as the year-round warm, sunny beaches in the north of the country, or the contrast in the south with its rainy, cold weather, but incomparable, natural beauty. Particularly attractive for tourists are the cities of Valparaíso, recently declared as international cultural heritage, as well as Viña del Mar with its international festival in February.

In Chile sind gleichgeschlechtliche Beziehungen seit 1998 legal. Das Schutzalter liegt bei 18 Jahren. Homosexuelle Kontakte dürfen allerdings nur privat stattfinden, da sie sonst als Erregung öffentlichen Ärgernisses angesehen und bestraft werden. Seit 1997 hat die Schwulenfeindlichkeit in Chile deutlich abgenommen, aber nach einer Studie der Universität in Chile ist sie immer noch eine der ernstzunehmendsten Arten der Diskriminierung. Seit 2001 hat in diesem Land eine Entwicklung begonnen, in deren Verlauf homosexuelle Männer in den Medien immer präsenter geworden sind. Diskriminierung und Absonderung werden in der Öffentlichkeit weiterhin verpönt. Da sich viele Prominente in den Medien geoutet haben, wird schwule Lebensart immer mehr akzeptiert. Darüber hinaus gibt es in Santiago auch immer mehr Schwulentreffs wie Bars, Diskos, Saunen und Hotels, die sich bis in den Norden, das Zentrum und den Süden des Landes ausbreiten: nach La Serena, Viña del Mar, Valparaíso und Valdiva. Im August 2011 brachte der konservative chilenische Staatspräsident Piñera einen Gesetzentwurf ein, das Homosexuellen die eingetragene Partnerschaft ermöglichen soll. Zwar unterstützen die linken Parteien generell diesen Kurs, müssten sich aber mit dem unpopulären Präsidenten an einen Tisch setzen. Zum Redaktionsschluss war nicht klar, ob diese Gesetzesinitiative den Kongress erfolgreich passieren wird.
In Chile gibt es viele Touristenattraktionen für jedermann: Die ganzjährig warmen, sonnigen Strände im Norden, oder im Kontrast dazu den Süden mit seinem regnerisch kalten Wetter, aber einzigartig natürlicher Schönheit. Für Besucher empfehlen sich vor allem die Städte Valparaíso, das vor kurzem zum internationalen Kulturerbe ernannt wurde, und Viña del Mar, wo im Februar ein internationales Festival stattfindet.

Au Chili, les relations entre personnes de même sexe sont légales depuis 1998. La majorité sexuelle est fixée à 18 ans. Les contacts homosexuels doivent néanmoins se dérouler dans le cadre privé car ils sont considérés comme un outrage public à la pudeur. Depuis 1997, l'homophobie a sensiblement baissé mais selon une étude de l'Université du Chili, elle est toujours une forme de discrimination à prendre très au sérieux.
Depuis 2001, le pays a commencé un processus d'ouverture où les homosexuels devraient être de plus en plus presents. Avec le coming out de nombreuses personnalités dans les medias, le mode de vie homo est de mieux en mieux accepté. En outre, de nouveaux lieux de rencontre gays ouvrent régulièrement à Santiago, tels bars, boîtes, saunas et hôtels qui se répartissent du nord au sud du pays : à La Serena, Viña del Mar, Valparaiso et Valdiva. En août 2011, le président conservateur chilien Piñera a déposé une proposition de loi de partenariat enregistré pour les homosexuels. Certes les partis de gauche vont en général dans ce sens mais ils ont dû aussi négocier avec le président impopulaire. Au moment de la clôture de la rédaction, il n'est pas sûr que cette proposition de loi soit votée par le congrès.
Le pays offre également de nombreuses attractions touristiques pour tout un chacun : les plages ensoleillées toute l'année au nord contrastant avec le temps humide et froid du sud avec sa beauté unique. Le visiteur se rendra dans les villes de Valparaiso, consacrée récemment patrimoine culturel de l'humanité, ainsi que Viña del Mar, où se déroule en février un festival international.

Desde 1998 son legales en Chile las relaciones sexuales entre homosexuales. La edad de consentimiento es de 18 años. Las prácticas sexuales deben efectuarse en lugares privados, pues de lo contrario se consideran como una ofensa a la „moral y las buenas costumbres", lo cual conlleva sanciones. Aunque desde 1997 la homofobia ha disminuido, sigue siendo la más grave de las discriminaciones, según estudios de la Universidad de Chile. Desde 2001 el país ha experimentado cambios que han permitido a los homosexuales ganar una importante presencia en los medios de comunicación, siendo rechazada, al menos a nivel público, la discriminación o la segregación. Gracias a los „outings" de conocidas figuras ante los medios, aumenta cada día más la aceptación del estilo de vida gay. Ello ha tenido como resultado que en la actualidad existan en Santiago variadas y numerosas ofertas de diversión para los homosexuales (bares y discotecas, saunas, moteles).Tales espacios han comenzado a extenderse al resto del país, en especial en La Serena (norte), Viña del Mar y Valparaíso (centro) y Valdivia (Sur). En agosto de 2011, el Presidente conservador Piñera presentó un proyecto de ley que permitirá a los homosexuales llevar a cabo uniones civiles registradas. Cierto es que, en general, los partidos de izquierda apoyan esta iniciativa, pero deberían sentarse a la mesa con el impopular presidente. Al cierre de la redacción no estaba claro aún si esta iniciativa legislativa sería aprobada con éxito por el Congreso.
A esas ofertas, se suman atractivos turísticos de interés general como playas cálidas durante todo el año en el norte del país, y climas fríos y lluviosos, pero de inigualable belleza vegetal, en el sur. Interesantes para visitar son Valparaíso, declarada recientemente Patrimonio de la Humanidad, y Viña del Mar que en febrero realiza un festival con destacados artistas internacionales.

In Cile i rapporti tra persone dello stesso sesso sono legali dal 1998. L'età legale per rapporti sessuali è di 18 anni. Contatti omosessuali tuttavia possono avvenire solo in privato poichè potrebbero turbare l'opinione pubblica e quindi puniti. Dal 1997 l'omofobia in Cile è diminuita significativamente ma secondo una ricerca dell'universita in Cile è comunque il tipo di discriminazione più frequente.

Dal 2001 i gay sono sempre più presenti anche nei mass media. La discriminazione viene deprecata pubblicamente. Anche grazie a molti vips che hanno fatto pubblicamente il coming out, l'omosessualità è sempre più accettata. Inoltre, a Santiago vengono aperti sempre più locali gay come discoteche, bar, saune ed hotel. Ad agosto del 2011 il Presidente della Repubblica, il conservatore Piñera, ha presentato un progetto di legge in favore delle unioni civili per gli omosessuali. I partiti di sinistra salutano positivamente questo nuovo corso, tuttavia, per dare realizzazione a questa iniziativa dovrebbero sedersi ad un tavolo con l'impopolare Presidente. A chiusura redazionale non è ancora dato sapere se questa iniziativa di legge riuscirà ad essere approvata dal Congresso.
Ci sono anche diverse attrazioni turistiche: le calde e soleggiate spiagge del nord ma anche il sud con la sua pioggia e il suo freddo ma anche con la sua naturale bellezza. Consigliamo particolarmente le città Valparaíso, da poco patrimonio culturale mondiale, e Vina del Mar, dove a febbraio ha luogo un festival internazionale.

INTERNATIONAL ORGANISATIONS

ACCIONGAY
San Ignacio 165 ✉ Santiago ☎ (02) 672 0000
LGBT Rights and HIV Prevention.

NATIONAL GAY INFO

Fundacion Savia (G)
Tegualda 1832 ☎ (02) 269 0937 💻 www.fundacionsavia.cl
National Foundation of People living with HIV and AIDS.

Vivo Positivo
San Isidro 367 ✉ Santiago ☎ (02) 635 9396
💻 www.vivopositivo.cl
National organization of PWA.

NATIONAL COMPANIES

Orpheus Travel Corporation Group (GLM)
Zurich 255 off.54, Las Condes, ✉ Santiago de Chile ☎ (09) 9731 9413
💻 www.myorpheustravel.com
Orpheus Travel is a gay and lesbian owned and managed South American Travel Corporation established to serve the LGBT community.

NATIONAL GROUPS

MOVILH
Coquimbo 1410 ✉ Santiago ☎ (02) 671 4855 💻 www.movilh.org

MUMS Mon-Fri 16-21.30h
Santa Mónica 2317 ✉ 8350574 Santigo ☎ (02) 671 4568
💻 www.mums.cl

Antofagasta ☎ 055

CAFES

Ciber Next (GLM) Mon-Thu 11-3, Fri & Sat 11-3 & Sun 15-1h
C/. Uribe 611 ☎ (055) 76 0884 💻 www.cibernext.260mb.com

DANCECLUBS

Underboys (! B D GLM S) Thu-Sun
Ave. Perez Zujovic 4800 💻 www.underboys.cl

CRUISING

Throughout Chile one should take care. Pickpockets active in many cruising areas.
-Plaza Colón (g MA r).

Arica ☎ 058

DANCECLUBS

Dancar (B D GLM S ST)
Avenida Comandante San Martin 322 ☎ 09 7847 0457
💻 www.discodancar.com

CRUISING

-Beach »El Laucho« (next to the Hotel Arica in the Avenida Costanera, early evenings)
-Plaza Colón (Square in front of City Hall and the Vicuña Square next to it, early evenings)
-Plaza Vicuña Mackenna, (early evenings).

Calama ☎ 056

DANCECLUBS

Fashion Discotheque (B D GLM PK S ST)
Ex-Ruta al Sol. Camino Vecinal 2450
💻 http://es-es.facebook.com/pages/Fashion-Discotheque/137017457432

Chillan ☎ 042

DANCECLUBS

Frida Kahlo (B D GLM S ST) Thu-Sat 22-?h
Isabel Riquelme 1118 💻 www.frida.cl

Concepción ☎ 041

DANCECLUBS

Diva's (B D GLM S) Fri & Sat 23.30-5.30h
Anibal Pinto 1661 *Between Heras & Rozas* ☎ (041) 52 0713
💻 www.divasdisco.cl
Two bars, own parking, regular events.

SAUNAS/BATHS

Uomo Spa (b DU FH G I m RR SA SB VS WO)
Sun-Thu 14-23 & Fri, Sat 15-23h
C/. Chacabuco 1159, Concepción *Between Orompello y Ongolmo*
☎ (041) 24 62874 💻 www.uomospa.cl
For those over the age of 18. No alcohol may be consumed on the premises.

SWIMMING

-Playa Blanca (G MA) (South of Concepción, approximately 1h by bus/car between Coronel & Lota).

CRUISING

-Plaza de la Independencia (g MA) (Corner Barros Arana/Aníbal Pinto)
-Paseo Peatonal Barros Arana & Aníbal Pinto (g MA) (busy after 21h).

Coquimbo ☎ 051

DANCECLUBS

Club Cosmos (D G)
Aldunate 502

Otsu (B D GLM PK S ST)
Avenida Las Palmeras 170 💻 www.otsu.cl

Vogue Club (D G)
Av. Los Lagos 1432 ☎ (09) 9 203 3846

Iquique ☎ 057

CAFES

Amnesia (B GLM M S SNU ST)
San Martin 119 ☎ (09) 8655 9846 💻 www.amnesiarestobar.tk

DANCECLUBS

CRBRO (B D GLM PK S ST)
Bajo Molle Km 7 *Camino Interior Costero s/n*
💻 www.facebook.com/group.php?gid=20214019098

La Serena ☎ 051

BARS

■ **Herrera** (B G)
Domeyko 578 🖳 www.facebook.com/ccherreralaserena

CRUISING

-Playa El Faro (g MA) (Dunes north of El Faro Monument).

Osorno ☎ 064

DANCECLUBS

■ **Play Bar** (B D GLM S ST)
Bulnes 928 🖳 facebook play.osorno

Puerto Montt ☎ 065

DANCECLUBS

■ **Adonis** (B D GLM S ST)
Avenida Angelmo 1856 🖳 www.twitter.com/adonispub

■ **Angels** (! B D GLM S ST)
Pacheco Altamirano 2507 🖳 www.fotolog.com/charlypubfiestas

Punta Arenas ☎ 061

DANCECLUBS

■ **Deliriuz** (B D GLM S ST)
Rio de los Siervos Km 5 🖳 www.facebook.com/d3liriuz?sk=info
Best known as „Los Torreones"

Rancagua ☎ 072

DANCECLUBS

■ **Medieval** (B D GLM S ST)
German Riesco 70 🖳 www.fotolog.com/medievaldisco

San Pedro de Atacama ☎ 055

RESTAURANTS

■ **Estaka. La** (B bf CC glm MA) 9-0.30h
Caracoles 259-b ☎ (055) 85 1201
Traditional food, meat and vegetarian dishes.

CRUISING

-Plaza de San Pedro (g).

Santiago ☎ 02

BARS

■ **Bar 105** (B GLM m) Thu-Sat 21.30-5h
C/. Bombero Núñez 105, Bellavista ☎ (02) 403 2990

■ **Dionisio** (B G) Wed-Sun 22-5h
Bombero Nuñez 111 ☎ (02) 737 6065

■ **Farinelli Bar y Espectaculos** (B GLM MA S ST) Tue-Sun 23-5h
Bombero Núñez 68, Recoleta ☎ (02) 732 8966 🖳 www.farinelli.cl
Shows on Fri & Sat from 23h.

■ **Pub Friend's** (B GLM M MA S ST) Wed & Thu 21.30-4, Fri & Sat -5h
Bombero Núñez 365, Bellavista ☎ (02) 777 3979 🖳 www.pubfriends.cl

■ **Vox Populi** (! B G M MA) Tue-Sat 22.30-5h
Ernesto Pinto Lagarrigue 364 *M° Baquedano* ☎ (02) 738 0562

CAFES

■ **Barabajo** (B GLM ST)
Erasmo Escala 2185 ☎ 697 1292 🖳 www.barabajo.cl

■ **Tomodachi** (GLM M) 10.30-23.30h
Jose Miguel de la Barra 432 *M° Bellas Artes* ☎ 638 4700
🖳 www.barriolastarria.com/cafeteria_tomodachi_barrio_lastarria.htm

DANCECLUBS

■ **Blondie** (D g MA)
Bernando O´Higgins 2897 local 104 🖳 www.blondie.cl

■ **Bokhara Club International** (AC B D GLM MC S ST) 23-?h
Pio Nono 430, Bellavista ☎ (02) 732 1050 🖳 www.bokhara.cl
Look for flyers for free entry.

■ **Bunker** (! AC B D GLM S ST VS) Fri, Sat & before public holidays 24-5h
Bombero Nuñez 159, Bellavista *Plaza Italia, M° Baquedano or Bellas Artes*
☎ (02) 737 1716 🖳 www.bunker.cl
Reportedly the biggest up-market gay disco in Santiago.

■ **Club 142** (B D GLM) 23.30-5h
Dardignac 142 *Corner Bombero Nuñez* 🖳 es-es.facebook.com/pages/club-142-ex-limon/119604594728653

■ **Club Miel** (B D glm S YC)
C/. Bilbao 465 Esquina Italia *M° Parque Bustamante Providencia*
☎ (02) 634 4347 🖳 www.clubmiel.cl

■ **Club Principe** (AC B D GLM MA S SNU ST) Mon-Sun 23.30-5h
Pio Nono 398, Bellavista ☎ (02) 777 6381 🖳 www.clubprincipe.cl

■ **Fausto** (! AC B D G MA S ST VS) Wed-Sun & before public holidays 23-?h
Av. Santa María 832, Providencia ☎ (02) 777 1041 🖳 www.fausto.cl
Beautiful wooden interior, various DJs. Fausto has been serving the community since 1980. Up-market.

■ **Nueva Cero** (B D GLM S SNU ST)
C/. Euclides 1204, San Miguel ☎ (02) 551 7298 🖳 www.nuevacero.cl
Largest gay disco in Santiago.

RESTAURANTS

■ **Ali Baba** (b glm M MA VEG) 12.30-17, 19-24h
Santa Filomena 102, Bellavista *M° Baquedano* ☎ (02) 732 7036
🖳 www.restaurantalibaba.cl
Middle Eastern and Arabian cuisine.

■ **Capricho Español** (! AC B CC GLM M MA OS RES s WL) 20-3h
Purísima 65, Bellavista *M° Baquedano* ☎ (02) 777 7674
🖳 www.caprichoespanol.cl
Spanish and international cuisine. Great food and friendly atmosphere. Most popular gay restaurant in Chile.

■ **Metropolitana** (! B GLM M)
Huerfanos 2897 ☎ (09) 9231 2441 🖳 www.metropolitanarestaurant.cl

SEX SHOPS/BLUE MOVIES

■ **Libreria Gallery** (g MA)
Merced 832-43, Centro *M° Sta. Lucia or U. De Chile* ☎ (02) 695 7137
Large selection of adult magazines and videos, and Santiago's gay magazine Lambda News.

SEX CINEMAS

■ **Cine Apolo** (G VS) 10-22h
Diagonal Cervantes 802, Subterraneo *City centre* ☎ (02) 632 7535

SAUNAS/BATHS

■ **Baños Metro** (AC b CC DR DU G GH MSG SA SB SL VS)
13-24, Fri & Sat -3h
Almirante Montt 471 *M° Bellas Artes* ☎ (02) 633 13 21
🖳 www.bañosmetro.cl
On two floors.

■ **Il Palatino** (DR MSG SA SB VR) 14-23.30h
Carmen 225 *M° Santa Lucia almost at the corner Curico in fronto of Blas Caña church* ☎ (02) 633 6421 🖳 www.ilpalatino.jimdo.com

■ **Sauna 282** (! AC B CC DR DU f FH G m MA MSG PI RR SA SB VS WH) Mon-Thu 13-1, Fri-Sun (non-stop)
Bellavista 282 *M° Bellas Artes, between Loreto & Patronato*
☎ (02) 777 1709 🖳 www.282cl
Three levels, cubicles available.

LEATHER & FETISH SHOPS

■ **Dimension** (cc G MA)
Monjitas 294, Centro *M° Bellas Artes* ☎ (02) 638 7718
Fashion, leather, videos, DVDs and sex shop.

TELECOMMUNICATION

■ **Liberaccion** (G)
Nataniel Cox 78 ☎ (02) 373 8132
🖳 www.wix.com/mancinicl/liberaccion#!
Gay cyber cafe.

■ **Scanner** (G) 24hrs
Nueva Los Leones 0120 🖳 www.escanner.jimdo.com
Gay cyber cafe.

DVD SHOPS

Please note that the commercial use of pornography is forbidden under Chilean law. Magazines and videos may be bought by adults (18 years and older) for private use only.

HOTELS

■ **Bed and Breakfast (Casa Moro)** (AC B bf CC GLM m OS) All year
C/. Corte Suprema 177 ☎ (02) 696 9499
🖳 www.bed-and-breakfast-santiago.cl

■ **Hotel del Patio** (BF CC H MA OS WI) All year
Pío Nono 61 *M° Baquedano* ☎ (02) 732 7571 🖳 www.hoteldelpatio.cl
Ten comfortable and modern, ensuite rooms. All rooms have LCD screen TVs, air-conditioning and central heating. Room rates include buffet breakfast.

■ **Julissa Palace** (B BF CC glm M OS VS WH) All year
Paseo Huérfanos 2293, Centro ☎ (02) 671 0565
The Julissa Palace has 46 rooms and is situated in the centre of downtown Santiago. Not a gay hotel but friendly and a great location.

■ **Hoteles Príncipe** (AC B BF CC glm M VS WH)
C/. Mac Iver nº 175 Piso 4, Of. 41 ☎ (02) 639 5491
12 rooms situated in the city centre.

HEALTH GROUPS

■ **REDOSS**
Melipilla 3432 ☎ (02) 736 55 42 🖳 www.redoss.cl
HIV Tests. Counselling. Education.

CRUISING

-Plaza Italia (g MA r) (Avenida Vicuña Mackenna corner Avenida Providencia, next to entrance of M° Baquedano and the Restaurante Prosit, after 22h, very busy on WE)
-Parque Metropolitano, near the Jardín Japones (lots of actions in the wood, days and night, AYOR police action)
-Plaza de Armas (g MA R) (Ahumada corner Compañía, after 21h)
-Avenida Providencia (g MA) (from 22h)
-Parque Bustamante from Bilbao or Tobalava (AYOR g MA T, after 23h)
-Parque Uruguay (AYOR g MA) (from Avenida Los Leones & Avenida Manuel Montt, along Mapocho river in Providencia, after 15h)
-Parque Gran Bretaña (AYOR g MA) (Between Avenida Providencia and Mapocho River, from Avenida Elcodoro Yáñez to Avenia Vicuña Mackenna in Providencia, after 21h)
-Cerro Santa Lucía (AYOR g MA R) (daytime only)
-Plaza Indira Gandhi (AYOR g R) (Avenida Santa María, next to the clinic INDISA and the Sheraton Hotel in Providencia, along the river and next to Plaza Indira Gandhi, after 15h, busy at night)
-Parque Forestal (AYOR g MA) (from Plaza Italia to Miraflores, along the river Mapocho in Santiago Centro, be very careful at night)
-Paseo Ahumada (g MA) (from the Alameda Bernardo O'Higgins to the Plaza de Armas in Santiago Centro, after 21h)
-Paseo Huérfanos (g MA) (from C/. Santa Lucía to C/. Bandera, Santiago Centro, after 21h).

Talca ☎ 041

DANCECLUBS

■ **Taboo** (B D GLM S ST)
Camino Antiguo a Pencahue Km 1, s/n ☎ (09) 6247 4052
🖳 www.taboo.cl

Valdivia ☎ 063

DANCECLUBS

■ **BlueQueen** (B D GLM S ST) Wed-Sat 23-?h
Caupolican Esq. Andwanter
🖳 www.facebook.com/profile.php?id=1655691515

GUEST HOUSES

■ **Aires Buenos** (b bf cc GLM H I m OS WO) All year
García Reyes 550 ☎ (063) 222 202 🖳 www.airesbuenos.cl

Valparaíso ☎ 032

CAFES

■ **Exodo** (B GLM) Wed-Thu 21.30-3.30 & Fri-Sat 22-4.30h
C/. Blanco Nº 298 ☎ (032) 223 1118
🖳 http://www.paganoindustry.cl/exodo/index.html

DANCECLUBS

■ **Babilonia** (B D GLM S ST)
Ecuador 57 ☎ (09) 8290 2849 🖳 Facebook babilonia discotheque

■ **Pagano** (! B D glm) Mon-Son 23-?h
C/. Blanco Nº 236. Esq Clave ☎ (032) 476 7475
🖳 : www.paganoindustry.cl/pagano/index.html

■ **Runway** (B D GLM S ST)
Yungay 2193 Esquina General Cruz ☎ (09) 9149 4274
🖳 http://www.facebook.com/profile.php?id=100001695784067&sk=info

CRUISING

-Plaza Victoria (g MA r) (17-24h)
-Avenida Pedro Montt (the two blocks leading to Plaza Victoria, late afternoon until late at night).

Viña del Mar ☎ 032

CAFES

■ **Openmind Cibercafé** (b GLM I m) Mon-Sat 12-1.30 & Sun 17-1.30h
C/. Von Schroeders Nº 27 🖳 www.openmindchile.cl

DANCECLUBS

■ **Divino** (! B D GLM S ST) Fri-Sat 24-?h
C/. Camino International Nº 530 *Recaña Alto*
🖳 nochedivino.blogspot.com
The largest gay club in Chile. Believed to be the largest gay club in South America. Up to 3000 people. Great shows. Mega-earthquakes proof.

TELECOMMUNICATION

■ **Vice Versa** (G) Mon-Sat 12-23h
Orompello 563 🖳 www.okviceversa.cl/cyber.html
Gay cyber cafe.

GUEST HOUSES

■ **Casa Olga** (AC b cc GLM m OS) All year
C/. 18 de Septiembre Nº 31 Esq. *Pasaje Olga - Recreo* ☎ (032) 318 2972
🖳 www.casa-olga.com

SWIMMING

-Los Marineros (G) (at the south end of Las Salinas, next to the Escuela Armamentos de la Marina Nacional).
-Dunas de Mantagua (G A) (north of Viña, between the beaches playa Ritoque and playa Roca Negra. Very popular. Take the bus P to Punta Piedra and exit at the beach between Concón and Quintero).
- Playa Luna (G NU). Chileís only legal nudist beach. In Horcon, 40km North of Viña del Mar. From Horcon harbourgh, walk North 4km. 50% gay. Very nice beach. Swimming safe.

CRUISING

-Calle Valparaíso (g MA) (main shopping area downtown, especially in the evening and late at night, near Samoiedo Cafe)
-Plaza Vergara (g MA) (busy at night).

China

Name: Zhongguo · Chine · Cina

Location: Eastern Asia

Initials: PRC

Time: GMT +8

International Country Code: ☏ 86

International Access Code: ☏ 00

Language: Mandarin Chinese or Putonghua

Area: 9,596,960 km² / 3,691,494 sq mi.

Currency: 1 Renminbi Yuan (RMB) = 10 Jiao

Population: 1,303,497,000

Capital: Beijing

Religions: Confucianism, northern Buddhism (Mahajana 100 Million), Taoism, Sunnite Moslem (14 Million)

Climate: The climate is extremely diverse and ranges from a tropical in the south, the Gobi desert region in the west and a sub-arctic climate in the north.

Important gay cities: Hong Kong and Shanghai

Homosexuality is not recognized in China. The age of consent is set at 14 for all. The spread of pornography to minors aged under the age of eighteen is punishable with imprisonment.

In mainland China, gay life often remains hidden because of the conservative traditional Chinese culture. Due to social and family pressure, most gay people living outside the major cities are still expected to marry and have children, while at the same time living a double life, hiding their gay life.

With the emergence of a liberated, sexually active gay community, the HIV figures in China are rising dramatically, creating unique challenges. AIDS education in China is complicated. Reliable statistics relating to the actual numbers of HIV infected men in China are not available - as many men do not identify themselves as homosexual. It is possible that as many as 4 percent of China's population (52 million people) are infected, due to the lack of knowledge about the virus. The Hong Kong based Chi Heng Foundation, which supports with AIDS orphans, teaches HIV prevention to gay men in China.

The government's policy toward the gay scene can be considered to be neutral. However, sometimes the gay scene is wrongfully accused of being involved with sex business, which the police treat harshly.

Offiziell gibt es in China keine Homosexualität. Das Schutzalter liegt einheitlich bei 14 Jahren. Die Verbreitung von Pornographie an Minderjährige unter 18 Jahren wird mit Gefängnis bestraft. Auf dem chinesischen Festland findet das schwule Leben, bedingt durch die traditionell konservative Kultur des Landes, noch immer im Verborgenen statt. Die meisten Schwulen außerhalb der größeren Städte geben dem Druck der Gesellschaft bzw. Familie nach und heiraten, haben Kinder und leben insgeheim ein Doppelleben.

Mit dem Entstehen einer befreiten, sexuell aktiven homosexuellen Gemeinschaft, steigen die Zahlen der HIV-infizierten in China drastisch. Die AIDS-Aufklärung in China ist ein kompliziertes Unterfangen mit besonderen Herausforderungen. Zuverlässige statistische Daten über tatsächlich HIV-infizierte Männer existieren in China nicht. Viele Männer identifizieren sich nicht als homosexuell. Schätzungsweise sind so-

gar 4 Prozent der chinesischen Bevölkerung (52 Millionen Menschen) wegen Unwissenheit über das Virus, infiziert.
Die in Hong Kong basierte Chi Heng Organisation unterstützt AIDS-Waisen und betreibt die HIV-Aufklärung bei Chinas Homosexuellen.
Die Regierungspolitik im Hinblick auf die Schwulenszene kann als neutral bezeichnet werden. Allerdings wird die Szene manchmal fälschlicherweise mit dem Sexgewerbe in einen Topf geworfen, welches von der Polizei streng verfolgt wird.

Officiellement l'homosexualité n'existe pas en Chine. La majorité sexuelle est fixée à 14 ans pour tous. La diffusion de pornographie à des mineurs de moins de 18 ans est punissable d'emprisonnement. Sur le continent chinois, la vie gay reste cachée du fait de la culture conservatrice traditionnelle du pays. La plupart des gays en dehors des grandes villes plient sous la pression de la famille ou de la société : ils se marient, ont des enfants et vivent une double-vie.
Avec la naissance d'une communauté homosexuelle active et libérée, le nombre de personnes infectées par le VIH a fortement augmenté. L'éducation sur le SIDA en Chine est une entreprise compliquée avec des enjeux particuliers.
Il n'existe pas en Chine de statistiques fiables sur les personnes atteintes du VIH. Beaucoup d'hommes ne s'identifient pas comme homosexuels. Selon des estimations, 4% de la population chinoise (52 millions de personnes) seraient infectées par ignorance du virus.
L'organisation Chi Heng basée à Hong-Kong assiste les orphelins du SIDA et soutient l'information sur le VIH chez les homosexuels chinois.
La politique gouvernementale est neutre envers la scène gay. Cependant la scène est parfois confondue par erreur avec la prostitution qui, elle, est fermement réprimée par la police.

La homosexualidad no existe oficialmente en China. La edad mínima para mantener relaciones sexuales está establecida en 14 años y la difusión de pornografía a menores de 18 años se castiga con penas de prisión. La vida gay en la China continental ha de ser llevada a cabo en la clandestinidad debido, en parte, a la cultura tradicionalmente conservadora del país. La mayoría de los hombres gays fuera de las grandes ciudades se ven obligados a ceder ante las presiones sociales y familiares para casarse y tener hijos, llevando así una doble vida secreta.
Con la aparición en China de una comunidad homosexual liberada y sexualmente activa, el número de infectados por VIH ha aumentado de forma pronunciada. La educación sobre el SIDA en China es una empresa complicada con problemas especiales.
En China no existen datos estadísticos fiables sobre el número de hombres infectados por VIH. Muchos hombres no se identifican como homosexuales y se estima que hasta un 4 por ciento de la población china (52 millones de personas) están infectadas debido a la ignorancia en relación al virus.
La organización Chi Heng, con base en Hong Kong, apoya a los huérfanos víctimas del SIDA y se encarga de expandir la educación sobre el VIH entre homosexuales chinos.
La política del gobierno en cuanto a la vida gay puede ser descrita como neutral, sin embargo, el ambiente gay se mete erróneamente en el mismo saco que la industria del sexo, la cual está estrictamente perseguida por la policía.

Ufficialmente in Cina l'omosessualità non esiste. L'età del consenso per i rapporti sessuali tra gay così come tra etero è di 14 anni. La diffusione della pornografia tra minorenni sotto i 18 anni è punibile con il carcere. Sulla terra ferma cinese, dove la cultura è di stampo tradizionalista e conservatrice, l'omosessualità non viene affatto vissuta con disinvoltura. La maggior parte dei gay che vive all'infuori dei grossi agglomerati cittadini cede alle pressioni familiari e sociali e quindi si sposano, fanno figli e conducono una doppia vita. Col crescere di una comunità omosessuale sessualmente più attiva e più libera cresce drasticamente anche il numero dei sieropositivi. Informare la gente sui pericoli dell'AIDS risulta essere in Cina un'impresa piuttosto difficile e complicata. In Cina non esistono dati statistici affidabili circa il numero di sieropositivi nel Paese. Molti uomini rifiutano di dichiararsi omosessuali. Con molta probabilità si stima che il 4% della popolazione cinese (52 milioni di persone) abbia contagiato il virus proprio a causa della disinformazione. La fondazione Chi Heng, con sede ad Hong Kong, si occupa di orfani affetti dall'AIDS e di fare campagne informative tra i gay cinesi. La politica del governo è abbastanza neutrale per quello che concerne la scena gay, tuttavia a volte si butta la scena gay nel calderone della prostituzione, che invece viene severamente perseguita.

Anshun ☎ 0412

CRUISING

-Jianshen Bath Hall
-Square in front of the railway station
-Xiaodongmen Park.

Baoding ☎ 0312

CRUISING

-Opposite Heibei Theater (Hebei Yingjuyuan).

Beijing ☎ 010

BARS

Alfa (AC B glm MA)
6 Xingfu Yi Cun Hutong ☎ 6413 0086
More gay on Fri.

Lantung Thai (B G MA OS)
LW-12 Solana Park, 6 Chaoyang Park Rd ☎ (010) 5905 6213
www.lantungbar.com
Boys night on Thu nights, popular in summer on large roof terrace. Attracts professionals, both expats and locals.

McQueen's (B g MA)
Tongli Studio, Sanlitun Rdoad *On the 4th floor* ☎ 6415 0388

Mesh (AC B g MA)
c/o The Opposite House, 1 Sanlitun Bei Rd, Sanlitun ☎ 6417 6688
www.theoppositehouse.com
Gay night on Thu.

Sobear (B D G I MA S WE)
B112, West Tower, Shangdu Soho, 8 Dongdaqiao St, Chaoyang District *1km north of the Yongan Li Station* ☎ (0159) 1050 8964
Bear bar.

Ten Bar (B d G MA S) 19-2h
Aihua Hotel, Tiantandong Li, Yi No 48 *50 m north of China Chess Academy, Yutingqiao North on South Second Ring Road* ☎ (010) 5120 5588
www.bjtenbar.com
Walk into the Xing Fu Hotel and go down the stairs on your left.

DANCECLUBS

Destination (AC B CC D G MA) Fri & Sat -4h
7 Gongti Xi Lu Rd, Chaoyang District *Near the Workers' Stadium*
☎ (010) 6551 5138 www.bjdestination.com
Modern decor, but expensive drinks. Cute and friendly staff. The most popular gay bar in Beijing at the moment.

RESTAURANTS

O Sole Mio (g M MA OS)
55 Xingfu Zhong Lu Jie Zuo Da Sha ☎ (010) 6417 7022
Simple Italian fare at reasonable prices. Outdoor seating in summer, 5 mins walk from Destination. Gay-friendly service from handsome waiters.

SAUNAS/BATHS

Batiya (b DU G m MSG S SA YC) 24hrs
82 Beijing Glory Mall North St (Bei Jing Guo Rui Gou Wu Zhong Xin

Bei Lu, Xuanwu district *M° Chongwenmen lines 2 and 5, take south east exit ,C', going south on Chongwenwai Da Jie, take first left (E) just before the Glory Mall, then 5 mins walk away, 2 elephant statues at the entrance* ☎ (010) 6717 7155 💻 www.bjbatiya.cn
Bring your own condoms.

■ **Feng Fan Wei Ye** (b DR DU G I m MSG RR SA WE WO) 11-2h
G/F Building 4, Xia Hong Miao, Guang An Men Wai, Xuanwu *From M° Fu Cheng Men line 2 catch bus 650 stop no. 9 in front of Hua Lian department store in direction of Xiao Hong Miao stop no. 21 - last stop; walk back 50 m to a building on your right with number 4 on it, and a row of shops on the ground floor* ☎ (010) 6346 5852
Also known as Tai Fan by locals, its original name. No over night stay possible. Bring your own condoms (cruisy!).

■ **Kai Yang** (b DR DU G m MA MSG PI SA SB) 8-24h, (Temporarily closed, need to check before going)
You An Men Wai Da Jie Dong San Tiao Yi Hao *Xuanwu district. Take a taxi and ask the taxi driver to call of directions* ☎ (010) 6356 4388
Directions: Beijing South Railway Station line 4, then 15 mins walk away going west; or take taxi to You An Men Wai Da Jie (second ring road south, you come off the second ring road at You An Men Qiao, going south), pass Macdonalds on your right hand side (W), past first traffic lights, then the sauna is down a narrow lane 50 m further on on your left (E) with an archway above the entrance.
Bring own condoms.

■ **Station Hall Spa** (b DR DU G I m MSG OC SA SB WE) 24hrs
A2 Ganyu Bystreet, Dong Dan North St, Dong Cheng District *M° Dengshikou line 5, take exit 'A', then 2 mins walk south, take right turn and go in entrance of Da Wan Hotel, go right down the stairs* ☎ (010) 6522 1069

MASSAGE

■ **SPA de Feng for Men only** (AC CC G MSG) 12-24h
Sunshine 100 C306, 2 Guanghua Road, Chaoyang District *Close to the China World Trade Centre, next to bonjour supermarket in Sunshine 100 building* ☎ (010) 8286 3879 💻 www.spadefeng.com
An upscale day-spa for men offers a wide selection of massages, waxing, facials, and spa packages. Cute therapists.

TRAVEL AND TRANSPORT

■ **ChinaMango Travel** (G)
☎ (0133) 5294 9596 💻 chinamango.blogspot.com
Professional officially licenced English speaking tour guide, offering personalised, discreet day and night tours, own car available for Beijing and other locations such as Chengdu, Pingyao, Xian and Xinjiang (Silk Road).

■ **Go Pink China** (GLM)
Huixin East Street, Chaoyang District ☎ (01) 371 872 97 98
💻 www.gopinkchina.com
„Go Pink China" offers fascinating city tours (Beijing, Shanghai & Xi'an) and national trips (Silk Road, Great Wall, Yangzi-River).

HOTELS

■ **Beijing YoYo Hotel** (BF H M) All year
10F Middle Section Of Sanlitun *Chaoyang district* ☎ (010) 641 733 88
💻 www.yoyohotel.cn
Very resonably priced hotel in a great location. Sichuan-style restaurant in the hotel.

■ **Hotel G** (AC B BF CC H m MA S) All year
A7 Gong Ti Xi Lu *Chaoyang district* ☎ (010) 655 236 00
💻 www.hotel-g.com
110 spacious, modernist rooms with a hint of glamour, a state-of-the-art gymnasium and two distinctive restaurants and bars offering superb food and a convivial atmosphere.

CRUISING

All these are AYOR, police patrols:
-Mudanyuan park near metro station
-Dongdan Park (beware of hustlers in extortion gangs)
-Outside main gate of Beida
-San Li He Park (opp. Diaoyutai guest house)
-Starbucks by Pacific Center
-University areas
-Near Wenhua He Yuyan Daxue.

Cangzhou ☎ 0317

CRUISING

-Long Distance Bus Terminal
-Opposite Jiuhe Hotel.

Changsha ☎ 0731

CRUISING

-Newspaper Post on May 1 Road
-Toilets near foreign language book shop.

Chengdu ☎ 028

BARS

■ **Beatles Bar** (B g MA)
67, 3rd Section Western First Ring Rd *Near Mianyang Hotel*

■ **Bian Zou (Variation Bar)** (B G MA S)
3/F 1st Club Jiuba, Hongxing Road Erduan
Cabaret.

■ **MC Club** (B D GLM MA OS S) 21-?h
1/F Haicheng Dasha, Tianxian Qiao Bei Rd *North street of Tianxian Bridge* ☎ (028) 8666 6029

■ **Mu Di Di (Destination)** (B G MA)
Ge Lin Pu Lan Te, 63 Huaxingdong Street
Karaoke.

SAUNAS/BATHS

■ **MC Sauna** (B DU G I MA MSG SB)
1/F Haicheng Bld *North street of Tianxian bridge* ☎ (028) 6603 8798

CRUISING

-Panda Square, near Shudu Bldg., Zongfu Rd.

Chongqing ☎ 0811

CRUISING

-Metropolitan Plaza shopping center attached to the Harbour Plaza Hotel
-Newspaper Wall (in the center of the walking mall).

Dalian ☎ 0411

CRUISING

-Jianmin Bath Hall
-Square in front of the Railway Station
-Zhongshan Park.

Fuzhou ☎ 0591

BARS

■ **Paradiso Café, Bar & Disco** (AC B D GLM M MA)
5.4 North Road *Near Fujian Sport Stadium, inside turn right*
European and Chinese food. Extensive wine list. Cute English-speaking staff.

CRUISING

-Small road between Dong Jie Kou post office and the Jin Min movie theater, best after 19h (g r YC)
-Toilet at Jiang Bing Park along Min river, best after 19h.

Guangzhou ☎ 020

BARS

■ **Bear Pub** (B G MA)
Liu Rong Bld, 61 Liu Rong Street ☎ (020) 6127 6012

■ **Rich-e** (B D g MA)
Tianhe Bld, 133 Ti Yu Xi Lu

■ **Velvet** (B D g MA)
1/F 403 International Electronic Mansion, Huanshi Dong Lu *Chinese Overseas Village* ☏ (020) 8732 7801

SAUNAS/BATHS

■ **Chuang Mei Li Jian Mei Zhong Xin** (B DU G MA RR SA SB) 18-?h
5/F 228 Haizhu Bei Lu *M° Simenkou* ☏ (137) 1177 7714

HOTELS

■ **Garden Hotel. The**
(AC B CC DU glm M MA MSG PI SA SB SOL WH WO) 9-23h
368 Huansi Dong Lu *City centre, 4 km from railways station*
☏ (020) 8333 2255 🖳 www.gardenhotel-guangzhou.com
Very large 5-star hotel complex. Not gay but some international airline crews stay here.

CRUISING

All these are AYOR:
-Beijing Rd
-Toilets at any foor at CITIC Plaza shopping mall (Tian-He District)
-Ji Nian Tang (underground station)
-Pearl Riverside near White Swan Hotel
-People's Park (gays usually hang out around the toilet on the west side of the park)
-Shamian Tennis Court
-Intersection of Zhongshan 4th Rd and Cangbian RD.

Guiyang ☏ 0851

CRUISING

- At People's Square around the Chairman Mao monument after dark. Very cruisy with YC.

Hangzhou ☏ 0571

BARS

■ **Jundu Club** (B D G MA S)
Near the intersection of Baochu Lu and Bei Shan Lu at the northern most shore of West Lake ☏ (0571) 8597 7186
Disco dancing starting about 22h, with karaoke going on before that. Crowd is a mix of locals and foreigners.

SAUNAS/BATHS

■ **Han Lin Chun** (B DR DU G MA MSG SA SB) 24hrs
Off Baochu Lu, between West Lake and Fen Qi Lu ☏ (0571) 8521 1745

Hankou ☏ 0451

CRUISING

-Xunlimen after dark to midnight near stop for Bus 703.

Harbin ☏ 041

SAUNAS/BATHS

■ **Mu Lian Hua** (B g SA WH)
115 Gong Le St, Dao Li District *Cnr. Jian Guo St*
Mixed crowd but seems quite active.

CRUISING

-Jiuzhan Park
-Yiman St
-Zhongshan Hotel
-The zoo, especially at the toilets.

Hong Kong

Location: Eastern Asia
Initials: HK
Time: GMT +8
International Country Code: ☏ 852 (no area codes)
International Access Code: ☏ 001 or 0080 or 009
Language: Chinese, English
Area: 1,092 km² / 414 sq mi.
Currency: 1 Hong Kong Dollar (HK$) = 100 Cents
Population: 7,061,200
Capital: Hong Kong
Religions: Christian majority; Buddhism; Confucianism
Climate: Tropical monsoon climate. Winters are cool and humid. Spring through summer is hot and rainy, fall warm and sunny.

Although gay rights in Hong Kong are slowly being implemented, such as the recently passed Domestic Violence Ordinance, which now also applies to gay couples, gay life still remains largely hidden or closeted due to the local conservative culture.
The main gay scene is located in Caseway Bay, Tsimshatsui and Mongkok. The most popular time for locals to go out is on Saturday night and evenings prior to a public holiday. The saunas are the most popular place for quick and uncomplicated sex. Most good saunas in Hong Kong provide free lube and condoms. The best time for a sauna visit is from 19-22h. Gay bars gay busy around midnight until the early morning. The Hong Kong Chinese generally prefer locals as opposed to the Chinese from Mainland China.
All drugs are illegal in Hong Kong and you can be searched by the police at any time. Prostitution is however legal in Hong Kong, unlike mainland China.
Gay events include the annual Gay Pride Parade in October and the Hong Kong Lesbian and Gay Film Festival and Mr. Gay Hong Kong Contest every November.

Obwohl homosexuelle Rechte in Hong Kong nun langsam eingeführt werden, wie die kürzlich verabschiedete Verordnung über häusliche Gewalt, die auch an homosexuelle Paare gerichtet ist, bleibt homosexuelles Leben wegen der lokalen konservativen Kultur noch größtenteils verborgen oder geheim. Die schwule Szene ist hauptsächlich in der Caseway Bay, Tsimshatsui und Mongkok ansässig. Die beste Zeit um auszugehen ist Samstagsnacht und Abende vor einem gesetzlichen Feiertag. Saunas sind die bevorzugten Orte für schnelle und unkomplizierte Sextreffen. Die meisten guten Saunas in Hong Kong stellen kostenloses Gleitgel und Präservative zur Verfügung. Die beste Zeit für einen Saunabesuch ist von 19 bis 22h. Schwule Bars werden erst gegen Mitternacht voll und bleiben oft bis zum Morgengrauen gut besucht. Die Hong Kong Chinesen bevorzugen im allgemeinen einheimische Männer im Gegensatz zu den Chinesen im Hauptland. Alle Arten von Drogen sind in Hong Kong verboten und Sie können durch die Polizei jederzeit gefilzt werden. Prostitution ist jedoch in Hong Kong, anders als auf dem Festland von China, nicht verboten. Die wichtigsten schwulen Veranstaltungen im Jahr sind die jährliche Gay Pride Parade im Oktober und die Lesbisch/Schwulen Filmfestspiele sowie den Mr. Gay Hong Kong Wettbewerb, die jeden November stattfinden.

Même si les droits des homosexuels s'établissent lentement comme le montre le décret récent sur les violences domestiques valable également pour les couples homosexuels, la vie homosexuelle reste en grande partie cachée ou dissimulée du fait de la culture conservatrice locale. La scène gay se concentre sur la Causeway Bay, à Tsimshatsui et Mongkok. Le meilleur moment pour sortir est le samedi soir et les soirées avant les jours fériés. Les saunas sont les lieux de prédilection des relations sexuelles rapides et faciles. La plupart des bons saunas à Hong Kong donnent des préservatifs et du gel. Le meilleur moment pour la visite d'un sauna est entre 19h et 22h. Les bars gays ne se remplissent souvent qu'à partir de minuit et restent pleins jusqu'au lever du jour. Les Chinois de Hong Kong, contrairement aux Chinois du continent préfèrent les autochtones.

Toutes les drogues sont interdites à Hong Kong et l'on peut se faire fouiller par la police à tout moment. Par contre la prostitution n'est pas interdite contrairement à la Chine continentale.
Les plus grandes manifestations gays sont la Gay Pride annuelle en octobre et le festival cinématographique gay et lesbien de même que le concours Mr. Gay Hong Kong qui se déroule en novembre.

Aunque se están empezando a introducir derechos para homosexuales en Hong Kong, como la legislación recientemente aprobada sobre la violencia doméstica, dirigida también a las parejas homosexuales, la vida homosexual se mantiene todavía oculta o en secreto debido, en gran parte, a la cultura local conservadora. El ambiente gay se localiza principalmente en la Bahía de Caseway, en Tsimshatsui y en Mongkok. Los mejores momentos para salir son los sábados por la noche y las noches previas a un día festivo. Las saunas son los lugares preferidos para encuentros sexuales rápidos y sin complicaciones. La mayoría de las saunas en Hong Kong disponen de lubricantes y condones gratuitos. El mejor momento para ir a una sauna es entre las 19 y las 22h. Los bares gays no se llenan hasta la medianoche y a menudo siguen abiertos hasta el amanecer. Los chinos de Hong Kong, a diferencia de los continentales, suelen preferir por lo general a los hombres locales.
Todos los tipos de drogas están prohibidas en Hong Kong, por esto la policía puede registrarle en cualquier momento. A diferencia de la China continental, la prostitución no es ilegal en Hong Kong.
Los principales eventos gays son el desfile anual del Orgullo Gay en octubre y el y el Festival de cine Gay/Lésbico así como el Mr. Gay Hong Kong Concurso tienen lugar cada Noviembre.

Sebbene ad Hong Kong i diritti degli omosessuali vengono pian piano affermandosi (come per esempio la recente ordinanza sulla violenza domestica estesa pure a coppie gay) l'omosessualità rimane comunque, a causa della forte cultura conservatrice, ancora un fenomeno per lo più nascosto o addirittura segreto. La scena gay si svolge soprattutto su Caseway Bay, Tsimshatsui e Mongkok. Il giorno migliore per uscire è il sabato sera o il giorno prima di una festa nazionale. Le saune sono i luoghi preferiti per incontri sessuali facili e veloci. La maggior parte delle saune in Cina mette a disposizione preservativi e lubrificanti gratis. Il miglior orario per andare in sauna è dalle 19 alle 22. I bar gay si riempono verso mezzanotte e rimangono pieni fino alle prime ore del giorno. Al contrario dei cinesi che abitano sulla terra ferma, i cinesi di Hong Kong preferiscono generalmente la gente del posto. Ad Hong Kong sono vietati tutti i tipi di droghe. La prostituzione invece, al contrario che sulla terra ferma, non è vietata. Le manifestazioni più importanti dell'anno sono il Gay Pride ad ottobre e il festival del cinema gay e lesbico come pure la competizione Mr. Gay Hong Kong a novembre.

NATIONAL PUBLICATIONS

DS (Dim Sum) Magazine
2/F, Qualipak Tower, 122 Connaught Rd West ✉ Hong Kong *Sai Ying Pun* ☎ 3150-8912 🖳 www.dimsum-hk.com
Hong Kong's first and only monthly gay lifestyle magazine. Q Guide is a map type gay scene directory published by DS Magazine.

NATIONAL GROUPS

AIDS Concern
5/F, Shau Kei Wan Jockey Club Clinic, 8 Chai Wan Rd., Shau Kei Wan ✉ Hong Kong ☎ 2898-4411 🖳 www.aidsconcern.org.hk
AIDS Concern is a registered charity that provides support services to people living with AIDS/HIV and HIV prevention education to gay men. Free HIV testing is available at local saunas.

Chi Heng Foundation
Box 3923, General Post Office ✉ Hong Kong ☎ 2517-0564 🖳 www.chihengfoundation.com
Organization that caters to AIDS prevention among MSM and sexual equality.

Hong Kong Aids Foundation
5/F, Shau Kei Wan Jockey Club Clinic, 8 Chai Wan Rd., Shau Kei Wan ✉ Hong Kong ☎ 2560-8528 🖳 www.aids.org.hk
A non-governmental social services organisation that supports those infected by HIV.

Horizons
Box 9837 ✉ Hong Kong ☎ 2815-9268 🖳 www.horizons.org.hk
A charity organisation that provides information, reference, education, counselling and referrals regarding sexual orientation issues in Hong Kong.

Rainbow of Hong Kong
Flat D, 7/F Lap Shun Bldg., 242 Nathan Rd, Jordon ✉ Hong Kong ☎ 2769-1069 🖳 www.rainbowhk.org
An organisation that promotes equal opportunities and sex education and to provide service to community needs with volunteer bases program.

Hong Kong – Hong Kong Island

BARS

Déjà Vu (AC B g P YC)
B/F, 41 Staunton St, Central ☎ 3481-9996
Small bar, hidden next to the temple in Soho.

Explode Bar & Karaoke (AC B CC G WE YC) 21-4h
9/F Jardine Centre, 50 Jardine's Bazzar, Causeway Bay *Across the street from SOGO department store* ☎ 2892-0993
Busy at weekends.

G Point (AC B G WE YC) Daily 21-4h
2/F Kingpower Commercial Bldg., 409-413 Jaffe Rd ☎ 2892-0993
Karaoke.

Lab. The (AC B G WE YC) 21-5h
3/F, Allways Centre, 468 Jaffe Rd, Causeway Bay *Back of Elizabeth House* ☎ 2838-1456
Friendly and trendy karaoke spot.

Psychic Jack Lounge (B CC G MA) Mon-Fri 19-3, Sat & Sun 21-3h
1/F, 30-32 Wyndham Street, Central ☎ 2868 6102
Former Works disco. Newly renovated. Sophisticated lounge. Newly introduced Happy Hours is from 7pm-10pm Monday to Friday.

Stroll (AC B G MA)
7 Mee Lun Street, Central *Near Gough Street* ☎ 2815 9005
Intimate bar.

Time (AC B CC G WE) 21-4h
B/F 65 Hollywood Rd., Central ☎ 2332-6565
Busy at weekends.

Volume (! B D G MA) Sun-Thu 19-2, Fri & Sat 19-4h
LG/F, 83-85 Hollywoood Road, Central *Corner of Hollywood Rd and Arberdeen Rd* ☎ 2857-7683 🖳 www.volume.com.hk
The most user-friendly bar as it's open and busy from around 21 to 3h most nights. Wednesday nights are the best - especially for the weekly free vodka offers for everyone until 20.30h!

Zoo (AC B CC G WE)
33 Jervois Street, Sheung Wan *Near Sheung Wan Market* ☎ 3583-1200
A bar on street level, visited by professionals after work. Busy at weekends

DANCECLUBS

Propaganda (P.P.) (! AC B CC D GLM MA VS)
Mon-Thu 21-3.30, Fri & Sat -5h
Lower Ground Floor, 1 Hollywood Rd., Central *MTR Central Station, opp. Central Police Station* ☎ 2868-1316
One of the largest gay bars/discos in Hong Kong. Busy from 1h.

SEX SHOPS/BLUE MOVIES

Comet (CC G) 15-22h
21/F Wah Hen Commercial Bldg., 381 Hennessy Rd., Wanchai *Next to Action Sauna* ☎ 2573-0902
Gay magazines, books, adult toys, swimwear and DVDs.

SAUNAS/BATHS

Action (! CC DR G I LAB NU RR SA SB SOL VS YC)
Sun-Fri 13-24, Sat & before public holidays 24hrs
1/F, Overseas Bldg., 417-421 Hennessy Rd., Causeway Bay *Causeway Bay MTR Exit B, above Hang Sheng Bank and next to Causeway Bay Fire Station* ☎ 2893-7027 🖳 www.hksauna.com
Hunk Spa is a large size sauna that is located right in the shopping district of Hong Kong. It has one of the largest nudist zones and Japanese Tatami (Sharing) for your own discovery. Discount for tourists. By ABC Gateway.

■ **Central Escalator (CE)** (AC B CC DR DU FC FH G I LAB M MSG RR SA SB SOL VS WH YC) 14-23h
2/F Cheung Hing Comm. Bld, 37-43 Cochrane Street, Central *M° Central Station, Exit D2, Lan Kwai Fong, Lyndhurst Terrace, above 7-eleven shop, opposite Lan Fong Yuen* ☎ 2581-9951 💻 www.gayhk.com/ce
Entrance from Gage Street, opposite „Park'n'Shops" main entrance. Centrally located popular sauna which attracts younger locals as well as international guests. Plenty of play spaces and free broadband internet access. Best from 14h daily. Free condoms and lube provided.

■ **Chaps** (AC B DR FC FH G m MA NU OS RR SA SB VS WH) 15.30-24, Sat -10h
Ground Floor, 15 Ming Yuen Western Street - North Point *MTR North Point, exit B1* ☎ 2570-9339

■ **Follow Me** (AC DU G SA SB VS) 24hrs
Shop B, G/F, 9 Old Bailey Street, Central *Enter at Stauton Street* ☎ 2810-0144

■ **Gateway** (! B CC DR FC FH G I LAB MA RR SA SB SOL VS WH) 14-1, Sat-Sun 13-2h
1/F, Kwong Ah Building, 114 Thomson Rd., Wan Chai *Wanchai MTR A3 Exit, next to Standard Chartered Bank and Hennessy Primary School* ☎ 2301-4500 💻 www.hksauna.com
The Flagship Sauna of ABC-gateway, the largest operator of men's saunas in Hong Kong.Gateway is an ultra-luxurious, comfortable and innovative spa with high standard of features such as individual LCD-TV in each room, extra large jacuzzi with hot and cold pool.

■ **My Way** (DU G MC SA SB SOL) 16-24, Sat 16 - Sun 24h non-stop
4/F, 340 Hennessy Rd., Wanchai ☎ 2574-9098
Special Discount for under 25

■ **QQ Fitness** (AC B DR DU G m OC SA SB VS) 24hrs
3/F King Dao Bldg, 14 Burrows Street, Wanchai *Near King Dao Theatre* ☎ 2527-7073 💻 www.geocities.com/qqsauna
Visited by mostly mature customers.

MASSAGE

■ **Dragonese Spa** (G MSG SB) 12-2h
18/F Bartlock Center, 3 Yiu Wa St., Causeway Bay ☎ 2893-0488 💻 www.dragonese-spa.com
Professional and friendly masseurs. Out calls available.

■ **Joy and Passion** (MSG) 15-24h
3/F United Bldg.,449 Hennessy Rd., Causeway Bay ☎ 2892-2853

■ **Prince Spa** (G MSG SB) 12-2h
Unit D, 4/F, Harvard Commercial Bldg., 105 Thomson Rd., Wanchai ☎ 2573-0233 💻 www.princesspa.com.hk

■ **Shanghai Onsen** (G MSG) 12.30-24h
22/F, Park Commercial Center, 180 Tung Lo Wan Rd., Causeway Bay *MTR Station Exit A1 next to Queen's College* ☎ 2573-4365 💻 www.shanghaionsen.com
Massage, rub-back, pedicure.

SWIMMING

-Middle Bay at South Bay Road. (Take bus from Central to Repulse Bay. Walk along the beach towards the South. Cruisy Sat afternoon and on Sunday. Action on the rocks between Middle Bay and South Bay. Wear good shoes because of the rocks)
-South Bay at South Bay Road
-Morisson Hill swimming pool in Oi Kwan Road, Wanchai
-Cheung Sha Beach, Lantau Island (Cruising between Upper and Lower Cheung Sha beaches and the one between the two beaches.

CRUISING

-Lan Kwai Fong public toilet and vicinity
-Ice House Street public toilet (Ice House street near Queen Road Central)
-Shing Wong Street public toilet (At the stairs on Hollywood Road, between Aderdeen Street and Man Mo Temple
-Middle Bay (Next to South Bay)
-South Bay and the beach in between South and Middle Bay
-California Fitness of Causeway Bay and Wanchai (In the steam rooms)
-Morrison Hill Road public swimming pool
-Times Square Shopping Mall (Top Floor Men's toilet and outside).

Hong Kong – Kowloon

BARS

■ **Boo Bar** (AC B G MA) Daily 20-5h
5/F, Pearl Oriental Tower, 225 Nathan Rd., Jordan *MTR Jordon Station Exit C1* ☎ 2736-6168 💻 www.boobarcom.hk
New bar opened in November 2010.

■ **New Wally Matt Lounge** (! AC B G I MA R) 17-4h
G/F, 5A, Hunphrey's Av, Tsim Sha Tsui *Tsim Sha Tsui MTR Station Exit A2* ☎ 2721 2568 💻 www.wallymatt.com
The only bar for foreigners where the staff speak English. Busy after 21h - especially at WE: Beware of money boys! Happy hour 17- 21h.

SEX SHOPS/BLUE MOVIES

■ **Male. Le** (G) 13-21h
Room B3, 2/F, Tsimshatsui Man., 83 Nathan Rd., Tsim Shat Sui ☎ 2368-8483
Gay magazines, books, magazine, adult toys, underwear, DVDs.

SAUNAS/BATHS

■ **ABC „All Boy Club"** (! AC CC DR f G I RR SA SB VS WH YC) 14-1h
6/F Cheong Hing Bldg, 72 Nathan Road, Tsim Sha Tsui *MTR Exit A2, About Citibank, entrance at Humphrey's Ave* ☎ 2301-4500 💻 www.hksauna.com
The premier sauna in town. It is an indulgence, a personal ritual, a comfortable and upbeat meeting place right in the tourist district in Hong Kong. Special promotion for tourists. By ABC-Gateway. The only sauna in Hong Kong that is equipped with sling and FF bench.

■ **Alexander 24 hours** (! CC DR F G I LAB MA RR SA SB SOL VS) 24hrs
1/F Wing Cheong Bldg., 404-412 Reclamation St. Mongkok *MTR Exit E1, Next to Langham Place Hotel and Langham Shopping Mall. Enter on Shan*

Tung St. ☎ 2148-0400 💻 www.hk-sauna.com
ABC-Gateway's ultra luxurious spa and sauna in Hong Kong. Alexander is specially crafted comfort for your enjoyment with the highest quality in every aspect. Extra large hot pool and maze in the steam room for your own discovery. Hot guy hard action 24hrs non-stop for you!

■ **Big Top** (DR SB) 15-24h
3/F Yuet Yuen Bldg., 17-19 Mongkok Rd, Mongkok *MTR Mong Kok Station Exit A2 – opposite the Dynasty Theatre* ☎ 2628-6196
Big Top is a new (opened July 2011) relatively compact sauna.In addition to a locker area and lounge, there is steam room, shower area, dark room and a number of relaxation cabins.

■ **Club Houzz** (DR g I RR SB) 15-24h
4/F Canton Plaza, 1125-1127 Canton Rd., Mongkok ☎ 3484-2770

■ **Colony** (B DR G m SA SB) 15.30-24, Fri & Sat -11, Sun 14.30-24h
2/F, 177 Prince Edward Road, West Kowloon *Above the beauty saloon* ☎ 3486-1342
New sauna opened in Jan 2010. Small and expensive.

■ **Double** (AC DU G MA SA SB SOL VS) 13-23h
8/F, Oriental House, 24-26 Argyle Street, Mongkok *MTR Mongkok Exit D3, Above Apple Shop* ☎ 2396-9595

■ **Galaxy** (AC b DR DU FC FH G M OC RR SA SB VR WH) 14-21h
5/F, Harilela Mansion, 81 Nathan Road, Tsim Sha Tsui *5th floor, next to Hyatt Regency Hotel, M° T.S.T-exit C2* ☎ 2366-0629
Large sauna frequently visited by mature and older crowd. Not luxuous at all (little bit dirty) but one of the few saunas where you can meet locals without making a date in advance.

■ **Hunter** (B DR G m MC SA SB) 24hrs
10/F Ko's House, 577 Nathan Road, Mong Kok *MTR Price Edward Station B2. Opposite Sino Center* ☎ 2138-8678 💻 www.huntersauna.com.hk
For members only, discount for young guys.

■ **KK Fitness** (AC B DR G m OC SA SB) 14-24h
16/F Block A, Fuk Lok Bld, 19-21 Jordan Rd *Near MTR at Yu Hwa Dept. Store on Nathan Road* ☎ 2388-3931
Mostly with mature/older crowd. Dinner is available on a daily basis.

■ **Ni-chome** (AC DU G m MA NU SA SB) 15-4h
8/F, Parmanand House, 51-52 Haiphong Road, Tsim Sha Tsui *MTR Exit C1* ☎ 2723-1881
All nude sauna.

■ **Rainbow** (DU G LAB MC SB VS)
14/F K.K. Centre, 46-54 Temple St, Yau Ma Tei *MTR: Yau Ma Tei - exit C* ☎ 2385-6652
Chubby crowded.

MASSAGE

■ **Eden Spa** (AC G MSG) 12-24h
9/F, Parmanand Hse., 51-52 Haiphong Rd., Tsimshatsui *MTR Exit A1* ☎ 2891-1284 💻 www.edenspa.com.hk
Former Poseidon Health Centre. Out calls available.

■ **Heaven Spa** (AC G MSG) 14-24h
7/F The Lamma Centre, 13-15 Parkes Street *Jordan MTR C2 Exit* ☎ 2736-7711
Easy to find and very clean, but very expensive! Also „special massages" (sensual ones) available. No credit card payments possible, only cash.

■ **Spa Homme** (AC G MSG) 14-24h
B1, 4/F Burlington House, 90-94 Nathan Road, Tsim Sha Tsui ☎ 3620-3420

SWIMMING

-Gold Coast Beach, Castle Peak Road (The gay area is at the end of the beach)
-Cheung Sha Beach, Lantau Island (Cruising between Upper and Lower Cheung Sha Beach).

CRUISING

-California Fitness Gyms in Mongkok, Tsimshatsui (In the steam rooms)
-Tsimshatsui Ocean Center toilet (3rd Floor outside men's toilet)
-Mongkok Road public toilet (Top floor men's toilet)
-Kowloon Park swimming pool (Changing room and shower area)

Kunming ☏ 0871

DANCECLUBS

■ **Top One Disco** (AC B D GLM m MA) 20h-late
Baita Street *Next to the Bolan Hotel*
Popular and cruisy in the evenings.

Lijiang ☏ 0888

BARS

■ **Dadawa** (AC B glm m MA)
Popular hang out, very mixed, cruisy later.

GUEST HOUSES

■ **Home Lijiang** (GLM I NR RWS) All year
30 Guang Yee Street ☏ 518 6023 🖳 www.homelijiang.net
Upscale boutique 10-room hotel in the Old Town of Lijiang. All rooms in Yunnan ethnical sytle with modern hygienic facilities, cable TV and free internet access.

Nanjing ☏ 025

BARS

■ **Red Bar (Hong Ba)** (B glm MA S)
Beijing East Rd ☏ (133) 2781 1472
■ **Zhongtian Yu Le Gong** (B g MA S)
Ping Jiang Fu Rd *Nearby the Confucian Temple shopping area*
☏ (137) 0147 0552

Qingdao ☏ 0137

BARS

■ **Dragon** (AC B cc D GLM H m MA S SNU ST t VS) Daily 19.30-4h
12 Gu Tian Lu *Xin Jia Zhuang Station* ☏ (0137) 9248 3550
Gay bar in the city centre, daily changing show programs, very friendly young staff.
■ **Yang Yang Yan Yi Ba** (B G MA S)
17 Chang Er Lu ☏ (0137) 9532 9595

Shanghai ☏ 021

China's international city, Shanghai, is home to a growing gay crowd from around China, Asia and the rest of the world. There are still a limited number of gay venues to choose from, despite the strides made since 1995. The scene changes rapidly, and the best way to find out what's happening is to get out there and talk to the locals and the foreign residents at the bars.

Shanghai beherbergt eine immer stärker aufblühende Community, die aus China, ganz Asien und dem Rest der Welt kommt. Trotz der Fortschritte, die seit 1995 erzielt wurden, gibt es nur wenige schwule Treffpunkte. Die Szene verändert sich sehr schnell. Am besten erkundigt man sich in den Lokalen bei einheimischen oder ausländischen Bürgern nach den aktuellen Highlights.

Shanghai héberge une très florissante communauté originaire de Chine, d'Asie et du reste du monde. Malgré des progrès réalisés depuis 1995, on trouve toujours peu de lieux de rencontre gay. La scène change très vite. Pour se renseigner sur les meilleures adresses de la scène, la meilleure solution est de demander aux habitants ou aux étrangers sur les lieux gays.

Shangai aloja a una floreciente comunidad proveniente de China, Asia y del resto del mundo. A pesar de los avances logrados desde 1995, aún hay muy pocos lugares de encuentro para los gays. La escena cambia con gran rapidez, por lo cual lo mejor es recabar información en los locales, entre los habitantes y los visitantes, sobre los puntos de mayor interés de la movida gay en el momento.

L'emergente community di Shangai è piuttosto internazionale: molti cinesi e asiatici in genere e persone dal resto del mondo. Nonostante i passi avanti che si sono fatti dal 1995, ci sono pochi punti di incontro per i gay. La scena cambia molto velocemente. È meglio quindi informarsi con la popolazione locale o straniera sul da farsi in città.

BARS

■ **9 Element** (AC B G MA S) 21-1h
9 Gaolan Lu *Junction of Sinan Lu; Metro Line 1, Shaanxi Nan Lu station*
☏ (133) 8605 8821 (mobile)
■ **Bobo's** (AC B D G MA S) 13-1h
1011 Qiujiang Street *3/F Chutian Hotel, near Huiwen Lu*
☏ (138) 1638 8565 (mobile) 🖳 www.bobosbar.com
Bear bar.
■ **Box. The** (AC B D GLM MA S) 19-2h
Oudeng Bowling Square, 10 Hengshan Lu (near Yongjia Rd) *Near M° line1, Hengshan Lu, exit 4* ☏ (021) 6474 8558 🖳 www.shthebox.com
■ **Cloud 9** (AC B G MC) 20.30-1h
Room 1, 406 Xinhua Lu ☏ (021) 5230 5979
Mainly Japanese customers.
■ **Eddy's Bar** (! AC B G MA) 20-2h
1877 Huaihai Zhong Road (near Tianping Road) ☏ (021) 6282 0521
Shanghai's longest operating and very popular gay night spot. Friendly owners and staff. Good place to find out what's going on in the local scene.
■ **Hunter Bar** (AC B G MA) 20-2h
86 Nanyang Road, Jingan District *Near The Hotel Portman Ritz Carlton, behind Nanjing Xi Lu/Xikang Lu* ☏ (021) 6258 1438
Off the street in a small lane, a small friendly bar tucked away in a residential area, mainly Chinese and Japanese crowd.
■ **K.M. Bar** (AC B G MC) 20-2h
276 Nanchang Road *Between South Maoming Rd and No.1 Ruijing Rd*
☏ (021) 6473 2121
Small venue with a local, older following. Visitors welcome.
■ **Kevin's** (B CC GLM m MA) 11-2h
No.4 Lane 946 ChangLe Road, JingAn District *Down the lane and through a small garden on the right* ☏ (021) 6248 8985 🖳 www.kevinssh.com
Pleasent place. Nice mixed crowd. Special low priced drinks at the weekend.
■ **OZNZ** (AC B glm m MA)
1153 Kaixuan Lu, Zhongshan Park ☏ (150) 0001 0275 (mobile)
■ **Rice** (AC B GLM MA) 20-1h
532 Fahuazhen Lu *Near Dingxi Lu* ☏ (021) 5230 8772
■ **Transit Lounge** (AC B G MA) 20.30-2h
141 Tai An Road, Chang Ning District *Near Hua Shan Lu*
☏ (021) 6283 3051 🖳 www.h5.dion.ne.jp/~pizzi5/tl-top.html
Elegant and sophisticated.

DANCECLUBS

■ **Club D2** (! AC B D GLM YC) Wed-Sat 20.30h-late
505 Zhong Shan Road South, The Cooldocks *Near Fu Xing Rd East*
☏ (021) 6152 6543 🖳 www.clubd2.cn
Hip and trendy club. 3 floors. One of hottest places to dance. Happy hour.
■ **Lai Lai Dance Hall** (AC B D G MC ST) Fri-Sun 19-21h
235 Anguo Road, 2nd floor *Near Zhoujiazui Rd, Hongkou district, metro line 4 Linping Rd, exit 2* ☏ (150) 2174 7399 (mobile)
Attracting more mature men.
■ **Shanghai Studio** (! AC B D GLM MA s VS) 21-3h
1950 Huaihai Middle Road, Unit 4 *Near Wukang Lu, opp. Tianping Rd, basement level* ☏ (021) 6283 1043 🖳 www.shanghai-studio.com
Popular. Unpretentious bar, converted bomb shelter with several rooms. One of the best clubs in Shanghai.
■ **Utoobar** (B D GLM MA)
288 Taikang Road 🖳 www.youtoobar.com

RESTAURANTS

■ **Simply Thai** (AC CC M NG OS) 11-22.30h
5C Dongping Lu ☏ (021) 6445 9551 🖳 www.simplythai-sh.com
Reservations recommended. Gay owned and operated, with friendly staff. A second restaurant is located at: Cnr Ma Dang & Xing Ye Rd, Xintiandi.

SAUNAS/BATHS

■ **Dingling Men's Club** (B DU G I m MA MSG P SA SB VS WH) 24hrs
775 Yanchang Middle Road, Zhabei District ☏ (021) 6152 6543
🖳 www.shdlclub.com
Probably the biggest gay sauna in Shanghai.

■ **Lian-Bang** (AC DR G MA MSG R RR WE WH) 24hrs
228 Zhizaoju Road, Lu-wan District ☏ (021) 6313-5567
This is one of Shanghai's most notorious and long standing gay bathhouses. Not exactly the cleanest, but definitely one of the most popular among the locals.
■ **Studio 2006** (B DU G m MA SA SB) 16-24, Fri-Sun 14-1h
1639 Huashan Rd., No. 10 ☏ (021) 5230 6916 🖳 www.studio2006.com.cn
Sophisticated men's sauna. Modern Asian decor in a labyrinth of a sexy play space.
■ **Yinxin** (b DU G m MA SB) 24hrs
6 Linping Rd., Hongkou ☏ (021) 6541 6530
Action in the showers and steam rooms. No overnight stays possible.

CRUISING

Commentary: Open air and public area cruising has slacked off as more gay venues have opened. Many rent boys frequent these locations, as well as thieves and plain clothes police. All places are AYOR!
-People's Square on the southeasteast side, near Xi Zang Zhong Lu
-Public Toilet in People's Square, in city center
-Da-mu-qiao (Great Wooden Bridge)
-Small Park (on Zhao-jia-bang Rd between Jiu-jiang Rd and Han-kou Rd).
-Public newspaper wall corner Nanjing Rd and Jiang-xi Mid Rd.

Shenyang ☏ 024

BARS

■ **Bar Place** (B G MA)
25 Caitajie, ShenYang-city ☏ (024) 8199

CRUISING

-Ba Yi Park (r)
-Lu Xun Park
-Along Nan canal (Park)
-Wan Liu Tang Park.

Shenzhen ☏ 0755

BARS

■ **Auld Lang Syne** (B G MA S)
2/F JinYuan Bld, 88 Song Yuan Rd, Luohu District ☏ (0755) 2588 7000
Busy on WE. Arrive before 22h.
■ **Why Not** (B D G MA)
2/F YunPeng Hotel, N3 Block Hongling Bldg, Hongling Nan Lu
☏ (0755) 2586 4798
Karaoke. Disco after midnight.

DANCECLUBS

■ **Barden-Barden Disco Club** (B D GLM S)
2/F No. 2033 Hong Ling Middle Rd *Opposite Shenzhen Humanity Hospital*
☏ (0755) 8241 8028
Hot dance mixes and shows nightly. Special events Fri-Sun. Karaoke 19.30-23, shows 23-0.30, disco from 0.30h-late.
■ **Ice Cream Disco** (B D GLM MA)
Huishang Mingyuan, Nanqing Street, Dong Men

SAUNAS/BATHS

■ **Yand Gang Sauna** (DU g MC SB VS WE) 24hrs
3/F 20333 Middle Hong Lim Rd., Fu Tain District *Across the street from Shenzhen Humanitarian Hospital* ☏ (0755) 2592-3353
Visit by local working class Chinese. Busy at weekends.

CRUISING

-Donghuan markets
-Train station
-Around Xindu Hotel main streets.

Suzhou ☏ 0512

BARS

■ **Deep Breath** (B G s YC)
93 ShuYuanXiang Rd *400 m west of the intersection of RenMin and Shi-Quan Rds* ☏ (0512) 6717 1060
Friendly atmosphere.

SAUNAS/BATHS

■ **Hai Xing** (DU G MA SA SB)
499 Zhu Hui Rd *About 1 km east of Sheraton, look for the blue vertical sign with red characters* ☏ (0512) 6519 5810
Best Fri & Sat evenings 18-24h.

CRUISING

-Suzhou Park, Gong Yuan Lu South off Gan Jiang Lu near small lake. Best WE early afternoon. Some hustlers.

Wuhan ☏ 027

BARS

■ **Dibao** (B d GLM MA)
Louyu Rd, Wuchang *Near the Wuhan Physical Exercise College*
☏ (134) 3719-1944
Friendly for foreigners.
■ **Mintiange** (B G MC)
Qianjin Wulu *Qianjin Five Rd, close to Jianghan Rd and Zhongshan Dadao*
■ **Romantic Life** (B GLM YC)
3-4 Jiangtan Park, Yangtze Riverside Esplanade, Hankou ☏ (027) 8278 9041
Friendly and popular gay bar on the Yangzi riverside. Busiest early on Fri & Sat.

SAUNAS/BATHS

■ **Han Lin Chun** (B DU G MA MSG SA SB)
3/F 25 Hai Shou Jie ☏ (133) 8751-7097
Private rooms available.

CRUISING

-Xunlimen, Hankou (nights).

Xiamen ☏ 0592

BARS

■ **Nong Qing Gan Wan Jiu Ba** (B D GLM MA)
G/F Da Tong Lu Xin Lu Jie *Street is a small intersection in downtown*
☏ (135) 9951 4790
Karaoke and disco bar.
■ **Raise** (B GLM MA S)
Back of Ming Fa Guang Chang Mall, Jia He Lu ☏ (0592) 520-1819

CRUISING

-Facilities at the ferry pier (r)
-Longyan facilities located on Xianbei Lu (close to the foot bridge)
-Lun Du, at the sea-front close to the pier (r).

Xian ☏ 029

BARS

■ **Club 21** (B GLM MA S)
21 East Lane 6, Heping Lu (Peace Rd) ☏ (029) 8744 5455
Friendly crowd of locals.
■ **In D** (B D G S)
Taibaoji Xiang *Inside Zhu Qu Men* ☏ 8762 6676
■ **Moon Palace** (B D G S YC)
Dong 7 Dao Xiang
Drag show, comedy skits and singers start to entertain nightly at 22.30h.

SAUNAS/BATHS

■ **Bei Ou Guan** (b DU G MA PI SB) 13-22h
123 Dong Xin Jie *50m east of Dong Xin Jie Night Market* ☏ (029) 8743 7015
Clean, comfortable, elegant, and good service.

Zhuhai ☏ 0756

BARS

■ **Blue Bar** (B G MA)
Shui Wan Lu No. 178, Zhuhai-Gongbei
Karaoke.

Colombia

Name: Kolumbien · Colombie
Location: Northwest coast of South America
Initials: CO
Time: GMT -5
International Country Code: ☏ 57 (omit 9 of area codes)
International Access Code: ☏ 009
Language: Spanish
Area: 1,141,748 km² / 439,735 sq mi.
Currency: 1 Columbian Peso (Col$) = 100 Centavos
Population: 44,915,000
Capital: Bogotá
Religions: 95% Roman Catholic
Climate: Tropical climate along the coast and eastern plains. The highlands are cooler.
Important gay cities: Bogota, Cali, Cartagena & Medellin

The age of consent in Colombia is 14 years of age. On 28 January 2009, the Constitutional Court of Colombia had ruled that gay and lesbian couples should enjoy the same rights as heterosexuals. A further ruling passed by the Constitutional Court in August 2011 is now giving the country's politicians two years' time for getting a law underway that provides homosexuals with the same status in civil partnerships as heterosexuals. If the Senate fails to find a solution by 2013, homosexuals will be able to have their partnerships registered before a notary. The conservative government meanwhile continues to insist that marriage should be the exclusive reserve of mixed-sex couples.
On the 6th March 2009 the human rights defender and LGBTI representative of the organisation Tinku, Álvaro Miguel Rivera was murdered in the city of Cali. This is the second murder of an LGBTI rights defender in Colombia in the past 13 months. Colombia Diversa, the leading LGBT rights organization in Colombia, was a driving force in this cause.
The gay scene in Bogotá is increasing in size. There are many gay venues in the city. An annual Gay Pride Parade takes place each June in Bogotá as well as in Medellin, and Cali. In November 2009 the first public event for sexual diversity in Cartagena took place. The security situation for tourists to Colombia has generally improved over the last five years. Nevertheless, it is presently advisable to avoid travelling in the Departaments Chocó, Putumayo, Nariño and Arauca in particular.

In Kolumbien liegt das Schutzalter bei 14 Jahren. Am 28. Januar 2009 entschied das kolumbianische Verfassungsgericht, dass schwule und lesbische Paare die gleichen Rechte wie Heterosexuelle genießen dürfen. Ein weitergehendes Urteil des Verfassungsgericht im August 2011 zwingt die Politiker dazu, innerhalb der nächsten zwei Jahre ein Gesetz auf den Weg zu bringen, dass Homosexuelle in einer Lebenspartnerschaft nicht schlechter gestellt werden dürfen als Heterosexuelle. Falls der Senat bis 2013 keine Regelung findet, können Homosexuelle ihre Partnerschaft beim Notar registrieren lassen. Die konservative Regierung besteht weiterhin darauf, dass die Ehe nur Mann und Frau vorbehalten sein soll.
Am 6. März 2009 wurde der Kämpfer für die Menschenrechte und LGBTI Vertreter der Organisation Tinku, Álvaro Miguel Rivera im Zentrum von Cali ermordet. Das war der zweite Mord an einem LGBTI Aktivisten Kolumbiens in den vergangenen 13 Monaten. Colombia Diversa, die führende LGBT Organisation Kolumbiens, war eine treibende Kraft für diese Gesetzesänderung.
Die Schwulenszene in Bogotá wächst derweil ständig. Es gibt viele schwule Treffpunkte in dieser Stadt. Es finden jährliche Gay Pride Paraden, jeden Juni in Bogotá, sowie in Medellin und Cali statt. Im November 2009 wurde die erste öffentliche Veranstaltung für die sexuelle Vielfältigkeit in Cartagena durchgeführt. Die Sicherheitslage in Kolumbien hat sich in den letzten fünf Jahren generell verbessert. Gegenwärtig wird allerdings von Reisen in die Departamentos Chocó, Putumayo, Nariño und Arauca abgeraten.

En Colombie, la majorité sexuelle est fixée à 14 ans. Le 28 janvier 2009, la Cour Constitutionnelle colombienne a décidé que les couples gays et lesbiens devaient disposer des mêmes droits que les hétérosexuels. Un arrêt plus large de la Cour Constituionnelle en août 2011 oblige les politiques à proposer une loi dans les deux prochaines années mettant les homosexuels en couple sur le même plan que les hétérosexuels. Au cas où le Sénat ne trouve aucun règlement, les homosexuels pourront enregistrer leur partenariat devant un notaire. Le gouvernement conservateur s'obstine à réserver le mariage aux couples homme-femme.
Le 6 mars 2009, Álvaro Miguel Rivera, défenseur des Droits de l'Homme et représentant de l'association LGBT Tinku, fut assassiné dans le centre de Cali. Ce fut le deuxième assassinat d'un activiste LGBT ces 13 derniers mois.
Colombia Diversa, la plus grande organisation LGBT du pays, est pour beaucoup dans ce changement législatif.
La scène gay à Bogotá est en développement constant. Les gays ont de nombreux lieux où se rencontrer. Tous les ans des Gay Prides ont lieu, en juin à Bogotá ainsi qu'à Medellin et Cali. En novembre 2009, la première manifestation publique pour la diversité sexuelle a eu lieu à Cartagena. Le niveau de sécurité en Colombie s'est amélioré ces cinq dernières années. Il est cependant déconseillé actuellement de se rendre dans les départements de Chocó, Putumayo, Nariño et Arauca.

En Colombia la edad mínima para mantener relaciones sexuales es de 14 años. El 28 de Enero de 2009, la Corte Constitucional de Colombia dictaminó que las parejas de gays y lesbianas deberían tener los mismos derechos que los heterosexuales. Una decisión ulterior por parte de la Corte Constitucional, en agosto de 2011, obligó a los políticos a incluir, en los próximos dos años, una ley que ofrezca a los homosexuales una forma de unión civil que sea equivalente a la heterosexual. Si no se presentara al Senado ninguna normativa en 2013, los homosexuales podrán registrar su unión civil ante notario. El gobierno conservador sigue insistiendo en que el matrimonio solo lo constituye un hombre y una mujer.
Álvaro Miguel Rivera, el activista pro derechos humanos y representante de la organización LGTBI Tinku, fue asesinado el 6 marzo de 2009 en el centro de Cali. Este fue el segundo asesinato de activistas LGTBI en Colombia en los últimos 13 meses.
Colombia Diversa, la organización LGBT más importante de Colombia, fue la fuerza impulsora de este cambio en la legislación.

Mientras tanto, el ambiente gay en Bogotá sigue creciendo constantemente. Hay muchos locales de ambiente gay en esta ciudad y también cuentan anualmente con desfiles del Orgullo Gay en Bogotá, Medellín y Cali cada mes de junio. En noviembre de 2009, el primer evento público de la diversidad sexual se realizó en Cartagena y, aunque por lo general la situación de seguridad en Colombia ha mejorado en los últimos cinco años, en la actualidad, sin embargo, se desaconseja viajar a los departamentos de Chocó, Putumayo, Arauca y Nariño.

In Colombia l'età del consenso è di 14 anni. Il 28 gennaio del 2009 la Corte Costituzionale della Colombia ha deciso che le coppie dello stesso sesso possono poter godere degli stessi diritti delle coppie eterosessuali. Un'altra sentenza della Corte Costituzionale si è spinta anche più in oltre: ad agosto del 2011, infatti, la Corte ha messo alle strette i politici intimandogli di mettere in cammino, entro i prossimi due anni, una legge che equipari le unioni omosessuali a quelle eterosessuali. Nel caso in cui il Senato non dovesse trovare un accordo entro il 2013, le coppie dello stesso sesso potranno far registrare la propria unione dal notaio. Il Governo conservatore continua ad insistere sull'esclusività del matrimonio tra un uomo e una donna.

Il 6 marzo del 2009 Álvaro Miguel Rivera, attivista per i diritti umani e rappresentante LGBT dell'associazione Tinku, è stato assassinato nel pieno centro di Cali. Si tratta del secondo assassinio di un attivista colombiano LGBT nel giro degli ultimi 13 mesi. Colombia Diversa, la più importante associazione LGBT del Paese, è stata decisiva per la suddetta modifica di legge.

La scena gay di Bogotá cresce costantemente e i luoghi d'incontro per i gay non mancano. Il Gay Pride si svolge ogni anno a giugno nelle città di Bogotá, Medellin e Cali. A novembre del 2009, a Cartagena, si è svolta per la prima volta una manifestazione per la diversità sessuale. Negli ultimi cinque anni la Colombia è diventata più sicura, tuttavia, attualmente, viene comunque sconsigliato di addentrarsi in dipartimenti come Chocó, Putumayo, Nariño e Arauca.

NATIONAL GROUPS

Colombia Diversa
Calle 30A No. 6 - 22 Oficina 1102 ✉ Bogotá ☎ (01) 483 12 37
www.colombiadiversa.org
The most important LGBT group in Colombia.

Liga Colombiana De Lucha Contra El Sida
Avenida 32, N° 14-46 ✉ Bogotá www.ligasida.org.co
A non-profit organisation fighting AIDS.

Barranquilla ☎ 958

BARS

Studio 54 (! B G MC S)
Carrera 54 N°. 72-154 ☎ (958) 348 9266
Popular bar with good shows.

SAUNAS/BATHS

Ambine Aqua Club
Carrera 44 # 79-201

Casablanca (G P SA SB) 14-22h
Carrera 46 No. 74-101 ☎ (958) 312 680 0537 (mobile)

Cielo. El (DU G P SA SB) 15-22h
Carrera 54 No. 46-53 ☎ (958) 379 89 59

SWIMMING

-Playa Bololo - 30 mins from Barranquilla.

CRUISING

-Plaza Colón
-Plaza Bolívar and Paseo Bolívar
-Centro Comercial Portal del Prado
-Centro Comercial Buenavista

Bogotá ☎ 1

BARS

Anonimos (B G MA)
Carrera 9a, N° 60-33/37, Chapinero
Not the best place in town but the best day to go is on Tuesdays.

Blues Bar (B G MA OS S SNU) Thu-Sun 8-3h
Calle 86a, N° 13a-30, Zona Rosa *Northern suburb* ☎ (1) 616 7216
Good music, especially on Fridays.

Café. El (B g MA)
Calle 59, N° 13-32, Chapinero ☎ (1) 249 6512

Chase (! B G MC)
Calle 58 Bis No. 8-45, Chapinero
High prices, otherwise a good place to visit. It is the best bar in Bogotá.

Dark Club Gay (! AC B CC D F G MA NU P S SNU VS WE)
Mon-Sat 22-4h
C/. 64, 13-35, 2° piso *Second floor* ☎ (01) 345 62 14
www.darkclubgay.com
Very large and busy with up to 200 guests. Good size and great layout. Nude dress code.

Estación Café (AC b cc G MA)
Calle 62 N° 7-13, Chapinero ☎ (1) 249 0662
A popular place. Reasonable prices and attractive surroundings.

Plataforma Star Bar (B g MC SNU)
Calle 63 N°. 13-11, Chapinero ☎ (1) 348 3566
Stripshows and more.

Punto 59 (B G MC)
Carrera 13 N°. 59-24 Interior 6, Chapinero *In the Centro Comercial Aquarium*

San Karma (B GLM MA) Mon-Sat & Sun 17-?h
Calle 59, N° 9-05, Chapinero ☎ (1) 210 3650
guiagaycolombia.com/sankarma

Vida Moderna (B G M MC)
C/. 59 N°. 9-43
Happy Hour 13-16h (30% off). Cocoktails, national and internation beers and warm dishes available. Karaoke and smoking area.

Village Café (B G MC)
Carrera 8 N°. 64-29, Chapinero ☎ (1) 346 6592
Small bar but great cocktails!

CAFES

Brokeback Mountain Café (b GLM m MA)
Carrera 9a, N° 60-25, Chapinero

Palo Santo (b glm m MA)
Carrera 13a, N° 79-20, Zona Rosa ☎ (1) 610 76 56

DANCECLUBS

Colosos (! B D G MA s) Thu-Sat 18.30-3h
Calle 60 N° 9-65 Interior 108, Chapinero ☎ (1) 255 9925
www.guiagaycolombia.com/colosos
A great place, especially for bears and their fans. Great music, a good variety of guests. Various events take place here.

Polo. El (B D GLM MA)
Calle 16, N° 7-71, Centro
Neighbourhood bar where everyone knows each other. The oldest gay bar in Bogotá.

Raices Musicales (B D GLM MC S)
Carrera 5, N° 18-40, Centro ☎ (1) 283 5146
Occasional strip shows.

Semaforo (B D G S VS) Thu-Sat 20.30-3h
C/. 21, N° 6-43, Centro ☎ (1) 341 7761
Not recommended!

Theatron de Pelicula (! AC B D G M MA P S VS WE) Sat 21-?h
C/. 58, N° 10-32, Chapinero *Bus Trasmilenio Estacion Calle 57*
☎ (1) 249 2092 www.theatrondepelicula.com
Strict door controls. Disco on three floors with 6 bars. The biggest club in the city. High recommended. Best on Fri & Sat nights.

■ **Titanic** (B D g)
Av. Caracas N° 40-43, Chapinero *second floor* ☎ (1) 288 9436
Bad and somewhat dangerous.

SEX SHOPS/BLUE MOVIES

■ **Monte Carlo Club** (G VS)
Calle 66, N° 10-81, Chapinero *2nd floor* ☎ (1) 249 6211
■ **Sex Videos 229** (DR g MA) Mon-Sat 11-20.30h
Av. Cr. 15 # 119 - 11 local 229 ☎ (311) 8499 7721

SEX CINEMAS

■ **Acuario's** (b G MA) 3.30-5.30h
Calle 25 Sur N° 69-57 ☎ (1) 261 5526
Horrible place and horrible opening hours!
■ **AS Video** (G VS)
Carrera 13, N° 61-47, Local S-126 Chapicentro ☎ (1) 507 7000
🖳 www.yacontactos.com
■ **Escandinavia Video** (B DR G MA NU VS) 11-23 & Fri -2h
Av. Caracas, N° 65-15, Chapinero *Between Calle 65 and 66*
☎ (1) 312 9680 🖳 guiagaycolombia.com/escandinavia
■ **Ibiza** (G MA VS) Wed-Sat 22-3h
C/. Carrera 9, 17-52, 2 Piso ☎ (1) 341 6116
Sex shop / video bar - without the bar! Poor hygiene.
■ **Pollos. Los** (AYOR B DR G MA P SNU VS) Daily 13-?h
Av. Caracas, N° 59-19, Segundo Piso, Chapinero *2nd floor*
☎ (1) 235 4945 🖳 guiagaycolombia.com/lospollos
Video bar and dangerous!
■ **Sky Sin Límites** (DR G NU R SNU VS) Daily 11-23h
Av. Caracas, N° 66-29, Chapinero *M° Las Flores, between C/. 66 & 67*
☎ (1) 211 2743 🖳 www.colombianito.co.nr/sky.htm
Not a sex cinema - more a brothel!

SAUNAS/BATHS

■ **Atlantix** (B DU G m MA MSG SA SB SNU WH) Daily 12-21h
Carrera 13, N° 78-47, Zona Rosa ☎ (1) 691 3415
🖳 www.guiagaycolombia.com/atlantix
■ **Babylon** (! B cc DR DU FH G m MA MSG RR SA SB SOL VS WH)
Mon-Sat 15-21.30, Sun 14-21.30h
Calle 73, N°14-32, El Lago, Zona Rosa *Close to financial centre. Transmilenio Calle 72* ☎ (1) 321 7385 🖳 www.babylonbb.com
Dark labyrinth, relaxing cubicles. Probably the best sauna in Bogota!
■ **Bagoas Club** (B CC DR DU G I m MSG SA SB SNU WH WO)
14-22, Fri 14-Sun 22h (non-stop)
Calle 69 N° 10-30 ☎ (1) 249 0163
🖳 www.guiagaycolombia.com/bagoas
Shows on Sun. 30 mins free internet. Smokers area and protected parking available.
■ **Baltimore** (b CC g m MSG SA SB SOL WH WO) 24hrs
Calle 33, esq. Carrera 15-17, Teusaquillo *M° Transmilenio Estacion Profamilia* ☎ (1) 288 6563
Reduced student rates.
■ **Casa Romana** (B DU G m MC MSG S SA SB VS WH) Daily 13-22h
Calle 35 N° 7-24, Santa Fe ☎ (1) 500 0128
🖳 www.turcocasaromana.com/espacios.htm
■ **Cómplices** (B D DR DU FH G I LAB MA MSG NU PI PP RR SA SB WE WH) Sun-Thu 14-23, Fri & Sat -0.30h
Carrera 13A N° 38-60, Teusaquillo *In Bogota's International Centre, beside National Park* ☎ (1) 340 0401 🖳 complicesspa.com
A real nudist sauna.
■ **Mediterraneo. El** (B DR DU G MSG SA SB SNU VS WH WO)
Daily 13-22h
Calle 66 N° 10-15, Chapinero ☎ (1) 500 1021
🖳 www.guiagaycolombia.com/elmediterraneo
■ **Touch Me** (B G MSG SA SB)
Transversal 18 No. 79-67 Local 5, Centro Comercial Los Heroes *Northern suburb* ☎ (1) 257 4761
Small but interesting! Nice masseurs.

■ **Turcos de la 57** (B DR DU f G MA MSG NU SA SB VS WH) Daily 13-22h
Carrera 8b, N° 57-32, Chapinero ☎ (1) 346 4331
🖳 www.guiagaycolombia.com/turcosla57
Popular among bears.

HOTELS

■ **Chapinero Place Hotel** (bf GLM I MA PK RWS RWT VA)
All year, 24hrs
Carrera 14 A N° 70-33 *Chapinero* ☎ (301) 268 78 97
🖳 www.gayhotelbogota.com
Located in the gay-friendly neighbourhood Chapinero, 7 blocks walk from the 13 Avenue where the best gay nightlife in the city can be found and also close to the downtown where are located the best and historical tourist attractions. Tours available with a gay guide around the city and surroundings.
■ **Hotel High Park** (bf GLM I M MA) All year
C/. 4, N° 58-58 ☎ (1) 483 3009 🖳 www.hotelhighpark.com
Probably the only gay hotel in Bogotá.

APARTMENTS

■ **Checkin Apartments Bogota** (CC glm H I RWS RWT VA)
All year
Carrera 11A, N°. 69-18/20 ☎ (313) 828 36 08 (mobile)
🖳 www.checkin.se/bogota
Trendy contemporary apartments in the area of Quinta Camacho and Nogal, close to the gay area. Two full apartments and three bedrooms.

CRUISING

All these areas are AYOR:
-Carrera 13 (between Calle 50 and 64
-Carrera 7 (between Calle 24 and 16)
-Calle 24 (between Carreras 7 and 13)
-Calle 19 (between Carreras 3 and 7)
-Centro Comercial, Hotel Tequendama
-Centro Comercial Unicentro at Carrera 15, Calle 122
-Parque Santander (Calle 16 between Carreras 5 and 7)
-Entrance of post office in Avianca Building between Carrera 7 and Calle 16. (centro)
-Biblioteca Luis Angel Arango (Calle 11 4-14, La Candelaria)
-Biblioteca Parque El Tunal (Calle 48b Sur 21-13, Tunjuelito)
-Biblioteca Virgilio Barco (Ak 60 Ac 63, Teusaquillo)
-Cafam Floresta Mundo Comercial (Carrera 68 96-50, Barrios Unidos)
-Centro Comercial Andino (Carrera 11 82-71, Chapinero)
-Centro Comercial Atlantis (Calle 81 Carrera 14, Chapinero)
-Centro Comercial Bulevar Niza (Ak 58 127 59, Suba)
-Centro Comercial Ciudad Tunal (Ak 58 127 59, Tunjuelito)
-Centro Comercial Gran Estacion (Calle 26 62-49, Teusaquillo)
-Centro Comercial Granahorrar (Avenida Chile 10-34, Chapinero)
-Centro Comercial Hacienda Santa Barbara (Carrera 7 115-60, Usaquen)
-Centro Comercial Iserra 100 (Ac 100 Tv 55, Barrios Unidos)
-Centro Comercial Plaza de las Americas (Kr 71 d 6 94 Sur, Kennedy)
-Centro Comercial Portal de la 80 (Transversal 100a 80a-20, Engativa)
-Centro Comercial Salitre Plaza (Carrera 68b 24-39, Fontibon)
-Centro Comercial San Martin (Carrera 7 32-16, Santa Fe)
-Centro Comercial Santafe (Autopista norte calle 183, Suba)
-Centro Comercial Terraza Pasteur (Carrera 7 23-56, Santa Fe)

Cali ☎ 2

BARS

■ **Baltimore** (B d G MC)
Calle 23CN N°. 3AN-58, Parque Versalles ☎ (2) 661 4954
Good music but no room to dance.
■ **Casa del Arte. La** (! B D G M MC S)
Calle 44 Norte N°. 4 n 31 ☎ (2) 310 4583409 (mobile)
Special events: Wed: film nicht with gay content, jazz and discount off wines, Thu: music from the 80ies, cocktails 2-4-1; Fri: contemporary pop music; Sat: high-energy dance music.

SAUNAS/BATHS

■ **Cali Club** (! B G MA SA SB)
Mon-Wed, Fri, Sun 14.30-2.30; Thu & Sat -21.30h
Calle 8 N° 26-61 ☎ (2) 554 1860
Thu & Sat mixed sauna after 21.30h.

■ **Metropolis Club** (B G MA SA SB VS)
Calle 22 Norte No. 2N-50 *On corner with Avenida Segunda Norte*
☎ (2) 661 3097

CRUISING

-Parque de Caicedo Calle 12 Carrera 4 (R)
-Cali River
-Avenida Colombia
-Avenida 6a Norte.
-Chipi Chape Shopping Center (Nice place to go cruising).

Cartagena ☎ 5

DANCECLUBS

■ **Código de Barras** (! B D G MC) 16-?h
Calle Estanco del Tabaco, N° 35-24, 2° Piso, Ciudad Amurallada

■ **Lincoln Road** (B D G S) Thu & Fri 22-4h
C/. del Porvenir N°. 35-18, Centro ☎ (5) 660 2790
Great shows.

■ **Studio 54** (B D G S) Thu-Sat 22-4h
Calle Larga Getsemaní No. 8b-98 ☎ (5) 664 3642
🖳 www.facebook.com/group.php?gid=21316905946

■ **Via libre** (B D G S) Sat 22-4h
Calle de la Soledad No. 9-52, El Centro
Is not the best disco in Cartagena but is the first disco in town.

HOTELS

■ **Casa El Carretero** (AC BF CC glm I OS PI RWT) All year
Calle del Carretero, Getsemani *City centre*
☎ (5) 300 660 4475 (mobile) 🖳 www.casaelcarretero.com

CRUISING

All these places are AYOR:
-Beach »Playa Boca Grande« (all day long)
-Carrera 2 (known as »Avenida San Martín«, Boca Grande)
-Beach close to Hotel Capilla del Mar, Boca Grande
-La Boca Chica (1h boat ride from pier in centre of town)
-La Boquilla beach near the airport with little restaurants)
-Under Clock Tower at the entrance to the old city (19-23h)
-Boccaquandu Beach near the Hollywood beach.

Cúcuta ☎ 7

BARS

■ **Punto G** (B D G S)
Centro Commercial Bolivar
The most famous disco in Cucuta.

CRUISING

-Avenida 0
-Avenida Simón Bolívar
-Calle17 (between Avenida 6 and Avenida 1)
-Parque Santander (after 18h).

Duitama ☎ 98

BARS

■ **New Samba Disco Bar** (B D g MA)
Carrera 21, N° 5-89 Avenida De Las Americas *behind Discoteca Casual*
☎ 311 218 5938 (mobile)

Manizales ☎ 6

BARS

■ **Dollar Club** (B g MC)
Av. Santander N° 59-87 *In front of the Estrella Centre* ☎ (6) 881 1204

DANCECLUBS

■ **Move Lounge** (B D G MA S)
Av. Santander No. 59-60 ☎ (6) 880 3127

Medellín ☎ 94

BARS

■ **Las Cabinas Sala de Internet** (B G I MC) 24hrs
Calle 53 N° 47-44, Centro *2nd floor* ☎ (94) 576 1720

■ **Sastreria. La** (B g MC) Mon-Thu -24, Fri & Sat -2h
C/. 57 N°. 45-63, Centro ☎ (94) 284 5703

DANCECLUBS

■ **Cantina De Javi. La** (B D G YC)
C/. 58, N° 47-18, Centro *Downtown* ☎ (94) 284 5370

■ **Ceres** (B D G MA)
C/. 56, N° 49-69, Centro *Downtown* ☎ (94) 512 1646
Be careful, surrounding area is unsafe at night.

■ **Sunset Disco** (AC B D g MC)
Calle 27 N° 43 F - 67 *Barrio Colombia* ☎ (94) 262 9473
Special events on Thu & Fri nights.

■ **Viva** (B D G MA S)
Calle 51 No. 73-100 *Centro comercial el diamante local 106*
☎ (94) 230 7489

SEX CINEMAS

■ **C & G House Club** (AC b m NU VS) Mon-Sat 14-, Sun 15-21h
Calle 47 N° 59 34, Prado Centro ☎ (94) 292 29 73
🖳 www.cyghouseclub.blogspot.com

SAUNAS/BATHS

■ **Barbacoas** (G SA SB)
Calle 57A N°. 46-47, Centro ☎ (94) 513 1074
Small but full of action!

■ **Club de Tobi** (! AK B DR DU f FC FH G GH LAB m MSG OS P PI RR SA SB SH SL SNU SOL VS WE WH WO YC) 12-22h
C/. 47, Bomboná 43-88, Centro *Near Parque, M° de San Antonio*
☎ (94) 239 7513 🖳 www.myspace.com/club_de_tobi
One of the best saunas in the country! With swimming pool, gynasium and sauna for 50 men or steam room for 70 men!

■ **Monte Caprino** (G SA SB)
Carrera 50, N° 60-47, Centro ☎ (94) 254 1578

■ **Tabomar** (b G SA SB SOL VS) Tue-Sun 10-20h
Carrera 45, 46-27 ☎ (94) 251 1295

CRUISING

-Carrera Junin between C/. 56 & 47
-Parque de Bolívar (R) (corner of Sayonara only)
-Avenida San Juan (R) (between Carreras 70 and 80; students)
-Loraita (male prostitution in the area of Universidad de Antioquia, Highway 51-49 and C/. 67-71)

Neiva ☎ 8

BARS

■ **Midas** (B g MA)
Carrera 2, N° 13-53

Pereira ☎ 6

BARS

■ **Magia Blanca Taberna** (B G MA)
Carrera 8 N° 25-69 ☎ (6) 334 7697

■ **Soho** (B G MC)
Carrera 6 N° 24-76 ☎ (6) 315 812 3649 (mobile)
Happy hour on Mon-Wed.

DANCECLUBS

■ **Super Club** (AC B CC D GLM M P S ST VS WE)
Thu & Fri 21-3, Sat -?h
C/. 23 N° 8-55 Local 302 P1 Centro Comercial Lago *Close to Plaza de Bolivar, opp. the Chambre of Commerce* ☎ (6) 333 0183
💻 www.corporacionsuperclub.com
Busy in the weekends with a nice good looking crowd dancing to Latin-house.

SAUNAS/BATHS

■ **Eqqus** (b DR G m MA MSG p SA SB VS) 14-22h
Carrera 5, N° 22 62, Risaralda *Between El Lago and Plaza Bolivar*
☎ (6) 334 4266 💻 www.eqqussauna.com
Clean and discreet. Friendly staff and masseurs.

Popayán ☎ 2

BARS

■ **Open Mind** (AC B D GLM m MA P VS WE) 18-3h
Carrera 9a 63N 48B, Bella Vista 💻 www.openmindbargay.jimdo.com

San Andrés Island ☎ 8

CRUISING

-Along Avenida Colombia (from Hotel Isleño to Hotel Aquarium; in the evening on the beach opposite Avenida Colombia).

Valledupar ☎ 952

BARS

■ **Babilonia** (B g MA)
Plaza Alfonso Lopez *At Compae Chipuco*

Costa Rica

Location: Central America
Initials: CR
Time: GMT -6
International Country Code: ☎ 506 (no area codes)
International Access Code: ☎ 00
Language: Spanish
Area: 51,100 km² / 19,730 sq mi.
Currency: 1 Costa Rica Colón (CRC) = 100 Céntimos
Population: 4,075,000
Capital: San José
Religions: 88% Roman Catholic, 8% Protestant
Climate: The dry season is from December to April. In the rainy season from May to November, it's sunny till the late afternoon, becoming cloudy and it often rains during the night.
Important gay cities: San José, Quepos/Manuel Antonio

Homosexual acts between men are not illegal according to the law. The age of consent is 18 for everyone. A new law exists since 1999 making discrimination against sexual and other minorities a punishable act. The National Insurance Institute has stated that same-sex couples can jointly apply for health and insurance policies, as well as for housing credits.
Costa Rica is a safe country for the gay tourist and enjoys a stable political climate and is a paradise for nature lovers. Almost a quarter of the entire country is a designated nature reserve zone. This country has, especially in the last ten years, become the most popular (gay-lesbian) location in central America. In San José and Quepos/Manuel Antonio the attitude of the general public towards homosexuality is mostly liberal.

Homosexuelle Handlungen zwischen erwachsenen Menschen sind dem Gesetz nach erlaubt. Das Schutzalter liegt einheitlich bei 18 Jahren. Seit 1999 existiert ein Gesetz, welches die Diskriminierung von sexuellen und anderen Minderheiten unter Strafe stellt. In Costa Rica hat der nationale „Dachverband der Versicherungen" beschlossen, dass homosexuelle Paare gemeinsam eine Krankenversicherung oder allgemeine Versicherungen abschließen und ferner zusammen einen Kredit, z.B. für einen Wohnungskauf, aufnehmen können.
Costa Rica gilt auch für Schwule und Lesben als sicheres Reiseland und erfreut sich einer stabilen politischen Situation. Das Land ist ein Paradies für Naturliebhaber. Über ein Viertel der Gesamtfläche steht unter Naturschutz. In den vergangenen Jahren hat sich Costa Rica zum absolut beliebtesten (schwul-lesbischen) Reiseziel Zentralamerikas entwickelt. Insbesondere in den homosexuellen Zentren San José und Quepos/Manuel Antonio toleriert die Gesellschaft Homosexualität weitestgehend.

Les relations homosexuelles sont légalement autorisées. La majorité sexuelle est fixée à 18 ans. Depuis 1999, une loi existe interdisant toute discrimination envers les minorités, sexuelles y compris. Au Costa Rica, la confédération des compagnies d'assurance a décidé que les couples homosexuels pouvaient contracter en commun une assurance, maladie ou autre, ainsi qu'un crédit, par exemple pour acheter un appartement. Le pays reste un paradis pour les fans de nature à l'état pur, pratiquement le quart de la superficie totale du pays est une réserve naturelle protégée. Depuis quelques années le Costa Rica est littéralement devenu la destination préférée des gays et lesbiennes en Amérique centrale, en particulier San José et Quepos/ Manuel Antonio, villes qui tolèrent la communauté homosexuelle.

Los contactos homosexuales entre personas adultas están permitidos según la ley. La edad de constentimiento es de 18 años para cualquier caso. Desde 1999 existe una ley que penaliza toda discriminación contra minorías sexuales o de otra clase. En Costa Rica, la „organización nacional de seguros" ha decidido que las parejas homosexuales podrán contratar de manera conjunta un seguro de enfermedad o un seguro general y así también poder solicitar juntos un crédito para, por ejemplo, la adquisición de una vivienda.
Costa Rica está considerado un destino turístico seguro y disfruta de una situación política estable. El país es un paraíso para los amantes

de la naturaleza. Casi una cuarta parte de su territorio está bajo protección natural. En los últimos años, Costa Rica se ha convertido en el destino turístico de Centroamérica más apreciado por gays y lesbianas; especialmente, en los centros homosexuales de San José y Quepos/Manuel Antonio, la sociedad tolera la homosexualidad de manera muy abierta.

Atti omosessuali tra persone adulte sono permessi dalla legge. L'età minima che consente il rapporto sessuale è di 18 anni. Dal 1999 esiste una legge che punisce le discriminazioni nei confronti delle minoranze, anche in base all'orientamento sessuale. In Costa Rica le assicurazioni hanno deciso che le coppie omosessuali possono adesso stipulare un'assicurazione comune e possomo anche chiedere un credito insieme (per esempio per l'acquisto di una casa).

La Costa Rica é ritenuta una meta turistica sicura, gode di una situazione politica stabile e rappresenta un vero e proprio paradiso per gli amanti della natura. Quasi un quarto della superficie totale é infatti protetta come parco naturale. Negli ultimi anni la Costa Rica é diventata una tra le mete turistiche gay e lesbiche preferite dell'America Centrale. L'omosessualitá é ampiamente tollerata dalla societá, soprattutto nei centri gay San José e Quepos/Manuel Antonio.

NATIONAL GAY INFO

gaycostarica.com (GLM)
☎ 824 8298 🖳 gaycostarica.com
Mainly for gay bears

NATIONAL PUBLICATIONS

Gente 10 Magazine (G)
PO Box 1910-2100 ✉ San José ☎ 2280-8886 🖳 www.gente10.com
Gente 10 is the gay magazine of Costa Rica, published bimonthly on the web. You can see it online in flash format or download it in pdf format.

SPECIAL INTEREST GROUPS

Ticosos (G)
✉ San José 🖳 www.ticosos.com
Gay bears association of Costa Rica.

Alajuela

BARS

Rick's (B CC D G M MA ST WE)
Wed- Thu18-2.30, Fri-Sat 18-3, Sun 16-midnight
La Garita *500m Este Casino Fiesta, carretera Heredia, in Río Segundo de Alajuela* ☎ 24412313
Popular local bar with shows.

RESTAURANTS

Casa Vieja (B CC DM GLM M PK) Mon-Sat 18-2, Sun 14-24h
500m from Montserrat church to the east, right behind the Internacional-Alajuela shopping mall ☎ 2440-8525
Very popular neighbourhood bar-restaurant.

SAUNAS/BATHS

Quinta Acrópolis (B G M MA NU OS PI) Sat & Sun
Rosario de Naranjo ☎ 2450-4353 ☎ 8843-7597 (mobile)
🖳 www.quintaacropolis.com
Sauna with outdoor pool and more.

Limón

HOTELS

Banana Azul (B BF CC GLM I M MA PI PK RWB RWS RWT VA)
24hrs
Puerto Viejo *Located 2km north of town on beach in Playa Negra, 200m north of Perla Negra Hotel* ☎ 2750-2035 🖳 www.bananaAzul.com
Website has all transport options from local bus to private driver. A gay-owned hotel open to both gay men and lesbians. 14 guestrooms.

Montezuma

GUEST HOUSES

Naturelodge Finca los Caballos (B BF CC GLM H I M MA MSG PI PK RWB RWS) Hotel closed in Oct. Restaurant open: 8-21h
On the southern tip of the Peninsula Nicoya *4km south of Cobano on the road to Montezuma* ☎ 2642-0124 🖳 www.naturelodge.net
Private, tranqill, romantic nature setting, horseback adventures. Gay owned & operated.

SWIMMING

-Playa Grande (NU) situated 25 mins south of Montezuma, is becoming an attraction for gay men.

Perez Zeledon

HOTELS

Las Aguas Jungle Lodge (AC B BF CC GLM I M PI RWS WH WO)
All year
Cana Blanca ☎ 2296-1880 🖳 www.LasAguas.com
Full service, located in the mountains of Costa Rica, jungle adventures and waterfalls galore. A unique experience. 8 guestrooms.

Quepos / Manuel Antonio

BARS

Bar Mogambo (gLm MA OS)
☎ 2777 6310
In the 2nd floor of Raphael's Terrazas. Great ocean view. Next to Hotel Costa Verde. Mostly gay men, good drinks.

■ **Republik Lounge** (AC B GLM MA) 18-2h, closed Tue
In front of Restaurant „Gran Escape", Quepos ☎ 2777-2120

DANCECLUBS

■ **Arco Iris** (D glm MA WE) Fri-Sat
■ **Liquid Lounge** (AC B CC D GLM M MA OS S) 21-3h
Manuel Antonio Beach nearby Hotel Karahe ☎ 2777-5158
THE gay disco in town.

RESTAURANTS

■ **Barba Roja** (B GLM M OS VEG) 7-22, Mon 16-22h
Carretera al Parque Nacional *Next to Los Altos* ☎ 2777-0331
American style, steaks and seafood. Every Sunday from 4 - 8 pm Gay Sunset Session at the Boat Deck.
■ **Café Milagro** (B glm M OS VEG) Daily 6-22h
Carretera al Parque Nacional *Opp. Hotel Casa Blanca* ☎ 2777-1707
🖳 www.cafemilagro.com
■ **Hacienda. La** (B CC GLM M MA)
Mon-Sat 17-22 (-23h in high season Dec-Apr)
Plaza Yara, Km 1.5 ☎ 2777-3473 🖳 www.lahaciendacr.com
■ **Raphael´s Terrazas** (B CC gLm M MA W)
Next to Hotel Costa Verde, Manuel Antonio ☎ 2777 6310
🖳 www.raphaelsterraza.com
THE gay restaurant in Manuel Antonio.

HOTELS

■ **Makanda By The Sea**
(AC B cc glm I M MA MSG OS PA PI PK RWB RWS VA WH) All year
Carretera al Parque Nacional *Road to Hotel Parador* ☎ 2777-0442
🖳 www.makanda.com
■ **Villa Roca** (! AC B BF CC GLM I MSG NU OS PI PK RWB RWS RWT VA WH) All year, office 7-21h
Apartado 143, Carretera al Parque Nacional *3 miles from Quepos and near M. Antonio National Park* ☎ 2777-1349 🖳 www.villaroca.com
10 double rooms and 5 apartments with bath, telephone, AC, refrigerator, safe, cable TV, WiFi and private terraces with the best ocean view. Infinity pool, sun terraces.

GUEST HOUSES

■ **Villa Nicolás** (AC BF CC GLM I OS PI PK RWB RWS WH) All year
Apartado 236, Puntarenas, Aguirre *4km from Quepos on main road and next to Si Como No Hotel* ☎ 2777-0481 🖳 www.villasnicolas.com
Nineteen guestrooms. Minimum stay applies.

Samara

GUEST HOUSES

■ **Casitas LazDívaz B&B** (BF glm I m MA OS PK RWB RWS)
Playa Sámara, Sector Matapalo *Playa Sámara, Guanacaste*
☎ 2656-0295 🖳 www.lazdivaz.com
A lesbian-run bed & breakfast right on beautiful Playa Sámara.

San José

GAY INFO

■ **Centro de Investigación y Promoción para América Central de Derechos Humanos (CIPAC)** (GLM)
Mon-Fri 8-19, Sat 11-16h
400 sur y 175 este de la Agencia del Banco nacional de San Pedro, Casa 2000 *Montes de Oca, de la Escuela Roosevelt, 200 sur 50 este.*
☎ 2280-7821 🖳 www.cipacdh.org
Human rights organization with special groups attending to the needs of the LGBT community.

BARS

■ **Bodega** (! B CC GLM MA)
Corner of Av. 9 and 1sr Street *San José Centro* ☎ 2248 2476
Very popular bar.
■ **Buenas Vibraciones** (gLm)
Avenida 14 *Between C/. 7 & 9* ☎ 2223-4573
Mostly lesbians.
■ **Cantábrico. El** (B GLM MA) Mon-Sat 15-24h
Av. 6, between C./ Central & 2 *Bus 74* ☎ 2221-5927
Best visited in early evening. Local neighborhood bar.
■ **Castilla Bar** (B gLm MA) 18-2.30h
475 m north to PLAZA DE LA CULTURA, San José centro ☎ 22210656
Mainly lesbian visited bar.
■ **El 13** (B CC G M MA)
200m to AyA del Paseo de los Estudiantes ☎ 2221 7228
🖳 el13cafebar.com
Very popular.
■ **Puchos Night Club** (B G MA S SNU ST) Mon-Sat 20-2h
Av. 11 & C./ 11 *Corner Av. 8 & 11th St.* ☎ 2256-1147
🖳 www.puchosnightclub.com
Amusing strip and drag shows on Fri & Sat.
■ **Tabu** (B CC D GLM M MA S ST WE) Tue-Sat 19-2, Sun 18-24h
Frente a Mudanzas Mundiales, Zapote *Opposite transports company „Mudanzas Mundiales"* ☎ 2253-1718
Local gay bar.
■ **TOP San José** (AC B G MA S) 16-2h
C/. Central *Between Av. 7 & 9. In front of Hotel Rivadavia, San Jose Centro*
☎ 2223-0004
Leather and bear bar.
■ **Werd** (AC B CC D G M MA S WE)
100 Metres Oeste de la Musmanni, Santa Ana Centro ☎ 2203-3624
Gay-friendly bar in Santa Ana with young crowd. DJs on WE and English speaking staff.

DANCECLUBS

■ **Avispa. La** (AC B D GLM m MA S VS) 20-3, Sun 17-2h, Mon closed
C/. 1 between Av. 8 & Av. 10 ☎ 2223-5343 🖳 www.laavispa.co.cr
Little sign. Downhill from Banco Popular on left side of the 1st street. Very popular for gays and lesbians, last Wed and second Fri women only.
■ **Bochinche. El** (! B CC GLM m MA ST VS WE)
Wed 20-2, Thu -3, Fri & Sat -4, Sun -3h
C/. 11 *Between Av. 10 & 12* ☎ 2221-0500
🖳 www.facebook.com/BochincheBarRestaurante
Restaurant service until one hour before closing. A fun place.
■ **Club O!** (! AC B D GLM m S YC) Wed-Sat 20-3h, closed Sun
C/. 2 y Avenida 14/16 *Between Av. 14 & 16* ☎ 2248-1500
🖳 www.clubohcr.com
Big club with 2 dancefloors. House and techno music. For your own security it is better to take a taxi.
■ **Energy Club** (B D GLM S YC) Wed-Sun 19.30 -?h
Paseo Colon beside Pizza Hut ☎ 2223-7594
■ **Azotea** (AC B D GLM S WH YC) Wed-Sun
La Uruca de Capris 250 al norte 🖳 www.hypnoticclubcr.com
New club with 8 private rooms with Jacuzzi for rent in the second floor.

RESTAURANTS

■ **Ankara** (B CC glm M OS S)
San José de la Montaña, Heredia *300 m south of the church* ☎ 2266-0303
■ **Café Mundo** (! AC B CC DM glm M MA OS VEG)
Mon-Fri 11-23, Sat 5-24h, Sun closed
Av. 9, C/. 15, house 1372 *Located in the historical district of Amón-Otoya*
☎ 2222-6190
One of the most celebrated gay-friendly restaurants serves creative international cuisine in a lovely former residence (with both indoor and outdoor dining).
■ **Esquina del Triángulo. La** (B CC d DM GLM H M MA OS PK RES S) 18-23h
Boulevard Rohrmoser (Hotel Colours) *In the Hotel Colours*
☎ 2296-1880 🖳 www.coloursoasis.com

SEX SHOPS/BLUE MOVIES

■ **XXX Adult World** (glm MA)
C/. 2, entre Avenidas 3 y 5 *Between Av. 3 & 5* ☎ 2221-7165

SAUNAS/BATHS

Hispalis (! B DR DU G m PI SA SB VS WH WO) 12-1h
Av. Segunda, 1762 *Between C/. 17 & 19, 75 m east of Museo Nacional*
☎ 256-9540 💻 www.clubhispalis.com
It is not that big but there are always visitors and action takes place in the big steam room or the labyrinth.

Sauna Paris (DR DU FH G GH MC SB) Daily, 24hrs
C/. 7 Avenida 7 *Look for a small French flag in the doorway*
☎ 2258 7254

HOTELS

Bohemian Paradise (AC CC glm m MA MSG WH)
C/. 3, Avenida 4 y 6 ☎ 2258-9683
Located only blocks from San Jose's shopping and cultural centre as well as the hottest gay discos, bars, and saunas. Friendly staff will help you to plan all types of tours.

Colours Oasis Resort (b BF CC d G I M MA MSG OS p PI PK RWS RWT SOL VA WH WO) All year, 8-21h
Boulevard Rohrmoser ☎ 2296-1880 💻 www.coloursOasis.com
Sample the gay nightlife or just lounge around at the poolside. Colours is a stylish boutique hotel, conveniently located.

Kekoldi (BF CC glm I OS RWS RWT VA) All year
Av. 9, between C/. 5 and 7 *Barrio Amón* ☎ 2248-0804
💻 www.kekoldi.com
Superior quality with ten elegant, well appointed guest rooms, with shower/ WC, telephone, cable-TV and safe, is located in the historic Barrio Amón of San José, about 200 m north of Parque Morazán.

GUEST HOUSES

Casa 69 (b BF GLM H I MA MSG OS p PA RWS RWT SA) All year
69 Calle 25 bis, Barrio California *Between Avenida Central and Ave. 2*
☎ 2256-8879 💻 www.casa69.com
An 8-room guest house close to gay scene and cultural places of interest.

Casa Rainbow Canyon (bf G MA NU PI) All year, 24hrs
Cope Street, Brazil de Santa Ana *Located between airport and downtown San Jose* ☎ 2249-4785 💻 www.casarainbowcanyon.com
Men only guest house.

CRUISING

The police carry out raids at the following cruising areas! All the cruising areas are dangerous at night!
-Parque Central, C/. Central and Avenida Segunda (especially at the Café Soda Palace and Perla Café)
-Parque Morazán (Avenidas 5a & 7a, C/. 5a and 7a) (r t) (in the woods) day and night
-Park La Sabana (busy at night) (between „Rohrmoser" and city; in the southwest, next to Municipal Stadium)
-Plaza de la Cultura (popular) (in front of the National Theatre and at the Plaza and also in the basement; between C/. 3 and 5; busy in the late afternoon and evening)
-Parque Nacional (Avenidas 1 and 3, C/. 15 and 19) in the afternoon.

Croatia

Name: Hrvatska · Kroatien · Croacia · Croatie
Location: Central Europe
Initials: HR
Time: GMT +1
International Country Code: ☎ 385 (omit 0 from area code)
International Access Code: ☎ 00
Language: Croatian
Area: 56,542 km² / 21,829 sq mi.
Currency: 1 Kuna (HRK) = 100 Lipa
Population: 4,443,000
Capital: Zagreb
Religions: 87% Catholic
Climate: Mediterranean and continental climate. Best time to visit is spring/summer (May-Sep) with the hottest temperatures in mid-summer (Jul & Aug).
Important gay cities: Zagreb, Rijeka

In Croatia center left political parties and their Members of Parliament advocate LGBT rights. Homosexuality is legal in Croatia since 1977. The age of consent is 14 years, equal for all people. Since 2003, when the Parliament adopted the Law of Same-sex Unions, gay couples can have limited rights, such as the right to legal regulation of property and mutual responsibility for financial support. In the last years legal protection has risen to a higher level, one of the most progressive in Europe. Today there are many laws that protect the rights of gays and lesbians: such as anti-discrimination clauses in the Labor code, Law on gender equality, higher education, asylum, media. Croatian Criminal code recognizes „hate crime", and Law on suppressing discrimination recognizes discrimination on the basis of sexual orientation, gender identity and gender expression. There are LGBT organizations in Zagreb and Rijeka. In 2005 the parliament rejected proposal for Registered Partnership, which would expand on the limited domestic partner law and allow both same-sex and different sex couples to register civil unions.
Whereas Gay Pride has been celebrated peacefully in Zagreb for many years, the first such event in Split in 2011 saw violent confrontations, with ca. 10,000 people attacking a group of 300 marchers. The violence drew sharp criticism from politicians at home and abroad, while the incident is putting Croatia's efforts to join the EU at risk.

In Kroatien treten die Mitte-Links-Parteien und ihre Abgeordneten für die Rechte der LGBT-Gemeinde ein. Homosexualität ist hier seit 1977 legal. Das Mindestalter liegt für alle bei 14 Jahren. Die Anerkennung unregistrierter Partnerschaften seit 2003 hat die rechtliche Lage gleichgeschlechtlicher Paare leicht verbessert, z. B. im Hinblick auf die Besitzstandsregelungen und gegenseitige finanzielle Unterstützung, während der gesetzliche Schutz in den letzten Jahren so stark ausgebaut wurde, dass er mittlerweile zu den progressivsten in Europa gehört. Mittlerweile gibt es viele Bestimmungen zum Schutz der Rechte von Schwulen und Lesben, darunter u. a. Antidiskriminie-

rungsklauseln im Arbeitsrecht und ein Gesetz zur Gleichstellung von Männern und Frauen, aber auch in der Hochschulbildung, den Medien und im Asylrecht. Das kroatische Strafrecht ahndet „Hassverbrechen" und das Antidiskriminierungsgesetz umfasst auch die sexuelle Orientierung, Geschlechtsidentität oder deren Ausdrucksformen. In Zagreb und Rijeka gibt es LGBT-Organisationen.
2005 hat das Parlament leider einen Gesetzesvorschlag für eingetragene Partnerschaften abgelehnt, der das momentane Lebenspartnergesetz erweitern und für hetero- und homosexuelle Paare gleichermaßen gelten sollte. Während in Zagreb schon seit vielen Jahren der CSD gefeiert wird, gab es im Jahr 2011 beim ersten CSD in Split gewalttätige Auseinandersetzungen. Dabei griffen ca. 10.000 Menschen die 300 CSD-Teilnehmer an. Die Gewalt wurde von der Politik im In- und Ausland scharf kritisiert, so gefährdet der Vorfall die Bemühungen Kroatiens um den Beitritt in die EU.

En Croatie, les partis de centre-gauche et leurs députés interviennent pour les droits de la communauté LGBT. L'homosexualité est légale depuis 1977. L'age légal est fixé à 14 ans pour tous. La reconnaissance des couples non-enregistrés depuis 2003 a légèrement amélioré la situation juridique des couples homosexuels, en particulier en matière de patrimoine et de soutien financier mutuel. Dans le même temps la protection juridique a été constamment étendue et fait partie des plus progressistes en Europe. Il existe désormais des directives de protection des droits des gays et lesbiennes, entre autres des clauses anti-discriminations en droit du travail et une loi pour l'égalité des hommes et des femmes, mais aussi dans l'éducation supérieure, les médias et droit d'asile. Le droit pénal condamne les crimes de haine et la loi contre les discriminations inclut l'orientation et l'identité sexuelles et leurs formes d'expression. Des organisations LGBT sont actives à Zagreb et Rijeka.
En 2005 le parlement a refusé une proposition de loi de partenariat qui aurait étoffé la loi actuelle sur le concubinage et aurait été valide aussi bien pour les couples hétéros ou homosexuels.
Alors qu'à Zagreb la Gay Pride est fêtée depuis des années, la première Gay Pride à Split en 2011 a été l'occasion de violents affrontements. Environ 10.000 personnes ont pris à partie les quelques 300 manifestants de la Gay Pride. La violence a été fortement critiquée par les politiques dans le pays et à l'étranger, l'incident pouvant compromettre les efforts de la Croatie de rejoindre l'UE.

En Croacia entran en juego los partidos políticos de centro-izquierda y sus representantes a favor de los derechos de la comunidad LGBT. La homosexualidad es legal desde 1977 y la edad mínima para mantener relaciones sexuales es de 14 años. El reconocimiento de las asociaciones no registradas desde el año 2003 ha mejorado ligeramente la situación jurídica de las parejas del mismo sexo, por ejemplo, con respecto a la legislación sobre la propiedad y el apoyo financiero mutuo. La protección jurídica se ha ampliado en los últimos años en tal medida que ahora es una de las más progresistas de Europa. Mientras tanto, existen numerosas disposiciones para proteger los derechos de gays y lesbianas, incluyendo las cláusulas contra la discriminación en el derecho laboral y una ley sobre igualdad entre hombres y mujeres, pero también en la educación superior, los medios de comunicación y el derecho de asilo. El derecho penal croata castiga los "crímenes de odio" y la ley contra la discriminación abarca, a su vez, la orientación sexual, la identidad de género o sus formas de expresión. En Zagreb y Rijeka existen organizaciones LGBT.
En 2005 el Parlamento rechazó una propuesta de ley para parejas registradas, la cual ampliaría la legislación vigente y aplicable tanto a parejas heterosexuales como homosexuales.
Mientras que en Zagreb se celebra desde hace muchos años la Marcha del Orgullo Gay, en 2011 tuvieron lugar enfrentamientos violentos durante la primera Marcha del Orgullo en Split. Este ataque enfrentó a unas 10.000 personas contra los 300 participantes de la Marcha del Orgullo. Este ataque recibió duras críticas tanto en el país como en el extranjero y el incidente amenazo también los esfuerzos de adhesión a la UE por parte de Croacia.

In Croazia, i partiti di centro-sinistra e i loro rappresentanti sono impegnati nella lotta per i diritti della comunità LGBT. L'omosessualità è legale dal 1977. L'età del consenso è, per tutti, di 14 anni. Il riconoscimento - dal 2003 - delle coppie di fatto ha leggermente migliorato la situazione giuridica delle coppie dello stesso sesso, ad esempio in relazione ai regolamenti sullo stato di proprietà e al reciproco sostegno finanziario. Negli ultimi anni la tutela giuridica si è estesa sempre di più, tanto da essere considerata, oggi, tra le più progressiste in Europa. Ci sono molte disposizioni a tutela dei diritti di gay e lesbiche, tra cui, le clausole antidiscriminatorie nel diritto del lavoro, una legge sulla parità tra uomini e donne,ma anche nel campo dell'istruzione superiore, dei media e in materia di diritto di asilo. Il diritto penale croato punisce i „crimini d'odio"; la legge antidiscriminazioni riguarda anche l'orientamento sessuale,l'identità di genere e le sue espressioni. A Zagabria e Rijeka ci sono organizzazioni LGBT.
Nel 2005, il Parlamento ha, purtroppo, respinto una legge per le unioni di fatto registrate, che avrebbe migliorato l'attuale legge sulle unioni civili riguardante gay ed etero.
Mentre a Zagabria già da diversi anni si festeggia il CSD, nel 2011, durante il primo CSD a Split, ci sono stati violenti tafferugli, durante i quali circa 10.000 persone hanno aggredito 300 manifestanti. La politica nazionale e internazionale ha aspramente criticato le violenze, mettendo in evidenza come questi incidenti mettano a repentaglio gli sforzi della Croazia per l'ingresso nell'Unione Europea.

NATIONAL GAY INFO

Croatia Gay Guide
www.friendlycroatia.com
Gay and lesbian tourist portal for Zagreb and Croatia. Gay guides, travel tips and travel news.

Gay.hr
www.gay.hr
The largest online gay media publication in Croatia. A community site supporting the LGBT population of Croatia. News and information on gay scene also in English (travel.gay.hr).

Queer.hr
www.queer.hr
Also large online gay media publication in Croatia. A community site supporting the LGBT population of Croatia.

NATIONAL GROUPS

Iskorak Mon-Fri 12-18h
Petra Preradoviceva 2 ✉ 10000 Zagreb ☏ (095) 475 6725
www.iskorak.org
Iskorak - Sexual and gender minorities center is a NGO that gathers LGBTIQ population. The center's mission is to fight against any discrimination.

Queer Zagreb
✉ 10000 Zagreb ☏ (091) 178 9972 www.queerzagreb.org
International festival of queer art.

HEALTH GROUPS

HUHIV/CAHIV
Medvescak 9 ✉ 10000 Zagreb ☏ (01) 4666 655 www.huhiv.hr

Brela ☏ 021

SWIMMING

-Punta Rata (g) (10-15 minutes walk from centre of Brela. Gay spot in the forest at the southernmost tip of the beach).

Cres ☏ 051

SWIMMING

-Beach (g) (after the auto-camp in the beginning of the bay)
-Martinscica (g) (take the road from Cres towards the island of Mali Losinj, near lake Vransko (Vransko jezero). The beach is to be found near the camping-site)
-Miholascica (g) (main beach near the tourist area).

Dubrovnik ☏ 020

BARS

■ **Caffe Bar Troubadour** (B NG)
Buniceva poljana 2
Unoffcial meeting place for gay men. The bar can be found at the square on the eastern end of the Old Town.

GUEST HOUSES

■ **Tihi Kut** (GLM H) Open from May-Oct
Ivana Matijasevica 6 ☏ (098) 758 879
free-du.t-com.hr/Mare-Ivanisin/
Tihi Kut offers two double bedrooms with bathroom to share. Use of the kitchen is also possible. Located in in Boninovo area within 10 minutes walk to the Old Town and just a few minutes walk to the beach.

SWIMMING

-Lokrum Island (MA) (take a ferry from the old harbour of Dubrovnik. At the end of nudist beach and the rocks on the south side. Action in woods behind the beach)
-Camp Solitudo (take bus 6 and get off at the last station, popular)
-Babin Kuk (from city centre by car. Between Hotel President and Argosy, under Hotel Argosy, follow footways. There is a nude beach and the cruising spot is on the cliff. Be careful).

Hvar Island ☏ 021

BARS

■ **Carpe Diem** (B NG) Daily during summer
Riva b.b. www.carpe-diem-hvar.com
A popular unofficial meeting place for gay men in summer. Popular! Located at the harbour.

DANCECLUBS

■ **Veneranda** (AC B NG YC)
Gornja cesta B.B. *Near Main Square* ☏ (098) 855 151
www.veneranda.hr

HOTELS

■ **Villa Nora** (BF H MA)
Petra Hektorovica bb ☏ (021) 742 498 www.villanora.eu

SWIMMING

-Sveti Jerolim Island (g MA) (Boat from the harbour of Hvar (city). Southwestern side of the island. Action in the bushes. Popular in summer.)

Kanegra ☏ 052

SWIMMING

-Beach near the Slovenian border on the southern coast of the Bay of Piran (MA WE) (Roads from Umag or Savudrija in Croatia or Portoroz. Action in the woods behind the nudist beach). Best way to arrive is through village Crveni vrh because through the campsite admission could be charged.

Karlovac ☏ 047

CRUISING

-Park near Korana River, behind Hotel Korana and the wooden bridge (evenings).

Kriz ☏ 01

CRUISING

-When going by car on the highway from Zagreb to Belgrade (Serbia), there is a rest area, called Kriz Novoselec, stop after Ivanic Grad. Sometimes action in the toilets.

Krk Island ☏ 051

SWIMMING

-Njivice (MA) (through village and auto-camp, enter forest by doors in fence, gay area 10-15 mins walk along sea shore)
-Baska (near camping-site Bunculuka)
-Krk (near the camping-site Politin)
-Punat Beach (MA NU), Camp Konobe, action in the woods behind the nudist beach.

Krvavica ☏ 021

SWIMMING

-Krvavica (g YC) (In Krvavica Village between Makarska and Baska Voda) Go to the main beach in Krvavica and turn left. Walk along the seashore, towards the rocks, and after approximately 150 m you will reach the gay area.

Nin ☏ 023

SWIMMING

-Zaton (g) direction to Nin(near the sea outside the camping-site). Sometime visited by gays during summer, now it is not as popular as before.

Osijek ☏ 031

BARS

■ **Posh** (B MA NG)
Kuhaceva ulica 10
Straight bar visited by some gays.

CRUISING

-Behind the Hotel Osijek
-City Park on the Drava.

Pisarovina ☏ 01

MEN'S CLUBS

■ **Red Hard Room** (AC B DR F G MA P VS WE) Fri & Sat 22-6h
Donja Kupcina 188 *30 km from Zagreb, towards Remetinec, Brezovica, Pisarovina* ☏ (098) 9625 464
Private house. Place for leather, rubber and uniform fans, skins or underwear fetishists. With sling, cabins and piss area. Special parties every Sat. Call for information.

Porec ☏ 052

SWIMMING

-Cervar Porata (G) (along the coast in the direction of Autocamp Ulika)
-White Bay/Bijela uvala (G) (4 km south of Pore, between Autocamp Bijela Uvala and Funtana)
-Sveti Nikola Island (opposite side of the main beach; head to to the western part of the island. Cruising along the seashore).

CRUISING

-Park Naftaplin, the park directly behind the Marina Porec. Busy after sunset especially at WE.

Primosten ☏ 022

HOTELS

■ **Stara Vila** (BF glm PA RWS RWT) May-Oct
Ribarska 14 ☏ (022) 570 154 www.staravila.de
The town is known for its old stone houses, cobbled streets and wonderful beaches, that are only a few metres from the hotel. English, German, Italian and Croatian spoken.

SWIMMING

-Beach (g) (in front of Hotel Marina Lucic)

Rab Island ☏ 051

BARS

■ **Celestina** (B GLM MA) 7-14 & 18-2h
Biskupa Draga 2 *Old town, opp. post office* ☏ (051) 213 406

■ **Sanda** (B GLM MA)
Donja ulica bb *Old town* ☏ (051) 725 764

SWIMMING

-Beach of the city of Rab (G MA) (by boat from the harbour. At the end of the nudist beach. Action in the woods)
-Frankj (G) (take a boat from Rab or a car to Suha Punta. Walk to the beach right next to Hotel Eva, turn left and at the end of the beach you will find the nudist area. You have to pay an entrance fee for the nudist area. When you have entered, walk through the woods and then turn right and walk approximately 300 m to reach the gay area which is told to be one of the most popular on the Croatian Rivera)
-Nudist beach at the end of the peninsula Frankj (take the boat from the harbour of Rab to the small island outside the city and then walk approximately 15 mins to get to the spot. One could also swim to the island. The shortest route is between two small bridges. Go to the end of the nudist beach).

CRUISING

-Park (between Hotel Istra and Hotel Imperijal)
-Park Dorka (small park in old town).

Rabac ☏ 052

SWIMMING

-Girandella (Nudist beach at the end of town, near hotel Girandella).

Rijeka ☏ 051

BARS

■ **Kosi Toranj - Lounge** (B g MA) 7-24h
Pul Vele crikve 1 *In the old town, near the Church of St Mary* ☏ (051) 336 214
The bar has a terrace and can be found in Old Town, near the leaning tower of the Church of St Mary of the Assumption.

DANCECLUBS

■ **Fun Academy** (B D glm s) Thu-Sun 22-5h
Preluk 1 *Bus 32 from Rijeka or Opatija to Preluk*
Especially gay Thu & Fri in summer.

SAUNAS/BATHS

■ **Aquateam** (AC b DR DU FC FH G GH I MA MSG OS RR SA SB SL VS WO) Sun-Thu 17-23, Fri & Sat -24h
Slavka Cindrica 9 *Close to City centre* ☏ (091) 511 0275 🖳 www.aquateam.hr
Close to the city centre, on the eastern side of river Rjecina.

GENERAL GROUPS

■ **LORI** (gLm) Office every day, 11-17h
Dolac 8 ☏ (051) 212 186 🖳 www.lori.hr
Website in Croatian only.

SWIMMING

-Bunker (G) (take bus 32 to Preluk, then walk back through the big curve, turn down to sea-shore)
-Medveja (g YC) (25 km west of Rijeka, on the Istrian peninsula, not far from Opatija and Moscenicka draga. The nude section is outside the village)
-Bivio (G) (take bus 1 from Rijeka. Get of at the last station then walk back some 100 m in direction of Rijeka, then turn down the steps and through the forest. Not very far from Bunker Beach).

CRUISING

-The Library of Rijeka University situated at Dolac 1, downtown Rijeka (near Hotel Bonavia). Look for guys sitting at the benches in the corridor on the first floor. Check out the toilets.
-beach at Rijeka, between Rijeka and Opatia at coastal street.

Rovinj ☏ 052

BARS

■ **Lobby** (B MA NG) 8-1h
Zdenac 6
Unofficial meeting place for gays.

APARTMENTS

■ **Apartments Porta Antica** (glm)
Vrata pod zidom 1 (office) ☏ (052) 811 315 🖳 www.portaantica.com
Four apartments with seaview on attractive locations in central Rovinj.

SWIMMING

-Punta Kriza (Cape Cross) or among gays often called Monsena. The most popular gay beach in Istria and northern Croatia. Can be found north/west of Rovinj, drive to Amarin (before called Monsena) camping-site. After roundabout take the dirt road to the right at the entrance to the Amarin resort. Go north along the sea until you reach the gay nudist area.
-Crveni otok (MA) (In the centre, near the temple). Not so popular as Monsena.

Selce ☏ 051

SWIMMING

-Selce Beach (NU) (At the end of the main beach, walk south approximately 10 minutes, in direction of Novi Vinodolski. The gay spot is when you can see the letters FKK written on some rocks).

Slavonski Brod ☏ 035

BARS

■ **Navigator** (B NG)
Korzo Main Street
Unofficial meeting place for gays. The bar can be found in the main shopping street called Korzo.

CRUISING

-Park next to the main railway station (Glavni kolodvor).

Split ☏ 021

BARS

■ **Ghetto** (B MA NG)
Dosud 10
Located within the palace walls, the combination of its location and atmosphere makes the Ghetto a great starting point for the evening.

■ **Teak** (B MA NG)
Majstora Jurja 11
Located in old part of the town.

DANCECLUBS

■ **Metropolis** (B D MA NG)
Matice Hrvatske 1 ☏ (021) 305110
Gays should be very discreet in this macho club; nevertheless said to be the unofficial meeting point for the G&L community in Split.

SWIMMING

-Duilovo (G) (take bus 15, then walk by the sea to the rocky end, between the Hotel Zagreb and the village of Stobrec). Most popular.
-Bikers Beach (by car via the Mestrovica Street in direction of the Oceanic Institute, turn left after 1 km, a small road leads to the beach. P. Near small white bus shelter go left to the beach. Be discreet. The beach is on the tip of the Marjan peninsula).

CRUISING

-Bacvice (from intercity bus station walk 200 m to a little park with a few benches. If a guy crosses the street to enter the park (called „Schwartzwald" by the local gay people) on the opposite side and disappears into the bushes, this could be a „signal" to you. Popular from around 19.30h or later in summer)

-Hotel Park (The whole area surrounding the hotel, including two parks, is very popular and cruisy. Most likely to meet somebody here is after midnight and WE) (AYOR)
-City Park (AYOR, near the monument)
-Main bus station and the park (AYOR) and beach behind (very active and popular).

Sibenik ☎ 022

SWIMMING

-Zablace (g MA) (The beach near Solaris camping-site. Walk by the seashore from Solaris camping centre towards Zablace camping centre. The gay spot is somewhere in the middle. Action in the bushes.)

Trogir ☎ 021

SWIMMING

-Beach (G) (walk to Hotel Medena. At the end of the hotel pavement begins a rocky beach. Action at the hill on the right side).

Umag ☎ 052

SWIMMING

-Polynezia (after the Village of Katoro, but before Zambratia. The best way to get there is to go to Zambratia and then walk from the small harbour to the beach. The gay spot is to be found in front of and on the peninsula).
-Kanegra-Crveni vrh (The beach is located between the campsite Kanegra and the village Crveni Vrh (Red Peak). Can be reached through campsite Kanegra through nudistic part in the direction of the village Crveni Vrh).

Varazdin ☎ 042

BARS

■ **Lavra** (b g MA)
Gajeva 17 *West of the city centre* 🖳 www.lavra.hr
■ **Piramida** (b g MA)
Bakaceva 2c *Near the park of the city centre*

SWIMMING

-Artificial Lakes (g) (to get there go by the road from Varaêdin to Koprivnica, popular).

CRUISING

-City park Mladost (Behind the national theatre. 22-24h in summer and 19-21h in winter.)

Veli Losinj ☎ 051

CRUISING

-Between Rovenska and Veli Losinj harbour.

Zadar ☎ 023

SWIMMING

-Puntamika (afternoons).

CRUISING

-Park near the Seamen College (evenings)
-Lenije Park near Bosuta.

Zagreb ☎ 01

BARS

■ **KIC club (Kulturno Informativni Centar)** (b GLM I MA OS) Mon & Sun 8-1h
Preradoviceva 5 *Near Flower square in the very centre*
A gay and lesbian friendly bar on the second floor. During the summer there is terrace on the street. Very popular and crowded. Smoking permitted.

■ **Vimpi** (b GLM I MA OS) Mon-Sat 8-1, Sun 9-1h
Prolaz sestara Bakovic 3 *Near Flower square and cinema Europa* ☎ (01) 4819 230
A gay and lesbian friendly bar in a small passage. During the summer there is outdoor terrace in the passage. Smoking permitted.

MEN'S CLUBS

■ **Denis** (b DR FC G I MA P SL VR) 14-24, Fri -1, Sat 15-23, Sun -24h
Mrazoviceva 9 *In the building on the ground floor* ☎ (098) 9313 836
🖳 www.denisclub.bloger.hr
Cruising-bar with few private cubicles. Sex parties every Saturday. Sometimes fetish parties.
■ **Mobilus** (b FC G GH I MA P VR VS) 15-23, Fri-Sun 16-24h
Ignjata Djordjica 10 *On the corner of Palmoticeva* ☎ (098) 1868 223
🖳 www.studio-mobilus.hr
In the apartment on the ground floor. Cruising-bar with few private cubicles.

DANCECLUBS

■ **Legacy Club** (B D glm MC) Thu-Sat 23-5h
36 Mesnicka St.
■ **Rush** (B D G MA) Thu-Sat 23-5h
Amruseva 10 *Centre of Zagreb, located close to the main square*

SEX SHOPS/BLUE MOVIES

■ **Lucky Bull** (AC CC g MA SH VS)
Mon-Fri 10-20, Sat 11-16h, Sun closed
Petrinjska 59 *City Centre, near Raiffeisen bank* ☎ (091) 1937 443
🖳 www.lucky-bull.hr
■ **Magic Market 1** (CC G MA VS) Mon-Sat 11-21h
Tuskanova 22 *Kvaternikov Square* ☎ (01) 465 07 35
🖳 www.magic-market.hr
■ **Magic Market 2** (AC CC MA VS) Fri & Sat 17-21h
Obrtnicki Prolaz 1 *City Centre* ☎ (01) 48 28 700 🖳 www.magic-market.hr

SAUNAS/BATHS

■ **David – Aquateam** (b DU FH G I MA p RR SA SB VS WO)
17-23, Fri & Sat -24h
ul. Ivana Broza 8a *Close to Sport Center Cibona* ☎ (091) 533 7757
🖳 www.sauna-aquateam.hr
One dry sauna and steam bath. Few cubicles and sling. Popular on weekends.

HOTELS

■ **Arcotel Allegra Zagreb** (AC B CC glm M OS PA PK RWS RWT SA SB VA WH WO) All year, 24hrs
Branimirova 29 *15 mins walk from main city square, 200 m from main railway station* ☎ (01) 4696-000 🖳 www.arcotelhotels.com/allegra

APARTMENTS

■ **FriendlyCroatia** (AC glm H I PA PK RWS RWT VA WO)
Check in at 12, Check out at 10h
Sermageova 9 *Zagreb centre* ☎ (091) 81 81 881 🖳 www.friendlycroatia.com
Private accommodation in Zagreb. Cosy apartments in the city centre. Online booking. Gay-friendly accommodation.

GENERAL GROUPS

■ **Zagreb Pride** (GLM)
Mestrovicev trg 2 ☎ (095) 9021 445 🖳 www.zagreb-pride.net
Festival Zagreb Pride take place in June every year.

SWIMMING

-Jarun lake (g MA NU) (Southern part of the eastern peninsula. Otok mladosti (Island of Youth), afternoons in summer only). Also at night near official nude beach along the path, throughout a year.

CRUISING

-Botanicki vrt/Botanical garden (g MA R) (Mihanoviceva Street. Mostly in the afternoon -20h. No sex possible. Meeting point only)
-Maksimir Park (g MA) (entrance from Bukovacka/Petrova Street. Western edge of the woods, late afternoon & evening)
-Bushes behind main bus station – Delete this, no more bushes there!
-Branimir's market place (Branimirova trnica) – public toilet
-Zrinjevac (meeting point on the south-eastern side).

Cyprus

Name: Kypros/Kibris · Zypern · Chypre · Chipre · Cipro
Location: Eastern Mediterranean Sea
Initials: CY
Time: GMT +2
International Country Code: ☎ 357 (south) and 90 (north)
International Access Code: ☎ 00
Language: Greek, Turkish
Area: 9,251 km² / 3,572 sq mi.
Currency: 1 Euro (€) = 100 Cents (south part). 1 Turkish Lira (TL) =100 Kurus
Population: 854,300
Capital: Nicosia (south part), Lefkosa (north part)
Religions: 95% Christ Orthodox
Climate: Mediterranean climate with hot, dry summers (Jun-Aug) and cooler, wet winters.
Important gay cities: Nicosia

In 2004 Cyprus joined the European Community, making life easier for the gay community. The EU directives do not tolerate discrepancy in any of the member states in regard to the treatment of homosexuals and heterosexuals. These differences, along with paragraph 171 were abolished before the new EU countries were accepted. Furthermore the age of consent was lowered from 18 to 17 years and raised for heterosexuals to 17. Nevertheless Cypriot society remains conservative.
The situation in the Turkish Republic of North Cyprus (controlled by the Turkish military) remains unclear although we made several attempts to obtain clarification from the Turkish authorities.

Die Aufnahme Zyperns in die Europäische Gemeinschaft im Jahr 2004 hat der dortigen Schwulengemeinde das Leben bedeutend leichter gemacht. Da die EU-Richtlinien in den Mitgliedsstaaten keine Abweichungen bei der Gleichstellung von Homo- und Heterosexuellen dulden, wurden diese vor dem Beitritt zur EU zusammen mit Artikel 171, der Analverkehr unter Strafe stellte, außer Kraft gesetzt. Außerdem wurde das Schutzalter für Homosexuelle von 18 auf 17 Jahre gesenkt und das für Heterosexuelle auf 17 Jahre angehoben. Die zypriotische Gesellschaft bleibt nichtsdestotrotz nach wie vor ziemlich konservativ.
Die Situation in der türkischen Republik des Nördlichen Zyperns (kontrolliert vom türkischen Militär) bleibt unklar, obwohl wir mehrere Versuche machten, Auskünfte von den türkischen Behörden zu erhalten.

L'entrée de la Chypre dans la Communauté Européenne en 2004 a facilité grandement la vie de la communauté gay locale. Vu que les directives européennes ne tolèrent dans les pays membres aucunes différenciations dans le traitement des gays et des hétérosexuels, les lois chypriotes non-conformes au droit européen dont l'article 171 qui punissait les relations anales ont été abrogées avant l'adhésion à l'UE. Deplus l'age légal pour les homosexuels est passé de 18 à 17 ans comme pour les hétérosexuels. La communauté chypriote reste cependant relativement conservatrice.
La situation dans la république de Chypre du Nord (contrôlée par l'armée turque) reste confuse, bien que nous ayons essayé de nous renseigner auprès des autorités turques.

La entrada de Chipre en la Unión Europea en el año 2004 facilitó de manera significativa la vida de la comunidad homosexual de la isla. Puesto que las directivas europeas no toleran en los estados miembros ningún tipo de contradicción sobre la equiparación de homosexuales y heterosexuales, todas fueron derogadas antes de la entrada a la UE junto con el artículo 171, que penalizaba el sexo anal. Además, la edad de consentimiento para los homosexuales se bajó de los 18 a los 17 años y para los heterosexuales se aumentó hasta los 17 años. Pese a todo esto, la sociedad chipriota sigue siendo igual que antes bastante conservadora.
Aunque se han hecho varios intentos para obtener información de las autoridades turcas, la situación en la República Turca del Norte de Chipre (controlada por las fuerzas armadas turcas) sigue sin estar clara.

L'ingresso di Cipro nell'Unione Europea avvenuto nel 2004 ha decisamente reso più facile la vita alla comunità gay del Paese. Poiché le direttive dell'Unione Europea non danno spazio a discriminazioni nell'ambito delle pari opportunità tra omosessuali ed eterosessuali, prima dell'ingresso nella UE si è provveduto ad eliminare queste discriminazioni, uno per tutti l'articolo 171 che penalizzava il sesso anale. Inoltre si è provveduto ad abbassare l'età del consenso per gli omosessuali da 18 a 17 e ad alzare quella per gli eterosessuali a 17.
La società cipriota rimane comunque abbastanza conservatrice.
La situazione nella Repubblica Turca di Cipro del Nord (controllata dalle milizie turche) rimane piuttosto confusa; i nostri numerosi tentativi di ricevere informazioni dalle autorità turche non ha portato grandi risultati.

NATIONAL GROUPS

Accept LGBT Cyprus
c/o NGO Support Centre, 27 Ezekia Papaioannou, Nicosia ✉ 1621 Nicosia 💻 www.acceptcy.org

North Part

Famagusta

SWIMMING

-Bedis Beach (between town and ruins; behind the bushes).

CRUISING

-City Walls (on top of main entrance to city. Climb up through the ramp way)
-Road from Port Gate toward Petek Pastanesi.

Kyrenia

BARS

Cream Bar/Club (AC B CC D G MA S)
56 Goksu Sokak *In car park around the corner to the Dome Hotel behind Ziraat Bankasi* ☎ 5428 556 264 💻 www.creamcyprus.com

A popular gay meeting space. A low-key location behind the harbour, warm relaxed staff and a Cypriot manager (with UK origin) ensures a safe platform for people to have a good time.

SWIMMING

-Kale arkasi (swimming behind the castle).

CRUISING

-Old Harbour Pier (Towards lighthouse. Pick up point is along the pier).

Nicosia / Lefkosia

CRUISING

-Kugulu Park (next to Kyrenia Gate)
-Arasta (Shopping centre towards the cathedral and market place, late at night)
-Oxi Square (transvestites, mainly non passive types) and the square's parking area and toilets.

South Part

Agia Napa

CRUISING

-Behind the Monastery (3 different places: the Hostel Gardens: cross the entrance behind Planet Bar and walk left at the dark side. Cruising after 1.30h. Another cruising place is the area between the road and Napia Star Hotel from 1.30 to 5.30h. The last cruising place is behind the monastery's hostel from 4.30h)
-Limanaki (Small Harbour): Cruising after 3h around the big beach at the end of the jetty
-Post Office: Some cruising after 1h at the square located at the Post Office and the public toilets.

Larnaca ☎ 04

DANCECLUBS

■ **Secrets Freedom Club** (AC B D DR GLM MA P S SNU VS WE) 21-4, Sat 23-4h, Mon & Tue closed
67, Artemidos Avenue *Larnaca Airport road* ☎ 99-455433
💻 www.secrets-freedom-club.com

CRUISING

-Phinikoudes (Day & Night along the coastal road but not frequently used).

Limassol ☎ 05

BARS

■ **Alaloum** (AC B D GLM MA S SNU ST T) 22-?h
1 Loutron Street, Old Town ☎ (05) 7 25 36 92 26
Best late at night.

CAFES

■ **Pi** (AC CC H NG OS) 10-24h
27 Kytiou Kyprianou, Palea Poli *Centre of the old town, in a restored building behind the town hall* ☎ (05) 253 419 44
Gay-friendly cafe/bar.

DANCECLUBS

■ **Escape FromUrself** (AC D GLM)
Makariou Avenue 81 ☎ 97757272
Very trendy.

GUEST HOUSES

■ **Rainbow Residence B&B** (AC BF G I M MA MSG RWB RWS RWT VA WH) All year
City Center *City, 6 mins from the beach* ☎ (05) 996 722 76
💻 www.rainbowresidence.com

SWIMMING

-Governors Beach: One of the most popular beaches for Gay people. Ignore the Touristy part of the beach and keep right at the end of the car park, after approximately ½ mile you will find another gravel car park. Park there and walk another ½ mile until you reach the white chalk Bays. Here you are, you can't miss it, people are cruising there all day long during the summer. Nudists welcome!
-Pissouri Beach: From the Highway, just head for the exit Pissouri Bay and continue until you get to a small roundabout. Turn left and park in the public car park. From there you can see the beach, once you have reached the beach, continue walking left and go straight until you hit some rocks, behind these rocks is where the very popular nudist beach starts. This part of the beach is frequented by plenty of gay guys which are there to top up the sun tan and some to have some daytime action.

CRUISING

-Dassoudi: At night the Dassoudi Beach area behind Pizza Hut turns into a very busy cruising area for gay men. If you are looking for some action at night, take a look, you might find what you are looking for. Please be careful as not all the people going for a nightly walk along the Dassoudi beach are gay.

Nicosia / Lefkosia ☎ 02

BARS

■ **Bastione** (B M NG s)
6, Athinas ave. *Near „green line" in old town* ☎ (02) 7 22 43 31 01
Busy late.

■ **Zoo Lounge** (B M MA NG) Daily
15 Stasinou avenue *Tafros area* ☎ (02) 7 22 45 88 11

CRUISING

-Eleftherias Square (cruising occurs peak times afternoons, late noon around 22h and then after 3h when clubs start closing. Drive up and down, follow the cars that stroll in the parkings, if they flash they are interested).
-D'avila parking (located opposite Zoo Lounge Bar, near the toilets. Meetings here happens on foot and by car).
-D'Avila municipal Garden, Constanza Bastion & Podocataro Parking by Salaminos Avenue and Old General Hospital Municipal Garden (parking areas considered safe due to the use of cars, gardens AYOR. On parking no serious attacks yet; some have occured in the gardens).
-Venetian Wall (Appart from an excellent military architectural unique design offers more pleasure for gay cruising during the night).

Paphos ☎ 06

BARS

■ **Different Bar. The** (B GLM H MA OS) 19-3.30h
Ayias Napas 4-7 *Paphos Aquarium* ☎ (06) 26 93 46 68
💻 www.differentbar.com
Very gay-friendly and meeting point of the Paphos' gays.

SWIMMING

-Spilies (Caves beach) tourist place used also as a cruising place before or after the caves.

CRUISING

-Castle (Cruising late at night at the marina in front of the castle)
-Pafos Baths (toilets and dressing rooms).

Czech Republic

Name: Ceská Republika · Tschechische Republik · République Tchèque · República Checa · Repubblica Ceca
Location: Central Europe
Initials: CZ
Time: GMT +1
International Country Code: ☏ 420
International Access Code: ☏ 00
Language: Czech
Area: 78,866 km² / 30,449 sq mi.
Currency: 1 Koruna (Kc) = 100 Haléru
Population: 10,234,000
Capital: Praha
Religions: 27% Catholic or Protestant
Climate: Moderate climate. Summers are warm, winters cold, cloudy and humid. Ideal months are May, Jun & Sept.
Important gay cities: Praha

Homosexuality was decriminalised in 1961. Laws against homosexual relations were repealed in 1990. The legal minimum age of consent (for heterosexual and homosexual relations alike) is 15 years (if no money is involved). Additionally, it is an offence to expose a minor (under 18) to the „danger of depravation" by enabling him an „idle or indecent life" or by seducing him into such a life.
The Czech parliament overrode the veto of the Czech president and voted in the domestic partnership law in May 2006. Gays and lesbians now have all the same rights as heterosexuals do, including the right to marry. The only exception is that they cannot adopt children.
Prague is a liberal city where many gay Czechs choose to live. There are no laws concerning tourists with HIV/AIDS but the intentional infection to any sexually transmitted disease is punishable according to § 189-190 of the Czech penal code with imprisonment of up to two years. Unintentional infection is also punishable with imprisonment for one year. Prostitution and the promotion of prostitution is legal, if the prostitute is at least 18 years old. Prostitution is however not accepted as a profession. The proliferation of pornography is illegal.
Czech society is generally liberal and open minded, perhaps because the church never had much influence within the society. This continues today, with a certain attitude of defiance. This liberal stand also covers sexuality and different lifestyles. The number of gay bars, clubs, cafes and accommodations is permanently growing.
A culture and film festival called Mezipatra has been taking place since 2002 in Prague. Prague's gay and lesbian scene is comparable with many western cities of the same size. Despite the extensive commercial gay scene and liberal Czech society, Prague had to wait until August 2011 for the first Gay Pride. Following its great success, Prague Pride is also to be continued next year. The Czech Crown will be still in use for the next couple of years. A change to the European currency the Euro is not planned in the near future.

Homosexualität steht seit 1961 nicht mehr unter Strafe und fortbestehende Gesetze, die gegen gleichgeschlechtliche Beziehungen diskriminierten, wurden 1990 endgültig außer Kraft gesetzt. Das gesetzliche Mindestalter (für hetero- und homosexuelle Beziehungen) ist 15 (sofern Geld keine Rolle spielt). Weiterhin stellt es ein Vergehen dar, Minderjährige (unter 18) der „Gefahr der Verwahrlosung" auszusetzen, indem man sie zu einem „müßigen oder unsittlichen Lebenswandel" verleitet oder ihnen einen solchen ermöglicht.
Im Mai 2006 hob das tschechische Parlament das Veto des tschechischen Präsidenten auf und verabschiedete ein Gesetz zur Anerkennung eingetragener Partnerschaften. Seither erfreuen sich Schwule und Lesben fast derselben Rechte wie Heterosexuelle, einschließlich des Rechts zu heiraten. Die einzige Ausnahme besteht darin, dass sie keine Kinder adoptieren dürfen.
Prag ist eine liberale Stadt, die viele schwule Tschechen zu ihrer Wahlheimat gemacht haben. Es gibt zwar keine spezifischen Bestimmungen für Touristen mit HIV/AIDS, doch die wissentliche Ansteckung mit einer sexuell übertragbaren Krankheit ist laut § 189-190 des tschechischen Strafgesetzbuches mit bis zu zwei Jahren Freiheitsentzug strafbar. Auch eine unbeabsichtigte Ansteckung kann mit Freiheitsentzug von bis zu einem Jahr geahndet werden. Die Prostitution und das öffentliche Anbieten sexueller Dienste sind legal, solange der Sexarbeiter/die Sexarbeiterin mindestens 18 Jahre alt ist, doch Prostitution wird nicht als Beruf anerkannt. Die Verbreitung von Pornographie ist hingegen illegal.
Die tschechische Gesellschaft ist generell liberal und freizügig, vielleicht weil die Kirche in ihr noch nie einen großen Einfluss ausgeübt hat, was sich heutzutage mit einer gewissen Aufsässigkeit fortsetzt. Diese liberale Einstellung erstreckt sich auch auf die Sexualität und unterschiedliche Lebensweisen. Die Zahl der schwulen Bars, Nachtclubs, Cafes und Übernachtungsmöglichkeiten ist in einem fortlaufenden Wachstum begriffen.
Seit 2002 findet in Prag ein Kultur- und Filmfestival namens Mezipatra statt. Die Lesben- und Schwulenszene Prags ist mit den entsprechenden Gegebenheiten in vielen westeuropäischen Städten gleicher Größe vergleichbar. Trotz der umfangreichen und kommerziellen Schwulenszene und der liberalen tschechischen Gesellschaft fand erst im August 2011 der erste CSD in Prag statt. Nach dem großen Erfolg soll der Prague Pride auch 2012 fortgeführt werden. Die tschechische Krone wird auch in den nächsten beiden Jahren als Zahlungsmittel in Verwendung bleiben, denn eine Umstellung auf die europäische Einheitswährung Euro ist in naher Zukunft nicht geplant.

L'homosexualité est dépénalisée depuis 1961 et les lois restantes qui discriminaient les relations de même sexe ont été définitivement abrogées en 1990. L'âge minimal légal pour les relations hétérosexuelles et homosexuelles est de 15 ans pour autant que l'argent ne joue pas un rôle. Cependant, l'exposition d' un mineur de moins de 18 ans à un „danger de déchéance" représente un délit lorsqu'on l'incite à une „conduite oisive et immorale" ou on lui rend possible une telle conduite.
En mai 2006 le parlement tchèque a levé le véto du président tchèque et a adopté une loi de reconnaissance d'un „pacs". Depuis lors, les gays et lesbiennes jouissent pratiquement des mêmes droits que les hétérosexuels, y compris le droit au mariage. La seule exception est qu'ils ne peuvent pas adopter d'enfants.

Prague est une ville libérale où beaucoup de gays tchèques ont élu domicile. Il n'existe certes pas de dispositions pour les touristes séropositifs, cependant la contamination intentionnelle par une maladie sexuellement transmissible est punie d'une peine de réclusion de deux ans maximum selon les paragraphes 189-190 du code pénal tchèque. Une contamination même involontaire peut être aussi punie d'une peine de réclusion d'un an maximum. La prostitution et l'offre publique de services sexuels sont légaux tant que le travailleur social est âgé d'au minimum 18 ans, cependant la prostitution n'est pas reconnue comme une profession. A l'inverse, la diffusion de la pornographie est illégale. La société tchèque est en général libérale et permissive, peut-être parce que l'église n'y a encore jamais trouvé une grande influence, ce qui qui se poursuit de nos jours avec une certaine insoumission. Cette attitude libérale se porte aussi sur la sexualité et sur les modes de vie différents. Le nombre de bars gays, boîtes de nuit, cafés et possibilités d'hébergement poursuit une croissance continue.
Un festival cinématographique et culturel nommé Mezipatra est organisé depuis 2002 à Prague. La scène gay et lesbienne à Prague est comparable à celles d'autres villes d'Europe occidentale de taille similaire. Malgré la scène gay foisonnante et commerciale et la société tchèque libérale, la première Gay Pride n'a eu lieu qu'en août 2011. Après ce grand succès, la Gay Pride continuera en 2012.
La Couronne tchèque va rester en usage ces deux prochaines années, le passage à la monnaie unique européenne n'étant pas prévu dans un futur proche.

La homosexualidad no está penada desde 1961 y las leyes existentes que discriminaban contra las relaciones homosexuales fueron abolidas definitivamente en 1990. La edad mínima legal (para relaciones heterosexuales y homosexuales) está en los 15 años (siempre que no haya dinero de por medio). No obstante, sigue siendo un delito el hecho de poner a los menores (menos de 18) en el „peligro del desaliño", en tanto que se los conduce a un „cambio de vida ocioso o inmoral" o bien se lo permiten.
En mayo de 2006 el Parlamento checo levantó el veto del presidente checo y aprobó una ley para el reconocimiento del registro de parejas. Desde entonces, gays y lesbianas gozan casi de los mismos derechos que los heterosexuales, incluído el derecho a casarse. La única excepción es que no les está permitido adoptar niños.
Praga es una ciudad liberal, que muchos gays checos han escogido como su ciudad de domicilio. No existen disposiciones específicas para turistas con HIV/SIDA, pero el contagio consciente de una enfermedad de transmisión sexual, según el artículo 189-190 del código penal checo, está castigado con una pena de privación de libertad de hasta 2 años. También el contagio sin intención puede ser castigado con una pena de privación de libertad de hasta un año. La prostitución y la oferta pública de servicios sexuales son legales, siempre que los trabajadores o las trabajadoras del sexo tengan al menos 18 años, aunque la prostitución no esté reconocida como profesión. La difusión de pornografía, por el contrario, es ilegal.
La sociedad checa es generalmente liberal y abierta, quizá porque la Iglesia nunca ha tenido una gran influencia, lo que todavía continua actualmente con cierta rebeldía. Esta postura liberal también se refleja en la sexualidad y en las formas de vida diferentes. El número de bars gays, clubes nocturnos, cafés y otras formas de ocio ha ido creciendo de manera continuada.
Desde 2002 se celebra un festival de cultura y cine en Praga, llamado Mezipatra. El ambiente gay-lésbico de Praga es comparable a la oferta de muchas ciudades europeas occidentales del mismo tamaño. A pesar de contar con una extensa y comercial comunidad gay y con una sociedad liberal, la primera Marcha del Orgullo Gay en Praga tuvo lugar en agosto de 2011. Tras su enorme éxito, esta Marcha volverá a tener lugar en 2012. La corona checa seguirá siendo aún en los próximos dos años la unidad monetaria de uso corriente, puesto que no está previsto un cambio a la moneda única europea (Euro) en un futuro cercano.

Nella Repubblica Ceca l'omosessualità è stata depenalizzata nel 1961. Le ultime disposizioni di legge contro l'omosessualità sono state abolite nel 1990. L'età del consenso è di 15 anni sia per i rapporti tra eterosessuali sia per i rapporti tra omosessuali. La suddetta età del consenso non vale per i rapporti sessuali nei quali ci sia stata una ricompensa in denaro. Infatti, è considerato un reato esporre un minorenne (al di sotto del diciottesimo anno di età) al „pericolo di depravazione" permettendogli o inducendolo ad „uno stile di vita ozioso o immorale".
A maggio del 2006 il parlamento della Repubblica Ceca ha approvato la legge sul riconoscimento delle unioni civili. Da allora i gay e le lesbiche godono di quasi gli stessi diritti di cui godono gli eterosessuali, compreso il diritto a sposarsi. L'unica eccezione consiste nel fatto che non è ancora consentito ad una coppia dello stesso sesso di adottare bambini.
Praga è una città molto liberale dove molti gay cechi decidono di trasferirsi. Non esistono precise disposizioni di legge per turisti portatori di HIV/AIDS, tuttavia secondo il paragrafo 189-190 del codice civile ceco, il contagio volontario di una malattia a trasmissione sessuale è punibile con una pena detentiva di massimo due anni. Il contagio involontario, invece, può essere punito con una pena detentiva di massimo un anno.
La prostituzione e la contrattazione pubblica di prestazioni sessuali sono legali solo se l'operatore/l'operatrice del sesso abbia compiuto il diciottesimo anno di età. Tuttavia questo lavoro non è ancora riconosciuto come professione. Mentre per quanto riguarda la pornografia, la sua diffusione è illegale.
Forse la società ceca è così liberale e così aperta perché la chiesa non ha mai avuto una grande influenza sul Paese. Questa tradizione continua ad essere portata avanti con una certa protervia. Questa attitudine liberale è riscontrabile anche nei confronti delle questioni di sessualità e nei confronti di stili di vita diversi. Il numero di bar gay, locali notturni, nightclub, caffè e servizi alberghieri gay è in costante aumento.
Tuttavia a Praga, dal 2002, si svolge un festival culturale e cinematografico che si chiama Mezipatra. La scena gay e lesbica di Praga, per opportunità, è ormai paragonabile a molte città europee occidentali di simile grandezza. Nonostante la vivacità della scena gay e nonostante l'apertura mentale della società ceca, il rimo CSD di Praga ha avuto luogo solo nell'agosto del 2011. Dopo il grande successo avuto, il Prague Pride riavrà luogo anche nel 2012. Poiché non è prevista nei prossimi anni l'adozione della moneta unica europea, la corona ceca rimarrà, ancora per alcuni anni, mezzo di pagamento ufficiale del Paese.

NATIONAL COMPANIES

Erotic City (CC G VS) Daily 9-21h
Na Belidle 63/1, Prague ✉ Prague 🖳 www.eroticcity.cz
With over 50 sex shops, this is the largest chain of sex shops in the Czech Republic.

Princ Press (G) Mon-Fri 10-18h
Komárkova 21 ✉ 148 00 Praha 4 ☏ 267 911 804 🖳 www.gayboy.cz
Publisher of gay porn magazines such as Princ, producer of gay porns (all in Czech).

Brno ☏ 5

GAY INFO

GayGuide.Net Brno (GLM)
🖳 www.brno.gayguide.net
Permanently updated Gay Guide. All emails are replied within 48 hours. English and German spoken.

BARS

Ácko (B glm M MA) Mon-Fri 11-24, Sat & Sun 15-24h
Starobrnenska 16/18 ☏ 603 398 273 🖳 www.acko-brno.cz
Bar/restaurant.

Dave's club (B GLM WI) 17-3h
Hybešova 8 ☏ 734 744 240 (mobile) 🖳 davesclub.cz
Newly opened in 2011.

Gibon Club (AC B DR F G m MA NU P VS) 17-2h
Pekarská 38 ☏ 543 246 677 🖳 gibon.ic.cz
Also sex shop. Naked party on Thu & Fri. Ring doorbell. Staff speaks English

H46 (B GLM M MA P R) 20-4h
Hybesova 46 *Tram 1/2 Hybesova, 10 mins from main railway station in direction fair area* ☏ 724 783 997 🖳 www.h46.cz
Oldest gay and lesbian bar in Brno. Busy from midnight.

MonRo (B glm OS) 9-20h
Cernopolni 33 ☏ 603 219 394 🖳 www.kavarnamonro.cz
Coffee house with 20 types of coffee. Summer terrace. Mixed crowd.

DANCECLUBS

Depo Club (B D GLM MA) Wed & Thu 18-2, Fri & Sat 21-6h
Pekarská 7 *Tram 5/6/12/13 Silingrovo Namesti* ☏ 777 733 901 (mobile)
🖳 www.depobrno.com

Richard Club (AC B D GLM I M MA P VS) Fri & Sat 20-6h
Luzova 29 *Zemedelska station, bus 93, tram 9/11* ☏ 533 312 952
🖳 www.richard.ic.cz

SAUNAS/BATHS

Palmas. Las (AC B DR DU FC G M MA P RR SA SB SH SOL VS WH) 16-3h
Galandauerova 17 *Kralovo Pole district, Bus 32 Srbska Street*
☏ 720 363 655 (mobile) 🖳 www.las-palmas.wz.cz
Small and very clean sauna, where one can also enjoy a light meal. The steam room is very small (3 men inside and it is crowded).

GENERAL GROUPS

STUD Brno Civic Association (G)
Bratislavska 31 ☏ 549 212 727 🖳 www.stud.cz
Community centre, queer library.

SWIMMING

-Brno Dam (NU beach). Transport: tram No 1, 3, 11 - ‚Bystrc-prístaviste' station, and ferry - ‚Osada' station.

CRUISING

-Ceská ulice
-Park in front of New Opera House
-Near Tesco department store
-Denisovy sady - Petrov hill.

Hostka ☏ 416

GUEST HOUSES

Penzion U Vikomta (AC B d g M NU OS P PI PK RWB SA ST WO)
All year, restaurant 10-22, bar 16-?h
Pod Nádrazím 281 ☏ 604 799 359 (mobile)
Inexpensive accommodation in Czech countryside. 3 rooms, all with shared bath. Czech or German spoken, but no English. Call for info about events.

Karlovy Vary ☏ 17

CAFES

Freedom Café (b glm) Mon-Fri 9-21h
Yugoslavska 3 ☏ 353 231 621 🖳 www.freedomcafe.cz
Cosy café/bar that attracts a gay/straight clientel.

Liberec ☏ 48

BARS

Marek (B D GLM MA) Fri & Sat 20-5h
Svernova 62 *Bus/tram Viadukt stop* ☏ 604 240 457 (mobile)

www.clubmarek.cz
Disco on Fri and Sat.

Most ☎ 35

GENERAL GROUPS

Most k Nadeji (GLM)
c/o Dum humanity, Jilemnického 1929 ☎ 476 104 877 (office)

Olomouc ☎ 68

BARS

Club Diva (B D GLM MA) Tue-Thu 20-2, Fri & Sat -5h
Pavelcákova 17 *Tram 1,2 center* ☎ 585 230 579
www.club-diva.websnadno.cz

Ostrava ☎ 69

BARS

Bar Ikarus (B G MA WI)
Mon-Thu 17 - ?, Fri & Sat 19- ?h, Sun closed
Nadrazni 34 *Downtown Tram 1/2/4/8/12 at Stodolni stop*
☎ 596 112 187 (moblie) www.barikarus.cz

Klub Bar Fiesta (Stara Fiesta) (B D GLM MA) Mon-Thu 16-24, Fri & Sat 19-3h, closed Sun
28 Rijna 59/239 *near the Opera House* ☎ 596 158 656
www.barfiesta.cz

MEN'S CLUBS

Beton (B CC DR F G MA P SNU VS) 16-4h
Bendlova 16 *Tram Marinska Namesti Bus 3 4 8 9 12 24 42*
☎ 596 617 609 www.beton-club.com
SM-equipment: cage, wooden cross, handcuffs, chains and sling.

GENERAL GROUPS

Klub Lambda
Vrsovcu 2/1147, Mariánské Hory ☎ 608 024 420 (mobile)

CRUISING

-In front of Hotel Ostrava Imperial (at New Church, námesti Národni).

Pardubice ☎ 40

BARS

Ptaci Klec (B D G MA S VS) Sat 20-?h
Ohrazenicka 310 *Trolleybus 2/3/4/11 Polabiny and Hradec stop*
☎ 723 923 237 www.diskoklec.cz
Saturday gay party, otherwise not gay.

Plzen ☎ 19

BARS

Club Misa (B D GLM MA p) Wed & Thu 21-24, Fri & Sat 21-5h
Cernicka 9-11 www.club-misa.cz
There's a bar, a place for the DJ, a dancefloor and 3 lounges.

Praha ☎ 2

Prague is an important gay centre in Eastern Europe, currently there are over 40 gay clubs, cafes, saunas and restaurants in Prague and this number is growing yearly. It is a liberal city where many gay Czechs choose to live. Czech society is open-minded and tolerant, perhaps because the church does not have much influence. Prague is one of the most beautiful cities in Europe, with 10 centuries of architecture, the world's largest castle complex and an Old Town Square out of a fairytale. Discover for yourself why the ancient Roman's named Prague „Mater Urbium", Mother of Cities. The Czech countryside is beautiful, with rolling hills, castles, medieval towns and mountains in the north and south. Brno, the second largest city, is developing a lively gay scene, with more than half a dozen gay cafes, clubs and saunas. A gay film festival called Mezipatra is held every November in both Prague and Brno.

Prag ist ein wichtiges Schwulenzentrum für Osteuropa mit momentan über 40 schwulen Nachtlokalen, Cafes, Saunen und Restaurants, und jedes Jahr kommen weitere hinzu. Es ist eine tolerante Stadt, die nicht nur viele schwule Tschechen anzieht. Die tschechische Gesellschaft ist generell aufgeschlossen und tolerant, wahrscheinlich weil die Kirche keinen großen Einfluss hat. Prag ist eine der schönsten Städte Europas mit Architektur aus 10 Jahrhunderten, dem größten Burgkomplex der Welt und einem Altstadtzentrum wie im Märchen. Entdecken Sie selbst, wieso die Römer Prag als „Mater Urbium", Mutter aller Städte, bezeichneten. Die tschechischen Landschaften sind wunderschön, mit sanften Hügeln, Schlössern, mittelalterlichen Städten und Bergen im Norden und Süden. In Brno, der zweitgrößten Stadt, entwickelt sich momentan eine lebendige Schwulenszene mit einer wachsenden Anzahl von schwulen Cafes, Nachtlokalen und Saunen. In Prag und Brno findet jeden November ein schwules Filmfestival namens „Mezipatra" statt.

Prague est un important centre homosexuel en Europe de l'Est et compte à ce jour plus de 40 cafés, boîtes, saunas et restaurants gays, nombre augmentant chaque année. Prague est une ville qui n'attire pas uniquement les gays tchèques, c'est également une des plus belles villes d'Europe offrant dix siècle architecture, le plus grand château-fort du monde et un centre-ville historique tout droit sorti d'un conte. Venez donc découvrir pourquoi les Romains nommaient Prague « Mater Urbium », la mère des villes. La société tchèque est de manière générale ouverte et tolérante, sans doute car l'Eglise y a peu d'influence. Les paysages tchèques sont magnifiques avec leurs collines, leurs châteaux, les villes médiévales et les montagnes au nord et au sud. A Brno, la deuxième ville du pays, un milieu gay est en train de s'installer et on y trouve en novembre, de même qu'à Prague, un festival annuel du film gay et lesbien, „Mezipatra".

Praga es un centro gay importante para Europa del Este, con más de 40 locales nocturnos, cafés, saunas y restaurantes, y cada año hay más. Es una ciudad tolerante que no sólo atrae a muchos gays checos. La sociedad checa en general es abierta y tolerante, probablemente porque la Iglesia tiene poca influencia. Praga es una de las ciudades más bonitas de Europa, con una arquitectura de 10 siglos, el mayor castillo del mundo y un centro antiguo de ensueño.
Descubra usted mismo por qué los romanos denominaron a Praga „Mater Urbium", la madre de todas las ciudades. Los paisajes checos son maravillosos, con suaves colinas, castillos, ciudades medievales y montañas en el norte y sur. En Brno, la segunda ciudad del país, está surgiendo un ambiente homosexual dinámico con un creciente número de cafés, locales nocturnos y saunas. En Praga y Brno se celebra cada mes de noviembre un festival de cine gay-lésbico llamado „Mezipatra".

Praga è un importante centro gay per l'Europa dell'est. La città conta più di 40 locali gay, caffè, saune e ristoranti, ed ogni anno se ne aggiungono dei nuovi. La popolazion ceca in generale è molto aperta e tollerante - probabilmente perché qui la chiesa non ha molto influsso sulle persone. Praga è una delle più belle città d'Europa con un'architettura di dieci diversi secoli. Il complesso del castello è uno dei più grandi del mondo ed il centro storico è letteralmente fiabesco. Scoprite voi stessi perché i romani chiamavano Praga Mater Urbim, cioè madre di tutte le città. A Brno, la seconda città più grande della Repubblica Ceca, si va sviluppando una scena gay sempre più vivace: i locali notturni, i caffè e le saune aumentano a vista d'occhio. In novembre, a Praga e a Brno si svolge ogni anno un festival del cinema omosessuale chiamato Mezipatra.

GAY INFO

GayGuide.Net Prague (GLM)
prague.gayguide.net
Permanently updated gay guide including reviews of all listed places. Information on gay-owned accommodation & gay-operated guided tours and airport transfers.

SHOWS

Tingl Tangl (AC B cc D glm M MA OS ST t WE)
Mon-Sat 11-23, Sun 10-22h
Karolíny Svetlé 12 ☎ 224 238 278 🖳 www.tingltangl.cz
Entertainment complex with a garden restaurant, cabaret, disco and cocktail bar. Great Czech and international dishes. Transvestite shows: Wed, Fri & Sat, mostly in Czech.

BARS

Angels Cafe (B g m YC) 17-1h, closed Sun
Vinohradská 30 *Tram 11 Italska stop, M° Muzeum* 🖳 www.angelscafe.cz
A good starting point before heading to other clubs. An intimate space, the staff is very attentive, and good quality beverages.

Club Temple & Little Temple Bar (AC B CC D G H M MA R SNU ST VS) 20-4h (Club), 12-22 (Bar)
Seifertova 32/3 *Tram 5/9/26 Husinecka stop, Night tram 55/58 Husinecka stop, 5 min walk from Metro C Hlavni Nadrazi* ☎ 222 710 773
🖳 www.clubtemple.net
Hustler bar with bar lounge. The club (former Pinocchio Club) is downstairs. Little Temple Bar (former) is a small cozy bar upstairs.

Fan Fan Club (AC B GLM MA) 17-2h
Dittrichova 5 *Trams 3/4/10/14/16-Palackeho Namesti; Metro Karlovo Namesti- exit in direction of Palackeho Namesti* ☎ 776 360 698 (mobile)
🖳 www.fan-club.cz
Trendy neighborhood bar, good place to meet new friends.

Friends Prague (! AC B D GLM S VS YC) 18-4h
Bartolomejska 11 ☎ 226 211 920 🖳 www.friendsprague.cz
200 m² of space, situated in Prague's down town area. Sound and video projection system. Wed & Sat parties with DJs.

Jampa Dampa (AC B GLM VS WE YC)
Mon-Thu 13-3, Fri & Sat 13-6h, Sun 18-1h
V Tuních 10 *Tram 4/6/10/16/22/23; Night tram 51/56/57 I.P. Pavlova stop; Metro I.P.Pavlova station* ☎ 739 592 099 (mobile)
🖳 www.jampadampa.cz
The most popular place for lesbians to hang out, especially on the weekends. 60% lesbian crowd then.

Klub 21 (B GLM MA P) Sun-Thu 18-24, Fri & Sat -2h
Rímská 21 ☎ 603 539 475 🖳 www.klub21.cz
Comfortable, nicely designed cellar bar with a relaxed atmosphere. Mostly young Czech audience, staff has limited English skills.

■ **KU Bar** (B glm MA) 19-4h
Rytirska 13 *Metro Mustek* ☎ 221 181 081 🖳 www.kubar.cz
Stylish trendy bar with cute waitstaff. Nightly DJ performances. Not gay but gay frequented.

■ **Latimerie Club Cafe** (B GLM MC) Daily 16-?h
Slezska 74 *Tram 10/16, night tram 51 Vinohradska Vodarna; M° Jiriho Z Podebrad* ☎ 224 252 049 🖳 www.latimerieclub.cz
Comfortably decorated club with a bar and table seating. Gets a mixed crowd and gets busy after 23h.

■ **Muzeum** (AC B glm MA) Mon-Fri 10-23, Sat & Sun 13-23h
Mezibranska 19 *50 meters from Metro Muzeum* ☎ 222 221 312
Cafe and bar near Wenceslas Square. Frequented by gays, especially between 17-23h.

■ **Piano Bar** (B G m MA) 17-?h
Milesovská 10 *Metro A Jiriho z Podebrad - Exit Námestí Jiriho z Podebrad, appr. 100 meter in TV-Tower-direction. Tram 11* ☎ 222 969 88 🖳 pianobar.sweb.cz
One of the very first gay bars in the Czech Republic. Mix of young and older, locals and tourists.

■ **Saints. The** (B CC GLM MA WI) 19-4h
Polská 32 ☎ 775 152 043 🖳 www.saintsbar.cz
Cosy and friendly English-speaking neighbourhood bar.

■ **Silwer Cafe and Bar** (B glm MA)
Mon-Thu 10-2, Fri & Sat 11-3, Sun 11-2h
Jungmannova Namesti 21 *M° Mustek, Trams 3/9/14/24 Vaclavske Namesti* ☎ 222 212 702 🖳 silwercafebar.cz
This cool, retro designed cafe attracts a mixed gay/straight good looking crowd.

■ **Club Strelec** (B G MC) 17-3h
Anglicka 616/2 ☎ 606 947 613 (mobile) 🖳 clubstrelec.com
Old fashioned Czech wine and beer pub attracting a mostly middle aged Czech clientele. Wednesdays popular with bears. Moved to new location in 2011.

■ **U Rudolfa** (B G OC) Mon-Fri 14-2, Sat & Sun 16-2h
Mezibranská 3 ☎ 605 872 492 (mobile)
Local Czech pub. A few foreign guests reported they did not feel welcome here, a few others like it. Cheap beer.

MEN'S CLUBS

■ **Alcatraz** (B DR F G M MA P S VS) 21-6h
Borivojova 58 *Tram 5, 9, 26, 55, 58 Lipanska* ☎ 222 711 458 🖳 www.alcatraz.cz
Modern sex club for uniforms, rubber & leather types. Naked parties every Thu and underwear parties every Sun. Fist parties two times a month. Popular.

■ **Drake's** (AC B CC DR G I MA MSG p R S SNU VS) 24hrs
Zborovská 50 *Metro Andel, Tram 6/22/23/ to Ujezd stop; Night tram 57/58 to Ujezd stop and 300 meters walk, corner of Petrinska* ☎ 257 326 828 🖳 www.drakes.cz
On 750 m² on 2 floors, enormous labyrinth, 40 cabins, small sex cinema, large bar area, sex shop, sling, cage and leather dungeon. Cover charge applies.

■ **Escape to Paradise** (AC B CC D G I MA R S SNU) Daily 21-4h
V Jáme 8 *Metro Muzeum and Mustek, close to Wenceslas Square; Tram 3/9/14/24-Vodickova* ☎ 606111177 (mobile) 🖳 www.escapeprague.eu
Escape To Paradise is right in the center of Prague, close to all the sites. Go-go dancers perform from 21h.

CAFES

■ **Alex Bistro** (B GLM M YC) 8-22, Sat 9-22, Sun -17h
Jecna 4 *Metro Karlovo Namesti; Trams 4 6 10 16 22 23 Stepanska stop; Night trams 51 56 57 59* ☎ 224 919 125 🖳 www.alexbistro.cz
Gay & lesbian friendly cafe and restaurant. Excellent burgers and sandwiches.

■ **Cafe-Cafe** (B CC M OS) 10-23h
Rytirska 10 *150 meter from metro station Mustek. Follow direction to Staromestke namesti, aka Oldtown square* ☎ 224 210 597 🖳 www.cafe-cafe.cz
Not really gay and mostly frequented by tourists.

■ **Erra Cafe** (B BF CC DM GLM M MA VEG) 10-24h
Konviktská 11 *Near Národní Třída, Metro B, Tram 22, 9, 18, 17, 6* ☎ 222 220 568 🖳 www.cafeerra.cz
Cosy place and very cute waiters. Recently renovated, relaxed atmosphere, good value snack meals with healthy and vegetarian options. Also a daily lunch menu.

■ **Kafírna U Ceského Pána** (B G MA WI) 14-23h
Kozí 858/13 *Metro A Station Staromestská, Tram 5, 14, 53 Dvorákovo nabrezi* ☎ 222 328 283 🖳 www.kafirna.wbs.cz
Small café-bar near the Jewish quarter.

■ **Q Café** (AC B CC GLM m MA S) 12-24h
Opatovická 166/12 *Tram 6/9/17/18/21/22-Narodni Trida; Metro Narodni Trida* ☎ 603 204 215 🖳 www.q-cafe.cz
Gay cafe and information desk.

■ **Sahara Cafe** (b g M MC) Mon-Fri 11-0.30, Sat 12-0.30, Sun 12-23h
Namesti Miru 6 *Tram 4/6/10/16/22/23-Namesti Miru: Metro Namesti Miru* ☎ 222 514 987 🖳 www.saharacafe.com
Stylish, sexy lounge cafe and restaurant, serving beverages, cocktails, salads, fresh pastas, grilled meats and yummy deserts. Moderately priced. A very cool new place to hang out in Prague, not gay, but gay frequented.

■ **Twin Café** (b m MC NG) Daily 8.30-21.30h
Novy Smichov Shopping Mall, Plzeňská 8 *Trams 4/7/20/14-Andel stop; Metro Andel* ☎ 257 324 413 🖳 www.twincafe.cz
Hip cafe serves coffees, drinks and light meals. Smart crowd of young good looking Czechs. Not gay but gay staffed.

DANCECLUBS

■ **Feno Man Club** (B D GLM I YC) Sun-Tue 17-5, Wed, Fri & Sat -9h
Blanicka 28 *M° Namesti Miru* ☎ 603 740 263 (mobile) 🖳 www.fenomanclub.cz
A bar with various seating areas, disco on weekends and Wednesdays. Attracts a mostly young Czech crowd. In the same neighbourhood as other popular venues.

■ **Lollypop @ Radost FX** (B D glm MA S)
Belehradska 120 ☎ 603 181 500 (mobile) 🖳 www.radostfx.cz
The gay party „Lollypop" is one of the most popular nights in this club. Travesty and/or strip shows. Check the webpage (www.radostfx.cz) for dates (irregular).

■ **On Club** (! AC B BF D DM DR GLM M OS S YC) 10-5h
Vinohradska 40/1789 *Metro: Namesti Miru station. Tram 11 to Vinohradska Trznice* ☎ 222 520 630 🖳 www.onclub.cz
Consists of a café with summer terrace, open daily from 10-17h, a daily disco open 21-5h with cruising areas, a chillout area, a club for special events, a VIP area and entrance.

■ **Stage Club** (AC B D GLM WI) 11-6h (café & restaurant) 20-6h (club)
Štěpánská 23, Praha 1 *Tram 4/6/10/16/22* ☎ 252 548 683
🖳 stageclub.cz
Modern and stylish, one of Prague's biggest gay venues. Restaurant serving Czech and International cuisine, open for lunch and dinner. Opened in November 2011.

■ **TERmix** (AC B D DR GLM MA VS) Wed-Sun 20-5h
Trebízského 4a, Vinohrady *Tram 11 Vinohradska Trznice stop; Metro A line Jiriho Z Podebrad* ☎ 222 710 462 🖳 www.club-termix.cz
This is a Western style club with a high-tech decor. Long bar, seating areas, small disco and dark-room with cubicles. No cover charge, no minimum consumption. Wed is Czech music night, their most popular night. Beware of draft sodas like the coke and tonic water, several guests reported stomach ache.

RESTAURANTS

■ **Casa Andina** (B glm M MA) 11-23, Wed-Sat 14-2h
Dusni 15 *Near Old Town Square, M° Staromestska* ☎ 224 815 996
🖳 casaandina.cz
Fine Peruvian cuisine.

■ **Celebrity Cafe** (AC B BF CC glm M MA OS WE)
Mon-Thu 8-1, Fri -2, Sat 10-2, Sun 12-24h
Vinohradská 40, Vinohrady ☎ 222 511 343 🖳 www.celebritycafe.cz
Summer garden. Great place next to the Valentino club and near Termix club.

■ **Noi** (AC B CC G I M MA) 11-1h
Újezd 409/19 *Tram stop Ujezd* ☎ 257 311 411 🖳 www.noirestaurant.cz
Fine Thai cuisine prepared by Thai chefs. Reasonably priced. Only serve lunch and dinner.

SEX SHOPS/BLUE MOVIES

■ **Erotic City Men's Shop** (G) Daily 9-21h
Zitna 43 🖳 www.eroticcity.cz
Large shop selling a huge selection of gay DVDs, sex toys, leather goods, and more. (There are no cubicles here for sex, it is just a shop.)

■ **Erotic City SM-Fetish** (CC F G) Daily 9-21h
Belidle 1 🖳 www.eroticcity.cz
All your fetish requirements and more.

■ **Heaven** (B BF CC DR DU G GH H I LAB RWT SH SL VR VS WI)
11-5, Sat & Sun 14-5h
Gorazdova 11 *M° Karlovo námestí* ☎ 224 92 12 82 🖳 www.heaven.cz
Very spacious establishment on 2 floors with a wide offer for the customer: bar, videotheque with 2000 DVDs, cinema, labyrinth, cabines, glory holes, sling and even showers. Also apartments available.

■ **Princ Sex Shop** (G MA) Mon-Fri 10-18h
Komárkova 21 *M° Roztyly* ☎ 267 911 804 🖳 www.gayboy.cz
Sex shop and publishers of ‚Princ Gay Sex Magazine' (monthly print porn magazine) and ‚Gay Kontakt' in Czech language (online).

ESCORTS & STUDIOS

■ **Gay Tailored Tours** (G MSG)
☎ (+ 36) 205 444 632 (mobile) 🖳 www.gaytailoredtours.com
World-wide escort and companion service. See: www.gaytailoredtours.com

SAUNAS/BATHS

■ **Babylonia** (B G I M MA MSG p RR SA SB SOL VS WE WH WO) 14-3h
Martinská 6 *Next to station of subway Narodni trida or Mustek.*
☎ 224 232 304 🖳 www.saunababylonia.cz
Very popular gay sauna in Prague on 500 m². Many tourists and young gays. Busy after 16,00.

■ **David Club** (AC b CC DR FC G I m MA MSG P RR SA SB SH SOL VS WH) Mon-Fri 9-23, Sat & Sun 11-23h
Sokolovska 44 ☎ 222 317 869 🖳 www.gaysauna.cz
Small, cosy and intimate. Local crowd.

■ **Labyrint** (B DR DU G GH MA MSG RR SA SB SH VS WH) 14-3h
Pernerova 4 🖳 www.saunalabyrint.cz
The newest gay sauna in Prague, opened in 2009. Wed naked parties.

■ **Marco** (AC B DR DU FC G M MA MSG OS P RR SA SB SH SOL VS WH) 14-3h
Lublanská 1917 ☎ 224 262 833 🖳 www.saunamarco.cz
Small, but popular.

■ **Sauna BonBon** (AC B DU G I M MA MSG p SA SB VS WH)
15-1, Fri-Sun -2h
Cernomorska 6 *M° Náměstí Míru, tram 4/22 Ruská* ☎ 777 146 068
🖳 www.saunabonbon.cz
Facilities small but all function well.

HOTELS

■ **Hotel Rainbow-Inn Prague** (B BF CC G MSG OS PK R SB SOL WH) All year, 24hrs
Zernovska 2/1195 *300m from M° Skalka - green line* ☎ 776 496 877
🖳 www.gayhotel-prag.com

ICON Hotel & Lounge. The (AC B BF CC DM H M MC NR OS PA PK RES RWS RWT VA VEG W WI WL) All year
V Jame, 1263/6 *Located in a quiet side street some 3-min walk from Wencesla's Sq./Na Prikope St. - Prague's main shopping/commercial boulevards, about 10 mins walk to the Old Town Sq. heart of the historical centre and about 10 mins walk to Vinohrady- Prague's gay quarter* ☎ 221634100 www.iconhotel.eu
Design hotel in the heart of the city, featuring trendy JET SET Restaurant, PlanetZen Thai Massage Centre and swedish Hästens beds. Winner of Trip Advisors Travellers' Choice™ 2011

Villa Mansland (B BF CC G I MA MSG OS PA PK R RWB RWS RWT S SA VA VS WH WO) All year
Stepnicná 9-11 ☎ 286 884 405 www.gay-hotel-prague.eu
Gay hotel in a villa with wellness and anti-aging programme, public restaurant, own taxi service. All 14 rooms (including two suites) with TV, BF on the terrace. WLAN in all the rooms.

GUEST HOUSES

Arcadia Residence (BF glm MA) All year
Hostivítova 3 ☎ 224 922 040 www.arcadiaresidence.com
All services of an hotel with the privacy of an apartment.

Charles Bridge Residence (bf CC H MA) All year
Mostecka 49/12 ☎ 257 532 627 www.charlesbridgeresidence.com
The accommodation is situated in an historic building just steps off one of Prague's most famous and picturesque landmarks, the Charles Bridge. The beautiful Charles Bridge Residence offers its guests a high standard of space and comfort and good value for money. The eight rooms are each with en-suite bathroom with shower, large screen sat-TV, direct dial telephone, refrigerator, safe, hairdryer and luxury natural linens and towels.

Prague Center Guest Residences (AC G RWS RWT VA WI) All year
☎ 728 428 050 (mobile) www.gaystay.net/PragueCenter
Prague Center Guest Residences has a selection of private apartments, from studio size to three bedrooms. The apartments are located in the centre.

Ron's Rainbow Guest House (BF G MA RWS RWT VA WH WI) All year
Bulharská 4 ☎ 271 725 664 ☎ 731 165 022 (mobile)
www.gay-prague.com
Whirlpool luxury & economy rooms with private bath/WC, free Wi-Fi access and more. Personal attention as well as insider tips are given by your native English-speaking host, Ron. 20-30% discounts available.

APARTMENTS

Holeckova Accommodation (BF cc g MA) All year
Holeckova 107 ☎ 602 250 929 (mobile) www.holeckova.net
Four holiday apartments very close to the city centre.

Toucan Gay Apartments (AC CC FH GLM I MA PA RES RWB RWS RWT T VA) All year
☎ 602 940 353 www.toucanapartments.com
Self-catering private apartments available in Praha 1, 2 & 3 from studio's to 1-4 bedroom apartments for all budgets.

HEALTH GROUPS

AIDS Centrum Infekcní odd Mon-Fri 8-14h
Klinika at the Bulovka Hospital, Budinova 2 ☎ 266 082 629

CSAP - Ceská Spolecnost AIDS Pomoc & Lighthouse
Mon 16-19, Wed 9-12h
Malého 3 ☎ 224 814 284 www.aids-pomoc.cz
Czech organization for AIDS-prevention and support for people with AIDS/HIV. HIV-testing and -counselling.

KHS - Kranská Hygienická Stanice Mon-Thu 13-18h
Dittrichova 17 ☎ 80 01-44 44 44 (helpline)
Free and anonymous HIV-tests Mon-Fri 8-12h.

Project Sance
Ve Smeckach 28 ☎ 602 229 395
Social working outreach project for male prostitutes.

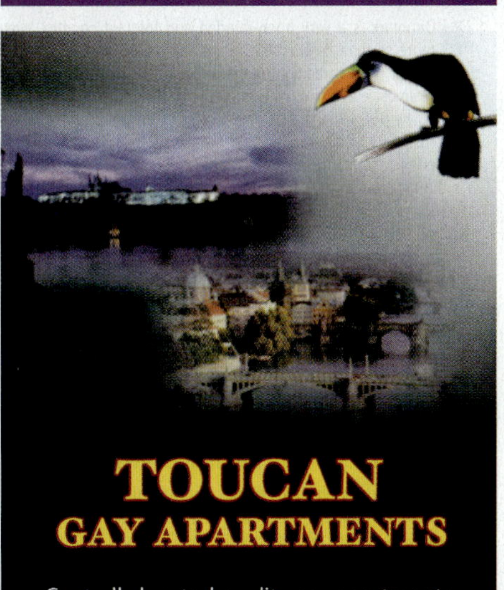

SWIMMING

-Seberak Lake (g) (take the subway to Kácerov, then a bus till Seberak (end station). From the bus stop walk to the opposite side of the lake)
-Sarka Lake (Dzba'n Lake) (g) (take the subway to Dejvicka the Tram 26 to the end station, walk down the path to the nudist lake, ca. 1 km)
-Plavecky Stadion Podolí ☞ SAUNAS.

■ **Plavecky Stadion Podolí**
Plavecky Stadion Podolí ☞ SAUNAS

CRUISING

All are very AYOR!
-Andel Shopping Center Bathrooms
-University for Economy Bathrooms.

Ustí nad Labem ☏ 47

BARS

■ **Martini Club** (B D GLM SNU) Mon-Fri 16-?, Sat & Sun 18-?h
Belehradská 19 ☏ 607 671 208

HEALTH GROUPS

■ **AIDS Centrum Ústí nad Labem** Call for appointment
Masarykova Nemocnice ☏ 475 682 602
Center offering treatment and prevention education for HIV/AIDS.

CRUISING

-Západni nádrazi (West Railway Station).

Denmark

Name: Danmark · Dänemark · Danemark · Dinamarca · Danimarca
Location: Northern Europe
Initials: DK
Time: GMT +1
International Country Code: ☏ 45 (no area codes)
International Access Code: ☏ 00
Language: Danish
Area: 43,098 km² / 16,639 sq mi.
Currency: 1 Danish Krone (dkr) = 100 Öre
Population: 5,416,000
Capital: København
Religions: 84% Protestant
Climate: Fairly mild climate. February is usually the coldest month and July/August the warmest.
Important gay cities: København

Denmark is a very open-minded and tolerant country, even more so than its liberal Scandinavian neighbours. To be a little „different" has a tradition and is part of life for the Danish. One accepts almost everything with humour. This attitude is reflected in national law. The national association of gays and lesbians (LBL) was founded in 1948 and was the first organisation of this kind which achieved the acceptance of anti-discrimination laws. In 1989 Denmark was the first country in the world to introduce same-sex partnership laws, now with the same rights as marriage, including adoption rights. In October 2011 the newly elected government of social democrat Helle Thorning-Schmidt, the first woman to become prime minister in Denmark, announced its intentions to open marriage, heretofore the exclusive reserve of heterosexuals, to lesbians and gays, including church weddings.
Most gay visitors head for Copenhagen, due to its lively gay scene and relaxed atmosphere. Other Danish cities such as Århus are charming and have a small gay scene. Apart from the cities, Denmark has an extensive coastline, which is very inviting for those looking to relax and go wandering. Discover this interesting country with its friendly and helpful inhabitants, who always have a humorous twinkle in their eye.

Dänemark ist ein sehr offenes und tolerantes Land, und das sogar noch mehr als seine ebenfalls sehr liberalen skandinavischen Nachbarn. Ein bisschen „anders" zu sein, hat schon fast Tradition und gehört für die Dänen einfach zum Leben dazu - man nimmt vieles sehr humorvoll. Diese Haltung spiegelt sich auch in den Gesetzen wider: Die nationale Vereinigung für Schwule und Lesben (LBL) wurde 1948 gegründet, war die erste Organisation dieser Art überhaupt und setzte schon früh Antidiskriminierungsgesetze durch. 1989 war Dänemark das erste Land der Welt, das gleichgeschlechtliche Partnerschaften einführte und nach und nach wurden diese eingetragenen Lebensgemeinschaften der Ehe gleichgestellt. Jetzt mit den gleichen Rechten wie die Ehe - inklusive Adoption. Im Oktober 2011 kündigte die neu gewählte Regierung von Sozialdemokratin Helle Thorning-Schmidt, die als erste Frau in Dänemark das Spitzenamt übernehmen konnte, an, die bisher nur für Heterosexuelle geltende Ehe für Schwule und Lesben zu öffnen. Dabei soll auch die kirchliche Trauung zugelassen werden.
Die meisten homosexuellen Besucher steuern in der Regel Kopenhagen an, was aufgrund der lebendigen Szene dort und der entspannten Atmosphäre in der Stadt nahe liegt. Auch andere dänische Städte, wie z. B. Århus, haben viel Charme und meist auch eine kleine Gay-Szene. Neben den Städten hat Dänemark auch endlose Küsten, die zum Erholen und Spazierengehen einladen. Entdecken Sie dieses interessante Land und seine freundlichen und hilfsbereiten Bewohner, die einem stets mit einem humorvollen Augenzwinkern begegnen.

Plus encore que ses voisins scandinaves, le Danemark est un pays libéral et très tolérant. Pour les Danois, être un peu „différent" fait partie de la tradition locale et de la vie- on prend souvent les choses avec humour. Cette tendance se reflète aussi dans législation: l'Union nationale pour les gays et lesbiennes (LBL), créée en 1948, était la première organisation du genre au monde. Elle a fait passer très tôt des lois anti-discriminatoires et en 1989, le Danemark était le premier pays au monde à permettre aux couples de même sexe de faire enregistrer leur partenariat. Les relations entre personnes de même sexe sont reconnues pour les homos comme pour les hétéros et garanti les mêmes droits que le mariage, y compris l'adoption. En octobre 2011, Helle Thorning-Schmidt, social-démocrate et première femme Ministre D'Etat, annonça d'ouvrir pour la première fois le mariage aux gays et lesbiennes. De même le mariage religieux doit être autorisé.

La plupart des touristes homosexuels se rendent à Copenhague pour son milieu très actif et son atmosphère détendue, mais d'autres villes, comme Århus, ne sont pas dénuées de charme et disposent d'un petit milieu gay. Outre ses villes, le Danemark dispose également de côtes à l'infini et ses habitants sympathiques vous accueilleront toujours avec un clin d'œil.

Dinamarca es un país muy abierto y tolerante, incluso más que sus igualmente liberales vecinos escandinavos. El hecho de ser „diferente" es casi como una tradición y para los daneses forma parte de la vida misma; se lo toman con sentido del humor. Esta actitud se refleja también en las leyes: la organización nacional para gays y lesbianas (LBL) se fundó en 1948 y fue la primera organización de este tipo que desde muy pronto reclamó leyes en contra de la discriminación. En 1989, Dinamarca fue el primer país del mundo que introdujo el registro de parejas del mismo sexo. el principio de que las parejas de hecho registradas, tanto homosexuales como heterosexuales, son legales y gozan de los mismos derechos que un matrimonio, incluso la adopción. En octubre de 2011, el nuevo gobierno de la socialdemócrata Helle Thorning-Schmidt, que fue la primera mujer en Dinamarca en tener el puesto más alto dentro del gobierno, anunció que la había abierto la legislación de uniones civiles, hasta ahora solo aplicable a heterosexuales, también para gays y lesbianas. Además, se permitirían las bodas por la iglesia.
La mayoría de homosexuales se dirigen principalmente a Copenhaguen por su dinámico ambiente gay y la atmósfera más relajada de la ciudad. Otras ciudades danesas como Ärhus también tienen mucho encanto y en la mayoría hay una pequeña zona gay. Aparte de las ciudades, Dinamarca dispone de costas interminables que invitan al descanso y al paseo. Descubre este interesante país y sus amables y hospitalarios habitantes, que siempre le reciben a uno con buen humor.

La Danimarca è un Paese aperto e tollerante e addirittura più liberale degli altri Paesi scandinavi. Per tradizione essere un po' „diversi" fà parte della vita dei danesi. Lo spiccato umore é una caratteristica dei danesi. Questa attitudine si rispecchia anche nelle leggi: la LBL (l'associazione gay e lesbica nazionale) é stata fondata nel 1948 e quindi la prima di questo genere. Già molto indietro nel tempo questa organizzazione é riuscita a imporre diverse leggi antidiscriminatorie. Nel 1989 la Danimarca fu il primo Paese che ha reso possibile la registrazione ufficiale per le coppie dello stesso sesso. Le convivenze registrate valgono sia per omosessuali che per eterosessuali con tutti i diritti che sono riconosciuti al matrimonio incluso il diritto di adozione. Nell'ottobre del 2011 il nuovo governo guidato dalla socialdemocratica Helle Thorning-Schmidt (prima donna a ricoprire questo ruolo) ha annunciato di voler aprire l'istituto del matrimonio alle coppie dello stesso sesso, e possibilmente, per chi lo volesse, con il rito religioso.
Copenhagen è molto visitata dai turisti gay, sia per la vivace scena sia per la rilassante atmosfera della città. Anche altre città danesi come per esempio Århus, hanno molto charme e solitamente anche una piccola scena gay. Oltre alle città, la Danimarca offre anche coste infinite che invitano il turista al relax e a lunghe passeggiate. Insomma, vale davvero la pena visitare questo interessante Paese e conoscere i suoi cordialissimi e affabili abitanti.

NATIONAL GAY INFO

Pride Radio DK
www.prideradio.dk
Danish LGBT net & FM-radiostation. Check website for details.

NATIONAL PUBLICATIONS

Out & About (GLM)
Oscar Pettifords Vej 27, 3.th. ☎ 40 93 19 77 www.outandabout.dk
Denmark's monthly gay and lesbian magazine. With an updated gay guide and gay map in English. The gay agenda in English is also available on mobile phone at mobil.outandabout.dk

PAN Bladet (GLM)
Nygade 7, 2 ✉ 1164 København K ☎ 33 36 00 82
www.panbladet.dk
Gay and lesbian web-magazine.

NATIONAL GROUPS

Hiv-Danmark
Skindergade 44, 2 ✉ 1159 København K ☎ 33 32 58 68
www.hiv-danmark.dk
The main organization for people with HIV.

LGBT Denmark - The Danish National Organisation for Gay Men, Lesbians, Bisexuals and Transgendered persons.
Nygade 7, 2 ✉ 1164 København K ☎ 33 13 19 48 www.lgbt.dk
Denmark's national organization for LGBT persons, founded in 1948. Local groups in all areas.

NATIONAL HELPLINES

AIDS-Linien Mon-Fri 9-20, Sat & Sun 11-15h
Skindergade 27, 2. th ✉ 1159 København K ☎ 33 91 11 19
www.aids-linien.dk
Anonymous counselling in Danish or English.

Ålborg

CRUISING

-Kildeparken (entrance from Vesterbro near toilets and Gammel Kaervej)
-Area of bushes and trees near race course (entrance up the slope from Skydebanevej just after the race course entrance; daytime, summer only).

Århus

BARS

Gbar (B D GLM LM MA) Wed 20-24, Thu -4, Fri & Sat -5h
Skolegade 28 ☎ 86 12 04 04 www.g-bar.dk
Popular gay bar in Århus.

SLM Århus – Men's Club (AC B CC DR F G I MA P VS)
Fri & Sat 22-3h, specials on 1st Fri, last Sat/month
Østbanetorvet 8 ☎ 86 19 10 89 www.slm-aarhus.dk
Leather bar on 2 floors for gay men only.

SEX SHOPS/BLUE MOVIES

Paradiset (b DR G I SA) 12-22h
Paradisgade 11 www.paradiset.pbio.dk

SAUNAS/BATHS

Joys (B DR DU G I NU P SA SL SOL) Gayclub only Sun 14-22h
Elkærvej 30 ☎ 604 180 99 www.joys.dk

FETISH GROUPS

SMil S/M Club (F g) Tue 20-22h
Postboks 198 ☎ 86 13 70 23 www.sado.dk
Leather & S/M group for hetero and gay men.

HEALTH GROUPS

STOP AIDS Mon-Fri 10-16h
Frederiksgade 76 A ☎ 86 12 88 00 www.stopaids.dk
Information and prevention regarding HIV and safe sex for gays.

SWIMMING

-Fløjstrup Stand.

CRUISING

-Mindeparken (Near Oddervej)
-Havnen Pier 3

-Tangkrogen (near Chr. Filtenborgs Plads, along the beach, summer after dark)
-Botanisk Have (main entrance to Den Gamle By at Eugen Warmings Vej).

Esbjerg

GENERAL GROUPS

■ **Es'gay'p** (B D GLM MA) See website for times
Nørrebrogade 102 *Bus line 1. Close to town center* 💻 www.esgayp.dk
Non profit organisation.

SWIMMING

-Houstrup Strand (G NU) (near Lønne. From the P walk 500 m in direction of the nude beach, very popular).

CRUISING

-City park/byparken (cruising near the water tower and the art museum)
-Vestkraftvej (at toilet and phone booth, best late evening and night)
-Molevej (at toilet).

Fakse Ladeplads

SWIMMING

-Beach on the „Feddet" (by the inlet of Præsto Fjord; after the P there is a nudist beach, and further on the beach is more action).

Fredericia

SWIMMING

-Trelde Næs
-The battlement »Volden«.

Grenaa

SWIMMING

-The island of »Anholt« (g) (very long and wonderful beach).

Herning

CRUISING

-P in Danmarksgade
-Toilets at the P behind supermarket Føtex on Bredgade.

Karrebæksminde

SWIMMING

-Beach on the Vesterhave side (turn to the right just before the bridge, after the P walk about 500m to the north-west).

København – Øresund

Copenhagen is the Mecca for gay men in northern Europe, many of whom come to the annual Gay Parade in August or the Copenhagen Gay & Lesbian Film festival in October, celebrating as one of the few in the world more than 20 years. The city is known for its fun and enjoyment of life. A plus is that most places are within walking distance. Despite the compactness the gay scene here is relatively large.
Copenhagen is a cheerful, open city fully of diversity with friendly inhabitants and an „unspoilt" and natural gay scene. Even on a dark and rainy winters day there are a range of shopping possibilities or cafés where one can simply relax. For those who seek adventure the train to and from Malmö /Sweden takes only 35 minutes, thanks to the new bridge between Denmark and Sweden, which opens a whole range of new possibilities in the Öresund-Region, an enrichment from which both cities can profit.

There is a new smoking policy in Denmark since May 2007. It is still possible to smoke at bars smaller than 40 m²! That means that Copenhagen's gay bars are divided into smoking and non smoking bars.

★ Kopenhagen ist das Schwulenmekka Nordeuropas. Besondere Attraktionen für schwule Besucher sind der jährlich im August stattfindende CSD und das „Copenhagen Lesbian & Gay Film Festival" im Oktober - eines der wenigen schwullesbischen Filmfestivals weltweit, die schon seit über 20 Jahren bestehen. Für Lebensfreude und Spaß ist die Stadt bekannt und da ist es von Vorteil, dass sich das meiste zu Fuß erkunden lässt. Trotz der Überschaubarkeit gibt es eine relativ große schwul-lesbsiche Szene.
Kopenhagen ist eine heitere, abwechslungsreiche und offene Stadt, mit sehr freundlichen Bewohnern und einer „natürlichen", ungekünstelten Szene. Selbst an einem dunklen, regnerischen Wintertag gibt es ausgiebig Gelegenheit zum Shoppen und Relaxen in einem der vielen Cafés. Und wer mag, kann nun auch in nur 35 min mit dem Zug nach Malmö/Schweden fahren. Dank der Brücke zwischen Dänemark und Schweden eröffnen sich ganz neue Möglichkeiten für die Öresund-Region, von der die beiden Städte profitieren und sich gegenseitig bereichern.
In Dänemark gilt seit Mai 2007 ein neues Rauchergesetz, wonach nur noch in Lokalen mit einer Größe bis zu 40 m² geraucht werden darf. Somit sind Kopenhagens Gay-Bars nun in Raucher- und Nichtraucherbars unterteilt.

✱ Copenhague est la capitale gaie du nord de l'Europe. Les touristes gays apprécieront tout particulièrement la Gay Pride au mois d'août et le „ Copenhagen Lesbian & Gay Film Festival „ en octobre - un des rares festivals du film gay et lesbien au monde à exister depuis déjà plus de 20 ans.
La ville est connue pour sa joie de vivre et un grand avantage réside dans le fait que, dû à sa taille, on peut s'y déplacer à pied. Malgré la taille restreinte de la ville, le milieu gay et lesbien est relativement important ; il est en outre resté très simple et „naturel".

København

EAT & DRINK
- Can Can – Bar 16
- Centralhjørnet – Bar 14
- Cosy Bar – Bar 6
- Jailhouse CPH – Bar 3
- Kafe Knud – Café 12
- Masken Bar – Bar 7
- Men's Bar – Bar 4
- Never Mind – Bar 2
- Oscar – Café 17
- Vela – Bar 23

NIGHTLIFE
- Be Proud – Danceclub 5
- Club Christopher – Danceclub 11
- SLM Copenhagen – Men's Club 18

SEX
- Amigo – Sauna 8
- Copenhagen Gay Center – Sex Shop/Blue Movies 24
- EP-video – Sex Shop/ Blue Movies 9
- Men's Shop – Sex Shop/ Blue Movies 25

ACCOMMODATION
- Carsten's Guest House & Holiday Apartments – Guest House 20
- Mayfair Hotel – Hotel 15

OTHERS
- SM-Shop – Leather & Fetish Shop 3
- STOP AIDS – Health Group 13
- Wonderful Copenhagen Tourist Information 22

Copenhague est une ville aux multiples facettes et ses habitants sont tolérants et sympathiques. Même pendant les courtes journées pluvieuses d'hiver, on peut faire les boutiques ou se détendre dans un des nombreux cafés. Et pour ceux qui le désirent, un train relie Malmö en Suède en seulement 35 minutes. Grâce au pont reliant le Danemark à la Suède, de nouvelles perspectives s'ouvrent à la région d'Öresund, enrichissant ainsi les deux villes.
La loi sur l'interdiction de fumer est en vigueur au Danemark depuis mai 2007, et il n'est plus autorisé de fumer que dans les établissements ne dépassant pas 40 m² de superficie. Les bars gais de Copenhague sont donc divisés entre fumeurs et non-fumeurs.

Copenhagen es la meca gay del norte de Europa. Los eventos más atractivos para cualquier visitante homosexual son la Marcha del Orgullo Gay, que se celebra anualmente en agosto, y el Festival de Cine Gay-lésbico en octubre, uno de los pocos festivales de cine gay-lésbico del mundo que existe desde hace más de 20 años.
La ciudad es conocida por su alegría de vivir y sus fiestas y la mayor ventaja es que se puede visitar casi todo a pie. Pese a esto, hay un ambiente gay-lésbico bastante grande.
Copenhaguen es una ciudad abierta y llena de distracciones, con unos habitantes muy amables y un ambiente muy „natural", poco artificial. Incluso en un día oscuro y lluvioso de invierno, se puede ir tranquilamente de compras o relajarse en uno de los muchos cafés. Y quien quiera, puede ir en tan sólo 35 minutos en tren a Malmö, Suecia. Gracias al puente entre Dinamarca y Suecia, se han abierto nuevas oportunidades para la región de Öresund, de la que disfrutan las dos ciudades y se complementan mutuamente.
En Dinamarca, desde mayo de 2007, entró en vigor una nueva ley antitabaco según la cual sólo se puede fumar en locales de hasta 40 m ². Por lo tanto, los bares gays de Copenhagen ahora están divididos en bares de fumadores y de no-fumadores.

Copenhagen è una sorta di mecca gay dell'Europa del nord. Attrazioni di particolare rilevanza per turisti gay sono l'annuale CSD che si svolge ad agosto e il Copenhagen Lesbian & Gay Film Festival nel mese di ottobre; il suddetto festival è uno dei pochi festival del cinema gay che esiste giá da 20 anni.
La città è nota per gli svaghi che offre e una cosa molto confortevole è il fatto che la maggior parte delle attrazioni si possono visitare girando a piedi. Nonostante la limitata estensione della città, la scena gay e lesbica è piuttosto grande.
Copenhagen è una città molto varia e aperta con degli abitanti molto cordiali ed affabili. La scena è molto tranquilla e „genuina". Persino negli invernali scuri giorni di pioggia ci sono tantissime possibilità per fare shopping o per rilassarsi in uno dei numerosissimi cafè. E chi desidera può andare a Malmö (in Svezia) in soli 35 minuti di treno. Grazie al ponte tra la Danimarca e la Svezia si aprono nuove prospettive per la regione dell'Öresund.
Dal maggio del 2007 vige una legge sul fumo nei locali pubblici che prevede il divieto di fumo nei locali pubblici di dimensione superiore ai 40 mq. I locali gay di Copenhagen sono quindi suddivisi in locali per fumatori e locali per non fumatori.

GAY INFO

Copenhagen Gay Life
www.copenhagen-gay-life.dk
Copenhagen's own network and chamber of commerce for gay businesses and organizations.

CULTURE

Meet Gay Copenhagen (CC GLM MA)
27 21 80 65 www.meetgaycopenhagen.dk
To discover Danish gay culture, you have the opportunity to visit gays or lesbians at their homes who will prepare a dinner for you and be your hosts. Also special arrangements and gay walking tours.

MIX COPENHAGEN – LesbianGayBiTrans Film Festival
Tagensvej 85F 33 93 07 66 www.cglff.dk
Festival period: Mid to late October.

TOURIST INFO

Wonderful Copenhagen Tourist Information
Vesterbrogade 4c 70 22 24 42
www.visitcopenhagen.com/gay
Ask for the Copenhagen Gay map at the counter.

BARS

Can Can (AC B CC GLM MA)
Sun-Thu 14-2, Fri & Sat -5h
Mikkel Bryggers Gade 11/ Lavendelstræde *50 m to Town Hall*
33 11 50 10
Friendly small gay bar in the centre of the city.

Centralhjørnet (AC B G MA S) 12-2h
Kattesundet 18 / Lavendelstræde 33 11 85 49
www.centralhjornet.dk
Oldest gay bar in Copenhagen. Relaxed „down-to-earth" atmosphere.

Cosy Bar (B D G MA) Sun-Thu 22-6, Fri & Sat -8h
Studiestræde 24 33 12 74 27
www.cosybar.dk
Popular and cruisy. One of the oldest bars in Copenhagen. Best in the early hours of the morning. Small dancefloor.

■ **Intime** (B MA NG WE) 18-2h
Allégade 25a, Frederiksberg District *Take bus N°14 or 15* ☎ 38 34 19 58
💻 www.cafeintime.dk
Friendly, old fashioned piano bar. Happy-hour 18-21h. Live music Mon-Sat 21.30-1.30h; jazz Sun 20-24h.

■ **Jailhouse CPH** (AC B CC GLM M MA S WE)
Sun-Thu 15-2, Fri & Sat -5h
Studiestræde 12 ☎ 33 15 22 55
💻 www.jailhousecph.dk
A concept bar and restaurant on 2 floors. Very friendly, uniformed waiters. Restaurant on the 1st floor. Very popular bar with events once a month.

■ **Masken Bar** (B GLM I MA) 14-3, Fri & Sat -5h
Studiestræde 33 ☎ 33 91 09 37 💻 www.maskenbar.dk
Bar on 2 levels. Attracts both young and mature men as well as lesbian customers.

■ **Men's Bar** (B f G MA) 15-2, happy hour 15-21h
Teglgårdstræde 3 ☎ 33 12 73 03 💻 www.mensbar.dk
Men only. Friendly atmosphere. Free brunch 1st Sun/month.

■ **Never Mind** (AC B CC D FC GLM MA) 22-6h
Nørre Voldgade 2 ☎ 2193 7625 💻 www.nevermindbar.dk
Late night bar, dancing

■ **Vela** (B gLm MA) Wed & Thu 20-24, Fri & Sat 20-5h
Victoriagade 2-4 ☎ 33 31 34 19 💻 www.velagayclub.dk
Lesbian bar in the location of an old „Red Light Strip Bar".

MEN'S CLUBS

■ **SLM Copenhagen**
(AK B CC DR DU F FC G GH LAB MA NR P SL VR VS) Fri & Sat 22-4h
Lavendelstræde 17c *Near town hall square, in the back yard*
☎ 33 32 06 01 💻 www.slm-cph.dk
SLM Copenhagen is Scandinavia's largest leather club. Two levels with bar, darkroom, mazes, slings, piss room, etc. Check the website www.slm-cph.dk for details and special events.

CAFES

■ **Kafe Knud** (G m MC) Tue-Thu 16-22h
Skindergade 21 ☎ 33 32 58 61 💻 www.hiv-danmark.dk
For people affected by HIV and AIDS and their friends.

■ **Oscar** (B CC GLM M MA OS) Kitchen 12-22, bar -2h
Rådhuspladsen 77 ☎ 33 12 09 99 💻 www.oscarbarcafe.dk
Situated near town hall, it is a good mix of café, bar & lounge. Stylish hang-out. Happy hour 17-21, DJ Fri. Non smoking.

DANCECLUBS

■ **Club Christopher** (AC B D GLM OS YC) Fri 23-5, Sat 24-5h
Knabrostræde 3 💻 www.clubchristopher.dk
Located in former premises of the legendary Pan Club. Danceclub on two floors.

■ **Roccos Mansion @ The White Room** (B D DR G MA)
1st Sat/month 23-6h
Høkerboderne 18-22 ☎ 33 93 50 40
💻 www.facebook.com/JohnnieIversen

RESTAURANTS

■ **Jailhouse CPH** (AC B CC GLM M MA S WE)
Sun-Thu 15-2, Fri & Sat -5h
Studiestræde 12 ☎ 33 15 22 55 💻 www.jailhousecph.dk
A concept bar and restaurant on 2 floors. Very friendly, uniformed waiters. Restaurant on the 1st floor. Very popular bar with events once a month.

SEX SHOPS/BLUE MOVIES

■ **Copenhagen Gay Center** (CC DR F G I MA MSG R RR SA VS)
10-22, Fri & Sat 10-24h
Istedgade 34-36 ☎ 33 22 23 00 💻 www.copenhagengaycenter.dk
Dry sauna with 36 lockers, 4 cinemas and shop with a large selection of the latest gay DVDs together with the latest in international gay magazines, sex toys and leather gear.

■ **Men's Shop** (CC G MA) Mon-Sat 10-22, Sun 12-20h
Viktoriagade 24 *Behind Central Station* ☎ 33 25 44 75
💻 www.mensshop.dk
Large sex/lifestyle shop for gay men with all kinds of toys, underwear, books, pharmacy, DVDs (regular and porn), leather and rubber items. English and German speaking staff, gay tourist information.

SAUNAS/BATHS

■ **Amigo** (B DR G I MA MSG R RR SA SB SH SOL VS)
12-7, Fri & Sat -8h
Studiestræde 31A ☎ 33 15 20 28 💻 www.amigo-sauna.dk
Sauna on 800 m². 3 floors with lots of cubicals, dark rooms, several video rooms as well as sling rooms and mazes. Not always clean and the staff is not always friendly. Shop in reception area.

■ **Body Bio** (AC DR G I MA SA t VS) 12-1h
Kingosgade 7 *Bus 6a, Vesterbrogade exit Kingosgade*
💻 www.bodybio.dk
Rather small cruising place with cinemas, cabins, mazes, dark rooms, sling and glory holes. Mixed crowd.

■ **Copenhagen Gay Center** (CC DR F G I MA MSG R RR SA VS)
10-22, Fri & Sat 10-24h
Istedgade 34-36 ☎ 33 22 23 00 💻 www.copenhagengaycenter.dk
Dry sauna with 36 lockers, 4 cinemas and shop with a large selection of the

latest gay DVDs together with the latest in international gay magazines, sex toys and leather gear.

LEATHER & FETISH SHOPS

■ **SM-Shop** (F g) 11-17.30, Fri -19, Sat 11-14h, closed Sun
Studiestrade 12 ☎ 33 12 79 12 🖳 www.sm-shop.dk
Situated in the heart of the latin quarter of Copenhagen. Bisexual, heterosexual, homosexual? The important thing is that you are sexual.

HOTELS

■ **Mayfair Hotel** (BF glm H I M PA RWS RWT) All year
Helgolandsgade 3 *2 mins from central train station* ☎ 70 12 17 00
🖳 www.choicehotels.dk

GUEST HOUSES

■ **Carsten's Guest House & Holiday Apartments**
(b BF CC G I m MA NR OS RWT) All year, reservations 9.30-21h
Christians Brygge 28 *5th floor* ☎ 33 14 91 07
🖳 www.carstensguesthouse.dk
Centrally located, 5 mins. walk to gay scene. Own key, shared bath, kitchen and laundry. Rooftop parties in summer. 10 rooms in the guesthouse and 10 bed-dormitory (hostel), 2 additional holiday apartments also in the city centre available.

GENERAL GROUPS

■ **Copenhagen Gay & Lesbian Chamber of Commerce**
(GLM MA)
🖳 www.copenhagen-gay-life.dk
Issuer of the Copenhagen Gay Map.

HEALTH GROUPS

■ **Stop Aids** Mon-Fri 10-16h
Amagertorv 33, 3rd floor ☎ 33 11 29 11 🖳 www.stopaids.dk
A non profit organization, supported by the government promoting AIDS awareness.

SWIMMING

-Bellevue Strand (Public beach 8 km north of Copenhagen city, used by many gay men; especially the northern part of the beach against the wall)
-Frederiksberg Svømmehal (g MA pi sa sol) (7-21, Sat 7-16, Sun 9-16h. Helgesvej 29, 2000 Frederiksberg; take bus N°2A Metro Frederiksberg), discreet cruising possible only in the „lux section"
-Tisvilde Strand (Public beach in North Sjælland (Sealand). Go by train E to Hillerød, then change to private railroad for Tisvildeleje. The beach is about 2 km from the station; pass the 🅿 and go 1-2 km further west).

CRUISING

-Ørstedsparken (Centrally located between Nørre Voldgade and Nørre Farimagsgade. Action during the day but mostly nights, ayor)
-Amager Fælled (🅿 at Lossepladsvej/Artillerivej, NU daytime and summer evenings) (OC)
-Utterslev Mose (Motorway 16 from the city, after the lakes there is a parking lot on the right. Cross the lawn, action is spread over a large area in the bushes. Daytime and summer nights) (YC)
-Charlottenlund Skov (take the S-train to Charlottenlund Station) and pass under the railway into the wood in direction of the castle; the action is usually between the castle and the Danmarks Akvarium in the evenings and at night)
-Tisvilde Strand (pass the large carpark and go 1-2 km further on where there is nude sunbathing and action in dunes and forest behind)

Kolding

BARS

■ **Lobito** (B D GLM MA) Thu 19-22, Sat 22-2h
Dyrehavegårdsvej 38,1 *1st floor* ☎ 75 54 10 23 🖳 www.lobito.dk

Kongerslev

GUEST HOUSES

■ **Svanfolk Bed & Breakfast** (BF CC GLM H I MA OS PK RWS WI) All year
Svanfolkvej 15, Svanfolk *30 km south of the city of Aalborg*
☎ 98 13 15 31 🖳 www.svanfolk-bb.dk
Svanfolk Bed & Breakfast is a former farmhouse situated in the beautiful area of East Himmerland, North Jutland, with some gay beaches nearby. There are two double rooms with private bathrooms. Other two double rooms and one single room share a bathroom. Gay owned.

Nykøbing

SWIMMING

-Marielyst Strand (near the nude area).

Odense

CAFES

■ **Lambda** (b GLM m MA) Thu-Sat 18-24h
Brogade 3 ☎ 32 12 62 45 🖳 www.lambda.dk

SEX SHOPS/BLUE MOVIES

■ **Videoshoppen** (g VS) Mon-Sat 10-24, Sun 12-22h
Vindegade 110

SEX CINEMAS

■ **Sexkino** (g MA VS) Mon-Sat 11-22h
Vesterbro 15 ☎ 66 13 19 84 🖳 www.pleasureandpain.dk
Sexshop, dvd sale, kino.

SWIMMING

-Hverringe Strand (nude bathing near Kerteminde. About 2km on the road along the »Nordstranden« in direction of Hverringe Slot. The entrance to the beach is at the 🅿 in the »Hverringe-skoven«).
-Park „Munke Mose" (along the river, evening and night).

Skagen

HOTELS

■ **Finns Hotel Pension** (BF GLM M MA OS RWS)
Open: 1 May-23 Sep 2012
Østre Strandvej 63 *Close to the beach* ☎ (+45) 98 45 01 55
🖳 www.finnshotelpension.dk
Five double and one single room. Some have private bath. There is a common living-room with library and no television, a common dining-room and a nice garden. Fantastic hosts.

GUEST HOUSES

■ **Skagen B&B** (BF glm I OS PK RWB RWT VA)
Open: Jun 25-Aug 25
Fyrbrovej 9 *Near Sønderstrand beach & the lighthouses* ☎ 98 44 60 17
🖳 www.skagenbb.dk

SWIMMING

-Beautiful long beach on the west coast (g)

Slagelse

SWIMMING

-Egerup strand between Korsør and Skælskør
-🅿 at Egerup strand, walk 600 m in a northerly direction.

CRUISING

-Picnic area on the motorway Slagelse, both sides.

Ecuador

Name: Equateur
Location: Northwestern South America
Initials: EC
Time: GMT -5
International Country Code: ☏ 593
International Access Code: ☏ 00
Language: Spanish, Quechua
Area: 256,370 km² / 98,985 sq mi.
Currency: 1 US$ = 100 Cents
Population: 13,228,000
Capital: Quito
Religions: 91,6% Roman Catholic
Climate: Tropical climate along the coast that becomes cooler inland. The best time for the Galápagos Islands is from Jan-Apr (ideal time for snorkeling).

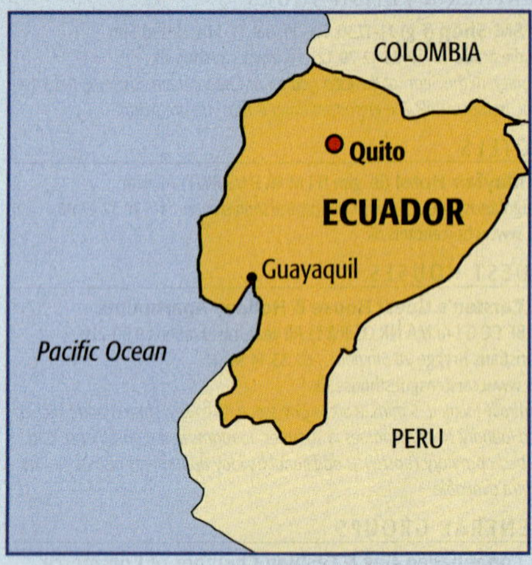

Up until 1997 homosexuality was considered a prosecutable offence in Ecuador. Nowadays the constitution sanctions non-discrimination on the basis of sexual preference, according to Ecuador's constitution § 2, Article 23, Number 3.
Nevertheless, the mentality of Ecuadorian society remains very catholic-conservative. Gay men and lesbians are not evident in everyday society, since homosexuality is still considered „perverse and insane".
At the end of August, 2007 the Secretary of Defense, Lorena Escudero, announced that the applicable constitutional articles regarding the prohibition of sexual discrimination in military were to be introduced. With this new law it is forbidden to dismiss soldiers from the army because of homosexual acts.
At present many groups are taking on different measures in order to obtain recognition and tolerance for the GLBT community rights.
The small and somewhat secluded gay scene in Ecuador is friendly and amusing, a mixture of different cultures like the country itself.
Tourists will find a vast diversity of climates and landscapes in Ecuador: jungle, snowy mountains, beaches, forests, old towns and modern cities. The capital city, Quito, was the first city in the world to be declared cultural heritage of the humanity by UNESCO. Since then Cuenca has been also declared a city of cultural heritage and is worth a visit. Loja is particular interesting for the ecological tourist and of course the Galápo Islands, also declared a natural heritage area.

In Ecuador galt Homosexualität noch bis 1997 als Strafdelikt. Mittlerweile fordert der Artikel 23 Absatz 3 der zweiten Verfassung Toleranz für Menschen jeglicher sexuellen Orientierung. Dennoch bleibt die Mentalität der Bürger Ecuadors streng konservativ-katholisch. Im alltäglichen Leben schrecken Schwule und Lesben vor ihrem Outing zurück, da Homosexualität immer noch als „pervers und krank" angesehen wird.
Zur Zeit ergreifen viele Vereinigungen verschiedene Schritte, um für Schwule, Lesben, Bisexuelle und Transgender Anerkennung und Toleranz durchzusetzen.
Ende August 2007 kündigte die Verteidigungsministerin Lorena Escudero an, dass der entsprechende Verfassungsartikel, der sexuelle Diskriminierung untersagt, in das Reglement des ecuadorianischen Militärs eingearbeitet werden soll. Damit wird verboten werden, dass Soldaten wegen homosexueller Handlungen aus dem Militärdienst entlassen werden können.
Ecuadors eingeschworene Szene ist klein, freundlich, humorvoll und setzt sich wie das Land selbst aus verschiedenen Kulturen zusammen. Touristen finden hier eine große Klima- und Landschaftsvielfalt: Es gibt tropische Vegetation, verschneite Berge, Strände, Wälder, alte und moderne Städte. Die Hauptstadt Quito wurde als erste Weltstadt von der UNESCO zum Kulturerbe erklärt, noch vor Cuenca und den Galapagos-Inseln. Ein Besuch von Lojas lohnt sich vor allem für den umweltliebenden Touristen.

En Équateur, l'homosexualité n'a été dépénalisée qu'en 1997. Depuis, le paragraphe 3 de l'article 23 de la deuxième constitution du pays exige des citoyens de se montrer tolérants envers toute personne et, ce quelle que soit son orientation sexuelle. Cependant, la mentalité des Équatoriens reste très influencée par le catholicisme et nombre de gays et lesbiennes hésitent à vivre au grand jour leur homosexualité, qualifiée encore de « perversion » et de « maladie ». De nombreuses organisations s'engagent pour obtenir plus de tolérance et de reconnaissance pour les gays, lesbiennes, bisexuels et transgenders.
La ministre de la Défense Lorena Escudero a annoncé fin août 2007 que l'article constitutionnel interdisant la discrimination sexuelle devait être incorporé au règlement de l'armée équatorienne. Il sera dorénavant interdit que des soldats puissent être renvoyés du service militaire pour cause de pratiques homosexuelles.
Le milieu gay est à l'image du pays lui-même : petit, accueillant, plein d'humour et multiculturel. Les visiteurs trouveront des climats et des paysages variés : de la végétation tropicale aux montagnes enneigées en passant par des forêts, des plages et des villes tantôt très anciennes, tantôt modernes. La capitale Quito a été la première ville à devenir patrimoine culturel de l'UNESCO, bien avant Cuenca et les îles Galapagos. Les touristes sensibles à l'écologie ne manqueront pas de visiter la ville de Loias.

Incluso hasta 1997 la homosexualidad era considerada una ofensa a perseguir en Ecuador. Actualmente la Constitución establece la no-discriminación en base a la orientación sexual, en virtud del título 2, artículo 23, punto 3 de la Constitución del Ecuador.
Sin embargo, la mentalidad de la sociedad del Ecuador sigue siendo muy católico-conservadora. Los hombres gays y lesbianas no son visibles en la sociedad actual ya que la homosexualidad se considera aún perversa e insana.
A finales de agosto de 2007 la ministro de Defensa, Lorena Escudero, anunció que el correspondiente artículo de la Constitución que prohíbe la discriminación sexual debería estar incorporado al reglamento militar ecuatoriano. De este modo se prohibiría que los soldados pudieran ser expulsados del servicio militar por actos homosexuales.
Sobre todo el ambiente gay de la capital, Quito, hasta hace muy poco limitado a tres zonas de cruising y un descuidado discopub, está viviendo un desarrollo muy positivo, y también los viajeros exigentes de Europa y Norteamérica encontrarán lugares de encuentro seguros y de un agradable diseño.

In Equador l'omosessualità fino al 1997 era considerata reato. Adesso l'articolo 23 comma 3 della seconda costituzione prevede tolleranza per persone di qualsiasi orientamento sessuale. Tuttavia la mentalità delle persone di questo paese rimane fondamentalmente cattolica e conservatrice. Gay e lesbiche sono reticenti nel fare il coming out poichè l'omosessuale viene ancora considerato „perverso e malato".
Alla fine del 2007 la ministra della difesa, Lorena Escudero, ha dichiarato che l'articolo della Costituzione che vieta la discriminazione fondantesi sull'orientamento sessuale dovrebbe entrare a far parte del regolamento del corpo militare affinchè i soldati non possano più essere licenziati a causa della loro omosessualità. Molte organizzazioni si stanno dando da fare per il riconoscimento e l'accettazione di gay, lesbiche, bisessuali e transgender. La scena dell'Equador è piccola, simpatica, divertente e piuttosto multiculturale, come d'altronde il resto del paese.
L'Equador offre ai turisti una moltitudine di paesaggi: molte montagne, vegetazione tropicale, spiagge, valli, città antiche e moderne. La capitale Quito è stata dichiarata dall'Unesco Patrimonio Culturale dell'Umanità nel 1978, ancor prima di Cuenca e le isole Galapagos. Ai turisti che amano la natura consigliamo di visitare la città di Loja.

NATIONAL GAY INFO

■ **gayecuador.com**
☏ (04) 239 05 98 🖳 www.gayecuador.com
Gay portal for Ecuador.

NATIONAL GROUPS

■ **Fundación Ecuatoriana Equidad** Mon-Fri 9.30-19h
Baquerizo Moreno E7-86 y Diego de Almagro, Quito ✉ Quito
☏ (02) 254 4337 🖳 www.equidadecuador.org
Non profit organization working on GLBT culture and GLBT health.

Ambato ☏ 03

BARS

■ **KarussoSalvation** (B MA NG)
Av. Víctor Hugo y Pareja Diezcanseco *Entrance Jefatura de Migración sector del Mall de los Andes* ☏ (03) 9582 3804
■ **Punto G bar** (B g MA)
Av. José Peralta Vía a Guaranda Km 1 Huachi Chico ☏ 095 886 958 (mobile)

CRUISING

-Terminal terrestre (toilets)
-Av. 9 de Octubre 22-?h
-Parque Centenario entre las 12 m. -18h
-Parque 12 de Noviembre (weekends, esp. toilets).

Cuenca ☏ 07

BARS

■ **Blues** (! B GLM)
Presidente Córdova S 5-84 y Hermano Miguel ☏ 087 748 365 (mobile)

CAFES

■ **Blues** (! B GLM)
Presidente Córdova S 5-84 y Hermano Miguel ☏ 087 748 365 (mobile)

DANCECLUBS

■ **Segunda Bacilus** (AC D g MC s)
Calle del Chorro 2-26 ☏ 283 37 11

CRUISING

-Parque Calderon (after sunset)
-Cine 9 de Octubre and the toilets (only when porn films shown)
-Turco del Balneario Rodas, Fri-Sun 14-?h.

Guayaquil ☏ 04

BARS

■ **Club Retro** (B d G) Thu-Sat 18-4h
Rocafuerte 709 e Imbadura, Mezzanine ☏ 0917 59914 (mobile)
■ **Queer Coffee & Club** (B GLM MA) Mon-Sat 17-?h
Baquerizo Moreno y P. Solano Esq.

DANCECLUBS

■ **Colors Disco** (B cc D G MA P ST) 22-4h
Corner Av. Orrantia y Av. Fco. Orellana *At Centro Comercial Kennedy Music* ☏ 0888 16688 (mobile)
■ **Vulcano** (AC B CC D MA S SNU ST) Thu-Sat 22-2.30h
Rocafuerte 419 y Padre aguirre ☏ (04) 2300 948
Still one of the best straight discos and the place to go on weekends.

RESTAURANTS

■ **Campanario.El** (g M MA) 12-16h
Alejo Lascano 1400 y Esmeraldas ☏ (04) 2282 917

CRUISING

-Promenade, Avenida 9 de Octubre
-Parque Centenario (ayor)
-Malecon 2000

Quito ☏ 02

BARS

■ **Dionisios** (B G MC PK S ST) Tue-Sat 21-2h
Manuel Larrea 1452 y Riofrío Quito, Pichincha *Manuel Larrea between the streets Checa and Riofrío, near Parque Ejido, access through outside stairs* ☏ (02) 255 5759
Friendly and popular. Thu-Sat cultural events. Also a disco area. Drag shows on Thu & Sat 22h.
■ **Naranjilla Mecánica** (B g MA) Mon-Sat 17.30-2h
Tamayo N22-43 y Veintimilla ☏ (02) 252 6468

DANCECLUBS

■ **Balzak OperaCLUB** (B D GLM MA S SNU) Thu-Sat 21-3h
C/. Toledo N22-326 y Lérida
■ **Blackout** (! AC B D GLM MA S SNU ST WE) Thu-Sat 22-2h
Baquedano 800 y Reina Victoria, Edif. Araucaria, planta baja *La Mariscal*
The „in" place now for the gay crowd, it gets a far better-looking crowd, from young and hip to elderly, and everything in between, and it is safer than the other place since they have a door-policy. It is nicer and with a more international atmosphere, and you can meet locals and foreigners. It is located half-a-block from Bohemio.
■ **Tercer Milenio (El Hueco)** (AYOR D GLM WE) Fri & Sat 22-2.30h
Baquedano 188 y Av. 6 de Diciembre, Mariscal
Eventhough it is popular among a certain crowd, it is not a safe place, specially for tourists! This disco is mostly a hangout for low-income people, hustlers and other people who are not advisable, so it is risky for locals, more so for foreigners!

SEX SHOPS/BLUE MOVIES

■ **Top Secret** (CC g) 10-13 & 14-19.30, Sun 10-16h
Tomás de Berlanga E5-32 e Isla Isabela ☏ (02) 243 0465
🖳 www.topsecretec.com
■ **Video Laser** (g MA S VS) Mon-Sat 14-21h
Versalles y Bolívia esquina, Centro Comercial American Center, Of 207
☏ (02) 254 1586
Gay videos are shown from Mon-Fri 19-21h.
■ **Videomaxxx** (B DR G MA VS) 12-20h, closed Mon & Tue
Av. América N27-84 y Selva Alegre, 2º piso ☏ (02) 256 6208

SEX CINEMAS

■ **Olympus** (AYOR DR G MA VS) 12-21h
C/. Cuero y Caicedo 734 y Av. América ☏ (02) 290 7571
🖳 www.quitogay.net/publicidad/olympus/olympus-index.htm

SAUNAS/BATHS

■ **Apolo** (DR FH G MA MSG RR SA SB SOL VS WH WO) 14-22, Fri 14-Sun 22h (non-stop)
San Ignacio 1027 y Gonzalez Suarez ☎ (02) 223 2014
On the ground floor there is a sauna, turkish room, jacuzzi, refreshment bar and TV. In the basement there is a porno video room and three private cabins.

■ **Azul** (B DR G GH MA MSG NU P RR SA SB VS WE WH WO) Mon-Fri 14-22, Sat & Sun 12-22h
C/. Mariscal Foch E9-36 y Av. 6 de Diciembre *Between Av. 6 de Diciembre and C/. Tamayo* ☎ (02) 222 1697
Clean, small sauna with an esoteric atmosphere. Soft drinks available. A nice place to meet people.

■ **Bambú Spa** (! B DU G LAB m MC MSG SA SB VR VS WH WO) Mon – Fri 14-22, Sat, Sun, & holidays; 11-22h
Robles E7-34 y Av. 6 de Diciembre ☎ (02) 254 29 98
💻 www.spa-bambu.com
The newest and best sauna in Quito.

■ **Jinetes** (AC B DR FH G MA MSG NU P RR SA SB VS WE WH) Mon-Fri 14-22, Sat & Sun 11-22h
Berlin 147 y 9 de Octubre ☎ (02) 254 2998
The oldest gay sauna in Quito. Soft drinks available. No private cabins. Popular.

TRAVEL AND TRANSPORT

■ **True Colors Travel** (glm) Mon-Fri 9-18h
Guayaquil N9-59 y Oriente, 2° Floor, Office 304 *Between Banco Central & Plaza del Teatro in the old town* ☎ (02) 295 5939
💻 www.galapagostraveller.com
Gay owned & operated. Specializes in Galapagos cruises.

HOTELS

■ **Cayman** (! AC b bf glm H I M OS)
Juan Rodriguez 270 y Reina Victoria ☎ (02) 256 7616
💻 www.hotelcaymanquito.com
Economic, comfortable and clean. Located in the very center of the restaurant and bar area.

GUEST HOUSES

■ **Casa Musa** (bf glm MA OS PI) All year
Tumbaco, El Arenal-La Esperanza, Pasaje Sombra Verde 88 *Off Autopista Interoceánica, 30 mins from downtown* ☎ 09 836 1260
💻 www.casamusa.com
B&B and apartments in a quiet and beautiful area.

CRUISING

After dark there is no area of Quito where it is safe to walk on the streets away from the main avenues. This particulary applies to any of the parks, the old town and the Mariscal area of the new town. Do not be tempted into unsafe places. Take a taxi everywhere you go.
-Avenida Patria along Parque El Ejido (but not in the park) across the street from the Colón Hotel (by daytime, in the new city centre, at night (AYOR) beware of the police!)
-Avenida Río Amazonas (R) (after sunset, near Hotel Hilton-Colón)
-La Moriscal (AYOR).

Egypt

Name: Misr · Ägypten · Egypte · Egipto · Egitto
Location: Northeastern Africa
Initials: ET
Time: GMT +2
International Country Code: ☎ 20
International Access Code: ☎ 00
Language: Arabic
Area: 1,002,000 km² / 385,227 sq mi.
Currency: 1 Egyptian Pound (Egypt£) = 100 Piastres
Population: 72,642,000
Capital: Cairo (Al-Qâhirah)
Religions: 90% Moslem (almost all Sunni)
Climate: Everywhere south of Cairo is uncomfortably hot in the summer months (Jun-Aug). Winter (Dec-Feb) is the best time to visit Luxor and Aswan.

It is no surprise that homosexuality is illegal in Egypt. Article 9(c) of Egypt's „Law on the Combating of Prostitution" forbids male homosexual conduct. This provision punishes the „habitual" practice of fujur („debauchery") and di`ara (prostitution /commercial sex) with up to three years' imprisonment, plus fines.

Ten years after the famous case „the Cairo 52," from May 2001, the situation in Egypt for gay men has not changed in the slightest. On the contrary – life has become more difficult and dangerous. Even after recent intervention from US politicians, the situation remains very alarming. Arrest and torture of homosexuals as well as men accused of being homosexual appears to be common practice. Support and sympathy can not be expected from family members. Islam is not just a religion but rather a way of life and gay life stands in contradiction to Islam. The dramatic upheavals which brought down the Mubarak government in spring 2011 have so far failed to show any signs that the lot of homosexuals is going to improve anytime soon. The situation continues to be unstable and uncertain, so that it remains to be seen how the political developments will turn out in the years to come.

The police continue to monitor gay chat rooms in Egypt and trap gay men by arranging a date with their unsuspecting victim.

Our advice: when you have to visit Egypt, please be extremely cautious. Don't use local chat rooms and be careful when visiting cruising areas. By using common sense you can keep out of trouble and enjoy this ancient culture and its people.

Es ist nicht sehr überraschend, dass die Homosexualität in Ägypten verboten ist. Artikel 9(c) des ägyptischen „Gesetzes zur Bekämpfung der Prostitution" untersagt gleichgeschlechtliche Handlungen zwischen Männern. Die Bestimmung bestraft die „Angewohnheiten" fujur (Ausschweifung) und di`ara (Prostitution/kommerzieller Sex) mit bis zu drei Jahren Freiheitsentzug und zusätzlichen Geldstrafen.

Zehn Jahre nach dem berühmt-berüchtigten Fall der „Kairo 52" im März 2001 hat sich die Situation für schwule Männer in Ägypten kein bisschen verbessert. Eher im Gegenteil – ihr Leben ist gefährlicher und schwieriger geworden. Sogar nach den jüngsten Interventionen amerikanischer Politiker bleibt die Lage bedrohlich. Die Verhaftung und Folter von Homosexuellen und Männern, die der Homosexualität beschuldigt werden, ist offensichtlich weit verbreitet. Auch von Familienmitgliedern kann man keine Unterstützung oder Sympathie erwarten. Der Islam ist nicht nur eine Religion, sondern eine ganze Lebensart, und das schwule Leben steht im Gegensatz zum Islam. Durch die dramatischen Umwälzungen, die im Frühjahr 2011 zum Sturz des Mubarak-Regimes geführt haben, gibt es noch keine Anzeichen für eine baldige Besserung für die Situation Homosexueller. Die Lage ist weiterhin instabil und unübersichtlich, so dass abzuwarten bleibt, wie sich die politische Entwicklung in den nächsten Jahren fortsetzen wird. Die ägyptische Polizei überwacht weiterhin schwule Chaträume und lockt schwule Männer in die Falle, indem sie sich mit ihren ahnungslosen Opfern verabredet. Unser Rat: Bei einem Besuch in Ägypten sollten Sie äußerste Vorsicht walten lassen. Greifen Sie nicht auf die örtlichen Chaträume zu und seien Sie sehr vorsichtig, wenn Sie in einschlägigen Gegenden cruisen gehen. Solange Sie sich auf Ihren gesunden Menschenverstand verlassen, werden Sie sich keinen Gefahren aussetzen und sich ungehindert an der geschichtsträchtigen Kultur und ihren Menschen erfreuen können.

Cela n'étonnera personne d'apprendre que l'homosexualité est interdite en Egypte. L'article 9(c) de la « loi de lutte contre la prostitution » prohibe les relations sexuelles entre hommes. La législation stipule que les « fuyur » (la débauche) et la « di'ara » (la prostitution) seront passibles d'une amende et d'une peine de prison pouvant aller jusqu'à trois ans.
Dix ans après le tristement célèbre épisode des « 52 du Caire « en mars 2001, la situation ne s'est pas améliorée du tout pour les gays en Egypte, au contraire: leur vie est devenue plus dangereuse et difficile encore et ce, malgré les récentes interventions de politiciens américains. L'arrestation et la torture d'homosexuels et d'hommes accusés d'homosexualité sont apparemment largement répandues. Aucun soutien ou sympathie n'est à espérer non plus de la part de la famille car l'islâm est une religion qui fait partie intégrante de la vie quotidienne et de la société et les modes de vie homosexuels sont à l'opposé de ses préceptes.
Une amélioration de la situation des homosexuels ne semble pas être proche du fait du profond bouleversement qui a conduit au printemps 2011 au renversement du régime de Moubarak. La situation restant instable et confuse, il ne reste qu'à attendre que le développement politique se poursuive dans les prochaines années.
La police continue de surveiller les chatrooms et tend des pièges aux gays en donnant rendez-vous à ses victimes qu'elle arrête ensuite. Il est donc recommandé d'être extrêmement prudent lors d'une visite en Egypte, de ne pas aller sur les chatrooms locaux et de faire attention sur les lieux de drague. Avec un minimum de bon sens et de prudence, vous pourrez profiter pleinement de la richesse culturelle de ce pays splendide et de ses habitants.

No sorprende mucho que la homosexualidad en Egipto esté prohibida. El artículo 9 (c) de la ìley egipcia para la lucha de la prostituciónî prohíbe las relaciones del mismo sexo entre hombres. La normativa penaliza las ìcostumbresî fujur (explotación) y diíara (prostitución o comercio sexual) con penas privativas de libertad de hasta 3 años y con sanciones económicas complementarias.
Diez años después del famoso caso ìCairo 52î en marzo del 2001, la situación para los homosexuales en Egipto no ha mejorado ni un poco. Al contrario, la vida es más peligrosa y difícil; incluso tras las recientes intervenciones de políticos americanos, la situación sigue siendo amenazante. Aumenta de forma clara el arresto y la tortura de homosexuales y de hombres a quienes se les culpa de homosexualidad. Uno tampoco puede esperar el apoyo o la simpatía de los miembros de la familia. El Islam no es sólo una religión sino también un completo estilo de vida, y la vida gay se contrapone al Islam.
Debido a los drásticos cambios acontecidos en la primavera de 2011 para derrocar al régimen de Mubarak, aún no existen señales de una rápida mejora en la situación de los homosexuales en este país. Esta situación sigue siendo inestable y confusa, por lo que queda por ver cómo evoluciona el desarrollo político en los próximos años.
La policía egipcia sigue controlando las salas de chat homosexuales y encarcelando a los hombres gays, víctimas inocentes, que deciden encontrarse con ellos sin saber que son policías encubiertos. Nuestro consejo: durante su visita a Egipto, deberá ser extremadamente cuidadoso. Evite acceder a las salas de Chat y sea extremadamente cuidadoso cuando visite las correspondientes zonas de cruising. Mientras utilice su sentido común, no correrá ningún peligro y podrá disfrutar sin problemas de una cultura memorable y de sus gentes.

Non sorprende il fatto che l'omosessualità in Egitto è vietata. L'articolo 9 (c) della legge egiziana per la lotta alla prostituzione vieta atti sessuali tra persone dello stesso sesso. La promisquità e la prostituzione vengono punite con una reclusione fino a tre anni più una pena pecuniaria.
Dieci anni dopo il famigerato caso del „Cairo 52" (in marzo del 2001) la situazione per gli omosessuali in Egitto non è minimamente migliorata anzi tutto il contrario: è peggiorata. Persino gli interventi di politici americani non hanno migliorato le cose: la situazione rimane ancora molto pericolosa. La tortura di omosessuali o presunti tali è ancora molto diffusa. Neanche da parte di familiari ci si puo aspettare sostegno o simpatie. L'Islam non è soltanto una religione bensì tutto un modo di vivere che comunque è opposto al modo di vivere degli omosessuali. Nonostante i drammatici sconvolgimenti che, nella primavera del 2011, hanno portato alla caduta del regime di Mubarak, non c'è ancora segno di alcun miglioramento della situazione degli omosessuali. La situazione continua ad essere così instabile e confusa che non rimane altro che aspettare la piega che prenderà la situazione politica nei prossimi anni.
La polizia continua a sorvegliare le chat rooms e intrappola i gay attraverso appuntamenti. Vi consigliamo quindi massima attenzione: cercate di evitare le chat rooms locali e state ben attenti quando andate a fare cruising. Affidatevi al buon senso e vedrete che non correrete pericoli, potendovi godetere, la ricca cultura storica di questo Paese.

NATIONAL GAY INFO

Gay Egypt
www.gayegypt.com
General information on the situation of LGBTs around Egypt.

Alexandria/El Iskandarya ☏ 03

CAFES

Al Togaria (b NG)
Corniche Street *Near the French Consulate, cnr. of the Corniche with Rue al Mokadam*
No sign, look for green awning between Nile Excelsior & French consulat.

Cairo Bus Station Cafe (g OS r YC)
Zaghoul Square

SEX CINEMAS

Ramses (AYOR MA r)
El Horrya Road *At El Nabi Danial Street*
Frequent police raids at this shabby place with an unfriendly management.

CRUISING

All AYOR
-Central (Misr) station and the park outside
-Saad Zaghloul Square
-Ramleh Square, Ramleh station (tram station), evenings

-Zahran city centre, also: Zahran Moul. Shopping Mall. On Thu evenings. 5 mins by taxi from Sidi Gaber station in Smoha area.
-San Stefano tram station toilets, evenings (20 stops from Ramleh station, red line N° 2)
-Stanley Bay, Stanley Bridge (evenings) and Sidi Bich (city beach), (limited cruising due to construction works)
-Syria Street in Rushdy area, night time
-Montuzah Park (13 km from the centre, discreet action in the afternoon)
-Nuzha Garden – close to the zoological gardens
-Sea side Cornish (mostly young students) from the city centre near the Cecil Hotel to the newly completed library. You might try in particular Al Togaria (near the French Consulate on the corner of the Corniche with Sharia Mokadam)
-Semouha Shopping Mall on Thursday evenings.

Assuan/Aswan

CRUISING

All AYOR:
-Boat landing and garden in front of Oberoi Hotel on Elephantine Island (at night)
-Cataract Garden (afternoons) and hotel swimming pool (entry for a small fee for non-hotel guests)
-Ramsis Square and station
-Around the city in the Nubian villages
-Kitchener's Island
-Municipal swimming pool, strictly for locals
-Swimming pool at the Cleopatra Hotel & the Basma Hotel's pool
-Ferial Gardens, southern end of the Corniche, between the Air Egypt offices and the Old Cataract Hotel.

Cairo/El Qâhira ☏ 02

BARS

■ **Harry's Bar** (B NG)
Cairo Marriott Hotel ☏ (02) 340 88 88
■ **Jackie's Joint** (B NG) 22-4h
Tahrir Square, Nile Hilton Hotel ☏ (02) 578 04 44
Attracts a mixed gay/straight crowd, the best time to go there is Thursdays when there is a DJ with house, trance and hip hop.
■ **Pub 28** (B NG)
28 Shagaret El Dorr St. Zamalek ☏ (02) 735 92 00
Pub with house music. Stays open until 2h.

CAFES

■ **Cafeteria Omu Kulsun** (b NG)
Very expensive regarding the local market.
■ **Roof Top Cafe at Nile Zamalek Hotel** (b NG)
Rush hour 9-10h.

DANCECLUBS

■ **Amonn Disco** (B D NG)
Sphinx Square, El Mohandessin *In Amnon hotel*
■ **Jackie's Joint** (B D NG) 21-5h
Corniche el-Nil (Nile Hilton Hotel) ☏ (02) 578 04 44
Smart dress is required. No cover before midnight. Cover charge applies after midnight includes two drinks. Be discreet.
■ **Saddle Up** (B D NG)
Mena House Hotel Complex
Very expensive entrance fee and drinks.

SEX CINEMAS

■ **Ali Baba** (AYOR NG) 12-?h
26 July Street
Run down place with hostile management towards gay men. Overpriced for tourists, no admittance in short trousers.
■ **Karim I and II** (AYOR NG)
5 Sharia Emad Ad-Din
■ **Radio** (AYOR NG)
24 Sharia Talaat Harb

SAUNAS/BATHS

■ **Hammam Behbel Bah** (AYOR NG) Men admitted after 21h
Sharia Behbel Bah *Off Klot Bek Street, Claude Bey Sharia, no sign, green front door*
Be discreet!
■ **Kalaoun / King Saleh Bazzar Hamamh** (AYOR NG SA SB) 10-19h
80 Elmoez Ldien Allah St. Elnahasen, Khan Al-Khalyly *A bit hidden, left of the entrance gate of Kalaoun-Hospital* ☏ (02) 589 27 47
■ **Nile Hilton** (AYOR NG SB)
Tahrir Square *On the Nile, next to the Egyptian Museum*
☏ (02) 578 06 84
Action takes place in the locker room and the steam bath, but be discreet!
■ **Suk Al Selah Hammam** (AYOR NG) Admission for men after 21h
Suk Al Selah Street *Near Al Saiyda Aisha Medan*
In a rather dangerous area.

CRUISING

All AYOR, police know about these cruising areas. Cruising at night only (unless otherwise indicated)
-Tahreer Square, down town Cairo, near KFC, rush hour at night after 21 or 22h
-Municipal swimming pool
-Talaat Harb Street, Qasr Nil Street (esp. soldiers)
-Hilton hotel (Tahreer Square) very cruisy
-Talaat Harb-Street/Tahreer Square
-Ferial Gardens
-Café Fishaawi, Khan El Khalili, El Hussein quarter
-Ramses Station, Square and Street / 26 July Street (also by car)
-Toilet of parking lot in front of the court building, during the day until 1h (near Al American bar)
-Corniche el Nil at the river in front of Nile Hilton
-Egyptian Museum
-Sharia Talaat Harb between Medan Talaat Harb and it's junction with 26 July Street
-Horreya Mall, on Sharia al-Ahram (al Ahram Street)
-Genena Mall in Naser City on Sharia Badrawi off Sharia Abbas El Akkad, busy on Thursday evenings
-Reception hall of Mariott Hotel & pool , zamalik area
-Buddha bar hotel, located at the Sofitel hotel in Zamalek
-Club 35 at Four Seasons hotel Giza crowded at weekends
-Mojeito bar at Hilton Ramsees hotel
-Gold's gym chain
-Smart gym in helioplolis city
-L'Aubergine pub in Zamalek at weekends

El Gouna / Hurghada ☏ 065

DANCECLUBS

■ **Piano, Piano** (AC B D g S)
Sharaton Road, Sakkala *In the Minamark Hotel* ☏ 15 24 14 84 84
New disco and show bar

Luxor/Al-Uqsur ☏ 095

BARS

■ **King's Head Pub** (B g MA)
Sharia Khalid Ibn Walid

CAFES

■ **Awaha** (AYOR b NG r)
Station Square *Opposite the station*
■ **Cafe @ Etap Hotel** (b MA NG)
Cornish
■ **ElTakia** (b MA NG)
Television Street

DANCECLUBS

■ **Sinouhe** (B D NG) 22-4h
Sharia Khalid Ibn Walid *Opposite the Sonesta*
Busiest on Thu.

HOTELS

■ **El Salam** (bf H)
Station Street ☎ (095) 37 25 17

■ **Hatshepsut** (B bf H)
Television, Main Street *On the outskirts* ☎ (095) 85 211

CRUISING

All AYOR
-The Corniche (from the Museum to the winter Palace Hotel)
-Park between Temple of Amon and Luxor Hotel
-Landing place for Nile river-boats
-Banana Island (at night)
-Train station and toilets (AYOR)
-Station St. (Sharia Mahatta).

Sharm el Sheikh ☎ 069

CAFES

■ **Hard Rock Cafe** (B NG)
Naama Bay

DANCECLUBS

■ **Bus Stop** (B D NG) After 24h
Naama Bay *In the Sanafer Hotel*

Siwa Oasis

CRUISING

All AYOR
-Cleopatra spring
-Fatnis Island, Abu Alif Bath
-Military area.

El Salvador

Location: Pacific coast of Central America
Initials: ES
Time: GMT -6
International Country Code: ☎ 503 (no area codes)
International Access Code: ☎ 00
Language: Spanish
Area: 21,041 km² / 8,124 sq mi.
Currency: 1 El-Salvador-Colón (¢) = 100 Centavos
Population: 6,881,000
Capital: San Salvador
Religions: 76% Catholic, 21% Protestant
Climate: Tropical climate. The best time to visit is in the dry season (Nov-Apr).
Important gay cities: San Salvador

In El Salvador's penal code there is no mention of laws punishing homosexuality. There are laws regarding „moral behaviour and good habits" which allow judges an extended field of interpretation. The age of consent is set at 18 years, regardless of sexual orientation. New laws have been introduced which set out to eliminate abuse of minors any street prostitution. In general the situation of gay men in El Salvador is comparative to that in many western countries. They do not enjoy any form of prominent understanding, but are tolerated. This tolerance is particularly evident in the large cities.
Every since 1996 a Gay Pride parade takes place each June. Bisexuality is common and in the larger cities you will find transvestites working as prostitutes at the roadside. In general discretion is advisable.
El Salvador, the smallest country in continental America, has a diversity of landscapes, from Pine forests to Palm-lined beaches, impressive volcanoes and crater lakes. Numerous archaeological sites offer a picture of life in pre-Columbian times and the sleepy villages prior to colonial times. The capital city San Salvador has several gay organizations as well as bars and discos and social groups.

In El Salvadors Strafgesetzbuch werden keine Bestimmungen gegen Homosexualität an sich erwähnt. Es gibt jedoch Gesetze über „moralisches Verhalten und gute Sitten", die den Richtern großen Ermessensspielraum geben. Das Mindestalter liegt bei 18 Jahren, unabhängig von der sexuellen Orientierung. In jüngster Zeit wurden neue Gesetze zur Eindämmung des Missbrauchs Minderjähriger und der Straßenprostitution erlassen. Generell ist die Situation der Schwulen in El Salvador mit der Lage der Homosexuellen in vielen westlichen Ländern vergleichbar. Sie genießen zwar keine übergroße Sympathie, werden aber toleriert. Diese Toleranz ist besonders in den größeren Ballungszentren spürbar.
Seit 1996 findet jedes Jahr im Juni eine Gay-Pride-Parade statt. Bisexualität ist weit verbreitet und in den Großstädten gibt es Transvestiten, die sich auf dem Straßenstrich als Prostituierte verdingen. Im Allgemeinen gilt: Diskretion ist geboten.
El Salvador, das kleinste Land Lateinamerikas, verfügt über eine sehr abwechslungsreiche Landschaft mit Kiefernwäldern und Palmenstränden, eindrucksvollen Vulkanen und Kraterseen. Zahlreiche archäologische Stätten geben einen Einblick in die vorkolumbianische Zeit und das Leben in den abgeschiedenen Dörfern vor der Kolonialzeit.
Die Hauptstadt San Salvador verfügt über mehrere Gay-Organisationen sowie über Bars, Discos und Vereine.

Le code pénal d'El Salvador ne mentionne pas l'homosexualité en soi. Il existe néanmoins des lois concernant le « comportement moral et les bonnes mœurs » qui laissent aux juges une grande marche de manœuvre laissée à leur appréciation. Indépendamment de l'orientation, la majorité sexuelle est fixée à 18 ans. De nouvelles lois ont été ajoutées récemment pour lutter contre le détournement

de mineurs et la prostitution de rue. La situation des homosexuels est, à El Salvador, comparable à celle dans nombre de pays occidentaux: la sympathie de la population locale envers eux reste certes limitée, mais ils sont tolérés, surtout dans les grands agglomérations. La bisexualité est largement répandue et on trouve dans les rues des grandes villes des travestis se prostituant. Il est généralement recommandé d'être discret. Depuis 1996, une Gay Pride a lieu chaque année en juin et la capitale, San Salvador, a plusieurs organisations et associations gays de même que des bars et des boîtes de nuit.
Le plus petit pays d'Amérique latine jouit d'un paysage des plus diversifiés avec des forêts de conifères, des plages bordées de palmiers, des volcans et des lacs de volcans. Les nombreux sites archéologiques donnent une impression de la vie dans les villes et villages précolombiens et à l'époque coloniale.

En el código penal de El Salvador no se menciona ninguna disposición en contra de la homosexualidad. No obstante, existen leyes sobre „el comportamiento moral y las buenas costumbres" que otorgan a los jueces un gran margen de arbitrariedad. La edad de consentimiento está fijada en los 18 años, independientemente de la orientación sexual. Recientemente se han aprobado nuevas leyes para la erradicación de los abusos a menores y de la prostitución en las calles. En general, la situación de los homosexuales en El Salvador es muy comparable a la situación de los homosexuales en muchos países occidentales. No despiertan una gran simpatía pero se les tolera. Esta tolerancia se percibe sobre todo en los grandes centros urbanos.
Desde 1996 se celebra cada año, en junio, una marcha para el Orgullo Gay. La bisexualidad está muy extendida y en las grandes ciudades hay transvestidos que se dedican a la prostitución en la calles. En general se mantiene la discreción.
El Salvador, el país más pequeño de Latinoamérica, tiene un paisaje muy variado con bosques de coníferas y playas con palmeras, volcanes impresionantes y lagos con cráteres. Muchos de los sitios arqueológicos son un claro testimonio de la época precolombina y de la vida de los pueblos antes del colonialismo. La capital, San Salvador, dispone de varias organizaciones gays así como bares, discotecas y asociaciones.

In El Salvador il codice penale non fa alcuna citazione circa l'omosessualità. Tuttavia le leggi sul „comportamento morale e buoni costumi" danno ai giudici un ampio margine di potere discrezionale. L'età del consenso è di 18 anni, indipendentemente dal tipo di orientamento sessuale. Recentemente sono state promulgate delle leggi per arginare l'abuso dei minorenni e la prostituzione. In generale, la situazione dei gay in El Salvador è paragonabile a quella dei gay in altri paesi occidentali. Non godono di particolare simpatia ma vengono tollerati. Questa tolleranza la si avverte ancor di più nei centri più grandi.
Dal 1996 ha luogo annualmente (a giugno) il gay pride. La bisessualità è molto diffusa e i travestiti si vendono per strada. Vi consigliamo di essere piuttosto discreti!
El Salvador è il Paese più piccolo dell'America latina e ha un paesaggio molto variegato: pinete, spiagge piene di palme, laghi vulcanici e impressionanti vulcani. I diversi siti archeologici testimoniano l'età precolombiana e la vita nei paesini più sperduti prima dell'età coloniale. Nella capitale San Salvador ci sono diverse organizzazioni e associazioni gay ma anche bar e discoteche.

San Salvador

BARS

Bluepoint (AC B CC G MA) Wed-Sat 21-2h
Prolongación Alameda Juan Pablo II *In disco Scape* ☎ 2261 07 24
www.scapedisco.com

DANCECLUBS

Fenix (AC B D G MA OS p R SNU) Mon-Sat 20.30-3h
Av. los Andes 2998, Colonia Miramonte

Scape (AC B CC D G MA S WE) Wed-Sat 21-2h
Prolongación Alameda Juan, Pablo Segundo *In Centro Comercial Juan Pablo Segundo, Local 311A* ☎ 2261 07 24 www.scapedisco.com
Upscale gay disco.

RESTAURANTS

Luna. La (AC B CC M MA NG OS) 12-2h
C/. Berlín 228, Urbanización Buenos Aires 3 ☎ 2259 13 75

Ventana. La (B CC M MA NG OS) 12-2h
C/. San Antonio Abad 2335, Colonia Centroamérica *In front of San Luis Mall* ☎ 2226 51 29

SAUNAS/BATHS

Body Club (B CC DR FC FH G LAB M NU OS PI RR S SA SB SOL VS) 12-22, Sun 10-22h
C/. los Abetos # 17, Col. San Francisco *Entrance via Blvd. Venezuela in Col. San Francisco, first entrance on the right*
A clean sauna with a great outdoor garden for sunbathing and relaxing. The only gay sauna in the country.

SWIMMING

-Majagual Beach
-La Libertad Beach.

CRUISING

-Metro Centro Mall (YC) (Centro Comercial, Boulevard de los Heroes) opposite the Hotel Camino Real, esp. near Mister Donuts and ADOC area
-Galerias Mall (esp. the Food Court toilets)
-Plaza Merliot in the Food Court
-Multiplaza Mall
-Gran Via Mall
-Segunda Avenida near „Hispanoamérica" transvestites
-1a Calle Pte. between Cefesa y El Central de Señoritas. This is several square blocks in area busy from around 19-24h. People cruise in cars, picking up men, some for money and some for free.
-Morazan Park/2nd Avenue (AYOR R)
-Boulevard Hipodromo (Zona Rosa)
-Acajutla Port (R)
-Sauna in Hotel Alameda and Crown Plaza Hotel (airline crews).

Suchitoto

HOTELS

Almendros de San Lorenzo. Los (AC B CC H M PI SOL) 7-22h
4ta. C/. Poniente 2B *Centro* ☎ 2335 1200 www.hotelsalvador.com
Small hotel with 6 guestrooms and a restaurant in the historical centre of the colonial town.

Estonia

Name: Eesti · Estland · Estonie
Location: Northeastern Europe
Initials: EST
Time: GMT +2
International Country Code: ☎ 372 (no area codes)
International Access Code: ☎ 00
Language: Estonian
Area: 45,227 km² / 17,413 sq mi.
Currency: 1 Euro (€) = 100 Cents
Population: 1,346,000
Capital: Tallinn
Religions: 23% Evangelical Lutheran and Russian Orthodox
Climate: Estonian winters (Dec-Mar) are servere. The best time to visit is spring (Apr & May) or summer (Jun-Sep).
Important gay cities: Tallinn

In Estonia consensual same-sex relationships involving adults are legal. The full age of consent is 18 years, (14-17 under pariental consent). Lesbians and gays in Estonia neither enjoy legal protection from discrimination, nor can they legally register their partnerships. A first bill introduced in parliament in 2008 was thrown out by the conservative government. Ministry of Justice sources are quoted as saying that another attempt will be made in 2012.

Estonia is one of countries with the highest growth rate in the number of new infections of HIV in the world. According to local records 38 percent of the new infections affect people under 20 years of age and 90 percent those under 30.

Society is generally open and accepting towards gays, yet walking hand in hand on streets is still unusual. There is a relatively large variety of gay venues available in Tallinn but not enough people to fill them. Therefore, gay life takes place at the weekend, when most clubs are open until very late.

In summer the scene gets busier and very international. Tallinn fills up with tourist all over the world outnumbering the locals. However, Estonians' so called „silent tolerance" makes it very easy to feel welcomed and part of local gay life which, after few drinks, does not appear to be as quiet as it might have seemed to be to start with.

The capital city Tallinn is, due to its fantastic seaside location, considered the most attractive city in the country and the old city centre was declared a World Culture Inheritance by the UNESCO.

Started in 2004, the annual Baltic Gay Pride tradition was introduced to Tallinn. It takes place every year in the middle of August and is called the „Moonbow Pride".

In Estland sind einvernehmliche gleichgeschlechtliche Beziehungen unter Erwachsenen legal. Das volle Schutzalter liegt bei 18 Jahren (und mit elterlicher Zustimmung zwischen 14 und 17 Jahren). In Estland gibt es für Lesben und Schwule weder gesetzlichen Antidiskriminierungsschutz noch die Möglichkeit einer gesetzlich eingetragenen Partnerschaft. 2008 wurde ein erster Gesetzesentwurf im Parlament durch die konservative Regierung zu Fall gebracht. Aus Kreisen des Justizministeriums ist zu hören, dass ein neuer Vorstoß 2012 unternommen werden soll.

Estland gehört zu den Ländern mit den höchsten Zuwachsraten von HIV-Neuinfektionen der Welt; dort wurden 38 Prozent der Neuinfektionen bei Personen unter 20 Jahren registriert und 90 Prozent bei Menschen unter 30.

Die Gesellschaft ist im Allgemeinen Schwulen gegenüber offen und tolerant eingestellt, aber Männer Hand in Hand auf der Straße sind noch immer ein ungewöhnlicher Anblick. Es gibt ein recht großes Ausgeh-Angebot für Schwule in Tallinn, aber leider wenige, die es nutzen. Schwules Leben findet hauptsächlich an den Wochenenden statt, wenn die Clubs besonders lange geöffnet haben. Im Sommer ist die Szene lebendiger und internationaler. Tallinn füllt sich mit Touristen aus aller Welt und diese übersteigen sogar die Anzahl der Einwohner. Die stille Toleranz der Esten macht es einem jedoch leicht, sich willkommen zu fühlen, Teil des schwulen Lebens zu werden, das nach ein paar Drinks auch gar nicht mehr so ruhig scheint, wie noch auf den ersten Blick.

Schwule werden vom Großteil der Bevölkerung ignoriert und leben ihre Sexualität mehr oder weniger im Verborgenen. Die estnische Hauptstadt Tallinn ist mit ihrer reizvollen Lage am Meer eine der schönsten Städte des Landes und die Altstadt ist zum UNESCO-Weltkulturerbe erklärt worden.

Entstanden im Jahr 2004, die jährliche baltische Gay Pride Parade findet Mitte August in Tallinn statt und wird der ÑMoonbow Prideì genannt.

La majorité sexuelle est fixée à 18 ans, mais elle peut être descendue jusqu'à 14-17 ans avec l'assentiment des parents. En Estonie, les gays et lesbiennes ne jouissent ni d'une loi anti-discriminatoire, ni d'un partenariat enregistré encadré par la loi. En 2008 une premières proposition de loi au parlement fut torpillée par le gouvernement conservateur. Selon des sources du Ministère de la Justice, une nouvelle tentative devrait être menée en 2012.

L'Estonie fait partie des pays ayant la plus forte augmentation du nombre de cas d'infection à VIH nouvellement diagnostiqués au monde : 38 % des nouveaux contaminés ont moins de 20 ans et 90 % ont moins de 30 ans.

La société est, d'une manière générale, plutôt tolérante envers les homosexuels, mais voir des hommes marcher main dans la main dans les rues est encore assez rare. Tallinn offre de nombreuses possibilités pour passer d'agréables soirées gays mais malheureusement bien peu qui en profitent. La vie gay se déroule plutôt le week-end quand les clubs restent ouverts plus longtemps. L'été, le milieu gay est plus animé et international. Tallinn se remplit alors de touristes venus du monde entier qui augmentent sensiblement le nombre d'habitants. La « tolérance tacite « des Estoniens permet à tout un chacun de se sentir bienvenu, de devenir part de la vie gay qui, après quelques verres, n'est plus aussi calme qu'elle y paraissait au premier abord.

En 2004, la tradition de la Gay-Pride baltique s'est également installée à Tallinn. Elle sera célébrée chaque année en août sous le nom de « Moonbow Pride « .

Les gays et lesbiennes sont généralement ignorés par le reste de la population et vivent leur sexualité plus ou moins cachés. La capitale estonienne, Tallinn, est avec sa situation en bord de mer, une des plus belles villes du pays.

En Estonia, las relaciones consentidas entre personas adultas del mismo sexo son legales. La edad de consentimiento en general está en los 18 años (y con el consentimiento de los progenitores entre 14 y 17 años). Los gays y lesbianas de Estonia no cuentan ni con una ley antidiscriminación ni con la posibilidad de un registro civil de parejas. En 2008, el primer esbozo de una ley semejante recibió la oposición del gobierno conservador en el Parlamento. En los círculos del Ministerio de Justicia, se escucha que en 2012 se llevará a cabo un nuevo ataque.
Estonia forma parte de los países con uno de los mayores porcentajes de crecimiento de nuevas infecciones del SIDA en el mundo. Aquí se registraron un 38 % de nuevas infecciones entre personas menores de 20 años y un 90 % entre personas menores de 30.
La sociedad, en general, se muestra abierta y tolerante hacia los homosexuales pero todavía no se ven hombres cogidos de la mano por las calles. En Tallin hay ya una oferta bastante amplia para los gays pero desgraciadamente hay pocos que lo utilizan. La vida gay se desarrolla básicamente los fines de semana, cuando especialmente los clubs abren hasta tarde.
En verano, el ambiente es más vivo e internacional. Tallin se llena de turistas de todo el mundo y sobrepasa el número de sus habitantes. La llamada „tolerancia silenciosa" de los estonios hace que sea fácil sentirse bienvenido y acogido, formar parte de la vida gay, lo que después de un par de copas ya no es tan tranquilo como parece.
Durante el año 2004 se implantó también en Tallin la tradición de la Marcha del Orgullo Gay del Báltico. Se celebra cada año en agosto, con el nombre de „Moonbow Pride".
Los homosexuales son, en su mayor parte, ignorados por la población y viven su sexualidad de manera más o menos clandestina. La capital estonia, Tallinn, con su magnífica situación enfrente del mar, es una de las más bellas ciudades del país y su parte antigua fue declarada patrimonio de la humanidad por la UNESCO.

L'età legale è di diciotto anni, tuttavia con il permesso dei genitori questa può variare tra i quattordici e i diciassette anni. In Estonia, per i gay e le lesbiche, non esistono né leggi antidiscriminatorie né la possibilità di un'unione civile ufficialmente riconosciuta. Nel 2008 il governo conservatore ha affossato in parlamento una proposta che andava proprio in questo senso. All'interno del Ministero della giustizia circolano voci circa la possibilità di un nuovo tentativo nel 2012.
L'Estonia è tra i paesi con la più alta percentuale di crescita di infezione da HIV nel mondo: sono stati registrati il 38% di infezioni tra la fascia di età sotto i 20 anni e il 90 % tra la fascia sotto i 30 anni.
La società, in generale, è piuttosto aperta e tollerante, tuttavia, l'immagine di due uomini che si tengono per mano in pubblico è ancora qualcosa di strano e insolito. A Tallinn l'offerta di posti e locali gay è piuttosto notevole, purtroppo però, sono in pochi coloro che sfruttano questa offerta. La scena gay è particolarmente vivace durante il fine settimana, durante il quale locali e discoteche restano aperti fino a tardi.
In estate la scena gay è più vivace ed internazionale che in altri periodi dell'anno: Tallinn si riempe di turisti da tutto il mondo, che addirittura, arrivano a superare il numero degli abitanti stessi. La „tacita tolleranza" degli estoni fa sì che ci si senta davvero benvenuti e che ci si integri facilmente all'interno della vita gay, che, dopo qualche cocktail, non è più così pacata come effettivamente potrebbe apparire in un primo momento.
Dal 2004 la tradizione del Gay Pride ha preso piede anche a Tallinn e viene celebrato annualmente nel mese di agosto con il nome di Moonbow Pride. Gli omosessuali vengono ignorati dalla maggior parte della popolazione e vivono la propria sessualità in maniera più o meno nascosta. La capitale estone Tallinn, con la sua affascinante posizione sul mare, è una delle più belle città del paese e il suo centro storico è stato dichiarato patrimonio culturale dall'UNESCO.

NATIONAL GAY INFO

GLIK – Estonian Gay & Lesbian Info Centre
Tue-Thu 16-20, Mon & Sat 10-14h
Tartu mnt. 29 ✉ 10128 Tallinn ☎ 645 4545 🖳 www.gay.ee

Pärnu

SWIMMING

-Beach of Pärnu (male nude beach).

Tallinn

TOURIST INFO

Tourism Tallin (NG)
Vabaduse väljak 7 ☎ 640 4411 🖳 www.tourism.tallinn.ee
Country information available in English, Russian, German, Finnish, Swedish and Estonian.

BARS

Chill-Out (B glm MA)
Fri & Sat 18-?h (occasionally also open on weekdays)
Roosikrantsi 3 *Back entrance, downstairs*
Turkish style bar with a small dancefloor and a friendly atmosphere. Two small private rooms allow some action behind closed doors.

G-Punkt (AC B D GLM M S VS WE YC) Tue-Thu 18-1, Fri & Sat 20-6h
Pärnu Mnt 23 *Back entrance, same building as sauna Club 69*
☎ 644 05 52
Looks like a lounge café with dance floor. Disco on Wed, Fri & Sat after 22h (YC).

X Baar (AC B CC d gLm M MA WE) 16-1, Fri & Sat -3h
Väike-Karja 1 *About 50 m from Angel Club* ☎ 641 9478 🖳 www.xbaar.ee
Relaxed, discreet atmosphere. Small dancefloor and loud music late at night. New location. Many lesbians but some gay guys on Fri & Sat nights. On Fri & Sat people are usually arrive for party around 23h.

MEN'S CLUBS

Ring Club (AC B CC DR G I p S SA VS) Sun-Thu 20-6, Fri & Sat 23-6h
Juhkentali 11 *Bus 3/16/17/23/39-Hotel Olumpia* ☎ 6605 490
🖳 www.ringclub.ee
Popular cruising place and sexclub with sauna, cinema, bar and mazes.

SEX SHOPS/BLUE MOVIES

Malesecrets (AC CC DR G p VS) Daily 18-?h
Juhkentali 11 *Same address as Ring Club* ☎ 660 54 93
🖳 www.malesecrets.eu
Gay adult store. Also mail order.

SexMax (g MA VS) 24hrs
Tartu mnt. 62 *Close to the central bus station*
Video booths and rooms, gloryholes.

SAUNAS/BATHS

Club 69 (AC B CC DR f FC FH G m MA MSG p PI PP r RR SA SB SH SOL t VS WE WH) 16-2, Fri & Sat -7h
Sakala 24 *On corner of Pärnu mnt. & Sakala street, inside the yard at Sakala street behind the black gate, ring the doorbell in front of small gate*
☎ 660 48 30 🖳 www.club69.ee
A modern, discreet and very friendly place; attractive for both tourists and locals. Close to other gay venues and public transportation.

GUEST HOUSES

Tihase B&B (bf H I MA PK RWT) All year
Tihase 6a *2km from the Tallinn city* ☎ 683 17 75 🖳 www.tihase.ee
Gay-friendly guesthouse

FETISH GROUPS

Estonian Leatherman's Club (F G MC P)
PO Box 5705 🖳 www.lmc-estonia.visonhb.se
Private club. Parties by invitation.

HEALTH GROUPS

AIDS Information & Support Centre (AIDS-i Tugikeskus) 15-18, Sat 11-14h, Sun closed
Kopli 32 ☎ 641 31 65 www.tugikeskus.ee
Support for people with HIV/AIDS. Testing of HIV/STDS. Sex workers project.

SWIMMING

-Pirita Rand. Beach on the right side from beach station to the end of the beach (area before the stones and in forest). Northern section called Kaasiku near Merlvälja tee
-Klooga Rand, in the dunes (40 mins by train from Tallinn)
-Stromi Rand, on the left side form beach station, cruising in reeds.

CRUISING

-Harju Mägi-Park (entrance from Vabaduse Väljak, the best is Linda Monument)
-Toompea.

Tartu

BARS

Illusion Club (AC B D glm MA S WE)
Raatuse 97 ☎ 581 579 17 www.illusion.ee

SWIMMING

-Banks of Emajögi River (Beach on the end of Ujula street, opp. old town).

CRUISING

-Toomemägi
-Laululava (the song festival-field. Apr-Oct: Wed-Sat 19-22h).

Valgamaa

GUEST HOUSES

Kalda talu puhkekeskus (B BF glm H I OS PA PI PK SA VA) 24hrs
Iigaste Küla, Tölliste Vald *At the bank of Väike Emajogi* ☎ (076) 70 512
www.kaldatalu.ee
A small guest house which can accommodate up to 12 guests.

Fiji

Name: Viti · Fidschi · Fiyi
Location: South Pacific Ocean
Initials: FJI
Time: GMT +12
International Country Code: ☎ 679 (no area codes)
International Access Code: ☎ 00
Language: English, Fijian, Hindi
Area: 18,376km² / 7,056 sq mi.
Currency: 1 Fiji-Dollar ($F) = 100 Cents
Population: 848,000
Capital: Suva
Religions: 49% various Christian denominations, 32% Hindu, 7% Moslem
Climate: Tropical marine climate. Only slight seasonal variation in temperature. A dry season (May-Oct) is the best time to visit.

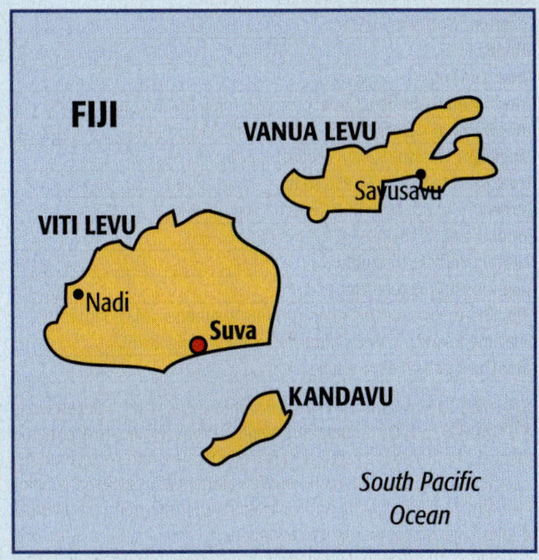

On the Fiji Islands the arrest gay men charged on sexual grounds have ceased. The unofficial age of consent is 16 years. Until recently homosexual actions were punishable. Even the „attempt" of homosexual action could be prosecuted. However, the government felt constrained to react to the tourism industry, which increases yearly by about 10%, particularly from Australia and New Zealand. In 2005 the arrest and conviction of an Australian caused a diplomatic incident.

Auf den Fidschi Inseln werden seit neuestem keine Schwulen mehr festgenommen, die einvernehmlichen Sex haben. Das inoffizielle Schutzalter liegt bei 16 Jahren. Bis vor kurzem waren homosexuelle Handlungen strafbar. Selbst der „Versuch" homosexueller Handlung wurde geahndet. Doch die Regierung sah sich gezwungen, auf die jährlich um ungefähr 10% steigende Tourismusindustrie, vornehmlich aus Australien und Neuseeland, zu reagieren. 2005 sorgte die Verhaftung und Verurteilung eines Australiers für Aufsehen.

Depuis peu, un homo ayant une relation sexuelle consentante ne peut plus être arrêté dans les Îles Fidji. La majorité sexuelle inofficielle est de 16 ans. Les relations homosexuelles étaient jusqu'à il y a peu répréhensibles devant la loi : même la « tentative » de relation homosexuelle était punie. Mais le gouvernement s'est vu obligé de réagir, étant donné la croissance annuelle d'environ 10% de l'industrie du tourisme, en provenance majoritairement d'Australie et de Nouvelle-Zélande. L'arrestation et la condamnation d'un Australien en 2005 notamment avait fait sensation.

En las islas Fiji, desde hace poco, ya no se arresta a los homosexuales que tiene sexo consentido. La edad de consentimiento oficiosa está en los 16 años. Hasta hace poco tiempo los actos homosexuales estaban penalizados, incluso el mero intento de actos homosexuales estaba perseguido. No obstante, el gobierno se vio obligado a reaccionar ante la creciente industria turística que cada año aumenta en un 10%, especialmente gracias a Australia y Nueva Zelanda. En 2005 el arresto y proceso de un australiano despertó la opinión pública.

Nelle isole Fiji, secondo una disposizione introdotta recentemente, il sesso tra due persone consensienti dello stesso sesso non è più punibile. L'età del consenso inufficiale per avere rapporti sessuali è di 16 anni. Fino a poco tempo fa, gli atti omosessuali erano perseguibili dalla legge. Persino l'intenzione di commettere atti omosessuali prima veniva punita. Tuttavia il governo si è visto costretto a reagire ai flussi di turismo che crescono annualmente di circa il 10% e che provengono principalmente dall'Australia e dalla Nuova Zelanda. Nel 2005, infatti, la carcerazione e la condanna di un australiano ha destato molto scandalo.

Nadi

CRUISING

-Bathrooms at bus station. Look at signs on walls (which were quite recent). Of course, cruising is AYOR due to local customs and laws.

Suva

BARS

■ **O'Reilly's** (AC B CC D glm S WE) Mon-Sun 16-1h
5 McArthur Street *Opp. Suva City library* ☎ 331 2884

DANCECLUBS

■ **Lucky Eddie's / Urban Jungle** (B D g)
217 Victoria Parade *Above O'Reilly's Bar*
■ **Traps** (B D g) Mon-Sat
305 Victoria Parade ☎ 312 922

RESTAURANTS

■ **Bad Dog Café** (AC CC g M WE)
Mon-Wed 11-23, Thu-Sat -1, Sun 17-23h
McArthur Street/Victoria Parade *Next to O'Reilly's* ☎ 331 2968

APARTMENTS

■ **Town House Apartments** (AC B g M)
3 Forster St., Central Suva ☎ 300 00 55
Rooms with private baths.

Taveuni

GUEST HOUSES

■ **Maravu Plantation Resort** (AC BF glm MC OS) All year
West Coast Road ☎ 888 0585 🖳 www.maravu.fiji-resort.net
14 bungalows in a tropical garden. Gay-friendly
■ **Qamea Resort** (AC B CC H I M MC RWB RWS WH) All year
PA Matei ☎ 888 0220 🖳 www.qamea.com
Transfer from Matei airport and a short car ride followed by a boat to the island.

Finland

Name: Suomi · Finnland · Finlande · Finlandia
Location: Northern Europe
Initials: FIN
Time: GMT +2
International Country Code: ☎ 358 (omit first 0 of area codes)
International Access Code: ☎ 00, 990, 994 or 999
Language: Finnish (92%), Swedish (5,6%)
Area: 338,144 km² / 130,558 sq mi.
Currency: 1 Euro (€) = 100 Cents
Population: 5,228,000
Capital: Helsinki/Helsingfors
Religions: 85% Protestant
Climate: The warmer weather in spring & summer (May-Sep) is the best time to visit. Summer attraction is the midnight sun.
Important gay cities: Helsinki

The age of consent is 16 for homosexuals and heterosexuals in Finland. Discrimination against homosexuals is a criminal offence. The law of registered partnership came into force in 2002, according to which male/male and female/female registered couples have almost all the rights and obligations that married heterosexual couples have except the right to adoption.
In Finland a lively debate regarding same-sexual marriage is taking place and the Ministry of Justice is currently investigating how a new marriage law could be implemented. This law would offer the same rights to all married couples regardless of the gender and same-sexual couples would be entitled to, among other things, the right to adoption of a person not belonging to the family. The election in April 2011 put the "True Finns", a right-wing populist party, in power as a coalition partner with 19%, thanks to their massively Eurosceptic campaign. As some politicians of this party have drawn attention to themselves with very homophobic statements, same-sex marriage is not to be expected in the near future. Nevertheless, no influence on the ecclesiastical wedding for same-sexual couples would apply as the church decides itself who it may marry.
General attitude towards gays and lesbians is tolerant, at least in big cities and among younger people. Every major city has a more or less active gay organization, which almost all are part of the state-supported national organization SETA. Travelling in Finland is quite expensive but easy with good train and flight connections.

Das Schutzalter liegt nun einheitlich bei 16 Jahren in Finnland. Diskriminierungen von Homosexuellen werden als strafbare Delikte geahndet. 2002 trat das Gesetz für eingetragene Partnerschaften in Kraft, das schwulen und lesbischen Paaren fast alle Rechte und Pflichten von verheirateten Heterosexuellen – mit Ausnahme des Adoptionsrechtes – zubilligt. In Finnland wird lebhaft über die gleichgeschlechtliche Ehe diskutiert und das Justizministerium diskutierte 2010, wie ein neues Ehegesetz in die Wege geleitet werden könnte. Dieses Gesetz würde allen Ehepaaren unabhängig von dem Geschlecht der Ehepartner die gleichen Rechte zuerkennen und gleichgeschlechtliche Paare bekämen u.a. das Recht zur Adoption einer nicht zur Familie gehörigen Person. Durch die Wahlen im April 2011 kamen die „Wahren Finnen", eine rechtspopulistische Partei, auf Grund eines massiven EU-kritischen Wahlkampfes mit 19% als Koalitionspartner in die Regierung. Mit einigen sehr homofeindlichen Aussagen fielen einzelne Politiker dieser Partei negativ auf, so dass vorerst mit einer Öffnung der Ehe für Schwule und Lesben nicht gerechnet werden kann. Auf die kirchliche Trauung hätte die Zulassung einer gleichgeschlechtlichen Ehe jedoch keinen Einfluss, denn die Kirche entscheidet selbst, wen sie kirchlich traut.
Die Einstellung der Bevölkerung Lesben und Schwulen gegenüber ist tolerant – zumindest in den Großstädten und bei jungen Leuten. Jede

größere Stadt hat eine mehr oder weniger aktive Schwulengruppe, die fast immer zu der staatlich unterstützten landesweiten Organisation SETA gehört. Das Reisen in Finnland ist zwar recht teuer aber aufgrund der guten Zug- und Flugverbindungen bequem.

La majorité sexuelle a été fixée à 16 ans pour tous en Finlande. La discrimination des homosexuels est considéré comme un délit puni de poursuites. En 2002 fut activée la loi de reconnaissance des couples homosexuels, qui bénéficient désormais des même droits et devoirs que les couples mariés (hétérosexuels) hormis le droit à l'adoption.
En Finlande des discussions houleuses ont lieu a propos du mariage du même sexe et le ministère de la justice cherche une solution pour pouvoir lancer une loi. Cette loi accorderait aux couples de même sexe les mêmes droits, entre autres le droit à l'adoption d'une personne n'appartenant pas à la famille. Avec les élections en avril 2011, le parti populiste de droite « Les Vrais Finnois « est entré dans une coalition gouvernementale après une campagne électorale critiquant massivement l'UE. Quelques politiciens de ce parti se sont faits remarquer par des propos très homophobes laissant douter de l'ouverture du mariage aux gays et lesbiennes. Cette autorisation n'aurait pas d'influence sur le mariage religieux, l'église pouvant décider elle-même de marier ou non deux personnes.
La population est tolérante vis à vis des homos, du moins dans les grandes villes et chez les jeunes. Dans toutes les villes se trouvent des associations homos, qui font presque toujours partie de la SETA, l'organisation nationale soutenue par l'État. Voyager en Finlande est certes cher mais l'accessibilité en avion ou train est très aisée.

En Finlandia la edad de consentimiento se establece ahora a los 16 años para todos. Las discriminaciones en contra de los homosexuales son castigadas como delitos penales. En 2002 entró en vigor la ley de parejas de hecho que otorga a las parejas gay-lésbicas casi todos los derechos y obligaciones de un matrimonio heterosexual, exceptuando el derecho de adopción. En Finlandia ha tenido lugar un activo debate en relación al matrimonio entre personas del mismo sexo; el Departamento de Justicia aclara actualmente cómo se puede llevar a cabo una nueva ley sobre el matrimonio. Esta ley reconocería los mismos derechos a todas las parejas independientemente del sexo de los cónyuges. De esta forma, se le reconocería a las parejas del mismo sexo, entre otras cosas, el derecho a adoptar a una persona no perteneciente al seno de la familia. Con las elecciones en abril de 2011 llegaron al poder los "Verdaderos Finlandeses", un partido populista de derechas que debe su éxito a la campaña electoral de protesta masiva contra la UE con un 19% de sus socios de coalición en el gobierno. Algunos políticos de este partido llamaron la atención de forma negativa a raíz de declaraciones homófobas, así que por ahora no se puede contar con la apertura del matrimonio para gays y lesbianas. La aprobación del matrimonio entre personas del mismo sexo no tendría ningún efecto sobre el matrimonio canónico, ya que la iglesia decide por sí misma a quién le otorga la bendición nupcial.
La actitud de la población hacia los gays y lesbianas es tolerante, por lo menos en las grandes ciudades y con la gente joven. En cada ciudad relativamente grande existe una asociación de homosexuales más o menos activa, que casi siempre pertenecen a la organización nacional SETA, con apoyo del estado. Viajar a Finlandia puede ser muy caro pero gracias a sus buenas comunicaciones en tren y avión muy cómodo.

L'età legale per avere rapporti sessuali è di 16 anni, per tutti in Finlandia. Discriminazioni nei confronti di gay vengono ritenute come delitti passibili di pena. Nel 2002 è entrata in vigore la legge per la registrazione dell'unione civile, che accorda a coppie lesbiche e gay quasi tutti i diritti e doveri che hanno anche coppie etero sposate, fatta eccezione per il diritto di adozione.
In Finlandia si è avviato un vivace dibattito sul matrimonio tra persone dello stesso sesso. Il Ministero della Giustizia sta infatti lavorando ad

nuova legge sul matrimonio. Questa legge riconoscerebbe a tutte le coppie – indipendentemente dal sesso dei coniugi – gli stessi diritti; le coppie dello stesso sesso otterrebbero, tra le altre cose, anche il diritto di adottare una persona non appartenente alla famiglia. Alle elezioni dell'aprile del 2011 il partito nazional-populista "Veri Finlandesi" (Perussuomalaiset), grazie ad un'intensa campagna antieuropeista, ha conquistato il 19% dei consensi, entrando così come partner di coalizione nel governo. Se si considera che alcuni membri di questo partito si sono già negativamente distinti per le loro dichiarazioni inequivocabilmente omofobe, è quanto mai superflua la speranza di una apertura del matrimonio alle coppie dello stesso sesso. Questa legge non avrebbe nessuna influenza sul matrimonio religioso, poiché, in questo campo, la chiesa decide autonomamente.
La popolazione finlandese è tollerante nei confronti di gay e lesbiche, almeno nelle grandi città e tra i giovani. Ogni grande città ha un gruppo gay, più o meno attivo, che fa parte quasi sempre dell'organizzazione nazionale SETA, sostenuta dallo Stato. Viaggiare in Finlandia è caro, ma molto comodo, grazie agli ottimi collegamenti ferroviari ed aerei.

NATIONAL GAY INFO

guys.fi (GLM MA)
www.guys.fi
the most comprehensive gay index in Finland with online community.

SETA – Seksuaalinen Tasavertaisuus ry (GLM)
Mon, Wed-Fri 10-14, Tue 10-13h
Mannerheimintie 170 A 4 ✉ 00300 Helsinki ☎ (09) 681 25 80
www.seta.fi
National LGBT organization. Member organisations are located throughout Finland.

NATIONAL COMPANIES

Baffin Books Oy
PL 15 ✉ 02771 Espoo www.baffinbooks.com
Online LGT bookstore, selling books, videos, DVDs and magazines.

NATIONAL GROUPS

Finnish AIDS Council
Unioninkatu 45 C 1 ✉ 00170 Helsinki ☎ (020) 74 65 700
☎ (020) 74 65 705 (Hotline: Mon-Fri 9-16h)
www.aidscouncil.fi

Helsinki ☎ 09

Helsinki is a fantastic city with a small but interesting gay scene. The lesbian scene in the city is very visible. All the bars and clubs are open to women too, even the Hercules nightclub. The only place where gay men can mix amongst themselves is Finland's only gay sauna „Vogue".
Helsinki Pride takes place at the end of June each year and is a political demonstration without the commercial side found at many other European Pride events. The parade ends in the Kaivopuisto Park where there is a stage and many live acts.
Tip: a Helsinki Card is a must for those on a short city break.

Helsinki ist eine fantastische Stadt mit einer kleinen, aber interessanten Schwulenszene. Die Lesbenszene ist in dieser Stadt sehr wahrnehmbar. Alle Bars und Nachtlokale stehen auch Frauen offen, sogar der Nachtklub „Hercules". Der einzige Ort, an dem schwule Männer ganz unter sich bleiben können, ist Finnlands einzige Schwulensauna namens „Vogue".
Der CSD von Helsinki findet jährlich Ende Juni statt und ähnelt einer politischen Demonstration; ohne die kommerzielle Seite, die viele andere europäische CSD-Events charakterisiert. Der Umzug endet im Kaivopuisto-Park, wo auf einer Bühne mehrere Liveauftritte stattfinden.
Tipp: Wenn Sie nur für einen Kurzbesuch in der Stadt sind, ist ein Helsinki-Ticket unerlässlich.

Helsinki est une ville fantastique avec un milieu gay petit mais intéressant. Le milieu lesbien est bien visible dans cette ville : tous les bars et les boîtes sont ouverts aux femmes, même le « Hercules ». Le seul endroit où les hommes sont entre eux est l'unique sauna gay de Finlande, le « Vogue ».
La Gay-Pride de Helsinki se déroule chaque année fin juin et ressemble à une manifestation politique sans l'aspect commercial qui caractérise tant d'autres Gay-Pride européennes. Le défilé s'achève au parc Kaivopuisto où plusieurs représentations live ont lieu.
Notre conseil : si vous ne faites que visiter brièvement la ville, achetez un Helsinki-Ticket !

Helsinki es una ciudad fantástica, con un ambiente gay pequeño pero interesante. El ambiente lésbico en esta ciudad es muy perceptible. Todos los bares y locales nocturnos están también abiertos a las chicas, incluso el club nocturno „Hercules". El único lugar en el que los gays pueden estar totalmente solos es la única sauna gay de Finlandia llamada „Vogue".
La Marcha del Orgullo Gay de Helsinki tiene lugar cada año a finales de junio y parece una manifestación política; sin la parte comercial, que caracteriza a muchas de las marchas y eventos gays de Europa. La Marcha finaliza en el Parque Kaivopuisto, donde se celebran varios espectáculos en directo.
Consejo: Si está en la ciudad sólo por un corto periodo, es imprescindible el Helsinki-Ticket.

Helsinki è una città fantastica con una piccola ma interessante scena gay. La scena lesbica in questa città è abbastanza consistente. Tutti i bar e i locali notturni sono aperti anche alle donne…persino il locale notturno Hercules. L'unico posto nel quale uomini omosessuali possono rimanere tra loro, è l'unica sauna gay della Finlandia Vogue.
Il Christopher Street Day di Helsinki si svolge annualmente ed assomiglia molto ad una manifestazione di tipo politico; manca infatti il lato

commerciale che invece è più che presente nei Christopher Street Day di altre cittá europee. La parata finisce al Kaivopuisto-Park, dove è allestito un palco per eventi dal vivo di vario genere.

Un consiglio: se vi trovate in cittá per una breve visita vi converrá comprare l' Helsinki-Ticket.

GAY INFO

Helsingin seudun SETA ry (GLM) Mon, Wed-Fri 10-14; Tue 10-13h
Mannerheimintie 170 A 4 ☎ (09) 681 25 80 www.heseta.fi
Very active gay and lesbian rights organization. Ask about their various services.

BARS

Fairytale (B glm I MA) Mon-Fri 16-2, Sat & Sun 14-2h
Helsinginkatu 7 *M° Sörnäinen* ☎ (09) 870 32 26 www.fairytale.fi
Internet access available. Happy hour daily until 20h.

Fenix (B GLM m MA S) 14-2h
Eerikinkatu 14 ☎ (09) 672 307 www.ravintolafenix.com
Games and shows in the evenings.

Hugo's Room (AC B CC GLM I M MA OS) 12-2, Sun 14-2h
Iso-Roobertinkatu 3-5 ☎ (09) 698 01 80 www.hugosroom.fi
Lounge- and musicbar.

Lost & Found (AC B CC D glm m MA NR s) Daily 20-4h
Annankatu 6 ☎ (09) 680 10 10 www.lostandfound.fi
The only hetero-friendly gay night club with occasional shows in Helsinki. Get lost, be found and let yourself be entertained in a relaxed atmosphere. Frequent guest artists, live music and stage shows in two floors. Fully licenced. Visitors must be over 24.

Mann's Street (AC B cc d G MA) Sun-Thu 14-2, Fri & Sat -4h
Mannerheimintie 12 A2 *2nd floor* ☎ (09) 612 11 03
www.mannsstreet.com
Karaoke bar. 1st Sat/month men's dance.

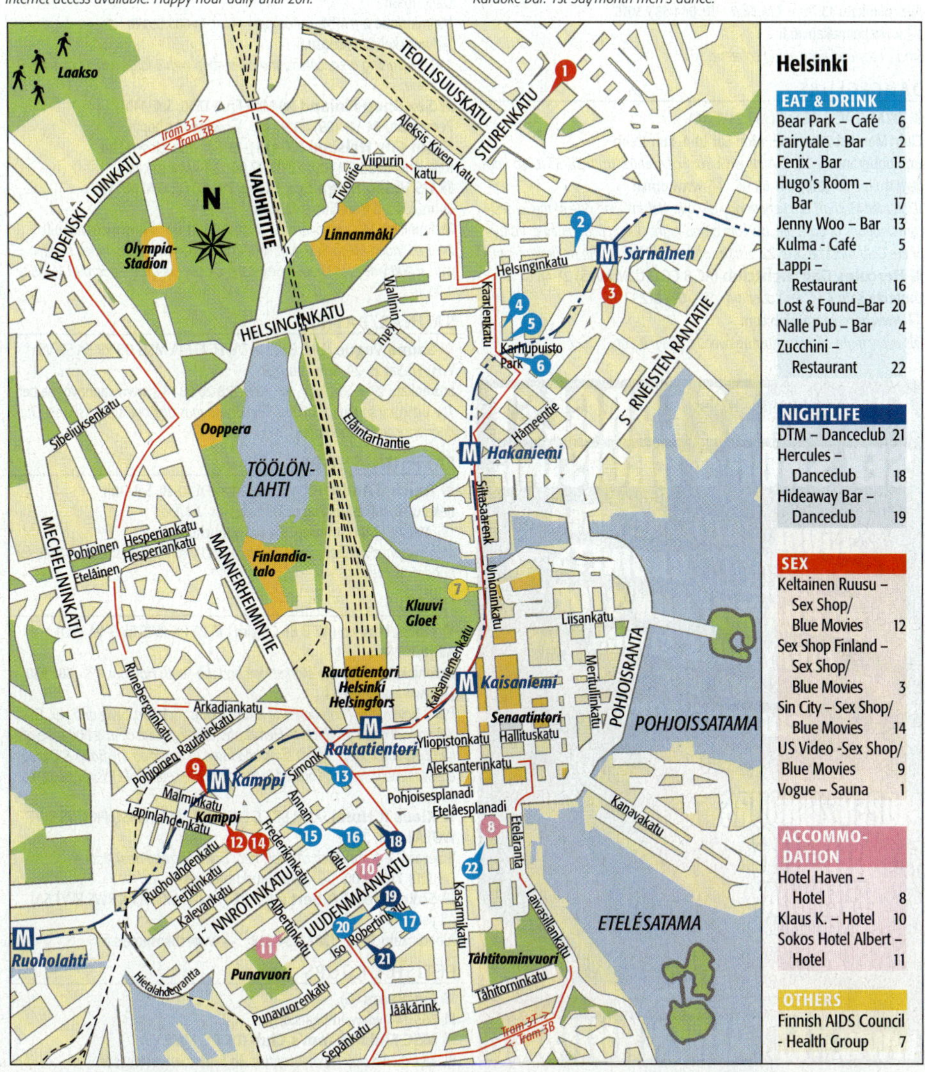

■ **Nalle Pub** (B CC GLM MA OS) 15-2h
Kaarlenkatu 3-5 ☏ (09) 701 55 43
A cosy gay pub in Kallio for socialising. Many Lesbians. Happy hour: 15-18h.

■ **Vatican** (B d glm MA s) Mon-Tue 11-23, Wed- Fri 11-4, Sat 18-4h
Simonkatu 6 🖳 www.vatican.fi
Stylish bar.

CAFES

■ **Bear Park Café** (BF CC FC GLM M MA OS PA WI)
Apr-Oct 8-20h; closed on rainy days
Karhupuisto – Fleminginkatu *Next to Kallio's church, tram 1A/3B/9*
☏ 044 576 06 79 (mobile) 🖳 www.bearparkcafe.net
Cosy summer cafeteria in the glorious Bear Park. Over 60 years old kiosk serves coffee, ice cream, fresh Finnish sweet pastries and soft drinks.

■ **Kulma** (b bf CC glm I m MA) 9-19, Sat & Sun 10-18h
Agricolankatu 13 *Tram 1,1A,3B,9* ☏ 044 533 3016
🖳 www.kulmakahvio.fi
Small, cosy and easy going cafeteria.

DANCECLUBS

■ **DTM** (! AC B CC D GLM I S WE YC)
Club: Mon-Sat 22-4; café: Mon-Sat 10-4, Sun 13-4h
Iso Roobertinkatu 28 *10 mins walk from city centre; tram 3B/3T to Iso Roobertinkatu* ☏ (010) 841 69 96 🖳 www.dtm.fi
„Don't tell Mama!" is a very trendy disco in Helsinki and one of the largest combinations of gay café, bar, disco and night club in Scandinavia. Visitors of the Club must be over 22, visitors of the café before 18h no limit of age.

■ **Hercules Gay Nightclub** (AC B CC D GLM MA S) 21-4h
Lönnrotinkatu 4 *M° Rautatientori* ☏ (09) 612 17 76
🖳 www.herculesgayclub.com
DJs every night. Visitors must be over 24 on Fri & Sat.

■ **Hideaway Bar** (AC B CC D glm MA S) 23-4h
Annankatu 6 *Downtown* ☏ (09) 680 10 10 🖳 www.lostandfound.fi
Downstairs disco of ‚Lost & Found' restaurant. Visitors must be over 24.

RESTAURANTS

■ **Lappi** (B CC GLM M MA) Mon-Fri 12-, Sat 13-22.30h
Annankatu 22 ☏ (09) 645 550 🖳 www.lappires.com
Original specialities from Lapland. Very popular but also expensive, especially the drinks. Friendly staff.

■ **Zucchini** (AC CC GLM MA OS VEG) Mon-Fri 11-16h
Fabianinkatu 4 *City centre* ☏ 622 29 07
Small nice restaurant in the city centre, serving vegetarian dishes, coffee and pastries.

SEX SHOPS/BLUE MOVIES

■ **Keltainen Ruusu – Yellow Rose** (AC cc DR f G MA T VS)
Daily 10-6h
Malminrinne 2-4 *M°/bus Kamppi* ☏ (09) 685 55270
🖳 www.keltainenruusu.fi
350 m² cruising area, cabins and a sex shop with a large variety of items on offer.

■ **Sex Shop Finland** (g) Mon-Fri 9-17.30, Sat -14h
Pengerkatu 24 ☏ (09) 71 97 02 🖳 www.sexshop.fi

■ **Sin City Helsinki** (CC g) 11-19, Sat -16h, closed Sun
Kalevankatu 26 ☏ (09) 70 02 92 04 🖳 www.sincity.fi

■ **US Video Mega Sex Store** (AC CC DR G M MA VS)
24hrs, closed from Sun 9-Mon 9h
Malminkatu 24 *Kamppi area* ☏ (09) 73 71 90 🖳 www.usvideo.fi
24/6 US Video Mega Sex Store with Cruising Cinema Area, Video booths with 16000 videos to choose, Sex store. Closed Sundays 9.00am to Monday 9.00am

SAUNAS/BATHS

■ **Sauna Vogue** (! AC B cc DR DU FC G MA MSG OS RR SA SB VS WH) Fri-Sat 15-24, Sun-Thu -23h
Sturenkatu 27 A *5th floor* ☏ (09) 728 20 08 🖳 www.saunavogue.net
The only gay sauna in Finland. Two dry saunas and one steam sauna. Outdoor enclosed seating area.

FASHION SHOPS

■ **Touch d'André** (CC glm YC) Mon-Fri 10-20, Sat -18h
Itäkatu 1b, Itäkeskus Piazza *M° Itäkeskus, 1st floor*
☏ 400 79 12 94 (mobile) 🖳 www.touchdandre.fi
Men's apparel boutique close to Helsinki city center with stylish clothing for handsome men.

HOTELS

■ **Hotel Haven** (AC B BF CC glm I M PA PK RWS RWT VA WO)
All year, 24hrs
Unioninkatu 17 *Next to Market Hall and the South Harbour* ☏ 681 930
🖳 www.hotelhaven.fi
Hotel Haven has 3 categories of luxury rooms: Comfort, Style and Lux. Enjoy the aromatic spa products of Elemis and envelop yourself in a bathrobe of fine Egyptian cotton. Watch films and listen to music on the Bang & Olufsen entertainment system. Located in the attractive setting of Helsinki's Market Square.

■ **Klaus K Hotel** (AC B BF CC D GLM H I M MA MSG PK RWS RWT WO) All year, 24hrs
Bulevardi 2-4 *1km from city hall, near tram, bus and train station*
☏ (20) 770 47 00 🖳 www.klauskhotel.com

■ **Sokos Hotel Albert** (AC B BF glm I M MC PA PK RWS RWT SA)
All year
Albertinkatu 30 ☏ (20) 1234 638 🖳 www.sokoshotels.fi

FETISH GROUPS

■ **Fin-Bears** (G)
PL 863 🖳 www.fin-bears.org

■ **MSC Finland-Tom's Club** (DR F G MA P VS)
PL 48 *No own club room – contact via tel or form on website*

☎ (09) 45 677 94 44 (mobile) 💻 www.mscfin.fi
Member of ECMC and ToE. Club for fetish gay men into leather, boots, uniforms, rubber, motorcycling or bondage & S/M. Also gays for sport fetish. Big yearly ECMC event Finlandization every summer end of July.

HEALTH GROUPS

■ **Positiiviset ry – HIV-Finland** Mon-Fri 9-16h
Paciuksenkaari 27 ☎ (09) 692 54 41 💻 www.positiiviset.fi
Organization for those with or those affected by HIV and AIDS.

HELP WITH PROBLEMS

■ **Pro-tukipiste** Mon-Fri 10-16 and by appointment, drop-in services Mon & Thu 12-16h
Vilhonkatu 4 B 20 *City centre* ☎ (09) 2512 730 💻 www.pro-tukipiste.fi
Pro-tukipiste offers professional low threshold social support, health care services and legal advice for people involved in sex work. Services are free of charge and anonymous.

SWIMMING

-Pihlajasaari (G NU) (Island 15 mins by boat from Merisatama, the most southern part of town)
-Uimastadion (g pi sa). Outdoor pools near the Olympic Stadium, open mid May to mid Sep
-Yrjönkatu Swimming Hall (! g PI SA SB NU). Swimming hall in Art Deco Style, with real finnish sauna! Tue, Thu, Sat – men only, most of men are swimming without swim gear,
Homepage: www.hel2.fi/liv/eng/yrjonkatu.html

CRUISING

-Mäntymäki (AYOR) (P and park near Olympic Stadium)
-Laakso (in the Keskuspuisto/central park behind the race track, evenings)
-Last P highway 6 from Porvoo (→ Helsinki)
-Stockmann department store (2nd & 5th floor), during daytime.

Joensuu ☎ 013

GAY INFO

■ **Joensuun seudun seksuaalinen tasavertaisuus Hobiles ry** (GLM)
PL 164 ☎ (0400) 201 498 💻 www.hobiles.fi
Parties once or twice a month, see www.hobiles.fi for details.

BARS

■ **Wanha Jokela** (AC B BF glm H M MA S)
Torikatu 26 ☎ (013) 12 28 91 💻 www.ravintolawanhajokela.fi
Popular among locals, intellectuals and artists.

SWIMMING

-Linnulahti (NG) (popular beach during summer, lots of young people, ☞ cruising)
-Aavaranta (MA NG) (popular beach during summer).

CRUISING

-Linnuanlahti (summer only, the rocks behind the trees to the right of the beach, very cruisy when sunny)
-Virkistysuimala Vesikko (MA NG) (very cruisy weekday nights).

Juankoski ☎ 017

GUEST HOUSES

■ **Seppo's Year Round Cottage** (AC DU g OS PA PK RES RWT SA VA) All year
Juanlammentie 17 *Distance from Kuopio airport approx.50km, Kuopio railway station approx.65km, skiing area Tahko Resorts approx 37km, situated next to a lake* ☎ (0)500 577044
4-6 beds with a living room, fully equipped kitchen, 2 rooms, toilet, bathroom, sauna, fireplace and TV, all in same building. Also a separated small sleeping summer cottage with 2 beds. Swimming area with a boat.

Jyväskylä ☎ 014

BARS

■ **Hemingway's** (B g m) Sun-Tue 12-2, Wed-Sat 12-3h
Kauppakatu 32 ☎ (014) 61 47 06

DANCECLUBS

■ **Club Kaappi** (B D glm MA)
Ilokivessä Keskussairaalantie 2 💻 www.jklseta.fi
Check www.jklseta.fi for exact dates.

GENERAL GROUPS

■ **Jyväskylän Seta ry** (GLM MA T) Thu 18.30-20, helpline Wed 19-21h on number 045 – 638 9540.
Vapaudenkatu 4 *Kumppanuustalo, B-building – 1st floor*
☎ (014) 310 06 60 (office) ☎ (045) 638 9540 (helpline, mobile)
💻 www.jklseta.fi
Jkl Seta's office will move to new premises in the beginning of February 2012. New address is: Matarakatu 6 in a new civil action centre. CLUB CLOSET parties in Ilokivi.

CRUISING

-Harju Park (in the centre)
-Taulumäki (hill beside lake Tuamiojärvi).

Kortteinen ☎ 017

GUEST HOUSES

■ **Seppo's Summer Cottage** (DU FH g OS PA PK RES RWT SA VA) Open May to Sept
Vaikkojoentie 36 *Distance from Kuopio airport approx.60km, Kuopio railway station approx.75km. Situated next to a typical Finnish lake in a peacefull countryside* ☎ (0)500 577044

Mariehamn ☏ 018

BARS

■ **Alvas** (B glm) 18-3h
Ålandsvägen 42 ☏ (018) 161 41

■ **Hotel Arkipelag** (B glm M)
31 Strandgaten ☏ (018) 140 20 www.hotellarkipelag.com
Wed & Fri disco, other days live music.

CRUISING

-Lilla Holma Island.

Oulu ☏ 08

BARS

■ **Becksu** (B CC D G MA WE) Fri & Sat 22-4h
Asemakatu 20 ☏ (08) 522 13 37 www.barbecksu.fi

SEX SHOPS/BLUE MOVIES

■ **Sex-Market** (g) Mon 10-20, Tue-Thu -18h
Pakkahuoneenkatu 32 ☏ (08) 37 92 21
Gay section with magazines, videos etc.

GENERAL GROUPS

■ **Oulun SETA ry** (GLM)
☏ (040) 836 95 69 www.oulunseta.fi
Parties mostly in Kruunumakasiini, Puusepänkatu 6. Check homepage for date and time. Hotline on Mon 19-20h.

CRUISING

-Oritkari park, busy 16-19h (3 km south-west of centre).

Pori ☏ 02

GENERAL GROUPS

■ **Porin Seudun SETA ry** (GLM) Wed 18-21h (helpline)
PL 261 ☏ (02) 231 03 34 (helpline) www.poseta.net
Parties 1x/month.

Rovaniemi ☏ 016

BARS

■ **Pub Paha Kurki** (B glm)
Koskikatu 5 ☏ (016) 31 72 30

■ **Pub Tupsu** (B glm) Sun-Thu 21-1, Fri & Sat -2h
Hallituskatu 24 ☏ (016) 34 58 38

RESTAURANTS

■ **Maxim's** (B D glm M)
Koskikatu 11 ☏ (016) 31 30 72

GENERAL GROUPS

■ **Rovaniemen seksuaalinen tasavertaisuus – SETA ry** (GLM)
PL 1216 *Valtakatu 22, 2nd floor* www.rovaniemenseta.fi
See website for details. Office open Wed 18-20h.

Tampere ☏ 03

DANCECLUBS

■ **Mixei** (AC B CC D DR GLM I MA S SL VR WE)
Tue-Thu 20-2, Fri-Sat 22-4h
Itsenäisyydenkatu 7-9 *Near Tampere railway station* ☏ (03) 222 03 64
www.mixei.com
Nightclub on two floors. Established in 1990, Mixei is the oldest gay club in Finland, and the only one in Tampere. Occasional shows, check website www.mixei.com or Facebook page.

GENERAL GROUPS

■ **Tampereen SETA ry** (GLM)
Kuninkaankatu 15 A, 2nd floor ☏ (03) 214 87 21
www.treseta.fi
Local member organization of Seta, promoting rights of LGBTI people.

HEALTH GROUPS

■ **AIDS tukikeskus, Tampere** Hotline: Mon-Fri 10-15.30h
Aleksanterinkatu 29A ☏ (0207) 465 709 (hotline)
www.aidscouncil.fi

CRUISING

-Park Eteläpuisto (Park at the southern end of Hämeenpuisto and the area at the lakeside, in the evening).

Turku ☏ 02

BARS

■ **suXes** (! AC B CC d GLM I m MA S) Daily 19-2h
Yliopistonkatu 9 (courtyard) *300 m from Market Place, opp. Hotel Centro, entrance in the courtyard* ☏ (02) 231 01 01 www.suxes.fi
Occasionally live music and dancers. Fri & Sat: disco, Thu & Sun: „Queer Karaoke".

GENERAL GROUPS

■ **Turun Seudun SETA ry** (GLM)
Rauhankatu 1 c B 22 ☏ (02) 250 06 95 www.tuseta.fi
Parties mostly in Club (Humalistonkatu 8) see webpage for date and time. Office open Tue 12-18, Wed and Thu 15-18h.

SWIMMING

-Ruissalo Saaronniemi (g NU) (nudist beach on the island of Ruissalo behind the camping area)
-Samppalinna (g pi sa) (outdoor swimming pool)
-Turun Ulimahalli (g NU pi sa) (men only Tue, Thu, Sat 13-20, best after 17h, Rehtorinpellontie 4).

CRUISING

-Urheilupuisto (sporting park, around the ponds and cliffs near the upper sand field. From sunset untill late at night).

Vaasa ☏ 06

BARS

■ **Ernst. Café** (B glm M) 17-1h
Hietasaarenkatu 7 ☏ (06) 317 85 56

■ **Fontana** (B D glm) Wed-Sat 22-4h
Hovioikeudenpuistikko 15 ☏ (06) 280 04 00
www.fontanaclub.com

■ **Streetbar** (b glm MA)
Hovioikeudenpuistikko 15

CAFES

■ **Kaffehuset August** (b glm)
Hovioikeudenpuistikko 13 ☏ (06) 320 05 55

GENERAL GROUPS

■ **Vaasan SETA ry** (GLM)
PL 162 ☏ (040) 521 01 30 www.vaasanseta.fi
Parties mostly in Club Fenix (Restaurant Thai House 20-2h, Vaasanpuistikko 17) See webpage for parties. Hotline on Sun 13-17h.

CRUISING

-Ahvensaari (behind the ice-rink)
-Uimahalli (g) (indoor swimming-pool, Hietalahdenkatu 8, Tue & Thu evenings best).

France

Name: Frankreich · Francia
Location: Western Europe
Initials: F
Time: GMT +1
International Country Code: ☏ 33 (omit the first 0)
International Access Code: ☏ 00
Language: French. Regional languages (Basque, Breton, Alsacian, Catalan, Corsican, Occitanian)
Area: 543,965 km² / 209,971 sq mi.
Currency: 1 Euro (€) = 100 Cent
Population: 62,200,000
Capital: Paris
Religions: 79% Roman Catholic, 8% Moslem
Climate: Generally summers are mild and winters cool. Along the Mediterranean winters are mild and summers hot.
Important gay cities: Lyon, Nice, Paris, Toulouse

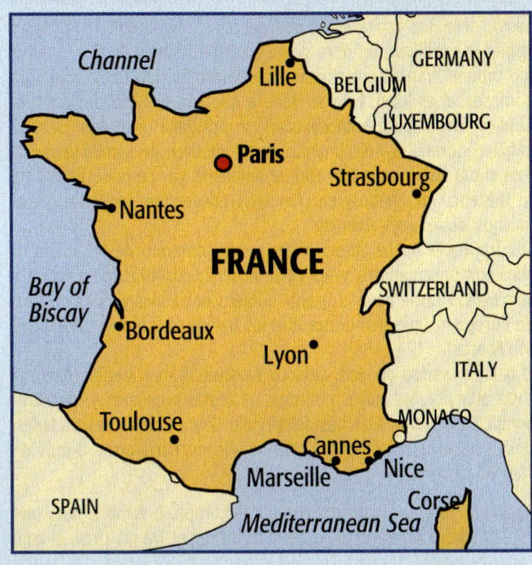

France – ideally situated in the heart of Europe – has always been a popular gay travel destination. Homosexuality was legalized more than 20 years ago and the age of consent is 15. France has since made significant progress concerning the issue and a little under ten years ago introduced the civil partnership act Pac allowing same-sex couples to register, without, alas, granting them the same rights married couples enjoy.
The adoption law has not yet been resolved. The battle for lesbian and gay marriage experienced a major setback in January 2011 after the Constitutional Court of France ruled the prohibition of same-sex marriage to be lawful because a similarly defined, recognized legal status is in the court's opinion already available to homosexuals in the form of the Pacs, deemed to also enable a normal family life.But discrimination based on one's sexual identity is now prohibited by law. As a consequence, gay life has been released from its ghetto existence and many openly gay locations can now be found everywhere in France.
The mastery of foreign languages is not one of the strengths of the French, but they are charming and show off their home country and its temptations with pride. In a European comparison, France has the largest number of saunas and sex clubs, proving once again that the French live their sexuality very freely.
The country is famous for its varied landscapes, Mediterranean and Atlantic coastlines, clothing optional beaches, traditional festivals and cuisine. Gay Pride events take place in various cities. The Paris Gay Pride has been attracting around 700,000 people for years.

Frankreich – im Herzen Europas gelegen – ist schon immer ein beliebtes Reiseziel für Schwule gewesen. Homosexualität ist hier seit über 20 Jahren legal und das Schutzalter beträgt 15 Jahre. Was Homosexualität angeht, hat Frankreich wichtige Fortschritte gemacht und vor fast 10 Jahren wurde das Pacs (Partnerschaftsgesetz) verabschiedet. Dieses Gesetz ermöglicht allen Paaren, sich eintragen zu lassen, ohne aber die gleichen Rechte wie bei einer Ehe einzuräumen. Das Adoptionsgesetz ist noch nicht verabschiedet und in jüngster Zeit wird auf höchsten Ebenen über eine Öffnung der Ehe für gleichgeschlechtliche Paare diskutiert. Im Januar 2011 haben die Bestrebungen, die Ehe für Schwule und Lesben zu öffnen, einen herben Dämpfer erhalten, nachdem der oberste französische Gerichtshof festgestellt hat, dass das Verbot der Homo-Ehe rechtmäßig ist, da mit dem Pacs eine ähnlich gelagerte anerkannte rechtliche Stellung für Homosexuelle zur Verfügung stehe, die ein normales Familienleben ebenso ermögliche. Diskriminierung aufgrund der sexuellen Identität steht nun gesetzlich unter Strafe. Damit ist das schwule Leben aus seinem Ghetto-Dasein befreit und man findet überall in Frankreich viele offen schwule Locations.
Die Beherrschung von Fremdsprachen ist nicht die Stärke der Franzosen, aber sie sind charmant und zeigen ihre Heimat und ihre Verlockungen mit Stolz. Frankreich hat in Europa die größte Anzahl an Saunen und Sexcubs und belegt damit, dass Franzosen ihre Sexualität frei leben.
Das Land ist berühmt für seine abwechslungsreichen Landschaften, die Mittelmeer- und die Atlantikküste, die FKK-Strände, die traditionellen Feste und die Kochkunst. Gay Prides werden in unterschiedlichen Städten veranstaltet. Seit Jahren zieht die Pariser Gay Pride ca. 700.000 Menschen an.

Idéalement située, au cœur de l'Europe, la France est depuis toujours une destination de choix pour les touristes gays. L'homosexualité y est légale depuis plus de vingt ans et la majorité sexuelle est fixée à 15 ans pour tous. La France a fait de gros progrès en matière d'homosexualité et a, il y a presque 10 ans, adopté le pacs qui permet aux couples de tous les sexes de se faire enregistrer, sans pour autant leur donner exactement les mêmes droits que le mariage. La loi sur l'adoption n'a pas encore été votée et des discussions aux plus hauts niveaux laissent espérer l'ouverture du mariage aux couples homosexuels. En janvier 2011 les efforts pour ouvrir le mariage aux gays et lesbiennes ont subi un revers après que la Haute Courte de Justice française ait constaté que l'interdiction du mariage homosexuel est légitime car le Pacs ouvre déjà une situation de droits aux homosexuels reconnue leur permettant une vie familiale normale.
L'homophobie et les actes en découlant sont désormais punis par la loi. L'homosexualité ne se vit plus uniquement dans des ghettos et il y a beaucoup de lieux gays qui s'affirment au grand jour.
Les Français ne brillent pas par leur maîtrise des langues étrangères, mais ils sont charmants et montrent avec fierté leur patrie et ses attraits. La France a de loin le plus de saunas et de sexclubs en Europe montrant que les Français vivent leur sexualité librement. Le pays est célèbre pour ses paysages variés, la Méditerranée, la côte atlantique, les plages naturistes, les fêtes traditionnelles et l'art culinaire. Une Gay Pride a lieu dans différentes villes, celle de Paris rassemble, fin juin, environs 700 000 personnes depuis plusieurs années.

Francia – ideal situada en el corazón de Europa – siempre es un destino turístico preferido para los homosexuales. La homosexualidad aquí es legal desde hace más de 20 años y la edad de consentimiento está en los 15 años. En lo que se refiere a la homosexualidad, Francia ha realizado importantes avances y hace casi 10 años que se aprobó la Pacs (ley de parejas de hecho). Esta ley permitió a todas las parejas que se registrasen pero desgraciadamente no se equipararon los mismos derechos que al matrimonio. La ley de adopción no se ha aprobado aún y se ha debatido recientemente a niveles más altos acerca de la apertura del matrimonio a parejas del mismo sexo. Las aspiraciones de legalizar el matrimonio para gays y lesbianas recibieron un duro golpe en 2011 después de que el máximo tribunal francés determinase que la prohibición del matrimonio homosexual es legal. Esto se debe a que con el PACS, un estatuto jurídico similar para homosexuales, se posibilita un estado de vida familiar ìnormalî. La discriminación por motivos de identidad sexual está ahora bajo pena. Con ello, el ambiente gay se pudo liberar de su existencia de ghetto y en Francia se encuentran por todas partes muchos locales gays abiertos.

Los franceses no se caracterizan por su dominio de los idiomas, pero son encantadores y les gusta enseñar con orgullo su patria y atractivos. Francia tiene el mayor número de saunas y clubs de sexo de Europa, lo que demuestra que los franceses viven su sexualidad con libertad.

El país es famoso por sus variados paisajes, el mar Mediterráneo, la costa atlántica, las playas nudistas, las fiestas populares y la gastronomía. Se celebran Marchas del Orgullo Gay en diferentes ciudades. Desde hace años la Marcha del Orgullo en París atrae a más de 700.000 personas.

La Francia, situata nel cuore dell'Europa, è sempre stata una meta molto importante per il turismo gay. Da già circa 20 anni l'omosessualità è legale e l'età del consenso è di 15 anni. La Francia ha fatto importanti passi avanti per quello che concerne l'omosessualità. Già 10 anni fa in Francia sono stati approvati i Pacs, i patti civili di solidarietà. Questa legge permette a tutte le coppie di essere riconosciute come tali, tuttavia senza la garanzia degli stessi diritti delle coppie unite dal matrimonio. La legge sulle adozioni non è stata ancora emanata. Da poco, nelle sfere alte del potere, si è cominciato a discutere di un'eventuale apertura del matrimonio alle coppie omosessuali. Nel gennaio del 2011 la lotta per l'apertura del matrimonio alle coppie gay e lesbiche ha subito un grave colpo: infatti la Corte Suprema francese ha deciso che il divieto del matrimonio omosessuale è pienamente legale, affermando che i Pacs rappresentano già una forma legalmente riconosciuta che permette agli omosessuali di condurre una normale vita familiare.

Le discriminazioni che riguardano l'identità sessuale sono punibili legalmente. Gli omosessuali non vivono più nel ghetto di prima, al contrario, adesso in Francia si trovano dappertutto location dichiaratamente e apertamente gay. I francesi non si contraddistinguono certo per le loro capacità linguistiche, piuttosto per il loro fascino. I francesi vi mostreranno il loro Paese con molto orgoglio. La Francia ha il maggior numero di saune gay e locali a luci rosse, e questo non fa altro che dimostrare l'attitudine piuttosto aperta dei francesi nei confronti del sesso.

La Francia è famosa per la varietà dei suoi paesaggi, per il Mar Mediterraneo, per la costa Atlantica, per le sue spiagge per nudisti, nonché per le sue feste tradizionali e la sua nota arte culinaria. I gay pride vengono organizzati in diverse città del Paese. Da anni il gay pride parigino attira più di 700.000 persone.

NATIONAL PUBLICATIONS

Sensitif
7, rue de la Croix-Faubin ✉ 75011 Paris ☎ 01.43.71.49.92 💻 www.sensitif.fr
Free, monthly gay magazine.

Têtu (G)
6bis rue Campagne-Première ✉ 75014 Paris ☎ 01.56.80.20.80
💻 www.tetu.com
The number one gay magazine in France (publ. 11x/year). A very stylish and sometimes activist newsmagazine with a supplement with personals and gay addresses in France, Switzerland and Belgium. Also Têtu Plage (publ. July), Têtu Voyage (publ. 2x/year) and online. Available worldwide.

Tribu Press / Tribu Move
c/o SARL Tribu Press, 79 rue du Chemin Vert ✉ 75011 Paris
☎ 01.48.06.57.17 💻 www.tribumove.com

NATIONAL PUBLISHERS

Groupe Illico
99 rue de la Verrerie ✉ 75004 Paris 💻 www.e-llico.com
Publishes the bimonthly free magazine Illico for Paris.

NATIONAL COMPANIES

Clair Production (G VS)
B.P. 111 ✉ 1360 Aix-en-Provence Cedex 01 ☎ 04.42.21.00.00
💻 www.clairproduction.com
Gay erotic videos, DVD-production, mail-order and casting.

French Art (AC CC G MA) 10-19h
64 rue de Rome ✉ 75008 Paris *M° Rome, Europe* ☎ 01.45.22.57.35
💻 www.cadinot.fr
Cadinot's famous shop.

Pink TV
20/22 rue de Turenne ✉ 75002 Paris ☎ 01.55.80.77.17 💻 www.pinktv.fr
Private gay TV via satellite (music, cinema, news, culture, travel and x-films).

NATIONAL GROUPS

Aides
14 rue Scandicci, Tour Essor ✉ 93508 Pantin Cédex ☎ 01.41.83.46.46
💻 www.aides.org
Organization fighting against HIV/AIDS. There are local branches of Aides in all major cities. Contact them or check their website for details on addresses and phone numbers.

Inter-LGBT (GLM MA T)
5, rue Perrée ✉ 75003 Paris ☎ 01.53.01.47.01 💻 www.inter-lgbt.org
Oraganization with over 50 participation groups in and around Paris fighting against discrimination. Organizes „Le Printemps des Assoces" & „La Marche des Fiertés" every year.

Syndicat National des Entreprises Gaies (SNEG)
12 rue des Filles du Calvaire ✉ 75003 Paris ☎ 01.44.59.81.01
💻 www.sneg.org
Also co-ordinates AIDS-prevention for the gay/lesbian community.

COUNTRY CRUISING

-A6 Paris ⇆ Lyon
P de Nemours (direction Paris)
P de Villabe (between Fontainebleau and Evry, direction Paris)
Exit Chalon-sur Saône, direction Monteau-les-Mines (in the forest)
-A7 Lyon ⇆ Marseille
P de la Combe Tourmentée (before Vienne Reventin)
P de la Grande Combe (at the end near the toilets, evenings)
P d'Orange (⇆ Le Cres et Coudoulet)
-A8 Aix-en-Provence ⇆ Nice
P Aire de Briguière
-A9 Nîmes → Montpellier (P) de Saint-Aunès
P de Saint-Aunès, km 91.5, direction Nîmes/Montpellier, day and night)
-A31 Lyon ⇆ Metz
P de Boncourt (between Nuit St Georges and Dijon)
P de Corgoloin (after Beaune, direction Nancy)
P de Flagey Echezeaux (between Dijon and Nuit St Georges)
-A50 Marseille ⇆ Nice
P de Sanary Saint-Cyr
P de Vidauban
-A61 Toulouse ⇆ Villefranche de Lauragais
P de Renneville
P de Baziège
-A63 Bordeaux ⇆ Belin-Béliet
P de Cestas
-RN7 Roanne ⇆ Lyon
P des Estivaux (8 km from Roanne)
-RN10 Bordeaux ⇆ Paris
P de Saint Appoline (after Cloyes, direction Chartres)

P de Maine de Boixe
P de Bedenac
-RN71 Troyes ⇆ Dijon
P between Fouchère and Virey sous Bar (evenings)
-RN137 Nantes ⇆ Rennes
P de Puceul (south of Nozay, both directions)
P between Rochefort and La Rochelle
-RN141 Limoges ⇆ Angoulême
P Bourganeuf
-RN147 Mirebeau ⇆ Loudun
P les Scevolles

Agen

CRUISING

-Quais de la Garonne
-Jardin Gayan
-Le Gravier
-Bords de la Garonne (after pont du canal)

Aigues-Mortes

HOTELS

Hotel Canal (AC B BF CC GLM H I M MA OS PI PK RES RWS RWT SOL VA W) All year, reception 7-22h
440 route de Nîmes *City centre and station SNCF 200m away*
☎ 04.66.80.50.04 www.hotel-canal-aigues-mortes.com
Designer hotel. Beaches 5 km. Visa card accepted.

GUEST HOUSES

Villa Fleur de Sel
(AC B BF FC G H MA NU OS p PI PK RES RWT VA W WH) All year
4 rue St. Vincent de Paul ☎ 04.66.73.30.37 www.villafleurdesel.com

APARTMENTS

Villa Deylof (FC G H I MA NU OS PI PK RES RWB RWS RWT VA)
La Malamousque, Chemin de Jarret *15 mins from the beach*
☎ 06.08.28.73.53 www.villadeylof.fr
Four studios to rent. 30 mins from Montpellier, Nîmes and Arles.

Aix-en-Provence

BARS

Bastide du Cours (AC B CC d g M MA OS)
43-47 Cours Mirabeau ☎ 04.42.26.10.06 www.bastideducours.com
Happy Days. Le
Place Richelme ☎ 04.42.21.02.35
Mediterranean Boy (b GLM MA VS) 21.30-2h
6 Rue de la Paix ☎ 04.42.27.21.47 www.med-boy.com

SAUNAS/BATHS

Aix Sauna Club (AC B DR DU FC FH G LAB MA NU p SA SB VR) 12-20.30h
8bis, rue Annonerie Vieille *City centre, between Rue Aude & Rue Bedarrides* ☎ 04.42.27.21.49
Very discreet sauna on 3 floors.

CRUISING

-Le Réaltor
-P down the Avenue Jules Ferry (near the kindergarten, until the railway bridge)
-Cours Mirabeau
-Parc Jourdan (AYOR) (day and night).

Aix-les-Bains

CRUISING

-Plage de Brison-St-Innocent
-Parc des Thermes

-Petit-Port
-Esplanade du Lac (Avenue du Grand Port)
-Cours Mirabeau
-Parc Jourdan (day and night)

Albi

BARS

■ **Triome** (AC B CC D GLM MA p S ST T WE) 22-2, Fri & Sat -4h
4 rue des Grenadiers *City centre* ☎ 05.63.43.50.07 🖳 www.letriome.fr
Gay owned. Frequented by gays. The perfect place to spend a good time.

RESTAURANTS

■ **Oscar Saint-Loup** (CC DM gLm M MA OS PA RES VEG WL) All year
8 rue Roquelaure ☎ 05.67.67.42.96 🖳 www.oscarbysaintloup.com
Very popular. Busy all week, reservation necessary. Gay owned. Beautiful place.

HOTELS

■ **Hôtel les Pasteliers** (AC BF CC gLm H I PK RES RWS RWT WH WI) All year
1-3 rue Honoré de Balzac ☎ 05.63.54.26.51
🖳 www.hotellespasteliers.com
Gay owned. Located in the center of the city. Some rooms with Jacuzzi. Very friendly.

Ambilly

SAUNAS/BATHS

■ **King Sauna** (AK B cc d DR DU FC FH G m MA P RR SA SB SH SL t VS WH) 14-23; Mon, Wed & Sun -20; Fri & Sat -1h
39, rue Jean-Jaurès, Immeuble l'Impérial *10 mins from Genève, near Annemasse, in front of Town Hall* ☎ 04.50.38.68.12
🖳 www.kingsauna.com
350 m² sauna with S/M room, sling and St Andrew's Cross.

Amboise

GUEST HOUSES

■ **Château de Perreux** (BF glm MA OS PI PK RWB RWS VA) All year
36 rue de Pocé *In Nazelles-Négron* ☎ 02.47.57.41.50
🖳 www.chateaudeperreux.fr
The château has 5 standard double rooms and 4 double room suites. All bedrooms with WC and bath, most of them with shower too. Two suites with balcony. Eric and Rodolphe invite you to „live the life of the château". An attractive reception hall, guest dining table and even a seminar room.

Amiens

CRUISING

-🅿 Montjoie (between Amiens & St-Fuscien)
-Behind Hatoie-Tivoli

Angers

SAUNAS/BATHS

■ **Maine. Le** (b DR DU FC FH G GH I LAB m MA RR SA SB SH SL VS WH) 14-23, Fri & Sat -24, Sun -21h
6, rue Valdemaine *Bus-Ralliement* ☎ 02.41.20.30.16
🖳 www.saunalemaine.com

■ **Tropic. Le** (AK b CC DR DU FC FH G I m MA NU p SA SB VS WH WO) Mon, Thu & Sun 14-24; Tue & Wed -23; Fri & Sat -1h
144-146 rue Larevellière ☎ 02.41.60.39.74 🖳 www.letropic.com
Gay on Tue, Wed, Fri and the weekend.

CRUISING

-Jardin des Plantes (day)
-Jardin du Mail

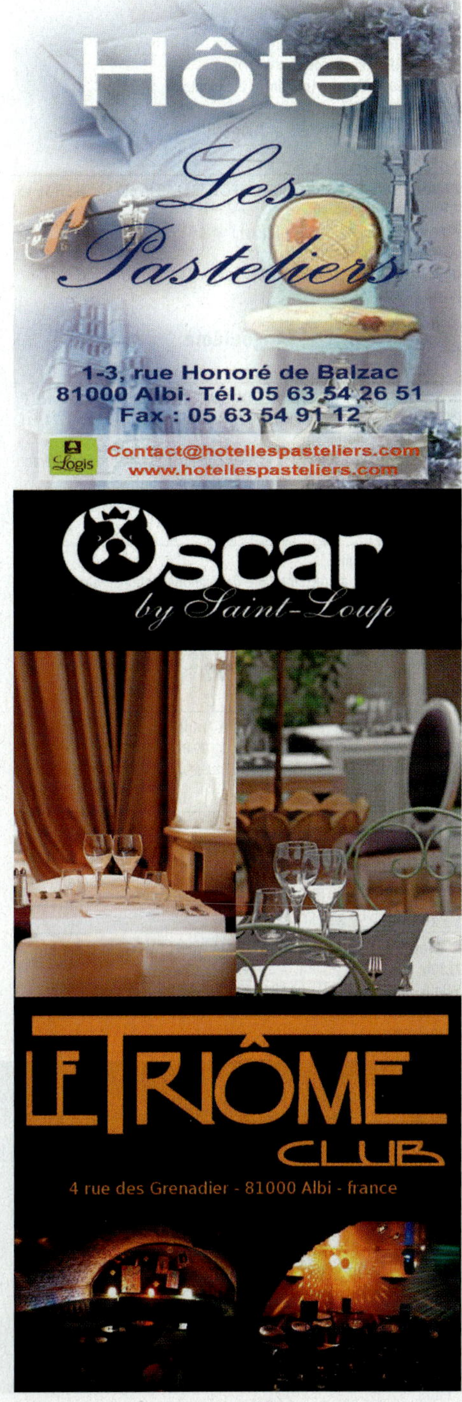

-Place de La-Rochefoucault
-Place du Maréchal-Leclerc
-Place du Tertre
-Château (Esplanades du Pont-Ligny)
-Montée Saint-Maurice (in front of the fountain)

Anglet

SAUNAS/BATHS

■ **Beaulieu. Le** (AC b CC DR DU FC G GH LAB m MA SA SB SH SL VS WH) 14-24, Fri & Sat -4h
27, rue de Beaulieu *Quartier St Jean* ☎ 05.59.58.20.39
🖳 www.lebeaulieu.com
Large sauna with regular S/M nights. Free parking for clients. Tue and Thu hetero and gay mixed.

Angoulême

SAUNAS/BATHS

■ **Sauna Prado** (! AC AK B CC DR DU FC FH G GH I LAB M MA NU P PK RR SA SB SH SL SOL T VR VS W WH) Mon-Wed 13-1,Tue- Thu -24, Fri 12-2, Sat 14-4, Sun 14-24h
16 Avenue de l'Etang des Moines *In La Couronne, 3 km from Angoulême*
☎ 05.45.62.08.08 🖳 www.sauna-prado.com
Very clean and beautiful sauna with mixed days. Large cabines.

CRUISING

-Jardin Vert (at night)
-RN 141/ Forêt de la Braconne/ Aire des Lignons (national road to Limoges), 10 km east of Angoulême. Busy at all times
-RN141 /Aire de Trottechien, 6km from Angoulême (during the day).

Annecy

BARS

■ **La vie en rose** (B FC G MA OS PA T) Tue-Sun 16-2 / Winter: 17-1h
13, rue Royale / passage des sorbiers ☎ 09.81.04.43.83
Straight-friendly and centrally located. Terrasse busy in summer.

MEN'S CLUBS

■ **Private Club** (G SL) Fri-Sun 23-5h
808 Route des Ponts ☎ 06.62.86.23.24 (mobile) ☎ +41.76.260.46.37
🖳 privateclub.onlc.fr
New gay sex club.

SEX SHOPS/BLUE MOVIES

■ **Magic Eden** (AC B CC FC G GH MA PK SH T VS W) Mon-Sat 10-21.30h
5 Boulevard Bellevue ☎ 04.50.67.69.75 🖳 www.magic-eden.com
Sexshop, cabines, sextoys, underwear. You can get information about gay life in Annecy.

SAUNAS/BATHS

■ **Octopus Sauna** (! AC AK B CC DR DU FC FH G GH I LAB M MA MSG NU p P RR SA SB SL VR VS WH)
Mon-Wed 13-24, Thu & Fri 13-21, Sat 14-3, Sun 14-23h
15, rue de Narvik ☎ 04.50.57.48.26
🖳 www.octopus-sauna.com
400 m² sauna with hammam. Mixed Mon, Tue & Fri but still very gay. Very clean and pleasant atmosphere.

■ **Oxygène** (B DR DU FC FH G GH m MA P RR SA SB SL VR VS WH)
Mon-Thu (G) 13.30-20.30, Fri 14-1, Sat & Sun 14-20h
12, avenue de la Mandallaz *Near Banque de France* ☎ 04.50.51.16.05
🖳 www.oxygenesauna.com
Sauna on 300 m².

CRUISING

-Toilets in the square near the post office
-Parc aux Oiseaux (near 🅿 Sainte Claire, on the banks of the Thiou)
-🅿 Basilique de la Visitation (ayor, bashers reported) (at night, popular, also car cruising)

Annemasse

BARS

■ **Double Jeu** 18-2, Fri & Sat -3h
4 rue Faucille ☎ 04.50.84.12.32 🖳 www.club-doublejeu.fr

Antibes

RESTAURANTS

■ **Incontournable. L'** (AC B CC GLM M MA)
9-15 & 18-0.30h
7 rue James Close ☎ 04.92.94.07.31

SEX SHOPS/BLUE MOVIES

■ **Eroshop Antibes** (AC CC f G VS) 10-23h
6 rue Vauban *Near port* ☎ 04.93.34.09.04
The only daytime cruising place. Big screen video room with DVDs.

HOTELS

■ **Relais du Postillon. Le** (B BF CC glm H I MA OS RWS RWT)
Restaurant: 8-23h, closed Mon evening
8 Rue Championnet *In old town, close to post office & beach*
☎ 04.93.34.20.77 🖳 www.relaisdupostillon.com
Restaurant, bar and hotel.

CRUISING

-The garden of the railway station
-Phare de la Garoupe
-Fort Carré
-Remparts du Port-Vauban (evenings)

Aramon

HOTELS

■ **Mas de Pougnadoresse** (AC bf GLM M NU OS PI PK RWS SA SB)
Route de Montfrin N° 126 *15 mins outside of Avignon* ☎ 04.66.59.43.42
🖳 www.masdepougnadoresse.com
Beautiful small hotel with clothing optional garden/pool area.

Argelès-sur-Mer

BARS

■ **Exotik Café** (B d GLM MC S)
8, allée J. Aroles ☎ 06.03.60.53.13

DANCECLUBS

■ **Pot-Chic. Le** (AC B CC D DR GLM MA OS p SNU T VS)
Fri-Sun and before public holidays 23-?h, Jul & Aug: Mon-Sun
Centre Commercial Costa Blanca, Bd de la Mer *25 km from Perpignan*
☎ 04.68.81.08.86 🖳 www.lepotchic.com

SWIMMING

-Tancande (NU) (between Cap Rederis & Abeille near Banyuls, summer only)
-River Tech (on the street from Argeles Plage Nord to St. Cyprien, P before and after the brigde over the river Tech)

Arles

GUEST HOUSES

■ **Mas du Petit Grava** (BF glm I MA OS PI PK RWS WO)
Mar-Oct/ Dec-Jan 8-19h
Quartier Saint Hippolyte *In Moulés, near Arles* ☎ 04.90.98.35.66
🖳 www.masdupetitgrava.net
18th century Provence farmhouse, completely renovated.

Arnay-le-Duc

BOOK SHOPS

■ **Art du Livre. L'** (g) Tue-Sun 10-12, 14-18h
37 rue César Lavirotte *Autoroute A6, exit Pouilly-en-Auxois*
☎ 03.80.90.20.46 🖳 www.didiergodard.fr
Antique and 2nd hand books, postcards, big section with gay and lesbian literature in French and English.

Assigny

GUEST HOUSES

■ **Fistinière. La** (BF DU F G MA NR NU OS P PI PK RES SL SOL W WE)
All year. Parties at WE only
Les Amelots ☎ 02.48.73.83.09 🖳 www.lafistiniere.fr
For FF fans. Rate includes apéritif, buffet supper available during the party and brunch the following day.

Auch

HOTELS

■ **Chateau les Charmettes**
(AC B BF CC glm H I MA MSG OS PI PK RWS RWT SOL VA WH WO)
21, route de Duran *70 km from Toulouse* ☎ 05.62.62.10.10
🖳 www.chateaulescharmettes.com

Auxerre

SAUNAS/BATHS

■ **KLS Sauna. Le** (AK b DR DU G GH MA OS SA SB SL)
Mon-Sat 12-19, Sun 14-20h
8 rue Denis Papin ☎ 03.86.42.76.87 🖳 www.lekls.fr

CRUISING

-St Germain forest (RN 77)
-Parc de Roscoff

Avignon

MEN'S CLUBS

■ **Cage. The** (B G MC OS P S) Fri-Sun 23-5h
1 Avenue des Sources ☎ 04.90.27.00.84 🖳 www.thecage.fr

CAFES

■ **Cid. Le** (B CC glm m MA)
11 Place de l'Horloge ☎ 04.90.82.30.38 🖳 www.lecidcafe.com

DANCECLUBS

■ **Esclave. L'** (! AC B CC D DR G MA p S ST VS) Open all year from 23-5h, winter: closed Mon (except before public holiday)
12, rue du Limas ☎ 04.90.85.14.91 🖳 www.esclavebar.com
One of the best gay places in Avignon.

RESTAURANTS

■ **Palais Royal. Le** (AC B CC d glm M OS S) 10-15 & 18-1h
Palace de L'Amirande 🖳 www.palaisroyal.net
Restaurant-cabaret-music hall

SEX SHOPS/BLUE MOVIES

■ **Body House** (AC CC glm MA VS) Mon-Sun 10-20h
199 Av. de Fontvert, Le Pontet ☎ 04.90.32.69.04 🖳 www.body-house.com
500 m² area.

SAUNAS/BATHS

■ **Exes** (AC B CC DR DU FC FH G GH I LAB MA NU SA SB SL T VR VS W WH) 12-22h, WE -24h
4, boulevard Saint Michel *Near railway station* ☎ 04.90.85.06.03
🖳 www.sauna-exes.com
Sauna on 300 m².

HOTELS

■ **Au Saint Roch – Hôtel et Jardin**
(AC B BF cc glm OS PA RWB RWS RWT) Mon-Sun 8-21h
9 rue Paul Mérindol *In historic centre, 5 mins from train station*
☎ 04.90.16.50.00 🖳 www.hotelstroch-avignon.com

■ **Cube Hôtel** (AC BF CC glm I OS PK RWB RWS RWT)
Daily, 7.30-20.30h
Impasse du Rhône *Bus 10 & 11* ☎ 04.90.25.52.29 🖳 www.cubehotel.fr

■ **Ferme. La** (AC B BF CC glm M MC MSG OS PI) 7-23h
110, Chemin des Bois – Île de la Barthelasse ☎ 04.90.82.57.53
🖳 www.hotel-laferme-avignon.com

■ **Lotus Tree. The** (B BF G I M MA NU OS PI PK RWB RWS RWT VA WO)
All year
La Micocoule *45 mins from Avignon, 60 mins from Nîmes*
☎ 04.66.82.76.09 🖳 www.thelotustree.com
Four double rooms and two studios with WC, bath, balcony, sat-TV, safe & own key. English, French, German, Swedish, Italian spoken. Many sport activities on offer.

GUEST HOUSES

■ **Agavi** (BF glm H M MC MSG OS PI RWS RWT) All year
Place de l'Eglise, Saint Christol de Rodières ☎ 04.66.82.65.59
🖳 www.agavi.fr
One double room and one suite. Near many local wine farms.

■ **Cigale en Provence. La** (bf cc glm H I MA MSG PA PK RWS VA)
Closed Nov-Feb
Grand rue, Mormoiron *Between Avignon and Le Mont Ventoux*
☎ 04.90.61.91.51 🖳 www.la-cigale.de

■ **Mas de la Treille** (BF CC glm H I OS PA PI PK RWS SOL WH)
All year
630 Chemin St. Maurice *In Saint-Laurent-des-Arbres, near Avignon*
☎ 04.66.50.62.29 🖳 www.lemasdelatreille.com
Luxurious property located in the famous Lirac vineyards, with 5 bedrooms, jacuzzi, pool and wonderful gardens. One separate doubleroom with a private swimming pool and jacuzzi is also available.

CRUISING

-Between the bridges Bompas & de Taracon (day & night, popular)
-City-wall (between Gate St. Michel and rue de la République)
-Champfleury Park (behind the station; AYOR in summer)
-La Durance River at Bompas, 20 mins drive SE of Avignon. Follow signs „Cavaillon", right after bridge over the TGV tracks turn into big unmarked, dirt parking lot (night), from there very bumpy road to right (day).

Bayonne

MEN'S CLUBS

■ **45, Le** (B G SL WI) Wed-Sun 21-2h
45, Boulevard Alsace-Lorraine ☏ 05.59.29.83.50 💻 www.le-45.fr

SAUNAS/BATHS

■ **Sauna S64, Le** (G) Sun-Thu 14-24, Fri & Sat -2h
70, Boulevard Alsace-Lorraine ☏ 05.59.64.84.52
💻 www.s64-sauna-bayonne.com

Berck

BARS

■ **3 Corbeilles. Les** (B CC d glm m MA S) 9-2 h
22 Bld. de Boulogne ☏ 03.21.09.12.99
■ **Terminus Bar Boys** (B cc G M MA ST)
Chemin des Anglais ☏ 03.21.09.19.81
■ **Welcome** (B glm MA OS) 11-1, WE -2h
6 Avenue du Général de Gaulle ☏ 03.21.09.31.00

SWIMMING

-In the dunes of „Le Terminus" beach
-Beach in the north of the town (G NU)

Bergerac

BARS

■ **BG. Le**
8, rue Cadillac ☏ 05.53.22.84.48

SAUNAS/BATHS

■ **Sauna de la Gare. Le** (b DU FC G MA MSG SA SB VS WH)
12-1, Sun -20h, closed Mon
20, Boulevard Santraille ☏ 05.53.27.35.64 💻 www.lesaunadelagare.fr

CRUISING

-Parc Jean-Jaurès (night)
-Eglise Notre-Dame (WC)
-Rives de la Dordogne (behind the dam, in summer)

Berrias

GUEST HOUSES

■ **Bastide Bleu Provence**
(AC B CC glm H I M MA MSG NU OS PA PI PK RWS RWT SA WO) All year
Place de l'Eglise *8 km from Vans, 1 hour from Nîmes* ☏ 04.75.39.58.02
💻 www.bastidebleuprovence.com

Besançon

MEN'S CLUBS

■ **Bar. Le** (B CC DR G I MA NU SA SB VS) 20-1, WE 21-2h, closed Mon
15 Rue Vignier *Central city* ☏ 03.81.82.01.00 💻 lebar.info

CAFES

■ **Théâtre. Café du** (b glm M MA OS WE)
8-1, Fri & Sat -2h, Sun closed
3 Rue Mairet *Near opera/theatre, bus-Granvelle* ☏ 03.81.82.04.12
💻 www.cafe-du-theatre.com

DANCECLUBS

■ **Privé. Le** (B CC D DR GLM MA P S T VS) 23-5h, closed Sun & Mon
1 Rue Antide-Janvier ☏ 03.81.81.48.57

SAUNAS/BATHS

■ **Club LG** (AC B DR DU FC FH m MA RR SA SB VS) 14-21, Thu-Sat -23h
14, rue d'Alsace *Between rue de la République et rue Bersot*
☏ 03.81.61.90.00 💻 www.saunalg.com
■ **Reservoir. Le** (AK b DR DU FC G GH LAB MA RR SA SB SL VS WH)
14-21, Fri & Sat -23h
1, rue Charles Fourier 💻 www.lereservoir.info

CRUISING

-Le Parc Micaud (night, at the border of Doubs river)
-Square Elisée-Cusenier
-Parc du centre-ville
-🅿 St.Paul (Night)
-Jardin des Senteurs
-🅿 Pont de la République (Corner of bridge and avenue Gaulard. Night and day)

Béziers

BARS

■ **Michel Ange. Le** (AC B D DR g MA P S VS) Thu-Sat 22.30-1h
47, rue du Midi ☏ 04.67.49.20.78
■ **New Kephren** (AC B CC d DR G MA p S SNU VS) Tue-Sun 22-4h
5 rue André Nougaret ☏ 04.67.49.02.20

SAUNAS/BATHS

■ **Kheops. Le** (AC b DR DU FC G GH LAB MA MC P RR SA SB SL VS WO)
12-20h
5, rue Berlioz *Near Allée Paul Riquet* ☏ 04.67.49.31.37
Clean and friendly sauna on 300 m².

GUEST HOUSES

■ **Domaine Bonne Vigne** (b bf G NU OS PI PK RWB RWS RWT VS) All year
Route de Béziers, Montady *5km from Béziers, 15 mins from gay beach*
☏ 04.67.49.35.16 💻 chambres.hote.pagesperso-orange.fr
Private naturist pool. Six rooms all with own bathroom.
■ **Sandeh** (glm I MA OS PA RWS VA) All year
12 Avenue de Fontes, Neffiès *Between Montpellier & Béziers, route D15. 3,5 km from Roujan* ☏ 04.67.24.09.81 💻 www.guesthouse-sandeh.com
2 double-rooms and 2 apartments, gay-owned.

SWIMMING

-Beach at Serignan (dunes between nudist camping site naturiste and trees)
-Also ☞ Fleury d'Aude

CRUISING

Biarritz

BARS

■ **Bobar. Le**
29, rue Gambetta ☏ 05.59.24.16.17
■ **Eleven** (B G) 16-2h
11, rue du Helder ☏ 05.59.67.72.34 💻 eleven-bar.com
■ **Excuse. L'** (B g MA)
11, rue du Helder ☏ 05.59.24.22.39
■ **Guet Apens. Le** (B cc GLM MA) 17-2h
2 Avenue Serano ☏ 05.59.24.39.66

DANCECLUBS

■ **Caveau. Le** (B G MA p) 22.30-5h
4, rue Gambetta ☏ 05.59.24.16.17

RESTAURANTS

■ **QG. Le** (AC B G M MA) 18-2h
49, Avenue de Verdun *Cnr. Rue de la Cité* ☎ 05.59.22.39.94
💻 leqg-biarritz.jimdo.com

GUEST HOUSES

■ **Moulin de Lassalle** (bf G I MA NU OS PI PK RWB RWS SOL VA)
All year
1895 route de Castets, Linxe *Between Bordeaux and San Sebastian, station Dax* ☎ 05.58.42.00.67 💻 www.moulindelassalle.fr
Five rooms with shower or bath/WC. Traditional country house in magnificent surroundings. Very gay atmosphere.

SWIMMING

-Miramar Beach (towards lighthouse, under cliffs)
-Port-Vieux Beach

CRUISING

-Chémin du Pavillon chinois (Chilberta's wood)
-Phare de Biarritz
-Last bus stop ligne 1 Hôtel de Ville
-Place Bellevue

Biscarosse

GUEST HOUSES

■ **B&B Minerve** (GLM I MA OS PK RWS) All year
65 Avenue de Lattre de Tassigny *In Gujan-Mestras, at the Bassin d'Arcachon* ☎ 06.61.46.79.82 💻 chambre.hotes.gays.free.fr
Two nights minimum stay applies.

Blaye

HOTELS

■ **Sauvageonne. La** (AC B bf glm m PI PK RWS RWT SA VA WH)
All year
2 les Mauvillains ☎ 05.57.32.92.15 💻 www.relax-in-gironde.com
Very nice place. Good value for money.

Blois

HOTELS

■ **Côté Loire** (b BF cc glm H I M MC OS PA RWS RWT)
Closed in Jan, restaurant closed Sun & Mon
2 Place de la Grève ☎ 02.54.78.07.86 💻 www.coteloire.com
Five minutes from the castle and from the town centre, on the bank of Loire river.

CRUISING

-Promenade Edmond Moulin
-🅿 Jardin des Lices
-Foret de Russy (route de Vierzon)

Bordeaux

BARS

■ **Babylon. Le** (AC B D GLM MC S T VS) 22.30-5h
96, rue Notre-Dame ☎ 05.57.87.00.82 💻 www.lebabylon.com
Karaoke Tue-Thu.

■ **Bateau Ivre, Le** (AC B CC D FC GLM MA VS W) 18-2h
1, rue Fénelon *Ligne B Grand Théatre*
New bar. Monthly event with new decoration. Special events on Tue & Thu. Facebook: Le Bateau Ivre Bordeaux

■ **Codebar** (AC B CC DR F FH G I LAB MA NU p S SL VS)
In summer: Mon-Sat 21-2h, in winter see website
34 rue de Cursol *Ligne A Musée d'Aquitaine* ☎ 06.79.20.53.17
💻 www.codebar-bdx.com
New owner and renovated. Sun naked sex party & fetish. Very popular.

■ **Go West, Le** (AC B CC D FC G MA PA S SNU ST VS W) 18-2h
3 Rue Duffour Dubergier *Ligne A & B Hôtel de Ville*
💻 legowest.com
Party atmosphere.

■ **Ours Marin, L'** (GLM) 17-2h
2 rue des Boucheries ☎ 05.57.30.84.07 💻 www.loursmarin.com
New bar. Straight-friendly. Typical french concept with possibility to meet around a drink and consume foie gras.

■ **QG de Monbadon, Le** (AC B CC FC G I MC p T VS) 18-2h
43 rue Lafaurie de Monbadon *Between Place Gambetta and Place Tourny*
☎ 05.56.81.37.98 💻 www.leqgdemonbadon.fr
Reopened. Straight-friendly. Sun: Tapas for free. Great cocktail menu.

■ **Trou Duck. Le** (AC B CC d GLM MA OS) 18-2h
rue ds piliers de tutelle ☎ 05.56.57.26.87
Bar Disco Funk 80's wiht video projection

■ **Velvet. Le**
6, rue Louis-Combes ☎ 05.56.51.00.79

MEN'S CLUBS

■ **Sous-Marin. Le** (AC AK B CC D DR DU F FC G GH M MA NU SL T VS)
Fri-Sat 22-?h
36, rue Menière ☎ 05.57.30.84.07 💻 www.lesousmarin.com
Intimate new bar. Hot sex area and dancing atmosphere.

■ **Traxx-Elix** (b CC DR G MA p VS) Mon-Thu 15-24, Fri & Sat 21-4h
38bis rue Arnaud Miqueu *Tram C-St Catherine* ☎ 05.56.44.03.41
💻 elix75.free.fr
400 m2 area

DANCECLUBS

■ **Shine Club** (AC B CC D DR F G M MA MSG NU P S VS) 24-4h
3-5, rue Cabanac ☎ 05.57.99.16.47 💻 www.shineclub.fr

RESTAURANTS

■ **Jacomo** (B CC GLM M MA PA VEG WL)
19, rue de la Devise
Extra large pizzas. Very popular for its food and reasonable prices.

■ **L'Antre de Peggy** (B CC d glm M MA OS S T) 11.45-15 & 18.45-?h
45-47, rue de la Devise ☏ 05.56.48.26.71

SAUNAS/BATHS

■ **Container. Le** (AC AK B CC DR DU FC FH GLM I LAB MC NU p RR SA SB SH T VR VS W WH) Mon-Thu 12-1, Fri -4, Sat & Sun 13-1h
69, cours Le Rouziec ☏ 05.57.54.88.06
New opened. 2 Jacuzzis, smoker room, large cabines. Friendly staff.

■ **Saint. Le** (AK B DR DU FC G P RR SA SB SL VS WH) 13-2h
39, rue Saint Joseph *tram C place Paul Doumer* ☏ 05.56.79.16.00
💻 www.saunalesaint.fr.fr
Straight gay & bi. Small sauna with warm atmosphere. Free drinks.

■ **Sauna Hugo** (B CC DR DU FC FH G GH I LAB M MA MSG NU p P RR SA SB SL T VEG VR VS W WE WH) 13-23 & Sun, Fri & Sat -2h
9, rue de l'Observance *Tram-Porte de Bourgogne* ☏ 05.56.31.50.01
💻 www.saunahugo.com
Centrally located. Large area and good decorated. Clean and crowded. Very nice staff. Professional massages. 500m²

■ **Sauna Saint-Jean** (B CC DR DU F FC FH G GH I LAB M MA MSG NU p P RR SA SB SH SL T VR VS WH)
Mon-Thu 13-1, Fri -2, Sat 14-2, Sun -1h
7, rue de Tauzia *Tram B-Tauzia* ☏ 05.56.94.02.06
💻 www.saunasaintjean.com
One of the latest saunas in Bordeaux. Young and dynamic team will help you to relax in an enjoyable ambiance. Theme parties every day of the week: including Blacklight (Mon), Bear

■ **Thiers** (AC B CC DR DU FC FH G GH I LAB M NU P PI RR SA SB SH SL VEG VS WH YC) 12-1, Fri -4, Sat 13-4, Sun 13-1h
329,Avenue Thiers *Bus 2/4, Pont Saint Emilion, tram A Galin*
☏ 05.56.32.00.63 💻 www.sauna-thiers.com
Well equipped, busy during WE.

CRUISING

-Parc des Expositions
-Bois de Bordeaux (de Bruges) (AYOR) (along the lake)
-Les jardins de Mériadeck (night)
-Ecole de la Santé Navale (park in front of the school Renaudel)
-Place d'Arlac (AYOR).

Bourges

BARS

■ **Jeremstar Café** (B D G)
2, Avenue Jean-Jaurès ☏ 06.70.92.35.46
💻 jeremstar.fr/jeremstar-cafe-en8.html

DANCECLUBS

■ **Q, Le** (D G)
10, Place Henri-Mirpied ☏ 02.48.24.80.58
💻 fr-fr.facebook.com/pages/discotheque-le-Q-bourges/322671833113

SAUNAS/BATHS

■ **L'Osmose** (B CC DR glm m MA NU S SA SB WH)
3, rue Mably ☏ 02.48.24.36.60

CRUISING

-RN 76 (20 km-Bourges, direction Moulins)
-🅿 Palais des Congrès (in the evening)
-🅿 du Lac d'Oreon
-Place Séracourt

Brest

BARS

■ **Happy Cafe. Le** (B CC GLM MA) Tue-Sun 18-2h, closed Mon
193 rue Jean Jaurès ☏ 02.98.33.62.93

■ **Maison. La** (B cc GLM m MA) Wed-Sun 17-1h
52 rue de l'Amiral Nicol ☏ 02.98.45.02.58

MEN'S CLUBS

■ **Corpus, Le** (B gLm SL) Tue & Wed 20-1h
65, rue Victor Hugo ☏ 02.98.44.30.55 💻 www.corpus-bar.fr

RESTAURANTS

■ **Fondue des Lys** (B glm M MA) Closed on Sun
40, rue de Lyon ☏ 02.98.43.42.77
Gay in the evening.

SAUNAS/BATHS

■ **Pink** (AC AK B DR DU FC G GH I LAB MA NU SA SB SL VS WH)
12-22.30, Fri -1, Sat 13-23.30, Sun -22.30h
35, rue Duperré *St. Martin* ☏ 02.98.80.68.57 💻 www.pink-sauna.com
NU on Mon-Thu evenings.

FASHION SHOPS

■ **Ebene** (g)
6, rue Ttienne Dolet ☏ 02.98.44.28.64
Men's fashion.

SWIMMING

-Plage de Keremna (2 km de Tréflez)
-Plage de Trézien (NU) (Plouarzel)
-Plage du Phoque /Le Conquet (NU).

CRUISING

-Jardin Kennedy (AYOR) (day and night)
-Jardin Maréchal Juin
-Cours d'Ajot
-Bois de Keroual (Penfled) 🅿 beware of police controls
-Aire du St. Servais
-Aire du Pont-de-Buis
-Phare du Portzic 🅿.

Brive-La-Gaillarde

SAUNAS/BATHS

■ **Cantou 19. Le** (AC G MA NU SA SB WH)
12-24, Fri & Sat 14-2, Sun -20h
10, rue Auguste Comte ☏ 05.55.88.33.47

Caen

BARS

■ **Excuse. L'** (B G MA p) Tue-Sat 23-3.30h
20 rue Vauquelin ☏ 02.31.38.80.89

MEN'S CLUBS

■ **Apollon. L'** (AC CC DR F G MA NU VS)
Mon-Thu 17-2h, Fri & Sat -3, 2nd Sun/month -21h
16 rue Varignon ☏ 02.31.93.00.82 💻 www.lapollon.com
Also sex shop.

DANCECLUBS

■ **Pink, Le** (D GLM) Fri & Sat 23-7h
54, rue de Bernières ☏ 02.31.50.05.25 💻 www.clubthepink.com

SAUNAS/BATHS

■ **Arc en Ciel** (b d DR DU FC G GH LAB MA RR SA SB SL WH WO)
Mon-Thu & Sat 13-20, Sat 14-20h
17, rue Varignon – 8, impasse Dumont ☏ 02.31.93.19.00
💻 www.club-arc-en-ciel.com

■ **Open Sauna. L'** (B CC DR DU FC FH G GH I LAB M MA MSG NU OS PI RR SA SB SL SNU VS WH) 13-1h
10, rue de Courtonne *Next to Hotel Mercure* ☏ 02.31.28.99.60
💻 www.lopensauna.com
Sauna with a large swimming pool, parties on some Saturdays. Clean and busy.

CRUISING

-🅿 of the castle
-Place Royale (garden)

-Plage de Franceville (15 mins from Caen, motorway direction Cabourg)
-Promenade Fossé St-Julien
-Promenade du Long du Cours
-Quartier du Vaugeux

Camelas

GUEST HOUSES

Mas d'en Coste (AC BF G I MA NU OS PI PK RWS RWT WO) All year
Hameau Politg *In Camelas, 20 km south-west from Perpignan*
☎ 04.68.53.66.40 www.masdencoste.com
3 double rooms with shower/WC, sat-TV, video, radio and own key, bf. incl. Rural location near Spanish border. Ideal for naturists.

Cannes

BARS

Charly's Bar. Le (AC B CC G I MA OS) 18-2.30h
5, rue du Suquet ☎ 04.97.06.54.78 www.pubcharlysbar.com
Cocktail bar.

Night. Le (AC B CC D GLM MA S SNU ST VS) Wed-Sun 21.30-5h
52 rue Jean Jaurès ☎ 04.93.39.20.50 www.night-club-cannes.com
Theme nights and younger crowd.

Pink. Le
81, Rue Félix Faure ☎ 04.93.38.53.18

Sparkling 4U. Le (! AC B d G M MA) 6-2.30h
6 rue des Frères Pradignac ☎ 04.93.39.71.21 www.sparklingforyou.com
Stylish bar and restaurant, very popular.

Vogue. Le (AC B CC glm MA p) 19-2.30h
20 rue du Suquet *Centre* ☎ 04.93.39.99.18 levoguebar-cannes.com

Zanzi Bar (AC B CC G MA OS) Daily 18-4h
85 rue Félix Faure ☎ 04.93.39.30.75 www.lezanzibar.com
One of the oldest gay bars in France, established since 1936. Legendary!

DANCECLUBS

Disco 7 (AC B D GLM MA S T) 23.30-?h
7 rue Rouguière ☎ 04.93.39.10.36
Trans shows at 2h.

RESTAURANTS

Barbarella (AC g M MA)
16, rue Saint-Dizier ☎ 04.92.99.17.33

Domino. Le (CC g M MA OS) Tue-Sat 12-14.30 & 19-23h
7 rue du Pré ☎ 04.92.98.07.87 franck.valmage.neuf.fr
Located in the „Le Suquet", the gay district of Cannes in the old part of the town. Traditional French cuisine.

SEX SHOPS/BLUE MOVIES

Parad'x (AC CC g MA VS) Daily 11-24h
13, rue des Mimosas ☎ 04.92.59.12.42 www.parad-x.com
Gay movies, rental and video shows and very good selection of products. Mon+Thu Gay only.

Video Sex (AC CC g MA VS) 10-24h
6 Rue Jean Jaurès *Near main station* ☎ 04.93.68.91.82

SAUNAS/BATHS

Sauna Le 9 (AC B CC DR DU FC FH G I LAB MA OS RR SA SB SH SOL VS WH) Mon-Sat 12.30-20h, Sun & before public holidays 14-20h
8 Chemin de l'Industrie *5 mins to Cannes, behind Castorama*
☎ 06.17.94.29.24 www.saunale9.com
Clean and discreet sauna where women are allowed. Coffee and lube for free.

Thermes Marins de Cannes
(AC b CC glm H M MA MSG OS PI SA SB SOL WH WO) 9-19h
47 rue Georges Clemenceau ☎ 04.92.99.73.10
www.lesthermesmarins-cannes.com

HOTELS

Hotel Croisette Beach (AC B BF CC glm H m MA OS PI SA SOL)
13 rue du Canada *50 m from la Croisette Centre Villa* ☎ 04.92.18.88.00
www.croisettebeach.com

Hôtel La Villa Tosca (AC b BF CC glm H MA MSG RWB RWS RWT) Closed from 21 Nov-25 Dec
11 Rue Hoche *2 mins from station, 5 mins from beach* ☎ 04.93.38.34.40
www.villa-tosca.com
22 rooms with sat-TV, safe & mini-bar. Quote Spartacus for a free breakfast.

CRUISING

-La Croix des Gardes
-Plage de la Batterie (between Cannes and Golfe Juan, around the service station, AYOR at night)
-Beach Ile Ste-Marguerite (NU, at the east side, near Ile St. Honoré)
-Square Carnot
-Square Frédéric-Mistral (beach)
-Boulevard de la Croisette (in the evening)

Cap-d'Agde

BARS

Casa Nueva (B glm M MA NU OS T) 17-3h
Colline 5, Port Nature *Quartier Naturiste* ☎ 04.67.26.08.15

Comptoir. Le (B GLM M) 9-15 & 18-1h, closed Sun & Mon
11 Boulevard du Soleil *Near cathedral* ☎ 06.80.24.70.70

Ilur (AC B CC D GLM MA) 9-2h
16, quai de la trirème ☎ 04.67.30.83.21

Look. Le (B CC G MA NU OS S T) 17-1, Summer -2h
2, Boulevard des Matelots *Opposite Port Nature V* ☎ 04.67.26.30.42

Mangoustan. Le (B G) Closed in winter
38 Quai de la Trinquette ☎ 04.67.01.59.48

SAUNAS/BATHS

Preambule (AC B DR G I M MA SA SB VS WH) Daily 12-4h
52, rue de la Gabelle *At the port* ☎ 04.67.93.75.24
www.preambule.info
New sauna with theme evenings.

HOTELS

Gil de France (AC B BF CC glm H I M MC MSG OS PI PK RWS RWT SA SB VA WH) All year
10 Avenue des Alizés *15 km from Beziérs airport* ☎ 04.67.26.77.80
www.capdagde-hotel.fr

GUEST HOUSES

Villa Littoral (B BF G I m NU OS PI PK RWS RWT SOL VA WH WO) Open Mar-Oct
10 Rue du Littoral – Grau d'Agde *40 mins from Montpellier, 5 mins from Cap d'Agde* ☎ 04.67.21.46.69 www.villalittoral.com
Five guest rooms. Near the naturist beaches.

SWIMMING

-Plage du Barbecue
-Marseillan plage (G NU) (Between Sète and Cap d'Adge, to be reached via N112. Pass junction Cap d'Agde and follow next junction to the right, direction Marseillan plage. The access to the dunes is strictly forbidden (Jul & Aug only), frequent police controls)
-Plage de Roche Pongue (at night).

Carcassonne

BARS

Cafe de Nuit. Le (AC g MA) 17-3h
31 boulevard Omer Sarraut ☎ 04.68.25.90.26

HOTELS

Relais Royal (B BF CC glm H I M MA OS PA PI PK RWS RWT VA)
8 rue Maréchal Clauzel, Mirepoix *In Mirepoix, approx. 40 km from Carcassonne* ☎ 05.61.60.19.19 www.relaisroyal.com
Five rooms, 3 suites, private parking and shuttle service. 10% discount for Spartacus-Readers

GUEST HOUSES

■ **Domaine aux Quat'Saisons. Le** (B BF glm I M MA OS PI PK RWS S VA) All year
26 ave Georges Clémenceau, Rieux-Minervois *60 mins south of Toulouse, 20 mins east of Carcassonne* ☏ 04.68.24.49.73
💻 www.southoffrancehotel.com
Traditional wine estate in the heart of Minervois. 5 luxuriously designed bedrooms and great facilities. Only 40 mins. drive to the gay beaches.

■ **Hauts de Fontgrande. Les** (bf glm H I MA MSG OS p PI SOL) All year
Chemin des Anglais *10 mins taxi drive from railway station and airport, bus service from city centre* ☏ 06.72.66.08.13
💻 www.leshautsdefontgrande.com
The location of these 3 rooms, looking upon the medieval valley town of Carcassonne is one of the best. The swimming pool is very pleasant in a lovely garden between vineyards.

■ **Villa De Mazamet. La** (AC BF CC GLM I M OS PI PK RWS RWT) All year
4 rue Pasteur, Mazamet *40 km north of Carcassonne* ☏ 06.25.50.56.91
💻 www.villademazamet.com
All rooms are ensuite with original parquet flooring, individual marble fireplace, a flat screen TV, DVD Player, iPod docking station & WiFi. Start your evening with a cocktail in the garden or lounge, before dining on the regions finest and freshest ingredients.

Carnac

DANCECLUBS

■ **Appalooza. L'** (AC B CC D DR GLM MA OS P S VS WE) Fri & Sat 24-6h
Route de Quiberon ☏ 06.09.04.01.60 💻 www.appalooza.com

Cassis

SWIMMING

-Calanque de Port-Pin (NU)
-La Pointe Cacau
-Cap Canaille (NU) (go east from the town, direction Route des Crêtes, there's a non marked steep way to a P. On the beach turn east. Gay at the end of the nude beach)

Caux

GUEST HOUSES

■ **Stone House B&B. The** (AC bf glm H I MA OS RWS) Closed 15 Nov-15 Jan
38 Boulevard Anselme Nougaret *5 mins from the beautiful town of Pezenas & 25 mins from the beach / mountains* ☏ 04.67.21.60.42
💻 www.thestonehouse.com
The village of Caux is set amongst the vineyards, offering the perfect quiet get-away for anyone looking to relax and explore the ‚real' south of France.

Chalon-sur-Saône

BARS

■ **Purgatoire. Le** (B CC GLM MA S ST T) Tue-Thu 10.30-1, Fri & Sat 10.30-3h, closed Sun & Mon
2 Porte de Lyon *Between 2 Mai de Saône and Hotel de Ville*
☏ 03.85.48.38.34
With cabaret and dinner shows. Day and night bar with entertainment on Fridays.

■ **Templiers. Les** (AC CC DR MA P) 19-2, Fri & Sat -3h, Mon closed
9 Place Saint Jean de Maizel *Between Espace d'Arts & Hôtel de Ville*
☏ 03.85.48.09.79

RESTAURANTS

■ **P'tit Lou. Le** (AC B bf CC d g M MA) Tue-Sun 9.30-14.30 & 15.30-22h, closed on Mon and Thu / Sun afternoon
17 Route de Dole, Damerey ☏ 03.85.47.58.09 💻 leptitlou.blogspace.fr
Pub in American style, restaurant in Parisian style. 10 types of Whiskey and 20 types of beer.

SAUNAS/BATHS

■ **Anteus** (B CC DR DU FC FH G MA MSG SA SB VS) Gay: Mon, Wed, Thu, Sun 14-20; Mixed: Tue 14-22 & Fri 14-22h, closed Sat
4, rue des Cornillons *Enter pedestrian zone at Place de la Mairie, then take the 3rd street to your left* ☏ 03.85.48.82.68 💻 www.sauna-anteus.com

Chambéry

RESTAURANTS

■ **Valentino. Le** (B DM glm M MA RES) 10-14.30 & 18-23h
711 Avenue de Lyon *5 mins from centre* ☏ 04.79.69.57.55
💻 www.ifrance.com/levalentino/valentino.htm

SAUNAS/BATHS

■ **Sun Beach** (AC B CC DR DU FC FH g GH LAB MA NU RR SA SB SH SL SOL VS WH WO)
Mon & Tue 13-21, Wed & Thu -22, Fri -24, Sat 14-1, Sun -22h
242, rue Jules-Bocquin *North of the centre, near the stadium*
☏ 04.79.62.12.29 💻 www.sunbeachclub.com
Private parking.

Chamonix

BARS

■ **Tof** (AC B CC D glm MA) Mon-Sat midnight-5h
158 Place Edmond Desailloud *Place de Chamonia Sud*
☏ 04.50.53.45.28 ☏ 06.07.63.46.03
Bar & disco. Also theme nights.

HOTELS

■ **Hotel Liberty Mont Blanc** (B BF cc d glm H I M MSG PA PI PK RWB RWS RWT SA VA WH)
Out of the season 11-16h, closed 3 weeks in Nov and 2 weeks in May
734, av. du Mont d'Arbois, Saint Gervais Les Bains *Between Chamonix and Megeve, 60 mins from Geneva airport* ☏ 04.50.93.45.21
💻 www.liberty-mont-blanc.com

Charleville-Mézières

BARS

■ **Ascott. L'** (B g MC)
23, rue Bourbon ☏ 03.24.33.39.83

CRUISING

-Pond of Bairon (at the beach)
-Square Bayard
-Square du Mont-Olympe

Clermont-Ferrand

BARS

■ **Marais, Le** (B GLM) Thu-Sun 20-2h
49, rue Fontgiève ☏ 04.73.40.06.56 💻 lemaraisclermont.skyrock.com

DANCECLUBS

■ **Sitges** (B cc D DR GLM MA p VS) 22-5h
3 Place Gilberte Perrier ☏ 06.71.64.03.98 💻 monsite.wanadoo.fr/SITGES

SEX SHOPS/BLUE MOVIES

■ **Eroshop** (CC GLM MA T VS) Mon-Sat 9.30-20h
23, rue Ballainvilliers ☏ 04.73.92.47.06 💻 www.eroshop63.fr

SAUNAS/BATHS

■ **Salins. Les** (AC B DR DU FC FH G LAB m P RR SA SB SH SOL VS WH WO YC) 14-24, Tue -19, Fri & Sat -2, Sun 15-24h

1, rue Montpela-Bujadoux *Close to Place des Salins & bus station*
☎ 04.73.29.26.10 💻 www.sauna-les-salins.fr
Clean & friendly sauna on 850 m² with maze. Shows on public holidays.

■ **Sauna d'Italie** (b DU G m SA SB VS)
Tue, Fri & Sat 13-1; Wed & Thu -20h
4, avenue d'Italie ☎ 06.16.62.57.89 💻 sauna-d-italie.com

■ **Sauna Le Viaduc** (B CC f g I MA NU SA SB VS)
12 rue des près bas ☎ 04.73.29.21.38

CRUISING

-Square de la Jeune Résistance
-Jardin Lecoq
-Place de la Poterne
-Nouvelles Galleries
-Place des Bughes
-Square Blaise-Pascal

Colmar

BARS

■ **Capt ,n Cafe** (B cc GLM MC S SNU)
19-3h, closed Mon-Wed
6 Rue des Trois Epis ☎ 03.89.24.05.36

SAUNAS/BATHS

■ **Gingko** (DU g MC RR SA SB VS) Sun-Thu 14-22, Fri -24, Sat -1h
31, rue des Jardins ☎ 03.89.23.13.82 💻 www.club-ginkgo.com

Compiègne

BARS

■ **Saint-Clair. Le** (B CC glm m MA OS S) 11-1, Wed-Sat -3h
8 Rue des Lombards ☎ 03.44.40.58.18

CRUISING

-La Faisanderie
-Le Quai Fleurant-Agricola (at the motorway exit Ressons)
-Place du Château
-Ressons-sur-Matz (at the motorway exit in direction of Amiens in the bushes)
-Carrefour du Puits-du-Roy

Corse

Corse – Bastia

DANCECLUBS

■ **Club Privé L'Énigme** (B D GLM MA SNU T)
Mon-Wed 23-5, Thu-Sat -10h
1 rue pino ☎ 04.20.03.57.56

SEX SHOPS/BLUE MOVIES

■ **Extrem' Vidéo** (AC CC g MA VS) 11-2h
1 Boulevard Auguste Gaudin *Centre* ☎ 04.95.31.91.44
💻 www.coresex.com
A mixed store with a wide range of gay videos & DVDs and accessories.

SWIMMING

-Barcaggio (before villiage, leave D 253 and walk 2 km east)
-Villages naturistes (50 km on the east coast, a licence is required to gain access)

CRUISING

-Café des Platanes
-Jardin Romieux
-Place De Gaulle
-Place Saint-Nicolas (after 21h, AYOR)

Corse – Corbara

SWIMMING

-Baie de Gienchetu (take the small train along the coast, first stop after Ile Rousse)
-Plage de Calvi

Dax

HOTELS

■ **Capcazal de Pachiou** (AC bf glm MA OS PK RWS) All year
606 Route de Pachiou *Near Pau* ☎ 05.58.55.30.54
💻 www.capcazaldepachiou.com
Chateau from the 17th century with 3 suites and two bedrooms.

CRUISING

-Allée du Bois du Boulogne (AYOR) (at night)
-Cathédrale
-Ancienne Gendarmerie
-Parc des Arènes

Dijon

MEN'S CLUBS

■ **Peub Club** (AC B CC DR DU F FC G GH I MA NU P SH SL VS)
Wed – Sat 21-?, Sun 16-? winter open at 22h
4 bis, rue de Serrigny ☎ 09.54.85.21.00 💻 www.peub-club.asso.fr
Sun naked party.

DANCECLUBS

■ **Paradise. Le** (AC B CC D DR DU FC GLM I MA P VS W)
Wed-Sat 23.30-5h
23 rue paster ☎ 06.06.75.11.69 💻 www.bartheparadise.com
Newly opened. Straight-friendly. Free entrance. Cocktail menu. For special events see website: www.bartheparadise.com

Wooz. Le (B CC D FC GLM MA p T VS) Wed-Sat 20-5h, Thu & Sun 20-2h
11, rue du Docteur-Albert-Remy *100m railway station* ☎ 03.80.43.90.61
lewooz.com
Free entrance. Straight-friendly. 2 bars. Large dancefloor. Smokers room. See webpage for special events: lewooz.com

SEX SHOPS/BLUE MOVIES

Librairie Érotique (AC CC FC G GH MC SH VS)
12-20, Sat & Sun 14-20h
64 Rue Berbisey ☎ 03.80.30.74.09
2 floors, 10 video cabines

SAUNAS/BATHS

Bossuet. Le (! B CC D DR DU FC FH G GH I LAB M MA NU p PI RR SA SB SH SL T VS WH) Gay: 12-18.30 mixed -1 & on We -2h
3bis, rue du Jardin des Plantes *5 mins from railway station*
☎ 03.80.53.06.28 www.sauna-bossuet.com
One of the biggest saunas in the Bourgogne with 700 m² on 2 floors. Evenings and Saturdays mixed gay and straight. Crowded and nice staff.

Relaxe, Le (B DR DU FC FH G M MA p RR SA SB VR VS) 14-20h
97, rue Berbisey *Hôpital Général/1er Mai* ☎ 03.80.30.14.40
www.lerelaxe.fr
A gay landmark in Dijon since 1980.

FITNESS STUDIOS

Energy Fitness (B CC DU g MA SA SB SOL) Mon-Fri 9-21, Sat 9-18h
9, rue des frères Montgolfier ☎ 03.80.52.73.73
www.energyfitness.fr
Well equipped gym.

GUEST HOUSES

Chateau Les Roches B&B (b BF CC glm m MA PK RWB RWS)
All year
Rue de Glanot, Mont Saint Jean *Located close to the A6, around 50 km west of Dijon* ☎ 03.80.84.32.71 www.lesroches-burgundy.com
This boutique hotel is located in the heart of Burgundy. A very peaceful area, ideal for a romantic get-away. If you like nature, history, art, food and wine you will like it here. Five spacious double bedrooms with private bath and satellite TVs, decorated with both antique and contemporary furnishings.

CRUISING

-Parc de l'Arquebuse
-Les Allées du parc (Cours du Général-De-Gaulle)
-P du Lac Kir

Douarnenez

SWIMMING

-Le Rheum (between St.Jean & Sables-Blancs beach, late at night)
-Dunes (12 km from Douarnenez; during the summer season cruising day and night; low season only from 12 to 14h)
-Les Roches blanches (at the edge of the bay, pass along the path of the customs officials)

Dunkerque

SAUNAS/BATHS

Pied Marin. Le (AC b CC DR DU FC FH G I LAB m MA MSG P RR S SA SB SH SL SOL VS WH) Sun, Mon, Wed & Thu 14-22.30; Tue, Fri & Sat -24h
2, rue du Nouvel Arsenal *10 mins walk from station* ☎ 03.28.51.16.54
www.lepiedmarin.fr
Sauna on 400 m² (2 floors).

CRUISING

-Dunes de Lefrinkouke (at the right side of the dyke)
-Behind St.Martin church
-Passerelle de la Douane (in the evening).

Epernay

GUEST HOUSES

Epicuriens. Les (BF H I M MC RES RWB RWS RWT) All year
9, rue Jean Thévenin *Marne* ☎ 03.26.51.26.30
www.les-epicuriens-epernay.com
Overnight price includes breakfast and a bottle of champagne.

Epinal

RESTAURANTS

Restaurant Le Belcour (AC B glm LM M OS PK RES S ST)
Call for show times
3,5 rue de Turenne, Saint-Nabord ☎ 03.29.62.49.97
www.lebelcour-restaurant.com
Hotel Belcour welcomes you all year round to their charming property. Just next door, you will be able to come to new strength in a traditional restaurant. A dinner show with drag queens is one of the highlights at the weekends.

Etretat

GUEST HOUSES

Jardin Gorbeau (bf CC glm H I M RWS RWT) All year
27 rue Adolphe Boissaye *20 m from the beach* ☎ 02.35.27.16.72
www.gorbeau.com
B&B in a beautifully restored 1824 house with garden, just 50 meters from the stunning beach. 5 suites, private baths, salons, video library. Gay owned.

Evian les Bains

HOTELS

Hôtel Les Cygnes (B BF cc glm I M MA PA PK RWB RWS RWT)
All year, 7-23h
8, Avenue de Grande Rive *On the shore of Leman Lake*
☎ 04.50.75.01.01 www.hotellescygnes.com
38 bedrooms with a personal touch. all equipped with Sat-TV and WI-FI, seminar rooms, private beach and pontoon, lounges, bar, car-park and playroom. Enjoy the charm of the terrace at the water's edge under the vine arbour; the cosy lounges and especially the tasty and refined cooking.

Evreux

SAUNAS/BATHS

Equatorial Sauna. L' (B DR DU FC FH G GH LAB M MC NU RR SA SB SL VR VS WH) Mon-Thu 13-22, Fri-Sun -24h
9bis rue Georges Bernard *Behind the Town Hall* ☎ 02.32.36.79.61
www.lequatorialsauna.com
Very populare with special events such as nude night, youngster night etc.

Golfe-Juan

SWIMMING

Plage de la Batterie (near service station between Cannes and Golf Juan, popular nudist beach)

Gourin

DANCECLUBS

Starman. Le (B D DR GLM H MA OS p s T) Gay on Sat 24-6h
4 Rue de la Gare ☎ 02.97.23.66.78 www.starman-club.fr
Disco and private hotel.

Grenoble

BARS

Code. Le (AC B cc GLM MA p) 18-1h
9 rue Étienne Marcel ☎ 04.76.43.58.91 lecodebar.skyrock.com
An ideal place to start off your evening.

CAFES

■ **Saint-Germain. Le** (B glm MC WE) Cafe: 8-17, Bar: 17-?h
146 cours Berriat
Gay and lesbian guests mostly on Fri & Sat nights.

DANCECLUBS

■ **George-V**
124, cours Berriat ☎ 06.62.15.16.22
🖳 www.discotheque-grenoble.com
■ **Luna. La**
94, cours Jean-Jaures

RESTAURANTS

■ **Mix. Le** (B g M MC OS)
4 place des Gordes ☎ 04.76.44.81.22

SAUNAS/BATHS

■ **Oxygène** (B DR DU FC FH G GH m MA P RR SA SB VR VS WH)
13.30-20.30, Fri 14-1, Sat & Sun 14-20h (mixed at WE)
24, rue Mallifaud *Tram ‚Albert 1er de Belgique'* ☎ 04.76.87.30.00
🖳 www.oxygenesauna.com
Modern interior.
■ **Saint-Ferjus. Le** (b DU FC FH G MA SA SB SH VS) 14-21, Fri -23h
22, rue Saint Ferjus *Next to Place de Verdun* ☎ 04.76.54.13.70
🖳 sauna.stferjus.free.fr
Popular sauna with free parking.

CRUISING

-Monument des Diables bleus
-Hôtel-de-Ville (night)
-Parc de l'Ile-Verte
-Rue Malherbe (garden)
-Champs-sur-Drac (summer)
-Etangs de St-Egrève (summer)
-Parc Paul-Mistral
-Parc Foch
-Place Victor-Hugo

Grignan

BARS

■ **Greco. Le** (B CC D DR GLM H M MA OS p PI s VS)
Disco: Fri & Sat 23-5h, summer Fri-Sun
Le Fraysse (Hamlet) on the D4 ☎ 04.75.46.51.66
Pool in summer. Accommodation available.

Haguenau

BARS

■ **Fanatik Underground** (B CC D GLM m P S)
Sun-Thu 21-3, Fri & Sat -4h, closed Tue
5 Marché aux Bestiaux ☎ 03.88.73.05.42
🖳 www.fanatikunderground.fr

Hossegor

BARS

■ **Tilt. Le** (AC B CC G S YC) 22-3h
366 Avenue du Touring Club ☎ 05.58.41.71.34

HOTELS

■ **Barbary Lane**
(B BF cc glm I M MA OS PA PI PK RWB RWT SOL VA WO) Closed Jan & Feb
156 Avenue de la Côte d'Argent ☎ 05.58.43.46.00
🖳 www.barbary-lane.com
Logis de France. 10% discount for Spartacus readers, except for high season Jul-Aug.

Hyères

SWIMMING

-Plage du Bau Rouge (in Carqueiranne, take D86)
-Rochers de Gien (NU) (Côte sud-ouest)
-Plage des Salins (last beach; the restaurant »Chez Pimpin« marks the entrance to the nude section). Easy access from Miramar (La Londe les Maures beach) on foot.

Ile-du-Levant

GUEST HOUSES

■ **Villa l'Eglantine** (AC GLM MC NU OS RWS) 1 Apr-30 Sep
Corniche l'Arbousier *6 mins from the seaside, 1 min from village*
☎ 06.70.79.49.72 🖳 www.villaeglantine.com
Located on naturist island, rooms & apartments to rent. Basic accommodation in a large villa. 6 rooms, 15 studios (with kitchen).

APARTMENTS

■ **Résidence l'Escapade** (B bf glm I MA MSG NU OS PA PI RWB RWS SA SOL WO) All year
Domaine Naturiste *Between the harbour and Place du Village*
☎ 04.94.05.93.45 🖳 www.escapade-levant.com
5 studios with ensuite shower/WC, kitchenette and own keys.
■ **Villa Marie-Jeanne** (B GLM I MC NU PI RWB RWS RWT SA WO) May-Sep
Domaine Naturiste d'Héliopolis *30 mins by boat from Hyères, near Nice*
☎ 04.94.05.99.95 🖳 www.villamariejeanne.fr
Studios, apartments and lofts on an idyllic island for nudists. Discount for those under 30 years.

CRUISING

-Ile-du-Levant (behind the castle, evening)
-Jardin Denis

La Baule (Brittany)

BARS

■ **Aventure. L'** (B CC GLM I MA OS P) 17-?h
153 avenue de Lattre-de-Tassigny *Close to Casino and Hotel Royal*
☎ 06.83.41.69

La Ferté-Gaucher

GUEST HOUSES

■ **Fontaine aux Loups. La** (B BF glm M OS PA PI PK RWS VA WH) All year
12 km from La Ferté Gaucher by D215 direction Montmirail
☎ 01.64.03.76.76 🖳 www.fontaine-aux-loups.org
Country retreat 1 hour from Paris.

La Roche-sur-Yon

BARS

■ **Bar Chez Papy's** (AC B cc d GLM MA P T)
22-3.30h, closed Sun & Mon
10 Place de la Résistance ☎ 02.51.62.71.93

La Rochelle

BARS

■ **Eden Café**
29, rue St Jean du Pérot ☎ 05.46.29.16.03

DANCECLUBS

■ **Douche. La** (AC B CC D DR G MA P)
Thu-Sun & before holidays 23-5h
14 Rue Léonce Vieljeux *Near the Vieux Port and Grosse Horologe*
☎ 05.46.41.24.79 🖳 www.douche.fr.fm

Two bars and a shower open to everyone in front of the dance floor. Regular foam parties.

■ **Tuxedo Café** (B cc D glm MA) 23-5h
Place de la Préfecture ☎ 05.46.50.01.22

SEX SHOPS/BLUE MOVIES

■ **Book Sex Shop** (g VS)
Tue-Sat 10.30-12.30 & 14.30-20, Mon 14.30-20h
6 Rue des Bonnes Femmes ☎ 05.46.41.51.83

SAUNAS/BATHS

■ **Atlantis. L'** (B cc DR DU FC FH G m MA RR SA SB SL VS)
14-21, Fri -1, Sat 15-1, Sun -21h
12, rue de l'Arsénal *Near Vieux Port, behind Quai Maubec*
☎ 05.46.41.15.89 💻 www.sauna-atlantis.com
Free snacks and drinks.

■ **Tom et Jules** (AC B DU G NU SA SB VS WH)
Mon, Tue & Thu 14.30-19.30; Fri 21.30-2; Sat 15-19.30h
2 Blvd. Aristide Rondeau *Port Neuf* ☎ 05.46.35.40.66 💻 tometjules.com
Gay on Tue, Thu & Sat only.

SWIMMING

-Le Marouillet (12 km from La Rochelle)
-Beach St-Jean-des-Sables (8 km from La Rochelle)

CRUISING

-Casino (public garden, evening)
-Rue Thiers (afternoon and evening)
-Bridge de Chagnolet
-Le Marché couvert (Rue Thiers)
-P de la Tour carrée (close to the ocean)

La Valette-du-Var

SAUNAS/BATHS

■ **Rainbow. Le** (AC DR DU G I SA SB VS)
12.30-20, Sun and before public holidays: 14-20h
Chemin Paul Madon 9 Espace Frioul *In industrial zone in direction Leroy Merlin, next door to planetX sex shop* ☎ 06.12.16.74.60
💻 www.saunalerainbow.com
Gay sauna located in the industrial area of La Valette-du-Var. Fully air-conditioned, easy access from the motorway (exit 5) with free parking.

Laval

BARS

■ **Autoreverse. L'**
1, rue des Cheveaux ☎ 02.43.56.77.02

■ **Charivari. Le**
32, Grande Rue ☎ 02.43.56.09.86

Le Freney d'Oisans

HOTELS

■ **Cassini. Le** (AC B BF glm I M PK RWS RWT VA) All year
Le Village *Near Alpe d'Huez* ☎ 04.76.80.04.10 💻 www.gayski.fr
A charming hotel. All ten rooms are en-suite with bath or shower.

Le Havre

BARS

■ **Castel.Le** (B CC D G LM MA p ST T W) 21-2h
75 rue guillemard 💻 www.lecastelbar.com
New straight-friendly gay bar with DJ. Hollywood glamour in white and black decoration.

RESTAURANTS

■ **Case à café. La** (B CC DM GLM M MA RES VEG W WL) 10.30-14, 17.30-22.30h / closed Sun & Sat midday
2, rue de Turenne ☎ 02.35.43.21.90 💻 www.la-case-a-cafe.com
Specials: pizzas and salads. Gay owned with friendly staff.

SAUNAS/BATHS

■ **Dédale.Le** (AC AK B CC DR DU FC FH G GH LAB MA NU RR SA SB SL VR VS WH) Mo-Thu & Sun 14-21, Fri & Sat -24h
98, rue Jean-Jacques Rousseau ☎ 02.77.00.00.84
💻 www.saunagaynormandie.com
Cruising and wellness area are separated. Mousse party each first Sat of the month. Mixed day on Thur and Fri night. Naked on Mo.

■ **Hot Way** (b DR DU FC FH G GH I m MA p PP RR SA SB SH VS WH) 14-20h
60, rue Dauphine *St. François district, bus-Notre Dame* ☎ 02.35.22.58.52
💻 www.hotway.fr
Two floors. Gay only on Mon & Tue.

SWIMMING

-Ste. Adresse Beach (NU) (at the end near airport)
-Tilleul Beach (23 km from Le Havre towards Etretat, after the rocks)

CRUISING

-Forest of Montgeon (AYOR) (in the vicinity of the Château d'Eau)
-Place Danton

Le Mans

BARS

■ **Arc-En-Ciel** (AC B CC DR GLM MA T VS) 17-2h, closed Mon
2 rue Dorée *Between Place de l'Eglise & Eglise St. Benoît*
☎ 02.43.23.80.16 💻 monsite.wanadoo.fr/bararcenciel

■ **Phoenix. Le**
108, rue Nationale ☎ 06.37.54.90.36

CAFES

■ **Palace** (B CC D GLM p S) 18-4h, Mon closed
101 avenue du Général Leclerc *Near train station* ☎ 02.43.87.09.36
Danceclub and bar.

DANCECLUBS

■ **Babylone. Le** (B D G MA P) Tue-Sun 17-4h
151 rue Nationale ☎ 02.43.78.08.02 💻 babylone72.free.fr
Upstairs is the sexclub „Le K-Chô".

SEX SHOPS/BLUE MOVIES

■ **Sex Shop de la Gare** (AC CC DR g MA T VS) 10-22, Sun & public holidays 15-20h
21 Bd de la Gare ☎ 02.43.24.31.16
A backroom downstairs.

SAUNAS/BATHS

■ **Delta** (B DU G I MA MSG SA SB SL WH) Mon 13.30-20, Wed & Thu -24, Fri -22.30, Sat -2, Sun -24h
263 Boulevard Carnot ☎ 02.43.23.26.81 💻 www.deltasaunaclub.fr

CRUISING

-Esplanade des Jacobins (night)
-Jardin de Tessé (Avenue de Paderborn)
-Place de Pontlieue (WC)
-P Tertre
-P Cormier

Les Menuires

RESTAURANTS

■ **Medz'é-ry. Le** (AC B CC DM glm LM M MA NR OS PA PK RES S ST VEG WL) Open every day in winter season, otherwise open every lunchtime and with reservation only for the evening & WE.
Quartier de Preyerand, Les Menuires ☎ 04.79.08.16.74
💻 cabaret.le.medzery.free.fr
The only cabaret in „Les 3 Vallées" skiresort

Les Sybelles - La Toussuire

HOTELS

Principauté de Comborcière
(B CC D GLM M MA OS PA PK SA SOL WH) Reception: 7-2h
1 route des Champions ☎ 04.79.83.09.20 💻 www.comborciere.com
A gay skiing resort in the French alps. Also a bar, restaurant and disco.

Leucate

SWIMMING

-Beach of Leucate (NU) (north of the straight-families' beach, under the cliffs of Cap Leucate)
-Northern beach of the villages Ulysse and Aphrodite

Lille

GAY INFO

J'en suis, j'y reste - Centre Gay & Lesbien de Lille
Wed 18.30-22, Fri 20-22, Sat 15-18h
19 Rue de Condé *M° Porte d'Arras* ☎ 03.20.52.28.68
💻 www.jensuisjyreste.org

BARS

Miss Marple. Le (! B CC GLM MA)
18, rue de Gand ☎ 03.20.39.85.92
Very popular and crowded, especially at the weekend.

Vice Versa (B CC FC G I MA PA ST T W WL) 15-3, Sun 16-3h
3 rue de la Barre ☎ 03.20.54.93.46
Large café style. Nice place to have a drink and meet friends in a cool atmosphere. DJ on FR and Sat.

MEN'S CLUBS

Sling. Le (! b DR F G MA NU VS WE)
Wed 14-2; Fri 14-3; Sat 20-4; Sun 14-1h; closed Mon, Tue, Thu
32, rue Jean Jaures *M° Porte de Valenciennes* ☎ 03.20.58.04.97
💻 www.lesling.com
300 m², 3 floors, glory-holes, slings, darkroom, prisons, cabines, 88 lockers, exhibition areas and wet areas. The only gay sex club in the north of France.

DANCECLUBS

Tchouka Club. Le (B cc D GLM s) 22-4h
80 rue Barthelemy De Lepaul ☎ 03.20.14.37.50
💻 www.tchoukaclub.org
Very crowded. Special parties at the weekend and gay Tea Dance on Sundays. Not busy before midnight.

SEX SHOPS/BLUE MOVIES

Cinesex (AC CC g VS) 10-23, Sun 12-23h
41 Rue des Ponts-de-Comines ☎ 03.20.06.25.83

Cube. Le (AC AK CC DR FC G GH LAB MA NU p RR SH SL T VR VS)
Mon-Thu 9-24, Fri & Sat -1, Sun 12-24h
5 ter rue du Vieux Faubourg *Near train station* ☎ 03.28.07.98.95
💻 www.cubelille.fr
Sex shop on 2 levels with sex cinema, sling, cubicles, gloryholes, and labyrinth.

Sex Center (AC CC g s VS) 10-23h
41 Rue des Ponts de Comines *M° Rihour* ☎ 03.20.06.25.83

SAUNAS/BATHS

Bains. Les (B CC DM DR DU FC FH G GH I LAB M MA MSG NU OS PI RR SA SB SOL VEG VR VS WH WO)
12-24, Fri 12-1,Sat 14-1, Sun 14-24h
52, rue de Cambrai *M° Porte de Valenciennes* ☎ 03.20.53.02.02
💻 www.lesbains.fr
Popular and cruisy sauna on 1200 m² and 4 levels. The extensive facilities and the laid-back atmosphere make it an experience.

Lokal. Le (AC B CC DR DU FC FH G GH I LAB M MA NU P RR SA SB SOL VR VS WH) Mon-Fri 12-24, Sat & Sun 14-24h
95bis, rue du Molinel *Centre, near station Lille-Flandres*

☎ 03.20.30.67.85 💻 www.lelokal.com
Big area. Wed: Mixed day. 2nd Sat in month: naked. Friendly staff and same owner as Sauna Les Bains.

Soho (B BF CC DM DR DU FC FH G GH I LAB M MA MSG NU OS p RR SA SB SOL VEG VR VS W WH WL) 12-24, Fri & Sat -1, Sun 4-1h
10 rue de la Madeleine *300 m from train station* ☎ 03.20.07.87.00
💻 www.saunasoho.com
1200m², free solarium. Free brunch on sun. Entrance ticket available all day long. Very popular and crowded. Friendly staff.

CRUISING

-Bois de Boulogne (ayor) (Forest of Boulogne; at the north end, behind the football stadium along the canal and in the groves; at night also on the P of the avenue Mathias-Delobel)
-P of the Communauté Urbaine de Lille (near the roundway, late in the evening)
-Bois de Phalempin (Forest of Phalempin, south of Lille, go 15 km on the A1 highway, leave it at exit Seclin and then take the road D8)
-Groves in the northern part of town Boulevard Robert-Schumann (go by car direction St.André; esplanade)
-Square de la Porte-de-Roubaix (AYOR)
-Vauban garden
-Stade Gimonprez-Jooris (AYOR OC)
-University campus (in the vicinity of the library).

Limoges

SAUNAS/BATHS

Éros Limoges (AC b CC DR DU FC FH G m p RR SA SB SH SOL VS WH YC) Sun & Mon 14-2, Tue-Thu -4, Fri & Sat -5h
8, rue Jean Jaurès *Close to town hall* ☎ 05.55.32.74.48
Two establishments at the same address, one gay, one mixed. Also sex-shop.

CRUISING

-Lac d'Uzurat
-Bois de la Bastide (AYOR)
-Garden of l'ancien Palais de l'Évéché
-Champ de Juillet (AYOR T)
-P Cora (Route de Paris)
-Place de la Cathédrale (AYOR)

Logonna Daoulas

GUEST HOUSES

■ **Domaine de Moulin Mer** (B bf cc glm I m PK RWB RWS) All year
34 route de Moulin Mer *Next to the port of Moulin Mer*
☎ 02.98.07.24.45 💻 www.domaine-moulin-mer.com
Fantastic manor house, located on a peninsula, completely refurbished 2007.

Lorient

BARS

■ **Drôle de..., Le** (B CC G MA T) Tue-Sun 19-1h
26 rue Jules Legrand ☎ 02.97.21.08.73
A discreet bar close to the centre.

SEX SHOPS/BLUE MOVIES

■ **Espace Broadway** (AC CC g VS)
11-20, Mon 13-23, Fri 11-23h, closed Sun & Aug
15 Rue Poissonnière ☎ 02.97.21.81.64 💻 www.broadway80.com
Also information on the local gay scene. 10% reduction for Spartacus readers.

■ **Marc Dorcel Store** (CC F) 10-20, Fri & Sat -21h
Z.I de Manebos, rue Rouget de lisle, Lanester ☎ 02.97.89.26.05
💻 www.dorcelstore.com
The first Marc Dorcel Store in France with a large selection of gay products.

SAUNAS/BATHS

■ **Korosko. Le**
(AC B CC DR DU FC FH G LAB m MA RR SA SB SH SL SOL VS WH)
Gay: Tue, Wed & Thu 14-1, Mon & Sun -24, Sat -20; mixed: Fri 14-2h
18, rue Lazare Carnot *Near harbour* ☎ 02.97.35.07.50 💻 www.lekorosko.fr
Sauna with big jacuzzi, labyrinth and a sling. The Korosko crew invites its clientele to a night of fun and adventure in their 450 m² sauna. Friendly venue with fun and cruisy visitors.

CRUISING

-Sport complex of Moustoir
-Jardin Le Faoudic (Place Anatole-le-Braz, harbour)
-Ile de Groix (beach on the west coast)
-Kaolins (nudist beach)

Luchon

HOTELS

■ **Panoramic** (b BF CC glm MA PK RWB RWS RWT)
All year, reception: 7.30-21h
6 avenue Carnot ☎ 05.61.79.30.90 💻 www.hotelpanoramic.fr

Lyon

BARS

■ **Apothéose. L'**
4, Rue Saint Claude ☎ 04.78.28.11.50

■ **Bagat'Telles**
18, rue des Capucins ☎ 06.18.52.48.70
💻 www.gayinlyon.com/guide/bagatelles-bar

■ **Broc Bar, Le** (AC B CC GLM M MA OS PA T WL)
Tue-Sat 7-1, Sun 10-21 & Mon 7-22h
20 rue Lanterne ☎ 04.78.30.82.61
Very popular bar with terrasse. Breakfast, aperitif and cocktail. Nice atmosphere.

■ **Cap Opéra** (AC B cc GLM m OS s) 14-3, Sun 16-3h
2 Place Louis Pradel *Near Opera* ☎ 04.72.07.61.55

■ **Forum** (AC B cc GLM MA OS p) 17-1, Fri & Sat -3h
15 rue des Quatre Chapeaux *M° Cordeliers* ☎ 04.78.37.19.74

■ **Matinee Bar** (AC B CC GLM MA S WE) Tue-Thu 11-23, Fri & Sat -1h
2/4, Rue Bellecordière ☎ 04.72.56.06.06 💻 www.matineebar.net

■ **Ruche, La** (AC B CC FC G MA OS p T W WL) 17-3h
22, rue Gentil ☎ 04.78.37.42.26
Popular bar with friendly staff. Great variety of cocktails.

■ **XS Bar** (AC B CC FC G MC OS PA T VS WL)
Mon-Thu 17-2, Fri & Sat 17-4, Sun 18-2h
19 rue Claudia ☎ 09.62.16.69.92
New small straight-friendly bar with nice staff and atmosphere. Terrasse open all year long. Separate room for smokers.

MEN'S CLUBS

■ **1er Sous-Sol** (B CC DR FC G GH LAB M MC NU P RR SH SL T VR VS W)
14-4, Fri & Sat -7h
7 rue Puits-Gaillot *M° Hôtel de Ville* ☎ 04.72.28.34.75
Cruising bar on 2 floors. 16 different rooms and 3 labyrinths in the 1000m² bar. Beautiful design and centrally located.

■ **BK69** (AC B CC DR DU F FC G MA MSG NU P S SL VR VS) Wed-Sat 19-?, Sun 17-? / Summer 21-?h
1, rue de Thou *M° Croix Paquet* ☎ 09.53.01.24.85 💻 www.bk69.fr
Very popular in France. Ideal for enjoying company and sex. The staff is very friendly. Lot of events: see website.

■ **Men Club. Le** (AC AK B CC DR DU F FC G MA NU P RR S SL VS)
Thu-Sat 21-3h
2 cours d'herbouville ☎ 04.72.07.04.70 💻 www.lemenclub.com
Renovated small and intimate bar to get quick sex with 4 slings.

■ **SMAC** (AK B CC DR DU F FC G MC NU p P SL VS)
Winter: Thu-Sat 20-?, Sun 16-? / Summer: 21-?
30, rue Burdeau *M° Croix Paquet* ☎ 04.72.08.58.89
💻 www.smac69.com
Men's club with 2 floors and 3 slings. Thu golden shower, first and third Sun mixed. See website for special events.

Station B (! AC B CC D DR FC G GH MC OS VR VS W)
Wed, Thu, Sun 18-2; Fri & Sat -3h
21, place Gabriel Rambaud *M° Hôtel de ville, close to Place desTerreaux*
☎ 04.78.27.71.41 🖳 www.stationb.fr
Bear & butch bar with regular events. Very crowded, specials on WE.

Trou. Le (! AC AK B CC DR DU F FC G GH LAB MA NU p SH SL VR VS)
Sun-Thu 14-3, Fri & Sat -6h
6 rue Romarin *M° Hôtel de Ville* ☎ 04.78.39.98.69
🖳 www.letrou.fr
Video labyrinth, sling, dungeon, stockade, showers, fist, hood, St Andrew's cross and a small shop. Best late at WE. Good service. See www.letrou.fr for special events.

DANCECLUBS

Bloc. Le
67, rue de Raincy

Div1 (AC B CC D GLM MA p ST T VS) Sun 24-7h
6 rue Rivoli
Only gay on Sun but popular with travesty show. 2 dancefloors.

DV 1 (AC B CC D glm MA p ST t) 24-6h, closed Mon & Tue
6 rue Roger Violi *M° Croix Paquet, near Hôtel de Ville* ☎ 04.72.07.72.62
No entrance fee. 80's bar and dance floor. Level 2: Electro & House.

Marais. Le
14, Rue Thomassin

Pink's. Le (AC B CC D GLM MA p T VS) 23-?h
38, rue de L'arbre Sec ☎ 04.78.29.18.19

United Café (AC B cc D GLM MC p s SNU) Daily 22.30-5h
Impasse de la Pêcherie *Between N°10 & 11 Quai de la Pêcherie*
☎ 04.78.29.93.18 🖳 www.united-cafe.com
Still a popular place. Regular events. See their website for more information: www.united-cafe.com

RESTAURANTS

■ **Gargotte La** (AC B glm M MA OS) 12-13.50 & 20-23h
15, rue Royale ☏ 04.78.28.79.20 🖳 www.resto.fr/lagargotte

SEX SHOPS/BLUE MOVIES

■ **Dog Klub** (CC f G MA) Tue-Sat 12-20h
12, rue Romarin ☏ 04.72.00.92.04 🖳 www.dogklub.com

■ **Major Videostore** (CC G VS) Mon-Sat 14-21, public holidays 16-21h
2 Place des Capucins *M° Hôtel de Ville, near Place des Terreaux*
☏ 04.78.39.09.28
Large selection of DVDs/videos. Sale and rental. Also accessories and gadgets.

SAUNAS/BATHS

■ **Bellecour. Le**
(AC B CC DR DU FC FH G GH M NU OC P RR SA SB SL VR VS) 12-22h
4, rue Simon Maupin *M° Bellecour, off Rue de la République, opp. Bar du Centre, 1st floor* ☏ 04.78.38.19.27 🖳 sauna.bellecour.free.fr
Popular welcoming sauna, frequented by more mature men.

■ **Double Side** (AC B CC DR DU FC FH G GH I LAB M MA MSG NU P RR SA SB SH SL SOL VR VS W WH) 12-23, Fri & Sat -5h
8, rue Constantine *M° Hôtel de Ville, near Place des Terreaux*
☏ 04.78.29.85.22 🖳 www.doubleside.fr
750m². Very clean and good concept of design and services. 3rd Sat very popular bear day. See web for special events.

■ **Men Avenue** (B G MA SA SB) Mon-Sat 13-20h
4, rue des capucins ☏ 06.09.94.23.48 🖳 www.avenueomecs.com

■ **Oasis sauna**
(B CC DR DU FC FH G GH I MC NU P RR SA SB SL T VR VS WH) 12-20h
2, rue Coustou ☏ 04.78.28.02.21 🖳 www.saunaoasis.com
Renovated sauna with 3 floors. Very friendly owner. Highly frequented by married men.

■ **Suncity Lyon** (B CC DR DU G M MA PI RR SA SB VS WH WO)
Sun-Thu 13-3h
3 rue Sainte Marie des Terreaux *M° Hotel de Ville* ☏ 04.72.10.02.21
🖳 www.suncitylyon.com
The largest sauna in Lyon with 2000m² which opened in September 2009. The same owners as the famous Sun City sauna in Paris.

FASHION SHOPS

■ **Dessous d'apollon. les** (CC G MA SH) Mon 14-19, Tue-Fri 12-19h
20, rue Constantine *M° Hôtel de ville* ☏ 04.72.00.27.10
🖳 www.inderwear.com
Underwear, swimwear, sportswear, loungewear. Biggest choice with 3000 references and a lot of brands.

HOTELS

■ **Hôtel Le Patio des Terreaux** (AC BF CC glm M MC PK RWS RWT VA) All year
9, rue Sainte-Catherine *2 mins walk from the Town Hall & Opera House*
☏ 04.78.28.11.01 🖳 www.lepatiodesterreaux.fr
A wonderful hotel in the centre of Lyon, only two minutes walk from the town hall and the opera house. Twenty tastefully decorated rooms with all the modern facilities you would expect from an upper class hotel.

CRUISING

-Gare SNCF Part-Dieu
-Quais du Rhône (left side between Pont Morland & Pont de l'Université and especially in front of the sauna on Quai Jean Moulin and under the bridges, less popular, but also cruisy on the right side)
-Quais de la Saône (Quai St Vincent, Pêcherie, St Antoine)
-Parc de Parilly (WE)
-Parc de la Tête d'Or (botanical gardens & zoo, AYOR, reported assaults)
-Parc de Gerland (car park and football field)
-Place Arisitide Briand
-Place Guichard
-Place Antonin Jutard
-Place du Maréchal Lyautey
-Place du Prado
-Tennis courts in Gerland (22-4h summers; from avenue Leclerc, drive south, past Mercure Hotel, then straight (3 km) to Port Edouard Heriot, park on the left, crawl through holes in fence onto the sports grounds)

Mâcon

CRUISING

-Quai des Marans
-Quai Lamartine (above the Saône-river)

Marcingny

PRIVATE ACCOMMODATION

■ **Centre d'art contemporain** (G H I RWS RWT VA) All year
2 Place du Prieure, Paray-le-Monial *In the center of the village, behind the church* ☏ 03.85.25.11.03
Two fully equipped studios. The hosts are a German/Portugese gay couple.

Marseille

BARS

■ **Bazar. Le** (AC B D glm MA S)
90, Boulevard Rabatau

■ **Drôles 2 Dames. Les** (B gLm MA S VS)
Mon-Thu 19-24, Fri & Sat 19-2h
40, rue Ferrari *Located in Plaine, centre of Marseille* ☏ 06.85.48.54.25
With 70s Deco.

■ **Polikarpov** (AC B CC d glm OS VS) 8-2h
24 Estienne D' orves *M° Vieux Port* ☏ 04.91.52.70.30

■ **Un Tout Petit Monde** (AC B CC glm M) 9.30-18h, We closed
10 Bd Garibaldi *M° Noialles* ☏ 06.91.54.08.98
Gay friendly teesalon in Marseille

MEN'S CLUBS

■ **FSMC – Le Mineshaft** (AC b DR F G MA P VS)
Fri & Sat 23-?, 1st Sun/month 15-?h
28 rue Mazagran ☎ 04.91.48.49.34 🖳 www.lemineshaft.com
Leather sex-club with strict dress code (leather, jeans & latex).

■ **Trash. Le** (AC B CC d DR f G MA p S SNU VS) Sun, Mon, Wed, Thu 21-2; Fri & Sat 22-2h
28, rue du Berceau *M° Baille* ☎ 06 78 40 45 68
🖳 www.trash-bar.com
Sling, labyrinth, St. Andrew's cross, water sports facilities and showers. Various theme nights.

CAFES

■ **Caffe Noir** (AC B BF CC d GLM m MA OS S) Mon-Fri 8-20, Sun 16-24h
3, rue Moustier *M° Noailles, parking Julien* ☎ 04.91.04.08.66
🖳 cargo-club.fr
luxury decoration, music and great ambient

DANCECLUBS

■ **Baby. Le**
2, rue André Poggioli ☎ 06.16.72.78.94

■ **Mare au Diable. La** (B CC D G MA OS p s VS WE)
Fri & Sat and before holidays 23-?h
Chemin de Bon Rencontre, Allauch ☎ 04.91.68.24.10
🖳 lamareaudiablemarseille.fr
In a suburb of Marseille. Car or taxi required.

■ **New Cancan. The** (AC B CC D DR GLM p SNU ST VS WE)
Thu-Sun 23-?h
3-7 Rue Sénac *M° Réformés/Noailles* ☎ 04.91.48.59.76
🖳 www.newcancan.com
Popular gay disco in Marseille. Show every night.

■ **Spartacus. Le** (B D GLM MA ST)
Plan de Campagne ☎ 06.63.00.33.90 🖳 www.spartacus-club.com

RESTAURANTS

■ **Buvards. Les** (B CC glm M MC) Mon-Sat 10-2h, Sun closed
34 Grad'Rue *M° Vieux Port* ☎ 04.91.90.69.98
French cuisine.

■ **Casa No Name** (GLM M MA) Tue-Sat 19-?h
7, rue André Poggioli, 6ème ☎ 04.91.47.75.82 🖳 www.casanoname.com

■ **Danaides. Les** (B CC GLM I M MA OS) 7-22.30h
6, square de Stalingrad ☎ 04.91.62.28.51 🖳 www.lesdanaides.fr

SEX SHOPS/BLUE MOVIES

■ **E Shop** (AC b CC DR f MA p VS) 14-?h, Sun closed
11 rue Moustier *M° Noailles* ☎ 04.91.33.51.70

■ **Eros Center** (AC CC DR f G MC T VS) 9.30-24h
5 Boulevard Garibaldi *M° Noailles, corner of Canebière/Cours Lieutaud*
☎ 04.91.92.72.30 🖳 www.eroscenter13.com
Cruising on 650 m², 3 cinemas, labyrinth and cabines.

SAUNAS/BATHS

■ **Cargo** (AC B CC d DR DU FC G M MA NU P PI RR SA SB SH VS WH) 14-21, Fri & Sat -2, Sun 12-2h
7-9 rue Moustier *M° Noailles, parking Julien* ☎ 04.91.33.45.62
🖳 cargo-club.fr
A big gay sauna in the mediterranean.

■ **Club XY** (AC B CC DR DU FC G I M MA MSG PI SA SB SH SOL VS WH) Sun-Thu 12-24, Fri & Sat -2h
66, rue Montgrand *M° Estrangin-Prefecture, near the law courts*
☎ 04.91.04.68.36 🖳 www.xy-leclub.com
Very clean place with newspapers and WiFi free of charge.

■ **JL Olympic** (B CC DR DU FC FH G LAB m MA SA SB SOL VS)
12-20.30, Tue & Fri-Sat -24h
28, rue Jean Roque *M° Noailles* ☎ 04.91.47.35.61
Sauna on 3 floors with a maze.

■ **MP Sauna** (B CC DR DU f FC FH G m RR SA SB SH SL SOL VS WH)
12-22, Sat -24h
82 La Canebière *M° Noailles* ☎ 04.91.48.72.51
One of the larger gay saunas in Marseille.

■ **Salvator** (b DR DU FC FH G SA SB SL VS WH) 12-20.30h
20, boulevard Louis Salvator *M° Prefecture* ☎ 04.91.42.99.31
On 3 floors and over 300 m².

TRAVEL AND TRANSPORT

■ **Gayvasion** (GLM MA) Mon-Sat 9-18.30h
89, Avenue des Roches ☎ 04.91.14.20.20 🖳 www.gayvasion.com

GUEST HOUSES

■ **B&B Romain & Pascal** (BF GLM H I m MA OS PK RES RWT) All year
33, rue Falque *M° Castelanne* ☎ 06.77.94.34.50
🖳 www.bnbromainpascal.com
In the city centre of Marseille. A truely comfortable place to stay with great hosts.4 rooms and 6 studios

■ **BnB les Amis de Marseille** (B BF GLM I M MA OS PK RWS VA) All year
84 rue de Lodi Bât F *5 mins from bus and metro stops* ☎ 06.74.89.66.26
🖳 www.bnblesamisdemarseille.com
Located in a peaceful corner in the centre of the city, one stop from Gare Saint Charles. Close of the old harbour, shops, beaches and inlets. Big terrace with panoramic view.

PRIVATE ACCOMMODATION

■ **Petit Jardin. Le** (AC bf glm I MC OS RWB RWS) 17-20h
136, chemin du Vallon de l'Oriol *M° Vieux Port* ☎ 04.91.52.69.65
🖳 www.petitjardin.eu

SWIMMING

-Les Calanques de Sugiton (20 mins walking after the Luminy University parking)
-Plage du Mont Rose (direction Ponte Rouge, after Prado beach; follow Avenue Montredon, turn to the right at the chapel to get to the P in front of the beach; to get there by bus, take N° 21)

-Les Gaudes (east of Marseille)
-Madrague de Montredon (NU) (beach)
-Plage du Ponteau (In Martigues, north-west of Marseille, NU at the rocky beach).

CRUISING

-Place Sébastopol
-Rue George, Square Sidi-Brahim, Blvd Sakakini, Blvd Chave
-Canebière (sex-shop-galerie)
-M° Vieux-Port
-Parc Borely (P IBM). Dangerous at night (AYOR).

Maussanne

GUEST HOUSES

■ **Gay Holidays In France** (B BF CC GLM I M MA PI PK RWB RWS RWT WO) All year
Chemin du mas D'Isoard ☏ 04.90.43.30.59
🖳 www.gayholidaysinfrance.co.uk
Large heated pool, 5 en-suite bedrooms with UK satellite TV.

Menton

CRUISING

-The high Jetty along the old harbour (especially at night in summer)
-Avenue Winston Churchill (especially at night in summer)

Metz

SAUNAS/BATHS

■ **Blue Club** (b DR DU FC FH G NU SA SB VS) 14-22h, closed Tue
8, rue Sebastien Leclerc *200 m from SNCF station* ☏ 03.87.18.09.40

CRUISING

-Bon Secours (close to the hospital)
-Ile aux Moines
-Ile aux Papillons
-Ile de Saulcy
-Passage du Sablon
-Square de Luxembourg
-P „La Croue" (motorway Strasbourg-Paris)

Millau

CRUISING

-Jardin de la Gare (Avenue de la République towards Cahors)
-Quai de la Tonnerie (banks of Tarn).

Mimizan

CRUISING

-Public garden behind the church Mimizan Bourg (summer only)
-P Remembert (beach, summer only)

Montargis

RESTAURANTS

■ **Oh Terroir** (AC B CC g M MC) Tue-Sat 11.45-14 & 19-22h
44, rue J. Jaures ☏ 02.38.89.07.57 🖳 www.ohterroir.com

CRUISING

-Forest of Montargis (go in the direction of Nemours; the action is in front of the Château d'Eau)
-Forest between Lorris and Sully s/Loire (D 961, at approx. 6km after Lorris at the right side, action in the forest and at the P)

Montluçon

CRUISING

-Avenue Marx-Dormoy (gas station Mobil)
-Avenue de la Gare
-Esplanade du Vieux Château
-Jardin Wilson
-P du quai Louis-Blanc
-Place Pierre-Petit
-Bords du Cher/Parc des Expositions

Montpellier

PUBLICATIONS

■ **LOM**
BP 90011 ☏ 04.67.07.39.43 🖳 www.mps-mag.com

BARS

■ **B6 Bar** (AC B CC d DR G MA OS VS) Wed-Sat 18-1h
6, rue Cope Cambes ☏ 04.67.56.61.08 🖳 www.bearscave.fr
Former Bear's cave bar.
■ **Café de la Mer** (B GLM I MA OS) 8-1, Sun & holidays 15-1, Jul-Aug -2h
5 Place du Marché-aux-Fleurs ☏ 04.67.60.79.65
■ **Heaven. Le** (AC B CC d GLM MA) 18-1h
1 rue Delpech ☏ 04.67.60.44.18 ☏ 08.99.02.56.11
🖳 www.facebook.com/group.php?gid=39515069359
■ **Men's. Le** (AC B CC d GLM MA OS S T)
Daily 18-1h (in summer until 2h)
26 rue de Candolle *Tram Louis Blanc* ☏ 04.67.66.21.95
Theme evenings, on two floors.

MEN'S CLUBS

■ **Chantier. Le** (AC cc DR f G MA VS) 15.30-5, Sat 20-5, summer 17-5h
25-27 Rue J.J. Rousseau *Near Jardin des Plantes* ☏ 04.67.60.91.98
Sling, cabines, glory holes and labyrinths on 2 floors on 200 m².

DANCECLUBS

■ **Moom** (! AC B CC D DR FC G MA p T) Tue-Sat 00.30-6, Sun 1.30-7h
3, rue Collot *Near Jean Jaures place*
New straight-friendly danceclub. Centrally located. Very popular. Friendly party atmosphere.

■ **Pam. Le** (AC B D DR G P s ST T) Fri & Sat 23-6h
Parc D'issanka *20 km from Montpellier* ☎ 04.67.78.71.38
Shows on Fri & Sun.

■ **Studio. Le** (CC D DR GLM MA VS) Daily 24-7h
Route de palavas, Lattes ☎ 04.67.64.70.00 🖳 www.leStudioo.com

RESTAURANTS

■ **Cigales. Les** (cc G M MA)
Closed Sun afternoon & Mon, in winter closed Sun-Mon
1 rue des Teissiers *Near St Roch church* ☎ 04.67.68.48.34
Cuisine from the Provence. View in the kitchen. Historic dining hall in the basement for receptions.

■ **Coquille. La** (AC B bf CC glm M MA OS) 7.30-1h. Sun closed
1 Plan du Palais *Centre* ☎ 04.67.60.47.97 🖳 www.restolacoquille.fr
Café-restaurant.

■ **Jardin Restaurant. Au** (AC B CC DM glm M MA OS RES VEG WL)
Wed-Sun 12-14, 19-22.30
4, rue Philippy *In pedestrian zone* ☎ 04.67.66.14.17
🖳 www.aujardinrestaurant.fr

■ **Volodia. Le** (b CC g M MA S) Tue-Fri 12-14 & 19-22.30, Fri & Sat 19-24h
29, rue Jean Jacques Rousseau ☎ 04.99.61.09.17
🖳 www.volodiarestaurant.com
A trip back into the past.

SEX SHOPS/BLUE MOVIES

■ **Rex Vidéo** (AC CC g MA) Mon-Thu 10-midnight, Fri & Sat -1h
9 rue Cheval Vert ☎ 04.67.58.39.59
A second shop is at 12, rue Bayer, Montpellier.

SAUNAS/BATHS

■ **36 Sauna. Le** (AC B BF CC DR DU FC FH G GH I LAB M MA MSG NU p RR SA SB SL VR VS W WH) 12-1, Sun 5-1h (until 2h in summer)
36, rue Bourrély ☎ 04.67.59.83.14 🖳 www.sauna-le36.com
A very cruisy sauna on 600 m² and 2 floors frequented primarily by middle-aged men looking for action. Very clean and friendly. Breakfast offered on Sun.

■ **Koncept** (AC B BF CC DR DU FC FH G I LAB m MA MSG P RR SA SB SH SL VS WH WO) Mon-Sat 12-1 (-2 in summer), Sun 5-1h
10 avenue de Lodève ☎ 04.67.58.25.27 🖳 www.konceptsauna.fr
One of the biggest saunas in the region, 500 m² on 2 floors. Each Wed shower party, Tue campus party, First Fri/month bear party, Fourth Fri/month „Trash-Koncept Party".

■ **Sauna de la Gare** (b CC DU FC FH G m MA RR SA SB SL SOL VS) 12-1h
8, rue Levat *Near railway station* ☎ 04.67.58.61.42
Popular sauna with a sling room.

FASHION SHOPS

■ **Village. Le** (CC G MA) 12-19h, closed on Sun
3, rue Fournarié *Historic Centre* ☎ 09.54.34.91.70
Underwear, swimwear and streetwear.

HOTELS

■ **Arceaux** (AC b BF CC glm I M MA OS PA RWB RWS RWT)
All year, reception 7-1h
33-35, Boulevard des Arceaux *City centre* ☎ 04.67.92.03.03
🖳 www.hoteldesarceaux.com

■ **Guilhem. Le** (AC B BF CC DU FC FH GLM H I M MA NR OS PA PK RES RWS RWT VA) All year
18 rue Jean-Jacques Rousseau *Near Palais de Justice, bus 16 exit Peyrou, tram exit Albert 1er* ☎ 04.67.52.90.90 🖳 www.leguilhem.com
Rooms with phone, TV and mini-bar in the historic centre. BF until 13h. Located right in the historical centre of Montpellier, only a few steps from the Promenade du Peyrou.

■ **Hotel d'Aragon** (AC BF CC GLM H PK RES RWS RWT VA WI)
All year
10 rue Baudin *Montpellier Saint Roch Railway Station – 0,5 km, Montpellier Airport – 10 km* ☏ 04.67.10.70.00 🖳 www.hotel-aragon.fr
A haven of elegance, French charm and peace. Warm environment and sophisticated atmosphere with modern technology (Flat screen TV, free Internet WiFi). A non-smoking hotel.

GUEST HOUSES

■ **4 étoiles, Les** (BF DU GLM H I MA NR OS p PK RES RR RWS RWT VA)
all year
3, rue Delmas *Centrally located* ☏ 04.67.02.47.49
🖳 www.les4etoiles.com
4 22m² rooms designed by different famous designers. Gay owned. Kitchen and piano at disposition.

■ **Cinq & Sept** (AC B CC G I M MA MSG OS p PI PK RWS RWT WO)
All year
5 & 7 Ave Henri Mas *50 mins from Montpellier* ☏ 06.32.86.57.52
🖳 www.cinqetsept.com
Exclusive gay guest house run by an English gay couple. 5 luxurious suites in an 18th century ,Maison Bourgeoisie' around a heated pool and garden ,summer kitchen' with lounge area and bar.

■ **Patio34. Le** (AC B BF CC g MA OS PI SA SOL WH WO)
25 Av. Moulin deTourtourel ☏ 04.67.27.46.03 🖳 www.lepatio34.fr
5 rooms and 4 apartments.

■ **Villa Ragazzi** (B BF DM DU FC G H I M MA MSG NU OS p PI PK RES RR RWB RWS RWT VA VEG) Mar-Oct
2 Impasse des Chênes Verts *Between Nîmes & Montpellier*
☏ 04.66.88.93.72 🖳 www.villaragazzi.com
Close to the beach l'Espiguette. There is a great outdoor bar next to the pool where „pool afternoons" are organised and naked sunbathing is permitted.

SWIMMING

-Beach (between Théâtre de la Mer and La Corniche)
-Beach of Grand Travers (NU) (between la Grande Motte & Carnou)
-Beach of Aresquiers/Frontignan (NU) (after parking lot ca. 2 km towards Palavas)
-Au Bois Joli (on the left side of the nudist camping site)
-Villeneuve les Maguelonne

CRUISING

-Beaux-Arts garden
-Around University Hospital
-Montmaur forest (on the way to Mende, near the ice rink, the zoo and the university)
-Parcours de Santé de Bois Joli
-Place des Arceaux (car cruising)
-Le Polygone
-Le Grand Travers, Dunes between roads D62 and D59 east of Carnon-Plage (early evening)
-La Promenade du Peyrou (lower level, no action possible).

Morlaix

CRUISING

-Viaduc (in the evening)
-Aire de Douron (on the RN 12, popular)
-Aire Saint-Servais (on the RN 12, between Morlaix & Brest, near Landivisiau. Popular)

Mulhouse

BARS

■ **Spart Bar** (B g MA OS p) 22-4h, closed Tue
50 Rue de l'Arsenal *Old town* ☏ 03.89.45.40.72 🖳 www.spartbar.fr

DANCECLUBS

■ **Jet 7 club**
47, rue de la Sinne ☏ 06.66.02.34.03 🖳 www.jet7club.fr

SAUNAS/BATHS

■ **Digitale** (b DU FC g MC PI RR SA SB)
Sun & Mon 14-22, Tue-Fri -23, Sat -24h
11, rue Lamartine *On corner with rue de la Sinne* ☏ 03.89.46.12.45
🖳 www.club-digitale.com
Not a gay sauna. Mixed sauna.

■ **Sauna Club LG** (B DR DU FC FH G m MA RR SA SB SL VS) 14-23; Mon, Wed & Sun -21h
8, quai D'Oran *Near central station, opp. Hotel Ibis* ☏ 03.89.36.01.02

Nancy

BARS

■ **Place. La** (AC B cc d glm MA s) 22-4h
7 Place Stanislas ☏ 03.83.35.62.63

■ **Unik. L'**
9, rue Jean Lamour ☏ 03.83.36.95.52 🖳 www.unikbar.com

SEX SHOPS/BLUE MOVIES

■ **Xshop Club 87** (AC b DR f G MA VS) 11-1, Sun 14-21h
87, rue Jeanne D'Arc *Bus Place de la Croix de Bourgogne, tram Mondésert*
☏ 03.83.28.67.70 🖳 www.xshop-nancy.com

CRUISING

-Aire de Villers-Clairieu (A33 ⇆, very popular, all day)
-On the banks of the Canal de la Marne
-Parc de la Pépinière (near the Caserne Thiry)
-Place Stanislas

Nantes

BARS

■ **203 Bar** (B GLM MC) Mon 19-2, Tue-Sun 15-2h
8 rue des Carmelites ☏ 09.81.71.93.49

■ **Casa Loca. La**
1, rue Kervégan ☏ 06.61.91.79.72

■ **Ferry. Le** (B GLM M) 10-15, 17.30-2h
15 rue du Bâtonnier Guinaudeau *In front of Pont Anne de Bretagne*
☏ 02.40.73.59.79
Also restaurant.

■ **Petit Marais. Le** (B CC GLM MC VS) 17-2h
15 rue Kervégan ☏ 02.40.20.15.25

■ **Plein Sud. Le** (B CC FC G I MA OS PA WL) 15-2h
2 rue Prémion *100m from cathedral* ☏ 02.40.47.06.03
24 years old bar. Friendly staff. Perfect place to take an aperitif with friends. Good prices. Direct view of the castle.

MEN'S CLUBS

■ **Autre Quai. L'** (AC B d F G MA P SOL VS) 22-4h
68 Quai de la Fosse *Tram Chantier Naval* ☏ 02.40.71.68.05
🖳 www.lautrequai.com
With slings and cabins.

■ **Block Men** (B DR G MA VS) 19-4h
3 rue Ogée ☏ 02.40.12.16.87 🖳 www.blockmen.blogspot.com
With cabins and a labyrinth.

DANCECLUBS

■ **Temps d'Aimer. Le** (AC cc D GLM MA ST) 24-7h
14 rue Alexandre-Fourny ☏ 02.40.89.48.60 🖳 www.letandem.com

RESTAURANTS

■ **Comptoirs d'armorique. Les** (CC DM GLM m PA RES SH)
Tue-Sat 16-22h
55, rue du Maréchal Joffre ☏ 06.86.17.03.45
🖳 comptoirsdarmorique.blogspot.com
Between a restaurant and a wine shop. Restaurant offers national wines and seasonal products.

SEX SHOPS/BLUE MOVIES

■ **Boîte à Films. La** (AC DR G MA T VS) 10-2, Sun 12-1h
16bis Allée du Commandant-Charcot *Near train station*
☎ 02.40.37.03.03
Tue: gay evening, Thu: darkroom evening.

SAUNAS/BATHS

■ **Aqua Sauna Club. L'** (AC AK B CC DR DU FC FH G GH I LAB M MA MSG NU p P RR SA SB SH SL SOL VR VS WH) 13-1, Sat 14-2, Sun -1h
8, quai de Turenne *Opp. Hospital CHU* ☎ 02.40.74.67.62
💻 www.aqua-sauna.com
Very pleasing place on two floors in a warm atmosphere with smoking room. Mon and Fri after 21h: mixed sauna, not just gay men!

■ **Steamer. Le** (AC AK B CC FC FH G GH I LAB M MA NU P PI RR SA SB SH SL SOL VR VS WH) 14-1, Mon -20, Sat -2h
4bis, rue Baron *Near Palais des Congrès and CHU* ☎ 02.53.45.79.75
💻 www.lesteamer.com
Very clean & nice design. Large pool, jacuzzi & cruising area on two floors. Friendly staff.

CRUISING

-Galerie Beaulieu
-🅿 Beaujoire (near the stadium)
-Place Louis-XVI (Cours St.Pierre, St.André)
-Parc de Procès (at night)
-Square Elisa-Mercoeur (Allée Baco, near the bus terminal)
-Beaulieu (at the far end of Ile-aux-Tours)
-Along the river Erdre (in the bushes behind the university buildings)

Narbonne

CRUISING

-Pont de l'Avenir
-Jardin du palais du travail
-Cours Mirabeau
-beach of St Cyprien.

Nevers

BARS

■ **Soft** Tue-Sun 22-2h
10, rue du champ-de-Foire ☎ 03.86.23.96.90
💻 http://www.facebook.com/pages/Nevers-France/Soft-music-bar/132609891201?v=info

RESTAURANTS

■ **Tandem Café** (B CC g H M) Tue-Sat 8-20h
7, place Guy Coquille 💻 www.tandemcafe.fr

SAUNAS/BATHS

■ **Equatorial sauna Nevers, L'** (B DR DU FH G GH LAB M MA NU OS PK RR SA SB SL VR VS WH)
13.00-20, Wed, Thu & Sun -22, Fri & Sat -24h
4ter, rue de la Passière *Near railway station Nevers* ☎ 03.86.59.55.56
💻 www.lequatorialsauna.com
Renovated and new owner. Most popular sauna of the region.

CRUISING

-Parc Roger Salengro (at night)
-Banks of the Loire (especially Chemin du Ver-Vert, outside of town, all day)
-Porte du Croux

Nice

BARS

■ **Civette du Cours. La** (B glm MC OS)
1, cours Saleya ☎ 04.93.80.80.59
The best place to sit outside, to see and be seen!

■ **Fard. Le** (AC B CC GLM OS YC) 18-2.30h, closed on Mon
25 Prommenade des Anglais *Between the Palais de la Mediterranee & Le Negresco* ☎ 04.93.80.63.40 💻 www.lefard.com
A new gay bar on the beach front. Friday house music starting at 21h. Saturday is electro music, with guest DJs and Sunday is theme parties with music from the 60s to 90s.

■ **Glam. Le** (AC B CC GLM M MA p ST VS WE) Fri-Sun 22.30-2.30h
6, rue Eugène Emanuel *City centre* ☎ 06.60.55.26.61
💻 www.leglam.org
Gallery, lounge and café on two floors with vernissages and live DJ. Best at WE.

■ **L'Hypnotic Café** (B CC d GLM MA)
2, rue Rusca ☎ 04.93.89.46.25

■ **Six. Le** (AC CC GLM MA P) 22-3.30h, closed Mon
6 rue Raoul Bosio *Near the opera and Marché aux Fleurs*
☎ 04.93.62.66.64 💻 www.le6.fr
Mister Gay 2010 is working here as a barman!

■ **Smarties** (AC B CC D G I MA OS) 18-2.30h
10, rue Defly *City centre* ☎ 04.93.62.30.75 💻 www.nice-smarties.com
Happy hour Mon 18-21h.

■ **ThyJeff's Café** (B GLM MA) 8-21h, closed Sun
7 rue Emmanuel Philibert *At Place du Pin* ☎ 04.93.55.25.35
💻 www.thyjeff.fr

MEN'S CLUBS

■ **Eagle** (AC AK B DR G MC NU p SL SNU VS) 21-2.30h
18bis rue Emmanuel Philibert *At the harbour* ☎ 04.93.26.35.30
🖳 www.eagle-nice.com

■ **Malabar Station** (! AC CC DR DU F G MA p S T VS)
21.30-2.30h
10 rue Bonaparte *Between the Port de Nice and Place Garibaldi*
☎ 09.51.18.53.52 🖳 www.malabar-station.com
Cruising bar with 8 cabins and showers. Sun/underwear Party, 1st Sun/month naked party. Terrasse open at WE.

■ **Morgan** (AC B CC d DR F G m MA MSG P S SNU VS)
22-2.30h and 4h at WE
3, rue Claudia *100 m of the english promenade* ☎ 06.31.60.37.13
☎ 06.08.77.39.87 🖳 www.morganclub.fr

DANCECLUBS

■ **Blue Boy. Le**
9, rue Jean-Baptiste Spinetta ☎ 04.93.44.68.24

RESTAURANTS

■ **Autre chose** (BF DM G M MA OS PA T VEG WL)
8, rue Bonaparte ☎ 04.93.14.49.01
90% of the diners are gay. There is always a very good atmosphere. Owned by a very crazy, gay- friendly woman, who takes part in the local gay events.

■ **Côté Marais** (DM glm M MA OS RES WL) 20-23h
4 rue du Pontin *Old town* ☎ 04.93.80.95.39
Traditional French cuisine.

■ **Domino. Le** (! AC B CC DM GLM LM M MA OS PA RES T WE)
20 rue Bonaparte ☎ 04.93.55.99.01
New. Gay owned. Concept: 5 € for 1 drink and cold buffet. Very crowded and friendly staff. Delicious cuisine.

■ **Pierre Bise. La** (AC CC GLM M MC OS T) 20-?h
5, rue Barillerie ☎ 04.93.53.44.94 🖳 www.lapierrebise.com

■ **Pinxcho** (AC B bf CC glm M MC OS)
7 rue Bonaparte *Near place Garibaldi* ☎ 04.93.89.81.83
🖳 www.pinxcho.com

■ **Rubis. Le** (AC B CC g M MA OS)
36, Boulevard Risso ☎ 04.93.26.92.88 🖳 www.lerubis.fr

■ **Tart'arts** (AC B BF CC DM G I M MA OS PA RES VEG W WL)
9, rue Bonaparte ☎ 04.93.89.90.54
Very friendly gay owned new restaurant. Very popular and good tasting food. Organise many gay events.

SEX SHOPS/BLUE MOVIES

■ **G.I. Sex Shop** (AC CC DR f G MA VS)
10-24, Sun & public holidays 14-20h
8 rue Descente Crotti *Place Masséna/Vieille Ville/near Palais de Justice*
☎ 04.93.80.29.49 🖳 www.gi-sexshop.com
Videos, gadgets and cruising on 4 floors. Big screen cinema and latest DVDs.

SAUNAS/BATHS

■ **7. Le** (AC B DR DU FC FH G LAB m MA RR SA SB SH VS WH) 13-21h
7, rue Foncet *Near Poste Wilson, bus 7/15* ☎ 04.93.62.25.02
Popular sauna on three floors with maze.

■ **Bains Douches**
(AC B DR DU FC FH G LAB M MA NU p RR SA SB VR VS WH) 13-22h
7, rue Gubernatis *Near Place Masséna, bus Félix Faure* ☎ 04.93.80.28.26
A large sauna on three floors with a big whirlpool and many cublicles free of charge. Reasonably priced entrance fees. Condoms and lube available for free.

■ **Block. Le** (! b CC DR DU FC FH G GH I LAB MA p SA SB SL VR VS)
Mon-Thu 20-4, Fri & Sat -7, Sun 14-4h
10-12 rue Jules Gilly *Near Cours Saleya* ☎ 04.93.80.18.55
🖳 www.sauna-cruising-nice.com
New renoved sauna and sex club on 3 floors. No alcohol available. Very friendly staff. beautiful jacuzzi.

Nice
EAT & DRINK
Civette. La – Bar 4
Côté Marais – Restaurant 9
Domino – Restaurant 11
Fard. Le – Bar 3
Glam – Bar 2
Pierre Bise. Le – Restaurant 6
Pinxcho – Restaurant 15
Six. Le – Bar 7
NIGHTLIFE
Eagle – Men's Club 13
Malabar Station – Men's Club 14
SEX
7. Le – Sauna 5
Block. Le – Sauna 10
G.I. – Sex Shop/Blue Movies 8
ACCOMMODATION
Connexion – Hotel 1
Baie des Anges
Plages
Le Château
Port
Phare
Gare Nice Ville
Place Masséna
Place Garibaldi
Théâtre/Acropolis
Promenade des Anglais
Quai des Etats-Unis
Quai Rauba
Quai Lunel
Quai Papacino
Boulevard de Frank Pilatte
Bd. de Stalingrad
Boulevard de Riquier
Rue de la République
Rue Barla
Cassini
Rue Emanuel Philibert
Boulevard Russo
Avenue Gallieni
Boulevard Carabacel
Boulevard Dubouchage
Rue Blacas
Avenue Felix Faure
Boulevard Jean Jaurès
Rue de la Prefecture
Rue Droite
Rue Raoul Bosio
Avenue Jean Médecin
Rue de Paris
Avenue Notre Dames
Avenue Marechal Foch
Av. Clemenceau
Avenue Thiers
Boulevard Victor Hugo
Rue du Marechal Joffre
Rue de la Liberté
Rue de la Buffa
Rue de France
Rue du Congres
Rue de Rivoli
Boulevard Gambetta
Ave Gambetta
Rue St. Philippe
Rue des Potiers
Rue Bottero
Avenue des Fleurs
F. Grosso

■ **Cercle. Le** (B CC DR DU F FC FH G I LAB M MA MSG NU p RR SA SB SH SL VS WH) Mon-Fri 13-24, Sat 14-4, Sun -22h
16 avenue Clement Ader *Tram-Gorbella* ☎ 04.93.51.88.39
🖳 www.gay-sauna-nice.com
800m2 area. mixed sauna. Relaxed atmosphere, spacious, clean and hygienic. Special event nights for Swingers, Foam Parties, Naked nights and more. Sun sex parties are very popular.

BODY & BEAUTY SHOPS

■ **BCM Concept store** (AC CC DU G MA MSG SH)
6, rue Bonaparte ☎ 09.50.41.99.31 🖳 www.bcm-conceptstore.fr
Combination of a concepstore with different english designers and a beauty welness shop offering facials and body care.

FASHION SHOPS

■ **BCM Concept store** (AC CC DU G MA MSG SH)
6, rue Bonaparte ☎ 09.50.41.99.31 🖳 www.bcm-conceptstore.fr
Combination of a concepstore with different english designers and a beauty welness shop offering facials and body care.

HOTELS

■ **Connexion** (AC AK BF CC F G H MA p RES RWS RWT SL VA WI)
Reception: 9-20h
65 rue de la Buffa *City centre* ☎ 04.93.88.99.46
🖳 www.connexionhotelnice.com
First 100% gay hotel at the French Riviera. Ideally located in the centre of Nice and 100 m from a gay beach.

GUEST HOUSES

■ **Absolu Living Nice** (AC CC GLM I MA MSG OS PA PI RWB RWS RWT SOL VA) All year, 10-19h
7 rue Jules Gilly ☎ 04.93.87.30.64 🖳 www.absoluliving.com
45 stylish apartments situated in the heart of the „Bay of the angels", the center of Nice.

■ **Eden Bleu. L'** (AC b bf G I m MA NU OS PI PK RWB RWS RWT SOL VS) All year
17, Chemin des Myrtes, Beaulieu-sur-Mer *Located between Nice & Monaco* ☎ 04.93.01.21.15 🖳 www.edenbleu.net
Three double rooms with shower/WC, TV/DVD, mini-bar and own key. Reservation required.

■ **Mas des Oliviers** (b BF cc glm I MA NU OS PI PK RWB RWS VA WO) All year, check in from 16.30h onwards
350, Chemin de Crémat ☎ 04.93.52.22.60
🖳 www.masdesoliviers-nice.com
Gay owned B&B on the hills over Nice, 10 minutes drive from airport. 4 large rooms, pool, TV room, terraces, tennis nearby. Cannes & Monaco 25 minutes drive.

■ **Relais du Peyloubet** (BF GLM I MA OS p PI PK RES RWB RWS RWT SOL VA WH) All year, reception 17-19h
65 Chemin de la Platière *In Grasse, 15 km from Nice* ☎ 06.16.90.67.39
🖳 www.relais-peyloubet.com
Traditional country house, bf incl. warmed swimmingpool.

APARTMENTS

■ **Tart'arts** (AC CC DU FC G H I M OS PA RES RWB RWS RWT VA VEG)
9, rue Bonaparte ☎ 04.93.89.90.54
Located in the gay street center of the city. Flat 40m² and 15m² terrasse. For guests there is a special price for dinner in the restaurant downstairs.

SWIMMING

-Coco Beach/Cap Nice (NU) (Bus at harbour to Coco Beach, small staircase down, climb rocky beach to the left)
-Jetée du port (NU)
-Near the lighthouse (NU)
-Plage des Pissarelles (500 m before Cap d'Ail, on the road to Monaco).

CRUISING

-Aire de Briguières
-Aire du Piccolaret

-Around the lighthouse (day and evening, all year)
-Parc Ferber / Promenade des Anglais
-Parc du Château
-Rue Masséna, Avenue Jean-Médecin (afternoon)
-Square Alsace-Lorraine.

Nîmes

BARS

■ **Cathédral. Le** (B d GLM MA s) 14-24h
Place des Carmes ☎ 06.64.80.04.38 🖳 www.lacathedral-bar.com

DANCECLUBS

■ **Lulu Club** (! AC CC D DR G MA P SNU VS) Fri & Sat 1-7h
10 Impasse de la Curaterie *5 mins walk from the station*
☎ 04.66.36.28.20 🖳 www.lulu-club.com
See their website for more information on events and parties.

RESTAURANTS

■ **5 Sens** (b CC DM glm M MA OS PA VEG WE WL)
12-14.30 & 19-22.30h
44 Boulevard Gambetta *Near to Coupule des Halles* ☎ 04.66.23.31.97

SEX SHOPS/BLUE MOVIES

■ **X Center**
27, boulevard Talabot

SAUNAS/BATHS

■ **Nîmes Club Sauna** (AC AK B CC DM DU FC FH G I LAB M MA NU P p RR SA SB SL SOL VR VS WH) Daily 12-24h
7/9, rue Fernand-Pelloutier *Behind Carré d'Art* ☎ 04.66.67.65.18
🖳 www.nimesclubsauna.fr
Sauna with shop. Theme nights last Sat/month 24-7h. Free solarium. Entrance ticket available all day long.

■ **Sauna Fahrenheit 212** (AC B CC DR DU FC FH G LAB M MA MSG PI RR SA SB VS WO) 12-24h
1606, avenue Marechal Juin *1 km from the autoroute exit Nîmes-Ouest*
☎ 04.66.38.24.76 🖳 www.fahrenheit212.fr
Very unfriendly place.

CRUISING

-Boulevard Jean-Jaurès
-Gorges du Gardon, at Collias (25 km) NE of Nimes via motorway Nîmes-Uzès (at 🅿 Gardon, Pont St. Nicolas then walk about 1-2 km in direction to the river, also nude bathing)
-Jardin La Fontaine (afternoon, evenings)
-Le Grau du Roi
-Plage de l'Espiguette.

Niort

BARS

■ **Insomnia. L'**
222, rue de Ribray ☎ 05.49.73.50.01

CRUISING

-Halles (🅿 du Moulin du Milieu)
-Jardin des Plantes
-Petit bois de la Tranchée (2 km from Niort, take road N 10 direction Bordeaux)
-Place St-Jean
-Place de la Brèche.

Orange

HOTELS

■ **Hôtel le Louvre** (AC B BF CC glm I M MA OS PA PI PK RWS RWT) All year
89 Avenue Frédéric Mistral ☎ 04.90.34.10.08
🖳 www.hotel-louvre-orange.com
Rooms with bath or shower/WC, mini-bar, phone, TV, bf at additionnal charge.

GUEST HOUSES

■ **Mas Julien. Le** (AC B BF glm H I M MA OS PA PI PK RWS WH WO) All year
704 Chemin de Saint Jean *5 km from Orange and Chateauneuf du Papes, 25 km from Avignon, Airport* ☎ 04.90.34.99.49
🖳 www.mas-julien.com
Five-room hotel in the Provence.

■ **Villa Aurenjo** (BF H I) All year
121, rue François Chambovet – BP 136 ☎ 04.90.11.10.00
🖳 www.villa-aurenjo.com
In the heart of the Antique Roman City of Orange, this beautiful gayfriendly residence sits amidst one hectare of enclosed grounds through which a creek flows, filled with magnolias, olive trees, and hundred-year old sycamores. There is a pool and tennis court as well.

Orléans

CRUISING

-Quai St-Laurent
-La Source (take the road RN 20, you find it on the right side behind the hospital; crossing in front of the Novotel)
-Bois de Semoy

Paris

Paris is famous for its breathtaking architecture and cultural lifestyle, thanks to the many museums and theatres as well as the romantic historical centre on the river Seine. Each year over 36 million tourists visit the French metropolis. Paris is a cosmopolitan and extremely tolerant city, open to the gay and lesbian lifestyle. Here you will find everything on offer: from bars, gay saunas, sex clubs or other meeting places for gay men. The annual Gay Pride is one of the largest of its kind in Europe, where even the gay mayor of Paris is a participant. Discover and enjoy the exciting gay life of Paris, until recently only in the „Marais" area, where most of the initial gay places were to be found. Nowadays the gay scene is spread out throughout the city.
Even though the bars are often open until the early hours of the morning, take into account that the Métro (underground) has no service between 1am and 5.30am and a taxi or night bus is the alternative. Even though the weather is sometimes somewhat grey and rainy, Paris remains one of the more important travel destinations for gay men.

Paris ist berühmt für seine atemberaubende Architektur und sein kulturelles Leben dank der zahlreichen Museen und Theater sowie seines romantischen historischen Zentrums an der Seine. Jedes Jahr kommen über 36 Millionen Touristen in die französische Metropole. Paris ist weltoffen und äußerst tolerant und schwulen Lebensformen sehr aufgeschlossen. Hier findet der Besucher alles im Überangebot: Ob Bars, schwule Saunen, Sexclubs oder sonstige Treffpunkte für Gays. Jedes Jahr findet hier einer der größten Gay Prides in Europa statt, an dem auch der schwule Pariser Bürgermeister teilnimmt. Entdecke und genieße das aufregende schwule Leben in Paris, lange Zeit nur mit dem Bezirk „Marais" verbunden, wo anfangs die meisten schwulen Lokale gegründet wurden. Mittlerweile hat sich die schwule Szene und Kultur über die gesamte Stadt verbreitet. Auch wenn die Bars bis früh in den Morgen geöffnet bleiben, ist zu bedenken, dass die Metro zwischen 1h und 5.30h nicht in Betrieb ist und man auf Taxi oder Nachtbus angewiesen ist. Zwar ist das Wetter manchmal grau und regnerisch, dennoch bleibt Paris eines der wichtigsten Reiseziele für Schwule.

Paris est célèbre pour son architecture époustouflante, son centre-ville historique romantique au bord de la Seine ainsi que sa vie culturelle des plus riches offrant aux touristes de nombreux musées et théâtres. Chaque année, plus de 36 millions de touristes visitent cette

Parc de Monceau
Boulevard de Batignolles
Rue de Rome
Rue de Clichy
Rue Blanche
Rue de Londres
Gare St-Lazare
Boulevard Pereire
Rue Pierre Demours
Avenue Niel
Avenue de Wagram
Boulevard de Courcelles
Rue du Faubourg Saint-Honoré
Boulevard Malesherbes
Boulevard Haussmann
Rue La Boétie
Av. de la Grande Armée
Arc de Triomphe
Place Charles de Gaulle
Avenue de Friedland
Avenue Foch
Avenue Victor Hugo
Avenue Kléber
Avenue Marceau
Avenue George V
Avenue des Champs Elysées
Rue de Ponthieu
Palais de l'Elysée
Avenue Gabriel
Opéra
Bvd. des Capucines
Rue Saint-Honoré
Rue de Rivoli
Av. Raymond Poincaré
Avenue d'Iéna
Grand Palais
Place de la Concorde
Musée d'Art Moderne
Cours la Reine
Jardin des Tuileries
Place du Trocadéro
Palais de Chaillot
Pont des Invalides
Pont Alex III
Pont de la Concorde
Quai des Tuileries
Place de la Résistance
Quai d'Orsay
Avenue de New York
Quai Anatole France
Bvd. St-Germain
Rue de l'Université
Pont d'Iéna
Rue Saint-Dominique
Pont Royal
Q. Voltaire
Seine
Quai Branly
Tour Eiffel
Avenue Bosquet
Boulevard de la Tour-Maubourg
Rue de Grenelle
Avenue de la Bourdonnais
Pont de Bir-Hakeim
Champ de Mars
Hôtel des Invalides
Boulevard des Invalides
Rue de Varenne
Boulevard St-Germain
Boulevard Raspail
Avenue de Suffren
Avenue de Tourville
Avenue de la Motte
Ecole Militaire
Avenue de Lowendal
Avenue de Ségur
Avenue de Breteuil
Rue de Babylone
Boulevard de Grenelle
Rue de Sèvres
Rue du Cherche Midi
Rue de Rennes
Rue Fondary
Rue du Commerce
Av. Emile Zola
Rue Chambronne
Boulevard Garibaldi
Place de Breteuil
Rue de Vaugirard
Byd. Montparnasse
Place du 18 Juin 1940
Rue Lecourbe
Square St-Lambert
M
1
2
3
4
5
10
13
16

Paris – City
EAT & DRINK
48 Condorcet. Le – Restaurant 9
Petit Batignolles. Le – Bar 5
NIGHTLIFE
Boys Video Club – Men's Club 18
Entre deux Eaux – Men's Club 13
Mec Zone. Le – Men's Club 8
Queen – Danceclub 10
SEX
Atlantide – Sauna 17
King – Sauna 4
Mykonos – Sauna 7
Steamer – Sauna 3
ACCOMMODATION
Francois 1er – Hotel 1
Hidden – Hotel 16
Hôtel le 20 Prieuré – Hotel 14
Keppler – Hotel 2
Paname – Hotel 15
See map A
See map B
Place Pigalle
Bvd. de Rochechouart
Boulevard de la Chapelle
Gare du Nord
Gare de l'Est
Boulevard de Magenta
Rue du Faubourg St-Denis
Rue du Faubourg Poissonnière
Rue N.D. de Lorette
Rue La Fayette
Rue J. B. Pigalle
Place du Colonel Fabien
Av. Jean Jaurès
Boulevard de la Villette
Hôpital Saint-Louis
Quai de Valmy
Quai de Jemmapes
Rue de la Grange
Rue du Faubourg St-Martin
Rue du Fauborg du Temple
Avenue Parmentier
Rue Saint Maur
Bvd. St-Martin
Place de la République
Bvd. J. Ferry
Bvd. R. Lenoir
Avenue de la République
Rue Oberkampf
Rue Réaumur
Rue de Turbigo
Rue Beaubourg
Rue du Temple
Rue de Rambuteau
Forum des Halles
Centre Pompidou
Archives Nationales
Rue Saint-Honoré
Musée du Louvre
Pont des Arts
Quai des Tuilleries
Pont Neuf
Q. de Conti
Q. de G. Augustins
Malaquais
Palais de Justice
Rue de Rivoli
Rue des Fr. Bourgeois
Quai Hôtel de Ville
Rue St-Antoine
Notre Dame
Quai de la Tournelle
Place de la Bastille
Opéra de Paris Bastille
Rue du Fbg. St-Antoine
Boulevard Voltaire
Rue du Chemin Vert
Rue de la Roquette
Quai Henri IV
Avenue Daumesnil
Rue de Bercy
Quai de la Rapée
Gare de Lyon
Pont d'Austerlitz
Quai d'Austerlitz
Gare d'Austerlitz
Seine

Paris – Map A Les Halles

EAT & DRINK

Alexander's – Bar	4
Aux Trois Petits Cochons – Restaurant	21
Champmeslé. Le – Bar	7
Lézard – Café	20
Loup Blanc. Le – Restaurant	22
Marc Mitonne – Restaurant	17
Pig'z – Restaurant	23

NIGHTLIFE

Club 18 – Danceclub	8
Next – Men's Club	18

SEX

Euro Men's Club – Sauna	3
Gym Louvre – Sauna	15
Hammam Boulevards – Sauna	2
IDM – Sauna	1
Suncity – Sauna	24
Til't – Sauna	12

ACCOMMODATION

Apartment4Gay – Apartments	26
Louvre Richelieu – Hotel	9

OTHERS

Abraxas – Piercing & Tatoo	13

capitale française extrêmement tolérante. Les gays y trouveront des bars, des saunas, des sexclubs et d'autres lieux de rencontre. Chaque année a lieu une des plus grandes Gay Pride d'Europe à laquelle participe le maire parisien. Si, autrefois, ce n'était que dans le « Marais » que l'on trouvait la grande majorité des lieux gays parisiens, on en trouve entre-temps dans toute la ville. Même si la plupart des bars restent ouverts jusqu'au petit matin, il ne faut pas oublier que le métro ne roule pas entre 1h00 et 5h30 du matin et que seuls les bus de nuit et les taxis permettent de regagner ses pénates. Le temps est certes parfois gris et pluvieux, mais Paris reste une des destination les plus importantes pour les homos.

París es conocido por su maravillosa arquitectura y la vida cultural gracias a sus museos y teatros así como su romántico centro histórico en el Sena. Anualmente llegan más de 36 millones de turistas a la metrópolis francesa. París está abierta al mundo, es tolerante y diversa con la vida homosexual. Aquí el visitante encontrará de todo: desde bares, saunas gays, clubs de sexo u otros puntos de encuentro gays. Cada año se celebra una de las mayores fiestas gays de Europa, en la que también participa el alcalde homosexual de la ciudad.
Descubre y disfruta del excitante ambiente gay de París, hasta hace poco sólo asociado al barrio del „Marais", donde al principio abrieron la mayoría de locales gays. Entretanto el ambiente y la cultura gay se extendió por toda la ciudad. Aunque los bares están abiertos hasta la madrugada, recuerda que el metro no funciona entre la 1h y las 5h30 y deberás tomar un taxi o el autobús nocturno. El clima puede ser a veces gris y lluvioso pero París sigue siendo uno de los destinos gays más importantes.

Parigi è famosa per la sua architettura mozzafiato, per la sua vita culturale, per i suoi numerosi musei e teatri e per il suo romantico centro storico sulla Senna. La metropoli francese è visitata ogni anno da più di 36 milioni di turisti. Parigi è una metropoli cosmopolita, tollerante e molto aperta nei confronti dell'omosessualità. Qui i turisti troveranno una vastissima offerta: bar, saune gay, locali a luci rosse e molti altri luoghi di incontro per gay. Ogni anno si svolge a Parigi uno dei gay pride

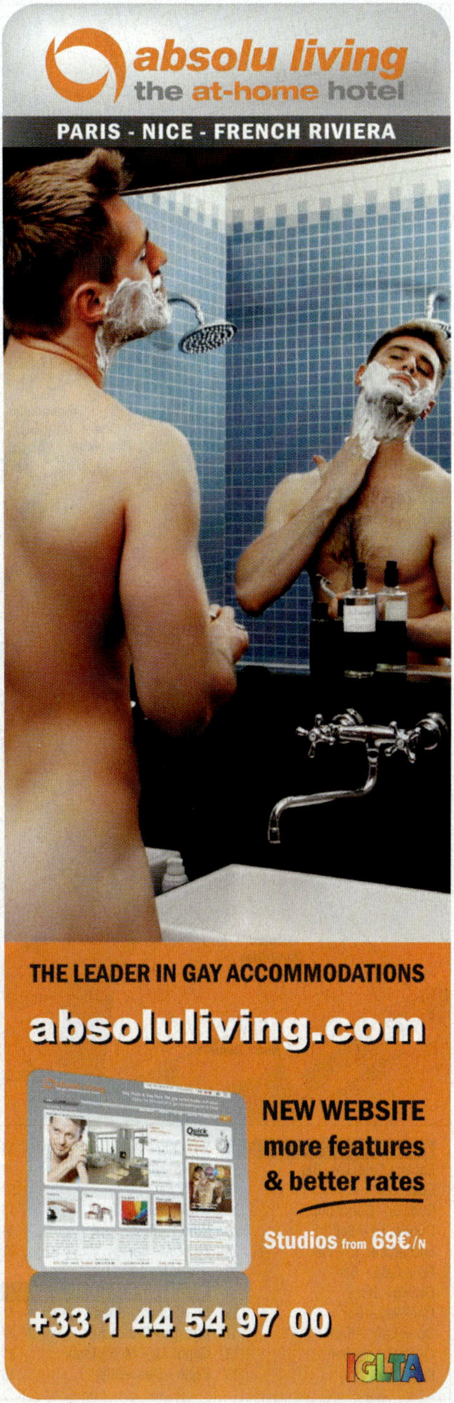

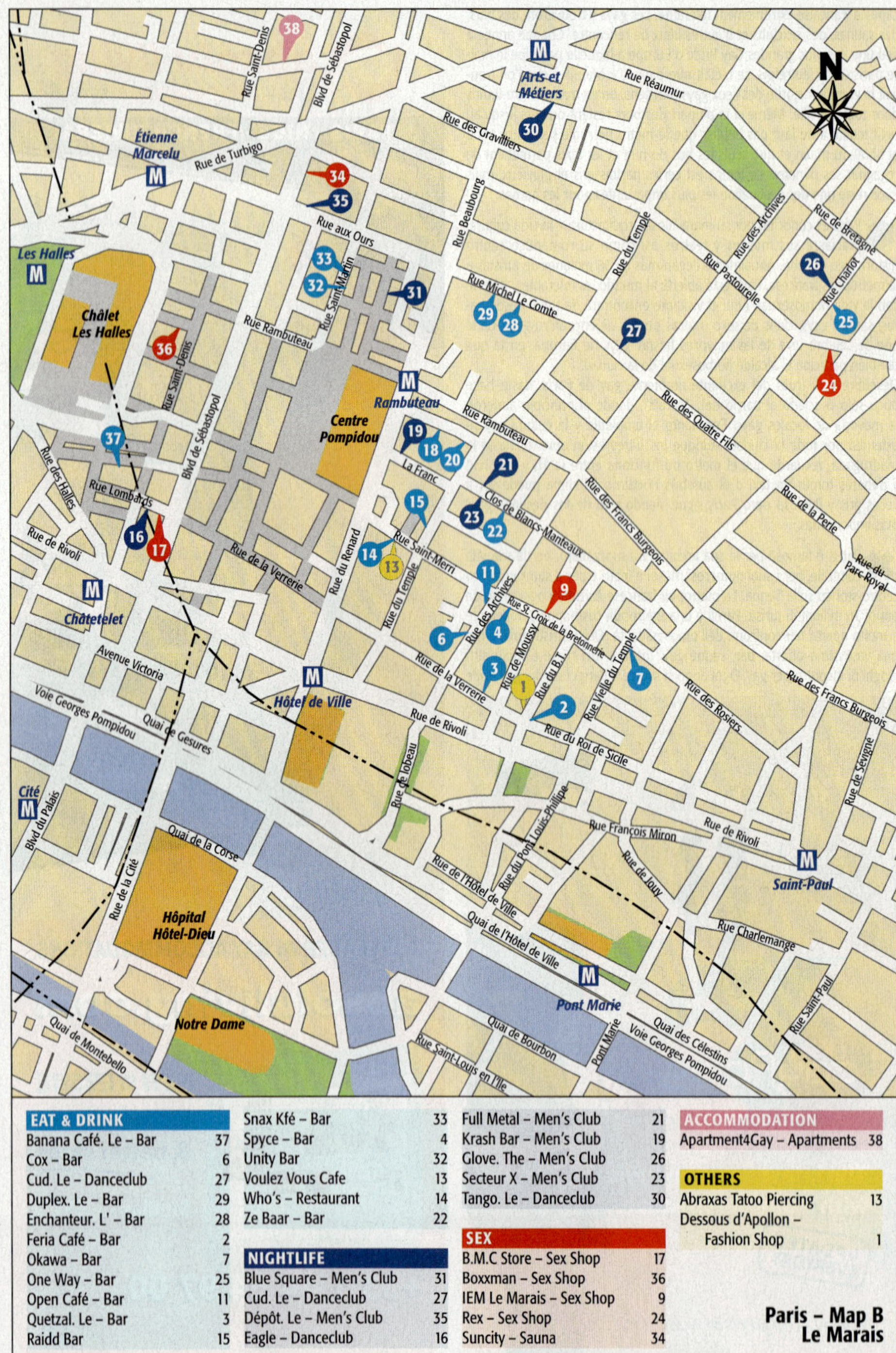
N
Arts et Métiers
Étienne Marcelu
Les Halles
Châlet Les Halles
Centre Pompidou
Rambuteau
Châtetelet
Hôtel de Ville
Cité
Hôpital Hôtel-Dieu
Notre Dame
Pont Marie
Saint-Paul
Rue Saint-Denis
Blvd de Sébastopol
Rue Réaumur
Rue des Gravilliers
Rue de Turbigo
Rue aux Ours
Rue Beaubourg
Rue du Temple
Rue des Archives
Rue de Bretagne
Rue Pastourelle
Rue Charlot
Rue Michel Le Comte
Rue Saint-Martin
Rue Rambuteau
Rue des Quatre Fils
Rue des Halles
Rue Lombards
Rue de Rivoli
La Franc
Clos de Blancs-Manteaux
Rue des Francs Burgeois
Rue de la Perle
Rue du Parc Royal
Rue Saint-Merri
Rue du Renard
Rue de la Verrerie
Rue St. Croix de la Bretonnerie
Rue de Moussy
Rue du B.T.
Rue Vieille du Temple
Avenue Victoria
Voie Georges Pompidou
Quai de Gesures
Rue du Roi de Sicile
Rue des Rosiers
Rue de Sévigne
Rue de Lobeau
Rue du Pont Louis-Phillipe
Rue François Miron
Blvd du Palais
Quai de la Corse
Rue de la Cité
Rue de l'Hôtel de Ville
Rue de Jouy
Rue Charlemange
Quai de l'Hôtel de Ville
Rue Saint-Paul
Quai de Montebello
Quai de Bourbon
Rue Saint-Louis en l'Ile
Pont Marie
Quai des Célestins
EAT & DRINK
Banana Café. Le – Bar 37
Cox – Bar 6
Cud. Le – Danceclub 27
Duplex. Le – Bar 29
Enchanteur. L' – Bar 28
Feria Café – Bar 2
Okawa – Bar 7
One Way – Bar 25
Open Café – Bar 11
Quetzal. Le – Bar 3
Raidd Bar 15
Snax Kfé – Bar 33
Spyce – Bar 4
Unity Bar 32
Voulez Vous Cafe 13
Who's – Restaurant 14
Ze Baar – Bar 22
NIGHTLIFE
Blue Square – Men's Club 31
Cud. Le – Danceclub 27
Dépôt. Le – Men's Club 35
Eagle – Danceclub 16
Full Metal – Men's Club 21
Krash Bar – Men's Club 19
Glove. The – Men's Club 26
Secteur X – Men's Club 23
Tango. Le – Danceclub 30
SEX
B.M.C Store – Sex Shop 17
Boxxman – Sex Shop 36
IEM Le Marais – Sex Shop 9
Rex – Sex Shop 24
Suncity – Sauna 34
ACCOMMODATION
Apartment4Gay – Apartments 38
OTHERS
Abraxas Tatoo Piercing 13
Dessous d'Apollon – Fashion Shop 1
Paris – Map B
Le Marais

LES DESSOUS D'APOLLON
UNDERWEAR-SWIMWEAR-SPORTSWEAR-LOUNGEWEAR
PARIS
Le Marais
M° Hôtel de Ville
15 rue du Bourg Tibourg
Tél. : +33 (0)1 42 71 87 37
Du lundi au samedi
11h - 20h
Dimanches et jours fériés
14h - 20h
LYON
Les Terreaux
M° Hôtel de Ville
20 rue Constantine
Tél. : +33 (0)4 72 00 27 10
Lundis 14h - 19h
Du mardi au vendredi
12h - 19h
INDERWEAR.COM
MEN UNDERWEAR EXPERTS SINCE 2005

più grandi d'Europa, al quale prende parte anche il sindaco (gay) di Parigi. La vita gay di Parigi, fino a poco tempo fa, si concentrava esclusivamente nel quartiere „Marais", il quartiere appunto dove sono stati fondati i primissimi locali gay. Adesso, invece, la scena gay si è un po' estesa in tutta la città. Anche se i bar rimangono aperti fino all'alba, bisogna ricordare che la metropolitana chiude all'1:00 per poi riaprire alle 5:30 e che quindi vanno tenuti in considerazione il taxi e i bus notturni. Sebbene il tempo sia a volte grigio e piovigginoso, Parigi rimane comunque una delle mete più importanti dal punto di vista gay.

GAY INFO

Centre LGBT de Paris Mon-Sat 16-20h
63, rue Beaubourg *M° Bastille/Voltaire/Ledru-Rollin* ☎ 01.43.57.21.47
www.centrelgbtparis.org
Meeting place for many GLBT-groups (contact them for information) and information about HIV/AIDS. Also with a shop, café and library.

PUBLICATIONS

2X magazine
32, Boulevard de Strasbourg ☎ 01.45.15.90.10 www.2xparis.fr
Bi-monthly free gay magazine with an extensive calendar of events. Available at gay venues. Also a free gay map of Paris is available.

SHOWS

Chez Michou (B glm M MA ST)
20.30-?, show 22.45h, closed May 1st and Aug 1st-31st
80 rue des Martyrs *M° Pigalle* ☎ 01.46.06.16.04
www.michou.com
Famous dinner-spectacle in Montmartre.

BARS

Alexander's (AC B CC F G OC) 18-2h
2 rue de Marivaux *M° Richelieu-Drouot/4 Septembre, opp. Opéra Comique*
☎ 01.42.96.40.79
Specials every day. Happy hour 18-23h.

Au Mange-Disque (B cc GLM MA S) Sun & Mon 17-2, Tue-Sat 11-2h
15 rue de la Reynie ☎ 01.48.04.78.17 www.au-mange-disque.com

Banana Café. Le (! AC B CC GLM MA OS S SNU T) Daily 18-?h
13 rue de la Ferronnerie *M° Châtelet /Les Halles, exit Place Ste Opportune*
☎ 01.42.33.35.31 www.bananacafeparis.com
Extravagant bar with many theme parties. Happy hour 18-21h.

Bar du Kent'z (B GLM MA) 14-2h
2 rue Vauvilliers *M° Châtelet* ☎ 01.42.21.01.16
www.facebook.com/group.php?gid=10220530775

Bar du Palmier (AC B CC D G I m OS VS YC) 14-6h
16 rue des Lombards *M° Châtelet/Les Halles* ☎ 01.42.78.53.53
Good atmosphere, cocktail bar.

Bears' Den (AC B CC d f G MC VS) 16-2, Fri-Sat -6h
6 rue des Lombards ☎ 01.42.71.08.20 www.bearsden.fr
Bears, daddies and friends.

Champmeslé. Le (B GLM MC) 16-4h
4, rue Chabanais *M° Pyramides* ☎ 01.42.96.85.20
www.lachampmesle.com
One of the oldest gay bars in Paris.

Cox (! AC B F FC G I LM MA OS) Mon-Thu 17.30-2, Fri-Sun 16.30-2h
15 rue des Archives *M° Hôtel de Ville* ☎ 01.42.72.08.00
www.cox.fr
Very popular and busy with a tougher crowd (skins, uniform and leather fans). Happy hour from 18-21 h.

Duplex. Le (B CC G MA) 20-2h, Fri & Sat -4h
25 rue Michel le Comte *M° Rambuteau* ☎ 01.42.72.80.86
Bar with little or no action, but a friendly crowd.

Enchanteur. L' (B GLM MA) 8-2h
15 rue Michel le Comte *M° Rambuteau* ☎ 01.48.04.02.38

Feeling. Le (B G MA) 17-2h
43 rue Ste Croix de la Bretonnerie *M° Hôtel de Ville* ☎ 01.48.04.70.03
Small, run down bar.

Feria Café (B g MC)
4, rue du Bourg-Tibourg *M° Hôtel de Ville* ☎ 01.42.72.43.99

YOU'RE
GONNA
LOVE
THIS PLACE
HOT SHOWER SHOW
DJ PERFORMANCES
www.raiddbar.com
23 RUE DU TEMPLE
75004 -PARIS
JOIN US ON FACEBOOK
LE RAIDD

Freedj. Le (AC B CC D FC G LM MA OS S VR) 19-3h
35, rue Sainte-Croix de la Bretonnerie *M° Rambuteau, Hôtel de Ville*
www.freedj.fr
Concept based of good music, DJ, 3 floors. A good place to take a drink and to dance.

Imprévu. L' (B GLM OS YC) 12-2h
7-9, rue Quincampoix *M° Châtalet* ☎ 01.42.78.23.50
www.imprevu-cafe.com

Interface (AC CC G MC) 16-2, 16-4h at WE
34 rue Keller *M° Bastille/Ledru Rollin/Voltaire* ☎ 01.47.00.67.15
Neighbourhood bar with happy hour 18-21h.

Marronniers. Les (B GLM M MA OS) 9-2h
18 rue des Archives *M° Hôtel de Ville* ☎ 01.40.27.87.72
Busy café, popular with the gay community.

Micmanbar (B CC DR FC G MC VR VS)
24 rue Geoffroy l'Angevin *M° Rambuteau* ☎ 01.42.74.39.80
One of the oldest bar of Le Marais. Convivial and friendly.

Okawa (AC B DM glm LM M MA NR PA S ST VEG) 11.30-2h
40 rue Vieille du Temple *M° Hôtel de Ville/St Paul, cnr Rue des Rosiers*
☎ 01.48.04.30.69 okawa.fr

One Way (AC B DR f G MA VS) 17-2h
28 rue Charlot *M° République* ☎ 01.48.87.46.10
Friendly atmosphere, cruising bar especially for bears. Happy hour 19-21h.

Open Café (! B CC G M MA OS VS) 11-2, Fri & Sat 11-4h
17 rue des Archives *M° Hôtel de Ville, cnr. rue Ste Croix de la Bretonnerie*
☎ 01.48.87.80.25 www.opencafe.fr
Modern place with a circular bar and a great terrace (also used in winter), a classic in the Marais. Happy hour for beers on tap 18-22h, brunch on Sat and Sun.

Petit Batignolles. Le (B bf cc g m MA) 19-5h
36 rue des batignolles *M° Rôme/ Place de clichy* ☎ 01.49.94.15.64

Petite Vertu. La (B g MC) Tue-Fri 11.30-2, Sat 17-2, Sun 14-18h
15 rue des Vertus ☎ 01.48.04.77.09 www.baratatta.com
Happy hour Tue-Fri 18-20h.

Pietons. Les (B CC GLM M OS) 12-2h
8, rue des Lombards *M° Hôtel de Ville* ☎ 01.48.87.82.87
www.lespietons.com

Pop In (B CC d glm YC) 18.30-1.30h
105 rue Amelot *M° Filles du Calvaire* ☎ 01.48.05.56.11
www.myspace.com/pop_in
Alternative and inexpensive bar with pop live music. 4th Sat/month gay parties.

Quetzal. Le (AC B G MA OS) 17-5h
10 rue de la Verrerie *M° Hôtel-de-Ville* ☎ 01.48.87.99.07
www.facebook.com/profile.php?id=100001503831448
Two bars.

RAIDD BAR (AC B CC G MA S SNU) 20-5h
23 rue du Temple *M° Hôtel de Ville* ☎ 01.53.01.00.00
www.raiddbar.com
Shower show daily. Popular with a tougher gay crowd. Great barmen!

Snax Kfé (B CC gLm I M MA OS PA RES W) 9-24h, Fri & Sat -2h
182, rue Saint Martin *M° Etinne-Marcel* ☎ 01.40.27.89.33
www.snaxkfe.fr
A great bar / Restaurant with an excellent Brunch and good lunch menu.

Spyce Bar (AC B CC G MA NR S)
23, rue Sainte-Croix de la Bretonnerie *M° Hôtel de Ville*
www.spycebar.com
Opened in 2010. Good looking barmen and every night a different music concept with DJ. Friendly and popular. Crowded every night!

Tout Arrive (B G MC)
16 rue de la Verrerie *M° Hôtel de Ville* ☎ 01.42.77.15.12

Tropic Café (B CC GLM m MA OS) 12-5h
66 rue des Lombards *M° Châtelet. Opp. Amazonial, cnr. Rue Ste Opportune* ☎ 01.40.13.92.62 www.tropic-cafe.com
Fri-Sun DJ with live music. Happy hour daily from 18-21h.

Unity Bar (B GLM MC WI) 16-2h
176, rue Saint Martin *M° Etienne-Marcel* ☎ 01.42.72.70.59
unity.bar.free.fr

■ **Wolf Bar** (AC B DR G MC OS) 17-2h
37 rue des Lombards *M° Châtelet* ☎ 01.40.28.02.52
💻 www.wolfparis.com
Bar for bears and wolves with nice terrace outside,music and back room.

■ **Ze Baar** (AC B CC G M MA) 17.30-2h
41, rue des Blancs Manteaux *M° Rambuteau/ Hôtel de Ville*
☎ 01.42.71.75.08
One bar on the ground floor, Lounge in the 2. floor.

MEN'S CLUBS

■ **Blue Square** (AC B D DR G MC P S ST t VS) Daily 17-2h
8, rue Brantôme *M° Rambuteau* ☎ 01.40.29.08.89
Cruising bar in the heart of the gay district. Different „soirées thematiques", Shows and tea dance on Sun.

■ **Boy's Video Club** (B DR F G GH MA NU p SL VR VS) 12-2h
8, rue de Nice *M° Charonne* ☎ 09.53.92.55.86
300m², Glory holes, slings, cabines and 2 cinemas.

■ **Bunker. Le** (B G MC)
150 rue Saint-Maur *M° Goncourt* ☎ 01.43.57.33.82
💻 www.bunker-cruising.com

■ **Club 88** (AC B CC DR G MA NU S VS) 20-2h
88, rue St-Denis *M° Les Halles* ☎ 01.44.82.63.00

■ **Dépôt, Le** (! AC B CC D DR G NU SNU VS YC) 14-7, Sat & Sun -8h
10 rue aux Ours *M°4 Etienne Marcel, bus 29 Sébastopol*
☎ 01.44.54.96.96 💻 www.ledepot-paris.fr
One of the most popular cruising bars in Paris with a huge labyrinth in the basement. Lots of cabins and theme parties every night on 1400m².

■ **Eagle. The** (! AC B CC D DR F G LAB MA OS S VR VS)
18-5, Fri & Sat -7h, closed Mon
33 bis rue des Lombards *M° Chatelet* ☎ 01.42.33.41.45
💻 www.eagleparis.com
Two bars, 2 darkrooms, maze and more. Happy hour for beer 18-23h. For more information see: www.eagleparis.com

Entre deux Eaux (AC B CC DR G M MA NU p SNU VS)
Sun-Thu 16-2, Fri & Sat -6h
45, rue de la Folie Méricourt *M° Oberkampf, St. Ambroise*
☎ 01.43.57.76.46 🖳 www.barentredeuxeaux.com
A 100% naked bar.

Full Metal (AC B CC DR F G MA NU P VS) 17-4, Fri & Sat -6h
40 rue des Blancs Manteaux *M° Rambuteau/Hôtel de Ville*
☎ 01.42.72.30.05 🖳 www.fullmetal.fr
Crowd gets cruisier late at night. Clean and friendly place. Where the action is.

Glove. The (AC b cc DR f G MA P)
Wed 20-2, Thu 17-2, Fri 23-?, Sat 17-22 & 23-?, Sun 17-?h, closed Mon & Tue
34 rue Charlot *M° Saint-Sébastien Frossart* ☎ 01.48.87.31.36
🖳 www.th-glove.com
Two slings, many special parties such as nudist, piss, sportswear etc. For those into fisting.

Impact. L' (AC B CC DR G H MC NU P VS)
Mon, Tue, Thu 20-3, Wed & Sat 22-6, Sun 15-3h
18 rue Greneta *M° Etienne Marcel* ☎ 01.42.21.94.24 🖳 www.impact-bar.com
Sex-Club 100% naked: Give your clothes up in upstairs bar and head downstairs. Darkroom, cabins, glory holes, sling & bed for sex-parties etc. Very clean and friendly. Also apartment for rent.

Krash Bar (! AC B CC DR F FC G GH LAB MA NU p SL VS)
Mon-Thu 15-5, Fri 15-7 , Sat 14-7, Sun 14-5h
12 rue Simon Le Franc *M° line 1-Hotel de Ville, 11- Rambuteau*
☎ 01.48.87.45.80 🖳 www.Krashbar.com
Popular. 2 floors, naturist night Sat, underwear on Sun. Special evenings see website.

Mec Zone. Le (B DR F G GH MA NU SL VS) 21-6, Sat-Sun 14-6h
27 rue Turgot *M° Anvers* ☎ 01.40.82.94.18 🖳 www.meczone.fr
Hard cruising bar on 2 floors with cabins and sling. Neighbourhood crowd.

Micmanbar (B CC DR FC G MC VR VS)
24 rue Geoffroy l'Angevin *M° Rambuteau* ☎ 01.42.74.39.80
One of the oldest bar of Le Marais. Convivial and friendly.

Next (AC B DR DU F FC G GH LAB MA MSG RR S VR WI)
Mon-Thu 12-3, Fri-Sun 24hrs
87 rue Saint-Honoré *M° Louvre-Rivoli / Les Halles* ☎ 06.81.95.05.87
🖳 www.lenext.fr
Cruising bar on two floors with naked and underwear parties. See website for more information: www.lenext.fr

Secteur X (AC B CC DR f G I MA NU p s VS) Mon-Thu 17-4, Fri -6, Sat 15-6, Sun -4h
49, rue des Blancs Manteaux *M° Hotel de Ville* ☎ 09.50.39.50.85
🖳 www.secteurx.fr
Smoking area. Specials apply.

Transfert. Le (AC B CC DR F G MA p VS) 24-?h
3 rue de la Sourdière *M° Tuileries* ☎ 01.42.60.48.42
🖳 www.letransfert.com
Hard cruising bar. Strict dress code: leather, uniform, jeans, latex. Popular with golden shower lovers.

TX (B CC DR G VS YC) 21-3, Fri & Sat 21-5, Sun 16-24h
40 rue Godefroy Cavaignac *M° Voltaire* ☎ 01.43.79.06.38
🖳 www.txcruisingbar.com
Sling room too.

CAFES

Lézard (B glm M MA OS) 9-2h
32 rue Etienne Marcel *M° Etienne Marcel, cnr. Rue Tiquetonne*
☎ 01.42.33.22.73
Small and packed at lunchtime 12-16h.

Stuart Friendly (AC b cc G M MA MC)
Mon closed, Tue-Thu 12-23, Fri & Sat 12-24, Sun 11.30-18h
16 rue Marie Stuart *M° Etienne Marcel* ☎ 01.42.33.24.00
🖳 www.stuartfriendly.fr
Very nice place with very good food and nice people. Non-smoking and straight-friendly!

Voulez Vous (AC B CC G M MA VS) Dayly 11-14, Fri & Sat 11-16h
18 rue du Temple *At le Marais. M° 1, 11- Hotel de Ville* ☎ 01.83.62.22.90
🖳 cafevoulezvous.com

DANCECLUBS

Bains Douches. Les (B D GLM m P VS YC) Sun-Mon 23-?h
7 rue du Bourg-l'Abbé *M° Etienne Marcel, cnr Bd de Sébastopol*
☎ 01.48.87.01.80
Very posh and trendy place on 2 floors, regular gay parties on Sun & Mon. Check local press.

Club 18 (AC B CC D G MA P) Every Fri, Sat and before a public holiday from midnight -?h
18 rue de Beaujolais *M° Palais Royal, directly behind the Jardin du Palais Royal* ☎ 01.42.97.52.13 💻 www.club18.fr
Small club on 2 floors with nice atmosphere & mainstream music. Crowd is mainly around 30 years old.

Cud. Le (! AC B CC D G MA P S SNU) 19-?h
12, rue des Haudriettes *M° Rambuteau* ☎ 01.42.71.56.60
💻 www.cud-paris.com
Great nightclub close to the Centre Pompidou / Forum Les Halles.

Insolite. L' (AC B CC D G MA WE) 23-5, Fri & Sat -6h
33 rue des Petits Champs *M° Pyramides* ☎ 01.40.20.98.59
Small danceclub.

Mix (B D GLM MC)
24 rue de l'Arrivée *M° Montparnasse* ☎ 01.56.80.37.37
The most popular gay tea dance in Paris on Sunday.

Queen Club (! B D G P S YC) Sun 24-6h
102 Av. des Champs Elysées *M° George-V* ☎ 01.53. 89.08.90
💻 www.queen.fr
Previously a 100% gay club but now gay on Sundays only.

Scène Bastille. La (B D G MA)
2bis, rue des Taillandiers *M° Voltaire* ☎ 01.48.06.12.13
3rd Sat/month „Eyes Need Sugar" (G) 23.30-?h. Also other gay nights, check press for details.

Tango. Le (B D GLM MA WE) Fri & Sat 22.30-5, Sun 18-23h
13 rue au Maire *M° Arts-et-Métiers* ☎ 01.42.72.17.78
💻 www.boite-a-frissons.fr
Don't expect mainstream or techno! Renowned for La Boîte à Frissons (ballroom music) on Sat. Friendly mixed crowd, no stress or absurd prices.

RESTAURANTS

48 Condorcet. Le (B glm M) Mon-Sat 19-24h, closed on Sun
48 rue Condorcet *M° Anvers* ☎ 01.45.26.98.19
💻 www.48condorcet.com

4pat (! BF CC DM G M MA PA RES T VEG) 12-2h
4 rue Saint Merri *M° Rambuteau* ☎ 01.42.77.25.45
💻 www.restaurant-4pat.com
Great decoration and good quality of food. Festive atmosphere. Very popular. Mention Spartacus when dining here.

Artishow. L' (B g M MC S)
3 cité Souzy *M° Rue des Boulets* ☎ 01.43.48.56.04
💻 www.artishowlive.com
Very friendly place with a good show.

Au Diable des Lombards (AC B CC GLM M MA OS VS WL) 10-2h
64 rue des Lombards *M° Châtelet Les Halles* ☎ 01.42.33.81.84
💻 www.diable.com
Historical place, famous gay restaurant in central Paris. Happy Hours from 18-20h. Busy every day. Musical video ambiance. Great brunches. Very busy at WE. Mostly American and mixed food.

Aux Trois Petits Cochons (AC b DM GLM M MA RES VEG WL) 19.30-1h
31 rue Tiquetonne *M° Etienne-Marcel* ☎ 01.42.33.39.69
💻 www.auxtroispetitscochons.fr
Last order at 24h.

Chant des Voyelles. Le (B cc glm M MA OS)
11-15 & 18-24, summer 11-24h
4 rue des Lombards *M° Châtelet/Hôtel de Ville* ☎ 01.42.77.77.07
An open-minded and friendly restaurant, Le Chant des Voyelles is not a specifically gay restaurant, but due to the convenient location attracts a lot of gay locals, especially in the evening. Weather permitting, you can enjoy the liveliness of the Marais on the outdoor terrace.

CUD
Night Bar - Paris
find us on Facebook / CUD or CUD Night Bar
CUD - 12 rue des Haudriettes - FR-75003 PARIS

■ **Coupe-Gorge. Le** (B CC GLM MA) Mon-Fri 12-14, Mon-Sun 19-24h
2 rue de la Coutellerie *M° Hotel de Ville* ☎ 01.48.04.79.24
www.coupegorge.com
Modern french cuisine.

■ **Dos de la Baleine. Le** (AC CC g M) Tue-Fri 12-14, 19.30-0h
40 rue des Blancs Manteaux *M° Rambuteau* ☎ 01.42.72.38.98

■ **Gai Moulin. Le** (CC DM GLM M WI WL) 12-24h
10 rue Saint-Merri *M° Hôtel de Ville* ☎ 01.48.87.06.00
www.le-gai-moulin.com
Traditional French cuisine.One of the oldest restaurants in the Marais.

■ **Gossip** (AC B CC DM G M MA OS RES VEG VS) 11-2h
16 rue des Lombards ☎ 01.42.71.36.83 www.gossipcafeparis.fr

■ **Loup Blanc. Le** (bf CC glm M MA PA VEG WL) 19.30-?, Sun also brunch 11-16.30h
42 rue Tiquetonne *M° Les Halles/Etienne-Marcel, pedestrian area*
☎ 01.40.13.08.35 www.loup-blanc.com
Famous meat and fish specialities. Friendly gay staff.

■ **Marc Mitonne** (B CC GLM LM M MA OS RES S VEG WL) 12-15, 18-24h, closed Sun & Mon afternoon
60 rue de l'Arbre Sec *M° Louvre-Rivoli* ☎ 01.42.61.53.16
www.marc-mitonne.com
Cosy restaurant in a traditional Parisian basement, free aperitif for Spartacus readers.

■ **Monsieur Sans-Gêne** (B cc DM GLM M MA OS VS) 12-2h
122 rue Oberkampf *M° Ménilmontant/Parmentier* ☎ 01.47.00.70.11
www.sansgene.fr
Located in the up and coming Oberkampf district. Happy hour 18-20 & 23-24h.

■ **Pig'z** (CC G M MA WE) 19.30-24h, closed Mon
5, rue Marie Stuart *M° Etienne-Marcel* ☎ 01.42.33.05.89

■ **Snax Kfé** (B CC gLm I M MA OS PA RES W) 9-24h, Fri & Sat -2h
182, rue Saint Martin *M° Etinne-Marcel* ☎ 01.40.27.89.33
www.snaxkfe.fr
A great bar / Restaurant with an excellent Brunch and good lunch menu.

■ **Trois. Le** (AC CC GLM M MA OS) 12-14.30 & 20-24h, closed on Mon
3 rue Ste Croix de la Bretonnerie *M° Hôtel-de-Ville, cnr. Rue Vieille du Temple* ☎ 01.42.74.71.52 www.letrois.com
Charming place with a quiet terrace and great food.

■ **Who's** (AC B CC G I LM M MA RES VEG W WL)
14 rue Saint-Merri *M° Rambuteau* ☎ 01.42.72.75.97
www.whoswooparis.fr
Newly opened. Straight-friendly. Cocktail bar with fresh fruit, Tapas and French cuisine. Reasonable prices. Open all night. New york style decoration.

SEX SHOPS/BLUE MOVIES

■ **B.M.C Store** (AC CC g MA VS) Daily 10-1h
21 rue des Lombards *M° Châtelet-Les Halles / Hôtel de Ville*
☎ 01.40.27.98.09 www.bmc-store.com
Sex shop, sale and rental of videos & DVDs and accessories. Good choice. Also cubicles. Online shop: www.bmc-store.com

■ **Boxxman** (AC CC FC G GH MA VS) Daily 10-24h
2, rue de la Cossonnerie *M° Châtelet les Halles, cnr. Blvd de Sébastopol*
☎ 01.42.21.47.02 www.boxxman.fr
Accessories and gadgets, rental and sale of videos. Cruising area in the basement with cinema, cabins & internet access. Underwear shop.

■ **IEM Le Marais (Men-Shop)** (G MA VS) Mon-Thu 13-20, Fri & Sat -21, Sun 14-20h
16 rue Ste Croix-de-la-Bretonnerie *M° Hôtel de Ville* ☎ 01.40.18.51.51
www.iem.fr

■ **newmillenium.fr** (CC G M MA) 11.30-20h, closed Sun & Tue
37 rue Jean Pierre Timbaud *M° Oberkampf/Parmentier*
☎ 01.40.21.30.23 www.newmillenium.fr
One of Europe's largest gay DVD Selection. Also toys, fetish equipment and magazines. Also mail order. See: www.mentools.eu

■ **Rex** (f G MA VS) 13-20h, closed Sun
42 rue de Poitou *M° Saint-Sebastien-Froissart* ☎ 01.42.77.58.57
www.rex-fetish.com
Tailor-made leather and latex clothes.

■ **RoB** (CC G MA) Mon-Sat 11.30-20h
8 Square Ste. Croix de la Bretonnerie *M° Hôtel de Ville*
www.rob-paris.com
Shop for leather, sextoys etc.

■ **Vidéovision** (AC CC G MA VS) Mon-Sat 12-20h
62 rue de Rome *M° Europe /Rome* ☎ 01.42.93.66.04 www.cadinot.fr
This is one of the Cardinot stores. In addition to Cadinot productions, you can buy products from other studios.

■ **Yanko** (AC CC G MA VS) 11-1, Sat-Sun & public holidays 14-1h
10 Place de Clichy *M° Place de Clichy* ☎ 01.45.26.71.19
Videos, DVDs, cinemas and cubicles. for sale, for hire, for viewing.

■ **Zone 02/RoB Paris** (G MC VS) Mon-Sat 11.30-20h
8, square Ste-Croix de la Bretonnerie *M° Hotel de Ville*
www.rob-paris.com

SAUNAS/BATHS

■ **Atlantide Sauna** (AC AK B CC DR DU F FC FH G GH MA NU P RR SA SB SL T VS W) Daily 12-22h
13, rue Parrot *100 m from M° Gare de Lyon* ☎ 01.43.42.22.43
www.atlantide-sauna.com
Newly renovated. Gay, bi and straight. Very clean, design and a lot of details for sex play.

■ **Bains d'Odessa. Les** (AK b CC DR DU FC FH G GH I LAB MA MSG p PI RR SA SB SL VS WO) Daily 12-22h
5, rue d'Odessa *M° Montparnasse Bienvenue, exit N°6* ☎ 01.40.47.83.43
www.lesbainsdodessa.com
It's very quiet place inside a 19th century building. Friendly staff and very clean.

■ **Bains Montansier** (AC B DR DU FC FH G M MA MSG p RR SA SB SH SOL VS WH) 12-20, Sat & Sun 9.30-20h
7, rue de Montreuil, Vincennes *M° Château de Vincennes / RER Vincennes*
☎ 01.43.28.54.03 www.montansier.fr
A good quality sauna in Vincennes, in eastern Paris. Meeting point for bears and friends.

■ **Euro Men's Club**
(AC B DR DU FC FH G m MA PI RR SA SB SOL VS WH) 12-21h
8/10, rue Saint Marc *M° Bourse/Grands Boulevards* ☎ 01.42.33.92.63
e-m-c.fr
Lots of action in the afternoon as it is situated in a business area. More mature crowd.

■ **Gym Louvre Sauna** (AC B CC DU FC FH G GH I M MA MSG SA SB SH VS WO) 9-2, Sun & holidays 12-2h
7bis, rue du Louvre *M° Louvre-Rivoli / Les Halles* ☎ 01.40.39.95.01
www.gymlouvre.com
Clean and modern sauna attached to a fitness club. One of the biggest gay body building gyms in France (1500 m²) with professional coaches, massage, protein bar and dietetic advice. Furthermore the wellness facilities are not only very spacious but also very beautiful and well frequented.

■ **Hammam Boulevards** (g NU SA SB) Mon & Wed 12-22, Fri 12-20h
23, rue des Jeûneurs *M° Grands-Boulevards* ☎ 01.48.01.03.05
www.hammamboulevard.com
A traditional Hammam. Only for men on Mon, Wed & Fri.

■ **IDM** (AC AK B CC DR DU FC FH G GH I m MA MSG NU RR S SA SB SL SNU VS WH WO) Daily 12-1h
4, rue du Faubourg Montmartre *M° Grands Boulevards*
☎ 01.45.23.10.03 www.idm-sauna.com
A place in town with real action! Under 35 years reduced entrance fee.

■ **Key West** (b DR DU FC G GH m MA P SA SB SOL VS WH WO) 12-1h
141, rue La Fayette *M° Gare du Nord* ☎ 01.45.26.31.74
www.keywestsauna.com
Big, beautiful and popular.

■ **King Sauna** (AC B DR DU FC FH G M MC P RR SA SB SH VS)
Mon-Fri 12-6, Sat & Sun 13-7h
21, rue Bridaine *M° Rome / Place de Clichy* ☎ 01.42.94.19.10
www.kingsauna.fr
Very popular. All amenities are in an impeccable state and the owners and staff know how to take care of their visitors. Not the biggest or most flashy sauna in the world, but good value for money, kind service and men for all tastes!

Mykonos. Le (B DR DU FC FH G MA NU P RR SA SB SL VS)
12-24h
71, rue des Martyrs *M° Pigalle, bus 56, 67* ☎ 01.42.52.15.46
www.everyoneweb.fr/sauna.mykonos.paris.fr
100 % naked.

Riad. Le (b CC DR DU FC FH G m MA MSG NU PI RR SA SB VS)
12-1h
184, rue des Pyrénées *M° Gambetta, bus 26 Ramus, 5 mins from Porte de Bagnolet* ☎ 01.47.97.25.52 www.le-riad.com
Big Hammam, traditional Moroccan interior. Try their famous mint tea or take a relaxing massage.

Steamer-Paris. Le (B CC DU FC FH G GH M MA MSG NU RR SA SB SL VS) Mon-Tue & Thu-Fri 13-21, Wed 13-23, Sat & Sun 15-21h
5, rue du Dr Jacquemaire Clémenceau *M° Commerce / Vaugirard*
☎ 01.42.50.36.49 www.lesteamer.fr

Suncity (! AC B cc DR DU FC G m MA p PI SA SB VS WH WO)
Daily 12-6h
62, boulevard de Sébastopol *Next to Le Depot, M° Etienne Marcel, bus 38, 47* ☎ 01.42.74.31.41 (infoline) www.suncity-paris.fr
A very big sauna on 4000 m² on 3 floors. Indian decor, a cosy atmosphere and exceptionally good-looking men make it a great experience not to be missed! See: www.suncity-paris.com

Til't Sauna (AC B CC DR DU FC FH G M MA NU SA SB SL VS)
Daily 12-7h
41, rue Sainte-Anne *M° Pyramides, M° Palais Royal / Musée du Louvre*
☎ 01.42.96.07.43 www.tiltsauna.com
Three levels, two slings, snack-bar, happy hour (18-21h), several events, English spoken. Sat & Sun naked party. Very popular night sauna.

BOOK SHOPS

Mots à la Bouche. Les (CC GLM) 11-23, Sun 13-21h
6 rue Ste Croix de la Bretonnerie *M° Hôtel de Ville* ☎ 01.42.78.88.30
www.motsbouche.com
Paris famous gay bookshop with an enormous stock of gay literature. Ask for catalogue: librairie@motsbouche.com

Violette and Co. (cc GLM MA) Tue-Sat 11-20.30, Sun 14-19h
102 rue de Charonne *M° Charonne/Faidherbe-Chaligny*
☎ 01.43.72.16.07 www.violetteandco.com/librairie
Bookstore on 80 m² with homosexual literature, CDs and DVDs. Violette and Co has an emphasis on lesbian issues and a quiet mezzanine for exhibitions and meetings with authors.

FASHION SHOPS

Boy'z Bazaar Collections-Basics (AC CC G)
Mon-Thu 12-20.30, Fri-Sat 12-22, Sun 13-20.30h
5 rue Ste Croix de la Bretonnerie ☎ 01.42.71.94.00
www.boyzbazaar.com
The largest gay fashion store in Paris.

Dessous d'apollon. les (AC CC G SH)
Mon-Sat 11-20, Sun 14-20h
15, rue du Bourg-Tibourg *M° Hôtel de ville* ☎ 01.42.71.87.37
www.inderwear.com
Underwear, swimwear, sportswear & lounge wear. Big choice: 3000 references. Lots of famous brands.

PR & PHOTOGRAPHY SERVICES

Vincent Desauti
3, avenue de Taillebourg ☎ 06.09.91.63.95 (mobile)
www.vincent-desauti.com
Do you need a photgrapher in Paris? Contact Vincent. For more information see: www.vincent-desauti.com

TRAVEL AND TRANSPORT

Absolu Living (cc GLM)
236, rue St. Martin ☎ 01.44.54.97.00 www.absoluliving.com
Inbound tour operator for gays and lesbians visiting France. Special packages, tours, hotel arrangements and also gay events.

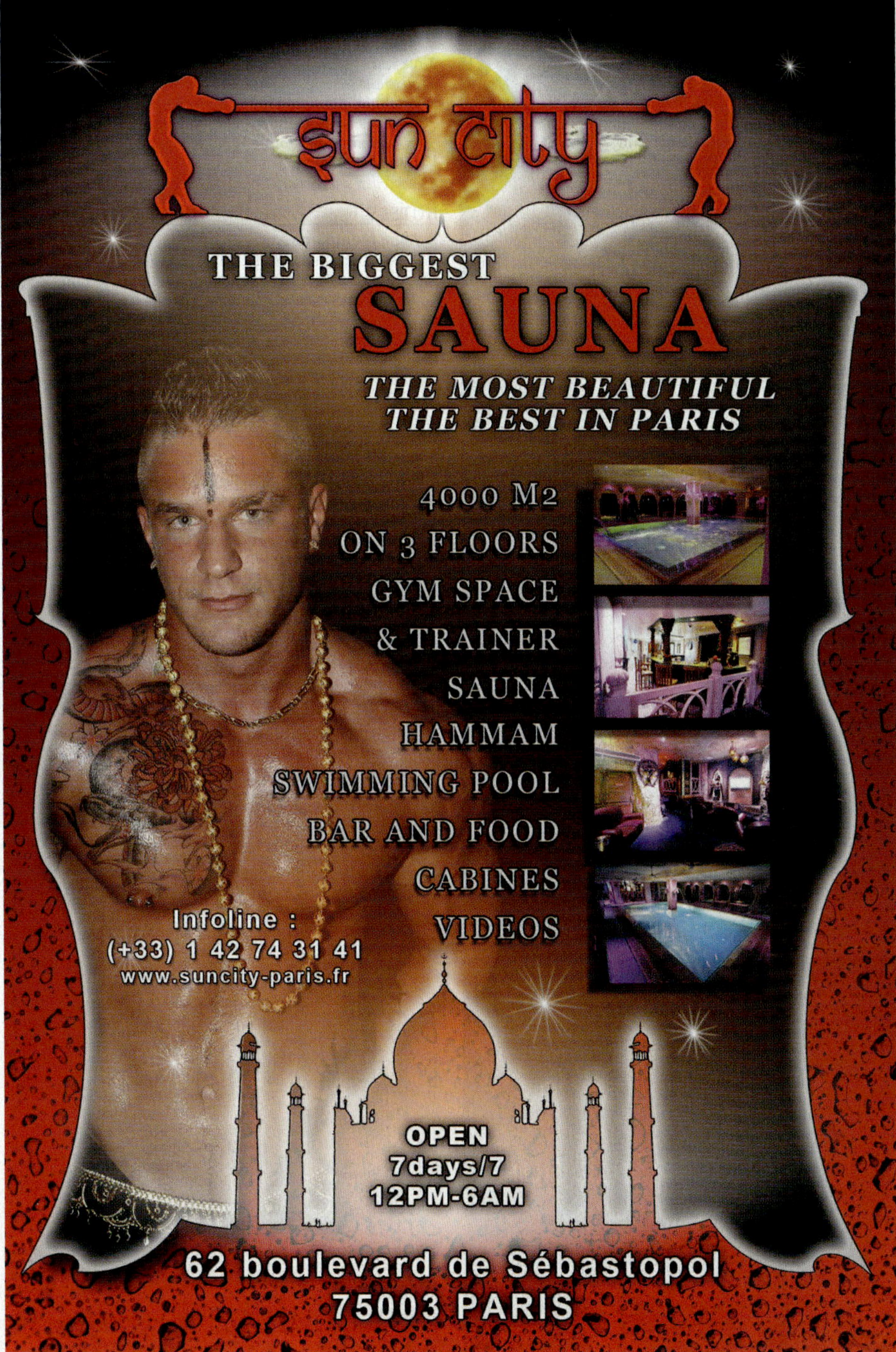

sun city
THE BIGGEST
SAUNA
THE MOST BEAUTIFUL
THE BEST IN PARIS
4000 M2
ON 3 FLOORS
GYM SPACE
& TRAINER
SAUNA
HAMMAM
SWIMMING POOL
BAR AND FOOD
CABINES
VIDEOS
Infoline :
(+33) 1 42 74 31 41
www.suncity-paris.fr
OPEN
7days/7
12PM-6AM
62 boulevard de Sébastopol
75003 PARIS

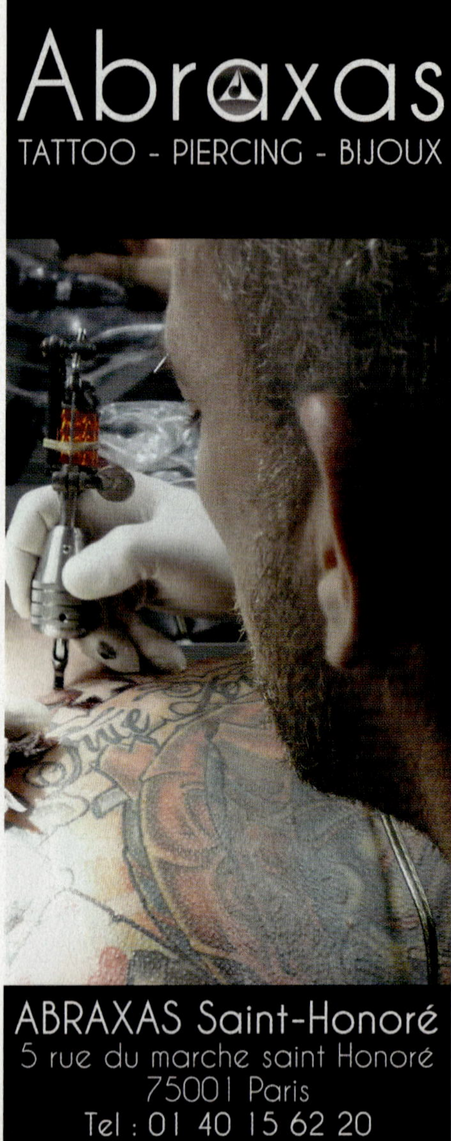

TATTOO/PIERCING

Abraxas Beaubourg (AC CC glm T YC)
Mon 11-20, Tue-Thu -21, Fri & Sat -22, Sun 13-20h
9, rue Saint Merri *M° Hôtel de Ville or Rambuteau. Opp. Georges Pompidou centre, Beaubourg* ☎ 01.48.04.33.55 🖳 www.abraxas.fr
Very professional and clean.

Abraxas Saint Honore (AC CC glm) Daily 10-20h
5, rue du Marché Saint-Honoré *M° Tuileries* ☎ 01.40.15.62.20
🖳 www.Abraxas.fr
A second, new store. For more information see www.Abraxas.fr

HOTELS

Abba Montparnasse
(AC B BF CC FH gLm H I MA RES RWS RWT VA VEG W)
20bis rue de la Gaîté *M° Montparnasse*
🖳 www.abbamontparnassehotel.com
IGLTA member. Gay friendly hotel 60m from Montparnasse. All rooms with bath. Room service available.

Beaumarchais (AC BF CC H I RWS RWT VA) All year
3 rue Oberkampf *M° Filles du Calvaire/Oberkampf, near the Marais and the Bastille* ☎ 01.53.36.86.86 🖳 www.hotelbeaumarchais.com
All rooms with bath/shower and WC, sat-TV, phone, WIFI and hair dryer. Payment possible with VISA, MC, Amex, traveller's cheques and cash in Euros.

François 1er (AC B BF CC glm H M MA OS RWS RWT) All year
7 rue Magellan *M° George V* ☎ 01.47.23.44.04
🖳 www.hotelfrancoispremier.com
Luxury 4-star-hotel in the „golden" district of Avenue des Champs Elysées, Avenue Montaigne and Avenue Georges V. Equipped with modern conveniences and beautiful fabrics.

Hidden Hotel (AC B BF CC GLM I MC PA RWS RWT VA) 24hrs
28 rue de l'Arc de Triomphe *Arc De Triomphe, near Champs Elysees, Metro line 1, 2, 6* ☎ 01.44.55.03.57 🖳 www.hidden-hotel.com
A fantastic, non smoking hotel, smokers terrace at bar, wine cocktail and beer menu at bar with snacks. Excellent breakfast buffet. Concierge service.

Unusual and very attractive accommodation. Great location and very friendly staff.

■ **Hotel du Vieux Saule** (AC bf CC glm H I PA RWS RWT SA) All year, 24hrs
6 rue de Picardie *M° République, Filles du Calvaire, Arts et Metiers and Temple* ☎ 01.42.72.01.14 🖳 www.hotelvieuxsaule.com

■ **Hôtel Jules & Jim**
(AC B BF CC H I MA NR OS RES RWS RWT VA W WL WO) All year
11, rue des Gravilliers *M° Arts & Métiers* ☎ 01.44.54.13.13
🖳 www.hoteljulesetjim.com
Some of the 23 guestrooms offer stunning views over the roofs of Paris.

■ **Hôtel le 20 Prieuré. Le**
(AC B BF CC GLM MC RES RWS RWT WI) All year
20 rue du Grand Prieuré *M° République/ Oberkampf* ☎ 01.47.00.74.14
🖳 www.hotel20prieure.com
A boutique hotel with 32 guestrooms. An excellent location.

■ **Jardins du Marais. Les** (AC B BF CC DU FH GLM H I M MA OS PA PK RES VEG W WL) All year
74 rue Amelot *M° Saint-Sébastien-Froissart/Richard Lenoir* ☎ 01.40.21.20.00
☎ 01.40.21.21.40 (reservations) 🖳 www.lesjardinsdumarais.com
4 stars. Hotel on both sides of the private Paris street. Designers decoration. Very good restaurant.

■ **Keppler** (AC B BF CC DU glm H I M MA MSG NR PA PI RR RWS RWT SA SB VA WO) All year
10 rue Kepler *M° Georges V, near Les Champs Elysées* ☎ 01.47.20.65.05
🖳 www.keppler-paris-hotel.com
Spacious rooms and suites as well as five exquisite suites with balcony and Eiffel Tower exclusive views. Fantastic accommodation and wonderful location. True luxury in Paris!

■ **Louvre Richelieu** (bf CC glm H MA RWS VA WI) All year
51 rue de Richelieu *M° Pyramides/Palais Royal* ☎ 01.42.97.46.20
🖳 www.louvre-richelieu.com
This gay-friendly one-star hotel is located next to the Louvre and near the Marais. It has 14 rooms with radio, phone and bathroom. The multilingual staff is keen to help you find your way in the gay scene. Simple, but worth recommending.

■ **Mas Cocoon. Le**
(B bf GLM M MA NU OS PA PI PK RWS RWT SA SOL WO) All year
32, Hameau de Trémainville, Chenou *One hour from Paris*
☎ 01.64.29.45.37 🖳 www.le-mas-cocoon.com
Relaxing and Cocooning Gay in a Country House in the south of Paris. This gay guesthouse has a heated indoor pool, a conservatory, sauna, solarium, fitness centre, cinema on the premises, fireplace, billiards room, sun terrace and garden all in Provence style.

■ **Paname** (BF cc H I OS) All year
64 rue Crozatier *M° Ledru-Rollin* ☎ 01.43.44.22.50
🖳 www.panamehotel.com
A new hotel near the gay area. See the details on their new website.

GUEST HOUSES

■ **Absolu Living** (CC GLM RWB RWS RWT VA) All year
236 rue St. Martin *M° Etienne Marcel* ☎ 01.44.54.97.00
🖳 www.absoluliving.com
Superior stylish apartments at various locations, short or long term rental.

APARTMENTS

■ **Apartment 4 Gay** (AC CC G)
18, rue Greneta ☎ 01.40.26.63.48 🖳 www.apartment4gay.com

■ **Friendly Frenchy** (bf GLM I MA MSG RWS RWT VA) All year
38 Avenue Jean Jaures *Near Buttes Chaumont, Canal St. Martin*
☎ 01.43.54.37.64 🖳 www.bbb4bbb.ifrance.com

■ **Gay Accommodation Paris** (G MA) All year
271, rue du Faubourg Saint Antoine ☎ 01.43.48.13.82
🖳 www.gayaccommodationparis.com
Long or short-term rentals of apartments, studios centrally located in various parts of the city.

■ **Marais Flat** (AC GLM I MA PK RWS RWT VA WO) All year
26, rue Pierre Lescot *Marais Montorgueil* ☎ 06.32.56.57.27 (mobile)
🖳 www.maraisflat.com
Two luxurious and furnished apartments (sleeps 2-4 people) rented by gay couple.

■ **My City Flat** (G) Office open Mon-Fri 9.30-20h
236 rue St Martin ☎ 01.42.78.01.58 🖳 www.mycityflat.com
The leading Paris lodging agency, in the heart of the Marais.

■ **Parismarais.com** (GLM RWS RWT VA)
45, rue Charlot 🖳 www.parismarais.com
Parismarais.com : the luxury booking center and travel guide for the most exclusive gay-friendly boutique hotels in Paris'gay district – best rates garanteed direct with each hotel reception. Download for free the Marais maps in English.

CRUISING

-Jardin des Tuileries/Quai des Tuileries 75001 (popular)
-Square de la Tour Saint Jacques 75004
-Square Sully Morland 75004
-Champs de Mars 75007 (Near l'Ecole Militaire, nights)
-Gare Saint-Lazare 75008 (level -1, next to Metro exit)
-Gare de l'Est 75010 (near Café Taverne)
-Gare du Nord 75010 (in front of platform N° 10)
-Quai du Canal Saint-Martin 75010 (promenade downstairs Quai de Valmy, unter the bridge. M° Jaures, popular)
-Bois de Vincennes 75012 (South Route de la Tourelle parking, popular)
-Place de la Nation 75012 (in the centre, popular)
-Port de la Gare 75013 (water level in front of Quai François Mauriac. Near the Bibliothèque Nationale de François Mitterand, popular, (ayor)
-Gare Montparnasse 75015
-Place du Paraguay/Place du Maréchal de Tassigny 75016 (M° Porte Dauphine. At night)
-Porte Dauphine 75016 (on the side of the Russian embassy)
-Porte de Maillot 75016 (near the monument of De Lattre)
-Trocadéro 75016
-Square des Batignolles 75017
-Parc des Buttes-Chaumont (AYOR) 75019 (roundabout, nights, popular but be aware of bashers)
-Cimetière du Père Lachaise 75020 (southern side).

Pau

BARS

■ **DK bar** (B d GLM m MA S SNU) Mon-Sat 18-2, Sun 15-2h
6, rue René Fournets ☎ 05.59.83.92.78
🖳 www.dkbar.com

■ **Station des Artistes. La** (B cc G MA p ST) 18-2h
8 Rue René Fournets ☎ 05.59.27.43.34
■ **Why Not** (B cc g MA)
Rue A. de Lassence ☎ 05.59.27.43.34

SAUNAS/BATHS

■ **Lokal, Le** (G GH SA SB SH SL VR VS WH) Sun-Thu 12-24, Fri & Sat 12-3h
3, rue Duboué ☎ 05.59.84.69.85 💻 www.le-lokal.fr
Sauna, sex shop and sex club.
■ **Sauna Eros Pau** (AC B CC DR DU FC FH g LAB MA P RR SA SB SL VS WH) Mon, Wed & Sun 14-2h
8, rue René Fournets *Hedas area* ☎ 05.59.27.48.80
💻 www.sauna-eros.net
Also female clientele. Gays are still welcome.

CRUISING

-Bois de Pau (for those with time on their hands)
-Boulevard Barbanègre
-Cour de la Gare de Marchandises (soldiers!)
-Parc Beaumont
-Parc Nitot
-Place de Verdun
-🅿 Souterrain des Halles
-Place Marguerite-Caborde.

Périgueux

DANCECLUBS

■ **Key Largo**
29, rue de Ludovic-Trarieux

CRUISING

-Garden of „la Tour de Vesone" (daytime only)
-Garden of „des Arènes" (daytime only)
-Parc Aristide-Briand (evening)
-Facilities Rue St-Front

Perpignan

BARS

■ **Calle Hot Cho** (AC B GLM M MA OS p S ST)
19-2h, Mon & Tue closed
8bis, av Palais des Expositions ☎ 04.68.52.82.35 💻 www.ubaclub.com

MEN'S CLUBS

■ **Backstage Cruising Bar** (AC B CC DR F G MA p P VS) 18-2h
1 rue Pierre Puiggary ☎ 06.20.58.26.11 💻 backstage.perpignan.com
Newly opened. Large cruising bar.

DANCECLUBS

■ **Uba Club** (AC B CC D DR GLM MA P S SNU ST WE)
Thu-Sun 0.30-5h
5, Bd Mercader ☎ 04.68.80.44.48
💻 www.facebook.com/profile.php?id=100001747936462

CRUISING

-Passage Rive-Gauche
-Place Bistan
-Route de Canet (dangerous in the evening)

Poitiers

BARS

■ **Sixties**
1, rue des Quares-Roues ☎ 05.49.52.19.44

DANCECLUBS

■ **George-Sand. Le**
25, rue Saint-Pierre-le-Puellier

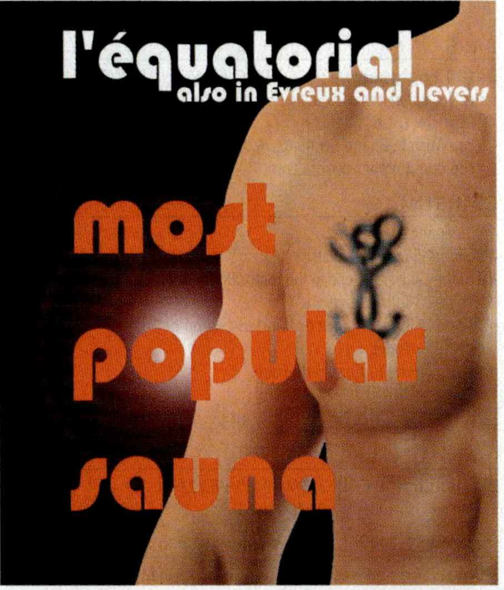

SAUNAS/BATHS

■ **Equatorial sauna Poitiers, L'** (AC B DR DU FC FH G GH LAB M MA NU OS PK RR SA SB SL VR VS WH) Mon-Tue 13-20, Wed-Thu & Sun -24, Fri & Sat -2h
56 Boulevard Pont Achard *8 min walk from central station*
☎ 05.49.41.77.67 💻 www.lequatorialsauna.com
New owner and renovated. Most popular regional sauna with special young day on Sat.

CRUISING

-Avenue du Recteur-Pineau (campus Rabelais)
-Garden/Jardin de la Villette (evening)
-Garden/Jardin des Coloniaux (evening)
-Parc de Blossac

Poussan

DANCECLUBS

■ **Le Pam** (AC B D DR G OS P s ST T) Fri & Sat and before public holidays 23-6h, also Sun in Juli and August
Parc D'issanka *20 km outside Montpellier* ☎ 04 67 78 71 38
Shows on Fri and Sun.

Pressigny les Pins

GUEST HOUSES

■ **Gay Resort „Le vieux Donjon"** (b bf cc G I M MA MSG NU OS PA PI PK RWS RWT SA SB SOL VA VS WE) 8-24h
6, place du Bourg, Montarois *113 km from Paris, Road No.7 exit Pressigny*
☎ 02.38.94.97.56 💻 www.gayresort.fr
„Vieux Donjon" is the first gay resort near Paris, located in a small village in an old residence with park, swimming pool, steam sauna and five guestrooms. Ideal for a romantic weekend with possible visits of the castle area and the vineyards.

Quimper

BARS

■ **100 Logiques. Le** (B CC d DR GLM MA OS P VS WE) 14-1h
9 rue des Réguaires *Behind the post office* ☎ 02.98.95.44.69

■ **Cupidon. Le**
52, rue Aristide-Briand ☎ 06.83.76.06.23
🖳 cupidon-quimper.skyrock.com

CRUISING

-Keradennec (forest)
-Public garden of the theatre
-🅿 at the Glacière (close to the footbridge)
-Place de La-Tour-d'Auvergne
-Place de la Tourbie (place de l'Ancien-Champ-de-Foire)
-Place du Guéodet
-Place du Nouveau-Champ-de-Foire

Reims

DANCECLUBS

■ **Club Lilas** (B CC D G M MA P t VS WE) 23-4h
75 Rue de Courcelles ☎ 03.26.47.02.81

SAUNAS/BATHS

■ **Lotus. Le** (AK B DR DU FC FH G GH I LAB m MA RR SA SB SH SL VS WO) 14-22, Fri -1, Sat -23h
33, rue de Witry ☎ 03.26.07.06.75 🖳 www.sauna-lotus.com

CRUISING

-🅿 near swimming-pool (AYOR)
-Place Drouet-d'Erlons
-Jardins de la Patte-d'Oie (AYOR) (at night)
-Parc Léo-Lagrange (in front of the stadium; at night)
-Place du Boulingrin (facilities close to the monument)

Rennes

BARS

■ **Anathème. L'**
2, rue Capitaine Dreyfuss ☎ 02.99.63.91.12 🖳 www.anathemecafe.fr

■ **Embleme. L'**
24, rue d' Antrain ☎ 02.99..38.71.88
🖳 l-embleme-bar.populus.org/rub/5

■ **M Station** (B G MA) 18-1h
4 Rue Saint Thomas ☎ 02.99.79.00.69

■ **Regards d'Ailleurs**
36bis, rue Dupont-des-Loges ☎ 02.99.31.86.47
🖳 regards.d.ailleurs.over-blog.com

MEN'S CLUBS

■ **Cosmos. Le** (AC DR F G MA NU P VS) 22-3, Fri & Sat -6h
21, rue Saint-Malo ☎ 02.23.21.18.76
🖳 lecosmos.blog4ever.com/blog/index-30676.html

DANCECLUBS

■ **Batchi. Le** (B D GLM MA) 0.30-5h, closed Mon
35 Rue Vasselot ☎ 02.99.79.62.27

■ **Espace. L'** (B cc D glm) Tue-Thu 24-5, Fri-Sun 23-6h
45 Boulevard de la Tour d'Auvergne ☎ 02.99.30.21.95

SEX SHOPS/BLUE MOVIES

■ **Cupidon** (CC G MA) 9-24, Sun 15-22h
4 avenue Louis Barthou ☎ 02.99.31.02.72
Also video rental, French and US brands.

SAUNAS/BATHS

■ **California** (AC B cc DR DU FC FH G GH I LAB m MA RR SA SB SH SL SOL VS WH WO) 12-1, Tue & Fri -20, Sat & Sun 13-1h
7, rue de Léon *5 mins from railway station and town hall, M° République / Gare* ☎ 02.99.31.59.81 🖳 www.saunacalifornia.com
Sauna on 500 m² and three floors. 1st and 3rd Thu/month foam party, 2nd and 4th Thu/month „Noir et Naturiste" night. New S/M cabin. Mon 20h naked nite. Also a boutique with gay articles.

CRUISING

-Parc de Bréquigny (behind the park and in the toilets of the Maison des Jeunes et de la Culture)
-🅿 Kléber
-Les Gayeulles (at the 🅿)
-Etangs d'Apigné (5 km from the centre, first to the right after the main pond; in the bushes at the 2nd pond)
-Le Champ de Mars (roundabout)
-Place des Lices (WC des Halles)
-Le Contour de la Motte (square and WC)
-Boulevard Magenta (square and WC near the former police station)
-Place Le Bastard
-Le Thabor (botanical garden).

Rochefort

BARS

■ **Stand By. Le**
51, rue du Docteur-Peltier ☎ 05.46.88.45.72

CRUISING

-Monument Pierre-Loti
-L'ex-Jardin de la Marine (after 22h, stop between Rochefort-BA 721)

Rouen

BARS

■ **Acte. L'** (B D FC G I MA OS PA T) Mon-Sat 18-2h
5, rue ecuyère *near grande Horloge* ☎ 06.62.04.00.10
New straight-friendly bar. Happy hour Thu-Fri at 18-20h and Mon all night long. Modern white decoration.

■ **XXL Bar & Club** (AC B CC D DR FC G MA p P VS W)
19-4, Fri & Sat -5h, closed Mon & Thue
25-27 rue de la Savonnerie *Near the cathedral* ☎ 02.35.88.84.00
Oldest gay cocktail bar. Monthly theme parties, house music in the basement. See facebook for events.

MEN'S CLUBS

■ **City Club, Le** (! AK B D DR DU FC G GH LAB MA NU P RR SL T VR VS) Sun-Wed 14-20, Thu-Sat 14-24h
12, rue Saint Etienne des Tonneliers *Near Halles aux Toiles*
☎ 02.77.76.87.82 🖳 www.cityclubrouen.com
400m² renovated cruising area with labyrinth and large cinema screen. Discrete exit. Very friendly staff.

■ **Club 66** (cc DR g MA VS) 12-2h
66 rue Bouvreuil ☎ 02.35.70.44.83
Sex-club and -shop on 3 floors. Also video rental.

■ **Kox. Le** (! AK B CC DR DU FC G GH LAB MA NU p P RR SL T VR VS)
Mo, Thu, Fri 14-2, Sat & Sun 18-2h
4, impasse des Hauts Mariages *M° Hôtel de Ville, Quartier St. Maclou*
☎ 02.32.08.40.66 🖳 www.le-kox.com
New opened and very popular. For special party see website. Big cruising area.

SEX SHOPS/BLUE MOVIES

■ **Liberty X** (AC CC FC GH GLM MA SH VR VS) 10.30 -24h
65, rue de la République *Near Hotel de Ville* 🖳 www.libertyx.fr
Discrete entrance. Shop with videos, sextoys, underwear & more.

SAUNAS/BATHS

■ **8. Le** (AC B DR DU f FC FH G SA SB SOL VS)
13-21, Sat-Sun 14-21h
8, place Saint-Amant ☎ 02.35.15.06.29

■ **Rive droite. La** (B CC DR DU FC G GH LAB M MA NU OS P PI PK RR SA SB SL VR VS WH) 12-24, Fri & Sat -2h
177 route de Paris *2km from Rouen* ☎ 02.32.12.56.29
💻 www.lerive-droite.com
New 700m² sauna. Exceptional decoration in small village style. Big hamam. Very relaxing.
■ **Square. Le** (b G MA SA SB) 13-20h
39, rue Saint Nicolas ☎ 02.35.15.58.05 💻 lesquare.chez.com

CRUISING

-Woods near Novotel (next to Faculté de Médicine, at the southern exit of the city in direction Paris)
-Square Verdrel and Rue du Baillage (near Rue Jeanne d'Arc)
-Left side of the Seine river/Rive gauche de la Seine (near Jeanne d'Arc bridge)
-P Aire parking de Bord
-P Robert-le-Diable
-Forêt de la Londe
-Forêt-Verte
-Port maritime
-Rue Henri-Dumont

Royan

BARS

■ **Chez Papy's** (B g MA)
10, place de la Résistance ☎ 02.51.62.71.93

SWIMMING

-Plage de la Bouverie. Bring own drinks as there is no restaurants/shops nearby
-Plage de la Palmyre
-Plage de la Grande Côte
-Royan Beach
-Plage de la Cèpe.

Saint Gervais Les Bains

HOTELS

■ **Hotel Liberty Mont Blanc** (B BF CC D GLM I M MSG PA PI PK RWB RWS RWT SA VA WH) Out of the season 11-16h, closed 3 weeks in Nov and 2 weeks in May
734, av. du Mont d'Arbois, Saint Gervais Les Bains *Between Chamonix and Megeve, 60 mins from Geneva airport* ☎ 04.50.93.45.21
💻 www.liberty-mont-blanc.com

Saint-Etienne

BARS

■ **L'R Flag** (B CC GLM MA p) Tue-Sat 13.30-1, Sun 18-1h
27 rue Charles De Gaulle ☎ 04.77.38.56.18
Two steps from the town centre, situated on the main centre line of the town.
■ **Zanzy Bar. Le** (B CC G m MA)
12-1.30, Sat 14-1.30h, closed Sun & Mon
44 rue de la Résistance ☎ 04.77.41.67.90

CAFES

■ **Brasserie L'Oreck's** (AC CC glm M OS) 9-1h
68 Cours Fauriel ☎ 04.77.25.62.82

SAUNAS/BATHS

■ **130. Le** (AC B DR DU FC FH G MA SA SB SH VS WH)
13-20, Fri & Sun -22h
3, rue d'Arcole *Tram-Jean Jaurès, near town hall* ☎ 04.77.32.48.04
Popular small sauna. Clean and friendly, busiest in the afternoon.
■ **Galaxy. Le** (B DR DU g GH MA SA VS) 13-20h
108, rue des Alliés ☎ 04.77.25.77.55

CRUISING

-Plaine Achille P of the tennis club, behind the Palais des Spectacles. Day & night, popular. Be careful, the street is a dead end.
-Sorbiers („La Buanderie", at the end of Sorbiers in direction of Saint-Chamond, behind a right turn there is a small path on the left that heads up into a forest. Between 13-18h, MC)
-Jardin des Plantes
-Place Anatole-France
-Place Carnot
-Place Villeboeuf

Saint-Flour

DANCECLUBS

■ **Liberty Night** (AC B CC D glm P S SNU YC) 22.30-5h
16 Place de la Liberté *Auvergne, A 75, Sortie 28* ☎ 04.71.60.35.87

Saint-Malô

BARS

■ **Aux Anges** (G MA VS) Mon-Sat 10.30-24, Sun 14.30-20.30h
7, rue Godard ☎ 02.99.82.01.20

SEX SHOPS/BLUE MOVIES

■ **Sex Shop Saint Malo** (CC MA VS) 10.30-12.30 & 14-20h
4, rue Puits aux Braies ☎ 02.99.56.01.51

SAUNAS/BATHS

■ **Brigantin, Le** (B DR FC G MA MSG PI PK SA SB VR VS WH)
Sun-Tue & Thu 14-22.30, Wed & Sat 14-20, Fri 14-1h
22, Avenue du Général Ferrié ☎ 02.99.19.72.95
💻 www.saunalebrigantin.fr

GUEST HOUSES

■ **Bay Ouest** (B BF G I MC NU OS PA PI PK RWB RWS RWT SA VA VS)
All year
Saint Séliac *In Québriac, near Mont Saint Michel and Rennes*
☎ 02.99.23.07.23 💻 www.bayouest.com
A 100% gay guest house, 4 guestrooms near nude gay beaches. Clothing optional around the pool.

CRUISING

-Parc Bel-Air
-Jardin du Cavalier
-Les Remparts
-Place Vauban
-Square Canada

Saint-Maur

CAFES

■ **Terres Noires. Les** (b BF CC g MA OS) 7-22, Sat -19h, closed Sun
80 av d'Occitanie, Zone Commerciale Saint Maur Cap Sud *Zone Commerciale Cap Sud* ☎ 02.54.27.00.64 💻 lesterresnoires.free.fr

Saint-Nazaire

BARS

■ **Betty's. Le**
75 Rue Albert de Mun 💻 bettysbar.skyrock.com

CRUISING

-Hôtel de Ville (WC)
-Cirque de Chemoulin (beach between St.Marc and Ste.Marguerite)
-Tharon-Plage (beach Sables d'Or)
-Parcours Vitta Vittel (especially in the evening)
-P Parc Paysager
-Avenue de Plaisance (in the evening)

Saint-Quay-Portrieux

SWIMMING

-Au Vieux-Bourg (NU) (nudism in a few smaller bays; take the exit to the small village of Pourry)
-Le Val-André (NU) (vast beaches which also welcome nudists; between Pleneuf-Val-André and Ville-Berneuf)
-Plage de Lortuais (north of the village, behind the cape of Erquy; wonderful landscape)

Saint-Tropez

DANCECLUBS

■ **Esquinade. L'** (AC CC GLM MA P SNU T)
23.30-6h, winter only Fri & Sat
2 rue du Four *Near Place de la Mairie* ☏ 04.94.56.26.31

RESTAURANTS

■ **Chez Les Garçons** (B g M MA OS) All year
13 rue du Cépoun San Martin ☏ 04.94.49.42.67
Very attractive, small restaurant decorated in pink, white and grey. The cuisine is delightful and refined. Continue the party in the bar with a gay disco.

HOTELS

■ **Kube** (AC B CC D GLM I M MA MSG OS PI PK RWB RWS RWT)
All year, 24hrs except Nov – mid Dec.
Route de St.Tropez, Gassin 🖳 www.designhotels.com
New Designhotel with 41 guest rooms and suites, arranged in four freestanding buildings along the perimeter of the resort gardens and pools. 10 mins from Downtown St.Tropez.

CRUISING

-Le Port (L'Escalet, alongside the maritime cemetery)
-Tour des Muscadins and Citadelle
-Beaches in Ramatuelle (Club 55, Aqua Club).

Saintes

BARS

■ **Salamandre. La** (B CC g MA) 18-2h, closed Mon
11 Quai de la République ☏ 05.46.74.20.33

SEX SHOPS/BLUE MOVIES

■ **Sex-Shop** (AC CC DR g MA VS)
10-19.15h, closed Sun & holidays
12 Quai de la République ☏ 05.46.74.51.72
One gay cinema.

Seignosse

RESTAURANTS

■ **Loom** (B G M MC OS) Tue-Sun
1 avenue Jean Moulin ☏ 05.58.43.31.39
🖳 www.leloom.fr
Restaurant with cocktail bar and outdoor garden area.

Sète

BARS

■ **Éros Café** (B g MA)
29, quai de Lattre-de-Tassigny ☏ 04.67.18.23.26

CRUISING

-Quai de la Résistance-Rue F. Mistral
-Beach (between the Théâtre de la Mer and la Corniche)
-Môle Saint-Louis
-Quai du Port

Soissons

DANCECLUBS

■ **Django. Le** Fri & Sat 23-5, Sun 22-3h
8 Avenue de l'Aisne ☏ 06.36.08.30.54
🖳 djangogayclub.e-monsite.com

Strasbourg

BARS

■ **Golden Gate. Le** (B g MC OS) Gay party on Wed
63, rue du Fossé des Tanneurs ☏ 03.88.75.72.98
■ **Irish Times**
19 Rue Sainte-Barbe ☏ 03.88.32.04.02

MEN'S CLUBS

■ **Antracte** (AC B CC DR F FC G GH LAB MA NU p RR SL T VR VS)
Mon-Thu 12-24, Fri & Sat 14-1, Sun 16-21h
2a, rue Moll *150 m from main station* ☏ 03.88.32.61.86
🖳 www.antracte.fr
Gay sex club. Every Sun „Naked Sex Party" 16-23h. Entrance fee applies. Very clean & friendly.

CAFES

■ **Salon de Thé Grand'Rue** (b glm MC)
Mon-Sat 9-18.45h, closed Sun
80 Grand Rue ☏ 03.88.32.12.70
Gay owned and cosy.

DANCECLUBS

■ **Off Shore** (B CC D GLM YC)
43, Route de Bischwiller, Bischheim ☏ 03.88.81.05.43
■ **So Divine** (AC B D GLM MA S VS WE) Thu 15-?, Fri & Sat 21-?h
3 rue du Marais Vert ☏ 06.67.11.57.29
🖳 so-divine.com

RESTAURANTS

■ **Au Petit Tonnelier** (AC b CC DM glm M MA OS PA RES t WL)
Daily 12-14, 19-22.30h
16 Rue des Tonneliers *City centre, tram Langstross/Grand Rue*
☏ 03.88.32.53.54 🖳 www.aupetittonnelier.com
Gay-friendly. Fresh market products. Last order 22.30h.
■ **Petit Ours** (CC glm M MA NR PA VEG WL) 12-14 & 19-23h
3 rue de l'Ecurie *300 m from the cathedral* ☏ 03.88.32.13.21
🖳 www.resto-petitours.com

SEX SHOPS/BLUE MOVIES

■ **Tentation** (cc G VS) 13-21h, closed Sun
16 Grande Rue ☏ 03.88.32.95.51

SAUNAS/BATHS

■ **Atrium Sauna** (AC B cc DU FC FH G M MA OS RR SA SB SOL VS)
Mon-Fri 14-23, Fri -2, Sat -3, Sun -22h
Schulstraße 68, D – 77694 Kehl *5 mins from Strasbourg, A5, KA-Basel, exit Appenweier* ☏ (+49 78) 51 48 27 05 (Germany)
🖳 www.sauna-atrium.net
Mixed on Tue & Wed.
■ **Equateur** (B CC DR DU FC FH G GH LAB MC NU p P RR SA SB VS)
13-23, Wed & Thu -19, Sat 14-23, Sun 14-19h
5, rue de Rosheim *300 m from the railway station* ☏ 03.88.22.25.22
🖳 www.sauna-equateur.net
Small sauna with nice staff. Opportunity to get intimate and easy sex. Mixed on Fri.
■ **H2O** (B CC DR DU FC FH G M MA NU p RR SA SB VS)
Mon-Thu 14-23, Fri -1, Sun -22h
22, rue de Bouxwiller *Near Place de Haguenau* ☏ 03.88.23.03.19
🖳 www.sauna-h2o.net
On 300 m². Mo & Thu mixted day.

HOTELS

■ Comfort Hotel Strasbourg
(B BF CC glm H I M OS PA PK RWS RWT VA) All year
14, rue des Corroyeurs *Tram stop Montagne Verte* ☎ 03.88.29.06.06
🖳 www.comfort-strasbourg.com
The hotel has 66 rooms, all with private shower, WiFi and sat-TV. It is situated in an exceptional spot at the gates of the Old Strasbourg. Original architecture in quiet, green surroundings and a warm welcome with a sense of service. A friendly welcome and great service.

CRUISING

-Parc de la Citadelle (ayor)
-Sentier de la Craponnière (at the beginning of the Route de Koenigshoffen)
-Les Gravières (direction Port du Rhin, north of Strasbourg)
-Porte Blanche (near Rue du Banc de la Roche, besides family garden) (AYOR)
-Little wood (between Route des Romains and highway besides Parc des Glacis).

Tarbes

RESTAURANTS

■ Entente. L' (B CC DM GLM H LM M PK RES S VEG WL)
Mon-Thu 7-2, Fri & Sat -3h
19 Place d'Astarac, Tournay *Near autoroute A64; and possibility airport of Tarbes or Pau or Toulouse* ☎ 05.62.35.70.27
🖳 www.restaurant-lentente.com

CRUISING

-Massay (the garden at the museum, daytime)
-Place du Foirail (AYOR) (by night)

Thonon-les-Bains

BARS

■ Tiffany's. Le (B CC G P) 19-3h, closed Mon
6 Place du 8 Mai 1945 ☎ 04.50.71.88.91

HOTELS

■ Côté-Sud Leman (B BF CC glm H I M MSG OS PA PK RWS RWT VA YC) All year
6, rue du Pamphiot *Lake Geneva, 30 mins from Geneva, 20 mins from Evian* ☎ 04.50.70.36.70 🖳 www.hotel-thonon.com

Toulon

BARS

■ Lampa. La (B CC G OS YC) 20-2h
117 Quai de la Sinse ☎ 04.94.09.35.90
■ Texas (AC B CC GLM MA P) 18-1, May-Sep -3h
377 Avenue de la République *Next to town hall* ☎ 04.94.89.14.10
🖳 www.texasbargay.com

MEN'S CLUBS

■ Meet X (AC AK B DR F FC G GH LAB MA NU p SL VR VS WE)
Mon-Wed 12-21, Thu & Fri -1h, Sat-Sun 14-21h / Oct-Jun: Sun 14-20h
19 rue Picot, 1st floor *Near Place de la Liberté* ☎ 04.94.09.38.74
🖳 www.meetxtoulon.com.
Cubicals and smoking room. No alcohol served. 3 video rooms. On 150m².

DANCECLUBS

■ Boy's Paradise (B D DR G MA P s SNU VS)
24-5, Fri & Sat 23-?h
1 Bd. Pierre Tosca *Opp. SNCF station* ☎ 04.94.09.35.90
🖳 www.boysparadise83.com
Large disco on 3 floors, no cover charge on Mon-Tue & Thu (except holidays). Regular strip & foam parties. See www.boysparadise83.com

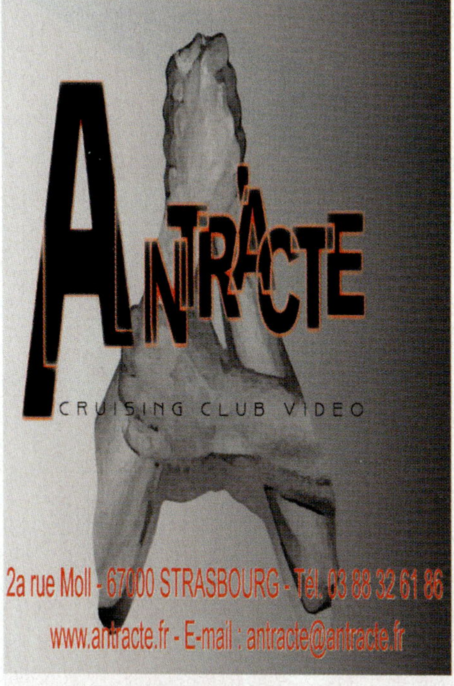

SEX SHOPS/BLUE MOVIES

■ Zone X (AC CC G I MA NU VS) 12-21, Fri & Sat -2h
24 Rue Garibaldi *Near Centre Commercial Mayol, opp. Portes d'Italie*
☎ 04.94.22.36.42 🖳 www.zonextoulon.fr
Nude Fri 20-2h, Sun 12-20h, underwear Sat 20-2h.

SAUNAS/BATHS

■ Blue Hot (b DR DU FC FH G LAB MA RR SA SB SH SL VS WH WO)
12.30-21, Sat & Sun 14-21h
16, place Vincent Raspail *Near Av. le la Republique* ☎ 04.94.91.49.55
🖳 www.blue-hot.fr
Friendly sauna on 300 m².

GUEST HOUSES

■ Quatre Saisons. Les (B CC glm H I m MA OS PA PI PK RWS SOL VA) All year
370 Montée des Oliviers, Route du Brûlat *In Le Castellet, 20 km from Toulon* ☎ 04.94.25.24.90 🖳 www.lesquatresaisons.org
One cottage with all possible amenities. 1 apartment and 5 guestrooms with shower or bath and WC.

SWIMMING

-Beach of Jonquet (from La Seyne Sur Mer take the road to Cap Sicié, the beach is located behind Fabregas)
-Beach of Mourillon

CRUISING

-Avenue Auguste-Berthon
-Jardin du Mourillon
-Place de la Porte-d'Italie
-Port de Bandol
-La Bedoule (motorway Toulon-Marseille)
-Square Alexandre-III (jardin centre ville)
-Fort du Cap Brun
-Place du Théâtre (at night ayor).

Toulouse

BARS

Bear's. Le (AC B CC DR G MA p VS WE)
Wed-Sun 19-2, Sat & before public holidays 19-5h
20, rue des sept troubadours *Close to Place Wilson and main station*
☎ 05.61.62.87.21 💻 www.bears-toulouse.com

Paradise Café. Le (B cc glm m MC OS) 8-21h, closed on Sun
3 Rue des Tourneurs ☎ 05.61.53.68.37

Quinquina. Le (B CC G OS) 12-24h, closed Sun
26 rue Peyras ☎ 05.61.21.90.73

MEN'S CLUBS

Grand Cirque. Le (! AC B DR G MA OS S VS) 19-2, Sat -4h
14 Boulevard Riquet ☎ 05.61.62.84.14 💻 www.legrandcirque.com
Cruising bar with sling, glory holes, labyrinth and cabins. Some theme nights and shows. See www.legrandcirque.com

DANCECLUBS

Kléo. Le
1, av. du Grand-Ramier 💻 www.le-ramier.com

Rleo, Le (B CC D G OS P S ST T YC)
18 Avenue du Grand Ramier *M° St.Michel Palais de Justice*
☎ 05.62.67.63

Shanghaï. Le (B D DR g MA P T VS) 23-?h, closed Mon & Tue
12 rue de la Pomme ☎ 05.61.23.37.80 💻 www.shanghai-leclub.com

RESTAURANTS

Beaucoup (AC B cc glm M MA OS) 10-2, Sat 11-5, Sun 11-2h
9 Place du Pont Neuf *Centre* ☎ 05.61.12.39.29 💻 www.beaucoup.fr

Café Culturel Folles Saisons (B g M MC)
197, route de Saint-Simon ☎ 05.61.62.84.14 💻 www.follessaisons.org
Bar & restaurant.

Jardins de l'Ambassade, Les (AC B CC d glm M MA OS S WL)
Mon-Fri 12-14.30 + 18-2, Sat+Sun 18-5h
22 Boulevard de la Gare ☎ 05.62.47.24.73
A private garden restaurant in the former consulate of Austria. A great atmosphere with fireplace and excellent cuisine.

SEX SHOPS/BLUE MOVIES

Boîte à Films. La (g VS) 10-2h
23 rue Denfert-Rochereau ☎ 05.61.62.76.75

Lynx Vidéo (AC CC DR g MA VS) 10-2h
2 rue Lafon *Near SNCF station, cnr. rue Bertrand de Born*
☎ 05.34.41.63.28
Cinemas (one gay), private cabins, videos and accessories.

Storix / Spartacus (AC CC G MA VS)
Mon-Thu 11-22, Fri-Sat 11-23h
29 rue Héliot *M° Jean Jaurès* ☎ 05.61.63.63.59 💻 www.storix.fr
A very large choice of gay products: DVDs (new titles each week), underwear and more. A good address in Toulouse.

SAUNAS/BATHS

Colonial. Le (! AC B CC DR DU FC G LAB M MA MSG NU RR SA SB SL VR VS WH) Sun-Thu 12-1, Fri & Sat 12-3h
8 place belfort *M° Matabiau-SNCF or Jean-Jaurès* ☎ 05.61.63.64.11
💻 www.lecolonial-sauna.com
No cover on Tue for guests under 25 years. Newly renovated with 500m² and smokers room. Friendly staff and busy all week. For special events see website.

KS. Le (! AC B BF CC DR DU FC FH G GH LAB M MC MSG RR SA SB SL VS WH WI) 12-2, Sun 5-2h nonstop
6, rue Saint-Ferréol *Near train station* ☎ 05.61.62.13.61
💻 www.ks-sauna.com
A very popular clean sauna. Naturist day 1st and 3rd Sat/month. Entrance tickent valid all day.

Pharaon. Le (AC B CC DR DU FC FH G LAB M MA MSG PI RR SA SB SL SOL VS WH WO) 12-1h
43, avenue de la Gloire *M° Gare Matabiau* ☎ 05.61.20.70.90

www.lepharaontoulouse.com
Luxurious sauna on 700 m² and 2 floors.

HOTELS

Albert 1er (AC BF CC GLM M MC RWS RWT WI) All year, 24hrs
8, rue Rivals *M° Capitole* ☎ 05.61.21.17.91 www.hotel-albert1.com
Located in a quiet street in the heart of Toulouse, the hotel is within short walking distance of Place du Capitole and the city's major points of interests. Very gay friendly.

Cuq en Terrasses (AC B BF CC DM GLM H I M MA OS PA PI PK RES RWS RWT SOL VA VEG) Open from 1st Apr-31st Oct.
Cuq Chateau, Cuq Toulza *35 km from Toulouse* ☎ 05.63.82.54.00
cuqenterrasses.com
Gay owned hotel and restaurant in an typical small french village.

GUEST HOUSES

A Nousto (BF G M OS PI PK RWB RWS VA) All year
13 rue de la Chapelle *110 km from Toulouse in the Pyrénées*
☎ 05.61.89.45.56 www.anousto.fr
Two guestrooms in former farmhouse. Dinner upon request using local produce. Also fully equipped mobile home available as well as converted barn for 30 people for hire.

■ **Coté Tarn** (BF cc G MSG NU OS PI PK RWS RWT) All year
Presbytère de Saint Pierre, Salvagnac *Train station Montauban is 28 km away* ☏ 06.07.10.29.99 ▭ www.cotetarn.com
■ **Domaine de Gilède. Le** (BF DU GLM H NU OS PI PK RES RWS WI) All year
Route de Dremil, „En Gilède" *15 mins drive from the Place du Capitole in Toulouse* ☏ 05. 61.83.92.32 ☏ (0)6 11 88 65 74 (mobile)
▭ chambreshotesgilede.free.fr
3 guestrooms, each one of an individual bathroom and WC. Heated pool.
■ **Masestival** (AC B BF G I M MSG NU OS PI PK RWS RWT VEG WO) All year
Le clôt *35 km from Toulouse* ☏ 05.63.70.99.53 ▭ www.masestival.com
Guest house 100% Gay. „Pass Piscine".

CRUISING

-Place Saint-Aubin
-Cours Dillon (AYOR) (very popular, day & night, especially between 18-23h)
-Géant Casino Mirail (all day action in the bushes, very mixed)
-Jardin des Plantes (in the afternoon)
-Les Quais (AYOR) (Port de la Daurade, Beaux-Arts)
-Saint Aubin (21-2h)
-Ile du Ramier (very popular)
-Behind Théâtre Garonne (Digne de la Garonne, Rue du Château d'Eau).

Tours

BARS

■ **Equivoque. L'** (AC B CC G MA) 19-2h
22 rue George Sand *Centre* ☏ 02.47.61.70.07 ▭ equivoque-bar.com
■ **Glasgow Bar** (B g m MC) Tue-Sun 16-2h
23 rue Lavoisier ☏ 02.47.66.59.21
■ **P'tite Chose. La** (AC B CC GLM S ST YC) 17-2h, Sun closed
32 rue de la Grosse Tour *Bus 4,10, „Grand Marché"* ☏ 02.47.76.00.09
▭ www.lapetitechose.com
Bar lounge with cocktails.
■ **Sagitaire. Le**
130, rue Colbert ☏ 02.47.64.89.48

MEN'S CLUBS

■ **Stud. Le** (B CC DR f G MC OS P VS) 21-2h, closed Mon
84 rue Colbert *Near cathedral* ☏ 02.47.66.62.70 ▭ thestud.free.fr

DANCECLUBS

■ **Gl. Le**
13, rue Lavoisier ▭ giclub.fr

SEX SHOPS/BLUE MOVIES

■ **Miroir des Hommes** (AC DR GLM MA VS) 9-2h
34 rue Michelet ☏ 02.47.61.13.38 ▭ perso.wanadoo.fr/mbt/miroir.htm
Videos and individual cabins. 15 projection rooms.

SAUNAS/BATHS

■ **Thermes Grammont. Les** (b DR DU FC FH G GH LAB m MC MSG NU SA SB SL VS WH) 15-22, Wed -24, Fri 12-20, Sat -2h
22 avenue de Grammont ☏ 02.47.05.49.24 ▭ www.sauna-tours.com

HOTELS

■ **Château des Ormeaux** (BF glm I OS PI PK RWS) All year
24, Route de Noizay, Nazelles *In Amboise, 20 mins from Tours*
☏ 02.47.23.26.51 ▭ www.chateaudesormeaux.fr
Château des Ormeaux has 5 guest rooms. View on some of the most magnificent landscapes of the Loire Valley. Facilities in the vicinity, e.g. horse riding, canoeing, tennis courts, 18-hole golf course, sailing tours on traditional Loire boats.

GUEST HOUSES

■ **Villa Marguerite. La** (BF CC G) All year, reception 17-20h, closed Nov. 12th – Dec. 1st, Jan. 7th – Feb. 5th
8 quai de la République et 20 rue Sully, Montrichard *40 km from Tours*
☏ 02.54.32.76.67 ▭ www.lavillamarguerite.fr
Guesthouse in the Loire valley in the middle of all the royal cattles of France. Pick-up service available.

CRUISING

-Quai d'Orléans (AYOR) (around the library, at night)
-Jardin du Musée
-Jardin des Prébendes d'Oé
-Bois de la Ville-aux-Dames (5 km west of Tours direction Montlouis)
-Square Prosper-Mérimée

Trégueux

SAUNAS/BATHS

■ **Hot Box** (B CC DU FC G MA NU PI SA SB SH VR VS WH)
Mon-Thu 12-24, Fri & Sat 12-2, Sun 13-1h
15, Avenue Pierre-Mendès-France ☏ 02.96.73.61.19 ▭ www.hot-box.fr

Troyes

CRUISING

-Behind the hospital
- „The Swiss Valley" (the park beside the Boulevard Gambetta, close to the railway station, in the afternoon and at night)
-Beach of Villepart (On the bank of the river Seine; take road RN 71 in direction to Dijon, exit Bréviande, left hand; after office hours).

Urbes

GUEST HOUSES

■ **Volets Bleus Alsace Vosges. Les** (BF glm I MA OS PK RWS RWT SA) All year, 17-23h
20, rue du Brisgau *40 km from Mulhouse* ☏ 06.76.74.58.83
▭ www.lesvoletsbleusalsacevosges.fr
Beautifully restored house with garden & 2 guestrooms as well as a guest suite. Minimum 2 nights stay applies.

Uzès

GUEST HOUSES

■ **Marronniers. Les** (BF glm H m MA OS PI PK RWS RWT) All year
Place de la Mairie *12 km from Uzes, North-West of Avignon*
☏ 04.66.72.84.77 ▭ www.lesmarronniers.biz

Valence

BARS

■ **Ambigu. L'** (B g m MA)
13 Avenue Gambetta ☏ 04.75.43.90.53

DANCECLUBS

■ **Avant-Garde. L'** (AC cc D glm)
19, rue Faventines ☏ 04.75.42.90.70

SAUNAS/BATHS

■ **Double Side** (AC B CC DR DU FC FH G GH I LAB M MA NU P p RR SA SB SH SL VR VS W WH) 13-23, Fri & Sat -1h
38, rue de L'Isle ☏ 04.75.42.93.23 ▭ www.doubleside.fr
Friendly 650m² sauna.
■ **Hylas Club Sauna** (AC b DR DU f FC FH G MA p RR SA SB SL VS WH) 13-21h, closed Tue
40, avenue de Verdun *Bus 8-Sully, in the Polygone commercial centre*
☏ 04.75.56.03.62 ▭ www.hylas-sauna.fr
On 200 m² with two floors with sling.

CRUISING

-Parc Jouvet

-Rue des Musiques
-Rue G.Rey, Jardin de l'Ancienne-Préfecture
-Gorges du Doux
-Barrage de Charmes-sur-Rhône (on the east side)

Valenciennes

CRUISING

-Aire d'Hordan (both sides of the motorway Valenciennes-Paris)
-Parc de la Rhonelle
-Parc Froissart (close to P Charles de Gaulle (22-2h)
-Soccer field (22-2h)
-Aire de Millonfosse

Vichy

SAUNAS/BATHS

■ **Anthares Sauna Club** (AC b DR DU FC G LAB M MA p RR SA SB SH SL VS WH WO) 14-20, Fri-Sun -24h, closed Tue
164, avenue des Graviers *Near Camping d'Abrest* ☎ 04.70.32.89.38
www.anthares-sauna.com

CRUISING

-Parcs d'Allier
-Pont-Barrage
-Serbannes forest
-Les Iles
-Place de la Poste (Boulevard des Etats-Unis/Rue d'Italie)
-Quatre-Chemins (in the nightlife-area)

Villersexel

GUEST HOUSES

■ **Manoir Saint-Pierre** (bf GLM MA PI SA) All year
23 rue François de Grammont ☎ 03.84.63.41.62
www.manoirsaintpierre.fr

French Polynesia

Name: Polynésie Française · Französisch-Polynesien · Polinesia Francesa
Location: South Pacific
Initials: TAH
Time: GMT -10
International Country Code: ☎ 689 (no area codes)
International Access Code: ☎ 00
Language: French, Tahitian
Area: 4,167 km² / 1,359 sq mi.
Currency: CFP-Franc
Population: 246,000
Capital: Papéete (Tahiti)
Religions: 54% Protestants, 30% Roman Catholic
Climate: Jun-October is the drier and cooler period, the best time to visit. The weather gets warmer and more humid between Nov-May.

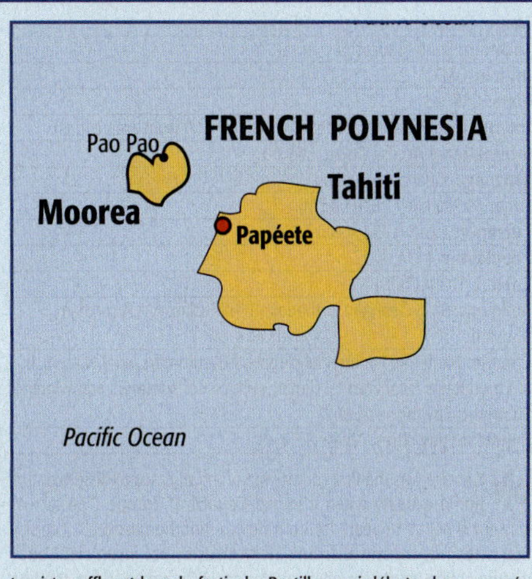

Here the French laws regarding homosexuality apply. The age of consent is set at 15 years for all. There are no gay organizations or groups, but at the same time no evident discrimination of homosexuals. The largest of the around 115 islands is Tahiti. The capital city Papéete has around 30.000 inhabitants. The Tahitians are polite and open minded and positive towards foreigners, who wish to discover the beauty of the islands. Most tourists are attracted to the island for the annual „Bastille" festival which start on the 14th of July and continue for at least 3 weeks.

Es gelten die französischen Gesetze zur Homosexualität. Das gemeinsame Schutzalter liegt bei 15 Jahren. Es gibt zwar keine schwulen Netzwerke aber ebenfalls keine Vorkommnisse von Diskriminierung gegenüber Homosexuellen. Die größte der ca. 115 Inseln Polynesiens ist Tahiti. Die Hauptstadt Papéete hat 30.000 Einwohner. Die Tahitianer sind höflich, aufgeschlossen und freuen sich über jeden Besucher, der die Schönheit der Inseln entdecken möchte. Die meisten Touristen kommen während der „Bastille"-Festivals auf die Insel, die jeweils am 14. Juli beginnen und drei Wochen andauern.

La réglementation concernant l'homosexualité est la même que pour la France. La majorité sexuelle est néanmoins fixée à 15 ans pour tous. Il n'existe pas d'associations gays mais pas de discrimination envers les homosexuel(le)s non plus. La plus grande des quelques 115 îles, Tahiti, a pour capitale Papeete, qui compte 30 000 habitants. Les Tahitiens sont amicaux, tolérants et apprécient les visiteurs venus découvrir les beautés de leurs îles. La plupart des touristes affluent lors du festival « Bastille » qui débute chaque année le 14 juillet et dure trois semaines.

Aquí rigen las leyes franceses sobre la homosexualidad. La edad de consentimiento general está fijada en los 15 años. No hay en realidad ninguna comunidad gay pero tampoco se dan casos de discriminación hacia los homosexuales. La mayor de las 115 islas de la Polinesia es Tahití. La capital, Papéete, tiene 30.000 habitantes. Los tahitianos son gente educada, abierta y se alegran de poder recibir a cualquier visitante que quiera descubrir la belleza de las islas. La mayoría de turistas llegan a la isla durante el festival „Bastille", que se inicia el día 14 de julio y dura tres semanas.

Riguardo all'omosessualità valgono le stesse leggi francesi. L'età del consenso è di 15 anni per tutti gli orientamenti sessuali. Non ci sono organizzazioni gay, ma d'altronde non ci sono neanche casi di discriminazione nei confronti dell'omosessualità. Tra le 115 isole della Polinesia Francese, Tahiti è la più grande. La capitale Papéete ha 30.000 abitanti. Gli abitanti di Tahiti sono molto cordiali e molto aperti nei confronti dei turisti. La maggior parte dei turisti viene per il festival Bastille che comincia il 14 luglio e dura tre settimane.

Rotaova – Fakarava

GUEST HOUSES

■ **Raimiti** (CC GLM M MC RWS) All year
Tetamanu ☎ 71 07 63 🖳 www.raimiti.com
Nine guestrooms.

Tahiti – Mahina

SWIMMING

-Pointe Vénus beach (from the harbour take Le Truck N° 60 to Mahina).

Tahiti – Papéete

BARS

■ **Piano. Le** (B D g MA S ST T)
Rue des Écoles *City centre* ☎ 42.88.24
A very popular mixed gay/straight club with drag shows each night.

RESTAURANTS

■ **Corbeille d'Eau. La** (B g M)
Boulevard Pomare, B.P. 20 215 ☎ 43.77.14
French cuisine.

CRUISING

-Beach south of Maeva Beach Hotel (Lots of Mahoos and Raerae)
-The way from the main road to the Bel Air Hotel (bushes on the left)
-Park Bougainville near post-office (MA) (locals in their cars about 21h)
-Around the cathedral (at night, R)
-At the beach of former Hyatt-hotel (take the bus to Mahina or Papenoo, stop at the seasideface, follow the beach to the right to the club-houses of the hotel and a bit further along the rocks (NU possible).

Tahiti – Papenoo

SWIMMING

-Surf Beach (WE YC), mainly locals
-Beach 21 km from Papéete (exactly at point kilométrique 21).

Georgia

Name: Sakartvelo, Georgien, Géorgie
Location: South Caucasus
Initials: GEO
Time: GMT +3
International Country Code: ☎ 995 (omit 0 from area codes)
International Access Code: ☎ 00
Language: Georgian, Russian
Area: 69,700 km²/ 26,911 sq mi.
Currency: 1 Lari (GEL) = 100 Tetri
Population: 4,474,000
Capital: Tbilisi (Tiflis)
Religions: 84% Georgian Orthodox, 10% Muslim, 4% Armenian Apostolic
Climate: Moderate continental climate, hot summers, cool winters. In the mountains a continental climate with colder summers and winters. Subtropical by the seaside.
Important gay cities: Tbilisi (Tiflis)

Georgia was the first country in South Caucasus to decriminalize homosexuality when it joined Council of Europe. The age of consent is set at 16 years for both hetero- and homosexuals. Legislation does not contain discriminatory clauses, yet insufficient anti-discrimination legislation often creates gaps. Georgia also has the first LGBT organization in the region and is known as most open-minded country compared to others in the region. A so-called Russian LGBT website Gay.Ru known for its opposition to the openness and public manifestations of LGBT community in Russia, expressed its full loyalty to the military intervention which current Russian authorities launched against independent Georgia.
This is not the first time when the site Gay.Ru demonstrates its full loyalty to the current political regime in Russia. In 2006 it was regularly used for attacks against the conduct of Gay Pride march in Moscow. Moreover, the site of Mr. Mishin regularly publishes materials that openness of homosexuals and coming-out are not useful and necessary for sexual minorities in Russia. According to the site, it will only create additional problems for gays and lesbians.

Georgien hat bei seiner Aufnahme in den Europarat als erstes Land des Südkaukasus die Homosexualität legalisiert. Das Schutzalter für Homo- und Heterosexuelle liegt bei 16 Jahren. Die Gesetze enthalten zwar keine diskriminierenden Klauseln, schützen aber nur ungenügend vor Diskriminierung, was die vorhandenen Rechtslücken offenbart. Georgien hat außerdem die erste LGBT-Organisation der Region und ist im Regionalvergleich als das aufgeschlossenste Land bekannt. Das sich selbst als LGBT-Website bezeichnende Internetangebot Gay.ru, bekannt dafür, in Russland gegen offene und freiheitliche Manifestationen der LGBT-Gemeinde zu opponieren, hat dem Militäreinmarsch der gegenwärtigen russischen Machthaber in das unabhängige Georgien seine volle Unterstützung ausgesprochen.
Dies ist nicht das erste Mal, dass die Website Gay.ru dem jeweiligen politischen Regime Russlands unerschütterliche Treue schwört. Schon im Jahr 2006 war sie regelmäßig für Angriffe auf die geplante Veranstaltung eines CSD-Aufmarsches in Moskau genutzt worden. Darüber hinaus veröffentlicht das von Edvard Mishin betriebene Internetangebot auch Beiträge, die den Nutzen und die Notwendigkeit eines offenen Umgangs mit der Homosexualität bzw. des Coming-Outs für sexuelle Minderheiten in Russland in Frage stellen. Wenn man der Webseite glauben schenkt, würde dies für die Schwulen und Lesben nur zusätzliche Schwierigkeiten bringen.

La Géorgie est le premier pays au sud du Caucase à avoir légalisé l'homosexualité et ce lors de son entrée au Conseil de l'Europe. La majorité sexuelle est fixée à 16 ans pour tous. Les lois ne contiennent certes aucune clause discriminatoire, mais elles ne pro-

tègent pas non plus ou insuffisamment de la discriminations et laisse nombre de vides juridiques.
Le site web Gay.ru se disant gay et lesbien est connu pour son opposition aux manifestations ouvertes et libérales de la communauté gay et lesbienne en Russie et a soutenu ouvertement l'intervention militaire de la Russie en Géorgie, pourtant indépendante.
Ce n'est pas la première fois que le site web Gay.ru voue une foi inébranlable au régime politique russe. Déjà en 2006, il a été utilisé régulièrement pour attaquer l'organisation d'une marche gay et lesbienne à Moscou. Qui plus est, ce site édité par Edvard Mishin publie également des articles qui remettent en cause l'utilité et le nécessité d'une ouverture en matière d'homosexualité ou du coming-out pour les minorités sexuelles en Russie. Si l'on en croit le site, ceci ne ferait qu'accroître les difficultés pour les gays et lesbiennes.

Georgia fue el primer país del Cáucaso en legalizar la homosexualidad cuando entró a formar parte del Consejo de Europa. La edad de consentimiento para homosexuales y heterosexuales está en los 16 años. Las leyes no contienen ninguna cláusula discriminatoria pero protegen sólo insuficientemente contra las discriminaciones, lo que conlleva lagunas legales.
La oferta de Internet autodenominada como web LGBT Gay.ru, conocida por oponerse en Rusia a las manifestaciones libres y abiertas de la comunidad LGBT, declaró su total apoyo a la invasión militar de las actuales fuerzas rusas a la Georgia independiente.
No es la primera vez que esta web Gay.ru jura fidelidad absoluta al régimen político ruso de turno. Ya en el año 2006 la utilizaron de manera regular para atacar la planeada celebración de la marcha del Orgullo Gay en Moscú. Además, esta oferta de Internet a cargo de Edvard Mishin también publica artículos que cuestionan el provecho y la necesidad de un entorno abierto con la homosexualidad o las minorías sexuales de Rusia. Si alguien otorga credibilidad a esta página web, sólo conllevará más dificultades para gays y lesbianas.

La Georgia, in conseguenza della sua entrata nel Consiglio d'Europa, è stato il primo paese del Caucaso del sud a legalizzare l'omosessualità. L'età del consenso per gli omosessuali e per gli eterossuali è per entrambi di 16 anni. Le leggi non contengono clausole che favoriscono la discrimanazione, tuttavia sono insufficenti: ne consegue che spesso si constata una vero e proprio vuoto legislativo.
Il sito gay.ru, autonominatosi sito LGBT e conosciuto in Russia per essersi opposto a delle aperte e libere manifestazioni della comunità LGBT, ha espresso il suo supporto all'incursione delle truppe militari russe nello Stato indipendente della Georgia.
Questa non è la prima volta che il sito gay.ru giura la sua fedeltà al regime politico di turno. Già nel 2006 il suddetto sito è stato usato per attaccare la manifestazione in occasione del CSD. Inoltre il sito amministrato da Edvard Mishin pubblica degli interventi che mettono in discussione l'utilità e il beneficio che può risultare da un rapporto aperto con l'omosessualità o dal coming-out da parte delle minoranze sessuali in Russia. Se si dovesse stare ai dati del sito, ciò causerebbe ai gay e alle lesbiche del Paese solo ulteriori difficoltà.

NATIONAL PUBLICATIONS

„ME" Magazine
www.inclusive-foundation.org/home
First Georgian LGBT quarterly magazine mostly in Georgian, has English resume. Provides information on human rights, health, art and culture and the main topics for the issue – coming out, lesbian and transgender issue, etc.

NATIONAL GROUPS

Inclusive Foundation
Tbilisi ☎ 32 20 66 55
www.inclusive-foundation.org
The first openly LGBT rights organization in Georgia and in South Caucasus, ILGA member. Main areas of work is advocacy and lobbying information and public awareness campaigns, study and research, empowerment of LGBT community, HIV/AIDS and STI prevention.

Batumi

CRUISING

-Alley between boulevard and beach
-Beach close to the lighthouse in pishcheviki area
-Around old railway station.

Tbilisi ☎ 032

BARS

Success (B CC D M MA NG R) 12-?h
3, Vashlovanis Street *In Perovskaia district*
Casual cruising bar, frequently visited by straight people.

CAFES

Cafe Kala (B I M MA NG s)
8-10, Erekle II Street *In Chardin area* kala.ge
Good Georgian food, many artistic people hanging out, live jazz performances, frequented by gay people.

Cafe. Le (B M MA NG)
4, Vashlovani Street *Opp. the Success bar in Perovskaia district*
Quite place with European cuisine. Friendly staff.

Rue Chardin 12 (B M MA NG)
12, Chardin Street *In old town Chardin area*
One of the most popular dining out places. A place to sit and be seen in a heart of old town. The smallest street in Tbilisi is home for number of upscale places that attract many community people. One can also find many other cafes in this area.

RESTAURANTS

Kopala (B M MA NG OS)
8-10 Chekhov Street *On the left bank of old town*
☎ (032) 32 77 55 20 (reservations) kopala.ge
Belleview terrace. Hotel restaurant with extensive menu and good service. Terrace offers one of the best views of the old town.

Meidani (B M MA NG)
2, Right Bank *In Chardin area*
☎ (032) 32 30 30 30 (reservations)
mgroup.ge
Upscale restaurant, very friendly. Offers traditional and fusion cuisine. Has chillout section with Kalian.

FITNESS STUDIOS

Vake Fitness (g MA PI SA SB SOL)
49b, Chavchavadze Avenue vakefitness.ge
Huge fitness complex with gym, olympic swimming pool, spa, sauna, gymnastics, solarium etc. Upscale workout place.

HOTELS

Sheraton Metekhi Palace
(AC B CC D H I M MA MSG NG OS PI SA WH WO)
All year
20, Telavi Street ☎ (032) 77 20 20
www.starwoodhotels.com/sheraton
Luxury hotel with 182 rooms with data port, safe, TV, phone, mini-bar and bathroom phone. Cruisy sauna.

CRUISING

-Underpass in front of the circus (dangerous)
-Rustaveli Ave. daytime cruising.

Germany

Name: Deutschland · Allemagne · Alemania · Germania
Location: Central Europe
Initials: D
Time: GMT +1
International Country Code: ☏ 49 (omit 0 from area codes)
International Access Code: ☏ 00
Language: German
Area: 357,093 km² / 137,847 sq mi.
Currency: 1 Euro (€) = 100 Cents
Population: 82,469,000
Capital: Berlin
Religions: 30% Roman Catholic, 29% Protestant
Climate: Winters can be quite cold and summers are generally warm and humid. Best time for a visit is from April to October.
Important gay cities: Berlin, Köln, München, Hamburg, Frankfurt/Main

The civil partnership law passed in Germany in 2001 as yet fails to provide equal rights, particularly in a number of tax- and civil service-related matters and in the area of joint adoption. However, the new coalition government CDU/CSU and the FDP has announced in the coalition contract to want to change this. Since 2005 the surviving relative's care and the so-called "stepchild" adoption have been made law. We will however, have to wait for common adoption rights. No likelihood of agreement here at present. Since 2006 there is also a rather tentative general parity act providing gay men and lesbians with some protection from discrimination in industrial and civil law. The state itself continues to discriminate against homosexuals in its tax laws and civil service law unchanged, but has meanwhile been forced to alter a number of regulations found to be unconstitutional by high court decisions. Notable is a comment by the Federal Constitutional Court in 2009 that no disadvantage for alternative partnerships is derivable from the "special protection of marriage" anchored in the constitution. The general age of consent in Germany is 16.

Germany has had a flourishing LGBT-infrastructure for decades. The large communities in Berlin, Cologne, Hamburg or Munich include countless associations, companies, bars and nightclubs. Even medium-sized cities have their own gay scenes. But acts of anti-gay violence still occur and discrimination persists, especially in industrial law and the Catholic Church, or from arch-conservative politicians. Even if in last decades the acceptance of gay-lesbian lifestyles has perceptibly increased, unfortunately homophobia, on the other hand, appears to be increasing. The important years of educational and acceptance work of the lesbian and gay federation (LSVD) and other organizations has decisively contributed to an increase in acceptance. Recently however the LSVD must increasingly undertake anti-homophobia work.

The Bavarian Alpine region in the south with king Ludwig's romantic castles and the beer capital Munich, the North and Baltic Sea beaches with their offshore islands, the Rhine valley to the west featuring medieval fairy-tale castles and the carnival centres Cologne, Mainz and Düsseldorf, and finally the Saxon east and its capital Dresden, called the "Florence on the Elbe" river, are all classic travel destinations that also attract many lesbians and gay men.

Deutschland hat seit 2001 ein Lebenspartnerschaftsgesetz, das eingetragenen Homopaaren noch keine gleichen Rechte bringt. Vor allem sind viele steuer- und beamtenrechtliche Regelungen noch nicht umgesetzt. Die neue Regierungskoalition aus CDU/CSU und FDP hat aber im Koalitionsvertrag angekündigt, dies ändern zu wollen. Geregelt sind seit 2005 auch die Hinterbliebenenversorgung und die Stiefkindadoption. Das gemeinsame Adoptionsrecht aber wird wohl weiterhin auf sich warten lassen. Seit 2006 gibt es ein stellenweise etwas zaghaftes Allgemeines Gleichstellungsgesetz, das Lesben und Schwule im Arbeits- und auch Zivilrecht ein wenig Schutz vor Diskriminierung gewährt. Völlig irreführend aber ist der Name des Gesetzes, denn das Ziel ist nicht die Gleichstellung. Zudem richtet es sich nur an die Bürgerinnen und Bürger sowie die Wirtschaft. Der Staat selbst setzt die Diskriminierung von Homosexuellen im Steuer- und Beamtenrecht unverändert fort, musste aber auf Grund von höchstrichterlichen Entscheidungen mittlerweile einige Gesetze umändern, da sie für verfassungswidrig erklärt wurden. Bemerkenswert ist ein Hinweis des Bundesverfassungsgerichtes von 2009, das aus dem im Grundgesetz verankerten „besonderen Schutz der Ehe" keine Benachteiligung alternativer Lebensgemeinschaften gefolgert werden darf. Das gemeinsame Schutzalter liegt in Deutschland bei 16 Jahren.

Seit Jahrzehnten hat Deutschland eine florierende lesbisch-schwule Infrastruktur. Zu den großen Homogemeinden in Berlin, Köln, Hamburg oder München gehören unzählige Vereine und viele Firmen, Kneipen oder Nachtlokale. Selbst in mittelgroßen Städten hat sich eine schwule Szene etabliert. Manchmal kommt es aber immer noch zu antihomosexuellen Gewalttaten und auch zu Diskriminierungsfällen, etwa im Arbeitsrecht oder durch Kündigungsdrohungen der Katholischen Kirche für eingetragene Lebenspartner, durch verbale Entgleisungen katholischer Bischöfe oder stockkonservativer Politiker. Auch wenn in den letzten Jahrzehnten die Akzeptanz schwul-lesbischer Lebensweisen spürbar zugenommen hat, so scheint andererseits leider die Homophobie wieder auf dem Vormarsch. Die wichtige, jahrelange Aufklärungs- und Akzeptanzarbeit des Lesben- und Schwulenverbandes (LSVD) und anderer Organisationen haben zum Akzeptanzschub entscheidend beigetragen. Seit einiger Zeit aber muss der LSVD wieder verstärkt Antihomophobiearbeit leisten.

Die Alpenregion im bayrischen Süden mit den Schlössern des romantischen Königs Ludwig und der Biermetropole München, die Nord- und Ostseestrände mit vorgelagerten Inseln, das Rheinland im Westen mit den mittelalterlichen Märchenburgen und den Karnevalshochburgen Köln, Mainz und Düsseldorf sowie der sächsische Osten mit der auch Elb-Florenz genannten Hauptstadt Dresden sind allesamt klassische und auch bei Lesben und Schwulen sehr beliebte Reiseziele.

Depuis 2001, l'Allemagne dispose d'une loi de reconnaissance des couples qui n'offrent pas encore aux couples gays les mêmes droits, en particulier fiscaux, d'adoption ou pour les fonctionnaires.

Dans son contrat de coalition, la nouvelle coalition gouvernementale CDU/CSU et FDP a cependant signalisé vouloir changer cela. Depuis

2005 la couverture du conjoint survivant et l'adoption de l'enfant du conjoint sont réglementées. Le droit commun d'adoption risque encore de se faire attendre.

Depuis 2006, une loi d'égalité de traitement protége les gays en droit civil et du travail. Cette loi trompe car il ne s'agit pas véritablement d'égalité et ne s'applique qu'aux citoyens et à l'économie. L'Etat lui-même continue d'appliquer des discriminations pour les homosexuels en matière de droit fiscal et de la fonction publique mais a dû modifier quelques lois déclarées inconstitutionnelles par la Haute Cour de Justice. Une indication de la Cour Constitutionnelle Fédérale en 2009 est particulièrement remarquable en affirmant que la „protection particulière du mariage" ancrée dans la Constitution ne peut conduire à un préjudice des autres formes de vie commune. La majorité sexuelle est fixée à 16 ans pour tous.

La scènes gay fleurit depuis des décennies. Les plus grandes communautés sont Berlin, Cologne, Hambourg et Munich avec d'innombrables associations, entreprises, bars... Même dans les villes moyennes, une scène se développe. Cependant on continue toujours de répertorier des violences homophobes ou des discriminations, par exemple en droit du travail ou par l'église catholique qui menace de licenciement ses employés lors de l'enregistrement du partenaire, lors de dérapages verbaux d'évêques et hommes politiques ultra-conservateurs.

Même si ces dernières décennies l'acceptation des gays et lesbiennes a sensiblement augmenté, d'un autre côté malheureusement l'homophobie semble progresser. Les campagnes d'information et d'acceptation de la Lesben- und Schwulenverbandes (LSVD, fédération gay et lesbienne) et d'autres organisations ont largement contribué à cette acceptation croissante. Depuis quelques temps la LSVD doit de nouveau mener des campagnes contre l'homophobie.

La région des Alpes dans le sud, en Bavière, avec les châteaux du romantique roi Louis II et Munich, sa métropole de la bière ; les plages et les îles de la Baltique et de la Mer du Nord ; la Rhénanie à l'ouest, ses châteaux forts moyenageux et ses carnavals à Cologne, Mayence et Düsseldorf ; sans oublier la Saxe à l'est et sa capitale Dresde: des classiques très appréciés des touristes gays.

La ley de parejas de hecho, vigente en Alemania desde 2001, deja un vacío legal en áreas como los regimenes de impuestos, la reglamentación de derechos de funciones públicas o el derecho de adopción.

El nuevo Gobierno de coalición del CDU/CSU y el FDP, ha anunciado en su acuerdo de coalición su deseo de cambiar esto. Ya en 2005 quedaron reguladas las pensiones de invalidez y la adopción de hijastros, pero el derecho de adopción conjunto aún tendrá que esperar.

Desde 2006 protege en cierto modo a gays y lesbianas contra la discriminación laboral asegurando sus derechos civiles. Pero el nombre de esta ley es engañoso, pues va dirigido a la economía y los ciudadanos en general, perpetuándose de esta manera la discriminación hacia los homosexuales. El propio Estado mantiene la discriminación de los homosexuales en el Derecho Tributario y Funcionarial sin modificaciones, pero ha tenido que cambiar algunas leyes debido a decisiones del Tribunal Supremo, ya que estas fueron declaradas inconstitucionales. Cabe destacar una indicación de la Corte Constitucional Federal de 2009 consagrada en la constitución, la ìprotección especial del matrimonioî, en la que se estableció que no se puede discriminar a las convivencias conyugales alternativas. La edad de consentimiento sexual se encuentra en Alemania en los 16 años de edad.

Alemania cuenta con una gran oferta de vida gay: Berlín, Colonia, Hamburgo o Munich cuentan con todo tipo de asociaciones, compañías, bares y locales nocturnos. Incluso en ciudades no tan grandes se puede encontrar zonas de ambiente gay.

La percepción de gays y lesbianas en Alemania es en general positiva y esto se debe, en parte, al trabajo realizado durante años por las asociaciones de gays y lesbianas en educación sexual y en integración social.

Aunque la aceptación de los estilos de vida de gays y lesbianas haya crecido de manera significativa en décadas recientes, lamentablemente la homofobia parece estar de nuevo en auge. Son importantes, los años de trabajo en educación y aceptación por parte de la Asociación de Lesbianas y Gays (LSVD por sus siglas en alemán) y otras organizaciones, ya que estas han contribuido en gran medida a la aceptación de la homosexualidad en la sociedad alemana actual. Sin embargo, hace ya tiempo que la LSVD tiene que reforzar su labor social en trabajos contra la homofobia.

La región de los Alpes al sur de Baviera, Munich, la cuna de la cerveza, las playas del Báltico y del mar del norte, Renania, con sus fantásticas ciudades medievales; el carnaval de Colonia, Maguncia y Dusseldorf, así como el este sajón, con la ciudad de Dresde son algunos de los clásicos destinos turísticos preferidos por la comunidad gay en Alemania.

Dal 2001 la Germania dispone di una legge sulle cosiddette unioni registrate che però non garantisce alle coppie omosessuali uguali diritti. Molti regolamenti che riguardano le tasse, il diritto amministrativo e il diritto di adozione rimangono ancora inapplicati.

La nuova coalizione di governo formata da CDU/CSU e FDP ha già però annunciato una modifica. Dal 2005 esistono anche leggi che regolano la reversibilità della pensione per il partner rimasto in vita e l'adozione dei figliastri. Per la comune adozione, invece, bisognerà ancora aspettare.

Nel 2006 è entrata in vigore una timida legge per la parificazione, che offre un minimo di tutela da discriminazioni anche a gay e lesbiche particolarmente nell'ambito del diritto di lavoro e del diritto civile. Lo Stato continua però a discriminare gli omosessuali nel diritto tributario e nel diritto amministrativo. In Germania lo Stato continua a perpetrare discriminazioni nei confronti degli omosessuali nel campo fiscale; tuttavia grazie a delle sentenze della Corte Costituzionale, la Germana si è vista costretta ad adeguare delle leggi dichiarate anticostituzionali. Degna di nota è la decisione della Corte Costituzionale tedesca del 2009 che ritiene che la distinzione tra unione solidale e matrimonio non possa essere giustificata dalla protezione particolare del secondo, sottolineando che lìistituto del matrimonio può essere tutelato senza che sia necessario svantaggiare lìuno o lìaltro stile di vita. L'età del consenso è di 16 anni.

Già da decenni in Germania c'è una scena gay e lesbica molto strutturata. Nelle grandi comunità omosessuali di Berlino, Colonia, Amburgo e Monaco ci sono tantissime organizzazioni, aziende, pub e locali notturni. Una scena gay si va strutturando anche nelle città medio-grandi. Si registrano ancora atti di violenza e di discriminazione a sfondo omofobo sui posti di lavoro o sottoforma di minacce di licenziamento da parte della chiesa cattolica, o ancora sottoforma di deviazioni verbali di vescovi cattolici o di politici ultraconservatori.
Sebbene negli ultimi decenni l'apertura nei confronti dell'omosessualità sia sensibilmente aumentata, purtroppo anche i casi di omofobia stanno altrettanto aumentando. A questa apertura hanno sicuramente contribuito i notevoli sforzi dell'associazione gay e lesbica tedesca LSVD e di altre organizzazioni. Da un po' di tempo, però, la LSVD si vede costretta ad occuparsi nuovamente di campagne antiomofobia. Mete turistiche classiche molto amate anche da gay e lesbiche sono le zone alpine nel sud della Baviera con i castelli del romantico Re Ludovico, la metropoli della birra, Monaco, le spiagge del Mar Baltico e del Mar del Nord con le tante isole antistanti, la Renania con i suoi castelli fiabeschi e con le roccaforti del carnevale Colonia, Magonza e Düsseldorf e infine la Sassonia con il suo capoluogo di Regione Dresda, chiamata anche Firenze sull'Elba.

NATIONAL GAY INFO

■ **Akademie Waldschlösschen** (GLM H)
Mon-Fri 8.30-12.30, Wed 15-18h
Waldschlößchen 1 ✉ 37130 Reinhausen *13km south east from Göttingen*
☎ (05592) 92 770 🖳 www.waldschloesschen.org
Conference hotel offering seminars, conferences and workshops for gays and lesbians. Please ask for free programme leaflet.

NATIONAL PUBLICATIONS

■ **Adam**
Foerster Media, Sprendlinger Landstraße 120 ✉ 63069 Offenbach
☎ (069) 83 10 22 🖳 www.foerstermedia.com
National monthly glossy.

■ **blu** (GLM)
Sophienstraße 8 ✉ 10178 Berlin ☎ (030) 443 19 80 🖳 www.blu.fm
Monthly gay magazine available for free at gay venues. Regional editions.

■ **Dreamboys**
c/o Bruno Gmünder Verlag GmbH, Kleiststraße 23-26 ✉ 10787 Berlin
☎ (030) 615 00 30
Monthly publication: erotic photography of young men and stories. 76 pages. € 9,95 / CHF 18,70. Subscription price € 89,95 (12 issues/year plus 2 special issues).

■ **Du&Ich**
c/o Jackwerth-Verlag, Tempelhofer Ufer 11 ✉ 10963 Berlin
☎ (030) 23 55 39 0 🖳 www.du-und-ich.net
National gay magazine, published bi-monthly.

■ **gaylife Magazin**
Garschargerstraße 20 ✉ 42899 Remscheid ☎ 089 / 453 44 376
🖳 www.gaylife24.com
Gay website with infos and news

■ **Macho**
c/o Bruno Gmünder Verlag GmbH, Kleiststraße 23-26 ✉ 10787 Berlin
☎ (030) 615 00 30
Monthly gay mazagine with many hunks and erotic stories. 76 pages. € 9,95 / CHF 18,70. Subscription price € 89,95 (12 issues/year plus 2 special issues).

■ **Männer**
c/o Bruno Gmünder Verlag GmbH, Kleiststraße 23-26 ✉ 10787 Berlin
☎ (030) 615 00 30 🖳 www.m-maenner.de
Germany's leading gay lifestyle magazine. Monthly publication with news, articles, reviews, interviews and photographs on around 100 pages.

■ **Mate**
c/o Sergej Medien- und Verlags-GmbH, Sophienstrasse 8
✉ 10178 Berlin ☎ (030) 44 31 98 35 🖳 www.mate-magazine.com
Quarterly gay lifestyle magazine in German.

■ **Porn Up**
c/o Bruno Gmünder Verlag GmbH, Kleiststraße 23-26 ✉ 10787 Berlin
☎ (030) 615 00 30 🖳 pornup.tv
Hardcore magazine with hot photo series every month from 6 cutting edge films on 76 pages, plus a free porn DVD with a full length hardcore film (12 issues/year plus special issues). Only € 12.95 / CHF 27 / US$ 16.95.

■ **Spartacus Traveler**
c/o Bruno Gmünder Verlag GmbH, Kleiststraße 23-26 ✉ 10787 Berlin
☎ (030) 615 00 30 🖳 www.spartacustraveler.com
Magazine for the gay traveller. 4 editions per year, 74 pages. In German only. Annual subscription € 11,95.

NATIONAL PUBLISHERS

■ **Bruno Gmünder Verlag**
Kleiststraße 23-26 ✉ 10787 Berlin ☎ (030) 615 00 30
🖳 www.brunogmuender.com
Publisher of SPARTACUS International, national editions, BERLIN VON HINTEN guide book, MÄNNER-magazine, SPARTACUS TRAVELER-magazine, DREAMBOYS-magazine, MACHO-magazine, PORN UP-magazine, fiction, non-fiction, photo books, DVD and video sale. Two shops in Berlin, one in Cologne, one in Hamburg and one in Munich.

■ **Himmelstürmer Verlag**
Kirchenweg 12 ✉ 20099 Hamburg ☎ (040) 64 88 56 08
🖳 www.himmelstuermer.de

■ **Männerschwarm Verlag**
Lange Reihe 102 ✉ 20099 Hamburg ☎ (040) 430 26 50
🖳 www.maennerschwarm.de

■ **MATTEI Medien**
Norbertstraße 2-4 ✉ 50670 Köln ☎ (0221) 390 66 – 0
🖳 www.mattei-medien.de
Publishers of local magazines „rik" and local gay guides.

Ich will Männer!
MÄNNER
10 JAHRE HOMOEHE
BEL AMI PRIVAT
Zu Besuch bei George Duroy und seinen Jungs
LADY GAGA
GLEE-STAR CHRIS COLFER
EXKLUSIV
GEORGE MICHAEL
BEST OF GAY POP
Die heißesten Songs, die schwulsten Heteros, die coolsten Newcomer
CHRIS HEMSWORTH
UNSER NEUER FILMGOTT: DER MANN MIT DEM HAMMER AUS THOR
GLAMOUR, SEX, SKANDALE
CHRIS EVANS
HEISSER BRUDER
Hollywoods homofreundlichster Superstar
EXKLUSIV
BEN COHEN
Der Rugby-Star über seinen Kampf gegen Homophobie im Sport
DU SCHWULE SAU!
INTERVIEW
HUGH JACKMAN
VERBOTENE LIEBE
DIE TOP 50
DANIEL CRAIG
SCHWUL IN DER TÜRKEI
JAHRES-HOROSKOP 2012

■ **Querverlag**
Akazienstraße 25 ✉ 10823 Berlin ☎ (030) 78 70 23 39
🖳 www.querverlag.de
Publisher of gay and lesbian fiction and non-fiction.

NATIONAL COMPANIES

■ **b.i.m.p. / eurogay**
Mittelweg 141 ✉ 20148 Hamburg ☎ (040) 21 00 65 60
🖳 www.eurogay.de
Gay information, community tools and lifestyle.

■ **Beate Uhse**
Gutenbergstraße 12 ✉ 24941 Flensburg ☎ (0461) 99 66 0
🖳 www.beate-uhse.ag
Germany's largest chain of sex shops with branches throughout Europe. Also mail order.

■ **Bruno's Mail Order**
Zeughofstraße 1 ✉ 10997 Berlin ☎ (030) 61 50 03 81
🖳 www.brunos.de
Fiction, non-fiction, photo-books, videos, calendars, CDs, DVDs. Free catalogue.

■ **Cazzo Film GmbH & Co KG**
Adalbertstraße 5 ✉ 10999 Berlin ☎ (030) 69 50 52 45
🖳 www.cazzofilm.com
Producers of high quality German porn films.

■ **Communigayte**
Buchwaldstraße 42 ✉ 63303 Dreieich ☎ (06103) 87 060 87
🖳 www.communigayte.de
Agency for gay marketing and advertising.

■ **Friends Medien** (GLM MA)
Max-Eyth-Str. 22 ✉ 71686 Remseck ☎ 07146 286330
🖳 www.gaymap.info
Publisher of worldwide Friends The Gaymap, Go Friends rewards program and Navigaytor Hoteldirectory.

■ **Gay Tantra**
☎ (030) 26344515 🖳 www.gay-tantra.de
Internatioal seminars, retreats and trainings.

■ **Heinz & Horst**
Hauptstraße 26 ✉ 10827 Berlin ☎ (030) 69 50 86 14
🖳 www.heinzundhorst.de

■ **Janssen Versand**
Pariser Straße 45 ✉ 10719 Berlin ☎ (030) 881 15 90
🖳 www.galerie-janssen.de

■ **Männer Natürlich** (G) Mon-Sat 11-20h
Im Mühlenbach 81 ✉ 53127 Bonn ☎ (0228) 254 434
🖳 www.maenner-natuerlich.com
Organizer of gay group tours.

■ **Queer.de** (GLM MA)
c/o Queer Communications GmbH, Rengsdorfer Str. 2 ✉ 51105 Köln
☎ (0221) 355 337 25 50 🖳 www.queer.de
Germany's gay news and entertainment site.

■ **SHAPE.FM** (GLM YC)
Geisbergstraße 29 ✉ 10777 Berlin ☎ (030) 8182 108 0
🖳 www.shape-fm.de
Dancemusic nonstop – 24/7!

■ **Sling King** (F)
Otto-Schill-Str. 10 ✉ 04109 Leipzig ☎ (0163) 441 32 83 (mobile)
🖳 www.slingking.eu

■ **Tom on Tour**
Postfach 14 01 63 ✉ 80451 München 🖳 www.tomontour.de
Internet travel portal.

■ **Wurstfilm**
Hauptstraße 26 ✉ 10827 Berlin *U-Kleistpark* ☎ (030) 69 50 56 02
🖳 www.wurstfilm.com
Producer of gay porn films.

NATIONAL GROUPS

■ **Deutsche AIDS-Hilfe e.V.** (glm MA)
Wilhelmstraße 138 ✉ 10963 Berlin ☎ (030) 690 08 70
🖳 www.iwwit.de
The Deutsche AIDS-Hilfe has been doing prevention and information campaigns since the early 80's. Branches and offices can be found throughout the country. Please contact them for information regarding addresses and services.

■ **ILGA-Berlin**
c/o Hartmut Schönknecht, Elberfelder Straße 23 ✉ 10555 Berlin
☎ (030) 392 53 11 🖳 www.ilga-europe.org, www.ilga.org

■ **LSVD – Lesben- und Schwulenverband in Deutschland e. V.** (GLM MA) Office hours Mon-Thu 10-17, Fri -16h
Pipinstraße 7 ✉ 50667 Köln *Near Heumarkt* ☎ (0221) 925 96 10
🖳 www.lsvd.de
Gay & lesbian umbrella organization for Germany. Call for info about local LSVD-groups. Emergency helpline Mon & Fri 19-21h ☎ 19-228.

COUNTRY CRUISING

-A1 (E47) Hamburg → Puttgarden P »Stapelfeld« after exit Ahrensburg, wood
-A1 (E22) Bremen → Lübeck Road house »Hamburg-Stillhorn«
-A1 (E31), A3 (E35), A4 (E40) Kölner Ring all P
-A1 (E37) Bremen → Dortmund Raststätte »Münsterland« (Wood behind road house. (Mon only)
-A1 (E37) Bremen → Osnabrück P »Mahndorfer Marsch« after Bremer Kreuz, popular -4h
-A1 (E37) Dortmund ⇆ Bremen between Hamm-Bergkamen and Hamm-Bockum/Werne
-A1 (E422) Trier → Saarbrücken 1st resting place → Saarbrücken (15 mins past Trier)
-A2 Bottrop → Oberhausen (P between »Bottrop« and »Oberhausen-Sterkrade«)
-A2 Hannover → Minden P between »Porta Westfalica-Veltheim« and »Paderborn-Sennelager« (day and night in the wood)
-A215 Hamburg ⇆ Kiel, P Rumohr, exit Blumenthal (sunbathing)
-A3 (E35) Wiesbaden → Köln P past »Niedernhausen«
-A3 (E42) Frankfurt → Nürnberg P past »Offenbach« P past »Seligenstadt«
-A3 (E42) Frankfurt → Würzburg Roadhouse „Weiskirchen" Raststätte
-A3 (E42) Wiesbaden → Würzburg P between »Frankfurter Kreuz« & »Frankfurt-Süd«
-A3 Passau ⇆ Regensburg P between „Hengersberg" & „Igensbach"
-A3 → Neatherlands P Stockweg, between exits 15 and 16
-A4 (E40) Chemnitz ⇆ Glauchau P »Rabensteiner Wald« wood behind the road house
-A4 (E40) Köln → Aachen P between »Eschweiler« & »Weisweiler«
-A4 Köln ⇆ Aachen P between Kerpen and Buir and between Aachener Kreuz and Aachen-Zentrum
-A4 Köln ⇆ Olpe (MA) P Hasbacher Höhe, 24h
-A4 Köln ⇆ Olpe P Mörkepütz
-A5 (E35) Darmstadt → Karlsruhe P past »Kreuz Walldorf« P past »Bruchsal«
-A5 (E451) Darmstadt ⇆ Frankfurt P Langen in both directions after »Langen/Mörfelden«
-A5 Basel → Karlsruhe P before exit Offenburg (P Schutter)
-A5 Karlsruhe → Basel P before Exit Lahr (P Unditz)
-A5 Frankfurt → Heidelberg P Fliegwiese (22-?h)
-A5 Heidelberg → Mannheim (Weinheim. WC)
-A6 (E50) Saarbrücken ⇆ Kaiserslautern P St. Ingbert, Silbersandquelle, Kahlenberg & Homburger Bruch
-A6 Mannheim → Heilbronn P past »Kreuz Walldorf« P near Heilbronn
-A6 Saarbrücken → Mannheim P between Landstuhl and Kaiserslautern-Einsiedlerhof
-A6 Stuttgart ⇆ Heilbronn 1st P past Neckarsulm
-A7 (E45) Kassel ⇆ Fulda P between »Guxhagen« & »Melsungen«
-A7 Flensburg → Hamburg P Hüsby between »Schleswig/Schuby« & »Schleswig-Jagel«
-A7 Hamburg ⇆ Kolding P »Altholzkrug« & »Handewitter Forst«
-A7 Hamburg → Flensburg P Sielsbrook between »Bad Bramstedt« and »Neumünster-Wittorf«
-A7 Hamburg ⇆ Quickborn P »Bönningstedt«

-A7 Ulm ⇆ Hittisstetten 1st 🅿 past Kreuz Hittisstetten (evening until 24h)
-A8 Saarlouis ⇆ Pirmasens 🅿 »Kutzhof« between »Kreuz Saarbrücken« & »Heuweiler«
-A8 München → Salzburg, 3 km after the exit „Felden", 🅿 with WC, underpath towards the Chiemsee
-A8 München → Salzburg, 🅿 before exit Aibling
-A9 München ⇆ Nürnberg 🅿 between »Manching« & »Langenbruck«
-A93 München-Regensburg, 🅿 Elsenburg or Siegenburg on both sides, that are connected by a bridge
-A23 Oldenburg → Wilhelmshaven🅿 Varel
-A24 (E26) Berlin → Hamburg 🅿 »Hahnenkoppel« (past »Witzhave«. WC & Wald (F) Thu)
-A28 (E234) Bremen → Bremerhaven 🅿 after the garbage disposal factory
-A29 Oldenburg → Wilhelmshaven 🅿 between „Varel-Obenstrohe" & „Varel-Bockhorn"
-A30 (E30) Osnabrück ⇆ Amsterdam 🅿 between „Lotte" & „Ibbenbüren/Laggenbeck"
-A31 Bottrop ⇆ Schüttorf 🅿 Dorsten-Holsterhausen
-A33 Paderborn 🅿 Paderborn-Elsen
-A33 Paderborn → Bielefeld 🅿 zwischen Paderborn-Schloss Neuhaus & Paderborn-Sennelager 🅿 Teutoburger Wald
-All 🅿 along the A33 between Bielefeld and Paderborn (also in the other direction). Especially the last 🅿 before the A2 (before the exit Hövelhof) large cruising area in the woods
-A42 Bottrop → Oberhausen 🅿 between »Bottrop« & »Oberhausen-Sterkrade« 🅿 »Castrop-Bladenhorst«
-A42 Dortmund ⇆ Gelsenkirchen 🅿 Castrop-Rauxel-Bladenhorst
-A43 Wuppertal → Münster Raststätte »Hohe Mark« & 🅿 »Haltern« & 🅿 »Speckhorn«
-A44 Aachen ⇆ Düsseldorf 🅿 Im Tunnel between Aachen-Brand and Aachener Kreuz
-A44 Kassel-Dortmund ⇆ 🅿 Am Baunsberg (Baunatal)
-A45 🅿 Dortmund-Marten (both sides) 🅿 Dortmund-Hoyensburg (both sides)
-A45 🅿 Universitätsstraße (opp. exit Dortmund-Eichlinghofen)
-A46 🅿 between Kreuz Hilden and Haan-Ost (both sides)
-A46 Düsseldorf ⇆ Heinsberg 🅿 »Herrather Linde«
-A48 Koblenz → Trier, first 🅿 after Koblenzer Kreuz
-A48 Trier → Koblenz 🅿 between Kreuz Koblenz and Koblenz Nord, at night only
-A49 Kassel ⇆ Fritzlar 🅿 Scharfenstein-Gudensberg
-A52 Düsseldorf ⇆ Mönchengladbach Raststätte »Cloerbruch« (on each side at the end in wooded area)
-A52 Möchengladbach → Düsseldorf 🅿 »Wolfskull«
-A57 (E31) Köln → Neuss 🅿 past »Köln-Chorweiler«
-A57 🅿 Kamp-Lintfort
-A57 Düsseldorf → Krefeld 🅿 Geißmühle (evenings)
-A59 🅿 between Düsseldorf-Garath and Monheim-Bamberg (both sides)
-A62 Pirmasens ⇆ Landstuhl 🅿 »Sickinger Höhe«
-A66 Parkplatz 🅿 between exit Gelnhausen West and Gelnhausen Ost
-A67 (E451) Frankfurt → Mannheim 🅿 between »Lorsch« & »Viernheimer Dreieck«
-A71 🅿 Schmira direction A4. Fri-Sat from 21h
-A73 Nürnberg ⇆ Erlangen 🅿 past »Eltersdorf« (in the wood)
-A81 (E41) Stuttgart ⇆ Heilbronn 🅿 »Kälbling« between »Mundelsheim« & »Pleidelsheim«
-A81 (E41) Stuttgart ⇆ Singen 🅿 »Eschachtal« (AYOR) (between »Rottweil« and »Villingen-Schwenningen«. Pedestrian subway)
-A115 (E51) Potsdam ⇆ Berlin, exit Babelsberg 🅿 „Parforceheide" and „Stern" in the nearby forest
-A480 (Gießener Ring) Marburg -Kassel-Eisenach 🅿 »Am Silbersee« (toilets/WC), 1300 m after exit »Wettenberg«, busy after sunset till dawn (WE -6h)
-A480 (Gießener Ring) Wetzlar-Limburg-Dortmund 🅿 »Am Pützenfeld« (toilets/WC), 1800 m before exit, busy after sunset till dawn (WE -6h)
-A661 Frankfurt ⇆ Darmstadt 🅿 between »Offenbach-Taunusring« & »Offenbacher Kreuz«

MAIL ORDER

Fun 24 Online (G SH)
☎ +49 179 998 10 90 (Germany) ☎ +45 36 95 03 70 (Denmark)
www.fun24-online.com

Aachen ☎ 0241

CAFES

Labyrinth (B BF glm M MA OS) 12-1h
Pontstraße 156 ☎ (0241) 355 95

DANCECLUBS

Ahoi Club @ Apollo Kino & Bar (B D G MA) 2nd Sat/month 23-?h
Pontstraße 141-149 www.ahoi-club.de

SEX SHOPS/BLUE MOVIES

Erotixx (AC b DR G MA VS) 9-1, Sun 14-24h
Gasborn 17 *City, near Kaiserplatz* ☎ (0241) 206 35
www.erotixx24.eu
2 cinemas, 16 cabins in club, 1000 programs, DVD sales.

Euro Video Aachen (AC DR g I MA VS) Gay films: Tue & Thu 11-24, Fri 19-24, Sat 22-?h
Steffensplatz 4 *Near Adalbertsteinweg, Amtsgericht* ☎ (0241) 912 80 70
www.euro-video-aachen.de

CRUISING

-University cafeteria (Mensa), in the basement
-Kármán-Auditorium
-Bus station in the Petersstraße
-Saarstraße/"Ehrenmal" (ayor r, popular).

Aalen ☎ 07361

CAFES

Cafe Dannenmann (b glm m MA)
Alter Kirchplatz 8
Mixed crowd, many gays.

CRUISING

-Bucher-Stausee, after dark, near the DLRG house, Rainau
-Cabin at the VFR-Stadium, 400m direction cemetery on the left 50m into the forest
-Limes Therme, Sat & Sun
-🅿Tiefen Stollen in Aalen-Wasseralfingen, mostly Sun after 20h.

Ahrenshoop ☎ 038220

HOTELS

Künstlerquartier Seezeichen (B BF cc glm H M MA MSG OS PA PK RWB RWS RWT SA SB SOL WO)
Dorfstraße 22 *On the beach* ☎ (038220) 6797-0
www.seezeichen-hotel.de
Gay-friendly hotel directly on the beach.

Altenau ☎ 05328

HOTELS

Haus Waldfrieden (b BF g M MA OS PA PK RWS SA) All year
Bürgermeister-Breyel-Weg 1-3 ☎ (05328) 14 50 252
www.waldfrieden-altenau.de
Hotel with long running club-bar and sauna. 15 guestrooms.

Augsburg ☎ 0821

BARS

Fegefeuer (B d GLM MA ST) 20-3, Fri & Sat -5h
Ludwigstraße 34 ☎ (0821) 508 9817 www.fegefeuer-augsburg.de
Drag-shows on special events.

CAFES

■ **Centro** (B glm MA OS) 9-24, Sun 10-24h
Maximilianstraße 35 *Moritzplatz* ☏ (0821) 51 33 69

DANCECLUBS

■ **Lovepop @ Kantine** (B D GLM MA) Sat 22h-open end, various dates
Am Exerzierplatz 25a, 💻 www.lovepop.info
Special gay parties, see www.lovepop.info

■ **Club Ideal** (B D GLM MA OS S)
Göggingerstraße 26-28 ☏ (0821) 58 96 007 💻 www.club-ideal.de

SEX SHOPS/BLUE MOVIES

■ **Inkognito** (AC CC DR g MA VS)
Mon-Thu 12-24, Fri & Sat -2, Sun & public holidays 14-22h
Theaterstraße 6 *Next to Stadttheater* ☏ (0821) 15 36 52
💻 www.inkognito-augsburg.de
With gay cinema and cabins.

■ **Triebwerk** (DR glm MA VS) Sun-Thu 12-2, Fri & Sat -4h
Bahnhofstr. 21 ☏ (0821) 2193 9750 💻 www.triebwerk-kino.de

SWIMMING

-Auensee near Kissing, below the barrier on the north shore (also cruising in the nearby forest)
-Kaisersee, near the Airport, nudist-area
-Lechbarrage 23, good spots along the river Lech, follow either from parkinglot left hand side a small pathway to the peninsula or right hand side along the shorewalk.

CRUISING

-Park ,Rotes Tor' after 24h
-Autobahnsee – 2nd parking lot (evenings)
-Schwedenstiege (part of the medieval city walls) south of Stephingerberg to Karmelitenmauer
-Wertach/Schwimmschulstraße heavy cruising (AYOR)
-Wolfzahnau, on the gravelisland, under the MAN-Bridge over the river Lech.

Bad Saarow ☏ 033631

HOTELS

■ **Esplanade Resort & Spa** (AC B BF glm I M MA MSG PI RWB RWS SA SB SH SOL) All year
Seestraße 49 ☏ (033631) 4320 💻 www.esplanade-resort.de
Exclusive wellness-resort on the banks of a peaceful lake within a 50 minutes drive from Berlin city.

Baden-Baden ☏ 07221

SEX SHOPS/BLUE MOVIES

■ **Video Sex Shop** (b glm MA VS) daily 09.30-1.30 & 2.30-7h
Lichtentaler Straße 44 ☏ (07221) 26 539

SWIMMING

-Baggersee Krieger, Söllingen, nude swimming on the northern shore of the lake (also cruising in the forest)
-Petersee, near golf-course (also cruising near parkinglot or along the path direction lake).

CRUISING

-DRK Clinic, park behind the Caracalla Thermal Bath, under the bridge (upper part of the park)
-Kurpark near the Tennis-courts, Ludwig-Wilhelm-Straße, mostly on weekends after 21h
-Augustaplatz facilities, toilet coin operated, very clean.

Bamberg ☏ 0951

BARS

■ **Galerie am Stephansberg** (B glm m MA OS) 19-?h, Mon closed
Unterer Stephansberg 5 *Stephanskirche* ☏ (0951) 560 00
Small and rustic wine-pub for students and artists. Some gays around.

■ **m lounge** (AC B D GLM I MA OS S ST) Sun-Thu 20-2, Fri & Sat 20-5h
Schranne 7 ☏ (0171) 362 9554 (mobile)
DJs on weekends, Fri & Sat gay party.

CRUISING

-Am Kranen (under the bridges)
-Underground garage at Karstadt department store
-Wanderparkplatz in Litzendorf
-Wegemann-Ufer underneath the Marien-Bridge.

Bansin ☏ 038378

HOTELS

■ **Villa von Desny** (BF glm M MA OS PK RWB RWS RWT VA WH)
All year
Strandpromenade 4 *On the island Usedom* ☏ (038378) 24 30
💻 www.villa-von-desny.de

Bayreuth ☏ 0921

SEX SHOPS/BLUE MOVIES

■ **Joy Erotik-Paradies** (DR g MA VS) Mon-Sat 10-23h
Bahnhofstr. 17 ☏ 220 80 30 💻 www.joy-bayreuth.com
Gay day on Sun.

CRUISING

-P Albrecht-Dürer-Straße
-Park near Festspielhaus.

Berlin ☏ 030

Berlin is certainly always worth a visit, also bearing in mind that Berlin as a place of residence for people from all over world is becoming more and more popular. It is the most inexpensive capital city in Western Europe and slowly becoming the gay capital of Europe! Highlights in the events calendar for Berlin include the Easter meeting for bears and friends, the Folsom Street party, the Hustler Ball and of course the many large sex parties which take place here. See the events calendar at the back of this guide for further details.
Berlin's gay scene is spread out across two main districts called Schoeneberg and Prenzlauer Berg and has two alternative, smaller epicentres in the less commercial Kreuzberg and the younger, somewhat student oriented Friedrichshain.

Mit Sicherheit ist Berlin immer eine Reise wert. Doch auch als Wohnort erfreut es sich bei Menschen aus der ganzen Welt zunehmender Beliebtheit. Berlin ist nicht nur eine der preiswertesten Metropolen, sondern entwickelt sich auch immer mehr zur Schwulenhauptstadt Europas! Nicht zuletzt durch ihren offen schwulen Bürgermeister und dessen Satz „Berlin ist arm, aber sexy" ist die Stadt bekannt geworden.
Zu den Höhepunkten des Berliner Eventkalenders zählen das Ostertreffen für „Bears" und ihre Freunde, das Folsom Street Festival, der Hustler Ball und natürlich die vielen Sex- und Fetishpartys, die hier regelmäßig stattfinden. Termine sind dem Veranstaltungskalender am Ende dieses Reiseführers zu entnehmen.
Das heutige Berlin ist aus vielen Dörfern und Städten rund um die alte preußische Königsresidenz zusammengewachsen. Jeder Bezirk hat daher einen eigenen Charakter und ein eigenes Zentrum. Dies gilt zum Teil auch für die schwule Szene, die sich hauptsächlich auf die Bezirke Schöneberg und Prenzlauer Berg sowie zwei alternative Nebenzentren – das linke, unkommerzielle Kreuzberg und das junge, studentische Friedrichshain – verteilt.

Berlin vaut toujours le détour et même de plus en plus de personnes des quatre coins du monde s'y installent. Berlin est non seulement une des métropoles les moins chères mais devient aussi la capitale gay européenne ! Son maire gay et sa phrase célèbre „ Berlin est pauvre mais sexy „ ont aussi fait parler de la ville.
Parmi les moments forts de l'année berlinoise, on trouve la rencontre de Pâques pour les „ bears „ et leurs amis, la Folsom Street, le Hustler Ball et bien-sûr les nombreuses et régulières soirées sexe et fétichistes. Les dates

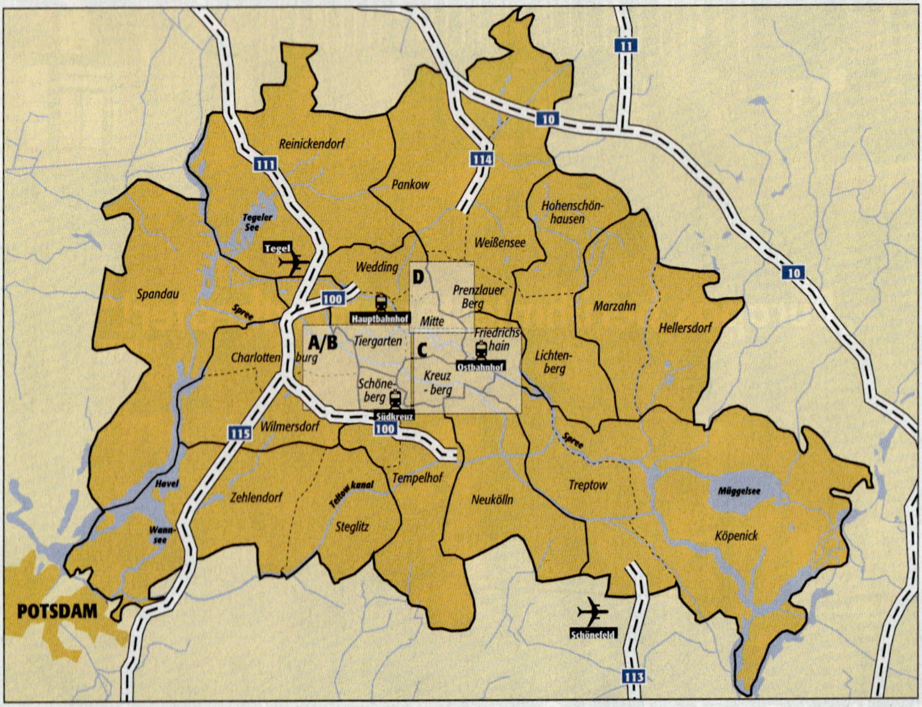

Reinickendorf
Pankow
Hohenschön-hausen
Tegeler See
Tegel
Weißensee
Wedding
D
Prenzlauer Berg
Spandau
Spree
Hauptbahnhof
Mitte
Marzahn
Hellersdorf
A/B
Tiergarten
Friedrichshain
C
Ostbahnhof
Charlottenburg
Lichtenberg
Schöneberg
Kreuzberg
Südkreuz
Wilmersdorf
Spree
Havel
Zehlendorf
Teltow kanal
Tempelhof
Neukölln
Treptow
Müggelsee
Steglitz
Köpenick
Wannsee
POTSDAM
Schönefeld
11
10
111
114
100
115
113

sont indiquées dans le calendrier des événements à la fin de ce guide. Le Berlin d'aujourd'hui est issu de beaucoup de villages et villes autour de l'ancienne résidence royale Prusse. Chaque quartier a son propre caractère et son propre centre. Ceci est vrai en partie aussi pour la scène gay qui se partage principalement entre les quartiers de Schöneberg et Prenzlauer Berg ainsi que deux centres annexes alternatifs – Kreuzberg, non-commercial et à gauche politiquement, et Friedrichshain, plus jeune et étudiant.

Berlín es claramente una de esas ciudades que siempre merece la pena visitar. Pero incluso como residencia permanente disfruta de una popularidad mundial en continuo aumento. Berlín no es sólo una de las ciudades más baratas, sino que además se está convirtiendo en la capital gay de Europa. Su alcalde abiertamente gay y la frase „Berlín es pobre pero sexy" son sólo una de las razones que han hecho famosa a esta ciudad. Entre los puntos destacados del calendario de eventos de Berlín se incluye la reunión de Semana Santa para „osos" y amigos, el „Folson Street Festival", el „Hustler Ball" y, por supuesto, las fiestas de sexo y fetiche que tienen lugar con frecuencia en la capital alemana. Puede encontrar todas las citas en el calendario de eventos al final de esta guía.
Berlín se ha consolidado a través de muchos pueblos y ciudades en torno al antiguo palacio real prusiano, es por esto que cada barrio tiene su propio carácter y, por lo tanto, su propio centro. Esto se puede observar, también en parte, en el ambiente gay berlinés, el cual gira en torno a dos barrios principales: Schöneberg y Prenzlauer Berg y a dos barrios alternativos: Kreuzberg (anticomercial y de izquierdas) y Friedrichshain (joven y estudiantil).

Sicuramente Berlino è una città che vale assolutamente la pena visitare. Berlino diventa sempre più popolare anche come meta per gente che vuole andarci a vivere. La città non è solo una delle metropoli più economiche d'Europa, ma sta anche diventando anche la capitale gay europea. La città è anche diventata nota per il suo sindaco gay che ha anche pronunciato la famosa frase „Berlino è povera, ma sexy". Tra gli highlights del calendario gay di Berlino ci sono l'incontro pasquale per gli orsi, il Folsom Street Festival, l'Hustler Ball e naturalmente i molti

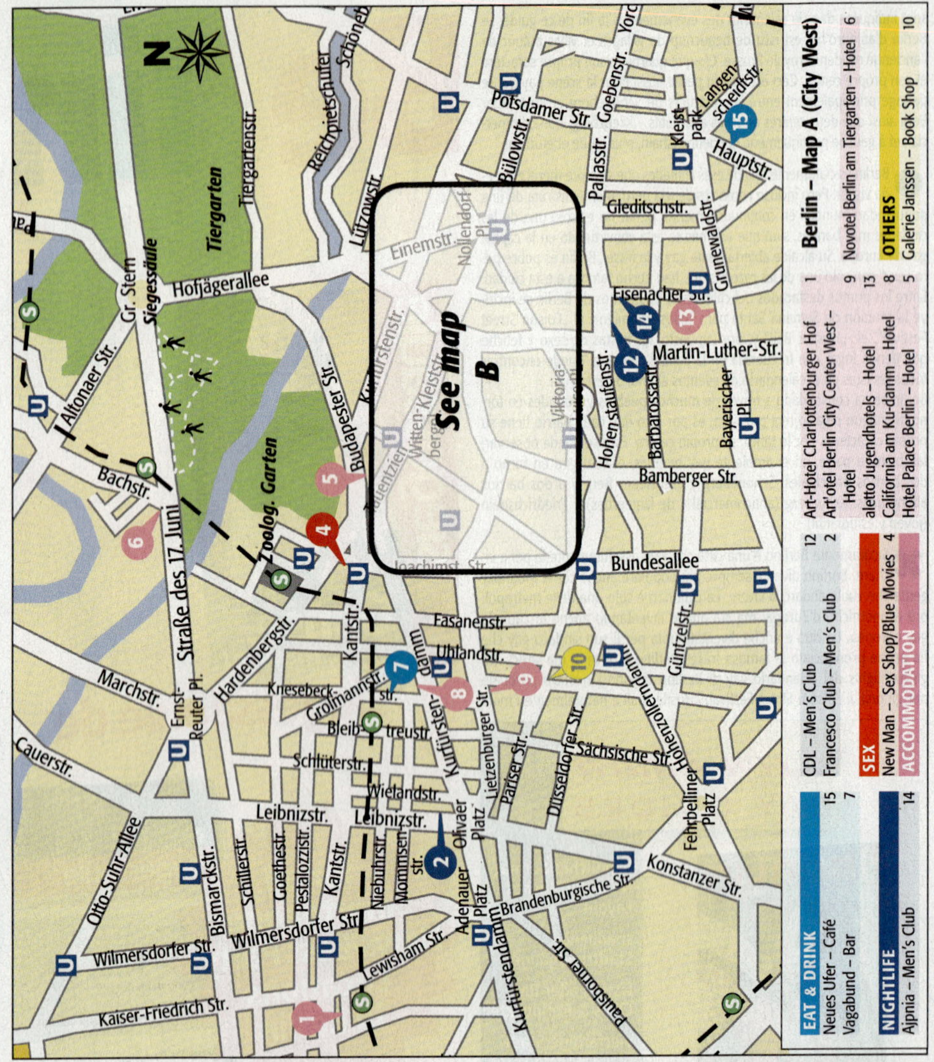

sex e fetish partys che si svolgono a scadenza regolare. Gli appuntamenti sono riportati sul calendario degli eventi alla fine di questa guida.

La Berlino di oggi continua a crescere agglomerando molti paesini e città della zona limitrofa alla vecchia residenza del Re di Prussia. Ogni quartiere ha un suo proprio carattere e un suo proprio centro. Questo vale in parte anche per la scena gay che per lo più è dislocata nei quartieri di Schöneberg e Prenzlauer Berg. Ci sono inoltre due centri gay più piccoli: uno è a Kreuzberg, zona rossa e alternativa e l'altro è a Friedrichshain, zona con molti studenti e con un pubblico più giovane.

GAY INFO

AHA-Berlin e. V. – Lesben und Schwulen-Zentrum (b G I MA S ST)
Monumentenstraße 13 ☎ 8962 7948 www.aha-berlin.de
Gaylesbian group in new location. Every 2nd Friday/month sexparty „erotikparty" from 21h until open end. See website for details.

Mann-O-Meter e. V. – Berlins schwules Info- und Beratungszentrum (B G I MA NR WI) Tue-Fri 17-22, Sat & Sun 14-20h
Bülowstraße 106 ☎ (030) 216 80 08
www.mann-o-meter.de
Also emergency phone and coffee shop. Health service and help with problems (HIV/AIDS).

PUBLICATIONS

Berlin von hinten
c/o Bruno Gmünder Verlag GmbH, Kleiststraße 23-26 ☎ (030) 615 00 30
www.brunogmuender.com
The ultimate city guide book about Berlin in English and German. 176 pages of information about Germany's capital: history, city tours, maps for better orientation, tourist information, tips and of course a complete directory of the best gay addresses in Berlin. In full colour throughout with discount entry!

Siegessäule
c/o Jackwerth Verlag, Tempelhofer Ufer 11 ☎ (030) 235 53 90
www.siegessaeule.de
Berlins leading free monthly gay-lesbian magazine with an extensive calendar and website. In German only.

TOURIST INFO

Berlin Tourism Daily 8-22h
Main Station, Ground Floor ☎ (030) 25 00 25 www.visitBerlin.de
Hotels, ticktes, information. Further offices: Neues Kranzler Eck, near Zoo/Kurfürstendamm, (10-20, Sun -18h); Brandenburg Gate, South Wing, (10-18h).

BARS

Akzept 21 (B G MA WI)
Wisbyer Str. 3 ☎ (030) 99192697 www.akzept21.de

Angels (AC B G MA R SNU) Daily 20h-open end
Courbierestraße 13 www.angelsberlin.de
Gay bar with table dance, erotic shows, sex shows. Former Club S.

Bärenhöhle (B f G MA OS) 16-6, Sat 20-4, Sun 18-4h
Schönhauser Allee 90 ☎ (030) 44 73 65 53
www.baerenhoehle-berlin.de
Cosy small bar. Wed: „Happy Hour".

Barbie Bar (B GLM MA OS) Sun-Thu 15-24, Fri & Sat 17-3h
Mehringdamm 77 ☎ (030) 69 56 86 10 www.barbiebar.de
Sun and public holidays „Cake & Cookies".

Barbie Deinhoff's (B D glm MA OS S) Mon-Sun 19-?h
Schlesische Straße 16 www.barbiedeinhoff.de
Alternative crowd, music: electro & punk.

Besenkammer (AC B G m MA) 24hrs
Rathausstraße 1 ☎ (030) 242 40 83
Tiny, but friendly bar. One of the two still existing gay bars of former East-Berlin. Smoking allowed!

Betty F*** (B G MA s t) 21-?h
Mulackstraße 13 www.bettyf.de

Bierhof Rüdersdorf (B d g I M MA OS) Mon-Sat 17-?, Sun 9-?h
Rüdersdorfer Straße 70, Am Wriezener Bahnhof ☎ (030) 29 36 02 15
www.bierhof.info
Beergarden in Summer with large open air area, small function room (Kantine), occasional parties (all year) especially on last Friday/month „Pet Shop Bears".

Blond (AC B BF CC GLM I MA OS) 10-4h
Eisenacher Straße 3a ☎ (030) 664 03 947 www.blond-berlin.de
Bar with guesthouse. Free jukebox and wlan.

Blue Boy Bar (B G m MA p R) 24hrs
Eisenacher Straße 3a ☎ (030) 218 74 98 www.blueboy-berlin.de
Rent bar, crowded after 3h.

Bull (B d DR f G MA S VS) 24hrs
Kleiststraße 35 ☎ (030) 960 857 60 www.bull-berlin.de

Café Adam (B BF GLM I MA OS) Mon-Thu 10-2, Fri 10-Mon 4h (non-stop)
Kleiststraße 7 ☎ (030) 23 62 47 00
Cozy bar in the former Stork's.

Drama (B BF GLM OS YC) Daily 14-?h
Mehringdamm 63 ☎ (030) 67 46 95 62 www.rikart.de/drama

Dreizehn (B G MC OS p) 24hrs
Welserstraße 27
A small, local bar.

Eldorado (B GLM I MC OS R s) 24hrs
Motzstraße 20 ☎ (030) 84 31 69 02 www.eldoradoberlin.de

Flax (AC B BF glm m S YC) Tue-Thu 17-3, Fri & Sat -6, Sun 10-3h
Chodowieckistraße 41 ☎ (030) 44 04 69 88 www.flax-berlin.de
Cocktail bar with house music. Popular with youngsters. Karaokeshows, Sun brunch-buffet.

Golden Finish (B GLM m MA) 20-?h
Wrangelstraße 87 www.goldenfinish.de

Hafen (! B G MA s t) 20-?h
Motzstraße 19 ☎ (030) 211 41 18 www.hafen-berlin.de
A landmark in the gay scene. Trendy and popular. Regular events. Every Monday night „Quizzorama" quiz show.

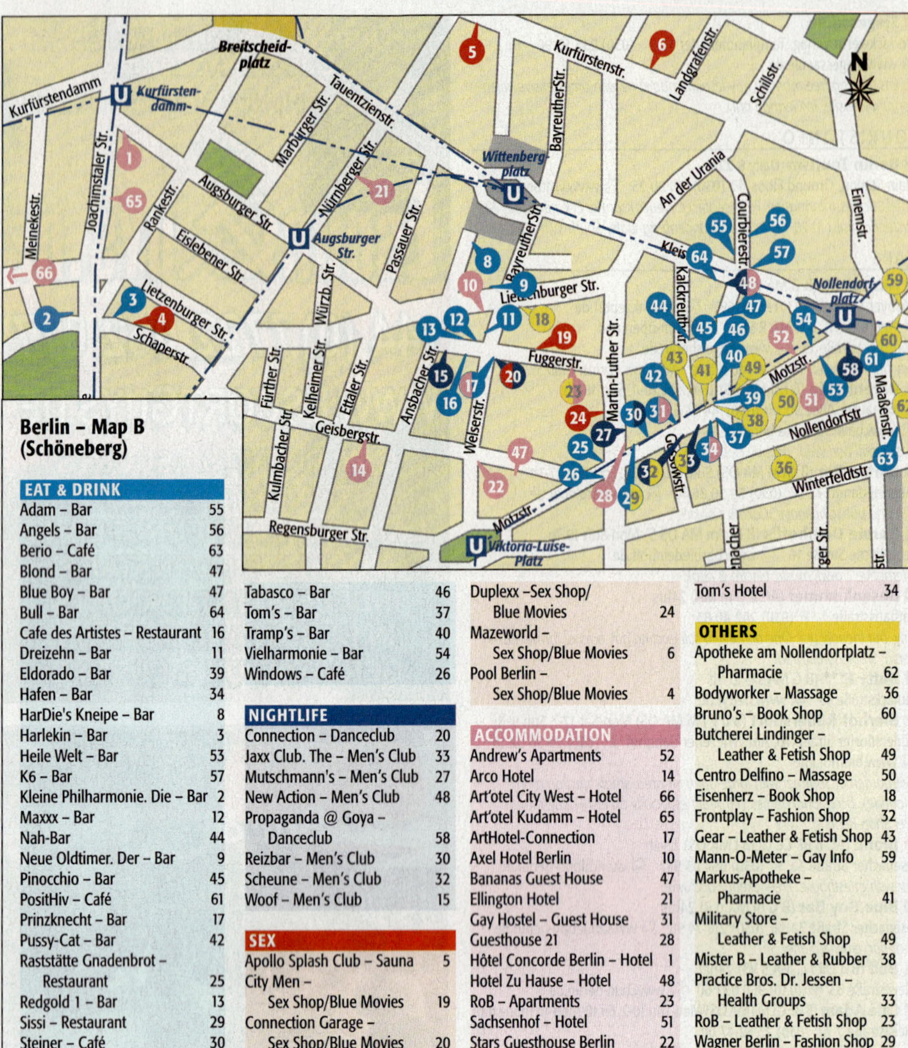

Berlin – Map B (Schöneberg)

EAT & DRINK

Adam – Bar	55
Angels – Bar	56
Berio – Café	63
Blond – Bar	47
Blue Boy – Bar	47
Bull – Bar	64
Cafe des Artistes – Restaurant	16
Dreizehn – Bar	11
Eldorado – Bar	39
Hafen – Bar	34
HarDie's Kneipe – Bar	8
Harlekin – Bar	3
Heile Welt – Bar	53
K6 – Bar	57
Kleine Philharmonie. Die – Bar	2
Maxxx – Bar	12
Nah-Bar	44
Neue Oldtimer. Der – Bar	9
Pinocchio – Bar	45
PositHiv – Café	61
Prinzknecht – Bar	17
Pussy-Cat – Bar	42
Raststätte Gnadenbrot – Restaurant	25
Redgold 1 – Bar	13
Sissi – Restaurant	29
Steiner – Café	30
Tabasco – Bar	46
Tom's – Bar	37
Tramp's – Bar	40
Vielharmonie – Bar	54
Windows – Café	26

NIGHTLIFE

Connection – Danceclub	20
Jaxx Club. The – Men's Club	33
Mutschmann's – Men's Club	27
New Action – Men's Club	48
Propaganda @ Goya – Danceclub	58
Reizbar – Men's Club	30
Scheune – Men's Club	32
Woof – Men's Club	15

SEX

Apollo Splash Club – Sauna	5
City Men – Sex Shop/Blue Movies	19
Connection Garage – Sex Shop/Blue Movies	20
Duplexx –Sex Shop/ Blue Movies	24
Mazeworld – Sex Shop/Blue Movies	6
Pool Berlin – Sex Shop/Blue Movies	4

ACCOMMODATION

Andrew's Apartments	52
Arco Hotel	14
Art'otel City West – Hotel	66
Art'otel Kudamm – Hotel	65
ArtHotel-Connection	17
Axel Hotel Berlin	10
Bananas Guest House	47
Ellington Hotel	21
Gay Hostel – Guest House	31
Guesthouse 21	28
Hôtel Concorde Berlin – Hotel	1
Hotel Zu Hause – Hotel	48
RoB – Apartments	23
Sachsenhof – Hotel	51
Stars Guesthouse Berlin	22
Tom's Hotel	34

OTHERS

Apotheke am Nollendorfplatz – Pharmacie	62
Bodyworker – Massage	36
Bruno's – Book Shop	60
Butcherei Lindinger – Leather & Fetish Shop	49
Centro Delfino – Massage	50
Eisenherz – Book Shop	18
Frontplay – Fashion Shop	32
Gear – Leather & Fetish Shop	43
Mann-O-Meter – Gay Info	59
Markus-Apotheke – Pharmacie	41
Military Store – Leather & Fetish Shop	49
Mister B – Leather & Rubber	38
Practice Bros. Dr. Jessen – Health Groups	33
RoB – Leather & Fetish Shop	23
Wagner Berlin – Fashion Shop	29

■ **Hardie's Kneipe** (AC B f G I MC t) 12-24, Fri & Sat -2h
Ansbacher Straße 29 ☏ (030) 23 63 98 42
🖳 www.hardieskneipe-berlin.de
Popular with a more mature crowd.

■ **Harlekin** (B G M MC OS) 16-late, Sun 14h-late
Schaperstraße 12-13 ☏ (030) 218 25 79 🖳 www.harlekin-bar-berlin.de
Small neighbourhood bar.

■ **Heile Welt** (AC B GLM MA) 18-4h
Motzstraße 5 *U-Nollendorfplatz* ☏ (030) 21 91 75 07

■ **Himmelreich** (AC B GLM MA OS S) 18-3, Sat & Sun 14-3h
Simon-Dach-Straße 36 ☏ (030) 29 36 92 92
🖳 www.gay-friedrichshain.de/himmelreich
Tue: Women's Lounge, Wed: „2-4-1", WE: cake buffet.

■ **Incognito** (B d GLM MA S ST T) Summer: 15-4, winter: 18-4h
Hohenstaufenstraße 53 *Cnr. Martin-Luther-Str.* 🖳 www.incognito-berlin.de
Regular travesty shows at weekends.

■ **K6** (B d G MA OS S) Mon-Sat 16-1, Sun 12-1h
Kleiststraße 3-6 ☏ (030) 23 62 69 84 🖳 k6berlin.de

■ **Kleine Philharmonie. Die** (B GLM m MA S) 19-?h, closed Mon
Schaperstraße 14 ☏ (030) 88 72 74 83
🖳 www.diekleinephilharmonie.eu

■ **Mangelwirtschaft** (B glm I m MA OS VS) Mon-Sat 10-22, Sun 12-20h
Paul-Robeson-Str. 42 ☏ (030) 60 40 57 67
🖳 www.mangelwirtschaft.com
Combined Bar/Café and laundry. Opening times are for laundry only, bar closes later.After 21h smoking allowed.

■ **Marienhof** (B GLM s YC) 18-?h
Marienburger Straße 7 ☏ (030) 675 15 494
🖳 www.marienhof-berlin.de

■ **Marietta** (B g MA) 10-2, Sat & Sun 10-4h
Stargarder Straße 13 ☏ (030) 43 72 06 46 🖳 www.marietta-bar.de
Gay and popular on Wed.

PRINZKNECHT

Berlin – Map C (Kreuzberg & Friedrichshain)

EAT & DRINK

Barbie Bar	23
Barbie Deinhoff's – Bar	15
Bierhof Rüdersdorf – Bar	2
Drama – Bar	24
Golden Finish – Bar	6
Himmelreich – Bar	10
Monster Ronson's Ichiban Karaoke - Bar	12
Melitta Sundström – Café	25
Möbel Olfe – Bar	20
Rauschgold – Bar	27
Roses – Bar	18
Sanatorium 23 – Bar	5
Sarotti – Café	29
Sofia – Bar	14
Südblock – Café	30
Zum Schmutzigen Hobby – Bar	31
Ficken 3000 – Men's Club	22
Große Freiheit No 114 – Men's Club	4
Kit Kat Club – Danceclub	1
lab.oratory – Men's Club	3
Panoramabar – Danceclub	3
Quälgeist – Men's Club	28
SchwuZ – Danceclub	25
SO 36 – Danceclub	17
Triebwerk – Men's Club	21

NIGHTLIFE

Berghain – Danceclub	3
Club Culture Houze – Men's Club	16
Die Busche – Danceclub	13

SEX

Boiler – Sauna	32
Dark Zone – Sex Shop/ Blue Movies	21
Erotixx – Sex Shop/ Blue Movies	11

ACCOMMODATION

Art'otel Mitte	8
Hotel Sarotti-Höfe	29

OTHERS

Schwules Museum – Culture	26
BKA – Shows	32

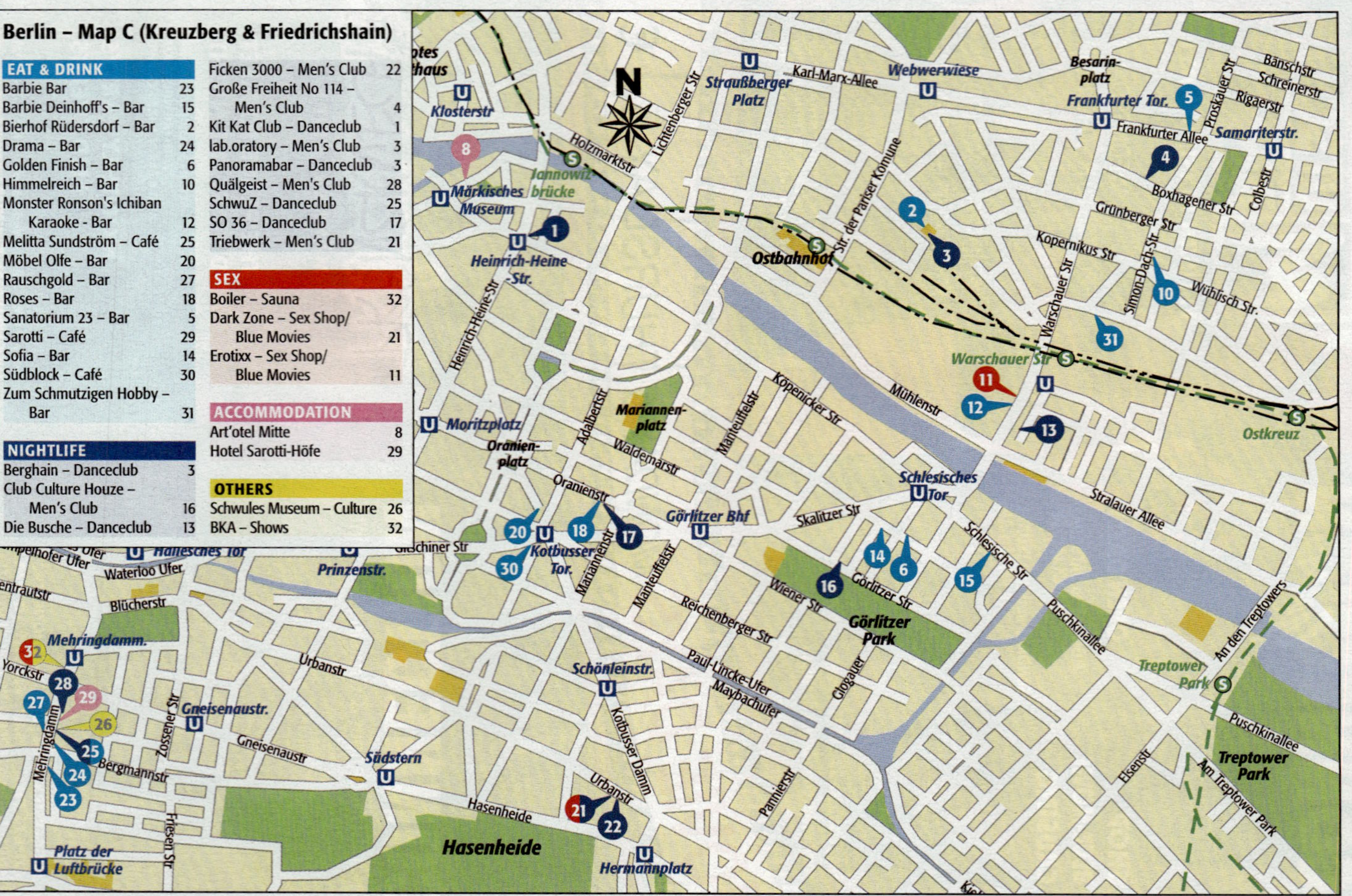

Maxxx (B f G I MC OS VS) Mon-Thu 18-?, Fri-Sun 18-4h
Fuggerstraße 34 ☏ (030) 21 00 52 84 🖳 www.maxxx-berlin.de

Möbel-Olfe (B GLM MA) 18-?h, closed Mon
Reichenberger Straße 177 ☏ (030) 23 27 46 90
🖳 www.moebel-olfe.de
Alternative and very mixed crowd.

Monster Ronson's Ichiban Karaoke (B D GLM MA S) 19-?h
Warschauer Straße 34 ☏ (030) 89 75 13 27
🖳 www.monsterronsons.de
Karaoke bar with six private cabins, Sun Liquid Brunch, Mon Fag Bar.

Nah-Bar (B GLM MA s) Fri, Sat, Mon, Tue 18-?h
Kalckreuthstaße 16 ☏ (030) 31 50 30 62 🖳 www.nah-bar.com

Neue Oldtimer. Der (B G MA OS) 16-?h
Lietzenburger Straße 12 ☏ (030) 23 62 06 54
For older men looking for young guys and vice versa.

Perle (B GLM M MA OS WE) Tue-Sun 19-?h
Sredzkistraße 64 ☏ (030) 49853450 🖳 www.bar-perle.de
Stylish bar, neither trashy nor overstyled. Classical and modern cocktails, selected spirits. Especially busy on thursdays.

Pinocchio (B G MA OS R) Sun-Thu 14-2, Fri & Sat -4h
Fuggerstraße 3 ☏ (030) 23 62 03 33 🖳 www.pinocchio-berlin.com
Rent bar.

Prinzknecht (! AC B DR f G MA OS s VS) 16-3h
Fuggerstraße 33 *U-Wittenbergplatz, next to Connection disco*
☏ (030) 236 274 44 🖳 www.prinzknecht.de
Large & popular. Check www.prinzknecht.de for special events. Packed on Wednesday night (2-4-1) from 19-21h. Mixed crowd, good music. Outdoor seating in summer.

Privatleben (B GLM MA OS) Daily 18-?h
Rhinower Straße 12 ☏ (0176) 61 16 92 49 🖳 www.privatleben-berlin.de

Puff (B GLM MA s) Daily 20-?h
Kalckreuthstraße 10
Sometimes live DJ.

Pussy-Cat (B d GLM m OS p t) 18-6h
Kalckreuthstraße 7 ☏ (030) 213 35 86 🖳 www.pussycat-berlin.de

Rauschgold (B GLM MA t) 20-?h
Mehringdamm 62 ☏ (030) 78 95 26 68 🖳 www.rauschgold-berlin.de

Redgold 1 (B G MA OS) 19-4h
Fuggerstraße 34 ☏ (030) 23 63 12 66 🖳 www.redgold1.de

Roses (! B GLM MA t) 21.30-5h
Oranienstraße 187 ☏ (030) 615 65 70
Popular and trashy. Once you've squeezed your way in to this place, you'll never want to leave.

Sanatorium 23 (B glm H I MA RWB RWS RWT W) 17-?h
Frankfurter Allee 23 *Frankfurter Tor* ☏ (030) 42 02 11 93
🖳 www.sanatorium23.de
Trendy café-bar-lounge-gallery with a very mixed crowd and DJ's on the weekend.

Schoppenstube (B D G M MA OS p S)
Tue-Thu 21-?, Fri-Sun 22-?h, closed Mon
Schönhauser Allee 44 ☏ (030) 442 82 04 🖳 www.schoppenstube.de
One of the two still existing gay bars of former East-Berlin.

Sharon Stonewall. The (B GLM I MA) 20-?h, closed Mon
Kleine Präsidentenstraße 3 *S-Hackescher Markt* ☏ (030) 24 08 55 02
🖳 www.sharonstonewall.com
Nice and stylish bar – smoking allowed.

Silverfuture (B glm MA) Sun-Wed 14-2, Thu-Sat -3h
Weserstraße 206 *U Hermannplatz* ☏ 7563 4987
Kings and Queens and Criminal Queers – very indie and undergroundy.

Soap (AC B d GLM I m MA OS)
Mon-Thu 10-24, Fri-1, Sat 12-1, Sun -24h
Eisenacher Straße 116 *U-Nollendorfplatz*
New and stylish cocktail bar in the gay district of Schöneberg. Smokers and chill-out lounge. Live DJs.

Sofia (B d GLM MA) 9-?, Sat 11-?, Sun 20-?h
Wrangelstraße 93 🖳 www.sofia-berlin.blogspot.com
Trashy and very unusual bar with a living-room atmosphere.

Berlin – Map D (Prenzlauer Berg & Mitte)
EAT & DRINK
Bärenhöhle – Bar 3
Besenkammer – Bar 41
Betty F*** – Bar 36
Der Hahn ist tot – Restaurant 30
Flax – Bar 25
Ganymed Brasserie Berlin – Restaurant 35
November – Café 22
Perle – Bar 23
Privatleben – Bar 12
Schall & Rauch – Café 13
Sharon Stonewall – Bar 32
Sonntags-Club – Café 9
Stiller Don – Bar 11
Trauerspiel – Bar 14
Villis Bierbar – Bar 7
NIGHTLIFE
Bonito @ Tresor – Danceclub 42
Chantal's House of Shame @ Bassy – Danceclub 29
Cocks Berlin – Men's Club 1
Darkroom – Men's Club 8
GMF @ Weekend – Danceclub 39
Greifbar – Men's Club 10
Irrenhouse @ Geburtstags-club – Danceclub 28
Kino International – Danceclub 40
Kit Kat Club – Danceclub 43
Stahlrohr 2.0 – Men's Club 6
SEX
Duplexx – Sex Shop/ Blue Movies 16
Gate – Sauna 46
Treibhaus – Sauna 16
XXL-Berlin – Sex Shop/ Blue Movies 2
ACCOMMODATION
Arcotel John F – Hotel 45
Arcotel Velvet – Hotel 34
East Side Pension – Guest House 21
Greifswald – Hotel 27
Hotel4Youth – Hotel 4
miniloftmitte – Apartments 33
Myer's – Hotel 26
Park Inn Berlin Alexanderplatz– Hotel 38
Radisson Blu Hotel – Hotel 44
Schall & Rauch – Hotel 13
Winters Hotel 47
OTHERS
Bruno's – Book Shop 15
Leathers – Leather/ Fetish Shop 17
MonGay @ Kino International – Cinema 40
Rubber Factory Berlin – Leather & Fetish Shop 24
Trüffelschwein – Fashion Shop 37
N
Bornholmer Str
Wisbyerstr
Arnim-platz
Schönhauser Allee
Stargarder Str
Humann-platz
Wichertstr
Gleimstr
Pappelallee
Prenzlauer Allee
Helmholtzplatz
Mauer-park
Eberswalder Str
Danziger Str
Kastanienallee
Kollwitz-platz
Zionskirchplatz
Senefelder Platz
Prenzlauer Allee
Greifswalder Str
Nordbahnhof
Invalidenstr
Brunnenstr
Zinnowitzer Str
Chausseestr
Torstr
Rosenthaler Platz
Rosa-Luxemburg-Platz
Am Friedrichshain
Volkspark Friedrichshain
Oranienburger Tor
Linienstr
Auguststr
Mollstr
Luisenstr
Oranienburger Str.
Oranienburgerstr
Weinmeisterstr
Karl-Liebknecht-Str
Otto-Braun-Str
Friedrichstr
Reinhardtstr
Monbijou Park
Hackescher Markt
Alexanderplatz
Museums-insel
Fernseh-turm
Schillingstr
Friedrichstr
Spandauerstr
Grunerstr
Alexanderstr
Straußberger Platz
Dorotheenstr
Unter den Linden
Klosterstr.
Lichtenberger Str
Branden-burger Tor
Behrenstr
Gertraudenstr
Holzmarktstr
H.-Arendt-Str
Mauerstr
Französische Str.
Jannowitz-brücke
Wilhelmstr.
Stadtmitte
Hausvogtei-platz
Märkisches Museum
Mohrenstr
Mohrenstr.
Leipziger Str
Spittelmarkt
Köpenicker Str

■ **Stiller Don** (B GLM m MA OS) 20-?h
Erich-Weinert-Straße 67 ☎ (0172) 182 01 68
Popular night on Mon.

■ **Südblock** (B bf D GLM m MA OS S ST) 10-21h, longer on events
Admiralstr. 1-2 *U-Kottbusser Tor* ☎ 609 41 853
🖳 www.suedblock.org
New venue with Café, Beer-garden and partylocation. Check www.suedblock.org for details.

■ **Tabasco Bar Berlin** (AC B G I m MA OS P R S SNU)
Mon-Thu 18-6, Fri 18-Mon 6h (non-stop)
Fuggerstraße 3 ☎ (030) 214 26 36 🖳 www.tabascobar.de
Rent bar, crowded on WE.

■ **To Be Free** (B GLM MA S) 15-?, Sat & Sun 16-?h
Brunsbütteler Damm 5 ☎ (030) 328 998 88 🖳 www.to-be-free.net

■ **Tom's** (! B DR G m MA p S VS) 22-6h
Motzstraße 19 ☎ (030) 213 45 70 🖳 www.tomsbar.de
Very cruisy. Popular Mon (2-4-1). Thu „Hand Made" live DJ, techno & house. A must when visiting Berlin.

■ **Tramp's** (AYOR B DR f G MA) 24hrs
Eisenacher Straße 6

■ **Trauerspiel** (B DR G MA) 20-3h
Milastraße 7 ☎ (030) 447 67 89

■ **Vagabund** (B d g MC OS P T) 17-?h
Knesebeckstraße 77 ☎ (030) 881 15 06
Running for over 30 years now. Crowded after 3h in the morning. Expensive.

■ **Vielharmonie** (B CC GLM m MA) 18-?h
Motzstraße 8 ☎ (030) 306 47 302 🖳 www.vielharmonie-berlin.com
Nice and stylish cocktailbar. Good place to start the evening.

■ **Villis Bar** (AC B g MA) 20-3h
Greifenhagener Straße 45 ☎ (030) 44 71 90 81 🖳 www.villis-berlin.de
Wed 20-24h happy hour, Sun all cocktails € 4.

■ **Zum Schmutzigen Hobby** (B GLM MA OS s ST) 18-?h
Revalerstr. 99 *U1 Warschauer Strasse* 🖳 www.ninaqueer.com
Legendary Bar of Berlin's infamous trash and glamour queen Nina Queer. Now at new location. Wed 21h „Glamourquizzz".

MEN'S CLUBS

■ **Ajpnia** (B DR G MA NU VS) Wed 19-2.30, Sat 21-?h
Eisenacher Straße 23 ☎ (030) 21 91 88 81 🖳 www.ajpnia.de

■ **Böse Buben** (B DR F G MA p VS) Wed 16-24, Fri & Sat 21-4h
Sachsendamm 76-77 *S-Schöneberg, yellow rear building in the courtyard*
☎ (030) 62 70 56 10 🖳 www.boese-buben-berlin.de
S/M, spanking, every dress code welcome. Walk through the gateway and go to the yellow 3-story house in the back of the inner courtyard.

■ **CDL** (B DR G MA P VS) 19-3, Fri & Sat 21-4, Sun 15-1h
Hohenstaufenstraße 58 ☎ (030) 32 66 78 55 🖳 www.cdl-club.de
Some days with dresscode. Wed & Sat naked only, bar with cruising area and darkroom with sling.

■ **Club Culture Houze** (AC B d DR f G m MA p VS)
Mon 19-?, Wed-Sat 20h-open end
Görlitzer Straße 71 *U1-Görlitzer Bahnhof* ☎ (030) 61 70 96 69
🖳 www.club-culture-houze.de
Bar on 2 floors with playground and shower. Special theme parties. Mixed on Wed, Thu & Sun.

■ **Cocks Berlin** (B DR F G MC p VS) 22-?, Wed & Sun 20-?h
Greifenhagener Straße 33 ☎ (030) 447 349 02 🖳 www.cocksberlin.de
Daily motto parties. Big darkroom with sling and bath tub.

■ **Darkroom** (B DR F G MA) 22-?h
Rodenbergstraße 23 🖳 www.darkroom-berlin.de
Wed: „underwear party", Fri: „naked sex party", Sat: „golden shower party".

■ **Factory** (AC b CC DR f G MA p VS) 12-?h
Schliemannstraße 38 ☎ (030) 442 77 86 🖳 www.leathers.de
New Sex-Club with bar.

■ **Ficken 3000** (B d DR f G MA p t VS) 22-?h
Urbanstraße 70 ☎ (030) 69 50 73 35 🖳 www.ficken3000.com
Not just for a quickie, also with a small dancefloor and comfortable seating. Can get full at WE after clubs close. Very mixed crowd.

■ **FickstutenMarkt @ Dragon-Room of the KitKat-Club**
(DR G MC P) Monthly event; entrance Mares: 17.30-18.30, entrance Stallions: 19-20h
Köpenicker Strasse 76 *Near U „Heinrich-Heine-Straße"*
Private event. Willing mares offer themselves to stallions without ever seeing their faces. Check rules and for further information see website.

■ **Francesco Club** (B d DR f G MA P S VS WE) Wed-Sun 21-?h
Leibnizstraße 34 *S/U-Zoologischer Garten, U-Wilmersdorfer Straße*
☎ (030) 346 60 280 🖳 www.francesco-club.de

■ **Greifbar** (AC B DR G MA p VS) 22-6h
Wichertstraße 10 ☎ (030) 444 08 28 🖳 www.greifbar.com
Mon Beck's Night (half price for Beck's beer).

■ **Große Freiheit No 114** (AC B DR FC G LAB MA S VR VS)
Tue-Sun 22-6h
Boxhagener Straße 114 ☎ (030) 29 77 67 13 🖳 www.grosse-freiheit-114.de
Wed „2-4-1" all night long. Thu DJ-night, Fri „Molle & Korn" special. Monthly special like „Porno-Karaoke". Specials like „Sneaker-Sex-Party" and others.

■ **Jaxx Club. The** (AC b CC DR G MA P VS) 12-3, Sun 13-3h
Motzstraße 19 ☎ (030) 213 81 03 🖳 www.thejaxx.de
Private club with strict door checks. Popular, especially Tue and WE.

■ **Laboratory** (! B DR DU F G LAB MA P s SL) T
hu 21-23, Fri & Sat 22-24, Sun 16-18h
Am Wriezener Bahnhof 🖳 www.lab-oratory.de
*Men-only sex club in an old substation which also houses the danceclubs „Berghain" and „Panoramabar". You have two hours to enter the sexparties, then the doors close to avoid the „when will my prince arrive"-syndrom! Sometimes dresscodes depending on themes (Sneaker, Yellow, Fist etc.). Wide-ranging darkrooms featuring all kinds of sex equipments like slings, jailhouse, wet-area, showers and locker room. Thu: „Naked Sex Party", Fri: „Friday F***" Sat & Sun: themed sex parties. Check website for actual details: www.lab-oratory.de*

■ **Mutschmanns Fetish-Cruising-Point** (AC B DR F G MA P VS)
Wed 23-?; Fri, Sat and before public holidays 22-?h
Martin-Luther-Straße 19 ☎ (030) 21 91 96 40
🖳 www.mutschmanns.de
Especially popular with the leather & fetish crowd. Special theme parties. Check www.mutschmanns.de for details. Entrance fee includes one drink.

New Action (AC B D DR F G MA P S VS WE)
Mon-Thu 22-5, Fri & Sat -7, Sun 17-5h
Kleiststraße 35 www.newactionberlin.de
Newly renovated, new owner and still very cruisy. Best after 1h and open late. sundays different sex parties. please observe dresscode.

Quälgeist (B DR DU F FC G MA P SL W)
Tue 20-1 (entrance 20-22), Fri & Sat 22-? (entrance 22-24), So 15-21h
Mehringdamm 51, 4th court 788 57 99 www.quaelgeist-berlin.de
Non-profit SM club in a location which meets all desires: St. Andrew's cross, slings, racks, bondage beds, pulleys, wet cell and more... different themed sex parties – see website for details.

Reizbar (B DR G MA p VS) 20-4, Fri & Sat -6h
Motzstraße 30 www.reizbar-berlin.de

Scheune (B DR F G MA p VS) 21-7, Fri & Sat -9h
Motzstraße 25 (030) 213 85 80 www.scheune-berlin.de
Naked Sex Party Sun 17.30-21h, popular, lots of hardcore action.

Stahlrohr 2.0 (B DR f G MA p VS) 22-6, Sun 18-6h
Paul-Robeson-Straße 50 (0170) 803 76 91 www.stahlrohr-bar.de
Every day a different theme.

Triebwerk (B DR f G MA p VS)
Mon, Thu-Sat 22-?, Tue & Wed 20-?, Sun 16-?h
Urbanstraße 64 (030) 69 50 52 03 www.triebwerkberlin.com
Tue, Wed, Fri & Sun: ‚Naked- & Underwear Sex Party', Sat: ‚Naked-Party', Mon ‚2-4-1', Thu: ‚Cruising Night'.

Woof Berlin (B DR F G MA) Mon-Sat 22-4, Sun 21-2h
Fuggerstraße 37 *U-Wittebergplatz* www.woof-berlin.com
Visit website for further details.

CAFES

Berio (B BF GLM M MA OS) Mon-Thu 7-24, Fri -1, Sat 8-1, Sun -24h
Maaßenstraße 7 *U-Nollendorfplatz* (030) 216 19 46 www.cafeberio.de
Large café on two floors in the gay area. Very popular, outdoor seating in summer.

Impala (AC B GLM OS WI) Mon-Fri 7-20, Sat&Sun 9-20h
Maaßenstrasse 5 *U Nollendorfplatz* (030) 2191 3812
www.impala-coffee.com
Delicious coffees, own roast. Gay owned and operated.

Impala (B D GLM MA OS WI) Mon-Fri 7-20, Sat 8-20, Sun 9-20h
Schönhauser Allee 173 (030) 40 50 54 85
www.impala-coffee.com
Delicious coffees – own roast. Gay owned and operated.

Impala (B D GLM MA WI) Mon-Fri 7-20, Sat&Sun 9-20h
Pappelallee 1 (030) 24 63 78 66 www.impala-coffee.com
Delicious coffees – own roast. Gay owned and operated.

Melitta Sundström (B BF D GLM m MA OS T) 13-4, Sat 10-Sun 4h
Mehringdamm 61 (030) 692 44 14
Best on Sat. Also a gay bookstore. Entrance to SchwuZ Disco.

Neues Ufer (B bf GLM H m MA OS s) 11-2h
Hauptstraße 157 (030) 78 95 79 00

November (! B BF GLM M MA OS VEG WE WI) 10-2, Sat & Sun 9-2h
Husemannstraße 15 *Near Kollwitzplatz* (030) 442 84 25
www.cafe-november.de
Popular bar-restaurant with moderate prices. Breakfast à la carte -16h, German-Austrian cuisine, well-known for its Schnitzel.

PositHIV (AC B GLM I MA OS)
Tue, Thu, Fri, Sun 15-23; Wed 13-23; Sat 18-?h
Bülowstrasse 6 (030) 216 86 54 cafepositiv.aidshilfe.de
For PWA/HIV and their friends.

Café Bar Sarotti-Höfe (B BF CC glm I M MA NR OS WL) daily 7-?h
Mehringdamm 57 *near cnr. Bergmannstraße* 600 3168 0
www.hotel-sarottihoefe.de
Trendy café in the gay-area of Kreuzberg. Fabulous cakes! Ideal to start the evening at. Happy Hour for cocktails from 18-20h, Smoker's-lounge Mon-Thu from 15, Fri-Sun from 18h. Sat+Sun Brunch 11-15h.

Schall & Rauch (B BF CC glm H M MA RWS RWT t WE)
8-12, Thu-Sat -?h
Gleimstraße 23 *S/U-Schönhauser Allee* (030) 443 39 70
www.schall-und-rauch.de
Schall & Rauch café and city hotel with 2 stars and 28 rooms. All rooms with shower/WC, TV and phone. Café: Cocktail hour daily 20-23h. Very large breakfast buffet on Sat & Sun.

Sonntags-Club Café (b GLM I MA OS S T VS) 18-24h
Greifenhagener Str. 28 (030) 449 75 90 www.sonntags-club.de

Steiner (B BF G M MA OS) Tue-Sun 9-19h, Mon closed
Motzstraße 30 (030) 23 63 09 00
One of the most attractive gay cafés in Berlin. Ambience in traditional style. Good coffees and teas. Delicious breakfasts, soups, quiches and homemade cakes. Excellent location in the gay scene.

Südblock (B bf D GLM m MA OS S ST) 10-21h, longer on events
Admiralstr. 1-2 *U-Kottbusser Tor* 609 41 853 www.suedblock.org
New venue with Café, Beer-garden and partylocation. Check www.suedblock.org for details.

Vanille & Marille (glm m MA) March-October 11-23h
Hagelberger Straße 1 *Near Mehringdamm* 78 95 47 31
www.vanille-marille.de
Small but best ice-cream parlour in Kreuzberg. Gay owned and operated.

Windows (B GLM m MA OS) 9-1h
Martin-Luther-Straße 22 (030) 214 23 94 www.cafewindows.de

DANCECLUBS

Berghain (! B D DR f G m MA OS P S WE) Sat 24h-Sun afternoon
Am Wriezener Bahnhof www.Berghain.de
Legendary club, voted best club of the world in 2009 by the readers of DJ Mag. Huge location in a former substation with 2 Clubs (Panoramabar & Berghain). See www.berghain.de for details. Strict door policy and controls.

Bonito @ Tresor (B D GLM MA)
1st Wed/month 23.59h-open end
Köpenicker Straße 70 www.tresorberlin.de
Queer houseparty in the world famous technoclub.

Busche. Die (B D GLM S YC) Wed 22-5, Fri & Sat -7h
Warschauer Platz 18 *Near Oberbaumbrücke* (030) 296 08 00
www.diebusche.de *(in German only)*
Discount entry available with club card.

Chantal's House of Shame @ Bassy
(B D GLM MA S ST t) Thu 23-?h
Schönhauser Allee 176a *U Senefelder Platz*
www.myspace.com/chantalshouseofshame
Dragshow at 2h.

Connection Club Berlin (B D DR f G MA VS)
Fri, Sat and before public holidays 22-?h
Fuggerstraße 33 (030) 218 14 32 www.connection-berlin.com
See www.connection-berlin.com for program details.

GMF (! AC B D GLM MA OS ST T) Sun 23-5.30h
Alexanderstraße 7 @ *Weekend-Club, U-Alexanderplatz*
(030) 28 09 53 96 www.gmf-berlin.de
The most popular T-Dance in town, great DJs, stylish club in the 12th and 15th floor with a roof terrace. Crowded by fashion victims, but friendly and open-minded.

Homopatik (B D G MA WE) 3rd Fri/month
Markgrafendamm 24 c @ *Club About:Blank, S-Ostkreuz*
www.aboutparty.net

Hustlaball (! AC B D DR DU F FC G GH LM MA MSG NU OS P PI S SL SNU ST T VR VS WE)
Köpenicker Straße 76 *U Heinrich-Heine-Str* www.hustlaball.de
Legendary Gay-Porn-Party in the famous Kit Kat Club on October 19th 2012.

Irrenhouse @ Geburtstagsklub (B D DR GLM S T YC) 3 rd Sat/month 23h-late
Am Friedrichshain 33 www.ninaqueer.com

Kino International (B D GLM t WE YC) 1st Sat/month 23h-late
Karl-Marx-Allee 33 *U-Schillingstraße* (030) 24 75 60 11
First Sat/month Klub International 23h-late. Popular with a younger crowd, a little less flashy than the GMF, attracts lots of students.

Kit Kat Club (B D DR F glm MA NU OS P PI S t W WE) Fri & Sat 23-8, Sun 8-18h
Köpenicker Straße 76 *U Heinrich-Heine-Str* (030) 21 73 68 41
www.kitkatclub.de
Theme nights with dresscode, see: www.kitkatclub.de for details.

What? (B D GLM MA)
Karl-Liebknecht-Straße 11 www.loreley.li
Different themed gay partynights such the R&B event „Peaches&Cream".

Panoramabar (B D glm MA P) Fri & Sat 24-?h
Am Wriezener Bahnhof www.berghain.de
Same entrance as Berghain, good houseclub with mixed (50:50) crowd. Fri normally separated from main club Berghain (closed then). On Sat both clubs connected.

Piepshow @ Kit Kat Club (! AC B D DR G MA NU OS P PI WE)
4th Fri/month 23h-open end
Köpenicker Straße 76 www.kitkatclub.org
Probably the best monthly party in town, where gay and straight boys party together, women allowed. Tolerance is a must. Parties often last until Saturday afternoon.

Propaganda Party (B D G S YC) 2nd Sat/month 23-?h
Nollendorfplatz 5 @ *Goya* (030) 84 41 55-0
www.propaganda-party.de
Popular. See website for further details.

SchwuZ (! AC B D GLM MA S ST t) Wed 22.30-?, Fri & Sat 23-?h
Mehringdamm 61 (030) 62 90 88-0 www.schwuz.de
An institution in Kreuzberg with a tradition of over 35 years. Basement location with 2 dancefloors, 3 bars and a cocktail lounge. Sat disco (pop, house, disco, electro & retro) and parties like „Madonnamania" or „Popkicker". Fri: non-mainstream programme (rock, indie), Wed specials like Wong, Populärmusik or Daenzgedoens. Also drag-shows.

SO36 (AC B D GLM MA S ST)
Oranienstraße 190 (030) 61 40 13 06 www.so36.de
A mixed and more alternative crowd than other clubs. The most popular parties are Sun „Café Fatal" (ballroom dancing) 19-2h, „Gayhane" (homo-oriental dancefloor) and „Kiezbingo". Check www.so36.de for the exact program.

Spy Club @ Cookies (B D GLM MA) 4th Sat 23-6h
Friedrichstraße 158 *S/U Friedrichstraße* www.spyclub.de
Check www.spyclub.de for details.

RESTAURANTS

Cafe des Artistes (B DM g MA VEG WL) Mon-Sat, closed on Sun
Fuggerstr. 35 *U Wittenbergplatz* ☎ 236 35 249

Cocotte. La (B CC G M MA) 18-1, kitchen -23h
Vorbergstraße 10 ☎ (030) 78 95 76 58 💻 www.lacocotte.de
French cuisine. Seasonal menu, occasional expositions.

Der Hahn ist tot (B DM M MC NG OS RES VEG WL) 19-1h
Zionskirchstraße 40 *U-Rosenthaler Platz* ☎ (030) 657 06756
💻 www.der-hahn-ist-tot.de
French & German cuisine. Delicious 4-course-set-menues at reasonable prices. Gay managed and owned restaurant.

Ganymed Brasserie Berlin
(AC B CC DM M MC NG OS RES VEG WL) 12-24h
Schiffbauerdamm 5 *U-Friedrichstraße* ☎ (030) 28 59 90 46
💻 www.ganymed-brasserie.de
Excellent service. French cuisine.

Kesselhaus Sarotti-Höfe (B CC DM glm M MA PA VEG W WL)
Tue-Sun 18-24h
Mehringdamm 55 *U Mehringdamm* ☎ (030) 600 316 80
💻 www.kesselhaus-sarottihoefe.de
Gay owned and operated stylish restaurant with award winning German cross-over cuisine in the old boilerhouse of the famous Sarotti chocolate factory.

More (B BF CC DM GLM I M MA NR OS PA RES VEG WL)
Breakfast 9-17, business lunch 12-17, dinner 17-24h
Motzstraße 28 *U-Nollendorfplatz* ☎ (030) 23 63 57 02
💻 www.more-berlin.de

Mädchen ohne Abitur (B glm M MA VEG)
Daily 18-2h, kitchen open until midnight
Körtestraße 5 *U7-Südstern* ☎ 616 258 60
Gay managed and owned restaurant.

Raststätte Gnadenbrot (AC B DM GLM M MA OS PA s VEG) 9-2h
Martin-Luther-Straße 20a ☎ (030) 21 96 17 86
💻 www.raststaette-gnadenbrot.de

Sissi (B BF DM GLM H M MA OS VEG)
12-22.30h, full menu available all day
Motzstrasse 34 *Between U-Nollendorfplatz & U-Viktoria-Luise-Platz*
☎ (030) 21 01 81 01 💻 www.sissi-berlin.de
One of the best austrian cuisines in town. Excellent wines and beers. Very small and cosy place with an oven in winter and a see-and-be-seen terrace during summer months.

unsicht-Bar (B glm M MA) Daily 18-?h
Gormannstraße 14 *Mitte, near Torstraße* ☎ (030) 2434 2500
💻 www.unsicht-bar-berlin.de
Germany's first dark restaurant. A completely new experience.

Zsa Zsa Burger (AC B glm M OS VEG)
Motzstraße 28 ☎ (030) 21913470
New and stylish burger-restaurant.

SEX SHOPS/BLUE MOVIES

City Men Shop & Video (CC DR G MA VS) 11-1, Fri & Sat -2h
Fuggerstraße 26 ☎ (030) 218 29 59 💻 www.city-men.net

Connection Garage (CC DR f G GH MA p VS)
10-1, Sun & public holidays 14-1h
Fuggerstraße 33 ☎ (030) 218 14 32
💻 www.connection-berlin.de/shop/
Sex shop with a very large crusing area. Cubicles with porn films and glory holes.

Dark Zone (G MA VS) 13-1h
Urbanstraße 64 ☎ (030) 61 20 36 37 💻 www.darkzone-berlin.eu
Sex cinema with video sales, large cruising area and video cabines.

Duplexx (! b DR G MA VS) 12-3h
Schönhauser Allee 131 ☎ (030) 48 49 42 00 💻 www.duplexx.eu
Popular sex shop with a second shop in Schöneberg.

Duplexx (AC b G MA P VS) 12-3h
Martin-Luther-Straße 14 ☎ (030) 23 63 18 84 💻 www.duplexx.eu
A spin-off of the popular & successful Duplexx in Prenzlauer Berg.

Erotixx (AC b DR GLM MA T VS) 13-1h
Warschauer Straße 38 ☎ (030) 31 16 65 74 💻 www.erotixx24.eu
Shop, video cabins, SM-room, cruising world, glory holes. DVD sale.

■ **Mazeworld** (AC B DR F G MA T VS) 12-5h
Kurfürstenstaße 79 ☎ (030) 23 00 32 51 💻 www.maze-world.eu
A sex shop with separate sling, cabines, glory holes and playrooms.

■ **New Man** (AC CC DR G MA r VS) 10-0.30, Sun 12-0.30h
Joachimstaler Straße 1-3 ☎ (030) 88 68 32 89

■ **Pool Berlin** (DR G MA VS) 12-22, Sun 15-21h
Schaperstraße 11 ☎ (030) 214 19 89 💻 www.pool-berlin.de

■ **XXL-Berlin** (DR F G GH LAB MA SL VR VS) 12-3h
Bornholmer Straße 7 ☎ (030) 32 89 82 22
💻 www.xxl-berlin.de

SAUNAS/BATHS

■ **Apollo Splash Club** (AC AK B CC DR DU FC G GH I LAB m MA MSG p PP RR s SA SB SH SL SOL VR VS WH WO)
Mon-Thu 12-7, Fri 12-Mon 7h (non-stop)
Kurfürstenstraße 101 *U-Wittenbergplatz* ☎ (030) 213 24 24
💻 www.apollosplashclub.de
The largest sauna in Berlin. New cruising labyrinth and wet area. On two floors with extensive sauna facilities. 60 private rooms with TV & video. Former Apollo Sauna Club Brasil. Foam parties!

■ **Boiler** (! B BF CC DR G M MA MSG PI SA SB VS WH)
Mon-Thu 12-6, Fri-Mon 12-6h (non-stop)
Mehringdamm 34 *U6/7-Mehringdamm* ☎ 57 707 175 1
💻 www.boiler-berlin.de
Brand new gay sauna in the heart of the gay district of Kreuzberg.

■ **Gate Sauna** (AC B bf CC DR DU FC G m MA MSG p RR SA SB SL SOL VS WH) 11-7, Fri 11-Mon 7h (non-stop)
Hannah-Arendt-Str. 6 *Near cnr. Wilhelmstraße and Brandenburger Tor, U-Mohrenstraße/S-Unter den Linden* ☎ (030) 229 94 30
💻 www.gate-sauna.de
Special days for youngsters, couples and bears. A large bar area. Sling room and a dark room area with a matress. Very cruisy in the steam sauna. Popular among tourists.

■ **Treibhaus** (AC B bf DR DU FC G m MSG p PP RR SA SB SH SOL VS WH YC) 13-7, Fri 13-Mon 7h (non-stop)
Schönhauser Allee 132 *S/U-Schönhauser Allee* ☎ (030) 448 45 03
🖳 www.treibhaussauna.de
Frequented by a younger crowd. Very busy on Sun.

MASSAGE

■ **Bodyworker** (G MA MSG) Mon-Sat 12-24h
Nollendorfstraße 26 ☎ (030) 23 63 83 25
🖳 www.bodyworker-berlin.de
Classic, erotic and even Tantra massages. Big team.

■ **Centro Delfino – Massage & Kosmetik** (CC GLM MA MSG)
Mon-Fri 11-22, Sat-Sun 12-22h
Nollendorfstraße 20 ☎ (030) 342 45 88
🖳 www.centro-delfino-berlin.de
Many different kinds of massages and facial treatments.

■ **Centro Delfino Akademie** (glm MSG) Mon-Fri 9-21, Sat 11-18h
Krumme Str. 10 *Im Stadtbad Charlottenburg* ☎ (030) 347 045 96
🖳 www.centro-delfino.de/massageschule.html
Massage education service.

■ **Die Wohlfühler** (glm MA) Mon-Fri 8-21, Sat 10-20, Sun 12-20h
Kollwitzstrasse 75 ☎ 4030 1334 🖳 www.diewohlfuehler.de
Cosmetic treatments, massages, wellness and more.

■ **Gay Love Spirit** (G MA MSG)
Paul Lincke Ufer 33 ☎ (030) 34 625 266 🖳 www.gaylovespirit.de
Massage, Tantra, Sex Coaching and more. Workshops in Europe. Tel: (0163) 686 39 30 (Berlin) & (0163) 686 39 56 (Cologne).

■ **Gay-Tantra Oase** (G MSG p SB WH) 10-22h
Bundesallee 156 *S-Ringbahn/U9 Bundesplatz* ☎ (030) 26 344 515
🖳 www.gay-tantra-oase.de
Discover the first-class massages in a sophisticated ambience.

■ **Just Men Berlin** (CC G MA MSG S) daily, 12-23h
Fuggerstraße 24 *U-Wittenbegplatz* ☎ (030) 346 646 48
🖳 www.just-men-berlin.de
Every 2 Months art exhibition with new international artist, Papenberg Underwear.

■ **Massage-Harmonie** (CC G MA PK)
Mon-Sun 10-21h, by appointment only
Brüder-Grimm-Gasse 4 *Potsdamer Platz Arkaden*
☎ (0)175 37 73 705 (mobile) 🖳 www.massage-harmonie.de
From the classical massage to Lomi Lomi Nui Hawaiian Massage, Aroma oil massage and foot reflexzone massage.

SHOWS

■ **Bar Jeder Vernunft** (B glm M MA S ST)
Schaperstraße 24 ☎ 883 1582 🖳 www.bar-jeder-vernunft.de
Theatre in a circus-tent. Great atmosphere. Check-out website for program!

■ **BKA-Berliner Kabarett Anstalt** (B glm m MA S)
Tickets: Mon-Fri 10-18, Sat 15-18h
Mehringdamm 34 ☎ (030) 202 20 07 🖳 www.bka-theater.de
Gay and gayfriendly institution in Berlin, many drag-performances or other gay artists. Theatre under the roof!

■ **Chamäleon Varieté**
Hackesche Höfe *S-/M-Tram-Hackescher Markt, U-Weinmeisterstraße*
☎ (030) 40 00 590 🖳 www.chamaeleonberlin.com

■ **Friedrichstadt-Palast** (AC B CC GLM MA)
Friedrichstraße 107 *S-/U-Friedrichstraße* ☎ (030) 2326 2326
🖳 www.show-palace.eu
Strapping young men under larger than life showers, sexy warriors with rock hard abs, hard bodied sailors and, of course, its legendary chorus line – with "Yma – too beautiful to be true", Friedrichstadt-Palast each night presents Berlinís hottest and most spectacular show on the worldís largest theater stage.

■ **Theater im Keller** (B CC g MA ST) Daily 18h-open end
Weserstraße 211 ☎ (030) 623 14 52 🖳 www.tikberlin.de
Theatre the size of a living room with regular travesty-shows. Shows start Thu-Sat 20h, Sun 19h.

CHAMÄLEON
Das Theater in den Hackeschen Höfen

Tipi am Kanzleramt (B glm M MA S t)
Tickets office Mon-Sat 12-19, Sun 15-18h
Große Querallee ☎ (030) 39 06 65 50 💻 www.tipi-am-kanzleramt.de
Shows of many german celebrities. Check website for the complete programme. Shows start Tue-Sat 20, Sun 19h.

CINEMA

MonGay @ Kino International (B GLM MA)
Mon 22, bar from 21h
Karl-Marx-Allee 33 ☎ (030) 24 75 60 11 💻 www.yorck.de
This cult cinema with its GDR-splendor interior shows gay/lesbian films every Monday night (Look for „Mongay" in every city calender).

Xenon (B GLM MA VS)
Kolonnenstraße 5-6 *S Julius-Leber-Brücke* ☎ (030) 78 00 15 30
💻 www.xenon-kino.de
Small cinema, but it shows GLBT-related movies every night.

CULTURE

Beate Uhse Erotik Museum (CC glm) 9-24, Sun 11-24h
Joachimstaler Straße 4 ☎ (030) 886 06 66 💻 www.erotikmuseum.de

Schwules Museum (! GLM) 14-18, Sat -19h, Tue closed
Mehringdamm 61 ☎ (030) 69 59 90 50 💻 www.schwulesmuseum.de
Permanent exhibition on the history of homosexuality and LGBT issues in Germany plus changing exhibitions: widely ranging topics, such as special historic and biographical themes, culture, art and everyday life of homosexuals through 200 years of history. Rich archive and library, accessible to the public (weekday afternoons or by appointment).

GIFT & PRIDE SHOPS

Dildoking (CC g) Mon-Sat 10-19h
Feldtmannstraße 23-25 ☎ (030) 34 35 30 55 💻 www.dildoking.de
Mail order with sale from the stock; you will get 10% of discount by buying directly in the Berlin shop.

Herrlich (glm MA) Mon-Sat 10-20h
☎ 784 5395 💻 www.herrlich-online.de
Gift shop for men.

BOOK SHOPS

Bruno's (! CC G MA) Mon-Sat 10-22, Sun 13-21h
Bülowstraße 106 ☎ (030) 61 50 03 85 💻 www.brunos.de
Bruno's gay store in Schöneberg with a huge selection of books, DVDs (also rental), toys, magazines, photobooks, underwear and pride articles. Ultimate gay shopping on 450 m² in the middle of the gay area.

Bruno's (CC G MA) Mon-Sat 10-22, Sun 13-21h
Schönhauser Allee 131 ☎ (030) 61 50 03 87 💻 www.brunos.de
Bruno's gay store in Prenzlauerberg with a huge selection of books, DVDs (also rental), toys, photobooks, underwear, magazines and pride articles.

Eisenherz Buchladen (! CC GLM MA) Mon-Sat 10-20h, closed Sun
Lietzenburger Straße 9a *near Wittenbergplatz* ☎ (030) 313 99 36
💻 www.prinz-eisenherz.com
A Berlin institution and oldest gay bookshop in town. Broad selection of books, magazines and DVDs in German, English & French for gays, lesbians & transgender.

Galerie Janssen (AC CC GLM MA) 11-20, Sun 14-20h
Pariser Straße 45 ☎ (030) 881 15 90 💻 www.galerie-janssen.de
Men's art gallery and book shop.

FASHION SHOPS

Corino for men (CC g MA SH) Mon-Fri 12-19, Sat 11-16h
Winterfeldtstraße 52 ☎ (030) 806 111 71 💻 www.corino4men.com

Frontplay (CC G MA) Mon-Fri 12-20, Sat 11-19h
Motzstraße 25 ☎ (030) 627 042 70 💻 www.frontplay.com
Fred Perry, Lonsdale, Ben Sherman and more.

Laden 114 (G MA) Mon-Thu 12-20, Fri&Sat -21h
Eisenacher Straße 114 ☎ (030) 2363 9373

Trüffelschwein (g) Mon-Sat 12-20h
Rosa-Luxemburg-Straße 21 ☎ (030) 70 22 12 25
💻 www.trueffelschweinberlin.com
Delicious menswear.

■ **Wagner Berlin** (CC G) Mon-Sat 12-20h
Motzstraße 32 ☏ (030) 28 59 83 05 💻 www.wagnerberlin.com
High-quality shirts, sweaters and underwear and swimwear from kinky to chic, all designed by Karl-Heinz Wagner.

LEATHER & FETISH SHOPS

■ **Blackstyle** (CC F G MA) Mon-Wed 13-18.30, Thu-Fri -20, Sat 11-18h
Seelower Straße 5 ☏ (030) 44 68 85 95 💻 www.blackstyle.de
Latex wear creation, leather, toys and mail-order.

■ **Butcherei Lindinger** (cc F G) Mon-Fri 14-20, Sat 12-20h
Motzstraße 18 ☏ (030) 20 05 13 91 💻 www.butcherei-lindinger.de
Tailormade leather- and fetishwear, individually designed articles (accessoires, toys and pumps) and accessories. Sterile atmosphere of a butchery.

■ **Gear Berlin** (CC F G I MA) Mon-Sat 12-20h
Kalckreuthstraße 13 *U-Nollendorfplatz* ☏ (030) 23 63 51 34
💻 www.gearberlin.com
Stylish Premium Brand Fetish Store – over two floors – with a wide range of Leather, Rubber, Sport and Urban Gear!

■ **Leathers – Lederwerkstatt Berlin** (F GLM MA T) Mon-Sat 12-20h
Schliemannstraße 38 *U-Eberswalder Straße, near Helmholtzplatz*
☏ (030) 442 77 86 💻 www.leathers.de
Leather tailoring.

■ **Leathers Shop** (CC F GLM MA T) 12-24h
Schliemannstraße 38 *U-Eberswalder Straße* ☏ 442 77 86
💻 www.leathers.de
Leather, fetish and sex shop.

■ **Military Store** (CC F G) Mon-Sat 12-19h
Eisenacherstraße 114 ☏ (030) 23 63 27 55 💻 www.military-store.de

■ **Mister B – Leather & Rubber** (CC F G MA)
Mon-Fri 12-20, Sat 11-20h
Motzstrasse 22 ☏ (030) 21 99 77 04 💻 www.misterb.com
Leather and rubber wear. Toys, magazines, cards and DVDs. Also mail order: www.misterb.com

■ **RoB – Berlin** (CC F G MA) Mon-Sat 12-20h
Fuggerstraße 19 ☎ (030) 21 96 74 00 🖳 www.rob-berlin.de
Handmade leather and rubber clothing. Very good reputation. Toys, videos. Also mail order on www.rob-berlin.de

■ **Rubber Factory Berlin** (F GLM) Mon-Fri 10-18, Sat -16h
Danziger Straße 52 ☎ (030) 440 337 68 🖳 www.rubber-factory.com
Manufacturer of high quality latex rubber clothing.

■ **Sling King** (G MA)
Eisenacherstrasse 115 ☎ 3462 2652 🖳 www.slingking.eu
New fetish shop in the heart of the Schöneberg bermuda triangle.

PHARMACIES

■ **Apotheke am Nollendorfplatz** Mon-Fri 8.30-20, Sat 9-17h
Maaßenstraße 3 ☎ (030) 216 34 53
🖳 www.apotheke-am-nollendorfplatz.de

■ **Markus Apotheke** Mon-Fri 8.30-20, Sat 9-14h
Motzstraße 20 ☎ (030) 21 47 93 90 🖳 www.markusapotheke-berlin.de

TRAVEL AND TRANSPORT

■ **movin' queer berlin** (GLM)
Liegnitzer Str. 5 ☎ (030) 618 69 55 🖳 www.movinqueer.de
Providing an individual stay in Berlin – accomodation, culture, sightseeing, tips.

■ **Over the Rainbow** (CC GLM MA) Mon-Fri 10-19, Sat 11-16h
Knesebeckstraße 89 ☎ (030) 318 05 80 🖳 www.overtherainbow.de
Queer travel agency.

HOTELS

■ **Aletto Jugendhotel** (BF H I NG PA PK RWS RWT YC) all year
Tempelhofer Ufer 8/9 ☎ 259 30 48 0 🖳 www.aletto.de

■ **Aletto Jugendhotel** (BF H I NG PA PK RWS RWT YC) 24hrs
Grunewaldstraße 33 *U7-Eisenacher Straße, U4-Bayrischer Platz, M°Bus 46, 3 mins walk to gay scene* ☎ (030) 21 00 36 80 🖳 www.aletto.de
All rooms with shower, WC, TV and radio. No age limit at this youth hostel.

■ **andel's Hotel Berlin**
(AC B BF CC glm I M MC PA PK RWS RWT SA SB WH WO) All year, 24hrs
Landsberger Allee 106 *S-Landsberger Allee* ☎ (030) 453 053 0
💻 www.andelsberlin.com
New gayfriendly hotel with nice views.

■ **Arco Hotel** (BF CC GLM I MA OS PA PK RWS RWT VA) All year
Geisbergstraße 30 *U-Wittenbergplatz, near KaDeWe department store*
☎ (030) 23 51 48-0
💻 www.arco-hotel.de
Hotel & Apartments – right in the gay area. 3 star comfort, operated by friendly owners, cosy terrace.

■ **Art'otel Berlin City Center West**
(AC B CC glm M MA RWS RWT WI) All year, 24hrs
Lietzenburger Straße 85 *U-Uhlandstraße* ☎ (030) 887 77 70
💻 www.artotels.com
Art-exhibition and hotel combined.

■ **Art'otel Berlin Ku'damm**
(AC B BF CC glm I M MA PA PK RWS RWT) daily, 24hrs
Joachimstalerstraße 28-29 *U9/1-Kurfürstendamm* ☎ (030) 88 44 70
💻 www.artotels.com
Art and living combined in Berlin's city-west.

■ **Art'otel Berlin Mitte**
(AC B BF CC glm I M MA PA PK RWS RWT VA) All year, 24hrs
Wallstraße 70-73 *U2-Märkisches Museum* ☎ 240 62 0
💻 www.artotels.com
Centrally located.

■ **Art-Hotel Charlottenburger Hof**
(B BF CC glm I M MA OS PA PK RWS RWT VA) All year
Stuttgarter Platz 14 *U-Wilmersdorfer Straße / S-Charlottenburg*
☎ (030) 32 90 70
Central location close to Kurfürstendamm. All rooms with bathroom, some with Jacuzzi, as well as computer and internet access for free, digital TV, DVD player/radio. Easily reachable from all airports by public transport. Bar/ restaurant is open 24 hrs.

ArtHotel Connection
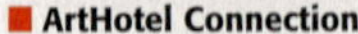
(BF CC f G I m MA MSG RWS RWT VA) All year, reception 8-22h
Fuggerstraße 33 *U-Wittenbergplatz* ☏ (030) 210 21 88 00
www.arthotel-connection.de
Located in the centre of the gay scene. 17 rooms, some with sling. Special equipped SM-apartments. Free WLAN. Under new ownership, all rooms were renovated in 2009.

Axel Hotel Berlin (B glm I M MA PI RWS RWT SA SB VA WH WO)
All year
Lietzenburger Straße, 13/15 *U-Wittenbergplatz* ☏ (030) 210 028 93
www.axelhotels.com
Axel Hotel Berlin is the third hotel of Axel Hotel's chain. There are 86 guestrooms (including superior rooms and a suite), restaurant, gym, sauna, jacuzzi and pool. In the heart of the gay area. Ideal for cosmopolitan gay travelers and businessmen. Also Restaurant „Kitchen by Axel".

California am Kurfürstendamm
(AC B BF CC H M MSG NG OS PK RR RWB RWS RWT SA SB SOL VEG WI WL WO) All year
Kurfürstendamm 35 *U-Uhlandstraße/S-Savignyplatz* ☏ (030) 88 01 20
www.hotel-california.de
4-star hotel. Central location. 160 rooms & suites with all modern amenities and an in-house steak restaurant.

spartacus traveler
DAS SCHWULE REISEMAGAZIN!
Viermal im Jahr mit Reportagen über interessante Reiseziele und Tipps für den perfekten schwulen Urlaub.
Im Abo (4 Ausgaben) für nur € 2,99 pro Heft, statt € 3,95 am Kiosk!
Gleich bestellen unter www.spartacus.de/traveler
Foto: Joan Crisol für ES Collection

■ **Ellington Hotel Berlin**
(AC B BF CC glm I M MA OS PA RWS RWT S VA WO)
All year, restaurant 11.30-23h
Nürnberger Straße 50-55 *U-Wittenbergplatz, U-Augsburger Straße*
☎ (030) 68 31 50 🖳 www.ellington-hotel.com
Landmarked building from the Golden Twenties. 285 rooms, design-hotel, restaurant „Duke" with international crossover-cuisine, open show kitchen and summer terrace.

■ **Esplanade Resort & Spa**
(AC B BF glm I M MA MSG PI RWB RWS SA SB SH SOL) All year
Seestraße 49, Bad Saarow ☎ (033631) 4320
www.esplanade-resort.de
Exclusive wellness-resort on the banks of a peaceful lake within a 50 minutes drive from Berlin city..

■ **Greifswald** (bf CC glm I MA OS PA RWS RWT VA) All year, 24hrs
Greifswalder Straße 211 *Prenzlauer Berg, tram 4* ☎ (030) 442 78 88
🖳 www.hotel-greifswald.de
Intimate private hotel in the trendy district Prenzlauer Berg. All rooms with shower/WC, TV, phone and WLAN.

■ **Hôtel Concorde Berlin**
(AC B BF CC glm H I M MSG PA PK RWS RWT SA SB SOL WO) All year
Augsburger Straße 41 *U-Kurfürstendamm, U-Zoologischer Garten*
☎ (030) 800 999 25 🖳 www.concorde-hotels.com/concordeberlin
A 5-star superior hotel, combining the arts, architecture and design with the savoir vivre, the higher French art of enjoying life, located on the famous Kurfürstendamm, only a few minutes walk away from the KaDeWe department store and the „Gedächtniskirche".

■ **Hotel Hansablick** (B BF CC H I MA NG PA PK RWS RWT WO)
All year
Flotowstaße 6 *S-Tiergarten, U-Hansaplatz* ☎ (030) 390 48 00
🖳 www.hansablick.de
Quiet and central located at the edge of Tiergarten. All rooms with shower, WC, TV, radio, safe and mini bar.

■ **Hotel Palace Berlin** (AC B BF CC g H I M MA MSG PA PI PK RWS RWT SA SOL WH WO) All year
Budapester Straße 45 *Near Gedächtniskirche and Kurfürstendamm, U-Zoologischer Garten/Wittenbergplatz, S-Zoologischer Garten* ☎ (030) 25 02 0 💻 www.palace.de
282 luxury rooms and suites, furnished and equipped with everything today's traveller needs. It has an excellent reputation as Berlin's private gourmet and convention hotel.

■ **Hotel Sarotti-Höfe**
(B BF cc glm I M OS PA PK RWB RWS RWT VA W) All year
Mehringdamm 57 *U-Mehringdamm, near event airport Tempelhof* ☎ (030) 600 3168 – 0 💻 www.hotel-sarottihoefe.de
Stylish and friendly gay-owned and operated hotel in the middle of the gay-scene of Kreuzberg.

■ **Hotel Zu Hause** (BF F GLM I RWS RWT) All year
Kleiststraße 35 *Gay area of Schöneberg* ☎ 0160 98313148 (mobile) ☎ 2362 5222 💻 www.hotelzuhauseberlin.de
Your home away for home. In the heart of Berlin's gay neighborhood Schöneberg.

■ **Hotel4Youth** (B BF CC glm m MA OS) 24hrs
Schönhauser Allee 103 *U-Schönhauser Allee* ☎ (030) 446 77 83 💻 www.Hotel4youth.de
Situated in a typical Berliner courtyard, this hotel is in the middle of the Prenzlauer Berg district, close to the local gay scene. All rooms are with all the modern conveniences.

■ **Myer's** (B BF CC glm H I M OS RWS RWT SA VA) All year
Metzer Straße 26 *U-Senefelder Platz* ☎ (030) 44 01 40 💻 www.myershotel.de
A 3 star private hotel with flair in a historic building in the heart of the trendy district Prenzlauer Berg. All rooms with bath/WC, telephone, fax, TV, radio, hair-dryer..

■ **NH Berlin Mitte** (AC B BF CC g M MA SA SB SOL WO) All year
Leipziger Straße 106-111 *U2-Stadtmitte* ☎ (030) 206 207 90 💻 www.nh-hotels.com

Being on top of the city life. Here on the Kurfürstendamm, not far from the Schöneberger Kiez, they know how to live the French way. Purist aesthetics give the almost extravagantly large rooms a very special atmosphere. Elegant interior design is merged with contemporary art to create a real feeling of savoir vivre. You, too, can experience your personal piece of France right in the heart of Berlin.

■ **Novotel Berlin am Tiergarten**
(AC B CC GLM M MA MSG PA PK RWS RWT SA SB SOL VA WO)
All year
Straße des 17. Juni 106-108 *S-Tiergarten* ☎ (030) 600 350
🖳 www.novotel.com
Trendy hotel close to the large city park „Tiergarten".

■ **Park Inn Berlin Alexanderplatz**
(AC B CC H I M MSG SB WO) All year, 24hrs
Alexanderplatz 7 *S/U-Alexanderplatz, next to TV Tower* ☎ (030) 23 89-0
🖳 www.parkinn-berlin.de
Berlin's biggest city hotel (four stars) with more than 1.000 Rooms on 37 Floors. Right in the heart of Mitte, not far from the gay venues in Prenzlauer Berg.

■ **Radisson Blu Hotel**
(AC B BF CC H I M MA MSG PI SA SB WI WO) All year
Karl-Liebknecht-Straße 3 *700 m from Alexanderplatz, directly on the river Spree and opposite Berlin cathedral* ☎ (030) 23 82 80
🖳 radissonblu.de/hotel-berlin
The contemporary designed hotel in purist style is centrally located in Berlin-Mitte.

■ **Sachsenhof** (B BF CC glm RWS RWT VA) All year
Motzstraße 7 *U-Nollendorfplatz* ☎ (030) 216 20 74
🖳 www.Hotel-Sachsenhof-Berlin.de
Moderately priced and at a central location in the gay area. 32 double rooms, 17 single rooms, all with bath/shower/WC, TV, phone and heating.

■ **Schall & Rauch** (B BF CC glm H M MA RWS RWT t WE)
8-12, Thu-Sat -?h
Gleimstraße 23 *S/U-Schönhauser Allee* ☎ (030) 443 39 70
🖳 www.schall-und-rauch.de
Schall & Rauch café and city hotel with 2 stars and 28 rooms. All rooms with shower/WC, TV and phone. Café: Cocktail hour daily 20-23h. Very large breakfast buffet on Sat & Sun.

■ **Tom's Hotel** (B CC G I MA NR PK RWB RWS RWT VA WI WO) All year
Motzstraße 19 *U-Nollendorfplatz* ☎ (030) 219 666 04
💻 www.toms-hotel.de
Guests receive a Hotel-Pass, which entitles you to exclusive offers in the gay scene; including discounts on dinner, shopping, clubbing and the sauna.

■ **Winter's Hotel Berlin Im Spiegelturm** (AC B BF CC H I M MA) all year, 24hours
Freiheit 5 *S-Stresow* ☎ (030) 330 980
💻 www.winters-hotel-berlin-spiegelturm.de
115 rooms, spacious, modern design, Wlan, air-condition, Breakfast buffet and dinner in the Panorama restaurant on the 16th floor with its breathtaking view.

■ **Winter's Hotel Gendarmenmarkt** (AC B BF CC H I MA NR OS PK RWB RWS RWT W) All year
Charlottenstraße 66 ☎ (030) 206050-0
💻 www.winters-hotel-berlin-gendarmenmarkt.de
Excellent location at the beautiful Gendarmenmarkt in the fashionable Mitte-District within walking distance to Friedrichstaße, Potsdamer Platz and the famous Brandenburg Gate.

■ **Winter's Hotel Berlin Mitte am Checkpoint Charlie** (B BF CC H I MA NR PK RWS RWT) All year
Hedemannstraße 11-12 *U-Kochstraße* ☎ (030) 319 86 18-0
💻 www.winters-hotel-berlin-mitte.de
Behind a historical facade with modern hotel interior. 112 design rooms each with multifunctional flatscreen and spacious safe.

■ **Winter's Hotel Berlin City Messe** (B BF CC H I M MA NR PK RWB RWS RWT) All year
Rudolstädter Straße 42 *S/U-Heidelberger Platz* ☎ (030) 897 83-0
💻 www.winters.de
Many rooms in different categories for the budget-minded traveller: 16 apartments with kitchen, 82 3-star-rooms and 36 2-star-rooms with shared showers and 3 conference rooms.

GUEST HOUSES

Bananas Guesthouse (G I RWT) All year
Geisbergstrasse 41 *U Nollendorfplatz, U Viktoria-Luise-Platz*
(030) 219 61 768 www.bananas-berlin.com
New Gay Guesthouse, centrally and quiet location, within minutes to the gay area. 10 rooms with WiFi. 4 large bathrooms to share.

Blond Guesthouse (bf CC GLM I MA RWT) All year
Eisenacher Straße 3 *U-Nollendorfplatz* 664 03 947
www.blond-berlin.de/guesthousestart.html
Guesthouse in the Schöneberg gay area. The two rooms share a shower/WC.

Eastside Pension (CC GLM I MA PA RWT VA) 24hrs
Schönhauser Allee 41 *U-Eberswalder Straße* (030) 43 73 54 84
www.eastside-pension.de
Four rooms with TV & private bathroom.

Garden Guest Houze (G I MA OS RWS RWT WO) All year
Görlitzer Straße 71 *U-Görlitzer Bahnhof* 251 78 89
www.garden-houze.de
Belongs to Club Culture Houze sexclub. A quiet oasis at the Görlitzer Park with rooms and apartments.

Gay Hostel (G I NR PK WI YC) All year, reception 10-24h
Motzstraße 28 *U-Nollendorfplatz* (030) 219 666 04
www.gay-hostel.de
Guests receive a Hostel-Pass, which entitles you to exclusive offers in the gay scene.

Guesthouse 21 (bf G I MA) All year
Martin-Luther-Straße 21 *U-Nollendorfplatz* (0173) 388 47 86
www.guesthouse21.de

Stars Guesthouse Berlin
(BF CC GLM I MA PA PK RWB RWS RWT VA) 7-24h
Welserstrasse 10-12 *U-Viktoria-Luise-Platz* (030) 210 14 5 14
www.stars-guesthouse.com
13 rooms with private or shared bathroom and 10 apartments. Located in the gay centre and very close to the shopping facilities of Kurfürstendamm.

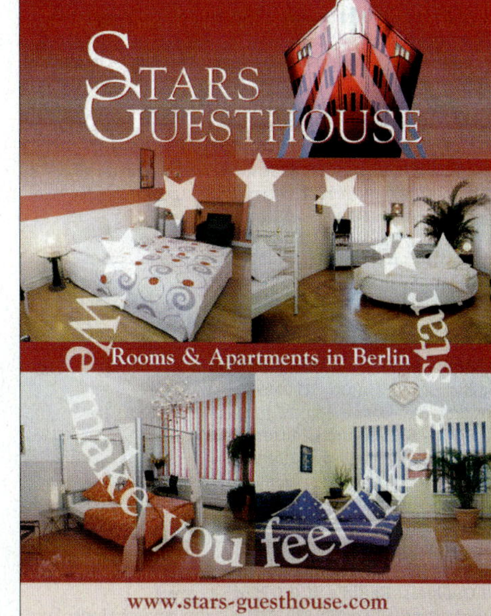

APARTMENTS

Berlin City Lounge (glm MA) All year
Friesingerstraße 17a *U-Winterfeldplatz* (030) 885 521 10
www.apartment-berlin-online.com
Two apartments (second apartment in Gleditschstraße 36) in the centre of the gay scene. In a quiet and green ambiance. Each apartment can accommodate a max. of 4 people.

Miniloftmitte (CC H I) Daily, 24hrs
Hessische Straße 5 *Near main station* (030) 847 10 90
www.miniloft.com
Stylish and modern apartments.

Andrew's Apartments (GLM I MA) All year
Motzstraße 10 *U-Nollendorfplatz* 9599 4862
www.andrews-apartments.de
4 different types of apartments in Berlin Schöneberg, all in the gay area around Nollendorfplatz, all with free WI-FI, fully equipped kitchen and bathroom.

RoB Leather Apartments Berlin (CC F G I MA) Mon-Sat 12-20h
Fuggerstraße 19 *U-Wittenbergplatz* (030) 21 96 74 00
www.rob-apartments.de
Two fully furnished apartments with own playroom/dungeon, only few steps away from the leather scene. Free internet access.

■ **Tom's Apartments** (DU G I MA PK RES RWS RWT WI) All year
Motzstrasse 19 *U-Nollendorfplatz* ☎ (030) 21966604
🖳 www.toms-group.de
Centrally located apartments for 1 to 4 people. Directly in the gay area and near the famous KaDeWe.

PRIVATE ACCOMMODATION

■ **Enjoy Bed & Breakfast** (BF G H MA) 9-22h
Bülowstraße 106 ☎ (030) 23 62 36 10 🖳 www.ebab.com
Worldwide private accommodation service €20-30 per person/night. More than 5.000 beds in 979 cities and 53 countries.

GENERAL GROUPS

■ **Magnus-Hirschfeld-Gesellschaft**
Chodowieckistraße 41 ☎ (030) 441 39 73 🖳 www.magnus-hirschfeld.de

FETISH GROUPS

■ **Berlin Leder und Fetisch e.V.** (F G MA)
Postfach 304152 ☎ (030) 215 00 99 🖳 www.blf.de
For all gay men who are interested in the leather and fetish scene.

■ **BOG – Biker ohne Grenzen.** (F G MA)
Perleberger Str. 59 🖳 www.bogberlin.de
Club for bikers, leather & fetish friends. Organizes bike-tours and partys .

■ **Böse Buben** (F G MA)
Sachsendamm 76-77 ☎ (030) 62 70 56 10
🖳 www.boese-buben-berlin.de
S/M-group. See website for info.

■ **Quälgeist Berlin e. V.** (F G P) Fri-Sat evening
Mehringdamm 51 ☎ (030) 788 57 99 🖳 www.quaelgeist-berlin.de
S/M-group. See website for info.

■ **Spreebären** (F G MA)
Landshuter Straße 1 ☎ (030) 21 96 73 53 🖳 www.spreebaeren.de
Social group for bearded and hairy men and their admirers.

HEALTH GROUPS

■ **Berliner Aids-Hilfe e. V.** (BF GLM MA)
Mon 12-18, Wed 12-14.30 (anonymous HIV test), Thu & Fri 12-15h
Einemstraße 11 ☎ (030) 885 64 00 🖳 www.berlin-aidshilfe.de

■ **Dr. Heiko & Dr. Arne B. Jessen & Dr. Luca Daniel Stein** (glm MA)
Mon-Fri 9-13; Mon, Tue, Thu 16-19; Sat, Sun & public holidays 11-14h
Motzstraße 19 ☎ (030) 235 10 70 🖳 www.praxis-jessen.de
Gay family doctors. Also English & French spoken.

■ **Pluspunkt** (G MA)
Greifenhagener Str. 52 ☎ (030) 44 66 88 0 🖳 www.pluspunktberlin.de
Help for people with HIV, testing, counselling and more.

HELP WITH PROBLEMS

■ **GLADT** Mon-Fri 10-18h
Kluckstraße 11 ☎ (030) 26 55 66 33 🖳 www.gladt.de
Organisation of queer immigrants, mostly from Turkey.

■ **LSVD Berlin-Brandenburg e.V.**
Kleiststraße 35 ☎ (030) 22 50 22 15 🖳 www.berlin.lsvd.de
Legal advice service: every 1st Thursday/ month from 17h.

■ **Maneo – Schwules Überfalltelefon und Opferhilfe** (GLM MA) 17-19h
c/o Mann-O-Meter, Bülowstraße 106 ☎ (030) 216 33 36
🖳 www.maneo.de
Hotline and service for gay victims of violence.

SWIMMING

-Stadtbad Wilmersdorf (Mecklenburgische Straße 80) has re-opened (especially interesting on Monday evenings)
-Strandbad Müggelsee (S-Friedrichshagen, tram-Fürstenwalder Damm/ Müggelseedamm)
-Halensee (S-Halensee bus-Rathenauplatz. Not the lido but the lawn beside Halenseestraße at Rathenauplatz)
-Teufelssee (S-Grunewald, then a 15 mins walk or 🅿 at end of Teufelsseechaussee, crowded in summer)
-Grunewaldsee (Bus M19 to »Hagenplatz« then take Königsallee to the the lake)
-Strandbad Wannsee (! S-Nikolassee, then take bus-shuttle to Strandbad, gay area is far right behind the nude section).

CRUISING

-Tiergarten near Strasse des 17.Juni around „Neuer See", especially in the tabletennis-area and „Löwenbrücke"
-"Tuntenwiese" (! at Siegessäule/Großer Stern, between Hofjägerallee and Straße des 17. Juni, U-Hansaplatz, bus 100/187) naked sunbathing and day-time cruising
-Grunewald (F) (at 🅿 Pappelplatz/Auerbachtunnel)
-Preußenpark (public toilets, U-Fehrbelliner Platz)
-Volkspark Friedrichshain (at »Märchenbrunnen«) (AYOR)
-Volkspark Wilmersdorf (around the toilets)
-Park at U Turmstraße Berlin-Moabit (AYOR)
-Viktoriapark Berlin-Schöneberg.

Bielefeld ☎ 0521

BARS

■ **Muttis Bierstube** (AC B CC d GLM I MA) 20-3, Fri & Sat -5h
Friedrich-Verleger-Straße 20 ☎ (0521) 618 16 🖳 www.muttis-bierstube.de

DANCECLUBS

■ **Magnus Party @ Hechelei** (B D GLM YC) 1st Sat/month 22.30-4h
Ravensberger Park 6 *Bus 21/22/29-Ravensberger Park*
☎ (0521) 96 68 80 🖳 www.triebwerk-der-club.de

RESTAURANTS

■ **Tres** (B GLM M MA) Daily 14-?h
August-Bebel-Straße 86a *Centre* ☎ (0521) 96 77 399
🖳 www.tres-bielefeld.de
BF on Sat, Sun and public holidays 5-11h.

SEX SHOPS/BLUE MOVIES

■ **Novum** (g VS) 9-22h
Eckendorfer Straße 60-62 ☏ (0521) 32 39 00 💻 www.novum-erotik.de

SAUNAS/BATHS

■ **Sauna 65** (B DR FC G LAB m MA OS PP RR SA SB SL SOL VS WE WO) 15-2h, Sat & Sun 14-2h
Niedermühlenkamp 65 *Near youth centre Kamp* ☏ (0521) 656 59
💻 www.sauna65.de
With a winter garden and terrace.

BOOK SHOPS

■ **Buchladen Eulenspiegel** (g MA) Mon-Fri 9-18.30, Sat 10-16h
Hagenbruchstraße 7 ☏ (0521) 17 50 49
💻 www.buchladen-eulenspiegel.de

CRUISING

-University Bielefeld (ground floor, sectors C0, S0, T0)
-Ravensberger Park, Heeper Street near the school building (evenings).

Binz ☏ 038393

HOTELS

■ **Rugard Strandhotel** (! B BF H M MA MSG PI RR RWB RWS RWT SA SB WO) All year (check in from 15, check out to 11h)
Strandpromenade 62 ☏ (038393) 560 💻 www.rugard-strandhotel.de
Wellness and vitality at its best is offered by the 5 star Royal Spa beach hotel Rugard with its congenial mix of Roman bathing culture, Asian spa elements and exclusive cosmetics.

Bocholt ☏ 02871

BARS

■ **Ramonas Wunderbar** (B GLM MA) Wed-Sun 20-5h
Osterstraße 27 ☏ (02871) 2923913
💻 www.facebook.com/ramonaswunderbar

Bochum ☏ 0234

GAY INFO

■ **Rosa Strippe e. V.** (GLM MA) Mon-Thu 16-18h
Kortumstraße 143 *Metro U35 Rathaus Nord* ☏ (0234) 640 46 21
💻 www.rosastrippe.de
Meeting point for various GLM groups and gay-counselling.

BARS

■ **Coxx** (B G MA VS) 20-3h, Mon closed
Ehrenfeldstraße 2 ☏ (0234) 33 72 96
■ **Orlando** (AC B BF CC GLM I M MA OS) 10-1, Fri & Sat -2h
Alte Hattinger Straße 31 *Schauspielhaus* ☏ (0234) 342 42
💻 www.orlando-bochum.net
■ **TeddyPierre** (B g M MA) 17-1h, closed Tue
Poststraße 43 ☏ (0234) 338 89 71
Bistro with German & French cuisine.

CAFES

■ **freiRAUM** (b GLM YC) Mon & Fri 16-22h
Kortumstraße 143 *Metro U35, Rathaus Nord* ☏ (0234) 6404621
💻 www.freiraum-bochum.de
Cafe for young lesbians and gays aged 14-27.

DANCECLUBS

■ **BO-YS** (! AC B D GLM YC) 1st Sat/month 22-4h
c/o Kulturzentrum Bahnhof-Langendreer, Wallbaumweg 108 *S1 S-Bochum-Langendreer* ☏ (0234) 6404621 💻 www.bo-ys.de
Very popular, with 2 dancefloors.
■ **Stargate** (AC D DR f G S SNU VS YC) Fri & Sat 23-?h
Hans-Böckler Str. 12 *City-Passage* ☏ (0234) 138 88 💻 www.stargate-club.de
■ **Zarah & Leander** (AC B D GLM YC)
c/o Kulturzentrum Bahnhof Langendreer, Wallbaumweg 108 *S1 S-*

Bochum-Langendreer ☏ (0234) 194 46 💻 www.zarahundleander.de
One of the most popular gay parties in this region, 2 dancefloors. See www.zarahundleander.de for exact dates.

SEX SHOPS/BLUE MOVIES

■ **Erotikshop Wolf** (AC CC G GH VS)
Mon-Fri 9.30-21, Sat 10-20, Sun 14.30-20h
Bongardstraße 2
■ **Life Erotica** (b DR f g MA VS) 9.30-24, Sun 10-24h
Rottstraße 16 ☏ (0234) 162 71 💻 www.ralfskontaktbar.de

CRUISING

-Ruhruniversität (Building GA 04 Nord)
-Dahlhausen 🅿 of railway museum
-🅿 Kemnader Brücke Nord
-Bochum-Riemke – toilets on market place
-Kortumpark / Aralpark, Wittener Straße (opp. Main Post Office).

Bodenmais ☏ 09924

GUEST HOUSES

■ **Villa Montara Bed & Breakfast** (B BF cc glm H I m MC MSG OS PA PK RWB RWS RWT SA VA) All year
Rechenstraße 38 *300 m from train station* ☏ (09924) 1015
💻 www.gaybayern.com
Gay-friendly guesthouse in the mountains „Bayrischer Wald" with a beautiful panorama view. 10 mins from skiing region „Großer Arber". Cosy & modern rooms.

Bonn ☏ 0228

BARS

■ **Boba's** (AC B d G MA p) 20-3h
Josefstraße 17 *Near Kennedybrücke* ☏ (0228) 65 06 85 💻 www.bobasbar.de

Copain. Le (B GLM MA WE) 17-?h
Thomas-Mann-Straße 3a *Near main station* ☎ (0228) 63 99 35

CRUISING

-Hofgarten (ayor) (behind the university at river Rhine; »Am Alten Zoll«)
-Dornheckensee (Bonn-Ramersdorf, summer only).

Bottrop ☎ 02041

SEX SHOPS/BLUE MOVIES

Erotique (DR g GH VS) 10-22, Sun 16-22h
Essener Straße 19 ☎ (02041) 77 61 22 🖳 www.erotique-bottrop.de

CRUISING

-Stadtgarten (near Quadrat)
-BAB-Parking
-Park in Beckendahl (evening)
-Halde Batenbrock (Tetraeder Beckstraße).

Braunschweig ☎ 0531

BARS

Knochenhauer (B glm M MC OS) 18-?h
Alte Knochenhauer Str. 11 ☎ (0531) 480 35 03 🖳 www.knochenhauer.net
Modern, lifestyle cocktail bar which serves meals, too. Sexy waiters!

DANCECLUBS

GaySensation @ Stereowerk (B D GLM MA)
Böcklerstr. 30-31 🖳 www.gaysensation-braunschweig.de
Check www.gaysensation.de for dates.

SWIMMING

-Island in Salzgittersee (Lawn on the hill, summer only)
-Kennelbad (summer only)
-Bienroder See (NU).

Bremen ☎ 0421

BARS

Friends (B GLM I m MA) Mon-Thu 19-1, Fri & Sat -3, Sun 16-1h
Rembertistraße 32 *3 mins from main station* ☎ (0421) 258 18 60
🖳 www.friends-bremen.de

König Lounge (AC B d GLM m MA S) 17-?, Sat 12-?h, closed Sun
Ostertorswallstraße 68 ☎ (0421) 223 12 73 🖳 www.koeniglounge.de

La Vie (B GLM MA) Sun-Thu 18-1, Fri & Sat 18-?h
An der Weide 24 ☎ (0421) 515 71 99

Queens (B G R VS YC) 20-?h
Außer der Schleifmühle 10 *Near main train station* ☎ (0421) 32 59 12
🖳 www.queens-bremen.de

Rendezvous (B G MA ST) 18-2h, closed Mon
Elisabethstraße 34 *Cnr. Bremerhavener Straße* ☎ (0421) 38 31 59
🖳 www.rendezvous-bremen.de

Schwarzer Hermann (B g I m MA OS) 18-2h, closed Thu
Hohenlohestraße 4-6 ☎ (0421) 62 65 681
🖳 www.schwarzerhermann.de

MEN'S CLUBS

Bronx (cc DR F G MA p VS) 22-?h
Bohnenstraße 1b *Crn. Gertrudenstraße* ☎ (0421) 70 24 04
🖳 www.bronxbremen.de

Zone 283 (B DR F G MA p) Fri & Sat 22-3h
Kornstraße 283 ☎ (0421) 53 20 99 🖳 www.zone283.de
Leather bar.

CAFES

Kweer (B GLM MA s) 1st Tue/month 20-24, Fri 20-24, Sun 15-18h
Theodor-Körner-Straße 1 ☎ (0421) 70 00 08
🖳 www.ratundtat-bremen.de
Lesbian café every 3rd Sat 20-?, Sun: cake.

DANCECLUBS

Bittersweet @ Römer (B D glm MA) 1st Fri/month 22-?h
Fehrfeld 31 ☎ (0421) 794 65 98 🖳 www.roemer-bremen.de

Downtown (B D G MA) Fri & Sat 23-?h
Außer der Schleifmühle 49 *Near main station* ☎ (0421) 334 72 70
🖳 www.downtown-hb.de
Happy Hour 23-24h and Karaoke.

Tom's Welt (D DR G MA p R SNU ST VS)
Außer der Schleifmühle 10 *Close to the main rail station*
☎ (0421) 32 59 12 🖳 www.queens-bremen.de
Occasional only.

SEX SHOPS/BLUE MOVIES

Men's Seven (AC b CC DR f G MA VS)
15-23h, closed Sun and public holidays
Am Dobben 7 *Tram 1/4/10-Rembertistraße* ☎ (0421) 32 36 87

Movie's Eventhouse (AC cc DR G I OS r VS) 9-1, Fri 9-Mon 1h
An der Weide 25 *Near main station, opp. post office*
☎ (0421) 337 81 79
Playroom, lounge, cruising and parties. Also information about the scene in Bremen.

SAUNAS/BATHS

■ **Perseus** (B DR DU G m MA MSG SA SB VS WO) 16-24h, closed Mon
Waller Heerstraße 126 *Near train station* ☎ (0421) 38 51 00
🖳 www.perseus-sauna.de
A clean and not flashy sauna on 600 m².

LEATHER & FETISH SHOPS

■ **HM-LEDER** (CC F G MA p) Mon-Fri 14-19, Sat 12-16h and by appointment
Neukirchstraße 18 *Near central train station. Bus 26/27*
☎ (0421) 37 14 30 🖳 www.hm-leder.com
Large selection of leather, rubber, uniforms, toys, magazines, accessories and DVDs. Also mail order.

HEALTH GROUPS

■ **AIDS-Hilfe Bremen**
Sielwall 3 ☎ (0421) 33 63 63-0 🖳 www.aidshilfe-bremen.de
Rapid HIV testing.

SWIMMING

-Unisee (south east of the beach, near facilities and dunes. Evenings: in the WC & dunes and in a small forest north east)
-Mahndorfer See (between lake and motorway).

CRUISING

-P Oldenburger Straße (ayor r) (under the fly-over Hochstraße, opposite Arbeitsamt).

Bremerhaven ☎ 0471

BARS

■ **Dreams** (B G H MA ST) 19-2, Fri & Sat 19-?h, Sun closed
Hopfenstraße 6 ☎ (0471) 941 81 43 🖳 www.dreams-bhv.de
1st Sat/month drag shows.

■ **Rudelsburg** (B GLM MA ST T) 19-?h
Goethestraße 1 *Tram „Am Leher Tor"* ☎ (0471) 440 82
1st Sat/month drag shows.

Chemnitz ☎ 0371

CAFES

■ **Rainbow** (B glm M MA OS) Tue-Thu 19-1, Fri & Sat -?h
Hartmannstraße 7 *Schmidtbankpassage, city centre* ☎ (0371) 909 95 75

DANCECLUBS

■ **Club FX** (B D GLM MA) Every 2nd Sat 22-?h
c/o Fuchsbau, Carolastraße 8 *Near main railway station*
☎ (0371) 67 17 17 🖳 www.clubfx.de

SAUNAS/BATHS

■ **Clubsauna Outside** (B DR DU G GH I LAB M MA MSG RR SA SB SH SL SOL VS WH) 15-23, Fri & Sat -24h, Tue closed
Reineckerstraße 64 ☎ (0371) 520 48 60 🖳 www.clubsauna-outside.de
Sauna on 500 m² and two floors. Video & DVD shop, also rental. Toys and underwear available.

BOOK SHOPS

■ **Conrad & Paul** (glm MA) Mon-Fri 10-18, Sat -16h
Rosenhof 23 *Central city, near Rosenhof* ☎ (0371) 57 37 882

CRUISING

-Kassbergauffahrt (tunnel at Fabrikstraße)
-Central tram stop (tunnel, 8-18h)
-Schlossteichpark (Promenadenstraße between Kurt-Fischer-Straße and Müllerstraße, popular).

Darmstadt ☎ 06151

BARS

■ **Queer** (B GLM YC) Mon-Sat 20-3, Sun -5h
Schulstraße 15 ☎ (0177) 243 8189

DANCECLUBS

■ **Schlosskeller** (b D GLM YC)
1st, 3rd and 5th Sun/month 22h-open end
Hochschulstraße 1 ☎ (06151) 163117
🖳 www.schlosskeller-darmstadt.de
Alternative student party, many lesbians.

SEX SHOPS/BLUE MOVIES

■ **Heguwa Erotikshop** (glm VS) Mon-Sat 10-22h
Ludwigstrasse 8 *1st. floor* ☎ (06151) 24233 🖳 www.sex-sinne.de
Eroticstory with gay section, cruising area and cinema with gloryholes.

BOOK SHOPS

■ **Thalia Buchhandlung** (glm MA) Mon-Sat 9.30-20h
Luisenstraße 20 / Schuchardtstraße 8 ☎ (06151) 91 85 00
Including Bruno Gmunder depot.

Dortmund ☎ 0231

GAY INFO

■ **KCR-Dortmunder Lesben- und Schwulenzentrum** (GLM I MA s) Thu 20-23h
Braunschweiger Straße 22 *U-Münsterstraße* ☎ (0231) 83 22 63
🖳 www.kcr-dortmund.de

BARS

■ **Burgtor Club** (B D G MA ST VS) 15-1, Fri -3, Sat 19-5, Sun -1h
Burgwall 17 ☎ (0231) 57 17 48 🖳 www.burgtorclub.com

■ **Heimes – jetzt erst recht** (B GLM I M MA OS)
12-1, Sat & Sun 10-1h
Ludwigstraße 4-6 *Next to concert hall* ☎ (0231) 120 63 54
🖳 www.heimes-dortmund.de

■ **Zaubermaus** (B G MA r) 16-?h
Kielstraße 32b ☎ (0231) 395 49 50
🖳 www.zaubermaus-dortmund.de

MEN'S CLUBS

■ **Amigo** (B DR G MA VS) 15-1, Fri & Sat -4h
Schwanenwall 26 🖳 www.amigo-do.de

■ **Boots Club. The** (B DR F G MA P VS) Sun-Thu 21-2, Fri & Sat -5h, Tue closed
Bornstraße 14 ☎ (0231) 476 63 96 🖳 www.thebootsclub.de
Dresscode leather! Cruisy atmosphere with bondage, S/M and more. Every 2. Fri/month is Sportsgear Night Party.

CAFES

■ **Chokolat** (b glm)
Neuer Graben 74

DANCECLUBS

■ **Smalltownboys @ Nightrooms** (B D GLM YC)
Last Sat/month 22.30-?h
Hansastraße 5-7 🖳 www.smalltownboys.de

SAUNAS/BATHS

■ **Fontäne** (B DR DU FC G m MA SA SB SH SL VS)
13-21h, Tue & Thu closed
Leuthardstraße 9 ☎ (0231) 524 600 🖳 www.sauna-fontaene.de
Moved to new location.

■ **Jumbo Center**
(B cc D DR FC G M MA MSG OS PI RR SA SB VS WH WO) 13-1h
Dammstraße 44 ☎ (0231) 880 58 53
Large, nice relaxation area. Dark area can very cruisy.

BOOK SHOPS

■ **Litfass – Der Buchladen** (CC glm) Mon-Fri 10-20, Sat -14h
Münsterstraße 107 *U-Münsterstraße* ☎ (0231) 83 47 24
🖳 www.litfass-gaybooks.de
General bookshop with gay section.

FASHION SHOPS

■ **Mr B & Demask** (CC F GLM MA) Mon-Fri 11-19, Sat -16h
Hamburger Str.120 ☎ 108 7117 🖳 www.demask-dortmund.de
Fashion, leather and fetish store on 400 m². 70 m² Mister B Store-In-Store.

CRUISING

-Westpark (entrance Ritterhausstraße, popular)
-Kaufhof, Westernhellweg
-University (Audimax, downstairs facilities on the same level where the parking area is)
-Facilities in Wal-Mart's Café, Wulfshofstraße (Dortmund Oespel).

Dresden ☎ 0351

GAY INFO

■ **Gerede – Homo, Bi und Trans e.V.** (b D GLM MA OS T VS)
Office: Mon-Fri 8-16, youth group: daily 15-21h
Prießnitzstraße 18 *Neustadt, Tram 11-Diakonissenkrankenhaus*
☎ (0351) 802 22 51 🖳 www.gerede-dresden.de
Meeting point for various gay and lesbian (youth) groups.

SHOWS

■ **Carte Blanche** (B glm M ST t) Wed-Sun 17-?h (May-Aug), 18-?h (Sep-Apr)
Prießnitzstraße 10 *Linie 11-Diakonissenkrankenhaus* ☎ (0351) 20 47 20
🖳 www.carte-blanche-dresden.de
Also restaurant and cocktail bar „Zora".

BARS

■ **Boys** (B CC G H m MA WE) 20-3, Fri & Sat -5h
Alaunstraße 80 *Scene district, Dresden-Neustadt* ☎ (0351) 563 3630
🖳 www.boys-dresden.de
■ **Queens** (! AC B D DR GLM MA S SNU ST) 20-5h
Görlitzer Straße 3 *Neustadt* ☎ 01520-9109940 (mobile)
🖳 www.queens-dresden.de

MEN'S CLUBS

■ **Bunker** (B DR f G MA p) Fri & Sat 22-3h
Prießnitzstraße 51 *Dresden-Neustadt, corner Bischofsweg*
☎ (0351) 441 23 45 🖳 www.lederclub-dresden.de
Dresscode for special events and parties, Fri & Sat open for everyone..

CAFES

■ **Kontakt** (b GLM I S T YC) 15-21h
Prießnitzstraße 18 *Neustadt, tram 11-Diakonissenkrankenhaus*
☎ (0351) 802 22 51 🖳 www.gerede-dresden.de
Popular international meeting point for young gays, lesbians, bis and trans people. Open, cosy, chilly atmosphere with friendly international staff.
■ **Valentino** (b glm MA) Sun-Thu 15-1, Fri & Sat -3h
Jordanstraße 2 ☎ (0351) 889 49 96 🖳 www.valentino-dresden.de

DANCECLUBS

■ **Disco Woanders @ Bärenzwinger** (B D GLM MA WE)
Bruehlscher Garten 1 *City Centre* ☎ (0351) 89 96 08 98
🖳 www.discowoanders.de
Party that takes place once a month. Check www.discowoanders.de for info.
■ **Queens** (! AC B D DR GLM MA S SNU ST) 20-5h
Görlitzer Straße 3 *Neustadt* ☎ 01520-9109940 (mobile)
🖳 www.queens-dresden.de
■ **sHe Party** (B D GLM MA)
c/o Metronom Club, Louisenstraße 55 🖳 www.she-party.de
See www.she-party.de for details.
■ **Think Pink Party @ Spinnerei Strasse E®** (B D DR GLM MA)
Werner Hartmann Str. 2 ☎ (0351) 89 96 08 98
🖳 www.dresden-ist-pink.de
Party that takes place once a month. Check www.dresden-ist-pink.de for info.

RESTAURANTS

■ **Lila Soße** (B CC DM glm M MA OS VEG WL)
Alaunstraße 70 *Kunsthof* ☎ (0351) 803 6723

SEX SHOPS/BLUE MOVIES

■ **Duplexx** (b DR G MA VS) Daily 15-3h
Förstereistraße 10 *Tram 7/8-Louisenstraße* ☎ (0351) 658 89 99
🖳 www.duplexx.eu
Cruising cinema, private cabines, big choice of DVDs, videos and toys. Four further Duplexx locations in Berlin, Munich and Stuttgart.
■ **Erotic-World** (AC g MA VS) Mon-Sat 9-23h
Tharandter Straße 84 *Dresden-Löbtau, direction Freital*
☎ (0351) 427 27 23

SAUNAS/BATHS

■ **Man's Paradise**
(AC B DR DU G m MA MSG OS p PI RR S SA SB SOL VS WH) 12-1h
Friedensstraße 45 *Neustadt* ☎ (0351) 802 25 66
🖳 www.mans-paradise.de
Sauna on 640 m² with s/m area. Terrace 600 m².

BOOK SHOPS

■ **Leselust** (glm) 11.30-19.30, Sat 10.30-14.30h, closed Sun
Louisenstraße 24 *Near station Neustadt* ☎ (0351) 404 50 46
🖳 www.leselust-dresden.de

HOTELS

■ **art'otel Dresden** (AC BF H M RWS RWT WI WO) All year
Ostra Allee 33 *S Dresden Mitte, near Zwinger* ☎ (0351) 4922 0
🖳 www.artotels.com

■ **Pullman Dresden Newa** (AC B BF CC glm H I M MA PA PK RWS RWT SA VA WO) All year
Prager Straße 2 c *Near main station, only a few min from the historical city*
☎ (0351) 4814-109 🖳 www.pullman-dresden-newa.com
Four-star hotel, centrally located. 319 rooms with modern interior, shower/WC, sat-TV, phone and safe. Style, design, feel-good-atmosphere and professional service.

PRIVATE ACCOMMODATION

■ **City Cottage Dresden** (glm I MA PK RWS RWT VA) All year
Louisenstraße 11 *Dresden-Neustadt* ☎ (0351) 799 6218
🖳 www.city-dresden.de
A two-floor cottage with lounge, TV and CD player, fully equipped kitchen and seperate bedroom. Sleeps up to 4 people. Non-smoking property.

SWIMMING

-Auensee (NU MA) (near Moritzburg)
-Tongrube Auer (On the road from Dresden to Großenhain, just after the village of „Neuer Anbau" there is a small parking area. Here you will find a small lake called „Gewandert").

CRUISING

-Kiesgrube Dresden-Leuben (NU MA) (Tram 2/12-Lasallestraße. Walk up the Salzburger Straße to the 🅿, go through the gate, after the second gate to the right, cruising and tanning)
-Altmarkt/Webergasse/Wallstraße (small wood)
-Marienbrücke (in summer)
-Roßthaler Straße

Duisburg ☎ 0203

BARS

■ **Harlekin** (B G m MA p s) 18-2, Fri & Sat -?h
Realschulstraße 16 ☎ (0203) 262 44 🖳 www.gayworld-duisburg.de

■ **Rainbow** (B glm MA OS) 10-1h
Friedrich-Wilhelm-Platz 4a ☎ (0203) 317 63 10
More gay in the evenings.

■ **Senftöpfchen** (B d glm MA) Tue-Sun 17-24h
Röttgersbachstraße 89 ☎ (0203) 50 12 45 🖳 www.senftoepfchen.com
With bowling alley.

MEN'S CLUBS

■ **Gay World** (B DR G MA VS) 10-2, Fri & Sat -5h
Krummacherstraße 44 ☎ (0203) 940 86 18
🖳 www.gayworld-duisburg.de
Maze with St. Andrews cross. Also a shop. From 18h connected to the „Harlekin"-bar.

DANCECLUBS

■ **Warm Up** (B D GLM MA S) 3rd Fri/month 22-?h
c/o HunderMeister, Dellplatz 16a ☎ (0203) 279 53 🖳 www.akdulus.de

SEX SHOPS/BLUE MOVIES

■ **Erlebniskino** (DR g VS) Mon-Sat 9-24, Sun 13-23h
Friedrich-Wilhelm-Straße 97 *Near central railway station*
☎ (0203) 285 47 19 🖳 www.erlebniskinos.com
Also glory holes. Various cabines with TV for 2 and more people.

■ **Madison** (DR g MA VS) 9-24, Sun 13-23h
Kasinostraße 4a

CRUISING

-Kantpark (behind museum → Realschulstraße)
-Kleiner Park (Mercatorstraße/main station)
-Town hall Hamborn (WC).

Düsseldorf ☎ 0211

PUBLICATIONS

■ **Exit**
c/o Exit Medien GmbH, Sternstraße 49 ☎ (0211) 41 66 74-40
🖳 www.inqueery.de
Gay magazine for Northrhine-Westfalia. Moved from Essen to Düsseldorf.

BARS

■ **Aroma** (B GLM MA OS) 9-1h
Oststraße 124 *U-Oststraße* ☎ (0211) 367 71 17
🖳 www.aroma-duesseldorf.de

■ **Bel Air** (AC B GLM MC r s) 9-?h
Oststr. 116 🖳 www.clubbelair.de
New gay bar and café near main-station. Smoking allowed.

■ **Café Seitensprung** (AC B GLM I m MA S) 18-1h, closed Mon
Grupellostraße 5 *U-Oststraße* 🖳 www.seitensprung-cafe.de

■ **Club Levent** (B d GLM M MA) Mon-Thu 17-5, Fri 17-open end, Sat 17-Mon 5h non-stop
Grupellostraße 32 *U-Düsseldorf Hbf*

■ **Comeback** (B G m MA R) 14-1, WE -5h
Charlottenstraße 60 *U-Oststraße, entrance Bismarckstraße*
☎ (0211) 17 54 989

■ **El Sombrero** (B d GLM MC R) daily 14-?h
Grupellostr. 7 ☎ 364 365 🖳 www.club-sombrero.de
One of the oldest gay-bars in town. Smoking allowed.

■ **Galapagoz** (B G I M MA OS VS) 15-1, Fri & Sat -3h
Klosterstraße 68a *U-Oststraße* ☎ 0172 2774635 🖳 www.galapagoz.de

■ **Hotspot** (B GLM MA) 15-1, Fri & Sat -?h
Bismarckstraße 56a ☎ (0211) 977 133 13 🖳 www.cafe-hotspot.de

■ **Ludwigs Bier & Brot** (B bf glm m MA) 18-5h
Mertensgasse 11 *Old town* ☎ (0211) 159 71 44
🖳 www.ludwigs-bier-und-brot.de
Breakfast available Sat & Sun 6-9h.

■ **Musk** (AC B DR G MA) 22-3, Thu-Sat -6h
Charlottenstraße 47 *Near main station, U-Oststraße* ☎ (0211) 46 15 08

■ **Nähkörbchen** (B GLM MA) 18-?, Sat 12-?, Sun 15-?h, closed Mon
Hafenstraße 11 *Tram Benrather Straße* ☎ (0211) 323 02 65
🖳 www.karins-naehkoerbchen.de

■ **Piranha** (AC B GLM m MA OS s)
Mon-Thu 19-1, Fri & Sat -3h, Sun closed
Bilker Allee 110 *S-Bilk, opp. Flora* ☎ (0211) 178 031 56
🖳 www.cafepiranha.de
Nice neighborhood bar, smoking allowed.

■ **Theater Stube** (B G MA) 14-?, Sat & Sun 12-?h
Luisenstraße 33 ☎ (0211) 37 22 44

■ **Wilma Next Generation** (B G MA) 20-5h
Charlottenstraße 60 *Near main station, corner Bismarckstraße, next door to „Comeback" Bar* ☎ (0178) 341 86 15
Small cozy pub for young and old.

DANCECLUBS

■ **Amitabha @ Berolina Bay** (AC B CC D G MA S t)
3rd Sat/month 23-?h
Berliner Allee 46 *Near main station* ☎ (0211) 875 04 27
🖳 www.amitabha-club.de

■ **Gay Happening** (B D G MA S) 1st Sat/month 22-5h
Königsallee 28-30 *@ Checker's* 🖳 www.internationalgayhappening.de
Check www.internationalgayhappening.de for details.

■ **Gayhappening** (B D GLM MA S) Sat on various dates
Bahnstraße 13 *@ Nachtresidenz* 🖳 www.gayhappening.de
Long running party. Check www.gayhappening.de for details.

■ **Joice @ Ufer 8** (B D G S)
Rathausufer 8 🖳 www.joice-duesseldorf.de
Unregular dates.

■ **K1 Club** (AC B D DR GLM MA S) 22h-open end
Bismarckstraße 93 *Entrance Karlstraße* ☎ (0211) 875 14 375
🖳 www.k1-duesseldorf.de
Popular. Mon Karaoke.

■ **Mandanzz @ Stahlwerk** (B D GLM MA) 2nd Sat/month 23-?h
Ronsdorfer Straße 134 *Cnr. Lierenfelderstraße* www.mandanzz.de

■ **Schamlos** (B D GLM M MA OS S T) 5th Sat/month
Fichtenstraße 40 *@ zakk* ☎ (0211) 875 04 27
www.schamlos-party.de
Check www.schamlos-party.de for exact dates.

SEX SHOPS/BLUE MOVIES

■ **New Man** (G VS)
Graf-Adolf-Straße 69

■ **Sexmesse** (g VS) 9-24, Sun & holidays 15-24h
Kölner Straße 24 ☎ (0211) 35 47 89

SAUNAS/BATHS

■ **Condor Wellness Sauna** (AC B CC DR G I M MA MSG OS PP RR s SA SB VS WE WH) 12-23, Fri & Sat -6h
Luisenstraße 129 *Near central train station* ☎ (0211) 37 39 73
www.condor-sauna.de
800 m² modern sauna on two floors with large terrace, garden and a bio-sauna.

■ **Phoenix** (! b cc DR DU FC G I m MSG OS p RR SA SB VS WH YC) 12-6, Fri 12-Mon 6h (non-stop)
Platanenstraße 11a *Bus 834-Hermannplatz, tram 709-Wetterstraße, S-Flingern* ☎ (0211) 66 36 38 www.phoenixsaunen.de
Very clean sauna on two floors with a decoration full of fantasy. Also Centro Delfino massage studio.

MASSAGE

■ **Centro Delfino** (CC G MA MSG) 14-22, Sat & Sun 13-23h
c/o Phoenix Sauna, Platanenstr. 11a *Close to main station*
☎ (0211) 66 36 38 www.centro-delfino.de
Massage studio in a gay sauna, holistic style, ayurveda, trad. thai massage, classic style, If you don't use the sauna, you don't have to pay extra entrance fee. Just ask for massage at the desk.

BOOK SHOPS

■ **Book XXX** (G) Mon-Fri 10-23, Sat -21h
Bismarckstraße 86 ☎ (0211) 35 67 50 www.bookxxx.eu
Books, films, hardcore.

HOTELS

■ **Hotel Friends Düsseldorf** (B BF CC glm H I MC PA PK RWS RWT) All year, 24hrs
Worringer Straße 94-96 *3 mins walk from main station*
☎ (0211) 17 93 090 www.hotel-friends-duesseldorf.de
Located in the heart of Düsseldorf, close to main station and city centre. 24h bar, 2 lounges, W-LAN for free and more.

■ **Hotel Windsor** (H RWB RWS RWT)
Grafenberger Allee 36 *Near to Düsseldorf's Zoo area and station Wehrhahn* ☎ 91 46 80 www.windsorhotel.de
Very traditional and aristocratically Hotel with fine english and antique furniture, personal service. Highly decorated in English style. Hundred year old town house.

■ **Sir & Lady Astor** (H RWB RWS RWT)
Kurfürstenstraße 23 *500m to main train station, 10mins walk to Königsallee, 18mins walk to Old Town* ☎ (0211) 17 33 70
www.sir-astor.de
All 20 guestrooms are fully equipped as a 3 star superior hotel.

SWIMMING

-Angermunder Baggersee / Kalkumer Baggerloch
-Düsseldorf-Himmelgeist (south of the city), P (near church, from there 20 minutes walk south to the river Rhine, popular).

CRUISING

-Graf-Adolf-Platz (toilets)
-Kirchplatz
-Nordpark (until 21h)
-Hanielpark (until 16h)

-Hofgarten, Area Rhein/Inselstraße and Oper, Inselstr.(best 22-1h, popular)
-Schwanenspiegel Elisabethstraße/Haroldstraße (paths around the pond -23h)

Erding ☏ 08122

SAUNAS/BATHS

■ **Therme Erding** (NG SB WO) 10-23, Sat, Sun & public holidays 9-23h
Thermenallee 1 ☏ (08122) 22 70 -100
Not a gay sauna but in Europe's largest water park. There is an unofficial gay night every last Wednesday of the month.

Erfurt ☏ 0361

GAY INFO

■ **SwiB-Zentrum** (GLM M MA S VS) 19-24h
Windthorststraße 43a *Near main station* ☏ (0361) 346 22 90
erfurt.aidshilfe.de/swib
Gay info centre, switchboard. Home of the SwiB-Café open Tue-Fri 19-24, Sun 15-20h.

MEN'S CLUBS

■ **OX's Clubkeller** (B DR F G m MA s VS) Sat 21-4h
Windthorststraße 43a *Near main station* ☏ (0361) 346 22 90
www.tlc-erfurt.de

SEX SHOPS/BLUE MOVIES

■ **Pleasure Shop** (AC CC glm MA VS) Mon-Sat 9-24, Sun 12-24h
Schillerstraße 55 ☏ (0361) 22 555 85
■ **Pleasure Shop II** (CC GLM MA VS) Mon-Sat 9-24, Sun 12-24h
Weimarische Straße 34 ☏ (0361) 211 54 02

CRUISING

-Willy-Brandt-Platz (in front of and behind the railway station in the city park)
-Johannesstraße (Kaufmannskirche to Alhambrakino via Hertie). AYOR but interesting after 23h at WE
-Domplatz (in the small park nearby).

Erlangen ☏ 09131

DANCECLUBS

■ **Colours** (AC B D GLM OS VS YC) 2nd Fri/month 22-4h
c/o E-Werk, Fuchsenwiese 1 *Near main railway station*
☏ (09131) 800 50 www.e-werk.de
Check www.e-werk.de for partydates. Formerly known as „Pink Friday".

CRUISING

-Friedrich-List-Straße (Underpass)
-P at Friedrich-List-Straße/Haus des Handwerks.

Essen ☏ 0201

PUBLICATIONS

■ **Fresh** (GLM MA)
c/o Verlag Tropilis UG, Kopstadtplatz 21 ☏ (0201) 74 71 61 81
www.fresh-magazin.de
Monthly gay-newspaper for the rhur-region.

BARS

■ **Barbados** (B GLM MA s) 20-?h, closed Mon
Steelerstraße 83 *Tram 103/109-Hollestraße* ☏ (0201) 17 14 07 06
New bar.
■ **Gentle M** (B d GLM m MA S) Daily 18-1.30h
Kettwiger Straße 60 *Near city hall* ☏ (0201) 821 73 33
www.gentlem-essen.de
Karaoke, occasional parties.
■ **Im Briefkasten** (B G M MA) 11-2h
Hachestraße 21 ☏ (0201) 23 00 81

■ **Im Büro** (B G MA) 20-?h
Viehofer Platz 14

■ **Zum Pümpchen** (B G m MA) 20-?h
Kopstadtplatz 23 ☎ (0201) 45 29 829
www.radio-rosa-rauschen.de/puempchen.htm

MEN'S CLUBS

■ **Drexx** (B D F FC G MA) Wed 19-1, Fri-Sat 22-5, Sun 16-24h
Rheinische Straße 60 *U-Berliner Platz or U-Rheinischer Platz*
www.drexx.de
Check website for the exact opening hours and dresscode

CAFES

■ **Vielfalt** (b GLM YC) Mon 16-24, Fri 18-24h
Kleine Stoppenberger Straße 13-15 ☎ (0208) 302 73 58
www.cafe-vielfalt.de
Advice center with café.

DANCECLUBS

■ **Glamourdome @ Zeche Carl** (B D GLM MA)
4th Sat/month 22-?h
Wilhelm-Nieswandt-Allee 100 www.glamourdome.de

RESTAURANTS

■ **Seitenblick** (B BF DM glm M OS VEG WL) 9-23, Fri & Sat -24h
Trentelgasse 2 *Near Grillo-Theater* ☎ (0201) 815 58 49
www.seitenblick-essen.de

SEX SHOPS/BLUE MOVIES

■ **Eros Boutique Essen** (AC DR G MA VS)
10-22, Sun & public holidays 16-22h
Klarastraße 19 *Opp. Rüttenscheider Markt* ☎ (0201) 78 83 21
www.gay4play.de

■ **Man Moviethek** (G r VS) 12-1, Fri & Sat -4, Sun 14-1h
Vereinstraße 22 ☎ (0201) 20 30 10

SAUNAS/BATHS

■ **Phoenix** (! AC AK b BF CC DR F FC G I LAB M MA MSG p PI RR SA SB SL SOL VS WH) 12-6, Fri 12-Mon 6h (non-stop)
Viehoferstraße 49 *U-Viehoferplatz* ☎ (0201) 248 84 03
www.phoenixsaunas.de
Very well equipped sauna with pedicure and free Turkish Hamam massage. Also Centro Delfino massage centre.

■ **St.Tropez-Wellness-Sauna** (B CC DR f G I m MA MSG OS PP RR s SA SB SOL VS WE WH) 12-23, Fri & Sat -7h
Maxstraße 62 *700 m from main station* ☎ (0201) 32 25 41
www.st-tropez-sauna.de
1000 m² sauna on 3 floors with large terrace, garden and bio-sauna.

MASSAGE

■ **Centro Delfino – Massage Kosmetik** (CC G MA MSG)
14-22, Sat & Sun 13-23h
c/o Phoenix Sauna, Viehofer Straße 49 ☎ (0201) 24 88 403
www.centro-delfino.de
Massage studio in a gay sauna, holistic style, ayurveda, trad. thai massage, classic style and hamam treatments. If you don't use the sauna, you don't have to pay extra entrance fee. Just ask for massage at the desk.

TRAVEL AND TRANSPORT

■ **ITR Reisen/Pink Elephant Safaris** (G)
Bahnstr. 11 ☎ (0201) 1700 890
www.pink-elephant-safaris.de
The gay way to Africa.

GENERAL GROUPS

■ **Essen-X-Point** (GLM MA)
Varnhorststraße 17 ☎ (0201) 105 37 17 www.essen-x-point.de
General information, AIDS counselling & meeting point for various groups and activities.

CRUISING

-Helbingstraße/Frau-Bertha-Krupp-Straße (2 parking lots)
-University Essen (library, foyer, toilets)
-Helbingbrücken (near main station)
-Porscheplatz (station, toilets).

Flensburg ☎ 0461

DANCECLUBS

■ **Schwulen- und Lesbendisco** (B D GLM MA s)
1st & 3rd Sat/month 22-4h
c/o K.u.K. Volksbad, Schiffbrücke 67 ☎ (0461) 16 00 100
www.sl-disco.de

SWIMMING

-Holnis near Glücksburg (NU, past Glücksburg 3km further, then follow the signs to the »Strand«)
-Campusbad on Tue, Wed & Fri 16h (Thomas-Fincke-Straße 19).

CRUISING

-City centre, by „Sankt-Jürgen-Treppe".

Frankfurt/Main ☎ 069

Those who visit Frankfurt will be reminded of an American city rather than a European City, as it is the only city characterised by its sky scrapers. This city of superlatives has the largest airport in continental Europe, the highest sky scraper in Europe and the world famous fair and exhibition centre, and all the most important German banks can be found here. Nevertheless only 650.000 people live here. This is noticable when one visits the local, small but welcoming gay scene. One always encounters many foreigners here, and in contrast to many other large European cities, it is easy to strike up a conversation over a beer or glass apple wine. The tourist attractions in this city, completed demolished during the war, include the Römer, the opera house the Gothic Emperor's Dome and the Paul's Church – making Frankfurt one of Germany's most historical cities. Other recommendations include the Kunsthalle Schirn, the Architecture Museum and the Städel. The large Christopher Street Parade and its parties take place from the 13th to 15th July 2012.

Wer Frankfurt besucht, wird gewiss eher an eine amerikanische als an eine europäische Stadt erinnert, denn sie ist als einzige durch eine fantastische Hochhaus-Skyline geprägt. Diese Stadt der Superlative besitzt den größten kontinentaleuropäischen Flughafen, das höchste Hochhaus Europas, die berühmteste Messe und ist Sitz der europäischen Zentralbank sowie aller bedeutenden deutschen Banken. Trotz allem wohnen hier nur rund 650.000 Einwohner – das merkt man auch, wenn man die recht überschaubare aber liebenswürdige schwule Szene besucht. Durch den internationalen Charakter der Stadt trifft man immer auf eine Menge Touristen und Auswärtige und im Gegensatz zu anderen großen europäischen Metropolen, ist hier ein Gespräch mit Fremden bei einem Glas Bier oder Apfelwein leicht herzustellen.
Die touristischen Ziele dieser, im Krieg komplett zerstörten und etwas nüchtern wieder aufgebauten Stadt sind der Römer, die Oper, der gotische Kaiserdom und die Paulskirche, die Frankfurt zu einer der geschichtsträchtigsten Orte Deutschlands machen. Unter den Museen ist die Kunsthalle Schirn, das Architekturmuseum und das Städel zu empfehlen. Die Feierlichkeiten rund um den CSD finden vom 13. – 15. Juli 2012 statt.

Francfort rappelle plus une ville américaine plutôt qu'européenne avec à l'horizon tant de hauts buildings. Cette ville des superlatifs a le plus grand aéroport d'Europe continentale, la plus haute tour d'Europe, les salons les plus connus et est le siège de la Banque Centrale Européenne et des principales banques allemandes. Malgré cela, elle ne compte que près de 650.000 habitants et la scène gay est de taille limitée mais très accueillante. De part son caractère international, on rencontre toujours des touristes et des personnes de passage. Et contrairement à

d'autres métropoles européennes, on lie facilement contact ici autour d'un verre de bière ou de cidre.
Les sites touristiques de cette ville pratiquement complètement détruite pendant la guerre et reconstruite sans grandes ambitions sont le bâtiment Römer, l'opéra, la cathédrale impériale gothique et l'église St-Paul qui font de Francfort un des lieux les plus emprunts d'histoire en Allemagne. Parmi les musées, la galerie d'art Schirn, le musée d'architecture et l'institut d'art et galerie municipale Städel – affectueusement surnommé le „ Städel „ - sont recommandés. Les festivités autour de la Gay Pride (CSD) ont lieu du 13 au 15 juillet 2012.

Para los que visitan Fráncfort, esta les recordará más a una ciudad norteamericana que a una ciudad europea, ya que se caracteriza por su panorama urbano plagado de rascacielos de gran altura. Esta ciudad de superlativos cuenta con el mayor aeropuerto de la Europa continental, el rascacielos más alto de Europa, la feria más famosa y es también sede del Banco Central Europeo y de los principales bancos alemanes. A pesar de todo, aquí sólo viven alrededor de unos 650.000 habitantes, lo cual también se nota al visitar el ambiente gay, amable pero bastante manejable. Debido al carácter internacional de la ciudad, no es raro encontrar aquí una gran cantidad de turistas y extranjeros, y, en contraste con otras grandes ciudades europeas, entablar una conversación con desconocidos mientras se bebe una cerveza o una sidra no es tarea difícil.
Los destinos turísticos de esta ciudad, completamente destruida durante la guerra y que se reconstruyó de una manera un poco más sobria, son el Römer (edificio del Ayuntamiento de Fráncfort), la Ópera, el Kaiserdom (la torre gótica) y la . Estos hacen de Frankfurt uno de los lugares históricos más importantes de Alemania. De entre los museos se recomienda la sala de Artes Schirn, el Museo de Arquitectura y el Städel. Las celebraciones relacionadas con el CSD tendrán lugar del 13 al 15 de julio de 2012.

Francoforte dà più l'impressione di una città americana che di una città europea. Infatti la città è caratterizzata dal bellissimo profilo dei suoi grattacieli. Francoforte è la città dei superlativi: infatti qui vi è l'aeroporto internazionale più grande d'Europa, il grattacielo più alto d'Europa, la fiera più famosa d'Europa, ed è anche la sede della Banca Centrale Europea nonché sede delle più importanti banche tedesche. Tuttavia Francoforte è una città di solo 650.000 abitanti circa: questo lo si percepisce anche dalle dimensioni della scena gay. Il carattere spiccatamente internazionale di Francoforte fa sì che in giro per la città si incontrino sempre tantissimi turisti e stranieri. Al contrario che in altre grandi metropoli europee, a Francoforte è molto facile entrare in contatto con la gente del posto, specialmente davanti ad un bicchiere di birra o di sidro.
A causa della distruzione che la guerra ha portato, Francoforte non è una città ricchissima dal punto di vista architettonico. Tra le mete turistiche più importanti, degne di nota sono il Römer (il Municipio), l'Opera, il Duomo gotico e la Chiesa di San Paolo. Fra i musei più importanti vi consigliamo di visitare il Kunsthalle Schirn, il Museo dell'Architettura e lo Städel. Le feste del CSD si svolgeranno tra il 13 e lil 15 luglio del 2012.

GAY INFO

AG 36: Gay Infoline (GLM MA)
Tue-Thu 11-17, cafe open from 19h
Alte Gasse 36 *U/S-Konstablerwache* ☎ (069) 29 59 59 (infoline)
www.ag36.de
Information about the gay scene in Frankfurt by mail or phone.

PUBLICATIONS

GAB – Das Gaymagazin (GLM) Mon-Fri 9.30-17.30h
Kaiserstraße 72 ☎ (069) 274 04 20 www.inqueery.de/gab
Monthly magazine for gay events in the Frankfurt area. Available for free at gay venues.

BARS

AG 36: Switchboard (B GLM MA) Tue-Sat 19-24, Sun 14-23h
Alte Gasse 36 *U/S-Konstablerwache* ☎ (069) 28 35 35
www.ag36.de
Meeting point for various GLM groups Info café for AIDS-Hilfe Frankfurt. Info material available (Popular).

Bananas (B d GLM MA) 10-24, Sun -21h
Schäfergasse 42 *Near Zeil* ☎ (069) 804 365 03
New and cozy gay bar in the neart of the city.

Birmingham Pub (B g m MA OS p) Mon-Sat 11-6, Sun 12-6h
Battonnstraße 50 *S/U-Konstablerwache* ☎ (069) 28 74 71
www.birmingham-pub.com
Regular pub at daytime, gay after 21.30h, popular very late.

Central (AC B GLM MA) 20-2, Fri & Sat -3h
Elefantengasse 13 *S/U-Konstablerwache* ☎ (069) 29 29 26
Classic type of urban bar. Stylish design but relaxed atmosphere. Great cocktails. Mixed Thursdays, happy hour 20-21h

Comeback (AC B G M MA R) 18-?h
Alte Gasse 33-35 *S/U-Konstablerwache*
Well established rent bar.

Halo (B G YC) Mon-Fri 18-?, Sat & Sun 15-?h
Alte Gasse 26 ☎ (069) 133 87 90

Krawallschachtel (B g MA R) 20-?, additionally Tue-Sat 12-19h
Alte Gasse 24 ☎ (069) 21 99 91 29
Old fashioned rent-bar in the bermuda triangle.

B
A
N
See Map B
Frankfurt / Main
Main
Eschenheimer Anlage
Bleichstr.
Petersstr.
Alte Gasse
Vilbeler Str.
Brönnerstr.
Stephanstr
Gr. Friedberger Str.
Schäfergasse
K.-Adenauer-Str.
Hammelsg.-Porzellanhofstr.
Stiftstr.
Zeil
Konstabler Wache
Musterschule
Grüne-burgweg
Hebelsstr.
Mercatorstr.
Friedberger Landstr.
Gaußstr.
Von Bethmann Park
Friedberger Anlage
Eschenheimer Landstr.
Eschenheimer Tor
Hochstraße
Börse
Börsenstraße
Große Eschenheimer Str.
Seilerstraße
Klapperfeldstr.
Heiligkreuzgasse
Konrad Adenauer Str.
Hauptwache
Taunus-anlage
Neue Mainzer Str.
Töngesgasse
Kurt Schumacher Straße
Battonnstraße
Roßmarkt
Große Taunusstr.
Berliner Straße
Pauls-kirche
Dom/Römer
Römer
Dom
Fahrgasse
Taunusanlage
Mainzer Landstr.
Weserstr.
Taunusstr.
Kaiserstr.
Gallusanlage
Mainkai
Willy Brandt Platz
Karlstr.
Moselstr.
Hauptbahnhof
Münchner Str.
Untermainkai
Eiserner Steg
Alte Brücke
Ignatz Bubis Brücke
Sachsenhäuser Ufer
Gutleutstraße
Wilhelm Leuschner Str.
Untermainbrücke
Elisabethenstr.
Dreieichstraße
Walter Kolb Straße
Schweizer Str.
Paradiesgasse
Holbeinsteg
Schaumainkai
Unter der Friedensbrücke
Speicherstraße
Gartenstraße
Schweizer Platz
Friedensbrücke
Stresemannallee
Theodor Stern Kai
Kennedyallee
Waldmannstr.
Uni-Klinik
Stresemann-allee

EAT & DRINK
Bananas 32
Birmingham Pub – Bar 27
Central – Bar 15
Comeback – Bar 17
Exil – Restaurant 6
Größenwahn – Restaurant 9
Krawallschachtel – Bar 18
Lucky's LM27 – Bar 20
Monte Carlo – Bar 33
Piper Red Lounge – Bar 12
Pulse – Restaurant 12
Switchboard – Bar 11
Tangerine – Bar 16
Taverne Amsterdam – Restaurant 1
Zum Schwejk – Bar 25
Zur Hexe – Bar 10
NIGHTLIFE
CK – Danceclub 21
Club 78 @ Unionhalle – Danceclub 34
Stall – Men's Club 26
SEX
Amsterdam – Sauna 1
Jerome – Sex Shop/Blue Movies 5
Metropol – Sauna 29
New Man – Sex Shop/ Blue Movies 4
New Man @ WOS – Sex Shop/Blue Movies 2
Saunawerk – Sauna 36
Skyline – Sex Shop/Blue Movies 30
ACCOMMODATION
Concorde – Hotel 3
Downtown – Hotel 19
Holiday Inn – Hotel 37
OTHERS
AG 36 – Gay Info 11
AIDS-Hilfe – Gay Info 39
Centro Delfino – Massage 29
Oscar Wilde – Book Shop 14
Our Generation 40

■ **Lucky's Manhattan LM27** (AC B CC GLM I MA OS)
15-1, Fri & Sat-open end
Schäfergasse 27 *S/U-Konstablerwache, in gay area* ☎ (069) 284 919
💻 www.luckys-lm27.com
Elegant lounge on 1st floor. Tuesday popular karaoke night. Smoker's lounge upstairs

■ **Maxroom** (AC B cc d G m MA S ST t VS)
12-1, Fri & Sat -5, Sun 14-1h
Wallstraße 22 *Near Affentorplatz in Sachsenhausen*
💻 www.maxroom.eu
Irregular parties such as Madonnamania, Bad Tasteparty, etc.

■ **Monte Carlo** (B G MA) Mon-Fri 19-?, Sat & Sun 17-8h
Alte Gasse 34 ☎ (069) 207 365 86
Cosy nightbar.

■ **Na und?** (B G MA) Sun-Thu 20-1, Fri & Sat -2h
Klapperfeldstr. 16 ☎ (069) 297 288 41

■ **Piper Red Lounge** (AC B CC D GLM I m MA OS)
18-1, Fri & Sat -5h
Bleichstraße 38 *Enter through Pulse Restaurant* ☎ (069) 13 88 68 02
💻 www.piper-red-lounge.de
Part of the Pulse complex.

■ **Tangerine** (B GLM m MA) 17-4h
Elefantengasse 11 ☎ (069) 28 48 79
Local pub.

■ **Zum Schwejk** (! B f G MA)
Mon 16-1, Tue-Thu 12-1, Fri-Sat -3, Sun 19-1h (winter: 15-1h)
Schäfergasse 20 *S/U-Konstablerwache* ☎ (069) 29 31 66
💻 www.schwejk.net
A Frankfurt institution, extremly popular pub. Party atmosphere esp. at the weekends.

■ **Zur Hex** (B GLM MA OS p) 21-10h
Elefantengasse 11 ☎ (069) 13 37 69 53
Tiny, camp bar. Busy late at night.

MEN'S CLUBS

■ **Grande Opera** (B D DR F g MA NU P SNU VS)
Christian-Pleß-Straße 11-13, Offenbach *Hassia Factory*
💻 www.grande-opera.de
Fetishparties with strict dresscodes, see www.grande-opera.de for more info.

■ **Stall** (! AC B F G MA VS) 22-4h, Fri & Sat -open end
Stiftstraße 22 *U-Eschenheimer Tor* ☎ (069) 29 18 80
💻 www.stall-frankfurt.de
One of the oldest leather bars in Germany.

DANCECLUBS

■ **CK Club** (! AC B D DR GLM MA S WE) Fri & Sat 22h-open end
Alte Gasse 5 *U-Konstablerwache*
Formerly known as C5, completely remodeled and reopened in 2009 with new and extraordinary party concepts like „Killer Cow", „Lockerroom" and many more. Friday „Queerbeet" on one floor, Sat „Another Level" parties with 2 dancefloors and Lasershow.

■ **Club78** (B D GLM MA) 22-6h
Hanauer Landstrasse 188 *@ Unionhalle, Tram 11 Schwedlerstrasse*
☎ (06109) 508439 💻 www.club78.de
Disco-Party with music from the 70's, 80's and 90's in it's 16th year.

■ **CocoonClub** (AC B CC D g m MA S) 3rd Sat 22-6h on irregular dates!
Carl Benz Strasse 21 *S-Dieselstrasse* ☎ (069) 900200 💻 www.cocoon.net
FAKE Party every 3rd Sat. See www.envymyparty.de for dates!

■ **Pulse** (! AC B BF CC D DM GLM I M MA NR OS PA VEG WL)
10-1, Fri & Sat -4h
Bleichstraße 38a *U/S Konstablerwache* ☎ (069) 13 88 68 02
💻 www.pulse-frankfurt.de
Elegant large bar & restaurant on 2 floors. WE 22-3h nightclub in the ballroom.

RESTAURANTS

■ **Exil** (B cc DM glm M MA OS PA RES WL) Mon-Sat 18-2h
Mercatorstraße 26 *Bus-Hessendenkmal* ☎ (069) 44 72 00

www.exil-frankfurt.de
French & Mediterranean cuisine. Reservation recommended.

Grössenwahn (glm M MA OS) Sun-Thu 16-2, Fri & Sat 16-1h
Lenaustrasse 97 ☎ (069) 599 356 www.cafe-groessenwahn.de
Popular mixed restaurant in the Nordend, excellent cuisine, reservation recommended.

Pulse (! AC B BF CC D DM GLM I M MA NR OS PA VEG WL) 10-1, Fri & Sat -4h
Bleichstraße 38a *U/S Konstablerwache* ☎ (069) 13 88 68 02
www.pulse-frankfurt.de
Elegant large bar & restaurant on 2 floors. WE 22-3h nightclub in the ballroom.

Taverne Amsterdam (B G M MA s VEG VS)
Tue-Sat 13.30-1 Sun-22h, closed Mon
Waidmannstraße 31 *S-Stresemannallee* ☎ (069) 631 33 89
Excellent traditional German & Hessian cuisine until 21.30h. Located in the Amsterdam Sauna, free entrance for restaurant guests.

SEX SHOPS/BLUE MOVIES

Jerome (AC DR G MA VR VS) Mon-Sat 11-23, Sun 15-23h
Elbestraße 17 *S/U-Hauptbahnhof* ☎ (069) 25 39 79
www.jerome-frankfurt.de
Sun naked party from 12-15h

New Man (CC DR F G MA VS) 9-24, Sun & holidays 12-24h
Kaiserstraße 66 *S/U-Hauptbahnhof, 1st floor* ☎ (069) 25 36 97

Skyline (CC F G MA) Mon-Sat 10-22h
An der Staufenmauer 5 *S/U-Konstablerwache* ☎ (069) 21 93 93 00
www.skylineworld.de
One of Europe's largest gay video stores. Also DVDs, books, magazines, toys and fetish equipment available. 10% discount on shop articles with skyline-membercard.

SAUNAS/BATHS

Amsterdam Clubsauna (B DR DU G M MA MSG OS RR s SA SB SOL VS WH) 13.30-23, Sun -22h, closed Mon
Waidmannstraße 31 *Sachsenhausen, S 3/4, tram 15/19/21-Stresemannallee*
☎ (069) 631 33 71 www.clubsauna-amsterdam.de
Popular and friendly sauna on 4 floors. Very good food at reasonable prices. Free buffet every last Fri/month.

Metropol-Sauna (AC B BF cc DR DU f G I LAB M MA MSG p R RR SA SB SOL VS WO) Mon-Thu 12-4, Fri 12-Mon 4h (non-stop)
Große Friedberger Straße 7-11 *U-Konstabler Wache, 2nd floor*
☎ (069) 4300 1680 www.metropol-sauna.de

Saunawerk (AK B DR G GH I LAB M MSG OS P PI RR SA SB SL VS WH) Mon-Thu 12-3, Fri 12-Mon 3h (non-stop)
Eschersheimer Landstraße 88 *U-Grüneburgweg* ☎ (069) 90 50 09 70
www.saunawerk.com

MASSAGE

Centro Delfino @ Metropol-Sauna (CC G MA MSG)
Daily 15-23h
Große Friedberger Str. 7-11 *U-Konstabler Wache* ☎ (069) 43 00 16 80
www.centro-delfino.de
Massage studio in a gay sauna.

BOOK SHOPS

Oscar Wilde Buchhandlung & Mail Order (AC CC GLM MA)
11-19, Sat 10-16h, closed Sun
Alte Gasse 51 *S/U-Konstabler Wache* ☎ (069) 28 12 60
www.oscar-wilde.de
Friendly staff. Books, magazines, CDs, DVDs and accessories.

HOTELS

Downtown Hotel Frankfurt (B BF CC glm I MA OS RWS RWT)
All year
Schäfergasse 27 *U/S-Konstablerwache* ☎ (069) 21 97 68 90
www.downtown-hotel-frankfurt.com
Modern hotel in the middle of Frankfurt's gay bermuda triangle. All rooms with small kitchen and own bath/WC.

■ **Holiday Inn Frankfurt City-South** (AC B BF CC glm H I M MA PA PK RWB RWS RWT SA SB VA WO) All year
Mailänder Straße 1 *Sachsenhausen* ☎ (069) 68 02 0
💻 www.frankfurt-hi-hotel.de
Large 4-star superior hotel with all modern amenities. All rooms are bright with sat-TV, phone, cosmetic mirror, large writing table, minibar, internet connection, safe and hairdryer.

■ **Hotel Concorde** (AC B BF CC glm H I MSG PK RWS RWT) All year
Karlstr. 9 *Opp. main station* ☎ (069) 242 42 20
💻 www.hotelconcorde.de
The Concorde Hotel with its unique interior design in the heart of Frankfurt is an ideal location for all business and pleasure trips.

■ **Monte Cristo** (B BF CC glm H I M PA PK RWS RWT VA) All year
Bieberer Straße 61 ☎ (069) 981 95 732
💻 www.hotelmontecristo.de
Located in the heart of Offenbach, a suburb of Frankfurt.

■ **Winter's Hotel Offenbacher Hof** (B BF CC H I M MA NR PK RWB RWS RWT SA SOL WO) All year
Ludwigstraße 33-37, Offenbach am Main *10 mins from Downtown; S1, S2, S8,S9-Ledermuseum* ☎ (069) 829 82-0 💻 www.winters.de
In a former leather factory, centrally located. 73 spacious rooms and junior suites, each one with classic design, electronic safe and WLAN.

APARTMENTS

■ **Winter's Eurotel Boardinghouse**
(B BF CC H I MA NR PK RWS RWT) All year
Friedhofstraße 8, Offenbach am Main *10 mins from Downtown; S1, S2, S8, S9-Offenbach Ost* ☎ (069) 982 42-0 💻 www.winters.de
69 comfortable apartments (27-37 qm), centrally located. Ideal for long term stays.

GENERAL GROUPS

■ **Kuss41** (b GLM m YC) Tue 17-23, Wed-Fri 17-22h
Kurt-Schumacher-Straße 41 *Near S/U-Konstablerwache*
☎ (069) 297 236 56 💻 www.kuss41.de
Gay-Lesbian youth centre.

■ **LSVD Hessen – Lesben und Schwulenverband in Deutschland – Landesverband Hessen e.V.**
Postfach 170341 ☎ (069) 94 54 96 16 💻 www.hessen.lsvd.de
Meeting every 2nd Friday/month at 19:15h at Lesbisch-schwules Kulturhaus Frankfurt (LSKH).

HEALTH GROUPS

■ **AIDS-Hilfe Frankfurt eV** (GLM MA) Mon-Thu 10-13 & 14-17h
Friedberger Anlage 24 *U-Konstabler Wache* ☎ (069) 405 86 80
💻 www.frankfurt-aidshilfe.de
Information, advice, help and connections – confidentially, anonymously and free of charge.

HELP WITH PROBLEMS

■ **AG 36: Counselling** (GLM MA) Mon 19-21h and by appointment
Alte Gasse 36 *U/S-Konstablerwache* ☎ (069) 29 59 59
💻 www.ag36.de

■ **KISS – Kriseninterventionsstelle für Stricher** (g R t YC)
Mon-Wed 13.30-16.30, Thu 16-20h
Alte Gasse 32 *S/U-Konstablerwache* ☎ (069) 29 36 71
💻 www.frankfurt.aidshilfe.de
Council for hustlers.

SPECIAL INTEREST GROUPS

■ **Our Generation e.V.** (GLM YC)
Mon 14-21, Tue & Thu 14-20, Wed & Fri 14-18h
Kurt-Schumacher-Str. 41 💻 www.kuss41.de
Gay-Lesbian youth-group. New center „KUSS41" open Tue-Fri 17-22h, call for more info!

CRUISING

-Airport toilets (Section C)

-U-Konstablerwache (MA) (B-level, near Entrance U6/U7 direction Heerstraße. 12-21h, AYOR)
-U-Nordwestzentrum (MA) (12-16h)
-U-Bockenheimer Warte
-U-Alte Oper (during the day only)
-Grüneburgpark (near August-Siebert-Straße)
-Friedberger Anlage (Park near Odeon, AYOR).

Freiburg ☎ 0761

GAY INFO

■ **Rosa Hilfe e.V.** (GLM MA) Café Fri 21-1h
Adlerstr. 12 ☎ (0761) 251 61 www.rosahilfefreiburg.de

BARS

■ **Freiburg-Bar und Restaurant** (AC B D glm M)
11-2, Fri & Sat -3, Sun 16-2h
Kaiser-Joseph-Str. 278 *3 mins from Martinstor* ☎ (0761) 70 48 618
www.freiburg-bar.net
Look for more www.freiburg-bar.net. Very nice 70s Lounge.

■ **Gareçons. Les** (B BF glm I M MA MSG OS S) 6.30-1, Sun 8-1h
Bismarckallee 7 *In the main station* ☎ (0761) 292 72 20
www.lesgarecons.de
Sun 15-18h live piano, Wed evening „Leuchtend Rosa", cocktail happy hour 18-20h.

■ **Josfritzcafé** (B BF GLM MA OS)
Mon & Thu 10-2, Tue & Wed 10-24, Fri & Sat 10-3h, Sun closed
Wilhelmstraße 15/1 ☎ (0761) 300 19 www.josfritzcafe.de
Different theme nights.

■ **Sonderbar** (AC B G MA OS) 18-2h
Salzstraße 13 *100 m from Bertolds-Brunnen, direction Schwabentor*
☎ (0761) 339 30 www.sonderbar-freiburg.de

DANCECLUBS

■ **Club Deluxe** (B D G MA)
www.clubdeluxe.info
Irregular parties in the Freiburg area. Check website for further information.

■ **Klub Kamikaze** (B D glm MA)
Oberlinden 8 *Near Schwabentor* www.klubkamikaze.de
Gayfriendly danceclub. Sometimes gayparties. Check www.klubkamikaze.de for program.

■ **Parabel** (D GLM MA S ST) Fri+Sat 22-?h
Universitätsstraße 3 *near Martinstor, pedestrian-mall* www.parabelclub.de
Location for 2 different gay-parties: FriGAY every 2nd Fri/month and Loversclub every last Sat/month.

■ **SchwuLesDance** (! B D GLM WE YC) On Sat, irregularly
Waldseestraße 84 ☎ (0761) 736 88 www.schwulesdance.com
Popular. Check www.schwulesdance.com for exact dates.

SAUNAS/BATHS

■ **RG1** (B cc DR DU g I m MA MSG OS RR SA SOL VS WE WO)
14-23, Fri & Sat -3h
Ziegelhofstraße 230 ☎ (0761) 514 61 93 (mobile)
www.rg1-saunaclub.de
Erotic show every month.

■ **Thermos Club** (B DR DU G M MA RR SA SB VS)
Tue-Fri 16-23, Sat & Sun 14-23h, closed Mon
Lehener Straße 21 *Near central station* ☎ (0761) 27 52 39
www.thermos-club-sauna.de
On two floors on 300 m². Use of the cubicles and sling room on the 1st floor is included in entrance price.

HOTELS

■ **City Hotel Freiburg** (AC BF CC H I MA OS P PA RWB RWS RWT)
Weberstrasse 3 ☎ 0761 38 80 70 www.cityhotelfreiburg.de

■ **Hotel am Rathaus** (BF CC glm H I MA PA PK RWS RWT VA)
Reception 7-24h
Rathausgasse 4-8 *In pedestrian zone* ☎ (0761) 29 61 60

www.am-rathaus.de
Comfortable and elegant rooms, free internet access and CDs/DVDs. Close to interesting bars and restaurants as well as to the tourist sights of the city. Non-smoking hotel.

■ **Parkhotel Adler** (B bf CC glm H I M MA MSG PA PI PK RWS RWT SA SB SOL WH WO) All year
Adlerplatz 3, Hinterzarten *Take the train from Freiburg to Hinterzarten, the hotel is located 5 mins from the station* ☎ (07652) 127 0
www.parkhoteladler.de

HEALTH GROUPS

■ **MSM-Prävention der AIDS-Hilfe Freiburg e.V**
Büggenreuterstraße 12 ☎ (0761) 1514664-0
www.aids-hilfe-freiburg.de

SWIMMING

-Baggersee Niederrimsingen (g NU) (B 31 exit Gündlingen) or Bus-Gündlingen, cruising/action in the wood behind the nude beach)
-Opfinger Baggersee (NU) (in the wood behind the nudist area)
-Nimburger Baggersee (NU) (BAB 5 approach Freiburg Nord. The whole length of south and west side).

CRUISING

-Colombi Park (opposite of Colombi Hotel, at night, popular)
-Bertoldsbrunnen (public toilets).

Friedrichshafen ☎ 07541

DANCECLUBS

■ **Danceclub Fortuna** (B D GLM MA) Sat 22-5h
Anton-Sommer-Straße 7 www.danceclub-fortuna.de
Straight danceclub with regular gay-events. See www.danceclub-fortuna.de for dates.

Füssen ☎ 08362

HOTELS

■ **Hotel Hirsch** (b CC glm H I M MA PA PK RWB RWS RWT VA)
All year, closed in Jan
Kaiser Maximilian Platz 7 *Centre* ☎ (08362) 939 80
www.hotelfuessen.de
Romantic hotel in the vicinity of the famous bavarian castles.

Fulda ☎ 0661

BARS

■ **Coyote Cafe Fulda** (AC B CC g M VS) 10-24, Fri & Sat -1h
Bahnhofstraße 27 *Near main station* ☎ (0661) 833 99 77

CAFES

■ **Café Palais Fulda (Palais Buttlar)** (B glm m YC)
Bonifatiusplatz 1
Nice and stylish café in a former bank.

GENERAL GROUPS

■ **Schwullesbische Organisation Fulda e.V.** (B d GLM MA S)
Wed 20h-open end, 4th Wed 18-20h youthgroup
Künzeller Straße 15 *Entrance in the courtyard* ☎ (0661) 901 4447
www.schwulesbi-fulda.de
GLM Group in Fulda, organizes the „Queer Lounge" on Wednesdays and irregular theme parties on weekends. Also youthgroup meetings every 4th wednesday 18-20h.

Gelsenkirchen ☎ 0209

BARS

■ **My Way** (B GLM MA OS s) Mon-Sat 8-?, Sun 15-?h
Hauptstraße 31 ☎ 155 2557 www.myway-ge.de
Every 1st Fri/month Karaoke 19-1h.

■ **Number One Lounge** (B GLM MA) Wed-Sun 20h-open end
Sellhorststraße 6-10 *10 mins walk from main station*
☎ (0209) 3842 0992 www.numberone-ge.de

SEX SHOPS/BLUE MOVIES

■ **Gaykino „Höhepunkt"** (DR F G MA VS) 10-23, Sun 16-23h
Wanner Straße 133 ☎ (0209) 255 80 www.gay-hot.de
Always the latest films. A good place to „come" together.

■ **LGS** (CC F glm I MA T) Mon-Fri 9-18.30, Sat 9-16h
Bochumer Straße 76 ☎ (0209) 222 14 www.lgs-gelsenkirchen.de
Leather, rubber, sex shop.

■ **Sex Palast** (AC CC DR G GH MA VS) 10-22, Sun 16-22h
Hochstraße 30 *Buer* ☎ (0209) 361 38 15
www.sexpalast-gelsenkirchen.de/gaystart.htm

GENERAL GROUPS

■ **Point. The** (b GLM m YC)
Wed 17-22 Café, Thu 14.30-16.30 Point to Talk, Thu 16.30-21h Café
Wildenbruchstr. 13 *2 mins walk from main station* ☎ (0209) 120 93 68
www.thepoint-gelsenkirchen.de
Youth Centre.

Gera ☎ 0365

DANCECLUBS

■ **Queer Life Party** (B D GLM YC) Monthly on Sat 22-5h
c/o Sevenclub, Bahnhofsplatz 6 *at Hauptbahnhof*
www.queerlifeparty.de
Small, but popular. Located in Sevenclub at Hauptbahnhof..

Gießen ☎ 0641

BARS

■ **Bel Ami** (B GLM MA) Sun-Thu 20-1, Fri -open end, Sat -5h
Liebigstraße 17 *Between new postoffice and railroad Xing Frankfurterstraße*
☎ (0641) 971 7190

■ **Bonaparte** (B d GLM m MA OS SNU ST) Mon-Thu 19-1, Fri-Sun -5h
Liebigstraße 66 *Bus 3, Stop Ebelstraße* ☎ (0641) 756 49
www.club-bonaparte.de
Oldest gaybar, a bit trashy but well-worth a visit.

DANCECLUBS

■ **Musikkeller Haarlem** (B D GLM) Thu 21h-open end
Schanzenstraße 9 *Near brewery ‚Brauhaus Alt'*
www.gay-and-friends.de
Every Thursday gay parties with oldies and hits of today.

Görlitz ☎ 03581

GENERAL GROUPS

■ **Schwubs – die SchwuLesBische Initiative für die Oberlausitz** (B D GLM MA) 2nd & 3rd Sat/month
Postfach 300 533 ☎ (0162) 671 46 34 (mobile) www.schwubs.info
At various locations. Schwubs-Parties, regulars' table in Görlitz, Zittau and Bautzen, Sundays swimming in Ober-C, GayLesbian Swim Fun, GörLs-Lesbian Group, literature salon „Metropolis".

Göttingen ☎ 0551

MEN'S CLUBS

■ **Club Luna** (B d DR G m MA SA SB SNU ST T WH)
1st & 3rd Fri/month 20-?h
Maschmühlenweg 50 ☎ (0551) 503 66 00 www.club-luna.de

DANCECLUBS

■ **Mandance Reloaded @ Musa** (B D GLM MA)
Hagenweg 2a www.mandance-reloaded.de
Check www.mandance-reloaded.de

SEX CINEMAS

Downtown (b DR F G MA VS) 11-22, Fri & Sat -1, Sun 15-21h
Große Breite 10 ☎ (0551) 205 30 60 💻 www.Downtownkino.de
Bar/lounge, DVD rental and sex-cinema with cruising area.

SWIMMING

-Baggersee Rosdorf (take B 27 direction Friedland, after the Reinshof right (no cars), then continue for ca. 1-2 km. On the south side of the Baggersee, only in summer)
-Badeparadies
-Freibad am Brauweg.

Hagen ☎ 02331

SEX SHOPS/BLUE MOVIES

Cinebar (DR g MA VS) 9.30-24, Sun 12-24h
Hindenburgstraße 22 *Near main train station* ☎ (02331) 37 15 51
Cinema and sex shop.

Halle/Saale ☎ 0345

PUBLICATIONS

Homo sum Daily 17-22h
c/o BBZ „lebensart" e. V., Oleariusstraße 9 ☎ (0345) 202 33 85
💻 www.bbz-lebensart.de
Quarterly free gay magazine.

DANCECLUBS

Dance Bar pe1 (AC B D glm m MA S SNU ST WE)
Großer Sandberg 10 *10 mins from train station, buslines 10,2,5 to „Markt"*
☎ (0162) 803 12 71 (mobile) 💻 www.pe1disco-halle.de
See www.pe1disco-halle.de for gay events.

Gayschorre (AC B D GLM M P S VS YC) 2nd Sun/month
Philipp-Müller-Straße 78 *Tram-Rannischer Platz* ☎ (0345) 21 22 40
💻 www.gayschorre.de

CRUISING

-Waisenhausring/Hansering (near Leipziger Turm, -24h, popular)
-FKK-Kanal/nude swimming (obere Aue, B 80 Angersdorf → Wörmlitz, popular)
-Steintor
-Thälmann-Denkmal (park).

Hamburg ☎ 040

Hamburg is the second largest city and the most important seaport of Germany. As a harbour metropolis it was formally as important as Rio de Janeiro, Shanghai and Cape Town, and the liberality of the Hanseatic city is deeply anchored in the city's history.
Hamburg has two equally large gay centres. Saint Pauli is maybe the biggest red light district in Europe. In the midst of female prostitution and sex shops around the infamous Reeperbahn there is also a varied gay scene: ranging from the hotels with rent boy bars, cruising cinemas up to smart bars. Similarly the scene is mixed in Saint Georg: around the Lange Reihe one can find cafés, bars, the leather scene, sex shops, rent boy bars as well as the most attractive gay sauna in Hamburg.

Hamburg ist die zweitgrößte Stadt und wichtigster Seehafen Deutschlands. Als Hafenmetropole wurde es über Generationen in einem Atemzug mit Rio de Janeiro, Shanghai und Kapstadt genannt, und die Liberalität der Hansestadt ist tief in ihrer Geschichte verankert.
Hamburg hat zwei etwa gleich große schwule Zentren. In St. Pauli befindet sich der vielleicht größte Rotlichtbezirk Europas. Im Dickicht von weiblicher Prostitution und Sexshops um die berüchtigte Reeperbahn gibt es auch eine vielfältige schwule Szene: vom Hotel mit Stricherbar über Cruisingkinos bis zur schicken Bar. Ähnlich gemischt ist die Szene in St. Georg: Um die Lange Reihe herum findet man Cafés, Bars, die Lederszene, Sexshops und Stricherbars sowie Hamburgs schönste Gay-Sauna.

Hambourg est la deuxième plus grande ville et le principal port d'Allemagne. A travers les générations, cette métropole portuaire fut comparée à Rio de Janeiro, Shanghai et au Cap, et le libéralisme de la ville hanséatique y est profondément ancré.
Hambourg a deux centres gays de taille presque égale. A St. Pauli se trouve probablement le plus grand quartier chaud d'Europe. Outre la prostitution féminine et les sex-shops au tour de la rue „ Reeperbahn „, on trouve une scène gay diverse, des hôtels avec prostitués, des cinémas pornos, des bars chics. La scène à St. Georg est tout aussi variée : le long de la rue „ Lange Reihe „ se trouvent des cafés, bars, la scène cuir, des sex-shops et bars à tapin et aussi le plus beau sauna gay de Hambourg.

Hamburgo es la segunda ciudad más grande y el principal puerto marítimo de Alemania. Como ciudad portuaria se la ha comparado durante generaciones con ciudades del mismo calibre como Río de Janeiro, Shanghai y Ciudad del Cabo. La generosidad de la ciudad hanseática está profundamente arraigada en su historia.
El ambiente gay en Hamburgo cuenta con dos epicentros de más o menos el mismo tamaño. En St. Pauli se encuentra el que probablemente sea el barrio rojo más grande de Europa y, en la espesura de la prostitución femenina y de los sexshops alrededor de la infame calle Reeperbahn, también un variado ambiente gay. Aquí encontrará desde hoteles con bar de alterne para hombres, cines porno o bares de lo más modernos. Igualmente variado es el ambiente en St. Georg, aquí podrá encontrar todo tipo de cafés, ambiente „leather", sexshops y bares de alterne, así como las mejores saunas gay de Hamburgo.

Amburgo è la seconda città più grande della Germania ma anche città portuale più importante del Paese. Come città portuale, per generazioni Amburgo, è stata messa alla stregua di Rio de Janeiro, Shanghai e Città del Capo. L'apertura della città portuale è saldamente ancorata alla storia della città. Amburgo ha due centri gay. A St. Pauli vi è probabilmente il più gran quartiere a luci rosse d'Europa e nel fitto della prostituzione femminile e dei sexshops, nella famigerata Reperbahn, c'è anche una variopinta scena gay: bordelli, cinema per il cruising e bar molto chic. Altrettanto variopinta è la scena di St. Georg: nella zona attorno alla Lange Reihe ci sono caffè, bar, la scena leather, sexshops, bar con prostituti e la sauna gay più bella della città.

GAY INFO

■ **Hein & Fiete** (G I) Mon-Fri 16-21, Sat -19h
Pulverteich 21 ☎ (040) 24 03 33 🖳 www.heinfiete.de
Information on HIV/AIDS.

■ **Magnus-Hirschfeld-Centrum** (b GLM m MA)
Café: Mon-Thu: 17.30-23, Fri -?, Sat closed, Sun 15-20h
Borgweg 8 ☎ (040) 27 87 78 00 🖳 www.mhc-hamburg.de
LGBT-Centre, meeting-point for various groups, councelling, café with beverages and small snacks, lesbian library.

■ **Querbild e.V.**
Schanzenstr. 45 ☎ (040) 348 06 70
🖳 www.lsf-hamburg.de
Organisers of the Hamburg Lesbian and Gay Film Festival.

PUBLICATIONS

■ **Hinnerk** Mon-Fri 10-18h
Steindamm 11 ☎ (040) 28 41 150 🖳 www.hinnerk.de
Hamburg's leading monthly free gay magazine.

■ **Schwulissimo**
Lübecker Straße 1, Altertower ☎ (040) 25 30 68 80
🖳 www.schwulissimo.de
Monthly appearing free gay magazine.

SHOWS

■ **Pulverfass Cabaret** (AC B g M SNU ST) Sun-Thu 19.30-?, Fri & Sat 19-?h; 1st show 20.30, 2nd 23.30, 3rd (Sat only) 2.30; Teatro Lounge 17-?h
Reeperbahn 147 ☎ (040) 24 78 78 🖳 www.pulverfasscabaret.de
The Birdcage at Reeperbahn, à-la-carte dinner served during the show; with restaurant Teatro Lounge in the foyer of the theatre.

■ **Schmidt Theater & Schmidts Tivoli**
(! AC B CC glm m MA OS S) Tickets 12-19h
Spielbudenplatz 24-28 ☎ (040) 31 77 88 -0 🖳 www.tivoli.de
One of the most famous cabarets in Germany. Some disco events. See local press.

BARS

■ **Angie's Nightclub** (B CC glm S WE) Wed-Sat 22.30-?h
Spielbudenplatz 28 ☎ (040) 31 77 88 11 🖳 www.tivoli.de
Many cocktails, live music.

■ **Bellini** (! B G MA) 18-2, summer: 19-2h
Danziger Straße 63 ☎ (040) 28 00 36 89 🖳 bellini-bar-hamburg.de
Very popular & stylish.

■ **Crazy Horst** (B BF CC g m MA) 21-4, Fri & Sat -6h
Hein-Hoyer-Straße 62 ☎ (040) 319 26 33 🖳 www.crazyhorst.com

Hamburg – St. Pauli

EAT & DRINK
Angies Nightclub – Bar 13
Café Sittsam – Café 1
Crazy Horst – Bar 3
Freudenhaus – Restaurant 5
Olivia Jones – Bar 9
Piccadilly – Bar 14
Prinzenbar – Bar 17
Toom Peerstall – Bar 4
Wunderbar – Bar 6

NIGHTLIFE
136° - The Club – Danceclub 8
Pulverfass Cabaret – Show 11
Sportplatz – Men's Club 2

SEX
Homo-Kino-Hamburg – Sex Shop/Blue Movies 12
Mystery Hall – Sex Shop/Blue Movies 7

OTHERS
Boutique Bizarre – Leather & Fetish Shop 20
Schmidt Theatre & Schmidts Tivoli – Show 16

ACCOMMODATION
East – Hotel 19

erotica
BOUTIQUE
BIZARRE
365 TAGE 10H – 02H
REEPERBAHN 35 20359 HAMBURG ST PAULI
+49-40-3176969-0 WWW.BOUTIQUE-BIZARRE.DE
LACK LEDER LATEX DESSOUS UNDERWEAR DVD LITERATUR EROTICTOYS ACCESSOIRES

■ **Cube** (B G m MA) 19-?h
Lange Reihe 88 ☎ (040) 24 87 07 07 🖳 www.cube-hamburg.de
Small, modern and minimalist cocktail bar, smoking allowed.

■ **Extratour** (B CC GLM m MA OS S T) Sun-Thu 11-4, Fri & Sat -5h
Zimmerpforte 1 ☎ (040) 24 01 84 🖳 www.gaybar-extratour.de
Local pub in a basement.

■ **Generation Bar** (B d G m OS s YC) 17-2, Fri & Sat -4h
Lange Reihe 81 ☎ (040) 28 00 46 90 🖳 www.generation-bar.de
Chic and popular with a very young crowd. Single parties, karaoke, happy hour daily 17-21h.

■ **Glanz & Gloria** (BF glm m MA OS) Wed-Sun 18-?h
Spielbudenplatz 28 ☎ (040) 31 77 88 10
🖳 www.glanz-und-gloria-bar.de

■ **Neue Baustelle @ Ahoi** (B d GLM YC) 2nd Sat/month 21-?h
Hafenstraße, Balduintreppe 🖳 www.schwule-baustelle.org
Alternative gay party.

■ **Olivia Jones Bar** (B GLM MA) Thu-Sat 20-?h
Große Freiheit 35 🖳 www.olivia-jones.de
Bar by Hamburg's most famous drag queen Olivia Jones.

■ **Piccadilly** (B G MA) 20-4h, closed Thu
Silbersacktwiete 1 ☎ (040) 319 24 74

■ **Pick Up** (AYOR B G MA R)
Zimmerpforte 2 ☎ (040) 2801738
Gay rent bar, beware of pickpockets.

■ **Prinzenbar** (B D g MA s)
Kastanienallee 20 ☎ (040) 317 88 35 🖳 www.prinzenbar.net
Kitschy and somehow overblown place, sometimes location for gay parties.

■ **Strada. La** (B G m MA R S ST WE) Mon-Fri 6-5h, WE 24hrs
Rostocker Straße 8 ☎ (040) 41 28 61 52 🖳 www.lastrada-hamburg.de
Large rent bar.

■ **Thomaskeller** (B G m MA r) 16-?h
Rostocker Straße 14 ☎ (040) 235 45 080
Small bar located in the basement. Few rent boys around.

DVDs und noch viel mehr!
In unseren Stores hast Du immer eine Riesenauswahl an Fashion, Büchern und Filmen. Zum Beispiel die besten Erotiklabel.
BelAmi
FALCON STUDIOS.COM
LUCAS ENTERTAINMENT.COM
RAGING STALLION STUDIOS
CAZZO
Bruno's
Alles, was Mann braucht.
BERLIN: Nollendorfplatz/Bülowstr. 106, U Nollendorfplatz BERLIN: Schönhauser Allee 131, Tram Milastr./ U Eberswalder Str. HAMBURG: Lange Reihe/Danziger Str. 70, U Hbf, Metrobus 6 Gurlittstr.
KÖLN: Kettengasse 20, U Rudolfplatz MÜNCHEN: Thalkirchner Str. 4/Fliegenstr. 7, U /Tram Sendlinger Tor

■ **Toom Peerstall** (AC B d GLM MA OS) 20-?h
Clemens-Schultz-Straße 43 ☎ (040) 28 51 72 05 💻 www.toom-peerstall.de

■ **Willi's am Rathaus** (B f G m MA OS) Mon-Sat 12-24, Sun 15-24h
Rathausstraße 12 ☎ (040) 32 67 95 💻 www.willis-hamburg.de
Friendy, local pub.

■ **Wunderbar** (! AC B D G MA WE) Sun-Thu 22-4, Fri & Sat -7h
Talstraße 14 ☎ (040) 317 44 44 💻 www.wunderbar-hamburg.de
Trendy and popular. Disco at WE.

■ **Zzzischer** (B glm m MA) 20-2h
Sillemstraße 53 ☎ (040) 55 77 51 95 💻 www.zzzischer.de

MEN'S CLUBS

■ **Cage, The** (AK B DR F G SL) Tue, Wed & Sun 22-, Thu 21-2, Fri-Sat 21-?h
Lincolnstr. 6 *opening Summer 2012, near Reeperbahn*
☎ (040) 520 15 737 💻 www.gaygetter.com/g4/venues/thecage
No dresscode, all fetish welcome.Rubber, leather, sports...

■ **Contact** (B DR F G MA p) Mon-Thu 20-2, Fri & Sat 20-open end, Sun 18-2h
Danziger Straße 51 ☎ (040) 55 50 26 97 💻 www.contact-bar.de
New fetish bar, in formerly „Strictly Men" location. Daily specials.

■ **FickstutenMarkt Hamburg @ S.L.U.T. Club** (DR P)
Rostocker Strasse 20 💻 www.fickstutenmarkt.com
Please check the rules and FAQ's at website.

■ **Slut Club Hamburg** (B D DR DU F G GH LAB MA P SH SL VR VS)
Wed & Thu 20-?, Fri & Sat 22-?, Sun 18-?h
Rostocker Straße 20 💻 www.slutclub.de
Cruising area on 2 floors. Dress-code applies on all SLUT Events and parties.

■ **Sportplatz** (B CC d DR f G MA VS) 20-?h
Talstraße 10-12 *S/U-Reeperbahn* ☎ 85 85 81
💻 www.hamburg-sportplatz.de
Cruising bar with darkroom, cabins, sling. Check website for special events. No dresscode!

■ **Tom's Saloon** (! B CC DR F G MA VS) 22-5, Fri & Sat -?h
Pulverteich 17 ☎ (040) 280 30 56 💻 www.toms-hamburg.de
Very popular, not only at the weekend.

CAFES

■ **Café SittsaM** (B F glm M MA) 18-?h
Wexstraße 42 ☎ (040) 31 79 26 09 💻 www.cafe-sittsam.com
SM Café. Check www.cafe-sittsam.com for parties and events.

■ **Dementy** (b D glm MA)
Mon-Thu 17-23, Fri -?, Sat 20-1, Sun 15-22h
Borgweg 8 *U-Borgweg* ☎ (040) 27 87 78 01
Café in Magnus Hirschfeld Centrum (gay communications and advisory centre).

■ **Gnosa** (! BF DM GLM M MA OS PA VEG)
Sun-Thu 10-24, Fri & Sat -1, kitchen open until 23.30h
Lange Reihe 93 ☎ (040) 24 30 34 💻 www.gnosa.de
Very popular, especially because of the great cakes. An institution in Hamburg.

■ **Kyti Voo** (B bf d GLM m MA OS) 9-24, Sat & Sun 10-24h
Lange Reihe 82 ☎ (040) 28 055 565 💻 www.Kytivoo.de
In the heart of gay szene, with big outdoor terrace. Cocktail lounge.

■ **Spund** (B BF G M MA) 10-24, Sun 15-24h
Mohlenhofstr. 3 ☎ (040) 32 65 77
Still running strong since 3rd of September 1974.

■ **Uhrlaub** (B BF CC glm M MA OS) 8-2h
Lange Reihe 63 ☎ (040) 280 26 24 💻 www.cafeuhrlaub.de

DANCECLUBS

■ **136° – The Club** (AC B CC D G YC) Sat 23-?h
Reeperbahn 136 *entrance next to „Ritze"* 💻 www.136grad.com
Hamburg's gay club in the heart of the famous red light district St. Pauli. International DJs, mainly playing house and electro-style.

■ **Camp 77 @ Neidclub**
Reeperbahn 25 💻 www.camp77.com

■ **Daniel's Company** (B D GLM)
Kreuzweg 6 ☎ (040) 249 610 💻 club.daniels-company.de

■ **Gay Factory @ Fabrik** (! B D GLM MA s)
Barnerstraße 36 ☎ (040) 39 10 70 💻 www.gayfactory.de
Check www.gayfactory.de for exact dates.

■ **Kir** (B D glm MA) Mon 22-?; Wed, Fri, Sat 23-?h
Barnerstr. 16 ☎ (040) 438 041 💻 www.kir-hamburg.de
Wave and gothic club for the alternative crowd. G mainly on Wed (Love pop) & 3rd Fri/month.

■ **Lovepop @ Kir Club** (B D GLM YC)
Wed 23-open end, 2nd Fri 23h-open end
Barnerstrasse 16 💻 www.lovepop.info
Special Gay-Dance event. See www.lovepop.info for details.

RESTAURANTS

■ **Dorf. Das** (CC GLM M MA NR OS VEG WL) 18-24, Sun 17-24h
Lange Reihe 39 *S/U-Hauptbahnhof* ☎ (040) 24 56 14
💻 www.restaurant-dorf.de
Cozy restaurant with antique furniture. German cuisine served.

■ **Freudenhaus** (B cc glm M MA S VEG WL)
Open from 18, kitchen open until 24h
Hein-Hoyer-Straße 7-9 ☎ (040) 31 46 42
💻 www.stpauli-freudenhaus.de
Good German cuisine, big portions.

■ **Sonntag's** (AC B glm M MA OS) 11-24, kitchen 11-14.30 & 18-23h
Schmilinskystraße 19 ☎ (040) 24 60 83
Bistro-Restaurant with German and international cuisine.

SEX SHOPS/BLUE MOVIES

Erotikheaven (AC CC DR F G MA T VS) 8-1h
Steindamm 14 ☎ (040) 280 563 92 www.mensheaven.de
Sex shop and cruising.

Homo-Kino-Hamburg (AC CC DR f G MA VS) 24hrs
Talstrasse 8 ☎ (040) 31 24 95

Mystery Hall (AC CC DR F G MA VS) 24hrs
Talstraße 3-5 ☎ (040) 31 79 05 70 www.mysteryhall.de
Gay sex cinema and sex shop.

New Man Plaza (CC DR G MA VS) 9.30-0.30, Sun 11-0.30h
Steindamm 2 ☎ (040) 24 54 16
Slings & cubicles. Very modern.

SAUNAS/BATHS

Apollo (B DR DU FC G m MA MSG PP RR SA SB SOL VS WO) 12-22h
Max-Brauer-Allee 277 *U/S-Sternschanze* ☎ (040) 43 48 11
www.apollosauna.de
Sauna on two floors.

Centro Delfino @ Men's Heaven Spa
(AK B DR DU FC FH G GH I LAB M MA MSG RR SA SB SL SOL VS) 13-1h
Steindamm 14 *Near main station* ☎ (040) 280 563 94 www.mensheaven.de
The newest sauna in Hamburg.

Dragon (! AC B CC DR DU FC G GH I LAB M MA MSG OS RR SA SB SH SL VEG VR VS WH) 13-24, Fri 13-Sun 24h (non-stop)
Pulverteich 37 *U/S-Hauptbahnhof, 2 mins from main station*
☎ (040) 24 05 14 www.dragonsauna.com
Busy bathhouse on two floors with a nice design. Very popular with men of all ages. Friendly and helpful crew completes the relaxed ambiance in Asian style on 1600 m². Women on Thu, too.

BOOK SHOPS

Bruno's (! CC G MA) Mon-Sat 10-21h
Danziger Straße 70 ☎ (040) 98 23 80 81 www.brunos.de
Bruno's gay store in Hamburg with a huge selection of books, DVDs (also rental), toys, magazines, undwerwear and pride articles.

Männerschwarm (CC GLM MA S W) 11-20, Sat 10 -18h, closed Sun
Lange Reihe 102 ☎ (040) 43 60 93 www.maennerschwarm.de
Excellent gay/lesbian bookshop (since 1981). Also a wide range of gay and lesbian DVDs, comics and magazines.

FASHION SHOPS

SCUBS (G) Mon-Sat 11-20h
Lange Reihe 30-32 *Near Central Station* ☎ (040) 46 00 78 58 www.scubs.de
Wide range of underwear and streetwear! Brands: Aussiebum, XTG, Bikkembergs, Diesel, Fred Perry, ES Collection, Armani

LEATHER & FETISH SHOPS

Boutique Bizarre (AC CC F GLM S T) 10-2h
Reeperbahn 35 ☎ (040) 31 76 96 90 www.boutique-bizarre.de
With 1400 m² one of the largest leather & fetish shops in Europe. Erotic art-exhibitions in the basement.

Mr. Chaps (CC F G H MA) Mon-Fri 11-19, Sat 11-18h
Greifswalder Straße 23 ☎ (040) 24 59 79 www.mr-chaps.de
Tailor made fashion in leather and latex. Sales of toys, rubber, leather, boots, gloves, uniforms, DVDs and second-hand stuff. Offer also a apartment for rent.

HOTELS

■ **East Hotel** (AC B BF CC d glm I M MA MSG PA PK RWS RWT SA SB SOL WO) All year, 24hrs
Simon-von-Utrecht-Straße 31 *U3-St.Pauli or S1-Reeperbahn*
☎ (040) 30 99 30 🖳 www.east-hamburg.de
Stylish new hotel close to the gay area in St.Pauli.

■ **Galerie-Hotel Sarah Petersen**
(B BF glm I M MA OS RWB RWS RWT VA) 8-23h
Lange Reihe 50 ☎ (040) 24 98 26 🖳 www.ghsp.eu

■ **Hotel Adria** (bf glm I MA PA RWS RWT VA) 24hrs
Ellmenreichstraße 24 *St. Georg, near central railway station*
☎ (040) 24 62 80 🖳 www.gaytel.de

■ **Hotel Baseler Hof**
(B BF CC glm H I M MA MSG RWS RWT SA SB SOL WO) 24hrs
Esplanade 11 *U1/B112/B5-Stephansplatz, U3-Rathaus, S1/S21/DB Dammtor, near Dammtor station* ☎ (040) 359 060 🖳 www.baselerhof.de
Central location near city hall, shoppings malls, Alster, State Opera House, Reeperbahn and St. Georg, with restaurant and wine bar Kleinhuis.

■ **Kieler Hof** (H I RWS RWT) All year
Bremer Reihe 15 *Near main railway station* ☎ (040) 24 30 24
🖳 www.kieler-hof.de
Gay-friendly hotel with reasonable prices in the heart of St. Georg, the gay district.

■ **Village** (B BF CC GLM MA PA RWS RWT VA) All year
Steindamm 4 *at main station in the gay area* ☎ (040) 480 64 90
🖳 www.hotel-village.de
Twenty rooms and 4 apartments. Most rooms with shower/WC, balcony, phone, fax, sat-TV, radio, heating and own key. Pets allowed.

GUEST HOUSES

■ **Gay Resort Altes Land** (b bf G M MA OS PK RWT VS) All year
Am Elbdeich 25, Jork-Borstel *Approx. 7 km southwest of Hamburg at the river Elbe, Bus 150 to Cranz-Elbdeich, train stop Neukloster*
☎ (04162) 90 87 60

Four individually furnished rooms in a beautiful, quietly situated house very close to the Elbe river.

SWIMMING

-Eichbaumsee (g NU) (Moorfleeter Deich at Allermöhle)
-Boberger See (g NU) (Bergedorfer Straße at Billstedt, very popular in summer)
-Alsterschwimmhalle (Mondays), Ifflandstraße 21, U-Lohmühlenstraße (PI).
-Kellinghusenbad (NG OS PI SA SB SOL) Goernestraße 21, U-Kellinghusenstraße.

CRUISING

-Volkspark (Around the Dahliengarten)
-University (Philosophenturm, basement, popular)
-Stadtpark, Blindengarten, Südring corner Hindenburgstraße (ayor MA) (U-Borgweg) Very popular at all hours, at night
-Planten und Blomen (Dammtordamm/Gorch-Fock-Wall. Up to Gustav-Mahler-Park (BAT House), evenings)
-Jakobi-Park (Wandsbeker Chaussee, Hamburg-Eilbeck, U-Ritterstraße)
-Rosengarten (Elbchaussee corner Hohenzollernring).

Hamm ☎ 02381

BARS

■ **Monsche** (B GLM MA) 20-1, Fri & Sat -?h, closed Sun & Mon
Werler Straße 95 ☎ (02381) 33 84 307 🖳 www.monsche-hamm.de

SEX SHOPS/BLUE MOVIES

■ **Pegasus** (g MA) 12-19, 1st Sat/month 10-14h, closed Sun
Werler Straße 95 *Near hospital* ☎ (02381) 54 02 40
🖳 www.pegasus-erotik.de
Also mail order.

CRUISING

-Ostenallee/Exerzierplatz
-Werler Straße/Alleestraße
-Chattanmoga-Platz (across Stadtsparkasse)
-🅿 at Wasser- und Schiffahrtsamt.

Hannover ☎ 0511

BARS

■ **Bouche. La** (AC B D G M MA OS S) Fri & Sat 20-?h
Weißkreuzestraße 20 *Same location as Le Fiacre* ☎ (0511) 342 337
🖳 www.lefiacre.de

■ **Burgklause** (AC B G m MC) 18-?, Sat 13-?h
Burgstraße 11 ☎ (0511) 32 11 86
A cosy and plush meeting place.

■ **Destille** (B glm M MA OS) 10-3, Fri & Sat -4h
Im Moore 3 ☎ (0511) 701 03 43 🖳 www.destille-hannover.de
Pub and sports bar. 3 TVs and Large Screen.

■ **Fiacre. Le** (AC B CC DR G H M MA OS R s VS) 14-?h
Weißekreuzstraße 20 *Near central station* ☎ (0511) 34 23 37
🖳 www.lefiacre.de
Long running rent bar. Also accommodation and restaurant.

■ **Martinos** (B G MA OS S SNU ST T)
Sun-Thu 17-3, Fri & Sat -5h
Gretchenstraße 16 *S3/7-Sedanstraße/Lister Meile* ☎ (0511) 388 33 01
🖳 www.martinos-hannover.de
Smoking pub.

■ **Odeon Café** (B d GLM M MA) Tue-Thu 22-5, Fri & Sat 19.30-?h
Odeonstraße 5 *Near main train station* ☎ (0511) 374 39 00
Warm food till morning available.

CAFES

■ **Fire Bar** (B glm M MA) 16-1, Sat & Sun 9-1h
Knochenhauer Straße 30 *Altstadt* ☎ (0511) 215 75 57
🖳 www.fire-bar.de
Café-bar-lounge with an extensive buffet.

■ **Konrad** (BF GLM m MA OS) Sun-Thu 10-24, Fri & Sat -1h
Knochenhauer Straße 34 *S-Markthalle/Kröpcke/Steintor*
☎ (0511) 32 36 66 💻 www.cafekonrad.de
■ **Lulu** (AC B glm M MA) 9-1, Fri & Sat -2h
In der Steinriede 12 *Wedekindplatz* ☎ (0511) 66 77 98
■ **Mezzo** (B BF glm m MA OS) 9-2, Fri & Sat -3, Sun & Mon -24h
Lister Meile 4 *RaschplatzñPavillon* ☎ (0511) 314 966
💻 www.cafe-mezzo.de

DANCECLUBS

■ **Fever** (AC B CC D GLM YC) Wed, Fri & Sat 22-?h
Mehlstraße 1c *200 m from main station* 💻 www.fever-club.de
Modern little club in the heart of Hannover. Entrance free of charge.
■ **Hannover Gay Night** (B D GLM YC)
c/o Agostea, Rundestraße 6 💻 www.hannover-gay-night.de
See website www.hannover-gay-night.de for details.
■ **Luder Park @ Pavillon am Raschplatz** (B D GLM MA)
Lister Meile 4 💻 www.luder-park.de
See www.luder-park.de for details.
■ **Schwule Sau** (B D GLM s YC) Fri & Sat 21-?h
Schaufelder Straße 30a ☎ (0511) 700 05 25
💻 www.schwulesauhannover.de
Non-profit club with the popular and packed Sau Party (!) on 2nd Fri/month. Call for information on parties and activities.
■ **Slide Club** (B D GLM MA)
Scholvinstr. 12 💻 www.slide-club.de
Check www.slide-club.de for dates.

SEX SHOPS/BLUE MOVIES

■ **Beate Uhse** (AC b CC DR g MA VS W) Mon-Sat 9-21h
Kleine Packhofstraße 16 ☎ 3538516 💻 www.beate-uhse-filialen.com
400 m² cruising area. Dark-town cinema.
■ **Irrgarten** (AC B D f G m MA VS) 10-4, Fri 10-Mon 4h (non-stop)
Reitwallstraße 4 *U-Steintor* ☎ (0511) 76 35 255
💻 hannover-irrgarten.de
Buffet on weekends, S/M room, showers, aquarium, doctor room, 2 cinemas, 13 cabins. For special events check hannover-irrgarten.de
■ **Joe's Dark and Play Rooms** (AC B DR f G I MA S VS) 11-1, Fri & Sat -6h
Odeonstraße 6 *Near central railway station* ☎ (0511) 169 06 64
Very large and modern sex shop: showers, bar, sex-parties.

SEX CINEMAS

■ **No Limit** (AC B DR f G MA MSG p r SNU t VS WE) Mon-Thu 10-4, Fri 10-Mon 4h (non-stop)
Reuterstraße 2 *U-Steintor* ☎ (0511) 898 28 30
Special gay parties and male strip contests.

HOUSE OF BOYS

■ **Royal House of Boys** (G)
Podbielskistr. 18

SAUNAS/BATHS

■ **Vulkan** (AK B DR G LAB M MA MSG OS p PP RR SA SB SL VS WH) 14-23, Fri 13-Sun 23h (non-stop)
Otto-Brenner-Straße 15 *Tram-Steintor, near Klagesmarkt, entrance Hausmannstraße* ☎ (0511) 151 66 💻 www.vulkansauna.de
A sauna with a long tradition on 3 floors. Also accommodation.

CRUISING

-Zauberwald, Eilenrieder Stadtwald at the zoo (at night)
-🅿 at Pänner-Schuster-Weg (at night).

Heidelberg ☎ 06221

BARS

■ **Rickys Beach** (B GLM) 16-?h
Vangerowstr. 24 ☎ (06221) 652 90 21

DANCECLUBS

■ **UnheilBar** (B D GLM MA)
c/o Karlstorbahnhof, Am Karlstor 1 💻 www.unheilbar.org
Gay parties. See www.unheilbar.org for dates.

HEALTH GROUPS

■ **Aids Hilfe Heidelberg e.V.** (glm MA) Mon & Fri 11-13, Wed 16-18
Rohrbacher Str. 22 ☎ (06221) 16 17 00 💻 www.aidshilfe-heidelberg.de
Regenbogencafé every Tuesday 16-19h.

Heilbronn ☎ 07131

BARS

■ **Bleriot** (B glm MA) Tue-Thu 21-2, Fri & Sat -3, Sun 16-1h
Stuttgarter Str. 11 ☎ (07131) 644 6633
Mixed Bar with gay events.
■ **Club Cousteau** (AC B D GLM MA S WE) 21-3, Fri & Sat -4h
Karlstraße 25 ☎ (07131) 62 71 54 💻 www.club-cousteau.de
■ **Libre Café Bar** (B d glm YC) Sun-Thu 18-1, Fri & Sat -3h
Frankfurter Straße 26 *Near the main train station* ☎ (07131) 9190 562
💻 www.libre-heilbronn.de

RESTAURANTS

■ **In's Kistle** (b glm M MA) 11.30-23h
Wilhelmstr. 13 ☎ (07131) 898 7420 💻 www.kistle.select24.de
Nice gayfriendly restaurant with local cuisine.

HOTELS

■ **RM Plaza Heilbronn** (AC B BF CC H M MA MSG OS) All year
Moltkestraße 52 *City centre, near theatre* ☎ (07131) 98 90
💻 www.rm-plaza-heilbronn.de

Hof ☎ 09281

BARS

■ **Schnürsenkel** (B d GLM m MC OS WE) 18h-open end, closed Mon
Fabrikzeile 1 *Near Hofbad* ☎ (09281) 446 13

SEX SHOPS/BLUE MOVIES

■ **Sex-Shop** (glm MA)
Klosterstr. 30 ☎ (09281) 2931
Videos, DVDs, toys – no cinema!

Hückelhoven ☎ 02433

HOTELS

■ **Hotel Friends Niederrhein** (b BF CC H I MA) All year, 24hrs
Berresheimring 1 ☎ (02433) 83 70 💻 www.hotel-friends.de
Located near Düsseldorf. 24h bar, lounge, W-LAN & parking for free and more.

Husum ☎ 04841

SEX CINEMAS

■ **Kino 29** (DR G VS) 12-24h, Sun closed
Maas 29 *Opp. slaughterhouse* ☎ (04841) 66 91 99
Cruising area with glory holes, shop with videos, DVDs and toys.

Ingolstadt ☎ 0841

SPECIAL INTEREST GROUPS

■ **Romeo & Julius** (GLM YC) Wed 20-22h
c/o Bürgerhaus Alte Post, Kreuzstraße 12 ☎ (0841) 1 37 32 62
💻 www.romeo-julius.de

CRUISING

-Hindenburgpark (very busy after sunset)
-Near Nordbahnhof
-Franziskanerstraße (OC) (behind Neues Rathaus -19h).

Iserlohn ☏ 02371

BARS

■ **Why Not** (AC B D GLM m MA S t) 18-3, Fri & Sat -5h
Viktoriastraße 1 *City centre, behind Kaufland* ☏ (02371) 120 02

Jena ☏ 03641

BARS

■ **Central** (B glm MA) 19-?h
Markt 23 ☏ (03641) 44 10 44

Kaiserslautern ☏ 0631

DANCECLUBS

■ **Umgekramt** (B D GLM YC)
3rd Fri of every other month (Jan, Mar, etc.) 22-?h
c/o Universität Kaiserslautern, Kramladen, Gebäude 46
www.umgekramt.de
Cheap and popular with students.

SEX SHOPS/BLUE MOVIES

■ **Peepshow & Sexshop Erotic Heaven** (glm m MA VS)
Wagnerstraße 12 ☏ (0631) 340 7225?
Straight peepshow, but also gay-section.

CRUISING

-P Frachtstraße (near station).

Karlsruhe ☏ 0721

BARS

■ **Club Tropica** (B D G m MA r SNU) Sun-Thu 20-5, Fri & Sat 21-5h
Bunsenstraße 9 *Tram Hübschstraße* ☏ (0177) 477 2651
Strip show once a month.

■ **Prinz S** (B GLM MA) 17-1, Fri & Sat -3h
Zähringerstraße 15 *Old town* ☏ (0721) 91 54 599
www.prinz-s.de

MEN'S CLUBS

■ **Culteum** (B D DR F GLM MA)
Essenweinstr. 9 *Citycenter/Oststadt* ☏ (0721) 966 3860 culteum.de
Gay and lesbian Party. Special gay-fetishparties. Check www.rubclub.de

CAFES

■ **Café & Bistro XXX** (B GLM OS YC) 2nd Sun 18-24h
Zähringerstraße 10 *Studierendenzentrum Z10*
Alternative event for gay/lesbian students, reasonable prices.

DANCECLUBS

■ **Liebstöckel** (B D glm YC)
Wed 21-open end, Fri & Sat 21h-open end
Kaiserstraße 21 liebstoeckel-ka.de
Gayfriendly Techno & Houseclub.

■ **Mystery** (B D GLM MA)
Pfannkuchstraße 16 @ *Nachtwerk Musikclub in Daxlanden-Mühlburg*
www.mystery-party.de
Gay parties. Check www.mystery-party.de

■ **Pink Clubbing** (B D GLM MA) Wed 22-?h
c/o Club Stadtmitte, Baumeisterstraße 3 ☏ (0721) 354 63 81
www.die-stadtmitte.de
House, Elektro, RnB.

■ **Queerdance @ Gotec** (B D GLM MA)
Gablonzerstraße 11, Mühlburg *Tram N€euter Straße*
www.schrill-im-april.de
See www.schrill-im-april.de for details.

■ **Rosapark** (B D GLM MA)
Erzbergstaraße 113 @ *Nachtflieger, near Westbahnhof* www.rosapark.de
Check www.rosapark.de for details.

RESTAURANTS

■ **Café Creativ Cuisine** (DM glm MA) Mon-Fri 9.30-18.30h
Klauprechtstraße 41 ☏ (0721) 66 55 364 www.cafecreativ-cuisine.de

SEX SHOPS/BLUE MOVIES

■ **Bluemovie** (AC DR G MA VS)
11-22.30, Sun & public holidays 14-22.30h
Kaiserstraße 33-37 *Opp. University* ☏ (0721) 937 58 58
www.bluemovie.de
4 rooms with gay films, darkroom, St. Andrew's cross and even a confessional for naughty boys.

■ **Revolt Shop Joe & Chris** (DR G MA VS) Mon-Sat 10-24h
Sedanstaße 8 ☏ (0721) 151 66 28
3 cinemas, current DVDs for rent and on sale, magazines, toys etc.

SAUNAS/BATHS

■ **Saunaland Aquarium** (! B CC DR DU FC G I LAB m MA MSG OS RR SA SB SOL VS WH) 15-24, Sat & Sun 14-24h
Bachstraße 46 *Tram 2/5-Philippstraße, entrance in the backyard*
☏ (0721) 955 35 33 www.aquarium-sauna.de
Large sauna with more than 600 m², beautifully designed with cabines and cruising area. Very popular.

SWIMMING

-Epple-See (g MA NU) (7 km from the city near Rheinstetten-Forchheim)
-Baggersee Leopoldshafen (near Eggenstein-Leopoldshafen).

CRUISING

-Nymphengarten (AYOR) (near Landesmuseum, Kriegsstraße, at night)
-Rheinhafen (action in the small park on the other side of P.

Kassel ☏ 0561

BARS

■ **b2 barlounge** (B gLm MA S) Mon-Sun 19-open end
Germaniastraße 13 ☏ (0561) 766 3737 www.b2-bar.de
Lesbian gayfriendly bar.

■ **Bel Ami** (B G M MA OS S) Sun-Thu 18-1, Fri & Sat 18-3h, Tue closed
Kölnische Straße 93 ☏ (0561) 288 80 90 www.belami-kassel.de
1st Sat/month sepcial events.

■ **Frisch & Frech** (B GLM MA) Mon-Sat 10-22h
Kirchweg 47 *Cnr. Wilhelmshöher Allee* ☏ (0561) 970 15 60
Cafe/bar/lounge in the city. After 18h smoking permitted!

■ **Queerbeet** (B f GLM MA OS) Mon-Thu 18-1, Fri & Sat 18-3, Sun -1h
Wilhelmshöher Allee 116 *Tram-Kirchweg* ☏ (0561) 766 89 79
www.queerbeet-kassel.de

■ **Suspekt Café-Bar** (B GLM MA MSG)
Tue-Thu, Sun 13-1, Fri & Sat -2h
Fünffensterstraße 14 *Near city hall* ☏ (0561) 10 45 22
www.cafe-suspekt.de

DANCECLUBS

■ **Sinnlust** (B D GLM MA) Sat, irregular dates
Bahnhofsplatz 1 @ *Gleis 1* ☏ (0561) 766 42 40 www.gleis1.eu
Popular gay party on irregular dates (every 6 weeks)

SEX SHOPS/BLUE MOVIES

■ **Pleasure Shop II** (AC CC DR GLM MA T VS)
9-23, Sun & public holidays 14-23h
Hedwigstraße 5 *Near Königsplatz* ☏ (0561) 70 36 801

SAUNAS/BATHS

■ **Sauna im Pferdestall**
(AK B DR G H I m MA MSG PA PK RR RWT SA SB SOL VA VS WO)
15.30-23, Fri & Sat -24, Sun & public holidays 14-22h
Erzberger Straße 23-25 *Near main railway station, city centre*
☏ (0561) 168 01 www.gay-in-kassel.de
Also accommodation. Free parking space available. Cruising on 400 m² on 2 floors.

CRUISING

-Kulturbahnhof (R)
-University (Cafeteria (mensa), at „Menü 2")
-Weinberg (Henschelgarten)
-P Messehallen (AYOR)
-P Konrad-Adenauer-Straße (last P before highway exit).

Kehl ☎ 07851

BARS

■ **Glouglou** (B CC G H MA OS p S VS) 18h-open end
Marktstraße 6 *Bus 21 from Strasbourg* ☎ (07851) 95 55 13
www.glougloubar.de

■ **Rick's Club** (B d glm MA)
Graudenzerstr. 6 ☎ (07851) 48 12 12 www.rickskehl.de
Mixed Bar with irregular gay events. Franco-arabic ambience. Bar open daily, club only Fri & Sat from 22h.

SAUNAS/BATHS

■ **Atrium Sauna** (AC B cc DU FC FH G M MA OS RR SA SB SOL VS)
14-23, Fri -2, Sat -3, Sun -22h
Schulstraße 68 *Bus CTS 21; 5 mins from Strasbourg, near the church*
☎ (07851) 48 27 05 www.sauna-atrium.net
Mixed on Tue & Wed

Kempten ☎ 0831

DANCECLUBS

■ **Village Club** (B D GLM MA) last Sat 21h-open end
Bleicherstrasse 35 @ *14Club* ☎ (0160) 90 333 995
www.villageclub-kempten.de
Rainbowparty @ 14Club www.villageclub-kempten.de

Kiel ☎ 0431

BARS

■ **Birdcage** (B GLM m MA OS) 20-2, Fri & Sat -4h
Rathausstraße 10 *Near Rathaus & Opernhaus* ☎ (0431) 696 73 73
www.birdcage-kiel.de

■ **Hanging Garden. The** (B glm m MA) 19-?h
Waitzstraße 91 *Near University* ☎ (0431) 56 58 33
www.hanging-garden.de

■ **Harlekin** (B d GLM MA) 20-4h
Kirchhofallee 38 ☎ (0431) 636 48 www.harlekinbar.de

DANCECLUBS

■ **Gaylirium Event @ X-Club** (B D GLM MA) 2nd Fri/month 22-?h
Legienstraße 40 www.gaylirium-event.de

■ **Tiffy Club @ Nachtcafé** (B D GLM MA) 3rd Sat/month 22-?h
Eggerstedtstraße 14 www.tiffy-club.de

SEX SHOPS/BLUE MOVIES

■ **WOS-Markt** (CC DR G MA) 10-24, Sun 12-24h
Schuhmacherstraße 31

CRUISING

-Schrevenpark (popular)
- P Rumohr on A215, both directions.

Koblenz ☎ 0261

BARS

■ **Shake Hands** (B glm m YC)
Firmungstraße 35
Every Friday meeting of the SJK (gay youthgroup) Koblenz. On other days mixed crowd.

■ **Vogue Lounge & Club** (B D GLM MA OS S ST)
17-?h, club: Fri & Sat 22-?h
An der Liebfrauenkirche 12 ☎ (0261) 30 97 64 www.vogue-koblenz.de

MEN'S CLUBS

■ **Achterspannerhof** (B BF DR F G H I MA MSG NU OS P SA VS)
Wed 18-1, Fri 19-2, Sat -3h
Achterspannerhof 1 *Kobern-Gondorf* ☎ (02625) 95 76 01
www.der-achterspannerhof.de
Private atmosphere on a farm. Overnight stays or even holidays are possible.

SEX SHOPS/BLUE MOVIES

■ **Gay in the City** (AC b DR f G MC T VS)
Mon-Thu 10-24, Fri & Sat -1, Sun 13-22h
Wallersheimer Weg 12-14 *In Lützel, close to the Rheinkaserne*
☎ (0261) 9888 5861
Gay shop, video, movies, cruising, bar and darkroom.

HOTELS

■ **Hotel Friends Mittelrhein** (b BF CC H I m MA PI) All year, 24hrs
Im Wenigerbachtal 8-25 *8 km from Koblenz main station*
☎ (02622) 88 40 www.hotel-friends-koblenz.de
Located near Koblenz and surrounded by beautiful nature. 2 Restaurants, 24h bar, lounge, W-LAN & parking for free & more.

■ **Hotel Merkelbach**
(B BF CC GLM H I M OS PA PK RWB RWS RWT VA) All year
Emser Str. 87 *Quarter Pfaffendorf* ☎ (0261) 97 44 10
www.hotel-merkelbach.de
This gay owned house is a well-tended 3-star hotel, directly situated at the river Rhine with cosy restaurant and an excellent german cuisine. The hotel offers one apartment and 14 cosy guestrooms, partially with large balcony overlooking the Rhine. All rooms are equipped with shower, WC, hairdryer, direct-dial telephone and cable-TV. Wireless internet access (WiFi) is available in the whole hotel.

Köln ☎ 0221

Cologne Gay Pride on July 8th, 2012, will probably be one of the largest gay pride celebrations in Germany, but it's not necessarily the high point of the city's party calendar. This is because Cologne – including gay Cologne – celebrates its famous carnival in February, when virtually the whole city joins in the fun – approximately 1 million inhabitants. Local gay life centres on two, almost neighbouring districts. The stretch of old town between „Heumarkt" and „Alter Markt" features bars for a more mature crowd and the leather and fetish scene, whereas the area around Rudolfplatz caters to a younger, trendier clientele. Cologne can get very crowded at weekends, but during the week some bars are empty sometimes almost.
Cologne's not very numerous but impressive tourist attractions include the cathedral, a splendidly atmospheric Gothic building, and a number of Romanesque churches of great art historical interest. Culture oriented visitors will also greatly enjoy the rich offer of museums (including the fantastic Museum Ludwig) and private galleries the city's international reputation as an important art location lives on.

Am 8. Juli 2012 findet in Köln der CSD statt. Doch auch wenn der Kölner einer der größten CSDs ist, ist er nicht unbedingt der Höhepunkt der Feiersaison. Denn Köln – auch das schwule Köln – hat im Februar den Karneval, und durch ihn zeigen die Kölner, dass sie feiern können. Dabei ist die Stadt am Rhein mit etwa einer Million Einwohner von überschaubarer Größe. Das schwule Leben konzentriert sich in zwei nicht weit voneinander entfernten Zentren. Das eine befindet sich in der Altstadt zwischen dem „Heumarkt" und dem „Alter Markt" und bietet Lokale für ältere Herren und die Leder- & Fetischszene. Um den Rudolfplatz befindet sich die jüngere, schickere Szene. Köln ist am Wochenende überfüllt, an den Wochentagen sind die Lokale jedoch häufig recht leer.
Köln hat ein paar herausragende Sehenswürdigkeiten: Der Kölner Dom ist ein Bauwerk der Hochgotik mit ungeheurer Wirkung, und viele romanische Kirchen sind von großer kunsthistorischer Bedeutung. Kunstinteressierte werden reichlich zu tun haben durch die Fülle an Museen (etwa das phantastische Museum Ludwig) und privaten Galerien, die Köln zu einem weltweit bedeutenden Kunstzentrum machen.

La Gay Pride aura lieu le 8 juillet 2012 mais, bien qu'elle soit une des plus grandes du monde, elle n'est néanmoins pas forcément l'apothéose de la saison festive qui commence dès février avec le carnaval. Cette ville d'environ un million d'habitants est compacte. Le milieu gay se concentre autour de deux centres peu éloignés l'un de l'autre. L'un se situe dans la vieille-ville entre le Marché au foin et le Vieux marché et offre des bars pour le public d'un certain âge et pour les adeptes du cuir et des fétiches. Autour de la Rudolfplatz, on trouve un milieu jeune et chic. Cologne est pleine à craquer le week-end mais le reste de la semaine, les bars sont presque vides. Elle a certes peu de curiosités, mais elles en sont d'autant plus spectaculaires : La cathédrale, une construction gothique des plus impressionnantes, ainsi que ses nombreuses églises romanes sont des chefs-d'œuvre de l'architecture. Il existe également un grand nombre de musées et de galeries privées qui font de Cologne un des plus importants centres artistiques au monde.

El 8 de julio del 2012 se celebrará en Colonia la Fiesta del Orgullo. Aunque sigue siendo una de las mayores fiestas, no es precisamente el punto álgido. Colonia, también conocida como gay Colonia, celebra Carnaval y aquí es donde los coloneses saben divertirse.
La ciudad del Rin, con un millón de habitantes, es una ciudad de tamaño medio. El ambiente gay se concentra en dos centros no muy lejanos el uno del otro. Uno está en el casco antiguo, entre Heumarkt y Alter Markt, y hay locales para mayores y para los amantes del cuero y fetichismo. En la Rudolfplatz se encuentra el ambiente más joven y moderno. Colonia está muy lleno los fines de semana y entre semana los locales están más bien vacíos.
Colonia tiene pocos pero grandes atractivos turísticos: la Catedral es un edificio gótico enorme y sus diversas iglesias románicas tienen un gran valor artístico. Todos los interesados en el arte se verán recompensados con la variedad de museos (entre ellos, el fantástico museo Ludwig) y galerías privadas, que hacen de Colonia uno de los centros mundiales del arte.

Il 8 luglio del 2012 si svolge a Colonia il più grande Christopher Street Day (Gay Pride) tedesco. A febbraio si festeggia qui il carnevale, grazie al quale gli abitanti di Colonia hanno davvero ben imparato cosa vuol dire saper festeggiare.
Colonia si affaccia sul Reno ed ha circa un milione di abitanti. La vita gay ha due centri principali che non distano molto l'uno dall'altro: il primo si trova presso la Rudolfplatz (per un pubblico più giovane e anche più trendy), mentre il secondo si trova nella città vecchia (raggiungibile a piedi da Rudolfplatz) tra l'Alten Markt e Heumarkt, (per un pubblico è un po' meno giovane). Ad Heumarkt si ritrova la scena leather e la scena fetish. Durante il fine settimana Colonia è davvero molto affollata, mentre durante la settimana non è raro trovare i locali letteralmente vuoti.
Colonia ha poche attrazioni turistiche ma in compenso le poche attrazioni sono di eccellente qualità. Alcuni esempi sono lo spettacolare Duomo gotico e molte chiese romaniche di grande importanza storica ed artistica. Gli appassionati dell'arte saranno ben lieti di visitare gli innumerevoli musei (per esempio il museo Ludwig) e le gallerie private che hanno reso Colonia uno dei centri artistici più importanti al mondo.

GAY INFO

■ **anyway – Jugendzentrum für Lesben, Schwule und deren FreundInnen** (B GLM I M YC)
Tue-Thu 17-22, Wed 17-22 (L), Thu 17-22h (G)
Kamekestraße 14 ☎ (0221) 577 77 60 🖳 www.anyway-koeln.de
Only for people under 27 years, various groups and activities.

■ **Centrum Schwule Geschichte e.V.** (GLM) Call for an appointment
Postfach 270308 ☎ (0221) 52 92 95 🖳 www.csgkoeln.de
Exhibitions, lectures and gay sightseeing. Library.

■ **Checkpoint** (GLM MA) 17-21, Fri & Sat 14-19, Sun -18h, closed Mon
Pipinstraße 7 ☎ (0221) 92 57 68 68 🖳 www.checkpoint-cologne.de
Gay and lesbian centre for information in Cologne. Also pride articles, books and magazines. HIV testing Wed+Thu 19-22h.

PUBLICATIONS

■ **BOX – Deutschlands Magazin für schwule Männer** 11-16h
Christianstraße 52 ☎ (0221) 954 13 12 🖳 www.box-online.de
Monthly free gay info magazine.

■ **RIK**
Norbertstraße 2-4 ☎ (0221) 39 06 60 🖳 www.rik-magazin.de
Monthly gay magazine for Cologne. Featuring gay news, information, addresses, classifieds, dates. For free in gay venues.

SHOWS

■ **Star-Treff** (B g ST) 19.30-?, Fri & Sat 18-3h, closed Mon-Wed
Turiner Straße 3 ☎ (0221) 25 50 63 🖳 www.startreff-cabaret.de
Good travesty shows, reservation recommended.

BARS

■ **Altstadtpub** (B G MA R) 11-3h
Unter Käster 5-7 ☎ (0221) 277 48 68 🖳 www.altstadtpub.com
Rent bar.

■ **Backbord** (B G m MC R) 11-1h
Steinweg 4 ☎ (0221) 258 14 79
Rent bar.

■ **Barcelon** (B G MA OS) 18-1, Fri & Sat -3, Sun 15-1h, closed Mon
Pipinstraße 3 🖳 www.facebook.com/barcelon.colonia

■ **Bastard** (B BF cc GLM MA OS) 11-2, Fri -3, Sat -5h
Friesenwall 29 ☎ (0221) 420 77 77
Trendy and friendly backyard bar with a great shady terrace; sunny roofgarden on top. Delicious snacks, popular in the evenings; sometimes DJs.

■ **Baustelle 4 U** (AC B f G m MA) Mon-Sun 19-3h
Pipinstraße 5 ☎ (0221) 258 17 83
Cologne local. Elderly gents in the early evenings, later on a popular late night meeting place for young and old.

■ **Beim Sir** (B GLM m MC OS) 12-6, Sun & Mon -1h
Heumarkt 27-29 ☎ (0221) 25 68 35 🖳 www.beim-sir.de

■ **Blue Lounge** (AC B d gLm MA WE)
Sun, Wed, Thu 21-2; Fri -4; Sat -5h
Mathiasstraße 4-6 ☎ (0221) 271 71 17 🖳 www.blue-lounge.com
Lounge with dance floor and DJs Fri & Sat.

spartacus traveler
DAS SCHWULE REISEMAGAZIN!
Viermal im Jahr mit Reportagen über interessante Reiseziele und Tipps für den perfekten schwulen Urlaub.
Im Abo (4 Ausgaben) für nur € 2,99 pro Heft, statt € 3,95 am Kiosk!
Gleich bestellen unter www.spartacus.de/traveler
Foto: Joan Crisol für ES Collection
MIAMI GAYS & GLAMOUR
SEOUL GANZ SCHÖN QUEER
KO SAMUI
KALIFORNIEN
HONGKONG
ANDALUSIEN
GRAN CANARIA
WINTER PRIDE
NEW YORK
AUF ANDY WARHOLS SPUREN

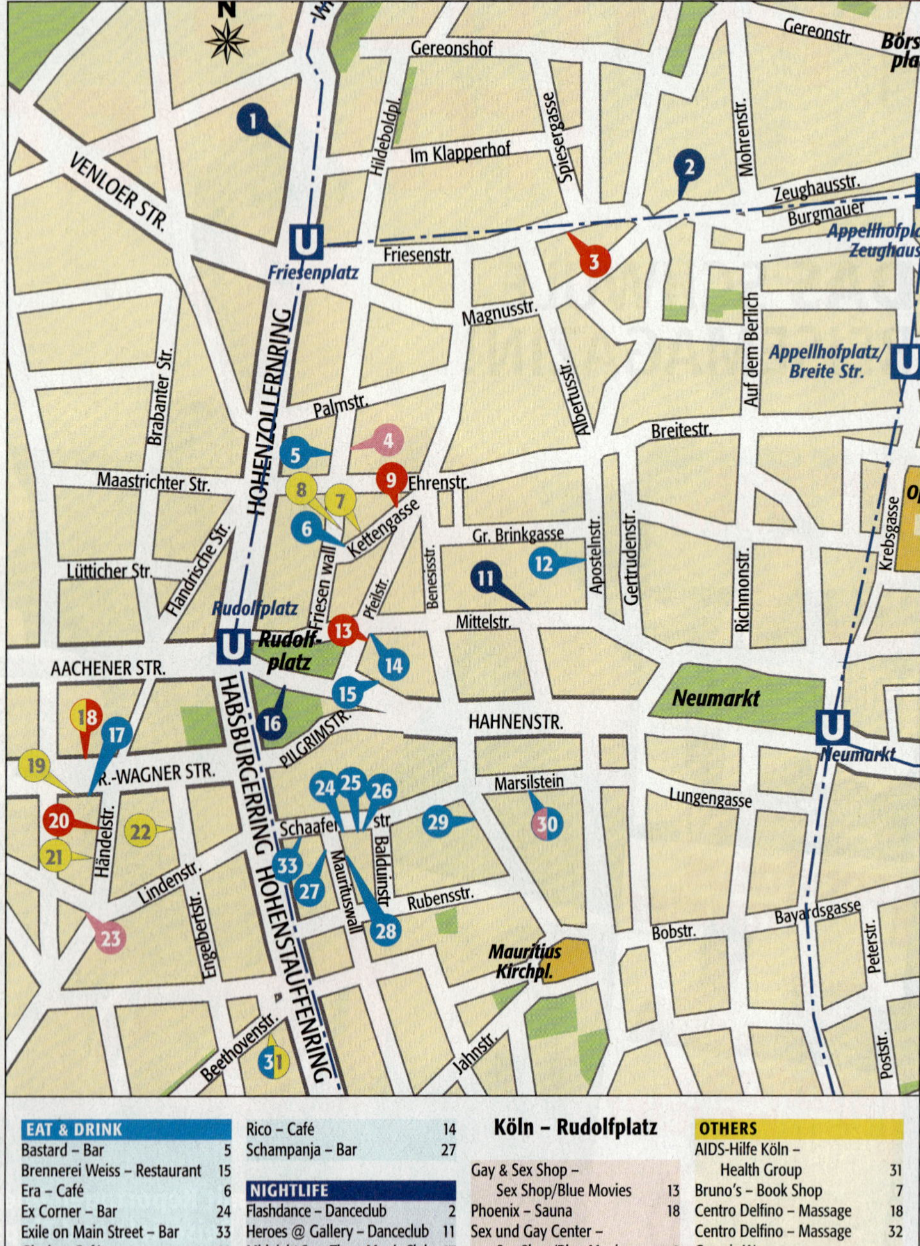

Köln – Rudolfplatz

EAT & DRINK

Bastard – Bar	5
Brennerei Weiss – Restaurant	15
Era – Café	6
Ex Corner – Bar	24
Exile on Main Street – Bar	33
Gloria – Café	12
Iron – Bar	26
Ix Bar	28
Marsil – Bar	30
Maxbar – Bar	29
Mumu. Die – Bar	25
Regenbogen-Café	31
Rico – Café	14
Schampanja – Bar	27

NIGHTLIFE

Flashdance – Danceclub	2
Heroes @ Gallery – Danceclub	11
Midnight Sun. The – Men's Club	17
Nightkomm/Greenkomm – Danceclub	1

SEX

Babylon Cologne – Sauna	3
Faun. Der – Sauna	20
Gay & Sex Shop – Sex Shop/Blue Movies	13
Phoenix – Sauna	18
Sex und Gay Center – Sex Shop/Blue Movies	9

ACCOMMODATION

Astor Aparthotel – Hotel	4
Barceló – Hotel	16
Chelsea – Hotel	23
Marsil – Guest House	30

OTHERS

AIDS-Hilfe Köln – Health Group	31
Bruno's – Book Shop	7
Centro Delfino – Massage	18
Centro Delfino – Massage	32
Cosmic Ware – Leather & Fetish Shop	22
Dome Fetish – Leather & Fetish Shop	21
Mate Wear – Fashion Shop	8
Mega-Gay-World – Leather & Fetish Shop	19

Bruno's

Alles, was Mann braucht.

BERLIN: Nollendorfplatz/Bülowstr. 106, U Nollendorfplatz **BERLIN:** Schönhauser Allee 131, Tram Milastr./ U Eberswalder Str. **HAMBURG:** Lange Reihe/Danziger Str. 70, U Hbf, Metrobus 6 Gurlittstr. **KÖLN:** Kettengasse 20, U Rudolfplatz **MÜNCHEN:** Thalkirchner Str. 4/Fliegenstr. 7, U /Tram Sendlinger Tor

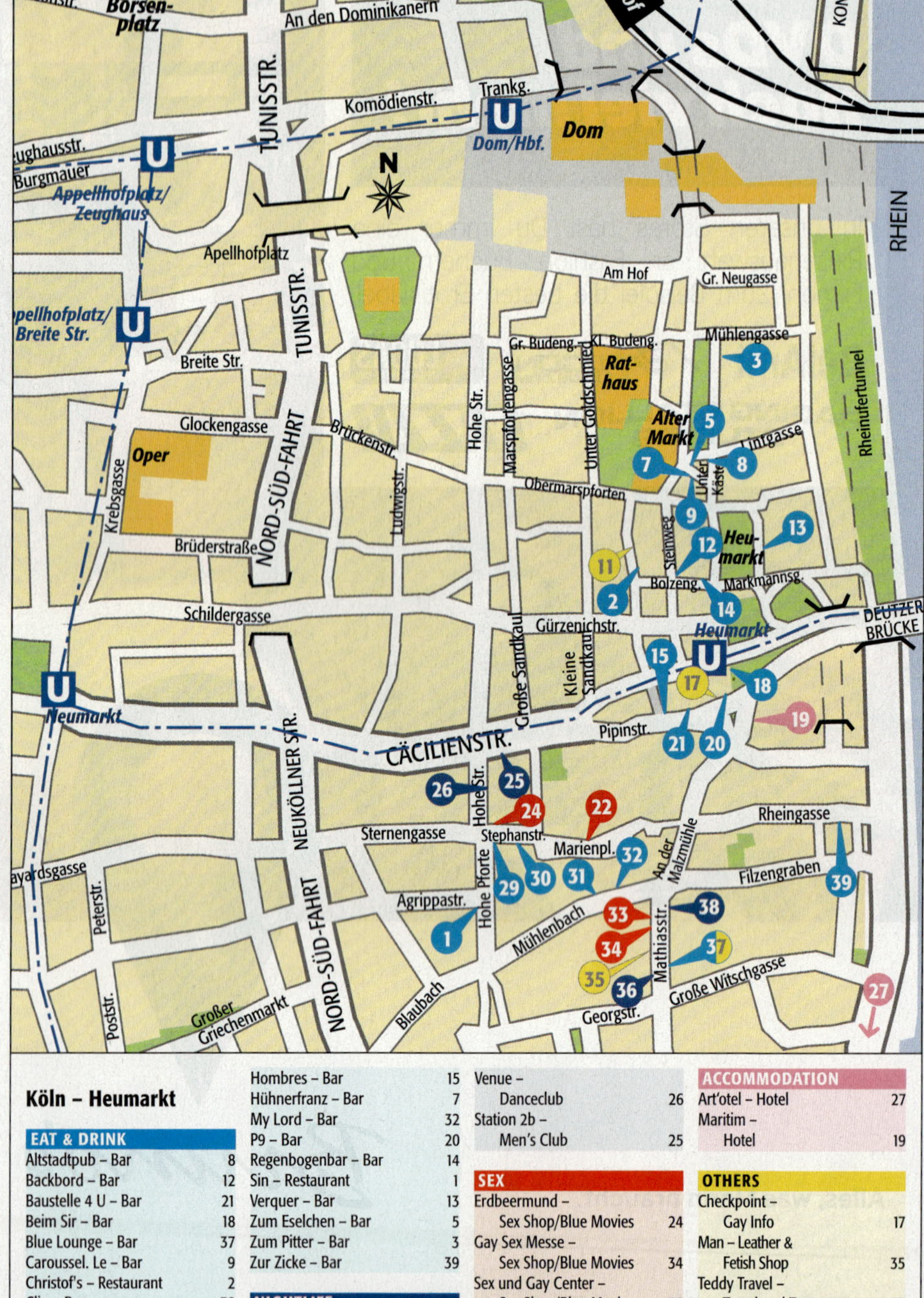

Köln – Heumarkt

EAT & DRINK	
Altstadtpub – Bar	8
Backbord – Bar	12
Baustelle 4 U – Bar	21
Beim Sir – Bar	18
Blue Lounge – Bar	37
Caroussel. Le – Bar	9
Christof's – Restaurant	2
Clip – Bar	30
Cox Cologne – Bar	31
Edelweiß – Bar	29
Hombres – Bar	15
Hühnerfranz – Bar	7
My Lord – Bar	32
P9 – Bar	20
Regenbogenbar – Bar	14
Sin – Restaurant	1
Verquer – Bar	13
Zum Eselchen – Bar	5
Zum Pitter – Bar	3
Zur Zicke – Bar	39

NIGHTLIFE	
Boners – Men's Club	38
Deck 5 – Men's Club	36
Venue – Danceclub	26
Station 2b – Men's Club	25

SEX	
Erdbeermund – Sex Shop/Blue Movies	24
Gay Sex Messe – Sex Shop/Blue Movies	34
Sex und Gay Center – Sex Shop/Blue Movies	33
Vulcano – Sauna	22

ACCOMMODATION	
Art'otel – Hotel	27
Maritim – Hotel	19

OTHERS	
Checkpoint – Gay Info	17
Man – Leather & Fetish Shop	35
Teddy Travel – Travel and Transport	37
Bodyworker – Massage	11

■ **Carrousel, Le** (B d G MA) 20-?h
Alter Markt 4-6 *Entrance Hühnergasse* ☎ (0221) 4734440
💻 www.lecarrousel.de

■ **Casino Eck** (B G MA S) Mon-Fri 16-?, Sat 11-?h, Sun closed
Kasinostraße 1a *Corner Stephanstraße* ☎ (0221) 23 24 42
💻 www.casino-eck.de

■ **Clip** (B D G MA) Tue, Thu, Fri & Sat 21-?, Sun 12-2h
Stephanstraße 4 *U-Heumarkt* ☎ (0221) 80 15 89 68
💻 www.clip-cologne.com
At the old location of Chains; Tue & Thu Karaoke.

■ **Cox** (B G MA)
Sun, Tue-Thu 20-1; Fri & Sat -3h; closed Mon except holidays
Mühlenbach 53 ☎ (0221) 240 04 19 💻 www.cox-cologne.com
The bar for bears and butch men.

■ **Edelweiß** (B G MA) 17-1, Fri & Sat -3, closed Mon
Stephanstraße 2 ☎ (0221) 219 03 34

■ **Ex Corner** (B G MA) 19-?h
Schaafenstraße 57-59 ☎ (0221) 233 60 60 💻 www.excorner.de
One of the few bars in town that are full all week. Happy hour 21-22h, best time: 22-24h, at weekends all night.

■ **Exile on Main Street** (B G m MA) 18-2, Fri & Sat -5, Sun 15-2h
Schaafenstraße 61a *U-Rudolfplatz* ☎ (0221) 67 77 05 78
💻 www.exile-cologne.de

■ **Hombres** (B GLM m MA) Wed-Mon 18-open end, Tue closed
Vor St. Martin 12 ☎ (0221) 258 23 47 💻 www.hombres-cgn.de
Neighbourhood bar with summer terrace

■ **Hühnerfranz** (AC B G m MA R WE) 6-4, Fri-Sun -?h
Hühnergasse 2-7 ☎ (0221) 25 35 36
Rent bar. Early morning breakfast from 6h.

■ **Iron** (AC B G m MA WE) 20-?h, closed Mon
Schaafenstraße 45 ☎ (0221) 801 40 95 💻 www.iron-bar.de
Daily happy hour. Cocktail bar.

■ **Ix Bar** (AC B CC d G m MA S) Daily 18-?h
Mauritiuswall 84 ☎ (0221) 233 60 60 💻 www.ixbar.de
Mon Cocktail Happy Hour. Every Sat Best of Clubsounds.

■ **Kattwinkel** (B GLM MA OS s) 18-?, Sun & public holidays 15-?h
Greesbergstraße 2 ☎ (0221) 13 22 20 💻 www.kattwinkel-cologne.de
Cosy bar with very friendly staff.

■ **Marsil** (B GLM H MA RWS RWT VA) Bar: Fri & Sat 22-5h, closed Sun-Thu
Marsilstein 27 ☎ (0221) 469 09 60 💻 www.marsil.de
Sophisticated crowd in a beautiful plush bar with theme evenings, DJs and cocktails. Popular at weekends. Eight apartments with WC/shower, kitchen & cable TV.

■ **Maxbar** (B GLM MA) Tue-Thu 20-2, Fri & Sat -4, Sun 19-?h, closed Mon
Am Rinkenpfuhl 51 💻 www.max-bar-cologne.de

■ **Mittelblond** (B glm m MA S) 17-?h, closed Mon & Tue
Schwalbengasse 2 ☎ (0221) 17 07 40 88
💻 www.mittelblond-kulturkneipe.de

■ **Mumu. Die** (B GLM YC) 18-?h
Schaafenstraße 51 💻 www.die-mumu.de
Young bar in the bermuda-triangle. Former location of „Café Huber".

■ **My Lord** (AC B G M OC)
Mon, Wed & Thu 16-1, Fri & Sat -3, Sun 14-1h, closed on Tue
Mühlenbach 57 ☎ (0221) 23 17 02 💻 www.barmylord.de
Long running bar for older gents and their admirers.

■ **P9** (B GLM m MA r) 14-?, WE 24hrs
Pipinstraße 9 💻 www.p9cologne.de

■ **Rambutan** (B G MC) 10-?, Sat & Sun 8-?h
Seidenmacherinnengässchen 1 ☎ (0221) 272 48 86
Former Rathausglöckchen.

■ **Regenbogen** (AC B G MA) 16-10h
Bolzengasse 7 ☎ (0221) 169 241 26 💻 www.regenbogen-em-bölzjen.de
After hour, great darkroom and cruising area. Men only from 22h. Weekend 2 bars.

■ **Sasch's** (AC B glm M MA VS WE) 21-?, Sun 19-23h, closed Mon
Wetzlarer Straße 2 ☎ (0221) 887 54 71 💻 www.saschs-bar.de
Jazz, Soul, Blues. Videoclips on WE.

■ **Schampanja** (B G MA s) 20-?h
Mauritiuswall 43 ☎ (0221) 240 95 44 💻 www.schampanja-koeln.de
■ **Verquer** (AC B GLM OS) Mon-Fri 14-24, Sat & Sun 12-?h
Heumarkt 46 ☎ (0221) 257 48 10
■ **Zum Eselchen** (B GLM MA T) 17-3h
Alter Markt 8 ☎ (0221) 271 28 13 💻 www.zum-eselchen.de
■ **Zum Pitter** (B GLM MA) 12-1, Fri & Sat -?, Sun 11-1h
Alter Markt 58-60 ☎ (0221) 54 81 60 00 💻 www.zum-pitter-cologne.de
■ **Zur Zicke** (B G MA s) 18-24, Fri & Sat 20-3, Sun 16-23h, closed Mon
Rheingasse 34 ☎ (0221) 240 89 58 💻 www.zur-zicke.de

MEN'S CLUBS

■ **Boners** (AC B DR F G MA P SL VS)
Mon 19-1, Tue-Thu 21-2, Fri & Sat 22-5, Sun 15-3h
Mathiasstraße 22 ☎ (0221) 24 35 41 💻 www.boners-cologne.com
Different theme nights, check www.boners-cologne.com for details. Sun „Naked Tea Time" 15-22h.
■ **Deck 5** (B DR f G MA VS) 22-5h
Mathiasstraße 5 ☎ (0221) 271 79 73 💻 www.deck-5.de
Best very late at night (after 1.30h). In the morning one of the horniest places in town, but not to be recommended for aesthetics. smoking allowed.
■ **Midnight Sun Köln** (B DR f G MA P VS) 22-5h
Richard-Wagner-Straße 25 ☎ (0221) 283 59 39
💻 www.midnightsun-koeln.de
Check website www.midnightsun-koeln.de for theme nights.
■ **Station 2b** (B D DR F G MA NU VS)
Wed & Thu 19-1, Fri & Sat 22-4, Sun 15-21h
Pipinstraße 2 💻 www.station2b.com
Fetish club with different theme nights every week.

CAFES

■ **Café Latte** (b GLM M MA NR VEG)
Mon-Thu 10-22, Fri -3, Sat 15-3, Sun -22h
Schaafenstr. 49 ☎ (0221) 16867277 💻 www.latte-koeln.de
Coffee-specialties, baguettes, soups, toasts, cakes and more.
■ **Era Cafe & Bar** (AC B bf G I M MA OS) 10-1h
Friesenwall 26 ☎ (0221) 169 344 30 💻 www.cafe-era.de
Modern & chic. Smoking allowed!
■ **Gloria** (AC B D glm MA S WE) Mon-Sat 11-23h, club: 23-6h
Apostelnstraße 11 ☎ (0221) 66 06 30 💻 www.gloria-theater.com
Café in the foyer, theatre/danceclub for various events in the back.
■ **Morgenstern** (B BF GLM I M MA OS) 10-22.30h, closed Mon
Friesenwall 24d *U-Rudolfplatz*
■ **Regenbogen-Café** (b GLM m MA) Mon-Fri 9-17h
Beethovenstraße 1 💻 www.aidshilfe-koeln.de
Positive-Café for concerned people and their friends. Breakfast 9-11h, lunch 12-14h.
■ **Rico** (AC B g m MA OS) Sun, Mon, Wed-Fri 10-20; Sat 9-20h
Mittelstraße 31-33 ☎ (0221) 240 53 64 💻 www.cafe-rico.de

DANCECLUBS

■ **Flashdance @ Zeughaus24** (B D GLM MA) 1st Sat/month 22-?h
Zeughausstraße 24 ☎ (0221) 943 94 91 💻 www.zeughaus24.de
70's and 80's music.
■ **GreenKomm @ Nachtflug** (! AC B D GLM MA) 1st Sun/month 6-17h
Hohenzollernring 89-93 💻 www.greenkomm.de
Very popular after hour party with many visitors from Benelux and France. Please check www.greenkomm.de for line-up and information
■ **Heroes** (B D G S YC) Fri 23-5h
Mittelstraße 12 *@ Gallery, U-Rudolfplatz* 💻 www.heroes-cologne.de
■ **Nightkomm** (AC B D GLM MA) 3rd Sat/month 23-5h
Hohenzollernring 89-93 *@ Starz* 💻 www.nightkomm.de
Please check www.nightkomm.de for the latest information. Smoking allowed!
■ **Pleasure Control @ Vanity Club & Cuisine** (B D GLM)
Hohenzollernring 16 💻 www.plx-party.de
Located at former Lulu Club.
■ **Sexy** (B D G MA OS) 4th Sat/month 23-?h
c/o Opernterrassen, Offenbachplatz an der Oper 💻 www.sexy-cgn.de
Check www.sexy-cgn.de for dates!

■ **Venue** (AC B D GLM MA S t) Fri+Sat 23-5h + b4 public holidays
Hohe Straße 14 ☎ (0221) 270 88 680 💻 www.venue-cologne.de
Various events like Poptastic, HomOriental, Gay Students Night and Gaycademy.

RESTAURANTS

■ **Brennerei Weiss** (AC B BF GLM M MA NR OS s VEG) Mon-Thu 15-1, Fri -3, Sat 13-?, Sun 14-1h
Hahnenstraße 22 ☎ (0221) 94 65 53 13 💻 www.brennereiweiss.de
■ **Christof's** (B glm M MA VEG WL) Tue-Sat 11.30-15, 18.30-23; Sun 11-15h, closed Mon
Martinstraße 32 ☎ (0221) 27 72 95 30 💻 www.christofs-restaurant.de
■ **Diner's** (AC BF glm M MA OS) Mon-Sat 8-20, Sun 12-18h
Neumarkt 16 ☎ (0221) 25 70 66 9 💻 www.diner-s.de
■ **Sin** (b glm M MA) Tue-Fri 11.30-24, Sat & Sun 10-24h, Mon closed
Hohe Pforte 9-11 ☎ (0221) 606 085 82

SEX SHOPS/BLUE MOVIES

■ **Erdbeermund Gay Store** (G MA VS) 9-24, Sun 12-24h
Stephanstraße 7-9 ☎ (0221) 240 20 34 💻 www.erdbeermund.de
Video Cabins. Cruisy atmosphere.
■ **Gay & Sex Shop** (G MC) 9-1, Sun and holidays 12-24h
Pfeilstraße 10 ☎ (0221) 25 62 78
■ **Gay Sex Messe** (DR G MC VS) 10-1, Sun & holidays 12-1h
Mathiasstraße 13 ☎ (0221) 271 67 93
A shop with 2 small cinemas.
■ **Sex und Gay Center** (DR G MA VS) 10-1h
Kettengasse 8 ☎ (0221) 258 09 18

HOUSE OF BOYS

■ **Valentino** (AC B G MA MSG p R SNU VS WE WH) 15-1, Fri & Sat -2.30h
Altenberger Straße 13 ☎ (0221) 13 70 79 💻 www.valentino.de
Last and only house of boys in cologne.

SAUNAS/BATHS

■ **Babylon Cologne** (! AK B cc DR FC G GH I LAB M MA MSG OS p PI RR SA SB SL VS WH) 12-6, Fri 12-Mon 6h (non-stop)
Friesenstraße 23-25 *U-Friesenplatz* ☎ (0221) 420 745 77
💻 www.babylon-cologne.de
One of the most beautiful saunas in Europe, completely rebuilt and enlarged play and fetish area downstairs; big open air pool.
■ **Faun. Der**
(AC B DR DU FC G I LAB M MC MSG OS p PP RR SA SB SL SOL VS) 12-1h
Händelstraße 31 *Near Rudolfplatz* ☎ (0221) 21 61 57
💻 www.faunsauna.de
Clean and relaxed sauna with a summer terrace. Bio-sauna.
■ **Phoenix** (AK b bf CC DR FC G GH I LAB m MA MSG OS p RR SA SB SL SOL VS WH) 12-6, Fri 12-Mon 6h (non-stop)
Richard-Wagner-Straße 12 *U-Rudolfplatz* ☎ (0221) 258 11 71
💻 www.phoenixsaunen.de
1200 m² on 2 floors. Also bio sauna and caldarium. Thu is Wellness Day. Special prices apply before 13h.
■ **Vulcano** (B DR FC FH G m MSG OC p PP RR SA SB VS) 11-22, Sat -8h
Marienplatz 3-5 *U-Heumarkt* ☎ (0221) 21 60 51
💻 www.sauna-vulcano.de
Friendly & clean. Admission includes two towels, sauna sandals and soap. Extras offered include medical massage and pedicure.

MASSAGE

■ **Am Mediapark Wellness Lounge** (CC G MA MSG NU SOL)
Mon-Sat 12-22h
Spichernstraße 71 ☎ (0221) 270 96 999 💻 www.wellnesslounge.me
Massages & Tantra from experienced, empathic masseurs in a feel good atmosphere.
■ **Bodyworker** (G MA MSG) 12-24h
Martinstraße 26 *U-Heumarkt, near old town hall, 10 mins walk from main station* ☎ (0221) 420 79 97 💻 www.bodyworker.de
■ **Centro Delfino – Massage & Kosmetik** (CC GLM MA MSG)
Mon-Fri 12-22, Sat -20h
Schaafenstraße 65 *U-Rudolfplatz* ☎ (0221) 320 19 418

www.centro-delfino.de
Many kinds of massages and facial treatments.

■ **Centro Delfino @ Phoenix Sauna** (CC G MA MSG)
Sun-Thu 13-23, Fri & Sat -4h
Richard-Wagner-Straße 12 *U-Rudolfplatz* ☎ (0221) 258 11 71
www.centro-delfino.de
Massage and cosmetics in gay Phoenix sauna.

■ **Zeus Studio** (G MSG)
Martinstr. 26 ☎ (0221) 420 7997 www.zeusmassage.de

BOOK SHOPS

■ **Bruno's** (! CC G MA) Mon-Sat 10-21h
Kettengasse 20 ☎ (0221) 272 56 37 www.brunos.de
An absolute must in Cologne! Bruno's is filled with books & magazines, DVDs, underwear, condoms & lubricants, pride articles and everything else the gay heart desires.

FASHION SHOPS

■ **Mate Wear** (G MA)
Mon-Tue 13-19, Wed 17-20, Thu & Fri 12-19, Sat 12-18.30h
Friesenwall 29 *U-Rudolfplatz* ☎ (0221) 258 98 84 www.mate-wear.de
Casual- and underwear for men.

■ **Menssecret.com** (CC GLM)
☎ (07751) 8980935 www.menssecret.com
International mailorder company. Jeans, Sportswear, Swimwear, T-Shirts, Tanks, Underwear, Accessoires. Store only in Zürich.

LEATHER & FETISH SHOPS

■ **Cosmic Ware** (CC F glm MA t) Tue-Fri 12-18.30, Sat 11-15h
Engelbertstraße 59-61 ☎ (0221) 240 12 01 www.cosmic-ware.de
Rubber, S/M and fetish store.

■ **Dome Fetisch** (CC F G MA) Mon-Fri 12-19, Sat 12-18h
Händelstraße 27 ☎ (0221) 923 42 09 www.dome-fetisch.de
Many specials, from XXS till XXXL Latex, Leather, Cockrings, etc. Large selection of toys.

■ **Man** (F G MA) 17-20, Fri 15-20, Sat 11-16h, closed Tue & Sun
Mathiasstraße 9 ☏ (0221) 240 74 08 🖳 www.man-cologne.de
Leather, boots, military and streetwear, also custom-made & extra large sizes.

■ **Mega-Gay-World** (f GLM I MA) Mon-Sat 12-23h
Richard-Wagner-Straße 27 *U-Rudolfplatz* ☏ (0221) 27 16 27 41
🖳 www.mega-gay-world-com
DVDs, magazines, toys, leather/fetish wear.

TRAVEL AND TRANSPORT

■ **Teddy Travel** (GLM) 9.30-18.30, Sat 10-13h, Sun closed
Mathiasstraße 12-14 ☏ (0221) 21 98 86 🖳 www.teddytravel.com
Travel agent and tour operator. Ask for their catalogue.

HOTELS

■ **Art'otel Cologne** (AC B BF CC glm I MA MSG PA RWS RWT SA) All year, 24hrs
Holzmarkt 4 ☏ (0221) 80 10 30 🖳 www.artotelcologne.com
Stylish new Art-Hotel in the city center directly on the river.

■ **Astor Aparthotel** (B BF CC H I NG PK RWS RWT SA) All year except between Dec 23th and Jan 2nd
Friesenwall 68-72 *U-Friesenplatz/Rudolfplatz* ☏ (0221) 20 71 20
🖳 www.hotelastor.de
Friendly private hotel in the gay district. 19 single rooms, 24 doubles, all rooms with shower/WC, cable-TV, phone & safe, 7 apartments with kitchenette (min. stay 14days).

■ **Barceló Cologne City Center** (AC B BF CC GLM I M PA PK RWS RWT SA SB VA VEG W WI WO) All year
Habsburgerring 9-13 *U-Rudolfplatz* ☏ (0221) 22 80
🖳 www.barcelocolognecitycenter.com
Gayfriendly hotel directly in the gay bermuda-triangle.

■ **Chelsea** (B BF CC glm H M MA OS PA PK RWB RWS RWT) All year
Jülicher Straße 1 *U-Rudolfplatz* ☏ (0221) 20 71 50
🖳 www.hotel-chelsea.de
Popular private hotel. Breakfast at the Café Central. Dinner at the elegant restaurant on the premises.

■ **Hotel Friends Köln** (b BF CC glm I MA PA PK RWS RWT)
All year, 24hrs
Roggendorfstraße 23-25 *10 mins drive from city centre*
☏ (0221) 67 11 880 🖳 www.hotel-friends-koeln.de
Located north of Köln, close to Leverkusen. 24h bar, lounge, W-LAN and parking for free and more.

■ **Hotel Royal** (B bf CC H I MA NG OS PA PK RWB RWS RWT VA)
All year
Hansaring 96 *Near central station* ☏ (0221) 91 40 18
🖳 www.hotel-royal-koeln.de
34 rooms with radio, cable TV, phone, mini-bar, bath and WLAN.

■ **Ludwig** (AC BF H I MA NG PK RWB RWS RWT VA)
Closed 22 Dec-2 Jan
Brandenburger Straße 24 *U-Hauptbahnhof* ☏ (0221) 16 05 40
🖳 www.hotelludwig.de
Cosy 3-star-hotel only a few steps away from the Cologne Cathedral.

■ **Maritim** (AC B CC DU FH H I M MSG NG NR PA PI PK RR RWB RWS RWT SA SB SOL WO) All year
Heumarkt 20 *U-Heumarkt* ☏ (0221) 202 70
🖳 www.maritim.de
Gay-friendly luxurious hotel with 454 rooms and suites, also smoking rooms available. Special CSD-offers upon request.

New Yorker. The (AC B BF CC glm I m MSG OS PA PK RWB RWS RWT SA SOL VA WO) All year
Deutz-Mülheimer-Straße 204 *U-Stegerwaldsiedlung, near exhibition center*
☎ (0221) 473 30 www.thenewyorker.de
Design hotel. All 40 rooms with bathroom, TV, telephone, mini-bar, internet access, also conference rooms. With a lovely garden.

Senats Hotel (B cc H I M RWS RWT)
Open all year except 21st Dec until 1st Jan
Unter Goldschmied 9-17 *Near main station* ☎ (0221) 206 20
www.senats-hotel.de
All rooms with own bath/shower/WC, mini-bar, hairdryer, phone, cable TV and WLAN.

GUEST HOUSES

Marsil (B GLM H MA RWS RWT VA)
Bar: Fri & Sat 22-5h, closed Sun-Thu
Marsilstein 27 ☎ (0221) 469 09 60 www.marsil.de
Sophisticated crowd in a beautiful plush bar with theme evenings, DJs and cocktails. Popular at weekends. Eight apartments with WC/shower, kitchen & cable TV.

pinkhomecologne (GLM I MA OS RWT VA)
Domstraße 64 *Near main station and cathedral*
☎ 172 759 59 20 (mobile) www.pinkhomecologne.de
Four stylish apartments (single/double), modern interior, cable-TV, full equipped kitchen, dining room and terrace. 2 shared bathrooms, WC/shower, centrally located, near gay-area. Separate apartment also available.

GENERAL GROUPS

Schwules Netzwerk NRW e. V. Tue & Thu 9-17h
Lindenstraße 20 ☎ (0221) 257 28 47
www.schwules-netzwerk.de

HEALTH GROUPS

AIDS-Hilfe Köln / Regenbogencafé (b g m MA)
Mon-Fri 9-17h, Sat & Sun closed
Beethovenstraße 1 ☏ (0221) 20 20 30 www.aidshilfe-koeln.de
Rainbow-Café for HIV+ and their friends, lunch served from 12-14h. Phone councelling Mon-Thu 19-21h.

HELP WITH PROBLEMS

RUBICON – Beratungszentrum für Lesben und Schwule (GLM MA)
Rubensstraße 8-10 ☏ (0221) 27 66 999-0 www.rubicon-koeln.de
Counselling Mon & Tue 14-18, Wed & Thu 10-18h.

SPECIAL INTEREST GROUPS

Bartmänner Köln e. V. / Bears of Cologne (F G MA)
PF 30 02 21 www.bearscologne.de
Group for hairy/bearded men and their admirers. Meetings 1st and 3rd Mon at „Verquer". Bear weekend in May „Bärenjagd". In Nov/Dec „Bear Pride Week"with election of „Mr Bear Germany", the biggest bear party in Europe.

SPORT GROUPS

Sport Club Janus e. V. (GLM MA) Office Mon 17-19h
Mittelstraße 52-54 ☏ (0221) 925 59 30 www.sc-janus.de
A large variety of sports activities, also various parties.

SWIMMING

-Bleibtreusee (g NU) (near Brühl)
-Agrippa-Bad (swimming pool) (Agrippastraße)
-Aqualand (Mon, Wed 18-23h, MA NU).

CRUISING

-U-Deutz-Kalker-Bad, (near body-building studio & student residences, MA)
-Aachener Weiher, along the railway lines or in the bushes along Universitätsstraße (AYOR) (day and night, popular)
-Cranachwäldchen – Niehl, by the Rhine north of the Mühlheimer Brücke (nu)
-Herkulesberg, Subbelrather Straße – near the bridge to Mediapark
-P Phantasialand BAB 553 near Brühl (F MA).

Konstanz ☏ 07531

BARS

EIN-Blick (B glm M MA) Tue-Fri & Sun 17-1, Sat -3h
Hofhalde 11 ☏ (07531) 551 88
Gayfriendly bar.

The Lounge (B GLM MA)
Theodor-Heuss-Straße 5 *Bus-Sternenplatz* ☏ (0173) 3257 939

VIP (B glm m MA OS) 11-14 & 17-?, kitchen -24h, winter evening only
Bodanstraße 15 ☏ (0162) 495 81 20 (mobile)

CAFES

Gay Café (B GLM YC) Wed 16-18h
Universitätsstrasse 10 *Room H301A, University* www.gay-cafe.de

Schmitt's (B BF glm M MA OS T) 10-1, kitchen 10-23h
Hieronymusgasse 2 ☏ (07531) 69 19 03 www.schmitt-s.de

Krefeld ☏ 02151

DANCECLUBS

Jogis Top Inn (B D glm MA) Fri, Sat & before holidays 22-5h
Neue Linner Straße 85 ☏ (02151) 65 73 43

Leipzig ☏ 0341

GAY INFO

Rosa Linde e.V. (GLM MA T) 19-22h, closed Mon
Lange Straße 11 ☏ (0341) 879 69 82 www.rosalinde.de

BARS

Havanna-Club (B GLM MA) 17-3; Sat, Sun & public holidays 19-3h
Goethestraße 2 ☏ (0341) 99 99 701 www.havanna-club-leipzig.de

MEN'S CLUBS

■ **Cocks** (AC B DR f G I MA P S VS) 19-3, Fri & Sat 21-5h
Otto-Schill-Straße 10 *Near Thomaskirche & Rathaus, tram 2,8,9*
☎ (0341) 22 54 03 06 💻 cocks-bar.com
Popular music bar with a very big and cruisy darkroom maze with sling.

■ **FickstutenMarkt Leipzig @ COCKS-Bar** (DR P)
Otto-Schill-Strasse 10 💻 www.fickstutenmarkt.com
Check the rules and FAQ's at website.

CAFES

■ **Apart** (B d glm H I m MA) 16-2, Sun -24h
Reichsstraße 16 *5 mins walk from main railway station*
☎ (0341) 962 80 46 💻 www.cafe-apart.de
Inner city cafe. Chill-out music, friendly service.

DANCECLUBS

■ **Nachts im Kaufhaus** (B D GLM MA)
Every 2nd Sun / month from 21h
Neumarkt 9

SEX SHOPS/BLUE MOVIES

■ **X Club** (B DR F G I MA NU R S T VS) 15-23h
Sternwartenstraße 14 *Between Ringkaffee and Bayrischer Bahnhof*
☎ (0341) 224 89 55 💻 www.gay6kino.de
Sex labyrinth on 2 floors, 250 m² with solo & double cabins. Daily ticket includes coffee & sparkling wine.

SEX CINEMAS

■ **United – Gay Cruising Kino** (AC B DR G I m MA VS)
Mon-Fri 13-21, Sat & Sun 15-21h
Otto-Schill-Straße 10 *Tram 2/8/9 Neues Rathaus* ☎ (0341) 961 42 46
💻 www.united-gay.com
Big cruisy darkroom labyrinth with sling. Free internet access.

SAUNAS/BATHS

■ **Clubsauna Stargayte** (! AC AK B DR G GH I LAB M MA MSG OS p RR SA SB SH SL SOL VS WH WO) Mon-Thu 12-2, Fri 12-Mon 2h (non stop)
Otto-Schill-Straße 10 *Near Rathaus and Thomaskirche, tram 2/8/9 Neues Rathaus* ☎ (0341) 961 42 46 💻 www.stargayte.de
One of the biggest saunas in Europe on two floors with 2 steam rooms, 2 whirlpools, 4 dry saunas & a cruisy darkroom labyrinth. Stargayte serves a very mixed hot crowd in a very laid back atmosphere.

SWIMMING

-Kulkwitzer See (B 87 Leipzig-Markranstädt, northern side)
-Ammelshainer Seen (A 14 → Dresden to »Naunhof«, cruising between the two lakes)
-Nauhofer See.

CRUISING

-Clara-Zetkin-Park (at Verkehrsgarten, Klingerweg/Nonnenweg, popular)
- Naunhofer See

Lemgo

CRUISING

-🅿 Regenstorplatz (Regentorstraße, day and night)

Limburg ☎ 06431

GENERAL GROUPS

■ **SchwulLesbischer Stammtisch Limburg e.V.** (GLM MA)
Cup Lahn e.V., PO Box 1648 💻 www.cup-lahn.de
Local glm-group, meetings at the „Batzewirt" Kornmarkt, Limburg Oldtown every 2nd and 4th Tuesday from 20h.

CRUISING

-Municipal hall (covered parking and around)
-Facilities at the Dome.

Lindau ☎ 08382

BARS

■ **Why Not** (B d GLM MA s t) Sun-Thu 20-1, Fri & Sat -3h
Bei der Heidenmauer 9 ☎ (0176) 2070 4123
Gaylesbian parties and bar.

RESTAURANTS

■ **Hoyerbergschlößle** (g M) Tue 18-?, Wed-Sun 12-14 & 18-?h
Hoyerbergstrasse 64 ☎ (08382) 25 29 5 💻 www.hoyerberg.de

Lörrach ☎ 07621

GENERAL GROUPS

■ **RainbowStars e.V.** (GLM MA) Wed
c/o Nellie Nashorn / Tumringerstr. 249
💻 www.rainbowstars.de
Group for gay-lesbian-transgender people. Also coming out group for youngsters. Meetings on Wednesdays at Nellie Nashorn, 1st floor.

Ludwigshafen ☎ 0621

DANCECLUBS

■ **Gays & Friends in Heaven** (AC B CC D GLM m MA S t)
2nd Fri/month 22h-open end
c/o Klangfabrik @ Club / Diskothek Ludwiq, Yorckstraße 2 *Opp. shopping mall „Walzmühle"* ☎ (0621) 122 847 10 💻 www.heaven-party.de
Probably the biggest friday event in Rhein-Neckar-area, approx. over 1.000 guests.

SAUNAS/BATHS

■ **Atlantis-Sauna**
(B CC DR DU FC FH G M MSG NU OC OS PI RR S SA SB SOL VS)
Gay: Tue-Thu 15-24; Fri -3; Sat, Sun & public holidays 13-1h; closed Mon
Wöllnerstraße 10 *Next to railway station Rheingönheim*
☎ (0621) 54 59 01 37 💻 www.atlantis-sauna.de
Very clean and popular sauna with large garden, accommodation and wellness area. Gay only from Tue-Sun. Thu & Fri „nude days". Summertime BBQ.

■ **Dagobert Sauna** (AC B DU glm MA RR SA)
Tue, Wed, Fri 16-24, Sat 15-24, Sun 15-23h
Dagobertstraße 8 *Munderheim* ☎ (0621) 577 966
💻 www.dagobert-sauna.de

Lübeck ☎ 0451

BARS

■ **CC Chapeau Claque** (B CC d GLM I MA s WE)
Tue-Thu 19-1, Fri & Sat 21-4h, Sun & Mon closed
Hartengrube 25-27 *City centre* ☎ (0451) 773 71 💻 www.cchl.de
Since 1978.

■ **Cole Street** (B GLM m MC S) Tue-Sun 9-?h
Beckergrube 18 💻 www.colestreet.de

■ **Flamingo-Gay-Bar** (B G MA OS R) 15-?h, closed Wed & Sun
Marlesgrube 58 *In the heart of the old town* ☎ (0451) 70 48 36
💻 www.gayromeo.com/Flamingo-Gay-Bar
Plushy bar.

SEX SHOPS/BLUE MOVIES

■ **Gay Kino Lübeck** (AC CC DR G MA VS)
Mon-Thu 9-23, Fri & Sat -24, Sun 12-23h
Lederstraße 2-4 ☎ (0451) 70 69 50

CRUISING

-Wallstraße (up to the Holstentor (r) and 🅿 at river Trave)
-Katzenberg (ayor r) (between Possehl and Stadtgraben)
-Mühlentorteller
-Burgtorteller (Gustav-Radbruch-Platz).

Lüneburg

SWIMMING

-Kalkbruchsee (NU)
-Volgershalle (behind Fachhochschule für Wirtschaft, north west side)

CRUISING

-Am Werder/Lüner Straße
-Graalwall
-Bardowicker Stadtmauer/Liebesgrund (22-?h).

Magdeburg ☎ 0391

BARS

Gummibärchen (AC B GLM m MA s) 19-1h
Liebigstraße 6 *Tram-Hasselbachplatz* ☎ (0391) 543 02 99
www.gaybaerchen.de

MEN'S CLUBS

Mens Club (B DR G MA P VS) Mon, Fri & Sat 22-?h
Liebigstraße 9a www.mens-club.info

DANCECLUBS

Boys 'n' Beats (B D G m MA OS) Wed-Sat 20-?h
Liebknechtstraße 89 *Bus/tram-Westring* www.boysnbeats.de

SEX SHOPS/BLUE MOVIES

Gay und Eroticshop (DR G MA r VS) Mon-Fri 10-20, Sat -15h
Bernburger Straße 1a *Near Hauptstraße* ☎ (0391) 401 29 43

GENERAL GROUPS

LSVD Sachsen-Anhalt (b GLM l m MA)
Mon 18-20, Wed 19-21h
Walther-Rathenau-Str 31 *Near Universitätsplatz* ☎ (0391) 54 32 569
www.sachsen-anhalt.lsvd.de
Different groups and activities, see website for details. Gay bashing helpline ☎ 0391 19228.

SWIMMING

-Neustädter See (NU) (S-Rothensee/Eichweiler)
-Freibad Süd (bushes near the open air theatre).

CRUISING

-Glacis Anlagen (Adelheidring, between Diesdorfer Straße and Liebknechtstraße, popular)
-Klosterbergegarten (street to the Sternbrücke)
-Fürstenwallanlage am Dom, facilities.

Mainz ☎ 06131

BARS

Bar jeder Sicht (AC B bf d GLM m MA S ST) Tue-Sat 18-?, Sun 11-?h
Hintere Bleiche 29 *Between Münsterplatz and Neubrunnenplatz*
☎ (06131) 554 01 65 www.sichtbar-mainz.de
Sunday brunch. Also community centre with counselling upon request. Meeting point of local all gay groups/associations.

Chapeau (AC B GLM MA) 17-?h
Kleine Langgasse 4 ☎ (06131) 22 31 11 www.chapeau-mainz.de
Small, cosy bar.

DANCECLUBS

Kulturcafé (Q-Kaff) (B D GLM OS YC)
every 2nd & 4th Fri 22h-open end
Johann Joachim Becher Weg 5 *On the campus of Uni Mainz*
☎ (06131) 392 4063 www.kulturcafe-mainz.de
Location of „Warm in's Wochenende"-Party. Nice school-like alternative party on two dancefloors, many local students and crowd from Frankfurt and Wiesbaden. Reasonable prices.

SEX SHOPS/BLUE MOVIES

Crazy Video Show (DR G MA VS) 9-23, Sun 13-22h
Dominikanerstraße 5 ☎ (06131) 214 750

SAUNAS/BATHS

Bluepoint (! B DU FC G l m MA MSG RR SA SB SH VS WO)
Tue-Sun 12-24h, Mon closed
Frauenlobstraße 14 *Near main train station* ☎ (06131) 972 48 00
www.bluepointsauna.de
Very nice sauna in a kind of ancient catacomb with great illumination evoking a pleasant atmosphere. Special youngsterparties see www.bluepointsauna.de for details.

CRUISING

-Rheinhalle (Green Bridge)
-Rosengarten
-University Mainz, facilities in the Re-Wi Building, daytime.

Mannheim ☎ 0621

BARS

Café Klatsch (AC B G m MA OS) 18-3, Sun 16-3h
Hebelstraße 3 *Near National theater* ☎ (0621) 156 10 33
klatsch-mannheim.de
Great atmosphere, nice staff.

Club Action (B d GLM MA)
22-5, Sat & Sun after hour from 6h-open end
Am Ring U5, 13 ☎ (0621) 15 34 35 www.club-action-disco.de
Medium sized cellar club. Cool after hours an Sat & Sun morning. Heterofriendly.

Lello (B glm M MA OS) 14-1, Fri & Sat -3, Sun -24h
Berliner Straße 17 ☎ (0621) 370 9000 www.cafe-lello.de
Recently renovated, good wine selection.

■ **Rosanellis** (B GLM MA) 20.30-2, Fri & Sat 21-5h
S2, 16 ☏ (0621) 178 56 90 🖳 www.rosanellis-bar.de
small and trashy bar.

■ **XS** (AC B G r) 11-1, Sun 14-1h
N 7,9 *Near central station* ☏ (0621) 158 29 59

MEN'S CLUBS

■ **FickstutenMarkt Mannheim @ Jails (MS Connexion)** (DR G P)
Angelstrasse 33 🖳 www.fickstutenmarkt.com

■ **Jail's** (! B D DR F G MA NU VS) Fri-Sun 21-?h
Angelstraße 33 *Next to MS Connexion* ☏ (0621) 854 41 46
🖳 www.jails-mannheim.de
300 m² darkroom area.

CAFES

■ **Kußmann** (B GLM MA OS) Mon-Thu 10-1, Fri -3, Sat 11-3, Sun 14-1h
T6, 19 *Near Nationaltheater* ☏ (0621) 397 42 70 🖳 www.cafe-kussmann.de

DANCECLUBS

■ **Himbeerparty** (B D GLM MA OS) Last Sat/month 22h-open end
Alte Feuerwache, Brückenstraße 2 🖳 www.himbeerparty.de
Very popular party. Check www.himbeerparty.de for details.

■ **MS Connexion** (B BF CC D DR f GLM MA S SNU ST T VS WE) 2nd Sat/month 23h-open end
Angelstraße 33 ☏ (0621) 854 41 44 🖳 www.msconnexion.com
Now straight club – only gay parties every 2nd Sat/month Gaywerk on 5 dancefloors, chillout, cruising, smoking and outdoor areas. Monsterparties on xmas, easter and whitsunday „Mega Gay Werk". .

■ **Zwei** (AC B D G m MA WE) Sat 22-5h
T6, 14 *Near National-Theatre* 🖳 www.ponyclub-mannheim.de
New gay danceclub in the former „T6 Club". Hosts „Ponyclub" Parties every Sat.

SEX SHOPS/BLUE MOVIES

■ **Binokel** (AC DR F G MA VS) Mon-Sat 12-23, Sun 15-23h
J2, 18 *Near Market* ☏ (0621) 22 117 🖳 www.binokel-gaykino.de
Not to be confused with straight restaurant Binokel!

■ **Cruising Point** (DR G SH VR) Mon-Fri 12-24, Sat -3, Sun 15-24h
Mittelstr. 15 ☏ (0621) 36 407 🖳 cruisingpoint-mannheim.de

■ **Studio 7** (AC DR f G I MA VS) 11-24, Sat 11-6, Sun & holidays 16-24h
Heinrich-Lanz-Straße 32 *Tram-Tattersaal, near the main train station*
☏ (0621) 44 93 06

SAUNAS/BATHS

■ **Atlantis**
☞ *Ludwigshafen.*

■ **Galileo City Sauna** (AC B DR DU FC FH G GH I LAB M MA MSG NU OS RR SA SB SH SL VS) 13-1; Fri, Sat & before holidays -8h
O7, 20 *Tram-Wasserturm / Kunsthalle / Tattersall, opp. Saturn*
☏ (0621) 178 64 09 🖳 www.nachtsauna.com
Popular sauna for gays and bisexuals on 3 floors, close to the main train station. Unusual design with a mixed crowd. Spacious steam bath with great design. Summer: open air terrace and „cinema-playground".

BOOK SHOPS

■ **Andere Buchladen. Der** (GLM) Mon-Fri 10-19, Sat -16h
M 2, 1 ☏ (0621) 217 55 🖳 www.der-andere-buchladen.de
Books, magazines, DVDs, CDs, pride articles.

GENERAL GROUPS

■ **CSD Rhein-Neckar e.V.** (GLM MA)
M2 1 🖳 www.csd-rhein-neckar.de
Group organizing the CSD Parade on August 11th 2012.

CRUISING

-Schlosspark (behind university, very popular at dusk)
-Friedrich-Ebert-Brücke (tunnel)
-Wasserturm (facilities)
-Neuer Messeplatz (WC).

Marburg ☏ 06421

BARS

■ **Hugo`s** (B glm m MA)
Gerhard-Jahn-Platz 21a ☏ (06421) 13000

■ **Schwule Theke im KFZ** (B GLM MA) Mon 21.30-1h
Schulstraße 6 *Citycenter, near Rudolfsplatz* ☏ (06421) 13898
Oldest gay meeting point in town, since 1977. Alternative place for gay parties and hang-outs. Lots of students.

DANCECLUBS

■ **Adam's Sin** (AC B D GLM YC) 2nd Sat/month 22h-open end
Bahnhofstr.31a Gleis 1a 🖳 www.adams-sin.de
Popular club night, lots of students. Various locations

CRUISING

-Schülerpark (near railway line and river Lahn)
-Bürgerpark (near youth hostel).

Meuspath (am Nürburgring) ☏ 02691

HOTELS

■ **Rennhotel am Nürburgring**
(B BF CC H M MA MSG PK RWS RWT WI) All year
Nordstrasse 1 *Neben der Grand-Prix-Strecke und der „Nürburgring-Nordschleife"* ☏ (02691) 93 510 60 🖳 www.rennhotel.de
Charming Hotel at the Nürburgring-Nordschleife. Two mins by car to GP route. Great breakfast buffet, public bar „bRENNBAR" with more than 30 sorts of whiskey and snacks.

Mülheim a.d. Ruhr ☏ 0208

SAUNAS/BATHS

■ **Ruhrwellness** (AC B CC DR FC FH G I M MA MSG NU OS PI PP RR SA SB SH SOL VS WH WO) 10-24, Sat 10-7h
Sandstraße 154 *S-Mühlheim-West* ☏ (0208) 302 48 11
🖳 www.ruhrwellness.de
Every 2nd Fri/month Youngster Party. Friendly, bright sauna with wellness offers on Wed and Sat.

GENERAL GROUPS

■ **Enterpride** (b GLM m YC)
Mon 15-22, Tue 18-24, Thu & Sun 18-24h
Wertgasse 37 *City centre, in front of the protestant hospital*
☏ (0208) 302 73 58 🖳 www.enterpride.de
Youth-Centre.

■ **Switchboard** (B BF D GLM MA)
Sandstraße 158 ☏ (0208) 412 59 21 🖳 www.the-switchboard.de
Sun 10-?h brunch, Wed music café 18-?h. Also „Generation-Café". Check Homepage for details.

München ☏ 089

Munich is famous for the October festival, BMW and its beer gardens. The conservative, catholic influence still remains present, although this influence is diminishing. The Mayor of Munich Christian Ude leads the Christopher Street Parade, allows the rainbow flags to be flown from the town hall and offers his workplace (the town hall at Marien Square) as the venue for the large CSD party. Culturally Munich has also much to offer: two opera houses, the Philharmony, many theatres, impressive museums (Technical Museum, Old and New Pinakothek, Modern Pinakothkek), an attractive city centre with the enourmous English Garden and the noble Maximilian Street.

München ist für das Oktoberfest, BMW und seine Biergärten bekannt. Der konservativ-katholische Einfluss ist zwar immer noch spürbar. Der Bürgermeister Christian Ude führt seit Jahren den CSD an und lässt die Regenbogenflagge vor dem Rathaus hissen. Auch heute noch stellt er seinen altehrwürdigen Amtssitz am Marienplatz für die

große CSD-Party zur Verfügung. Auch kulturell hat München ein großes Angebot: zwei Opernhäuser, die Philharmonie, viele Theater, prächtige Museen (Technikmuseum, Alte und Neue Pinakothek, Pinakothek der Moderne), eine schöne Innenstadt mit dem riesigen Englischen Garten und die edle Maximilianstraße.

Munich est connue pour la fête de la bière, ses Biergärten et BMW. L'influence conservatrice et catholique est certes toujours sensible. Le maire Christian Ude conduit la Gay Pride depuis des années et hisse le drapeau arc-en-ciel devant la maire. Aujourd'hui encore il met à la disposition sa noble mairie sur la Marienplatz pour la grande soirée de la Gay Pride, appelée CSD en Allemagne. Au niveau culturel, Munich a beaucoup à offrir : deux opéras, la philharmonie, beaucoup de théâtres, de magnifiques musées (musée de la technique, Alte Pinakothek, Neue Pinakothek), un beau centre-ville avec l'énorme jardin Englischer Garten et la très chic rue Maximilian.

Munich es famoso por el Oktoberfest, BMW y por sus cervecerías al aire libre. Aunque se puede sentir la influencia católica conservadora. El alcalde Christian Ude conduce el desfile del Orgullo Gay e iza la bandera del arco iris delante del Ayuntamiento muniqués y, a día de hoy, sigue incluso poniendo la sede del ayuntamiento, en la Marienplatz, a disposición de las celebraciones del CSD. Culturalmente Munich tam-

bién tiene mucho que ofrecer: dos óperas, una Filarmónica, incontables teatros, espléndidos museos (el museo de tecnología, la antigua y nueva Pinacoteca, la Pinacoteca de Arte Moderno), un hermoso centro urbano con el inmenso Jardín Inglés y la elegante calle de Maximilianstrasse.

Monaco è conosciuta per la festa della birra (Oktoberfest), per la BMW e per i suoi Biergärten. Tuttavia l'influenza cattolica e conservatrice della Regione è ancora abbastanza forte. Il sindaco Christian Ude è testimonial del CSD e in quest'occasione lascia sventolare la bandiera arcobaleno dal Municipio e mette anche disposizione i prestigiosi spazi dell'edificio a Marienplatz per le grandi feste del CSD. Monaco offre tanto anche dal punto di vista culturale: due teatri dell'Opera, sontuosi musei come per esempio il Museo della Scienza e della Tecnica, detto anche Deutsches Museum, la Vecchia e la Nuova Pinacoteca, la Pinacoteca del Moderno, un bellissimo centro città con un enorme Giardino Inglese e l'elegantissima Maximilianstraße.

GAY INFO

Gay Touristoffice (GLM MA)
Tumblingerstraße 1 ☏ (089) 4423 7037 www.gaytouristoffice.com
Hotel and Tourbookings, tickets, bike- and car-rental. Onlinebookings or through the office.

Sub-Schwules Kommunikations- und Kulturzentrum (B G MA s) 20-1, Sun 19-22h
Müllerstraße 43 ☏ (089) 260 22859 www.subonline.org
Centre for communication, information, counselling & groups. Also gay library, help with problems and health service.

PUBLICATIONS

Leo (GLM MA)
c/o querformat GmbH, Augsburgerstraße 6 ☏ (089) 55 29 716-33
www.leo-magazin.de
Monthly city gay magazine available for free at gay venues.

BARS

Alexander's (AC B G m MA R) Daily 18-?h
Utzschneiderstraße 4 ☏ (089) 260 54 98 www.cafe-bar-alexanders.de
Well established rent bar.

Bar Jeans (B f GLM MA VS) Sun-Thu 21.30-5h, Fri & Sat -open end
Blumenstrasse 15 ☏ (089) 26 43 23

Bau (! AC B CC DR F G m MA OS S VS) 20h-open end
Müllerstraße 41 ☏ (089) 26 92 08 www.bau-munich.de
Popular, very cruisy.

Bei Carla (B gLm M MA OS) Tue-Fri 16-?, Sat 18-?
Buttermelcherstr. 9 ☏ (089) 41 87 41 68 www.bei-carla.de
Many Lesbians, gays welcome.

Colibri (B G m MA T) 11-2, Fri & Sat 14-4h
Utzschneiderstraße 8 ☏ (089) 260 93 93
Tiny bar.

Cook (B F G MC) 20-1, Sat -3h
Augsburger Straße 21 ☏ (089) 26 59 95 www.cook-munich.de

Drei Glöcklein (B G MA) 15-3, Sat & Sun 11-3h
Hans-Sachs-Straße 8 ☏ (089) 26 61 75
A small, friendly bar for heavy drinkers.

Edelheiß (AC B f G m MA) 15-1, Fri & Sat -3h
Pestalozzistraße 6 ☏ (089) 26 54 53 www.edelheiss.de
Rustic bar and a popular pub for bearded men and bears.

Jennifer Parks (B GLM MA OS) Thu 21-1, Fri+Sat -4h
Holzstraße 14 ☏ (0176) 200 78 461 (mobile)
www.jennifer-parks.com
New and trendy bar with relaxed atmosphere.

Marktklause (B G m MA R) 16-2, Fri & Sat -3h
Frauenstraße 20 ☏ (089) 29 90 76
Rent boy bar.

Pimpernel (B D g MA t) 22-6h
Müllerstraße 56 ☏ (089) 45 23 86 02
www.pimpernel-muenchen.de
Late night bar, a bit rough. Used to be more gay in the past but still worth a visit when everything else closes.

BelAmi®
ENTERTAINMENT
Wholesale requests for Europe: www.brunogmuender.com/distribution
Love is
in the Air

München

EAT & DRINK

Name	No.
Alexander's Bar & Café	11
Bar Jeans	62
Bau – Bar	42
Beim Franz – Restaurant	29
Café am Hochhaus – Café	40
Café im Sub – Bar	43
Cook – Bar	49
Colibri – Bar	12
Deutsche Eiche – Restaurant	19
Drei Glöcklein – Bar	31
Edelheiss – Bar	54
Emiko – Restaurant	18
Filmwirtschaft	64
Jennifer Parks – Bar	1
Kr@ftakt – Café	59
Marktklause – Bar	15
Morizz – Restaurant	24
Moro – Restaurant	38
Nil – Café	65
Pop As – Bar	52
Prosecco Schlagerbar	46
Rendezvous – Bar	56
Rubin – Café	55
Rubico – Restaurant	28
Stacherias – Café	2
Sunshine Pub – Bar	23
Unantast "Bar"	51
Zur Feuerwache – Bar	22

NIGHTLIFE

Name	No.
Bergwerk – Danceclub	55
Blub Club @ Pacha – Danceclub	7
Camp – Men's Club	48
Energie – Men's Club	10
Garry Klein @ Harry Klein – Danceclub	21
Hanoi – Danceclub	39
NY Club – Danceclub	8
Ochsengarten – Men's Club	44

SEX

Name	No.
Atlantic City – Sex Shop/Blue Movies	3
Buddy Shop – Sex Shop/Blue Movies	14
Deutsche Eiche – Sauna	19
M54 – Sauna	56

ACCOMMODATION

Name	No.
Belle Blue – Hotel	5
Carat Hotel Munich – Hotel	50
Cortina – Hotel	16
Deutsche Eiche – Hotel	19
hotelmüller – Hotels	58
Louis HH – Hotel	18
Pension Eulenspiegel – Hotel	61
Pension Gärtnerplatz – Guest House	25
Pension Seibel – Guest House	13

OTHERS

Name	No.
Bruno's – Book Shop	60
Kunstbehandlung – Culture	41
Mongay @ Atelier – Cinema	4
Savage – Leather & Fetish Shop	26
Spexter – Leather & Fetish Shop	56

Pop As (B f G MA) 21-?h
Thalkirchner Straße 12 ☏ (089) 260 91 91 www.pop-as.de
Clubhouse of MLC e.V. Any help for members of ECMC-clubs.

Prosecco Schlagerbar (! B D GLM MA ST T)
Thu-Sat 21-?h, open before & on holidays, Sun-Wed closed
Theklastraße 1 *near Viktualienmarkt* ☏ (089) 230 323 29
www.prosecco-munich.de
Very busy at WE with live DJ, until early morning. Mixed party crowd, but very gay.

Rendezvous (B cc GLM m MA OS) Daily 16-?h
Müllerstraße 54 ☏ (089) 260 41 25
Western style bar.

Sunshine Pub (B G m MA r) 6-3h
Müllerstraße 17 ☏ (089) 260 93 54
Small and run down pub, a late night meeting place.

Unantast „Bar" (B glm MA) 17-?h
Thalkirchner Straße 16 ☏ (089) 260 74 69
Half a dozen stools around a wooden bar, the tiniest bar imaginable. For heavy drinkers.

Zur Feuerwache (B bf G m MA) 11-24, Fri -3, Sat 5-3, Sun -24h
Blumenstraße 21a ☏ (089) 260 44 30
www.bar-zur-feuerwache.de
Friendly local pub for beer drinkers. Sun 6-14h Weißwurst Breakfast.

MEN'S CLUBS

Camp (B DR f G MA P) 20-2, Fri & Sat -3h
Reisingerstraße 15 ☏ (089) 23 23 08 30

Energie (AC B DR G I MA NU P VS) 20-4, Sun 16-20h
Maistraße 63 ☏ (0176) 26 77 01 42
Gay naked party bar.

Ochsengarten (AC B F G MA P) 22-3h
Müllerstraße 47 ☏ (089) 26 64 46 www.ochsengarten.de
Dark and old-fashioned leather bar, local club of MLC.

CAFES

Café am Hochhaus (AC B D glm MA OS p)
Tue-Sat 20-3, 1st+3rd Sun/month 20-3h
Blumenstraße 29 ☏ (089) 890 58 152
www.cafeamhochhaus.de
Also Sunday T-dance „Queer-Sunday", see website for more info.

Café im Sub (! B G MA s) 19-23, Fri & Sat -24h
Müllerstraße 43 ☏ (089) 260 30 56 www.subonline.org
Newly renovated café in the gay centre.

Café Loony (B GLM MA) Mon-Sat 9-1, Sun -18h
Augustenstrasse 112 ☏ (089) 579 33757

Filmwirtschaft (B GLM MA OS) 14.30h-open end
Sonnenstrasse 12 @ *Atelier Cinema* ☏ (089) 215 88 880

Glück (B bf gLm M MA OS) 15-1h
Palmstraße 4 ☏ (089) 201 16 73
Many lesbians.

Kraftakt (AC B BF CC GLM I M OS YC) 10-1, Fri & Sat -3h
Thalkirchner Straße 4 ☏ (089) 21 58 88 81 www.kraftakt.com
Café, bar, restaurant, Internet.

Nil (B GLM M MA OS S) 15-3h
Hans-Sachs-Straße 2 ☏ (089) 23 88 95 95 www.cafenil.com

Petit (b G m MA) 15-22h
Marienstraße 2 ☏ (089) 29 56 72

Rubin (b glm M MA) 15-1, Fri & Sat -3h
Thalkirchner Straße 10 ☏ (089) 97 34 94 13 www.cafe-rubin.de

Stacherias (B glm M MA) Mon-Fri 10-24, Sat 9-1, Sun 10-22h
Karlsplatz 8 ☏ (089) 51 50 59 30 www.stacherias.de

DANCECLUBS

Bergwerk @ Flashbox (B D GLM MA)
Thalkirchner str. 10 *opp. Kr@ftakt* ☏ (089) 5487 4539?
www.flashbox.me
New party in town on irregular dates. Watch out for flyers or check website

■ **Blub Club** (B D glm MA S)
Maximiliansplatz 5 @ *Pacha* www.blubclub.com
For 20 years now the hottest mixed party in town, with cool house beats by DJ Cambis & friends! Very gayfriendly! See website for partydates.

■ **Candyclub** (B D GLM MA S)
2nd Sat/month @ Rote Sonne + 4th Fri/Month @ Orange House 23-?h
Maximiliansplatz 5 www.candyclub.de
Long running alternative and independent party for gays, lesbians and friends. Check www.candyclub.de for dates and locations.

■ **Popparty** (AC B CC D GLM S YC)
Sonnenstrasse 25 @ *NY Club* www.facebook.com/PopParty

■ **Hanoi** (AC B D GLM ST T WE YC)
Fri, Sat & before public holidays 22h-open end
Theklastraße 1 *Near Viktualienmarkt* ☎ (089) 23 00 04 96
Large dancefloor, lounge and several bars.

■ **GarryKlein @ Harry Klein**(B D GLM MA S) Wed 23-5h
Sonnenstraße 8 *Stachus @ harryklein club* ☎ 4028 7400
www.harrykleinclub.de
New midweek gay-party with house and techno.

■ **NY Club** (AC B cc D DR GLM MA S WE)
Fri, Sat and before public holidays 23-open end
Sonnenstraße 25 ☎ (089) 6223 2152 www.nyclub.de
Lounge-Dance-Cruise at the No.1 Dance-Club in Munich.

RESTAURANTS

■ **Beim Franz** (B DM G M MA OS) 18-1h, closed Mon
Holzstraße 41 ☎ (089) 260 75 47 www.beimfranz.de
Excellent Bavarian cuisine.

■ **Brenner** (B bf CC glm M MA)
Mon-Thu 8.30-1, Fri & Sat 8.30-2, Sun 9.30-1h
Maximilianstraße 15 ☎ (089) 45 22 880 www.brennergrill.de
Fashionable restaurant with great cuisine!

■ **Cube** (B glm M MA OS) Tue-Sat 18h-open end, holidays closed
Bruderstraße 6 ☎ (089) 121 911 92 www.lifestyle-gastronomie.de
Stylish and gayfriendly restaurant.

■ **Deutsche Eiche Restaurant**
(B BF CC DM G I M MA NR OS RES VEG WE WL) 7-1h
Reichenbachstraße 13 ☎ (089) 23 11 6661 www.deutsche-eiche.com
In the building of the sauna & hotel with the same name. Large restaurant with Bavarian & international cuisine.

■ **Emiko** (AC B cc glm MC NR RES VEG WL) Daily 18-23.30h
Viktualienmarkt 6 ☎ (089) 4111 908 111 www.louis-hotel.com

■ **Lotus Lounge** (B glm M MA) 17-23h
Hans-Sachs-Straße 10 ☎ (089) 2189 9755 www.lotuslounge.eu
Gayfriendly Thai-restaurant in the heart of the gay „Glockenbach"-quarter.

■ **Melcher's** (glm M MA OS) Mon 18-23, Tue-Thu 11-23, Fri -1, Sun -23h
Buttermelcherstraße 21 ☎ (089) 2424 3705 www.das-melchers.de

■ **Morizz** (AC B cc DM GLM M MA NR OS s VEG WL) 19-2, Fri & Sat -3h
Klenzestraße 43 ☎ (089) 201 67 76 www.morizz.com
Cocktails and Thai cuisine.

■ **Moro** (B G M MA OS RES VS)
Mon-Fri 17-1; Sat, Sun & public holidays 11-1h
Müllerstraße 30 ☎ (089) 23 00 29 92 www.moro-munich.com
Sun & holidays brunch 11-15.30h. International & Bavarian cuisine. Popular.

■ **Regenbogen** (b GLM M MA s) Mon-Fri 11.30-14, Tue-Fri 17-23h
Lindwurmstraße 71 ☎ (089) 54 33 31 02
www.muenchner-aidshilfe.de
Restaurant-Café for people with HIV/AIDS and their friends. Good food for little money.

■ **Restaurant N° 5** (B glm M MA)
Mon-Fri 11.30-14.30 + 18-24, Sa 18-24h
Thierschstraße 5 *Isartorplatz* ☎ 2421 6150 www.nummer-5.com
Excellent upscale cuisine.

■ **Rubico** (B glm M MA) Tue-Sat 18.30-1h
Klenzestraße 62 ☎ (089) 20 20 78 28 www.rubico.de

■ **Sax** (AC B BF glm M MA OS S WI WL)
Hans-Sachs-Str. 5 ☎ (089) 26 88 35 www.sax-muenchen.de
Gayfriendly Bar and Restaurant in the heart of munich's gay Glockenbach quarter.

■ **Wirtshaus zum Isartal** (AC B BF DM glm I LM M MA NR OS PA PK S VEG WL) 11-1, Sat & Sun 10-1h
Brudermühlstraße 2 ☎ (089) 77 21 21
💻 www.wirtshaus-zum-isartal.de

■ **Zum Alten Markt** (B glm M MA OS) Mon-Sat 11h-midnight
Dreifaltigkeitsplatz 3 *Near Viktualienmarkt* ☎ (089) 29 99 95
💻 www.zumaltenmarkt.de
Traditional restaurant in the heart of the city. Old wooden interior. Bavarian cuisine of high standard.

SEX SHOPS/BLUE MOVIES

■ **Atlantic City** (AC B G MA S VS)
Mon-Thu 9-2, Fri & Sat 9-5, Sun & holidays 11-2h
Schillerstraße 3 ☎ (089) 59 42 91
Man's Planet on 1st floor (G). Part of the Beate Uhse sex department store.

■ **Buddy Shop** (DR G VS)
Shop: Mon-Tue 12-19, Wed-Fri -24, Sat 11-24, Sun 14-20h
Rumfordstraße 11a ☎ (089) 3265 4912 💻 www.buddy-muenchen.de
Special price for those aged under 27.

■ **Duplexx** (G MA VS) 10-1h
Theresienstraße 130 ☎ (089) 5795 2648 💻 www.duplexx.eu
Cruising club with 12 cabins and 128 programs. Large selection of DVDs.

■ **Erotixx** (GLM m MA t VS) Mon-Thu 10-1, Fri & Sat -3, Sun 14-24h
Poccistraße 2 ☎ (089) 74 64 09 05
💻 www.erotixx24.eu
2 cinemas (straight/gay) and cabins. DVDs for sale and rent.

■ **Follow Me** (cc DR f G MA VS) 10-19.30, Sat -15.30h, closed Sun
Corneliusstraße 32 *U1/U2-Frauenhoferstraße* ☎ (089) 202 12 08

HOUSE OF BOYS

■ **Marcel's Gesellschafterteam München MGM** (B G R)
☎ (089) 39 86 39 💻 www.mgm-muenchen.de
More than 30 young men available. Long running escort service.

SAUNAS/BATHS

■ **Deutsche Eiche** (AC B BF CC DR DU FC G GH I LAB M MC MSG NU OS RR SA SB SH SL SOL T VS WH)
Mon-Thu 12-7, Fri 14-Mon 7h (non-stop)
Reichenbachstraße 13 *Near Gärtnerplatz, tram 17/18* ☎ (089) 23 11 660
💻 www.sauna.deutsche-eiche.com
Fully equipped sauna on 4 floors.

■ **Herren Sauna** (B DR DU G OC p SA) Mon-Sat 11-19h, closed on Sun & public holidays
Dachauer Straße 9a *On the corner Marsstraße, 5 mins from main station*
☎ (089) 515 189 16 💻 www.herrensauna.com
Meeting place for mature men and their admirers. Basic facilities.

■ **M54 Saunaclub** (AC AK b DR FC G GH I LAB m MSG RR SA SB SL SOL VS WE YC) 12-3, Fri & Sat -8h
Müllerstraße 54 *U-Sendlinger Tor* ☎ (089) 89 05 82 16
💻 www.muenchengaysauna.de
Mon: partner day (2-4-1), 1st Thu/month: „foam party", Wed: Happy hour (reduced entrance fee before 18h).

■ **Schwabinger MEN Sauna** (B CC DR DU FC G LAB m MA MSG p RR S SA SB SL SOL ST VS WO) 15h-open end
Düsseldorfer Straße 7 *U2-Scheidplatz / U3-Bonnerplatz*
☎ (089) 307 23 42 💻 www.mensauna.de
Light-spectrum & infrared saunas. Very intimate erotic massages.

MASSAGE

■ **Massage Munich** (AC CC GLM MA MSG)
Daily 9-24h (also on public holidays)
Tal 30, 4th floor *U Marienplatz* ☎ +49 175 – 617 52 55
💻 www.massage-munich.com
full body massage – sensual and medical, tantric, gentle touch

■ **Massage Team München** (CC GLM MA MSG) 10-24h
Buttermelcherstraße 4 ☎ (089) 23 68 45 44
💻 www.massageteammuenchen.com
Massage and cosmetic studio, holistic style, ayurveda, trad. thai massage, classic style, hot stone and cosmetic treatments, solarium.

CINEMA

■ **Mongay @ Atelier** (GLM MA) Mon 21.15h-?
Sonnenstraße 12 ☎ (089) 59 19 83 💻 www.city-kinos.de
Movies with a gender-related theme.

CULTURE

■ **Kunstbehandlung KG** (AC CC GLM MA s)
Mon-Fri 12-14 & 16-20, Sat 11-20h & by appointment, closed on Wed
Müllerstraße 40 ☎ (089) 260 53 99 💻 www.kunstbehandlung.de
Gallery with gay art.

BOOK SHOPS

■ **Bruno's** (! CC G MA) Mon-Sat 10-20h
Thalkirchner Straße 4 ☎ (089) 97 60 38 58 💻 www.brunos.de
Bruno's trendy gay store in Munich with a huge selection of books, DVDs (also rental), toys, underwear, magazines and pride articles.

FASHION SHOPS

■ **Seba's Fashion** (GLM MA) Mon-Fri 11-19, Sat -16h
Angertorstraße 7 ☎ 260 18 005 💻 www.seba-fashion.de
Sportswear, underwear, bathing suits, accessories and more.

LEATHER & FETISH SHOPS

■ **Diburnium Store** (CC G MA) Tue-Fri 15-20, Sat 12-20h
Thalkirchner Straße 5 ☎ (089) 23 88 88 32 💻 www.diburnium.com
Big selection of toys, tools and clothes and online shop. Own workshop for repairs.

■ **Savage Leder** (F g) 11-19h, closed Wed & Sun
Reisingerstraße 5 ☎ (0172) 823 98 50 💻 www.savageleather.com

■ **Spexter** (AC CC DR F G I MA VS) Mon-Sat 10-20h
Müllerstraße 54 ☎ (089) 26 02 48 64 💻 www.spexter.com
Centrally located, popular and well equipped sex-toy-store with a huge selection of leather, rubber and uniforms. Also Bruno Gmünder Depot and organizer of various fetish events.

HOTELS

Belle Blue (AC BF CC GLM I MC PA PK RWS RWT) Reception: 6.30-24h
Schillerstraße 21 *5 mins walking distance from Central station Hauptbahnhof and 15 Minutes from city centre-Marienplatz* ☏ (089) 550 62 60
www.hotel-belleblue.com
A completely rebuilt and renovated hotel offering you a unique and refreshing atmosphere centrally situated in Munich. Free Wifi, city map and complimentary coffee or tea.

Carat Hotel & Apartments (AC B CC glm I MA PA PK RWS RWT) 24hrs
Lindwurmstraße 13 *U-Sendlinger Tor* ☏ (089) 23 03 80
www.carat-hotel-muenchen.de
Gay-friendly property in the main gay area. Free breakfast and wlan.

Cortiina (B glm H I MA RWS RWT)
All year, check in from 15, check out to 12 (Sun to 13h)
Ledererstrasse 8 *Zwischen Viktualienmarkt, Marienplatz und Maximilianstrasse* ☏ (089) 2422 49 0 www.cortiina.com
New design hotel in the heart of the old town close to gay areas.

Deutsche Eiche (AC B BF CC GLM I M MA PK RWS RWT) All year
Reichenbachstraße 13 *Near Gärtnerplatz, tram 17/18-Reichenbachplatz*
☏ (089) 2311 660 www.deutsche-eiche.com
Central location. All 36 rooms with shower/WC, TV and phone. Restaurant and gay-sauna (reduced entrance-fee) also in the building. New: luxury suite (55 m²), separate apartment (55 m², across the street).

Louis Hotel (AC B cc glm I M MSG PA RWS RWT SA VA WO) All year
Viktualienmarkt 6 *U-Marienplatz* (089) 4111 90 80 www.louis-hotel.com

Moosbeck Alm All year
☏ (08867) 912 00 www.moosbeck-alm.com
☞ *Rottenbuch.*

Müller (BF CC glm I PA PK RWS RWT VA) Reception 6-23h
Fliegenstraße 4 *U-Sendlinger Tor, 100 m from hotel* ☏ (089) 232 38 60
www.hotel-mueller-muenchen.de
Small and sophisticated hotel in the main gay area. The hotel is a 3-star city hotel with a friendly atmosphere and individual service.

Pension Eulenspiegel (BF cc glm I MA PK RWS RWT VA)
Müllerstraße 43a *U-Sendlinger Tor* ☎ (089) 26 66 78
www.pensioneulenspiegel.de

Winter's Hotel München Am Hauptbahnhof
(BF CC H m MA NR RWS RWT WI) all year, 24hours
Arnulfstraße 12 ☎ (089) 55139 www.winters.de
Centrally located at the Munich main station, only a few meters away from town hall, Stachus, Hofbräuhaus and other well known sights.

GUEST HOUSES

Pension Gärtnerplatz (BF cc glm H I PK RWB RWS RWT) All year
Klenzestraße 45 *U-Fraunhoferstraße* ☎ (089) 202 51 70
www.pensiongaertnerplatz.de
A small, family-run hotel located in the centre of Munich, located between the old city center and the river Isar. All the guestrooms are non-smoking with a private bath, telephone, satellite-TV as well as WLAN-access. A rich breakfast is available with assorted, mostly local organic products from the surrounding areas.

Pension Seibel (AC BF CC glm m MA RWS RWT VA)
All year, reception 7-22h
Reichenbachstraße 8 *Viktualienmarkt, U/S-Marienplatz*
☎ (089) 231 91 80 www.seibel-hotels-munich.de
Simple Hotel in the heart of the gay scene.

FETISH GROUPS

■ **MLC München e.V.** (F G MA P)
Postfach 33 01 63 ☎ (089) 38 89 94 99
🖳 www.mlc-munich.de
The „Münchner Löwen Club" is one of the largest non-profit leather and fetish organizations in Europe. More than 100 events per year. Regular fetish parties at „UnderGround" (MLC club location), at the Starkbierfest (Mar) and the Oktoberfest (Sep).

HEALTH GROUPS

■ **Münchener Aids-Hilfe** Mon-Thu 10-16, Fri -14h
Lindwurmstraße 71 *U3/U6-Goetheplatz* ☎ (089) 54 333 0
🖳 www.muenchner-aidshilfe.de
HIV counselling and testing.

SWIMMING

-Ismaning bridge (between Garching & Ismaning)
-Englischer Garten (g NU) (Schönfeld Wiese at Eisbach)
-Großhesseloher Brücke (1 km north of the bridge between river Isar and the channel. P at Conwentzstaße, cross the channel on the pedestrian bridge. Cruising to the right, around sunset)
-Pupplinger Au (WE) (Near Wolfratshausen, follow the signs to „Klärwerk Weidach", where the rivers Isar and Loisach meet)
-Pucher Meer, west of Munich. On the slopes at the back of the naked sunbathing area (FKK) which is popular with many gay men.

CRUISING

-Englischer Garten (Entrance at Lerchenfeldstraße/Prinzregentenstraße proceed to the bridge, lots of action) Stay away from the childrens playground as there are many police raids here – unfriendly police!
-Luitpoldpark (facility at Scheidplatz, cruising on the hill)
-Following underground stations: U-Max-Weber-Platz, U-Stieglmaierplatz, U-Westendstraße,
U-Theresienwiese (popular),
-Kolumbusplatz
-Odeonsplatz
-Innsbrucker Ring
-Toilets at Lerchenauer See.

Mühlhausen ☎ 03601

BARS

■ **Nische** (AC B g m MA) Mon-Sat 15-24, Sun 16-22h
Schaffentorstraße 26 *Near centre* ☎ (03601) 42 41 07

Münster ☎ 0251

GAY INFO

■ **KCM Schwulenzentrum Münster eV** (b D G I MA) Wed 20-24h
Am Hawerkamp 31 ☎ (0251) 66 56 86 🖳 www.kcm-muenster.de
See www.kcm-muenster.de for party information.

BARS

■ **Café Garbo** (B glm I M MA OS) 15-1, Sun 10-23h
c/o Cinema, Warendorfer Straße 47 ☎ (0251) 30 300
🖳 www.cinema-muenster.de
■ **Na und** (B d G MA) 21-?h, closed Mon
Sonnenstraße 43 *Bus-Bült* ☎ (0251) 430 13 🖳 naund-ms.de

DANCECLUBS

■ **Emergency-Party** (B D GLM OS YC) 2nd Sat/month 23-?h
Am Hawerkamp 31 *Near KCM and Münsterland Hall at Fusion Club*
🖳 www.emergency-party.de
Greatest monthly party event in Münster for gays, lesbians and their friends.
■ **Navigaytion @ Go-Go Roseclub** (B D GLM MA)
1st Fri/month 22-?h
Servatiiplatz 1 *Close to main station* ☎ (0251) 45726
🖳 www.gogo-roseclub.de

SEX SHOPS/BLUE MOVIES

■ **Erotik World** (g MA VS) Mon-Sat 10-24, Sun 11-24h
Wolbecker Straße 1
Gay cabins.
■ **Erotikuss** (AC CC G MA VS) Mon-Fri 11.30-19.30, Sat 12-17h
Mauritzstraße 20 *Opp. Karstadt-Sport* ☎ (0251) 51 14 61

SAUNAS/BATHS

■ **Insel. Die** (B CC DR DU FC G M MA MSG OS p PI RR s SA SB SH SL SOL VS) 13-24, Sat -3h
Geringhoffstraße 46-48 *MS-Süd, Mecklenbeck, bus-Mersmannstiege*
☎ (0251) 78 64 58 🖳 www.dieinselsauna.de
1000 m² sauna with jail, erotic jungle, golden shower area, sling, play area, and lots of special events.

SWIMMING

-Gelmer (NU) (canal bridge „KÜ", unused part of the Dortmund-Ems-canal)
-"Hügel" (hill): Promenade, corner Kreuzschanze/Buddenturm from 23h on.

Mönchengladbach ☎ 02161

BARS

■ **Highlight** (AC B GLM MA OS p) 21-2, Fri -3, Sat -5h, closed Tue
Gasthausstraße 68-70 ☎ (02161) 272 37 16 🖳 www.highlight-mg.de
■ **Liberty** (B d GLM MA) Wed 20-3, Fri & Sat -5, Sun 17-3h
Aachener Straße 24 *Old market* ☎ (02161) 17 93 81
🖳 www.liberty4u.de

SEX SHOPS/BLUE MOVIES

■ **New Man im WOS-Markt** (CC DR G MA VS) 10-24, Sun 12-24h
Hindenburgstraße 201 *Opp. main railway station* ☎ (02161) 92 66 60

Neubrandenburg ☎ 0395

GAY INFO

■ **Begegnungszentrum Initiative Rosa-Lila** (GLM I MA T) Tue, Wed, Thu 14-18, 1st Sat/month 11-14; Counselling: Tue 14-18 & Thu 9-11h
Neustrelitzer Straße 71 *Centre, near Friedrich-Engels-Ring*
☎ (0395) 563 86 30 (Meetingcentre) 💻 www.rosalila.de
Gay and lesbian centre with big library (7000 books), counselling, information and shop. Different groups and activities.

BARS

■ **Papagei** (B d GLM H MA) Tue-Sat 18-1h
Morgenlandstraße 25 *Jahnviertel, next to station, 5 mins to town centre*
☎ (0395) 566 51 57 💻 www.papagei-gaybar.de
3rd Sat/month disco.

GUEST HOUSES

■ **Nobel-Hobel Pension** (B BF GLM M MA PA RWS RWT)
Morgenlandstraße 25 *Jahnviertel, next to station, 5 mins to town centre*
☎ (0395) 566 51 57 💻 www.pension-nobel-hobel.de

CRUISING

-Wallabschnitt (Friedländer Tor → Fangturm)
-Tollensee (summertime).

Nürnberg ☎ 0911

PUBLICATIONS

■ **NSP – Lesbischwules Magazin für Nordbayern** (GLM)
Breite Gasse 76 ☎ (0911) 42 34 57 11 💻 www.n-s-p.de
Gay info-website.

SHOWS

■ **Paradies Revue Theater** (B CC glm MA ST)
Shows 20.30h, Sun & Mon closed
Bogenstraße 26 ☎ (0911) 44 39 91 💻 www.paradies-cabaret.de
Plushy ambience and good shows. Reservation from 18.30h.

BARS

■ **Alt Prag** (B G MA) 11h-open end, Sun & public holidays 15-24h
Hallplatz 29 ☎ (0911) 24 33 41
Tiny, rusty bar.

■ **Bas. La** (B GLM m MA OS R) 11-open end
Hallplatz 31 ☎ (0911) 22 22 81 💻 www.einfachso-nürnberg.de
Rent bar.

■ **Bert's** (B GLM m MA)
Mon & Tue 19-1, Fri & Sat -2, Sun 15-1h, closed on Wed & Thu
Wiesenstraße 85 ☎ (0911) 43 13 555 💻 www.berts-nuernberg.de

■ **Einfachso** (B GLM MA) 18h-open end
Klaragasse 28 💻 www.einfachso-nürnberg.de
Small rustic bar.

■ **Kloster** (B d GLM MA S) Sun-Fri 17-1, Sat 14-3h
Obere Wörthstraße 19 ☎ (0911) 20 99 75 💻 www.das-kloster.eu
No mainstream bar!

■ **Petit-Café** (B G MA) 22-5h
Hinterm Bahnhof 24 ☎ (0911) 454 118
Smoking club.

■ **Pigalle Schlagerbar** (B GLM MA)
Sun-Mon, Wed+Thu 19-2, Fri & Sat -3h
Pfeifergasse 2a ☎ (0911) 234 2603 💻 www.pigalle-schlagerbar.de

■ **Salon Regina** (B glm MA) 10-1h
Fürther Straße 64 ☎ 929 1799 💻 www.salonregina.de

■ **Savoy** (B G m MC OS) 19-3, Fri & Sat 20-4h, closed Sun & Mon
Bogenstraße 45 ☎ (0911) 45 99 45 💻 www.savoy-nbg.de

■ **Smiley** (B GLM MA) Wed-Sun 20-2h
Johannesgasse 59 ☎ (0911) 660 40 43 💻 www.smiley-bar.de

■ **Toy Bar** (B DR GLM MA VS) Mon-Sun 18-5h
Luitpoldstraße 14-16 ☎ 241 9600

MEN'S CLUBS

■ **Am Pranger** (B DR F G MA p) 20-3, Fri & Sat -4, Sun 16-3h
Ottostraße 4 💻 www.pranger-nbg.de

■ **F*Bar** (B DR F G MA p) Wed & Thu 21-2, Fri & Sat -4h
Ottostraße 28 ☎ (0911) 237 504 09 💻 www.f-bar.de

CAFES

■ **Balazzo Brozzi** (B d GLM M MA OS S)
Mon-Sat 9-23, Sun -21h, closed every first Mon in month
Hochstraße 2 ☎ 288 482 💻 www.balazzobrozzi.de

■ **Cartoon** (B GLM I m MA OS) 11-1, Fri & Sat -2, Sun 14-1h
An der Sparkasse 6 ☎ (0911) 22 71 70 💻 www.cafe-cartoon.de

■ **Fatal** (B BF GLM M MA OS) 9-1h
Jagdstraße 16 ☎ (0911) 39 63 63
Becomes more gay in the evening.

■ **Literaturhaus-Café** (B glm M MA S) 9-1h
Luitpoldstraße 6 ☎ (0911) 234 26 58 💻 www.literaturhaus-nuernberg.de
Stylish and large café with good breakfast and meal-selection, also lots of books and magazines to choose from and relax.

■ **Neue Zentrale** (B bf GLM M OS YC) 9-1h
Hans-Sachs-Gasse 10 ☎ (0911) 24 13 14 💻 linda-neue.de/zentrale

■ **Treibhaus** (B GLM M MA)
Mon-Wed 8-1, Thu+Fri -2, Sat 9-2, Sun 9.30-1h
Karl Grillenbergerstraße 28 ☎ 223 041 💻 www.cafe-treibhaus.de

■ **Zeit & Raum** (B BF glm m MA OS) 9-2h
Wespennest 2 ☎ (0911) 227 406 💻 www.zeiti.net
Stylish french-oriental breakfast-cafe.

DANCECLUBS

■ **Parkcafé** (B D GLM MA OS)
Berliner Platz 9 ☎ (0911) 5974 485 💻 www.parkcafe.com
Home of the parties „Pink Friday" and „Pink Saturday" on irregular dates. See www.parkcafe.com for details.

■ **Pink Monkeys Club** (B D GLM MA S) Sat 23h-open end
Innere Laufer Gasse 11 @ *Panicroom*
Entry from 21yrs or older, check out website for dates: www.pinkmonkeys-club.de

■ **Rosa Hirsch** (B D f GLM MA S VS WE)
Vogelweiherstraße 66 @ *Hirsch* ☎ (0911) 42 94 14
💻 www.der-hirsch.de
Regular queer parties, check www.rosawebworld.de for details.

■ **Rosa Planet** (B D GLM MA S)
Klingenhofstraße 40 @ *Planet* 💻 www.rosawebworld.de
3 floors. Details on www.rosawebworld.de

■ **Schlampenfest** (B D GLM MA S)
Josephsplatz 10 @ *Nachtcafé Planet Earth* 💻 www.schlampenfest.de
Funny gay party on various dates. See www.schlampenfest.de for details.

RESTAURANTS

■ **Eleon** (B DM glm H M MA NR OS PA VEG WL) 17-1h, closed Mon
Wiesentalstraße 1 ☎ (0911) 419 36 62 💻 www.eleon-online.de
Traditional greek food.

■ **Estragon** (CC GLM M MA S) 11-23, Sat & Sun 17-23h, closed Mon
Jakobstraße 19 ☎ (0911) 241 80 30 💻 www.estragon-nuernberg.de
Mediterranean cuisine.

■ **Gasthaus Pegnitztal** (DM glm M MA OS RES VEG WL) Mon-Fri 11.30-15 & 17.30-23, Sat 17.30-23, Sun 11.30-23h
Deutschherrnstraße 31 ☎ (0911) 26 44 44
💻 www.gasthaus-pegnitztal.de
Traditional and vegetarian cuisine. Party service available. Sun breakfast brunch. Also party service.

■ **Palais Schaumburg** (B glm M MA OS) Sun-Fri 11.30-1, Sat 14-1h
Kernstraße 46 ☎ (0911) 260 043 💻 www.palaisschaumburg.de

■ **Tibet** (B glm M MA) 17-1h
Johannisstraße 18 ☎ (0911) 300 07 54 💻 www.cafe-tibet.de

■ **Wacht Am Rhein** (B GLM M MA) 24-open end
Klaragasse 22 ☎ 226 475 💻 www.die-wacht.de
Late night restaurant and bar. Kitchen open 24-3h.

SEX SHOPS/BLUE MOVIES

■ **In Man im Stage 2000** (DR G MA VS) 17-5h
Luitpoldstraße 12 ☎ (0911) 240 57 39
Gay cruising in the basement.

■ **New Man im WOS** (AC CC DR G MA VS) 10-24, Sun 12-24h
Luitpoldstraße 11 ☎ (0911) 20 34 43
Nice cruising, some younger gays also.

■ **Video-Club 32** (CC DR G MA VS) 14-22h
Tafelfeldstraße 32 ☎ (0911) 44 15 66
Very small and intimate video shop with crusing area.

SAUNAS/BATHS

■ **Chiringay** (B BF CC DR DU FC G m MA MSG OS p RR SA SB SH SOL VS) 14-24, Fri & Sat -8h
Comeniusstraße 10 *U-Hauptbahnhof* ☎ (0911) 44 75 75
🖳 www.chiringay-nuernberg.de
Nice sauna on 2 floors, smoking permitted, open air terrace.

■ **Saunaclub 67** (b DR FC FH G GH MA p RR SA SL SOL VS WO) 13-24, Fri 13-Sun 24h (non-stop)
Pirckheimerstraße 67 *North of the city, tram 9, bus 46/47-Maxfeldstraße, entrance in courtyard* ☎ (0911) 35 23 46 🖳 www.sauna67.de

MASSAGE

■ **abi vital Massagepraxis & Pension** (glm MA) by appointment
Amalienstraße 15 ☎ (0911) 33 66 15
Different types of professional (medical) massage, physiotherapy, psychological counselling & hypnosis. Gay literature & gay info available.

CONDOM SHOPS

■ **Condomeria. La** (cc g) Mon-Sat 10.30-19h
Ludwigstraße 57 ☎ (0911) 23 27 84 🖳 www.lacondomeria.de

GENERAL GROUPS

■ **Fliederlich** (GLM) Cafe Sun 14-17.30h
Breite Gasse 76 ☎ (0911) 19 446 (Wed 19-21h) 🖳 www.fliederlich.de

FETISH GROUPS

■ **Nürnberger Lederclub e.V. (NLC)** (b DR F G MA P)
1st Sat/month, entry 21-23h
Schnieglinger Straße 264, Keller ☎ (0911) 891 75 28
🖳 www.nlc-nuernberg.de
Keller party once a month; check out www.nlc-nuernberg.de for detailed information.

SWIMMING

-Freibad Langsee (NU) (S-Mögeldorf, direction Freibad Langsee, there is a nudist meadow)
-Birkensee (NU) (along the street from Schwaig to Diepersdorf near highway crossing Nürnberg an der Straße von Schwaig nach Diepersdorf)
-Freizeitbad „Palm Beach".

CRUISING

-Municipal park (summer only)
-Rosengarten (r, opp. opera house, popular)
-Main railway station (ayor R, also in subway)
-U-Plärrer
-U-Frankenstraße (also WC in fornt of the Frankencenter, near the bus station, 6-24h)
-U-Maximilianstraße (WC, afternoon)
-In Fürth, near Nürnberg, U-Jakobinenstraße.

Oberhausen ☎ 0208

DANCECLUBS

■ **Bang!** (B D GLM YC) 3rd Sat/month 22-?h
c/o Jugend- und Kulturzentrum Druckluft e.V., Am Förderturm 27 *Near main railway station* ☎ (0208) 85 24 54 🖳 www.bang.de
On 3 floors, mainstream music.

SEX SHOPS/BLUE MOVIES

■ **Gaykino Höhepunkt** (CC DR G MA VS)
9.30-23, Sun and public holidays 16-23h
Nohlstraße 25 ☎ (0208) 810 61 42 🖳 sexshop-oberhausen.de/gay.html

CRUISING

-Bero-Zentrum
-Grillopark (near main railway station & Schwartzstraße)

Oeversee ☎ 04630

HOTELS

■ **Genießer Hotel Historischer Krug** (b BF CC d H I M MSG NG OS PA PI PK RWB RWS RWT s SA SB SOL WH) All year
Grazer Platz 1 *9 km south of Flensburg* ☎ (04630) 94 00
🖳 www.historischer-krug.de
Four star hotel located on Flensburg's doorstep, with excellent connections to Hamburg, Sylt and Denmark. An oasis for gourmets and wellness fans.

Offenbach ☎ 069

SEX SHOPS/BLUE MOVIES

■ **Josefines Sexkino** (DR g VS) Mon-Sat 9-23.30, Sun 12-23.30h
Platz der Deutschen Einheit 3 🖳 www.josefines-sexkino.de

Offenburg ☎ 0781

BARS

■ **Tabu** (AC B D F GLM m MA) Thu & Sun 20-1, Fri-Sat 21-?, Mon-Tue closed
Hauptstraße 102 ☎ (0781) 742 43 🖳 www.tabu-gayclub.de

SEX SHOPS/BLUE MOVIES

■ **Erotik-Kino-Center** (AC CC G MA T VS)
9.30-24, Sun and public holidays 16-24h
Unionrampe 6 *Near main station* ☎ (0781) 235 53
🖳 www.erotik-kino-center.de
With a great gay section.

■ **Novum** (b glm MA)
Marlener Straße 3a *Next to Club OM* ☎ (0781) 639 3144
Sex-cinema with glory holes.

Oldenburg ☎ 0441

BARS

■ **Hempels Kneipencafé** (B GLM MA T)
Mon (GLM) 20.30-24, Thu (L) 20-23, Fri (GLM) -24h
Ziegelhofstraße 83 *At „Lesben- und Schwulenzentrum"*
☎ (0441) 777 59 90 🖳 www.naund-oldenburg.de

■ **Schwarzer Bär** (AC B D DR f G MA p WE)
Bar: Tue-Thu 21-?, disco: Fri-Sat 21-?h
Donnerschweer Straße 50 *100 m from main station, northern exit*
☎ (0441) 885 07 37 🖳 www.schwarzerbaerol.de

DANCECLUBS

■ **Alhambra** (B D G MA)
Hermannstraße 83 ☎ (0441) 144 02 🖳 www.alhambra.de
Regular gay parties on Saturdays: „Rosa Disco" (see www.naund-oldenburg.de), „Männerfabrik" (F, see www.maennerfabrik. de) and „Homophilias". Check www.alhambra.de for party details.

■ **EX²** (AC B D glm MA WE) Fri & Sat 22-5h
Stau 39-41 *Near main railway station* ☎ (0162) 300 76 57
🖳 www.ex-oldenburg.de
No entrance fee or minimum consumption. Danceclub on 2 levels. Sometimes privat parties. Check www.ex-oldenburg.de for details.

SAUNAS/BATHS

■ **K13 Club Sauna** (B DR DU G m MSG OS RR S SA SB SOL VS)
15-24, Sat 14-Sun 24h (non-stop)
Klävemannstraße 13 *Opposite main railway station* ☎ (0441) 998 74 99
🖳 www.k13-sauna.de

CRUISING

-Park behind the theatre
-Cäcilienpark
-Bar 28
-Blankenburger See (southside)

Osnabrück ☏ 0541

BARS

■ **Confusion** (B GLM) Tue-Thu 19.30-2, Fri-Sun 19.30-?h
Pottgraben 27 ☏ (0541) 350 44 88 🖳 www.confusion-online.eu
■ **Mecs** (B G MA) 20-2, Fri -3, Sat -?, Sun 19-24h, closed Mon
Pottgraben 27 ☏ (0541) 350 44 88 🖳 www.mecs-online.de

CAFES

■ **Larimar** (B DM GLM M MA VEG)
Mon-Thu 11.30-14 & 17-22.30, Fri 16-22.30, Sun 14-22.30h
Hermannstraße 6 *Cnr. Spindelstraße* ☏ (0541) 506 38 03
🖳 www.cafelarimar.de

DANCECLUBS

■ **Gay Rose Club** (B D GLM MA) 3rd Sat/month 22-?h
Rosenplatz 23 *In the renovated cinema Rosenhof* ☏ (0178) 326 08 48
🖳 www.gay-rose-club.de
■ **OS-Gay-Night @ Five Elements** (B D G YC)
1st Sat/month 22.30-?h
Hamburger Straße 20 🖳 www.os-gay-night.de

SEX SHOPS/BLUE MOVIES

■ **Men's Life Erotik Shop** (AC DR f G MA VS) Mon-Thu 11-23, Fri & Sat -24, Sun 14-24h
Möserstraße 39 *100 m from railway station* ☏ (0541) 202 08 46
🖳 www.menslife.de

CRUISING

-Raiffeisenpark (ayor) (opposite main station & P across the street, popular)
-Gertrudenberg/Bürgerpark (near Hasetorbahnhof around Rosengarten, popular WE nights).

Paderborn ☏ 05251

BARS

■ **Susis Unverschämt** (B d GLM m MA p S ST WE) Wed-Sun 19-?h
Franziskanergasse 4 *Near Franziskaner Church* ☏ (05251) 73 02 02

Passau ☏ 0851

BARS

■ **Selly's** (B GLM M MA OS) Mon-Thu 19-1, Fr 19-3, Sat 14-3, Sun 14-24h
Bratfischwinkel 5 ☏ (0851) 934 78 44 🖳 www.sellys.de

GENERAL GROUPS

■ **L.u.S.T. (Der Lesben- und Schwulentreff an der Uni Passau)** (GLM YC)
Innstrasse 41 ☏ (0851) 5090 🖳 www.students.uni-passau.de
Write an eMail to get more infos.

CRUISING

-town hall
-Innpromenade (between Innsteg & Krankenhaus evenings)
-Facilities at main station (ayor).

Pforzheim ☏ 07231

SEX SHOPS/BLUE MOVIES

■ **Bal-d-amour** (DR g MA VS) 10-23, Sun 15-23h
Westliche Karl-Friedrichstraße 129 *Near Messplatz* ☏ (07231) 768 94 54
🖳 www.bal-d-amour.de
■ **Erotik Point** (CC DR g MA VS) 10-23, Sun 14-23h
Am Waisenhausplatz 26 *Town centre, beside theatre* ☏ (07231) 35 67 39
🖳 www.erotikpoint.info
Cruising area and glory holes.

CRUISING

-Municipal hall & Theatre (Enzufer)
-Schloßpark (across main station)
-Turnplatz
-Meßplatz
-Grösseltal, on B294 direction Bad Wildbad, 2km after Birkenfeld left turn, direction Engelsbrand, after the bridge P on the left hand side
-Kaufland, upper parking-deck after 20h
-Wilferdinger Höhe, on the public P next to supermarket, evenings after 22h.

Potsdam ☏ 0331

BARS

■ **Leander** (B CC glm I MA OS VS) 12.30-2.30h
Benkertstraße 1 *Tram Nauener Tor, Dutch quarter* ☏ (0331) 58 38 408
🖳 www.leander-potsdam.de
■ **Quartier** (B glm MA)
Charlottenstraße 29 ☏ (0331) 280 59 40
„Kreuz & Quer"-Party (GLM) once a month. Ring for info.
■ **Unscheinbar** (B glm MA)
Friedrich-Ebert-Straße 118 ☏ (0331) 270 06 42

CRUISING

-Colonnade at the Friedenskirche (Park Sanssouci)
-Bassinplatz (near the houses)

Ravensburg ☏ 0751

BARS

■ **Deluxe** (B d GLM m MA) Wed & Thu 19-24, Fri & Sat 20-3, Sun 18-24h
In der Höll 35 *Next to Oase* ☏ (0751) 354 5619
Cozy gaybar with special events and themeparties.

HEALTH GROUPS

■ **AIDS Hilfe Bodensee Oberschwaben** (glm MA)
Frauenstrasse 1 ☏ (0751) 354 072

Recklinghausen ☏ 02361

SEX SHOPS/BLUE MOVIES

■ **Erotikshop Wolf** (AC CC g VS) 10-21, Sun 14-21h
Dortmunder Straße 1 ☏ (02361) 456 01

CRUISING

-Am Neumarkt (Recklinghausen Süd), toilets at Marktplatz (take bus 205 from main railway station to Neumarkt)
-Rathauspark (OC)
-Erlbruckpark (at town hall)
-Parking at Freibad Mollbeck

Regensburg ☏ 0941

BARS

■ **Jeans** (AC B f GLM MA s) Sun-Thu 21-1, Fri & Sat 21-3h
Glockengasse 1 ☏ (0941) 517 82

CAFES

■ **Allora!** (B GLM M MA) Mon-Sun 10-1h
Engelburgergasse 18 *Near Arnulfplatz* ☏ (0941) 584 07 83
🖳 www.allora-regensburg.de
■ **Café Schierstadt** (B GLM MA)
An der Schierstadt 1 ☏ (0941) 8700 762

DANCECLUBS

■ **Scala Club** (B D GLM MA S) Various dates
Gesandtenstraße 6 www.scalaclub.de
Every Thursday „GayDay" from 23-3h, every last Sat „SaturGay" party check www.scalaclub.de for more infos.

SEX SHOPS/BLUE MOVIES

■ **Erotic Markt** (glm MA VS) Mon-Sat 9-24, Sun 12-24h
Franz Hartelstraße 6 *A3 exit University Regensburg* ☎ (0941) 7849 36610
■ **Erotik-Planet** (b g MA VS) 11-23h
Friedenstraße 14 *Opp. arcades* ☎ (0941) 750 1225

CRUISING

-Der Wackel (Park at Albertstraße. Near main railway station, 22-?h)
-P Neue Bahnhofsstraße/Margaretenstraße
-Vor der Grieb (opposite »Sudhaus«, -18h)
-City park (Prüfeningerstraße, -18h)
-University (at Audimax, entrance K)

Reutlingen ☎ 07121

BARS

■ **Club Apollo e.V.** (B d GLM MA) Wed & Fri 20.30-24h
Dachsweg 2 *Near Hofbühlhalle* ☎ (07121) 157 25
www.apollo-club-reutlingen.de
Cosy meetingplace for clubmembers and their friends.

GENERAL GROUPS

■ **schwubert** (GLM MA) 1st and 3rd Wed from 19.30h
Unter den Linden 23 *@ Café Nepomuk* www.schwubert.de
Gay-Lesbian group in Reutlingen near Stuttgart. Also organiser of irregular gaylesbian partyevents.

Rosenheim ☎ 08031

RESTAURANTS

■ **Jägerstüberl** (b d f glm m MA s) 13-?, Sun and public holidays 20-?h
Nicolaistraße 13 *Town centre* ☎ (08031) 346 65
www.jaegerstueberl-rosenheim.de

CRUISING

-Park at Loretowiese, facilities.

Rostock ☎ 0381

BARS

■ **b sieben** (B GLM MA) 18-?h
Am Burgwall 7 *Northern historic city* ☎ (0381) 3644 959 www.bsieben.de
■ **Klönstuv** (B glm m MA) 20-?h
Am Leuchtturm 18 *Opp. „Hotel am Leuchtturm"* ☎ (0381) 519 24 95
www.kloenstuv.de

DANCECLUBS

■ **Studentenkeller** (B D GLM MA)
Universitätsplatz 5 www.schwules-rostock.de
„Gay Keller Parties". Check www.schwules-rostock.de for info.

SAUNAS/BATHS

■ **Nordic Steam** (B DR DU G MA RR SA SB SH SOL VS)
Mon & Wed 11-24, Fri & Sat 18-2h
Badstüber Straße 3 ☎ (0381) 25 22 39 95 www.nordic-steam.de
Small, but clean and friendly.

GUEST HOUSES

■ **Unser Bauernhof** (BF G m MA NU OS PA RWS SA) All year
Stralsunder Chaussee 36 *Wiepkenhagen, 40 km from Rostock, 30 km from Stralsund* ☎ (03 82 25) 304 18 www.regenbogenkate.de
Farm house 20 km from the sea. Five rooms with shared, one with private bath, mini-bar, phone, heating, own key. Parking and TV-room. Take advantage of the sauna.

SWIMMING

-Markgrafenheide (! NU) (from Warnemünde take the car ferry to Hohe Düne, from there go 5 km to Markgrafenheide, then to the camping ground P. Go further on foot for ca. 20 mins, on the beach go 20 mins to the east)
-Warnemünde (10 mins west of tower 6 of the DLRG)
-Elmenhorst (road to the beach, to P then 10 mins to the west, at the rocky beach)
-Strand Diedrichshagen (between Stolteraa and Diedrichshagen/Hundestrand).

CRUISING

-Wall (MA) (between Kröpeliner Tor & Rosengarten)
-University (in main building, ground floor, popular).

Rottenbuch ☎ 08867

HOTELS

■ **Wellness Landhotel Moosbeck Alm** (B BF CC FH glm I M MA MSG NU OS PA PI PK RR RWB RWS RWT SA SB SOL VA WE) All year
Moos 38 *70 km from Munich, between Füssen & Munich, 1.5 km from Rottenbuch* ☎ (08867) 912 00 www.moosbeck-alm.de
Popular gay destination in upper Bavaria. The hotel features 20 rooms, a „Tuscan" wintergarden, boccia and a badminton court. In winter sledge-riding and skiing. Peaceful location with 17.000m² parklands.

Saarbrücken ☎ 0681

BARS

■ **Madame** (B GLM I MA WE) 18-?, Sun 15-?h
Mainzer Straße 4 ☎ (0681) 329 63 www.madame-saarbruecken.de
■ **Mademoiselle** (B GLM I MA) 21-?h
Mainzer Straße 8 ☎ (0681) 390 44 45
■ **Pegalle** (B d GLM MA ST) 19-3h
Bahnhofstraße 1 *30 km NW of Saarbrücken* ☎ (0176) 86 00 99 84
Bar/Lounge with two areas, open for gays/bi/swinger/trans.

MEN'S CLUBS

■ **Boots** (AC B D DR F G MA P S VS) 22-5h
Mainzer Straße 53 ☎ (0681) 614 95 www.bootssb.de

CAFES

■ **History Bistro** (B glm M MA) 15-1h, closed Mon
Obertorstraße 10 ☎ (0681) 390 85 82

DANCECLUBS

■ **Big Ben** (AC B D DR G m MA p ST VS WE) 18.30h-open end
Försterstraße 17 *Near town hall, in the Nauwieser Quarter*
☎ (0175) 44 79 344 www.bigben-sbr.net
■ **GAYS @ blau** (B D DR GLM MA S) 1st Sat 23h-open end
Am Steg 3 *at the Blau Niteclub* www.blau-niteclub.de
Check www.blau-niteclub.de
■ **Heaven @ Seven** (B D GLM MA)
Futterstraße 5-7 www.seven-sb.de
Gay Partyevent once a month, check www.seven-sb.de for details.
■ **Warme Nacht @ Garage** (B D GLM MA) 2nd Sat/month 22-?h
Bleichstraße 3 www.warme-nacht.de

SAUNAS/BATHS

■ **XL Sauna & Lounge** (B CC d DR DU FC G GH I m MA MSG NU OS P RR SA SB SL SOL VS) Sun-Thu 14-23, Fri -2, Sat -8h
Brebacher Landstraße 15 ☎ (0681) 958 16 83 www.xl-sb.de

Schöllnach ☎ 09903

GUEST HOUSES

■ **Mühle. Die** (b BF G NU SA SOL) All year
Englfing 3 ☎ (09903) 562 www.gay-muehle.de
About 30km from Passau, small guest house in the Bavarian Forest with a private atmosphere.

Schömberg ☏ 07084

HOTELS

■ **Haus am Kurpark** (BF cc glm H I MSG OS PA PK RWB RWS RWT) 8-20h
Parkstraße 13 *Behind town hall, next to park* ☏ (07084) 927 80
🖳 www.hotel-hausamkurpark.de
All 40 rooms with balcony, own bath, sat-TV, free W-LAN. Ideal for biking-tours in the Black Forest. Gay owned and only about 60 km southwest of Stuttgart.

Schwerin ☏ 0385

BARS

■ **Saitensprung** (AC B d DR GLM M MA p) 20-?h, Mon-Wed closed
Von-Thünen-Straße 45 ☏ (0385) 71 29 67

DANCECLUBS

■ **Gay Party @ Benno B.** (b d G MA)
Franz-Mehring-Straße 40 *Cnr. Severinstraße, near Central Station*
🖳 www.hot-n-queer.de
Check www.hot-n-queer.de for exact dates.

■ **QueerZone** (B D GLM MA WE) 1st Sat/month 22h-?
Mecklenburgstr. 8 *@ Club M8* ☏ (0385) 555560
🖳 www.QueerZone.de

GUEST HOUSES

■ **Historischer Forsthof zu Zapel** (B BF G I M MA MSG NU OS PA PK RWS RWT SA SB VA VS) All year
Trammer Straße 5 *15 km from Schwerin* ☏ (03863) 522 797
☏ (0152) 531 461 53 (mobile) 🖳 www.gay-gaestehaus.de

GENERAL GROUPS

■ **Klub Einblick e.V.** (b GLM MA) Tue-Sat 17-?
Lübecker Str. 48 ☏ (0385) 55 55 60 🖳 www.klub-einblick.de

SWIMMING

-Schweriner See (Zippendorfer beach)
-Vorbecker See (Bus 6 from Hermann-Duncker-Straße to Vorbeck)
-Kaninchenwerder in the Schweriner See (NU) (take the »Weißen Flotte« ferry from Schloßbrücke or Tippendorf).

CRUISING

-Westuferpromenade Ziegelsee (Dr.-Hans-Wolf-Straße, evenings in summer).

Siegen ☏ 0271

GAY INFO

■ **andersROOM – Lesbischwules Zentrum in Siegen Schwule Initiative Siegen eV** (B d GLM MA s)
Mon-Wed 13-16h, Thu 16-18h
Freudenberger Straße 67 ☏ (0271) 532 97 🖳 www.andersroom.de
Fri: YC (16-27 years) 20-22, Gay-Helpline: Mon 14-16, Thu: 16-18h.

BARS

■ **Incognito** (AC B GLM H MA S) Tue-Sat 20h-late
Hundgasse 12 *At the town hall* ☏ (0271) 575 23
Also guesthouse (www.siegen-uebernachtung.de).

SWIMMING

-Biggesee, official nudist beach towards Attendorn and inofficial nudist beach near Schnüttgenhof pub
-Stadtbad am Löhrtor, discreet cruising on Tue (men only in the straight sauna).

CRUISING

-University, Hölderlin-building, 3rd floor next to the café
-town hall (facilities)
-Schlosspark (parking lot and public facilities).

Sindelfingen ☏ 07031

SEX SHOPS/BLUE MOVIES

■ **Sexteufel** (g) 9-24, Sun 16-24h
Vaihingerstraße 10 *Opp. city hall* ☏ 879 598 🖳 www.sexteufel.info
Cabins with glory holes.

Stralsund ☏ 03831

HOTELS

■ **Hotel Amber** (B BF glm I MA PA PK RWS RWT VA) All year, bar busy from 22h
Heilgeiststraße 50 ☏ (03831) 28 25 80
The cellar bar in this gay owned hotel is the meeting point for the local gay community. Every Wed & Fri „Rainbow Night".

Stuttgart ☏ 0711

GAY INFO

■ **Weissenburg – Schwul/lesbisches Zentrum** (AC b d GLM m MA) Mon-Wed & Fri 19-22, Thu 17-22, Sun 15-22h
Weißenburgstraße 28a *U-Österreichischer Platz* ☏ (0711) 640 44 94
🖳 www.zentrum-weissenburg.de

PUBLICATIONS

■ **Schwulst** (GLM MA)
c/o Buchladen Erlkönig, Nesenbachstraße 52 ☏ (0700) 72 49 85 78
🖳 www.schwulst.de
Magazine for gays and lesbians in Baden-Wurttemberg.

BARS

■ **Alte Münze** (B glm MA r)
Willy-Brandt-Straße 23 *Planetarium, U-Staatsgalerie*

■ **Baou Baou** (B glm MA) 20-0.30h
Gerokstraße 53 ☏ (0711) 24 03 71

■ **Bernstein** (B D GLM M MA) Tue-Sun 16-2h
Pfarrstraße 7 ☏ (0711) 726 91 69 🖳 www.bernstein-stuttgart.de

■ **Boots** (AC B DR f G MA VS) 19-2, Fri & Sat -3h
Bopserstraße 9 ☏ (0711) 236 47 64 🖳 www.boots-stuttgart.de

■ **Finkennest** (AC B G I m MA MSG r SNU T)
Mon-Fri 16-2, Sat-Sun-4h
Weberstraße 11d *Near „Feuerwache Süd"* ☏ (0711) 248 32 48

■ **Goldener Heinrich** (B G MA)
Leonhardstraße 3

■ **Jakobstube** (B GLM MA r) Sun-Thu 10-2, Fri & Sat 10-3h
Jakobstraße 6 *U-Rathaus* ☏ (0711) 23 54 82 🖳 www.jakobstube.de
Cosy und rustic location.

■ **Magnus** (B GLM MA S) 18-6h
Rotebühlplatz 4 *Near Kronprinzstraße* ☏ (0711) 223 89 95
🖳 www.magnus-stuttgart.de
Karaoke 22-6h.

■ **Monroe's Pub** (B GLM MA OS) 12-5, Sun 15-5h
Schulstraße 3 *Near Rathaus, upstairs* ☏ (0711) 226 27 70
🖳 www.cafe-monroes.de

■ **Ruben's** (AC bf GLM m MA S SNU ST) 11-1, Fri & Sat 9.30-3h
Geißstraße 13 🖳 www.rubens-home.de
Nice bar and cafe in the old town of Stuttgart, In-location!

MEN'S CLUBS

■ **Eagle** (AC B DR F G MA P VS) 21-2, Fri & Sat -3h
Mozartstraße 51 *U Österreichischer Platz* ☏ (0711) 640 61 83
🖳 www.eagle-stuttgart.com
See www.eagle-stuttgart.com for special theme nights.

■ **GOK** (B d DR F G MA NU P VS WE)
Fri, Sat & before holidays 2h-open end
Gutenbergstraße 106 *Cnr. Rötestraße, city west* ☏ (0711) 601 457 45
🖳 www.gok-stgt.de
Private sex parties.

Treffpunkt Kellergewölbe (B CC DR F G m MA OS P VS)
2nd & last Sat/month 20.30-4h
Blumenstr. 29 *U-Olgaeck* ☏ (0711) 23 33 33 23 www.gay-keller.de
Check www.gay-keller.de for partydates and events. Also location for ero. gen parties!

CAFES

Graf Eberhard (AC B BF CC glm M MA OS)
Sun-Thu 6-24, Fri & Sat -2h
Nesenbachstraße 52 *S-Österreichischer Platz, U-Stadtmitte*
☏ (0711) 24 20 25
Very popular gay cafe. Try the homemade cakes.

Grand Café Planie (B GLM M MA OS) Sun-Thu 8-1, Fri & Sat -2h
Charlottenplatz 17 ☏ 292 553

Pfiff (B GLM M MA) Mon, Tue, Thu-Sat 11.30-14 + 17.30-1h
Bebelstr. 85 *U9 and U4 direction Botnang, stop Vogelsang* ☏ 505 30 980
www.pfiff-stuttgart.de

Zimt & Zucker (B GLM M OS YC) Tue-Fri 12-18, Sat-Sun 10-18h
Weissenburgstr. 2c ☏ 9127 5198

DANCECLUBS

Gaydelight (B D GLM MA)
☏ (0711) 47 03 162 www.gaydelight.de
Several parties in different locations. Check www.gaydelight.de for details.

Kings Club (KC) (B D GLM ST YC) Fri & Sat 22-?, Sun -6h
Calwer Straße 21 *Entrance Gymnasiumstraße* ☏ (0711) 226 45 58
www.kingsclub-stuttgart.de

Laura's Club & Café (B D GLM MA) daily 14-?h
Lautenschlagerstr. 20 www.laurasclub-stuttgart.de
One of the citie's oldest clubs. Thu Karaoke from 21, Fri-Sat dance night from 22h.

Lovepop @ Lehmannclub (AC B D GLM MA)
2nd Sat/month 22-?h
Seidenstraße 20 *U14,4,9, Bus 42/43 Berliner Platz, former Bosch-Area, Basement* ☏ (0711) 806 0910 www.lovepop.info
Special Gay-Event since 2007. See www.lovepop.info for details.

Therapy (B D GLM MA S) Fri on irregular dates
Büchsenstraße 11 *@ AER-Club* www.therapy-party.de
Special Gay-Party in Stuttgart. See website for dates and details.

RESTAURANTS

Bianco e Nero Ristorante (cc DM glm M MC OS VEG WL)
Tue-Fri & Sun 12-14.30 & 18-22.30, Sat 18-22.30h, closed on Mon
Kirchheimer Straße 64a *Sillenbuch* ☏ (0711) 907 54 19
www.biancoenero.de
Very personal and friendly service, exclusive dining experience

SEX SHOPS/BLUE MOVIES

Blue Box (AC DR F G I MA T VS)
Mon-Wed 9-24, Thu-Sat 9-4, Sun 10-24h
Steinstraße 15 *U-Rathaus* ☏ (0711) 470 48 41
www.blueboxstuttgart.de
Cinema and cruising on 2 floors, also cabins. Themed days; 1st Tue/month: TV and female underwear fetish.

Crazy Video Show (G SH VR)
Mon-Thu 9-24, Fri & Sat 9-1, Sun 11-24h
Rotebühlplatz 1 ☏ (0711) 35 14 200

Insider Video (CC G MA) Mon-Sat 12-21.30h
Böblinger Straße 185 *U-Bihlplatz* ☏ (0711) 649 40 23
www.insider-video.de
Large variety of gay DVDs, toys, leather & magazines.

HOUSE OF BOYS

Skyboys (CC G MA) Sun-Thu 10-24, Fri & Sat -2h
Steinstraße 15 *4th floor* ☏ (0711) 414 817 59 www.skyboys.de

SAUNAS/BATHS

Pour Lui (AC AK B DR FC G GH LAB M MA MSG RR SA SB SL VS)
12-2, Sat -3h
Schmidener Straße 51, Bad Cannstatt *Opposite of Hotel Mercure*
☏ (0711) 900 53 91 www.pour-lui.de
Small and intimate.

Viva (B DR FC G GH I M MA MSG RR SA SB SOL VS)
14-24, Fri & Sat -2h
Charlottenstraße 38 *U-Olgaeck* ☏ (0711) 236 84 62
www.vivasauna.de
Spacious sauna with a clean and professional atmosphere. Smokerlounge

BOOK SHOPS

Erlkönig (CC GLM s) Mon-Fri 10-13.30 & 14.30-19, Sat 10-18h
Nesenbachstraße 52 *S/U-Stadtmitte/Rotebühlplatz/Österreichischer Platz*
☏ (0711) 63 91 39 www.gaybooks.de
Books, magazines, cards, CDs, pride articles and lubes. Also mail order.

DVD SHOPS

G-Point (G m) Mon-Sat 11-23h
Rotebühlstraße 163 *S-Schwabstraße* ☏ (0711) 912 716 17
DVD-rental, toys, magazines

HOTELS

Haus am Kurpark
☞ *Schömberg.*

GUEST HOUSES

Gästehaus Ziegler (B BF CC G I MA RWS RWT VA) All year
Blumenstr. 29 *U-Olgaeck* ☏ (0711) 233 33 30
www.hotel-ziegler.com
Nine rooms, buffet breakfast included. Reservation required. Irregular gay parties in the basement.

HEALTH GROUPS

Landesleiter MSM Projekt Gentle Man
Haußmannstraße 6 ☏ (0761) 151 46 64-0 www.gentle-man.eu

CRUISING

-Unterer Schloßgarten (near the Rossebändiger/fountain)
-Mittlerer Schloßgarten (P Planetarium (R), near Café am See, by night only)
-TV tower in Stuttgart-Degerloch (behind the news stand, popular, MA).

Trier ☏ 0651

BARS

Palette (B G m MC p s) 20-4h
Oerenstraße 13b *Near Pauluskirche* ☏ (0651) 426 09
Mixed age bar, friendly barkeeper, nice „living-room"-atmosphere.

Werner's (AC B glm WE) 21-3h
Jüdemerstraße 28 ☏ (0651) 761 08

Winkel. De (B GLM m MA OS) 18-1, Fri-Sat -2h, Sun closed
Johannisstraße 25 *Bus 81/82/83 Karl-Marx-Haus* ☏ (0651) 436 18 78

CAFES

SCHMIT-Z Café (AC B d GLM I m MA OS s)
Café Tue & Thu 15-19, Fri 21-2, Sun 16-20h
Mustorstraße 4 *Bus 2/6/82/87-Mustorstraße* ☏ (0651) 425 14
www.schmit-z.de
Helpline Sun 20-22h.

DANCECLUBS

Homo Sapiens (B D GLM YC)
Zurmaienerstraße 114 www.exhaus.de
Gaylesbian party of the youthgroup. Well established but only 3 partydates per year. Check www.exhaus.de for details.

Homosphère – Gay and Lesbian Party (D GLM MA)
Sep-Jun 3rd Sat/month
☏ (0172) 524 93 64 www.schmit-z.de
Check www.schmit-z.de for locations, partydates and other details.

SEX SHOPS/BLUE MOVIES

Boutique Amour (g MA VS)
Karl-Marx-Str. 70a
Filthy but with gloryholes. In the cinema no gay-films.

Pleasure Shop (DR glm MA VS)
Karl-Marx-Str. 87-89
Sexshop with gay-section, sex-cinemas on 3 screens, integrated video-cabins, many gay guests.

BOOK SHOPS

Gegenlicht (glm) Mon-Wed 9.30-18.30, Thu-Fri -19, Sat -16h
Glockenstraße 10 ☏ (0651) 765 80
www.gegenlicht-buchhandlung.de

GENERAL GROUPS

SchwuFo (G YC) Tue 20h
SCHMIT-Z, Mustorstraße 4 ☏ (0651) 425 14 www.schwufo.de
Local youthgroup

CRUISING

-Palastgarten between Kurfürstliches Palais and Kaiserthermen (r)
-Nells Park
-Mehringer Höhe.

Tübingen ☏ 07071

CRUISING

-Park am Neckar (near Alleenbrücke, at night)
-Public toilets in the university cafeteria (Mensa 1, entrance Wilhelmstraße, 12-14h)
-Stadtpark (between Derendinger Allee and Anlagensee)
-Old Botanical Garden (Wilhelmstraße)
-Bus station (subway Europaplatz)

Ulm ☏ 0731

BARS

4-Friends (B D GLM m MA S) 19-1, Fri & Sat -3h
Brückenstraße 3 *Near Congress Center Maritim Hotel, to Neu-Ulm over the river Danube* ☏ (0731) 97 71 638

Gaybar-Ulm (B DR GLM MA)
Tue & Thu 21-2, Fri & Sat 21-3, Sun 21-2h, Fri-Sun men only!
Erenäcker 18 *In suburb Wiblingen, formerly known as „Wiblinger Eck"*
☏ (0731) 403 7830 www.gaybar-ulm.de
Gaybar in Ulm with darkroom on weekends.

CRUISING

-Rosengarten (underneath Adlerbastei from 22h)
-Donauhalle, tram 1, end station Friedrichsau (during the day)
-Waldbaggersee Senden (summer, all day)
-Herdbrücke

Unna ☏ 02303

DANCECLUBS

Doppelherz @ Lindenbrauerei (B D GLM YC)
2nd Sat/month 23-?h
Massener Straße 33-35 ☏ (02303) 25 11 20
www.lindenbrauerei.de

Villingen-Schwenningen ☏ 07720 & 07

BARS

Club 46a (B D GLM MA) Fri & Sat 21-4, Sun 20-1h
Dauchingerstraße 46a ☏ (07720 & 07721) 639 09

Life pur (B GLM m MA) 18-1, Fri & Sat -3h, Mon closed
Bärengasse 20

SEX SHOPS/BLUE MOVIES

Wali Filmpalast (B DR f g MA VS) Mon-Sat 11-1, Sun 16-1h
Waldstraße 13 ☏ (07720 & 07721) 578 14 www.wali-kino.de

SAUNAS/BATHS

Pfeffermühle (AC B DR DU FH G m MA OS PP RR S SA SB VS)
15-22, Sat & Sun 14-22h, Tue closed
Tuttlinger Str. 4 *Mühlhausen, bus-Mühlhausen/Ried*
☏ (07720 & 07721) 56 69
www.gaysauna-pfeffermuehle.de
Three floors sauna located in a tastefully decorated house. Open air terrace in the garden.

Weimar ☏ 03643

BARS

Warm Up (B G I MA) 19-?h
Ernst-Thälmann-Straße 42 *5 mins from main station*
☏ (03643) 900 777

CRUISING

-Park an der Ilm (between Burgplatz and Platz der Demokratie)
-Wittumspalais

Westerland – Sylt ☏ 04651

BARS

Deja Vue (AC B d glm MA S)
Strandstraße 6-8

Gatz auf Sylt (AC B g MA) 12-?, winter 16-1h
Strandstraße 10 *Pedestrian area* ☏ (04651) 210 06

Nanu (AC B D G MA T) 21-4h
Strandstraße 23 *Pedestrian area* ☏ (04651) 928 01 24
Probably the most crowded gay bar on Sylt.

DANCECLUBS

■ **Kleist-Casino (KC)** (AC B D f GLM MA p r s) 20-?h
Elisabethstraße 1a *Town centre* ☎ (04651) 242 28
🖳 www.kc.gay.disco.sylt.site.ms

SAUNAS/BATHS

■ **Steam Beach Club** (AC B cc DR DU FC G I m MA s SA SB SOL VS)
Tue -Sun 14-24h, closed Mon
Bötticherstraße 3 *5 mins from railway station* ☎ (04651) 83 52 49
🖳 www.steam-sauna.de
Also bio sauna.

HOTELS

■ **Marin-Hotel-Sylt** (BF H MA NG PA RWS RWT) All year
Elisabethstraße 1 *Cnr. Strandstraße* ☎ (04651) 928 00
🖳 www.marinhotel.de
Situated 5 km from the airport. Rooms are partly equipped with kitchenette. All have own bath/WC, TV and phone.

GUEST HOUSES

■ **Haus Hallig** (BF glm I m MA OS PK RWS RWT) All year
Danziger Straße 9 ☎ (04651) 242 13 🖳 www.haus-hallig.de
All rooms with bath/WC. Free WLAN in guest house. Also apartments available.

APARTMENTS

■ **Hussmann Ferienwohnungen** (glm MA)
Andreas-Dirks-Straße 14 ☎ (04651) 836 330 🖳 www.hussmann-sylt.de
40 completely furnished apartments. Central location, close to bars.

Wiesbaden ☎ 0611

BARS

■ **Kuckucksnest** (B glm MA OS) 11.30-open end, Sun 13h-open end
Wilhelmstraße 52 *Entrance on Burgstraße* ☎ (0611) 528 05 00

■ **Robin Hood** (B CC GLM I m MA OS)
12-open end, Sun 15h-open end
Häfnergasse 3 ☎ (0611) 30 13 49 🖳 www.robin-wi.de
Bistro with internet access.

■ **Trend** (AC B f GLM m MA OS) 19-2h
Am Römertor 7 ☎ (0611) 37 30 40 🖳 www.trend-wi.de

SEX SHOPS/BLUE MOVIES

■ **Adam & Eva** (DR g VS) Mon-Sat 10-22h
Rheinstraße 27 ☎ (0611) 580 6766
Mixed erotic shop with cinema and darkroom.

SAUNAS/BATHS

■ **Club-Sauna** (B DR DU G M MA p SA SB SL VS) 14-23h, Tue closed
Häfnergasse 3 *Drei-Lilien-Platz* ☎ (0611) 30 55 74
🖳 www.clubsauna-wi.de
Relatively small, but on three floors.

CRUISING

-Wilhelmstraße/Warmer Damm (WC)
-Reisinger Anlagen (ayor r) (in front of railway station, at night)
-Park Friedrich-Ebert-Allee / Rhein-Main-Halle
-Kurpark/Kurhaus (WC)

Wilhelmshaven

SWIMMING

-Hooksiel-Campingplatz (g MA NU) (left side, best at WE)
-Klein Wangerooge/Banter See (Coming from the P, take the first path to the left. Best time 12-20h, summer only)

CRUISING

-Adalbertplatz/Köhler Park (r)

Wismar ☏ 03841

GENERAL GROUPS

■ **SchuLZ e.V.** (GLM MA)
Mon, Thu 9-12.30, Tue 18-20, Wed, Sun 15-20h
Mühlenstraße 32 *Centre, near harbour* ☏ (03841) 21 47 55
🖳 wismar.aidshilfe.de
Café & library Sun 15-20h.

SWIMMING

-Wohlenberger Wieck
-Ostseebad Boltenhagen
-Insel Poel
-Zierow
-Hohenwieschendorf (Near Grankow)

CRUISING

-Am Lindengarten at Rostocker Tor (by day)

Wolfsburg ☏ 05361

CAFES

■ **Zum Tannenhof** (AC BF CC glm m MA OS s ST)
Mon-Fri 17.30-23, Sat 10-23, Sun 10-15h
Kleiststraße 49 *Near city centre* ☏ (05361) 86 15 86
🖳 www.tannenhof-wolfsburg.de

CRUISING

-Park at the Großen Schillerteich near playground area (evenings)

Wuppertal ☏ 0202

BARS

■ **Keller Club (KC)** (AC B GLM MC)
19-1, Fri & Sat -3h, closed Sun
Schloßbleiche 32 *Elberfeld, entrance Wirmhof* ☏ (0202) 45 55 35
■ **Marlene** (B glm MA) 19-?h, closed Mon
Hochstraße 43 ☏ (0202) 31 64 28

CAFES

■ **Café Creme** (AC B bf glm M MA) 8-24, Fri & Sat -?h
Briller Straße 3 ☏ (0202) 304 363
■ **Espresso & More** (B BF glm I M MA OS) Mon-Sat 9.30-?h
Schöne Gasse 6 ☏ (0202) 976 67 66

SAUNAS/BATHS

■ **Theo's Sauna Club** (B DR DU G M MC MSG OS PP RR SA SB SOL VS WH WO) 14-22, Sat & Sun 13-22h, closed Tue
Uellendahlerstraße 410 *Elberfeld, bus-Uellendahl Friedhof*
☏ (0202) 70 60 59 🖳 www.theos-sauna.de

Würzburg ☏ 0931

GAY INFO

■ **WuF-Zentrum** (B GLM MA OS VS)
Nigglweg 2 ☏ (0931) 41 26 46 🖳 www.wufzentrum.de
Details on www.wufzentrum.de, Thu open evening, 2nd Tue Literature, 4th Tue gaming night, 4th Sat movie night, 2nd & 4th Sun coffee party, 3rd Sat 40+ night.

BARS

■ **BB – Treffpunkt für Freunde** (B GLM MA) 19-?h
Burkarderstaße 12 *Near the old main-bridge* ☏ (0931) 359 07 91
Smoking permitted.

DANCECLUBS

■ **Gay Disco** (B D f GLM OS YC) 1st Sat/month 22-3h
c/o Cafe Ludwig, Kaiserstraße 5 *5 mins from main station*
☏ (0931) 412 646 🖳 wufzentrum.de
■ **Gay Disco @ Posthalle Würzburg** (B D GLM)
every first Sat/month 22-?h
Bahnhofplatz 2 ☏ (0931) 412646 (WuF-Zentrum) 🖳 www.wufzentrum.de
New location for popular Gay Disco Würzburg organized by WuF-Zentrum.
■ **gay.licious @ Suzie Wong** (B D GLM MA)
Last Fri/month 22h-open end
Friedrich-Rätzer-Straße 4, Schweinfurt *30 km NE of Würzburg*
☏ (09721) 188 133 1 🖳 www.suzie-wong-sw.de
■ **gay.volution** (B D GLM YC) 3rd Fri/ month 22-05h
c/o Zauberberg, Veitshöchheimer Str. 20 *Opp. Cinemaxx*
☏ (0931) 329 26 80 🖳 www.junx4you.de
Half-price entrance fee before 23h.

SAUNAS/BATHS

■ **Alibi-Club-Wellness-Center**
(B DR DU FC G GH I LAB M MA MSG RR SA SB SH SOL VS)
Tue-Fri 16-1, Sat & Sun 14-1h, closed on Mon (except public holidays)
Nürnberger Straße 88 *Industriegebiet Ost, bus 26-Israelitischer Friedhof*
☏ (0931) 299 85 58 🖳 www.alibi-sauna.de
Sauna on 600 m² with regular events. Admission until 24h. Very nice, clean and elegant.

LEATHER & FETISH SHOPS

■ **Werkstatt. Die**
Seinsheimstraße 11 ☏ 178 1865 182 🖳 www.Leder-1.de
Leather clothing and articles made to order.

SWIMMING

-Sommerhäuser Badesee (Road B 13 to Ochsenfurth/Ansbach. At Sommerhausen to P Wildpark. Along gardens to the lake (20 mins)
-Baggerseen Dettelbach- und Hörblach- (approx. 20 km east of Würzburg on the B22 motorway, large flooded quarrys (Baggerseen) with nudist area)
-Sandermare, Virchowstraße, public indoor-pool, from 17h, contacts in the showers
-Nautiland, public indoor-pool, best midweek 18-22h, mens-shower and facilities.

CRUISING

-Ringanlagen (near Sanderring/Amtsgericht)
-Husarenpark (Ringpark between Husarenstraße & Rennweger Ring, after 21h)
-Kriegerdenkmal, in the adjacent park after 22h
-Ludwigsbrücke, P and facilities, midday and evenings
-Grombühl, facilities near tram-station (drugstore)
-Sanderring, facilities in the park near Ottostrasse
-Rue de Galopp, Rennwegerring after dark
-Sternplatz, facilities, filthy but action possible, esp. before noon
-Zoo Stadium, facilities.

Zwickau ☏ 0375

SAUNAS/BATHS

■ **cTs – Thermo Club Sauna** (AC B DR DU FC G LAB m MA p RR SA SB SOL VS WH) 15-24, Fri & Sat -2h, Tue closed
Leipziger Straße 40 *Near Neumarkt* ☏ (0375) 29 60 10
🖳 www.thermoclubsauna.de

CRUISING

-Schwanenteichanlagen (evenings)
-Kaufland (WC next to the bakery)

Zwiesel ☏ 09922

CAFES

■ **Cafe Gloria** (B glm MC OS S ST)
Sun & Wed 13-18, Thu-Sat 13-17 6 19-1h
Theresienthal 13 ☏ (09922) 80 45 170 🖳 www.cafe-gloria.de
New cafe owned and run by a local trans-star!

Gibraltar

Name: Gibilterra
Location: South Europe
Initials: GBZ
Time: GMT+1
International Country Code: ☏ 350 (no area codes)
International Access Code: ☏ 00
Language: English, Spanish
Area: 6.5 km² / 2.5 sq mi.
Currency: 1 Gibraltar Pound (Gib£) = 100 Pence
Population: 28,759
Religions: 85% Catholics; Muslims, Anglicans
Climate: Mediterranean climate. Winters are mild, summers warm.

In September 2000, the Equality Rights Group GGR was founded by Felix Alvarez in order to change the social and legal situation of sexual minorities in Gibraltar. Up until then, gay issues were met with silence and treated as a taboo. Many changes have occurred since then: GGR has become Gibraltar's prime human rights organisation, with British and European Members of Parliament amongst its supporters, providing expertise on human rights in Gibraltar to the European Commission. From the 4 political parties in Gibraltar today 3 of them have pro-gay rights policies, whilst the Government party is in the throes of internal change on this issue. Today, Gibraltar is more open to sexuality issues than back in 2000. But the law has hardly changed: the age of consent for homosexuals is 18 whilst for heterosexuals it is set at 16 years of age. Civil partnership rights do not exist, nor do gays have legal protection against discrimination. Whilst it is rare for a gay person to be discriminated against in shops, hotels or restaurants there is, nonetheless, no legal protection as such. Gibraltar still has some way to go before it achieves the standards gay people can expect today in the majority of European countries. In general, ordinary Gibraltarians are mostly tolerant and accepting people, although somewhat conservative in attitude.
Gibraltar is full of history – whether Roman, Islamic, medieval Spanish or 18th Century British – from World War II with secret tunnels deep in the Rock, to charming colonial side streets, amazing views to the Mediterranean and Atlantic and a magical medieval Moorish castle perched on the Rock. A visit to Gibraltar is a must when in southern Spain or Morocco.

Im September 2000 gründete Felix Alvarez die Equality Rights Group GGR, um die soziale und rechtliche Situation sexueller Minderheiten in Gibraltar zu verbessern. Bis dahin wurden Belange Homosexueller verschwiegen und tabuisiert. Seit damals hat sich jedoch viel verändert: Mit Unterstützung britischer und europäischer Politiker entwickelte sich die GGR zur wichtigsten Menschenrechtsorganisation Gibraltars, die ihre Erkenntnisse über die Menschenrechtslage in Gibraltar an die Europäische Kommission weiterleitet. Drei der vier politischen Parteien Gibraltars verfolgen inzwischen eine homosexuellenfreundliche Politik, während die Regierungspartei diesen Wandel noch nicht ganz vollzogen hat. Gibraltar ist heute gegenüber sexuellen Fragen zwar offener als im Jahr 2000, doch die Gesetze haben sich kaum verändert. So liegt das Schutzalter für Homosexuelle bei 18 Jahren, für Heterosexuelle jedoch bei 16 Jahren. Es existiert weder ein Partnerschaftsgesetz noch genießen Homosexuelle gesetzlichen Schutz vor Diskriminierung bei Eigentumsfragen. Auch wenn Homosexuelle z.B. in Geschäften, Hotels oder Restaurants nur selten diskriminiert werden, besteht für sie doch noch kein Rechtsschutz. In Gibraltar muss noch einiges unternommen werden, damit der Standard erreicht wird, den Homosexuelle heutzutage in den meisten europäischen Staaten vorfinden. Im Allgemeinen sind die Bewohner Gibraltars jedoch sehr tolerant, wenngleich auch recht konservativ.
Gibraltar ist reich an Geschichte, geprägt von Rom, dem Islam, dem mittelalterlichen Spanien oder seit dem 18. Jh. vom Britischen Empire, und es bietet Vieles: von geheimen Felsgängen aus dem Zweiten Weltkrieg über bezaubernde koloniale Gässchen, atemberaubende Ausblicke auf das Mittelmeer, den Atlantik und sogar die Afrikanische Küste bis hin zum „Moorish Castle", einer auf dem Felsen thronenden maurischen Burg aus dem Mittelalter. Gibraltar ist ein idealer Zwischenstopp im Rahmen einer Reise durch Südspanien oder auf dem Weg nach Marokko.

Felix Alvarez a fondé en septembre 2000 le Equality Rights Group GGR afin d'améliorer la situation sociale et juridique des minorités sexuelles à Gibraltar. Jusque là, les intérêts des homosexuels étaient ignorés et tabouisés. Depuis, beaucoup a changé : Avec le soutien de politiciens britanniques et européens, le GGR est devenue l'organisation des droits de l'Homme la plus importante de Gibraltar, qui transmet à la Commission Européenne ses conclusions sur la situations des droits de l'Homme à Gibraltar. Trois des quatre partis politiques de Gibraltar poursuivent désormais une politique favorable aux homosexuels, alors que le parti gouvernemental n'a pas encore complètement pris le train en marche. Gibraltar est certes plus ouvert aux questions sexuelles qu'en 2000 mais les lois n'ont pratiquement

pas changé. C'est ainsi que la majorité sexuelle pour les homosexuels est de 18 ans alors qu'elle est fixée à 16 ans pour les hétérosexuels. Il n'existe aucune loi sur un quelconque partenariat, et de même les homosexuels ne bénéficient d'aucune protection légale contre les discriminations dans les questions de propriété. Même si les homosexuels sont rarement discriminés par exemple dans les commerces, les hôtels ou les restaurants, il n'existe encore aucune protection légale. Il reste donc encore à faire à Gibraltar afin d'y atteindre le standard dont bénéficient les homosexuels dans la plupart des pays européens. Les habitants de Gibraltar sont en général très tolérants bien qu'assez conservateurs.
Gibraltar a une histoire riche, imprégnée de Rome, de l'islam, de l'Espagne médiévale ou, depuis le 18e siècle, de l'Empire britannique, et a beaucoup à proposer : Des sentiers secrets de la Seconde Guerre Mondiale aux ravissantes ruelles coloniales, des magnifiques vues sur la Méditerranée et sur l'Atlantique jusqu'au „ Moorish Castle „, une superbe citadelle maure médiévale perchée sur un éperon rocheux. Gibraltar est aussi une halte idéale dans le cadre d'un voyage en Espagne ou sur la route vers le Maroc.

En septiembre de 2000, Felix Alvárez fundó el grupo Equality Rights Group GGR para mejorar la situación social y jurídica de las minorías sexuales en Gibraltar. Hasta entonces se negaban y se escondían las necesidades de los homosexuales. A partir de entonces ha cambiado mucho: con el apoyo de los políticos británicos y europeos, el GGR se ha convertido en la organización de derechos humanos más importante de Gibraltar, que informa de sus conocimientos sobre la situación de los derechos humanos en Gibraltar a la Comisión Europea. Tres de los cuatro partidos políticos de Gibraltar siguen una política favorable a los homosexuales, mientras que el partido del gobierno todavía no ha puesto en práctica este cambio. Gibraltar está hoy más abierto a los temas sexuales que en el año 2000 pero las leyes apenas han cambiado: así la edad de consentimiento para los homosexuales está en los 18 años, para los heterosexuales en los 16 años. No existe ni una ley de registro de parejas ni tampoco una protección jurídica anti-discriminación para los temas de propiedades. Aunque raramente se produce algún tipo de discriminación en los establecimientos comerciales, hoteles o restaurantes, todavía no existe ninguna protección jurídica. En Gibraltar aún quedan cosas por hacer para poder alcanzar el nivel que los homosexuales disfrutan en los demás países europeos. En general, los habitantes de Gibraltar son muy tolerantes, aunque también pueden ser muy conservadores.
Gibraltar es rico en historia – aquí dejaron su huella tanto los romanos, como el Islam, la España medieval o desde el siglo XVIII el imperio británico- y tiene mucho que ofrecer: desde los pasadizos secretos en la roca de la II guerra mundial hasta las fantásticas callejuelas coloniales, las impresionantes vistas al Mediterráneo y al Atlántico o el ìcastillo moroî, un impresionante castillo situado en la cima de una roca de época medieval. Gibraltar es una parada ideal durante un viaje por España o de camino a Marruecos.

A settembre del 2000 Felix Alvarez ha fondato l'Equality Rights Group GGR ai fini dell'equiparazione sociale e giuridica delle minoranze sessuali a Gibilterra. Prima di questa iniziativa, invece, le cause degli omosessuali erano considerate tabù e quindi venivano completamente taciute. Adesso la situazione è molto cambiata. Con il supporto di politici britannici ed europei, la GGR è diventata una delle organizzazioni per i diritti umani più importanti di Gibilterra. Inoltre la GGR corrisponde i suoi rapporti sulla situazione dei diritti umani alla Commissione Europea. Attualmente, tre dei quattro partiti politici di Gibilterra perseguono una politica molto attenta ai diritti degli omosessuali; il partito di governo, invece, rimane restio a questi cambiamenti. È vero che oggi Gibilterra per quello che riguarda la sessualità è molto più aperta rispetto al 2000, tuttavia le leggi non sono per niente cambiate. Un esempio tra tutti è l'età del consenso: per gli omosessuali è di 18 anni mentre per gli eterosessuali è di 16 anni. Inoltre non esiste nè un regolamento per le coppie di fatto nè una tutela in tema di discriminazione nel diritto di proprietà. Anche se succede molto raramente che gli omosessuali vengono discriminati per esempio in negozi, alberghi, ristoranti, ecc., qualora questo dovesse comunque verificarsi, l'omosessualità non è tutelata da leggi antidiscriminatorie. Per quanto riguarda i diritti degli omosessuali, a Gibilterra, ancora, c'è molto da fare per il raggiungimento dei parametri vigenti nella maggior parte degli Stati europei. Tuttavia, anche se piuttosto conservatrice, la poplazine di Gibilterra si mostra abbastanza tollerante.
Gibilterra è molto ricca di storia (si pensi all'Impero Romano, l'Islam, la Spagna medioevale, l'impero Britannico dal XVIII secolo in poi) ed ha davvero tanto da offrire: i misteriosi corridoi scavati nelle rocce risalenti alla seconda guerra mondiale, incantevoli stradine coloniali, stucchevole panorama sul Mediterraneo e sull'Atlantico e il bellissimo „Moorish Castle", castello medioevale in stile moro che troneggia sulle rocce. Gibilterra è, insomma, una tappa intermedia ideale nel contesto di un viaggio in Spagna o in Marocco.

Gibraltar

BARS

Charlie`s Hole in the Wall (B g MA) 20-3h
5 Castle Street *Opp. post office* ☎ 735 94
Gay-owned and famous with the British Navy, tourists and locals alike.

GENERAL GROUPS

Equality Rights Group GGR (G MA) Wed only
c/o Charlie's Hole-in-the-Wall, 5 Castle Street *Opp. post office, up lane and steps* ☎ 735 94 (after 20h) equalityrightsggr.blogspot.com
Contact and further information through Charles from Charles' Hole-in-the-Wall or through the infoline.

Greece

Name: Ellâs · Griechenland · Grèce · Grecia
Location: Southeastern Europe
Initials: GR
Time: GMT+2
International Country Code: ☎ 30
International Access Code: ☎ 00
Language: Greek
Area: 131,957 km² / 50,949 sq mi.
Currency: 1 Euro (€) = 100 Cents
Population: 11,104,000
Capital: Athina
Religions: 97% Greek Orthodox
Climate: Moderate climate. Winters are mild and wet, summers hot and dry.
Important gay cities: Athens, Mykonos, Thessaloniki

Greece might not be a gayís paradise everywhere but there are places, cities, beaches and islands that you can really feel beautiful and very welcomed. Greeks have a totally different approach to gay people depending on their generation, with younger Greeks been really relaxed and open minded.

In the wake of the existential financial crisis besetting Greece, the introduction of an officially recognized same-sex partnership is now being considered. This would also serve economic interests amongst concerns about Greece having in recent years fallen out of favour as a travel destination with gays and lesbians, known to boost tourism, partly because of the stateís discrimination against homosexuals.

Greece is inexpensive (with the exception of Mykonos), uncomplicated and safe. The Greeks are a warm and hospitable people and you can expect to encounter very few problems on account of your sexuality. The age of consent in Greece is 17, the same as for heterosexuals.

Gay life on the islands is focused on Mykonos, particularly if you are looking for fun, crowded beaches and hot nights. Of course beaches available for gay cruising can be found also on other islands such as Santorini, Kriti, Rodos, Corfu and Skiathos that lately is staring being more attractive to many gay tourists. On the mainland the scene is generally more conservative but there are also a few places for gay cruising and beaches for gay fans of the Mediterranean nature.

Against all odds the country that everyone is expecting to emerge after this financial crisis will refer to a really modern and new faced Greece that all the problems and the anxieties of the past will be buried under the sandy beaches and be burnt under the eternally bright Greek sun.

Griechenland mag zwar nicht überall das reinste Schwulenparadies sein, doch es gibt viele Orte, Städte, Strände und Inseln, wo man sich wirklich wohl und herzlich willkommen fühlen kann. Die Einstellung der Griechen zur Homosexualität hängt stark von der betreffenden Generation ab. Jüngere Einheimische gehen meist sehr entspannt und aufgeschlossen damit um.

Im Zuge der existenziellen Finanzkrise Griechenlands gibt es auch Überlegungen, eine staatlich anerkannte Lebenspartnerschaft für Homosexuelle einzuführen. Das hat durchaus ökonomische Interessen, da man sich Sorgen darüber macht, dass Schwule und Lesben als bewährte Touristenmagneten dem Land als Reiseziel in den letzten Jahren zunehmend den Rücken kehren, auch aufgrund der Diskriminierung von Staats wegen.

Griechenland ist preiswert (mit Ausnahme von Mykonos), unkompliziert und sicher. Die Griechen sind ein warmherziges und gastfreundliches Volk, in dem Sie mit Ihren sexuellen Vorlieben nur selten auf Schwierigkeiten stoßen werden. Das Schutzalter liegt bei 17 Jahren für Hetero- und Homosexuelle gleichermaßen.

Das schwule Leben der Inseln ist größtenteils auf Mykonos konzentriert, besonders wenn man vorwiegend an Spaß, gut besuchten Stränden und heißen Nächten interessiert ist. Aber auch die Inseln Santorini, Kreta, Rhodos, Korfu und Kos, die in jüngster Zeit für viele schwule Touristen immer attraktiver geworden sind, verfügen über eigene Strände für entsprechende Freizeitvergnügen. Und obwohl die Szene auf dem Festland generell etwas konservativer eingestellt ist, gibt es auch hier Cruising-Gegenden und Strände für schwule Liebhaber der mediterranen Naturlandschaften.

Irgendwie erwarten alle, so unwahrscheinlich es auch klingt, dass aus dieser Finanzkrise ein wirklich modernes Griechenland hervorgehen wird, das ein neues Ansehen genießt, und dass die Ängste der Vergangenheit von den Sandstränden begraben und vom ununterbrochen im ganzen Lande herrschenden Sonnenschein hinweggebrannt werden.

La Grèce n'est peut-être pas partout un paradis pour les gays mais il y a des endroits, des villes, plages et îles où l'on se sent bienvenus. Les Grecs ont une approche totalement différente sur les gays selon leur génération, les jeunes Grecs étant décontractés et ouverts d'esprit.
Dans le sillage de la crise financières existentielle que traverse la Grèce, il est prévu d'introduire un partenariat homosexuel officiellement reconnu. Ceci n'est pas sans arrière-pensée économique, la Grèce étant tombée dans l'estime des gays et lesbiennes, connus pour stimuler le tourisme, en raison des discriminations menées par l'Etat contre les homosexuels. La Grèce n'est pas chère (à l'exception de Mykonos), pas compliquée et sûre. Les Grecs sont accueillants et hospitaliers et vous ne devriez rencontrer que peu de problèmes en raison de votre sexualité. La majorité sexuelle est fixée à 17 ans en Grèce, comme pour les hétérosexuels.
La vie gay sur les îles se concentre sur Mykonos, en particulier si vous cherchez des plages bondées et fêtardes ou des nuits chaudes. Bien-sûr il existe des plages pour le cruising gays sur d'autres îles comme Santorin, la Crète, Rhodes, Corfou et Skiathos devenus plus intéressantes pour les touristes gays ces derniers temps. Sur le continent, la scène est généralement plus conservatrice mais il existe tout de même des lieux de drague et des plages gays pour les amateurs de la nature méditerranéenne.
Contre tout attente, le pays qui sortira de la crise financière sera une Grèce veritablement moderne avec un nouveau visage laissant derrière lui tous les problèmes et anxiétés du passé enfouis sous les plages de sable fin et brûlés au soleil éternel grec.

Puede que Grecia no sea un paraíso gay en toda su extensión, pero hay lugares, ciudades, playas e islas, en las que uno realmente se puede sentir bello y bienvenido. Los griegos tienen una visión de la homosexualidad que depende totalmente de un factor generacional. Por lo general, los jóvenes griegos son relajados y tolerantes.
A raíz de la crisis existencial financiera que afecta a Grecia a día de hoy, se está considerando la introducción de un reconocimiento oficial de las parejas del mismo sexo. Esto también atendería a intereses económicos dadas las crecientes preocupaciones en Grecia por haber caído en desgracia en los últimos años como destino turístico para gays y lesbianas, conocidos por impulsar el turismo, en parte debido a la discriminación del Estado contra los homosexuales. Grecia es un país asequible (con la excepción de Mykonos), sencillo y seguro. Los griegos son gente amable y hospitalaria, y puedes esperar encontrar muy pocos problemas en relación a tu sexualidad. La edad de consentimiento sexual en Grecia es de 17 años de edad, la misma que para los heterosexuales.
La vida gay en las islas gira en torno a Mykonos, especialmente si lo que buscas es diversión, playas abarrotadas y noches calurosas. Por supuesto, también pueden encontrarse playas disponibles para el cruising gay en otras islas como Santorini, Kriti, Rodos, Corfu y Skiathos, las cuales últimamente se están convirtiendo en destinos mucho más atractivos para los turistas gays. En la península griega el ambiente gay es, generalmente, más conservador, pero también se cuenta con algunas zonas de cruising gay y con playas para los aficionados gays a la naturaleza mediterránea.
Contra todo pronóstico, a este país, por el que todo el mundo espera a que resurja de la crisis financiera, se lo conocerá como una muy moderna y nueva Grecia en la que todos los problemas y las angustias del pasado se habrán enterrado en las playas de arena, quemándose bajo el eterno sol brillante de Grecia.

La Grecia non è certo un paradiso gay in terra, ma è anche vero che ci sono luoghi, città, spiagge e isole bellissime nelle quali ci si può sentire molto ben accolti. I greci, a seconda della generazione della quale fanno parte, hanno un approccio molto diversificato con le persone gay; i più giovani, per esempio, hanno una mentalità molto aperta. La Grecia è una meta turistica economica (ad eccezione di Mykonos) e sicura. I greci sono un popolo accogliente e ospitale. È raro che in Grecia si possano avere problemi a causa del proprio orientamento sessuale. L'età del consenso in Grecia è di 17 anni, sia per omosessuali che per eterosessuali. Nelle isole la vita gay si concentra prevalentemente a Mykonos, soprattutto se si è alla ricerca di divertimento, spiagge affollate e notti calde. Naturalmente le spiagge a disposizione per il cruising gay si possono trovare anche su altre isole come Santorini, Creta, Rodi, Corfù e Skiathos, che ultimamente si sta sempre più rivelando meta sempre più ambita dai turisti gay. Sulla terraferma la scena è generalmente più arretrata, ma anche qui non mancano comunque i luoghi d'incontro per il cruising e le spiagge gay per gli amanti dei paesaggi mediterranei. Nonostante tutte le difficoltà, il paese che tutti si aspettano emergere dopo la crisi finanziaria, diventerà una realtà moderna pronta ad affrontare nuove sfide e capace di seppellire tutte le angosce e i problemi del passato sotto la sabbia delle sue spiagge per poi essere bruciati sotto il suo sole luminoso.

NATIONAL GAY INFO

gayguide.gr (GLM MA)
www.gayguide.gr
Online Greek gay map.

NATIONAL PUBLICATIONS

Antivirus
PO Box 8143 10010 Athina 693 2101127 www.avmag.gr
Bi-monthly equal rights free magazine (in Greek only).

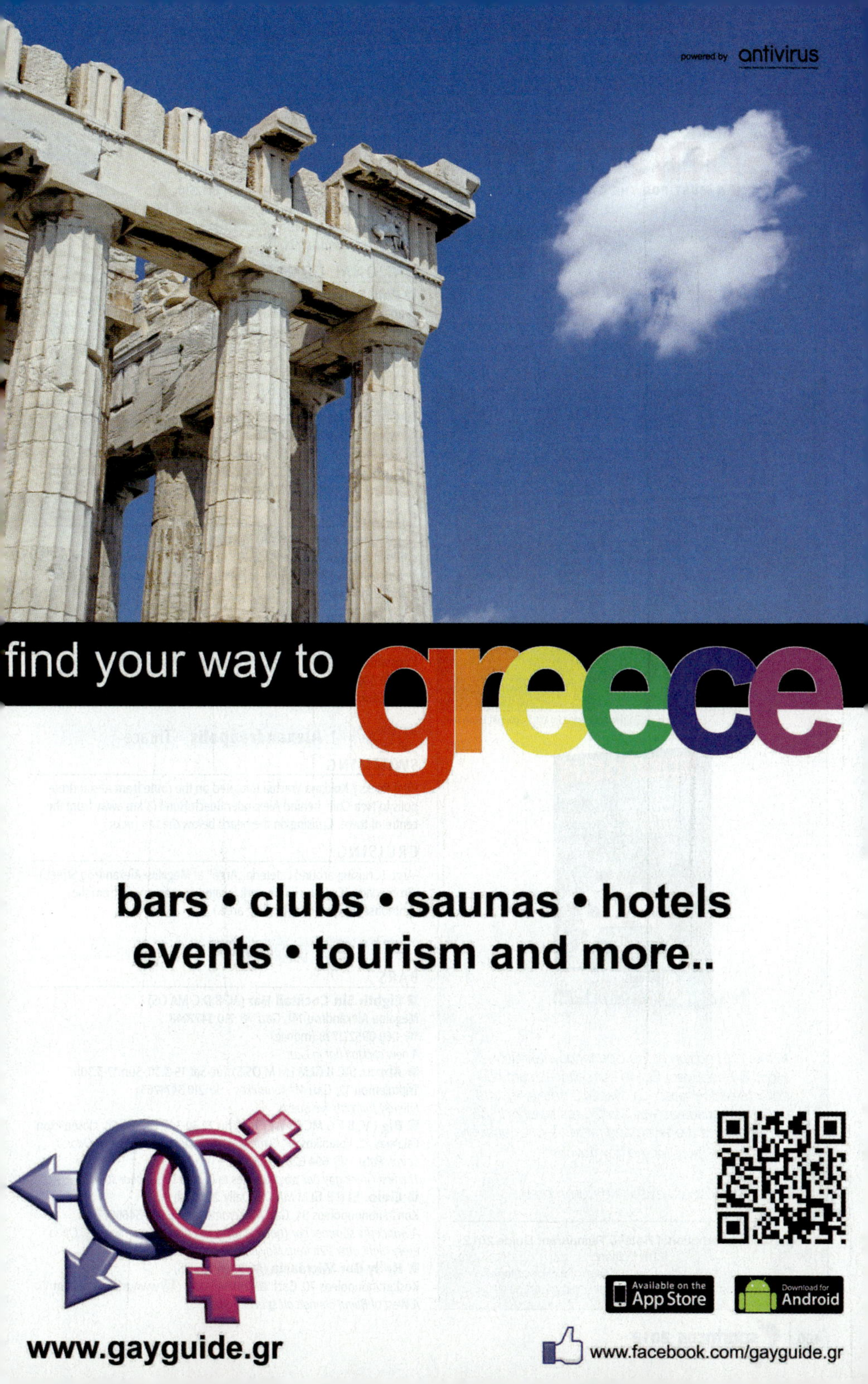

■ **City Uncovered**
Zaimi 45 ✉ 106 82 Exarchia, Athina *Athens city centre* ☎ 210 3830784
Gay & lesbian free magazine. Includes a section in English and a Greek gay guide.

■ **DeonGuide**
Arapaki 91 ✉ 17675 Athina ☎ 211 0112510
The annual free gay travel magazine & guide of Greece & Cyprus. Includes travel destination features & articles. Published in beginning of June. Also, available in digital format.

NATIONAL COMPANIES

■ **Paul Sofianos Creations**
Arapaki 91 ✉ 17675 Athina ☎ 211 0112510 💻 www.paulsofianos.net
Gay info, business promotion, publications, guides, gay tourism and gay event's promotion. Info by phone daily 9-21h. Creator of the websites: gay-greece.gr and gayholidays.gr

NATIONAL GROUPS

■ **Greek Transgendered Support Association (S.Y.D.)**
💻 www.transgender-association.gr

■ **O.L.K.E.** Tue, Wed, Fri 18-20h
Halkokondili 25 ✉ 10432 Athina ☎ 694 7434353 💻 www.olke.org
Gay & lesbian community of Greece. Information by phone.

GAY INFO

■ **gaygreece.gr** (GLM MA) Mon-Sat 10-21h
c/o Paul Sofianos Creations ☎ 211 011 2510 💻 www.gaygreece.gr
News site & gay tourism guide of Greece & Cyprus, event calendar, travel services and more.

HEALTH GROUPS

■ **Act Up DRASE Hellas** Mon-Fri 10-20h
Konstantinou Manou 11 ✉ 11633 Pangrati, Athina *Centre*
☎ 210 3305 500
Information and support for people with or affected by HIV and AIDS.

Alexandroúpolis – Thrace

SWIMMING

-Red Rocks / Kokkina Vrachia (Situated on the route from Alexandroupolis to Nea Chili, behind Alexander Beach Hotel (3 km away from the centre of town. Cruising on the beach below the red rocks.)

CRUISING

-Argo (Cruising around cafeteria „Argo" at Megalou Alexandrou Street.)
-Promenade (Cruising in the park located at promenade from the lighthouse up under the parking area.)

Athina

BARS

■ **Eighth Sin Cocktail Bar** (AC B D G MA OS)
Megalou Alexandrou 141, Gazi ☎ 210 3477048
☎ 069 0952 2798 (mobile)
A new cocktail bar in Gazi.

■ **Almaz** (AC B GLM LM M OS S) Tue-Sat 19-3.30, Sun 17-3.30h
Triptolemou 12, Gazi *M° Keramikos* ☎ 210 3474763
Friendly bar with live guests.

■ **Big** (AC B F G MC VS WE) Tue-Thu 22.30-3, Fri & Sat -5h, closed Mon
Falaisias 12, Votanikos *M° Keramikos, near the cross roads Iera Odos & Spirou Patsi* ☎ 694 628 28 45
The first Greek gay bar which aspires to coil the Greek bear scene.

■ **Cielo. El** (! B GLM MA OS) Daily 20.30-4h
Konstantinoupoleos 84, Gazi *M° Keramikos* ☎ 210 3460677
A wonderful summer bar (open terrace) just above Kazarma Club. Open every night after 22h from May until September.

■ **Holly Bar Micraasia** (AC B MA NG OS)
Kostantinoupoleos 70, Gazi ☎ 210 3469139 💻 www.micraasia.com
A West of Beirut Lounge art space.

■ **Kinky Cafe** (AC B GLM MA) Tue-Sat 16-?, Sun 18-?
Megalou Alexandrou 24 *Metro Metaxourgio* www.kinkycafe.gr

■ **Koukles Show Club** (AC B D GLM S ST T WE)
23-?h, closed Mon & Tue and in August
Zan Moreas 32 & Sungrou ave., Koukaki ☎ 694 7557443
www.koukles-club.gr
Entrance fee applies. Drag shows on Friday & Saturday night.

■ **maYOR** (AC B GLM OS) 22-4h, closed Mon & Tue
Persefonis 33, Gazi *M° Keramikos* ☎ 210 3423066
Stylish lounge bar with roof terrace.

■ **My Bar** (AC B D GLM M MA S WI WL) 22-?, Sun 20-?h
Kakourgiodikou 6 & Athinas, Psirri *M° Monastiraki* ☎ 695 5263015
www.mybar.gr
Stylish cocktail bar in a happy atmosphere and friendly service.

■ **NyLon Bar** (AC B D gLm OS YC)
Damokleous 10, Gazi ☎ 211 4052389

■ **Philipp Champagne Bar** (AC B GLM MA)
Wed-Sat 21-4 / Sun 17-?h
Tompazi 4, Psirri *Metro Monastiraki* ☎ 2130325624
www.philipp-bar.com

■ **Polihromo** (AC B G OC OS) 19-?h, closed Mon & Tue
Lempesi 12 & Tsokri Sq., Makrigianni *M° Akropoli* ☎ 210 9241574
www.polihromo.gr
Place for mature men and their admirers.

■ **Taxidi** (AC B gLm LM M MA OS) 20-?h, closed Mon & Tue
Zagreos 23 & Konstantonoupoleos 46, Gazi *M° Keramikos*
☎ 693 7286999 www.myspace.com/taxidicafebar

■ **Trap** (AC B G MC) 19.30-?h, closed Tue
Koritsas 15 & Konstantinoupoleos 123, Votanikos
☎ 210 9222248
Café-bar with nice Greek music and excellent service by Elias.

■ **Vise Versa** (AC B D GLM MA) Fri & Sat 22.30 – ?, Sun 21-?
Konstantinoupoleos 84, Gazi *1st floor* ☎ 210 3460677

MEN'S CLUBS

■ **Fc_uk** (AC DR F FC G GH MA NR p S SL VR) Sun-Thu 21-3, Fri & Sat 21-6h
Keleou 3, Gazi *M° Keramikos* www.fc-uk.gr
Athens fetish cruising point.

CAFES

■ **Blue Train** (AC B GLM I LM MA OS VS WI) Daily 19.30-?h
Konstantinoupoleos 84, Gazi *M° Keramikos* ☎ 210 3460677
Beautiful meeting place for enjoying coffee, juices, drink & sweets next to the train rails.

■ **Del Sol** (AC B I M NG OS WI YC) 8-?h
Voutadon 44, Gazi ☎ 210 3418169

■ **Myrovolos** (AC B gLm LM M MA OS) 16-?h
Giatrakou 12, Keramikos *M° Metaxourgio* ☎ 210 5228806

■ **Rages** (AC B GLM LM M MA OS WI) 19.30-?h
Konstantinoupoleos 82, Gazi *M° Keramikos* ☎ 210 3452751

■ **Rooster** (AC B BF G I M MA OS WI) 8-?h
Agias Irinis sq. 4, Monastiraki ☎ 210 3224410
All day cafe-bar.

DANCECLUBS

■ **Bear Code** (AC B D F G MA WE) Thu-Sun 23-?h
Konstantinoupoleos 8, Gazi *M° Keramikos* ☎ 6948883241
www.bearcode.gr
Dance club for bears and admirers.

■ **Eight Sin @ Basement** (AC B D G MA) Closed in summer
Megalou Alexandrou 141, Gazi ☎ 210 347 7048 ☎ 069 0952 2798 (mobile)
New popular gay club. No entry fee applies.

■ **Fou** (AC B D F GLM MA S SNU VS WE) 23.30-6h
Keleou 8 & Iera Odos, Gazi *M° Keramikos* ☎ 210 3466800
www.fouclub.gr
International pop, house, alternative dance & also Greek hits from 3 DJs. On stage go-go dancers, strippers, wet live shows on Sat night, regular special events with guest porn stars.

Athens

EAT & DRINK	
8th Sin – Bar	15
Almaz – Bar	16
Big Bar	28
Blue Train- Cafe	23
Cielo Summer. El – Bar	23
Del Sol Cafe	11
Holly Bar Micraasia	21
Jamon Pintxos – Restaurant	25
Kinky Cafe	25
Marmita – Cafe-Restaurant	2
MaYor – Bar	14
Myrovolos – Cafe-Restaurant	10
NyLon – Bar	29
Philip Champagne Bar	30
Rages – Cafe	26
Rooster – Cafe	1
Schweinchen Dick – Restaurant	3
Ta Koutalakia – Restaurant	6
Trap Bar	13
Vise Versa	23

NIGHTLIFE	
Fou – Danceclub	18
FouClub	18
Fc_uk – Men's Club	22
Moe Club	20
Noiz Club	26
S-Cape Club	27
Sodade Club	17
Spray Club	31

SEX	
Alexander Sauna	19
Attraxx – Sex Shop	9
Eroxx DVD – Sex Shop	5
Flex Sauna	6

ACCOMMODATION	
Alexander Apartments	19
Athinaikon Hotel	24
Dorian Inn Hotel	32
Eridanus Hotel	8
Mc Queen Hotel	3

■ **Glee – the club** (AC B D G MA S SNU WE)
Thu-Sun 23 – ?, Sun 21-?h
Dinokratous 19 *Kolonaki* ☏ 697 7161806
A new danceclub in Athens.

■ **Lamda Reloaded** (AC B D DR G MA S SNU WE) Thu-Sun 23-?h
Lembesi 15 & Sungrou ave., Makrigianni *M° Acropolis* ☏ 210 9224202
The oldest gay club of Athens for more than 17 years now. Renovated in 2008 offers a large dancing ground floor and as well as a large cruising basement with darkroom.

■ **Moe** (! AC B D GLM MA S SNU ST VS WE) 24-8h
Keleou 1-5 & Iera Odos str., Gazi *M° Keramikos* ☏ 6955 263015
To ultimate dance club in town that specializes in cheerful Greek music. Friendly environment. Drag shows, strip-shows & happenings at the weekends.

■ **Noiz** (AC B D gLm MA S WE) 23-4h
Konstantinoupoleos 78 & I. Odos, Gazi *M° Keramikos* ☏ 210 3424771
www.noizclub.gr
The most popular lesbian club in Athens.

■ **S-Cape into an Army Academy**
(! AC B D GLM OS S SH VS WE YC) Daily 23-?h
Megalou Alexandrou 139 & Iera Odos, Gazi *M° Keramikos*
☏ 210 3411003 www.s-capeclub.gr
Athens biggest gay club divided into lounge and dance areas. All kind of music depending on time and mood. An open lounge area is available from May until Sep. Mon Karaoke.

■ **Sodade** (! AC B D G MA VS WE) 23-4, Fri -6, Sat -6.30h
Triptolemou 10, Gazi *M° Keramikos* ☏ 210 3468657
One of the most famous gay dance clubs in two different stages, front with mainstream successes & laser show and back with progressive house music. Packed at the weekend.

■ **Spray Club** (AC B D gLm MA WE) Sun-Thu 10.30-? / Fri & Sat 11-?
Odysseos 14 & Kolonou 76 *Metro Metaxourgio*

RESTAURANTS

■ **Jamon Pintxos** (AC B I M MA NG OS WI WL)
Mon-Sat 16-?, Sun 14-?h
Elasidon 15 & Dekelion, Orfeos 46, Gazi *M° Keramikos* ☏ 210 3464120
www.jamon.gr
Gourmet snack bar with fine Mediterranean products, wine and international beer.

■ **Marmita** (AC B G M MA)
Koristas 19 & Melenikou, Votanikos ☏ 210 3479906 ☏ 210 3412185
Traditional cafe from the good old days.

■ **Palia Athina. I** (! AC g M MA) 11-?h, closed Sun
Nikis 46, Plaka *M° Acropolis* ☏ 210 3245777
They offer the most traditional Greek cuisine in Plaka, the historical area of Athens. Delicious homemade meals, a variety of appetizers, fresh fish, steaks and salads.

■ **Prosopa** (AC g M MA OS) 20-?h
Megalou Vasiliou 52 & Konstantinoupoleos 4, Rouf *M° Keramikos*
☏ 210 3413433 www.prosopa.gr
High class stylist & friendly restaurant.

■ **Schweinchen Dick** (AC M MA NG OS)
Lakhou 9-11, Gazi ☏ 6937 83556
German food with original sausages.

■ **Ta Koutalakia** (AC M MC NG)
Tue 18-24 / Wed-Sat 13.30-24/ Sun 13-18h/ Mon closed
Thermopilon 39, Metaxourgio *M° Metaxourgio* ☏ 210 5224512
☏ 697 2030610 www.koutalakia.gr
Traditional Greek restaurant.

SEX SHOPS/BLUE MOVIES

■ **Attraxx** (! AC DR FC G GH I LAB MA RR SH VR VS) 12-3, Fri & Sat -6h
Iakchou 36, Gazi *50 m from M° Keramikos* www.attraxx.gr
Comfortable cruising area with luxury private cabins with adult movies projection monitors in combination with complex labyrinth, dark rooms, glory holes & vinyl scenes.

■ **Eroxxx DVD** (AC CC G VS) Mon-Fri 10-22, Sat & Sun -20h
Stadiou 61 *2nd floor, near Omonia Square*

SEX CINEMAS

■ **Olympic Cinema** (AC g MA VS) 8.30-2.30h
Filonos 88, Piraeus *Near Agios Nikolaos* ☏ 210 4294701
The only adult cinema in Piraeus with cruising at the toilets lobby.

HOUSE OF BOYS

■ **Fantastiko** (AC B G MA R) 23-?h
Aristotelous 37 *Near Vathis Square* ☏ 210 8819720

■ **Sammi's** (AC B G MA R) 22-?h
Filis 34 *Victoria sq., M° Victoria* ☏ 210 882 21 34

■ **Test Me** (AC B G MC R) 23-?h
Pipinou 62 & Aristotelous *Agios Panteleimon* ☏ 08 22 60 29

SAUNAS/BATHS

■ **Alexander Sauna** (! AC B CC D DR DU F FC FH G GH H I LAB M MA MSG NR NU OS p PK RR RWT S SA SB SH SL SNU ST VR VS WH)
Mon-Thu 18-3, Fri 18-8, Sat 16-8, Sun 16-3h
Megalou Alexandrou 134 & Iera Odos Str, Gazi *M° Keramikos*
☏ 210 6980282 ☏ 69 369 59 134 (mobile)
www.alexandersauna.gr
The most popular Sauna in town. Located in Gazi, the hot gay area in Athens. Relax and enjoy cruising in a unique, modern and youthful atmosphere.

■ **Flex Sauna** (AC B CC DR DU G I MA OS p SA SB SOL WE WH WO)
Sun-Thu 14-3, Fri & Sat 14-7h
6, Poliklitou Str. at Vissis Str, Monastiraki *M° Monastiraki – Lines 1 & 3*
☏ 210 3210539 ☏ 210 3210876
www.myspace.com/flexsaunagym
Athens Sauna on 4 floors located in the city center of Athens.

■ **Ira Baths (Hera)** (DR DU G MSG OC SA SB)
Wed-Mon 11ñ20, Tue closed
Zinonos 4, Omonia *M° Omonia. In the arcade* ☏ 210 5234964
A small sauna in the basement of the building. Mostly mature men.

BOOK SHOPS

■ **Colourful Planet** (GLM p)
9-21h, Sat 9-18h, closed Sun & on bank holidays
6 Antoniadou & Patission *Near the Archaeological Museum*
☏ 210 8826 600 www.colourfulplanet.gr
The only gay bookshop/publishing house, covering all the Greek gay literature, and Greek and foreign gay press. Helpful staff. The bookshop is on the mezzanine.

TRAVEL AND TRANSPORT

■ **GayHolidays.gr** (GLM)
☏ 211 0112510 www.gayholidays.gr
The 1st gay & lesbian travel site, with tour packages for Greece & abroad, special packages for world biggest gay events & personal travel packages with care for individual gay & lesbian travelers.

HOTELS

■ **Athinaikon Hotel** (AC BF H I NG PA RWS RWT) All year
Evripidou 40, Psirri ☏ 210 3215657 www.athhotel.com
Central hotel in low rates with quality services.

■ **Dorian Inn** (AC B BF CC H I M NG OS PA PI RWB RWS RWT)
All year
Pireos 15-19, Omonia www.dorianinnhotel.com
One of the most accessible hotels in the historic center of Athens.

■ **Eridanus** (AC B BF H I M NG OS PK RWS RWT SA WO) All year
Piraeus 78, Keramikos *M° Keramikos, 10 mins walk* ☏ 210 5205360
www.eridanus.gr
An elegant & luxurious 5-star hotel located near the main gay area in Athens.

■ **Mc Queen Hotel** (AC B BF CC I NG OS RWB RWS RWT WO)
All year
Kastorias 24 *Votanikos. M° Metaxourgio or M° Keramikos, 10 mins walk*
☏ 213 0099099 www.mcqueen.gr
Mc Queen Hotel is a 5-floor modern building. It's the ideal hotel for those who are visiting Athens.

APARTMENTS

Alexander Apartments (AC CC DR G I RWS RWT SA SB WH WI)
All year
Megalou Alexandrou 134 & Iera Odos, Gazi *M° Keramikos, 5 mins walk*
☎ 06936959134 (mobile) ☎ 2106980282 www.alexander-apartments.gr

Apartment Dora (AC G I RWB RWT)
Ifikratous 6 *Pangrati* www.apartmentdora.com
Α spacious apartment with two bedrooms that can host up to four persons, a living room with TV, DVD & stereo, private bathroom and a fully equipped kitchen.

HEALTH GROUPS

Positive Voice Mon-Fri 9-17h
Anafis 2 ☎ 210 8627572 www.positivevoice.gr
The association of people living with HIV in Greece Positive Voice was founded in 2009 to combat the spread of HIV, and to fight the social and economic impact of the disease.

SWIMMING

-Dikastika (Marathonas): Rocky beach at Marathonas, shortly after the famous beach of the Schinias. Easy to find. Take the left turn just before the end of the Schinias beach. Over the hill, turn right at first corner (very sharp and downhill). In about half a km you can park and walk to the right until you reach the sea.

-Kineta's Panorama: On the national road Athens – Corinth, turn right after the third tunnel, the indication „Kineta-Panorama" and follow the road that leads to the beach. Reaching the road is still only left the Suna hotel. Park there and continue walking along the coast (towards Athens). The beach is big enough, so after 20 minutes Cana will find the first and several gay nudist swimmers. The beach is sand and stone and stretches along the sea.

-Legrena (KAPE – Sounio): Located about 64 km from the center of Athens along the coastal road from Athens to Sounion. When you arrive almost at the 64th km to a left turn, you will see a sign „KAPE" on your right. Follow the dirt road for about 500-600 meters and at the end of the road you will see a small clearing. Park your car there and walk to the end. If you intend to sit for long enough, you can get the necessary from the canteen there. Opposite there steps that will lead to the first beach. On your right you will find some rocks, go there and to follow the small path that is formed. After a big rock is a small beach. If you find it easy point, then make sure you get there early and stay until the beautiful sunset.

-Limanakia (Vouliagmeni): Rocky beach suitable for nudism and cruising but not recommended to anyone seeking quality. Located after Lake Vouliagmeni direction to Varkiza and you can go with the E22 express bus (starting point: Academy) for Saronida and stop at the 3rd stop Limanakia or the tram to Glyfada and from there by express bus E22.

-Mavro Lithari: A nudists beach with less gay cruising but better quality. Located after Saronida, on the way to Anavissos, just before the EOT School of Tourism, on the right side. Not visible from the road. Park your car, jump the protective railings and go down by the stairs that leads to the beach.

-Riba's (Varkiza): In the coastal Athens – Sounion after Varkiza, down the avenue you will find many nudists and gay couples. He has pretty good beach, although access is difficult.

CRUISING

-Larisis Railway Station (Discreet gay cruising in the toilets during the day time but you must be careful because apart of gays, there are a lot of straight people, too)

-Votanikos (At Agiou Policarpou str. of Votanikos from the area of „Urban Busses Depot" up to the road Orpheus and little below for gay cruising with car & truck drivers during the afternoon and evening hours)

-National Gardens (Discreet gay cruising only during day time in the public toilets and around them)

-Pedio Areos Park (left and behind the statue of ‚Athina' in the areas beside Alexandras ave. and towards the Court buildings in the afternoon and evening hours; around the toilets at day time) AYOR

-Peloponnisou Railway Station (Discreet gay cruising in the toilets especially after 16h with greeks and foreign young men)

-Zappion Park (in the evening hours on left and right side of the fountain) (AYOR).

Chalkidiki – Macedonia

SWIMMING

-Afytos: Small beach on the east side of the Kassandra peninsula. It has two main beaches, but the end left after the rock is a small cove nudist suitable for gay cruising.

-Agios Mamas: excellent 3km sandy beach with a nude bathing. Beyond the two beach bars near the watchtower, there was just a scattering of people – a few couples and single men (a few of them gay), mainly nude.

-Kalamitsi: From the main beach, walk a few metres until you see a path which leads you over a small hill with bushes. After 10 minutes you will see the nudists beach suitable for gay cruising. It is sandy with many tents and clear water.

Cyclades Islands

Cyclades Islands – **Amorgos**

SWIMMING

-Agia Anna: From the bus stop there is a path on the left leading to a beach with a church. After 50 m, turn right and after a rocky trail, 250 m away, you will find a nudists beach with plenty of gay cruising.

Cyclades Islands – **Folegandros**

APARTMENTS

Anemomilos Apartments (AC BF CC H M OS PA PI PK RWB RWS RWT WI) May – Sep
☎ 22860 41309 www.anemomilosapartments.com
A complex with comfortable & fully equipped kitchenette studios & apartments.

SWIMMING

-Agios Nikolaos, Livadaki Beach: main nudist beach

Cyclades Islands – **Milos**

HOTELS

■ **Del Mar Hotel** (AC BF CC DU H OS PA PK RWB RWS RWT WI)
May 1 – Oct 15
☎ 22870 41440 🖳 www.delmar.gr

SWIMMING

-Agios Ioannis: Very secluded, on the West side of the Island it is rather difficult to reach. When the main road finishes, add 6 km of dirt road as far as to the monastery that gives the name to the beach, then go on foot on a steep rocky road for 10-15 minutes. You reach the first of three connected beaches. The real beauty are the second and the third ones with golden sand, turquoise waters, wonderful colourful rocks.
-Fyriplaka: The nudist part is after the rocks on the farthest western end of the beach (beyond the giant rock). Crystal clear waters and a very impressive landscape. The road is bumpy, and an ugly factory stands 2 km before the beach – don't be misled, it is the right direction!
-Paleochori: One of the best beaches in Greece. It is very long with 3 sections. The northernmost section after some fallen rocks is the one where you can swim nude. The nudist part, is at your left after the rocks, when you stand looking at the sea where you will notice some gay nudists, too.
-Triades: After you park your car, Walk down the easy path and you're on the first beach. Walk across the beach and then a little up the hill and then again a little walk down you reach the second beach. If you do this thing once more you reach the third beach. There you may find nudists and some gays.

Cyclades Islands – **Mykonos**

Mykonos is a truly unique island, combining the warmth, beauty and hospitality for which Greece is famous for with a whole host of gay venues to suit all tastes and ages. While most guys flock to the busy beaches of Super Paradise and Elia followed by an all night session in town, it is possible to take a break from this hectic social life. There are many less discovered parts of the island worth exploring, including some secluded coves and several laid back resorts; for an unforgettable mix of Greek culture be sure to visit the ancient ruins at Delos.
Wild nights, steamy beach life, sexy guys (and beautiful architecture!) – all the ingredients you need for a hot, fun-packed vacation.

Mykonos ist eine wirklich einzigartige Insel, auf der sich die Sonne, Schönheit und Gastfreundschaft, für die Griechenland berühmt ist, mit einer riesigen Vielfalt an Szenetreffs für jede Altersgruppe und jeden Geschmack vereinen.
Die meisten Männer strömen zwar tagsüber an die populären Strände Super Paradise und Elia und ziehen bis in die frühen Morgenstunden durch die Stadt, es ist aber auch durchaus möglich, sich vom hektischen Treiben zurückzuziehen. Es gibt unzählige weniger bekannte Gegenden auf der Insel, deren Entdeckung sich lohnt, darunter einige abgelegene, kleine Buchten und mehrere sehr entspannte Urlaubsorte. Wer einen unvergesslichen Einblick in die griechische Kultur nehmen möchte, sollte einen Besuch der antiken Ausgrabungen auf Delos nicht vergessen. Wilde Nächte, ein äußerst erotisches Strandleben, geile Männer (und wunderbare Architektur!) – was könnte man mehr erwarten für einen heißen, mit Spaß und spannenden Begegnungen nur so vollgepackten Urlaub?

Mykonos comble tous les voeux des vacanciers: des nuits excitantes, des plages débordantes d'activité, des mecs sexy et une superbe architecture. Les plages de Super Paradies et de Elia attirent nombre d'hommes qui, le soir venu, vont ensuite faire la fête en ville. Les touristes désirant s'éloigner de ce tumulte iront plutôt visiter les régions plus calmes de l'île où l'on trouve des baies retirées et plusieurs lieux d'hébergement. L'impressionnante culture grecque est présente dans les ruines de Délos.
Mykonos dispose d'un milieu gay pour tous les âges et tous les goûts. C'est une île vraiment unique qui jouit d'un climat chaud, d'une nature très belle et de l'hospitalité grecque.

Mykonos es realmente una isla única, en la que se unen el calor humano, la belleza y la hospitalidad por la que Grecia es tan conocida con la gran variedad de puntos de encuentro gay para cualquier gusto o grupo de edad. La mayoría de hombres se dirigen durante el día a las populares playas Super Paradise y Elia y por la noche están hasta las primeras horas de la mañana por la ciudad; de todos modos, también se puede escapar de este ambiente tan agotador. Hay incontables zonas poco conocidas en la isla que merecen ser descubiertas, entre ellas algunas pequeñas y apartadas calas y varios lugares muy relajantes. Quien quiera llevarse un inolvidable recuerdo de la cultura griega, no debe olvidar la visita a las antiguas excavaciones arqueológicas de Delos.
Noches salvajes, el erótico ritmo de vida en la playa, hombres guapísimos (y una arquitectura maravillosa!) – ¿qué más se puede pedir de unas vacaciones calurosas?

Mykonos è un'isola particolarissima dove si possono ritrovare tutte le caratteristiche per le quali la Grecia è conosciuta e cioè cordialità, bellezza e calore; tutto questo in combinazione con una vastissima scelta di locali e luoghi di incontro per tutti i gusti e per tutte le età. Durante il giorno, la maggior parte dei gay affluisce numerosa nelle note spiagge Super Paradise ed Elia per poi ritrovarsi in città fino all'alba. Ma a Mykonos è anche possibile fare una vita più „ritirata" per così dire. Ci sono tantissime zone sull'isola che sono meno conosciute e che vale davvero la pena visitare: tra queste alcune piccole baie che sono piuttosto nascoste e quindi difficili da raggiungere e molte altre località turistiche per turisti che cercano un po' di tranquillità. Per i turisti in cerca di cultura, da non perdere sono le antiche rovine di Delos. Notti selvagge, una vita da spiaggia più che erotica, uomini da sballo... e un' architettura bellissima! ...cosa ci si potrebbe aspettare di più da una vacanza?

PUBLICATIONS

Mykonos Gay Guide & Cyclades
☏ 211 0112510 💻 www.gaymykonos.gr
The annually gay guide of Mykonos & rest of Cyclades island publishing every year (at the end of May) with free distribution in Mykonos, rest of Cyclades, Athens & Thessaloniki.

BARS

Elysium Sunset Bar (! B G M MA OS PI) 10-?h (Jun-Sep)
Area School of Fine Art *At Elysium Hotel* ☏ 22890 23952
The swimming pool of the well known Elysium Hotel open for the public. Don't miss the unique sunset shows!

Kastro Bar (B MA NG) May-Oct 12-3h
Paraportiani *Next to Paraportiani church* ☏ 22890 23072
💻 www.kastrobar.gr
Since 1976 Kastro Bar is the Hot Spot in Mykonos to start your night.

Le Vent (B GLM M MA OS) All day (May-Oct)
Super Paradise Beach ☏ 6933 118152
💻 www.facebook.com/profile.php?id=100001179499828&sk=wall

Lola (B GLM MA OS) All year 19-?h
Zanni Pitaraki 4 & Mitropoleos streets *Limni area* ☏ 22890 23072

Montparnasse – The Piano Bar (B GLM LM MA S)
Late April-Oct 19-3h
24 Agion Anargyron Street ☏ 22890 23719 💻 www.thepianobar.com
Celebrating our 30th season in 2012. Let us tempt you with our classic and contemporary cocktails, along with nightly performances by our amazing lineup of cabaret entertainers.

Porta (AC B D GLM MA OS s) Apr-Oct 21-3h
Porta area *Behind Nikos Tavern* ☏ 22890 27087

DANCECLUBS

Babylon (B D G MA OS)
Summer: daily 22-?h, winter: WE & bank holidays only
Old harbour *Waterfront to Paraportiani*

In the town's seaside picturesque corner, near the famous Paraportiani church, with seating area outside on the pier. Babylon bar gathers every night one of the most colourful crowds on the island.

■ **Cavo Paradiso** (B D NG OS PI) May-Sep 24-9h
Opp. Paradise Beach ☎ 22890 26124 💻 www.cavoparadiso.gr
A famous club with guest deejays. Mostly gay in Sep.

■ **Jackie O'** (B D G MA OS ST) 22-? h
Old Harbour *Waterfront to Paraportiani* ☎ 22890 79167
💻 www.jackieomykonos.com
Popular gay bar & club in Mykonos plays all kinds of dance music and offers unique comedy drag shows by the famous Brazilian showman Joe William.

■ **Pierro's Bar by Manto** (AC B D GLM OS ST YC) May-Sep 22.30 – 4h
Mantoyianni Street *Agia Kyriaki, near Pierros* ☎ 22890 22177
For the past three decades until today, parties, great music, good drinks, drag shows and a joyous atmosphere are what make talented artists, designers, actors and models put "Pierrois" on the world map.

Mykonos

EAT & DRINK	
Avra – Restaurant	14
Bakalo – Restaurant	13
Catari – Pizzeria	20
Elysium Sunset – Bar	19
Fato A Mano – Retaurant	8
Kastro – Bar	3
Kounelas Fish Tavern – Restaurant	9
Lola – Bar	5
Montparnasse – The Piano Bar	4
Nikos Tavern – Restaurant	7
Porta – Bar	6

NIGHTLIFE	
Babylon – Danceclub	1
Jackie O' – Danceclub	2
Pierros – Danceclub	15

ACCOMMODATION	
Elysium – Hotel	18

OTHERS	
Mykonos Accommodation Centre	12
Sabbia – Fashion Shops	10

RESTAURANTS

■ **Avra Restaurant** (! AC B GLM M OS VEG) May-Oct 12-?h
27 Kalogera Street ☎ 22890 22298 💻 www.avra-mykonos.com
Greek and international seafood cuisine, efficient service, intimate atmosphere and reasonable prices, satisfying even the most demanding customers.

■ **Bakaló Greek Eatery** (AC CC G M MA OS VEG WI)
Apr-Oct 19-?h
☎ 22890 78121 💻 www.bakalo.gr
Newly born gay owned Greek eatery in downtown Mykonos, fresh local ingredients, traditional home cooking, trendy retro decor, friendly service and ...prices!

■ **Catarí Pizzeria** (AC B CC G M MA OS WI) Apr-Oct 16.30-?h
Near Leto Hotel ☎ 22890 78571 💻 www.catari.gr
Cool gay owned pizzeria where you dine under palm trees; enjoy crispy Neapolitan pizzas, sip sensational cocktails or indulge in all time home made pastas!

■ **Fato a Mano** (B CC M MA NG OS PK VEG) May-Oct Daily 12-2h
Meletopoulou Square, Chora *Limni Area* ☎ 22890 26256
💻 www.fatoamano.gr
Unique and delicious tastes with emphasis of the cuisine of Thessaloniki (North Greece), a list of carefully selected wines, excellent and friendly service. Minimalistic interior and exterior.

■ **Fish Tavern Kounelas** (b M MA NG OS PK VEG)
Evenings from 20 Apr-15 Oct only
Svoronoy *Near Porta Bar* ☎ 22890 28220
The freshest fish in Mykonos. Choose your fish and have it grilled immediately. This small restaurant with its charming courtyard is a tip from the locals. Winner of many awards. Good and very friendly service.

■ **Nikos Tavern** (CC G MA OS) Apr-Oct 12-?h
Agias Monis sq. ☎ 22890 28220
A traditional fish tavern with home-made meals & fresh fishes open day & night (lunch & dinner) with many gay tourists.

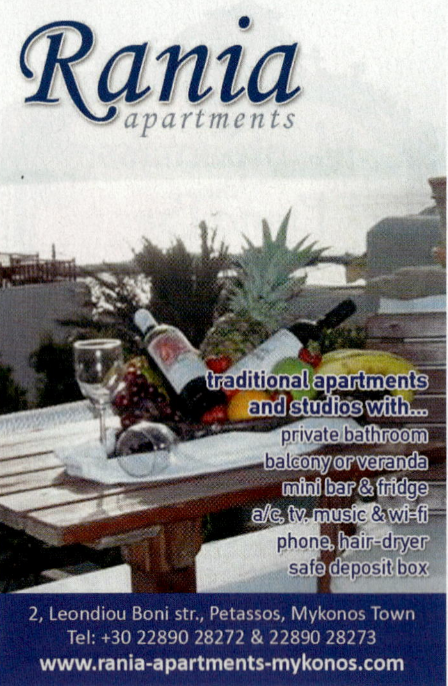

FASHION SHOPS

Sabbia Summerwear
Agiou Gerassimou 8 ☎ 22890 79284

TRAVEL AND TRANSPORT

Mykonos Accommodation Center (AC CC GLM MA)
8.30-22.30, winter: 8.30-22, Sun -12h
Enoplon Dynameon No.10 *1st floor, above Nautical Museum*
☎ (22890) 23160 ☎ 23408 🖳 www.mykonos-accommodation.com
Gay-friendly travel agency. Reservations for all hotels, apartments, villas, excursions, cruises, car rental on Mykonos plus all similar travel services for the surrounding Cycladic Islands (Santorini, Paros, Naxos, Syros, Tinos, Ios) and Athens.

HOTELS

Elysium (AC B BF CC GLM I M MSG NU OS PA PI PK RWB RWS RWT SA SB WH WO) May-Oct
Area School of Fine Art *150 m from the central bus station*
☎ 22890 23952 🖳 www.elysiumhotel.com
Exclusive gay 1st class hotel with swimming pool (nudism is allowed), pool bar, open-air Jacuzzi, spa, gym, sauna & steam room.

Golden Star
(AC B BF CC GLM I m MSG OS PI RWS RWT SA WH WO) May-Oct
Sotiraki *150m from the central bus station* ☎ 22890 23883
☎ 22890 24922 🖳 www.goldenstarhotel.gr
A 4 star hotel with 29 well-decorated rooms and 3 luxury suites, all of which have private balconies or terraces and a variety of conveniences. Pool (with hydro-massage) and pool bar. Rent-a-car and bike services. Located 200 m away from the beach and within walking distance to the centre of town.

Kouros Hotel & Suites (AC BF glm H I M MSG PI WO) Apr-Oct
Tagoo ☎ 22890 25381 🖳 www.kouroshotelmykonos.gr
With its exceptional Mykonian architecture, Kouros Hotel & Suites is one of the most charming hotels in Greece. All the rooms and suites of Kouros boutique hotel in Mykonos, Greece offer an astonishing sea view and a breathtaking Cyclades sunset.

Mykonos Star (AC B BF CC glm H I M PI) Open from Apr-Oct
Agios Sostis ☎ 22890 24032 🖳 www.mykonos-star.com

Spanelis (AC BF CC glm H I m OS PK RWS RWT) May-Oct
Tangoo *Near Old Port* ☎ 22890 23081 🖳 www.spanelishotel.com

Tharroe of Mykonos
(AC B BF glm H I M MA PA PI PK RWB RWS RWT SA SB VA WO) May-Oct
Angelica Street *900 m from center of town* ☎ 22890 27370-4
🖳 www.tharroeofmykonos.gr
A deluxe hotel and spa, renovated in 2007, located on the top of a small hill, offering panoramic view of the Aegean Sea and breathtaking sunsets. A brilliant blend of traditional Mykonian architecture with sophisticated luxury influences and modern facilities.

Villa Konstantin (AC BF GLM I OS PI RWS) All year, 24hrs
Agios Vassilios *700 m from Mykonos Town* ☎ 22890 26204
🖳 www.villakonstantin-mykonos.gr
Warm and inviting „home from home" Guest House with private studios and apartments set in a peaceful location with stunning views and quick access to Town and the nightlife.

APARTMENTS

Anchor Apartments (H)
Downtown ☎ 22890 24457 🖳 www.anchormykonos.com

Pinelopi Villa (AC CC NG OS) April – October
Limni Choras ☎ 22890 23159 🖳 www.villapinelopi.gr

Rania Apartments (AC B CC GLM NR OS RWT WI) All year
2, Leondiou Boni Street *Petassos area* ☎ 22890 28272 ☎ 22890 28273
🖳 www.rania-apartments-mykonos.com
It's built according to the traditional Cycladic architectural style. The hospitable management and friendly staff provide all-inclusive services.

Yakinthos Residence
(AC CC DM DU MA NG OS PI PK RWB RWS RWT W) May – Sep
Panormos *Panormos Bay* ☎ 22890 29183
🖳 www.yakinthos-residence.gr
A privately owned complex of 11 traditionally built suites and studios, located in Panormos Bay.

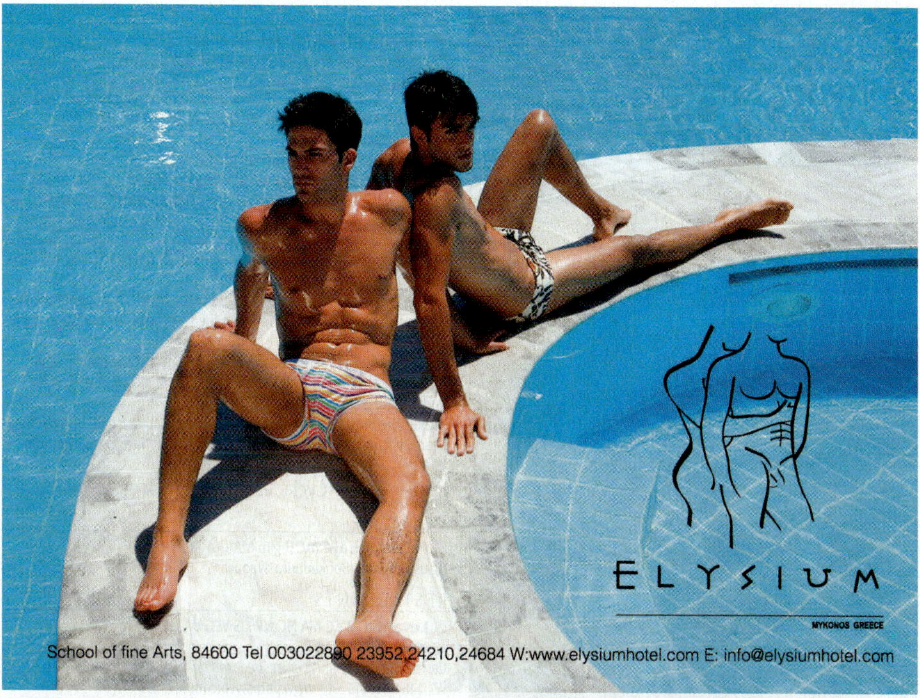
ELYSIUM
MYKONOS GREECE
School of fine Arts, 84600 Tel 003022890 23952,24210,24684 W:www.elysiumhotel.com E: info@elysiumhotel.com

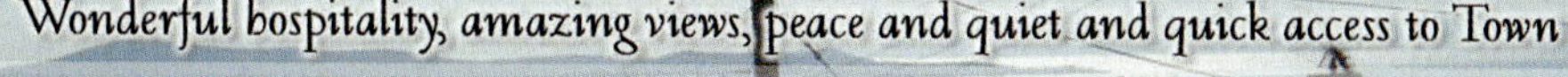

Wonderful hospitality, amazing views, peace and quiet and quick access to Town
VILLA KONSTANTIN offers an alternative to the usual hotel. Our self-catering apartments and studios allow you to experience a 'Home-Away-From-Home' feel but at the same time caters to all your needs!
VILLA KONSTANTIN
Agios Vassilios, Mykonos, Greece :: Tel: +30 22890 26204 & + 30 694 4777674 :: Fax: +30 22890 26205
FB: Villa Konstantin - Mykonos :: E: info@villakonstantin-mykonos.gr :: W: www.villakonstantin-mykonos.gr

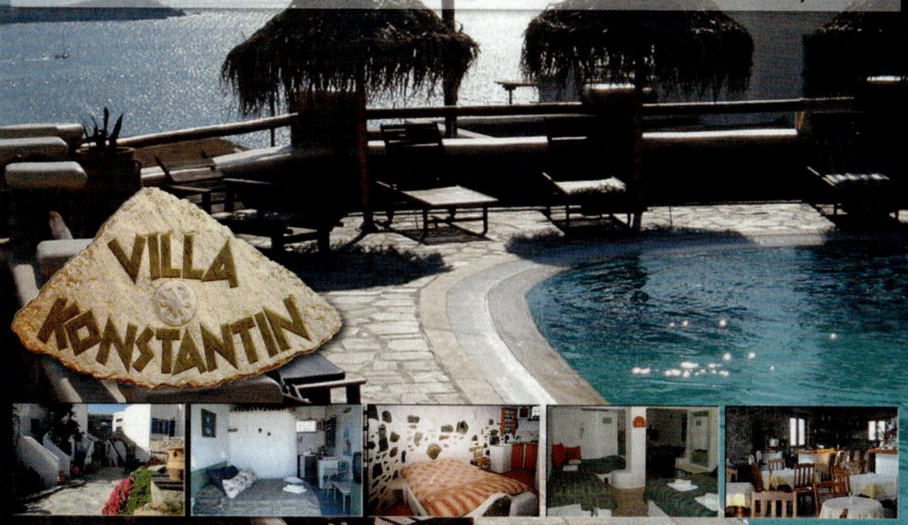

SWIMMING

-Elia Beach: It's a favourite of gay sun worshippers, it can be reached by bus or by boat from the harbour, otherwise take the bus to Plati Yiallos, and from there the little fishing boat will take you .The nudists part is on the right side, while on the right and immediately within the next two gulfs you will meet only gay swimmers and there is a lot of cruising on the rocks. You can also go by road to the nearby beach Argari and walk on the cliffs to the left of the beach until you reach gay men and the first bay with gay swimmers.
-Paranga Beach: Gay cruising around the rocks on the south side of the beach.
-Super Paradise: Super Paradise Beach is located right next to Paradise Beach and is reachable by taxi-boat (regular boat services are available from Platis Yialos) and local bus. It's the most famous gay beach of Greece with a lot of gay cruising, gay fun & nudism on the right part of it.

CRUISING

-Panagia Paraportiani church (An 800 years old church with a lot of gay cruising around it in the evening & late at night but mostly after the bars closing)
-Public toilets (at the waterfront, beside the harbor, on the way to Paraportiani church).

Cyclades Islands – **Naxos**

BARS

Babylonia (B GLM MA) 21-4.30h
Chora Naxos *On the seafront near the harbour*
☎ 69764 92350
On the 1st floor with balcony. Look for the rainbow flag.

Notos (B GLM MA) 21-4.30h
Chora Naxos *At Ancient Agora*

CAFES

Captain's (B MA NG) Apr-Oct, all day
Chora Naxos *Back of City Hall* ☎ 22850 22820

HOTELS

Three Lakes Hotel (AC BF DU H OS RWB RWS RWT WI)
April – October
☎ 6977 33 57 77 www.hotelthreelakes.gr
A marvelous holiday complex with a wonderful view of the Aegean Sea, located on the West coast-side in Agios Prokopios, near Naxos Town.

SWIMMING

-Agia Anna: If you walk to the southern edge of the beach, you will meet gay swimmers and nudists.
- Agios Prokopios: At the northern end of the beach rocks penetrate the sea and create a unique scenery. It is the first choice for nudists and gay tourists.
- Maragas: A lovely sandy beach, situated almost at the middle of the west coast of the island, at the northern edge of a cove. It is ideal for nudism and gay cruising.
-Plaka: The most beautiful beach of the island, at the south of Agia Anna beach. It is nearly deserted and so offered for nudism and gay cruising.

Cyclades Islands – **Paros**

BARS

Fotis Art Café (AC B glm MA OS) Apr-Oct 19-?h
Agios Dimitrios-Boukadoura, Naousa ☎ 6944 426431

RESTAURANTS

Levantis (B CC MA NG NR OS VEG WL)
18.30-0.30h, May-Oct
Castro Parikia *Central market street, in Parikia's old town*
☎ 22840 23613 www.parosweb.com/levantis

Open Garden (B MA NG OS) Apr-Oct, daily 19-24h
River Road *Potami* ☎ 22840 51433
Enjoy a serene dinner from a Belgian-Greek chef, in the minimalist cool white and blue modern environment that host also special live music events each year.

HOTELS

Hermes Hotel (! AC BF G MSG OS RWB RWS RWT WI) Apr-Oct
☎ 22840 21217 www.hotelhermes.gr
Very friendly with massage on offer by the owner.

GUEST HOUSES

Anthippi Guest House
(AC B BF CC DU H M OS PA PI RWS RWT WI) Apr-Oct
Kakapetra ☎ 22840 21601 ☎ 694 4549935 (mobile)
www.anthippi.com
Self-catering studios & apartments for up to 4 persons each, hosted in a traditional farmhouse.

SWIMMING

-Langeri: Beautiful, wide, sandy beach near Naousa. The smallest beach on the northeastern edge of the island with few swimmers. You can go by boat from Naousa in 15 minutes.

Cyclades Islands – **Santorini**

BARS

Murphy's (AC B D G MA) Mar-Nov
Fira ☎ 22860 22248
Friendly typical Irish Pub.

DANCECLUBS

Tropical (AC B D G MA)
Fira ☎ 22860 23089
Popular for gay tourists.

HOMERIK POEMS
apartments & suites
Firostefani, 84700 Santorini, Cyclades, Greece
Tel: +30 22860 24661 - 3 • Fax: +30 22860 24660
WWW.HOMERICPOEMS.GR

HOTELS

Homeric Poems Apartments & Suites
(AC B BF CC FH glm H I M MA OS PI RWB RWS RWT WI) Apr-Oct
Firostefani ☎ 22860 24661 ☎ 22860 24663
www.homericpoems.gr
Each apartment with furnished balconies with magnificent view, bathtub, hairdryer-accessories, Fully equipped kitchenette with cooking utensils, fridge, mini bar, safe deposit box and daily maid service.

SWIMMING

-Koloumpos, in the turn that is apartments „Soulis", park your car and you go down the path to the shore, reaching in the shore, you turn left and you walk for about 100 meters (by the shore) until you reached in the centre of gay department of the beach
-Vlychada, a beautiful beach with the best sunset (worth to see it!), the beach is extended in enormous distance and our information says to us that there is some discreet gay cruising to utmost where exist also a few nudists (even if it is difficult their locate them).

Cyclades Islands – **Syros**

SWIMMING

-Delphini: A very long beach near Kini village half occupied by nudists (discreet gay cruising)
-Orneos Galissa: Just below Agias Pakou church and only 5 mins away from Galissa main beach is this gay nudists beach with some gay cruising.

CRUISING

-Dock Bay: Discreet gay cruising during night time at the harbour, in front of the Customs Office.

Dodecanese Islands

Dodecanese Islands – **Astypalea**

SWIMMING

-Tzanaki: A bay over some rocks to the left of Livadi beach, 20 m long, with many nudists and some gay men.

Dodecanese Islands – **Kos**

DANCECLUBS

Hamam Club (AC B D G MC OS)
Akti Kountouriotou 1 *Platanos*
Very popular & friendly club.

Kyttaro Club (AC B D G MC OS)
Alexandrou Diakou 6 ☎ 693 2273029 www.facebook.com/kyttaroclub

SWIMMING

-Alykes, a nudists sandy beach at Tigaki, after you reach in Tigaki taxi station, you turn coastally to left, you pass and old gate and you end at the parking space on the right.

CRUISING

-Archaeological site: Cruising in the evening hours at the entry of archaeological site, (Ippokratous street), dark but safe place for acquaintances with Greeks and foreigners
-Taxi station: Discreet gay cruising in the evening at the small park above the taxi station.

Dodecanese Islands – **Patmos**

HOTELS

Skala Hotel (AC B BF CC DU H OS PA PI PK RWB RWS RWT WI)
Apr-Oct
Seafront ☎ 22470 31343 ☎ 22470 34034 www.skalahotel.gr

SWIMMING

-Petra Grikou: At the very end of Grikos main beach there is a wonderful rock situated over the sea, gay cruising on this rock, in the caves and at the beach that is located at the next gulf (NU).

Dodecanese Islands – **Ródos**

BARS

Berlin (AC B D G MA) 22-?h
Orfanidou Street 4 *New Town* ☎ 22410 32250
The popular gay bar is under new management and renovated.

Red and Blue (AC B D G MA S SNU ST T)
21-?h, closed Mon (winter only)
Er. Stavrou 2 (ex- I. Metaxa) *Old town* ☎ 22410 32661
www.wix.com/gaybarredandblue/gaybar-red-and-blue

Theatro Bar (B D GLM MA) 23-?h
Miltiadou 5 *Old Town*

SAUNAS/BATHS

Turkish Baths (G MA) Mon-Sat
Arionos sq. *Old town*

TRAVEL AND TRANSPORT

Triton Holidays (CC NG)
Nikolaou Plastira 9 ☎ 22410 21690 www.tritondmc.gr
A well established Travel Agency (since 1961), that specializes in incentives, congresses, conferences, all travel services and accommodation in Dodecanese islands.

SWIMMING

-Faliraki nudist beach (15 mins by bus from Rhodos, walk to right about 2 km along the beach to third cove)
-Beaches near Thermes Kalitheas (on the rocks near Pinewood area, right side from the small family beach).

CRUISING

-Knights Castle (Cruising in the park next to castle)
-Windmills Harbour: Cruising with cars and pedestrians near the three windmills and on the road from Mandraki to harbour.

Evia – Sterea Ellada

SWIMMING

-Hiliadou Beach: A very well known beach for nudists with some gay cruising (on the right side of the main beach), located in the middle of Evia, after Glyfada village.

Ilia – Peloponnese

SWIMMING

-Kaiafa: The left side of this very long sandy beach is ideal for nudism and the small woody area at the end of the beach is used as a gay cruising place
-Lintzi: At Lintzi main beach, after the canteen, there are nudists and some gay cruising.

Ioannina – Epirus

CRUISING

-Litharitsia Park: Gay cruising at the area behind ‚Merarhia'
-Molos: Gay cruising during the night time beside the lake.

Ionian Islands

Ionian Islands – **Ithaca**

SWIMMING

-Sarakiniko: Situated at the eastern side of Vathi and you can reach by boat from the Skinos bay as well as by car. Setting off from the small central port, you will follow a path on the left side till you find a magnificent reserved bay, ideal for gay couples and cruising.

Ionian Islands – **Kefalonia**

HOTELS

■ **Fiscardo Bay Hotel** (AC B BF CC DU H M OS PA PI PK RWB RWS RWT WI) May – Oct
☎ 26740 41295 ☎ 210 9841461 🖳 www.fiscardobay.com
This superb small boutique hotel is located a short stroll from the famous Fiscardo waterfront with its taverns, restaurants and shops.

SWIMMING

-Antisamos: Located near Sami and there is some gay cruising at the last gulf
-Avithos: Located after Argostoli airport and on the left side of the main beach, after the end, cross some rocks and then you will find a nudist beach with a lot of gay cruising
-Koroni: A nudists beach, on the way to Skala, with a lot of gay cruising on the left and right edges
-Lassi: Small gulfs for nudism and discreet gay cruising, before Makris Yalos
Myrtos: A famous beach for nudism with some gay cruising on its right edge
-Skala: Gay cruising with locals & tourists (English, Italian & German) after the rocks you see on the right side of the main beach
-Xi: Located north of Lixouri & Paliki areas and is well-known for its red sand, if you walk to the right edge of the beach, after the rock, you will find a nudism beach with a lot of gay cruising.

Ionian Islands – **Kérkyra (Corfu)** – Kérkyra

BARS

■ **Fagins** (B MA NG OS ST)
Sidari *Opposite Alkion Hotel*
Gay-friendly English bar with recurrent drag queen shows.
■ **Zanzibar** (B MA NG OS ST)
Pelekas ☎ 693 6443799
A cozy small bar in the heart of Pelekas.

RESTAURANTS

■ **Elia** (G M OS)
Mirtsiotissa Beach
■ **Giannis Taverna** (g M MA OS)
Anemomilos ☎ 26610 31066
■ **La Famiglia** (glm M MC OS)
Maniarisi Arlioti 16 ☎ 2661 030270

GENERAL GROUPS

■ **Gay Corfu Info**
☎ 6970 541764 🖳 www.gaycorfuinfo.com
A non profit website with the most updated gay information for Corfu Island.

CRUISING

-Anemomylos (Cruising during night time at the park and during day time around the toilets)
-Spaniada (Cruising after 22h at the main square of the town (upper side) just beside the main entrance of the old castle with many locals and some tourists).

Ionian Islands – **Kérkyra (Corfu)** – Mirtiotissa

SWIMMING

-Almyros: Located on the north side of the island, behind Acharavi village. Bypass the lake, cross over the bridge and you will find a beach with a lot of gay cruising (nudist area)
-Issos: Located on the north side of the island, after Acharavi village, after the lake, cross over the bridge and you will find a beach with a lot of gay cruising
-Mirtiotissa: A nudists beach near Pelekas village with a lot of gay cruising (mostly on the rocky side of the beach).

Ionian Islands – **Kythira**

SWIMMING

-Kaladi: Two bays with a large rock separating them, nudist beach and right endless caves to explore.
-Melidoni: A small picturesque beach in the southwest of the island, the most beautiful island with fine sand and fresh water. Ideal also for nudists.

Ionian Islands – **Lefkada**

SWIMMING

-Mylos Beach: A beautiful beach located between Kathisma and Agios Nikitas. To get to the mill you can either take a boat from the beach of Agios Nikitas or walk. If you decide to walk, we must start from the main pedestrian street in Agios Nikitas, and turn to close the tavern Poseidon (there is a sign to Millos). It is about 15-20 minutes walking on a path that climbs the hill that separates the two beaches. Walk left and you will find gay nudists and swimmers.
-Pefkoulia: Beautiful beach, 2.5 km north of the village Agios Nikitas. On the right side of the beach, where the trees stop at the beach, there is some liberal camp. Walk even further you will find several gay and nudist swimmers.

Ionian Islands – **Zakynthos**

SWIMMING

-Dafni: A nice beach with some gay cruising
-Vrontonero: Popular nudist beach with locals & Italian tourists and gay cruising.

Kalamata – Peloponnese

SWIMMING

-e-Filoxenia: The rocky part of the beach after the e-Filoxenia Hotel is ideal for nudism & gay cruising.
-Kalo Nero: On the west coast of the Peloponnese, some kilometres north of Kyparissia, there is the village called Kalo Nero. From about 2 km on the north of the last houses the beach is nearly deserted for distance of more than 5 km and is ideal for nude bathing and gay cruising at the end of the beach.
-Romanos Beach: One hour west of Kalamata and about 10 km from Pylos on the road to Kiparisia. The beach is easy to find. Cross the village Romanos, follow the signs to the beach, past the parking and ride alongside the beach. At the end of the road you find a beautiful long beach. The beach is visited mainly by Greek men and there is gay cruising in the dunes.
-Voidokilia Beach: Situated after Pylos and a gulf with a a big lagoon of murky water and is suitable for nudism.

Katerini – Macedonia

SWIMMING

-Korinos: From Katerini beach drive all to the left along the beach. Korinos is about 6km from that point. Along the way there is a clear view of the beach connecting Paralia and Korinos, which offers opportunities for nudism and gay cruising.
-Neoi Poroi: Located 20-30 minutes drive south of Katerini, the coastal road. Walk 500 meters south along the beach until the end of the buildings and the bend. Frequented by a few gay (near the reeds) & straight nudists & couples.
- Olympic Beach (Katerinoskala): From Katerini (or the highway) follow the road to Paralia. Just after the railway the road splits. Take the right direction which leads to Olympic beach after 7km. When you reach the beach, drive left to the end of the buildings and park. Walk for about 5-10 min and there is a beach with mixed gay & straight nudists.

Kavala – Macedonia

SWIMMING

-Ammolofi (Nea Peramos): At 25 km from the town of Kavala, across the Egnatia Odos, and 1 km from New Peramos there is the famous Ammolofi Beach (3 km legth). Three huge bays delimit the dunes, the first bay is suitable for gay cruising and more free situations.
-Eleftheron Thermals: Situated near the main road from Kavala from Thessaloniki, 46 km from Kavala. In panels for Thermals, go straight and after 1-2 kms before a abandoned small outpost, turn right on a dirt road leading to the beach. Hang straight & gay nudists.

CRUISING

-Faros: At Panagia area, around the castles of Faros, there is a path with steps to the beach with some gay cruising during the evening time
-Park: Gay cruising beside the swimming pool and at promenade close to the old fishing boats.

Kriti Island

Kriti – Chania

CAFES

■ **Dyo Lux Revolution** (AC B GLM m MA OS) Daily 9-3h
Sarpidonos 8 *Near the east old venetian port* ☎ 28 210 52 515

HOTELS

■ **Halepa Hotel** (AC BF CC H PI) All year
Eleftheriou Venizelou 164 ☎ 2821028440 💻 www.halepa.com
Located close to the center of town and blends the charm and personality of yesterday with the amenities and technology of today.

APARTMENTS

■ **Athina Luxury Villas** (AC BF cc H PI) All year
Xamoudochori Platanias ☎ 2821 020960 ☎ 2821 096300
💻 www.athinavillas.gr
■ **Marianna Luxury Apartments** (CC PI) All year
Almirida, Apokoronas ☎ 28210 92509 ☎ 697 4827178
💻 www.almyrida-apartments.gr
A brand new complex of 4 air-conditioned maisonettes with a swimming pool, all with large living room, full kitchen equipment, bathroom, WC and bedrooms with balconies that can accommodate 2-5 persons each.

SWIMMING

-Agioi Apostoloi: Cruising at the rocky left & right side of the main beach
-Georgioypolis Beach: One the way to Rethymnon, after Georgioupoli, turn to the 1st parking space to the left and drive to the beach, stop at 100-200 m and go to this part of beach that there some gay cruising at the sand-dunes
-Macherida Beach: In Tarsanas, Akrotiri, 13 km from Chania, rocky with small, sandy bays (NU).

CRUISING

-Agoras Square: Discreet cruising around public toilets.

Kriti – Heraklion

BARS

■ **Desire Club** (AC B D glm MA) Daily
Esplanande (onshore avenue)
■ **Eros** (AC B D G MA OS S) Apr-Oct: 20-4, Fri & Sat -6; Nov-Mar: from 23h
Emmanouel Tsagaraki, Malia *Hersonissos, on the road between Malia Port and the cemetery, opp. Yiannis Manos Hotel* ☎ 699 6462022
💻 www.erosbarcrete.com
Busiest on Sat.
■ **Pagopiion** (AC B g MC) All day
Agiou Titou square ☎ 2810 346028
■ **Take Five** (AC B g MA) All day
Arkoleontos 7 ☎ 2810 226564

SWIMMING

-Anisaras: A nudists beach at Hersonissos
-Gournes: Gay nudists use the section that is far away from the little port and the shower facilities, the beach is also used as gay cruising place
-Karteros: A beautiful beach at Agios Ioannis (at the end of the airport, Nea Alikarnasos) with gay cruising back of the rocky area
- Kommos: To reach Kommos beach you'll have to follow the road towards „Matala", when you reach the small village of „Pitsidia" slow down and look at your right so you won't miss the turn to Kommos beach, follow the road until you meet a crossroad, the road to your right goes straight to the beach and if you feel lucky you might find some good parking there as well, the two small hills at the right of the excavations area are the cruising area (having the excavations area at your left go up on the hill to your right)
-Lido: Nudists use the beach behind the swimming pool; gay cruising area at the reeds
-Malia: A famous beach for nudism with a lot of tourists and gay cruising at the rocky area
-Sarantari: A nudists beach with gay cruising at Hersonissos.

CRUISING

-Ammoudara: In the evening at the beach in the backyard of „Carrefure", around the parking area on the way to the beach
-Georgiadis Park: close to Eleftherias square, 100 m from the center of the town
-Kazatzakis Momentum: Plastira street
-Behind Pagkritio Stadium and close to Yofiros river.

Kriti – Hersonossos

BARS

■ **Roze Maandag** (! AC B D GLM I MA OS PA PK WE WI) 20-2h
C. Parlama Str. / Filonidou Zotou Str. *Centre* ☎ (28970) 21563
💻 www.rozemaandag-kreta.com
Roze Maandag(Pink Monday) is the first and only gay bar in Hersonissos, Crete!

APARTMENTS

■ **Villa Ralfa** (BF GLM H I MA MSG NR NU OS PK RES RWB RWS RWT WI) All year
Villa Ralfa *3km from Port Hersonissos, 25km from Heraklion Airport*
☎ 694 710 2573
Self contained apartment, lesbian and gay homestay with double bed.

Kriti – Lasithi

SWIMMING

-Agia Fotia: A beautiful beach near Ierapetra village that is used discreetly as gay cruising place
-Finikodasos Vai: One of the most beautiful beaches in Greece with gay cruising on the left and on the right side.

Kriti – Rethymno

HOTELS

■ **Creta Mare** (AC BF cc M) All year
Plakias ☎ 28320 32239 💻 www.cretamareplakias.com

SWIMMING

-Ammoudi: A nudist beach on the road to Plakia village with some gay cruising
-Arsaniou Monastery: On the way to Rethymno town, from the old national road, at Arsaniou Monastery area (after El Greco Hotel and the bridge), turn to the right at the first dirt road, park your car and walk to the beach for nudism and gay cruising
-Mikro Ammoudaki & Klisidi: In between Ammoudi & Damnoni beaches, on the way to Plakia (S. Rethymno), there are these two small gulfs that offered for nudism & gay cruising.

CRUISING

-Harbour: Cruising during night time at the new marine.

Loutraki – Peloponnese

CRUISING

-Perivolakia Central Square
-Michanikou Beach (below infantry camp)
-Milokopis (1km from waterfall).

Nafplio – Peloponnese

SWIMMING

-Karathonas: Located near Arvanitia and it's suitable for nudism & gay cruising.

North Aegean Islands

North Agean Islands – **Chios**

SWIMMING

-Mavra Volia (Nudist beach with some gay cruising that takes place at Emporios village)
-Porto Loubino Mersinidi (Gay nudist beach near Vrontados village, close to the Monastery)
-Daskalopetra (An ideal beach for nudism and some gay cruising).

North Agean Islands – **Ikaria**

APARTMENTS

■ **Cavos Bay** (AC BF CC NG OS PI) Apr-Oct
Faros Armenistis ☎ 22750 71381-3

SWIMMING

-Drakano: Famous sandy small beach with some nudists and cruising on its left side.

North Agean Islands – **Lesvos** – Eressos

BARS

■ **10th Muse** (B BF gLm OS) 9-?h
Main Square, Skala ☎ 22530 53287

■ **Aqua** (B D GLM OS VS) 20-?h
Skala
The well known „Fuego Bar" with a billiard's hall, video projections, karaoke nights and special women only parties.

■ **Mariana** (B gLm OS) All day
Skala
The oldest and most proud lesbian café / bar of Eressos Beach.

DANCECLUBS

■ **Naos** (B D GLM) 23-?h
Skala
The only disco in Eressos. Located on the road from Eressos Beach to Skala.

RESTAURANTS

■ **Margaritari** (GLM M OS) All day
Skala ☎ 22530 53042
Ideal place for snacks and sweets. Located by the sea on the best spot of Skala Eressos.

■ **Saranis** (GLM M MA) All day
Skala
High quality european restaurant at Sappho Hotel.

North Agean Islands – **Lesvos** – Molyvos

BARS

■ **Molly's** (B GLM MC OS)
Molivos Harbour ☎ 22530 71539
Molly's Bar is located in an old fisherman's house in the narrow street at the entrance to picturesque Molivos Harbour. The bar is open every evening during the main holiday season (end April to mid October) for drinks, cocktails, coffee and bar snacks.

SWIMMING

-Eftalou Beach: A nudists beach with gay cruising near Molivos. Pass on foot the thermals and the taverns and after 500 meters is the main beach with a lot of straight swimmers. Gay swimmers and nudists exist at the end of the main beach.

North Agean Islands – **Lesvos** – Mytilene

CRUISING

-Mytilene's Park: Cruising during the evening hours near the theatre.

North Agean Islands – **Limnos**

SWIMMING

-Thanos: A nudists beach with some gay cruising.

North Agean Islands – **Samos**

BARS

■ **Kalimera** (AC B g)
Kokari ☎ 22730 92568

RESTAURANTS

■ **Blue Chairs** (AC glm M)
Vourliotes ☎ 22730 93311

■ **Galazio Pigadi** (AC glm M)
Vourliotes ☎ 22730 93480

■ **Nireas** (AC glm M)
Kokkari

CRUISING

-Tsamadou beach (g NU) (An ideal beach for nudism, the gay cruising area with natives and soldiers is located at the rocky side of the beach).

Patra – Peloponnese

DANCECLUBS

■ **YMCA DanceFloor II** (! B D GLM MA S) Thu-Sat 23-?h
Kanari 90, Psila Alonia ☎ 698 2940534
A beautiful club with perfect decoration, music, shiny dancefloor, hot shows, amazing dancers and DJ's.

SWIMMING

-Akrata: 10 km beyond Akrata village (direction to Egio), at the old national road, there is a beautiful beach with a lot of gay cruising, located 5-7 km after a bridge, left & right of parking area
-Kalogria (Eastern Beach): The most famous beach in the area with gay nudist and only 35 km west of Patras (near Araxos), after the parking area at the main beach head to the hill, follow the path next to the „Nun's Castle" and finally you are right at the gay section of the beach
-Kalogria (Western Beach): Go towards Kalogria beach and turn left after the woods and again left at the first dirt road, you will meet gay nudists after the parking area (left side)
-Kastelokampos: A nudist's beach with many gay people and cruising, right next to Achaia Beach Hotel
-Kounoupeli Hyrmini Baths: The beach at Hyrmini Baths is suitable for nudism and some gay cruising.

CRUISING

Patras is a closed society and gays prefer to meet each other in friendly venues, beaches and some cruising spots. So, if you meet a gay man from this area, ask him to meet also his friends and everything will develop smoothly.
-Port, by the pier: Discreet cruising during evening times at promenade with „straight" and natives
-KTEL (long distance bus terminal): cruising at the parking area late at night & in the toilet's during all day
-Mili: Discreet gay cruising late at night around the streets at Myloi (before KTEL).

Piraeus – Sterea Ellada

SEX CINEMAS

■ **Olympic Cinema** (AC g VS) 8-3h
88 Filonos Street ☎ 210 429 47 01
Cruisy area is in the toilets.

Preveza – Epirus

SWIMMING

-Artolithia: Driving to Parga, turn left at the sign „to Riza beach". Going down the hill, turn left at the first junction you will find and drive until you reach the beach (about 5-10 minutes). The left part of the beach is suitable for naturists and discreet gay cruising.
-Kanali Beach: Leaving from Preveza, about 10 Km on the way to Igoumenitsa you will find a camping and then the hotel Kanali on the right. At that point there is an interchange. You turn left and after 100m distance you turn left again and park there (there is a cafeteria). When you reach the beach, walk to the left for 3-5 minutes and you will find a few nudists straight & gay men and straight couples.

Sporades Islands

Sporades Islands – Skiathos

BARS

■ **De Facto** (AC B CC D G MA) May-Sep 20.30-?h
Grigoriou E' ☎ 24270 22068
🖳 www.skiathosinfo.com/business/defactobar.htm
The only gay bar in the island of Skiathos. It is located in the town (behind the main church of Treis Ierarches) and it's every night the „meeting point" for the all gay tourists of the island.

HOTELS

■ **Mandraki Village** (AC B BF CC glm M MC) All year
Koukounaries ☎ 24270 493014 🖳 www.mandraki-skiathos.gr

SWIMMING

-Banana Beach (nudist beach next to Kokounaries Beach; buses from town; take bus to last stop, then walk right over a small hill and through an olive grove)
-Tsougrias Island (take the boat from Skiathos, approximately hourly departures).

Sporades Islands – Skyros

SWIMMING

-Papa to Homa: The beach is situated just below the huge rock Skyros Town (Castle). It's a beautiful and quiet beach unofficial nudist with big and clean sand. There is also a cave and some rocks. The only way to get to the beach is via steep paths (due to landslides) from both the left and the right side of the beach.

Sparti – Peloponnese

SWIMMING

-Vathi: Cruising and nudism at the left side of the main beach, after the camping area.

Thessaloníki

PUBLICATIONS

■ **Screw**
🖳 screwmagazine.blogspot.com
Gay & lesbian free newspaper (in Greek only).

BARS

■ **Bar Me** (AC B D G MC VS) 23-3h
Agiou Mina 3 *Near Ladadika-Tsimiski Street* ☎ 2310 554099
■ **Bigaroon** (AC B CC GLM MA OS VS) 10.30-3.30h
44 Pavlou Mela Street *Diagwnios area* ☎ 2310 267 727 🖳 www.bigaroon.gr
■ **Eli Ela / Presante** (AC B D GLM MA) 12-3h
Vironos 5 *Diagonios* ☎ 2310 270233
■ **Stretto** (AC B d g MA) 7-4h
18 Karolou Diehl ☎ 2310 275 159

CAFES

■ **En Technes** (AC B gLm LM MA OS WI) 11-3h
Navmachias Ellis
Very popular all day cafe-bar with nice music and live guests.

DANCECLUBS

■ **Shadow Club** (! AC B D G MC SNU VS WE) Mon-Sat 22-4, Sun 5-8h
Peristeriou 4, Salonica *Ladadika* ☎ 6976 001001
With influences from London, while keeping a traditional architecture in mix with video shows and loud dance music, is the ultimate fun in the city!
■ **Da.Da Fresh** (AC B D gLm MA WE) Thu-Sat 23 – ?
Navmachias Ellis 4, Ladadika
Mainly lesbian bar.
■ **Enola** (AC B D GLM MC) 22-?h
Valaoritou 19 *2nd floor* 🖳 www.enola.gr

SEX SHOPS/BLUE MOVIES

■ **Blue Vision** (AC CC DR G MA S VS) 12-2, Fri & Sat -5h
6 Afroditis Street *Near the railway station, back of Holiday Inn Hotel*
☎ 2310 534844 🖳 www.bluevision.gr
14 cabins, glory holes, 3 cinema areas, sex shop.

SEX CINEMAS

■ **Laïkon** (g r VS) 10-4h
Monastiriou 7 *Near Vardari Square*
■ **Theano** (g r VS) 10-1h
Konstantinoupoleos 75, Botsari

■ **Vilma** (g r VS) 10-23h
Gladstonos 5, Vardaris

SAUNAS/BATHS

■ **Splash** (AC B FH G LAB M MA NU OS RR SA SB VS WH)
Sun-Thu 19-3, Fri & Sat -7h
Afroditis 23, Vardaris *4th & 5th floors* 🖳 www.splashsauna.gr
Popular sauna in 2 floors with Jacuzzi, steam room, cabins, labyrinth, TV rooms, snack bar, chill out area & roof garden.

HOTELS

■ **Avalon Hotel** (AC B BF CC DU G M MA OS PA PI PK RWB RWS RWT WI)
Airport area, Thermi ☎ 2310 46270 🖳 www.avalonhotel.gr
A 4-star hotel with warm and friendly atmosphere with luxury and quality.

■ **Colors Hotel** (AC DU G MSG RWB RWS RWT WI)
Valaoritou 21 ☎ 2310 5022 🖳 www.colorshotel.gr
Brand new 4-star hotel with comfortable spacious rooms & fully equipped with kitchenettes apartments that can accommodate up to 4 persons.

■ **Galaxy Art Hotel** (AC B BF DU G M OS RWB RWS RWT WH WI)
Merkouri 1, Oreokastro ☎ 2310 696142 🖳 www.galaxyarthotel.gr

■ **Plaza Art Hotel** (AC B DU G MA RWS RWT WI)
Pageou 5, Ladadika ☎ 2310 520120 🖳 www.hotelplaza.gr
Warm and friendly atmosphere at Thessaloniki's traditional Ladadika.

GENERAL GROUPS

■ **Co-Operation Against Homophobia (CAH)** (GLM MA)
51 Filippou ☎ 6999 249000
This Thessaloniki-based organisation, founded in 1995, fights homophobia mostly through lobbying and various consciousness raising activities.

SWIMMING

-Navagio (Shipwreck): An excellent sandy beach with dunes in Epanomi, and a nude bathing area with some gay cruising at the end of the cape, about 1 km away from the beach bars. While you walking towards to the left, you encounter more and more nudists and large groups of mostly male / gay nudists.
-Nea Iraklia: Before arriving in the village Nea Iraklia, (you will see it on a hill in front of you), turn left at a vineyard, drive straight through towards the sea, once there turn right and drive till you see a white pavilion. The part from the pavilion and for about 300m to the left is frequented by nudists, and to the end also by many gay locals.
-Nea Kalikratia: Rocky and hard to reach nudists beach with a lot of gay cruising.

CRUISING

All are AYOR:
-Small park next to Hotel Macedonian Palace
-Streets and small park around central train station (Michalikalou Street)
-Sappho's Street (back of Monastiriou at Vardaris) (R T)
-Behind the Judical court and the basketball ground.

Volos – Thessalia

HOTELS

■ **Leda Beach** (AC BF CC FH I M MSG NG OS PA PI PK RES RWB RWS RWT SB WH WO) Apr-Oct
Horto *Pilio* ☎ 24210 38008 🖳 www.ledahotel.gr
It consists of houses constructed in Pelion architectural style all looking on to the sea and the small islands of Pagassetic Gulf. These houses have rooms, studios, apartments, suites and independent villas.

SWIMMING

-Melani: A nudist beach located next to Potistika area, the left side is used as a gay cruising area
-Paradise Beach: The most famous beach for nudists in the area, located 15 km distance from Volos and after Koropi Beach, for discreet gay cruising follow the narrow path that drives you to the first beach and walk at the end to the left, near the rocks
-Plakes: The third bay after Volos Naval Club is suitable for gay acquaintances.

Greenland

Name: Kalaallit Nunaat · Grönland · Groenland · Groenlandia
Location: Greenland is located between the Arctic and Atlantic Oceans, east of the Canadian Arctic Archipelago.
Time: GMT
International Country Code: ☎ 299
Language: Greenlandic (Kalaallisut) and Danish
Area: 2,166,086 km² / 836,109 sq. mi
Currency: 1 Danish Krone (dkr) = 100 Öre
Population: 56,452
Capital: Nuuk (Godthåb)
Climate: Greenland has an Arctic climate. Winters can be severe and the summers comparatively mild, particularly in areas which are sheltered from the prevailing winds. Precipitation, mostly snow, is moderately heavy around the coast. The north of the country, and much of the interior, enjoys true Arctic weather, with the temperature only rising above freezing for brief periods in the summer.

Greenland is, by area, the world's largest island that is not a continent. It is the least densely populated dependency or country in the world.
In 1953, Greenland became a county, in principle on equal terms with the other Danish counties. Greenlandic opposition to Danish administration contributed to the introduction of home rule in 1979. Thanks to the ties with Denmark, Greenland was actually the fourth country in the world to establish a registered domestic partner law in 1996.
Over a thousand participants to part in the first Pride event in Nuuk last May, turning it into the second largest demonstration in the nationís history.

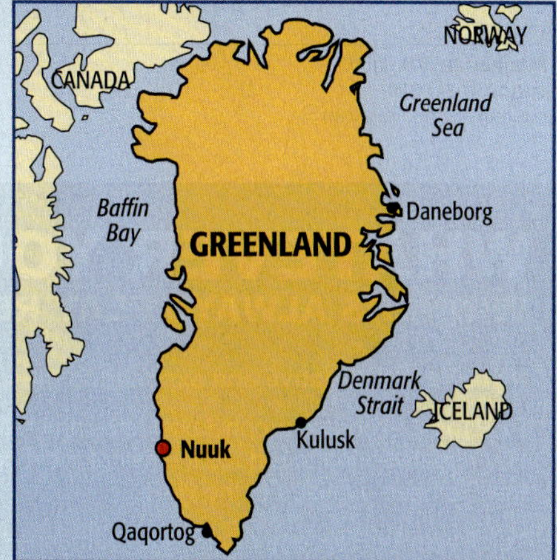

There are very few places where gay men can meet in Greenland. This is mainly due to the sparse population as well as the long and dark winters and the lack of roads, boat being the most popular method of transportation in Greenland.Internet has become the most popular means of making contact. There is only one gay-friendly location in Nuuk.

Bei Grönland handelt es sich nicht nur um die größte Insel der Erde, die kein Kontinent ist, sondern auch um das am dünnsten besiedelte Land bzw. Verwaltungsgebiet der Welt, denn seit 1953 gilt Grönland nicht mehr als Kolonie, sondern als weiterer Landkreis Dänemarks, der den anderen prinzipiell gleichgestellt ist. 1979 führte der Widerstand der Grönländer gegen die Dänische Verwaltung dann zur inneren Autonomie. Dank der Verbindung mit Dänemark war Grönland 1996 sogar das vierte Land der Welt, in dem eingetragene Partnerschaften eingeführt wurden.

Anlässlich des ersten CSD in Nuuk kamen letzten Mai über tausend Teilnehmer zusammen, was die Veranstaltung zur zweitgrößten Demonstration machte, die je im Land stattgefunden hat.

In Grönland gibt es nur wenige Orte, an denen sich schwule Männer treffen können. Das hängt vorwiegend mit der niedrigen Besiedelungsdichte zusammen, aber auch mit den langen, dunklen Wintern und dem Mangel an Straßen, denn in Grönland sind Boote das Transportmittel erster Wahl. So hat sich das Internet zum beliebtesten Medium der Kontaktanbahnung entwickelt. In Nuuk gibt es nur eine schwulenfreundliche Location.

Le Groenland est non seulement la plus grande île du monde qui ne soit pas un continent mais aussi le pays ou zone d'administration à la densité la plus faible au monde, car le Groenland n'est plus une colonie du Danemark mais une circonscription indépendantes des autres. En 1979 la résistance des Groenlandais contre l'administration danoise conduisit à une autonomie interne. Grâce au lien avec le Danemark, le Groenland fut le quatrième pays au monde à mettre en place le mariage homosexuel.

Lors de la première Gay Pride à Nuuk en mai dernier, plus de mille participants en ont fait la deuxième plus grande manifestation qu'il y ait eu dans le pays.

Au Groenland il n'existe que peu d'endroits où les gays puissent se rencontrer. Cela vient surtout du fait de la faible densité mais aussi des longs et rudes hivers et du manque de routes; le bateau étant le moyen de transport de prédilection. Par conséquent, Internet est devenu le moyen de contact le plus important. À Nuuk, il n'existe qu'un seul lieu gay-friendly.

Cuando hablamos de Groenlandia no sólo hablamos de la isla más grande del mundo, que no sea un continente, sino también del país/área administrativa menos poblada del mundo, ya que desde 1953 Groenlandia deja de ser una colonia y pasa a convertirse en una región autónoma de Dinamarca. En 1979, la resistencia de los groenlandeses contra la administración danesa condujo a la autonomía. Gracias a la relación con Dinamarca, Groenlandia fue, en 1996, el cuarto país del mundo en el que se introdujeron políticas para el registro de parejas.

Con ocasión de la celebración del primer CSD en Nuuk, se reunieron en mayo pasado más de mil participantes, que hicieron que el acontecimiento se convirtiese en la segunda mayor manifestación que ha tenido lugar en el país.

En Groenlandia, hay pocos lugares de encuentro para hombres gays. Esto se debe, principalmente a la baja densidad de población, a los largos y oscuros inviernos, y también a la falta de carreteras; en Groenlandia los barcos son el medio de transporte por excelencia. Es por esto que Internet se ha desarrollado como el medio de comunicación favorito dentro de la comunidad. Nuuk sólo cuenta con un local gay friendly.

La Groenlandia non è solo l'isola più grande del mondo che non costituisce continente, ma anche il paese più scarsamente popolato. Dal 1953 la Groenlandia non è più una colonia, bensì un distretto della Danimarca ugualmente equiparato agli altri. Nel 1979 la resistenza della sua popolazione nei confronti dell'amministrazione danese ha portato all'autonomia. Grazie al rapporto con la Danimarca, nel 1996 la Groenlandia è stato il quarto paese al mondo ad aver introdotto le unioni registrate. Al primo CSD, svoltosi a Nuuk lo scorso maggio, hanno partecipato più di mille persone, facendo di questa manifestazione la seconda manifestazione più grande che sia mai stata organizzata in Groenlandia. In Groenlandia ci sono solo pochi luoghi dove i gay si possono incontrare. Ciò ha a che fare, per lo più, con la scarsa densità di popolazione, ma anche con i bui inverni e la scarsità di strade, visto che in Groenlandia il mezzo di trasposto di prima scelta è la barca. È anche per questo che internet è diventato un mezzo di comunicazione fondamentale per allacciare contatti. A Nuuk c'è solo un locale gay friendly.

Nuuk

DANCECLUBS

Manhattan (B D glm YC)
Imaneq 30 ☎ 34 80 80
The only gay-friendly club in town.

HOTELS

Hotel Hans Egede (BF CC I M NG RWB RWT)
Hotel Hans Egede A/S, Postboks 1049 ☎ 32 42 22 www.hhe.gl
The hotel has 140 modern rooms and 10 well-equipped hotel apartments each with a kitchen, a bathroom and laundry facilities. There is free access to 12 tv channels in all rooms and apartments – and if you stay in polar class or in a suite, three hours of wireless internet is included in the room price.

Guam

Location: Pacific Ocean
Initials: GU
Time: GMT +10
International Country Code: ☏ 1 671 (no area codes)
International Access Code: ☏ 011
Language: Chamorro, English
Area: 549 km² / 212 sq mi.
Currency: 1 US Dollar (US$) = 100 Cents.
Population: 166,090
Capital: Hagatna
Religions: 90% Catholic
Climate: Tropical marine climate. The dry season lasts from Jan-Jun, the rainy season from Jul-Dec. There's little seasonal temperature variation.

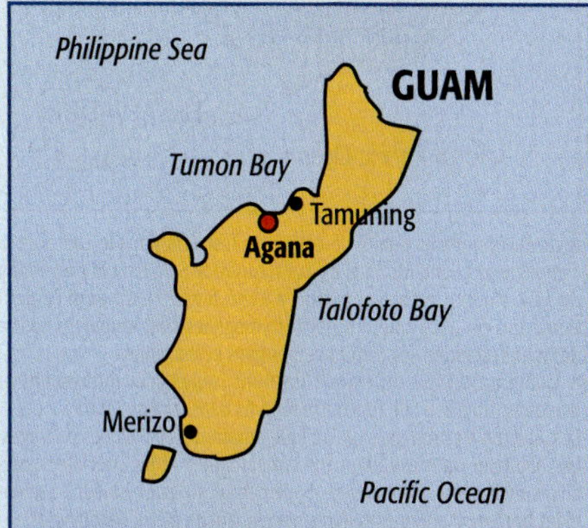

Although no juridical information is available, it is mentioned in Internet that the age of consent is generally 16 years of age.

Zwar liegen uns keine juristischen Informationen vor, allerdings ist dem Internet zu entnehmen, dass das Schutzalter generell bei 16 Jahren liegt.

Nous ne possédons certes pas dìinformations juridiques, mais on sait à travers Internet que la majorité sexuelle est fixée à 16 ans.

No disponemos de ninguna información jurídica; no obstante gracias a Internet se desprende que la edad de consentimiento en general está en los 16 años.

Anche se non disponiamo di notizie di natura giuridica, apprendiamo da internet che l'età del consenso è generalmente di 16 anni.

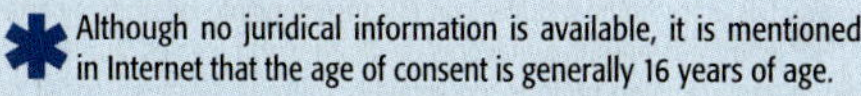

Agaña

GENERAL GROUPS

Guam Friends
P.O. Box 1861 ☏ 649 94 54
A, non-profit organization aimed chiefly at helping visitors discover gay Guam.

Tumon

BARS

Club Denial (B g MC SNU)
☏ 646-2526
Amateur strip night on Wednesdays.

CRUISING

-Ypao Beach Park (21-2h).

Guatemala

Location: Central America
Initials: GCA
Time: GMT -6
International Country Code: ☏ 502 (no area codes)
International Access Code: ☏ 00
Language: Spanish
Area: 108,889 km² / 42,042 sq mi.
Currency: 1 Quetzal (Q) = 100 Centavos
Population: 12,295,000
Capital: Ciudad de Guatemala
Religions: 80% Roman Catholic; 19% Protestant
Climate: The dry season (Nov-May) is the best time, weather-wise, to visit Guatemala.

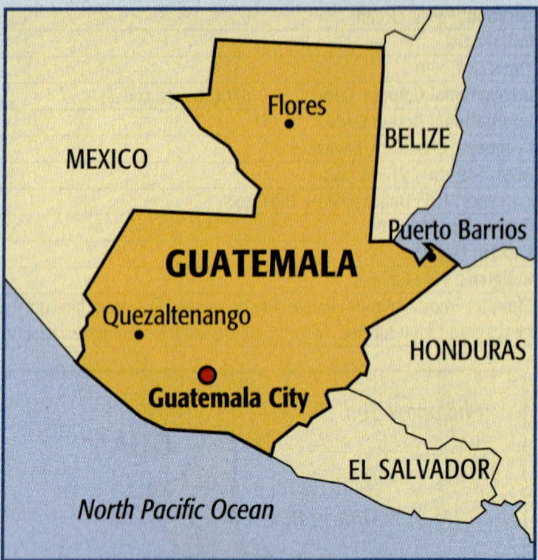

Homosexual acts between consenting men over the age of eighteen are legal. However, we have received conflicting reports on the actual social conditions for gay men. The shortcomings in human rights issues in Guatemala remain a major problem and Guatemala is light years away from some of its neighbours regarding the rights of minority groups and gay rights!
On October 18, 2008, a teargas bomb was thrown into a meeting being held by two local organizations Amigos contra el Sida and Asociación Gay de Samayac who organised an event called „Our Gay Beauty" in Samayac Suchitepéquez. The event itself was focused on HIV prevention in the context of the campaign by the Global Fund to Fight AIDS. No one was seriously injured. This is the second time in 2008 that teargas bombs were used to attack events held by the LGBTI community.
There is a small but interesting gay scene in Guatemala City and a few other locations throughout the country. Guatemala is a truly beautiful country with some spectacular landscapes. The people are extremely friendly and the local dishes and specialities are delicious. There are beautiful, isolated beaches and ancient cultures, just waiting to be discovered.

Homosexuelle Handlungen im gegenseitigen Einvernehmen zwischen zwei Männern über 18 sind legal. Allerdings haben wir beunruhigende Nachrichten über die soziale Situation für Schwule erhalten. Die unzureichende Achtung der Menschenrechte in Guatemala ist ein ernstes Problem und in Bezug auf die Anerkennung von Minderheiten und Rechten für Homosexuelle ist es von seinen Nachbarländern Lichtjahre entfernt.
Am 18. Oktober 2008 wurde in Samayac Suchitepéquez eine von den beiden örtlichen Organisationen Amigos contra el Sida und Asociación Gay de Samayac unter dem Titel „Our Gay Beauty" organisierte Veranstaltung mit einer Tränengasbombe angegriffen. Bei dieser Veranstaltung, die im Rahmen der Kampagne des Globalen Fonds zur Bekämpfung von Aids stattfand, ging es um die HIV-Prävention. Glücklicherweise wurde niemand ernsthaft verletzt. Somit wurde im Jahr 2008 schon zum zweiten Mal Tränengas für Übergriffe auf Veranstaltungen der LGBT-Gemeinde eingesetzt.
Es gibt eine kleine, aber interessante Szene in Guatemala City und einige wenige Treffpunkte in den restlichen Landesteilen.
Guatemala ist ein wahrhaft schönes Land mit phantastischen Landschaften. Die Menschen sind außergewöhnlich freundlich und die einheimischen Spezialitäten sind köstlich. Es gibt einzelne schöne einsame Strände und antike Kulturen, die darauf warten, entdeckt zu werden.

Les rapports homosexuels sont légaux entre adultes consentants de plus de 18 ans. Néanmoins, des nouvelles inquiétantes nous sont parvenues quant à la situation sociale des gays : le non-respect des droits de l'Homme au Guatemala est un sérieux problème qui situe le pays à plusieurs années lumière de ses voisins en matière de reconnaissance des minorités et d'égalité de droits pour les homosexuels.
Le 18 octobre 2008 à Samayac (Suchitepéquez), la manifestation „Our Gay Beauty" organisée par les deux associations locales Amigos contra el Sida et Asociación Gay de Samayac a été attaquée par une bombe à gaz lacrymogène. L'objet de cette manifestation dans le cadre de la campagne du Fond Mondial de Lutte contre le Sida était la prévention du VIH. Heureusement personne n'a été blessé. C'est ainsi la deuxième fois en 2008 que des gaz lacrymogènes sont employés contre des manifestations des communautés gays et lesbiennes.
A Guatemala City, on trouve un petit milieu gay intéressant et quelques rares lieux de rencontre répartis dans le reste du pays.
Le Guatemala est un pays magnifique offrant de fantastiques paysages. Les habitants sont extrêmement sympathiques et les spécialités culinaires délicieuses. On trouvera également des plages isolées et splendides bordant d'antiques cultures n'attendant qu'à être découvertes.

Los actos homosexuales con el consentimiento de ambas partes entre dos hombres mayores de 18 años son legales. Sin embargo, hemos recibido noticias inquietantes sobre la situación social de los homosexuales en este país. El insuficiente respeto a los derechos humanos en Guatemala es un problema muy serio y en cuanto al reconocimiento de las minorías y los derechos de los homosexuales está todavía a años luz de sus países vecinos.El 18 de octubre de 2008, en Samayac Suchitepéquez, una de las dos organizaciones de Amigos contra el Sida y la Asociación Gay de Samayac fue atacada con una bomba de gas lacrimógeno, durante la celebración organizada bajo el título „Nuestra belleza gay". Este acto que se celebraba en el marco de la campaña del Fondo Global para la lucha contra el SIDA trataba sobre la prevención del HIV. Afortunadamente nadie salió gravemente herido. Con ello, se utilizó en el año 2008 por segunda vez gas lacrimógeno para ataques contra las manifestaciones de la comunidad LGBT.

Gli atti omosessuali tra uomini maggiorenni e consenzienti sono legali. Tuttavia, ci sono pervenute notizie contrastanti circa la reale condizione sociale dei gay. Il rispetto dei diritti umani in Guatemala è davvero un problema. Anche per quello che riguarda i diritti delle minoranze e degli omosessuali, il Guatemala è rimasto indietro anni luce rispetto ai paesi vicini.
Il 18 ottobre del 2008 a Samayac Suchitepéquez la manifestazione „Our Gay Beauty", organizzata dalle due organizzazioni locali „Amigos contra el Sida" e „Asociación Gay de Samayac" è stata attaccata con del gas lacrimogeno. La suddetta manifestazione si è svolta nel contesto della campagna del fondo globale per la lotta contro l'Aids e quindi si occupa di campagne di prevenzione contro l'HIV. Per fortuna non ci sono stati feriti gravi, sebbene è da registrare che già per ben due volte nel 2008 è stato usato il gas lacrimogeno per attaccare eventi organizzati dalla comunità LGBT.

NATIONAL COMPANIES

George's Travel Club
www.georges-travelclub.com
Gay travel services for travel in Guatemala.

NATIONAL GROUPS

APAES/Solidaridad 8-18h
2a. Avenida 11-40, zona 1 Guatemala City 232 7649
Association for the prevention and assistance of people with AIDS.

OASIS
3a. Avenida 9-57 Zona 1 Ciudad de Guatemala 2232-9808
A cultural centre and café. Aim of this organization is the prevention of HIV/AIDS as well as the defence of the rights for gay men and women, sex workers and transexuals.

Antigua

RESTAURANTS

Fridas (b glm M MA) 13.30-24h
5 Av. Norte, Calle del Arco 7832 0504
Popular. Bar loosely based on artist Frida Kahlo. The specialty of the house is Mexican cuisine.

Sabe Rico (! B GLM MC OS VEG) Daily 8-21h
6 Av. Sur N° 7 *One and a half block from Central Park* 7832 0648
www.saberico.com.gt
Known as the secret garden. Enjoy natural products especially the homemade fruit ice-cream made with yogurt without preservatives. Another speciality is their handmade chocolate.

Sobremesa (B CC G M) 11-22, Sun 12.30-20h, closed Tue
4ta Calle Oriente N° 4 *Northeast corner of Central Park* 7832 3231
www.alexferrar.com
One of the few gay-friendly establishments in Antigua. Restaurant with lovely art gallery and reasonable prices. Owner helps to give information about other gay-friendly places.

GUEST HOUSES

Casa Azul (b glm PI SA WH)
4 Av. Norte N° 5 *Town centre* 7832 0961
Ten attractive rooms with minibar and cable TV.

CRUISING

-Main Square
-Plaza de Armas
-Around the famous archway.

Atitlán

HOTELS

Casa Palopó (AC b BF glm M OS PI PK RWB RWS) All year
On the shores of Lake Atitlán 5773 7777 7762 2270
www.casapalopo.com
Nine bedroom villa overlooking the lake Atitlán with views of three volcanoes. Pool, boat rides across the lake. Gay-friendly with excellent food.

Isla Verde (B BF cc H M MA MSG S SA SOL) All year, 24hrs
Santa Cruz La Laguna, Solola *From the Tzanjuyu dock in Panajachel take a boat to private dock at Isla Verde* 5760 2648
www.islaverdeatitlan.com
8 cabins with breathtaking views over lake Atitlán.

Ciudad de Guatemala

BARS

Black & White Bar (B CC D DR G MA SNU ST VS) Wed-Sat 19-1h
11 Calle 2-54, Zona 1 5904 1758 www.blackandwhitebar.com
The music, decor, cocktails and lighting all appear in black and white tones.

Café del Callejon (! glm m MA WL) Tue-Sat 17-24h
10 Avenida A 4-74, zona 1. 5202 4055
A great cafe-bar with great atmosphere. Well worth a visit!

Club Five (5) (B cc G SNU VS WE) Thu-Sat 19-4h
Ruta 1 5-13, 3° Nivel- Zona 4
A nice modern bar. Well worth a visit!

Encuentro. El (B G m MA) Mon-Sat 17-24h
5 Av. N° 10-52 zona 1, C.Comercial Capitol, Local 229 *3rd floor* 2232 9235
Nice place with a friendly atmosphere, best early evenings. The evening starts here!

K1 Coffee Bar & Restaurant (B g m MA) Tue-Sat 18-24h
3 Av. 6-26, Zona 1

MEN'S CLUBS

SO 36 Sexclub (B DR G MA S SNU VS) Daily 16-22h
5a Calle 1-24, Zona 1, Centro Histórico Norte 2251 2583
www.clubso36.com
Cruising place. Facebook: SO36 Guatemala.

CAFES

Café Ciber Pl@ce (AC B GLM I m) 8-20, Sun 10-20h
4 Av. N° 11-10, Zona 1 2232 2660
www.gayguatemala.com/anunciantes/cyberplace/index.html

Café de la Ermita (B g m MA) Mon-Fri 7-16.30, Sat 8-15h
9 Av. N° 13-19, Zona 1 *Centro Histórico* 2220 7992
www.gayguatemala.com/anunciantes/ermita/index.htm

DANCECLUBS

Rouge Downtown (B cc DR G SNU VS WE) Thu-Sun 19-1h
4a Calle 5-30, Zona 1 5801 7369 www.guatemalagayguia.com
A great bar with modern atmosphere. Well worth a visit!

Genetic (AC CC D GLM MA OS P S SNU ST VS WE) Fri & Sat 19-1h
Ruta 3 3-08 Zona 4 *Cnr. of Via 3* 2332 2823
www.guatemalagayguia.com
The biggest and most popular disco.

RESTAURANTS

Arrin Cuan (b glm LM M OS RES VEG) Daily 11-23h
5 Av. N° 3-27, Zona 1 *At 3. Calle* 2238 0242 www.arrincuan.com
For an authentic Guatemalan meal.

SAUNAS/BATHS

Dansei Sauna (B DR G MA SB VS) 14-19, Fri & Sat -24h, closed Tue
7 Av. N° 1-13 Zona 2 2238 4834

Il Colliseum Menës Club (B G LAB m MA P SB VS)
17 Calle „A" 7-40, Zona 10 2368 3584 www.ilcoliseummensclub.com

Sauna Urbano Spa (b G m MA SA SB VS)
3 Calle „A" 9-19 „a", Zona 1 4141 2041 www.saunaurbanospa.com
Massage for free on Wed & Fri.

CRUISING

-La Calle del Amor (love street) 7th street between 2nd and 5th Avenues, at night – (ayor)
-Cerrito del Carmen (park) afternoons
-Parque Central (central park) afternoons
-Tikal Futura Shopping Mall where the Hotel Hyatt is
-Los Próceres Shopping Mall in Zona Viva.

Panajachel

BARS

Circus Bar (B CC M MA NG S) 12-24h
15 C/. 2-77 Zona 10 *Opp. disco Chapiteau. zona viva Panajachel*
7762 0374 www.circusbar.com.gt
Live music.

Puerto Barrios

HOTELS

Hotel Puerto Libre (AC B BF CC H M MC OS PI PK RWS RWT) All year
Km. 292 Ruta al Atlántico *At the crossroad to Santo Tomas de Castilla*
7979 9188 7979 9189 www.hotelpuertolibre.com
Gay-friendly. 50 rooms.

SWIMMING

Playa Sand Bay – 19 Calle Final, Marina Lidimar www.playasandbay.com
Weekends 8-18hrs (gay-friendly).

Honduras

Location: Central America
Initials: HN
Time: GMT -6
International Country Code: ☎ 504 (no area codes)
International Access Code: ☎ 00
Language: Spanish; English
Area: 112,492 km² / 43,277 sq mi.
Currency: 1 Lempira (L) = 100 Centavos
Population: 7,048,000
Capital: Tegucigalpa
Religions: 90% Catholic
Climate: The coastal lowlands are warm year-round. The mountainous interior is cool and rainy from May-Oct. On the Caribbean coast rain showers are very common all year round.

Consenting homosexual acts between men to more than 18 years are permitted according to the law, however, the ban of same-sexual marriage and adoption is set in the constitution since 2005. Attacks on transvestites is a frequent and re-occurring problem. There have been no efforts to create any anti-discriminatory regulations and police or military raids are often part of everyday life. This negative situation arose with the outcome of AIDS.

Einvernehmliche homosexuelle Handlungen zwischen Männern über 18 Jahren sind dem Gesetz nach erlaubt, jedoch ist seit 2005 das Verbot von gleichgeschlechtlicher Ehe und Adoption in der Verfassung verankert. Und es kommt immer wieder zu brutalen Übergriffen auf Transvestiten. Es gibt keine Bestrebungen, Antidiskriminierungsregelungen einzuführen; Polizei- und Militärrazzien stehen auf der Tagesordnung. Diese negative Situation herrscht seit dem Auftreten von AIDS.

Les relations homosexuelles consentantes entre hommes de plus de 18 ans sont autorisées par la loi, cependant depuis 2005 líinterdiction díunion homosexuelles et líadoption du fait d'homosexuel(les) sont inscrites dans la loi. Et les travestis sont toujours victimes díagressions brutales. Personne n'est à l'abri des discriminations et des chicanes de la police et de l'armée, par exemple, qui „visitent" régulièrement les lieux gais. Ces conditions existent depuis l'apparition de l'épidémie du SIDA.

Los actos homosexuales de mutuo acuerdo entre hombres mayores de 18 años están permitidos según la ley, pero desde 2005 en la Constitución se ha establecido la prohibición del matrimonio y adopción para las personas del mismo sexo. Continúan produciéndose brutales ataques a los transexuales. No hay aspiraciones para reformas legislativas y se sabe que militares y policías molestan a los gay con frecuencia. Esta situación se agravó con la problemática del SIDA.

l'età legale per rapporti sessuali è di 18 anni, sia per omosessuali. Il sesso tra due omosessuali maggiorenni consensienti non è punito dalla legge. Tuttavia, dal 2005, è saldamente ancorato alla costituzione il divieto di matrimonio ed adozione per due persone dello stesso sesso. Inoltre aumentano sempre più le aggressioni ai travestiti. Non esiste neppure il proposito di emanare una legge contro la discriminazione dei gay. Si parla invece di ripetute violenze contro i gay da parte della polizia e dei militari. Questa situazione esiste da quando si conosce l'AIDS.

La Ceiba

GUEST HOUSES

Casa Cangrejal B&B (AC BF H OS WI) All year
Km 10 Rio Cangrejal Road *30 mins from La Ceiba airport* ☎ 2408-2760
www.casacangrejal.com
Jungle B&B Hotel.Four guestrooms, with private bath and hot water Gay-friendly accommodation.
Natural swimming holes,bar,games room. Hiking, rafting, horseback riding.

Diving Pelican Inn (AC H OS RWS RWT)
184 Playa Helen ☎ 3369-2208 www.divingpelicaninn.com
Two guestrooms. Gay-friendly accommodation near the beach. Airport/bus/ferry pickup-drop off available at additional charge.

San Pedro Sula

HOTELS

Best Western Gran Hotel Sula (BF CC H M MA NG PI WO)
1 Calle, 3-4 Avenida *In front of Central Park* ☎ 545 2600
www.hotelsula.hn
Not a gay hotel but very practical when visiting this city. 8 floors and 115 guest rooms.

CRUISING

-Park in city centre (AYOR)
-Near the railway tracks (AYOR).

Tegucigalpa

CRUISING

All cruising areas are AYOR
-Parque Central (around the cathedral)
-Plaza Miraflores
-Mall Multiplaza.

Hungary

Name: Magyarország · Ungarn · Hongrie · Hungria · Ungheria
Location: Central Europe
Initials: H
Time: GMT+1
International Country Code: ☏ 36 (omit 0 from area code)
International Access Code: ☏ 00
Language: Magyar (Hungarian)
Area: 93,030 km² / 35,920 sq mi.
Currency: Forint (Ft)
Population: 10,107,000
Capital: Budapest
Religions: 64% Roman Catholics; 23% Protestant
Climate: Spring can be wet (May & Jun). Summer is warm and long. The best time to visit is Jul & Aug. The wettest month is Nov. Winter is cold and bleak.
Important gay cities: Budapest

Since September 2002 there are no longer any anti-sodomy laws as such in Hungary and the age of consent is 14, both for gays/lesbians and heterosexuals. Same-sex marriage is not possible, but gays and lesbians – just like heterosexuals – can enter into domestic partnerships, which cannot and do not need to be registered, (for a specific purpose, one can ask for a certificate from the local government).
Following repeated attempts, civil partnerships became available to Hungarian homosexuals on 01.07.2009. But the right-wing conservative Fidesz Party, that has meanwhile come into power with a two-thirds majority in parliament, used this opportunity to introduce far-reaching, constitutional amendments. These also include the explicit exclusion of same-sex marriages in the new constitution, because it defines marriage as an exclusively heterosexual partnership.
During the past few years an interesting and lively gay scene emerged in Hungary, but due to the increase in Nationalist anti-gay violence, gay life is still hidden and open displays of affection are not visible. After Budapest had seen violent confrontations during the 2008 Pride Parade, the 2009 event went peacefully, thanks to extensive security precautions. But sadly homosexuals were violently attacked by neo-Nazis on the day after the 2011 Pride Parade, which had been protected by police blockades. The police sided with the right-wingers, who claimed to have been attacked by gays and lesbians.
No positive changes are apparently to be expected in the political and social situation of homosexuals in the near future. A study published in 2011 comes to the conclusion that homosexuals are resented by a large majority of Hungarians.
If you dial a cell phone number in Hungary on a local landline phone you need to use the dialling code 06.

Seit September 2002 gibt es in Ungarn keine Gesetze gegen schwulen Sex mehr, und das Schutzalter für Homo- und Heterosexuelle liegt einheitlich bei 14 Jahren. Gleichgeschlechtliche Ehen sind nicht möglich, aber Schwule und Lesben können – ebenso wie Heterosexuelle – eine häusliche Lebensgemeinschaft bilden.
Nach einem wiederholten Anlauf gilt seit 01.07.2009 in Ungarn die eingetragene Lebenspartnerschaft für Homosexuelle. Seit 2010 regiert jedoch die rechtskonservative Fidesz-Partei mit einer Zweidrittelmehrheit im Parlament und nutzte die Gelegenheit, weitreichende Verfassungsänderungen zu beschließen. Darunter fällt auch, dass explizit in der neuen Verfassung die Homo-Ehe ausgeschlossen wird, da sie die Ehe ausschließlich als Lebensgemeinschaft zwischen Mann und Frau definiert.
In den letzten Jahren hat sich in Ungarn eine interessante und lebendige schwule Szene entwickelt. Wegen der Zunahme von nationalistischen, antihomosexuellen Gewalttaten findet homosexuelles Leben aber noch immer im Verborgenen statt. In der Öffentlichkeit sieht man daher keine schwulen Paare, die ihre Zuneigung zeigen.

Nachdem es schon 2008 in Budapest zu gewalttätigen Auseinandersetzungen während der Pride Parade kam, gab es 2009 auf Grund großer Sicherheitsvorkehrungen keine Auseinandersetzungen. Leider gab es am Tag nach der Pride Parade 2011, die selbst durch Polizeiblockaden abgesichert wurde, tätliche Übergriffe durch Neonazis auf Homosexuelle. Die Polizei ergriff Partei für die Rechten, die angaben, von Schwulen und Lesben attackiert worden zu sein.

In naher Zukunft scheint sich die Lage für Homosexuelle politisch und gesellschaftlich nicht zum Positiven zu verändern. Eine 2011 herausgegebene Studie kommt zum Ergebnis, dass Homosexuelle von einer großen Mehrheit der Ungarn abgelehnt wird.
Wenn Sie innerhalb Ungarns wohnen und ein Telefon verwenden, um eine Mobilnummer zu wählen, müssen Sie vor dieser Nummer die 06 wählen.

Depuis septembre 2002 il n'y a plus de lois homophobes dans le pays, et la majorité sexuelle est fixée pour tous à 14 ans. Il est toutefois probable qu'elle sera remontée dans le futur.
Les mariages entre personnes de même sexe ne sont pas autorisés, mais une sorte de partenariat existe toutefois. Celui ne doit ni ne peut être enregistré (mais dans certains cas, la mairie peut faire établir un certificat de partenariat). Le partenariat enregistré pour les homosexuels existe en Hongrie depuis le 01/07/2009. Cependant le parti conservateur de droite Fidesz est au gouvernement depuis 2010 avec une majorité des deux tiers au parlement et en profite pour modifier en profondeur la Constitution. Ainsi le mariage homosexuel est explicitement exclu dans la nouvelle constitution en définissant le mariage comme un partenariat entre homme et femme uniquement.
Ces dernières années, une scène gay et lesbienne intéressante s'est développée en Hongrie. Du fait d'une augmentation des actes de violence nationaliste, anti-homosexuelle, la vie homosexuelle reste toujours dissimulée. En public, les couples gays ne montrent pas visiblement leur affection.
Après des altercations violentes à Budapest en 2008 lors de la Pride Parade, des mesures de sécurité plus importantes ont permis d'éviter toute altercation en 2009. Malheureusement le lendemain de la Pride Parade 2011, elle-même sécurisée par un cordon policier, des actes de violence ont eu lieu par des néonazis sur des homosexuels. La police prit parti pour les personnes de l'extrême-droite qui alléguèrent avoir été attaquées par des gays et lesbiennes.
Dans un avenir proche, la situation des homosexuels ne semble pas s'améliorer en politique et dans la société. Une étude menée en 2011 arrive au résultat que la majorité des Hongrois rejette l'homosexualité. Si vous êtes en Hongrie et que vous souhaitez appeler un numéro de portable, vous devez composer le 06 avant ce numéro.

Desde septiembre de 2002 no hay ya ninguna ley en contra del sexo entre homosexuales y la edad de consentimiento tanto para los homosexuales como los heterosexuales está unitariamente establecida a los 14 años. No obstante, podría aumentarse pronto para todos. Los matrimonios del mismo sexo no son posibles pero gays y lesbianas pueden fundar una „vida en común" igual que los heterosexuales. Desde el 1 de julio de 2009 y tras repetidos esfuerzos, Hungría cuenta con la opción de uniones civiles para homosexuales. Sin embargo, desde 2010, el partido de derechas Fidesz, que gobierna con una mayoría de dos tercios en el Parlamento, ha tenido la oportunidad de adoptar cambios de gran alcance constitucional. Esto ha supuesto también la exclusión del matrimonio homosexual en la nueva constitución, ya que se ha definido al matrimonio exclusivamente como la unión civil entre un hombre y una mujer.
En los últimos años se ha estado desarrollando en Hungría una interesante y animada vida gay. Aún así, debido al aumento de actos violentos de origen nacionalista y anti-homosexual, la vida gay permanece todavía oculta. Es por esto que las muestras de afecto en público por parte de parejas gays no son visibles.
Tras los actos de violencia producidos en Budapest durante la Marcha del Orgullo Gay en 2008, dichos actos no volvieron a tener lugar en 2009 gracias a las estrictas medidas de seguridad. Desafortunadamente, un día después de la Marcha del Orgullo Gay de 2011, cuya seguridad se garantizó gracias a las barreras formadas por el cuerpo policial, se produjeron ataques físicos a homosexuales por parte de neo-nazis. La policía se alió con los derechistas que afirmaban haber sido atacados por gays y lesbianas.
La situación política y social para los homosexuales en un futuro próximo no parece que vaya a cambiar a mejor. Un estudio publicado en 2011 llega a la conclusión de que la homosexualidad es rechazada por una gran mayoría de la sociedad húngara. Si usted vive en Hungría y desea utilizar un teléfono para llamar a un móvil, deberá marcar el prefijo 06 antes de dicho número de teléfono.

Dal settembre 2002 non esiste più alcuna legge contro rapporti omosessuali e l'età legale per avere rapporti sessuali è ora, per tutti, di 14 anni. Questa tuttavia potrebbe presto venire aumentata sia per etero che per omosessuali. Matrimoni gay non sono possibili, ma gay e lesbiche possono, come gli eterosessuali, dare vita ad una convivenza. Dopo un ripetuto tentativo, dal primo di luglio del 2011 sono finalmente entrate in vigore le unioni civili per gli omosessuali. Tuttavia, dal 2010, a governare è il partito conservatore Fidesz, che gode della maggioranza di due terzi dei seggi in parlamento e che ha colto, quindi, l'occasione di apportare modifiche di vasta portata alla Costituzione. Tra queste modifiche vi è l'esplicita esclusione dei matrimoni omosessuali dalla Costituzione poiché il matrimonio viene definito come esclusiva unione tra uomo e donna.
Negli ultimi anni in Ungheria è andata sviluppandosi una scena gay molto vivace e interessante. A causa di una crescente ondata di violenza di stampo nazionalista e omofobo, la vita gay continua a svolgersi in maniera piuttosto nascosta. Proprio per questo non si vedono coppie gay che si scambiano effusioni in pubblico. Dopo i violenti scontri della Pride Parade di Budapest del 2008, nel 2009, grazie a severe misure di sicurezza, non si sono verificati tafferugli di alcuna sorta. Invece, nel 2011, il giorno dopo la Pride Parade, facilitata dai blocchi di polizia, si sono verificate aggressioni fisiche da parte di neonazisti nei confronti degli omosessuali. La polizia si è schierata con i neonazisti che sostenevano, invece, di essere stati, loro, aggrediti dai gay e dalle lesbiche. Non sembra che nel prossimo futuro la situazione politica e sociale sul fronte omosessuale possa vedere dei miglioramenti. Uno studio pubblicato nel 2011 rivela che l'omosessualità viene deprecata dalla grande maggioranza degli ungheresi.
Se vivete in Ungheria e volete chiamare un numero di cellulare è necessario digitare lo 06 prima del numero.

NATIONAL GROUPS

Háttér Support Society for LGBT in Hungary Info and helpline 18-23h
PO Box 50 1554 Budapest (01) 329 33 80 www.hatter.hu
Founded in 1995. With its 70 members, Háttér (meaning 'background') runs several projects: a hotline, which is a counselling and information line, a HIV/AIDS prevention project (supported by the National AIDS Committee), a gay/lesbian archive and a free legal aid service for gays, lesbians, bisexuals and transgendered people.

Budapest 01

Budapest „Paris of the East" has always been known as a gay metropolis in Eastern Europe. Beside bars, dance clubs, the famous baths and the cruising spots, there are politically active gay and lesbian groups operative in counselling and socialising activities, gay orientated AIDS-prevention, publication of gay papers and broadcasting gay radio magazines. A gay switchboard takes care of the wishes and enquiries of gay tourists before, during and even after their stay. Since 1997 an annual Gay Pride event takes place in Budapest.
All the gay places, except some baths, are in the centre of Budapest's Pest side, in the V., VI., VII. and IX. district. Buda is hilly and residential; Pest is flat and the lively part of the city. Major tourist sights are the Parliament, the Heroes Square, Opera, Basilika, Castle district, Matyas church, Fisherman's Bastion. The gay scene is not very differentiated: Everyone goes to the same bars and clubs, no matter what age or preferences. There are not certain bars for certain gay sub-cultures (e.g. leather, rent boys, „chubbies", Asians etc.). The public transportation in Budapest is very good and in almost every street you will find 24-hour food stores. Some of the gay accommodation even has air conditioning, although it's not

really needed. April and October usually still have nice, sunny weather when other parts of Europe are cold. Hungary is predominately a catholic country and a bit conservative. The city of Budapest is very attractive and a must to visit!

Budapest, das „Paris des Ostens", war schon immer die schwule Metropole Osteuropas. Neben Bars, Discos, den berühmten Bädern und den Cruisingplätzen haben Gruppen und Organisationen politische Aktivitäten und Ansätze einer schwulen Community entwickelt, beraten, führen AIDS-Prävention durch, verlegen Zeitschriften und produzieren schwule Radiomagazine. Ein „Gay Switchboard" kümmert sich um das Wohlbefinden schwuler Touristen vor, während und nach ihrer Reise. Seit 1997 findet alljährlich ein Gay Pride statt.
Alle schwulen Adressen, mit Ausnahme einiger Bäder, befinden sich im Zentrum des Stadtteils Pest, im V., VI., VII. und IX. Bezirk. Buda ist eine hügelige Wohngegend; Pest ist der ebene, lebendige Teil der Stadt. Zu den wichtigsten Sehenswürdigkeiten gehören das Parlamentsgebäude, der Heldenplatz, die Oper, die Basilika, der Schlossbezirk, die Matayas-Kirche und die Bastion der Fischer. Die schwule Szene ist nicht sonderlich vielfältig: Männer aller Altersgruppen und Vorlieben gehen in dieselben Bars und Clubs. Es gibt keine speziellen Bars für bestimmte schwule Vorlieben (Leder, Stricher, „Bären", Asiaten usw.).
Der öffentliche Nahverkehr in Budapest ist sehr gut und in fast jeder Straße finden sich Lebensmittelgeschäfte, die rund um die Uhr geöfffnet sind. Im April und Oktober ist das Wetter meist angenehm, während es in anderen Gegenden Europas kalt ist. Ungarn ist ein überwiegend katholisches und etwas konservatives Land. Budapest ist eine faszinierende Stadt und auf jeden Fall eine Reise wert.

Budapest (le „Paris de l'Est") a toujours été la métropole homo de l'Est. En plus des bars, discothècques, bains renommés et lieux de rencontre, des groupes et des organisations ont développé des activités politiques et les prémices d'une communauté homo. Ils conseillent et pratiquent la prévention contre le SIDA, ils publient des revues et produisent des magazines gais à la radio. Un „Gay Switchboard" s'occupe du bien-etre des touristes, pendant et après leur voyage. Depuis 1997, un „Gay Pride" a lieu une fois par an.
Toutes les adresses homos repertoriées, hormis certains bais, sont au centre-ville de Pest, dans les V., VI., VII. et IX arrondissements. Buda est la partie résidentielle de la ville bâtie sur des colllines, Pest est son opposée, la partie vivante de la ville. Parmi les curiosités de la ville, le Parlement, la place des Héros, l'Opéra, la Basilique, le quartier des châteaux, l'Eglise Mataya et le bastion des pêcheurs. Le milieu homo n'est pas particulièrement varié: les hommes de tous âges et toutes préférences confondues vont dans les même bars et clubs. Il n'y a pas de bars spécialisés à Budapest.
Le réseau de transports en communs est efficient, dans pratiquement chaque rue de la ville des épiceries sont ouvertes en continu. Certains lieux d'hébergment gay sont équipés de climatiseurs. En avril et octobre, le temps est agréable alors que dans beaucoup d'autres villes il fait déjà froid. La Hongrie est majoritairement catholique et particulièrement conservatrice. Budapest est une ville fascinante qu'il ne faut pas manquer.

Budapest, que se conoce también como el París del Este, siempre fue una metrópoli gay en Europa Central. Aparte de bares, discotecas, los famosos baños y sitios de cruising han surgido múltiples grupos y organizaciones, que defienden los intereses de la comunidad gay, desarollan actividades políticas, aconsejan, trabajan en la prevención del SIDA, públican revistas y producen programas de radio. Para los turistas homosexuales se creó un „Gay Switchboard", que se encarga del bienestar del visitante, antes, durante y despúes de su estancia en Hungría. Desde 1997 se organiza anualmente un Gay Pride.
Todas las direcciones gays, exceptuando algunos baños, se encuentran en el centro de Pest, en los distritos V., VI. , VII. , y IX. Buda es más una montañosa zona residencial; Pest es la parte plana y animada de la ciudad. Entre sus atractivos destacaríamos el Parlamento, la plaza de los héroes, la Opera, la basílica, el distrito del palacio, la iglesia de Mataya y el bastión de los pescadores. El ambiente homosexual no es especialmente variado: hombres de distinta edad y gustos van a los mismos bares o clubes. No hay bares especiales para los distintos gustos de los gays (leather, osos, prostitución, asiáticos, etc.)
El transporte público en Budapest es muy bueno y en casi todas las calles hay tiendas de comestibles que abren las 24 horas. Algunos alojamientos para gays disponen incluso de aire acondicionado, aunque en realidad tampoco es necesario. En abril y octubre, el clima todavía es agradable, cuando en otras zonas de Europa hace frío. Hungría es mayoritariamente un país católico y un poco conservador. Budapest es una ciudad fascinante que merece la pena visitar.

Gir da sempre Budapest („Parigi dell'oriente") c la metrepoli gay dell'est. A parte i bar, le discoteche, i famosi bagni e le possibilitr per il cruising, gruppi e organizzazioni hanno sviluppato delle attivitr politiche e iniziato a stabilire una comunitr gay. Tra le diverse iniziative sono da elencare i servizi di consulenza e di prevenzione contro l'AIDS, la pubblicazione di riviste e la mandata in onda di trasmissioni gay nelle radio locali. Un „gay switchboard" si occupa del benessere dei turisti gay prima, durante e dopo il loro viaggio. Dal 97 ogni anno ha luogo un Gay Pride.
La maggior parte dei locali gay si trova nel centro di Pest, nel V, VI, VII e IX rione. Buda è infatti una collina residenziale; Pest è la parte pianeggiante e vivace della città. Tra le attrazioni turistiche vanno annoverati il Parlamento, la Piazza degli Eroi, l'Opera, la Basilica, il castello, la chiesa Matayas e i Bastioni dei Pescatori.
La scena gay non è particolarmente varia: uomini di ogni età e dalle diverse preferenze si recano negli stessi bar e club. Non ci sono bar per particolari „passioni" gay (leather, orsi, etc.)
I mezzi pubblici di Budapest sono molto ben organizzati e praticamente in ogni via ci sono negozi d'alimentari, aperti 24 ore al giorno. Il clima è anche in aprile ed ottobre molto piacevole.
L'Ungheria è un paese cattolico e abbastanza conservatore. Budapest è una città affascinante e vale la pena visitarla.

GAY INFO

GayGuide.Net Budapest (GLM)
☎ 30 932 3334 (mobile) 💻 budapest.gayguide.net
Permanently updated gay guide including reviews of all listed places. Information on gay-owned accommodation & gay-operated guided tours.

BARS

Action Bar (AC B DR G MA R S SNU VS WE) 21-4h
Magyar utca 42 *Near to M°3 Kálvin tér, tram 47/49; bus 9/15/83/109/115/909/914* ☎ (01) 266 91 48 💻 www.action.gay.hu
Gay basement bar with a strongly frequented back & video room. Fridays live sex shows at 0.45h. Saturdays „Oral Academy" at 0.45h. Not easy to find. A door to a cellar with a „A"

Mystery Bar (AC B G I m MA p) Sun-Thu 12-2, Fri & Sat 12-4h
V, Nagysándor József utca 3 *M° Arany János utca, near US-Embassy*
☎ (01) 312 14 36 💻 www.mysterybar.hu
Small pub with 3 internet terminals. Free Wifi Internet access (bring your laptop).

Why Not Café & Bar (B glm MA) 10-5
Belgrad rakpart 3-4 *At the Danube river; tram 2/2A/47/49; bus 15/83/115/979/979A; near M° Kalvin Ter* ☎ (01) 780 45 45
💻 whynotcafe.hu
Coffee shop during daytime and bar at night. A gay friendly cafe on the river side by Szabadsag Bridge with a terrace from March to October. Former name: Cafe Mylord.

Funny Carrot (AC B G MA) 19-6h
Szep utca 1/b *Between M° Astoria and M° Ferenciek tere*
☎ (06) 70 625 75 51 (mobile) 💻 www.funnycarrot.hu
Downtown gay bar. Former Darling Bar.

Habroló Bisztró (AC B G I m MA PA WI)
Mon-Fri 9-4 Sat & Sun 10-4h
V, Szép utca 1/b *Near M° Astoria and Ferenciek Ter; night bus 921, 973, 914, 950, 979* ☎ (01) 9506644 💻 www.habrolo.hu
Small gay bar that attracts locals. No entrance fee. No minimum consumption. Next door to Funny Carrot.

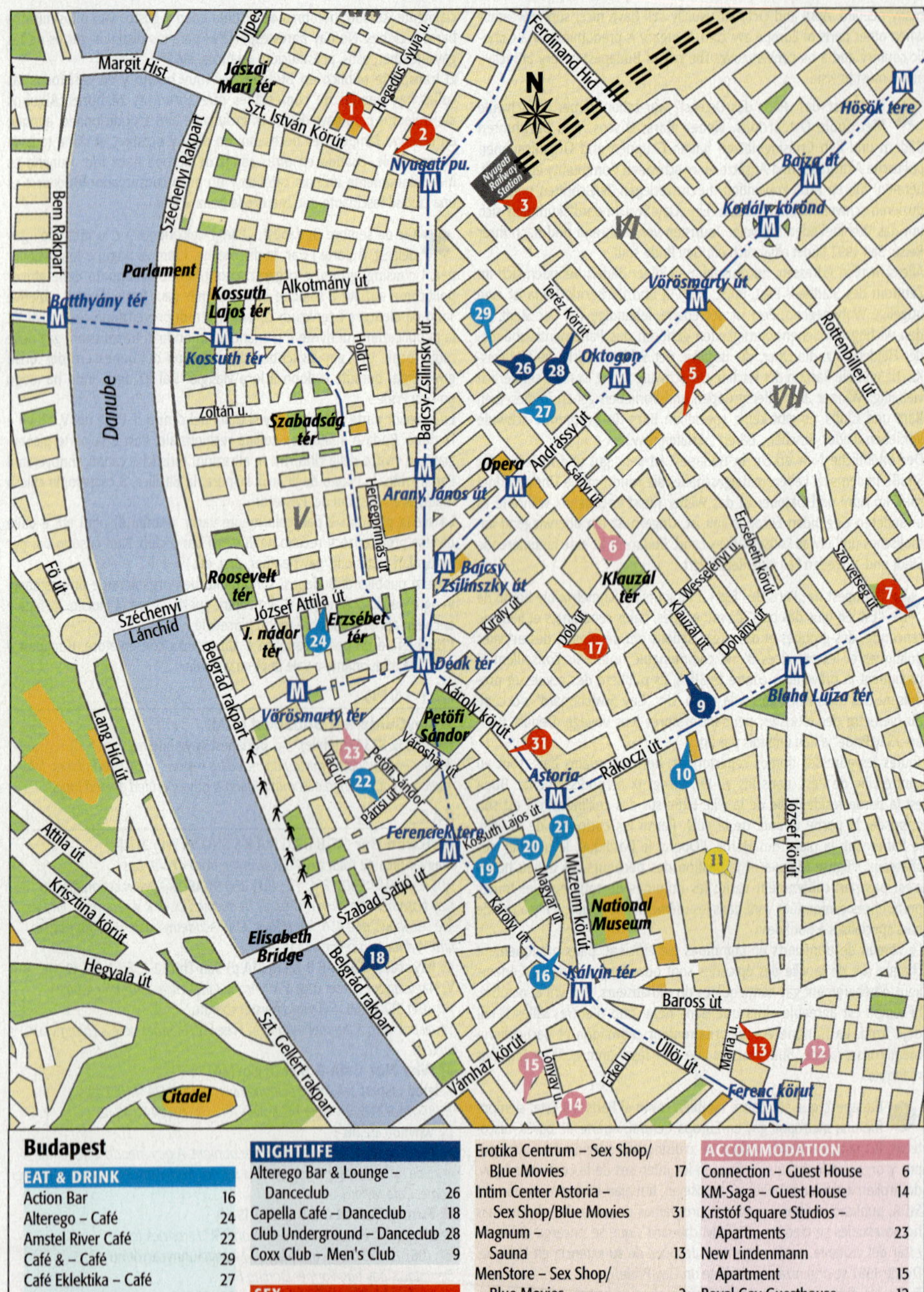

Budapest

EAT & DRINK

Action Bar	16
Alterego – Café	24
Amstel River Café	22
Café & – Café	29
Café Eklektika – Café	27
Mystery Bar – Bar	25
Funny Carrot – Bar	19
Habroló Bisztró – Bar	20
Pizzeria Club '93 – Restaurant	10
Ruben – Restaurant	21

NIGHTLIFE

Alterego Bar & Lounge – Danceclub	26
Capella Café – Danceclub	18
Club Underground – Danceclub	28
Coxx Club – Men's Club	9

SEX

Amour Videómozi Sex Shop. L' – Sex Shop/Blue Movies	5
Erotik Mozi Video Center – Sex Shop/Blue Movies	1
Erotika Centrum – Sex Shop/ Blue Movies	17
Intim Center Astoria – Sex Shop/Blue Movies	31
Magnum – Sauna	13
MenStore – Sex Shop/ Blue Movies	2
Metro Sex Shop – Sex Shop/ Blue Movies	2
Vénusz Shop – Sex Shop/ Blue Movies	7

ACCOMMODATION

Connection – Guest House	6
KM-Saga – Guest House	14
Kristóf Square Studios – Apartments	23
New Lindenmann Apartment	15
Royal Gay Guesthouse	12

OTHERS

Black Dream – Leather & Fetish Shop	11

■ **Monte Christo** (B G) Mon-Sun 15-?
Victor Hugo u. 5 ☎ (070) 410-2199 (mobile) 💻 www.montechristo.hu

MEN'S CLUBS

■ **Coxx Club** (AC AK B DR DU F G GH I LAB M MA NU RWT SH SL VR VS)
Sun-Thu 21-4, Fri & Sat -5h
VII, Dohány utca 38 *Corner to Nagydiófa utca, near to M° Astoria and M° Blaha Lujza tér, bus 7 – Urania, trolley bus 74* ☎ (01) 344 48 84
💻 www.coxx.hu
In the basement on 400 m². Three bars, large cruising area, jail, sling room, hardcore movies etc. Weekly special parties (military cruising night, nude sex party)

CAFES

■ **Alterego Café** (b glm M MA) 19-3h
Erzsebet ter 1 *M° Deak Ter* ☎ 703454302 (mobile)
💻 www.alteregoclub.hu
Alterego Cafe owned and operated by Alterego Club (See Danceclubs). Mondays, Thursdays and Saturdays Karaoke at 22h. No entrance fee. No minimum consumption.

■ **Amstel River Café** (AC B BF g M MA OS) 12-24h
V, Párizsi utca 6 *M° Ferenciek tere/Vörösmarty tér* ☎ (01) 266 43 34
Popular, gay-friendly café and restaurant downtown. Friendly staff, good food, reasonable prices and nice atmosphere.

■ **Café &** (B GLM m MA) Mon-Thu 10-2, Fri 10-4, Sat 16-4h
Dessewffy utca 30 *M° Arany Janos utca; tram 4-6, trolleybus 70/72/73/78; nightbus 906/914/923/950* 💻 www.cafeand.hu
Cafe and bar near Alterego and Cafe Eklektika. Home-made pastries and baguettes, wide range of alcoholic beverages and soft drinks. Gay owned and operated with gay staff.

■ **Café Eklektika** (B GLM I M MA) 10-24, Fri & Sat 12-24h
Nagymezo utca 30 *60 m from the corner Nagymezo utca and Andrassy utca* ☎ (01) 266 12 26 💻 www.eklektika.hu
Moved from Semmelweiss utca to Nagymezo utca. Nice gay-friendly, lesbian-owned cafe and restaurant. International and Hungarian kitchen with daily specials for reasonable prices. Breakfast served from 9-12h at weekdays and between 12-18h at the weekends.

DANCECLUBS

■ **Alterego Bar & Lounge** (B D GLM MA S) Fri & Sat 22-5h
Dessewffy utca 33 *M° Oktogon and Arany János stations*
☎ 70345 43 02 (mobile) 💻 www.alteregoclub.hu
In a basement. 3 bars, some sofas, a dance floor and a stage for shows. Retro parties, Diva nights. Entrance fee, no drink included.

■ **Capella Café** (B D DR glm m MA OS SNU ST) 21-4h
V, Belgrád rakpart 23 *M° Ferenciek tere* ☎ 70295 95 07 (Mobile)
💻 www.capellacafe.hu
Staff mostly gay, but bar attracts mainly a straight crowd. Gay on Wed. Daily disco. Entrance fees apply. Shows at 24 and 1h. Beautiful interior.

■ **Club Underground** (B D gLm MA ST)
Mon, Tue & Thu 11-0h, Fri & Sat 11-5h
Dohany utca 22-24 ☎ 20 261 8999 (mobile)
💻 www.clubunderground.hu
Small disco with shows. Mainly lesbian.

RESTAURANTS

■ **Fenyögyöngye** (B glm M MA) 12-23h
II, Szépvölgyi út 155 *Bus 65 from Kolosy tér* ☎ (01) 325 97 83
💻 www.fenyogyongye.hu
Reservation recommended. Off the beaten track, but with great Hungarian cuisine. Call ahead as they sometimes have private parties.

■ **Pizzeria Club ,93** (AC B glm M MA NR OS) 12-24h
VIII, Vas utca 2 *Between M° Astoria & Blaha Lujza tér* ☎ (01) 338 11 19
💻 www.club93pizza.hu
Very small non-smoking restaurant, popular with gays and lesbians. Tables outside during summer.

■ **Ruben** (AC B CC GLM M MA) 12-24h
Magyar utca 12-14 *Near M° Ferenciek tere and Astoria* ☎ (01) 266 36 49
💻 www.rubenrestaurant.hu
Located in the heart of the city, in a quiet street. Modern gay-friendly restaurant with Hungarian and international cuisine. Full menu in English, German and Italian.

SEX SHOPS/BLUE MOVIES

■ **Amour Videómozi Sex Shop. L'** (AC DR g MA VS) 10-22h
VI, Király utca 72 *Tram 4/6 Király utca* ☎ (01) 342 15 59 💻 www.szex-shop.hu
Videos, cabins with gloryholes, 1 cinema (43 seats), magazines, toys. Gay films 16-22h.

■ **Connection Bt** (CC g) Mon-Fri 11-21, Sat -15h, Sun closed
Berzsenyi D. utca 3 *Bus 7/78-Berzsenyi utca* ☎ (06) 209 591761 (mobile)
💻 www.connectionbt.hu
Wide selection of gay DVDs, dildos, JoyDivision and WET lubricants. Free Budapest gay map and programs.

■ **Erotik Mozi Video Center** (AC DR g MA VS) Mon-Sat 9-2, Sun 14-2h
XIII, Hegedüs Gyula utca 1 ☎ (01) 320 40 05 💻 www.erotikcenter.hu
One gay cinema, one straight.

■ **Erotika Centrum** (AC DR g VS)
Mon-Sat 10-22, Sun 12-18h; cabins/bar Mon-Sat 14-22, Sun 12-18h
VII, Dob utca 11 *M° Astoria* ☎ (01) 351 1000 💻 www.tuttifrutti.hu
Also Tutti Frutti Sex Shop. See: www.tuttifrutti.hu

■ **Intím Center Astoria** (g) 9-20h
V, Károly körút 14 ☎ (01) 317 09 18
Mostly straight audience, but has cabins for rent if you need one.

■ **MenStore** (AC F G I WI) Mon-Fri 14-19h
Szent István krt. 24 *Tram 4/6, Near Nyugati West Railway Station*
☎ (01) 239 46 66 ☎ (70) 32 77 777 (mobile) 💻 www.gaydvd.hu
The only exclusiv gay sex shop in Hungary.

■ **Metro Sex Shop** (G MA) Mon-Sat 10-19, Sun 12-19h
Nyugati pályaudvar, Railway Station *In the passage*

■ **Vénusz Shop** (g) Mon-Fri 10-19h
VIII, Rákoczi út 69 *M° Keleti pu., Bus 7* ☎ (01) 313 48 25

ESCORTS & STUDIOS

■ **Gay Tailored Tours** (G MSG) 12-24h
City centre ☎ 205 444 632 (mobile) 💻 www.gaytailoredtours.com
Outstanding world-wide escort and companion service. See: www.gaytailoredtours.com

SAUNAS/BATHS

■ **Gellért Bath** (DU MA MSG NG OS PI SA SB SOL) 6-19, Sat & Sun -17h
XI, Kelenhegyi út 4-6 *Bus 7, Tram 18/19/47/49* ☎ (01) 466 61 66
The architecturally beautiful bath was built in 1918 in Art Nouveau style. Pool and outside area are cruisy in the summer. Separate male/female areas; pool is mixed. The most expensive bath house in the city. Not a sauna in the traditional gay sense.

■ **Király Bath** (DU g MA MSG r RR SA SB)
Daily 9-20h (entrance until 19h)
II., Fö utca 82-84 *Tram 4, 6, Bus 6, 26 to Margaret bridge, on the Buda side, then walk or take bus 60, 86 for one stop direction Battyány tér*
☎ (01) 202 36 88
Turkish bath built in the 15th century. Since May 2011 no more ,men only' days. It was very cruisy for decades.

■ **Magnum** (! B CC DR DU f FC G GH I LAB m MA MSG RR S SA SB SL SNU SOL VS WH WO) Mon-Thu 13-24, Fri -4, Sat 13-Mon 1h (non-stop)
VIII., Csepreghy utca 2 *Corner Mária utca, M° Ferenc körút, tram 4/6, bus 83, nightbus 906, 923, 966, 979* ☎ (01) 267 25 32
💻 www.magnumsauna.com
Budapest's biggest (550 sqm) and busiest gay sauna with full gym. Popular with all age groups. Busy all days, but especially Mon, Wed and weekends. Naked party every Fri at 10pm. Free internet and Wifi.

■ **Szauna 69** (B CC DR DU FC G GH I M MA MSG NR P RR SA SB VR VS WH WI) Sun-Thu 13-1, Fri 13-2, Sat 13-6h
IX, Angyal utca 2 *Boraros ter, M2 Corvin negyed, Tram 4/6 Mester utca stop*

light No. 2 above the door ☏ (01) 210 17 51 💻 www.gaysauna.hu
The place to be in Budapest! Very popular sauna among young men every day. Clean and hygenic.
English speaking friendly staff. A big gay sauna on 500 m²..

■ **Széchenyi Spa** (! DU MC NG OS PI) 6-19h
XIV., Állatkerti krt. 11. *M° Széchenyi fürdo* ☏ (01) 321 03 10
💻 www.szechenyibath.com
One of the largest bathing complexes in Europe! The first thermal baths on the Pest part of the city. Wonderful buildings in New Baroque style. Outdoor bathing is very popular, especially in winter. A wonderul collection of different types and temperatures of water in indoor pools. A must when in Budapest!

LEATHER & FETISH SHOPS

■ **Black Dream** (AC F G I PA) Tue-Fri 12-20, Sat -17h
Mária utca 9 *M° Blaha Lujza* ☏ (01) 266 7485 💻 www.blackdream.hu
High quality and hightech gay, fetish and SM goods. Also internet shop.

HOTELS

■ **art'otel Budapest** (AC BF H M RWT WI WO) All year
Bem Rakpart 16-19 ☏ (01) 487 9 487 💻 www.artotels.com

■ **Mamaison Hotel Andrássy** (B BF CC glm H M MA PK RWS RWT VA) All year
Andrássy út 111 ☏ (01) 462 2190 💻 www.andrassyhotel.com
The 5 star Mamaison Hotel Andrássy Budapest is an elegant upscale boutique hotel, located in the most exclusive Embassy neighbourhood just off Pest's Andrássy Avenue. With spacious, beautifully designed rooms and suites. Book 30 hotel rooms and get the main meeting room free of charge.

GUEST HOUSES

■ **Connection** (b BF CC glm I PA PK RWS RWT VA)
All year, reception 24hrs
VII, Király utca 41, 1st floor, doorbell 24 *Tram 4/6, trolley 70*
☏ (01) 267 71 04 💻 www.connectionguesthouse.com

Gay-friendly guesthouse with seven double and two single rooms with shared as well as private bathrooms. All room rates include a buffet breakfast and free internet access as well.

■ **KM-Saga** (BF glm MA RWS RWT VA) All year
V, Lónyai utca 17, 3rd Floor, Door N° 1 *Near National Museum, M° Kálvin tér* ☎ (01) 217 19 34 💻 www.km-saga.hu
Gay-owned, discreet guest-house. All rooms with cable TV, telephone, own/shared baths. 5 rooms.

■ **Kristóf Square Studios** (AC G I PA RWB RWS RWT VA) All year
V, Kristóf tér *M° Vörösmarty tér / Deak Ferenc tér, 40m off Vaci Street* ☎ 309323334 (mobile) 💻 gaystay.net/KristofSquare
Studio apartments with private bathrooms, kitchenettes, mobile phones, AC, free Wifi internet, safety boxes and elevator. 150 m to the river Danube, 40m to famous Vaci Street.

■ **Royal Gay Guesthouse** (G MSG) All year; check-in by appointment
Kisfaludy utca 28/A *M° Ferenc körút* ☎ (06) 30 685 26 43 (mobile) 💻 www.budapest-gayguide.com
Two spacious apartments (150 m² each) with five sleeping rooms. Conveniently located near downtown area; gay owned and gay operated.

APARTMENTS

■ **Boyduo** (G I RWT)
Ráday utca 41 ☎ (06) 20 965 77 80 (mobile) 💻 twokeys.tk

■ **Dembinszky Street Apartment** (GLM I PA RWS RWT VA) All year
VII., Dembinszky utca *M° Keleti station* ☎ 309323334 (mobile) 💻 gaystay.net/Dembinszky
One bedroom apartment for up to 4 persons with living room, kitchen, bath, mobile phone, safety box, Sat TV. Pest side (all gay venues are on the Pest side). Free gay map.

■ **Gay Guesthouse and Apartments** (G)
Andrássy utca 27 ☎ (06) 30 685 26 43 (mobile) 💻 www.budapest-gayguide.com

■ **New Lindenmann Apartment** (B BF CC GLM I MA MSG p RWS RWT VA) All year, 24hrs
IX, Csarnok tér 3-4 *City centre* ☎ (06) 70 583 28 08 (mobile) 💻 www.gaybeach.hu
Each apartment or studio has its own bathroom and a double bed. One apartment is equipped with a kitchenette.

■ **Rozsa Street** (G I PA RWS RWT VA) All year
Rozsa utca *Trolley Bus lines 73, 74 and 76* ☎ 309 32 33 34 💻 gaystay.net/Rozsa
Renovated, newly furnished. Near gay bars & clubs on the Pest side. Living room, well equipped kitchen, bathroom, mobile phone, Sat TV, free Wifi, safety box. For 1-4 persons.

■ **Vas Street Studio** (AC G PA RWS RWT VA) All year
Vas utca *Between Astoria Square and Blaha Luijza Square* ☎ 309 32 33 34 💻 gaystay.net/Vas
Bright and quiet gay owned studio apartment with bathroom, kitchenette, mobile phone, safety box, Sat TV, gas heating, elevator. Walking distance to gay bars and clubs.

HEALTH GROUPS

■ **Anonym AIDS Tanácsadó Szolgálat** (GLM)
Mon & Wed 17-20, Tue & Fri 9-12h
XI., Karolina út 35/b *Bus 212* ☎ (01) 466 92 83 💻 www.anonimaids.hu
Anonymous AIDS Association.
Aims: HIV prevention, consulting and testing of HIV, Syphylis, Hepatitis B and C free of charge and anonymous. Results received within 7 days.

■ **Szent Sebestyén Kft.** Wed 19-21h
VI, Podmaniczky u. 27, groundfloor, Apt 10 *Near Nyugati pu.* ☎ 30 254 7378 (moblle)
Anonymous testing for HIV and STDs and advice.

CRUISING

-Promenade along the Danube on the Pest side (Duna-korzó) (G R) (between Március 15. tér and Mariott Hotel. Beware of hustlers) 17-23h
-Népliget (AYOR R) (Peoples Park, behind the Planetarium and especially next to the area of the old ruins. 19-0h. At the back of the park along the railways. 16-19h. Also car-cruising at the road around the park)
-The little park north off Margaret bridge on the Buda side, 19-23h
-Cruisy toilets at Nyugati and Ferenc krt. Metró stop; some, but not only rent boys; best time 10-18h
-Westend City Center, toilets on all floors, most popular: The toilet on the ground floor near Match Supermarket.

Debrecen ☎ 052

DANCECLUBS

■ **Club Zeus** (B D G MA)
Domb utca 1 *First floor, at the ‚Kaptar Music Pub'* ☎ 202 574 541 (Charlie, mobile) 💻 www.clubzeus.hu
Regular gay parties. Check website for dates.

CRUISING

-Toilets at main railway station
-Park near Thermal Furdo.

Eger ☎ 036

GUEST HOUSES

■ **Anna Guest House** (DU NG) 24h
Joo Janos utca 30 ☎ (36) 419390 💻 annavendeghaz.hu
Gayfriendly guest house 15 min walking from historical downtown. Double rooms with shower, WC, TV (34 cabel programs) and balcony.

CRUISING

-Népkert (Park between the bus station and Basilica)
-Lake with nudist area close to a spring
-Egerszalók, a village 6km south-west from Eger (reached by coach), famous hot springs; cruising area is at the hilltop, around the nudist area
-Park near train station, between Dr. Münnich Ferenc u. & Klapka György u.

Gyor

CRUISING

-Toilet in the railway station.

Miskolc

CRUISING

-Tapolca swimming pool (in summer)
-Plaza Department Store (area of Cafe Woodoo).

Nyiregyháza ☎ 042

BARS

■ **Together For Each Other In Eastern Hungary** (B D GLM m MA SNU ST WE)
Belso körút 31 ☎ 20 365 8767 (mobile) 💻 www.egymasert.com
(Együtt Egymásért Kelet-Magyarországon Egyesület) Association that runs a GLBT community center (for all ages) with bar, video room, dance floor, gym, workshop- and meeting rooms. During the summer garden area, swimming pool, grill parties. Regular health care programs and culture events. Disco every weekend and free movies every second weekend. (Free) Accommodation for the weekends. Free dating service by phone for anyone from the north-east counties of Hungary.

CRUISING

-Petofi square and park (park between the bus station and railway station).

Pécs ☎ 072

DANCECLUBS

■ **Club Mediterran** (B D GLM MA) Sat
Verseny utca 29 ☎ 702 99 77 52 (mobile) 💻 www.clubmediterran.info
Parties usually Sat nights.

CRUISING

-Szent István tér (in front of cathederal)
-Barbakán kert (near cathederal).

Siófok

CRUISING

-Park between the railway station and the church
-Street behind Hotel Europe (summer only).

Sopron ☎ 099

HEALTH GROUPS

AIDS Segély Alapítvány
PO Box 217 ☎ 99 788 435 (Mon-Fri 17-20)
www.aidsinfo.hu
The AIDS Aid Foundation offers anonym and free HIV Tests every Thu 17-20h. Also runs a gay group Homofil.

Szeged

CRUISING

-Main railway station (2nd floor)
-Széchenyi tér (near Main Post Office).

Szombathely

CRUISING

The park in front of the Savaria Museum on Széll Kálmán utca (5 minutes walk from the railway station).

Iceland

Name: Island · Islande · Islandia · Islanda
Location: near Artic Circle in North Atlantic Ocean
Initials: IS
Time: GMT
International Country Code: ☎ 354 (no area codes)
International Access Code: ☎ 00
Language: Icelandic
Area: 103,000 km² / 39,768 sq mi.
Currency: 1 Icelandic Crown (ISK) = 100 Aurar
Population: 292,000
Capital: Reykjavík
Religions: 95% Evangelical Lutheran, 3% Protestant
Climate: Summer is short and winters are cold and windy. Many places close from Aug-Apr.
Important gay cities: Reykjavik

In Iceland the general age of consent is 14. The Icelandic gay community is small but very active and has achieved wide public acceptance, as well as having many rights enforced by laws. As a result same sex couples with legally registered partnerships are allowed to assume care and custody of their partner's children. There are further wide-reaching anti-discrimination laws. Ever since the parliament of Iceland has unanimously granted homosexuals the right to marry in 2010, the country has been one of the few in the world where lesbians and gays enjoy exactly the same rights as heterosexuals.
Jóhanna Sigurðardóttir became the world's first openly lesbian head of government after the prime minister had had to resign because of the global financial crisis, which has hit Iceland particularly hard. Sigurðardóttir and Jónína Leósdóttir were the very first couple to become married once the new law on gay marriage had come into power.
In recent years there have been virtually no acts of homophobic violence. As well as their manifestly democratic position, another reason for the levels of tolerance could be that amongst the limited Icelandic population, almost everyone has a gay relative or friend.
A commission set up by the Icelandic Prime Minister has been tasked with further liberalising aspects of discrimination. Under consideration are full adoption rights for lesbian and gay parents equal to those of straight couples, the possibility of church weddings, and access for lesbians to artificial insemination. For homosexuals Iceland already has one of the most advanced systems of jurisdiction in the world.
Iceland is the second largest island in Europe, but has only 292,000 inhabitants, 67% of whom live in Reykjavic. The landscape is wild, craggy and vibrantly coloured, with black lava rocks, red sulphur, shimmering blue geysers, waterfalls, rivers, glaciers, fjords, and green valleys.

Das Schutzalter für alle Menschen in Island ist 14. Die isländische Gay Community ist klein, aber sehr aktiv und hat inzwischen eine breite gesellschaftliche Akzeptanz erreicht sowie viele gesetzlich verankerte Rechte durchgesetzt. So ist es gleichgeschlechtlichen Paaren mit gesetzlich eingetragener Partnerschaft erlaubt, das Sorgerecht für die Kinder des Partners/der Partnerin zu übernehmen. Ferner gibt es weitreichende Antidiskriminierungsgesetze. Seit 2010 hat das isländische Parlament mit keiner einzigen Gegenstimme die Ehe für Homosexuelle geöffnet, so dass Island als eines der wenigen Länder weltweit die Rechte Homosexueller vollkommen denen Heterosexueller gleichgestellt hat.
Seit 2009 regiert die erste offen lesbische Regierungschefin Jóhanna Sigurðardóttir, nachdem in Folge der weltweiten Finanzkrise, die Island besonders hart traf, der isländische Premier zurücktreten musste. Nachdem das Gesetz zur Öffnung der Ehe für Schwule und Lesben in Kraft trat, war Sigurðardóttir und Jónína Leósdóttir das erste Paar, das sich trauen ließ.
Gewaltakte gegen Homosexuelle gab es in den letzten Jahren so gut wie überhaupt nicht. Neben der ausgeprägten demokratischen Tradition könnte ein Grund dafür darin liegen, dass bei der geringen Anzahl an Isländern fast jeder homosexuelle Verwandte oder Freunde hat.
Eine Kommission, die vom isländischen Premierminister eingesetzt wurde, hat sich zur Aufgabe gesetzt, diskriminierende Aspekte in den Gesetzen weiter zu liberalisieren. Es sind ein völlig gleichgestelltes Adoptionsrecht von schwulen und lesbischen Paaren wie bei heterosexuellen Paaren, die Möglichkeit zur kirchlichen Heirat und das Recht zur künstlichen Befruchtung von lesbischen Frauen im Gespräch. Aber

schon jetzt hat Island in Bezug auf Homosexualität eine der fortschrittlichsten Rechtssprechungen der Welt.
Island ist zwar die zweitgrößte Insel Europas, aber hier leben nur 292.000 Menschen, 61% davon in Reykjavik. Die Landschaft ist wild, zerklüftet und farbenprächtig mit schwarzem Lavagestein, rotem Schwefel, ihren heißen, bläulich schimmernden Geysiren, Wasserfällen, Flüssen, Gletschern, Fjorden und grünen Tälern.

La majorité sexuelle est fixée à 14 ans pour tous en Islande. La communauté gay est petite mais très active et est désormais largement acceptée par la population. Les Gays et lesbiennes jouissent également de droits légaux : les couples de même sexe peuvent se faire enregistrer, et obtenir ainsi la garde de l'enfant de leur conjoint(e) ; diverses lois anti-discriminatoires ont également été adoptées. Depuis 2011 le parlement islandais a ouvert le mariage aux homosexuels à une seule voix contre, l'Islande est ainsi un des rares pays au monde à accorder intégralement les même droits aux homosexuels qu'aux hétérosexuels.
Depuis 2009, la première chef de gouvernement ouvertement lesbienne Jóhanna Sigurðardóttir est au pouvoir après la démission du premier ministre en raison de la crise financière mondiale qui a particulièrement touché l'Islande. Après l'entrée en vigueur de la loi sur l'ouverture du mariage aux gays et lesbiennes, Sigurðardóttir et Jónína Leósdóttir furent le premier couple à se marier.Outre la forte tradition démocratique du pays, le nombre réduit d'Islandais joue sans doute un rôle puisque ici, tout le monde ou presque a un parent ou ami homosexuel.
Une commission mise en place par le Premier ministre a été chargée de supprimer d'autres aspects discriminatoires de la législation existante. Le droit à l'adoption peu importe l'orientation sexuelle, le mariage à l'église et le droit à l'insémination artificielle de lesbiennes sont ainsi en discussion. Mais même dans son état actuel, la législation islandaise est déjà une des plus progressistes au monde. L'Islande est peut-être la deuxième île d'Europe en superficie, mais elle n'a que 292 000 habitants dont 61 % vivent à Reykjavik. Le paysage est sauvage, crevassé, haut en couleur avec ses roches volcaniques noires, son souffre rouge, ses geysers bleu scintillant et autres chutes d'eau, ses rivières, glaciers et fjords ainsi que ses vallées vertes.

La edad de consentimiento para todo tipo de personas en Islandia está en los 14 años. La comunidad gay islandesa es pequeña pero muy activa y ha conseguido una aceptación muy amplia en la sociedad así como muchos derechos legales. Así pues, se permite ya el registro de parejas del mismo sexo, el derecho de tutela para los hijos del compañero o compañera. Además existen amplias leyes antidiscriminatorias. Desde 2010, el Parlamento islandés legalizó, sin ningún voto en contra, el matrimonio homosexual, por lo que Islandia se ha convertido en uno de los pocos países en todo el mundo que cuenta con derechos para homosexuales totalmente equiparables a los de los heterosexuales.
Desde 2009 gobierna el país Johanna Sigurðardóttir, la primera Presidenta abiertamente lesbiana, quien tomo el cargo como consecuencia de la crisis financiera mundial que afectó a Islandia de forma especialmente dura, lo que provocó, en consecuencia, que el primer ministro islandés tuviera que dimitir. Después que la ley del matrimonio homosexual entrase en vigor, Sigurðardóttir y Jónína Leósdóttir fueron la primera pareja en casarse.
En los últimos años no se produjeron actos de violencia contra los homosexuales. Aparte de su asentada tradición democrática, también podría deberse a que ante el bajo número de islandeses, casi todos tienen un pariente o amigo homosexual.
Una comisión, que fue creada por el primer ministro islandés, tiene como misión liberar a las leyes de todos aquellos aspectos discriminatorios. Se habla actualmente de un derecho de adopción equiparado totalmente para parejas gays y lesbianas así como también para las heterosexuales, la posibilidad de matrimonio eclesiástico y también el derecho de inseminación artificial para las mujeres lesbianas. Incluso ahora mismo, Islandia tiene una de las jurisdicciones del mundo más avanzadas en cuanto a la homosexualidad.
Islandia es la segunda isla más grande de Europa pero aquí sólo viven unas 292.000 personas, 61% de ellas en Reykjavik. El paisaje es salvaje, escarpado y lleno de colores con fuentes de lava negra, azufre rojo, géisers azules y calientes, saltos de agua, ríos, glaciares, fiordos y valles verdes.

In Islanda l'età del consenso è per tutti di 14 anni. La comunità gay islandese è piccola ma così attiva da raggiungere un largo consenso sociale come anche molti diritti. Infatti qui è stata introdotta la convivenza registrata per le coppie dello stesso sesso e il diritto di custodia per i bambini del partner. Inoltre ci sono delle buone e dettagliate leggi antidiscriminatorie. Dal 2010 il Parlamento islandese ha approvato all'unanimità il matrimonio omosessuale. Con questo ulteriore passo l'Islanda risulta essere uno dei pochi Paesi al mondo ad avere equiparato pienamente i diritti degli omosessuali a quelli degli eterosessuali.
Dopo le dimissioni del Premier islandese a causa della crisi finanziaria mondiale, dal 2009 a governare il Paese è Jóhanna Sigurðardóttir, la prima lesbica dichiarata a coprire questo ruolo. Dopo che è entrata in vigore la legge sui matrimoni omosessuali, Sigurðardóttir e Jónína Leósdóttir sono state le prime ad unirsi in matrimonio.
Negli ultimi 20 anni sono stati rarissimi gli atti di violenza nei confronti di omosessuali. Un motivo per questo potrebbe essere la lunga tradizione democratica dell'Islanda ma anche il fatto che considerato il bassissimo numero di abitanti islandesi, quasi tutti gli omosessuali hanno parenti o amico.
Il capo del coniglio islandese ha istituito una commissione che ha lo scopo di correggere ulteriormente aspetti discriminatori nelle leggi islandesi. Per adesso si discute anche sulla possibilità di istituire il diritto di adozione paritario per omosessuali ed eterosessuali, sulla possibilità di matrimonio in chiesa e sul diritto di inseminazione artificiale per donne lesbiche. L'Islanda ha già comunque, per quanto riguarda l'omosessualità, una delle legislazioni più liberali del mondo.
L'Islanda è la seconda isola più grande d'Europa, anche se qui vivono solo 292.000 persone; di questi, il 61% vive a Reykjavik. Il paesaggio è abbastanza selvaggio, frastagliato e saturo di colori: il nero della lava, il rosso dello zolfo, il verde delle valli, il blu dei geyser, delle cascate, dei fiumi, dei ghiacciai e dei fiordi.

NATIONAL PUBLICATIONS

Samtakafréttir (GLM)
Pósthólf 1262 ✉ 121 Reykjavik ☏ 552 7878
www.samtokin78.is
Newsletter published by Samtökin ,78 four times a year.

NATIONAL GROUPS

Samtökin ,78 (GLM)
Laugavegur 3 ✉ 101 Reykjavik *4th floor* ☏ 552 7878
www.samtokin78.is
The Icelandic organization of lesbians and gay men.
The national gay rights organization.
Runs a gay centre with café & gay library in Reykjavik.

Reykjavik

Reykjavic is an interesting city with a small but active gay scene. The best time to visit is either in August, when the Gay Pride takes place, or in September and October when the tourists have gone and the prices have been reduced. Iceland is generally expensive. The gay scene is busy on Friday and Saturday nights only and it starts late, with bars open until 6am and later. The locals are extremely friendly and English is spoken by everyone.

Reykjavik ist eine erstaunlich moderne Stadt, die dank der Energieversorgung aus Wasserkraft und Erdwärme eine der saubersten der Welt ist. Es gibt viele farbenfroh gestaltete Holzhäuser, die im Sonnenschein in allen Farben des Regenbogens strahlen. Der Name Island ist ein wenig irreführend, denn die Winter sind hier erstaunlich mild. Dennoch ist das Klima unbeständig und die beste Reisezeit ist Juni/Juli, um die Mitternachtssonne zu bestaunen.

Reykjavik est une ville étonnamment moderne qui, grâce à son énergie hydraulique et géothermique, est une des plus propres du monde. Les maisons de bois sont souvent richement colorées et le soleil leur donne líaspect díun arc-en-ciel. Le nom de lîle est quelque peu déroutant car les hivers y sont relativement doux. Cependant, le temps est changeant et la meilleure période pour visiter la ville est en juillet/août pour y admirer le soleil de minuit.

Reykjavic es una ciudad sorprendentemente moderna que, gracias a sus fuentes de energía provinentes del agua y del calor de la tierra, es una de las ciudades más limpias del mundo. Hay muchas casas de madera de diferentes colores que a la luz del sol brillan con todos los colores del arco iris. El nombre de Islandia puede conducir a error pues los inviernos son sorprendentemente suaves. Sin embargo, el clima es muy inestable y la mejor época para visitarlo es entre junio y julio, para poder apreciar así el sol de medianoche.

Reykjavik è una città molto moderna che grazie all'energia idroelettrica e all'energia ricavata dal calore geotermico è una delle città meno inquinate del mondo. Ci sono molte case di legno colorate, che quando splende il sole, riflettono tutti i colori dell'arcobaleno. Il nome Islanda è un po' ambiguo visto che gli inverni qui sono paradossalmente miti. Tuttavia il clima è abbastanza variabile e i mesi migliori per ammirare il sole di mezzanotte sono giugno e luglio.

GAY INFO

Reykjavik Gay Center (b CC GLM MA) Mon & Thu 20-23.30, Oct-Apr also Sat 13-17h
Laugavegur 3 *4th floor* ☎ 552 7878 www.samtokin78.is
Rainbow room café and gay library. Meeting place for gay groups: ‚AA group' meets Tue 21h, parents' supporting group 2nd Wed/month at 20h, youth group Sun 20-23h, transsexual supporting group the 1st Wed/month at 21h.

TOURIST INFO

Elding Whale Watching (b CC g m MA) Office: 8-17h
Aegisgardur 7, Reykjavik harbour ☎ 555 3565 www.elding.is
A gay-friendly company offering whale watching, sea angling and sailing – based in Reykjavik. Also organizers of special gay cruises.

BARS

Barbara (B D GLM MA)
Laugavegur 22

Kaffibrennslan (b glm M MA) Mon-Thu & Sun 11-1, Fri & Sat -3h
Pósthússtræti 9 ☎ 561 3600
A huge range of beers on offer, also fast foods.

Rainbow Room (! AC b CC GLM MA s) Mon & Thu 20-23.30h
c/o Reykjavik Gay Center, Laugavegur 3 *4th floor*
Cosy and friendly. Foreigners welcome.

MEN'S CLUBS

MSC Iceland (b CC DR F G MA P VS) Fri & Sat 23-3h
Laugavegur 28 *Entrance from street through passage and back door*
☎ 562 1280 www.msc.is
Men only, dresscode: leather, jeans, uniforms.

RESTAURANTS

Fjöruborðið (AC B CC LM M NG PK) 12-?h
Eyrarbraut 3A, Stokkseyri *About 20 mins by car from Reykjavik*
☎ 483 1550 www.fjorubordid.is

Við Tjörnina „By the Pond" (AC B CC DM H M MC NG RES WL)
Templarasund 3 ☎ 551 8666 www.vidtjornina.is

BOOK SHOPS

Ida (cc) 9-22h
Laekjargata 2a *Old downtown* ☎ 510 5001 www.ida.is
Gay owned. Merchandise partly gay themed.

TRAVEL AND TRANSPORT

KGB Tours (CC GLM)
Mosabarði 14 ☎ 554-1827 www.kgbtours.is
Trolltours, introduction of folklore. Bird watching, daytours from Reykjavik greater area or tours all around the island.

HOTELS

101 Hotel (BF H M WO) All year, office: Mon-Fri 9-17h
Hverfisgata 10 ☎ 580 0101 www.101hotel.is

Hotel Phoenix (AC BF CC GLM H I MA PK RWS RWT) All year
Laugavegur 140 *100m from the main bus station Hlemmur* ☎ 511 5002
www.phoenix.is
Gay-owned, non-smoking hotel with 9 guestrooms. Spartacus readers get 15% discount off the room rates for bookings made directly with the hotel.

APARTMENTS

Guesthouse Galtafell (CC H I OS)
Laufásvegur 46 ☎ 551 4344 www.galtafell.com

Room with a View (AC CC GLM I MC NR PK RWS RWT SB VA WI) All year
Laugavegur 18 *Main street* ☎ 896 2559 www.roomwithaview.is
40 self-catering apartments with cooking facilities, Many of the apartments have access to an outdoor roof-top which is perfect for Northern Lights or midnight sun.

HEALTH GROUPS

Alnæmissamtökin á Íslandi Mon-Thu 12-16h
Hverfisgata 69 ☎ 552 8586 www.aids.is
The AIDS-organization of Iceland.

SPORT GROUPS

St. Styrmir FC (G) Practise: Wed & Sun 20-22h
Fífan Sports Complex, Dalssmára 5, Kópavogur *Kópavogur is a suburb of Reykjavik* ☎ 663 8317 www.ststyrmir.is
Styrmir Football Club is a group of gays and a number of straight friends in Iceland who get together couple of hours twice a week to play football.

SWIMMING

-The bay near the „Pearl" is ideal for swimming as warm water is pumped into the bay water.

CRUISING

-The wooded area around the „Pearl", you need to go there by car (G MA).

India

Name: Bhárat · Indien · Inde
Location: South Asia
Initials: IND
Time: GMT +5.30
International Country Code: ☏ 91
International Access Code: ☏ 00
Language: Hindi and English
Area: 3,287,263 km² / 1,229,737 sq mi.
Currency: 1 Indian Rupee (INR) = 100 Paise
Population: 1,094,583,000
Capital: New Delhi
Religions: 81% Hindu, 12% Moslem, 2.5% various religious minorities
Climate: Oct-Mar tend to be the most pleasant months throughout the country. In the south, the monsoon weather makes Jan-Sep more pleasant. In northeastern India the best time is from Mar-Aug. In Kashmir and the mountainous regions it is best from May-Sep. The deserts and northwestern Indian Himalayan regions best from Jan-Sep.
Important gay cities: Bangalore, Mumbai, New Delhi

On the 30th June 2009 the Delhi High Court overturned a 148-year-old colonial law criminalizing consensual homosexual acts. Section 377 of the India Penal Code was amended but continues to govern non-consensual penile non-vaginal sex and penile non-vaginal sex involving minors. The age of consent is set at 18 years of age. This amendment to the Indian Penal Code was brought about due to the efforts by the NAZ Foundation (India) Trust, a sexual health organization based in New Delhi, who filed the petition to change Section 377 in 2000.

India's newly emerging LGBT communities, along with changing gay scene in larger cities such as Delhi is an exciting development, in which gay nights are becoming more and more popular in several discos and bars.

New Delhi's second Gay Pride Parade took place on the 28th June 2009. Homosexuality in Indian society remains however a taboo even though several, famous Bollywood actors have supported a liberalisation. The clout of the religious influence was demonstrated in October 2011, when pressure from Hindu and Catholic groups forced the government of the federal state of Goa to shelve plans for marketing it as a gay-friendly part of India. A number of politicians have also further stoked resentments towards homosexuals on occasions.

It is possible that as a result of this amendment to the law in India, neighbouring countries such as Bangladesh, Sri Lanka, Malaysia and Singapore will follow and amend their laws too, which are still based on outdated, British colonial law.

Am 30. Juni 2009 schaffte das Oberste Zivilgericht Delhis ein 148-jähriges Kolonialgesetz, das homosexuelle Handlungen kriminalisierte ab. Paragraf 377 des Strafgesetzbuches Indiens wurde geändert, bleibt aber für nicht im gegenseitigen Einvernehmen durchgeführten Verkehr und Sex mit Minderjährigen bestehen. Das Schutzalter liegt bei 18 Jahren. Diese Änderung im indischen Strafgesetzbuch wurde dank der Anstrengungen des NAZ Fundament erreicht. NAZ ist eine in Neu Delhi beheimatete Gesundheitsorganisation, die bereits im Jahr 2000 gerichtlich beantragte, den Paragraf 377 zu ändern.

Mit der kürzlich gegründeten LGBT Organisation Indiens, und dem Wandel der schwulen Szene in den größeren Städten, nimmt Indien eine aufregende Entwicklung, in der schwule Nächte in mehreren Diskos und Bars immer populärer werden.

Die zweite Gay Pride Parade Neu Delhis fand am 28. Juni 2009 statt. Homosexualität in der indischen Gesellschaft bleibt jedoch ein Tabu, obwohl mehrere berühmte Bollywood Schauspieler eine Liberalisierung unterstützt haben. Wie groß der religiöse Einfluss ist, zeigte sich im Oktober 2011, als die Regierung im Bundesstaat Goa auf Druck von katholischen und hinduistischen Gruppen Pläne zurückziehen musste, Goa als schwulenfreundlicher Teil Indiens zu vermarkten. Auch manche Politiker schürten vereinzelt weiter Ressentiments gegen Homosexuelle. Es ist zu hoffen, dass infolge dieser Gesetzesliberalisierung in Indien, benachbarte Länder wie Bangladesch, Sri Lanka, Malaysia und Singapur diesem Beispiel folgen und ihre Gesetze, die noch auf dem überalterten britischen Kolonialgesetz beruhen, anpassen.

Le 30 juin 2009, la cour suprême de Delhi a abrogé une loi coloniale vieille de 148 ans qui criminalisait les actes homosexuels. L'article 377 du code pénal indien a été modifié mais reste valable pour les relations sans consentement mutuel avec un mineur. La majorité sexuelle est fixée à 18 ans. Cette modification du code pénal indien a été réalisée grâce aux efforts du NAZ Fundament. Le NAZ est un organisme de santé originaire de New Delhi qui déjà en 2000 avait demandé l'abrogation de l'article 377.

Avec la fondation récemment de l'association LGBT indienne et la transformation de la scène gay dans les plus grandes villes, l'Inde promet de développer une scène nocturne particulièrement excitante avec des boites et des bars au succès grandissant.

La deuxième Gay Pride de New Delhi a eu lieu le 28 juin 2009. L'homosexualité dans la société indienne reste un tabou bien que plusieurs acteurs célèbres de Bollywood aient soutenu une libéralisation. Preuve de la forte influence religieuse, le gouvernement a dû reculer en octobre 2011 sous la pression de groupes catholiques et hindous et ne mettra pas en avant Goa comme une région accueillante pour les gays. Quelques politiciens isolés aussi attisent des ressentiments envers les homosexuels.

Il reste à espérer qu'avec la libéralisation des lois en Inde, des pays voisins tels que le Bangladesh, Sri Lanka, Malaisie ou Singapour suivront le même chemin et moderniserons leurs lois basées sur des lois coloniales britanniques obsolètes.

El 30 de junio de 2009 el Tribunal Superior de Delhi abolió una ley colonial de 148 años de antigüedad que criminalizaba los actos homosexuales. El artículo 377 del Código Penal Indio fue modificado, pero sigue estando vigente en casos de relaciones sexuales sin consentimiento mutuo y en casos de sexo con menores de edad. La edad mínima para mantener relaciones sexuales en India es de 18 años. Este cambio en el Código Penal de la India se ha logrado gracias a los esfuerzos de la Fundación Naz, una organización de salud de Nueva Delhi, que ya en el año 2000 presentó una moción ante un tribunal para modificar el artículo 377.

Con la recién formada organización LGBT india y el cambio del ambiente gay en las grandes ciudades, la India comienza a desarrollarse tímidamente convirtiendo a sus noches, discotecas y bares gays en destinos cada vez más populares.
El segundo desfile del Orgullo Gay de Nueva Delhi tuvo lugar el 28 de junio de 2009. La homosexualidad en la sociedad india sigue siendo un tabú, aunque varios famosos actores de Bollywood han apoyado la liberalización. La gran influencia que ejerce la religión en este país se hizo evidente en octubre de 2011 cuando el gobierno del estado de Goa se vio obligado a retirar, debido a la presión de grupos católicos e hindúes, su plan de comercializar Goa como un estado gayfriendly de la India. Algunos políticos avivan de forma esporádica el resentimiento en contra de los homosexuales. Es de esperar que tras la anulación de estas leyes en la India, países vecinos como Bangladesh, Sri Lanka, Malasia y Singapur sigan su ejemplo ajustando también sus leyes, la cuales aún dependen de la anticuada legislación colonial británica.

Il 30 giugno del 2009 la Suprema Corte Civile di Delhi ha abrogato una legge coloniale di 148 anni fa che criminalizzava gli atti omosessuali. L'articolo 377 del codice penale indiano è stato modificato in tutte le sue parti tranne che per il sesso non consenziente e per il sesso con i minorenni. L'età del consenso è di 18 anni. Le modifiche nel codice penale indiano sono state raggiunte grazie agli sforzi compiuti dalla NAZ, un'associazione a Nuova Delhi che si occupa di salute e che già nel 2000 si appellò alla Corte per modificare l'articolo 377. L'India si sta sviluppando in maniera molto interessante: da poco è nata la prima organizzazione LGBT del Paese e la scena gay prende sempre più piede nelle grandi città. Le serate gay, organizzate nelle discoteche o nei bar, diventano sempre più popolari. Il 28 giugno del 2009 si è svolto il secondo Gay Pride di Nuova Delhi. Sebbene molti famosi attori di Bollywood abbiano spinto verso uno sdoganamento dell'omosessualità, il fenomeno rimane nella società indiana ancora un tabù. La forte influenza religiosa la si è potuta toccare con mano nell'ottobre del 2011, quando il governo si è visto costretto, in seguito a forti pressioni di gruppi cattolici e induisti, a rinunciare alla sponsorizzazione di Goa come meta turistica più gay-friendly dell'India. Il risentimento contro l'omosessualità è stato ulteriormente alimentato anche dai politici. Si spera solo che a seguito di queste impronte più liberali nella legge, i Paesi vicini seguano l'esempio modificando le obsolete leggi che si rifanno ancora alla legge coloniale britannica.

NATIONAL COMPANIES

Creative Travel India
Creative Plaza, Nanakpura, Moti Bagh, New Delhi 110021 ✉ 110021 New Delhi ☎ (011) 687 22 57 🖳 www.travel2india.com

Indjapink
Lajpat Nagar 1 ✉ 110019 New Delhi 🖳 www.indjapink.co.in

NATIONAL GROUPS

infosem The India Network For Sexual Minorities
🖳 www.infosem.org
The India Network For Sexual Minorities is a collective national effort by sexual minorities to ensure equality for themselves in all spheres of life, free from discrimination.

Naz Foundation India Trust
A – 86 East of Kailash ✉ 110 065 New Delhi ☎ (011) 2691 0499 🖳 www.nazindia.org
One aspect of Naz India caters to improve prevention, awareness, and education on the one hand, and to care, support and therapy on the other for those with HIV/AIDS.

Alwar

CRUISING

-City Palace and Museum Complex near State Bank of India
-Company Garden around sunset
-Jaikrishna Club, area around the tennis courts after 18.30h.

Aurangabad

CRUISING

-Siddharth Garden, around main bus stand.

Bangalore ☎ 80

GENERAL GROUPS

Good As You Helpline Tue & Fri 19-21h
c/o Swabhava, 4th floor, No. 1 ☎ (080) 547 5571 🖳 www.goodasyou.in
A supportive and safe social space for LGBT people and other sexuality-minorities.

Sangama
No 9, ABABIL Patil Cheluvappa Street, JC Nagar ☎ (080) 2341 6940 🖳 www.sangama.org
LGBT drop-in center, library, outreach.

CRUISING

-Majestic Bus Stand (ayor)
-Corporation Bus Stop (ayor)
-Corporation Library (Kubban Park extension) (ayor)

Bhopal

CRUISING

-Ghandi Park Area near the public toilet, best after 17h
-T.T.Nagar, near the city bus stand
-Public Park in front of the Lily Theater (cinema hall).

Chennai (Madras) ☎ 44

GENERAL GROUPS

Social Welfare Association for Men – SWAM
12/5 Natarajan Street, Balakrishna Nagar, Jafferkhanpet ☎ 2371 2324

CRUISING

-Marina Beach, gay corridor near to the north of the Anna Swimming Pool, after 19h
-Kannage Silai Beach near swimming pool, look for lover's path, best after 19h, especially Sun many students
-Ideally Mambalam, best after 18h, many civil servants.

Ernakulam (Cochin)

CRUISING

-Cochin GCDA, very cruisy, best during late afternoons to midnight, popular with people under 45 & many students
-Subash Chandra Bose Park, also known as just Subash Park (MA R), mostly students after dark between 20-22h.

Goa

CRUISING

-Barga Beach near Andrew's and Lucky Star beach shacks, gays gather here for sea and sunbathing
-Goa Madgaon, big circular public garden right at city centre, best from 17h till late at entire length of beach from Calangute to Baga, especially near Tito's (R WE)
-Panaji park in Campal, on main road leading to Miramar beach, on the river side of the road, go to area with trees with dimly lit promenade along the beach edge, best times are in the evening, from 17h.

Hyderabad – Secunderbad

CRUISING

-Public gardens – meeting place for Kothi's (feminine bottoms) and Hijra's.

Jaipur – Rajasthan ☎ 141

HOTELS

Umaid Bhawan (AC bf CC glm H M PI RWB RWS RWT WE) All year
D1-2A, Behind Collectorate, (Via) Bank Road, Bani Park
☎ (0141) 220 1276 www.umaidbhawan.com

GUEST HOUSES

Umaid Mahal (AC BF CC glm H M MA PI RWB RWS RWT) All year
C-20 / B-2 Bihari Marg, Jai Singh Highway, Bani Park *Opp. Lane of K.P. Automotives* ☎ (0141) 220 1952 www.umaidmahal.com

Jaisalmer ☎ 2992

HOTELS

Jeet Villa (AC BF H I RWS RWT)
C.V. Singh Colony *Railway station 500m, Bus Station 100m, near to airport*
☎ (02992) 252 727 ☎ (9929) 296 969 (mobile)
Modern conveniences and traditional golden sand stone carving. Hotel organises camel safaris.

Monsoon Palace (AC BF GLM H I MA MSG PK RWB RWS RWT VA) All year
On Fort Vyasa Para *On the wall of the fort* ☎ (2992) 254 317
www.monsoonpalacejsm.com
Hotel Monsoon Palace is situated within the ancient walls of the Jaisalmer Fort. The building is about 600 years old and designated a Heritage Hotel for its authentic architecture.

GUEST HOUSES

Hotel Fifu (AC bf glm H I m MA MSG OS RWB RWS RWT VA) All year
Opposite Nagar Palika, Bera Road *10 mins walk from the centre of town, free pick up to Jailsalmer railway station* ☎ (2992) 254 317
www.hotelfifu.com
It is a gay-friendly place with open-minded staff. The rooms have all the modern amenities you would expect. Offers Organised Camel Safaris in the quite area of Thar Desert.

Jodhpur – Rajasthan ☎ 291

GUEST HOUSES

Durag Niwas (AC bf H M MA MSG NG OS RWS) All year
1st Old Public Park, Raika Bagh *Between the Meharangarh Fort and the Umaid Bhavan Palace* ☎ (291) 513 1560 www.durag-niwas.com
Great gay-friendly guesthouse with 11 basic rooms. Excellent hospitality, free cooking lessons, Ayurvedic massages, horse riding, Thar-Desert safaris and tours to Bishnoi village available as well as airport transfers. A real insider tip.

Kolkata (Calcutta) ☎ 33

HOTELS

Park Hotel (AC B BF CC D H M MA MSG OS PI SA SB WH WO) All year
17 Park Street *City centre, near markets and entertainment complex*
☎ (033) 2249 9000 www.theparkhotels.com
Very friendly and cute staff. The hotel sauna is a cruisy area. Very popular with locals and foreigners.

GENERAL GROUPS

Integration Society
P. O. Bag No. 794 A, Kolkata ☎ (033) 3112 9922
Visibility and communication. Organizes Gay Pride comemorating Stonewall Riots Day since 1999; events, plays, animations, music, dance, debate, exhibition, parties, etc. Also carrying research based studies.

HELP WITH PROBLEMS

SAATHII Helpline Mon, Wed & Fri 15-18h
☎ (033) 2334 7329 www.saathii.org

Mumbai (Bombay) ☎ 22

PUBLICATIONS

Bombay Dost
105A Veena Beena Shopping Center *Near Bandra Station*
☎ (022) 618 7476 bombay-dost.pbwiki.com
Newsletter of the LGBT-group „The Humsafar Trust". Quarterly gay magazine.

BARS

Voodoo Club (B d g m MA R)
Colaba *Near Gateway of India, & end of seawall/Radio Club, turn right*
Gay night Sat. Cover charge applies. The first gay club in India. Rather dingy and sleazy.

DANCECLUBS

Lets Scream (B CC D G MC NR P) Sat 21-?h
249 P D'Mello Road *Next to Jahaz Bhuvan,Ballard Pier*
Entrance fee includes 2 drinks. No sex and absolutely no drugs on the premises! Smoking only outside allowed. Music is a mix of Bollywood as well as English Rock.

Salvation Star (B D GLM MA)
www.salvationstar.com
Regular LGBT parties. Check website for details.

GIFT & PRIDE SHOPS

Azaad Bazaar (AC CC GLM MA) 13-21h, closed Mon
Junction of 16th & 33rd Road, Bandra (West) *Bandra Train Station – West*
☎ (099) 3021 2636 www.azaadbazaar.com
Azaad Bazaar is India's first and only LGBT Pride shop.

GENERAL GROUPS

GayBombay
www.gaybombay.org
Events put up on website. Meets every 1st, 3rd and 5th Sunday/month; organizes filmfests, treks, Indian festival celebrations. Parties held every fortnight at different clubs.

Humsafar Trust. The (GLM T)
Mon-Fri 11-20, 2nd & 4th Sun/month 16-20h
4th floor, Municipal Market Building, Nehru Road, Vakola *Santa Cruz East, near Vakola Mosque and Vakola Market* ☎ (022) 2667 3800
www.humsafar.org
Drop in center, counseling, STI treatment, HIV testing, queer library, support group for HIV+. Capacity building and networking with other MSM / Gay and Transgender groups.

CRUISING

-Gateway of India, along seawall from Gateway to Arthur Bunder Street, evenings (MA R)
-Around Voodoo Club, Sat at the corner from the end of the seawall, when the club goes all gay
-Chowpatty near Dadar
-Local railway trains at peak hours (both central and western lines) – ask local gay men about the „2 by 2 compartment".

New Delhi ☎ 11

BARS

Peppers (AC B g MC) Tue from 22.30h
Chanakayapuri *Next to Chanakya Cinema, behind the Egyptian Embassy Former „Pegs and Pints", gay on Tuesday nights only. Cover charge coupons for a couple of small drinks/beer, always busy after 22.30h. Nice cross-section of people. Located in the centre of Delhi in a quiet neighbourhood, very near Nehru Park (see Cruising).*

Polka Bar (AC B CC d g M MA)
Hs-4, Kailash Colony Market, Greater Kailash ☎ 6464 0882
Gay on Saturday night only.

DANCECLUBS

Amigo (B D glm MA)
3, Local Shopping Centre, Masjid Moth, Greater Kailash 2 *community centre*
Frequently gay on saturdays.

RESTAURANTS

Orange Hara (AC B CC glm M MA) 12-?h
Southern Park Mall *behind Select City Walk* ☎ 4059 7538/39
🖳 www.orangehara.com
Indian kitchen with kebabs, curries, roti and bar. Gay on most Saturdays.

SAUNAS/BATHS

Sauna Fitness Spa at Hyatt Regency Hotel (AC B CC DU M MA MSG NG OS PI SA SB WH WO)
Bhikaji Cama Place, Ring Road ☎ (011) 2679 1234
Straight institution, but popular with some trendy gay men.

MASSAGE

Kalph Kaya (AC G MA MSG SB WE) 9-21.30h
19 Sant Nagar, East of Kailash *Off the outer ring road at Nehru Place*
☎ (098) 1090 7129
Very basic set-up.

TRAVEL AND TRANSPORT

GoPink Asia (G SH)
Arjun Nagar 7 Kotla *Near Toyota Showroom* ☎ +33 970440360 (France)
☎ +1 305 517 7887 (USA) 🖳 www.gopink.asia
Offers unique guided vacations for gay men.

Indjapink (G MA)
B-91, 1st Floor Lajpat Nagar ☎ 4652-9883 🖳 www.indjapink.co.in
First and only gay travel agency in India. Custom-taylored gay tours, private arrangements and local guides.

GENERAL GROUPS

Humrahi
c/o Naz Foundation India Trust, A – 86 East of Kailash *Andrews Gunj*
☎ (011) 2691 0499 🖳 www.nazindia.org
The Naz Foundation has a further group: The Milan Project (milanproject@hotmail.com)

CRUISING

-Dhaula Kuan bus stand & garden opposite to the Dhaula Kuan Defence Services Officers Institute, popular with soldiers; gardens are directly situated on road towards National Airport leading from Dhaula Kuan intersection (r)
-Interstate Bus Terminal (ISBT) near Kashmiri Gate in Old Delhi, all day (ayor MA)
-In front of McDonalds, the one at Inner Circle, Connaught Place facing the Metro Station built on what was the Central Park; the oldest public cruising area, busy throughout the week, peaking at Friday and Saturday, best during evenings, from after dusk to 22-23h; you can sit around under the small trees, and watch the guys walk up and down
-Jahanpanah Forest with plenty of bushes and benches around to have fun even in broad daylight, best near the Chiragh Delhi fly-over between 16-18h and Sun afternoon (r)
-Nehru Park; the area of this large and beautiful park that's opposite the 5-star Ashok Hotel, the park is fenced, so look for the pedestrain entrance flanked by a parking area brimming with cars and 2 wheelers with men looking up each other before entering the park, popular, best Sat & Sun evening, opp. Ashoka Hotel including the rope bridge and surrounding gardens, best between 19-21h
-India Gate Lawns.

Pune (Poona) ☎ 20

HOTELS

Celebrity Country Club (AC B g M MA MSG PI SA SB WO)
6 Bund Garden Road *Near Akashwani, Pune Sholapur Road*
☎ (020) 8400 8386.

Kapila (AC B H M MA NG OS)
174 Dhole Patil Road *Off Wadia College Road, 5 mins from station*
☎ (020) 2612 1272
Good hotel with beautiful gardens.

CRUISING

-Junglee Maharaj along Junglee Maharaje Road, pick-up only, evenings from 18-21h (MA)
-Bus stop at Gandharv, all day (MA)
-Bund Garden (Lover's Garden), evenings after dusk, best benches under big tree
-Sambhaji Park, close to Decccan on Jungli Maharaj Road, evenings
-Boardwalk east of city, late evenings and night time.

Surat

CRUISING

-Chaupati, best by riverside area
-Sneh Milan Garden during afternoon
-Dutch Garden in Nanpura Surat.

Thiruvanandapuram ☎ 471

SEX CINEMAS

Sree Bala Cinema (g MC) Shows at 14.30 & 18.30h
Mahathma Gandhi Rd, Pazhavangadi *After petrol station, one block from Saj Lucia Hotel*
Go to the the very back of the balcony and wait until the lights go off.

Trivandrum

SWIMMING

-Kovalam Beach, about 15km from the city. Very clean with many great restaurants, gift shops and Ayurvedic clinics. Best of all, are the loads of nice, friendly guys walking and playing on the beach. Some are hustlers, but most are just ready to chat.

Udaipur – Rajasthan ☎ 294

CAFES

Edelweiss (CC GLM)
73, Gangaur Ghat ☎ (0294) 0941 423 3573
German bakery and coffee shop.

RESTAURANTS

Savage Garden (B CC GLM MC)
22, Inside Chadpole ☎ (0294) 242 5440
The restaurant Savage Garden was created by two locals and a German tour guide, whose first enterprise together was a German bakery called Café Edelweiss. Savage Garden is located in an old 18th century house which was lovingly restored using traditional techniques and local craftsmanship. The courtyard, painted in a dark Majorelle blue and decorated with a Moorish fountain and cusped arches, reflects the influence of Islamic culture found from Spain to India.

GUEST HOUSES

Tiger. The (B BF cc glm M MSG PA RWB RWS RWT SA SB WO)
All year
33, Gangaur Ghat ☎ (0294) 2420430 🖳 www.thetigerudaipur.com

Varkala ☎ 470

GUEST HOUSES

Villa Jacaranda All year
Temple Road West ☎ (470) 261 02 96 🖳 www.villa-jacaranda.biz
Gay-friendly guesthouse of very high standard. Rooms are very clean, pleasantly furnished in a quiet location, one minute from the beach. Great breakfast (served on a private veranda) by smiling staff.

Indonesia

Name: Indonesien · Indonésie
Location: Southeast Asia
Initials: RI
Time: GMT +7/+8/+9
International Country Code: ☏ 62 (omit 0 from area codes)
International Access Code: ☏ 001 or 008
Language: Bahasa Indonesia. English as language of commerce
Area: 1,912,988 km² / 738,608 sq mi.
Currency: 1 Rupiah (Rp.) = 100 Sen
Population: 217,588,000
Capital: Jakarta
Religions: 87% Moslem
Climate: Tropical climate that is hot and humid. The best time to visit is in the dry season (May-Oct).
Important gay cities: Bali, Jakarta

Unlike in many other Muslim counties, Indonesia is relatively tolerant of homosexuality. This does not apply in the devoutly Muslim province of Aceh, where the Sharia laws apply. No laws exist that specifically prohibit homosexuality. The age of consent for sexual acts is set at 18.
As in many countries in South East Asia, homosexuality is a part of everyday life. Even in the media several prominent gay or transsexual people exist. Nevertheless this subject is low key and not openly talked about. Fanatical Muslim groups have been known to attack gay men, e.g. at an anti-AIDS meeting in Solo, where the participants were attacked by a masked band of several hundred people.
Legal guidelines regarding HIV/AIDS do not exist. This is surprising as AIDS is a major problem in most countries in the region. Those infected with AIDS travelling to Indonesia can possibly be refused entry or threatened with quarantine.
There is a gay scene with bars and clubs in Jakarta, Surabaya, Jogyakarta and other large cities as well as Bali. Another possible meeting places are the many juice-bars in the flashy shopping centres in all the larger cities.

Anders als in anderen muslimischen Ländern ist die indonesische Gesellschaft relativ tolerant in Bezug auf Homosexualität. Dies gilt in der Provinz Aceh nicht, denn dort werden die Sharia Gesetze angewandt. Es gibt aktuell keine Gesetze, die Homosexualität verbieten. Das Schutzalter für sexuelle Handlungen liegt bei 18 Jahren. Wie in anderen Ländern Südostasiens ist sie integraler Bestandteil des Alltags, es gibt sogar Prominente in den Medien, deren Homo- oder Transsexualität bekannt ist. Dennoch wird das Thema totgeschwiegen und nur im Verborgenen gelebt. Es gibt aber auch fanatisch-muslimische Tendenzen mit Übergriffen auf Schwule, z.B. auf eine Anti-AIDS-Kundgebung in Solo, deren Teilnehmer von einigen hundert Maskierten überfallen wurden. Erstaunlicher Weise gibt es keine rechtlichen Regelungen die sich mit HIV/AIDS befassen, obwohl dies, wie in den meisten Ländern der Region, ein großes Problem ist. Bei der Einreise von betroffenen Personen muss jedoch mit Einreiseverweigerung bis hin zur Quarantäne gerechnet werden. Es gibt in den größeren Städten wie Jakarta, Surabaya und Jogyakarta und natürlich im touristisch erschlossenen Bali, eine entwickelte schwule Szene mit Bars und Clubs. Ansonsten trifft man sich auch an den Saft-Bars in schickeren Einkaufszentren größerer Städte.

Contrairement à d'autres pays musulmans, la société indonésienne est relativement tolérante envers l'homosexualité. Ceci ne vaut pas pour la province d'Aceh où les lois de la Sharia sont en vigueur. Il n'existe actuellement aucune loi qui interdise l'homosexualité. La majorité sexuelle est fixée à 18 ans. Comme dans d'autres pays d'Asie du Sud-Est, celle-ci fait partie intégrante du quotidien, il existe même des personnalités dans les médias dont l'homosexualité ou transsexualité est connue. Cependant le sujet reste passé sous silence et n'est vécu que dissimulé. Mais il existe aussi des tendances islamiques avec des attaques contre les gays par exemple lors d'une manifestation contre le SIDA à Solo où des participants ont été pris à partie par une centaine de personnes masquées.
De façon étonnante, il n'existe aucune mesure légale concernant le VIH ou le SIDA bien que le problème y soit important, comme dans la plupart des pays de la région.
Lors de l'entrée dans le pays, les personnes concernées peuvent se voir interdire l'entrée sur le territoire ou contraint à une quarantaine.
Il existe dans les villes importantes comme Jakarta, Surabaya et Yogyakarta et bien-sûr dans la région touristique de Bali une scène gay développée avec des clubs et des bars. Dans les autres cas, on se rencontre dans les bars à jus de fruits des élégants centres commerciaux des plus grandes villes.

A diferencia de otros países musulmanes, la sociedad de Indonesia es relativamente tolerante respecto a la homosexualidad. Esto no es aplicable en la provincia de Aceh, ya que allí se cumple con las leyes de la Sharia. Actualmente no hay leyes que prohíban la homosexualidad. La edad mínima para mantener relaciones sexuales es de 18 años. Como en otros países del Sudeste Asiático esto es una parte integral de la vida cotidiana, incluso hay celebridades en los medios de comunicación de las que se conoce su homosexualidad o transexualidad. Sin embargo, este es un tema ignorado y sólo se vive en secreto. A pesar de esta relativa calma, aquí pueden encontrarse fanáticos musulmanes que centran sus ataques contra los homosexuales, como es el caso de la manifestación contra el SIDA en Solo, en la que cientos de hombres enmascarados atacaros a los participantes.
Sorprendentemente no hay normativas jurídicas que traten el VIH / SIDA, aun siendo este, como en la mayoría de los países de la región, un problema importante.
A la hora de entrar en el país, las personas afectadas deben contar, sin embargo, con la denegación de entrada en la frontera o incluso con una entrada en cuarentena.
En las grandes ciudades como Yakarta, Surabaya y Jogyakarta y por supuesto en la turística Bali se puede encontrar un ambiente gay desarrollado con bares y clubes. Por lo demás, otros puntos de encuentro son los bares de zumos en los centros comerciales más elegantes de ciudades más grandes.

Diversamente che in altri Paesi islamici, la società indonesiana è relativamente tollerante nei confronti dell'omosessualità.

Questo non vale per la provincia di Aceh, dove ancora si pratica la legge della Sharia. Non esistono leggi che vietano l'omosessualità. L'età del consenso è di 18 anni. Come in altri Paesi del sud est asiatico l'omosessuale è parte integrante della vita quotidiana; molte persone dello spettacolo sono risaputamente omosessuali o transessuali. Nonostante ciò il tema non viene affrontato e l'omosessualità viene vissuta di nascosto. C'è anche un certo fanatismo musulmano che opera violenza nei confronti dei gay: infatti, a titolo di esempio, durante una manifestazione contro l'AIDS svoltasi a Solo, i manifestanti sono stati aggrediti da un centinaio di persone mascherate. Non ci sono regolamentazioni legali per quanto riguarda l'HIV e l'AIDS; questo stupisce visto che l'HIV e l'AIDS costituiscono un grave problema nella maggior parte dei Paesi dell'area. Alle persone colpite da questa infezione potrebbe essere rifiutato l'ingresso nel Paese e potrebbero anche essere messe in quarantena. Una vera e propria scena gay con bar e discoteche la si trova a Jakarta, a Surabaya, a Jogyakarta e naturalmente nella turistica Bali. In alternativa ci si può incontrare nei juice bar dei centri commerciali.

TOURIST INFO

Jawa Barat = West Java
Jawa Tengah = Central Java
Jawa Timur = East Java
Sumatera Utara = North Sumatra
Sumatera Barat = West Sumatra
Sulawesi Selatan = South Sulawesi (Celebes)
Sulawesi Utara = North Sulawesi (Celebes)
Kalimantan Timur = East Borneo
Kalimantan Selatan = South Borneo
Irian Jaya = West Papua
Jakarta and Yogyakarta are separate districts on Java
Bengkulu is a separate district on Sumatra.

Bali

Badung – Bali ☎ 0361

APARTMENTS

■ **Tamu Seseh** (AC BF CC GLM M MA OS PI RWS RWT) All year
Jalan Pantai Seseh, Banjar Sogsogan, Gang Sentul, Cemagi *20 mins from Seminyak* ☎ (0361) 742 7810 💻 www.tamuseseh.com

Buleleng – Bali ☎ 0361

HOTELS

■ **Bali au Naturel** (AC B BF CC DM DU GLM I M MA MSG NR NU OS PI RR RWB RWS RWT SA VEG WH) All year; check in at 14h and check out time at 12h
Jalan Pantai, Buleleng ☎ (361) 4736 568 💻 www.baliaunaturel.com
Gay-owned and managed resort designed by passion and love. It provides luxurious and alternative accommodation to nudist-lovers, men and women, gay and straight.

Denpasar – Bali ☎ 0361

TRAVEL AND TRANSPORT

■ **Dive the Rainbow** (GLM)
Jl. Drupadi 23 b, Seminyak-Kuta ☎ (817) 974 7268 (mobile)
💻 www.dive-the-rainbow.com
Professional dive service. Introductory diving as well as internationally valid certificates.

■ **Gaya Dewata** (G)
Jl. Sakura IV No. 8 💻 www.GayaDewata.com

CRUISING

-Renon Park (t), Jalan Tukad Musi (21-24h)
-Jalan Gatot Subroto Barat / Jalan Gunung Catur VI (The housing Complex, an unfinished Real Estate), (10-17h, no lights in the evening)
-Lapangan Puputan (football field) (r t); 20-24h.

Kerobokan – Bali ☎ 0361

MASSAGE

■ **Antique Spa** (b CC g MA MSG OS) 10-22 (last reservations 20h)
Jalan Lestari, Br. semer, Umalas *10 mins drive to Seminyak*
☎ (0361) 73 98 40 💻 www.antiquebali.com
16 massage rooms, open bathtub, gallery. Pick-up services is available from Kuta, Tuban and Nusa Dua.

TRAVEL AND TRANSPORT

■ **Unseen Bali** (GLM MA)
Jalan Umaalas Klecung 10 ☎ (0361) 4736568 💻 www.unseenbali.org
Gay owned travel agency, specialised in gay and gay-friendly travel in Bali.

HOTELS

■ **Antique Villa And Spa** (AC bf cc glm H MA MSG RWB RWS VA) All year
Jalan Dukuh Indah, Br.semer, Umalas ☎ (0361) 73 98 40
💻 www.antiquebali.com
A gay-friendly property. The staff has been trained to cater for gay guests. Only 10 minutes walk to the nearest gay bars and shopping area.

■ **Spartacvs Exclusive Member Hotel** (AC B BF CC G I M MA MSG P PI PK RWB RWS RWT S VA WH WI) All year
Jln. Pura Telaga Waja Petitenget *Near Petitenget Temple, take road from Living Room restaurant towards Sentosa Villas* ☎ (0361) 738 944
💻 www.spartacvsbali.com
Spartacvs is an exclusive all gay male only member hotel with 12 rooms consisting of standard, deluxe, deluxe pool, superior garden & superior pool. 5 minute walk to gay beach.

GUEST HOUSES

Villa Layang Bulan (BF G M MA MSG NU PI) All year, 24hrs
Jalan Batu Belig, Gang Daksina 10b *Seminyak, North Kuta*
☎ (0812) 46 367 527 💻 www.villalayangbulan.com
Villa Layang Bulan is an all male, clothing optional resort. The resort has private and dorm rooms.

Kuta – Bali ☎ 0361

TRAVEL AND TRANSPORT

Gay Bali Tours (GLM MA) 9-17, Sat 9-13h, Sun closed
Jl. Griya Anyar 76 A, Br. Kajeng-Suwung – Tuban *Bali airport*
☎ (0361) 788 6627 💻 www.bali-rainbows.com
Professional tour operator for the LGBT community. Organizes accommodations, tours and more.

Hanafi Dharma – Tour Specialist 9-24h
Jl. Raya Kuta No. 1 E *In front of Pasar Pagi Kuta, downtown*
☎ (0361) 756 454 💻 www.hanafi.net
Gay travel agency, english speaking driver and guide only for Indonesia, especially the Bali region.

HOTELS

Villa Karisa (AC b BF CC H m MA MSG PI) All year
Jl. Drupadi 100X, Seminyak ☎ (0361) 73 93 95 💻 www.villakarisabali.com

GUEST HOUSES

Laki Uma Villa (AC B BF G I MA MSG NU OS PI PK RWB RWS SA SB VA VS WH) All year
Jl. Umalas-Kerobokan ☎ (0361) 4736568 💻 www.lakiumavilla.com
All-male villa with 4 guest rooms. Probably the only gay-only, clothing-optional resort in South-East Asia.

Umah Watu Villas (AC B BF CC GLM OS PI PK RWS VA WI) All year, 24hrs
27C. Jl. Sari Dewi, Basangkasa, Seminyak *Approx. 300 m from Legian Surf Beach, behind the Oberoi Hotel* ☎ (0361) 73 10 06
💻 www.umahwatu.com
Seminyak Area peacful and tranquil location,set in the rice paddies. Walking distance to beach. Close to local gay venues,restaurants, clubs and bars.

SWIMMING

-Beach north of where Jalan Pantai meets the beach
-Kuta beach (r AYOR) (Northern part, be discreet).

CRUISING

-Ganesha-Oberoi beach (1km north of „Resor Seminyak", r), Legian beach (All along the beach)
-Kuta beach (r), All along the beach (18-23h).

Legian – Bali ☎ 0361

HOTELS

Court Yard Hotel & Apartments (AC B bf CC glm H I M MA OS PI PK RWS RWT VA) All year
Jl. Werkudara No. 14 ☎ (0361) 75 02 42 💻 www.balicourthotel.com
Modern style. Centrally located. 5 mins walk to legian beach.

Seminyak – Bali ☎ 0361

BARS

Bali Joe (B G MA OS r S ST)
Jl. Dhyana Pura, Abimanyu Arcade 8 ☎ (0361) 730 931
Popular bar with locals and tourists alike.

Birdcage Bali (B G)
Jl. Dhyana Pura – abimanju Arcade 7 💻 birdcagebali.com
New bar.

Bottoms Up (AC B G m MA T) 19-3h
Dhyana Pura Street 10 *Jln Caplak Tanduk 10*
💻 bottomsupseminyak.webs.com

Club Cosmo Bali (AC B D GLM m MA OS S SNU ST T WE)
Mon-Thu 16-3, Fri-Sun -4h
Jl. Dhyana Pura Gosha Plaza 8-9 ☎ (0361) 738 696
Two show stages with entertainment starting 10pm till 1am. Many male dancers, gogo boys, pole dancers, drag queens.

Facebar (AC B D G MA S ST) 20-3h
Jalan Dhyana Pura *Off Jalan Raya Seminyak*
Popular. Drag shows and muscle men in g-strings doing bartop dancing at 23h.

Mixwell Bar'n'Lounge (B g MA OS ST) 19-2h
Jalan Dhyana Pura 6 ☎ (0361) 73 68 64
Chill-out place.

RESTAURANTS

Gado Gado (B glm M MA OS) 8-24h
Jalan Dhyana Pura 99 *Beach front* ☎ (0361) 37 69 66
💻 www.gadogadorestaurant.com
Open-air restaurant.

KuDéTa (AC b bf glm M MA) 8-2h
Jalan Laksmana 9 *In the Oberoi district, between the Legian and Oberoi Hotel* ☎ (0361) 73 69 69 💻 www.kudeta.net

Lucciola. La (B CC glm M MA OS) 9-24h
Jalan Kayu Aya Beach (beach front), Oberoi *End of Jln Dhyana Pura*
☎ (0361) 73 08 38
Very popular for lunch on the beachfront or afternoon chillout.

Mades Warung (B BF CC glm I M MA OS) 10-24h
Jalan Raya Seminyak *In the heart of Seminyak* ☎ (0361) 75 30 39
💻 www.madeswarung.com

Waroeng Bonita (B glm M MA MSG) 7-24h
Jalan Petitenget 2000X ☎ (0361) 731 918 💻 www.bonitabali.com
Pretty garden restaurant serving fabulous Indonesian and western dishes. Also home of Bonita's Spa, massages available.

MASSAGE

Banana Spa Bali (G MSG) 10-22h
20 Jalan Drupadi ☎ (0361) 213 5525 💻 www.bananaspabali.com

HOTELS

Villa Bali Asri (AC BF CC DU FH I MA NG PI PK RWS RWT SA VA VEG WI) All year
Jl. Sari Dewi 39, Seminyak-Oberoi ☎ (0361) 735 444
💻 www.villabaliasri.com
A group of 11 luxury villas each with swimming pools, 2 minutes walk from the beach, 5 minutes walk from the best restaurants and gay bars.

GUEST HOUSES

Green Chaka (BF G MA MSG NU PI) All year
Petitenget 41 *Next to gay beach of Seminyak* ☎ (08133) 700 2625
💻 www.greenchaka.com
Men only rooms and suites. Balinese garden and high-end Indonesian contempory design.

Mango Villa (AC B BF FH G M MA MSG OS PI PK RWS RWT WI)
Jalan Drupadi 69 *Located on Jalan Drupadi directly opposite the famous Banana Spa Bali* ☎ (0361) 212 9200 💻 www.fruitvillasbali.com
Mango Villa comprises of two spacious bedrooms with luxurious queen-size 4 poster beds. It can be rented out as a 2 bedroom Villa or each of the bedrooms can be rented separately.

Phil's Place (AC BF CC G m MSG PI) All year, 24hrs
Jalan Plawa, Gang Melati 40 ☎ (0821) 4724 7101 💻 www.philsbali.com
Five bedroom villa, exclusively for gay men.

Space at Bali Villas (! AC B BF CC glm M MC OS PI PK RWB RWS RWT VA) All year
Jl Drupadi 8 *Off Jl Laksmana. Gay street 15 mins walk* ☎ (0361) 731 100
💻 www.spaceatbali.com

Villa Angelo (AC BF CC G I MC NU OS PI PK RWB RWS RWT VA) All year
Jl. Raya Seminyak 26d *2 blocks from the beach* ☎ (0361) 84 7576 2
💻 www.baligayguesthouse.jimdo.com

APARTMENTS

■ **Downtown Villas Bali** (AC bf CC H M MA MSG PI WO)
Jalan Pura Dalem 9d ☎ (0361) 736 464 🖳 www.downtownbali.com
Nine luxuriously appointed villas in the heart of Seminyak.

CRUISING

- Beach at restaurant Kantina near W Hotel

Ubud – Bali ☎ 0361

GUEST HOUSES

■ **Bhanuswari Resort & Spa** (AC GLM M PI RWB RWS) All year
Jl. Tengkulak ☎ (0361) 947 831 🖳 www.bhanuswariresort.com

Java

Bandung – Jawa Barat

CRUISING

-Merdeka Street (nights)
-Dago Plaza, 61-63 Jalan H Juanda
-Jalan Sumatra at night
-Bandung Indah Plaza (g r), Jalan Merdeka 56, near McDonald's or in the basement car park facility, late afternoon and nights (R)
-Istana Plaza at Jalan Pasir Kaligi/Rajajaran (g)
-Town Square at Jalan Dalam Kaum (opp. the central mosque), two facilities at opposite ends (AYOR)
-Cipaku swimming Pools are very cruisy especially on Wed.

Bogor – Jawa Barat ☎ 0251

BARS

■ **Karaoke Mulia** (B glm) Sat
Taman Topi, Kapt. Muslihat Street

DANCECLUBS

■ **Spectrum Discoteque** (B D glm MA)
Jalan Pajajaran *Near to Hotel Pangrano III* ☎ (0251) 25 70 57

CRUISING

-In front of Hotel Salak
-In front of the Istana Palace, day and night
-Jambu Dua Mall (main entrance stair), (YC)
-Taman Topi, Park (YC), opp. the Central Police Station (19-22h, WE)
-RRI (Radio Republik Indonesia) – in front of the offices.

Jakarta ☎ 021

BARS

■ **Comedy Cafe Indonesia** (B d glm M MA S) 10-24h
Plaza Festival, GF-06 Jl HR Rasuna Said C-22 ☎ (021) 526 32 18
Popular with local gays and lesbians. They serve Indonesian and European food.

■ **Matra** (B d gLm)
Grand Mentang Hotel, Jalan Matraman Raya
Mostly lesbian, but also young gay men on Sat mornings.

■ **Red Square** (B glm M MA)
Plaza Senayan Arcadia, Jl. Asia Afrika ☎ (021) 57 90 12 81
Chic Vodka bar with fabulous cocktails.

DANCECLUBS

■ **Apollo**
Bellagio Boutique Mall UG Level, Jl. Mega Kuningan Barat VII
☎ (021) 91 30 84 23 🖳 www.apolloclub-jakarta.com

■ **Stadium** (B D glm MA)
Just off Jl. Hayam Wuruk, Kota *Up from the Moonlight Discotheque*
Popular on Fri & Sat nights, but be discreet. Drug oriented, be careful.

SAUNAS/BATHS

■ **9M** (b DU G m MSG RR SA SB VS WH WO) 11-24h
Jalan Talang Betutu 4 *Near Hyatt Hotel* ☎ (021) 3192 4467
Meeting place for the gay community. Indonesian, Thai, Swedish massage from man to man.

■ **Millenium Sauna and Fitness Centre**
(b g MA MSG PI SA SB SOL WH)
3 Jalan Fachrudin ☎ (021) 230 36 36
Many visitors are gay and the sauna and steam room is very popular especially among Chinese men.

■ **Mulia** (B FH g M MSG OS PI SA SB SOL WH WO)
6-22; massage & treatment from 7h
Jalan Asia Afrika, Senayan *Business district* ☎ (021) 574 77 77
🖳 www.hotelmulia.com
Sauna in first class hotel. Best after 20h. Be discreet.

HOTELS

■ **Putri Duyung Cottage** (AC b CC H MA)
Taman Impian Jaya Ancol, Jalan Lodan Timur No. 7
☎ (021) 68 01 08

CRUISING

-Lapangan Banteng (R AYOR) (Park opp. Hotel Borobudur), don't go down from car and only talk to people on the other cars, not to the pedestrians
-Ambassador Mall (cruisy at lunch hours and adter 17h)
-Pasar Festival lower level (R, cruisy after 17h)
-Block M Plaza and Terminal (Kebayoran Bari district)
-Sogo (Plaza Indonesia/Grand Hyatt Hotel/Hotel Indonesia circle, day and night)
-Ancol swimming pool (under the waterfall Sun)
-Sarinah shopping centre (ground floor, at McDonald's)
-Kuningan Swimming Complex, Pasar Festifal Jalan Rasuna Sahid (r) (17-20h)
-Java Department store (Djakarta Theatres), opposite Sarinah, near Pizza Hut (r)
-Jalang Jaksa, hostel street for back packers (24/7) (r).

Jember – Jawa Timur

CRUISING

-Town Square (alun-alun) (at night t)
-"The Warung", small restaurant in alley in front of station, after 21h.

Kediri – Jawa Timur

CRUISING

-In front of the Brawijaya stadium (at night, best on Sat)
-In front of the Kowak swimming pool.

Malang – Jawa Timur ☎ 0341

BARS

■ **Bale Barong** (B g MA) Tue 22-?h
Jl. Panglima Sudirman

■ **My Place** (B glm) Sat
c/o Kartika Prince Hotel

CRUISING

-Lobby Mandala Theatre, Sat night.

Mojokerto – Jawa Timur

CRUISING

-Town Square (alun-alun) (next to the military police building, at night).

Pasuruan – Jawa Timur

CRUISING

-North Town Square (alun-alun) (t, at night)
-Banyubiru baths (17 km from Pasuran, sun daytime)
-Makam Gunung Gangsir, Bangil (T, Fri).

Ponorogo – Jawa Timur

CRUISING

-Town square (alun-alun) (next to the banyan tree on the south side, along the sidewalk between the West & East squares, best Sat night 20-?h).

Salatiga – Jawa Tengah

CRUISING

-Jalan Sudirman (Sat night)
-Near Salatiga Plaza (nights).

Semarang – Jawa Tengah

CRUISING

-Menteri Supeno Street
-Simpang Lima Field (near Citraland, nights).

Sidoarjo – Jawa Timur

CRUISING

-Town Square (alun-alun) (near the public telephones beside the Mahkota cinema and the street next to it, sat night best)
-Larangan Market.

Solo / Surakarta – Jawa Tengah ☏ 031

CAFES

■ **Saraswati** (b glm m MA)
Novotel Slamet Riyadi

DANCECLUBS

■ **Legenda Discotheque** (B D glm MA)
Jalan Pasar Besar
Best on Sat night.

CRUISING

-Jurung Park (river side)
-Park behind Pasar Legi (t)
-Slamed Ryiady, near BTPN Bank
-Sriwedari Park (also the parking lot behind, night).

Surabaya – Jawa Timur ☏ 031

DANCECLUBS

■ **Calypso** (B D glm MA) Sun
Kenjeran Amusement Park (Pantai Ria Kenjeran)
■ **Station Top Ten** (b D glm MA)
6/F Plaza Tunjungan, Jalan Tunjungan
Best on Fri & Sat.
■ **Vertical 6** (B d g MA)
c/o J.W. Marriott Hotel, Jl. Embong Malang
More gay on WE nights.

SAUNAS/BATHS

■ **Atlas Clark Hatch** (b g MSG OS SA WO)
Jalan Darma Husada Indah Barat ☏ (031) 594 5466
Mostly Chinese and local customers.
■ **Klub Primalaras** (B G M MSG OS SA SB WH WO) 14-22h
Darmo Grande Site
Local crowd and international guests.
■ **Sheraton Health Club** (B g M MSG OS PI SA SB SOL WH) 6-22h
Embong Malang 25-31 *Tunjungan Place at central business district*
☏ (031) 546 80 00

SWIMMING

-Water Park (b g m MSG OS SA WO), Jln Kenjeran (Mon 13-18h)
-Pasar Atom at Jln Bunguran.

CRUISING

-Taman Remaja Surabaya (r T) (Amusement Park next to Surabaya Mall, Jalan Kusuma Bangsa, Thu open-air drag show)
-Gunung Sari at Jln Irian Barat (opposite the Patra Hilton Hotel) (T)
-Jalan Irian Barat (T)(21-24h)
-Tunjungan Plaza (shopping centre, evenings)
-Plaza Surabaya (r), Shopping centre
-Pattaya, cruising riverside (r t), Jalan Kangean opp. ‚Monumen Kapal Selam' (22-24h).

Yogyakarta ☏ 0274

BARS

■ **Hugo's** (b d glm MA)
Jalan Laksda Adisucipto *Near parking area of Sheraton Hotel*
Trendy café club with live music and DJ. Upmarket place with many gays on Sat.

HOTELS

■ **Dusun Jogja Village Inn** (AC CC glm M MA PI WO) 24hrs
Jalan Menukan 5, Karangkajen *In front of Radio Yasika FM-bus N°2 from bus Station* ☏ (0274) 37 30 31 💻 www.jvidusun.co.id
Stylish & full of character. Good food and music.

CRUISING

-Alun alun in front of the Kraton or Sultan's Palace
-Malioboro Mall, popular with local gays, 15-19h.

Kalimantan

Balikpapan – Kalimantan Timur ☏ 0542

SAUNAS/BATHS

■ **Dusit Hotel Sauna** (B g M MSG OS SA SB SOL WO) 18-21h
Jalan Jend. Sudirman *East of the city, in the basement* ☏ (0542) 420 150
Best Tue-Thu 18-20h.

CRUISING

-Lapangan Monumen, Jalan Jend Sudirman (after 21.30h, many gay locals)
-Jalan Gunung Pasir (T), after 23h.

Pontianak

CRUISING

-Taman Alun Kapuas, Park (in front of Military office) (after 19h).

Samarinda

CRUISING

-Patung Pesut Mahakam, Park (Mon 21-24h)
-Mesra Indah Mall, 2nd floor, (r)(Sat 18-21h)
-Citra Niaga (CN)
-Terapung Discotique, (Mon 21-24h).

Lombok

Senggigi ☏ 0370

BARS

■ **Berry's** (B g M MA)
Jl. Raya ☏ (0370) 818 0520 9736
Gay-owned.

CAFES

Pojok (B glm M MA)
Jl. Raya

RESTAURANTS

Bai Bar & Grill (AC B glm M OS VEG WL) 7-23h
Jalan Raya Mangsit *At Qunci Villas* ☏ (0370) 69 38 00
www.quncivillas.com
Happy hour 17-19h. Indonesian & international cuisine.

Bumbu Café (b glm M s)
Jl. Raya ☏ (0370) 818 540 989
Excellent Thai cuisine. Gay owned.

HOTELS

Qunci Villas (AC B BF CC GLM M OS PI RWB RWS RWT) All year
Jalan Raya Mangsit *10 mins north of Senggigi Beach town*
☏ (0370) 69 38 00
www.quncivillas.com
20 units with all modern comforts. Breakfast is served either on the bedroom veranda or at the Bai Bar & Grill Restaurant. 15-meter beachfront pool.

Riau Islands

Batam – Riau ☏ 0778

CAFES

Noname Café (b g m MA)

DANCECLUBS

Ozon Discotheque (B D g MA)
Pacific Discotheque (B D g MA)

CRUISING

-Batu Ampar harbour (Sat nights)
-In front of BCA from (22-5h)
-Plaza 21, Tanjung Pantun-Jodoh (14-22h)
-Bus stop in front of Permata Bank (22-3h)
-Bukit Senyum (Smiling Hill), nights
-Centrepoint Shopping Centre
-Jalan Cut Nya Dhien, near Education and Culture office (g) (night).

Sulawesi (Celebes)

Makassar – Sulawesi Selatan ☏ 0423

DANCECLUBS

Botol (AC B CC D glm MA r S WE)
Jl. Somba Opu 235 *In Quality Hotel*

M Club (AC B D glm MA r)
Jl. Panakkukang Mas Bl F/66

CRUISING

-Makassar Theater jalan Bali (Sat night)
-Karebosi Field (at night)
-Losari Beach (at night)
-Makassar harbour (t) (at night)
-Makassar harbour (t) (after sunset).

Manado – Sulawesi Utara

CRUISING

-Pasar 45 (station and terminal complex) (t) at night
-Near the Balai Wartawan & Arta Pusara Bank (at night)
-People's Unity Park (Taman Persatuan Bangsa) (t).

Rantepao – Tana Toraja ☏ 0423

TRAVEL AND TRANSPORT

PT. Emerald Indonesia tours & travel (CC GLM I PK SH W)
Mon-Fri 9-18, Sat 10-15h, Sun closed (by appointment only)
Jl. Monginsidi No. 1 ☏ (0423) 25100 www.go2indo.com
Gay-friendly travel agency. For tours, hotel reservations, flights, airport transfers, boat-tickets and guides within Indonesia.

HOTELS

Toraja Prince
(AC B BF cc glm H I M MA MSG PI PK RWB RWS RWT S VA) All year
Jalan Jurusan Palopo KM4 *Centre of Toraja, near the traditional market „Pasar Bolu"* ☏ (0423) 214 07
64 rooms. All rooms with bath/WC, TV, radio, mini bar.

GUEST HOUSES

Tongkonan Layuk Lion (bf glm RWB RWS RWT) 14-22h
Near to main street to catch local bus/taxi ☏ ((0423)) 25100
layuklion.webs.com
Eco-lodge in Toraja. Balinese style bathrooms and balconies facing the traditional Tongkonan village. Surrounded by tropical forests & emerald green mountains.

CRUISING

-Palu Plaza Shopping centre (t) (after 21h till morning)
-Palu Studio Cinema (t) (during last movies).

Sumatra

Bandar Lampung – Lampung ☏ 0752

DANCECLUBS

Oya Discotheque (B D glm MA) Sat
Yos Sudarso Street, Sukaraja, Telukbetung

CRUISING

-Tanjungkarang district, around the monument in front of the Golden Movie House (Bioskop Golden) and between Pemuda Street and the main crossroads (nighttime)
-Near King Supermarket, Tanjungkarang Plaza (daytime).

Medan – Sumatera Utara ☏ 061

DANCECLUBS

Retrospective (B D g MA) Sat
c/o Capital Building, Jl. Putri Hijau *Beside Deli Plaza*

Tobasa (B D g MA) Sat
c/o Hotel Danau Toba International, Jl. Imam Bonjol

CRUISING

-Jalan A. Yani
-London Boulevard (near the post office PTP)
-Jalan Iskander Muda (T)
-Jalan Pal Merah (T)
-Medan Mall at Jln Haryono M.T (R)
-Taman Ria Amusement Complex (after 19h)
-Swimmingpool at the Tiara Hotel, Jl. Cut Mutia.

Padang – Sumatera Barat ☏ 0751

DANCECLUBS

Bumi Minang Pub (B D g) Sat night after 21h
c/o Hotel Bumi Minang

CRUISING

-Imam Bonjol Park (between 21h and dawn) (T)
-Minang Plaza (10-21h)

-Padang Theater, all hours
-President Music Room
-Taman Melati (Aditiawarman Museum Complex, near the Utama Theater at the Taman Budaya).

Palembang – Sumatera Selatan ☏ 0711

DANCECLUBS

■ **Mega Bintang Disco** (b D g)
c/o Hotel Darma Agung, Jalan Sudirman *On the road to the airport*

CRUISING

-Internasional Plaza (top floor in the cinema lobby, 15-19h)
-Jl. Dr Wahidin (Topaz area, near Kambang Iwak, nightly) (T)
-Outside the Telkom office on Jl. Merdeka, near Tugu Monpera, between the post office and Garuda cinema (20-22h)
-Tugu Monpera Monument on Jl. Merdeka (opposite Mesjid Agung, nightly) (T)
-Outside Wartel Dahlia (Jln Letkol Iskandar 902a, opposite the Internasional Plaza, 19-21h)
-Lumban Tirta public swimingpool (next to Sporthal on Jl. P.O.M IX, Saturdays and Sundays).

Pekanbaru – Riau

CRUISING

-Atrium of Plaza Citra (21-24h)
-Café Plaza Citra (g) 20-22h)
-Jin Cut Nya Dhien (next to the Education & Culture Deepdikbud Building) (21-24h).

Iran

Name: Îrân · Irán
Location: Middle East
Initials: IR
Time: GMT +4
International Country Code: ☏ 98
International Access Code: ☏ 00
Language: Persian (official), Turkish, Kurdish, Luri
Area: 1,648,000 km² / 636,294 sq mi.
Currency: 1 Rial (Rl) = 100 Dinars
Population: 67,006,000
Capital: Tehrān (Teheran)
Religions: 99% Muslim
Climate: Summer (Jun-Aug) has very high temperatures and is the most unpleasant time to visit. The best time is spring (Apr-Jun) and autumn (Sept-Nov).

Homosexuality is illegal according to Article 110 of the Penal Code. The Deputy Attorney General of Iran declared in October 2008 that judicial authorities would put a moratorium on the death penalty for juveniles. The moratorium will take effect immediately, with plans to seek final parliamentary approval.
A ban on juvenile execution would be an important human rights development for sexual minorities where often young Iranian men have been executed as juveniles after being charged with sodomy and other sexual crimes. This is a positive step toward improving human rights in Iran.
Historically, Iranian Courts have interpreted Article 49 of the Islamic Penal Code in a way that allows them to impose the death penalty on children. Although Article 49 states that children are not criminally liable, judges often use existing laws to define the age of adulthood as 15 for boys and just 9 for girls. In June 2010 a prominent Iranian lawyer Mr. Mohammad Mostfaii reported that about 100 young people in Iranian jails waiting to be executed for crimes they committed as juveniles.
But a recent announcement by judicial authorities defines juveniles as those under age 18, and says that the maximum penalty for all crimes committed by juveniles is life in prison, which can be reduced to 15 years in jail with parole.
The change comes after significant opposition to the death penalty for minors was voiced in Iran itself. Nobel Peace Prize winner Shirin Ebadi has been an outspoken critic of child executions, speaking up against this inhumane practice at national and international forums and representing juvenile defendants in court.

Homosexualität ist Artikel 110 des Strafgesetzbuches zufolge verboten. Der stellvertretende Generalstaatsanwalt des Iran ließ im Oktober 2008 verlauten, dass die Justizbehörden ein Moratorium über die Vollstreckung der Todesstrafe an Jugendlichen verhängen wollen. Das Moratorium tritt sofort in Kraft, die endgültige Absegnung durch das Parlament ist in Planung.
Ein Verbot der Hinrichtung Jugendlicher würde besonders für Angehörige sexueller Minderheiten eine deutlich bessere Menschenrechtssituation darstellen, denn viele iranische Jugendliche sind bereits des Analverkehrs und anderer sexueller Gesetzesübertretungen beschuldigt und gehängt worden. Für den Iran würde dies einen riesigen Fortschritt bei den Menschenrechten darstellen.
Bisher haben die iranischen Gerichte Artikel 49 des islamischen Strafrechts auf eine Weise ausgelegt, die ihnen die Verhängung der Todesstrafe für Kinder ermöglicht. Obwohl Artikel 49 Minderjährige eigentlich von strafrechtlicher Verfolgung freistellt, wenden die Richter oft bestehende Gesetze an, um männliche Jugendliche ab 15 und weibliche Jugendliche sogar schon ab 9 Jahren für strafmündig zu erklären. Im Juni 2010 berichtete der bekannte iranische Rechtsanwalt Mohammad Mostfaii, dass in iranischen Gefängnissen ungefähr 100 Menschen wegen Vergehen, die sie als Jugendliche begangen haben, auf ihre Hinrichtung warten.
Im Gegensatz dazu definiert die Verlautbarung der Justizbehörden alle Personen unter 18 Jahren als minderjährig und sieht gleichzeitig als Höchststrafe für alle von Minderjährigen begangenen Vergehen lebenslangen Freiheitsentzug vor, der auf Entlassung nach 15 Jahren mit Bewährung reduziert werden kann.

Der Sinneswandel ist eine Folge des beachtlichen Widerstands gegen die Vollstreckung der Todesstrafe an Minderjährigen im Iran selbst. Die Nobelpreisträgerin Shirin Ebadi hat die Hinrichtung von Kindern immer wieder scharf kritisiert, sich in nationalen und internationalen Foren gegen diese unmenschliche Praxis ausgesprochen und persönlich die Verteidigung jugendlicher Angeklagter vor Gericht übernommen.

Le procureur général adjoint de l'Iran a laissé entendre en octobre 2008 que les autorités judiciaires décrètent un moratoire sur l'exécution de la peine de mort pour les adolescents. Le moratoire entre immédiatement en vigueur, l'adoption définitive est en projet au parlement.

Une interdiction des exécutions de mineurs représenteraient une situation bien meilleure pour les minorités sexuelles, car beaucoup de jeunes Iraniens ont été condamnés et pendus pour des relations anales et d'autres transgressions sexuelles. En Iran, cela représenterait un pas important pour les Droits de l'Homme.

Jusqu'à présent les cours de justice iraniennes ont interprété l'article 49 de telle sorte que la pendaison d'enfants est possible. Bien qu'en fait l'article 49 exempte les mineurs de poursuites pénales, les juges utilisent souvent des lois existantes pour déclarer légalement et pénalement responsables les garçons dès 15 ans et pour les filles même dès 9 ans. En juin 2010 le fameux avocat iranien Mohammad Mostfaii rapportait qu'environ 100 personnes attendent leur pendaison pour des faits perprétrés dans leur adolescence.

Contrairement à cela, le communiqué récent des autorités judiciaires définit toute personne de moins de 18 ans comme mineure et prévoit parallèlement une peine de prison à vie pour tous les actes commis par des mineurs avec possibilité de mise en liberté après 15 ans avec sursis.

Cette volte-face fait suite une opposition considérable au sein-même de l'Iran contre la mise en oeuvre de la peine de mort contre des mineurs. La Prix Nobel Shirin Ebadi a toujours critiqué virulemment l'exécution de mineurs en s'exprimant dans des forums internationaux contre les pratiques inhumaines et a défendu en personne de jeunes prévenus devant les tribunaux.

La homosexualidad está prohibida, según el artículo 110 del código penal. El fiscal general de Irán hizo saber en octubre de 2008 que las autoridades judiciales querían imponer una moratoria en la ejecución de la pena de muerte para los jóvenes. La moratoria entró en vigor enseguida, y está prevista la ratificación definitiva a través del Parlamento.

La prohibición de la ejecución de jóvenes representaría una clara mejora en la situación de derechos humanos, especialmente para las minorías sexuales, puesto que muchos jóvenes iranís fueron declarados culpables por practicar sexo anal y otras infracciones sexuales y después ahorcados. Para Irán esto significaría un gran avance en la situación de los derechos humanos.

Hasta ahora, los tribunales iranís interpretaron el artículo 49 del código penal islámico de tal manera que incluso era posible imponer la pena de muerte para menores. Aunque el artículo 49 en realidad libera a los menores de la ejecución penal, los jueces aplican a menudo esta legislación para declarar culpables a chicos menores a partir de los 15 años e incluso a chicas menores a partir de los 9 años. En junio 2010 el conocido abogado iraní Mohammad Mostfaii informó que en las cárceles iranís esperan su ejecución más de 100 personas por actos cometidos cuando eran menores de edad.

Contrariamente, las declaraciones de las autoridades judiciales definen a todas las personas menores de 18 años como jóvenes y prevé a su vez que la pena máxima para los delitos cometidos por menores sea la privación perpétua de libertad, que puede reducirse a 15 años con vigilancia. Este cambio de orientación es consecuencia de la contínua oposición contra la aplicación de la pena de muerte a menores en Irán. La premio Nobel Shirin Ebadi ha criticado siempre de manera enérgica la ejecución de menores, se ha declarado en contra de esta práctica inhumana en foros nacionales e internacionales y se ha ocupado de la defensa de jóvenes demandados ante los tribunales.

Secondo l'articolo 110 del codice penale, l'omosessualità è vietata. Nell'ottobre del 2008 la magistratura iraniana dichiarava che le autorità competenti fossero in procinto di attuare una moratoria sulle pene capitali che riguardano i minorenni. La moratoria è entrata subito in vigore e adesso si aspetta l'ultima parola del parlamento. Un divieto delle esecuzioni penali rappresenterebbe un miglioramento della situazione dei diritti umani per gli appartenenti ad una fascia sessuale minoritaria poichè molti giovani iraniani sono stati già condannati e impiccati per aver praticato sesso anale e per aver commesso altri reati di tipo sessuale. Questo, quindi, rappresenterebbe per l'Iran un grandissimo passo avanti verso i diritti umani.

Fino ad adesso i tribunali iraniani hanno applicato l'articolo 49 del codice penale islamico in una maniera tale da consentire l'esecuzione capitale anche di bambini. Sebbene l'articolo 49 esenta i minorenni da persecuzione penali, i giudici usano spesso le vigenti leggi in maniera tale da permettere condanne penali su ragazzi che abbiano già compiuto il 15° anno di età o su ragazze che addirittura abbiano compiuto il 9° anno di età.

Nel 2010 giugno l'avvocato Mohammad Mostfaii dichiarava che nelle carceri iraniane circa 100 persone aspettano la loro pena capitale per reati che hanno commesso quando erano minorenni. Di contro delle autorità di giustizia definisce minorenni tutte le persone che non abbiano compiuto il 18° anno di età e allo stesso tempo prevede per gli stessi come pena massima l'ergastolo, che può essere ridotto ad una pena di 15 anni di libertà condizionata con successivo rilascio.

Quest'aria di cambiamento è una conseguenza della implacabile contrarietà espressa dalla società civile iraniana contro le esecuzioni capitali esercitate sui minorenni. Il premio Nobel Shirin Ebadi ha, da sempre, severamente criticato le esecuzioni capitali dei minorenni definendole pratiche disumane, partecipando a forum nazionali ed internazionali e prendendo personalmente la difesa di questi giovani in tribunale.

NATIONAL GROUPS

Iran Leathermen (F G)
Site in Persian and English.

Iranian Railroad for Queer Refugees (IRQR)
414-477 Sherbourne Street, Toronto, Canada
(+1 (416)) 548 4171 (Canada) www.irqr.net

By documenting and reporting cases of torture, persecution, execution and other human rights violations that occur in Iran on a regular basis, the IRanian Queer Railroad (IRQR) has helped remove any international doubt about the dismal situation of queers in Iran. From advocacy for asylum seekers to direct financial support of refugees in dire need, IRQR has aided hundreds of Iranian queers since its inception.

Ireland

Name: Éire · Irland · Irlande · Irlanda
Location: West Europe in North Atlantic Ocean
Initials: IRL
Time: GMT
International Country Code: ☏ 353 (omit 0 from area code)
International Access Code: ☏ 00
Language: Irish (Gaelic) and English
Area: 70,273 km² / 21,137 sq mi.
Currency: 1 Euro (€) = 100 Cents
Population: 4,159,000
Capital: Dublin / Baile Atha Cliath
Religions: 88% Roman Catholic, 3% Anglican
Climate: Summers are warm (Jul-Aug). Many places in small towns close from Oct-Mar (until Easter).
Important gay cities: Dublin

The age of consent is 17 for homosexuals as for heterosexuals in Ireland.
On the 19th of July, 2010 the President of Ireland, Mrs. Mary McAleese, signed the Civil Partnership Act. The law means for many thousand of men and women a strengthening and security of their civil rights.
In January 2011, Senator David Norris launched his campaign for the presidency and was long considered a strong contender for winning the election, which would have given the Irish the first gay head of state in history. But Norris increasingly came under pressure in connection with earlier statements on paedophilia and was finally forced to concede in summer that, 15 years earlier, he had asked the Israeli authorities for leniency regarding a former lover who had been convicted for sex with a minor. At the election in October 2011, Norris only gained 6.2 % of first votes.
An annual Gay Pride Festival takes place in Dublin, Cork and Galway as well as the famous gay and lesbian Film Festival every August bank holiday in Dublin. Also the annual Alternative Miss Ireland competition is held in Dublin where the winners of regional heats battle it out for the crown. Held in March each year, this is the highlight of the gay calendar and the event is hosted by Ireland's leading drag artiste Panti. For exact dates, please see our Events Calendar for at the back of this guide. A lively gay scene has developed in Dublin and Cork and be sure to check out the infamous drag shows in The George bar in Dublin.

In Irland liegt das Mindestalter für hetero- und homosexuelle Handlungen bei 17 Jahren. Am 19. Juli 2010 hat Irlands Staatspräsidentin, Frau Mary McAleese, den „Civil Partnership Act" unterzeichnet. Das Gesetz bedeutet für viele tausende Männer und Frauen eine Verstärkung und Absicherung ihrer Bürgerrechte.
Im Januar 2011 bewarb sich der Senator David Norris um das Präsidentenamt und galt lange Zeit als aussichtsreicher Favorit, diese Wahl für sich entscheiden zu können. Damit hätten die Iren das erste Mal in der Geschichte ein schwules Staatsoberhaupt bekommen. Jedoch geriet Norris zunehmend wegen früherer Aussagen zum Thema Pädophilie unter Druck und musste letztlich im Sommer einräumen, dass er 15 Jahre zuvor die israelischen Behörden bat, seinem Ex-Freund Milde zu gewähren, nachdem dieser wegen Geschlechtsverkehrs mit einem Minderjährigen verurteilt wurde. Norris errang bei der Wahl im Oktober 2011 nur 6,2% der Erststimmen.
In Dublin, Cork und Galway finden jedes Jahr CSD-Veranstaltungen statt. Dublin verfügt darüber hinaus noch über ein schwul-lesbisches Filmfestival am verlängerten „Bank Holiday"-Wochenende im August. Weiterhin gibt es den „Alternative Miss Ireland"-Wettbewerb in Dublin, wo die Gewinner der regionalen Vorentscheidungen um die Krone kämpfen. Der jeden Mai stattfindende Wettbewerb ist einer der Höhepunkte des schwulen Kalenders und wird von Irlands führendem Travestiestar Panti moderiert. Die genauen Termine sind dem Eventkalender am Ende dieses Reiseführers zu entnehmen. In Dublin und Cork hat sich eine lebendige Schwulenszene entwickelt. Auf keinen Fall verpassen sollten Sie die berüchtigten Travestieshows in der Dubliner Bar „The George".

En Irlande, la majorité sexuelle est fixée à 17 ans pour les hétérosexuels et les homosexuels. Le 19 juillet 2010, la Présidente de la République d'Irlande, Mme Mary McAleese, a signé le « Civil Partnership Act ». La loi signifie pour des milliers d'hommes et de femme un renforcement et une protection de leurs droit civils.
En janvier 2011 le sénateur David Norris s'est porté candidat à l'élection présidentielle et semblait avoir le plus de chance de remporter l'élection. Les Irlandais auraient eu ainsi le premier Chef d'Etat homosexuel de leur histoire. Cependant du fait de ses déclarations passées sur la pédophilie, Noris fut soumis à des pressions et dut admettre l'été dernier qu'il avait demandé 15 ans auparavant aux autorités israëliennes d'être clémentes avec son ex-ami Milde après que celui-ci fut condamné pour des relations sexuelles avec un mineur. Norris n'a obtenu que 6,2 % des voix lors de l'élection en octobre 2011.
Dublin et Cork disposent díun milieu gay très animé et le bar travesti The George à Dublin est à voir absolument. A Dublin, Cork et Galway se déroulent des Gay-Pride chaque année. Cíest également à Dublin quía lieu pendant le week-end férié en août un festival gay et lesbien et, en mai, un concours de „Alternative Miss Ireland", animé par la star des travestis irlandais Panti et où les vainqueurs des concours régionaux se disputent la couronne. Vous trouverez les dates exactes à la fin de ce guide, dans notre agenda.

En Irlanda, la edad de consentimiento para heterosexuales y homosexuales está en los 17 años. Mary McAleese, presidenta de Irlanda, firmo el 19 de julio de 2010 la ìLey de Unión Civilî. Esta ley significa para muchos miles de hombres y mujeres el fortalecimiento y la protección de sus derechos civiles.
En enero de 2011, el senador David Norris, candidato a la presidencia, era considerado como uno de los favoritos para ganar las elecciones. Si así hubiera sido, los irlandeses habrían conseguido, por primera vez en la historia, tener un Jefe Estado gay. Sin embargo, Norris se vio sometido a una intensa presión a causa de declaraciones previas sobre la pedofilia y, finalmente, en verano tuvo que admitir que, hace 15 años, le rogó a las autoridades israelíes que le concedieran el indulto a su ex novio tras haber sido declarado culpable de mantener relaciones sexuales con un menor de edad. En las elecciones de octubre de 2011, Norris consiguió tan solo el 6,2% de los votos.

En Dublín, Cork y Galway tienen lugar anualmente Marchas del Orgullo. Dublín celebra además un festival de cine gay-lésbico en agosto. También se realiza en Dublín la competición „Miss Ireland Alternativa", donde participan los ganadores de los concursos regionales. Esta competición, que se celebra cada mes de mayo, es uno de los platos fuertes del calendario gay, dirigido por la conocida travesti irlandesa Panti. Para saber las fechas exactas, véase el calendario de eventos al final de esta guía. En Dublín y Cork surgió un ambiente gay dinámico. No debe perderse los famosos shows de travestis en el bar dublinés „The George".

✖ In Irlanda l'età del consenso è di 17 anni sia per eterosessuali sia per omosessuali. Il 19 luglio del 2010 la Presidente della Repubblica irlandese Mary McAleese ha firmato il iCivil Partnership Acti. Per molte migliaia di uomini e donne, questa legge rappresenta il rafforzamento e la tutela dei loro diritti civili.
Nel gennaio del 2011 il senatore David Norris si è candidato a Presidente e per molto tempo è stato considerato come il candidato favorito. Se così fosse stato sarebbe stata la prima volta della storia che gli irlandesi avrebbero avuto un presidente gay. Tuttavia Norris è caduto sempre più sotto pressione a causa di vecchie dichiarazioni in tema di pedofilia. In estate, infatti, ha dovuto ammettere che 15 anni fa ha pregato le autorità israeliane di condannare il suo ex partner, che aveva avuto un rapporto sessuale con un minorenne, ad una pena meno severa. Alle elezioni dell'ottobre del 2011 Norris è riuscito a raccogliere solo il 6,2% dei mandati diretti.
A Dublino, a Cork e a Galway si svolge ogni anno il CSD. Dublino ospita inoltre un festival di cinema gay e lesbico che si svolge durante un finesettimana di agosto. In più, Dublino ospita anche la competizione alternative miss Ireland, nella quale i vincitori delle preliminari regionali si contendono la corona. La competizione di maggio è uno degli appuntamenti clou nel calendario gay in Irlanda e viene presentato dalla star travestita iralndese Panti. Per ulteriori informazioni circa gli appuntamenti del calendario gay potete consultare le ultime pagine di questa guida. A Dublino e a Cork è andata sviluppandosi una scena gay molto vivace. Da non perdere sono i famigerati show di travestiti nel bar The George a Dublino.

NATIONAL GAY INFO

■ **queerid.com** (GLM MA)
🖳 www.queerid.com
Gay website with infos on every city.

NATIONAL PUBLICATIONS

■ **Gay Community News** (GLM) Mon-Fri 9-17h
Unit 2, Scarlett Row, West Essex Street, Temple Bar ✉ Dublin 8
☎ (01) 671 90 76 🖳 www.gcn.ie
Ireland's free monthly gay and lesbian magazine.

■ **gay-ireland.com** (GLM MA)
🖳 www.gay-ireland.com

NATIONAL GROUPS

■ **Equality Authority**
2 Clonmel Street ✉ Dublin 2 ☎ (01) 417 33 33 🖳 www.equality.ie

■ **GLEN (Gay & Lesbian Equality Network)**
Fumbally Lane ✉ Dublin 8 ☎ (01) 473 05 63 🖳 www.glen.ie
GLEN works for change in legislation and social policy in Ireland to advance equality for lesbian, gay and bisexual (LGB) people. Since 1988 GLEN has played a pivotal role in work done to dismantle legal discrimination, to promote equality and safeguard human rights.

Cork ☎ 021

GAY INFO

■ **Gay Information Cork** Mon-Thu
8 South Main Street *At „The Other Place"* ☎ (021) 430 48 84
🖳 gayprojectcork.com
Information, support, education on sexual health issues for gay men.

■ **Other Place. The** (B D GLM I MA S) Café: 13-22, Sat -19h, closed Sun
8 South Main Street *Upstairs* ☎ (021) 427 84 70 🖳 www.gayprojectcork.com
City center community & resource center.

BARS

■ **Instinct @ The Oyster** (AC B d GLM MA S t WE)
18-24, Fri-Sun -2h, closed Mon & Tue
Meet Market Lane *Off Patrick Street, next door to English Market*
🖳 www.bebo.com/InstinctBarCork
Gay bar full of trendy young men.

■ **Loafers** (B GLM MA) 17-23.30, Fri-Sun 16-0.30h
26 Douglas Street 🖳 www.bebo.com/loaferscork

DANCECLUBS

■ **Freakscene @ Gorbys & G2** (B D glm YC) Wed 23-5h
Oliver Plunkett Street ☎ (021) 425 42 80 🖳 www.freakscene.com
Alternative party place after closing time.

■ **Rubys** (B D GLM MA) Fri 23-?h
Hanover Street 🖳 www.bebo.com/RubysN7

■ **Sinners @ Chambers** (B D GLM MA) Wed 22-?h
Washington Street 🖳 www.bebo.com/SinnersC

SAUNAS/BATHS

■ **Mykonos Cork** (b DU FC G I MA MSG SA WH)
13-1, Fri & Sat -6h
40 MacCurtain Street ☎ (021) 450 37 77
🖳 www.mykonossaunacork.com
Small sauna, but clean. Massage and waxing on offer. They also offer therapeutic, sports, reflexology and deep tissue massage by a qualified masseur.

GUEST HOUSES

■ **Emerson House / New Cork B&B**
(BF cc GLM I MA OS PA PK RWS RWT VA WO) All year
2 Clarence Terrace, Summer Hill North *Off Mac Curtain Street*
☎ 86 834 0891 (mobile) 🖳 www.emersonhousecork.com

■ **Rolf's Country House & Restaurant**
(B BF CC glm M MA OS PA PK RWB RWS RWT) All year
Baltimore ☎ (028) 202 89 🖳 www.rolfscountryhouse.com
Seaside resort with 14 ensuite rooms and 4 guest cottages, restaurant & wine bar.

HEALTH GROUPS

■ **Southern Gay Mens Health Project** (GLM)
Mon-Sat 11-17.30h
8 South Main Street ☎ (021) 427 84 70
🖳 www.gayhealthproject.com

CRUISING

-Lower Quays (Lapp's Quay, Anderson's Quay, Anderson's Street, action mainly at night, after the clubs close)
-Bus station toilets (Parnell Place, from 12h)
-The Marina (head down the Centre Park Road, and turn left at the end, (mainly car cruising) and beside Páirc Uí Chaoimh)
-Merchant's Quay public toilets (located just by the river, NOT situated in Merchant's Quay Shopping Centre) (OC)
-Fitz Patrick park (WE).

Derry ☎ 028

BARS

■ **Pepe's Bar & Angels Nightclub** (B D GLM I MA OS SNU ST) 20-2h
64 Strand Road ☎ (+44 28) 71 374 002 (UK)
Wed karaoke.

Dublin ☎ 01

It may not have the largest gay and lesbian scene in the world, but Dublin is nevertheless a lively, cosmopolitan, European capital city. A real advantage of the small scene is that almost all places of interest are within 10 minutes walk of one another, many being grouped in and around the South Great George's and Dame Street and across the river Liffey to Ormond Quay.

Auch wenn sie nicht gerade die größte Schwulen- und Lesbenszene der Welt aufweisen kann, ist Dublin doch eine lebhafte und weltoffene europäische Hauptstadt. Der größte Vorteil der eher kleinen Szene liegt darin, dass fast alle interessanten Anlaufpunkte nur 10 Gehminuten voneinander entfernt liegen, viele davon in oder bei der South Great George Street und der Dame Street sowie von der gegenüberliegenden Seite des River Liffey bis zum Ormond Quay.

Dublin ne possède certainement pas la plus grande scène gaie et lesbienne du monde mais est néanmoins une ville cosmopolite européenne très vivante. L'avantage de ce milieu assez petit réside dans le fait qu'il suffit de 10 minutes à pied pour parcourir les endroits intéressants, la plupart se situant autour des South Great George's et Dame streets et de l'autre côté de la rivière Liffey sur le quai Ormond.

No es que tenga el mayor ambiente homosexual del mundo, pero Dublín es, no obstante, una capital europea animada y muy cosmopolita. Una gran ventaja de un ambiente tan pequeño es que todos los sitios de interés se encuentran a diez minutos de distancia – siempre andando. La mayoría de ellos se encuentra en la calle South Great George's and Dame y sus alrededores así como, al otro lado del río Liffey, hacia Ormond Quay.

Anche se non può proprio vantare la più grande scena gay e lesbica del mondo, Dublino è una capitale europea vivace e cosmopolita. Il grosso vantaggio di una scena piuttosto ridotta sta nella distanza minima, ca. 10 min. a piedi, che separa tra loro quasi tutti i luoghi di spicco, molti dei quali si trovano in South Great George Street e in Dame Street o nelle vicinanze immediate, nonché sul lato opposto del River Liffey fino a Ormond Quay.

GAY INFO

Gay Switchboard Dublin Mon-Fri 19-21h
Carmichael House, North Brunswick Street *City centre* ☎ (01) 872 1055
www.gayswitchboard.ie

Outhouse Community and Resource Centre (b GLM m MA) Mon-Fri 10-21, Sat 13-17, Sun 15.30-19h
105 Capel Street *Junction of Parnell & Chapel St* ☎ (01) 873 4932
www.outhouse.ie

BARS

Dragon (B G YC) 17-2.30, Tue & Wed -23.30, Sun -23h
64/65 South Great Georges Street ☎ (01) 478 1590
Dublins most funky gay pub, about 50m up fom the George. Its very modern with 2 levels and good sounds.

Front Lounge. The (B CC D GLM S) 12-23.30, Fri -2.30, Sat 15-2.30, Sun -23.30h
33/34 Parliament Street *Across the road from Dublin Castle* ☎ (01) 670 4112
The Front Lounge is the most stylish gay bar in Dublin city. Be sure to see Ireland's best drag queen April Showers in action on Tuesday night for Panti's Casting Couch, a hilarious mix of karaoke and quick comments. All free admission.

George. The (! AC B CC D f G M MA ST T)
12.30-23.30, Wed-Sat -2.30, Sun -1h
89 South Great George Street ☎ (01) 478 2983
www.thegeorge.ie
Popular bar/club with a great atmosphere. Bingo in the George on Sun at 22h has become an institution. Hosted by Shirley Temple Bar accompanied by Dolly. Another must-see is Space-N-Veda on Wed nights, hosted by Veda Beau Reves & Davina Divine (formed a band called Lady Face). A funny mix of everything from candy-pink pop to dark moody drag. Unmissable and free before 20h.

Pantibar (B G MA S)
Mon-Wed 17-midnight, Thu-Sat 17 -2.30, Sun 15-23.30h
7-8 Capel Street ☎ (01) 874 07 10 pantibar.com
There is a good show on a Thursday night and it is always busy. Half price drinks all day on Sunday.

CAFES

Stage Door Cafe.The (B BF GLM M OS)
Mon-Fri 8-22, Sat & Sun 9-22h
10-12 East Essex Street, Temple Bar
www.facebook.com/pages/Stage-Door-Café/148389536216
Good, trendy path side cafe. Friendly staff.

DANCECLUBS

Furry Glen @ Pantibar (B D G MC) 3rd Sat/month 22-2.30h
7-8 Capel Street www.thefurryglen.com
An extremely popular night. The Furry Glen is a club night aimed at the Bear community & its admirers.

Mother (AC B D GLM) Sat 23-?h
2 Lord Edward Street @ *Copper Alley Night Club in the Arlington Hotel Temple Bar*
Saturdays SynthPop & Electro club. Strictly over 21 only!

Sunday Social (AC B D GLM MA OS) Sun 21-?h
9 Sycamore Street @ *The Sycamore Club, above Purty kitchen, Temple Bar* ☎ 474 3942
Gay Sunday Tea-Dance on Dublin's most fabulous roof top terrace with sweet sounds from DJ Rocky T Delgado.

RESTAURANTS

Juice (B g M MA)
South Great George's Street

SEX SHOPS/BLUE MOVIES

Basic Instincts (AC CC DR GLM MA VS)
10-21, Fri & Sat -18.30, Sun 12-18h
8, Eustace Street *Temple Bar, City Centre* ☎ (01) 633 4400
The complete adult / fetish store. Open 7 days. Basement cruise cinema (all day pass out's).

Condom Power (AC CC glm MA) Mon-Sat 9-18, Thu -20h
57 Dame Street *Basement, opp. Phillips Shop* ☎ (01) 677 8963
www.condompower.ie

SAUNAS/BATHS

Boilerhouse. The (AC b BF CC DR DU FC FH G M MA RR SA SB SH SL SOL VS WH) Mon-Thu 13-6, Fri 13-Mon 6h (non-stop)
12 Crane Lane *Next to Olympia Theatre, off Dame St.* ☎ (01) 677 3130
www.the-boilerhouse.com
Expensive gay sauna.

Dock. The (BF CC DR FC FH G I M MA MSG RR SA SB SH SOL VS WE) Mon-Thu 10-6, Fri 10-Mon 6h (non-stop)
21 Upper Ormond Quay *Same entrance as guesthouse „Inn On The Liffey"* ☎ (01) 677 0828 www.innontheliffey.com
A really great place.

BOOK SHOPS

Books Upstairs (CC glm) Mon-Fri 10-19, Sat -18h
36 College Green *Opposite Trinity College* ☎ (01) 679 6607
www.booksirish.com
Friendly, quiet store across from Trinity College with a selection of gay and lesbian books to choose from.

GUEST HOUSES

Inn on the Liffey (bf CC GLM I MA RWS RWT SA VA)
All year except 25 Dec
21 Upper Ormond Quay *City centre* ☎ (01) 677 0828
www.innontheliffey.com
11 rooms. Only gay B&B in Dublin. Access to the Dock Sauna included in the price.

Merchant House. The (AC CC GLM I M RWS RWT VA) 9-21h
8 Eustace Street *Temple Bar* ☎ (01) 633 4447
www.themerchanthouse.eu
Luxurious suites to 5 star standard, only a few minutes walk from the gay area.

HEALTH GROUPS

■ **Dublin AIDS Alliance** (GLM MA) 9.30-17.30h
53 Parnell Square *City centre* ☎ (01) 873 3799 🖳 www.dublinaidsalliance.ie

SWIMMING

-Forty Foot (g NU)
-Seapoint (g) (close to Forty Foot).

CRUISING

-Balbriggan railway station (toilets)
-Toilets in Killiney Hill Park
-Palmerston Park, at night, walkway through park and inside park, climb over railing AYOR
-Martello Tower at Seapoint, on coast road between Blackrock and Dun Laoghaire, at night in summer mostly but milder winter too, behind Martello Tower, around rocks and along coast line.

Galway ☎ 091

BARS

■ **Dignity Bar West** (B G MC S) Wed-Sat 21-?h
34 Shop Street *Near Eyre Square Shopping Centre* ☎ (091) 530 701
🖳 www.dignitybar.com

■ **Stage Door** (B GLM MA S) 22.30-11.30, WE -11h
Wood Quay *City centre* ☎ (091) 564 868

DANCECLUBS

■ **Eden @ The Warwick Hotel** (B D GLM YC) Fri 23-?h
Salthill 🖳 www.edenexperience.com

Kilkenny ☎ 056

RESTAURANTS

■ **Motte Restaurant. The** (CC DM glm M MA NR p PK RES VEG WL) Wed-Sat 19-21.30h (last orders), closed Sun-Tue
Plas-Newydd Lodge, Inistioge, Co. Kilkenny *25 km from the city*
☎ (056) 775 865 5

Limerick ☎ 061

BARS

■ **31 Thomas St** (B CC D GLM m MA S SNU ST VS)
15-24, Thu & Fri -1, Sat -2.30, Sun 17-23h
31 Thomas Street ☎ (061) 404 643 🖳 www.31thomasst.ie

■ **La Boutique @ Dolan's** (ac B BF CC D GLM M MA OS S WE)
Dock Road ☎ (061) 314 483 🖳 www.bebo.com/laboutiquelimerick
A twice monthly night of gay dancing. Check www.bebo.com/laboutiquelimerick for dates.

GUEST HOUSES

■ **Glocca Morra B&B** (BF CC GLM PK RWS) All year
Ogonnelloe/Scarriff *8 kms outside of Killaloe/Ballina* ☎ (061) 923 172
🖳 www.gloccamorra.com
Glocca Morra is a 4 star Failte Ireland approved B&B and has four bedrooms all en-suite.

Waterford ☎ 051

BARS

■ **Dignity** (B d GLM MA S) 18-?h
John Street *Opposite the corner with Waterside Street* ☎ (051) 879 631
🖳 www.dignitybar.com
A second bar now open in Galway.

DANCECLUBS

■ **Bubble** (B D GLM MA) 1st Fri/month 24-?h
c/o The Forum, The Glen ☎ (087) 949 92 29
Regular theme nights.

Israel

Name: Yisra'él/Isra'il · Israël · Israele
Location: Middle East
Initials: IL
Time: GMT+2
International Country Code: ☏ 972 (omit 0 from area code)
International Access Code: ☏ 00, 012, 013, 014, 015, 018
Language: Modern Hebrew (Ivrit), Arabic, English and Russian are widely spoken
Area: 20,991 km² / 8,473 sq mi.
Currency: 1 New Shekel (NIS) = 100 Agorot
Population: 7,200,000
Capital: Jerusalem (Yerushalayim)
Religions: 76% Jewish, 20% Moslem, 2% Christian
Climate: The best time to visit is spring/fall. Apr-May/Sept-Oct). Summer (June-Aug) is quite warm along the coast, cooler in Jerusalem. Winter is mild along the coast, but it can snow in Jerusalem.
Important gay cities: Tel Aviv

In Israel 16 is the legal age of consent. Israel's gays and lesbians typically enjoy freedoms similar to their counterparts in European countries. This has included civil partnerships for homosexuals since 2002. In legal terms they are on an equal footing with heterosexual marriage in many respects, including the option of benefiting from tax privileges, granted by a 2006 decision of the Supreme Court, or the right to adopt. The country of Israel is hence playing a pioneering role in the Near East where homosexual equality is concerned.
Tel Aviv holds a festive annual gay parade, rainbow flags can be seen around the city and there is a city-funded community centre for gays. However not everything is as harmonious as it seems. In 2005, an ultra-Orthodox protester stabbed three marchers at a Jerusalem Gay Pride Parade. In 2008 a member of the ultra-Orthodox Shas party commented in parliament that earthquakes were divine punishment for homosexual activity. The worst attack against the gay community in Israel took place on the 2nd August 2009, where a masked gunman killed two people at a centre for gay youth in Tel Aviv. Eleven people were wounded, four of them critically.
Despite these isolated attacks, Gay Pride has grown into a large-scale event in Tel Aviv over the years, drawing as many as 100,000 visitors by 2011, which can indeed be considered an indication of societal acceptance.
The lesbian and gay protest march in Jerusalem cannot be compared to the celebrations in Tel Aviv. In 2011 the Gay Pride here was merged with other demonstrations critical of social conditions in Israel, leading to a much more pronounced political element than in Tel Aviv.

Das Schutzalter liegt bei 16 Jahren. Schwule und Lesben in Israel genießen die gleichen Freiheiten wie in vielen europäischen Ländern. So gibt es seit 2002 die eingetragene Partnerschaft für Homosexuelle. Rechtlich sind diese in vielen Teilen der heterosexuellen Ehe gleichgestellt, so können Homosexuelle seit einem Urteil des Obersten Gerichts im Jahr 2006 Steuerprivilegien geltend machen oder das Recht der Adoption in Anspruch nehmen. Israel ist damit das Land im Nahen Osten, das im Bereich der Gleichstellung für Homosexuelle eine Vorreiterrolle einnimmt. Tel Aviv veranstaltet jährlich eine festliche Gay Pride, Regenbogen-Fahnen sind überall in der Stadt zu sehen und es gibt ein von der Stadt gefördertes Gemeindezentrum für Homosexuelle.
Es ist jedoch nicht alles so harmonisch wie es scheint. 2005 wurden zwei Teilnehmer beim Jerusalem Gay Pride verletzt, weil ein orthodoxer Jude mit einem Messer um sich gestochen hatte. 2008 kommentierte ein Mitglied der ultraorthodoxen Shas Partei im Parlament, dass ein Erdbeben Gottesstrafe für die homosexuelle Tätigkeit sei. Der schlimmste Angriff gegen die homosexuelle Gemeinschaft in Israel fand am 2. August 2009 statt. Ein maskierter Bewaffneter tötete zwei Menschen vor einem Zentrum für die homosexuelle Jugend in Tel Aviv. Elf Menschen wurden verletzt, vier davon schwer.
Trotz der vereinzelten Übergriffe hat sich der Gay Pride in Tel Aviv über die Jahre hinweg zu einem großen Event entwickelt, dem 2011 mittlerweile 100.000 Besucher beiwohnen, das durchaus als Zeichen gesellschaftlicher Anerkennung gesehen werden kann.
Der Protestmarsch der Schwulen und Lesben ist in Jerusalem nicht mit den Feierlichkeiten in Tel Aviv zu vergleichen. Im Jahr 2011 wurde der Gay Pride mit anderen Protestmärschen, die die sozialen Bedingungen in Israel anprangern, zusammengeführt, so dass hier der politische Protest weitaus stärker zum Ausdruck gebracht wird als in Tel Aviv.

La majorité sexuelle est fixée à 16 ans. Les gays et lesbiennes en Israël jouissent des mêmes libertés que dans beaucoup de pays européens. Ainsi le partenariat enregistré existe depuis 2002 pour les homosexuels. Celui-ci est en grande partie similaire au mariage, ouvrant ainsi les même avantages fiscaux depuis un jugement de la Haute Court de Justice en 2006 et le droit à l'adoption. Israël joue pour cela un rôle de précurseur pour les droits des homosexuels au Proche Orient.
A Tel-Aviv est organisée chaque année une Gay Pride festive, des drapeaux arc-en-ciel sont visibles partout dans la ville et il existe même un centre communautaire soutenu par la ville pour les homosexuels. Tout n'est cependant pas si harmonique que cela paraît. En 2005 deux participants à la Gay Pride de Jérusalem ont été blessés par un juif orthodoxe armé d'un couteau. En 2008, un membre du parti ultra-orthodoxe Shas a commenté qu'un tremblement de terre était un acte divin contre les activités homosexuelles. L'attaque la plus grave contre la communauté homosexuelle en Israël a eu lieu le 2 août 2009. Un homme masqué et armé a tué deux personnes dans un centre pour les jeunes homosexuels de Tel-Aviv. Onze personnes ont été blessées, dont quatre grièvement. Malgé des actes isolés , la Gay Pride de Tel Aviv devient avec les années un grand événement avec 100.000 visiteurs en 2011, signe d'une reconnaissance sociale. La marche de protestation des gays et lesbiennes à Jérusalem n'est pas comparable aux festivités de Tel Aviv. En 2011, la Gay Pride s'est combinée à d'autres marches de protestation contre les conditions sociales en Israël exprimant ainsi une protestation fortement plus politique qu'à Tel Aviv.

La edad mínima para mantener relaciones sexuales es de 16 años. Los gays y lesbianas gozan aquí de las mismas libertades que en muchos países europeos. Desde 2002 existe un registro de uniones civiles para homosexuales que es legalmente similar, en mu-

chos aspectos, al matrimonio heterosexual. Desde el fallo de la Corte Suprema en 2006, los homosexuales pueden hacer valer su derecho a los beneficios fiscales o a la adopción. De esta forma Israel se convierte en un país pionero en Oriente Medio respecto a la igualdad de derechos para los homosexuales.
Tel Aviv, organiza anualmente una celebración del Orgullo Gay, donde las banderas del arcoíris están presentes por todas partes y hay incluso un centro para la comunidad gay financiado por la ciudad. Lamentablemente, no todo es tan armonioso como parece. En 2005, dos participantes del Orgullo Gay en Jerusalén resultaron heridos por un judío ortodoxo que les agredió con un cuchillo. En 2008, un miembro del partido ultra-ortodoxo Shas comentó en el Parlamento que un terremoto había sido el castigo de Dios por la actividad homosexual. Aún así, el peor ataque contra la comunidad homosexual israelí tuvo lugar el 2 de agosto de 2009. Un hombre armado y enmascarado mató a dos personas en un centro para las juventudes gays en Tel Aviv. Once personas más resultaron heridas, cuatro de ellas de gravedad. A pesar de los ataques esporádicos, la Marcha del Orgullo Gay en Tel Aviv se ha convertido en los últimos años en un gran evento que ya en 2011 contó con unos 100.000 visitantes, lo que, sin duda, puede interpretarse como un signo de aceptación social. La marcha de protesta de gays y lesbianas en Jerusalén no puede compararse con las celebraciones en Tel Aviv. En 2011, la Marcha del Orgullo Gay confluyó con otras marchas de protesta que denunciaban las condiciones sociales en Israel, es por esto que aquí el carácter de protesta política adquiere un contraste que se expresa con mucha más fuerza que en Tel Aviv.

L'età del consenso è di 16 anni. I gay e le lesbiche in Israele godono delle stesse libertà dei gay e delle lesbiche di molti Paesi europei. Nel 2002 sono state introdotte le unioni civili per gli omosessuali. Giuridicamente le unioni civili tra omosessuali sono molto simili ai matrimoni tra gli eterosessuali, infatti dopo una sentenza del 2006 della Corte Suprema è possibile avvalersi di alcuni privilegi fiscali e del diritto di adozione. Israele è, quindi, il Paese pioniere del Medio Oriente in tema di equiparazione omosessuale.
Ogni anno a Tel Aviv si svolge il Gay Pride. Girando per la città non è difficile vedere sventolare bandiere arcobaleno. Il comune sovvenziona anche un centro per omosessuali. Tuttavia la situazione non è così rosea come si potrebbe pensare. Nel 2005, al Gay Pride di Gerusalemme, un ebreo ortodosso ha cominciato ad accoltellare tutto quello che aveva attorno ferendo così due partecipanti. Nel 2008 un membro del partito ultraortodosso Schas, durante una seduta in parlamento, affermava che il terremoto fosse una pena divina per gli atti omosessuali. Il più feroce attacco contro la comunità omosessuale in Israele ha avuto luogo il 2 agosto del 2009, quando un uomo a volto coperto ha ucciso due persone in un centro per giovani omosessuali a Tel Aviv. Undici persone sono state ferite e quattro di queste in maniera grave. Nonostante sporadiche aggressioni, nel corso degli anni il Gay Pride di Tel Aviv è divenuto un grande evento che nel 2011, per esempio, contava già 10.000 visitatori. Ciò può essere visto come un chiaro segno di riconoscimento sociale.
La marcia di protesta di gay e lesbiche di Gerusalemme sono cosa ben diversa dalle feste di Tel Aviv. Nel 2011 il Gay Pride di Gerusalemme è stato organizzato insieme alle altre marce di protesta che denunciano le condizioni sociali in Israele; unendo la forza di tutte le proteste si è data molta più voce alla protesta politica di Gerusalemme, risultando anche più accesa della protesta a Tel Aviv.

NATIONAL COMPANIES

Gay Way (CC GLM) All year, 8-20h
32 Ben Yehuda Street ✉ Tel-Aviv *12th floor* ☎ 54-5430340
🖳 www.gaywaytlv.com

NATIONAL GROUPS

Aguda. The – Israeli GLBT Association (GLM) Sun-Thu 9.30-18h
28 Nachmani Street ✉ 61290 Tel Aviv ☎ (03) 620 55 90 🖳 www.glbt.org.il
The first GLBT organisation in Israel (est. 1975). Central association and information center. Branches in all larger cities (except for Jerusalem/see: JOH). Diverse groups meet here. In charge of the annual Gay Pride during June.

New Family – The Organization for the Advancement of Family Rights Sun-Thu 9-17h
34 Nachmani Street ✉ 65795 Tel Aviv ☎ (03) 566 05 04
🖳 www.newfamily.org.il
Established in 1998, The New Family Organization specializes in the legal rights of same-sex families. An experienced staff of lawyers assists thousands of couples each year on an array of issues including common-law marriage, parental rights, adoption, inheritance and establishing legal status for foreign partners.

The Israel Project
Jerusalem Technology Park, Malha, 1 Agudat Hasport Hapoel Rd.
✉ 96951 Jerusalem ☎ 02-6236427 🖳 www.theisraelproject.org
TIP is an international non-profit organization devoted to educating the press and the public about Israel while promoting security, freedom and peace, providing accurate information about Israel. TIP is not related to any government or government agency.

NATIONAL HELPLINES

Israel AIDS Task Force AIDS hotline: Mon-Thu 20-22h
18 HaNatziv Street ✉ 61572 Tel Aviv *Corner of Beit Hillel, Montefiore area*
☎ (03) 561 30 00 🖳 www.aidsisrael.org.il
Anonymous testing center Sun-Wed 17-20, Fri 10-13h. Rapid testing available.

Be'er Sheva

CRUISING

-Independence Park (Gan HaAtzmaut (Old City, near the mosque)), friendly park, great to meet the locals for conversation and more; opportunity to socialize also with local Bedouins
-Park opposite Municipality, next to Yotvata Restaurant.

Eilat ☏ 07

GENERAL GROUPS

Aguda. The
Shilan House, Rubin Center *Near municipal library*
In charge of the annual Gay Pride during June. Info for the Gay Pride: www.gayisrael.org.il and phone (050) 366 66 32.

CRUISING

-Beach at the new lagoon behind the Herod's Hotel
-Offira Park (near Teddy's Pub)
-Um Rashrash Park (near Mul Yam shopping mall and Red Rock Hotel)
-Park HaYovel (beside the court of justice and vis-à-vis tourist center).

Haifa ☏ 04

CAFES

Mandarin (B g M) 8.30-24, Fri & Sat -1h
129 HaNasi Blvd. *In the back yard of Carmel Center* ☏ (04) 838 08 03
Puzzle (! AC B BF CC GLM M OS) Sun-Fri 10-?, Sat 16-?h
21 Massada Street *Hadar* ☏ (04) 866 0879

HOTELS

Colony Hotel Haifa. The (AC B BF glm I MC MSG NR OS PK RWS RWT) All year
28 Ben-Gurion Boulevard *In the German Colony* ☏ 04-8513344
www.colonyhaifa.com
A boutique hotel offering 40 luxurious rooms and mini-suites of the highest design standards. Excellent location.

SWIMMING

-Atlit (G NU) (summer only, 1 km north of Atlit, 0,5 km north to the naval army base)
-Dru Beach (south of Haifa).

Jerusalem ☏ 02

GAY INFO

Jerusalem Open House for Pride and Tolerance (JOH). The (Ha-Bayit Ha-Patuach) (GLM I) Sun-Thu 10-17h
2 HaSoreg Street, 1st floor ☏ (02) 625 05 02 www.joh.org.il
Jerusalem's GLBT center. Also meeting place for various groups: transgenders, international group (in English), bisexuals, parents, politics and Gay Pride initiatives. Incl. a library and a coffee corner. HIV testing clinic available free of charge at 7 Ben Yehuda Street, 2nd floor. Sundays 18-20h.

BARS

Van Gogh Bar (AC B CC d g m MA ST) Sat-Thu 21-?, Fri 22-?h
3 Coresh Street *Back of Central Post Bldg., corner of Shlomtzion HaMalka Street* ☏ (050) 339 15 50
Mon 23-?h: Drag Queen Shows.

CAFES

Tmol Shilshom (AC B BF CC M NG)
9-1h, closed Sat daytime, opens again Sat evening
5 Solomon Street *Nahalat Shiva Pedestrian Mall, entrance through back alley at 11 Solomon Street* ☏ (02) 623 27 58 www.tmol-shilshom.co.il
Gay-owned and gay-friendly. European cuisine (fish & vegetarian). Bookshop, Kosher restaurant and a good starting place in the Holy City.

GUEST HOUSES

Diana's House (AC BF G I OS PA RWB RWS WH WO) All year
10 Hulda HaNeviah Street *Musrara/City center, behind Jerusalem's City Hall*
☏ (02) 628 31 31 assaf.adiv.googlepages.com/diana_gay
1st Gay B&B in Israel (est. 1989). 10 mins walk to the Old City, tourist attractions and the gay scene. Special features include a whirlpool with a spectacular view on Mt. Olives and the Dome on the Rock. Warm hospitality, animals allowed. Wireless Internet. Minimum of 3 nights required.

CRUISING

-Independence Park (Gan HaAtzmaut) (r) 24h (near Sheraton Plaza Hotel, popular especially evenings, where secular Jews or Arabs meet orthodox Jews and/or tourists, a rare melting point in this city)
-King David Park (behind the hotel, activity mainly at dusk, ayor)
-Central bus station (men's restrooms, pedestrian tunnel -18h).

Tel Aviv ☏ 03

With its fine restaurants, stock and diamond exchanges, shopping opportunities, beach, clubs, universities, and museums, Tel Aviv is not only the financial capital of Israel, but also its cultural hub. As the international community is waiting for the result of final diplomatic status talks vis-à-vis Jerusalem, most countries have located their embassies in Tel Aviv. With a population of just under 400,000, the greater metropolitan area boasts over 1.5 million inhabitants, and on weekends, Tel Aviv is the night life centre for all of Israel. As an immigrant society, its creative expression has absorbed numerous cultural and social influences, as the traditions of each group mix with those of other groups, confront Israel's recent history and life in the context of the middle east, and blend together to create a new culture unique to Israel in general and Tel Aviv in particular.
Unlike the spiritual, ancient, holy city of Jerusalem, Tel Aviv (founded in 1909) is a modern city. Though much of the city's buildings are built in the plain cement style of the 1950's and 1960's, many buildings from the 1930s have recently been renovated to their original splendour. With the unique abundance of „Bauhaus" (International Style) buildings, in 2003 UNESCO recognized the „White City" of Tel Aviv as a World Heritage Site. During the month of June, Tel Aviv hosts numerous gay pride activities, many of them funded by the local municipality. As the GLBT cultural centre of the country, the ever-expanding annual pride parade attracts an audience of many thousands, lots of them non-gay – a sign of the growing tolerance towards gays in Tel Aviv.
The gay scene spreads out from the bars and pubs of the Nahalat Binyamin district to the large dance clubs at the old Tel Aviv port. The highlights are parties that take place once a week at various locations (get the latest information in the bars, as it changes constantly).

Mit seinen erlesenen Restaurants, Einkaufsmöglichkeiten, Stränden, Clubs, Universitäten und Museen ist Tel Aviv nicht nur das Finanzzentrum Israels, sondern auch der kulturelle Mittelpunkt des Landes. In seiner Eigenschaft als Immigrantengesellschaft vereint die Bevölkerung der Stadt zahlreiche kulturelle und soziale Einflüsse, wobei sich die Traditionen unterschiedlichster Gruppen vermischen, der jüngsten Geschichte Israels sowie der Umgebung des Nahen Ostens zuwiderlaufen und miteinander zu der besonders für Tel Aviv einzigartigen Kultur verschmelzen. Im Gegensatz zu Jerusalem ist Tel Aviv (gegründet 1909) eine moderne Stadt und an den Wochenenden das landesweite Zentrum des Nachtlebens. Mit ihrer reichhaltigen Fülle an Bauhaus-Architektur ernannte die UNESCO 2003 die „Weiße Stadt" Tel Avivs zum Weltkulturerbe.
Jedes Jahr im Juni finden in Tel Aviv zahlreiche Gay-Pride-Aktivitäten statt, von denen viele die Unterstützung der Stadtverwaltung erhalten. Als kulturelles Zentrum der GLBT-Gruppen Israels zieht die immer beliebter werdende jährliche Pride Parade viele tausend Zuschauer an, darunter auch viele Nicht-Homosexuelle – ein Zeichen für die wachsende Toleranz gegenüber Homosexuellen in Tel Aviv.
Die Schwulenszene erstreckt sich von den Bars und Pubs des Nahalat-Binyamin-Distrikts bis hin zu den großen Danceclubs im alten Hafen Tel Avivs. Die Höhepunkte sind die einmal pro Woche an verschiedenen Orten stattfindenden Parties (die neuesten Informationen erhält man in den Bars, da es immer wieder Veränderungen gibt).

Avec ses restaurants raffinés, ses possibilités de shopping, ses plages, ses clubs, ses universités et ses musées, Tel-Aviv est non seulement le centre financier d'Israël mais aussi le centre culturel du pays. Issue de l'immigration, la population de la ville concentre de nombreuses influences culturelles et sociales, les traditions des différents groupes ayant plutôt tendance à se mélanger, à l'encontre de la tendance de l'histoire récente d'Israël aussi bien que de celle de son environnement proche-oriental. Et en fusionnant, ces influences diverses font la particularité unique de la culture de la ville. Au contraire de la

ville sainte Jérusalem, Tel-Aviv (fondé en 1909) est une ville moderne et durant le weekend elle est le centre de la vie nocturne pour tout le pays. Avec sa profusion d'architecture de style Bauhaus, l'UNESCO a élevé en 2003 la „ ville blanche „ au rang de patrimoine culturel mondial.
Chaque année en juin ont lieu à Tel-Aviv de nombreuses activité liées à la Gay Pride qui ont le soutient de la municipalité. En tant que centre culturel des groupes GLBT d'Israël, la populaire Gay Pride attire chaque année de plus en plus de public, dont de nombreux non-homosexuels : un signe de la tolérance grandissante à l'encontre des homosexuels à Tel-Aviv. La scène homo va des bars et des pubs du quartier de Nahalat Binyamin Distrikts jusqu'aux grands clubs du vieux port de Tel-Aviv. L'apothéose sont les parties hebdomadaires qui ont lieu à différents endroits (et comme des modifications de dernière minute ont toujours lieu, c'est dans les bars qu'on obtient les infos les plus actuelles).

Con sus selectos restaurantes, tiendas, playas, clubs, universidades y museos, Tel Aviv no es sólo el centro financiero de Israel sino también el centro cultural del país. En su calidad de sociedad de inmigrantes, la población de la ciudad reúne en si misma varias influencias culturales y sociales, a la vez que se mezclan las tradiciones de diferentes grupos, refleja la historia reciente de Israel así como la atmósfera del Próximo Oriente y se integra en la especialmente peculiar cultura de Tel Aviv. Al contrario que la ciudad santa de Jerusalén, Tel Aviv (fundada en 1909) es una ciudad moderna y durante los fines de semana el centro del ocio nocturno. Gracias a la gran cantidad de arquitectura de la Bauhaus, en 2003 la UNESCO declaró la ìCiudad Blancaî de Tel Aviv Patrimonio de la Humanidad.
Cada año en junio se celebran en Tel Aviv numerosas actividades para el Orgullo Gay, de las cuales muchas tienen el apoyo de la administración municipal. Como centro cultural de los grupos GLBT de Israel, la cada vez más popular Marcha del Orgullo atrae a miles de participantes, entre ellos muchos heterosexuales – un signo de la creciente tolerancia hacia los homosexuales en Tel Aviv.
El ambiente homosexual se extiende desde los bares y pubs del distrito de Nahalat Binyamin hasta las grandes discotecas del viejo puerto de Tel Aviv. Los eventos más importantes son las fiestas que se celebran una vez por semana en distintos sitios (se puede consultar la información más actual en los bares, ya que siempre hay modificaciones).

Con i suoi pregiati ristoranti, con le molte possibilità di shopping, con le sue spiagge, discoteche, università e musei, Tel Aviv si conferma non solo centro finanziario bensì anche centro culturale del Paese. Nella loro peculiarità di società di migranti, gli abitanti di Tel Aviv nascondono diverse influenze sociali e culturali. Le tradizioni si fondono a quelle dei gruppi più disparati. Sono le tradizioni della più recente storia di Israele come anche le tradizioni della confinante area mediorientale: tutto questo fondersi di culture rende Tel Aviv una città particolarissima. Al contrario della città santa, Gerusalemme, Tel Aviv fu fondata nel 1909 e quindi è una città moderna, che durante il fine settimana diventa la culla della vita notturna di tutto il Paese. La „città bianca" di Tel Aviv è stata dichiarata città di patrimonio dell'umanità UNESCO per il suo tesoro di architettura Bauhaus.
Ogni anno a giugno a Tel Aviv si svolgono tantissime attività e manifestazioni collegate al Gay Pride. Molte di esse vengono sovvenzionate dall'amministrazione comunale. Il Pride annuale è l'highlight culturale della comunità GLBT israeliana e diventa sempre più popolare attirando molte miglia di spettatori tra i quali figurano tanti eterosessuali. Questo è un segno lampante della crescente tolleranza nei riguardi dell'omosessualità in città come Tel Aviv.

BARS

Apolo (AC B CC D DR G MA) 21-?h
46 Allenby Street apolo.b144sites.co.il

Beef @ Fight Club (B D DR f G m MA) Tue 22-?h
32 Ben Yehuda Street
www.facebook.com/group.php?gid=92284705938
For bears, butch men and their admirers.

Espressobar Rothschild (B G m MA) Daily -24h, except Fri
8 Rothschild Boulevard
Tiny bar.

Evita (! AC B CC GLM I m MA OS S ST VS) Daily 20-4h
31 Yavne Street ☎ (03) 566 95 59
A trendy, well designed interior and a friendly warm atmosphere. Mixed crowd but mostly gay men. One of the hottest gay places in Tel Aviv. Great for dinner. Drag shows on Tuesdays.

Shpagat (AC B CC G MA NR) 21-?h
43 Nahalat Binyamin Street
Wednesday more lesbian crowded.

MEN'S CLUBS

Mess @ Dungeon (AC B CC D DR F G MA SL) Sat 22-?h
12 Hasharon Street
Fetish party for men only. Sex shows.

Sinsa Pilla (AC B DR G MA) Daily 11-?h
Lilenbloun 20 ☎ (077) 201 88 23
Modern bar in a Coffeehouse style. Also used as „after-party" location.

DANCECLUBS

3some (AC B D GLM MA S) every 2nd Fri 23.30-?h
17 Ben Avigdor Street
Features some of the most popular local DJs.

Arisa (AC B D GLM MA S) Thu 23.30-?h
Gay partyevent on various dates, once a month with Arabic and Oriental music. Check local flyers for details.

Beef Jerky @ Zizi Club (B D DR F G MA)
7 Carlebach Street www.facebook.com/group.php?gid=92284705938
Monthly party for butch men.

Big Boys @ Theatre Club (B D G MC) Every 2nd Fri 24-?h
10 Yerushalayim Avenue, Jaffa
Theme parties.

Cheesecake @ Breakfast Club (AC B CC D GLM MA)
Thu 23.30-?h
6 Rotschild Boulevard
Underground house party on two floors.

Chong @ Shlager (AC B CC D GLM YC) Sat from 22.30h
4 Kaplan Street
Dj Adi Dgani spins uplifting music. The first 100 people arriving to the event will get a free chaser. Age: 18+

Communist @ Lilienblum 25 (AC B CC D G OS YC) Sun from 22.30h
25 Lilienblum Street
Rock, Punk and Pop music for gays. Free entrance.

Disturbia @ Flight Club (AC B CC D GLM YC) Every Sat
32 Ben Yehuda Street
Hip Hop and hits.

Dreck @ Storage (AC B D GLM MA S) Wed 23-4h
Dizengoff 98 *2nd floor*
Hip hop, pop and electro parties, music concerts, fashion shows etc.

Eurovision Night @ Evita (B CC D GLM M S) Sun 22-?h
31 Yavne Street ☎ (03) 566 95 59
Every Sun, free entry.

FFF Line @ HaOman 17 Megaclub (B D DR G MA S) Fri 24-?h
88 Abarbanel Street *In Florentine neighborhood*
The famous long running FFF (Friendly Freedom Friday) party takes place twice a month.

Forever Tel Aviv @ TLV (B D DR G MA) Once a month, Fri 24-?h
Famous circuit party held once a month with star DJs and guests.

Glam-ou-Rama @ Comfort 13 (B D GLM MA) Fri 24-?h
Comfort 13 🖳 www.glam-ou-rama.co.uk/telaviv
Best of kitch, pop, happy 80's, 90's.

Hangover @ Lima Lima (AC B CC D GLM YC) Tue from 22.30h
42 Lilienblum Street
House, hits and pop music, free entrance.

Menstream (B D G MA) 2nd Thu 23-?h
Lilienblum 24
House party. Lower cover b4 0.30h

Notorious Gay. The (B CC D G MA OS) Mon 20-5h
c/o Lima Lima bar, 42 Lilienblum Street @ *Lima Lima Bar* ☎ (03) 560 09 24
Hip Hop and Rap music. Free entry.

PAG @ Zizi (AC B D G MA s) every 2nd Fri 0-?h
Carlebach 7 ☎ (03) 687 80 90
Hip crowd, underground atmosphere, beautiful people.

Roof @ Gag (AC B CC D G OS) Tue from 23h
24 Saíadia Gaon Street
The beautiful venue, on the roof, consists of 2 areas: indoor with full air-con and open with 2 bars, overlooking the city. Free entrance.

Stootz @ Breakfast Club (AC B CC D GLM YC) Tue from 22.30h
6 Rothschild Street
Pop hits with sleazy touch. Free entrance till midnight.

RESTAURANTS

Orna & Ella (CC glm M MA)
33 Shenkin Street ☎ (03) 620 47 53

SEX SHOPS/BLUE MOVIES

Sexy Shop (AC CC DR F G MA VS)
Sun-Wed 11-24, Thu -4, Fri 11-16 & 23-5, Sat 18-4h
150 Dizengoff Street ☎ (03) 523 17 96 🖳 www.sexyshop.co.il
Israel's major gay sex shop. Gay books, guides and photo albums. Staff helpful with info about the Tel Aviv scene. Also gay labyrinth & cinema.

Sisters (gLm)
63 Frishman Street ☎ (03) 527 07 04 🖳 www.sisters.co.il
Women's sex shop.

SAUNAS/BATHS

Paradise (! AC B CC D DR DU FC G GH I M MA MSG p RR RWT S SA SB SH SL VR VS WH) Sun-Thu 12-6, Fri 19-Sun 6h (non-stop)
75 Allenby Street *Ground floor, bus 4* ☎ (03) 620 21 88
🖳 www.saunaparadise.co.il
Cosy & intimate. Popular among a mixed crowd (israeli, soldiers, Arabs, Russians). Very central location. Admission with unlimited stay. Friday nights: best DJs with greatest club hits.

Sauna City (B DR DU FC G GH I m MA MSG RR SA SB SH SL VS WE) Sun-Wed 12.30-24, Thu -5, Fri 23-6, Sat 15-2h
113 Hashmonaim Street ☎ (03) 624 11 48 🖳 www.sauna-city.com
Large & modern sauna on 2 floors. Oriental design. Popular especially in the afternoons (MC) and at the weekend (YC).

TRAVEL AND TRANSPORT

Gay Way (GLM MA)
☎ 54 5430 340 🖳 www.GaywayTLV.com
Gay travel agency for in- and outgoing tours in Israel (Tel aviv).

GayIsrael.org.il (cc G) Sun-Thu 9.30-18h
28 Nachmani Street ☎ (03) 620 55 90 🖳 www.gayisrael.org.il
Everything you need to know about your gay vacation in Israel.

Kenes Tours (CC) Sun-Thu 8-18, Fri -14h
PO Box 56, Ben Gurion Airport ☎ (054) 678 78 72

Ofakim Tours (cc G)
82 Menachem Begin Road ☎ (03) 761 07 13 🖳 www.ofakim.co.il

Ronen Lev
36 Hibat Zion Street, Ramat-Gan ☎ (052) 545 46 64 (mobile) ☎ 619 4284
Licensed gay tour guide/driver who will be happy to serve gay men/lesbians who decide to come to the Holy Land.

HOTELS

Brown TLV Urban Hotel (AC BF cc glm H I M MC MSG OS PA PK RES RWS RWT S SOL W WH) All year
25 Kalisher Street *5 mins walk from Rothschild and Neve Tzedek quarter, 10 mins walk to the beach* ☎ (03) 717 0200 🖳 www.browntlv.com
A gay-friendly, boutique hotel located in the heart of Tel Avivís gay area, next to most major gay nightlife establishments. 30 stylish yet affordable guestrooms.

GUEST HOUSES

Pink House TLV (AC BF G I MA RWB RWT VA) All year
10 Najara Street *On the corner with Raban Gamliel Street*
☎ (054) 233 09 32 🖳 www.pinkhousetlv.com
Small gay guest house in the centre of the city with 5 private rooms. The ONLY gay guest house in Tel Aviv.

APARTMENTS

Ben Yehuda Apartments (AC CC GLM MA RWS VA)
Office: 9-17, reservations: 8-22h
119-121 Ben Yehuda Street *Located 5 mins walk from the Hilton Gay Beach*
☎ (03) 522 93 93 🖳 www.tel-aviv-rental.co.il

GENERAL GROUPS

White Hotline – There's Someone to Talk To
Sun-Thu 19.30-22.30h
28 Nachmani Street ☎ (03) 620 55 91
Information and assistance over the phone or face to face over a cup of coffee.

SWIMMING

-Hilton Beach (g MA) (at HaYarkon Street, mainly north of the Hilton Hotel, right off Independence Park, opposite the eagle statute that is located on the top of the cliff, summer only)
-Ga'ash Beach, summer only; approx. 10km north of Tel Aviv, near Kibbutz Ga'ash (NU) (Right below the Wingate Institue).

CRUISING

-Independence Park (Gan HaAtzmaut) & Hilton Beach (! AYOR MA) One of the most popular meeting places in Israel for socializing and more especially after dusk
-Gan HaRakevet (pedestrian tunnel connecting bus and train stations and in the adjacent parks, 24h)
-Shape Fitness Club – gay friendly gym, very popular, 75 Hayarkon Street, Tel Aviv
-Dizengoff Center, top floor (north end) men's restroom, next to Jimmy Fitness Club
-Tel Aviv new central bus station, men's restroom
- P Tel Aviv University, in front of the entrance to the Diaspora Museum
- P Gan HaChashmal (AYOR, R), at night; mostly hustlers, also in the surrounding area.

spartacus traveler
DAS SCHWULE REISEMAGAZIN!
Viermal im Jahr mit Reportagen über interessante Reiseziele und Tipps für den perfekten schwulen Urlaub.
Im Abo (4 Ausgaben) für nur € 2,99 pro Heft, statt € 3,95 am Kiosk!
Gleich bestellen unter www.spartacus.de/traveler
Foto: Joan Crisol für ES Collection

Italy

Name: Italia · Italien · Italie
Location: Southern Europe
Initials: I
Time: GMT +1
International Country Code: ☎ 39
International Access Code: ☎ 00
Language: Italian
Area: 301,336 km² / 116,303 sq mi.
Currency: 1 Euro (€) = 100 Cents
Population: 57,573,000
Capital: Roma
Religions: 91% Roman Catholic
Climate: Predominantly Mediterranean climate. Alpine climate in the far north, the south is hot and dry.
Important gay cities: Milano, Bologna, Firenze, Roma, Viareggio

The legal situation offers a uniform age of consent for hetero and homosexual relations of 14 years (16 years regarding so-called authority persons).
Berlusconi may have gone, making room for what is referred to as a government of experts, meant to stave off the financial crisis with the same majority in parliament, but for homosexuals in Italy, no improvements are anywhere in sight. Instead the new government includes a number of homophobes toeing the Vatican line so that Italy will just have to wait a little longer for an anti-discrimination law or the legal emancipation of same-sex partnerships. Europride 2011 in Rome with over half a million visitors and Lady Gaga heading the line-up was a great success in spite of that.
Italy, an extremely popular tourist attraction, is divided into a northern and central parts, in which the gay scene is extremely lively – at least in the large cities like Milan, Rome and Bologna this is the case, and the south, where the commercial influence is extremely weak. In many establishments you require a so-called „club pass" (for example the Uno Club Card from Arcigay) in order to gain access. These can be purchased on site.
In summer gay life concentrates at the beach, above all in Torre del Lago in the Toscana, but recently also in the Salento in southern Apulia (Gallipoli) and between Siracusa, Catania and Taormina in Sicily. In summer in the cities there is often not that much going on. To assist with orientation it is important to know that Italy is divided into 20 regions.

Die Gesetzgebung sieht ein einheitliches Schutzalter von 14 Jahren (von 16 Jahren gegenüber so genannten Autoritätspersonen) für hetero- wie homosexuelle Beziehungen vor.
Zwar ist Berlusconi als Premier verschwunden und hat einer sogenannten Expertenregierung Platz gemacht, die mit der gleichen parlamentarischen Mehrheit die Finanzkrise abwenden soll, doch sind für Homosexuelle in Italien keine Verbesserungen in Sicht. Vielmehr gehören der neuen Regierung einige vatikantreue Homogegner mehr an, so dass Italien weiterhin auf ein Anti-Diskrimierungsgesetz und auf die rechtliche Gleichstellung homosexueller Partnerschaften warten muss. Dennoch war der Europride 2011 in Rom mit einer halben Million Teilnehmer/innen und Lady Gaga als Topact ein großer Erfolg.
Italien mit seiner großen touristischen Anziehungskraft ist geteilt in den nördlichen Teil plus Zentrum, wo die schwule Szene zumindest in den großen Städten sehr lebendig ist (vor allem in Mailand und Rom oder in Bologna) und den Süden, wo das kommerzielle Angebot äußerst dürftig ist. In viele Einrichtungen kommt man nur mit „Clubausweis" (oft die Uno Club Karte des Arcigay) herein, der vor Ort ausgestellt wird. Im Sommer findet schwules Leben eher am Meer statt, vor allem Torre del Lago in der Toscana, aber neuerdings auch im Salento im südlichen Apulien (Gallipoli) und zwischen Siracusa, Catania und Taormina in Sizilien, in den Städten ist dann oft nicht mehr so viel los. Für eine bessere Orientierung sind die Ortschaften Italiens den 20 Regionen zugeordnet.

La législation prévoit la majorité sexuelle à 14 ans pour tous (et à 16 ans face aux personnes d'autorité) aussi bien pour les relations hétérosexuelles qu'homosexuelles.
Certes Berlusconi n'est plus premier ministre et a fait place à un gouvernement composé d'experts qui devront désamorcer la crise financière mais la situation des homosexuels en Italie ne devrait pas s'améliorer. Au contraire des opposants aux gays fidèles au Vatican composent ce gouvernement et l'Italie devra encore attendre avant d'obtenir une loi contre les discriminations ou une loi de partenariat homosexuel. Cependant l'Europride 2011 à Rome fut un grand succès avec un demi-million de visiteurs et la prestation de Lady Gaga.
L'Italie dans son ensemble est une des destinations touristiques les plus importantes au monde et pourtant le fossé nord-sud reste béant : tandis qu'on trouve au nord et au centre des centres industriels et commerciaux riches, ce qui se reflète également dans les milieux gays des grands centres urbains (Milan, Rome mais aussi Bologne et bien d'autres villes), le sud reste pauvre, son milieu gay étant quasiment inexistant. De nombreux bars et boîtes exigent la présentation de la carte de membre Uno ou Arcigay, que l'on peut acquérir directement sur place. En été la vie gay se concentre plutôt en bord de mer, en particulier à Torre del Lago en Toscane, mais aussi depuis peu dans le Salento dans le sud de la Région des Pouilles (Gallipoli) et entre Syracuse, Catania et Taormina en Sicile. Les villes au contraire sont plus calmes en été.
Pour une meilleure orientation, les villes sont rangées dans leurs 20 régions respectives.

La legislación establece la edad de consentimiento sexual en los 14 años de edad (16 años de edad para las aquí llamadas personas de autoridad) tanto para las relaciones heterosexuales como para las homosexuales.
Aunque Berlusconi ha dejado su cargo como Primer Ministro y ha dado paso al conocido como Gobierno de Expertos, que con la misma mayoría parlamentaria debería evitar la crisis financiera, sin embargo, no hay mejoras a la vista para los homosexuales italianos. En vez de esto, algunos fieles al Vaticano contrarios a los homosexuales pertenecen al nuevo Gobierno y, de esta forma, Italia debe continuar esperando por una ley antidiscriminación y por la igualdad jurídica de las parejas homosexuales. Sin embargo, el Euro Pride de 2011en Roma

fue un gran éxito gracias a su medio millón de participantes y a Lady Gaga como actuación estelar. Italia tiene un gran atractivo turístico y está dividida entre la parte norte y el centro, donde al menos en las grandes ciudades el ambiente gay es muy dinámico (principalmente en Milán y Roma pero también en Bolonia y otras ciudades) y la parte sur, donde la oferta comercial es muy insuficiente. En muchos locales sólo se accede con un „carnet de socio" (normalmente con el carnet del Uno Club Arcigay), que puede ser expedido allí mismo.

La vida gay en verano, como es natural, se ve desplazada hacia la costa, aquí cabe mencionar Torre del Lago en la Toscana, aunque últimamente son también populares lugares como Salento, al sur de Apulia (Gallípoli), y las zonas de Siracusa, Catania y Taormina en Sicilia. En las ciudades la vida gay en verano es casi nula. Para una mejor orientación, las localidades de Italia están clasificadas en 20 regiones.

✖ La legge prevede la stessa età del consenso sia per i rapporti eterosessuali che per i rapporti omosessuali: è in genere di 14 anni e sale a 16 anni se uno dei due partner ha una qualche forma di autorità o ascendente sul/la partner più giovane.

Berlusconi si è dimesso da capo del governo lasciando spazio ad un governo di tecnici che dovrebbe affrontare la crisi finanziaria con la stessa maggioranza parlamentare di prima. Gli omosessuali italiani non hanno comunque di che gioire, infatti del nuovo governo fanno anche parte dei soggetti molto vicini al Vaticano, che sono anche piuttosto omoscettici e dai quali non ci si può certo aspettare né una legge contro le discriminazioni né una equiparazione delle unioni tra persone dello stesso sesso. Sembra proprio che l'Italia dovrà ancora aspettare per questo. Di contro però, l'Europride 2011 di Roma, con il suo mezzo milione di visitatori e Lady Gaga come ospite principale, è stato un grandissimo successo.

Il paese, che conserva un indubbio fascino turistico, è diviso tra una zona settentrionale e centrale in cui la vita glbt è più viva, almeno nei grandi centri (in particolare Milano e Roma, ma anche Bologna ed altre città), ed una meridionale in cui il circuito commerciale è assai limitato. In molti locali gay si accede solo con tessera (rilasciata in loco), spesso Arcigay.

In estate la vita gay si sposta per lo più verso le coste, soprattutto a Torre del Lago (in Toscana), ma recentemente anche nel Salento, (al sud della Puglia vicino a Gallipoli) e tra Siracusa, Catania e Taormina. D'estate le città spesso si svuotano ed hanno ben poco da offrire. Ai fini di facilitare la consultazione, abbiamo associato le singole località alle regioni di appartenenza.

NATIONAL GAY INFO

■ **Agedo** Thu 15-17.30h
☎ 02 54 12 22 11 💻 www.agedo.org
Italian association of parents of lesbians and gays.

■ **ANLAIDS-Associazione Nazionale per la Lotta Contro l'AIDS** Mon-Fri 9-17h
Via Giolitti 42 ✉ 00187 Roma ☎ 06 47 46 60 31
💻 www.anlaids.it
National coordination of ANLAIDS. Gives information about AIDS-organizations in Italy.

■ **Arcigay Nazionale-Italian Lesbian & Gay Association**
Mon-Fri 14.30-19h
Via Don Minzoni 18 ✉ 40121 Bologna ☎ 051 64 93 055 💻 www.arcigay.it
Head office of Arcigay, the only national organization of Italy with 45 local sections and over 70 recreative clubs: information, gay archive, videos, meetings.

■ **Arcitrans** (T) Infoline: Wed 20-22h
c/o CIG, Via Bezzecca 3 ✉ 20135 Milano ☎ 02 54 12 22 27
💻 www.arcitrans.it
National association of transsexuals, transgender and drags.

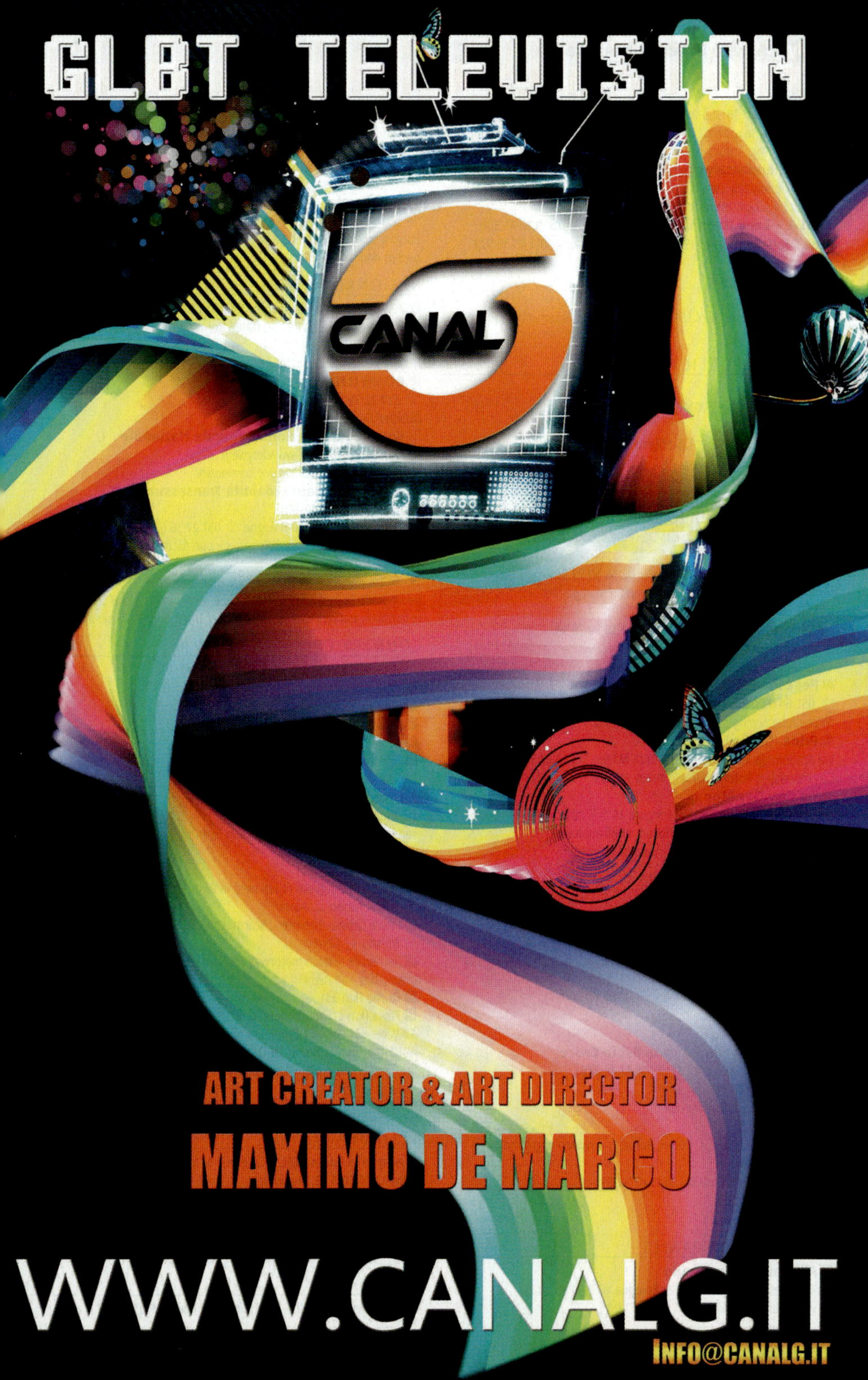
GLBT TELEVISION
CANAL
ART CREATOR & ART DIRECTOR
MAXIMO DE MARCO
WWW.CANALG.IT
INFO@CANALG.IT

AZ Gay
Via dei Vascellari 48 ✉ 00153 Roma 🖳 www.azgay.it
New guide to the main GLBT activities in Italy containing also a list of professionals, lawyers, doctors and other services.

GayFriendlyItaly.com
🖳 GayFriendlyItaly.com
Information on gay events and gay life for travellers.

LILA – Lega Italiana Lotta contro l'AIDS 9.30-13.30h
Corso Regina Margherita 190/e ✉ 10152 Torino ☎ 011 43 10 922
🖳 www.lila.it

Radio DeeGay.it
🖳 www.deegay.it
The first webradio for the GLBT community. Music, information and entertainment.

NATIONAL PUBLICATIONS

CANAL G
Arco della Pace 15 ✉ 00186 Roma 🖳 www.canalg.it

Clubbing
Via Sammartini 23 ✉ 20125 Milano ☎ 339 38 76 398
🖳 www.gayclubbing.it
Available in gay venues, information about gay scene.

Gay.it
Via Ravizza 22/e ✉ 56121 Pisa ☎ 050 31 55 51 🖳 www.gay.it
Main gay internet platform in Italy: news, shopping, travels etc.

Guide Magazine
Via Sassetti 10 ✉ 20124 Milano ☎ 02 36 50 79 94
Monthly gay guide available together with LUI in gay venues.

LUI
Via Sassetti 10 ✉ 20124 Milano ☎ 02 36 50 79 94
🖳 www.luimagazine.com
Monthly gay magazine available in gay venues.

Pegaso
☎ 051 64 93 055 🖳 www.arcigay.it/pegaso
Three-monthly magazine published by Arcigay.

Pride (G) Mon-Fri 14.30-19.30h
Via Antonio da Recanate 2 ✉ 20124 Milano ☎ 02 87 38 48 43
Gay monthly in Italian available in gay venues.

Up City Gay Map
c/o Echo Communication, Via Porpora 14 ✉ 20133 Milano
☎ 02 83 60 200 🖳 www.echocommunication.eu
Gay city maps for the most important Italian cities.

NATIONAL PUBLISHERS

Dito e la Luna. Il
Casella Postale 10223 ✉ 20110 Milano ☎ 02 52 20 97 43
🖳 www.ilditoelaluna.com
Gay-lesbian publisher.

Echo Communication (G)
Via Porpora 14 ✉ 20131 Milano ☎ 02 83 60 200
🖳 www.echocommunication.eu
Publisher of Up City Maps.

Edizioni Libreria Croce di Fabio Croce
Via Noto, 23 ✉ 00182 Roma ☎ 06 47 46 780
🖳 www.edizionicroce.com
Publisher of homosexual literature.

Playground
Via Napoleone III, 86 ✉ 00185 Roma 🖳 www.playgroundlibri.it

ZOE edizioni
C.P. 7149 ✉ 47100 Forlì ☎ 0543 47 32 35
🖳 www.zoeedizioni.it
Books for gays & lesbians.

NATIONAL COMPANIES

All Male Studio Group
Via Ezio Cesarini 4/A ✉ 40129 Bologna ☎ 340 88 28 217
🖳 www.allmalestudio.com
Production of gay videos. Casting by appointment. www.aboutgay.com: contacts and information for gay men, www.club18shop.com: online shop with probably the lowest prices in Europe.

Co.Sta Media Group
Via Melzo 19 ✉ 20129 Milano ☎ 02 29 51 0681
Wholesale for sex and video shops.

Cool-Made
☎ 333 37 00 455 🖳 www.cool-made.com
Booking and events agency: Parties, shows, go-go boys, performers, drag queens and more in North and central Italy.

NATIONAL GROUPS

Associazione Radicale ‚CERTI DIRITTI' 8.30-21h
Via di Torre Argentina 76 ✉ 00186 Roma ☎ 06 689 791
🖳 www.certidiritti.it
National association for GLBT rights close to the Radical Party.

BDSM Italia (glm)
☎ 327 22 79 607 🖳 www.bdsmitalia.org
National Bondage and SM Association.

Key We Associazione Culturale Nazionale
☎ 02 890 383 69 🖳 www.keywe.it
National association for the gay community.

MIT – Movimento Identità Transessuale
Mon-Thu 10-18, Fri 10-14h
Via Polese 15 ✉ 40120 Bologna ☎ 051 27 16 66 🖳 www.mit-italia.it
Political advocacy and psychological support for transgenders.

Orsi a Zonzo
☎ 347 46 39 986 (infoline) 🖳 www.orsiazonzo.it
Bears group organization: meetings and parties in clubs and saunas mainly in northern and central Italy. Organizer of Mister Bear & Chaser Italia.

COUNTRY CRUISING

-A1 (E35) Milano ⇆ Roma
-P Chiaravalle (km 80)
-P Fontanellato (km 96,5)
-P Crostolo (km 135)
-P Castelfranco (km 177)
-P Firenze Nord (facilities) (km 280)
-P Scandicci much action, northbound only
-A11 Firenze ⇆ Mare
-P Altopascio (AYOR, police controls)
-service area Versillia nord, direction Firenze
-A31 Padova ⇆ Valdastico
-P at the exit Thiene
-P at Canale Langosco (1 km west of River Ticino)
-A5 (E 25) Torino → Aosta
-P Pietra Grossa (between „Scarmagno" & „S. Giusto")
-A7 Milano ⇆ Genova
-P Serravalle Scrivia: motorway A7 Genova – Milano, dir. Milano (truck drivers, day and night)
-P Dorno (km 33)
-P Pavia (km 17) southbound only
-A8 Varese-Milano, P Brughiera. ‚Esso' facilities.
-A91 Fiumicino → Roma, P Q8 Gas Station (km 15) near Parco De' Medici (very cruisy day&night, in the stalls and in the garden behind station)

Agrate Brianza – Lombardy

RESTAURANTS

Acqua e Farina (AC b CC glm H M MC OS PA PK WL)
Daily, 12-14.30 & 18.30-midnight
via Dell' Artigianato 4 *About 20 km northeast of Milan* ☎ 039 68 93 022
🖳 www.acquaefarina.net

Airole – Liguria

SWIMMING

-Fiume Roya Beach (NU) (100 m from Roman bridge).

gay

CRUISING
-Via Madonna (only during the summer).

Alba – Piemonte

HOTELS
Cascina di Villa Due. La (b BF glm H M MA OS PI PK RWB RWS RWT SOL VA WO) All year
Via Oltretanaro, 16, Log. Gabetti *Autostrada A6 exit Mondovi/ Cheraseo/ Alba 15 km* ☎ 0173 77 62 77 💻 www.cascinadivilladue.it
Holidays in the countryside of Italy in the Piemont-region. Good restaurant, where the owners cook.

CRUISING
-Piazzale della S.A.U.B. (near the level crossing, at night)
-Piazza Tanaro (NU): square on the right side of the Tanaro river, just after the bridge of the road from Alba to Neive (Sat and Sun afternoon).

Alessandria – Piemonte

CRUISING
-Lungotanaro Magenta (by car, at night, also side streets).

Ancona – Marche

GAY INFO
Arcigay Arcilesbica Caleido
Via Vittorio Veneto 11 ☎ 071 20 30 45

HELP WITH PROBLEMS
Anlaids Regione Marche
Piazza del Plebiscito 2 ☎ 071 20 21 166

CRUISING
-Via Panoramica, zona Passetto (by night, by car and by foot in the gardens)
-Via Panoramica (at the end of the street in direction of the forest).

Aosta – Valle d'Aosta

GAY INFO
Arcigay Articolo 3 (GLM) Wed 20.30-22.30h
Via J.C. Mochet 7 ☎ 329 68 62 948
💻 arcigayaosta.blogspot.com

GUEST HOUSES
Neiges d'Antan. Les (AC B BF glm M PI RWS RWT WO) All year
Crêt Perrères ☎ 0166 94 87 75 💻 www.lesneigesdantan.it
Ten rooms with four-star-standards, furnished with wonderful larch-wood panels and floors. All rooms offer plenty of space and comfortable relaxing area. Refrigerator, safe, flat panel LCD-TV, DVD-player and stereo system. Luxury class bathrooms with stone and teakwood.

CRUISING
-Mura Romane (also at the P on the right of the railway station)
-Strada per l'autoporto valle d'Aosta (truckers, sometimes police patrols)
-Laghetti di Quart/Brissogne (you can see the lakes from the motorway, as you approach the exit (Autostrada A5 Torino-Aosta), near the camping site Du Lac, be careful).

Arco – Trentino-Alto Adige

GUEST HOUSES
Da Gianni (AC BF H M MC PA PK) All year
Via San Marcello nr. 21 *5 km from Garda Lake* ☎ 0464 51 64 64
💻 www.dagianni.it
A small, family-run bed and breakfast. In operation since 1962.

Arezzo – Toscana

GUEST HOUSES
Massa. La (CC glm I OS PI RWB RWS SA VA WH WO)
Località Vertelli 21, Castel San Niccolò *30 km from Arezzo* ☎ 0575 57 27 42 ☎ 333 11 01 226 (mobile) 💻 www.lamassa.tuscany.it
Detached villa with pool and spectacular views. Gym with sauna and hot tub. Free wireless internet.

APARTMENTS
Casa Gemelli (H I PI)
Casa Gemelli 14 *Casteluccio, 7 km from Arezzo* ☎ +49 7272 9291002 ☎ +49 174 2142143 (mobile) 💻 www.casa-gemelli.de
House for 4 and 6 persons fully equipped with swimming pool. Weekly rental (Sat to Sat).

Asti – Piemonte

SWIMMING
-Lungo Tanaro (NU) (pass S. Fedele in direction of the bridge, behind the bridge there is a sign-post to the paths, which all end at the beach).

CRUISING
-Bus station, beside railway station, young people and soldiers, afternoon and night).

Bari – Puglia

GAY INFO
Arcigay Liberi di Essere Liberi di Amare
Via Zara 13/15 ☎ 080 21 46 195 💻 www.arcigaybari.it

SEX SHOPS/BLUE MOVIES
Europa92 (g)
Via Pisanelli 16/18 ☎ 080 54 25 990 💻 www.europa92.com

SAUNAS/BATHS
Millennium Bath (AC B DR G I MA OS P SA SB VS WH)
15.30-23h, Mon closed
Via Adriatico 13 ☎ 080 53 42 530 💻 www.millenniumbath.com
A very pleasant sauna on two floors. During the summer there is access to an outdoor terrace. There is a dark room and private rooms for more intimate encounters. Uno Club Card required.

CRUISING
-Lungomare Nazario Saurio (R) (on the pier, in summer, mixed)
-Fiera del Levante (T) (by car only)
-Facoltà di Lettere e Filosofia (near post office, behind Piazza Re Umberto)
-Public park (between the universities)
-Lungomare (t) (towards San Giorgio)
-Stadio San Nicola.

Bassano del Grappa – Veneto

CRUISING
-Via Chilesotti (at night)
-Viale Venezia (barracks area)
-Viale Monte Grappa (R, t).

Bergamo – Lombardia

GAY INFO
Arcigay Cives
☎ 320 57 77 517 💻 www.arcigaybergamo.it

BARS
Divina Fashion (AC B glm YC) 20-2, Sun & Mon closed
Via S. Caterina 1e *Near Accademia Carrara* ☎ 035 21 84 21
💻 www.bardivina.it

■ **Mamo's** (B GLM MA S) 17-2h, Mon closed
Via Baschenis 13/A ☎ 035 27 00 14 🖳 www.mamos.it
Tue: Karaoke, Wed: Kartomamos, Thu: Single Party.

SAUNAS/BATHS

■ **City Sauna Club. The** (! AC B CC DR DU FC FH G GH LAB m MA MSG P PI RR SA SB SOL VS WH) Sep-May 14-2, Jun-Aug 15-2h, closed Tue
Via della Clementina 8 / Via Borgo Palazzo *Bus 4/7/8* ☎ 035 24 04 18
🖳 www.thecitysauna.com
One of Europe's biggest and most attractive gay saunas. Free condoms. Uno Club card required.

CRUISING

- -P hospital Gavazzeni, Via Gavazzeni (by car, at night)
- -Piazzale Malpensata (T)
- -Piazzale Cimitero (at night by car)
- -Riverside along the river ‚Serio' at Grassobbio near the airport (afternoon & evening).

Biella – Piemonte

CRUISING

- -Giardini alpini d'Italia: gardens near Via Vernato
- -Giardini pubblici: city park, next Via Garibaldi
- -Viale Carducci: behind the hospital (at night).

Bologna – Emilia Romagna

The university town Bologna with its 400,000 inhabitants is not as well known as Milan or Verona, it is however, always – also for the gay tourist – well worth a visit.
Here are the headquarters of the Arcigay, the most important LGBT federation are in Italy, and the very active regional publisher Cassero: regular parties take place in the attractive rooms of a former salt works. In addition Cassero organizes the Gender cooper festival every November. In tolerant Bologna a disproportionately high number of lesbians and gay men can be found. There are three saunas, including the biggest sauna in Italy, a gay bookstore and different clubs and bars.
Bologna is known for his more than 38 km long arcades and offers many other tourist highlights like two skew towers Asinelli and Garisenda, the landmarks of the city as well as the basilica San Petronio.

Die Universitätsstadt Bologna ist mit ihren knapp 400.000 Einwohnern zwar weniger bekannt als Mailand oder Verona, doch allemal – auch in schwuler Hinsicht – eine Reise wert. Hier befindet sich das Hauptquartier des Arcigay, des wichtigsten LGBT-Verbandes in Italien, und der regionale Ableger Cassero ist sehr aktiv: In den wunderschönen Räumen einer ehemaligen Saline finden regelmäßig Partys statt, zudem organisiert der Cassero jeden November das Gender Bender Festival. Im toleranten Bologna leben überproportional viele Lesben und Schwule, es gibt drei Saunen, darunter die größte Italiens, eine schwule Buchhandlung und verschiedene Clubs und Bars. Bologna ist bekannt für seine über 38 km langen Arkaden und bietet viele andere touristische Highlights wie die zwei schiefen Türme Asinelli und Garisenda, die Wahrzeichen der Stadt, und die Basilika San Petronio.

La ville universitaire de Bologne avec se près de 400.000 habitants est certes moins connue que Milan ou Vérone, mais mérite un voyage, aussi d'un point de vue gay. On trouve ici le quartier général de Arcigay, la plus grande association LGBT de l'Italie, et la branche locale Cassero est très active : dans les magnifiques locaux d'une ancienne saline, des soirées sont organisées, en outre le Cassero organise en novembre le Gender Bender Festival. Dans la ville tolérante de Bologne vivent un nombre dispropoortionné de Gays et Lesbiennes, il existe trois saunas, dont le plus grand d'Italie, une librairie gay et divers bars et boîtes. Bologne est connue pour ses arcades de 38 km et offrent beaucoup d'autres attractions touristiques comme les deux tours penchées de Asinelli et Garisenda, les emblêmes de la ville, et la basilique San Petronio.

La ciudad universitaria de Bolonia, con sus casi 400.000 habitantes, es menos conocida que las de Milán o Verona, sin embargo -también en lo que a vida gay se refiere- vale la pena visitarla . En Bolonia se encuentran la sedes de Arcigay, la organización LGBT más importante de Italia, y de la asociación Cassero, muy activa y conocida por sus fiestas, como las que organiza en las salas de una antigua salina, además de por el Gender Bender Festival que se celebra cada noviembre. Bolonia es una ciudad tolerante en la que, en proporción, viven un gran número de gays y lesbianas. Aquí se pueden encontrar tres saunas, las más grandes de Italia, una librería de temática gay y diversos bares y clubes. Bolonia es también conocida por sus arcadas de mas 38 Km. de extensión, pero también ofrece otros lugares de interés turístico como las torres inclinadas de Asinelli y Garisenda, símbolos de la ciudad, o la basílica de San Petronio.

Può anche essere vero che la città universitaria Bologna (400.000 abitanti) sia meno conosciuta di Milano o Verona, tuttavia vale davvero la pena venirla a visitare, anche per la sua vivace scena gay. Qui vi è anche la sede centrale dell'Arcigay (la più importante organizzazione LGBT in Italia) e anche la sede della sua attiva propaggine regionale, il Cassero. Nei meravigliosi spazi di una ex salina si svolgono regolarmente delle feste; una di queste è il Gender Bender Festival, organizzata dal Cassero ogni novembre. Nella tollerante Bologna ci vivono proporzionalmente davvero tanti gay e tante lesbiche; ci sono tre saune (una delle quali è la sauna più grande d'Italia), una libreria gay e molti bar e discoteche. Bologna è conosciuta per i suoi 38 km di portici e per le sue attrazioni turistiche, come per esempio le due torri inclinate che, rispettivamente, portano il nome Asinelli e Garisenda e la Basilica di San Petronio.

GAY INFO

Arcigay Il Cassero 9-19, 21-24, helpline Mon-Fri 20-23h
Via Don Minzoni 18 ☎ 051 09 57 200 ☎ 051 09 57 215 (helpline)
www.cassero.it
Gay & lesbian centre: cultural lectures, theatre, politics, counselling and bar. „Welcome Group" on Sun, every two weeks 18-20h.

Friendly Bologna
☎ 327 97 65 726 www.friendlybologna.it
Gay info for Bologna: Hotels, restaurants, clubs, houses, shops, gay culture, events, travels, people and gay lifestyle.

CULTURE

Centro di Documentazione Il Cassero
Mon-Fri 10-13, 14-19, Mon 21-24h
Via Don Minzoni 18 ☎ 051 09 57 214 www.cassero.it/doc
Gay and lesbian archive.

Gender Bender Festival
c/o Il Cassero, Via Don Minzoni 18 ☎ 051 09 57 221
www.genderbender.it
International festival conceived to recognize and decipher the swift changes in gender related imagery: visual arts, movies, music, theatre and literature, one week at the end of October.

BARS

Barattolo Café (AC B bf glm m OS YC) 7.30-2.30h, Sun closed
Via Borgo di S. Pietro 16/A *centre* ☎ 348 98 82 874 (mobile)
www.barattolocafe.com
Alternative bar with many gay & lesbian students. Fri special events.

Godot Wine Bistrot (AC B CC GLM m MA OS) Wed & Sat 19-24h
Via Santo Stefano 12/B *Piazza Santo Stefano* ☎ 051 26 29 71
☎ 347 63 89 505 (mobile)
Aperitivo (buffet and drinks) gay on Wed and Sat.

Stile Libero (AC B GLM m MA) Sun 19-23h, closed Aug
Via Lame 108/A ☎ 335 54 14 131
Cocktail bar and food (aperitivo) with DJs.

MEN'S CLUBS

Bar't (AC B DR f MA s) 22.30-5, Fri & Sat -6h, Mon closed
Via Polese 47/A ☎ 051 24 39 98 www.bartclub.net
Cruising bar. House DJ Fri & Sat. Uno Club card required.

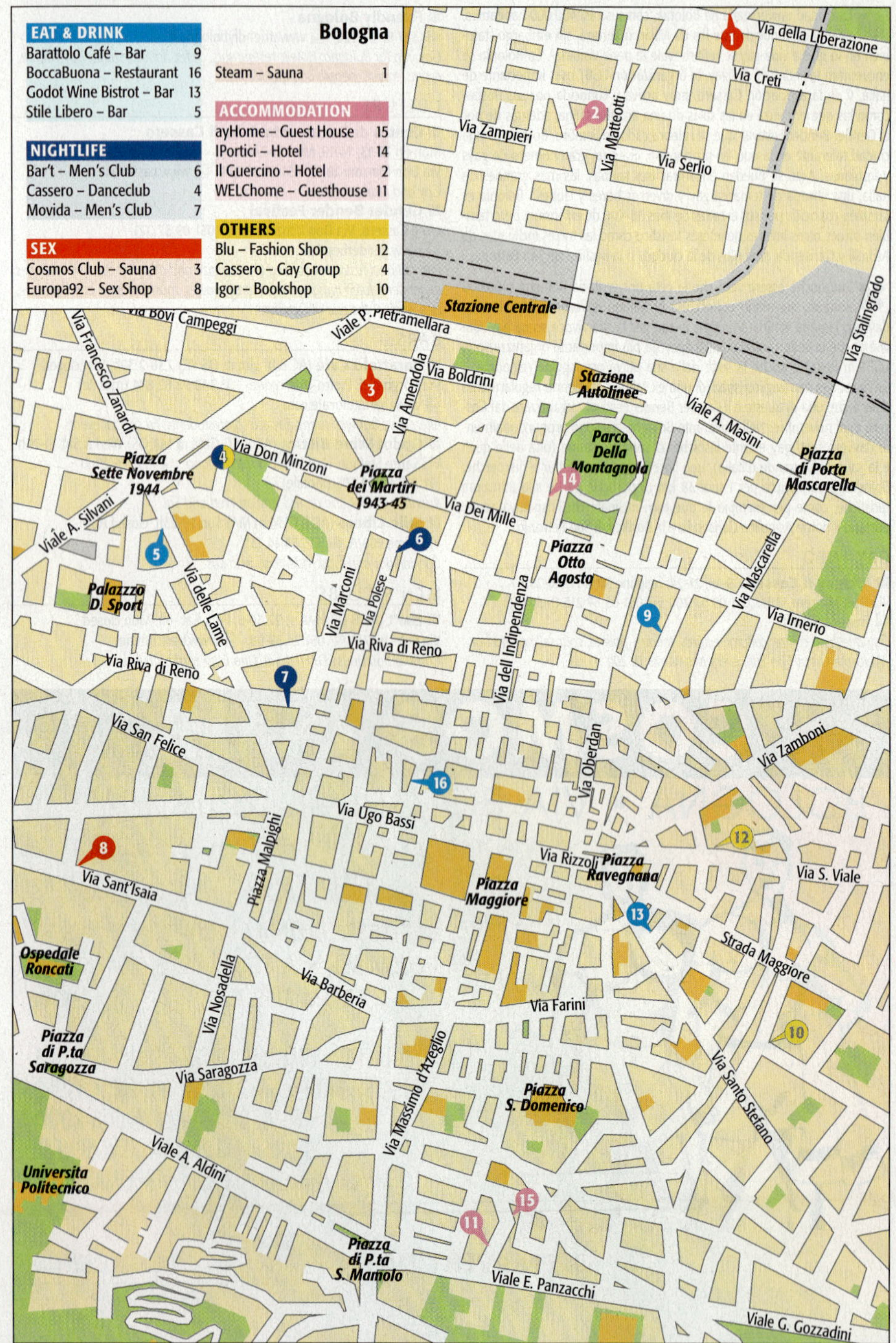
Bologna
EAT & DRINK
Barattolo Café – Bar 9
BoccaBuona – Restaurant 16
Godot Wine Bistrot – Bar 13
Stile Libero – Bar 5
Steam – Sauna 1
ACCOMMODATION
ayHome – Guest House 15
IPortici – Hotel 14
Il Guercino – Hotel 2
WELChome – Guesthouse 11
NIGHTLIFE
Bar't – Men's Club 6
Cassero – Danceclub 4
Movida – Men's Club 7
OTHERS
Blu – Fashion Shop 12
Cassero – Gay Group 4
Igor – Bookshop 10
SEX
Cosmos Club – Sauna 3
Europa92 – Sex Shop 8
Via della Liberazione
Via Creti
Via Zampieri
Via Matteotti
Via Serlio
Stazione Centrale
Via Stalingrado
Via Bovi Campeggi
Viale P. Pietramellara
Via Francesco Zanardi
Via Boldrini
Via Amendola
Stazione Autolinee
Viale A. Masini
Parco Della Montagnola
Piazza di Porta Mascarella
Piazza Sette Novembre 1944
Via Don Minzoni
Piazza dei Martiri 1943-45
Via Dei Mille
Viale A. Silvani
Piazza Otto Agosto
Via Mascarella
Via delle Lame
Via Marconi
Via Polese
Via dell Indipendenza
Via Irnerio
Palazzo D. Sport
Via Riva di Reno
Via San Felice
Via Oberdan
Via Zamboni
Via Ugo Bassi
Via Rizzoli
Piazza Ravegnana
Via S. Viale
Via Sant'Isaia
Piazza Malpighi
Piazza Maggiore
Strada Maggiore
Ospedale Roncati
Via Nosadella
Via Barberia
Via Farini
Piazza di P.ta Saragozza
Via Saragozza
Via Massimo d'Azeglio
Via Santo Stefano
Piazza S. Domenico
Viale A. Aldini
Universita Politecnico
Piazza di P.ta S. Mamolo
Viale E. Panzacchi
Viale G. Gozzadini

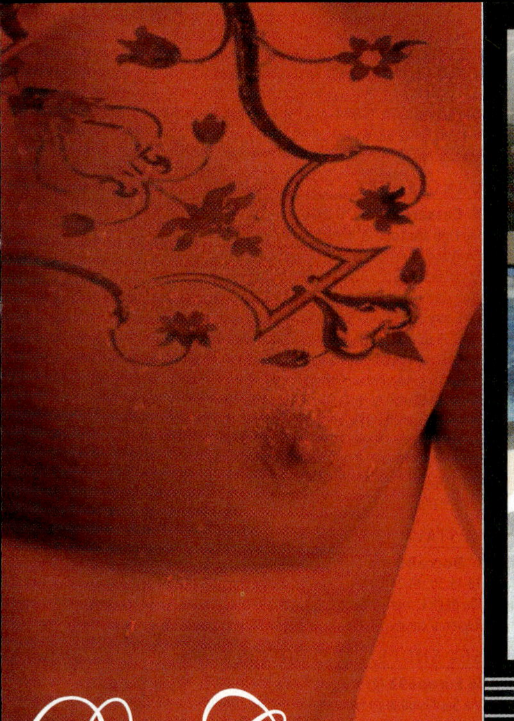

Via del tipografo 2
40138 Bologna

Movida (AC B DR G MA VS) 21-5h
Via San Felice 6B ☎ 051 23 25 07
On Saturday special parties (leather ecc.).

DANCECLUBS

Cassero. Il (! AC B d GLM MA P s) Wed-Sun 23-5h
Via Don Minzoni 18 *10 mins from railway station* ☎ 051 09 57 200
Arcigay club in a beautiful former silo: Wed queer disco. Thu lesbian night, Fri different parties, Sat house music (glm). First Fri/month bear night. Uno Club card required.

Easy Staff (AC B D GLM S YC) Fri, Sun & public holidays 23-4h
☎ 339 62 78 524 www.gaybologna.com
Gay parties in Bologna in different locations. Mainstream & house music. See www.gaybologna.com

Red Club (AC B CC D DR G MA NR OS PI) Sat 23-6h
Via del Tipografo 2 *Bus 14b stop „Via del Muratore", „Suburbana" train direction „Roveri", stop „Roveri", by car Tangenziale exit 10 „Roveri"*
☎ 335 813 03 94 www.discoredclub.com
Mainstream dancefloor with big cruising. In summer attached to swimming pool of Black Sauna. 2 darkrooms. Uno Club card required.

RESTAURANTS

BoccaBuona (AC CC GLM VEG)
12-15:30, 19-24h, closed on Tuesday evening
Via degli Usberti 5 *Centre* ☎ (0039) 051 221750 ☎ 349 2279135
Regional cuisine to affordable prices. Mixed crowd with some gays.

SEX SHOPS/BLUE MOVIES

Europa92 (g)
Via Sant'Isaia 80/b (centre) ☎ 051 64 92 998 www.europa92.com

SAUNAS/BATHS

Black (! AC B DR DU G LAB M MA MSG OS P PI RR SA SB SOL VS WH) 14-2, Fri & Sat -3h
Via del Tipografo 2 *Bus 14b, stop „Via del Muratore". „Suburbana" train direction „Roveri", stop „Roveri". By car Tangenziale exit 10 „Roveri"*
☎ 339 279 75 10 www.blacksauna.com
Probably the best sauna in Italy at the moment. Special price 14-15h & for under 26 years old. Free condoms. Recently renovated cabins. Uno Club Card required.

Cosmos Club (AC B DR DU FH G m MA MSG NU P RR SA SB SOL VR VS WH) 12-0.30, Fri -1, Sat -2h
Via Boldrini, 16 interno *Near main railway station, in the courtyard through the iron gate. Look for green light over bell* ☎ 051 25 58 90
ENDAS card required. Smoking zone on site.

Steam (! AC B CC DR DU FC G GH LAB M MA P PP RR SA SB SL VS WH) 14-1, Fri & Sat -2h
Via Ferrarese 22-i *10 mins from railway station, near Piazza dell'Unità, bus 25, 27* ☎ 051 36 39 53 www.steamsauna.it
Discount for under 26 and after 21h. Uno Club card required.

FITNESS STUDIOS

Fitlife (g) Mon-Fri 9.30-22.30, Sat 10-20, Sun 11-14h
Via Andrea Costa 131/2 ☎ 051 74 59 252 www.fit-life.it

BOOK SHOPS

Igor (G) Mon-Fri 9.30-13, 15.30-19.30, Sat 10.30-13.30, 15.30-19.30h
Via San Petronio Vecchio 3 ☎ 051 22 94 66
www.facebook.com/igor.libreria
Gay bookshop. Art exhibitions and book presentations in the centre of Bologna.

FASHION SHOPS

Blu (AC CC) Mon-Sat 10-13, 15-19:30h
Via San Vitale 34 B/C *Close to the two towers* ☎ 051 272754
Stylish clothes in the centre of Bologna.

HOTELS

Hotel Il Guercino (AC B BF CC GLM H I M OS PA PK RWB RWS RWT VA WH WO) All year

Via Luigi Serra 7 *Bus 10/25/27* ☎ 051 369 893 🖳 www.guercino.it
Beautiful rooms with SAT-TV. Wireless internet. Also restaurant & bike rental. Summer breakfast terrace outside & new fitness room and jacuzzi.

■ **I Portici Hotel Bologna** (AC B BF CC glm I M MA PA PK RWS RWT S ST) All year, 24hrs
Via Indipendenza, 69 *Near main station* ☎ 051 421 85
🖳 www.iporticihotel.com
I Portici Hotel is probably the most stylish and elegant hotel in town with a great fusion between classic and contemporary ambiance. Reflecting the most refined taste for art in all the hotel's public areas, bedrooms, lounge bar, restaurant and theatre. Unique in town with a glorious past and magnificent liberty decorations, Eden Theatre is alive with events and shows taking place throughout the year.

GUEST HOUSES

■ **ayHome B&B** (BF glm I RWT) All year
Via Savenella, 2 *In the Zone Tribunale* ☎ 051 588 30 75
🖳 www.aygroup.it
Gay owned bed&breakfast centrally located.

■ **WELChome** (glm)
Via Savenella 26 *City centre* ☎ 347 30 60 852 🖳 www.italianoabologna.com
One private room in the centre of Bologna. Special services: Italian lessons, cultural activities and Italian cooking.

GENERAL GROUPS

■ **Key We Associazione Culturale Nazionale**
☎ (0039) 02 890 383 69 🖳 www.keywe.it
National association for the gay community.

CRUISING

-🅿 Via della Manifattura, between Via Stalingrado/Via Ferrarese (by car, at night)

Bolzano/Bozen – Trentino-Alto Adige

GAY INFO

■ **Centaurus** Infogay: Tue 20-22, Lesbian Line: Thu 20-22h
Via Galileo Galilei 4A ☎ 0471 97 63 42 (infoline) 🖳 www.centaurus.org
Also youth group. Library with gay films open on Sat 21-24h.

BARS

■ **Bossanova** (AC B GLM m) Tue-Sat 17-1, Sun 18-1h
Via Cappuccini 8/a ☎ 347 45 75 846
Food & drinks.

■ **Centaurus (Arcigay/Arcilesbica)** (B GLM m MA)
Sat 21-24h
Via Galileo Galilei 4A ☎ 0471 97 63 42 🖳 www.centaurus.org
Bar inside the gay association.

SAUNAS/BATHS

■ **Exit** (B CC D DR DU g M MA MSG p RR SA SB SOL VS WH)
Tue, Thu, Fri 18-0.30, Sat & Sun 14-0.30h
Via Visitazione – Mariaheimweg, 2 ☎ 347 47 00 645 (italian)
☎ 338 25 95 189 (german) 🖳 www.sauna-exit.it
Menu available. Subscribe for the newsletter of events under: sauna@exitcenter.it

HOTELS

Kuhn (AC B BF glm H M OS PA PI PK RWB RWS RWT SA) All year
Via Bolzano – Bozner Straße 18 *Settequerce-Terlano, 5 km from Bolzano*
☎ 04 71 91 75 02 💻 www.hotel-kuhn.it
Rooms with shower/WC, sat-TV, own key, hair dryer & phone. Pets allowed.

Maciaconi
☞ *Val Gardena*

SWIMMING

-Africa at river Talvera (G MA NU) (take road to Sarnthein/Sarentino, 4 km from Bozen turn right at village Sill and drive to end of road. From there, walk 500 m up the river, busy Sat/Sun).

CRUISING

-Parco Petrarca, near Ponte Talvera/Talfer bridge, around the small lake.

Brescia – Lombardia

GAY INFO

Arcigay Orlando (G) Helpline: Fri 21-23h
Via Valerio Paitone 42 ☎ 030 47 601 (helpline) 💻 www.arcigaybrescia.it

BARS

Re Desiderio (B CC G m MA) 19-1h, closed Mon
Vicolo Lungo 11 *Next to Piazza del Foro* ☎ 328 33 98 538
💻 www.redesiderio.com

DANCECLUBS

Out Limits (AC B D DR GLM OS) Fri & Sat 23-5h
Via Ugo Foscolo 2, Paderno Franciacorta *Highway A4 MI-VE exit „Ospitaletto". 2km from the exit.* ☎ 030 65 75 36 💻 www.outlimits.it
2 dancefloors: House and mainstream music. Fri gLm, Sat Glm

Trap (B D DR F G MA NU OS P VS) Fri & Sat 23-4h
Via Castagna 55 *Exit A4 Brescia Ovest, direction Dogana*
☎ 328 45 23 880 (infoline) 💻 www.trapmad.it
Fri boys & girls, also naked cruising floor upstairs. Sat dresscode. House music.

SEX SHOPS/BLUE MOVIES

Europa92 (g)
Via dei Mille 22/3 ☎ 030 37 58 459 💻 www,europa92.com
Sex shop with new viedeocabins.

Hot (g) Mon 14-20, Tue-Sat 10-20h
Via Mandolossa 144 ☎ 030 37 33 076 💻 www.hotsexyboutique.it
Gay DVDs, fetish wear and vast offer of erotic items. Further store at Via P.Superiore, 74; Tel: 030 26 29 130.

Magic America (AC G) 10-12.30 & 15-20h
Via Oberdan 20/c *Zona Caserma Pompieri* ☎ 030 39 84 53
💻 www.magicamerica.it

CRUISING

-Breda zone
-Via Torrelunga and Via Spalto S. Marco (behind the jail)
-Giardini del Castello (AYOR) (in the parks close to S. Pietro church; evening and day)
-Viale Italia (R T) (after 23 h)
-Zona Industriale (MA YC) (Via Grandi/Via Perotti, by car, weekdays after 21, WE after 13 h).

Brunico/Bruneck – Trentino-Alto Adige

SWIMMING

-River Ahr between Gais and Uttenheim, by bike and on foot.

Capri – Campania

HOTELS

Floridiana. La (AC B glm H M OS PA PI RWB RWS RWT WO) All year
Via Campo Di Teste, 16-I ☎ 081 83 70 166 💻 www.lafloridiana-capri.com

SWIMMING

-Grotta dell'Arsenale, underneath Via Krupp.

Casatenovo – Lombardia

RESTAURANTS

San Mauro (AC B CC glm H M MC OS PA PK WL)
Daily from 12-14.30 & 18.30-midnight
Via de Gasperi 82 *Near Milano, Monza and Lecco* ☎ 039 9202601
💻 www.sanmauroweb.it

Caserta – Campania

CRUISING

-Palazzo Reale (very AYOR) (in the gardens)
-Viale Carlo III (at night, by car).

Castel di Sangro – Abruzzo

GUEST HOUSES

Tiglio Bed & Breakfast. Il
(B BF CC GLM H I M PA PK RWB RWS RWT VA WI) 8-10.30h
Via XX Settembre 132-136 *Centre of the city* ☎ 08 64 84 72 76
💻 www.bebiltiglio.it
Rooms with phone and TV. Internet access. En-suite bath room.

Cecina Mare – Toscana

DANCECLUBS

Aftersun (D glm OS) May-Sep: Thu-Sun 24-6h
Via della Forestale, Loc. Capocavallo ☎ 0586 62 00 34
Open air beach disco. Mainstream and house music. Mixed.

RESTAURANTS

Da Bruno (AC B CC g M OS)
11-15, 18-24h; Tue closed in low season; completely closed from Nov-March
Viale della Repubblica 200 ☎ 0586 62 21 81
Restaurant & Pizzeria. Specialities of the Mediterranean coast.

SWIMMING

-Beach between Cecina Mare and Bibbona (south of Andalù Beach), action in the bushes. Also cruising by car in the night (ayor).
-Beach Oasi di Bolgheri: Marina di Bibbona, go in direction of Camping-site Il Gineprino and leave the car in the parking. Action is at the end of the public beach, direction south.

Como – Lombardia

SEX CINEMAS

Italia (AC B g MC) 15-?h
Via Marchesi 6 *Ponte Chiasso* ☎ 031 53 01 35
Gay films for sale.

CRUISING

-Circle around soccer stadium (after 22h)
-Railway station (AYOR)
-Main road between Lomazzo-Turate, wood on the right side (day and night by car).

Cosenza – Calabria

GAY INFO

Arcigay EOS Mon-Sat 16-20h
c/o Casa delle Culture, Corso Telesio 29 ☎ 347 76 00 480
💻 www.arcigay.it/cosenza

Cremona – Lombardia

GAY INFO

■ **Arcigay „La Rocca"** Sun 20-23h, closed Aug
c/o Arci, Via Speciano 4 *Bus 1, near the Dome* ☎ 338 50 15 488
🖳 www.arcigaycremona.it

DANCECLUBS

■ **Notte Praga** (AC B CC D G MA S WE) Fri & Sat 22-4h
Viale Po' 129D *Highway A21 Piacenza – Brescia, exit Cremona/Castelvetro*
☎ 349 37 63 150 (mobile) 🖳 www.nottepraga.com
Friday 90's dancefloor, Sat with naked gogo dancers. See the homepage www.nottepraga.com

SEX SHOPS/BLUE MOVIES

■ **Adamo ed Eva – Sex Shop** (AC CC g VS)
Mon 15-20, Tue-Sun 10-20h
Via Rosario 56 *Tangenziale-Fiera near Boschetto* ☎ 0372 23 407
🖳 www.sexyshopadamoedeva.it
■ **Mela Proibita. La** (g) Closed Mon
Galleria Kennedy 12 ☎ 0372 36 118 🖳 www.lamelaproibita.it
Gay video/DVD section.

CRUISING

-Via Lungo Po Europa (near the camping site)
-Foro Boario (near Stadium, by night).

Crotone – Calabria

CRUISING

-Viale Regina Margherita.

Cuneo – Piemonte

GAY INFO

■ **Arcigay Figli della Luna**
Via Amedeo Rossi 12
🖳 www.arcigaycuneo.altervista.org

CRUISING

-Dogana dei Camion: Corso De Gasperi (in the evening)
-Parco Caduti Divisione Alpina (at night)
-Parco Monviso (near railway station)
☞ Garda.

Desenzano del Garda – Lombardia

BARS

■ **Sisi Bar** (B glm) 18-3, summer 20h-all night, closed Tue
Vicolo Duomo 13/A *Near the dome* ☎ 030 91 40 085
🖳 www.sisipub.com

DANCECLUBS

■ **Art Club** (AC B CC D GLM OS S YC) Wed, Fri-Sat 22-4h
Via Mella 4 ☎ 030 91 27 285 🖳 www.artclubdisco.com
New location close to Splash Sauna. Check www.artclubdisco.com
■ **Big Mama's** (AC B CC D gLm m MA OS S)
Thu 21.30-2, Fri & Sat 22-4, Sun 19-2h
Via Mapella 7, Lonato del Garda *Exit Desenzano on highway A4, follow signs ‚Lonato'. After exactly 2 km on the right hand* ☎ 347 15 09 452
🖳 www.bigmamas.it
Mainly lesbians. Mixed music, two dancefloors and summer dancefloor.

SEX SHOPS/BLUE MOVIES

■ **C'est La Vie** (CC g) Daily 10-22h
Viale Marconi 130 ☎ 030 99 11 784
Dvds, gadgets and toys.

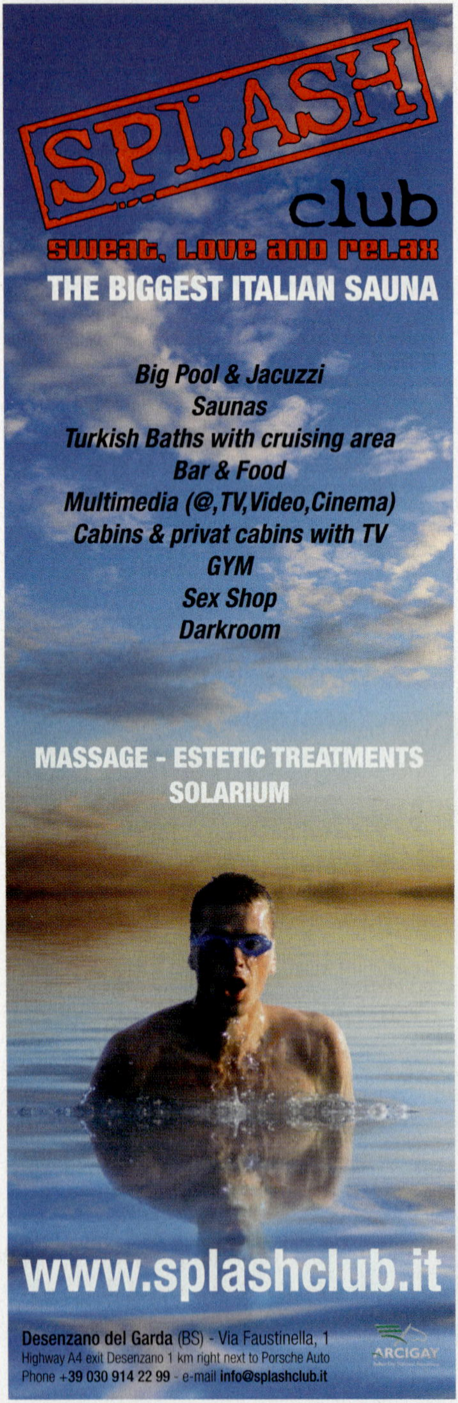

SAUNAS/BATHS

■ **Splash Club** (! AC B CC DR DU FC G GH I LAB M MA MSG OS P PI RR SA SB SH SL SOL VS WH WO) 14-1, Sat -2, Sun -24h
Via Faustinella, 1 *On highway A4 Venezia-Milano, exit „Desenzano del Garda", direction Mantova, first exit, first street right, straight up till the sign, next to Porsche* ☎ 030 914 22 99 🖳 www.splashclub.it
Largest sauna of northern Italy. Internet point & smoking area. Sexshop inside the sauna! Tue 2 for 1, Thu special entrance fee, Wed special entrance fee for those under 26. Uno Club Card required.

HOTELS

■ **San Filis** (AC B BF CC glm H M MSG OS PA PI RWS VA) All year
Via Marconi, 5, San Felice del Benaco *15 km from train station Desenzano*
☎ 0365 625 22 🖳 www.sanfilis.it
San Filis is situated in the old part of San Felice del Benaco, a typical romantic village on the western shore of lake Garda, which is about 800 m away. The hotel is a typical 16th century building, recently refurbished.

GUEST HOUSES

■ **B&B Relais San Michele**
☞ *Garda*

SWIMMING

-Punta del Vò (rocky beach on road 572, 1 km from the village, daytime only)
-Rocca di Manerba (G NU) (take the road to Salò, turn off at Moniga del Garda (centro) and follow the signs)
-Parco naturale to the end of the road (but don't follow the signs „Manerba del Garda"!) Then take via Marinello on foot to the beach (15 mins).

CRUISING

-Punto del Vò (afternoon above the road, night at 🅿).

Fano – Marche

BARS

■ **Caffè degli Scomposti** (B bf CC GLM M MA)
7.30-2h, closed Sun
Via San Francesco 45 *Near central station* ☎ 0724 80 86 51

Ferrara – Emilia Romagna

GAY INFO

■ **Arcigay Arcilesbica Circo Massimo**
Via Contrada della Rosa 14 ☎ 0532 24 14 19
🖳 www.circomassimo.org

SEX CINEMAS

■ **Mignon** (g)
Porta S. Pietro 18 ☎ 0532 76 01 39

DECORATION

■ **Food Designer** (G)
☎ 0346 682 1737
Creative and artistic presentation of mouth-watering cusine. Professional catering for parties, exhibitions and special events. Avialable throughout ITALY and Europe upon request. Impress your friends or business partners with this unique catering company.

SWIMMING

-Lido delle Nazioni, in the northern part towards the lake, NU & activity in the woods.

CRUISING

-Alla Giarina: S. Maria Madalena (on the dam over the river Po, by car night & day)
-Le Mura (wall 200 m from railway station, ayor)
-In front of restaurant Al Doro, Via Padova (by car at night).

Firenze – Toscana

Florence is one of the most important art centres world wide. Nowhere else in the world can one find such a collection of buildings, paintings and sculptures from the Gothic, Romanesque and especially Renaissance periods. Here one can find the cathedral and one of the most important painting collections in the world. The capital of the Tuscany has around 400,000 inhabitants and therefore a small but interesting gay scene. Due to a tolerant climate the first gay locations were established many years ago. The bars have an international flair and are mostly within walking distance of each other. The whole of the inner city is a traffic free zone, so it is highly recommended not to travel here by car, or if you do, to park the car outside the city. Gay run or gay-friendly accommodations (especially in Arezzo, Siena and Saturnia) offer tranquillity for those looking for it, but also serve as a great base as does Torre del Lago – the gay hotspot in summer, which is only one hour away by car. Florence is truly a must. Book your hotel early as accommodation is difficult to obtain even in the low season.
Please note that the house numbers run in a parallel system: business addresses have mostly a red (occasionally blue) house number, with a „R" after the number. All other house numbers are black.

Florenz ist eine der wichtigsten Kunststädte weltweit: Nirgends sonst auf der Welt existiert eine derartige Dichte an Bauten, Bildern und Skulpturen der Gotik, Romanik und vor allem der Renaissance. Hier befinden sich u. a. der Dom und die Uffizien, eine der bedeutendsten Gemäldesammlungen der Welt. Die Hauptstadt der Toskana hat ca. 400.000 Einwohner und dementsprechend eine kleine, aber feine Schwulenszene. Aufgrund ihres toleranten Klimas sind hier schon früh die ersten schwulen Einrichtungen entstanden. Nach einem neuen Gesetz der Region Toscana sind Schwule dort vor Diskriminierung geschützt. Die ganze Innenstadt ist zudem verkehrsberuhigt, weshalb es sich empfiehlt, nicht mit dem Auto anzureisen oder es außerhalb zu parken.
Von Florenz aus lassen sich viele Touren in die landschaftlich reizvolle Umgebung starten. Von Schwulen geführte oder schwulenfreundliche Landhäuser (siehe hierfür vor allem Arezzo, Siena und Saturnia) können denen, die es ruhiger mögen, als Ausgangsbasis dienen, aber auch das trubelige Torre del Lago als schwuler Sommertreffpunkt ist nur eine Stunde entfernt. Florenz ist vor diesem Hintergrund also auch für den schwulen Touristen ein Muss! Hotels sollten jedoch möglichst frühzeitig gebucht werden, da es nicht nur zu den Stoßzeiten (wie zu Ostern) schwierig ist, freie Betten zu ergattern.
Zu beachten sind die beiden parallelen Hausnummerierungen: Kommerzielle Einrichtungen haben meist eine rote (selten: blaue) Hausnummer (ein „R" hinter der Nummer), ansonsten ist die Hausnummer schwarz.

Florence est une des villes artistiques les plus importantes du monde: nulle part ailleurs sur la terre existe un telle densité de monuments, de peintures et de sculptures gothiques, romanes, mais avant tout de la Renaissance. On trouve dans la ville entre autres la cathédrale et la Galerie des Offices, une des plus importantes collections d'art du monde. La capitale de la Toscane dénombre env. 400,000 habitants et offre en conséquence une petite mais intéressante scène gay. En raison de son climat tolérant, des etablissements gays se sont ouvert ici assez tôt. Les bars sont dotés d'un flair international et sont tous accessibles à pied. La circulation dans le centre ville est limitée et il est conseillé de garer sa voiture à l'extérieur.
En partant de Florence, on peut faire de nombreuses excursions dans les magnifiques alentours. Si vous désirez plus de calme entre chacune d'entre elles, vous pourrez louer une maison de campagne auprès de propriétaires gays ou gay friendly (voir en particulier Arezzo, Sienne et Saturnia) mais la très animée Torre del Lago, lieu de rencontre gay en été, n'est également qu'à une heure de trajet.
Il faut faire attention à la numérotation des maisons : les établissements commerciaux ont un numéro rouge (parfois bleu), avec un „R" derrière le numéro, sinon les numéros sont en noir.

Florencia es una de las ciudades del arte más importantes en todo el mundo: en ningún otro lugar existe una tal concentración de edificios, pinturas y esculturas del arte gótico, románicao y, especial-

mente, del Renacimiento. Aquí están entre otros, la Catedral y la „Galería de los Oficios", una de las colecciones de pintura más importantes del mundo. La capital de Toscana tiene unos 400,000 habitantes y, por tanto, una pequeña pero refinada comunidad homosexual. Gracias al clima de tolerancia en la ciudad, se instalaron desde hace tiempo los primeros locales homosexuales. Los bares tienen un ambiente muy internacional y se puede llegar de uno a otro muy bien a pie.
En toda la ciudad antigua está restringido el tráfico, por ello recomendamos no viajar con el coche, es decir, mejor aparcar el vehículo fuera de la ciudad.
Desde Florencia se pueden iniciar muchas rutas por los maravillosos paisajes de su entorno. Algunas casas de huéspedes regentadas por homosexuales o consideradas tolerantes (véase aquí especialmente Arezzo, Siena y Saturnia) pueden ser un buen punto de partida para aquéllos que les guste la tranquilidad; además, la población de turismo gay en verano de Torre del Lago está sólo a una hora. Debe prestarse atención a la numeración paralela de las casas: los locales comerciales tienen en genereal un número rojo (en ocasiones azul) y una „R" detrás del número; de lo contrario, el número es negro.

Firenze è tra le città d'arte più importanti del mondo: non esiste altro posto, infatti, con una tale concentrazione di edifici, dipinti e sculture in stile gotico, romanico e, soprattuttto, del Rinascimento. Qui si trovano, tra le altre cose, il Duomo e gli Uffizi, una delle pinacoteche più prestigiose del mondo. Il capoluogo toscano ha circa 400,000 abitanti e la scena gay, quindi, non è grande ma raffinata. Grazie ad un clima cittadino tollerante, i primi locali gay sono sorti già molti anni fa. I bar hanno un'atmosfera internazionale e sono quasi sempre raggiungibili a piedi. Tutto il centro città è zona pedonale, quindi si consiglia di non viaggiare con la macchina o al limite posteggiarla fuori la città. Da Firen-

ze si possono intraprendere diverse escursioni per le numerose località dell'affascinante campagna toscana. A chi piace una vacanza un po' più tranquilla consigliamo dei casolari di campagna a gestione gay (vedi p.e. Arezzo, Siena e Saturnia) come punto di partenza; ma anche la vivace Torre del Lago, punto d'incontro per gay, è solo ad un'ora di distanza. Bisogna fare attenzione alla parallela numerazione civica: attività commerciali hanno in genere un numero rosso (più raramente blu) e una „R" dietro al numero, altrimenti i numeri civici delle abitazioni sono neri.

GAY INFO

■ **Azione Gay e Lesbica „Finisterrae"** (GLM) Mon-Thu 18-20h
Via Pisana 32/34r ☎ 055 22 02 50 💻 www.azionegayelesbica.it
Gay and lesbian political association. Meeting, library. Monthly parties, shows. Health consultations. Touristic information.

BARS

■ **Piccolo Cafè. Il** (AC B GLM MA) 20-3h
Via Borgo Santa Croce 23/R *Centre* ☎ 055 20 01 057
💻 www.facebook.com/piccolocafefirenze
Nice, small bar in a new style. DJ on Fri & Sat. Crowd outside in summer.

■ **Y.A.G** (AC B CC GLM I S VS YC) 21-3, Sun 17-3h
Via de' Macci 8r *Near Santa Croce church* ☎ 055 24 69 022
💻 www.yagbar.com
Video & music bar, very crowded. Huge video screen. Happy hour Sun 17-22h.

MEN'S CLUBS

■ **Crisco** (AC B DR F GLM MA P S VS)
22.30-3, Fri & Sat 23-4h, closed Sun & Tue
Via S. Egidio 43r 💻 www.criscoclub.it
Cruising bar, parties with DJ in the weekend. Mon naked/underwear party, last Thu/month La Roboterie, famous electro/techno party

■ **Fabrik** (AC B d DR f G MA OS P SNU VS) 22-3, Fri & Sat -4h, Mon closed
Via del Lavoro 19, Calenzano *Ca. 15 km from Florence, next to train station Calenzano, bus 2. Highway A1 exit Calenzano, after exit right, at the fourth round-a-bout left and after tunnel right, Fabrik is on the left side*
☎ 349 89 06 645 (infoline) 💻 www.fabrikfirenze.it
Cruising in a huge former factory with garden and video room. Sat disco. Discount for under 25. Every third Sat/month Bears Troops. Uno Club Card required.

■ **Hard Bar 85** (AC B CC DR F G M MA P VS WE) 21-3, Fri & Sat -6h
Via Guelfa 85/R *Near railway station, city centre* ☎ 055 264 54 61
💻 www.hardbar85.eu

DANCECLUBS

■ **Tabasco Disco Gay** (AC B CC D DR G MA S SNU VS WE)
22.30-?h, closed Mon
Piazza Santa Cecilia, 3 *Inside Signoria Square* ☎ 055 21 30 00
💻 www.tabascogay.it
One of the first gay places in Italy. Wed bisex!

■ **Testardamente** (D GLM YC)
c/o Auditorium Flog, Via M. Mercati 24 b ☎ 055 22 02 50
Monthly parties on Fri. Crowded. Info from Azione Gaylesbica.

RESTAURANTS

■ **Munaciello** (AC B CC DM glm LM M MA S VEG WL) Daily 19.30-1h
Via Maffia 31 33R ☎ 055 28 71 98 💻 www.munaciello.it
Restaurant in a former horse stable. Napolitan restaurant & pizzeria, fish specialities. Wed live Neapolitan music.

Semolina (AC CC GLM M OS VEG)
19:30 – 24, Fri-Sun also 12-15h
Piazza Ghiberti 87R *close to Yag Bar* ☏ (0039) 055 2347584
Nice restaurant with Mediterranean and Florentine cuisine. Mixed crowd & outdoor space.

SAUNAS/BATHS

Florence Baths
(AC B CC DR DU G M MA MSG PI SA SB SOL VS WE WH) 12-2h
Via Guelfa 93/R *Near railway station, city centre* ☏ 055 21 60 50
www.florencebaths.it
Outdoor pool from May to September.

FITNESS STUDIOS

Klab (g WO) Mon, Wed, Fri 7.30-22,
Tue & Thu 9-22, Sat -18, Sun 10-14h
Via dei Conti 7 *Near Piazza S. Lorenzo*

BODY & BEAUTY SHOPS

Domina (AC CC glm) 9-18h, Mon closed
Via 27 Aprile 53-55r ☏ 055 49 48 48
Hair and style for men and women.

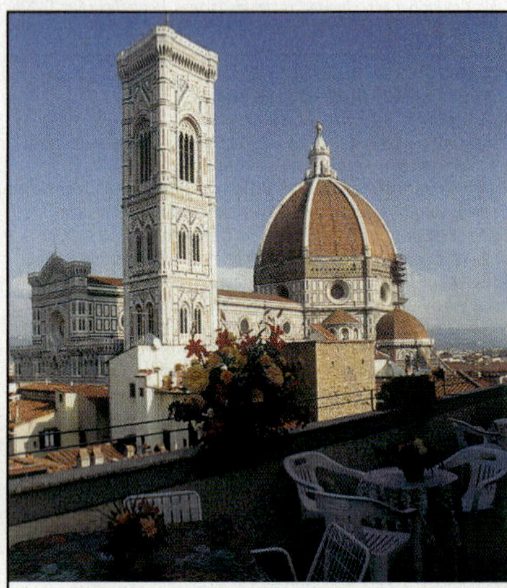

TRAVEL AND TRANSPORT

Florence by Bike (CC glm)
April-Oct: 9-19.30; Nov-March: 9-13, 15.30-19.30h, Sun closed
Via San Zanobi 120R ☎ 055 48 89 92 💻 www.florencebybike.it
Bike rental for tours in and around Florence.

HOTELS

Alamanni (AC B GLM I PK RWS RWT VA WI) All year
Via Luigi Alamanni 35 *Close to railway station* ☎ 055 265 84 09
💻 www.hotelalamanni.com
18 rooms with private bath and sat-TV. Free car parking and wireless internet for Spartacus readers. Also booking of Gemini Studios.

Cellai Boutique Hotel (AC B BF CC GLM H I OS RWS RWT WI)
All year
Via 27 Aprile 14 *Centre of Firenze* ☎ 055 48 92 91 💻 www.hotelcellai.it
Centrally located 4-star-boutique-style charming hotel. 18th century building with an intimate winter garden, library, terrace. For art and design lovers.

Globus (AC bf CC glm I PK RWS RWT VA) 24hrs
Via S. Antonino, 24/black *5 mins from train station* ☎ 055 21 10 62
💻 www.hotelglobus.com
All 23 rooms with bath, Sky-TV and phone. Complimentary breakfast. Free wireless DSL connection. Completely renovated. Friendly staff.

Masaccio (BF H M RWS RWT) All year
Via Masaccio 228 *Centre* ☎ 055 57 81 53 💻 www.hotelmasaccio.net
Small clean hotel with restaurant centrally located. Rooms with and without own bathroom.

Medici (BF CC GLM OS PA RWB RWS RWT) All year
Via de Medici, 6 ☎ 055 28 48 18 💻 www.hotelmedici.it
Rooms with phone. Own/shared bath. BF incl. Beautiful roof garden. Apartments upon request. Gay owned.

GUEST HOUSES

1900 Artevita (AC BF CC glm I)
Viale Raffaele Sanzio 2 *15 min by foot from the centre, bus 12, 6*
☎ 347 12 52 290 (mobile) ☎ 349 64 34 924 (mobile)
💻 www.1900artevita.com
Rooms with tv, safe and private bathroom. Free wireless internet. Gay owned.

Bears & Breakfast (BF G MA WI) All year
Via S. Giovanni Bosco 14 *Bus 6/14A/14B/14C – Autostrada Firenze Sud – Stazione Campo di Marte* ☎ 055 66 03 38
💻 www.bearsandbreakfast.com
B&B in a quiet residential area close to the center. Comfortable beds and a big shower box. Gay-friendly ambience. Maps and guides available.

■ **Bed and Breakfast di Piazza del Duomo** (BF H)
Via Oriuolo 49 ☏ 055 28 50 18 🖳 www.duomorooms.com
B&B close to Duomo and gay venues.

■ **Dei Mori Bed & Breakfast** (AC BF CC glm I MC RWS)
All year
Via Dante Alighieri 12 *Between the Duomo and Signoria square*
☏ 055 21 14 38 🖳 www.deimori.com
Own key. Non-smoking hotel, small and friendly. Free wireless internet. Early booking advisable. Gay managed. Also museums & restaurants reservations.

■ **MR My Resort Firenze** (AC CC glm I OS RWS RWT SB WH)
All year
Via delle Ruote 14A *One block from Piazza San Marco and Galleria dell'Accademia* ☏ 055 28 39 55 🖳 www.mrflorence.it
Cosy, chic and gay friendly. In the rooms glam and glitter accents accompany precious materials such as crystal, mirrors, velvet.

APARTMENTS

■ **Gemini Studios** (AC BF CC glm RWS VA) All year
Viale Fratelli Rosselli 55 *Close to railway station* ☏ 055 29 52 50
🖳 www.inflorence-apartments.com
Modern furnished and fully equipped one-bedroom accommodations, 10 studios with modern comfort for 2-4 persons.

■ **Suite Santa Croce Florence**
Via dei Benci 10 *near Piazza Santa Croce* ☏ 335 22 12 64 (mobile)
🖳 www.santacrocebedflorence.it

PRIVATE ACCOMMODATION

■ **Borghetto. Il** (AC G OS PI)
Via degli Alberi 60, Montaione *50 km from Florence* ☏ 0571 58 24 02
🖳 www.tuscanyitalianhome.com
A nice, cosy villa for up to 6 people in the Tuscan hills between Firenze, Siena and Pisa. Sat-TV and equipped kitchen. Rental for the weekend or the whole week.

GENERAL GROUPS

■ **Arcigay Il Giglio Rosa** Fri 16-20h
Via di Mezzo 39/R ☏ 055 01 23 121
🖳 www.arcigayfirenze.it

■ **Key We Associazione Culturale Nazionale**
☏ 02 890 383 69 🖳 www.keywe.it
National association for the gay community.

FETISH GROUPS

■ **BearsKing** (F G)
🖳 www.bearskingitalia.com
Parties for bears in all Italy. Special events in Florence.

SWIMMING

-Piscina Costoli (swimming pool, facilities and showers; best late afternoon; be discreet).

CRUISING

-Campo di Marte stadium, Via Malta (by foot at night)
-Viale Lincoln-Washington (on the bike path from „Ponte della Vittoria" to „Ponte all'Indiano" at night on foot or by bike 🅿 behind disco Meccanó, ayor)
-Highway Florence-Rome A1 (🅿 between Firenze Sud/Incisa, both directions)
-Petrol station Florence North-Florence South A1. „Scandicci", both directions
-Parking Motel Agip, exit Firenze Nord.

Foggia – Puglia

CRUISING

-Porta Manfredonia (T)
-Piazza Cavour (at night)
-Viale XXIV Maggio
-Railway Station (R) (also in the gardens and on the square to the right of the station)
-Viale della Stazione.

Gaeta – Lazio

SWIMMING

Arenauta Beach (better known as „Spiaggia dei 300 Gradini"). Half way between Rome & Naples. 3 km from Gaeta on the SS213 coastal road „Flacca". Parking is not allowed on the coas'tal road. By rail / bus: From Formia train station take the Cotral bus line to Sperlonga-Terracina (Mon-Sat). Request the stop „Le Scissure". The nudist area is between „L'ultima Spiaggia" and „Le Scissure". Action in rocky coves. Nudism is tollerated here but not legal.

Gallarate – Lombardia

SAUNAS/BATHS

■ **New Flug** (AC B G m MC RR SA SB VS WH) 15-1h, Sat closed
Strada Pradisera 58, Ingresso Azalee B *Near Malpensa airport*
☏ 0331 24 59 59 🖳 www.newflug.org
Uno Club card required.

Gallipoli – Puglia

GUEST HOUSES

■ **Lune Saracene B&B** (BF G MA NU)
Open from 1 April to 31 October
Contrada Capoccia Scorcialupi ✉ 74020 Maruggio (TA) *S.P.122 Litoranea Salentina angolo 6a via* ☏ 333 7351904 🖳 www.lunesaracene.it
Lunesaracene is the ideal place to discover the magic Apulia.
Our house, near the sea, is at the center of the main tourist itineraries ranging from the Valle d'Itria to Salento.

APARTMENTS

■ **Casa Nina** (glm OS)
☎ 0583730170 ☎ 3666854281 (mobile) www.tuscanysalentoholidays.com
Beautiful property in Puglia in the historic center of small village of Specchia, between Gallipoli and Lecce. Casa Nina is divided into four separate apartments but can also be used as a single house, for up to 15 people.

SWIMMING

-Spiaggia Libera (From Gallipoli go to Ugento. Action in the pine forest on the right 1 km behind the Hotel Costa Brada)
-Fico d'India (between Porto Cesarea and S. Catarina, cliffs down at the kiosk).

Garda – Veneto

GUEST HOUSES

■ **Relais San Michele** (b BF glm I M PA PK RWS RWT)
Località Cason degli Ulivi, 11, Rivoli Veronese *5 km from Garda Lake, 20 km from Verona, only 1 km from highway A22 exit Affi/ Lago di Garda sud*
☎ 045 732 81 42 www.relaissanmichele.it
Gay owned, friendly & nice place with a wonderful garden overviewing a canal next to the lake of Garda. Relaxed atmosphere, house built in 1844, recently renovated, ideal for romantic holidays. Restaurant in the house.

SWIMMING

-Punta S. Viglio at Baia delle Sirene, at the end and on the right side of the nudist beach, action day and evening, in summer only (take the APT Bus 62-64, stop at S. Viglio).

Genova – Liguria

GAY INFO

■ **Arcigay L'Approdo** Helpline: Thu from 14-17 & 21-23h
Vico Mezzagalera 3 ☎ 010 56 59 71 ☎ (347) 0011818 (mobile)
www.arcigaygenova.it
Thu: Free legal counseling from 14 to 17h and free phone counseling from 21 to 23h.

BARS

■ **Aqua Club** (AC B DR MA VS) Thu-Sat 21.30-2h
Salita Salvatore Viale 15/R *Bus 20/30/18, near Via XX Settembre*
☎ 010 58 84 89
Cruising bar.

■ **Cage. La** (AC B d G m MA P) 21-2h, closed Mon
Via Sampierdarena 167/R *Bus 20/1* ☎ 010 645 45 55 (infoline)
Disco bar. Arci Card required. Next to Virgo Disco.

MEN'S CLUBS

■ **Lussurian Club** (AC B DR G GH LAB MA SNU VR)
Thu 22-2.30, Fri & Sat 22-5.30, Sun 15-2h
Via Sanpierdana 112r *bus 20/1* ☎ 010 403 05 22 www.lussurian.it
New cruising bar. Uno Club card required.

DANCECLUBS

■ **Virgo** (AC B D DR GLM S) Sat 23.30-4.30h
Via Carzino 11/13 R *Exit Genova Ovest, parking Magazzini del Sale*
☎ 347 81 51 451 www.virgoclub.com
House & mainstream music with animation and show.

SEX CINEMAS

■ **Centrale** (g) Daily 10-24h
Via S. Vincenzo 13/R ☎ 010 58 03 80

SAUNAS/BATHS

■ **Aqua Club** (AC B DR DU G m MA P RR SA SB VS WH)
15-21h, closed Tue
Salita Salvatore Viale 15/R *Bus 20/30/18, near Via XX Settembre*
☎ 010 58 84 89
Uno Club card required. Special prices on Mon. The sauna adjoins a cruising bar.

HOTELS

■ **Helvetia** (AC B bf CC GLM H I MC OS PA PK RWB RWS RWT VA) 24hrs
Piazza Nunziata 1 *M° Gramsci* ☎ 010 24 65 468
www.hotelhelvetiagenova.it
33 rooms with shower/WC, mini-bar, own key, phone, TV and fax. Free WI-FI internet point. No smoking. Visitors and pets allowed. Totally renovated.

■ **Hotel Cairoli** (AC B BF CC glm I MSG PA RWS RWT VA WO)
All year
Via Cairoli, 14/4 *Near Piazza della Nunziata* ☎ 010 246 14 54
www.hotelcairoligenova.com
The huge rooms are inspired by famous modern and contemporary art and offer all comfort. Free Wifi access & internet point.

GENERAL GROUPS

■ **Key We Associazione Culturale Nazionale**
☎ 02 890 383 69 www.keywe.it
National association for the gay community.

HEALTH GROUPS

■ **LILA – Lega Italiana Lotta contro l'AIDS** Mon-Fri 9-12, 13-15h
☎ 010 24 62 915

SWIMMING

-Pieve Ligure (take the gate 200 m from the railway station, go down over the bridge and go to the sea climbing over the fence on the right hand (NU))
-Varigotti (near Savona, from Noli in direction of Varigotti, beautiful nudist beach is under the tower, find the way up and the rope to go down).

CRUISING

-Mura delle Cappucine and Giardini Coco (gardens, (ayor), near Galliera hospital, by car and by foot at night)
-Punta Vagno (Giardini Govi, near the water clearing plant Corso Italia, mainly in summer by foot by day and at night).

Gorizia – Friuli – Venezia Giulia

BOOK SHOPS

■ **Libreria Equilibri** (g)
Via del Seminario 8 ☎ 0481 53 21 28

HEALTH GROUPS

■ **Centro Malattie sessualmente trasmesse**
Mon-Fri 8-14, Sat 8-12h
Via Mazzini 7 ☎ 0481 59 28 19
Anonymous HIV tests and other STD.

Grosseto – Toscana

GAY INFO

■ **Arcigay Leonardo Da Vinci** Helpline: Thu 16-20h
Via Parini 7/e ☎ 0564 49 05 65 🖳 www.grossetogay.it
■ **Friendly Maremma**
☎ 0564 49 05 65 🖳 www.friendlymaremma.it
Association to promote gay and gayfriendly locations of the region.

GUEST HOUSES

■ **La Tana dei Lupi** (B glm M)
Via del Corso, Montorgiali *17 km from Grosseto* ☎ 0564 58 02 21
🖳 www.latanadeilupi.com
Romantic ancient house with excellent panoramic views in the Tuscan hills. Rooms with sat-TV, private bath and Wi-Fi. Also restaurant on site.
■ **Valdonica Vineyard Residence & Winery**
(AC BF CC G I MA OS PI WO)
Via Dogana 1, Sassofortino *35 km from Grosseto* ☎ 0564 567 251
🖳 www.valdonica.com
Valdonica is a great landhouse residence & winery in the beautiful rolling hills of Tuscany, not far from the Mediterrean Sea. Worldwide wine delivery, winery tour & degustation. Free Wifi.

SWIMMING

-Marina di Alberese (wonderful natural landscape, many gays, crowded)
-Marina di Grosseto (along the SS 322 „delle Collacchie", 3 miles south of Castiglione delle Pesciaia, near „Le Marse" camping).

Ischia – Campania

HOTELS

■ **Capizzo** (AC CC H M OS PI SOL) 8 Apr-14 Oct
Via Provinciale Panza 189, loc. Citara *500 m from the sea*
☎ 081 90 71 68 🖳 www.hotelcapizzo.it
34 rooms with private bathroom, AC, phone, sat-TV, fridge, safe and sea view. Also thermal swimming pool (32°C) and garden. Small pets allowed.
■ **Residence Villa Ravino** (CC glm MSG OS PI SOL WH WO)
Via II Mura (Loc. Citara) ☎ 081 99 77 83 🖳 www.ravino.it

CRUISING

-Harbour in Porto on the left side near lighthouse
-Maronti beach behind Hotel La Jondola.

Ivrea – Piemonte

CRUISING

-Parking Pietra Grossa (motorway A5 Torino – Aosta, direction Torino, between Scarmagno and S. Giorgio Canavese)
-Piazza del Rondolino, close to Cinema Sirio (by car).

L'Aquila – Abruzzo

GAY INFO

■ **Arcigay Massimo Consoli**
☎ 339 87 94 768

Latina – Lazio

CRUISING

-Railway station (Piazzale del Palazzetto dello Sport)
-Viale Michelangelo
-Via dei Mille.

Livorno – Toscana

GAY INFO

■ **Arcigay Il Faro**
Piazza della Libertà 14, Cecina (LI) ☎ 320 81 71 758
🖳 www.arcigaylivornese.it

SWIMMING

-Sassoscritto (NU) on the cliffs (9 miles south of Livorno, near restaurant Sassoscritto, at km 304 marker on the Aurelia road).

CRUISING

-Piazza Dante (r) (in front of railway station at night)
-Zona industriale Picchianti (highway exit Livorno Centro. Follow centre indications. At the Circus, drive to Picchianti Industrial Area. In the open area, at night)
-Lungomare dell'Ardenza (on the seaside, near Bagni Fiume, south of the Naval Academy, in the afternoon and at night, on foot, on the seaside and on the steps).

Lucca – Toscana

MEN'S CLUBS

■ **Catch Club** (B cc D DR F G m MA NU P S SNU VS) Wed-Sun 16-4h
Via di Poggio II 29, Ponte San Pietro ☎ 0583 32 70 34
☎ 347 357 0204 (mobile) 🖳 www.catchclub.it
Uno Club card required. Wed half price, Thu masked event, Fri live sex. Discount entry for those under 25 years.

DANCECLUB

■ **RMX** (AC B CC D DR GLM S ST YC) Oct-Apr Sat 23-5h
c/o HUB, Via di Poggio II 29, Ponte San Pietro *Bus 12 from railway station*
☎ 0583 327034 ☎ 345 13 47 346 (mobile) 🖳 www.rmxdisco.it
Two dancefloors with house and mainstream with drag shows.

GUEST HOUSES

■ **Gemma di Elena. La** (BF glm I PA PK RWB RWS RWT VA) All year
Via della Zecca 33 *Centre* ☎ 0583 49 66 65
🖳 www.virtualica.it/gemma

CRUISING

-Hospital, Via Delano Roosevelt and streets nearby (by car at night)
-Porta Elisa (inside of the city walls, near the ramparts, on the right side of the city gate, on foot).

Malcesine – Veneto

SWIMMING

-Scogli delle Gallerie (State road to Riva del Garda, park your car at the last tunnel before Torbole. Then follow the path and go to the little beaches, nudity, action on the paths).

Mantova – Lombardia

GAY INFO

■ **Arcigay La Salamandra**
Piazza Tom Benetollo 1 ☎ 0376 28 53 218 🖳 www.arcigaymantova.it

SEX SHOPS/BLUE MOVIES

■ **Tuttisensi** (g MA VS) Closed Mon 9.30-12-30h
Via Vivenza 60 *Near the Sub-ring* ☎ 0376 26 35 02

GUEST HOUSES

■ **B&B Al Mincio** (BF H) All year, closed Jan 15th-Feb 28th
Stradello Croce 43 *Located near Mantova within the Mincio River Park*
☎ 0376 302 519 💻 www.bbalmincio.it
Ideally located for visiting art and cultural towns like Mantova, Verona, Modena and Ferrara. Ideal for a romantic stay in a cosy place. 40 km from the famous Garda lake.

■ **Guesthouse Virgiliana** (BF glm I OS)
Via Frizzi 2 ☎ 0376 27 03 08 ☎ 347 45 00 980 (mobile)
💻 www.guesthouse-virgiliana.it
Gay owned guesthouse. Rooms with private bath, tv and balcony. Bike rental.

CRUISING

-Piazzale Palazzo Te (at night)

Mariano Comense – Lombardia

RESTAURANTS

■ **Riso Amaro** (AC b CC glm H M MC OS PA PK WL) Mon-Sat 12-14.30 & 19-midnight
via Milano *20 km from Milan* ☎ 031 750 997 💻 www.risoamaro.it

Merano/Meran – Trentino-Alto Adige

CRUISING

-Gilf-Promenade between Ponte Romano/Steinerne Steg and Ponte Tappeiner.

Milano – Lombardia

Milan is well known as a bustling media and fashion city. People work hard and when they go out in the evening they want to be seen. With this background it is hardly surprising that Milan shares with Rome the title of the gay capital of Italy. Also the good chance of finding work attracts many gay people to the country's financial capital. What's on offer is equally great. The scene has become more differentiated in recent years and now has something to offer for virtually every taste: youngsters meet at "Vogue Ambition" and "Mama-Off" on Fridays or at Borgo for "Join the Gap" on Sundays, "Pourhomme" at Magazzini Generali is the place to be on Saturdays, while the leather crowd and bears congregate in "Company".
Sauna-lovers will find much to enjoy here and whoever is after sex only will get lucky in Milan in no time at all. Several permanently well-attended cruise bars (Cruising Canyon, Flexo, Illumined) are located near the Stazione Centrale, unless of course one prefers to visit one of the themed sex parties such as the "Naked Party" in "Depot".
One of Milan's specialties is its "Aperitivi" in the early evening, where you can help yourself to a drink from the buffet.
From a gay point of view Milan is certainly worth a visit. Although the bars and clubs are spread out across the city, most of them can be reached by underground train which runs until midnight.

Mailand ist bekannt als frenetische Mode- und Medienstadt. Man arbeitet viel und will sich dann abends zeigen. Vor diesem Hintergrund verwundert es kaum, dass sich Mailand mit Rom den Titel schwule Hauptstadt Italiens teilt. Doch auch die hohe Wahrscheinlichkeit, hier eine Arbeit zu finden, lockt viele Schwule in das wirtschaftliche Zentrum des Landes. Dementsprechend groß ist das Angebot. Die Szene hat sich in den letzten Jahren differenziert, sodass für fast jeden Geschmack etwas dabei ist: Junges Publikum trifft sich freitags bei „Vogue Ambition" und bei „Mama-Off" oder sonntags im Borgo bei „Join the Gap", samstags sind die Magazzini Generali „Pourhomme" angesagt, die Ledermänner und Bären treffen sich hingegen im „Company". Saunaliebhaber kommen voll auf ihre Kosten, und auch wer lediglich Sex sucht, wird in Mailand leicht fündig: In der Nähe der Stazione Centrale gibt es mehrere stets gut besuchte Cruisingläden (Cruising Canyon, Flexo, Illumined), oder aber man geht auf spezielle Sexpartys wie z. B. auf eine Naked Party im Depot.
Eine Besonderheit Mailands sind seine „Aperitivi" am frühen Abend: Zu einem Drink kann man sich am Buffet bedienen. Mailand ist also unter schwulen Gesichtspunkten eine Reise wert. Und die Lokale sind, obwohl sie über die ganze Stadt verteilt sind, bis Mitternacht meist gut mit der U-Bahn erreichbar.

Milan est célèbre pour ses défilés de mode et ses medias. Les gens travaillent beaucoup et se montrent le soir. Il n'est donc pas étonnant que cette ville se dispute avec Rome le titre de capitale gay du pays. Mais c'est peut-être la forte probabilité d'y trouver du travail qui attire nombre de gays à Milan, centre économique de l'Italie. La scène s'est diversifiée ces dernières années: un publique jeune se retrouve le vendredi au « Vogue Ambition » et « Mama-Off » ou le dimanche dans le Borgo au « Join the Gap », le samedi les Magazzini Generali « Pourhomme » sont courus alors que les types cuir et bear se retrouvent au « Company ». Les amoureux des saunas en ont pour leur argent et celui qui recherche un plan baise saura facilement trouver ce qu'il lui faut : Il y en a plusieurs bons pour la drague et bien fréquentés dans les environs de la Stazione Centrale (Cruising Canyon, Flexo, Illumined), ou alors on va dans des parties spéciales comme par ex. une Naked Party au „Depot".
Une particularité milanaise sont ses „aperitivi" en début de soirée : pour une boisson, on peut se servir au buffet. Díun point de vue gay, Milan mérite aussi un séjour. Bien que les bars soient éparpillés dans toute la ville, ils sont pour la plupart faciles à atteindre jusquía minuit avec le métro.

Milán es conocida por ser la frenética ciudad de la moda y los medios. Se trabaja mucho y luego, por la noche, uno quiere salir. Ante estas razones, no sorprende que Milán comparta con Roma el título de la capital gay de Italia . También las múltiples posibilidades de encontrar un trabajo atrae a muchos gays hacia el centro económico del país. En consecuencia, la oferta es grande. El ambiente gay se ha diferenciado mucho en los últimos años, por lo que siempre se encuentra algo para casi todos los gustos: el público más joven se reúne los viernes en el "Vogue Ambition" y en el "Mama-Off" o los domingos en el Borgo junto al "Join the Gap", los sábados se anuncia la Magazzini Generali "Pour Homme", por el contrario, los aficionados al cuero y los osos se encuentran en el "Company".
Los amantes de la sauna se divertirán y aquellos que sólo busquen sexo, en Milán lo encontrarán fácilmente: cerca de la estación central hay varios locales de ligue muy concurridos (Cruising Canyon, Flexo, Illumined) o bien se puede ir a fiestas especiales como a una naked party en "Depot".
Una especialidad de Milán son sus "aperitivi" de media tarde: junto con la bebida, puede uno disfrutar del bufet.
Milán, en el aspecto gay, merece la pena un viaje. Aunque los locales están repartidos por toda la ciudad, por lo general están bien comunicados en metro hasta la medianoche.

Milano è famosa come frenetica città della moda e dei mass media. Qui si lavora molto e di sera ci si vuole mettere un pò in mostra. Milano insieme a Roma si contende il titolo di capitale gay dell'Italia. Ad attirare molti gay nella capitale economica d'Italia è la buona probabilità di trovare un lavoro. Altrettanto buona è l'offerta. Negli ultimi anni la scena gay di Milano si è andata sempre più differenziando. Oggi Milano offre infatti qualcosa per tutti i gusti. Il pubblico giovane si incontra il venerdì da "Vogue Ambition" o da "Mama-Off", la domenica al Borgo al "Join the Gap". Sabato sono molto in voga i Magazzini Generali "Pourhomme"; gli orsi e gli amanti del leather si incontrano invece al "Company". Gli amanti delle saune gay ameranno questa città. Chi cerca del sesso troverà sicuramente qualcosa a Milano: nei pressi della stazione centrale ci sono diversi locali per il cruising che sono sempre ben frequentati (Cruising Canyon, Flexo, Illumined) o sex party a tema come per esempio il naked party al Depot. Una specialità di Milano sono gli aperitivi in prima serata: bevendo un aperitivo ci si può spesso servire al buffet.
Dal punto di vista gay, vale davvero la pena visitare Milano. Anche se i locali sono un po sparsi per la città, sono ben raggiungibili fino a mezzanotte con la metropolitana.

GAY INFO

Centro di Iniziativa Gay (CIG) Mon-Fri 15-20h
Via Bezzecca 3 ☎ 02 54 12 22 25 www.arcigaymilano.org
Helpline: ☎ 02 54 12 22 27 (Mon, Tue, Thu, Fri 20-23h). Political and cultural activities, conferences, international library and archive, anti-Aids programme, gay pride, school group. Sun welcome group 15.30-19.30h. Contact for gay sports groups.

SHOWS

Zeligay Cabaret (AC B GLM m MA OS S) Fri 21-?h
Viale Monza 140 *M° Gorla* ☎ 02 25 50 121 (for reservations)
From Oct to May: Dragshow on Fri with famous comedians. Visit www.areazelig.it for the programme.

CULTURE

Biblioteca, Videoteca, Centro di Documentazione Omologie Mon, Wed, Fri 15-20; Wed 21-23; Sun 16-18h
c/o C.I.G., Via Bezzecca 3 ☎ 02 541 22 225
www.arcigaymilano.org
Books, videos, library & documentation centre.

BARS

Afterline (AC B D GLM MA P SNU) 21-2, Fri & Sat -3h, Sun closed
Via Sammartini 25 *M° Stazione Centrale* ☎ 339 38 76 398
www.afterline.eu
Fri Go-go-boys, Fri & Sat DJ.

Beerbanti. I (B glm) 8-2h, closed Sun
Via A. Solari 52 ☎ 02 42 29 76 12

G-Lounge (AC B bf CC d glm m MA OS)
8-3, Sat & Sun 18-3, Mon 8-22h
Via Larga 8 *M° Duomo, bus 60* ☎ 02 80 53 042
www.glounge.it
Trendy cocktail bar with DJ. Happy hour 18-21h.

Lelephant (AC B glm m) 18.30-2h, Mon closed
Via Melzo 22 *Metro Porta Venezia* ☎ 02 29 51 87 68
Nice bar with many gays. Good pre-dinners (aperitivi). Popular on Wed.

Club 23 (AC B CC G M MA) 22-?h, Mon closed
Via Sammartini 23 *100 m from the railway station, M° Centrale*
☎ 333 89 12 029 (mobile)
Bar next to Afterline and XLine. Special events. Free membercard.

Mono Bar (AC B GLM m MA OS) Tue 18.30-1, Wed & Thu 18.30-1.30, Fri & Sat 18.30-2, Sun 18.30-1h, Mon closed
Via Lecco 6 *M° Porta Venezia* ☎ 339 48 10 264
www.myspace.com/monomilano
One of the most crowded bars at the moment. Good aperitivo (pre-dinner) in the early evening.

Next Groove Café (AC B glm m MA r) 12-2h
Via Sammartini 23 *M° Stazione Centrale* ☎ 348 74 44 957 (mobile)
Day & night bar in the gay street of Milan with some hustlers.

rha bar (AC B GLM m OS) 19-2h, Mon closed
Via Alzaia Naviglio Grande 150 *Navigli district, tram 2* ☎ 393 971 95 61
www.rhabar.it
Lounge offering cocktails & aperitivi (pre-dinners) 19-21.30h. Wed-Sat with DJ, Sat & Sun large buffet, Thu live music. Exhibitions, various events.

MEN'S CLUBS

Company Club (AC B DR F G P VS WI) 21.30-2, Fri & Sat -6, Sun 19-2h
Via Benadir 14 ☎ 347 32 31 073 (mobile) www.companyclub.org
Equipped darkroom. Popular on Fri & weekend with DJ. Thu karaoke. Sun aperitivo with buffet. Welcome bears, leather, chubbies, daddy & chaser and friends. No fashion. Smoking area.

Cruising Canyon (! AC CC DR G MA P VS)
16-8h, Fri 16-Mon 8h (non-stop)
Via G. Paisiello 4 *M° Loreto/Piola* ☎ 02 20 40 42 01
www.cruisingcanyon.com
Very popular large cruising area on 3 floors. Uno Club card required.

AFTERLINE
YOUR FAVOURITE GAY
BAR in MILAN
ITALIA 2011
Foto di Luca Guadagni

Milano
EAT & DRINK
Beerbanti. I – Bar 9
G-Lounge – Bar 4
Rhabar – Bar 15
NIGHTLIFE
Barbarella Club – Danceclub 1
Bomberos – Danceclub 11
Cockette = That's All – Danceclub 8
Company Club – Men's Club 13
Flexo Club – Men's Club 12
HD – Danceclub 10
Plastic – Danceclub 8
Playroom – Danceclub 13
Mama-Off – Danceclub 3
SEX
Fenix – Sauna 12
Royal Hammam – Sauna 11
Thermas – Sauna 7
OTHERS
Centro di Iniziativa Gay – Gay Group 5
Downtown – Fitness Studio 14
Get Fit – Fitness Studio 6
N
See map B
Viala Jenner
Viale Marche
Maciachini
Viale Zara
Zara
Sondrio
Viale Lunigiana
Staz. Merci
Via Bassi
Stazione Centrale
Cimitero Monumentale
Via C. Farini
Garibaldi F.S.
Via De Castillia
Via M. Gioia
Piazza Duca D'Aosta
Gioia
Centrale F.S.
Via Monviso
V. Crispi
B. Pta. Nuova
V. Montello
Piazza Repubblica
Moscova
Via Moscova
Repubblica
Bast. Pta. Venezia
Via Bertani
Giardini Pubblici
ParcoSempione
Turati
Via Pagano
Lanza
Via Pontaccio
Corso Venezia
Castello Sforzesco
Cadorna
Palestro
Prefettura
Buonarotti
Pagano
Conciliazione
Cairoli
Via Broletto
Monte-napoleone
Wagner
Corso Vercelli
Corso Magenta
Via Carducci
Via Manzoni
San Babila
Viale Bianca Maria V.
Cordusio
Duomo
Duomo
S. Ambrogio
Viale Papiniano
Via de Amicis
Via Torino
Missori
Universita
Via Franc. Sforza
S. Agostino
Via Foppa
Corso Italia
Crocetta
C.Colombo
C.Simonetta
P.ta Genova F.S.
Via Vigevano
Ple. XXIV Maggio
Corso Porta Romana
P.ta Romana
Viale Beatrice D'Este
Ripa di Porta Ticinese
S. Gottardo
Via Tabacchi

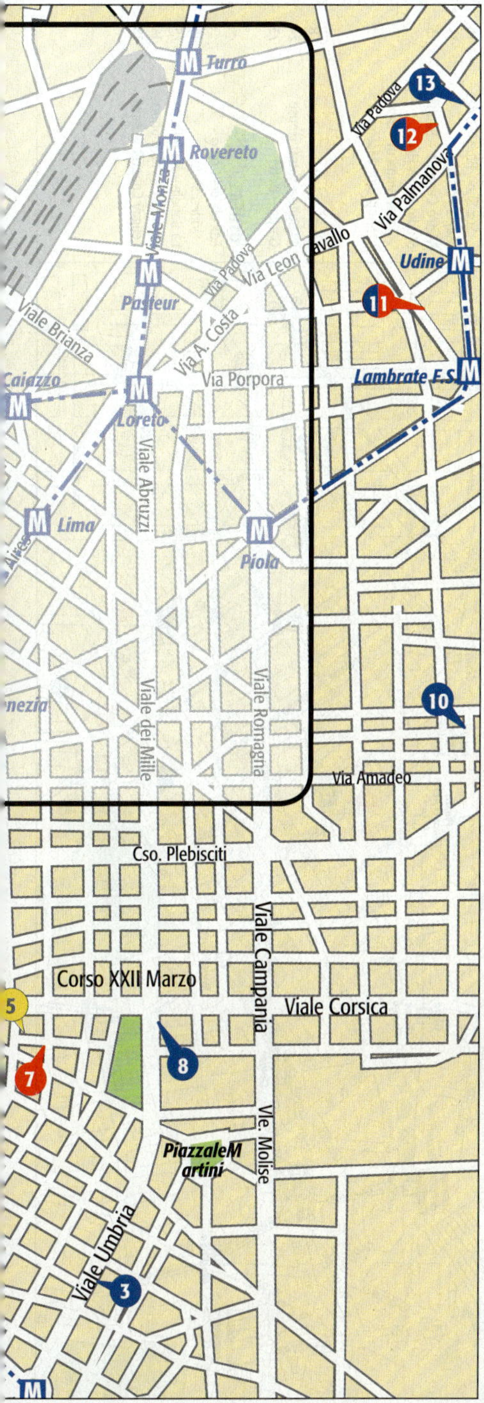

Turro
Rovereto
Viale Monza
Via Padova
Via Palmanova
Via Leon Cavallo
Udine
Pasteur
Via Padova
Via A. Costa
Viale Brianza
Caiazzo
Via Porpora
Lambrate F.S.
Loreto
Viale Abruzzi
Lima
Piola
Viale dei Mille
Viale Romagna
Via Amadeo
Cso. Plebisciti
Corso XXII Marzo
Viale Campania
Viale Corsica
Vle. Molise
PiazzaleM artini
Viale Umbria

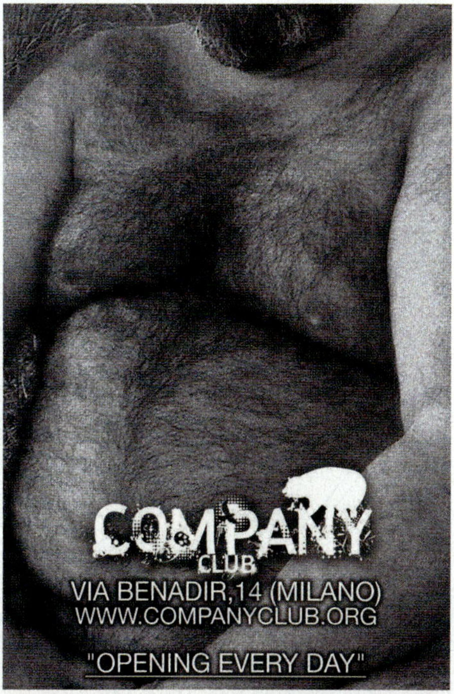

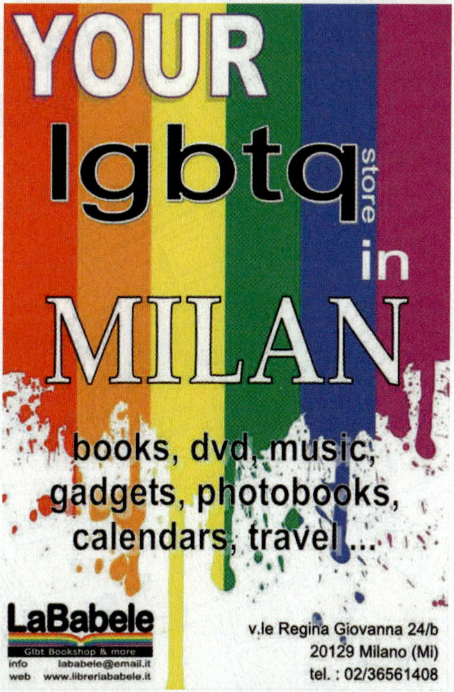

Milano – Map B
EAT & DRINK
Afterline – Bar 4
Chiar di Luna – Restaurant 2
Grani & Braci – Restaurant 20
Lelephant – Bar 12
Club 23 – Bar 5
Mono – Bar 1
Next Groove Café – Bar 5
NIGHTLIFE
Barbarella – Danceclub 10
Cruising Canyon – Men's Club 9
Depot – Men's Club 19
Illumined – Men's Club 17
XClub Cruising – Men's Club 4
SEX
Erotika Video Shop – Sex Shop/Blue Movies 13
Europa92 – Sex Shop/Blue Movies 16
Magic – Sauna 11
Metrò Centrale – Sauna 3
Studio Know How Entertainment – Sex Shop/Blue Movies 7
ACCOMMODATION
Charly – Hotel 8
44 suite – Guest House 24
Garda – Hotel 23
OTHERS
Edicola del Corso – Video Shop 15
La Babele – Bookshop 25
Oberdan – Video Shop 14
Zeligay Cabaret – Show 18
Stazione Centrale
Piazza IV Novembre
Piazza Duca D'Aosta
Piazza Luigi di Savoia
Centrale
Gioia
Garibaldi
Stazione di Porta Garibaldi
Repubblica
Giardini Pubblici
Venezia
Turati
Moscova
Zara
Sondrio
Maciachini
Caiazzo
Loreto
Lima
Piola
Pasteur
Rovereto
Turro
Ospedale
Viale Monza
Viale Zara
Corso Buenos Aires
Viale Monte Santo
Bastioni Porta Venezia

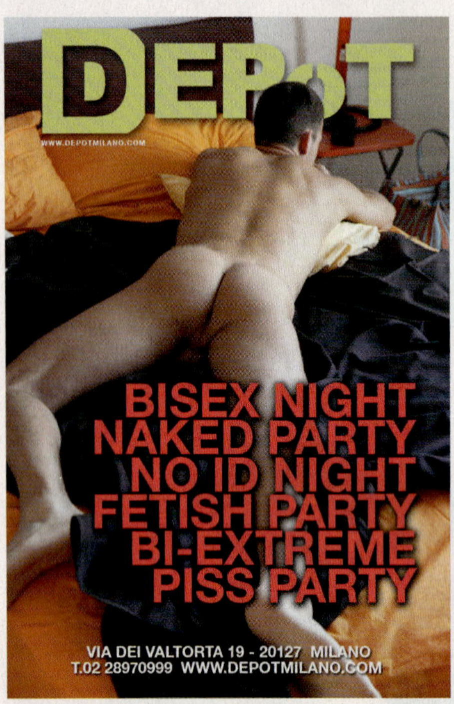

■ **Depot** (AC B CC DR F G MA P S VS)
Mon-Wed 22-3, Fri & Sat 22-open end, Sun 15-22h. Thu closed.
Via dei Valtorta 19 *M° Turro* ☎ 02 28 97 09 99
💻 www.depotmilano.com
Cruising bar on 2 floors. Mon bisex, Tue „No ID" party, Wed, Fri & Sun Naked/Underwear party. Sat changing program. Smoking area. Key We card required.

■ **Flexo Club** (AC B CC DR f G MA NU OS P VS)
21-?, Fri & Sat -7, Sun 15-?h, Mon closed
Via Oropa 3 *M° Cimiano* ☎ 02 26 82 67 09
💻 www.flexoclub.it
Cruising bar next to sauna Metrò Cimiano. Tue & Thu 21-?h naked party, Sun 13-21h lounge. Smoking zone, summer garden.

■ **Illumined** (AC B CC DR f G m MA P SNU VS) Daily, 24hrs
Via Napo Torriani 12 *M° Centrale* ☎ 02 66 98 50 60
💻 www.club-illumined.com
Cruising bar on 3 floors. Hardcore zone in the third floor, special parties (naked, fist, fetish). Uno club card & passport required.

■ **Transfer** (B D G MA PI VS WE)
Via Breda 158 ☎ 02 4966 3786 ☎ 346 750 5875 (mobile)
💻 www.transferdisco.it
Transfer has two levels: upstairs there is a bar and cruising area, downstairs you find the disco, video room, swimming pool and jacuzzi.

■ **XClub Cruising** (AC B BF DR G m MA r SNU VS)
22-6, Mon & Tue closed
Via Sammartini 25 *M° Stazione Centrale* ☎ 02 67 07 06 83
💻 www.xclubmilano.com
Cruising bar with cabins. Wed naked party, Thu orgia party, Fri sex live show, Sat show. Uno Club card required.

DANCECLUBS

■ **Barbarella Club** (AC B D G MA S WE) Sat 23.30-?h
c/o Shocking Club, Bastioni di Porta Nuova 12 *M° Porta Garibaldi*

☎ 345 26 53 431 (mobile) 💻 www.barbarellaclub.com
House & electronic music.

■ **Bomberos** (AC B CC D G MA S) Sat 23-5h
Via Plezzo 16 *Exit Tangenziale Lambrate* ☎ 02 21 55 800
Disco club in a location next to the sauna Royal Hammam.

■ **Cockette** (AC B D G MA) Fri midnight-5h
c/o Plastic, Viale Umbria 120 *Tram 12/24, bus 92*
💻 www.cocketteparty.com
Hetero-friendly, alternative party for bears and friends. Techno and acid house. See www.cocketteparty.com

■ **HD** (AC B D G MA S WE) 23-5h
Via Tajani 11/Via Caruso *Bus 61, entrance Via Caruso*
☎ 02 71 89 90
Mon go-go boys, cabaret show on Tue, Fri: strip & disco, Sat: disco, trash & 80ties music. Popular at WE.

■ **Join the Gap** (! AC B D GLM M YC)
Sun 20.30h restaurant and show, disco from 22h
c/o Borgo del Tempo Perso, Via Fabio Massimo 36
☎ 02 54 12 22 25
The most crowded party in town, better known as „Borgo". Mainstream, R&B, house music on different dancefloors. The night starts with a dinner.

■ **K O Club** 22-3. Fri & Sat -6h
Via Resegone 1 ☎ 339 77 97 450 💻 www.koclubmilano.com

■ **Mama-Off** (AC B D GLM S WE YC) Fri 23-?h
c/o Cafe Atlantique, Viale Umbria 42 *Metro Lodi*
☎ 345 1347346 (infoline) 💻 www.mamamiadisco.it
New Friday night organized by Mama Mia Crew of Torre del Lago (Viareggio). Mainstream & house music.

■ **Nuova Idea International** (AC B D GLM M MA OS S T) Sat 22-5h
Via Alcide de Gasperi 14, Corsico *Corsico, between Lorenteggio and Ikea, close to Roadhouse* ☎ 02 39930955 ☎ 333 4816780
💻 www.lanuovaidea.com
Two dance halls, drag shows, striptease. Italian music, mainstream & house. See www.lanuovaidea.com. New location.

■ **One Way Club** (AC B D DR f G MA P VS) Sat 23-4.30h
Via Felice Cavallotti 204, 20122 Sesto S. Giovanni *M° Sesto-Marelli, Sesto Rondo* ☎ 02 24 21 341 💻 www.oneway.it
Mainstream music. Also parties for bears. Uno Club card required.

■ **Plastic** (B D GLM MA) Thu-Sun 23-?h
Viale Umbria 120 *Tram 12/24, bus 92* ☎ 02 73 39 96
💻 www.thisisplastic.com
3 dancefloors with house & electronic music.

■ **Playroom** (AC B D DR G MA OS P VS) Fri & Sat 22.30-5h
Via Derna 26 ☎ 347 32 31 073 (mobile) 💻 www.companyclub.org
New disco club close to Company with cruising area. International DJs in the weekend. Uno Club card required.

■ **Pourhomme** (AC B D GLM S WE YC) Sat 23-5h
c/o Magazzini Generali, Via Pietrasanta 16 ☎ 333 66 56 658
💻 www.pourhomme.tv
Gay party in Milan in one of the most famous clubs. Mainstream & house music, young crowd. See www.pourhomme.tv

■ **Vogue Ambition** (AC B D GLM YC) Fri 23.30-4h
c/o Black Hole, Viale Umbria 118 ☎ 339 13 87 983 (mobile)
☎ 348 86 17 420 (mobile)
New gay party event on Fri. Mixed music and young crowd.

RESTAURANTS

■ **Chiar di Luna** (AC B CC gLm M MA S)
12-15h, 18.30-2h, closed Mon evening
Via Borsieri 14 *M° Garibaldi; bus 31/82* ☎ 02 68 85 54 35
Pizzeria and more. In the evening pub with pool table and tabletop football. Fri/Sat DJ & live music. Mainly lesbians.

■ **Grani & Braci** (AC b CC glm M OS PA PK WL) Daily 12-14.30 & 19-24h
via Carlo Farini / Via Giuseppe Ferrari ☎ 02 3663 7422
💻 www.graniebraci.it
Huge restaurant close to the new fashion district. Steak house & pizzeria.

SEX SHOPS/BLUE MOVIES

Erotika Video Shop (g) Mon-Sat 9-21, Sun 13.30-19.30h
Via Melzo 19 *Cnr. Buenos Aires* ☎ 02 29 52 18 49
www.sexerotika.it

Europa92 (g)
Via G.B. Sammartini 25 ☎ 02 66 98 24 48 www.europa92.com
Sex shop with videocabins.

Studio Know How Entertainment (G) 9.30-19.30h, Sun closed
Via Antonio da Recanate 7 *M° Centrale F. S.* ☎ 02 67 39 12 24
Gay articles, videos.

SAUNAS/BATHS

Alexander's Club
(AC B DR DU F G m MA MSG R SA SB SOL VS) 13-1h
Via Pindaro 23 *M° Villa S. Giovanni* ☎ 02 25 50 220
www.alexandersauna.net
Two floors. The right place for lovers of S/M.

Fenix Sauna (G MA P)
Via Oropa 3 *M° Cimiano* ☎ (02) 28510528
Former Metro Sauna Cimiano. At the same building as gay cruising club Flexo.

Magic (B DU G m MSG OS R SA SB SOL VS) 12-24h
Via Maiocchi 8 *4th floor* ☎ 02 29 40 61 82

Metrò Milano Centrale (AC B cc DR DU f FC FH G I LAB m MSG P RR SA SB SOL VS WH YC) 12-2, Sat -3h
Via Schiaparelli 1 *M° Centrale* ☎ 02 66 71 90 89 www.metroclub.it
Popular and hygenic sauna on 3 floors. Uno Club card required.

Royal Hammam (! AC B CC DR DU FC FH G M MA MSG OS P PI RR SA SB SOL VS WH) 12-2, Fri -3, Sat 12- Mon 1h non stop
Via Plezzo 16 *Railway station & M° Lambrate* ☎ 02 26 41 21 89
www.royalhammam.com
Huge, friendly and very popular sauna with a swimming pool and all the usual amenities as well as great decor. Next door to disco Bomberos. Uno Club card required.

Thermas (AC B DR DU FC FH G m MA SA SB WH WO)
12-24, Fri & Sat -2h, closed Mon
Via Bezzecca 9 (in the courtyard) *Tram 9/12/23/27/29/30, bus 60/62/73/84 – Cinque Giornate from M° Duomo* ☎ 02 54 50 355
www.thermasclub.com
Hygienic, relaxed sauna and friendly atmosphere. Jacuzzi and Turkish bath. Special discount for those under 26 years of age, after 20h and on Tuesday. Free buffet Sun from 18h.

FITNESS STUDIOS

Down Town (g) Mon-Fri 7-23, Sat & Sun 10-20h
Piazza Diaz 6 *M° Duomo* ☎ 02 86 31 181

Get Fit (g PI) Mon-Thu 7-23.30, Fri 9-23.30, Sat & Sun 10-20h
Viale Piacenza 4 *M° Porta Romana* ☎ 02 54 69 900

BOOK SHOPS

Babele. La (CC GLM)
Mon 15.30-20, Tue-Sat 10.30-20, Sun 15.30-20h
Viale Regina Giovanna 24/B *Near Corso Buenos Aires, Metro Porta Venezia, Bus 5/33* ☎ 02 36 56 14 08 www.libreriababele.it
Libreria Babele is back again with new owners: Books, magazines, DVDs, fotography, art, clothes, gadgets and more. Also mail order at www.libreriababele.it.

DVD SHOPS

Edicola del Corso (g) 24hrs
Corso Buenos Aires 9 *Cnr. Viale Tunisia* ☎ 02 29 53 01 03
www.edicolaccia.com
International videos, DVDs & magazines.

Oberdan (g) 24hrs
Piazza G. Oberdan, Ang. Via Tadino ☎ 02 29 53 15 09
www.edicolaccia.com
International videos, DVDs & magazines.

HOTELS

■ **Charly** (B BF CC glm I OS PK RWB RWS RWT)
24hrs, closed in August
Via Settala 76 *M° Lima 2/3, tram 1/33/60, 3 mins from central station*
☏ 02 204 71 90 💻 www.hotelcharly.com
Gay-friendly comfortable hotel with eighteen rooms in two villas, centrally located in the heart of Milan. All rooms have shower, some their own bath, balcony or terrace. Discount for Spartacus readers.

■ **Garda** (AC B BF CC H) Open all year except Christmas
Via Napo Torriani 21 *Close to central station* ☏ 02 66 98 26 26
💻 www.hotelgardamilan.com
Rooms with private bath, sat-TV, minibar and safe. Please book through the homepage. Discount for Spartacus users: Promocode SPAR4LESS

GUEST HOUSES

■ **44 suite** (AC bf CC g I)
Via Vitruvio 44 ☏ 02 49 45 80 49 💻 www.44suite.com
Small bed & breakfast centrally located. Rooms with bathroom, sat-TV, wireless internet and minibar. Gay owned and managed.

GENERAL GROUPS

■ **Agedo** Thu 14.30-17.30h
Via Bezzecca 4 ☏ 02 54 12 22 11
Association of parents of lesbians and gays.

■ **Key We Associazione Culturale Nazionale**
☏ 02 890 383 69 💻 www.keywe.it
National association for the gay community.

■ **Sportello Trans**
Via Boifava 60/A ☏ 02 89 51 64 64
💻 www.alainrete.org/sportellotrans.html
Support for transsexuals and transgender.

HEALTH GROUPS

■ **Anlaids** Helpline on Wed 18-20h
Via Monviso 28 ☏ 02 33 60 86 80

■ **ASA – Associazione Solidarietà AIDS** Mon-Fri 10-19h
Via Arena 25 *M° S. Agostino* ☏ 02 58 10 70 84 💻 www.asamilano.org
Information, advice, psychological and legal advice, self-help groups for HIV-positives, documentation centre.

SPECIAL INTEREST GROUPS

■ **Gay Statale**
c/o Università, Via Festa del Perdono 3 💻 www.gaystatalemilano.it
Gay students group. Cultural activities, parties & events.

SWIMMING

-Vigevano-River Ticino (On Milano-Vigevano road, 30 km, P at bridge; walk for about 2 km southwards down east bank; action everywhere and NU)
-Cassano d'Adda (30 km from Milano): River Adda beach, follow paths from Cassano-Rivolta road
-Piscina ‚Romano' (Via Ponzio, Metro-Piola, in summer).

CRUISING

-Cimitero Monumentale, Piazza Baiamonti, at night (ayor R T)
-Piazza Trento (R)
-Ortomercato/Via Monte Cimone (r by car, at night)
-Parco Nord (from Via Fulvio Testi before reaching Mc Donalds turn to the left into Via Fabrizio Clerici, the first street right), by night, popular (ayor)
-Public gardens Palestro (metro Porta Venezia), near kindergarten 17-23h
-Industrial zone, from Viale Forlanini, behind airport Linate, right hand at the entrance of village Canzo (busy)
-La Fossa (Viale Zola along the northern railway, cruisy day and night). La Fossa (Viale Emilio Zola along the northern railway, cruisy day and night, ayor)

Modena – Emilia Romagna

GAY INFO

■ **Arcigay Matthew Shepard** Mon 21-23h
Via IV Novembre 40/A ☎ 348 76 69 298 (infoline)
🖳 www.arcigaymodena.org

CRUISING

-Giardino Ducale
-A1 Milano → Roma P Castelfranco at km 177
-Under Cialdino flyover (Viale Monte Kosica, Via Dogali, coach station)
-Via Minutara in front of Aeronautica Militare
-P New Palasport
-Viale dello Sport (facilities outside Iperoop)
-P at public swimming pool Pergolesi.

Napoli – Campania

When visiting Italy a trip to Naples is a must. Naples is unlike the rest of Italy: it is chaotic, loud, sincere and at the same time full of contradictions and charm. Many myths are told about Naples and unusual things can happen in this city on the Vesuv, leaving an everlasting impression. Even from a gay point of view Naples is unconventional. An „Arabian" attitude towards homosexuality exists here: of importance is whether one is active or passive and not whether one is homo or heterosexual. Piazza Bellini is a good starting point at night to discover the scene. Here is the meeting point for the youth and the gays.
Party locations change frequently, so the best thing to do is check out what's happening on the night by word of mouth, or call the information lines to find out. Also useful is the homepage: www.napoligaypress.it. Most locations can be reached by foot. Be careful however, and do not carry many valuables around with you. Naples is quite dangerous at present!
From the harbour city of Naples there are ferries travelling between the islands of Ischia, Procida and Capri. The famous city of Pompeii and the wonderful Amafian coast (especially worth mentioning is Positano) are further attractions, not far away and well worth a visit.

Bei seinem Italientrip sollte man Neapel auf keinen Fall auslassen. Neapel unterscheidet sich vom Rest Italiens, ist chaotisch, laut, herzlich, gleichzeitig voller Widersprüche und voller Charme. Viele Mythen ranken sich um Neapel, doch sind tatsächlich ungewöhnliche, bisweilen absurde Erlebnisse nicht selten und die Stadt am Vesuv hinterlässt schnell einen bleibenden Eindruck.
Auch in schwuler Hinsicht ist Neapel außergewöhnlich: Ein „arabischer" Umgang mit Homosexualität ist weit verbreitet, nicht homo oder hetero, vielmehr aktiv oder passiv ist dabei das Unterscheidungsmerkmal. Piazza Bellini ist abends ein guter Ausgangspunkt, um die Szene zu erkunden. Hier treffen sich die jungen Leute – und die Schwulen. Partylocations wechseln häufig und man sollte am besten nachfragen, was nachts gerade angesagt ist oder auch die Infolines anrufen. Hilfreich ist auch die Homepage: www.napoligaypress.it. Vieles ist zu Fuß erreichbar, jedoch sollte man vorsichtig sein und nicht zu viele Wertgegenstände mit sich rumschleppen. Napoli ist gerade ziemlich gefährlich!
Von der Hafenstadt Neapel fahren Fähren auf die Inseln Ischia, Procida und Capri. Auch die Ausgrabungsstätte von Pompei und die wunderschöne amalfitanische Küste (vor allem Positano ist zu empfehlen) sind nicht weit und lohnen einen Ausflug.

Naples reste un passage obligé pour tout séjour en Italie. La ville se différencie du reste du pays : elle est chaotique, bruyante, chaleureuse, à la foi pleine de contradictions et de charmes. Beaucoup de mythes existent sur Naples et il est vrai que l'ont peut y faire des expriénces inhabituelles, parfois absurdes, qui laissent un souvenir indélébile. Naples est aussi originale d'un point de vue homosexuel : une conception plutôt proche du monde arabe y règne, où la difference n'est pas tant entre homos et hétéros mais plutôt entre actifs et passifs. La Piazza Bellini est un bon point de départ pour sortir le soir. Ici se retrouvent les jeunes et les gays. Les lieux de fête changent fréquemment et il vaut mieux demander quels clubs sont en ce moment à la mode ou se renseigner par téléphone. La page web est aussi utile : www.napoligaypress.it On peut se déplacer dans la ville à pied mais il est recommandé de rester prudent et de ne rien emporter de valeur avec soi. Naples est en ce moment relativement dangereuse. Depuis le port de Naples, il est possible de se rendre sur les îles d'Ischia, de Procida, et de Capri. Le site des découvertes archéologiques de Pompei et la côté magnifique amalfitaine (en particulier Positano) ne sont pas loin et méritent le détour.

En cualquier viaje a Italia, Nápoles es una ciudad que por ningún caso se debe dejar de visitar. Nápoles se distingue mucho el resto de Italia: es caótica, ruidosa, cordial y a su vez también llena de contrastes y de encanto. Se oyen todavía muchos mitos y tópicos sobre Nápoles pues, en realidad, suceden aún muchas cosas poco usuales y absurdas, pero la ciudad al lado del Vesubio sigue impresionando rápidamente. Desde el punto de vista homosexual, Nápoles también es excepcional: existe mayoritariamente un comportamiento „árabe" con respecto a la homosexualidad, es decir, no se trata de ser „homo" o „hétero" sino más bien de ser activo o pasivo como una característica diferenciadora. La Piazza Bellini es el mejor sitio para empezar la noche y para informarse sobre el ambiente. Aquí se ecnuentran la genete joven y los homosexuales. Las fiestas cambian a menudo y por eso es mejor preguntar dónde se encuentra los más de moda o bien llamar a las líneas de información. 1. La página principal es también de gran ayuda: www.napoligaypress.it
Se puede ir a muchos sitios a pie, sin embargo se debe ir con cuidado y no llevar consigo muchos objetos de valor iNápoles es bastante peligroso actualmente!
Desde el puerto de Nápoles salen diferentes „ferries" en dirección a las ilsas de Ischia, Procida y Capri. La famosa ciudad de Pompeya o la impresionante costa amalfitana (especialmente os recomendamos Positano) son dos lugares que valen la pena visitar.

Durante un viaggio in Italia, Napoli è assolutamente da non perdere. È una città diversa dal resto del paese, caotica, rumorosa, generosa, piena di contradizzioni e di fascino. Esistono numerose leggende su Napoli ed in effetti, fare esperienze bizzarre o al limite dell'assurdo, non è cosa rara in questa città ai piedi del Vesuvio, che anche in poco tempo si imprime fortemente nella memoria del visitatore.
Anche nell'ottica gay, Napoli è insolita: un atteggiamento „di tipo arabo" verso l'omosessualità è molto diffuso, dove ciò che fa la differenza non è tanto l'essere omosessuali o eterosessuali, quanto attivi o passivi. Piazza Bellini la sera è un buon punto di partenza per scoprire cosa succede in giro. Qui, infatti, si ritrovano i giovani e anche i gay. Le location dei party cambiano spesso, quindi è meglio informarsi sul posto circa il da farsi oppure si può chiamare la infoline. Utile è anche il sito: www.napoligaypress.it Molti posti si possono visitare a piedi, tuttavia bisogna stare attenti a non portare con sè molti oggetti di valore. Di questi tempi Napoli è molto pericolosa.
Dal porto di Napoli partono i traghetti per le isole di Ischia, Procida e Capri. Anche gli scavi di Pompei e la meravigliosa Costa Amalfitana (consigliamo particolarmente Positano) non sono lontani. Vale davvero la pena andarli a visitare.

GAY INFO

■ **Arcigay Antinoo** 16-21h
Vico San Geronimo 17 *M° Dante, bus R2* ☎ 081 5528815
☎ 349 7584462 (mobile) 🖳 www.arcigaynapoli.org
Helpline & information about gay life, political and cultural groups, information about HIV, prevention campaigns. Free health & legal assistance (send mail). Open bar 16-21h

■ **NapoliGayPress**
🖳 www.napoligaypress.it
Informations about gay life in Naples and the region Campania.

BARS

■ **Bar Fiorillo** (B GLM OS) 6-4h
Via Santa Maria di Costantinopoli 88 ☎ 081 459 905
Gay meeting point directly at Piazza Bellini.

■ **Caffè Intra Moenia** (AC B bf CC glm M MA OS) 10-2h
Piazza Bellini 70 *M° Cavour/M° Montesanto* ☎ 081 29 09 88
💻 www.intramoenia.it
Bar and bookshop at Piazza Bellini (the gay meeting point).

■ **Delirious** (AC B GLM) 19-5h, closed on Mon
Via Santa Chiara 16 ☎ 331 152 13 17
New small gay lounge bar in the centre. Happy hour 19.30-21h

MEN'S CLUBS

■ **Basement. The** (B DR F G GH LAB MA NU S SL SNU VS) Wed-Sun 22-?h
Via Atri 36b *Centre* ☎ 081 19252174 ☎ 348 0977856
💻 www.thebasement.it
New cruising place n the centre of Naples. See the websit for special events.

■ **Depot** (! AC B CC DR G MA P VS)
Tue-Thu 22-3, Fri & Sat -5, Sun -3h (Oct-May 15-3h), Mon closed
Via della Veterinaria 72 *Near Piazza Carlo III* ☎ 081 78 09 578
💻 www.depotmilano.com
Uno Club card required. Smoking area. Crusing area with cubicals and a sling room. Entrance fee includes one drink and the cloakroom fee. Wed naked party. See www.depotmilano.com

DANCECLUBS

■ **Freelovers** (AC B D GLM MA) Thu & Sat 23-?h
☎ 338 33 34 769 (mobile)
Group organizing parties on thursdays and saturdays. Call for informations.

■ **Macho Lato** (AC B D G m MA P S) Fri 22-4, Sat 23-5, Sun 22-2h
Via Abate Minichini 62 *Near Piazza Carlo III & Piazza Ottocalli*
☎ 081 78 03 062 💻 www.macholato.it
New dance club in Naples, good atmosphere. Tek-house and dance music.

SEX CINEMAS

■ **Agorà** (AC b DR g MA r t) 10-22h
Via Guantai Nuovi 4/6 *Near the harbour, M° Piazza Dante, bus 201*
☎ 081 55 24 893

■ **Argo** (G M MA R T) 9-22h
Via Alessandro Poerio 4 ☎ 081 55 44 764 💻 www.cinemaargo.com
Many rent boys and transsexuals. Recently renovated, very crowded.

SAUNAS/BATHS

■ **Blu Angels**
(AC B DR DU FC FH G LAB M MA MSG P PI RR SA SB VS WH) 13-22h
Centro Direzionale Isola A/7 *From railway station walk along the Centro Direzionale, opposite side of the street from Fiat showroom on the corner, cross the street leading to the highway, go up the stairs, round the corner on the right* ☎ 081 56 25 298 ☎ 081 56 25 035
💻 www.saunabluangels.com
This sauna is not easy to find, tucked away in a shopping precinct. Three floors, maze, HIV-info. Large hot tub, stream room and rest rooms. On three floors, with cubicles on the top floor. The steam room is where the action is. Upstairs is also a video room for smokers. Condom in your key chain available free upon arrival. Fri: bears/leather night. Uno Club card required.

HOTELS

■ **Chiaja Hotel de Charme** (AC B BF CC glm H I PA RWS RWT VA)
All year, at night you must ring to get in
Via Chiaja 216 *Near Piazza del Plebiscito, 1st floor* ☎ 081 41 55 55
💻 www.napleshotelsdecharme.com
Charming traditional hotel, close to the Royal Palace and the main shopping street. On a pedestrain street. Gay-friendly and very comfortable.

■ **Decumani Hotel de Charme**
(AC BF CC glm H I OS PA RWS RWT)
All year, at night you must ring to get in
Via San Giovanni Maggiore Pignatelli 15 *Centre, near Piazza del Gesù e Monastero di Santa Chiara, Metro Piazza Dante* ☎ 081 55 18 188
💻 www.napleshotelsdecharme.com
Charming hotel in the heart of the historical part of Naples. The Hotel is located in the former 18th century residence of Cardinal Sisto Riario Sforza. Wonderfull hall with frescos. Free wireless internet. Website promo-code GSP78 for special Spartacus discounts.

GENERAL GROUPS

Key We Associazione Culturale Nazionale
☏ 02 890 383 69 💻 www.keywe.it
National association for the gay community.

ATN Napoli
☏ 333 77 40 209 (mobile)
Group for transsexuals.

HEALTH GROUPS

Ospedale San Paolo
Via Terracina 219 ☏ 800 01 92 54 (free toll)
Free & anonymous hiv test.

SWIMMING

See also Sperlonga and Sorrento
-Marechiaro Beach (from via Posillipo-via Marechiaro; mixed in the rocks)
-Pozzuoli, in the rocks behind the port
-Spiaggia di Cuma, near Licola (t)

CRUISING

-Agnano, entrance parking in front of ippodrome, by car at night very busy
-Centro Direzionale, near Holiday Inn (at night, on foot) (r)
-Corso Meridionale (R)
-Via Brin (AYOR) (by car, busy)
-Via Brecce to S. Erasmo (Gianturco district): by car at night
-Railway station Piazza Garibaldi (R)
-Capodimonte Park (AYOR) (morning and afternoon)
-Piazza Bellini (meeting place in summertime at night).

Novara – Piemonte

CRUISING

-Bastioni: park around Castle Visconteo, at the toilets near the central post office (on foot)
-Parco dell'Allea (on foot at night)
-Via Raffaello Sanzio: also in the gardens in front of police station and in the parking lot (at night)
-Via Regaldi (by car at night).

Padova – Veneto

GAY INFO

Arcigay Tralaltro Tue 21-23.30, Wed 18-20h
Corso Garibaldi 41 ☏ 049 876 24 58 💻 www.tralaltro.it
Information on HIV, prevention, support as well as political and cultural activities.

Radio Gamma Cinque Mon 19.30-21.30h
Antoniana 66 ☏ 049 700700 /838 ☏ 049 700838
💻 www.radiogammacinque.it
Gay radio broadcasting on 94,0 Mhz or in streaming audio on the site. In Italian language only.

Tanti Lati Latitanti (G) Mon 19.30-21.30h
Via Antoniana 66 *Radio Gamma 5 94,0 Mhz for the region of Veneto*
☏ 049.700700 ☏ 3347102672 SMS 💻 www.radiogammacinque.it
Gay broadcasting in Italian.

PUBLICATIONS

Tralaltro
Via S. Sofia 5 💻 www.tralaltro.it
Online news for the GLBT community of the north-east of Italy.

BARS

Anima Drinks & More (AC B GLM m OS S YC)
21-2h, Mon & Tue closed
Via Vicenza 15 ☏ 348 72 64 713
Busiest bar for the moment in Padova.

Bertelli's (AC B glm M MA) Mon-Sat 18-24h, closed Sun
Via A. Gritti 3/a *Near Piazza Delle Erbe* ☏ 347 880 97 66

Tiratardi (AC B glm m) 18-2h, closed Sun and Aug
Via Palermo 20 *Bus 5/near Bassanello* ☏ 049 65 20 83
💻 www.tiratardipub.it

Xchè No Cafe' (B d GLM MA OS) 18-2h, Mon closed
Via A. Manzoni 4 *Near Prato della Valle* ☏ 049 68 77 75
Disco/bar. Special parties once a month.

MEN'S CLUBS

Dopolavoro Mario (AC B DR G)
Via Longhin 129 ☏ 366 409 33 27 (mobile)
New cruising bar.

Flexo Club (AC B CC D DR f G I m MA NU OS P SNU VS)
22-?, Fri & Sat -7h, Mon & Tue closed
Via Turazza 19, Int.1 *900 m from the railway station, exit A 4 Padova Est, bus 9 & 18* ☏ 033 973 79 579 💻 www.flexoclub.it
Disco (house/mainstream) Sat. Sun Karaoke & Dragqueens. First Sat/month bears night. Smoking area & Internet available. Uno Club card required.

Hot Dog (AC b DR G MA NU SNU VS) 21-?, Sat & Sun 15-?h
Via Turazza 19, Scala A *Bus 9/18* ☏ 338 66 65 207
💻 www.hot-dog-club.com
Naked/underwear parties every day. Check www.hot-dog-club.com. Uno Club Card required.

Officina (AC B D DR f G MA P S SNU VS) Wed-Sun 22-3h
Via Volta 1/7, Limena *Basement of The Block* ☏ 348 45 00 418
💻 www.clubOfficina.com
Thu: naked party, Sat: only naked, special price for The Block. Equipped fist zone with shower. Leather parties. Uno Club card required. Check out if Officina in 2011 is still there.

DANCECLUBS

Padova Pride Village (B D GLM I M MA OS VEG)
Tue-Thu & Sun 20-2, Fri 20-3, Sat 20-4h (6. 7. – 2.9.2012)
c/o Fiera di Padova, entrance from Via Goldoni ☏ 349 40 29 364 (info)
💻 www.padovapridevillage.it
Huge outdoor summer event in summer time (July – September): bars, restaurants, concerts, dancing, shopping and meeting in the centre of Padova.

SAUNAS/BATHS

Metro Padova Sauna (AC B cc DR FC FH G GH LAB M MA MSG OS P RR SA SB SOL VS WH WO) 14-2h
Via Turazza 19, int. 1 *Bus 9/18-Piazzale Stanga Stop* ☏ 049 80 75 828
💻 www.metroclub.it
Very cruisy and popular sauna on 500 m². Uno Club card required. Also gym-space.

BOOK SHOPS

Libreria Feltrinelli 9-19.30h
Via S. Francesco 7 ☏ 049 87 54 630 💻 www.lafeltrinelli.it

GENERAL GROUPS

Key We Associazione Culturale Nazionale
☏ 02 890 383 69 💻 www.keywe.it
National association for the gay community.

CRUISING

-Inceneritore (lungargine San Lazzaro): from Via Turazza into Via S. Fidenzio, straight on, after the motorway bridge turn right (night & day, by car, crowded)
-Via Manzoni /Giardini di Pontecorvo (AYOR)
-Via Loredan/Via Marzolo, zona universitaria (R)
-Via Tommaso Grossi.

Parma – Emilia Romagna

DANCECLUBS

Andromeda (AC B D GLM MA) Sat 23-?h
Via Gramsci 5, Soragna *30 km north-east from Parma* ☏ 0524 59 72 04

SWIMMING

-Taro beach (after the bridge over the Taro River, walk towards Monte)

CRUISING

-River/fiume Parma (right-hand side)
-Parco Ducale (in summer)
-Mercati Generali (R T) (after 23 h)

Pavia – Lombardia

GAY INFO

Arcigay Coming Aut
Via Siro Comi 11 ☎ 346 69 27 476 🖳 www.coming-aut.it

SWIMMING

-Lido di Pavia (NU) (P Lanche)
-Pieve del Cairo (River Agogna: on the road from Pieve del Cairo to Sannazzaro de Burgondi, turn right before bridge over river, continue for 400 m. Beach by the waterfall, mixed).

CRUISING

-Customs depot (AYOR) (Via Donegana, truckers)
-Old railway bridge over river Ticino (until 3h)
-Strada Persa (by car until 3h)
-Via Rismondo (around castle at night, on foot and by car)

Perugia – Umbria

GAY INFO

Arcigay Arcilesbica Omphalos Fri 21.30-23.30h
Via della Pallotta 42 *Near Piazza IV Novembre* ☎ 075 57 23 175
🖳 www.omphalospg.it

BARS

Omphalos (B D GLM MA OS ST WE) Fri & Sat 22-4h
Via Antonio Fratti 18 ☎ 075 57 23 175 🖳 www.omphalospg.it
3 floors and terrace. Run by Arcigay. Uno Club card required.

HOTELS

Villa di Missiano (glm PI PK RWS RWT WH) All year
Via Gramsci 51, Panicale ☎ 075 83 73 18 🖳 www.villadimissiano.it
Six elegant suites, each one comprises a double bedroom, en-suite bathroom, lounge and kitchen.

CRUISING

-Via Monte Malbe: parking and in the park (by day, OC)
-Via Ripa di Meana (by car and by foot in the gardens, at night).

Pesaro – Marche

GAY INFO

Arcigay Agorà
☎ 389 97 25 980

SWIMMING

-Beach between Pesaro and Fano (NU).

CRUISING

-Piazza Matteotti (parking, by car at night)

Pescara – Abruzzo

GAY INFO

Jonathan- diritti in Movimento (GLM MA T)
Mon 21-23, Sat 17-19h
Via Palermo 41 ☎ 347 61 63 26 0 🖳 www.alinvolo.org
GLBT association.

BARS

Phoenix (AC B d GLM) Wed-Sun 22.30-3, Sat disco 23-5h
Via Caravaggio 109 ☎ 085 73 689 🖳 www.phoenixclub.it
Uno Club card required.

MEN'S CLUBS

David Cruising Bar (AC DR G LAB MA VS)
Thu, Fri & Sun 21.30-1, Sat -2h
Via Palermo 41 *Centre* ☎ 340 770 83 24
New cruising bar. Uno Club card required.

CRUISING

-Porta Nouva station
-Piazza Salotto
-Piazza Maggio

Peschiera del Garda – Veneto

SEX SHOPS/BLUE MOVIES

Secret Paradise (CC g) Mon-Sat 10-20, Sun 15-20h
Via XX Settembre 43, Cavalcaselle *2 mins from highway exit Peschiera del Garda* ☎ 045 64 02 471
DVDs, gadgets and toys.

Piacenza – Emilia Romagna

GAY INFO

Arcigay L'Atomo
Strada Malchioda 39 ☎ 346 68 77 021 🖳 www.arcigay.it/piacenza

BARS

Pick Up (B glm)
Via Campo Sportivo Vecchio

SEX SHOPS/BLUE MOVIES

Erotika Video Shop (g)
Mon 15.30-19.30, Tue-Sat 10-13 & 14-19.30h
Via XXIV Maggio 104/D ☎ 0523 40 15 74 🖳 www.sexerotika.it
Two further stores in Milano.

SWIMMING

-Beach by the river Po (direction Piacenzo-Milano follow signs to C. San Sisto, park your car and walk to the area below the motorway bridges)

CRUISING

-Girone del Vescovo (under the bridges and motorway-P, also along the river)
-Piazza della Cittadella
-Bar Bologna (in front of the bar, opposite the railway station)
-Viale S. Ambrogio
-Monumento al Pontieri (R T) (on the square)
-P Fiorenzuola motorway exit
-Lungo Po (meetings between Nino Bixio swimming pool and Via da Feltre)
-Lungo la Foce del Trebbia (YC)

Pinerolo – Piemonte

CRUISING

-Piazza Canova (MA) (evenings)

Pisa – Toscana

GAY INFO

Arcigay Pisa (GLM) Mon, Tue & Fri 18-20h
Via S. Lorenzo 38 ☎ 050 55 56 18 www.arcigaypisa.it
Helpline 199 44 45 92 (Mon 16-20h).

BARS

Colors (! AC B d GLM m s YC) Oct-May: Wed-Sun 21.30-2h
Via Mossotti 10 *Near Ponte di Mezzo* ☎ 050 50 02 48
www.colors.fm
Disco/bar. Uno Club card required.

Colors Disco Pub (AC B D GLM S ST YC)
Tue-Sat 22.30-2, Sun 18-2.30h (October-May)
via Mossotti *centre, 200m from Ponte di Mezzo*
☎ 393 22 39 322 (mobile) www.colors.fm
Wed dragshow, Thu karaoke, DJ in the weekend, Sun mainly lesbians. Uno Club card required.

MEN'S CLUBS

Catch Club
☞ Lucca.

DANCECLUBS

Mamamia
☞ Viareggio.

My Keta (AC B D GLM S ST YC) Fri 22.30-4.30h (October-April)
c/o Akua Keta (ex Carmilla), Via Sancasciani 8 *500m from Colors*
☎ 393 22 39 322 (mobile) www.myketa.it
Mainstream music with dragshow. Free entry.

RMX
☞ Lucca.

SAUNAS/BATHS

Siesta Club 77 (AC DR DU FC G I MA PP RR SA SB VS WH)
Sep-May: 15-24, Jun-Aug: 17-24h
Via di Porta a Mare 26 *500 m from railway station* ☎ 050 22 00 146
www.siestaclub77.com
Sauna on three floors. Uno Club card required.

HOTELS

Abitalia Park Resort (AC B H I M PI)
Via Caduti del Lavoro 46 ☎ 050 78 46 444
www.abitaliaparkresort.it
Luxurious hotel with pay and sat-TV, free wireless internet, restaurant, American bar on the panoramic terrace and outside swimming pool.

GUEST HOUSES

Casa Madrigal (GLM I MA OS VA) All year
Via Porta a Mare 13 *Near sauna Siesta Club 77, 5 mins walking from the railway station, 10 mins from the leaning tower* ☎ 050 23 161
www.casamadrigal.it
Own key, free internet.

Podere Paterno (AC G I M OS PI)
Via Podere Paterno 204 *40 km from Pisa* ☎ 328 70 24 781
www.poderepaterno.it

APARTMENTS

Podere La Vitalba (glm PA PI PK) All year
Via Provinciale del Montevaso km 19 ☎ 32 81 92 03 59
www.poderelavitalba.it
An 16th century cottage with a garden in the countryside. 3 Apartments with 3 double rooms, own kitchen and TV. 2 bathrooms. 20 km from the sea.

SWIMMING

-Tirrenia (g NU) (Beach to the south of Camp Darby's beach)
☞ Torre del Lago.

CRUISING

-Giardini Scotto (OC) (afternoon)
-Lungarno Guadalongo (along Arno river, by car and at foot at night).

Pistoia – Toscana

GAY INFO

Arcigay La Giraffa
☎ 347 69 26 658

Pompei – Campania

COUNTRY CRUISING

Railway station, square in front of Villa dei Misteri (by foot and by car, ayor)

RESTAURANTS

■ **Principe. Il** (AC B CC glm M OS) 12-15h, 19.30-23.30h
Piazza Bartolo Longo 8 *Attached to archeological site* ☎ 081 85 05 566
www.ilprincipe.com

Pordenone – Friuli-Venezia Giulia

DANCECLUBS

■ **Heaven Club** (AC B D DR GLM MA SNU VS) Wed, Fri & Sat 22-4h
Via Friuli 16 ☎ 347 6840333 www.heavenclub.it

APARTMENTS

■ **Casa Colonica** (AC glm OS)
Casore del Monte, Marliana *16 km from Pistoia*
Huge villa on three floors to rent.

Positano – Campania

CAFES

■ **Brezza. La** (AC B BF CC D G I M MA OS) 10-3h (Apr-Dec)
Via del Brigantino 1 ☎ 089 87 58 11
Cocktail bar, snacks, happenings & parties. Internet point & Wi-Fi to good prices. Buffet 18-21h (May-Sep)

RESTAURANTS

■ **Next2** (B G M MA OS) 19-1h
Via Pasitea 242 ☎ 089 812 3516 www.next2.it
Great restaurant with mediterrean cuisine & cocktail bar.

■ **Tre Sorelle. Le** (GLM M MA)
12.30-16, 19-24h (closed some weeks in winter)
Via del Brigantino 27/29 ☎ 089 87 54 52
www.letresorellepositano.it
Fine restaurant on the sea promenade. Seafood, pasta and great wines.

DECORATION

■ **Soso** (CC) 9.30-13h, 16-22h
Via Pasitea 51 ☎ 089 87 53 27
Traditional ceramic interior design & gifts. The owner is happy to give informations about gay life in Positano.

HOTELS

■ **Hotel Montemare Positano**
(AC B BF CC GLM H M MA OS PK RWB RWS RWT)
Open from April-October
Via Pasitea 119 ☎ 089 87 50 10 www.hotelmontemare.it
Spectacular views over Positano. Southern Italian cuisine in the restaurant „Il Capitano" (open 12-15, 19-24h)

■ **Poseidon** (AC B BF CC GLM H I MSG OS PA PI PK RWB RWS RWT SA SOL WO) 19 Apr-30 Oct 2012
Via Pasitea 148 ☎ 089 81 11 11
www.hotelposeidonpositano.it
Luxurious hotel with wellness centre with massages, turkish bath, gym and solar shower. Meeting room. Parking available on extra charge. Pets allowed.

■ **Punta Regina** (AC B BF CC H I MA OS RWS RWT WH)
Via Pasitea 224 ☎ 089 81 20 20 www.puntaregina.com
Beautiful panorama from the terrace with a whirlpool.

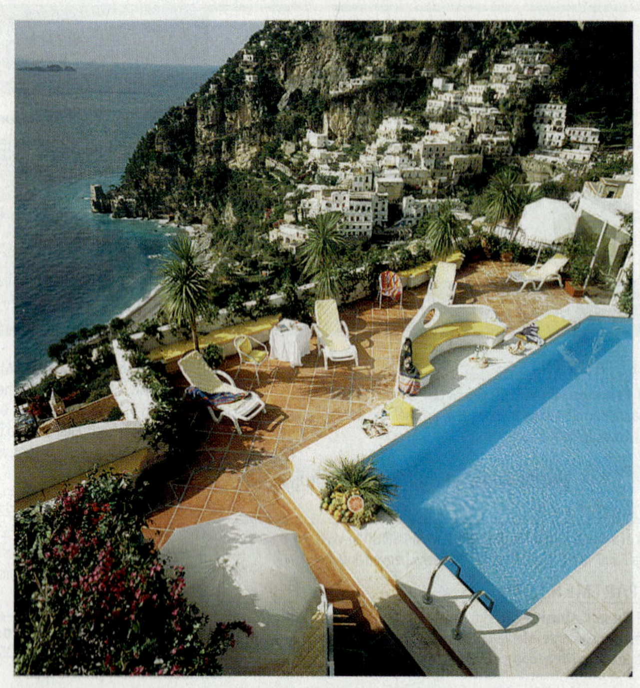

■ **Reginella** (AC B bf CC glm H I PK RWB RWS RWT VA) March-Nov.
Viale Pasitea 154 ☎ 089 875 324 🖳 www.reginellahotel.it
All rooms with own bath, TV and view over the sea. Affordable prices. Parking service.

■ **Villa Franca** (AC B BF CC glm H I M MSG OS PI RWB RWS RWT SA SB SOL WO) All year
Viale Pasitea, 318 ☎ 089 87 56 55 🖳 www.villafrancahotel.it
Luxurious hotel with swimmingpool with view over Positano and the sea. Wellness centre and restaurant with fine Mediterranean cuisine. Very gay-friendly.

■ **Villa Gabrisa** (AC BF CC glm H I M MA OS PA RWS RWT VA)
All year. Reception 8-20; restaurant 12.30-14.30, 19-23h
Via Pasitea 227 ☎ 089 81 14 98 🖳 www.villagabrisa.com
Family run hotel with 2 suites and 7 double rooms all with sea view. Mini-bar, phone, fax, safe, sat-TV, pay-TV and WiFi connection. Pets and visitors allowed.

APARTMENTS

■ **Villa Casa Bianca** (AC G I OS SB)
Via Oratorio 4 *6 km from Positano* ☎ 339 42 44 097
🖳 www.casabiancaholiday.com
Beautiful apartment for up to 4 persons (weekly rental: Sat to Sat). Two bathrooms and turkish bath inside. Wireless internet included. Parking available on request.

SWIMMING

-Fornillo beach, right side (g)

Prato – Toscana

FASHION SHOPS

■ **Aivy Lab** Mon 15.30-19.30, Tue-Sat 9.30-13 & 15.30-20h
Via G. Garibaldi 77 ☎ 0574 07 12 30 🖳 www.aivy.it
Fashion shop, accessories, men's underwear, book corner (photography, fashion and gay-lesbian books). Information on the gay scene.

CRUISING

- Interporto: around the lake by foot and by car (at night)
- Piazza della Stazione: by day and night (ayor)
- Parco di Galceti: Parking in front, at night.

Ravenna – Emilia Romagna

SEX SHOPS/BLUE MOVIES

■ **Cactus** (G SH)
v.le G. da Verazzano 24, Lido di Classe ☎ 0544 948 207
☎ 0338 7731 480 🖳 www.sexyromagna.com/cactushome.asp
Small gay-friendly sex shop.

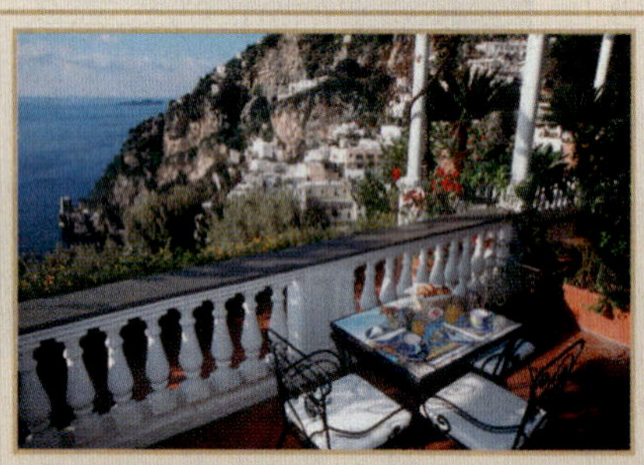

HOTELS

■ **Tosco Romagnolo** (AC B CC H M MSG PI SA SOL WH WO)
All year
Piazza Dante 2, Bagno di Romagna *In front of the thermal bath*
☎ 0543 91 12 60 💻 www.paoloteverini.it
Wellness hotel with all comforts in the hills near Ravenna.

■ **Zeus** (AC glm M OS)
Via F.lli Vivaldi 66 *In Lido di Classe* ☎ 0544 93 91 72 💻 www.zeushotel.it
Near the gay beach. Friendly atmosphere. Special events in summer.

GUEST HOUSES

■ **I Gigli Bed & Breakfast** (bf glm)
Via Romea 96 *Ten mins walk to town centre* ☎ 346 019 69 95
💻 www.gigliravenna.com
Four guestrooms, some with private bathroom.

SWIMMING

-Lido di Classe (NU) (between Ravenna and Cervia, free beach north of the kiosk bearing the same name. Large pine forest. Gay zone of the beach is near the river surrounding the beach itself, in the northern area)
-Lido di Dante (NU) (free beach beyond the campsites, on the right; dunes and pine trees).

CRUISING

-Public gardens (ayor R) (Viale S. Baldini, at night)
-Piazzale and Viale Farini (R)
-Piazza Mameli (R)
-Via Rocca ai Fossi (R)
-Lido di Classe (gay area begins north along the dunes after ca. 200 m down to river Bevano, cruising also in the pine-tree wood, mainly at night; also at parking right to the river)
-Lido di Dante (NU).

Rimini – Emilia Romagna

GAY INFO

■ **Comitato Provinciale Arcigay di Rimini „Alan Mathison Turing"**
Via Bergamo, 2 💻 www.arcigay.it/rimini

CAFES

■ **Fuera** (B GLM m OS S YC) Apr-Oct 17-6h
Piazzale Gondar 1 *Infront of beach number 89* ☎ 338 46 55 512
💻 www.fuera.it

DANCECLUBS

■ **Classic Club** (AC B D GLM MA WE) Sat 24-?h
Via Feleto 15 ☎ 335 58 54 640 (mobile) 💻 www.clubclassic.net
Uno Club card required.

■ **Enigma Labirint Club** (AC B D DR G MA S) Wed, Fri-Sun 23-?h
Via Ausa 173 ☎ 0541 72 94 01 💻 www.enigmalabirintclub.com
New cruising danceclub on 500 m². Uno Club card required.

RESTAURANTS

■ **Osteria dal Minestraio** (AC B glm M MA OS)
Viale G. D'Annunzio 12 ☎ 0541 64 41 27 💻 www.osteriadalminestraio.com
Many different pasta dishes and extensive wine list.

SEX SHOPS/BLUE MOVIES

■ **Sexy Moon** (g)
Via Nazionale Adriatica 23 ☎ 0541 95 36 08 💻 www.sexycactus.com

HOTELS

■ **Hotel des Nations** (AC B BF CC H MA MSG OS SA SOL WH WO)
All year
Lungomare Costituzione 2 *Near the beach and the harbor*
☎ 0541 64 78 78 💻 www.lgbt-friendly.it
Beach hotel with 30 rooms with own shower/WC, own key, mini-bar, safe, phone and TV. Small pets allowed, reservation required.

■ **Hotel Migani Spiaggia B&B** (BF glm I OS PK RWS)
Open from 15 Apr-30 Sep
Via Vincenzo Monti 7 *Centre, 100 m from the beach* ☎ 0541 385 450
💻 www.hotelmigani.com
Gay-friendly hotel in a cosy atmosphere close to the sea. Free Wifi, 5% discount for Spartacus readers. Also rooms for 4/5 persons available.

GUEST HOUSES

■ **Casa Madana** (BF GLM MA)
Viale Giumbo 26/A *Rimini Torre Pedrera* ☎ 328 22 89 088 (infoline)
💻 www.casamadana.com

SWIMMING

-Along the sea/Lungomare Libertà (Viale Ceccarini area)
-Ponte Marano beach, between Rimini and Riccione.

CRUISING

-Behind Hotel Savioli (winter, by car and on foot)
-Viale Vittorio Emanuele (at night, by car and on foot in the gardens next to Bombo Bar)
-South Rimini/Rimini sud (at Miramare, between Centro Talasso Terapico and Colonia Bologna).

Riva del Garda – Trentino-Alto Adige

CRUISING

-Beach between „Punta Lido" and „Sabbioni Beach" (at night)
-Cruisy beach (NU) (take road to Torbole-Malcesine. Then take small stairs just at the end of the 5th tunnel behind Torbole.)

Roma – Lazio

Hardly a tourist will fail to fall victim to the fascination of this eternal city with its countless churches, monuments and art treasures. And even if one cannot really draw comparisons to the nightlife in other major cities, gay tourists are still bound to get their moneyís worth. Instead of a gay neighbourhood as in Madrid or Paris, the small, highly frequented Gay Street directly next to the Coliseum, besides its bars and an ice cream parlour also boasts a shop catering to the needs of not only gay men, as well as a gay bed & breakfast.
In summer the Gay Village in the south of Rome opens its gates. Every evening different parties and concerts take place with several thousand guests. However, also during the rest of the year one can go out every evening, dancing is, however, more popular at the weekend. The different locations are spread out all over the city. Those in the centre are often accessible by foot. A special experience is to explore Rome on a scooter and thereby to remain flexible especially at night. A visitor to Rome has a vast choice of accommodation choices on offer, from gay bed & breakfast guesthouses to gay-friendly, 4-star hotels.
From Rome it is only just 30 kilometres to Ostia and the sandy beaches, very popular with gays and further to the south at the Mediterranean Sea.

Kaum ein Tourist wird sich der Faszination der ewigen Stadt, seiner unzähligen Kirchen, Monumente und Kunstschätze entziehen können. Das Nachtleben anderer Metropolen sollte zwar nicht der Maßstab sein, der schwule Tourist kommt dennoch auf seine Kosten. Statt eines Schwulenkiezes wie in Madrid oder Paris bietet die kleine, stark frequentierte Gay Street direkt neben dem Kolosseum immerhin neben seinen Bars und einer Eisdiele auch einen Laden für die Bedürfnisse nicht nur des schwulen Mannes und ein schwules Bed&Breakfast.
Im Sommer öffnet weiterhin das Gay Village im Süden Roms seine Pforten: Jeden Abend unterschiedliche Parties und Konzerte mit mehreren Tausend Besucher/-innen.
Doch auch das restliche Jahr kann man jeden Abend ausgehen, Tanzen ist meist am Wochenende angesagt. Die verschiedenen Locations sind über die ganze Stadt verteilt, jedoch im Zentrum oft auch zu Fuß erreichbar. Ein besonderes Erlebnis ist es, Rom mit dem Motorroller zu erkunden und somit auch nachts flexibel zu bleiben. Dem Rom-Besucher stehen inzwischen eine Vielzahl an Übernachtungsmöglichkeiten zur

Auswahl: vom schwulenfreundlichen 4-Sterne-Hotel bis zum schwulen Bed&Breakfast.
Von Rom aus sind es nur knapp 30 Kilometer bis nach Ostia und den auch von Schwulen stark frequentierten Sandstränden weiter südlich am Mittelmeer.

Aucun touriste n'échappe à la fascination de la ville éternelle, ses innombrables églises, monuments et trésors artistiques. La vie nocturne n'est certes pas comparable à d'autres métropoles, cependant le touriste gay y trouvera son compte. Au lieu d'un quartier gay comme à Madrid ou à Paris, la Gay Street, petite rue fortement fréquentée située tout à côté du Colisée, propose tout de même des bars, un glacier et aussi un magasin pour les besoins non seulement des gays et un bed&breakfast gay. glaces, un magasin pour les besoins pas seulement des gays et aussi un bed&breakfast gay.
En été au sud de Rome, le Gay Village ouvre ses portes: tous les soirs, différentes soirées et concerts avec des milliers de visiteurs.
Toute l'année on peut aussi sortir tous les soirs, on danse plutôt le week-end. Les différents endroits sont dispersés à travers toute la ville, cependant dans le centre ils sont souvent accessibles à pied. Une expérience toute particulière: la découverte de la ville en Vespa et ainsi rester flexible la nuit.

Une quantité d'hébergements sont accessibles aux touristes: du 4 étoiles gay-friendly au bed&breakfast gay.
Seulement 30 kilomètres séparent Rome d'Ostia et des plages de sable fortement fréquentée par les gays plus au sud en bord de Méditerranée.

Pocos turistas escapan a la fascinación de la Ciudad Eterna, a sus numerosas iglesias, sus monumentos y sus tesoros artísticos. La vida nocturna de otras ciudades no debería ser el criterio que siga el turista gay. En lugar de un barrio gay, como el de Madrid o el de París, la pequeña y muy frecuentada Calle Gay junto al Coliseo ofrece, además de sus bares y heladerías, una tienda para las necesidades de, no únicamente, el hombre gay y un Bed&Breakfast.
En verano abre también sus puertas en el sur de Roma la llamada Gay Village: todas las noches tienen lugar diferentes fiestas y conciertos con varios miles de visitantes.
Pero el resto del año también se puede salir de fiesta todas las noches. Aún así, se suelen reservar las fuerzas para el fin de semana. La mayoría de los locales se encuentran distribuidos por toda la ciudad, pero a menudo en el centro se puede llegar a pie de uno a otro. Una experiencia única es la de explorar Roma en moto y así también mantenerse abierto y a tono para cuando caiga la noche. Los visitantes de Roma tienen a su disposición un amplio abanico de posibilidades en lo que a alojamiento se refiere: desde hoteles gay-friendly de 4 estrellas hasta Bed&Breakfast para gays.
Desde Roma hay sólo unos 30 kilómetros hasta la ciudad de Ostia y más hacia el sur en el Mediterráneo las playas de arena altamente frecuentadas por homosexuales.

Nessun turista si può sottrarre al fascino della città eterna, delle sue numerose chiese, dei suoi numerosi monumenti e dei suoi tesori artistici. La vita notturna di altre metropoli non dovrebbe certo essere un metro di giudizio per Roma, tuttavia i turisti gay troveranno sicuramente qualcosa che fa per loro. Invece di un intero quartiere gay come a Madrid o a Parigi, a Roma c'è una piccola e molto frequentata Gay Street, sita direttamente di fronte al Colosseo e dove si possono trovare bar, gelaterie, un Bed&Breakfast gay e un negozio per le esigenze di gay e non.
Ogni estate il Gay Village, a sud di Roma, apre ogni sera le sue porte alle feste più disparate e a concerti frequentati da diverse migliaia di persone. Anche durante il resto dell'anno c'è molta vita notturna. Le discoteche sono frequentate per lo più durante il fine settimana. I locali sono sparsi un po' per tutta la città, e quelli del centro sono facilmente raggiungibili a piedi. Un'esperienza particolare è quella di esplorare Roma in scooter, che permette, tra l'altro, di muoversi anche di notte. Ormai a Roma ci sono un'infinità di possibilità di pernottamento: dall'hotel a 4 stelle molto gay friendly, fino al Bed&Breakfast gay. Ostia e le spiagge un po' più a sud, frequentate anche da gay, distano da Roma solo circa 30 chilometri.

GAY INFO

Circolo di Cultura Omosessuale Mario Mieli
Mon-Fri 11-18h
Via Efeso 2/a *M° San Paolo* ☎ 06 54 13 985
☎ 800110611 Rainbow Line 🖳 www.mariomieli.org
Helpline, counselling, welcome & cultural group, HIV-tests, Support for people with AIDS. Call for information on activities. Also Agedo – Gays & lesbians parents organization (Mon 17-19h). Helpline for transsexuals (Lili) Mon 14-16.30h.

Gay Center Mon, Wed, Thu & Sat 16-20h
Via Zabaglia 14 (Testaccio) *M° Piramide* ☎ 800 713 713 (free gay helpline)
☎ 06 64 50 11 02 🖳 www.gaycenter.it
New center formed by Arcigay Roma, ArciLesbica Roma, Nps (network for people with hiv) and Azione Trans

PUBLICATIONS

AUT
c/o Circolo Mario Mieli, Via Efeso 2a ☎ 06 54 13 985
🖳 www.mariomieli.org
Monthly gay magazine for politics, culture and roman gay scene. Available not only in gay bars.

BARS

■ **Coming Out** (AC B GLM M MA OS S) 7:30-2h
Via S. Giovanni in Laterano 8 *M° Colosseo, in front of the Colosseum*
☏ 06 70 09 871 💻 www.comingout.it
First gay bar and restaurant open during day time in the recently established „Gay Street", crowded pub and cocktail bar in the night. Recently renovated.

■ **Garbo** (AC B GLM M MA) 22-?h, Mon closed
Vicolo di Santa Margherita 1/A *Trastevere district* ☏ 06 58 12 766
💻 www.garbobar.com

■ **Hangar** (AC B DR f G I MA P SNU VS)
Mo, Wed-Sun 22.30-2.30h, closed Tue
Via in Selci 69 *M° A Via Cavour/M° B Piazza Vittorio, near the Colosseum*
☏ 06 48 81 397 💻 www.hangaronline.it
Porn films on Mon, Striptease on Thu. Rome's first cruising bar open since 1984. Free entrance, Uno Club card required. Smoking area on site.

■ **My Bar** (AC B BF CC GLM M MA OS) 8.30-2h
Via S. Giovanni in Laterano 12 *M° Colosseo, in front of the Colosseum*
☏ 06 70 04 425 💻 see facebook
Typical Roman bar with breakfast, lunch and dinner. In the day gay-friendly, in the evening gay. Next to Coming out in the small „Gay Street".

■ **Skyline** (AC B DR G I LAB MA P S SNU VS) 22.30-4h
Via Pontremoli 36 *San Giovanni, opp. post office, Metro S. Giovanni*
☏ 06 70 09 431 ☏ 328 11 61 668 (mobile)
💻 www.skylineclub.it
2 bars, video room, „smoking room" as well as a labyrinth with cabins. Mon Naked Party. Crowded.

MEN'S CLUBS

■ **Eagle Club** (AC B d DR F G MA P S SNU VS)
Tue-Thu & Sun 22-3h, Fri & Sat 22-6h, closed Mon
Via Placido Zurla 68 *Pigneto district, M° Termini-Giardinetti: stop Alessi*
💻 www.eagleclubroma.com
New bear, leather and muscle club. Disco on WE.

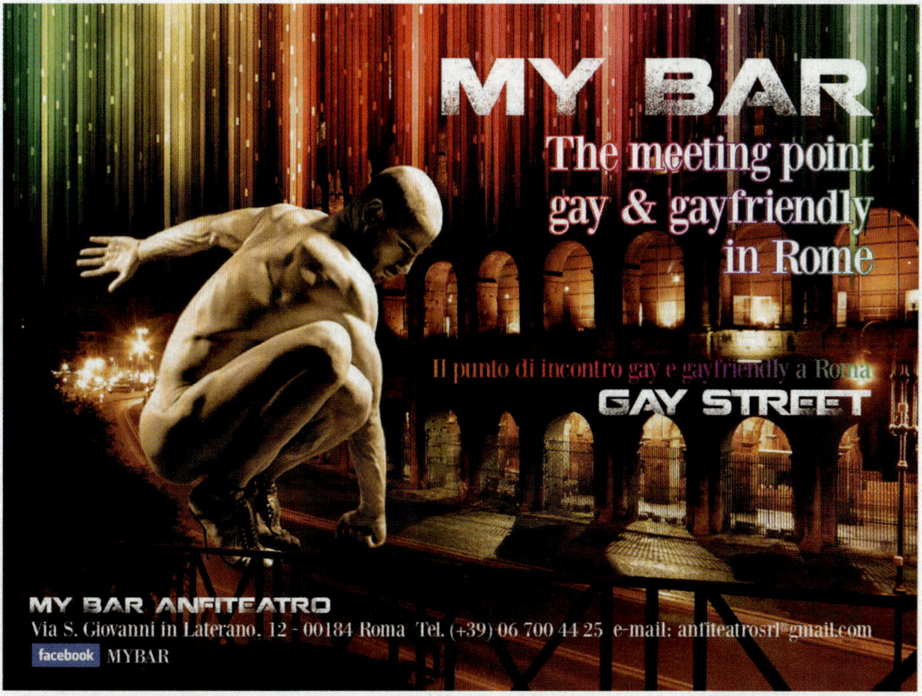

Roma –Map A
EAT & DRINK
Anima e Sapori – Restaurant 17
Dolci e Doni – Restaurant 30
Edoardo II – Restaurant 29
Focaccia. La – Restaurant 35
Garbo – Bar 28
Osteria Vecchio Pegno – Restaurant 34
Skyline – Bar 13
NIGHTLIFE
Alibi. L' – Danceclub 25
Eagle – Men's Club 2
Frutta e Verdura – Danceclub 19
Gate – Men's Club 14
Gorgeous I Am – Danceclub 23
K Sex Club – Men's Club 8
Omogenic – Danceclub 16 & 25
SEX
Cobra – Sex Shop/Blue Movies 4
EMC - Europa Multiclub – Sauna 9
EMC's Bear Den – Sauna 26
Studio Know How – Sex Shop/ Blue Movies 27
Flaminio
Lepanto
Ottaviano
Piazza del Popolo
Galoppatoio
Spagna
Piazza di Spagna
Barberini
Piazza del Risorgimento
Piazza Cavour
Castello S. Angelo
VATICANO
Piazza S. Pietro
F. Tevere
Palazzo d. Quirinale
Fontana di Trevi
Piazza Navona
Campo dei Fiori
Piazza Venezia
Monumento a Vit. Emanuele II
Staz. S. Pietro
Villa Abamelek
Monte Gianicolo
Isola Tiberina
Foro Romano
S. Maria in Trastevere
Monte Palatino
Museo di Roma
Circo Massimo
Piazza di Porta Capena
Porta Portuense
Piazza A. Toja
Mattatoio
Piramide Ostiense
Staz. Roma Ostia-Lido
Piazza Partigiani
Staz. Roma Trastevere
Vle. delle Milizie
Via Cola di Rienzo
Via Crescenzio
Via dei Coronari
Corso Vittorio Emanuele
V. d. Botteghe Oscure
V. d. Plebiscito
V. del Corso
V. Tomacelli
V. del Condotti
V. d. Tritone
Vle. d. Muro Torto
Vle. d. Trinita dei Monti
Lung. Michelangelo
Lung. Castello
Lung. Tor di Nona
Lung. Vaticano
Lung. in Sassia
Galleria PR. A. Savoia
Lung. Gianicolense
Lung. dei Sangallo
Lung. d. Farnesina
Lung. d. Tebaldi
Lung. d. Vallati
Lung. d. Cenci
Lung. Sanzio
Lung. Anguillara
Lung. Aventino
Lung. Testaccio
Via Arenula
Viale Trastevere
Vle. Glorioso
Via Portuense
V. di S. Michele
Via Marmorata
V. Giov. Battista
V. Galvani
Vle. M. Gelsomini
Vle. Piramide Cestia
Vle. Aventino
Vle. Campo Boario
Viale Marco Polo
V. del Porto Fluviale
V. P. Matteucci
Via dei Cerchi
Via del Circo Massimo

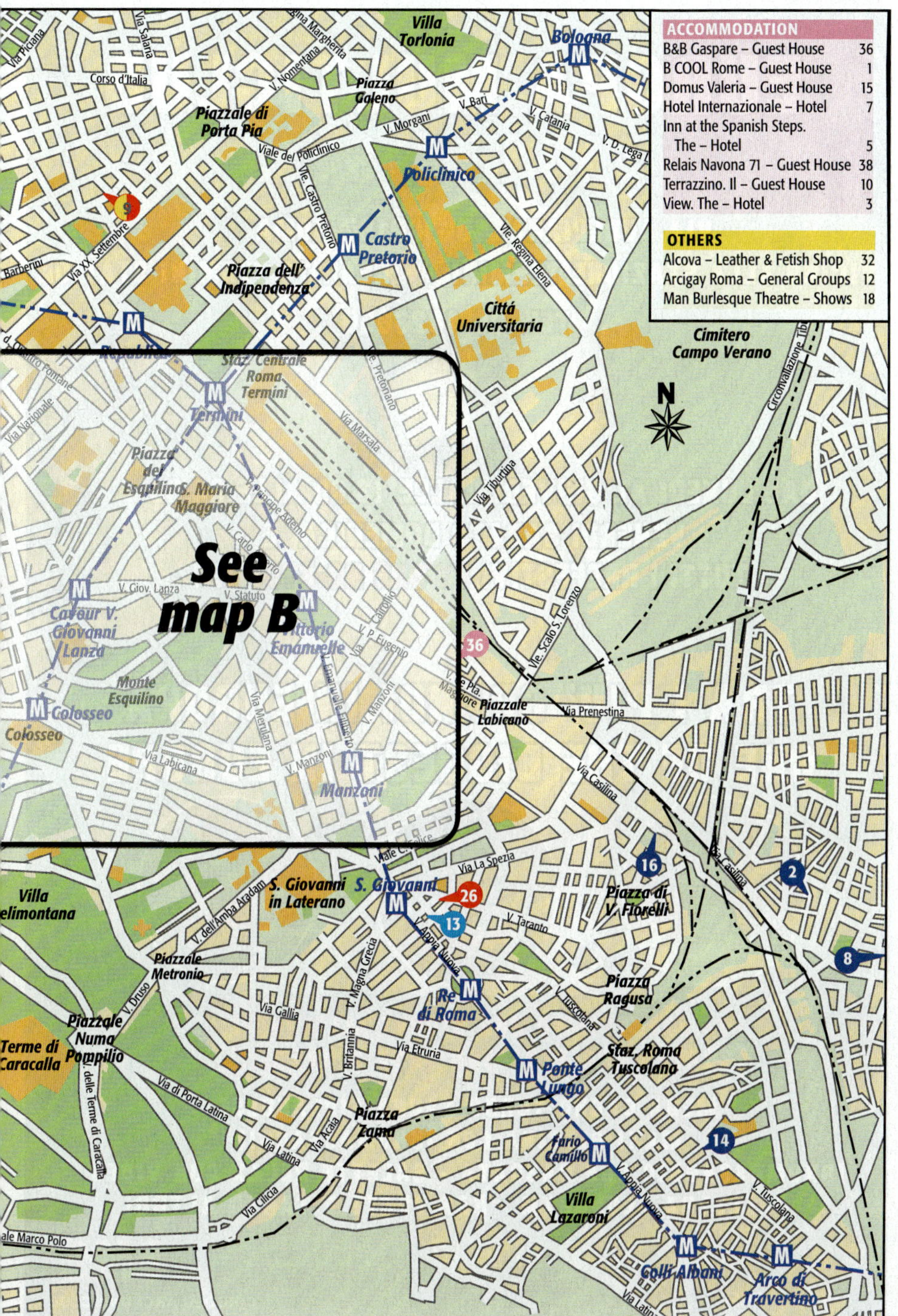
ACCOMMODATION
B&B Gaspare – Guest House 36
B COOL Rome – Guest House 1
Domus Valeria – Guest House 15
Hotel Internazionale – Hotel 7
Inn at the Spanish Steps. The – Hotel 5
Relais Navona 71 – Guest House 38
Terrazzino. Il – Guest House 10
View. The – Hotel 3
OTHERS
Alcova – Leather & Fetish Shop 32
Arcigay Roma – General Groups 12
Man Burlesque Theatre – Shows 18
See map B
Villa Torlonia
Bologna
Piazza Galeno
Piazzale di Porta Pia
Policlinico
Castro Pretorio
Piazza dell' Indipendenza
Città Universitaria
Cimitero Campo Verano
N
Staz. Centrale Roma Termini
Termini
Repubblica
Piazza dei Esquilino
S. Maria Maggiore
Cavour V. Giovanni Lanza
Colosseo
Monte Esquilino
Manzoni
Piazzale Labicano
S. Giovanni in Laterano
S. Giovanni
Villa Celimontana
Piazzale Metronio
Piazzale Numa Pompilio
Terme di Caracalla
Re di Roma
Ponte Lungo
Piazza di V. Fiorelli
Piazza Ragusa
Staz. Roma Tuscolana
Piazza Zama
Furio Camillo
Villa Lazaroni
Colli Albani
Arco di Travertino
Via Salaria
Corso d'Italia
V. Nomentana
Viale del Policlinico
V. Morgagni
V. Bari
V. Catania
Vle. Castro Pretorio
Vle. Regina Elena
Via XX. Settembre
Via Marsala
Via Tiburtina
Vle. Scalo S. Lorenzo
Via Prenestina
Via Casilina
Via Nazionale
V. Giov. Lanza
V. Statuto
Via Merulana
Via Labicana
V. Manzoni
Via La Spezia
V. Taranto
V. Appia Nuova
V. Tuscolana
Via Gallia
Via Etruria
V. Magna Grecia
V. Britannia
V. Druso
Via di Porta Latina
Via Latina
Via Acaia
Via Cilicia
V. delle Terme di Caracalla
Circonvallazione Tib.
Viale Marco Polo
Via Latina

Roma – Map B

EAT & DRINK

- Carbonara. La – Restaurant 23
- Città in Fiore – Restaurant 21
- Coming Out – Bar 16
- Hangar – Bar 18
- Ice Cream Bears – Café 27
- Forchetta d'Oro. La – Restaurant 1
- My Bar – Bar 26
- Sitar Indian Restaurant 25

SEX

- Apollion – Sauna 15
- Cobra – Sex Shop/Blue Movies 11
- Mediterraneo – Sauna 14

ACCOMMODATION

- Ares Rooms – Guest House 19
- Best Place – Guest House 7
- Best Western President – Hotel 12
- Dimora Storica Urbana – Hotel 10
- Enjoy Rome – Guest House 5
- Inn at the Roman Forum. The – Hotel 28
- Labelle – Hotel 20
- Morgana – Hotel 8
- Royal Court – Hotel 4
- Royal Santina – Hotel 9
- RomeBed – Guesthouse 2
- 2nd Floor – Guesthouse 3

OTHERS

- Bici & Baci – Travel & Transport 13 & 22
- Quiiky – Travel & Transport 29
- First – Fitness Studio 6
- Hydra II – Fashion Shop 24
- Souvenir Rainbow – Bookshop 2

■ **Gate** (AC B DR F G MA NU P SNU VS) 22-3, Fri/Sat -4h
Via Tuscolana 378/380 *Near S. Giovanni, Metro Furio Camillo, bus 55 Notturno from Termini* ☎ 347 61 23 752 (mobile) ☎ 348 57 93 760 (mobile) 💻 www.gateroma.it
New cruising bar with cabins and leather room. Mon & Wed free entry, Tue naked, Wed naked bears party, Sun naked vs. underwear. Uno Club card required.

■ **Il Diavolo Dentro** (AC B DR F G LAB MA NU P SL SNU VS) Tue & Thu & Sun 16-21, Wed 16-2, Fri/Sat 22-4h
Largo Itri 23 *At the level of Via Prenestina 239* ☎ 392 490 72 71 (mobile) 💻 www.ildiavolodentro.com
Uno Club card required. On summer the club organizes a naked/orgy vacation in an isolated Villa with swimming pool.

■ **K Sex Club** (AC B DR G MA P VS) 22-4h
Via Amato Amati 6/8 *10 mins from the terminal station, bus 105, night bus 18N* ☎ 06 21 70 12 68 ☎ 349 58 76 731 (mobile) 💻 www.ksexclub.it
Wed & Sun Naked. Uno Club Card required.

CAFES

■ **Ice Cream Bears** (AC B GLM MA) 11-3h
Via S. Giovanni in Laterano 120 ☎ 335 72 99 569
💻 www.myspace.com/icecreambears
Ice cream served by two bears in the small Roan „Gay Street".

DANCECLUBS

■ **Alibi** (AC B D GLM MA OS S WE) Sat 23-?h
Via di Monte Testaccio, 44 ☎ 348 770 8433
„Tommy" Dance Party in the traditional gay club Alibi.

■ **Amigdala** (D GLM) Sat 23-?h
☎ 392 09 29 671 💻 www.amigdalaqueer.it
Queer parties with electronic music in different locations.

■ **Crazyball Festival** (B D GLM MA S)
☎ 334 81 82 654 (infoline) 💻 www.crazyballfestival.com
First international GLBT festival organized by SplashRoma from 12th to 15th July 2012. Four days of fun with five parties, international guests, many performances and more surprises in various locations in Rome.

■ **Frutta e Verdura** (AC B D DR G MA P S t) Sun 4.30-10h
Via di Monte Testaccio 94 ☎ 347 87 97 063 (infoline)
💻 www.fruttaeverdura.roma.it
Gay afterhour with two darkrooms in the early morning. Smoking area. Uno Club card required.

■ **Gay Village** (B D GLM M MA OS S)
Jun-Sep, Thu-Sat 20.30-4, free entry 20.30-21.30h
Via delle Tre Fontane / Parco del Ninfeo *M° B Magliana, night bus 96N*
☎ 340 75 38 396 (infoline) 💻 www.gayvillage.it
Bars, restaurants, shops, concerts, shows and bars in an artificial village. See www.gayvillage.it for daily programme.

■ **Gloss** (AC B CC D GLM M OS S SNU ST YC)
Thu 22.30-4.30h
c/o Alibi, Via di Monte Testaccio 44 *M° Piramide* ☎ 347 66 08 332
💻 www.gloss.it
Young crowd, mainstream music.

■ **Gorgeous I Am** (AC B D DR GLM M OS S) Oct-June: Sat 23-5h
c/o Alpheus, Via del Commercio 36 ☎ 340 75 38 396
💻 www.gorgeousroma.it
Mainstream, house and revival music on 6 dancefloors. More information see www.myspace.com/gorgeousroma

■ **Muccassassina** (B D DR GLM S YC) Fri 22.30-5.30h (Oct-Jun)
c/o Qube, Via di Portonaccio 212 *Bus 409, night bus 17N from Roma Tiburtina M° B* ☎ 06 54 13 985 💻 www.muccassassina.com
Very popular. Danceclub on three floors run by Mario Mieli.

■ **Omogenic** (AC B D GLM M) Fri 23-4h
c/o Alibi, Via di Monte Testaccio 44 *Metro Piramide* ☎ 340 75 38 396
💻 www.gayvillage.it
Disco, black & house music. Good prices.

■ **Splash Roma** (AC B CC D GLM OS S WE YC)
Sat 23-5h, First Sun/month, 19-1h
c/o Room26, Piazza Guglielmo Marconi 31 *M° B Magliana*
☎ 334 81 82 654 (infoline) 💻 www.splashroma.it
T-Dance Party with international DJs, performances and hot go-go-boys, house & pop dancefloor. Outdoor garden for smoking and chilling. For further special "One night events" check the homepage..

■ **Subwoofer** (B D DR f G MA)
💻 www.subwooferbears.com
Bear parties, every last weekend/month.

RESTAURANTS

■ **Anima e Sapori** (B GLM MA) 11-24h
Via di Tor Millina 17a/18 *Piazza Navona* ☎ 06 68 13 62 79
💻 www.animaesapori.com
Traditional Roman Cuisine.

■ **Carbonara. La** (B glm M) 12.30-14.30 & 20-24h
Via Panisperna 214 *Monti district* ☎ 06 48 25 176
💻 www.lacarbonara.it
Good Roman cuisine in a nice atmosphere, bar with excellent cocktails, open until 2h. Restaurant discount for Spartacus readers!

■ **Città in Fiore** (B DM glm M VEG WL) 11-15.30, 18-0.30h, Tue & Wed in the evening only
Via Cavour 269 *Metro Cavour* ☎ 06 48 24 874
Chinese restaurant with many gay diners.

■ **Dolci e Doni** (AC B BF CC GLM M) 11-24, Nov-March -23h
Via delle Carrozze 85b *Close to the Spanish Steps, M° Spagna*
☎ 066 992 5001
Tea room and cocktail bar with lunch and dinner.

■ **Edoardo II** (AC B DM GLM M MA OS P S VEG WL)
19-1h, closed Tue
Vicolo Margana 14 *Piazza Venezia* ☎ 06 69 94 24 19
💻 www.edoardosecondo.com
The only explicitly gay restaurant in Rome with Mediterranean cuisine & pizza. Dining also outside in a nice and relaxed atmosphere.

■ **Focaccia. La** (AC B CC DM glm M OS VEG WL) 11-2h
Via della Pace 11 *Near Piazza Navona* ☎ 06 68 80 33 12
💻 www.lafocaccia.com
Restaurant and pizzeria.

■ **Forchetta d'Oro, La** (g M OS) 11-15 & 17-1h, Fri at lunch closed
Via San Martino ai Monti 40 *M° Cavour & Matro Vittorio Emanuele, bus 40/64/70/71/75/714, night bus 40N* ☎ 06 48 91 31 53
Typical Roman cuisine to good prices.

■ **Osteria Vecchio Pegno** (glm M MA RES VEG WL) 11.30-15 & 19-24h, Wed closed
Vicolo Montevecchio 8 *Near Corinari Street* ☎ 06 68 80 70 25
💻 www.osteriadelpegno.com
Traditional Roman cuisine – and not just Pizzas, which are served at lunch-time only.

■ **Sitar Indian Restaurant** (AC CC GLM M MA)
12-15 & 19-24h, closed Mon for lunch
Via Cavour 256A *Opp. M° Cavour* ☎ 06 890 267 10
☎ 348 25 44 943 (mobile) 💻 www.sitar-roma.org
Gay friendly Indian restaurant. 10% discount for Spartacus readers.

SEX SHOPS/BLUE MOVIES

■ **Cobra** (g VS) Mon-Sat 9.30-20h
Via Giovanni Giolitti 307/313 *M° Piazza Vittorio E.* ☎ 06 37 51 73 50
💻 www.sexyshopcobra.it
Underwear, magazines, retail and rental of gay videos.

■ **Cobra** (g VS) Mon-Sat 9-20h
Via Barletta 23 *M° Ottaviano* ☎ 06 37 51 73 50
🖳 www.sexyshopcobra.it
Underwear, magazines, retail and rental of gay videos.

■ **Cobra** (g VS) Tue-Sat 9.30-20h
Via Aurelio Cotta 22/24 *M° Numidio Quadrato* ☎ 06 37 51 73 50
🖳 www.sexyshopcobra.it

■ **Studio Know How** (GLM) 10.30-20h, Sun & Mon closed
Via di San Gallicano 13 *Trastevere district* ☎ 06 58 33 56 92

SEX CINEMAS

■ **Ambasciatori** (g r VS)
Via Montebello 101 *M° Termini* ☎ 06 49 41 290

SAUNAS/BATHS

■ **Apollion** (
AC B CC DR DU FC FH G GH m MA MSG p PI RR SA SB VS WH) 14-23h
Via Mecenate 59/a *M° Piazza Vittorio / Colosseo* ☎ 06 48 25 389
🖳 www.apollionsauna.com
Smoking zone. Uno Club card required.

■ **EMC – Europa Multiclub** (AC B CC DR FC FH G I m MSG P PI PP RR S SA SB SOL VS WH WO YC) 13-24, Fri 13-Sun 24h (non-stop)
Via Aureliana 40 *Near railway station, M° Republica* ☎ 06 48 23 650
🖳 www.europamulticlub.com
Big sauna on 1500 m². Parties on Fri and Sat at 24h „Light parade": music, steam, foam and dark labyrinth. Big hammam with water and light games. Swimming pool with back massage and cromo-therapy. Kneipp-foot massage in salt water. Smoking zone. Uno Club card required.

■ **EMC's Bear Den** (AC B CC DR G M MA MSG P SA SB VS WH) 13-24, Fri 13-Sun 24h (non-stop)
Via Pontremoli 28 *M° S. Giovanni, close to Skyline Bar* ☎ 06 70 45 00 22
🖳 www.emcbear.com
Brand new sauna for bears & friends. 3 whirlpools. Relax rooms in oversize. Check out www.emcbear.com

■ **Mediterraneo**
(AC B DR DU FC G LAB m MA MSG P RR SA SB VR VS WH) 13-23h
Via Pasquale Villari, 3 *M° Manzoni / Vittorio Emanuele / Colosseo, bus 16, 714 between Via Merulana and Via Labicana* ☎ 06 77 20 59 34
🖳 www.saunamediterraneo.it
Sauna on three floors. Special price for those under 26. Best times daily from 15-21h. Uno Club card required.

■ **Terme di Roma Internazionale** (AC B DR DU FC FH G LAB M MA PP RR SA SB VS WH) 12-23h; Mon & Tue (G), Wed-Sun mixed
Via Persio 4 *Bus 765 from M° Arco di Travertino, district Quarto Miglio/Via Appia Nuova* ☎ 06 71 84 378
Sauna with a big maze, quite far from the centre. Mon & Tue (G), Wed-Sun mixed.

FITNESS STUDIOS

■ **EMC – Europa Multiclub** (G WO) 13-24, Fri 13-Sun 24h (non-stop)
Via Aureliana 40 *Near railway station, M° Republica* ☎ 06 48 23 650
🖳 www.europamulticlub.com
Fitness in the gay sauna.

■ **First** (g WO) Mon-Fri 8-23, Sat & Sun 10-21h
Via Giovanni Giolitti 44 *M° Termini* ☎ 06 47 82 63 00

TRANSVESTITE / SHOWS

■ **Man Burlesque Theatre** (GLM ST) every Sun 21.30h
Piazza di Santa Chiara 14 *Near Pantheon*
☎ (0039) 06 687 55 79 (info & reservations) 🖳 www.canalg.it
Show every Sun at 21.30h in the Palazzo Santa Chiara Theatre, open from 21h.

■ **Reversman** (GLM SNU) every Mon 21.30h
c/o Teatro Campo d'Arte, Via dei Cappellari 93 *Near Campo dei Fiori*
Unique Man Stripshow. For info and reservation: reversman@canalg.it

BOOK SHOPS

■ **Souvenir Rainbow** (GLM) 12-24h, every day
Via San Giovanni in Laterano 26 *next door to Coming Out and My Bar, metro Colosseo* ☎ 06 97 84 57 55 🖳 www.souvenirsouvenir.eu
Everything you need: books, guides, gadgets, dvds, toys, presents etc.

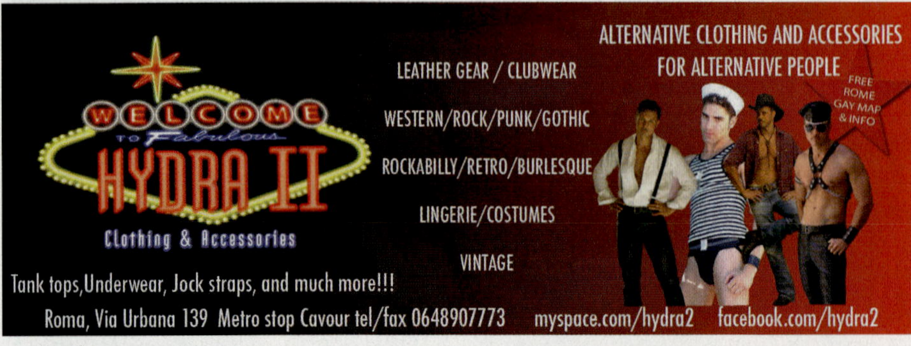

FASHION SHOPS

■ **Hydra II** (F GLM) Mon 15-21, Tue-Sat 11-21h
Via Urbana 139 *M° Cavour, Monti district* ☎ 06 48 90 77 73
💻 facebook.com/hydra2
Clubwear, rock, punk, goth, retro, burlesque and leather gear.

LEATHER & FETISH SHOPS

■ **Alcova** (AC f g) 10-20, Mon 15-20h, closed Sun
Piazza Sforza Cesarini 27 (off Corso Vittorio Emanuele II) *5 mins from Piazza Navona/Campo dei Fiori* ☎ 06 68 64 118 💻 www.alcova.biz
Lingerie, clubwear, fetishwear etc.

TRAVEL AND TRANSPORT

■ **Airport Transfer Rome**
☎ 338 93 18 904 (mobile) 💻 www.airporttransferrome.com
Door-to-door service between Airport Fiumicino, Ciampino & Civitavecchia port and Rome.

■ **Bici&Baci** Daily 8-19h
Via Cavour 302 *Near Foro Romano, M° Colosseo* ☎ 06 94539240
☎ 06 94538713 💻 www.bicibaci.com
Scooter rental in the centre of Rome. Good prices.

■ **Bici&Baci** Daily 8-19h
Via del Viminale 5 *Close to railway station Termini* ☎ 06 4828443
☎ 06 48986162 💻 www.bicibaci.com

■ **Luca Gay Guide** (G) All year
💻 www.gay-guide-rome.com
Private gay tour guide in Rome.

■ **Quiiky** (GLM)
Via della Consulta 52 ☎ 06 455 958 85 💻 www.quiiky.com
Italian Gay & Lesbian Tour Operator, member of IGLTA

HOTELS

■ **Aris Garden** (AC B BF CC H I M MA OS PI SA SB WO)
Via Aristofane, 101 *Between EUR and Ostia, 7 km from Fiumicino airport*
☎ 06 52 36 24 43 💻 www.rosciolihotels.com
Luxurious hotel between Rome and the beaches. 12.000 qm sportive area: pool, tennis playground, soccer, gym. WIFI and Pay-TV. Pick up upon request.

■ **Best Western President** (AC B BF CC H I M MA) All year
Via Emanuele Filiberto 173 *M° Vittorio Emanuele, near Colosseum*
☎ 06 77 01 21 💻 www.rosciolihotels.com
Four-star hotel with 192 modern rooms with own bath or shower/WC, mini-bar, phone, fax, TV and modem. Reservation required, pick-up service possible, bf incl. WIFI.

■ **Best Western Universo**
(AC B BF CC glm H I M MA OS PA RWB RWS RWT SA SB WO) All year
Via Principe Amedeo 5/B *M° Termini* ☎ 06 47 68 11
💻 www.rosciolihotels.com
Four-star hotel with 199 rooms and 15 suites with own bath or shower/WC, mini-bar, phone, modem and radio. Reservation required, pets allowed. WIFI. Pay-TV. Pick-up service upon request.

■ **Claridge** (AC B BF CC H I M MA OS PA SA SB WO) All year
Viale Liegi 62 *Parioli district, tram 3/19, bus 52/53/360* ☎ 06 84 54 41
💻 www.rosciolihotels.com
Four-star hotel with 93 rooms with bath or shower/WC, mini-bar, safe, phone, fax, modem, TV and radio. WIFI. Reservation required, pets allowed. Pick-up service upon request.

■ **Dimora Storica Urbana** (AC b BF CC glm MSG SA SOL WH WO) All year
Via Urbana 35 *between railway station Termini and Colosseum, metro Cavour* ☎ 06 99 70 99 45 🖳 www.dimorestoricheroma.com
Comfortable rooms with all ameneties. Spa with sauna, whirlpool and fitness room in the basement. Located in a nice area near gay venues.

■ **Hotel Internazionale** (AC B bf CC glm H I OS PA RWS RWT) All year
Via Sistina, 79 *50 m from Piazza di Spagna, 500 m from Trevi fountain* ☎ 06 69 94 18 23 🖳 www.hotelinternazionale.com
Rooms with sat-TV, free WI-FI, minibar and safe. See www.mygemhotels.com for further hotels.

■ **Inn at the Roman Forum. The**
(AC B BF CC glm H I OS RWS RWT) All year, 24hrs
Via degli Ibernesi 30 *Metro Colosseo* ☎ 06 69 19 09 70
🖳 www.theinnattheromanforum.com
Luxurious, sophisticated hotel with archeological sight inside the hotel. Beautiful views over the Foro Romano from the terrace.If you mention Spartacus you will get upgrade.

■ **Inn at the Spanish Steps. The**
(AC B BF CC glm H I OS RWS RWT) All year, 24hrs
Via dei Condotti, 85 *M° Spagna* ☎ 06 69 92 56 57
🖳 www.atspanishsteps.com

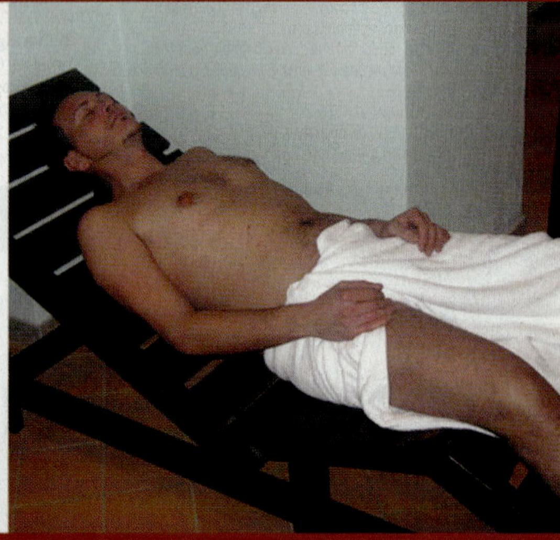

b-cool rome
GAY FRIENDLY
B&B - BOUTIQUE HOTEL
A cool place for cool people
Confort and Relax for your holiday in Rome
phone 06 45504533
mobile 333 8449796
info@b-cool.eu
www.b-cool.eu

Exclusive hotel with a terrace overlooking the Spanish steps.If you mention Spartacus at the moment of reservation you will get a free upgrade and a gift.

■ **Labelle** (AC BF CC glm PA RWS RWT) All year
Via Cavour 310 *M° Colosseo/Cavour* ☎ 06 67 94 750 🖳 www.hotellabelle.it
Also triple and quadruple rooms. All rooms are with own bath or shower and fridge. Discount for Spartacus readers.

■ **Morgana** (AC B CC glm H I RWS RWT) All year, 24hrs
Via Filippo Turati, 33 *Near Stazione Termini* ☎ 06 446 72 30
🖳 www.hotelmorgana.com
The Morgana is centrally located. If you mention Spartacus at the moment of reservation you will get a free upgrade and a gift.

■ **Panama Garden** (AC B CC glm H I PA RWS RWT) All year, 24hrs
Via Salaria 336 *Near Villa Ada and Priscilla catacombs* ☎ 06 855 25 58
🖳 www.hotelpanamarome.com
If you mention Spartacus at the moment of reservation you will get a free upgrade and a gift.

■ **Royal Court** (AC B CC glm H I RWS RWT) 24hrs
Via Marghera 51 *Near Stazione Termini* ☎ 06 44 34 03 64
🖳 www.morganaroyalcourt.com
Centrally located.If you mention Spartacus at the moment of reservation you will get a free upgrade and a gift.

■ **Best Western Premier Royal Santina** (AC B BF CC glm H I M MA OS PA RWB RWS RWT) All year
Via Marsala 22 *M° Termini* ☎ 06 44 87 51 🖳 www.rosciolihotels.com
Four-star hotel with 118 rooms with bath or shower/WC, mini-bar, phone, TV, radio, fax and modem. WIFI. Reservation required, pets allowed. Pick up service.

■ **View at the Spanish Steps. The**
(AC B bf CC glm H I RWS RWT) All year
Via dei Condotti, 91 ☎ 06 69 92 56 57 🖳 www.theviewatthespanishsteps.com
Beautiful, luxurious penthouse with great view over the Spanish steps.If you mention Spartacus at the moment of reservation you will get a free upgrade and a gift.

GUEST HOUSES

2nd Floor (AC BF GLM I MC RWB RWS RWT) All year, 24hrs
Via San Giovanni in Laterano, 10 *100m from the Colosseum*
☎ 333 411 86 20 💻 www.2floorgay.it
New stylish gay guesthouse in the „gaystreet" of Rome with view over the Colosseum. Comfortable rooms with own bath and all modern ameneties, free WiFi access included.

Ares Rooms (BF CC GLM I PA RWS RWT VA) All year
Via Domenichino 7, scala A *Near railway station Termini. M° Cavour & M° Vittorio Emanuele, bus 40/64/70/71/75/714, night bus 40N*
☎ 06 474 45 25 💻 www.aresrooms.com
Eight rooms with and without own bathroom, with tv. Centrally located, gay owned and managed. Pets allowed. Information about the gay scene available. Reception 24hrs.

B&B Gaspare (AC BF GLM I) All year
Via Balilla, 16 *M° Vittorio Emanuele, 500 m from Termini railway station*
☎ 06 64 82 16 60 💻 www.bbgaspare.com
Rooms with private bathroom, kitchenette & TV. Wifi access. Internet available. Own key. Reservation required. Pets allowed.

B-COOL Rome (AC BF GLM I RWS RWT) All year
Via Famagosta 4 *Metro A Ottaviano, close to Vatican and San Pietro*
☎ 333 8449796 ☎ 06 45504533 💻 www.b-cool.eu

Bedfiora (H OS PA RWB RWS) All year
Via Balilla 20 *Close to Porta Maggiore and central railway station Termini*
☎ 06 648 214 09 ☎ (347) 0769 084 (mobile) 💻 www.bedfiora.it

Best Place (b BF G I MA NR RWS)
Via Turati 13 *3 mins walk to Termini Station*
☎ 329 21 32 320 (mobile) 💻 www.bestplace.it
Rooms with private bath and TV. Reservation required.

Domus Valeria (AC BF CC H M MSG OS)
Via del Babuino 96 *A few steps from the Spanish Steps, metro Spagna*
☎ 339 2326540 💻 www.domusvaleria.it
Three nice rooms in an apartment directly at the Spanish Steps. Gay owned.

Enjoy Rome Bed & Breakfast
(AC B BF CC glm I MA PA PK RWS RWT VA) All year
Via Dell'Esquilino 38 *City centre* ☎ 06 976 148 48
💻 www.enjoyromebb.com
Stylish and comfortable guesthouse. Free non-alcoholic drinks. Gay information available. Every room with a free laptop and WiFi access. Special rates for Spartacus readers.

Il Terrazzino (AC BF CC glm I)
Via Cesare Pascarella 12 *Trastevere district, railway station Trastevere, tram 8, bus 3, 170, H from Termini* ☎ 339 65 17 084 (mobile)

☎ 348 95 13 314 (mobile) 🖳 www.ilterrazzinobandb.it
Three rooms in a private apartment. Free wireless internet, breakfast also possible in the room. Owned by a nice lesbian couple.

■ **Relais Navona71** (AC BF CC G)
Piazza Navona, 71 ☎ 06 68 96 915 🖳 www.navona71.it
6 Bedrooms with bath, 4 with a direct view of Piazza Navona. All the rooms with air conditioning, PC and wireless access, small refrigerator, safe, hair dryer, TV, LCD.

■ **RomeBed** (AC H RWT WI) All year
Via Emanuele Filiberto 109 *near Piazza Vittorio Emanuele, Metro Manzoni*
☎ 339 1580615 🖳 www.romebed.com
Huge rooms in a private apartment in the center of Rome, close to railway station Termini.

GENERAL GROUPS

■ **Arcigay Roma** Mon-Sat 16-20h
Via Zabaglia 14 *Testaccio district, M° Piramide* ☎ 06 64 50 11 02
🖳 www.arcigayroma.it
Volunteer group fighting against homophobia and HIV.

■ **Key We Associazione Culturale Nazionale**
☎ (0039) 02 890 383 69 🖳 www.keywe.it
National association for the gay community.

FETISH GROUPS

■ **CoMoG**
🖳 www.comog.it
Coordination of gay & lesbian motorbikers.

■ **Leather Club Roma (LCR)** (F G)
🖳 www.lcroma.com

■ **Rome Bear Week** (F G)
☎ 347 32 31 073 🖳 www.RomeBearWeek.com
Organizer of the Rome Bears Week in the beginning of January.

HEALTH GROUPS

■ **LILA – Lega Italiana Lotta contro l'AIDS** Mon-Fri 10-13 & 14-17h
Via Bradano 6 *Near Corso Trieste* ☎ 06 88 48 492 🖳 www.lilalazio.it

SPECIAL INTEREST GROUPS

■ **Associazione di Volontariato Libellula** (MA T) Tue 19-21.30h
Piazza Vittorio Emanuele II, 2 ☎ 06 44 63 421 🖳 www.libellula2001.it
Association of transexuals, transgender and drags.

SWIMMING

-Beach south of Ostia, take train to C. Colombo then bus 7 (nice dunes; by car: from Lido di Ostia in direction Anzio, after km-sign 8; by bus: Bus 7 from C. Colombo till you see the gay flags, beach bar Stabilimento Balneare Settimo Cielo)
-Beach at Cerenova (at km 46 on Via Aurelia).
-Spiaggia di Campo di Mare in Cerveteri (arrive by car at the end of Viale Mediterraneo, corner Lungomare dei Navigatori Etruschi,
enter the beach and the ditch on the right side, after 800 m naturist gay beach/cruising in the reeds).

CRUISING

-Colosseo Quadrato (Metro Magliana, gardens near Bar Palombini, in the evening, crowded AYOR)
-Piazza Belle Arti „Valle Giulia", in front of National Gallery of Modern Art, opposite hustlers, by car and on foot (r)
-Monte Caprino (in the evening/at night, gates are closed, so only cruising at the bottom of the hill, ayor)
-Villa Borghese, Galoppatoio (evening)
-Via dei Colli della Farnesina, Parco di Montemario, behind the Ministry for foreign affairs (during the day)
-Via di Fioranello/Via Appia Antica: from Raccordo Anulare for one kilometre Via Appia Nuova in direction Ciampino airport. Before the airport right hand (by car, all day and night, busy).

Salerno – Campania

GENERAL GROUPS

■ **Arcigay Marcella di Folco**
Piazza Vittorio Veneto 2 ☎ 089 25 42 42 ☎ 331 64 01 985
🖳 www.arcigaysalerno.it
Meeting every Thu 17-20h.

SWIMMING

-Pontecagnano: Lido Arenella, northern part (NU), in wintertime cruising in the woods (by day and night).

CRUISING

-Seafront
-Stadio Arecchi, Piazzale dello Stadio (by car, at night, ayor)
-Giardini Teatro Verdi (T).

San Benedetto del Tronto – Marche

SWIMMING

-Punta Nina (beach between Pevaso and Benedetto, behind Pensione Il Contadino).

CRUISING

-Railway Station
-Cinema delle Palme (garden behind the cinema, at night)
-Muro del Pianto (garden behind Roxy Hotel, at night).

Sardegna

Sardegna – Cagliari

GAY INFO

■ **Associazione Culturale ARC** Help & Infoline Wed 20-23h
Via Puccini 51 ☎ 347 29 19 800 (help & info) 🖳 www.associazionearc.eu
Small festival of gay and lesbian films, HIV prevention.

BARS

■ **Ciringuito Loungebar** (B glm MA)
Only in summer (June-September)
Lungomare Quartu Sant'Elena *some km outside of Cagliari, near the compass* ☎ 348 58 76 314 (mobile)
Beachbar with shows.

■ **Rainbow Café** (B GLM MA OS ST) 19-2h, Mon closed
Via Rossini, 16 ☎ 347 60 78 384 (mobile)
Only gay bar in Cagliari town. Shows on Wed.

DANCECLUBS

■ **Go Fish** (AC B CC D GLM I ST) Thu & Sat 24-4.30h
Via G.B. Venturi 12/14 *Opp. Viale Marconi* ☎ 348 58 76 314 (mobile)
💻 www.go-fish.it
Thu: cabaret and disco, Sat: disco.

SEX SHOPS/BLUE MOVIES

■ **Sixtynine** (g)
10-13, 17-20.30h, Sun closed (in winter also closed on Mon morning)
Via Baylle 69 *centre* ☎ 070 66 95 50 💻 www.sixtynine.it
Only sex shop in Sardegna with gay items.

GUEST HOUSES

■ **Gabbiani. I** (glm H I OS PA RWT VA) All year
Largo Carlo Felice 36 *100 m from harbour and harbour*
☎ 07 06 65 976
Two double rooms in an old palazzo in the city centre with old furniture.

■ **Open B&B** (AC BF G I MA RWB RWS RWT) All year
Via Sonnino 147 ☎ 070 650358 (mobile) 💻 www.openbb.it
Two double rooms with bathroom and private balcony with wonderfull views. Shopping facilities, restaurants and pubs in walking distance.

■ **Terrazza sul Porto. La** (AC BF H I OS) All year
Largo Carlo Felice, 36 ☎ 339 876 0155 (mobile)
💻 www.laterrazzasulporto.com
Rooms with and without private bathroom. Beautiful terrace with great view on the roof. 10% discount for Spartacus readers. Gay owned.

GENERAL GROUPS

■ **CGIL – UffIcio Nuovi Diritti** Mon 17-19h
☎ 070 27 97 270
Gay and lesbian rights at work. Help against discrimination.

■ **CGIL – UffIcio Nuovi Diritti** Mon 17-19h
☎ 070 27 97 270
Gay and lesbian rights at work. Help against discrimination.

SWIMMING

-Cala Fighera, Cala Mosca (g NU) (5 km from Cagliari, Bus N°11, under the casern, on the rocks)
-Terra Mala (G NU) (20 km from Cagliari, on the way to Villasimius, last bus stop, turn left and walk 700 metres along the shore)
-Piscina Rei (Monte Nai), swimming pool, on the dunes.

CRUISING

-Piazza Matteotti (in front of the railway station, all day, AYOR)
-P Stadium S. Elia (especially after 20h) (AYOR)
-P Fiera, Piazza Marco Polo/via C. Colombo (after 20h) (AYOR)
-Lighthouse Cala Mosca (daytime).

Sardegna – Olbia Costa Smeralda

GUEST HOUSES

■ **Villa Torcis Boutique B&B** (AC BF CC G H M MSG OS PI SOL)
Loc. Li Crineddi 1, Telti *15 km from Olbia* ☎ 339 11 36 277 (mobile)
💻 www.villatorcis.it
Gay owned beautiful landhouses in a large property with oak and olive trees. Rooms with private bath, Sat tv, dvd, frigobar and daily roomservice. Dinner available. Italian, English, Portuguese, Spanish and French spoken.

Sardegna – Oristano

SWIMMING

-Marina di Arborea (G MA NU) (Strada mare 29)
-Is Arenas beach (from Oristano take the direction of Cuglieri, turn at the camping Nurapolis, walk around 2 km on the beach at the end of the P on the left side).

CRUISING

-Torre Grande pine trees wood, after Orbia direction Cagliari (by car and on foot).

Sardegna – Sassari

GENERAL GROUPS

■ **Movimento Omosessuale Sardo (MOS)** (B GLM I MA)
Mon-Fri 18-23h
Via Rockfeller 16/c ☎ 079 21 90 24
💻 www.movimentomosessualesardo.org
Political and cultural centre for gays, lesbians and transexuals. Helpline and information, bar, internet point

SWIMMING

-Porto Ferro (NU) near Alghero (at the end on the right on the rocks, cruisy)
-Maria Pia, Alghero beach (last part on the trees side direction Fertilia).

CRUISING

-Corso Giò Maria Angioi (r t) (from 22h, on foot or by car)
-Quarto pettine (zona Platamona) (winter by car, summer also by foot)
-Railway station (and the place in front at night)raus

Sasso Marconi – Emilia Romagna

HOTELS

■ **Triana e Tyche. Albergo** (AC CC glm MSG PA PK RWB RWS RWT VA) Closed from 24 Dec-7 Jan
Viale J.F. Kennedy 9 *700 m from station* ☎ 0516 75 16 16
💻 www.atethotel.it
Special rates for long stays and for Spartacus readers.

CRUISING

-Exit A1 Sasso Marconi, turn left, direction ‚Piccolo Paradiso', after the bridge turn left, along the river (at daytime).

Saturnia – Toscana

GUEST HOUSES

■ **Quercia Rossa B&B** (AC BF glm H I M OS PA PI PK RWS RWT VA) All year
Santarello 89, fraz. Montemerano ☎ 0564 62 95 29
💻 www.querciarossa.net
Charming B&B between Roma and Siena, close to Saturnia's cascades and thermal baths. Large rooms with own key, bath and TV.

SWIMMING

-Cascades with hot thermal water (entrance of Saturnia), many gays at the weekends.

Savona – Liguria

SWIMMING

-Varigotti, castello (up the hill with the small castle beside the tunnel, on the left side to the sea; the left bay is interesting).

CRUISING

-Loano (seaside from railway station Loano in direction Borghetto, P ex-railway stop near Piazza del Popolo, at night).

Senigallia – Marche

DANCECLUBS

■ **Pensiero Stupendo** (AC B D DR GLM MA OS P S SNU ST VS WE)
Fri & Sat 23-?h
Strada della Bruciata km 7,2 *At residential centre „Le Piramidi" direction Monterado, after 7 km on the left* ☎ 347 07 79 266
www.pensierostupendo.net
Disco club with big cruising area and cabins. Uno Club card required.

SAUNAS/BATHS

■ **Velluto**
(AC B DR DU FC FH G GH I LAB M MA MSG p RR SA SB VS WH) 15-24h
Marzocca di Senigallia, S.S. Adriatica Sud, 184 *300 m from train station Marzocca* ☎ 340 77 08 324 (mobile)
450 m² on two floors. Uno Club card required.

SWIMMING

-Spiaggia delle Piramidi: Senigallia nord, in front of the shopping centre Il Maestrale (From the parking place by foot along the river to the beach)

CRUISING

-Marotta, Spiaggia delle Vele: after the bridge to the right. Cruising between camping and Le Vele complex (by night, by car and on foot)
-Railway Station (toilets)

Sesto Fiorentino – Toscana

BARS

■ **BK** (B glm m MA)
Via Alfieri 95 ☎ 055 42 18 878

Sicilia

Sicilia – Agrigento

GAY INFO

■ **Arcigay Ganimede**
☎ 349 78 22 930 www.arcigayagrigento.it

GUEST HOUSES

■ **Camere a Sud** (AC BF H I)
Via Ficani 6 ☎ 349 63 84 424 www.camereasud.it
Gayfriendly B&B. All rooms equipped with bathroom, TV and air conditioning. Internet point and Wi-Fi.

SWIMMING

-Località San Leone (NU)
-Le Dune (last bus stop)
-Eraclea Minoa Beach, near Ribera (very beautiful & crowded).

CRUISING

-Bus parking (behind Astor cinema)
-Piazza Vittorio Emanuele (in front of main post office)
-Viale della Vittoria (at bus stop)
-Piazza Fratelli Rosselli (R)
-Villa Communale.

Sicilia – Catania

GAY INFO

■ **Arcigay Catania**
Viale Kennedy 80 ☎ 348 35 34 116 www.arcigaycatania.it

■ **Centro di Iniziativa Gay Trans Lesbica Open Mind**
17-20h
☎ 348 47 29 236 www.openmindcatania.ilcannocchiale.it
Independent group working since 1990 for sexual orientation and gender politics. Organizer of the Catania Pride GLTB.

MEN'S CLUBS

■ **Codice Rosso** (AC B DR F G MA P SNU)
Tue-Thu & Sun 22-2, Fri & Sat 22-4h
Via Conte Ruggero 48 *Between Piazza Vittorio Emanuele II and Piazza Trento* ☎ 333 86 26 925 www.codice-rosso.it
Sun naked/underwear.

DANCECLUBS

■ **Café Noir** (AC B D DR GLM m S SNU ST WE YC)
Fri 24-5h (October-May)
Via Domenico Tempio 60 *In front of the port*
Danceclub with 2 dancefloors. Young crowd.

■ **Cappannine. Le** (AC B D DR GLM M OS S SNU ST WE YC)
Fri & Sun 24-5h (Jun-Sep)
Viale Kennedy, Lidi Playa ☎ 347 95 48 021
3 dancefloors: House, mainstream & revival. Also bungalows to rent.

■ **Pegaso's Disco Club** (AC B D GLM MA P S SNU ST VS WE)
Sat 23-6h (Oct-May), Jun-Sep Thu, Sat, Sun 23-?h
Viale Kennedy 80 ☎ 095 73 57 268 www.pegasos.it
In summer outdoor with swimming pool and outside cruising. Shows on Thu & Sun. Uno Club card required. Beware of the Transsexuals!

RESTAURANTS

■ **Neva** (AC B BF CC GLM M MA OS) 10-3, Sun 18-3h
Piazza San Francesco d'Assisi 5 *Centre* ☎ 095 31 55 45
www.pegasos.it
Restaurant and pizzeria with Mediterranean cuisine and American bar.

SAUNAS/BATHS

■ **Mykonos** (B DR FC G I m MSG OS RR SA SB SOL VS WH WO)
Tue-Sun 15.30-22.30h
Via Platamone, 20 ☎ 095 531 355 www.saunamykonos.it
Large and popular venue with extensive facilities, free internet. Friendly staff.

■ **Terme di Achille** (AC B DR DU FC FH G GH I LAB M MA MSG PI PP RR S SA SB VS) Tue-Sun 15-24h, closed on Mon
Via Tezzano 13 *Near the main train station* ☎ 095 746 35 43
🖳 www.termediachille.it
Clean, nice sauna. Smoking area and internet point.

BOOK SHOPS

■ **Libreria Gramigna**
Via S.Anna 19 ☎ 095 32 75 58

HOTELS

■ **Romano House** (AC BF CC glm I OS) All year
Via Di Prima, 20 ☎ 095 59 67 558 🖳 romanohouse.it

■ **Romano Palace** (AC BF CC glm I OS) All year
Viale Kennedy ☎ 095 59 67 111 🖳 www.romanopalace.it

■ **Villa Romeo** (AC BF CC G I OS RWT SOL WI) All year
Via Platamone 8 *Near central train station* ☎ 095 53 47 14
🖳 www.hotelvillaromeo.it
Renovated gay-friendly hotel near gay venues. Rooms with Sat & Sky TV, safe and free internet access. Parking available.

GUEST HOUSES

■ **Amenano Bed & Breakfast** (AC BF G I)
Via Bicocca 24 *Centre, between Piazza Duomo and Piazza Università*
☎ 095 32 07 87 🖳 www.amenano.it
Huge rooms with own bath, TV and internet access for up to 4 persons. Gay owned.

■ **Rossocorallo B&B** (AC H RWS WI) All year
Via Umberto I, 56 *Historical centre of Catania* ☎ 095 0930212
☎ 3409845453 🖳 www.bebrossocorallo.it
Rooms with private bathroom, air condition, equipped with all facilities in the main shopping street Via Umberto I.

CRUISING

-Railway Station (ayor r t): 22-3h
-Piazza Grenoble (by car only)
-Villa Bellini (toilets in the town park, only afternoon)
-Porto (harbour, near the lighthouse, by car at night AYOR).

Sicilia – Cefalù

HOTELS

■ **Hotel-Museum Atelier Sul Mare**
(AC B BF CC glm I M OS PA PK RWB RWS s SA VA) All year
Via Cesare Battisti 4 *Castel di Tusa* ☎ 0921 33 42 95
🖳 www.ateliersulmare.it
Hotel and museum combined. Rooms with bath or shower/WC, mini-bar, phone, sat-TV, own key. Pets & visitors allowed at reasonable prices. Arts exhibitions and pottery courses throughout the year.

Sicilia – Lipari Island

RESTAURANTS

■ **Filippino** (AC B CC GLM H M MA OS) 12-15, 19.30-23h
Piazza Mazzini ☎ 090 981 10 02 🖳 www.bernardigroup.it
Fine Aeolian cuisine which is praised widely both by Italien and international. Elegant dining setting catering to a more sophisticated clientele. Authentic home made products such as bread, pasta, pastries and ice cream.

APARTMENTS

■ **A Tana** (DU glm MA OS RWB RWS RWT SH)
Filicudi ☎ 349 7891728 🖳 www.atana.it

Sicilia – Messina

GAY INFO

■ **Arcigay Makwan**
☎ 388 36 35 992 🖳 www.arcigaymessina.altervista.org

SWIMMING

-Capo Scaletta: from Messina in direction Catania (15 km) to Giampilieri, in the cliffs (NU)
-S. Saba: from Messina in direction Palermo (20 km, Bus N. 81), in the cliffs (NU), very busy.

CRUISING

-Harbor area (R)
-Piazza Cavallotti mainly by car, but also on foot in the streets nearby.

Sicilia – Milazzo

SWIMMING

-Tono: from Tono on the cliffs in direction of Capo Milazzo.

CRUISING

-🅿 „Bazia" A 20 Palermo – Messina between exits Falcone and Barcellona, only by car.

Sicilia – Modica

SWIMMING

-From the Marina in Modica take the road in direction Marina di Ragusa, about 2 km before Sampieri turn left in the direction of an abandoned factory with a large brick chimney. There is a parking area and the beach can be reached on foot. Gays are found in the middle of the beach, at the foot of the dunes.

Sicilia – Noto

GAY INFO

■ **Tourguide Alessandro**
Noto ☎ 0367 549 1786 (mobile)

Alessandro will help you find your way around in Sicilia. He will find you on the gay beach in Noto.

APARTMENTS

Triskeles Guest House (glm) All year
Vico Etna 12 ☎ 094 256 581
A fantastic location, near the old city centre. A very comfortable apartment with 2 rooms. Near the gay beach.

SWIMMING

-Eloro Paradise Beach: on the other side of Noto Lido. Follow the signs to Scavi Eloro. Take the dirt road (around 500m) to the private parking area and go over the rocks on the left end of the beach to the next bay. The gay beach is on the far right side with crusing in the dunes.

Sicilia – Palermo

GAY INFO

Arcigay Palermo
Piazza S. Anna 18

BARS

Caterina Pub (B glm OS YC) 18.30-2.30, Fri & Sat -4h, closed Mon
Via Squarcialupo 19/23 ☎ 333 25 14 175
Trendy mixed bar with many lesbians and also gays in the centre of Palermo.

Exit (AC B d G MA OS) 22.30-3h, closed Tue & Fri
Piazza S. Francesco di Paola 39/40 *Between Teatro Politeama and Teatro Massimo* ☎ 348 78 14 698 (Infoline) 💻 www.exitdrinks.com

Via di Mezzo (B glm OS YC) Winter 17-1, summer 19-1h
Via S. Oliva 20/22 *Near Teatro Politeama and Exit bar* ☎ 091 60 90 090

DANCECLUBS

Rise Up (AC B D GLM OS S WE YC) Fri 24-4.30h
Via Ugo La Malfa 95 *industrial district, 100m before the shopping centre Auchan* ☎ 348 78 14 698 (infoline)
Only gay danceclub in Palermo. Outside cruising area. Taxi best option to reach the club.

RESTAURANTS

Al Viale (AC B BF CC glm M OS) 8-1.30h, Mon closed in winter (Sep-Jun), Sun closed in summer (Jun-Sep)
Via Archimede 189 / Via Libertà *Centre, near Politeama* ☎ 091 60 90 133
Mediterrean cuisine and cocktail bar.

BOOK SHOPS

AltroQuando (g)
Via Vittorio Emanuele 143 ☎ 091 61 14 732

GUEST HOUSES

BB22 Bed and Breakfast (AC B BF CC glm I)
Largo Cavalieri di Malta, 22 *Near Piazza S. Domenico* ☎ 091 61 11 610 💻 www.bb22.it
Stylish guesthouse. Rooms with sat-TV, safe and minibar with own bath. Wireless internet.

SWIMMING

-Balestrate (cruising wood)
-Barcarello/Sferracavallo Beach (after walking 45 mins on the rocks).

CRUISING

-Foro Italico public garden (day and night, AYOR)
-Parco della Favorita, behind the Ippodrome (day and night)
-Via Lincoln (r).

Sicilia – Ragusa

GAY INFO

Arcigay Ragusa
☎ 333 988 40 67

CRUISING

-Kamarina beach (near Club Med)
-Playa Grande (between village and mouth of River Irminio, left of disco La Fazenda, also on the beach below)
-Square in front of railway station and side streets
-Sampieri beach (opposite Pisciotto, walking along the beach from Via Miramare or turn right at the first traffic light on provincial road 66 from Sampieri direction Marina di Modica).

Sicilia – Sciacca

GUEST HOUSES

B&B da Lulo e Gagà (H)
Vicolo Muscarnera 9 ☎ 0925 866 64

Sicilia – Siracusa

GAY INFO

Arcigay Siracusa
☎ 333 606 53 67

HOTELS

Piccolo Hotel Casa Mia
Corso Umberto I 112 *Centrally located, close to Ortigia* ☎ 0931 46 33 49 💻 www.bbcasamia.it

GUEST HOUSES

Frescura. La (AC B BF CC GLM MSG OS)
Via per Floridia 50 *6 km from Siracusa in the countryside* ☎ 338 940 19 37 💻 www.lafrescura.com
La Frescura is an ancient country house dating back to the 17th century. All guestrooms are en suite, and some of them self catering.

APARTMENTS

Residence Levante (AC glm MA OS PK RWB RWS RWT VA) All year
Via Nizza 49 *Island Ortigia, historic centre, airport Catania* ☎ 0931 21 369 💻 www.residencelevante.com
4 apartments for rent.

SWIMMING

-Eloro Beach (take the exit Noto/Lido di Noto from A18 and follow signs for Eloro (dirt road); after the bridge under the railway turn right; by foot cross river Tellaro; gay beach is behind the hill).

CRUISING

-Via di Natale.

Sicilia – Stromboli

HOTELS

Sciara. La (B BF CC H M OS PI SOL) Apr-Oct
Via Soldato Cincotto ☎ 090 98 60 04 💻 www.lasciara.it
All rooms have telephone, private bath and balcony.

Sirenetta Park Hotel. La (AC B BF CC H M PI) 31 Mar-31 Oct
Via Marina 33 ☎ 090 98 60 25 💻 www.lasirenetta.it
Beach location, all rooms have phone, private bath and balcony.

SWIMMING

-Marina Lunga Beach

Sicilia – Taormina

BARS

Irish Pub O'Seven (AC B CC glm M MA OS)
11-3h, Mon closed (only from Oct to Mar)
Corso Umberto, Largo La Farina 6 *Behind Torre dell' Orologio* ☎ 0942 24 980
Irish pub with Sicilian cuisine. Cocktail bar.

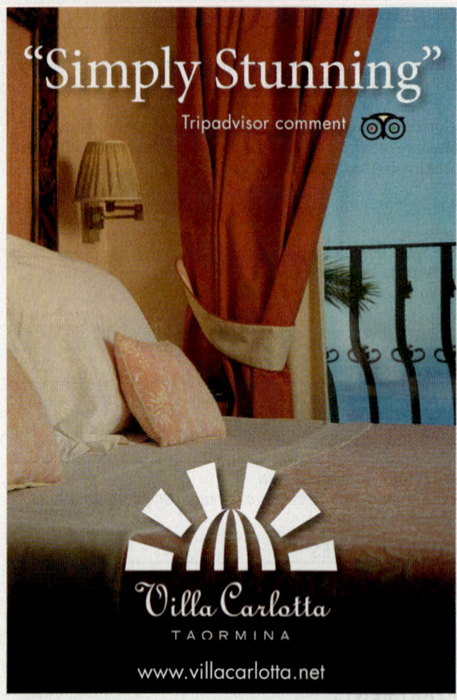

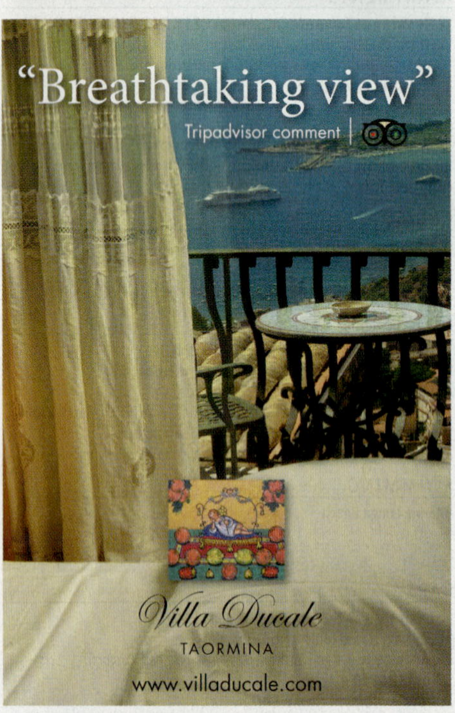

■ **Re del Sole** (B g m MA OS) May-Oct
Spisone Strada Statale 114 ☎ 0942 62 53 85
Beach bar near the gay beach „Rocce Bianche". Restaurant service until 16h.

■ **Sunkisses** (B BF G M OS) 9-19h (May-Oct)
Strada Statale 114, km 40 ☎ 0942 37 111
Beach bar at the nice gay beach Fondaco Parrino.

HOTELS

■ **Hotel Villa Carlotta** (AC B BF cc glm H I M MA MSG PA PI PK RWB RWS RWT SOL VA) All year
Via Pirandello, 81 ☎ 0942 626058 🖳 www.villacarlotta.net
A small luxury hotel in the centre of Taormina overlooking the Mediterranean sea.

■ **Villa Ducale** (AC B BF CC H I m MA OS WH)
Via Leonardo da Vinci 60 ☎ 0942 28 153
🖳 www.villaducale.com
Boutique hotel with 17 rooms and all ameneties. Great panoramic terrace.

GUEST HOUSES

■ **Isoco** (AC B BF GLM I M MSG OS PA PK RWB RWS RWT VA WH) Mar-Dec
Via Salita Branco 2 *Central, near Porta Messina* ☎ 0942 236 79
🖳 www.isoco.it
Beautiful view of the coast. Rooms with TV, mini-bar, safe and radio. Garden with whirlpool. New roof sundeck. Every day dinner at 20h (reservation before 12h). Free internet.

SWIMMING

-Rocce Bianche (G MA NU) (take any beach bus, the gay beach is at the white rocks between Re del Sole and Caparena)
-Fondaco Parrino (G MA NU) (Strada Statale 114, near Capo S. Alessio Siculo. Take bus direction Messina, step out at Camping Paradise).

CRUISING

-Corso Umberto (at night).

Sicilia – Trapani

HOTELS

■ **I Mulini Resort Trapani** (AC B BF CC H I M OS PI)
Lungomare Dante Alighieri Erice Mare *2 km from the centre*
☎ 0923 58 41 11 🖳 www.imuliniresort.it
Luxurious hotel directly at the Mediterrean sea at the beautiful Western part of Sicily. The rooms offer every comfort. Sailing school, windsurf and kitesurf rental on site.

CRUISING

-Beach Scogliera delle Vergini.

Siena – Toscana

GAY INFO

■ **CIGS – Centro Interculturale GLBT Senese** (B D GLM MA OS PI s) Wed 21.30-23h
Via Massetana Romana 18 ☎ 0577 28 89 77 🖳 www.gaysiena.it
Infoline, counselling, weekly meetings, shows & exhibitions.

HOTELS

■ **Arcobaleno** (AC B bf CC glm I M MA OS) All year
Via Fiorentina 32 *Near Porta Camollia & railway station* ☎ 0577 27 10 92
🖳 www.hotelarcobaleno.com
19 rooms with own key, cable TV, phone, fax, safe, mini-bar, internet connection and own safe. Panoramic terrace, parking and garage. 5% discount for Spartacus readers, pets allowed.

■ **Pia Dama. La** (AC BF CC H I PI SOL)
Località Poggiolo 98, Sinalunga *50 km from Siena* ☎ 0577 63 20 05
🖳 www.lapiadama.it
Hotel in a castle with large pool, garden and relax rooms.

GUEST HOUSES

Castello Montelifré (G OS PI WH)
Montelifré *38 km from Siena* ☎ 034 9606 4453
🖳 www.castellomontelifre.it
4+1 quite spartan double rooms in a huge, fascinating structure.

San Bruno Relais (BF H) All year
Via Di Pescaia 5/7 *400m from the centre of Montepulciano*
☎ 0578 716222 🖳 www.sanbrunorelais.com
Small boutique hotel in the heart of Tuscany. Ideal for relax and food/wine tasting. Close to Siena and Montalcino.

Valdonica Vineyard Residence & Winery
☞ *Grosseto – Toscana.*

CRUISING

-Via A. Sclavo, P Palasport (at night by car)
-Superstrada Siena-Firenze P between the exits Siena Nord and Siena-Acquacalda (after 22h)
-Superstrada Siena -Firenze, dir. Firenze. P after exit Poggibonsi Nord
-P in front of Golden Bar (Via Fiorentina).

Sondrio – Lombardia

CRUISING

-Via Samaden and Zona Agneda (evenings, by car).

Sorrento – Campania

GUEST HOUSES

Casale Antonietta B&B (AC B glm M) All year
Via Trav. Pantano 3 *Bus A or the blue bus line* ☎ 081 878 26 49
🖳 www.casaleantonietta.com

SWIMMING

-Bagni Regina Giovanna (popular)
-Capo di Sorrento, on the cliffs.

CRUISING

-Villa Communale (at night; also at the end of the viale)
-Piazzetta V. Veneto (in the gardens)
-Stazione Circumvesuviana (facilities)
-Piazza del Monumento.

Sperlonga – Lazio

GUEST HOUSES

B&B of Dreams (BF G M OS PI) All year
Contrada San Simone 24, Vallecorsa *Highway Roma – Napoli, exit Frosinone. Also pick-up from railway station of Castro, 18 km from Sperlonga*
☎ 347 17 42 517
B&B in the countryside between gay beach „300 Scalini" and the mountains. Dinner available.

SWIMMING

-300 Scaline (NU g): 10 km from Sperlonga in direction Gaeta. From the sign „ultima spiaggia" take the path down.

Spessa Po – Lombardia

SWIMMING

-Along River Po (g MA NU r) (afternoons).

Spresiano – Veneto

SWIMMING

-Ponte della Priula (NU) (between Treviso and Conegliano, on River Piave; coming from Treviso after the bridge „Ponte della Priula" turn right, after the railway after 500 m turn right again. Action by foot on the right. Also in winter)

Taranto – Puglia

SWIMMING

-Scogliera delle Donne Maledette (NU) (San Vito – Lido Bruno, 7 km from Taranto, way for ‚Sun Bay', romantic spot; also known as Le Conchette)
-Cancello Rosso (NU) (Lama, close to the supermarket ‚Tidy dei fiori', red entry, 200 m to the left up to the tower).

CRUISING

-Seafront of Taranto (at night, AYOR)
-Viale Virgilio (R T) (at night)
-Parco della Rimembranza and parking nearby
-Ponte Punta Penn (T) (near Caserma Aeronautica, AYOR at night).

Tarquinia – Lazio

CRUISING

-Piazza Cavour (evenings)
-Tarquinia Lido (near Porto Clementino, all day in the summer).

Terni -Umbria

CRUISING

-Giardini Via Lungonera Savoia
-Viale Fonderia
-Stadium Libero Liberati
-Corso Tacito.

Torino – Piemonte

GAY INFO

Arcigay Ottavio Mai
Via Fàà di Bruno 2 ☎ 011 19 70 31 45 🖳 www.arcigaytorino.it

Contatto
☏ 011.4364066 💻 www.contattoglbt.it
Helpline for gays, lesbians, bisexuals and transgender.

Maurice – Circolo Culturale Gay Lesbico Bisessuale Transgender Queer Mon-Sat 14-18 h
Via Stampatori 10 ☏ (011) 52 11 116 💻 www.mauriceglbt.org
Cultural group, gayline, meetings, information about gay life, entertainment, lesbian, transgender & youth group. Also library and archives, lectures, videos.

Tuttaltrastoria (! GLM)
💻 www.quore.org/friendly-piemonte/tuttaltra-storia
One of the best gay tours around. See where the local and international gay and lesbian people lived in this beautiful city.

CULTURE

Fondazione Sandro Penna (glm MA p S) Mon-Fri 9-13h
Via S. Chiara 1 ☏ 011 52120 33 💻 www.fondazionesandropenna.it
Library, gay press, cultural centre, archive. Call for appointment.

BARS

Shortbus Wed-Sat 18.30-2.30h
Via Gaudenzio Ferrari 5/i ☏ 011 27 63 987 💻 www.shortbuscafe.it

MEN'S CLUBS

Tunnel Club (AC B DR G I MA NU VS) Tue-Thu 21-2, Fri 21-4, Sat 21-6, Sun 15-2h
Via Sordevolo 7/B ☏ 345 59 48 018 💻 www.gayromeo.com/tunnelclub
Cruising bar with equipped labyrinth and relax rooms. Free internet point and smoking room. Tue Bisex night, Thu Naked party. Arci card required.

XXX Cruising Bar (AC B DR G MA NU s VS) Sat 22-?h
Via Messina 5/D ☏ 011 28 42 63
💻 www.011saunaclub.it/xxx/english/index.html
Naked party on Sat.

CAFES

Extreme
Via San Massino 31 ☏ 392 71 32 209 💻 www.myspace.com/extremecafe

DANCECLUBS

Centralino-Dietrich. Il (AC b D GLM MA s SNU) Fri-Sun 24-4h
Via delle Rosine 16/A ☏ 335 53 49 808 (Infoline)
Drag show on Fri, strip on Sun. DJ Superpippo.

Folies Scandal. Les
c/o Chalet, Viale Virgilio 25 ☏ 347 58 11 687 💻 www.pqdisco.it

Queever (B CC D GLM m MA S) Sun 19.30-2h
c/o La Gare Disco Club, Via Sacchi 65 *Three blocks from the central station*
☏ 393 18 98 307 💻 www.queever.it
An early-night club, with good food and beverage included in the entrance fee, relaxed atmosphere and mixed gay and lesbian crowd, in the largest club in town. With Drag shows.

RESTAURANTS

Guscio. Il (AC g M) 19-23h, closed Mon
Via Postumia 17/B *M° Piazza Massana* ☏ 011 20 75 484
Mediterrean cuisine. Delivery service.

La Linea Continua (AC B glm M) 12-15, 19.30-1h
Via Massena 68 *Near railway station Porta Nuova* ☏ 011 50 96 288
💻 www.hotelbostontorino.it
Piemontese Cuisine and vast offer of wines.

Zi' Barba (AC B CC glm M MA) 18-2h, closed Mon
Via S. Pellico 13/E *Bus 67, tram 18* ☏ 011 65 83 91
Also a great wine bar and pub.

SAUNAS/BATHS

011 Sauna Club (! AC B DR DU G LAB m MA p PI SA SB SL VS WH) 14-2, Sat -6, Sun & public holidays -1h
Via Messina 5/D *Largo Regio Parco, tram 18, bus 63* ☏ 011 28 42 63
💻 www.011saunaclub.it
Large sauna on 700 m² with a big maze and hardcore film area. Not the friendliest, although the action is good. Sat. after 24h special Naked Party. Uno Club card required.

Garage Club
(AC B DR DU FC G LAB m MA MSG p RR SA SB VS WH) 14-1h
Corso Stati Uniti, 35 *Near train station „Porta Nova"* ☏ 346 300 66 12
💻 www.garageclub.it
Mon, Wed & Fri naked party from 22h.

BOOK SHOPS

Libreria Luxemburg (AC CC g MA) Mon-Sat 8-19.30, Sun 10-13, 15-19h
Via Battisti 7 *Centre* ☏ 011 56 13 896
International book-shop. Gay friendly information, videos and gay literature.

HOTELS

Art Hotel Boston (AC B BF CC glm I M OS PK RWS RWT) All year
Via Massena 70 *Tram 15/16, bus 4/14* ☏ 011 50 03 59
💻 www.arthotelboston.it
Art hotel with 63 double, 23 single rooms and 5 suites with specially designed furniture and decoration. All rooms with AC, sat & pay TV and wireless internet. Buffet breakfast included. The restaurant La Linea Continua is open every day for lunch and dinner.

Napoleon (AC B BF CC GLM I OS PA PK RWS RWT VA) All year
Via XX Settembre 5 *On the third floor of a historic building in the center of Turin, near Piazza Castello* ☏ 011 561 32 23
💻 www.hotelnapoleontorino.it
All rooms with bath, TV, fridge and breakfast. Gay men welcome: 20% discount for Spartacus readers.

NH Ambasciatori (AC B BF CC H M MA RES RWS RWT VEG WL) All year
C.so V. Emanuele 104 ☏ 011 57521 💻 www.nh-hotels.com
The stylish ambience, modern décor and streaming light available in the hotel's 199 guest rooms and conference center.

GUEST HOUSES

B&B Casablanca (BF GLM PK RWB RWS WI) All year
Via Noé 4 *Centre, close to Duomo and central market* ☏ 011 7650432
☏ 338 4707839
Double, triple and quadruple rooms in a gay-friendly atmosfere. Some rooms with separate entrance. Free Wifi, affordable prices.

Binôt (bf glm I OS PA PK RWS RWT VA) All year
Via E. Dominici 8 *29 km from Torino* ☏ 347 28 01 145 💻 www.binot.it
Renovated 19th century farmhouse immerse in an attractive countryside. Comfortable rooms furnished with family antiques with TV and WiFi. Gay owned.

PRIVATE ACCOMMODATION

L'Orangerie (AC BF CC GLM)
Via del Carmine 8 *Near Porta Susa railway station* ☏ 338 80 41 945
💻 www.lorangerie.splinder.com
One suite to up to 4 persons.

HEALTH GROUPS

Anlaids Mon Wed Fri 15-19h
Via C. Botta 3 ☏ 011 43 65 541 💻 www.anlaids.it
Prevention and information.

Arcobaleno Aids
Via Caprera 46/d ☏ 011 36 30 87 💻 www.spazzi.org

LILA – Lega Italiana per la Lotta contro l'AIDS
Corso Regina Margherita, 190/e ☏ 011 43 10 922 💻 www.lila.it

SPECIAL INTEREST GROUPS

Altra Communicazione. L' 10-18h
Corso Principe Oddone 3 ☏ 011 53 48 88 💻 www.tglff.com
Organizers of the gay & lesbian film festival (19.-25.4.2012).

SWIMMING

-Chivasso at Orco river (NU): A4 Torino-Milano, exit Chivasso Ovest, direction Chivasso, after the bridge along the railway turn left to Prato-regio. Stop before the small tunnel under the highway. Cruising in the wood and along the river. From 14h till dark. Also in winter.

CRUISING

-Corso Marche (near corner Regina Margherita in gardens) (in the afternoon, ayor, police raids)
-From Corso Unione Sovietica turn right to public road Stupinigi direction Orbassano. First and second P on the right hand.
-Lumini, Cimitero Monumentale, Lungo Dora Colletta, Parco Crescenzio (by car and on foot, night and day, mainly in summer)
-Parco del Valentino (also car-cruising)
-Parco delle Vallere, Moncalieri: left side of Corso Trieste, at the side of the entry for the highway to Savona/Piacenza (by bike, on foot, daytime only).

Trento – Trentino-Alto Adige

GAY INFO

■ **Arcigay Trentino 8 Luglio** (glm MA) Thu 20.30-22.30h
Largo Nazario Sauro 11 *Club is on the 2nd floor, entrance near the chinese restaurant* ☎ 348 14 47 151 🖳 www.agtrentino.org

CRUISING

Piazza Venezia: by foot, at night

Treviso – Veneto

GAY INFO

■ **Arcigay Queerquilia**
Via Pisa 13/b ☎ 340 34 11 244 🖳 www.queerquilia.it

DANCECLUBS

■ **Gold** (AC B CC D DR G OS P S SNU VS WE YC)
Via Leonardo da Vinci 4 ☎ 334 3165316 🖳 www.discogold.it
■ **Time 2 Move** (B D GLM MA) Fri-Sun
Via Leonardo da Vinci 4 *In Godega di Sant'Urbano – Veneto*
☎ 347 63 44 163 🖳 www.timetomove.it

RESTAURANTS

■ **Hostaria Vecchia Malvasia** (AC B GLM M MA OS) Tue-Sun 17.30-2h
Via Trevisi 29 *Behind Piazza dei Signori* ☎ 0422 41 15 00
Only gay-lesbian bar in Treviso.

SAUNAS/BATHS

■ **Hobby One** (AC B DR DU FC G GH LAB m MA MSG OS P RR SA SB SOL VS WH) Tue-Sat 16-1h (summer: 18-1h)
Via Leonardo Da Vinci 4, Godega di Sant'Urbano *Industrial zone, behind Manhattan discotheque* ☎ 0438 38 82 56 🖳 www.hobbyone.it
Video in the Finnish sauna. Uno Club card required.

CRUISING

-Parking lot at the hospital (car-cruising in the evening only)
-Ponte di Piave (15 km from Treviso: under the bridge; in summer swimming during the day).

Trieste – Friuli-Venezia Giulia

GAY INFO

■ **Arcigay Arcilesbica Arcobaleno** Thu 16-17h
Via Pondares 8 ☎ 040 63 06 06 🖳 www.arcigay.it/trieste
Helpline & chatline (on homepage): Mon 20.30-22h

BOOK SHOPS

■ **Libreria in der Tat** (glm)
Via Diaz 22a ☎ 040 30 07 74 🖳 www.indertat.it

GUEST HOUSES

■ **Canovella B&B** (BF glm RWS RWT) All year
Aurisina 153/F1 *Località Ginestre, 5min from gay-beach Costa dei Barbari*
☎ 040 202 41 53 🖳 www.canovella.it

SWIMMING

-Beach resort „Bagno alla Lanterna" (glm): Molo Fratelli Bandiera, bus 8 (May-Sep)
-Costa dei Barbari (glm NU) Sistiana (opp. bar Costa dei Barbari. From carpark walk down hill then to the left.

CRUISING

-Molo Audace (pier opposite Piazza Unità-late evenings)
-Viale Romolo Gessi (nights only, from Campo Marzio up the hill on viale Romolo Gessi. All the hillside and gardens on the right)
-P on the SS14 from Triest direction Venedig at km 137,5 just before reaching Sistiana (hidden entrance on a curve, seaside).

Tropea – Calabria

SWIMMING

-Beach at Santa Domenica (rocky beach between spiaggia formicoli and spiaggia riendi).

CRUISING

-Piazza Vittorio Veneto (public gardens)
-Corso Vittorio Emanuele (till late at night).

Udine – Friuli-Venezia Giulia

GAY INFO

■ **Arcigay Nuovi Passi**
Via T. Deciani 89/135 ☎ 340 31 44 203 🖳 www.arcigay.it/udine
Also Helpline 0432 52 38 38 Wed & Fri. See: www.chatamica.it

CRUISING

-Cormor Park, behind the parking
-Piazza I Maggio, under the castle
-Partidor, industrial area, near the „Mercato Ortofrutticolo", by car
-Stadio Friuli, parking, by car
-Torrente Torre, via Cividale, under the bridge (after the bridge direction Cividale, turn left and after 200m left again) (NU).

Val Gardena – Trentino-Alto Adige

HOTELS

■ **Alpin Garden Wellness Resort** (AC B BF CC GLM H I M MSG OS PA PI PK RWB RWS RWT SA SB SOL VA WH WO)
Via Skasa 68 *In Ortisei/St. Ulrich* ☎ 0471 79 60 21 🖳 www.alpingarden.com
Small hotel with a big whirlpool and gourmet restaurant.
■ **Maciaconi Hotel & Residence** (B BF CC glm H M MA OS PA RWB RWS RWT SA SB SOL WH WO) All year
Via Plan da Tieja 10 *Gröden, approx. 40 km from Bolzano airport*
☎ 0471 79 35 00 🖳 www.hotelmaciaconi.com
Comfortable gay-friendly hotel with a good restaurant (Pizzeria Maciaconi Appetit – CC YC). Fashion shop on the premises. Also apartments.
■ **Sporthotel Platz** (B BF CC H I M MA OS PI SA SOL WH) Closed 15 Oct-15 Dec & 15 Apr-15 May
Via Bulla 12 ☎ 0471 79 69 35 🖳 www.sporthotelplatz.com
■ **Wolkenstein** (B BF CC D H M OS PI SA SB SOL WH)
Via Plan da Tieja 14 ☎ 0471 77 22 00 🖳 www.wolkenstein.it

Varazze – Liguria

HOTELS

■ **Coccodrillo** (AC B BF CC glm H I M OS PA PI PK RWB RWT SOL) All year
Via Sardi 16 ☎ 019 93 20 15 🖳 www.coccodrillo.it

SWIMMING

-Piani d'Invrea: from P at the exit A10 ‚Varazze' to the sea by foot (direction Savona). The beach is near the first ex-railway tunnel (NU), cruising in the forest behind.

Varese – Lombardia

DANCECLUBS

■ **Zsa Zsa** (AC B D GLM m S) Thu-Sun 20-4h
Via Felice Orrigoni 7 ☎ 349 1734 234 (mobile) 💻 www.zsazsa.it

CRUISING

-Piazzale Kennedy (AYOR R) (police)
-North Railway Station (AYOR R) (police).

Varzi – Lombardia

CRUISING

-Piazza della Fiera (evenings).

Venezia – Veneto

BARS

■ **Devil's Forest Pub** (AC B GLM M WI) 11-1h
Calle dei Stagneri 5185 *San Marco 5185, between San Marco Square and Rialto bridge* ☎ 041 5200623 💻 www.devilsforestpub.com
Coffee bar in the afternoon, later wine & cocktail bar. Lunch and dinner available. Free WiFi hotspot

CAFES

■ **Grom** 11-24h
Dorsoduro 2761 *Campo San Barnaba, boat Nr.1, stop Cà Rezzonico*
☎ 041 09 91 751
Great ice cream next door to Ristoteca Oniga.

DANCECLUBS

■ **Glitter** (AC B DR G VS) Fri & Sat 22.30-4h
Via delle Macchine 41/43 *1km from railway station Mestre*
☎ 041 921247 💻 www.glitterdisco.com
Disco bar in Mestre. Uno Club card required.

RESTAURANTS

■ **Bistrot de Venise** (AC B CC DM glm M MA NR OS PA RES S VEG WL) Daily; wine bar 10-1h, restaurant 12-15, 19-1h
San Marco 4685, Calle dei Fabbri *Near Piazza S. Marco*
☎ 041 523 66 51 💻 www.bistrotdevenise.com
Classic and historical Venetian cuisine. Very good selection of wines. Art expositions. Special dining rooms dedicated to famous Venetian celebrities of the 18th century: Goldoni, Vivaldi and Casanova.

■ **Centrale Restaurant Lounge**
(AC B CC DM glm LM M RES VEG WL) Daily 18.30-2h
S. Marco, Piscina Frezzaria, 1659 *Close to Teatro La Fenice*
☎ 041 29 60 664 💻 www.centrale-lounge.com
Stylish restaurant and lounge bar, international glamourous flair, dinner until late.

■ **Da Mamo Trattoria & Pizzeria** (B DM glm M VEG WL)
12-15.15 and 19.15-22.30h
Calle Stagneri 5251, San Marco *Close to Rialto Bridge* ☎ 041 523 65 83
💻 www.damamo.it
A few steps from the Rialto Bridge and San Marco Square. Venetian cuisine and pizza, reasonable prices.

■ **Ganesh Ji** (AC glm M OS)
12.30-14, 19-24h. In wintertime closed on Wed.
Fondamenta Rio Marin 2426, San Polo *near railway station* ☎ 041 71 98 04
Indian restaurant. Also take away.

■ **Ristoteca Oniga** (AC CC DM glm M MA OS RES WL) 12-15, 19-24h, closed Tue
Dorsoduro 2852 *Campo San Barnaba. Boat number 1. Stop: Cà Rezzonico* ☎ 041 52 24 410 💻 www.oniga.it
A restaurant with a wine bar. Reservation advisory. See www.oniga.it

SAUNAS/BATHS

■ **Metrò Sauna Venezia** (AC B cc DR DU FC FH G GH I LAB m MA MSG OS P RR SA SB SH SOL VS WH) 14-2h
Via Cappuccina 82/b, Mestre *500 m from the railway station Mestre, bus 2/7 from Venezia* ☎ 041 538 42 99 💻 www.metroclub.it
Supplementary space with terrace. Relax cabins. Uno Club card required.

TRAVEL AND TRANSPORT

■ **Lido on Bike** (GLM) 9-19:30h (Mar-Oct)
Gran Viale Santa Maria Elisabetta 21 ☎ 041 5268019 💻 www.lidoonbike.it
Gay-friendly bike rental to discover Lido and its nice beaches.

HOTELS

■ **Antica Locanda Sturion** (AC cc glm H I PA RWB RWS RWT) All year
Calle del Sturion – San Polo 679 ☎ 041 523 62 43
💻 www.locandasturion.com
Beautiful, small and elegant hotel near Ponte Rialto. Some rooms with view over the Grand Canal.

■ **Casa Verardo** (AC B CC H I OS) All year
Castello 4765 *Near Campo S. Felippo e Giacomo, Piazza San Marco, waterboat San Zaccaria* ☎ 041 52 86 127 💻 www.casaverardo.it
Historical residence with small garden and solarium terrace. Some rooms overlook the canal. Wi-Fi.

■ **Hotel Al Codega** (AC B BF CC glm H I RWS RWT)
San Marco 4435 *San Marco* ☎ 041 241 32 88
🖳 www.alcodega.it
Between San Marco and Rialto. Waterbus 1/2 (stop Rialto). New charming hotel centrally located in a small quiet courtyard.

■ **Locanda Barbarigo** (AC BF cc glm H RWS RWT) All year
Fondamenta Barbarigo, San Marco 2503/A *Close to San Marco Square*
☎ 041 241 36 39 🖳 www.locandabarbarigo.com
In a Venetian Palazzo of the 17th century, some rooms with view over the channel. 10% discount for Spartacus readers.

■ **Residenza San Maurizio** (AC BF cc H)
Via Calle Zaguri 2625, San Marco *At Campo San Maurizio, close to Piazza San Marco, waterbus 1 „Giglio"* ☎ 041 52 89 712
🖳 www.residenzasanmaurizio.com
Very comfortable rooms in Venetian design with private bathroom, sat-TV and safe. 10% discount for Spartacus readers.

GUEST HOUSES

■ **Alle Guglie B&B**
(! AC B BF DU FH G H I MA NR OS PA RWB RWT VA WI)
Calle Del Magazen, Cannaregio 1308 *5 mins from railway station, 15 from Rialto, water boat stop: Guglie, San Marcuola*
☎ 320 36 07 829 🖳 www.alleguglie.com
Cozy and elegant B&B in the historic centre of Venice, one nice doubleroom with breakfast two steps from railway station. Lively area. Gay owned.

■ **Ca' Bonvicini** (AC b BF CC GLM I RWS) All year
Santa Croce 2160 *waterbus 1 ,San Stae', 5min from Ponte Rialto*
☎ 041 27 50 106 🖳 www.cabonvicini.com
Charming guesthouse with 6 double rooms offering phone, Sat TV, minibar and wireless internet. Own bathroom.

■ **Casa de Uscoli** (AC glm I MA RWS RWT) All year
San Marco 2818 *Next to Accademia delle Belle Arti*
☎ 348 26 36 677 🖳 www.casadeuscoli.com
A small B&B on the Grand Canal with 4 guest rooms. Also organizes cultural events. Gay-friendly. Gay owned.

■ **Friendly Venice** (BF H RWS RWT)
San Marco 2947 *Campo Santo Stefano, few steps from Accademia, waterboat Accademia* ☎ 380 3893585
🖳 www.friendlyvenice.hostelvenice.net

■ **Fujiyama** (AC B CC glm H I OS RWS RWT VA) All year
Dorsoduro 2727A *Near Campo Santa Margherita, water boat nr.1: stop Ca' Rezzonico* ☎ 041 724 10 42
🖳 www.bedandbreakfast-fujiyama.it
Bed & breakfast with own key, rooms with sat-TV, own bathroom and safe. Free wireless internet. Tea room open from 14-20h (Mon-Fri, in winter also on Sun). Gay owned.

SWIMMING

-Caorle: Spiaggia della Brussa
-Eraclea Mare: Laguna del Morto (NU), very cruisy
-Lido di Venezia: Alberoni (NU), cruising in the dunes and in the forest
-Lido di Venezia: San Nicolò (in the dunes).

CRUISING

-San Marco (along the fence of the Royal Gardens next to the Piazza along the water front. Mostly in warm months from 22h)
-Under the overpass between Mestre and Marghera (ayor YC): Via Elettricità (off Via Fratelli Bandiera) and side streets, especially near the truck scale, also street along the canal next to the ship yard. Busy after dark
-Via Ca'Marcello, Mestre (occasionally at night by car).

Ventimiglia – Liguria

SWIMMING

-Balzi Rossi (Coming from Ventimiglia through the first tunnel, P before the gas station, go down, pass under the railway line, to the left).

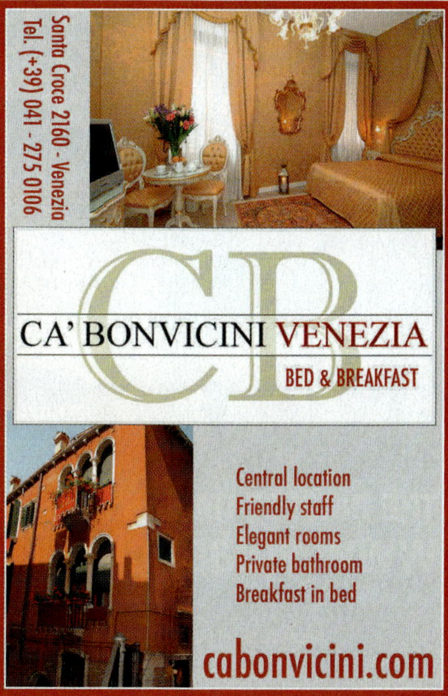

Verbania-Pallanza

HOTELS

■ **Grand Hotel Majestic** (AC B BF CC GLM H I M PA PI PK RWB RWS RWT SA WO) Open from 6 Apr -7 Oct 2012
Via Vittorio Veneto 32 *Lago Maggiore* ☎ 0323 509 711
🖳 www.grandhotelmajestic.it
Once a former summer residence of the nobility, nowadays an extremely gay-friendly luxury hotel (Small Luxury Hotels of the World). Today more then ever with all imaginable comforts and pure relaxation.

Vercelli – Piemonte

CRUISING

-Piazza Mazzini (occasionally police patrols).

Verona – Veneto

GAY INFO

■ **Arcigay Arcilesbica Pianeta Urano** Helpline Mon-Fri 20-24h
Via Gela 9 ☎ 045 81 06 253 🖳 www.arcigayverona.org

■ **Circolo Pink – Centro di Iniziativa e Cultura Gay Lesbica Bisessuale Transgender Verona**
Via Scrimiari 7 ☎ 045 80 12 854 (Helpline)
🖳 www.circolopink.it
GLBT-centre. Mon 21-23h cultural activities, Sat 16-18h Welcome Group, Fri 19-21h Transexual Group.

BARS

■ **Al Semaforo** (B G MA r)
Summer: 20-2, Winter: 19-2h, closed Mon
Via Unitá d'Italia 100 *S. Michele* ☎ 045 97 64 01

CAFES

Lucla' Café (AC B bf CC G M MA OS) Mon-Fri 7-2h, Sat & Sun 18-2h
Via M. Bentegodi 4/A *Near the Arena, pedestrians exit from parking Arena*
☎ 345 22 90 250 🖳 www.luclacafe.it
In daytime mixed café with breakfast and lunch, from 19h mainly gay pub.

Mada Café (B BF glm m) Mon-Sat 7.30-20, Sun 14-20h
Via Teatro Filarmonico 7 *Close to Arena* ☎ 340 56 20 034

p3 (B glm m YC) 19-2h, closed Tue
Vicolo Amanti 6 *Near Arena* ☎ 333 80 86 404 (info)

DANCECLUBS

Romeo's Club (AC B CC d DR G m MA P s VS)
Tue-Sun 23-2, Fri & Sat -4h
Via Nicoló Giolfino 12 *Area Porta Vescovo-Bus 11/12/13*
☎ 340 96 60 487 (Infoline) 🖳 www.romeosclub.it
Disco bar with labyrinth. Tue & Thu naked, Wed cinema, Sun karaoke, Fri & Sat D (mainstream). One Sat/month bears party. Uno Club card required.

Skylight (AC B D DR G m MA OS P Pl s SNU) Sat 23-4.30h
Via Fontanelle 28, S. Bonifacio ☎ 045 76 12 587
🖳 www.skylightdisco.com
A4 Milano-Verona, exit Soave/S. Bonifacio. Outside turn left, direction S. Bonifacio. After 2.5 km right, direction Legnago. After 3 km.

RESTAURANTS

Al Bracere (AC B glm M OS) 12-15 & 18.30-1h
Via Adigetto 6/a *Centre* ☎ 045 59 72 49
Great restaurant in the centre of Verona, close to the Arena.

SEX SHOPS/BLUE MOVIES

Europa92 (g)
Vicolo Fossetto 3 ☎ 045 80 09 714 🖳 www.europa92.com

Prima o Poi Mon-Sat 9-20h
Corso Milano 51 ☎ 045 81 87 000
Dvds, gadgets and toys.

SAUNAS/BATHS

City Sauna Club (AC B CC DR G m MA MSG SA SB SOL VS WH)
14-2, (Jun-Sep) 15-2h
Via Giolfino 12 *Porta Vescovo, Bus 11/12/13* ☎ 045 52 00 09
Free condoms available. Uno clubcard required but availabe there.

Splash Club
☞ *Desenzano del Garda (BS).*

CRUISING

-C.O.N.I. (Via Basso Acquar: streets around the gyms, as far as Alfa Garage, only at night by car)
-Industrial zone (coming from „Verona Sud" turn left behind „Metro" in direction Alpo, in the tunnel from Via Roveggia at night by car)
-Lazzaretto (a little bit outside from district Porto S. Pancrazio, on the bridge over the Adige, turn left and walk along the Adige to the ruins of the old military hospital, in the afternoon in summer)
-Via B. Avesani: in the end of the street in the bushes on the left (busy, at night).

Viareggio – Toscana

The Mediterranean seaside resorts from „Friendly Versilia" Viareggio and Torre del Lago have developed in the past few years into an important attraction for gay tourists in summer. The beach „La Lecciona" has been a favourite gay beach for over 20 years, and due to the support from the city administration over the last several years a gay infrastructure has emerged with bars, restaurants, discos and gay events. Between June and August all hell breaks loose (thousands of gay men in the high season in August). A gigantic event is the Mardi Gras in August. In contrast the pre- and late season quiet, apart from the weekends.
There are various options for overnight stays. Virtually all the hotels are located in Viareggio, whereas gay bed & breakfasts can be found in the directly adjoining Torre del Lago, the centre of the gay nightlife.

Die Mittelmeerorte der „Friendly Versilia" Viareggio und Torre del Lago haben sich seit einigen Jahren zu einem bedeutenden Anziehungspunkt für schwulen Sommertourismus entwickelt. Zwar wird der Strand „La Lecciona" schon seit über 20 Jahren von Schwulen besucht, doch gibt es mit Unterstützung der Stadtverwaltung erst seit einigen Jahren eine schwule Infrastruktur mit Bars, Restaurants, Diskotheken und Veranstaltungen. Zwischen Juni und August ist inzwischen die Hölle los (Zehntausend Schwule in der Hochphase Mitte August), ein Riesenspektakel ist der Mardi Grasso im August. Demgegenüber ist es in der Vor- und Nachsaison bis auf das Wochenende eher ruhig.
Direkt vor Ort gibt es unterschiedliche Übernachtungsmöglichkeiten: Fast alle Hotels befinden sich in Viareggio, während man im direkt angrenzenden Torre del Lago, dem Zentrum schwulen Nachtlebens, schwule Bed & Breakfasts finden kann.

Les stations balnéaires de la sympathique Versilia, Viareggio et Torre del Lago se sont érigées depuis quelques années en destinations privilegiées pour les gays en été. Certes la plage de la Lecciona est connue des gays depuis de plus de vingt ans. Pourtant cela ne fait que six ans qu'existent des infrastructures gays : bars, restaurants, discothèques et manifestations spéciales, grâce au soutien de la municipalité. Entre juin et août, c'est la folie (milliers de touristes gays, l'an dernier en août). „Mardi gras", au mois d'août, est un spectacle à voir absolument. Le reste de l'année est plutôt calme, mis à part le week-end.
Il existe directement sur place différentes possibilités d'hébergement: Presque tous les hôtels se trouvent à Viareggio, alors qu'on peut trouver juste à côté à Torre del Lago, le centre de la nuit homo, des bed & breakfast gays.

Los lugares mediterráneos de la „simpática Versilia", Viareggio y Torre del Lago, se han convertido desde hace algunos años en punto de atracción significativo del veraneo gay. La playa de „La Lecciona" era ya muy concurrida por los homosexuales desde hace más de 20 años pero ahora, con el apoyo de la administración municipal, se ha creado una infraestructura gay de bares, restaurantes, discotecas y otros actos. Entre junio y agosto hay mucha actividad (mil de gays en

la temporada alta, a mediados de agosto), el mayor espectáculo es el Mardi Grasso en agosto. Por el contrario, antes y después de temporada está bastante tranquilo, incluso los fines de semana.
Allí directamente hay diferentes posibilidades de alojamiento: casi todos los hoteles se encuentran en Viareggio, mientras que en la cercana Torre del Lago, el centro de la vida nocturna gay, se pueden encontrar Bed & Breakfasts gays.

Da alcuni anni i centri balneari della „Friendly Versilia" Viareggio e Torre del Lago sono i centri turistici più amati dai gay nei mesi estivi. La spiaggia „LaLecciona" è meta privilegiata di „sirenetti" gay già da 20 anni. Da alcuni anni però, con l'aiuto dell'amministrazione comunale, è stata creata un'infrastruttura gay con bar, ristoranti, discoteche e diversi manifestazioni. Tra giugno ed agosto è molto visitata (10.000 gay si aggirano da queste parti nel periodo di metà agosto), con il Mardi Grasso come spettacolo di punta in agosto. D'altra parte Viareggio è piuttosto tranquilla nel periodo preestivo e in bassa stagione, eccetto il fine settimana.
A Viareggio si trovano diversissime possibilità di pernottamento: quasi tutti gli alberghi sono in città, mentre nella confinante Torre del Lago, centro della vita notturna gay, si possono trovare molti bed & breakfast.

BARS

Adagio (B GLM m MA OS s) Apr.-Sep. 17-4, Oct.-Mar. Thu-Sun 21-1h
Viale Europa 9, Torre del Lago ☎ 392 92 32 446
www.adagiolounge.com
Spectacular lounge on 2 levels with large terrace; quiet and relaxing atmosphere. Lounge music. Famous for ist excellent cocktails. Open all year.

Baddy (AC B BF CC GLM M MA OS S ST)
May-Sep: 11-2, Oct-Apr: Thu-Sun 21-2h
Viale Europa 9, Torre del Lago ☎ 346 99 52 338 (mobile)
www.baddy.tv
Bar with snacks and buffet (aperitivo) on the roof. On Fri & Sat drag queen restaurant „Bigodini".

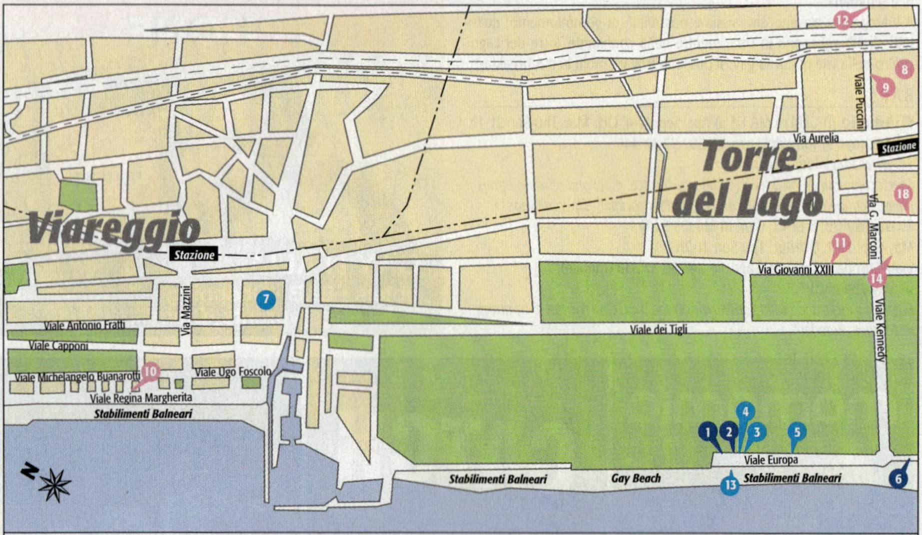

Viareggio
Torre del Lago
Stazione
Via Aurelia
Viale Puccini
Via G. Marconi
Via Giovanni XXIII
Viale Kennedy
Viale dei Tigli
Viale Europa
Via Mazzini
Viale Antonio Fratti
Viale Capponi
Viale Michelangelo Buonarotti
Viale Ugo Foscolo
Viale Regina Margherita
Stabilimenti Balneari
Gay Beach

Viareggio / Torre del Lago

EAT & DRINK

- Adagio – Bar 3
- Baddy – Bar 4
- Lucciola. La – Restaurant 7
- Dune LGTB Beach – Café 13
- Priscilla – Bar 5

NIGHTLIFE

- StupidA – Danceclub 1
- Frau – Danceclub 6
- Mama Mia – Danceclub 2

ACCOMMODATION

- Adam's Garden – Guest House 18
- Caffeletti – Guest House 11
- Christian & David's Guest House 14
- Le Villi – Guest House 9
- Libano – Guest House 8
- Palace – Hotel 10
- Villa Ricordi – Guest House 12

■ **Priscilla** (B GLM m MA S ST t) Jun-Aug: Tue-Sun 8-4h, closed on Mon (in July & Aug also open). Sep-May: Tue-Thu 11-19, Fri-Sun 8-3h
Viale Europa 19, Torre del Lago ☏ 0584 341 804
☏ 337 25 33 46 (mobile) 🖳 www.priscillacaffe.it
Gay bar with shows and cabaret. Fri-Sun dragshow from 22h, from June-August every day. Only place to buy cigarettes on the beach!

CAFES

■ **Mama Dune Beach** (B GLM M YC) 9-19h, May-Sep
Viale Europa 5, Torre del Lago *In front of Mama Mia*
☏ 392 62 62 642 (mobile) 🖳 www.mamadunebeach.it
Gay-lesbian beach bar with WI-Fi, deck chairs and sun beds, warm showers and volleyball. Meals available at luch time and drinks availabe all day.

MEN'S CLUBS

■ **Catch Club**
☞ Lucca.

DANCECLUBS

■ **Frau** (AC B D glm MA t) Fri-Sun 24-6h
Viale Europa, rotonda, Torre del Lago ☏ 0584 34 22 82
🖳 www.fraumarleen.com
House club, only few gay men. Quite expensive.

■ **Mama Mia** (! B CC D F GLM M S YC)
May-Sep 18-4, Oct-Apr Thu-Sun 21-2h
Viale Europa 5, Torre del Lago *Road along the sea*
☏ 345 13 47 346 (mobile) 🖳 www.mamamiadisco.it
Crowded disco/bar with drag show and disco (mainstream and revival) at the weekend in summer. Also appetizers (aperitivi) mainly on Sat & Sun afternoon.

■ **RMX**
☞ Lucca.

■ **StupidA** (AC B D GLM M YC) April-September:
Mon-Thu 18-2.30, Fri-Sun -4h. October-March: Fri-Sun 22.30-3.30h
Viale Europa 1, Torre del Lago *ex-Boca Chica* ☏ 393 223 93 22 (mobile)
🖳 www.stupida.tv
Aperitivo and disco in the end of Viale Europa. Mainstream music, gog-go boys, dragshows etc. Next door to the restaurant RistoStupid.

RESTAURANTS

■ **Lucciola. La** (B CC glm M) 19-23h, Tue closed
Via Pucci 80 ☏ 0584 96 16 23
Restaurant & pizzeria with a gay staff. Fish specialities.

HOTELS

■ **Palace** (AC B BF CC GLM H I M OS RWS RWT)
Lungomare / Via Flavio Gioia, 2 ☏ 0584 461 34
🖳 www.palaceviareggio.com
Luxurious hotel with a beautiful roof garden facing the sea.

GUEST HOUSES

■ **Adam's Garden B&B** (AC BF G I OS)
Via Mazzini 93/a, Torre del Lago *400 m from railwaystation*
☏ 331 280 9363 🖳 www.adamsgarden.it
A gay-owned B&B with 2 large suites, 4 rooms and a garden.

■ **B&B „Le Villi"** (AC B BF CC GLM M MA OS PA RWS RWT)
25 Apr-15 Oct
Viale Puccini 178, Torre del Lago *In the centre of Torre del Lago close to Museo Puccini* ☏ 0584 34 03 55 🖳 www.levilli.com
All rooms with own bath, air conditioning, TV, fridge and safe. Dinner available. Free bikes.

■ **Caffeletti** (AC BF G I MA OS)
Via Pardini 34/c, Torre del Lago ☏ 347 196 46 85 (mobile)
🖳 www.caffeletti.com
Closest B&B to the beach. All rooms with AC, security box, TV and own bath. Access to nice, small garden. Free wireless internet.

■ **Christian & David's Guesthouse** (glm OS)
Via Colombo 35, Torre del Lago ☏ 347 54 78 190 (mobile)
Quiet place in a natural reservation very close to gay locations. English, German, French & Spanish spoken.

Libano (AC BF G I M MA OS PK RWS RWT VA WO) All year
Via Tabarro 23, Torre del Lago ☎ 0584 35 03 22
💻 www.bedandbreakfast-libano.it
Rooms with sat-TV, safe and fridge. In the new floor under the roof also rooms with balcony. Free wireless internet. Bike-rental. Dinner upon request. Transfer from airport / train station. Small gym on site.

Locanda al Colle (AC BF GLM I PA PI PK RWB RWS) Apr-Oct
Via La Stretta 231 *Capezzano, 20 mins from the gay beach by car, 30 mins from Pisa airport* ☎ 0584 915 195 💻 www.locandaalcolle.it
Maison de Charme in the hills. Heated swimming pool of salted water. Two times/week dinner available, lunch on request. Free wireless internet.

Valdonica Vineyard Residence & Winery
☞ *Grosseto – Toscana.*

Villa Ricordi B&B (BF CC GLM OS PA PK) All year
Viale Giacomo Puccini 230 *Torre del Lago.* ☎ 339 5894702
☎ 338 3323203 💻 www.villaricordi.it
Quiet place with a large garden, near to the lake and close to the center of Torre del Lago. Good prices.

SWIMMING

-"La Lecciona" beach, at the end of Viale Europa.

CRUISING

-Via Zara (R) (by car and on foot by night, also areas in the vicinity and in the pine wood)
-Torre del Lago: at the end of Viale Europa, near the beach in the forest (evening/night).

Vicenza – Veneto

CRUISING

-Railway Station (AYOR) (at night, also in the areas nearby, e.g. in the Campo Marzio gardens)
-P Largo Bologna (at night by car or on foot), Motorway A31 „Valdastico"
-P Villa Tacchi (both sides day & night)
-P Thiene (both sides day & night).

Viterbo – Lazio

SEX SHOPS/BLUE MOVIES

Cobra (g VS) 10-19.30h, Sun & Mon closed
Via Enrico Fermi ☎ 0761 34 62 89 💻 www.sexshopcobra.it
Three further stores in Rome.

CRUISING

-Piazza Gramsci
-Bagnaccio
-Bullicame Park.

Japan

Name: Nippon · Japon · Japón · Giappone
Location: Between Sea of Japan & western Pacific Ocean
Initials: J
Time: GMT +9
International Country Code: ☏ 81 (omit 0 from area code)
International Access Code: ☏ 001, 0061 or 0041
Language: Japanese. English (commercial language)
Area: 377,837 km² / 145,831 sq mi.
Currency: 1 Yen (¥) = 100 Sen
Population: 127,764,000
Capital: Tokyo
Religions: 80% Buddhist or Shinto
Climate: Spring (Mar-May) is cherry blossom season. Autumn (Sep-Nov) is an ideal time to travel, with pleasant temperatures and the autumn colours. Winter (Dec-Feb) can be very cold.
Important gay cities: Tokyo, Osaka

Homosexual acts in private between consenting adults are not illegal. The reasons for this may be rooted in Japanese history. Over 200 years ago, Samurai warriors commonly practiced sodomy („shudo") and recognized it as a superior kind of love. During the Meiji era, under the influence of Christianity, homosexual activities were discouraged, though still not made illegal. At present, the general social attitude is a version of „don't ask, don't tell." In April 2011, Taiga Ishikawa became the first openly gay politician to be elected to a seat in a Tokyo ward assembly. He intends to champion greater openness in the treatment afforded homosexuality in schools. But Taiga Ishikawa also wants to promote registered partnerships in parliament in future. Sex with minors, 17 and under, is strictly prohibited by laws in each prefecture.

Current gay social activities are growing. The gay parade in Sapporo is held every September, while the parade in Tokyo is on hold for the time being. There are also gay street fairs in Nagoya (June) and in Shinjuku Ni-chome in Tokyo (August). The Tokyo International Lesbian & Gay Film Festival is held every July in Tokyo.

Many gays lead a double life due to pressures imposed by family, workplace, and society. The increasing number of HIV-positive men is another serious problem. NPO/ NGO groups are actively working to encourage gays to practice safer sex. Gay information centres in Tokyo („akta") and Osaka („dista") also encourage safer sex practices.

Gay tourists are frequently less than welcome because of the language barrier and a possible disregard of Japanese customs. Gay bars are often declared „members only" to deter heterosexuals. Gay establishments can be difficult to find. Most urban addresses consist of the district name and three numbers, for example a bookstore at Shinjuku 2-12-3. From this you know the store is in the Shinjuku district, in the second section. Within the second section, the store is on block twelve and is in the third building on that block. To help you, there are occasional green signs giving the district and the section of the district on lampposts and electric poles. Each building displays a blue plate with the exact address.

Freiwillige, private homosexuelle Handlungen zwischen Volljährigen sind nicht strafbar. Der Grund dafür ist wahrscheinlich in der japanischen Geschichte zu finden. Vor über 200 Jahren praktizierten die Samurai-Krieger gewohnheitsmäßig Analverkehr („shudo") und betrachteten ihn als höhere Form der Liebe. Während der Meiji-Periode wurde zwar aufgrund des christlichen Einflusses von homosexuellen Handlungen abgeraten, diese wurden jedoch nicht unter Strafe gestellt. Momentan gleicht die gesellschaftliche Einstellung vorwiegend einer Version von „nicht fragen, nichts sagen". Im April 2011 ist trotz des weiter bestehenden Tabus ist mit Taiga Ishikawa erstmalig ein offen schwuler Politiker in ein Tokioter Bezirksparlament gewählt worden. Er will sich dafür stark machen, dass das Thema Homosexualität an den Schulen offener behandelt werden soll. Auch für eingetragene Partnerschaften will Taiga Ishikawa im Parlament künftig werben. Sex mit Minderjährigen (17 und jünger) ist in allen Präfekturen strengstens verboten.

Die aktuelle Entwicklung des schwulen Soziallebens ist erfreulich. In Sapporo findet jeden September eine Parade statt, während das jährliche Schwulenfest in Tokio momentan zu pausieren scheint. Es gibt aber auch in Tokio schwule Straßenfeste in Nagoya (Juni) und in Shinjuku Ni-chome (August). Außerdem findet hier jeden Juli das Tokyo International Gay & Lesbian Film Festival statt. Viele Schwule werden durch den Druck von Familie, Arbeitsplatz und Gesellschaft in ein Doppelleben gezwungen. Ein weiteres ernsthaftes Problem ist die Zunahme an HIV-Infektionen unter Männern. Politisch unabhängige Interessengruppen sowie schwule Informationszentren arbeiten intensiv daran, schwule Männer zum „safer sex" zu bewegen.

Wegen der Sprachbarriere und möglicher Missachtung von japanischen Gebräuchen sind schwule Touristen oft nicht gern gesehen. Schwulenbars werden häufig mit „members"only deklariert, um Heterosexuelle abzuschrecken. Schwule Lokale sind oft sehr schwer zu finden. Die meisten urbanen Adressen bestehen aus dem Namen des Stadtteils und drei Zahlen wie z.B. für einen Buchladen in Tokyo: Shinjuku 2-12-3. Die erste Zahl bedeutet, dass sich das Geschäft im 2. Stadtviertel von Shinjuku befindet. Die zweite und dritte Zahl geben den dortigen Häuserblock (12) und das Gebäude (3) selbst an. Als Orientierungshilfe gibt es gelegentlich grüne Schilder an Laternenpfählen und Strommasten, die Stadtteil und Stadtviertel angeben. An den Häusern selbst befinden sich dann blaue Plaketten mit der exakten Adresse.

Les relations homosexuelles privées entre majeurs consentants ne sont pas passibles de peine. L'histoire japonaise en est peut-être la raison : il y a plus de 200 ans, les Samurais pratiquaient régulièrement le « chudo », la pénétration anale, et le considéraient comme la forme suprême de l'amour. Pendant la période Meiji, l'influence chrétienne a voulu dissuader des rapports homosexuels sans pour autant les interdire. Aujourd'hui, on préfère ne pas parler de son homosexualité et beaucoup mènent une double vie pour assurer la paix sociale et familiale. Malgré le tabou ambiant, Taiga Ishikawa est le premier homme politique ouvertement gay a être élu dans un parlement de circonscription de Tokyo. Il veut s'engager à ce que le sujet de l'homosexualité soit abordé ouvertement dans les écoles. Taiga Ishikawa souhaite également discuter du partenariat enregistré

au parlement. Les relations homosexuelles entre adultes consentants ne sont pas un délit et la majorité sexuelle est fixée à 17 ans.
L'évolutions actuelle de la vie sociale gay est réjouissante. A Sapporo se déroule en septembre chaque année une parade alors que la fête gay annuelle de Tokyo semble actuellement faire une pause. Il existe cependant à Tokyo aussi des fêtes de rue, à Nagoya (juin) et à Shinjuku Ni-Chome (août). De plus, le Festival International du Film Gay et Lesbien de Tokyo a lieu en juillet chaque année. Beaucoup de gays se voient enfermer dans une double-vie sous la pression de la famille, du travail et de la société. Un autre problème est l'augmentation des contaminations au VIH et plusieurs organisations de Tokyo et d'autres grandes villes du pays incitent les homosexuels au safer sex.
Les touristes gays sont souvent mal-vus en raison de barrières linguistiques et de possibles non-respects des coutumes japonaises. Les bars sont souvent déclarés « members only » pour décourager les hétérosexuels. Le lieux gays sont souvent difficiles à trouver car la plupart des adresses sont constituées du nom de l'arrondissement et de trois nombres comme par exemple pour une librairie de Tokyo : Shinjuku 2-12-3. Le premier nombre (2) correspond à l'arrondissement de Shinjuku, le deuxième le bloc de maison (12) et le troisième l'immeuble (3). On trouve parfois des panneaux verts aux lampadaires ou poteaux électriques indiquant l'arrondissement et le quartier ; les maison quant à elles portent des plaquettes bleues où figure l'adresse complète.

Los actos homosexuales voluntarios entre mayores de edad no están penalizados. Los motivos se pueden encontrar en la historia japonesa. Hace más de 200 años, los "samurai" practicaban regularmente el sexo anal ("shudo") y lo consideraban la forma suprema del amor. Durante el periodo "meiji" se desaconsejaban las prácticas homosexuales debido a la influencia cristiana pero no estaban penalizadas. Actualmente, la posición de la sociedad es generalmente la de "no preguntar y no decir nada". En abril de 2011, a pesar de la existencia de tabúes al respecto, se eligió por primera vez en un parlamento del distrito de Tokio a un político abiertamente gay, su nombre es Taiga Ishikawa. Ishikawa quiere hace campaña para que la homosexualidad se trate abiertamente en las escuelas. En el futuro, Taiga Ishikawa también quiere hacer campaña en el Parlamento a favor de las parejas registradas. El sexo con menores (17 años) está prohibido en todas las prefecturas.
La evolución actual de la vida gay es admirable. En Sapporo, se celebra cada septiembre una marcha gay, mientras que en Tokio parece que la fiesta gay anual ha finalizado provisionalmente. Sin embargo, en Tokio también se celebran fiestas en la calle Nagoya (junio) y en Shinjuku Ni-chome (agosto). Además, en Tokio se celebra cada julio el festival internacional de cine gay-lésbico.
Muchos homosexuales se ven obligados a llevar una doble vida por la presión familiar, laboral o social. Otro problema importante es el crecimiento de las infecciones por VIH entre los hombres. Algunos grupos políticos independientes así como centros de información gay están trabajando activamente para fomentar el sexo seguro entre los gays.
Debido a la barrera del idioma y al posible desconocimiento de las costumbres japonesas, los viajeros gays son a menudo mal vistos. Los locales gays suelen presentarse a menudo como "solo para miembros", para evitar la entrada de heterosexuales. Los locales gays son a menudo difíciles de encontrar. En la mayoría de direcciones figura el nombre del barrio y tres números como, por ejemplo, en una tienda de Tokio: Shinjuku 2-12-3. El primer número indica que la tienda está en el 2º distrito de Shinjuku. El segundo y tercer número indican el bloque de casas (12) y el edificio (3). Como orientación pueden encontrarse a veces carteles verdes en las farolas y palos eléctricos que le indicaran el distrito o barrio. En las casas hay carteles azules con la dirección exacta.

I rapporti omosessuali volontari tra maggiorenni non sono punibili. Forse il motivo è da ritrovare nella storia del Giappone. Più di 200 anni fa, infatti, i samurai praticavano il sesso anale (shudo) e identificavano in questo tipo di sesso la forma più alta d'amore. Durante l'era Maiji, forse a causa dell'influenza cristiana, queste pratiche vennero deprecate tuttavia non punite. Attualmente l'attitudine sociale nei confronti degli omosessuali sembra essere quella del „non domandare e non dire niente". Ad aprile del 2011, nonostante il forte tabù che continua a persistere nella società giapponese, con Taiga Ishikawa è stato eletto per la prima volta (anche se in un parlamento circoscrizionale di Tokyo) un politico dichiaratamente gay. Il politico ha dichiarato di voler impegnarsi affinché il tema dell'omosessualità venga trattato apertamente nelle scuole. Anche per le unioni civili, dichiara il politico, non mancherà il suo impegno. Il sesso con i minorenni (sotto i 17 anni) è severamente vietato.
A Sapporo, ogni settembre ha luogo un corteo. Tokio offre feste gay rionali come quella di Nagoya (a giugno) e di Shinjuku Ni-chome (ad agosto). Inoltre ogni luglio si svolge il Tokyo International Gay & Lesbian Film Festival.
Molti gay sono obbligati spesso dalle circostanze sociali a condurre una doppia vita. L'aumento di infezioni da HIV rappresenta un grave problema. Organizzazioni non governative indirizzano i propri sforzi alla sensibilizzazione di omosessuali al sesso sicuro.
A causa della barriera linguistica e della possibile violazione degli usi e costumi dei giapponesi, spesso i turisti gay non sono visti di buon occhio. I bar gay adottano spesso la politica del ‚members only' con lo scopo di scoraggiarne l'entrata agli eterosessuali.
Spesso è molto difficile trovare i locali gay. Molti indirizzi civici sono composti dal nome del quartiere più 3 cifre, come per esempio l'indirizzo di una libreria a Tokyo: Shinjuku 2-12-3. Il primo numero significa che il negozio si trova nella seconda circoscrizione del quartiere Shinjuku. Il secondo e il terzo numero indicano corrispettivamente l'isolato e l'edificio stesso. A volte ai pali delle lanterne e della corrente potrete trovare dei cartelli verdi atti ad un migliore orientamento: questi indicano il quartiere e la circoscrizione nei quali ci si trova. Nei palazzi e negli edifici poi si ritrovano dei cartelli blu con l'indirizzo in dettaglio.

NATIONAL PUBLICATIONS

Badi
Shinjuku KM Building, 1-14-5 ✉ Tokyo – Shinjuku-ku
☎ (03) 3350-3922 🖳 www.badi.jp
Monthly gay magazine with a history of many years.

Samson
Kaimeikan, PO BOX 66, Ueno Post Office, Ueno ✉ Tokyo, Taito-ku
☎ (03) 3841-2901
A monthly gay magazine for chubby and chasers.

NATIONAL PUBLISHERS

G-project Co., Ltd.
2F Kusafuka Bldg. 5-4 Araki-cho ✉ 160-0007 Tokyo – Shinjuku-ku *2nd floor* ☎ (03) 5269-1880 🖳 www.gproject.com
Publisher of the magazines G-men (the best selling gay magazine in Japan) and SM-Z (the only gay SM magazine in Japan).

NATIONAL GROUPS

Bear Club of Japan (BCJ) (G)
Contact only via Internet ✉ Tokyo 🖳 www.bearclubofjapan.org
Non-profit, semi-social gay organization. International membership.

NATIONAL HELPLINES

Tokyo AIDS Telephone Service
✉ Tokyo ☎ (0120) 085-812 (english, 24 hours)

Fukuoka ☎ 092 & 093

BARS

Air Roll (B G MA) 20-5h
B1F, Nakanishi Bldg, Kiyokawa, Chuo-ku ☎ (092) 531-8035
🖳 hp.did.ne.jp/airroll-top

■ **Bros** (B G m MA) 21.30-3h
4-9-4 Sumiyoshi, Hakata-Ku ☏ (092) 411-6523
Foreigners welcome but no English spoken.
■ **Dungaree** (B G MA) 21h-, Closed Tue
4-13-14, Sumiyoshi, Hakata-ku ☏ (092) 473-0825
■ **Gab** (B G MA) 21-4h
4-9-4, Sumiyoshi, Hakata-ku ☏ (092) 411-6533 🖳 gabai.x.fc2.com
■ **Hachibankan** (B G) 20-3, Sat -4h, closed Wed
4-15-3, Sumiyoshi, Hakata-ku ☏ (092) 473-2525
■ **Selfish** (B G MA) 20-4h, closed Tue
3F Meitengai Bldg, 5-16 Konyamachi, Kokurakita-ku
☏ (093) 533-0722
■ **Sichimencho** (B G MA) 20-3, Sun & holiday 21-8h, closed Mon
4-13-15 Sumiyoshi, Hakata-ku ☏ (092) 441-9037

SEX SHOPS/BLUE MOVIES

■ **Hakata Anzu-ya** (g) 12-3h
1F, Taihei Bldg, 5-17-14, Sumiyoshi, Hakata-ku ☏ (092) 412-3925

SAUNAS/BATHS

■ **Business Inn Kokura** (B DU G m OS PI SA SB VS WO) 24hrs
B1, Tagawa Bldg. Kyo-machi 4-5-1, Kokurakita-ku ☏ (092) 551 1400
■ **Golgo** (B DR DU G m OS PI SA SB VS WO) 17-5, Sat and the day before holiday 15-11, Sun and holiday 15-5h
2F, 4-15-3 Sumiyoshi, Hakata-ku *Off Sumyoshi-Dori*
☏ (092 & 093) 413-5227
Very friendly staff and especially good on Fri & Sat nights. Lots of action in the darkroom.
■ **RED** (DR DU G) 18-6h
3F, Tamiya Bldg, 3-7-9 hakataekimae, Hakata-ku ☏ (092) 483-7115
🖳 redjk.web.fc2.com

CRUISING

-Higashi Koen Park
-Shingu Beach (10 mins walk from Seitetu Shingu station).

Hamamatsu ☏ 053

SWIMMING

-Nakatajima beach, take bus N°19 from main station, get off at the terminus, walk 20 mins down the road. At the small hotel called Car Road turn towards the beach (G, popular at WE in summer).

CRUISING

-Wajiyama Koen (park) after 22h.

Hiroshima ☏ 082

BARS

■ **Gout Temps** (B G MA) 20-?h, closed Sun
4F, No.2 Tsuda Bldg, 3-4 Ebisu-cho, Naka-ku ☏ (082) 247-8624
🖳 www.gout-temps.net

CRUISING

-Kyohashigawa Ryokudo Park.

Kagoshima ☏ 099

BARS

■ **Buzz R** (B G MA) 20-4h
3F, Nichi Bldg, 9-39, Yamanokuchi-cho ☏ (099) 227-2002
🖳 www7b.biglobe.ne.jp/~buzz-r
■ **Ken's Bar** (B G MA) 21-?h
2F, Taguchi Bldg, 10-17, Yamanokuchi ☏ (099) 223-0598
🖳 kens-bar.com/pc/index.htm
■ **Koguma** (B G MA) 18.30-1.30h
2F, Kadotamabekkan, 10-18, Hinoguchi-cho ☏ (099) 3154

Kanazawa ☏ 076

BARS

■ **RMX** (B G MA) 20-2h, closed Sun
2F Pent House, 2-30-2, Kata-machi ☏ (076) 262-0881
🖳 www4.nsk.ne.jp/~rmx/rmx/RMX.html
■ **Shinjugai** (B G MA) 20-4h
3F, Nozaki Bldg, 1-8-7 Kata-machi ☏ (076) 205-7867
🖳 www.spacelan.ne.jp/~mayo

CRUISING

-Ekimae Cinema
-Spa Fukuyu (2nd floor in the rest room).

Kobe ☏ 078

CRUISING

-Basement of Kobe Shimbun Kaikan Building
-Suma (Shioya Beach).

Kumamoto ☏ 096

BARS

■ **Bar Ken Ken** (B G MA) 20-5h, closed Mon
3F, Aiai Bldg, 1-6-7, Shimodori ☏ (096) 351-1919
🖳 www.kenkenken.com/kenken-top.html

Kyoto ☏ 075

BARS

■ **Apple** (AC B G MA) 19-4h
3F Kobayashi Kaikan, Kiyamachi Dori, Shijo ☏ (075) 256-0258
🖳 apple1985.web.fc2.com
Friendly. Foreigners welcome. Mostly older crowd.

■ **masa-masa** (B G MA) 20-2h
225, Sento-cho, Nishikiya-machi, Shimogyo-ku ☎ (075) 344-6737
🖳 www.kyoto-masamasa.com
■ **Metro** (B g MA s T)
Marutamachi-Kawabata *Keihan Marutamachi Station, Exit 2, in the basement* ☎ (075) 752-4765 🖳 www.metro.ne.jp
Gay on last Fri of month is Diamond Night – gay night and drag queen show. Mixed crowd, also straights.
■ **Shu's** (B G MA) 20-3h
2F, No 13 Street, Higashi Hairu, Shijo Agaru, Kiyamachi *Hankyu Railways-Kawaramachi Station, near Takashimaya department store. From Shijo street, go north, 3rd alley to the right. 5th floor* ☎ (075) 251-6792
Very friendly. Foreigners welcome. Mostly older crowd.

Miyazaki ☎ 098

BARS

■ **Wishplus** (B G MA) 20-2h
2F, Seizan Bldg, 8-5, Chuodori ☎ (0985) 65-7868
🖳 x102.peps.jp/wishmiyazaki

Nagasaki ☎ 095

BARS

■ **BanBan** (B g) 19-3h, closed Wed
2F, Kuraoka Bldg, 1-1 Kashima, Karashima ☎ (095) 822-9703
🖳 www1.odn.ne.jp/~cev88650/BANBAN

SWIMMING

-Miyazuri beach (30 mins from town by bus)

Nagoya ☎ 052

BARS

■ **Hips** (B G MA) 20-3h, closed Wed & Thu
1F Tokyo Bld, 4-11-10 Sakae Yonchome, Naka-ku ☎ (052) 265-0904
■ **Puffin** (B G MA) 18-24h
2F, Gyoennishi Bldg, 1-7-4, Sakae, Naka-ku ☎ (052) 203-5534
🖳 www.puffin-nagoya.com

Narita

BARS

■ **Skinpray** (AC B D DR G MA) 18-3h
508 O11 building, 2nd floor, Kami-cho, Chiba *5 mins walk from Narita town train station, walk down Omote Sando Street towards the temples*
Attracts local guys who want to meet foreign visitors and airline staff. Bilingual personnel.

CRUISING

-Natita JR Station (go out the west exit. This leads to New Narita-City. Go down the stairs. There are 3 curb-side bus stops. By N°2 there is a WC. During the rush hour (18-20h) lots of cruising takes place there between train & bus. If you're staying in a hotel nearby, an invitation might be easily accepted. Alternately go out the east exit, turn left and 20 m along the building there is another WC).

Nigata ☎ 025

BARS

■ **JaJa** (B G MA) 20-2h, closed Tue
2F Ekimae Ing. Bld. 1-2-26 Benten *Near Niigata Station*
☎ (025) 241-8074 🖳 www.geocities.jp/giraudjaja

CRUISING

-Yamanoshita beach park. Many gay people in the summer.

Okayama ☎ 086

BARS

■ **Orb** (B G MA) 19-?h
203 Sansei Bldg, 1-11-5, Tamachi, Kita-ku ☎ (086) 221-0901
🖳 www.orb-bar.com/top.htm

Okinawa ☎ 098

BARS

■ **Ankh** (B G MA) 20-2h
2F Pomp Bldg. 2-8-21 Makishi ☎ (098) 864-5912 🖳 ankh.to
Friendly atmosphere with no Karaoke. A second branch in Asagaya, Tokyo.
■ **Snack Resort** (B G MA) 20-4h
2F Nakayoku-tuboya Bldg, 1-9-11, Tsuboya ☎ (098) 869-2754
■ **Sunshin** (B G MA) 21-3h, closed Tue, Wed
2F, 3-10-3, Makishi, ☎ (098) 97870438
🖳 k.fc2.com/cgi-bin/hp.cgi/OKINAWA-SUNSHIN

SAUNAS/BATHS

■ **Pineapple House** (B DR DU G M OS PI SA SB VS WO) 13-11h
4F 2-17-44 Makishi ☎ (098) 867-9952

SWIMMING

-Naminoue beach (near Tomari harbour, cruisy).

CRUISING

-Yogi Park (near Naha's prefectural library, hospital and main police office)
-Bus terminal (afternoon)

Osaka ☎ 06

Osaka has the second largest gay scene in Japan. Visitors can orientate themselves with the help of the Magazine „Kansai Scene", which sometimes lists gay or gay friendly establishments. Gay areas are located in Doyama-Cho and Kamiyama-Cho (not far from JR Osaka and Hankyu Umeda stations).This area is often referred to as Kita (north area). Nanba and Shinsekai are referred to as Minami (south area). The largest area is Kita with and is the most welcoming to gay foreigners. Gay events or nights are sometimes held at famous straight clubs as well. The local gay bookshops often have fliers about events.

Osaka hat die zweitgrößte Schwulenszene Japans. Die Zeitschrift „Kansai Scene" gibt Auskunft über schwulenfreundliche oder rein schwule Lokale und hilft Besuchern so bei ihrem Einstieg ins Nachtleben. Die schwule Szene findet man in Doyama-Cho und Kamiyama-Cho (unweit der JR Osaka und Hankyu Umeda Bahnhöfe). Diese Gegend wird auch oft Kita (Nordstadt) genannt. Nanba und Shinsekai werden dagegen als Minami bezeichnet (Südstadt). Das größte Gebiet ist die Nordstadt, die auch am meisten für den schwulen Reisenden zu bieten hat. Auch Hetero-Clubs organisieren schwule Veranstaltungen oder Partys. In den schwulen Buchläden liegen oft Flyer für solche Events aus.

Osaka a le deuxième milieu gay du Japon. Les quartiers gays se trouvent à Doyama (près de la gare d'Umeda), Nanba et à Shinsekai. Doyama est le plus grand et celui qui est le plus ouvert aux touristes gays. Tous les week-end ont lieux dans les boîtes de nuit gays des spectacles. Le magazine « Kansai Scene » vous donne des informations sur les bars gays et gays friendly et guide les touristes dans leurs virées nocturnes.
Le milieu gay se trouve à Doyama-Cho et Kamiyama-Cho (près des gares de JR Osaka et de Hankyu Umeda). Cette région est souvent également appelée Kita (quartier nord). Nanba et Shinsekai portent, par contre, le nom de Minami (quartier sud). Le quartier nord est plus grand et a le plus à offrir aux touristes gays. Certains clubs hétéros organisent des soirées gays et pour s'y retrouver, on peut consulter les prospectus qui sont souvent déposés dans les librairies.

Osaka tiene el segundo ambiente gay más grande de Japón. La revista local „Kansai Scene" da información necesaria sobre los locales gays y sirve de buena introducción a la vida nocturna para los turistas.
El ambiente gay se encuentra en los distritos de Doyama-Cho y Kamiyama-Cho (cerca de las estaciones de JR Osaka y Hankyu Umeda). Esta zona se la denomina a menudo también Kita (Norte). En cambio, Nanba y Shinsekai se las llama Minami (Sur). La mayor parte está en el norte, que es donde hay más oferta para los turistas gays. Los locales heterosexuales también organizan eventos o fiestas para gays. En las librerías gays se encuentran a menudo las entradas para este tipo de eventos.

Dopo quella di Tokyo, la scena gay di Osaka è la seconda più grande del Giappone. La rivista locale „Kansai Scene" dà informazioni circa i locali gay friendly e i locali prettamente gay, aiutando così i visitatori al primo approccio con la vita notturna della città.
La scena gay di Osaka si concentra nella zone di Doyama-Cho e Kamiyana-Cho (non molto lontano dalle stazioni JR Osaka e Hankyu Umeda). Questa area viene spesso chiamata Kita (al nord della città). Invece Nanba e Shinsekai vengono chiamate Minami (il sud della città). Il quartiere più grande è la zona nord che ha anche la maggior offerta per i turisti gay. Anche le discoteche non prettamente gay organizzano eventi e party gay. I flyer per questi party li trovate nelle librerie gay.

GAY INFO

Kansai Scene (G)
Sakuragawa 1-4-29 2F *Osaka, Naniwa-ku* ☎ (06) 556-0022
www.kansaiscene.com
A monthly, bilingual, free magazine packed with articles, reviews, listings and classifieds. Also gay places.

BARS

Bacchus (B GLM m MA) Mon-Fri 20-2, Sat -?h, closed Sun, except when Mon is a public holiday
3F Daini-Shouei Kaikan, 6-14 Doyama-cho, Kita-ku *3rd floor, next to Hotel Trevi* ☎ (06) 6361-2366 www.geocities.jp/osaka_bacchus
English speaking staff.

Shift (B G MA) 20-3h
2F, Kirishima Leisure Bldg, 8-18, Doyama-cho, Kita-ku ☎ (06) 6311-1303
shiftosk.web.fc2.com
Elegant bar with several choice of wines

Boo8 (B G MA) 18-23.30h, closed Tue
3F Mize Bldg, 4-6-2, Namba, Chuo-ku homepage2.nifty.com/boo8

Breast (B G MA) 19-5h
2F, Pearl Leisure Bldg, 1-6-4, Doyama-cho, Kita-ku ☎ (06) 6366-7188
breast-do.com
Spacious bar with Karaoke.

Gin Rockets (B G MA) 19-?h
105 Matsumoto Leisure Bldg, 8-18, Doyama-cho, Kita-ku
☎ (06) 6313-1239 ginrockets.web.fc2.com

Grandslam (B G MA) 20-5h
1F, Dai2 Matsueikaikan, 6-14, Doyama-cho, Kita-ku ☎ (06) 6362-8077
www.grandslam-osaka.com/index2.php
Show time by gogo boys on weekend.

Hysterics (B GLM YC) 20-5h
16-10 Doyama-cho *Suite 6 Kuei Dai-Ni Leisure Bld* ☎ (06) 6365 9996
www.ponpy.com/hysterics/index01.htm

Kuro (B GLM MC) 18.30-2h, closed Sun & Holidays
OK Bld 16-6 Doyama-cho, Kita-ku *Near the entrance of Doyama-cho gay area* ☎ (06) 6313-4665
Oldest gaybar in town, make sure you go into the right one with the blue sign (another bar with same name and green sign)!

Leibniz (B GLM MA) 19.30-2h
201 Dai 2 Matsueikaikan, 6-14, Doyama-cho, Kita-ku *Same building as Motoba and Cafe J²* ☎ (06) 6362 0239

Lupu (B GLM MA) 20-5h, closed Wed
Kansai-Chuo Bldg., Bekan 1/F, 101 15-2 Doyama-cho, Kita-ku
☎ (06) 6364 1357 lupu.atspace.com
Lesbian run mixed bar.

Marriage (B GLM YC) 20-5h
401 Kyuei Leisure Bld, 16-10 Doyama-cho ☎ (06) 6311 1588

Physique Pride Osaka (! B CC G YC) 20-2h
1F Sanyo-kaikan, 8-23 Doyama-cho, Kita-ku *Osaka Kita*
☎ (06) 6361-2430 www.physiqueprideosaka.com
Friendly gay bar for foreigners and their admirers. English spoken. No cover charge.

Popeye (B G YC)
3F Daiichi Shoei Bld, 6-15 Doyama-cho, Kita-ku ☎ (06) 6315-1502
popeye-osaka.hp.infoseek.co.jp

Red White (B G MA) Mon-Thu 20-24, Fri & Sat -2h, closed Sun
3F, Matsumoto Leisure Bldg, 8-18, Doyama-cho, Kita-ku
☎ (06) 6364-1009 www.hamq.jp/i.cfm?i=91827364

Town Space H2 (B G MA)
5F, GT Town, 4-3-16 Namba, Chuo-ku ☎ (06) 6644-0809
www.geocities.co.jp/HeartLand-Oak/9795

Zakoza (B G MA) 18-24h, closed Tue
3F, Harmanos Bldg, 2-3-23, Dotonbori, Chuo-ku ☎ (06) 7501-7212
zakoza.x.fc2.com/zakoza/Welcome.html

CAFES

Cafe de Jumpin' Jumpin' (Cafe J²) (B GLM m YC)
☎ (06) 6363 3367 www.cafe-jj.com
Friendly and relaxed place with cute staff. Special events.

Do With Café (B GLM M MA ST)
B1 Jyuraku Bld, 9-23 Toganochyo, Kita-ku ☎ (06) 6312 1788
Upscale venue often has drag events and draws a mixed crowd of all ages.

DANCECLUBS

Explosion (! B D G s YC) 20-4, Sat & before public holidays -5h
B1 Sanyo-Kaikan, 8-23, Doyama-cho, Kita-ku *Hankyu Umeda/JR Osaka Station* ☎ (06) 6312-5003 www.ex-osaka.com
English-speaking staff. Often holds gay events.

Jack in the Box (B D G MA) 21-5h, closed Thu
B1 Daikichi Bldg. 12-12, Doyama-cho, Kita-ku *Osaka-Kita*
☎ (06) 6361-3271 www.jack-box.com
Disco and club, gay events.

SEX CINEMAS

Higashi Umeda Rose Theater (GLM MA VS)
17-8, Doyama-cho, Kita-ku *close to the gay bars in Doyama-cho*
☎ (06) 6312-1856
Gay movies, plus occasional „Young Rose Guy Show".

SAUNAS/BATHS

Daikichi (AC DR G MA S SA) 24h
12-12, Doyamacho, Kita-ku ☎ (06) 3270 www.jack-box.com/daikichi

Hokuoukan (! B DU FC FH G LAB M OS PI SA SB SOL VS WH WO) 16-24h
14-10 Doyama-cho Kita-ku *Center of gay north area Doyama*
☎ (06) 6361-2288 www.hokuoukan.jp
Most famous in Osaka. Foreigners should speak some Japanese. Different rates depending on your age. When entering, ask reception for the blue code number to enter the Blue Zone area for people under 40. ID required. Also accommodation and food available.

Ranger (AC G MA S) 16-5h
Nakatsu, Kita-ku *1 min from MRT Nakatsu station exit 2* ☎ (06) 8986
www.ranger-osaka.jp

Royal Sauna (AC G MA MSG SA)
1-2-4 Ebisuhigasi Naniwa-ku, Osak-shi ☎ (06) 6643-0001
www.sauna-royal.jp

CRUISING

-Act III shopping area and facilities, near the gay bars in Doyama-cho.
-Sakuranomiya Park, across from Sakuranomiya Station on the Loop Line, south of the bridge, after midnight.

Sapporo ☏ 011

BARS

■ **Reboot Sapporo** (B G MA) 20-3h, closed Sun & Holidays
5F, Dai 2 Keiwa Bldg, Nishi 3 Chome, Minami 6 Jo, Chuo-ku
☏ (011) 513-1010 🖳 www.bar-reboot.jp

■ **Buena Vista** (B G MA) 20-3h
2F SA Bldg. Nishi-rokuchome, Minami-gojo, Chuo-ku ☏ (011) 561-6122
🖳 buenavista.dayuh.net

■ **Club Nostalgie** (B G MA) 20-3h
2F SA Bldg. Nishi-rokuchome, Minami-gojo, Chuo-ku ☏ (011) 812-8350
🖳 www13.ocn.ne.jp/~club-nos

■ **Crews** (B g MA) 19-3h
3F SA Bldg, Nishi-rokuchome, Minami-rokujo, Chuo-ku
☏ (011) 512-9389
Table tennis event every Sunday.

■ **Dan** (AC B G m MA) 20-3h
Minamig Nishi 6,3F Dai6 Asahi-kanko Bld *M° Susukino Station*
☏ (011) 562-4005 🖳 www2.ocn.ne.jp/~dan123/index.htm
Staff speaks some English.

■ **Hearty@Cafe** (B G MA) 20-3, Fri & Sat -4h
2F, Daiichi Family Bldg, Nishi 7 Chome, Minami 5 jo, CHuo-ku
☏ (011) 530-6022

■ **Non Stop** (B G MA) 20-3h
3F, SA Bldg. Nishi-rokuchome, Minami-gojo, Chuo-ku
☏ (011) 530-6336

CRUISING

-Odori Park (Nishi 11-chome)
-Sapporo Railroad Station
-Yuraku Cinema
-Sauna in the basement of Hotel Line.

Sendai ☏ 022

BARS

■ **Ajito** (B G MA) 18h-
3F, Lion Sendaikan Bldg, 2-8-3, Kokubun-cho, Aoba-ku
☏ (022) 215-0605 🖳 www5f.biglobe.ne.jp/~ajito

■ **Ant Lion** (B G MA) 19-3, Fri & Sat -5h
4F, Lemon Shato Bldg, Kokubun-cho, Aoba-ku ☏ (022) 263-7188
🖳 pksp.jp/bar-antlion

Tokyo ☏ 03

Tokyo has the largest gay scene of the country. Foreigners can orientate themselves with help of the magazines „Metropolis Tokyo" and „Tokyo Night Life" both written in English. There are several gay areas including Shinjuku-nichome, Shinbashi, Ueno, and Asakusa. Shinjuku-nichome, largest gay area, is the most welcoming to gay foreigners. It is also where the Tokyo Rainbow Festival is held annually on a Sunday in August.

Tokyo hat die größte schwule Szene des Landes. Ausländische Besucher können sich mit Hilfe der englischsprachigen Stadtmagazine „Metropolis Tokyo"und „Tokyo Night Life" orientieren. Es gibt verschiedene Schwulengegenden wie z.B. Shinjuku-nichome, Shinbashi, Ueno und Asakusa. Shinjuku-nichome, die größte, ist schwulen Touristen gegenüber am aufgeschlossensten. Hier findet auch alljährlich an einem Sonntag im August das Tokio Rainbow Festival statt.

Tokyo dispose du plus grand milieu gay du pays. Il y a plusieurs quartiers gays comme par exemple Shinjuku Ni-Chome, Shinbashi, Ueno et Asakusa. Shinjuku Ni-Chome, est le plus grand quartier gay et celui qui est le plus ouvert aux touristes. C'est là qu'a lieu, chaque année en août, la « Tokio Rainbow Festival ». Les touristes étrangers peuvent s'y retrouver plus facilement en consultant les magazines en anglais « Metropolis Tokyo » et « Tokyo Night Life ».

Tokyo dispone del ambiente gay más grande del país. Los visitantes extranjeros podrán orientarse bien con la ayuda de las revistas en inglés „Metropolis Tokyo" y „Tokyo Night Life". Hay diferentes zonas gays como, por ejemplo, Shinjuku-nichome, Shinbashi, Ueno y Asakusa. Shinjuku-nichome, la mayor, es la más abierta hacia los turistas gays. Aquí se celebra cada año en un domingo en agosto el festival gay de Tokyo.

A Tokyo c'è la scena gay più grande del Giappone. I visitatori stranieri potranno orientarsi in questa città con l'aiuto di due riviste locali in lingua inglese: „Metropolis Tokyo"e „Tokyo Night Life". Ci sono molti quartieri gay come per esempio Shinjuku-nichome, Shinbashi, Ueno e Asakusa. Shinjuku-nichome è il quartiere gay più grande e per il turisti gay la più praticabile. Qui si svolge ogni anno alla fine di agosto (di domenica) il „Tokyo Rainbow Festival".

MEN'S CLUBS

■ **Gate In** (b G YC) 12-23.45h
5F, Nakatsubo Bldg, 1-7-10, Yaesu, Chuo-ku *on 5th floor*
☏ (03) 3245 0707 🖳 www.joinac.com/gatein
Young gay nudist cruise spot.

■ **Roppongi Inch** (b G YC)
3 Chome, Roppongi, Minato-ku *Roppongi Stn, exit 3, right-turn, cross the road at first traffic jct then turn right. walk a few blocks until Irish pub Hobgoblin. Left on that street, right at the first alley, left at the next alley. Club located on 2nd floor in the last building, behind a bar called Lost Angels Lots of hot, in-shape 20-30yo guys , customers over 40 are allowed in only on Fridays.*

SAUNAS/BATHS

■ **TREFF** (AC B DR DU G M MC P SA SB WH) 12-23h
4F Fukutomi Bld, 2-13-24, Minato-ku, Akasaka *M°Akasaka Station Exit No 5, near the ANA Intercontinental Tokyo* ☏ (050) 1563-8431
Sex club for foreigners and their admirers. Daytime discount from 12-15h on weekdays. Naked day on Sat, Sun and holiday. Other days Speedos or underwear.

CRUISING

-Yamanote line railway, cruising in the last carriage of the train.
-Facilities (toilets):
BYGS Building, Shinjuku Ni-Chome used to be cruise central, but now security has mounted cameras in all the facilities and cut peep holes in the bottom of the toilet stall doors!
Hibiya Park, facilities next to Police box
My City, Shinjuku Station, B/1 shops & B/2 parking garage
Shibuya Station, near exits
Shibuya Station, Tokyu Toyoko-Ten Department Store, all levels from train station to the roof
Shinjuku Station, East Exit inside ticket gate
Shinjuku Station, near JR ticketing office 1/F
Shinjuku Station, West Exit near ticket gate
Ueno Station, near exits
-Shinjuku Ni-Chome, small park in the heart of gay area, rentboys, strange people, afternoon to late evenings (AYOR)
-Shinjuku Ni-Chome, small „garden" in B/1 BYGS Building
-Sumida Park, at the river in Asakusa, fetish Japanese costume cruising and late evening action
-Starbucks, Shinjuku San-Chome, very cruisy due to proximity to the gay scene.

Tokyo – Minato-ku ☏ 03

BARS

■ **Bingo!** (AC G MC) Mon-Sat 19-23.30h
3F Dai 2 Daiko Bldg, 4-10-6, Shimbashi, Minato-ku ☏ (03) 3437-3435
🖳 www.pu3.fiberbit.net/bingo

■ **Bravo!** (B G MA) 18-24h
6F, Kokura Bldg, 2-11-8, Shinbashi, Minato-ku ☏ (03) 3503-8805
🖳 www.ne.jp/asahi/bravo/bravo/framepage9.html

■ **Koguma** (B G MA) 19-1, Sat and day before holiday 20- 1h, closed Sun
2F Sogo Bldg.4-18-4 Shimbashi, Minato-ku ☎ (03) 3431-3088

■ **TACTICS Shimbashi** (B G MA) 18-24, Fri -5h, closed Sun
3F, Princess Ichibankan, 3-22-3, Shinbashi, Minato-ku
💻 www2c.airnet.ne.jp/tactics/shinbashi/top2.html

■ **Town House Tokyo** (B G MA) 18-2, Sat 16-24h
6F, Cortire, 1-11-5, Shimbashi, Minato-ku ☎ (03) 3289-8558
💻 www13.ocn.ne.jp/~t_h_tky

DANCECLUBS

■ **Warehouse** (B G MA)
B1F10-14-5 Azabu ☎ (03) 6230-0343 💻 www.a-warehouse.net
Holds a monthly gay mix club night called The Ring.

SAUNAS/BATHS

■ **Junction** (B DR DU G M MA SA SB VS WH) 13-24h
3F Tanakawa Bld 4-20-3 Tanakawa, Minato-ku *4 mins walk from JR Shinagawa Station, Family Mart on 1F* ☎ (03) 3448-9077
💻 www.junction-s.com

TRAVEL AND TRANSPORT

■ **Magnet Tours** (GLM SH)
2F Sereno Nishishinbashi bldg. 2-11-14 Nishishinbashi
☎ (03) 3500-4819 💻 www.magnettours.jp
Focused specifically on LGBT tours.

Tokyo – Shibuya-ku ☎ 03

BARS

■ **GATE** (B G MA)
B1, Social Dogenzaka, 1-14-9, Dogenzaka, Shibuya-ku ☎ (03) 6416-4747
💻 www.gatetokyo.jp/top.htm

■ **[kéivi!]** (B G M MA) 18h-
4F Yoshino Bldg., 17-10 Sakuragaoka-cho, Shibuya-ku ☎ (03) 3462-9200
💻 www.keivi.com

■ **Mango Mango** (B G M MA) 19-1h
3F Shibuya Johnson Bldg., 17-12 Sakurayaokacho, Shibuya-ku
☎ (03) 3464-3884 💻 www.mango-mango.com
Bar in Thai style.

■ **Shibuya 246** (AC B G M MA) Daily 18-2h
4F, Shimizu Bldg, 2-7-4 Dogenzaka, Shibuya-ku *3 mins walk from Shibuya Station* 💻 246.o.007.jp
Newest gay bar in Shibuya.

MEN'S CLUBS

■ **BABYLON Tokyo** (DR G S) 14h-
3-5F, Sendagaya Bldg, 5-30-9, Sendagaya, Shibuya-ku ☎ (03) 7619
💻 http://www.babylon-tokyo.com/bt.html
Stylish cruising space with 3 floors.

Tokyo – Shinjuku-ku ☎ 03

NATIONAL GAY INFO

■ **akta** (GLM) 16-22h
Daini Nakae Bldg N° 301, 2-15-13 *Shinjuku-Gyoenmae Station*
☎ (03) 3226-8998
Gay community center & information about HIV/STDs.

NATIONAL PUBLICATIONS

■ **G-Men**
2F Kasafuka Bldg 5-4 Araki-cho *2nd floor* ☎ (03) 5269-1800
💻 g-men.co.jp
Japan's most read gay magazine.

BARS

■ **Advocates Cafe Tokyo** (B GLM MA OS) 18-4h
1F, Dai-7 Tenka Bldg. 2-18-1 Shinjuku, Shinjuku-ku ☎ (03) 3358-3988
💻 advocates-cafe.com
Remains one of the best places to start the evening and meet locals and foreigners alike (since it's open-air, it's also one of the easiest bars to find).

■ **Alamas Café** (B d GLM M MA ST WI) Mon-Thu 18-2, Fri+Sat -5, Sun 15-0h
1F, 2-12-1, Shinjuku, Shinjuku-ku *Garnet Building* ☎ (03) 3358 3988
💻 www.alamascafe.net
New location with DJ and Dragshows on Weekends. Friendly staff, english spoken. Free WiFi

■ **BAR Soi 2** (B G MA) 20h-
7F, Yamahara Heights, 2-12-15, Shinjuku, Shinjuku-ku ☎ (03) 3350-5119
Asian taste bar

■ **Bridge** (B G I MA NR OS) 20-2, Fri & Sat -4h
6F, SENSHO Bldg, 2-13-16, Shinjuku, Shinjuku-ku ☎ (03) 6423-7384
💻 www.bar-bridge.com/index2.html
Stylish and nice bar with balcony.

■ **DNA** (B G MA)
1F Musasino Bldg., 2-13-14 Shinjuku, Shinjuku-ku ☎ (03) 3341-4445
Opens earlier than most clubs, good starting place.

■ **Dragon Men** (B GLM MA) 18-3, Fri & Sat -5h
1F, Stork Nagasaki Bldg., Shinjuku 2-11-4 ☎ (03) 3341-0606
💻 clubdragon.jpn.org
Spacious bar which attracts a good mix of locals and foreigners, both male and female. English spoken.

■ **Fuji** (B G MA) 20-3h; Sat, Sun & day before holidays -5h
B1 Saint Four Bldg. 2-12-16, Shinjuku, Shinjuku-ku *Basement N° 104*
☎ (03) 3354-2707
One of the most popular bars for tourists. Karaoke with many songs in English.

■ **Gatten** (B G MA) 20-2h, closed Mon
6F, New Futami Bldg, 2-12-14, Shinjuku, Shinjuku-ku ☎ (03) 3350-8815
💻 k1.fc2.com/cgi-bin/hp.cgi/gten

■ **GB Tokyo** (! B G MA VS) 20-2, WE -3h
B1 Shinjuku Plaza Bldg. 2-12-3 Shinjuku, Shinjuku-ku *Basement of a hotel*
☎ (03) 3352-8972 💻 gb-tokyo.tripod.com
All nationalities welcome. Sign „GB" on sidewalk. English speaking staff.

■ **King of College since 1977** (B CC G MA R) 12-1h
2F Sakagami Bldg 2-14-5 Shinjuku, Shinjuku-ku *2nd floor*
☎ (03) 3352-3930 💻 www.kocnet.jp
English spoken. Mainly host boys. Call our English-speaking manager for further details.

■ **Kinsmen** (B GLM MC) Tue-Thu & Sun 19-1, Fri & Sat 19-3h, closed Mon
2F Homebase Bldg., 2-18-5 Shinjuku, Shinjuku-ku *On the 2nd floor of a corner building* ☎ (03) 3354-4949 💻 www11.ocn.ne.jp/~kinsmen
Comfortable atmosphere with jazz and R&B music.

■ **Ku Su O** (B G MA) 20-4, Sat & day before holidays, Sun & holidays -5h
3F Sunflower Bldg, 2-17-1 Shinjuku, Shinjuku-ku *3rd floor*
☎ (03) 3354-5050

■ **La tanya** (B G I MA) 19-2, Fri & Sat -4h
6F, Yamahara Heights, 2-12-15, Shinjuku, Shinjuku-ku ☎ (03) 6457-4232
💻 www.la-tanya.com
Stylish and elegant bar

■ **LOGOS** (B G MA) 20-2, Fri & Sat -5h
2F, Dai 33 Kyutei Bldg, 2-11-7, Shijuku, Shinjuku-ku ☎ (03) 3225-1881
💻 www.geocities.jp/logos_hp
Karaoke Bar

■ **Monsoon** (B GLM YC) 15-6h
6F, Shimazaki Bldg, 2-14-9, Shinjuku, Shinjuku-ku *across the street from Advocates, on the 6th floor* ☎ (03) 0470
💻 www.geocities.co.jp/Foodpia-Celery/3441
Funky hang-out for 20-something queers and their friends.

■ **Paradise Cafe** (B G MA) 19-4h
3F, Fujii Bldg, 2-13-16, Shinjuku, Shinjuku-ku ☎ (03) 3341-0626

■ **Rehab Lounge Tokyo** (B d GLM MA S) 19-2, Fri & Sat -3h
2F Sensho Bld, 2-13-16 Shinjuku, Shinjuku-ku ☎ (03) 3355 7833
💻 www.rehabloungetokyo.com

■ **Tac's Knot** (B G MA) 20-2h
202 Nagatani Take 8, 3-11-12 Shinjuku, Shinjuku-ku ☎ (03) 3341-9404
🖳 www.asahi-net.or.jp/~km5t-ootk/tacsknot.html
Gay art exhibitions.

■ **TACTICS Shinjuku** (AC G MA) 20-2, Fri & Sat -4h
1F Villa Heights, 2-7-3, Shinjuku, Shinjuku-ku ☎ (03) 3355-6669
🖳 www2c.airnet.ne.jp/tactics/shinjyuku/top.html

■ **TANKTOP** (B G MA) 20-6h
5F, Dai 7 Tenka Bldg, 2-18-1, Shinjuku, Shinjuku-ku ☎ (03) 3350-8066
Karaoke Bar

■ **the CLUBHOUSE** (B G MA) 15-3h
3F, Daiichi Tamaya Bldg, 3-6-11, Shinjuku, Shinjuku-ku
☎ (03) 3225-9946 🖳 www.theclubhouse.jp

■ **Usagi** (B glm MA)
Smoke-free bar, mixed but attracts a large gay crowd.

■ **WORDUP BAR** (B G MA)
2F, TOM Bldg, 2-10-7, Shinjuku, Shinjuku-ku ☎ (03) 3353-2466
🖳 http://wordup.que.jp/

MEN'S CLUBS

■ **BodyBreath!** (DR G MA S) 24h
near Shinjuku Gyoen station ☎ (03) 6457-8500 🖳 www.bodybreath.jp/jp

■ **Dock** (DR G MA NU) 21-4h
B1F Dai-2 Seiko Bldg. 2-18-5 Shinjuku, Shinjuku-ku ☎ (03) 3226-4006
Different theme nights. Very small darkroom. Expensive.

DANCECLUBS

■ **Annex. The** (B D GLM MA) 19-3h
1F Futami Building, 2-14-11 Shinjuku, Shinjuku-ku ☎ (03) 3356-5029
🖳 www.arty-farty.net
Same owners as Arty Farty (swap parties with one entrance fee). Long bar and dim cruise space at the rear.

■ **Arch** (B D GLM MA ST) Fri-Sun
B1F, Dai-2 Hayakawaya Bldg., 2-14-6 Shinjuku, Shinjuku-ku
☎ (03) 3352-6297 🖳 www.clubarch.net
Theme parties, drag divas, underground beats. Sat men only. Some women-only parties as well.

■ **Arty Farty** (B CC D GLM MA) 19-3h
3F, Kyutei Bldg No.33, 2-11-7 Shinjuku, Shinjuku-ku *2nd floor*
☎ (03) 5362-9720 🖳 www.arty-farty.net
Still the most popular dance club for both men and women in the neighborhood. Same owners as The Annex (swap parties with one entrance fee).

SEX SHOPS/BLUE MOVIES

■ **Lumiere** (CC G) 11-7h
1F Sunflower Bldg., 2-17-1 Shinjuku, Shinjuku-ku *1st floor*
☎ (03) 3352-3378 🖳 www.rumie-ru.jp
Gifts, books, magazines, videos; large selection.

SAUNAS/BATHS

■ **24 Kaikan Shinjyuku** (AC B DR DU FC FH G M MA OS SA SB SOL VS WH WO) 24hrs
2-13-1 Shinjuku, Shinjuku-ku *From Shinjyuku station subway take the exit C8. The sauna is about 400 m from there but not easy to find. 24 Kaikan is in front of the long side of Shinjyuku park* ☎ (03) 3354-2424
🖳 www.juno.dti.ne.jp/~kazuo24/english/english.htm
Hotel and sauna with 7 floors. Very modern and very clean. A little quiet during the WE. Foreigners welcome.

■ **HX** (B DR G MA SA SB) Mon-Thu 15-10, Fri 15-Mon 10h (non-stop)
1F UI Bld, 5-9-6, Shinjuku, Shinjuku-ku *From Ni-Chome, take Nakadori Street north, cross Yasukuni Dori and turn right across from MOS Burger. HX is on the 1st floor of a residential building. There is a small sign at the door handle* ☎ (03) 3226-4448

MASSAGE

■ **Kenshindo Seitai** 15-5, Fri-Sun 13-6h
2F, Dai 2 Kosei Bldg, 2-18-5, Shinjuku, Shinjuku-ku ☎ (03) 5919-2382
🖳 www.ksd-tokyo.net
Chinese style massage.

■ **KOC MASSA** (G MSG) 12-1h
2F, Sakagami Bldg, 2-14-5, Shinjuku, Shinkuku-ku *Inside King of College*
☎ (03) 3352-3930 💻 www.koc-massa.com/en/index.html
Oil massage by young male therapist.
40 min. JPY 8,000, 70 min. JPY 11,000, 90 min. JPY 13,000, 120 min. JPY 16,000

HEALTH GROUPS

■ **HIV to Jinken Jyoho Centre** (glm) 2nd & 4th Sun/ month 19-21h
☎ (03) 5259-0750

Tokyo – Taito-ku ☎ 03

BARS

■ **Korian Gokai** (B G MA) 19-24, Sun 17-24h
5F, Biko Bldg, 4-10-17, Higashiueno, Taito-ku ☎ (03) 5828-1448
💻 korian5f.web.fc2.com
■ **Omusubi** (B G MA) 18-2h, closed Thu
4F, Shatou Ueno, 7-10-5, Ueno, Taito-ku ☎ (03) 3847-0087
💻 omusubichan.sakura.ne.jp/menu.php
■ **Smile** (B G MA) 20-4.30h, closed Sun
1F, NKYM Heights, 7-5-6, Ueno, Taito-ku ☎ (03) 3841-7355
💻 smileueno.takara-bune.net
■ **Tohenboku** (B G MA) 18-2, Fri & Sat -6h
101 Shato Ueno, 7-10-5, Ueno, Taito-ku ☎ (03) 3841-1786
💻 www.touhen-boku.com

SAUNAS/BATHS

■ **24 Kaikan Ueno** (AC B DR DU G M MA OS SA SB SOL VS WH WO) 24hrs
1-8-7 Kita-Ueno, Taito-ku *Take the Hibiya subway to Iriya Station and take exit 1. Cross two streets to the beginning of elevated highway. Follow the street under the highway during 300 m. 24 Kaikan is just on the left side* ☎ (03) 3847-2424
💻 www.juno.dti.ne.jp/~kazuo24/english/english.htm
Hotel and sauna with 11 floors, probably the biggest gay sauna in Tokyo. Sun-bathing area on the rooftop. Foreigners are welcome. Free condoms available.

Tokyo – Toshima-ku ☎ 03

SAUNAS/BATHS

■ **Jinya** (B DU G M MA OS SA SB VS WH WO) 24hrs
2-30-19 Toshima-ku, Ikebukuro Ni-Chome *Use Ikebukuro station, take West Exit or C1 Exit. Find Love Motel with very big neon 10 Yen sign*
☎ (03) 3931-0186
Foreigners are welcome. Also accommodation.

Yokohama ☎ 045

BARS

■ **BEAST** (B G MA) 19-4h
201 Kagami Bldg, 1-6, Noge-cho, Naka-ku ☎ (045) 241-7661
💻 pksp.jp/be-st
■ **Club Teppei** (B G MA) 18-2, Weekend -5h
2-20, Miyagawa, Naka-ku ☎ (045) 251-6518
💻 www.hamq.jp/i.cfm?i=clubteppei
■ **Mixbar TROY** (B G MA) 19-4h, closed Sun
502 Shion Fukutomicho, 504 Higashidori, Fukutomi-cho
☎ (045) 262-3834 💻 kannnai-mixbar-troy.jimdo.com
■ **MONS** (B G MA) 19-24, Fri & Sat -2h
302 Lions Mansion Nogeyama Koen, 3-63-1, Miyagawa-cho, Naka-ku
☎ (045) 334-8988 💻 mons-web.com
Newly opened on Sep, 2011. There is no Karaoke, so enjoy the conversation with local people.

Jordan

Name: al-Urdunn · Jordanien · Jordanie · Jordania · Giordania
Location: Middle East
Initials: HKJ
Time: GMT +2
International Country Code: ☎ 962
International Access Code: ☎ 00
Language: Arabic, English
Area: 89,342 km² / 35,461 sq mi.
Currency: 1 Jordan-Dinar (JD) = 100 Piastres
Population: 5,759,732
Capital: Amman
Religions: 92% Moslem (Sunnites), 6% Christian
Climate: The best time to visit is spring/fall (Apr-Oct). Summer (July, August) is quite warm in the desert, cooler in Amman. Winter is mild along the Dead Sea , but can snow in Amman.

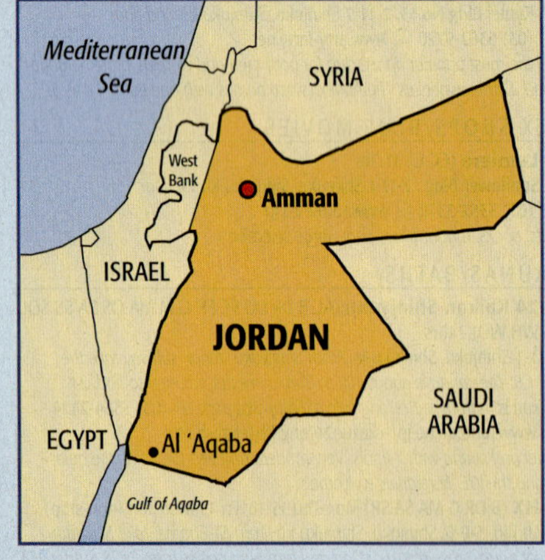

Homosexuality is officially legal in Jordan, however, gay men can still become victims of honorary murder. Although in many countries in the Middle East, one observes physical closeness between men in public, this should not in any way be confused with being homosexual. A gay scene does exist but unlike that in neighbouring Israel or Lebanon, it is often very secret, isolated, and in many cases relies on internet to arrange contacts. As Jordan is quite computer literate, it is easy to make contact over the internet with gay men. You can meet most single guys, as well as numerous migrant Iraqis at the cruising places listed below. It's important to remember, here as everywhere: rely on eye contact and behave decently. All the meeting places we give here are not purely gay; even so, it will immediately be obvious to the visitor who is gay, that all these men are apparently sitting around randomly and waiting for someone.

Jordan is a modern, friendly, western-orientated country, with many contradictions. In many parts of Amman you often get the impression that you are in Europe, but at the next corner you could discover a real taste of the Orient and meet with people who have been educated in a very traditional way. Amman itself is a new city. It is built on several mountains and it's often confusing for the tourist to find their way around. The streets wind in incomprehensible directions between the mountains and the valley. For orientation purposes use the Circles (ring roads), of which there are seven, the outer one is similar to a motorway.

Homosexualität ist in Jordanien offiziell legal, doch schwule Männer können immer noch Opfer von Ehrenmorden werden. Wie aber in vielen Ländern des Orients sind körperliche Nähe zwischen Männern in der Öffentlichkeit präsent, wobei dies nicht mit Homosexualität verwechselt werden darf. Die jordanische Homo-Szene existiert, anders als im benachbarten Israel oder im Libanon, nur sehr verstreut, teils im Geheimen und nutzt inzwischen oftmals die Mittel der Informationstechnologie, um Kontakte herzustellen. Da die technischen Standards recht hoch sind, ist es durchaus möglich, über's Internet Kontakte zu Mittelschicht-Schwulen zu knüpfen. Den Großteil der einfachen Bevölkerung, wie auch die zahlreichen eingewanderten Irakis trifft man allerdings eher an den unten angegebenen Cruising-Points. Hier gilt, wie immer: Augenkontakt und dezentes Auftreten! Alle angegebenen Treffpunkte sind nicht rein schwul, wenngleich es dem Besucher sofort ins Auge springen wird, warum all diese Männer so scheinbar zufällig dort sitzen und warten.
Jordanien ist ein modernes, westlich orientiertes, dabei freundlich gebliebenes Land mit großen Widersprüchen. Während man in großen Teilen Ammans das Gefühl hat, in Europa zu sein, begegnet einem um die nächste Ecke der Orient und eine oft auch sehr traditionell eingestellte Bevölkerung. Amman an sich ist eine junge Stadt. Da die Stadt auf mehreren Bergen gebaut wurde, ist die Straßenführung für den Fremden schwer nachzuvollziehen, da die Straßen sich, anders als bei anderen großen Städten, auf unverständlichen Umwegen zwischen Berg und Tal schlängeln. Als Orientierung dienen die Circles (circle road), von denen es 7 gibt, wobei die äußersten eher Autobahnen gleichen.

L'homosexualité est officiellement légale en Jordanie, mais les hommes homosexuels peuvent toujours être victimes de crimes d'honneur. Comme dans les autres pays orientaux, les relations entre hommes, faites de contacts corporelles sont courantes en public, ce qui ne doit pas être confondu avec l'homosexualité. Un milieu homo existe en Jordanie, différent de celui de ses voisins le Liban et Israël. Officiellement les homosexuels n'existent pas en Jordanie. Au mois de mars dernier, la nouvelle loi sur l'orientation sexuelle ne les a pas non plus pris en compte comme groupe existant au sein de la population.
La Jordanie est à la fois un pays moderne et orienté vers l'Occident et qui reste en même temps plein de contradictions. Alors que dans certains des quartiers d'Amman on pourra avoir l'impression d'être en Occident, dans d'autres l'Orient jaillira à nouveau et sera perceptible surtout à travers une population restée très traditionnelle En soie Amman est une ville très jeune. De par sa topographie, ville construite sur des collines, la circulation paraît de prime abord incompréhensible pour l'étranger, l'obligeant souvent à faire des détours entre vallées et collines pour aller d'un quartier à un autre. Pour s'orienter les routes de ceintures ont été créées (Circle Road), il y en a 7, la septième étant plus une autoroute qu'une route.

La homosexualidad en Jordania es legal oficialmente pero los homosexuales todavía pueden ser víctimas de crímenes por deshonor. Como en muchos otros países de Oriente, el contacto corporal entre los hombres en público está muy presente, aunque ésto no debe confundirse con homosexualidad. El ambiente en Jordania existe, al contrario que en Israel o Líbano, de manera muy dispersa, en parte en secreto y actualmente ayudan mucho las nuevas tecnologías para abrirse paso. Como el nivel tecnológico medio está bastante avanzado, es posible establecer contacto a través de Internet con homosexuales de clase media. La mayoría de la población así como los numerosos inmigrantes iraquíes se reúnen más bien en los puntos de cruising debajo indicados. Aquí impera, como siempre, el contacto visual y una imagen decente! Todos los sitios indicados no son puramente gay, si bien a cualquier visitante le llamará la atención el porqué todos esos hombres parece que estén casualmente allí sentados esperando.
Jordania es un país moderno, orientado hacia Occidente, agradable y con grandes contrastes. Mientras que en algunas zonas de Amman uno tiene la sensación de estar en Europa, a la vuelta de la esquina uno se encuentra con Oriente y una población todavía muy tradicional. Amman es en sí una ciudad joven. Como la ciudad fue construida entre diversas colinas, la estructura de las calles puede resultar difícil de entender para los extranjeros puesto que éstas, a diferencia de otras grandes ciudades, serpentean de manera incomprensible entre las colinas y el valle. Como orientación se pueden seguir las rondas (circle road), de las que hay 7, aunque las más exteriores se asemejan más a una autopista.

Ufficialmente, l'omosessualità in Giordania è legale, tuttavia può succedere ancora che gli omosessuali siano vittima di omicidi d'onore. Come però spesso succede nei paesi orientali, i contatti fisici tra uomini in pubblico sono presenti, anche se ciò non può essere inteso come atteggiamento omosessuale. Una scena gay esiste ma a differenza dei vicini paesi Israele e Libano è però ancora nascosta e si avvale per lo più delle moderne tecnologie per poter stabilire contatti. In Internet si può facilmente avvicinare una popolazione gay di livello mediamente alto, mentre la normale popolazione, della quale fanno parte anche gli iracheni trasferitisi in Giordania, si trova nei sottostanti punti d'incontro. I primi contatti si stabiliscono con sguardi discreti. I seguenti punti d'incontro non sono solo per gay.
La Giordania è un paese moderno, occidentalizzato, ospitale e con molte contraddizioni. Mentre in molti quartieri di Amman si ha la sensazione di essere in Europa, basta girare l'angolo per trovarsi improvvisamente in Oriente ed imbattersi in una popolazione decisamente tradizionale. Amman è una città relativamente giovane. Essendo stata costruita su più colline, il tracciato stradale è, per lo straniero, difficile da comprendere. Per un più facile orientamento seguite i Circles (circle road), in tutto sette.

GAY INFO

Gay Middle East
www.gaymiddleeast.com
Gay info on what's happening in Jordan and throughout the Middle East.

Al Aqaba ☎ 03

CRUISING

-Along the Corniche
-At the harbour, near the military barracks
-King Boulevard between Days Inn and Alcazar hotels.

Amman ☎ 06

CINEMA

Revoli (AYOR MA NG R) Until 18h
Omar al Mukhtar Street (Quraysh) No 37 *Opposite the Church of the Saviour*

CAFES

b@c in Abdoun (AC B BF CC DM I RES VEG WE)
10 Omar ibn Ikrimah Street *Abdoun* ☎ (962) 5923036

Books @ Café (AC B CC DM GLM I M MA OS T VEG WE)
Omar Ibn Al Khattab Street #12 First Circle *In the historic neighborhood of Jabal Amman* ☎ (06) 465-0457 booksatcafe.com
Restaurant, Bar, Coffee shop and bookstore, crowded during weekends.

SAUNAS/BATHS

Al Pasha Turkish Bath (AYOR CC MA MSG NG NU SA SB)
1st Circle, Mahmoud Ali Taha Street ☎ (06) 463 30 02
Definitely not a gay sauna, but a very pleasurable middle-eastern experience. A few gays go there.

TRAVEL AND TRANSPORT

Lebtour.com (GLM H MA)
☎ (+961) 3 004 572 www.lebtour.com
LebTour is the first and only LGBT-dedicated tour operator for tourists and travellers visiting Lebanon, Syria & Jordan. Member of the ILGTA, LebTour cooperates with the most renowned LGBT associations and companies in the country. LebTour organises hotel accommodation, tour guiding, night clubs/parties, as well as many pioneer events.

CRUISING

All AYOR – police raids
-Park in front of old Roman Amphitheatre – many Iraqis looking to earn an extra Dinar or two (r), pleasant
-Hashimiya Square (R) (in front of Amphitheatre and Odeon)
-Toilets at the taxi station next to the Amphitheatre (no sex possible in the toilets, but only a 3 mins walk to the mini-bus station)
-Toilets next to the Mini-Bus-Station, sex on the premises is possible here, no guards
-Toilets at Hashimiya Square (in front of the Amphitheatre park), discreet action possible.

Kazakhstan

Name: Kasachstan · Kazajstán · Kazakistan
Location: Central Asia
Initials: KZ
Time: GMT +6
International Country Code: ☎ 7
International Access Code: ☎ 8 (wait for tone) 10
Language: Kazakh, Russian
Area: 2,724,900 km² / 1,052,089 sq mi.
Currency: 1 Tenge (T) = 100 Tiin
Population: 14,994,000
Capital: Astana
Religions: 47% Moslem, 44% Russian Orthodox
Climate: Summers are extremely hot and winters bitterly cold, spring (Apr-Jun) and autumn (Aug-Oct) are the best seasons to visit Kazakhstan.

Homosexuality is legal. Age of consent is 16 for homo- and heterosexual sex. Civil code describes marriage as union man and woman, so gay marriage is impossible, just as some other civil partnership for same sex partners.
Ever since the Republic of Kazakhstan gained independence there is growing tolerance towards sexual minorities. However, it is to be noted that this is only applicable to the biggest city of Kazakhstan, Almaty, and a few of the regional centres. Even there it is not advisable to display homosexual behaviour outside the bars and clubs listed in this guide. In rural areas, homophobic attitudes remain widespread.

Homosexualität ist legal. Das Schutzalter ist 16 für homosexuelle und heterosexuelle Beziehungen. Das Zivilrecht beschreibt die Ehe jedoch als Partnerschaft von Mann und Frau, so dass eine schwule Ehe genauso unmöglich ist wie einige andere Formen der eingetragenen Partnerschaft für gleichgeschlechtliche Paare.
Seit die Republik Kasachstan politische Unabhängigkeit erreicht hat, nimmt die Toleranz gegenüber sexuellen Minderheiten stetig zu. Allerdings muss man hier anmerken, dass sich diese Entwicklung bisher vorwiegend auf Almaty, die größte Stadt Kasachstans, und einige regionale Ballungsgebiete beschränkt. Doch sogar an diesen Orten ist es nicht ratsam, sich außerhalb der in diesem Reiseführer angegebenen Bars und Klubs offen schwul zu verhalten. In den ländlichen Gegenden ist die Schwulenfeindlichkeit nach wie vor weit verbreitet.

L'homosexualité est légale et la minorité sexuelle est fixée à 16 ans pour tous. Le code civil définit cependant le mariage comme l'union entre un homme et une femme rendant ainsi impossible le mariage homosexuel de même que d'autres formes de partenariat enregistré pour les couples de même sexe.
Depuis que la République du Kazakhstan a obtenu son indépendance, la tolérance envers les minorités sexuelles n'a cessé d'augmenter mais il convient de préciser que cette évolution ne concerne qu'Almaty,

la plus grande ville du Kazakhstan et quelques autres grands centres régionaux. Et même dans ces agglomérations, il est conseillé de ne pas montrer son homosexualité autre part que dans les bars et boîtes énumérés dans ce guide. Dans les régions rurales, l'homophobie est en outre toujours très répandue.

La homosexualidad es legal. La edad de consentimiento está fijada en los 16 años para relaciones homosexuales y heterosexuales. El derecho civil, no obstante, describe el matrimonio como la unión de hombre y mujer con lo cual el matrimonio homosexual sigue siendo igual de imposible como cualquier otra forma de parejas de hecho del mismo sexo.
Desde que la república de Kazajstán alcanzó la independencia política, va creciendo la tolerancia hacia las minorías sexuales. Sin embargo, cabe destacar que esta evolución hasta ahora sólo se limita a Almaty, la mayor ciudad de Kazajstán, y a algunas otras regiones densamente pobladas. De todas maneras, en estos lugares no se aconseja mostrarse de manera muy abierta fuera de los bares y clubs indicados en esta guía. En las zonas rurales, la intolerancia hacia los homosexuales está todavía muy extendida.

L'omosessualità è legale. L'età legale è di 16 anni sia per rapporti eterosessuali sia per rapporti omosessuali. Il diritto civile tuttavia definisce come matrimonio il rapporto tra uomo e donna escludendo così il matrimonio omosessuale ma anche qualsiasi forma di uonione registrata tra persone dello stesso sesso.
Da quando la Repubblica del Kazakistan ha raggiunto l'indipendenza, la tolleranza nei confronti delle minoranze sessuali cresce costantemente. Tuttavia c'è da evidenziare che questo fattore di tolleranza si limita, fino ad adesso, prevalentemente ad Almaty, la città più grande del Kazakistan, e ad alcuni agglomerati urbani. Ma anche in questi posti non è consigliabile assumere un comportamento apertamente gay al di fuori dei bar e clubs riportati in questa guida. Nelle zone di provincia l'omofobia è molto diffusa.

NATIONAL GAY INFO

Gay.kz
www.gay.kz
Gay portal of Kazakhstan. Information about gay life, gay organization, health, psychology, society, sub-culture and more. Acquaintance, chat, message board. Most articles presents in Russian. Only some information in English.

NATIONAL GROUPS

Adali Public Fund
Almaty ☎ 701 338 46 47
Non-governmental, non-profit organization for the prevention of HIV/AIDS and other STDs and also human rights watch and lawyer and psychologist hotline for LGBT.

GALA (Gay and Lesbian Alliance) (GLM) 10-18h
Ermekova 29/3 100009 Karaganda ☎ 3212 43 00 04
Organization for the prevention of HIV/AIDS and other STDs among sexual minorities. Also promotes gay rights and fights homophobia.

Almaty / Alma Ata ☎ 3272

CAFES

Art (B GLM m MA)
Satpaeva-Dzhandosova street *Opposite the Metro Bowling Club*

DANCECLUBS

Da Freak (B D NG YC) Thu-Wed 23-6h
40 Gogol Street *Park of 28 Guardsmen-Panfilovtsy, in the same building as restaurant „Zhuldyz"* ☎ (3272) 73 13 37
Not a gay place, but many gay people come here to dance.

Sirius Club (glm) 23-?h
Gogol Street *On the corner of Pushkin St*

VIP (B D glm MC)
Raimbek Avenue *On corner of Rozybakiev St*
In a blue building along south part of Raimbek Ave. Blue light decorations at the entrance

Kenya

Name: Kenia
Location: East Africa
Initials: EAK
Time: GMT +3
International Country Code: ☎ 254
International Access Code: ☎ 00
Language: English & Swahili (both official), numerous indigenous languages
Area: 582,646 km² / 224,960 sq mi.
Currency: 1 Kenyan Shilling (K.Sh.) = 100 Cents
Population: 34,256,000
Capital: Nairobi, Mombasa, Malindi,Lamu
Religions: 38% Protestant, 28% Roman Catholic, 26% indigenous beliefs
Climate: The hottest months are Jan & Feb. The rainy season is Apr-May and Nov-Dec.

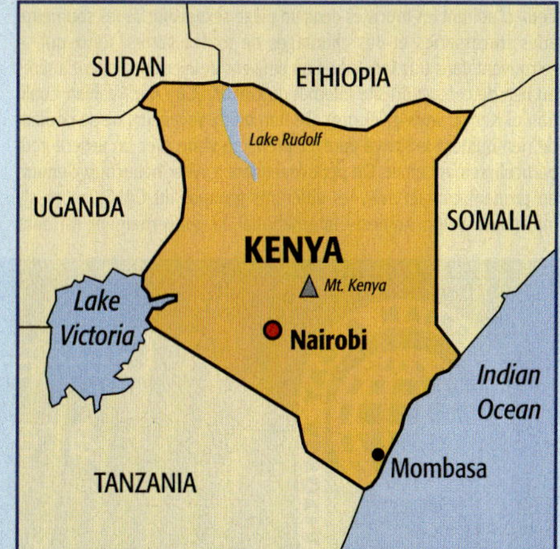

Homosexual acts are illegal and those caught are severely punished. The paragraphs 162-165 of the Kenyan penal code list these acts as „carnal acts against the order of nature", punishable by a minimum of 5 and up to a maximum of 14 years imprisonment. For a prosecution to be possible, the two have to be caught red handed in the act. Kenya being a tourist country, the police have formed an unholy union with some male prostitutes who lure gay tourists into sex, and then they are faced with a chain of extortion and blackmail. If one finds oneself (invariably), then one should seek support from GALCK (Gay and Lesbian Coalition of Kenya, www.galck.org) through the contacts of their website. Many unsuspecting gay people visiting Kenya for the first time leave with a bitter taste but if they do their research and connect through the various groups in GALCK, a lot of pain would be avoided. At present the government of Kenya is failing to protect the lives of citizens in its custody, according to Amnesty International. The subject of homosexuality is strictly taboo and is not discussed anywhere in literature, politics or in the media. A generally accessible gay infrastructure does not exist to our knowledge. The bars listed below are not gay meeting places but are rather mixed addresses where one has a better chance of meeting „gay" people.

Homosexuelle Handlungen sind illegal und werden hart bestraft. Die Paragraphen 162-165 des kenianischen Strafgesetzbuches bezeichnen sie als widernatürlichen Geschlechtsverkehr und ahnden sie mit Haft zwischen mindestens fünf und höchstens 14 Jahren. Um eine Anklage zu ermöglichen, müssen beide während des Geschlechtsakts in flagranti erwischt werden. Im Reiseland Kenia ging die Polizei dazu eine teuflische Allianz mit einigen männlichen Prostituierten ein: Sie locken Touristen in die Sexfalle, wonach diese dann Schikanen und Erpressungen ausgesetzt werden. Wer selbst in eine solche Situation gerät, kann über die Kontakte auf der Website von GALCK (Gay And Lesbian Coalition of Kenya, www.galck.org) Unterstützung finden. Viele ahnungslose homosexuelle Kenia-Reisende verlassen das Land nach dem ersten Besuch mit einem bitteren Beigeschmack. Wer aber mit den verschiedenen Gruppen von GALCK Kontakt aufnimmt und sich dort informiert, kann sich viel Ärger ersparen. Laut Amnesty International gelingt es der kenianischen Regierung momentan nicht, das Leben der eigenen Bürger zu schützen. Homosexualität als Thema ist in Kenia ein großes Tabu und wird nirgends in Presse, Literatur und Politik diskutiert. Eine allgemein zugängliche schwule Infrastruktur existiert unseres Wissens nicht. Die unten angegeben Bars sind keine Schwulentreffpunkte, sondern gemischte Adressen, wo man eine etwas größere Chance hat, einen Schwulen kennenzulernen.

Au Kénia, l'homosexualité est un délit qui est sévèrement puni. Conformément aux articles 162 à165 du code pénal kénian, les « actes charnels contre nature » peuvent vous coûter cher: entre 5 et 14 ans de prison. Pour permettre une inculpation, les deux personnes concernées doivent être prises en flagrant délit durant l'acte sexuel. Dans un pays touristique tel que le Kenya, la police n'a pas hésité àconclure une alliance diabolique avec quelques prostitués masculins : Ceux-ci attirent les touristes dans un piège sexuel afin de les soumettre àdes tracasseries et des chantages de toutes sortes. Ceux qui se retrouvent dans une telle situation peuvent trouver un soutient auprès du lien de contact du site Internet du GALCK (Gay And Lesbian Coalition of Kenya, www.galck.org). De nombreux voyageurs ne se doutant de rien quittent le Kenya après la première visite avec un arrière-goût particulièrement amer. On peut cependant s'éviter beaucoup d'ennuis en prenant contact avec les différents groupes du GALCK et en s'y informant. Selon Amnesty International, le gouvernement est dans l'incapacité de garantir la protection de certains citoyens. L'homosexualité est un sujet tabou au Kénia. On n'en parle jamais dans la presse, la littérature ou en politique. Il n'y a pas vraiment d'infrastructure gaie. Les bars mentionnés ci-dessous ne sont pas vraiment des lieux gais. Ce sont plutôt des adresses mixtes où on aura un peu plus de chance de rencontrer quelqu'un qu'ailleurs.

Las actividades homosexuales son ilegales y son objeto de duras sanciones. Los artículos 162-165 del código penal keniano las califican de „actos carnales contra el orden de la naturaleza" y son sancionados con penas de prisión que van desde 5 hasta 14 años. Para poder interponer una demanda, es necesario que ambos sean descubiertos in flagranti durante el acto sexual. En Kenia, la policía además mantiene una alianza diabólica con algunos hombres que ejercen la prostitución, de tal modo que éstos provocan a los turistas para mantener relaciones sexuales y así pueden chantajearlos y presionarlos. Aquél que cayera en una situación similar, puede encontrar el apoyo necesario gracias a los contactos de la página web GALCK (Gay And Lesbian Coalition of Kenya, www.galck.org). Muchos turistas homosexuales sin experiencia dejan el país después de la primera visita con mal sabor de boca. No obstante, quien contacta con diversos grupos de GALCK y se informa, puede ahorrarse situaciones desagradables. Según Amnistía Internacional, el gobierno de Kenia de momento no logra ni tan siquiera proteger la vida de sus ciudadanos. En Kenia la homosexualidad es un tema completamente tabú y no se debate ni en la prensa ni en las obras de carácter literario, ni en la vida política. Que nosotros sepamos, tampoco existe una infraestructura gay. Los bares que citamos a continuación no son sitios de ambiente, sino direcciones mixtas, donde quizás haya posibilidad de algún tipo de contacto.

Gli atti omosessuali sono illegali e duramente puniti. I paragrafi 162-165 del codice penale del Kenya, li definiscono come „atto carnale contro l'ordine della natura" punibili con la prigione da cinque a quattordici anni. Si può essere accusati solo qualora si sia colti in flagrante durante un rapporto sessuale. Nel turistico Kenya la polizia si è messa d'accordo con la prostituzione maschile per far cadere i turisti nella trappola, per poi umiliarli e ricattarli con delle estorsioni. Se vi doveste capitare di trovarvi in simili situazioni vi potete rivolgere al sito di GALCK (Gay And Lesbian Coalition of Kenya, www.galck.org) cliccando sulla voce „contatti". Molti turisti gay ingenui che visitano il Kenya per la prima volta, lasciano il paese con l'amaro in bocca. Ci si può risparmiare davvero molte noie se, invece, si contattano i gruppi del GALCK e ci si informa anticipatamente sulla situazione locale. Secondo Amnesty International, il governo del Kenya non è al momento in grado di tutelare la vita dei suoi cittadini. L'argomento dell'omosessualità costituisce un tabù mai discusso nella letteratura, dai politici e nei mass-media. Per quanto ne sappiamo, non esiste una infrastruttura gay generalmente accessibile. I bar indicati qui sotto non possono essere considerati dei punti d'incontro gay, ma dei luoghi dove si può avere almeno una piccola possibilità d'incontrare qualcuno.

NATIONAL COMPANIES

■ **Exclusive Gay Travel** (GLM MA)
Muiri Lane Off Langata Road Karen ✉ 859 – 00502 Nairobi
☎ 734 512 412 💻 www.exclusivegaytravels.com
Travels, accommodation and car hire in East Africa.

■ **Makatini Travel** (GLM)
PO Box 5608 ✉ 80401 Diani Beach ☎ (73) 537 42 71
💻 www.makatini.com
GLBT tourist guide in Kenya. Service is available by reservation only.

GAY INFO

■ **gaykenya.com** (GLM)
Address upon request ✉ Nairobi ☎ (020) 242 6060
💻 www.gaykenya.com
Gay Kenya is a Human Rights Advocacy group for LGBTI Kenyans. Founded in 2004.

GENERAL GROUPS

■ **Gay and Lesbian Coalition of Kenya** (GLM MA)
P.O Box 13005-00100, Nairobi ☎ 20-242-6060 💻 www.galck.org
Their mission: to promote recognition, acceptance and defend the interests and rights of LGBTI organizations and their members including their health rights.

Kisumu ☎ 35

DANCECLUBS

■ **Club. The** (B D NG P WE YC) Wed, Fri-Sat 21-?h
c/o Hotel Royal
Hotel Royal is a wonderful old English hotel, nothing gay but an interesting place to meet locals.

Lamu ☎ 73

HOTELS

■ **Kijani House** (AC B BF CC H M NG PI) Closed May and June
P.O. Box 266 ☎ ((020)) 2435700 ☎ (0)725 545264 (mobile)
💻 www.kijani-lamu.com
A small, friendly hotel right on the seafront in Shella.

Malindi ☎ 72

BARS

■ **Il Fermento** (B D MA NG) 23-?
Piano bar frequented by fashionable Italian crowd.

CAFES

■ **Karen Blixen Café** (B BF MA NG)
THE meeting place in Malindi in the morning hours up to 13h for a capuccino, juice or breakfast.

DANCECLUBS

■ **Stardust** (! AC B D MA NG WE) 24-?
Very popular with both residents and tourists!

■ **Stars and Garters** (B D MA NG S WE) 23h-open end

RESTAURANTS

■ **Lena Joint** (B d M MA NG)
Very popular by locals for their Njama Choma (roasted beef or chicken).

■ **Lorenzo's** (b M MA NG) Open for dinner only
International ambiance in a luxury setting; excellent service and large menu.

■ **Old Man and The Sea. The** (H M)
Small restaurant; good value for money. Pleasent atmosphere.

■ **Rosada** (H M OS) lunch only
Lunch in a beautiful setting; sun beds to be hired at bar service.

TRAVEL AND TRANSPORT

■ **Tourist Promotion** (G MA) 24 hours
☎ (726) 311 555 (mobile) 💻 www.localtourismkenya.com
All gay safaris and interaction with locals. Taylormade arrangements and accommodation in privates villas, boutique hotels and beach apartments. Also incoming travel-service and villas in Nairobi.

HOTELS

■ **Scorpio Villas** (AC B BF CC d I M MA NG OS PI S)
☎ (72) 631 15 55
Beach hotel within walking distance from Malindi old town and the Golden Mile with restaurants, cafés, discos and shops.

PRIVATE ACCOMMODATION

■ **Coast Villa** (AC BF G I M MA OS PI)
☎ (0726) 311 555 (mobile)
The private villa has 4- bedrooms and a pool. Next to the beach and Malindi Marine Park. DeLuxe accommodation with privacy is guaranteed. With own cook, house staff & security.

■ **Malindi Villa** (BF glm MC) All year
Address upon request *10 mins from town centre* ☎ (72) 631 15 55
💻 www.cinetourism.net
Stay with a gay friendly couple from Holland and Germany who have been living in Kenya for 25 years.

Mombasa ☎ 41

BARS

■ **Bob's open bar and restaurant** (B M MA NG S)
12h-open end
Popular after 21h.

■ **Tamarind Dhow** (B CC NG)
An old seagoing Dhow (large boat) sailing around the port of Mombasa, dinner set menu, life band.

DANCECLUBS

■ **Black Havana** (B D NG WE YC) 24-?

■ **Tembo Disco** (B D MA NG WE) 24h-open end
Situated on the Mombasa-Malindi road, 25 mins from town
💻 tembodisco.de
Mixed crowd of Europeans and Kenyans of all ages.

RESTAURANTS

■ **Pirates** (B D M MA NG WE) 23-?h
Situated on the Mombasa-Malindi road – bamburi, 30 mins from town
💻 tembodisco.de
Open air restaurant and disco, frequented by tourists and locals.

■ **Tamarind** (B CC M NG OS) 12.15-14.30, 18.45-22.15h
Sino Road *Near Old Nyali Bridge* ☎ (41) 47 17 47
Upmarket open air restaurant with view on Mombasa old town and port, specialized in seafood.

TRAVEL AND TRANSPORT

■ **Makatini Travels** (cc GLM) 24hrs
PO Box 940, Diani Beachm, South Coast *38km from Mombasa*
☎ (72) 627 96 41 💻 www.makatini.com
Main GLBTI travel/tour operator in Kenya, offering also safaris.

HOTELS

■ **Sunset Villa** (AC B BF glm I PA PI RWB RWS VA WH) All year
PO Box 5386, Diani Beach *32km south of Mombasa* ☎ (41) 717 010 670
💻 www.sunsetdianivilla.com

APARTMENTS

■ **Tamarind Village** (AC B BF CC I M NG OS PI WO)
☎ (41) 47 46 00 💻 www.tamarind.co.ke
A nice apartment with spacious rooms in a quiet residential area (Nyali) not too far from Mombasa nightlife and points of interest.

CRUISING

- Low profile along Mama Ngina Road – often in cars – and in the discos (R).

Nairobi ☏ 2

BARS

■ **Gypsy Bar** (B MA NG) 17h-open end
Woodvale Grove, Westlands *Near the Landmark Hotel*
A good place to meet locals and white people. Be discreet.

■ **Olives Bar** (AC B CC D GLM MA) 20-6h
Viking house, Westlands Nairobi *In the suburbs, take a taxi from city centre.*
First openly gay bar in Nairobi.

■ **Spiders Pub** (B MA NG) Fri & Sat 22-3h
Ronald Ngala Street
A good place to meet locals.

DANCECLUBS

■ **Pavement** (B D M MA NG OS)
Westview Center, Sports Rd, Muthangari *Opposite the casino and the mall*
☏ (2) 20 4442357
Mixed ages on Thu nights with Salsa live band, on Fri nights clubbing with younger crowd.

■ **Secrets bar & lounge** (B d g M MA OS)
Utalii lane *Utalii lane, View Park Towers ground floor opp. Alliance francaise*
☏ (2) 020 250 8866 💻 www.secretsnairobi.com
VIP lounge bar and late night dining. Sometimes all-gay parties.

■ **Taco´s** (B D g OS YC)
Kimathi Street
Younger gays on the verandah, beer sold by the dozen, 21 yrs or older policy applies.

RESTAURANTS

■ **Carnivori** (AC B CC M NG OS) 12-14.30, 18.45-22.15h
Langata Road, PO Box 566 85 ☏ (2) 50 17 79
African specialities (roast meats with salads and sauces).

■ **Tamarino** (AC B CC M NG) 12-14, 18.30-22h
Harambee Avenue *National Bank Building*
☏ (2) 33 89 59
International and African specialties (seafood).

CRUISING

-Kenyatta Avenue, around GPO
-Intercontinental Hotel, City Hall Way, (especially Sun afternoon)
-Sarit Centre, Westlands (lower ground floor).

Korea-South

Name: Taehan Min'guk · Südkorea · Corée du Sud · Corea del Sur · Corea del Sud
Location: Eastern Asia
Initials: ROK
Time: GMT +9
International Country Code: ☏ 82 (omit 0 from area codes)
International Access Code: ☏ 001 or 002
Language: Korean
Area: 99,313 km² / 38,325 sq mi.
Currency: 1 Won (W) = 100 Chon
Population: 48,082,000
Capital: Seoul
Religions: 28% Protestants, 21% Buddhist, 23% Confucians (an ethical code, not a religion)
Climate: Moderate climate with heavier rainfall in the summer than in winter.
Important gay cities: Seoul

Homosexuality is not mentioned in the penal code from South Korea. The general age of consent is 13, but same sex relations are taboo in Korea. Same-sex marriages have not been „socially and culturally" recognised, following a ruling in 2004. There is a general lack of knowledge in the society about homosexuality. Despite this social „outlawing" there is a small bar and club scene for gays and lesbians. There are examples of exclusion from school, or the loss of jobs for gays in Korea. In school books homosexuality is barely mentioned, or if so, then negatively. Homosexuality is considered to be a disaster within the family. When in 2003 a famous TV presenter came out, there was public outrage and because of this many gay Koreans decided to hide their sexual preference. Men holding hands is common between friends and should not be confused with gay gestures.
Having been one of the 54 states supporting a UN resolution against discrimination on the grounds of sexual orientation in December 2006, the South Korean government removed the attributes „sexual orientation" and „gender identity" from the planned anti-discrimination law, bowing to pressure from conservative Christian groups. Another seven attributes, such as „nationality" and „mother tongue" were also struck off this list at the same time.
As recently as summer 2007, the Korea Tourist Organization (KTO) still pursued a programme trying to position the country as a „must-see" destination in eastern Asia. The second edition of the English language gay and lesbian travel guide „Utopia Guide" appeared at the same time. So while homosexual travellers are made to feel welcome in commercial terms, native gays and lesbians can hardly expect to be treated with respect in the near future, not to mention attaining legal rights.

Homosexualität findet im Strafgesetzbuch von Südkorea keine Erwähnung. Das allgemeine Schutzalter liegt bei 13 Jahren. Gleichgeschlechtliche Liebe ist in Korea bis heute ein Tabu und Homosexualität ist in der Bevölkerung allgemein unbekannt. Gleichgeschlechtliche Hochzeiten werden nach einem Urteil aus dem Jahre 2004 „sozial und kulturell" nicht anerkannt. Zwar gibt es in Seoul eine kleine Bar- und Disco-Szene für Schwule und Lesben, gesellschaftlich wird Homosexualität jedoch geächtet. Dies kann bis zum Schulverweis oder dem Verlust des Jobs führen. In Schulbüchern wird Homosexualität gar nicht oder nur diskriminierend erwähnt. Besonders in der Familie ist Homosexualität eine Katastrophe. Als sich im Jahre 2003 ein bekannter TV-Moderator outete, gab es noch große Empörung in der Gesellschaft. Schwule Koreaner ziehen es daher vor, ihre schwule

Neigung zu verbergen. „Händchenhalten" unter Männern kommt zwischen Freunden häufig vor und sollte nicht als schwule Geste missverstanden werden.
Nachdem Südkorea im Dezember 2006 zu den 54 Staaten zählte, die eine UNO-Resolution gegen die Diskriminierung aufgrund sexueller Ausrichtung unterstützten, hat die Regierung auf Druck konservativer christlicher Gruppen das Merkmal „sexueller Ausrichtung" und „Geschlechtsidentität" wieder aus dem geplanten Antidiskriminierungsgesetz gestrichen. Weitere sieben Merkmale, wie „Nationalität" und „Muttersprache" wurden ebenfalls entfernt.
Noch im Sommer 2007 ist die Korea Tourism Organization (KTO) in die Offensive gegangen und versucht, sich als „Must-See"-Reiseziel in Ostasien zu positionieren. Parallel erschien die zweite Auflage des englischsprachigen schwul-lesbischen Reiseführers „Utopia-Guide".
Kommerziell werden homosexuelle Reisende also gerne in das Land geladen, doch mit Respekt, geschweige denn Rechten können die einheimischen Schwulen und Lesben in nächster Zeit kaum rechnen.

Il n'est pas fait mention de l'homosexualité dans le code pénal de Corée du sud. La majorité sexuelle est fixée à 13 ans pour tous. L'amour entre personnes de même sexe est aujourd'hui encore un tabou dans la société coréenne. Les mariages homosexuelles ne sont pas reconnus que ce soit « socialement ou culturellement » selon un arrêté de 2004. Il existe certes un petit milieu gay à Séoul, mais l'homosexualité est toujours proscrite et peut mener à un renvoi de l'établissement scolaire ou la perte de l'emploi. Dans les manuels scolaires, l'homosexualité n'est pas mentionnée ou seulement en termes discriminants. La situation au sein de la famille est catastrophique. Lorsqu'un célèbre présentateur télé a fait son coming out en 2003, la population a réagi avec indignation. Les homosexuels coréens préfèrent donc vivre leur homosexualité en secret. Les hommes se tiennent souvent la main dans la rue en signe d'amitié mais il ne faudrait pas y voir un geste homosexuel.
Après que la Corée du Sud ait fait partie en décembre 2006 des 54 États ayant soutenu la résolution de l'ONU contre les discriminations en raison de l'orientation sexuelle, le gouvernement a, après pression de groupes chrétiens conservateurs, rayé du projet de loi anti-discriminations la mention « orientation sexuelle » et « identité sexuelle ». Sept autres mentions ont été expurgées elles aussi, comme celle de « nationalité » ou de « langue maternelle ». L'office du tourisme coréen (KTO) était encore allé à l'offensive durant l'été 2007 en essayant de se positionner comme une destination obligée en Extrême-Orient. Parallèlement paraissait la deuxième édition du guide de voyage homo-lesbien anglophone « Utopia-Guide ». Les voyageurs homosexuels sont donc conviés avec respect à visiter le pays, mais les homos et lesbiennes locaux peuvent encore moins espérer plus de droits dans un avenir proche.

La homosexualidad no aparece mencionada en el código penal de Corea del Sur. La edad de consentimiento general está fijada en los 13 años. El amor entre personas del mismo sexo sigue siendo un tabú en Corea. Según una sentencia del año 2004, no se reconocen ni social ni culturalmente los matrimonios entre personas del mismo sexo. En Seul hay un pequeño ambiente gay con bares y discotecas pero la sociedad rechaza la homosexualidad. Esto puede conducir a un expediente escolar o incluso a la pérdida del trabajo. En los libros escolares, la homosexualidad no aparece o bien se menciona de manera discriminatoria. Especialmente en las familias la homosexualidad representa una catástrofe. Cuando en el año 2003 un conocido presentador de televisión salió del armario, causó una gran indignación en la sociedad. Los gays coreanos prefieren mantener escondida su tendencia sexual. El hecho de pasear dos hombres cogidos de la mano es habitual y no está considerado como un gesto homosexual.
Después que Corea del Sur perteneciera al grupo de 54 estados que en diciembre de 2006 apoyara la declaración de la ONU contra la discriminación por motivos de orientación sexual, el gobierno ha cedido a las presiones de los grupos cristianos conservadores y ha eliminado la característica de „orientación sexual" y „identidad sexual" de la legislación antidiscriminación prevista. Otras siete características como „nacionalidad" y „lengua materna" también fueron igualmente eliminadas.
En verano de 2007, la Organización de Turismo de Corea (CTO) emprendió la ofensiva para intentar posicionarse como destino turístico del Sudeste asiático. Paralelamente se publicó la segunda edición de la guía gay-lésbica de viajes en inglés „Utopia-Guide".
Comercialmente, los turistas homosexuales son bienvenidos al país, pero con respeto, por no hablar de que los gays y lesbianas locales apenas podrán contar con unos derechos próximamente.

L'omosessualità non viene citata nel codice penale della Corea del Sud. L'età del consenso è di 13 anni. Il sesso tra coppie dello stesso sesso è tutt'ora un tabù. I matrimoni tra coppie dello stesso sesso, secondo una sentenza del 2004 non vengono riconosciute ne socialmente ne culturalmente. Anche se a Seul c'è un piccola scena gay con dei bar e delle discoteche, socialmente l'omosessualità viene deprecata. L'omosessualità può portare all'espulsione dalla scuola o addirittura al licenziamento.
Nei libri scolastici, l'omosessualità non viene completamente citata e se citata, viene descritta in maniera molto negativa. In famiglia la situazione per gli omosessuali è quasi catastrofale. Un presentatore televisivo, in seguito al suo coming out nel 2003, ha destato molto sconcerto nella società. I gay in Corea del Sud preferiscono vivere la propria omosessualità di nascosto. Tenersi per mano è una cosa piuttosto normale tra amici e quindi non va interpretato come gesto omosessuale.
Dopo che la Corea del Sud, nel dicembre del 2006, è stato uno dei paesi ad aver appoggiato la risoluzione delle Nazioni Unite contro la discriminazione in base all'orientamento sessuale delle persone, adesso, invece, il governo attuale, dietro pressioni di gruppi conservatori cristiani, ha rimosso dalla proposta di legge sulle discriminazioni, la dicitura „orientamento sessuale" e „identità sessuale". Sono state cancellate anche altre sette diciture come per esempio „nazionalità" e „madrelingua".
Nell'estate del 2007 la Korea Turism Organization (KTO) è andata all'offensiva cercando di affermarsi come meta turistica fondamentale nell'Asia orientale. Nello stesso tempo è stata pubblicata, in inglese, la seconda edizione della guida turistica gay e lesbica Utopia Guide.
I turisti omosessuali, per motivi meramente commerciali, sono i benvenuti nella Corea del Sud, tuttavia i gay del posto devono ancora aspettare molto tempo prima di vedersi trattare con rispetto, e ancora più tempo per vedersi riconoscere dei diritti.

NATIONAL PUBLICATIONS

Buddy (GLM)
PO Box 776, Chongno-Gu, Kwanghwa-Moon ✉ Seoul
☏ (0505) 938 7979 www.buddy79.com
Gay and lesbian focused lifestyle magazine. Since 1998. Sadly only in Korean.

NATIONAL GROUPS

Korea Queer Culture Festival
5F, DongKum B/D, 197-1, Myo-dong Jongno-gu
✉ 110-370 Seoul ☏ (0505) 303 1998 www.kqcf.org

Korean Sexual Minority Culture and Rights Center (GLM)
5/F Samhueng Building, 256-2 Hangangno, 2-Ga Yongsan-Gu ✉ Seoul
www.kscrc.org
First help centre for minorities (gay, lesbian, bi-sexual, transgender) and HIV+ people and others.

Kwangju ☏ 062

BARS

Fantasia (B g MC)

Pyung Hwa (Little Peace) (B G m MA)
Khum Nam No *Near river*
Run down place frequented by the cruisy crowd. Friendly and helpful staff.

CRUISING

-Kum Nam No Shopping Cente. Toilets. Evenings till very late.

Pusan ☎ 051

BARS

Club One (B g m YC) 19-5h
Behind Hyundai Department Store *M° Beomildong* ☎ (051) 631 8559
Reasonable prices and free snacks. Foreigners welcome.

G-Men (B g m MA)
Behind Hyundai Department Store *Beomildong area*
Tiny but friendly bar.

Zip (B g l m MA)
Behind Hyundai Department Store *Beomildong area* ☎ (051) 645 3625
Gay magazines available.

SAUNAS/BATHS

Double (B FC G l m MA SA SB) 24hrs
4/F of sae-rah-mik (ceramic tile) Blvd *In Beomildong, opposite Sahmil Cinema* ☎ (051) 633 1611
Foreigners welcome. Lube and condoms provided.

Ho Chim Song (B DR g m PI SA SB WO) 24hrs, closed Sun
Dong Nae *Short walk from M° Somyon, behind North-east Building at Somyon Ratary*
Not exclusively gay, but a must-see. A huge, well-known bathing complex with pools, caves and birds. Obviously, this place is popular with gays. Best between 14-18h, action in dark relax room.

K (B G m MC SA SB VS)
Beomildong area; M° Jwacheon-dong, Exit 3 ☎ (051) 642 7715
Welcomes foreigners. Busy on Fri and Sat nights.

Otoko (B G l m MA SA SB VS)
Jwacheondong *M° Jwacheondong, exit 5. Walk the small road. Look for the sign that says Membership Club 3rd Floor*
Big and clean sauna.

CRUISING

-Park in the center of town on a hill.

Seoul ☎ 02

BARS

Almaz (B g MA)
136-6 Iteawon 1, Dong Young-San Gu *Homo Hill* ☎ (02) 3785 0834

Always Homme (B G MA)
Yongsan-ku, Itaewon *Opp. Why Not?* ☎ (02) 798 0578
Famous and friendly bar with nice design. Meeting point before going out „Why not".

Barcode (B CC G MA) 19.30-4h
177-1 Myo-dong, Jongno-gu *M° Jongno-3GA, exit 3 or 8; 2nd floor of the building beside Family Mart* ☎ (02) 3672 0940
Barcode is a very popular western style bar in Seoul and very friendly, foreign travelers gain information about Koreas gay scene there.

Bliss (B d G MA) 12-?h
72-32 Itaewon, Yongsan-Ku *Shopping area, 150 m from Hamilton Hotel* ☎ (02) 749 7738
Very stylish establishment with sofas, exclusive decor, big windows with a view to a Japanese garden.

Butler QAF (B G MA)
132-2 Ikseon-dong, Jongro-gu ☎ (02) 747 8591
Beer, wine and cocktails.

Men's Club (B f G MC)
Jong Ro 3 Ga ☎ (02) 764 5640
Western style shot bar for bears and friends.

Pulse (B D G MA)
132-16 Itaewon Dong, Yongsan-gu ☎ (02) 749 3370
Upscale gay bar and lounge.

Queen (B GLM MA)
Yongsan-ku, Itaewon *M° Itaewon, exit 3* ☎ (02) 793 1290
Busy after 22h, packed on WE. Managed by a gay Australian guy.

Queer (B D GLM m MA S)
33-17 B1 Changcheon-dong, Seodaemun-gu ☎ 333 9225
💻 www.queer-bar.com
English speaking staff.

Soho (B glm MA)
Yongsan-ku, Itaewon *Homo Hill* ☎ (02) 797 2280
English speaking staff.

DANCECLUBS

Trance (AC B cc D G m MA S ST T WE)
136-42 Itaewon-dong, Yongsan-Gu, Itaewon *Near fire station up the hill, left at Kings Club into narrow street* ☎ (02) 797 3410
Best late till mornings. Friendly, cruisy. Cute English speaking staff. Locals and foreigners.

Why Not? (! B D GLM YC)
137-4 Yongsan-ku, Itaewon *Itaewon station* ☎ (02) 795 8193
Young crowd, good place to meet English speaking men. Reasonable prices, handsome staff in a smaller disco playing House, Trance and Electro music.

RESTAURANTS

Our Place (B g M MA)
Itaewon *Same building as Equus sauna*
Gay owned.

Sanchon (g M MA S) 11.30-22h
14 Kwanhoon-Dong Chongro-Gu ☎ (02) 735 0312
💻 www.sanchon.com
Korean cuisine.

SEX CINEMAS

Jong Gak dvd theater (AC DR G m MA P VS WE) 12-24, Fri & Sat -6h
71-5 Jong Ro 2 Ga, Jong ro gu *M° Jong Gak station, gate 12* ☎ (070) 7715 2335
Gay movies and meeting place.

SAUNAS/BATHS

Adam (b DR DU g l MA RR SB VS WH) 24hrs
M° Sinseoldong, between exit 2 and 3, entrance marked with a neon hot spring sign ☎ (02) 921-6990

Equus (B DR DU F G MA MSG) Mon-Fri 17-?h, WE 24hrs
4F/ 736-15 Hannam Dong, Yongsan-Gu *M° Itaewon, exit 3; next to fire station, Equus sign on the building, 3rd floor* ☎ (02) 793 6227
💻 www.equuszone.com
More a cruise box than a sauna, very small and limited facilities. 3rd & 5th Fri/month is a GoGo Boy show. Dress code: Wed: Slave & Master, Thu: Mask & Nude Party.

Hyundai (g MA PI SA SB) 24hrs
Cheongnyangni/Chongyangni *Across from Hamilton Hotel, then head to the next small street on the left*
At the farmers market walk on the right hand side to a building with a sign with steam coming out of a rock and a barber's pole (like a hot soup-cup). Hyundai is the second building with this icon. Best time is early mornings or afternoons. Not the cleanest sauna.

Mun Hwa (B DR G m MA SA SB WH) 24hrs
Chongno 3-Ga *M° Chongno 3-GA, exit 1. Walk down the little passageway besides Lotteria all the way to the end, than turn left and follow the barber poles. The entrance to Mun Hwa is near the end of the little passageway at the third barber pole* ☎ (02) 747-0623
This place is a bit run down.

Prince (b DU G l MA RR VS) 24hrs
At Shinchon Station, 200 m from exit 8 ☎ (02) 334 8245
💻 www.princetel.co.kr
More a cruising club than a sauna. Foreigners welcome.

MASSAGE

■ **Bodyguardshop** (cc G MSG s) 24hrs
142-3 Itaewondong, Yongsangu *On the 1st floor* ☎ (02) 793 1587
💻 www.bodyguardshop.com
The only gay massage shop in Korea.

CRUISING

-Tapkol Park (popular late afternoon, on right side OC, near monument YC)
-Namsan Park (between the Hilton and the Hyatt, nights)
-Around Homo Hill all day.

Taegu ☎ 053

BARS

■ **Mask** (B g MA)
Near Dongtaegu Station ☎ (053) 756 1040
Helpful and friendly English speaking owner.
■ **Rookie. The** (B g MA)
Dong-Gu *In an alley between Babylon Sauna and Daegu Bank*
■ **Tombo** (B g MA)
Near Dongtaegu Station; behind Dunkin Donuts ☎ (053) 745 5425
English speaking staff. Welcoming to foreigners.

Kosovo

Location: South-eastern Europe
Initials: RKS
Time: GMT +1
International Country Code: ☎ 381
Language: Albanisch, Serbisch
Area: 10.887 km²
Currency: 1 Euro (€) = 100 Cents
Population: 2.126.708
Capital: Priština
Religions: 90% Muslims, 5% Serbian orthodox, 5% others

The age of consent in Kosovo is 16, regardless of sexual orientation and/or gender, according to the Criminal Code Art.192 from 2004.In March 2006, Kosovo no longer considered homosexuality as a mental disorder. Violence and discrimination is experienced daily by people with same sex references. Any public display of homosexual desire or behaviour on the street or in parks can still be dangerous. There is a tiny gay scene, as homosexuality is considered quite abnormal by the majority of the locals. The Swedish and Dutch embassies sometimes sponsor local LGBT activities.

Laut Artikel 192 des Strafgesetzbuches von 2004 beläuft sich das Mindestalter in der Republik Kosovo unabhängig von der sexuellen Orientierung für beide Geschlechter auf 16 Jahre. Seit März 2006 wird Homosexualität im Kosovo auch nicht mehr als psychische Störung betrachtet. Trotzdem erfahren Menschen mit gleichgeschlechtlichen Vorlieben hier täglich Diskriminierung und Gewalt. Jegliche öffentliche Zurschaustellung homosexuellen Verlangens oder Verhaltens auf den Straßen oder in den Parks kann immer noch gefährlich sein. Da die Bevölkerung des Landes Homosexualität mehrheitlich als abartig betrachtet, gibt es nur eine winzige Schwulenszene. Die Botschaften Schwedens und Hollands sponsern gelegentlich lokale Aktivitäten der LGBT-Gemeinde.

L'âge de consentement est fixé à 16 ans au Kosovo, indépendamment de l'orientation sexuelle et/ou du genre, conformément au Code Pénal art. 192 de 2004. Depuis mars 2006, le Kosovo ne considère plus l'homosexualité comme un trouble mental. Les homosexuels vivent au quotidien la discrimination et la violence. Le fait d'exposer un comportement ou un désire homosexuel en public reste dangereux. Il existe une minuscule scène gay, du fait que l'homosexualité est toujours considérée comme anormale par les habitants. Les ambassades suédoise et néerlandaise sponsorisent de temps en temps des activités LGBT locales.

La edad de consentimiento sexual en Kosovo, independientemente de la orientación sexual y /o del sexo, es de 16 años, de acuerdo con el Código Penal Art.192 de 2004. En marzo de 2006, en Kosovo dejó de considerar la homosexualidad como un trastorno mental. Las personas con preferencias sexuales por el mismo sexo experimentan a diario la violencia y la discriminación, y cualquier exhibición pública de deseo o comportamiento homosexual en la calle o en parques aún pueden ser peligrosa. El ambiente gay es reducido debido a que la mayoría de sus habitantes consideran la homosexualidad como algo muy anormal. Las embajadas de Suecia y Holanda patrocinan a veces actividades locales LGBT.

Secondo l'articolo 192 del 2004 l'età del consenso in Kosovo è di 16 anni a prescindere dall'orientamento sessuale e/o di genere. A marzo del 2006 il Kosovo ha ufficialmente smesso di considerare l'omosessualità un disturbo mentale. Le violenze e le discriminazioni nei confronti degli omosessuali sono all'ordine del giorno. Qualsiasi tipo di ‚espressione omosessuale' in strada o nei parchi può ancora avere risvolti pericolosi. Considerando che l'omosessualità è vista ancora come qualcosa di anormale, la scena gay si può considerare un fenomeno del tutto marginale. A volte le ambasciate svedesi e olandesi sponsorizzano attività LGBT a livello locale.

Pristina ☎ 01

HOTELS

■ **Hotel Aldi** (AC B CC MC NG RWB RWT) All year
Cagllavica 303 ☎ (01) 38 548 802 💻 www.hotelaldi.com
Not a gay place but gay-friendly and no problem for gay men to stay here.

Kyrgyzstan

Name: Kirgisistan · Kirghizie · Kirguistán
Location: Central Asia
Initials: KS
Time: GMT + 5
International Country Code: ☎ 996
International Access Code: ☎ 00
Language: Kirgisish and Russian
Area: 199,900 km² / 77,184 sq mi.
Currency: 1 Kirgisistan-Som (K.S.) = 100 Tyin
Population: 5,144,000
Capital: Biškek (Bishkek)
Religions: 75% Sunnite, 20% Russian Orthotox
Climate: Summer is extremely hot in the lowlands. Jul & Aug are the best months to visit the mountain regions.

Homosexuality was legalized on January 1, 1998, repealing the old Soviet article 121,1 which made homosexuality illegal. Article 130 of the new Criminal Code legalizes homosexual acts unless they involve „force" or „the threat of force" or „take advantage of the weakness of the victim." We have no information regarding the age of consent for homosexuals.
Kyrgyzstan is doing more than most Central Asian republics to encourage tourism due to the fact that tourism is one of the few things it has to offer to the outside world.
There are no examples of fantastic architecture or numerous cultural events but the people are friendly and very keen to meet foreigners. The gay scene is limited to a few bars in the capital city Bishkek.

Am 1. Januar 1998 wurde Homosexualität legalisiert. Dadurch wurde der alte Artikel 121,1 abgeschafft, der Homosexualität als illegal bezeichnete. Artikel 130 des Strafgesetzbuches legalisiert gleichgeschlechtliche Sexualkontakte, sofern sie „ohne Gewalt" oder „deren Androhung" stattfinden und „die Schwäche des Sexualpartners nicht ausnutzen". Leider liegen uns über das schwule Schutzalter keine Informationen vor.
Kirgisistan ist vor allem auf seinen Tourismus angewiesen und bemüht sich daher mehr als die anderen Staaten Mittelasiens, Reisende ins Land zu holen. Zwar gibt es keine prächtige Architektur und kulturellen Veranstaltungen, aber die Menschen sind freundlich und Ausländern gegenüber sehr aufgeschlossen. Die Szene beschränkt sich auf einige Bars in der Hauptstadt Bishkek.

Depuis l'abolition de l'article 121,1 le 1er janvier 1998, l'homosexualité est légale en Kirghizie. L'article 130 du code pénal ne pénalise ainsi pas les rapports homosexuels obtenus « sans user de la force », « sans menace d'user de la force » et « sans utiliser à son profit la faiblesse du partenaire sexuel ». Malheureusement, la majorité sexuelle pour les homosexuels n'a pu nous être donnée.
La Kirghizie dépend essentiellement de son tourisme et s'efforce donc plus que les autres états d'Asie centrale d'attirer des touristes sur son sol. L'architecture n'est certes pas monumentale et les activités culturelles plutôt minces, mais les gens sont sympathiques et ouverts aux étrangers. Le milieu gay se résume à quelques bars dans la capitale Bichkek.

El 1 de enero de 1998 fue legalizada la homosexualidad. Con ello se derogó el antiguo artículo 121,1 que consideraba ilegal la homosexualidad. El artículo 130 del Código Penal legaliza los contactos sexuales entre personas del mismo sexo siempre que sean "sin violencia" o "sin amenazas" y que "no se abuse de la inferioridad del otro".
Desgraciadamente no disponemos de información sobre la edad de consentimiento para los homosexuales. Kirguistán depende sobre todo del turismo y por eso se esfuerza mucho más que otros estados de Asia Central en atraer turistas a su país.
Quizá no tenga una fantástica arquitectura y eventos culturales pero la gente es amable y muy abierta hacia los extranjeros. El ambiente se limita a algunos bares en la capital, Bishkek.

Il primo gennaio del 1998 l'omosessualità è stata legalizzata: l'articolo 121 comma 1, che considerava l'omosessualità un reato, è stato quindi abolito. L'articolo 130 del codice penale legalizza i contatti sessuali tra persone dello stesso sesso se questi avvengono „senza violenza", „senza minacce" e se „non si sfrutta la debolezza del partner sessuale". Purtroppo non abbiamo informazioni circa l'età legale per i rapporti sessuali. Il Kirgisistan profitta molto del turismo e, più di altri paesi dell'Asia centrale, si da molto da fare per attirare turisti.
Non ci sono particolari attrazioni architettoniche e manifestazioni culturali, ma le persone sono molto cordiali e ospitali con i turisti. La scena gay si limita ad alcuni bar nella capitale Bishkek.

Bishkek

BARS

■ **Mayak** (B D GLM MA p ST) 21-4h
Square Ala-Too *Central Square, east side. Under the arches* ☎ 66 26 86
Former Nautilus restaurant. Entrance fee applies. Show time (transvestite) Fri-Sun 24-1h. A bar for gays and lesbians only, a „face control" applies at the door. 80% gay. Busy from about 23h.

■ **Spiders** (B G MA)
Cnr Prospekt Chuy & Shopokova Street *At the intersection in Ploshad Pobedy*
Mainly young crowd.Less than 50% gay.

DANCECLUBS

■ **Gvozd** (D g MA P)
Mon, Wed, Fri & Sat 10-1h
Corner of Manas Street & Chyi Avenue *West side of Filarmonia*
☎ 555 761773
New mixed club. Some gay men come here. The manager (Victoria) sends SMS messages to gay men she has on the list about the upcoming events.

CRUISING

- On Erkindik boulevard from Toktogula Street to Chui Avenue (early evening).

Laos

Name: Sathlanalat Paxathipatai Paxaxôn Lao
Location: South East Asia
Initials: LAO
Time: GMT +7
International Country Code: ☏ 856
International Access Code: ☏ 14
Language: Lao, English
Area: 236,800 km² / 91,429 sq mi
Currency: 1 Kip = 100 Att
Population: 5,792,000
Capital: Viangchan (Vientiane)
Religions: 58% Buddist, 34% local religions
Climate: The best time to visit is from Nov-Feb. The rainy season is from Jul-Oct.

Homosexuality is not forbidden, but sexual activity is considered to be a violation of the traditional way of life, and as a result is not officially recognized. Laotian gays live discreetly without any real trouble or discrimination, even in steady relationships. Many of these relationships end abruptly after years together, as a result of family pressure to force people into traditional heterosexual relationships.

Prostitution and drug use is strongly forbidden in Laos and can result in immediate imprisonment for everyone involved. Even the most minor contact between foreigners and Laotians is seen as prostitution, and talking about it with the all-powerful and completely corrupt police force is pointless. Shared accommodation in hotels for same sex couples is generally trouble-free, especially if both parties are foreigners. Also full-on sex between men is often not linked with homosexuality, as gays are generally only identified as being effeminate.

The country with the Mekong running through it, and high country covered in rainforests is a year round travel destination, both beautiful and interesting, with less rain in the months of July and August.

Throughout the country the local population is very friendly, and they are mostly easy-going towards foreigners. Discreet gay holiday-makers may get to have a number of unexpected insights into local daily life.

Homosexualität ist nicht verboten, sexuelle Handlungen werden als Verstoß gegen die traditionelle Lebensweise verstanden, und daher offiziell nicht zur Kenntnis genommen. Laotische Schwule leben unauffällig, eher unbehelligt, kaum diskriminiert und meist in festen Partnerschaften, die oft durch familiären Druck nach Jahren abrupt enden, um die Partner in traditionelle heterosexuelle Verbindungen zu zwingen.

Prostitution und Drogenmissbrauch sind in Laos grundsätzlich verboten und können für alle Beteiligten umgehende Gefängnisstrafen zur Folge haben. Bei engeren Kontakten zwischen Laoten und Ausländern wird meistens Prostitution unterstellt. Diskussionen mit der allgewaltigen und korrupten Polizei sind zwecklos. Gemeinsame Hotelübernachtungen sind für gleichgeschlechtliche Paare normalerweise problemlos, besonders, wenn beide aus einem anderen Land stammen. Auch handfeste sexuelle Handlungen zwischen Männern werden oft nicht mit Homosexualität in Verbindung gebracht – als Schwule werden oft nur feminin wirkende Männer bezeichnet.

Das vom Mekong durchströmte Land hat beachtliche, mit Regenwäldern bewachsene Höhen. Laos ist ein ganzjährig interessantes und angenehmes Reiseziel mit wenigen Regenstunden in den Monaten August und September.

Die einheimische Bevölkerung ist durchweg sehr freundlich und besonders gegenüber Ausländern meistens nachsichtig. Diskreten schwulen Reisenden können sich viele unerwartete Einblicke in den laotischen Alltag eröffnen.

L'homosexualité n'est pas interdite, uniquement considérée comme manquement aux règles de vie traditionnelles. Les gays laotiens vivent plutôt tranquillement leur vie, sans discriminations, la plupart du temps en couple ; beaucoup d'entre eux sont toutefois contraints par la famille à se marier et construire une famille au sens traditionnel du terme.

La prostitution ainsi que l'usage de drogues sont interdits et peuvent mener à des peines d'emprisonnement cela pour toute individu mêlé de prêt ou de loin. Des contacts trop rapprochés entre Laotiens et étrangers peuvent être consideré comme de la prostitution. Essayer de discuter avec la police toute puissante et corrompue est sans espoir. Prendre une chambre d'hôtel avec une personne de même sexe ne pose pas de problème lorsque les deux individus ne résident pas dans cette ville. Deux hommes qui se tiennent par la main ne seront pas considérés comme homos, seuls les hommes efféminés le sont.

Le pays du Mékong connaît un climat pluvieux. Le Laos est une destination attractive toute l'année durant ; la saison sèche s'étend d'août à septembre.

La population locale est particulièrement aimable et indulgente envers les touristes. Les gays sachant rester discret pourront découvrir au quotidien maintes choses de la culture laotienne!

La homosexualidad no está prohibida, pero los actos sexuales son considerados como una agresión al modo de vida tradicional y por ello no se reconocen oficialmente. Los homosexuales de Laos viven de manera discreta, bastante tranquilos, apenas discriminados y a veces en relaciones de pareja estables, que la mayoría de las veces, por presiones familiares, acaban repentinamente después de años para obligarles así a una unión heterosexual tradicional.

La prostitución y el consumo de drogas están por lo general prohibidos en Laos y pueden conllevar penas inmediatas de cárcel para todos los implicados. Los contactos entre ciudadanos de Laos y los extranjeros se presumen normalmente como prostitución. En este caso, una discusión con la violenta y corrupta policía no tiene sentido. Alojarse conjuntamente en un hotel no acostumbra ser para las parejas del mismo sexo ningún problema, especialmente si los dos proceden de otro sitio. Tampoco los actos puramente sexuales entre hombres son considerados a menudo como homosexualidad; sólo se califica de homosexual a aquellos hombres de apariencia femenina.

Este país surcado por el Mekong tiene alturas considerables con selvas frondosas. Laos es un destino turístico interesante y agradable todo el año, con pocas lluvias entre los meses de agosto y septiembre. La población local es muy amable y en su mayoría muy tolerante con los extranjeros. Los discretos visitantes gays podrán disfrutar de muchas inesperadas impresiones de la vida cotidiana en Laos.

L'omosessualità non è vietata, atti sessuali sono considerati un affronto al tradizionale modo di vivere e quindi non vengono considerati. I gay del Laos vivono nell'ombra indisturbati e non discriminati. Talvolta vivono relazioni fisse che vengono però poi sciolte dalle rispettive famiglie che impongono legami eterosessuali.
La prostituzione e l'uso di stupefacenti sono vietati dalla legge, la cui trasgressione porta alla carcerazione. Rapporti intimi tra laotiani e stranieri vengono ritenuti atti di prostituzione. Non porta a nulla cercare di ragionare con la polizia locale. Il pernottamento comune in albergo di una coppia di turisti gay non ha costituito mai problemi. Gay vengono considerati solo gli effeminati. Atti sessuali particolarmente „robusti" tra uomini non vengono collegati con l'omosessualità.
Il paese attraversato dal fiume Mekong ha montagne molto alte con foreste tropicali. Laos è una meta turistica interessante durante tutto l'anno. I mesi con meno precipitazioni sono agosto e settembre.
La popolazione locale è molto ospitale soprattutto col turista straniero. I turisti gay particolarmente discreti potranno entrare in contatto con particolari aspetti della quotidianità del Laos.

Luang Prabang

BARS

■ **Blue Ice** (AC B D G H MC S) 18-24h
Kingkitsarath Road, Ban Watsene *Walking distance from the main street Sakkarine Road on the Nam Khan river* ☏ 020 775 591 91

■ **Maylek Pub** (AC B D glm M MA) 10-24h
Corner of Kitsarath Settathirat Rd and Visunnarat Rd *Near Dara Market*
Trendy night spot also attracting the gay crowd after 22h. Relaxed atmosphere. Many cocktails. Check flyer for occasional DJ parties. Cute staff.

DANCECLUBS

■ **Duang Jampa** (AC B D glm M MA) 21.30-24h
Ban Viengham *Out of city centre at Vat Visoun, over the river, near Talat Matthahip, about 1,5 km out of town* ☏ 071 212 677
Large, comfortable, Lao style disco. Can be very cruisy. Be discreet. Best after 23h and at WE.

■ **Muang Xou** (AC B D glm m MA OS) 21-24h
Phou Vao Road *Out of city centre past Vat Visoun, over the river, near Talat Matthahip, about 700 m out of town*

RESTAURANTS

■ **House Restaurant & Bar. The** (B H M MA NG OS) 8.30-23.30h
Phousi Road 10, Ban Aphai Village *At the bottom of Mount Phousi near Nam Khan River* ☏ 071 255 021
🖳 www.facebook.com/thehouselaos?v=info
A trendy place in Luang Prabang. Huge terrace and garden. Belgian Chef with 28 years experience makes tasty European Asian Fusion Food.

HOTELS

■ **3 Nagas** (AC BF CC H M MA)
Centre of the Old Town ☏ 071 252 079 🖳 www.3nagas.com
This 4-star hotel offers superior rooms designed in an Asian style.

■ **Apsara** (AC BF CC H M MA)
Kingkitsarath Road, Baan Wat Sene ☏ 076 342 160
🖳 www.apsararesidence.com

■ **Rama** (AC B CC glm H M MA MSG OS RWB RWS RWT VA) 24hrs
Ban Visoun, Visonnarath Road *South of bus station* ☏ 071 212 247
🖳 www.ramahotel.net
30 guestrooms with modern amenities. 5 % discount with internet reservation. Five mins walk to the Mekong or Namkhan river.

■ **Villa Santi Hotel & Resort** (AC B CC H M MA MSG OS PI WO) All year
Royal Sakkarine Road, Ban Wat Sene, PO Box 681 *Near Wat Sene Temple* ☏ 071 253 470 🖳 www.villasantihotel.com
Probably the most luxurious boutique hotel resort in Laos.

CRUISING

-At Mekong river after dark
-Dara Market.

Vientiane

DANCECLUBS

■ **Lak Song** (AC B CC D glm m YC)
100 Luangprabang Road *Town centre, nightclub at Sene Souk Hotel* ☏ 021 213 375
Loud, popular. Best between 22-23h.

RESTAURANTS

■ **Europe** (AC B CC glm M MA) 11-23h
086 Ban Saphanthong Neua, Phonsavanh Rd *Near Fontain Nam Phu* ☏ 414 086
Swiss, Italian, French and Asian cuisine.

■ **Moon the Night** (B glm M MA OS)
Thanon Kamkon *Near Novotel, at banks of Mekong river* ☏ 021 217 073
Inexpensive Lao restaurant with great view across the Mekong river to Thailand.

HOTELS

■ **Lane-Xang** (bf H MA)
Fa Ngum Road *On the banks of the river Mekong* ☏ 021 214 100

GUEST HOUSES

■ **Heuan Lao** (b H m MA OS) 7-22h
055 Ban Simoung *Off Buddha Park, Shell Station or Lao Express Bus Station. Walking distance to centre and markets* ☏ 021 216 258
Clean guest house with 12 rooms. Relaxed, very friendly atmosphere.

CRUISING

The whole city is a possible cruising area. Some popular points are:
-The park along the river, as well as the well known Nam Phu fountains (many rent boys and lady boys, quite a safe place but be discreet)
-Outdoor boxing school beside the river.

Latvia

Name: Latvija · Lettland · Lettonie · Letonia · Lettonia
Location: Northeast Europe
Initials: LV
Time: GMT +2
International Country Code: ☏ 371
International Access Code: ☏ 00
Language: Latvian, Russian
Area: 64,589 km² / 24,938 sq mi.
Currency: 1 Lats (Ls) = 100 Santims
Population: 2,301,000
Capital: Riga
Religions: 55% Lutheran, 24% Roman Catholic, 9% Russian Orthodox
Climate: Spring and summer (Apr-Sep) are the best times to visit. Winter weather (Nov-Mar) can be extreme.
Important gay cities: Riga

Sexual acts between persons of the same sex are not illegal in Latvia. Criminalization of consensual sexual acts between adult men was repealed in 1992 just after Latvia regained independence from the USSR. The age of consent is 16 for all sexual acts. Relationships between persons of the same-sex are not legally recognised in Latvia. Moreover, same-sex marriage in banned by the Civil Code (since 1991) and the Latvian Constitution now defines marriage as a union between a man and a woman (since 2005). The 1999 proposal for a law on registered partnership for same-sex partners introduced at the Latvian parliament was rejected at the Committee stage, even before plenary debate.

Sexual orientation discrimination in employment is banned since 2006. Latvia was the last member of the European Union to introduce such ban as required by the EU. Initially the Latvian parliamentarians deleted sexual orientation from the Labour Law. The President of Latvia refused to sign their decision and sent it back for reconsideration.

While there is increasing visibility of gay community and social acceptance of homosexuality in Latvia, some public opinion polls remains relatively negative. The Church takes a leading role in anti-gay sentiment. Cardinal Janis Pujat described homosexuality as an „unnatural form of prostitution that must not be ennobled by such things as a gay marriage". In his opinion, EU-membership has sexualized society and homosexuals are now taking advantage of that. He called on his fellow countrymen to demonstrate against the 2007 Parade, which approximately 100 of them did. A few days later, 500 people attended the demonstration and nobody was injured, although one should add that the police completely shielded the demonstrators, who were evacuated in buses at the end. Amnesty International and various members of the European parliament support the Latvian gay movement and hence the country's democratization, as democracy not only means that the majority decides, but that minorities are also respected!

In Latvia you will discover a wealth of fascinating history, culture and nature. While the gay life and gay rights are still being built and fought for – you also can be part of this important development by visiting Latvia.

In Lettland sind gleichgeschlechtliche Handlungen nicht strafbar. Einvernehmlicher Sex zwischen erwachsenen Männern wurde 1992 legalisiert, kurz nachdem Lettland die Unabhängigkeit von der UdSSR erlangt hatte. Das Mindestalter für alle sexuellen Handlungen liegt bei 16. Gleichgeschlechtliche Beziehungen genießen jedoch keinerlei Rechtsstatus. Außerdem untersagt das Zivilrecht seit 1991 gleichgeschlechtliche Ehen und das lettische Grundgesetz definiert die Ehe neuerdings (seit 2005) als Beziehung zwischen Mann und Frau. Die 1999 im Parlament eingebrachte Vorlage eines Partnerschaftsgesetzes für gleichgeschlechtliche Paare wurde noch vor der eigentlichen Plenardebatte im Beratungsstadium abgelehnt. Diskriminierung am Arbeitsplatz aufgrund der sexuellen Orientierung ist seit 2006 gesetzeswidrig. Bei der Umsetzung dieses von der EU geforderten Verbots war Lettland das Schlusslicht unter den Mitgliedsstaaten. Ursprünglich hatte das Parlament die sexuelle Orientierung ganz aus dem Arbeitsrecht gestrichen. Doch der Präsident von Lettland verweigerte seine Zustimmung und forderte eine Überarbeitung.

Obwohl die lettische Schwulenkultur immer sichtbarer wird und sich zunehmender Toleranz erfreut, sind einige Umfrageergebnisse nach wie vor ziemlich negativ. Vorreiter der Antischwulenbewegung sind die Kirchen. Kardinal Janis Pujat bezeichnete Homosexualität als „unnatürliche Form der Prostitution" und sie dürfe nicht durch Dinge wie der Homo-Ehe geadelt werden. Seiner Meinung nach hat die EU-Mitgliedschaft die Gesellschaft sexualisiert, und das nützten die Homosexuellen jetzt aus. Er forderte seine Mitbürger dazu auf, gegen die CSD-Parade 2007 zu demonstrieren, was ungefähr 100 taten. Wenige Tage später nahmen 500 an der Parade teil und niemand wurde verletzt. Allerdings schirmte die Polizei die Demonstranten vollständig ab und am Ende wurden sie in Bussen evakuiert. Amnesty International und verschiedene europäische Parlamentarier unterstützen die Schwulenbewegung in Lettland und damit die Demokratisierung des Landes, denn Demokratie bedeutet nicht allein, dass die Mehrheit entscheidet, sondern auch dass man Minderheiten achtet.

In Lettland gibt es eine faszinierende, reiche Geschichte, Kultur und Natur zu entdecken. Momentan wird noch für die Rechte der hiesigen Schwulen, deren Kultur sich im Aufbau befindet, gekämpft. Durch einen Besuch des Landes können Sie Ihren Beitrag zu diesem Kampf leisten.

Les relations sexuelles sont légales entre adultes consentants depuis 1992 en Lettonie, peu après l'indépendance du pays et la majorité sexuelle est fixée à 16 ans pour tous. Cependant, les relations homosexuelles ne sont pas reconnues juridiquement : le code civil interdit depuis 1991 le mariage homosexuel et la loi fondamentale lettonne définit depuis 2005 le mariage comme l'union entre un homme et une femme. Une proposition de loi déposée au parlement en 1999 instaurant un partenariat enregistré pour les couples de même sexe a été refusée et ce avant même le début des débats, pendant l'étape de consultation.

Depuis 2006, la discrimination professionnelle liée à l'orientation sexuelle est un délit et la Lettonie a été un des derniers pays-membres à appliquer cette directive européenne. Le parlement avait même supprimé l'orientation sexuelle du droit du travail mais le président letton a refusé de donner son accord et exigé une reformulation.

Bien que la culture gay lettonne soit de plus en plus visible et jouisse d'une tolérance grandissante de la part de la population, les résultats de certains sondages restent négatifs. Les églises sont les précurseurs des mouvements homophobes. Le cardinal a décrit l'homosexualité comme une « forme de prostitution non naturelle ne devant pas être anoblie par le biais de trucs genre le contrat civil « . L'adhésion à l'EU a selon lui sexualisé la société, ce qu'exploiteraient les homosexuels. Il a encouragé de plus ses concitoyens à manifester contre la Gay Pride 2007, ce que firent environ 100 personnes. Peu de jours après, 500 participèrent au défilé et personne ne fut blessé. Ceci dit, la police protégeait complètement les participants, qui furent tous évacués en bus à la fin. Amnesty International et différents parlementaires européens soutiennent le mouvement gay en Lettonie et par là-même la démocratisation du pays, puisque la démocratie ne signifie pas que la majorité décide, mais aussi que l'on prête attention aux minorités !
La Lettonie dispose d'une histoire fascinante et d'une culture très riche, sans compter les magnifiques paysages. Rendre visite à ce pays, c'est donc non seulement visiter un pays passionnant mais aussi aider la culture gay et lesbienne locale à s'installer.

En Letonia las relaciones homosexuales no están penalizadas. El sexo entre hombres adultos fue legalizado en 1992, después de que Letonia consiguiera la independencia de la URSS. La edad de consentimiento para cualquier relación sexual está en los 16. Las relaciones homosexuales, sin embargo, no disfrutan de ningún status jurídico. El derecho civil prohíbe desde 1991 los matrimonios homosexuales y la Constitución letona, desde 2005, define el matrimonio como relación entre hombre y mujer. La propuesta de ley de parejas, presentada ante el Parlamento en 1999, fue rechazada incluso antes de llegar al Pleno en la fase de toma en consideración.
Las discriminaciones en el trabajo con motivo de la orientación sexual son ilegales desde 2006. Durante la aplicación de esta directiva exigida por la UE, Letonia fue el más reacio entre los estados miembros. Originariamente, el Parlamento había eliminado la orientación sexual del derecho laboral, pero el presidente de Letonia se negó a prestar su conformidad y exigió una revisión.
Aunque la cultura homosexual letona está cada vez más presente y goza de mayor tolerancia, algunos resultados de encuestas muestran todavía una imagen bastante negativa.
Las iglesias son las que promueven el movimiento homófobo. El cardenal Janis Pujat considera la homosexualidad como una „forma antinatural de prostitución y no debe ser ensalzada con cosas como el matrimonio homosexual". Según su opinión, la entrada a la UE ha sexualizado a la sociedad y eso es lo que aprovechan ahora los homosexuales. Exigió a sus conciudadanos que se manifestaran en contra de la Marcha Gay del 2007, lo que hicieron unas 100 personas. Días más tarde, 500 personas participaron en la manifestación y nadie salió herido. Sin embargo, la policía protegió completamente la marcha y al final se les evacuó a todos en autobuses. Amnistía Internacional y diferentes parlamentarios europeos apoyan el movimiento gay en Letonia y con ello la democratización del país ya que democracia no significa sólo que la mayoría decide sino que también se tiene en cuenta a las minorías!
Letonia ofrece una rica historia, cultura y naturaleza. De momento, todavía se lucha por los derechos de los homosexuales, cuya cultura sigue construyéndose. Con una visita a este país puede prestar su ayuda a la lucha.

In Lettonia gli atti sessuali tra persone dello stesso sesso non sono più punibili. L'atto sessuale consensuale tra uomini adulti è stato legalizzato nel 1992, poco dopo che la Lettonia raggiunse l'indipendenza dall'Unione Sovietica. L'età del consenso per tutti i tipi di atti sessuali è di 16 anni. I rapporti tra persone dello stesso sesso non sono oggetto di nessun tipo di legislazione. Dal 1991 il diritto civile vieta il matrimonio tra persone dello stesso sesso. Dal 2005 la costituzione definisce il matrimonio come rapporto tra uomo e donna. Il testo di legge per le unioni tra persone dello stesso, presentato nel 1999, è stato bocciato ancor prima del dibattito plenario.
Dal 2006 è vietata ogni forma di discriminazione al posto di lavoro. Nei tempi di attuazione di questa legge antidiscriminazione, richiesta tra l'altro dall'Unione Europea, la Lettonia è stata il fanalino di coda dei paesi membri. Originariamente il parlamento aveva completamente omesso l'orientamento sessuale dal diritto del lavoro; tuttavia il presidente della Repubblica si è rifiutato di firmare chiedendo una modifica della legge. Sebbene la cultura omosessuale acquisti sempre più visibilità, i risultati di alcuni sondaggi sono ancora molto deludenti. Capi indiscussi del movimento omofobo sono le chiese. Il Cardinale Janis Pujat ha definito l'omosessualità come „forma contro-natura di prostituzione che non va nobilitata attraverso il matrimonio omosessuale". Secondo l'opinione del Cardinale, l'adesione all'Unione Europea ha ‚sessualizzato' la società e la comunità omosessuale sta cercando di approfittarne. Lo stesso Cardinale ha esortato i suoi connazionali a manifestare contro il gay pride del 2007. È riuscito a raccogliere tra le sue fila circa 100 persone. Pochi giorni dopo ha avuto luogo la parata, durante la quale non ci sono stati incidenti di nessun genere. Tuttavia la polizia ha garantito lo svolgimento della manifestazione serrando la stessa ed evacuando, alla fine, i manifestanti su degli autobus. Amnesty International e diversi parlamentari europei sostengono attivamente il movimento gay in Lettonia. Questo aiuta anche la democratizzazione del Paese, se si considera il fatto che democrazia non significa solo il volere della maggioranza ma anche il rispetto delle minoranze.
La Lettonia è ricchissima di storia e di cultura. La natura qui è tutta da scoprire. Al momento, in questo paese, si combatte molto per i diritti degli omosessuali, la quale cultura si sta lentamente affermando. Visitando la Lettonia offrirete sicuramente un contributo a questa lotta.

NATIONAL GROUPS

Mozaika
Gertrūdes iela 19/21 ✉ 1010 Riga 🖳 www.mozaika.lv
Alliance of lesbian, gay, bisexual and transgender people and their friends. Leading LGBT right organisation in Latvia.

Riga

BARS

Golden Bar & Club (AC cc D f glm MA) Mon-Wed 18-4, Thu-Sun -5h
Gertrudes iela 33/35 *Centrally located* ☎ (371) 2550 5050
🖳 www.goldenbar.lv
First chillout lounge in Riga. Large and good cocktail selection. Very friendly staff. Free internet at the bar. Unofficially gay. One of the few places for gay men during the day in Riga.

CAFES

Dorian Gray (B cc glm MC S) Daily 12-1h
1 Maza Muzeja iela (I-1) ☎ 2914 77 24 (mobile)
Serves a mix of European cuisine and Latvian homey meal traditionals. Cultural space and bar at night. On Tue special thematical events, Thu movie days, also live music and other performances on different weekdays.

Skapis (b BF glm MA)
Aspazijas bulvaris 22

DANCECLUBS

Essential (B D glm m MA)
Skolas street 2 ☎ 371 6724 2289 🖳 www.essential.lv
Mixed crowd, local gays love this club, top DJ-acts, see www.essential.lv for details.

XXL Club (! AC B CC D DR F G MA P r SNU VS) 18-7h
A. Kalnina iela 4 *Near the railway station Marijas iela, in the city centre*
☎ 921 08 41 🖳 www.xxl.lv
Popular gay club, decorated with Tom of Finland drawings. Bar and danceclub with excellent shows. Friendly staff and excellent place to start to discover Riga's gay life. For more details see: www.xxl.lv

SEX SHOPS/BLUE MOVIES

Kupidon Plus (g VS) 10-22.30h
A. Caka 72 ☎ 731 34 60
Large cinema on ground and 1st floor with five differnt rooms and four cubicles with glory holes.

Labi (g VS) Gay videos daily 10-19h
Lacplesa 47 ☎ 728 66 41
Small cinema with 2 rooms.

SAUNAS/BATHS

Varaviksne (! B DR DU FC FH G MA MSG RR SA SB VS WH)
Sun-Thu 15-2; Fri & Sat -7h
Alfreda Kalnina iela 4 ☎ 67 28 34 85 www.xxl.lv/sauna
The first gay sauna along with the best club XXL and hotel „Centrum". Best time to visit is Fri & Sat after 22h.

HOTELS

Gay Hotel Centrum (B G MA RWS RWT SA VA) All year
A. Kalnina iela 4 *Same building as gay club „XXL"* ☎ 728 32 87
www.gayhotel.lv
The first gay guest house along with the best sauna and bar in the Baltic. One luxury suite and four standard bedrooms. Hotel guests have free entry to the XXL Bar.

SWIMMING

-Kalngale (g) (take the train direction Saulkrasti and get off at Kalngale, then walk 30 mins along the beach to the north)
-Incupe (g NU) (take the train direction Saulkrasti and get off at Incupe, then walk 30 mins along the beach to the south)
-Lielupe (g) (take the train direction Jurmala and get off at Lielupe, then either walk 45 mins along the beach to the east (to the right), until you reach the river or take the bus 1 direction Uzvara until the last stop. Walk 20 mins to the north).

CRUISING

-The Square (in front of the university main building, opp. to Raina bulvaris 19)
-Arkadijas parks (AYOR) (Tram 10, near the toilets in the park)
-Grizinkalns (AYOR) (Park at Pernavas iela/J. Asara iela).

Lebanon

Name: Lubnan · Libanon · Liban · Líbano
Location: Middle East
Initials: RL
Time: GMT +2
International Country Code: ☎ 961
International Access Code: ☎ 00
Language: Arabic
Area: 10,452 km² / 4,015 sq mi.
Currency: 1 Lebanese Pound (L£) = 100 Piaster
Population: 4,000,000
Capital: Beirut
Religions: 60% Muslim, 40% Christian
Climate: Mediterranean climate. Winters are mild to cool and wet, summers hot and dry. The mountains experience heavy winter snowfall.
Important gay cities: Beirut

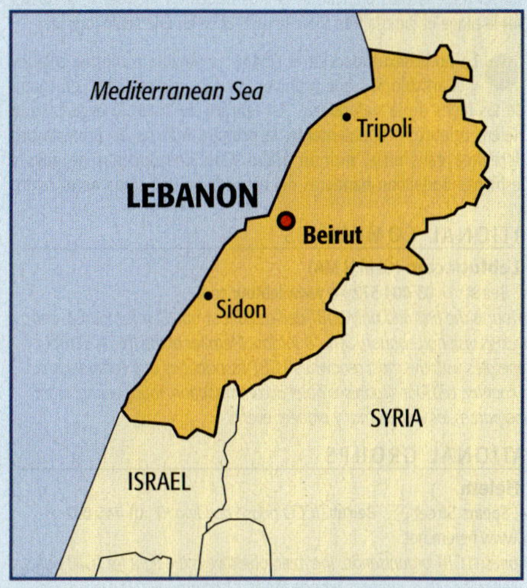

Legally homosexuality is prosecutable under article 534, however, this penal law is not implimented since decates, however, affectionate behavior in public places is not advised.
The situation for gay men in Lebanon has improved significantly in the past few years. And recently Beirut hosted the IGLTA FAM TRIP to start promoting itself as an LGBT regional destination.
Gay bars and clubs operate freely and an LGBT centre has been created to cater to all the needs of the community.
Despite the aftermath of the 2006 conflict with Israel much of the country is safe and the Lebanese people are extremely friendly and hospitable. Lebanon is a fast changing country and is inherently capable of recovering from any challenges. Each time you visit this vibrant society, it will be like visiting a different country with new experiences.
Lebanon is a country to be visited during all seasons; you can ski in some of the best, soft snow in the world, go to the beach, and party all night long all in the same day.
Because of the historical ethnic mix between European, Mediterranean, Middle Eastern groups and the whole spectrum in between, Lebanese men offer an appealing variety.
If you wish to see the amazing and fascinating result of East meets West; then Beirut is the place to be. Beirut is many cities in itself; it only takes a moment to find what fits you best. Beirut is the largest city and the most liberal urban centre in the country, the last big city in European terms before the desert!

Homosexualität ist laut Gesetzesartikel 534 strafbar und verbietet sexuelle Beziehungen die „gegen die Naturgesetze" sind. Im Februar 2009 veranstaltete die Organisation Helem wahrscheinlich den ersten Protestmarsch für homosexuelle Rechte in der arabischen Welt. Fast zwei Dutzend Schwuler und Lesben schwenkten Regenbogenfahnen auf einem Platz in der Innenstadt Beiruts. Mit Plakaten forderten sie mehr Rechte für Homosexuelle. Sie protestierten gegen die Polizei, die zwei Schwule verprügelte, die beim Sex in der Öffentlichkeit erwischt wurden.
In den letzten Jahren hat sich die Lage der schwulen Männer im Libanon jedoch deutlich verbessert. Schwulenbars und -discos können ungestört betrieben werden und ein erst kürzlich eingerichtetes LGBT-Zentrum kümmert sich um alle Belange der Schwulengemeinde.
Trotz der Nachwirkungen der jüngsten Konflikte mit Israel ist ein Großteil des Landes sicher für Reisende. Das libanesische Volk ist äußerst aufgeschlossen und gastfreundlich. Der Libanon wandelt sich in einem rasanten Tempo und ist aus eigener Kraft fähig, jegliche Herausforderung zu bewältigen. Bei jedem erneuten Besuch dieses abwechslungsreichen Landes wird es Ihnen so vorkommen, als seien Sie in ein ganz anderes Land gefahren, das völlig neue Erfahrungen

für Sie bereithält. Der Libanon ist zu allen Jahreszeiten eine Reise wert: man kann hier auf dem besten, weichsten Schnee der Welt Ski fahren, Zeit am Strand verbringen und die Nacht durchfeiern, und das alles an einem einzigen Tag.

Selon l'article 534, l'homosexualité est un délit et les relations sexuelles « contre nature « sont interdites. En février 2009, l'organisation Helem a organisé probablement la première marche pour les droits des homosexuels dans le monde arabe. Près de deux douzaines d'homosexuels et lesbiennes ont brandis des drapeaux arc-en-ciel dans le centre ville de Beyrouth. Avec des affiches demandant plus de droits pour les homosexuels, ils ont protesté contre la police qui a frappé deux gays surpris à faire l'amour en public.
2010, Bertho Makso de LebTour, a preparer la premiere campagne de promotion pour promouvoir Beyrouth en tant que destination de tourism LGBT en invitant l'association IGLTA (international gay and lesbian travel association).
Malgré les récents conflits en 2006, avec Israël et leurs conséquences, une grande partie du pays est sûre pour les voyageurs. Les Libanais sont extrêmement ouverts et hospitaliers. Le Liban se transforme très rapidement et est capable de relever tous les challenges par soi-même. A chaque nouvelle visite du pays, vous aurez l'impression d'en visiter un autre. Le Liban peut être visité toute l'année : on peut y faire du ski sur la neige la plus blanche et la plus douce du monde, se prélasser sur la plage et faire la fête toute la nuit, et ce en une seule journée.

La homosexualidad en el Líbano es punible conforme a la ley y al artículo 534 que prohíbe las relaciones sexuales „en contra de las leyes de la naturaleza". En febrero de 2009, la organización Helem celebró, probablemente, la primera marcha de protesta pro derechos gays en el mundo árabe. Casi dos docenas de gays y lesbianas ondeaban banderas del arco iris en una plaza en el centro de Beirut. Con pancartas exigieron más derechos para la comunidad gay y protestaron contra los policías que golpearon a dos hombres homosexuales, que habían sido sorprendidos teniendo relaciones sexuales en público.
A pesar de las consecuencias del reciente conflicto con Israel, la mayor parte del país es seguro. El pueblo libanés es extremadamente abierto y hospitalario. El Líbano se transforma a gran velocidad y es capaz de superar cualquier dificultad. En cualquier nueva visita que realice se dará cuenta que este país tan variado le ofrecerá otras experiencias. El Líbano merece la pena ser visitado en todas las épocas del año: se puede ir a esquiar con la mejor y más suave nieve, tumbarse en la playa y salir de fiesta por la noche: todo esto en un solo día!

L'articolo 534 vieta i rapporti sessuali che vanno „contro le leggi della natura" e quindi anche l'omosessualità. A febbraio del 2009 l'organizzazione Helem ha organizzato probabilmente la prima marcia di protesta nel mondo arabo per i diritti degli omosessuali. Una ventina di gay e lesbiche sventolavano bandiere arcobaleno in una piazza del centro di Beirut. Gli striscioni della manifestazione chiedevano più diritti per gli omosessuali. Inoltre si è protestato contro la polizia che ha picchiato due gay perché trovati a fare sesso in pubblico.
Nonostante le conseguenze del recente conflitto con Israele, si può comunque viaggiare per la maggior parte del paese in maniera piuttosto sicura. Il popolo libanese è molto aperto ed accogliente. Il Libano si sta trasformando molto velocemente ed è una paese che riesce ad affrontare ogni sfida con le proprie forze. Quando fate un'escursione in questo paese molto eterogeneo, avrete l'impressione di visitare volta per volta paesi differenti. Si può fare una vacanza in Libano in qualsiasi stagione: è possibile trascorrere vacanze bianche, trascorrere le giornate in spiaggia e godersi le vita notturna...e tutto questo lo si può fare nell'arco di un solo giorno.

NATIONAL COMPANIES

Lebtour.com (GLM H MA)
✉ Beirut ☎ 03 004 572 💻 www.lebtour.com
LebTour is the first and only LGBT-dedicated tour operator for tourists and travellers visiting Lebanon, Syria & Jordan. Member of the ILGTA, LebTour cooperates with the most renowned LGBT associations and companies in the country. LebTour organises hotel accommodation, tour guiding, night clubs/parties, as well as many pioneer events.

NATIONAL GROUPS

Helem
174, Spears Street ✉ Beirut *ZICCO house building* ☎ 01 745 092
💻 www.helem.net
Lebanese LGBT organisation, the main objective is the fight for LGBT rights, as well as health awareness among the LGBT community. The word „Helem" is the Arabic acronym of Lebanese Protection for LGBTQ. It is also the Arabic word for „dream."

Marsa Sexual Health Center
Mexico street, near Hagazian University, Clemenceau ✉ Beirut *Myrtom House building, 2nd floor* ☎ 1737 647
The main objective of the centre is to provide social, psychological, and medical services to all sexually active individuals in Lebanon regardless of gender, age, and sexual orientation in complete confidentiality. Services include free voluntary testing and counselling (VCT) for the detection of HIV1/2, Hepatitis B and C using the rapid test.

Meem
✉ Beirut 💻 www.meemgroup.org
Meem is a community of and for LBTQ women in Lebanon. Female part of Helem. LBTQ is defined as women who self-identify as lesbian, bisexual, transgender (including male-to-female and female-to-male), queer, in addition to women questioning their sexual orientation.

Raynbow
💻 www.raynbow.net
Raynbow is a Lebanese Gay group committed to empowering LGBT activism in Lebanon through fund raising and media awareness. Raynbow has launched the „Lebanese LGBT Media Monitor" on Facebook in June 2009 to spread awareness about LGBT issues and recruit straight allies.

FETISH GROUPS

Bear Arabia (! F G MA RES)
✉ Beirut ☎ 3004572 💻 www.beararabia.org
Bear Arabia is the first bear community of the Middle East, hosting bear themed events and social activities in Lebanon and the rest of the Middle East, Turkey & Armenia.

HEALTH GROUPS

SIDC (Soins Infirmiers et Développement Communautaire)
Youssef Karam Street ✉ Beirut *Daou bldg, 1st floor* ☎ 1480714
💻 www.sidc-lebanon.org
SIDC's mission is to meet the health needs of the youth, elderly and the most vulnerable individuals and groups in Lebanon through community empowerment.

Beirut

BARS

Dark Box (AC B CC GLM M MA R ST T WE) 19-2h, closed Mon
Monot Street Street, Ashrafie *Middle of Monot Street, opp. Facebook cafe*
Mostly known for being the transexual bar or Beirut (transgenders, escorts, and queens).

Society Lounge & Bar (AC B CC F GLM M MA) 19-2h
Hamra area – beside the Cavalier Hotel *Facing the main entrance of Cavalier Hotel*
Cozy & small. Perfect place for a drink before you start your nightclub experience with friends or a new date.

Life Bar (AC B CC F GLM m MA) 19-2h
Liban Street, Tabaris, Ashrafieh *Behind SNA building*
Lesbian bar, owned and operated by women. Best time to go Wed, Thu and Sat.

■ **Ob La Di** (AC B CC F GLM M MA) 19-2h
Mar Maroun Street, Gemayzeh
Small yet it's being a nice hanging out spot.

■ **Posh** (AC B CC F GLM M MA) Thu-Sun 23- 5h
Antelias *Antelias Highway – after Jal el Dib's bridge, turn richt after Total petrol station. Bar on your right 100m from highway*
Not central located but very cosy bar that get transformed into a small dancing club around midnight. The place deserve to be visited, especially its attracting the Bear community from around the country.

■ **Wolf** (AC B F G MC) 19-2h, closed Mon
Mankhoul Street, Hamra *Near the American University and St Mary's orthodox church* ☏ 3 002 965
🖳 www.wolfbars.com
Bears and wolves bar. See website www.wolfbars.com for directions.

CAFES

■ **Colombiano** (CC I NG OS)
Ashrafieh *Sassine Roundabout*
Usually gay people go there mostly to use internet.

■ **Columbus** (AC I MA NG)
Sassine Square – In ABC shopping mall *Top floor*
This branch of Columbus café, located on the top floor of ABC shopping mall is becoming a new gathering place for the gay community.

DANCECLUBS

■ **B 018** (B D GLM P PK) Sat & Sun 2-?h
Forum De Beyrouth (Quarantina) 🖳 www.b018.com
An after hour Techno/House music. Crowd usually mixed, including LGBT. However, single men sometimes are not allowed to enter, especially on Sat nights. High quality drinks but expensive.

■ **Ghost Bar** (AC B D G MA)
Beirut *Sin el Fil – Dekweneh highway, behind the Freeway center*
Operated by the same staff as the former Acid. Great place to meet new friends and enjoy the LGBT scene of Beirut. Crowded on both Fri & Sat.

■ **Le BOY** (AC B D G MA R SNU T)
Port De Beyrouth *Not far from Beirut harbour close to the Beit el Kataeb main office* ☏ (961) 76744295
Le Boy will host int'l & local resident DJs, as well as int'l branded parties from all over the world on a regular basis! Music style will range from all types of dance music.

RESTAURANTS

■ **Bardo** (! AC B BF CC GLM I LM M MA RES VEG WE) Daily 7-2h
Clemenceau Street, Sanyeh area *Opp. Haigazian university*
Open every day for breakfast, lunch and dinner. A mixed cuisine restaurant with Lebanese and far eastern food like Chinese and Vietnamese.

■ **Mayrig** (! AC B BF CC M MA NG RES VEG) All day
Mar Mekhael Street *Beside the Mar Mekael Church*
Armenian Restaurant – serving a fine Armenian cuisine.

■ **Walimat** (AC B BF CC DM M MA NG RES VEG) 12-2h
Makdessi Street – Hamra *In the Lobby of The Marble Town Hotel*
Open every day for lunch and dinner. Traditional Lebanese cuisine is served; typical restaurant for warm up before partying. Themed evenings on Sat.

SEX CINEMAS

■ **Khayyam** (AYOR DR g MA VS WE)
Jeanne d'Arc, Hamra
Cinema showing old films and straight porn. Best for cruising on Sun afternoons.

■ **Morocco** (AYOR DR g MA VS WE)
Mar Doumit str. Sin el Fil – Nabaa *Same location as Plaza*
Movie theatre showing old movies – straight porn and mainstream films. Cruising and pick-up area for men. Some action on the balcony and in the bathrooms.

■ **Plaza** (AYOR DR g MA VS WE)
Mar Doumit str. Sin el Fil – Nabaa
Very busy and most attractive crowd on Sun afternoons.

■ **Royal** (AYOR DR g MA VS WE)
Cornish el Nahr *Burj Hammoud area, on Nabaa side*
Movie theatre showing old American and international movies: straight porn and mainstream films. Some action on the balcony, bathrooms used as darkroom.

SAUNAS/BATHS

■ **Nuzha** (FH G MA MSG RR SA SB) 24hrs
Zukak el Blat *Walking distance from downtown area, located beside the "Ring" Bridge*
The oldest hammam in Beirut, centrally located. Soap and oil massage on offer. Extras like soap, shampoo, massage and scrub are paid on top of the entrance. Tipping is expected.
BE DISCREET – as lately it has been reported that the owner isn't tolerating gay action in his Bathhouse.

■ **Shehrazad** (DR FH G MA MSG RR SA SB WH)
Daily 14-2h
Burj Hammoud *On the 2nd entrance beside Burj Hammoud football standium, Burj hammoud area*
Modern style bathhouse with cruising amongst customers; crowded during weekends. Be discreet! Extras like soap, shampoo, massage and scrub are paid on top of the entrance. Tipping is expected.

FITNESS STUDIOS

■ **Fitness Zone** (AYOR CC DU FH NG PK WO)
Hamra *Crowne Plaza Hotel – ground floor*

MASSAGE

■ **8ieme Spa and Tea Lounge. Le**
(AC CC FH MSG NG OS RES SOL)
Rome Street *Immeuble Maktabi, rue de Rome, rond-point* ☎ 1378018
💻 www.le8eme.com
A tea & spa lounge located in the heart of Beirut.
Le 8ieme thé boutique and lounge, is fully dedicated to Mariage Frères selections of tea.
Eden spa, also part of le 8ieme, was inspired from the virtue of tea leaves. Clientele receives an exclusive range of treatments including sodashi facials & body wraps, nail care, make up and professional massages.

TRAVEL AND TRANSPORT

■ **Lebtour.com** (GLM H MA)
☎ 03 004 572 💻 www.lebtour.com
Hotel booking and tour guiding services for Lebanon, Jordan and Syria as well as Packages to Turkey, Armenia and beyond. Reservations: minimum one week in advance.

HOTELS

■ **Grey. Le** (BF CC H M MC MSG NG RES RWS RWT WH WI)
All year
Martyrs' Square ☎ (01) 971 111
💻 www.campbellgrayhotels.com

CRUISING

All AYOR! Be discreet and specify clearly what you want and whether money is involved:
-Industrial area – Jdeideh – Dekweineh, not far from the new bridge high way – Dekweineh – Ashrafieh
-Rawshe Cornish – cruising is frequent on the Cornish, take care of the escorts and thieves, and police controls, lots cross the fences in front of the famous pigeon rock; there inside the bush some may have sex – recently some incidents were reported – so please take care.
-Dbayeh – Marina Cornish – Beirut side, not far from the Golden Beach Resort. Take care of the escorts and thieves, and police controls. Late night, the place is partly gay.
-Ramlet el bayda open beach Beirut
-Tyre Open beach, south of Lebanon

Tripoli

SAUNAS/BATHS

■ **Al Abed** (AYOR FH MA MSG NG RR SA SB) 9-21h
Ancient Gold Souk *Not far from the Soap Khan*
Very old bathhouse, dating from the Ottoman Empire, in an over 500 year-old building. It is one of the best Hammams in Lebanon, located in the tourist area of the old part of Tripoli. This Hammam offers Lebanese bathing tradition: people gather, meet and sometimes cruise. Al Abed Turkish bath offers a steam room and sauna, some bathing cells and for sure an unforgettable massage!

CRUISING

-Al Mina Cornish – Tripoli – cruising is frequent on the Cornish, take care of the escorts & thieves, and police controls.

Liechtenstein

Location: Central Europe
Initials: FL
Time: GMT +1
International Country Code: ☎ 423 (no area codes)
International Access Code: ☎ 00
Language: German
Area: 160 km² / 62 sq mi.
Currency: 1 Swiss Franc (sfr) = 100 Rappen
Population: 34,000
Capital: Vaduz
Religions: 83% Catholic, 7% Protestant
Climate: Continental climate. Winters (Nov-Mar) are cold with frequent snow or rain. Summers are cool to moderately warm and humid.

In the penal code from Liechtenstein, § 205, point 4 states "when the age of the perpetrator is not more than three years older than the age of the minor and none of the conditions mentioned in paragraph 3 apply, the perpetrator is not punishable according to paragraph 1 & 2, unless the minor is under the age of 13". Note: there is no differentiation made between homo- and heterosexuals.
On 24.10.2007, the parliament supported the introduction of registered partnerships by a majority vote and the corresponding bill was passed.

Das liechtensteinische Strafgesetzbuch, § 205, Abs. 4, sieht Folgendes vor: „Übersteigt das Alter des Täters das Alter der unmündigen Person nicht um mehr als drei Jahre und ist keine der Folgen des Abs. 3 eingetreten, so ist der Täter nach Abs. 1 und 2 nicht zu bestrafen, es sei denn, die unmündige Person hat das zwölfte Lebensjahr noch nicht vollendet." Anmerkung: Es wird nicht zwischen Homo- und Heterosexuellen unterschieden.
Am 24.10.2007 sprach sich der Landtag mehrheitlich für die Einführung der Eingetragenen Partnerschaft gleichgeschlechtlicher Paare aus, und die entsprechende Gesetzesvorlage wurde angenommen.

Le paragraphe 205, alinéa 4 du code pénal du Liechtenstein prévoit ceci : « si l'âge de l'inculpé ne dépasse pas celui de la personne mineure de plus de trois ans et si aucune des suites de l'alinéa 3 n'est survenue, l'inculpé n'est pas condamnable selon les alinéas 1 et 2 sauf si la personne mineure a 12 ans et moins. « Remarque : il n'est fait aucune différence entre homosexuels et hétérosexuels.
À partir du 24/10/2007 le parlement s'est majoritairement déclaré pour l'introduction d'un contrat de partenariat pour les couples de même sexe et la proposition de loi correspondante a été admise.

GERMANY
LIECHTENSTEIN
Vaduz
AUSTRIA
SWITZERLAND
ITALY

El código penal de Liechtenstein, en su artículo 205 párrafo 4, establece lo siguiente:
„Si la edad del autor no supera en tres años la edad del menor y no concurren ninguna de las consecuencias del párrafo 3, no se puede penalizar al autor según los párrafos 1 y 2, a menos que el menor no haya cumplido los 12 años." Nota: No se distingue entre homosexuales y heterosexuales.
El 24 de octubre de 2007 el Parlamento se declaró de forma mayoritaria a favor de la introducción del registro de parejas del mismo sexo y así se admitió el correspondiente proyecto de ley.

Il codice penale del principato del Lichtenstein, § 205 paragrafo 4 prevede che se l'età del maggiorenne non supera di 3 anni l'età del minorenne e se non sussiste nessuna conseguenza descritta nel paragrafo 3, il maggiorenne, secondo il pragrafo 1 e 2 non è punibile tranne nel caso che il minorenne non abbia compiuto il dodicesimo anno di età. È da notare che non sussiste alcuna differenza di trattamento tra omosessuali ed eterosessuali.
Il 24 ottobre del 2007 la maggioranza del parlamento si è espressa a favore dell'introduzione del registro per le unioni civili per coppie dello stesso sesso, e quindi approvato il progetto di legge.

Schaan

GENERAL GROUPS

■ **Verein für Schwule und Lesben (FLay)** (GLM MA)
Postfach 207 ☎ 769 3529 🖳 www.flay.li

HEALTH GROUPS

■ **FA6 – Fachstelle für Sexualfragen und HIV-Prävention**
Mon-Fri 9-12h
Im Malarsch 4 ☎ 232 0520 🖳 www.fa6.li

Lithuania

Name: Lietuva · Litauen · Lituanie · Lituania
Location: Northeast Europe
Initials: LT
Time: GMT +1
International Country Code: ☏ 370
International Access Code: ☏ 8 (wait for tone) 10
Language: Lithuanian, Russian
Area: 65,3101 km² / 25,174 sq mi.
Currency: 1 Litas (LTL) = 100 Centas
Population: 3,414,000
Capital: Vilnius (Wilna)
Religions: 80% Roman Catholic
Climate: Spring & summer (May-Sep) are the best times of year to travel in Lithuania.

The age of consent in Lithuania is 14, as specified by the Lithuanian Criminal Code §153. LGBT Pride events have been banned during the last 10 years.

In January 2009 Lithuania's Parliament approved a censorship bill that sharply curbs the spreading of public information that lawmakers say could harm the mental, physical, intellectual and moral development of youngsters. The bill prohibits any information that encourages homosexual, bi-sexual or polygamous relations. The bill came into effect in March 2010.

On the 1st July 2008 the new version of the equal treatment law came into force. The new version of this law extends clearly the range of the discrimination reasons which are to be fought. Six reasons for discrimination: age, gender, sexual orientation, disability, descent, race or ethnic affiliation and religion or conviction, are complemented with a further six inadmissible grounds for discriminations: belief, language, nationality, descent, social standing and approach to life.

Both the law regarding equal rights between man and woman as well as the equal treatment law, determine the basic rules of the public life in Lithuania.

Lithuania is a wonderful country for travellers, with a capital that invites exploration in place of mere sight-seeing. The gay scene in Vilnius is relatively small but not without its very own charm, just as most aspects of the city and the country. The travel season lasts all year round, even if late spring and summer are the most pleasant periods.

Das Schutzalter in Litauen liegt gemäß §153 des Strafgesetzbuches bei 14 Jahren. Alle LGBT Demonstrationen wurden in den letzten 10 Jahren verboten.

Im Januar 2009 bewilligte Litauens Parlament ein Zensurgesetz, wonach das Verbreiten öffentlicher Informationen eingeschränkt wird, was der geistigen, physischen, intellektuellen und moralischen Entwicklung von Jungendlichen schaden könnte.

Das Gesetz verbietet jegliche Informationen, was homosexuelle, bisexuelle oder polygame Beziehungen ermutigen könnte. Die Regelung trat im März 2010 in Kraft.

Am 1. Juli 2008 ist eine neue Fassung des Gleichbehandlungsgesetzes in Kraft getreten. Darin erweitert der Gesetzgeber die Bandbreite der zu bekämpfenden Diskriminierungsgründe noch einmal deutlich. Die sechs Diskriminierungsgründe Alter, Geschlecht, sexuelle Orientierung, Behinderung, Abstammung, Rasse bzw. ethnische Zugehörigkeit und Religion bzw. Überzeugungen sind nun um sechs weitere unzulässige Diskriminierungen ergänzt worden: Glaube, Sprache, Nationalität, Abstammung, sozialer Status und Lebensanschauungen. Zusammen mit den gesetzlichen Regelungen zur Gleichberechtigung von Mann und Frau bestimmt nun das Gleichbehandlungsgesetz die Grundregeln des öffentlichen Lebens in Litauen.

Für Reisende ist Litauen ein wunderschönes Land mit einer Hauptstadt, die man eher erkundet als besichtigt. Die schwule Szene in Vilnius ist klein, hat aber einen eigenen Charme, so wie die meisten Seiten der Stadt und des Landes. Das ganze Jahr ist Reisezeit, wenngleich Spätfrühjahr und Sommer am angenehmsten sind.

L'article 153 du code pénal fixe à 14 ans la majorité sexuelle. Toutes les manifestations LGBT ont été interdites ces 10 dernières années.

En janvier 2009 le parlement lituanien a voté une loi de censure censée limiter la diffusion d'information pouvant porter préjudice au développement mental, physique, intellectuel et moral de la jeunesse.

Cette loi interdit toutes les informations qui pourraient encourager les relations homosexuelles, bisexuelles ou polygames. Cette loi entre en vigueur en mars 2010.

Le 1er juillet 2008 une nouvelle constitution est entrée en vigueur. Celle-ci élargit sensiblement le domaine de la lutte contre les discriminations. Aux six discriminations (âge, sexe, orientation sexuelle, handicap, origine, race ou appartenance ethnique et religieuse ou convictions) s'ajoutent six nouvelles: croyance, langue, nationalité, origine, statut social et philosophie.

Les deux lois, celle sur l'égalité hommes-femmes ainsi que celle de l'égalité de traitement, règlent la vie publique en Lituanie.

La Lituanie est pour les voyageur un magnifique pays avec une capitale qu'on explore plus que l'on ne la visite. La scène gay de Vilnius est réduite mais a un charme particulier, tout comme la plupart des facettes de cette ville ou celles du pays. On visite le pays toute l'année, même si la fin du printemps et l'été sont les plus agréables.

La edad mínima para mantener relaciones sexuales en Lituania queda establecida en el Código Penal en 14 años de edad. Todas las manifestaciones LGBT en este país han sido prohibidas durante los últimos 10 años.

En enero de 2009 el Parlamento lituano aprobó una ley de censura que restringe la difusión de información pública que pueda perjudicar el desarrollo mental, físico, intelectual y moral de los jóvenes.

La ley prohíbe cualquier información que pueda alentar a relaciones homosexuales, bisexuales o polígamas. Está normativa entraría en vigor en marzo de 2010.

El 1 de Julio de 2008 entró en vigor la nueva ley antidiscriminación que amplia claramente el margen de actuación a la hora de establecer la lucha contra sus causas.

Las seis causas de discriminación son: la edad, el género, la orientación sexual, la discapacidad, el origen y la religión. Pero otras opiniones complementan esta lista con otras seis causas inadmisibles de discriminación como: el credo, el idioma, la nacionalidad, la procedencia, el estatus social y los estilos de vida.

Tanto la ley de igualdad de derechos entre hombre y mujer, como también la ley general de igualdad de trato, determinan las normativas fundamentales de la vida pública de Lituania.

Para los turistas Lituania es un país maravilloso, con una capital más para descubrir que visitar. El ambiente gay en Vilnius es pequeño pero tiene un encanto propio, al igual que la mayoría de caras de la ciudad y del país. Todo el año es bueno para viajar si bien primavera y verano son las temporadas más agradables.

Secondo l'articolo 153 del codice penale lituano l'età del consenso è di 14 anni. Durante gli ultimi 10 anni tutte le manifestazioni LGBT sono state vietate. A gennaio del 2009 il parlamento lituano ha approvato una legge censoria che impone una serie di vincoli allo scambio di informazioni che potrebbero danneggiare lo sviluppo mentale, fisico e intellettuale degli adolescenti. La legge vieta qualsiasi messaggio che potrebbe incoraggiare rapporti omosessuali, bisessuali o poligami. La suddetta legge entrerà in vigore a marzo del 2010.

Nel 2005 il parlamento lituano ha approvato una modifica di legge che vieta ogni tipo di discriminazione (originaria dall'orientamento sessuale) sul posto di lavoro, nel campo della formazione e nelle graduatorie per l'assegnazione di una casa.Il primo luglio del 2008 è entrata in vigore una nuova versione della legge sulle pari opportunità. La nuova legge estende sensibilmente lo spettro di forme di discriminazione da combattere.

Le sei forme di discriminazione già riconosciute sono: età, sesso, orientamento sessuale, disabilità, razza/origine etnica, e religione/convinzioni personali. Adesso se ne aggiungono altre sei: credo religioso, lingua, nazionalità, provenienza, status sociale e ideologia.

Ambedue le leggi, la legge sulle pari opportunità tra uomo e donna e la legge antidiscriminatoria, dettano le regole fondamentali della vita pubblica in Lituania.

Dal punto di vista turistico la Lituania è davvero uno splendido Paese. La sua capitale, Vilnius, è piccolina ma ha uno charme molto particolare come del resto la gran parte del Paese. Si può visitare la Lituania durante tutto l'anno, tuttavia i periodi migliori rimangono la tarda primavera e l'estate.

NATIONAL GROUPS

LGBT Centre @ Lietuvos Geju Lyga (LGL) (GLM MA) Mon-Fri 9-18h
Jaksto 22-15 ✉ 01105 Vilnius ☎ (05) 261 0314 💻 www.lgl.lt
Lithuanian Gay League is a national nonprofit, nongovernmental organization uniting homosexual, bisexual, and transgender persons, a member of the International Lesbian and Gay Association (ILGA) since 1994. Lithuanian gay league is an advocacy organization dedicated to fighting homophobia and discrimination based on sexual orientation and gender identity. Through education, support, and representation of the LGBT community, LGL promotes an inclusive social environment for gay men, lesbian women, bisexual and transgender persons.

Lithuanian Positive Group
8-16.45, Fri -15.45, closed Sat & Sun, Hotline: Mon-Fri 9-18h
Subaciaus str. 116-23A ✉ 11343 Vilnius ☎ (5) 233 0111 💻 www.aids.lt
Support group for HIV+ people with AIDS.

Kaunas ☎ 37

CRUISING

-Laisves Aleja
-Vilniaus Gatve
-Park near bus station
-Ramybes Park

Klaipėda ☎ 46

BARS

Naktine Ledi (B D GLM M MA WE) Mon-Thu & Sun 22-3, Fri & Sat 22-6h
Silutes Ave. 21 ☎ (699) 55 940 💻 www.naktineledi.com
Monday until Thursday and Sunday free entry, Showevents on Friday and Saturday.

SWIMMING

-Smiltyne (NU) (male nude beach, left side)

Vilnius ☎ 5

MEN'S CLUBS

New Men's Factory (AC B D glm P PI SA SB SNU ST VS WE YC)
Fri & Sat 22-6h
Sevcenkos str. 16 (10 corpus) ☎ (699) 85 009 💻 www.mensfactory.lt
Biggest and trendiest night club which evolved from a former gay club. Now more known as gay friendly with a mixed crowd. Famous dance parties on weekdays. Special separate room for smokers and a big maze of rooms on the lower level.

DANCECLUBS

Soho club (AC B CC D DR GLM MA PK S ST VS WE)
Thu 22-4 (free entry), Fri & Sat 22-7h (with entry fee)
Svitrigailos str. 7/16 *On center street from Vilnius airport 3 km, near Centrum Hotel* ☎ 69939567 💻 www.sohoclub.lt
Cosy, renovated (2011) nightclub which is very popular with local LGBT commmunity. Themed evenings, special shows and pop concerts on weekdays. Good music, reasonably priced drinks

SAUNAS/BATHS

Gay sauna Glamour (AC DR DU G LAB MA PI SA SB WH) Sun 19-24h
Sevcenkos str. 16 i Vilnius ☎ 67271172 (mobile) 💻 www.gayclub.lt
Gay night club New Men's Factory

Luxembourg

Name: Lëtzebuerg · Luxemburg · Luxemburgo · Lussemburgo
Location: Western Europe
Initials: L
Time: GMT +1
International Country Code: ☎ 352 (no area codes)
International Access Code: ☎ 00
Language: French, German, Lëtzebuergesch
Area: 2,586 km² / 998 sq mi.
Currency: 1 Euro (€) = 100 Cents
Population: 453,000
Capital: Luxembourg-City
Religions: 95% Roman Catholic
Climate: Mild winters and cool summers.

The age of consent for heterosexuals as well as homosexuals in Luxembourg is set at 16 (Penal Code Article 372 to 378 from 1992). In addition a partnership law came into force in November 2004 in which gay couples in Luxembourg can register their partnership. This „Déclaration de Partenariat" does not imply marriage rights, but simply a registration of the partnership with tax and retirement benefits. Luxembourg has a small gay scene, concentrated in the attractive capital city.

Seit 1992 liegt das Schutzalter für Heterosexuelle und Homosexuelle in Luxemburg gleichermaßen bei 16 Jahren (Artikel 372 bis 378 des Strafgesetzbuches). Außerdem ist im November 2004 ein Partnerschaftsgesetz in Kraft getreten, das gleichgeschlechtlichen Paaren nun auch in Luxemburg ermöglicht, sich registrieren zu lassen. Die „Déclaration de Partenariat" bedeutet allerdings keine Gleichstellung mit der Ehe, sondern ermöglicht den amtlich anerkannten Partnern lediglich steuerliche Vergünstigungen sowie gemeinsame Kranken- und Rentenversicherung. Luxemburg hat eine kleine schwule Szene, die vor allem in der reizvollen Hauptstadt zu finden ist.

Selon les articles 372 à 378 du code pénal luxembourgeois en vigueur depuis 1992, la majorité sexuelle est fixée à 16 ans pour tous. En outre, une loi passée en novembre 2004 reconnaît les couples de même sexe et leur permet de faire enregistrer leur partenariat. Mais la « déclaration de partenariat » ne signifie cependant pas une reconnaissance des droits au même titre que le mariage: elle octroie aux couples enregistrés des droits fiscaux ainsi qu'une couverture sociale commune concernant la maladie et la retraite. Le Luxembourg dispose d'un petit milieu gay se concentrant principalement dans sa capitale du même nom.

Desde 1992, la edad de consentimiento para heterosexuales y homosexuales en Luxemburgo está en los 16 años de igual manera (artículo 372 a 378 del código penal). Además, en noviembre del 2004 entró en vigor una ley de parejas en Luxemburgo que autoriza el registro de las parejas del mismo sexo como tal. La llamada „Déclaration de Partenariat" no significa sin embargo una equiparación con el matrimonio, sino que sólo autoriza a las parejas así registradas ciertas bonificaciones fiscales así como poder tener una seguridad social común. Luxemburgo tiene un ambiente gay pequeño que sobre todo se localiza en su fantástica capital.

In Lussemburgo, dal 1992, l'età del consenso (Art. 372-378 del codice penale) è di 16 anni per tutti (eterosessuali ed omosessuali). Inoltre a novembre del 2004 è entrata in vigore una legge che permette alle coppie dello stesso sesso di registrare la loro unione. La „déclaration de partenariat" non dà comunque gli stessi diritti di cui godono le coppie eterosessuali sposate, ma si limita a riconoscere vantaggi per quello che riguarda le tasse, la sanità e le pensioni. Nel Lussemburgo c'è una piccola vita gay che si concentra soprattutto nella affascinante capitale.

NATIONAL GAY INFO

■ **Rosa Lëtzebuerg a.s.b.l** (GLM MA T)
60, Rue des Romains ✉ 2444 Bonnevoie ☎ 26 19 00 18
💻 www.gay.lu
Gay site in French, German and Lëtzebuergesch; publisher of the quarterly newsletter „La Pie qui Chante."

Bascharage

BARS

■ **Flowers** (B glm M MA)
182 Blvd JF Kennedy ☎ 26 50 12 22

Esch/Alzette

BARS

■ **Mojo Bar** (B CC glm MA S) Mon-Thu 14-01, Fri-Sun -03h
29, Rue du Commerce

Frisange Grand Duché de Luxembourg

HOTELS

■ **Hôtel Restaurant de la Frontiere** (AC B cc glm M MC OS)
All year
52, rue Robert Schuman ☎ 23 615 💻 www.hoteldelafrontiere.lu

Luxembourg

GAY INFO

■ **Cigale – Centre d'Information Gay et Lesbien** (GLM MA T) Mon & Tue 13-17, Wed 16-20, Thu 13-19h
60 rue des Romains ☎ 26 19 00 18 💻 www.cigale.lu
Counselling, information and leisure activities.

BARS

■ **Banana's** (B glm m MA OS) 9-1h
9 Av. Monterey *Near Place d'Armes* ☎ 46 15 11
💻 www.bananas.lu

■ **Bar Lounge Evidance** (B CC GLM MA S)
Mon-Thu & Sun 17-1, Fri-Sat -3h
7 Rue du Palais de Justice ☎ 26 86 47 55

■ **Color's** (B BF cc glm M MA) 8-1h
5 rue Chimay *Near place d'Armes* ☎ 26 20 28 03 🖳 www.colors.lu
Cuisines Italienne, Française, Végétarienne.

■ **Chez Mike** (AC B D GLM MA S WE) Wed 20-2, Fri & Sat 21-3h
30 Av. Emile Reuter

■ **Petit Manoir. Le** (CC GLM MA S) 17-1, Sun 14-1h
24 rue de l'Eau ☎ 26 26 21 90

■ **Red & Black** (B CC GLM MA S)
Mon-Thu 7-1, Fri -3, Sat 18-3h, Sun closed
11 rue Aldringen ☎ 27 47 83 83

■ **What Else Bar** (B D G MA ST T)
17-1, Fri -3, Sat 18-3, Sun 18-1h, closed Mon
7, rue du Palais de Justice

CAFES

■ **Café Chez Madame Sansgêne** (B CC GLM MA) Mon closed, Tue-Thu 11-1, Fri-Sat -3, Sun 18-1h
11 rue Aldringen

SEX SHOPS/BLUE MOVIES

■ **Cinema XXX** (AC CC G MA T VS)
Mon-Thu 10-1, Fri & Sat -3, Sun & public holidays 15-1h
3 rue du Fort Wedell *Near station* ☎ 48 58 36
Video booths (gay, bi, trans programs).

■ **Erotic Video Center** (g VS) 11-24h
15 rue de Reims ☎ 48 14 55 🖳 www.erotic-shop.lu

■ **Sex Center** (CC f g MA T VS)
Mon-Fri 10-22, Sat 13-20h, Sun & public holidays closed
60 rue de Fort Neipperg *Near main station* ☎ 26 18 74 78
With gay cinema. Video booths.

HEALTH GROUPS

■ **Stop AIDS Now asbl** 8-12, 14-18h
94 Blvd G. Patton ☎ 40 62 51 🖳 www.aids.lu

CRUISING

-City Park (AYOR) (near the pond)
-🅿 Parking Kockelscheuer (AYOR) (evenings, but frequent police controls).

Remich

SAUNAS/BATHS

■ **Nº 1** (B DR G MA OS SA SB SOL VS WO) 14-20h, Mon closed
22 rue de la Gare *E29 east from Luxembourg City on the border heading toward Saarbrucken. Opp church with parking 50 m away* ☎ 26 66 06 12
🖳 www.sauna-n1.com

HOTELS

■ **Auberge des Cygnes** (BF CC glm M OS s) 10-1h
11 Esplanade *Overlooking the river „Moselle" in the middle of the Esplanade* ☎ 23 69 88 52
Hotel with a good restaurant. All rooms with shower and WC.

Macedonia (FYRoM)

Name: Makedonija · Mazedonien · Macedoine
Location: Southern Central Europe
Initials: FYR
Time: GMT + 1
International Country Code: ☎ 389 (omit 0 of area codes)
International Access Code: ☎ 00
Language: Macedonian, Albanian, Turkish, Bosnian
Area: 25.173 km² / 48391.34 sq mi.
Currency: 1 Denar (MKD) = 100 Deni
Population: 2,034,000
Capital: Skopje
Religions: Macedonian Orthodox (70%), Muslims (35%), other (3%)
Climate: Temperate climate. The best weather for a visit is from June to August.

✱ Homosexuality in Macedonia is legal and the age of consent is 16 although legal provisions which regulate the age of consent do not discuss specifically whether they refer to heterosexuals or homosexuals. In such a case, Macedonian experts believe, this can be interpreted in a way that the age of consent for same-sex relations is also 16. Changes to the law regarding homosexuality do not reflect a raised public awareness, nor are they an act of goodwill on the part of the Macedonian law and decision makers. It was in the process of becoming full member of the Council of Europe that Macedonia was „forced" to change its Criminal Law in a way that it would no longer discriminate against same-sex conduct and that its provisions on sexual offences would no longer distinguish between heterosexual and homosexual acts.

The Macedonian LGBT movement is organized and led by the Centre for Civil and Human Rights, based in Skopje. This civil association was the very first – and so far the only one in Macedonia – that openly deals with the rights of sexual minorities.

In August 2002 this Centre, in collaboration with the Macedonian Helsinki Committee, carried out the first official and recorded research into public opinion regarding homosexuality. The results of this research show that in Macedonia it is still a wide-held standpoint that homosexuality is something abnormal – an illness or psychological disturbance that directly violates traditional and family values.

It is recommended to avoid displays of affection in public even in places which might seem to be gay-friendly.

★ In Mazedonien gilt Homosexualität als legal, und das Schutzalter liegt bei 16 Jahren, wobei die gesetzlichen Bestimmungen keinen Unterschied zwischen Hetero- oder Homosexuellen machen. Mazedonienkenner interpretieren dies so, dass auch das Schutzalter für schwullesbische Beziehungen bei 16 Jahren liegt.

Gesetzesänderungen hinsichtlich Homosexualität spiegeln leider weder eine gesteigerte öffentliche Toleranz wider, noch sind sie ein Zeichen des guten Willens der Gesetzgeber und Entscheidungsträger des Landes.

Als Mazedonien vollwertiges Mitglied des Europarates wurde, musste das Land sein Strafgesetz in folgender Weise abändern: Es durfte gleichgeschlechtliche Kontakte nicht länger diskriminieren, und die Bestimmungen über sexuelle Vergehen sollten keinen Unterschied mehr zwischen hetero- und homosexuellen Menschen machen.
Die LGBT-Bewegung wird vom Zentrum für Zivil- und Menschenrechte organisiert und geleitet. Es hat seinen Hauptsitz in Skopje und ist das allererste und bisher auch einzige in Mazedonien, das sich offen mit den Rechten sexueller Minderheiten befasst.
Im August 2002 hat dieses Zentrum in Zusammenarbeit mit dem mazedonischen Helsinki-Komitee die erste offizielle und niedergelegte Studie über Homosexualität durchgeführt.
Ergebnisse zeigen, dass Homosexualität in Mazedonien immer noch als anormal und als Krankheit oder psychologische Störung gilt, die traditionelle und familiäre Werte verletzt. Daher empfiehlt es sich, auch an scheinbar schwulenfreundlichen Orten zurückhaltend zu sein und weder Küsse auszutauschen noch Händchen zu halten.

L'homosexualité est légale en Macédoine, et l'age légal s'établit à 16 ans. Le législateur ne fait pas la différence entre hétérosexuels ou homsexuels. Les connaisseurs de la Macédoine interprêtent de cette façon que l'age légal de 16 ans vaut aussi pour les relations homosexuelles. Les changements législatifs en matière d'homosexualité ne reflêtent malheureusement pas une plus grande tolérance publique, et ne sont pas non plus un signe de la bonne volonté du législateur et des décideurs du pays. Lorsque la Macédoine est devenue membre à part entière du Conseil de l'Europe, la Macédoine a dû modifier sa loi pénale : les contacts entre personnes du même sexe ne devaient plus être discriminés et les mesures en matière de comportement sexuel ne devaient plus faire la différence entre hétérosexuels et homosexuels.
Le mouvement LGBT est organisé et dirigé par le Centre pour les Droits Civils et de l'Homme. Son siège est situé à Skopje et est le premier et jusqu'à présent le seul mouvement qui s'occupe ouvertement des droits des minorités sexuelles.
En août 2002 ce Centre a conduit avec le comité macédonien Helsinki le premier rapport officiel sur l'homosexualité.
Les résultats montrent que l'homosexualité en Macédoine est toujours perçue comme anormale ou comme une maladie ou un désordre psychologique qui va à l'encontre des valeurs traditionnelles et familiales. Il est par conséquent conseillé de se comporter de manière réservée même dans des lieux qui paraissent « gay-friendly », et de ne pas s'embrasser ou se donner la main.

La homosexualidad en Macedonia es legal y la edad de consentimiento es de 16 años, sin embargo las leyes referentes a este tema no definen si esta disposición es para heterosexuales o para homosexuales. Al respecto, los expertos juristas del país anotan que en todo caso se debe entender que las relaciones entre personas del mismo sexo están autorizadas a partit de los 16 años. Las reformas legales con respecto a la homosexualidad no despiertan particular interés entre la sociedad macedonia, ni son motivo de la benevolencia por parte de los legisladores y políticos macedonios. Fue en aras del ingreso de Macedonia al Consejo Europeo como miembro de plenos derechos, que este país se vió obligado a modificar el Código Penal a fin de que no se siguiera discriminando la homosexualidad y que las previsiones en materia de delitos sexuales no hicieran más distinciones entre hetrosexuales y homosexuales.
El movimiento LGBT está organizado por el Centro de Derechos Civiles y Humanos, ubicado en Skopje. Esta organización es la primera, y hasta el momento la única, que trata abiertamente la temática de los derechos de las minorías sexuales. En agosto de 2002 el Centro , en colaboración con el Comité Macedonio de Helsinki, llevó a cabo la primera investigación de campo y sondeo de opinión pública sobre la homosexualidad en Macedonia. El resultado de esta investigación mostró que en este país todavía se considera que la homosexualidad es anormal -deficiencia física o perturbación psicológica- y que atenta contra los valores tradicionales de la familia. Ante tal situación, se aconseja evitar en público toda manifestación de orientación homosexual, aún en los lugares que parezcan ser tolerantes hacia los homosexuales.

In Macedonia l'omosessualità è legale e l'età minima per avere rapporti sessuali è di 16 anni senza distinzione tra omosessuali ed eterosessuali. Le leggi riguardo l'omosessualità rispecchiano la situazione piuttosto arretrata del paese. Quando la Macedonia é entrata a far parte del Consiglio d'Europa il suo codice penale ha subito diversi cambiamenti: non saranno più tollerate discriminazioni nei confronti dei rapporti omosessuali e riguardo ai rapporti sessuali non si fa piú distinzione tra omo ed etero.
Il movimento LGTB viene diretto dal centro per i diritti umani e civili; ha sede a Skopje ed è la prima e sola organizzazione in Macedonia che lotta apertamente per i diritti delle minoranze sessuali. In agosto del 2002 il suddetto centro, in collaborazione con il Comitato Helsinki, ha presentato il primo ufficiale studio sull'omosessualità. Il risultato testimonia che l'omosessualità in Macedonia è ancora considerata una malattia o un disturbo psicologico che va contro i valori tradizionali e familiari. Quindi vi consigliamo di essere discreti evitando di tenervi per mano o di scambiare affettuosità anche in locali gay friendly.

Bitola ☎ 047

CAFES

■ **Deep** (B NG OS)
Sirok sokak *In the pedestrian zone in the town centre*
Other possibilities in the same area are: Millennium and Iguchi Cafés.

DANCECLUBS

■ **Rascekor** (B D MA NG)

RESTAURANTS

■ **De Niro** (M NG)
Sirok sokak *Pedestrian zone*

Kumanovo ☎ 031

CAFES

■ **Intermezzo** (B NG OS)
Town Square
Other cafés at town square where you might find gay men are Corsso, Zafir and Candy Shop. All these cafés have OS in summer only.

DANCECLUBS

■ **Club** (B D NG)
In the summer this disco is located at the town square.

■ **Linka** (B D NG)
Ivo Lola Ribar Street (Nagoricki sokak)

RESTAURANTS

■ **Blue** (B NG OS)
3rd MUB Blvd *Corner of Narodna Revolucija street*

■ **Copacabana** (B M NG OS)
Ilindenska Street *Opposite the „Garnizon" building*
Another restaurant in the same building where you might meet gay men is called Laguna on the 1st floor.

■ **Fransh** (B M NG OS)
Narodna Revolucija Street *Next to the town library*

HOTELS

■ **Mimoza** (b M MA NG)
Trgovski Centar Building Complex *In the town centre, at the beginning of the „Zelen Rid" district*
Please be discreet when bringing guests back to the hotel.

■ **Rim Pariz** (B M NG)
On 3rd MUB Boulevard *In the central town area, corner of Narodna Revolucija street*

CRUISING

-Outside the central town area, in the town park, near the bus station, evenings (AYOR).

Skopje ☎ 02

BARS

■ **Damar** (B glm MC OS s)
Stara Charshija *In the old part of the town*
Gay-friendly bar with Beer garden. Try their Mojito. Very very tasty. Also interesting during the daytime.

■ **G Bar** (B GLM MA) 12-24, Fri & Sat -1h
Bulevard Mito-Hadjivasilev Jasmin 2 *Situated on the back of the Museum, known as the Old Railway Station, next to the Ramstore Mall*

■ **St. Patrick Irish Pub. The** (B BF NG OS)

■ **VirusCaffe** (B glm MC)
Bul.Sveti Kliment Ohridski br 52 ☎ 71222014 (mobile)
🖳 www.facebook.com/viruscaffe

CAFES

■ **Izlet Kafe** (b LM MC NG OS S)
Nikola Trimpare, Kapistec *Next to Hotel Queens in the ‚Zebra' mall*
Coffee bar with great garden. The owner speaks English.

■ **New Age** (B glm MA OS)
Kosta Sakov 9 *Behind „Kuzman Josifovski Pitu" student dorms*

■ **Orient House** (B glm MA)
Ivo Lola Ribar 49 *Near Bulgarian and Croatian Embassies; the site is also known as „Mlin Balkan"*

DANCECLUBS

■ **Collosseum** (D MA NG)
Near British Embassy, opposite „Josip Broz Tito" High School
🖳 www.colosseum.com.mk

■ **Fabrique. La** (D MA NG) Summertime only

■ **Kafe Bony** (B D glm MC) Sun 24-6h
🖳 www.facebook.com/kafeboni
Gay party every Sunday.

RESTAURANTS

■ **Pelister** (M NG OS)
Macedonia Square *In the City Square, officially called the Macedonia Square* 🖳 www.pelisterhotel.com.mk/uk_restoran.htm

SEX SHOPS/BLUE MOVIES

■ **Crvenkapa** (g MA VS)
Please be discreet.

■ **Valijant 1** (g) Mon-Fri 13-22, Sat-Sun 13-20h
Bul: Kuzman Josifovski Pitu 28a/15 *In the passage; in the „Star Aerodrom" district, U-T.C.Skopjanka* ☎ (02) 246 02 06 🖳 www.valijant.com.mk
DVDs and toys. Please be discreet.

■ **Valijant Sex Centar** (g) Mon-Fri 13-22, Sat-Sun 13-20h
Bul: Partizanski Odredi 3 *Underground, near Café Bar Mr. Jack*
☎ (02) 246 02 06 🖳 www.valijant.com.mk
Some gays in cinema, please be discreet.

CRUISING

-City centre, on the left bank of the river Vardar. It begins on the quay of the river Vardar under the „Goce Delcev" bridge near the main bus station; then it goes downstream towards the MNT and ends with the clearing encircled by the MNT, the village bus station, the MANU and the „Kiril i Metodij" primary school. (AYOR)

Madagascar

Name: Madagaskar
Location: Southeast Africa
Initials: MG
Time: GMT +3
International Country Code: ☎ 261 (omit 0 from area codes)
International Access Code: ☎ 00
Language: Malagasy, French
Area: 587,041 km2 / 226,597 sq mi
Currency: Malagasy Ariary (MGA)
Population: 18 606 000
Capital: Antananarivo
Religions: 50% traditional religion, 40% Christians
Climate: Wet season from Jan-Mar when roads are often unpassable.

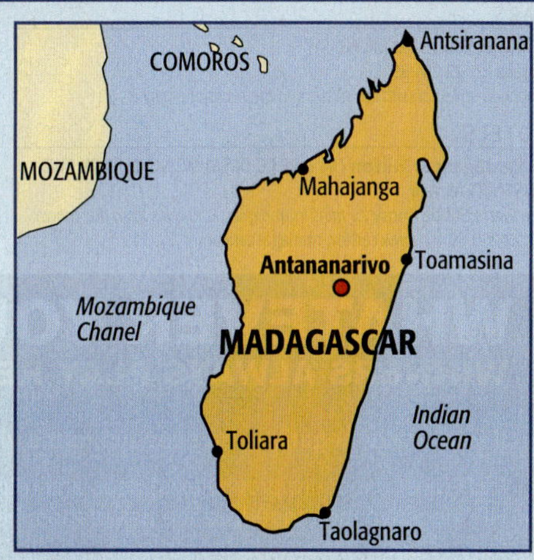

Madagascar is the fourth largest island of the world, situated in the Indian Ocean. It is a unique island not only in regard to its biodiversity – with lemurs and chameleons the best known representatives – but also due to the culture strongly influenced by Asian people. Indonesian sailors discovered the island and started settling the still uninhabited island in 6th century. Today, 18 million people are living on the island which was colonized by the French for 164 years. Madagascar got independent in 1960.
Homosexuality is nearly not visible in Madagascar and as such more or less unknown. No legislation concerning same sex relations are existent, means also, that homosexuality is not illegal. On the other hand, cross-dressing does exist, even in remote areas, but these people are not regarded as homosexuals.
Age of consent is 21 and prostitution with minors is persecuted. No explicitly gay places exist, but Hilton Hotel and Mojo Club are popular, also for gays to meet and socialise.

Madagaskar ist die viertgrößte Insel der Erde und liegt im Indischen Ozean. Die Einzigartigkeit des Landes ist nicht nur in seiner Artenvielfalt begründet – zu deren bekanntesten Vertretern die einheimischen Lemuren und Chamäleons zählen – sondern auch in dem starken asiatischen Kultureinfluss: die noch unbewohnte Insel wurde im 6. Jahrhundert von indonesischen Seefahrern entdeckt und besiedelt. Mittlerweile leben 18 Millionen Menschen auf Madagaskar,

das vor seiner Unabhängigkeit im Jahr 1960 164 Jahre lang unter französischer Kolonialherrschaft gestanden hatte.
Homosexualität ist hier so gut wie unsichtbar und mehr oder weniger unbekannt. Da es keine gesetzlichen Regelungen im Hinblick auf gleichgeschlechtliche Beziehungen gibt, ist sie jedoch auch nicht illegal. Darüber hinaus gibt es hier sogar in abgelegenen Gegenden Männer, die Frauenkleider tragen, doch diese werden nicht als homosexuell angesehen. Das Schutzalter liegt bei 21 und die Prostitution Minderjähriger wird strafrechtlich verfolgt. Es gibt zwar keine ausdrücklich schwulen Einrichtungen, doch das Hilton und der Mojo Club sind als Treffpunkte auch unter den Schwulen beliebt.

Madagascar est la quatrième plus grande île au monde et est située dans l'Océan Indien. La singularité de ce pays vient non seulement de sa biodiversité tels ses variétés de caméléons et ses lémuriens mais aussi de la forte empreinte culturelle asiatique: l'île encore inhabitée au 6ème siècle fut découverte et colonisée par des marins indonésiens. De nos jours, 18 millions de personnes vivent à Madagascar qui fut pendant 164 ans colonisée par la France et obtint son indépendance en 1960.
L'homosexualité est quasiment invisible et plus ou moins inconnue. Les relations de même sexe ne sont pas légiférées, ni illégales. De plus dans des régions reculées, il existe des hommes qui portent des habits de femmes, cependant ils ne sont pas considérés comme homosexuels. La majorité légale est fixée à 21 ans et la prostitution des mineurs est poursuivi pénalement. Il n'existe certes pas de lieux explicitement gays mais l'hôtel Hilton et le Mojo Club sont appréciés des gays.

Madagascar es la cuarta isla más grande del mundo y está situada en el océano Índico. La singularidad de este país no se debe únicamente a su biodiversidad, cuyos máximos representantes son los lémures y camaleones autóctonos, sino también a la fuerte influencia cultural que ha heredado de Asia: la isla estuvo deshabitada hasta el siglo VI cuando fue descubierta y colonizada por marineros indonesios. A día de hoy viven 18 millones de personas en Madagascar, la cual, antes de su independencia en 1960, se mantuvo durante 164 años bajo el dominio colonial francés. La homosexualidad es aquí prácticamente invisible y en mayor o menor grado desconocida. Dado que tampoco existen disposiciones legales con respecto a las relaciones entre personas del mismo sexo, la homosexualidad no es ilegal en este país. Además, existen zonas remotas en las que incluso se pueden encontrar hombres que se visten con ropas de mujer, pero a estos no se les considera homosexuales.
La edad mínima para mantener relaciones sexuales es de 21 años, en consecuencia, la prostitución de menores de edad es perseguida por la ley. Si bien no hay establecimientos abiertamente gays, el Hilton y el Mojo Club son los lugares de encuentro favoritos también para hombres gays.

Il Madagascar è la quarta isola più grande del mondo e si trova nell'Oceano Indiano. L'unicità del paese non è rappresentata solo dalla sua biodiversità – gli esempi più significativi sono i lemuri e i camaleonti locali – ma anche dalla forte
influenza culturale asiatica: l'isola, ancora piuttosto disabitata, è stata scoperta e conquistata nel VI secolo dai marinai indonesiani. Dopo 164 anni di colonizzazione francese, il Madagascar raggiunge l'indipendenza nel 1960. Oggi in Madagascar vivono circa 18 milioni di persone. L'omosessualità è, qui, pressoché invisibile e più o meno sconosciuta. Poiché non esistono norme che regolano le relazioni tra persone dello stesso sesso, non esistono neanche espliciti divieti. Nelle aree più sperdute ci sono addirittura uomini che indossano abiti da donna, ma questi comportamenti non vengono considerati omosessuali.
L'età del consenso è di 21 anni e la prostituzione minorile viene perseguita penalmente. Non esiste nessun tipo di locale o organizzazione espressamente gay, anche se l'Hilton e il Mojo Club sono due punti di ritrovo molto amati dai gay.

Antananarivo ☏ 020

BARS

Mojo Bar (B LM MC NG S)
Isoraka ☏ 22 254 59
European-style bar with live music and the occasional gay visitor.

HOTELS

Madagascar Hilton (AC B BF CC DM M MC NG OS PI PK RWB RWS RWT) All year
Rue Pierre Stibbe Anosy *25 mins from airport & 10 mins from downtown*
☏ 22 260 60 www.carlton-madagascar.com
From outside an unattractive hotel and not the best place for a long stay. Convienient and free airport shuttle. One of the only places where gay men can be found.

Saint-Marie ☏ 057

GUEST HOUSES

Adonys Eden Lodge (glm M MA OS RWB RWS SH)
All year
Ankarena La Grotte *10 mins from airport, on the beach* ☏ 205 790 649
☏ 326 401 946
Gay owned and operated lodge with private cabins directly on the beach!

Malaysia

Name: Persekutan Tanah Malaysia · Malaysie · Malasia · Malesia
Location: Southeast Asia
Initials: MAL
Time: GMT +8
International Country Code: ☏ 60 (omit 0 from area code)
International Access Code: ☏ 00
Language: Malay, English, Chinese, Tamil
Area: 329,733 km² / 127,320 sq mi.
Currency: 1 Malayan Ringgit (RM) = 100 Sen
Population: 24,894,000
Capital: Kuala Lumpur
Religions: 60% Muslim, 20% Buddhist, 9% Christian, 6% Hindu
Climate: Tropical climate. Avoid the rainy season (Nov-Jan) on Malaysia's east coast if you want to enjoy the beaches.

Malaysia stands under heavy influence of Islam and homosexuality is technically illegal: with a punishment for homosexual acts (oral/anal) of up to 20 years imprisonment. As foreigner you need not fear these drastic measures. It is also surprising that under these conditions a gay scene has developed. Due to discretion the police and the general public tend to ignore its existence. Even a gay organization exists, however with little support. Prostitution is forbidden but widely exists.

The leader of the opposition party in Malaysia, Anwar Ibrahim, was arrested in July 2008, accused of sodomy with a 23-year-old male aide. Under Malaysian law, even consensual sodomy is punishable by up to 20 years in jail if convicted. He rejoined Malaysia's Parliament in October 2008, following his goal to become Prime Minister.

The „Seksualiti Merdeka" (freedom of sexuality) festival, held annually to promote diversity since 2008, was banned in November 2011 after politicians and religious Muslims had denounced it as „immoral". It looks as if the opponents of the festival saw a need for the ban after the festival had generated greater media attention by way of a PR campaign in the previous year.

Despite these restrictions one can have a wonderful holiday in Malaysia, the people are generally extremely friendly and the infrastructure is well developed. Much of the country is mountainous, tropical rain forest and rice paddies. The islands of Penang (Pearl of the East), Langkawi and Pangkor as well as the east coast peninsula have the most attractive beaches in the entire far-east region.

Malaysia ist ein islamisch geprägtes Land und Homosexualität ist illegal: homosexuelle Handlungen (Oral-/Analsex) können mit bis zu 20 Jahren Gefängnis und öffentlichem Auspeitschen bestraft werden. Als Ausländer hat man diese drakonischen Strafen allerdings kaum zu befürchten. Überhaupt ist es erstaunlich, wie unter diesen Bedingungen in den Städten eine verhältnismäßig vielfältige Szene entstehen konnte. Deren Diskretion macht es der Öffentlichkeit und der Polizei leicht, sie zu ignorieren. Es gibt sogar einige schwule Organisationen, die jedoch keine große Unterstützung erfahren. Prostitution ist verboten.

Anwar Ibrahim, der Fraktionsvorsitzende der malaysischen Oppositionspartei, wurde im Juli 2008 verhaftet und der „Sodomie" mit einem 23-jährigen Assistenten beschuldigt. Im malaysischen Recht kann nachgewiesener Analverkehr mit bis zu 20 Jahren Freiheitsentzug bestraft werden. Im Oktober 2008 ist Ibrahim jedoch wieder in das Parlament eingezogen und verfolgt somit weiter sein Ziel, Premierminister zu werden.

Seit 2008 fand jährlich das Festival „Seksualiti Merdeka" (Freiheit der Sexualität) statt, das Vielfalt propagierte. Im November 2011 wurde das Festival jedoch verboten, nachdem Politik und religiöse Muslime dieses Event als „unmoralisch" verurteilten. Das Verbot scheint offenbar in den Augen der Kritiker notwendig zu sein, seitdem das Festival im Vorjahr durch eine PR-Aktion eine größere Medienaufmerksamkeit erzeugte.

Trotz dieser Einschränkungen kann man in Malaysia einen tollen Urlaub verbringen, da die Malaysier sehr freundliche und offene Menschen sind und durch die gut funktionierende Infrastruktur das Reisen recht komfortabel ist. Einen großen Teil des Landes machen Berge, tropische Regenwälder und Reisfelder aus. Die Inseln Penang („Perle des Ostens"), Langkawi und Pangkor sowie die Ostküste der malaysischen Halbinsel bieten einige der schönsten Strände des Fernen Ostens.

La Malaisie est un pays d'influence musulmane où la prostitution est interdite et l'homosexualité un délit: les rapports homosexuels (oraux et anaux) sont passibles d'une peine de prison pouvant aller jusqu'à 20 ans assortie de flagellation publique. Un étranger n'a cependant pas à redouter de telles peines draconiennes. Il est assez étonnant de constater que malgré ce climat d'oppression, un milieu gay relativement diversifié a pu s'établir dans les villes. Sa discrétion lui garantit de rester ignoré de la police et du public. Il existe même quelques organisation gays qui ne jouissent néanmoins pas d'un grand soutien.

Anwar Ibrahim, le président du groupe parlementaire de l'Oppositon malaisienne, a été incarcéré en juillet 2008 et accusé de « sodomie » avec un assistant de 23 ans. En droit malaisien, une relation sexuelle anale prouvée est passible d'une peine d'emprisonnement de 20 ans maximum. En octobre 2008. M. Ibrahim a pu retourner au Parlement et poursuivre son ambition de devenir Premier Ministre.

Depuis 2008 le festival « Seksualiti Merdeka » (Liberté de sexualité) se déroule tous les ans et propage la diversité. En novembre 2011 cependant, le festival fut interdit, des politiciens et des musulmans religieux jugeant immoral cet événement. L'interdiction semble manifestement être nécessaire aux yeux des détracteurs depuis que le festival a attiré un intérêt médiatique plus important l'année précédente suite à une opération de communication. La situation des homosexuels est donc toujours aussi précaire, même si après l'enregistrement de leur déposition les hommes ont été relâchés.

Malgré ces restrictions, la Malaisie est une destination superbe et les Malais sont des gens sympathiques et tolérants: la bonne infrastructure du pays rend le voyage en outre assez confortable. Le paysage est surtout constitué de montagnes, de forêts tropicales et de rizières. Les îles de Penang (« perle de l'océan »), Langkawi et Pangkor ainsi que la côte orientale de la presqu'île de Malacca ont quelques unes de plus belles plages d'Extrême-Orient.

Malasia es un país islámico y la homosexualidad es ilegal: las prácticas homosexuales (sexo oral y anal) pueden ser castigadas con penas de cárcel de hasta 20 años y con flagelaciones públicas. No obstante, como extranjero, no debe temerse por estas penas tan drásticas. Sorprende todavía como, bajo estas condiciones, existe en las ciudades un cierto ambiente muy variado. La discreción hace que tanto la población como la policia lo ignoren. Hay incluso algunas organizaciones gays que, sin embargo, no reciben apenas apoyos. La prostitución está prohibida.
Anwar Ibrahim, el presidente del grupo parlamentario del partido de la oposición en Malaysia, fue arrestado en julio de 2008 y acusado de „sodomía" con un asistente de 23 años. Según el derecho malayo, el sexo anal puede ser castigado con una pena de hasta 20 años de privación de libertad. En octubre de 2008, no obstante, el Sr. Ibrahim volvió a sentarse en el Parlamento y sigue con su objetivo de convertirse en primer ministro.
Desde 2008 tiene lugar anualmente el festival "Seksualiti Merdeka" (la libertad de la sexualidad), que promueve la diversidad. En noviembre de 2011, el festival fue prohibido después de que políticos y religiosos musulmanes declararán este evento como "inmoral". Las facciones críticas han considerado esta prohibición como necesaria desde que el año pasado el festival recibiera una mayor atención de los medios gracias a una campaña de relaciones públicas.
Pese a estas limitaciones, en Malasia se puede disfrutar de unas buenas vacaciones ya que los malayos son un pueblo muy amable y abierto y gracias a una infraestructura bastante buena, el viaje puede resultar muy cómodo. La mayor parte del país está compuesto por montañas, selvas tropicales y campos de arroz. Las islas de Penang (la Perla de Oriente), Langkawi y Pangkor así como la costa oriental de la península malaya tienen unas de las playas más bonitas del Lejano Oriente.

La Malaysia è un Paese islamico e l'omosessualità è vietata: gli atti omosessuali (sesso anale e orale) possono essere puniti fino a 20 anni di carcere e con flagellazione pubblica. Per gli stranieri, tuttavia, non sussiste il pericolo per queste punizioni così severe. Quello che stupisce è come qui sia riuscita a svilupparsi una scena così variopinta in queste condizioni così ostili. Forse la discrezione di questa scena è un motivo per non essere risultati visibili alla polizia e in pubblico. Ci sono addirittura alcune organizzazioni gay che però non hanno molto sostegno. La prostituzione è vietata.
Anwar Ibrahim, capo del gruppo parlamentare del maggior partito di opposizione in Malesia, è stato arrestato con l'accusa di avere praticato ‚sodomia' con un assistente ventitreenne. In Malesia il comprovato rapporto anale può costare fino a venti anni di carcere. In ottobre del 2008 Anwar Ibrahim è ritornato in parlamento e continua a perseguire il suo scopo: diventare primo ministro.
Dal 2008 si svolgeva annualmente il festival „Seksualiti Merdeka" (Libertà Sessuale), un festival attraverso il quale si intendeva promuovere la diversità. A novembre del 2011 il festival è stato vietato in seguito alle pressioni da parte della politica e dei fondamentalisti islamici che deprecavano l'evento definendolo ‚immorale'. Secondo i critici il divieto era necessario, poiché l'anno precedente, il festival, tramite un'iniziativa di pubbliche relazioni, aveva attirato molte attenzioni da parte dei mass media.
Nonostante queste limitazioni, in Malaysia si possono comunque trascorrere delle bellissime vacanze. La gente qui si distingue per la sua cordialità e apertura nei confronti dei turisti. L'infrastruttura turistica è piuttosto efficiente. Il paesaggio della Malaysia è costituito prevalentemente da montagne, risaie, foreste pluviali e tropicali. Le isole di Penang („Perla dell'Est"), Langkawi, Pangkor e la costa orientale della penisola offrono alcune delle più belle spiagge dell'estremo Oriente.

NATIONAL GROUPS

■ **PT Foundation** (G MA T) Mon-Fri 9-18h
7C-1, Jalan Ipoh Kechil (off Jln Raja Laut) ✉ 50350 Kuala Lumpur *Off Jalan Raja Laut* ☎ (03) 4044 4611 🖳 www.ptfmalaysia.org
Previously known as Pink Triangle Malaysia. Community-based, voluntary non-profit organization providing HIV/AIDS education, prevention, anonymous tests, care and support programmes, gender and sexuality counseling, support groups and empowerment programmes. Reaches out to gay men, transgenders, sex workers, drug users and PLHIV. Counselling hotline from 19.30-21.30 (Monday-Fri, except public holidays)
phone: 03-4044 5455 / 5466

Alor Setar (Kedah) ☎ 04

CRUISING

-Hospital Alor Setar Car Park (from stadium/Merdeka garden it is only 3 minutes walk diagonally across the big roundabout, very close to hospital car park area; be discreet. Quite a busy place after dark)
-Bidara Pool (next to the KFC in Jalan Stadium)
-Merdeka Garden inside and along road, near the benches (at night)
-Stadium Darul Aman. Near entrance to Maksak gym, opp. Merdeka Garden. (At night, AYOR)
-Shopping Centers: City Point (old wing) groundfloor, Sentosa, 1st. and 2nd. floor facilities, Star Parade, groundfloor facility.

Bukit Mertajam

CRUISING

-The garden on the hill inside Taman Bukit Indah (beside St. Annes) at night
-Taman Hwa Seng (just opp. mini market beside Jln Rozhan, around the Alma, Bukit Mertajam area), river beside playground, after 20h.

Butterworth ☎ 0749

SAUNAS/BATHS

■ **U 2** (B DR G M MSG SB VS) Mon-Thu 19-24h, Fri-Sun 17-24h
71A & B, Jln Perai Empat, Bandar Perai Jaya *Behind the Megamall*
☎ 016 498 0895
Mainly Malay and Indian guests, with a mix of body types from young sports to chubs.

CRUISING

-Ampang Jajar Garden near Permatang Pauh, noon-5pm, young Malay and Chinese guys
-Park between old British Fortress and city hall, after 22h (AYOR, R), beware of police decoys
-Swimming pool in Seberang Jaya, on Sat & Sun.

Georgetown ☎ 04

BARS

■ **Bagan Lounge** (B glm MA) 15-2, Fri & Sat -3h, closed Sun
Bagan, 18 Jln Bagan Jermal *Near Gurney Drive* ☎ (04) 226 4977
🖳 www.32atthemansion.com
Cozy and relaxing ambience.

■ **Beach Blanket Babylon** (B D GLM m MA)
32 Jalan Sultan Ahmad Shah *Opp. the E&O Hotel* ☎ (04) 2638 101
Swanky design on two levels. Good snacks and desserts. Gents night every Sunday.

■ **Color pub and lounge** (B glm m MA ST)
Jalan Larut *Near the Royal Hotel* ☎ (04) 604 226 7888
No cover charge.

RESTAURANTS

■ **Perut Rumah** (glm M MA OS) 11-22.30h
17 Jln Kelawei ☎ (04) 227 9917

In a restored 100-year-old mansion not far from Gurney. Gay-owned and specializing in Peranakan cuisine.

CRUISING

-Fitness at Gurney Plaza 7th floor, some chinese gays in the steam bath and dry sauna, action possible but be discrete
-Gurney Plaza Shopping Center, facilities at ground floor (men only)
-Komtar Shopping Mall, facilities on 2nd floor and up
-Batu Feringghi Beach near the International Hotel after 16h and back of the Ship restaurant
-Tanjung Bunga beach, between Paradise hotel/International School and at the rocks at the end, especially afternoons and early evenings
-Midlands Park Shopping Center (One Stop Complex), outside KFC and facilities on ground- and 1st floor
-Penang Youth Park, facilities near the shop and area behind shops with tables to play checkers, afternoon from 14-17h
-Moon Gate near the entrance of Penang Botanical garden (popular with joggers during the day) and near the waterfall
-Permata swimming pool at Farlim, Air Hitam (best after 17h).

Ipoh (Perak)  07

CAFES

■ **Friend's Café** (glm m MA OS)
Ipoh Garden East
Nice place to hang out.

MASSAGE

■ **DMAN Male Massage** (GLM MA MSG)
1/F 94-A Jln Raja Ekram *near Rega-Lodge Hotel* ☎ 012 517 7677
The one and only gay-owned and managed business in Ipoh. Teakwood ambience with 9 individual, spacious rooms, offering quality full-body massage. Clean and well-kept. Good selection of trained masseurs.

CRUISING

-Birch Memorial Clock Tower, Old Town and surrounding car park. Mostly late at night after the nearby food center closes. Stretches down to the double storey car park below
-Garden in front of Ipoh Railway Station, around and near the fountain. Very cruisy at night
-The Railway Station
-Ipoh Club Padang in front of St Michael School
-JUSCO Ipoh, 2 Jln Teh Lean Swee. Shopping center is cruisy on weekends and during public holidays, the garden in front is busy after 8pm until morning, especially on holidays
-The swimming pool at the Ipoh Stadium has some gay cruising.

Johor Bahru ☎ 07

BARS

■ **AJ** (B glm m MA)
77 Jln Perisai, Taman Sri Tebrau ☎ (07) 334 9604
Karaoke Bar, Pub & Café.

■ **Warung Idaman** (B g MA)
1 Susur Larkin Perdana
Karaoke bar, popular with the locals.

RESTAURANTS

■ **Riz's** (B glm M MA OS) Tue-Thu 18-1, Fri & Sat -3h
No.134 Jalan Dato' Sulaiman, Taman Century ☎ (607) 335 9904
🖳 rizscafe.multiply.com
Popular with local gays. Nice and romantic. The owner is very creative.

SAUNAS/BATHS

■ **Maze. The** (B cc DR G LAB m P SB WH WO) 16-23, WE 14-23h
77A & 79A Jalan Perisai, Taman Sri Tebrau *Opp. Crystal Crown Hotel*
☎ (07) 335 5680 🖳 www.themazejb.net
Busy sauna with TV-lounge and private cabins. Nice Jacuzzi. Wed: discount for youngsters, Thu: crowded with Indians.

■ **People Like Us Spa Sanctuary** (B DU G I MA MSG OS RR SA SB WH) Daily 15-2h
7 Jln Tun Abdul Razak Susur 1/1 *Opposite Zen Zeng Hotel*
☎ (07) 227 1069 🖳 plu1069.com
Gay bath house in a secluded spot near the Danga Mall on 2 floors.

■ **V Gym Spa Centre** (B DR DU G I MA MSG NU RR SA SB VS WH WO) Mon-Fri 13-23, Sat & Sun 11-23h
8-02 & 8-03 Jln Permas 10/5, Bandar Baru Permas Jaya
☎ (07) 607 387 3733 🖳 www.vgym-spa.com
Clean and spacious men's club.

MASSAGE

■ **Artemis Traditional Massage** (AC b cc G MA MSG)
38A Jalan Abiad, Taman Tebrau Jaya ☎ (07) 335 2262
Very good men-to-men massage. Ordinary traditional massage and Urut Batin provided, special male potency massage.

■ **Home Massage Gallery** (G MA MSG)
10 Jln Camar 10, Taman Perling ☎ (07) 235 2369
🖳 gardenhome.moonfruit.com
Offering quality massage and luxurious full body scrub. Nice tropical garden with fountains. Call to make an appointment.

CRUISING

-Lido Beach at the war memorial, just opposite Pusat Islam, and along the beach
-MPJB Pool in the early evening after 17.30h
-Sungai Segget near traffic circle with fountain and nearby car park (near UMNO complex, west of the water). Late night, especially weekends.

Kota Kinabalu – Sabah ☎ 088

BARS

■ **Q Bar** (AC B cc D GLM MA ST) 20-1, Sat & Sun -2h
Jln Gaya 50 ☎ (088) 230 722
Bar with pool table and small dance floor. Gay owned.

■ **Shenanigans** (AC B CC D glm MA)
B/F Hyatt Hotel ☎ (088) 318 888
Popular nightspot with handsome gay men.

■ **Upperstar** (AC B D glm MA OS)
Jln Datuk Salleh Sulong *Opp. Hyatt Hotel*

CRUISING

-Fitness at Hyatt Regency Hotel, some local gays in the sauna, action possible but be discrete
-Fitness at Promenade Hotel
-All along the road in front of the KFC bandaran which is located directly opposite the only cinema in the city (T)
-Centrepoint shopping center
-Long distance bus terminal at night, transgenders
-Hyatt Hotel entrance, pedestrian pathway connecting Jln Datuk Salleh Sulong to Wisma Merdeka is very cruisy. Sit in Mosaic café at one end or hang out near the shopping mall entrance at the other end
-Prince Philip Park, Tanjung Aru (near the pond and the circle with fountain, late night, some hustler decoys – AYOR)
-Anjung Senja hawker centre, waterfront opposite the Promenade Hotel, evenings.

Kuala Lumpur ☎ 03

BARS

■ **Palace Bar** (B GLM M S YC)
Block N, Jalan 3/93A, Off Batu 2 1/2 Jalan Cheras *opp. Payathin Food Court* ☎ (03) 9205 6280 🖳 www.palacebar.blogspot.com
Mostly gay crowd here at this contemporary, friendly and relaxed bar, lounge and karaoke.

■ **Vogue Pub & Bar** (B glm m MA ST)
46G Jln Metro Pudu 2 *off Jln Yew* ☎ (03) 9222 6168
Gay show every Sat night.

CAFES

BJBS (b g MA)
G/F 115, Jalan 3/93, Taman Miharja Cheras
Meeting and cruising point for local gays.

Café Café (b glm M MA) 18-24h
175 Jalan Maharajalela ☏ (03) 2141 8141 🖳 www.cafecafekl.com
Gay owned and staff, high-drama decor, mainly French and Italian meals.

Coffee Klub (B GLM m MA OS)
Plaza Berjaya, Jln Imbi
Coffee specialties, and snacks like satays and noodles. Owner welcomes all gays, especially chubs and their admirers.

Khun Bear Café (B G m MA s) 18-1h, closed Tue & Wed
2/F G97, 97-1 Jln 3/93 (off Jln Lombong), Taman Miharja, Cheras
☏ (03) 9200 6133
Crowd is primarily Asian chubs and their admirers.

DANCECLUBS

Blue Boy (AC B D G MA s) 22-3h
54 Jalan Sultan Ismail *Entrance off Jalan Sultan Ismail, behind Pizza Hut*
☏ (03) 242 1067 🖳 www.blueboy-kl.com
Packed on Fri & Sat nights.

Enigma (AC B D gLm m MA) 18h-open end
23-1 Plaza Danau 2, Jln 4/109F, Taman Danau Desa *Club is accessed by a stairway and entry door on first landing is unmarked* ☏ (03) 7987 9211
Lesbian-owned club and only pub in town that caters largely for women. It's a safe and friendly high-style atmosphere, with bar, pool table, and private lounge nooks for intimate conversations.

Frangipani (AC B glm MA) Monday closed
25 Changkat Bukit Bintang ☏ (03) 2144 3001
World-class club. On Fridays a very busy and popular gay location in KL.

Marketplace (! AC B G MC) Sat nights
4A, Lorong Yap Kwan Seng ☏ (03) 2166-0752
🖳 www.marketplacekl.com
Cool view of Petronas Towers. Hot house beats. Rooftop chill-out space (popular).

Queen Club. La (AC B D G YC) Wed-Sun 21-3h
5 Jln P. Ramlee ☏ (017) 325 9985
Disco on two floors.

RESTAURANTS

69 Bistro (AC B glm M MA) Mon-Fri 16.30-1.30, Sat & Sun 14-1.30h
No 14.Jalan Kampung Dollah,Off Jalan Pudu ☏ (03) 2144 3369
🖳 www.69bistro.com.my
This gay-owned restaurant is a living tribute to the 60s with its mod prints, retro-flavored furniture, vintage fabrics and several antique pieces. Horoscope and tarot card readings available daily from 18h-midnight.

Rahsia (B CC glm M MA WE) Mon-Fri 12-24, Sat & Sun 16-24h
13 Jalan Damai *Off Jalan Aman / Tun Razak, near Crown Princess Hotel / Empire Tower* ☏ (03) 2144 0059 🖳 rahsia-kl.com
Ethnic charm meets cosmopolitan chic: Rahsia is located in a 60's bungalow surrounded by green. The ambience is invigoratingly peaceful, yet stylish. Complimentary Cosmopolitan cocktails and 50 % off beers and spirits daily 16-20h.

SAUNAS/BATHS

101 Spa & Beauty (b DR G m MSG SA SB)
Daily from 15h-open end
7-1, Jln 5/91, Taman Shamelin Perkasa ☏ (03) 016-6446727
In the Shamelin/Cheras area.

Chakran (b DU G H M MA MSG NU OS RR SA SB VS WH)
Mon-Thu 14-23, Fri-Sun 12-23h
1/F 22A-B Jln Padang Belia, Brickfields *Sentral Monorail Station or Tun Sambathan Monorail Station, look for the YMCA. After 7Eleven look for shop #22* ☏ (03) 345 7178
Sauna on 3 floors. Friendly staff and management keep up the high quality of this men's social club.

Day Thermos (AC b DR DU G I LAB m MA MSG RR SA SB WO)
14-23h
40-6A Jalan Sultan Ismail *Around the cnr. from Blue Boy*
☏ (03) 2144 9648 🖳 www.daythermos.com
Very clean and friendly to foreigners with a great location.

Kakiku (b DU G I m RR SA SB VS WH WO) Mon-Fri 17-24, Sat & Sun and before public holiday 14-24h
2/F 109-2, Jln Cerapu 1, Cheras *At Sang Kee Restaurant*
☏ (03) 9282-5303

Mandi Manda (B DR DU G I LAB m MA OS RR SA SB)
Mon-Fri 17-24, Sat 14-24, Sun -23h, last admission 23h
31 Jalan 109E, Desa Business Park, Taman Desa *Off Old Klang Road*
☏ (03) 7980 3900 🖳 www.mandimanda.com

Otot-Otot (! AC b DR DU G I m MA MSG OS P RR S SA SB SNU VS WH WO) Mon-Fri 17-24, Sat & Sun 13-24h
7a 2nd floor, Jalan Ipoh Kechil *Off Jalan Raja Laut, the Star PWTC LRT station, „Chow Kit Monorail" and KTM train station „Putra commuter" are within walking distance* ☏ (03) 4044 3369 🖳 www.otot2.com
Look for mailbox with name. Do not mix with nearby mainstreet Jalan Ipoh. A great gym/sauna with clean and open atmosphere. Big steam room and several dark rooms.

Senjakala spa for men (AC b CC DU g M MA MSG OS SB WH WO) Daily 12-24h
20 Jalan Pudu Raya *Near Pudu Raya Terminal* ☏ (03) 2031 8082
🖳 www.senjakala.com
Services include massage, body work and skin care. Very friendly and helpful staff, great choice of massage styles and body work. „Extra services" from the therapists are not allowed to provided for. Spot-checks by the authorities take place regularly.

Senses (AC B DR DU G I m MSG OC RR SA SB VS)
2/F 27-2 & 3 Jln Tun Sambanthan 4 *Turn left from tun Sambantham Monorail Station and walk down the covered walkway next to the school yard. Keep going across the intersection and look for Sentral Bistro restaurant in shop on the left. Stairwell with a sign overhead Blind TMC Centre. Go to 2nd floor to unmarked glass door entrance*
☏ (03) 2260 6018
Popular and friendly. Clean and well-managed. The friendly crowd is more mature with plenty of uncles and chubs

Sentral Massage & SPA (B DU g m MA MSG RR SA SB VS)
11-23h
1/F Jalan Thamby Pillai, Brickfields *Next to ‚Super Blind Massage'*
☏ (03) 2260 1018
Popular with masculine, mature men, chubs and their admirers.

FITNESS STUDIOS

California Fitness (g MA WO)
3/F Lot T-011, Midvalley Megamall, Mid Valley City ☎ (03) 2284 3833
Cruisy gym and busy men's sauna (be discreet!).

MASSAGE

Absolute Massage (G MSG SA) 12-20h
Jalan PJU 8/1, Metropolitan Square, Damansara Perdana Petaling Jaya *Petaling Jaya* ☎ (019) 273 9660 🖳 absolutesauna.tripod.com
Massage by stocky and mature male masseurs. Hotel outcall massage possible

Aromadamai Day Spa (AC b G MA MSG SB)
21A Tingkat 2, Jalan Tun Sambanthan 4, Brickfields ☎ (019) 377 3358
Aromatherapy massage, floral and herb bathes.

Touch. A (AC G MSG WE) 14-23h
1/F 23C Jln Desa Jaya, Taman Desa *1st floor* ☎ (03) 7981 0136
🖳 www.atouch.com.my
Small, quiet and clean. Great environment.

HOTELS

Seasons View (AC B BF cc H M MA)
61 Jalan Alor *Off Bukit Bintang, near Blue Boy Club* ☎ (03) 2145 7577
🖳 www.seasonsview.com
Small budget hotel with friendly staff. No problem with overnight friends.

GUEST HOUSES

Pondok Lodge (AC b glm I m MA OS) All year
20-2C Jalan Changkat Raja Chulan *Bukit Bintang District*
☎ (03) 2142 8449 🖳 www.pondoklodge.com
Good standard budget accommodation and basic, traditional Malay living with a beautiful roof garden. Near tourist attractions. Internet access, TV-lounge with movie nights.

Pujangga Homestay (AC b glm I m MA PK) All year
21 Jalan Berangan off Jalan Nagasari *Near Istana Hotel. Monorail Jin Raja Chulan or Sultan Ismail* ☎ (03) 2143 1279
🖳 www.pujangga-homestay.com
Small, gay-friendly guest house.

Westover Lodge (AC H I) All year, 24hrs
No. 4, 2nd Floor, Medan Pasar *2 mins walk from Masjid Jamek & Pasar Seni Station* ☎ (03) 2070 1286 🖳 www.westoverlodge.com
A friendly guest house located in the heart of Kuala Lumpur's famous China Town.

SWIMMING

The following public pools can be interesting for the gay visitor:
-Bandar Tun Razak, Cheras (swimming pool and park. Best after sunset)
-Chin Woo Stadium pool (near Chinatown) ore gays after 5pm
-MPPJ pool, Kelana Jaya (Showers, locker rooms. Be discreet)
-Pandamaran swimming pool complex, after 19h in the shower room, many naked guys.

CRUISING

All are AYOR:
-Sungei Wang Plaza, Jalan Bukit Bintang (commercial centre between Hotel Apoll and Regent Hotel, 3rd floor)
-Kota Raya (shopping complex on Jalan Chen Lock)
-Taman Permaisuri Park (next to football stadium)
-Central Market (toilets on ground floor) ans area between back entrance and bridge, watch out for security-staff!
-Low Yat Plaza, Bukit Bintang
-Sunway Pyramid shopping mall (toilets)
-Shopping Malls in Bukit Bintang: Star Hill Shopping Center (opp. Regent Hotel) especially on highher floors, KL Plaza, from The Coffee Bean to the facilities, Low Yat Plaza, IT mall buzzing with young computer nerds, Pavilion, for brand kings and label queens, Sungei Wang Plaza, on top floor, near the Reliance. Beware of pickpockets
-Bintang Walk (the whole Jalan Bukit Bintang, starting at Marriott Hotel until Lot10 and Jln Alor's hawker Food street) is KL's mayor cruising area nicknamed the „Catwalk" especially in the evenings
-Railway Station Park (after dark, T)
-Cheras Shopping Mall facilities
-AmCorp Mall, ground- and 1st. floor facilities
-Basketball court park, Jln BP 1/5, Bandar Bukit Puchong, Puchong District, a cruising place for many gays at night, esp. after 22h
-between old Subang International airport and Petaling Jaya, about 8km from KL City Center, behind the Kelana Jaya Stadium, by the lake, very cruisy with more upscale locals, after dark till very late
-Aquaria Shopping Center, leading to the underground passage to KLCC, the facility is a meeting place, especially after work
-Endah Parade, cruisy facilities in the upper floors, week-days and after office hours
-Wisma Rampai facilities in Sri Rampai are quite cruisy, within the office building, quite safe and not many people.

Kuantan ☎ 09

BARS

Cocoloco (AC B CC glm M MA)
Teluk Cempedak *Part of Hyatt Regency Hotel Complex*

SWIMMING

-Tekluk Cempedak Beach (best at night)
-Megamall Shopping Centre, Toilets on 1st, 2nd & 3rd Floor (AYOR).

Kuching – Sarawak ☎ 082

BARS

Grappa (B GLM MA)
Jalan Padungan *Next to Planet Sambal*
Mixed club. Most are young MSM/TG during Wednesday, Friday and Saturday.

Planet (B glm MA)
3rd Mile, Jln Rock
Karaoke Bar, mostly mature Chinese crowd.

CAFES

Khaturistiwa (B D glm m OS YC) 24hrs
Mostly young Chinese crowd.

Starbucks Coffee (b glm m MA)
The Spring
Opened in Jan 2008 and quickly drawing a gay crowd.

The Gallery Arts and Café (B glm YC)
Riverbank Suite *Jln Tunku Abdul Rahman*
Popular on weekends.

FITNESS STUDIOS

Hilton Kuching Gym (MSG NG SA SB)
Jalan Tunku, Abdul Rahman
Great Steam Room, be discreet!

MASSAGE

Borneo Traditional Massage (glm MA)
Muara Tabuan ☎ (082) 016 888 9956
Native traditional massage by well trained male masseurs, call for appointments, in- and outcall.

SWIMMING

-KMC public swimming pool, Padungan district (mixed crowd, be discreet. Best in evening)
-Setampak swimming pool (very cruisy in the evenings)
-Waterworld, in the housing estate of BDC Stampin area, formerly Stampark swimming-pool, mixed crowd (be discreet), very cruisy in the evenings.

CRUISING

All are AYOR:
-Sarawak Museum (back garden, track up hill, after 19h)

-Kuching Water Front (some foreigners, from 21h until late)
-Kuching Reservoir Park, Jalan Taman Budaya (best at WE between 15-19h)
-Sarawak Plaza (toilets on ground level)
-Wisma Satok (toilets on 1st floor)
-Wisma Saberkas (toilets on ground floor)
-The Spring Shopping Centre, facilities
-Boulevard Shopping Centre, facilities
-Travillion area, several Bars & Cafés (Amoebar, Barzing & Jungle) YC.

Langkawi ☎ 04

BARS

■ **Chime** (B D glm MA)
Teluk Nibong Pulau *in the Sheraton Hotel*
Can be interesting on Mon. Locals and tourists.

■ **Enigma** (B D GLM MA)
Jalan Pantai Tengah *in the Aseania Hotel*
Mixed disco.

■ **Sunba** (B glm MA)
Pantai Tengah
Mixed pub with retro music and live band. Very gay friendly staff.

CAFES

■ **Atira Cyber Cafe** (b glm m MA)
Kuah Town

Melaka ☎ 06

CRUISING

-Old Padang Park between St. Paul's Hill and A&W restaurant (best after 23h; AYOR MA r WE).

Miri – Sarawak ☎ 085

BARS

■ **Cherries Berries** (AC B D m YC)
Pelita Commercial Center *Near the Grand Palace Hotel.*
Young crowd. Mixed venue, popular with gay tourists.

Maldives

Name: Malediven · Maldives · Maldivas · Maldive
Location: South-Asia
Initials: MV
Time: GMT +5
International Country Code: ☎ 960 (no area codes)
International Access Code: ☎ 00
Language: Maldivian Divehi (official language)
Area: 298 km² = 115.06 sq mi.
Currency: 1 Rufiyaa (Rf) = 100 Laari
Population: 329,000
Capital: Male
Religions: Sunni Muslim (almost 100%)
Climate: Dry season between December and April. In November & April water clarity is ideal for diving.

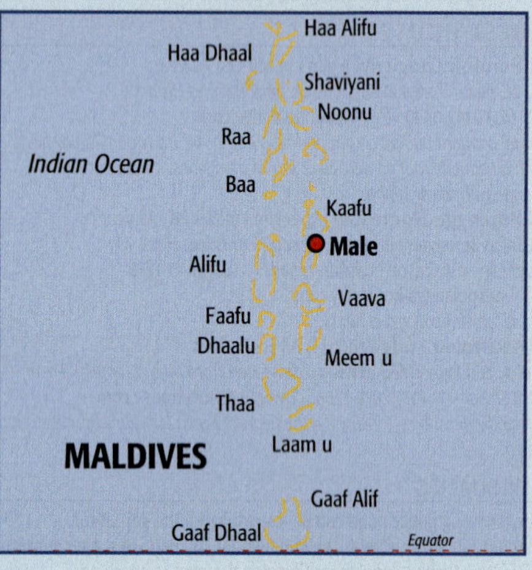

The Indian penal code applies on all the Island of the Maldives and according to this code, homosexuality is illegal. For gay couples visiting the islands we recommend you act discreetly. The Maldive Islands are not for those looking for entertainment. They are a group of small islands with probably the best beaches in the world, ideal for those who wish to relax. Water sports as well as diving are further attractions on offer on these paradise islands.

Das indische Strafgesetzbuch gilt für alle Inseln der Malediven und betrachtet Homosexualität als Delikt. Schwulen Pärchen, die die Inseln besuchen, empfehlen wir daher, sich diskret zu verhalten. Ein Aufenthalt auf den Malediven ist nicht für Touristen zu empfehlen, die das große Spektakel suchen. Die kleinen, paradiesischen Inseln sind allerdings ideal zum Entspannen und haben die wahrscheinlich schönsten Strände der Welt. Abgesehen davon kann man hier auch hervorragend Tauchen und Wassersport treiben.

Le code pénal indien est valable sur toutes les îles des Maldives et pénalise l'homosexualité. Nous recommandons donc aux couples gays qui visitent ces îles de rester discrets. Ceux qui recherchent le grand spectacle ne le trouveront pas aux Maldives : les petites îles paradisiaques offrent plutôt le repos, sans doute les plus belles plages du monde et la possibilité de pratiquer la plongée sous-marine ainsi que divers autres sports aquatiques.

El Código Penal de la India es válido para todas las islas Maldivas y éste considera la homosexualidad como un delito. Recomendamos a las parejas homosexuales que visiten estas islas que se comporten de forma discreta. No es recomendable una visita a las Maldivas para aquellos turistas que busquen grandes espectáculos. No obstante, estas pequeñas y paradisíacas islas son ideales para relajarse y probablemente tienen las playas más bellas del mundo. Aparte de esto, aquí también se puede bucear y practicar deportes acuáticos.

Il codice penale dell'India vale per tutte le isole delle Maldive; secondo il codice penale, l'omosessualità è considerata un delitto. Quindi consigliamo alle coppie gay che visitano queste isole di comportarsi in maniera discreta. Le Maldive non sono un posto per chi cerca „action", tutt'altro, le paradisiache isole offrono una vacanza all'insegna del relax. Nelle Maldive ci sono fantastiche spiagge che probabilmente sono anche le più belle del mondo. Inoltre, le isole sono famose per le innumerevoli possibilità che offrono dal punto di vista degli sport acquatici e per l'immersione.

Emboodhu Finolhu

RESTAURANTS

Quench Restaurant (M MA NG)
☎ 324 571
Dishes such as Nasi Goreng, Chicken Maryland, Fish Kebab and Maldivian hot and spicy dishes.

HOTELS

Taj Exotica Resort and Spa (AC B BF M MA NG OS PI RWB RWS RWT WO) All year
PO Box 20117 ☎ 442 200 🖳 www.tajhotels.com
64 palm-thatched villas, beach villas with private plunge pools, and lagoon villas on stilts with their own private sun deck. All modern conviences. Resort for discreet gay couples.

Rahdhebai Magu

RESTAURANTS

Farivalhu Restaurant (M MA NG)
☎ 317 755
Interesting diners can sometimes be found here.

Malta

Name: Malte
Location: South Europe
Initials: M
Time: GMT+1
International Country Code: ☎ 356 (no area codes)
International Access Code: ☎ 00
Language: Maltese, English
Area: 315,6 km² / 122 sq mi.
Currency: 1 Euro (Euro) = 100 Cents
Population: 404,000
Capital: Valletta
Religions: 95,4% Roman Catholic
Climate: Mediterranean climate. Winters are mild and rainy, summers hot and dry.

Malta has no sodomy laws; however sex with minors is punishable if the minor himself/herself or his/her parents file a complaint with the police. The age of sexual consent is 18.
Malta's recent inclusion into the EU has promoted some improvements, such as the introduction of new regulations against sexual orientation discrimination in the workplace. These resolutions however still fall short of the full implementation the corresponding European Directives. Further gay-friendly legislation do not exist as yet. There is no partnership/civil union law, or legislation protecting sexual minorities for example.
On the social level however, things have been improving. Malta now has an active gay lobby and visibility of gay issues in the media is on the increase and is generally given positive coverage. Incidents of gay bashing are almost non-existent and the harassment on the basis of sexual orientation is also minimal.

In Malta gibt es keine Gesetze gegen den Geschlechtsverkehr unter Männern, aber sexuelle Handlungen mit Minderjährigen sind strafbar, wenn der/die Minderjährige selbst oder seine/ihre Eltern bei der Polizei Anzeige erstatten. Das sexuelle Mindestalter liegt bei 18 Jahren.
Die kürzlich erfolgte Aufnahme Maltas in die EU hat einige Verbesserungen gebracht wie beispielsweise die Verabschiedung neuer Bestimmungen, die eine auf der sexuellen Orientierung basierende Diskriminierung am Arbeitsplatz verhindern sollen. Diese Gesetze bleiben allerdings weit hinter einer vollen Implementierung der betreffenden europäischen Richtlinien zurück. Bisher bestehen keine weiteren schwulenfreundlichen Gesetzesinitiativen. Es gibt zum Beispiel weder gesetzliche Regelungen für Partnerschaften bzw. eheähnliche Verhältnisse noch solche zum Schutz sexueller Minderheiten.
Auf sozialer Ebene hat sich die Lage allerdings deutlich verbessert. Malta verfügt mittlerweile über eine aktive Schwulenlobby, und die Sichtbarkeit schwuler Belange in den Medien steigt bei einer generell positiven Berichterstattung. Es gibt so gut wie keine Fälle von Gewalt gegen Schwule, und Belästigungen wegen der sexuellen Orientierung kommen ebenfalls selten vor.

Il n'existe pas de loi concernant l'homosexualité masculine à Malte mais le détournement de mineur est un délit et les parents ou le/la mineur(e) peuvent porter plainte. La majorité sexuelle est fixée à 18 ans. L'intégration de Malte à l'Union Européenne a apporté quelques améliorations comme par exemple un texte empêchant la discrimination fondée sur l'orientation sexuelle sur le lieu de travail. Ces lois restent malgré tout largement en deçà des directives européennes et aucune loi n'est prévue pour améliorer la situation des homosexuel(le)s maltais, comme par exemple un partenariat enregistré ou une protection des minorités sexuelles.
Au niveau social, la situation s'est par contre largement améliorée : Malte dispose désormais d'un lobby gay et la visibilité des homosexuel(le)s a augmenté dans les médias et les reportages sont généralement positifs. Il n'y a pratiquement pas de cas d'agression envers les gays et le harcèlement est également plutôt rare.

En Malta no existe ninguna ley contra las relaciones sexuales entre hombres pero los actos sexuales con menores están penalizados, si el mismo menor o sus progenitores lo denunciasen a la policia. La edad de consentimiento está fijada en los 18 años.
La reciente incorporación de Malta a la Unión Europea ha supuesto algunas mejoras como, por ejemplo, la aprobación de nuevas disposiciones que deberán evitar cualquier discriminación en los puestos de trabajo basada en la orientación sexual. Estas leyes, sin embargo, todavía quedan lejos de la plena ejecución de las directivas europeas en este ámbito. Hasta ahora no existe aún ninguna iniciativa legislativa a favor de los homosexuales. Así pues, no hay ni normativas legales sobre las parejas de hecho o relaciones similares ni tampoco leyes que protejan las minorías sexuales.

En el aspecto social, la situación ha mejorado bastante. Malta dispone de un grupo de presión homosexual activo y ha aumentado la visibilidad de los homosexuales en los medios de comunicación con una actitud generalmente positiva hacia ellos. Apenas se producen agresiones a homosexuales y raramente hay molestias u ofensas por razón de la orientación sexual.

A Malta non ci sono leggi che riguardano i rapporti sessuali tra uomini, tuttavia i rapporti sessuali con minorenni sono perseguibili nel caso in cui gli stessi o i rispettivi genitori facciano una denuncia. L'età del consenso è di diciotto anni.
Il recente ingresso di Malta nell'Unione Europea ha portato alcuni miglioramenti come per esempio la ratifica di alcuni accordi che tutelano le discriminazioni (riguardanti gli orientamenti sessuali) sul posto di lavoro. Rispetto alle direttive europee queste leggi tuttavia non sono applicate in maniera completa. Fino ad adesso non sono state portate avanti altre iniziative di legge che tendono a migliorare la situazione dei diritti omosessuali. Non ci sono infatti regolamentazioni legislative riguardanti le coppie o le convivenze tra persone dello stesso sesso ne riguardanti la tutela delle minoranze sessuali.
Sul campo sociale, tuttavia, molte cose sono notevolmente migliorate. Adesso a Malta c'è una comunità gay molto attiva e la tematica omosessuale viene trattata dai mass media con accezioni sempre più positive.
Non ci sono casi di violenza nei confronti di omosessuali e le molestie nei confronti di particolari orientamenti sessuali sono molto rari.

NATIONAL GAY INFO

Gaymalta (GLM)
www.gaymalta.com
Gaymalta is a reference point for all the Maltese gay community and tourists visiting Malta.

NATIONAL GROUPS

Malta Gay Rights Movement (GLM MA) National Gay Helpline 21 43 00 06 (Mon, Wed, Fri 18-21h)
32, Parish street, Mosta ✉ MST 2021 Malta ☎ 21 43 00 09
www.maltagayrights.org
The Malta Gay Rights Movement is a non-governmental and non-profit organisation which was started in June of 2001.

Gozo – Gharb

RESTAURANTS

Salvina's (AC B BF CC glm H LM M MSG NR OS PI PK RES SA VEG WH WL) Restaurant: 12-15, 18-22, bar: 10-15, 18-1h
21 Frenc Ta'L-Gharb Street *Behind Gharb-Church* ☎ 21 55 25 05
Good food and friendly atmosphere.

Gozo – Marsalforn

SWIMMING

-San Blas Bay (direction Nadur. Sometimes NU but then AYOR)

Malta – Bugibba

CRUISING

-All along the sea front from Buggiba to Qawra Point.

Malta – Mgarr

SWIMMING

-Gnejna Beach and Pembroke Beach (Take bus 47 from Valletta, from Bugibba bus 51, from Sliema bus 652. Stop off at Ghajin Tuffieha Bay and walk through the narrow passage. NU on rocky plateau, many caves for action. AYOR, robbery reported, leave your valuables at the hotel!)

Malta – Mqabba

PRIVATE ACCOMMODATION

Vacanza Maltija (ac CC G MA OS PI)
www.gay-holiday-malta.com
Old Maltese farmhouse for rent.

Malta – Sliema

GUEST HOUSES

Soleado Guesthouse (AC B bf glm I M MSG OS PI RWB RWS RWT SA SB VA VS WH WO) All year
15, Ghar Id-Dud Street *Near German Embassy, Bus 11/12/13 Valletta and X2 from Airport* ☎ 21 33 44 15 www.soleadomalta.com
Gayfriendly guest house. 10% discount for Spartacus readers.

CRUISING

-Yacht marina Gardens in Gzira. Very popular. WE. Action in the bushes
-Tower Road (area near the Tower, overlooking Independence Gardens & Exiles Beach)
-Tigne Point (walk down Qui-Si-Sana Place and follow the rough track beyond the Crown Plaza Hotel towards Fort Tigne)

Malta – Valletta

BARS

Tom Bar (B G M MA) 11.30-14.30 (lunch, Oct.-March), 20.30-1h, closed Mon
1 Crucifix Hill, Floriana *Floriana, in walking distance from Valetta Terminus* ☎ 21 25 07 80 www.tombarmalta.webs.com
Two floors. Downstairs is the latest dance/club music. Very friendly staff.

SEX CINEMAS

City Light Cinema (AYOR DR G MA VS WE) 9-20h
56, St. John Street
Movie theatre showing straight Erotic movies; some action takes place discreetly.

APARTMENTS

Vallettastudios (glm I MA RWB RWS RWT VA) All year
63 Battery Street ☎ 21 25 17 48 www.vallettastudios.com
Two studios with kitchen and living/bedroom.

SWIMMING

-White Rocks (active after 14h), take bus 68 from Valletta to Bahar-Ic-Caghaq (NU).

CRUISING

Rent-boys operate in some cruising areas. Before taking someone with you, be sure to establish the nature of the transaction beforehand to avoid misunderstandings.
-Valletta Bus Terminal (in public toilet)
-Commonwealth Air Forces Memorial (car park)
-Porte de Bombes (Jubilee Gardens). Take the path on the left (facing the gate) leading along the ditch behind the trees. This is a daytime cruising area (AYOR at night).
-Gzira Garden, Gzira area
-Offshore Cafe, known to be a gathering place but the place itself is not gay.

Mauritius

Name: Maurice · Mauricio
Location: Southwestern Indian Ocean
Initials: MS
Time: GMT +4
International Country Code: ☏ 230
International Access Code: ☏ 00
Language: English, French, Creole
Area: 2,040 km² / 794 sq mi.
Currency: 1 Mauritius Rupie (MR) = 100 Cents
Population: 1,243,000
Capital: Port Louis
Religions: 50% Hindu, 26% Christian, 17% Muslim, 5% others
Climate: Tropical climate. Winter (Jul-Sep) is the best time to visit with less rain and humidity. The hottest time in summer (Jan-Apr) is very hot & humid with possible cyclones. Dec-Mar is the best time for diving, when the sea is clearest.

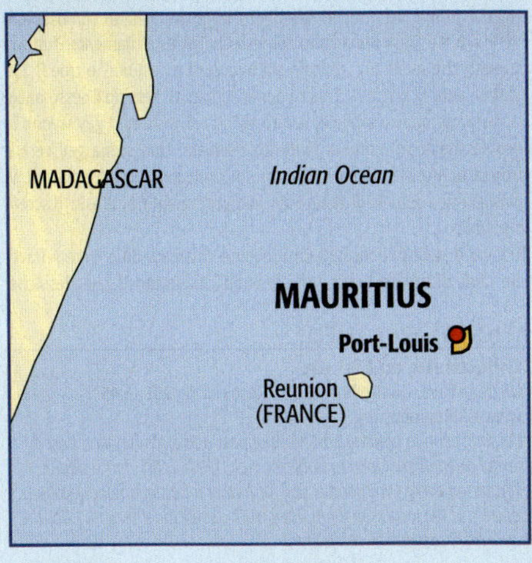

At a first glance, no law seems to exist which prohibits homosexuality. The laws however, do not directly apply to homosexuality. Worth mentioning is however in the paragraph 250 (5 years imprisonment for sodomy). Gays in Mauritius lead a secluded life. A real gay scene does not exist. Many men marry or lead double lives. Generally speaking inconspicuous conduct in public is recommended. Yet the free „Blue-Ocean-Travel" brochure with its stronger focus on lesbian and gay tourists has recently appeared. Even if its promotional efforts are more strongly addressed to couples, rather than single gay travellers hoping for sexual adventures with natives. Mauritius, the brochure suggests, is a wonderful travel destination for possible honeymoons. The first Mauritian Gay Pride (the Rainbow March, organized by „the Collectif Arc en Ciel"), was held in Rose Hill in May 2006 and attracted around 600 people. This group is right now advocating for the recognition of LGBT rights in the Mauritian law.
More than 200 Mauritian gays took part in a smaller version of gay Pride in June, called „The March of Gay Visibility", which according to the organisers was a great success despite the island's non recognition of homosexuality as a sexual orientation.

Auf den ersten Blick gibt es kein Gesetz, das Homosexualität verbietet. Die Gesetze nehmen keinen spezifischen Bezug auf Homosexualität. Zu erwähnen ist allerdings der „Sittlichkeits-Artikel" 250 (fünf Jahre Gefängnis auf Sodomie). Selbst freiwilliger Analverkehr ist demnach sittenwidrig. Gays führen auf Mauritius ein zurückgezogenes Leben, und eine richtige Szene gibt es nicht. Manche heiraten oder führen ein Doppelleben. Grundsätzlich wird ein unauffälliges Verhalten in der Öffentlichkeit empfohlen. Allerdings ist die kostenlose „Blue Ocean Travel" Broschüre erschienen, die verstärkt um schwule und lesbische Touristen wirbt. Diese Werbung richtet sich mehr an Paare, als an den alleinreisenden Homosexuellen mit Hoffnung auf sexuelle Abenteuer mit Einheimischen. Mauritius, so die Broschüre, eignet sich wunderbar als Reiseziel für etwaige Flitterwochen. Der erste CSD von Mauritius überhaupt (die Regenbogenparade, organisiert von der Gruppe „Collectif Arc en Ciel") konnte im Mai 2006 in Rose Hill stattfinden und hat etwa 600 Besucher angelockt. Die genannte Organisation setzt sich weiterhin für die rechtliche Gleichstellung der LGBT-Gemeinde auf Mauritius ein.
Im Juni haben über 200 schwule Mauritier unter dem Motto „Marsch für schwule Sichtbarkeit" an der abgespeckten Version eines CSD teilgenommen. Von ihren Organisatoren wurde die Demonstration angesichts der mangelnden Anerkennung, die der gleichgeschlechtlichen Liebe als sexueller Orientierung auf der Insel entgegengebracht wird, als Riesenerfolg gewertet.

A première vue, il n'existe aucune loi interdisant l'homosexualité et les textes n'en font même pas mention. Néanmoins, l'article 250 concernant le « respect des bonnes mœurs » condamne la sodomie même entre adultes consentants à 5 ans de prison. Les gays de l'île vivent donc leur homosexualité secrètement et il n'y a pas de milieu gay. Il est donc recommandé de rester discret. En outre est parue la brochure « Blue Ocean Travel « qui fait une publicité plus forte à destination des touristes homos et lesbiennes. Cette pub s'adresse plus aux couples qu'aux homos voyageant seuls et désirant des aventures sexuelles avec les autochtones. Selon la brochure, l'île Maurice est particulièrement adaptée aux éventuels voyages de noce.
La première Gay-Pride de l'île Maurice (la Rainbow March, organisée par le groupe « Collectif Arc-en-ciel « a néanmoins pu avoir lieu en mai 2006 à Rose Hill et a attiré 600 visiteurs. L'organisation continue de s'engager pour l'égalité des droits de la communauté LGBT de l'Île Maurice.
En Juin, plus de 200 Mauriciens gays ont défilé lors d'une gay pride allégée sous la devise « Marche pour la Visibilité homosexuelle « . Les organisateurs ont qualifiée la manifestation d'énorme succès, du fait de la faible reconnaissance apportée sur l'île à l'amour entre personnes de même sexe et à l'orientation sexuelle.

Al primer vistazo parece que no hay ninguna ley que prohíba la homosexualidad. Las leyes no hacen referencia específica a la homosexualidad. Sólo cabe mencionar el llamado „artículo 250 de la tradición" (5 años de cárcel por sodomía). Incluso el sexo anal voluntario está contra las normas. Los gays en Mauricio llevan una vida retirada y no existe un ambiente propiamente. Algunos se casan o llevan una doble vida. En general se recomienda un comportamiento discreto en público. En efecto, se ha publicado la revista gratuita „Blue Ocean Travel", que va orientada claramente a turistas gays y lesbianas. Esta publicación se dirige más a parejas, que a homosexuales solteros con esperanzas de encontrar una aventura sexual con la gente del lugar. Mauricio, según la publicación, es justamente un destino turístico fantástico para una semana de luna de miel.
La primera marcha del Orgullo Gay de Mauricio (la „Marcha del Arco Iris", organizada por el grupo „Collectif Arc en Ciel") pudo celebrarse en mayo de 2006 en Rose Hill y atrajo a unos 600 participantes. La mencionada organización sigue defendiendo la equiparación legal de las comunidades LGBT en Mauricio.
Más de 200 gays mauricianos participaron en junio en una descafeinada versión del Día del Orgullo Gay bajo el lema „Marcha por la Visibilidad Gay". Los organizadores de la manifestación, dada la falta de reconocimiento que tienen en la isla el amor entre parejas del

mismo sexo, como también la orientación sexual, la han considerado un autentico éxito.

A prima vista non ci sarebbero leggi che vietano l'omosessualità. Le leggi non citano l'omosessualità esplicitamente. Tuttavia va detto che esiste un „articolo sui buoni usi e costumi" e cioè il 250 (cinque anni di prigione previsti per la sodomia). Persino il sesso anale va, secondo questo articolo, contro gli usi e i costumi. I gay vivono la loro sessualità in maniera piuttosto riservata. Una scena gay vera e propria non esiste. Alcuni si sposano o conducono una doppia vita. Vi consigliamo, quindi, di tenere un comportamento piuttosto discreto in pubblico.

Tuttavia è stata pubblicata una brochure chiamata Blue Ocean Travel che viene distribuita gratis e che fa pubblicità tra turisti gay e lesbiche. Questa pubblicità è indirizzata più alle coppie che agli omosessuali single che viaggiano con la speranza di avventure sessuali con la gente del posto. La brochure precisa che le isole Mauritius sono una meta turistica ideale per le lune di miele. A maggio del 2006, nel quartiere di Rose Hill, ha avuto luogo il primo CSD (la „parata dell'arcobaleno", organizzata dal gruppo Collectif Arc en Ciel) delle Mauritius. Al corteo hanno partecipato circa 600 persone. L'organizzazione Collectif Arc en Ciel continua ad impegnarsi per la parificazione legale della comunità LGBT nelle Mauritius.

A giugno più di 200 gay delle Mauritius hanno partecipato ad una versione ridotta del CSD, con lo slogan „marcia per la visibilità gay". Considerato il fatto che sull'isola l'amore tra persone dello stesso sesso non viene riconosciuto, la manifestazione è stata ritenuta dagli organizzatori un grande successo.

NATIONAL GAY INFO

Collectif Arc en Ciel. Le
57 Av. de la Faye, Quatre Bornes ✉ Rose Hill ☏ 251 16 45
www.lalitmauritius.org
First organisation to fight against homophobia and discrimination based on sexual orientation. Open to public on Sat 11-15h. LGBT dance parties are organised every two months. Call for further information and locations. Organisers of the local Gay Pride. They work closely together with PILS, the national AIDS prevention company.

Grand Baie

BARS

Banana Beach Club (CC m MA NG OS S WE) Mon-Sat 11.30-2, Sun 6-?h
Coastal Road *Next to Caltex petrol station* ☏ 263 03 26
www.bananabeachclub.com
Garden bar with live music at WE. Very popular with tourists.

Bob Marley (B d glm OS r S ST t)
Route la Salette
Ask locals for directions.

Enfants Terribles. Les (B d m MA NG OS WE) Wed-Sun
Pointe aux Cannoniers
Somewhat stylish clientele.

DANCECLUBS

Buddha Club. The (B D MA NG WE) Wed-Sun 22h-open end
Coastal Road *Next to Star Dance Disco*
On Friday and Saturday with 3 dancefloors. Smart-casual dress is required.

N'Gyone (B D MA NG OS WE)
Royal Road *Rivière du Rempart* ☏ 263 7664
Innovative and stylish decoration. Guest DJs, outside bar and a nice crowd.

Star Dance Nightclub (B D MA NG)
Coastal Road *Next to Buddha Club*

Zanzibar (B D MA NG) Mon-Sat 23-5h
Royal Rd North of Town Centre ☏ 263 3265
Small disco with mostly mainstream music and sometimes Techno.

CRUISING

-Mont Choisy gay beach during the day and crusing on weeknights only. On weekends crowded with families.

Pereybere

SWIMMING

-Pereybere public beach.

Phoenix

SEX CINEMAS

Phoenix palace (glm MA) Movies at 14.30 and 20h
Royal road
A place where gays meet and have sex. Saturday is more popular. Only straight porn movies.

Port Louis

BARS

Shooters Sports Pub & Grill (B glm M MA OS)
Le Caudan Waterfront *First Floor, L'Obervatoire* ☏ (230) 210 9737
www.shooters-resto.com
Popular sports bar and restaurant.

CAFES

Keg & Marlin Bar (B m MA NG) 12h till late
Block AG1-AG8, Les Docks Building *Waterfront* ☏ 211 68 21
Chic and nice! Offers draught beer, several drinks and some nice snacks. Open every day, best on Fridays.

HEALTH GROUPS

PILS – Prévention Information Lutte contre le SIDA
Mon-Fri 9-16.30h
21bis J. Nehru Street ☏ 210 70 75
PILS is the only NGO in Mauritius working exclusively in the fight against HIV/AIDS and has been doing so since 1996. They have a hotline: ☏ *800 50 01, Mon-Fri 9-20h. They work closely together with the Collectif Arc en Ciel.*

Quatre Bornes Town

BARS

Choice Palace (B M MA NG OS)
Bar and live music by a bunch of guys playing guitars on Saturdays. Also very good B-B-Q available!

DANCECLUBS

Indigo (B D GLM MA)
Royal Road
They organise gay parties sometimes, around every 2 months. Check with the locals for dates or just stop by and ask.

Rose Hill

DANCECLUBS

Saxophone. Le (B D MA NG WE)
Beau Bassin ☏ 465 30 21
Playing good music, probably the best in Rose Hill. Fridays and Saturdays.

Trou-aux-Biches

SWIMMING

-Trou aus Biches Public Beach (next to Trou aux Biches Hotel)
-On most of the northern beaches (Pereybere, Grand Baie, Mont Choisy, Trou aux Biches) one could find boys cruising around. However hustlers are also frequent.

Mexico

Name: México · Mexiko · Mexique · Messico
Location: Southern North America
Initials: MEX
Time: GMT -6/ -7/ -8
International Country Code: ☏ 52
International Access Code: ☏ 00
Language: Spanish
Area: 1,953,162 km² / 756,061 sq mi.
Currency: 1 Mexican Peso (mex$) = 100 Centavos
Population: 103,089,000
Capital: Ciudad de México
Religions: 90% Roman Catholic, 5,2% Protestant
Climate: Oct-May is the most pleasant time to visit. May-Sep can be hot and humid, particularly in the south, and inland temperatures drop to freezing from Dec-Feb.
Important gay cities: Acapulco, Guadalajara, Mexico City, Puerto Vallarta

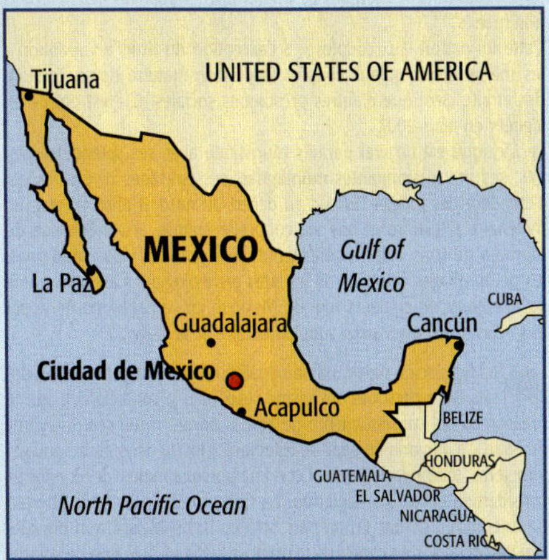

The legislation in Mexico does not punish relations between persons of the same sex, on condition that both consenting individuals are over the age of majority. Any sexual relation with a person under 12 years is considered rape, for both hetero and homosexuals. The age of consent is 18 years for women and men. The constitution protects the freedom of sexual preferences. In a Catholic country like Mexico prejudice towards homosexuality still exists. Such reactionary Catholic values have taken a run-up since the conservative government came into power in 2001. Nevertheless a general atmosphere of tolerance reigns, at least in the big cities. In June 2003 the Federal Law Against Discrimination was approved, which includes sexual minorities and creates a National Council to eradicate all traces of discrimination.

In May 2009, Puerto Vallarta's city council repealed Article 40, Section XIV of the misdemeanours code, which defined immorality to include: „public practices that indicate the development of an abnormal sexual life." This law enabled police abuse including the arrest of gay men and lesbians for simple acts of affection, such as holding hands.

Both the regional parliament of the northern Mexican state Coahuila and Mexico City's town council have passed a law affording the partnerships of same-sex and unmarried heterosexual couples a legal status.

This law gives couples the same legal rights as married couples, apart from the right to adoption, including inheritance and pension rights as well as other social rights. This law came into effect in March 2007.

Mexico is a tourist paradise: wonderful beaches, impressive mountains, vast landscapes from the jungle in the south to the desert in the north, a millennial historical past and the melting of three different cultures into a very dynamic and coloured society. Big, exciting, modern cities, fascinating small colonial villages and rich archaeological areas make of this country a living museum. Last but not less, the authentic Mexican cuisine makes a visit to Mexico a must!

In Mexiko sind gleichgeschlechtliche Kontakte und Beziehungen unter der Bedingung erlaubt, dass beide Partner volljährig sein müssen. Sowohl für Hetero- als auch Homosexuelle gilt jeglicher sexueller Kontakt mit einer minderjährigen Person als Missbrauch.

Das Schutzalter liegt bei Frauen und Männern bei 18 Jahren, und die Freiheit, sexuelle Neigungen auszuleben, wird von der Verfassung geschützt.

In einem katholischen Land wie Mexiko hat man gegenüber Homosexualität immer noch Vorurteile. Seitdem die konservative Regierung 2001 an die Macht kam, haben reaktionäre katholische Ansichten wieder zugenommen. Trotzdem gibt es wenigstens in den großen Städten eine tolerante Grundstimmung. Im Juni 2003 wurde das Bundesgesetz gegen Diskriminierung angenommen, das sich sexueller Minderheiten annimmt und die Bildung eines Nationalrates vorsieht, der jegliche Ansätze von Diskriminierung schon im Keim ersticken soll.

Im Mai 2009 hob der Stadtrat von Puerto Vallarta den Artikel 40, Paragraf XIV des Strafgesetztes auf, der das öffentliche Praktizieren von abnormalen sexuellen Handlungen verbot. Dieses Gesetz ermöglichte der Polizei den Missbrauch, einschließlich der Verhaftung von Schwulen und Lesben wegen einfacher Zeichen der Zuneigung, wie Händchen halten oder einem Kuss in der Öffentlichkeit.

Das Regionalparlament des nordmexikanischen Staates Coahuila und das Stadtparlament von Mexiko-City haben ein Gesetz verabschiedet, mit dem die Partnerschaften für gleichgeschlechtliche und unverheiratete Heterosexuelle Paare legalisiert werden. Das Gesetz gibt Paaren – bis auf das Adoptionsrecht – eheähnliche Rechte in Fragen des Erb- und Rentenrechts sowie andere soziale Leistungen. Das Gesetz ist im März 2007 in Kraft getreten.

Mexiko ist ein echtes Paradies für Touristen und hat wunderschöne Strände, eindrucksvolle Berge, weite Landschaften vom südlichen Dschungel bis zur Wüste im Norden, eine tausendjährige Geschichte und eine lebhafte und bunte Gesellschaft, die aus der Mischung von drei verschiedenen Kulturen entstanden ist. Pulsierende moderne Großstädte, faszinierende kleine Kolonialdörfer und archäologische Fundorte machen das Land zu einem lebenden Museum. Schon allein die mexikanische Küche lohnt einen Besuch.

Au Mexique, les rapports et relations homosexuels sont légaux si les deux partenaires sont majeurs. Le détournement de mineurs est aussi bien pour les hétérosexuels que les homosexuels un délit. La majorité sexuelle est fixée à 18 ans pour les femmes et les hommes et le droit de vivre son orientation sexuelle est ancré dans la constitution.

Dans un pays catholique comme le Mexique, les préjugés négatifs envers l'homosexualité sont monnaie courante et depuis l'élection en 2001 du gouvernement conservateur, de tels propos se font à nouveau entendre. Néanmoins, une loi a été adoptée en juin 2003 qui protège les minorités sexuelles, et prévoit la création d'un comité national devant étouffer dans l'oeuf toute forme de discrimination.

En mai 2009 le conseil municipal de Puerto Vallarta a abrogé l'article 40, paragraphe XIV du code pénal qui interdit la pratique publique de relations sexuelles anormales. Cette loi permettait à la police l'emprisonnement de gays et lesbiennes seulement pour des signes d'affection comme se donner la main ou s'embrasser en public.

Le parlement régional de l'État du Coahuila dans le nord du Mexique et le parlement de la ville de Mexico ont adopté une loi légalisant le partenariat pour les couples de même sexe et pour les hétérosexuels non mariés.
Cette loi octroie aux couples « à l'exception du droit à l'adoption « les même droits qu'aux couples mariés en matière de succession, de retraite ainsi que d'autres prestations sociales. Elle est entrée en vigueur en mars 2007.
Le Mexique est un vrai paradis touristique avec ses splendides plages, ses impressionnantes montagnes, ses paysages diversifiés qui s'étendent des jungles du sud au désert du nord. Il offre en plus un millénaire d'histoire et une vie culturelle animée et variée issue du mariage de trois cultures différentes. Les grandes villes modernes, les petits villages coloniaux et les sites archéologiques associés à une société haute en couleurs font du Mexique un véritable musée vivant et sa cuisine est une raison supplémentaire de le visiter.

La legislación mexicana no penaliza en modo alguno las relaciones entre personas del mismo sexo, bajo la condición de que se realicen con el consentimiento de ambas partes y que sean mayores de edad. La mayoría de edad se establece a los 18 años para hombres y mujeres, toda relación sexual con una persona menor de 12 años es considerada como una violación. La Constitución protege la libertad de orientación sexual. En un país católico como México aún prevalecen los prejuicios en contra de la homosexualidad. Este tipo de valores reaccionarios han cobrado impulso desde que el gobierno conservador asumió el poder en 2001. De cualquier forma reina una atmósfera de tolerancia, al menos en las grandes ciudades. En junio de 2003 se aprobó la Ley Federal Contra la Discriminación, que incluye a las minorías sexuales, y se creó un Consejo Nacional para combatir las expresiones de discriminación.
En mayo de 2009, el Ayuntamiento de Puerto Vallarta anuló el artículo 40 de la sección XIV del Código Penal, que prohibía la práctica pública de actos sexuales anormales. Esta ley permitió abusos por parte de la policía, incluida la detención de gays y lesbianas a causa de un simple signo de afecto, como ir agarrado de las manos o besarse en público.
El Parlamento regional del estado mexicano del norte Coahuila y el Parlamento de la ciudad de México han aprobado una ley, mediante la cual se legalizan las parejas de hecho, tanto las parejas del mismo sexo como las parejas heterosexuales no casadas.
La ley otorga a las parejas (hasta el derecho de adopción) los mismos derechos que un matrimonio en cuestiones de derecho sucesorio, derecho a pensión así como otras prestaciones sociales. Está nueva ley entró en vigor en el marzo de 2007.
México es un paraíso turístico: playas maravillosas, impresionantes montañas, vastos paisajes que abarcan desde las selvas en el sur hasta los desiertos en el norte, un pasado histórico milenario y la fusión de tres diferentes culturas en una sociedad dinámica y diversa. Grandes ciudades modernas, pequeños pueblos coloniales y grandes áreas arqueológicas hacen de este país una museo viviente. Y finalmente, pero no menos importante, la auténtica cocina mexicana merece una visita a México!

In Messico i rapporti dello stesso sesso sono permessi solo se entrambi i partner sono maggiorenni. Rapporti con minorenni sono vietati sia per omosessuali che per eterosessuali. L'età legale per i rapporti sessuali è di 18 anni per entrambi i sessi e l'espressione del proprio orientamento sessuale è tutelata dalla costituzione.
Essendo un paese cattolico, in Messico, ci sono ancora molti pregiudizi nei confronti dell'omosessualità. Da quando nel 2001 il Messico ha scelto un governo di destra, le reazioni omofobe cattoliche nei confronti dell'omosessualità sono aumentate. Nel giugno del 2003 è stata approvata una legge antidiscriminazione che tutela le minoranze sessuali.
A maggio del 2009 la giunta comunale di Puerto Vallarta ha abrogato l'articolo 40, paragrafo XIV del codice penale che vietava la pratica di atti sessuali deviati. Questa legge permetteva alla polizia di sbattere in galera gay e lesbiche anche per semplice scambio di affettuosità come per esempio il tenersi per mano o il baciarsi in pubblico.
Il parlamento regionale dello Stato settentrionale Coahuila e il parlamento municipale di Città del Messico hanno approvato una legge che riconosce le coppie dello stesso sesso e le coppie di fatto eterosessuali. La suddetta legge garantisce alle coppie dei diritti che sono molto simili a quelli del matrimonio, come per esempio il diritto ad ereditare, la reversibilità della pensione e molti altri diritti sociali e civili. Eccezione viene fatta per il diritto di adozione. La legge è entrata in vigore a marzo 2007.
Il Messico è un vero paradiso per i turisti: ci sono meravigliose spiagge, bellissime montagne, paesaggi sconfinati (dalla giungla al sud fino al deserto al nord). Il Messico ha mille anni di storia e la sua popolazione è davvero molto variopinta: è il risultato di 3 diverse culture. Vivaci e moderne città, piccoli affascinanti paesini coloniali e i siti archeologici fanno del Messico un vero e proprio museo. La sola cucina messicana è comunque un buon motivo per il viaggio.

NATIONAL PUBLICATIONS

Homópolis (GLM)
Vidal Alcocer 56, colonia Centro ✉ 06020 Ciudad de México
☎ (55) 5704-3927 ☎ 5704-6175 🖳 www.homopolis.com.mx
Fortnightly LGBT magazine and guide. For free at LGBT venues.

Rola Gay (G)
Adolfo Prieto 1920, Col. Obrera ✉ 64010 Monterrey, NL
☎ (081) 8340-0366 🖳 www.rolaclub.com
Monthly publication with information about the gay venues in the whole country. For free in main gay locations. Edition: 30,000 issues/month.

NATIONAL COMPANIES

Babylon Tours 9-18h
Versalles 16 Piso 2, Col Juarez ✉ 06600 Ciudad de México
☎ (055) 5705-1900 🖳 www.babylontours.com.mx
Gay travel agency.

Acapulco – Guerrero ☎ 744

BARS

Parranderías (B GLM SNU) 23-?h
Av. Cuauhtémoc *On Colonial Progresso, around corner from Hotel Palacio, opp. Sears*

Plaza del Mariachi (B G m MA OS SNU ST) 22-4h
C/. Legazpi y Diego Hurtado de Mendoza *On the beach*
Becomes more gay from 1h. Check out pool hall next door and taxi-washing boys in parking lot (AYOR).

DANCECLUBS

Cabaré-Tito Beach (! B D GLM S SNU) Fri-Sat 21-?h
Privada de Piedra Picuda 17 ☎ (744) 484 7146

Factory Demas (B D GLM S SNU) 22.30-?h
Av. De los Deportes 11, Zona Dorada *Behind Pizza Hut on the Costera*
☎ (744) 484-1800
🖳 www.facebook.com/pages/DEMAS-FACTORY/221610136231
Shows (T) on Wed & Sat at 4.30h.

Picante Acapulco (AC B CC D DR G MC R S SNU ST VS) 21-5h
C/. Piedra Picuda 16 *Behind Carlos & Charlies* ☎ (744) 484-2342
Stripper show every night. Cover charge includes one free drink. Great dancers.

Relax (AC B D GLM r SNU T VS) 22-?h, closed Mon-Wed
C/. Lomas del Mar 4 *Off Costera M. Alemán near La Tortuga Restaurant*
☎ (744) 484-0421
Entrance fee includes a drink. Best on Sat night. WE drag & strip shows. Also small bar downstairs with porn videos and a dark toilet area.

■ **Savage** (AC B D GLM MA T VS) 22.30-?h
Av. De los Deportes 10, Zona Dorada *Behind Pizza Hut on the Costera, next door to Moons* ☎ (744) 484-1800 💻 www.facebook.com/savage.acapulco
Shows (T) on Wed & Sat at 1.30h and 3.30h. Same location as Factory Demas.

■ **Zoom** (AC B D GLM S SNU) Bar Wed-Sat 21-?h & Disco Fri-Sat 22-?h
Av. De los Deportes 110 *In front of Pizza Hut Calinda & the restaurant La Mansión* ☎ (744) 484 22 55 💻 www.zoom-acapulco.com

RESTAURANTS

■ **Bistroquet. Le** (b CC glm M OS VEG WL) 18-23.30h
C/. Andrea Doria 5 / Costa Azul *Opp. Oceanic 2000 building, 1/2 block from Main Av.* ☎ (744) 484-6860 💻 www.lebistroquet.com
French and International cuisine.

■ **Tortuga. La** (B glm M) 11-24h
C/. Lomas del Mar 5 *Behind Relax* ☎ (744) 484-6985
Wonderful Mexican food in a great garden location. Excellent service and authentic Mexican dishes. Not to be confused with the Tortuga Hotel on the Costera.

HOTELS

■ **Villa Tiffany** (CC G MA PI)
C/. Villa Vera 120 ☎ (744) 294-7849
In gay area, close to bars and gay beach.

GUEST HOUSES

■ **Casa Condesa** (AC B CC G I M MA MSG NU OS p PI PK RWS RWT SOL) All year
Bellavista 125, Fracc. Farrallón ☎ (744) 484-1616 💻 www.casacondesa.com
Private retreat only a two block walk to the best that Acapulco has to offer.

■ **Villa del Angel Guesthouse Acapulco** (AC BF glm H m MA PI RWS RWT VA) All year, 24hrs
C/. Playa de Hualtulco No. 2, Colonia San Nicolas de las Playas *Coyuca de Benetiz* ☎ (744) 444-4499 💻 www.casadelangelacapulco.com
On the beach two blocks from the resort El Parador del Sol.

■ **Villa Roqueta** (AC B BF CC g M MSG NU OS p PI RWB RWS RWT SA WH WO) All year
C/. San Marcos, 24 Las Playas *On the cliffs of Acapulco* ☎ (744) 294-7849 💻 www.gayhotelsacapulco.com
The former estate of Gloria Gaynor now is a luxurious guesthouse.

CRUISING

-The gay beach here is called „La Condesa" and is near the „Fiesta Americana Hotel". Cruising also takes place on the far end of the beach, where you have to climb over the rocks. The water here is usually not clean enough to swim.
-Beto's Beach (near Condesa, Chichifos)
-Pie de la Questa (BA Beach about 13km south)

Aguascalientes – Aguascalientes ☎ 449

BARS

■ **Caporal. El** (B G MC) Wed-Sun
Av. de la Convención 910 *Near the Cinema Av. Plus* ☎ (449) 918-0702

■ **Mandiles** (D GLM p) Fri-Sat 22-3h
Av. López Mateos 730 Poniente *Near Convención de 1914, between Chabacano & Aguacate* ☎ (449) 918 153 281

CRUISING

Both AYOR:
-Plaza Principal (g YC)
-Plaza de Toros.

Cabo San Lucas – Baja California Sur ☎ 624

GUEST HOUSES

■ **Posada Chabela** (AC b bf CC glm I M MA MSG p PI RWS WO) All year, check in: 14:30h
#11 Calle Tropical / Lomas de Costa Azul *Km 28½ Transpeninsular Cabo a San Jose* ☎ (624) 172-6490 💻 www.posadachabela.com

Cancún – Quintana Roo ☎ 998

BARS

■ **Cafe d' Pa** (B glm M MC)
Av. Alcatraces *Near C/. Gladiolas*
Colourful street front bar & restaurant with a comfortable, homely feel. Creative menu with crepes.

■ **Picante** (AC B d G MA r SNU VS) 21-5h
Av. Tulúm 20 – Plaza Galerías *North of Av. Uxmal past McDonald's & Banco Confia* ☎ (998) 845-5587 💻 www.picantebar.com
A small video bar with a tiny dance floor. Also occasional drag and strip shows. All-male clientele of good-looking macho men.

■ **Sabor** (B glm MC S ST)
Av. Yaxchilan 12 *Next to Placita restaurant*
Dark but friendly cabaret with nightly drag shows featuring Spanish stars. Live music and mixed visitors.

DANCECLUBS

■ **Karamba** (B D GLM MA S WE) Thu-Sun 22.30-6h
Av. Tulúm 87, Esq. Azucenas. SM 22 *Opposite city hall. Bus lines 1 & 2* ☎ (998) 884-0032 💻 www.karambabar.net
Attracts a mixed (male/female) crowd and lots of international visitors. Good dance music and hot go-go boys. Every Wednesday drag shows.

■ **Risky Times** (B D glm MC) 2-8h
Av. Tulúm *At Av. Coba*
Many locals who finish work come here at around 2h.

HOTELS

■ **Aristos Cancún** (B glm M MA PI)
Blvd Kukulkán Lt. 42 ☎ (998) 883-0011
With private beach.

■ **Hotel Margaritas** (AC B BF CC H I M OS PI) All year
Av. Yaxchilan No 41 Sm 22 *Close to the bus station, in downtown Cancun* ☎ (998) 881-7870 💻 www.margaritascancun.com

SWIMMING

-Playa Delfines (southern end of the hotel zone). Police raids in the bushes (AYOR).
-Beach near Club Med (AYOR)
-Playa Chac Mool (r)
-Playa del Carmen (g) (50 mins by bus, walk left along the beach north)
-Caesar Park Beach (G).

CRUISING

-Av. Tulum (late)
-Delfines Beach (south end of hotel zone, Kukulcan Blvd km17 from 6 to 8h)
-Palapas Park, downtwon Cancun, one block east of Tulum Av., between 21-midnight.

Chihuahua – Chihuahua ☎ 614

BARS

■ **Chido's** (B G) ?-23h
C/. 6, Num. 300 *Right of Hotel Maceyra*

DANCECLUBS

■ **No Name Bar** (! B D GLM) Thu-Sat 21-3h
Av. Universidad 2307 *naer to Pancho Villa Glorieta* ☎ (614) 218 0107 💻 www.nonamebar.com

CRUISING

-Plaza de la Constitución
-Plaza Hidalgo

Ciudad de México – D. F. ☎ 55

The former Tenochtitlan is one of the biggest cities in the world, with more than 19 million inhabitants. 1,525 km² of steel, stone, glass, vegetation, people, music, light, life, history, all that at 2,240 meters above sea level, surrounded by mountains and snow covered volcanoes Popocatépetl and Ixtlaxihuatl. Impossible to see everything it all in just one visit!

The busiest gay area is the „Zona Rosa", mainly at Amberes street, close to the city centre: trendy bars, sophisticated restaurants, chic boutiques and gift shops, – a relaxed atmosphere in the middle of the city rush. In the old city centre, around the Alameda Park, are some of the traditional gay meeting points. La Marcha LGBT (Pride) takes place on the last Saturday in June.

The south of the city is worth a visit: Coyoacán, San Angel – „Bazar del Sábado", Xochimilco, soul of the colonial past. The Campus of the Universidad Nacional Autónoma de México is a must. If you are a keen visitor of museums, the city offers the biggest and the best conglomerate of museums in Latin America. Be sure not to miss a visit to the Museo de Antropología!

Mit über 19 Millionen Einwohnern ist das frühere Tenochtitlan eine der größten Städte der Welt. Sie liegt 2.250 m über dem Meeresspiegel, wird von Bergen und den schneebedeckten Vulkanen Popocatépetl und Iztlaxihuatl umrahmt und besteht aus 1.750 Quadratkilometern Stahl, Fels, Glas, Vegetation und Menschen.

Das lebendigste Schwulenviertel ist die „Zona Rosa" in der Nähe des Stadtzentrums. Es lockt Besucher mit schicken Bars, feinen Restaurants, Boutiquen und Geschenkläden und lädt in einer entspannten Atmosphäre inmitten der Stadt zum Verweilen ein.

Im alten Stadtzentrum in der Nähe des Alameda Parks findet man einige der traditionellen Schwulentreffs. Der LGBT-Pride „La Marcha" findet am letzten Samstag im Juni statt.

Auch der Süden der Stadt lohnt einen Besuch: Coyoacán, San Angel mit dem „Bazar del Sábado", der die koloniale Vergangenheit des Landes widerspiegelt.

Ein Besuch der Universität Nacional Autónoma de México ist empfehlenswert. Die Stadt hat außerdem die größten und schönsten Museen Lateinamerikas. Besonders ein Besuch des anthropologischen Museums lohnt sich!

Avec plus de 19 millions d'habitants, l'ancienne Tenochtitlan est une des plus grandes villes du monde. Située à 2,240 km au dessus du niveau de la mer et entourée de montagnes, dont les deux volcans enneigés Popocatépetl et Iztlaxihuatl, elle est constituée de 1,525 km² d'acier, de pierre, de verre, de végétation et de personnes.

Le quartier gay le plus animé est le « Zona Rosa » principalement dans la rue Amberes, près du centre-ville qui offre aux visiteurs bars chic, restaurants fins et boutiques de goût pour passer un moment tranquille tout en restant en pleine ville.

Dans le vieux centre-ville près du parc Alameda, on trouve quelques uns des lieux gays traditionnels. La LGTB-Pride (La Marcha) a lieu le dernier samedi de juin.

Une visite au sud de la ville (Coyoacán, San Angel avec son « Bazar del Sábado » rappelant le passé colonial du pays), et de l'université Nacional Autónoma de México s'imposent également. La ville dispose des plus grands et riches musées d'Amérique latine, et son musée d'anthropologie est passionnant!

La antigua Tenochtitlan es una de las mayores ciudades del mundo, con más de 19 millones de habitantes. 1,525 km² de acero, piedra, cristal, vegetación, gente, música, luz, vida, historia, todo a 2,240 metros sobre el nivel del mar, rodeado de montañas y los volcanes nevados Popocatépetl e Ixtlaxihuatl. Imposible verlo todo en tan solo una visita! La principal área de vida gay es la Zona Rosa, principalmente en la calle de Amberes, cerca del centro de la ciudad: bares modernos, restaurantes sofisticados, elegantes boutiques y tiendas de regalos, todo ello en una atmósfera relajada en medio del estrés urbano. En el antiguo centro de la ciudad, al rededor del Parque de la Alameda, se encuentran algunos de los tradicionales puntos de reunión gay. La Marcha LGBT (orgullo gay) tiene lugar el último sábado de junio.

El sur de la ciudad merece una visita: Coyoacán, San Angel -Bazar del Sábado, Xochimilco, son alma del pasado colonial. El Campus de la Universidad Nacional Autónoma de México es ineludible. Si es usted fanático de los museos, la ciudad ofrece el mayor y mejor conglomerado de museos de toda América Latina. Por ningún motivo se pierda el Museo de Antropología!

Con più di 19 milioni di abitanti, Città del Messico è una delle città più grandi al mondo. Si trova a 2,240 km al di sopra del mare ed è circondata da montagne e vulcani innevati (Popocatépetl e Iztlaxihuatl). Il quartiere gay più vivace è „Zona Rosa", principalmente della strada Amber, nei pressi del centro: qui vi sono bar piuttosto chic, eleganti ristoranti, boutique e negozi di articoli da regalo che invitano a gironzolare per il centro città.

Nel centro storico, vicino al parco Alameda, vi sono un paio di locali gay un po' più tradizionali. Il pride LGBT (La Marcha) si svolge l'ultimo sabato del mese di giugno. Anche il sud della città è molto interessante: da vedere sono il Coyoacán e San Angel con il „bazar del sábado" che rispecchia il passato coloniale del paese.

Vi consigliamo anche una visita all'università Nacional Autónoma de Mexico. Inoltre a città del Messico ci sono i più grandi e più bei musei di tutta l'America latina. Di particolare interesse è il museo antropologico.

NATIONAL GROUPS

Comunidad Cristiana de Esperanza (GLM)
Dr. Río de la Loza 170, 2 piso *M° Balderas*
☎ (04455) 1473-3826 (mobile)
Exclusive Christian group for the GLBT community.

CULTURE

Centro Cultural de la Diversidad Sexual (GLM I M MA)
Tue-Sat 15-22.45, Sun 13-20.45h
C/. Colima 267, Col. Roma *Between Insurgentes Sur and C/. Tonala*
☎ (55) 5514-2565 💻 www.diversidadsexual.com
A cultural centre with cafe, internet, sale of books and magazines as well as a library. Meetings for young gay men Thu 20h, transvestites on Wed+Fri 19h, gay men Tue+Thu 20h and lesbian club Sun 15h.

Urban Fest (GLM MA)
💻 www.urbanfest.net
Organiser of Gay Films Festivals

BARS

Taller. El (B d G MC) Daily
C/. Florencia 37-A *Zona Rosa, between Londres and Hamburgo*
☎ (55) 5533 4984
Very crowded, very friendly, good music and cruisy place. Also disco „El Taller" in the same building.

42nd Street (B GLM I MA) Mon-Sat 14-4h
C/. Amberes 4, Zona Rosa ☎ (55) 5208-0352

Lollipop (B cc d DR G SNU) Fri-Sat 21.30-?h
C/. Amberes 14, Zona Rosa 💻 www.boybarclub.com

Gayta. La (ac B cc d G m MA) Sun-Mon 13-24, Fri-Sat 13-2h
C/. Amberes 18, Zona Rosa *Next to The Pussy Bar* ☎ (55) 5207-7626
💻 lagayta.hi5.com
Beside the Pussy Bar sharing an open wall between the lesbian and gay bars.

Lipstick (AC B CC D GLM m MA S t WE) Wed-Sat 22-6h
C/. Amberes 1 Esq. Paseo de la Reforma *Zona Rosa* ☎ (55) 5514-4920
💻 www.facebook.com/pages/Lipstick/30564869562
Cover charge applies. Each day a different theme and DJ as well as special shows.

Lugar Roshell. El (B d GLM m S SNU) Mon-Sun
C/. Lorenzo Boturini 440, esquina Sur 79 *Lorenzo Boturini, between Congreso de la Unión and La Viga* ☎ (55) 5768 1317
💻 hwww.ellugarderoshell.com

Oasis (B G MA s) Daily
C/. República de Cuba 2-G *Centro Histórico*
Slightly more elegant than the Vienna Bar next door. Jukebox and many small tables. Sometimes shows. Staff very friendly.

Papi (! B CC GLM MA S) Mon-Wed 15-1.30, Fri-Sun -5h
C/. Amberes 18, Zona Rosa *Corner at Estrasburgo* ☎ (55) 5208 3755
💻 www.papifunbar.com

Play Bar (B CC GLM MA) Thu-Sat 21-4h
C/. Oaxaca No. 130, Col. Roma *Few blocks from M° Sevilla*
☎ (55) 5207-4314

Pride (B CC GLM MA) Tue-Sat
C/. Alfonso Reyes 281, Col. Condesa ☎ (55) 5516 2368

Pussy Bar. The (ac B cc d GLM m r S YC) 13-2h
C/. Amberes 18, Zona Rosa, Col Juarez del Cuahutemoc *M° Insurgentes*
☎ (55) 5207-7626 💻 lagayta.hi5.com
Little bar in the gay district that opens and gets crowded early.

Tom's Leather (B CC DR G MA SNU VS)
C/. Insurgentes Sur 357, Col. Condesa ☎ (55) 5564-0728
💻 www.toms-mexico.com
Special events see www.toms-mexico.com.

Viena. El (AYOR B G MA) Mon-Sun
C/. Republica de Cuba 3, Centro Historico

MEN'S CLUBS

Casita I. La (DR G MA NU VS) 24hrs
Viaducto Miguel Aléman 72, Col. Algarín *Between Bolivar and 5 de Febrero* ☎ (55) 5519-8842 💻 www.lacasita.com.mx
You don't know México if you don't visit La Casita – claims the owner.

Casita II. La (DR G MA NU VS) 24hrs
C/. Insurgentes Sur 228, Col. Roma *Between Durango and Colima*
☎ (55) 5514-4639 💻 www.lacasita.com.mx
See commentary to La Casita I.

CAFES

■ **Le Cirque Nuit Bar** (CC GLM m MA) Mon-Sun 10-23h
C/. Amberes 12-B ☎ (55) 5445-8332
Coffee shop in the heart of the Zona Rosa, main gay centre of the city. The profits from café support the activities of the Bgay Bproud Foundation.
■ **Cafe y Salud VIHDA** (b GLM MA) Mon-Fri
C/. Gumersindo Esquer 34 ☎ (55) 5740-3402
■ **Virreinas** (GLM MA) Tue-Sun
Av. México 54. Col. Santa Cruz Atoyac *Between C/. Parroquia & C/. Eje 8, behind the Plaza Universidad* ☎ (55) 5601-7460

DANCECLUBS

■ **Ansia. El** (AC B CC D G MA ST) Thu-Sat 21.30-3h
C/. Insurgentes Sur 1391, Col. Insurgentes Mixcoac *In Centro Armand* ☎ (55) 5611-6118
Cover charge includes one drink.
■ **Babylon** (D MC WE) Thu-Sat 21-3h
Hamburgo 96 *M° Insurgentes. Zona Rosa* ☎ (55) 5758 2271
Electro and pop music with guest DJ's and very busy on weekends.
■ **Botas Bar** (D GLM MC WE) Thu-Sat 21-3h
Niza 45 *M° Insurgentes. Zona Rosa* ☎ (55) 1321-2239
Upstairs is only for women. Downstairs is for men. Table-dance, go-go dancers. Also private upon request!
■ **Cabare-Tito Fusion** (B CC D GLM MA S SNU T) Wed-Sun 17-?h
C/. Londres No. 77, Col. Juárez *Zona Rosa half block from Insurgentes* ☎ (55) 5511-1613 💻 www.cabaretito.com/portal
■ **Cabaré-Tito Neón** (B D GLM MC S) Mon-Sun 18-?h
C/. Londres 161-20A, Zona Rosa *In Plaza del Angel* ☎ (55) 5514 9455 💻 www.cabarétito.com
■ **Cabaré-Tito ANIWAY** (B D GLM S) Thu-Sat
C/. Monterrey 47, Col Roma 💻 www.cabarétito.com
(Thu lesbianight)
■ **Chango** (B CC D GLM MA) Thu-Sat 22-5h
Río Chiquito s/n, Col. El Cerrito *North of the metropolitan area; a taxi takes around 45 mins from Zona Rosa* ☎ (55) 5872-3234
■ **La Bomba VIP** (B D GLM) Wed, Fri & Sat
C/. Florencia 67, Zona Rosa ☎ (55) 5525 8523
■ **Hibrido Night Club** (B CC D GLM MA S) Fri-Sat 22-4, Sun 19-4h
C/. Londres 161, 2° Piso, Zona Rosa *At Plaza del Angel* ☎ (55) 5511-1197 💻 hibridonightclub.com.mx
■ **Kashbah** (B D GLM MA WE) Thu-Sat 21-3h
Insurgentes Sur 234 *M° Insurgentes. Zona Rosa. At the corner Colima*
It offers a very sophisticated and glamorous show in Las Vegas stile. Here everybody is welcome!
■ **Ken** (B D G MA WE) Thu-Sat 21-3h
Medellín 65 *Near to Glorieta de las Cibeles* ☎ (55) 4612-1755
One of the best gay-pop clubs in the city frequented by men between 20-30. Electronic and pop music.
■ **La Purísima** (! B D G MA WE) 21-3h
Cuba 22 *M° Allende. Zona Rosa*
Right in the center of the city is one of the most successful clubs. Frequented by crowds around 20-30 although the area is not very secure.
■ **Las Tortugas** (D G MC WE) 21-3h
Calle 65 y 67 No. 4 *M° Zaragoza* ☎ (55) 5758-2271
Very busy bar, specially on weekend. Not very secure since the area is on the outskirts of the city. Much going on with younger crowd.
■ **Liverpool 100** (AC B CC D GLM MA S ST) Fri-Sat 21-4h
C/. Liverpool 100, Col. Juárez *One block from Zona Rosa crossing Insurgentes* ☎ (55) 5208-4507 💻 www.liverpool100.com
■ **Living** (B cc D GLM S) Fri & Sat
C/. Bucarelli 144, Col. Juarez ☎ (55) 5512 7281
💻 www.living.com.mx
One of the biggest and best clubs in Mexico!
■ **Marrakech. El** (D G MC WE) 21-3h
Cuba 18 *M° Allende. Zona Rosa*
Situated in the center of the city. It is one of the most visited discos. Specially frequented by crowd between 20-30. The area it's not very secure but the place is highly recommended.
■ **New Cine Club** (B D GLM S) Thu-Sat
C/. Colón 1 *M° Hidalgo, near Plaza Solidaridad* ☎ (55) 2243 1258
■ **New Vaquero** (D G MC WE) 21-3h
Florencia 35, local B *M° Insurgentes. Zona Rosa* ☎ (55) 5525-3332
💻 www.facebook.com/pages/New-Vaquero/189360754442187
■ **Nicho** (D G MC WE) Thu-Sat 21-3h
Londres 182 *M° Insurgentes. Zona Rosa*
■ **Pink Paradise** (D G MC WE) Fri-Sat 21-3h
Eje 3 Oriente corner Av. Ermita *M° Escuadron 201. At the corner Av. Ermita*
■ **PK** (B D G MC WE) Thu-Sat 21-3h
Hamburgo No. 75 ☎ (55) 4981 184 💻 www.pkclub.mx
Electro and pop music with guest DJ's and very busy on weekends.

RESTAURANTS

■ **12:30** (AC B CC D GLM I M MA OS) Mon-Sat 11-4, Sun 12-24h
C/. Amberes 13, Zona Rosa ☎ (55) 5514-5971
On three floors with restaurant, bar and area for private events.

SEX SHOPS/BLUE MOVIES

■ **Erotika** (CC g VS) 10-22, Fri & Sat -24, Sun 13-20h
Genova 20, local 3 *M° Insurgentes, Zona Rosa* ☎ (55) 5340-3790
💻 www.erotikasexshop.com
Private cabins for gay porn videos.

SAUNAS/BATHS

■ **Baños Finisterre** (DU FH g MA MSG SA SB) 7-21, Sun 6 -15h
C/. Manuel Maria Contreras 11, Col. San Rafael *M° San Cosme, at the exit turn left. Three streets on the other side of the Pte de Alvarado* ☎ (55) 5535-3543
This is a typical bath house, where men go to relax and get a massage. Not a typical sauna in the European sense. A very unique experience. You can take men back to your room. Mainly frequented by locals. Wonderful head-to-toe massage available. Your shoes get polished as part of the service.
■ **Baños Mina** (DR G MA MSG SB) 6-22.00h
Mina 10 *Just off Reforma near Alameda Park* ☎ (55) 5512 9910
A little tacky but a great place to meet men of all ages.
■ **Baños Rocío** (g SA SB)
C/. Tlalpan 1165 ☎ (55) 5539-8830
■ **Baños San Juan** (g MA MSG SA SB)
C/. López 120 *M° Salto de Agua* ☎ (55) 5521-3376
■ **Baños San Juan** (B g SA SB) 7-20.30h
Lopez 120 *Metro Salto del Agua Station* ☎ (55) 5535-8759
■ **Baños Señorial** (b DU g MSG SA SB) 6-20, Sun -15h
Isabel la Católica No 92, Centro *Centro, M° Isabel la Católica* ☎ (55) 5709-0732
Nice sauna with steam and dry-heat rooms.
■ **Club Body Insurgentes** (G MC SA SB WE) Daily 11-22h
Insurgentes Centro No. 14 *M° Revolución. Corner Puente de Alvarado* ☎ (55) 5514-4477
■ **SO.DO.ME** (! B CC DU G m MA MSG NU P RR S SA SB VS WE WH)
Tue-Wed 16-24, Thu 16-4, Fri 16-Sun 23h
Mariano Escobedo 716, Col. Anzures *Between Hotel Fiesta Americana and Hotel Camino Real* ☎ (55) 5250-6653 💻 www.sodome.com.mx
Best sauna in town, a must!
■ **Toalla Valle. La** (DR DU G MA MSG NU RR SA VS WO) 7-23h
Cda. de Sánchez Azcona 1724, Col. Del Valle *Next to Felix Cuevas* ☎ (55) 5524-8530 💻 www.latoalla.com.mx
A second „Toalla" sauna. See the comments for La Toalla VIP.
■ **Toalla VIP men club. La** (B DR DU G MA NU SA SB VS WO) 24hrs
Alvaro Obregón 259, Col. Roma *Between Valladolid and Medellin* ☎ (55) 5511-0686 💻 www.latoalla.com.mx
This sauna combines two possibilities: to explore bodies and to take a bath.

FITNESS STUDIOS

■ **Club San Francisco** (G MA SB WO) 6.15-22.45h
Rio Tiber 36 *M° Line. 1 Sevilla and near from La Diana* ☎ (55) 5525-1894
💻 www.clubsanfrancisco.com.mx
One of the most popular gyms in México City for men only.

BOOK SHOPS

■ **Armario Abierto. El** (CC glm) Mon-Sat 11-21h
C/. Agustin Melgar 25, Colonia Condesa ☎ (55) 52 86 0895
🖳 www.elarmarioabierto.com
Bookstore dedicated to sexual health and sexuality education, with GLBT section, including condom and sex toys store.

■ **Voces en Tinta** (AC CC GLM I m MA S t WE)
10-21, Thu-Sat -22, Sun 12-19h
Niza 23-A Zona Rosa Delegacion Cuauhtemoc *Between Reforma and Hamburgo* ☎ (55) 55 33 7116 🖳 www.vocesentinta.com
Special events from Thu-Sat.

CONDOM SHOPS

■ **Condomaniacos** (cc GLM)
C/. Amberes 57, Zona Rosa ☎ (55) 1686 3961

FASHION SHOPS

■ **Boutique Sodoma** (CC GLM) Mon-Sun 12-21h
Estrasburgo No. 31 – A, Col. Juárez *Almost at the corner of C/. Amberes, a few steps from Papi Bar and next door to Rainbowland*
🖳 http://es-es.facebook.com/pages/BOUTIQUE-SODOMA-ZONA-ROSA/199578333415439
Designer clothes.

■ **Open Desires** (CC GLM)
C/.Álvaro Obregón 130. Local. 10.B *Near Metrobus Alvaro Obregón*
☎ (55) 5584 4627
Underwear and swim suits for men.

GIFT & PRIDE SHOPS

■ **Rainbowland** (CC GLM) Mon-Sat 11-20h
Estrasburgo No. 31, Col. Juárez *Almost at the corner of C/. Amberes, a few steps from Papi Bar and next door to Sodoma Boutique*
☎ (55) 52-08-94-67 🖳 www.rainbowland.com.mx
Pride articles, souvenirs, etc.

HOTELS

■ **Hotel de Cortes** (B CC H I M MA MSG) All year
Av. Hidalgo 85 *M° Hidalgo* ☎ (55) 5518-2181
🖳 www.boutiquehoteldecortes.com

■ **Red Tree House. The** (AC B BF CC OS)
C/. Culiacan 6, Col. Condesa *Between Amsterdam & Campeche St.*
☎ (55) 5584 3829 🖳 www.theredtreehouse.com

GUEST HOUSES

■ **6M9 Guesthouse** (b bf CC G MA PI SA SB WH WO) Reception: 8-22h
Marsella 69, Col. Juarez *M° Insurgentes* ☎ (55) 5208-8347
🖳 www.6m9guesthouse.com.mx
Gay guesthouse in Mexico City for men only. Breakfast, complimentary drinks, jacuzzi, steam room, gymnasium, WIFI, DVD library. Close to gay scene.

■ **Casa Comtesse** (B BF glm I MC PK RWS RWT VA) All year
C/. Benjamin Franklin, 197 *Col. Condesa, between Altata and Ometusco*
☎ (55) 5277-5418 🖳 www.casacomtesse.com
Eight personalized rooms, all with private bath. Condesa is a trendy and animated neighbourhood with parks, gay bars, restaurants and clubs.

■ **Casa Roma** (AC BF glm H I M OS PK RWB RWS RWT VA) All year
C/. Aguascalientes 174, int 102, Colonia Condesa *M° Chilpancingo, between Chilpancingo and Culiacán* ☎ (55) 4006 9199
🖳 www.casaromadf.com
Casa Roma is a large apartment with 3 guestrooms, located in the trendy district of La Condesa, close to many bars and restaurants. A Mexican or Continental breakfast is available in your room or in the dining-room. Local guides are available upon request.

■ **Condesa Haus** (BF CC G H I M MA) all year
C/. Cuernavaca No. 142, Col. Condesa *Between Campeche and Alfonso Reyes* ☎ (55) 5256-2494 🖳 www.condesahaus.com
Old fashion boutique hotel with five rooms in a very nice neighborhood, five minutes from the Zona Rosa. Personal attention from the owner. Every now and then expositions or cocktails for young writers, painters, etc.

GENERAL GROUPS

■ **AVE de México** (glm MA) Mon-Sat 11-20h
Querétaro 246 3er piso *M° Chilpancingo, line 9*
☎ (55) 1054-3212 ▭ www.avedemexico.org.mx
Civic organization for the development of projects & programs for vulnerable social groups. Support group for homosexual parents & children. „Diversitel", hotline on sexual diversity. „La Condonería", condom store.

HEALTH GROUPS

■ **CAPPSIDA** (b GLM MA) Mon-Fri
C/. Gumersindo Esquer 34 ☎ (55) 5740-3402 ▭ www.cappsida.org.mx
Specialized attention to persons with VIH. Meeting of groups.

CRUISING

SAFETY TIP: Do not stop a taxi on the streets. Ask in the hotel to call you a radio taxi or look for a taxi stand (sitio). Be careful whom you take back to your hotel room. Parks late at night can be very dangerous.
-Alameda Parque (AYOR), Avenida Juarez
-Chapultepec Bosque (Park), Castle Hill
-Parque Hundido (AYOR).

Ciudad Juárez – Chihuahua ☎ 656

BARS

■ **Club Padrino** (B D GLM)
C/. Santos Degollado N
■ **Escondida. La** (B GLM M)
C/. Ignacio de la Peña 366, Oeste *Around the corner from Olímpico*
■ **G & G** (B d g S SNU) 21-3h
Av. Lincoln 1252 *Córdoba-Américas*
Strippers at WE.
■ **Nebraska** (B glm M r)
C/. Mariscal 251 *Centre*
Rough neighbourhood.
■ **Olímpico** (B GLM) 12-2h
Av. Lerdo 210 Sur *City centre*

Ciudad Nezahualcóyotl – Estado de México ☎ 058

DANCECLUBS

■ **Spartacu's** (B D DR MC S SNU ST WE) Fri-Sat 21-9h
Av. Cuauhtémoc 8, Col. Maravillas ☎ (55) 5701-0204
▭ www.discospartacus.com
Is a very popular place with a terrace and a huge dark-room. The travesty & stripper shows are highly recommended. Since the area is not secure is better to go there with a group.

Coacalco – Estado de México ☎ 058

DANCECLUBS

■ **Heaven Coacalco** (B D G S SNU ST WE) Fri-Sat 21-6h
Eje 8 No. 26, Col. Sta.María *Near to Av. López Portillo* ☎ (55) 2474-3245
Music for all tastes. Very popular in the area. It presents shows with special guests. Strippers and transvestites.
■ **Opuestos** (D G MC SNU ST WE) Fri-Sat 21-6h
Eje 8 s/n, Col. Sta.María *Near to Av. López Portillo* ☎ (55) 2474-3245
Music for all tastes. Very popular in the area.

Coatzacoalcos – Veracruz ☎ 921

BARS

■ **Collage** (B D GLM MA SNU ST) Fri-Sat 22-2h
Av. John Spark #110 *Over the Malecon Costero* ☎ (921) 142-2122
Cover charge.

DANCECLUBS

■ **Habana. La** (B D GLM S SNU) Fri-Sat: 22-?h
C/. Ignacio de la llave 403, Col. Centro

Córdoba – Veracruz ☎ 271

CRUISING

-Mercado/Market Juárez, Calles 7 & 9 (g WE YC)
-Sidewalk cafés on El Portal Zevallos.

Cozumel – Quintana Roo ☎ 987

GUEST HOUSES

■ **Alfonso's Villa** (g MA OS WH)
C/. 9 Sur, 248 *60 mins ferry ride to the island* ☎ (987) 872-3309
▭ www.geocities.com/viladiua
Lush gardens and jacuzzi. Kitchen available. Within walking distance of center of San Miguel and ferry to Playa del Carmen.

Cuautitlán Izcalli – Esdado de México

DANCECLUBS

■ **Gay-Sha** (B D G MC WE) Fri-Sat 21-6h
Av. Jorge Jiménez Cantú 419 Altos, Col. San Isidro
☎ (04455) 1340-3773 (mobile)
Since it is not situated in Mexico City is better to go there if you are in town and with a group. It is not very secure. Electro music.

Cuernavaca – Morelos ☎ 777

BARS

■ **Barecito** (B g MC)
C/. Comonfort 17 *Opp. Morrow* ☎ (777) 314-1425
■ **Oxygen** (AC B D GLM m MA OS S SNU ST VS WE) Fri & Sat 22-?, Thu 21-24h film
Av. Vincente Guerrero 1303 ☎ (777) 317-2714

DANCECLUBS

■ **Casa del Dictador. La** (B D glm MC)
C/. Jacarandas, 4 *Opp. Av. Zapata* ☎ (777) 317-2377
■ **Coco Bar 18** (B D g MC)
Av. Vicente Guerrero 907 A, Col.Prados de Cuernavaca ☎ (777) 377-8205

SAUNAS/BATHS

■ **Tepoz Spa** (b DR DU FC G I LAB M MA MSG OS PI PP RR SA SB SOL VS WE WH) Sat & Sun 11-21.30h
Carretera San Andres de la Cal #69, Tepoztlan *7 km from Cuernavaca*
☎ (739) 395-8457 ▭ www.TepozSpa.com
Outside of Tepoztlan, entrance next to Gallaecia, a large events center.

GUEST HOUSES

■ **Casa Alex y Ariel** (BF G MA)
Paseo Cancún, 84 *Quintana Roo* ☎ (777) 310-3261
■ **Casa del Angel** (b glm I M MA MSG PI RWS RWT) All year, 8-22h
C/. Clavel 18, Colonia Satelite ☎ (777) 512-6775
▭ www.hotelangelmexico.com
■ **Casa la Condesa** (BF glm MA)
C/. Morelos 29, Acapantzingo, col. Amplicacion ☎ (777) 318-8757
▭ www.morelosweb.com/arcoiris
■ **Nuestra B & B. La** (BF GLM I MC PI)
C/. Mesalina 18 ☎ (777) 315-2272
Four guestrooms run by two American ladies.

CRUISING

-Zocalo/Plaza Morelos/Jardín Juárez
-Market (Sun)

Culiacán – Sinaloa ☎ 667

DANCECLUBS

■ **Equal** (B D GLM S)
C/. Buelna 846 A, Centro ☎ (667) 716 17 73 ▭ www.equalculiacan.com

■ **Mistery Lounge** (B D G OS S SNU) Wed-Sun
C/. Rosales 254 Centro

SEX SHOPS/BLUE MOVIES

■ **Ramses** (CC GLM)
C/. Francisco Villa N° 87, Col. Centro ☎ (667) 712 29 60
🖳 www.sexshopramses.com

Ecatepec – Estado de México ☎ 057

BARS

■ **Cabaré-Tito Dubaih** (B GLM) Thu-Sat
Carr. Lecheria-Texcoco Km 45 *Col. Ampliación del Carmén*
🖳 www.cabaretito.com

Ensenada – Baja California Norte ☎ 646

BARS

■ **Scandalosas** (AC B D GLM MA VS) 20-?h
Blvd. Costero *North end of Blvd Costero next to Sanborn's & Cinemark theaters*

DANCECLUBS

■ **L. A. Studio** (B D G MA VS) 20-?h
Blvd Costero *North end of Blvd Costero across from Sanborn's & Cinemark theaters* ☎ (646) 76-1440

Guadalajara – Jalisco ☎ 33

Guadalajara is a large, thriving, cosmopolitan city (the second largest in Mexico with more than four million inhabitants) with more than 500 years history. It is an important symbol of the Mexican spirit, being the home of Tequila, Mariachis and Charro riding. Past and present live together in this city, also known as the „city of the roses". Unfortunately, due to the influence of the Catholic church, Guadalajara has to continually fight against traditional values, intolerance and old fashioned clichés.
Nevertheless, the gay scene keeps growing in this city and it is considered the most prosperous city in Mexico with more than 20 gay bars, modern discos and saunas, as well as their own gay radio program. Puerto Vallarta, which is close to Guadalajara (3 hours by car), offers also a wide range of gay venues and makes this area the „gay belt" of Mexico.

Guadalajara ist eine große, pulsierende Stadt und mit über vier Millionen Einwohnern Mexikos zweitgrößte Metropole, die über 500 Jahre Geschichte in sich vereint.
Sie spiegelt die mexikanische Mentalität von Tequila, Mariachis und Charroreiten wider. Die Vergangenheit und die Gegenwart gehen in dieser Stadt, die auch als die „Stadt der Rosen" bekannt ist, Hand in Hand. Leider muß Guadalajara wegen des großen Einflusses der katholischen Kirche immer noch gegen tradierte Wertvorstellungen, Intoleranz und altmodische Klischees kämpfen.
Trotzdem gedeiht die dortige Szene prächtig und gilt als die größte und bunteste Mexikos. Sie hat mehr als 20 Schwulenbars, moderne Diskos und Saunen und sogar ein schwules Radioprogramm. Puerto Vallarta ist nur 3 Autostunden von Guadalajara entfernt und gilt mit seinen zahlreichen Szenetreffs als „Schwulengürtel" Mexikos.

Guadalajara est une grande ville dynamique au passé historique de cinq siècles et avec plus de 4 millions d'habitants, c'est la deuxième ville du Mexique.
Elle est le reflet de la mentalité mexicaine avec sa tequila, ses mariachis et ses charros. Le passé et le présent marchent main dans la mains dans cette ville connue également sous le nom de « ville des roses ». Malheureusement, Guadalajara continue de subir la grande influence de l'Église catholique qui propage des idées traditionnelles, l'intolérance et des clichés d'un autre temps.
Néanmoins, le milieu gay s'y développe merveilleusement et est devenu le plus grand et le plus riche du Mexique. Il possède plus de 20 bars, boîtes modernes et saunas et dispose même d'un programme de radio. Puerto Vallarta n'est qu'à trois heures en voiture de Guadalajara et, avec ses nombreux lieux gays, cette ville fait figure de « cordon gay » du Mexique.

Guadalajara es una gran ciudad, floreciente y cosmopolita (la segunda ciudad más grande del país con más de 4 millones de habitantes) con más de 500 años de historia. Es un importante símbolo del espíritu de México, por ser la tierra del tequila, los mariachis y la charrería. Pasado y presente conviven en esta ciudad, también conocida como la „ciudad de las rosas". Desafortunadamente debido a la influencia de la iglesia católica, Guadalajara tiene que luchar continuamente contra los valores tradicionales, la intolerancia y anticuados clichés.
De cualquier forma, la escena gay crece constantemente en la ciudad y es considerada la más próspera en el país, con más de 20 bares gay, además de discotecas y saunas modernas, así como un propio programa de radio. Puerto Vallarta, muy cerca de Guadalajara (3 horas en coche) ofrece también una amplia oferta de lugares gay, lo que convierte a esta zona en el cinturón gay de México.

Guadalajara è una città con più di 4 milioni di abitanti ed è la seconda città più grande del Messico (dopo città del Messico) con più di 500 anni di storia.
Il passato e il presente in questa città, chiamata anche „città delle rose", convivono armoniosamente. A causa della forte influenza della chiesa, l'intolleranza e i pregiudizi sono piuttosto diffusi. Nonostante ciò, la scena gay qui, è la più grande e la più variopinta di tutto il Messico. Ci sono più di 20 bar, discoteche molto moderne, saune e addirittura una radio gay. Puerto Vallarta è a sole 3 ore di macchina da Guadalajara, ed è nota per i suoi numerosi locali gay.

GAY INFO

■ **Aquí estamos** (G)
🖳 www.aquiestamos.com
Web site for the Guadalajara gay community, with useful information about the gay life in the city and other important gay centres in Mexico.

■ **Guadalajara Gay Radio** (G) Fri 24h
104.3 FM Red Radio Universidad Guadalajara
🖳 www.gdlgayradio.com
Gay radio station.

BARS

■ **Arizona Saloon** (B G MA S SNU) Wed-Sun 22.30-3h
Av. de la Paz 1985, Zona Rosa *At Chapultepec, Zona Rosa*
☎ (33) 3827-1274

■ **California's** (! B G MC NR) 18-3, Sat 17-5h
C/. Pedro Moreno 652 *At 8 de Julio* ☎ (333) 614-3221
Hansom guys and cheap drinks. Normally packed!

■ **Cantina Tí@s** (AC B d GLM MA VS WE) 8-1h
C/. Degollado 138, Centro *Opp. Hotel Universo. Bus Turquesa, 45, 214 „Cantina" style.*

■ **Caudillos** (B D G M YC)
Wed, Fri & Sat 17-6, Mon, Tue, Thu & Sun 17-4h
C/. Prisciliano Sánchez 407 *At Ocampo* ☎ (33) 3613-5445
Disco bar with a restaurant. Every day beer 2-4-1, Wed beer is 3-4-1.

■ **Ciervo. El** (B G MA)
C/. 20 de Noviembre 797 *At Los Angeles* ☎ (33) 3619-6765

■ **Circus Club** (B D GLM I S WE) Fr- Sat 21-5h
C/. Galeana 277, Centro *Corner of Prisciliano Sánchez* ☎ (33) 13-0299
🖳 www.grupocircus.com
Cyber café, boutique, jugglers performance.

■ **EQuilibrio** (! AC B D glm) Mon-Sun
C/. Ocampo 293 *Corner Miguel Blanco* 🖳 www.rutacaudillos.com

■ **Kike's Bar** (B g MA S) Wed-Mon 16-3h
Colón 440, Las Nueve Esquinas *Between Leandro Valle & Nueva Galicia, Las Nueve Esquinas*

■ **Link Bar** (B G MC OS) Tue-Sun 19-3h
Av. La Paz 2199, Zona Rosa ☎ (33) 31-3840
Four areas: terrace lounge, main bar, garden terrace and VIP lounge. Mon: live music, Tue: games night, Sun: afternoon brunch buffet.

■ **Maskara's** (! B G m MA) 8-2h
C/. Maestranza 238, Col. Centro *At Prisciliano Sánchez, two blocks from Degollado Theatre* ☎ (33) 613-81-0

■ **Prisciliana. La** (B glm MA) Mon-Sun 17-3h
Prisciliano Sánchez 395, Centro Histórico *Near Mision Carlton Hotel* ☎ (33) 3562-0725

■ **Via Plata** (B G M MA OS) 21-2, WE -4h
Av. de la Paz 2121-C *Sector Juárez* ☎ (33) 3616-1207

CAFES

■ **Pancho Jr. Los** (B D glm MA r) 9-2h
C/. Galeana 180 A *2nd floor* ☎ (33) 3613-5325

■ **Vida Caffé** (B G m MC)
Avenida Hidalgo 81-a ☎ (33) 118 11834
A new cafe with snacks and sandwiches.

DANCECLUBS

■ **7Sins** (B D DR GLM SNU) Fri-Sat 22-?h
C/. Pedro Moreno 532, Zona Centro *Corner at Donato Guerra* ☎ (33) 3658 0713

■ **Angel's** (AC B CC D G M MA S SNU WE) Fri-Sun 22-4h
C/. López Cotilla 1495-B, Colonia Americana *Between Av. Chapultepec & Marsella* ☎ (33) 3615-2525

■ **Light Kiss** (! B CC D GLM S SNU) Tue-Sun 21-?h
C/. Hidalgo 838 *Col. Centro Histórico*
The biggest gay club in Guadalajara .

■ **Monica's** (! B D glm m S SNU ST YC) Tue-Sun 22-5h
Av. Álvaro Obergón 1713 *Sector Libertad, between C/. 68 & 70* ☎ (33) 3643-9544 🖳 www.monicasdisco.com
Popular after midnight. Drag & strip shows Fri-Sun. No sign, look for canopy under a big palm tree.

■ **Mr. Tom's. El** (AC B CC g M MA OS VS WE) 13-3h
C/. Madero 111, Centro *Close to Hotel San Francisco. Bus 330* ☎ (33) 3614-8326
Live music Fri-Sat.

■ **Passion Club** (B D GLM MA S ST)
C/. Ocampo 268, Centro ☎ (33) 1197-1762 (infoline)
Call for information regarding the party programme.

■ **Sexy's** (B D GLM MA S) 18-3h
C/. Degollado 273, Centro *Next door to San Francisco Plaza Hotel Show 22.30h.*

■ **SOS Club** (D GLM OS S ST) 21-3h, closed Mon
Av. La Paz 1413, Zona Centro *Sector Hidalgo* ☎ (33) 3826-4179
Established in 2002 and still going strong! Drag and live sex shows at WE. Wed, Thu & Sun no cover charge and cheap beer, Fri & Sat cover charge includes two beers or one drink. Strip shows on Fri & Sat.

■ **Taller. El** (! B D G S YC) 22-5h
C/. 66 N° 30, Col. Reforma *Bewteen C/. Gigantes Eje & 12 de Octubre* ☎ (33) 3826-9812

RESTAURANTS

■ **Chata. La** (AC B BF cc M NG RES VEG)
Av. Corona 126, Zona Centro *Between Av. Juarez & López Cotilla* ☎ (33) 3613-0588 🖳 www.lachata.com.mx
Not a gay restaurant but truly worth a visit. Wonderful Mexican cuisine. There is always a crowd waiting for a table at this very popular restaurant.

SEX SHOPS/BLUE MOVIES

■ **Erectus** (g) Mon-Sat 12-21h
Marsella 126, Zona Rosa *Between Vallarta & López Cotilla* ☎ (33) 3848-4360 🖳 www.erectus.com.mx

■ **Ninfa** (F glm WE) Mon-Sat 11-20h
C/. Corona 181, local 1207, piso 2 *Bus 214, 258, 629, Turquesa & Platino* ☎ (33) 3613-6977

SAUNAS/BATHS

■ **Academia. La** (b DU FH G MA MSG P RR SA SB WE WO) 9-21h
Prisciliano Sánchez 484, Centro *Between Donato Guerra & Enrique González. Bus 45, 142, 214* ☎ (33) 3124-1154 🖳 www.gaygdl.com/directorio/academia
Rather run down but otherwise action-packed. Remember to bring your own condoms.

■ **Baños La Fuente** (! B DU G MA MSG SB VS WO) 12-21h
C/. Manuel Acuña 1107 *Between Nicolás Romero & Gregoria Davila* ☎ (33) 3826-3618
Two steam rooms and one darkroom. Basic but lots of action. There are no lockers, only cubicles.

■ **Renacer Day Spa** (! B DU FH G I m MA MSG OS p PP RR SA SB SOL WH WO) 12-22h
Amado Nervo 106, Col. Ladrón de Guevara *Close to Av. Americas & Av. Mexico* ☎ (33) 3616-4441 🖳 www.renacerdayspa.net
Sauna with European standards. Most expensive sauna in the city. Great garden to relax in and good facilities. Best day is Wed (partner day; 2-4-1). Manicure, pedicure and massage available.

HOTELS

■ **Casa Alebrijes** (BF CC G I MA PK RWS RWT VA WI) All year
Libertad 1016, Colonia Centro *Located in the historic centre and centre of gay nightlife area* ☎ (33) 3614-5232 🖳 www.casaalebrijes.com
Boutique hotel for gay men and women, 2 suites and 7 rooms.

■ **Hostel Lit** (bf CC G m MA MSG SA) Hostel 7-23h, reception 24h
C/. Degollado, 413, Col. Centro ☎ (33) 1200 55 05 🖳 www.hostel-lit-guadalajara.com
Located in the heart of historic Guadalajara and the gay village. Gay clubs, bars and saunas are within a few blocks. All the sights and some of the best restaurants in Jalisco are on the doorstep. Affordable, clean hostel with singles, doubles and dormitories dedicated to gay clients.

■ **La Perla** (AC BF G I OS RWS RWT VA) All year
Prado 128, Colonia Americana ☎ (33) 3334-9673 🖳 www.LaPerlaGdl.net
Gay owned and operated. The hotel offers one or two staff members of the staff to guide you through near gay bars and clubs.

■ **San Francisco Plaza** (BF cc glm M MA) All year
C/. Degollado 267, Col. Juárez *Centre* ☎ (33) 3613-8954
A wonderful, small hotel with comfortable rooms. Not far from some gay bars and the nightclub. Traditional or European breakfasts available.

GUEST HOUSES

■ **Casa Venezuela** (BF cc G MA) All year, 24hrs
Venezuela 459, Colonia Americana *Near city centre* ☎ (33) 3826-6590 🖳 www.casavenezuela.com.mx
Casa Venezuela a restored colonial house within easy walking distance of many gay bars, restaurants and saunas. Gay owned.

■ **Escape B&B** (bf G I MA NU OS RWS RWT VA WO) All year
Enrique Gonzalez Martinez 446, Zona Centro ☎ (33) 3613-4140 🖳 www.escapeguadalajara.com
An economical bed and breakfast located in the center of the historical area of Guadalajara.

GENERAL GROUPS

■ **Homo Sapiens, A. C.** (GLM)
Apartado Postal 1-1796 🖳 www.geocities.com/homosapiensac
Human rights group also dealing with questions regarding HIV and AIDS.

CRUISING

All AYOR:
-Plaza Tapatía (near Degollado theatre)
-Calle Pedro Moreno.

Guanajuato – Guanajuato ☎ 415

DANCECLUBS

■ **Bule** (B D DR G SNU VS) Sat 22-3h
Mar Báltico 125 esq. Alfredo Valadez, Col. Rinconada del Sur. Leon ☎ (477) 761-9228 🖳 www.bule-club.com

■ **Whoopees** (B D GLM S) Thu-Sat
C/. Manuel Doblado 39 *near to Plazuela del Ropero* ☎ (415) 737 0327

■ **Wish Garden** (! B D GLM S) Mon-Sun
C/. Tepetapa 78 ☎ (415) 732 4659

CRUISING

-Zócalo (Jardín de la Unión opposite Teatro Juárez)
-C/. Pedro Moreno / C/. Morelos / Av. Chapultepec / Av. Donato Guerra.

Irapuato – Guanajuato ☎ 462

BARS

■ **Blanco y Negro** (B D g) Thu-Sun
Av. Ejército Nacional 890 ☎ (462) 4-2381

DANCECLUBS

■ **Pedro's Lounge Room** (B D GLM S SNU) Mon-Sun
C/. Ocampo 21 *Corner of Ave. Guerrero* ☎ (462) 113 7704

Ixtapa Zihuatanejo – Guerrero ☎ 753

BARS

■ **Splash** (B f g MA VS) 12-24h
C/. Ejido *Corner of C/. Vicente Guerrero, in front of Comermex bank*
☎ (753) 4-0880

Jalapa – Veracruz ☎ 228

BARS

■ **Cabaret Xalapa** (AC B D GLM MA) Wed-Sat 21.30-3.30h
Francisco Javier Clavijero # 4, Col. Centro Histórico
🖳 cabaretbarxalapa.blogspot.com

■ **Disco Mix Kloset** (B D DR GLM MA S SNU ST) Wed-Sun 21-3h
Chapultepec 2-A, Col. Los Laureles *Cose to Pepsi*
Go-gos, drag queens, promotions every day.

■ **Kiss** (B D GLM MA) Thu-Sat 21.30-3.30h
Callejon González Aparicio #2, Col. Centro Histórico *Close to Café Lindo*

DANCECLUBS

■ **Secret** (B D GLM SNU) 22-?h
C/. Ruiz Cortines 1384

CRUISING

-Parque Juárez (AYOR)
-Jardines del Agora (centro next to Parque Juárez; AYOR)

La Paz – Baja California ☎ 612

HOTELS

■ **Hotel Mediterrane** (AC B BF cc glm I M MC OS PK RWB RWS RWT VA) All year
C/. Allende 36 *Located in the city centre. 20m from Malecón*
☎ (612) 125-1195 🖳 www.hotelmed.com
The rooftop terrace overlooks the Malecon, the waterfront promenade where Paceños greet the day, and everyone stops to watch the spectacular sunsets.

León – Guanajuato ☎ 477

BARS

■ **Amigo. El** (B g) ?-24h
Belisario Domínguez 423 P. B.

■ **Ego** (AC B D GLM S SNU) Fri-Sun
Mar Báltico 125, Col. Rinconada del Sur *At Alfredo Valadez* ☎ (477) 161-8038

■ **G Bar** (B D G MC OS) Daily 18-2h
Madero 226, Centro Histórico *Corner of Gante* ☎ (477) 716-3695
🖳 www.labizantina.com
Opened in 2005, this bar/cafe is a place to unwind after work. In the most beautiful part of town.

■ **Movida. La** (B G MC) 10-24h
Belisario Domínguez 417 *2nd floor* ☎ (477) 714-2141

DANCECLUBS

■ **Biza Club** (B D G YC) Wed, Fri & Sat 22-3h
C/. 20 de Enero 204, Centro Histórico *Next door to Inmaculada Church*
☎ (477) 716-3695 🖳 www.labizantina.com
A gay club since 1998. For those over 18 years only. Dress code fashion, urban and casual/trendy. House Room & Pop Room music. Check out the events: www.labizantina.com

■ **Heaven** (B D GLM S) Fri-Sat
Av. de las Torres 5300 ☎ (477) 273 32 04 (mobile)
🖳 www.heavenclub.com.mx

■ **Madame Disco Club. La** (B D G MC S ST T) Thu-Sun 22-3h
Blvd Lopéz Mateos, 1709, Col. Los Gavilanes ☎ (477) 716-3695
🖳 www.labizantina.com
A great disco welcoming transvestites as well as gay men over the age of 18.

SAUNAS/BATHS

■ **Baños Altamar** (DU g SA SB) 8-20h, closed Mon
27 de Septiembre, Col. Obregón *Corner of C/. Julián de Obregón*
☎ (477) 713-3446
This is not a gay-dedicated facility so discretion is advised. Don't forget to bring your sandals, just for hygiene purposes. Ask for „vapor general" at the entrance to go to the commune showers and steam room. Otherwise you will be given a private, boring cubicle.

CRUISING

-Market (Mon & Tue)
-Zocalo near and around the fountain.

Manzanillo – Colima ☎ 314

BARS

■ **Evolution** (B g MA) Tue-Sat 19-3h
Blvd Miguel de la Madrid H. 1550, Zona Hotelera
Fri & Sat drag show.

CRUISING

-Plaza Santiago and Playa Santiago
-La Perlita
-El Jardín
-Plaza San Pedrito
-Zona Roja

Mazatlán – Sinaloa ☎ 669

BARS

■ **Pepe Toro** (! AC B D GLM MA ST WE) Thu-Sun 21.30-4h
Av. de las Garzas 18, Zona Dorada *In front of restaurant Guadalajara Grill*
☎ (669) 9144176 🖳 www.pepetoro.com

■ **Vitrolas** (AC B GLM m MA S VS WE) Tue-Sun 18-2h
Heriberto Frías 1608, Centro Histórico *Between Angel Flores St. & 21 Marzo* ☎ (669) 985-2221 🖳 www.vitrolasbar.com

CAFES

■ **Panamá Restaurant Pastelería** (b glm m MA)
Av. de las Garzas / Ave Camerón Sábalo

DANCECLUBS

■ **Passion Club** (B D GLM SNU) Fri-Sun
Av. Playa Gaviotas N° 417 *Zona Dorada* 🖳 www.fotolog.com/passion_club

HOTELS

■ **Old Mazatlán inn** (AC B BF CC D glm M OS PI S) All year
C/. Pedregoso 18 ☎ (669) 981-4361 🖳 oldmazatlaninn.com

CRUISING

-Beach, walk from Valentino's to the El Pollo Soco restaurant

Mérida – Yucatán ☎ 999

BARS

■ **Pancho's Club** (B g MA)
Av. Juárez 33

■ **Scalivur** (B G MA) Thu-Sun 22-3h
C/. 4-B X 39-A No. 308 Cól. San Camilo II ☎ (999) 108-2046

DANCECLUBS

■ **Angeluz** (B CC D GLM S SNU) Wed-Sun 23-?h
Km 7 C/ Mérida-Umán *near PEMEX-house* ☎ (999) 217-5233
www.angeluzclub.com
has the feel of Miami

■ **Kabuki's** (B D glm MA ST) Thu-Sat
Av. Jacinto Canek 381 *Near C/. 59A, west of C/. 124, along the Corralón*
Drag shows.

■ **Pride Disco** (B CC D G S SNU) Wed-Sat
C/. Anillo Periférico Mérida *200m from Puente de Umán*
☎ (999) 946-4401 www.pridedisco.com

GUEST HOUSES

■ **Angeles de Mérida B & B** (AC BF CC GLM I m MSG PI RWS RWT VA) All year
C/. 74-A, 494-A x 57 y 59-A *Between 57 & 59-A St* ☎ (999) 923-8163
www.angelesdemerida.com
Gay owned and gay friendly. Antique Mexican colonial style Hotel with a beautiful private garden available to guests. Professional, attentive staff.

■ **Casa Ana B & B** (AC H MA OS PI) All year
C/. 52 #469 *Between C/. 51 & C/. 53* ☎ (999) 924-0005
www.casaana.com
Guesthouse with four rooms, all with private bathrooms. Very reasonable prices.

■ **Posada Santiago** (AC bf CC GLM MA PI)
All year, reception 10-20h
C/. 57, No. 552, x 66 y 68 *Airport 5 miles away* ☎ (999) 928-4258
www.posadasantiagomx.com
Gay owned and operated 4-room guesthouse. 18-foot tall privacy fence. Roof top sunning area.

PRIVATE ACCOMMODATION

■ **Casa San Juan** (AC BF GLM)
C/. 62, N° 545A, Centro *Historical centre* ☎ (999) 986-2937
www.casasanjuan.com

CRUISING

-Zócalo (Parque Central)
-Santa Lucía Park (after 16h)
-Calle 60 (between Zócalo and Santa Lucía Park)
-Cinema Premiere.

Mexicali – Baja California Norte ☎ 686

BARS

■ **Babylon's** (AC B GLM MA VS) Wed-Sat 21-?h
Blvd. Morelos 475 *½ block south of Lerdo*
Adjoining Internet café open daily.

■ **Mirage** (AC B GLM MA ST) 21-?h
Av. Zaragoza *Downtown on Zaragoza, 1 block west of Morelos*

■ **Tare Bar** (AC B D GLM MA SNU T WE) 21-3h
Av. Jalisco y Calle Tercera 1098, Col. Pueblo Nuevo *In front of Hospital de las Californias*
Miss Mexicali Gay Award takes place here every November 19th.

■ **Taurino. El** (B D GLM MA R) 18-?h Mon closed
Av. Juan de Zuazúa 480 *At Avenida José María Morelos*
Late bar.

DANCECLUBS

■ **Life** (AC D GLM MA)

CRUISING

-Chapultepec Park (centre)
-San José Steam Baths (AYOR).

Monterrey – Nuevo León ☎ 81

BARS

■ **Akbal** (AC B CC d G MA OS VS WE) Tue-Sun 20-2h
Abasolo 870, Planta Alta, Casa del Maíz *Between Diego de Montemayor & Dr. Coss. Bus 1, 4, M° Zaragoza* ☎ (81) 1257-2986
www.akballounge.com
Trendy bar in an old factory warehouse.

■ **Between** (AC B gLm MA S VS) Wed-Sat 21-?h
Eugenio Garza Sada 2121, Col. Roma */Between Junco de la Vega & Atenas*
☎ (81) 8358-7035
Lesbian bar.

■ **Brut 33** (B G MC) Wed-Sat
C/. Madero Pte, 2213 *Between C/. Degollado & Edison* ☎ (81) 4444-8428
www.brut33.com
Opened in 2009.

■ **Divas** (B GLM MA SNU ST WE) Wed-Sat 22-h?
C/. Zaragoza/Isaac Garza *City centre*

■ **Dorados de Villa** (AC B GLM MA OS WE) Wed-Sat 19-1h
Treviño 1813, Col. Obrera

■ **Evolution** (AC B D G MA SNU ST VS WE) Fri & Sat 21-?h
Espinoza 345 *Between C/ Juan Méndez & Jiménez* ☎ (81) 8465-5882
A disco for cowboys, that opens only Fri & Sat for men only.

■ **Kloster. El** (AC B g MA R T WE) G after 22h
Av. Benito Juárez 916 *Between C/. Arteaga & Madero*

■ **Taurus. El** (B G WE YC) 11-1h
C/. Arteaga 117, Poniente *Between Colegio Civil & Juaréz*

■ **Vongolé Terraza** (B GLM MC) Wed-Sat 21-?h
Eugenio Garza Sada 2121, Col. Roma *Terrace on Between's 2nd floor*
☎ (81) 8358-7035 www.vongoleterraza.com
Between is lesbian crowd and Vongolé mixed crowd.

MEN'S CLUBS

■ **Casita. La** (AC cc DR G NU S SB SNU VS)
Mon-Sat Summer 19-3.30 and Winter 20-3.30h
C/. Allende 943, Ori, *San Diego de Montemayor* ☎ (81) 8345 1104
www.lacasitamonterrey.com

DANCECLUBS

■ **BabyShower** (AC B D G MA SNU ST VS WE) Sat 22.30-7h
Ocampo 433 Pte. Centro ☎ (81) 8881-5632
www.babyshowerdisco.com

■ **Casa Lola. La** (B D glm MA) Thu-Sat 23-?h
C/. Padre Mier N° 867 *Between Porfirio Diaz and Vallarta*
☎ (81) 8343-6210 www.lacasadelola.com

■ **Extremo** (D G MA S) 19-2h, Wed & Thu closed
Av. Fidel Velazques 318 *200m north of Pulga Mitras*
Strip shows on Sat.

■ **Kasting-Mty** (B D glm) Thu-Sat 21.30-?h
C/. Padre Mier N° 318 *Between Cuauhtemoc and Pino Suárez*
☎ (81) 8343-9470 www.kasting-mty.com

■ **Parking** (B D GLM S) Wed-Sat 22-?h
C/. Allende 120, Oriente, Centro
www.facebook.com/pages/Parking-Club/94869607410

SAUNAS/BATHS

■ **Baños Stic** (DU g MA SA SB) 6-22, Sun 8-16h
Heroes del 47 / Carlos Salaza ☎ (81) 8375-7690
Mixed sauna where discretion is advised. Try to get a cabin with a number above 20, as the higher numbers are at the back, away from the attendants.

■ **Sparta Sauna & Gym** (B DU G SA SB VS WH WO) Daily, 12-24h
Alvaro Obregón 107 *Between Modesto Arreola and Aramberri*
☎ (81) 1739-3111 www.spartamty.com

Before 16h students with ID pay half price. Tue: 2 x 1(locker), Fri:"Password Day" check out the web page on Thu to get the password for Fri. With ithe code you get a discount and you will be able to leave the sauna and come back as you wish on that day.

GIFT & PRIDE SHOPS

■ **Closet de Kika. El** (GLM)
Tue & Sun 1130-20, Wed-Sat 11.30-23.30h
C/. Allende 118 *Between Guerrero & Juárez*
www.elclosetdekika.com

CRUISING

-Zona Rosa-Plaza Hidalgo (from 17-21h)
-Sanborns, Zona Rosa news stand
-Galerías Monterrey Shopping Mall (public bath)
-C/. Padre Mier / Av. Juárez & Av. Cuauthémoc
-Villa de Santiago (WE) (La Boca Lake área)
-C/. Morales.

Morelia - Michoacán ☎ 443

BARS

■ **Amnesia Happy Bar** (B GLM MA) Tue-Sat 18.30-2.30h
C/. Gertrudis Bocanegra No. 905, Col. Ventura Puente *Corner of Av. Lázaro Cárdenas* ☎ (443) 312-1578
■ **Beered** (B GLM MA) Fri-Sun 18-23h
Vicente Barroso No 44 – A, Col. Félix Ireta *Next to gas station Ventura Puente*
■ **Mama No Lo Sabe** (B D GLM MA S) Thu-Sat 22-3h
C/. Aldama 116, Col. Centro *Corner Garcia Obeso* ☎ (443) 189-9447
■ **Open Mind** (B D GLM MA S SNU ST) Wed-Sat 22-3h
Av. Madero Poniente No. 1790 ☎ (443) 327-5372
■ **Salamanders** (B D GLM MA S SNU ST) Wed-Sun 22-3h
C/. Aquiles Serdán No. 227, Centro Histórico ☎ (443) 218-1171
Go-gos.

DANCECLUBS

■ **Con la Rojas** (b D G MA) 23-2h, Sun-Wed closed
C/. Aldama 343, Centro Histórico ☎ (443) 312-1578

Nuevo Laredo - Tamaulipas ☎ 867

BARS

■ **Gusano** (B g) ?-2h
C/. Dr. Mier 2908 ☎ (867) 2-2075

DANCECLUBS

■ **Soho** (B D g MA)
Jesús Carranza 115, Centro *Two blocks from bridge N°2*

Oaxaca - Oaxaca ☎ 951

BARS

■ **Chinampa. La** (B g m MA) Daily 11-1h
C/. Bustamente 605 *North of Periférico* ☎ (951) 2-3133
Very cheap beer. Very relaxed atmosphere. Located half a block from the Cine Rio – a place to meet people.
■ **Rinconada del Carmen. La** (B g MC) Daily 7-?h
Privada 14 de Julio 212, Col. 5 Señores
Mexican cantina with snacks, beer and lots of University students.

MEN'S CLUBS

■ **Costa. La** (B G MC SNU) Sat & Sun 21-?h
16 de Septiembre 517, col. 5 señores

DANCECLUBS

■ **502 / Numerito. El** (B D g T YC) Wed-Sat 22.30-?h
C/. Porfirio Díaz 502, Centro ☎ (951) 51-6602
Wed karaoke, Thu juke-box, Fri & Sat danceclub.

SAUNAS/BATHS

■ **Baños La Fuente** (b DU g MA RR SA SB)
Sun-Thu 7-19, Fri & Sat -2h
C/. 20 de Noviembre 1021, Centro *Between Periférico & Moctezuma*
☎ (951) 516-5668

Orizaba - Veracruz ☎ 272

BARS

■ **Clyo Club** (B g MA) Thu-Sat 21-?h
Camino Nacional N. 125 *At C/ Santo Domingo* ☎ (272) 722-0578
■ **Sky Drink** (B D g SNU ST) Wed-Sat
Madero Norte 1280
Drag & strip shows on Sat.

Playa del Carmen - Quintana Roo ☎ 984

BARS

■ **Playa 69** (AC B D DR G S SNU YC) Mon-Sat 10.00-14 & 17-21, Sun Closed
Av. 5a #156 *Between 4th and 6th street behind the 7-11 store*
☎ (984) 134-7799
No cover charge.

DANCECLUBS

■ **Bloo** (AC D G MA NU ST)
C/. 6 *Near Av. 20*

RESTAURANTS

■ **Jacobi's Restaurant-Bar** (B CC G MA) 8-24h
C/. 22 / Av. 10 *Corner of C/. 6, between Av. 10 & 5* ☎ (984) 873-1876

HOTELS

■ **Aqualuna** (AC B BF cc H MA MSG) All year
Av. 10 & 14th *Close to the 5th Av. and all its reataurants, bars and shops and one block away from C/. 12, where the nightlife is* ☎ (984) 873-1013
■ **Le Rêve Hotel & Spa** (AC B BF CC GLM I M MA MSG OS PA PI RWB RWS RWT WO) All year
Playa Xcalacoco Fraccion 2A ☎ (984) 109 5660
www.hotellereve.com
Romance, peace and secludedness combined with impeccable service.

Puebla - Puebla ☎ 222

BARS

■ **Cigarra. La** (B G MA s) Mon-Sun 18-3h
C/. 5, Centro Histórico *At Poniente corner of C/. 7 Sur* ☎ (222) 343-4390
Video bar.
■ **Oxi_gn** (B d GLM m) Wed-Sun 19-?h
C/ 5 Oriente, Col Analco

CAFES

■ **Encuadre. El** (G I M MA S VS) Mon-Sat 17-23h
14 Oriente 1414-A, Zona de Monumentos *Close to the convention centre / Church of San Francisco* ☎ (222) 236-3957
Art exhibits, theatre, movie nights, and other LGBT cultural events.
■ **Franco's Coffee & Beer** (G MA)
C/. 5 Oriente No. 402, Barrio de los Sapos ☎ (222) 232-3409
■ **Mariposa** (GLM MA)
4 Sur No. 705
■ **Quimera** (GLM MA)
C/. 3 Oriente No. 611, Barrio de los Sapos
■ **Schmetterling** (GLM MA)
14 Sur No. 3509, Anzures ☎ (222) 194-4555

DANCECLUBS

■ **Agora** (B D GLM MA)
14 Sur No. 3509, Anzures ☎ (222) 576-2349

■ **Eclectica** (B D GLM MA S ST) Thu-Sat 20-3h
9 Poniente No. 2317, Col. Rivera Santiago *One block from Av. Juárez, corner of 25 Sur* ☎ (222) 482-8086
■ **Franco's Bule Bar** (B D GLM) Tue-Thu
C/. 5 Oriente 402, Barrio de los Sapos ☎ (222) 232-3409
💻 www.francosdisco.com
■ **Franco's Disco Club** (B D GLM) Fri & Sat
C/. 3 Oriente 1403, Col. Analco ☎ (222) 246-1639
Same owners as Franco's Bule Bar.
■ **Garrotos Disco Club** (! B D GLM S) Fri & Sat 21-3h
22 Oriente 602, Col. Xenenetla *Near Blvd 5 de Mayo, opp. Gigante*
☎ (222) 242-4232
■ **Keops** (B D GLM SNU ST YC) Thu-Sun 22-3h
14 Poniente 101, San Andrés Cholula *12km from Puebla, at C/. 5 de Mayo*
☎ (222) 247-0368
■ **Soberbia. La** (B D GLM)
C/. 3 Oriente 611, Barrio de los Sapos ☎ (222) 294-2785

SAUNAS/BATHS

■ **Baños Las Termas** (! DR DU G MA MSG OS SA SB SOL VS WH WO) 8-20, Sat 8-21, Sat 10.30-Sun 15h (non-stop), Mon closed
C/. 5 de Mayo 2810 ☎ (222) 232-9562
💻 www.garotosdisco.com/termas.htm
One of the few Mexican gay saunas with a safe and cosy atmosphere. Frequented by both locals and tourists who want to relax and have fun. There is a wonderful sun terrace on the top floor of this three floor sauna. The sauna is very well equipped and the staff are extremely friendly. The latest videos are shown and the steam room is large and very hot. Condoms are sold here but best is to bring your own.

CRUISING

-Zócalo/Plaza de la Constitución
-CAPU (bus station)
-Casa de la Cultura (5 oriente No. 5)

Puerto Vallarta – Jalisco ☎ 322

BARS

■ **Amigos. Los** (B G m OS R) 18-4h
C/. Carranza 219 *Zona Romantica* ☎ (322) 222-7802
Friendly locals & some rentboys.
■ **Amor Bar** (B D GLM MA)
C/. Lazaro Cardenas 271 ☎ 222-7427
Delicious martinis and refreshing cocktails with local and guest dj's, fabulous music, great atmosphere, and comfortable sitting areas.
■ **Antropology Male Strippers Bar** (AC B G MA SNU) 21-4h
C/. Morelos 101, Plaza Río Cuale *At the bridge* ☎ (322) 221 6380
💻 www.antroplogypv.com
Continous strippers shows from 21-4h. The strippers hustle the crowd very aggressively for drinks and a „private visit" upstairs.
■ **Apache's Bar** (B GLM M OS) daily 17-2h
C/. Olas Altas 439 *At Rodríguez, adjacent to Apache's Bistro* ☎ (322) 222 4004
Lively sidewalk cocktail bar. Mature mixed gay/lesbian crowd. Lesbian owned.
■ **Bar Frida** (B GLM MA R) 13-2h
C/. Insurgentes 301 *At Venustiano Carranza* ☎ 222 3668
Popular. Some hustlers, or „Chichifos" as they are called in Puerto Vallarta. Also serves food.
■ **Casanova Show Lounge** (AC B CC g S SL) 22-?h
C/. Lázaro Cárdenas 302
Continuous Stripper shows. Mixed gay men and straight women.
■ **Diva's** (B GLM MA) 14-2h
C/. Francisco Madero 388
Small and cosy bar with jukebox and tables. Popular with locals, Mexican cantina-style bar. Gay owned.
■ **Fuego Bar & Bites** (B CC M MA OS)
Corner of Pulpito/Amapas ☎ 222-2114
Fuego is a casual bar in the beach area with upstairs and sidewalk seating. Pub bar style food, to tide you over, this is a great place to see and be seen.
■ **Garbo's Piano Bar & Jazz Lounge** (AC B GLM MA S) 17-2h
Pulpito 142 at Olas Altas
Very popular with locals & tourists. Upscale and elegant, gay owned. Live music on weekends
■ **La Bola Bar** (AYOR B CC DR G I MC NU OS PI R SB SOL VS WE WH) 10-24h
C/. Pilitas 174 *Courtyard of Vallarta Cora Hotel*
☎ 223-2815 💻 www.vallartacora.com
Poolside bar. Jacuzzi and darkroom area. Popular and very cruisy.
■ **No Borders Bar** (AC B GLM) Tue-Sat 17-2h
C/. Libertad 221 *Corner of Júarez* ☎ (322) 136 8775 (mobile)
💻 www.noborderspv.com
Western styled bar.
■ **Noche Bar/Lounge. La** (! AC B CC glm MA)
C/. Lázaro Cárdenas 263 ☎ 222-3364 💻 www.lanochepv.com
Very Popular, classy, table-service bar, Great Martini's. Gay-owned.
■ **Sama Martini Lounge** (AC B G MA OS) 18-1h
C/. Olas Altas 510, Zona Romántica ☎ (322) 221-6380
💻 www.samapv.com
Luxurious and elegant sidewalk seating.
■ **Stereo Bar** (AC B CC GLM) 21-4h
C/. Lázaro Cardenas 267 *Zona Romántica*
Young and hip crowd.
■ **Vallarta Cora** (AYOR B CC DR G I MC NU OS PI R SB SOL VS WE WH) 10-23h
C/. Pilitas 174, Col. Emiliano Zapata *At Vallarta Cora Hotel*
☎ (322) 223-2815 💻 www.vallartacora.com
Poolside bar. Jacuzzi and darkroom area. Popular and very cruisy.

CAFES

■ **Coffee Cup. The** (GLM m MA)
C/. Rodolfo Gomez 146 *At Olas Altas* ☎ (322) 222-8584
THE gay coffee shop.
■ **Cyber Smoothie** (AC glm M MSG)
C/. Rodolfo Gomez 111 ☎ (322) 223-4784
The attractive owner is also a massage therapist.
■ **Heart Coffee** (AC B bf CC F glm)
C/. Basilio Badillo 419 ☎ (322) 222-0828
Great ambience.
■ **San Angel** (bf CC F glm M MA OS)

DANCECLUBS

■ **Balcones** (AC CC D G MA S SL T WE) 22-6h
C/. Juarez 182, Centro ☎ 222-4671
Outdoor terrace, two stories, dance floor, go-go boys, Drag shows. Gay owned
■ **Club Mañana** (! AC B D G M OS PI S ST YC) 15-6, disco 22-?h
C/. Venustiano Carranza, 290 ☎ (322) 222-7772 💻 www.manana.mx
Large dance club with multiple areas including patio, dance floor, pool, indoor lounges.
■ **Paco's Ranch** (! D G MA S SL T WE) 10-6, disco 22-?h
Av. Ignacio L. Vallarta 237 ☎ (322) 222-1899 💻 www.pacosranch.com
Great drink prices, a truly tacky drag show in Spanish (that the locals love), dance floor, and a nice cantina space with pool table.

RESTAURANTS

■ **Agave Grill** (B CC g M) Mon-Sat 12-23.30, Sun 17-23.30h
C/. Paseo Diaz Ordaz 589 ☎ (322) 222-2000 💻 www.agavegrillpv.com
■ **Apaches Bistro** (B CC GLM M) 17-2h
C/. Olas Altas 439 *At Rodríguez, adjacent to Apache's Bar*
☎ (322) 222 4004
Martini & cocktail bar. Happy hour daily 17-19h.
■ **Archie' Wok** (AC B CC F T) 17-23.30h
C/. Francisca Rofriguez 130 ☎ (322) 222-0411
Oriental food from various cuisines
■ **Arrayán. El** (! B CC glm M OS) Wed-Sun 17.30-23h, Tue – closed
C/. Allende, 344 *Centro* ☎ (322) 222-7195 💻 www.elarrayan.com.mx
Voted best traditional Mexican food in town three years running. Moderate prices. Try the Margaritas Arrayán. Lesbian owned.

■ **Barcelona** (AC B CC F T) 16-23h
C/. Matamoros & 31 de Octubre *Downtown* ☎ (322) 222-0510
🖳 www.barcelonatapas.net
Spanish Tapas.

■ **Café Bohemio** (B CC GLM M OS) 17-23h
C/. Rodolfo Gomez 127 ☎ (322) 223-4676
Great food at moderate prices. Gay owned.

■ **Café des Artistes** (! AC B CC F g T) 18-0h
C/. Guadalupe Sanchez 740 *Downtown* ☎ (322) 223-3228
Gourmet Mexican and French dining

■ **Coco Tropical** (B BF GLM M) Daily. 12-23.30h
C/. Basilio Badillo 101, Playa de los Muertos ☎ (322) 222-5485
🖳 www.cocotropical.com

■ **Gilmar** (B CC GLM M OS) daily 11-23.30h
C/. Madero 418, Col. Zapata ☎ (322) 223-9707
🖳 www.gilmarrestaurant.com

■ **Joe Jack's Fish Shack** (B CC GLM M OS) 12-23h
Basilio Badillo 212 ☎ (322) 222-2114
Authentic and delicious fish & chips!

■ **No Way, José** (B GLM M MC OS RES) Tue-Sun 16-23.30h
C/. 5 de Febrero 260 ☎ (322) 223-2853 🖳 www.nowayjosemx.com
A recognition from Virtual Vallarta's Reader's Choice Awards

■ **Palapa. La** (B DM F GLM LM M OS PA RES T VEG WL) 19-22.30h
C/. Pulpito 103, Col. Emiliano Zapata ☎ (322) 222-5225
🖳 www.lapalapapv.com
Commentary: Beach side fine dining. Seafood

■ **Piazzeta. La** (B CC F g)
C/. Olas Altas 143 ☎ (322) 222-0650 🖳 www.lapiazzettapv.com
Italian cuisine

■ **Red Cabbage** (AC B F g)
C/. Rivera del Rio 204A ☎ (322) 223-0411
🖳 www.redcabbagepv.com
Popular, traditional Mexican food.

■ **The Swedes** (AC B BF CC g)
C/. Pulpito 154 *Zona Romantica, corner of Olas Altas* ☎ (322) 223-2353
🖳 www.theswedes.info
Swedish Food. Gay owned

■ **Trattoria Michel** (AC B CC G)
C/. Olas Altas 507 *Cnr. Rodolfo Gomez* ☎ (322) 223-2060
🖳 www.trattoria.com.mx
Traditional Italian recipes. Homemade Pasta – Freshly cooked with love. Gay owned. Al Fresco Sidewalk dining with a streetview

■ **Trio** (! AC B CC glm M OS) 18-23.30h
C/. Guerrero 264 *Two blocks from main square* ☎ (322) 222-2196
🖳 www.triopv.com
Fine dining, rave reviews.

FITNESS STUDIOS

■ **Gold's Gym** (AC g MSG SA SB WH) 6-23, Sat 8-20, Sun 10-14h
Plaza Genovesa *North of downtown* ☎ (322) 224-4040
🖳 www.goldsgymmexico.com/franquicias.php
Huge, state-of-the-art facility. Take a taxi or bus from gay area.

EDUCATION SERVICES

■ **Spanish Experience Center**
República de Chile #182 *Col. Cinco de Diciembre* ☎ (322) 223-5864
🖳 www.spanishexperiencecenter.com
Learn Spanish and experience the culture of Mexico!

FASHION SHOPS

■ **Best Underwear & Beachwear** (CC)
C/. Rodolfo Gomez 115 – L2 ☎ (322) 222-5128
🖳 www.best4upv.com

■ **Liquid Men** (AC CC)
C/. I.L. Vallarta 274-A ☎ (322) 223-3165

HOTELS

■ **Abbey Hotel** (AC B bf GLM H MA MSG PI T WH)
C/. Pulpito 138 ☎ (322) 222-4488 🖳 www.abbeyhotelvallarta.com

■ **Blue Chairs Beach Resort** (AC B cc G m MA OS PI RWB RWS RWT S SNU ST VA) All year
#4 Malecon Y Playa los Muertos ☎ (322) 222-5040
🖳 www.hotelbluechairs.com
Blue Chairs has 40 guestrooms and two restaurants. Please beware when booking via Internet – better to book directly with the hotel!

■ **Blue Seas** (AC B bf CC g MA MSG PI)
C/. Malecon 1 Esq. Abedul Col. Emiliano Zapata ☎ (322) 223-1521
🖳 www.blueseaspuertovallarta.com

■ **Casa Boana Torre Malibu** (AC g OS PI PK RWB RWS RWT VA) All year. Office 9-17h
Amapas 325, Col. Emiliano Zapata ☎ (322) 222-0999
🖳 www.boana.net

■ **Casa Cúpula** (AC B BF CC GLM I M MA MSG PA PI PK r RWB RWS RWT S VA WH WO) All year, 24hrs
Callejon de la Igualdad 129 ☎ (322) 294-0942
🖳 www.casacupula.com
Boutique hotel for gay men and their friends. Now with nine rooms and five suites available for rent.

■ **Mercurio Hotel** (AC B bf CC GLM MC OS PI RWS RWT VA) All year
Francisco Rodríguez 168, Col. Emiliano Zapata ☎ (322) 222-4793
🖳 www.hotel-mercurio.com
The Mercurio Hotel is an excellent choice of accommodation in Puerto Vallarta. Close to the beach and the gay scene with a wonderful pool. A tranquil place to relax after a loud and hectic night out. Enjoy your breakfast at the pool. Popular poolside Mercurio Bar open from 15-23h. All rooms with own bathroom.

■ **Vallarta Cora** (AC B G M MA MSG NU OS PI PK RWB RWS RWT VA WH) All year
C/. Pilitas 174, Col. Emiliano Zapata *At Playa de los Muertos*
☎ (322) 223-2815 🖳 www.vallartacora.com
Hotel & popular bar. Clothing optional. Men only.

GUEST HOUSES

Casa Aventura Vallarta (AC BF G I MC OS PI RWS RWT)
All year
C/. Jacarandas 551, Alta Vista ☏ (0322) 222 1175
☏ +1 954 519 2085 (USA) 💻 www.casaaventuravallarta.com
Gay owned guesthouse for men only, close to the beach and bars. Luxury studios and hotel rooms, rooftop pool, sundeck with ocean view.

Casa Dos Comales (AC BF glm PI RWS VA) All year
C/. Aldama 274 ☏ (322) 223-2042 💻 www.casadoscomales.com
Gay-friendly B & B with eight apartments.

Casa Fantasia (BF G MA OS PI RWB RWS RWT) All year
Pino Suarez 203, Col. Emiliano Zapata *Near Rio Quale* ☏ (322) 223-4035
💻 www.casafantasia.com

Hacienda B & B. La (AC B BF G H OS PI RWS RWT) All year
C/. Milán 274 *Colonia Versalles* ☏ (322) 225-0358
💻 www.pavoreal.com

Villa David (AC B BF CC G I NU OS PI RWB RWS RWT VA WH) All year
C/. Galeana 348 *At C/. Miramar* ☏ (877) 832 3315
💻 www.villadavidpv.com

Villa Viva Vallarta (AC bf CC G MSG PI WH) All year
Villas Altas Garza Blanca #210 *Km 7 Carr.a Barra de Navidad Zona Hotelera* ☏ (+1 702) 474-0264 💻 www.gaypuertovallartahotel.com
Spacious three bedroom Villa for gay men only.

APARTMENTS

Casa de los Arcos (AC B BF CC G OS PI RWB RWS RWT) All year
C/. Hortencia 168, Col. Alta Vista ☏ (322) 222-5990
💻 www.casadelosarcos.com

Puerto Vallarta Rentals Premier Vacations (PVRPV) (CC GLM)
Francisca Rodríguez 140 ☏ (322) 222-5990 💻 www.pvrpv.com
Gay-owned vacation apartment rental agency.

CRUISING

-Gay beach at south end of Playa Los Muertos
-In the rocks at the far south end of Playa los Muertos (afternoon, early evening; AYOR)
-Plaza Lazaro Cardenas, near Club Paco Paco (late nights; AYOR)
-Most streets in the South End (gay neighborhood) are cruisy later in the evening, but some caution is advised, as many attractive young guys are hustlers.

Querétaro – Querétaro ☏ 442

DANCECLUBS

Creación Nuevo Milenio. La (B D) Fri & Sat
Monte Sinaí No 113 ☏ (442) 13-5190

CRUISING

-Alameda (AYOR)
-Zócalo/Plaza Obregón/Plaza de la Constitución (AYOR)

San Luis Potosí – San Luis Potosí ☏ 444

BARS

Sheik Disco Bar (B CC D GLM MA SNU ST T) Fri-Sat 22-?h
Prolongación Zacatecas 347 *Fracc. San Juan* ☏ (444) 812-7457
💻 www.sheikdisco.com

MEN'S CLUBS

Gremio. El (AC DR F G MA VS) 19-3h
C/. San Luis 480, Centro *Between C/. Allende & C/. Damian Carmona*
☏ (444) 812-7985 💻 www.gremiosanluis.com

San Miguel de Allende – Guanajuato ☏ 415

GUEST HOUSES

Susurro (AC b BF glm I OS PI)
C/. Recreo, 78 💻 www.susurro-sma.com

Tampico – Tamaulipas ☏ 833

BARS

Bilbao (B glm)
Francisco I. Madero Oriente / A. Serdán Sur

Tropicana (B glm)
C/. de General López de Lara Sur

Tecate – Baja California Norte

BARS

Acapulco (B D GLM ST T) 20-?h
Blvd Universidad *Just north of Av. Nuevo León*
Beer bar.

Tijuana – Baja California Norte ☏ 664

GAY INFO

Baja Mexico Gay (BMG)
💻 groups.yahoo.com/group/Baja_Mex_Gay
The bilingual (English & Spanish) Yahoo group Baja Mex Gay (BMG) provides abundant up-to-date information. See also www.facebook.com/BajaAdvisor.

LGBT Community Centre Thu 17-20h
C./ Artículo 123, N° 7648, Suite 7 *In the centre* ☏ (664) 685-9163
💻 forums.delphiforums.com/gaybaja

BARS

Colibri. El (B G MA VS) 16-?h

DF (B G MC R) 10-?h
Plaza Santa Cecilia 781 *At 1st & Revolución*
Late bar.

Hawaii (AC B D G MA SNU) 10-?h
Plaza Santa Cecilia *At 1st & Revolución*

Ranchero. El (AC B D G MA R T VS) 10-?h
Plaza Santa Cecilia 769 *Near C/. Primera, between Revolución & Constitución*

Taurino. El (B D G MC R ST) 10-2, Fri & Sat -5h
Av. Niños Héroes 579 *Zona Norte, between C/. 1 and Constitución, 1 block west of Revolución* ☏ (664) 685-2478

Villa Garcia (AC B D GLM ST) 20-?h
Corner 1st / Revolución, Plaza Santa Cecilia ☏ (664) 685-3534

DANCECLUBS

Caguamamas (AC B D GLM MA ST VS) 20-?h
Plaza Viva Tijuana, Colonia Federal *One block west of the U.S./Mexico San Ysidro border crossing*
Also club Exitasis at the same location.

Club Tropicazo (B D GLM MA ST) 21-?h, closed Mon
6th Av. *¼ block west of Revolución*

Equipales. Los (B D g S T) Thu-Sun 21-3h
C/. 7 / Galeana 8236 *Zona Centro, opp. Jai Alai Palace* ☏ (664) 688-3006
Gay after 22h.

Medusas (AC B D GLM MA) 19-?h
Av. Revolución 1380 *Near 7th*

Mike's (B D G S ST VS) 17-5, Thu -3h, closed Wed
Av. Revolución 1220 *Corner of C/. 6A* ☏ (664) 685-3534

SAUNAS/BATHS

Baños Vica (b DU g MA MSG SA SB) 7-20h
Diaz Ordaz 1535 *Near mercado Tijuana Tianguis* ☏ (664) 622-0386
Not totally gay, though it sometimes seems that way. Be discreet to a point and the other men will make themselves understood.

SWIMMING

-Rosarito Beach, B.C.N. (half an hour south of Tijuana)
-Along the coast from Playas Tijuana to Punta Bandera.

CRUISING

-Near Noa Noa & El Taurino

-Park at América parking (in heart of Zona Norte at 1981 C/. 3a)
-Revolución (from C/. 2 to 8)
-Calle 4 (from Constitución across Revolución to Madero)
-Calle 7 (from Revolución to Madero)
-Crea park (across the river from the Hotel Camino Real, in the Zona Río) in the toilets
-Plaza Santa Cecilia (AYOR; by night)
-Plaza Río Shopping Centre (g WE YC; area near central arcade cafeteria).

Torreón – Coahuila ☎ 871

BARS

■ **Eclipse** (B D G YC)
Blvd Constitución y R. Corona ☎ (871) 716-5251 🖳 www.baregeo.com

Tulum – Quintana Roo ☎ 984

HOTELS

■ **Adonis Tulum Riviera Maya Gay Resort & Spa**
(AC B BF CC D DM DU FH G I LM M MA MSG NR OS PI PK RES RR RWB RWS RWT S SA SB SH VEG WH WO) All year, 24hrs
Carretera Federal Playa-Tulum ☎ 800 040 76 72
🖳 www.adonistulum.com
All-suites small luxury gay-only resort located on Mexico's beautiful and coveted Tulum Riviera Maya.

Tuxtla Gutiérrez – Chiapas ☎ 961

BARS

■ **Ice Lounge & Bar** (B cc D GLM S SNU) Thu-Sat 22-?
Boulevard Belisario Domínguez KM. 1089 *Plaza Galerias No. 8*
☎ (961) 166 5615

■ **Liberty** (B CC D GLM S SNU) Thu-Sat 22-?h
Boulevard Belisario Domínguez No. 2235 *Col. Jardines de Tuxtla*
☎ (961) 185 1251

■ **Pink Ambient Club** (B d GLM)
Boulevard Belisario Domínguez 850
☎ (961) 169 5101

■ **Sandy's** (B glm T)
C/. 9 Sur / 8 Poniente

DANCECLUBS

■ **Feeling** (B CC D GLM S) Thu-Sat 22-?
Boulevard Belisario Domínguez KM ☎ (961) 192 8872

CRUISING

-Plaza Belisario Domínguez

Veracruz – Veracruz ☎ 229

BARS

■ **Why not L Club** (B gLm) Fri-Sat 22-3h
Av. Independencia Norte 19-A, Col. Centro *Beside Luxuex*

DANCECLUBS

■ **After** (! B cc D GLM) 13-?h
Av. Independencia 924, Centro Histórico *corner to Emparan*
☎ (229) 932 4935

■ **Antique 924** (AC B CC D GLM MA P) Tue-Sat 22-5h
Independencia 924, Col. Centro *Close to La Antigua, corner of Emparan*
☎ (229) 150-8804 🖳 www.nueve24.blogspot.com

■ **Cabaret** (AC B CC D GLM MC P S SNU YC)
Thu-Sat 22-5h
Av. Juárez # 219, Col. Centro *Between 5 de Mayo and Independencia, in front of Telcel* 🖳 www.cabaretveracruz.com
Happy hour 21-3h, no cover charge.

■ **Luxueux** (D G S SNU) Fri+Sat 22-4h
Av. Independencia Norte 19-A, Col. Centro *At C/. Padilla*
☎ (229) 915-1420
Go-go dancers at the weekends.

■ **Remeber's** (AC B D gLm MA P S) Wed-Sun 21-5h
Callejon Mártires de Tlapacoyan #40, Col. Centro *Between Aquiles Serdan and Mario Molina, almost infront of Cathedral*

■ **Yesterday** (AC B CC GLM M MA) Tue-Sun 20-3h
Aquiles Serdán 517, Col. Centro Histórico *Between Independencia and Zaragoza* ☎ (229) 931-2465

RESTAURANTS

■ **Bodeguita. La** (AC CC glm M MA S) 13-18h
Juan de Grijalva, 436 *Fracc. Reforma*
💻 www.labudeguitaveracruz.com

GUEST HOUSES

■ **Casa de la Luz** (AC glm MC OS)
C/. Bernardino Aguirre 15, Tlacotalpan *Two hrs from Veracruz*
☎ (288) 884-2331 💻 www.casadelaluz-mexico.com
Two rooms for rent on a daily basis and a furnished apartment for rent by the day, week, or month. Shared bath with the owner.

Zacatecas – Zacatecas ☎ 492

DANCECLUBS

■ **Juana Gayo** (D GLM MA) Wed-Sat 22-5h
C/. Feria Zacatecana ☎ (492) 105-2849

■ **Scandalo's** (D GLM MA S) Fri & Sat 21-3h
Feria Zacatecana, Terraza 4 ☎ (492) 922-0805

Zipolite – Oaxaca ☎ 951

GUEST HOUSES

■ **Casa Sol** (BF G MA PI) 24hrs
Arcolris #6, Col Arroyo 3 💻 www.casasolzipolite.com

■ **Cósmico. Lo** (H M MC NG OS) Tue-Sun 8-16h
Aptdo. postal 36 *On the beach* 💻 www.locosmico.com/en
Huts are made out of natural materials, great beachside restaurant. A great place to unwind.

SWIMMING

Playa Camarón is a rocky cove at the west end of Zipolite behind Shambala. This is the only nude beach in Mexico and the small cove underneath the Shambala cottages. Take care when swimming. The current is very dangerous.

Moldova

Name: Republica Moldova · Moldawien · Moldavie · Moldavia
Location: Southeast Europe
Initials: MD
Time: GMT +2
International Country Code: ☎ 373
International Access Code: ☎ 00
Language: Moldovan (Romanian), Russian, Gagauz (Turkish dialect)
Area: 33 800 km² / 87 542 sq. miles
Currency: 1 Moldau-Leu (MDL) = 100 Bani
Population: 4,206,000
Capital: Chisinau
Religions: Russian-Orthodox
Climate: The best months to visit are from April to October.

✱ The Soviet law prohibiting homosexuality was abolished in 1995 and it is legal to be gay. Although homosexuality is not punishable in Moldova, many homosexuals behave discreetly. The age of consent is 14 years for everyone, straight or gay. The passing of this very recent legislation sheds light on the fact that Moldova is moving towards progression in the area of civil rights for sexual minorities.
Socially, gay men still find themselves having to hide their sexuality from close friends and family. But, in the context of socializing with other gay men, significant progress has been made. Thanks to the establishment of GenderDoc-M, the only NGO advocating for the rights of sexual minorities in Moldova, an information network has been established. While in the past it seemed the only place to meet another gay man was the public toilets, now Moldovan gays can meet at the centre, attend regular disco parties, attend gay film nights, visit the centre's website (www.lgbt.md) and chat room, receive counselling, and benefit from many other services.
The town council of Cishinau, the Moldovan capital, prohibited a Gay Pride Parade repeatedly in 2007. The Parliamentary Assembly of the Council of Europe subsequently advised the Moldovan government that all minorities need to be guaranteed equal rights and due respect.
The public still looks away from gay men, either choosing to pretend they don't exist or avoiding the subject in entirety. Assaults and other forms of violence do occasionally occur but can be avoided with discreet behaviour. As far as nightlife, some owners of Chisinau's hopping nightclub scene have welcomed and out rightly solicited gay men. A majority of club owners however, feel that devoting their clubs solely to gay people will drive away business from other clientele. Nonetheless, the centre arranges disco parties with select club owners for the gay community only. At least one club, considered the best in Chisinau, is known to have an owner very supportive and sympathetic to the gay cause.
The people of Moldovia are extremely friendly and often very good looking. The Dollar/Euro exchange rate is high, making eating out, nightlife and hotel accommodation inexpensive for tourists. The Genderdoc-M Center offers all sorts of useful information about Moldova.

★ Homosexualität ist heutzutage legal, denn das sowjetische Gesetz, das schwulen Sex unter Strafe stellte, wurde 1995 abgeschafft. Trotz Straffreiheit verhalten sich viele Schwule in Moldawien sehr diskret. Das Schutzalter für Homo- und Heterosexuelle liegt einheitlich bei 14 Jahren. Diese noch recht neue gesetzliche Regelung macht deutlich,

dass sich Moldawien auf dem Gebiet der Bürgerrechte für sexuelle Minderheiten auf einem sehr fortschrittlichem Weg befindet.
Im Alltag müssen Schwule ihre sexuelle Orientierung oft noch vor engen Freunden und der Familie verbergen. Aber die Kontaktaufnahme zu anderen Schwulen ist deutlich einfacher geworden. Dank des GenderDocM, der einzigen landesweiten Organisation für die Rechte sexueller Minderheiten, konnte ein Informationsnetz eingerichtet werden. Während früher öffentliche Toiletten als einzige Möglichkeiten schienen, Gleichgesinnte zu finden, können sich jetzt die Schwulen im Land im GenderDoc-Zentrum treffen, regelmäßige Disko-Partys oder schwule Filmnächte besuchen. Außerdem steht ihnen die Website und der Chat offen (www.lgbt.md), um sich beraten zu lassen und von vielen anderen Diensten zu profitieren.
2007 hat die Stadtverwaltung der moldawischen Hauptstadt Chisinau die CSD-Parade erneut verboten. Der Parlamentarische Rat Europas forderte daraufhin die Regierung Moldawiens dazu auf, allen Minderheiten gleiche Rechte und gebührenden Respekt zuzusichern. Die Öffentlichkeit nimmt Schwule noch immer nicht zur Kenntnis – entweder indem man vorgibt, dass es keine gäbe oder das Thema komplett meidet. Überfälle oder andere gewaltsame Übergriffe kommen gelegentlich vor, können aber durch diskretes Verhalten vermieden werden.
Einige Besitzer von Chisinaus wilder Nachtclub-Szene heißen Schwule ausdrücklich willkommen und werben um sie als Besucher. Dennoch glaubt die Mehrheit der Clubbesitzer, andere Gäste würden ausbleiben, wenn man sich den Schwulen als Zielgruppe zuwende. Nichtsdestotrotz veranstaltet der Verein mit ausgewählten Clubbesitzern Disco-Parties nur für Schwule. Zumindest von einem Club, der als der beste in Chisinau gilt, weiß man, dass der Besitzer schwule Anliegen wohlwollend unterstützt.
Die Einwohner von Moldawien sind sehr freundlich und gut aussehend. Der Dollar/Euro hat eine hohe Kaufkraft; Essen, das Nachtleben und die Hotelunterkunft sind günstig. Im Zentrum des GenderdocM erhält man alle wissenswerten Informationen über das Land.

La loi soviétique interdisant l'homosexualité a été renversée en 1995 et jusqu'à aujourd'hui, il est tout à fait légal d'être gai. Bien que, par conséquent, l'homosexualité ne soit pas reprehensible en Moldavie, plusieurs homosexuels choisissent de se comporter discrètement. La majorité sexuelle est de 14 ans pour tous, tant homo qu'hétéro. L'entrée en vigueur très récente de cette loi démontre que la Moldavie s'oriente vers le progrès en termes de droits civils pour les minorités sexuelles. Socialement parlant, les hommes gais on encore à cacher leur sexualité de leur parents et amis proches mais, pour ce qui est de socialiser avec d'autres hommes gais, des avancées remarquables ont été faites. Grâce à l'aide de GenderDoc-M, la seule ONG défendant les droits des minorités sexuelles en Moldavie, un réseau d'information a été mis sur pied. Tandis que dans le passé on aurait pu croire que le seul endroit pour rencontrer un autre homme gai était les toilettes publiques, les gais moldaves peuvent maintenant se rencontrer au centre, participer à des partys disco régulières, à des représentations de films gais, visiter le site web du centre (www.lgbt.md). En 2007 l'administration municipale de la capitale moldave Chisinau a de nouveau interdit le défilé de la Gay Pride. Sur ce, le Conseil Parlementaire européen a exigé du gouvernement moldave que des droits identiques et le respect qui leur est dû soient assurés à toutes les minorités.
Le public ignore toujours les hommes gais, faisant semblant qu'ils n'existent pas ou évitant le sujet tout simplement. Il arrive que certains hommes soient attaqués ou subissent d'autres formes de violence mais le tout peut être évité avec un comportement discret. Pour ce qui est de la vie nocturne, certains propriétaires de l'énergique scène de nuit de Chisinau ont souhaité la bienvenue a certains hommes gais, lorsque proprement sollicités. Néanmoins, le centre arrange des partys disco avec certains propriétaires de clubs selects pour la communauté gaie seulement. Il y a au moins un club, considéré comme étant le meilleur de Chisinau, dont le propriétaire est reconnu comme étant très sympathique à la cause gaie.

Actualmente la homosexualidad es legal pues la ley soviética que penalizaba el sexo homosexual fue derogada en 1995. A pesar de esta liberación, muchos homosexuales actúan todavía de manera discreta. La edad de consentimiento tanto para homosexuales como para heterosexuales se establece a los 14 años. Esta nueva normativa legal muestra claramente que Moldavia está avanzando en el ámbito de los derechos civiles de las minorías sexuales. En la vida cotidiana, los gays deben esconder todavía su orientación sexual ante los amigos o la familia pero el contacto con otros homosexuales se ha vuelto mucho más fácil. Gracias a GenderDocM, la única asociación nacional en defensa de los derechos de las minorías sexuales, se ha creado una red de información. Mientras antes los baños públicos eran la única posibilidad de conocer a otros gays, ahora pueden reunirse en el centro local de GenderDocM, organizar regularmente fiestas o noches de cine gay. Además también pueden acceder a la página web y al chat (www.lgbt.md) para asesorarse y aprovechar otros servicios.
En 2007 la administración municipal de la capital moldava Kischinau ha prohibido de nuevo una marcha gay. El Consejo de Europa exigió por ello al gobierno de Moldavia que deben garantizarse los mismos derechos y el debido respeto a todas las minorías.
La sociedad todavía no reconoce a los homosexuales: o pretenden que no existen o se evita el tema completamente. Ocasionalmente ocurren agresiones violentas pero pueden evitarse mediante un comportamiento discreto.
Algunos propietarios de los locales nocturnos de Chisinau admiten expresamente a los gays e incluso hacen propaganda de ello. Sin embargo la mayoría de los propietarios de estos clubes cree que algunos clientes podrían dejar de ir a su local si se dedicaran exclusivamente al público gay. A pesar de esto, la asociación organiza fiestas-discoteca sólo para gays entre algunos clubes seleccionados. Al menos se sabe de un club, supuestamente el mejor de Chisinau, cuyo propietario apoya la causa homosexual.

Oggi come oggi l'omosessualità è legale, poichè la legge sovietica che prevedeva una pena per sesso gay, è stata abolita nel 1995. Ciò nonostante, in Moldavia, molti gay si comportano ancora in modo molto discreto.
L'età legale per rapporti sessuali etero ed omosessuali è di 14 anni. Tutto ciò mostra come il paese si stia muovendo su un percorso di progresso, almeno per quanto riguarda i diritti civili per le minoranze sessuali.
Nel quotidiano molti gay devono ancora nascondere a parenti ed amici i loro orientamenti sessuali. Ma le occasioni di entrare in contatto con altri omosessuali sono aumentate. Grazie al GenderDocM, l'unica organizzazione nazionale per i diritti delle minoranze sessuali, è stata infatti creata una rete d'informazione.
Mentre prima i bagni pubblici sembravano l'unica possibilità per incontrare altri gay, ora ci si può trovare nel centro GenderDoc, in discoteca oppure prendere parte alle serate cinematografiche organizzate dall'associazione. Oltre a ciò si può usare la Website e la linea chat (www.lgbt.md) per consigli d'ogni genere e molto altro ancora.
Nel 2007 l'amministrazione municipale della capitale della Moldavia, Chisinau, ha vietato ancora una volta la sfilata del Christopher Street Day. Il Consiglio Europeo ha reagito esortando la Moldavia al rispetto delle minoranze e all'osservanza dei loro diritti. I gay non vengono considerati pubblicamente; o si afferma che ciò non esiste o si evita di affrontare il tema. Non mancano purtroppo di tanto in tanto attacchi violenti nei loro confronti, evitabili però attraverso un comportamento discreto.
Alcuni proprietari di night club in Chisinaus invitano apertamente il pubblico gay a frequentare i loro locali, ma sono anche convinti che il rivolgersi esclusivamene a tale clientela escluderebbe altri ospiti. Ciò nonostante vengono organizzati party danzanti per soli gay. Gli abitanti della Moldavia sono molto ospitali ed affascinanti. Il dollaro/euro è molto forte sul mercato; mangiare, fare vita notturna e il pernottamento sono molto economici per il turista. Nel centro GenderDocM si ricevono le informazioni fondamentali riguardanti il paese.

Chisinau ☎ 22

GAY INFO

■ **Information Center GenderDoc-M** 14-18h
Str. 31 August 1989, 24 B / C. P. 317 *Close to corner at Str. Ciuflea, the two-floor peach coloured house with a wooden door and blue roof*
☎ (22) 54 44 20 🖳 www.lgbt.md
The only organization in Moldova to advocate for LGBT rights. Has an extensive collection of books, DVDs and videotapes available for beneficiaries. Organizes Pride events every year in May. Be sure to check the center's website for an updated list of news, local events, etc.

DANCECLUBS

■ **Bodhi** (B D GLM MA) Thu 21-?h
Str. Ismail, 84/3 ☎ ((22)) 288861 ☎ 288863 🖳 www.lgbt.md
Every Thursday. The only disco for the LGBT community.

■ **Studio Nightclub** (B D MC NG)
Bucuresti Street 68 ☎ (22) 22 80 80 🖳 www.md4ever.com/studio
Gay-friendly

■ **City Nightclub** (B D MC NG)
31 August 1989 Street, 115 ☎ ((22)) 22 25 08
🖳 www.md4ever.com/city
Gay-friendly disco.

■ **Star Track** (B D glm m MA)
Kiev 7 Street
Gay-friendly danceclub. Military Pub is in the same building (1st floor).

CRUISING

-Park, close to the „Valaea Morilor" lake. Benches to the left from the alley behind the National Art University
-Parcul Morarilor located on Kogalniceanu street.

Mongolia

Name: Monggol Ulus · Mongolei · Mongolie
Location: Central Asia
Initials: MNG
Time: GMT +7 / +8 / +9
International Country Code: ☎ 976
International Access Code: ☎ 00
Language: Khalkha Mongol
Area: 1,565,000 km² / 604,247 sq mi.
Currency: 1 Tugrik (Tug) = 100 Mongo
Population: 2,515,000
Capital: Ulaanbaatar (Ulan-Bator)
Religions: 90% Buddhist
Climate: Country of extremes with Ulan-Bator being the coldest capital city in the world. Temperatures in the Gobi Desert range between + 40° C in summer and – 30° C in winter.

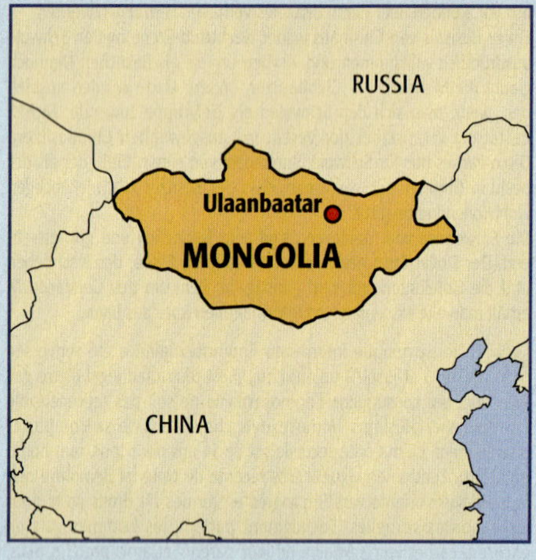

Although sexual interactions between homosexual adults in Mongolia are not forbidden, it is seldom possible to openly live in a different way to the majority of the population. Since 2007 some activists who formed and registered an organisation called „Lesbian, Gay, Bisexual and Transgender Centre" (LSBT) in Ulaanbaatar. This Lesbian, Gay. Bisexual and Transgender Centre in Ulaanbaatar is the first non-governmental organisation in Mongolia, which aims to change the social, legal and institutional situation regarding questions concerning discrimination, persecution and violence, which the LSBT community in Mongolia has suffered from for years.

Zwar sind einvernehmliche homosexuelle Handlungen zwischen Erwachsenen in der Mongolei nicht strafbar. Dennoch ist es kaum möglich, offen „anders" zu leben als die Mehrheit der Bevölkerung.
Seit 2007 bemühen sich einige Aktivist(inn)en eine LSBT-Organisation mit Namen „Lesbian, Gay, Bisexual and Transgender Centre" in Ulaanbaatar registrieren zu lassen. Das „Lesbian, Gay, Bisexual and Transgender Centre" in Ulaanbaatar ist die erste Nichtregierungsorganisation in der Mongolei, die sich für einen sozialen, rechtlichen und institutionellen Wandel einsetzen wird, wenn es um Fragen der Diskriminierung, Verfolgung und Gewalt geht, die LSBT seit Jahren in der Mongolei erfahren.

Les relations homosexuelles entre adultes consentants sont certes légales en Mongolie mais il est à peine possible de vivre sa différence par rapport à la majorité de la population. Depuis 2007 quelques activistes de l'association LGBT « Lesbian, Gay, Bisexual and Transgender Centre » essaie de se faire enregistrer à Oulan-Bator. Celle-ci est la première ONG en Mongolie à s'engager pour un changement sociale, juridique et institutionnel en matière de discrimination, persécution et violence auxquelles la communauté LGBT est confrontée en Mongolie depuis des années.

En Mongolia las relaciones homosexuales consentidas entre adultos no son punibles. Aun así, es impensable llevar un estilo de vida que sea „distinto" al de la mayoría de la población. Desde 2007 un grupo de activistas ha puesto todo su empeño en registrar una asociación en Ulán Bator bajo el nombre „Lesbian, Gay, Bisexual and Transgender Center". Dicho Centro en Ulán Bator sería la primera organización no gubernamental de Mongolia que promueva el cambio social, jurídico e institucional en cuestiones de discriminación, persecución y violencia que las personas LGBT sufren en Mongolia desde hace años.

Sebbene in Mongolia i rapporti omosessuali tra persone consenzienti non siano penalmente perseguibili, non è comunque possibile vivere apertamente la propria „diversità".
Dal 2007 alcuni attivisti si stanno dando da fare per far registrare ad Ulaanbaatar un'organizzazione LGBT col nome di „Lesbian, Gay, Bisexual and Transgender Centre". Il „Lesbian, Gay, Bisexual and Transgender Centre" di Ulaanbaatar sarà la prima ONG della Mongolia che lavorerà per una svolta sociale, legale e istituzionale impegnandosi nella lotta alla discriminazione, alla persecuzione e alla violenza che da anni vessano il mondo LGBT in Mongolia.

NATIONAL GAY INFO

Youth Health Center for Gay Men
Door 317, Tsetsee Gun Institute, UNDP St, Baga Toiruu ✉ Ulaanbaatar ☎ (090) 152 576
Information centre for safe sex and general health.

NATIONAL COMPANIES

Mongolian Rainbow Tours
PO Box 20A/2 ✉ 210644 Ulaanbaatar 💻 rainbowtoursmn.blogspot.com
Explore Mongolia with this gay-owned company.

NATIONAL GROUPS

Tavilan (GLM)
PO Box 405 ✉ 210644 Ulaanbaatar ☎ (095) 156-075
Mongolia's first gay and lesbian's human rights group, Tavilan (Eng=Destiny), formed in spring 1999 as a result of „police harassment and improper sentencing procedures that violated civilian rights." Meanwhile Tavilan opened a small office in central Ulaanbaatar to begin building an organization to counter such problems.

HEALTH GROUPS

We Are Family-Mongolia Sexual Health and Rights (GLM MA)
☎ 9998 4852
Providing information on HIV/AIDS for gay men and working to change the social understanding of sexuality and to prevent sexual violence against the local LGBT community.

Ulaanbaatar

CAFES

Dave's Place (b M MA NG)
East side of the Sukhbaatar Square
British gay-friendly café.

Millies Café (glm M MA OS)
West side of the Choijin Lama Museum *In front of the Sukhbaatar Square* ☎ 328 264
Gay friendly and popular place for lunch. Excellent steak sandwiches, lasagna, and lemon pie.

DANCECLUBS

Flower Night Club (B D GLM MA)
UB Palace *Opp. Sukhbaatar Square*
Twice a month there is a LGBT party.

SAUNAS/BATHS

The Sauna @ Flower Hotel (m MA MSG NG NU OS PI SA SB)
Bayanzurkh Duureg, Zaluuchuud Avenue-18 *Near Ikh Toiruu* ☎ 458 330
Japanese-style bathhouse on the first floor of the hotel. Some Locals go here to meet visitors. Be discreet!

TRAVEL AND TRANSPORT

Mongolian Rainbowtours (GLM MA)
P.O. Box-20A/2 ☎ 9914 7365 💻 rainbowtoursmn.blogspot.com
Gay-owned company offering a variety of options to explore Mongolia and the Gobi Desert. Wildlife trekking and hiking, bird watching, horse and camel riding, ancient monasteries are just some of the services they arrange.

CRUISING

-In front of the State Department store downtown (AYOR).
-G&L Secret Street where local gays get together at night. It is on the east side of the state department store on the way to Ard cinema (west side of Ard cinema). There is a fountain in the middle of the street garden (AYOR).

Montenegro

Name: Crna Gora · Montenegro · Monténégro
Location: South-eastern Europe
Initials: ME
Time: GMT +1
International Country Code: ☎ 381
International Access Code: ☎ 99
Language: Montenegrinish (official language), Crna Gora (local)
Area: 13,812 km² / 39,449 sq mi.
Currency: 1 Euro (€) = 100 Cents
Population: 608,000
Capital: Podgorica (Montenegro)
Religions: 75% Serbian-Orthodox, 15% Muslim
Climate: On the coast and in central parts is a Mediterranean climate with hot summers and rainy, clod winters. Snow in the mountains, depending on the altitude.

The age of consent for homo- and heterosexual activities in Montenegro has recently been amended to 18 years for all. Discrimination against gay men and lesbians does not exist, according to the law. Homosexuality is however a social taboo – as a result the gay scene is hidden. The former meeting places (parks, train stations) are loosing popularity due to the presence of internet. Especially young gay men in Montenegro make out dates via the gay internet sites such as Smokva (Croatian site) or Gayserbia (Serbian and English site). Efforts to hold a first Pride event in Montenegro in 2011 foundered because of substantial safety concerns on the part of the organizers after attacks on gays and lesbians in the run-up.

Das Schutzalter für homo- und heterosexuelle Handlungen liegt in Montenegro seit kurzem einheitlich bei 18 Jahren. Rechtliche Diskriminierung gibt es für Schwule und Lesben nicht. Homosexualität ist aber ein gesellschaftliches Tabu, sodass eine Szene nur im Verborgenen existiert. Die früher üblichen Kontaktpunkte (Parks, Bahnhöfe) treten seit Erfindung des Internets immer mehr in den Hintergrund.

Vor allem junge Schwule treffen sich in Montenegro heutzutage in der Regel über die einschlägigen Homepages wie Smokva (kroatische Seite) und Gay-Serbia (serbisch/englischsprachige Seite).
Bemühungen, einen ersten CSD 2011 in Montenegro zu veranstalten, scheiterten an erheblichen Sicherheitsbedenken seitens der CSD-Organisatoren, nachdem es im Vorfeld zu Übergriffen gegen Schwule und Lesben kam.

La majorité sexuelle a été fixée il y a quelques temps à 18 ans pour les hétérosexuels comme pour les homosexuels. Il n'existe aucune forme de discrimination juridique envers les gays et les lesbiennes, mais l'homosexualité est un sujet tabou de sorte que le milieu gay reste caché. Depuis l'apparition d'Internet, les anciens lieux de rencontre tels les parcs et les gares ont été relégués au second plan et les jeunes gays monténégrins se retrouvent de nos jours plutôt sur des sites Internet comme www.smokva.com (site uniquement en croate) ou www.gay-serbia.com (site en serbe et en anglais).
Les tentatives d'organiser la première Gay Pride en 2011 au Monténégro ont échoué du fait de fortes réserves en matière de sécurité de la part des organisateurs après des actes de violence contre des gays et lesbiennes.

La edad de consentimiento para relaciones heterosexuales y homosexuales fue establecida hace poco de modo unitario en los 18 años. No existe discriminación legal hacia gays y lesbianas. La homosexualidad sigue siendo un tabú social, por lo que sólo existe cierto ambiente gay de manera escondida. Los puntos de encuentro habituales anteriormente (como parques y estaciones) son ahora cada vez más escasos desde la aparición de Internet. Hoy en día, los jóvenes gays se citan por lo general a través de las páginas web como Smokva (página croata) y Gayserbia (página serbia) – las dos están sólo en la lengua local.
En Montenegro, los esfuerzos para organizar una primera Marcha del Orgullo Gay en 2011 no llegaron a buen puerto debido a los significativos problemas de seguridad planteados por los organizadores de la Marcha tras los ataques sufridos contra gays y lesbianas.

L'età del consenso in Montenegro è di 18 anni sia per eterosessuali che per omosessuali. Dal punto di vista della legge non sussiste alcun tipo di discriminazione per gay e lesbiche; tuttavia l'omosessualità rappresenta una sorta di tabù sociale. Una scena gay esiste, tuttavia in maniera piuttosto „sotterranea". Dall'avvento del web i tradizionali luoghi di incontro e cruising (parchi, stazioni, ecc.) vengono frequentati sempre più di rado. I gay e specialmente i giovani gay si incontrano adesso tramite homepage come Smovka (pagina croata) e Gayserbia (pagina serba) che tuttavia sono accessibili solo in lingua locale. Gli sforzi per organizzare il primo CSD (2011) in Montenegro sono stati vani, poiché già fin dai primi momenti ci sono state avvisaglie di aggressioni nei confronti di gay e lesbiche; ciò ha portato gli organizzatori del CSD a disdire la manifestazione per gravi problemi di sicurezza.

Podgorica ☏ 81

BARS

■ **OGP** (B LM MC NG OS WI) Mon-Sat 9-3, Sun 17-3h
Balšićeva 57 ☏ 68 56 82 84
Live R&B, funk and rock music on Wed & Thu. A meeting place for some gay men.

CAFES

■ **Berlin Cafe** (B MC NG OS)
24 Njegoševa *In center of Podgorica*
Officially, there are no gay places in Podgorica but there are few cafes or bars where you can find gay people. This is one of them.

SWIMMING

-Uvala Ratac (Ratac cove near Sutomore – nudist beach)
-Plaza Mogren (Mogren beach), Budva.

CRUISING

-Park opposite Hotel Crna Gora (AYOR)
-Ratac Beach in summer.

Ulcinj

SWIMMING

-Along the beach (12km!)
-Camping area of »Ada« (NU)

Morocco

Name: Al-Magrib · Marokko · Maroc · Marruecos · Marocco
Location: Northwestern Africa
Initials: MA
Time: GMT
International Country Code: ☏ 212
International Access Code: ☏ 00 (wait for tone)
Language: Arabic, Berber Dialects, French
Area: 458,730 km² / 172,413 sq mi.
Currency: 1 Dirham (DH) = 100 Centimes
Population: 29,824,000
Capital: Rabat
Religions: 99 % Muslims (80% Sunnite Muslems)
Climate: Mediterranean climate, hot in the interior. In the lowlands the cooler months are from Dec-Feb.

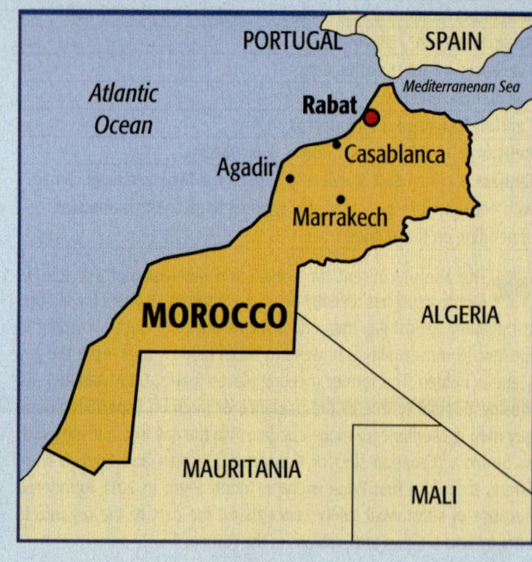

According to article 489 of the Penal Code homosexuality in Morocco is illegal and can be punished with anything from 6 months to 3 years imprisonment and a fine of 120 to 1200 Dirhams – or even more. The „Arab spring" had also taken hold of Morocco in 2011, forcing King Mohammed VI into action. A constitutional reform elaborated subsequently promises freedom of opinion and social equality for women, amongst other aspects. But the measures initiated

so far to make the country more democratic continue to stall because the military, judiciary and Islamic institutions are de facto still controlled by the king. The Islamic party PJD emerged as the clear winner from early elections held in November. There are no indications as yet that homosexuality will be legalized.
Nevertheless, homosexual activity is fairly common, especially in the holiday resorts. Relationships are often visibly displayed and money often plays a role where sex is involved. In the community homosexuality remains a taboo and is considered immoral. The rejection of affluent western tourism and the immoral developments is on the increase. Islamic fundamentalists have also become noticeably more aggressive towards gay men in recent years, no doubt also due to the increase in prostitution. Blackmail and arrests are on the increase again correspondingly. Even the mere suspicion that one may have had sex can be enough. In addition, young native men may be followed by the police, who will then beat information on the goings-on in hotel rooms or private holiday apartments out of them. We can therefore only advise you to proceed with caution! In June 2004 the editor of a local newspaper was sentenced to 6 months imprisonment because of his article which he published describing a homosexual holiday affair of the current Minister of Finance. The reason for his arrest was that the editor failed to adhere to foreign currency regulations in 1994. As he could not immediately settle a fine of 3 million Dirhams, he was incarcerated.
Safety warning: kidnappings in the centre of the country are not uncommon.

Homosexualität ist illegal und wird gemäß Artikel 489 des Strafgesetzes mit 6 Monaten bis 3 Jahren Haft und einer Geldbuße von 120 bis 1200 Dirhams bestraft. Der „arabische Frühling" hatte 2011 auch Marokko erfasst und König Mohammed VI. zum Handeln gezwungen. Eine Reform der Verfassung wurde erarbeitet, die unter anderem Meinungsfreiheit und die soziale Gleichstellung der Frau beinhaltet. Die bisher eingeleiteten Schritte zu mehr Demokratisierung im Land sind jedoch weiterhin zögerlich, denn de facto hat der König weiterhin die Macht über Militär, Justiz und islamische Einrichtungen. Im November fanden vorgezogene Parlamentswahlen statt, aus denen die islamische Partei PJD als Sieger hervorging. Bisher zeigen sich keinerlei Anzeichen, dass Homosexualität legalisiert wird. Dennoch – Homosexualität ist inzwischen weit verbreitet, vor allen in den Urlauberregionen. Beziehungen werden häufig „offen" geführt und meist spielt Geld beim Sex eine Rolle. Gesellschaftlich ist Homosexualität immer noch ein Tabu und gilt als unmoralisch. Die Abneigung gegen den westlichen Wohlstandstourismus und seine manchmal peinlichen Auswüchse vergrößert sich zunehmend. Auch ist der fundamentalistische Islam in den vergangenen Jahren immer feindseliger gegen Schwule vorgegangen. Dazu trug offensichtlich auch die enorme Prostitution bei. Erpressungen und Verhaftungen haben dementsprechend wieder zugenommen. Allein der Verdacht, dass man Sex gehabt hat, kann ausreichen. Einheimische junge Männer werden teilweise auch von der Polizei verfolgt und Informationen darüber, was sich in Hotelzimmern, oder privaten Ferienwohnungen abgespielt hat, werden aus ihnen herausgeprügelt. Also passt ein bisschen auf euch auf! Im Juni 2004 wurde der Herausgeber einer regionalen Zeitung zu 6 Monaten Gefängnis verurteilt, da dieser über die homoerotischen Urlaubseskapaden des Finanzministers geschrieben hatte. Als Grund wurde dessen Missachtung von Devisenbestimmungen in 1994 aufgeführt. Da er keine 3 Mio. Dirhams Strafe zahlen konnte wurde er kurzerhand inhaftiert. Ferner wird vor einem erhöhten Sicherheitsrisiko (Entführungen) im Landesinnern gewarnt!

Au Maroc, l'homosexualité est un délit et est passible de peines de 6 mois à 3 ans de prison et d'une amende de 120 à 1200 dirhams selon l'article 489 du code pénal. Le «Printemps Arabe» a déferlé sur le Maroc en 2011 et a poussé le roi Mohammed VI à l'action. Une réforme de la Constitution a été élaborée et comprend la liberté d'expression et l'égalité sociale de la femme. Les premiers pas vers plus de démocratie sont toujours hésitants car le Roi détient toujours le pouvoir sur l'armée, la justice et les institutions musulmanes. En novembre des élections législatives avancées se sont tenues et le parti islamique PJD en est sorti vainqueur. Jusqu'à présent aucun signe n'indique que l'homosexualité sera légalisée.
Néanmoins, l'homosexualité est très largement répandue, notamment dans les régions touristiques. Les relations sont souvent libres et le rapport sexuel est généralement associé à l'argent. Dans la société, l'homosexualité est toujours tabouisée et perçue comme immorale. L'aversion envers le tourisme occidental et ses déformations parfois honteuses grandit de plus en plus au sein de la population. L'islâm fondamentaliste progresse également et son animosité envers les gays s'est accrue ces dernières années, le grand nombre de prostitué(e) s y contribuant sans aucun doute. En conséquence, chantages et arrestations ont à nouveau augmenté. Rien que le soupçon d'avoir eu une relation sexuelle peut suffire. De jeune marocains peuvent être pistés par la police dans le but de leur extorquer sous la violence des informations concernant ce qui s'est passé dans des chambres d'hôtel ou dans des appartements de vacances privés. Faites donc un peu attention ! En juin 2003, le gérant d'un journal local a été condamné à 6 mois de prison pour avoir publié un article sur les escapades homoérotiques du ministre des finances. Le motif invoqué était son non-respect du règlement sur les monnaies et comme il ne pouvait pas payer l'amende de 3 millions de dirhams, il a été aussitôt incarcéré. En outre, la plus grand prudence est recommandée à l'intérieur du pays car des enlèvements peuvent s'y produire.

La homosexualidad es ilegal y en virtud del artículo 489 del código penal está castigada con una pena de 6 meses hasta 3 años y una sanción económica de 120 hasta 1200 dirhams. La "Primavera Árabe" también llegó a Marruecos en 2011, forzando la mano del Rey Mohammed VI. Se llevó a cabo una reforma de la constitución, que incluía, entre otras, la libertad de opinión y la igualdad social de la mujer. Los pasos tomados hasta ahora hacia una mayor democratización del país son, sin embargo, irresolutos, ya que el rey sigue teniendo de facto el poder sobre el ejército, la justicia y las instituciones islámicas. En noviembre se llevaron a cabo elecciones parlamentarias anticipadas, en las que el partido islámico PJD se alzó victorioso. Hasta ahora no se han dado ningún tipo de señales que indiquen que la homosexualidad pediera llegar a ser legalizada en este país.
Sin embargo, la homosexualidad está ahora muy extendida, sobre todo en las regiones turísticas. Se mantienen relaciones a menudo de manera „abierta" y la mayoría de las veces siempre con dinero de por medio. Socialmente, la homosexualidad continua siendo un tabú y está considerada inmoral. Las posiciones en contra del turismo occidental y sus a veces penosas consecuencias se están incrementando. También el fundamentalismo islámico, en los últimos años, ha expresado siempre su repulsa hacia los homosexuales. A ello, se añade también la enorme prostitución. Han aumentado las presiones y los arrestos. Sólo la mera sospecha que se ha practicado sexo puede ser suficiente. La polícia incluso persigue en parte a los jóvenes locales y les saca información sobre lo que ha sucedido en la habitación de hotel o en apartamentos de alquiler privados. Por tanto, itened un poco de cuidado! En junio del 2004, fue sentenciado el editor de un periódico regional a 6 meses de prisión por haber publicado las escapadas de vacaciones homoeróticas del ministro de finanzas. Como motivo presentaron el incumplimiento de las normativas de divisas en 1994. Como no pudo pagar la sanción de 3 millones de dirhams, fue encarcelado enseguida. Además, debemos advertir del riesgo para la seguridad (secuestros) en el interior del país.

L'omosessualità è illegale e viena punita dall'articolo del 489 del codice penale con una pena detentiva che va dai sei ai tre anni più una pena pecuniaria (dai 120 ai 1200 Dirham).
La „primavera araba" ha coinvolto anche il Marocco e ha costretto il Re Mohammed VI ad aprire delle trattative. In seguito è stata riformata la Costituzione nella quale, tra le altre cose, è stata introdotta la libertà di opinione e l'equiparazione dei diritti della donna. Tuttavia le riforme

di ampio respiro democratico sono tutt'ora ancora molto timide, poiché, di fatto, è il Re che continua ad avere il potere sull'esercito, sulla giustizia e sulle istituzioni islamiche. A novembre si sono svolte le elezioni anticipate dalle quali è uscito vincitore il partito islamico PJD. Ad oggi non ci sono ancora motivi per pensare che l'omosessualità venga decriminalizzata.

Tuttavia, l'omosessualità è molto diffusa specialmente nelle zone turistiche. I rapporti vengono vissuti in maniera piuttosto „aperta" e nella maggior parte dei casi i soldi hanno un ruolo fondamentale nei rapporti. Nella società l'omosessualità è ancora un tabù e viene considerata immorale. Il rifiuto nei confronti del turismo occidentale cresce sempre di più. Negli ultimi anni l'Islam fondamentalista è diventato sempre più intollerante nei confronti degli omosessuali. A contribuire a questo crescente odio è stato anche l'aumento della prostituzione. Le estorsioni e le catture sono di nuovo aumentate. Può già bastare il sospetto di copulazione tra omosessuali per avere problemi con la legge. I ragazzini marocchini vengono, a volte, anche perseguitati dalla polizia al fine di raccogliere informazioni su quello che è avvenuto nelle camera d'albergo o nelle case di villeggiatura con i turisti. Per raccogliere queste informazioni i ragazzini vengono anche picchiati. Quindi vi preghiamo di fare particolare attenzione. In giugno del 2004, l'editore di un giornale regionale è stato condannato a sei mesi di prigione perchè questi aveva riferito delle avventure omoerotiche del ministro degli esteri. Poichè l'editore non poteva permettersi di pagare i 3 milioni di Dirhams, è stato arrestato immediatamente. Vi consigliamo, inoltre, di stare attenti nel muovervi per le parti centrali del Paese: il rischio di rapimenti è alto!

NATIONAL PUBLICATIONS

Mithly
☎ 618 877 894 💻 www.mithly.net
Online magazine in Arabic and French

Agadir ☎ 028

BARS

Techno Bar. The (B d g YC) 21-4h
Boulevard du 20 Août, Secteur B *In the Hotel Carribean Village Agador*
Mixed crowd, mainly young gays.

CAFES

Fontaine. La (B g MA OS)
Av. Hassan II *Downtown, in town centre*
Very chic sidewalk café where everybody meets, especially in the afternoon. Pick-up place with a lot of flirting. No direct contact with the boys, play with the eyes and they will follow you – if you want and have somewhere to go!

DANCECLUBS

Salammbo (B D MC NG WE) Sat & Sun
Boulevard du 20 Aout *In Caribbean Village Agador* ☎ (028) 84 71 01
A club where young gays come for dancing and which is cruisy. The ‚keyword' here is discretion. Don't trust everybody and be aware that not all of them are gay even if they pretend to be.

RESTAURANTS

Etoile d'Agadir (B g M MA OS s)
Place Lahcen ou Brahim Tamri *Just in front of Cinema Sahara, at the old city Talborjt* ☎ (028) 97 90 57
Nice traditional restaurant with a mixed crowd, mostly gay. Outside seating. It's easy to get in contact with the boys that pass by. Gay-friendly owner.

Mezzo Mezzo (B g M MA OS)
Av. Hassan II *Downtown, beside La Fountain*
Italian style restaurant, where the chic crowd meets, only open in the evenings. Pretentious cuisine, not cheap, but nice atmosphere.

HOTELS

Caribbean Village Agador (B BF D M MA NG OS PI RWB RWS RWT)
Boulevard du 20 Aout *West coast* ☎ (028) 84 71 01
A comfortable 3-star hotel, offers good value for money. It is located in the town center and the beach is only a 500 m walk away. The hotels night club is the local meeting point for gay men. The entrance is located just outside the hotel. Note that it is not possible to take someone in your hotel room.

Résidence Lahoúcine (bf H MA)
1, rue d'Oua ☎ (028) 84 82 54
You can bring in visitors. Get your own key and come and go as you like. Be careful as police checks are possible.

CRUISING

All meeting points AYOR:
-Along Av. Hassan II (Café Uniprix (R) and Cafe Mokkar), Mohamed V (Hotel Anezi) (YC, best time mid-afternoon/early evening) Active!
-In front of all the cinemas (afternoons are best, but there is not that much action here anymore)
-Souks Agadir and Inezgane
-Inezgane (8km from Agadir; beach at mouth of River Sousse; main beach between P.L.M. Hotel Dunes d`Or and la Douche; municipal showers).

Asilah

CRUISING

-There is a well-known market every Sunday in a village about 3km from the coast where you may find some action with locals.

Casablanca ☎ 02

CINEMA

Lutetia (AYOR MA) 14.30-23h
Near Prince Moulay Abdallah *Downtown*
Movie house with two floors. The toilets on the ground floor can be interesting.

BARS

Fleurs. Les (B MA NG OS r) 11-24h
A good starting point to meet the locals.

DANCECLUBS

Village. Le (B D g m r) 22-3h
Corniche. Ain Diab *Ask taxi driver for directions*
Probably the only disco in Casablanca where you are likely to find gay men. Western & local music.

CRUISING

-Café in the front of the Hyatt Regency Hotel
-Parc de la Ligue Arabe. AYOR, police.

El Jadida

CRUISING

-The three principal cafés facing the Municipal Theatre in Place Mohamed V
-Beach 2km north of the Hotel Maharba
-Street from Place Mohammed V to Hotel Bruxelles
-Beach road to Houzia Beach (about 3 to 4km north from El Jadida).

Fes

CRUISING

-Boulevard Gardens in the Medina (near the Bartha Museum)

Marrakech ☏ 024

CAFES

Negociants. Les (B g MA)
110, Av. Mohamed V – Angle Blvd Mohamed Zerktouni
Sidwalk café with a mixed crowd.

SAUNAS/BATHS

Hammam Essalama (AYOR MA SB) 10-23h
Daoudiate

HOTELS

Dar Soukaina (AC B glm I M MA RWS) All year except from 4th to10th Jan.
19 Derb El Ferrane, Riad Laarouss ☏ (024) 44 736 054
www.darsoukaina.com

GUEST HOUSES

Riad Arahanta (AC glm I MA) All year
14, Derb Tizougarine, Dar el Bacha ☏ (024) 42 63 90
www.arahanta.isuisse.com
Clean and central riad with gay owners from Scotland. Gay clientele and no reception. Reasonable prices. Good location.

Riad Dar Mouassine (b BF CC H M MA MSG OS p PI SOL) All year
148 deb Snane, Mouassine *Airport Transfer service* ☏ 05 24 44 52 87
www.darmouassine.com
Gay owned. Charm Morrocan Riad guest house with 7 rooms, swimming pool, garden, solarium. 5 min to Djemaa El Fna. French, German and English spoken.

Riad Dar Tinmel (AC bf H I MC MSG NG OS PI RWS WI) All year
4 Derb Chorfa Seghir *Start from Jemaa el Fna main square: when facing the Argana Café, take the street on its left handside. Go all the way of that street until a T junction with „Café Bougainvilliers". Turn left and after 15m left again* ☏ (0)6 61 08 20 42 inforiads@gmail.com
A very comfortable and tastefully decorated Riad with plunge-pool in the courtyard. A quiet oasis amids the hustle of the busy city.

CRUISING

-Av. Mohamed V
-Place Jemma El Fnaa
-Piscine Municipale (behind Hotel Palais Badia)
-Piscine de la Koutoubia.

Rabat

CRUISING

-Sidi Moussa Beach (by day)
-Theatre square (late evenings) AYOR, police
-Jardin d'Essai, Ave An Nasr.

Tangier/Tanger ☏ 09

BARS

Café Pilo (B NG)
Rue de Fés
Crowded in the early morning!

SWIMMING

-Atlas Beach
-Coco Beach
-Mustapha Beach Club
-Neptuno
-In front of Café Sherazade
-In front of Soleil Lounge.

CRUISING

-All the cafés in the Petit Socco, a small, lopsided square in the Medina, particularly the Café Central. The entire sea front promenade (Av. d'Espagne and Av. des F.A.R.). Safe enough by day, but it has become a very dangerous area at night and should be avoided (muggings). It is also advisable not to visit the Medina area unaccompanied at night.
-Bazaar Kinitra
-Rue du Mexique (especially the lower end, 19-?h).

Myanmar

Name: Myanma Pye
Location: Southeast Asia
Initials: MYA
Time: GMT +6.30
International Country Code: ☏ 95
Language: Burmese, English
Area: 676 552 km² = 261,969 sq mi.
Currency: 1 Kyat (K) = 100 Pyas
Population: 50,004,000
Capital: Yangon (Rangoon)
Religions: 87% Buddist, 6% Christian, 4% Muslim, 4% other
Climate: Myanmar has a tropical climate with three seasons; the hot season between April and May; the monsoon between June and October and the cool season between November and March.

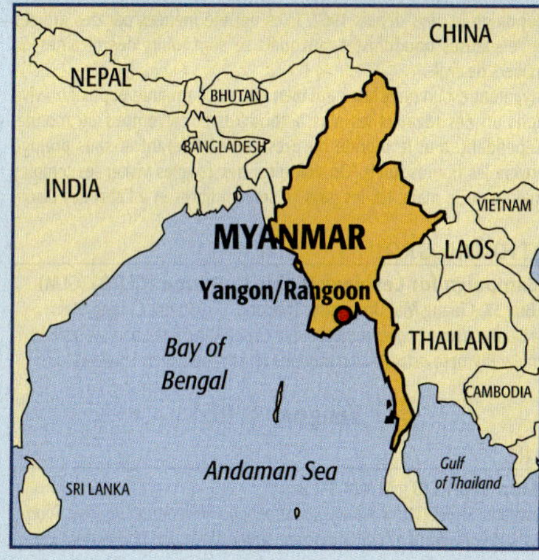

✱ Male homosexual relations are illegal according to the Penal Code 1882-88. There have been no reports of any recent prosecutions under this legislation and a social tolerance towards homosexuality prevails. There is no gay scene as such most gay life takes place in public places. In this respect, Myanmar customs are more like those in India than its south-eastern neighbour, Thailand. Cruising is popular.

International tourism has massively declined since autumn 2007, when the demonstrations of many months running were suppressed, partly by the use of force. The marches had initially concerned drastic fuel price increases, but soon grew into a protest movement against the military regime in power since 1962. Their leaders were Buddhist monks and nuns, who were quickly joined by tens of thousands of civilians.

Myanmar is a unique and fascinating destination where you will find a charming, kind and gentle people unfortunately terrorised by one of the world's most corrupt political regimes. Nevertheless tolerance towards homosexuality exists and there appears to be little social prejudice. Gays were very open, it's possible to see obvious gay couples visiting temples together and holding hands.
Most locals are fascinated by foreigners and its very easy to strike up conversations and to meet other „singles".

Sexuelle Kontakte unter Männern sind in Myanmar illegal nach den Strafgesetzen 1882-88. Allerdings gab es bisher keine Verurteilungen aufgrund dieser Gesetzgebung und es herrscht eine große Toleranz gegenüber Homosexualität vor. Da es keine richtige Szene in Myanmar und keine reinen Schwulenbars gibt, finden die meisten Begegnungen an öffentlichen Orten statt.
Der internationale Tourismus ist seit Herbst 2007 sehr stark zurückgegangen, nachdem die monatelangen Demonstrationen teilweise gewaltsam beendet wurden. Die Demonstrationen richteten sich Anfangs gegen die drastische Erhöhung der Treibstoffpreise und weiteten sich bald gegen das seit 1962 herrschende Militärregime aus. Geführt wurden sie von buddhistischen Mönchen und Nonnen, denen sich bald Zehntausende andere Zivilisten anschlossen.
Myanmar hat als faszinierendes Land eine freundliche und charmante Bevölkerung, die unter einem Regime lebt, das zu den weltweit schlimmsten und korruptesten gehört. Dennoch sind fast alle tolerant und unbefangen zu Homosexuellen. So sieht man auch Pärchen Hand in Hand die Tempel besuchen. Schwule fühlen sich hier frei und unbelästigt. Auch Fremden gegenüber ist man sehr kontaktfreudig, kommt schnell ins Gespräch und man trifft auch leicht andere „Alleinstehende".

Selon la loi 1882-88, le rapport sexuel entre hommes est un délit au Myanmar. Néanmoins, il n'y a eu jusqu'à présent aucune condamnation se référant à ce texte et on observe une grande tolérance envers l'homosexualité. Comme il n'existe pas de véritable milieu gay dans ce pays, et pas de bars strictement gays, les rencontres ont lieu dans les lieux publics. Les habitudes ne sont pas celles de la Thaïlande et on a plutôt tendance à draguer comme en Inde.
Le tourisme international a particulièrement baissé depuis l'automne 2007, après que les manifestations qui duraient depuis des mois aient été réprimées en partie dans le sang. Ces manifestations étaient tout d'abord dirigées contre l'augmentation drastique des prix des carburants, puis s'étaient ensuite tournées contre le régime militaire qui dirige le pays depuis 1962. Elles ont été menées par des moines et religieuses bouddhistes, auxquels se sont joints des dizaines de milliers de civils.
Myanmar est un pays fascinant bien que sa charmante population vive dans un des régimes les plus autoritaires et corrompus du monde. Cependant, tout le monde ou presque est tolérant et sans préjugé envers les homosexuels. On voit ainsi des couples visiter les temples main dans la main. Ici, les gays se sentent libres et à l'abri des discriminations. Il est facile d'entrer en contact avec la population locale et de rencontrer d'autres « célibataires ».

Los contactos sexuales entre hombres en Myanmar son ilegales, según las leyes penales 1882-88. No obstante, no se ha dado ninguna sentencia condenatoria con motivo de esta legislación y reina una gran tolerancia hacia la homosexualidad. Como en Myanmar no hay precisamente una zona gay ni bares específicamente para gays, la mayoría de encuentros se realizan en lugares públicos. Las costumbres se parecen más a las de la India que a las de Tailandia y se va más de „cruising".
El turismo internacional ha disminuído mucho desde otoño de 2007, después que las manifestaciones que duraban ya meses fueran disueltas en parte con violencia. Las manifestaciones, en un principio, se convocaron contra el drástico aumento de precios del petróleo y posteriormente se extendieron contra el régimen militar imperante desde 1962. Los monjes y monjas budistas fueron quiénes las iniciaron pero pronto también se unieron a ellos millares de civiles.
Myanmar es un país fascinante y sus habitantes son amables y encantadores, a pesar de vivir en uno de los regímenes más corruptos y duros del mundo. Sin embargo, casi todos son tolerantes y abiertos con los homosexuales. Así se pueden ver a parejas cogidas de la mano visitando el templo. Los gays se sienten libres y no se les molesta. También les gusta mucho hablar con los extranjeros, se puede entrar en conversación con ellos rápidamente y se encuentran fácilmente a otros „solitarios".

Nel Myanmar (conosciuto in coccidente ancora sotto il nome di Birmania), secondo le leggi del codice penale 1882-88, i rapporti sessuali sono illegali. Tuttavia non ci sono stati ancora sentenze inerenti a questo divieto poichè nei confronti dell'omosessualità c'è qui molta tolleranza. Visto che non esiste una vera e propria scena gay nè locali prettamente gay, gli incontri avvengono prevalentemente nei luoghi pubblici. Gli usi sono più simili a quelli dell'India piuttosto che a quelli della Tailandia, con la differenza che qui si fa più crusing.
Dall'autunno del 2007, da quando le manifestazioni protrattesi per alcuni mesi sono state violentemente represse, il turismo internazionale è diminuito significativamente. Inizialmente i manifestanti hanno protestato contro l'aumento dei prezzi del greggio. In un secondo momento, tuttavia, si è arrivati a protestare contro il regime militare stabilitosi nel 1962. Le manifestazioni sono state guidate dai monaci buddisti ai quali si sono affiancati migliaia di altri civili.
Il Myanmar è un Paese molto affascinante con una popolazione molto affabile che purtroppo vive sotto uno dei più corrotti regimi del mondo. Nei confronti dell'omosessualità, la popolazione del Myanmar è molto tollerante: non è raro vedere coppie omosessuali che si tengono per mano quando si va a visitare i templi. Insomma, qui, da omosessuali ci si sente piuttosto liberi e indisturbati. Ma anche nei confronti degli stranieri la gente è molto aperta e non è difficile scambiare qualche parola o incontrare altri singles.

NATIONAL GROUPS

■ **Campaign for Lesbigay Rights in Burma (CLRB)** (GLM)
PO Box 37, Chiang Mai University, Thailand ✉ 50202 Chiang Mai
Exile Burma human rights organization. Organises confidential workshops with gay Burmese activists who manage to go regularly to Thailand.

Yangon ☎ 01

BARS

■ **Lion World** (B g M MA) 9-23h
Anawyatar Street *Cnr. of Anawyatar Street and Shwedagon Pagoda Road*
Enjoy a great view of all cruising action on the street and bridge from the upstairs balcony. At evenings many gays hang around near the entrance.

■ **Silver Oak Café** (B glm m MA)
83/91 Bo Aung Kyaw Street *Two blocks from The Strand* ☎ (01) 299 993
The front are Ko Ko's hair stylists. Small club with live music, handsome and very friendly staff in the back. Enjoy local food and drinks. Best after 20h.

■ **Strand Bar. The** (B M MA NG OS)
92 Strand Road *Part of The Strand Hotel* ☎ (01) 243 377
The place where usually the trendy and upper locals meet on Friday nights. Some gay men. Luxurious and friendly venue. Pool table. Happy hour applies.

■ **YGN Bar** (B glm MA S) Fri
c/o Yangon International Hotel, 330 Ahlone Rd.
New gayfriendly party on Fri nights.

CAFES

■ **365 Café** (B glm M OS YC) All year, 24hrs
Alan Pya Pagoda Street *Next door to the Thamada Hotel, in front of the Rail Road Station*
Always busy with the youth of the new Myanmar middle class. Also frequented by Myanmar and Western gays.

■ **Ko Ko's** (B GLM m MA)
9 Sayar San Rd *Near Mr. Guitar, Bahan Township*
The first gay café and bar in Myanmar. Ko Ko is a famous hair-stylist with five hair salons around Yangon.

■ **Ritz Café** (b g MC)
296/1 Shwedagon Pagoda Rd, Dagon Twp *Downtown Yangon*
☎ (01) 253-680
A small quiet place for food, drink, and talk. Western and Asian food. Very gay friendly.

DANCECLUBS

■ **BME II** (B D glm H m MA OS)
c/o Yangon International Hotel, 330 Ahlone Rd.
A mixed friendly crowd and the gay men just blend in with them. Some cute Burmese guys go here. Busiest on Fri and Sat nights as early as 10pm (occasional crackdowns order most clubs to close by midnight).

■ **Pioneer @ Yuzana Garden Hotel** (AC B D glm m t WE YC)
Alan Paya Pagoda Rd *Opp. La Pyayt Wun Plaza and The Grand Plaza Park Royal Hotel*
Best at WE or on public holidays with lively young and trendy crowd, some gay men. All other nights the place is deserted.

RESTAURANTS

■ **Lavender** (B glm M MA)
179/181 Botataung Pagoda Rd *four blocks east of city hall* ☎ Yangon
Gay-friendly. In the evening gay and lesbian couples show up.

■ **Monsoon** (B glm M MA)
85-87 Theinbyu Rd *east of city hall about six blocks*
Expensive, but the food is good and the waiters cute. Very gay-friendly.

CRUISING

-Kandawgi Lake park, vicinity of Kandawgi Hotel (AYOR)
-Aungsan National Sports Stadium, surrounding restaurants
-Thein Gyi Zay Bridge at crossing of Anawyater Street and Shwedagon Pagoda Road. Evenings between 19-21h, young men
-Fitness area at Olympic swimming pool for local gay people. Poor facilities but cute young men
-Mahabandoola Park area, at night
-Mr. J. Donuts (Shwe Bon Htar St at Dagon Centre) day and early evenings (by eye contact only) R
-Rock Heart cafe on top of the FMI center
-Scott's Market, around small terrace with coffee corner at the far-right end
-Inya Lake park
-Sule Paya Rd starting about 5pm at an outside tea shop. Facing the front of Café Aroma there are two cinemas to your right (south). Next to the 2nd cinema is the tea shop with a blue awning. Every evening, but especially on weekends.

Namibia

Name: Namibie
Location: South West Africa
Initials: NAM
Time: GMT +2
International Country Code: ☎ 264
International Access Code: ☎ 09
Language: English, Afrikaans, Native Languages & German
Area: 824, 292 km² / 318,694 sq mi.
Currency: 1 Namibia Dollar (N$) = 100 Cents
Population: 2,031,000
Capital: Windhoek
Religions: 62% Protestant, 17% Catholic
Climate: Desert climate that is hot and dry. Rainfall is sparse and erratic. Autumn (Apr-Sep) is the best time to visit Namibia.

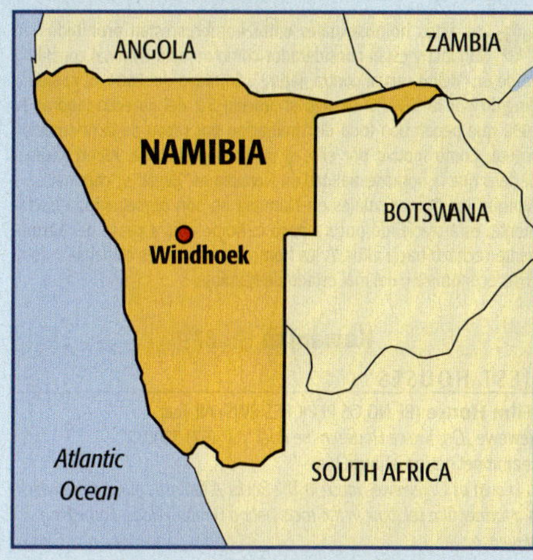

In Namibia male homosexuality is illegal, based on the common law offence of committing „an unnatural sex crime". In May 2004 the clause 5 (2), in employment rights from 1992 in which discrimination based on sexual orientation was forbidden, was struck from the records by the SWAPO government. The reason for this move was given by Albert Kawana, the Minister of Justice, who stated that homosexuality in Namibia is „illegal" and „criminal". Although no direct persecution of homosexuals exists in Namibia there is a growing sense of homophobic hostility as a result of the extensive discussions against homosexuality. Homosexuals in Namibia are held responsible for the economic stagnation and misery in the country.
In 2006, the Ministry of Safety and Security even prohibited the distribution of condoms in prisons, as this „would be tantamount to an invitation to maintain homosexual relations". According to UN data, one in five Namibians (more than 21%) is infected with the HIV virus. Many gay men are forced to lead double lives and marry. Many gay people simply live with the new situation and the hostility.
Nevertheless Namibia is a wonderful country to visit with a variety of activities on offer such as following the trail of the desert elephants, river rafting on the Kunene River or game watching in luxury safari lodges in the Kalahari.

Homosexuelle Handlungen zwischen Männern sind in Namibia verboten und werden als strafbare Ausübung eines „widernatürlichen Sexualverbrechens" betrachtet. Im Mai 2004 wurde Artikel 5(2) des Arbeitsrechts von 1992, der Diskriminierung aufgrund der sexuellen Orientierung unter Strafe stellte, von der SWAPO-Regierung außer Kraft gesetzt. Als Grund dafür gab Justizminister Albert Kwana an, Homosexualität sei in Namibia „illegal" und „kriminell".
Obwohl Homosexuelle in Namibia nicht direkt verfolgt werden, macht sich wegen der andauernden Stimmungsmache gegen sie langsam eine schwulenfeindliche Atmosphäre breit. Den einheimischen Homosexuellen wird die Schuld am wirtschaftlichen Niedergang und schlechten Zustand Namibias gegeben.
2006 wurde sogar die Verteilung von Kondomen in Gefängnissen vom Ministerium für Sicherheit abgelehnt, da es einer „Aufforderung zur Fortführung homosexueller Kontakte" gleichkäme. Nach Angaben der Vereinten Nationen ist in Namibia jeder Fünfte mit dem HI-Virus infiziert (mehr als 21%). Viele schwule Männer sehen sich gezwungen, ein Doppelleben zu führen und zu heiraten. Die meisten Schwulen versuchen einfach, mit der veränderten Situation und den neuen Anfeindungen zu leben.

Trotz alledem ist Namibia ein wunderbares Urlaubsziel, das interessante Betätigungsmöglichkeiten bietet wie z. B. Wildbeobachtung in luxuriösen Safarihütten in der Kalahari, Floßfahrten auf dem Fluss Kunene oder Ausflüge auf den Spuren der Wüstenelefanten.

En Namibie, les relations homosexuelles sont considérées comme des « crimes sexuels contre-nature « et sont donc interdites. En mai 2004, le gouvernement SWAPO a supprimé du droit du travail l'article 5(2) datant de 1992, qui punissait la discrimination fondée sur l'orientation sexuelle. Le ministre de la justice, Albert Kwana, a justifié cette décision par le fait que l'homosexualité est » illégale » et « criminelle » en Namibie.
Bien que les homosexuels namibiens ne soient pas directement poursuivis par la justice, l'ambiance homophobe croît, soutenue par le climat politique et social rendant les homosexuels responsables du déclin économique et du mauvais état de la Namibie.
En 2006 la distribution de capotes dans les prisons a même été interdite par le ministère de la Sécurité, prétextant que ça équivaudrait à une « incitation aux contacts homosexuels « . En Namibie, d'après les informations des Nations Unies, une personne sur cinq est infectée par le virus HIV (plus de 21%).
De nombreux homosexuels se voient obligés d'avoir une double-vie et de se marier. La plupart des gays essaient simplement de vivre avec la nouvelle situation et les nouvelles animosités.
Malgré tout, la Namibie est une magnifique destination qui propose de nombreuses activités telles les safaris-photos dans le Kalahari, des descentes en radeau sur le fleuve Kunene ou des excursions sur les traces des éléphants du désert.

Los actos homosexuales entre hombres están prohibidos en Namibia y están considerados como un acto criminal constitutivo de un "delito sexual contra natura". En mayo del 2004, el gobierno dirigido por la SWAPO derogó el artículo 5.2 del derecho laboral de 1992 que penalizaba toda discriminación por razón de la orientación sexual. Como motivo por ello, el ministro de Justicia, Albert Kwana, declaró que la homosexualidad en Namibia es "ilegal" y "criminal".
Aunque los homosexuales en Namibia no son perseguidos directamente, está creciendo poco a poco la homofobia a causa del permanente rechazo hacia ellos. A los homosexuales se les culpabiliza de la crisis económica y del mal estado de Namibia.
En 2006 el Ministerio de Seguridad llegó a denegar la distribución de condones en las cárceles pues equivalía a un „fomento de la continuidad de los contactos homosexuales". Según datos de las Naciones Unidas, una quina parte de la población de Namibia está infectada con el virus VIH (más de un 21%).
Muchos hombres homosexuales se ven obligados a llevar una doble vida y a casarse. La mayoría de homosexuales intentan simplemente sobrevivir con la nueva situación y las nuevas hostilidades.
A pesar de todo, Namibia es un destino turístico maravilloso pues ofrece muchas actividades interesantes como, por ejemplo, observar la vida salvaje en lujosas cabañas de safari por el Kalahari, excursiones en balsa por el río Kunene o bien en busca de las huellas de los elefantes del desierto.

In Namibia i rapporti omosessuali tra uomini sono vietati e vengono considerati „crimini sessuali contronatura". Nel maggio del 2004 l'articolo 5 (2) del diritto del lavoro risalente al 1992 che puniva la discriminazione basata sull'orientamento sessuale, è stata abrogata dal governo Swapo. Il Ministro della Giustizia Albert Kwana ha motivato la sua decisione affermando che l'omosessualità in Namibia è „illegale" e „criminale".
Sebbene gli omosessuali in Namibia non vengano direttamente perseguitati, lentamente si sta diffondendo un'atmosfera omofoba. Agli omosessuali locali viene data la colpa del declinio finanziario e della pessima situazione nella quale si trova la Namibia.
Nel 2006 il ministero della sicurezza ha persino vietato la distribuzione di preservativi nelle carceri, poiché ciò, secondo il ministero, sarebbe stato percepito come un „invito alla pratica omosessuale". Secondo le Nazioni Unite, in Namibia un quinto della popolazione è infetto da HIV (più del 21%). Molti uomini omosessuali sono costretti a fare una doppia vita e quindi anche a sposarsi. La maggior parte dei gay cercano di convivere con la nuova situazione creatasi e conseguentemente con questa atmosfera ostile. Nonostante tutto, la Namibia è una meta turistica molto affascinante che offre interessantissime opportunità di svago come per esempio i safari nel Kalahri, durante i quali si può osservare la natura da lussuriose capanne oppure escursioni in zattere sul fiume Kunene o itinerari alla ricerca delle orme degli elefanti del deserto.

Kamanjab ☎ 67

GUEST HOUSES

Film House (BF NG OS PI PK RES RWS) All year
Onjewewe *„Onjowewe House-in-the-Rock"* ☎ (67) 330032
namibnet.net/oasehouse.htm
Also known as Onjewewe House In The Rocks. A fantastic guesthouse which was a former film set, built in the rocks near a Himba Village. Something very unique.

Otjiwarongo ☎ 67

GUEST HOUSES

Okonjima (AC B glm M PI PK RWS) All year
P.O Box 793 *Half way between Windhoek and the Etosha National Park on the B1* ☎ (067) 687 032 www.okonjima.com
Probably the most luxurious lodge in Namibia. This is much more than just a lodge. Okonjima is also home to The Africat Foundation which provides a rehabilitation-and-release and relocation programme for Namibia's Cheetahs and Leopards.

Swakopmund ☎ 64

BARS

Tavern Bar (B LM NG) Daily 20-5h
2 Theo Ben Gurirab Avenue
Not gay but popular with local gays and the only place which is open so late.

GUEST HOUSES

Secret Garden Guesthouse. The (AC BF cc glm H I m OS PA PK RWS VA) All year
36 Bismarck Street *Opp. Europa Hof hotel* ☎ (064) 404 037
natron.net/tour/secretgarden
All rooms face onto a secluded courtyard. There are also 2 luxury suites with private balcony. Breakfast is included in all rates. Refreshments provide in all rooms.

Tsumeb ☏ 67

HOTELS

Kempinski Mokuti Lodge Etosha (AC B glm M PI PK RWS RWT WO) All year
PO Box 403 ☏ (067) 229 084 www.kempinski-mokuti.com

Windhoek ☏ 61

BARS

Joe's Beer House (B cc DM M NG VEG WL)
Mon-Thu 16-late, Fri-Sun 11-late
160 Nelson Mandela Avenue ☏ (061) 232-457
Popular with many tourist, some of them gay. Enjoy a Zebra or an Ostrich steak. A great place to socialise.

RESTAURANTS

Luigi & The Fish (B cc M NG OS VEG WL) 18-22h
90 Sam Nujoma Drive *Klein Windhoek, on the way to the airport*
☏ (061) 228 820
The restaurant is quite large with a number of different areas. Seafood is the speciality but game is also available. Not a gay place but gay men can often be found dining here.

TRAVEL AND TRANSPORT

Namibia JJ Tours (GLM)
Cauas Okawa 30, Outjo District, Kunene Region *At Etosha National Park*
☏ (81) 42 411 14 www.namibiajjtours.com

CRUISING

-In front of Kalahari Sands Hotel (bus station)
-Wernhil shopping center (upper level toilets)

Nepal

Name: Népal · Nepál
Location: Central Asia
Initials: NEP
Time: GMT+5
International Country Code: ☏ 977
International Access Code: ☏ 00
Language: Nepali, Maithili, Bhojpuri (Bihari)
Area: 147,181 km² = 54,363sq mi.
Currency: 1 Nepalese Rupee (NPR) = 100 Paisa
Population: 26,591,000
Capital: Kathmandu
Religions: 90% Hindu (state religion), 5% Buddist, 3% Muslim
Climate: Three different climate zones. The valleys are hot in summer and very cold in winter.

Homosexuality is not illegal in Nepal. There is no law against homosexuals in the civil code of Nepal, but paragraph 4, § 16 of Nepal's civil code punishes „any kind of unnatural sex" with up to one year imprisonment. This law has been abused as justification for the arrests of men who have sex with men and transgender people. Foreigners can get expelled for committing homosexual acts. Even though gay activists supported the 2006 Maoist rebel protests against the dictatorial king Gyanendra, who consequently agreed to the devolution of power, the Maoists have called for the repression of homosexuality. In their opinion, homosexuality is „a by-product of capitalism".
Particularly metis – i. e. male-to-female transsexuals – are being victimized by the police. There are reports that even owning a single condom was sufficient reason for an arrest.
On the 21st December 2007, the Supreme Court of Nepal issued a directive order to the Government of Nepal to recognize third gender (LGBT) according to their gender identity and protect sexual and gender minority rights. On the issue of same sex marriage, the Court issued a directive order to form a seven member committee to conduct a study on practises adopted by other countries and international practice on same sex marriage.

Homosexualität ist in Nepal nicht verboten, und es gibt im nepalesischen Zivilrecht auch kein ausdrücklich schwulenfeindliches Gesetz, aber Artikel 16, Paragraph 4 des bürgerlichen Gesetzbuches von Nepal sieht für „jegliche Art unnatürlichen Sexualverhaltens" Haftstrafen von bis zu einem Jahr vor. Diese Bestimmung wird missbräuchlich als Rechtfertigung für die Verhaftung von Männern herangezogen, die Sex mit anderen Männern oder Transsexuellen hatten. Ausländer können wegen homosexueller Handlungen des Landes verwiesen werden.
Nachdem Homo-Aktivisten 2006 noch an der Seite der maoistischen Rebellen gegen den diktatorisch regierenden König Gyanendra protestiert hatten und dieser dann in Folge der Machtteilung zustimmte, setzen sich die Maoisten nun für die Unterdrückung von Homosexuellen ein. Homosexualität sei ein „Nebenprodukt des Kapitalismus" hieß es. Besonders Metis – Mann-zu-Frau-Transsexuelle – sind der Verfolgung durch die Polizei ausgesetzt. Es wird berichtet, dass allein der Besitz eines Kondoms ausreichte, um inhaftiert zu werden.
Am 21. Dezember 2007 hat der oberste Gerichtshof von Nepal die hiesige Regierung angewiesen, das so genannte dritte Geschlecht (LGBT) der jeweiligen Geschlechtsidentität entsprechend anzuerkennen und die Rechte sexueller bzw. geschlechtsbezogener Minderheiten zu schützen. Zum Thema gleichgeschlechtlicher Ehen wies der Gerichtshof die Bildung eines siebenköpfigen Ausschusses an, der die diesbezüglichen internationalen Regelungen bzw. die Handhabung in anderen Ländern untersuchen soll.

Au Népal, l'homosexualité n'est pas un délit et le droit civil népalais ne contient pas de loi homophobe, mais le paragraphe 14 de l'article 16 du code civil prévoit une peine de prison d'un an maximum pour « tout rapport sexuel contre nature ». Cette loi est détournée par la police pour justifier l'arrestation d'hommes ayant eu un rapport sexuel avec d'autres hommes ou avec des transsexuels. Les étrangers peuvent dans ce cas être expulsés du pays.
Après que des activistes homosexuels aient protesté en 2006 aux côtés des rebelles maoïstes contre la dictature du roi Gyanendra et que celui-ci ait finalement accepté un partage du pouvoir avec ces derniers, les maoïstes se prononcent maintenant pour la répression

des homosexuels. L'homosexualité serait désormais un « sous-produit du capitalisme ».
Des homos se voient obligés d'avouer en public des actes de nature sexuelle pour finir en détention plusieurs années, durant lesquelles ils sont maltraités et violés. Ce sont particulièrement les transsexuels qui sont dans la ligne de mire de la police. On rapporte que même seule la possession de capotes suffise à se faire arrêter.
Le 21 décembre 2007 la plus haute Cour de Justice du Népal a ordonné au gouvernement du pays de reconnaitre le « troisième sexe » (gay, lesbien, trans) correspondant à l'identité sexuelle respective et de protéger les droits des minorités sexuelles ou relatives au sexe. Pour ce qui est du mariage des personnes de même sexe, la Cour de Justice a demandé la formation d'une commission de sept personnes qui doit étudier les réglementations internationales à ce sujet et l'application dans d'autres pays.

La homosexualidad en Nepal no está prohibida y en el derecho civil del Nepal tampoco hay ninguna ley expresa contra la homosexualidad pero el artículo 16, párrafo 4 del código civil nepalí prevé para „aquellos actos sexuales contra natura" penas de hasta un año. Esta disposición pues se utiliza de forma abusiva como justificación para el arresto de hombres que mantienen relaciones sexuales con otros hombres o con transexuales. Los extranjeros pueden ser expulsados del país por actos homosexuales.
Después de que activistas homosexuales en el 2006 protestaran todavía del lado de los rebeldes maoístas en contra del gobierno dictatorial del rey Gyanendra y aprobaran luego el reparto de poder, ahora los maoístas están a favor de la sumisión de los homosexuales. Dicen que la homosexualidad es un „producto addicional del capitalismo"
Los homosexuales se ven parcialmente obligados a practicar sexo en lugares públicos, por lo que está prevista una pena de prisión, en la que se les pega o también se abusa de ellos. La polícia persigue especialmente a los metis (transexuales de hombre a mujer). Se comenta que sólo la mera posesión de un condón basta para ser detenido.
El 21 de diciembre de 2007 el tribunal supremo de Nepal ordenó al gobierno estatal a reconocer al llamado tercer sexo (LGBT) la identidad sexual correspondiente y a proteger los derechos de las minorías sexuales. En cuanto al tema del matrimonio homosexual, el tribunal supremo ordenó la formación de una comisión de siete miembros, que debería estudiar la regulación internacional y la práctica sobre este asunto en otros países.

L'omosessualità in Nepal non è vietata. Il diritto civile del Nepal non ha delle leggi espressamente omofobe, sebbene l'articolo 16, paragrafo 4 del codice civile nepalese prevede pene detentive fino ad un anno per „qualsiasi tipo di comportamento sessuale innaturale". Questo articolo viene abusato come pretesto per arrestare transessuali o uomini che hanno rapporti sessuali con altri uomini. Gli stranieri possono essere espulsi dal Paese per omosessualità. A dispetto di questa situazione legislativa piuttosto discriminatoria, nel 1998, due donne sono riuscite a sposarsi.
Dopo che, nel 2006, gli attivisti omosessuali hanno protestato a fianco dei ribelli maoisti contro il Re Gyanendra (che ha governato il paese come un dittatore), adesso i maoisti si impegnano per la repressione degli omosessuali arrivando ad affermare che l'omosessualità è un „subprodotto del capitalismo".
Gli omosessuali vengono spesso obbligati ad ammettere di aver avuto rapporti sessuali in luoghi pubblici per poi essere arrestati e quindi picchiati e violentati. Specialmente i Metis (uomini gay travestiti da donna) sono particolarmente perseguitati dalla polizia. Si dice che basti il possesso di un preservativo per essere arrestati.
Il 21 dicembre del 2007 la corte suprema del Nepal ha esortato il governo di riconoscere il cosiddetto terzo sesso (LGBT), la rispettiva identità sessuale e di tutelare i diritti delle minoranze sessuali e di genere. Per quanto riguarda i matrimoni tra persone dello stesso sesso è stata istituita una commissione di sette persone che ha il compito di prendere in esame i regolamenti internazionali su questo tema e monitora sulla loro applicazione.

NATIONAL GAY INFO

Trekking Through Nepal
Thamel ✉ Kathmandu ☎ (985) 108 41 87
Dinesh is a local trekking and tour guide, who can help you plan your trip to Nepal.

NATIONAL COMPANIES

Aasha Nepal Travels and Tours
Thamel, P.O. Box 8975 EPC 5415 ✉ Kathmandu *Next to Dexo Music Center, near Marcopolo Student Guest House* ☎ (01) 422 87 68
www.aashanepal.com.np
Operating in Nepal since 2001, exclusively for gay travellers.

NATIONAL GROUPS

Blue Diamond Society Drop-in centre 10-17, STD clinic Sat 11-13h
Shiv Bhakta Marg-344, Khursani Tar, Lazimpat ✉ Kathmandu *Near Shangri La Hotel* ☎ (01) 444 33 50 www.bds.org.np
Nepal's only gay organization. See website for activities and support on offer. Sunil has been elected into the local parliament in 2008. Also publisher of weekly magazine „Blue Diamond weekly".

Kathmandu ☎ 01

BARS

Café Mitra (b MA NG)
Thamel, near Hotel Pisang / Tara Guest House ☎ (01) 425 9015
Cosy lounge, gay-friendly.

Maya (b MA NG)
Thamel, opp. KC restaurant ☎ (01) 441 0371
Cocktail bar frequented by some gay people.

CAFES

Himalayan Java (b BF glm M MA)
Tridevi Marg *Thamel entrance* ☎ (01) 1 442 25 19
www.himalayanjava.com

DANCECLUBS

Babylon Discotheque (B D glm MA)
Sundhara ☎ (01) 424 8755
Mixed crowd.

Club Platinum Disco (B D glm MA)
c/o Hotel Yak And Yeti, Durbar Marg *In the Hotel Yak and Yeti*
☎ (01) 424 89 99 www.yakandyeti.com
Here the son-in-law of former King Gyanendra Shah, was arrested from the same Disco on August 7 2010 for breaking the midnight deadline for discotheque-goers.

Fire Club (B D MA NG)
Thamel district *on 1st Floor under the Reggae Bar*
A disco/pub frequented by some gays esp. on Fridays. Very friendly and full of fun. To go there, ask for the Reggae bar (everybody knows it). Best time is around 23h.

RESTAURANTS

Jatra Restaurant and Bar (B CC M MA NG OS RES WI) 14-22h
J. P. Road, Thamel ☎ (01) 4256622
Restaurant with live music. Jatra has 2 floors with a nice garden.

Oriental Dynasty Restaurant (M MA NG) 24hrs
Darbar Marg ☎ (01) 422 2515

HOTELS

Vaishali (AC B BF CC H M MA NG) All year
PO Box 206, Thamel ☎ (01) 413 968 www.vaishalihotel.com
A luxury hotel with all the modern comforts. Host of the „3D" (Diwali, Drag, Dance) Extravaganza Party.

GUEST HOUSES

International Guest House (BF M MA NG)
GPO 7060, Thamel *North west Thamel* ☎ (01) 425 2299
www.ighouse.com
45 rooms in the centre of the touristic area of Kathmandu.

Netherlands

Name: Nederland · Niederlande · Pays-Bas · Paises Bajos · Paesi Bassi
Location: Western Europe
Initials: NL
Time: GMT +1
International Country Code: ☏ 31 (omit 0 from area code)
International Access Code: ☏ 00
Language: Dutch, Frisian
Area: 41,526km² / 16,164 sq mi.
Currency: 1 Euro (€) = 100 Cents
Population: 16,282,000
Capital: Amsterdam, Den Haag (Government and Royal Residence)
Religions: 33% Roman Catholic, 25% Protestant, 4,4% Moslems
Climate: Moderate and marine climate. Summers are cool, winters mild.
Important gay cities: Amsterdam, Rotterdam, Den Haag

The Netherlands is considered to be one of the most tolerant countries in the world. Discrimination on the basis of religion, philosophy, political persuasion, race, sex or any other ground, is forbidden according to a civil right that is found in Article 1 of the constitution. Moreover homosexuality has been sanctioned for almost a century. Nowadays education concerning homosexuality is more or less standard practice in schools, which contributes to recognition and mutual understanding. In 2001 Holland had the world première of becoming the first country where civil marriage was instituted for people of the same sex. Meanwhile a law has been adopted in which homosexual couples are allowed to adopt children. The age of consent is 16 in Holland.
From 2008, a Dutch insurance company will be the first in the world to offer health insurance specifically addressing gay requirements. The insurance package jointly developed with the Lesbian and Gay Association COC includes additional „pink elements" such as guaranteed treatment in gay-friendly hospitals and special home care support, naturally with a particular focus on HIV.
The social climate for homosexuals is most agreeable in the Urban Agglomeration of Western Holland (the city triangle between Amsterdam, Rotterdam and Utrecht). The gay-scene is well represented in this area, although gay cafes are found practically everywhere in the Netherlands. Like in most European countries, problems with homophobia can be encountered in very small, rural towns.

Die Niederlande gelten allgemein als eines der tolerantesten Länder der Welt. Diskriminierung wegen des Glaubens, der Lebensanschauung, politischen Ansichten, ethnischen Herkunft, sexuellen Neigungen oder aus jedem anderen Anlass ist einem in Artikel 1 des Grundgesetzbuches verankerten Zivilrecht zufolge untersagt. Außerdem ist gleichgeschlechtlicher Sex hier seit fast hundert Jahren straffrei. Heutzutage sind Bildungsmaßnahmen zum Thema Homosexualität an den Schulen fast alltäglich geworden, was deutlich zum gegenseitigen Verständnis und Respekt beiträgt. Im Jahr 2001 war Holland das erste Land weltweit, in dem gleichgeschlechtliche Paare ihre Partnerschaften amtlich registrieren lassen konnten. Mittlerweile wurde darüber hinaus ein Gesetz erlassen, das homosexuellen Paaren die Adoption von Kindern erlaubt. Das Schutzalter liegt in Holland bei 16 Jahren. Seit 2008 bietet ein niederländisches Versicherungsunternehmen als weltweit erstes eine speziell für homosexuelle Bedürfnisse ausgerichtete Krankenversicherung an. Das Versicherungspaket wurde gemeinsam mit dem Schwulen- und Lesbenverband entwickelt und beinhaltet zusätzliche "rosa Elemente", wie die Garantie auf Behandlung in homofreundlichen Krankenhäusern, besondere Hilfe für die Pflege zu Hause, und natürlich werde ein besonderes Augenmerk auf HIV gelegt. Am angenehmsten ist das soziale Klima für Homosexuelle im Ballungsgebiet von Westholland (das Städtedreieck Amsterdam, Rotterdam, Utrecht). In diesem Landstrich ist die Schwulenszene besonders gut vertreten, es gibt aber auch praktisch überall sonst in den Niederlanden schwule Cafes.

Les Pays-Bas sont toujours considérés comme un des pays les plus tolérants du monde. La discrimination reposant sur l'appartenance religieuse, les modes vie, la tendance politique, l'appartenance ethnique, l'orientation sexuelle ou toute autre discrimination sont interdites par l'article 1 de la loi fondamentale. En outre, les relations homosexuelles sont légales depuis près d'un siècle et l'homosexualité est un thème abordé à l'école, incitant ainsi à la compréhension et au respect réciproques. En 2001, la Hollande était le premier Etat au monde à permettre aux couples de même sexe de se faire enregistrer. Depuis, une loi est passée permettant aux couples homosexuels d'adopter des enfants. La majorité sexuelle est fixée à 16 ans.
À partir de 2008 c'est une société d'assurance néerlandaise qui proposera pour la première fois une assurance maladie spécialement adaptée aux besoins des homosexuels. Le pack assurance a été développé conjointement avec la fédération des homosexuels et lesbiennes et contient des éléments additionnels très „ arc-en-ciel „, comme la garantie d'un traitement dans des établissements hospitaliers favorables aux homosexuels, des aides de soins à domicile particulières et, bien-sûr, une attention particulière concernant le HIV.
C'est dans l'agglomération de Hollande occidentale, entre Amsterdam, Rotterdam et Utrecht, que le climat social est le plus agréable : le milieu gay y est particulièrement bien implanté, mais il y a presque partout au Pays-Bas des bars gays.

Los Países Bajos están considerados generalmente uno de los países más tolerantes del mundo. Según el derecho civil, está prohibida toda discriminación por razones religiosas, modos de vida, opiniones políticas, raza, orientación sexual o cualquier otro motivo, lo que aparece en el artículo 1 de la Constitución. Por ello, el amor entre parejas del mismo sexo no está penalizado desde hace casi un siglo. En las escuelas se han introducido medidas de formación sobre la homosexualidad para fomentar la comprensión y el respeto mutuos. En el 2001, Holanda fue el primer país del mundo que permitió el registro oficial de parejas del mismo sexo. Entretanto se aprobó una ley que autoriza la adopción a las parejas homosexuales. La edad de consentimiento en Holanda está en los 16 años.
A partir del 2008 una empresa de seguros holandesa ofrecerá por primera vez en el mundo un seguro de enfermedad dirigido a cubrir las necesidades de los homosexuales. Este paquete asegurador se creó

junto con la ayuda de la asociación de gays y lesbianas y contiene otros „elementos rosa" complementarios tales como la garantía de tratamiento en hospitales tolerantes, ayuda especial para los cuidados en casa y naturalmente se presta una atención especial al VIH.
La actitud social ante los homosexuales es más agradable en Holanda Occidental (el triángulo urbano de Amsterdam, Rotterdam, Utrecht). En esta zona, el ambiente gay está muy bien representado pero en casi todos los rincones de Holanda existen cafés para homosexuales.

I Paesi Bassi sono conosciuti come uno dei Paesi più tolleranti del mondo. Ogni tipo di discriminazione in base all'appartenenza religiosa, alle idee politiche all'appartenenza ad una certa razza o ad una particolare tendenza sessuale etc. è vietata dall'articolo numero 1 della costituzione. L'omosessualità nei Paesi Bassi non è più punibile da già quasi un secolo. Nelle scuole, il tema dell'omosessualità è inserito nei programmi ministeriali per l'istruzione come contributo ad un reciproco rispetto e ad una reciproca tolleranza. Con una legge emanata già nel 2001, l'Olanda può vantarsi di essere il primo Paese al mondo che ha reso possibile la registrazione ufficiale delle convivenze tra coppie dello stesso sesso. Adesso è passata anche una legge che permette l'adozione anche a coppie omosessuali.
L'età del consenso è di 16 anni.
Dal 2008, un'assicurazione privata olandese lancerà la prima assicurazione sanitaria al mondo che si orienterà sui fabbisogni della comunità omosessuale. Il pacchetto assicurativo è stato studiato e progettato di comune accordo con diverse associazioni omosessuali e lesbiche e prevede cosiddetti „elementi rosa", come per esempio il diritto di farsi curare in ospedali gay-friendly, incentivi per la cura a casa e naturalmente una particolare attenzione al tema dell'HIV.
Nell'Olanda occidentale e cioè nel triangolo compreso tra Amsterdam, Rotterdam e Utrecht, il clima sociale per quanto riguarda l'omosessualità è particolarmente positivo. In questa zona la scena gay è molto attiva anche se in tutto il resto del Paese non è mai difficile trovare locali gay.

NATIONAL GAY INFO

■ **COC Nederland** 9.30-17h
Postbus 3836 ✉ 1001 AP Amsterdam *Visiting address: Nieuwe Herengracht 49, Tram 7, 9 and all metrolines Waterlooplein station*
☎ (020) 623 45 96 💻 www.coc.nl
Founded in 1946 and the largest Dutch LGBT-organization. Publisher of Expreszo. Central office of local COC organizations around the country. COC Netherlands has consultative status by the ECOSOC NGO Committee.

■ **Ihlia – Homodok** (GLM MA) Daily 12-17h
Oosterdoksstraat 143 ✉ 1011 DL Amsterdam *In Amsterdam Public Library, near Central Station* ☎ (020) 523 08 37 💻 www.ihlia.nl
Archives, library and info-centre.

NATIONAL PUBLICATIONS

■ **Expreszo**
c/o COC Netherlands, Postbus 3836 ✉ 1001 AP Amsterdam
☎ (020) 623 45 96 💻 www.expreszo.nl
Bi-monthly magazine of ca. 84 pages for young gays and lesbians.

■ **Gay & Night**
Postbus 10428 ✉ 1001 EL Amsterdam ☎ (020) 78 81 360
💻 www.outmedia.nl
Gay monthly magazine available at gay venues. Bi-lingual (Dutch & English). Features information on parties, venues, events, art, books, etc. Extensive listing of addresses and city map.

■ **GK Magazine (De Gay Krant)** Mon-Thu 8.30-17, Fri -12.30h
Postbus 10 ✉ 5680 AA Best ☎ (0499) 39 10 00 💻 www.gk.nl
National gay newspaper for the Netherlands. In Dutch only.

■ **Gay News**
Postbus 76609 ✉ 1070 HE Amsterdam ☎ (020) 679 15 56 (advertising)
💻 www.gaynews.nl
English-Dutch magazine with reports and reviews on all aspects of gay life in the Netherlands.

■ **winq.**
P.O. Box 3291 ✉ 1012 DK Amsterdam ☎ (020) 305 3825 💻 www.winq.com
Holland's leading gay lifestyle magazine.

NATIONAL COMPANIES

■ **Artemedia** Mon-Fri 10-17h
Eerste Boerhaavestraat 1 ✉ 1091 RZ Amsterdam ☎ (020) 320 52 50
💻 www.Artemedia.nl
DVD mail order.

■ **Duizendpoot Gay Advertising**
Postbus 17402 ✉ 1001 JK Amsterdam ☎ (020) 528 61 87
💻 www.dp-communications.com
Specialized in gay advertising, promotion & events. Advertising campaigns in all major gay magazines throughout Europe.

■ **Oscar's** (CC GLM)
Postbus 4325 ✉ 7320 AH Apeldoorn 💻 www.oscarsshop.nl
Internet bookshop, mailorder.

COUNTRY CRUISING

Route A1 (E8)
-Hengelo-Amersfoort-Amsterdam km 28.9 (Section betweeen Baarn and Huizen. De Witte Bergen. Take the exit for Soest at km 28.9, but continue on the parallel road towards Amsterdam, until you see the sign for the motel-restaurant, turn left at top of exit road, park at the end of the short road. Walk through the area of trees and sand on the left at the end of the road)
-km 21.6 (Section near Naarden. P without name. In cars and adjacent bushes, mainly at night, but some daytime possibilities)
-Amsterdam-Amersfoort-Hengelo km 20.6 (P without name. Section near Naarden. In cars and bushes, day and evening. Not very busy)
-km 27.8 (Section between Huizen and Baarn. De Witte Bergen. Take the exit for the motel-restaurant, turn left of top of exit road, drive over the bridge crossing the motorway, park at the end of the short road. Walk through the area of trees and sand on the left at the end of the road)
Route A7 (E22)
-Veenborg in the direction Groningen P after Hoogezand and Groningen / Drachten by petrol stations „Oude Riet" and „Mienscheer"
Route A27 (E37)
-Breda-Almere, P Bosberg, km 90.2 (Section near Hilversum. In cars and in adjacent forest. Main area is in the trees ahead of P-area, turn left after you climb through hole in fence)
-km 96.8 (De Witte Bergen. Section Hilversum-Almere. Take exit onto A1, direction Amsterdam. Take next exit from A1 (restaurant). Turn left at stop of exit road, park at the end of the short road. Walk through the area of trees and sand on the left at the end of the road)
Route A28 (E35)
-Amersfoort-Zwolle-Groningen, Laakse Strand (Take exit Nijkerk and follow direction Lelystad-Almere. Over the bridge and turn into loop road which takes you under the same bridge. 2.5 km further turn left at sign Laakse Strand. At end of road you will find cruising in the big P; evenings. Same P is also good for nude beach (NG) in the daytime)
-Strand Horst (Follow »Strand« direction. At several Ps, left or right, is cruising. Evenings best)
-P Section Zwolle-Harderwijk (near Zwolle)
-P Glimmermade (Section Assen-Groningen, 7 km south of Groningen, off northbound carriageway)
Route A58
-Breda-Tilburg P Leikant (near Gilze, follow pathway to wooded area, very popular)
-P „Witte Molen" 7 km south of Groningen
Route A67 (E34)
-Antwerpen-Duisburg, Section in the Netherlands. Formerly E3, now with new number E34, km 46.2, P Leysing (Parked cars, and a hole in the fence leading to forest area, day and night)
-P Oeienbosch, km 15.2 (Parked cars, and adjacent forest area, day and night)

-km 9.5, E3 Strand (Leave motorway and follow signs either E3 Strand or E3 Plas. You have to pay to go in. Sunbathing, swimming, cruising. Mixed. Sunny days only)
-P Beerze, km 0.2 (Parked cars, and adjacent forest. This is the last P in the Netherlands before the Belgian border. Day and night)
Route A79
-Maastricht-Aachen, P Keelbos
-Aachen-Maastricht, P Ravenbos
Route N2 (E9)
-Liege-Utrecht (De Baan behind Makro, Gagel, in section Eindhoven-Best) Route A4 (E10)
-Amsterdam-Den Haag (at Amsterdam end of motorway, Nieuwe Meer, beach behind Eurohotel, days and evenings)
Route N228 (E37)
-Amersfoort-Maarn (Section to south of Amersfoort, near Leusden. Den Treek recration area, by Trekerpunt, day and evening, before dark. Leave N228 at km 4.9 and follow the P signs. Use either P or explore woodland area.) Route A12 (E35)
-Arnhem → Utrecht, P 't Ginkelse Sand
-117.2 P Grysoord (between Arnhem and Ede, north side)
Route A1
-81.3 P (South side)
-N345 P Bussloo (turn left at km 7.7, 9km east of Apeldoorn)
-48.4 on N31 (South side, between Appelscha and Smilde, 15-20h)
Route A29 Rotterdam ⇆ Bergen op Zoom
-P between exits Numansdorp and Oud-Beyerland
A 28 (E232) Zwolle ⇆ Meppel
-P between exists Ommen and Nieuwleusen

Edam ☎ 0299

GUEST HOUSES

■ **Bed & Breakfast Edam** (BF glm H I MA OS) All year
Jacob Tonissenstraat 14 *16 kms north of Amsterdam* ☎ (0299) 742440
💻 www.bed-breakfast-edam.com
Three guestrooms with a possibility to sleep 9 people. Special discounts for longer stays.

Alkmaar ☎ 072

SEX SHOPS/BLUE MOVIES

■ **Erotheek** (g VS) 11-22, Sat -18h, closed Sun
Koningsweg 17 ☎ (072) 515 77 15
■ **HT Cinema** (f G VS) 11-23h
De Laat 4 ☎ (072) 515 66 17

GENERAL GROUPS

■ **COC Alkmaar** (AC B D GLM S) Every Thu 20-24, every Sat 22-2.30, 2nd Fri/month: 19-02.30h (women only).
Bierkade 14 A ☎ (072) 511 16 50 💻 www.cocalkmaar.nl
Cosy bar/disco and information and support center. Thu bar (MA), Sat bar/disco (YC, MC), 1st Sun/month bar/disco (MA).

CRUISING

-Park Bolwerk (centre)
-Molen van Piet
-P Geestmerambacht (Alkmaar-Schagen, southern parking, take paths to nudist beach area, sunset and after dark, be discreet)

Almere ☎ 036

RESTAURANTS

■ **Den Enghel** (B GLM M MA) Tue 11-23, Wed & Thu -1, Fri -3, Sat -4, Sun 15-23h, closed Mon
Zadelmakerstraat 57 ☎ (036) 530 44 75 💻 www.denenghel.com
Menu changes regularly, often events take place. See website www.denenghel.com for details.

CRUISING

-Zilverstrand (NU) (at Hollandse Brug, take exit Muiderzand direction Zilverstrand from Route A6. Last part of nudist area is gay)

Amersfoort ☎ 033

SEX SHOPS/BLUE MOVIES

■ **Erotica Amersfoort** (AC CC DR G GH T VS) Mon-Fri 12-22, Sat 12-18h
Coninckstraat 4-6 ☎ (033) 4756235 💻 www.eroticcinema.nl
Sexshop, Cinema, Cruising area, Darkroom

GENERAL GROUPS

■ **WHAM, Werkgroep Homosexualiteit Amersfoort** (B GLM MA) Wed & Fri 21-24h
Hendrik van Viandenstraat 13 a/b ☎ (033) 461 26 54
💻 www.wham-amersfoort.nl
Wed: café 21-24h. See website for events on Fri.

CRUISING

-Den Treek recreation area (road Amersfoort-Maarn, near Trekerpunt)
-Plantsoen-West (between Koppelpoort and Stadhuis)
-Birkhoven (at the sand pits)

Amsterdam ☎ 020

For centuries the extremely tolerant climate in Holland has had a magnetic appeal to gay men all over the world. After all, where in the world can a gay couple walk hand in hand or smoke a joint in the streets without repercussions? The gay scene is well represented in this former seventeenth century harbour city with it picturesque canals and bridges, that give it its unique place in world architecture. The four most important gay areas are situated in the centre, within walking distance from each other: the Reguliersdwarsstraat (trendy), the Amstel („Bruin Cafe"-athentic dutch pub), the Warmoesstraat (leather) and the Kerkstraat. Yearly Amsterdam has a number of large-scale gay-events. There are several street parties on Queensday (April 30) and the Roze Wester festival at the homo-monument, next to the Westerkerk. Every first weekend of August the Amsterdam Pride takes place. The Canal Parade on Saturday forms the highlight of the festivities and is the only gay-parade on water in the world.

Das extrem tolerante Klima Hollands zieht schon seit Jahrhunderten Schwule aus aller Welt an. Wo sonst kann ein Schwulenpärchen unbelästigt auf der Straße Hand in Hand laufen oder einen Joint rauchen? In dieser größtenteils im 17. Jahrhundert entstandenen Hafenstadt mit den malerischen Kanälen und Brücken, die ihr einen besonderen Platz in der Weltarchitektur sichern, ist die Schwulenszene gut repräsentiert. Die vier wichtigsten Schwulengegenden befinden sich in Laufweite voneinander im Stadtzentrum in der Reguliersdwarsstraat (trendy), am Amstel („Bruin Cafe" – authentische holländische Kneipe), der Warmoesstraat (Leder) und in der Kerkstraat. In Amsterdam finden Jahr für Jahr einige große Gay Events statt. Es gibt gleich mehrere Straßenfeste am Königinnentag (30. April) sowie das Roze Wester Festival am Homosexuellenmahnmal neben der Westerkerk. Und am ersten August-Wochenende findet der Amsterdam Pride statt. Die Kanalparade am Samstag bildet den Höhepunkt der Feiern und ist weltweit die einzige Schwulendemo, die auf dem Wasser stattfindet.

La tolérance hollandaise attire depuis toujours des homos du monde entier. Dans quelle autre ville peut-on se tenir par la main ou fumer un joint sans être dérangé ? Dans cette ville portuaire datant essentiellement du XVIIe siècle, avec ses canaux et ses ponts pittoresques lui garantissant une place au patrimoine architectural mondial, le milieu gay est formidablement bien représenté. Les quartiers gays se trouvent dans le centre et sont accessibles à pied : la Reguliersdwarsstraat (très tendance), au bord de la Amstel, la Warmoestraat (cuir) et la Kerkstraat. A Amsterdam se déroulent tous les ans les plus importantes manifestations gays : plusieurs kermesses gays pour le 30 avril (Koninginnedag) et

pour le Roze Wester Festival au monument commémoratif de la déportation homosexuelle près de la Westerkerk ; la première semaine d'août a lieu l'Amsterdam Pride dont la „Canal Parade" du samedi est la seule manifestation gay aquatique au monde.

El ambiente tolerante de Holanda atrae desde hace siglos a homosexuales de todo el mundo. ¿Dónde si no puede una pareja gay pasear cogidos de la mano sin ser molestados o bien fumar droga? Esta ciudad portuaria, surgida en su mayor parte en el siglo XVII, con sus pintorescos canales y puentes que le aseguran un puesto privilegiado dentro de la arquitectura mundial, acoge una comunidad gay muy amplia. Las cuatro áreas gays más importantes se encuentran en el centro de la ciudad, en la Reguliersdwarsstraat (moderno), en el Amstel (con el „Bruin Café", un auténtico bar holandés), la Warmoesstraat (cuero) y en la Kerkstraat. En Amsterdam se celebran cada año diferentes eventos gays. Hay varias fiestas en la calle para el Día de la Reina (30 de abril) y para el Festival Roze Wester, en el monumento de los homosexuales, al lado de la Westerkerk. Y el primer fin de semana de agosto se celebra la Marcha del Orgullo Gay. El desfile por los canales del sábado representa el punto álgido de la fiesta y es la única manifestación gay del mundo que se celebra sobre el agua.

Il clima particolarmente tollerante dell'Olanda attira già da centenni gay da tutto il mondo. Da quale altra parte del mondo una coppia omosessuale può camminare indisturbata mano per mano o fumare una canna per strada. Amsterdam è una città portuale per lo più formatasi nel XVII secolo. Con i suoi pittoreschi ponti e canali, si è assicurata un posto privilegiato nell'architettura mondiale. Qui la scena gay si concentra in 4 zone principali e tutte e quattro si trovano al centro e sono facilmente raggiungibili a piedi l'una dall'altra. Queste sono la Regulierswarsstraat che rappresenta la scena trendy, la zona sull'Amstel („Bruin Cafe" – autentico pub olandese), la Warmoesstraat (scena leather) e la Kerkstraat. Ad Amsterdam si svolgono ogni anno diversi happenings gay. Il 30 aprile, per il compleanno della regina, hanno luogo diverse feste rionali in tutta la città. Altre feste di quartiere si svolgono anche durante il Roze Wester Festival. Il primo fine settimana di agosto è il giorno dell' Amsterdam Pride. La Kanalparade, che si svolge di sabato, è l'highlight del fine settimana ed è l'unico corteo omosessuale in tutto il mondo a svolgersi sull'acqua.

NATIONAL GAY INFO

Stichting Homo-Monument
Argonautenstraat 55-1 *Monument location: On Westermarkt, near Anne Frank House and Western Church, Tram 1/2/5/13/17/20* ☎ (020) 626 71 65
www.homomonument.nl
The monument for gays and lesbians was erected in 1987 by the Dutch gay community. Originally aimed to be a place for remembrance and warning, it is also nowadays a place for mourning about deceased friends and to celebrate that it is great to be gay or lesbian.

GAY INFO

Gay & Lesbian Switchboard (GLM MA)
Mon, Wed, Fri 12-18; Tue & Thu -22; Sat & Sun 16-20h
Postbus 15830 ☎ (020) 623 65 65 www.switchboard.nl
Information and support by phone for gays and lesbians, opening hours of the STD-clinic, gay tourist-information or the latest production in the gay theatre? Switchboard knows it all.

Pink Point (CC GLM MA) 10-18h
Westermarkt *Tram 13/14/17 Westermarkt* ☎ (020) 428 10 70
www.pinkpoint.org
The world's first gay and lesbian information kiosk, also has a great selection of queer souvenirs and gifts. Next to the Homomonument and in front of the Westerkerk.

CULTURE

Amsterdam Sexmuseum (glm MA) daily 9.30-23.30h
Damrak 18 *Near central station* ☎ (020) 622 83 76
www.sexmuseumamsterdam.nl
Presentation on public and private aspects of sex.

TOURIST INFO

Amsterdam Tourist Board Centraal Station (glm)
8-20, Sun 9-17h
Perron 2 B, Centraal Station *This office is located at platform 2 B inside Central Station and always very busy*
☎ (0900) 400 40 40 www.visitamsterdam.nl
The Tourist Board also has offices at Schiphol Airport (arrival desk 40), Leidseplein 1 and Stationsplein 10.

BARS

Amistad (bf CC G H I m) 12-24h
Kerkstraat 42 *In Amistad Hotel* ☎ (020) 624 80 74 www.amistad.nl
Internet café, very popular gay spot.

Amstel Fifty Four (! B G OC OS S) 16-1, Fr & Sat -3h
Amstel 54 *Corner Halvemaansteeg* ☎ (020) 623 42 54
www.amstelfiftyfour.nl
Traditional and long-established gay bar – formerly known as Amstel. Easy going, with popular Dutch music. Weekly karaoke and new video system.

Argos (! AC B DR F G MC) 22-3, Fri & Sat -4h
Warmoesstraat 95 *Near central station* ☎ (020) 622 65 95
www.argosbar.com
Popular long-established leather bar. Very friendly staff, check the local press for special events.

■ **Bleu** (B GLM MA OS) 16-1, Fri & Sat -3h
Geldersekade 111 ☏ (020) 77 60 210 💻 www.cafebleu.nl

■ **Bump** (AC B D GLM m MA S)
17-1, Fri & Sat -3h, closed Mon & Tue
Kerkstraat 23 ☏ 624 821 077 💻 www.barbump.nl
Large bar with two floors, two bars and dance floor. Clubby bar downstairs and cocktail – gentlemans bar upstairs.

■ **Cafe 't Mandje** (B d GLM MA) Tue 20-1, Wed & Thu 16-1, Fri & Sat 14-3, Sun -1h
Zeedijk 63 ☏ (020) 622 5375 💻 www.cafetmandje.nl

■ **Café Chez René** (AC B FC G YC) 18 -3, Fri & Sat -4h
Amstel 50 *Near Rembrandtplein and Muntplein* ☏ (020) 4203388
💻 www.chez-rene.nl
Every day happy hour 23-24h.

■ **Cafe Rouge** (AC B G MA) 16-1, Fri & Sat -3h, closed Mon & Tue
Amstel 60 ☏ (020) 420 98 81 💻 www.caferouge.nl
Cosy and a little old fashioned Cafe Rouge remains a very popular place to hang out and have a chat.

■ **Club Stereo** (B d MA NG) 16-1, Fri & Sat -3h, closed Mon & Tue
Jonge Roelensteeg 4 ☏ (020) 770 40 37 💻 www.clubstereo.nl
Happy hour 18-19h.

■ **Cozy Bar** (B d G l m MA S ST WE) 16-1, Fri & Sat -3h
Sint Jacobsstraat 8 💻 www.cozybar.nl
A gay bar owned and operated by an American.

■ **Cuckoo's Nest. The** (AC B DR F G MA OS VS)
13-1, Fri & Sat -2h
Nieuwezijds Kolk 6 ☏ (020) 627 17 52 💻 www.cuckoosnest.nl
Best in the afternoon. A good place to start a horny day.

■ **Dwarsliggertje, 't** (B)
Reguliersdwarsstraat 105 💻 www.hetdwarsliggertje.nl

■ **Engel Next Door. De** (B d G m MA)
Tue 15-20, Wed-Thu 16-23, Fri 12-1, Sat 15-3h
Zeedijk 23/25 ☏ (020) 4276 381 💻 www.deengelnextdoor.nl

■ **Engel Van Amsterdam. De** (B D G MA OS)
13-1, Fri & Sat -3h
Zeedijk 21 ☏ (020) 427 63 81 💻 www.engelamsterdam.nl

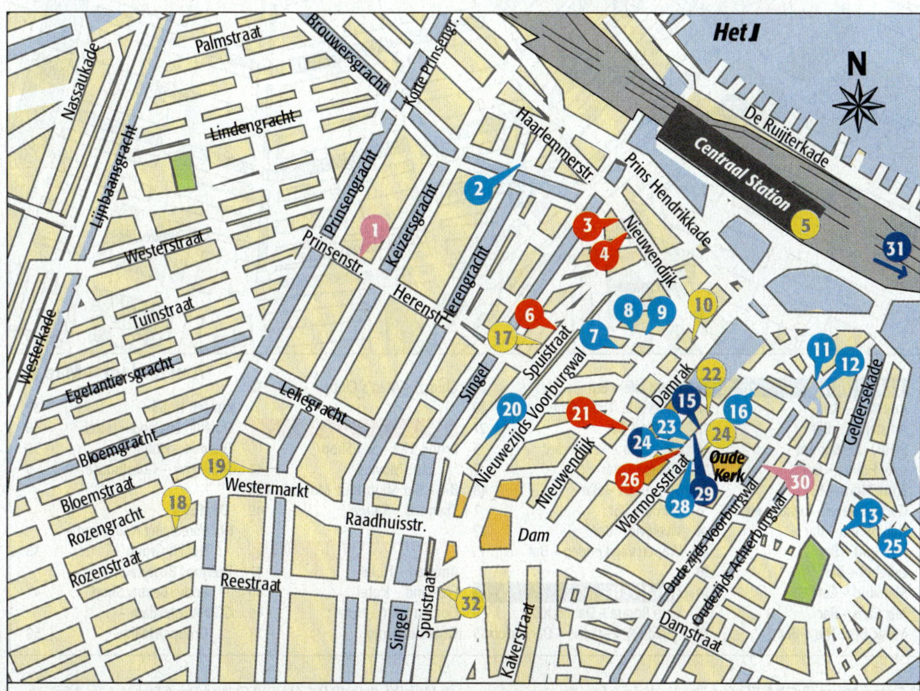

Amsterdam – Map A

EAT & DRINK	
Argos – Bar	28
Barderij. De – Café	11
Belhamel. De – Restaurant	2
Bleu – Bar	13
Boven – Café	24
Cozy Bar – Bar	8
Cuckoo's Nest – Bar	7
Getto – Restaurant	16
Hemelse Modder – Restaurant	25
Prik – Bar	20
Queens Head. The – Bar	12
Web. The – Bar	9

NIGHTLIFE	
Dirty Dick's – Men's Club	15
Eagle. The – Men's Club	29
Fuxxx – Danceclub	24
Warehouse @ BG – Danceclub	31

SEX	
Amsterdam Gayshop – Sex Shop/Blue Movies	6
Adonis – Sex Shop/Blue Movies	26
Alfa Blue – Sex Shop/ Blue Movies	4
Boysclub 21 – House of Boys	6
Drake's – Sex Shop/Blue Movies	21
William Higgins Le Salon – Sex Shop/Blue Movies	3

ACCOMMODATION	
Anco – Hotel	30
Truelove – Guest House	1

OTHERS	
Amsterdam Sexmuseum – Culture	10
Amsterdam Tourist Board Centraal Station – Tourist Info	5
Black Body – Leather & Fetish Shop	17
Boekhandel Vrolijk – Book Shop	32
COC Amsterdam – General Group	18
Mister B Leather & Rubber – Leather & Fetish Shop	24
Mister B Piercing Studio – Tattoo/Piercing	24
Pink Point – Gay Info	19
RoB Accessories – Leather & Fetish Shop	22

Amsterdam – Map B

EAT & DRINK

Amistad – Bar	47
Amstel 54 – Bar	17
BIHP – Restaurant	1
Café Rouge – Bar	22
Entre Nous – Bar	23
Garlic Queen – Restaurant	6
Habibi Ana – Bar	4
Hot Spot – Bar	8
Lellebel – Bar	30
Mankind – Café	34
Mix Café – Bar	16
Music Box. The – Bar	25
Night Life – Bar	27
Otherside. The – Café	10
Reality – Bar	21
Saturnino – Restaurant	5
Sultana – Bar	6
Spijker. De – Bar	48
Taboo – Bar	7
Vivelavie – Bar	29
Wapen van Londen – Bar	15

NIGHTLIFE

Club Roque – Danceclub	9
Rapido @ Paradiso – Danceclub	35
Church – Men's Club	32

SEX

Bronx. The – Sex Shop/ Blue Movies	43
B-1 – Sex Shop/Blue Movies	14
Thermos – Sauna	49

ACCOMMODATION

Amistad – Hotel	47
Freeland – Hotel	40
Golden Bear – Hotel	46
Orlando –Hotel	31
Prinsen Hotel	37
Quentin England – Hotel	36
Quentin – Hotel	39
Triple Five – Guesthouse	3

OTHERS

HIV Vereniging Nederland – Health Group	38
Thermos Beatysalon – Body&Beauty Shop	42
GGD Amsterdam – Groups/Health	50

■ **Entre Nous** (B G WE YC) Sun-Thu 21-3h, Fri & Sat -4h
Halvemaansteeg 14 ☎ (020) 623 17 00
Pop hits and disco music draw a somewhat younger, easy going crowd into the bar.

■ **Eve** (AC B CC d GLM M MA OS) Sun-Thu 16-1, Fri & Sat 16-3h
Reguliersdwarsstraat 44 *Behind the flower market, tram 1/2/5*
☎ (020) 689 70 70 🖳 www.eve-amsterdam.com
Former Arc.

■ **Getto** (B CC f GLM I M MA S VEG VS) Tue-Thu 16-1, Fri & Sat -2, Sun 16-24h
Warmoesstraat 51 *Near Central Station & red light district*
☎ (020) 421 51 51 🖳 www.getto.nl
Trendy lounge/cocktail bar also serving snaxs and home infused vodkas. Cocktail Happy Hour Tue-Sat 17-19h, Sundays „Bubble Bash! Changing art expositions, Themed events and Dj's.

■ **Habibi Ana** (B D G MA S VEG) Wed-Thu & Sun 19-1, Fri & Sat -3h
Lange Leidedwarsstraat 93 🖳 www.habibiana.nl
Cosy gay bar with Arabian music.

■ **Havana** (B G)
Reguliersdwarsstraat 17-19 🖳 www.barhavana.nl

■ **Hot Spot Café** (AC B d GLM MA S ST T VS) Mon 21-3, Tue-Thu & Sun 20-3, Fri & Sat -4h
Amstel 102 *Next to Rembrandt square* ☎ (020) 622 83 35
🖳 www.hotspot-cafe.nl

■ **Leeuwtje. 't** (B G m MC) Sun-Tue, Thu: 15-1, Fri & Sat -3h
Reguliersdwarsstraat 105
An new small gay bar with a beergarden.

■ **Lellebel** (AC B glm MA ST T) Mon-Thu 21-3, Fri & Sat 20-4, Sun 15-3h
Utrechtsestraat 4 *Tram 4/9/14 stop Rembrandtplein* ☎ (020) 427 51 39
🖳 www.lellebel.nl

Drag-transvestites café with shows, Karaoke and other in-house specialities. Tuesday is Karaoke night and Friday is Open podium – go and have fun.

■ **Ludwig II** (B G)
Reguliersdwarsstraat 37 ☎ (020) 625 3661 🖳 www.ludwigzwei.nl
New gay cocktail bar. See www.ludwigzwei.nl for more information.

■ **Mix Café** (AC B glm MA) Sun-Thu 20-3, Fri & Sat -4h
Amstel 50 ☎ (020) 420 33 88 🖳 www.mixcafeboxtel.nl
Dutch and pop music, gay and straight mixed crowd. For special events check website www.mixcafe.nl.

■ **Mon Ami** (B G MC) Tue 17-open end, Wed & Thu 17-1,Fri -3, Sat 16-3, Sun -1h, closed Mon
Amstelstraat 34 🖳 www.cafemonami.nl
Daily happy-hour.

■ **Montmartre** (! B F GLM S ST YC) Sun-Thu 17-1, Fri & Sat -3h
Halvemaansteeg 17 ☎ (020) 620 76 22 🖳 www.cafemontmartre.nl
Dutch, dance and pop music and a good mix of guests make this bar one of the most popular in Amsterdam.

■ **Music Box. The** (AC B CC G MA R) 21-3, Fri & Sat -4, Sun 16-3h, Mon closed
Paardenstraat 9 *Near Rembrandtplein* ☎ (020) 620 41 10
Hustler bar.

■ **Night Life** (B G R) 20-3, Fri & Sat -4, Sun 17-3h
Paardenstraat 7 ☎ (020) 420 92 46
Hustler bar.

■ **Prik** (AC B GLM I M MA OS S) Sun-Thu 16-1, Fri & Sat -3h
Spuistraat 109 *Close to Dam square and central station* ☎ (020) 320 00 02 🖳 www.prikamsterdam.nl
Snacks, Cocktails & DJs. Lots of special events, check website www.prikamsterdam.nl.

■ **Queens Head. The** (AC B d f G MA S) Sun-Thu 15-1, Fri & Sat -3h
Zeedijk 20 *Near central station* ☎ (020) 420 24 75 🖳 www.queenshead.nl
Traditional bar with spectacular view over the red-light district. Nice mixed crowd, Tue from 22h bingo night.

■ **Reality** (B G MA) 20-3, Fri & Sat -4h
Reguliersdwarsstraat 129 ☎ (020) 639 30 12
Popular black and white bar, latin music. Hot & tropical!

■ **Soho** (AC B D G MA OS S) 17-1, Wed & Thu -3, Fri & Sat -4, Sun -3h
Reguliersdwarsstraat 36 *Near flower market* 🖳 www.cafe-soho.nl

■ **Spijker. De** (AC B DR G MA VS) 16-1, Fri & Sat -3h
Kerkstraat 4 *City centre* ☎ (020) 620 59 19 🖳 www.spijkerbar.nl
Cosy brown bar with pool table, pinball machine and a fireplace. Very popular with local residents. Close to gay hotels.Porn videos and an upstairs darkroom. Happy hour 5pm-7pm.

■ **Sultana** (B D GLM MA OS) Mon-Thu & Sun 19-3, Fri – Sat -3h
Reguliersdwarsstraat 21 🖳 www.sultanabar.nl
New oriental gay bar for guys. Downstairs for drinks, upstairs for Arabic music.

■ **Taboo** (AC B CC D G M MA VS) Sun-Thu 18-3, Fri & Sat 16-4h
Reguliersdwarsstraat 45 ☎ 06 533 946 86 🖳 www.taboobar.nl
A popular gay bar in the main trendy gay street of Amsterdam. Offers a large smoking area with comfortable seats and coutches. An extended cocktail menu is available.

■ **Vivelavie** (AC B gLm I M) 16-1, Fri & Sat -3h
Amstelstraat 7 *Near Rembrandt square* ☎ (020) 624 01 14 🖳 www.vivelavie.net

■ **Wapen van Londen. Het** (AC B CC G OS YC) Sun, Tue-Thu 16-1, Fri & Sat -2h
Amstel 14 ☎ (06) 15 39 53 17 🖳 www.hetwapenvanlonden.nl

■ **Web. The** (AC B DR F G M VS) 14-1, Fri & Sat -2h
Sint Jacobsstraat 4-6 ☎ (020) 623 67 58
Action in this horny bar starts in the afternoon. Busiest on Sun. DJs Wed, Fri-Sun. Porn videos. Every Wed night the Web hosts a dildo lottery.

MEN'S CLUBS

■ **Church** (AC B D DR F FC G MA S ST) Tue& Wed 20-24, Thu 22-4, Fri & Sat 22-5, Sun 16-20 & 22-4h, closed Mon
Kerkstraat 52 *Near Leidsestraat, tram 1/2/5* ☎ (020) 4210392 🖳 www.clubchurch.nl
Club with changing (mainly erotic) themes every night. Tue kinky, Wed naked, Thu dance, Fri underwear party, Weekends changing themes.

■ **Dirty Dicks** (AC B DR F G GH MA p SL VR) Sun-Thu 23-3, Fri & Sat -4h
Warmoesstraat 96 *Near Central Station* ☎ (020) 623 96 04 🖳 www.dirtydamsterdam.com
Naked dark and Golden shower parties. See homepage for details.

■ **Eagle. The** (AC B DR F G MA p) 22-4, Fri & Sat -5h
Warmoesstraat 90 ☎ (020) 627 86 34
1st Sun/month: FF Party (15-21h)
Cruisey men-only leather bar. Besides the usual darkroom the Eagle sports a pool table with an adjustable sling above it.Can get extremely crowd.

■ **fuxxx** (AC B D DR F G GH LAB MA NR p SL VR WE) Thu & Sun 23-4, Fri & Sat -5h
Warmoesstraat 96 ☎ (020) 456 45 879 🖳 www.clubfuxxx.com
Club FUXXX is the new dance and cruise club, at the old location of the former club Cockring. Large cruising area on two floors.

■ **Sameplace** (B DR F G) Mon 20-1h
Nassaukade 120 🖳 www.sameplace.nl
Mondays only: sex parties for men.

CAFES

Barderij. De (B G MA) 12-1, Fri & Sat -3h
Zeedijk 14 ☏ (020) 420 51 32

Boven (b G WE) Fri-Sat 13-19, Sun -18h
Warmoesstraat 71 ☏ (020) 42 83 000 💻 www.rob.eu
Day time cafe upstairs at Rob's leather shop. Recently there is an exhibition with drawings.

Mankind (B GLM M MA OS WI) Mon-Sat 12-23h
Weteringstraat 60 ☏ (020) 638 47 55 💻 www.mankind.nl
Friendly gay bar/café with canal view in museum quarter. Snacks served; free wireless internet access.

Otherside. The (B G m) 11-1h
Reguliersdwarsstraat 6 ☏ (020) 625 51 41
💻 www.theotherside.nl
One of those special coffee shops you'll find only in the Netherlands, good place to hang out and have a joint.

DANCECLUBS

Club Roque (B D GLM YC) Fri & Sat 23-5h
Amstel 178 💻 www.clubroque.nl

Rapido @ Paradiso (AC B CC D G MA S)
Weteringschans 6 ☏ (020) 624 51 18 💻 www.clubrapido.com
Irregular dates on Sun 15-2h. Please check www.clubrapido.com for the latest information. Amsterdam's hottest dance event.

Trut (B D GLM MA) Sun 22-3h
Bilderdijkstraat 165 ☏ (020) 612 35 24 💻 www.trutfonds.nl
Very popular. Queue early as the club fills quickly.

Warehouse @ BG (AC B CC D G MA S) Sat 23-5h
Oosterdokskade 3 *Near central station* ☏ (020) 624 51 18
💻 www.clubrapido.com
Irregular dates on Sat 23-5h. Please check www.clubrapido.com for the latest information. Uplifting House with loads of energy.

RESTAURANTS

Belhamel, De (AC B CC GLM M MA OS RES)
18-22, Fri+Sat -22.30h
Brouwersgracht 60 *Five mins walk from Central Station*
☏ (020) 622 10 95 💻 www.belhamel.nl
Lunch is served between 12h-16h

BIHP (B CC glm M MA VEG) 18-22.30h
Keizersgracht 335 *Tram 1/2/5-Keizersgracht* ☏ (020) 622 45 11
💻 www.bihp.nl
Gay-friendly affordable, trendy restaurant/bar. Kitchen open until 22.30h. Easy music, international cuisine. Every two months different exhibitions.

Eve (AC B CC d GLM M MA OS) Sun-Thu 16-1, Fri & Sat 16-3h
Reguliersdwarsstraat 44 *Behind the flower market, tram 1/2/5*
☏ (020) 689 70 70 💻 www.eve-amsterdam.com
Former Arc.

Garlic Queen (AC B CC glm M MA RES VEG WL)
Reservations 18-20h, Mon-Tue closed
Reguliersdwarsstraat 27 ☏ (020) 422 64 26
💻 www.garlicqueen.nl
Every meal contains garlic, even the desserts!

Getto (B CC f GLM I M MA S VEG VS)
Tue-Thu 16-1, Fri & Sat -2, Sun 16-24h
Warmoesstraat 51 *Near Central Station & red light district*
☏ (020) 421 51 51 💻 www.getto.nl
Trendy lounge/cocktail bar also serving snaxs and home infused vodkas. Cocktail Happy Hour Tue-Sat 17-19h, Sundays „Bubble Bash! Changing art expositions, Themed events and Dj's.

Hemelse Modder (CC DM GLM M MA OS VEG)
Mon-Sun 18h-open end
Oude Waal 11 *Close to Central Station* ☏ (020) 624 32 03
💻 www.hemelsemodder.nl
West-European kitchen and friendly staff. Recommended for value and variety. Great food!

■ **Old Highlander** (B glm M OS RES VEG) Sun-Thu 12-1, Fri & Sat -3h
Sint Jacobsstraat 8 *Tram 1/2/5, Nieuwezijds Kolk* ☎ (020) 420 83 21
Scottish cuisine, breakfast all day!

■ **Saturnino** (B GLM M MA VEG) 12-24h
Reguliersdwarsstraat 5H *Tram 1/2/5* ☎ (020) 639 01 02
Italian cuisine in the middle of the gay area. Very popular. Always crowded.

SEX SHOPS/BLUE MOVIES

■ **Adonis** (AC CC DR G MA VS) 10-1, Fri-Sun -3h
Warmoesstraat 92 ☎ (020) 627 29 59
Bookshop, erotic toys and DVDs.

■ **Alfa Blue** (CC G MA VS) Daily 9-24h
Nieuwendijk 26 *Near Central Station* ☎ (020) 627 16 64 💻 www.alfablue.com

■ **Amsterdam Gayshop** (CC DR G MA SNU VS) 11-1h
Spuistraat 21 *Near Central Station* ☎ (020) 625 87 97
💻 www.adonis-4men.info

■ **B-1 Sexshop** (AC CC DR G MA VS) 9-24, Sun 12-24h
Reguliersbreestraat 4 ☎ (020) 623 95 46 💻 www.b1sex.nl
With a gay cinema and a labyrinth.

■ **Bronx. The** (CC DR G VS) Daily 10-22h
Kerkstraat 53-55 ☎ (020) 623 15 48 💻 www.bronx1976.com
Also mail order. Large collection of DVDs.

■ **Drake's of LA** (AC CC DR G VS YC) 9-22h
Damrak 61 *200 m south of Central Station* ☎ (020) 627 95 44
💻 www.drakesdirect.com
Adult store plus gay cinema with 23 DVD cockpits and glory holes/peep holes upstairs!

■ **William Higgins Le Salon** (AC CC DR G LAB VS YC) 9-22h
Nieuwendijk 22 *Near Central Station* ☎ (020) 622 65 65
💻 www.lesalonamsterdam.nl
Gay sex super market including large maze and cinema/DVD cockpits!

HOUSE OF BOYS

■ **Boysclub 21** (AC B CC G I MSG SNU VS WH) 13-1, Fri & Sat -2h
Spuistraat 21 *Above 4 Men* ☎ (020) 622 88 28 💻 www.boysclub21.nl
International boys, three standard rooms, one VIP-room with spa, free strip/sexshows.

SAUNAS/BATHS

■ **Damrak** (b G m MA MSG SA SB SOL WH) Daily 12-21h
Damrak 54 *10 mins walk from Central Station* ☎ 622 60 12
💻 www.saunadamrak.com

■ **Thermos Sauna Day & Night** (! AC B CC DM DR DU FC G I M MA MSG NU OS PI RR SA SB SH SL SOL VR VS WH WI WO) 12-8h
Raamstraat 33 *Tram 1/2/5-Leidseplein* ☎ (020) 623 91 58
💻 www.thermos.nl
Huge sauna on five floors with restaurant, private cabins, roof terrace, beauty salon and hair dresser. Voted most popular sauna in the Benelux for the last ten years. Very clean facilities and friendly staff.

BODY & BEAUTY SHOPS

■ **Cuts and Curls Hairstyling** (CC F GLM MA)
Tue-Thu 10-20, Fri & Sat -19h
Korte Leidsedwarsstraat 74 *Near Rijksmuseum* ☎ (020) 624 68 81
💻 www.cutsandcurls.nl
Hairstylist and barber for rough types, specialist in hair colouring.

■ **Thermos Beautysalon** (AC CC GLM MA MSG NR SH WI) 13-20h
Raamdwarsstraat 5 *Entrance through Thermos Sauna and/or from the street* ☎ (020) 623 91 58 💻 www.thermos.nl

Hairstyling, body and facial cosmetics, waxing, massage. Sale of underwear and swimwear.

BOOK SHOPS

American Book Center. The (CC g)
Mon-Wed, Fri & Sat 10-20, Thu -21, Sun 11-18.30h
Spui 12 *Tram 1/2/5/9/14/16/24/25* ☎ (020) 625 55 37 www.abc.nl
English language gay section on the 2nd floor, literature, magazines, travel books.

Boekhandel Vrolijk (! CC GLM)
Mon-Fri 11-18, Sat 10 -17, Sun 13-17h
Paleisstraat 135 *Near the Royal Palace* ☎ (020) 623 51 42
www.vrolijk.nu
Multilingual gay & lesbian literature, DVDs and photo books. International magazines, soft porn magazines and art films. Also mail order at www.vrolijk.nu

GIFT & PRIDE SHOPS

Gays & Gadgets (CC GLM MA) Daily 11-20, Sun 12-20h
Spuistraat 44 *Tram Nieuwezijds Kolk* ☎ (020) 330 14 61
www.gaysandgadgets.com
Gifts, cards and extraordinary souvenirs of Amsterdam and its gay life. Extensive information and tickets for all parties available.

LEATHER & FETISH SHOPS

Black Body (AC CC F G) Mon-Sat 11-19, Sun closed
Spuistraat 44 *Tram Nieuwezijds Kolk* ☎ (020) 626 25 53
www.blackbody.nl
Specializes in rubber. More than 500 rubber clothing models in stock. Also large leather, sportswear and toys collection. Online shop: www.blackbody.nl

Demask (F g) 10-19, Thu -21, Sun 12-17h
Zeedijk 64 ☎ (020) 620 56 03 www.demask.com
Rubber and leather shop with gallery.

■ **Mister B Leather & Rubber** (CC F G MA)
10.30-19, Thu -21, Sat 11-18, Sun 13-18h
Warmoesstraat 89 *Near central train station* ☏ (020) 788 30 60
🖳 www.misterb.com
Leather and rubber wear, toys, tattoos and piercings. Magazines, cards and DVDs. Also mailorder: www.misterb.com

■ **RoB** (CC F G) Mon-Sat 11-19h, Sun 13-18h
Warmoesstraat 71 ☏ (020) 428 30 00 🖳 www.rob.eu
Hand-made leather and rubber clothing. Very good reputation. Toys, videos, cards. Also mail order.

■ **Robin and Rik Leermakers** (CC G)
Mon 14-18.30, Tue-Sat 11-18.30h
Runstraat 30 *City centre* ☏ (020) 627 89 24
Hand-made own leather collection.

MAIL ORDER

■ **Artemedia** (G) Mon-Fri 10-17h
Eerste Boerhaavestraat 1 ☏ (020) 320 52 60 🖳 www.artemedia.nl
DVD mail order. UK, Europe & Worldwide.

TATTOO/PIERCING

■ **Mister B Tattoo & Piercing Studio** (CC F G MA)
10.30-19, Thu -21, Sat 11-18, Sun 13-18h
Warmoesstraat 89 *Near Central Station* ☏ (020) 788 30 60
🖳 www.misterb.com
Always safe and best quality tattoos & piercings wherever you want.

HOTELS

■ **Amistad Hotel & Apartments** (BF CC G I M RWS RWT VA)
All year
Kerkstraat 42 *City centre* ☏ (020) 624 80 74
🖳 www.amistad.nl
Gay owned and operated hotel with very friendly and helpful staff.

■ **Anco** (B BF CC F G m MA RWS RWT VA) Bar: 9-22h, hotel: 24hrs
Oudezijds Voorburgwal 55 ☏ (020) 624 11 26 🖳 www.ancohotel.nl
Close to the leather bars. Some rooms with shared shower/WC, cable TV and 24hrs gay video service. Just a short walk to the city's famous leather scene. Different room categories with shared/own bath.

■ **Freeland** (bf CC glm I MA RWB RWS RWT VA) All year
Marnixstraat 386 *Leidseplein, tram 1/2/5* ☏ (020) 622 75 11
🖳 www.hotelfreeland.com
Pascale and Rick offer you an open-minded and cosy atmosphere in their fine hotel in the middle of the gay-scene in Amsterdam. All 15 rooms are ensuite and have a phone, TV/DVD & WiFi. This clean hotel is „hetero-friendly". Local information is available from friendly staff. Freeland is registered as a pink point.

■ **Golden Bear** (BF CC F GLM I MA RWS RWT VA)
All year, reception 8-22h
Kerkstraat 37 *Tram 1/2/5-Prinsengracht* ☏ (020) 624 47 85
🖳 www.goldenbear.nl

■ **Orlando** (BF CC GLM RWT) All year
Prinsengracht 1099 *Near Rembrandtplein, tram 4 stop Frederiksplein*
☏ (020) 638 69 15 🖳 www.hotelorlando.nl
Luxurious hotel in a 17th century canal house. The seven rooms are each tastefully designed with bath/shower, TV, minibar and phone. Very close to most of the gay venues.

■ **Prinsen Hotel** (B BF CC glm I MA OS RWS RWT VA) All year
Vondelstraat 36-38 ☏ (020) 616 23 23 🖳 www.prinsenhotel.nl
A friendly hotel with 45 rooms, centrally located. All rooms have en-suite bathrooms, phone, TV, safe and hairdryer.

■ **Quentin** (B BF CC glm MA OS)
Leidsekade 89 *Tram 1/2/5-Leidseplein* ☏ (020) 626 21 87
🖳 www.quentinhotels.com

■ **Quentin England** (b BF CC g MA OS)
Roemer Visscherstraat 30 ☏ (020) 689 23 23 🖳 www.quentinhotels.com

GUEST HOUSES

■ **Adriaen van Ostade B&B** (AC BF GLM I PK RWB RWS RWT VA WI) All year
Van Ostadestraat 66 *In the midst of trendy De Pijp area*
☎ (020) 673 71 57 🖳 www.ostadebb.com
Total privacy with all amenities in a totally renovated building.

■ **Kien Bed & Breakfast Studios** (bf glm I RWB RWT) All year
Tweede Weteringdwarsstraat 65 *400m from Rijksmuseum*
☎ (020) 428 52 62 🖳 www.marykien.nl
Stylish apartments right in the centre of Amsterdam. WiFi and self service breakfast included.

■ **Triple Five** (AC b GLM I m MA)
Prinsengracht 555 ☎ (020) 428 38 09 🖳 www.triplefive.nl

■ **Truelove** (CC GLM H I MA NR RWS RWT WI) All year
Prinsenstraat 4 *Near Central Station* ☎ (020) 320 25 00
🖳 www.truelove.be
Guest house & antique shop.

APARTMENTS

■ **Flatmates Amsterdam** (cc glm I MA RWB RWS RWT VA) All year, 9-18h
Kruithuisstraat 18 (office) *City centre* ☎ (020) 620 15 45 🖳 www.flatmates.nl
Apartments, studios, house boats and guest houses. Gay owned. 30 different properties in the city centre.

GENERAL GROUPS

■ **COC Amsterdam** (GLM MA)
Rozenstraat 14 ☎ (020) 626 30 87 🖳 www.cocamsterdam.nl
Gay rights movement, daily info-coffee-shop, home for several groups and organizations. See website for information on regular parties.

■ **Gay and Lesbian Association (GALA)** (GLM)
Postbus 15815 ☎ (020) 676 23 17 🖳 www.gala-amsterdam.nl
Organizes parties, the „Roze Wester Festival" at the Gay Monument on Queensday (April 30th); Liberation Day (May 5th) and during Amsterdam Pride.

HEALTH GROUPS

■ **AIDS Fonds** (glm) Mon-Fri 14-22h
Keizersgracht 390 ☎ (020) 626 26 69 🖳 www.aidsfonds.nl
AIDS- & STD-helpline.

■ **GGD Amsterdam (STI Clinic)** (G MA) By appointment only
Weesperplein 1 ☎ (020) 555 58 22 🖳 www.gezond.amsterdam.nl
STI check by appointment only. Look for more information on the website: www.gezond.amsterdam.nl

■ **HIV-Vereniging Nederland** (glm) 9-17h, closed Sat & Sun
Eerste Helmersstraat 17 ☎ (020) 616 01 60 🖳 www.hivnet.org
Association that safeguards the interests of people with HIV & AIDS (medical, welfare, juridical, social, assistential, representational). Saturday HIV-café. Anonymous counselling by phone Mon-Fri 14-22h ☎ (020) 689 25 77.

CRUISING

-Vliegenbos, Meeuwenlaan (AYOR) (Amsterdam Noord)
-Vondelpark at the rose-garden (very popular at night)
-Oosterpark
-Sarphatipark (busy at night)
-De Oeverlanden Park. Take tram 2 and get off before the last stop, then walk south (bashers – AYOR).

Apeldoorn ☎ 055

SEX SHOPS/BLUE MOVIES

■ **Video Station** (DR g MA VS) Mon-Fri 13-22, Sat & Sun 12-18h
Stationsdwarsstraat 120 *Near the train and bus station Apeldoorn centre*
☎ (055) 522 11 81 🖳 www.videostation.nl

SAUNAS/BATHS

■ **Tutti Frutti** (B DR DU G GH m MA RR SA SH SL VS) Mon-Sat 10-23, Sun 12-23h
Marktstraat 15 *Near market place, opp. salvation army* ☎ (055) 522 42 73
🖳 www.tuttifruttisauna.nl
Shop, sauna & cinema.

Arnhem ☎ 026

BARS

■ **Cafè Capella** (B d GLM) Wed & Thu 21-1, Fri & Sat -2, Sun 16-2h, closed Mon & Tue
Nieuwstraat 66 🖳 www.capellacafe.nl

■ **Café Xtra** (B GLM MA) Thu 20-1, Fri -2, Sat 14-2, Sun 21-2h
Rijnkade 3 ☎ (026) 442 31 61 🖳 www.cafextra.nl

CAFES

■ **Spring** (B GLM m MA OS) 16-1, Thu-Sun -2h
Bovenbeekstraat 5 *Near central station* ☎ (026) 442 50 36
🖳 www.cafespring.nl
Not gay owned anymore, but operated by a very open-minded and gay-friendly couple. Mixed crowd.

SAUNAS/BATHS

■ **Steamworks** (B DR DU FC FH G LAB M MA MSG PI RR SA SB SH SL SOL VS WH) 12-1, Fri & Sat -2h
Roermondsplein 32 *5 mins from central station* ☎ (026) 442 33 43
🖳 www.steamworks.nl
Voted in 2008 as the best gay sauna in the Netherlands. The aim is to maintain a special balance between relaxation, sex and style. The atmosphere is trendy. Enjoy a weekend in Arnhem with a special Weekend Package available with Hotel Haarhuis.

GENERAL GROUPS

■ **COC Midden-Gelderland** (B D GLM I MA) Mon & Tue, Fri 12.30-18, Thu 12.30-18 & 19-21h, Wed closed (except holidays)
St. Catharinaplaats 10 ☎ (026) 442 31 61 🖳 www.diverzo.nl
Advice, information and shop for gays and lesbians. Café on Saturdays and Sundays. Check website for our activities!

CRUISING

-Meinderswijk (in summer only)
-Carpoolplace Wolfheze (A12)
-Park Sonsbeekpark (near westside entrance at Zijpendaalseweg, evenings and nights)
-Rozendaalsebos

Assen

CRUISING

-Asserbos 15-20 (city park, directly behind ice rink)
-P Snelweg (Assen-Noord/Assen-West, by small petrol station off Assen-West)
-A28 (E35) Assen-Groningen (P Glimmenade, 7km south of Groningen, off north-bound carriageway)
-De Moere (NU) (12 km southeast of Assen, lake on west-side, 14-20h)

Bergen aan Zee

CRUISING

-Beach near Pile 36 and nude area between piles 31 and 32

Bergen op Zoom ☎ 0164

GENERAL GROUPS

■ **COC Bergen op Zoom** (GLM)
Blokstallen 4 ☎ (0164) 25 42 35 www.cocbergenopzoom.nl

Best ☎ 0499

BARS

■ **Manus** (B G MA) 11.30-2 h
Nieuwstraat 92

CRUISING

-De Baan (behind Makro, Gagel)
-Route E9 (Eindhoven/Best)
-Kriekampen (A58 dir. Tilburg).

Breda ☎ 076

BARS

■ **Café 't Piggenhuys** (B GLM MA s) 19-2, Sat & Sun 17-2h, closed Mon
Nieuwstraat 19 ☎ (076) 571 87 73 www.piggenhuys.nl
■ **V Bar** (AC B D GLM MA) 20.30-2, Sun 17-2h, closed Mon & Tue
Halstraat 30 ☎ (076) 521 67 02 www.barv.nl

CRUISING

-Valkenberg (City park opposite Central Station)
-Liesbos (near E10)
-Kalix Berna (A27 direction Utrecht)
-Galgewaard (A27 direction Breda, popular)
-Lage Aard (A58 direction Tilburg-Breda, unofficial nude area)
-Galderse Meren (NU, YC) recreation area 7km south of Breda. Northern lake.

Callantsoog

CRUISING

-Sand dunes near nudist beach (direction Petten; also Pile 16)

Delft ☎ 015

BARS

■ **DWH (Delftse Werkgroep Homoseksualiteit)** (ac B d GLM MA) Wed & Sun 21-1, Thu & Fri 22-2h
Lange Geer 22 *Near station, opp. Legermuseum* ☎ (06) 1431 2546
www.dwhdelft.nl
Women's night 4th Sat/month; movies Wed; youngster evening Thu 21-2h.

Den Bosch / 's Hertogenbosch ☎ 073

BARS

■ **Club Chez Nous** (AC B D GLM MA s) 22-3, Fri & Sat -4h
Vughterstraat 158 ☎ (073) 614 25 92
■ **Kabberdoes** (B d GLM) Wed & Thu, Sun 16-2, Fri & Sat -4h, closed Mon & Tue
St. Josephstraat 6-8 ☎ (073) 612 36 65 www.kabberdoes.nl

SEX SHOPS/BLUE MOVIES

■ **B-1 Sexshop** (CC DR G H MA SNU VS) 11-23.30, Sat 12-23.30, Sun 13-23.30h
Vughterstraat 89 ☎ (073) 613 33 01 www.b1sex.nl

GENERAL GROUPS

■ **COC Noordoost Brabant** (GLM MA)
Sint Barbaraplein 6 te Oss ☎ (0412) 62 66 66
www.cocnoordoostbrabant.nl

CRUISING

-Park Hekellaan
-Tennisbaan-Hekellaan (evening)
-Engelermeer(NU), A59 Den Bosch – Waalwijk exit De Vutter.

Den Haag / 's Gravenhage ☎ 070

BARS

■ **Basta Café** (AC b GLM I MA S) Mon 17-24, Fri & Sat 21-1h
Scheveningseveer 7 *Near Palace Noordeinde* ☎ (070) 365 90 90
www.cochaaglanden.nl
■ **Boss. The** (B DR F G MA NU VS) 21-1, Fri & Sat 21.30-?, Sun 17-?h
Rijswijkseweg 536 *Between Laakkwartier & Rijswijk* ☎ (06) 19 19 43 91
www.the-boss.nl
Fetish bar with different sex parties every night. All gay except Thu: mixed partners night.
■ **Cafe 't Achterom** (B GLM MA) 16-1, Fri & Sat -3h, closed Mon & Tue
Achterom 22 A ☎ (070) 360 59 35 www.cafeachterom.nl
■ **Duijnstee** (B GLM MA) 14-1h
Halstraat 10 ☎ (070) 365 3145 www.cafe-duijnstee.nl
■ **Hans en Brietje** (B D GLM MA) Thu & Sun 22-4, Fri & Sat -5h
Herenstraat 13a www.hansenbrietje.nl
■ **Landman. De** (B g MA) Sun-Wed 16-1, Thu-Sat -2h
Denneweg 48 *Near Central Station, behind Hotel des Indes*
☎ (070) 346 77 27 www.cafedelandman.nl
■ **Stairs** (B DR F G MA) Fri & Sat 23-2h
Nieuwe Schoolstraat 11 *Close to Central Station* ☎ (070) 364 81 91

MEN'S CLUBS

■ **Club Ron** (AC B CC DU f FC FH G m MA MSG NU P RR S SA SOL WH) Mon-Fri 15-24h
Laan van Meerdervoort 506 *Tram 3/12, exit Gouden Regenstraat*
☎ (070) 310 67 65 www.clubron.nl
Exclusive men's club. Wed afternoon „slave orgy". Member of the Excellent Group which stands for luxury, hygiene and comfort.

CAFES

■ **De Klap** (b DM glm M MA WL) 10-23h
Koningin Emmakade 118A ☎ (070) 345 4060 www.deklap.nl

SEX SHOPS/BLUE MOVIES

■ **Sexshop Hans** (g MA VS)
Herengracht 24a ☎ (070) 360 05 93
Cabins, books, DVDs, tools.

SAUNAS/BATHS

■ **Blue River** (B DR DU FC G M MA MSG OS PI PP RR SA SB SH SOL VS WH) 17-23, Sat 14-23, Sun -22h
Valkenboslaan 181-191 *Tram 2/12, bus 13/14* ☎ (070) 364 64 07
www.blueriver.nl

■ **Fides** (B DR DU FC FH G m MA PP SA SB VS) 13-23h
Veenkade 20 *Tram 17 from Central Station, exit Noordwal*
☎ (070) 346 39 03 🖳 www.saunafides.nl
Clean and friendly sauna in the centre of The Hague. Two SB and one SA. Snacks available between 17-20h.

BOOK SHOPS

■ **American Book Center. The** (CC g) Mon 11-19, Tue & We, Fri 10-19, Thu -21, Sat -18, Sun 12-18h
Lange Poten 23 *Centre, near Plein & Parliament* ☎ (070) 364 27 42
🖳 www.abc.nl
General bookstore with gay section in English. Second store is in Amsterdam.

GENERAL GROUPS

■ **COC Haaglanden** (GLM) Wed 17-23, Thu 21-2h
Scheveningseveer 7 *Near palace Noordeinde* ☎ (070) 365 90 90
🖳 www.cochaaglanden.nl
Every Thursday multicultural disco.

CRUISING

-Meer en Bos
-Zuiderpark
-Het Haagsebos-Leidsestraatweg (AYOR R) (near station)
-De Scheveningsebosjes-Jacobsweg in the dunes near the bunker (sometimes police controls, very busy)

Den Helder

CRUISING

-Kennedypark
-Churchillpark
-Dunes left from strandslag Duinoord
-Park Quelderduyn, Schooterweg

Deventer ☎ 0570

GENERAL GROUPS

■ **COC Deveter e.o.** (AC B D GLM MA S WE) Thu 21-24, Fri & Sat 22-2, Sun 21-24h
Brink 64a ☎ (0570) 61 91 49 🖳 www.cocdeventer.nl
Also café. See website for schedule and info.

Dordrecht ☎ 078

CRUISING

-De Merwelanden (near Spaarbekken)
-Weizigtpark (close to central station).

Eindhoven ☎ 040

BARS

■ **Genestho** (B GLM MA) Tue-Thu 19-2, Fri -4, Sat 15-4, Sun -2h; closed Mon
Stratumsedijk 21 ☎ (040) 212 26 37 🖳 www.genestho.eu
■ **Queen's Pub** (B GLM MA) 20-2, Sun 16-2h
Lambertusstraat 42 ☎ (040) 244 25 06
🖳 www.freewebs.com/queenspub

DANCECLUBS

■ **Club Pecheur** (AC B D GLM p S VS WE YC) 21-2, Fri & Sat -4h, closed Tue & Wed
Stratumsedijk 37 ☎ (040) 211 44 40 🖳 www.clubpecheur.com
During weekdays mixed ages from 18-60, on weekends mostly younger crowd 18-29.
■ **Pallaz Club** (AC B D G MA S ST) 21-2, Fri & Sat -4h, closed Mon & Tue
Stratumsedijk 14 *200 m from the town hall* ☎ (040) 211 17 14
🖳 www.pallaz.com

SAUNAS/BATHS

■ **Jaguar** (AC b DR DU FC FH G GH I m MA OS PP RR s SA SB VS WO) Mon-Sat 12-24, Sun 13-20h
Ledeganckstraat 1 *Bus 19-Medisch Centrum Maxima* ☎ (040) 251 12 38
🖳 www.saunajaguar.com
A friendly place with free soup from 17h. Free parking in the vicinity. Bears day last Fri/month.
■ **Tibet** (b DR DU G m MA OS PI PP SA SB SOL WH) 12-2h
Antoon Coolenlaan 10 ☎ (040) 292 01 99 🖳 www.sauna-tibet.nl

GENERAL GROUPS

■ **COC Eindhoven / Pand 54** (B GLM OS S) 1st Thu/month (YC), 3rd Sun/month (OC)
Prins Hendrikstraat 54 ☎ (040) 245 57 00 🖳 www.coceindhoven.nl
Café Pand 54 (B f GLM MA OS): Tue 21-24, Fri -1, Sun 18-22h.

CRUISING

-Ekkerswijer (between Son and Eindhoven)
-Dommelplantsoen (Elzentlaan/Jan Smitzslaan/Anne Frank plantsoen)
-E3 plas (NU) (between Eersel and Vessem)
-De Baan (behind Makro; Gagel, E9 Eindhoven)

Emmen

SWIMMING

-Rietlandenplas (g NU) (in summer on WE or weekdays late)

CRUISING

-Marktplein (near Stadhuis)
-Bargeresbos (right and left side)

Enschede ☎ 053

BARS

■ **Gay centre 't Bölke** (! AC B D DR DU FC FH GH GLM I LAB M OS PI PP RR S SA SB SH SL SOL T VS WH YC) Mon-Thu 12-24, Fri -2, Sat -9, Sun 13-24h
Molenstraat 4-6-8 *Near railway station* ☎ (053) 434 13 41
🖳 www.bolke.nl
Large gay entertainment complex with a sauna with swimming pool, restaurant, bar and dance club. Foam parties.
■ **Stonewall** (B GLM MA) Thu 20-23, Fri 21-2, Sat 15.30-2, Sun 15.30-20.30h
Walstraat 12-14 ☎ (053) 431 70 14 🖳 www.stonewall.nl

CAFES

■ **Stonewall** (AC B d GLM MA OS S) Thu 20-23, Fri -2, Sat 15.30-2, Sun -20.30h
Walstraat 12-14 ☎ (053) 431 70 14 🖳 www.stonewall.nl

DANCECLUBS

■ **Gay centre 't Bölke** (! AC B D DR DU FC FH GH GLM I LAB M OS PI PP RR S SA SB SH SL SOL T VS WH YC) Mon-Thu 12-24, Fri -2, Sat -9, Sun 13-24h
Molenstraat 4-6-8 *Near railway station* ☎ (053) 434 13 41
🖳 www.bolke.nl
Large gay entertainment complex with a sauna with swimming pool, restaurant, bar and dance club. Foam parties.

SEX SHOPS/BLUE MOVIES

■ **Videotheek Amsterdam** (G VS) 11.30-23h
Molenstraat 14-16 ☎ (053) 433 74 01 🖳 www.videotheekamsterdam.nl

SAUNAS/BATHS

■ **Gay centre 't Bölke** (! AC B D DR DU FC FH GH GLM I LAB M OS PI PP RR S SA SB SH SL SOL T VS WH YC) Mon-Thu 12-24, Fri -2, Sat -9, Sun 13-24h
Molenstraat 4-6-8 *Near railway station* ☎ (053) 434 13 41
🖳 www.bolke.nl
Large gay entertainment complex with a sauna with swimming pool, restaurant, bar and dance club. Foam parties.

CRUISING

-Volkspark
-Vliegveld, Veldschoterweg
-Het Rutbeek (5km southwest of Enschede, follow cycle path east side, 15-20h).

Gouda

CRUISING

-Bus station
-Houtmansplantsoen (near band stand)
-IJsselpark

Groningen ☏ 050

CULTURE

Gallery MooiMan (G) Fri-Sun 14-18h
Noorderstationsstraat 40 *200 m from railway station Groningen-Noord* ☏ (050) 571 03 94 www.mooi-man.nl
The largest figurative male-art gallery in the world (commentary of the magazine The Art of Man, USA).

BARS

Café Decadent (B GLM MA) 16-2, Thu-Sat -?h
Gelkingestraat 56 ☏ 311 22 40 www.cafe-decadent.nl
News Café (AC B CC D g M OS WE)
Waagplein 5 ☏ (050) 311 18 44 www.newscafe.nl
Rubio. El (B GLM MA OS s T) 16-3h
Zwanestraat 26 ☏ (050) 314 00 39 www.elrubio.nl
Friendly bar where everybody can find his place.

CAFES

Ons Moeke (b GLM m MA) 12-21, Sun 16-21h, closed Tue
Paterswoldseweg 42 *Near city centre* ☏ 31 46 625
www.onsmoeke.com

DANCECLUBS

Golden Arm. De (B D DR GLM MA P) Fri & Sat 24-6h
Hardewikerstraat 7-9 ☏ (050) 313 16 76 www.goldenarm.nl

SEX SHOPS/BLUE MOVIES

Videotheek 3000 (G VS) 12-23h
Ged. Zuiderdiep 130 ☏ (050) 314 42 21 www.videotheek3000.nl

SAUNAS/BATHS

Pakhuisje 't. (B CC DR DU FC FH G M MA MSG PP RR SA SB SH SOL VS WH WO) Tue-Sun 14-23, Sat -2h, Mon closed
Schuitenmakersstraat 17 ☏ (050) 312 92 88 www.pakhuisje.nl
Intimate sauna on four floors. Friendly staff, nice bar with a cosy atmosphere and good facilities.Newly renovated.

CRUISING

-De Reitemakersrijge
-Bushes west of the Zernikelaan
-Behind the Kernfysisch Versnellers Instituut
-Behind Main Post Office
-Noorderplantsoen
-P „Glimmermade" E35 (A28) Assen (Groningen, north-bound)
-Hoornseplas (south, near road Haren, Groningen)
-Nude beach (action until late).

Haarlem ☏ 023

NATIONAL PUBLICATIONS

Proud Magazine (G)
Zijlweg 133a ☏ (023) 576 3014 www.proud-magazine.nl
New gay magazine in full colour. At least 5 issues (incl. 1 pride issue) per year in dutch and english.

BARS

Gay Café Wilsons (B d DR G I m MA s WE) Mon 20-1, Thu 17-1, Fri & Sat -4, Sun 17-23h, closed Tue & Wed
Gedempte Raamgracht 78 *Near the theatre* ☏ (023) 532 58 54
www.wilsons.nl

SEX CINEMAS

Roxy Sex Theater (DR g VS) 12-24h
Kleine Houtstraat 77 ☏ (023) 532 51 39 www.roxysextheater.nl

CRUISING

-Spaarnwoude forest, near the Westhofbos. Outside the village of Spaarndam, north of Haarlem
-Haarlemmerhout (park, Hertenkamp) after dark
-Bolwerk (behind the station) after dark

Harderwijk ☏ 0341

BARS

Entre Nous (B d GLM) 20-1, WE -2h
Smeepoortenbrink 18 ☏ (0341) 41 20 75

Heerlen – Landgraaf – Kerkrade ☏ 045

BARS

Splash NY (AC B D GLM MA OS) Thu 21-2, Fri & Sat 21-5, Sun 15-2h
Kempkensweg 7 *Near railway station* ☏ (06) 22 28 34 59
www.splash-ny.eu

SEX SHOPS/BLUE MOVIES

Erotiek Discount Centre (CC DR G MA S VS) 10-22h, closed Sun
Willemstraat 13 ☏ (045) 571 06 87

SAUNAS/BATHS

Alexandre (AC B DR DU FC FH G M MA OS RR SA SB VS WH) Thu-Sun 15-23h
Heerlenseweg 143 *In the region Aachen – Parkstad Limburg – Maastricht* ☏ (045) 533 17 16 www.sauna-alexandre.eu
Spacious new sauna.
Sauna Joe (b CC DR DU FC FH G I m MA PI RR SA SB VS WH WO) 13-1, Fri & Sat -3h, closed Tue
Nieuwstraat 110 *Herzogenrath* ☏ (045) 535 06 65 www.sauna-joe.nl

Hengelo ☏ 074

BARS

Vogue (B g) Thu & Fri, Sun 22-4, Sat -6h
Veldbleekstraat 4 ☏ (074) 250 83 08

Hilversum ☏ 035

BARS

So What (AC B GLM MA OS) Mon, Wed, Thu, Sun 16-2, Fri & Sat -3h; closed Tue
Noorderweg 72 ☏ (035) 683 10 03

SEX SHOPS/BLUE MOVIES

Erotica Hilversum (AC DR DU F G MA NR NU SH SL T VS) Sat -18h, closed Sun
Vaartweg 24c ☏ (035) 621 97 85 www.eroticcinema.nl
Sexshop, cinema, cruising area, darkroom,gloryholes.

Hoek van Holland

CRUISING

-Nudist beach between piles 116110 and 116360 (Rechtzeestraat, between two camping areas opposite 's Gravenzande)
-Maasvlakte.

Hoorn

CRUISING

-🅿 De Koggen (A7 from Purmerend to Hoorn)
-🅿 ABC (after 16h)
-Westerdijk (near De Hulk, summer only)

Leeuwarden ☏ 058

GENERAL GROUPS

■ **COC Friesland** (GLM) Mon-Fri 13-17h
Maria Anna Straatje 5-7 *Five mins from the station* ☏ (058) 212 49 08
💻 www.cocfriesland.nl
With café, also open on Fri & Sat 21-2h.

CRUISING

-Groene Ster (2nd 🅿 behind the golf club)
-Forest on the north side of the Groningerstraatweg (near farm & the Otterpark)
-De Kleine Wielen
-Ringerspark
-City park (near museum Prinsentuin, evenings and nights)

Leiden ☏ 071

CAFES

■ **Gaycafé De Roze Beurs** (AC B GLM I MA OS S ST) Sun 17-1, Mon, Wed 19-1, Thu-Sat 19-2h; closed Tue
Oude Singel 128 *Near main shopping street* ☏ (071) 528 06 80
💻 www.derozebeurs.nl

GENERAL GROUPS

■ **COC Leiden** (AC B d GLM MA WE) Café Fri 22-3, Sat 22-4h
Langegracht 65 *Centre, ten mins from central station* ☏ (071) 522 06 40
💻 www.cocleiden.nl
Fri & Sat bar/disco, last Sun/month 17-21h women only.

Lelystad

CRUISING

-🅿 Zuigerplaspark (north of town, near the railway)
-🅿 Larserbos (NU) (between Lelystad & Harderwijk, also small nudist beach 10 mins from 🅿 Larserbos)

Maastricht ☏ 043

BARS

■ **Nexxt** (B GLM MA) Thu 12-24, Fri -2, Sat 14-3, Sun 14-24h
Kommel 8 ☏ (043) 851 90 71 💻 www.grandcafenexxt.nl

SAUNAS/BATHS

■ **Gay Sauna Maastricht** (AC B DR DU FC FH G m MA MSG OS PI PP RR SA SB SOL VS WO) 13-24h
Kelmonderhofweg 51 *In Beek-Kelmond, ca. 10km north of Maastricht*
☏ (046) 449 00 15 💻 www.gaysaunamaastricht.nl
Built in a reconstructed and monumental farm. Intimate yet luxurious atmosphere and a mixed gay crowd.

HOTELS

■ **Quartier Bassin** (BF CC glm MC) All year
Boschstraat 55 *City centre* ☏ (043) 350 00 88
💻 www.quartierbassin.nl

GENERAL GROUPS

■ **COC Limburg** (B GLM MA) Café: Fri 17-24, Sat -0.30, Sun -23; Info-center Wed 14-16, Thu 20-21.30h
Bogaardenstraat 43 ☏ (043) 321 83 37 💻 www.coclimburg.nl
COC-Café Rosé and gay/lesbian info center.

CRUISING

-Plateau Sint Pietersberg
-Oudenhof
-Mgr. Molenpark (at Sint Lambertuslaan in Villapark).

Niekerk ☏ 0594

CAMPING

■ **Heerenborgh. De** (G MA NU PI) May-Sep
Niekerkerdiep 1 *Between Grootegast and Zuidhorn, end of Havenstraat*
☏ (0594) 50 34 46 💻 www.deheerenborgh.nl
Caravan and camping site for gay men only.

Nijmegen ☏ 024

BARS

■ **Café Meermin** (B glm MC OS T) 16-1h, closed Mon
Bloemerstraat 2 *Centre* ☏ (024) 323 61 00
Open for 10 years now. Gay owned. 2nd Thursday/month Transsexual Café.

■ **Mets** (B d GLM MA) 14-2, Sat 12h-open end
Grotestraat 7 *Centre* ☏ (024) 323 95 49 💻 www.cafe-mets.nl
Many lesbians.

■ **Plak. De** (B D GLM M MA) 12-23h
Bloemerstraat 90 ☏ (024) 322 27 57 💻 www.cafedeplak.nl

MEN'S CLUBS

■ **Chaps** (AC B DR F G MA p VS) Thu-Mon 21-2h
2e Walstraat 96 ☏ (024) 360 42 72 💻 www.chaps-nijmegen.nl
Mon & Thu dresscode: underwear, shoes or T-shirt only.

CAFES

■ **Plak. De** (B D GLM M MA) 12-23h
Bloemerstraat 90 ☏ (024) 322 27 57 💻 www.cafedeplak.nl

SAUNAS/BATHS

■ **Azzurra** (AC B DR DU FH G M PP RR SA SB SNU SOL VS WH YC) 12-24, Fri & Sat -2h
Van Heemstraweg 57, Beuningen *Near Nijmegen* ☏ (024) 684 18 08
💻 www.gaysaunaazzurra.nl

BOOK SHOPS

■ **Feeks. De** (GLM) 10-18, Thu -20, Sat -17, Mon 13-18h
Van Welderenstraat 34 ☏ (024) 323 93 81 💻 www.feeks.nl
Gay and lesbian bookshop. Free catalogue upon request.

SWIMMING

-Berendonck and Bisonbaai (nudist beaches on the banks of the river Waal)

CRUISING

-Kelfkenbosch (near Traianusplein)
-Goffertpark (only evenings around the parking lot)
-De Elsthof-forest along grootstalseweg (only daytime)

Putte ☏ 0164

SEX SHOPS/BLUE MOVIES

■ **B-1 Sexshop** (CC DR G H MA SNU VS) Mon-Sat 10-22h
Antwerpsestraat 56 ☏ (0164) 60 34 08

Roermond ☏ 0475

BARS

■ **Brunke. 't** (B d GLM MA) Mon, Thu, Sun 21-2, Fri & Sat -3h
Sint Nicolaasstraat 2 ☏ (0475) 33 29 23 💻 www.brunke.nl

SAUNAS/BATHS

■ **Dingeman** (B FC FH G m MA OS RR SA SB SOL VS WH) 13-24h
Willem II Singel 14 *Near railway station* ☏ (0475) 33 62 36
Sauna with a terrace and occasional parties.

Rotterdam ☏ 010

BARS

■ **Bliss** (B G)
Van Oldebarneveltstraat 88 🖳 www.blissbarlounge.com
■ **Gay Cafe Bonaparte** (B d GLM MA t) 22-6h
Nieuwe Binnenweg 117 ☏ (010) 436 74 33 🖳 www.cafebonaparte.nl
Gay Bar/Cafe with mixed clientele
■ **Jef's Cafe** (B GLM MA) 15-23, Wed & Thu -1, Fri & Sat -2h
Posthoornstraat 9 🖳 www.jefscafe.nl
■ **Keer Weer** (AC B GLM m p s) Mon-Thu 16-6, Fri-Sun 15-6h
Keerweer 14 *Near Binnenwegplein/1e Westblaakhof* ☏ (010) 413 12 17
🖳 www.keerweer.nl
■ **Loge 90** (AC B G I MA) 12-2, Fri & Sat -3h
Schiedamsedijk 4 ☏ (010) 414 97 45 🖳 www.loge90.nl
■ **Lusten** (B d GLM M MA) 17-1, Fri & Sat -2h, closed Sun
Schiedamsedijk 9 a ☏ (010) 414 85 77 🖳 www.cafelusten.com
■ **Regenboog. De** (AC B CC D GLM MA) Wed-Sun 16-2h
Van Oldenbarneveltstraat 148 A *Near Central Station and town hall*
☏ (010) 51 38 98 68 🖳 regenboogrotterdam.hyves.nl
One of the best gay bars in town. Wed karaoke night. Always a party. Friendly staff.
■ **Strano** (B GLM) 16-1, Fri & Sat -4h
Van Oldenbarneveltstraat 154 ☏ (010) 412 58 11 🖳 www.cafestrano.nl

MEN'S CLUBS

■ **Gay Play** (B DR F G MA) Mon-Thu 12-1, Fri -2, Sat 20 -2, Sun 15-20h
's Gravendijkwal 92 ☏ (010) 225 17 25 🖳 www.gay-play.nl
Different theme parties Fri, please check dates and times at www.gay-play.nl.

CAFES

■ **Apollo** (b GLM YC) Fri 18-2, Sat 21-2h
Schiedamsesingel 175 🖳 www.apollo-rotterdam.nl
Young crowd night Fri (under 26).
■ **Cafe Praag** (b GLM MA) Fri & Sat 21-2h
Schiedamsesingel 175 ☏ (010) 414 15 55 🖳 www.cocrotterdam.nl
Café for gays and lesbians at COC Rotterdam. COC night for young gays 3rd Thu/month 21-2h.

DANCECLUBS

■ **Gay Palace** (B D f GLM m MA ST T) Sat 23-5.30h
Schiedamsesingel 139 ☏ (010) 414 14 86 🖳 www.gay-palace.nl
Make sure not to be late, this place usually gets packed after 24h. Sat party night with Dj Rinaldo and Friends. See website www.gay-palace.nl for information on special events.

RESTAURANTS

■ **Engels** (B g M MA OS) 9-24h
Stationsplein 45 *Next to central station* ☏ (010) 411 95 50
🖳 www.engels.nl
Tourist info cafe.

SEX SHOPS/BLUE MOVIES

■ **Erotheek Schiedam** (DR g MA VS) 11-22, Sat -21, Sun 12-17h
Rotterdamsedijk 411-413, Schiedam *In the suburbs, Tram Koemarkt*
☏ (010) 427 04 24 🖳 www.erotheekshop.nl
Large selection of adult novelties and gay movies.
■ **Gaytoys** (cc G) Mon-Fri 12-20, Sat -18h
Keerweer 10 *M° Beurs/Churchillplein* ☏ (010) 411 35 22
🖳 www.gaytoys.nl

SAUNAS/BATHS

■ **Spartacus** (B DR DU FH G M MA OS RR SA SB SOL VS WH) 13-6h
's Gravendijkwal 130 *Tram 4, exit Nieuwe Binnenweg, 2nd floor*
☏ (010) 436 62 85 🖳 www.saunaspartacus.nl
Intimate and friendly sauna. A great roof terrace where there is plenty of action going on in the summer. The relaxed, mixed gay crowd is sure to build up some steam. For those who get hungry the Spartacus crew offers a variety of meals.

GENERAL GROUPS

■ **COC Rotterdam** (GLM) Café Fri & Sat 21-2h
Schiedamsesingel 175 *In the same street as Gaypalace.* ☏ (010) 414 15 55
🖳 www.cocrotterdam.nl

CRUISING

-Bergse Bos
-Zevenhuizerplas
-Kralingsebos
-Museumpark Booymans van Beuningen (rozentuin) (AYOR)
-Under Willemsbrug
-Zuiderpark
-Het Park
-Nudist beach and dunes Hoek van Holland

Sluis ☏ 0117

SEX SHOPS/BLUE MOVIES

■ **B-1 Sexshop** (cc g H MA VS) 10-21h
Nieuwstraat 5 ☏ (0117) 46 17 47 🖳 www.b1sex.nl
Two more shops in Sluis: one in the Nieuwstraat 16-18 (open from 9-18h) and one in Kapellestraat 27 (open from 9-23h).

Stadskanaal ☏ 0599

HOTELS

■ **Hotel-Restaurant Stadskanaal** (B BF CC glm H M OS) All year
Raadhuisplein 30 *Groningen is 30 mins by car* ☏ (0599) 65 06 99
🖳 www.hotel-stadskanaal.nl
Close to the Hondsrug Hills and at short distance from the fortified town of Bourtange, the Regional Historic Center, the Star Historic Railway, Pagedal sports complex, the village of Borger and surrounding boglands. Picknick baskets and bicycles are for hire. 40 rooms and two suites with all modern comfort.

Terneuzen ☏ 0115

BARS

■ **Café Teut** (B GLM OS YC) Thu-Sun 16-?h
Zeestraat 11-13 *In Axel, between Terneuzen & Antwerp* ☏ (0115) 56 69 66

Tilburg ☏ 013

BARS

■ **Café de Lollipop** (AC B D GLM MA OS S WE) Thu-Sat 14-4, Sun 14-2, Mon 14.30-2h, Tue & Wed closed
Paleisring 25 ☏ (013) 535 52 39 🖳 www.delollipop.nl
■ **Cafe Rosé** (b glm MA) Thu 20-?, Fri-Sun 14-?h
Stadhuisstraat 17 ☏ (013) 544 51 18
■ **Popcorn** (B D GLM MA) Tue & Wed 16-2, Thu-Sat 14-4, Sun -2h
Paleisring 19 🖳 www.depopcorn.nl
■ **Wijn. De** (B d gLm MA) Thu & Fri 19-4, Sat 16-4, Sun -2h
Stadhuisstraat 17 ☏ (013) 544 51 18 🖳 www.dewijn.nl

CAFES

■ **Popcorn** (B D GLM MA) Tue & Wed 16-2, Thu-Sat 14-4, Sun -2h
Paleisring 19 🖳 www.depopcorn.nl

SEX SHOPS/BLUE MOVIES

■ **Candy Shop** (AC B DR g H MA OS) Mon-Fri 12-24, Sat -18h
Korvelseweg 215-217 *Willem II football stadium* ☏ (013) 543 23 94
■ **Gay Cinema Candy** (AC B DR G MA OS VS) 10-24, Sun 14-24h
Korvelseweg 217 ☏ (013) 543 23 94

SAUNAS/BATHS

■ **Victory** (B DR DU FC FH G m MA NU OS PI PP RR SA SB SOL VS WH) Daily 12-24h
Bosscheweg 284 *Take bus 9 or 140 from central station*
☏ (013) 468 43 43 🖳 www.victory-massage.com

GENERAL GROUPS

■ **COC Tilburg** (G MA)
Postbus 36 ☎ (06) 29 26 20 36 (mobile) 💻 www.coctilburg.nl

CRUISING

-Wilhelminakanaal Biest-Houtakker
-A58 Breda-Tilburg, P Leikant (near Gilze)
-Wilhelminapark
-Luis Bouwmeesterplein.

Utrecht ☎ 030

BARS

■ **Bodytalk** (! AC B D F G M MA OS p S ST VS WE) Mon-Thu 17-2, Fri -5, Sat 16-5, Sun -3h
Oudegracht 64 *Centre, near central station* ☎ (030) 231 57 47
💻 www.bodytalk.org
Waterfront terrace in summer, trendy bar (cellar) on weekends.

■ **U-Bar** (AC B d GLM m MA VS WE) Fri & Sat 21-3h
Oudegracht 64 ☎ (065) 422 77 61 💻 www.u-bar.nl

DANCECLUBS

■ **enSuite on Saturday** (B D GLM YC) Sat 23-5h
Oudegracht aan de Werf 97 *Down the stairs, at waterside*
💻 www.en-suite.nl

■ **PANN @ Tivoli** (D GLM S YC) 3rd Sat/month 22-4h
Oudegracht 245 *Seven mins walk from trainstation Utrecht Central*
💻 www.pann.nl
Biggest party in the city for all sexual identities. Music from the 80ies to the 2000+.

■ **Rits – Le Club le Plus Queer** (B D GLM YC) Fri 23-4h
c/o K-Sjot, Oudegracht 157, water level *Centre, near Stadhuisbrug*
💻 www.clubrits.nl
Various themes and DJs.

SEX SHOPS/BLUE MOVIES

■ **Davy's Erotheek** (AC CC DR F GLM MA VS) 10-23, Sat 11-20h, closed Sun
Amsterdamsestraat 197 ☎ (030) 244 09 75
Gay on Wed & Fri.

BOOK SHOPS

■ **Savannah Bay** (GLM) Mon 13-18, Tue-Fri 10-18, Thu -21, Sat 10-17, 1st Sun/month 13-17h
Telingstraat 13 *Near square Neude & town hall, next to cinema 't Hoogt*
☎ (030) 231 44 10 💻 www.savannahbay.nl
Books, DVDs, cards and gadgets.
Specialized in gay, lesbian and transgender literature. Most books are in English.

GENERAL GROUPS

■ **COC Midden-Nederland** (G MA)
Postbus 117 ☎ (030) 231 88 41 💻 www.cocmiddennederland.nl

CRUISING

-Museumbrug, Prinsesselaan
-Sterrenwacht (at the end of Nieuwegracht)
-Hogelandse Park (near Museumlaan, 19-24h)

Venlo ☎ 077

SEX SHOPS/BLUE MOVIES

■ **B-1 Sexshop** (CC DR g H MA SNU VS) Mon-Fri 9.30-22, Sat -19h
Maaskade 15 ☎ (077) 354 25 85 💻 www.b1sex.nl
Sex shop with labyrinth & gay cinema.

Wageningen ☎ 0317

GENERAL GROUPS

■ **Homogroep Wageningen @ De Wilde Wereld** (B D GLM MA S) 1st Sat/month 22.30-3h
Burgtstraat 1 ☎ (06) 1675 8923 💻 www.shoutwageningen.nl
Disco 1st Sat/month at De Wilde Wereld, Burgtstraat 1, 6701 DA Wageningen.

Wieringerwerf ☎ 02272

SAUNAS/BATHS

■ **NCC Gaynight** (AK B DR DU FC FH G GH M MA p RR SA SB SL VR VS) Parties twice a month: Mon 19-24 & Sun 16-23h
Zuiderdijkweg 12 *40 mins by car from Amsterdam* ☎ (06) 30 33 32 73
💻 www.nccgaynight.com
Drinks, snacks, towels, condoms and lube included in entrance fee. Once a month a safe sex party. Several playrooms, a sling and sauna for gay and bisexual men only. Check website

Zandhuizen ☎ 0561

CAMPING

■ **Vlegel. De** (G MA NU OS PI) Apr-Oct
Oldeberkoperweg 23 ☎ (0561) 43 31 13 💻 www.devlegel.nl
Camping site for gay men.

Zandvoort ☎ 023

BARS

■ **Zicht op Zee** (B D G M MA S t) 16-24h
Boulevard Barnaart 10 ☎ 681 307 328
Bar and restaurant at the (north) boulevard, overlooking the sea and beach.

HOTELS

■ **Hoogland** (B BF CC GLM I OS PA PK RWB RWS RWT WH) All year
Westerparkstraat 5 *Near nude beach and town centre* ☏ (023) 571 55 41 💻 www.hotelhoogland.nl
Located in a quiet area near the centre of Zandvoort. The beach is only two minutes and the centre of town three minutes walk away. A creative hotel for guests who are looking for comfort and service. 30 guestrooms with shower/WC, TV/VCR, radio, CD player, room safe and phone.

SWIMMING

-Zuidstrand (go by bike or 40 mins by foot along the beach. The gay beach is near the nude beach. Cruising in the dunes behind the beach, also known as Het Flessenveld)

Zwolle ☏ 038

GENERAL GROUPS

■ **COC Zwolle** (B D GLM MA S)
Kamperstraat 17 ☏ (038) 422 44 03 💻 www.coczwolle.nl
See www.coczwolle.nl for details.

New Caledonia

Name: Nouvelle Calédonie · Neukaledonien · Nueva Caledonia · Nuova Caledonia
Location: Nouvelle-Calédonie
Initials: NC
Time: GMT +11
International Country Code: ☏ 687 (no area codes)
International Access Code: ☏ 00
Language: French
Area: 19,103 km² / 7,358 sq mi.
Currency: 1 Franc (CFP) = 100 Centimes
Population: 209,222
Capital: Nouméa
Religions: 59% Catholic, 17% Protestant
Climate: Tropical climate. Avoid the cyclone season (Nov-Apr).

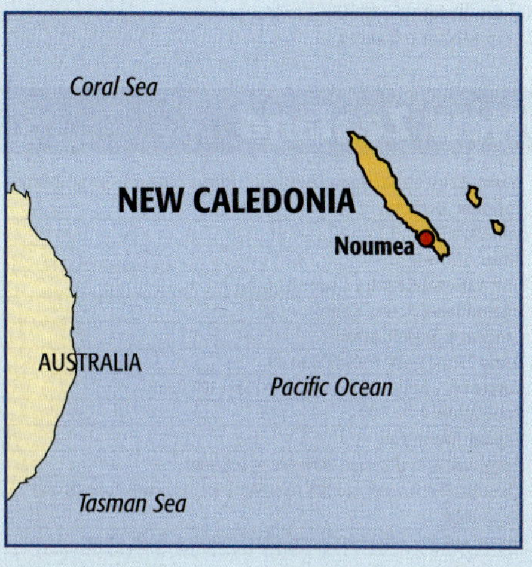

(☞ France.)
Homosexuality is legal in New Caledonia. The French penal code is in effect here. The equal age of consent of 16 was introduced in 1982. However, the newly introduced partnership laws in France („PaCS") – a registered partnership which applies to both lesbian and gay as well as to straight couples, do not apply in New Caledonia.
The island New Caledonia is not a classical gay destination, but is developing a small gay scene with bars and clubs in the capital city. The island is a tropical paradise and is the third largest of the South Pacific islands with white, sandy beaches lined with coconut palms and aquamarine lagoons. Nude bathing is however illegal.

(☞ Frankreich.)
Homosexualität ist in Neukaledonien nicht strafbar, es gelten die Strafbestimmungen Frankreichs. Das Schutzalter liegt seit 1982 bei 16 Jahren. Allerdings ist die in Frankreich eingeführte eingetragene Partnerschaft für Schwule, Lesben und Heteros hier nicht anerkannt. Neukaledonien ist zwar kein klassisch schwules Urlaubsziel, aber immerhin hat sich eine kleine Szene mit Bars und Clubs in der kleinen Hauptstadt entwickelt. Neukaledonien ist ein traumhaftes Reiseziel und die drittgrößte Insel im Südpazifik mit weißen Stränden und Palmen, tropischer Vegetation und Lagunen rund um das Eiland. Nacktbaden ist allerdings nicht gestattet.

Actuellement, le droit penal français est applicable (☞ France).
En Nouvelle Calédonie, la législation française est en vigueur: l'homosexualité n'est donc pas un délit et la majorité sexuelle est fixée depuis 1982 à 16 ans pour tous. Néanmoins, le pacs, qui autorise en France les homosexuel(le)s et les hétérosexuel(le)s à faire enregistrer leur partenariat, n'est pas reconnu. La Nouvelle-Calédonie et sa capitale ne sont certes pas des destinations habituelles pour les touristes homos mais il existe cependant un petit milieu gay comportant des bars et des boîtes. La Nouvelle-Calédonie est une destination de rêve et ses plages de sable fin, ses palmiers, sa végétation tropicale et ses lagunes font de la troisième plus grande île du Pacifique-sud un havre de paix où le naturisme n'est pourtant pas autorisé!

El Código Penal francés (☞ Francia) es vigente en Nueva Caledonia.
La homosexualidad en Nueva Caledonia no está penalizada pues rigen las normativas penales de Francia. La edad de consentimiento está desde 1982 en los 16 años. Sin embargo, aquí no está reconocido el registro de parejas de hecho para gays, lesbianas y heterosexuales como sucede en Francia. Nueva Caledonia y su capital no son precisamente un destino turístico clásico para los gays pero de todos modos se ha desarrollado un pequeño ambiente con bares y clubs en su pequeña capital. Nueva Caledonia es un destino paradisíaco y es la tercera isla más grande del Pacífico Sur, con blancas playas y palmeras, vegetación tropical, lagunas alrededor de las islas. El nudismo, sin embargo, no está permitido.

E'in vigore il codice penale francese (☞ Francia).
L'omosessualità in Nuova Caledonia non è legale e valgono le stesse regole che in Francia. Già dal 1982 l'età del consenso è di 16 anni. Tuttavia la legge introdotta in Francia sulle convivenze registrate per eterosessuali, omosessuali e lesbiche qui non è riconosciuta. È vero che la Nuova Caledonia non è una delle tipiche mete per il turismo gay, ma negli ultimi anni nella piccola capitale, Noumea, si è comunque creata una piccola scena gay con bar e locali notturni. La Nuova Caledonia è una meravigliosa meta turistica e la terza isola più grande nel Sud Pacifico. Qui vi si trovano bianchissime spiagge, una vegetazione tropicale e molte lagune. Ricordiamo infine che, qui, fare il bagno nudi non è permesso.

NATIONAL GROUPS

Homo-Sphère (GLM)
team meeting @ Malecon Bar 1st Tue/month 19h
4 rue Pallu de la Barrière, Vallée du tir ✉ BP 16868- 98803 Nouméa
☏ 97 62 64 💻 www.homosphere.asso.nc
Association for gays and lesbians in New Caledonia.

Nouméa

DANCECLUBS

Luna. La (B D glm YC)
Near Place Des Cocos (Coconut Square) *Opposite Le Saint Herbert*
Le Luna has a great atmosphere and is generally packed on a Sat night – it's a favourite hang out for the locals and cruise ship crew.

MV Lounge (B cc D glm PK WE)
Wed 21-3, Thu -4, Fri & Sat 22-4, Sun 18-22h
Baie des Citrons ☏ 274 646 💻 mvlounge.com
The gayest place in Nouméa.

FITNESS STUDIOS

Master Club (AC g WO)
83, Rte de l'Anse Vata ☏ 24 18 12

HOTELS

Mocambo (bf cc glm m)
46 bis, Rue Jules Garnier, Grand Terre *Baie des Citrons* ☏ 26 00 77
Somewaht tired decor and for one night is this hotel ok.

SWIMMING

-Plage de Nouville (G NU) (between Cimetiere de Nouville and Kuendu Hotel).

CRUISING

-Baie des Citrons
-Around Brandshell (late evenings)
-Quartier Latin (AYOR R T)
-Avenue James Cook (R T)
-Fort Tereka

New Zealand

Name: Neuseeland · Nouvelle Zélande · Nueva Zelandia · Nuova Zelanda
Location: Oceania
Initials: NZ
Time: GMT +12
International Country Code: ☏ 64
International Access Code: ☏ 00
Language: English, Maori
Area: 270.534 km² / 104,628 sq mi.
Currency: 1 New Zealand Dollar (NZ$) = 100 Cents
Population: 4,061,000
Capital: Wellington
Religions: 61% Christian, 30% Maori religions
Climate: The warmer months (Nov-Apr) are busy with tourists and locals alike.
Important gay cities: Auckland, Christchurch & Wellington

The big legal changes in New Zealand have come in the last generation. In 1986 gay sex was decriminalised with the age of consent set at 16. Discrimination on the ground of sexual orientation was outlawed, removing the fear of being rejected just because of what you are. And now, after the Civil Unions Act and Relationships Act were passed in 2004/2005, same-sex relationships have been given a legal status.
New Zealand's awesome landscapes, lush forests, amazing wildlife and pleasant climate make it a haven for many outdoor activities, and a great place to unwind. New Zealand society is diverse, sophisticated, and multicultural, and the honesty, friendliness, and openness of Kiwis will impress you. A great advantage of New Zealand is that all of its diverse physical, cultural, and artistic landscapes are so close to each other! New Zealanders have a unique and dynamic culture, with European, Maori, Pacific and Asian influences.

Der tiefgreifende gesetzliche Wandel wurde erst in der jüngsten Generation Neuseelands vollzogen. 1986 wurde schwuler Sex entkriminalisiert (das Mindestalter liegt bei 16 Jahren). So kann man endlich ohne ständige Furcht vor Verhaftung lieben und leben. Die Diskriminierung auf Grund der sexuellen Orientierung wurde vor zwölf Jahren verboten. Niemand muss jetzt noch Ablehnung fürchten, nur weil er ist was er ist. 2004/2005 wurde dann gleichgeschlechtlichen Beziehungen durch ein Partnerschaftsgesetz Rechtsstatus eingeräumt. Die Neuseeländer akzeptieren, dass es jüngst legalisierten und gegen Diskriminierung geschützten Menschen auch möglich sein sollte, einander zu lieben, einen Namen für diese Beziehung zu haben, sie feierlich mit einer Zeremonie zu begehen und erforderlichenfalls rechtswirksam zu belegen.
Atemberaubende Landschaften, üppige Wälder, eine erstaunliche Tierwelt und das angenehme Klima prädestinieren Neuseeland geradezu für viele Freiluftaktivitäten und als großartigen Ort der Entspannung. Die neuseeländische Gesellschaft ist bunt gemischt, niveauvoll und multikulturell; die Aufrichtigkeit, Freundlichkeit und Offenheit der Kiwis wird Sie beeindrucken. Dass diese vielfältigen physischen, kulturellen und künstlerischen Landschaften so nah beieinander liegen, ist dabei ein großer Vorteil! Die einzigartige und dynamische Kultur Neuseelands vereint europäische Einflüsse mit von den Maori geprägten und asiatisch-pazifischen Elementen.

En Nouvelle-Zélande, de profondes transformations se sont produites ces dernières années. En 1986, le rapport homosexuel a été dépénalisé (la majorité sexuelle est fixée à 16 ans) ce qui permet de vivre et d'aimer sans la perpétuelle peur de se faire arrêter. Il y a 12 ans, la discrimination liée à l'orientation sexuelle a été interdite. Personne ne peut donc être refusé pour ce qu'il est. Depuis 2004-2005, enfin, les couples de même sexe peuvent se faire enregistrer. Les Néo-zélandais acceptent que les personnes depuis peu légalisées et protégées de la discrimination puissent s'aimer, donner un nom à cette relation et la consacrer par une cérémonie ainsi que, le cas échéant, la faire valoir au moyen de papiers légaux. Des paysages à couper le souffle, des forêts luxuriantes, une faune surprenante et le climat modéré prédestinent la Nouvelle-Zélande aux activités de plein-air ainsi qu'à la détente sous toutes ses formes. La société néo-zélandaise est multiculturelle, haute en couleurs et cultivée ; l'honnêteté, la sympathie et l'ouverture d'esprit des „Kiwis" vous impressionnera. Un autre atout est sans aucun doute que les paysages physiques, culturels et artistiques se côtoient. La culture néo-zélandaise est unique en son genre et très dynamique : elle rassemble les influences européennes, Maoris, pacifiques et asiatiques.

El radical cambio legislativo empezó a notarse primero en las jóvenes generaciones de Nueva Zelanda. En 1986 se descriminalizó el sexo entre homosexuales (la edad mínima está en los 16 años). Así finalmente ya se puede amar y vivir sin miedo permanente ni penalización. La discriminación por motivos de orientación sexual fue abolida hace 12 años. Nadie debe entonces temer ningún rechazo, sólo porque uno sea como es. En el 2004/2005, se otorgó a las parejas del mismo sexo un rango legal con la aprobación de la ley de parejas. Los neozelandeses aceptan que las personas que están protegidas legalmente y contra la discriminación pueden también quererse, deben tener un nombre para su relación, deben poder celebrarlo en una ceremonia y poder tener eficacia jurídica.
Paisajes fascinantes, bosques enormes, una fauna sorprendente y un clima agradable son los mejores ingredientes de Nueva Zelanda para realizar actividades al aire libre y un lugar ideal para el relax. La sociedad neozelandesa es muy variada, elegante y muticultural; seguro que su honestidad, amabilidad y hospitalidad le impresionarán. Que estos variados paisajes, tanto físicos, culturales como artísticos estén tan cerca es una gran ventaja! La dinámica y única cultura de Nueva Zelanda reúne influencias europeas con la cultura maorí y elementos asiáticos.

L'età del consenso in Nuova Zelanda è di 16 anni. Il cambio determinante in ambito legislativo è stato completato solo negli ultimi tempi. Nel 1986 gli atti sessuali tra persone dello stesso sesso sono stati decriminalizzati. Così, è possibile vivere ed amare senza la costante paura di essere incriminato. La criminalizzazione in base all'orientamento sessuale delle persone è stata vietata 12 anni fa. Adesso nessuno rischia di essere rifiutato per essere quel che è. Tra il 2004 e il 2005 è stata emanata una legge che ha dato il via libera alle unioni civili anche tra coppie dello stesso sesso. I neozelandesi accolgono positivamente i cambiamenti legislativi che permettono anche agli omosessuali di amarsi liberamente, di poter definire questo rapporto, di poterlo festeggiare con una cerimonia e se necessario di poterlo dimostrare legalmente.
La Nuova Zelanda offre paesaggi che lasciano a bocca aperta, fitte foreste, un'impressionante fauna e un piacevole clima; tutto questo fa della Nuova Zelanda un posto ideale per il relax e per attività all'aria aperta. La società neozelandese è molto mista, colorata e multietnica. La sincerità, la cordialità e l'apertura dei Kiwis vi lasceranno impressionati. La particolarissima e dinamica cultura neozelandese unisce gli influssi europei agli elementi asiatici e pacifici dei Maori.

NATIONAL GAY INFO

Lesbian & Gay Archives of New Zealand (LAGANZ) (GLM MA)
PO Box 11-695, Manners Street ✉ Wellington *At Alexander Turnbull Library* ☎ (04) 474 30 00 🖳 www.laganz.org.nz
Research library and national lesbian/gay archives.

New Zealand Gaystay (GLM) 24hrs
3/186 Chester Street East ✉ Christchurch ☎ (03) 379 96 64
🖳 www.gaystay.co.nz
Group of gay-hosted B&B or homestay accommodation around New Zealand. See www.gaystay.co.nz to get information about each property.

NATIONAL PUBLICATIONS

Express (GLM) Mon-Fri 9-17h
c/o Cornerstone Publications Ltd, 166 Richmond Road, Grey Lynn
✉ 1021 Auckland *First floor* ☎ (09) 361 01 90 🖳 www.gayexpress.co.nz
Express is New Zealand's GLBT magazine and website. They inform, support and strengthen the GLBT community New Zealand wide by reporting on relevant people, places, stories and events. Express has been published since 1998, to date the longest, and now the only GLBT publication in the country.

NATIONAL COMPANIES

Gay Tours New Zealand
P.O. Box 39029, Harewood ✉ 8545 Christchurch ☎ 03 741 5071
🖳 www.gaytours.co.nz

NATIONAL GROUPS

New Zealand Aids Foundation (National Office)
(GLM MA) Mon-Fri 9-17h
31-35 Hargreaves Street, Ponsonby ✉ 1141 Auckland ☎ (09) 303 31 24
🖳 www.nzaf.org.nz
Prevention/education, anonymous, confidential, free HIV testing and counselling, support services for people with HIV/AIDS.

North Island

Auckland ☎ 09

Auckland is the largest city in New Zealand and has a large Polynesian population. It is a clean, modern city with excellent restaurants, hotels and tourist services. Auckland is built around two harbours and a number of extinct volcanic hills with lush greenery and fine beaches. The inner city suburbs of Ponsonby, Grey Lynn, Mt. Eden and Parnell have significant gay populations. Most bars and clubs are located in Karangahape Road („K" Road) Ponsonby Road or Downtown. Ponsonby is well known for its restaurants and wine bars.

Auckland ist die größte Stadt Neuseelands mit vielen polynesischen Bewohnern. Sauber und modern ist diese Stadt, die exzellente Restaurants, Hotels und touristische Dienstleistungen bietet. Mehrere erloschene Vulkane und erstklassige Strände umgeben Auckland, das an zwei Buchten entstand. Die Vororte Ponsonby, Grey Lynn, Mt. Eden und Parnell haben einen beachtlichen Anteil an schwuler Bevölkerung. Die meisten Bars und Clubs liegen in der Karangahape Road (auch K-Road genannt), der Ponsonby Road oder Downtown. Ponsonby ist bekannt für seine Restaurants und Weinlokale.

Auckland est la plus grande ville de Nouvelle Zélande. La majorité des Aucklandais est d'origine polynésienne. La ville est moderne, propre et jouit d'une excellente infrastructure touristique (hôtels, restaurants, services). Auckland a été construite sur d'anciennes collines volcaniques, au bord de deux baies. Les arrondissements du centre-ville Ponsoby, Grey Lynn, Mont Eden et Parnell revêtent un intérêt particulier pour le touriste gay. La plupart des bars et boîtes se situent dans la Karangahape Road, nommée « K » Road, dans la Ponsonby Road et dans le centre-ville. Ponsonby est également célèbre pour ses restaurants et ses bars à vin.

Auckland es la ciudad más grande de Nueva Zelandia. Lo primero que llama la atención es la gran concentración de población polinesia. La ciudad es limpia y moderna y ofrece excelentes restaurantes, hoteles y servicios turísticos. Auckland se encuentra entre encantadoras playas y varios volcanes, que ya no son activos. La mayoría de los bares está situada en la Karangahape Road (también llamada „K" Road), en la Ponsonby Road o en Downtown. Ponsonby es conocida por sus restaurantes y vinaterías.

Aukland, la più grande città della Nuova Zelanda, ha una grande comunità polinesiana. È una città moderna e pulita con eccellenti ristoranti, hotel e servizi turistici; è costruita intorno a due porti ed a numerose colline vulcaniche, in mezzo ad una vegetazione lussureggiante ed a spiagge incantevoli. I distretti centrali Ponsonby, Grey Lynn, Mt.Eden e Parnell hanno una rilevante comunità gay. La maggior parte dei bar e delle discoteche si trovano nella Karangahape Road (chiamata anche „K" Road), nella Ponsonby Road o nel Downtown. Ponsonby è famosa per i ristoranti e le enoteche.

SHOWS

■ **Caluzzi** (B CC glm M ST)
461 Karangahape Road ☎ (09) 357 07 78 🖳 caluzzi.co.nz
Drag cabaret show with dinner.

BARS

■ **Lola** (B d GLM MA) 10-?h
212 Ponsonby Road
Be who you are, love who you are. Happy hour 15-17h.

■ **Club Seven** (B d GLM MA) 10-?h
243 Karangahape Road *Cnr. Pitt St*
Happy hour 16-20h. Former Naval & Family Hotel.

■ **Urge** (! B CC d F G MA VS WE) Thu & Fri 21-3, Sat 21-4h
490 Karangahape Road ☎ (09) 307 21 55 🖳 www.urgebar.co.nz
Urge Bar has been a part of the Auckland Gay community for 13 years, making it the longest running gay men's bar in the country. No-attitude masculine space catering towards the Bear, Rugged, Masculine, Leather crowd & their admirers...

MEN'S CLUBS

■ **Basement** (AK B CC DR DU F FC G GH I LAB M MA PK RR S SH SL VR VS) Mon-Thu 12-12, Fri & Sat 12-2, Sun 13-12h
12 Canada Street *Down Drive* ☎ (09) 302 22 50
🖳 www.basementnz.com
The only gay adult shop in Auckland with the cruisiest little cruise sex club. Fetish nights and underwear parties.

■ **Lateshift Men's Cruise Club** (AC B bf CC DR G m MA VS) 19-3, Fri & Sat -10h
Level 2, 25 Dundonald Street, Newton *Corner of Basque Rd, look for blue light outside. Not on the roadside, down some stairs in a regualr office building* ☎ (09) 373 26 57 🖳 www.lateshift.co.nz
Fetish playrooms, extensive maze and cubicals, pool table, pinball, cable TV. Free breakfast at the weekend. Entrance fee applies.

CAFES

■ **Barretta Espresso** (b g MC) Mon-Fri 7-15h
Charles Davis Building, Shop 7, Beresford Rd ☎ (09) 309 23 65
Probably the best coffee in town.

■ **Garnet Station** (b glm m)
85 Garnet Road, Westmere ☎ (09) 360 5320
Lesbian run with Chiasso coffee, organic and gluten-free cakes and pastries.

■ **Kamo** (B CC GLM m MA S) Tue-Sat 16-21h
382 Karangahape Road ☎ (09) 377 23 13

DANCECLUBS

■ **Family** (AC B cc D GLM MA S ST WE) Thu-Sat 22-6h
270 Karangahape Road 🖳 www.familybar.co.nz
Karaoke and drag shows. The biggest and most popular location on K-Road. See www.familybar.co.nz for events.

RESTAURANTS

■ **Finale Restaurant & Cabaret** (B cc GLM M MA ST) 18.30-24h
350 Karangahape Road ☎ (09) 377 48 20
🖳 www.totaltravel.co.nz/link.asp?fid=572495

■ **SPQR** (B glm M MC NR OS VEG WL) Daily 12-?h
150 Ponsonby Road ☎ (09) 360 17 10 🖳 www.spqrnz.co.nz
Very popular. A great place to see and be seen. Good Italian food and NZ wines. Probably the best gay-friendly restaurant on Ponsonby Road.

SEX SHOPS/BLUE MOVIES

■ **Basement** (AK B CC DR DU F FC G GH I LAB M MA PK RR S SH SL VR VS) Mon-Thu 12-12, Fri & Sat 12-2, Sun 13-12h
12 Canada Street *Down Drive* ☎ (09) 302 22 50 🖳 www.basementnz.com
The only gay adult shop in Auckland with the cruisiest little cruise sex club. Fetish nights and underwear parties.

■ **D.vice** (CC f glm MA) 11-18, Sun -17h
27 Ponsonby Road, Ponsonby ☎ (09) 376 55 99 🖳 www.dvice.co.nz
Quality sex gear for adventurous, everyday people! Lingerie, leather and PVC clothing, party gear and sex toys for both women and men.

■ **Den. The** (CC DR f G MA VS) Sun-Thu 11-24, Fri & Sat -3h
348 Karangahape Road ☎ (09) 307 91 91 🖳 www.theden.co.nz
Gay magazines, videos, leather, adult toys and more. Cruising lounge, video rooms, play areas. Other stores: 440 Khyber Pass, Newmarket; 27 Barry's Point Road, Takapuna and 16 Wyndham Street, City.

■ **Erox Adult Store** (CC f G MA) Thu-Sun 24hrs, other nights -?h
474 Karangahape Road *Near gay bars and clubs.* ☎ (09) 366 64 99
🖳 www.eroxadult.com
Cruisy theatre with booths.

SAUNAS/BATHS

■ **Centurian** (! B CC DR DU FC G GH LAB m MA RR SA SB SH SL SOL VS WH WO) Mon-Thu 12-2, Fri & Sat 11-6, Sun -2h
18 Beresford Square, Newton *Off Pitt Street, bus stop: Karangahape Rd*
☎ (09) 377 55 71 🖳 www.centuriansauna.co.nz
Decorated in a Roman style. New Zealand's largest and busist gay sauna. Exceptionally clean and well maintained premises on Two floors: huge screen and three level theater, maze, sky movies, three porn rooms.

■ **Club Westside** (B CC DR DU f FC G LAB m MA RR SA SB SL VS WH WO) Tue-Thu 12-2, Fri 12-Mon 2h (non-stop)
37-39 Anzac Av. *1st floor, above OUT! bookshop* ☎ (09) 377 77 71
🖳 www.out.co.nz
Oldest gay sauna in Auckland. When will this place be renovated?

■ **Wingate Club** (AC cc DR DU FC FH G GH I LAB m MA OS P PI RR SA SB SH VS WH WO) 12h-open end
76 Wingate Street, Avondale *Behind the Avondale Racecourse along the banks of the Whau River, approx. 800 m from bus stop Great North Rd*
☎ (09) 828 09 10 🖳 www.wingateclub.co.nz
Suburban country club atmosphere.

TRAVEL AND TRANSPORT

■ **Travel Desk NZ** (glm) 8-20h
37-39 Anzac Avenue *In central buisness district* ☎ (09) 377 90 31
NZ's only complete travel agency. Agents available outside business hours.

GUEST HOUSES

■ **Brown Kiwi. The** (B CC glm MA OS) Daily 8-12 & 14-19h
7 Prosford Street, Ponsonby *5 min by bus to city center* ☎ (09) 378 01 91
🖳 www.brownkiwi.co.nz
Two floor colonial home, five mins from beach. 4 to 6 beds dormitories or four double rooms. Shared bath and kitchen.

■ **Moana Vista B&B** (BF CC GLM I MA OS PK RWB RWS RWT) All year
44 Queens Drive, Oneroa, Waiheke Island *Close to Oneroa and hekerua Bay beaches* ☎ (09) 3722282 🖳 www.moanavista.co.nz
Gay owned and operated.

GENERAL GROUPS

■ **Rainbow Youth** (GLM YC) Mon-Fri 10-17.30h
281 Karangahape Road ☎ (09) 376 41 55 🖳 www.rainbowyouth.org.nz
Work with GLBT, Takataapui and Fa'afafine young people (under 27 years). Has a drop-in centre, an education program and runs eight social/support groups.

HEALTH GROUPS

■ **Body Positive Inc** (GLM MA)
1/2 Poynton Terrace, Newton ☎ 0800 448 5463 ☎ 09 309 3989
Founded by and and run for people with HIV/AIDS. Welcoming all people living with HIV and AIDS in New Zealand.
Body Positive Inc. breaks down isolation and builds a sense of community while advocating on behalf of HIV+ people on a national level.

■ **New Zealand AIDS Foundation @ Burnett Centre** (glm)
1/3 Poynton Terrace, Ponsonby ☎ (09) 309 55 60 🖳 www.nzaf.org.nz
Free confidential HIV testing. Gay related counselling & practical support for people living with HIV/AIDS.

HELP WITH PROBLEMS

■ **GenderBridge** (MA T)
Mon 14-19, Tue 13-18 + 19.30-22, Sun 19.30-22h
☎ 0800 844357 🖳 www.genderbridge.org
Incorporated society established to provide support for transgendered people and their friends & family.

■ **OUTLine NZ** (GLM MA) Mon-Fri 10-21, Sat+Sun 18-21h
☎ (09) 309 3268
Free, confidential telephone counselling service for the rainbow community New Zealand wide. They are here to listen, provide information and to help you with your issues.

SPECIAL INTEREST GROUPS

■ **Gay Auckland Business Association (GABA)** (GLM)
PO Box 30 92 ☎ (09) 489 64 33 🖳 www.gaba.org.nz
Association of gay and lesbian business & professional people.

SWIMMING

-St. Leonard's Beach. (Catch bus to Takapuna, e.g. Long Bay Bus 839, and walk south; walk down the steps at the end of St. Leonard's Road; left is the predominantly gay swimming area)
-Long Bay (30km north of the city, reached by Long Bay Bus 839; gay area is 5 min. walk around rocks at the northern end, labelled Pohutakawa Bay)
-Ladies Bay (Catch 769 Glendowie bus along waterfront to St Heliers, ladies Bay is next beach to South. Follow road along cliff until you reach path heading down to beach).

CRUISING

All AYOR:
-Student Union Building (basement)
-Avondale (Roxbard Road)
-Newton Road (New North Road at shopping centre)
-Parnell Rose Gardens
-Western Springs Park at night (police!)
-Zoo car park
-High Street (below car park)
-Lake Pupuke, park near Milford shopping centre (at night)
-Domain (around Winter Gardens area)
-Long Bay/Pohutakawa Bay (most cruising in bushes around cliff at north end of the beach)
-Ladies Bay (in bushes behind the Gentlemen's Bay beach around headland)
-Toilets at Sentinel Beach (evenings) in summer only.

Bay of Islands/Northland ☎ 09

GUEST HOUSES

■ **88 Lodge B&B** (BF CC GLM I OS PI PK RWB RWS RWT) All year
88 Koropewa Road, Kerikeri RD 2 *Central to Bay of Islands and all Northland, complimentary transfers to local airport & coach terminal*
☎ (09) 407 82 88 🖳 www.88lodge.co.nz
Luxury B&B in the beautiful countryside of Kerikeri and central to Bay of Islands and Northland. En-suite or private bathroom, TV and DVD, fridge etc. Chris and Geoff's unique and original approach has created this luxury B&B to meet the needs of the discerning gay visitor to this lovely part of New Zealand.

■ **Baystay B&B Paihia** (BF GLM I M OS PK RWS RWT WH) All year
93A Yorke Road *3 mins out of Paihia, the centre of the Bay of Islands*
☎ (09) 402 75 11 🖳 www.baystay.co.nz
Relax and unwind. Spectacular panoramic river views from deck. Complimentary gourmet breakfast for 2 included. Close to all tourist attractions.

■ **Orongo Bay Homestead** (B CC GLM I M MA MSG OS PK RWB RWS RWT SA) All year
45 Aucks Road, RD 1, Russell *Five mins drive from historic Russell, Bay of Islands* ☎ (09) 403 75 27 🖳 www.thehomestead.co.nz
Luxurious, historic house with fine dining. Three rooms with bath/WC, hairdryer and heating.

■ **Wairoa Valley Quality B&B** (BF GLM OS PK RWB RWS RWT)
All year
59D Harmony Way – Riddell Road, Kerikeri *5 mins from Kerikeri town*
☎ (09) 407 99 77 💻 www.wairoavalley.co.nz
Set in bush, streams and gardens. The accommodation for a maximum of four people is completely separate from the house and has own lounge and large bedroom with en-suite bathroom.

Hamilton ☎ 07

BARS

■ **Shine** (B D GLM MA S) Thu-Sat 20-?h
161 Victoria Street ☎ (07) 839 31 73
💻 www.facebook.com/group.php?gid=100506264577

CAFES

■ **Angels** (B glm m MA OS)
1009 Heaphy Terrace, Fairfield ☎ (07) 853 7960
Gay owned & operated cafe.

SAUNAS/BATHS

■ **Guyz** (B DR DU FC FH G I LAB m RR SA SB SH VS WH) 16-24h, closed Mon
856a Victoria Street ☎ (07) 839 52 22 💻 www.guyz.co.nz

CRUISING

All are AYOR!
-Garden Place
-Memorial Park (also known as Parana Park)
-Victoria Lake (near miniature railway)
-Towpath near Waikato River
-Rowing Club Public Toilets (late afternoon/evenings)
-Hamilton Lake toilets.

Havelock North ☎ 06

GUEST HOUSES

■ **Ngatahi Lodge** (! bf CC FC FH G I MA NU OS PK RWB RWS WH)
All year
172 St. Andrews Road *Between Hastings & Havelock North*
☎ (06) 877 15 25 💻 www.ngatahi.com
You need to relax? This is the place! Beautiful gay retreat, clothing optional. Enjoy the new lounge and the views across the pond to Te Mata Peak. Probably the best gay-only accommodation in New Zealand.

Napier ☎ 06

BARS

■ **Take Five** (B cc glm M MA) 16-?h
189 Marine Parade ☎ (06) 835 40 50
Wine and gourmet bar in an arty atmosphere with jazz music.

GUEST HOUSES

■ **Ormlie Lodge** (AC B BF CC glm M MSG OS PA RWB RWS RWT SA VA WH WO) All year
17 Omarunui Road, Taradale *Situated mid-way between Napier and Hastings* ☎ (06) 844 57 74 💻 www.ormlielodge.co.nz
Six spacious luxury suites, all with ensuites and access to private balcony.

PRIVATE ACCOMMODATION

■ **Napier Hill Homestay** (bf GLM M MA MSG OS RWS RWT WH)
All year
11 Seapoint Road, Bluff Hill *Napier Hill* ☎ (06) 835 71 18
💻 www.clivesquare.com/welcome.htm

■ **Ridgetop B&B** (bf CC GLM I PK RWT) All year
Napier Hill ☎ (06) 835 74 02 💻 www.gaystay.co.nz/ridgetop.htm
Modern, two-storey house with a large garden and extensive sea views. Laundry and pick-up service available.

CRUISING

-Marine parade (near coloured fountain)
-Anderson Park (Auckland Road-Green Meadows)
-Spriggs Park (Hardinge Road).

New Plymouth

SWIMMING

-Back Beach (behind Paratutu, New Plymouth during summer)

Palmerston North ☎ 06

BARS

■ **Club Q** (B D GLM MC) Fri & Sat 22-3h
Jersey Lane *Located at the far end of the Square Edge courtyard, off Fitzherbert Avenue* ☎ (06) 358 53 78 💻 www.malgraclubq.org.nz

Rotorua ☎ 07

BARS

■ **Shampers** (B GLM MA) Wed-Sat 17h-open end
1207 Eruera Street ☎ (07) 07 349 4891

GUEST HOUSES

■ **Central B&B** (BF G MC OS PI PK WH) All year
4a Carnot Street *Ten mins walk to town* ☎ (07) 346 08 95
💻 www.gaystay.co.nz/centralb&b.htm
A super location and extremely friendly hosts. Close to the local sights. A secluded, peaceful home with a geothermally heated hottub. Great gardens and attractive accommodation. Clothing optional pool area. Call for address.

CRUISING

-The Domain (Lakeside Park)

-Kerosene creek (natural hot water stream and swimming pool)
-Kuirau Park, lake front.

Ruakaka

SWIMMING

-Uretiti Beach: there is a gay area to the left (NU) with a cruising area in the dunes.

Tauranga

CRUISING

-Memorial Park
-Tauranga Domain (Hamilton/Cameron Road).

Waipu ☎ 09

GUEST HOUSES

The Trading Post (BF G I m MA MSG NU OS PA PK RWB VA WO)
4 Connell Road, rd2 *80 km from Auckland, off Nova Scotia Road*
☎ 432 0121 www.thetradingpost.net.nz
Farmhouse, nude beach nearby.

Wairarapa ☎ 06

RESTAURANTS

Tin Hut. The (B H M MA NG S) Tue-Sun 11-?, 17.30-?h, closed Mon
State Highway 2, Tauherenikau ☎ (06) 308 96 97 www.tinhut.co.nz
The Tin Hut retains the comfortable, friendly atmosphere of the traditional Kiwi country pub.

Wanganui

CRUISING

-P-area of the Olympic Swimming Pool (by the yacht harbour).
-Uretiti Beach (NU) (go onto the beach from the car P and turn right, keep walking until you are out of the mixed area).

Wellington ☎ 04

The capital of New Zealand is located at the southern tip of the North Island and although known as the „Windy City", because of the fresh breezes, it enjoys a mild climate. It is a culturally rich city with many museums, art galleries, and restaurants. There is a strong live music scene, lots of cafes and good restaurants. Being a university town, has a lively gay scene, which now includes a Gay Pride Week in early September. Wellington is worth visiting!

Die Hauptstadt Neuseelands liegt an der Südspitze der Nordinsel und ist zwar wegen der steifen Brise als „Windy City" bekannt, hat aber ein eher mildes Klima. Die Stadt verfügt über ein reichhaltiges Kulturangebot mit vielen Museen, Galerien und Restaurants. Es gibt hier auch eine lebendige Live-Music-Szene, unzählige Cafés und Feinschmeckerrestaurants. Da Wellington Universitätsstadt ist, befindet sich hier auch eine äußerst belebte Schwulenszene, die mittlerweile jährlich Anfang September eine Gay-Pride-Week zelebriert. Wellington ist immer einen Besuch wert!

La capitale de la Nouvelle-Zélande se situe à la pointe sud de l'Ile du Nord et est connue sous le nom de „windy city" en raison de la brise qui y souffle sans discontinuer. Son climat est malgré tout assez doux. La ville dispose d'une grand choix culturel avec de nombreux musées et galeries, ainsi que des lieux de spectacle où l'on joue de la musique live mais également d'innombrables cafés et restaurants pour gourmets. Wellington, en tant que ville estudiantine, a un milieu gay extrêmement vivant qui célèbre chaque année début septembre une Gay Pride Week. C'est donc une ville vaut largement le détour!

La capital de Nueva Zelanda está situada en la punta sur de la Isla del Norte y es conocida como la „Ciudad del Viento" debido a sus fuertes brisas pero tiene, sin embargo, un clima suave. La ciudad dispone de una rica oferta cultural con muchos museos, galerías y restaurantes. También hay aquí una cierta corriente de música en directo, incontables cafés y restaurantes de lujo. Como Wellington es una ciudad universitaria, también existe un ambiente gay bastante dinámico, que celebra cada año a principios de septiembre la Semana del Orgullo Gay. ¡Wellington siempre merece la pena visitarla!

La capitale della Nuova Zelandia si trova all'estremo sud dell'isola del nord e, considerato il forte vento, è anche conosciuta come „windy city"; tuttavia a Wellington predomina un clima piuttosto mite. La città offre molti eventi culturali, molti musei, gallerie e ristoranti. La musica dal vivo qui ha una particolare importanza. Inoltre ci sono molti cafè e ristoranti per i palati più sensibili. Poiché Wellington è anche una città universitaria, la scena gay qui è molto vivace. Annualmente all'inizio di settembre si svolge il gay pride. Insomma vale sempre la pena fare un salto a Wellington.

GAY INFO

Gay Wellington Helpline (GLM MA) 19.30-21.30h
PO Box 11 372, Manners Street ☎ (04) 473 78 78
www.gaywellington.org
Information about events, venues, gay groups & accommodation; telephone helpline.

BARS

Club Ivy (B D GLM MA OS)
13 Dixon Street www.clubivy.co.nz
Club Ivy is Wellington's only Gay, Lesbian, Bisexual, Intersex & Transexual Bar & Nightclub.

Fringe Bar (B glm MA) Mon-Thu 6-?, Fri & Sat 8.30-?h
119 Cuba Street *Cnr. Vivian Street* ☎ (04) 251-0589

S & M's Cocktail Bar and Lounge (B CC D GLM MA) Tue-Thu, Sun 17-?, Fri & Sat -3h
176 Cuba Street ☎ (04) 802 53 35 www.scottyandmals.co.nz
An intimate, two-level gay cocktail lounge. Themed evenings include pool table events, handle club and Karaoke. Regular shows, camp bongo every Wednesday DJ every WE.

SAUNAS/BATHS

Checkmate (B CC DR DU FC G GH I m MA NU P RR SA SB SH SL VS WH) Sun-Thu 12-2, Fri & Sat -4h
15-19 Tory Street, City ☎ (04) 385 65 56
www.checkmatesauna.co.nz
TV lounge, pool table, cruise area and internet access.

Emperors Bar Sauna (AC B CC DR DU FC G LAB M MA MSG S SA SB VS WH) 11-2, Fri & Sat -6, Sun & Mon -24h
5 Wigan Street, Te Aro *off Taranaki ST* ☎ (04) 3854212
www.emperorsbathhouse.co.nz
New gay bathhouse that holds events such as underwear parties or occasional BDSM parties.

BOOK SHOPS

Unity Books (glm MA) Mon-Thu 9-18, Fri -17, Sat 10-17, Sun 11-16h
57 Willis Street ☎ (04) 499 42 45 www.unitybooks.co.nz

PRIVATE ACCOMMODATION

Koromiko Homestay (CC G I MA OS) 24hrs
11 Koromiko Road, Highbury *Near central Wellington* ☎ (04) 938 65 39
www.koromikohomestay.co.nz
Accommodation for gay men and their friends, two doubles and one single room.

HEALTH GROUPS

New Zealand Aids Foundation Wellington (Awhina Centre) Mon-Fri 9-17h
Level 1, 187 Willis Street ☎ (04) 381 66 40 www.nzaf.org.nz
Free confidential, anonymous HIV testing, information, support and counselling.

SWIMMING

-Breaker Bay (at Wellington Harbor entrance; catch bus 3 to last stop and walk either up through Pass of Branda or take coast trail around Point Dorset)
-Paekakariki Beach (20 mins out of Wellington North, State Highway 1, entrance to QEII park opposite railway crossing. Drive down to beach P 6).

CRUISING

-Lower Hutt (near river, Council offices and park)
-Thorndon Road
-Cenral Park, Brooklyn Rd, just up from Willis Street (after dark)
-PParamata, SH1 just past the Mobile Service Station. Toilets are sometimes busy.

Whangarei

SWIMMING

-Uretiti Beach (MA NU) (Travel 30 km south from Whangerei. Uretiti is well sign posted on the East Coast. Gay section is at south end of beach).

South Island

Christchurch ☎ 03

GAY INFO

Gay Information Line 19-21h free information phone
PO Box 25 165 ☎ (03) 379 94 93
Information on local events, places and groups.

BARS

Cruz (B D GLM MA ST WE) Wed-Sat 19-?h
90 Lichfield Street ☎ (03) 379-2910 www.cruz.co.nz

SAUNAS/BATHS

Menfriends (AC AK B CC DR DU F FC G GH I LAB M MA NR OS P PK RR SA SB SH SL VR VS WH) May-Sep: Mon-Wed 11-1, Thu -2, Fri 11-Mon 1; Oct-Apr: Mon-Wed 11-2, Thu -3, Fri 11-Mon 2h
To be advised ☎ (03) 377 1701
www.menfriends.co.nz
A sauna for men with cruise option and adult shop on two floors. This is a well run professional venue with friendly and helpful staff. Very popular with locals. The venue was destroyed in February's earthquake and will re-open early 2012. Phone venue for update and location details or visit website.

BOOK SHOPS

altsexcafe.com @ Menfriends (F G MA)
Sun-Wed 10-1, Thu -2, Fri & Sat 24hrs
Post earthquake store re-opens Feb 2012 *Location to be announced*
☎ (0 3) 377 1701 www.altsexcafe.com
Large range of adult products with a focus on BDSM toys and supplies. A one stop shop in Christchurch for the active guy as well as an online shop

GUEST HOUSES

Designer Cottage B&B (BF CC GLM MA MSG OS) All year
53 Hastings St,reet, West. Sydenham *20 mins walk from CBD at the heart off Sydenham. Off Colombo street at Sydenham Park & Mc Donald*
☎ (03) 377 80 88 www.designercottage.co.nz
Experience one of the few heritage cottages left after the 2011 Christchurch Earth quake. Twenty mins walk to Cathedral Square. Close to cruise areas and venues.

Midhurst Farm (BF G I MA) All year
268 Bethels Road, RD4, Springston ☎ (03) 329 5287
www.midhurstfarm.yolasite.com
A quiet gay farm stay in a rural farmhouse. One guest room in the house suitable for one or two people. Comfortable, relaxed atmosphere. Free broadband internet, dinner by arangement.

HEALTH GROUPS

NZAF South Te Toka 9-17h
269 Hereford Street ☎ (03) 379 19 53 www.nzaf.org.nz
New Zealand AIDS Foundation: support, information for the GLBT Community, HIV-testing, counselling for those infected and affected by HIV/AIDS.

CRUISING

All are AYOR:
-Malvern Park (Innes Road)
-North Hagley Park (Park Terrace, between Peterborough & Salisbury Streets), near a small shelter at night.
-Brighton Pier (New Brighton Beach)
-Denton Park (Sports Pavillion)
-Hagley Park (Armagh Street Entrance of changing shed)
-Jellie Park (Greers Road)
-Manchester Street Car Park (Manchester Street)
-North Beach Surf Pavillion (in changing shed)
-St. Albans Park (Madras street around changing shed)
-Wordsworth Street (next Colombo Street Corner)
-Waimairi Beach (1km north of the Surf Club in dunes)
-Spencer Park (along the sand dunes).

Dunedin ☎ 03

SAUNAS/BATHS

Bodyworks 127 (B cc DR DU FC G I LAB m MA P RR SA SB SL SOL VS WH) Mon & Tue, Thu 17-24, Wed & Sun 14-24, Fri & Sat 14-2h
127 Lower Stuart St ☎ (03) 477 82 28 bodyworksnz.com

GUEST HOUSES

Belmont House (BF CC DU GLM H I MA OS PK RES RWS RWT VA WI) Check in from 15h
227 York Place, City Rise *700m from centre of city* ☎ (03) 477 37 13
www.belmonthouse.co.nz
Gay owned and operated. Close to the centre of town.

CRUISING

-Smailles Beach
-St.Clair Beach (at sand dunes and by Barnes Memorial Lookout)
All AYOR:
-Dowling Street (opp. Queens Gardens)
-Albany Street (near George Street)
-Jubilee Park (Queens Av.).

Invercargill

CRUISING

All AYOR
-Town Hall (back of Tay Street)
-Queens Park Gardens (Kelvin Street side)

Nelson ☎ 03

GENERAL GROUPS

Spectrum (Nelson) Inc. Thu 19.30-22h
P. O. Box 4022 *In Franklyn Street* ☎ (03) 545 22 84
www.spectrum.org.nz
Social and support group for gay and bisexual men.

Oamaru ☎ 03

GUEST HOUSES

Homestay Oamaru (bf glm I m OS)
14 Warren Street ☎ 434 14 54 www.bellview.co.nz
Three guestrooms.

Queenstown ☏ 03

SPORT GROUPS

■ **Gay Ski Week**
🖳 www.gayskiweeknz.com
See website for more information.

CRUISING

-Waterfront Jetty (city centre)

Takaka ☏ 03

GUEST HOUSES

■ **Autumn Farm** (BF G I M MA MSG NU OS PI PK RWB S) All year
37 Central Takaka Road *100 km west of Nelson* ☏ (03) 525 90 13
🖳 www.autumnfarm.com
Four comfortable double bedrooms, and two double cabins (shared/own bath). Backpackers welcome, clothing optional. Camper and motor homes welcome.

Nicaragua

Location: Central America
Initials: NIC
Time: GMT -6
International Country Code: ☏ 505
International Access Code: ☏ 00
Language: Spanish; English
Area: 120,245 km² / 49,998 sq mi.
Currency: 1 Córdoba (C$) = 100 Centavos
Population: 5,149,000
Capital: Managua
Religions: 59% Roman Catholic, 24% Protestant
Climate: The best time to visit the Pacific or central regions is early in the dry season (Dec & Jan).

On November 14, 2007, the Nicaraguan national assembly passed a new penal code. On the 9th July 2008 the new Nicaraguan Penal Code came into force. Article 240 has finally been banned. This article defined sexual activities between consenting, homosexual adults as „sodomy" and was an offence, subject to punishment. This amendment to the penal code was achieved by local human rights groups as well as amnesty international and the Hirschfeld-Eddy-Stiftung.

Am 14. November 2007 hat die nikaraguanische Nationalversammlung ein neues Strafgesetzbuch verabschiedet. Am 9. Juli 2008 ist das neue Strafrecht Nicaraguas in Kraft getreten. Artikel 240, der freiwillige sexuelle Handlungen zwischen erwachsenen Homosexuellen als „Sodomie" und strafbaren Gesetzesverstoß definierte, ist dabei endlich gestrichen worden. Diese Änderung im Strafrecht wurde von örtlichen Menschenrechtsgruppen in Zusammenarbeit mit amnesty international und der Hirschfeld-Eddy-Stiftung ermöglicht.

L'assemblée nationale du Nicaragua a adopté le 14 novembre 2007 un nouveau code pénal. Le nouveau droit pénal du Nicaragua est entré en vigueur le 9 juillet 2008. L'article 240, qui considérait les relations sexuelles consentantes entre homosexuels majeurs comme „sodomie" et comme une infraction pénale, a enfin été supprimé. Ce changement du droit pénal a été rendu possible grâce à l'intervention de groupes des droits de l'homme locaux en coopération avec Amnesty International et la fondation Hirschfeld-Eddy.

El 14 de noviembre de 2007, la Asamblea Nacional de Nicaragua aprobó un nuevo código penal. El 9 de julio de 2008 entró en vigor el nuevo derecho penal de Nicaragua. El artículo 240, que definía las relaciones sexuales voluntarias entre homosexuales adultos como „sodomía" y una infracción penal, fue finalmente derogado. Esta modificación en el derecho penal fue posible gracias al trabajo de los grupos de derechos humanos locales, en cooperación con Amnistía Internacional y la fundación Hirschfeld-Eddy.

Il 14 novembre del 2007 l'Assemblea Nazionale ha approvato un nuovo codice penale. Il 9 luglio del 2008 è entrato in vigore il nuovo codice penale del Nicaragua. L'articolo 240, che definiva i rapporti sessuali tra omosessuali adulti e consenzienti come un atto di ‚sodomia' e come reati punibili dalla legge, è stato finalmente eliminato. Questo cambiamento nel diritto penale è stato possibile grazie ad associazioni locali che si battono per i diritti umani e grazie alla collaborazione con Amnesty International e la fondazione Hirschfeld-Eddy.

León

BARS

■ **Bar Camaléon** (! AC B D G m S YC) Thu-Sun
Iglesia La Recolección 85 *In the center close to Teatro Municipal*

Granada

BARS

■ **Omix** (B G MA SNU) Tue–Fri 17-24, Sat-Sun -2h
Iglesia la Merced *1 1/2 cuadras al norte,Diagonal from El Club*
☏ 8744 28 65 🖳 www.gaynicaragua.org
Male strippers on Sat.

HOTELS

■ **Joluva Nicaragua** (AC BF cc GLM I MA MSG PA PI RWS RWT VA) All year
C/. Cuiscoma *Close to bus station* ☏ 2552 05 55
🖳 www.facebook.com/guesthousejoluva
Joluva has three rooms and one apartment, all with a private bathrooms, catering to the gay and lesbian traveller. Helpful and friendly staff.

■ **Kekoldi de Granada** (AC b BF CC glm H I MA RWB RWS RWT VA) All year
C/. El Consulado, N° 315 *350 m west from Central Park Colonial, historic city* ☏ 2552 41 06 🖳 www.kekoldi-nicaragua.com
Located in the heart of the oldest city in the Americas, with a private garden, beautiful architecture with colonial and indigenous elements, light and

colourful. Twelve rooms with AC, TV, wireless internet access. Other Kekoldi Hotels in Costa Rica see: www.kekoldi.com.

■ **La Islita Boutique Hotel** (AC B BF CC GLM H MA)
De la Alcaldía 2 C. al Lago 2 C. al Sur ☎ 2552 74 73 💻 www.laislita.com

GUEST HOUSES

■ **Casa Capricho** (AC BF CC H MSG PI) All year
C/. El Arsenal, 401 *Behind Convent San Francisco on Arsenal*
☎ 2552 84 22 💻 www.casacapricho.com

Managua

BARS

■ **Club Tabu** (! AC B D G MA p r S) Thu-Sun 23-?h
Costado este Mansión Teodolinda *Across from Parking INTUR*
☎ 2244 17 48 ☎ 8420 21 41 💻 www.barclubtabu.com
Main gay bar in Managua. A dancefloor and two bars. Also a karaoke bar upstairs. Take a taxi home. Do not walk around in the city at night.

DANCECLUBS

■ **Disco Bar "Q"** (! AC B D G m S YC) Thu-Sun
Calle 27 de Mayo *About 6 blocks from Club Tabu*
There is a dancefloor and 2 bars. The music is a mix of latin-techno and latin pop.

■ **Lollypop** (! AC B D G m S YC) Daily, Sun Happy hour 16-21h
Hotel Crown Plaza 2 C. Sur 2 C. Oeste 1/2 C. Norte ☎ 8966 45 97
☎ 8688 16 01 💻 www.lollypopnic.com
Crowded at the weekend.

GUEST HOUSES

■ **Thats the Magic of It** (AC bf CC H m MA MSG)
De la Optica Nicaraguense, 2 cuadras arriba *Downtown*
☎ (305) 891 23 10 💻 thatsthemagicofitbb.vpweb.com

■ **Viva Nicaragua Hotel** (AC BF CC H MSG PI) All year
Carretera Masaya (Km 14) *Turn right to km 17 1/2 Carretera Ticuantepe*
☎ 2276 7059 ☎ 8743 3700 💻 www.vivanicaraguaguesthouse.com

CRUISING

ATTENTION: beware of thieves and pickpockets
-Central Park (AYOR)
-Inside the ruins of the cathedral (AYOR)
-Park near A.C. Sandino Stadium (sidewalks around Laguna di Tiscapa)
-Plaza de la Revolución
-Near mausoleum of Carlos Fonseca (AYOR)
-Gardens near Teatro Rubén Darío
-Camino de Oriente (Fri-Sun between Lobo's Jack and Infinito)
-Parque de las Piedrecitas (AYOR at night)
2nd floor of Shopping Center "Metrocentro" during opening hours

Norway

Name: Norge · Norwegen · Norvège · Noruega · Norvegia
Location: Northern Europe
Initials: N
Time: GMT +1
International Country Code: ☎ 47 (no area codes)
International Access Code: ☎ 00
Language: Norwegian
Area: 323,759 km² / 125,049 sq mi.
Currency: 1 Norwegian Kroner (nkr) = 100 Øre
Population: 4,623,000
Capital: Oslo
Religions: 85,7% Protestant (Lutherian state Church)
Climate: Norway is at its best in summer (May-Sep). Between late May and late July is the so-called „midnight sun" evident especially north of the Artic Circle.
Important gay cities: Oslo

The age of consent in Norway is 16 years of age. On the 11th June 2008 the Norwegian Parliament voted overwhelmingly to approve a bill, despite opposition from the Christian Democrats and Progress Party, which recognizes both partners in a marriage as equal parents and gives lesbian couples the same access to „medically assisted reproduction" as opposite-sex couples. Passage of the law makes Norway the sixth country in the world to approve same-sex marriages.
The Norwegian scene is concentrated in the cities of Oslo, Bergen and Trondheim, and here you will find exclusively gay bars. In smaller towns it is common for the discos to hold a gay/lesbian night once a week. The atmosphere here is, however, so gay-friendly that gays and lesbians are socialising more and more with straight people, to the point that mixed meeting places are gradually becoming the norm.
Norway has one very interesting and professional gay publication: the news & entertainment magazine »Blikk«.

In Norwegen liegt das Schutzalter bei 16 Jahren. Am 11. Juni 2008 hat das norwegische Parlament, trotz des von den Christdemokraten und der Fortschrittspartei geleisteten Widerstandes, mit überwältigender Mehrheit einen Gesetzesentwurf angenommen, der beiden Ehepartnern die Elternschaft garantiert und lesbischen Paaren den gleichen Zugang zur „medizinisch unterstützten Fortpflanzung" verschafft, wie heterosexuellen Ehepartnern. Die Verabschiedung dieses Gesetzes macht Norwegen zum sechsten Land der Welt mit einem geschlechtsneutralen Ehegesetz.
Die Szene des Königreiches konzentriert sich auf die Städte Oslo, Bergen und Trondheim. Hier gibt es reine Schwulenkneipen. Ansonsten, in den kleineren Städten, ist es nicht unüblich, dass allgemeine Discos einen wöchentlichen »Schwulen- und Lesbentag« pflegen. Da jedoch das gesellschaftliche Klima so schwulenfreundlich ist, gibt es kaum Berührungsängste zwischen Schwulen, Lesben und Heteros und allmählich werden gemischte Treffpunkte die Regel. Norwegen hat eine außerordentlich interessante und professionelle Zeitschrift für Schwule: das populäre Nachrichten- und Freizeitmagazin „Blikk".

En Norvège, la majorité sexuelle est fixée à 16 ans. Le 11 juin 2008, malgré l'opposition des chrétiens démocrates et du parti du progrès, le parlement norvégien a accepté avec une large majorité,

INGEN
ER SOM
ALLE
ANDRE
NOBODY IS LIKE EVERYBODY ELSE!
Norway's gay-lesbian monthly magazine. Daily news: blikk.no
BLIKK

une proposition de loi qui garantit la paternité aux deux conjoints et qui permet le même accès à la „ reproduction médicalement assistée „ aux couples de lesbiennes qu'aux couples mariés hétérosexuels. L'adoption de cette loi fait de la Norvège le 6ème pays au monde d'une loi matrimoniale indépendante du sexe.
Oslo, Bergen et Trondheim sont les principales villes gaies du pays. On y trouve des bars exclusivement gais. Sinon, dans les petites villes, des boîtes de nuit organisent régulièrment une fois par semaine une „soirée gaie et lesbienne". La Norvège est un pays homophile où on peut vivre sa différence au grand jour. Résultat : les gais et les lesbiennes sont de plus en plus intégrés au reste de la population. Les lieux de rencontre mixtes sont devenus la règle. En Norvège, il y a une excellente revue gaie : le magazine d'information et de divertissement „Blikk".

Homosexuales y heterosexuales son iguales ante la ley. El 11 de Junio 2008 el Parlamento noruego aprobó con una abrumadora mayoría, y a pesar de la oposición de Demócrata Cristianos y del Partido Progresista, un proyecto de ley que garantiza la paternidad de ambos cónyuges y el mismo acceso a la „reproducción asistida" que se da a parejas heterosexuales para parejas de lesbianas. La aprobación de esta ley ha convertido a Noruega en el sexto país del mundo con una ley de matrimonios de género neutral.
El «ambiente» gay del reinado noruego se concentra en las ciudades de Oslo, Bergen y Trondheim -en estas ciudades hay bares exclusivamente gay. Por lo demás, es bastante habitual que discotecas de ciudades pequeñas organicen un «Día de los gays y lesbianas» una vez por semana. Por otro lado el clima social noruego es de lo más afable hacia los homosexuales. Los gays y las lesbianas suelen mezclarse cada vez más con los heterosexuales y lentamente sitios de reunión mixtos son los más habituales.
Noruega tiene una revista para gays extraordinariamente bien hecha e interesante: La revista de actualidades y entretenimiento „Blikk".

L'età legale per avere rapporti omosessuali è di 16 anni. Nonostante la dura opposizione della Democrazia Cristiana e del Partito del Progresso, l'11 giugno del 2008 il parlamento della Norvegia ha recepito a grande maggioranza un progetto di legge che garantisce a entrambi i partner il diritto ad essere genitori e alle coppie lesbiche l'accesso alla fecondazione assistita. Con l'approvazione di questa legge la Norvegia è il sesto paese al mondo ad avere introdotto una legge matrimoniale parificatoria.
La vita gay norvegese si concentra nelle città di Oslo, Bergen e Trondheim, dove troverete dei locali esclusivamente gay. Altrimenti, nelle piccole città, è spesso abitudine, per le discoteche, di avere una notte alla settimana per gay e lesbiche. Da quando l'atmosfera generale in Norvegia è così favorevole ai gay e pochi di essi nascondono la loro omosessualità, i gay e le lesbiche si uniscono sempre di più e con sempre meno difficoltà agli eterosessuali e i luoghi d'incontro misti stanno diventando sempre più comuni. La Norvegia vanta una rivista gay molto interessante e valida: la rivista di notizie e intrattenimento „Blikk".

NATIONAL GAY INFO

Gaysir (GLM MA)
Arbeidergata 2 ✉ 0159 Oslo ☎ 40 00 15 25 💻 www.gaysir.no
One of Norway's largest GLBT websites and online communities, including a list of events for all the major cities of Norway.

LLH Landsforeningen for lesbisk og homofil frigjøring (GLM MA) By appointment
Valkyriegata 15 ✉ 0153 Oslo ☎ 23 10 39 39 💻 www.llh.no
The national gay/lesbian rights organization. Local groups located nationwide.

NATIONAL PUBLICATIONS

Blikk (GLM)
Youngs gate 6 ✉ 0181 Oslo ☎ 22 33 44 55 💻 www.blikk.no
Norway's largest gay/lesbian magazine. Published monthly. Daily updated news online.

NATIONAL GROUPS

■ **Kirkens SOS** (MA NG) 24h
Tøyenkirken, Herslebs gata 43 ✉ 0578 Oslo
☎ 22 57 89 00 💻 www.kirkens-sos.no
Kirkens SOS can be found in major cities throughout the country. See www.kirkens-sos.no for addresses.

HEALTH GROUPS

■ **Helseutvalget for homofile (Norwegian Gay Health Committee)**
Skippergata 23 ✉ 0154 Oslo ☎ 23 35 72 00 💻 www.helseutvalget.no

Ålesund – Møre og Romsdal

CRUISING

-Borgernes vei (tour path behind the Aksla)
-Byparken (Town park)
-Kaiområdene (Harbor areas).

Arendal – Tromöysundet

RESTAURANTS

■ **Chaos og Tapas** (B glm M MA)
Langbryggen 7 ☎ 40 000 703 💻 www.chaosogtapas.com
Gayfriendly restaurant

Bergen – Hordaland

BARS

■ **Fincken** (B GLM m MA WE)
Wed-Thu 19-1.30; Fri, Sun -2.30; Sat 20-2.30h
Nygårdsgate 2 A ☎ 55 32 13 16 💻 www.fincken.no
Café during the day and pub in the evening.

CAFES

■ **Opera** (B glm M) 12-1h
Engen 24 *Next to the theatre* ☎ 55 23 03 15

SAUNAS/BATHS

■ **Tropic** (b DU g MA MSG RR SA SOL WH) 11-21, Fri & Sat 12-18h
Nye Sandviksvei 48 A ☎ 55 32 65 33

GENERAL GROUPS

■ **Studentgruppen Uglez** (GLM YC) 2nd Fri/month 19-24h
Olav Kyrresgate 49-53, Det Akademiske Kvarter *2nd floor in the students' house* 💻 www.uglez.uib.no

CRUISING

-Rasmus Meyers Allé
-Skoltegrunnskaien (near ships).

Drammen – Buskerud

CRUISING

-Spiraltoppen (WC near the old canons)
-🅿 by Damtjern.

Kristiansund – Møre og Romsdal

CRUISING

-Storsand (down the steep hills around Kringsjå, then down to the rocks, summertime).

Oslo

With only half a million inhabitants, Oslo is one of the smallest capitals in Europe, and is surrounded by amazing nature at its best. The city has an excellent infrastructure and using the public transport system you can cross the whole town and get to the wilderness or one of the islands in the inner Oslo Fjord in less than twenty minutes. Holmenkollen, Oslo's largest ski centre, with its ski jump, is the best-known symbol of the city and is illuminated at night. During the short Nordic summer, life is enjoyed to the full and the whole of Oslo is out and about. The gay scene is certainly small here, but really interesting and friendly, and compared to other cities, very laid-back.

Mit nur etwa 500 000 Einwohnern ist Oslo eine der kleinsten Hauptstädte Europas und ringsum von phantastischer Natur umgeben. Die Stadt hat eine sehr gute Infrastruktur, mit den öffentlichen Verkehrsmitteln kommt man in weniger als 20 Minuten durch die ganze Stadt, in die Wildnis oder auf eine der Inseln des inneren Oslofjords. Oslos großes Skizentrum Holmenkollen mit der Skisprungschanze ist wohl das bekannteste Wahrzeichen Oslos und nachts sogar beleuchtet. Im kurzen, nordischen Sommer wird das Leben in vollen Zügen genossen, und ganz Oslo ist auf den Beinen. Die Schwulenszene ist zwar klein, aber sehr nett und familiär und im Vergleich zu anderen Großstädten sehr entspannt.

Avec ses quelques 500 000 habitants, Oslo est une des plus petites capitales européennes. Entourée d'une nature fantastique, la ville dispose d'une excellente infrastructure et les transports en commun vous mèneront en 20 minutes maximum où vous voudrez, que ce soit en pleine nature ou sur une des îles du fjord d'Oslo. Holmenkollen, le plus grand centre de ski de la ville avec son tremplin de saut à ski éclairé la nuit est sans doute un des symboles les plus connus d'Oslo. L'été nordique est certes court mais il se savoure sans modération et toute la population le fête dignement jusque tard dans la nuit. Le milieu gay est petit mais l'ambiance est agréable et, comparé à d'autres grandes villes, très détendue.

Oslo, con sus 500.000 habitantes, es una de las capitales de Europa más pequeñas y está rodeada de una naturaleza maravillosa. La ciudad dispone de una muy buena infraestructura de transporte público; en menos de 20 minutos uno puede cruzar toda la ciudad, ir a paisajes agrestes o bien visitar una de las islas del fiordo interior de Oslo. El mayor centro de ski de Oslo, Holmenkollen, con sus instalaciones para saltos, es una de las atracciones de Oslo y está incluso iluminado por la noche. Actualmente, el verano nórdico se disfruta ya a lo grande y todo Oslo está en la calle. El ambiente homosexual es en efecto pequeño pero muy agradable, familiar y, comparado con el de otras grandes ciudades, mucho más relajado.

Con i suoi 500.000 abitanti Oslo è una delle più piccole capitali europee. La città è circondata da una natura spettacolare. Oslo dispone di un'ottima infrastruttura: con i mezzi di trasporto pubblici, in meno di 20 minuti, si attraversa tutta la città, o si può andare in aperta campagna o in una delle isole dell'Oslofjorden. Il centro sciistico di Oslo „Holmenkollen" con il suo trampolino di lancio è il simbolo più conosciuto di Oslo e rimane illuminato pure durante la notte. La breve estate nordica viene vissuta molto intensamente e tutta Oslo è fuori per strada. La scena gay è piccola ma molto carina e familiare e rispetto ad altre grandi città anche molto rilassante.

BARS

■ **Bob's Pub** (B glm MC) Daily 12-2.30h
Grønland 3 ☎ 22 17 25 21
Traditional and gayfriendly pub with friendly service.

■ **Elsker** (AC B CC D GLM M ST YC) 15-1, Thu-Sat -3h
Kristian IVs gate 9 *Opp. Theatre, T-Stortinget* ☎ 22 41 66 08
Newly remodeled, cozy interior promoting urban charm. Extensive menu, reasonable prices. Disco on Fri & Sat. Dragshows on Wed & Sun.

■ **London Pub & Club** (! B d GLM MC) Daily 15-3h
C. J. Hambros Plass 5 *Entrance in Rosenkrantzgate* ☎ 22 70 87 00
💻 www.londonpub.no
Oslo's oldest existing gay bar. A little bit worn but charming, attracting mature men. Popular all day, all year. Mainly gay. Billiard, Jukebox, two bars.

■ **SO** (B D gLm MA) Wed,Thu,Fri, Sat 18-3h
Arbeidergata 2 💻 www.so-oslo.no
Lesbian Bar with dancefloor

■ **The Villa** (B d glm MA) Fri & Sat 23-3.30h
Møllergata 23 💻 www.thevilla.no
Straight and gay underground music bar

MEN'S CLUBS

■ **SLM Oslo** (AC b d DR F G MA p) 2nd Sat/month 23-3h
Rådhusgata 28 *Tram 12/13/19-Kongensgate, entrance from Nedre Slottsgata* ☎ 41 444 666 💻 www.slmoslo.no
Entrance fee. ECMC members half price. Dress code enforced, frequent theme parties, contact post@slm-oslo.no

DANCECLUBS

■ **Fire Club** (B D GLM MA OS p s)
Youngstorget 2 💻 www.facebook.com/groups/2315307286/
Fire Club is a trendy rooftop bar and nightclub open during the warm months. Beginning in mid-April.

RESTAURANTS

■ **Ett Glass** (B CC DM glm M MC S VEG WL) Mon-Thu 11-1, Fri 11-3, Sat 12-3 & Sun 12-1h
Karl Johans gate 33 *Entrance via Rosenkrantz gate* ☎ 22 33 40 79
💻 www.ettglass.no
Great bar! Enjoy lunch until 18h, dinner, sandwiches, snacks, good wine and drink in this intimate and warm, gay-friendly establishment.

SEX SHOPS/BLUE MOVIES

■ **Duo shop** (cc glm MA) Mon-Fri 11-20, Sat+Sun 12-18h
Prinsensgate 6 ☎ 22 33 4444 💻 www.duoshop.no
Gay and lesbian sexshop. DVD, prideproducts, leather, toys, lubes, books and more.

■ **GI Shop** (glm) Mon-Thu 10-22, Fri -19, Sat -15, Sun 14-20h
Rosteds gate 2 ☎ 22 20 37 36 💻 www.gishop.com

■ **Shop 66** (G) Mon-Fri 11-19, Sat 11-17h
Helgesensgate 66 ☎ 22 37 64 88 💻 www.shop66.no
Gay and SM sexshop

SAUNAS/BATHS

■ **Club Hercules** (AC B CC DR DU FC FH G LAB M MA SA SB SL SOL VS WH) Sun-Thu 15-2, Fri & Sat -8h
Storgaten 41 ☎ 22 11 11 13 💻 www.gsauna.com
Oslo's biggest gay sauna on four floors. TV rooms, maze and sling room. Very pleasant atmosphere with many bear Vikings. Spotlessly clean.

BOOK SHOPS

■ **ARK Egertorget** (CC glm MA) Mon-Fri 9-20, Sat 10-18h
Øvre Slottsgt 23/25 💻 www.ark.no
Gay and lesbian books are available on lower level.

■ **Tronsmo Bøker & Tegneserier** (CC glm MA) 10-17, Thu 9-18, Sat -16h, closed Sun
Kristian Augustsgate 19 ☎ 22 99 03 99 💻 www.tronsmo.no

HOTELS

■ **Park Inn by Radisson Oslo** (AC B BF CC glm I M RWS RWT)
All year
Øvre Slottsgate 2c *10 mins walk from Oslo Central Sation* ☎ 22 400 100
💻 www.parkinn.com/hotel-oslo

GENERAL GROUPS

■ **LLH Oslo og Akershus – Landsforeningen for lesbiske homofile bifile og transpersoner** (GLM MA) Mon-Fri 9-16h
Valkyreigata 15 *Entrance Slemdalsveien, T Majorstuen* ☎ 22 60 6860
💻 www.llh.no/oslo
The gay/lesbian rights organization. Umbrella organization for various interest groups; also offers many sport activities.

■ **Skeiv Ungdom** (GLM YC)
Valkyriegata 15 ☎ 23 10 39 36 💻 www.skeivungdom.no
LGBT youth organisation. Organise the Jafnadr – the Nordic queer youth festival every year.

SWIMMING

-Homolulu gay beach (! NU) (Close to Paradisbukta. Take Bus 30 from centre to the last stop (Bygdøy). Go along the small path on the right side of the parking lot) When coming from the bus, you pass a bay with a sandy beach, and on your left hand side. Just after a house, the path follows a fence down to a narrow pebble beach. If you walk closer to the edge you'll spot the sunbathers. Lots of cruising happening in the woods to the right in summer.
-Langøyene (NU) (Take the boat from Vippetangen to Langøyene, then go straight on until you pass a kiosk. Take the small path to the gay nude area)
-Svartskog (NU) (Close to Sognsvann, pass Ingierstrand continue to the nudist beach).

CRUISING

-Ekeberg (sporting hut toilets)
-Tryvannstårnet (the toilets at the parking lot)
-Tøyenbadet (public bath, in the sauna and the showers)
-Bislet Bad (public bath, in the sauna and the showers)
-Galgeberg (Jordalsgate, near Jordal Amfi. Take bus 37 from centre. Best around midnight)
-Sognsvann (Toilets/parking place and outdoors in the woods. Take the subway, 2nd car park from station, day and night)
-Frognerparken (behind the Monolitt statue, evening and night. Bird-boxes filled with lubricants and condoms!)
-Stensparken (on the top behind ‚Blæsten', evening and night)
-Vervenbukta (around the parking area).

Stavanger – Rogaland

BARS

■ **MaMi Open Mind** (AC b d GLM MA S)
Tue-Fri 18-1.30, Sat 15-1.30, Sun 19-1.30h
Bakkekata 16 *Located in the center of Stavanger, next to Øvre Holmegate*
💻 www.hotstavanger.no

■ **Sting** (B CC D glm m MA OS s ST) Wed-Sat 23-3.30h
Valberget 3 *Valberg Taarnet* ☎ 51 89 38 78 💻 www.cafe-sting.no
Café-bar, restaurant & nightclub. Sun jazz-café.

DANCECLUBS

■ **Hot Open Mind** (AC B D GLM MA S WE) Fri & Sat 23-3.30h
Skagen 25-27 *Tårngalleriet* ☎ 94195978 💻 www.hotstavanger.no
Gay & lesbian night club.

CRUISING

-Orrestranden (summer)
-Skansekaien (from Victoria Hotel to Hurtigbåtterminalen)
-Bjergstedskaien (from Englansterminalen to the parking place by the grove, after dark).

Tønsberg – Vestfold

CAFES

■ **Don't tell Mama** (GLM MA) Tue-Thu 19-22h
Halfdan Wilhelmsen allé 1b *Near town hall* ☎ 33 31 06 10

Tromsø – Troms

BARS

■ **Mirage. Le** (B CC GLM m YC) 12-2, Fri & Sat -3, Sun 14-2h
Storgate 42 ☎ 77 68 65 36
Popular with students.

CAFES

■ **Verdensteateret** (B glm m MA)
Storgata 9
Gayfriendly café-bar

Trondheim – Sør-Trøndelag

BARS

Brukbar / Supa (B D glm m MA)
Munkegata 26 www.brukbar.no
Gayfriendly café-bar with dance floor

DANCECLUBS

Metro (B CC d GLM M MA WE) Wed 21-2, Thu -1, Fri & Sat 22-3h (D)
Kjøpmannsgate 12 ☏ 73 52 05 52
The only gay-lesbian disco in Trondheim, disco at WE.

Panama

Location: Southern Central America
Initials: PA
Time: GMT -5
International Country Code: ☏ 507 (no area codes)
Language: Spanish; English
Area: 75,517 km² / 29,761 sq mi.
Currency: 1 Balboa (B/.) = 100 Centésimos (US$ is used)
Population: 3,232,000
Capital: Panamá City
Religions: 85% Roman Catholic
Climate: Tropical climate that is hot, humid and cloudy. Rainy season from May to January and dry season that from January to May.

Homosexuality is not illegal in Panama. No laws prohibiting consensual homosexual relations exists. No anti-discrimination legislation exists in Panama. Discrimination against gays still exists. An example is an executive decree dating back to 1949 in which gay sex in public is punishable by a fine or 1 year imprisonment. Gays and lesbians are banned from the armed forces and police. Article 39 of the constitution forbids the creation of „companies, associations or foundations" that are „contrary to moral or legal order". This has been used to refuse registration of gay organisations. Nevertheless in 1996 Panama's first lesbian and gay organisation Asociación Hombres y Mujeres Nuevos de Panama (AHMNP) was founded.
In the last couple of years a few bars and clubs catering for gay men have opened. This is a positive sign that things are slowly changing in Panama. The Asociacion Hombres y Mujeres Nuevos de Panama (AHMNP), visited the National Assembly of Deputees (Asamblea Nacional de Diputados), the equivalent of a Congress or Parliament, in September 2005, and presented their Office of Citizen Participation (Oficina de Participacion Ciudadana) a proposal of law which would ban any type of sexual orientation and/or gender identity based discrimination. In 2005 the first ever Parade for Sexual Diversity (Marcha por la Diversidad Sexual), their own version of a Gay Pride Parade, was held in Panama. In 2006, Panama was one of 54 states supporting a UN resolution against discrimination on the grounds of sexual identity.

Homosexualität ist in Panama nicht verboten. Es gibt keine Gesetze gegen einvernehmliche homosexuelle Beziehungen und Kontakte. Allerdings gibt es immer noch diskriminierende Gesetze, wie zum Beispiel das Verbot von öffentlichem Sex, auf den eine Strafe von 500 Dollar oder ein Jahr Haft steht – im Gegensatz zu Sex bei Heterosexuellen. Schwule und Lesben werden auch vom Militär und der Polizei schlechter behandelt. Artikel 39 der Satzung untersagt die Gründung von Firmen, Verbänden und Vereinen, die „unmoralisch" und „gesetzwidrig" sind. Er wurde in der Vergangenheit oft zur Nichtbewilligung von Schwulen- und Lesbenorganisationen herangezogen. Bisher fehlt auch eine Antidiskriminierungsgesetzgebung. Seit 1996 tritt aber die nichtstaatliche AHMNP in Panama-City für die Rechte Homosexueller in diesem Land ein.
In den letzten Jahren entwickelte sich in der Hauptstadt eine kleine, lebendige Szene, und einige Discos und Bars öffneten. In Anbetracht der erwähnten Diskriminierungen ist ein allmählicher Wandel hinsichtlich der Toleranz und Gelassenheit in der Gesellschaft festzustellen. Die Asociacion Hombres y Mujeres Nuevos de Panama (AHMNP) hat im September 2005 die Abgeordneten-Versammlung (Asamblea Nacional de Diputados), was einem Kongress oder Parlament entspricht, besucht und hat deren Kanzlei für Bürgerbeteiligung (Oficina de Participacion Ciudadana) einen Gesetzesvorschlag unterbreitet, der jede Art von Diskriminierung aufgrund von sexueller Orientierung und/oder geschlechtlicher Identität unter Strafe stellen soll.
2005 wurde die allererste Parade der sexuellen Vielfalt (Marcha por la Diversidad Sexual), einer eigenen Version des CSDs, in Panama abgehalten.
Im Dezember 2006 gehörte Panama zu den 54 Staaten, die eine UNO-Resolution unterstützten, die sich gegen Diskriminierung aufgrund sexueller Identität richtet.

L'homosexualité n'est pas un délit entre adultes consentants au Panama. Par contre, des lois homophobes sont toujours en vigueur qui interdisent par exemple d'avoir un rapport sexuel en public, tout contrevenant pouvant être puni d'une amende de 500 dollars ou d'une peine de prison d'un an. Le rapport hétérosexuel en public, lui, n'est pas concerné par cette loi. La police et l'armée malmènent également les gays et lesbiennes et l'article 39 interdit la création d'entreprises, d'associations et de groupes jugés „immoraux" et „illégaux", ce qui a servi par le passé à interdire des organisations gays et lesbiennes. Il n'existe également pas de loi anti-discriminatoire. A Panama, l'organisation AHMNP s'engage néanmoins pour les droits des homosexuels du pays. Ces dernières années, un petit milieu gay très vivant, composé de bars et de boîtes, s'est développé dans la capitale ce qui, vu la discrimination ambiante, est un tournant dans la société et annonce plus de tolérance et d'acceptation.
L'association „Hombres y Mujeres Nuevos de Panama" s'est rendue a l'" Assemblea Nacional de Diputados", correspondant à l'Assemblée Nationale ou au Congrès, et a déposé au bureau des affaires sociales (Oficina de Participacion Ciudadana) un projet de loi qui interdirait toute forme de discrimination fondée sur l'orientation et/ou l'identité sexuelle. En 2005, la toute première Gay Pride (Marcha por la Diversidad Sexual) s'est déroulée à Panama.
En décembre 2006 le Panama fait partie des 54 États soutenant la résolution de l'ONU qui condamne la discrimination pour cause d'identité sexuelle.

La homosexualidad no está prohibida en Panamá. No existe ninguna ley en contra de las relaciones o contactos homosexuales consentidos. No obstante, existen todavía algunas leyes discriminatorias como, por ejemplo, la llamada prohibición de sexo público, para la que está prevista una sanción de 500 dólares o el arresto por un año, al contrario de lo que ocurre con el sexo entre heterosexuales. En el ejército y en la policía se sigue maltratando a gays y lesbianas. El artículo 39 de la Constitución prohíbe expresamente la creación de empresas, asociaciones u organizaciones que sean inmorales o contrarias a la ley y en el pasado se utilizó dicho artículo para denegar la autorización a las organizaciones gay-lésbicas. Hasta hoy, todavía falta una legislación anti-discriminación. Desde 1996, la organización no gubernamental AHMNP de la Ciudad de Panamá actúa en defensa de los derechos de los homosexuales.

En los últimos años, se ha creado en la capital un cierto ambiente gay, pequeño pero dinámico, y han abierto algunas discotecas y bares. Además, teniendo en cuenta las discriminaciones mencionadas, se observa poco a poco un cierto giro en la sociedad hacia la tolerancia.

La Asociación de Hombres y Mujeres Nuevos de Panamá (AHMNP) visitó en septiembre del 2005 la Asamblea Nacional de Diputados, lo que correspondería al Parlamento o Congreso, y propuso a su Oficina de Participación Ciutadana un proyecto de ley para penalizar cualquier tipo de discriminación por razón de la orientación sexual y/o identidad sexual. En el 2005 se organizó la primera Marcha por la Diversidad Sexual en Panamá, una versión de la Marcha por el Orgullo Gay.

En diciembre de 2006 Panamá pertenecía al grupo de 54 estados que apoyó una resolución de la ONU que declaraba la no-discriminación por razón de la identidad sexual.

L'omosessualità a Panama non è vietata. Non ci sono leggi contro contatti o rapporti omosessuali. Tuttavia ci sono leggi piuttosto discriminatorie come per esempio il divieto di sesso in pubblico, che viene punito con una multa di 500 dollari o un anno di detenzione. Questo invece non sussiste per gli eterosessuali. Gay e lesbiche vengono trattati peggio anche dalla milizia e dalla polizia. L'articolo 39 dell'ordinamento vieta la fondazione di aziende, associazioni e organizzazioni „illegali" ed „immorali": questo articolo è stato usato, in passato, per vietare la fondazione di organizzazioni gay e lesbiche. Fino ad ora mancano delle leggi antidiscriminatorie. Dal 1996 l'organizzazione non governativa AHMNP, è impegnata nella lotta per i diritti degli omosessuali in questo Paese.

Negli ultimi anni nella capitale è andata sviluppandosi una piccola scena gay con bar e discoteche. Per quello che riguarda la tolleranza nei confronti dei gay, si avverte un costante miglioramento. A settembre del 2005 l' AHMNP (Associacion Hombres y Mujeres de Panama) ha partecipato all' assemblea parlamentare (Asamblea Nacional de Diputados), che è il corrispettivo di un Senato o di un Parlamento, ed ha presentato all'ufficio per la partecipazione cittadina (Oficina de Participacion Ciudadana) una proposta di legge che mira a punire ogni tipo di discriminazione che si basi sull'orientamento e/o sull'identità sessuale. Nel 2005, a Panama, ha avuto luogo, per la prima volta, il corteo della diversità sessuale (Marcha por la Diversidad Sexual) che è una versione nostrana del CSD.

A dicembre del 2006 Panama è stato uno dei 54 Stati che ha appoggiato la risoluzione dell'ONU che si impegnava a combattere la discriminazione basata sull'orientamento sessuale.

NATIONAL GROUPS

■ **Asociación Hombres y Mujeres Nuevos de Panamá**
Mon-Fri 10-17h
Via España Edificio Orion 4to. piso oficina 4-D
✉ Ciudad Panamá *Edificio del Almacen y Sastreria La Fortuna*
☎ 264-2670
Panama's national non-profit organization for gay men, lesbian women and all sexual minorities. Founded in 1996. Political lobby for legal equality & social justice, as well as social and cultural events. Regional chapters in the provinces of Colon and Chiriqui. AIDS advocacy, information and counselling. Meetings Tue 18.30h (Panama City only). Now with own clinic where gay men and sexual minorites in general can take an HIV test without any fear of being treated discriminatorily. Panama's first such clinic, geared specifically towards this particular population. Non-biased, friendly.

Bocas del Toro

HOTELS

■ **Solarte del Caribe Inn** (H I M MC OS RWS) All year
Isla Solarte, ☎ 6 488 4775
Seven rooms wonderful views of the tropical rainforest.

Chiriquí

GUEST HOUSES

■ **Boquete River Inn** (b GLM H I MA OS PI PK RWS WO) All year
Apdo. 0413-00092, Boquete ☎ 720 4385
🖳 www.boqueteriverinn.com
Fully-equipped cabins and B&B nestled in mountain-side greenery on a secluded plateau. Spectacular views. Heated pool, volleyball, gym, and trails.

■ **Purple House Hostel** (ac bf glm MA) 24hrs
C/. C Sur, Av. Sexta Oeste ☎ 774 4059
🖳 www.purplehousehostel.com
The only backpackers place. Many services to tourists, including free internet, central location, book exchange, family atmosphere, free tea & coffee, kitchen use possible, fully equipped living room, private or shared baths.

La Venta

GUEST HOUSES

■ **Tógo B&B** (BF G MA OS WI) All year
Calle La Venta, Playa Blanca, Farallon *Close to the Decameron Hotel*
☎ 6534-9106 (mobile) ☎ 993-3393 🖳 togopanama.com
90 mins drive from Panama City. Gay owned and operated. 5 guestrooms.

Panamá City

BARS

■ **Boite Saoco** (AYOR B G MA)
C/. 21 de Enero, Calidonia *Behind Burger King* ☎ 212 0098

■ **Caracoles** (AYOR B G MA)
Av. 1, Monte Oscuro, San Miguelito ☎ 261 6706

■ **Escape** (B GLM)
El Dorado *Next to Pizza Hot diagonally opposite to Blockbuster*

■ **Madrid. La** (AC AYOR B G MA) ?-23h
C/. 12 y Santa Ana Plaza *Old city, opp. Mansion Dante, behind the Pio Pio Restaurant*

■ **Tropical (La Chinitos)** (AC AYOR B G MA)
C/. 12, Av. B, Santa Ana Plaza *Old city, behind the Coca Cola Restaurant and next to the Colón Hotel*
Attended by a mostly gay clientele, however the owners don't care about the community itself.

DANCECLUBS

■ **Bar Discoteca** (B D glm MA)
Av. J / C/. 9

■ **BLG** (AC B CC D G MA S SNU ST) Wed-Sat 22-5h
Vía Transismica *Next to Petro Autos, in front of McDonalds*
🖳 www.farraurbana.com
Wednesday is the most popular night. No tables or chairs. It is also a little hard to find. It is about 10m off Uruguay street on a side street (no street sign) with no sign on the building. Follow the young men to find the place. Very busy but a very young crowd (18-25).

■ **Icon** (B D GLM)
Antiguo Depósito de Tumba Muerto *Go the street Calle Juan Pablo II down*

SEX SHOPS/BLUE MOVIES

Exxxclusive Video Sex Shop (G VS)
Hotel Venezia, Av. Perú, Local 1B ☎ 6631 5175

SEX CINEMAS

Cine El Dorado (AC AYOR g OC VS)
Av. Central, C/. 12 – Plaza Santa Ana
Very run down but action from 10-20h. Bring your own condoms!

Cine Tropical (AC AYOR OC VS) 12.30-20.30h
C/. Estudiante y C/. Monteserin *Close to Instituto Nacional* ☎ 262 2714
Straight porno movies, but gay sex within premises. Bring your own condoms!

Cine Variedades (AC AYOR g OC VS)
C/. 12 *Right next to Santa Ana Church* ☎ 228 2091
Mixed porno movies (from straight to gay) from Tue-Thu. Gay sex within premises. Bring your own condoms !

SAUNAS/BATHS

Esparanto Spa (DR G MA OS P SA SB VS WH) 18-24h
C/. 73, No. 14-32
Sauna in a small apartment building. Great design and layout, somewhat improvised. Friendly staff. Busy.

Saunas Men
Edificio Metropolis, Planta Baja *In front of Crown Plaza Hotel*

GUEST HOUSES

Balboa Inn (B bf CC glm M MA OS PA WI)
Las Cruces ☎ 314 1520 🖳 www.thebalboainn.com

Casa Buddy Panama B&B (bf G NU PI) All year, 7-3h
Via Cincuentenario, Duplex crema, cas 5B, Coco del mar
☎ 6741 8719
3 rooms.

APARTMENTS

Cuatro Tulipanes. Los (AC BF cc glm H I MA RWB RWS RWT)
All year
Av. Central *Between C/. 3 and C/. 4* ☎ 211 0877
🖳 www.loscuatrotulipanes.com
Hotel style service in seven unique historic apartments.
All apartments are fully restored and of a very high standard.

CRUISING

-Av. 4 de Julio (not far away from the Smithsonian Institute (R T)
-Av. Cuba (between C/. 29 and C/.42; AYOR R)
-Via Vennetto. Side street, by Hotel El Panama, across the street from Via España. Very cruisy, especially by the young college types (YC)
-Via España. From Blockbuster Video to Hotel El Panama. Especially at night and inside the Rey Supermarket, which is open 24hrs.
-C/. 50. From Athens Pizza restaurant to Plaza New York shopping plaza. Bus stops are the main spots
-Plaza Porras (AYOR)
-Av. central (close to Hotel Intercontinental)
-Parque Legislativao (around the Plaza 5 de Mayo)
-Veracruz beach, Sat & Sun. Mixed, but very cruisy (WE).

Paraguay

Location: Central South America
Initials: PY
Time: GMT -4
International Country Code: ☎ 595
International Access Code: ☎ 00
Language: Spanish, Guaraní (mostly bilingual)
Area: 406,752 km² / 157,047 sq mi.
Currency: 1 Guaraní (G) = 100 Céntimos
Population: 5,899,000
Capital: Asunción
Religions: 89,5% Roman Catholic, 6% Protestant
Climate: Varied climate from moderate in the east to quite dry in the far west. The coldest month is July.

Homosexuality is not mentioned in any legislation in Paraguay. The minimum age of consent for homosexuals is 16. If a judge, however, considers the accused to be „perverse" because of his homosexuality, this can have an influence on his sentence.
The right to express ones opinion and the freedom from discrimination on grounds of sexual orientation are set in the international agreement, on which the Article 25 and 46 from the countries constitution are based and supported by further national policies.
In Paraguay there is nowadays not only several LGBT organisations. Since 2003 there is also a national gay internet site paraboi.com

Homosexualität wird in der paraguaianischen Gesetzgebung nicht erwähnt. Das Schutzalter für Homosexuelle liegt bei 16 Jahren. Allerdings kann ein Richter, wenn er das Schwulsein eines Täters als „pervers" erachtet, diesen Umstand als strafverschärfend werten.
Das Recht auf Meinungsfreiheit und darauf, nicht wegen seiner sexuellen Orientierung diskriminiert zu werden, sind zusammen mit der allgemeinen Pressefreiheit eindeutig in den internationalen Abkommen verankert, die von der Landesverfassung (Artikel 25 und 46) und zahlreichen weiteren nationalen Regelungen unterstützt werden.
In Paraguay gibt es mittlerweile nicht nur verschiedene Organisationen der LGBT-Bewegung, sondern seit 2003 auch ein erstes Schwulenportal im Internet namens paraboi.com

L'homosexualité n'est pas mentionnée dans le droit paraguayen. La majorité sexuelle est fixée à 16 ans pour les homosexuels, mais un juge peut décider que l'homosexualité d'un inculpé constitue une circonstance aggravante. La liberté d'opinion et la non-discrimination en raison de l'orientation sexuelle, ainsi que la liberté de la presse, sont fortement ancrées dans les traités internationaux et sont repris par la constitution du pays (Articles 25 et 46) et de nombreuses autres réglementations nationales.
Il existe désormais au Paraguay non seulement diverses organisations LGBT mais aussi depuis 2003 un premier portail internet gay: paraboi.com

La homosexualidad no aparece mencionada en la legislación paraguaya. La edad de consentimiento para los homosexuales está fijada en los 16 años. Sin embargo, un juez podría considerarla como agravante de la pena, si valorase la homosexualidad del autor como algo „perverso".El derecho a la libertad de expresión y, por lo tanto, el no ser discriminado por la orientación sexual están claramente consagrados, junto con la libertad de la prensa, en acuerdos internacionales que son compatibles con la Constitución del Estado (artículos 25 y 46) y con numerosas convenciones nacionales.
En Paraguay no sólo existen ahora diferentes organizaciones del movimiento LGBT, sino que desde 2003 cuentan también con el primer portal de Internet para gays llamado paraboi.com

L'omosessualità non viene citata nelle leggi di questo Paese. Per gli omosessuali, l'età del consenso è di 16 anni. Tuttavia se il giudice ritiene l'omosessualità dell'imputato „perversa", può inasprire la pena.
Il diritto alla libertà di opinione, il diritto a non essere discriminato a causa del proprio orientamento sessuale e la libertà di stampa sono espressamente sanciti negli accordi internazionali che sono riconosciuti e promossi dalla Costituzione del paese (articolo 25 e 46) e da altri regolamenti nazionali.
In Paraguay ormai oltre ad esserci molte organizzazioni LGBT, dal 2003 c'è anche un portale gay chiamato paraboi.com

NATIONAL GAY INFO

■ **Paraboi.com** (G)
✉ Asunción 💻 www.paraboi.com
Paraguay's first gay web portal, founded in 2003. Has info on clubs, hotels, cinemas and cruising locations. Has a chat room that has become a popular place to hook-up for Paraguayan gays. Also has an informative page in English.

■ **Somosgay** (b G m) Sun-Thu 10-22, Sat 10-24h
C/. Manduvirá 367 ✉ Asunción *Between Chile and Alberdi*
☎ (21) 446 258 💻 www.somosgay.org
Information about the gay scene in Paraguay.

NATIONAL GROUPS

■ **Aireana** (GLM)
Eligio Ayala 907 c/Tacuary, Asunción ✉ Asunción ☎ (21) 447 976
💻 www.aireana.org.py
Lesbian activist Group that sponsors the annual LGBT film festival in Asuncion in the Centro Cultura de Espana Juan de Salazar [usually in July or August], as well as other activities for the community.

■ **GAGL-T Grupo de Accion Gay, Lésbico y Transgenero**
☎ (981) 520 157
One of the earliest gay rights groups in Paraguay, financed by a Spanish NGO

■ **Panambí – Asociación de travestis, transgéneros y transexuales**
☎ 981 334 137
Activist group for trans rights.

■ **ParaGay**
Cerro Cora 1564 ✉ Asunción *Between Perú and Irrazabal* ☎ (021) 232-821
Non-profit organisation aiming to fight homophobia and make homosexuals seen and heard in the Paraguayan culture.

Asunción ☎ 21

BARS

■ **Elixir** (B GLM) Tue-Sun 20-4h
Colon 219 e/pte Franco y Palma *Between Franco and Palma*
Karaoke bar.

■ **Friend's Club** (AC B DR g MA P s VR VS) 12-24h
Chile 932 C/. Piribebuy *1st floor. Near Hotel Excelsior*
☎ 0984 840 518 (mobile)

■ **Frogus** (B GLM OS) Mon-Sat 20 -3h
Estrella 852 *Between Montevideo and Ayolas*
Karaoke bar with open air patio.

■ **Serafina. La** (B gLm MA)
Eligio Ayala 907
Also home of a feminist cultural centre and a café. Place mostly for lesbians.

■ **Toctoc** (B g MC P) Mon-Thu 18-3, WE -5h
C/. Colon 999 *In front of Armelle Grand Hotel* ☎ (21) 444 700
A straight bar with karaoke and a disco where one can go and pick up guys. Entrance fee after midnight.

DANCECLUBS

■ **Coyote** (B D g MC P) Wed 19-?, Fri & Sat 23-?h
Sucre 1655 c/ San Martín ☎ (21) 662 816 💻 www.coyote.com.py
Upmarket, hetero disco where some gays can be found.

■ **Hollywood Dance** (AC B D GLM YC) Fri-Sat from 23.59-?h
Independencia Nacional c/ Teniente Fariña *Former Cine Cosmos*
☎ (982) 488 652 (mobile) ☎ 906 494 (mobile)
With capacity for 1500 people, 3 dance floors on three different levels and an exclusive „Mega VIP" room where you can reserve your own private booth. This is Asuncion's largest and most upscale gay disco. It has a parking.

■ **Trauma Pub** (B D DR GLM MA T VS) Fri & Sat
25 de Mayo 760 casi Antequera
Disco bar with 3 floors (1st floor dancefloor & bar, 2nd floor – bar, 3rd floor porn cinema & darkroom). Entrance fee costs extra if you want to use the cinema and darkrooms). Very mixed place with gays, lesbians and transsexuals.It attracts the roughest crowd of all the gay bars (the travestis are known for being especially fierce) so be careful with possesions as thefts of wallets and backpacks are common.

SEX CINEMAS

■ **Cine Gay** (G MA)
Curupayty entre Cerro Cora y Azara *If you turn on Azara, it is the third building between Azara & Cerro Corra on the right hand side in an old house, with a tall gray railing on the porch, carpark and open door, next to an orange building. Closer to Azara than to Cerro Cora there is no sign Cinema with gay XXX-films. Irregular opening hours.*

■ **Cine Guaraní** (AYOR NG) 20-?h
Eusebio Ayala *In front of Club Guaraní*
Cinema with straight XXX-films.

■ **Pera Video Club. La** (G) Daily from 14h
Rca . Argentina Nº 55
Young, gay men. Individual and double cabins. Cinema XXX.

■ **Video Bar** (b DR g) Daily 12-3h
Curupayty 563 *At C/.Cerro Cor* ☎ (21) 234 166
Two cinemas: one gay, one straight. You can buy beer or soft drink at the entrance.

■ **Video Bar Gay** (DR G VS) Daily 10-21h
Chile 932 1er. piso c/ Piribebuy
Close to the Hotel Excelsior, on the same block. Look for a closed door with a sign that says "Abierto". You enter and go to the first floor. It has two video rooms, a meeting room and dark room. Small but clean.

SAUNAS/BATHS

■ **945 Sauna Club** (b DR DU G m MA MSG PI RR SA SB VS) 14-22, Sat -24h
Tte. Fariña 945 e/ Parapiti y EE UU *Between Estados Unidos & Parapiti streets* ☎ (21) 0971 727 651 💻 www.sauna945.com
Popular sauna with roof garden and a little pool on the roof. Friendly staff.

■ **Gl'uomi** (B DR G MSG SA SB VS) 9-21h
Acá Carayá Nº 162 C/. Mcal. López ☎ (21) 206 340

■ **Menstetic** (B DR DU G LAB MSG RR SA SB VS WO YC) 14-22h
C/. 14 de Mayo Nº 865 *Between C/. Piribebuy and Humaita*
☎ (21) 0981 14 💻 mensteticsauna.com

TRAVEL AND TRANSPORT

■ **Mburucuya Travel & Leisure** (GLM) Thu-Sat 9-16h
C/. Manduvirá 367 *Near C/. Chile* ☎ (21) 446 258 💻 www.somosgay.org
A travel agency specialized in gay and lesbian travel.

HOTELS

Cecilia (AC B BF CC H M MC NG RES RWS RWT)
Estados Unidos 341 ☎ (21) 202 222 www.hotelcecilia.com.py
No unregistered guest allowed.

Rio (RWS)
Parapiti 1643 casi 5ta avenida ☎ 370 598
Same sex couples are allowed but must leave ID at reception.

Sheik (G H RWS)
Tacuary c/ Azara ☎ (21) 4 97 262
Same owners as Sauna 945. Exclusively gay.

CRUISING

-Mall Excelsior
-Shopping Multiplaza Km. 5 Eusebio Ayala Km 5.
-Mcal Lopez Shopping. Charles de Gaulle corner of Quesada (bathroom in the third floor)
-Shopping Mall Villamorra. Charles de Gaulle corner of Mcal Lopez
-Plaza de la Democracia. Oliva between Nuestra Señora and Independencia Nac (AYOR)
-Plaza de la Libertad. Oliva between Chile and Nuestra Señora (AYOR)
-Plaza Uruguaya. 25 de Mayo w / Antequera (AYOR)
-C/. Cerro Cora / Oliva / O'leary / Chile (AYOR). Mainly escorts and „taxiboys"
-Escalinata Antequera Antequera between Fulgencio R Moreno and Manuel Dominguez.
-Behind the Sportivo Luqueño 3 blocks Calle Carlos Antonio Lopez, and the Plaza Mariscal López.

Peru

Name: Perú · Pérou
Location: Western Coast of South America
Initials: PE
Time: GMT -5
International Country Code: ☎ 51 (omit 0 from area code)
International Access Code: ☎ 00
Language: Spanish, Quechua
Area: 1,285,216 km² / 496,222 sq mi.
Currency: 1 New Sol (S/.) = 100 Céntimos
Population: 27,968,000
Capital: Lima
Religions: 92% Roman Catholic 3% Protestant
Climate: The highlands are best from Jun-Aug, and the beaches Dec-Mar. The rainy season is Dec-Mar.
Important gay cities: Lima

Homosexual acts among consenting adults are legal. An exception was made for all military and police personnel, who could be punished with between 60 days to 20 years imprisonment or discharge from the forces but the Constitutional Court has declared that ruling as unconstitutional and ordered that it must be changed. Homosexuality can also be used as grounds for separation or divorce. Laws meant to protect »public morals« are often used against lesbians and gays. Society's attitude towards homosexuals is generally hostile and is heavily influenced by the Catholic Church. In the 1980's the founding of the organisation „Movimiento Homosexual de Lima" (MHOL) managed to bring about at least a slight change in the way the media treated homosexuality.

Einvernehmliche homosexuelle Handlungen zwischen Erwachsenen sind legal. Eine Ausnahme besteht für Angehörige des Militärs und der Polizei, die bei homosexuellen Handlungen eine Strafe von 60 Tagen bis 20 Jahren Gefängnis erhalten oder aus dem Dienst entlassen werden. Das Verfassungsgericht hat diese Regelung jedoch für verfassungswidrig erklärt und fordert eine Gesetzesänderung. Homosexualität wird als Trennungs- oder Scheidungsgrund anerkannt. Gesetze, die die „öffentliche Moral" betreffen, werden oft gegen Lesben und Schwule angewandt. Die allgemeine Einstellung der Bevölkerung gegenüber Schwulen ist feindselig und wird zusätzlich von der katholischen Kirche verschärft. Die Gründung der Organisation „Movimiento Homosexual de Lima (MHOL)" hat in den 80er Jahren zumindest einen leichten Wandel zu einer wohlwollenderen Darstellung gleichgeschlechtlicher Lebensweisen in den Medien bewirkt.

Au Pérou, les relations sexuelles entre adultes consentants ne sont pas un délit, sauf pour les membres de la police ou de l'armée qui, eux, risquent, selon les circonstances, 60 jours à 20 ans de prison, accompagnés d'un licenciement sec. La cour constitutionnelle a cependant déclaré ce règlement anticonstitutionnel et réclame une modification de la loi.
L'homosexualité est une raison officielle de séparation ou de divorce. Les lois protégeant la «morale publique» sont fréquemment utilisées contre les gais et les lesbiennes.
Les Péruviens sont, dans l'ensemble, plutôt homophobes et l'Eglise catholique ne fait rien pour arranger les choses. Le MHDL, „Movimiento Homosexual de Lima" a été fondé au début des années 80. C'est grâce à lui que les choses ont pu bouger, surtout dans les médias.

Las relaciones homosexuales por acuerdo mutuo entre adultos son legales. Se excluyen a miembros de las fuerzas armadas y de la policía, que pueden ser condenados desde 60 días hasta 20 años de cárcel o pueden ser separados del cargo, el tribunal Constitucional no obstante ha declarado inconstitucional esta regulación y exige una modificación jurídica.
La homosexualidad es reconocida como motivo de separación o divorcio. También se aplican leyes con respecto a la «moral pública» en contra de las lesbianas y los gays. La opinión pública es generalmente hostil e influenciada sobre todo por la iglesia católica. El «Movimiento Homosexual de Lima (MHOL)» inició en los años 80 por lo menos un cambio leve en la representación de formas de vida homosexuales en los medios de comunicación.

Gli atti omosessuali fra adulti consenzienti non sono illegali. Un'eccezione viene fatta per appartenenti alle forze militari e alla polizia, dove l'omosessualità può essere punita con la reclusione da 60 giorni fino a 20 anni o l'espulsione dal corpo. La Corte di giustizia ha ritenuto questa regolamentazione incostituzionale e quindi chiesto una modifica. L'omosessualità può anche essere usata per le cause di separazione o di divorzio. Le leggi concernenti la „pubblica moralità" vengono spesso usate contro persone lesbiche e gay. Il comportamento generale della società verso gli omosessuali è ostile e pesantemente influenzato dalla presenza della Chiesa Cattolica. La costituzione del „Movimiento Homosexual de Lima (MHOL)" negli anni ottanta ha contribuito a cambiare l'opinione dei mass-media riguardo allo stile di vita di coppie dello stesso sesso.

NATIONAL GAY INFO

■ **Deambiente.com**
☏ (01) 9793-7660 💻 www.deambiente.com
Portal for Peruvian gay people with forums, articles, surveys, contacts and guides.

NATIONAL COMPANIES

■ **Amerika Viajes y Turismo** (GLM) Mon-Fri 9-13 & 15-19, Sat 9-13h
Av. el Sol #948 Oficina 321 ✉ Cusco *In Centro Comercial Cusco Sol Plaza* ☏ (084) 930-1520 💻 www.gaytravelperu.com
Experienced tour operator. Provides information about gay tourist services for all destinations in Peru, specially for the city of Cusco. First travel agency in Peru dedicated exclusively to the Gay Community.

NATIONAL GROUPS

■ **Movimiento Homosexual de Lima (MHOL)** (GLM) Mon-Fri 9-13 & 16-20, Sat 19-22h
Mariscal Miller 828 Jesús María ✉ Lima
☏ (01) 433-5314 💻 www.mhol.org.pe
Gay and lesbian group established in 1982. Postal address: MHOL, PO Box 110289, Lima 11.

Arequipa ☏ 09

MEN'S CLUBS

■ **Casanova Club** (B DR G MA p VS) Daily 14-22h
Av. Jorge Chavez 612 *Opp. Estadio Melgar* ☏ (09) 960-0981

DANCECLUBS

■ **Open Night** (B CC D GLM MA S SNU) Wed-Sun 22-5h
Calle Tronchadero 209, ☏ (09) 600-0981

GUEST HOUSES

■ **Casa Arequipa** (BF H MC)
Av. Lima 409, Vallecito ☏ (09) 5428-4219 💻 www.arequipacasa.com
B&B with seven guestrooms. Complimentary full breakfast included in rate. Near Plaza de Armas. Staff speaks Spanish and English.

SWIMMING

-Jaime Baños (Golfo 208, Miraflores).

CRUISING

-Plaza de Armas at night. Be careful of organised groups of thieves.

Cuzco ☏ 084

HOTELS

■ **Apus. Los** (AC BF cc H I RWS) All year
Atocsaycuchi 515 ☏ (084) 264 243 💻 www.losapushotel.com
Gay-friendly accommodation under Swiss management. Free breakfast and transportation to and from the airport.

Lima ☏ 01

BARS

■ **Jarrita. La** (AC B D G M MC S) Daily 19-?h
Jr. Camana 949, Cercado de Lima *Near Av. Wilson and Plaza San Martin*
☏ (01) 98 991-6391 💻 www.lajarrita.com
Bar and restaurant.

CAFES

■ **Bohemia** (B g M MA OS) Mon-Fri 13-24, Sat 13-2, Sun 13-18h
Av. Santa Cruz 805, Ovalo Gutiérrez, Miraflores ☏ (01) 446-5240
💻 www.bohemiacafe.com

■ **Café Café** (! AC B BF CC g M MA OS WE) 18-1h
Av. Mártir Olaya, 250, Miraflores *At Parque de Miraflores* ☏ (01) 445-1165

DANCECLUBS

■ **80Divas** (AC B CC D DR G MA r S SNU ST VS)
17-1, Fri & Sat -5, Sun 18-1h, closed Mon
Av. Petit Thouars 2677, Lince ☏ (01) 99 937-9555 💻 www.80divas.com

■ **Athenas Disco** (b D GLM ST YC) Thu-Sun 23-7h
Av. Nicolas de Pierola 716, Centro *Three blocks from Plaza San Martin*
The place is small and as hot as a sauna, but it is popular with a young crowd.

■ **Cueva. La** (! B d GLM S T) Wed-Sat 23-?h
Av. Aviación 2514, San Borja ☏ (01) 9789-9125
💻 www.gayperu.com//lacueva
First gay disco to open in Lima. Located in a safe district about 15 mins by taxi from Miraflores. Show on Fri & Sat at 3h. Popular and definitely worth a visit. Crowd older than 35 and shows somewhat difficult to see when packed.

■ **Laberynto** (B D f G m MA MSG p S SNU ST VS WE) 16-6h
Jr. de la Union 1088 *Downtown Lima, near San Martin Plaza*
☏ (01) 51 623-0006 (mobile) 💻 www.minotauroclub.com
Gay club, very popular with local drag queens and transvestites. Shows Fri & Sat, but Sat is the best day.

■ **Legendaris** (! B cc D GLM MC S) Thu-Sun 23-?h
C/. Berlin 363, Miraflores ☏ (01) 446-3455
💻 www.gayperu.com/legendaris
Bars (cute barmen!) on both floors. Very popular. The most lavishly decorated club in Lima. Fri Strippers' shows, Sat fascinating Las Vegas-style revues, and frequent theme parties all year. Cover charge on Fri & Sat, but entrance is free until 23h.

■ **Punto G** (AC b D GLM MA S SNU VS) Wed-Sun 22-?h
Pasaje Santa Luisa, Lote 4, Urb. Santa Leonor *In Trujillo* ☏ (01) 44 959-9909

■ **Sagitario** (B D G) Daily 22-10h
Av. Wilson 869 Cercado *Located in a very unsafe district, so you must come and go by taxi* ☏ (01) 424-4383 💻 www.gayperu.com/sagitariodisco
One of the oldest gay discos in Lima centre. Busy every night. Cruise bar on the balcony overlooking the main dance floor. Although the official name of that Avenue has been changed to Garcilaso de la Vega, people still call it Wilson. Tell the taxi driver „Wilson at intersection with Jiron Quilca." There is no sign outside but you can recognize the place by the line of taxis in front of the door.

RESTAURANTS

■ **Tranquera. La** (AC B glm M MA) 12-24, Sun 12-23h
Av. Pardo 285, Miraflores ☏ (01) 447-5111
💻 www.restaurantelatranquera.com
A steak-house with a sensational mixed grill. The Parilla is a must.

SAUNAS/BATHS

■ **240 Baños Turcos** (! AC B cc DR DU FH G m MA MSG p RR SA SB VS WE) 15-23, Sat 15-8, Sun -22h
Jiron Tarma 240, Cercado *Jiron Tarma is on the other side parallel of Paseo colon, also called Av. 9 de Diciembre* ☏ (01) 332-4370
A Finnish sauna, two Turkish saunas and porno video room upstairs. Nine private cabins and male masseurs. Clean and well-maintained. Not a very safe area to walk in at night, so you better come and go by taxi. Busy from 16h. Sat open all night. Here is where the action is!

■ **Baños Tívoli** (B DR DU G MSG NU P SA SB SNU VS WH WO) 14-22h
Av. Petit Thouars 4041, San Isidro ☏ (01) 222-1705
💻 www.gayperu.com/saunativoli
Located in a safe district, only a short taxi or bus ride from Miraflores. Two Finnish saunas, two steamrooms, three private two-men jacuzzis, male masseurs, and nine private cabins are available there. This clean and well-maintained sauna is more popular after 18h. With four paid entries the 5th is free.

■ **Oupen** (AC B DR DU G m MA MSG p SA SB VS WO) Daily 15-23h
Av. 28 de Julio 171, Miraflores *Next to Radisson Hotel* ☎ (01) 242-3094
💻 www.gayperu.com/oupensauna
Modern and exclusively gay. Two Finnish saunas, two steamrooms, male masseur, gym, cafeteria, porno video room and about twelve private cabins. It is very clean and well-maintained. 2-4-1 Mon-Fri.

■ **Sagitario** (b DU G I MA MSG SA SB VS WH) 11-?, Sun 6-?h
Rufino Torrico 936, Centro *Behind Sagitario Disco* ☎ (01) 433-1424
💻 www.gayperu.com/saunasagitario

■ **Sauna 69** Mon-Fri & Sun 14-23, Sat 14-?h
Emilio Fernández 782 *Near to 9 Paseo de la República – Canal 7*
☎ 331-2819

■ **Sauna Ozono**
Av. del Ejército 1233 *1/2 block from Estadio Bonilla, by Pacific Hotel*
☎ 221-5471

TRAVEL AND TRANSPORT

■ **Gay Adventures Peru** (CC GLM MA p T)
Bajada Balta 131 OF 9, Second Floor, Miraflores *Half a block from Kennedy Park* ☎ (01) 726-7513

HOTELS

■ **Domeyer Hostel** (CC GLM MA) All year
Jr. Domeyer 296, Barranco ☎ (01) 247-1413
Close to local bars and restaurants. Laundry service as well as airport transfers available.

■ **Hostal de las Artes** (H I MA NG RWS RWT) All year
Jiron Chota 1460 *Near Av. España, Centro* ☎ (01) 433-0031
English, German, Dutch and Spanish spoken. Also airport transfer upon request. 16 guestrooms.

■ **VIP Hotel** (glm RWT VA) 24hrs
Jr. Salaverry 569, Magdalena del Mar *Between block 39 and 40 on Av. Brasil* ☎ (01) 462-4722 💻 www.peruesgay.com/hostalvip
Discrete and comfortable Hotel.

■ **VIP Imperial** (b cc glm MA MSG) 24hrs
Jr. Tomas Ramsey 130, Magdalena del Mar ☎ 592-3057
💻 www.peruesgay.com/hostalvip/imperial.htm
Close to local bars, restaurants and in an extremely safe neighbourhood. Laundry service as well as airport transfers available. 30% discount for Spartacus guests.

GUEST HOUSES

■ **Mansion San Antonio** (AC B BF CC G m MA PI WH WO) All year
Av. Tejada, 531, Miraflores ☎ (01) 445-9665
💻 www.mansionsanantonio.com
First class gay accommodation.

HEALTH GROUPS

■ **Vía libre** Mon-Fri 9-13, 14-18, Sat 9-13h
Jr. Paraguay 478 *Plaza Bolognesi square, between Paseo Colón & Av. Alfonso Ugarte* ☎ (01) 203-9900 💻 www.vialibre.org.pe
NGO for HIV, AIDS, STD prevention and health services for people with STD, HIV & AIDS.

CRUISING

ATTENTION: All areas are AYOR, thieves and pickpockets are found here:
-Av. Nicolás de Piérola (also known as Colmena)
-Plaza San Martín (R)
-Parque El Olivar (R T; near library)
-Avenida J. Prado Oeste cuadra 1, San Isidro
-Parque Kennedy, Av. Benavides cuadra 4, Miraflores (be careful of pickpockets and thieves!)
-Parque Pedro Ruiz Gallo, Lince
-Parque Salazar (at the end of Av. Larco, Miraflores).

Trujillo ☎ 044

SAUNAS/BATHS

■ **H2O** (B CC G M MA MSG SA SB SOL VS WE WO) 15.30-23h
Cavero y Muñoz 322, Urb. Las Quintanas *Two blocks away from Gran Chimu coliseum* ☎ (044) 475 108

Philippines

Name: Pilipinas · Philippinen · Filipinas · Filippine
Location: Southeastern Asia
Initials: RP
Time: GMT +8
International Country Code: ☎ 63
International Access Code: ☎ 00
Language: Philippino, English
Area: 300,000 km² / 115,830 sq mi.
Currency: 1 Philippine Peso (P) = 100 Centavos
Population: 81,617,000
Capital: Manila
Religions: 84% Roman Catholic
Climate: Tropical and marine climate. The northeast monsoon lasts from Nov-Apr, the southwest monsoon from May-Oct. Mar-May is hot and dry. Jun-Oct is rainy. Nov-Feb is cool.
Important gay cities: Manila

There is no prohibition on homosexuality in the Philippines. The age of legal consent is 18. Philippine law prohibits public scandals -regardless of whether the perpetrators are homosexual or not. The Anti-Discrimination Act (Bill 956 from the House of Representatives) is an act prohibiting discrimination on the basis of sexual orientation and gender identity and lists penalties for violations of this act. Sadly this bill is still at the committee level and is still under debate. There are several, LGBT organisations in the Philippines and gay life is generally quite open, although the majority of the population is Roman Catholic.

Wonderful beaches, fantastic scenery, friendly people and mouth-watering cuisine are just a few reasons to visit this fantastic country.

Auf den Philippinen ist Homosexualität nicht verboten. Das gesetzliche Schutzalter liegt bei 18 Jahren. Die Gesetzgebung der Philippinen verbietet jedoch die Erregung öffentlichen Ärgernisses – unabhängig davon, ob die Beteiligten homosexuell sind oder nicht. Das geplante Anti-Diskriminierungsgesetz (Gesetzesvorlage 956 des Repräsentantenhauses) soll die Diskriminierung aufgrund der sexuellen Orientierung und Geschlechtsidentität eindämmen und sieht bei Gesetzesverstößen entsprechende Strafmaße vor. Doch leider befindet sich die Gesetzesvorlage immer noch auf der Ausschussebene und wird weiterhin debattiert.

In den Philippinen gibt es gleich mehrere LGBT-Organisationen, und das schwule Leben findet generell recht offen statt, obwohl die Bevölkerung mehrheitlich römisch-katholisch ist.

Es gibt also noch mehr Gründe für einen Besuch dieses Landes als „nur" die wunderbaren Strände, fantastischen Landschaften, freundlichen Menschen und das köstliche Essen.

L'homosexualité n'est pas interdite aux Philippines. L'âge de protection légale est fixée à 18 ans. La législation des Philippines interdit cependant l'outrage public à la pudeur – que les personnes en cause soient homosexuelles ou pas.

La loi anti-discriminatoire prévue (projet de loi 956 de la Chambre des Représentants) doit limitée la discrimination en raison de l'orientation et de l'identité sexuelles et prévoit des mesures pénales dans le cas d'infraction à cette loi. Malheureusement ce projet de loi reste bloqué au niveau d'une commission et continue d'être débattu.

Aux Philippines on trouve même plusieurs associations gay et lesbiennes et la vie homosexuelle est vécue ouvertement, bien que la majorité de la population est d'obédience romaine-catholique. Il y a encore d'autres raisons de visiter le pays: les plages magnifiques, les paysages fantastiques, les personnes accueillantes et la merveilleuse nourriture.

En las Filipinas la homosexualidad está prohibida. La edad de consentimineto legal está en los 18 años. La legislación de Filipinas prohíbe la provocación por escándalo público, independientemente de si los implicados son o no homosexuales.

La ley antidiscriminación prevista (propuesta legislativa 956 de la Cámara de Representantes) debería enterrar la discriminación por razón de la orientación sexual e identidad sexual y están previstas las sanciones penales correspondientes por infracciones a la ley. No obstante, la propuesta legislativa se encuentra desgraciadamente aún en la fase de comisiones y se sigue debatiendo.

En las Filipinas existen varias organizaciones LGBT y el ambiente gay se vive en general de manera bastante abierta, a pesar de que la población sea mayoritariamente católica. Hay por tanto muchos otros motivos para visitar este país y no sólo por sus fantásticas playas, hermosos paisajes, gente amable y su deliciosa gastronomía.

Nelle Filippine l'omosessualità non è vietata. L'età del consenso è di 18 anni. La legislazione delle Filippine vieta tuttavia l'offesa alla pubblica decenza, indipendentemente dal fatto che chi è coinvolto sia omosessuale o no.

La proposta di legge contro le discriminazioni (progetto di legge 956 del parlamento) dovrebbe limitare le discriminazioni in base all'orientamento e all'identità sessuale e prevede, in caso di non osservanza della legge, un corrispondente grado di pena. Purtroppo però il progetto di legge è ancora sul tavolo della commissione e continua ad essere dibattuto.

Nelle Filippine ci sono molte organizzazioni LGBT, e sebbene la maggioranza della popolazione sia cattolica, la vita gay ha una dimensione piuttosto aperta. Ci sono quindi molti motivi per visitare questo Paese e non „solo" per le meravigliose spiagge, i fantastici paesaggi, le cordialissime persone e il buonissimo cibo.

NATIONAL PUBLICATIONS

■ **Outrage** (GLM)
Manila ✉ Manila ☎ 928 785 4244 🖳 www.outragemag.com
The first and only online publication for the Filipino gay, lesbian, bisexual, transgender, queer, intersex(GLBTQIA) community

Baguio City ☎ 74

BARS

■ **Cloud 7** (B D G MA SNU)
B/F Naguilan Inn, 444 Naguilan Rd, Baguio City
Dancers perform from 21.30-3h. Some strip all the way. Admission is Peso 150 (US$3.50) and will be applied to your drink bill.

DANCECLUBS

■ **Friday's** (B D g YC)
Unit 4,5,6 Nevada Square, 1 Loakan Rd *Near the entrance gate of Camp John Hay* ☎ (74) 092 8401 2868
Very nice and cozy bar. Most popular dance club for the young crowd.

■ **Thunderbird** (B D G MA SNU)
KM3 Naguillan Rd
Dancers perform from 21.30-3h.They all strip at midnight.

CRUISING

All are AYOR:
-Mines View Park
-Sessions Road
-Burnham Park, best between 23-4h, r
-Centennial Park (in front of City Hall).

Boracay ☎ 36

BARS

■ **Beachcomber** (B D GLM MA OS)
Station 1, white beach ☎ (36) 288 31 57

■ **Café Duo** (B g m MA) 18h-open end
Manggayad, Malay Aklan *Near Lorenzo Beach Resort, near boat station no 3* ☎ (36) 634 26 39
Very friendly owner who will direct you, where the gay people like to go.

■ **Coco Loco** (B d glm MA)
Malay Aklan *near Boracay Beach* ☎ (36) 288 3028

■ **Summer Place** (B D GLM MA)
White Beach ☎ (36) 288 31 44 🖳 www.summerplaceboracay.com
Nice place to go with someone to chat, drink and cuddle. Very friendly staff. Reasonable prices.

DANCECLUBS

■ **Sulu Star** (B D GLM MA OS)
White Beach *Southern end of White Beach, across from Boat Station #3 and above the Sulu Thai restaurant*
Karaoke competitions. Popular with gays. Nightly sing-along contests, with disco dancing after midnight.

HOTELS

■ **Flora East Resort & Spa** (AC B BF CC I M MSG OS PI RWB RWS RWT SA) All year
Sitio Sugod, Manocmanoc, Malay, Aklan ☎ (036) 288 1450
🖳 www.flora-east.com
This exclusive cliff-top resort and spa is the perfect place to stay.

■ **Nigi Nigi Nu Noos Beach Resort** (AC B BF CC H I M MA MSG) 7-23h
PO Box 11, Kalibo Aklan *At the beachfront* ☎ (36) 288 31 01
🖳 www.niginigi.com
Twenty rooms all with cable-TV, shower/WC, balcony/terrace and safe. Room service and own key available. Scuba diving and sailing possible.

■ **Nigi Nigi Too Beach Resort** (AC B BF CC H MSG NG) 6-24h
White Beach, Balabag, Malay, Aklan *At the beachfront* ☎ (36) 288 3150
🖳 www.niginigitoo.com
Fifteen rooms all with cable television, hot and cold shower, balcony. Room service and own key available. Scuba diving and sailing possible.

■ **Paradise BoraGay Hotel** (B BF GLM M MA OS PI) All year
Tulubhan, Maly, Aklan *near the former dock 3* ☎ (36) 288 5124
🖳 www.boragay.com
Well established hotel run by a german couple. In 2010 re-opened under new name and now fully dedicated to the gay traveler. Hidden but still close to nightlife.
■ **Villa Sunset Boracay** (AC b bf cc glm H MA MSG PI) Daily 6-22h
Sitio, Manggayad, Balabag, Malay, Aklan ☎ (36) 288 56 66
🖳 www.villa-sunset-boracay.com
Cosy and private budget boutique hotel, located in the middle of one of the world's best tropical beaches, Boracay. Two mins walk from the main beach.

GUEST HOUSES

■ **Rainbow Rooms** (AC B GLM I MA OS RWS RWT)
Angol, Station 3 ☎ 263 70 77 🖳 www.gayboracay.com
Gay guesthouse with private studio apartments on the beach.

CRUISING

-Southern part of the white beach at the rocks (daytime & sunset, AYOR).

Cagayan de Oro ☎ 88

BARS

■ **Navigator** (B d G r SNU)
Osmena St *near Discovery Hotel and Limketkai Mall* ☎ (88) 856 5628
Strip Club, on Fri and Sat special singing and performing events.
■ **Tubby's** (AC B D g m MA r S SNU) 20-4h
Rizal Gomez Street 63-927 *Close to Divisoria* ☎ (88) 394 9121
Gay bar with KTV VIP-rooms, darts, billards, shows all night long, cute lads and more.

CAFES

■ **The Park Café** (B glm MA OS)
A favourite hangout for gays.

DANCECLUBS

■ **1150 Club** (B D G MA OS)
Pabaya Delores Street *In front of the Dynasty Court Hotel*
Favored by the GLBT of Cagayan de Oro. Crowded after 23.30 and until closing at 3 or 4h. Heavy cruising.

CRUISING

All AYOR:
-Divisoria Downtown
-Gaisano Mall
-Limketkai Mall
-McArthur Park, popular around this area. Not difficult to meet someone, some of them are young and well educated
-Opol Beach
-Ororama Megacenter
-Pelaez Sports Center
-The Site, Limketkai Rosario Arcade. Most gays hang around here on weekends.
-SM Mall.

Cebu City ☎ 32

BARS

■ **Doce Bar** (B g MA)
Mango Avenue *Uptown Cebu, near Fuente Osmena*
A cozy place in Cebu where you can hang out and meet good guys.
■ **Milkman** (B d g MA SNU)
Del Roario Ave, Guizo
Smallest and friendliest of Cebu's bars. They show slightly more than other bars.
■ **Naughty Ka Restobar** (B d g MA)
#11 Cuenco Ave *Beside Sentinel Condominium*
■ **Navigator** (B d glm MA)
Cabahug Rd *5-minute walk north of Jollybee*
Attracts many Korean women as well as gays.

■ **The Host 78** (B g MA SNU)
Maxilom Ave *between Mango Park Hotel and Mango Plaza*
No sign on the outside, just a white door in a vaguely castle-like wall. Poor lighting and expensive by local standards. Cebu city regulations mean their dancers show less than in Mandaue.

DANCECLUBS

■ **Club Juliana** (B D glm MA OS)
Mango Square
recently becoming a good place due to rising numbers of gays coming here.
■ **Vudu** (B cc D glm MA OS)
Crossraods Mall, Banilad ☎ (32) 234 0836
🖳 www.facebook.com/VUDUcebu
The premiere nightclub in the city. It gets cruisy sometimes.

SEX CINEMAS

■ **Eden Theater** (g MC VS)
Colon St
■ **Ultravistarama Theater** (g MA VS)
Legaspi St

CRUISING

All are AYOR:
-Arcade at Pelaez & Colon intersection
-Ayala complex, across from Harrison Plaza and Robinson Mall
-Cebu Coliseum Roller Skating (afternoon and evening)
-Fuente Osmena skating rink at night
-Maroco Beach, Dumlob Talisay (13km from Ceby City, at nearby pool)
-South Expressway Bus Terminal (late night)
-University of Visayas, Colon St.

Davao ☎ 82

BARS

■ **Boyztown** (B D GLM MA OS)
Ponciano Reyes St. *Madraso, Adrazo Compound*
Best place to go!
■ **Dokidoks** (B D glm MA OS s)
F. Torres Street
■ **Rizal Promenade** (B d glm MA OS WE)
Rizal Street *Downtown*
At least 10 bars offering acoustic live bands, music and discos. Some are very gayfriendly.

CRUISING

All AYOR:
-Boulevard Strip
-Gaisano Mall
-Ilustre Avenue
-Lawaan Theater
-Rizal Promenade, Mi Piace
-Victoria Plaza.

Manila ☎ 2

SHOWS

■ **White Bird Disco Theater and KTV** (B D glm M MA OS S ST)
715 Boulevard Galleria, Roxas Boulevard Paranaque City ☎ (632) 851-2089
All-male entertainment bar. Shows and entertainment nightly.

BARS

■ **Bassilica** (B glm m S)
1855 Pilar Hildago Lim Street, Malate ☎ (2) 522 6210
Weekly theme changing sing-along bar with shows. Inexpensive.
■ **Big Papa Bar** (AC B CC d G MA MSG S SNU ST T WE) Mon-Sun 21-4h
2315 Aurora Blvd Tramo, Passay City ☎ (2) 854 4100
Macho dancer bar with private rooms for side shows.
■ **Clarke Quay Comedy Bar** (B GLM M MA OS S)
405 Lopes St, San Joaquin ☎ 7821-6858
Sing-along bar with two nightly performances with gay entertainers.

■ **Club Adonis** (AC B cc GLM MA R SNU T) 19-3h
18 Timog Av., Quezon City ☏ (2) 925 5919
■ **Club Hercules** (AC B cc GLM MA R SNU T) 19-3h
2256 Tramo St, Pasay City
■ **Comic Lab** (AC B cc GLM M MA R S T) 19-3h
1718 J Bocobo Street, Malate *Near Robinsons Mall* ☏ (2) 526 2730
■ **El Notre** (B D glm M MA OS S)
1810 Orosa St ☏ 9296-6937
Acoustic gigs Mon-Sat on 2nd floor, free karaoke on groundfloor.
■ **Gigolo** (B glm MA) 19-3h
76 A Timog Av., Quezon City *Near GMA-7* ☏ (2) 925 5918
■ **Jail House Rock** (AC B cc GLM MA R S) 19-3h
65-B Scout Tobias St., Quezon City
■ **Library. The** (AC B cc GLM M MA R S T) 18-3h
1779 Adriatico Street, Malate *Near Remedios Circle, Malate* ☏ (2) 522 2484
Mixed but popular with local celebrities and gay love sing-alongs and stand-up comedy. Entertaining hosts. Best after 22h.
■ **Messrs** (AC B cc DR G m MA VS)
34-B Stanford Street, Cubao, Quezon City ☏ (2) 439 2405
■ **O Bar** (AC B CC D G m MA ST) 21-?h
1800 M. Orase Street, Malate *Cnr. J. Nakpil Street* ☏ (2) 522 2796
Gay bar. Transvestite shows on Tue & Sun. Sexy ledge dancers Wed-Sat.
■ **O Bar** (B GLM m MA OS)
Ortigas Home Depot, Julia Vargas Ave *Ortigas Center*
Second branch of this bar in town.
■ **Punchline Comedy Bar** (AC B cc GLM MA S T) 19-3h
Quezon Av., Quezon City
■ **Soulmate** (AC B cc D glm m MA OS R SNU T) 20-2h
690 NS Amoranto Street, Quezon City ☏ (2) 712 3662
Also rooms by the hour. Former Club 690.
■ **Steel Bar** (B glm)
Scout Tobias, Quezon City *At Timor Av.*
■ **Vanilla & Tonic Bar** (B g m MC s)
Esquinita on Sgt. Esguerra St., Quezon City *Near the TV Studios ABS & CBN*
Gay-friendly bar. Most patrons from TV station due to the location. Bar shows and light meals.

CAFES

■ **3rd X Café** (B glm M MA OS)
82 Tirona Hi-way, Mabolo, Bacoor
Gay-friendly. Good music and food.
■ **Campus Diner** (B glm M OS YC)
Taft Avenue *Half way between Quirino Avenue and Vito Cruz Stations, not far from De La Salle University*
During the day an eating place for students, by night it turns into a karaoke bar.
■ **Jefz Café** (B G)
1811 Leon Guinto Street, Malate *Ground level of Hotel Solanie*
☏ (2) 524 8643

DANCECLUBS

■ **Bed** (AC B D GLM MA S ST t WE) Wed-Sat 22-?h
Unit 8, Maria Orosa Street, Malate *Cnr. Julio Nakpil St., entrance to courtyard on Orosa St between Synder and Sonata, door between Mafia and the other establishment is Bed* ☏ (2) 563 3045 🖳 www.bed.com.ph
Wild and raunchy on two floors with own bars and DJs. Friendly and cute staff is serving moderately priced drinks. Entrance fee includes one drink. Jam packed after midnights at WE. No food, mostly drinks.

RESTAURANTS

■ **People's Palace** (b CC glm M) 12-14.30, 18-23h
Greenbelt 3, Ayala Center Makati *Ground floor* ☏ (2) 729 2888
🖳 www.peoplespalacethai.com
Upscale Thai restaurant, attracting a trendy crowd. There is a chic outdoor lounge with wide settees where patrons can drink before or after meals.

SEX CINEMAS

■ **Alta** (AYOR g MA VS)
Aurora Blvd, Quezon City ☏ (2) 911 0475
■ **Remar Cinema Cubao** (AYOR G VS)
Aurora Blvd, Quezon City *Near Gateway*
This cinema is cleaner, bigger and well-ventilated in comparison to the others. To meet younger men, pay P$110 for the deluxe (upper part) of the cinema and you can also cruise downstairs. The lower and cheaper area (P$80) is mostly for mature men and you may not be allowed to cruise upstairs.

SAUNAS/BATHS

■ **Club Bath Philippines** (AC B DR DU G I LAB M MA OS P RR S SB SH VS WI WO) Mon-Thu 18-2, Fri -3, Sat & Sun 15-3h
2456 F. B. Harrison Blvd, Pasay City *Cnr. Valhalla St, near Pasay City Sports Complex & Pasay City Hall* ☏ (2) 833 2866
Especially Thu, Sat & Sun, busiest after 20h. The oldest gay bath house in Manila with private rooms, dressing rooms and a snack bar. Entrance only with valid ID!
■ **Epitome** (B DR DU G LAB m MA RR SA SB ST VS WH WO)
Mon-Thu 19-2, Fri & Sat 20-3, Sun 15-3h
1922 Leon Guinto Street, Malate *Near Remedios Street, off Taff Av.*
■ **Fahrenheit Café & Fitness Center** (AC B D DU G LAB m MA P S SB SH SNU ST VS WE WH WO) 20-3h
1204 E. Rodriguez Sr. Av., Brgy. Mariana, Quezon City *Quezon City, in front of Tri-Palace Hotel* ☏ (918) 900 8002 (mobile)
🖳 www.Fahrenheitcafe.com
Crowded weekend dancefloor and monthly pageants, singing contests and guest male performances.
■ **Queeriosity Palace** (AC B DR DU G I MSG SB VS WH)
Sun-Thu 18-2, Fri & Sat -3h
1946 F.B. Harrison Street, Pasay City *Cnr with Epifanio Delos Santos Av*
☏ (02) 527 8337 🖳 www.queeriosity.com
Manila's newest gay sauna.
■ **Sanctuario** (B g l m MSG RR SA SB VS WH) Sun-Thu 15-24, Fri+Sat -3h
1829 Jorge Bocobo St, Malate
An old house recently converted into a brandnew spa, catering for both men and women (straight). Cruising is prevalent within the wet area, there is a central courtyard with lap pool, open air hot tub. Showers are not well maintained but décor is quite rustic. Choice of either male or female masseurs; male masseurs can be enticed to be more daring in massage service.

FITNESS STUDIOS

■ **Hardcore Gym** (g MA WO)
185 Ronquillo Bld, Kaingin, Balintawak Q.C. *Near the Royal bus stop on Edsa* ☏ (2) 415 1510
Gay-friendly gym, clients include police, guards, macho dancers, and discreet gays.

MASSAGE

■ **Amanjaya Spa** (glm MA MSG SB)
103A Hillcrest Condominium, 1616 E. Rodriguez Sr. Ave ☏ 386-5401
Gay-owned venue to relax and indulge. They offer all types of massage and reflexology, body scrubs and a Turkish bath. Package services available. Attendants are all trained and skilled masseurs.
■ **Braveheart Men Spa** (g MA MSG)
1091 Quezon Ave, Barangay Sta. Cruz
☏ 994-6804 or (091) 7510 2565 mobile
Gay-owned body spa massage.
■ **Cicada Spa** (glm MA MSG) 24 hrs
97 Gil Puyat Ave *Cnr South Super Highway, beside Cash n Carry Mall*
☏ 889-3716
Gay-owned. Trained masseurs and masseuses providing Swedish massage, shiatsu, foot massage and scrub, and more.

HOTELS

■ **Tropicana Apartment Hotel** (AC B cc g M MSG PI SA)
1630 L. M. Guerrero Street, Malate ☏ (2) 525 5555
In easy walking distance to many local gay spots. Also serviced apartments for daily, weekly and monthly rent available.

APARTMENTS

Baywatch Luxury Condos (GLM M MA OS PI RWB RWS RWT SA WO) All year, 24hrs
☎ (+63) 919 490 1330 www.baywatch1403.com
Gay-owned studio apartment with breathtaking view of Manila Bay. A first class accommodation in the center of Malate, Manila's nightlife district.

SWIMMING

-Rizal, public swimming pool (not always very clean) on the Rizal Colliseum, near La Salle University. A lot of young, good looking University guys and serious swimmers
-ULTRA, Merlaco Avenue, inside the University of Life, Pasig City. University guys and serious swimmers, with lots of young, hunky men.

CRUISING

All are AYOR:
-Harrison Plaza Shopping Center, 2nd floor (R) (14-20h, students)
-Amihan Gardens, Makati (evenings)
-Robinson's Commercial Center, Metro Adriatico Street
-Makati Stock Exchange
-Old Mill Theatre (in the lobby, afternoons)
-Mehang Gardens (evenings)
-Roxas Blvd near corner Buendia Av. and „Boom na Boom"
-Aurora Gardens (opposite Congress Building in Rizal Park)
-Greenbelt Cinemas in Makati (daytime)
-At side of Delta Theater, Quezon Av., Quezon City (R)
-Around Araneta Coliseum at Cubao, Quezon City (R)
-Ali Mall shopping centre, Quezon City (R)
-Farmer's market shopping centre, Quezon City (R)
-S.M.City, West Avenue, Quezon City
-Eliptical Rd, Quezon City Memorial Park near Aristocrat Restaurant parking lot
-Quezon Memorial Circle Quezon City (after midnight)
-Shangri La Plaza, facilities
-Starbucks, Festival Mall, regular group of gays who chat on Internet meet here on Tue
-UP Circle, hot spot. Busy from 18-22h (at curfew). Near the naked statue on the right side where cruisers usually ‚chill out'
-QC Circle from 19-23 and from 4h onwards (especially when it's dark) at the ‚hill' near the ballroom dancing studio.

Puerto Galera – Mindoro

CRUISING

All AYOR:
-East end of White Beach, walking towards Minolo Bay, in the bushes
-The rocks on the other end of White Beach, towards Aninuan Beach, afternoons.

Poland

Name: Polska · Polen · Pologne · Polonia
Location: Eastern Europe
Initials: PL
Time: GMT +1
International Country Code: ☎ 48
International Access Code: ☎ 0 (wait for tone) 0
Language: Polish
Area: 312,685 km² / 120,727 sq mi.
Currency: 1 New Zloty (Zl) = 100 Groszy
Population: 38,165,000
Capital: Warszawa
Religions: 95% Roman Catholic
Climate: Continental climate. The best time to visit is late spring (May & Jun) or late summer (Jul-Sep).
Important gay cities: Warsawa, Tricity (Gdansk, Gdynia, Sopot)

The age of consent for all in Poland is 15 and was introduced in 1932. The Polish Constitution prohibits discrimination on all grounds. Marriage is restricted to a man and a woman only. Poland joined the European Union on the 1st of May 2004 and adopted anti-discrimination provisions laid down by EU directives. Since January 2008 Poland is part of the Schengen Zone.
Prime Minister Jaroslaw Kaczynski was finally voted out of office in 2007 and the new government was formed by Donald Tusk's Civic Platform (PO).
While the government of Donald Tusk had shown inertia where gay and lesbian equality was concerned, first indications of a small shift towards greater openness in this area of Polish politics nonetheless exist. In 2011, the Polish parliament saw its very first introduction of a registered partnership bill, presented by opposition party SDL. And when Tusk was re-elected in October of the same year, the left-wing populist Ruch Palikota, whose agenda includes the introduction of same-sex civil partnerships, also achieved a respectable result.
In recent years, the Gay Pride Parades have either been prohibited or were confronted with hostile counter-demonstrators if they did go ahead. The era of prohibitions at least is now over. On July 17 2010 the EuroPride took place in Warsaw with over 10 000 participants who marched through out the streets of Poland's capital. There was no violence. There are three Pride Festivals (with Pride Marches) in Poland: in April in Krakow called Queer May in June in Warsaw called Equality Days and in November in Poznan – Equality and Tolerance Days. The gay scene is mainly located Warsaw, although some other large cities like Krakow, Lodz, Poznan, Wroclaw and Gdansk have an emerging gay scene.

Das Mindestalter in Polen ist 15 und wurde schon 1932 eingeführt. Das polnische Grundgesetz verbietet Diskriminierung aus jeglichen Gründen, definiert die Ehe jedoch als ausschließlichen Bund zwischen Mann und Frau. Mit seiner Aufnahme in die Europäische Union am 1. Mai 2004 hat sich Polen zur Umsetzung der in den EU-Richtlinien stipulierten Antidiskriminierungsbestimmungen verpflichtet. Seit Januar 2008 gehört das Land auch zum Schengen-Gebiet.
Nach der Abwahl des Premierministers Jaroslaw Kaczynski im Jahr 2007 ist die neue Regierung von Donald Tusk und seiner Bürgerplatt-

form-Partei PO gebildet worden. Während die Regierung von Donald Tusk bei dem Thema Gleichberechtigung für Schwule und Lesben untätig blieb, gibt es dennoch erste Anzeichen einer kleinen Bewegung in Richtung einer Öffnung auf diesem Gebiet in der polnischen Politik. Die Oppositionspartei SLD hat 2011 erstmalig einen Gesetzentwurf zur Gleichberechtigung Homosexueller in das polnische Parlament eingebracht. Bei der Wiederwahl von Tusk im Oktober desselben Jahres errang die linkspopulistische Ruch Palikota einen Achtungserfolg, die unter anderem die Einführung von homosexuellen Lebenspartnerschaften auf ihrer Agenda hat.
In den letzten Jahren sind CSD-Veranstaltungen entweder verboten worden oder mussten sich andernfalls auf feindselige Gegendemonstranten gefasst machen. Die Zeit der Verbote scheint jetzt wenigstens vorbei zu sein: am 17. Juli 2010 hat der EuroPride mit über 10.000 Teilnehmern in der Hauptstadt Warschau stattgefunden, und das ganz ohne gewaltsame Übergriffe.
In Polen gibt es drei CSD-Veranstaltungen: „Queer May" in Krakau im April, die Warschauer „Gleichstellungstage" im Juni und im November die „Gleichberechtigungs- und Toleranztage" in Posen. Die Schwulenszene ist vorwiegend in Warschau konzentriert, entwickelt sich jedoch langsam auch in anderen Städten wie Krakau, Lodz, Posen, Breslau und Danzig.

Depuis 1932, la majorité sexuelle est fixée à 15 ans depuis 1932. La constitution polonaise interdit les discriminations en tout genre mais définit le mariage uniquement comme lien entre homme et femme. Avec son entrée dans l'UE le 1er mai 2004, la Pologne s'est engagée à adhérer aux directives anti-discriminations. Depuis janvier 2008, elle appartient à l'espace Schengen.
En 2007, le premier ministre Jaroslaw Kaczynski a dû passer le relais à Donald Tusk et son parti citoyen PO. Alors que le gouvernement de Donald Tusk sur le thème de l'égalité des droits pour les homosexuels et lesbiennes est resté inactif, des premiers signes d'ouverture dans ce sens se font sentir dans la classe politique polonaise. Le parti d'opposition SLD a pour la première fois présenté une proposition de loi sur l'égalité des droits des homosexuels devant le parlement polonais en 2011. Lors de la réelection de Tusk en octobre de la même année, le parti populiste de gauche Ruch Palikota a remporté une victoire considérable et porte dans son programme, entre autres, l'instauration d'un partenariat enregistré homosexuel.
Ces dernières années, les Gay Pride ont été soit interdites, soit elles ont fait face à des contre-manifestants hostiles. Le temps des interdictions paraît terminé tout du moins: le 17 juillet 2010, l'Europride a accueilli plus de 100.000 participants dans la capitale, sans acte de violence.
Il existe trois manifestations gays en Pologne: « Queer May » à Cracovie en avril, les « journée de l'égalité » à Varsovie en juin et en novembre les « journées de l'égalité et de la tolérance » à Poznan. La scène gay est majoritairement concentrée à Varsovie mais se développe lentement dans d'autres villes comme Cracovie, Lodz, Poznan, Wroclaw et Gdansk.

La edad mínima en Polonia es de 15 años y está vigente desde 1932. Su Constitución prohíbe la discriminación por cualquier motivo, pero define el matrimonio como la unión exclusiva entre hombre y mujer. La anexión a la UE el 1 mayo de 2004 le obliga a aplicar las directrices europeas contra la discriminación. Desde enero de 2008 también pertenece al espacio Schengen.
El nuevo gobierno de Donald Tusk y su partido Plataforma Cívica PO se formó en 2007 tras la destitución del primer ministro Jaroslaw Kaczynski. Mientras que el gobierno de Donald Tusk no hizo nada en cuanto a la igualdad de derechos para gays y lesbianas, en la actualidad hay señales de movimiento hacia una pequeña apertura en esta área de la política polaca. El partido de la oposición, el SLD, introdujo en 2011 por primera vez en el Parlamento polaco un proyecto de ley sobre la igualdad de derechos para los homosexuales. Con la reelección de Tusk, en octubre de ese mismo año, el populista de izquierda Ruch Palikota consiguió una victoria pírrica que le ha llevado a incluir en su agenda, entre otras, la introducción de las uniones civiles entre homosexuales.
En los últimos años se han prohibido o cancelado eventos del orgullo gay debido al ambiente hostil de las contra manifestaciones. Esta situación llega ahora a su fin: el 17 de julio 2010 tendrá lugar en Varsovia el Europride, con más de 10.000 participantes y sin ataques violentos.
En Polonia hay tres eventos de orgullo gay: "Queer May" en Cracovia (abril), "Días de Igualdad" en Varsovia (junio) y "Días de Igualdad de Derechos y Tolerancia" en Poznan (noviembre). El ambiente gay está principalmente en Varsovia, aunque se desarrolla también lentamente en ciudades como Cracovia, Lodz, Poznan, Breslavia y Gdansk.

L'età del consenso è di 15 anni e vige già dal 1932. La costituzione polacca vieta qualsiasi tipo di discriminazione e, tuttavia, definisce il matrimonio come unione esclusiva tra uomo e donna. Col suo ingresso nell'Unione Europea, l'1 Maggio 2004, la Polonia si è impegnata ad attuare le direttive antidiscriminatorie dell'UE. Da gennaio del 2008, il paese è entrato a far parte dell'area Schengen.
Dopo la destituzione del primo ministro Jaroslaw Kaczynski nel 2007 Donald Tusk e il suo partito Piattaforma Civica (PO) hanno formato il nuovo governo. Mentre il governo di Donald Tusk non ha fatto niente in tema di equiparazione per gay e lesbiche, nella politica polacca si manifestano, invece, dei primi segnali di apertura da parte di un piccolo movimento. Il partito di opposizione SLD ha presentato per la prima volta nel 2011 un progetto di legge sull'equiparazione dei diritti degli omosessuali. Le elezioni di ottobre dello stesso anno, oltre alla rielezione di Tusk hanno visto anche il considerevole successo del Ruch Palikota, un partito di sinistra che, tra le altre cose, ha nel suo programma l'introduzione delle unioni civili per gli omosessuali.
Negli ultimi anni i CSD sono stati o espressamente vietati o avversati da ostili contromanifestazioni. Adesso il tempo dei divieti sembra essere finito: il 17 luglio nella capitale, Varsavia, ha avuto luogo l'EuroPride, che contava più di 10.000 partecipanti e che si è svolto in maniera del tutto pacifica. In Polonia ci sono tre CSD: ad aprile il „Queer May" di Cracovia, a giugno le „giornate dell'uguaglianza di Varsavia" e a novembre „le giornate dell'uguaglianza e della tolleranza" a Poznan. La scena gay si concentra soprattutto a Varsavia, e lentamente si va estendendo verso altre città come Cracovia, Lodz, Poznan, Wroclaw e Danzica.

NATIONAL GAY INFO

Fellow.pl – Gay & Les Dating
www.fellow.pl
Gays and lesbians profiles.

gay.pl – Polish Gay Portal (G)
601 243 444 (mobile) english.gay.pl
Information about gay life, venues and accommodation in Poland in Polish and English. News, personals, profiles, gay guide to Poland, detailed information on Warsaw and Cracow. Also erotic section with Polish models.

Gejowo – Your Rainbow Portal
www.gejowo.pl
News, culture, lifestyle, personals. Information about gay life and gay venues in Poland in Polish.

innastrona (GLM)
www.innastrona.pl
News, culture, lifestyle, personals. Information about gay life and gay venues in Poland in Polish, English and German.

NATIONAL PUBLICATIONS

Adam
P.O. Box 47, Poznan 60-957 Poznan 66 (061) 842 74 70
Biggest national gay magazine with interviews, stories, pictures, personals with gay films on DVD.

AYOR
ul. Majowa 5 lok. 57, Warszawa 03-395 Warszawa (022) 811 88 38
Free gay magazine with guide.

Gejzer
ul. Orzechowa 25, Warszawa ✉ 02-244 Warszawa ☎ (022) 886 56 60
🖳 www.pinkpress.pl
Gay magazine and distributor.

NATIONAL COMPANIES

MasterColt – Leather Art (G)
ul. Zlotoryjska 9/35 ✉ 53-614 Wroclaw 🖳 www.mastercolt.pl
High quality toys, leatherwear and sex shop items.

NATIONAL GROUPS

Campaign Against Homophobia (KPH)
ul. Zelazna 68, Warszawa ✉ 00-866 Warszawa ☎ (022) 423 64 38
🖳 www.kph.org.pl
Largest gay and lesbian organisation in Poland fighting against homophobia. Central office of local KPH organisations around the country. Local groups of KPH are located in Warsaw, Torun, Trojmiasto (Tricity), Wroclaw, Slask (Silesia), Szczecin and several other cities. Wide range of activities.

Zjednoczenie na Rzecz Zyjacych z HIV/AIDS „Pozytywni w Teczy"
ul. Targowa 44 lok 1/1A, Warszawa ✉ 03-377 Warszawa
🖳 www.pozytywniwteczy.pl
HIV/AIDS gay info and help.

Bydgoszcz ☎ 52

BARS

Przystań (B D GLM MA) Fri & Sat 20-6h
ul. Warminskiego 17 ☎ 507 46 62 29 (mobile)

Red Art (B D GLM MA) Sun-Tue, Thu closed, Wed 18-2, Fri & Sat 20-4h
Dworcowa 72 *Entrance from the gate and yard of Matejki street #2*
☎ 609 715 910 (mobile)

Chorzów Batory ☎ 32

SAUNAS/BATHS

Therma Silesia (B CC DR DU G I p SA SB VS WO YC) 15-24, Sat 15-3h, Sun closed
ul. Lesna 10 *10 km from Katowice, entrance from Zelazna Street*
☎ (032) 246 79 19 🖳 www.gaysauna.pl
Three levels on 400 m²; two bars, three saunas, darkroom, TV, private rest areas, free internet, jaccuzzi. Clean, great atmosphere.

Debki

SWIMMING

-Debki Beach (AYOR G NU YC; approx. 65 km from Gdansk, the road ends in the village of Debki and from there walk west through the woods, over a covered wooden bridge and on for approx. 2 km along the beach).

Gdansk ☎ 58

BARS

Que Pasa (B D glm) 17-?h
Chmielna 101 ☎ 782 961 257 (mobile)
A gay-friendly pub/club.

SWIMMING

-Stogi (AYOR NU) (Tram N°8 to the roundabout in Stogi. Walk along the beach about 1.5 km to the right. Gay beach is right after the nude one)
-Chalupy/Debki.

CRUISING

-Main railway station Gdansk-Glowny
-Small park at the student's club »Zak« corner of Waly Jagiellonskie/ Hucisko-evenings and nights (AYOR).

Gdynia ☎ 58

SEX SHOPS/BLUE MOVIES

Pink Shop (g) 10-22h
ul. Zygmunta Augusta 9 ☎ (058) 661 11 30
Movies, toys, accessories and gay section.

SAUNAS/BATHS

Electro (B DR DU G H I p SA SB VS) 16-23h
ul. Inzynierska 52 Gdynia-Orlowo *Near SKM train station* ☎ 600 606 944
New sauna on 2 levels.

CRUISING

All are AYOR:
-Railway station Gdynia-Glówna
-Gdynia-Kolibki (NU) (take the City-train to Sopot/Kamienny Potok, walk approx. 300m in the direction of Gdynia, past a camping ground to the gas station then take the path on the right to the sea)
-Plac Kaszubski
-Skwer Kosciuszki (near the cinema, in front the White Fleet Harbor)
-Skwer Plymouth.

Katowice ☎ 32

BARS

Blue Box (B DR G I MA) Mon-Thu 16-2.30, Fri & Sat 17-5.30, Sun 17-2.30h
ul. Krzywa 2 ☎ (032) 206 82 34 🖳 bluebox.katowice.pl

MEN'S CLUBS

Fan Club (AC B CC DR G P VS YC) Sun-Thu 13-2, Fri & Sat -3h
ul. Kordeckiego 3 *Near main train station* ☎ 505 778 620 (mobile)
🖳 www.gayclub.pl
The only bar with darkrooms in the Silesia (Slask) district.

SEX SHOPS/BLUE MOVIES

Ars Amandi (G)
ul. Poniatowskiego 19 ☎ 501 545 068 (mobile)
DVDs, videos and erotic articles.

Pink Shop (g VS) 10-22h
ul. Piastowska 3 ☎ (032) 258 58 68
Movies, toys, accessories, and video cabins.

SAUNAS/BATHS

Tropicana Sauna Club (! B CC DR DU G I M MA p SA SB SOL VS WH) Mon-Thu 12-24, Fri 14-6, Sat 16-6, Sun 16-24h
ul. Mariacka 14 *City centre, 500 m from the railway station* ☎ (032) 206 94 10
🖳 tropicanasauna.republika.pl
Sauna on two floors. Bar, sauna, steam room, jacuzzi, cabins, TV room & internet.

Koszalin ☎ 94

BARS

Oscar (B DR GLM MA) 12-?h
ul. Matejki 5

Kraków ☎ 12

GAY INFO

GayGuide.Net Cracow (GLM) Hotline 16-20h
☎ (+36 309) 32 33 34 🖳 gayguide.net/Europe/Poland

MEN'S CLUBS

Blue XL (AC B CC DR F G H I LAB MA P S SL SNU ST T VS) 19-?h
ul. Jozefa Dietla 85, Srodmiescie *At the corner of Josefa Dietla / Starowislna Street* ☎ (012) 421 64 89 🖳 www.bluexl.pl
Safe-sex parties with private entry from the back. Also B&B. Friday & Saturdy Private Underwear Sex Parties.

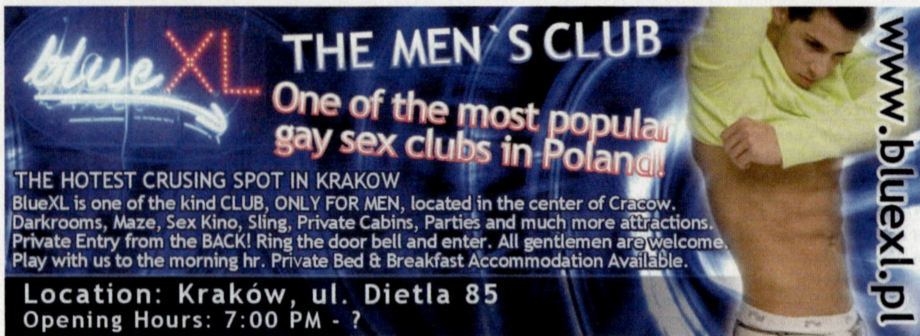

■ **Ciemnia Cruising Bar** (B DR G MA P VS)
Sun-Thu 20-2, Fri -4, Sat -5
Krowoderska 31 *Turn on right next to the hostel entrance,then see the black gate with Ciemnia logo at the end of the passage, ring bell, entrance to the celler* ☎ 0692 651 311 (mobile) 💻 www.ciemnia.com.pl
The only sex cruising bar in Krakow. Regular most popular underwear and naked parties usually on the first and third Saturday of the month. Also other theme dress-code parties.

■ **XLLL Fetish Underwear Party** (AC B CC DR F G m P VS WE YC)
Fri 22-6, Sat -7h
ul. Jozefa Dietla 85 *Above the Gay Bar BlueXL* ☎ (692) 116 412 (mobile) 💻 www.bluexl.pl
Dresscode underwear or nothing but shoes only a must.

CAFES

■ **Club Oko Cafe** (B GLM MA)
ul. Wegierska 1 *Tram 3/6/8/13/24; 50 m from Rynek Podgorski* ☎ (012) 423 59 79 💻 www.cluboko.pl
Small photo gallery with three rooms, which organizes monthly exhibitions. Sat 19h „Strange Opera Evening" with live opera music.

DANCECLUBS

■ **Cocon** (AC B D DR G OS) Thu, Fri-Sun 21-?h
ul. Gazowa 21 *Old Jewish district Kazimierz, right on the bank of Vistula River. Walking distance from the Old Town* ☎ (012) 632 22 96 💻 www.klub-cocon.pl
The biggest gay disco in Cracow, karaoke on Thu, oldies on Fri, house party on Sat. Cocon offers 2 big dance floors, 3 bars and a summer garden.

■ **Fresh** (B D GLM MA p S SNU ST WE) Thu & Sun 21-2, Fri & Sat 21-? h
Krowoderska 31 *Entrance in the passage near Girafe hostel, black doors on the left, doorbell*
Modern dance club, special events.

■ **LaF** (AC B D DR gLm OS) Thu 18 -?, Fri & Sat 20-?h
Pl. Wolnica 7 ☎ 601 272 902 💻 www.lafklub.pl
Mixed gay and lesbian place. Lots of girls.

SEX SHOPS/BLUE MOVIES

■ **Black & White** (CC DR glm MA VS) 11-22h
ul. Westerplatte 3 *Near central station* ☎ (012) 429 20 91
Video cabins, cinema and shop.

SAUNAS/BATHS

■ **Spartakus** (AC b DR DU G I m MC OS RR SA SB WO)
11-23, Sun 14-21h
ul. Konopnickiej 20 *Opp. Wawel Castle, bus 114, 119* ☎ (012) 266 60 22 💻 spartakus.queer.pl
Clean and friendly sauna on three floors, popular with a middle aged crowd. Internet available in the lounge and a sundeck in summer. A unique opportunity to sunbath completely nude in center of the city with a view on Vistula river. The steam room is particularly popular. The staff is very friendly and speaks English and German.

APARTMENTS

■ **Fineapartment.pl** (H)
ul. Krowoderska 58 / 18 ☎ (012) 631 32 50 💻 www.fineapartment.pl

■ **Noce** (glm H) Mon-Fri 10-18, Sat 10-14h
ul. Radziwillowska 29/1 *Across Dworca Glównego* ☎ (012) 422 63 62 💻 www.noce.pl
German, English, French, Russian and Polish speeking staff. Office in Kraków.

SWIMMING

-Kryspinow Beach (G nu) (at the artificial lake in Kryspinow, near Balice Airport. Bus 192 and then a 15 mins walk).

CRUISING

-Planty (AYOR R) (Park around the old town, especially at the side of the central station).

Lodz ☎ 42

DANCECLUBS

■ **Ganimedes Dyskoteka** (B CC D DR GLM MA MSG P S SNU ST T)
Daily from 20h. Disco Fri & Sat from 21h
ul. Piotrkowska 140 *City Centre; Entrance also from Lub Roosvelta 10* ☎ (042) 42 236 57 17 💻 www.ganimedes.net
Club (gay and lesbian mixed) on two floors.

■ **Narraganset** (! B D DR GLM S ST T VS) Fri 20-5 & Sat -6, Pub open daily from 20-?h
ul. Gdanska 129 *Downtown* ☎ 601 317 758 (mobile) 💻 narraganset.pl
Big disco with drag queens behind the bar. Entrance fee applies. Popular place with a big darkroom. Now with a bar open daily from 20h.

SEX SHOPS/BLUE MOVIES

■ **Erotic Land** (AC b CC DR G MA VS) 10-21h, Sun closed
ul. Piotrkowska 48 ☎ (042) 630 26 91 💻 www.eroticland.pl
Also at Piotrkowska 82 and ul. Sienkiewicza 35, Kosciuszki 28. Sex shops with video rooms.

■ **Pink Shop** (g VS) 10-22h
ul. Rzgowska 26/28 ☎ (042) 681 20 65

■ **Videoland** (B CC DR GLM MC VS) 10-22h
ul. Kosciuszki 28 ☎ (042) 630 26 91

SAUNAS/BATHS

■ **Ganimedes Sauna** (B CC DR DU FH G GH m MA MSG P SA SB VS WH) 15-?, Sun from 14h
ul. Roosevelta 10 *The sauna is under Ganimedes club, but the entrance is from the parking lot at Roosevelta 10* ☎ 519 382 210 (mobile) 💻 www.ganimedes.net

APARTMENTS

■ **Arrivia B&B** (bf H)
ul. Narutowicza 24/34 ☎ (042) 661 01 00 💻 www.arrivia.pl

CRUISING

-Plac Dabrowskiego in front of the Opera House
-Park Zdrowie (Al. Unii)
-Park Moniuszki (Ulica Nartowicza/Ulica Armi Ludowej).

Lublin

CRUISING

-Plac Litewski.

Poznan ☎ 61

BARS

■ **Elektrownia** (B DR G MA)
Sun & Tue 20-6, Mon & Wed -5, Thu -7, Fri & Sat -10h
Sw. Marcin 23 ☎ 607 259 702 (mobile) 💻 clubelektrownia.blogspot.com

■ **Hallo Cafe** (B G MA p VS) 14-?h
ul. Rybaki 22

MEN'S CLUBS

■ **Eagle club** (B DR G MA P VS)
Mon-Thu 15 -2, Fri & Sat 5-6, Sun 20-2h
ul. Rybaki 13 A ☎ 507 969 885 💻 www.eagleclub.pl
Cinema and darkrooms. Former Klub Heros.

■ **Klub Dark Angels** (B D DR F G I MA S SNU)
Mon-Thu 18-2, Fri+Sat -5h
ul. Garabary 54 ☎ 061 853 88 62 💻 www.clubdarkangels.com

■ **Pokusa-Kino** (B DR G MA p VS)
Mon & Wed 10-5, Tue -6,Thu -7, Fri-Mon open non-stop
Sw. Marcin 23 ☎ 607 259 702
💻 pl-pl.facebook.com/people/Kino-Pokusa/100001082719146
Cinema and darkroom.

DANCECLUBS

■ **Voliera** (B D DR G MA) Tue, Fri & Sun 21-?h
ul. Garbary 112 *Near coffee house Astra* ☎ 607 505 258
Onsite parking. Big bar, dark room and VIP room.

SAUNAS/BATHS

■ **Amigo Sauna Club** (AC B DR DU G I M MA MSG p RR SA SB SOL VS WE) Mon-Thu 16-22, Fri & Sat -24h, Sun closed
Osiedle Lecha 120 *Back side of drugstore, next to Outpatient Clinic, tram 1, 5, 17- Osidle Czecha* ☎ 61 872 24 48 💻 www.amigosauna.pl
Located outside the city centre, but very popular.

HOTELS

■ **IBB Andersia Hotel** (AC B BF CC H I MSG PI RR SA SB SOL WH WO)
Plac Wladyslawa Andersa 3 *Andersa Square* ☎ (061) 667 80 00
💻 www.andersiahotel.pl
Luxury hotel with restaurant, spa and workout amenities.

APARTMENTS

■ **Extravaganza Apartments** (H)
ul. Rybaki 13 ☎ 504 891 243

SWIMMING

-Biskupice (g NU) (from Poznan go to Gniezno to the lake of Kowalkie).

Sopot ☎ 58

BARS

■ **Retromaniak** (B D glm) 19-?h. Mon closed
ul. Niepodleglosci 771 *Turn after Ruch Kiosk, opp. Europa Hotel*
☎ 512 898 423 (mobile) 💻 retromaniak.com.pl

DANCECLUBS

■ **Club sixty9** (AC B CC D GLM I MA S ST VS)
Sun-Thu 18-23, Fri & Sat 21-5h
Kosciuszki 68a ☎ 58 717 21 74 (mobile)
💻 www.sixty9.pl
The club is located in an old fashioned house in a residential area of Sopot.

■ **Elton** (B CC D GLM m MA S ST VS) Fri & Sat 21-5h
ul. Sportowa 1 *Located near SKM city train station*

Szczecin ☎ 91

BARS

■ **Inferno-Club** (AC B CC D GLM H I MA P S VS WE)
Wed, Fri & Sat 21-5h
ul. Wojska Polskiego 20 ☎ 509 092 621 (mobile)
☎ 91 488 40 54 💻 www.inferno-club.pl
Fashionable place, well stocked bars and large dancefloor, House Music played by well-known Djs from Poland and abroad.

MEN'S CLUBS

■ **Club Enigma** (B D G MA p)
Daily from 20-1 (Wed from 18.30) Fri & Sat -3h
ul. Wielka Odrzanska 24/25 *In the courtyard* ☎ 692 55 20 70 (mobile)
💻 www.enigmapub.pl
Men only.

CRUISING

-Plac Brama Portowa & Planty (near Plac Zwyciestwa).

Torun ☎ 56

DANCECLUBS

■ **Incognito Avangard** (B D G MC ST)
Mon-Thu 18-24, Fri & Sat 18-6h, Sun closed
ul. Jeczmienna 13 ☎ 785 047 423 (mobile)

CRUISING

All are AYOR:
-Plac Rapackiego
-Park near Club Wodnik (evenings).

Warszawa ☎ 22

Warsaw is Poland's largest city and the main economic, cultural and educational centre. The city spans the Wisla (Vistula River), and all of the main tourists sites are on the left bank, while the right bank contains the increasingly fashionable Praga district. Warsaw has the biggest gay scene and is the most open city for gays and lesbians in Poland. More and more clubs and cafes are gay-friendly.

Warschau ist Polens größte Stadt und auch das wichtigste Wirtschafts-, Kultur- und Bildungszentrum. Die Wisla fließt mitten durch die Stadt. Die wichtigsten touristischen Einrichtungen liegen am linken Ufer, während sich das zunehmend in Mode kommende Viertel Praga am rechten Ufer befindet. Warschau hat die größte Schwulenszene und ist die offenste Stadt für Schwule und Lesben in Polen. Immer mehr Clubs und Cafes sind lesben- und schwulenfreundlich.

Varsovie est la plus grande ville du pays et représente également son centre économique, culturel et universitaire. La Vistule partage la ville en deux : sur la rive gauche, on trouve les principales attractions touristiques tandis que le quartier « Praga » se développe sur la rive droite et devient un quartier des plus tendance. Varsovie a la plus grande scène gay et est la ville la plus ouverte pour les homos et les lesbiennes en Pologne. De plus en plus de clubs et de cafés ont une attitude ouverte vis-à-vis des gays et des aux lesbiennes.

Varsovia es la ciudad más grande de Polonia y también el centro económico, cultural y profesional más importante. El río Wisla transcurre por el centro de la ciudad. Las localizaciones más turísticas se encuentran en la orilla izquierda, mientras que el creciente barrio de moda, Praga, está situado en la orilla derecha. Varsovia tiene el ambiente gay más grande y es la ciudad más abierta para gays y lesbianas en Polonia. Cada vez hay más clubs y cafés abiertos a gays y lesbianas.

Varsavia è la città più grande della Polonia ma anche il centro economico e culturale più importante del paese. La Vistola scorre attraverso il centro della città. Le attrazioni turistiche più importanti si trovano sulla riva sinistra, mentre il quartiere Praga – una zona che sta diventando sempre più trendy – è situato sulla riva destra. Varsavia ha la più grande scena gay di tutta la Polonia e ne è anche la città più aperta. Sempre più club e bar diventano gay-friendly.

NATIONAL COMPANIES

■ **gaywarsaw.pl** (GLM MA)
www.gaywarsaw.pl
Polish gay website.

BARS

■ **City** (B GLM I S) 16-2h
Al. Jana Pawla II 43a paw 28b www.clubcity.pl
■ **Lodi Dodi** (B DR G I) Sun-Thu 18- 24, Fri & Sat 18-?h
ul. Wilcza 23 *Next to the police station* www.lodidodi.pl/en
■ **Rasko** (AC B CC d GLM MA S SNU ST WE) 17-3h
ul. Burakowska 12 ☎ 22 838 01 30 www.klubrasko.pl
Cafe/bar/disco near to Arcadia shopping centre. Mixed gay/lesbian young crowd.

MEN'S CLUBS

■ **fanTOM** (! B DR G MA p) Mon-Thu 14-2, Fri -4, Sat -4, Sun 16-2h
ul. Bracka 20 a *Entrance from the yard of Bracka 20, left gate to the club, right to the sauna – 3rd door, ring doorbell* ☎ (22) 828 54 09
www.fantomwarsaw.com
With more than fifteen years the oldest gay establishment in Poland. Bar, gay sex shop, sex club and sauna in one. The place is busy every day, not only at the weekends. If you are looking for sex definitely the no.1 in Warsaw.

■ **Wild Club** (B DR f G H MA P VS)
Tue-Thu 19-? (till the last guest) Fri-Sun 21-?h
ul. Chlodna 39 lok.3 ☎ 791 851 175
www.wild.waw.pl
Two levels, dresscode, theme parties (naked, underwear, fetish), security. See www.wild.waw.pl for details.

CAFES

■ **Bastylia** (B glm MA)
ul. Mokotowska 17 *Near pl. Zbawiciela* ☎ (22) 825 01 57
Gay-friendly creperia, run by lesbians.

DANCECLUBS

■ **Galeria** (B D GLM MA ST) 18-?h
Plac Mirowski 1 ☎ (22) 850 41 55
Bar with little dancefloor and drag queen shows. Faktoria Milorda – gay/lesbian theatre – shows on Mondays.
■ **Glam Club** (B D GLM MA)
ul. Zurawia 22 *M° Centrum* ☎ 510 631 740
pl-pl.facebook.com/pages/GLAM-CLUB/113850325306747
Gay-friendly place. Check website for dates.
■ **Hunters Club** (AC B CC D G MA S SNU WE)
Fri 21-4, Sat 18-6, Sun 21-3h
ul. Jasna 1 www.huntersclub.pl
New gay club with gogo-boys in downtown Warsaw.
■ **M25** (B D glm MA)
ul. Minska 25 www.m25.waw.pl
Gay-friendly place, not open every weekend. Electro music. Check website for dates.
■ **Toro** (! AC B D DR GLM S ST) 20-5h, Mon closed
ul. Marszalkowska 3/5 *Entrance from Zoli Street* ☎ (22) 825 60 14
www.toro.waw.pl
Bar and disco in the centre on 2 floors. Local atmosphere. Large darkroom. Yes, the disco really starts at 20h! At the weekends the most popular gay/lesbian disco in town. Cover charge on Fri & Sat – 15 zl, On Sun cover charge – 20 zl – drink as much beer as you want.

SEX SHOPS/BLUE MOVIES

■ **Bizzariusz** (g OC VS) 10-22, Sat 10-18h, Sun closed
ul. Nowogrodzka 46/15a *Close to Warszawa Central Station*
☎ (22) 622 11 79 www.wamper.pl/bizzariusz.php
The only erotic movie theatre in Warsaw, gay-friendly, gay movies shown in the small hall, also video booths and sex shop. Quite sexy and cruisy.
■ **Pink Shop I** (g VS) 10-22h
Al. Jana Pawla II 46/48 – Pawilon 1A *Three stops from central station with any tram or bus towards Zoliborz* www.gayshop.com.pl/index.php
Movies, toys, accessories and video room.
■ **Pink Shop II** (g VS) 10-22h
ul. Chmielna 104 *100 m from railway station* ☎ (22) 654 16 68
www.gayshop.com.pl/index.php
Movies, toys, accessories and video room.
■ **Pink Shop III** (g VS) Mon-Fri 9-21h
ul. Orzechowa 25 ☎ (22) 499 99 26

SAUNAS/BATHS

■ **fanTOM** (B CC DR DU FC G MA MSG p SA SB SH VS WH)
Mon-Sat 14-24, Sun 16-24h
ul. Bracka 20 a *Tram 7/9/25-Smyk shopping centre, in the yard on the right gate, 3rd door* ☎ (22) 828 54 09 fantomwarsaw.com
The only gay everyday-sauna. Also sex shop. Best time from 18-22h. Complementary free entrance to fanTOM club, which is on the other side of the underground. Very popular. This is where the action is.
■ **Club Sauna Galla** (B DU G MA RR SA)
Mon-Thu 14-23, Fri -1, Sat 12-1, Sun -23h
ul. Ptasia 2 ☎ (22) 652 19 86
www.saunagalla.com
■ **Heaven Sauna** (AC B CC DR DU FC G I LAB m MA MSG RR SA SB VS WO) Mon-Thu 14-24, Fri 14-3, Sat 13 – Sun -24 (non-stop)

ul. Waliców 13 *City centre* ☏ (22) 620 02 55
🖳 www.heavensauna.pl

LEATHER & FETISH SHOPS

■ **reFForm Fetish Store** (CC F GLM)
13-18, Sat 14-18h, Sun closed
Prosta 2/14 ☏ 501 199 919 🖳 www.refform.pl
This new outlet displays and sells a comprehensive range of products.

GUEST HOUSES

■ **Friends** (BF G MSG RWS RWT VA) All year
ul. Sienkiewicza 4 *Close to M° Centrum, rail station Centralny, Palace of Culture & Science* ☏ 601 243 444 (mobile infoline)
The only gay guesthouse in Warsaw. Directly in the centre and the middle of the gay scene. Three rooms with private shower. Reservations via email or telephone required in advance.

GENERAL GROUPS

■ **Lambda Warszawa Association & Information and Support Centre** Gay switchboard, Tue-Sat 18-21h
ul. Zurawia 24 A ☏ (022) 628 52 22
🖳 www.lambdawarszawa.org
Gay & lesbian organization, info and helpline, also several support groups.

■ **Parada Rownosci**
ul. Gustawa Morcinka 20/4 ☏ (0888) 666 999 (mobile)
🖳 www.paradarownosci.eu
Organisation Team of Warszawa Gay Pride.

CRUISING

-Park Skaryszewski-Praga AYOR
-Plac Trzech Krzyzy (Park close to Ulica Ksiazeca, at night). AYOR
-Dworzec Centralny (Central railway station) – toilets in the underground near to Zlote Tarasy shopping centre
-Zlote Tarasy shopping centre.

Wroclaw ☏ 71

BARS

■ **H2O Caffe** (B D GLM MA)
Tue & Wed 20- 2, Thu -4, Fri -5, Sat -6, Sun -?h, Mon closed
ul. Zelwerowicza 16/18 *Near Music Academy, tram 0/10/12/14 or bus 127/135/144 – Imaja P.* ☏ (071) 359 27 70 🖳 h2o-wroc.eu
Popular danceclub with karaoke on Tue and Thu.

MEN'S CLUBS

■ **Cactus Klub** (B DR G MA VS WE) 18-2, Fri & Sat 18-5h
ul. Zelwerowicza 18a ☏ 512 370 348 (mobile)
🖳 www.cactusclub.pl

DANCECLUBS

■ **Coffee Planet** (B D glm YC)
Rynek Starego Miasta *Passage under the blue sun*
☏ (071) 796 45 40 🖳 www.coffeeplanet.pl
Gay-friendly disco at weekends.

SEX SHOPS/BLUE MOVIES

■ **Pink Shop** (g VS) Mon-Sat 10-22, Sun -17h
ul. Biskupia 10/10b
🖳 www.pinkshop.pl/gej_index.htm
Movies, toys, accessories and video room.

SWIMMING

-Opatowicka Isle (behind the zoo).

CRUISING

-Ulica Swidnicka (opposite the opera)
-Opposite Palace of Justice
-Hanka Sawicka Park
-Wzgórze Polskie (near Panorama Raclawicka).

Portugal

Name: Portugal Portogallo
Location: Southwest Europe
Initials: P
Time: GMT
International Country Code: ☏ 351 (no area codes)
International Access Code: ☏ 00
Language: Portuguese
Area: 92,345 km² / 35,654 sq miles
Currency: 1 Euro (€) = 100 Cents
Population: 10,549,000
Capital: Lisboa
Religions: 88% Roman Catholic
Climate: A mix of Atlantic and Mediterranean climates, cooler and wetter in the north and warmer and drier in the south.
Important gay cities: Lisboa, Porto

In strictly catholic Portugal the parliament approved the homosexual marriage proposal at the beginning of January 2010. This approval is a triumph in ultra-conservative Portugal.
The age of consent is 16 in Portugal. Gays and lesbians are highly accepted and take part in Portuguese society, often mixing with heterosexuals in bars and clubs. There are several organizations up and down the country which are dedicated to various gay and lesbian interest groups and produce the weekly radio broadcast „Vidas Alternativas". The Gay Pride events in Lisbon and Porto enjoy ever growing popularity and the Lisbon gay and lesbian film festival is one of the best in Europe. Portugal is a very beautiful country and the birthplace of the very first empire to open up to globalization. The country has a rich historical heritage and features outstandingly attractive landscapes, as well as a multi-faceted coastline. The Portuguese language and culture can be encountered around the world, from Brazil to Goa. Portugal is currently becoming increasingly popular as a gay destination offering eccentric Lisbon, one of Europe's most magnificent cities, baroque Porto, surrounded by historically grown small towns and the unique wine-growing regions Douro and Vinho Verde, the Algarve with its breathtaking coast and pleasant climate, the incomparably beautiful islands of Madeira and the Azores, plus numerous historic towns, and last but not least the delicious cuisine and first-rate wines.

Im streng katholischen Portugal hat das Parlament Anfang Januar 2010 für die Einführung der Homosexuellenehe gestimmt. Die Abstimmung ist ein großer Erfolg im erzkonservativen Portugal.
In Portugal liegt das Schutzalter bei 16 Jahren. Schwule und Lesben erfahren in Portugal eine hohe Akzeptanz und sind ein Teil der Gesellschaft, in Bars und Discos mischen sie sich oft unter Heterosexuelle. Es gibt mehrere Organisationen in ganz Portugal, die sich verschiedenen schwulen und lesbischen Gruppen widmen und das wöchentliche Radioprogamm „Vidas Alternativas" auf die Beine stellen. Die Gay Prides in Lissabon und Porto erfreuen sich wachsender Beliebtheit und das Lissabon International Gay and Lesbian Filmfestival zählt zu den besten Europas.
Portugal ist ein wunderschönes Land und die Wiege des ersten Weltreichs, das sich der Globalisierung öffnete. Das Land ist reich an Geschichte und besitzt außerordentlich reizvolle Landschaften und eine vielgestaltige Küste. Die portugiesische Sprache und Kultur sind in aller Welt anzutreffen, von Brasilien bis nach Goa. Portugal erfreut sich heute wachsender Beliebtheit als schwules Reiseziel: das exzentrische Lissabon, eine der prachtvollsten Hauptstädte Europas, das von historisch gewachsenen Städtchen und den einzigartigen Weinbaugebieten Douro und Vinho Verde umgebene, barocke Porto, die Algarve mit ihrer atemberaubenden Küste und dem angenehmen Klima, die unvergleichlich schönen Inseln Madeira und die Azoren sowie zahlreiche historische Städte und nicht zuletzt die köstliche Küche und die hervorragenden Weine.

Au Portual, pays en soi très catholique, le parlement a voté début janvier 2010 l'instauration du mariage gay. Ce vote est une grande victoire dans ce pays ultra conservateur.
La majorité sexuelle au Portugal est fixée à 16 ans. Gays et lesbiennes bénéficient au Portugal d'une bonne acceptation générale et sont une partie intégrante de la société, ils se mélangent souvent aux hétérosexuels dans les bars et les boîtes. Il existe plusieurs organisations dans tout le Portugal qui s'adressent à différents groupes gays et lesbiens et qui mettent sur pied le programme radio hebdomadaire „Vidas Alternativas". Les Gay Pride à Lisbonne et Porto sont de plus en plus populaires et le Festival International du Film Gay et Lesbien compte parmi les meilleurs d'Europe. Le Portugal est un pays magnifique et le berceau du premier empire planétaire et ouvert à la mondialisation. Le pays possède une histoire très riche, de superbes paysages ainsi que des côtes très variées. La langue et la culture portugaises se retrouvent de part le monde, du Brésil jusqu'à Goa. Le Portugal bénéficie d'une popularité grandissante en tant que destination gay : L'excentrique Lisbonne, une des villes européennes les plus magnifiques, l'historique et baroque Porto entourée des vignobles hors-pairs du Douro und Vinho Verde, l'Algarve avec ses côtes à couper le souffle et son agréable climat, les îles à la beauté incomparable de Madère et des Açores de même que de nombreuses villes chargées d'histoire, sans parler d'une savoureuse gastronomie et d'excellents vins.

A principios de enero de 2010 el parlamento portugués votó a favor de la introducción del matrimonio homosexual. Esta votación significa un gran éxito para un país tan conservador e incondicionalmente católico como Portugal.
En Portugal la edad de consentimiento está en los 16 años. Homosexuales y lesbianas disfrutan en Portugal de una gran aceptación y forman parte de la sociedad, en los bares y discotecas se mezclan a menudo con los heterosexuales. Existen muchas organizaciones en todo Portugal que se dedican a diferentes grupos gay-lésbicos y que elaboran el programa radiofónico „Vidas Alternativas". Las Marchas del Orgullo en Lisboa y Porto tiene un éxito creciente y el festival internacional de cine gay-lésbico de Lisboa es uno de los mejores de Europa. Portugal es un país fantástico y es la cuna del primer imperio mundial que se abrió a la globalización. El país es rico en historia y posee paisajes extraordinariamente bonitos y una costa muy variada. La lengua y cultura portuguesas se hallan en todo el mundo, desde Brasil a Goa. Portugal goza hoy de un creciente éxito como destino turístico gay – la excéntrica Lisboa, una de las capitales más fantásticas

de Europa, la barroca Porto, con su núcleo histórico y rodeada de las zonas vinícolas del Douro y Vinho Verde, el Algarve con sus impresionantes costas y agradable clima, las incomparables islas de Madeira y las Azores así como otras ciudades históricas, sin olvidar su deliciosa gastronomía y los fantásticos vinos.

All'inizio di gennaio del 2010 il Parlamento del cattolicissimo Portogallo ha votato in favore dell'introduzione delle unioni omosessuali. Il risultato del voto è stato un enorme successo per un Paese ultraconservatore come il Portogallo.
L'età del consenso è di 16 anni. Gay e lesbiche sono ben integrati nella società portoghese. Nei bar e nelle discoteche non è raro vederli perfettamente integrati tra gli eterosessuali. In Portogallo ci sono molte organizzazioni che si dedicano ai diversi gruppi omosessuali e lesbici. Inoltre la comunità omosessuale ha messo su un programma radio settimanale chiamato Vidas Alternativas. I gay pride a Lisbona e a Porto diventano sempre più popolari e il festival internazionale del film gay e lesbico si attesta tra i migliori d'Europa. Il Portogallo è un paese magnifico e culla del primo impero mondiale che si aprì alla globalizzazione. Il paese è ricco di storia e di paesaggi molto suggestivi. Le sue lunghe coste sono molto variegate. La lingua e la cultura portoghese hanno conquistato il mondo: dal Brasile fino allo stato di Goa. Il Portogallo diventa meta sempre più amata da turisti gay. Il Portogallo ha davvero molto da offrire: l'eccentrica Lisbona, una delle più splendide capitali europee, circondata da cittadine ricche di storia e dai vigneti Douro e Vinho Verde, la barocca Porto, l'Algarve con il suo piacevolissimo clima e con la sua costa mozza fiato, le bellissime isole Madeira e le Azzorre, molte città storiche e non ultima l'ottima cucina e il buon vino.

NATIONAL PUBLICATIONS

Com' Out (GLM MA)
☎ 213 805 048 💻 www.com-out.pt
Stylish three-monthly gay magazine.

Jornal PÚBICO (GLM)
☎ 9650 86300 💻 www.jornal-pubico.blogspot.com

Revista KORPUS (GLM)
Apartado 22868 ✉ 1147-501 Lisboa ☎ 9650 86300
💻 www.revista-korpus.blogspot.com
Publisher of Lisbon Gay Guide.

NATIONAL COMPANIES

Be Travel Group All year
Av. D. João II, Lote 1.02.2.2 C – 1° andar ✉ 1990-095 Lisbon
☎ 211 106 006
Providing the best offers for the LGBT markets. Co-operations around the world with the best gay tour operators.

NATIONAL GROUPS

ILGA-Portugal (B GLM I MA) Wed-Sat 18-23h
Rua de São Lázaro, 88 ✉ 1150 Lisboa ☎ 218 873 918
💻 www.ilga-portugal.pt
Organizer of Gay Pride. The Lesbian and Gay Community Center has legal, medical, psychological and HIV counselling (by appointment) as well as a small bookstore, cafeteria and internet access.

Liga Portuguesa Contra a SIDA
Rua Crucifixo, 40 ✉ 1100-183 Lisboa *4th floor* ☎ 213 225 575
💻 www.ligacontrasida.org

Opus Gay Associação/Association (GLM I)
Rua da Ilha Terceira, 34 ✉ 1000-173 Lisboa *2nd floor* ☎ 213 151 396
💻 www.opusgay.org
Opus Gay Association has legal, psychological, HIV and religious assistance, internet cafe as well as a „dog and cat sitter" service.

Rede Ex Aequo (GLM)
Rua de São Lázaro, 88 ✉ 1150-333 Lisboa ☎ 968 781 841
💻 www.rea.pt/forum
LGBT groups in all Portugal. Informations in schools about sexual orientation and gender identity.

Albufeira – Algarve

BARS

Best Of (AC B D GLM MA S SNU ST) Winter: Tue-Sat 22-?, Summer: 22-?h
Centro Comercial Arcadas, Praia dos Aveiros, Oura *400m from the main strip* ☎ 963 568 505
Sophisticated decoration with sofas and a large outdoor sitting area.

DANCECLUBS

Pride Disco (AC B CC D GLM MA S ST) July/August: every day 23-7, Sep-June: Wed-Sun 23-7h
Av. Sá Carneiro, Vilanova Resort Lote 1-B 1° Andar
☎ 963 686 142 (mobile) 💻 www.pride-disco.com
Gay disco with shows and other events.

SAUNAS/BATHS

Thermas Pride – Spa for Men (! AC AK B DR DU G LAB MA MSG P RR SA SB VS WH) 20-4h
Av. dos Descobrimentos, Lote 21 *Five mins from Albufeira Center, next to the Fire Station* ☎ 963 686 142 (mobile)
💻 www.thermas-pride.com
Only gay sauna in Algarve; located near bars and nightlife.

HOTELS

Vila Galé Praia (AC B BF CC glm H M MA OS PI RWS RWT SA SB WH) All year
Praia da Galé, Lote 33 – Apartado 2204 ☎ 289 590 180
💻 www.vilagale.pt
SPARTACUS readers get 25% discount of the rack-rate (Code Price: SPTS06). Bookings by mail, fax or telephone.

GUEST HOUSES

Thermas Pride – Guest House (AC B BF G I PK RWB RWS RWT SA VA) All year, 24hrs
Av. dos Descobrimentos, Lote 21 *Next to fire station, in front of city hall*
☎ 963 686 142 (mobile) 💻 www.thermas-pride.com
Three double rooms and one suite; free access to the gay-sauna for male guests.

SWIMMING

Armação de Pêra: Praia Grande and sand dunes

CRUISING

-Centro Comercial Modelo (in the day)
-Montechoro, Pastelaria „Martinique"
-Av. connecting Montechoro & Oura beach

Braga – Minho

HEALTH GROUPS

Dispensario de Higiene Social Mon-Fri 9-12h
Largo Poulo Osorio ☎ 25 327 041
Ask for AIDS Help Group.

CRUISING

-Bom Jesus do Monte (in the park)
-Sta. Barbara Gardens
-Av. dos Combatentes (Avenue).

Caminha – Minho

SWIMMING

-Praia do Moledo, between public beach of „Praia de Âncora and Caminha; from [P] of Praia de Âncora by foot through the nice wood (! NU)

Carvoeiro – Algarve

GUEST HOUSES

■ **Casa Marhaba** (B BF G I M MA NU OS PI PK RWS VA VS WH) Apr-Sep
Rua de Benagil, Carvoeiro *50 km west from Faro Airport* ☎ 282 358 720
🖳 www.casamarhaba.com
Friendly and private guesthouse with four double bedrooms and one triple bedroom (all with en-suite bath), set in one acre of land in a rural area, near to the beach.

Coimbra – Beira – Litoral

CAFES

■ **Pigalle** (B g r YC) 7-21h
Av. Sá da Bandeira 123/125 ☎ 239 826 559
Students meeting place.

CRUISING

-Shopping Centre Sofia
-Railway Station (Coimbra A)
-Praça da République
-University Stadion (Santa Clara)
-Baixa
-South Rio Mondego (parking right hand side of the river).

Costa da Caparica – Estremadura

APARTMENTS

■ **Caparica Beach Apartments** (CC glm MSG)
Av. Movimento das Forças Armadas, 34 ☎ 914 176 969
🖳 www.casadobairro.pt
Four to six persons per unit; three mins walk from the beach. Gay owned.

SWIMMING

-Costa da Caparica, Beach (Praia) 17, 18, 19 (AYOR G NU); best place beach 19, stay away from the bushes after dark. Take the bus in Praça de Espanha to Costa da Caparica and then the small train (only in summer), at the end of the main pedestrian street, by the water front, to the beach No 17/19, last train returns at around 18h or take the ferry from M° Cais do Sodré to Cacilhas and then the bus 127 to Fonte da Telha (walk approx. 500 meters to right side of the beach to Praia 19). Last bus back at about 23h. By car: take the bridge „25 de Abril" in Lisboa, follow the sign to Costa da Caparica, at the end of the motorway on the second set of traffic lights turn left; follow that road for aprox 2 km until the first curve to the left; then turn right into the small dusty road go always straight-on until the end 🅿 Beach 17.

Estoril – Estremadura

SWIMMING

-Piece of waste land along coast road (AYOR at night) (between Av. Fausto de Figueredo and Hotel Atlântico, facing towards the sea; 10-18h)
-Piscina Tamariz, swimming pool (take train from Lisboa to Cascais; pool is opposite railway station Estoril).

CRUISING

-Terrace near clock and above restaurant on promenade (AYOR)
-Behind railway station.

Faro – Algarve

BARS

■ **Gayvota** (AC B D GLM MA S SNU ST T) 23-7h
Trvessa de São Pedro, 10 ☎ 919 014 794 🖳 gayvotabar.blogspot.com

GUEST HOUSES

■ **Casa Charneca** (AC B BF GLM I MSG NU OS PI PK RWB RWS RWT SA WH WO) All year
Sítio de Charneca 502 A, Santa Barbara de Nexe *EVA bus-line. 500 m to Faro and Loulé Road* ☎ 289 992 842 🖳 www.casacharneca.com
This luxurious guesthouse is tucked into the hills of Santa Bárbara de Nexe near Faro. From your balcony or from the terrace by the pool where you'll enjoy breakfast, you will have the most amazing views of the Algarve coast. Yet, you will be within minutes of the Algarve's most beautiful beaches as well as many of its finest restaurants, bars and clubs.

SWIMMING

-gay beach between Quinta do Lago and Faro Island beaches.
-Praia do Cavalo Preto (between Vale do Lobo and Quarteira. It is a generously sized gay beach, with a large stretch of sand and dunes, and a bush area north of the dunes where cruising takes place).

CRUISING

-Jardim Manuel Bivar (garden), near the marina
-Near the Miracoles (gambling house)
-Parking behind Hotel Eva
-Park at end of Quarteira nearest to Vale do Lobo (walk along the beach or cliff top in direction of Vale do Lobo; after the 2nd red sandstone cliff, you'll see dunes with bushes, within sight of Vale do Lobo; cruising and discreet action in the bushes).

Figueira da Foz – Beira Litoral

CRUISING

-Around the Casino and adjacent streets
-Beaches to the south at Gala (from camp site walk 5-10 mins through woods and dunes, when reached ocean walk left)

Lagos – Algarve

BARS

■ **Alo** (AC B D GLM M MA S WE) 14-2h
Rua Soeiro da Costa 21

■ **Luisol** (B G MA p) 21-2h
Rua de São José, 21 ☎ 282 761 794

RESTAURANTS

■ **Restaurante O Cangalho** (B G M MC OS ST) 12.30-15 & 18.30-22h. Closed Mon & last 2 weeks of Nov & Jan
Barão de São João *Next to Lagos Zoo* ☎ 282 687 218
🖳 www.cangalho.com
Two different styles in two different rooms: rustic or tropical. Extensive menu with local dishes. Shows on Tue (Fado) and Sat (drag show).

GUEST HOUSES

■ **Terramar** (b GLM MA OS PK RWB) All year
Rua C.I.C.A. 5, Lt. 30 ☎ 282 782 313 🖳 www.gay.holidayslagos.com
Two double rooms with shared bathroom.

APARTMENTS

■ **Quinta Santo Phunurius** (glm MA OS PI)
Estrada Atalaia Apartado 730 *15 mins by foot from down town*
☎ 282 081 182 🖳 www.studiophunurius.iowners.net
Apartments suitable for two to 12 people.

SWIMMING

-Meia Praia (dune are near the Palmares Golf) opposite side to Lagos after the Marina (NU)
-Praia das Furnas in a place called Figueira (road between Lagos and Vila do Bispo)
-Praia dos Pinheiros (200m before old Lagos lighthouse turn to the left and follow path to cove (NU)
-Praia Barranco do Martins (close to lighthouse at Ponta da Piedade)
-Praia Canavial (500m right of Praia Barranco do Martins)

CRUISING

-Promenade along the river
-Meia Praia beach in the late evening
-Parking close to courtbuildings (Tribunal)
-Parking about 100m above harbour entry, after nightfall

Funchal – Madeira

BARS

■ **Trendy Lounge Bar** (AC B CC D G M MA S)
Rua de Santa Maria, 23 *Old part of Toen Funchal* ☎ 915 164 267
🖳 www.bas-fond.com/texto.asp?id=22&nivel=1
Cocktail bar located in old part of Funchal. Every week DJ's and several live acts.

DANCECLUBS

■ **Arquipélagos** (AC B CC D DR g m MA S ST WE) 22-2, Sun 21-2h
Rua Mary Jane Wilson, 10 ☎ 965 197 195

CRUISING

-Santa Catarina Park (AYOR) (at Av. do Infante)
-Av. Arriaga (ayor) (stay in the lighted areas)
-Facilities at Anadia shopping mall.
-Facilities at Marina shopping mall.
-Along the sea wall
-Beach Poças do Governador (Lido zone).

Leiria – Beira Litoral

BARS

■ **Blue Angel** (B G MA ST) 22-2h
Rua Dom Afonsa Henriques, 30
■ **Why not?** (B d G MA s ST)
Casal da Cortiça, Barreira ☎ 912 091874

CRUISING

-Parque de Jardim central
-Square near Mercado Municipal (City Market)

Lisboa

Lisbon is one of Europe's grandest and most scenic capitals. Its metro region has 3 million people and is spread over a wide area around the huge Tagus river estuary from elegant Cascais to romantic Sintra and the castle towns of Palmela and Setubal. Lisbon dates back to the Phoenicians, Greeks and Romans and was the world's richest city in the 16th century following the discovery of the sea route to India by Vasco da Gama in 1498, a voyage that historians regard as marking the beginning of the modern era.
Lisbon, with wonderful museums, art galleries and monuments is one of the trendiest European cities with a vibrant night life (gay, African, Brazilian or alternative) mostly around Bairro Alto, Principe Real and Avenida 24 de Julho/Alcantara quarters, and very modern design and fashion and architecture in some of Europe's best shopping malls and Park of Nations (Metro: Oriente).
Lisbon is surrounded by a fantastic coastline, north and south. Caparica beach is Europe's most beautiful gay beach (take the beach train and get off at the stop before the last) and a bit further south Meco beach is a treat (you need a car to get here) and for great scenery Arrábida National Park, Tróia fabulous endless beach (with a gay section) and the beaches along the Sintra coast (Guincho, Praia Grande and Ericeira).

Lissabon zählt zu den beeindruckendsten und schönsten Hauptstädten Europas. In ihrem Einzugsgebiet, das sich großflächig von Cascais zum romantischen Sintra und Setubal erstreckt, leben 3 Millionen Menschen. In Lissabon gibt es wunderschöne Museen, Kunstgalerien und Denkmäler. Außerdem gehört sie zu den Städten mit dem angesagtesten Nachtleben in den Stadtteilen Príncipe Real und Bairro Alto (schwul, afrikanisch, brasilianisch oder alternativ). Es gibt ein wöchentliches schwules Radioprogramm. Bars, Discos und Geschäfte mit sehr modernem Design, das einzigartige Designmuseum im Kulturzentrum von Belém oder das Tiles/Azulejos Museum. Innovative Architektur kann man auch in einigen erstklassigen Einkaufszentren und dem Parque das Nações, dem früheren Expogelände von 1998, bewundern. Im Norden und Süden ist Lissabon von phantastischen Küsten umgeben.
Der Strand von Caparica gehört zu den schönsten schwulen Stränden Europas. Etwas weiter südlich ist der Strand Meco ein echtes schwules Juwel – man braucht allerdings ein Auto. Landschaftlich besonders reizvoll sind Arrábida, Tróia (mit einem schwulen Strand) und die Strände entlang der Küste von Sintra (Guincho, Praia Grande und Ericeira).

Lisbonne est l'une des plus charmantes et des plus pittoresques des capitales d'Europe. Sa région métropolitaine compte trois millions d'habitants et s'étend sur une vaste surface de Cascais aux romantiques Sintra et Setubal. Lisbonne, avec ses merveilleux musées, monuments et galeries d'art est une ville branchée avec une vive scène nocturne (gaie, africaine, brésilienne et alternative), une émission de radio gaie hebdomadaire dans les quartiers Príncipe Real et Bairro, un design très moderne (bars, discos, boutiques et le tout particulier Musée du Design au Centre Culturel de Belém ou encore le musée de tuiles Azulejos) ainsi qu'une architecture incroyablement innovatrice dans certains des meilleurs galeries d'Europe et enfin Parque das Nações, l'ancien site de l'Expo ,98. Lisbonne est entourée d'une splendide côte au nord et au sud. La plage de Caparica est la plus belle plage gaie d'Europe, vous avez également un peu plus loin au sud la plage de Meco, également charmante (seulement accessible en auto) et pour de magnifiques paysages, Arrábida, Tróia (inclut une plage gaie) et les plages le long de la côte de Sintra (Guincho, Praia Grande et Ericeira).

Lisboa es una de las mayores capitales de Europa con más de 3 millones de habitantes. La ciudad se expande hacia las regiones de Cascais, Sintra, Palmela y Setubal. Lisboa con maravillosos museos, grandes restaurantes y atmósfera agradable es a su vez una ciudad moderna con una escena vibrante (gays, africanos, brasileños y alternativos) en los barrios de Príncipe Real y Barrio Alto. Existe un programa de radio gay semanalmente. Hay bares, discotecas y establecimientos con un diseño muy moderno, el singular museo del diseño en el Centro Cultural de Belém o el Museo de Azulejos. También se puede admirar una arquitectura innovadora en algunos centros comerciales exclusivos y

en el Parque das Nações, el antiguo recinto de la Expo 1998. Lisboa está rodeada por el norte y el sur de fantásticas playas.
Caparica es una de las playas gays más bonitas. Más hacia el sur, está la playa Meco, una auténtica joya para los gays, pero se necesita automóvil.
En cuanto al paisaje, Arrábida, Tróia (con una playa gay) y las playas a lo largo de la costa de Sintra (Guincho, Praia Grande y Ericeira) son especialmente atractivas.

Lisbona è tra le città più belle ed impressionanti d'Europa. Nel suo territorio, che si estende da Cascais sino alla romantica Sintra e Setubal, vivono 3 milioni di abitanti. Ci sono splendidi musei, gallerie d'arte e monumenti. Oltre a ciò è tra le città con la più vivace e rinomata vita notturna nei quartieri Príncipe Real e Bairro Alto (gay, africani, brasiliani...). Una volta a settimana va in onda un programma radiofonico gay. Bar, discoteche e negozi dal moderno design, il particolarissimo museo del design nel centro culturale di Belém o il Museo Tiles/Azulejos. L' Architettura contemporanea si può ammirare in alcuni centri commerciali di prima classe e nel Parque das Nações, la zona dell'Expo 1998. Lisbona è circondata a sud ed a nord da splendide costiere.
La spiaggia di Caparica è una delle spiagge gay più belle d'Europa. Più a sud c'è la spiaggia Meco, un vero gioiello per ogni gay; ci vuole però un auto per raggiungerla. Particolarmente affascinanti sono poi Arrábida, Tróia (con una spiaggia gay) e le spiagge lungo la costa di Sintra (Guincho, Praia Grande e Ericeira).

BARS

Baliza (b g m MA WE) Mon-Fri 13-2, Sat 16-2h, Sun closed
Rua da Bica de Duarte Belo, 51-A *At Elevador da Bica, Tram 28*
☎ 213 478 719 🖳 balizacafebar.blogspot.com

Bar 106 (AC B cc G MA) 21-2h
Rua de São Marçal, 106 *M° Rato, near Príncipe Real Park, Bus 58*
☎ 213 427 373 🖳 www.bar106.com
Good information point for gay venues. Wed Wacko Party, Thu Dice Party and Sun message Party (popular).

Favela chic (B GLM MA) Sun-Thu 20-2, Fri & Sat -3h
Rua Diário de Notícias, 66 ☎ 967 076 739
DJs from Thu-Sat.

Fiéis ao Bairro (B glm YC) daily 21-2h
Tv da Espera, 42-A *Bairro Alto, M° Baixa-Chiado, Bus 58, 100*
Cocktail bar.

Luz Nocturna Bar (AC B D GLM WI YC) Mon -Sun 15 -4h
Praça das Flores, 62 ☎ 91 884 16 62

Portas Largas (! B GLM MA)
Sun-Thu 19-2, Fri, Sat & before public holidays 19 -3h
Rua da Atalaia, 105 *M° Baixa-Chiado, Bairro Alto, Bus 58, 100*
☎ 21 346 63 79
Very popular, ancient Bairro Alto-bar, often live music.

Primas Bar (B GLM M YC) Mon-Thu 22-2, Fri & Sat -3h
Rua da Atalaia, 154 ☎ 21 342 19 42

Purex Club (B D GLM WE)
Sun, Tue -Thu 22 -2, Fri & Sat 22 -3h, Mon closed
Rua das Salgadeiras, 28 ☎ 213 421 942
🖳 www.myspace.com/purexclub

Sétimo Céu (AC B GLM MA S)
Mon -Thu 22-2, Fri & Sat -3h, Sun Closed
Travessa da Espera, 54 *M° Baixa-Chiado, Bairro Alto, Bus 58, 100*
Famous cocktail bar.

SS-Bar (AC B GLM M MA S SNU ST) Mon-Sat 21-4h
Calçada da Patriarcal, 38 *M° Rato, near Príncipe Real Park, Bus 58, 100*
☎ 21 347 0335
Entrance fee incl. minimum consumption applies. Shows on Fri & Sat.

Tr3s (B F G M MA) 16-2h
Rua Ruben António Leitão 2A ☎ 213 463 012
🖳 www.tr3slisboa.com
New bear bar.

WoofLX (B G MC) Mon -Sun 22 -4h
Rua da Palmeira, 44B ☎ 213 468 418 🖳 www.wooflx.com
Cozy bear bar.

MEN'S CLUBS

Labyrinto (AC B CC DR F G MA NU P VS) Mon-Sat 21-2, Sun & public holidays 16-2h
Rua dos Industriais, 19 *M° Cais do Sodré* ☎ 21 390 32 00
☎ 964 002 325 (mobile) 🖳 www.labyrinto.com
Cruising bar at walking distance of main gay venues. Naked, underwear & fetish parties. See www.labyrinto.com

WoofX (DR G GH MC VR) Mon -Sun 22 -4h
Rua Manuel Bernardes 2-B *M° Rato, near Príncipe Real Park, Bus 58*
☎ 21 394 04 80
New kinky bear bar.

CAFES

BS Café (B g)
Rua da Imprensa Nacional, 116 B/C

Mar Adentro Café (AC B BF CC GLM I M MA) 8-23, Sat 13.30-1h, Sun closed
Rua do Alecrim, 35 *M° Baixa Chiado* ☎ 213 469 158
Very interesting combination: restaurant, café and bookshop at the same time.

Lisboa

EAT & DRINK

- Alfaia – Restaurant 16
- Baliza – Bar 30
- Bar 106 – Bar 10
- Bota Alta – Restaurant 21
- BS Café – Café 6
- Café Luso – Restaurant 15
- Favela Chic – Bar 24
- Fieis ao Bairro – Bar 27
- Marais. Le – Café 31
- Portas Largas – Bar 20
- Primas – Bar 14
- Restaurante Trivial – Restaurant 2
- Sétimo Céu – Bar 26
- Sete Luas – Bar 3
- SS – Bar 5
- WoofLX – Bar 12

NIGHTLIFE

- Bricabar – Danceclub 8
- Finalmente – Danceclub 11
- Frágil – Danceclub 17
- Labyrinto – Men's Club 34
- Trumps – Danceclub 7
- WoofX – Men's Club 9

SEX

- Sertório – Sauna 4
- Spartakus – Sauna 23
- Trombeta Bath – Sauna 28
- Viriato Ginásio – Sauna 1

ACCOMMODATION

- Anjo Azul – Hotel 19
- Casa de Lisboa – Apartments 32
- Casa Do Bairro – Guest House 33
- Casa Do Patio – Guest House 35
- Pensão Globo – Hotel 13
- Pensão Luar – Guest House 22
- Ribeira Tejo Boutique – Guest House 36

■ **Marais. Le** (AC B GLM I M MA)
Mon-Thu 17.30-2, Fri/Sat -4, Sun 13-23h
Rua de Santa Catarina, 28 *M° Baixa-Chiado, close to panoramic view point Adamastor* ☎ 21 346 73 55
Cocktail bar & free internet point. Sat free buffet, Sun brunch, every day happy hour 17.30-19.30h.

DANCECLUBS

■ **Bric** (AC B CC D DR G MA p SNU ST)
Fri, Sat & before public holidays 23.30 -6h
Rua Cecílio de Sousa 84 *Near Príncipe Real Park, Bus 58, 100, M° Rato*
☎ 213 428 971 💻 facebook.com/briclx
Cruising bar. Fri & Sat also Danceclub (entrance fee).

■ **Finalmente** (! AC B D GLM MA p ST T)
1-6, show every night at 3h
Rua da Palmeira, 38 *M° Rato, near Príncipe Real Park, Bus 58, 100, 790*
☎ 213 479 923
Very popular. Shows every night. Monday is amateur night.

■ **Frágil** (AC b CC D glm MA p WE) 23.30-4h
Rua da Atalaia, 128 *Bairro Alto, Bus 58, 100; opposite to Bar Portas Largas*
☎ 213 469 578
Mixed club with house and electronic music.

■ **Kremlin** (AYOR B D glm)
Escadinhas da Praia, 5
Criminal and violent surroundings. Be careful!

■ **Lux-Frágil** (AC B D glm MA) Thu-Sat 23-6h
Av. Infante D. Henrique- Armazém A / Warehouse A *At Tagus bank between Cais da Pedra and Sta. Apolónia Station* ☎ 2188 20890
💻 www.luxfragil.com
Famous mixed club for house, electro & techno music.
See www.fragil.com.pt

■ **Maria Lisboa** (B D GLM MA ST) Fri & Sat 23-?h
Rua das Fontaínhas, 86 ☎ 213 622 560

■ **Trumps** (! AC B CC D GLM S WE YC)
Fri, Sat & before public holidays 23.45-6h
Rua da Imprensa Nacional, 104-B *M° Rato, near Príncipe Real Park, Bus 58, 100* ☎ 213 951 135 💻 www.trumps.pt
Best and biggest gay club in Lisbon. Consists of three bars and two dance floors. Live music show Fri at 2h.

RESTAURANTS

■ **Alfaia Restaurante** (AC CC GLM M VEG WL) 12-2, Sun 18-2h
Travessa da Queimada, 22 *Bairro Alto, M° Baixa-Chiado, Bus 58, 100* ☎ 213 461 232 💻 www.restaurantealfaia.com
Traditional Portuguese cuisine: various fish dishes, meat dishes and salads and an extensive range of sweet desserts on offer. Another speciality is the rich selection of wines.

■ **Be gold** (AC CC glm M) 19-1, Sun also 12-15h
Rua da Rosa, 151 *Bairro Alto* ☎ 213 465 285
Nice stylish restaurant with Italian and Portuguese cuisine. Brasilian feijoada on Sundays at lunch. Smoking room.

■ **Bota Alta** (AC B CC glm M) Mon-Fri 12-14.30 & 19-22.45, Sat 19-22.45h
Trav. Da Queimada 37/Rua da Atalaia 122 *M° Baixa-Chiado, Bairro Alto, in front of Portas Largas* ☎ 21 342 79 59
Typical portuguese cuisine.

■ **Café Luso** (AC B CC DM GLM LM M MA NR S VEG WL) Daily 19.30-2h, shows start at 20.30h (folklore & Fado) and 22.30h (only Fado)
Travessa da Queimada, 10 *Bairro Alto, M° Baixa-Chiado, Bus 58, 100* ☎ 21 342 2281 💻 www.cafeluso.pt
Restaurant with typical Fado and folklore live music. Dinner and show, including Fado singing. Later at night there are less tourists.

■ **Trivial Restaurante** (B cc M MC NG VEG WL) Mon-Sat 12.30-15 & 20h-midnight
Rua da Palmeira nº 44-A *Principe Real* ☎ 21 347 35 52
Friendly restaurant with pleasant atmosphere. First stop before visiting local bars in the Principe Real. Modern, Portuguese cuisine is served.

SEX SHOPS/BLUE MOVIES

■ **Espaço Lúdico Sex Shop** (cc g MA)
Mon-Sat 10-14 & 15-1.45, Sun 17-24h
Rua do Conde Redonde, 82 ☎ 213 155 094

SEX CINEMAS

■ **Cinebolso** (g)
Rua Actor Taborda, 27 *M° Saldanha*
Hetero porno cinema.

SAUNAS/BATHS

■ **Sauna Spartakus** (AC B DR DU LAB MA p SA SB VS WH) 12-9h
Largo Trindade Coelho 2 *Bairro Alto, Bus 58, 100. Hidden in the building no.2. Ring the bell!*
Charming old sauna on 4 floors that seems to be a labyrinth. Also frequented in the night.

■ **SaunApolo 56** (AC B DR DU F G GH H LAB M MA MSG S SA SB SL VS W) Sun-Thu 12-3, Fri/Sat & before public holidays 12-8h
Rua Luciano Cordeiro 56a *M°-Marques de Pombal* ☎ 926 136 808 ☎ 218 282 854 💻 www.saunapolo56.pt
A new concept for a sauna/bathclub/spa in Lisbon. Mainly for the gay crowd, but it's also open for lesbians, transgenders and hetero swingers. Fully equipped for handicaped people.

■ **Sertório** (AC B DR DU F G LAB M MA MSG p S SA SB SOL VS WH WO) Mon-Sat 15-8, Sun -24h
Calçada da Patriarcal, 34 *Near Príncipe Real Park, Bus 58, 100, M° Rato* ☎ 213 470 335

■ **Trombeta Bath** (! AC B CC DR DU G LAB MA SA SB SL VR VS)
Sun-Thu 12-3, Fri & Sat 12-5h
Rua do Trombeta 1c *Bairro Alto* ☎ 216 095 626 💻 www.trombetabath.com
The sauna is located in the heart of the gay district, approx. 350 m² large.

■ **Viriato Ginásio**
(B DR DU f FC FH G LAB m MA MSG OS PI SA SB SOL VS WH WO)
13-2h
Rua do Telhal, 4-B *M° Avenida* ☎ 213 429 436
One of the biggest steam baths in the country. A large video room. Best in the afternoon. Huge outside area.

GIFT & PRIDE SHOPS

■ **Alfaia Garrafeira** (CC GLM MA) Daily until midnight
Rua Diário de Notícias, 125 ☎ 213 433 079
www.garrafeiraalfaia.com
Portuguese wines & specialties.

TRAVEL AND TRANSPORT

■ **Be Out** (GLM) All year
Av. Dom João II, Lote 1.02.2.2C – 1° Andar Ed. Nascente
Parque das Naçōes ☎ 211 106 000
www.facebook.com/pages/Be-Out-The-Art-of-Travel/176516759072279
Providing the best offers for the LGBT markets. Co-operations around the world with the best gay tour operators.

HOTELS

■ **Hotel Anjo Azul** (AC CC G MA PA RWB RWS VA)
All year, 24hrs
Rua Luz Soriano, 75 *M° Baixa-Chiado, Bus 58, 100; Bairro Alto near São Luis Hospital* ☎ 213 478 069 ☎ 213 467 186
www.anjoazul.com
A renovated 19th century townhouse, set on a narrow street in Bairro Alto, within walking distance from most of the gay bars and discos. 10% discount for Spartacus readers (cash).

■ **Hotel Pouso dos Anjos** (BF CC G MA OS RWB RWS)
all year, 24hrs
Rua dos Anjos, 31 *M° Intendente, tram 28, bus 34, 40, 60; near Italian Embassy* ☎ 213 572 759 www.pousodosanjos.com
Friendly, not exclusively gay hotel, tastefully decorated and reasonably priced. 32 rooms, many with recently renovated private bathroom.

■ **Solar Dos Mouros** (AC CC GLM H MSG RWS RWT) All year
Rua do Milagre de Santo António, 6 *Near Castelo de Sao Jorge, Tram 28, Bus 37, M° Rossio, Baixa-Chiado* ☎ 21 885 49 40
www.solardosmouros.com

GUEST HOUSES

■ **Casa Do Bairro B&B**
(AC B BF CC GLM I MSG OS RWB RWS RWT VA) All year
Beco do Caldeira, 1 – (Rua Fernandes Tomas) Santa Catarina
☎ 91 417 5969 guesthouselisbôn.com
Seven comfortable rooms, all with private bathroom, and two apartments. Centrally located and only five mins. walk from the gay area in Bairro Alto. Gay owned & operated. English, German, Portuguese and French spoken. Free Wi-Fi and internet point.

■ **Casa do Pátio** (AC BF H I NG OS RWS RWT) All year
Travessa da Caldeira 19, Patio das parreiras porta 20 ☎ 914 176 969
☎ 913 303 963 guesthouselisbon.com/casadopatio
8 guestrooms, located at Santa Catarina, a very typical and quiet neighbourhood, just 5 minuts walking distance from Bairro Alto and Chiado. Private bathroom, full breakfast.

■ **Pensão Globo** (AC B GLM RWB RWS VA) All year, 24hrs
Rua do Teixeira, 37 *M° Baixa-Chiado, Bus 58, 100; Bairro Alto, opp. São Pedro de Alcântara gardens* ☎ 213 462 279 ☎ 213 432 106
www.pensaoglobo.com.pt
Located in a small and peaceful old city street, very close to the cable car station for Elvador da Glória. Rooms with private WC. 10% discount for Spartacus readers.

■ **Pensão Luar** (glm MA) All year, 24hrs
Rua das Gáveas, 101 *M° Baixa-Chiado, Bus 58, 100; Bairro Alto, near Largo de São Roque* ☎ 213 460 949 www.pensaoluar.com
Simple, but comfortable rooms with private WC, telephone and TV. 10% discount for Spartacus readers.

■ **Ribeira Tejo Boutique Guest House** (AC H NG RWB WI)
Travessa de São Paulo 5 ☎ 914 176 969
guesthouselisbon.com/ribeiratejo
From the Ribeira-Tejo you can reach all beautiful things to worth seeing and visiting in Lisbon because the Cais do Sodre interface station is only a 2 minute walk.

APARTMENTS

■ **Casas de Lisboa Apartments** (CC GLM I MSG) All year
Bairro Alto ☎ 91 417 6969 ☎ 91 330 3963
guesthouselisbon.com/casasdelisboa
Short-term rental apartments with a full hotel service through other guest houses from the same group. Centrally located. 5 min walk from the gay area Bairro Alto. Gay owned.

■ **Lisbon Experience Apartments** (GLM I MA RWT VA) All year, 24hrs
Central Lisbon ☎ 21 397 1367 ☎ 96 680 7297 (mobile)
www.lisbonexp.com
All apartments are centrally located near the main gay venues. Very friendly staff! Reservations upon internet or phone.

HEALTH GROUPS

■ **Associação Abraço** 10-13, 14-19h
Largo José Luís Champalimaud 4 *Bairro Alto, M° Baixa-Chiado, Bus 58, 100* ☎ 21 799 750 0 www.abraco.org.pt

■ **Centro de Saúde** 18-22h
Rua de São Ciro, 36 ☎ 213 957 993 www.sida.pt
HIV/AIDS Tests and counselling. Easier for EC nationals with health cards.

■ **Checkpoint LX** Mon-Fri 12-20h
Tv. Monde do Carmo 2 ☎ 910 693 158 www.checkpointlx.com
Free HIV tests. Appointment requested.

■ **Grupos Apoio e Auto-Ajuda** 14-20h
Rua de São Paulo, 216 *1st floor A* ☎ 213 422 976

SWIMMING

Beaches south of Lisbon:
- ☞ Costa da Caparica and Sesimbra
Beaches west of Lisbon
- ☞ Estoril

CRUISING

-Príncipe Real Park (very late at night after closing the bars)
-Railway station of Oriente (M° Oriente), crowded
-Belém (at the riverside in Belém near ferry-station Fluvial, by car, AYOR, R)
-Estação Rodoviária (Bus Main Station of Lisbon) at Arco do Cego (Av. António José de Almeida, M° Saldanha)
-Campo Grande (M° Entre Campos, best place near the pool / AYOR, R)
-Cidade Universitária (University, near medical Faculty; near Av. Prof. Gama Pinto by car, AYOR, R)
-Parque Eduardo VII. (closed to M° station Parque, AYOR, r)
-Shopping-Centers (on WC's): Amoreiras (toilets next to Boss store, Bus 58), Armazens do Chiado (top floor toilets), Atrium Saldanha, Saldanha Residence (M° Saldanha), Colombo (near Casa Havaneza & Benetton, M° Colégio Militar – Luz)
-Parque das Nações, Garcia da Orta Garden (M° Oriente, AYOR)
-outside Lisboa: ☞ Estoril.

Nazaré – Beira Litoral

SWIMMING

-Praia do Norte (ca. 5km north of Nazaré)
-Praia do Salgado (3km from Nazaré)
-Praia Vale Furado (Légua)

Pedrogao Pequeno

GUEST HOUSES

■ **Truelove Resort Portugal** (AC BF G M OS PI)
Outro Monte
☞ *see Serta*

Peniche – Beira Litoral

SWIMMING

-Dunes between Peniche and Baleal -80 km north of Lisboa is the fishing town Peniche (bus from Sol Expresso in Lisboa). Best Jun-Sep.

CRUISING

-Parkings in Peniche
-Parkings in Baleal.

Portimão – Algarve

SWIMMING

-Praia do Submarino (between Alvor and Praia da Rocha. You can park the car near the road and walk inside the woods till you see the sea. Look for the area marked Zona Verde and also check the abandoned farm house on the beach side of fence; take shoes and use only low tide!)

CRUISING

-Park and cafés near the railway station
-Praça da República-Square
-Casa Inglesa-Coffe Shop (at night).

Porto – Douro Litoral

Porto is the major city in the Northwest of the Iberian Peninsula and its gay hub, has in its metro region 2 million people, and was declared by UNESCO a world heritage city. Porto is blessed with wonderful perspectives along the Douro river and the sea promenade at Foz quarter. Porto has a great heritage of baroque churches, medieval quarters (Ribeira), great museums (Serralves Museum of Contemporary Art is a must and Soares dos Reis Museum of Fine Arts) and, of course, the cellars of legendary Port Wine. Porto is an ideal starting point to discover the Douro vineyards (Europe's first demarcated wine region and declared world heritage) and Minho province.

Porto ist mit 2 Millionen Menschen in ihrem Einzugsgebiet die größte Stadt und schwules Zentrum im Nordwesten der iberischen Halbinsel. Die Stadt wurde von der UNESCO zum Weltkulturerbe erklärt. In Porto hat man – entlang des Flusses Douro und der Meerpromenade im Bezirk Foz – eine herrliche Aussicht. In der Stadt gibt es beeindruckende historische Zeugnisse: Barockkirchen, mittelalterliche Viertel (Ribeira), hervorragende Museen (das Serralves Museum für zeitgenössische Kunst ist ebenso wie das Soares do Reis Kunstmuseum unbedingt einen Besuch wert) – und natürlich die Weinkeller des legendären Portweins. Porto ist ein idealer Ausgangspunkt, um die Douro Weinberge, Weltkulturerbe und erstes abgegrenztes Weinanbaugebiet Europas, sowie die Provinz Minho (Braga, Guimarães and Viana) zu erkunden.

Porto est la ville principale de même que le centre gai du nord-ouest de la péninsule ibérique. La région métropolitaine compte deux millions d'habitants. Porto fut déclarée ville du patrimoine mondial par l'UNESCO. La ville compte de splendides panoramas le long du fleuve Douro et de la promenade du quartier Foz. Porto dispose d'un grand héritage d'églises baroques, de quartiers médiévaux (Ribeira), de grands musées (le Musée d'Art Contemporain Seralves, à ne pas manquer, et le Musée des Beaux-Arts Soares dos Reis) et, bien sûr, les caves du légendaire vin de Porto. Porto est un point de départ idéal pour découvrir les vignobles du Douro (première région vinicole démarquée de l'Europe et également déclaré patrimoine mondial) et la province de Minho.

Porto es, con sus dos millones de habitantes en el área metropolitana, la ciudad más grande y el centro gay del noroeste de la península ibérica. La ciudad fue declarada Patrimonio Cultural de la Humanidad por la UNESCO. En Porto se puede disfrutar, a orillas del río Douro y desde el paseo marítimo en el distrito de Foz, de una magnífica vista. En la ciudad hay impresionantes testimonios históricos: iglesias barrocas, un barrio medieval (Ribeira), museos excelentes (el Museo Serralves de arte contemporáneo y el museo de arte Soares do Reis merecen una visita) y naturalmente las bodegas del legendario vino de Porto. Porto es un punto de partida ideal para descubrir los viñedos del Douro, patrimonio cultural de la Humanidad y primera zona vinícola delimitada de Europa, así como las ciudades de Braga, Guimarães, Viana, Aveiro, Vila do Conde y Ponte de Lima.

Porto è, con i suoi 2 milioni d'abitanti, nel suo bacino idrografico, la città più grande e il centro gay a nord-ovest della penisola iberica. L'UNESCO ha dichiarato la città Patrimonio Culturale Mondiale. Da Porto si ha una meravigliosa vista, soprattutto lungo il fiume Douro e sul lungomare nel quartiere Foz. In città si possono ammirare splendide testimonianze storiche: chiese barocche, quartieri medievali (Ribeira), splendidi musei (il museo Serralves d'arte contemporanea è, come d'altronde il museo d'arte Soares do Reis, assolutamente da vedere) e, ovviamente, le enoteche del leggendario vino Porto. Porto è l'ideale punto di partenza per scoprire i vigneti di Douro, Patrimonio Culturale Mondiale, e la provincia Minho (Braga, Guimarães e Viana).

BARS

■ **Bears Cave** (AC B cc DR f G M MC MSG S VS) 17-2h
Rua de Alexandre Herculano, 183 *Near Praça da Batalha and Teatro São João* ☎ 915 009 788
Restaurant-bar, dedicated to the bear culture, but everybody is welcome.

■ **Glamour** (AC B cc D GLM MA p S ST t) Wed-Sun 23-5h
Rua do Bonjardim, 836 ☎ 912 717 277

CAFES

■ **Atelier** (AC B glm M OS)
9-19, 21-1.30, Fri/Sat -2.30h. Mon night closed
Rua Dr Barbosa de Castro, 58 – Cordoaria *250m from Clerigos Tower, in front of Boys'r'us Club*

■ **Café Lusitano** (B D GLM M S) 22-2, Fri/Sat -4h, Sun closed
Rua José Falção, 137 ☏ 222 011 067
Popular gay bar in the centre of Porto.

DANCECLUBS

■ **Boys'r'us Club** (AC B D GLM p ST YC) Wed & Sun 22.30-2.30, Fri & Sat -4h. Mon, Tue & Thu closed
Rua do Dr. Barbosa de Castro, 63 *250m from Clerigos Tower*
☏ 917 549 988 (mobile)
Popular bar on two floors, dance floor downstairs: house, pop and mainstream.

■ **Pride Bar** (B D g S YC) Fri-Sun 24-5, in July & August also Wed 24-5h
Rua do Bonjardim, 1121 ☏ 225 096 205 ☏ 91 836 9861 (mobile)
Crowded disco with young gays.

SEX SHOPS/BLUE MOVIES

■ **Casa d'Eros** (AC CC f glm MA) Mon-Sat 11-19.30h.
Rua Firmeza, 570 *Close to City Hall* ☏ 223 406 202
💻 www.casaderos.com

SAUNAS/BATHS

■ **Spartakus** (b DR DU FC FH G m MA OS RR SA SB SOL VS WH) 14-9h
Rua do Bonjardim 628 *M° Trindade* ☏ 22 202 40 21
Large sauna with interior garden of 700 m². Smoking room.

■ **Thermas 205** (B DR DU G MA SA SB VS WH) 14-4, weekend 14-9h
Rua das Guedes de Azevedo, 205 *M° Trindade* ☏ 222 057 533
💻 www.thermas205.net

SWIMMING

-Praia do Castelo do Queijo
-Vila Nova de Gaia, Praia do Cabodelo (where the Douro ends and the Atlantic Ocean begins)

CRUISING

-Av. dos Aliados (near Praca da Libertade, at night)
-Brasilia shopping Center
-Praça D.João I (at night)
-Praça Mouzinho de Albuquerque (at night)
-São Bento Railway Station (busy, day & night at the toilets)
-Trindade Station (daytime)
-Castelo do Queijo (at night)
-Rotunda da Boavista (in the evening)

Póvoa de Varzim – Douro Litoral

SWIMMING

-Praia do Vila do Conde

São Pedro de Moel

SWIMMING

-Praia Velha – Old beach (North of São Pedro)
-Praia das Pedras Negras – Black Stones beach (north between Praia Velha and Vieira de Leiria)

Serta

GUEST HOUSES

■ **Truelove Resort Portugal** (AC BF G I M OS PI PK RWS RWT) All year
Outro Monte, Pedrogao Pequeno *50 km southeast of Coimbra*
☏ 968 291 641 💻 www.truelove.be
Three double rooms with private bathroom, sat TV, radio and kitchen use. Heated pool. Breakfast included, dinner on request.

Sesimbra – Estremadura

SWIMMING

-Praia do Meco (g NU) (from Lisbon in direction Lagoa de Albufeira. Then the road to Alfarim, before entering the village turn left, before camping-site enter the sand road through the pine trees until you find a 🅿)

Setúbal – Estremadura

SWIMMING

-Albarquel
-Arrábida camping
-Coelhos
-Figueirinha
-Galapagos
-Peninsula de Troia (NU) (15 mins from camping).

CRUISING

All cruising areas are AYOR
-Centro Comercial do Bonfim
-Estação Central de Autocarros (central bus station)
-Praça do Bocage (R)
-Rua dos Ourives
-Rua Antão Girão.

Silves – Algarve

PRIVATE ACCOMMODATION

■ **Quinta do Caçapo** (B BF g OS PI WO)
Franqueira 402/L ☏ 282 332 747

Sintra – Estremadura

GUEST HOUSES

■ **Casa Buglione** (BF glm I MSG OS PI PK RWB RWS RWT)
Closed Dec to Mar
Estrada Nova, 95 – Azoia, Colares *Lead to village centre. In front of the restaurant called „Refugio da Roca" enter the Estrada Nova and drive to Nr. 95* ☏ 962 969 471 💻 www.casabuglione.com

■ **Quinta do Corvo** (bf CC glm MA NU OS p PA PI PK RWB RWS RWT VA) All year, 24hrs
Quinta do Corvo, Colares *Outside Lisbon, 10km from Sintra, 15km from Cascais* ☏ 219 291 841 💻 www.quintadocorvo.eu
Six romantic apartments in an old farm area with a great garden; breakfast service.

Tavira – Algarve

GUEST HOUSES

■ **Quinta Escola Primária** (BF G MA OS) All year
Monte da Fuzeta, C.P. 903 D *12km from Tavira* ☏ 281 326 613
Tranquil countryside location.

SWIMMING

-Praia da Ilha de Tavira (Tavira Island beach)

CRUISING

-The small park along the river (Rua José Pires Padunha)
-Between Tavira and Vila Real de Santo António in Manta Rota (cruising and nudist gay beach).Walk approx. 500m from parking lot towards the dunes near the old village of Cacela Velha. Cruising in the dunes.

Tomar – Ribatejo

GUEST HOUSES

■ **Casa Wladival** (AC b BF CC g m MC MSG NU OS SOL WH WO)
All year, 24hrs
Rua da Barca, s/n, Dornes *30 km from Tomar* ☏ 962 049 148
💻 www.casawladival.com
This is a paradise for lovers of water sports and fishing.

CRUISING

-Tomar, Jardim da Azenha – Azenha Garden
-Ourém, Castle zone (outside Tomar, near Fátima).

Viana do Castelo – Minho

CRUISING

-Praia do Cabedelo/Cabedelo Beach. Take the ferry to the town beach then walk.
-Praia do Rodenho (between Praia do Cabedelo and Praia da Amorosa).

Vidigueira – Alto Alentejo

GUEST HOUSES

■ **Quinta da Fé** (AC B BF CC GLM M MA MSG OS PI WO)
All year, 8.30-24h
Estrada de Alcaria, Taipinhas *24 km north of Beja* ☎ 284 434 105
🖳 www.quintadafe.com
Beautiful and recently renovated farm located in the calm and relaxing countryside.

Vila Nova de Famalicão – Minho

CRUISING

-Centro Comercial Aro
-Jardim Dona Maria II.

Vila Nova de Milfontes – Baixo Alentejo

GUEST HOUSES

■ **Casa Amarela** (glm H OS RWS RWT) All year
Rua D. Luis Castro e Almeida *120km south of Lisbon* ☎ 283 996 632
🖳 www.casaamarelamilfontes.com
Seven rooms all with private bath/WC, very gay-friendly.

SWIMMING

- Praia do Malhão (exit Brunheiras 5km north from V. N. de Milfontes)
- Praia do Carreiro da Fazenda (Dunes between Village and Lighthouse on the Atlantic Side)
- Praia dos Aivados (located north of Praia do Malhão, south part)
- Praia das Furnas (south bank of Rio Mira; Rock's zone).

CRUISING

- Av. Marginal from castle to lighthouse.

Vila Real de Santo António – Algarve

SWIMMING

-Monte Gordo beach (3km from Vila Real de Santo Antonio).

CRUISING

-Av. along the river
-Between Tavira and Vila Real de Santo Antonio in Manta Rota (cruising and nudist gay beach). Walk approx. 500m from parking lot towards the dunes near the old village of Cacela Velha. Cruising in the dunes.

Vilamoura – Algarve

DANCECLUBS

■ **Pride Disco** (D G) Fri, Sat & before public holidays 23 -6h
Ed. Verona, sector 2 🖳 www.pride-disco.com

SWIMMING

- Praia do Cavalo Preto (between Vale do Lobo and Quarteira. It is a generously sized gay beach, with a large stretch of sand and dunes, and a bush area north of the dunes where cruising takes place)
- Park at end of Quarteira nearest to Vale do Lobo (walk along the beach or cliff top in direction of Vale do Lobo; after the 2nd red sandstone cliff, you'll see dunes with bushes, within sight of Vale do Lobo; cruising and discreet action in the bushes).

Reunion

Name: Réunion · Reunión · Riunione
Location: Indian Ocean
Initials: REU
Time: GMT +4
International Country Code: ☎ 262 (no area codes)
International Access Code: ☎ 00
Language: French
Area: 2,512 km² / 970 sq mi.
Currency: 1 Euro (€) = 100 Cents
Population: 706,300
Capital: St. Denis
Religions: 92% Catholic
Climate: Tropical climate which moderates with the elevation. Cool and dry from May-Nov, hot and rainy from Nov-Apr.

The Réunion Islands are a French „Département d'Outre Mer". Legislation concerning homosexuality is the same as in ☞ France. The flight from Mauritius to the Réunion Islands takes only about a half an hour. The landscape is so beautiful that the trip is certainly worth it. Contrary to other destinations in the area, there is no violence towards homosexuals on the island. Reunion Island is a small paradise, where tradition and family values still run strong. It's difficult for the locals (Creoles) to come out, because they are surrounded by their relatives, but they believe that diversity is a positive cultural value. On the other hand, French and foreign homosexuals do not pose a problem, even when it is comparatively visible.

Réunion ist ein französisches »Département d'Outre-Mer«, die gesetzliche Situation entspricht der in ☞ Frankreich. Von

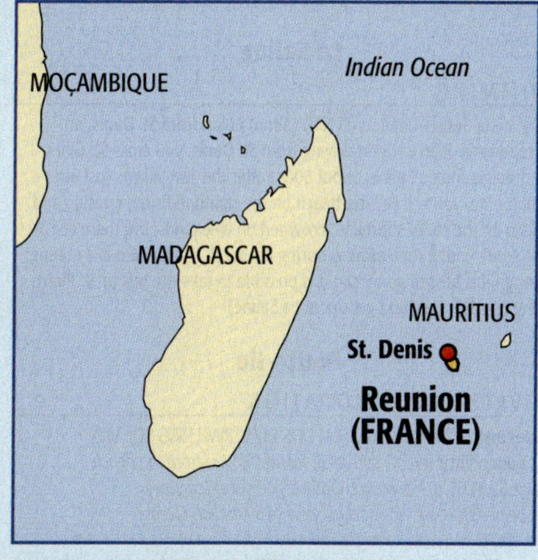

Mauritius aus dauert der Flug dorthin nur eine halbe Stunde, und die Landschaft ist so schön, dass sich ein Besuch allemal lohnt.
Im Gegensatz zu anderen Reisezielen in dieser Region gibt es auf der Insel keine Gewalt gegen Homosexuelle. Réunion ist ein kleines Inselparadies, in dem traditionelle Werte und Familie sehr groß geschrieben werden. Man muss sich bewusst sein, dass Réunion zwar vielleicht nichts

für sexuelle Begegnungen, aber trotzdem ein geeignetes Reiseziel für Schwule ist. Die Einwohner beweisen immer öfter eine gewisse Toleranz gegenüber Schwulen und Lesben, da auch gemischte Paare zwischen Kreolen (einheimischen) und Franzosen vom Kontinent entstehen.

La Réunion est un département français d'outre-mer. La législation y est donc la même qu'en ☞ France métropolitaine. Depuis l'île Maurice, le vol ne dure qu'une demi-heure. Le paysage est magnifique. A voir absolument! Au contraire des autres destinations touristiques de la région on n'observe pas à la Réunion de violences contre les homosexuels. La Réunion est une petite île paradisiaque où les valeurs traditionnelles ainsi que la famille sont importantes. Étant donné qu'ils vivent au sein de leurs familles il est difficile pour les autochtones de déclarer leur homosexualité, mais ils voient dans la diversité une valeur culturelle positive. D'autre part, les homosexuels français et étrangers ne relèvent aucun problème, même dans le cas d'une visibilité relative. Il faut cependant être conscient que la Réunion n'est pas une destination de rencontres sexuelles mais reste une destination touristique appropriée aux homosexuels. Les réunionnais faisant preuve, de plus en plus, d'une certaine tolérance envers la communauté gay et lesbiennes étant donnés que des couples mixtes créoles/métropolitains se forment.

Reunión es un «Département d`Outre-Mer» (Departamento de Ultramar) francés, por lo tanto la situación legal corresponde a la de Francia. El vuelo desde Mauritius hasta las Islas Reunión dura solamente media hora y el paisaje es tan bonito, que una visita merece sin duda la pena. Uno debe ser consciente que Reunión no es un destino turístico para mantener contactos sexuales pero sigue siendo un destino adecuado para los gays. Sus habitantes muestran cada vez más a menudo una cierta tolerancia hacia la comunidad gay-lésbica, puesto que existen parejas mixtas entre criollos (locales) y franceses del continente.

Reunione è un „Département d'Outre Mer", la situazione legale corrisponde a quelle della ☞ Francia. Il volo da Mauritius fino alle Isole Reunion dura solo mezz'ora, quindi vale la pena andarci. Diversamente dagli altri paesi di quest'area, sull'Isola della Riunione (chiamata anche Réunion) non si registra violenza contro i gay. L'Isola della Riunione è un piccolo paradiso dove i valori tradizionali e la famiglia hanno un peso particolare. Per gli abitanti, i creoli, è molto difficile dichiarare la propria omosessualità, tuttavia vedono la diversità come valore culturale positivo. Gli omosessuali francesi e stranieri non sono tema di scandalo neanche quando assumono comportamenti piuttosto espliciti. Sebbene l'isola della Riunione sia una meta piuttosto adatta per il turismo gay, bisogna comunque tener presente che non è la meta ideale per trovare del sesso. Gli abitanti del luogo si mostrano sempre più tolleranti nei confronti della comunità gay e lesbica, e questo è sicuramente dovuto al fatto che si formano sempre più spesso coppie miste tra creoli (gli abitanti) e francesi.

Etang Salé

GUEST HOUSES

La Buddha Case (ac bf GLM MA OS PI)
62 chemin Bois de Nèfles ☏ 06.92.61.47.36

La Possession

HOTELS

Lodge Roche Tamarin. Le (B BF H M OS WH)
142 chemin Bœuf Mort ☏ 02.62.44.66.88
www.villagenature.com

La Saline

SWIMMING

-Plage de la Souris-Chaude (G NU) (about 60km from St. Denis, on the road to St. Pierre; when driving from St. Denis, you cross St. Gilles, L'Hermitage and La Saline; about 600m after this last village, just after a small bridge, you will see the beach on the righthand side; cruising and nudism on the rocky shoreline; crowded on weekends, but there are always some young men around during the week, even when it is raining; although it is best to go by car, it is possible to take the bus to St. Pierre on the coastal route and get out at La Saline)

Petite-Ile

PRIVATE ACCOMMODATION

Veremer B&B (AC BF GLM I OS PI PK RWB RWS SOL VA)
40 Chemin Vitry *Ten mins from St. Pierre, two km from the beach*
☏ 02.62.31.65.10 www.chambre-gite-veremer.com
Gay owned B&B with spectacular view of the Indian Ocean.

Saint-Gilles

DANCECLUBS

Le Klub (B D glm MA OS)
2 Mail de Rodrigues

Le Loft (B D glm m MA OS) Fri-Sat
70, Avenue de Bourbon

Saint-Denis

BARS

Moda Café (B NG YC)
75 rue Pasteur ☏ 02.62.41.33.41

CAFES

Le Zanzibar Café (B GLM M MA OS)
41 Rue Pasteur

DANCECLUBS

Boy's. Le (B D GLM MA)
108 rue Pasteur

SEX SHOPS/BLUE MOVIES

Adult Video Show (AC CC g MA VS) 9-20.30h
15 rue Amiral-Lacaze *Barachois* ☏ 02.62.41.15.05
www.adultvideoshow.re

CRUISING

-Promenade de la piscine du barachois (at night)
-Jamaïque-picnic area (AYOR)
-Black sand beach of l'Etang Salé
-Souris Chaude beach in the evenings and also during the day. Attention: police occasionally in dunes.

Saint-Pierre

BARS

Cherwaine's. Le (B CC D glm MA WE) Mon-Sat 20-2h
6 rue Auguste Babet *In the centre, close to city hall* ☏ 02.62.35.69.49
cherwaine.free.fr
Gay-owned karaoke bar.

RESTAURANTS

Vieux Bardeau. Le (b glm M MA)
Route Nationale 3 / 24ème kilomètre ☏ 02.62.59.09.44
www.levieuxbardeau.fr

TRAVEL AND TRANSPORT

Cilaos Aventure (glm)
12 chemin de la chapelle ☏ 06.92.66.73.42 (mobile)
www.cilaosaventure.com

GUEST HOUSES

■ **Villa Belle** (AC bf G m MSG OS PI SB SOL WH) All year
45 rue Rodier ☎ 06.92.65.89.99 💻 www.villabelle.net

Trois Bassins Littoral

APARTMENTS

■ **Dalon Plage. Le**
(AC GLM NU OS PA PI PK RWB RWS RWT VA WH WO) All year
4 RN 1 Souris-Chaude *In the middle of the west coast close to RN 1 and the places of interest* ☎ 02.62.34.29.77
💻 pagesperso-orange.fr/ledalon
Gay owned accomodation. Fully equipped, luxury bungalows available with sea views. Friendly welcoming, on the gay nudist beach „Souris Chaude". 10% reduction with Spartacus!

Romania

Name: România · Rumänien · Roumanie · Rumania
Location: Southeastern Europe
Initials: ROM
Time: GMT +2
International Country Code: ☎ 40 (omit 0 from area codes)
International Access Code: ☎ 00
Language: Romanian
Area: 238,391 km² / 92,043 sq mi.
Currency: 1 Leu (ROL) = 100 Bani
Population: 21,634,000
Capital: Bucuresti
Religions: 87% Romanian Orthodox, 5% Roman Catholic
Climate: Moderate climate. Cold winters and warm summers.
Important gay cities: Bucuresti

The age of consent in Romania for homosexuals is set at 15 years. In June 2001 the government in Romania passed a new law repealing Section 200, referring to sex related offences, in order to eliminate any discrimination based on sexual orientation from the Romanian Penal Code. The President has since signed this law into effect. Romania joined the European Union as a full member on January 1, 2007. Romania will not adopt the Euro as it's currency until at least 2014. Romania remains a country with entrenched homophobia. Discretion is advised for gay and lesbian travellers.
The „diversity march" provided the finale of the cultural event „GayFest 2007" held in Bucharest in June. Approximately 300 demonstrators were protected by 400 police who arrested over 100 protesters opposing the demonstration. It is assumed that the extremely right-wing association „Noua Dreapta" („New Right") organized the counter-demonstration; in addition, the Romanian Orthodox Church castigated the „sinful behaviour" of homosexuals in nationwide prayer events. The IGLHRC (International Gay and Lesbian Human Rights Commission) programme manager also lamented that the Romanian authorities tolerate neo-fascist symbols that are as prohibited in Romania as they are in virtually all other European countries.
Nevertheless, cultural attitudes are slowly beginning to change, and a small gay and lesbian scene is emerging, especially in the capital, Bucharest. The Romanian Orthodox Church and the state are losing some of their control, as young Romanians become more liberal-minded and westernised. Romania is a country of beautiful landscapes, monasteries, mountains and historic cities. Gay and lesbian visitors will be rewarded with genuine hospitality and friendliness. The area of Romania known as Transylvania is a particularly magical destination.

Das Schutzalter für Homosexuelle liegt in Rumänien bei 15 Jahren. Im Juni 2001 verabschiedete die rumänische Regierung ein neues Gesetz, um jegliche Diskriminierung aufgrund sexueller Neigungen aus dem rumänischen Strafgesetzbuch zu entfernen. Die neue Verordnung sollte den Paragraphen 200 abschaffen. Dieser bezog sich auf die Bestrafung von Sexualdelikten. Durch seine Unterschrift hat der Präsident dieser Verordnung Gültigkeit verliehen. Am 1. Januar 2007 ist Rumänien zwar Vollmitglied der europäischen Gemeinschaft geworden, doch die Einführung des Euro wird frühestens 2014 stattfinden. Schwulenfeindlichkeit ist in Rumänien immer noch tief verwurzelt, weshalb sich schwullesbische Reisende diskret verhalten sollten.
Der „Marsch der Vielfalt" bildete im Juni den Schlusspunkt der Kulturveranstaltung „GayFest 2007" in Bukarest. Die etwa 300 Demonstranten wurden von 400 Polizisten beschützt, die über 100 Gegendemonstranten festnahmen. Man geht davon aus, dass der rechtsextreme Verein „Noua Dreapta" (Neue Rechte) die Gegenveranstaltung organisierte, außerdem richtete sich die rumänische orthodoxe Kirche mit landesweiten Gebetsveranstaltungen gegen das „sündige Verhalten" Homosexueller. Der Programmmanager des IGLHRC (International Gay and Lesbian Human Rights Comission) beklagte zudem, dass die rumänischen Behörden neo-faschistische Symbole tolerierten, die sowohl in Rumänien, als auch in nahezu allen restlichen europäischen Ländern verboten sind.
Trotzdem verändern sich die bisherigen Einstellungen langsam, so dass vor allem in der Hauptstadt Bukarest eine kleine schwullesbische Szene heranreift. Da die rumänische Jugend sich an den Gegebenheiten im Westen orientiert und immer aufgeschlossener wird, verlieren die rumänisch-orthodoxe Kirche und der Staat an Einfluss.
Rumänien ist ein Land mit wunderschönen Landschaften, Klöstern, Bergen und historischen Städten. Besonders das berühmte Transsilvanien ist ein geradezu magisches Reiseziel.

En Roumanie, la majorité sexuelle est fixée à 15 ans pour les homosexuels. En juin 2001, le gouvernement a fait passer une nouvelle loi qui élimine du code pénal toute forme de discrimination fondée sur l'orientation sexuelle. La nouvelle législation devait supprimer le paragraphe 200 qui pénalisait les délits sexuels.
Depuis le premier janvier 2007, la Roumanie est certes membre de l'Union Européenne, mais l'introduction de l'euro ne pourra se faire au plus tôt qu'en 2014.
L'homophobie est toujours bien enracinée en Roumanie et il est recommandé de se montrer discret. La „Marche de la diversité" a clôturé la manifestation culturelle „Gay Fest 2007" à Bucarest en juin.

Les quelques 300 participants étaient protégés par 400 policiers qui ont arrêté 100 contre-manifestants. On suppose que l'association d'extrême-droite „Noua Dreapta" („Nouvelle Droite") est à l'origine de la contre-manifestation, tandis que l'Église Orthodoxe roumaine organisait dans tout le pays des prières collectives contre le „comportement pécheur" des homosexuels. Le manageur du IGLHRC (The International Gay and Lesbian HumanRights Comission) déplorait en outre que les autorités roumaines toléraient des symboles néo-fascistes qui non seulement sont normalement interdits en Roumanie même, mais aussi dans presque tous les autres pays européens.

Néanmoins, les choses évoluent lentement de sorte que, dans la capitale Bucarest surtout, un petit milieu gay se développe peu à peu. Les jeunes Roumains s'orientant de plus en plus vers l'ouest et devenant plus tolérants, l'Église roumaine-orthodoxe et l'État perdent de leur influence. La très célèbre Transylvanie est un lieu magique à voir absolument.

La edad de consentimiento para los homosexuales en Rumania es de 15 años. En junio de 2001, el gobierno rumano aprobó una nueva legislación para apartar cualquier discriminación por razón de la orientación sexual del código penal rumano. La nueva normativa debería derogar el artículo 200, que se refiere a la penalización de delitos sexuales. A través de su firma, el presidente ha dado validez a esta normativa. Desde el 1 de enero de 2007 Rumanía es miembro de pleno derecho de la Unión Europea pero la entrada del euro se realizará como muy pronto en el 2014.

La intolerancia hacia los homosexuales continúa muy arraigada en Rumania, por lo que recomendamos a los turistas gays y lesbianas que se comporten de forma discreta. La „Marcha de la Diversidad" supuso el punto final del evento cultural „GayFest 2007" de junio en Bucarest. Los casi 300 manifestantes fueron protegidos por más de 400 policías, que detuvieron a más de 100 contramanifestantes. Se cree que la asociación de extrema derecha „Noua Dreapta" („Nuevos Derechos") fue quien organizó esta contra-manifestación; además la iglesia ortodoxa rumana dirigió pregarias a todo el país en contra del „comportamiento pecaminoso" de los homosexuales. El director del programa IGLHRC (The International Gay and Lesbian HumanRights Comission) se quejó además que las autoridades rumanas toleraron símbolos neofascistas que están prohibidos tanto en Rumanía como también en el resto de estados europeos.

No obstante los anteriores prejuicios cambian poco a poco, de tal modo que en la capital, Bucarest, está naciendo un cierto ambiente gay-lésbico. Como la juventud rumana se orienta hacia las costumbres de Occidente y cada vez son más abiertos, la Iglesia rumano-ortodoxa y el Estado va perdiendo su influencia. Rumanía es un país de paisajes fantásticos, claustros, montañas y ciudades históricas. Especialmente la tan conocida Transilvania es un destino turístico mágico.

L'età legale per i rapporti sessuali è di 15 anni. Nel giugno del 2001 il governo rumeno ha varato una nuova legge che vieta qualsiasi tipo di discriminazione in base agli orientamenti sessuali. La nuova legge ha praticamente abolito il paragrafo 200 riguardante le punizioni per i reati sessuali. Con la sua firma, il Presidente, ha così messo in uso la legge. L'uno gennaio del 2007 la Romania entrerà a far parte a tutti gli effetti dell'Unione Europea, tuttavia l'euro verrà introdotto non prima del 2014. L'omofobia in Romania è però ancora molto radicata e per questo consigliamo di comportarcisi in maniera discreta.

La marcia della diversità è stata la manifestazione di chiusura del GayFest 2007 svoltasi in giugno a Bucarest. I circa 300 manifestanti sono stati scortati da 400 poliziotti, 100 contro-manifestanti sono stati arrestati. Si dà per scontato che ad organizzare la contro-manifestazione sia stata l'organizzazione di estrema destra Noua Dreapta (Nuova Destra). Inoltre la chiesa ortodossa rumena ha organizzato raduni di preghiere in tutto il Paese contro il „comportamento peccaminoso" degli omosessuali. Il program manager dell'IGLHRC (The International Gay and Lesbian HumanRights Comission) denunciava il fatto che le autorità rumene continuano a chiudere un occhio sulla simbologia neofascista che è vietata sia in Romania che nella maggior parte degli altri paesi europei. Ma nonostante ciò si fanno piccoli passi avanti riguardo al tema omosessualità: nella capitale Bucarest cresce pian piano una scena gay. Poiché la gioventù rumena si orienta sempre più verso i costumi occidentali, la chiesa ortodossa e la chiesa perdono sempre più voce in capitolo. La Romania è un paese con meravigliosi paesaggi, monasteri, montagne e città storiche. Di particolare interesse turistico sono le magiche atmosfere della Transilvania.

NATIONAL COMPANIES

Queer.ro (CC G)
✉ Bucuresti 🖳 www.queer.ro
Online mail order site. Spartacus also sold here.

Tymes Tours (g) All year
Str. Lisabona 7/1A, Apt. 6 ✉ RO300603 Timisoara *Piata Victoriei / Victory Square* ☏ (0256) 203 015 🖳 www.tymestours.ro
Active tours, sightseeing tours and special interest tours throughout Romania.

NATIONAL GROUPS

Accept Association (GLM) 10-18h
CP 34-56 ✉ Bucuresti ☏ 252 16 37 🖳 www.accept-romania.ro
Romanian non-government organization that defends and promotes the rights of LGBT's on the national level.

Arad

CRUISING

-Strandul de pe Mures, Gara de Nord.

Bacau

CRUISING

-Gara CFR, Parcul Trandafirilor.

Braila

CRUISING

-Parcul Monument
-Parcul Central

Brasov ☏ 0268

DANCECLUBS

Club V (B D DR f GLM MA S) Fri 22-5, Sat -6h
Str. Vasile Lupu Nr. 30 ☏ (0727) 006 521

La Feri (B D DR GLM S) Sat 22-6h
Str. Ion Neculce nr. 11B *At the city border, take a taxi from railway station* ☏ (07) 22 88 44 83 (mobile, ask for Feri)
Sat gay parties with occasional shows.

CRUISING

-Piata Sfatului
-Central Park (entrance opp. City Hall)
-Central Garden (in front of Aro Hotel)

Bucuresti ☏ 021

DANCECLUBS

French Kiss Club (B D G MA) Fri & Sat
Strada Balcesti nr. 9 ☏ 0786 688 846

Soho (! B D GLM m MA) Fri & Sat 23-05h
Str. Selimber 1 *Next to saint george church* ☏ (021) 0733 74 85 02 🖳 www.soho-studio.ro
A very cool place to hang out. Special theme nights, expect a nice crowd, door policy is strict: dress up! Check www.soho-studio.ro for details.

SWIMMING

-Municipal Bath »Grivita« (g pi) (for men Wed, Fri & Sat 10-18, Sun 7-12h, opp. Orthodox church)
-Hotel Turist (pi) (Bd. Poligrafiei nr. 1-5)

-Hotel Bucuresti (pi) (Calea Victoriei)
-Tei Toboc Beach.

CRUISING

All are AYOR !
-Titan Park (especially at the north-west side of the park)
-Magheru Blvd (between University and Romana Circle)
-Piata University (public men's room in the subway/underground concourse)
-Opera Park (popular)
-Herastrau Park (entrance from Romanian Television)
-Bucur Obor and Parcul Operei parks
-Calea Victoria 37 (near main post office, right from the entrance)
-Pedestrian underground Blvd Republici and Blvd Balcescu
-Park Cismigiu (entrance Bulvar, Magureanu and Brezo Street)

Cluj-Napoca ☎ 0264

BARS

■ **Zig Zag** (B GLM MA) Fri & Sun 21-?, Sat 23-?h
Bv. 21 Decembrie 1989 nr. 8 💻 www.myspace.com/521737512
Music pub.

CRUISING

-Central Park (Parcul Central or Parcul Mare in Romanian. Opp. Hungarian Theatre, evening cruising, especially on the river side near to the boat lake)
-Expo Transilvania (dark area near Expo Transsilvania. Popular with residents of the Marasti district).

Constanta ☎ 0241

BARS

■ **Soul Cafe** (B GLM S) Wed-Sun 22-?h
Blvd Tomis 28 ☎ 07 45 47 75 06 (mobile)
☎ 0755.935.222 (mobile)
Trans-party on Saturday nights.

CRUISING

-Republica garden
-The Theatre Café (at the rear side of the Drama Theatre)
-The Luna park
-Mamaia resort (at the northern point on the way to Navodari, only in summer)
-Blvd Tomis 79 (in the park opp. Railway Bureau CFR)
-Stefan cel Mare/Mihai Viteazul Street (in pedestrian underground near the store »Tomis«)

Craiova ☎ 051

BARS

■ **Raul Cafe** (B GLM MA)
Str. Brestei Nr. 36

CRUISING

-Gara CFR.

Galati

CRUISING

-Parc Durbaca
-Stadionul Dunarea
-WC P-ta Centrala.

Iasi

CRUISING

-Parc Copou
-Parc Nicolina.

Sibiu

SWIMMING

-Ocna Sibiului (10km from Sibiu. Go by train from Sibiu Main Station to Ocna Sibiului. Go to »La lacuri«, an area with natural salt seas)

CRUISING

-Arini and Astra parks (during the day)
-Central park.

Timisoara ☏ 0256

DANCECLUBS

■ **Sauvage Club** (AC B D g M MA P S SNU ST T WE) Fri-Sat 23-5h
Str. Bredicean Nr. 2, (Piata Libertatii) *Tram 4/5, at Libertatii Square, centre Timisoara* ☏ (072) 105 92 00
Karaoke show Fri, Sat starts at 22h. Very central location in the heart of the city.

Russia

Name: Rossiya · Russland · Russie · Rusia
Location: East Europe and Northern Asia
Initials: RUS
Time: GMT +3...+12
International Country Code: ☏ 7
International Access Code: ☏ 8 (wait for tone) 10
Language: Russian
Area: 17,075,400 km² / 6,592,812 sq mi.
Currency: 1 Ruble (RUR) = 100 Kopeks
Population: 143,850,000
Capital: Moskva (Moscow)
Religions: 24 % Russian Orthodox, 15 % Muslims
Climate: Winters are cold, especially in the north east where there often severe snow falls. Summers are mild, although June and July can be extremely hot.
Important gay cities: Moskva, St. Petersburg

Homosexuality between consenting adults is legal with age of consent set at 16. Prostitution is legal for clients. Sex workers risk an administrative offence. Make sure you don't pick up anyone below the age of 18.
Being gay has become relatively safe in Moscow and St. Petersburg where the gay commercial scene is a little developed. In other cities, the gay life is at best underground or at worst non-existent. Often, it consists of public cruising areas, popular cafes or, occasionally small groups.
Russian Gay activist scene has received wide media coverage since 2005 when Project GayRussia lead by Nikolai Alekseev entered into a fight with the Mayor of Moscow who denied them the right to stage their first Gay Pride. Despite all bans, activists took the streets every May starting in 2006 provoking harsh reactions from fanatics.
But homosexuality remains a taboo subject, which is most of all to be blamed on the communists in the Soviet Union era. Current politics in Russia is still marked by attempts to curb the public relations efforts of gay activists with a raft of laws, despite the 2010 decision of the European Court of Human Rights.
Always carry your passport with valid visa and ensure that you are registered within 3 days of your arrival. Russia is a rewarding travel destination, although the travel industry is not yet client-focused outside main cities. Rich national cuisine, vivid countryside and diverse sightseeing opportunities will certainly make your visit memorable.

Einvernehmliche homosexuelle Handlungen zwischen Erwachsenen sind legal, das Schutzalter liegt bei 16 Jahren. Gewerblicher Sex ist für den Kunden legal, Sexarbeiter können wegen Ordnungswidrigkeit belangt werden. Stellen Sie sicher, dass potenzielle gewerbliche Sexpartner mindestens 18 Jahre alt sind.
In Moskau und St. Petersburg, wo die kommerzielle Schwulenszene schon etwas weiter entwickelt ist, kann man als Schwuler mittlerweile in relativer Sicherheit leben. In anderen Städten findet das schwule Leben bestenfalls im Untergrund oder schlimmstenfalls überhaupt nicht statt. Oft stellen öffentliche Cruising-Gegenden, beliebte Cafes und manchmal auch kleine Gruppen die einzigen Möglichkeiten dar, sich zu treffen.

Seit der Auseinandersetzung im Jahr 2005 zwischen der von Nikolai Alekseev geleiteten Organisation Gay Russia und dem Bürgermeister von Moskau, der widerrechtlich die Veranstaltung von Russlands erstem CSD-Marsch verboten hatte, wird auch international in den Medien über die schwule Aktivistenszene Russlands berichtet. Trotz aller Verbote haben Aktivisten seit 2006 jeden Mai eine Demonstration abgehalten, die bei fanatischen Gegnern auf schroffe Reaktionen stößt. Weiterhin gibt es durch die gegenwärtige Politik in Russland Bestrebungen, den Aktivisten mit einer Reihe von Gesetzen trotz des Urteils vom Europäischen Gerichtshof für Menschenrechte von 2010, in ihrer Öffentlichkeitsarbeit zu behindern.
Ausländische Besucher sollten sich immer streng an die Einreisebestimmungen halten. Russland ist ein lohnendes Reiseziel, die Tourismusindustrie außerhalb der Großstädte allerdings noch nicht besonders kundenorientiert. Die vielfältige russische Küche, abwechslungsreiche Landschaften und die unzähligen Sehenswürdigkeiten des Landes werden Ihren Besuch garantiert zu einem unvergesslichen Erlebnis machen.

Les relations homosexuelles consentantes entre adultes sont légales et la majorité sexuelle est fixée à 16 ans. Pour le client, la prostitution est légale mais le prostitué risque des poursuites pour trouble à l'ordre public. Assurez-vous que le potentiel partneraire sexuel „commercial" a au moins 18 ans.
A Moscou et St-Pétersbourg où la scène gay commerciale est déjà plus avancée, il est devenu possible pour les gays de vivre en relative sécurité. Dans les autre villes, la vie gay est dans le meilleur des cas confinée à la clandestinité ou dans le pire des cas n'existe même pas. Parfois les seules possibilités sont limitées à des lieux de cruising publics, des cafés et parfois quelques petits groupes.
Depuis les démêlés entre l'organisation GayRussia menée par Nikolai Alekseev et le maire de Moscou qui avait interdit la première Gay Pride, la scène gay russe a gagné sa place dans les médias internationaux. Malgré toutes les interdictions, les activistes tiennent depuis 2006 en mai une démonstration rencontrant de fortes réactions de la part d'opposants fanatiques. La politique actuelle en Russie continue d'entraver les activistes dans leurs campagnes de sensibilisation avec toute une série de lois, malgré le jugement de 2010 de la Cour Européenne de Justice pour les Droits de l'Homme.
Les touristes étrangers doivent observer strictement les conditions de séjour dans le pays. La Russie est une destination avantageuse, cependant l'industrie touristique est passablement développée en dehors des grandes villes. La riche cuisine russe, les paysages variés et les curiosités touristiques innombrables garantissent un séjour inoubliable.

Las relaciones homosexuales consentidas entre adultos son legales, la edad de consentimiento está en los 16 años. El sexo profesional es legal para los clientes pero los trabajadores del sexo pueden ser acusados por incumplimiento del orden. Asegúrese que los potenciales compañeros sexuales tengan al menos 18 años.
En Moscú y en San Petersburgo, donde las zonas comerciales del ambiente están un poco más evolucionadas, se puede vivir como homosexual con relativa seguridad. En otras ciudades la vida gay se halla, en el mejor de los casos, en la clandestinidad o bien, en el peor de los casos, no existe en absoluto. A menudo las únicas alternativas son las zonas públicas de ligue, cafés conocidos y a veces también en pequeños grupos.
Desde el conflicto del año 2005 entre la organización dirigida por Nikolai Alekseev GayRussia y el alcalde de Moscú, que prohibió ilegalmente la primera Marcha del Orgullo Gay en Rusia, se informa cada vez más en los medios de comunicación internacionales sobre la situación de los activistas gays de Rusia. A pesar de todas las prohibiciones, estos activistas vienen celebrando desde el 2006 cada mes de mayo una manifestación, que provoca encendidas reacciones de grupos opositores fanáticos. A pesar de la sentencia del Tribunal Europeo de Derechos Humanos de 2010, la política actual de Rusia sigue intentando obstruir, mediante una serie de leyes, el trabajo público de los activistas.
Los turistas extranjeros deben respetar las cada vez más estrictas disposiciones de entrada. Rusia es un destino turístico que merece la pena, aunque el sector turístico fuera de las grandes capitales no esté especialmente orientado al cliente. La variada gastronomía rusa, los entretenidos paisajes y los innumerables atractivos de este país seguro que harán del viaje una experiencia inolvidable.

I rapporti omosessuali tra adulti consenzienti sono legali e l'età del consenso è di 16 anni. Il sesso a pagamento è legale per il cliente mentre l'operatore o l'operatrice del sesso possono essere soggetti ad una sanzione amministrativa. Assicuratevi che l'operatore o l'operatrice del sesso abbia compiuto il 18° anno di età. A Mosca e a San Pietroburgo, dove le rispettive scene gay sono già piuttosto affermate, si può vivere la propria omosessualità in maniera piuttosto sicura. Nelle altre città, la vita gay si svolge, nella migliore delle ipotesi, nei sotterranei, nella peggiore delle ipotesi, invece, non esiste proprio. Spesso l'unica possibilità sono gli spazi pubblici per il cruising, famosi caffè e a volte piccole organizzazioni.
Da quando avvenne la lite tra il responsabile del sito GayRussia Nikolai Alekseev e il sindaco di Mosca, che nel 2005 ha vietato, contro la legge, la prima manifestazione del Christopher Street Day in Russia, le notizie sugli attivisti gay del Paese fanno il giro del mondo. Nonostante tutti i divieti, dal 2006, nel mese di maggio, gli attivisti gay sono riusciti ad organizzare delle manifestazioni avversate tuttavia da fanatici oppositori. Inoltre, gli attuali politici si stanno dando da fare per ostacolare ulteriormente le pubbliche relazioni degli attivisti, nonostante la sentenza della Corte Europea dei diritti dell'uomo del 2010.
I visitatori stranieri farebbero bene ad attenersi sempre alle condizioni d'ingresso per i turisti stranieri. Vale davvero la pena visitare la Russia, sebbene l'industria del turismo fuori le grandi città non sia ancora orientato verso la clientela estera. La varia cucina, i suggestivi paesaggi e le infinite attrazioni di questo Paese faranno della vostra vacanza un'esperienza indimenticabile.

NATIONAL GAY INFO

■ LGBT Human Rights Project GayRussia.Ru
✉ Moskva 🖳 www.GayRussia.ru
The main LGBT advocate group in Russia. Also a national gay website providing daily news updates. More than 400 articles in English about gay life in Russia. Organizer of Moscow Gay Pride Festival and the Russian International Day Against Homophobia (IDAHO). Founding member of the Gays Without Borders network.

NATIONAL PUBLICATIONS

■ BF (Best For)
✉ Moskva 🖳 www.bfmg.ru
Free magazine, in Russian only.

■ Coverboy
✉ Moscow 🖳 coverboy.ru
New Russian male photography magazine.

■ Kvir gay magazine
✉ Moskva ☏ (495) 783 00 55 🖳 www.kvir.ru
Available in a few book shops; in Russian only.

■ Pinx
✉ Moskva ☏ (495) 783 00 99
🖳 shop.gay.ru/books/pinx
Leaflet for Lesbians; in Russian only. Same distributor than „Kvir".

NATIONAL PUBLISHERS

■ LGBT Media Publishing
Published Russian version of several books about Oscar Wilde. Several photo book projects.

NATIONAL COMPANIES

■ Russian Version – Gay Video Internet Store
✉ Moskva 🖳 www.gayvideo.ru
Wide assortment of Russian, American and European gay and lesbian videos and CDs. Orders via internet, shipping worldwide.

Astrakhan – Astrakhan Region ☏ 8512

PUBLICATIONS

■ Prospekt (GLM)
A special gay section is included. Appears every Wed.

CAFES

■ Spektr (b glm MA)
3, Trusova ul.

DANCECLUBS

■ Dair (B D GLM MA) Sat 22-5h
Gay night on Sat only.

SWIMMING

-Nudist beach „eva plage" (when coming from the town, take the new „Novi most" bridge. At the middle of the bridge, head down on the right side, go along the Volga by the beach (ca 2km) until the „Kossa" turn in the Volga. Only in summer (May-Sep)

CRUISING

-Central station „Vokzal" (toilets on the outside, when leaving the station on the right)
-Esplanade situated on the right side of central station „Vokzal"
-Park Lenina (near „Novimost" bridge on the left, bus N°4/25/4A, tram N°1A, trolleybus N°1/3 exit „Dietski mir")
-Fraternity Park „Bratski sad" also known as „bliadski sad" (opp. the entrance of Krémelin d'Astrakhan)
-"Studientcheskaïa polyclinika" (toilets on the outside, bus N°4, exit „ulitsa kommunisticheskaïa")
-"Darwinskie" toilets (13 Darwin Street)

Chelyabinsk – Chelyabinsk Region ☏ 3512

RESTAURANTS

■ Grilliage (B d glm M ST)
Molodogvardeytsev Str. 31 ☏ (352) 741 22 51
Gay parties on Fridays.

CRUISING

- Kirova street, next to the Opera house, after 19h
- U Tanka (public park at the Komsomolskaya square) (g OC).

Ekaterinburg – Sverdlovskaya Region ☏ 343

DANCECLUBS

■ Kvartal – PRO (CC D DR glm M P S VS) Sat 23-6h
Belinskogo ul. 83 ☏ (919) 378 66 62
Dancing, sofa-zone, dark room. Video installations, low prices at the bar, show program, face-control.

■ Popova 6 (b glm WE) 22h-open end
Popova ul. 6

Irkutsk – Irkutsk Region ☏ 3952

TOURIST INFO

■ Mandarin Travel (glm MA)
10-20, Sat 11-16h, Sun closed
of. 6, Marata str, 38 ☏ (3952) 33 60 26
Gay-friendly travel services, individual trips, tickets, special programmes.

DANCECLUBS

■ Megapolis (B D g MA)
Ulitsa Ulan-Batorskaya 4 ☏ (3952) 42 64 10

Kaliningrad – Kaliningrad Region ☏ 4012

BARS

■ Selena Café-Bar (B glm WE)
Moskovsky prospekt 97 ☏ (4012) 43 43 39
Mostly gay after 23h.

Kazan – Tatarstan Republic ☏ 843

BARS

■ Provokatsia (B d G S) Thu-Sun 21-5h
Bratiev Kasimovyh Street 38 ☏ (843) 35 22 67
Disco, striptease, show balet, various competitions, big money prizes to win at weekends!

DANCECLUBS

■ Shura-Le Club (B G m SNU) 21-3h
Moskovskaya ul. 40 *Go into the arch, then up the stairs on the 2nd floor*
☏ (843) 260 70 40
This club is for those who like to sit in quiet atmosphere, entertainment starts around midnight.

CRUISING

-Square in front of Kamala theatre
-Park near the monument to Tukai.

Krasnodar – Krasnodar Region ☏ 8612

DANCECLUBS

■ Club Labris (b glm) lesbian party on Fri
c/o Cafe Reina, Krasnaya ul. 102 ☏ (8612) 918 981 78 82
🖳 www.clublabris.ucoz.ru
The first and unique club in the south of Russia created by girls and only for girls. See www.clublabris.ucoz.ru for details.

Moskva ☎ 499

Moscow, capital of Russia, was founded in 1147 and has a population of over 15 million inhabitants. Moscow is not only the business centre of Russia, but also home of the most flamboyant Russian gay venues, though the scene is not stable with venues changing frequently. Even though public attitude towards homosexuality in Moscow is quite tolerant, it is advisable to refrain from public display of affection (whereas e. g. kissing in the street, holding hands etc). The first gay pride festival took place in May 2006. On this occasion, several people were beaten by small nationalist groups coming from regions of Russia. Since then, gays attempted to organize the same event every May with the same result.

Die russische Hauptstadt Moskau wurde im Jahr 1147 gegründet und hat mittlerweile über 15 Millionen Einwohner. Moskau ist nicht nur das Geschäftszentrum Russlands, sondern beherbergt auch die schrillsten Schwulenlocations des Landes. Doch die Szene ist mit ihren ständig wechselnden Veranstaltungsorten sehr schnelllebig. Obwohl die Moskauer recht tolerant mit der Homosexualität umgehen, ist von öffentlichen Zärtlichkeitsbekundungen wie Küssen oder Händehalten abzuraten. Bei der ersten CSD-Demonstration der Stadt im Mai 2006 wurden mehrere Demonstranten von kleinen, nationalistisch gesinnten Gruppen tätlich angegriffen, die aus verschiedenen Regionen des Landes angereist waren. Seitdem wird hier alljährlich im Mai der Versuch unternommen, einen CSD zu organisieren – bisher leider immer mit den gleichen Folgen.

Moscou, la capitale russe, a été fondée en 1147 et compte aujourd'hui plus de 15 millions d'habitants. Moscou est non seulement le pôle commercial de la Russie mais comprend aussi les lieux gays les plus extravagants du pays: la scène est en mutation constante, avec des cafés, bars, boîtes qui changent en permanence. Bien que les Moscovites soient assez tolérants envers l'homosexualité, les gestes publics d'affection tels que baisers ou se tenir la main sont déconseillés. Lors de la première Gay Pride de la ville en mai 2006, plusieurs manifestants ont été attaqués violemment par de petits groupes à tendance nationalistes venus de différentes régions du pays. Depuis lors, chaque mois de mai, une Gay Pride est célébrée avec toujours les mêmes conséquences malheureusement.

La capital rusa se fundó en el año 1147 y ahora ya tiene más de 15 millones de habitantes. Moscú no es sólo el centro económico de Rusia sino que también alberga los locales gays más extravagantes del país, ya que el ambiente aquí es muy vivo, con locales que cambian constantemente de localización. Aunque los moscovitas son tolerantes con la homosexualidad, no aconsejamos hacer muestras de cariño en público como besarse o darse la mano. Durante la primera marcha del Orgullo Gay de la ciudad, en mayo de 2006, muchos participantes fueron agredidos por pequeños grupos de carácter nacionalista, que se habían trasladado desde diferentes regiones del país. Desde entonces cada mes de mayo se intenta organizar una marcha del Orgullo pero desgraciadamente siempre con las mismas consecuencias.

La capitale russa Mosca è stata fondata nel 1147 e conta adesso più di 15 milioni di abitanti. Mosca non è solo il centro finanziario della Russia ma anche il luogo che ospita i più estroversi locali gay del Paese. Tuttavia la scena gay è molto cangiante e le location cambiano costantemente. Sebbene i moscoviti siano abbastanza tolleranti nei confronti dell'omosessualità, vi sconsigliamo di scambiarvi effusioni di affetto in pubblico e quindi baciarsi o tenersi per mano. Nel maggio del 2006, durante la prima manifestazione in ambito del Christopher Street Day, molti manifestanti sono stati aggrediti da piccoli gruppi di ultranazionalisti arrivati di proposito dalle più diverse regioni del Paese. Da allora, tutti i mesi di maggio, si cerca di organizzare a Mosca una manifestazione in ambito del Christopher Street Day, che tuttavia ha sempre gli stessi risvolti.

GAY INFO

Telephone Hotline
☎ (499) 783 83 33
Free telephone hotline for men having sex with men.

BARS

12 Volt (! B gLm M S YC) 18-6h
Tverskaya St., 12, building 4 *M° Tverskaya, Pushkinskaya or Chekhovskaya*
☎ (495) 933 28 15 www.12voltclub.ru
Face control. Small place, often foggy with smoke. Possibility to dine. The DJ plays your music for an extra payment. Low prices. Mostly for lesbians.

7freedays (! AC B d GLM MA S VEG WI) 18-6h
Milyutinskiy pereulok, 6 bld 1 *M°Lubyanka* ☎ (495) 627 3101
www.7freedays.com
Russia's first GL-friendly bar. Cozy atmosphere, affordable bar, cultural events, exciting games, karaoke, your favorite movies, art-exhibitions, fashion and talk-shows.

ChubaBar Afterhours (Bar Vrednyh Privychek)
(B glm M SNU YC) 24hrs
Myasnitskaya St., 26a *M° Turgenevskaya* ☎ (495) 542 37 65
www.chubabar.ru
Gay afterparty Fri, Sat, Sun from 5am.

Club 69 (B GLM MA) Thu 19-6h, Fri-Sun 23-6h
Rozanova St., 4 *M° Begovaya* ☎ (495) 580 6927 www.club-69.ru
Opened in December 2008, designed in European minimalistic style. Karaoke. Wi-Fi for free. Not centrally located

Udar (B GLM M MA S) Thu-Sat 22-6h
Olimpiyskiy Prospekt, 16-1 *Olimpiyskiy stadium M° Prospect Mira*
☎ (495) 6883722 www.udarclub.ru
One of the best and the biggest lesbian clubs in Russia.

CAFES

Elf (B D G MC) 11-6h
Leningradski Prospekt, 23 *M° Belorusskaya or Dinamo* ☎ (495) 626 48 37
In the afternoon dining room of an office building. After 20h starts to work in a gay bar mode. Bear parties in cafe-bar „Elf" on Wed and Sat. Not centrally located.

Filial (GLM M MC) Mon-Wed 12-24, Thu-Sun 12-6h
Krivokolennyi per. 3, bld. 1 *M° Lubyanka* ☎ (495) 621 2143
www.filialmoscow.com
Ideal place for a meeting with friends, appointments and simply single suppers to itself in pleasure. Besides near to „Propaganda".

Nashe Café (B G MC S) 18-6h
Tverskaya 25/9 *M° Tverskaya* ☎ (495) 699 2683 www.nashe.su
In cafe two small halls – one for dialogue and the rest, the second for dances and the show program. Low prices.

DANCECLUBS

Baza (b d G m MA) Daily 11-6h
Milyutinskiy pereulok, 6 *M° Lubyanka* ☎ (495) 627 31 93
www.clubbaza.com
Very trashy place, small and poorly lighted. Drag shows at 3h.

Central Station (! AC B CC D DR F G M MA OS S SNU ST VS) 22-6h
Yuzhnyi Proezd 4 *M° Krasnye Vorota, opp. Hilton Hotel Leningradskaya*
☎ (495) 988 3555 www.centralclub.ru
The newest and biggest club in Moscow. Opened in continuation of „Three Monkeys" club and his own team. Sister club „Central Station" in St. Petersburg. Four levels, 2 bars, professional karaoke, dark room, two stages, European restaurant.

Charm (! B D DR glm MC RR S t) Daily 23-6, Fri-Sun 23-7h
Dubininskaya str. 69, bld 74 *M° Paveletskaya or Tulskaya*
☎ (495) 645-07-66 www.sharm.clubchance.net
Big, mixed club on two floors. For the first time in history club – toilet for males, females and transsexuals.
Many various halls

La Discoteque (B D g MA) Fri-Sat 23-6h
Niznij Susalnyj per. 5/5a *M° Kurskaya near Secret club* ☎ (495) 410 5452
www.discoteque.ru
Gay party sometimes.

Propaganda (B D g m MA P) Sun 23-6h
Bolshoi Zlatoustinskiy per, 7 *M° Kitai-Gorod* ☎ (495) 624 57 32
www.propagandamoscow.com
Gay parties only Sun 23-6h. Strict face and dress control.

■ **Secret** (! B D DR GLM OS S ST WE YC) 22-6h
Niznij Susalnyj per. 7, bld 8 *M° Kurskaya, near bar Kruzhka on Kazakova str.* ☎ (495) 649 1432 🖳 www.secret-club.ru
In the mix-club „Secret" there are two big dance-floors: 1st floor – House, 2nd floor – Euro-pop. Three bars, the summer patio, VIP zone, professional light and good sound. On the big stage on the ground floor, not only drag queens perform, but also stars of the Russian pop music. See www.secret-club.ru for details.

RESTAURANTS

■ **Lafonten** (AC B CC g LM M MA OS S) 12 – until last customer leaves
Dubininskaya, 30, Bldg 1 *M° Petrovsko-Razumovskaya* ☎ (499) 480 41 92 🖳 www.lafonten.ru
Nice and quiet, gay-friendly restaurant not in the city centre. Guitar and piano concerts in the evenings. Affordable prices.

SAUNAS/BATHS

■ **Mayakovka Spa**
(! AC B DR DU FH G MA MSG P RR SA SB VS WH WO) 17-6h
Oruzheynyi pereulok, 13, Bldg. 2 *M° Mayakovskaya, go along Garden Ring from Tverskaya St., turn left off bldg. 13* ☎ (499) 250 00 83 🖳 www.mayakovka.com
It may be the best sauna but it is not really modern or comfortable compared to Eurpean standards. Not really large – about 4000sq ft.

■ **Nashe Spa** (B M MC MSG RR SA SB) 24 hrs
2nd Paveletskiy proezd 5, bld 1. *M° Paveletskaya* ☎ (495) 728 1011 🖳 www.nashe.su
Modern gay complex the area of 500 sq. m consisting of: the Finnish sauna, the Turkish steam room, pool with a font, shower, the Restaurant hall, bar, relax rooms and more.

■ **Termas** (B DR DU FC G M MSG P PI PP R RR SA SB SOL VS WH) 14-6h
Sadovaya Spasskaya, 18 *M° Krasnye Vorota* ☎ (495) 500 20 77 🖳 www.termas.ru
Finish sauna, solarium, restaurant, VIP rooms. Massage available on the premises. Very friendly staff. Fri – club show! Private club, ask for entrance-pass in Mayakovka Spa sauna.

■ **Voda** (! AC b DR DU FH G m MA MSG OS p PI SA SB SH SNU SOL VS WH WO) 17-5h, Fri & Sat -7, Sun 17-5h
Yuzhnyy proyezd 4 *4 M° Krasnye Vorota, near Central Station club.* ☎ (499) 246 09 11 🖳 www.vodaspa.ru
Biggest gay sauna in Moscow, about 800 sq m.Popular and crowded. Western styled atmosphere and service. Two floors, sauna, cold swimming pool, Hammam, dark room, massage.

TRAVEL AND TRANSPORT

■ **Three Monkeys** (CC GLM) Mon-Fri 11-19h
Yuzhnyi proezd 4 *M° Krasnie Vorota* 🖳 www.tk3.ru
Assistance with gay guides, visas and accommodation. In and out tourism. English speaking staff.

GENERAL GROUPS

■ **Charities Aid Foundation (CAF)**
Myasnitskaya str. 24/7, bld. 1 *M° Turgenevskaya* ☎ (495) 792 59 29 🖳 www.cafrussia.ru/eng
British charity foundation extending support and offering legal assistance to NGOs, including gay and lesbian organizations.

CRUISING

Do not take anyone you may have picked up in a crusing area to your hotel room!
-Square round a fountain front of Bolshoi theatre (M° Teatralnaya)
-Kamergersky pereulok (M° Okhotny Ryad, Teatralnaya)
-Iliynsky Skver (M° Kitai-Gorod, very popular in the evening)
-Alexandrovsky Sad (M° Okhotny Ryad/Borovitskaya/Ploschad Revolutsii, the garden near the Kremlin walls
-Pushkinskaya Ploschad (M° Pushkinskaya/Tverskaya, the square around the Pushkin monument)
-Izmailovsky park (M° Izmailovsky par, two paths which leading to the clearing)
-GUM Department Store, in the facilities.

Murmansk – Murmansk Region ☎ 8152

DANCECLUBS

■ **Neon** (B D glm I MA) Wed-Sun 18-2h
Razina ul., 8 ☎ (8152) 24 23 06
Every Friday and Saturday showprogram.

HEALTH GROUPS

■ **Murmansk AIDS Center** 9-17h
Tralovaya ulitsa 47 *City center, opp. Sea College* ☎ (8152) 47 36 61

CRUISING

- Zolotoy Lev Café (Samoylovoy Ulitsa)
- Logovo Bar.

Nizhny Novgorod Nizhny Novgorod Region ☎ 831

DANCECLUBS

■ **STM Club** (B D G m p) Wed-Sun 23-5h
Rozhdestvenskaya, 20 *In the premises of Molodezhniy Bar* ☎ (951) 915 57 20

CRUISING

- Ploschad Minina (the alley to the right from the Dmitievskaya tower of the Novgorod Kremlin)

Novosibirsk – Novosibirsk Region ☎ 383

DANCECLUBS

■ **Pride** (AC D GLM m MA S SNU) 23-6h twice monthly
☎ (0923) 150 76 05
Probably the biggest gay party in Siberia, twice a month.

■ **Sky-Night** (AC B D GLM m MA WE) Fri-Sun 23-6h
Selezneva ul, 46 *M° Berezovaya Roscha*

TRAVEL AND TRANSPORT

■ **Joy Travel** (GLM)
Krasnij Prospect 54, of.405 ☎ (383) 21 35 62 🖳 www.joytravel.ru
Travel agency, also providing gay tours.

CRUISING

- Square in front of the Opera Theatre.
- Beach at Obskoye More in Akademgorodok.

Omsk – Omsk Region ☎ 3812

GENERAL GROUPS

■ **Pulsar** (GLM MA T) Helpline Tue & Sat 13-17h (Moscow time)
PO Box 2861 ☎ (03812) 38 52 55 🖳 www.pulsarrussia.ru
Also ☎ (03812) 28 52 55 – 24-hour help line.

Rostov-na-Donu – Rostov Region ☎ 8632

BARS

■ **777** (d glm MA) 18-6h
Bolshaya Sadovaya ul. 180-182
The cosy gay and lesbi-bar. Club music – electronic mixes.

■ **Moskovskiy** (B D glm M s)
Bolshaya Sadovaya ul. 62 *Across the street from the City Duma and Gorky Park, in the premises of restaurant Moskovskiy*
Showtime Sat.

DANCECLUBS

■ **Kamasutra** (D GLM M ST) 21-6h
Lermontovskaya ul., 233 B ☎ (863) 206 16 40 🖳 www.kamasutra-club.ru
The club's total area is 800m², with VIP-zone, every Fri and Sat stars of the travesty-collective of Russia perform.

■ **Pomada MIX** (B D GLM M S ST) Tue-Sun 21-5h
15 linia, 2 ☏ (919) 884 25 15 🖳 www.pomadaclub.ru
The most unusual and quickly developing club project „Pomada MIX" is a network of progressive clubs in the south of Russia for youngsters with „the expanded orientation". A lot of party-goers, freaks, most unusual and very interesting people. All week club parties. See website for details.

CRUISING

-Park of October revolution (At theatre square, behind Maxim Gorkiy-Theatre)
-fountain near the book House (Crossing of the Budennovsky prospekt and Bolshaya Sadovaya).

St. Petersburg ☏ 812

St. Petersburg, the cultural and gay capital of Russia, was founded on May 27, 1703 by emperor Peter the Great and has a current population of around 5 million inhabitants. Much effort was undertaken to revamp for the 300 year celebration, making the city even more attractive to foreign visitors.
St. Petersburg possesses not only the tourist treasures such as the Hermitage, Russian Museum and Imperial Palaces in the environs, but also home the scattered gay venues including night clubs, bars, saunas, seaside beaches and the officially registered in 1991 gay and lesbian Center „Krilija" – a first in Russian history.

St. Petersburg wurde am 27. Mai 1703 von Kaiser Peter dem Großen gegründet und ist heute mit etwa 5 Millionen Einwohnern Russlands schwule und kulturelle Hauptstadt. Für die 300-Jahr-Feier wurden weder Kosten noch Mühen gescheut, um die Stadt für ausländische Besucher noch interessanter zu gestalten.
Neben den touristischen Sehenswürdigkeiten wie der Eremitage, dem Russischen Museum und den Zarenpalästen der Umgebung hat das Zentrum von St. Petersburg noch einiges zu bieten: Zahlreiche schwule Treffpunkte wie Nachtclubs, Bars, Saunen, Badestrände und das „Krilija". Es ist das erste Center für Schwule und Lesben der russischen Geschichte und ist seit 1991 offiziell eingetragen.

Saint-Pétersbourg a été fondée le 27 mai 1703 par le tsar Pierre le Grand et avec ses 5 millions d'habitants, elle est aujourd'hui la capitale culturelle et homosexuelle du pays. Pour ses 300 ans, la ville a été rénovée pour la rendre encore plus attrayante aux touristes étrangers.
Outre les curiosités touristiques telles que le musée de l'Hermitage, le musée russe et les palais des tsars aux environs, le centre de Saint-Pétersbourg a beaucoup a offrir : de nombreux bars, boîtes, saunas et plages homos, sans oublier le « Kriliya », le premier centre gay et lesbien de l'histoire de la Russie, officiellement créé en 1991.

San Petersburgo fue fundada el 27 de mayo de 1703 por el emperador Pedro el Grande y actualmente es, con sus aproximadamente cinco millones de habitantes, la capital cultural gay de Rusia. Para la celebración del 300º aniversario, no se escatimaron ni esfuerzos ni gastos para que la ciudad fuera mucho más interesante para los turistas extranjeros.
Junto a los puntos de interés turístico como el Hermitage, el Museo Ruso y los palacios imperiales de los alrededores, el centro de San Petersburgo tiene todavía mucho que ofrecer: numerosos locales gays como clubes nocturnos, bares, saunas, playas y el „Krilija". Se trata del primer centro para los gays y lesbianas de la historia rusa y está inscrito oficialmente desde 1991.

San Pietroburgo fu fonfata il 27 maggio 1703 dall'imperatore Pietro il Grande e oggi con i suoi 5 milioni di abitanti è la capitale culturale e gay della Russia. Per il trecentenario della fondazione della città non si è badato a spese per abbellire la città agli occhi dei turisti.
Oltre alle attrazioni turistiche come l'Hermitage, il Museo Russo e i palazzi degli Zar, il centro di San Pietroburgo ha molto altro da offrire: diversi locali gay come discoteche, bar, saune, spiagge e la „Krilija" che è il primo centro per omosessuali nella storia della Russia ed è ufficialmente registrato dal 1991.

GAY INFO

■ **Excess Gay** (GLM)
🖳 www.xsgay.ru
Web site with informationon on gay life in St. Petersburg.

BARS

■ **Blue Oyster** (B cc D DR G m MA r t) 18-1h, Fri & Sat -8h
Lomonosova Ulitsa 1 *M° Nevsky Prospekt*
🖳 www.boyster.ru
Loud and busy on WE.

MEN'S CLUBS

■ **Bunker** (! AC B DR F G MA P SA SH VS) 16-6h
Naberezhnaya Reki Fontanka 90, bld 7 *M° Pushkinskaya, near hotel Kamea, Borodinskayastr. 11* ☏ (812) 764 28 23
🖳 www.bunkerspb.ru
A comfortable place with private cabins, showers and videos. The only cruising bar in St. Petersburg. Parties every Thu 20-24h.

DANCECLUBS

■ **Cabaret** (B D DR GLM m MA S ST WE) Fri-Sun 23-6h
Obvodnii Canal Emb. 181 *M° Baltiiskaya* ☏ (812) 575 45 12
🖳 www.cabarespb.ru
Drag shows after 2h in the morning. Very popular. 1000 m² area.

■ **Central Station** (! AC B D DR G I M MA S SNU ST VS)
18-6, Fri & Sat -10h
Lomonosova Ulitsa 1 *M° Nevsky Prospekt* ☏ (812) 312 36 00
🖳 www.centralstation.ru
3 floors, big dancefloor, karaoke room, restobar, 5 bars, dark room.

■ **Club. The** (! B D DR GLM p S ST VS YC) Thu-Sun 23-7h
Shcherbakov Pereulok, 17 *M° Dostoevskaya/Vladimirskaya* ☏ 912 11 69
🖳 www.the-club.fm
A new club in the city centre with weekly changing performances.

SAUNAS/BATHS

■ **Fitness Club** (AC B CC DR DU G I MA MSG SA SB SL SOL VS WO)
Daily 16-6h
Mokhovaya str. 47 *M° Nevskiy Prospect and M° Mayakovskaya*
☏ (812) 273 98 82 🖳 bunkerspb.ru/en/fitnesssauna
Small but comfortable sauna in the city center. The only gay sauna in the city! Don't be put off by the woman at the entrance who collect the entrance money.

TELECOMMUNICATION

■ **Cafe-Max** (B MA R) 24hrs
Nevsky Prospect 90/92 *M° Mayakovskaya* ☏ (812) 273 82 82
Internet-cafe on main street of the city. In the evening it's crowded with young gay boys, who come to check mails and have a bottle of beer with friends. Also popular among hustlers.

GENERAL GROUPS

■ **Krilija (Wings)** (G I MA) 12-22h
Box 108 *City center, M° Nevsky Prospekt/Gostinniy Dvor* ☏ (812) 312 31 80
🖳 www.krilija.sp.ru
Gay human rights center and ILGA member, providing city gay scene information, support, gay friendly accommodation, operating gay tourist agency.

HEALTH GROUPS

■ **City Anti-AIDS Center** (GLM MA)
179-a Obvodnil Canal *M° Baltiskaya* ☏ (812) 575 44 81
Anonymous HIV testing.

CRUISING

-Moskovyky Railway Station (M° Ploshchad Vosstania, main hall, facilities. As well as the facilities at the other four city railway stations)
-Small park Kat'kin Sadik near to the monument to Catherine the Great on the Nevsky Prospekt, next to the National Library (M° Gostinii Dvor), day and night, be careful.

Saratov – Saratov Region ☏ 8452

SAUNAS/BATHS

■ **Bath on the Ilinsky area** (g MA PI)
Chapaeva *Towards Avenue of Kirov*
Possibility to hook-up for the evening.

GENERAL GROUPS

■ **Krylia** (YC)
Cheluskintsev, dom 54, kv 6 ☏ (8452) 25 15 88
Center for Social Problems and Humanitarian Development of Children and Teenagers.

SWIMMING

-The Engelsky part of a city beach through the bridge Saratov-Engels on Volga (gay beach in Summer time).

CRUISING

-Square on street crossing Moscow (the central road) and Astrakhanskaya.

Sochi – Krasnodar Region ☏ 8622

DANCECLUBS

■ **Cabaret Mayak** (B D GLM M OS PI R S ST VS)
Sokolova ul, 1 *City centre to the right of hotel „Primorskaya"*
☏ (8622) 38 30 40 🖳 www.sochi-club.ru
One of the best and big clubs of the country (with more than 1000 m²). Two halls, a cabaret hall (250 people) and cruise-bar (100 people) with dark labyrinths, cabins and pool. Also a summer garden for 80 guests. Daily transvestite shows. Show acts on stage. Cruising bar.

■ **Pomada MIX** (B D GLM M S ST) Tue-Sun 21-5h
Chernomorskaya ul, 15 ☏ (8622) 918 099 44 89
🖳 www.pomadaclub.ru
The most unusual and quickly developing club project „Pomada MIX" is a network of progressive clubs in the south of Russia for youngsters with „the expanded orientation". Party-goers, freaks, most unusual and very interesting people. All week club parties.

CRUISING

-Sputnik Beach (AYOR NU) (shuttle bus 4 or 4C from the main bus station, Maly Akhun)
-Dagomys beach, (behind a beach of a hotel complex „Dagomys").

Tomsk – Siberian Federal District ☏ 3822

DANCECLUBS

■ **Contra Club** (B D GLM MC) Wed-Sun 22h-open end
Komsomolsky prospect, 68/2 ☏ (3822) 903 951 02 11
Show programms on Fri & Sat.

■ **The Center** (B D GLM WE) Thu-Sun 21h-open end
Obrub ul., 8a ☏ (3822) 51 53 00
300 m², original interior, parking. The club is located in the city centre.

CRUISING

-New cathedral square
-Vacation spots at White lake (Beloe Ozero)

Tver – Tver Region ☏ 4822

DANCECLUBS

■ **Prince** (B D P WE YC)
Levitana ul., 28 ☏ (4822) 72 54 22 🖳 www.prince-club.ru
Very glamourous club. There is a dark labyrinth and „a confidential" room. See www.prince-club.ru for details.

CRUISING

-Kazakov Square (on Sovetskaya ulitsa)
-Medical Academy Square (on Ploschad Revolutsii)
-Square near the monument to Krylov (near to eternal fire and Suvorov military cadet school).

Vladivostok – Primorya Region ☏ 4232

BARS

■ **Tetka** (b glm) 21-6h
Pologaya ul., 22 (2nd floor) ☏ (4232) 648 050
This unique and oldest gay bar is an institution in Vladivostok.

■ **Tribunal** (B D GLM m ST) 20-6h
Aleutskaya ulitsa 14a ☏ (4232) 51 53 30
🖳 www.gay.ru/vladivostok/tribunal
Karaoke.

DANCECLUBS

■ **Lu-Lu** (B D glm WE) 22-6h
Melnikovskaya ul., 101 ☏ (4232) 552 551
Big, spacious, comfortable. The club occupies over 500 m² and is arranged on two floors.

Voronezh – Voronezh Region ☏ 4732

SAUNAS/BATHS

■ **Sauna Voronezh** (b g m MA SA)
per. Slavy 6 *Near Central road service station on the Moskovsky prosp.*
Not gay but sometimes interesting for hookups. Be discreet!

HEALTH GROUPS

■ **AIDS Center** (glm MA)
Moskovsky Prospekt 109 ☏ (4732) 14 54 40

CRUISING

-Petrovsky garden

Serbia

Name: Srbija · Serbien ·Serbie ·Serbia ·Serbian
Location: South-eastern Europe
Initials: SER
Time: GMT +1
International Country Code: ☏ 381
Language: Serbian
Area: 88,361 km²
Currency: 1 Dinar (N. Din) = 100 Para
Population: 9,863,000
Capital: Belgrad
Religions: 70% Serbian Orthodox

The age of consent in Serbia is 14, regardless of sexual orientation and/or gender. In March 2009 the parliament approved a unified Anti-Discrimination Law which prohibited, among other things, discrimination on the basis of sexual orientation and transgender status in all areas.
But the new legal situation has so far failed to reduce the violence and discrimination daily experienced by people with same-sex preferences. Any public display of homosexual desire or behaviour on the street, in parks or non-gay clubs can still be dangerous.
Western-oriented groups in Serbia, who want to lead the country into the European Union, saw this cancellation as a setback. During the Gay Pride 2010 in Belgrade dozens of protesters from a right wing nationalist group clashed with marchers and police. Police used water cannon and tear gas to disperse the protesters. The 2011 Gay Pride in Belgrade was cancelled because of safety concerns, as had already happened in 2009, after 2010 had seen 5,000 police deployed to protect 1,000 Pride marchers from counter-demonstrators. Banning Gay Pride events also finds broad support in the population.

Das Schutzalter in Serbien liegt bei 14 Jahren für alle, unabhängig der sexuellen Orientierung und/oder des Geschlechts. Im März 2009 genehmigte das Parlament ein Antidiskriminierungsgesetz, das unter Anderem die Benachteiligung von Menschen wegen der sexuellen Orientierung oder des transgender Status auf allen Gebieten verbietet.
Diese neue Gesetzeslage hat bislang jedoch nicht die Gewalt und Diskriminierung verringert, die Menschen mit gleichgeschlechtlicher Neigung alltäglich erfahren. Die öffentliche Zurschaustellung homosexueller Zärtlichkeit oder gar Lust auf der Straße, in Parks oder in nicht-schwulen Clubs kann immer noch gefährlich sein.
Bei der Pride Parade 2010 in Belgrad, kam es zu gewalttätigen Auseinandersetzungen zwischen Dutzenden von Gegendemonstranten und den Teilnehmern bzw. der Polizei. Die Polizei setzte an verschiedenen Stellen entlang der Marschroute Wasserwerfer und Tränengas ein. Wie schon 2009 wurde auch 2011 der CSD in Belgrad auf Grund von Sicherheitsbedenken abgesagt, nachdem 2010 ein Aufgebot von 5.000 Polizisten eingesetzt werden musste, um 1.000 Teilnehmer vor Gegendemonstrationen zu schützen. Auch in der Bevölkerung erfährt ein Verbot des CSD große Zustimmung.

La majorité sexuelle est fixée à 14 ans pour tous en Serbie, indépendamment de l'orientation sexuelle ou/et du sexe.
En mars 2009 le parlement a adopté une loi antidiscriminatoire qui interdit entre autres les discriminations du fait de l'orientation sexuelle ou du statut de transgenre à tous les niveaux.
Cette nouvelle situation juridique n'a cependant jusqu'à présent pas diminué la violence et la discrimination que subissent les personnes attirées par celles de même sexe. L'ostentation publique d'un désir ou d'un comportement homosexuel dans la rue, dans les parcs ou dans les clubs non gays peut toujours s'avérer dangereuse.
Lors de la Gay Pride en 2010 à Belgrade, des altercations violentes ont eu lieu entre des contremanifestants et des participants ou contre la police. Tout comme en 2009, la Gay Pride a été annulée en 2011 pour des raisons de sécurité après l'usage de 5.000 policiers en 2010 pour protéger les 1.000 participants face aux contre-manifestants. La population elle-même soutient une interdiction de la Gay Pride.

La edad mínima para mantener relaciones sexuales en Serbia es de 14 años, independientemente de la orientación sexual y del género. En marzo de 2009 el Parlamento aprobó una ley la antidiscriminación que prohíbe, entre otras cosas, la discriminación por motivos de orientación sexual o condición de transgénero en todas las áreas.
Esta nueva situación jurídica no ha hecho disminuir hasta ahora la violencia y la discriminación que sufren diariamente las personas homosexuales. La muestra en público de tendencias o actitudes homosexuales en la calle, en parques o en clubs heterosexuales aún puede ser peligroso.
Durante el desfile del Orgullo Gay de 2010 en Belgrado hubo enfrentamientos violentos entre decenas de contra manifestantes, los participantes y la policía. Al igual que en 2009, también en 2011 se ha cancelado la Marcha del Orgullo Gay en Belgrado, por razones de seguridad, después de que en 2010 un contingente de 5.000 policías tuviera que proteger a 1.000 participantes a causa de las contramanifestaciones. La prohibición de la Marcha contó además con gran apoyo por parte de la población.

L'età del consenso in Serbia è per tutti di 14 anni, indipendentemente dal sesso e dall'orientamento sessuale. A marzo del 2009 il parlamento ha varato una legge antidiscriminatoria che vieta, tra le altre cose, anche qualsiasi tipo di discriminazione determinata dall'orientamento sessuale o dall'identità di genere.
A questo miglioramento legislativo, tuttavia, non ha corrisposto un miglioramento in termini di violenza e discriminazione su gente che, invece, è costretta a subirla ogni giorno a causa del proprio orientamento sessuale. L'esposizione pubblica di comportamenti omosessuali in strade, parchi o discoteche non gay può, quindi, essere ancora molto pericoloso.
Durante il CSD di Belgrado 2010 ci sono stati violenti scontri tra una dozzina di contro-manifestanti, manifestanti e polizia. Come era successo già nel 2009, anche nel 2011, a causa di problemi di sicurezza, è stata annullata la parata del CSD di Belgrado. Nel 2010, invece, c'è voluto un dispiego di 5.000 poliziotti per proteggere circa 1.000 manifestanti dai contromanifestanti. Un eventuale divieto del CSD nutre molto consenso anche tra la popolazione.

GENERAL GROUPS

■ **Queeria center** (GLM) Mon-Fri 11-19h
Kralja Milana 22/3 ✉ 11000 Belgrad
☎ (064) 192 49 12 💻 www.queeriacentar.org
National LGBT group working for tolerance and human rights for the homosexual community in Serbia. With Gay Straight Alliance they organize Belgrade Pride, see here www.parada.rs

Belgrad ☎ 011

GAY INFO

■ **Gayecho Web Info Portal** (GLM)
💻 www.gayecho.com
Gayecho is the most popular regional queer info portal that covers not only Serbia but also Bosnia, Montenegro and Croatia. Gay and lesbian info centre GLIC runs this portal. Portal includes daily news, queer theory, queer culture and art, personals, chat, forum and blog.

BARS

■ **Idiot** (B D glm YC)
Dalmatinska 13
One of the coolest bars in the city. Pleasant staff and reasonable prices.
■ **Kandahar** (B glm MA)
Strahinjica Bana 48 ☎ (064) 334 39 70
■ **Smiley** (B glm MA)
Terazije 3-5

CAFES

■ **Bizzare** (B MA NG)
Zmaj Jovina 25 ☎ (011) 303 38 70
A bar/cafe visited by gays, not gay place but friendly atmosphere.
■ **Cafe 24** (b GLM m MA) 18h-open end
Kajmakcalanska 22 *Cnr. Branka Krsmanovica, close to the red cross*
☎ (060) 70 70 777
■ **Espeho Café** (B GLM MA) 18h-open end
Centinjska 4 pasage *Between Buleva despota Stefana and Hilandarska*

DANCECLUBS

■ **Club Apartman** (B D glm YC)
Karadjordjeva 43
Gay-friendly club.
■ **Night club Pleasure** (B D GLM YC)
Kneza Milosa 9 ☎ (062) 899 68 78
The most popular gay and lesbian club in the city.

RESTAURANTS

■ **Supermarket** (B GLM M MA)
Višnjiceva 10
Gayfriendly restaurant.
■ **Zaplet** (b glm M MA)
Kajmakcalanska 2 ☎ (011) 11 2404 142
Gayfriendly restaurant.

GENERAL GROUPS

■ **Belgrade Bears** (f FC G MA)
☎ (062) 9 611 449 💻 www.belgradebears.webs.com
Belgrade bears is the first community of gay bear guys from Belgrade and Serbia, as well as all their fans. Parties are organized every 2-3 months.
■ **Gay Straight Alliance** (GLM)
Cika Ljubina 12/II ☎ 2624 608 💻 www.gsa.org.rs
■ **Spy** (GLM)
☎ 2452 241 💻 www.spy.org.rs
SPY – Safe Puls of Youth has also Drop-in centre, a place to get informed about health, have some coffee or even watch a movie.

CRUISING

All these places are AYOR:
-Usce Park (around Museum of Modern Art, at nights)
-Karadjordjev park (JNA Street, close to Slavija Square, opp. Sveti Sava Cathedral, at night)
-the island in the river Sava Ada Ciganlija, in summer also gay swimming

Novi Sad ☎ 021

BARS

■ **Nublu** (B NG)
Zarka Zrenjanina 12 ☎ 525 365 💻 nublunovisad.blogspot.com
Library and café club. Visited by gays and lesbians.
■ **Queen** (B G P) Fri-Sat 24-7h
c/o Novi Sad Hotel, Bulevar Jase Tomica bb *Opp. main station* ☎ 442 51

DANCECLUBS

■ **Coxx club** (B D G SNU WE)
V. Staica 33
Apply for membership on Gayromeo to enter the club or send email to: coxclub.ns@gmail.com
■ **Yellow club** (B D GLM WE YC)
Petrovaradinska Tvrdjava *Petrovaradin's fortress* ☎ (064) 9 234 678

SEX CINEMAS

■ **Arena** (g) 10-17h
Bulevar Mihajla Pupina *Behind hotel park*
Occasionally porn films.

GENERAL GROUPS

■ **Drop-In Centre** (GLM)
Maksima Gorkog 48 ☎ (062) 350 799 💻 www.jazas.rs
JAZAS Youths organization from Novi Sad runs Drop-in centre, a place to get informed about health, HIV and more.

CRUISING

-Garden in front of the railway station (AYOR; at night)
-Futoski park (Futoska street, behind hotel park, evenings)
-Becar Strand
-Kamenjar Beach
-Bus station (daytime)
-Spens shopping centre (ground floor).

Subotica ☎ 024

DANCECLUBS

■ **Enjoy Club** (B D DR GLM P WE)
☎ (064) 185 79 94
Every second Saturday is a party. Ask for parties calendar and club address on Gayromeo or Facebook or by email: info.enjoytheclub@gmail.com

CRUISING

-Park opposite main station (only evenings)
-Park opposite City Sport centre

Singapore

Name: Singapur · Singapour
Location: Southeast Asia
Initials: SGP
Time: GMT +8
International Country Code: ☏ 65 (no area codes)
International Access Code: ☏ 001
Language: English (official language), Mandarin, Malay, Tamil
Area: 647 km² / 239 sq mi.
Currency: 1 Singapore Dollar (S$) = 100 Cents
Population: 4,800,000
Capital: Singapore
Religions: 32% Buddhists, 22% Daoists, 15% Moslems, 13% Christians
Climate: Hot and tropical climate, humid with some rainy periods from mid August to mid Oct.

Notwithstanding a highly visible campaign in 2007 to rescind article 377A prohibiting anal and oral sex between males, said article remains in force, even if the prime minister himself declared it to be a mere symbol of „a conservative society" and made reassurances that homosexuals would not be prosecuted. Abolishing the law could give off the wrong signal at the moment, he continued, as it was only a question of time until homosexuals would also demand the right to marry and adopt children.
In recent years, the attitude in Singapore towards gay men has swung from extreme to extreme. From 2001 to 2004, it appeared as if the government's stance had softened, evidenced by events such as NATION (held on the eve of Singapore's National Day in August), recognised by Time Magazine and Wall St Journal as Asia's largest gay circuit party. However, this has changed since end of 2004 when the government has inexplicably hardened its position. Gay life still appears to be bubbling and very active, leading many visitors to comment that Singapore streets are „the cruisiest in all of Asia".

Trotz einer vielbeachteten Kampagne 2007 zur Aufhebung des Artikels 377A, der Anal- und Oralsex zwischen Männern verbietet, bleibt dieser in den Gesetzbüchern bestehen, auch wenn der Premierminister selbst dieses Gesetz lediglich zu einem Symbol einer „konservativen Gesellschaft" erklärte und versicherte, dass Schwule nicht verfolgt würden. Eine Abschaffung des Gesetzes könne allerdings derzeit als falsches Signal verstanden werden, da es nur eine Frage der Zeit wäre, dass Homosexuelle auch ein Recht zur Ehe und zur Adoption einforderten.
In den letzten Jahren hat sich die Einstellung gegenüber Schwulen in Singapur von einem Extrem ins andere gewandelt. Zwischen 2001 und 2004 schien die Haltung der Regierung aufgeweicht zu sein. Das zeigte sich am Nation-Fest am Vorabend des Nationalfeiertages im August: vom Time Magazine und Wall Street Journal wurde es damals als größte asiatische Schwulenparty gewürdigt. Allerdings fährt die Regierung seit Ende 2004 aus unerklärlichen Gründen wieder einen harten Kurs. Schwules Leben scheint noch immer sehr lebendig zu pulsieren und viele Besucher beschreiben die Straßen von Singapur als die „größte Cruisingmeile Asiens".

Malgré une campagne remarquée en 2007 concernant la levée de l'article 377A qui interdit et pénalise les relations sexuelles anales et orales entre hommes, celui-ci reste inscrit dans le code civil, même si le Premier ministre en personne a déclaré cette loi comme étant le symbole d'une „société conservatrice" et a assuré que les gays ne seraient pas poursuivis. Selon lui cependant, une abrogation de la loi n'est pas d'actualité et pourrait être actuellement comprise comme un mauvais signal, les homosexuels s'engageant alors dans la brèche jusqu'à exiger le droit à l'union et à l'adoption.
Ces dernières années, les mentalités concernant les gays à Singapour sont passées d'un extrême à l'autre. Entre 2001 et 2004, la position du gouvernement semblait s'être en effet adoucie comme le montre la Fête de la Nation célébrée en août, la veille de la fête nationale : le Time Magazine et le Wall St Journal l'ont consacrée « plus grande fête d'Asie ». Néanmoins, le gouvernement a repris sans raison claire une politique plus dure fin 2004. Cependant, la vie gay semble être toujours aussi animée et de nombreux touristes décrivent les rues de Singapour comme – le plus grand boulevard de drague d'Asie.

A pesar de una popular campaña en 2007 para la abolición del artículo 377A, que prohíbe el sexo anal y oral entre hombres, éste todavía continúa en los libros de leyes, incluso cuando el mismo primer ministro declaró que esta legislación era un símbolo de una „sociedad conservadora" y aseguró que no se perseguiría a los homosexuales. La supresión de la ley podría ser interpretada actualmente como una falsa señal pues se trataría sólo de una cuestión de tiempo hasta que los homosexuales también exijan el derecho al matrimonio y la adopción.
En los últimos años, la actitud hacia los homosexuales en Singapur ha cambiado de un extremo a otro. Entre 2001 y 2004 parece que la posición del gobierno se ha suavizado un poco, como muestra la fiesta Nation (que tuvo lugar en agosto, en la vigilia de la fiesta nacional del país): desde la revista Time hasta Wall Street Journal la calificaron como la mayor fiesta asiática. Sin embargo, desde finales del 2004, por motivos que desconocemos, el gobierno vuelve a tener una postura muy dura. No obstante, la vida gay parece que sigue tan vibrante como antes y muchos de sus visitantes continuan describiendo las calles de Singapur como las mejores para ligar de toda Asia.

Nonostante la massiccia campagna del 2007 contro l'articolo 377° che vieta il sesso anale ed orale tra persone di sesso maschile, la legge rimane comunque nel codice anche se il primo ministro stesso tiene a ribadire che questa legge è simbolo di una società conservatrice. Inoltre il primo ministro ha assicurato che l'omosessualità non è e non verrà perseguitata e che l'abolizione della legge potrebbe essere percepita come un falso segnale, visto che comunque, il diritto da parte degli omosessuali a sposarsi e ad adottare bambini è solo una questione di tempo. Negli ultimi anni l'atteggiamento nei confronti dei gay a Singapore è estremamente cambiato. Tra il 2001 e il 2004 l'atteggiamento del governo sembrava essersi „addolcito", come effettivamente si poteva notare alla festa della nazione (che ha luogo alla vigilia del giorno di festa nazionale in agosto); dal Time Magazine e dal Wall St. Journal veniva descritta come la più grande festa nell'area asiatica. Tuttavia, dalla fine del 2004, il governo ha cominciato, per motivi che non riusciamo a spiegarci, ad assumere un atteggiamento ostile. Ma nonostante la vita gay sembra comunque essere ancora molto attiva. Molti visitatori descrivono le strade di Singapore come „la più grande cruising area dell'Asia".

NATIONAL GROUPS

AfA (Action for AIDS)
35 Kelantan Lane ✉ 208652 Singapore ☎ 6254 0212 🖳 www.afa.org.sg
Non-profit AIDS organization which also organizes gay HIV+ support groups (Club Genesis) and MSM outreach programs.

PLU People Like US
✉ 911710 Singapore 🖳 www.plu.sg
Singapore's first organization for GLM.

Singapore

BARS

Backstage (AC B CC GLM OS T) 19-2, Fri & Sat -3h
13 A Trengganu Street *Near Chinatown MRT Station* ☎ 6227 1712
🖳 www.backstagebar.moonfruit.com
Broadway themed bar. Cosy with games room on the top level. Especially friendly to transgenders.

ebar (AC B d G MA) Mon-Sat 20-3h
57 Neil Road *Chinatown* ☎ 6324 2802
Gay Mandarin karaoke bar with nice crowd and friendly staff.

Lockerroom (AC B cc d f G m MA S VS) Mon-Sun 19-late
43 Neil Road, Chinatown *Near to Chinatown MRT Station or Tanjong Pagar MRT Station* ☎ 6221 7988 🖳 www.lockerroom.sg
Sports cafe & bar. Nice mix of locals, expats and visitors. Sunday is Beer & Bears day. Other theme nights apply.

Same Café Bar (AC B G MA) 19.30-?h
208 South Bridge Road *Chinatown* ☎ 9842 7849
Karaoke club that is especially welcoming to beefy guys, bears and chubs.

Tantric (AC B CC GLM MA OS) Sun-Fri 20-3, Sat -4h
78 Neil Road ☎ 6423 9232 🖳 www.backstagebar.moonfruit.com
Ethnic decor and an East-meets-West theme.

DANCECLUBS

Play (AC B CC D GLM YC)
Mon & Tue 19-24, Wed & Thu -2, Fri -3, Sat -4h, Sun closed
21 Tanjong Pagar Road ☎ 6227 7400 🖳 www.playclub.com.sg
A great club especially for the young and trendy.

Superstar (B D glm MA s) Sun nights only
Block C The Cannery, River Valley Road #01-02 to 05 *Clarke Quay, @ Zirca* ☎ 6333 4168 🖳 www.superstar.sg
Ultimate week closer/starter. Great party with live DJs.

Taboo (AC B CC D GLM MA)
Wed & Thu 20-2, Fri 22-3, Sat -4h, Sun-Tue closed
65/67 Neil Road *Opposite Tantric Bar, near Tanjong Pagar MRT Station*
☎ 6225 6256 🖳 www.taboo97.com
Features a two-storey club with attic: one for dancing with podiums and poles and one for chillout. Great music and glamour!

Zouk Club (! B D glm MA) Wed, Fri, Sat nights
17 Jiak Kim Street *Off Kim Seng Road* ☎ 6738 2988
🖳 www.zoukclub.com
Polysexual. Very popular as the must-visit Singapore institution. International DJs play here regularly.

RESTAURANTS

Eight Café & Bar (AC B CC glm M MA) 11.30-14 & 18.30-22h
8 Bukit Pasoh Road *MRT to Outram Park, green line* ☎ 6220 4513
Classic/fusion Asian cuisine.

Pont de Vie. Le (AC B CC g M MA) 12-14 & 18.30-24h
26 Kandahar Street *MRT to Bugis Green line* ☎ 6238 8682
🖳 www.lepontdevie.com
French/modern European cuisine.

SAUNAS/BATHS

Absolute (B DR DU G LAB MA RR SA SB WO)
Mon-Thu 15-24, Fri -8, Sat 12-8, Sun -24h
32A Pagoda Street *Entry on the ground floor to 2nd level* ☎ 6423 1632
🖳 www.absolute.sg
Clean and nice decor and friendly staff. Theme nights.

Club One Seven (AC b DR DU FC FH G I m MA OS P PP RR SA SB SH WH WO) Sun-Thu 11.30-23.30, Fri -7, Sat 12-7, Sun -23.30h
17 Upper Circular Road *Between Boat & Clark Quays, behind Riverwalk Apartments* ☎ 6223 0017 🖳 www.oneseven.com.sg
Full meals available. Theme days.
Popular with foreigners.

Hercules Club (B DR DU G I m MA RR SA SB WH)
Sun-Thu 10.30-24; Fri, Sat & eve of public holidays -2h
4 Jalan Klapa *Across the street from Keybox Sauna* ☎ 6296 1018
🖳 www.herculesclub.com.sg
Three floors of facilities. Theme nights such as chub and chaser, skin night, young night. Mostly Chinese locals.

Keybox (AC B DR DU G I MA RR SB WH WO)
Sun-Thu 13-23; Fri, Sat & before public holidays 13-10h
786, 788 & 790 North Bridge Road *Nearby MRT station Lavender*
☎ 6299 4121 🖳 www.keybox.com.sg

Queen Resort (AC cc G I M MA MSG OS RWB RWS RWT S SA SB VA WH WO) All year, 24hrs
325, New Bridge Road *Outside Outram Park MRT exit H Opp. Pearl Center*
☎ 6222 2292 🖳 www.queenresort.com
Queen Resort is an exclusively gay property with its own on-site gay sauna complex. Hotel guests have free access to the sauna. There are six different room types.

ShoGun (b DR DU G GH I LAB MA RR SB VS) 24hrs
51A, Pagoda Street, Pagoda House
Japanese style sauna and men.

10mens Club (AC b DR DU G I LAB MA MSG P RR SB)
13-23, Sat & Sun 12-23h
205/207 New Bridge Road 2nd Level *New location near people's park complex and MRT Chinatown* ☎ 6327 8870 🖳 www.tenmensclub.com
A multi-story cruising space.

FASHION SHOPS

SportsmenAsia Studio (GLM MA)
Mon-Fri 11.30-20.30, Sat & Sun 11-21h
01-02 The Platinum, 46 Upper Cross Street *Beside Hotel 81 Chinatown*
☎ 6327 4088 🖳 www.sportsmenasia.com
Sexy underwear, swimwear, sportswear and sex toys.

HOTELS

Hotel 1929 (AC B BF CC H M NG OS RWS RWT WH WI) All year
50 Keong Saik Road ☎ 6347 1929 🖳 www.hotel1929.com
Affordable, hip and trendy boutique hotel with designer furniture and fittings. In the heart of Singapore's gay village within walking distance to all the bars.

Inn at Temple Street. The (AC B bf glm I M MA PK RWS RWT SA VA WI) All year
36 Temple Street, Chinatown *Near the famous Pagoda & Trengganu Streets* ☎ 6221 5333 🖳 www.theinn.com.sg
42 rooms in old shop houses. Laundry service. Airport transfer. Close to many gay venues. Minimum stay of 2 nights is required with guarantee bookings.

Queen Resort (AC cc G I M MA MSG OS RWB RWS RWT S SA SB VA WH WO) All year, 24hrs
325, New Bridge Road *Outside Outram Park MRT exit H Opp. Pearl Center*
☎ 6222 2292 🖳 www.queenresort.com
Queen Resort is an exclusively gay property with its own on-site gay sauna complex. Hotel guests have free access to the sauna. There are six different room types.

Strand (AC B BF CC H M NG)
25 Bencoolen Street ☎ 6338 1866
🖳 www.strandhotel.com.sg
Close to the city and affordable. Ideal for budget travellers and quickies.

HEALTH GROUPS

Action for Aids (glm) Tue & Wed 18.30-20, Sat 13.20-15.30h
c/o DSC STD Clinic 02-16, 31 Kelantan Lane *Rowell Road* ☎ 6254 0212
🖳 www.afa.org.sg
AIDS information & education. Anonymous HIV testing.

■ **Oogachaga** (GLM MA)
Mon-Fri 10-18, Hotline: Tue-Thu 19-22, Sat 14-18h
41A Mosque Street *near Chinatown* ☎ 6268 6626 🖳 www.oogachaga.com
Counselling and Support Group activities. Sauna outreach and mature men projects.

SWIMMING

Public Pools. AYOR – Try your luck at many of Singapore's public pools where you will find hot hunky guys getting a tan, especially at weekends. Some of the following ones are particularly cruisy, but please be discreet, and try not to „do it" in the changing rooms where many have been caught.

CRUISING

All cruisings are AYOR:
-Orchard Road up and down, some R
-P in Chinatown behind Ann Siang Hill (on Amoy Street, weekend evenings)
-Public swimming pools at weekdays, afternoon till dusk
-Orchard Towers, Orchard Road (cruisy Sat and Sun afternoon)
-Lucky Chinatown, New Bridge Road, Chinatown
-Maxwell Road Hawker Centre, Tanjong Pagar Road (weekend evenings)
-Takashimaya Shopping Centre

Slovakia

Name: Slovensko · Slowakei · Slovaquie · Eslovaquia · Slovachia
Location: Central Europe
Initials: SK
Time: GMT +1
International Country Code: ☎ 421
International Access Code: ☎ 00
Language: Slovakian
Area: 49,034 km² / 18,932 sq mi.
Currency: 1 Euro (€) = 100 Cents
Population: 5,387,000
Capital: Bratislava
Religions: 69 % Roman Catholic
Climate: Moderate climate. Summers are cool, winters cold. The best time is from May-Sept.

As recently as 2004, the foreign minister still demanded guarantees that Slovakia would not have to legalize gay or lesbian marriages or even recognize same-sex partnerships registered in other countries. But in 2006, Slovakia was one of the 54 states supporting a UN resolution against discrimination on the grounds of sexual identity. Homosexuality is not illegal, and the legal age of consent is fifteen. In the last few years, the public opinion concerning homosexuality has undergone a considerable change. The gay scene in slowly emerging, especially in the capital city Bratislava, a city that features a beautifully restored old town, and an imposing castle overlooking the Danube river. Slovakia is a country of mountains, rolling hills, medieval towns and thermal spas. The high Tatras mountains provide opportunities for great hiking, skiing and scenic tourism.

2004 forderte der Außenminister noch eine Garantie, weder in anderen EU-Ländern geschlossene Eingetragene Partnerschaften noch schwul-lesbische Ehen in der Slowakei anerkennen zu müssen. Im Dezember 2006 gehörte die Slowakei zu den 54 Staaten, die eine UNO-Resolution gegen die Diskriminierung aufgrund sexueller Identität unterstützten.
Homosexualität ist nicht illegal. Das Schutzalter liegt bei 15 Jahren. Die öffentliche Meinung hinsichtlich schwuler Themen hat sich in den letzten Jahren positiv gewandelt. Die Schwulenszene bildet sich langsam, aber sicher, besonders in der Hauptstadt Bratislava.
Diese bietet darüber hinaus eine fantastisch restaurierte Altstadt und eine beeindruckende, hoch über der Donau gelegene Burg. Die Slowakei ist ein gebirgiges Land mit vielen steilen Tälern, mittelalterlichen Städten und Thermalquellen. Die Hohe Tatra bietet neben großartigen Landschaften auch hervorragende Möglichkeiten für Skiläufer und Bergsteiger.

En 2004 le ministre des Affaires étrangères exigeait encore la garantie de ne devoir reconnaître ni les partenariats homosexuels conclus dans les autres pays de l'Union Européenne ni les couples homosexuels en Slovaquie. En décembre 2006 la Slovaquie faisait partie des 54 États soutenant la résolution de l'ONU contre la discrimination en raison de l'identité sexuelle.
En Slovaquie l'homosexualité n'est pas un délit. La majorité sexuelle y est fixée à 15 ans. L'opinion publique est devenue beaucoup plus tolérante face aux homosexuels. Le milieu gay se développe lentement mais sûrement en Slovaquie, surtout dans la capitale Bratislava, qui dispose d'ailleurs d'un centre ville historique magnifiquement restauré et d'un incroyable château surplombant le Danube. La Slovaquie offre un paysage montagneux ponctué de nombreuses gorges abruptes, des villes médiévales et des sources thermales. Le Massif des Hautes Tatras offre la possibilité de faire des randonnées et du ski dans un décor absolument superbe.

En 2004 el ministro de Exteriores promovió todavía una garantía para no tener que reconocer en Eslovaquia aquellas parejas de hecho registradas en otros estados miembros de la UE ni a matrimonios gay-lésbicos. En diciembre de 2006 Eslovaquia pertenecía al grupo de 54 estados que apoyó una resolución de la ONU que declaraba la no-discriminación por razón de la identidad sexual.
La homosexualidad es legal. La edad de consentimiento es de 15 años. La opinión pública en relación a la homosexualidad ha experimentado un cambio radical en los últimos años. El ambiente homosexual va creciendo poco a poco pero seguro, especialmente en la capital, Bratislava, que además tiene un casco antiguo fantásticamente restaurado y un castillo impresionante con vistas al Danubio. Eslovaquia es un país montañoso con muchos monasterios, ciudades medievales y fuentes termales. La alta cordillera del Tatras ofrece unos paisajes maravillosos así como excelentes posibilidades para el esquí y la escalada.

Nel 2004 il ministro degli esteri ha chiesto delle garanzie per non avere l'obbligo di riconoscere né le unioni domestiche registrate, né i matrimoni tra persone dello stesso sesso, che invece l'UE riconosce. Nel dicembre del 2006, la Repubblica Slovacca è stato uno di quei 54 paesi che hanno sostenuto la risoluzione dell'ONU contro la discriminazione fondata sull'orientamento sessuale.

L'omosessualità non è illegale. L'età legale per avere dei rapporti sessuali è di 15 anni. Negli ultimi anni la gente ha cambiato molto la propria opinione sugli omosessuali. La scena gay va prendendo sempre più piede, specialmente nella capitale Bratislava che tra le altre cose offre un centro storico esemplarmente restaurato e un suggestivo castello con vista sul Danubio. La Repubblica Slovacca è un Paese prevalentemente montuoso, ricco di ripidi pendii frastagliati, città medioevali e sorgenti termali. I monti Tatras, oltre a spettacolari paesaggi offrono anche molte opportunità per gli amanti dello sci e dell'alpinismo.

NATIONAL GROUPS

■ **Ganymedes** (GLM)
Bjornsonova 3 ✉ 811 05 Bratislava 💻 www.ganymedes.info
Movement for equality of homosexual citizens in the Slovak Republic.

Bratislava ☎ 2

NATIONAL GAY INFO

■ **GayGuide.Net Bratislava** (GLM)
💻 bratislava.gayguide.net/
Permanently updated gay guide including reviews of all listed places.

BARS

■ **Club B Barbaros** (B GLM MA) Fri & Sat 21-4h
Vysoka 5219/14 *Near Hodzovo square and President's palace behind the Tatra Center*
Barbaros reopened in June 2009. Also known as ,Club B'.

■ **Be Happy** (B GLM MA) Mon-Thu 16-1, Fri -4, Sat 17-4, Sun -1h
Vysoka 4281/20 *Near Hodzovo square and President's palace behind the Tatra Center* 💻 www.gayclub.sk
Gay/Lesbian cafe and bar in the centre.

DANCECLUBS

■ **Apollon Gay Club** (! B D G H I P S SNU ST VS YC)
Mon & Tue 18-3, Wed -5, Thu -3, Fri & Sat 20-5, Sun 19-1h
Panenská 668/24 *Near Hodžovo square and President's palace*
☎ (905) 0948 900 093 (mobile) 💻 apollon-gay-club.sk
The longest running gay disco club of Slovakia. Two bars with young staff. Every Sun naked party only for men. Mon-Tue Karaoke party. Wed, Fri, Sat disco 22-05h. Thu Film club 20h. Also cafe and accommodation.

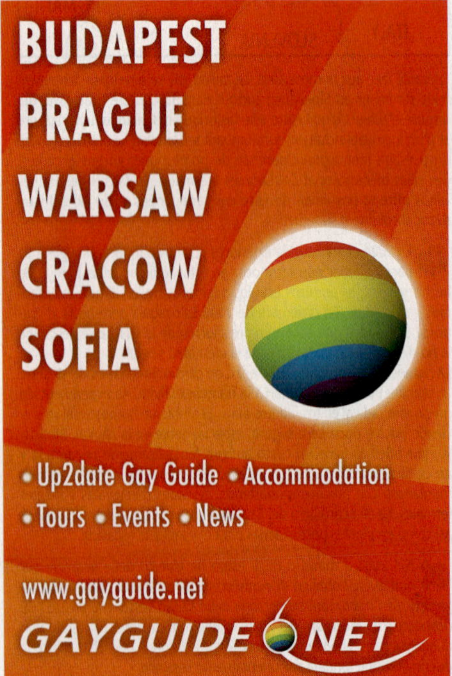

RESTAURANTS

■ **Restaurant Pension Nova** (b glm H M MA) 24hrs, restaurant 11-22h
Nová 2 *Near Vajnorska street, Tram 1/2/4 Odbojarov stop*
☎ (2) 2 44 45 13 40 💻 www.pension-nova.sk
Gayfriendly hotel and restaurant. Offers 6 double bed rooms and one apartment. Strictly non-smoking.

■ **Ufo** (B M NG) 10-23h
Nový Most ☎ (2) 62 52 03 00 💻 www.u-f-o.sk
Restaurant on top of the tower with great view over the city. Not gay. Popular with tourists. Expensive.

SAUNAS/BATHS

■ **Club Sauna Expert** (AC b DR DU G MA MSG p RR SA SB VS)
Mon-Thu 15-24, Fri & Sat -2h
Zivnostenská 2950/4 *Trolley bus 206, 10 mins walk from main station*
☎ (914) 914 10 57 17 (mobile) 💻 www.clubsaunaexpert.com
A middle sized and clean sauna (massage possible). 10 cabins. Bar upstairs.

SWIMMING

Lakes near Bratislava:
-Zlate Piesky – Lesik (last stop on the trams No. 2, 4)
-Rusovce.

CRUISING

-University Building / Safarikovo Námestie (VERY DANGEROUS)
-Jesenského Blvd
-Lido (between the Donua bridge and the bridge Apollo) (AYOR).

Košice ☎ 55

DANCECLUBS

■ **Marseille H(e)aven** (AC B D DR GLM I MA P S VS WE)
Mon-Thu 16-24, Fri-Sat 19-4, Sun closed
Hlavna 45 *In the centre* ☎ 069 201 83 80 💻 www.klubmarseille.sk

SAUNAS/BATHS

■ **Sauna Palma** (B G MSG PI SA SB) Men only Tue & Fri 16-24h
Sturova 33 *1st floor* ☎ (905) 38 49 64 (mobile) 💻 www.saunapalma-ke.sk
This sauna is open all week, but only on Tue and Fri are ,men only' days with gay audience.

Látky ☎ 45

HOTELS

■ **Royal** (B BF H I M OS PI SA SB WO)
Prašivá 4 ☎ 45 5376 329 💻 www.royalhotel.sk

Nitra ☎ 37

DANCECLUBS

■ **Prince Club** (B D DR GLM) Tue-Thu 16-1, Fri-Sat 18-4h
Dolnozoborska 8 ☎ 0949 608 362 💻 www.princeclub.sk
New gay club in a small historic city near Bratislava. Popular weekend place with gays from Bratislava and other Slovakian cities.

Vrutky ☎ 43

BARS

■ **Shanghai Club** (B D DR G VS) Sat 20-5h (gay party)
Dolná Kružná 23 ☎ 907 840 500 (mobile) 💻 www.shanghai.sk

Slovenia

Name: Slovenija · Slowenien · Slovénie · Eslovenia
Location: Central Europe
Initials: SLO
Time: GMT +1
International Country Code: ☏ 386 (omit first 0 from area code)
International Access Code: ☏ 00
Language: Slovenian
Area: 20,253 km² / 7,819 sq mi.
Currency: 1 Euro (€) = 100 Cents
Population: 2,001,000
Capital: Ljubljana
Religions: 58% Catholic, 4% Orthodox
Climate: Mediterranean climate on the coast, continental climate with mild to hot summers and cold winters in the east.

In Slovenia the age of consent is 15 years. The gay-lesbian movement has a long tradition here: in 1984 the first non-governmental organization „Magnus" was founded. In the same year the film festival in Ljubljana, with the same name, showing gay-lesbian films which has become an institution. This early commitment, which continued after the country gained independence in 1991 is a contradiction of the standpoint of the general public regarding homosexuality. Although the Slovenians are generally held to be tolerant and progressive, homophobia regularly emerges and many prominent people continue to hide their homosexuality. Public opinion is changing slowly. A contribution to this change is made by the annual Pride Parade.
In June 2005 the Law on Registered Same-Sex Partnership was passed. This law covers so-called property relations only, and includes the right/obligation to support socially weaker partner and only partly inheritance rights. It does not bring any rights in the area of social security (social and health insurance, pension rights), and it does not give the next of kin status to the partners.
Since joining the EU, this small country with its alpine landscape and middle European culture, has started attracting many tourists. From the fantastic mountains to the impressive Adrian coastline, everywhere is very close to the capital city Ljubljana which has a lot to offer with its cultural diversity.

In Slowenien liegt das allgemeine Schutzalter bei 15 Jahren. Die schwul-lesbische Bewegung hat dort eine recht lange Tradition: schon 1984 wurde die erste nichtstaatliche Organisation „Magnus" zum Schutze der Rechte Schwuler gegründet und im selben Jahr das gleichnamige Filmfestival in Ljubljana, das mit schwul-lesbischen Filmen schnell zu einer festen Institution wurde. Dieses frühe Engagement, das auch nach der Unabhängigkeit des Landes im Jahre 1991 anhält, steht im Widerspruch zu der gesellschaftlichen Haltung gegenüber Homosexualität. Zwar geben sich die Slowenen tolerant und fortschrittlich, aber gleichzeitig tritt Schwulenfeindlichkeit noch immer auf, und viele Prominente leben weiter ungeoutet. Die öffentliche Meinung wird nur langsam liberaler. Einen Beitrag dazu leistet möglicherweise die jährlich stattfindende Pride-Parade.
Im Juni 2005 wurde das Gesetz für eingetragene Partnerschaften verabschiedet. Es betrifft ausschließlich die vermögensrechtlichen Aspekte und umfasst zwar die Verpflichtung, sozial schwächer gestellte Partner zu unterstützen, jedoch nur eine teilweise Erbfolgeberechtigung. Es bringt weder neue Rechte im Sozialleistungsbereich (Sozial- und Krankenversicherung, Pensionsberechtigung), noch etabliert es einen verwandtschaftlichen Status zwischen den Partnern.
Spätestens seit dem EU-Beitritt zieht das kleine Land, in dem alpine und mitteleuropäische Kulturen und Landschaften aufeinander treffen, viele Reisende an. Von den phantastischen Bergen zu den beeindruckenden Küsten der Adria ist es nur ein Katzensprung, und auch die Hauptstadt Ljubljana hat kulturell einiges zu bieten.

En Slovénie, la majorité sexuelle est fixée à 15 ans pour tous. Le mouvement gay et lesbien y a longue tradition puisque c'est en 1984 que la première organisation non-gouvernementale pour le respect des droits des gay, „Magnus", a été fondée et le premier festival du film gay et lesbien s'est déroulé la même année à Ljubljana pour devenir rapidement une véritable institution. Cet engagement précoce qui a perduré après l'indépendance en 1991 s'inscrit en porte-à-faux avec la mentalité plutôt homophobe de la population. Certes, la Slovénie est un pays tolérant et progressiste, mais l'homophobie est encore sensible et nombre de célébrités préfèrent ne pas faire leur coming out. L'opinion publique se libéralise cependant lentement et la Gay Pride annuelle.
En juin 2005, la loi autorisant le partenariat enregistré a été adoptée. Elle ne concerne cependant que les questions financières et si elle oblige à soutenir le partenaire socialement plus défavorisé, elle n'implique que partiellement le droit à la succession. Elle n'octroie de nouveaux droits ni à la sécurité sociale ni à la retraite, et n'établit pas non plus de statut familial entre les partenaires.
Depuis l'adhésion de la Slovénie à l'UE, les touristes affluent encore plus nombreux pour goûter le charme, la culture et les paysages de cette république alpine aux bords de l'Adriatique. Les fantastiques montagnes et les impressionnantes côtes sont à deux pas de la capitale Ljubljana qui a beaucoup à offrir aux amateurs de culture.

En Eslovenia, la edad general de consentimiento está en los 15 años. El movimiento gay-lésbico tiene aquí ya una larga tradición: en 1984 se fundó la organización no-gubernamental para la protección de los derechos homosexuales „Magnus" y en el mismo año se creó el festival de cine gay-lésbico en Liubliana, que con sus películas gays pronto se convirtió en una institución. Este firme compromiso, que desde la independencia del país en 1991 continúa todavía vivo, se contradice con la actitud de la sociedad hacia la homosexualidad. Aunque los eslovenos procuran ser tolerantes y abiertos, todavía se producen actitudes intolerantes y muchos famosos permanecen en el armario. La opinión pública se va liberalizando poco a poco. Una buena contribución a ello es probablemente la Marcha del Orgullo Gay que se celebra anualmente.
En junio de 2005, se aprobó la ley de registro de parejas. Se trata exclusivamente de aspectos jurídico-patrimoniales y en ella se regula la obligación de prestar asistencia al compañero/-a necesitado pero solamente se establece parcialmente un derecho sucesorio. No introduce ni cambios en el campo social (seguridad social, seguro de

enfermedad o derecho a pensión) ni tampoco establece un status familiar entre los miembros de la pareja.
Desde la entrada en la UE, este pequeño país en el que se mezclan el paisaje y la cultura alpina con el mediterráneo, atrae cada vez más turistas. Desde sus fantásticas montañas hasta las impresionantes costas del Adriático hay sólo un paso y su capital, Liubliana, ofrece un buen ambiente cultural.

In Slovenia l'età del consenso è di 15 anni. Il movimento gay e lesbico in Slovenia ha una lunga tradizione: giá nel 1984 fu fondata la prima ONG per la tutela degli omosessuali „Magnus". E sempre nello stesso anno fu istituito l'omonimo festival cinematografico a Lubiana diventando successivamente un evento a scadenza regolare. Questo precoce impegno sul fronte omosessuale, che tra l'altro ha continuato a persistere anche dopo il raggiungimento dell'indipendenza, è in contrasto con la mentalitá della gente locale nei confronti dell'omosessualitá. I sloveni si mostrano piuttosto aperti e tolleranti nei confronti degli omosessuali ma allo stesso tempo ci sono ancora molti casi di omofobia e molte personalitá di rilievo non hanno ancora fatto il coming out. L'opinione pubblica va divendanto lentamente più liberale. Un rilevante contributo lo offre l'annuale Pride-Parade.
Dal suo ingresso nell'Unione Europea questo piccolo paese, dove la cultura e il paesaggio alpino e mitteleuropeo si fondono armoniosamente tra loro, attira ancora più turisti. Per arrivare dalle fantastiche montagne fino alle suggestive coste adriatiche ci si mette davvero poco. La capitale Lubiana ha anche molto da offrire dal punto di vista culturale.
In giugno del 2005 è stata approvata la legge per le unioni registrate. La legge si occupa prevalentemente degli aspetti patrimoniali e regola l'impegno al mantenimento dei partner finanziariamente più deboli; tuttavia per quello che riguarda l'eredità, questa viene garantita in maniera molto limitata. La suddetta legge, inoltre, non apporta ne novità dal punto di vista dei diritti nel campo del sistema sociale (previdenza sociale, assistenza sanitaria, diritto alla pensione) ne stabilisce uno stato di parentela tra le persone.

NATIONAL GAY INFO

■ **Slovenian Queer Resource Directory – SIQRD**
Kersnikova 4 ✉ 1000 Ljubljana 💻 www.ljudmila.org/siqrd
Information also in English.

NATIONAL GROUPS

■ **DIH – Društvo za integracijo homoseksualnosti**
Mon-Fri 16-18h
Slomškova 11 ✉ 1000 Ljubljana *Near railway station*
☎ (041) 56 23 75 (mobile) 💻 www.dih-drustvo.si
Association for integration of homosexuality.

■ **Legebitra** Mon-Fri 10-18h
Trubarjeva 76a, Preseren Square ✉ 1000 Ljubljana *City center, street starts behind the main statue of Preseren* ☎ (01) 430 51 44
💻 www.drustvo-legebitra.si
Legebitra is a Slovenian LGBT organization working against discrimination on the basis of sexual orientation and gender identity in Slovenia.

Banovci

CRUISING

Mixed saunas in which cruising is possible include:
-Sauna in Spa Olimia in Podcetrtek. See: www.terme-olimia.com
-Sauna in Terme Catez, in Catez. See: www.terme-catez.si
-Sauna in Terme Zrece, in Zrece. See: www.terme-zrece.si

Bled

CRUISING

-Beach between Toplice Hotel and the entrance to the bathing-place beneath Bled castle

Celje

CRUISING

-Mestni Park (across the Savinja river)
-Nudist beach by the river Savinja (close to the pebble islands)
-Sauna at Spa Lasko. 15 km from Gelje (mixed but cruisy)
-Promenade by the river Savinja, cruising around the Rafter statue, cross the bridge on the right side of the park (benches around playground on summer evenings)
- P „Lopata" on the highway Maribor – Ljubjana, around the toilets.

Ljubljana ☎ 01

GAY INFO

■ **Tiffany** (b D GLM MA)
Masarykova 24 *Inside alternative cultural center „Metelkova mesto"*
💻 www.ljudmila.org/siqrd
Alternative parties from time to time. AIDS prevention office and some other cultural activities in this former bar. See site www.ljudmila.org for the latest news.

CAFES

■ **Kafeterija Lan** (AC B glm MA OS)
Mon-Thu 9-24, Fri -1, Sat 10-1, Sun -22h
Gallusovo nabrežje 27 *Old town, between St Jacob's & Cobbler's bridges*
☎ (01) 426 50 35

■ **Monokel** (gLm MA S)
Masarykova 24 *City centre, 10 mins from railway/bus station*
💻 www.klubmonokel.com
Open only occasionally for special events.

■ **Open Café** (b gLm m MA S) Mon-Sat 9-24, Sun 16-22h
Hrenova 19 *Old town* ☎ (04) 127 01 27 💻 www.open.si
DJ nights on Fri, discussions, cultural events, sometimes concerts.

DANCECLUBS

■ **Inbox** (B D GLM MA)
224 Jurckova cesta 💻 www.inbox-club.si/
Irregular events called „Salomay party", every 2-3 months. .

■ **K4 Roza** (B D GLM MA) Sun 21-4h (closed during the summer), once a month on Sat
Kersnikova 4 💻 www.klubk4.org
Occasionally opened on Sat. See www.klubk4.org for details.

RESTAURANTS

■ **Julija** (b glm M MA) Mon-Sat 8-24, Sun 10-24h
Stari trg 9 ☎ (01) 425 64 63
Excellent food, wine and romantic environement. Across the street: Romeo with wide selection of excellent salads and tacos.

■ **Tomato** (AC B BF M MA NG OS)
Šubiceva ulica 1 ☎ (01) 252 75 55
Moderate prices and great meals. Salads, soups and more.

SAUNAS/BATHS

■ **Gymnasivm** (B DR DU FC G m MA OS P RR SA SB VS WE WO)
Summer: 17-23; winter: 15-22, Fri & Sat -23h
Ulica Pohorskega Bataljona 34 *Bus 6, 8 Smelt, 14 Mercator. Take the street opp. Domina Hotel. The sauna is a residential house at the second turning*
☎ (01) 534 24 85 💻 www.klub-libero.si
Mediterranean atmosphere on 300 m² and three levels, with music and food. Large private rooms at no extra charge. Excellent steam room and sauna.

HOTELS

■ **Fluxus** (cc glm OS) All year
Tomsiceva 4 *Near Parliament & Opera House* ☎ (01) 251 57 60
💻 www.fluxus-hostel.com

The Fluxus hostel is situated in the heart of the city centre. There are 16 beds in three different rooms – most with shared bathroom.

GENERAL GROUPS

■ **SKUC-Magnus** (G)
Metelkova 6
Gay group since 1984. Gay and HIV advocacy, HIV/STI prevention.

SPORT GROUPS

■ **Out In Slovenija** (GLM MA WO) Mon-Fri 9-18h or on request
Slomškova 11 ☎ (041) 56 23 75
First sports and recreational group for gays and lesbians in Slovenia. Activities include cycling, walking, swimming, badminton, bowling, camping, jogging, skiing and others.

SWIMMING

-Beach on the Sava river (500 m from the Chinese restaurant on the left bank. Popular all year).

CRUISING

-Tivoli Park P after sunset at the end of the parking space and in the woods behind the sport facilities and Hala Tivoli.
-Park (AYOR) (near the railway behind the petrol station on the Tivolska cesta) (all day-most busy after sunset).

Maribor ☎ 02

BARS

■ **Theater Café** (B glm MA) Sun closed
Slomškov trg *Next to the theatre*

SAUNAS/BATHS

■ **Terme Olimia** (AC B DU GLM M MA MSG NU PI RR SA SB SOL WH WO) 8-22h
Zdraviliška cesta 23 *60 km south of Maribor* ☎ (03) 829 70 00
💻 www.terme-olimia.com
Big spa with very large sauna-world. Not gay but mixed. In the evenings cruising in the special japanese sauna is possible.

HELP WITH PROBLEMS

■ **Lingsium** (GLM YC)
Galerija Media Nox, Židovski trg 12
Local LGBT youth group.

CRUISING

-Nudist beach on the „Maribor Island" (popular summer resort on the river Drava). City bus no. 15.
-City Park, the path past the Aquarium toward the Three Ponds; gets lively towards evening; only summer
-Sauna in terme „Fontana" (mixed) see: www.termemb.si
-First parking lot on the road from Maribor to Celje, approximately 1km after the exit to Fram.

Piran

SWIMMING

-Beach from Piran to Strunjan (NU) under the cliff in Piran and in Strunjan.

CRUISING

-Coast walk (at night)
-Main street along coast in Portoroz (at night)
-Sauna in Hotel Palace (mixed).

Ptuj

CRUISING

-City Park (epecially near Ribic-restaurant).

South Africa

Name: Suid-Afrika · Südafrika · Afrique du Sud · Sudáfrica · Sud Africa
Location: Southern Africa
Initials: ZA
Time: GMT +2
International Country Code: ☏ 27
International Access Code: ☏ 09
Language: English, Afrikaans, African languages
Area: 1,219,080 km² / 471,442 sq mi.
Currency: 1 Rand (ZAR) = 100 Cents
Population: 45,509,000
Capital: Cape Town (legislative capital); Pretoria (administrative capital)
Religions: 87% Christians
Climate: Ranging from hot and dry in summer to cold and wet in winter. Sub-tropical to Mediterranean climates.
Important gay cities: Cape Town, Johannesburg

Since 1 January 2008, the age of consent in South Africa is 16 years, regardless of sexual orientation and gender. No sodomy laws apply in South Africa, however sex with a male under the age of 19 is punishable with imprisonment of up to six years with or without a fine of up to 12,000 Rand.

Parliament passed the Civil Union Bill which was tabled in reaction to the Constitutional Court ruling of 1 December 2005 where the court ordered parliament to amend the definition of marriage from „a union between a man and a women" to „a union between two persons".

The Bill of Rights chapter of the Constitution of South Africa clearly outlaws, amongst others, any discrimination on the basis of sexual orientation, gender and marital status.

Safe sex is highly advisable as South Africa has the highest number of HIV infections in the world – 5 million.

Although the government downplays the statistics and denies that South Africa is the „crime capital of the world," this post-apartheid country still has one of the highest murder rates. The government banned publication of crime figures, because of „serious problems about the integrity and reliability of the statistics". Crime in South Africa is all too often accompanied by extreme violence involving guns. House robbers operate mainly in small groups, usually at night and normally hold up their victims with firearms.

Please note that all bars are forced by law to stop serving liquor at 02h00 in the morning. The bars do however still remain open until the early morning ± 03h00 to 04h00.

Homosexualität ist an sich nicht rechtsrelevant, doch gleichgeschlechtlicher Verkehr mit einem Mann unter 19 kann mit Freiheitsentzug von bis zu sechs Jahren und einer zusätzlichen Geldbuße von bis zu 12.000 Rand belegt werden.

Im November 2006 verabschiedete das Parlament ein Gesetz für eingetragene Partnerschaften, das in Reaktion auf einen Richterspruch des Verfassungsgerichts eingebracht wurde, der den Volkvertretern auftrug, die Definition der Ehe von „Beziehung zwischen Mann und Frau" auf „Beziehung zwischen zwei Personen" zu ändern.

Die in der südafrikanischen Verfassung garantierten Grundrechte untersagen unter anderem auch grundsätzlich jegliche Diskriminierung aufgrund der sexuellen Orientierung, des Geschlechts oder des Ehestands.

Zu Safer Sex muss in Südafrika noch eindringlicher geraten werden als anderswo, da das Land mit 5 Millionen HIV-Infizierten über die weltweit höchste Infektionsrate verfügt.

Auch wenn die Regierung die Statistik herunterspielt und nicht zugeben mag, dass Südafrika die weltweite „Kriminalitätshochburg" ist, weist das Land in den Zeiten nach der Apartheid immer noch eine der höchsten Mordraten der Welt auf. Die Regierung lässt die Veröffentlichung von Kriminalitätszahlen nicht mehr zu, was sie mit „schweren Problemen hinsichtlich der statistischen Vollständigkeit und Verlässlichkeit" begründet. In Südafrika geht die Kriminalität sehr oft mit extremer Waffengewalt einher. So bedrohen auch die vorwiegend in kleinen Gruppen auftretenden, nächtlichen Einbrecher ihre Opfer mit Schusswaffen.

Bitte beachten Sie, daß alle Bars vom Gesetz her gezwungen sind, den Alkoholausschank um 2 Uhr morgens einzustellen. Sie bleiben jedoch noch bis ca. 3- oder 4 Uhr morgens geöffnet.

Depuis le 1er janvier 2008, la majorité sexuelle en Afrique du Sud est fixée à 16 ans, indépendamment de l'orientation sexuelle et du sexe. L'homosexualité en soi ne figure pas dans les textes de loi, mais les rapports sexuels avec un homme de moins de 19 ans peuvent être punis d'une peine de prison de six ans assortie d'une amende pouvant atteindre 12 000 rands.

En novembre 2006, le parlement a ratifié la loi pour les partenariats enregistrés, répondant ainsi à une décision du tribunal constitutionnel demandant aux représentants du peuple de redéfinir le mariage comme une „union entre deux personnes" et non plus comme „l'union entre un homme et une femme".

Les droits fondamentaux garantis par la constitution sud-africaine interdisent entre autre toute forme de discrimination fondée sur l'orientation sexuelle, le sexe ou la situation maritale.

Avec ses 5 millions de séropositifs, le taux d'infection le plus élevé au monde, il est recommandé en Afrique du Sud plus qu'ailleurs de pratiquer le sexe sûr.

Même si le gouvernement sous-estime les statistiques et ne veut pas avouer que l'Afrique du Sud est la „championne de la criminalité", le pays accuse depuis la fin de l'Apartheid un des taux les plus élevés d'homicides de part le monde. Le gouvernement n'autorise plus la publication des chiffres de la criminalité en prétextant de „graves problèmes concernant l'intégrité et la fiabilité des statistiques". La criminalité en Afrique du Sud s'accompagne très souvent d'une extrême violence armée. C'est ainsi que des cambrioleurs opérant le plus souvent la nuit en petits groupes menacent leurs victimes avec des armes à feu.

Desde el 1 de enero de 2008 la edad mínima para mantener relaciones sexuales en Sudáfrica es de 16 años, independientemente de la orientación sexual y del género.

La homosexualidad en sí no es jurídicamente relevante pero una relación sexual con un hombre menor de 19 puede conllevar una

IT'S COMING

BIGGER THAN THE BIG 5
MR GAY
WORLD
2012

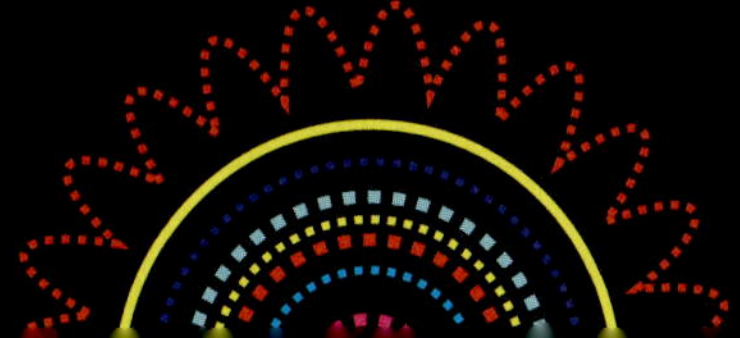

privación de libertad de hasta seis años y una sanción económica complementaria de hasta 12.000 Rands.
En noviembre de 2006, el Parlamento aprobó una ley para el registro de parejas de hecho que se presentó como reacción a una sentencia del Tribunal Constitucional que sirvió a los representantes del pueblo para modificar la definición de matrimonio como „relación entre hombre y mujer" en „relación entre dos personas".
Los derechos fundamentales garantizados en la Constitución sudafricana prohíben también, entre otros, cualquier discriminación por razón de la orientación sexual, sexo o el estado civil. En cuanto al sexo seguro, debe continuar el asesoramiento de manera intensiva pues el país, con 5 millones de casos de SIDA, posee la tasa de infecciones más alta del mundo.
Aunque el gobierno intente subestimar las estadísticas y no le guste admitir que Suráfrica es el bastión mundial de la criminalidad, el país sigue contando, todavía después de los tiempos del apartheid, con una de las mayores tasas de mortalidad del mundo. El gobierno ya no permite que se publiquen los datos de criminalidad, lo que provoca graves problemas en cuanto a la fiabilidad y corrección de las estadísticas. En Suráfrica la criminalidad se manifiesta con la violencia extrema de las armas. Por eso, los delicuentes nocturnos que mayoritariamente van en pequeños grupos amenazan a sus víctimas con armas de fuego.

✖ Dal 1° gennaio del 2008 l'età del consenso è di 16 anni, indipendentemente dal sesso e dall'orientamento sessuale. L'omosessualità in se non è rilevante dal punto di vista della legge e del diritto, pur tuttavia i rapporti omosessuali con partner che non abbiano compiuto il diciannovesimo anno di età sono punibili con una pena detentiva fino ai 6 anni e in alcuni casi anche una pena pecuniaria che può arrivare fino ai 12.000 Rand.
A novembre del 2006 il parlamento ha approvato una legge per la registrazione delle unioni di fatto, che ha esortato i rappresentanti del popolo a cambiare la definizione di matrimonio da „unione tra un uomo e una donna" in „unione tra due persone", attualmente viene discussa in Parlamento anche una legge per il riconoscimento delle unioni civili.
I principi fondamentali sanciti dalla costituzione sudafricana vietano ogni tipo di discriminazione che ha origine nella sessualità, nell'orientamento sessuale e nello stato civile degli individui.
Per quello che riguarda i rapporti protetti, in Sudafrica bisogna prestare un po' più attenzione rispetto che in altri paesi poichè qui la media delle infezioni da HIV è la più alta al mondo: si parla di cinque milioni di persone infette.
Anche se il governo gioca ad abbassare i numeri delle statistiche, non volendo quindi ammettere volentieri che il Sudafrica è la 'roccaforte' della criminalità, il Paese continua, negli anni del post-apartheid, a detenere uno dei record più alti per quantità di omicidi commessi. Il governo non permette più di pubblicare i dati e i numeri relativi ai crimini commessi nel Paese, giustificandosi dicendo che sussistono gravi problemi per quello che riguarda la completezza e l'affidabilità delle statistiche. In Sudafrica la criminalità si manifesta spesso durante la notte con atti di violenza estremi per mezzo di armi da fuoco per lo più da parte di piccoli clan.

NATIONAL PUBLICATIONS

Exit Newspaper
PO Box 28827, Kensington ✉ 2101 Johannesburg ☎ 011 622 2275
💻 www.exit.co.za
Monthly gay and lesbian newspaper, published mainly in English.

Gay Pages (G) Mon-Fri 9-16h
PO Box 1050, Melville ✉ 2109 Gauteng ☎ 011 726 1560
☎ 082 777 0830 (mobile) 💻 www.gaypagessa.co.za
Quarterly lifestyle magazine and gay business directory. South Africa's premier and largest gay publication. Established 1994.

NATIONAL COMPANIES

■ **Alternative Travel** (CC G) All year
PO Box 2409 ✉ 2118 Cresta ☎ 011 476 6999
💻 www.alternativetravel.co.za
Specialists for business people, adventurous adults and the LGBT community.

■ **Cape Info Africa - Travel & Tourism** Mon-Sat 8-18h
14 Cobern Street, De Waterkant ✉ 8000 Cape Town ☎ 021 425 6463
💻 www.pinksa.co.za

Addo - Eastern Cape

GUEST HOUSES

■ **Hopefield Country House & Guest Farm** (AC B BF CC glm I M MA OS PI PK RWS s VA) All year
Off the R336, Sundays River Valley *65 km from Port Elizabeth Airport*
☎ 042 234 0333
Six double rooms. 15 min from the world famous Addo Elephant national Park.

■ **Lemon3lodge** (AC B BF GLM H M MA OS PI VA) All year
Main Street R336 *Addo - Kirkwood* ☎ 042 230 1653
💻 www.lemon3lodge.co.za
Lemon3lodge is a modern and trendy 4 star guesthouse nearby Addo Elephant National Park. Surrounded by lemon trees and great mountain views.

Barrydale - Western Cape

GUEST HOUSES

■ **Barrydale. The** (B BF GLM I M MA OS PI PK RWB RWS VA WO)
All year
30 Van Riebeeck Street *In the Karoo, 90 mins from Cape Town*
☎ 028 572 1226 💻 www.thebarrydale.co.za

Tradouw Guest House (B BF GLM m OS PK RWB RWS) All year
46 Van Riebeeck Street *Situated on the Route 62 between Montagu and Swellendam*
☎ 028 572 14 34 www.tradouwguesthouse.co.za
The Tradouw Guesthouse is a perfect stopover on ones way to the Garden Route.

Bloemfontein

DANCECLUBS

Buzerant (B D G MC) Fri & Sat 21-4h
Orange Grove Farm, Fereirra Road ☎ 082 783 5684 (mobile)
The only gay club in Bloemfontein.

GUEST HOUSES

Emtonjeni Country Lodge (B BF CC H MA NU OS PI VS) All year
Hope Valley, Ferreira 9301 *Close to the Windmill Casino* ☎ 051 443 8030
☎ (0)823252824 (mobile) www.emtonjenicountrylodge.co.za
Gay owned and managed. 4 large guest rooms with beautiful views of the garden. All rooms have private entrance. Rooms are furnished in modern African style.

Hobbit. The (AC BF cc glm M MC OS PI RWS RWT)
19 President Steyn Avenue, Westdene ☎ 051 447 0663
www.hobbit.co.za
This luxury boutique hotel boasts professionally decorated rooms, all named after a specific Lord of the Rings character, all with mini bars, electrical blankets and a full range of high-quality amenities.

Boksburg – Gauteng

DANCECLUBS

Destiny (B D G MA S) Wed & Thu 19-1, Fri & Sat 19-4, Sun 19-1h
38 Market Street *Opposite Boksburg Lake* ☎ 079 305 9553 (mobile)

Ramp Divas (AC B D G MA S) Wed-Sun 19-2h
154 Anabella Street, Bartlett *Opp. East Rand Mall, off North Rand Rd* ☎ 072 123 1179 (mobile)
www.facebook.com/pages/Ramp-Divas/135639873171108
Student night on Thursdays. Saturday are grand party nights and Sundays with the Divine Drag Divas.

CRUISING

-Boksburg Lake (AYOR) (close to Boksburg/Benoni Hospital. Very active. The whole Boksburg/Benoni side of the lake is used. From Johannesburg, follow Main Street out into R-23 Motorway. Leave the Motorway at the Boksburg Exit to the right, pass large „Pick & Pay" Hypermarket. Continue past „Pick & Pay" (now on your left) until you reach Cason Road at a T-junction. Turn left. Continue until next set of robots (traffic lights), where you turn right into Trichardweg. Pass the Cinderella Prison. 30 yards beyond the subway, turn right. Park the car in the car park and stroll along the dam wall or over the footbridge)
-At „Pick & Pay", Hypermarket (9-17, Sat 9-13h) inside main entrance, 1st floor toilets).

Cape Town – Western Cape

Cape Town, known to its locals as the Mother City, is Africa's self-proclaimed gay capital. It also just happens to be one of the world's most beautiful cities: a cosmopolitan city nestled between the heights of Table Mountain and the Twelve Apostles and the superb beaches along the Atlantic Ocean.
If you are into natural beauty, try the view from Table Mountain or a wander through the Winelands (Stellenbosch, Franschhoek and Paarl). If beaches are your thing, check out Clifton 3rd, Camps Bay or the nudist Sandy bay. If it's shopping that turns you on, look no further than the Waterfront or the other proud members of Cape Town's Big Five shopping Centres. De Waterkant – Cape Town's Gay Village. Centrally situated and within walking distance of the City Centre and the V&A Waterfront, and a few minutes drive from the best beaches. If you want to sleep with, and/or eat, drink or shop around „family", then de Waterkant is a good choice! Cape Town has everything the gay traveller can want.

Kapstadt wird von den Einheimischen als Mutterstadt bezeichnet und ist Afrikas selbst ernannte schwule Hauptstadt. Es ist außerdem eine der schönsten Weltmetropolen, die zwischen den Anhöhen des Tafelberges, den Zwölf Aposteln und den zauberhaften Stränden des Atlantiks liegt.
Wer naturbelassene Schönheit liebt, sollte den Ausblick vom Tafelberg genießen oder durch das Weingebiet (Stellenbosch, Franschhoek und Paarl) wandern oder die Strände besuchen: Clifton 3rd, Camps Bay oder den FKK-Strand Sandy Bay. Shoppen kann man an der Waterfront oder in den anderen 5 großen Einkaufscentern von Kapstadt.
De Waterkant – die Schwulengegend von Kapstadt. Zentral gelegen in Laufweite vom Stadtzentrum und der Victoria and Albert Waterfront und nur wenige Fahrminuten von den besten Stränden entfernt. Wenn Sie also im „Kreis der Familie" übernachten und/oder essen, trinken bzw. shoppen möchten, dann ist De Waterkant eine hervorragende Wahl! Die Stadt hat wirklich alles, was der schwule Reisende begehrt.

Le Cap est le berceau de la nation pour les autochtones et pour les gays la véritable capitale du pays. C'est en outre une des plus belles métropoles du monde, trônant entre la montagne de la Table, les Douze Apôtres et les splendides plages de l'Atlantique.
Les amateurs de spectacles naturels ne manqueront pas d'apprécier la vue du haut de la montagne de la Table ou de faire une randonnée dans les vignobles de Stellenbosch, Franschhoek et de Paarl ou d'aller sur les plages de Clifton 3rd, Camps Bay ou la plage naturiste de Sandy Bay. De Waterkant est le quartier gay du Cap. Situé à proximité du centre-ville et de „ Victoria and Albert Waterfront", à quelques minutes en voiture des plus belles plages. Si vous voulez donc passer la nuit, manger, boire ou faire du shopping en famille, alors De Waterkant est un excellent choix ! La ville a tout ce qu'un voyageur homo peut désirer.

Ciudad del Cabo está considerada por sus habitantes como la Ciudad Madre y es la llamada capital gay de Africa. Además, es una de las metrópolis más bellas del mundo, situada entre las alturas de la Table Mountain y los Doce Apóstoles y las maravillosas playas del Atlántico.
Para aquellos que les guste la belleza paisajística, deben disfrutar de las vistas desde Table Mountain o bien caminar por la zona vinícola de Stellenbusch, Franschhoek y Paarl o ir a las playas: Clifton 3rd, Camps Bay o la playa nudista de Sandy Bay. De Waterkant – la zona gay de Ciudad del Cabo. Situada a poca distancia a pie del centro de la ciudad y del frente marítimo Victoria and Albert y sólo a unos cuantos minutos en coche de las mejores playas. Si quiere por tanto alojarse, comer, beber e ir de compras "al calor de la familia", De Waterkant es una fantástica elección! La ciudad tiene realmente todo lo que un turista gay podría desear.

Città del Capo, chiamata anche dalla gente del posto „Mother City", è la capitale gay del Sudafrica. Dal punto di vista paesistico Città del Capo è una delle metropoli più belle al mondo: si estende tra le alture dei promontori Table Mountain e Dodici Apostoli. È inoltre ricca di immense spiagge. Chi ama la natura e i paesaggi deve assolutamente salire sulla Table Mountain, fare un tour per i vigneti (Stellenbusch, Franschhoek e Paarl) e naturalmente visitare le bellissime spiagge (Clifton 3, Camps Bay o la spiaggia nudisti di Sandy Bay). Per lo shopping ci sono diverse possibilità tra cui il Waterfront e gli altri cinque centri commerciali della città.
De Waterkant è la zona gay di cittá del Capo. Si può raggiungere a piedi dal centro della cittá e dal Victoria and Albert Waterfront. Dalle migliori e più famose spiagge si può raggiungere in pochi minuti con i mezzi di trasporto. Se volete quindi pernottare, mangiare, bere, fare shopping „in famiglia", De Waterkant è la scelta che fa per voi. Insomma, Città del Capo offre davvero tutto quello che un turista gay può desiderare.

BARS

Beaulah Bar (B D gLm MC) Mon-Thu 17-2, Fri & Sat -4h
Corner Somerset Rd & Cobern St, Greenpoint ☎ 021 421 6798
www.beaulahbar.co.za
Friendly, mixed, men's and women's bar with live entertainment and dancing. Back in the same place after the building was torn down.

■ **Crew Bar** (! B D GLM MA OS) Mon-Sun 19-4h
30 Napier Street, De Waterkant ☎ 021 418 01 18
This bar combines stylish decor, gorgeous bartenders and the best in Cape Town music. There are front and back verandahs, dancefloors, a VIP bar and loads of sizzle!

■ **Venue. The** (AC B CC G MA) Mon-Sun 16-2h
24 Napier Street, De Waterkant ☎ 021 425 1782 🖳 www.thevenuect.co.za
Lounge and bar in the heart of the gay village of Cape Town. After works drinks & private functions.

MEN'S CLUBS

■ **Amsterdam Action Bar** (AC B DR G MA SNU VS) Daily 12h-late
10-12 Coburn Street, De Waterkant *Gay Village* ☎ 083 626 4615 (mobile)
🖳 www.amsterdambar.co.za
Two floors with the action upstairs, cubicles and more, downstairs daily drink specials and regular events.

■ **Bar Code** (! B DR F G OS P S VS) Sun-Thu 22-2, Fri & Sat -4h
18 Cobern Street, Green Point *Off Somerset* ☎ 021 421 5305
🖳 www.leatherbar.co.za
Cape Town's most popular leather bar. A must for all leather/jeans men. A downstairs bar and action on the upper floor/deck. Very friendly staff. Check their website for activities: www.leatherbar.co.za

■ **Bronx Action Bar** (AC B D GLM MA OS) Daily 20-4h
22 Somerset Road, Green Point *Cnr. Napier & Somerset Road opposite BP garage* ☎ 021 419 92 16 🖳 www.bronx.co.za
Bronx's consistent and energetic atmosphere has made it one of the top dance bars in Cape Town.

DANCECLUBS

■ **Navigaytion Night Club** (AC B D GLM MA)
Wed, Thu, Fri & Sat 23-6h
22 Somerset Road, Green Point ☎ 021 41 92 216
🖳 www.navigaytion.co.za
Navigaytion Nightclub is an underground party collective of like minded owner, djs, friends and clubbers.

■ **Stargayzer** (B D G MC) Wed, Fri & Sat 21-?h
12 Caxton Street, Parow ☎ 083 269 3236 (mobile)
Unpretentious, no attitude place.

RESTAURANTS

■ **Andiamo Deli-Restaurant-Bar** (B BF CC g M MA)
Mon-Sun 9-23h
Cape Quarter, 72 Waterkant Street, Green Point ☎ 021 421 1111
🖳 www.andiamo.co.za
Andiamo caters for breakfast, lunch and supper, cocktails and drinks. The food is straightforward and traditional Italian ranging from salads, tramezzinis and antipasti, to pizza, pasta, meat and seafood.

■ **Beefcakes** (B BF CC GLM M MC ST) Daily 11-23h
7 Sovereign Quay, 40 Somerset Rd *Greenpoint* ☎ 021 425 9019
🖳 www.beefcakes.co.za
Burger bar with good coffee and great drag shows.

■ **Blues** (AC B CC glm M NR OS PK VEG WL) 12h-late
The Promenade, Victoria Road, Camps Bay *Beachfront* ☎ 021 438 2040
🖳 www.blues.co.za
Seafood restaurant.

■ **Café Manhattan** (B BF CC GLM I M MA OS S) 10-1h
74 Waterkant Street, De Waterkant ☎ 021 421 6666
🖳 www.manhattan.co.za
Opened in 1994. The oldest gay owned and operated bar and restaurant in Cape Town.

■ **Five Flies** (CC DM glm M MA NR OS PK VEG WL)
Daily 12-15 & 18-23h
14-16 Keerom Street , City Bowl ☎ 021 424-4442 🖳 fiveflies.co.za
Renown for its artistic and delicious creations, which are presented together with some of the finest local wines.

■ **On Broadway** (GLM)
44 Long Street *Corner Hout Street* ☎ 021 424 1194
Theatre/restaurant

■ **Societi Bistro** (AC b BF cc glm M MA OS PK RES VEG WL)
Daily 9-23h
50 Orange Street, Gardens *Opposite the UCT art campus* ☎ 021 418 9483
🖳 www.societi.co.za
Sophisticated, cosmopolitan and trendy restaurant using seasonal produce and offering exceptional value. Cooking courses offered too.

■ **Soho** (AC B BF cc GLM M MC NR VEG) Daily 7.30-22.30h
49 Napier Street, de Waterkant *In the Village Lodge hotel*
☎ 021 421 9898 🖳 www.thevillagelodge.com
Authentic Thai cuisine from Chang Mai and Bangkok.

■ **What's On Eatery** (B BF cc glm M NR PK VEG WE WL) Mon 6.30-16, Tue-Fri 6.30-16 & 18-midnight, Sun 18-midnight
6 Watson Street *Between Loop Street and Bree Street* ☎ 021 422 5652
🖳 www.whatsoneatery.co.za
Located in a renovated Victorian town house. The deli is on the ground floor offering lunchtime specials and a full English breakfast.

SEX SHOPS/BLUE MOVIES

■ **Adult World** (g)
36 Riebeeck Street *Between Loop & Bree* ☎ 021 418 74 55
🖳 www.adultworld.co.za
Everyting erotic for adults.

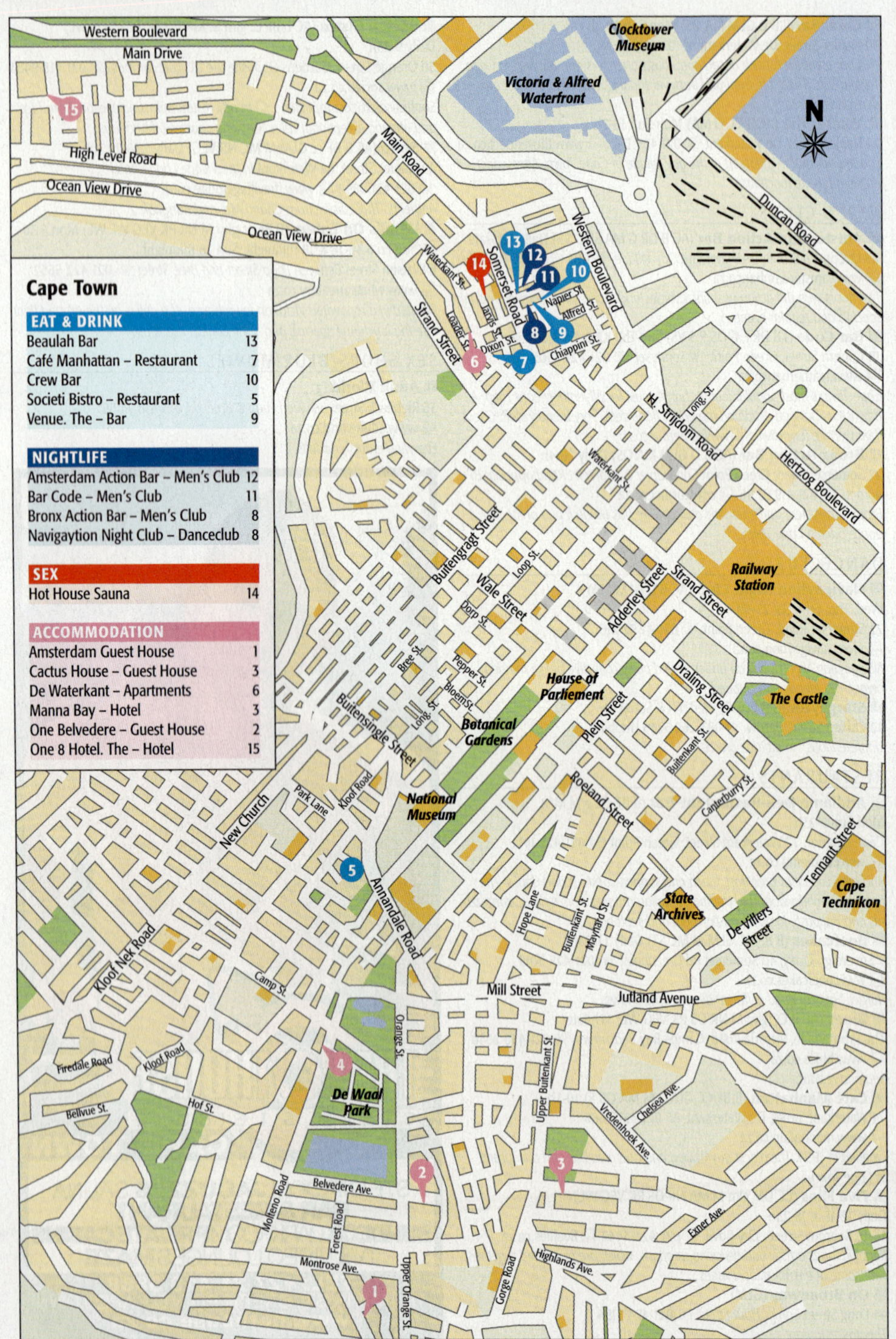
Western Boulevard
Main Drive
High Level Road
Ocean View Drive
Ocean View Drive
Clocktower Museum
Victoria & Alfred Waterfront
N
Main Road
Duncan Road
Western Boulevard
Somerset Road
Waterkant St.
Strand Street
Loader St.
Jarvis St.
Dixon St.
Napier St.
Alfred St.
Chiappini St.
H. Strijdom Road
Long St.
Hertzog Boulevard
Waterkant St.
Buitengragt Street
Loop St.
Wale Street
Dorp St.
Adderley Street
Strand Street
Railway Station
Bree St.
Pepper St.
Bloem St.
Long St.
Buitensingle Street
House of Parliement
Drailing Street
The Castle
Plein Street
Botanical Gardens
Buitenkant St.
Roeland Street
Canterbury St.
Park Lane
Kloof Road
National Museum
New Church
Tennant Street
Cape Technikon
Annandale Road
Hope Lane
Buitenkant St.
Maynard St.
State Archives
De Villers Street
Kloof Nek Road
Camp St.
Mill Street
Jutland Avenue
Orange St.
Firedale Road
Kloof Road
Hof St.
Bellvue St.
De Waal Park
Upper Buitenkant St.
Chelsea Ave.
Vredenhoek Ave.
Belvedere Ave.
Molteno Road
Forest Road
Exner Ave.
Montrose Ave.
Upper Orange St.
Gorge Road
Highlands Ave.
Cape Town
EAT & DRINK
Beaulah Bar 13
Café Manhattan – Restaurant 7
Crew Bar 10
Societi Bistro – Restaurant 5
Venue. The – Bar 9
NIGHTLIFE
Amsterdam Action Bar – Men's Club 12
Bar Code – Men's Club 11
Bronx Action Bar – Men's Club 8
Navigaytion Night Club – Danceclub 8
SEX
Hot House Sauna 14
ACCOMMODATION
Amsterdam Guest House 1
Cactus House – Guest House 3
De Waterkant – Apartments 6
Manna Bay – Hotel 3
One Belvedere – Guest House 2
One 8 Hotel. The – Hotel 15

■ **Wet Warehouse** (CC DR G MA VS) Mon-Sat 10-19, Sun & Public Holiday 13-19h
122A Longmarket Street *3rd Floor I.L. Rosenberg House* ☎ 021 424 7798
☎ 082 8899 898 (mobile)
Catering for gay & bisexual men only. DVD's and videos. Private video rooms. All day video lounge.

SEX CINEMAS

■ **Wet Warehouse** (CC DR G MA VS) Mon-Sat 10-19, Sun & Public Holiday 13-19h
122A Longmarket Street *3rd Floor I.L. Rosenberg House* ☎ 021 424 7798
☎ 082 8899 898 (mobile)
Catering for gay & bisexual men only. DVD's and videos. Private video rooms. All day video lounge.

SAUNAS/BATHS

■ **Hot House – Steam & Leisure** (! AC B CC DR DU FC FH G I LAB M MA OS p RR SA SB VS WH)
Mon – Wed 12-2, Thu 12-4, WE 24hrs (non-stop)
18 Jarvis Street, Green Point ☎ 021 418 3888 💻 www.hothouse.co.za
Trendy, modern sauna in gay village. Upmarket atmosphere with spectacular views from sundeck. A very large and clean sauna. One of the best saunas in Africa.

FITNESS STUDIOS

■ **Virgin Active** (g) Mon-Thu 5-22, Fri 5-21, Sat & Sun 6-21h
Bill Peters Drive, Green Point ☎ 021 434 0750 💻 www.virginactive.co.za
Clean locker room, steamroom, and sauna. 80% gay men but also families.

MASSAGE

■ **Deister Studio** (CC G MC MSG RES) Mon-Thu 9-22, Fri & Sat 8-?, Sun 10-21h
51 Monte Carlo Street ☎ 086 722 7455 ☎ 072 656 3608 (mobile)
💻 www.studio.deister.co.za
Professional full body massage, male waxing

FASHION SHOPS

■ **Cape Quarter** (AC B BF CC g M MA OS)
72 Waterkant Street, Green Point ☎ 021 421 0737
💻 www.capequarter.co.za
Probably the best shopping centre in Cape Town. A one-stop destination for excellent food and restaurants, unique lifestyle stores and Piazza entertainment.

TRAVEL AND TRANSPORT

■ **Friends of Dorothy Tours** (G)
PO Box 4859 ☎ 021 4651871 ☎ (0)83 555 6611 (mobile)
💻 www.friendsofdorothytours.co.za
Day tours for maximum of 7 passengers in and around Cape Town, including trips to penguins, Cape Point, Winelands, whales (in season). Private tours can be arranged.

■ **Karoo Biking** (CC G)
5 Howe Street, Observatory ☎ 021 447 4759
☎ 082 5 33 66 55 (mobile) 💻 www.karoo-biking.de
BMW Motorcycle tours and rentals in Southern Africa. ON road | OFF road & everything in-between.

HOTELS

■ **Glen Boutique Hotel** (AC B BF CC GLM I M MA MSG OS PI PK RWB RWS RWT S SA SB VA WH WO) All year
3 The Glen, Sea Point *Between High Level and Main Rd* ☎ 021 439 0086
💻 www.glenhotel.co.za
A luxurious and stylish, exclusively gay, 4-star boutique hotel.

■ **MannaBay Fine Boutique Hotel** (AC B CC glm I M MC OS PI PK RWB RWS RWT VS) All year
1 Denholm Road, Oranjezicht *On corner with Yeoville Rd* ☎ 021 461 1094
💻 www.mannabay.com
Cape Town's latest and most elegant boutique hotel with seven luxury suites. Gay owned and in the heart if the city.

■ **One 8 Hotel. The**
(AC B BF CC glm I m MSG PI PK RWB RWS RWT WH WO) All year
18 Antrim Road, Green Point *20 mins form the international airport*
☎ 021 434 6100 💻 www.theone8.com
Relax and enjoy the hospitality and atmosphere of this modern and intimate 4-star hotel, located close to the Waterfront, the gay village as well as fine restaurants and great beaches. Gay owned. Frequent seasonal specials available.

■ **Village Lodge Portfolio. The** (AC B BF CC GLM MA MSG PI)
All year, 24hrs
49 Napier Street, De Waterkant ☎ 021 421 8488
💻 www.thevillagelodge.com
The Village Lodge is a 15 bedroom boutique hotel and an in-house restaurant Soho where breakfast is served.

GUEST HOUSES

■ **27 Hudson** (AC BF CC G I MC PK) All year
27 Hudson Street ☎ 082 600 0219 (mobile) 💻 www.27hudson.com
Three guestrooms, two with en-suite bathroom.

■ **Amsterdam** (AC b BF cc G I NU OS PI PK RWS RWT SA SB VA WH)
All year
19 Forest Road *City Bowl* ☎ 021 461 8236 💻 www.amsterdam.co.za
Centrally located with stunning views. Completely renovated 8 double rooms with own bath/WC, TV, AC, video, phone and own key. Clothing optional in entertainment area. Full breakfast till noon. Full aircon/heating in all rooms. Winner of Exit & Diva Awards for best gay accommodation for many years running now.

■ **Antrim Villa** (cc g OS PI RWS) All year
12 Antrim Road, Greenpoint ☎ 021 433 2132
💻 www.antrimvilla.com

■ **Bickley House** (BF cc g I MC OS PI PK RWS) All year
17 Bickley Road, Sea Point ☎ 021 4347424
💻 www.bickleyhouse.com
Enjoy the big Scandinavian breakfast buffet every morning. Gay owned.

■ **Blackheath Lodge** (AC B BF CC GLM H I M MA MSG PI PK RWS RWT) All year
6 Blackheath Road, Sea Point ☎ 021 439 2541
💻 www.blackheathlodge.co.za
Gay owned guesthouse. 10 spacious double en-suite rooms.

■ **Cactus House** (b BF CC G NU OS PI RWB RWS RWT VA WH) All year
4 Molteno Road *Close to Mount Nelson in City Bowl* ☎ 021 422 5966
💻 www.cactushouse.co.za
The Cactus House is a spacious Victorian guesthouse, exclusively for gay men with emphasis on comfort and luxury. Centrally located within minutes from beaches/gay life. The bedrooms are tastefully decorated and the breakfasts are great!

■ **Chocolate Box Luxury Guest House** (G MC) All year
34 Chapman Avenue, Gordon's Bay ☎ 076 924 8614 (mobile)
💻 www.chocolateboxguesthouse.co.za

■ **David's** (BF CC G I MC OS RWS RWT SH WI) All year
12 Croxteth Road, Green Point ☎ 021 439 4649
☎ 083 255 9618 (mobile) 💻 www.davids.co.za
David's Cape Town guest house is in the trendy heart of Green Point and combines the ambience of classic style with modern chic.

■ **One Belvedere** (BF CC G I OS PI PK RWB RWS RWT SA SB WH) All year
1 Belvedere Avenue, Oranjezicht *City centre* ☎ 021 461 2442
☎ 083 344 0810 (mobile) 💻 www.onebelvedere.co.za
An exclusive, 4 stars (for excellent hospitality and service) gay guest house situated in a Victorian villa. The place to unwind, to relax and make friends. Close to all the hotspots and beaches. Within walking distance to the trendy and buzzing Kloof and Long Street. City and mountain views.

■ **Pink Rose Guesthouse & Spa** (AC b BF CC G I M MSG NU OS PI PK RWB RWT SA SB VA WH) All year, 8-22h
15 Lantana Street, Helderview *In Somerset West – 44 km from Cape Town*
☎ 021 855 5189 💻 www.pinkroseguesthouse.com
The Pink Rose Guesthouse & Spa is the first gay only guesthouse in the Winelands near Cape Town and is situated in a quiet residential area with striking views of the mountains.

■ **Purple House** (BF g I MC OS RWS RWT) All year
23 Jarvis Street, De Waterkant Village ☎ 021 418 2508
💻 www.purplehouse.co.za
The guest rooms are stylish and spacious.

■ **Shisa ! Guest Farm for Men Only**
See: Tulbagh – Western Cape *120km N.E. of Cape Town*
💻 www.shisafarm.com
☞ *Tulbagh – Western Cape.*

■ **Southern Comfort Guest Lodge** (AC BF g I MC OS PI PK RES RWS RWT)
27 Belmont Avenue, Oranjezicht ☎ 076 732 7280 (mobile)
☎ 021 4614500 💻 www.scomfort.co.za
Re-opened in October 2011 after extensive refurbishment. Gay-friendly accommodation. 5 guestrooms.

■ **Tom's Guest House** (cc G I MC OS PI RWS RWT) All year
44 Breda Street, Oranjezicht ☎ 021 465 3223
💻 www.tom-kapstadt.de
A very quiet and centrally located guesthouse 5 minutes away from Cape Town city centre.

■ **Villa Martini** (BF MC NG OS WH) All year
11 Milner Road, Sea Point ☎ 021 434 7953
This Tuscan styled Cape Town villa / guesthouse, nestling on the slopes of Signal Hill offers every convenience and comfort to the discerning traveller.

APARTMENTS

■ **Apartment 809 @ Seasons** (AC GLM I PI PK RWB RWS RWT VA WO) All year
47 Buitenkant Street, Zonneblom ☎ 028 272 9628
💻 www.bucacosud.co.za
A stylish fully equipped self catering apartment on the edge of the Cape Town CBD. Sleeping 2, in a one bedroom en-suite, but could accommodate a child or extra person (extra sleeping space in lounge, sofa bed). With HiFi, Plasma TV, linen and towels.

■ **De Waterkant Cottages** (AC CC GLM H I MA OS RWT)
Office hours: Mon-Fri 8-17.30. WE 10-15h
40 Napier Street, De Waterkant *City centre* ☎ 021 421 2300
💻 www.dewaterkantcottages.com

HEALTH GROUPS

■ **Health4Men** Mon-Fri 8-16.30h
24 Napier Street, Green Point *1st Floor, Anatoli Building* ☎ (021) 421 6127
💻 www.health4men.co.za
A gay men's sexual health centre (in Green Point) and clinic (in Woodstock) offering: free services including HIV testing, management and treatment, STI diagnosis and treatment, professional counselling, support groups, seminars, media production, lube and condom distribution.

■ **Triangle Project**
Mon-Fri 8.30-16h (Clinic Tue & Wed 18-20.30h)
Unit 29, Waverley Business Park, Dane St, Mowbray ☎ 021 448 3812
💻 www.facebook.com/pages/Triangle-Project/92804147303
A lesbian & gay service organisation providing a range of health, counselling and info services. Also a library, discussion & support groups, medical sevices and sexuality education.

SWIMMING

-Sandy Bay Beach (G NU) Cold water! (Take M6 to Hout Bay and leave in Llandudno)
-Clifton 3rd Beach (very nice beach).

CRUISING

-Sandy Bay, Llandudno. In the bushes on the far right hand side of Sandy Beach (!)

Darling – Western Cape

SHOWS

■ **Evita se Perron** (! b CC glm M MA S) Tue-Sun 10-16h
Darling Station, *55 mins from Cape Town* ☎ 022 492 2831 🖳 www.evita.co.za
Hosted by South Africa's most famous lady: Evita Bezuidenhout. The theatre/restuarant/bar, Boerasic Park & Evita's A en C (arts & crafts) are open Tue-Sun from 10-16h.

Dullstroom – Mpumalanga ☎ 013

HOTELS

■ **Walkersons Private Estate** (AC B BF CC g M MC MSG OS PI PK RES RR RWS RWT VEG W WH WL) All year
PO Box 185 *240km from Johannesburg and 185km from Kruger National Park* ☎ 013 253 7000 (reservations) 🖳 www.walkersons.co.za
25 luxury guestrooms, an excellent restaurant and the Amani Spa. Gay owned property.

GUEST HOUSES

■ **Kat-man-doo** (G M MA MSG OS PI RWB RWT S SA SB) Special weekends only
Bosman Street *2 hours drive from Pretoria* ☎ 078-569-6910 (mobile)
The newest, exclusive five star gay male resort in South Africa. gay weekends once a month for discerning gay males.

Durban – Kwazulu Natal

BARS

■ **Lounge. The** (AC B D DR GLM MA S SNU WE) Tue 20-? (G), Wed & Thu 20.30-?, Fri & Sat 21-?h, closed Sun & Mon
226 Mathews Meyiwa, Morningside *Stamford Hill* ☎ 031 303 9022
🖳 www.thelounge.za.org
Five bars, 3 dance floors and 2 outdoor balconies. Every Tue upstairs in the Red Bar is men only! Use separate „red door" entrance to the LEFT of the Main Entrance. No entry fee. Happy hour from 20-21h.

DANCECLUBS

■ **Bent Events** (B D gLm MA P S) Monthly or bi-monthly Fri 20-3h
16 Pitcairn Road, Carrington Heights ☎ 083 382 6655 (mobile)
🖳 www.bent.co.za
Vibrant and funny in safe, up-market areas. New: lesbian only parties every Friday!

■ **Origin** (B D GLM MC OS P) Fri & Sat 21-5h
9 Clark Road, Lower Glenwood *Near Gale Street* ☎ (031) 201 9959
🖳 www.theorigin.co.za
Four dance floors, various chill out areas, bars, balconies and a roof garden. Check their events calendar in Facebook.

RESTAURANTS

■ **Bean Bag Bohemia** (B g M MA OS VEG) Mon-Sat 10-1h
18 Windermere Road, Morningside ☎ 031 309 6019
🖳 www.beanbagbohemia.co.za
Restaurant, bar, „tea" garden. Cocktail special every Wed 16.30-19h, live entertainment. Gay managment and one waiter downstairs. A very mixed place to hang outs. Downstairs bar only.

■ **Spiga d'Oro** (cc DM g M MC NR OS PK RES VEG WL) Sun & Mon 7-12, Tue & Wed -2, Thu-Sat -3h
200 Florida Road, Morningside ☎ 031 303 9511
Prices are very reasonable and the restaurant is open till the early hours of the morning. A typical Italian pavement bistro.

SEX SHOPS/BLUE MOVIES

■ **Adult World** (AC CC DR MA VS) Mon-Sat 8-22, Sun & pub holidays 10-21h
114 Dr Pixley Kaseme St (West Street) ☎ 031 332 13 37
🖳 www.adultworld.co.za
Everything erotic for adults.

SEX CINEMAS

■ **Cine X** (AC DR G MA VS) Mon-Thu 9-20, Fri & Sat -21, public holidays & Sun 10.30-20h
16 Woodford Grove, Stamford Hill *Basement* ☎ 031 312 5277
For gay and bisexual men. DVD's for sale. „Pants-off" party on first Friday of every month 20-23h.

GUEST HOUSES

■ **African Rainbow Lodge** (AC b BF CC G I m MA NU OS PI PK RWS RWT S SA WH) All year
307 Helen Joseph Rd (formerly Davenport Rd), Glenwood *Central Durban* ☎ 031 202 3838 🖳 www.africanrainbowlodge.co.za
Six en suite rooms. Also self-catering. Near beaches and gay locations.

■ **Ammazulu African Palace** (BF cc GLM I MC OS PK RWB RWS RWT SA SB) All year
20 Windsor Road, Kloof *20 minutes from central Durban* ☎ 031 764 8000
🖳 www.ammazulupalace.com
A unique luxury lodge on the edge of the Kloof Gorge and Krantzkloof Nature Reserve. All ten rooms with tea/ coffee facilities and bar fridges

■ **Bordello. La** (BF CC G MA) All year
18 Windermere Road, Morningside *At Bean Bag Bohemia*
☎ 031 309 6019 🖳 www.beanbagbohemia.co.za
Boutique hotel right next door to the restaurant Bean Bag Bohemia.

■ **Durban View Gay Guesthouse** (AC B BF CC GLM I MA PI PK RWB RWS RWT VA WH) All year
16 Holstead Gardens, Musgrave *Berea suburb* ☎ 0837 033 329 (mobile)
🖳 www.durbanview.co.za
Gay guest house in Durban with superb city wide views from the roof-top sundeck and jacuzzi.

■ **Manaar House** (G) All year
16 Manaar Road ☎ (031) 5617902 ☎ 083-4434303 (mobile)
🖳 www.manaarhouse.co.za
Manaar House is situated in the beautiful coastal resort town of Umhlanga Rocks. Guests have the choice of staying in the bed & breakfast or choosing the self catering apartments.

■ **Rainsgrove Lodge** (BF G MC OS PK) All year
220 St Thomas Road, Berea ☎ 031 201 0855
B&B or self-catering accommodation

HEALTH GROUPS

■ **Durban Lesbian & Gay Community & Health Centre** (GLM)
Mark Lane *Between Pine and West Streets* ☎ (031) 301-2145
🖳 www.gaycentre.org.za
The Community Centre provides, personal, HIV/AIDS, sexual health and legal education, counselling and advise. Organisers of the Durban GLBT Pride event.

SWIMMING

ALL beaches in and around Durban are ideal for swimming. Please adhere to the warnings from the beach guards.
-Battery Beach – opposite Blue Waters Hotel (WE AYOR)
-Rachael Finlayson Baths in the showers, (g WE)
-Umhlanga Lagoon (NU).

CRUISING

All these areas are AYOR:
-Battery Beach (opposite Blue Waters Hotel and down the beach to the Snake Park, 24h)
-Beachfront (from Addington to North Beach, esp. at night)
-Virginia Airport behind the dunes and the parking lot
-Toilets at Buxtons Spar Centre, Umghlanga (during the day).

East London – Eastern Cape

DANCECLUBS

■ **Club Eden** (B D gLm MC) Wed 20-3, Fri & Sat 20-5h
Atlas Road, Arcadia ☎ 083 569 9158 (mobile)
🖳 www.getyourqueeron.com/east/category/Club%20Eden
The only gay place in East London.

PRIVATE ACCOMMODATION

B & B at the Castle (B BF glm I NU OS PA PI PK RWS RWT VA)
All year
13 Acacia Road, Beacon Bay *3 km from swimming / surfing beaches*
☎ 083 504 0888 (mobile) www.castlebandb.co.za
Self-catering apartments or B&B half way between Durban and Cape Town. Stunning pool and deck. Believe it or not, your host is Texan!

CRUISING

-Eastern Beach (beachfront)
-Esplanade area especially opposite the Quanza Marine Hotel or Osner Hotel
-Blue Lagoon Hotel carpark in Nahoon – after 16h and Nahoon Reef parking lot Fri & Sat after midnight
-Vincent Park Center – upstairs toilet.

Graskop – Mpumalanga

GUEST HOUSES

Flycatcher Castle (B BF glm M MC OS PI PK RWS RWT WO)
All year, reception 7-22h
PO Box 663 *5km from the famous God's Window* ☎ 013 767 11 14
www.flycatchercastle.com
The co-owners Michael and Manie welcome you in their home. Cosy, antique furnished suites with modern, sensual, open-plan bathrooms to enjoy an intimate sharing. Romantic 4-course dinners in Restaurant „Der Rosenkavalier", plenty of works of art celebrating the nude male. Private areas such as the Stargazer Deck and the solar heated plunge pool. Rated 5 Star grading offering exceptional quality and service.

Hermanus – Western Cape

RESTAURANTS

@365 Restaurant (AC B DM glm M RES VEG WL)
Tue-Fri 10-22, Sat 9-?, Sun 9-15h
365 Central Road, Pringle Bay *Between Cape Town & Hermanus*
☎ 028 273 8931
A funny place, full of gay people, but not actually gay. Fresh seafood dishes, succulent steaks, sumptuous venison, and good home-style cooking.

Tides. The
Clarence Drive (R44), Betty's Bay ☎ 028 2729835 (mobile)
Gay-friendly and great food.

GUEST HOUSES

Buçaco Sud (BF CC glm I MA OS PI PK RWB RWS RWT VA WE)
All year
2609 Clarence Drive, Betty's Bay ☎ 028 272 9750
www.bucacosud.co.za
Situated on the spectacular whale coast, close to Cape Town and winelands, great decor, stunning views.

Seemeeue. Die (AC BF GLM I M MA OS PA PI PK RWB RWS)
All year
60 Ghwarrie Crescent, Vermont *7 km from Hermanus, 110 km from Cape Town* ☎ 028 316 24 79 www.seemeeue.co.za
Cosy guesthouse, magnificent panoramic views over sea and mountains. Beaches, nature reserve. Whale-and shark boat trips nearby. Restaurant, intimate garden
German, French, Dutch, Afrikaans and English spoken.

Johannesburg – Gauteng

Johannesburg (Jozi, Jo'burg or eGoli) is the largest city in South Africa. The population (including Ekhuruleni, West Rand, Soweto and Lenasia exceeds 10 million people. Greater Johannesburg consists of over 500 suburbs covering an area of more than 1 645 km² (635 sq mi) and is the provincial capital of Gauteng. Jo'burg has the strongest economy of any metropolitan region in Sub-Saharan Africa. The city is one of the 40 largest metropolitan areas in the world and it is one of the six global cities of Africa. Johannesburg houses the Constitutional Court, is the source of a large-scale gold and diamond trade and the International Airport is the largest and busiest airport in Africa. Jo'burg has no distinctly gay area and venues are scattered from downtown, into the suburbs in and around Jozi. Public cruising had become extremely dangerous and were largely replaced by safe cruising venues and the internet. Travel with locals if possible and do not display yourself as being a tourist or openly expose your wealth.

Johannesburg (auch Jozi, Jo'burg oder eGoli genannt), Hauptstadt der Provinz Gauteng, ist die größte Stadt Südafrikas mit einer Gesamtbevölkerung von über 10 Millionen Menschen, wenn man Ekhuruleni, West Rand, Soweto und Lenasia mitrechnet, und einem mindestens 1.645 km² großen Ballungsgebiet, das über 500 Vorstädte umfasst. Johannesburg hat die stärkste Wirtschaftkraft aller afrikanischen Metropolregionen südlich der Sahara, zählt zu den 40 größten Ballungsgebieten der Welt und ist eine der sechs Weltstädte des afrikanischen Kontinents. Hier finden sich das Verfassungsgericht, der größte und verkehrsreichste Flughafen von ganz Afrika sowie das Zentrum des groß angelegten Handels mit Gold und Diamanten. In Ermangelung eines eigenen Schwulenkiezes sind die einschlägigen Anlaufpunkte jedoch über ganz Johannesburg verteilt, vom Zentrum bis in die Vorstädte. Da das öffentliche Cruisen hier äußerst gefährlich geworden ist, trifft man sich heutzutage lieber an sicheren Orten oder im Internet. Es wird geraten, sich möglichst in der Gesellschaft von Einheimischen zu bewegen, nicht als Tourist erkennbar zu geben, und seinen Wohlstand nicht öffentlich zur Schau zu stellen.

Johannesburg (aussi appelée Jozi, Jo'burg ou eGoli), capitale de la province de Gauteng, est la plus grande ville d'Afrique du Sud avec une population totale supérieure à 10 millions d'habitants, en prenant en compte Ekhuruleni, West Rand, Soweto et Lenasia qui regroupent une agglomération de plus 1.645 km² et plus de 500 villes périphériques. Johannesburg est le plus grand centre économique de toutes les régions métropolitaines africaines subsahariennes, fait partie des 40 plus grandes agglomérations au monde et est une des six plus grandes villes du continent africain. On y trouve la cour constitutionnelle, le plus important aéroport de toute l'Afrique ainsi que le centre du commerce du diamant et de l'or. Faute d'un quartier gay, les lieux gays sont dispersés dans toute la ville, du centre à la périphérie. La drague dans les lieux publics étant particulièrement dangereuse, on préfère se rencontrer de nos jours dans des lieux sûrs ou sur internet. Il est recommandé d'être en compagnie de locaux et de ne pas montrer que l'on est touriste, de même il faut éviter de montrer des signes de richesse.

Johannesburgo (también conocida como Jozi, Jo'burg o IGoli) es la capital de la provincia de Gauteng y con una población de más de 10 millones de habitantes es la ciudad más grande de Sudáfrica; si se cuenta con Ekhuruleni, West Rand, Soweto y Lenasia. Johannesburgo tiene un mínimo de 1.645 Kilómetros cuadrados de área metropolitana que incluye más de 500 barrios. Johannesburgo cuenta con la economía más fuerte de todas las áreas metropolitanas del África al subsahariana, se encuentra además entre las 40 aglomeraciones urbanas más grandes del mundo y es una de las seis metrópolis del continente africano. Aquí se encuentran el Tribunal Constitucional, el aeropuerto más grande y de mayor actividad de toda África, como también el centro de comercio a gran escala de oro y diamantes. Dada la ausencia de un barrio gay los puntos de encuentro correspondientes están dispersados por todo Johannesburgo, desde el centro hacia los suburbios. Ya que el cruising se ha vuelto extremadamente peligroso es preferible encontrarse hoy en día en lugares seguros o a través de Internet. Se aconseja moverse, en la medida de lo posible, en compañía de lugareños para evitar ser reconocido como turista y no exhibir ni hacer alarde de riquezas en público.

Johannesburg (chiamata anche Jozi, Jo'burg o eGoli), capoluogo della provincia Gauteng, è la città più grande del Sudafrica e conta più di 10 milioni di abitanti (considerando anche Ekhuruleni, West Rand, Soweto e Lenasia). Johannesburg è un agglomerato di almeno 1.645 km² che comprende più di 500 sobborghi. Johannesburg è l'economia più forte di tutta la zona al sud del Sahara, è uno dei 40 conglomerati più grandi al mondo ed è una delle sei metropoli del continente africano.

Johannesburg è sede della Corte Costituzionale, dell'aeroporto più importante di tutta l'Africa ed è anche centro del commercio di oro e diamanti. In mancanza di un quartiere prettamente gay, i punti di incontro per i gay sono sparsi su tutta la città, dal centro fino ai sobborghi della periferia. Poiché il cruising in luoghi pubblici è diventato molto pericoloso, adesso si preferisce incontrarsi in posti più sicuri o tramite internet. È consigliabile muoversi in compagnia di gente del luogo, non far capire di essere turisti e non ostentare in pubblico il proprio benessere.

BARS

■ **Babylon Bar** (B D G p PK YC) Wed, Fri & Sat 21-?h
198 Oxford Road, Illovo *In Oxford Centre*
Joburg's more intimate version of the Babylon club in Pretoria. Sexy barmen with stylish decor and crowd. Happy Hour 19-21h (2-4-1)

■ **LiquidChefs @ The Zone** (B g M MC OS VEG) Tue-Sun 11-2h
Tyrwhitt Avenue, The Zone 2, Rosebank *Next to Piza Vino*
☎ 011 447 6412 liquidchefs.co.za
Cocktails, sandwiches, snacks and more.

■ **Ratz** (AC B cc glm LM MA s) 18-2h
7th Street, Melville *Shop 9* ☎ 011 482 5593 www.ratz.co.za
A very gay-friendly iconic coaktail bar, with 80's disco hits.

■ **Simply Blue** (AC B CC D GLM m MA p S SNU) Fri & Sat 21h-late
36 Rogers Street, Selby, Booysens ☎ 082 544 7600 (mobile)
www.clubsimplyblue.com
A place for people of colour and those who appreciate colour. Tuesday night fever, Cheeky Fridays student nights, Sat free before 21h Resident DJ Charlie B. Clubnights: Thu – Sat and on eve of public holidays.

MEN'S CLUBS

■ **Factory. The** (B CC DR F G M MA NU p S VS) 12-6, WE 12-7h
6, Sixth Street, New Doornfontein *South of Ellis Park Stadium*
☎ 083 965 2227 (mobile)
Men-only, multi-level cruise bar. Dress code: fetish/leather gear or shoes and socks only. Also with a guesthouse The Factory B&B.

CAFES

■ **Amuse** (B g M MC OS VEG) Tue-Sat 16h-midnight
34 5th Street, corner 4th Avenue, Linden *Shop 12, Manlam court*
☎ 084 555 5252 (mobile)
A funky lounge – café – restaurant

DANCECLUBS

■ **Citrus Lounge** (B D g MC)
38 Rogers Road *Cnr Webber & Selby, downtown Jo'burg* ☎ 011 493 4887
www.citrus-lounge.co.za
Occational Theme Parties (Dates on www.citrus-lounge.co.za)

■ **Risque** (B D G MA) Wed, Fri & Sat
Corner Witkoppen and Main Road, Braynston ☎ 082 222 1562
www.risquelounge.co.za
Risqué is a stylish, up market venue with an avenue of palm trees leading to the entrance The club is open Wednesday to Saturday with different events every night – look out for the pole dancing on Saturdays!

■ **Simply Blue** (AC B CC D GLM m MA p S SNU) Fri & Sat 21h-late
36 Rogers Street, Selby, Booysens ☎ 082 544 7600 (mobile)
www.clubsimplyblue.com
A place for people of colour and those who appreciate colour. Tuesday night fever, Cheeky Fridays student nights, Sat free before 21h Resident DJ Charlie B. Clubnights: Thu – Sat and on eve of public holidays.

■ **V2 Experience** (AC B D glm MC) Fri & Sat 20-?h
c/o Lemon 8, 38 Roger Street, Selby *Corner of Roger & Weber St.*
Monthly parties attracting a very trendy clientele. See Facebook entry for party details.

RESTAURANTS

■ **Bell Pepper. The** (AC B CC glm M MA OS)
Lunch: 11-15, dinner from 18h
176 Queen Street, Kengsington ☎ 011 615 7531
Uncomplicated local and international cuisine.

Cafe Culture (B BF cc g M PK) Daily 11-?h
Straight Street, Sandton *In Pineslopes Shopping Centre*
☎ 082 894 6114 (mobile)
A bistro restaurant and cocktail lounge.

Dio Bacco (AC B CC GLM M MA OS) Tue-Sat 12-22, Sun 11-15h
48 The Avenue, Gardens *Norwood* ☎ 011 728 2826
Mediterranean gastronomic experience.

Doppio Zero (AC B BF CC glm I M MA) 7-22h
Corner Barry Hertzog & Gleneagles Road, Greenside ☎ 011 646 8740
www.doppio.co.za
Trendy coffee bar, breakfasts, continental bakery and pizzeria. 13 different coffee inspired beverages available.

Melon (AC B CC GLM M) Daily 12-23h
7th Street, Melville *Shop 9a* ☎ 011 482 9965
www.melon-restaurant.co.za
French cuisine, extensive wine list and reasonably priced meals.

Piccola Prima Donna (B CC glm M MA ST) Daily 12-15.30 & 18-22h
38 Grant Avenue, Norwood *Next to Fishmongers* ☎ 011 483 0089
Great pizzas. Drag shows on Tuesday nights.

SEX SHOPS/BLUE MOVIES

Adult World (AC CC DR MA VS) 9-13h
Jan Smuts Avenue 356, Craighall Park www.adultworld.co.za
Ramrods men only cruising area.

Adult World Cresta (AC cc DR G MA p VS)
260 Beyers Naude Drive, Blackheath ☎ 011 678 9996
www.adultworld.co.za
Everything erotic for adults.

Amour. L' (CC g) Mon-Sat 10.30-20, Sun -17h
Sandela Court c/o Oliphant and Levubu Roads, Emmerentia *Shop 1*
☎ 011 888 1888 www.dvdsexselect.co.za

Erotic Pleasure (G) Mon-Sat 9.30-22h
38 Grant Ave *Cnr Dorothy Road, 205 Tarquin House* ☎ 011 483 19 19
2 preview lounges and 6 preview booths.

Hustler Extreme (cc G) Mon-Sat 9-21, pub. Holidays and Sun 10-18h
Shop 10 Manlam Court, Corner 5th Street & 4th Avenue, Linden
☎ 011 782 1570 www.hustlerextreme.co.za
A large variety of DVD's, toys, enhancers and more.

SAUNAS/BATHS

Rec Room Johannesburg. The (! AC B CC DR DU FC FH G GH LAB M MA OS p SA SB VS WE WH) Mon-Thu 12-1, Fri & Sat 12-7, Sun 13-1h
Phoenix Centre, Malibongwe Drive, Randburg *100 m from the N1 Highway* ☎ 011 792 1288 www.recroom.co.za
The largest gay sauna in Johannesburg and possibly the entire South Africa.

LEATHER & FETISH SHOPS

Kinx Fetish (CC F) Tue-Fri 12-20, Sat 10-17, Sun 10-14h
Shop 1d, 7th Street, Melville *Go up 2nd Ave to 7 St. turn right, just past Nunos resturant is the new shop* ☎ 079 777 55 00 www.kinx.co.za
Mail order possible. Web sales worldwide.

TRAVEL AND TRANSPORT

AfricanFlamboyance (GLM MA RES) Daily 10-18h
☎ (0)73 142 8066 (mobile) www.africanflamboyance.com
AfricanFlamboyance is a LGBT focused Inbound Tour Operator & Destination Management Company based in Johannesburg South Africa.

GUEST HOUSES

12 Stars Lifestyle Guest House (BF CC glm I OS PK RWB RWS RWT) All year
7th Street, Melville ☎ 011 482 7979 www.12stars.co.za
Self catering, studio apartments with equipped kitchens and bathrooms with separate bath and shower.

33 on First (AC b BF CC glm I m MA OS PI PK RWS RWT) All year
33 First Avenue, Melville ☎ 011 726 7172 www.33onfirst.co.za
Six rooms, all with private bathrooms, cable television and tea/coffee making facilities.

Africa Centre Airport Leisure Hotel (AC B BF CC H I M OS PI WH)
65 Sunny Road, Lakefield, Benoni *Near OR International Airport*
☎ 011 894 4857 www.africacentrehotel.co.za
Self catering units available.

Agterplaas, Die (BF CC H I M OS)
66 Sixth Ave, Melville *Within 7km from major Johannesburg universities, nature reserve and trendy bars and retaurants* ☎ 011 726 8452
www.agterplaas.co.za

Akuwaiseni Guest House (B BF CC GLM I M MA PI PK RWB RWS RWT SB WO) All year
24 Wargrave Ave, Auckland Park ☎ (086) 722 7255 (mobile)
www.akuwaiseni.co.za
Akuwaiseni (the place of rest) has nine double rooms with a definite minimal/ethnic flavor all with Sat-TV and ceiling fans.

Graton (BF CC glm I OS PI PK RWS) All year
4a Oaklands Road, Orchards ☎ 011 728 23 40 www.graton.co.za
Gay run and gay ownewd guesthouse with 5 guestrooms.

Sleepy Gecko (AC b BF CC G H I m MSG OS PI) All year
84, 3rd Avenue, Melville ☎ 011 482 52 24 www.sleepygecko.co.za
10 meters away from 7th street the night time hub of Melville bars, restaurants and clubs. Close to all shopping centres and major businesses. Airport transfers possible upon request.

Space Guest House. The (BF cc DU GLM MA OS RWB RWT) All year
62, 5th Avenue, Melville *In the heart of trendy Melville* ☎ 011 482 7979
www.thespaceguesthouse.co.za
12 guestrooms with private entrances and many comforts.

Twin Oaks Losieshuis (b BF G I M OS S WH) 9-22h
Houghton ☎ 011 487 0964
Accommodation, wedding and spiritual venue, art gallery, photography and hair stylist. Stylise and compile tours in and around Gauteng and North.

CAMPING

Voëlkop Guest Farm (B BF cc d G m MA NU PI S SA SB WE) All year
PO Box 1303, Brits *80km from Pretoria on the road to Sun City*
☎ 012 254 1157 www.voelkop.co.za
One and half hour drive from Pretoria or Johannesburg. Male nudist Retreat past Hartebeespoort Dam in the direction of Sun City, near the town Makalowe. Drive through the town and turn right at the „cemetery" sign. Follow farm road to Voelkop gate. Self-catering chalets and camping- bring everything you need.

GENERAL GROUPS

GALA – Gay LGBTI Archive
PO Box 31719 *Ground floor, William Cullen Library, East Campus, University of Wits* ☎ 011 717 1963

CRUISING

-Johannesburg Botanical Gardens, car-cruising in and between parking just off Beyers Naude Drive and the Rose Garden (AYOR)
--Ramrods at Adult World Craighall Park.

Knysna – Western Cape

HOTELS

Turbine Boutique Hotel & Spa. The (AC B BF CC g I M MC MSG OS PI RWB RWS RWT SB VEG WL) All year
36 Sawtooth Lane, Thesen Islands ☎ 044 302 57 46
www.turbinehotel.co.za
Five star accommodation in a former power station with 17 guestrooms, 6 suites and one honeymoon suite.

GUEST HOUSES

Bliss (AC BF GLM MC PI PK RES) All year, 8-20h
12 Faure Street *Garden Route* ☎ 044 382 4569 www.bliss.co.za
Two comfortably separate, self catering units, and one B&B unit. Stunning views of the lagoon. Within walking distance of town.

■ **Trogon Guest House B&B** (BF GLM I MA OS PA PK RWB RWS VA)
All year, 8-20h
6 Boyce Close, Hunters Home *Knysna on the Garden route*
☎ 044 384 0495 🖳 mysite.mweb.co.za/residents/liewyk
Communal TV room.

SPECIAL INTEREST GROUPS

■ **Pink Loerie Promotions (pty) Ltd.** (GLM)
☎ 044 382 7768 🖳 www.pinkloerie.co.za
Organisers of the Pink Loerie Carnival – a gay/lesbian festival held from the 28th April to 1st May 2012 in Knysna.

Magaliesberg – Gauteng

HOTELS

■ **Quiet Mountain Country House**
(AC BF cc glm I M OS PI PK RWB RWS) All year
1 Berg Road, Hekpoort (North West Province) *60 mins from Johannesburg*
☎ 014 576 1258 🖳 www.quietmountain.co.za
All 7 guestrooms are ensuite. The rates include dinner, bed and breakfast. A minimum stay of 2 nights applies at weekends. Children and day visitors are not allowed.

Malelane – Mpumalanga

GUEST HOUSES

■ **River House Guest Lodge** (AC B BF GLM MC OS PI RWB RWS)
All year
Fish Eagle Bend *On the Southern Border of the Kruger National Park*
☎ 013 790 1333/1 🖳 www.riverhouse.co.za

McGregor – Western Cape

RESTAURANTS

■ **Karoux** (B DM glm M MC OS PA PK VEG WL)
Mon-Wed 18-?, Fri-Sun 12-?h, closed on Thu
42 Voortrekker Road *On the main street* ☎ 023 625 1421
🖳 www.karoux.co.za
Highly recommended for an intimate evening meal in cosy surroundings reminiscent of days gone by, Karoux is warmed by the fireplace in winter and promises to overflow onto the patio for al fresco dining on long summer evenings.

■ **Tebaldi's at Temenos** (AC B DM glm M OS PA PK VEG WL) Tue-Sun
Voortrekker Street *At Temenos Retreat* ☎ 023 625 1115
🖳 www.temenos.org.za
Named after the great Italian Opera prima donna, Renata Tebaldi, Tebaldi's celebrates the love of great food, great wine and great music. Enjoy a weekly evening menu offering seasonal and local produce as well as superb wine list offering wines of the region. Also a lunch menu.

GUEST HOUSES

■ **Temenos Retreat** (B cc glm M MA OS PI PK RWB RWS) All year

Voortrekker Street *20 km from Robertson in the picturesque village of McGregor* ☎ 023 625 1871 🖳 www.temenos.org.za
Self-catering cottages in extensive gardens with fireplaces and all amenities. Restaurant, library, swimming pool and wellness therapies available.

Mkuze – KwaZulu Natal

HOTELS

■ **Ghost Mountain Inn**
(AC B BF CC glm H I M MSG OS PI PK RWB RWS RWT SB WO) All year
Fish Eagle Road *3 hrs north of Durban, 5 hrs east of Johannesburg*
☎ 035 573 1025
🖳 www.ghostmountaininn.co.za
Situated beneath the legendary Ghost Mountain in Northern KwaZulu Natal, this Country Inn and Spa offers a variety of game, cultural safaris and boat rides in the vicinity.

Mossel Bay – Eastern Cape

HOTELS

Botlierskop (AC B BF CC glm M MC PK RWS) All year
PO Box 565 *25 mins from Mossel Bay* ☎ 044 696 6055
www.botlierskop.co.za
Botlierskop Private Game Reserve ensures its visitors of a unique safari experience. It is situated on the world renowned Garden Route. Easily located just off the N2 and an easy 30 minutes drive from George Airport or a 4-hour scenic drive from Cape Town.

Nelspruit / Mbombela – Mpumalanga ☎ 013

DANCECLUBS

Stables Club (B D glm MA OS S)
General Dan Pienar Avenue ☎ 013 755 4697 www.stablesclub.co.za

HOTELS

Nomndeni View Lodge (AC B BF CC G m MA PI S) All year, 24hrs
7 Beetle Walk, Steiltes ☎ (013) 013 744 91 89 www.nomndeni.co.za
Located in Nelspruit, surrounded by breathtaking views of the South Africa Lowveld. The lodge hosts various gay events and provides a retreat to all gay men.

Oudtshoorn – Western Cape

GUEST HOUSES

Adley House (AC b BF glm OS RWS W) All year
209 Jan van Riebeeck Road ☎ 044 272 4533
www.adleyhouse.co.za
Fourteen en-suite individually decorated rooms, with modern individual air conditioners, TV's, tea and coffee making facilities, fully stocked bar fridges, overhead fans, toiletries and also a daily laundry service.

Oulap Country House (B BF g M MA NR OS PI PK RWS) All year
PO Box 77 , De Rust *15km from De Rust on the R 341. 55km from Oudtshoorn* ☎ 044 241-2250 www.oulap.com
A gay-friendly guesthouse with 5 guestrooms. Dinner, bed and breakfast is available.

Port Edward – KwaZulu Natal

GUEST HOUSES

Ku-Boboyi River Lodge (B BF cc glm M OS PI PK RWB RWS VA) All year
PO Box 877 *Leisure Bay South* ☎ 072 222 77 60 (mobile)
www.kuboboyi.co.za
Six doubles, 5 singles and 2 suites, some with own bathroom. Visa and MasterCard accepted. Situated south of Durban, on the Hibiscus Coast, close to the Wild Coast.

Port Elizabeth – Eastern Cape

BARS

Italian Job (AC B GLM M S) Tue-Sun
19 Robson Street, Central *Off Rink Street* ☎ 041 5861720
☎ 073 7310 210 (mobile)
Gay bar and restaurant. Every Sunday night is karaoke night

DANCECLUBS

Aqua (B D GLM MA) Wed, Fri & Sat 20-4h
York & Prince Alfred Road, North End ☎ 072 057 7705 (mobile)
www.clubaqua.co.za
Port Elizabeth's premier gay nightclub.

APARTMENTS

Belvedere Cottages (G) All year 8-20h
15 Edward Street *Richmond Hill* ☎ (0)721171315
www.belvederecottages.co.za
Belvedere Cottages offers two self-catering, luxury 3-star cottages. Close to local gay scene.

CRUISING

-Beach near Oceanarium
-Park in front of Edward Hotel (Donkin Memorial)
-Lighthouse Hill (at night).

Robertson – Western Cape

TRAVEL AND TRANSPORT

Viljoensdrift Wines (NG)
Bonnievale Road (R317) ☎ 023 615 1901 www.viljoensdrift.co.za
Here you can take a boat trip with a picnic basket, enjoying the wonderul regional wines and food while sailing up the Brede River.

Soweto

GUEST HOUSES

Lebo's Soweto Backpackers (B BF cc H I M OS)
10823A Pooe Street, Orlando West ☎ 011 936 3444
www.sowetobackpackers.com/contact-us.html

Swellendam – Western Cape

GUEST HOUSES

Augusta de Mist (G MA) All year
3 Human Street *Just off the N2, 240km from Cape Town, or 160km from Mossel Bay* ☎ 0 28 514 2425 www.augustademist.com
One of the most beautiful guest houses in Swellendam, on South Africa's Garden Route. Experience stylish living on a large country retreat. Augusta de Mist is a luxury retreat

Tshwane / Pretoria – Gauteng

✱ The city's original name was Pretoria Philadelphia. Known as the Jacaranda City for all the spring purple blossom-bedecked trees which line its thoroughfares, Pretoria is a lovely, quiet and truly African city. It has a long, involved and fascinating history going back to the first Ndebele settlements in the 1600's. Apart from the many significant historical old buildings, fascinating museums and other attractions, you will find Pretoria's gay life vibrant and exciting. Post-apartheid Pretoria developed a strong Gay culture, several popular clubs, bars, saunas, guest houses and two exclusive male only farms, for those wishing to experience the African bush. Most locals speak English fluently. Commuter and main line trains from Pretoria Station link the city to all major centers in and outside the province but other forms of public transport are also available. Extensive changes are in progress at the station, as work is being done to accommodate the new Gautrain. The city has a subtropical climate with long, warm to hot summers and short moderately cool dry winters.

★ Pretoria ist eine reizvolle, ruhige, sehr afrikanische Stadt, die ursprünglich mal Pretoria Philadelphia hieß, heutzutage aber wegen der vielen Jacaranda-Bäume, die ihre Straßen säumen und im Frühling in ein malvenfarbiges Blütenmeer verwandeln, oft auch als Jacaranda City bezeichnet wird. Ihre lange, fesselnde und abwechslungsreiche Geschichte reicht bis ins 17. Jahrhundert zurück, als sich die ersten Ndebele hier niederließen. Neben vielen historischen Gebäuden, faszinierenden Museen und anderen Sehenswürdigkeiten findet sich hier auch eine quicklebendige Schwulenszene. Seit der Abschaffung der Apartheid hat sich in Pretoria eine eindrucksvolle Schwulenkultur entwickelt, mit zahlreichen gut besuchten Diskotheken, Kneipen, Saunen, Gästehäusern und sogar zwei ausschließlich Männern vorbehaltenen Farmen, die eine lebensnahe Erfahrung des afrikanischen Buschlands ermöglichen. Die meisten Stadtbewohner sprechen fliessend Englisch. Vom hiesigen Bahnhof aus, der momentan für den neuen Gautrain umgebaut wird, sind alle wichtigen Reiseziele in und außerhalb der Provinz gut mit dem Zug zu erreichen, andere öffentliche Verkehrsmittel sind jedoch ebenfalls vorhanden. Die Stadt hat ein subtropisches Klima mit langen, warmen bis heißen Sommern und kurzen, trockenen, nicht besonders kalten Wintern.

Pretoria, autrefois appelée Pretoria Philadelphia, est une ville calme très africaine et fascinante. Son surnom „ Jacaranda City „ est dû aux nombreux arbres de Jacaranda qui fleurissent à tous les coins de rues. Son histoire longue et envoutante commence au 17ème siècle avec l'installation des Ndébélés. On y trouve outre de nombreux bâtiments historiques, musées fascinants et autres attractions, une scène gay palpitante. Depuis la fin de l'apartheid, la culture gay s'y est fortement développée avec des boites, bars, saunas, hôtels et même deux fermes tenues exclusivement par des hommes qui offrent une expérience concrète du buschland africain. La plupart des citadins parlent couramment anglais. De la gare locale en phase d'aménagement pour le nouveau „ Gautrain „, toutes les destinations importantes de la province et de l'extérieur sont accessibles en train, d'autres moyens de transport public sont aussi présents. La ville a un climat subtropical avec un long été chaud voire torride et un court hiver sec et peu frais.

A esta encantadora y tranquila ciudad africana, originalmente llamada Pretoria Philadelphia, se la conoce a día de hoy como ciudad del Jacaranda, por los árboles de Jacaranda que inundan sus calles en primavera con flores color malva. Su larga, fascinante y variada historia se remonta al siglo XVII, cuando se asentaron aquí los primeros Ndebele.
Además de los muchos edificios históricos, museos y otras atracciones, también ofrece un vibrante ambiente gay. Desde la abolición del apartheid Pretoria ha desarrollado una cultura gay impresionante, con numerosas y concurridas discotecas, bares, saunas, hostales y hasta dos granjas reservadas exclusivamente para hombres, que permiten experimentar de cerca la Sabana africana. La mayoría de los residentes urbanos hablan inglés con fluidez. Desde la estación de tren local, actualmente en obras por el nuevo „Gautrain", tendrá acceso a todos los destinos importantes dentro y fuera de la provincia, aunque otros medios de transporte también están disponibles. La ciudad tiene un clima subtropical con veranos largos y cálidos/calurosos e inviernos cortos, secos y no especialmente fríos.

Pretoria è una tranquilla ed affascinante città africana che originariamente si chiamava Pretoria Philadelphia e che oggi, per i molti alberi di Jacaranda che ornano le sue strade, viene chiamata anche Jacaranda City. La sua lunga ed avvincente storia risale al XVII° secolo, quando i primi Ndebele cominciarono ad insediarvisi. Oltre ai molti edifici storici, ai bellissimi musei e alle altre attrazioni turistiche, Pretoria ha anche una scena gay molto vivace. Dalla scomparsa dell'apartheid a Pretoria è andata affermandosi un'importante cultura gay con discoteche molto frequentate, bar, saune, pensioni e addirittura due fattorie per soli uomini che permettono un incontro ravvicinato con il paesaggio naturale africano. La maggior parte degli abitanti di Pretoria parlano bene l'inglese. Tutte le mete turistiche più importanti dentro e fuori la provincia sono raggiungibili con il treno dalla stazione di Pretoria. La città ha un clima subtropicale con lunghe e calde estati e brevi e miti inverni.

BARS

Babylon (B D GLM MC PK) Sat 20-?h
Lenchen Ave N, Heuwel Avenue *Southlake Mall*
Centurion www.babylontheclub.co.za
An ultra modern funky dance floor with superb lighting and sound. Topless barmen

Detour Bar & Lounge (AC B CC D GLM MA OS s) Daily 17-late
680 Rubenstein Ave, Moreletapark *Pretoria East*
072 495 25 00 (mobile) www.detourlounge.com
Now the only gay club with entertainment licence and liquor licence with dancefloor.

Lounge Maximus (B GLM PK s WE)
57 Glenvillage North, Faerie Glen *Cnr Hans Strydom & Olympus Dr*
012 991 1110
Cocktail-bar with meals from 16h till late. Karaoke evening on Wed. Former Q-Bar & Lounge

Rasputin (B d G MC) 10-3h
642 Meyer Street *Wonderboom South* ☏ 084 404 1525 (mobile)
Bar with small dance floor. Local artists performing on Friday nights

MEN'S CLUBS

Camp David (AC B CC DR F FC G M MA NU P SL SNU VS) 12-5h
46 Selati Street, Alphen Park *Beneath the restaurant* ☏ 072 497 2500
www.campdavidbar.com
100% nude bar. Slings, free lube & condoms. Cinema and cruising area.

Friction Cruise Bar (B DR G NU S VS) Daily 18-?h
Park Centre, 680 Rubenstein Drive *Moreletapark* ☏ 072 497 2500
www.frictionbar.com
Men-only cruise bar. part of Detour Lounge.

DANCECLUBS

Babylon (B cc D GLM MC OS PK WE)
Lenchen Ave N, Heuwel Avenue ☏ 082 375 2412
www.babylontheclub.co.za
A large gay nightclub with secure parking, upstairs smoking area overlooking the dance floor.

Plum (B D G) Tue-Fri 17-2, Sat 20-2h
265 Hill Street ☏ 012 7513 519 plumpretoria.co.za

RESTAURANTS

Blue Crane (B BF CC glm M NR OS PK S WL) Mon 7.30-15, Tue-Fri -?, Sat 9-?, Sun -16h
Boshoff Street/Melk Street, New Muckleneuck *Near Brooklyn Square*
☏ 012 460 7615 www.bluecranerestaurant.co.za
Beautiful setting on a natural heritage site, the Austin Roberts Bird Sanctuary, surrounded by a lake with a lovely park – a stone throw away from Brooklynn Square. African fusion cuisine.

Charisma (AC B CC g M MA)
Breakfast: 7-9, lunch:12-14, dinner 18-21.30h
67 Albatros Street, Ninapark *Nestled on the northern slopes of the Magaliesberg* ☏ 012 54 24 449 ☏ 076 470 3173 (mobile)
www.CastaDiva.co.za
Open 7 days a week for breakfast, lunch and dinner.

Nuvo Cuisine Fine Dining (AC B CC G M MA) Tue-Sat 11-15.30 & 18-22, Sun 11-15h, Mon closed
823 Old Farm Road *Pretoria East, Faerie Glen* ☏ 012 9913396
www.nuvocuisine.co.za
Elegant, warm romantic ambiance. International favourites, with a strong French & italian influence served with South African flair. Gay owned and operated.

SEX SHOPS/BLUE MOVIES

Adam Adult Shop (G VS) 10-19h, closed Sun
179 Gordon Road, New Colbyn Center, Colbyn ☏ 012 342 4395
☏ 011 329 1165 (mail order)
Gay adult shop. Also mail order.

Adult World (AC CC DR G GH MA VR VS) 8-1h
534 Voortrekkers Road, Gezina ☏ 012 320 03 84
www.gaydvdsite.co.za
Very busy.

SAUNAS/BATHS

Sauna Boyz (AC B CC DR G M MSG s SA SB VS WH WO)
309 Lynnwood Road, Menlo Park ☏ 072 497 25 00 (mobile)
www.saunaboyz.com
New sauna which is designed and built as a copy of Babylon in Bangkok. There is a restaurant and gym for example. A great location!

FASHION SHOPS

Bone Wear (CC G) Mon-Fri 9-16.30, Sat 9-13h. Sun closed
355 Lynnwood Road ☏ 021 346 5050 www.bonewear.com
The new shop from South Africa's leading underwear and swimwear company.

GUEST HOUSES

222 Silver On Silver Oak Guesthouse
(AC b bf CC glm I m MA OS PI) All year
222 Silver Oak Avenue, Waterkloof ☏ 012 346 34 85
www.222onsilveroakguesthouse.co.za
Centrally situated in a peaceful surroundings of Waterkloof where the streets are lined with Jacaranda trees and the bird life is exceptional. The house is situated close to Brooklyn/Menlyn shopping centers, varies hospitals, universities and embassies. Luxurious suites and also self-catering units decorated classically with a modern chic.

Manfields All-Male Resort
☞ *Warmbaths (Bela Bela)*

TreeTops & Treats Guest House
(AC b BF CC g H I MA OS PI) All year
611 Leyds Street, Muckleneuk Hill *Near the Muckleneuk Telkom Tower*
☏ 012 343 86 19 www.treetopsandtreats.co.za
Be treated in the old splendour of a historical home in the tranquillity of warm hearted Pretoria.

Whistletree Lodge
(AC B BF CC glm H I M MA OS PI PK RWB RWS RWT SA VA) All year
1267 Whistletree Drive, Queenswood *Opp. Colbyn Valley Nature Reserve*

☎ 012 333 99 15 ☎ 012 333 99 16 🖳 www.whistletree.co.za
Five-star luxury accommodation and a tennis court with well appointed and lovingly decorated guestrooms. Ideally located, close to shopping and great, local restaurants and an ideal base when travelling to Kruger National Park. A heated swimming pool and sauna offer a further touch of luxury.

SPECIAL INTEREST GROUPS

■ **OUT Pretoria** Mon-Thu 8.30-17, Fri 8.30-14h
1081 Pretorius Street, Hatfield *Near the Union Buildings* ☎ 012 430 3272
🖳 www.out.org.za
Non-profit organisation specialising in mental and sexual health, research, mainstreaming and advocacy.

CRUISING

Public cruising especially around parks and toilets had become extremely dangerous for the outsider, as criminals have identified cruising tourists and even locals as soft targets. Rather use alternatives like video-areas at some adult shops or the internet.
All are AYOR:
-Springbok Park(corner of Hilda and Schoeman St, Hatfield)
-Burgerspark (opposite Holiday Inn Garden Court, van der Walt St.)
-Toilets at Lynn Ridge Mall (2nd floor)
-Hercules shopping center, off Van Der Hoff Rd
-Toilets on upper level of Pick & Pay (Frates Road, Gezina) beware of the security guards.

Tulbagh – Western Cape

GUEST HOUSES

■ **Shisa ! Guest Farm for Men Only**
(B BF CC G I M MA NU OS PI PK RWB RWS) Open Sep-Apr
PO Box 333 *Near Tulbagh, 120 km N.E. of Cape Town*
☎ 083 324 44 66 (mobile) (Joe) ☎ 083 954 44 28 (mobile) (Francois)
🖳 www.shisafarm.com
For gay men only. A stylish B&B in the Cape Winelands, 80 minutes from Cape Town. All the rooms are ensuite and have unspoilt mountain views. The historic village of Tulbagh, good restaurants and award-winning wine estates are close by.

Warmbaths (Bela-Bela)

GUEST HOUSES

■ **Manfields All-male Resort**
(B BF CC G I M MA NU OS PA PI PK RWS VA VS WH) All year
Limpopo Province *8km from Warmbaths aka Bela Bela* ☎ 083 399 0779
🖳 www.manfields.co.za
This all-male resort consists of ten 2 sleeper log cabins with en-suite facilities and a 6 sleeper bush camp with 3 canvas tens elevated onto wooden decks in its own little bush village. This is ideal for a group of friends to camp together and enjoy the outdoor life.

Welkom

DANCECLUBS

■ **Club Igo** (B D G MC) Wed-Sat
3 Alma Road *Next to the SPCA* ☎ 083 688 1189 (mobile)
The only gay place in Welkom.

Wilderness – Western Cape

GUEST HOUSES

■ **Wilderness Manor** (b BF cc g MC OS PK RWS RWT) 8- 23.30h
397 Waterside Road *On the Garden Route, 15km from George*
☎ 044 877 0264 🖳 www.manor.co.za
An elegant and refined colonial guest house, overlooking the beautiful Wilderness Lagoon, within easy and safe walking distance to beaches, restaurants and village shops.

Spain

Name: España · Spanien · Espagne · Spagna
Location: Southwest Europe
Initials: E
Time: GMT +1
International Country Code: ☏ 34
International Access Code: ☏ 00
Language: Spanish, (regional languages include: Catalan, Basque & Galician.)
Area: 504,782 km² / 194,884 sq mi.
Currency: 1 Euro (€) = 100 Cents
Population: 42,690,000
Capital: Madrid
Religions: 97% Roman Catholic
Climate: Ideal months to visit with excellent weather are May, Jun & Sep (plus Apr & Oct in the south). High summer with many Spanish and foreign tourists in Jul & Aug.
Important gay cities: Madrid, Barcelona, Ibiza, Sitges, Playa del Inglés (Gran Canaria), Benidorm, Sevilla, Torremolinos and Valencia

The general age of consent in Spain is 16, but if you're over 18 you should always be careful with younger guys. In summer 2005, when the socialist government amended the partnership laws, giving gay men equality in marriage, adoption and inheritance, leading to a stronger normalisation process. In November 2011, the conservative Partido Popular (PP) gained an absolute majority in parliament. Previous announcements cast doubts on the future of the same-sex marriage law introduced under Zapatero. Also uncertain is the Constitutional Court's ruling on an appeal against gay marriage already lodged by the PP beforehand.

The enormous forward drive in modernization over the last decades has lead to the realization that homosexuals are an important economic factor, with a result that tourists are rarely subject to discrimination, even in the most desolate provinces. Particularly in major cities (Madrid, Barcelona, Valencia, Seville) openly gay communities are developing at a meteoric rate, with an ever-wider and more varied scene. Please note that a place isn't necessarily gay just because it has a rainbow flag in the window!

Every year, more Gay Pride celebrations take place and at many traditional festivals, for example at Carnival in Tenerife and Cadiz, the Feria in Seville in April and at the Fallas in Valencia, you can experience gay life in all its hues, as part of the well-organized main events. If you drop all your defences in the heat of the moment, you obviously need to watch out. Even if he's laid back himself, a Spaniard thinks of his countrymen as very conservative, and above all he demands discretion in his own back yard. That famous Spanish passion has to be carefully unleashed behind closed doors.

For years gays have secured for ourselves the best resorts out of the many seaside places available: Ibiza, Sitges and Torremolinos are summer resorts, while the Canary Islands are much loved year-round destinations. And in recent years small gay guesthouses are springing up all around the mainland coast and on the islands away from all the noise, letting you get a breath of fresh air. It's no surprise that Spain is Europe's number one holiday destination!

Das allgemeine Schutzalter liegt in Spanien bei 16 Jahren. Wer jedoch über 18 Jahre alt ist, sollte mit Minderjährigen eher vorsichtig sein. Seit Sommer 2005 hat die sozialistische Regierung nun die völlige Gleichstellung der Homosexuellen in Ehe-, Adoptions- & Erbrecht umgesetzt, was zu einer immer stärkeren Normalisierung führt. Im November 2011 errang die konservative Partei Partido Popular (PP) die absolute Mehrheit im Parlament. Nach vorherigen Ankündigungen ist unklar, ob die unter Zapatero eingeführte Homo-Ehe angetastet wird. Zudem ist unsicher, wie das höchste Gericht über die bereits eingereichte Klage der PP zur Homo-Ehe bewerten wird.

Der enorme soziale Modernisierungsschub der letzten Jahrzehnte führt bereits seit einiger Zeit zur Entdeckung der Homosexuellen als

wirtschaftliches Potential, sodass man als Tourist selbst in der abgelegensten Provinz kaum mit Ressentiments und Diskriminierung zu rechnen hat. Insbesondere in den Großstadtzentren (Madrid, Barcelona, Valencia, Sevilla) entwickeln sich rasant und offen Gay-Communties mit einer immer breiter gefächerten Szene. Hier ist mittlerweile darauf zu achten, dass nicht überall Homo drin ist, wo Regenbogen drauf steht.

Jedes Jahr finden mehr Gay-Pride-Paraden statt und bei vielen Volksfesten, z. B. im Carnaval (vor allem in Teneriffa und Cádiz), der Feria de Abril (Sevilla) oder den Fallas (Valencia) kann man schillernde Blüten des bunten schwulen Lebens und mitunter gut organisierte Events erleben. Auch wenn im Festtaumel bisweilen alle Schranken fallen, ist Vorsicht unbedingt angesagt. Selbst sehr locker, hält der Spanier seine Landsleute für völlig konservativ und ist vor allem in der eigenen Nachbarschaft auf äußerste Diskretion bedacht. Die berüchtigte spanische Leidenschaft wird erst hinter sorgsam geschlossenen Jalousien entfesselt.

Von den zahllosen Zentren des Badetourismus haben sich die Homos die schönsten Plätze je nach Jahreszeit gesichert: Ibiza, Sitges und Torremolinos sind im Sommer, die Kanaren ganzjährig beliebte Ziele. Zusätzlich entwickeln sich in den letzten Jahren an fast allen Küsten und auf den meisten Inseln kleine Schwulenpensionen abseits des großen Trubels, die es erlauben, Landluft zu schnuppern. Nicht zufällig ist Spanien Europas Reiseland Nr.1!

En Espagne, la majorité sexuelle est fixée à 16 ans, mais le détournement de mineur est un délit.

En été 2005, le gouvernement socialiste a adopté un texte octroyant aux couples homosexuels les mêmes droits qu'aux couples hétérosexuels concernant le mariage, l'adoption et la succession, ce qui contribue à une normalisation sociale. En novembre le parti conservateur (Partido Popular, PP) a obtenu la majorité absolue au parlement. Après des annonces précédentes, il n'est pas clair si le nouveau gouvernement touchera au mariage gay introduit sous le gouvernement de Zapatero.De plus, le décision de la haute cour de justice est incertaine quant à la plainte du PP contre le mariage gay.

L'énorme élan de modernisation de ces dernières années avait déjà permis de faire découvrir les homosexuels comme un nouveau potentiel économique de sorte que les touristes n'ont à craindre aucune discrimination ni homophobie dans tout le pays et ce, même dans les provinces les plus reculées.

L'importante modernisation du pays dans les dernières décennies avait déjà découvert le potentiel économique des homosexuels et les touristes gays et lesbiennes ne sentiront que peu ou pas la discrimination, même dans les contrées les plus reculées du pays.

La grande vague de modernisation de ces dernières années a fait découvrir aux entrepreneurs le potentiel économique des gays, et les touristes ne craignent plus grand-chose aujourd'hui à vivre leur homosexualité au grand jour, même dans les régions reculées du pays. Des communautés gays se développent essentiellement dans les grandes villes (Barcelone, Madrid, Séville, Valence) et offrent un milieu gay diversifié. Il faut même faire attention, car tout ce qui porte un arc-enciel n'est pas forcément gay.

Chaque année ont lieu des défilés de la Gay-Pride et des fêtes populaires comme les carnavals de Ténériffe et Cadiz, la Feria de Abril à Séville, les Fallas de Valence, où l'on trouve des soirées gays bien organisées. Même si lors de ces fêtes tout semble permis, il vaut mieux rester prudent. Bien que très cool, les Espagnols restent conservateurs et il est plus prudent de se montrer discret. La célèbre passion espagnole ne se libère que derrière des persiennes soigneusement fermées.

Parmi les nombreux centres touristiques, les homos se sont réservés les meilleurs plages : on ira ainsi à Sitges, Ibiza et Torremolinos en été et à les îles Canaries toute l'année.

On trouve aussi presque partout sur la côte et sur la plupart des îles de petites pensions gays plus tranquilles et qui permettent de respirer l'air du pays. Pas étonnant donc que l'Espagne soit le premier pays touristique d'Europe !

La edad de consentimiento en España es de 16 años. Sin embargo, quien sea mayor de 18 años, debe ser prudente con los menores.

Desde verano del 2005, el gobierno socialista aplicó la total equiparación de los homosexuales en cuanto al derecho de matrimonio, de adopción y de sucesiones, lo que supuso una normalización cada vez mayor. En noviembre de 2011, el partido conservador Partido Popular (PP) consiguió la mayoría absoluta en el Parlamento. Tras previos anuncios, aun no está claro si la Ley del Matrimonio Homosexual, introducida por el Gobierno de Zapatero, será modificada. Además, también queda por determinar cuál será el veredicto del Tribunal Supremo sobre el recurso presentado por el PP en relación al Matrimonio Homosexual.

La enorme modernización social de las últimas décadas ya había conllevado el descubrimiento de la comunidad homosexual como un gran potencial económico, por lo que, incluso en las provincias más alejadas, muchas veces se acoge al turista homosexual sin resentimientos ni discriminación.

Así, la enorme modernización social de las últimas décadas ha supuesto un descubrimiento de la homosexualidad como un potencial económico más, de modo que apenas se pueden encontrar resentimientos o discriminación en las provincias más alejadas. Especialmente en los centros de las grandes ciudades (Madrid, Barcelona, Valencia, Sevilla) se están desarrollando rápida y abiertamente comunidades gays con un ambiente cada vez más diverso. Aquí, debe ahora tenerse en cuenta que no todo es gay donde aparece la banderita del arco-iris. Cada año tienen lugar más marchas del Orgullo Gay y en muchas de las fiestas populares, como por ejemplo en Carnaval (entre ellos, en Tenerife y Cádiz), en la Feria de Abril de Sevilla o en las Fallas de Valencia se puede encontrar ya un ambiente gay diverso y disfrutar de actos bien organizados. Aunque parezca que durante las fiestas caen todos los prejuicios, debe actuarse con prudencia. Muchos españoles son muy abiertos pero consideran a sus conciudadanos como muy conservadores y sobre todo, ante los propios vecinos, se intenta mantener la máxima discreción. La tan famosa pasión española se desata primero detrás de cortinas bien cerradas.

Entre los numerosos centros del turismo de playa, los homosexuales se han asegurado los sitios más bonitos según la estación del año: Ibiza, Sitges y Torremolinos son para el verano; las Islas Canarias son los destinos preferidos para todo el año. Además, en los últimos años, están surgiendo en casi todos los rincones de la costa y en las islas pequeñas casas de huéspedes para gays, alejados del jaleo y que permiten respirar aire fresco ¡No es casualidad que España sea el destino turístico número 1 de Europa!

L'età legale per i rapporti sessuali è per tutti di 16 anni. Tuttavia se si è maggiorenni si deve stare particolarmente cauti se si hanno rapporti sessuali con minorenni.

Dall'estate del 2005 il governo socialista ha attuato una completa parificazione degli omosessuali per quanto riguarda il diritto al matrimonio, il diritto di adozione e il diritto ereditario. A novembre del 2011 il partito conservatore Partido Popular (PP) è riuscito ad ottenere la maggioranza assoluta in parlamento. In seguito a precedenti dichiarazioni, non è ancora chiaro se il matrimonio omosessuale introdotto da Zapatero sarà messo in discussione. Inoltre, ad essere ancora incerto è anche il giudizio della Corte suprema sul ricorso del PP circa il matrimonio tra coppie dello stesso sesso.

Questo contribuisce ulteriormente alla completa normalizzazione del fenomeno. Questo ha provocato, da un lato, durissime reazioni da parte di ambienti conservatori, dall'altro, un Gay Pride senza precedenti a Madrid, dove si sono appunto festeggiati i positivi cambiamenti. L'enorme spinta modernizzatrice degli ultimi decenni aveva già spianato il terreno facendo scoprire l'omosessuale come potenziale economico e rendendo possibile agli omosessuali turisti di non sentirsi discriminati neanche nelle più isolate province del paese.

L'enorme spinta di modernizzazione degli ultimi decenni ha fatto scoprire gli omosessuali come potenziale economico. Da turista gay

ci si può addentrare nelle province più remote senza temere alcun risentimento o discriminazione da parte della popolazione. Il boom di modernizzazione degli ultimi decenni ha fatto scoprire l'omosessuale come potenziale economico e commerciale. Anche nel più sperduto paesino, ci si sente sempre piuttosto al sicuro e non si temono risentimenti o discriminazioni di alcun genere. Specialmente in grandi città come Madrid, Barcellona, Valenzia, Siviglia la scena gay cresce a vista d'occhio. Si deve però far attenzione a non credere che i posti che mostrano l'arcobaleno siano necessariamente gay. Ogni anno si svolgono diversi gay pride in tutto il paese. In altre feste popolari come per esempio il carnevale (Tenerife e Cádiz), la Feria de Abril (Siviglia), le Fallas (Valenzia) si può notare una vivace e colorata presenza di gay. Anche se di solito l'euforia della festa tende a non far sentire le inibizioni vi consigliamo comunque di stare attenti. Persino lo stesso spagnolo giudica il suo popolo come conservatore e soprattutto nel vicinato ci si deve comportare in maniera discreta. La famigerata passione spagnola la si può scoprire solo dietro le persiane.
I gay si sono „appropriati" dei posti turistici balneari più belli: Ibiza, Sitges e Torremolinos in estate e le Canarie tutto l'anno. Negli ultimi anni sono sorte molte pensioni gay un po' in tutto il paese compresa quasi tutta la costa e quasi tutte le isole – infatti non a caso la Spagna è il paese più visitato.

NATIONAL GAY INFO

Guía gay de Carreteras España (G)
Apartado 832 ✉ 37080 Salamanca ☎ 620 220 244 (mobile)
🖳 www.go.to/ruta
Updated national information about cruising and carcruising areas. Twice a year, there is a publication with road maps, aerial photos, nudist beaches and self aid information. The only cruising guide published in Spain.

NATIONAL PUBLICATIONS

Odisea
Palma 13, Local Izda ✉ 28004 Madrid ☎ 91 523 21 54
🖳 www.odiseaeditorial.com
Free gay monthly newspaper.

OMG (G)
Calle dos de Mayo, numero 4. piso 5 ✉ 28004 Madrid 🖳 www.omgod.es
Oh my God! is a high-class, glossy gay lifestyle amagzine. Available online too.

Qtravel
Av. Roma, 152. Entlo 1ª ✉ 08011 Barcelona ☎ 93 454 91 00
🖳 www.qtravel.es
Gay travel magazine published 4x a year.

Shangay
Apartado 4023 ✉ 28080 Madrid ☎ 914 451 741 🖳 www.shangay.com
Shanguide is a free gay paper listing all gay and so-called gayfriendly sites and venues in Spain

UXXS Magazine
☎ 630 23 93 17 🖳 www.uxxsmagazine.com

NATIONAL PUBLISHERS

Egales editorial
Cervantes, 2 ✉ 08002 Barcelona ☎ 93 412 52 61
🖳 www.editorialegales.com
Publishing house which specialises in gay and lesbian literature.

NATIONAL COMPANIES

Gay Homestays Office: Mon-Fri 9-18h
C/. D'en Taco, Sitges ✉ Sitges ☎ 93 811 4856
High quality, reasonably-priced, gay accommodation in over 40 European cities.

Jalifstudio (G) Mon-Fri 10-14.30, 16.30-20.30h
C/. Sant Vincenç, 5, baixos ✉ 08001 Barcelona *M° Sant Antoni*
☎ 93 443 91 44 🖳 www.jalifstudio.com
Jalif is the director and foptographer of porn movies; all produced in Spain with Spanish actors. Check www.jalifstudio.com for castings.

M. G. Triangulo Distribuciones S. L.
C/. Hortaleza, 62 ✉ 28004 Madrid *M° Chueca* ☎ 91 522 55 99
🖳 www.triangulodistribuciones.com
Distributors of SPARTACUS and Bruno Gmünder photo books in Spain. Oder by email: triangulo@triangulodistribuciones.com

NATIONAL GROUPS

Federación Española Colegas Mon-Fri 10-14 & 19-21h
C/. Carretas 33, 3° izq. ✉ 28012 Madrid ☎ 90 211 89 82
Publisher of magazine „Colega".

FELGTB Federación Estatal de Lesbianas, Gays, Transexuales y Bisexuales FELGTB
C/. Infantas, 40. 1° derecha ✉ 28004 Madrid ☎ 91 360 46 05
🖳 www.felgtb.org
LGBTB organisation for Spain as a whole.

Fundación Arena (GLM)
Balmes, 34 ✉ 08007 Barcelona ☎ 93 487 49 48
🖳 www.fundacionarena.com
Devoted to social activities within the gay scene; awards intenational prices for art and for literature every year.

Fundacion Triángulo
Pl San Leandro 10 ✉ 41003 Sevilla ☎ 661 010 173
Local groups in 8 cities.

Altea

BARS

Plaza. La (B G)

A Coruña / La Coruña

CAFES

Backstage (B D GLM MA S) Thu, Fri-Sat 23-4.30h
Caleixón da Estacada, 4 ☎ 675 957 847
Cocktails in a very nice ambience. The place for you to „come as you are".

SEX SHOPS/BLUE MOVIES

Fantasias (g VS) Mon-Sat 10-3, Sun -14 & 16-3h
C/. Fernando Macías, 9 ☎ 98 125 56 09 🖳 www.fantasiasxshop.com

SAUNAS/BATHS

Sauna Hamam (B DR DU FC FH G m RR SA SB SL VS WH) Sun-Thu 16-2h, WE-6h
Nueva Travesia Buena Vista 4 *In Los Castros* ☎ 625 253 315 (mobile)
Very clean and well equipped sauna, with sling and spacious cabins.

Alicante / Alacant

BARS

Café Français. Le (B GLM H m MA S) 11-2h
C/. Sant Pedro, 19 ☎ 966 880 281
🖳 www.gayromeo.com/lecafefrancais

Canibalpub (! AC B CC DR GLM MA S SNU ST VS WI) Mon-Sat 23-4h
C/. César Elguezábal, 26 *Near Plaza Nueva* ☎ 965 202 523
🖳 www.canibalpub.com

Divina (B G MA) Fri & Sat 23-4h
C/. Montegón, 7 ☎ 617 356 513 🖳 www.divinapub.com

Forat. El (B G MA) Thu-Sat 23-4h
Plaza Santa Faz, 4 *Behind townhall*
In business since 1974!

Grizzly (AC B d DR G MA VS) Mon-Fri 19-3, Sa 23-4 & Su 22-3h
C/. San Juan Bosco N° 6 *near Pza de Luceros/behind Diputación*
🖳 www.grizzlybar.com

Oh my God!
www.omgod.es
The real gay life style magazine
Oh my God!
IN APP STORE TOO
OH MY GOD IPAD
+ SPANISH
+ ENGLISH
+ CHINESE
Photography THOMAS SYNNAMON

■ **Paparazzi** (AC B d DR G MA s VS) 22-3.30h
C/. Gravina, 4 *Downtown* ☎ 96 521 67 28

MEN'S CLUBS

■ **Dark** (AC B DR F G MA p VS) 22-4h
Av. Ramon y Cajal, 9 *Opp. Parque de Canalejas* 💻 www.dark-alicante.es.tl
Thu 22-24h 2-4-1.

SEX SHOPS/BLUE MOVIES

■ **Pikante** (DR g VS) 10-3h
C/. San Fernando, 12 *Second entrance at C/. Rafael Altamira, 20*
☎ 96 514 48 22 💻 www.pikante.com
Cruisy. Cubicals with glory holes. Cinema upstairs with labrinth. A second shop at: C/. Rafael Altamira, 20.

■ **Sexyland** (DR F g) Mon-Sat 9.30-22.30, Sun 16-22.30h
C/. Segura, 18 ☎ 96 520 08 26 💻 www.fusionreaccion.es

SAUNAS/BATHS

■ **Basaky** (B DR DU G m MSG SA SB VS WH) Mon-Sun 15-22, Sat -23h
C/. Murcia 4 *Near train station*
☎ 96 638 76 76 💻 www.basakysauna.es
The newest and biggest sauna in Alicante: well designed and professionally operated. Always fresh fruit for the sauna guests available.

■ **Ipanema Termas** (AC B DR DU G m OS p PI SA SB VS WH YC) 15-22h
C/. Espronceda, 12 *Behind the bull ring, in front of tobacco factory*
☎ 67 784 0119

■ **Steam** (AC B DR DU f G GH I m MA NU SA SB VS WH) 15-24, Fri & Sat and before holidays -9h
C/. Cardenal Peyá 17 bajo *Near Station Renfe* ☎ 96 512 69 16
💻 www.saunasteam.es
Not the biggest, but modern and stylish sauna with a young and cruisy crowd. Special events each day.

GUEST HOUSES

■ **Finca La Cantera** (B BF GLM I M MA OS PA PI RWT VA) All year
C/. de las Cuevas Altas, 10 *40 mins from Alicante* ☎ 96 547 62 83

■ **Four Points Villa** (AC B BF CC G I M MA NU PI PK RWB RWS RWT VA WH) All year, 24hrs
Camino Noria de Sargueta, 85, Aspe *Approx. 7kms along the CV-847 and before Aspe* ☎ 965 492 020 💻 www.fourpointsvilla.com

■ **Gaywind Guesthouse** (AC GLM OS PA PK RWS RWT VA WO) All year, reception 10-23h
C/. Segura, 20 bajo *5 mins from train station* ☎ 650 718 353 (mobile)
💻 www.guesthousealicante.com
Apartments in a tasteful Mediterranean style.

GENERAL GROUPS

■ **Asociación Decide-T de lesbianas, gays, bisexuales y transexuales de Alicante**
C/. Labradores, 14 ☎ 657 35 32 38

SWIMMING

-Cabo de Las Huertas (NU) (take bus 22)
-Carabasi Beach (NU) (12km south of Alicante, late afternoons and evenings)
-Marina o Playa del Rebollo (NU) (entrance at Camping International de la Marina and Club Michel. Road N-332, Km 76)
-Urbanova (NU) (go in the direction of the airport. Entrance of the beach at Altet)
-Las Canas between Play de Altet and Urbanova (dunes between parking and beach).

Almería

DANCECLUBS

■ **Dracena Disco** (AC B D G MA SNU WE) 0-7h
C/. Benizalon s/n, Cortigo Grande ☎ 609 365 772
💻 www.dracenadisco.com

APARTMENTS

Casa de Angeles (B glm M MA MSG NU OS PI PK RWS RWT WO) All year
Urb. Cort. Las Negras, Parc 27 & 28 *30 mins from Almeria airport* ☎ 95 038 81 01
🖳 www.ourakcha.com/gay-casa-de-angeles-es-E205.html
Located in the nature park Cabo de Gata. Five mins walk to the beach. Two private apartments in a villa surrounded by very large gardens and a large swimming pool with hydro massage and private terraces. In a typical Spanish fishing village inside the national park. Close to gay nudist beaches.

Torremar Natura Complex (AC glm I MA NU OS PI RWB RWS RWT SOL VA WH) 24hrs
Av. Tortuga Boba, 3 ☎ 669 500 918 (mobile)
🖳 www.veraplaya-FKK.com
Vera-Playa is a gay-friendly nudist beach. You can walk nude on the streets all the way to the beach from your apartment! Bus service from Madrid. Train station in Murcia and Cartagena city. Transfer from the airport upon request.

GENERAL GROUPS

Co. Le. Ga. – Coletivo de Lesbianas y Gays de Almería (GLM) Mon-Wed 10-14, Thu-Fri also 17-20h
C/. Rueda López, 17, 1° Derecha ☎ 95 027 65 40
🖳 www.colegaweb.org
Meetings Thu 20.30h

Balearic Islands

Balearic Islands – Ibiza

In summer Ibiza is THE international meeting place, regardless of sexual orientation. From May to September the young and young at heart party here. In any case a colourful mix. Of course gays are very much integrated. The gay scene itself is particularly centred round the picturesque capital, especially in the old town and Figueretes. Here everything is within walking distance. Start the night with a stroll around the almost totally gay Calle de la Mare Deu (C/. de la Virgen), take a seat on the mixed terraces at the foot of the city walls, and move on to one of the mega-discos (which often have either gay bar or have specific gay events going on) or you can go up to the old town (Dalt Vila) for a dance or cruise around the bars. Thereafter cruising is possible at the cliffs with the Figueretes beach below. During the daytime the wonderful beach of Es Cavallet beckons, with cruising in the bushes behind the superb beach. If you're looking for a more peaceful time, you can find cosy guesthouses. Everything is easy to reach by bus and taxi services. Lately there is a direct boat connection between Figueretes and Es Cavallet.

Im Sommer ist Ibiza einer der Treffpunkte der internationalen Szene, egal welcher sexuellen Orientierung. Von Mai bis September feiert hier ein junges oder junggebliebenes, auf jeden Fall buntes Volk. Schwules ist selbstverständlich integriert, die schwule Szene im engeren Sinne konzentriert sich aber auf die malerische Hauptstadt, insbesondere auf die Altstadt und Figueretes, wo alles in kurzen Fußwegen erreichbar ist. Die Nacht beginnt mit einem Rundgang durch die fast ganz schwule C/. de la Virgen und setzt sich in den gemischten Terrassen am Fuße der Stadtmauer fort, von wo die einen in die Megadiscos (von denen viele entweder eine schwule Bar oder spezielle Gay-Events anbieten) und die anderen zu Tanz und Bars in die Oberstadt (Dalt Vila) weiterziehen. Danach gibt's noch die Felsen ganz oben und den Figueretes-Strand dahinter. Tags lockt der Traumstrand Es Cavallet mit cruisy Gestrüpp dahinter. Wer es beschaulicher mag, findet lauschige Pensionen. Alles ist gut mit Bussen oder Taxis verbunden. Neuerdings gibt es eine Bootsverbindung von Figueretes direkt nach Es Cavallet!

En été, Ibiza est le point de rencontre des gens branchés au niveau international, peu importe leur orientation sexuelle. De mai à septembre, la population est plutôt jeune et hétérogène. Les gays en font partie naturellement. Les endroits gays se concentrent tous dans la capitale de l'île, en particulier la vieille ville et Figueretes ou tout est aisément accessible à pied. La nuit débute par une balade sur le C./ de la Mare et C/. de la Mare Deu (C/. de la Virgen) quartier quasi exclusivement gay. Puis sur les terrasses autours des fortifications. Après, les uns iront plutôt dans les méga-discothèques (qui organisent souvent des soirées gay), les autres continueront leur quête dans les bars de la ville-haute (Dalt vila). Pour rencontrer des hommes les falaises tout en haut ou la plage de Figueretes sont recommandées. En journée, la plage paradisiaque d'Es Cavallet est propice aux rencontres. Pour ceux qui aspirent à la tranquillité, des maisons d'hôtes sont à proximité de la ville et reliées facilement par bus. Dernierement il y a une connection directe en bateau entre Figueretes et Es Cavallet.

En verano Ibiza es uno de los puntos de encuentro del ambiente internacional, independientemente de la orientación sexual. De mayo a septiembre se reúne aquí una población joven, o que lo aparenta, pero sin duda con mucho colorido.
Lo gay está integrado en el paisaje; el ambiente en un sentido más estricto se concentra sin embargo en la pintoresca capital, especialmente en el centro histórico y en Figueretes, donde todo está a poca distancia a pie. La noche empieza con un paseo a través de la casi por completo gay C/. de la Mare de Déu o de la Virgen y continúa en las terrazas a los pies de la muralla, desde donde algunos se dirigen a las mega-discos (de las cuales muchas o tienen un bar gay u ofrecen eventos especiales para gays, sin tener siempre éxito) y otros se van a los bares o discotecas de la ciudad (Dalt Vila) para continuar la fiesta. Después todavía quedan las rocas más arriba y la playa de Figueretes detrás. Durante el día, la maravillosa playa de Es Cavallet, con la zona de cruising, atrae a muchos. A quien le guste algo más contemplativo, también encontrará alojamientos más apacibles en Ibiza. Todo está bien comunicado en autobús o taxi. Ultimamente hay una conexion directa en lancha desde Figueretes a Es Cavallet.

Ibiza è, d'estate, uno dei luoghi d'incontro internazionale per qualsiasi tipo d'orientamento sessuale. Qui, da maggio a settembre, festeggia una popolazione giovane e variopinta. Il gay è perfettamente integrato, la scena omo si concentra però nel pittoresco capoluogo, particolarmente nella città vecchia e a Figueretes, dove tutto è raggiungibile a piedi. La notte comincia con una passeggiata lungo la C/. de la Mare Deu (C/. de la Virgen), quasi completamente gay, e prosegue sulle terrazze ai piedi della cinta muraria. Da qui alcuni si spostano nelle grandi discoteche (che offrono un bar o un party gay); altri vanno a ballare oppure nei bar della città alta (Dalt Vila) a cercare compagnia. Poi ci sono ancora la scogliera e la spiaggia Figueretes. Durante il giorno è la fantastica spiaggia gay Es Cavallet, con alle spalle cespugli adatti agli incontri, ad attirare i turisti. Chi ama la tranquillità trova senza difficoltà intime pensioni. Tutto è ben collegato con bus e taxy. C'è un collegamento in traghetto tra Figuretes e Es Cavallet!

TOURIST INFO

Oficina de Turismo Mon-Fri 8.30-13.30 & 17-19.30, Sat 9-18h
Plaza Antonio Riquer, s/n *Opp. Estación Marítima* ☎ 97 130 19 00

BARS

Angelo (AC B G m MA) 22-24h
C/. Santa Lucia, 12 ☎ 97 131 16 07 🖳 www.angeloibiza.com
rooftop terrace with sushi

Cube (B G I m MA OS) 19-4h
C/. Ramón Muntaner, 3 *Playa Figueretas* ☎ 97 139 91 66
🖳 www.facebook.com/CUBE.Ibiza
Former DJ's Bar; Indonesian food, Wi-Fi Internet access.

Dado (B G MA OS) Mon-Sun 21-3.30h, winter only Fri&Sat
Calle de la Virgen 40

Dome (B g OS YC) May-Sep 22.30-4h
C/. Via Alfonso XII, 5 ☎ 97 131 74 56 🖳 www.dome.es

Exis (B G) May-Oct
C/. de la Virgen, 57

JJ Bar (B f G MA OS) 22-4h all year
C/. de la Virgen, 79 ☎ 97 131 02 47 🖳 www.jjbaribiza.com

A
N
de Rosello
Ramon
Eugenio
Molina
Riambau
Cruz
Pl. José Pidal
Olozaga
Garuo
Mayor
Pl. Garijo
Opisbo Cardona
Jose Verdera
SA PENYA
La Virgen
Pl. Drasaneta
M.J. Mayans
Paseo Vara de Rey
Azara
A. Matutes
Antonio Palau
Amadeo
Pedrera
Anibal
Agricola
Soler
Rincon Muralla
Vicente Cuervo
Avda. Gen. Franco
Pl. Luis Tur y Palau
Pl. Desamparados
S. Benito
S. Carlos
Ignacio Riquer
Gen. Balanzat
Pl del Sol
S. Luis
Poniente
Pl. España
Juan Roman
Sta. Maria
DALT VILA
Pl. Catedral
Punta Ratjada
EAT & DRINK
Angelo – Bar & Restaurant 12
Can Soap – Restaurant 10
Dalt Vila – Restaurant 20
Dome – Bar 11
Exis – Bar 1
JJ Bar 3
JJX Bar 4
León Bar 5
Nada. La – Bar 8
Olivo. El – Restaurant 21
Portalón. El – Restaurant 19
Scala. La – Restaurant 15
SOAP – Bar 13
Waunas – Bar 25
NIGHTLIFE
Anfora Discoteca – Danceclub 18
Lola – Danceclub 24
Mad – Men's Club 9
Muralla. La – Men's Club 14
ACCOMMODATION
El Patio – Guesthouse 22
La Ventana – Hotel 16
Navila Aparthotel 23
Ibiza –Map A
OTHERS
Sa Majesté – Leather/Fetish Shop 22
B
N
C/ Navarra
C/ Ramon Muntaner
C/ d'Al Sabini
C/ del Archiduque
Luis Salvador
Pluig des Molins
C/ Luci Oculaci
C/ Galicia
C/ Formentera
C/ del Pais Vasco
C/ Asturias
Paseo de Ses
Playa de Figueretas
Paseo de Ses Pitiusas
Ibiza – Map B
EAT & DRINK
C.U.B.E. – Bar 30
Kitsch – Café 29
Magnus – Café 31
ACCOMMODATION
Cenit Apartments 26
Hotel Marigna 27

■ **JJX Bar** (AC B DR G MA OS VS) 22-4h
C/. de la Virgen, 64 ☎ 971 31 02 47 🖳 www.jjbaribiza.com
New bar opposite JJ Bar. Same atmosphere, same owner. Spacious darkroom instead of harbour view like in JJ.

■ **León Bar** (AC B G MA OS) 22-?h
C/. de la Virgen, 62

■ **Nada. La** (AC G m MA OS) 20-4h
C/. de la Virgen, 10 ☎ 97 131 12 26

■ **Soap** (! AC B G MC OS s ST) 22-4h
C/. Santa Lucia 23 *Next to old market*
🖳 www.facebook.com/profile.php?id=1686019232
Very popular pre-clubbing spot. Also open off season.

■ **Waunas** (B g MA OS) 20-?h
C/. d'Enmig, 9 ☎ 97 131 56 60

MEN'S CLUBS

■ **Mad Bar** (B d DR f G MA OS VS) 21.30-3.30h
C/. de la Virgen, 32
🖳 www.facebook.com/pages/MAD-Bar-Ibiza/89967699371
Spacious back zone, maze and glory holes.

■ **Muralla. La** (AC B DR F G NU P VS) 23-4h
Sa Carrossa, 3 *Dalt Vila / Old Town* 🖳 www.lamuralla-ibiza.com
Check website for current programme: www.lamuralla-ibiza.com

CAFES

■ **Chiringay** (B G M MA OS) Apr-Oct 9.30-21h
Playa Es Cavallet ☎ 97 118 74 29 🖳 www.chiringay.com
Furnished in bali style. Beach-shop Ibioca Swimwear label. Direct boat transfer from and to Figueretes.

■ **Kitsch** (B G MA OS) All year, : 21-3.30h
C/. Ramón Muntaner, 26 *Figueretas* ☎ 687 587 639 (mobile)
🖳 www.barkitschibiza.com

■ **Magnus** (B BF G M MA OS) Apr-Oct 10-2h
Puerto Deportivo Marina Botafoch *Figueretes, at the beachfront*
☎ 97 139 25 65 🖳 www.magnus-ibiza.com
To see and be seen! Hot meals all day.

DANCECLUBS

■ **Anfora Discoteca** (! AC B D DR G MA s VS) May-Oct 24-6h
C/. San Carlos, 7 *Dalt Vila* ☎ 97 130 28 93 🖳 www.anfora-disco.com
Two floors. lower cover b4 1am.

■ **Lola's** (B D DR GLM MA OS) 24-06h
Alfonso XII, 10 🖳 www.facebook.com/lolasibiza

RESTAURANTS

■ **All Café Bistro** (AC CC G M MA) 8-24h
Paseo de las Pitiusas 28 *Playa Figueretes* ☎ 971 301 925
🖳 www.apartamentosllobet.com

■ **Bistro. El** (CC G H M MA OS PA VEG WL) Apr-Oct 20-1h
Plaza Sa Carossa, 15 *Dalt Vila* ☎ 97 139 32 03
🖳 www.elbistrorestaurante.com

■ **Can'OA-Soap** (CC G M MA OS PA VEG) 21-1h (June-Sep.)
C/. Santa Lucia, 7b *Next to Soap Terrace* ☎ 971 194 680
Modern Mediterranean cuisine.

■ **Dalt Vila** (B CC g M MA OS) Apr-Oct 20-1h
Plaça de Vila, 3-4 *In Dalt Vila* ☎ 97 130 55 24
Basque and Catalan cuisine.

■ **Olivo. El** (AC b CC GLM M MA OS PA RES VEG WL) 19-1h
Plaza de Vila, 9 *Dalt Vila* ☎ 97 130 06 80 🖳 www.elolivoibiza.org
High quality French cuisine at reasonable prices and friendly staff.

■ **Portalón. El** (AC b CC G M MA OS WL) Daily 19-1h
Plaza Desamparados, 1-2 (Dalt Vila) ☎ 97 130 39 01 ☎ 97 130 08 52
Local and international cuisine.

■ **Scala. La** (AC CC GLM M MA OS RES) 20-?h, Tue closed
C/. Sa Carrossa, 7 *Dalt Vila* ☎ 97 130 03 83 🖳 www.la-scala.com
International cuisine. Nice terrace with fresh flower decoration.

FITNESS STUDIOS

■ **Fraile Gym** (AC b CC g WO) Mon-Fri 7-22.30, Sat 9-22.30, Sun 10-22.30h
C/. Aragón, 94 ☎ 97 139 06 80 🖳 www.frailegym.com

LEATHER & FETISH SHOPS

■ **Sa Majesté** (CC g SH) All year
67 Calle de la Virgen ☎ 971 93 12 66

HOTELS

■ **Casa Alexio** (AC B BF G I MA NU OS PI PK RWB RWS RWT VA WH) All year
C/. Kiwi, 39 *Talamanca* ☎ 639 632 522 (mobile) ☎ 971 314 249
🖳 www.alexio.com
This friendly and luxurious gay hotel with Jacuzzi and sunbathing terraces is located on a small hill overlooking the bay of Talamanca.

■ **Hotel & Restaurant La Ventana** (AC B cc glm I M) All year, reception 8-24h
Sa Carossa, 13 *Dalt Vila* ☎ 97 139 08 57 🖳 www.laventanaibiza.com
14 large rooms, 8 of which with a balcony.

■ **Hotel Marigna** (AC B BF CC GLM I m MA OS RWB RWS RWT SA VA WH) Open Apr-Oct
C/. Al Sabini, 18 *Figueretes* ☎ 97 139 99 42 🖳 www.hotelmarigna.com
All rooms at Hotel Marigna are ensuite, with bath/shower, phone, sat-TV. 24hrs reception. Bar open 10-24h. The hotel is situated at the Los Molinos hill.

■ **Navila Aparthotel** (AC b g MA OS PI) All year
C/. San Luis, 1 ☎ 97 139 05 73 🖳 www.navila.es
All rooms with bath, WC, phone, sat-TV, kitchen and big terraces with sea view.

■ **Torre del Canónigo, La** (B g MA)
C/. Mayor, 8 *Dalt Vila* ☎ 97 130 38 84 🖳 www.elcanonigo.com
Elegant, renovated hotel in a 14th century building.

GUEST HOUSES

■ **Finca Ibiza. La** (AC B BF G m OS PI PK RWB RWS RWT SA) All year, 24hrs
C/. del Cabussó 11, Sant Jordi *3km from Ibiza city centre* ☎ 97 130 10 04
🖳 www.lafinca-ibiza.com
Historic Finca, quiet and romantic with a beautiful tropical garden. Beautiful view of the landscape and the sea.

■ **Patio. El** (AC B BF G MA)
C/. de Santa Ana 21 ☎ 971 304 719 ☎ 626 122 552 (mobile)
Very private guesthouse in the middle of Ibiza Town.

■ **Vista Salinas** (AC b bf CC G m MA PI PK RWB RWS RWT) May-Oct
San Josep, Km 5 ☎ 97 141 02 23

APARTMENTS

■ **Cenit Apartments** (B g m PI)
C/. Archiduque Luis Salvador s/n. Los Molinos, Figueretas
☎ 97 130 14 04
💻 www.hotelcenit.com
Swimming pool on a roof terrace with a gay open-air bar and a great view onto the southern part of the island. Bar and pool freely accessible for non-residents, too.

GENERAL GROUPS

■ **Colectivo LGTB de Ibiza** (GLM) 18-20h
C/. Madrid 52 bajos 💻 www.colectivogayibiza.org

HEALTH GROUPS

■ **ALAS – Asociación de Lucha anti-SIDA de las Islas Baleares** Mon-Thu 8-15h
C/ Joan Planells nº11 ☎ 97 131 23 57 (AIDS-info)
💻 www.alas-baleares.com
HIV & AIDS info.

CRUISING

-Southwest corner at top of old city walls (above La Muralla Bar on opposite side of the street)
-Playa Figueretas (nights and early mornings after bar hopping)
-Rocas (entrance: tunnel oppostite of the town hall).

Balearic Islands – Mallorca – Palma de Mallorca

GAY INFO

■ **Mallorca Gay Map** (GLM)
Calle Fabrica 4141bjs ☎ 971 457 564
💻 www.mallorcagaymap.com
Mallorca's LGTB guide with all the hotspots of the island.

BARS

■ **Aries** (AC B d DR DU G MA MSG SA SB VR VS WH) 22-4h
C/. Porres, 3 *At Avenida Joan Miró* ☎ 97 173 78 99
💻 www.ariesmallorca.com
■ **Bruixeries** (B G MA)
C/. Estanc 9
■ **Divitt** (AC B G MA) 20-3h
Av. Joan Miró, 52 *near Plaza Gomila*
■ **Euphoria** (AC B CC d DR f G MA S) 24-5h, closed Tue
Calle Joan Miró, 54 *Near Plaza Gomila*
New design bar and club in Gomila.
■ **Yuppi Club** (AC B DR G I MA OS VS) 24-9h
Av. Joan Miró, 98
Free internet access.

MEN'S CLUBS

■ **Dark** (AC AK B DR f G GH MA NU p s SL VR VS) 16.30-2.30; Sat, Sun & before public holidays -10.30h
C/. Ticià, 22 *Near Plaza D'Espanya* ☎ 971 763 864
💻 www.darkpalma.com
Free entry -21.30h. Theme nights. Slings, glory holes and St Andrews Cross. First cruising bar in Palma. Check www.darkpalma.com for details.
■ **Horny** (B DR G NR OS VR) Daily 21-?h
Juan Miro 80 *Near Plaza Gomila*
A new cruising bar with 3 floors. Main floor music and videos, first floor a large cruising area with cabins, videos & dark room. Terrace with sea view for smokers. Happy Hour 20-22h.
■ **XY Cruising** Mon-Thu 18-2.30, Fri-Sun 18-10h
C/. Vinyassa, 23 💻 www.xyclubcruising.com

CAFES

■ **Can Miquel** (b G MA)
General Riera, 36

■ **Coto Bar Café** (AC B BF GLM M MA OS)
Mon-Fri 8-24, Sat 9-24h, in winter also Sun
Plaza Drassana, 12 *Near la lonja* ☎ 616 138 478 🖳 www.bar-coto.com
Nice café terrace. Breakfast and lunch with daily fresh products from the market; salads, vegetarian food.: also menu del día

■ **Flexas** (b GLM MA)
C/. Llotgeta 12

■ **Gruta, La** (b GLM MA OS)
C/ Sa Gruta n.14 bajos

■ **Kfé** (AC B bf GLM m MA) Summer 16-?h, winter 9-16,19-?h
Joan MIró 82 *Near Plaza Gomila* ☎ 622 653 759
🖳 kfejoanmiro.blogspot.com
Salads & Tapas all day. Famous for Mojitos.

■ **Lorca** (b GLM MA ST)
C/. Federico Garcia Lorca, 21

■ **Mandragora** (b MA NG)
C/. San Antonio de la playa 39

■ **Michel** (b G MA)
C/. Porras esquina Joan Miró *Gomila*

■ **Mokaccino Bistro** (b m MA)
C/. Dels Oms 7

■ **Si Vens** (b GLM MA)
C/ Federico Garcia Lorca, 21

■ **Unic** (b GLM MA ST)
C/ Gran Via Colón 18

DANCECLUBS

■ **Black Cat** (AC B D DR GLM MA S SNU ST WE) WE 24-6h
Av. Joan Miró, 75 🖳 blackcatdisco.blogspot.com
Good show, very popular. Best from 2h, shows at 3.30h.

■ **Demence Palma. La** (! AC B D DM GLM MA S t) Sat 24-6h
c/o Luna Palma, Plaza del Vapor, 4 *Sta. Catalina*

■ **Isi Pub** (D GLM YC)
Alvaró de Bazan 2

RESTAURANTS

■ **Amano** (! DM MA NG VEG)
Calle San Magin 70
Typical Mallorquin restaurant for „Pa amb oli".

■ **Diner I** (M MA NG)
C/. San Magi 23
Best Burgers in Town!

■ **Diner II** (M MA NG)
C/ Juan Maura Bisbe 5 *Plaza España*

■ **Horreo Veinti3** (! M NG OS VEG)
Calle Fabrica 23
Worth to visit! Especially in the summer with a great terrace!

■ **Pizzeria Benibazari** (M NG OS)
Cró. Can Tofol 10
Delicious pizzas in a relaxed atmosphere in the countryside.

■ **Sorrentos** (M MA NG)
Paseo Illetas 117

■ **Toque** (! B DM MA NG OS)
C/. Federico Garcia Lorca, 6 🖳 www.restaurante-toque.com
A wonderful Belgium restaurant with delicious food, great service and a large variety of beers!

■ **Twins Chill Out** (AC B CC G M MC S SNU ST T)
Daily 20-2.30h
C/. Rodriguez de Arias, 5 ☎ 695 454 693 (mobile)
🖳 www.twins-chillout.com
Chill ambience to start the night, to relax or for dinner and a Shisha. Check website for specials: www.twins-chillout.com.

SEX SHOPS/BLUE MOVIES

■ **Erotic Palace I** (SH)
C/. Fausto Morey, 2

■ **Erotic Palace II** (SH)
C/Gral, Ricardo Ortega, 3

Erotic Toy Stories (CC G VS) 10-14, 16.30-20h, Sun closed
Passatge Maneu, 10 ☎ 97 172 78 65

Lust (SH)
C/ Caputxines 5D *Plaza Mercat* 💻 www.lustuniverse.com

Picaro Cupido (SH)
C/. Conde de Barcelona, 25 💻 www.picarocupido.es

SAUNAS/BATHS

Aries (AC B d DR DU G MA MSG SA SB VR VS WH) 22-4h
C/. Porras, 3 *At Avenida Joan Miró* ☎ 97 173 78 99
💻 www.ariesmallorca.com

Spartacus Sauna (B DR DU G MA MSG PI SA SB SOL VS WO) 15-22h
C/. Sant Esperit, 8, baixos *Near Plaza Mayor* ☎ 97 172 50 07
💻 www.saunaspartacus.es
A clean sauna which is nicely decorated with art and sculptures. Popular. Special discount for -26 and military.

HOTELS

Aries (BF G M MA RWB RWS RWT VA) Daily 16-24h
C/. Porres, 3 *Av. Joan Miró, near Plaza Gomila* ☎ 971 737 899
💻 www.ariesmallorca.com
All rooms with shower, WC, AC, cable-TV. Sunroof terrace with shower & amazing bay view. Also bar & sauna for non-residents. Special weekend offers.

GUEST HOUSES

Can Teo BnB (cc DU GLM H MA NR OS RWB RWT WI) All year
Avenida Compte de Sallent, 19 *3rd floor, door 1* ☎ 670 875 264
💻 www.canteobnb.com
Clean guesthouse with 5 rooms. No breakfast service. Fully modernized rationalist style building with wood flooring, large kitchen and shared bathrooms.

Mythos Bed&Breakfast (DU FC GLM I PA RWB) Open all year
Calle Fábrica s/n *Santa Catalina* ☎ 971 100 628 ☎ 971 457 564
Very friendly atmosphere in trendy and bohemian Sta. Catalina area in Palma. Free Wifi.

APARTMENTS

Galeria
☎ +44 (0)1273 676696 (UK) 💻 www.gayholidayplaces.com

PRIVATE ACCOMMODATION

Son Jordi Nou (Private House) (AC glm H MA PI PK RWS SOL VA WH) All year
Camino de Son Jordi, s/n, Consell *20 mins by car to Palma. Station: Consell-Alaró* ☎ 610 257 241
Weekly rent from Sat to Sat. Big house with 6 rooms and private pool.

GENERAL GROUPS

Ben Amics – Asociación LGTB de les Illes Balears (GLM MA) Information Mon-Fri 9-15 and Thu-Fri 18-21h
Avinguda Alemanya, 13 ☎ 97 171 56 70 💻 www.benamics.com
AIDS-Prevention-Group. Lesbian-Group, Youth-Group, Christian-Gay-Group, Gay-ride-Week, Gay and Lesbian Film Festival (www.festivaldelmar.com). Social, judiciary, psychologic and sexologic advisory. Library.

HEALTH GROUPS

ALAS – Asociación de Lucha anti-SIDA de las Islas Baleares Mon-Thu 10-14, 17-20, Fri 10-14h
Plaza Cardenal Reig 4, 1°A ☎ 97 171 5566 (AIDS-info)
💻 www.alas-baleares.com
HIV- & AIDS-info, also publishes Fanzine ALAS.

SWIMMING

-Es Trenc (! g NU) (Take road to Campos del Puerto, then direction Colonia de Sant Jordi. Near restaurant El Ultimo Paraíso, approx. 50km from Palma)
-Playa de Illetas (g OC) (gay at the end, bus 3)
-Playa del Mago (NU) (in Portas Vells at the rocks, popular)
-Playa San Juan de Dios in Ca'n Pastilla (NU r)
-Playa Cala Aguua (NU) (rocky part north of the beach, cruisy in the forest)
-Ca'n Picafort (g) (Playa de Muro, action in the dunes between the two west side towers)
-Playa Cala Grand in Cala D'Or Centre (G)
-Playa San Carlos (g)
-Playa y Dique del Oeste (Porto Pi), Bus EMT n°1 (directo), 3 y 21
-Es Carnatge (Ca'n Pastilla), Bus EMT n°15
-Cala Blava (Final S'Arenal), Bus EMT n°23
-Playa de Muro (Ca'n Picafort) Inca, Autocares Bellver.

CRUISING

-Promenade at city walls beneath Cathedral (AYOR) (steps and gardens)
-Plaça de Espanya (AYOR R)
-Dique del Oeste (G) 24hrs. Bus 3. At end of Paseo Marítimo, also cruising by car, no swimming)
-Camino de Jesús (R) (near river, by car)
-El Bosque (S'Arenal), Bus EMT n°15
-La nina muerta (G) between Can Pastilla and Coll d'en Rabassa, near Hospital San Juan de Dios
-Snipers Bar, C/. Robert Graves 32, Gomila.

Balearic Islands – Mallorca – Playa de Palma

BARS

Dins sa Gàbia (AC B DR G MA VS)
22.30-?h, winter only WE
C/. Milán, 9 *Playa de Palma, near Balneario 1*

Sa Bota (B d DR f G MA s VS)
summer 22-4, winter 22.30-1h Wed-Sat
C/ Trasimé 73 *Near Balneario 12nd line*
STV every other week; Thu: Bears

Barcelona

Barcelona is the vibrant capital of Catalonia. Its distinctive culture is clearly seen in its art, language and way of life. Gay people are confident but not in a flashy way. The scene has everything you would expect from a major city. You'll find the oldest gay bars tucked away in the narrow alleyways of the old quarter around the Ramblas. In the nineteenth-century Eixample, laid out in a grid when the city was enlarged, you'll find the so-called Gaixample; here you'll find the most contemporary designer bars for modern gays, and, impressively, the first ever straight-friendly conference hotel! It's so modern in fact that with a few exceptions, bars and clubs are not exclusively gay. Everything is open to everyone, so that while the following listings are essentially gay, in fact there are many more available things to do, and these should be researched in bigger local publications. Lately, new sex clubs emerge in the area around the Poble Sec which complement well with the traditional cruising area of Montjüic.

Barcelona ist die vibrierende Hauptstadt Kataloniens, dessen alte, unverwechselbare Kultur sich in allen Künsten, der Lebensweise und der Sprache spiegelt. Schwules behauptet sich selbstbewusst, aber nicht schrill. Die Szene bietet alles, was von einer Metropole zu erwarten ist: In engen Altstadtgassen um die Ramblas verstecken sich die ältesten Homobars, in der schachbrettartig angelegten Stadterweiterung des 19. Jh. (Eixample) wächst seit Jahren unaufhaltsam das sogenannte Gaixample, wo zeitgeistig designte Lokalitäten moderne Homowelt bedeuten, wie das erste „straight-friendly" Kongresshotel eindrucksvoll beweist. Modern heißt, dass sich – abgesehen von Ausnahmen – die Locations nicht als ausschließlich schwul definieren. Alles ist offen für alles. Daher ist die folgende Liste als schwule Essenz eines in Wirklichkeit sehr viel breiteren Angebots zu lesen, das sich in lokalen Publikationen großformatig präsentiert. Neuerdings entstehen in der Gegend ums Poble Sec schwule Sexclubs, was eine gute Ergänzung zur klassischen Cruisingarea an den Hängen des Montjüic ist.

Barcelone est la capitale de la Catalogne dont la culture, ancienne et incomparable, se reflète dans les arts, le mode de vie et bien sûr dans la langue. Les gays sont sûrs d'eux sans être excentriques et la ville offre tout ce qu'on peut attendre d'une métropole : les plus vieux bars gays se cachent dans les ruelles de la vieille ville autour des Ramblas et dans le quadrillage de la ville moderne de Eixample construite au XIXè siècle, on trouve le Gaixample avec ses bars et boîtes au design résolument moderne dont l'exemple le plus marquant est peut-être le premier hôtel des congrès „straight-friendly". „Moderne" signifie aussi que les bars et boîtes ne sont pas exclusivement gays mais ouverts à tous. La liste ci-dessous est donc à prendre comme le condensé gay d'une palette bien plus large en réalité qui s'affiche dans les magazines locaux. Dernierement des nouveau sexclubs gay surgissent dans la zone du Poble Sec qui complementent avec la traditionelle zone de cruising du Montjüic.

Barcelona es la vibrante capital de Cataluña, cuya antigua e inconfundible cultura se refleja en todas las artes, su modo de vida y su lengua. Los homosexuales se muestran conscientes de serlo pero no son provocantes. El ambiente gay ofrece todo lo que se espera de una metrópolis: en las estrechas calles cerca de las Ramblas, se esconden los viejos bares gays, en la ampliación de la ciudad del s. XIX, en forma de tablero de ajedrez (Eixample), está creciendo sin parar desde hace años el llamado Gaixample, donde los locales de diseño representan el moderno mundo gay, como lo demuestra el primer e impresionante hotel „straight-friendly". En Barcelona, moderno significa que, salvo excepciones, los locales no se definen exclusivamente como gays. Todo está abierto para todos. Por esta razón, el siguiente listado debe entenderse como lo esencial del mundo gay, dentro de una oferta en realidad mucho más amplia que aparece en las publicaciones locales de gran formato. Ultimamente surgen nuevos sexclubs en la zona alrededor del Poble Sec, que complementa con la tradicional zona de cruising en Montjüic.

Barcellona è la vivace capitale della Catalogna. L'antica cultura di questa città si rispecchia nell'arte, nella lingua e nel modo di vivere. I gay sono qui piuttosto sicuri di se e non molto eccentrici. La scena offre tutto quello che ci si può aspettare da una metropoli: nelle antiche viuzze del centro storico vicino le ramblas ci sono i locali gay più antichi. Nell'estensione a scacchiera della città risalente al XIX secolo (Eixample) va ingrandendosi sempre più la cosiddetta Gaixample, dove i moderni locali in design simboleggiano un altrettanto moderno stile di vita gay; un esempio di questo stile di vita gay moderno è rappresentato dal primo Hotel congressi „straight-friendly". Moderno significa – salvo eccezioni – non definire i locali come esclusivamente gay. Tutto è aperto a tutti. Per questo la lista dei locali riportata in seguito è da considerare „l'essenza" di una più vasta offerta che può essere comunque approfondita leggendo le pubblicazioni locali. Recentemente nella zona di Poble Sec aprono locali a luci rosse gay, che rappresentano una buona alternativa alla classica zona di cruising ai pendii del Montjuic.

GAY INFO

Pink Point (AC GLM MA) Mon-Fri 11-24, Sat & Sun 15-24h
C/. Calabria, 96 *M° Rocafort* ☎ 93 426 23 12
Barcelona's information desk for any kind of gay and lesbian issues, i. e. discounts for gay/lesbian venues, info about beaches, transportation etc.

PUBLICATIONS

Info Gai (GLM)
c/o CGB, Ptge. Valeri Serra, 23 ☎ 93 453 41 25 🖳 www.colectiugai.org
Free bimonthly gay magazine issued by Col-lectiu Gai de Barcelona.

Lambda (GLM) 17-21h
Verdager i Callís, 10 ☎ 93 319 55 50 🖳 www.lambdaweb.org
Free quarterly publication. News from the group Casal Lambda, the gay scene, cultural and political articles, addresses, and personal ads.

Nois (G)
C/. Aribau, 168, entr. 1°, 1a ☎ 93 454 38 05 🖳 www.revistanois.com
Free monthly gay magazine in Spanish. Available at gay venues.

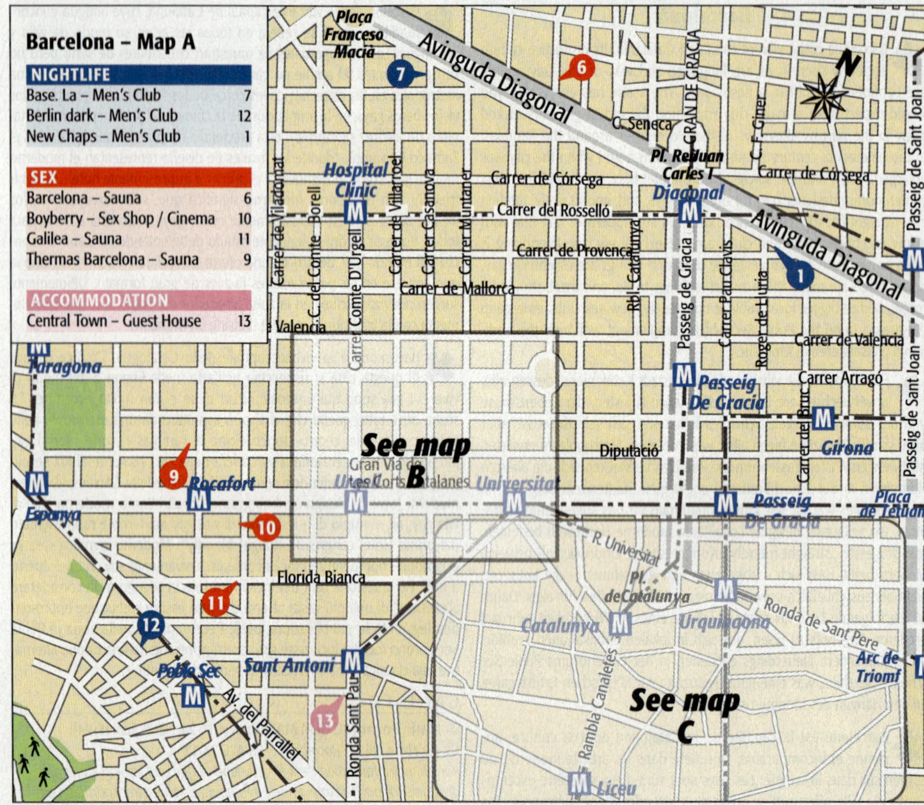

■ **Revista Gay Barcelona** (G)
Control C Media Network, SL, Av. Roma, 152 ☎ 93 454 91 00 🖳 www.gaybarcelona.net
Free magazine covering the gay scene in Barcelona, Madrid and more.

BARS

■ **Acido Oxido** (AC B DR f G H MA VS WE) 6-23h
C/. Joaquin Costa 61 local 1 *Near Plaza Universidad* ☎ 93 412 26 61
housemusic and great atmosphere

■ **Aire Sala Diana** (AC B D glm MA s) Thu-Sat 23-3h, (Jul & Aug: Mon closed)
C/. Valencia, 236 ☎ 934 515 812 🖳 www.arenadisco.com/frame.htm
Cafe, bar and club in one. Music from the 70's, 80's and 90's.

■ **Atame** (AC B d G MA S) 19-2.30h
C/. Consell de Cent, 257 *M° Universidad, between Muntaner and Aribau* ☎ 93 454 92 73
Live shows on Tue, Thu and Sun at 24h.

■ **Bacon Bear Bar** (AC B d F G m MA s) 18-3h
C/. Casanova, 64 *M° Urgell*
Former Ursus Planet.

■ **Black Bull Barcelona** (AC B G m MA VS) 16-3h
C/. Muntaner, 64 *M° Universidad* ☎ 654 047 677 🖳 facebook.com/blackbullbarcelona

■ **Bubble Boys** (B G) Thu-Sat 22-3h
Diputació, 174 🖳 www.bubbleboys.net
Pole Dance gay bar

■ **Butch Bar** (AC B CC d G MA OS S VS) Thu-Sat 24-3h
C/. Diputació 206 🖳 www.butchbear.es
Famous Tato from castro & Martin now with his new own bar

■ **Cangrejo Eixample. El** (AC B d G MA S) Thu-Sat 22.30-3h
C/. Villarroel, 86 *M° Urgell* 🖳 www.facebook.com/group.php?gid=42624997688
Special party 1st Thu/month; 2-4-1 before 24h.

■ **Concha. La** (B GLM MA T) 17-3h
C/. Guardia, 14 *M° Liceu* ☎ 93 302 41 18

■ **Cueva. La**
C/. Calábria, 91 🖳 lacuevabcn.wordpress.com

■ **Dacksy** (AC B CC G m) 17-2.30h
C/. Consell de Cent, 247 *M° Universidad*
Cocktail bar.

■ **Dietrich** (AC B d G MA S) 22-2.30h
C/. Consell de Cent, 255 *M° Universidad* ☎ 93 451 77 07 🖳 www.dietrichcafe.com
Daily shows from different artists.

■ **Lust** (AC B d G MC s WE) 20-3h
C/. Casanova, 75 *M° Universitat* ☎ 93 451 14 19
Bar and cafeteria.

■ **Moeam** (AC B CC d G MA OS) Daily 18-3h
C/. Muntaner 11 *M° Universitat, between Gran Vía & Sepúlveda* ☎ 659 229 033 🖳 www.moeembarcelona.com
Thu 19-22 free snacks & special rates.

■ **Museum** (AC B CC d G m MA S) 22-3h
C/. Sepulveda, 178 *M° Universitat* 🖳 www.facebook.com/group.php?gid=76075450223
music video bar, fri & sat pop with video dj. Thu -24h 2-4-1 for Spartacus readers.

■ **Nightberry** (AC B CC DR G MA S SNU VR VS) 18-2.30, Fri & Sat -3h
C/. Diputació, 161 *M° Urgell* 🖳 www.nightberry.es
Men only. Sexbar without dress code.

■ **People Lounge** (AC B CC G MC) 20-3h
C/. Villarroel, 71 *M° Urgell* ☎ 93 532 77 43 🖳 www.peoplebcn.com
Gentlemen's lounge for those over 25 years of age, preferring softmusic.

■ **Punto BCN** (AC B G MA) 18-2.30h
C/. Muntaner, 63 *M° Universidad* ☎ 93 453 61 23
🖳 www.arenadisco.com

■ **Sky Bar by Axel** (B g OS) 21-3h
c/o Axel Hotel Barcelona, C/. Aribau, 33 ☎ 93 323 93 93
🖳 www.axelhotels.com
The lounge-bar located on the hotel rooftop. Enjoy the cocktails or the pool whith spectacular views over the city.

■ **The Boss** (B d GLM YC)
C/. Consell de Cent, 245

■ **The Ground Bar by Axel** (AC B G MA) 10-3h
Axel Hotel, C/. Aribau, 33 *Gayxample, M° Plaza Universitat*
🖳 www.axelhotels.com
Hotel bar.

■ **Zelig** (AC B G m MA) 19-2, Fri & Sat -3, Mon closed
C/. Carme, 116 *M° San Antonio* ☎ 649 261 599 (mobile)
🖳 www.zelig-barcelona.com
DJs at weekends with music from 80ies to electro, techno and intelligent pop.

■ **Zeltas** (AC G MA) daily 23-3h
C/ Casanova, 75 ☎ 93 454 19 02
New gay bar with DJ.

MEN'S CLUBS

■ **Base. La** (AC B DR F G MA p VS) 22-3h
C/. Casanova, 201 🖳 www.labasebcn.com
Fri underwear, Wed & Sat naked.

■ **Berlin Dark** (AC B DR F G MA P VS) Tue-Sun 22.30-3.30h
Passatge Prunera, 18 *Metro Linea 3 – Poble Sec. near Av Paral.lel and C/. Tamarit* 🖳 www.berlindark.com
Strict dress code. Bar club hard & fetish, with slings, bath, dungeon, BDSM, shower, anal shower. Toys, condoms, lube for free. Check website.

■ **New Chaps** (AC B DR F G MA p s VS WE) 21-3, WE -3.30h
Av. Diagonal, 365 *M° Diagonal* ☎ 93 215 53 65
🖳 www.newchaps.com
Leather bar, Sun 19-22h happy hour.

■ **Open Mind** (AC B F G MA NU P)
Thu 23-4h, Fri -7, Sat 24-8, Sun 23-4, b4 public holidays 23-6h
C/. Aragon 130 *M° Urgell, corner of C/. Urgell* ☎ 93 451 04 79
🖳 www.openmindbcn.com

Barcelona – Map B

EAT & DRINK

Name	No.
Acido Oxido – Bar	42
Aire – Bar	7
Atame – Bar	10
Bacon Bear – Bar	36
Butch – Bar	38
Cangrejo – Bar	28
Castro – Restaurant	19
Dacksy – Bar	15
dDivine – Restaurant	2
Dietrich – Bar	11
Iurantia – Restaurant	33
Lust – Bar	37
Marquette – Restaurant	32
Moeam – Bar	41
Museum – Bar	44
Nightberry – Bar	35
Plata – Café	16
People Lounge – Bar	27
Punto BCN – Bar	13
Sazzerak – Restaurant	21
Theseo – Restaurant	46

NIGHTLIFE

Name	No.
Arena Sala Classic – Danceclub	3
Arena Sala Madre – Danceclub	5
Arena Sala V.I.P. & Sala Dandy – Danceclub	1
Metro – Danceclub	43
Open Mind – Men's Club	22

SEX

Name	No.
Buenos Aires – Sauna	23
Casanova – Sauna	30
Nerón – House of Boys	24
Nostromo – Sex Shop/Blue Movies	39

ACCOMMODATION

Name	No.
Absolut Centro Hostal – Guest House	29
Axel – Hotel	9
Barcelona City Centre – Guest House	6
Eos – Guest House	40

OTHERS

Name	No.
Boxer – Shop	31

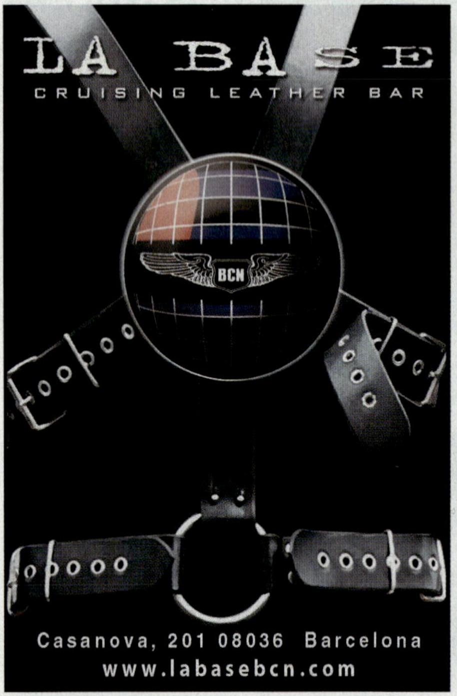

boyberry
C/CALABRIA 96
(METRO ROCAFORT)
OPEN 11h-24h
DISSABTES Y FESTIUS
15h-24h
CRUISING AREA / GLORYHOLES / DARKROOM / GAYMAP
PORN DVD'S / GAY THEMED FILMS / FREE MAGAZINES
OPEN 365 DAYS A YEAR / WWW.BOYBERRY.COM
nightberry
100% gay
c/DIPUTACIÓ, 161
(METRO URGELL)
Opened every day from
6pm to 2.30/3am
nightberry.es
BAR - DARKROOM - PORN SCREEN - CRUISING - CABINS

Private sex club. Membership posible per night, 3 months and year, ID necessary. Strict dress code. 2 levels with FF, watersports facilities, st andrews cross, slings etc. 2nd sat /2nd month FF, Sun 19-23 naked with mask (provided). check openmindbcn.com

CAFES

Plata Bar (AC B CC G MA OS) Daily 18-3h
C/. Consell de Cent, 233 *Corner Casanova* ☎ 93 452 46 36
Nightbar with dance music. Multi-lingual staff and outdoor seating throughout the year.

DANCECLUBS

Arena Sala Classic (AC B D G MA VS) 0.30-5h
C/. Diputació, 233 *M° Universidad* ☎ 93 487 83 42
www.arenadisco.com
Pop hispano music.

Arena Sala Dandy (AC B D G MA VS)
Fri-Sat & nights before public holidays 1-6h
Gran Via, 593 *M° Universidad* www.arenadisco.com
Fantastic dance music!

Arena Sala Madre (AC B D G MA S VS)
0.30-5h, Mon closed (Aug: all week)
C/. Balmes, 32 *M° Universidad* ☎ 93 487 83 42 www.arenadisco.com
Special theme parties Wed, Thu, Sun. Popular on Sundays.

Arena Sala VIP (AC B D G MA YC)
Fri-Sat & before public holidays 1-6h
Gran Vía, 593 *M° Catalunya/Universidad* www.arenadisco.com
International pop music.

DMen (AC B D DR G MA) Fri & Sat 24-6h
C/. Ronda de Sant Pere, 19-21 *M° Urquinaona* www.matineegroup.com
Lots of muscle boys.

Metro (! AC B D DR G S SNU ST VS YC)
Mon 1-5, Sun, Tue-Thu 12-5, Fri, Sat 12-6h
C/. Sepúlveda, 185 *M° Universidad* ☎ 93 323 52 27
www.metrodiscobcn.com
Sat 2h folk dancing on one dance floor.

RESTAURANTS

Cafeti. El (g M MA)
13.30-15.30, 20.30-23.30h, closed Mon & Sun evening
C/. Sant Rafael, 18 ☎ 93 329 24 19 www.elcafeti.com
Spanish cuisine.

Castro (AC B CC DM f GLM M MA PA VEG WL) 13-16 & 20-24h
C/. Casanova, 85 *M° Urgell* ☎ 93 323 67 84

dDivine (AC CC GLM LM M MA RES S T WL)
Mon-Fri 12-16, Wed-Sat 22-2h
C/. Balmes, 24 *Between C/. Diputacio & Gran Vía, M° Universidad/Plaça Catalunya* ☎ 93 317 22 48 www.ddivine.com

Iurantia (AC B CC G M MC)
Mon-Fri 13.30-16, Mon-Sat 21-24h, closed Sun
C/. Casanova, 42 *M° Urgell & Universidad* ☎ 93 454 78 87
www.iurantia.com
Creative Italian food. It's adviseable to reserve a table for dinner.

Kitchen by Axel (B g M MA)
c/o Axel Hotel Barcelona, C/. Aribau, 33 ☎ 93 323 93 93
www.axelhotels.com
Restaurant in Axel Hotel.

Marquette (AC CC G M MA) 13-16.30h, 20-2.30h, WE 20-3h
C/. Diputació, 172 *M° Urgell & Universidad* ☎ 93 162 39 05
www.marquettecaffe.com

Sazzerak (AC B CC G M MC) Sun-Mon & Wed-Thu 20.30-1, Fri-Sat -3h
C/. Consell de Cent, 211 ☎ 93 451 11 38
www.facebook.com/pages/Sazzerak/39725627187
Mediterranean cuisine & cocktail bar.

Theseo (B CC g M MA) 13-16.30, 21-23h closed Sun
C/. del Comte Borrell, 119 ☎ 93 453 87 96
Best evenings.

SEX SHOPS/BLUE MOVIES

Angelo, D' (G I MA P SH SNU VR VS)
C/. Enença, 218
Peep shows from 14-20h. & cubicles and 2 cinemas and more!

Boyberry Barcelona (AC CC DR G GH VR VS YC)
Mon-Fri 11-24, Sat & holidays 15-24h
C/. Calàbria 96, bajos ☎ 93 426 23 12
www.boyberry.com
16 fully equiped cabins with gloryholes and an LCD flat screen TV, always playing the hottest movies. Extensive DR behind the Sex-shop.

Erotixx (DR G GH SL) 10-24, Fri & Sat -3, Sun 14-24h
Avenida de Roma 153 *M° Hospital Clinico, corner C/. Casanova*
☎ 943 515 747 www.erotixx24.eu

Harmony Love (g MA VS) 9-14, 16-19h
Gran Via de los Corts Catalanes, 562 ☎ 93 405 33 00

NTM Nostromo (AC CC DR F G VS) 11-23, Sat & Sun 15-23h
C/. Diputació, 208 ☎ 93 451 33 23
www.facebook.com/group.php?gid=146976395323727
Parcours including high end glory holes; cabins.

Sestienda Gay Shop (AC CC DR G VS) 10-21h, closed Sun
C/. Rauric, 11 ☎ 93 318 86 76 www.sestienda.com
With glory holes & cubicles.

Skorpius (AC CC G MA) 10-24h
Gran Via de los Corts Catalanes, 384-390
☎ 93 423 40 40 skorpius.com

Zeus (AC CC DR G MA VS) 10-21h, closed Sun
C/. Riera Alta, 20 ☎ 93 442 97 95

HOUSE OF BOYS

American Boys (AC cc G R VS) 12-24h
Ronda Universidad, 23, 3°, 2B *U Plaza Catalunya* ☎ 93 317 00 47
www.chicosbcn.com
Top latin boys, mostly from Brasil.

■ **Neron** (CC G R t VS WH) 24hrs
C./ Consell de Ciento, 185, 3°, 2a *M° Urgell* ☎ 93 451 10 28
💻 www.nerondalila.com
Boys from 18 to 30. Also room-rental per hour.

SAUNAS/BATHS

■ **Barcelona** (B CC DR DU G M MA MSG PI RR SA SB SOL VS WH) 24hrs on weekends
C/. Tuset, 1 *Corner at Av. Diagonal* ☎ 93 200 77 16 💻 www.pases.com
Very clean and somewhat stylish sauna with cabins and many wellness facilities

■ **Bruc** (B DR DU FH G LAB m MSG OC RR SA SB VS WH WO) 11-22h
C/. Bruc, 65 *M° Passeig de Gracia / Girona* ☎ 93 487 48 14
Mainly frequented by daddies and their admirers.

■ **Buenos Aires** (B DR DU G MA MSG SA SB VS WH) 24hrs
C/. Urgell, 114 *On corner of Consell de Cent* ☎ 93 323 81 99
💻 www.saunabuenosairesbcn.com

■ **Casanova**
(! B DR DU FC G LAB M MA MSG r RR SA SB SOL VS WH WO) 24hrs
C/. Casanova, 57 ☎ 93 323 78 60 💻 www.pases.com
In the centre of Barcelona gay area. Very popular and busy at any time on any day.

■ **Condal** (B DR DU F FC G LAB m MA MSG PI SA SB SOL VS WH) 24hrs
C/. Espolsasacs, 1 *M° Catalunya. C/. Espolsasacs is a very small street*
☎ 93 317 68 17 💻 www.pases.com
popular sauna on 3 floors and whirlpool for twelve people, special s/m play-room for free large, video room with big screen, frequented by a mixed crowd.

■ **Corinto** (B CC DR DU FC G LAB M MA MSG SA SB SOL VS WH)
Mon-Thu 12-5, Fri-Sun 0-24h
C/. Pelai, 62 *At Plaça Catalunya* ☎ 93 318 64 22 💻 www.pases.com
Popular sauna with relaxed atmosphere, overloking busy Plaza Catalunya square and the Ramblas. Entrance via the Hotel Monegal, sauna on the first floor.

■ **Galilea** (B DR DU FC FH G I m MSG RR SA SB VS WH WO)
13-24, Fri-Sun 24hrs (non-stop)
C/. Calabria 59 *M° Rocafort* ☎ 93 426 79 05
A clean and busy sauna with a hot and friendly crowd.

■ **Thermas Barcelona** (AC B CC DR DU FC G m MA MSG PI R RR SA SB SOL VS WH WO) 24hrs
C/. Diputació, 46 *M° Rocafort* ☎ 93 325 93 46 💻 www.pases.com
Large sauna on three floors, frequented by a mixed crowd of mostly south americans (hustlers) and their admirers.

FITNESS STUDIOS

■ **Wellness Club 33** (AC CC DU GLM MSG PI RR SA SB SOL WH WO) Mon-Fri 7-23h, WE 10-23h
Axel Hotel, C/ Aribau, 33 *M° Universitat* 💻 www.axelhotels.com
The gym of Axel Hotel. Also for non-residents.

MASSAGE

■ **Gay Love Spirit** (G MA MSG)
💻 www.gaylovespirit.com
Massage, Tantra, Sex Coaching and more.

BOOK SHOPS

■ **Antinous** (B BF CC GLM) Mon-Fri 10.30-14, 17-21, Sat 12-14, 17-21h
C/. Josep Anselm Clavé, 6 ☎ 93 301 90 70 💻 www.antinouslibros.com
Also English book section and mail order.

■ **Cómplices** (GLM) Mon-Fri 10.30-20, Sat 12-20h
C/. Cervantes, 4 *M° Liceu* ☎ 93 412 72 83 💻 www.libreriacomplices.com
Also information about the gay scene.

FASHION SHOPS

■ **ES Collection**
Consejo de Ciento, 218 ☎ 610 728 760 ☎ 934515315 (mobile)
💻 www.escollection.es
Swimwear, underwear and athletic wear. Online shop and 13 stores world-wide, visit: www.escollection.es

■ **Ovlas** (AC G MA)
C/. Aribau, 31 *Opp. Axel Hotel* 🖳 www.ovlas.com

LEATHER & FETISH SHOPS

■ **Boxer Barcelona** (CC F G I MA) Mon-Sat 11-15 & 16-21h
C/. Diputació 167-169 *M° Universitat / Urgell* 🖳 www.boxerbcn.com
Sports, leather, toys, underwear and more. Spain's largest gay retailer.

HOTELS

■ **Axel Hotel Barcelona** (AC B BF CC GLM I M MA OS PI RWB RWS RWT SA SB SOL VA WH WO) All year
C/. Aribau, 33 *Gayxample, M° Plaza Universitat* ☎ 93 323 93 93
🖳 www.axelhotels.com
Luxury gay design hotel with 105 room and all modern facilities.

■ **California** (AC B BF CC GLM H I RWS RWT) All year
C/. Rauric, 14 *M° Liceu, corner with C/. Ferran near Ramblas Barcelona*
☎ 93 317 77 66 🖳 www.hotelcaliforniabcn.com
Centrally located. Rooms with bath, AC, phone and wifi, plasma tv, lift. Ask about special offers.

■ **RAS – Room Advice Service** (CC G) Mon-Fri 11-14, 17-20h
☎ 607 149 451 (mobile) 🖳 www.raservice.com
Reservations of hotels & apartments in Sitges & Barcelona (only hotels). English, French, German & Spanish spoken. CC necessary.

GUEST HOUSES

■ **Absolut Centro Hostal** (ac bf G RWB RWS) All year
C/. Casanova, 72 *M° Passeig de Gràcia / Universidad*
☎ 649 550 238 (mobile) 🖳 www.absolutcentro.com
Some rooms with private bath, all rooms with TV. Accommodation for up to four people per room.

■ **Baires** (cc glm PA RWB RWS VA) All year
C/. Avinyó, 37 Principal *5 mins from las Ramblas, M° Drassanes*
☎ 93 319 77 74 🖳 www.hostalbaires.com
A charming hostel right in the heart of the Gothic district of Barcelona near the beach and shopping facilities.

■ **Barcelona Centre Gay Accommodations** (AC GLM I OS) All year
C/. Tallers, 30/4 *M° Plaza Catalunya, close to the „Gayxample"*
☎ 616 474 651 (mobile) 🖳 www.barcelonacitygay.com
Four private rooms.

■ **Barcelona City Centre Hostel** (AC bf CC GLM I MA RWS RWT) All year
C./ Balmes 60, entresuelo *Next to Plaça Catalunya*
☎ 653 900 039 (mobile) 🖳 www.barcelonacitygay.com
See the website for special promotions. Very central location.

■ **Barcelona City North** (AC CC glm I PK RWB RWS RWT) All year
C/. Saragossa, 95-97. Entlo. 2a *city center* ☎ 653 900 039 (mobile)
🖳 www.barcelonacitycentre.com/north/lodging

■ **Barcelona City Ramblas** (AC cc glm I VA) 24hrs
Las Ramblas, 133, 3° *Plaza Catalunya* ☎ 653 900 039 (mobile)
🖳 www.barcelonacitygay.com/ramblas
Six double rooms with shared bathrooms. Visa and EC/Mastercard accepted.

■ **Barcelona City Urquinaona** (CC glm I MA RWB) All year
Bailen, 13 Pral. 1a *2 streets away from Estació del Nord bus staition*
☎ 653 900 039 (mobile) 🖳 www.barcelonacitygay.com/urquinaona

■ **Casa de Billy Barcelona** (glm H MA RWT) All year, 24hrs
Gran Via 420, 4-1 *M° Plaza España* ☎ 93 426 30 48
🖳 www.casabillybarcelona.com
Five bedrooms (two twin beds in each room) share three bathrooms.

■ **Central Town Gay Guest House** (AC BF CC DU G I MA OS RES RWB RWS RWT VA WI) 24 hours. Fees for late check-in apply.
Ronda San Pau, 51, 5, 2 *M° San Antoni* ☎ 93 442 70 57
🖳 www.centraltown.com
Centrally located near gay bars.

■ **Eddy Barcelona** (bf GLM MA) All year
C/. Girona, 46-3° 1a *Cnr. Gran Via* ☎ 932 456 013
🖳 www.eddybarcelona.com

Eos Guesthouse (AC BF GLM I OS RWS RWT) All year
Gran Vía de los Corts Catalanes 575 *M° Universitad, between Muntaner/Aribau* ☎ 93 451 87 72 🖳 www.pensioneos.com
Free internet access for guests. Breakfast until 13h. Friendly French owner.

Fashion House (AC BF CC glm I OS RWB RWT) All year
C/. Bruc 13 Principal *Between Ronda San Pere and C/. Ausias Marc*
☎ 637 904 044 (mobile) 🖳 www.bcnfashionhouse.com
Located a few steps away from the Paseo de Gràcia and Plaça Catalunya. The rooms are spacious and have air conditioning and private or shared baths. Also a beautiful 100m² terrace and a large living-room.

Hostal L'Antic Espai (AC b bf CC glm I m RWS RWT) All year
C/. Gran Vía de los Cortes Catalanes 660, Principal *M° Paseo de Gracia/Plaza de Catalunya* ☎ 93 304 19 45 🖳 www.lanticespai.com
All rooms have been decorated with unique furniture and equipped with the latest technology.

APARTMENTS

Absolu Living Barcelona (CC G) All year
☎ (+33) (0)1.44.54.97.00 (France) 🖳 www.absoluliving.com
Upscale, stylish apartments and beach apartments. Central location, unique, comfortable and with tasteful décor. Friendly staff with excellent knowledge of local scene.

Apartments bcn (AC CC GLM MC) All year
C/. Independencia, 350 ☎ 93 456 16 19 🖳 www.apartmentsbcn.com

Aramunt Apartments (AC glm MC RWB RWS RWT) All year
C/. Muntaner, 60 *M° Universidad* ☎ 93 268 33 88

Barcelona Pillow Apartments (AC cc glm) Mon-Fri 10-19h
Paseo Joan de Borbón, 47 apt. 3-1 ☎ 93 221 36 27
🖳 www.pillowapartments.com
Fully equipped comfortable apartments in the city centre. Discount for SPARTACUS readers with code 28 38 68 BCN!

Boxer Apartments (AC B BF GLM I OS PK RWS RWT) all year
C/. Diputació 167-169 *Corner C/. Casanova, M° Urgell/Universitat*
☎ 933 234 353 🖳 www.boxerapartments.com
Gay owned and operated by the boys of Boxer Barcelona. Also one fetish apartment avaible.

Domus Apartments Barcelona (cc H I)
☎ 687 694 818 (mobile) 🖳 www.domusapartments.com

GENERAL GROUPS

Acegal Assiciació Catalana d'Empreses per a Gais i Lesbianes (GLM) Mon-Fri 10-13, 16-20h
C/. Calabria, 96 ☎ 93 860 49 09 🖳 www.acegal.org
Catalan association of gay and lesbian businesses.

Casal Lambda (GLM) 17-21h
C/. Verdaguer i Callís, 10 ☎ 93 319 55 50
🖳 www.lambdaweb.org

CGB – Col-lectiu Gai de Barcelona (G)
Mon-Fri 19- 21.30, Fri & Sat 23-2h
C/. Passatje Valeri Serra, 23 *M° Plaça Universitat / M° Urgell*
☎ 93 453 41 25 🖳 www.colectiugai.org
A gay association based in Barcelona for many years now. La Kantina, a bar onsite, where you can meet gayactivists and their admirers

Coordinadora Gai-Lesbiana (GLM) 10-14 & 16-20h
C/. Violant d'Hongria, 156, bajos ☎ 93 298 00 29
🖳 www.cogailes.org
Publisher of „900Rosa". Free Information line ☎ 900 601 601 (18-22h).

FAGC – Front d'Alliberament Gai de Catalunya (GLM I MA) Mon-Fri 19-21h
C/. Verdi, 88 *Observatorio contra la Homofobia* ☎ 93 217 26 69
Publisher of rompearmarios.blogspot.com. See also www.observatoricontralhomofobia.org.

FETISH GROUPS

Associació Gai d'Òssos i Admiradors de Catalunya – BEARcelona (G) Meetings Wed 19h
c/o CGB, Ptge. Valeri Serra, 23 ☎ 93 54 31 25
🖳 www.bearcelona.org

HEALTH GROUPS

Departamento de Sanidad (glm)
Av. Drassanes, 17-21 *M° Universidad* ☎ 93 441 46 12
HIV-testing.

Stop Sida (G MA T) Helpline 10-14 & 16-18.30h
C/. Muntaner 121, entresuelo 1ª *L5, Parada Hospital Clínic*
☎ 93 452 24 35 (helpline) 🖳 www.stopsida.org
Helpline: 93 452 24 35

SWIMMING

-Platja de Chernobyl (g NU) (outside Barcelona near the Olympic City in S. Adrian de Besos. M° Sant Roc. The beach is behind the Tagra-factory. No bushes. Very popular. In winter car-cruising)
-Platja Mar Bella (g NU) (M° Ciudadela, then 2km on foot)
-Platja de la Barceloneta (g)
-Also at night, M° Poble Nou, then 10 mins to walk.

CRUISING

All are AYOR
-Station/Estación de Sants (very popular)
-San Andrés/Arenal Estación
-El Corte Inglés-Shopping Centre, Plaça Catalunya
-Parque de Montjuic (especially between Palau Nacional and C/. Lleida, very popular day and night)
-Park between Calle de Castillejos and Torre Agbar (M° Glòries)
-Plaça de Catalunya (R)
-Estación del Norte.

Benidorm

Benidorm is the jewel of the Costa Blanca, and is renowned for its wonderful Poniente beach, designated even by the UN as one of the seven most beautiful beaches in the world. The gay scene is concentrated in the old town between the two big beaches. A year round warm climate, which is reflected in a year round varied gay scene, as well as a wide range of leisure activities, for example the theme park „Terra Mitica", make Benidorm an appealing travel destination. You can enjoy yourself on the wonderful sandy beach, in the intimate gay bay, in the comfortable bars or leather bars, the drag shows, or just having coffee and cake in a café. According to people who have visited them, many of the bars identified in local publications as „gay-owned" are actually mixed places. For places to stay there is a range of possibilities for gay accommodation, from a basic but central hostel right in the middle of the gay scene to a peaceful guesthouse near the town. And if you are looking for the real Spain you'll find picturesque villages just a few miles inland.

Benidorm ist das Juwel der Costa Blanca und berühmt für seinen wunderschönen Strand Poniente, den selbst die UNO als einen der sieben schönsten Strände der Welt bezeichnet. Die schwule Szene konzentriert sich in der Altstadt zwischen den beiden großen Stränden. Ein ganzjährig mildes Klima, die ebenfalls ganzjährige, jedoch leider nicht immer abwechslungsreiche und sehr britische schwule Szene, sowie ein breites Spektrum an Freizeitangeboten (wie z. B. der Themenpark „Terra Mitica") machen Benidorm zu einem attraktiven Reiseziel. Mann vergnügt sich am belebten Sandstrand, in der lauschigen Nacktbadebucht, in Plüsch- oder Lederbars, bei Travestieshows oder Kaffee und Kuchen. Viele der in lokalen Publikationen als „gay-owned" bezeichneten Bars sind hinsichtlich ihres Publikums und ihres Angebots jedoch eher gemischt. Die schwulen Unterkunftsmöglichkeiten reichen vom einfachen, aber zentralen Hostal mitten in der Szene bis hin zum stilvollen Gästehaus im Umland. Wer das authentische Spanien sucht, findet wenige Kilometer im Hinterland malerische Dörfer.

Benidorm est le joyau de la Costa Blanca et est célèbre pour sa superbe plage de Poniente que l'ONU a clasée dans la liste des sept plus belles plages du monde. Le milieu gay est localisé dans la vielle ville entre les deux plages. Un climat tempéré toute l'année, la vie gay également active toute l'année ainsi qu'une large palette d'activités (comme le parc d'attraction « Terra Mítica ») font de Benidorm un des

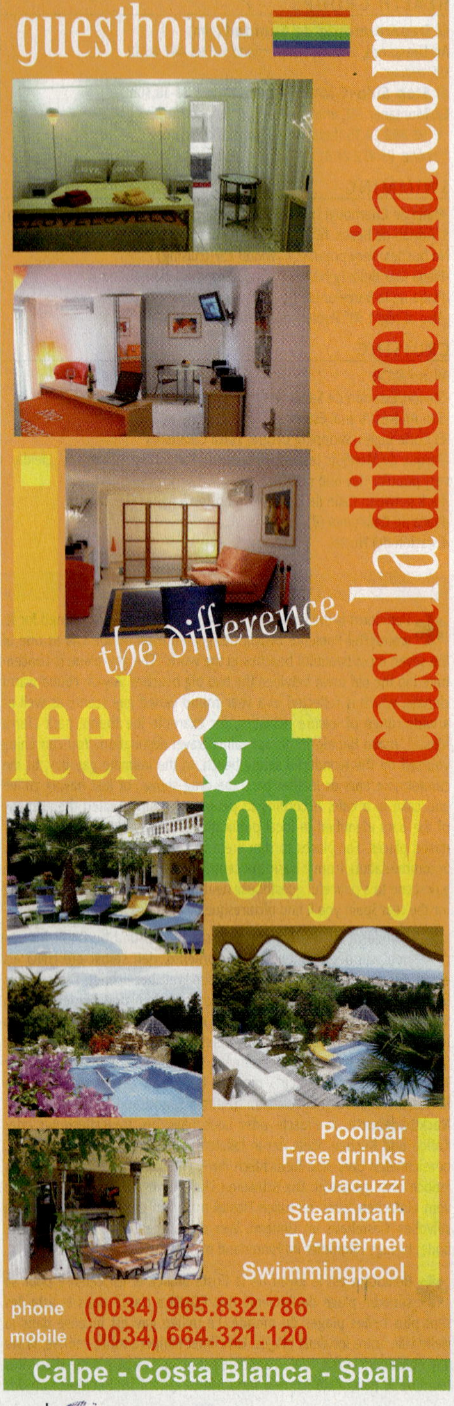

sites touristiques les plus intéressants. On ne manquera pas d'aller dans la crique réservée aux naturistes de la plage de sable fin très animée, dans les bars kitsch ou cuir, aux spectacles de travestis ainsi que dans les autres cafés. Nombre des bars qualifiés dans la presse locale de gays sont plutôt mixtes. On peut loger dans un des hôtels simples situés dans le ghetto, ou encore dans une pension cossue aux portes de la ville. À quelques kilomètres de la ville, on trouve des villages pittoresques qui vivent à l'heure de l'Espagne traditionnelle.

Benidorm es la joya de la Costa Blanca y famoso por la maravillosa playa de Poniente, considerada por la ONU como una de las siete playas más bellas del mundo. El ambiente gay se concentra en el barrio viejo, entre las dos grandes playas. Su clima suave durante todo el año, un ambiente gay muy variado y abierto también durante todo el año, así como una gran multitud de ofertas de ocio (como, por ejemplo, los parques temático de „Terra Mítica") convierten a Benidorm en un atractivo destino turístico. Para divertirse uno puede ir a la playa, siempre llena de gente, a la pequeña bahía para nudistas, a los bares de ambiente „leather", a un espectáculo de travestis o a un café. Muchos de los bares que aparecen en las publicaciones locales como „gay-owned" son sin embargo, teniendo en cuenta su público y oferta, más bien mixtos. Como alojamiento, hay una gran variedad de posibilidades, desde el sencillo pero céntrico hostal hasta la elegante casa de huéspedes en los alrededores de la ciudad. Aquellos que busquen la España más auténtica, pueden encontrar a unos kilómetros hacia el interior pueblos muy pintorescos.

Benidorm è un gioiello della Costa Blanca ed è famosa per la sua fantastica spiaggia Poniente che la stessa UNO definisce come una tra le sette più belle spiagge del mondo. La scena gay si concentra nel centro storico tra le due grandi spiagge. Il clima è mite tutto l'anno. La scena gay è molto varia. Le attività per il tempo libero sono notevoli (per esempio il parco „Terra Mitica"). Tutto questo fa di Benidorm una meta turistica molto amata. Ci si può divertire nella vivacissima spiaggia o si può andare in una più tranquilla cala gay o in un bar kitch, in un bar leather, ad uno show di travestiti o ad un semplice tavolino con caffè e dolce. Molti locali che vengono elencati nelle riviste locali come „gay" sono da considerarsi invece piuttosto misti. Per dormire ci sono moltissime possibilità per i gay: dal semplice ma centralissimo ostello (proprio al centro della zona gay) fino al più raffinato albergo un po' più fuori dal centro. Per chi ricerca la Spagna autentica, la si può trovare a pochi chilometri nei pittoreschi paesini dell'entroterra.

BARS

Bear's Bar (AC B DR F G MC VS) 22.30-4.30h
Plaza de la Constitución, 9 www.bearsbar.com
2 DR, sling & st. andrews cross

Chaplin (AC B G MA NU t) 22.30-5h
C/. San Vicente, 16 ☎ 680 169 807

Company (AC B G OS) 18-2h
C/. San Miguel, 16 ☎ 650 859 268

Eros (AC B CC DR F MA S SNU VS) 1-5h
C/. Santa Faz, 24 ☎ 96 585 37 06 realbenidorm.net/eros
Established in 1994 and still running strong!

J. J. Privat Bar (AC B DR G OC ST VS) 20-2h
Av. Uruguay, 4 www.jjprivatebar.com
English and Spanish spoken. Nice atmosphere for those looking for someone more mature.

Look. The (AC B d DR G MA S VS YC) 22-4.30h
C/. Santa Faz, 12 ☎ 96 680 16 89
Ask about special events.

Lovers (AC B d DR G MA VS) 21-4h
C/. Cuatre Cantons, 3 ☎ 666 743 377 (mobile)
www.gaybenidorm.com/lovers
Now with more cabins.

Mercury (AC B d DR f G MA s VS) 22.30-5h
C/. Alicante, 10 ☎ 96 680 67 30

Papagayo. El (AC B G MA) 22-2.30h
C/. Santa Faz 31 www.elpapagayobenidorm.com

People (AC B d DR G MA VS) 22-4h
C/. Santa Faz, 29 ☎ 96 586 00 92 www.gaybenidorm.com

■ **Pynk** (AC B D G MA S t) 13-2.30h
C/. de Palma 29 *Old town* ☎ 693 509 691 🖳 www.pynk-bar.com
Stylish gay music bar.
■ **Refuel Café Bar** (GLM I m MA OS) summer 9.30-21 & winter 10-19h
C/. San Pedro 10. Old Town *facing the harbour, parque elche*
☎ 966 831 010 🖳 www.realbenidorm.net/refuel.html
nice view on the harbour.
■ **Rich Bitch** (AC B d G MA S ST T) 21-?, shows 22-1h
C/. de Pal, 4 ☎ 666 055 906 (mobile) 🖳 www.richbitchshowbar.com

MEN'S CLUBS

■ **Eagle Bar Benidorm** (AC B DR F G MA VS) 16-4.30h
C/. Santa Faz, 5 *Old Town* ☎ 630 794 090
■ **Peppermint** (B DR F G MA) 23-4.30h
C/. San Vincente,11 ☎ 96 586 07 89 🖳 www.barpeppermint.com
Ask for apartments.

RESTAURANTS

■ **Paneil's** (AC CC G M MA) Tue-Sat 19-?h
C/. de la Palma, 12 ☎ 96 595 05 95 🖳 www.realbenidorm.net/paneils.html
Minimalistic design with clear lines and warm colors that create a relaxing atmosphere.

SAUNAS/BATHS

■ **Adonis** (AC B DR DU FC FH G MA MSG RR SA SB VS WH) 15-21.30h
Av. Venezuela, 4 *Edificio Narcea, near Gasolinera Isleta, Av. Jaime I*
☎ 96 585 79 58 🖳 adonissauna.galeon.com
■ **H2O Sauna Benidorm**
(AC B DR DU FC FH G MA MSG RR SA SB VS WH) 14-22h
C/. Tomas Ortuño, 46 *Old Benidorm, in city centre* ☎ 96 680 50 91
🖳 www.h2osauna.com
Busy and central sauna. Totally renovated. Great mix of tourists and residents.

HOTELS

■ **Babylon. The** (B cc GLM M) All year, 24hrs
C/. Alicante, 28 ☎ 965 865 019 🖳 www.babylonbenidorm.com
Traditional basic hotel in the old town of Benidorm right in the middle of the gay scene.
■ **Casa la Diferencia** (AC B BF CC DU G I m MA MSG NU OS PI PK RES RWB RWS RWT SB VA WH WO) All year, 24hrs
Canuta de Ifach 45 -A, Calpe *Situated in Calpe at the Costa Blanca near Benidorm between Altea and Denia* ☎ 96 583 27 86
☎ +34 664 321 120 mobile 🖳 www.casaladiferencia.com
Dutch owned and run, scenic views over bay.
■ **Queens** (AC B BF G M OS RWB RWS S VA) All year
Plaza Constitución, 5 ☎ 96 681 29 96 🖳 www.queensbenidorm.com
New rooftop terrace with great views over Benidorm and the coast.

GUEST HOUSES

■ **Casa Don Juan** (AC B bf cc GLM PA RWB RWS RWT VA) All year
C/. Santa Faz, 28 ☎ 96 680 91 65 🖳 www.gaybenidorm.com/casadonjuan
Bar and hotel.

APARTMENTS

■ **Casa Callas** (AC cc g MA PI) All year
Calle Haya 172, Moraira *Appr. 20 km from Benidorm* ☎ 96 574 90 84
🖳 www.casacallas.nl
Gay owned. English, Spanish, German and Dutch spoken.

SWIMMING

-La Cala (g MA NU) (Playa Poniente, by the rocks at the end of the beach. Popular, but dangerous)
-Rincon de Loix (g) (at the end of the beach)
-Playa Levante, in front of „Peter's Playa Bar" (popular)
-Playa Campomanes, ca. 10km north of Benidorm (g NU) (near 03590 Altea, take road Altea-Calpe, before tunnel, under Pueblo Mascarat)
-Playa Racó Conill (g NU) (bus to playa Finestrat, then walking in direction Alicante, up the hill and down to the beach and further on).

CRUISING

- Playa Ponente, on the beach in the arches under the promenade
- Illuminated Cross high up the hills above Rincón de Loix at the end of Playa Levante.

Bilbao

BARS

■ **Mykonos** (AC B DR G MA s SNU VS) 20-3.30h
C/. General Castillo, 4 ☎ 607 42 00 92
■ **Santu Bear. The** (AC B DR G MA s) 20-2h
C/. Dos de Mayo, 8 *Entrance C/. Lamana* ☎ 695 782 863 (mobile)

CAFES

■ **Luz Gas** (AC B GLM MA OS) Sun-Thu 15-1, Fri & Sat -3h
C/. Pelota, 4-6 ☎ 94 479 08 23

DANCECLUBS

■ **Balcón de la Lola** (AC B D g MA S WE) Fri 0-5h, Sat 11-16h
C/. Bailén, 10 ☎ 607 513 875 (mobile)

RESTAURANTS

■ **Txomin Barullo** (B g M) 18.30-23.30h
C/. Barrenkalle, 40 ☎ 944 152 788

SEX SHOPS/BLUE MOVIES

■ **Americans** (g VS) Mon-Sat 10-3, Sun 10-14 & 16-3h
C/. Nicolas Alcorta, 5 ☎ 94 470 34 92 🖳 www.fantasiasxshop.com
Cabins with glory holes.

■ **Fantasias** (g VS) Mon-Sat 10-3, Sun 10-14 & 16-3h
C/. General Eguía, 21-23 ☎ 94 410 16 56 🖳 www.fantasiasxshop.com
Second shop at C/. Niccolas Alcorte, 7 in Galería Centro Zabalburo, 1st floor. Cabins with glory holes.

SAUNAS/BATHS

■ **Ego** (! AC B CC DR DU F G GH I LAB m MA PP RR S SA SB SL SNU SOL VS WO) 15-24, Thu -1, Fri -9, Sat 15-24h
Nicolás Alcorta 3, bajo *Plaza Zabalburu, entrance in the Galería comercial, Calle Pop* ☎ 94 470 07 77 🖳 www.saunaego.com
Large friendly sauna with ample facilities on over 800m². Popular and very cruisy. Happy hour from 21h.

■ **Element** (b DR DU G m RR SA SB VS WH)
16-23, Fri 16-9, Sat 16-Sun 24h (non-stop)
C/. Particular de Costa, 8-10 *Near Plaza Zabalburu* ☎ 94 405 23 03
🖳 www.element.es
Very fashionable, well designed facility which is very clean. Each cubicle has its own temperature control and ventilation. Mainly good looking young men with no attitude can be found here.

GENERAL GROUPS

■ **Aldarte** (glm) Mon-Fri 10-13, & 17.30-21.30h
C/. Berastegi, 5-5º Dptos: 8 y 9 ☎ 94 423 72 96 🖳 www.aldarte.org
Centre for information, help with problems, archives.

■ **EHGAM** (GLM) Mon-Fri 20-22h
Escalinetas des Solokoetxe, 4 ☎ 94 415 07 19 🖳 www.ehgam.org
Gay library and archives. Radio programme „Giroan", 97.0 FM, Mon 20h. Friendly assistance for all sorts of problems. Gaylinea 900 700 719 (gay info hotline).

HEALTH GROUPS

■ **Comisión Ciudadana Anti-SIDA de Bizkaia** (glm)
Mo-Fr 9-14, 15-20h
C/. Bailén, 6 ☎ 94 416 00 55 🖳 www.bizkaisida.com/bizkaisida.htm
Information and services concerning AIDS.

SWIMMING

-Playa Larrabastera (La Salvaje) & Playa Arrigunaga (Algorta)

CRUISING

-Azkorri
-Park Casilda Iturriza

Burgos

CRUISING

-Pinares de Cortez (day and evening).
-El Empecinado (park at the river, gardens of La Isla).

Cádiz

BARS

■ **Pub Poniente** (AC B d G MA s t WE) 23-4h
C/. Beato Diego de Cádiz, 18 *Close to Plaza España* ☎ 95 621 26 97

HOTELS

■ **Hostal Playa Sur** (AC CC glm MA PK RWS RWT VA)
Mar-Nov, reception 8.30-23.30h
C/. Cervantes, 10, Conil de la Frontera *Nearest airports: Jerez 40, Sevilla and Gibraltar 90 mins* ☎ 95 644 16 01 🖳 www.hostalplayasur.com

CRUISING

-Playa de Cortadura (from the Edificio Alfa over the beach wall to the beginning of the beach; night and late night)
-Maritim Promenade (Victoria Beach; nights)
-Callejón del Blanco
-Playa de Candor (Rota). Left side of the nudist beach, behind abandoned military site.

Canary Islands

Canary Islands – Fuerteventura

BARS

■ **Jellyfish** (B CC D G M MA) Tue-Sun 10-14 & 17-2h, Sat -2.30, closed Mon
C/. Hibisco, 1 *Centro Comercial El Campanario. Next door to the bank Banesto* ☎ 691 910 010 🖳 barjellyfish.com
Gay night on Fri. The latest sounds direct from Global dance events.

HOTELS

■ **Barceló Corralejo Bay** (AC B BF CC H I M MSG NG OS PI PK RWB RWS RWT SA SB SH VEG WH WL) All year
Playa del Corralejo *5 mins walk from the centre of Corralejo*
☎ 928 53 5367 🖳 www.barcelo.com

SWIMMING

-Dunas de Corralejo (g NU) (between Puerto del Rosario and Corralejo)
-Playa Castillo, Caleta de Fuste (g MA NU).

Canary Islands – Gran Canaria – Las Palmas

BARS

■ **Bar Da Vinci** (AC B CC G m MA OS) 11-2h
C/. Ripoche, 6 *Near Parque Sta. Catalina* ☎ 92 826 98 67

■ **Madame. Le** (AC B d DR GLM YC) 21-3h, WE also 5-10h
C/. Nicolás Estévanez, 12 ☎ 92 822 19 66

■ **Sentido** (B GLM MA OS) 21-3h
C/. Mariana Pineda, 1

■ **Sidney** (B GLM MA OS) 19-3h
C/. Marinana Pineda, 7 ☎ 928 22 54 09

■ **Victors Copas** (B CC GLM M S ST) Tue-Sun 20-3.30h
C/. Dr. Miguel Rosas, 21 ☎ 928 271 584
🖳 www.victorscopashow.com

CAFES

■ **Gran Terraza Lolita** (! B bf g I m MA OS) 9-1.30h
Parque Santa Catarina, 7 ☎ 92 826 06 85
🖳 www.terrazalolitapluma.com
Very popular.

■ **Nuevo Río** (B G M MA OS r) 8-2h
Parque Santa Catalina 74 ☎ 92 822 30 48

DANCECLUBS

■ **Babylon** (AC B CC D g MA S) Tue-Sat 24-6h
C/. Martinez de Escobar, 37-39 *Near Station Catalina*
☎ 676 159 069 (mobile) 🖳 www.discotecababylon.com

■ **Faunos** (AC B D G MA r VS WE) 23-?h
C/. Dr. Miguel Rosas, 37, bajo ☎ 92 826 47 58

■ **Inolvidable** (AC B CC D GLM MC S SNU ST VS) Tue-Sun 22-5h
C/. Olof Palme, 38 *Near Plaza de la Victoria* ☎ 92 822 18 03
Shows (SNU) on Wed, (ST) on Fri.

RESTAURANTS

■ **Clandestino** (AC CC G M MA) 13-1h
C/. Doctor Miguel Rosas, 8 *Near Parque Sta. Catalina* ☎ 92 822 69 03
🖳 www.restauranteclandestino.com
Rather creative interpretation of international cuisine.

SEX SHOPS/BLUE MOVIES

■ **Jomatog** (CC g VS) Mon-Sat 10-2, Sun 16-24h
C/. Dr. Miguel Rosas, 4 ☎ 92 822 15 02 🖳 www.jomatog.es
Second branch (10-22h) in C/. Albareda, 30.

■ **Sala X** (g VS) 11-24h
C/. Tomás Miller, 51, bajo *Zona Puerto* ☎ 928 26 12 04

Bienvenidos a, welcome to Gran Canaria!
MASPALOMAS
GAYPRIDE
MASPALOMAS
GAYPRIDE
7-13
MAY 2012
www.gaypridemaspalomas.com

SAUNAS/BATHS

■ **Portugal** (AC B DR DU G MA MSG P SA SB SL VS) Daily 16-24h
C/. Portugal, 27 *Near La Playa de las Canteras* ☎ 928 227 284
www.saunaportugal.com
Two floors. Big darkroom, sling-room and restroom downstairs.

■ **Sauna Club** (B DR DU G MA MSG SA SB VS) 16-23h
C/. Tomás Miller, 55 ☎ 92 826 57 21

GENERAL GROUPS

■ **GAMÁ** (GLM MA T) Mon-Fri 8-15, 18-21h
C/. Tomas Morales 8, bajo *Near Parque San Telmo* ☎ 92 843 34 27
www.colectivogama.com
GAMÀ = Colectivo de Lesbianas, Gays, Transexuales y Bisexuales de Canarias.

CRUISING

-Parque Santa Catalina / C/. Ripoche (r)
-Parque Doramas
-Playa de las Canteras el Balneario
-Roques Muelle Deportivo
-Parque San Telmo
-Estación de Guaguas.

Canary Islands – Gran Canaria - Playa del Inglés/ Maspalomas

Playa del Ingles on the southernmost tip of Gran Canaria, with its notorious dunes at Maspalomas, is the Miami Beach of Europe. It's a meeting place for everyone wanting to enjoy the year round summer climate of the Canary Islands, which lie in a chain just off the coast of West Africa. From the desert sands a holiday paradise has been created, with constant sun, fine beaches and a full-on nightlife.
The gay Scene is concentrated on the Av. Tirajana, the Cita-Cente and especially the famous Yumbo-Centre, where men from all over the world go wild 365 days a year; from sophisticated restaurants to heavy sex clubs with slings and bathhouses etc. all needs can be met. The club hosts, who are just as international as their guests, are a great example of European unity. They jointly organize a Gay Pride with official blessing, which grows more and more stunning every year, and it's done with Northern European efficiency mixed with a southern warmth. Also carnival offers not only gay attractions even for those who think having seen everything already. Absolutely recommended is a trip to Las Palmas, with its typical Canary Island feel together with an urban Scene in the port area, which is also possible with a guided gay tour.

Playa del Inglés an der äußersten Südspitze Gran Canarias, mit seinen berühmt-berüchtigten Dünen von Maspalomas, ist das Miami-Beach der Europäer: Treffpunkt für alle, die im Winter das ganzjährig sommerliche Klima des vor Westafrika liegenden kanarischen Archipels zu schätzen wissen. Mitten aus dem Wüstensand enstand ein Ferienparadies mit beständiger Sonne, feinem Strand und einem intensiven Nachtleben. Die schwule Szene konzentriert sich auf die zentrale Av. Tirajana, das Cita-Center, vor allem jedoch auf das bereits legendäre Yumbo-Center, wo Männer aller Herren Länder wilde 365 Nächte im Jahr durchmachen. Von gepflegten Restaurants und Cafés bis hin zu harten Sexbars mit Slings, Badewannen etc. wird jedes Bedürfnis bedient. Die nicht minder internationalen Wirte sind ein Vorbild für die europäische Vereinigung: Gemeinsam (und mit offiziellem Wohlwollen) organisieren sie mit südlicher Glut und nordeuropäischer Effizienz einen Jahr für Jahr beeindruckenderen Gay Pride. Auch der traditionelle Karneval ist nicht nur aus schwuler Perspektive einen erlebnisreichen Aufenthalt für selbst jene wert, die meinen, auf GC schon alles zu kennen. Unbedingt zu empfehlen ist ein Ausflug nach Las Palmas. Für seine typisch kanarische und zugleich atlantisch-urbane Szene im Hafenviertel werden auch fachkundige schwule Führungen angeboten.

Située à l'extrême sud de l'île Grande Canarie, la Playa del Inglés avec ses fameuses dunes de Maspalomas, est la Miami-Beach des Européens. Lieu de rencontre pour tous ceux qui savent apprécier en hiver le climat d'été qui règne toute l'année sur cet archipel canarien devant l'Afrique de l'Ouest. Un paradis pour vacanciers au centre d'un désert constamment ensoleillé, une plage de sable fin et une vie nocturne trépidante. Le milieu gay se concentre autour de l'avenue centrale Tirajana, le Cita-Center, mais principalement autour du légendaire Yumbo-Center où des hommes originaires de presque tous les pays passent 365 nuits folles par an à faire la fête.
Des restaurants et cafés de qualité jusqu'aux sex bars hard avec des slings, des baignoires etc., il y en a pour tous les goûts. Les patrons pas moins internationaux sont un modèle de la réunification européenne : ils organisent chaque année ensembles (et avec la bienveillance officielle) des Gay Pride de plus en plus impressionnantes, avec une efficience nordique et une fougue méditerranéenne. Le carnaval offre des attractions pas seulement gays meme pour ceux, qui croient ayant connu déjà tout. Il est vivement conseillé de faire un saut à Las Palmas et le quartier du port, non seulement typiquement canarien mais aussi très urbain, ce qui se peut faire aussi en visite guidée gay.

Playa del Inglés, en la punta más meridional de Gran Canaria, con sus famosas dunas de Maspalomas, es el Miami Beach de los europeos. Es punto de encuentro de todos aquellos que saben apreciar en invierno el clima veraniego del archipiélago canario, situado enfrente de África. En medio de la arena del desierto se creó un paraíso vacacional con sol permanente, bonitas playas y una vida nocturna intensa. El ambiente gay se concentra en la avenida central de Tirajana, el Cita-Center y sobre todo en el ya legendario Yumbo-Center, donde hombres de todos los países disfrutan a lo grande las 365 noches del año. Desde los cuidados restaurantes y cafés hasta los bares de sexo más duros con correas, bañeras, etc. aquí se satisface cualquier deseo. Los no menos internacionales propietarios son un ejemplo de unificación europea. Juntos (y con el beneplácito oficial) organizan año tras año, con eficiencia norteña y fervor sureño, una marcha del Orgullo Gay impresionante. Tambien el carnaval ofrece atractivos no sólo gays, mismo para aquellos que piensan haber conocido ya todo. Se recomienda mucho una excursión a Las Palmas y al puerto (en bus directo Yumbo-Sta. Catalina), con su típico ambiente canario y urbano a la vez, que se puede disfrutar tambien en visita guiada gay.

Playa del Inglés, sulla estrema punta sud di Gran Canaria, con le sue rinomate dune di Maspalomas, è la Miami-Beach degli europei: punto d'incontro per tutti coloro che sanno apprezzare d'inverno il clima estivo dell'arcipelago delle Isole Canarie, di fronte all'Africa dell'Ovest. In mezzo ad un deserto di sabbia è sorto un paradiso turistico con sole costante, spiagge incantevoli e una vita notturna intensa. La scena gay si concentra nella centralissima Av. Tirajna (nel quartiere Cita-Center) ma in maniera particolare nel leggendario Yumbo-Center, dove uomini di ogni paese trascorrono 365 notti selvagge all'anno: dai ristoranti e caffè più curati fino ai più estremi sexbar con sling, vasca da bagno, etc... ogni desiderio viene soddisfatto.
Anche il tradizionale carnevale è interessante non solo per i gay, ma anche per quelli che credono di conoscere già tutto sull'isola. Vi consigliamo di fare un'escursione a Las Palmas con la sua scena tipica delle Canarie e un'atmosfera atlantico-urabana nella zona del porto, dove vengono anche offerte guide ai turisti gay.

PUBLICATIONS

■ **Guapo**
☎ 639 161 002 www.guapograncanaria.com

TOURIST INFO

■ **Patronato de Turismo**
www.grancanaria.com
Chamber of Tourism for Gran Canaria.

BARS

■ **Adonis** (B GLM MA OS) 12-2.30h
Yumbo Centro, Planta 1 *On level 1* ☎ 92 876 56 72
www.adonisworld.de
Popular.

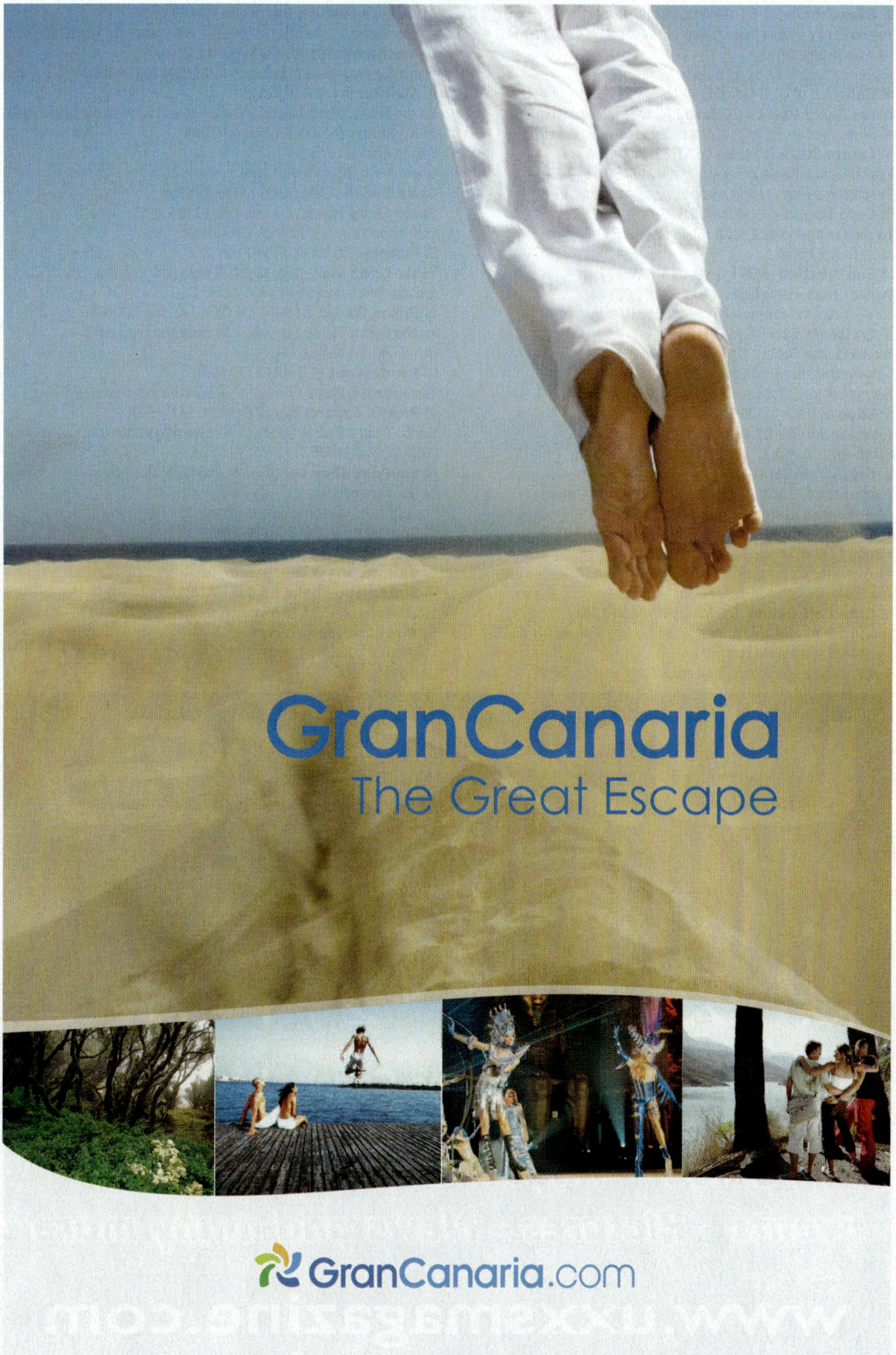

■ **Bärenhöhle** (AC B F G MA OS VS) 20-3h
Yumbo Centro, Planta Baja *On level , Local 151-9* ☎ 92 877 80 14
💻 www.beargc.de
You do not have to be a bear to be welcome here.

■ **Bulle. La** (B CC G I MA OS) 18-1h
Yumbo Centro, Local 131-26 *Planta 1* 💻 www.labullegc.com
stylish lounge-bar with large variety of belgian & international beers.

■ **Centre Stage** (B f G MA OS ST) 22-4h
Yumbo Centro, Planta 2 *On level 2* ☎ 92 877 90 64
Thu Leather & Feather party. All digital music & videos.

■ **Coco Loco** (B d GLM MA OS t) 23-?h
Yumbo Centro, Planta 2, local 261-15 *On level 2*
Music videos, karaoke.

■ **Construction** (B DR F G MA OS SNU VS) 22-4h
Yumbo Centro, Planta baja *On level 0*
Cabins, slings and Plasma porn screens. Live DJ every night.

■ **Cruise** (AC B DR F G MA VS) 23-6h
Yumbo Centro, Planta 2 *On level 2* ☎ 928 763 453
💻 www.cruisebaryumbo.com
Two darkrooms and two slings.

■ **Eden** (B G MA OS) 19-2h
Yumbo Centro, Planta baja *On level 0* ☎ 92 876 66 78
French day & night bar.

■ **Gio** (B G MA OS) 11-3h
Yumbo Centro, Planta 1 *On level 1* ☎ 690 700 834 (mobile)
💻 www.giobargrancanaria.com

■ **Gloryhole Mens Bar** (AC B DR F G MA OS VS) 23-?h
Yumbo Centro, Local 251-11 *Planta 2*
💻 www.gloryholemensbar.com
Private cabines with glory hole. No strict dress code.

■ **Gran Café Latino** (B G MA OS VS) 18.30-2.30h
Yumbo Centro, Planta Baja, local 121.04 *On level 0* ☎ 92 877 88 70
💻 www.grancafelatino.com
A cosy bar with a big terrace. Latino music and great cocktails.

■ **Jackie's Lesbian Bar** (B gLm MA OS) 18-3h
Yumbo Centro, Planta baja *On level 0* 💻 www.jackiesbar.gaycitymap.com

■ **Macho Macho** (AC B G MA OS s t) 22-4h
Yumbo Centro, Planta 2 *On level 2* ☎ 637 294 297 (mobile)

■ **Meicker** (B G MA OS) 20-3h
Yumbo Centro, Planta baja *Middle of the square* 💻 www.barmeicker.net

■ **Mykonos** (AC d G MA) daily 11-3.30h
Yumbo Centro *4th floor*
One of the oldest gay bars in town.

■ **Na Und** (B d GLM OC OS r S) 19.30-3.30h
Yumbo Centro, Planta 1 *On level 1* ☎ 92 876 30 55
Intergenerational, international, inspirational.

■ **Parrots** (B G MA OS S) 19-2.30h
Yumbo Centro, Planta Baja, 121/01 💻 www.parrots-group.com
Famous Parrots from Sitges finally also in GC.

■ **Prison Bar** (AC B DR F G MA OS VS) All year: 23.59-?h
Yumbo Centro, Planta 2 *On level 2* 💻 www.prison-bar.eu
DR with AC and bathtub, dogstation.

■ **Rendezvous** (B G MA OS) 19.30-3h
Yumbo Centro, Planta 1 *On level 1* 💻 www.bar-rendezvous.eu

■ **Ricky's Cabaret Bar** (B d glm OS S ST) 19-3h
Yumbo Centro, Planta1 *On level 1* 💻 www.rickyscabaretbar.com
Shows daily at 23.30h

■ **Sparkles Showbar** (B CC d G MA OS S) 19.30-3h
Yumbo Centro, Planta 2
Comedy dragshows on large open terrace. Tue, Wed & Fri 2 shows.

■ **Spartacus** (B G MA OS) 20-2.30h
Yumbo Centro, Planta 1 *On level 1* ☎ 92 876 65 40
💻 www.spartacus-gc.de

■ **Strand-apo-Theke** (! B G M MA NR OS) Mon-Sat 11-23h
C.C. Oasis – Local 35 & 36 *Near Faro, seafront* ☎ 928 141 296
💻 www.strand-apo-theke.com
The place to go after the beach. They play German hit songs and its very cosy and friendly.

Terry Show (B G MA OS ST) 22-?h
Yumbo Centro *On level 2*
Fri & Sat ST.

Wunderbar (B d G MA OS s VS) 20-2h, Wed closed
Yumbo Centro, Planta 1 www.wunderbar-island.com
famous for their cocktails & parties (esp. for Grand Prix Eurovision de la Chanson). GLAY-Award winner „Bar of the Year 2010"

MEN'S CLUBS

Basement Studios (AC B BF CC DR F G GH LAB m MA NU OS PI RWB RWS RWT SL VA WH) All year
Av. de los Estados Unidos, 37 *Opp. Yumbo Centre* ☎ 92 876 51 43
www.basementstudios.es
All bungalows with sling; garden with cabins, gloryholes, camouflage maze, dungeon. Day and week tickets available for non-residents.

Box. The (B DR f G MA OS VS) 23-4h
Yumbo Centro, Planta 2 *On level 2* www.theboxgc.com
Slings, piss room, glory holes, fisting bench, and cabins.

Bunker (AC B CC DR F G MA NU SNU VS) 22.30-5h
C.C. Yumbo, Planta 1 *Southeast corner* www.bunkergc.com

Cellar. The (B DR F G MA OS S VS) 22-?h
Yumbo Centro, Planta 1 *On level 1* www.thecellarmensbar.com
Underwear and naked bar with lots of horny men.

Chaps (AC B DR F G MA P VS) 22-3h
Centro Comercial Cita, Avenida de Francia *Basement, next to the lift*
www.chaps-grancanaria.com
Enlarged now double size. See the website for special events: www.chaps-grancanaria.com

Reds (B DR DU F G GH MA P SL VS) 21-4h
Avenida de Tirajana 17, Edif. Barbados II *100 m from Yumbo Center*
☎ (35100) 928 140 748 www.redsclub.es
New gay sex club on 160 m². Naked only on Mon, Wed, Sat & Sun.

CAFES

Café Wien (B g m OS) 9-19h
Centro Comercial Cita, Planta 2 *Upstairs* ☎ 92 876 0380

Mulato. El (AC B bf CC G I M MA OS PI) 11-23h
Avenida de Tirajana, 13 *One block from CC. Yumbo direction C.C. Cita*
☎ 928 767 344
Nice Café close to Yumbo Center – ideal to start your day or evening at!

Rainbow (B BF G M MA OS s VS) 10-3h
Av. de Tirajana 7 *Ed. Tenesor* ☎ 649 738 483 (mobile)
www.rainbow-bistro.de
Bistro-café. Breakfast, lunch, afternoon coffee & dinner. Homemade German food.

DANCECLUBS

Amigos (AC B D G MA OS S ST VS)
C.C. Yumbo, Planta 2

Babylon (AC B D DR G S ST VS) 22-6h
C.C. Yumbo, Planta 2

Heaven Gran Canaria (AC B D DR G MA S) 24-7h
Yumbo Centro, Planta 4 *On level 4* ☎ 92 877 17 30
One of the bigger clubs in Yumbo – open til late.

Mantrix (AC B D DR G MA OS VS) 2-6h
Yumbo Centro, Planta 4 *On level 4* www.level4men.com

RESTAURANTS

Bei Lelo (B CC GLM M OS VEG WL) 17-24h
Yumbo Centro, Planta 2a *On level 2* ☎ 92 877 29 24

Candela. La (B CC DM G M MA NR OS PA VEG WL) 18.30-24h
Yumbo Centro, Planta 2 *On level 2* ☎ 92 877 23 80
Spanish and Italian dishes as well as local specialities.

Dali's (AC B CC G M OS VEG) 18-23.30h, Mon closed
Yumbo Centro, Planta 2 *On level 2* ☎ 92 877 11 73
www.gaygrancanaria4u.com/restaurants/Dali.shtml
International & French cuisine.

Facecook (AC CC G M MA OS PA RES VEG WL) Daily 18-?h
Yumbo Centre, Planta 2 *Second floor* ☎ 92 877 60 69

■ **Merlín** (AC B CC G M MA NR OS PK RES VEG WL) 16-24h
Av. de Tirajana, 18 *Edificio Lenamar* ☏ 92 876 95 01

■ **Romeo** (CC DM G H MA OS PA RES) 17-?h
Av. de Tirajana, 24 *1/2 block from Yumbo* ☏ 928 767 629
Also apartments Iguazu to let.

■ **Valentine's** (CC G M MA OS VEG) 19-23, Tue closed
C.C. Yumbo, Planta 2 ☏ 928 760 403 🖳 www.restaurant-valentines.com

SEX SHOPS/BLUE MOVIES

■ **D. G.'s Pride Shop** (AC CC GLM) 16.30-1h
Yumbo Centro, Planta 2 *On level 1* ☏ 92 876 66 15
🖳 www.prideshop.info
DVDs, videos, rainbow articles and now also a video cubicle for up to three people.

■ **Jomatog** (CC G VS) Mon-Sat 10-22
Centro Comercial Nilo, Local 1057-1058 ☏ 92 876 36 41
🖳 www.jomatog.es

■ **Man's Lounge** (AC CC DR G MA VS WE) 16.30-2.30h
Yumbo Centro, Planta 1 *On level 1* ☏ 92 876 42 86
Videocabins and cinema; ticket valid for entire day, including one drink.

■ **Man's Plaza** 16.30-2.30
Yumbo Cantro, Planta baja ☏ 928 764 286
Video cabins.

SAUNAS/BATHS

■ **Heroes** (AC B CC DR DU G M MA MSG p SA SB VS WH) Daily 16-2h
Yumbo Centro, Planta 4 *On level 4* ☏ 92 877 47 70
🖳 www.level4men.com

■ **Nilo** (! B DR DU f FC G I M MSG NU RR SA SB SNU VS) 19-2h
Centro Comercial Nilo, Local 137 *End of isle in Nilo* ☏ 928 765 464
🖳 www.saunanilo.com
14 cabins with TV. Clean but cruisy with canarios and cute massage boys. Sat SNU and life-sex-show. Thu 2 for 1. -25y/o pay half price.

FITNESS STUDIOS

■ **Biceps Gym** (B CC GLM MA WO) Mon-Thu 10-24, Fri & Sat -22, Sun 16.30-22h
Av. de Tirajana 19, Aptos. Barbados II, local 23 ☏ 92 876 85 36
🖳 www.bicepsgym.es

MASSAGE

■ **Kumo Ki** (G MSG) 10-20h
☏ 686 044 474 (mobile) 🖳 www.facebook.com/roland.schwarz1
Reiki and massage service. Pick up service from hotel possible. Also guided tours of the island. For more information see Facebook: Roland Kumoki Schwarz.

BODY & BEAUTY SHOPS

■ **Golden Moments** (AC B CC G M MA OS) Tue-Fri 9-19, Sat 9-16h
Av. de Tirajana – Edif. Tenesor No. 6 *Between C.C. Yumbo and C.C. Cita*
☏ 928 77 22 06 🖳 www.golden-moments-gc.com

LEATHER & FETISH SHOPS

■ **RoB Cran Canaria** (CC G MC) Daily 14-22h
Yumbo Centro, Planta 4 *Above Farmacia* ☏ 928 771076

HOTELS

■ **Birdcage Resort** (AC B BF cc G H M MA MSG NU OS PI S VA WH) All year
C/. Egipto 10 *100m walk from Yumbo Centre* ☏ 928 764722
☏ +49 8938151778 (reservations) 🖳 www.birdcage-resort.com
Exclusive gay only resort. Suites with private garden. The only 4 star deluxe gay hotel on Gran Canaria.*

■ **Bohemia Suites & Spa** (AC B BF CC GLM I M MA OS PI) All year
Av. Estados Unidos 28 ☏ 92 876 00 58
🖳 www.bohemia-grancanaria.com
New designhotel opening in march 2012. Stylish and fashionable. no families, no kids. Fantastic roof terrace with views over beaches, dunes and all Playa del Inglés.

■ **Pasion Tropical** (B BF CC G I m MA NU OS PI PK RWB RWS RWT SOL VA WH WO) All year
C/. Las Adelfas, 6 *Urbanización San Agustín, 20m from beach*
☏ 92 877 01 31 🖳 www.pasion-tropical.com
The only gay resort by the sea in all Gran Canaria. Stylish intimate atmosphere, elegant-ethnic rooms, fantastic tropical garden. Spectacular ocean-front rooftop sundeck.

■ **Tropical La Zona** (B BF CC G I M NU OS PI RWT SOL WH WO) 24hrs
Av. Sargentos Provisionales 16 *Five mins walk from C.C. Yumbo*
🖳 www.tropicallazona.com
One of the best Bungalow-resorts for gay men-only in Maspalomas.

GUEST HOUSES

■ **Basement Studios** (AC B BF CC DR F G GH LAB m MA NU OS PI RWB RWS RWT SL VA WH) All year
Av. de los Estados Unidos, 37 *Opp. Yumbo Centre* ☏ 92 876 51 43
🖳 www.basementstudios.es
All bungalows with sling; garden with cabins, gloryholes, camouflage maze, dungeon. Day and week tickets available for non-residents.

■ **Beach Boys Resort** (I MSG PI RWT WH)
Avenida Touroperador Finnmatkat 6 ☏ 649 019 985
🖳 www.beachboysresort.com

■ **Jackies Guest House** (bf GLM MA OS PI)
C/. Isla de Lobos, 36, San Fernando ☎ 610 504 310
💻 www.jackiesguesthouse.com
Lesbian owned.

■ **Residence Gran Canaria. La** (AC cc G I MA MSG PI RWS RWT SOL WH) All year, 24hrs
C/. Inglaterra, 16 *250m from the beach and Yumbo Center*
☎ 667 452 541 (mobile) 💻 www.laresidencegrancanaria.com
5 delightful apartments in a quiet residential district in the centre of Playa del Inglés.

APARTMENTS

■ **Apartamentos Judoca Colors** (AC glm I PI RWB RWS RWT VA) Reception daily 8-16h
Av. Roma, 20 ☎ 92 876 07 85
A cosy complex of twelve double occupancy apartments, less than 50m from the beach.

■ **Bungalows Parque Sol** (G) Reception: 9-13 & 14-18h, closed Sun
Avenida Estados Unidos 43 *In front of Yumbo center* ☎ 928 765 753
💻 www.bungalowsparquesol.eu
Small bungalow complex with 18 bungalows with 2 separate bedrooms and 5 bungalows with 1 bedroom.

■ **Escape Club Gran Canaria** (AC B CC GLM I OS PI PK RWS RWT VA) 24hrs
Pasaje entre C/. Alemania & Inglaterra *5 mins walk to Jumbo Centre*
☎ 691 933 261 💻 www.escapeclubgc.com
Self-catering bungalow-complex in quiet residencial area. gay owned and operated. taylormade services on request.

■ **Tenesoya** (G PI) All year, reception Mon-Fri 10-14h
Av. de Tenerife 18 ☎ (+49) (0)221 21 98 86 (Germany)
💻 www.tenesoya.de
Cosy little gay men only bungalow complex with twelve bungalows, six with one and six with two bedrooms. 800 m walk to Yumbo Centre .

■ **Villas Blancas** (AC B BF CC G I M MSG NU OS PI RWS RWT S VA VS) All year, bistro from 18-22h
Av. T. O. Tjaereborg, Campo de Golf ☎ 90 216 81 69
💻 www.villasblancas.com
Beautifully furnished bungalows in a peaceful setting each with kitchen, AC, sat-TV and own bath. Around the swimming pool clothing is optional. Pool recently fully renewed. Airport transfer available.

HEALTH GROUPS

■ **Centro Médico Alemán** Mon-Sat 9.30-13.30, 17-19h, Summer only mornings
C.C.Varadero, A180 Meloneras *Near Faro Maspalomas* ☎ 928 141 538

CRUISING

-Maspalomas Sand Dunes (AYOR) (in the small bushes, very popular)
-P Charco Maspalomas (Car-cruising 19-4h).

Canary Islands – La Gomera

RESTAURANTS

■ **Montaña. La** (g M MC) All year
☎ 92 280 40 77
Original and home cooking. Meals made from ecological farm produce, using ancient recepies.

GUEST HOUSES

■ **Jardín las Hayas** (G H M MC OS) All year
Las Hayas Valle Gran Rey ☎ 92 280 40 77 💻 www.gomeranatural.com
Rural houses for rent.

Canary Islands – La Palma – Los Llanos de Aridane

BARS

■ **Luna. La** (B CC GLM I MA OS) 18-2h
C/. Fernández Taño, 26 *On the sunny west coast* ☎ 92 240 19 13
💻 www.LaLuna.moonfruit.com

Canary Islands – La Palma – Puntagorda

GUEST HOUSES

■ **Mar y Monte** (BF glm H OS RWB) All year
C/. Pino de la Virgen, 7b *Puntagorda* ☎ 92 249 30 67
💻 www.la-palma-marymonte.de
Five guest rooms in a non-smoking guesthouse.

Canary Islands – La Palma – Santa Cruz de la Palma

APARTMENTS

■ **Apartamentos La Fuente** (CC GLM I MA OS PA RWB RWS RWT VA) Mon-Fri 9-12, 17-20, Sat 9-12h
C/. Pérez de Brito, 49 *In the historic centre* ☎ 92 241 56 36
💻 www.la-fuente.com
Nine fully equipped apartments. Rental of further houses in the countryside.

SWIMMING

-Playa Los Cancajos (g MA NU) (South of Santa Cruz. Walk along the beach from Los Cancajos to the south in direction of the airport, climb over the rocks. After about 30 mins you reach the beach)
-Playa Cuatro Monjas (g MA NU) (South of Playa Naos. Follow road to south just behind Puerta Naos. Leave car near banana plantations, follow path down to the sea).

Canary Islands – Lanzarote – Puerto del Carmen

BARS

■ **Black & White** (B d G MA) 21-4h
Atlántico Centro, Av. de la Playa, 38

SWIMMING

-Playa Guasimeta (g nu)(behind the airport)
-Playa del Papagayo.

Canary Islands – Tenerife – La Laguna

GAY INFO

■ **tenerifegay.es**
💻 www.tenerifegay.es

SEX SHOPS/BLUE MOVIES

■ **Momentos Love Shop** (GLM)
C/ San Agustín, 7 💻 www.momentos-loveshop.com

HEALTH GROUPS

■ **Unapro** (glm MA) Mon-Fri 9-14 & 15-20h
Carrer Los Guanches, 3, 1° – Barrio Nuevo ☎ 92 263 29 71
💻 www.unapro.org
HIV/AIDS-group.

CRUISING

-Estación de Guaguas
- Avenida Ángel Guimerá Jorge, Cruz de Piedra (junto vías del Tranvía)

Canary Islands – Tenerife – Los Realejos

BARS

■ **Barca. La** (AC B g MA) 19-2h
C/. El Monturrio, 12 *Toscal-Longuera* ☎ 637 930 356 (mobile)

Canary Islands – Tenerife – Playa de las Américas

BARS

■ **Chaplin Bar** (AC DR G MA S) 22.30-6h
Centro Comercial Salytien *Next to Bingo, basement*
☎ 680 169 807 (mobile)
DJ at the weekend.

■ **Feelings Gay Bar** (AC D FC GLM MA PK S)
Avenida Rafael Puig Lluvina, C.C. Galaxia I *Semisótano*
■ **Ukelele** (B GLM) 22.30-3h
Paseo de la Habana, 11 – Lopcal 18 *Los Cristianos*

DANCECLUBS

■ **Discoteca Punto Zero** (AC D DR G MA) 22.30-6h
Centro Comercial Salytien *Next to Bingo, basement*
DJ at the weekend.

RESTAURANTS

■ **Ryan´s Bar & Grill** (AC B GLM M WL)
C.C. Pueblo Canario

APARTMENTS

■ **Flamingo Suites** (AC CC H OS PI)
Av. España S/N *Costa Adeje* ☎ 92 271 84 00
💻 www.flamingosuites.co.uk
■ **Playaflor Chill-Out Resort** (B cc G I M MSG PA PI RWS RWT VA WO) Reception: 9-1h
Av. Rafael Puig, 3 *100m from the beach* ☎ 92 278 96 24
💻 www.playaflor.com

SWIMMING

-Los Cristianos (NU) (via Santa Cruz by bus)
-Playa de la Tejita (g NU) (very popular day and night; between El Medano and Los Abrigos)

CRUISING

-Near Las Tejitas at Playa de la Montaña Roja. Also on the street between El Medano and Los Abrigos. P
-Paseo Maritimo in front of Geminis and the CC Salytien.

Canary Islands – Tenerife – Puerto de la Cruz

BARS

■ **Men's Club Dominique** (AC B G MC) 22-?h
C/. Santo Domingo, 11 ☎ 92 237 45 29
■ **New Robin. The** (B GLM LM MA)
C/. Valois, 16 *Edificio Belair*
■ **Tabasco** (AC B DR G MA OS VS) 22-3h
Av. Bethencourt Molina, 15

DANCECLUBS

■ **Anderson New Generation** (B d DR GLM MA VS) 23-5h
Avda. Bethencourt Molina, 24 bajo
■ **D'Espanto** (B d DR GLM MA OS VS) 23-4h
Av. Bethencourt Molina, 24 *Edificio Drago*
■ **Vampi's** (B D GLM MA S SNU ST VS) Tue-Sun 24-7h
Av. Bethencourt Molina, 24 *Edificio Drago* ☎ 92 236 88 51
💻 www.discovampis.com

RESTAURANTS

■ **Mil Sabores** (AC GLM M WL)
C/. Cruz Verde, 5

SAUNAS/BATHS

■ **Laurent** (AC B DR DU G m MA MSG NU RR SA VS WE WH) 16-22h, closed Mon
C/. Iriarte, 37 ☎ 646 876 740 (mobile)
■ **Sauna Babylon** (AC B DR DU FC FH G I MA MSG RR SA SB VS WH) Mon-Fri 14-22, Sat 14-Sun 8h (non-stop)
C/. Blanco, 34 – Bajos Edif. Isla *Close to Plaza del Charco* ☎ 92 237 26 10
💻 www.saunababylon.com
A big Jacuzzi was added in November 2010.

GUEST HOUSES

■ **Villa Maspalmeras** (B BF CC f G OS PI RWS RWT VA WO)
All year
Vista Panorámica, 20 (Santa Ursula) ☎ 92 230 26 07
💻 www.villa-maspalmeras-tenerife.com
Stylish guest house with apartments and rooms in beautiful gardens with pool overlooking Puerto De La Cruz.

CRUISING

-Estación de guaguas
-Montaña del Amor (La Paz)
-Playa Martiánez
-Avenida de Colón (day and night)
-Plaza del Charco
-Playa Jardín/Castillo San Felipe.

Canary Islands – Tenerife – Santa Cruz

BARS

■ **Blue Dreams** (B DR G MA s VS) 22-?, WE -5h
C/. San Miguel, 14 ☎ 92 227 45 06
■ **Copita. La** (B D FC GLM OS)
C./ Candelaria, 8 *Zona La Noria*
■ **Jet Lag** (D FC GLM OS)
C./ Candelaria, 6 (Zona La Noria)

DANCECLUBS

■ **Discoteca Cirkus Tenerife** (B D DR G MA ST) Thu-Sat 24-6h
C/ Gáldar, 2 💻 www.grupocirkus.com

SEX SHOPS/BLUE MOVIES

■ **Fresas y Pitangas** (GLM)
C/ La Rosa, 32 ☎ 922 034 414 💻 www.fresasypitangas.com
■ **Fussion Sex** (GLM SH VR)
C/. La Equis, 11
■ **Momentos Love Shop** (GLM)
C/ Robayna, 3 💻 www.momentos-loveshop.com

■ **Sex Shop Luna** (P)
San Vicente Ferrer, 75 ☎ 922 29 13 58 🖳 www.lunasexshop.es

SAUNAS/BATHS

■ **Sauna Acuario** (DR DU G LAB MSG P R SA SB WH) 14-22h
C/ Santiago Beyro, 9

GENERAL GROUPS

■ **Algarabía** (GLM MA) Mon-Fri 10-14 & Fri -20h
C/. Heliodoro Rodríguez González Nº 10. Local Izqdo
☎ 638 790 420 – 922 882 188 (mobile) 🖳 www.algarabiatfe.org
Check website for current program.

HEALTH GROUPS

■ **Centro Dermatológico** (glm) Mon-Fri 8.30-14h
C/. San Sebastián, 75 ☎ 92 227 93 97
Information and help concerning AIDS.

SWIMMING

-Las Teresitas (take bus 914)
-Dársena Pescadora (Los Rusos)
-Benijos.

CRUISING

-Zona intercambiador de transportes
-Parque García Sanabria (r)

Cartagena

SEX SHOPS/BLUE MOVIES

■ **Sexyland** (g) 10-12h, Sun closed
C/. Sagasta, 55 ☎ 96 852 60 87

Córdoba

BARS

■ **Siena** (B BF g M MA OS) 19-1h
Plaza las Tendillas s/n ☎ 95 747 30 05

HOTELS

■ **Cortijo La Prensa. El** (AC B CC glm I M PI WH WO)
Arroyo de las Tijeras, Nacimiento de Zambra, Rute 14960
☎ 606 313 532 🖳 www.elcortijo-laprensa.com

GENERAL GROUPS

■ **Colegas Córdoba** (GLM)
C/. Duque de Hornachuelos, 12 ☎ 95 749 27 79
🖳 www.colegaweb.org
Meetings Thu 20h, Video-Forum Fri 21h.

CRUISING

-Parks Victoria (northern part) and Diego de Rivas (popular day and night) (MA)
-Park at Guadalquivir, Av. del Alcazar (at San Rafael bridge, popular)
-Ferial (near C/. Teresa de Córdoba y Hoces; at night car cruising)
-Los Naranjos (at Mesquita, some men, days only)
-Main railway station, Ronda de Cercadilla

Denia

GUEST HOUSES

■ **Residencia Luz del Mar** (B BF CC G I OS PA PI PK RWB RWS RWT VA) All year, 9-20h
Careterra Denia – Javea Nr 10 *500m from city centre, opp. Nautic Club*
☎ 96 642 2781 🖳 www.luzdelmar.com
Five suites with private bathrooms. Suitable for groups up to 20 people. Transfer service from Alicante/Valencia upon request.

Elche

SEX SHOPS/BLUE MOVIES

■ **Exzess** (AC DR G) 10.30-14h, 17-21h
Plazoleta de l'Espart, 10 ☎ 966 614 030 🖳 www.exzess-sexshop.com

Figueres

BARS

■ **Natural Men** (B D DR GLM MA OS s VS WE) 22-6h
Centre Aduana, Poligono Enporda, Vilamalla ☎ 972 52 60 39

SAUNAS/BATHS

■ **Termas Sauna Sparta** (AC B DR DU FH G m MA MSG NU RR SA SB VS WH) 15-22.30, Sat 16-5h
C/. Requesens, 18 *Near the railway station* ☎ 97 251 17 05
Interestingly mixed crowd as the sauna is just 20 km from the French-Spanish border. Popular among locals and tourists.

Fuengirola

BARS

■ **Kudos** (AC B DR F G I MA S SNU VS)
underwearparty Sun 17-23h, Mon 23-?h
Avenida Nuestro Padre Jesús Cautivo, 4 *antigua Avd. Jesús Santos Rein*
☎ 67 894 58 83
One of the oldest gay bars in Fuengirola. Special party nights. Call for details.

RESTAURANTS

■ **Olivos. Los** (B CC g M MA)
Av. Ramon y Cajal *Corner of C/. Martinez catena* ☎ 95 258 63 79
A smart restaurant in the city centre. Great menu with traditinonal and modern Spanish cuisine.

CRUISING

-Paseo Marítimo (between Caracola Restaurant and London Pub, including elevated promenade opp. London Pub; especially in summer)
-Right from the old castle.

Gijón

BARS

■ **Cánovas** (AC B DR G MA S SNU WE) 22-8h
C/. Menéndez Pelayo, 32 ☎ 985 360 066
■ **Phashion** (AC B GLM VS WE YC) 19-5.30h
C/. Ezcurdia 40, bajo
■ **Es Collection Cocktail Club** (B GLM ST WE) 22-3.30, Fri & Sat -5.30h, closed Mon & Tue
Corrida 2 ☎ 699 139 085 (mobile)
Italian cocktail bar.

DANCECLUBS

■ **Versus** (AC B D DR GLM MA VS) 21-?h
Av. del Llano, 5 *At the end of Paseo Segovia*
■ **Zeus** (AC B D DR GLM MA WE) 21-8h
C/. La Playa, 17 ☎ 653 409 020 (mobile)

SEX SHOPS/BLUE MOVIES

■ **Fantasias** (g VS) Mon-Sat 10-3, Sun 10-14 & 16-3h
C/. Ezcurdia, 49 ☎ 98 513 37 43 🖳 www.fantasiasxshop.com

GENERAL GROUPS

■ **Xente Gai Astur** (GLM)
Av. Pablo Iglesia, 83 ☎ 98 522 40 29 🖳 xega.org/xega

CRUISING

-Parque de Isabela la Católica
-Paseo de la Playa de San Lorenzo

Girona

BARS

■ **In & Out Music Club** (AC B D DR GLM MA OS SNU WE)
Ctra. Figueras, 1 ☎ 97 263 06 01

SEX SHOPS/BLUE MOVIES

■ **erotic planet** (g VS)
Ctra. Nacional II, 62, bajo *Located in La Jonquera* ☎ 972 55 58 69
🖳 www.fusionreaccion.es

GUEST HOUSES

■ **eXus natur** (bf GLM MA MSG SA SOL WH) Reception 14-23h
C/. Ponent 8, Fontclara *40 km from airport Girona Costa Brava*
☎ 972 634 159 🖳 www.exusnatur.com

CRUISING

-Railway station
-Plaza de la Independencia
-La Rambla

Granada

BARS

■ **Ambient XXL** (AC B d DR G MA s VS)
Sun-Thu 22.30-3.30, Fri & Sat 22.30-4.30h
C/. Montalbán, 13
■ **Fondo Reservado** (B D G MA S ST) 22.30-4.30h, Mon closed
Cuesta Santa Inés, 4 ☎ 95 822 10 24
Bar and discotheque. Fri&Sat night Drag shows
■ **Pub Infra Rojo** (AC B CC D GLM H MA S) 23.30-3, Fri & Sat -4h
Plaza de los Lobos 9
■ **Rincón de San Pedro** (B GLM MA) 16-4, WE -2h
C/. del Darro, 12
■ **Sal. La** (B gLm MA) 22-4h
C/. Santa Paula, 11
■ **Six Colours** (AC B GLM MA S VS WE) 16-4, june-july 21-4.30h
C/ Tendillas de Santa Paula, 6 ☎ 95 820 39 95 🖳 www.sixcolours.com
■ **Templo del Flamenco** (B D glm M MA S)
C/ Pemaleros Alto 41 *Near Puerto Elvira* ☎ (625) 821 073
🖳 www.templodelflamenco.com
Gay owned and managed Flamenco Dance Bar in a cave.
■ **Tic Tac** (AC B DR G MA VS) 19-3.30, Fri & Sat -5h
C/. Horno de Haza, 19 ☎ 958 29 63 66

DANCECLUBS

■ **Status** (B D GLM MA) Fri&Sat 0-7h
C. de los Frailes 5
■ **Zoo** (AC B D f G S ST t YC) Thu-Sat 1.30-7.30h
C/. Moras, 2 *Behind Teatro Isabel la Católica* ☎ 687 757 538 (mobile)
Straight-friendly gay disco in the center of Granada. Mixed, young crowd. Gets busy when other bars close. No cover b4 3h.

RESTAURANTS

■ **Gayedra** (AC CC GLM M MA S WE)
Wed-Sat 13.30-16.30 & 21-0.30, Sun & Thu 21-0.30h, Mon closed
C/. Tendillas de Santa Paula, 6 ☎ 95 820 74 37 🖳 www.gayedra.com
Innovative and young kitchen, also vegetarian meals, exotic and seafood.
■ **Puerta del Vino** (AC B BF glm M MA OS WE)
Summer: 18-2, winter: 12-2h
Paseo de los Tristes, 5 ☎ 95 821 00 26
🖳 www.granadainfo.com/tapichuela/puerta.htm

SEX SHOPS/BLUE MOVIES

■ **Sala X Cinema** (AC B cc DR G I NU) 10.30-1h
C/. Séneca 1 ☎ 630 854 204 (mobile)
🖳 salaxgranada.blogspot.com

SAUNAS/BATHS

■ **Boabdil** (AC B DR DU FC FH G MA RR SA SB VS) 16-22h, Tue closed
C/. El Trevenque S/N *Ctra. Sierra Nevada, C/ EL TREVENQUE, S/N*
☏ 95 822 10 73 💻 www.saunaboabdil.com
Nice, friendly and clean sauna which attracts a mixed crowd.

■ **Géminis** (AC B G MA MSG SA SB) daily 16-22h
C. Santa Cruz 2 ☏ (958) 805126

GUEST HOUSES

■ **Antinous** (G)
C/. Animas, 2 *Corner Cuesta Gomérez* ☏ 95 822 50 21
Unique accommodation in an Andalusian house.

CRUISING

-Paseo de Basilios (at the border of the river Genil, popular car cruising at night)
-Estación de autobuses
-Camino de Puchil, near „Puleva" factory (car cruising or by bike, by day only)

Graus

HOTELS

■ **Mesón Bodegas de Arnés**
(AC B cc glm M OS PA PK RWB RWS RWT VA) All year
Cruce a Panillo s/n *1 km north of Graus, 200m from the crossing of A-139 to Benasque & the road to Valle de la Fueva, near Buddhist temple*
☏ 97 454 03 00 💻 www.bodegasdearnes.com
Fourteen rooms and suites, additional bed possible, own keys. Restaurant.

Huelva

BARS

■ **Artemisa** (B GLM MA) 22-3h
C/. Puerto, 1

■ **Taller. El** (B G MA) 23.30-4h
Av. Cristobal Cólon, s/n *Under the arches of Plaza de Toros*

GENERAL GROUPS

■ **Colegas Huelva** (GLM) Meetings Fri 19h
C/. San José, 35 ☏ 95 928 49 55

Huesca

APARTMENTS

■ **Casa Juez** (bf glm H MA MSG OS WE) WE & holidays
C/. Única, 5 ☏ 656 581 986 (mobile) 💻 www.casajuez.com
Three apartments and common social area.

CRUISING

-Central bus station (C/. del Parque)
-Municipal park
-Around Hospital Provincial

Jaén

BARS

■ **Noche. La** (B D GLM p S SNU WE) Tue-Sat 23-6h, closed Sun & Mon.
Av. de Andalucía, 22 ☏ 95 327 30 34

Javea

SWIMMING

-Torre d'Ambolo (g NU) (C/. al cabo de la Nau)
-Playa de la Cumbre del Sol (g NU)

La Herradura

CAFES

■ **Luciano** (B glm MC)
Paseo Andrés Segovia ☏ 655 840 035 (mobile)

DECORATION

■ **Eleven Creative** (GLM)
El Enclave 4, Las Palomas ☏ 95 864 09 85 💻 www.elevencreative.com

EDUCATION SERVICES

■ **Centro de Enseñanza de Español La Herradura** (GLM)
Urb. El Camping, bajo Nº 3 ☏ 95 864 05 28

■ **El Mar** (glm)
Plaza San José, 3 ☏ 95 864 00 93 💻 www.languagescool.com
Language school.

PROPERTY SERVICES

■ **Karcher** (glm)
Paseo Andres Segovia, 20 ☏ 95 882 78 11
💻 www.inmobiliariakarcher.com

HOTELS

■ **Hotel Restaurant La Tartana** (B BF cc glm M OS PI PK RWB RWS RWT VA) Open all year except two weeks in Jan
Urb. San Nicolás *From Malaga on N 340, 100m before traffic lights*
☏ 95 864 05 35 💻 www.hotellatartana.com
La Tartana has seven double rooms and a suite, all around a central courtyard with fountain. All doors and beams are from a 16th century convent. Many gardens and terraces to sit and relax. Entire place for hire for private parties. Great views of the sea. Gay-friendly property. Restaurant with terrace with scenic views of the sea.

APARTMENTS

■ **Costa Tropical Villas & Apartments** (AC GLM H MA)
Casa Mariposa, C/. Navarra, 3 ☏ 95 864 05 04
💻 www.costatropicalvillas.com
A family business specialising in renting a small number of quality properties, located in the beautiful Spanish village of La Herradura on the Coast of Granada in Andalucia.

SWIMMING

- Playa del Muerto – between La Herradura and Almuñecar. Turn off the N340 to the right (Cotobro), on the very end of the beach. Also cruising
-Playa del Cantarijan (NU) (road to the Mirador Cerro Gordo, following the sign to the beach. Down at the beach are two bars. Behind the rocks on the left handside is the nudist beach. Cruising in the mountain behind)
-Playa la Joya (NU) (behind Motril direction Almería before the lighthouse).

León

RESTAURANTS

■ **Girola. La** (AC B CC d f glm M MA NR OS PA WE) 13.30-16, 21-23.30h
C/. Ave María, 2 *Near the cathedral, corner of C/. San Lorenzo*
☏ 98 727 05 69

CRUISING

-Jardines del Paseo de Papalaguinda
-Plaza del Ganado

Lleida

SEX SHOPS/BLUE MOVIES

■ **Eurovisex Sex Shop** (G VS) 10-22h
C/. Cristóbal de Boleda, 15 ☏ 97 326 78 34

GENERAL GROUPS

■ **Col·lectiu EAGLE** (GLM) Mon & Wed 19-20.30h
C/. Artur Mor, 1 ☏ 653284774 💻 www.espaieagle.org
Open House GLT. Youth Time Activities

CRUISING

-Campos Elíseos
-Campo Escolar
-Castillo

-Estación de Renfe
-Plaza Noguerola
-Parque La Mitjana
-Estación Autobuses

Lloret de Mar

BARS

■ **G-Bar** (AC B G MA VS) Apr-Sep 22-3h
C/. Migdia, 44 *On the beachfront* ☎ 97 236 71 89
Former „Incógnito" bar.

DANCECLUBS

■ **Arena Costa Brava** (AC B CC D GLM MA S SNU ST VS WE) Oct-May Fri-Sun 0-5h, Jun-Sep open daily
Pº Camprodrón y Arrieta, 35 ☎ 97 236 64 21 🖳 www.arenadisco.com
■ **Bubu. La** (AC B D GLM MA p S T VS) Mon-Thu 23-3, Fri & Sat 23-3.30h
C/. Areny, 33 ☎ 97 237 03 02

SEX SHOPS/BLUE MOVIES

■ **Lloret Sex Center** (AC glm VS)
Mon-Sat 10-13.30 & 16-21, summer 10-22h
C/. San Tomás, 19 ☎ 97 237 04 43

SWIMMING

-Boadella beach (g NU) (Busy and cruisy. There is a ferry from the town hall to this mixed beach. Gay part is on the left side of the docks. Mixed on the right side)
-Passeig Maritim/Trav. Venecia (Mixed beach in front of the bars)
-La Aguadilla (Take the boat to Blanes 1 station. No sand, but many cliffs and rocks. The cruising starts after the last ferry has left)

CRUISING

-Around the castle
-Bus station (daytime)
-behind Boadella beach in the bushes (daytime, very cruisy)

Logroño

SEX SHOPS/BLUE MOVIES

■ **Sex Shop Eurovisex** (G VS) Mo-Sa 10-22 & Su 12-22h
C/. Barrera, 18 ☎ 94 121 05 58 🖳 www.eurovisex.com

GENERAL GROUPS

■ **GYLDA – Gays y Lesbianas de Aquí** (GLM) Tue & Fri 20-22h
C/. Huesca 61, Bajo ☎ 94 122 67 62 🖳 www.gylda.org

Madrid

Madrid is the sparkling capital of an empire on which once the sun never set. The former splendour of the stern Castillian city blends seamlessly with the noisy chaos of a modern European metropolis. In a central, formerly run-down area around the Plaza Chueca, a gay quarter has been growing and flourishing for years, which in terms of its variety and breadth, stands almost alone in the world. Chueca has virtually become a lifestyle, just as San Francisco's Castro Street was in its day. For the Gay Pride events more then a million people gather here. Tourists only need to leave Chueca to visit the splendid sights and museums around Madrid. Outside the quarter there are some saunas, several mixed clubs which are part of the alternative scene in Lavapies, and several places where harder sex clubs are growing up. Saunas are popular in the afternoon; bars get going after midnight, and clubs after 3am. The beautiful town parks of Retiro and Casa del Campo are cruisy and worth visiting throughout the day and night.

Madrid ist die glanzvolle Hauptstadt eines Reichs, in dem zeitweise die Sonne nie unterging. Die alte Pracht kastilischer Strenge paart sich mit dem lärmenden Chaos einer modernen europäischen Metropole. In einer zentralen, ehemals heruntergekommenen Gegend um die Plaza Chueca herum wächst und gedeiht seit Jahren ein schwules Viertel, das in Dichte und Vielfalt weltweit fast einzigartig ist. Chueca ist ebenso zum Begriff eines Lebensstils geworden, wie seinerzeit die Castro Street in San Francisco. Zur Gay-Pide-Parade versammeln sich hier mittlerweile mehr als 1 Mio. Menschen. Der Tourist muss Chueca nur verlassen, wenn er Interesse an den herrlichen Sehenswürdigkeiten und Museen in und um Madrid hat. Außerhalb des Viertels liegen einige Saunen, einige eher gemischte Bars der Alternativszene in Lavapiés und einige Locations der sich gerade formierenden Szene von härteren Sexclubs. Die Saunen sind nachmittags belebt, in den Bars beginnt das Leben ab Mitternacht, in den Discos ab 3h morgens. Ganztägig cruisy und sehenswert sind die schönen Stadtparks Retiro und Casa del Campo.

Madrid est la capitale majestueuse d'un empire où jadis le soleil ne se couchait jamais. Le faste et la rigueur castillane du passé s'associe au chaos bruyant de la métropole européenne moderne. Dans le quartier délabré mais central de la Plaza Chueca s'est installé il y a plusieurs années un milieu gay devenu depuis florissant au point de devenir, de par sa densité et sa diversité, unique au monde. Chueca désigne ainsi aujourd'hui un style comme auparavant Castro Street à San Francisco. Plus d'un million de personnes viennent à assister chaque année au spectacles grandioses des Gay Pride. Le visiteur désireux de visiter les curiosités touristiques et les musées doit quitter Chueca, mais il trouvera encore des saunas, des bars plutôt mixtes du milieu alternatif de Lavapiés et quelques clubs récemment ouverts et plus hard. On ira au sauna plutôt l'après-midi, dans les bars après minuit et en boîte après 3 heures du matin. Les parcs municipaux de Retiro et de Casa del Campo sont très beaux et on peut y faire des rencontres!

Madrid es la espléndida capital de un imperio en el cual antiguamente nunca se ponía el sol. La vieja suntuosa sobriedad castellana se une con el ruidoso caos de una metrópolis europea moderna. En una zona céntrica antes marginada, alrededor de la plaza de Chueca, está creciendo y expandiéndose desde hace años un barrio gay que, por su densidad y diversidad, es casi único en el mundo. Chueca es ya un concepto de estilo de vida, como en su día lo fue Castro Street de San

THE CAGE

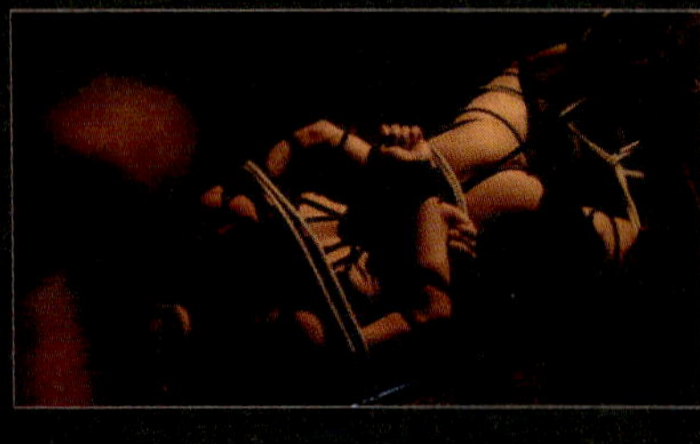

THE CAGE is a fetish bar. We are beyond the obvious. We try that everyone finds what they are looking for, and we like our patrons to be open and with imagination. And above all, participatory

Sex, however you like it, is important to us. But not the only thing. we can also appreciate the excitement in a chat or some laughs. Thats why we offer a play room but also today newspapers.

So you decide. Feel free and cage yourself in the atmosphere here, at The CAGE.

Tuesday

Customer's day

Friday

The Cage party

wednesday

Bondage session

Sunday

Private party

Check our blog for more info

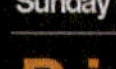

Thursday

Monthly Party

Check our blog for Thursday agenda

thecagemadrid.com // thecagemadrid.blogspot.com // San Marcos St. 11th

MADRID

Madrid – Map A

EAT & DRINK	
Cornucopia – Restaurant	22
El Rincon Guay – Bar	30
Museo Chicote – Bar	36
Tabata – Bar	26

NIGHTLIFE	
Angel. The –Danceclub	8
Attack Bar – Men's Club	13
Bangalá – Men's Club	33
Copper – Men's Club	6
Mad Hunter – Danceclub	2
Madness – Men's Club	32
Odarko – Men's Club	12
Paw. The – Men's Club	27
Shanghai – Danceclub	5
Strong Center – Danceclub	23

SEX	
Adán – Sauna	4
Adonis – House of Boys	28
Center – Sauna	25
Lavapies – Sauna	37
Octopus – Sauna	7
Paraíso – Sauna	1
Príncipe – Sauna	3

ACCOMMODATION	
Atrium Hostal – Hotel	17
Hostal Adriano – Hotel	29
Hostal Adria Santa Ana – Hotel	35
Hostal La Fontana – Hotel	16
Hostal La Zona – Hotel	14
Hostal Pizarro – Hotel	10
Hostal Puerta del Sol – Hotel	20

OTHERS	
Deffort – Shop	11
Open House – Health Centre	34

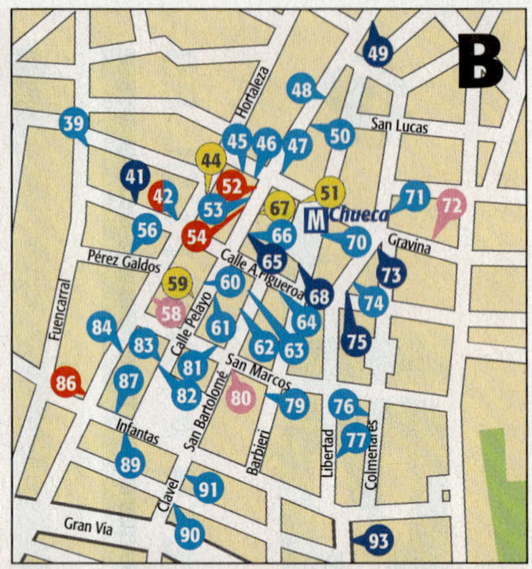

Madrid - Map B

EAT & DRINK

Armario. El - Restaurant	62
BAires - Café	46
Bears Bar	61
Bebop Café	70
Clip - Bar	45
Divina La Cocina - Restaurant	76
Colby - Restaurant	39
Cruising - Bar	56
D'mystic - Café	47
Enfrente - Bar	89
Figueroa - Café	42
FU3L - Bar	81
Hot - Bar	87
La Boheme - Bar	53
Leather - Bar	50
Lio - Bar	48
Liquid - Bar	79
LL Bar	60
Local - Bar	74
Mamá Inés - Café	84
Mangiami - Restaurant	83
Misadedoce - Bar	64
Momo - Restaurant	77
Paso. The - Bar	82
Rick's - Bar	91
Rimmel - Bar	71
Sama-Sama - Restaurant	63
Troje. La - Café	66
XXX Café	90

NIGHTLIFE

Black & White - Danceclub	73
Delirio - Danceclub	75
DLRO live - Danceclub	49
Eagle Madrid - Men's Club	65
Griffin's - Danceclub	93
Mito - Danceclub	41
Sachas - Danceclub	68

SEX

City Sex Store - Sex Shop	86
Cristal - Sauna	42
Men - Sauna	54
Play Sex Store	52

ACCOMMODATION

Ambiance Home Rooms - Private Accommodation	72
Dolcevita - Guest House	80
Hostal Hispano - Hotel	58

OTHERS

Berkana - Bookshop	44
Chueca Travel - Travel and Transport	51
Different Life. A - Bookshop	67
SR - Leather & Fetish Shop	59

Francisco. Para la manifestación del Orgullo Gay se reunen cada ano más de un millón de personas. El turista debe salir sólo de Chueca si quiere visitar además los fantásticos museos y otros puntos de interés de Madrid y sus alrededores. Fuera de este barrio, existen algunas saunas, algunos bares más bien mixtos del ambiente alternativo de Lavapiés y algunos locales del incipiente ambiente de sexo duro. Por la tarde, las saunas están más frecuentadas, en los bares la vida empieza a partir de la medianoche y en las discotecas, a partir de las 3 de la madrugada. Durante el día, los bonitos parques del Retiro y la Casa de Campo merecen una visita para el ligue (cruising).

Madrid è una meravigliosa città di un impero dove storicamente il sole non è mai tramontato. L'antico splendore del severo stile castigliano si accoppia armoniosamente al rumoroso caos di una moderna metropoli europea. Nella centrale Plaza Chueca, zona prima piuttosto fatiscente, c'è già da anni un quartiere gay che sta ingrandendosi sempre più e che per peculiarità e qualità è quasi unico al mondo. Chueca è diventato un sinonimo per un determinato stile di vita, come allora la Castro Street a San Francisco. In occasione del gay pride si contano qui più di un milione di persone. Il turista sente l'esigenza di lasciare la Chueca solo per andare a vedere i bellissimi monumenti e musei della città. Al di fuori del quartiere Chueca si trovano anche alcune saune; nella zona Lavapiés ci sono alcuni bar alternativi (per lo più misti). Inoltre sta crescendo sempre più una scena di locali hard (sexclubs). Le saune sono molto frequentate di pomeriggio. I bar cominciano a funzionare da mezzanotte in poi mentre le discoteche dalle 3 di mattina. Da vedere sono i parchi Casa del Campo e Retiro (specialmente per i turisti in cerca di cruising).

GAY INFO

Berkana, Libreria Bookshop (AC b CC GLM MA) 10.30-21, Sat 11.30-21, Sun 12-21h
C/. Hortaleza, 64 ☎ 91 522 55 99 🖳 www.libreriaberkana.com
Good information point for the gay scene. Free gay map of Madrid. Catalogue upon request. Also café.

Gay Inform / Linea Lesbos COGAM (GLM) Mon-Fri 17-21h
C/. Puebla 9, bajo ☎ 91 522 45 17 🖳 www.cogam.es
LGBT organization for Madrid.

PUBLICATIONS

Shangay (G)
Apartado 4023 ☎ 91 445 17 41 🖳 www.shangay.com
Free bimonthly gay paper listing all sites and venues in gay Madrid. Great information source on what's going on in the city.

BARS

A Noite (AC B d G MA R ST) 21-6; show 0.30h
C/. Hortaleza, 43 ☎ 91 531 07 15

Bears Bar (AC B F G MC VS) 18.30-2.30h, WE 3.30h
C/. Pelayo, 4 ☎ 647 50 30 33 🖳 www.bearsbar.net
BEARS BAR is located in the heart of the gay district of Chueca, is a meeting point for Bears, Chubs, Daddies, and Admirers.

Clip (B G MA) 20-2h
C/. Gravina, 8

Cruising (AC B D DR f G VS YC) 19-3, Fri-Sat -3.30h
C/. Pérez Galdós, 5 ☎ 91 521 51 43

Enfrente (AC B d DR f MC) 18h-?
C/. Infantas, 12 ☎ 687 791 462 (mobile)
🖳 www.facebook.com/pages/BAR-ENFRENTE/109737679050701
Same owners as Hot and Disco Angel.

FU3L (AC B CC d DR f G MA VS) 17-3, WE -3.30h
C/. San Marcos, 16 *M° Chueca* 🖳 www.fu3l.es
Bear bar, 2-4-1 with midnight special events Thu-Sun, check www.fu3l.es for current programme.

Hot (AC B DR F G MC s VS) 13-3h
C/. Infantas, 9
Small chatty upstairs bar. Darkroom with an open area and cubicles downstairs, not too dark. Special 2-4-1 daily from 18-24h.

La Bohème (AC B CC d GLM SNU ST) Wed-Sun 20.30-3.30h
C/. Pelayo, 31

Leather Club (B d DR f G MA VS) 18-3, Sat -3.30, summer 20-3h
C/. Pelayo, 42 ☎ 91 308 14 62 🖳 www.leathermadrid.es
Large maze like building with two darkrooms and several cubicles and cruising area, disco downstairs. No strict dresscode.

Lio (AC B d G MA) 20-2, WE -2.30h
C/. Pelayo, 58 🖳 es-es.facebook.com/barlio
241 all night. Owned & operated by bears.

Liquid (AC B CC G MA VS) Sun-Thu 21-3, Fri & Sat -3.30h
C/. Barbierri, 7 ☎ 91 523 28 08 🖳 www.liquid.es
Video bar; a great place to start the night with music videos.

LL Bar (B DR G MA S SNU VS) 18-?, show 23.30h
C/. Pelayo, 11 ☎ 91 523 31 21 🖳 www.interocio.es/LL/

Local (AC B CC d G YC) 17-3h
C/. Libertad, 28 ☎ 91 532 7610
DJ at the WE.

Misadedoce (AC B BF CC GLM M MA WE) Sun 17-2, Fri+Sat -2.30h
C/. Augusto Figueroa, 20 *Chueca* ☎ 91 522 82 88
Popular place of Chueca.

Mojito. El (B GLM MA) 21-2.30, Fri-Sat -3.30h
C/. del Olmo, 6 ☎ 915 311 141

Museo Chicote (AC B CC GLM M MA)
Gran Via, 12 ☎ 91 532 67 37 🖳 www.museo-chicote.com
Trendy and classic Cocktail bar from 1931. Art Deco Design and lots of famous people. Smart casual dress code.

Paso. The (AC B DR f G MA S VS) 18-3.30h
C/. Costanilla de Capuchinos 1 *M° Gran Vía / Chueca. At Plaza Vazquez de Mella* ☎ 91 522 08 88
Happy hour 2-4-1 daily 18-24h.Special show events on Fridays. Bears, chubbies chasers and admirers found here too. See their facebook page.

Rick's (B d G MA) 23-5.30, WE -?h
C/. Clavel, 8 ☎ 91 531 91 86
one of the classics to start the night. José Cobo is caring for his clients for more than 25 years by now

Rimmel (B DR G VS YC) 19-3h
C/. Luis de Góngora, 2

Rincon Guay. El (AC B bf CC GLM M MA OS) Daily 9-2h
C/. Embajadores, 62 *M° Lavapies/ Embajadores* ☎ (63) 061 93 77
🖳 www.facebook.com/pages/El-Rincon-Guay/72402289898
Cafeteria /Pub in the heart of Lavapies,open daily from 9-2h , nice place to have breakfast, a nice beer or tapas or to meet at any time the lost lover; wi-fi service. More info: www.elrinconguay.com

Tabata (B d G YC) Wed-Sat 23.30-?h
C/. Vergara, 12 ☎ 91 547 97 35 🖳 www.pubtabata.com

Tantalo
C/. Libertad, 14 ☎ 91 521 31 27 🖳 www.tantalo.es

Truco (AC B d gLm MA OS) Tue-Sun 16-3h
C/. Gravina, 10 ☎ 91 532 89 21

MEN'S CLUBS

800 Madrid (CC DR F G GH LAB m MA P S VS) Tue-Sun 13-24h
C/. de Cadarso, 3 ☎ 605 535 520 🖳 www.800madrid.com
Sex club with a contemporary art gallery on 300 m².

Attack (AC B CC DR F G MA NU P VS) Tue-Sun 21-3h
C/. Lavapies, 12 *M° Tirso de Molina/Lavapies*
🖳 www.attack-bar.com
Sex Club on two levels with cabins, st Andrew's cross, sling, cage, many toys and fetish gear for public use. Check website for current programme. English spoken.

BANGALÁ
EVERYDAY
NAKED PARTY
SEX CLUB
DARKROOM
GLORY HOLES
XXX PARTYS
VIDEOS...
C/DE LA ESCUADRA Nº1
METRO LAVAPIÈS-ANTÓN MARTÍN
WWW.BANGALAMADRID.COM

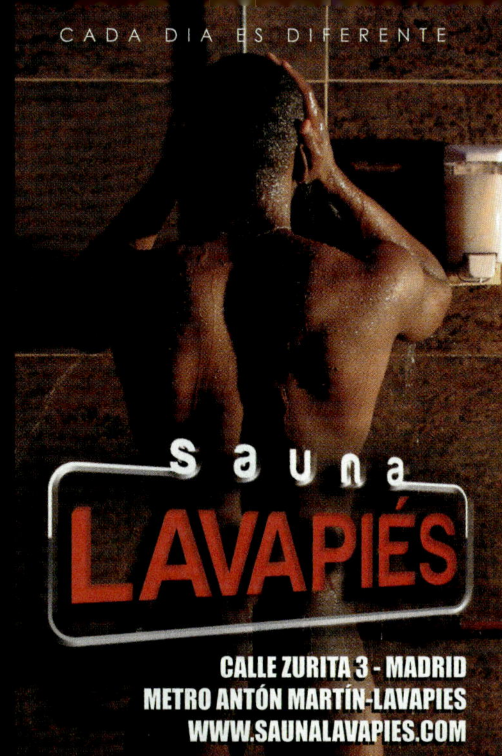
CADA DIA ES DIFERENTE
sauna
LAVAPIÉS
CALLE ZURITA 3 - MADRID
METRO ANTÓN MARTÍN-LAVAPIES
WWW.SAUNALAVAPIES.COM

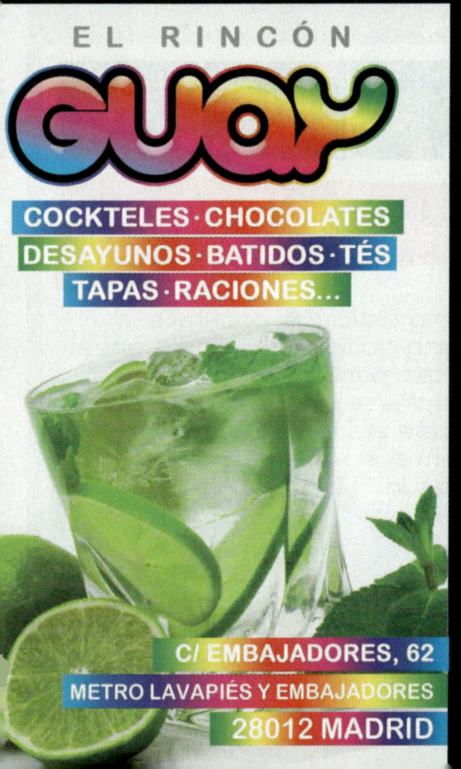
EL RINCÓN
GUAY
COCKTELES · CHOCOLATES
DESAYUNOS · BATIDOS · TÉS
TAPAS · RACIONES...
C/ EMBAJADORES, 62
METRO LAVAPIÉS Y EMBAJADORES
28012 MADRID

MAD
NESS
100% HOT MEN MEETING POINT
ENCUENTROS REALES
ZONA DE CRUISSING
GLORY HOLES • VIDEOS XXX
SLING • CABINAS
INTERNET GRATIS
Lunes fiestas especiales.
Martes, Miércoles, Jueves y Domingos de 16:00h a 24:00h.
Viernes, Sábados y vísperas de fiesta de 18:00 h a 02:00 h.
CALLE DE LOS TRES PECES, 30
METRO ANTON MARTIN Y LAVAPIES
28012 MADRID
WWW.MAD-NESS.ES

Bangalá (AC B DR G GH MA NU p VS) 21-3h
C/. Escuadra, 1 www.bangalamadrid.com
A nudist bar in Lavapie's multiracial atmosphere, open daily from 21:00 h. to 02:30 h, offers bar, video, cabins, glory holes, dark room, and wi-fi service. Different parties are held every day. For more information visit the web: www.bangalamadrid.com. Entrance ticket includes one drink.

Cage, The (F G)
San Marcos, 11 thecagemadrid.blogspot.com
New leather and fetish bar.

Copper (AC B DR F G MA P VS) 14-3h, Fr & Sa -3.30h
C/. San Vicente Ferrer, 34 www.copperbarmadrid.com
Naked or underwear. Improved installations: sling with mirror etc, free coffee.

Eagle Club (! AK B DR F G MA P SL VS) 18-3.30h
C/. Pelayo, 30 *Chueca* www.eaglespain.com
Special offers for beers and rinks from 6pm. Great music. Fetish bar with dress code and special party events on Wed-Fri. Porno videos. Bar for leather fetish, military, rubber, uniform, industrial, skin, sports and more.

Hell (B DR G MA P VS WE) Tue-Thu 22.30-2.30, Fri & Sat -3.30h
C/. de Buenavista 14 www.hellsexclub.com
Visit www.hellsexclub.com for tickets.

Into the Tank (! AC AK DR F FC G GH LAB MA SL VR VS)
☎ 915 229 251 www.intothetank.org
Big fetish event, organised several times a year by the Odarko's boys. Check www.intothetank.org or ask in Odarko Bar.

Madness (AC B DR G GH MA p SL VR VS WE WI) 16-24, WE 18-2h
C/. de los Tres peces 30 *M° Anton Martín / Lavapies. Bus 6, 26,32. In the center of Madrid next to the museum-area, in the heart of Lavapies*
www.mad-ness.es
Lavapie's new meeting point. No dress code, special opening hours from 16 to 24h and weekends from 18 to 02h with sling, cabins, dark room, cross of punishment, colts, free internet, videos and many more possibilities for your fantasies.

Odarko (AC B cc D DR F G MA p VS) Mon-Sat 22-4.30, Sun 18-4.30h
C/. Loreto y Chicote, 7 *Callao – Gran Via* ☎ 91 522 92 51
www.odarko.com
Strict dress code.

Paw. The (B CC DR G MC NU P VS) Mon-Sat 18-?, Sun 17-?h
C/. Calatrava, 29 ☎ 91 366 60 93 www.thepaw.es

Xtrem (B F G MC NU P) 18-3, Sat & Sun 14-3h
C/. Valverde, 3 *Entrance: C/ Desengaño nº 2*
Dress codes apply.

CAFES

B Aires (AC B CC GLM I m MA s) 15-2h
C/. Gravina, 4 ☎ 91 532 98 79
WiFi available.

Bebop (B BF G m OS) 9-2h, WE-2.30h
Plaza Chueca, 9 ☎ 915 219 879
Breakfast and cocktails.

D'Mystic (AC B BF CC G M) 9.30-2, Fri & Sat -2.30h
C/. Gravina, 5 *M° Chueca* ☎ 91 308 24 60

Figueroa (B GLM m MA) 12-1.30, Fri-Sat -2.30h
C/. Augusto Figueroa, 17 ☎ 91 521 16 73

Mama Inés (AC B BF G M MA) 9.30-1.30h
C/. Hortaleza, 22 *M° Gran Vía/Chueca* ☎ 91 523 23 33
www.mamaines.com
More BF variety, daily menu, homemade food, cocktails, fresh juice, ice cream, cakes, sandwiches and more.

Troje Café. La (AC B GLM m MA s) 17-2, WE -2.30h
C/. Pelayo, 26 ☎ 91 531 05 35

XXX Café (AC B BF CC G m MA s) 13-2, Fri-Sat 17-1, show Thu 23.30h
C/. Clavel ☎ 91 532 84 15

DANCECLUBS

Angel. The (B F G MA) Sun, Wed & Thu 24-6, WE -6.30h
C/. Campoamor, 11
The bears' disco. Wed, Thur & Sun entrance fee includes two drinks.

Black & White (B D G MA R SNU VS) Mon-Fri 20-5, Sat & Sun -6h
C/. Libertad, 34 ☎ 91 531 11 41 www.discoblack-white.net
Thu-Sun 3h ST.

Bunker Bears Club @ Sugar Cool (B D f G MA) Sat 24-6h
C/. Isabel La Católica, 6 ☎ 90 249 99 94

Cool (AC B CC D G MA S WE) Sat 24-6h
C/. Isabel la Católice, 6 ☎ 90 249 99 94
Stylish club with two dancefloors (big: house, smaller: disco) and a lounge.

Delirio (AC B CC D G MA S VS) 23-5.30h
C/. Libertad 28, Chueca ☎ 91 531 18 70 www.deliriochueca.com
Former „Truck" bar. Gogo boys daily.

DLRO Live (AC B CC D G MA ST) 23.30-2h, Fri, Sat, Sun – 5.30h
C/. Pelayo, 59 *M° Chueca*
more Delirio: cocktails, gogos, british pop & electronic music

Escape (AC B D GLM MA s) 0-6h
C/. Gravina, 13 ☎ 915 325 206 www.escapechueca.com
Check local press for events.

Griffin's (AC B D G MC S WE) 23-5, Fri & Sat -6h
C/. Marqués de Valdeiglesias, 6 ☎ 91 522 20 79
www.griffins.com.es
On three floors with bar, lounge and dancefloor.

Kluster @ Paddock (D f G)
Paseo de Recoletos, 16 klustermadrid.blogspot.com
Only +18 entrance.

L.O.A. (B D G MA)
C/. Madrid 3

Mad Hunter (AC B CC D f G MA S WE) Thu-Sun 24-6h
C/. Pelayo 80-82 *M° Chueca/ Alonso Martínez*
www.madhunterclub.com
Club in chueca with 2 dancefloors.

Mito (AC B D GLM MA r S t) 23-6.30h
C/. Augusto Figueroa, 3 ☎ 91 532 88 51 www.discomito.com

Priscilla (AC B CC D g MA) 19-3, Fri-Sat -5h
C/. San Bartolomé, 6 *M° Gran Vía*

■ **Sachas** (AC B D GLM OS r ST) Bar next door daily 20-3, disco only Thu-Sun 20-2.30h
Plaza Chueca, 1

■ **Shangai Club** (AC B CC D G MC S WE) Fri-Sat 24-6h
Costanilla de los Angeles 20 *M° Callao/ Opera/ Santo Domingo. Close to Plaza Santo Domingo* ☎ (91) 547 93 94 🖳 www.shangaiclub.com
For current programme check website.

■ **Space of Sound @ Macumba** (AC B CC D G S WE)
Sun 0-6h
Estación de Chamartín, s/n ☎ 90 249 99 94
🖳 www.spaceofsound.com
Gogo dancers on Sun. Further details see www.spaceofsound.com.

■ **Strong Center** (B D DR f G MA SNU) 24-6h
C/. Trujillos, 7 ☎ 91 541 54 15 🖳 www.strong-center.com

RESTAURANTS

■ **Armario. El** (AC CC DM GLM M MA WE) 13.30-16, 21-24h
C/. San Bartolomé, 7 *M° Chueca* ☎ 91 532 83 77
🖳 www.elarmariorestaurante.com
Superb food at lunchtime. The evening meals are very refined. Book ahead for dinner on Fri & Sat.

■ **Colby** (AC CC DM G M MA VEG WL) Mon-Thu 9.30-1.30, Fri-Sat 9.30-2.30, Sun 11.30-1, kitchen 10-24.30h
C/. Fuencarral, 52 *M° Tribunal* ☎ 91 521 25 54
🖳 www.restaurantecolby.com
The menu is extensive, with a choice between set menu and à la carte, with a range from pizzas to creative dishes with fish and meat. Second branch in C/. Vergara, 12, M° Opera. Third branch at 35, Paseo Imperial.

■ **Cornucopia** (AC CC DM g H M NR OS VEG WL) Daily 12-24h
C/. Navas de Tolosa, 9 ☎ 91 521 38 96
🖳 www.restaurantecornucopia.com
Creative cuisine which merges traditions and ingredients of different countries. Dining rooms are decorated with art exhibitions.

■ **Divina la Cocina** (AC CC DM GLM M MA RES WE WL) 13.30-16, 21-24, Fri & Sat -1h
C/. Colmenares, 13 ☎ 91 531 37 65 🖳 www.divinalacocina.com
Since more than ten years famous for its delicious cuisine and beautifully decorated desserts.

■ **Mangiami** (AC CC G M) 12-16.30 & 20-1.30h
Costanilla Capuchinos, 3 ☎ 91 521 32 77
Small, but stylish Pizzeria. Homemade Pizza, salads and deserts; also takeaway.

■ **Momo** (AC CC glm M) 14-16h, 21-24h
C/. Libertad, 8 ☎ 91 532 7348
Special set menus for lunch (11€), dinner (15€) and WE (17€)

■ **Samá-Samá** (AC CC GLM MA WE)
13.30-15.45 & 21.15-23.45h, closed Sun & Mon (evening)
C/. San Bartolomé, 23 ☎ 91 521 55 47
🖳 www.restaurantesamasama.es
Pleasant and relaxed atmosphere. Chillout and jazz music. Colonial decor. Friendly staff and excellent meals.

SEX SHOPS/BLUE MOVIES

■ **Amantis** (CC g) Mon-Sat 10.30-22, Sun 16.30-21h
C/. Pelayo, 46 ☎ 91 702 05 10 🖳 www.amantis.net

■ **B 43 Gay Shop** (CC G MA p)
11-14, 16-22, Sun 16-22; summer 11-14, 17-22, Sun 17-22h
C/. Barco, 43

■ **Chuecacenter** (CC F G) 11-14.30 & 17-21.30h
C/. Hortaleza, 31 ☎ 91 532 81 91
Sex shop with DVD's and much more!

■ **City Sex Store** (AC CC G) Daily 11-22h
C/. Hortaleza, 18 ☎ 91 181 27 23 🖳 www.citydvd.biz

■ **Fantasias** (g VS) Mon-Sat 10-3, Sun 10-14 & 16-3h
C/. Sta. Maria Micaela, 4 ☎ 91 599 42 10
🖳 www.fantasiasxshop.com

■ **Play Sex Store** (AC CC G VS)
Mon-Sat 11-21.30, Sun 12.30-21.30h
C/. Pelayo, 31 *M° Chueca* ☎ 91 523 08 41
With 35 films to view and 8 cubicals.

HOUSE OF BOYS

■ **Adonis Madrid** (AC b CC G MSG R VS) 24hrs
☎ 639 442 457
Always boys available. All rooms with showers/bathroom.

SAUNAS/BATHS

■ **Adán** (B DR DU G MA MSG PI R SA SB VS) 24hrs
C/. San Bernardo, 38 *M° Noviciado* ☎ 91 532 91 38
🖳 www.saunasmadrid.com
Many rent boys!

■ **Center** (b DR DU FH G m MSG RR SA SB SOL VS WO) 24hrs
Cuesta de Santo Domingo, 1 *M° Opera / Santo Domingo*
☎ 91 542 45 70
A really huge sauna which is not easily to fill with people. Some reports about dirty facilities.

■ **Cristal** (b DR DU G m MA MSG PI r SA SB VS) 15-3h
C/. Augusto Figueroa, 17 *M° Chueca* ☎ 91 531 44 89
🖳 www.saunasmadrid.com
Busy on WE.

Men (B DR DU FH G MA SA SB VS)
15-8, Fri 15.30-Mon 8h (non-stop)
C/. Pelayo, 25 ☎ 91 531 25 83 www.saunamen.es
Very small but at times cruisy though.

Octopus (AC B DR DU F G I MA MSG PI SA SB VS WH) 13-24h
C/. Churruca, 10 *M° Tribuna / Bilbao* ☎ 91 445 17 88
www.mundoplacer.com
A beautifully decorated sauna. International ambiance. English spoken. Discount with flyer.

Paraíso (AC B DR DU F FC G MA MSG PI SA SB SOL VS WH) 13-24, Fri 13-Sun 24h (non-stop)
C/. Norte, 15 *M° Noviciado / Plaza de España* ☎ 91 522 58 99
www.mundoplacer.com
A beautiful, fully air-conditioned sauna with a typical Spanish ambience. Internet service available. English spoken.

Premium Sauna (B DR DU G I MA SA SB WH) Mon-Fri 15-23, Sat, Sun & pub holidays 3-23h
C/. Costanilla de los Ángeles, 5 *Zona Opera* ☎ 911 155 411
www.premiumsauna.com

Príncipe (! AC B DR DU G I m MA MSG RR SA SB VS WH) 12-24h
C/. Travesía de Beatas, 3 *M° Noviciado / Plaza de España* ☎ 91 559 02 59
www.mundoplacer.com
A sauna for bears and their admirers. The staff are friendly. Lots of chill-out areas with sofas and a porn room. Clean and well maintained. Busy from 16h.

Puerta de Toledo (DU G OC RR SB) 14-24h
C/. Cuesta de las Descargas, 6 *M° Puerta de Toledo* ☎ 91 365 90 95
www.saunapuertadetoledo.com
Best before 19h. Clean, but very small gay sauna. Clientele mainly 40+.

Sauna Lavapies (B CC G MSG SA SB VS WH WI) 24hrs
C/. Zurita 3 *M° Anton Martín / Lavapies. Close to Reina Sofía Museum -Sol-Atocha-Lavapies area* www.saunalavapies.com
The only sauna in the neighbourhood. Open 24/7, it offers 400m2 for action: bar, turkish bath, Finnish sauna, Jacuzzi, relaxation cabins, massages, dark room and free internet.

FITNESS STUDIOS

V 35 (AC CC g YC) 8.30-23, Sat 10-22h, Sun closed
Valverde, 35 ☎ 91 523 93 52
Also rates per day.

BOOK SHOPS

Berkana, Libreria Bookshop (AC b CC GLM MA) 10.30-21, Sat 11.30-21, Sun 12-21h
C/. Hortaleza, 64 ☎ 91 522 55 99 www.libreriaberkana.com
Good information point for the gay scene. Free gay map of Madrid. Catalogue upon request. Also café.

Different Life. A (CC GLM) 10.30-21.30h
C/. Pelayo, 30 ☎ 91 532 96 52 www.lifegay.com
Books and DVD's.

Life Gay (G SH)
C/. Pelayo 30 ☎ 91 532 96 52 www.lifegay.com
Bookstore & sex shop.

LEATHER & FETISH SHOPS

Boxer Madrid (G SH)
C/. Pelayo 3

Deffort (AC CC F G) Mon-Sat, 1st Sun/month 17-21h
C/. Loreto y Chicote 10 ☎ 91 522 50 60 www.deffort.com
Men's store specialized in military, sports and fetish gear. Franklin&Marshall, Fred Perry, Ben Sherman, Schott NYC, etc

Industrial Gay. El (CC G)
C/. Hortaleza, 31 ☎ 91 532 81 91
Make and import clothing for the leather, army military and bears scene.

SR (F G) 11-14 & 17-21, Sun 16-21h
C/. Pelayo, 7 ☎ 91 523 19 64 www.sr-shop.com
Leather and fetish.

TRAVEL AND TRANSPORT

Chueca Travel (CC GLM) 10-13.30, 17-20h
C/. Gravina 25 ☎ 91 532 83 76 www.ctpviajes.com

HOTELS

Atrium Madrid (AC BF CC glm MA) All year
C/. Valverde, 3, 3ª planta, Chueca *M° Gran Vía* ☎ 91 523 47 78
www.atriummadrid.es

Hostal Adria Santa Ana (AC H RWS RWT WI) Check-in & reception desk 24 hours: C/. de la Cruz, 26, 4º piso (at Hostal Adriano)
C/. Nuñez de Arce 15 – 3º piso *Mº Sol* ☎ 91 521 13 39 ☎ 91 521 56 12
www.hostaladriasantaana.com
Great location and great prioe.

Hostal Adriano (AC CC glm I MA PK RWB RWS RWT VA) All year
C/. de la Cruz, 26, 4 *M° Sol* ☎ 91 521 13 39 www.hostaladriano.com
Only 150m from Puerta del Sol and Plaza Mayor. Completely refurbished. 22 bright and comfortable single, double, triple and quadruple rooms with private bathrooms and internet access.

Hostal Hispano (AC CC glm I OS RWB RWS RWT) All year
C/. Hortaleza, 38, 2° *M° Chueca/Gran Vía; bus 3,40,149* ☎ 91 531 48 71
☎ 91 531 28 98 www.hostalhispano.com
In the gay area. 21 guest rooms with bath/WC, phone & TV.

Hostal La Fontana (bf CC GLM I PA RWB RWS RWT VA) All year
C/. Valverde, 6, 1° *M° Gran Vía* ☎ 91 521 84 49
www.hostallafontana.com
17 rooms, 15 with bath/WC; bf incl.; internet, heating, ceiling-fans, .

Hostal La Zona (AC BF CC G I RWB RWS RWT VA) All year
C/. Valverde 7, 1° & 2° *M° Gran Vía* ☎ 91 521 99 04
www.hostallazona.com
Gay owned and run with WiFi throughout. Ten double bedded, and four twin-bedded rooms. All rooms have their own bathroom and TV. Non-smoking rooms and apartments available, too.

Hostal Odesa (AC CC G I MA RWS RWT WI) All year
C/. Hortaleza, 38, 3° Izda. ☎ 91 531 01 24 www.hostalsonsodesa.com
Twelve rooms with own bath, TV, Tel. Visa/Mastercard accepted. Safe & Fax service available. Also apartments.

Hostal Pizarro (AC BF CC GLM I OS PA RWS RWT WI)
Reception 8-22h
C/. Pizarro, 14, 1° *Noviciado, Callao, Gran Vía* ☎ 91 531 91 58
www.hostalpizarro.eu
Quality accommodation hostal in a modern building. 20 guestrooms with private baths, safe and more.

Hostal Puerta del Sol (AC BF cc GLM I M OS RWB RWS VA) All year
Puerta del Sol, 14, 4° *City centre* ☎ 91 522 51 26
www.hostalpuertadelsol.com

Oporto (cc glm) 24h
C/. Zorrilla 9, 1° ☎ 91 429 78 56 www.hostaloporto.com

GUEST HOUSES

Alaska Hostal (glm RWS RWT) All year
C/. Espoz y Mina, 7, 4° Derecha ☎ 91 521 18 45
www.hostalalaska.com

Casa Chueca (AC CC G I MC RWB RWS RWT VA) All year
C/. San Bartolomé, 4, 2°, izq. ☎ 91 523 81 27 www.casachueca.com

Chueca Pensión (cc glm I OS)
C/. Gravina, 4, 2°, dcha ☎ 91 523 14 73 www.chuecapension.com

Colors Host (AC CC DU glm H I RWB RWS RWT VA) Reception 24h
C./ Fuencarral, 39, 4°, izq. *M° Gran Vía, Tribunal* ☎ 915 214 646
www.colorshost.com
centrally located in the gay area, nicely furnished in bright colors, free WIFI, computer terminal, english spoken.

Dolcevita (cc glm I) All year
C/. San Bartolomé, 4, 3° *M° Chueca* ☎ 91 522 40 18
www.hospedajedolcevita.com
Most of the 19 guestrooms with private bathroom. Breakfast included in the room rate.

APARTMENTS

■ **Apartamentos Hispano** (AC CC G OS RWS)
C/. Hortaleza, 38, 2°, 8 ☎ 91 531 48 71 ☎ 91 531 28 98
🖳 www.hostalhispano.com
Apartments can accommodate 2, 3 or 4 people.

■ **Apartamentos Odesa** (AC cc G)
C/. Hortaleza, 38 – 3° Izda. ☎ 91 531 01 24
🖳 www.hostalsonsodesa.com

■ **Benignus** (AC B BF CC G I) 24h
C/. Valverde 4 *M° Gran Via* ☎ 638 853 802
🖳 www.apartamentosbenignusmadrid.com
Centrally located, fully equipped apartments in gay scene for up to 3 persons. Preferable reserve trough www.pases.es

■ **Chuecahome** (AC BF cc g I OS)
Plaza de Chueca,3 1°Exterior *M° Chueca* 🖳 www.chuecahome.com
Beautiful two bedroom-apartment, enjoy the charming view from the living room and the double bedroom balcony, both looking out onto Chueca Square.

■ **Accord Suites & Rooms** (glm I MA RWB RWS RWT VA) 24hrs
Valverde 32, 4° Izq. *M° Chueca* ☎ 91 522 96 37
Extended-stay residence. Minimum one week stay.

PRIVATE ACCOMMODATION

■ **Ambiance Home Rooms** (cc GLM)
C/. Gravina, 25 ☎ 617 731 355 (mobile) 🖳 www.chuecatravel.com
A small but attractive gay lodging with three double and two single rooms with private facilities.

GENERAL GROUPS

■ **Asociación RQTR** (GLM MA T VS) Mon-Fri 17-19.30h
Fac. CC. Políticas y Sociología, Universidad Complutense, Campus Somosaguas, Pozuelos ☎ 91 394 28 28 🖳 www.rqtr.org
Association for lesbians, gays, bisexuals and transsexuals.

■ **Colectivo Lesbianas, Gays, Transexuales y Bisexuales de Madrid (COGAM)** (GLM) Mon-Fri 17-21
C/. Puebla 9, bajo ☎ 91 522 45 17 🖳 www.cogam.es

HEALTH GROUPS

■ **Centro Medico Open House** (AC b CC GLM MSG) Mon-Fri 17-20h
C/. Atocha, 117, 1° ☎ 91 429 49 59 🖳 www.openhouse.com.es
General medicine & psychology, rapid diagnosis, relaxed atmosphere.

SWIMMING

- Piscina del Lago (Casa del Campo, M° Lago)
- Piscina La Elipa (M° Estrella, nudist sunterrace area)

CRUISING

-Estación de Chamartín (r)
-Estación de Atocha, Cercanía-station, WC entrepiso (very popular)
-FNAC (Plaza Calao, toilets 5th floor)
-Corte Inglés shopping centre 1.Sol, 2.Goya, 3.Castellana
-La Vaguada shopping centre (downstairs, next to the Disney shop, M° Barrio del Pilar. Popular)
-Parque del Retiro (near sports zone; popular daytime, at night AYOR. M° Atocha-Renfe)
-C/. del Almirante (R)
-C/. del Prim (R)
-Plaza de Toros, Monumental, Parking (M° Ventas, car-cruising from 22h, very popular)
-Av. de América (C/. de Cartagena, out of town, right side. Car-cruising from 22h, popular)
-Parque Atenas (at night)
-Templo de Debod (at night)
-Casa de Campo (in the surrounding wood of Teleférico (cable railway) ground parking. 24h. At night: AYOR)

Málaga

BARS

■ **El Carmen** (B G MA)
Plaza de la Merced 12 ☎ 952 210 924 💻 www.elcarmengaybar.com
■ **Reinas** (AC B GLM MA) Thu-Sun 23-?h
C/. Molina Lario, 5 ☎ 692 047 253
■ **Telón** (AC B bf G m MA OS) 10-3h
Plaza de la Merced, 18

CAFES

■ **Calle de Bruselas** (AC B BF g m MA OS) Sun-Thu 21-2, Fri & Sat 21-3h
Plaza de la Merced, 16 ☎ 95 260 39 48
■ **Flor de Lis** (AC B BF G m MA OS) 9.30-4, Sun 12-4h
Plaza de la Merced, 18 ☎ 95 260 98 19

SEX SHOPS/BLUE MOVIES

■ **Amsterdam** (AC g VS)
C/. Duquesa de Parcent, 1
■ **Pikante** (G VS) 10-3h
C/. Muelle de Heredia, 12 ☎ 95 222 15 83 💻 www.pikante.com
Cubicals with glory holes. Large range of DVDs as well as toys, leather and much more!
■ **Sex Shop** (g VS) 11-22h
Plaza Bailén, 2 ☎ 95 239 06 62

HOTELS

■ **Bandolero** (B glm I M PA PI PK RWB RWS RWT VA) Restaurant & bar closed on Tue
Avenida Havaral, 43, Júzcar *Eastern end of the village* ☎ 952 183 660
💻 www.hotelbandolero.com

GUEST HOUSES

■ **Donkey House. The** (AC bf CC GLM MA NU OS PI)
C/. Aptdo 85, Coin ☎ 95 245 17 29 💻 www.thedonkeyhouse.com
■ **Finca La Maroma** (G MA MSG PI SA WH WI WO) All year
Cerro Panadero s/n, Sedella *50 mins drive from Málaga* ☎ 958 069 030
💻 www.fincalamaroma.com
Finca La Maroma offers 6 luxurious self catering studio apartments for gay men and friends.

APARTMENTS

■ **Apartment Borzoi, Estepona** (AC cc g NU p) Office: Mon-Sat 10-22h
Casa 225, Los Llanos de Estepona ☎ 95 279 83 05
💻 www.borzoi.iowners.net
Two bedroom, one bathroom apartment in shared villa in a peaceful area of Estepona. Private pool, garden and chillout area.
■ **Finca Fénix** (AC glm I MA OS PI PK RWB RWS RWT VA WO)
Cuesta Del Río 26, Alora *Alora, 40km northwest of Málaga*
☎ 95 249 81 76 💻 www.fincafenix.com
Comfortable apartment with two double rooms and all modern amenities.

CRUISING

-Paseo del Parque (AYOR) (nights)
-Jardines de Puerta Oscura (AYOR r)
-Campo de Golf beach (8 km from Málaga and Torremolinos, car cruising at night)
-Train station (AYOR, r).

Marbella

BARS

■ **Boccacio Inn** (B G MA VS) 23.30-?h
C/. Puerto del Mar, 7 ☎ 95 277 5215
■ **Gruta. La** (AC B D G MA S)
Av. El Fuerte, Edf. Torre de Marbella
Gay friendly bar near beach of Marbella.

RESTAURANTS

■ **Garum** (B CC glm M MA VEG) Daily 11-24h
Paseo Maritimo / Av. de la Fontanilla ☎ 95 285 88 58
💻 www.garummarbella.com
restaurant on seafront with fantastic views and great food.

Murcia

BARS

■ **Bacus** (AC B DR G OC p ST VS) 19-2.30, show Sun 21.30h, Tue closed
C/. Isidoro de la Cierva, 5, B3 ☎ 616 338 355
💻 www.backvs.com/backvs.html
■ **Maricoco** (B GLM YC)
C/. Vitorio 5
■ **Piscis Disco Bar** (AC B D DR GLM MA p s VS) 22-4h, show Sun
C/. Enrique Villar, 13 ☎ 96 823 89 62
Disco, video, surprise shows. Popular.
■ **Sentio, El** (B GLM MA)
C/. Luisa Aledo 14
■ **Temperatura Ambiente** (B GLM MA)
C/. Victorio 9 *At the corner C/. Paco*
■ **Vie en Rose. La** (AC B DR G MA VS) 20-3h
Rincón de Santo Domingo, 7 ☎ 600 416 253

DANCECLUBS

■ **L.O.A.** (B D G MA)
C/. Madrid 3
■ **Metropol** (! AC B D DR GLM MA OS S SNU ST VS) Thu-Sun 2-6h
Ctra. Puente de Tocinos, C/. Portada s/n ☎ 96 824 85 00
💻 www.metropoldisco.com
Very large disco on three floors. Very popular in entire region, especially at WE. SNU on Fri, ST on Sun. All shows at 3h.

SEX SHOPS/BLUE MOVIES

■ **Master's** (g VS) 10-14, 16-22h
C/. Mariano Ruiz Funes, 5 ☎ 96 824 28 39
■ **Sexyland** (DR G VS) 10.30-1h
C/. Los Bolos, 1 ☎ 968 243 821 💻 www.fusionreaccion.es
New branch in Av. Gral. Primo de Rivera, 9.

SAUNAS/BATHS

■ **Nordik Sauna Masculina** (! B DR DU FH G MA RR SA SB VS) 14-21h
C/. Cartagena, 72 ☎ 96 825 91 20
💻 www.saunanordik.com/murcia.htm
■ **Ulises** (AK B DR DU FH G LAB MA SA SB SOL VS WH) 15.30-22, Sat -3h
C/. Madre Elisea Oliver Molina s/n *In front of the health care centre*
☎ 96 893 30 55 💻 www.saunaulisesmurcia.tk

BOOK SHOPS

■ **Libreria Encuentros** (AC CC GLM) 10-13.30 & 17-20.30h
C/. Mariano Vergara, 17 ☎ 86 807 82 05

GUEST HOUSES

■ **Almond Tree Villa** (BF GLM M OS PI PK RWS) Mar-Dec
Dip.Zarzalico, 1, Buzon 14, *5kms from Autovia A91 between Puerto Lumbreras and Velez Rubio* ☎ 606 202 963
💻 www.almondtreevilla.com
Experience the peace and tranquillity at this gay-friendly guesthouse in the countryside with fab views and clothing optional pool area. Great value gourmet meals with wine.

HEALTH GROUPS

■ **Consejería de Sanidad** (glm) Mo-Fr 9-14h
Ronda de Levante, 11 ☎ 96 823 51 41 💻 www.murciasalud.es
Anonymous HIV-testing.

CRUISING

- Monte de Fuensanta behind the Santuario Fuensanta between Akgezares & La Alberca in the hills, nice landscape & great sunsets!
-Paseo del Malecón (AYOR) (gardens, popular at night)
-C/. de Luis Fontes Pagan (car-cruising).
-El Corte Inglés shopping center.
-Central bus & train Station.

Oviedo

BARS

■ **Olympo** (AC B D DR GLM MA VS) 21-8h
C/. Campoamor, 19 ☎ 98 520 34 05
■ **Santa Sebe. La** (B d GLM MA) Thu-Sat 22.30-5.30h
C/. Altamirano, 6 ☎ 985 211 886 🖳 www.lasantasebe.com
■ **Versache's** (AC B d DR GLM MA S SNU ST WE) Mon-Thu & Sun 21-4, Fri-Sat 21-?h
C/. Campo Amor, 24 bajos ☎ 98 521 83 11

SEX SHOPS/BLUE MOVIES

■ **Fantasias** (g VS) 10-14 & 16-22h
C/. González del Valle, 6 *Galerías Pidal* ☎ 98 525 24 99
Another branch oft this Sexshop in C/. Gil de Jaz, 3.

SAUNAS/BATHS

■ **Boys-Sauna** (AC B CC DR DU G I LAB MSG SA SB SL VS WH) 16-23, Fri -5, Sat -8h
C/. Luis Braille, 1 *Opp. Facultad del Milán* ☎ 98 408 44 80
Well designed, clean and comfortable sauna in bright colours. Sling in one cabin. Free internet access and friendly service.

CRUISING

-C/. Dr. Fleming / C/. Marqués de Mohías (after dark)
-Parque del Invierno.

Pamplona/Iruña

BARS

■ **Alakarga** (AC B GLM MA) 23-6h
Plaza Monasterio de Azuelo, 1 ☎ 94 826 60 05

SEX SHOPS/BLUE MOVIES

■ **Haizegoa Amsterdam Sex Centre** (g VS) 10-15, 17-22h
Sancho Ramírez, 29 ☎ 94 817 72 99 🖳 www.haizegoa.com
■ **Sex Mil 1** (AC CC glm VS) 10-22h
C/. Virgen del Puy, 9 *Near Juzgado* ☎ 94 825 23 19 🖳 www.sexmil1.com

SAUNAS/BATHS

■ **Sauna Muscle Gym Men** (AC B CC DR DU G MA MSG SA SB SOL VS WO) 16-22, Fr 16-8 & Sa 16-22h
Plaza San Juan la Cadena 2, trasera ☎ 94 826 34 13

CRUISING

-Parque de la Taconera
-Plaza del Castillo
-Bus station (AYOR)

Platja d'Aro

SWIMMING

-Cala del Pi (G NU) (coming from Platja d'Aro take the Camino de Ronda. After 15 mins take the tunnel up hill)

Salamanca

CAFES

■ **Miranda** (B GLM MA)
Calle de San Mateo 6 ☎ 923 213 460

DANCECLUBS

■ **Kandavia** (B D MA NG)
C/. Bermejeros 16 ☎ 923 266 591

GENERAL GROUPS

■ **Unión pro derechos de Gais y Lesbianas de Castilla-León IGUALES**
Apartado 4004 ☎ 629 379 167 (mobile)
Publish their own bimonthly gay-lesbian magazine „Entre Iguales".

CRUISING

-Parque de Alamedilla (AYOR)
-Estación Renfe
-Central bus station
-Calzada de Medina, at the end of Paseo de la Estación (car-cruising in the evening)

Salou

BARS

■ **Adeene** (AC B cc D GLM MA OS S SNU ST T WE) 23-4h
C/. Bruselas, 11 ☎ 97 738 44 50
■ **Art Gallery** (AC B cc D DR GLM MA OS S SNU ST T WE) 23-4h
C/. Bruselas, 13 ☎ 97 738 36 00
■ **Dycken's Bar** (AC B GLM MA S WE) 23-4h, Show Fri & Sat
C/. del Sol, 72 *Near Plaza Venus* ☎ 97 738 14 99
Former Tres Coronas.
■ **Mar. La** (B d G SNU YC) 19-4h
C/. Penedes 24

San Sebastián

BARS

■ **Pub Dionis** (B G)
Igentea 2 ☎ 943 429 746
■ **Txirula** (B G)
San Martín 49

SAUNAS/BATHS

■ **Venconmen** (B CC DR DU FC G H M MA MSG p RR SA SB SH SOL VS WE) 16-22, Fri -8, Sat 16-Sun 22h (non-stop)
C/. General Jáuregui, 8 ☎ 94 344 61 16 💻 www.venconmen.net

GENERAL GROUPS

■ **GEHITU** (GLM I MA) Mon-Fri 9-13.30, 18-20, WE 18-20h
Arrasate, 51 3º Dcha, Donostia ☎ 94 346 85 16 💻 www.gehitu.net

SWIMMING

-Playa de la Concha (daytime)
-Playa de la Zurriola

CRUISING

-Playa de la Concha (at night)
-Rocas de Mompas

Santa Cristina d'Aro

DANCECLUBS

■ **Mas Marco** (B cc D DR G MA S SNU t VS) 23-5.30h
Ctra. Roca de Malvet, Km. 1 ☎ 972 837 740 💻 www.masmarco.es.tl
Free entrance, 1 compulsory drink.

Santander

BARS

■ **Colilla Queens** (B GLM MA)
C/ Sol 20
■ **Cool** (B MA NG)
C/. San Emeterio 3
■ **Trovador, El** (B GLM MA)
Santa Lucia 51

DANCECLUBS

■ **Dragón** (AC B D DR f G MA P S t VS WE) 23.30-6h
C/. Tetuán, 32 ☎ 94 222 10 63 💻 www.discodragon.es
Also restaurant with shows.

SAUNAS/BATHS

■ **Santander** (B DR DU FC FH GH m MSG RR SA SB VS) 18-24 (winter 16.30-23), Fri -24, Sat -2, Sun -23h
C/. Rosario de Acuña, 9-bajo ☎ 94 207 81 61
💻 www.saunasantander.com
Former „Havana Sun" sauna.

GENERAL GROUPS

■ **ALEGA Cantabria** (GLM) 10-13.30 h
C/. Rampa de Sotileza 8 entlo. izq Oficina 1 ☎ 942 214 049
💻 www.alega.org
Meetings Wed 20h. ALEGA = Asociación de Lesbianas, Gais, Transexuales y Bisexuales de Cantabria.

CRUISING

-Paseo Pareda (after 24h)
-Jardín Pareda (AYOR)
-Bus station
-Jardines de Piquío (nights)
-The dunes, on the beach
-Parking area at the playa Valdearenas in Liencres
-Auto stop A-8 heading to Bilbao, about 25km. In the toilets from 20-6h.

Santiago de Compostela

BARS

■ **Coffeepop** (B GLM)
Rúa de San Pedro 9
■ **Forum Club** (B GLM)
Rúa Travesa 4
■ **O Curruncho** (B GLM MA) Daily 19-2h
C/ Entremuros, 12 ☎ 981 576 778
Happy hour every day until 2h
■ **Tarasca** (B GLM)
C/ Entremuros, 13

SAUNAS/BATHS

■ **Azul 2** (b DR DU FH G MA SA SB VS) 16-4, Sat -7h
C/. Sánchez Freire, 4 ☎ 98 152 25 58 💻 www.royazul.com
Very clean sauna with friendly staff.

Segovia

BARS

■ **Amarote** (B g MA)
C/. Escuderos, 5

Sevilla

BARS

■ **Arte** (B G OC) 22.30-3?h, closed Sun
C/. Trastamara, 19
■ **Barón Rampante. El** (B G MA OS) 18-3, Fri & Sat 18-4h
C/. Arias Montano, 3
■ **Bosque Animado. El** (B g m MA OS S) Winter: Mon-Sat 16-?, Sun 12.30-?, Summer: 20-?h
C/. Arias Montano, 5,
■ **Habanilla Café** (AC d GLM M s T WE) 11-5h
Alameda de Hércules, 63 ☎ 95 490 27 18

■ **HM – Hércules Mítico** (AC B G m OS)
Cafeteria: 16-22 & Club: 22-?h
Alameda de Hércules, 93 ☎ 95 437 22 98

■ **Hombre y el Oso. El** (AC B DR F G MA VS)
22.30-2.30 & WE 22.30-3.30h
C/. Amor de Dios, 32
Three floors & two bars. Meeting point for bears.

■ **Isbiliyya** (B G MA S) 20-5h
Paseo de Colón 2 ☎ 95 421 04 60 🖳 www.sol.com/bar/isbiliyya
One of the most popular bars of the gay scene in Seville. Shows at 24h except Wed & Sat.

■ **Mirada. La** (AC B DR G MA r VS) 22-5h
C/. Luis de Vargas, s/n

■ **Neo 27. El** (AC B DR G MA R VS) 22-3h, WE -4h
C/. Trastamara, 27 ☎ 95 421 62 09
Also rooms for rent.

■ **Paseo. El** (AC B g MA OS) 23-?h
Paseo de Colón, 2 ☎ 95 422 50 34
Popular.

CAFES

■ **Cafe Hércules** (B G m MA OS) 9.30-2h
C/. Peris Mencheta, 15 ☎ 95 490 21 98

■ **Cafélatte** (AC B glm m s) 20-4h
C/. Jesús del Gran Poder, 83 *Near Alameda de Hércules*
☎ 95 490 46 07

DANCECLUBS

■ **Domm Disco** (D G) Fri & Sat 24-6h
Edificio Vilaser, Poligono Calonge, Av. Kansas City s/n

■ **Itaka** (! AC B D DR G MA ST VS) 22.30-?h
C/. Amor de Dios, 31
Wed & WE show 1h.

RESTAURANTS

■ **Naranja** (AC CC glm M MC)
Open for lunch & dinner, Tue closed
C/. Relator 21-b ☎ 622282644
🖳 www.cocinanaranja.blogspot.com

■ **Puerto Delicia Actividades & Restauracion** (AC B bf CC M MA OS WE) Mo-Fr 13-17 & 21-24, Sa 13-24 & Su 13-18h
Muelle de las Delicias, S/N. Modulo Sur ☎ 95 511 56 56
🖳 www.puertodelicia.es

SEX SHOPS/BLUE MOVIES

■ **Fantasias** (g VS) Mon-Fri 10-22, Sat & Sun 10-14 & 16-22h
C/. Sierpes, 48 ☎ 95 456 07 29 🖳 www.fantasiasxshop.com
A second store is at C/. Tetuán, 5.

■ **Intimate** (AC CC g VS) 11-1h
C/. Monsálvez, 5
Video cabins for two or more.

SAUNAS/BATHS

■ **Nordik** (AC B DR DU F G LAB m MA PI SA SB SOL VS WH)
12-23, Fri & Sat -7h
C/. Resolana, 38 *Bus C 1-4, C 13, C 14* ☎ 95 437 13 21
🖳 www.saunanordik.com/sevilla.htm
Welcoming staff. Two jacuzzis and a swimming pool. Darkrooms and a maze with cubicles and a gay porn cinema. Very popular on Sun.

■ **Termas Hispalis** (AC B CC DR DU FC FH G I LAB m MA MSG OS p PI PP RR SA SB SL SOL VR VS WE WH) 12-22, Sat & Sun -24h
C/. Céfiro, 3 *Bus 21, 24, 32: Corte Inglés Nervión* ☎ 95 458 02 20
🖳 www.pases.com
Very large, clean and beautiful sauna. The warm colours give it a cozy atmosphere. There is also a whirlpool for up to 16 men.

TRAVEL AND TRANSPORT

■ **Passion Tours** (G) Mon-Fri 9-14, 17-21h
C/. D. Alfonso el Sabio N°4, 1° ☎ 95 456 32 45
🖳 www.passiontours.com
Guided city tours, gay itineraries in Spanish, English, French & Italian.

HEALTH GROUPS

■ **Comité Ciudadano Anti-SIDA** (glm) Mon-Fri 10-14, 18-21h
C/. San Luis, 50 ☎ 95 437 19 58
Information and services concerning AIDS. Free condoms.

CRUISING

-Parque de María Luisa (evenings, also car-cruising)
-Plaza del Duque de la Victoria (r) (in front of El Corte Inglés)
-Parque del los Príncipes (until 21h, then AYOR) (at the end of Av. Rep. Argentina)
-Paseo de Colón (until 21h, then AYOR)
-Parque del Alamillo (between former AVE-train-station of the EXPO 92-ground and the river Guadalquivir)
-El Corte Inglés department store, Plaza del Duque, El Nervión
-Santa Justa rail station (right side)
-Bus station (C/. Torneo)

Sitges

Sitges combines the traditional look of an old fishing village with the established charm of a smart Catalan coastal resort, designed with amazing architecture in the Modernist style. Its proximity to the city of Barcelona (30 minutes by train) and its superbly conserved townscape, compared to other resorts on the Mediterranean, meant that it was discovered early on by gay holiday-makers. In the summer and at Carnival, Sitges turns into an international gay resort, offering first class hotels, restaurants and pavement cafes to one of the most the longest established, well-heeled gay clienteles looking for a complete scene to enjoy. At weekends it's full of Barcelona's gay population. The gay beach in the centre is given over body and swimwear fashion shows, and on the outlying parts of the beach with a cruising area behind, you can do

more than just look at the bodies. For honeymooners there are romantic gay guest houses set in the beautiful mountains behind the beaches.

★ Sitges verbindet die Tradition eines alten Fischerdorfs mit dem gediegenen Charme eines mondänen katalanischen Seebads mit herrlicher Modernismo-Architektur. Wegen seiner Nähe (30 Min. per S-Bahn) zur Metropole Barcelona und seinem – im Vergleich zu anderen Badeorten des Mittelmeers – vorbildlich erhaltenen Stadtbild ist es schon früh von schwulen Reisenden entdeckt worden. Im Sommer und im Karneval verwandelt sich Sitges heute in ein internationales schwules Seebad mit einer der eher wohlsituierten Klientel entsprechenden kompletten Szene mit erstklassigen Hotels und Restaurants, Bars, Caféterrassen etc. Über das Wochenende kommen viele Schwule aus Barcelona angereist. Der Strand im Zentrum wird im Sommer zur Körper- und Bademodenschau. Nicht nur gucken kann man am außerhalb gelegenen Nacktbadestrand mit dahinterliegendem Cruisinggelände. Für den Honeymoon sind in den wild-romantischen Bergen in Sitges' Umgebung hübsche Schwulenpensionen zu entdecken.

Sitges réunit en un même lieu la tradition d'un petit village de pêcheurs et le charme feutré d'une station balnéaire catalane à l'architecture Modernismo. Proche de la métropole de Barcelone (30 min. en RER) et relativement bien conservée, Sitges a été découverte relativement tôt par les gays. En été et pendant le carnaval, la ville se transforme en une station balnéaire gay avec une clientèle internationale plutôt aisée, ce que reflète le milieu avec ses hôtels de premier choix et ses restaurants, bars, terrasses de cafés etc. fréquentés le week-end aussi par les gays de Barcelone. La plage homo au centre devient en été lieu d'exhibition corporelle et de lingerie de bain. Et ceux qui ne veulent pas que regarder, peuvent se diriger vers la plage nudist plus à l'extérieur et son lieu de drague. Pour une lune de miel romantique, on pourrait aller dans une des pensions gays dans les montagnes de l'arrière-pays.

Sitges combina la tradición de un antiguo pueblo pesquero y el arraigado encanto de un mundano pueblo catalán de la costa con una preciosa arquitectura modernista. A causa de su proximidad a la ciudad de Barcelona (30 minutos en tren) y de su centro histórico, ejemplarmente conservado en comparación con otros pueblos de la costa mediterránea, Sitges pronto fue descubierto por los homosexuales. En verano y en Carnaval Sitges se transforma en un balneario gay internacional con un ambiente muy completo, con hoteles de primera clase, restaurantes, bares yterrazas, orientado a una clientela bien situada,. Los fines de semana es muy frecuentado por gays procedentes de Barcelona. La playa gay del centro se convierte en verano en una exhibición de bañadores y cuerpos atléticos. En la playa nudista situada en las afueras, con su zona trasera de cruising, no sólo se va a mirar. Para aquellos que van de luna de miel, en las salvajes y románticas montañas de los alrededores descubrirán románticos alojamientos para gays.

Sitges

EAT & DRINK

- Alma – Restaurant 26
- Amura – Bar 33
- Azul – Bar 8
- B.Side – Bar 14
- Beach House – Restaurant 30
- Bears' Bar 36
- Café Sitges – Café 32
- Candil. El – Bar 27
- Casablanca – Bar 28
- Celler Vell – Restaurant 12
- Comodín – Bar 23
- Dark Sitges – Bar 41
- Enfants Terribles. Les – Restaurant 16
- Horno. El – Bar 42
- Locacola. La – Bar 38
- Man Bar 11
- Orek's – Bar 34
- Parrots – Restaurant 44
- Parrots Pub – Bar 45
- Parrots Terrace 46
- Perfil – Bar 5
- Piano. El – Bar 13
- Prinz – Bar 25
- Privilege – Bar 39
- Queenz – Bar 37
- Trull. El – Restaurant 29
- 7. El – Bar 24

NIGHTLIFE

- Mediterráneo Danceclub 7
- Organic Club. The – Danceclub 35
- Trailer – Danceclub 22
- XXL – Danceclub 40

SEX

- Sitges – Sauna 4
- Parrots – Hotel & Sauna 43

ACCOMMODATION

- Hotel Alexandra – Hotel 2
- Antonio's Sitges – Guest House 47
- Hostal Termes – Hotel 3
- Hotel de la Renaixenca – Hotel 17
- Liberty – Hotel 6
- Los Globos – Hotel 46
- Outlêt – Apartment 19
- Parrot's – Hotel & Sauna 43
- Hotel Romàntic – Hotel 18
- Sitges Guest House 20
- Stay Sitges – Apartments 21

Sitges è una sintesi tra la tradizione di una paesino peschereccio con lo charme di una più mondana località balneare catalana con architettura „modernismo". Grazie alla sua vicinanza (30 minuti con il treno) con Barcellona – in confronto alle altre località balneari del mediterraneo – è stata scoperta ben presto dal pubblico omosessuale. In estate e a carnevale Sitges si trasforma in una località balneare internazionale gay con una clientela per lo più abbiente. La spiaggia gay in centro diventa in estate una vera e proprio sfilata di corpi e costumi da bagno. La spiaggia un po' più appartata offre anche uno spazio per il cruising. Per la luna di miele, nelle selvagge montagne dell'entroterra ci sono romanticissimi alberghetti gay.

TOURIST INFO

Agència de Promoció Turisme de Sitges
Sínia Morera, 1 ☎ 90 210 34 28 www.sitgestur.com

BARS

7. El 7 (AC B G MC s) 22-3h, in winter only WE
C/. Nou, 7 www.barseven.com

Amura (AC B DR G MA VS) 18-2.30h
C/. Sant Pere, 3

Azul (AC B G MA VS) 22-3h
C/. Sant Bonaventura, 10
Happy prices.

B. Side (AC B DR G MA s SNU VS) 21-3.30h
C/. Sant Gaudenci, 7
Happy hour 21-23.30h, in summer weekly naked parties.

Bears' Bar (AC B DR F G MA VS) 22-3h
C/. Bonaire, 17 ☎ 93 894 62 96 www.bearsbar.com
Two darkrooms with sling and St. Andrews cross.

Blondies (B GLM MA OS) 14-3h
C/. Puerto Alegre, 10 *At the beginning of San Sebastian Beach*
☎ 628 656 962 (mobile)
Former Phillip's Bar.

Candil. El (! AC B D DR G MA ST VS)
22-3, Fri & Sat -3.30h, Sun 19-3h, closed Oct-Jan
C/. Carreta, 9
Aperitivo & dragshow Sun 19h

Casablanca Cocktail & Art Bar (AC B G MC) 20-3h
C/. Pau Barrabeig, 5 ☎ 93 894 70 82
Daddies and admirers.

Comodín (AC B d G MA) 22-3, Fri & Sat -3.30h
C/. Tacó, 4 ☎ 93 894 16 98 www.facebook.com

Dark Sitges Bar DSB (AC B DR G MA S SNU VS)
22.30-3.30h, in winter 17-3h
C/. Bonaire, 14
Thu-Sun SNU in summer. regularly underwear parties

Horno. El (AC B DR F G MA VS) 17.30-3h
Juan Tarrida Ferratges, 6 ☎ 93 894 09 09 www.sitges4men.com/horno.htm
As one of only a few bars in Sitges to open its doors early in the evening, El Horno is still the place to go for a quiet drink after a long session on the beach.

Locacola. La (B G MA) 18-3h
C/. Bonaire, 35 www.lalocacola.com
Aperitifs and more.

Male à Bar. Le (AC bf D DR G m MA OS SNU VS)
23-?h, winter show on WE.
CC Oasis, Local 28
Irregular open end after hour bar.

Man (AC B DR F G MC p S VS) 22-3.30h
C/. Sant Bonaventura, 19
Underwear & naked parties. This bar has a hard industrial feel with chains, metal bars and discreet lighting creating a dark and cruisy atmosphere.

Orek's (AC B CC d DR GLM MA SNU VS) 22-3.30h
C/. Bonaire, 13
SNU in summer daily, in winter Fri & Sat only.

Parrots Pub (AC B BF F GLM MA OS S) 17-3h,
Plaza Industria, 2 www.parrotspub.com

Parrots Terrace (AC B BF GLM OS) 10-3h, breakfast -15h
Plaza Industria, 2/3 www.parrotspub.com

Perfil (B d f G MA s VS) 22.30-3-30h
C/. Espalter, 7 ☎ 656 376 791 (mobile)
www.facebook.com/perfilsitges

Piano. El (AC B cc d GLM MA S) 22-3.30h
C/. Sant Bonaventura, 37 ☎ 93 814 62 45
www.facebook.com/groups/114093131947
Friendly fun bar. Live music every night.

Prinz (AC G MA S SNU ST) 23-3.30h
C/. Nou, 4 *50m from City Hall* ☎ 93 894 67 36 www.prinzbar.com
SNU, ST or live sex show in summer daily except Mon, in winter Thu-Sat.

Privilege (AC B CC D DR G MA SNU) 22.30-3.30h (Apr-Oct only)
C/. Bonaire, 24 www.privilegesitges.com
SNU Wed, Fri and Sun.

Queenz (AC B CC D G MA S SNU VS) 22.30-3.30h
C/. Bonaire, 17 *Centre* www.barqueenz.com
Popular Music bar with daily shows and entertainment.

Romàntic (B BF CC glm M MA OS RWT SOL) All year
C/. Sant Isidre, 33 ☎ 93 894 83 75 www.hotelromantic.com
Hotel with Cocktail Bar in the Garden (open daily 9-0h).

CAFES

Café Sitges (AC B BF CC G M MA OS)
Mon 11-15, Tue closed & Wed-Sun 11-15, 18-?h
C/. Sant Pau (San Pablo), 32 ☎ 93 894 97 79 www.cafesitges.com
Quality gourmet coffee together with delicious snacks and food using quality ingredients and prepared on-site; good house wines. Affordable prices, cosy modern interior.

DANCECLUBS

Gay Beach Party @ L'Atlantida (B D G OS) Tue 24-?h (summer only)
www.gaybeachparty.com
Open-air party on a private beach. Free shuttle bus to the party from the Hotel Calipolis. See www.gaybeachparty.com for details.

EL HORNO
PUB

XXL
SITGES

Mediterráneo (AC B D G MA)
22-3.30h, Easter-May only Fri & Sat, closed Oct-Carnival
C/. Sant Bonaventura, 6
www.facebook.com/pages/Mediterraneo-sitges/130346303646455

Organic Club. The (AC B D DR G MA s) 2.30-6h
C/. Bonaire, 15 www.theorganicdanceclub.com

Trailer (AC B D G MA)
1-6h, in winter only WE and before public holidays
C/. Angel Vidal, 36

XXL (AC B d DR G MA VS) 23-3.30h, in winter only WE
C. Juan Tarrida 7 www.sitges4men.com
Lovers of dance music are well catered for on the ground floor with an in-house dj playing the latest funky house, disco and electro tunes. Contact: grupoxxl@yahoo.es

RESTAURANTS

Alma (B CC GLM M OS s) 20-?h, winter: closed Tue & Wed
C/. Tacó, 16 ☎ 93 894 63 87 *French cuisine.*

Ambassade. L' (AC CC DM M MC OS RES VEG W WE WL) Apr-Oct 12.30-17 & 19.30-2, winter: 12.30-17 & Fri-Sun 12.30-17 & 19.30-2h
16 Passeig de la Ribera ☎ 938 114 806

Beach House (AC bf CC G M MA OS) 18-2h, Nov-Dec closed
C/. San Pau, 34 ☎ 93 894 90 29 www.beachhousesitges.com
Also apartments available.

Celler Vell. El (AC CC glm M MA RES VEG WL) Mon-Thu 20.30-23, Fri-Sun 13-15.30 & 20.30-23h, closed on Wed
C/. Sant Bonaventura, 21 ☎ 93 811 19 61 www.elcellervell.com
Family run, traditional Catalan restaurant, tastefully decorated in a rustic, regional style in the old cellar of an ancient mansion.

Enfants Terribles. Les (AC CC G M MA) 20-23.30h; Sun & Mon closed in winter
C/. Sant Bartomeu, 40 ☎ 93 894 96 51
French cuisine, set menu for a fixed price. In summer on Wed dinner spectacle. Reservation recommended. Modernly designed interior.

Mezzanine (AC CC g M MA) 20h-?h
Espalter, 8 ☎ 93 894 99 40
French-Mediterranean cuisine.

Parrots Restaurant (CC G M MA) 19.30-24h
C/. Joan Tarrida, 18 ☎ 93 811 12 19 evening
www.parrotsrestaurant.com
Modern and fashionable restaurant in the gay scene. International cuisine with Swiss influence. Extensive wine list.

Trull. El (AC CC DM GLM M MA OS) 19.30- ?h, Wed closed
Carrer Mossén Félix Clará, 3 *Casco Antiguo* ☎ 93 894 47 05
www.facebook.com/pages/Restaurant-El-Trull-Sitges/171421862915576
International cuisine.

SEX SHOPS/BLUE MOVIES

Mask. The (AC CC g VS) 12-22, Fri & Sat -24h
C/. Bonaire, 22 ☎ 93 811 22 14

SAUNAS/BATHS

Parrots Sitges Sauna
(AC B CC DR DU FC G LAB MA MSG NU SA SB VR VS WH) May-Sep
Joan Tarrida, 16 *In same building as Parrots Sitges Hotel. Not part of hotel*
☎ 93 894 13 50 www.parrots-group.com
Open to all. Parrots Sitges Sauna: a safe and clean place to socialise and enjoy one another's company. Jacuzzi, Sauna, Steam Room, Cabins, Showers, Free Lockers.

Sauna Sitges (AC AK B DR DU f FC FH G GH LAB m MA MSG RR SA SB SL VS WE WH) Summer: 16-11, Winter: 16-22h
C/. Espalter, 11 ☎ 93 894 28 63 www.saunasitges.com
Free condoms and lube. Foam parties Tue, Fri & Sun, foam at 18h.

FASHION SHOPS

zak men (AC cc G) 10.30-14.30 & 16.30-21.30h
C/. San Francisco, Nº1 ☎ 93 810 26 27
Male Pret-a-Porter with latest trends in fashion, accessories, swimsuits, bags, watches, etc.

HOTELS

Globos. Los (AC B BF CC G I MA OS PA PK RWB RWS RWT VA) All year
Avda. Ntra. Sra de Montserrat, 43 ☎ 93 894 93 74
www.hotelsitgeslosglobos.com
50m from the beach. All rooms with private bath and balcony or private garden with beautiful views of sea and mountains. BF is served on terrace. Wi-Fi.

Hostal Termes (AC CC GLM OS) All year
C/. Termes, 9 ☎ 93 894 23 43 www.hostaltermes.com
Centrally located to gay bars and beach.

Hotel Alexandra (AC cc glm MA PA RWB RWS RWT VA)All year
C/. Termes, 20 ☎ 938 941 558 www.hotelalexandrasitges.com
Gay owned and operated.

Hotel de la Renaixenca (B BF CC G MA)
21 Mar-31 Oct, in winter only WE
C/. Illa de Cuba, 13 ☎ 93 894 84 60 www.hotelromantic.com
Elegant, bar also open to non-residents 19-23h.

Hotel Masia Sumidors
(AC B BF CC DM FH GLM M NR OS PI PK RWS VEG WI WL)
All year. Check-in: 14-20h. Closed Christmas & New Year
Carretera de Vilafranca Km. 4,6, Sant Pere de Ribes *10 mins drive from Sitges, 30 mins from Barcelona* ☎ 93 896 20 61
www.sumidors.com
Located in a national park. Easy access to Sitges and Barcelona. Nine guestrooms. Breakfast is served outside on the covered terrace. No TV but Wi-Fi, a place to relax.

Liberty (AC b CC GLM OS PA RWB RWS RWT VA) All year
C/. Illa de Cuba, 45 ☎ 93 811 08 72 www.libertyhotelsitges.com
Five storey house with large, bright rooms and apartments. Breakfast available until noon. Hotel Liberty is close to the gay bars, restaurants and the beach. Shuttle service available.

Parrots Sitges Hotel (AC BF FC GLM H I MA RWB RWS RWT VA) Feb-Oct
Joan Tarrida, 16 *In the centre of the historic town of Sitges just meters from the beach* ☎ 93 894 13 50 💻 www.parrotshotel.com
All rooms are en-suite with safe, fridge, phone and flat-screen TV. Parrots Sauna located in same building. Parrots VIP Promotion with reservations made via hotel website.

Pension Espalter Sitges (AC g I RWS RWT) All year
C/. Espalter, 11 *Same building as Sauna Sitges* ☎ 093 894 28 63 💻 www.pensionespalter.com

RAS – Room Advice Service (CC G) Mon-Fri 11-14, 17-20h
☎ 607 149 451 (mobile) 💻 www.raservice.com
Reservations of hotels & apartments in Sitges & Barcelona (only hotels). English, French, German & Spanish spoken. CC necessary.

Romàntic (B BF CC glm M MA OS RWT SOL) All year
C/. Sant Isidre, 33 ☎ 93 894 83 75 💻 www.hotelromantic.com
Hotel with Cocktail Bar in the Garden (open daily 9-0h).

Sitgesonline (CC G) Mon-Fri 11-14, 17-20h
☎ 607 149 451 (mobile) 💻 www.sitgesonline.com

GUEST HOUSES

Antonio's Sitges (CC GLM I PA PK RWB RWS RWT VA) All year
Passeig Vilanova, 58 *Three blocks from gay beach* ☎ 93 894 92 07 💻 www.antoniossitges.com
Just a few minutes walk away from centre and beaches. Ask for long term rates. Laundry service, safe in the room.

Sitges Guest House (ac CC G I) All year
2 mins walk from train station, from the gay beach and bars
☎ 666 325 974 (mobile) 💻 sitgesguesthouse.com
Read descriptions, view photographs and reserve your accommodation on-line.

APARTMENTS

Bonnois (GLM OS) All year
C/. Valencia 12, Apt. 6 ☎ 651 060 338 (mobile)

■ **Liberty** (AC b CC GLM OS PA RWB RWS RWT VA) All year
C/. Illa de Cuba, 45 ☎ 93 811 08 72 🖳 www.libertyhotelsitges.com
Five storey house with large, bright rooms and apartments. Breakfast available until noon. Hotel Liberty is close to the gay bars, restaurants and the beach. Shuttle service available.

■ **Outlêt 4 Spain** (CC GLM MA) Mon-Fri 10-18h
C/. Francesco Guma, 20 ☎ 938 102 711 🖳 www.outlet4spain.com
View and book accommodation online. Rooms, apartments, villas and hotels.

■ **Phillip's Apartments** 24h
C/. San Honorato, 20, 2°, 1a ☎ 938 973 764
Phillip from former Phillips Bar still renting out his nice apartments

■ **Sitges on the beach** (AC H MA OS PI RWB RWS RWT W WI)
Joan Salvat Papasseit 30 *Balmins Beach, 15 mins walk to Sitges train station* ☎ (+44) 7956 315 414 (UK) 🖳 www.sitgesonthebeach.com
Each of the 3 self-contained apartments has its own access. Swimming pool shared with neighbours.

■ **Stay Sitges** (CC GLM) Mon-Sat 9.30-18h
C/. San Sebastian, 46 ☎ 93 894 13 18 🖳 www.staysitges.com

PRIVATE ACCOMMODATION

■ **Gay Homstays** Office: Mon-Fri 9-18h
C/. D'en Taco ☎ 93 811 4856 🖳 www.gayhomestays.com
High quality, reasonably-priced, gay accommodation in over 40 European cities.

CRUISING

-Cruising during the day is popular in the forrest behind the nude beach (15 minute walk from club l'Atlantida. In the weekend (hot) local boys from Barcelona can be found in the forrest too.
-At night cruising is popular on the boulevard.
-The boulevard between Hotel Calipolis and further south is the gay cruising area in Sitges. Each night, the boys coming out from the bars and clubs try their luck on the beach.

Tarragona

BARS

■ **Casa del Loco. La** (B g OC) 21-3.30h
C/. del Sol, 72, Salou ☎ 97 738 1 592
Bears especially welcome.

Torremolinos

BARS

■ **21** (AC B DR G MA OS) 14-3h
C. C. La Nogalera, 21 ☎ 695 159 070
Italian owned & run.

■ **A Noite** (AC B D G MA R VS) 21-5h
C/. Danza Invisible, C. C. La Nogalera ☎ 95 205 35 92
Happy hour 2-4-1 -1h.

■ **Anfora** (B GLM MA OS) 23-?h
C. C. La Nogalera, 522

■ **Babu. La** (AC B G OS) 21.30-4h
C. C. La Nogalera, Local 203

■ **Bacchus** (AC B F G MA WE) 22-4h
Calle Nogalera, Local, 712
Oldest bears bar in town. Good Music. Porno videos. Bears, bar staff very friendly.

■ **Chessa** (AC B G MA OS) 18-2h, WE-4h
C. C. La Nogalera 408
■ **Contacto** (AC B G MA OS S VS)
Fri, Sat & public holidays 23-5h. In summer daily
C. C. La Nogalera 204
■ **Esquina. La** (B GLM MA OS) 20-2, WE -3h
Pueblo Blanco, 39 🖳 www.renesbartorremolinos.com
■ **Free Eagle** (AC B DR F G MA OS VS) 22-3, WE -4h
C. C. La Nogalera, 718 🖳 www.free-eagle.eu
Whole Bar half-darkroom behind closed doors, Sun topless, theme parties check
■ **Gato Lounge. El** (AC B G M MA OS) 10-2h
Paseo Maritimo del Pedregal 1 *in front of Beirola gay beach of Torremolinos, between hotel Melia costa del Sol and Santa Clara.* ☎ 951251509
🖳 www.elgatolounge.com
Stylish lounge bar, good food and wine, great terrace in front of gay beach of Torremolinos. Friendly staff. Also beach service.
■ **Help** (AC B DR G MA OS VS) Sun-Thu 22-2, Fri & Sat -3h
C. C. La Nogalera, Local 507
■ **Malú** (B GLM MA OS) 21-3h
C/. Danza Invisible, C. C. La Nogalera 1103 *Calle Danza Invisible Commercial Pueblo Blanco*
Running for more than 25 years now!
■ **Men's Bar** (B DR f G MA VS WE) 22-5h
C. C. La Nogalera, 714 ☎ 95 238 42 05
■ **Morbos** (B DR G MA OS SNU ST) 22-6h
La Nogalera, 113
Show 23h. Cruisy darkroom!
■ **Palmera. La** (B G m MA OS) 17-6h
La Nogalera, local 201-202
Early-evening bar.
■ **Pourquoi Pas?** (AC B GLM MA) 21-3, Fri Sat -4h
C. C. La Nogalera 703
■ **Timeless Bar** (AC B GLM m MA OS) 20-?h, Tue closed
C/. Casablanca, 9 ☎ 95 240 90 14
A great place to meet and enjoy a drink in a comfortable contemporary bar.
■ **Wow** (AC B G M MA OS) 22-?h
C. C. La Nogalera, local 701 ☎ 678 284 982 (mobile)
🖳 www.freewebs.com/gaywow
■ **XS** (AC B DR F G MA VS) 23-?h
C/. Nogalera 19 🖳 www.barxs.com
Fetish, videos, dark, sling room upstairs regular theme nights.

MEN'S CLUBS

■ **Privé** (AC B G MA OS p R VS)
C/. Casa Blanca 20
Rooms for rent with porn videos.

CAFES

■ **Cafe El Atrio** (AC B GLM MA OS WE) Summer 20-3h, Winter 18-2h
Casablanca nº 13 *Planta Alta* 🖳 www.cafeelatrio.eu
Pub-cafe in the center of Torremolinos, on the Nogalera, for coffee, a cocktail or a drink. It has a large terrace for smokers

DANCECLUBS

■ **Cruising** (AC B D DR G S SNU ST VS) 23-?h
C/. Danza Invisible, C. C. La Nogalera
Bears bar Ursus in basement.
■ **Kingdom** (AC B D GLM MA S ST WE) Wed-Fri 23-6, WE -7h
C/. Casablanca 15, C. C. Nueva Nogalera Pueblo Blanco ☎ 95 237 34 79
■ **Parthenon** (B D DR G MA OS S SNU ST VS) 23-6, WE -7h
C. C. La Nogalera, 716
■ **Passion** (AC B D glm) Fri/Sat 2.30-7h
Av Palma de Mallorca, 18 ☎ 66 514 45 99 🖳 www.passiondisco.com

RESTAURANTS

■ **Crema. La** (AC B CC DM glm M OS PA PK VEG WL) 18-24h, closed Thu
C/. Skal, 19, Urbanización la Roca ☎ 95 238 13 94
Spanish and international cuisine.
■ **Crepería Bahia** (AC B CC G M MA S) Tue-Sun 19-2h
Urb. Pueblo Blanco, Local 32-33 ☎ 95 240 90 64
Crepes, salads and pasta.
■ **Escalera. La** (AC CC DM GLM M VEG) 18.30-23h, Sun closed
C/. Cuesta del Tajo, 12 *End of C/. San Miguel* ☎ 95 205 80 24
International cuisine with menu in ten languages. Free Internet Hotspot.
■ **Poseidón** (B BF CC g M MA OS) 9.30-24, winter 9.30-18h
Paseo Marítimo, Playa del Lido 3 ☎ 95 238 00 40
Popular.
■ **Pouls** (CC G M MA OS) 18-1h
C/. Danza Invisible, La Nogalera ☎ 95 205 13 59
Steakhouse with a rustic atmosphere.

SAUNAS/BATHS

■ **Termasauna Miguel** (AC B DR DU FC FH G GH LAB m MA MSG OS PI RR SA SB VS WE WH) 14-24h
Av. Carlota Alessandri, 166 *10 mins from centre* ☎ 95 238 87 40
🖳 www.termasaunamiguel.es
1240m² sauna with pool, 2 Jacuzzis, maze of cabins, as popular as ever. Now also apartments available in package with free entry to the sauna.

BOOK SHOPS

■ **Contramano** (CC GLM)
Tue-Thu 10.30-14 & 18-22, Fri & Sat 10.30-14 & 18-2, Sun 18-22h
C/. Danza Invisible 3, C. C. La Nogalera, local 517 ☎ 95 240 92 76
🖳 www.tiendacontramano.com

PROPERTY SERVICES

■ **Inmobiliaria MIA** (AC GLM)
Mon-Fri 10-14 & 16.30-20.30, Sat 10-14h
C/ de la Cruz 32, Edif Hispania Bajo Izq ☎ 95 237 84 97
🖳 www.inmobiliariamia.com

HOTELS

■ **Guadalupe Hotel & Restaurant** (AC B CC G M OS PA RWB RWS RWT VA) Restaurant: 12-16 & 19-23h, Wed closed
C/. Peligro, 15 *Bajondillo, on the beach* ☎ 95 238 19 37
🖳 www.hostalguadalupe.com
All the rooms and apartments have their own bathroom. There is a delightful sunny roof patio. The restaurant is famous for vegetarian dishes and fresh home made specialities. Close to the local gay scene.
■ **Residencia Miami** (AC B CC glm I M MA OS PA PI RWS RWT) All year
C/. Aladino 14 *Close to gay district, 50m from the beach* ☎ 95 238 52 55
🖳 www.residencia-miami.com
A quiet and charming hotel.

SWIMMING

-Playamar at Restaurant/Bar El Poseidón (G)
-Campo de Golfo, near Hotel Guadalmar (G) (between Torremolinos and Málaga, ca. 8km from Torremolinos, daytime some cruising in the bushes; car-cruising at night)
-Torrequebrado (g NU) (Beach behind the casino between Torremolinos and Fuengirola in Benalmadena, 1st exit after casino and back to the beach. There (G) at the right side)
-Las Dunas (G NU) (Ca 30km west of Torremolinos, just past Cabo Pino. Narrow stony beach, but busy dunes and wood at the end of the beach in direction Marbella. P at bar (F g) »Las Dunas«)

CRUISING

-C/. San Miguel (the shopping mall with the sidewalk cafés: „Heladería San Miguel" & „Bar El Toro")
-Plaza Andalucía (R)
-In front of the bus station (r)

Torrevieja

BARS

■ **Newboy** (AC d DR G MA OS) Daily 21-?h, closed Sun in winter
C/. San Pablo, 12 ☎ 96 571 59 99

■ **Patio de Chueca. El** (AC B d f GLM m MA s t WE) 10-4h
C/. Apolo, 12 ☎ 666 196 399

CAFES

■ **Pink Mopy** (AC B d GLM m MA OS S SNU t) 10.30-?h
Rambla Juan Mateo Garcia, 8 ☎ 69 783 64 63 www.pinkmopy.com
Occasionally different events: Madonna nite, salsa music, chill out.

DANCECLUBS

■ **Boys Pub** (B D DR G MA VS) Summer 23-4, winter 22-4h (closed Mon)
C/. San Antonio, 38 ☎ 96 692 33 30 www.pubboys.com

SEX SHOPS/BLUE MOVIES

■ **Eros** (AC CC GLM VS) 10-1h
Av. Purísima 31, Playa del Cura ☎ 96 670 46 46
www.saferelax.com/eros-torrevieja

■ **Pacific Blue** (AC CC DR F G VS) 10-23h
C/. Miguel de Unamuno,9 ☎ 965 717 639

Valencia

GAY INFO

■ **Ibiza G News** (G)
c/o Grupo Ibigay, Maestro Gozalbo, 28, 5° ☎ 619 120 217 (mobile)
www.mucho-g.com
Free magazine published 4x a year, during the summer.

BARS

■ **ADN** (AC D GLM MA s WE) 22.30-3.30h
C/. Angel Custodi, 10, Barri del Carme ☎ 617 421 831 (mobile)
Disco-Pub.

■ **Café de la Seu** (! AC B CC d G I m MA OS) 18-2h
C/. Santo Cálz, 7 ☎ 96 391 57 15 www.cafedelaseu.com

■ **D'Angelo Pub** (AC B G p R VS) 20.30-9h
C/. Vilaragut, 5 *Next to Hotel Astonia*
Rooms for rent with yacuzzi & kingsize bed.

■ **Moratin** (AC B DR G MA R) 20-3h
C/. Moratin, 7 *M° Xativa* ☎ 626 507 486 (mobile)
3 Three rooms for rent. Video lounge upstairs with jacuzzi. Former Club Siete.

■ **North Dakota Saloon** (B f G MA) 20-3h
Plaça Margarita Valldaura, 1 ☎ 96 357 52 50

■ **Space by Venial** (AC B CC d G MA WE) Thu-Sun and before holidays 24-?h
Plaza Vicente Ibora, 4 bajos ☎ 96 391 73 56 www.venialvalencia.com
Predance del Venial. If you have drink here, you have free entry to Venial Disco. Except Sat.

■ **Ydeal Club** (AC B d G MA ST) Thu-Sun 23-3.30h
C/. Pepita, 2 *Near Deseo 54 Danceclub* ☎ 685 353 049 (mobile)
Predance pub with billard and chill sofas before you go to Deseo 54. Monthly special parties.

MEN'S CLUBS

■ **Cross** (AC B d DR f G MC NU s SNU VS) 20-3.30h, closed Mon & Tue
C/. Juan de Mena, 7 Bajo *Near Torres de Quart* ☎ 96 315 58 74
DJ on Thu-Sat, Wed & Sun: naked party.

■ **Hòmens Sex** (AC B d DR f G MA p S SNU VS WE) 12-3h
C/. Alacant, 11 *Next to Central station* ☎ 96 328 02 92

■ **Nuncadigono** (AC B CC DR f G MA P SNU VS) Mon-Wed 19-3, Thu-Sun 15-4h
C/. Turia, 22 ☎ 96 391 60 97
A former sauna with hot showers and slings. Underwear Party 3rd Thu/month, all other Thu Naked Party.

CAFES

■ **La vaca de guantiné** (AC B d G m MA S) Tue-Sun 18-?h
C/. Dr. Montserrat, 14bis *Near Torres de Quart* ☎ 96 338 22 90

■ **Q Art** (AC B CC GLM M MA ST) 10-1.30h
C/. Guillem de Castro, 80 *Near Torres de Quart* ☎ 96 391 61 15
Fine coffees, cocktails, and good Mediterranean food, all framed by a broad range of art exhibitions and musical performances.

■ **Sant Miquel** (AC B G M MA OS)
19.30-3, Fri-Sat -4.30h, Mon closed
Plaça Sant Miguel, 13 ☎ 96 392 45 96

■ **Som Com Som** (AC B d GLM YC)
C/. Cádiz, 75, Barrio de Ruzafa ☎ 96 332 66 48

■ **Trapezzio** (AC B G MA OS VS) 8-2h
Plaza Músico López Chavarri, 2 *Barrio del Carmen* ☎ 96 391 50 27
💻 www.trapezziocafe.com

DANCECLUBS

■ **Deseo 54** (AC B CC D G MA S SNU ST VS WE) Thu-Sun 1.30-7.30h
C/. Pepita, 15 💻 www.deseo54.com
Thu House music, Fri & Sat House/Electo, Sun Electro, Progressive. Check website www.deseo54.com for programme.

■ **Mogambo** (B D g YC) 24-5, Fri & Sat -7h
C/. Sangre, 9 *Near Plaza del Ayuntamiento*

■ **Venial** (B D GLM S VS YC) Thu-Sun 22-?h
Plaza Vicente Iborra, 4 ☎ 96 391 73 56

RESTAURANTS

■ **33 Lounge** (AC B CC M OS) Tue-Sun 12-16, 20-2h, Mon closed
C/. San Dionisio, 8 ☎ 96 392 41 61
Mediterranean cuisine.

■ **Bien Divina** (g M MA ST) 12-16, Sat & Sun 21-2h
C/. Martin el humano 3 ☎ 675 188 854 💻 www.biendivina.com

■ **Llantia Dorada. La** (AC B cc glm M MA S VEG)
Mon-Fri 13.30-1.30 & Sat 17-?h
C/. Hierba, 4 *Behind cathedral* ☎ 96 391 27 16

■ **Turangalila** (AC B CC DM GLM LM M RES S WL)
Mon-Fri 14-17 & Mon-Sat 21.30-?h
Avda, Maestro Rodrigo, 13 *City centre* ☎ 96 3472803 💻 www.turangalila.es
Dinner spectacles, reservation recommended, international cuisine.

SEX SHOPS/BLUE MOVIES

■ **Afro** (g) 9.30-22.30h, closed Sun
Gibraltar 1 ☎ 96 341 11 02

■ **Blue Rain, S. L.** (AC glm MA)
C/. Teruel, 5 ☎ 963 844 792 💻 www.bluerainsex.es

■ **Blue Sex Factory** (g VS) 9.30-22.30h
C/. Bailén, 38 ☎ 96 342 38 68 💻 💻 www.fusionreaccion.es

■ **Erotic planet** (g)
C/. Castellón, 12 ☎ 963 940 649 💻 www.fusionreaccion.es

■ **European Center** (g VS) 11-14 & 16.30-21.30h
Av. Constitución, 26 ☎ 96 347 44 27

■ **Evadan** (g)
C/. Matías Perelló, 14 ☎ 963 742 065 💻 www.fusionreaccion.es

■ **Holliwood** (g)
C/. Dr Zamenhoof, 5 ☎ 963 821 497 💻 www.fusionreaccion.es

■ **Magic Spartacus** (DR G GH MA VS)
C/. Bailén, 38 ☎ 96 342 38 68 💻 www.fusionreaccion.es

■ **Moncho Internacional** (DR G VS) 9.30-22.30h
C/. Dr. Zamenhoff, 15 ☎ 96 382 33 49 💻 www.fusionreaccion.es

■ **Sala X** (g R VS) 11-20h
C/. Alcoi, 3 *Behind station & Plaza de Toros*

■ **Spartacus** (DR G VS) 9.30-22.30h
C/. Flassaders 8, Centro ☎ 96 352 56 62 💻 www.fusionreaccion.es
Gay cabins upstairs.

SAUNAS/BATHS

■ **Magnus Sauna** (AC B DR DU FC G LAB m MSG PI RR SA SB SOL VR VS WH WO) 10-24, Sun 6-24h
Av. del Puerto, 27 *Bus 1/2/3/4* ☎ 96 337 48 92 💻 www.pases.com
Spectacular sauna with a big swimming pool and whirlpool for up to 10 people. Frequented by a hot mixed crowd. Worth a visit.

 **Olímpic**
(AC B DR DU FC G I LAB m MSG PI RR SA SB SOL VR VS WH WO) 14-24h
Vivons, 17 ☎ 96 373 04 18 💻 www.pases.com
Very large sauna on two floors. Maybe the most beautiful sauna in Spain. Giant whirlpool and a very large steam bath. Put this place on your to-do list!

■ **Thermas Romeo** (B DR DU FC FH G MSG R RR SA SB VS WH)
15-21h, closed Tue
C/. Pintor Gisbert, 5 ☎ 96 336 50 98

BOOK SHOPS

■ **Carácteres** (CC glm)
Mon-Fri 10-13.30 & 16.30-20, Sat 10-14 & 16-20, Sun 10-14h
Plaza de la Merced, 4 bajo izq ☎ 96 351 65 75
Bookshop specialised in literature with a lesbian/gay section (600 titles), art exhibitions, access to culturerelated websites (reserved to bookshop customers), coffee service.

GUEST HOUSES

■ **Casa Rural & Restaurant L'Almassera** (B BF CC GLM H I M MA NU OS PA PI PK RWS RWT SA SOL VA WE WO) All year
C/. Abadia, 20, Margarida – Planes, Alicante *In the mountains between Alicante & Valencia* ☎ 96 551 43 14 💻 www.cageauxfolles.eu
For mountain holidays.

■ **Villa Florencia** (AC B BF CC G MA PI WH) All year
14-Carretera de Barx, Marxuquera Alta, Gandia *5km from Gandia train station, pick-up can be arranged; 40 mins from Valencia Airport, 60 mins from Alicante Airport, 50 mins from Benidorm* ☎ 96 296 04 00
💻 www.gandiacasarural.com
Situated in the picturesque region of Valencia. Ideal for those seeking a base near a beautiful beach with options of hiking, biking & horseriding or just relaxing around the pool.

HELP WITH PROBLEMS

■ **Col-lectiu Lambda** (GLM YC) Mon-Fri 10-15, 17-22h
C/. Vivons, 26 bajo ☎ 96 334 91 21 💻 www.lambdavalencia.org
Info-pink-Hotline: 963 913 238 (Mon-Fri 17-21h).

SWIMMING

-Playa del Saler (NU) (take bus from Plaza Espanya to the end of the bus line, approximately 15km south of Valencia. Walk south on beach for 1-2km. Very cruisy near the forest)
-Playa de la Casa Negra (NU) (on the same bus line at the Golf Course Resort Hotel)
-Playa de Malvarosa de Corinto (G NU) (20 mins from Valencia to Sagunto, near hotel Torre Corinto).
-El Pinedo (NU) (cruising in the ruins of and old factory behind beach)

CRUISING

-Viveros (Jardins del Real) end of Alameda
-Billares Colón, C/. Lauria (R)
-Jardines del Turia (near Paseo de la Alameda)
-Paseo Alameda (also by car, at night)
-C/. Joaquín Ballester (r t) (also by car, at night)
-Jardines de Palacio de Congresos, park next to the Placio de Congesos.

Valladolid

BARS

■ **House Bar 1900** (AC B d G MA WE) 22-5, WE -6h
C/. Alarcón, 3, bajo *Near Plaza Mayor* ☎ 98 335 35 90
Thu-Sat with DJ. Fri & Sat show at 3h.

■ **Libertad 3** (AC B BF d G m MA S SNU) 8.30-4h
Bajada de la Libertad, 3 ☎ 98 335 63 83

DANCECLUBS

■ **Deja Vu** (B D GLM MA OS S) Daily from 18-?h
Plaza Tenerías 10

■ **Discoteca Roma** (B D GLM MA S)
Calle de San José 9

SEX SHOPS/BLUE MOVIES

■ **Eurovisex Sex Shop** (G VS) 10-22h
C/. Puente Colgante, 11 ☎ 98 322 13 42

SAUNAS/BATHS

■ **Capuchinos** (B DR DU FC G M RR SA SB SOL VS) 16-24, Fri -24 Sat -3h
C/. Capuchinos, 8 *Near bus terminal* ☎ 98 318 90 78

GENERAL GROUPS

■ **ALEGAVA – Asociación de Lesbianas y Gays de Valladolid** (GLM)
Plaza Carmen Ferreiro, 3, 1° aula 19 *Quarter San Pedro Regalado, last stop of bus 1* ☎ 646 941 032 (mobile)

CRUISING

-Central bus station
- P football stadium José Zorrilla (after dark)
-"Pinamar", in Pine woods next to stadium
-Playa de las Moreras
-Campo Grande (park closes at 24h or 22h in winter)
-Valsur shopping center (toilets)
-Zone Cerro de las Contiendas

Vigo

BARS

■ **7.4** (B g OS YC) Mon-Sat 23-4.30h. Winter Wed-Sat only
Rúa Arenal, 74 ☎ 98 612 89 59

■ **Plaff Café-Bar** (AC B D GLM MA OS S ST VS WE)
Tue-Thu 20-2, WE -4h, Mon closed
Oliva N° 8 *City centre, next to concathedral Colexiata, bus stop „Puerta del Sol"* ☎ 646 405 939 (mobile)

■ **Poper's** (AC B DR f G MA VS) 22.30-?h
Rúa Serafin Avendaño, 12 ☎ 88 611 79 88
■ **Roy Black** (B D DR G MA VS) 24-4h
Rúa Oporto, 12 ☎ 98 622 30 46

CAFES

■ **Tournasol** (AC B CC g m MC OS s) 12-1, Fri & Sat -3h
Rúa Roupeiro, 7 ☎ 98 612 89 59

SEX SHOPS/BLUE MOVIES

■ **Pikante** (g VS) 10-3, Sun 16-3h
C/. Príncipe, 22 *Galerías* ☎ 98 643 21 55 🖳 www.pikante.com
Second store C/. Paraguay, 5 in Vigo.

SAUNAS/BATHS

■ **Azul** (B DR DU G m MA SA SB SOL VS WO) 16-4h
C/. Roupeiro, 67 ☎ 98 622 82 92 🖳 www.royazul.com

GENERAL GROUPS

■ **Legais – Colectivo de Lesbianas e Gais de Vigo** (GLM MA) Fri 20-22h
Rua Real 4, 1° ☎ 630 061 399 (mobile)

SWIMMING

-Samil Beach/Praia Samil (g nu) (at the rocks)
-Barra Beach/Praia Barra (G)
-El Vao (G).

CRUISING

-Garden at Club Náutico
-Gardens at Arenal (behind Comandancia de Marina)
-Estación Renfe (railway station).

Vitoria

BARS

■ **Moët & Co** (AC B GLM MA) 19-3, Fri & Sat -3.30h
Calle de Los Mantelli, 1 *Corner C/. Los Herrán, 46* ☎ 94 528 93 33

GENERAL GROUPS

■ **Gaytasuna Colectivo Gay de Alava** (G)
C/. San Francisco 2, 1° ☎ 94 525 78 66 🖳 www.ehgam.org

HEALTH GROUPS

■ **Comisión Ciudadana Anti-SIDA de Alava** (glm)
Mon-Fri 9-14, 16-20h
C/. San Francisco, 2 – 1° ☎ 94 525 78 66

Zaragoza

BARS

■ **Fangorya Zaragoza** (B GLM MA) 22-?, Fri & Sat 24-?h
C/. Fita, 11 🖳 www.fangorya.com
■ **Imán** (B GLM MA) Thu 23.30-3.30, Fri & Sat -4.30h
C/. Fita, 1 *On corner with C/. de Martín Ruizanglada*
■ **Mick Havanna** (AC B DR F G I MA VS WE) 16-3, WE -5h
C/. Ramón Pignatelli, 7 *Av. Cesaraugusto* ☎ 97 628 44 50
🖳 www.mickhavanna.es.tl
■ **New Ebano** (B DR G MA VS)
C/. Peromarta Telesforo, 5 ☎ 97 643 10 00
■ **Paradys** (AC B D G MA VS)
Wed, Thu, Sun 18-3, Fri & Sat 23.30-4.30h
C/. García Galdeano, 4 ☎ 97 623 00 08
■ **Sandor** (B DR G MA VS) 21-4h
C/. Loscos, 13 ☎ 97 639 82 02
■ **Urano** (B D GLM MA) 23-?h
C/. Fita, 9 *Sector Gran Via*
■ **...Y Que?** (B GLM MA)
C/. Garcia Galdeano, 13

CAFES

■ **Madalena. La** (B GLM M MA OS)
C/. Mayor, 48 ☎ 97 639 19 52

DANCECLUBS

■ **Boy's** (AC B D G MA s VS) Thu-Sun 22-5h
C/. Dato, 18 ☎ 97 622 84 02
■ **Bunker** (B D G MA)
C/. Fita, 15 ☎ 97 615 81 81
■ **Oasis** (AC B g MA S ST T WE) 24-8h
C/. Boggiero, 28
Show Fri-Sat from 1.30h. Special events at e.g. gay liberation day.
■ **Spook** (AC B D G m MA S) 19-?h
C/. Arzobispo Domenech, 12 ☎ 97 622 04 73

RESTAURANTS

■ **Flor Restaurante** (AC B CC G M OS)
13.30-16 & 20.30-24h, Sun closed, Mon only evenings
C/. del Temple, 1 ☎ 97 639 49 75

SEX SHOPS/BLUE MOVIES

■ **Amor Amor** (g)
C/. Cesareo Alierta 4, pasaje Miraflores local 20
■ **Eurovisex Sex Shop** (g VS) 10-22h
C/. José Anselmo Clavé, 23-25 *Opp. train station* ☎ 97 643 26 39
New Shop in C/. Rioja 32.
■ **Pignatelli** (g VS) 10-22h
C/. Ramón de Pignatelli, 44 ☎ 97 643 71 99
■ **Tubo. El** (AC CC G MA VS) 10-22h
C/. Cuatro de Agosto, 15 *Near Bar El Plata* ☎ 976 297 113
🖳 www.eurovisex.com

SAUNAS/BATHS

■ **Nordik** (b DU FH G I m MSG PI RR SA SB SOL VS WH)
15-23, Sat also 1-7h
C/. Vidal de Canellas, 18 *Near Plaza Roma* ☎ 97 635 39 23
🖳 www.saunanordik.com/zaragoza.htm

GENERAL GROUPS

■ **LYGA – Lesbianas y Gays de Aragón** (GLM)
Mon & Fri 19-22h, Fri youth group
C/. San Vicente de Paul, 26, 2° ☎ 97 639 55 77

HEALTH GROUPS

■ **Comité Antisida, Asociacion de lucha antisida** (GLM)
C/. Pignatelli, 53 ☎ 97 643 81 35
Second address in C/. Boggiers 71.

CRUISING

-Plaza de los Sitios (at night)
-Estación El Portillo (at night).

Sri Lanka

Location: South Asia
Initials: CL
Time: GMT +6
International Country Code: ☎ 94 (omit 0 from area code)
International Access Code: ☎ 00
Language: Sinhalese,Tamil, English
Area: 65,610 km² = 25,332 sq mi.
Currency: 1 Sri Lanka Rupee (LKR) = 100 Cents
Population: 19,625,000
Capital: Colombo
Religions: 77% Buddhist, 8% Hindu, 9% Muslim, 7% Christian
Climate: Constant warm climate with most rain in May and Oct.

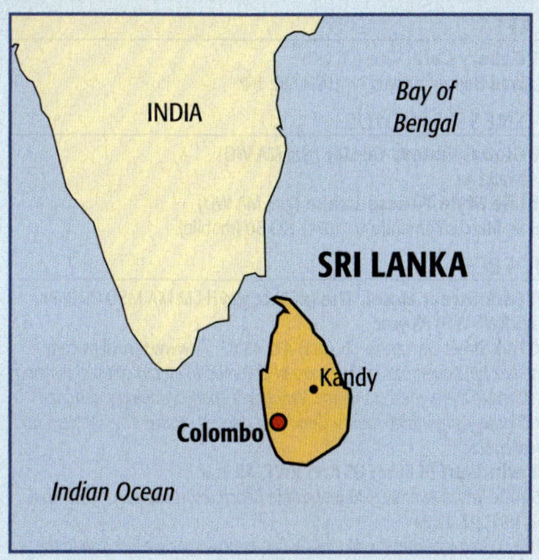

According to paragraph 365a, homosexuality is illegal in Sri Lanka. Gay men can be imprisoned for up to ten years when prosecuted. Although nobody has been prosecuted in court for 20 years, the situation in Sri Lanka is worrying, according to Amnesty International. The population is plagued by a rising number of abductions, illegal killings and children being recruited to the army.Yet in 2011, the Colombo Pride even „Equal Ground" could go ahead for the 7th time. It should be seen as a particularly resounding success that the celebrants included homosexuals as well as heterosexuals.

Nach dem Paragraphen 365a ist Homosexualität in Sri Lanka verboten. Schwulen Männern können bei Anklage bis zu zehn Jahren Haft drohen. Allerdings ist seit 20 Jahren niemand mehr gerichtlich belangt worden. Dennoch ist die Situation in Sri Lanka laut Amnesty International Besorgnis erregend. Steigende Zahlen von Verschleppungen, illegale Tötungen und Kindereinberufung plagen die Bevölkerung. Aber 2011 hat zum siebten mal der Colombo Pride „Equal Ground" stattgefunden. Als besonders großer Erfolg darf die Tatsache genannt werden, dass die Feiernden sowohl homo-, als auch heterosexuell waren.

Selon le paragraphe 365a l'homosexualité est interdite au Sri Lanka. En cas de poursuite, les hommes homosexuels risquent une peine de jusqu'à 10 de détention. En outre personne n'a été poursuivit en justice depuis 20 ans, mais la situation au Sri Lanka est particulièrement préoccupante. Un nombre croissant d'enlèvements, d'homicides et d'appels illégaux sous les drapeaux d'enfants rongent le pays. Mais en 2011 a eu lieu pour la 7em fois à Colombo la Gay Pride „Equal Ground". On peut noter comme un énorme succès le fait que parmi les fêtards se trouvaient aussi bien des homos que des hétérosexuels.

La homosexualidad está prohibida en Sri Lanka. Según artículo 365a, hombres gays pueden ser castigados con hasta diez años de prisión.
A pesar de que desde hace 20 años nadie más ha sido juzgado, la situación en Sri Lanka es, según Amnistía Internacional, preocupante. El creciente número de secuestros, de muertes ilegales y rapto de menores dañan a la población. No obstante, en 2011 se celebró por séptima vez el Orgullo Gay de Colombo „Equal Ground". Cabe mencionar especialmente como un gran éxito que los participantes fueran tanto homosexuales como heterosexuales.

Secondo il paragrafo 365a, l'omosessualità in Sri Lanka è vietata. I gay, in seguito ad una denuncia, possono anche rischiare fino a 10 anni di carcere. Tuttavia da più di 20 anni nessuno più è stato perseguitato penalmente. Amnesty International continua comunque a ritenere la situazione in Sri Lanka molto preoccupante. I numeri delle deportazioni e degli omicidi e non fanno altro che crescere. Nel 2011 ha avuto luogo, per la stimma volta, il Colombo Pride Equal Ground. Un grande successo che può essere annoverato all'Equal Ground è sicuramente quello di aver portato in piazza sia omosessuali che eterosessuali.

NATIONAL GROUPS

■ **Equal Ground** (GLM I) Mon-Fri 9.30-17.30h
20/1A Kassapa Road ✉ Colombo 5 ☎ (011) 251 29 77
💻 www.equal-ground.org
Focusing on the human rights of Sri Lanka's LGBTIQ communities. They are for the equitable status for all sexual orientations and gender identities and to eliminate the physical, emotional, spiritual and psychological abuse stemming from strict interpretations of gender and sexuality. They also offer a video & book library, safe space including dance classes, movie nights etc.

HEALTH GROUPS

■ **AIDSline** (GLM MA) Mon-Fri 16-20h
☎ (94-11) 485-7575
A telephone counseling service, open to gay men and women, launched in January 2000, by the AIDS Coalition for Care, Education and Support Services (ACCESS), offering free advice and guidance to callers seeking information on HIV/ AIDS and other sexual matters.

Aluthgama ☎ 034

RESTAURANTS

■ **Tropical Anushka-River-Inn** (B DM glm H M OS PA VEG) Daily
97 Riverside Road *On river Bentota* ☎ (034) 227 53 77
💻 www.anushka-river-inn.com
Hotel, bar and restaurant. Local gay information available from the owner.

CRUISING

-Beruwela, near Barberine-Hotel at the beach where reef starts (also swimming area)
-Beruwela, Sunshine-Restaurant (popular after 20h).

Colombo ☎ 011

BARS

■ **Bay Leaf** (AC B CC MA NG OS WE)
Gregory's Road ☎ (011) 269 59 20
Great bar, great food.

■ **Rhythm'n'Blues** (AC B cc D glm m MA)
Duplication Road ☎ (011) 536 38 59
Popular with the gay crowd. Live music every night with a great atmosphere!

CAFES

■ **Gallery Cafe. The** (CC NG)
2 Alfred House Gardens ☎ (011) 582 162

FITNESS STUDIOS

■ **Global Fitness Center** (glm MA WO)
3 Jawatta Av.
■ **Life Style Fitness Lanka** (glm MA WO)
45 Sir Marcus Fernando ☎ (074) 723 30 (mobile)

HOTELS

■ **Park Street Hotel. The** (AC B cc glm H I M MA MSG OS PI PK RWS RWT WO) All year
20 Park Street *City centre* ☎ (011) 472 43 63 💻 www.taruvillas.com
The first boutique hotel in the centre of Colombo in an old colonial building restored to the highest standards. Very gay-friendly. Stunningly designed and large, comfortable rooms. Good and discreet service. Fine Western and local cuisine.
■ **Windsurf** (B BF H I OS RWS RWT) All year
15-A De Soyza Avenue, Mount Lavinia *Beach resort suburb of Colombo* ☎ (01) 273 22 99
Only 50 m away from the Mount Lavinia beach and close enough to the Galle Road, Colombo's main road. 18 guestrooms.

HEALTH GROUPS

■ **Companions on a Journey** (G MA)
☎ (011) 485 15 35
An exclusively LGBT organization founded in 1995 and focusing their work in three main areas: advocacy for protection of rights of LGBT people and decriminalisation of consenting adult homosexuality; networking; and providing peer based outreach services. They operate two drop-in centers in Colombo and Kandy. In addition, they conduct film screenings, host reading room facilities and social get-togethers. They also provide peer counseling, STI/HIV testing and treatment and provide free condoms and information on STIs/HIV through peer outreach workers.

CRUISING

-Colombo public library toilet
-Wellawattha railway station and Wellawatta Beach (Police patrolling around 21h)
-Fort railway station toilet. (Buy train ticket first. All day, best late afternoon and WE)
-Fort Galle Face Green. Popular with locals and gays from outside, especially foreigners. (MA. Some Navy and Army)
-Dickmans Road (occasionally very cruisy. Some r from 20-24h walking along roadside)
-New Parliament Grounds at Battaramulla, Kotte. Heavy policed compound became the favorite cruising area, best between roundabout and bridge from 20h until late – except during Parliament sessions. (MA, some r)
-Liberty Plaza Shopping Mall, Kollupitiya, Colombo 3. Facilities upstairs at middle at center of complex
-Majestic City Shopping Complex, Bambalapitiya, Colombo 4, Galle Road. Busy second and third floors. Facilities are under supervision.
-Bambalapitya beach (behind Majestic City)
-Main Intercity Bus Stop in Colombo-Fort. Two toilets. (Very busy.)
-Government bus stand (outside, not in the Metro Inn building), a small busy washroom without cabins. Look and pick-up. No cabins.
-Behind Hotel/Casino near Katunayake airport. (Drive from Negombo road to the airport into small road). Popular with taxi drivers and customers at night
-Colombo Fort, facilities in the CTB government bus stand.
-Beaches (best after 15h)
-Mount Lavinia railway station. All day. Some „masseurs" (best to bring your own oil with you)

Galle ☎ 094

HOTELS

■ **Galle Fort** (AC B BF CC glm M PI RWS RWT) All year
28 Church Street ☎ (094) 932 870 💻 www.galleforthotel.com
With 14 suites and friendly staff this hotel offers guests the relaxed and beautiful experience of living in a grand colonial home.
■ **Kahanda Kanda** (AC B BF CC glm H I M MA MSG OS PI PK RWB RWS RWT VA WO) 24hrs
Angulugaha *30 mins from Galle* ☎ (094) 912 28 67 17
💻 www.kahandakanda.com
Luxurious boutique hotel with 7 individual suites in a 13 acre tea estate surrounded by jungle and overlooking Koggalla lake. Fantastically glamourous with great food and service.

Hikkaduwa ☎ 91

GUEST HOUSES

■ **Villa Tara** (glm H OS PI)
7 mins from the beach, in the jungle ☎ 776 326 879 (mobile)
💻 www.villatara.net
Apartment house. All guests will be picked up from the airport in Colombo.

Negombo ☎ 031

BARS

■ **Sherry Land Bar** (B GLM MA OS)
Ettukala
Famous outdoor bar and the best gay-friendly meeting place in Negombo.

CAFES

■ **Dolce Vita** (B GLM M MA OS)
Portuhota Rd *Enter through the Sea-Sands Guesthouse*
Gay-friendly italian coffee-shop. Good Tirami-su and ice-cream. Terrace with a fantastic view right beside the beach.

RESTAURANTS

■ **Bijou** (B GLM M MA OS)
Portuhota Rd ☎ (031) 531 9577
Run by the swiss couple Dolly & Augustin, Bijou is the place in Negombo for Europeans, swiss-asian cross-over cuisine.
■ **King Coconut** (B glm M MA OS)
Right at the beach with lots of locals and local food.
■ **Lords** (B GLM M MA OS)
80 B Poroutha Road *Beach Road* ☎ 777234721
Gay owned restaurant. The food and service is unique and well worth a visit. Lords is a nice, arty restaurant with an associated art gallery.

GUEST HOUSES

■ **Dickman Resort** (AC B BF G I M OS PI) All year
26/7 Poruthata Road – Sea Avenue *15 mins from Colombo International Airport* ☎ (031) 777 66 01 20 💻 www.dickmanresort.com
The Boutique Hotel provides eight exclusive rooms and suites, located around a charming Mango Garden and the pool. They supply airport limousine pick up service availability for 15 Euro with good and safe cars directly to Dickman Resort and Negombo.
■ **Gomez Place** (AC BF GLM I MA MSG NU OS PA PI PK RWB RWS RWT VA) All year
22/6b Poruthota Road, Ettukala *3 mins walk from the beach*
☎ (031) 227 68 27 💻 www.gomezplace.com
Seven room guesthouse located in Negombo, close to the beach and airport. All rooms en-suite with kingsize beds, minibar and kitchen.

CRUISING

-Negombo Bus Terminal, after 7:30pm until late
-Sunday in front of the 5-star „Beach Hotel." Walk down to Negombo Beach Park. Crowded with sweet, friendly people. Morning until noon and after 4pm. Don't go after 7pm

Sweden

Name: Sverige · Schweden · Suède · Suecia · Svezia
Location: Northwest Europe
Initials: S
Time: GMT +1
International Country Code: ☎ 46 (omit 0 from area code)
International Access Code: ☎ 00
Language: Swedish
Area: 449,964 km² / 173,731 sq mi.
Currency: 1 Swedish Crown (skr) = 100 Öre
Population: 8,992,000
Capital: Stockholm
Religions: 85% Protestant
Climate: Moderate climate in south with cold, cloudy winters and cool, partly cloudy summers, the north is sub-arctic.
Important gay cities: Stockholm

Sweden was the fifth European country, after the Netherlands, Belgium, Spain and Norway, to recognise same-sex marriage. Sweden, already a pioneer in granting same-sex couples the right to adopt children, is the first country in the world to allow homosexuals to marry in a church.

The situation for homosexuals in Sweden is two-sided. On one hand there is a great liberal spirit for which the country is renowned around the world. There are comprehensive anti-discrimination laws, registered partnerships with far-reaching rights which have been available for some time, and neither the age of consent (fifteen) nor the requirements to adopt children are any different for homosexuals. In addition there are generous public monies available to financially support gay organisations.

This tolerance is visible in everyday life in the larger towns of Sweden (although homosexuals are not exactly out on the streets), but in the countryside living an openly gay life is much harder, and there is occasional threat of violence. What many find surprising is the strictness of certain laws, for example the „buying of sexual services" where buying it rather than selling it is illegal (the buyer is the one committing the act, whereas the seller is the victim). The sale and use of Poppers is forbidden. You also risk prosecution if you fail to inform your sexual partner of your positive HIV status before having sex.

You may be surprised to always find restaurants in gay bars. This is because Sweden's restrictive alcohol laws make it virtually impossible to serve spirits in bars without food. In addition one can search in vain in the Swedish cities for gay saunas and sex clubs. With the emergence of HIV towards the end of the eighty these venues were abruptly closed by the government.

Schweden ist das fünfte europäische Land, nach den Niederlanden, Belgien, Spanien und Norwegen in dem Homosexuelle heiraten dürfen. Schweden, bereits ein Pionier in Bezug auf Adoptionsrechte für gleichgeschlechtliche Paare, erlaubt nun als erstes Land der Welt, dass Homosexuelle in einer Kirche heiraten können.

Die Situation für Homosexuelle in Schweden ist sehr zwiegespalten. Auf der einen Seite gibt es eine große Liberalität, für die das Land in aller Welt bekannt ist. Mag diese Toleranz in den größeren Städten des Landes im alltäglichen Leben spürbar sein (obwohl Homosexuelle auf der Straße kaum wahrnehmbar sind), so ist ein offen homosexuelles Leben auf dem Lande weitaus schwieriger und es kam immer wieder zu Gewaltakten. Was ebenfalls erstaunt, sind strenge Gesetze bezüglich des „Kaufs sexueller Dienstleistungen", wobei nur der Kauf illegal ist, nicht aber das Angebot (Käufer=Täter, Anbietender=Opfer). Der Gebrauch von Poppers ist untersagt.

Im übrigen macht man sich strafbar, wenn man einen Sexualpartner vor dem Sex nicht über seine HIV-Infektion aufklärt. Möglicherweise verwundert, dass es in schwulen Kneipen immer auch ein Restaurant gibt. Schwedens restriktive Alkoholpolitik macht den Ausschank von Spirituosen ohne gleichzeitiges Essensangebot in Lokalen so gut wie unmöglich.

Darüberhinaus sucht man vergeblich in den Städten nach schwulen Saunen und Sexclubs, denn mit Aufkommen der HIV-Problematik Ende der Achtziger Jahre wurden diese durch die Regierung alle kurzerhand geschlossen.

La Suède est le cinquième pays européen après les Pays-Bas, la Belgique, l'Espagne et la Norvège à autoriser le mariage gay. La Suède, déjà un pionnier en matière d'adoption pour les couples de même sexe, est désormais le premier pays au monde à autoriser les mariages gays dans une église.

La situation pour les homosexuels suédois peut sembler idéale: l'ouverture d'esprit des habitants est célèbre dans le monde entier, les lois anti-discriminatoires sont très élaborées, les couples de même sexe peuvent depuis longtemps se faire enregistrer, la majorité sexuelle est fixée à 15 ans pour tous et le droit à l'adoption est accordé aussi bien aux homos qu'aux hétéros. Des fonds publics soutiennent également les organisations gays. Néanmoins, cette tolérance se cantonne aux grandes villes et il est plus difficile de vivre son homosexualité au grand jour dans les campagnes et les actes de violence n'y sont pas rares. Etonnantes également les lois relativement strictes concernant „l'achat de services sexuels" qui prohibent l'achat mais pas l'offre et considèrent les prostitué(e)s comme des victimes et le client comme criminel. Poppers sont interdits.

Ne pas prévenir son partenaire avant le rapport sexuel de son infection au VIH est d'ailleurs puni par la loi. La présence d'un restaurant dans chaque bar gay peut surprendre mais elle est due à la loi restrictive ne permettant la distribution de boissons alcoolisées que dans les établissements où l'on sert également des plats.

La politique restrictive suédoise en matière d'alcool rend la vente d'alcool quasiment impossible sans une offre de restauration parallèle. De plus les saunas et sex-clubs sont inexistants dans les villes car avec la montée du VIH à la fin des années quatre-vingt, le gouvernement les a tout simplement fermés.

Suecia es el quinto país europeo, después de Holanda, Bélgica, España y Noruega en el que los homosexuales pueden contraer matrimonio. Suecia, pioneros incluso en términos de derechos de adopción para parejas del mismo sexo, se convierte ahora en el primer país del mundo en el que los homosexuales pueden contraer matrimonio por la iglesia.

La situación para los homosexuales en Suecia es bastante discrepante. Por un lado, existe una enorme libertad, por lo que el país es conocido en todo el mundo: Además, las organizaciones homosexuales se benefician de generosas subvenciones de dinero público para su apoyo financiero.
Si bien esta tolerancia se percibe claramente en la vida diaria de las grandes ciudades del país (aunque los homosexuales apenas se notan en la calle), llevar una vida homosexual abierta en el campo sigue siendo más difícil y pueden producirse incluso actos violentos. Lo que también sorprende son las estrictas leyes referentes a „la adquisición de servicios sexuales", aunque solamente la adquisición es ilegal y no la oferta (comprador = culpable, ofertante = víctima). El poppers está prohibido.También está penado el hecho de no decir a tu compañero sexual que eres seropositivo antes de practicar el sexo. Probablemente sorprenda que en muchos bares gays también haya un restaurante. La restrictiva política anti-alcohol de Suecia hace imposible que se puedan servir bebidas alcohólicas sin una oferta gastronómica alternativa.
La restrictiva política sobre el alcohol en Suecia hace prácticamente imposible la venta de licores en locales sin una oferta simultánea de alimentos. Además, buscará en vano en las ciudades saunas y clubes de sexo gay, ya que con el advenimiento de los problemas relacionados con el VIH estos fueron cerrados por el gobierno sin más preámbulos a finales de la década de los ochenta.

Dopo i Paesi Bassi, il Belgio, la Spagna e la Norvegia, la Svezia è il quinto Paese europeo che ha esteso l'istituto del matrimonio agli omosessuali. La Svezia, già Paese pioniere per quello che riguarda le adozioni omogenitoriali, adesso è anche il primo Paese al mondo a consentire il matrimonio in chiesa degli omosessuali.
La situazione per gli omosessuali in Svezia è molto ambigua. Da un lato c'è molta liberalità, per la quale la Svezia è famosa nel mondo. Inoltre lo Stato mette a disposizione fondi finanziari per le organizzazioni omosessuali. Tuttavia, anche se nelle grandi città si avverte una diffusa tolleranza, di contro, la realtà più provinciale dei paesini è, per gli omosessuali, più ostica tanto che spesso si verificano atti di violenza nei confronti degli stessi. Quello che inoltre stupisce, sono le severe leggi riguardo „l'acquisto di prestazioni sessuali". Tuttavia si deve tener presente che solo e soltanto l'acquisto è illegale e non l'offerta (acquirente = criminale, offerente = vittima). I popper sono vietati. Inoltre ci si rende punibili se non si informa il sex partner della propria infezione HIV. A causa della politica restrittiva sull'alcol, nei locali non è più possibile consumare superalcolici, se non abbinati al cibo. Inoltre è inutile andare alla ricerca di saune gay e sex club, poiché negli anni ottanta, col diffondersi dell'HIV, sono stati tutti chiusi dal governo.

NATIONAL GAY INFO

■ **qruiser.com** (GLM MA)
www.qruiser.com
Gay website for Scandinavia.

NATIONAL PUBLICATIONS

■ **Kom Ut**
Box 350 ✉ 101 26 Stockholm ☎ (09) 50 16 29 13 www.rfsl.se
Free LGBT newspaper (four issues/year) with articles on lgbt politics and life in Sweden and abroad. Published by RFSL, the Swedish Federation for Lesbian, Gay, Bisexual and Transgender Rights.

■ **QX** (GLM MA)
Box 17218 ✉ 104 62 Stockholm ☎ (08) 720 30 01 www.qx.se
Free monthly gay-lesbian newspaper with articles on lifestyle and gay life. Distributed for free at gay and gayfriendly venues.

NATIONAL GROUPS

■ **HomO – Ombudsman Against Discrimination on Grounds of Sexual Orientation** (GLM)
Box 3327 ✉ 070903 Stockholm ☎ (08) 50 88 87 80 www.homo.se
Information and advice for those who feel discriminated and preventive measures.

■ **RFSL** (GLM MA T) 10-15.30h (telephone)
Sveavägen 59 ✉ 113 59 Stockholm *City centre* ☎ 50 16 29 00
www.rfsl.se
The Swedish federation for gay, lesbian, bisexual and transgender rights. Local offices throughout the country that have small cafés, group meetings and LGBT-parties sometimes. See website for further information and addresses.

■ **SFQ Sveriges Förenade HBTQ Studenter**
Box 577 ✉ 114 79 Stockholm www.gaystudenterna.se
National organisation for LGBT student groups at Sweden's universities.

NATIONAL HELPLINES

■ **AIDSjouren** Mon-Fri 9-17h
Eriksberggatan 46 ✉ 114 30 Stockholm ☎ (08) 700 46 00
www.noaksark.org
Information about HIV and other sexually transmitted infections. Anonymously, confidentially and free of charge (if calling from inside Sweden).

GAY INFO

■ **gaymap.eu** (GLM MA)
www.gaymap.eu

Borås ☎ 033

GENERAL GROUPS

■ **RFSL-Borås** (D GLM MA) Disco & bar: Thu 18-23, Sat 22-2h (except July: Thu 22-2h)
Magasinsgatan 1 ☎ (033) 10 69 70 www.rfsl.se/boras

Eskilstuna

CRUISING

-Main road E20 P Rabyhed, 10km west of town
-Klippberget, 1km north of McDonald's, direction Torshalla.

Gävle ☎ 026

GENERAL GROUPS

■ **RFSL-Gävleborg** (b CC d GLM m MA t) Café: Mon & Wed 18.30-20.30; Pub: 3rd Sat/month 20-23; Disco: 1st Sat/month: 22-2h
Fjärde Tvärgatan 55 *Near Staffan Church in Brynäs* ☎ (026) 18 77 18
www.rfsl.se/gavleborg

Göteborg ☎ 031

BARS

■ **Gretas** (! B CC GLM M MA S ST) Tue-Thu 18-1, Fri & Sat 21-4h
Drottninggatan 35 *Brunnsparken* ☎ (031) 13 69 49 www.gretas.nu
Great bar that also serves delicious meals. At the same time nightclub on two floors with two dancefloors.

MEN'S CLUBS

■ **Wandas Gay Swing** (b DR G m MA SA VS)
Andra Långgatan 16 ☎ (031) 24 00 03 www.wandas.se
Swingers club with gay nights. See www.wandas.se for opening hours.

DANCECLUBS

■ **Gossip Bar & Kök** (B D glm MA) Mon-Thu 18-1, Fri & Sat -3, Sun 21-1h
Parkgatan 13 ☎ (031) 13 12 67 www.gossip.nu
Small and friendly bar with lounge and dance floor. No entry under 23 years. See www.gossip.nu for details.

■ **Queer** (D GLM MA S ST T) Last Fri/month 23-5h
c/o Park Lane, Kungsportsavenyn 36 ☎ (031) 20 60 58
www.cum.se

SEX SHOPS/BLUE MOVIES

■ **Future Erotica Nyhavn** (G MA VS) 10-22, Sun 12-22h
Lilla Drottninggatan 3 ☎ (031) 711 19 63 🖳 www.nyhavnerotica.se
DVD's, magazines and sex toys. DVD showrooms, cinema.

■ **Video Look** (G MA VS) 24hrs
Andra Långgatan 16 *Tram 3, 4, 9 – Masthuggstorget* ☎ (031) 12 55 71
Video club and sex shop.

■ **Videoshopen** (g MA VS) 10-23, Sun 12-23h
Färgfabriksgatan 3 *Hisingen Island, near Vågmästareplatsen*
☎ (031) 50 80 55 🖳 www.videoshopen.nu

GENERAL GROUPS

■ **RFSL-Göteborg** (GLM MA) Café: Sun 16-21, Wed 18-21; office open Fri 9-16h
Stora Badhusgatan 6 ☎ (031) 13 83 00 🖳 www.rfsl.se/goteborg
Local branch of the Swedish federation for gay and lesbian rights (RFSL).

SWIMMING

-Saltholmen. Seperate areas for men and women (g NU)
-Smithska udden (G)
-Stora Amundön (g) (nudist beach, in summer only).

CRUISING

-Slottskogen Park, cruising at the hill next to the tower, and hill between the tower and the parking (daily, all year).
-Kungsparken (night, all year).

Götene

CRUISING

-Blomberg (outdoor bath)
-Kungsparken (at night).

Halmstad ☎ 035

SEX SHOPS/BLUE MOVIES

■ **Kosmos Erotik** (DR g MA t VS) 12-21h
Laholmsvägen 25 ☎ (035) 12 71 73 🖳 www.kosmoserotik.se

SWIMMING

-Vilshärads Beach (NU)
-Heden, Hagön (NU)
-Mellbystrand, a very large beach, nudist area with cruising possibilities

CRUISING

-Norrekatts Park
-Heden, Hagön
-Mellbystrand in Laholm.

Helsingborg ☎ 042

SEX SHOPS/BLUE MOVIES

■ **Erocenter** (AC CC g MA T VS) 11-22h
Järnvägsgatan 27 *Centrally located* ☎ (042) 13 71 72

■ **Kosmos Erotik** (DR g MA t VS) 11-21h
Furutorpsgatan 73 ☎ (042) 14 16 16 🖳 www.kosmoserotik.se
DVDs, magazines, condoms, lubricant, massage oil and sex toys. DVD showrooms.

CRUISING

-Rosenträdgården (in the evening around the old fortress Kärnan)

Hemavan ☎ 0954

HOTELS

■ **Sånninggården** (B BF CC H I M MA OS SA) 10-22h
Dearna Klippen ☎ (0954) 330 00 🖳 www.sanninggarden.com
Hotel and Restaurant

Jönköping ☏ 036

CAFES

■ **Club 42 @ RFSL** (B GLM MA) Thu 19-21h
Norra Strandgatan 42 ☏ (036) 71 84 80 🖳 www.rfsl.se/jonkoping

Kristianstad ☏ 044

GENERAL GROUPS

■ **RFSL Kristianstad** (B D GLM MA) Pub: Fri 21-1h
Norra Kanalgatan 2 *Near Tivoliparken* ☏ (044) 10 65 90
🖳 www.rfsl.se/kristianstad

SWIMMING

-Yngsjö Naturbad (in summer only).

CRUISING

-Tivoliparken (between theater and baths, northern section at night all year).

Lund ☏ 46

CAFES

■ **Ebbas Skafferi** (B BF glm M MA)
Mon-Fri 8-21, Sat -18, Sun 9-18h
Bytaregatan 5 ☏ (46) 15 91 56 🖳 www.ebbasskafferi.com

SWIMMING

-Lomma (NU, 11km west of Lund, north of Lomma; between a square artificial lake and the sea)
-Högevalls badet (Stadsparken).

Malmö – Öresund ☏ 040

TOURIST INFO

■ **Malmö Turism** (glm) Mon-Fri 9-17, Sat & Sun 10-15h
Centralstationen *In central station* ☏ (040) 34 12 00
🖳 www.malmo.se/turist
Cross Øresund bridge between the Danish Copenhagen and the Swedish Malmö. It takes only half an hour by train or car. The Øresund region offers a varied selection of gay events.

CAFES

■ **Chez Madame** (b G MC) Mon-Fri 11-19, Sat & Sun 9.30-17h
Karlskronaplan 7

DANCECLUBS

■ **At Club** (B NG)
c/o Thap Thim, Västergatan 9
Best on Wednesdays.

■ **Tomboy Gayklubb** (B D GLM MA S) 22-3h
Bergsgatan 20 🖳 www.myspace.com/tomboygayklubb
Alternative queer club. Music varies from pop, rock, punk to electronica.

■ **Wonk** (B D GLM) Wed 20-24, Sat 23-4h
Adelsgatan 2 🖳 www.wonk.se
Bar and Nightclub with DJs and events.

SEX SHOPS/BLUE MOVIES

■ **Taboo** (AC CC DR g MA VS) Mon-Fri 11-22, Sat & Sun -18h
Södra Förstadsgatan 81 ☏ (040) 97 64 10 🖳 www.taboo.se

FETISH GROUPS

■ **SLM Malmö** (b DR F G MA P VS)
Sat 22-24h, sometimes Wed & Fri
Ystadsgatan 13 *Bus 2, 7, 8 – Smedjegatan*
☏ (040) 702 92 00 19 (club room during opening time)
🖳 www.slmmalmo.se
Leather club with special events and theme nights.

SWIMMING

-Ribersborg nudebeach NU (west part of the beach, close to the harbour for small boats)
-Ribersborg Kallbadhus NU (the old outdoor bathhouse 9-19h)
-Aq-va-kul (PI) (10-21h, Regementsgatan, opposite Slottsparken. Go to Turkish sauna on 2nd floor) Mon-Thu 9-21, Fri 9-20, Sat & Sun 10-18h, ☏ 30 05 40)

CRUISING

-Slottsparken ((between Kung Oscars väg and Mariedalsvägen)
-Pildammsparken (toilets)
-Aq-Va-Kul (especialy the Turkish bath), Regementsgatan 24
-Lernacken NU (cruising area on sunny days)

Piteå ☏ 0911

GENERAL GROUPS

■ **RFSL Nord** (B D GLM MA T WE)
Prästgårdsgatan 23 ☏ (0911) 925 70 🖳 www.rfsl.se/nord
Organizes events, parties and meetings in the Northern part of Sweden.

Stockholm ☏ 08

The beautiful so-called „Venice of the North" is situated on numerous islands between Lake Malaren and the Baltic. The city has never been destroyed in any wars. As a result it has a wonderful appearance which has grown up over the centuries. Stockholm is a wonderfully relaxed place surrounded by water, and still incredibly natural. The city is particularly beautiful in the summer months, when the long days and short nights give you plenty of time to get to know the city and its beautiful surroundings: the sculpture park, the „skerries" or the alleys in the old town with its colourful houses. Although the city's gay scene is small, it is friendly and lively.

Das Venedig des Nordens liegt unbeschreiblich schön auf unzählige Inseln verteilt an der Nahtstelle des langgezogenen Mälaren-Sees und der Ostsee. Die Stadt wurde nie zerstört und hat so ein über Jahrhunderte gewachsenes, wunderschönes Erscheinungsbild. Ein herrlich entspannter Ort mit viel Wasser und einer ungewöhnlichen Natürlichkeit. Besonders schön ist es in den Sommermonaten mit den langen Tagen, die einem viel Zeit geben, die Stadt und die Schönheiten der Umgebung kennen zu lernen: den Skulpturenpark Millesgården, die Schären oder die Gassen der Altstadt mit den bunten Häusern. Die schwule Szene der Stadt ist klein, aber freundlich und lebendig.

La Venise du nord s'étire magnifiquement sur d'innombrables îles à la jonction entre le lac Mälar tout en longueur et la Mer baltique. La ville n'a jamais été détruite et a ainsi pu évoluer harmonieusement au cours des siècles pour devenir ce lieu de sérénité au milieu des eaux. Les mois d'été sont particulièrement agréables et le soleil ne se couchant qu'à peine permet de visiter la ville et ses environs sans se presser. Le parc de sculptures Millesgården, l'archipel de Schären ainsi que les ruelles de la vieille ville avec leurs maisons colorées. Le milieu gay de Stockholm est petit mais agréable et vivant.

La Venecia del Norte está situada de una manera indescriptiblemente hermosa sobre varias islas en el punto de unión de un extenso lago y el mar Báltico. La ciudad nunca fue destruída y por eso conserva un aspecto maravilloso que ha ido creciendo a lo largo de los años. Un lugar fantástico y relajado, con mucha agua y una naturaleza poco habitual. La ciudad y sus bonitos alrededores son especialmente atractivos durante los meses de verano con sus largos días de luz que le permiten a uno tener más tiempo para visitarla: como el parque de esculturas Millesgärden o las callejuelas de la zona antigua con sus casitas de colores. El ambiente gay de la ciudad es pequeño pero agradable y dinámico.

Situata alla confluenza delle acque dolci del lago Malaren con quelle salate del Mar Baltico, la città (detta anche Venezia del Nord) domina un vasto arcipelago di isolotti. Stoccolma non è mai stata

distrutta, quindi il suo magnifico aspetto rispecchia una storia che va oltre i secoli. Stoccolma è una meravigliosa e tranquilla città con molta acqua e una naturalezza insolita. Particolarmente belli sono qui i mesi estivi con i loro lunghi giorni, che offrono molto tempo per conoscere la città e le bellezze dei dintorni: p.e. il parco delle sculture Millesgården o le viuzze della città vecchia con le loro caratteristiche case colorate. La scena gay è piccola ma molto cordiale e vivace.

TOURIST INFO

■ **Stockholm Tourist Center** (glm) 9-18, Sat 10-17, Sun -16h
Vasagatan 14 ☎ 08 508 28 508
🖳 www.visitstockholm.com/gay-lesbian
Publisher of the free „Stockholm Gay Guide".

BARS

■ **Babs Kök & Bar** (B GLM M MA) 17-1h
Birger Jarlsgatan 37 *M° Östermalmstorg, exit Stureplan. Pass Stureplan and continue Birger Jarlsgatan three blocks to cinema Zita* ☎ (08) 23 61 01
🖳 www.babsbar.se
Bar and restaurant. Delicious food and dizzy drinks served by friendly staff.

■ **Mälarpaviljongen** (B CC glm M MA VEG WL) 9-24h
Norr Mälarstrand 64, Kungsholmen ☎ (08) 650 87 01
🖳 www.malarpaviljongen.se
On the waterfront. Open April-September

■ **Roxy** (B CC GLM M MC) Sun, Tue-Thu 17-24, Fri & Sat 17-1h, Mon closed
Nytorget 6 *M° Medborgarplatsen, exit Folkungagatan* ☎ (08) 640 96 55
🖳 www.roxysofo.se
This is also a restaurant, very nice place for people around 30.

■ **Side Track** (! AC B CC f G M MA) Wed-Sat 18-1h
Wollmar Yxkullsgatan 7 *T-Mariatorget* ☎ (08) 641 16 88
🖳 www.sidetrack.nu
Also restaurant with excellent food and service. Great place!

■ **Torget** (B CC GLM M MA OS) Mon-Fri 16-1, Sat & Sun 13-1h
Mälartorget 13 *Opp. T-Gamla Stan* ☎ (08) 20 55 60
🖳 www.torgetbaren.com
Nice bar and restaurant with a kitschy boudoir interior and sometimes DJs.

CAFES

■ **Anna och Mats på Kungsholmen** (B glm m MA) 11-18h
Drottningholmsvägen 9 *M° Fridhemsplan*

■ **Chokladkoppen** (! AC bf GLM m MA OS) Daily 9-23h
Stortorget 18 *T-Gamla Stan* ☎ (08) 20 31 70
Beautiful in and outdoor seating. Close to the Royal Palace, in the heart of the historic old town. Cosy atmopsphere, delicious cakes, sandwiches and coffee or hot chocolate.

■ **Kafé Tjärlek** (B glm MA) 12-18h
Tjärhovsgatan 19 *M° Medborgarplatsen*
Café with Swedish cult music.

■ **Muren** (b CC GLM m MA) 10-22, Fri & Sat 10-23h
Västerlånggatan 19 *T-Gamla Stan* ☎ (08) 10 80 70
Gay-owned café. Ice cream bar during the summer.

DANCECLUBS

■ **Kinks & Queens @ Camarillo** (B D F GLM T) Sat 22-3h
Kungstensgatan 22 *M° Rådmansgatan* ☎ (08) 707 15 59 69
🖳 www.kinksqueens.com
Stockholm's fetish party. Dresscode is obligatory: minimum all black.

■ **Paradise** (B D GLM) Fri 22-3h
c/o Kolingsborg, Gula Gången, T-Slussen

■ **Patricia** (AC B CC D glm M MA OS S) Wed-Thu 17-1, Fr & Sat 18-5, Sun (G) -3h
Stadsgårdskajen 152 *T-Slussen* ☎ (08) 743 05 70
🖳 www.ladypatricia.se
Danceclub and good restaurant on quite a big ship. Fantastic location and always packed on Sundays!

■ **Zipper** (AC B D GLM I m MA OS) Sat 22-3h
Lästmakargatan 8 ☎ (08) 08 20 62 90 🖳 www.zippersthlm.com

RESTAURANTS

■ **Göken** (B CC GLM m MA OS) Lunch weekdays 11-14, dinner daily 17-1, brunch sundays 12-16h
Pontonjärgatan 28 *M° Fridhemsplan* ☎ (08) 654 49 28
🖳 www.goken.se
New owner. Busy gay restaurant and bar, crowded on weekends. Large outdoor seating in the summer.

■ **Monarki** (B CC DM GLM M MA VEG) 17-?h
Kungstensgatan 14 *Rådmansgatan, green line* ☎ (08) 400 20 406
🖳 www.monarki.eu
Nice restaurant and bar!

SEX SHOPS/BLUE MOVIES

■ **Basement. The** (CC DR G MA VS) 12-6, Fri & Sat -8h
Bondegatan 1b *T-Medborgarplatsen* ☎ (08) 643 79 10
Popular. Videos for sale & rent.

■ **Haga Video H56** (B DR GLM R T VS) 12-6h
Hagagatan 56 *T-Odenplan* ☎ (08) 33 55 44 🖳 www.hagavideo.com

■ **Manhattan** (DR G MA VS) Daily 12-6h
Hantverkargatan 49 *T-Rådhuset* ☎ (08) 653 92 10
🖳 www.ix.nu/manhattan
Very popular!

■ **US Video** (AC b CC DR G MA VS) 24hrs
Regeringsgatan 76 *T-Hötorget* ☎ (08) 545 158 30
🖳 www.usvideo.se
Popular darkroom. Large selection of erotica, toys, several cinemas and private rooms.

LEATHER & FETISH SHOPS

■ **Läderverkstan** (F glm MA) Mon-Fri 12-18h
Rosenlundsgatan 30 A *Södermalm* ☎ (08) 442 30 35
🖳 www.BDSMSHOP.se
Large variety of leather and toys in the gay backroom.

HOTELS

■ **Berns Hotel** (AC B D glm I M RWB RWS RWT SA WH) All year
Näckströmgatan 8 *Near Royal Palace and Old Town* ☎ (08) 566 322 00
🖳 www.berns.se

■ **Långholmen Hotel & Hostel** (B BF glm I M MA PK RWS RWT) All year
Kronohäktet, Box 9116 *On an island in city centre* ☎ (08) 720 85 00
🖳 www.langholmen.com
Great accommodation in a former prison on a picturesque island close to the city centre.

■ **Sheraton Stockholm Hotel** (AC B BF CC glm I M MC PA PK RWS RWT SA VA WO)
Tegelbacken 6 *Two minutes from the airport rail link* ☎ (08) 412 34 00
🖳 www.sheratonstockholm.com
Gayfriendly luxury-hotel right in the heart of town.

APARTMENTS

■ **Checkin Apartments** (cc glm PK RWT) All year
Oxenstiersgatan 33 *Centrally in Stockholm* ☎ (08) 658 50 00
🖳 www.checkin.se
All apartments are centrally located, close to the main gay venues. Furnished with Scandinavian design.

FETISH GROUPS

■ **SLM – Scandinavian Leather Men** (B D DR F G MA P VS) Wed 21-24, Fri & Sat 22-2h
Wollmar Yxkullsgatan 18 *T-Mariatorget, entrance at garage door*
☎ (08) 643 31 00 🖳 www.slm.a.se

HEALTH GROUPS

■ **Posithiva Gruppen** (G) Wed 18-24, Fri & Sat 19-24h
Tjurbergsgatan 29 *M° Skanstull, exit Allhelgonagatan* ☎ (08) 720 19 60
🖳 www.posithivagruppen.se
The Swedish organization for gay men with HIV/AIDS. Check website for info and events.

SWIMMING

-Frescati (G NU) (M° Universitetet, over the railway, left and through the woods)
-Kärsön (G) (M° Brommplan, bus to Kärsön, get of after the bridge at Brostugans Parking lot, walk right over the Island)
-Långholmen (G NU) (M° Hornstull, west side, cruising on the hill above the café)
-Solsidan (g NU) (M° Slussen, then train to Solsidan-Stop. Walk along Vårgårdsvägen until its end, then over the hill)
-North end of Kärsön Island (G NU) (bus from M° Brommaplan, get off at first stop after first bridge and walk around wheat field, then uphill through forest. Warm summer days until about 20h. Plenty of action)

Uppsala

SWIMMING

-Fjällnora (NU) (beach to the right)
-Centralbadet (NG pi sa)

CRUISING

-Stadsparken (public park northern part behind Flustret and next to Nedre Slottsgatan)

Växjö

CRUISING

-Linnéparken (evenings and nights in summer)
-Simhallen (best time Wed evenings, open until 22h)
-Jägargap.

Switzerland

Name: Schweiz · Suisse · Svizzera · Suiza
Location: Central Europe
Initials: CH
Time: GMT +1
International Country Code: ☎ 41 (omit 0 from area code)
International Access Code: ☎ 00
Language: German, French, Italian, Rhaeto-Romanic
Area: 41,285 km² / 15,940 sq mi.
Currency: 1 Swiss Franc (CHF) = 100 Centimes/Rappen
Population: 7,437,000
Capital: Bern
Religions: 41,8% Roman Catholic, 35,3% Protestant
Climate: Moderate climate that varies with the altitude. Winters are cold with snowy. Summers cool ocassionally very warm.
Important gay cities: Zürich, Lausanne

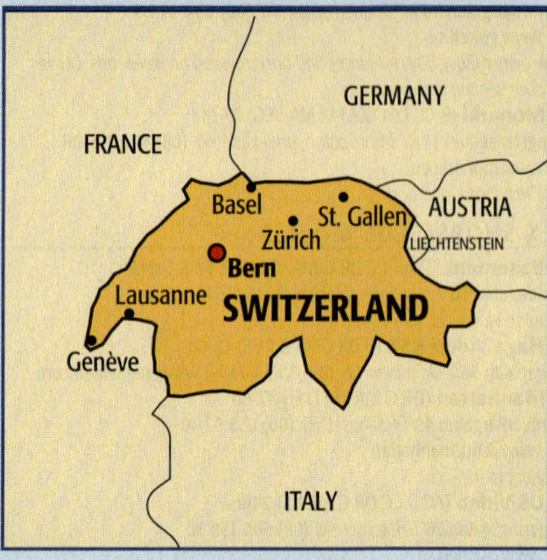

There are no special restrictions applying to gay sex in Switzerland. The age of consent is 16 years and applies to everyone. But there is no statutory protection from discrimination. Same-sex couples have been able to register since 2007, gaining almost the same rights as married partners. The law passed by referendum in 2005 however excludes them from adoption and medically assisted reproduction methods. 2011 saw Switzerland decide against granting homosexuals the same adoption rights as heterosexuals, thanks to the conservative majority in parliament.
Many lesbians and gay men lead an openly gay life in Switzerland without encountering any problems, even in rural areas. But there are still some aggressive homophobes left whom one should keep in mind while cruising outdoors or in gay areas late at night.
As a travel destination Switzerland has something for everyone, from ibex in the Alps to the boisterous party scenes located in Lausanne, Geneva and Zurich, the latter a little more prudish now since the authorities increasingly enforce their moral standards. Individual destinations in the Alps also cater to lesbian and gay tourists, but offer no gay life as such.
Switzerland is easiest seen by train, not all that cheap, but rewarding, as four different language and cultural regions (German, French, Italian, Rhaeto-Romanic) are combined in a very small area. Lakes Geneva and Constance, the Jura Mountains in the north and the almost Mediterranean Ticino in the south are all truly worlds apart.
Although Switzerland prefers to celebrate its insular status and continually tighten immigration laws, the presence of new cultures is hard to overlook and accompanied by the usual difficulties, but also by cultural and culinary benefits: the traditional Swiss Cervelat sausage and folk music have been joined by welcome rivals.

In der Schweiz gibt es keine besonderen Einschränkungen für gleichgeschlechtlichen Sex. Das Schutzalter 16 gilt einheitlich für alle. Ein gesetzlicher Diskriminierungsschutz fehlt dagegen. Seit 2007 können sich gleichgeschlechtliche Paare eintragen lassen. Sie erhalten damit fast die gleichen Rechte wie Ehepaare. Das 2005 in einem Referendum angenommene Gesetz schliesst die Paare aber von der Adoption und den Methoden ärztlich unterstützter Fortpflanzung aus. 2011 lehnte die Schweiz mit der konservativen Mehrheit im Parlament die Angleichung des Adoptionsrechts für Schwule an Heterosexuelle ab.
Viele Lesben und Schwule leben in der Schweiz ohne Probleme offen, auch in ländlichen Regionen. Neben der Toleranz gibt es auch aggressive Homophobie, der man sich beim outdoor-Cuising ebenso bewusst sein sollte, wie spät abends auf der Piste.
Das Reiseland Schweiz bietet für jeden Geschmack etwas, vom Rendez-vous mit Steinböcken in den Alpen bis zur ausgelassenen Party-Szene namentlich in Zürich, Lausanne und Genf. Ein bisschen prüder allerdings ist es in Zürich schon geworden, seit die Behörden vermehrt auf „Sitte und Anstand" pochen. Auch einzelne Alpen-Reiseziele setzen übrigens auf lesbischwule Touristen. Sie bieten aber kein Gaylife. Bereisen lässt sich die Schweiz bequem mit der Bahn. Das ist nicht ganz billig, aber es lohnt schon allein deshalb, weil die Schweiz auf sehr kleinem Gebiet vier Sprach- und Kulturregionen vereint (Deutsch, Französisch, Italienisch, Rätoromanisch). Genfer See und Bodensee sind erlebbar verschiedene Welten, ebenso die Hügelzüge des Jura im Norden und das Tessin im Süden, wo man beinahe schon das Mittelmeer riechen kann.
Obwohl die Schweiz immer wieder ihre Sonderstellung zelebriert, sich als Insel in der EU gefällt und ständig die Migrationsgesetze verschärft, ist die Anwesenheit neuer Kulturen nicht zu übersehen, einhergehend mit den üblichen Problemen, aber auch mit kulturellen und kulinarischen Bereicherungen: Die Schweizer Volkswurst Cervelat und die Ländlermusik haben willkommene Konkurrenz erhalten.

En Suisse il n'existe pas de restrictions particulières en matière de relation homosexuelle. La majorité sexuelle est fixée à 16 ans pour tous. Par contre, une loi anti-discriminatoire manque toujours. Les couples gays peuvent se faire enregistrer depuis 2007 et obtiennent presque les mêmes droits ques les couples mariés. La loi adoptée par référendum en 2005 exclut pour autant ces couples de l'adoption ou de la procréation médicalement assistée. En 2011, la Suisse avec sa majorité conservatrice au parlement a refusé l'ouverture aux homosexuels du droit d'adoption.
En Suisse beaucoup de gays et lesbiennes vivent ouvertement leur homosexualité sans problème, même à la campagne. Malgré la tolérance, on ne doit pas oublier les cas d'homophobie et d'agressions sur les lieux de cruising et de sortie. Tout le monde trouve son compte en Suisse, que ce soit les sorties dans la nature ou les soirée turbulentes de Zurich, Lausanne et Genève. Bien que Zurich soit devenue un peu plus prude depuis que les autorités réclament plus de décence. Quelques destinations alpines s'ouvrent même sur le tourisme gay sans pour autant offrir une véritable gay life.
On voyage facilement bien que assez cher en train, déjà pour découvrir sur une petite superficie quatre régions culturelles et linguistiques: allemande, française, italienne et rhéto-romane. Lac Léman et Lac de Constance: deux mondes différents à découvrir ; le massif du Jura au nord, le Tessin au Sud où l'on se croirait déjà au bord de la méditerranée. Bien que la Suisse cultive son exception d'isolation au milieu de l'UE et renforce constamment ses lois d'immigration, la présence de nouvelles cultures avec ses problèmes habituels est visible mais elles apportent aussi un enrichissement culinaire et culturel. Cette concurrence tombe à point pour le cérvelat et la musique alpine!

En Suiza no existe ninguna limitación especial para el sexo entre homosexuales. La edad de consentimiento de los 16 años rige para todos igual. Sin embargo falta una ley de protección contra la discriminación.

Desde el 2007 las parejas del mismo sexo ya pueden registrarse. Así obtienen casi los mismos derechos que los de un matrimonio. La ley que salió aprobada en un referéndum de 2005 excluyó no obstante a estas parejas de la adopción y de los métodos de reproducción asistida. En 2011, Suiza rechazó, con mayoría conservadora en el Parlamento, la equiparación de la ley de adopción para los homosexuales a la de los heterosexuales.

Muchas lesbianas y gays viven en Suiza sin problemas, de forma abierta, también en las regiones rurales. Junto a la tolerancia, también hay homofobia agresiva, hecho que debe tenerse en cuenta en zonas de ligue al aire libre o bien por la noche en algunas zonas de marcha nocturna.

Suiza, como destino turístico, ofrece algo diferente según los gustos, desde citas en los alpes con las cabras hasta zonas de ambiente abierto y distendido como en Zurich, Lausanne o Ginebra. Aunque Zurich se ha vuelto un poco más puritano, desde que sus autoridades llaman contínuamente a respetar el decoro y las formas. Algunos destinos alpinos piensan también en los turistas gay-lésbicos, si bien no tienen nada para la vida gay.

Viajar por Suiza se puede hacer cómodamente en tren o funicular. No resulta nada barato pero merece mucho la pena ya que Suiza reúne en una zona muy pequeña a cuatro regiones lingüísticas y culturales (alemán, francés, italiano y reto-románico). El lago de Ginebra y el lago de Constanza ya son en sí dos mundos distintos, al igual que las montañas del Jura, en el norte, o del Ticino en el sur, donde uno puede llegar casi al Mediterráneo.

Aunque Suiza se enorgullece todavía de su situación excepcional, al ser como una isla dentro de la UE y sigue restringiendo sus leyes migratorias, no debe despreciarse en absoluto la presencia de nuevas culturas, junto con los problemas habituales que conlleva pero también con la riqueza cultural y gastronómica que supone: la popular salsicha suiza „Cervelat" y la música popular tienen ahora una nueva competencia.

In Svizzera non esiste nessuna forma di discriminazione manifesta nei confronti dell'omosessualità. L'età del consenso è di 16 anni, sia per eterosessuali sia per omosessuali. Tuttavia non esiste una legge antidiscriminazioni.

Dal 2007 è possibile per le coppie dello stesso sesso farsi registrare e quindi essere riconosciuti. Questa forma di riconoscimento fa sì che le suddette coppie godano quasi degli stessi diritti delle coppie sposate. Una legge del 2005, tuttavia, esclude queste coppie dal diritto di adozione e dai metodi di procreazione assistita. Nel 2011, la Svizzera, con una maggioranza conservatrice al Parlamento, ha respinto il tentativo di equiparazione del diritto di adozione omosessuale a quello eterosessuale.

In Svizzera molte persone vivono la loro omosessualità senza problemi, anche nelle zone un po' più di provincia. Oltre ad esserci molta tolleranza ci sono anche casi di aggressione a sfondo omofobo dei quali bisogna tener conto quando si va in zone di cruising all'aperto o quando si esce di notte.

La Svizzera è una meta turistica che ha da offre davvero tanto: dagli incontri ravvicinati con gli stambecchi sulle Alpi, alla sfrenata scena notturna dei party di Zurigo, Losanna e Ginevra. Da quando però le autorità hanno deciso di puntare tutto sul decoro e il buon costume Zurigo è diventata un po' più pudica . Alcune mete di turismo alpino hanno scoperto il turismo gay, pur tuttavia non offrendo una vera e propria gay life.

All'interno della Svizzera ci si può muovere comodamente in treno. La Svizzera non è una delle mete più economiche da visitare, tuttavia vale la pena visitarla, già solo per il fatto che raccoglie in una così piccola area geografica ben quattro diverse zone linguistiche e culturali

(tedesca, francese, italiana e romancia). Il lago di Costanza e il lago di Ginevra sono due mondi a sé stanti, così come lo sono anche i tratti rotondeggianti dello Jura al nord e il Canton Ticino al sud, da dove si può già sentir l'odore del Mediterraneo.

Anche se la Svizzera si autocelebra sempre come caso particolare, si compiace di essere un'isola nell'Unione Europea e inasprisce continuamente le leggi contro l'immigrazione, bisogna comunque non sottovalutare la presenza di nuove culture, che è sì ovviamente collegata ai soliti problemi che ciò comporta, ma anche agli arricchimenti culturali e culinari: infatti, il salsicciotto arrostito del Cervelat (Volkswurst Cervelat) e la musica svizzera tradizionale (Ländlermusik) si trovano adesso in ben accetta concorrenza.

NATIONAL GAY INFO

360° (GLM)
36, rue de la Navigation ✉ 1200 Genève ☎ 022 741 00 70 💻 www.360.ch
Monthly gay magazine and website in French, published by 360° association, that organizes events and social forums. For sale in newsstands and in France & Belgium.

NATIONAL PUBLICATIONS

360° (GLM)
36, rue de la Navigation ✉ 1200 Genève ☎ 022 741 00 70 💻 www.360.ch
Monthly gay magazine and website in French, published by 360° association, that organizes events and social forums. For sale in newsstands and in France & Belgium.

Cruiser (GLM MA)
P.O. Box 72 ✉ 8034 Zürich ☎ 044 388 41 54 💻 www.cruiser.ch
Monthly gay newspaper with information about the gay scene in the German speaking part of Switzerland.

display (GLM)
display Media AG, Eichstraße 27 ✉ 8045 Zürich ☎ 044 313 15 05
💻 www.display-magazin.ch
Major Swiss monthly gay magazine, with articles about lifestyle, people stories, gay news and party guide.

gay.ch
Glattstegweg 95 ✉ 8051 Zürich ☎ 044 271 92 00 💻 www.gay.ch
Free lifestyle magazine with party guide, available in gay venues; also as online magazine www.gay.ch

Mannschaft (G)
Eigerstrasse 68 ✉ 3007 Bern ☎ 031 382 11 80
💻 ww.mannschaft-magazin.ch

NATIONAL COMPANIES

Flamingo Languages (GLM)
Bahnhofplatz 4 ✉ 8001 Zürich ☎ 044 397 17 00
💻 www.flamingolanguages.com
Language travel program designed especially for the gay and lesbian community.

Ikarus Entertainment
Postfach 50 ✉ 4153 Reinach ☎ 061 713 11 72
💻 www.ikarus-entertainment.com
Gay porn production company working in Switzerland as well as the rest of Europe.

Joy4Men (CC)
Thiersteinerstrasse 31-33 ✉ 4153 Reinach ☎ 061 713 11 72
💻 www.joy4men.ch
Mail order of gay DVD's and more.

NATIONAL GROUPS

AIDS-Hilfe Schweiz (AHS) (GLM) 8.30-12 & 14-17h
Konradstraße 20 ✉ 8005 Zürich *Next to main station* ☎ 044 447 11 11
💻 www.aids.ch
Prevention, information and counselling for people with HIV/AIDS. The AIDS-Hilfe has offices throughout the country, please check website or call for the exact addresses. See also www.drgay.ch for tips on sexual health.

Pink Cross – Schweizerische Schwulenorganisation (GLM MA)
Zinggstraße 16 ✉ 3001 Bern ☎ 031 372 33 00 💻 www.pinkcross.ch
The Swiss national gay organization.

COUNTRY CRUISING

-A1 Bern → Zürich P leave motorway at Mägenwil, then ca 500m on main road towards Brugg; P on both sides of the street, cruising in little forest. Also in other direction, best between 12-24h
-N1 Winkeln ⇆ Feldli Reitbahn P Moosmüli
-N1 Richtung/direction Baden-Zürich, in front of Zürich P Oberengstringen
-N1 Genève ⇆ Lausanne P between Morges & Aubonne
-N12 (E27) P behind Matran
-N14 Luzern ⇆ Zug, between Emmen-Süd & Gisikon Root P St.Katharina
-N2 Chiasso ⇆ Basel P Lugano Sud/Nord (both sides)
-N2 Chiasso ⇆ Basel P Mendrisio (both sides)
-N2 Chiasso ⇆ Basel P Ceneri Sud/Nord (both sides)
-N20 Nordring Zürich, both sides P Büsisee
-N9 Brig ⇆ Lausanne, exit 1km before Sion P in summer 17-24h

GAY INFO

gaymap.ch (GLM MA)
Genève www.gaymap.ch

queer.ch (GLM MA)
www.queer.ch
Swiss gaylife on the web.

TOURIST INFO

Switzerland Tourism
00800 100 200 30 (toll-free) MySwitzerland.com
Download a brochure on gay and lesbian travel to Switzerland or order a copy by calling the toll-free number.

DANCECLUBS

Purplemoon Party (B D GLM YC) 21.30-?h
Irregular gay party in various cities www.purplemoon.ch
Very popular with the young folks of the purplemoon chat page, 50% gay 50% lesbian. For more info see www.purplemoon.ch.

Arosa

HOTELS

Posthotel Arosa (AC B BF CC glm H M OS PI PK RWB RWS RWT SA SB SOL WH) All year
Oberseepromenade *Approx. 45 mins from Chur* 081 378 50 00
www.posthotel-arosa.ch

Baden

DANCECLUBS

GayRoyal (AC B D GLM M MA p S)
Sat on irregular dates 22h-open end
c/o Grand Casino, Haselstrasse 2 *near Mainstation*
www.gayroyal.ch
Irregular gay parties in the Grand Casino Baden, see www.gayroyal.ch for dates and details.

HOTELS

Best Western Hotel Du Parc
(AC B BF CC glm H I M MC OS PK RWS RWT) All year
Römerstrasse 24 056 203 15 15
www.duparc.ch
Charming and newly renovated 4-sta hotel. First-class restaurant and bar with live piano music. Baden is only 14 mins from Zurich and offers all advantages of a historic town.

Basel

GAY INFO

gaybasel.ch (GLM)
Postfach www.gaybasel.ch
Gay Website for the area.

TOURIST INFO

Basel Tourism Mon-Fri 9-18.30, Sat -17, Sun 10-15h
Aeschenvorstadt 36 *Stadt Casino @ Barfüsserplatz* ☎ 061 268 68 68
💻 www.basel.com
Info on Basel and it's rich cultural treasures. Other office in Railway Station SBB.

BARS

Besenkammer (B GLM MA) Thu-Sun 18-1h
Baselstraße 48, Reinach ☎ 061 711 97 50 💻 www.besenkammer.ch.vu

Elle & Lui (B DR GLM MA OS) 18-3h
Rebgasse 39 *Near Claraplatz* ☎ 061 692 54 79
1st Fri/month bears evening.

Storch (B g m MA OS) 6-24, Sat 8-?, Sun 10-?h
Hauptstraße 36, Reinach *Tram 11-Reinach Dorf* ☎ 061 711 86 86
💻 www.storch-reinach.ch.vu

Zischbar (B GLM MA OS) Tue 19.30-1h
c/o KaBar, Klybeckstraße 1b *Kaserne, near Claraplatz in Kleinbasel*
☎ 061 681 4717 💻 www.zischbar.ch
Very popular mid-week event.

DANCECLUBS

Annex (B D GLM OS YC) Gay on selected dates only
Binningerstrasse 14 *near Zoo* 💻 www.theannex.ch
Sometimes gayparties. Check www.theannex.ch for details and dates.

Gameboys (B D GLM S YC) Sat 22-?h on various dates only
Binningerstrasse 14 *@ Kuppel near Zoo* ☎ 061 564 66 00
💻 www.game-boys.ch
New irregular heterofriendly party at the legendary venue „Kuppel". 3-6 times a year. Check website for details.

Isola (B D GLM MA WE) see website for party dates
Clarastrasse 45 *@ Club EnVogue* ☎ 061 683 1535 💻 www.isolaclub.ch
Revival of the oldest gay club in switzerland, the legendary „Isola" – hosted by Club EnVogue

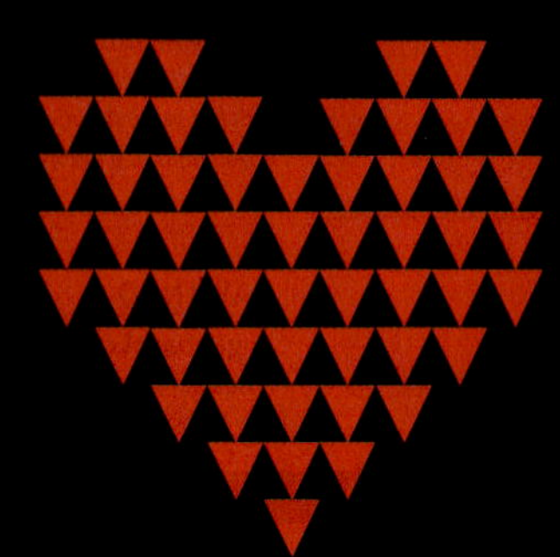

It's a man's world
Grenzacherstrasse 62
4058 Basel, Switzerland
info@sunnyday.ch
T. +41 (0)61 683 44 00
Mo – Do 12.00 – 23.00
Fr 12.00 – 05.00
Sa/So 14.00 – 23.00
www.sunnyday.ch
Sunnyday
Club Sauna/Shop
VEGAS

■ **Queerplanet** (! B D GLM MA) 22h-open end
Marktplatz 34 @ *Singerhaus* 💻 www.queerplanet.ch
Irregular gay party, 50 % gay 50 % lesbian. For more info see www.queerplanet.ch.

■ **Rainbow Gay** (B D GLM)
Level 31 Messeturm, Messeplatz 10 @ *Bar Rouge* 💻 www.colors-night.ch
Irregular gay-lesbian parties. Check www.colors-night.ch for schedule.

■ **Untragbar @ Hirscheneck** (B D GLM M MA S T WE)
Sun 21h-open end
Lindenberg 23 *near Wettsteinplatz* ☎ 061 692 73 33
Alternative gay event.

RESTAURANTS

■ **Hirscheneck** (B d GLM M MA)
Mon 14-0, Tue-Thu 11-0, Fri 11-1, Sat 14-1, Sun 10-0h
Lindenberg 23 *Tram 2-Wettsteinplatz, close to Theodorskirche*
☎ 061 632 73 33 💻 www.hirscheneck.ch
A small and very underground/alternative bar with local DJs. Hetero-friendly and gay/lesbian events. Also Brunch until 15h and special Dinner menu.

■ **Gareçons. Les** (B BF CC d DM glm M MA MSG NR OS PA PK S VEG WL) Mon-Thu 9-24, Fri & Sat -1h
Badischer Bahnhof, Schwarzwaldallee 200 *Train station: Badischer Bahnhof, Highway exit: Badischer Bahnhof* ☎ 061 681 84 88
💻 www.lesgarecons.ch
Tango Argentino every Monday. Every Sun „Rosa Sofa" 16-23h breakfast until 22h Also coffee and cake or cocktails.

SEX SHOPS/BLUE MOVIES

■ **6 New Shop** (CC G MA VS) Mon-Fri 12.30-21, Sat 12-20h
Feldbergstraße 82 ☎ 061 681 99 44 💻 www.6newshop.ch

■ **Gay-Mega-Store** (CC G MA OS) Mon-Fri 11.30-19.30, Sat 11-18h
Laufenstraße 19 *Tram station Münchensteinerstraße* ☎ 061 421 48 88
💻 www.gay-mega-store.ch
The biggest gay store in Switzerland with a wide range of products. Winner of the David-Award for „Best Gay Store in Europe".

SAUNAS/BATHS

■ **Sunnyday** (AC AK B CC DR DU F FC FH G GH I LAB M MA MSG p RR SA SB SH SL SOL VS WH WO) Mon-Thu 12-23; Fri -5; Sat, Sun & holidays 14-23; summer every day from 15h
Grenzacherstraße 62 *Near river Rhine, right bank, Wettsteinbrücke, in the basement of the building with supermarket Migros* ☎ 061 683 44 00
💻 www.sunnyday.ch
Modern and clean sauna with bio-sauna, daily foam party and a gay store.

BOOK SHOPS

■ **Arcados Gay info shop** (CC GLM MA)
Tue-Fri 13-19, Sat 12-16h
Rheingasse 67 *Tram 2-Wettsteinplatz/4, 6-Greifengasse* ☎ 061 681 31 32
💻 www.arcados.com
Magazines and books. New Blog on www.arcados.ch „thommens senf online".

HOTELS

■ **Teufelhof** (b CC glm M MA PA RWS RWT) Closed 23-27 Dec
Leonhardsgraben 47-49 *Tram 3 Musikakademie, near theatre*
☎ 061 261 10 10 💻 www.teufelhof.com

GENERAL GROUPS

■ **Homosexuelle Arbeitsgruppe Basel (habs)** (GLM)
Office Wed 19-21h
Postfach 1519 ☎ 061 692 66 55 💻 www.gaybern.ch
Consulting, information, politics, lobbying.

HEALTH GROUPS

■ **AIDS-Hilfe beider Basel** (GLM MA)
Mon, Wed-Fri 9-12, 13.30-17, Tue 9-12h
Clarastraße 4 ☎ 061 685 25 00 💻 www.ahbb.ch
Anonymous HIV/AIDS and Syphilis testing and councelling.

SWIMMING

-Northern shore of river Rhine (g NU) (between ferry station St Alban and facility at the Solitude, Schaffhauserrheinweg).

CRUISING

-Schaffhauserrheinweg (Near Stachelrain, at the stairs close to wooden-cabin) and Solitude Promenade
-Schützenmatt-Park (back part of Bundesplatz and near tram-station)
-Petersplatz (near Botanical Institute, Spalentor) facilities
-St.Alban Rheinweg between Farnsburger- and Eptingerstrasse
-Birsköpfli (in Birsfelden, near the river rhine) facilities.

Bern

BARS

Aux Petits Fours (B G MA) 18-0.30h
Kramgasse 67 *In the basement* ☎ 031 312 73 74

Blue Cat (B GLM I m OS) Tue & Wed 9-20, Thu-Sat -0.30, Sun 10-17h
Gerechtigkeitsgasse 75 *Near town hall* ☎ 031 311 07 29

Comeback (AC B CC d GLM M MA OS s)
Sun & Mon 18-0.30, Tue-Thu -2, Fri & Sat -3.30h
Rathausgasse 42 *Near town hall* ☎ 031 311 77 13 💻 www.comebackbar.ch

Samurai (AC B CC D GLM MA ST T WE)
Tue-Thu 18-1, Fri & Sat 21-3.30h, Sun & Mon closed
Aarbergergasse 35 *3 mins from main station* ☎ 031 311 88 03
💻 www.samurai-bar.ch
An institution in Bern. Expensive drinks but no cover-charge!

CAFES

Adriano's (B CC glm m MA OS)
Mon-Sat 7-0.30, Sun 10-0.30h
Theaterplatz 2 ☎ 031 318 88 31 💻 www.adrianos.ch

Villa Stucki (B GLM M MA) Mon-Fri 9-15, Tue & Thu 18-23h
Seftigenstraße 11 ☎ 031 371 44 40 💻 www.villastucki.ch
Fresh, homemade, seasonal – those are the characteristics of the lunch menu in Villa Stucki. Reservation recommended. Dinner of the gay group Bern every Wed 18.30h.

DANCECLUBS

Bad Boyz (B D GLM MA S WE) Sat 23-?h
Kramgasse 8 @ *Lounge Kapelle*
Gayevents with DJs and afterhour. Check www.gaybern.ch for dates.

DiscOriental (B D GLM MA) 1st Sat 20.30-3h
Kramgasse 6 💻 www.onobern.ch
Fram Bhangra to Rai – finest arabic music for gays, lesbians & friends. Check www.onobern.ch

Exzess (B D GLM MA) 1st Wed, free entry
Junkerngasse 1 @ *Sous-Soul*
Neo disco and elektroparty for gays and friends.

Gentle Boyz @ Du Théâtre (B D G MA S) Sat 22h-open end
Hotelgasse 10 💻 www.dutheatre.ch

Juliusparty (B CC D GLM M MA WE) 1st Sat/month 22-3.30h
Lorrainestrasse 2 @ *Restaurant Du Nord, Bus 20 station „Gewerbeschule"*
☎ 332 90 90 💻 www.juliusparty.ch

Liquido Club (B D GLM MA S SNU ST t) Sun 20-1h
Gewerbezone 2 *A1 exit Kerzers* ☎ (076) 262 08 55 💻 www.liquido.ch
Gay event „Gaymunity" on Sundays. Close to Bern.

Tolerdance (B D GLM MA) Every 4th Sat/month 22-?h
Neubrückstraße 10 @ *ISC Club* 💻 www.tolerdance.ch

Villa Kunterbunt (B D GLM MA) Sat 21-3.30h
Scheibenstrasse 72 *Bern Wankdorf*
Irregular gay-parties at the Graffitty.

RESTAURANTS

Lorenzini (B glm M MA OS) Reservations required
Hotelgasse 10 ☎ 031 318 50 67 💻 www.lorenzini.ch
To see and be seen italien restaurant, connected with club/lounge Du Théatre, host of Bubennacht party.

SEX SHOPS/BLUE MOVIES

■ **Cine 6** (g MA R VS) daily from 10h
Ryffligässlein *Between Spital- and Neuengasse, near Central Station*
2 Cinemas and many cabins. Rentboys.

■ **Loveland** (glm MA VS) Mon-Fri 10-18.30, Sat 10-16h
Gerechtigkeitsgasse 41 ☎ 311 70 70 🖳 www.peepstore.ch

SAUNAS/BATHS

■ **Al Peter's Sun Deck** (! B CC DU FC FH G GH I M MSG OS PP RR SA SB VR VS WH WO YC) 12-23h
Länggassstraße 65 *Entrance Schreinerweg 14, bus 12 -Uni Tobler*
☎ 031 302 46 86 🖳 www.sundeck.ch
For 29 years one of the best and most frequented gay baths in Switzerland, that constantly adjusts to the visitors' needs. Very clean, friendly staff and a new roof garden. Special events.

■ **Aqualis** (! B CC DR DU FC FH G GH I M MC MSG p PK PP RR SA SB SL SOL VR VS WH) Sun-Thu 12-23, Fri -3.30, Sat 14-23h
Brunnmattstraße 21 *Tram 6 BrunnhofTram 7+8 KV-Verband*
☎ 031 382 69 69 🖳 www.aqualis-sauna-club.ch
Modern and renovated sauna on 600 m², 1st Fri/month „Sneakers Party", 2nd Fri/month „Naked Party", 3rd Fri/month „Fist Party", 4th fri/month naked night (all 23-3.30h).

■ **Studio 43** (B DU f G OC OS SA SB SOL VS WO)
14-23h, closed 15th Jul-14th Aug
Monbijoustraße 123 *Tram 9-Wander* ☎ 031 372 28 27 🖳 www.studio43.ch
Popular sauna with bio-sauna and terrace in a courtyard.

TRAVEL AND TRANSPORT

■ **Hotelplan** Mon-Fri 9-18.30, Sat -15h
Hirschengraben 8 *Globus Reise Lounge* ☎ 031 328 08 88
🖳 www.hotelplan.ch/themen/gay-travel
Your travelagent: Daniel Gilgen-Sommermatter

Sauna
Aqualis
Da wo Mann sich trifft
Finnish Sauna
Large Steam bath
Whirlpool
Sling Room
Cabines
Crusing Areas
Gloryholes
Movies
Solarium
Bar and Snacks
Free Internet
Car Parking
every Friday Special Night
23h-3.3oh
Brunnmattstrasse 21 • 3007 Bern • Tel. 031 382 69 69
www.aqualis-sauna-club.ch

HOTELS

Belle Epoque (B BF CC glm H I M MA PA PK RWS RWT VA)
Gerechtigkeitsgasse 18 *10 mins walk from main station, 50m to Bus Stop „Nydeck"* ☏ 031 311 43 36 🖳 www.belle-epoque.ch
Wonderful small „Boutique Hotel" on one of the oldest and most beautiful streets in Bern. Formerly gay owned, the new proprietors keep the tradition and gladly welcome gay & lesbian travelers from all over the world.

Hotel La Pergola (BF cc glm I OS PA PK RWS RWT VA)
All year except 23.12 to 02.01
Belpstrasse 43 *10 mins walk to the cental train station and city centre* ☏ 031 941 43 43 🖳 www.hotel-lapergola.ch
Located in very peaceful surroundings. A very gay-friendly management and staff attend to all your needs.

GENERAL GROUPS

Homosexuelle Arbeitsgruppen Bern (HAB) (GLM MA)
Wed 19-21h (office)
Seftigenstraße 11 *In Villa Stucki* ☏ 031 311 63 53 🖳 www.gaybern.ch
Gay and lesbian organization for the region of Bern. Publisher of the „Berner Gayagenda" and „hab-info". Gay dinner „3Gang" Wed 19.30h.

CRUISING

-Allmend, behind Ice-stadium, nighttime
-Rosengarten near the bear-dungeon, in the park at night
-Grosse Schanze, Park above the main station, sometimes rentboys, after dark
-Bodenweid, at the forest behind sports-ground next to playgorund, after 22h, summer only
-Oberes Gerechtigkeitsgässchen (Spysi), facilities between Gerechtigkeitsgasse and Junkerngasse

Biel / Bienne

DANCECLUBS

Gaypirinha (B D GLM MA OS) Thu 17h-open end,free admission
Barkenhafen, Nidau @ *La Péniche* 🖳 www.gaypirinha.ch
Cool gay open-air event on the lake-shore in summer (July/August) only. Weather permitting!

SAUNAS/BATHS

Sauna Club XY (B DR DU G m RR SA SB VS) Daily 11.30-21h
Place de la Gare 7 *Close to the train station* ☏ 76 587 16 51 (mobile) 🖳 www.sauna-xy.ch

Brienz

HOTELS

Grandhotel Giessbach (B H M MA RWB RWS RWT)
Open from 20 Apr-21 Oct 2012
Above Lake Brienz, near Interlaken, by train and boat ☏ 033 952 25 25 🖳 www.giessbach.ch

Chandolin-Pres-Savièse

GUEST HOUSES

Grande Maison. La (BF cc glm I PA PK VA WH)
Check-in 17.30, check-out 12h
Route du Sanetsch 13 ☏ 027 395 35 70 🖳 www.lagrandemaison.ch
Six rooms and one suite in a 200 year old mansion, situated in the beautiful countryside of the Rhône Valley. Suite and one room with open fire place. Gay owned

Egerkingen

SAUNAS/BATHS

Cruising World (b DR DU g MA SA SB VS) 11-23, Sun 14-22h
Lindenhagstraße 3 ☏ 062 398 39 27 🖳 www.cruisingworld.ch
Mixed erotic sauna on 800 m².

Engelberg

HOTELS

Spannort Hotel & Restaurant
(BF CC glm H I M MA OS PK RWB RWS RWT SA) Tue-Sun 15-23h
Dorfstrasse 28 *Engelberg Valley, Titlis Ski-Area* ☏ 041 639 6020 🖳 www.spannort.ch
Traditional hotel with rustic interior, large restaurant and wine selection. Ideal for winter sports or hiking in the summer.

Fribourg

HELP WITH PROBLEMS

Sarigai, mixed homosexual association (B GLM MA S YC)
Tue 20-23h, location „2Seven"
27, av. Louis-Weck-Reynold, Case Postale 282 *Near Bern* ☏ 079 61 05 93 7 🖳 www.sarigai.ch

Genève

GAY INFO

Dialogai – Association Homosexuelle (B G MA)
Mon-Fri 9-17h
11-13, rue de la Navigation *Bus station Navigation or tram Môle* ☏ 022 906 40 45 (info) 🖳 www.dialogai.org
Many activities: Wed nights diner, parties Fri & Sat (call for info or see www.santegaie.ch). Movies on Sun evenings. Also location for the Café Off.

BARS

Boudoir de la Baronne. Le (B CC d G MA S SNU)
Wed-Sat 22-5h
3, rue Rossi ☏ 078 642 21 59
SNU on Fri, D on Sat.

Bretelle, La (B GLM m MA) 18-2h
17, rue des Etuves ☏ 022 732 75 96 🖳 www.labretelle.ch

■ **Concorde. La** (B G M MA OS R)
Mon-Fri 7-2, Sat 9-2, Sun 16-2h
3, rue de Berne *Below Cornavin railway station* ☎ 022 731 96 80
Young hustlers and old clients.

■ **Déclic. Le** (AC B CC D G S VS YC) Mon-Fri 17-2, Sat 21-2h
28, blvd du Pont d'Arve *Tram 12, 13, 16 Pont d'Arve, behind Chic Chicken*
☎ 022 320 59 14 💻 www.ledeclic.ch
Famous gay cocktail bar with over 70 specials. Oldest gay bar in Geneva. Young crowd.

■ **K-36** (B D GLM MA) Thu-Sat 22-5h
9, rue de Richemont 💻 www.k36.ch
Small club.

■ **Nathan** (B D GLM M MA S WE WI) Tue-Sat 20-2h
6, rue Baudit *Behind Cornavin railway station* ☎ 022 733 78 76
💻 www.swissgay.ch/nathan
Young crowd. A pillar in the gay community of Geneva.

■ **Phare. Le** (B GLM MA OS S) 15-2, Sun 17-24h
3, rue Lissignol ☎ 022 741 15 35 💻 www.le-phare.ch
Artistic events. Terrace in summer. Easy going. Alternative crowd.

■ **Ranch. Le** (B GLM MA) 16-2h
7 rue Sismondi ☎ 022 731 61 31

■ **Scandale. Le** (B GLM M YC)
24, rue de Lausanne ☎ 022 731 83 73 💻 www.lescandale.ch
Young mix crowd. Lounge. Fashion fans. Music downstairs.

MEN'S CLUBS

■ **Boy's Club** (B G) Wed-Sun 23-5h
22 Place Bémont ☎ 022 310 51 40

■ **Cruising Canyon** (b DR G MA SL) 17-4, Fri & Sat-6, Sun 15 -24h
15, rue Alfred-Vincent ☎ 022 731 81 15 💻 www.cruisingcanyon.ch

CAFES

■ **Aiglon. L'** (B CC d DM GLM M MA) Mon – Sat 8-2h, Sun closed
16, rue Sismondi ☎ 022 732 97 60 💻 www.laiglon.ch

■ **Livresse** (b GLM M MA) Mon 13-24, Tue – Thu 9-24, Fri -1, Sat 10-1h
5, rue Vignier ☏ 022 320 80 57 💻 www.livresse.ch
Library-café.

DANCECLUBS

■ **Garçonnière. La** (AC B CC D G M MA p S ST T VS WE WL) 19-5h
4bis, rue de la Rôtisserie ☏ 22 700 26 24 💻 www.lagarconniere.ch
Dinner show: Thu, Fri & Sat: 19-23h. Travesty shows at 23.30h and 3.30h.

RESTAURANTS

■ **Évidence. L'** (B G M MC OS) 9-14.30, 19-22h, closed Sun
13 rue des Grottes ☏ 022 733 6165
Gay managed. Excellent dessert buffet. Terrace in summer.

■ **Nid'Poule. Le** (AC B CC DM GLM M MA NR PA RES WL)
9-14.30, 19-22h, closed Sun
26, rue Adrien-Lachenal ☏ 022 735 59 49
Gay owned but nothing special.

SEX SHOPS/BLUE MOVIES

■ **Substation X-World** (! AC B CC DR f G I MA VS)
Mon-Sat 11-24, Sun & holidays 14-20h
14, rue de Neuchâtel *5 mins from the station* ☏ 022 900 14 69
💻 www.subinfo.biz
250 m² sex-shop, movies and sexclub on three floors. The basement is 100% gay with a giant screen, cubicles, sling, glory holes and labyrinth. Free web access for customers.

SAUNAS/BATHS

■ **Avanchets. Les** (B DR DU g GH LAB MA SA SB VS WH)
12-24, Fri -1, Sat -2, Sun -23h
Avenue de Baptista ☏ 022 796 90 66 💻 www.saunalesavanchets.com
Gay only on Sun.

■ **Bains de l'Est** (! B BF CC DR DU FC FH G GH I LAB M MSG PP RR SA SB SL SOL VS WH WO YC) 12-1, Fri & Sat -6, Sun 14-1h; Tue & Fri mixed
3, rue de l'Est *Tram 12/16/17, bus 1/6/8-Terrassière* ☏ 022 786 33 00
💻 www.bainsdelest.ch
Fully renovated. Foam party every Wed 20h. Also cabins and Hammam.

■ **Pradier** (b DU FC FH G MC RR SA SB SOL VS WH)
11.30-21, Sat -20h, Sun closed
8, rue Pradier *Near Cornavin railway station* ☏ 022 732 28 57
Small sauna.

■ **Sauna des Sources** (GLM MA MSG SA SOL VS WH)
Mon-Sat 11-22, Sun 13-22h (until 18h men only)
17, rue des Sources ☏ 022 320 04 63 💻 www.saunadessources.ch

HEALTH GROUPS

■ **Checkpoint** (glm) Mon 16-20, Thu 11-15h
11-13, rue de la Navigation *Bus station Navigation, tram Môle*
☏ 022 906 40 40 💻 www.dialogai.org
Quick HIV testing, STI screening, vaccination, counselling.

CRUISING

-Parc des Bastions (AYOR)
-Perle du Lac (park)
-Parc Geisendorf
-Parc Bertrand
-Toilet at Place Claparede
-Toilet at Place Dorciere
-Toilet at Rond point de Plainpalais
-Toilets of the University „Uni Dufour"
-Bains des Paquis in summer, on the lake, next to the sauna, on the jetty
-Vengeron beach in summer.

Glarus

CRUISING

-P in front of railway station
-Volksgarten near the fountain.

Ich will Männer!
MÄNNER 09.11
LADY GAGA
OUTLAWS IN MARLBORO COUNTRY?
GLEE-STAR CHRIS COLFER
EXKLUSIV
GEORGE MICHAEL
MÄNNER 05.11
SPECIAL
BEST OF GAY POP
Die heißesten Songs, die schwulsten Heteros, die coolsten Newcomer
CHRIS HEMSWORTH
10 JAHRE HOMOEHE
BEL AMI PRIVAT
Zu Besuch bei George Duroy und seinen Jungs
MÄNNER 04.11
SPECIAL
GLAMOUR, SEX, SKANDALE
CHRIS EVANS
HEISSER BRUDER
Hollywoods homofreundlichster Superstar
TORI AMOS
DER FEIND IN MEINEM BETT
BRASILIAN WAX
EXKLUSIV
BEN COHEN
Der Rugby-Star über seinen Kampf gegen Homophobie im Sport
DU SCHWULE SAU!
LUST AUF DROGEN
KEIN PARDON
INTERVIEW
HUGH JACKMAN
VERBOTENE LIEBE
MÄNNER 02.12
PORNOS BEI DER BUNDESWEHR?
SCHWULE BEIM FBI?
DIE TOP 50
MÄNNER 01.12
DANIEL CRAIG
BÖSE ALTE TUNTE
TRENNUNG ALS CHANCE?
SCHWUL IN DER TÜRKEI
JAHRES-HOROSKOP 2012

Interlaken

HOTELS

Derby (BF CC glm I M MA OS PA PI PK RWS RWT SA SB VA WO)
All year
Jungfraustraße 70 *Near town centre* ☎ 033 822 19 41
www.derby-interlaken.ch
Hotel under private management offering individual service. Centrally located with a quiet atmosphere. Free access to nearby swimming and fitness facilities.

Lausanne

BARS

Entrée, L' (AC B BF CC D GLM I M MA S ST VS)
Tue-Thu 17-24, Fri & Sat -2, Sun -1h, closed Mon

5, avenue de Tivoli *Next to Pink Beach Sauna* ☎ 021 312 80 00
www.bar-lentree.ch
Bar on two floors with DJs and lounge.

Saxo. Le (AC B CC F G MA S)
Wed, Thu & Sun 19-24, Fri -2, Sat 18-2h
3, rue de la Grotte ☎ 021 323 46 83 www.lesaxo.com

Yookoso (B CC glm MC) Tue-Fri 10-19, Sat 8.30-17h
18, rue de la Madeleine 18 *Above the hairdressers* ☎ 021 312 73 42

MEN'S CLUBS

Trafick (AC b CC DR F G MA NU p T VS)
12-23, Fri -24, Sat 11-24, Sun 15-21
22, av. de Tivoli *In the heart of the city, 5 mins from train station*
☎ 021 320 69 69 www.trafick.ch
Club on three levels with cabins, glory holes, play and sm room, maze etc. Theme schedule see www.trafick.ch. Located opp. Switzerland's largest and most popular sauna, the Pink Beach.

CAFES

Pur. Le (B CC glm I M OS YC) Mon-Fri 8-, Sat+Sun 9-?h
Rue du Port-Franc 17 ☎ 311 99 33 www.pur-flon.ch
Modern café with large summer terrace next to MAD club in the heart of Lausanne. Sat & Sun Brunch 11-16h.

DANCECLUBS

43&10 Club (! AC B CC D GLM MA)
Tue-Sat 23-5h, open on Sun only before public holidays
43, rue du Bourg *5 mins from central station* ☎ 021 320 43 20
www.lesbigay.ch
Also non-smoking area.

AYOR @ Amnesia (! B D GLM MA S YC) Sat 23-5h, various dates
Plage de la Voile d'Or, Vidy www.gay-party.com
Premium Gay & Lesbian Hetero-friendly fashion and party event. Check www.gay-party.com for details.

Jungle Gay Party (! AC B CC D DR GLM MA OS S SNU ST VS)
22-5h, only on public holidays
23, rue de Genève *@ MAD, centre of old town* ☎ 021 340 69 69
www.gay-party.net/jungle
Five x/year, very popular, mega-event on five floors. Check www.gay-party.net for details.

TRIXX (AC B CC D GLM MA OS P) Sun 23-5h
23, rue de Genève *@ Mad, center of old town, new and trendy Flon district*
☎ 021 340 69 69 www.trixx.ch
In the basement of Mad-Club, happy hour (2-4-1) from 23-24h. No entrance fee.

RESTAURANTS

Ma Mère m'a dit (AC B bf CC GLM M MA OS S)
Tue-Thu 9-14.30 & 17.30-24, Fri & Sat -1h; closed Sun
8, av. de Tivoli *Near Pink Beach Sauna* ☎ 021 312 69 69
www.mameremadit.ch

■ **ML16** (B CC G M MA OS) Mon-Fri 9-14.30 & 17.30-23h
16, av. Mont-Loisir ☎ 021 616 32 98 ■ www.ml16.ch
Very good food in an extremely friendly restaurant.

■ **Nautica. La** (B CC DM glm NR OS PA VEG WE WL)
Mon-Fri 7-24, Sat & Sun 10-1h
Chemin des Pêcheurs 7 *Lakeside, in the middle of the harbour*
☎ 021 616 12 12

■ **Open Café** (AC B BF cc GLM I M MA OS S)
Tue-Fri 10-15 & 17-24, Sat & Sun 17-24h
60, av. de Tivoli *In the gay street of Lausanne* ☎ 021 625 77 74
■ www.open-cafe.ch
Cosy place with good atmosphere and a terrace.

SEX SHOPS/BLUE MOVIES

■ **Garage. Le** (AC B CC DR F G MA VS) Shop 12-19, Sat 11-18, closed Sun. Club 12-23, Fri -24, Sat 11-24, Sun 15-21h
22a, av. de Tivoli *Bus 3 -Cecil, in front of Pink Beach Sauna*
☎ 021 320 69 69 ■ www.legarage.net
Boutique with magazines, books and more.

SAUNAS/BATHS

■ **New Relax Club** (b DR DU FC FH G GH m MA OS PP RR SA SB SOL VS WH) Gay from 12-18h
Galerie St. François A *City centre* ☎ 021 312 66 78
■ www.newrelax.ch
Gay in the afternoon only. Crowded on weekends.

■ **Pink Beach** (! AC AK B BF CC DR DU FC FH G GH H LAB M MA MSG NU PP RR S SA SB SH SL SOL VR VS WH WI WO)
12-23, Fri 12-3, Sat 12-Sun 23h (non-stop)
Avenue Tivoli, 7-9 *City centre, 5 mins walk from railway station near Chauderon Bridge* ☎ 021 311 69 69 ■ www.pinkbeach.ch
Switzerland's largest and „hottest" sauna on 2 floors with 1650 m².

■ **Top Club** (B DR DU FC FH G M MA MSG RR SA SB SOL VS WH WO)
14-23, Fri & Sat -24h
6, rue Belle-Fontaine *Opp. Bellefontaine parking* ☎ 021 312 23 66
■ www.topclub.ch

GIFT & PRIDE SHOPS

■ **Au petit q** (GLM I MA S) 12-19h, closed Sun
60, av. de Tivoli *In the gay street of Lausanne, next to Open Café*
☎ 021 312 29 29 ■ www.qshop.ch
Deco boutique selling books, DVDs, Gifts, Pride articles and more. Within the shop: Skin deep beauty and health care for boys, girls and other species.

TRAVEL AND TRANSPORT

■ **Hotelplan** Mon-Fri 9.30-18.30, Sat 9-17h
26, Rue de Bourg ☎ 021 341 71 00
■ www.hotelplan.ch/themen/gay-travel
Your travelagent: Jean-Luc Marion

TATTOO/PIERCING

■ **Skin Dream Tattoo** (AC CC GLM) 10-18h, closed Sun & Mon
5, av. de Tivoli *In the gay street of Lausanne. Bus stop Tivoli*
☎ 078 892 33 03 ■ www.skindreamtattoo.ch
Very professional and clean. A good choice. Skin deep beauty and health care for boys, girls and other species.

GUEST HOUSES

■ **Bernaldo B&B** (bf GLM MA) All year
Av. Harpe 47 ☎ 076 271 64 79 ■ www.bernaldo.ch
Gay owned.

■ **Rainbow Inn** (! CC G I MA OS PA PK RWB RWT SA VA VS)
All year
9, av. de Tivoli *Conveniently located next to the Pink Beach Sauna*
☎ 021 311 69 69 ■ www.rainbowinn.ch
Free admission to Pink Beach Sauna during your stay. Each room at the Rainbow Inn has its own individual style, equipped with TV. Reservations in advance are recommended. Check-in at Pink Beach.

Non Stop Weekend
From Saturday to Sunday
Xperience Night
Last Saturday of the month
Naked & more darkness from 9 pm
No Limit Night
2nd Friday of the month
Naked Sauna from 8 pm
Young Boys
Every Thursday & Friday
Under 30... entrance CHF 8.-
Twin Day
Every Monday
Two for One
SWISS QUALITY
I'm not into saunas,
but I love the Pink Beach
2 Floors
1650 m²
Tropical-Cruising-Area
Large Steam Bath
Finnish Dry Sauna
Whirlpool
Cold Water Pool
Dark & Play Rooms
Rest Cabins
Cinema & Labyrinth
Private Lavatory Room
Solarium
Wellness Massage
TV & Video Lounge
Bar & Snacks
Smoker Lounge
Free Internet
Own Guesthouse
PinkBeach
Switzerland's Best and Largest Sauna
Lausanne-Switzerland
Avenue Tivoli 7-9
www.pinkbeach.ch
+41 21 311 69 69
ETIENNE & ETIENNE

GENERAL GROUPS

■ **Vogay** (GLM MA)
☎ 021 653 00 59 💻 www.vogay.ch

SWIMMING

-Beach (1km from Morges access through the forest)
-Belle Rive Plage, end of sundeck

CRUISING

-Parc du Denantou (near Tour Haldimand)
-Promenade du Lac

Locarno

CAFES

■ **Maxway** (B BF H I MA NG OS) Tue-Sat 8.30-21h
via B. Rusca ☎ 091 751 29 36 💻 www.maxwaybar.ch
Italian style breakfast, selected wines.

SWIMMING

-Delta della Maggia (G NU) (between Locarno and Ascona river Maggia)
-Ponte Brolla Grotten (summer g NU) (2km out of Locarno in direction Centovalli-Valle Maggia, at Ponte Brolla in front of Maggia bridge to the right, path to the grotten, be careful, slippery!)

CRUISING

-Park near tennis court (both sides of the road along the Lago Maggiore, at night, on foot)
-Small park around Casino theatre

Lugano

BARS

■ **The Oc** (AC B CC glm M MA OS s) Tue-Sat 17-1h (19-23h also restaurant)
Via Cantonale, Magliaso *going from Magliaso in direction Pura, on the left side; train Lugano-Ponte Tresa stops in Magliaso* ☎ 091 60 65 157
New lounge bar. Mixed crowd, many gays.

SAUNAS/BATHS

■ **Gothic Sauna** (! B CC DR DU FC FH G GH I LAB m MA p PP RR SA SB SH SL SOL VS WH) Sun-Thu 14-23; Fri, Sat and before public holidays 14-1h
Vicolo Vecchio 3, Massagno *500 m from Lugano railway station, Massagno*
☎ 091 967 50 51 💻 www.gothicsauna.net
Very clean and popular sauna on three floors with original decoration and internet corner. Free condoms.

GUEST HOUSES

■ **Lugano Guest House** (B bf CC G OS WI) All year
Vicolo Vecchio 3, Massagno *Massagno, next to Gothic Sauna*
☎ 091 967 50 51 💻 www.gothicsauna.ch
Rooms with shower/WC, TV, radio and balcony. Free Wifi.

GENERAL GROUPS

■ **Imbarco Immediato** (GLM)
Via Colombi 1, Bellinzona ☎ 79 84 98 717 💻 www.imbarcoimmediato.ch
GLBT group of the region Ticino. Also organization of parties in different cities in and around Lugano. See their website.

HEALTH GROUPS

■ **Zonaprotetta**
c/o Aiuto Aids Ticino, Via Bagutti 2 ☎ 091 92 38 040
💻 www.zonaprotetta.ch
Prevention of HIV and support for people with Aids in the region of Ticino.

CRUISING

-Campo Marzio (Lugano-Cassarate close to the Lido)
-Parco Civico/Ciani (behind Mövenpick, closed 22.30h) (ayor)
-Central station (platform 1, in the toilets, ayor)

Luzern

BARS

■ **Uferlos – lesbischwules Zentrum** (B D GLM MA WE) Tue 20-0.30h
Geissensteinring 14 *Bus 4 from central train station* ☏ 041 360 14 60 🖳 www.halu-luzern.ch

DANCECLUBS

■ **Frigay Night** (B D GLM YC) 3rd Fri/month 22-4h
c/o The Loft, Haldenstraße 21 *Opp. Hotel National* ☏ 041 410 92 44 🖳 www.frigaynight.ch
Regular gay-event in Lucerne. Every 3rd Friday – see www.frigaynight.ch for more infos.

■ **Menergy** (B D G MA) Sat 22-5h, various dates
Inseliquai 12c @ *Nautilus Club* ☏ 041 211 07 05
🖳 www.menergy.ch
Irregular gay party. For more info see www.menergy.ch.

RESTAURANTS

■ **Sebastian's** (b CC glm M MA OS)
Mon-Sat 11.30-14, 18-23.30, closed Sun
Rütligasse 2 / Pfistergasse 3 *Near parking garage Kesselturm* ☏ 041 240 88 00 🖳 www.sebastians.ch

SEX SHOPS/BLUE MOVIES

■ **Erotic Store** (glm MA)
Bireggstraße 20a

SAUNAS/BATHS

■ **Cruising World** (b DR DU g MA SA SB VS) 11-22, Sun 14-22h
Staldenhof 3, Littau *Suburb of Luzern* ☏ 041 250 66 03
🖳 www.cruisingworld.ch
Not only gay.

■ **Discus** (! AC B DR DU FC G GH M MA PK RR SA SB SH SL SOL VS WH) open daily from 13-24h
Industriestrasse 10, Kriens *S4+5 Stopp Mattenhof or Bus 31 Stop Kuonimatt* ☏ 041 360 88 77 🖳 www.discus-sauna.ch
Sauna on 450 m², clean and friendly.

■ **Tropica** (B DR DU FC FH G m MC p PP SA SB SOL VS WH)
14-22, Fri -23h
Neuweg 4 *7 mins from train station* ☏ 079 335 77 44

HOTELS

■ **Best Western Hotel Rothaus Luzern**
(BF CC glm H I M OS PA RWS RWT) All year, 7-23h
Klosterstraße 4 ☏ 041 248 48 48
🖳 www.rothaus.ch

■ **Hotel Seeburg Luzern**
(B BF CC glm H I M MA OS PA PK RWB RWS RWT s) All year
Seeburgstraße 53-61 *Bus stop No. 24 in front of hotel* ☏ 041 375 55 55
🖳 www.hotelseeburg.ch
Welcoming atmosphere in the luxury of a 4-star hotel. Two nice bars in the hotel, occasionally events.

■ **Post Hotel Weggis – POHO** (AC B BF CC D GLM H I M MA MSG PA PI RWB RWS RWT S SA SB SOL WO) All year
Seestraße 8, Weggis ☏ 041 392 25 25 🖳 www.poho.ch
Gayfriendly lifestyle-hotel right next to Lake Lucerne.

SWIMMING

-Public baths at the lake (bathing enclosure with sun bathing area on the sun decks, near central station & Hotel Palace).

CRUISING

-Haldenstraße (by the side of Grand Hotel National)
-Inseli Promenade, Park Aufschütte am See (close to bath).

Montreux

SWIMMING

-Villeneuve (NU) (at the end of the beach).

Neuchâtel

CRUISING

-Jeunes Rives (path along the lake between university and harbour)

Olten

BARS

AM Bar & Lounge (AC B G m MA P S) 20h-open end
Klarastraße 1 *5 mins from main station* ☎ 079 340 45 52
💻 www.amlounge.ch

Silvaplana

HOTELS

Conrad (AC B I M MA OS PA RWB RWS RWT) All year
Via dal Farrer 1 ☎ 081 828 81 54 💻 www.hotelconrad.ch
Traditional and innovative 3star hotel in the scenic Engadin-region.

Sion

CRUISING

-Highway Martigny-Sion, last P before Sion
-Gardens near Banque Cantonale du Valais
-Near Église St. Guérin
-WC in underground P of Planta (Rue de Lausanne, afternoons).

St. Gallen

BARS

Nuts (B D GLM MA OS) Sun-Thu 19-24, Fr & Sat 20-2h
Linsebühlstraße 37/39 ☎ 071 222 0 666 💻 www.nuts-bar.ch

RESTAURANTS

Japan House Edo / Sushi-bar Wasabi (AC B CC glm M MA NR VEG WL) 11.30-14 & 17.30-23.30h
Engelgasse 11-15 *Near the market* ☎ 071 222 00 81 💻 www.edojapan.ch
Japanese restaurant.

Restaurant Bar Barolo (B DM glm M MA OS PA RES VEG WL)
Tue-Sat 11-23.30h, closed Sun & Mon
Schmiedgasse 1 *Next to the cathedral* ☎ 071 222 60 26
💻 www.restaurant-barolo.ch

SAUNAS/BATHS

Badehaus Mann o mann (! AC B CC DR DU F FC FH G GH I LAB M MA MSG RR SA SB SH SL SOL VS WH) 14-22.30, Fri & Sat -24h
St. Jakobstraße 91 *Central, bus 3 to Olma* ☎ 071 244 54 64
💻 www.mann-o-mann.ch
An excellent sauna with a stylish interior on 400 m². Very clean, modern and extremely popular! Permanent foam party in special foam room with adjacent rainshower. Special hamam-massage available.

Rainbow Men's Club (B DR DU FC FH G I m MA MSG RR SA SB VS) 14-22, Fri -24h
Augustinergasse 19 *Near main station and Marktplatz-bus 1, 3, 7, 11*
☎ 071 230 14 85 💻 www.rainbowmensclub.ch

St. Moritz

HOTELS

Misani (B bf CC D GLM H M MA) Dec-Apr
Via Maistra 70 *2km from St. Moritz Dorf* ☎ 081 839 89 89
💻 www.hotelmisani.ch
Designer hotel with three restaurants, nightclub and wine bar.

Uster

CRUISING

-Municipal park
-Quay Niederuster
-Lido Uster am Greifensee

Vevey

BARS

■ **Baretto, Il** (AC B CC G m MA OS) 17-1h, closed Mon
4, Place du Marché ☎ 021 921 22 81 🖳 www.baretto.ch

CRUISING

-Place du Marché
-Bois d'Amour
-Passage souterrain Placette

Windisch

BARS

■ **Louis Tropic Bar** (B GLM I M MA OS S SNU t YC) 18-24, Fri & Sat -2h, closed Tue
Zürcherstraße 21 *End of town, direction Baden* ☎ 056 442 51 34
🖳 www.tropicbar.ch

Winterthur

DANCECLUBS

■ **Lollipop** (B D glm MA) Fri 22h-open end, various dates
Untere Vogelsangstrasse 8 *Bolero Club Lounge* ☎ 052 209 09 90
🖳 www.lollipopparty.ch
Gay-friendly oldie & Schlagerparty in Winterthur and Zurich.

GENERAL GROUPS

■ **WILSCH – Winterthurer Lesben und Schwule** (B BF d GLM m MA s t) Thu 19.30-23h
Badgasse 8 *in the pedestrian zone* 🖳 www.badgasse8.ch
Winterthurs Gay and Lesbian Group. Sometimes Events. Every second Wednesday, the club is open for Lesbians only from 17.00h, on the second Saturday Dinner special from 17.00h

Yverdon

CRUISING

-P in front of railway station
-Plage d'Yvonnard (3km direction Estavayer-le-Lac).

Zürich

Zurich is with its round 400,000 inhabitants, a small, manageable metropolis with an astonishingly lively and modern gay scene. The days when Zurich was seen as a sterile finance city are a long gone. The gay scene locations are frequently open until the early hours of the morning. A registered, same-sex partnership contract was past by referendum with a 2/3 majority and the party scene has a good reputation not only because of the success of the „Zurich Pride" and the last remaining Techno parade in Europe which takes place on the 2nd Saturday in August.

At the beginning in 2008 a lower court declared sex in „public commercial rooms", meaning darkrooms in Zurich for illegal. Owners and gay organizations have contested this judgment. Up until the last minute before publishing this Spartacus the legal situation remains unclear.

With around 400,000 inhabitants Zurich is a small manageable city, yet it has a surprisingly lively and modern gay scene. The time when Zurich was known as just a super-clean financial town is long gone. Recently the bars have started staying open until early morning, registered same sex partnership laws were recently voted through by a two thirds majority in a referendum, and the Zurich party scene has a Europe-wide renown following the success of the CSD and the Street Parade (Techno Parade).

Zurich's gay scene is traditionally located in Kreis 1 in the old town around Niederdorf Street, east of the Limmat. A broader, more alternative scene is located in Kreis 4, and there is a new development of several dance clubs in a former industrial area in Kreis 5 near the Escher-Wyss square.

Zürich ist mit etwa 400.000 Einwohnern eine kleine, überschaubare Metropole mit einer erstaunlich lebendigen und modernen schwulen Szene. Die Zeiten, als Zürich noch als sterile Finanzstadt galt, sind längst vorbei: Die Lokale haben häufig bis spät in die Morgenstunden geöffnet, eine registrierte gleichgeschlechtliche Partnerschaft wurde durch eine Volksabstimmung mit einer 2/3 Mehrheit durchgesetzt und die Partyszene hat nicht nur wegen der Erfolge des „Zurich Pride" und der letzten in Europa noch stattfindenden Technoparade „Streetparade" am 2.Samstag im August europaweit einen guten Ruf.

Anfangs 2008 hat ein Gericht Sex in gastgewerblichen Räumen (Darkrooms) in Zürich für gesetzeswidrig erklärt. Betreiber und Schwulenorganisationen haben das Urteil mit Erfolg angefochten. So gibt es auch heute wieder in diversen Clubs Darkooms, die jedoch klar vom Getränkeausschank abgetrennt sind.

Zürichs schwule Szene befindet sich traditionell im Kreis 1 in der Altstadt rund um die Niederdorfstraße, östlich der Limmat. Eine weitere, etwas alternative Szene befindet sich im Kreis 4 südwestlich des Hauptbahnhofs. Seit einiger Zeit hat sich eine spannende Szene aus Dance- und Afterhour Clubs im Kreis 5, in einem ehemaligen Industrieareal in der Nähe des Escher-Wyss Platzes, etabliert.

Avec près de 400.000 habitants, Zurich est une métropole de taille moyenne avec une scène gay étonnement vivante et moderne. L'époque est révolue où Zurich était considérée comme un centre financier stérile. Les bars sont ouverts jusque tard dans la nuit, un référendum a entériné la loi sur le partenariat homosexuel enregistré avec une majorité des deux tiers et la scène nocturne jouit d'une bonne réputation dûe non seulement aux succès de la « Zurich Pride » et « Street Parade » le deuxième samedi d'août, la dernière technoparade se déroulant en Europe.

Début 2008 un tribunal a jugé illégal le sexe dans les bars (darkrooms) à Zurich. Les gérants et les organisations gays ont contesté avec succès le jugement. Dès lors on retrouve des backrooms dans différents clubs qui sont cependant bien séparés du comptoir.

La scène gay zurichoise est située traditionnellement dans le 1er arrondissement dans la vieille ville autour de la rue Niederdorf, à l'est de la Limmat. Une autre scène plus alternative se trouve dans le quatrième arrondissement au sud-ouest de la gare centrale. Depuis quelque temps une scène dynamique voit le jour dans le cinquième arrondissement dans une ancienne zone industrielle dans les environs de la place Escher-Wyss avec des boîtes et des afters.

Zurich es una ciudad pequeña y manejable que cuenta con unos 400.000 habitantes y con un ambiente gay sorprendentemente vivo y moderno. La época en que a Zurich se la consideraba un frío centro financiero ya ha quedado atrás: los locales están generalmente abiertos hasta altas horas de la madrugada, la unión registrada de parejas del mismo sexo se estableció por voto popular con una mayoría de 2/3 y el ambiente fiestero goza de buena reputación, no sólo por el éxito del "Zurich Pride", sino también por los últimos desfiles de música Techno celebrados en toda Europa, el „Street Parade" el sábado 2 de agosto.

A principios de 2008 un tribunal menor declaró ilegal la práctica de sexo en los „espacios de hosteleria", como los „cuartos oscuros" de Zurich. Los empresarios y las organizaciones de homosexuales impugnaron la sentencia pero, antes de la publicación de Spartacus, la situación jurídica todavía no estaba clara.

Zürich, con aproximadamente 400.000 habitantes, es una pequeña metrópolis fácil de visitar. Tiene un ambiente gay dinámico y moderno. Los tiempos en que Zürich estaba considerada como una ciudad financiera muy limpia ya han pasado: ahora los locales están abiertos a menudo hasta la madrugada, la legislación sobre parejas del mismo sexo se

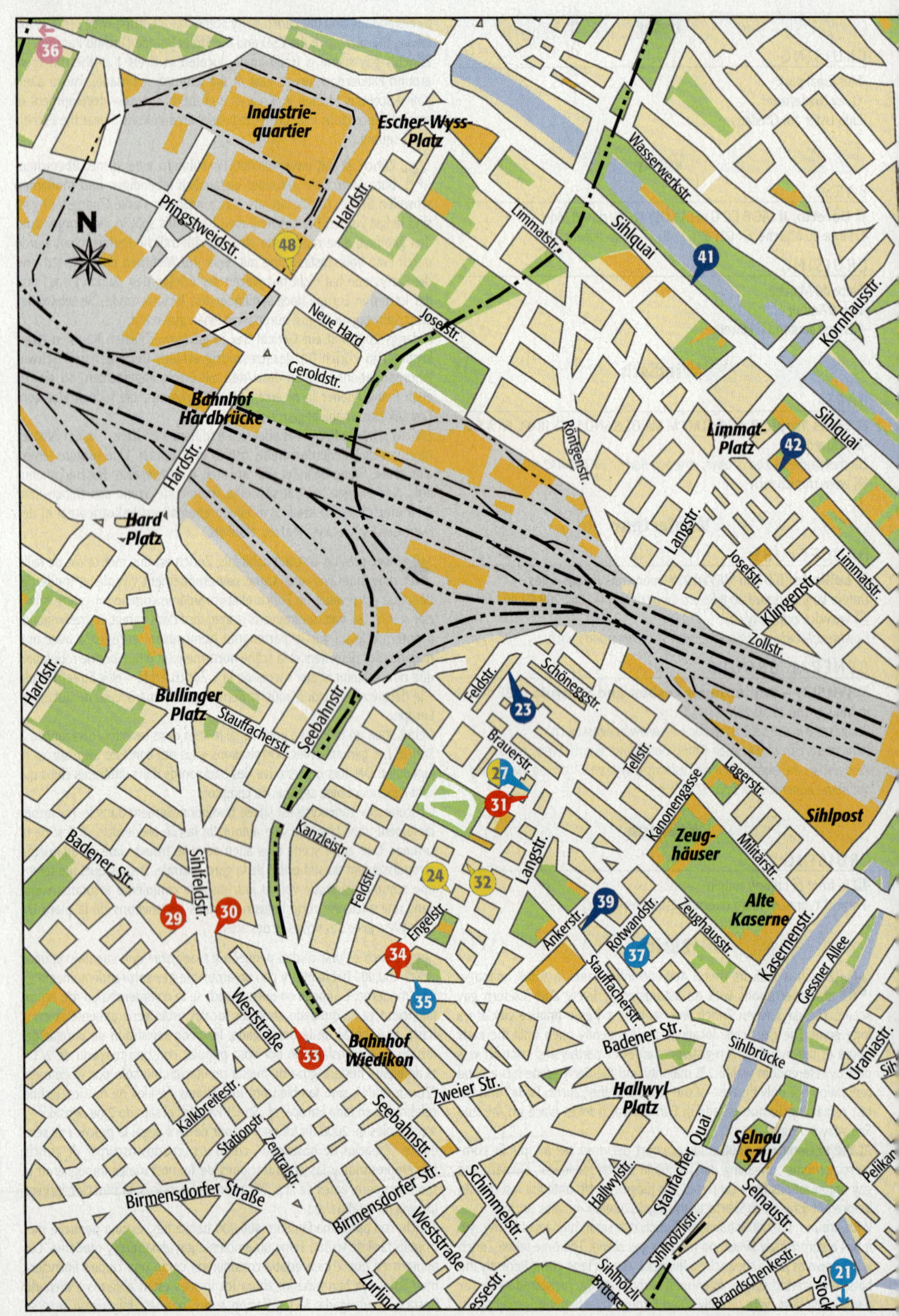
36
Industrie-
quartier
Escher-Wyss-
Platz
Wasserwerkstr.
Pfingstweidstr.
N
48
Hardstr.
Limmatstr.
Sihlquai
41
Neue Hard
Josefstr.
Kornhausstr.
Geroldstr.
Bahnhof
Hardbrücke
Röntgenstr.
Limmat-
Platz
42
Sihlquai
Hardstr.
Hard
Platz
Langstr.
Josefstr.
Klingenstr.
Limmatstr.
Zollstr.
Hardstr.
Feldstr.
Schöneggstr.
23
Bullinger
Platz
Stauffacherstr.
Seebahnstr.
Brauerstr.
Tellstr.
Lagerstr.
27
31
Sihlpost
Kanonengasse
Zeug-
häuser
Militärstr.
Kanzleistr.
Badener Str.
Sihlfeldstr.
24
32
Langstr.
Feldstr.
39
Alte
Kaserne
29
30
Ankerstr.
Rotwandstr.
Zeughausstr.
Kasernenstr.
Engelstr.
34
37
Gessner Allee
Weststraße
35
Stauffacherstr.
Badener Str.
Sihlbrücke
33
Bahnhof
Wiedikon
Uraniastr.
Zweier Str.
Hallwyl
Platz
Kalkbreitestr.
Seebahnstr.
Selnau
SZU
Stationstr.
Zentralstr.
Stauffacher Quai
Birmensdorfer Straße
Birmensdorfer Str.
Schimmelstr.
Hallwylstr.
Selnaustr.
Weststraße
Sihlhölzlistr.
Sihlhölzli
Brücke
Brandschenkestr.
21

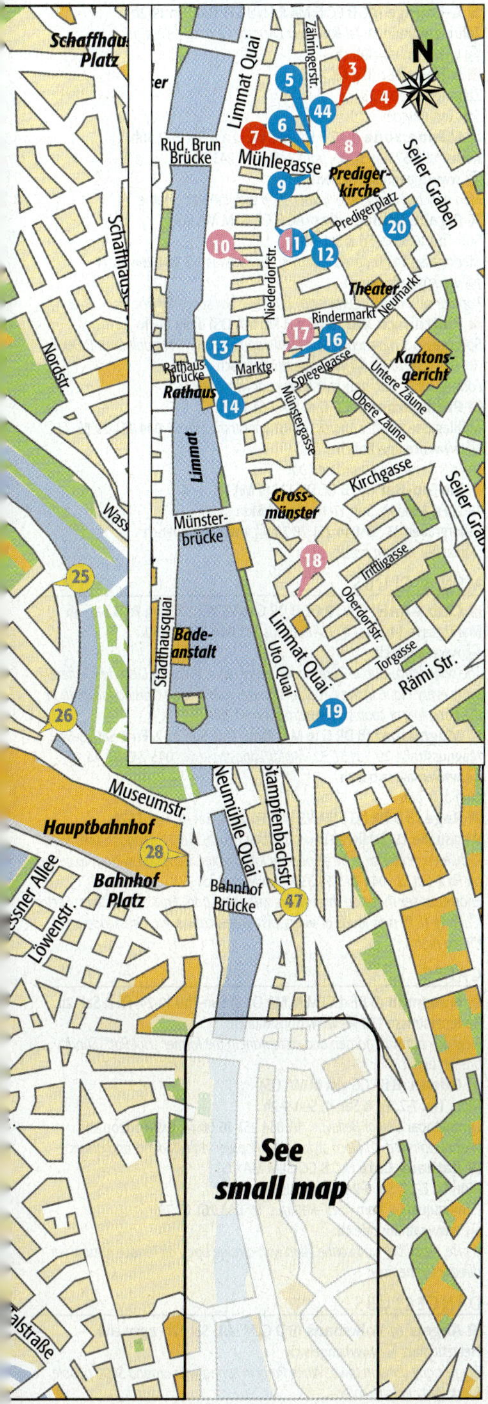

Zürich

EAT & DRINK

Acqua – Restaurant 21
Barfüsser – Bar 12
Cranberry – Bar 13
Daniel H. – Bar 37
Dynasty Club. The – Bar 5
G-Lounge – Bar 5
Huusmaa – Café 35
Männerzone – Bar 27
Marion – Restaurant 9
Odeon – Café 19
Pigalle – Bar 16
Platzhirsch – Bar 11
Predigerhof – Bar 6
Rathaus Café 14
Tagliatelle – Restaurant 44
Tip Top – Bar 20

NIGHTLIFE

Angels @ Volkshaus – Danceclub 39
Club AAAH! – Men's Club 17
G-Colors House – Danceclub 17
Heldenbar – Danceclub 41
Lollypop @ Xtra – Danceclub 42
Magnusbar – Men's Club 23
T&M Club – Danceclub 17

SEX

Apollo – Sauna 4
Erotik Factory – Sex Shop/ Blue Movies 29
Macho City Shop – Sex Shop/Blue Movies 3
Maxxx Erotic Discount – Sex Shop/Blue Movies 30
Moustache – Sauna 34
Mylord – Sauna 33
Paragonya – Sauna 7
Reno's Relax – Sauna 31

ACCOMMODATION

Adler – Hotel 10
Goldenes Schwert – Hotel 17
Helmhaus – Hotel 18
Platzhirsch – Hotel 11
Route 39 – Hotel 36
Scheuble – Hotel 8

OTHERS

AIDS-Hilfe Schweiz – National Group 24
Checkpoint – Gay Info 26
HAZ – Gay Info 25
Leonhards Apotheke – Pharmacy 47
Männerzone – Leather & Fetish Shop 27
Ministry of Kink – Leather& Fetish Shop 32
Pink Cloud – Travel & Transport 48
Zürich Tourism – Tourist Info 28

aprobó mediante una votación popular (mayoría de 2/3) y los éxitos de la Marcha del Orgullo Gay y de la Street Parade (Techno Parade) han aumentado su fama como ciudad europea de las fiestas.
El ambiente gay de Zürich se concentra en el Distrito (Kreis) 1, alrededor de la Niederdorfstrasse; en el Distrito 4, de carácter más alternativo y; algunas discotecas en el Distrito 5, una antigua zona industrial.

Zurigo è una piccola metropoli di circa 400.000 abitanti con una scena gay sorprendentemente vivace e moderna. Sono finiti i tempi in cui Zurigo veniva considerata una sterile città finanziaria: i locali sono spesso aperti fino a tarda mattinata, le unioni civili tra persone dello stesso sesso sono passate attraverso un referendum nel quale ha prevalso la maggioranza dei due terzi. La scena dei party di Zurigo gode di un'ottima fama: qui si svolgono infatti il celebre Zurich Pride e la Streetparade, l'ultimo corteo techno d'Europa, che si svolge ogni anno durante il secondo sabato d'agosto. All'inizio del 2008 un tribunale ha vietato, tramite sentenza, il sesso negli spazi pubblici commerciali (darkroom). I proprietari degli esercizi commerciali e le associazioni lgbt hanno impugnato con successo la sentenza. Così adesso nei club si possono ritrovare le darkroom, ben separate dalle teche dove vengono servite le bevande. La scena gay di Zurigo si concentra tradizionalmente nella prima circoscrizione, e cioè nel centro storico, intorno alla Niederdorfstrße, a est della Limmat. Nella quarta circoscrizione, a sudovest della stazione centrale, troviamo invece una scena un po' più alternativa. Mentre nella quinta circoscrizione, in una ex zona industriale vicino alla piazza Escher-Wyss, da un paio d'anni è andata affermandosi una scena notturna con molte discoteche e club per gli afterhour.

GAY INFO

Checkpoint Zürich (G MA) Mon, Wed & Fri 16-20h
Konradstraße 1 ☎ 044 455 59 10 www.checkpoint-zh.ch

gaycity.ch
www.gaycity.ch
Gay website for locations in the Niederdorf-area.

Homosexuelle Arbeitsgruppen Zürich (HAZ) (GLM MA)
Office: Wed 14-18, Library: Wed, last Thu & Fri 20-21.30h
Sihlquai 67 *Near central station* ☎ 044 271 22 50 www.haz.ch
Also tourist information centre.

CULTURE

Schweizerisches Schwulenarchiv (GLM) By appointment only
c/o Sozialarchiv, Stadelhoferstraße 21 ☎ 043 268 87 40
www.schwulenarchiv.ch
Swiss gay archives.

TOURIST INFO

Zürich Tourism (glm) Summer: 8-20.30, Sun 8.30-18.30, winter 8.30-19, Sun 9-18.30h
In the main railway station ☎ 044 215 40 00 www.zuerich.com
Hotel information and reservations: hotel@zuerich.com

BARS

Barfüsser (! AC B CC glm LM M MA OS PA RES s VEG)
Mon-Thu 11-24, Fri -2, Sat 14-2, Sun 15-24h
Spitalgasse 14 *Oldtown „Niederdorf", tram 4/15 Stop „Rudolf Brun Brücke"*
☎ 044 251 40 64 www.barfuesser.ch
Modern & chic Sushi Restaurant with a long bar, art-videos and leather sofas.

Cranberry (! AC B CC GLM MA OS) Sun-Wed 17-0.30, Thu -1, Fri & Sat -2h
Metzgergasse 3 *Tram 4, 15 -Rathaus* ☎ 044 261 27 72
www.cranberry.ch
Very popular trendy cocktail bar.

Daniel H. (B d glm m MC) Mon-Thu 17-24, Fri & Sat -2h
Müllerstraße 51 ☎ 044 241 41 78 www.danielh.ch
Alternative good homemade food served in stylish 60ies surroundings.

Dynasty Club. The (AC B CC D GLM H I MA OS S) 17-2h
Zähringerstraße 11 *Near central station* ☎ 044 251 47 56
www.dynastyclub.ch

G-Lounge (AC B CC G MA R SNU ST) Thu-Sun 19-2h
Zähringerstraße 11 *1st floor over Dynasty Club, same entrance*
www.dynastyclub.ch

Johanniter (B g MC)
Zähringerstrasse 33
Smokers lounge.

Männerzone (! AC B F G MC WE) Fri & Sat 21-2.30h
Kernstraße 57 *Bus 31, 33, tram 2* ☎ 043 243 30 43
www.maennerzone.com
Men-only bar next to the leather shop with the same name.

Pigalle Schlagerbar (AC B CC GLM MA OS S)
Sun-Thu 16.30-2, Fri & Sat -4h
Marktgasse 14 *Niederdorf, tram 4, 15 -Rathaus* ☎ 044 266 18 77
www.pigalle-bar.ch
Popular sing-along (Eurovision) bar. Juke box songs for free.

Platzhirsch Bar (B CC g H I m MA OS) daily 14-?h
Spitalgasse 3 *Hirschenplatz in Niederdorf, Tram 15+4 Rudolf Brun Brücke*
☎ 044 250 70 88 www.meinplatzhirsch.ch
Former Lobby Bar, now stylish new bar with hotel.

Predigerhof (B CC G m MA OS) 14-2h
Mühlegasse 15 *After Migros the 1st bar on the left* ☎ 044 251 29 85
www.predigerhof.ch
Long time running bistro and bar.

TipTop-Bar (AC B CC D GLM m MA S)
18-2, Fri & Sat -4, Sun 17-1h, closed Mon
Seilergraben 13 ☎ 044 251 78 20 www.tiptopbar.ch
Dance bar with hit music.

MEN'S CLUBS

Club AAAH! (! AC B CC D DR G m VS YC) 22.30-4, Fri & Sat -6h
Marktgasse 14 *Tram 4, 15 -Rathaus* ☎ 044 253 20 60
www.aaah.ch
The only dance club in Zürich open every night. With live DJs and a different party every night. In the G-Colours house, with a huge cruising labyrinth in the back, lots of cabins. Free admission till 23h.

Magnusbar (B DR G m MA) Mon, Thu, Sun 21-2, Fri & Sat 23-5h
Magnusstraße 29 *Bus 31, 32 -Militär/Langstraße* ☎ 043 243 90 43
www.magnusbar.ch
Men-only bar.

Rage (B D DR f G I MA VS WE) Fri 22-4, Sat -5, Sun 17-2h
Wagistraße 13, Schlieren *In a suburb of Zurich, bus 31 -Wagonfabrik, Train -Schlieren, entrance at large parking lot, private shuttles every hour to centre on Fri & Sat* ☎ 044 773 38 33 www.rage.ch
Enormous sex maze on three floors with three bars. Fri & Sat upstairs „Sector C" Party (F P) with loads of slings, piss areas, cabins, etc. Dresscode and theme nights.

CAFES

Huusmaa (B BF d GLM M MA OS s) Sun-Thu 10-24, Fri & Sat -2h
Badenerstrasse 138 www.huusmaa.ch
New gay bar with garden and restaurant in the former „Hot Pot". Sunday brunch buffet.

Odeon (B BF CC glm M MA OS)
Mon, Thu 7-2, Fri & Sat -4, Sun 9-2h
Limmatquai 2 *Near Bellevue* ☎ 044 251 16 50 www.odeon.ch
Well established Art Deco styled café. Popular with students and artists.

Rathaus Café (AC B CC GLM MA OS)
Mon-Fri 7-24, Sat 9-24, Sun 10-19h
Limmatquai 61 *Tram 4, 15 -Rathaus* ☎ 044 261 07 70
www.rathauscafe.ch
A nice, small bar and coffee shop with a huge open air terrace in summer directly by the river.

DANCECLUBS

Angels @ Volkshaus (B D GLM MA) Sat 22h- open end
Helvetiaplatz www.angels.ch
Biggest gay party in town: White Party in spring with around 3000 people, Black Party in fall/winter.

ZURICH PLACES // GAYCITY.CH

KREIS 1

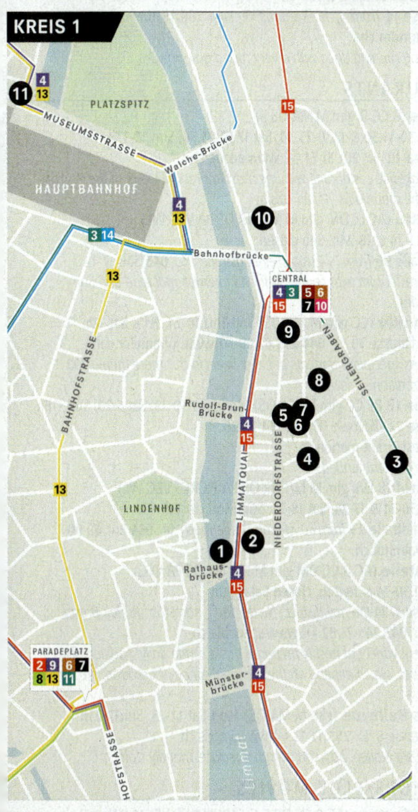

1 RATHAUS CAFÉ
BAR–CAFÉ
Limmatquai 61
www.rathauscafe.ch

2 CRANBERRY
BAR
Metzgergasse 3
www.cranberry.ch

3 TIPTOP BAR
SCHLAGER–DRINK–TREFF
Seilergraben13
www.tiptopbar.ch

4 BARFÜSSER
CAFÉ–BAR–SUSHI
Spitalgasse 14
www.barfuesser.ch

5 PARAGONYA
WELLNESS CLUB
Mühlegasse 11
www.paragonya.ch

6 PREDIGERHOF
BISTRO–BAR
Mühlegasse 15
www.predigerhof.ch

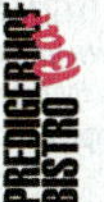

7 THE DYNASTY CLUB
3 BARS – 1 ENTRANCE
Zähringerstrasse 11
www.dynastyclub.ch

8 MACHO
CITY SHOP
Häringstrasse 16
www.macho.ch

9 JOHANNITER
RAUCHER LOUNGE
Zähringerstrasse 33
www.johanniter.com

10 LEONHARDSAPOTHEKE
Stampfenbachstr. 7
www.leonhardsapotheke.ch

11 CHECKPOINT
GESUNDHEITSZENTRUM
Konradstrasse 1
www.checkpoint-zh.ch
044 455 59 10

KREIS 3 / 4

12 MOUSTACHE
DIE SAUNA FÜR MÄNNER
Engelstrasse 4
www.moustache.ch

13 HUUSMAA
KAFI–MITTAGSTISCH–BAR
Badenerstrasse 138
www.huusmaa.ch

14 RENOS RELAX
CLUB SAUNA
Kernstrasse 57
www.renosrelax.ch

15 ROUTE 39
B&B AND APARTMENTS
Winzerstrasse 39
www.route39.ch

Design: bicorne.ch

■ **Aviator Layover Party** (B D G) Sat 22.30-?h
Kalanderplatz 6 *S4 Saalsporthalle, Tram 13* www.itraveller.ch
Popular party take place six times a year at different locations. A must for all travellers, airliners and tourist staff.

■ **Beefcake** (AC B D GLM MA S) Sat 22-?h on selected dates only
Badenerstrasse 109 @ *Plaza Klub* ☎ 542 90 90
www.plaza-zurich.ch
Nice location.

■ **Boyahkasha Party** (! B D G OS S YC)
www.boyahkasha.ch
Please see Website for Dates and more Info.

■ **Cabaret Club** (B D glm MA S) 23-?h
Geroldstrasse 15 www.cabaret.im
Gayfriendly danceclub. Sometimes gay-parties. See www.cabaret.im for details.

■ **Flexx** (B D DR GLM MA) Sat 23h-open end, irregular dates
Albulastrasse 38 @ *Loop 38* www.flexx-party.ch
New sportswear gay party-event. Check www.flexx-party.ch

■ **Heldenbar** (! B D G I m OS S YC) Wed 20-?h
Sihlquai 240 @ *Provitreff* www.heldenbar.ch
Cool midweek dance-lounge event. See website www.heldenbar.ch for details.

■ **Hive** (B D glm MA S) Wed-Sun 21-?h
Geroldstrasse 5 *near Escher-Wyss-Platz* www.hiveclub.ch
Gayfriendly danceclub, sometimes gayparties and concerts. See www.hiveclub.ch for details.

■ **Jackparty** (AC B D GLM MA S) Sat on selected dates only
Pelikanplatz @ *Kaufleuten, Festsaal* www.jackcompany.com
Legendary gay danceparty on two floors in the famous „Kaufleuten". See www.jackcompany.com for dates.

■ **Lollipop @ Xtra** (B D glm MA)
Fri 22h-open end, various dates
Limmatstrasse 118 www.lollipopparty.ch
Gayfriendly oldie & schlagerparty in Zurich and Winterthur. Check www.lollipopparty.ch for details.

■ **Misbehave @ Frieda's Büxe** (B D GLM MA) Thu 21-?h
Hohlstrasse 18 *near Albisriederplatz* www.misbehave.ch
Gay parties on Thu: see www.misbehave.ch for details.

■ **Offstream Party** (B D G MA) 22h-open end
www.offstream.ch
Irregular alternative gay party with rock and soul, indie and electronic music in different locations. For more infos see www.offstream.ch.

■ **Pfingstweide** (B D glm MA S) Sat 23-?h
Pfingstweidstrasse 12 www.pfingstweide.ch
21yrs and older only.

■ **Stairs Club** (AYOR B D glm MA)
Fri 23-8, Sat 23 – Sun 22h nonstop
Baslerstraße 50 *Top floor EKZ-Letzipark* www.stairsclub.ch
Electro/minimal sound, progressive underground party, mainly an after-hour place and some gays are always here. Entrance behind McDrive and Shell-station (Hohlstraße).

■ **T&M Club** (! AC B CC D GLM OS S ST VS YC)
Wed & Thu 21.30-3, Fri & Sat -6h
Marktgasse 14 *Tram 4, 15 -Rathaus* ☎ 044 266 1818
www.tundm.ch
Zurich's long running disco with a very mixed gay crowd.

RESTAURANTS

■ **Acqua** (B CC D glm M MA OS S)
Tue-Fri 11.30-14.30 & 17.30-23.30, Sat 17.30-23.30, Sun 10-17h
Mythenquai 61 ☎ 201 51 61 www.acqua.ch
Beautiful lakeside restaurant, with the most impressive views of the city, the lake and the mountains. Italian cuisine.

■ **Corretto** (AC cc DM glm M MA NR OS PA VEG WL)
Mon-Sat 11-14 & 18-24h, Sun closed
Seefeldstraße 96 *Tram 2/4 stop „Feldeggstraße"* ☎ 043 536 17 12
Little cosy restaurant with fiendly staff and international food and fine wine selection.

■ **Johanniter** (CC glm M MA OS) Sun-Thu 10-24, Fri & Sat -2h
Niederdorfstrasse 70 ☎ 044 253 62 00 www.johanniter.com
Typical Swiss specialties and lots of finest beers in this more than a 100 years old traditional place.

■ **Marion** (B BF CC glm M MA OS) Mon-Fri 7.30-23, Sat 5-23, Sun -18h
Mühlegasse 22 *Old town* ☎ 044 261 27 26
www.restaurant-marion.ch
Reservation recommended.

■ **Palmhof** (B DM glm M MA NR OS PA PK RES VEG WL)
Tue-Fri 11.30-14 & 17-24, Sat 18-24, Sun-Mon closed
Universitätsstraße 23 *Tram 10, station Haldenbach* ☎ 044 261 69 90
www.palmhof.ch

■ **Tagliatelle** (AC B CC DM glm M MA NR OS PA VEG)
Mon-Fri 11.30-14 & 18-22h, closed Sat & Sun
Mühlegasse 17 *In the gay district „Niederdorf", tramstop „Rudolf Brunn Brücke"* ☎ 043 243 71 82 www.scheuble.ch
Enjoy a great variety of freshly prepared pasta made daily. Additionally, artful menues, which depend on the seasonal range of products, are served each day.

■ **Yoojis Bellevue** (glm M MA OS) Mon-Sat 11-23, Sun17-23h
St. Urbangasse 8 ☎ 253 11 11 www.yoojis.ch
Freshest Sushi, Kaiten, beautiful summer terrace, friendly staff.

SEX SHOPS/BLUE MOVIES

■ **Erotik Factory** (AC B CC DR F G GH I MA VR VS) 10-24h
Badenerstraße 254 ☎ 044 241 11 63 www.erotikfactory.ch
Large shop on two floors and a sex area with cabins & glory holes.

■ **Macho City Shop** (CC G) Mon-Fri 11-20, Sat 10-17h
Häringstraße 16 *Near central station* ☎ 044 251 12 22
www.macho.ch
DVDs, toys, books, magazines. Also online shop: www.macho.ch

■ **Maxxx Erotik Discount** (AC CC g MA) 10-23h
Sihlfeldstraße 58 *Tram 2, 3 -Lochergut* ☎ 044 451 21 01
www.maxxx.ch

G
COLORS
the_house
www.g-colors.ch
THE ONLY
GAY DISCO
IN DOWNTOWN
ZURICH
OPEN EVERY NIGHT
TWO DANCEFLOORS
CHILLOUT ROOMS
CRUISING AREA
GAME ZONE
HOT SNACKS
LIVE SHOWS
LIVE DJS
FOR SPECIAL EVENTS VISIT
WWW.G-COLORS.CH
OR DOWNLOAD OUR APP
* WE NEVER
CLOSE
BEFORE 4
CLUB AAAH!
T&M
CLUB
LIVE DJ'S
PERFORMANCE
MARKTGASSE 14 | 8001 ZÜRICH

SAUNAS/BATHS

■ **Adonis** (b DU FC FH G m MC RR SA VS)
Mon-Sat 11.30-20h, closed on Sun
Mutschellenstraße 17 *Near Wollishofen, S-Brunau* ☎ 044 201 64 16

■ **Apollo** (b DU FC FH G m MC RR SA SB VS) 12-22h
Seilergraben 41 *5 mins from railway station* ☎ 044 261 49 52
Cozy sauna close to the gay scene and the university.

■ **GayAqua**
(AK B bf CC DR DU f FC FH G I LAB MA p RR S SA SB SH SL VS) 16-23h
Hertistrasse 24 *S8/14 to Station Wallisellen, bus 759 to „Herti"*
☎ 043 233 02 00 💻 www.gayaqua.ch
Mediterranean ambiance and a large choice of cocktails at the bar. Enjoy the heat of the „South Seas Sauna" or a wet adventure in the tropical steam room. Large cruising area for your pleasure including St. Andrew's cross, sling and video room with ongoing porn movies. Free internet station. This sauna is worth a visit.

■ **Moustache** (! AC B CC DR DU FC FH G GH LAB m MA MSG p PI PP RR s SA SB SH SL SOL VS WH) 11.30-23h
Engelstrasse 4 *4th floor, tram 2/3, bus 32 Kalkbreite* ☎ 044 241 10 80
💻 www.moustache.ch
Offers bio-sauna, a dry sauna, a large steam sauna and whirlpool. Large and comfortable cubicles. Popular place with the locals.

■ **Mylord** (B DR DU FC FH G MC MSG RR SA VS) Mon-Sat 13-22, Sun -19h
Seebahnstraße 139 *Tram 2, 3 -Kalkbreite* ☎ 044 462 44 66

Paragonya (! AC B CC DR DU G M MA R RR SA SB SOL VS WH) 11.30-23h
Mühlegasse 11 *Near main station, near river Limmat, in the Migros-building on the 1st floor, Tram 4 Rudolf-Brun-Brücke* ☏ 044 252 66 66
🖳 www.paragonya.ch
Clean and popular sauna on 440 m² on two floors. Many rent boys.

Reno's Relax (! AC B DR DU FC FH G I m MA MSG p PP RR SA SB SL SOL VS WH) Mon-Thu 12-23, Fri & Sat -7, Sun & holidays 14-23h
Kernstraße 57 *3rd floor, tram 8, bus 32-Helvetiaplatz* ☏ 044 291 63 62
🖳 www.renosrelax.ch
Popular sauna with foam room, bio sauna, two slings, „lovers swing". Very clean, stylish and perfect furnishings. Very friendly staff. Cubicles, as in all saunas in Switzerland, are free of charge.

BOOK SHOPS

Orell Füssli (GLM MA)
Bahnhofstrasse 70 *Tram Rennweg* ☏ 254 39 60 🖳 www.books.ch
Own gay section with a vast variety of gay books.

FASHION SHOPS

Menssecret.ch (CC G)
Store open Sat 11-15h and by appointment
Bremgartnerstrasse 51 ☏ 041 76 318 70 03 🖳 www.menssecret.ch
Swiss internet fashion store.
Sportswear, Jeans, Swimwear, Underwear, sexy Wear, Shoes, Accessories

LEATHER & FETISH SHOPS

Männerzone (AC cc F G MC) Tue-Fri 12-19, Sat -17h
Kernstraße 57 *Bus 31/33, tram 2* ☏ 043 243 30 43
🖳 www.maennerzone.com
Fri & Sat 21-2.30h bar for leather men, bears and others next to the shop.

Ministry of Kink (CC F G MA s) Mon-Fri 11-14, 15-20, Sat 10-17h
Engelstraße 62 *Tram 2, 3 -Kalkbreite, tram 8 -Helvetiaplatz*
☏ 044 241 28 22 🖳 www.kink-shop.ch
Leather, rubber, army and toys. DVDs for sale and for rent.

PHARMACIES

Leonhards Apotheke (CC glm MA) Mon-Fri 7.45-18.45, Sat 9-14h
Stampfenbachstrasse 7 ☏ 252 44 20 🖳 www.leonhardsapotheke.ch

TRAVEL AND TRANSPORT

Hotelplan Mon-Sat 9-20h
Einkaufszentrum Glatt ☏ 044 832 50 20
🖳 www.hotelplan.ch/themen/gay-travel
Your travelagent: Markus Uebelhart

Hotelplan Mon-Fri 8-20, Sat -17h
Bahnhofstrasse 151 *Wetzikon Züri Oberland Märt* ☏ 044 931 01 20
🖳 www.hotelplan.ch/themen/gay-travel
Your travelagent: Valentin Fürpass

Pink Cloud (GLM MA) Mon-Fri 9-19h
Hardstrasse 235 *@ Kuoni Travel* ☏ 274 15 55 🖳 www.pinkcloud.ch
Travel agency for the gay-lesbian community with own glbt-program and trained staff.

HOTELS

Designhotel Plattenhof (B CC glm I M PA PK RWS RWT VA)
All year
Plattenstraße 26 *Tram 5, 9 -Kantonsschule or 6 -Platte* ☏ 044 251 19 10
🖳 www.plattenhof.ch
Conveniently and centrally located in a residential area close to the old town.

Four Points by Sheraton Sihlcity Zürich (AC B BF CC H M OS PA PK RWS RWT VEG W WI WL) All year, 24hrs
Kalandergasse 1 *Train Saalsporthalle, Tram Sihlcity-North*
☏ 044 554 00 00 🖳 www.fourpointssihlcity.com

G-Hotel Goldenes Schwert (B CC D G I MA PA PK RWB RWS RWT VA) All year
Marktgasse 14 *Central, in Zurich old town & gay area* ☏ 044 250 7080
🖳 www.g-hotel.ch
The G-Hotel „Goldenes Schwert" is situated in the heart of Zurich's „Niederdorf" within walking distance to all the main city attractions.

Helmhaus (AC BF CC glm H I RWS RWT VA) All year
Schifflände 30 *Tram 4 Helmhaus, Limmatquai*
☏ 044 266 95 95 🖳 www.helmhaus.ch
The smallest 4-star hotel in the city with 24 rooms. Centrally located in the old-town, near gay bars, clubs and shopping. The rooms are modern and tastefully decorated.

Hotel Adler (B BF CC H I M NG PA RWS RWT) All year
Rosengasse 10 *At Hirschenplatz* ☏ 044 266 96 96
🖳 www.hotel-adler.ch
Centrally located 3-star hotel in the heart of the old town. Newly renovated rooms have bath/shower, phone, TV, radio, mini-bar. Internet-terminal in the lobby.

Hotel Platzhirsch (B BF CC glm I RWB RWS RWT) All year
Spitalgasse 3 *Walking distance from main train station, Tram 4 & 15*
☏ 044 250 70 88 🖳 www.meinplatzhirsch.ch
Brand new and chic hotel in Zurich's gay district Niederdorf. Free use of iPads in the lobby!

Leoneck
(AC B BF CC H I M MA OS RWB RWS RWT VEG W WI)
All year, 24hrs
Leonhardstrasse 1 *Near Central, Tram 10 Haldenegg*
☏ 044 254 22 22 🖳 www.leoneck.ch
Nice 3 star hotel close to Zürich's gay area Niederdorf.

Scheuble (B BF CC H I M NG PA PK RWB RWS RWT) All year
Mühlegasse 17 *Old town centre* ☏ 044 268 48 00
🖳 www.scheuble.ch
In a 19th century building in the heart of the gay scene. Rooms with all modern conveniences. With own restaurant „Tagliatelle".

Townhouse Boutique Hotel
(BF CC H I M OS PA RWS RWT VA W) All year
Schützengasse 7 *2 mins to main train station*
☏ 044 200 95 95 🖳 www.townhouse.ch
Brandnew stylish boutique hotel right in the city's shopping area.

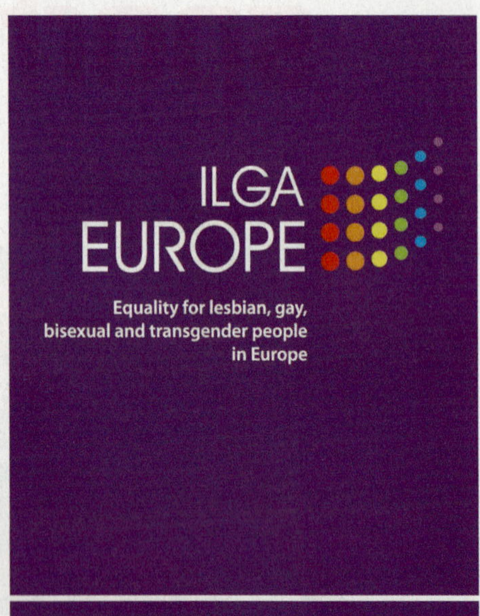

■ **Sorell Hotel Zürichberg**
(B BF CC glm I M OS PA PK RWB RWS RWT VA) All year
Orellistrasse 21 *Tram 6 -Zoo* ☏ 044 268 35 35 🖳 www.zuerichberg.ch
Thirty-six rooms in the historic section of the Designhotel and 30 rooms in the modern extension, which was skilfully blended into the natural surroundings.

GUEST HOUSES

■ **Route 39** (BF cc H I MA OS RWB RWS RWT) All year
Winzerstraße 39 *Tram 17 -Tüffenwies or bus 80-Hohenklingensteig*
☏ 044 822 20 70 🖳 www.route39.ch
3 Stylish furnished rooms, two with balcony, sunbathing on roof deck, free WiFi. Close to Werdinsel (nude river-beach). City centre reachable in 15 minutes by bus and train.

APARTMENTS

■ **Route 39 Apartments** (H OS RWB RWT WI) All year
Winzerstr. 65 *Hohenklingensteig, Bus Nr. 80 + 89 Tüffenwies, Tram Nr. 17* ☏ 044 822 20 70 🖳 www.route39.ch
Three stylish decorated and furnished apartments with either patio or balcony and complete kitchen and bathroom. For up to 4 people. 3 nights minimum stay. Check-In Winzerstr. 39.

HEALTH GROUPS

Zürcher AIDS-Hilfe (glm) Helpline Mon-Fri 14-17h
Kanzleistraße 80 ☏ 044 455 59 00 www.zah.ch

HELP WITH PROBLEMS

SafeBoy (G)
c/o Aids-Hilfe Schweiz, Postfach 1118 www.safeboy.ch
Information, counselling and meeting point for hustlers.

SPECIAL INTEREST GROUPS

Zurich Pride Festival (GLM MA)
www.zurichpridefestival.ch
Organiser of the CSD in Zurich.

SWIMMING

-Werd-Insel (G NU) (Hard to find: beach on a small island in the middle of River Limmat. Take tram 4 or Bus 80/89 to Tüffenwies. Go to the coloured wheel then to the end of the island)
-Strandbad Tiefenbrunnen (!), lawn in front of the men's lockers (G) summer only
-Bad Utoquai, left two sundecks men only (G)
-Schanzengraben swimming-pool at river Sihl (men only)
-Untere Letten (G,YC) Nostalgic wooden riverside bathhouse. locals, many gays in the afternoon, free entry.
-Obere Letten (MA) river-bathhouse on either side with bar and snacks. on the right hand side of the river rather gay and trendy people, free entry

CRUISING

-Park Arboretum at beginning of Mythenquai (at night, AYOR)
-Waffenplatzpark (F) (after midnight, 10 mins walk from train station Enge, popular)
-Obere Letten, near the river bathhouse on the right hand side

Taiwan

Name: T'ai-wan · Taïwa
Location: Off Mainland China
Initials: RC
Time: GMT +8
International Country Code: ☏ 886 (omit 0 from area code)
International Access Code: ☏ 002
Language: Chinese
Area: 36,006 km² / 13,901 sq mi.
Currency: 1 New Taiwan Dollar (NT$) = 100 Cents
Population: 22,689,000
Capital: T'aipei
Religions: 42% Buddhists; 34% Daoists; 3,6% Christians
Climate: Tropical and marine climate. The rainy season during southwest monsoon lasts from June to August.

Neither the term „homosexuality" nor the concept of an age of consent exist in Taiwanese legislation. Marriage is legal from the age of 18, and that too is the age people become fully accountable by law. Yet, legally, people become adult when they are 20 years of age.
Taiwan is claiming to be the first area in China to hold a gay rights parade, after the first such event took place in November 2003. The parade in Taipei with around 300 participants dressed in costumes, many with masks and carrying rainbow flags. The event was designed to promote the planned legalization of gay marriage proposed in October 2003, which has remained shelved since then. According to a survey carried out in April 2006, 75 % of the Taiwanese population accept homosexual relationships. A bill prohibiting discrimination at the workplace on the grounds of sexual orientation was passed in 2007.
Tolerance and acceptance are spreading very rapidly in Taiwanese society; the Pride Parade in October 2007 was attended by 10,000 to 15,000 people of virtually every persuasion. In the opening speech for Pride Week 2006, Taipei mayor Ma Ying-Jeou declared: „Tolerance is a necessary virtue for a world-class city...; Taipei is a multilayered city that is full of love, peace and tolerance."
The worldwide success of Taiwanese director Ang Lee's „Brokeback Mountain" was immediately followed by plans for a further three movies and twelve projects in 2006.

Es gibt in den taiwanesischen Gesetzen weder den Begriff Homosexualität, noch ein Konzept, das ein Schutzalter beinhaltet. Man darf zwar ab 18 heiraten und ist dann auch vollständig strafmündig, rechtlich volljährig wird man aber erst mit 20.
Taiwan ist die erste Region in China, in der eine Parade zur Durchsetzung schwuler Rechte stattgefunden hat. Sie wurde im November 2003 abgehalten. An der Parade in Taipeh beteiligten sich etwa 300 Männer, die Regenbogenflaggen schwenkten und Kostüme und Masken trugen. Die Veranstaltung sollte die Legalisierung der Homo-Ehe vorantreiben, die im Oktober 2003 vorgeschlagen wurde, seitdem allerdings auf Eis liegt. Einer Umfrage vom April 2006 zufolge akzeptieren 75% der Taiwanesen homosexuelle Beziehungen. 2007 wurde ein Gesetz verabschiedet, welches Diskriminierung am Arbeitsplatz aufgrund sexueller Orientierung verbietet.
Toleranz und Akzeptanz verbreiten sich in der taiwanesischen Gesellschaft sehr schnell, so nahmen an der Pride Parade im Oktober 2007 zwischen 10.000 und 15.000 Menschen verschiedenster Gruppen teil. Bei der Eröffnungsrede der CSD-Woche 2006 hatte der Bürgermeister von Taipeh, Ma Ying-jeou, erklärt: „Toleranz ist eine nötige Tugend für eine Weltklassestadt, Taipeh ist eine vielschichtige Stadt, die voll ist von Liebe, Frieden und Toleranz."
Nach dem weltweiten Erfolg des Films „Brokeback Mountain" des taiwanesischen Regisseurs Ang Lee wurden 2006 gleich drei weitere Filme produziert und zwölf Projekte geplant.

Ni le terme d'homosexualité, ni le concept de majorité sexuelle n'existent dans la législature taïwanaise. Le mariage est permis à compter de l'âge de 18 ans. C'est également à cet âge que les taïwanais deviennent pleinement responsable devant la loi. Pourtant, on ne devient majeur qu'à 20 ans. La peine de mort menace quiconque est trouvé coupable d'avoir commis des actes homosexuels lors de son service militaire.
Taiwan est la première région chinoise où un défilé en faveur des droits des gays et lesbiennes a en lieu. Il s'est déroulé en novembre

2003 à Taipei et a regroupé 300 personnes masquées et costumées, arborant le drapeau arc-en-ciel.
La manifestation avait pour but de donner un coup de pouce à la légalisation de l'union homosexuelle, proposée en octobre 2003 mais mise au placard depuis. Un sondage d'avril 2006 montre que 75% des Taiwanais acceptent les relations homosexuelles. Une loi a été promulguée en 2007 qui interdit toute discrimination sur le lieu de travail en raison de l'orientation sexuelle.
La tolérance et l'acceptation évoluent très rapidement dans la société taiwanaise, et c'est ainsi qu'en octobre 2007 ce sont entre 10 000 et 15 000 personnes de groupes les plus divers qui ont participé à la Gay Pride. Lors du discours d'ouverture de la Semaine de la Gay Pride de 2006, le maire de Taipeh, Ma Ying-Jeou, a déclaré que „ la tolérance est une vertu nécessaire dans une ville de classe mondiale (…) „, que „ Taipeh est une ville hétérogène pleine d'amour, de paix et de tolérance „.
Après le succès mondial du film „ Brokeback Mountain „ du réalisateur taiwanais Ang Lee, trois autres films ont été directement réalisés en 2006 et douze autres sont en projet.

En la legislación de Taiwan no aparece ni el término „homosexualidad" ni el concepto de „edad de consentimiento" para las relaciones sexuales. El matrimonio es legal a partir de los 18 años y en esa misma edad uno ya es responsable jurídicamente de sus actos. No obstante, la mayoría de edad se obtiene a partir de los 20 años. Quien, estando sirviendo en el ejército, se deje seducir por actos homosexuales, está amenazado con la pena de muerte.
Taiwan es la primera región de China en la que se celebró una marcha para la defensa de los derechos de los homosexuales. Tuvo lugar en noviembre de 2003. En la Marcha celebrada en Taipei, participaron unos 300 hombres vestidos con disfraces y máscaras que hacían ondear banderas del arco-iris. El acontecimiento debía dar paso a la propuesta de legalización del matrimonio homosexual, que fue tramitada en octubre de 2003, desde entonces no obstante está congelada. Según una encuesta de abril de 2006, el 75% de los taiwaneses aceptan las relaciones homosexuales. En 2007 se aprobó una ley que prohíbe cualquier discriminación en el puesto de trabajo por motivo de la orientación sexual..
Tolerancia y aceptación se extienden rápidamente en la sociedad taiwanesa, y así en la Marcha del Orgullo de octubre de 2007 participaron entre 10.000 y 15.000 personas de diferentes grupos. Durante el discurso de apertura de la Semana del Orgullo en 2006, el alcalde de Taipei, Ma Ying-jeou, declaró que: „La tolerancia es una virtud necesaria para una ciudad de categoría mundial...Taipeh es una ciudad con muchas caras, que está llena de amor, paz y tolerancia."
Después del éxito mundial de la película „Brokeback Mountain", del director taiwanés Ang Lee, en 2006 se produjeron otras tres películas y se planearon doce proyectos más.

Nella legislazione taiwanese non esiste l'espressione „omosessualità" e nemmeno il concetto di „età legale per rapporti sessuali". Ci si può sposare a partire dai 18 anni e si è completamente responsabili, eppure la maggiore età si raggiunge solo coi 20 anni.
Il Taiwan è il primo paese della Cina nel quale ha luogo una manifestazione per i diritti degli omosessuali. Il primo pride si è svolto nel 2003. Al gay pride di Taipeh hanno partecipato circa 300 persone che sventolavano bandiere arcobaleno e che indossavano costumi e maschere. La manifestazione intende anche promuovere la proposta di legge sui matrimoni tra persone dello stesso sesso che è stata annunciata nell'ottobre del 2003 ma che da allora è stata anche ‚congelata'. Secondo un sondaggio fatto in aprile del 2006, il 75% della popolazione ammette di accettare i rapporti omosessuali. Nel 2007 è stata emanata una legge che vieta le discriminazioni basate sull'orientamento sessuale sul posto di lavoro.
L'accettazione e la tolleranza cominciano a diffondersi piuttosto velocemente tra la popolazione. Al Pride Parade, in ottobre del 2007 hanno preso parte tra le 10.000 e le 15.000 persone appartenenti ai più diversi gruppi e strati della società. All'apertura della settimana del Christopher Street Day 2006 il sindaco di Taipeh, Ma Ying-jeou, dichiarava: „la tolleranza è una virtù fondamentale per una città cosmopolita (…). Taipeh è una città piena di diversità, di amore, di pace e di tolleranza".
Dopo il successo del film „i segreti di Brokeback Monuntain" del regista taiwanese Ang Lee, sono stati prodotti altri tre film e sono in corso altri dodici progetti.

NATIONAL PUBLISHERS

Goodguy
G&L Publishing Corporation, Suite 9, 11/F #20 Minchiuan West Road
✉ Taipei ☎ (02) 2541-1213
www.glorytw.com
Taiwanese gay magazine.

Tung Yen Wu Chi (Gay Speak Out)
PO Box 112-637 ✉ Taipei
Quarterly gay magazine.

Chai-Yi ☎ 05

BARS

Miracle (B GLM MA) 21-?h
4F 424 Min Chiuan Road *Between Min Sheng Street and Jung Yi Street, 100m from Zhong Zheng Park* ☎ (05) 216-7021

SAUNAS/BATHS

Chiayi Fitness Center (DU FC FH G I SA SB VS WO)
Fri 17-24, Sat & Sun 12-24h
B1 640 Chui-Yang Road *On same road as Far East & Shinguang Mitsukoshi department stores*
☎ (05) 222-3155

CRUISING

-Zhong Zheng Park between Bei-rong Street Guo-hua Street, Zhong-yi Street and Ming-quan Road.
-Zhong Shan Park near intersection of Qi-min Road, near train station.

Chang-Hua ☎ 04

BARS

Tureman (AC B G m MA)
2F 17 Kong-men Road *Near train station / Cultural Centre, 2nd floor*
☎ (04) 724-3131

SAUNAS/BATHS

Tian Qin (AC B DU G m MA SA SB VS WH WO)
26-12 Lane 324 Zhong-shan 2nd Road *300 m from train station, 3rd floor*
☎ (04) 722-4618

Hua Lien ☎ 03

SAUNAS/BATHS

Man Ho Chin Cho De (DR DU FC FH G I MC SB VS) Daily 17-3h
No. 99, Guóxìng 1st *Near train station. It is very discreet so look out for the building numbers* ☎ (03) 834-5381
Busy on Wed, Fri Sat & Sun nights. No English spoken. Razors, toothbrush and toothpaste as well as towels and condoms supplied for free.

CRUISING

-Zhong Shan Park, Guo-lian 1 Road near train station. Locals, all day

Kaohsiung ☎ 07

BARS

69 Bar (AC B GLM MA)
No. 69 Min-sheng 2 Rd *Near Made in Taiwan Bar*

■ **Cai Se Min** (B g)
5 Da Yong Street ☏ (07) 551-3757

■ **Da Heng Game** (B G MA)
8 Lane 56, Wu Fu 3rd Road ☏ (07) 215-5512
For mature men and their admirers.

■ **Made in Taiwan** (B glm M MA)
2-2 Yuzhu First Street ☏ (07) 282-8567
Friendly gay owned BBQ and beer bar. English speaking owner.

■ **Marui** (B GLM S YC)
120 Shing Tieb Road ☏ (07) 271-4523
Stylish gay-owned coffee shop with karaoke club downstairs. Gay magazines on sale. Monthly special shows.

■ **Possible** (B d g MA)
461 Chung Shen 2nd Road *2nd floor* ☏ (07) 330-3083
Cosy karaoke pub.

■ **Private Life** (B G M MC)
278 Chi Hsien 3rd Road ☏ (07) 561-1100
Friendly and helpful staff. Best on Fri & Sat nights.

SEX CINEMAS

■ **Kuo-gong** (G VS)
6F Da-you Street *Opp. Colorful Pan Pub*
Straight adult movies but mostly gay audience, busy facilities.

SAUNAS/BATHS

■ **Milky Way** (B DU G m OC SA SB VS WH WO)
253 Chi Shien 3rd Road, Yen Chen District *Near Shou Shin Cinema*
☏ (07) 532-5366

■ **Station** (B DR DU G m MA SA SB VS WO) 24hrs
226 Nan-Hwa Road ☏ (07) 235-4612
Many hunky types on five floors.

CRUISING

-Black Forrest (23-2h) diccicult to find, path through the trees that gets busy at night, busiest 23h-midnight, latest until 2h
-Lover River Park at He-xi Road between Zhong-zheng Bridge and Qi-xian Bridge. Busy at nights.

Keelung ☏ 02

SAUNAS/BATHS

■ **Fishing-Man** (B DU G m MA SA SB VS WO) 24hrs
2-56 Shen-ao-ken Road *Near Rui-fang „Beautiful World"-stop*
☏ (02) 2468-0946

Taichung ☏ 04

BARS

■ **Ai Qiao** (B g MA)
216 Cheng-gong Road ☏ (04) 221-1975

■ **Big Elephant** (B glm MA)
12 Tzu Yu Road, Sec. 2 *8th floor* ☏ (04) 222-4336

■ **Flower City** (B glm YC)
9 Tzu Yu Road, Sec. 2 *9th floor* ☏ (04) 220-0380

■ **Purple Grindery** (B g)
B, No. 60, Chung Shen Road ☏ (04) 220-2126

■ **Shin Chiao** (B g MC)
Shuang Shi Road, Lane 19, Sec. 1
Japanese style karaoke bar.

CAFES

■ **Sunny Park** (b glm M MA OS)
259-12 Xi-tun Second Road *Near Ming-liu Plaza, at Shang-Shi 5th lane*
☏ (04) 258-7425

RESTAURANTS

■ **Life Restaurant** (AC B glm M MA)
100 Xue-shi Rd *Next to Zhong-zheng swimming pool, inside Zhong-zheng Park, Bus 38 or 31, stop China Medical College* ☏ (04) 234 4145
It shares facilities with the swimming pool and gym so lots of things may be observed.

SEX CINEMAS

■ **Taichung Movie Theater** (G VS)
188 Gong-yuan Road ☏ (04) 202-3820
Mostly gay audience watching straight movies. Cruisy.

SAUNAS/BATHS

■ **Adam** (b DR DU G MA SA SB)
Shuang She Lu 1 Tuan, Sec. 1, 19 Siang 2 ☏ (04) 2220-1069
Primarily young men and their older admirers.

■ **Hon Hwa Gong** (B DR DU G m MA SA SB VS WH WO) 24hrs
145 Kuang Fu Road ☏ (04) 225-2665

CRUISING

-Taichung park at intersection of Gong-yuan Road and Shuan-shi Road
-Train Station.

Tainan ☏ 06

BARS

■ **Light** (B GLM MA WE)
72 Zhong-yi 3rd Road ☏ (06) 225 1781
Mostly gays, some lesbians and some straight women also. Friendly staff and helpful about the gay scene. Busiest Fri nights.

■ **Music Town Karaoke** (B d glm m MA)
9, 72 Huan-he West Road *Near Da-yong, Chinatown Theater/Shopping Complex, 11th floor* ☏ (06) 220-8800
On the left side of the lift. Friendly staff speaks some English.

■ **Nice Pub** (AC B GLM MA) 21-4h
2/F, 31 Kaishan, West Central Dist *Near Tainan Train Station*
☏ (06) 091 755 7957
Thai-style music and karaoke bar.

■ **Suck** (B GLM MA)
Min-chuan 2nd Road

RESTAURANTS

■ **Fu Low** (b glm M MA OS)
1-22 Sha Lin Road ☏ (06) 229-6535
Great open-air place with fresh sea food and local cuisine.

SAUNAS/BATHS

■ **Green House** (B DR DU G I M MA MSG RR SA SB VS)
147, Sec. 2 Chung Yi Road *5th floor* ☏ (06) 221-0108 🖳 greenlove.idv.tw
Some cabins allow individual activity, even sleeping, and free drinks are provided all time. Theme nights. Very busy on weekends, especially Sun noon.

CRUISING

-Zhong-shan Park, near Premier Hotel. Big and very cruisy all night.

Taipei/Taipeh ☏ 02

BARS

■ **Asakusaya** (B g MA)
63 Tian-jin Street *Opp. Cheng Du, 3rd floor* ☏ (02) 2511-3548

■ **Bear House** (B G MA) 21-5h
2/F No. 7 Lane 133, Linshen N. Rd *Jhongshan*
Japanese snack-style drinking bar popular with pandas (Asian bears) and their admirers.

■ **Café Dalida** (B g MA)
51 Lane 10, Chengdu Road *MRT Ximen station; in the Red Theater Plaza*
☏ (02) 2370-7833

■ **Cheng Du** (B g MA)
68 Tian-jin Street *Opp. Asakusaya, 3rd floor* ☏ (02) 2536-7377

■ **G-Mixi** (B G MA)
Red House, No. 51, Lane 10, Chengdu Rd ☏ (02) 2388 2069
Super-friendly bear bar and great place to get info on all things gay and bear in the city.

■ **Mori** (AC B G MA) 21-5h
2/F unit 7, 21 Lane 105, Jhonshan N. Road, Sec 1 *Next to Astor Hotel*
☏ (02) 2567-9039
Japanese drinking and karaoke bar.

■ **Red House** (GLM MA)
No. 51, Lane 10, Chengdu Rd
Cultural complex that houses a dozen or more gay and queer-friendly bars like G-Paradise, Siam House, BIGGYM, Mudan, G-2 and more. Lively most nights and packed on weekends.

■ **Scorpio Pub** (B d g) 19-4h
110-1 Hsin Sheng North Road, Section 1 *Between Chung Hsiao E. and Nanking E. Road, 1st floor* ☎ (02) 2562-5647
Entrance fee applies.

■ **Taiwan Club** (B G m MA)
B1F, No.8, Lane 39, Sec 2, Jhongshan N. Rd *Next to Grand Formosa Regent Hotel* ☎ (02) 2581-7068 💻 www.taiwanclub.com.tw
Gay karaoke lounge bar with Chinese, Japanese and English songs. Popular with bears. Closed Sun.

■ **Xiyan** (B G MA P)
B/1, 3 Lane 416, Linsen N. Road ☎ (02) 2561-0592
Karaoke spot with a local crowd.

CAFES

■ **Hours** (AC B GLM M MA) 14-23h, closed Tue
Alley 8, Lane 210, Roosevelt Rd, Section 3 *Next door to GinGin's gay shop and across from Love Boat* ☎ (02) 2364 2742

DANCECLUBS

■ **Fresh** (! AC B D GLM M MA OS S)
2/F No. 7, Sec. 2 Jinshan South S Rd *just south of Xinyi Rd, next to a Yoshinoya 24-hour Japanese restaurant* 💻 www.fresh-taipei.com
Gay venue on four floors: vegetarian restaurant and chill-out space, main bar and two lounge areas, dance space and rooftop garden terrace. Trendy and very popular, this club gets warmed up before midnight and runs until the morning hours.

■ **Funky** (! AC B D G WE YC) Sun-Thu 21-3.30, Fri & Sat -5h
10 Hang Chou South Road, Sec. 1 *Basement* ☎ (02) 2494-2162
Many foreigners and young men like to dance here especially on Fri night.

■ **Gstar** (AC B D GLM MA)
B/F 33 Songjian Rd ☎ (02) 2507 8186 💻 www.gstar-club.com
Time warp early-90s interior decor with lasers and black curtains. Taiwanese pop tunes.

■ **Jump** (AC B D glm MA)
B1 No. 8, Sec 1, Keelung Rd ☎ (02) 2762 9246
Regular gay nights and events for the hardcore party goer. Can get very packed.

■ **Luxy** (AC B D glm MA)
5/F No. 201, Jhongsiao E. Rd, Sec 4 *Central Taipei close to the MRT* ☎ (02) 095 590 4600 💻 www.luxy-taipei.com
Similar to the old „2F". A stylish, big club with occasional gay nights and a mixed crowd on other nights. Admission prices vary but there is a good calendar of events on their website www.luxy-taipei.com

■ **Xi-yan (Wedding)** (AC B D glm) 21-6h
3 Lane 416 Linsen North Road, Jhongshan District *Opp. Cosmed at intersection of Linsen North Road and Jia-zhou Street, "membership" sign at the door* ☎ (02) 2561-0592

RESTAURANTS

■ **Trendy's** (AC B GLM M MA)
2F No.114-4, Sec. 2, Wuchang Street *above 7/11 store* ☎ (02) 2314 6969
Gay-owned and staffed restaurant opened by the owners of So Young Men Spa, two floors above. Vibrant, contemporary Asian design and excellent service from the hunky waiters!

SAUNAS/BATHS

■ **Aniki Club** (! AC B cc DR DU G H I M MSG OS SA SB VS WH WO) 24hrs
B1, 20, Lane 353, Lin-sen N. Rd *Close to Gloria Prince Hotel* ☎ (02) 2564 1069 💻 www.aniki.com.tw
Gay-owned Aniki Club is a world-class, very stylish private recreational club for gentlemen who want to enjoy 5-star pampering with club services. Also 4 suites with individual shower room in each suite, providing hotel accommodation for overnight guests.

■ **Chuan Tang Hot Spring** (DU g MA PI SB) 24hrs
10, Alley 300, Singyi Rd, Yangmingshan Hot Springs *MRT Tamshui line, Shipai station* ☎ (02) 2874 7979
Not a gay place, but plenty of action and gays tend to be aggressively cruisy, especially in the dark steam room. Best after 22h as well as on Fri, Sat and Sun.

■ **Genghis Khan Club** (AC DR DU I MA RR SA SB SOL VS WH) 24hrs
5/F., 72 Zhong Xiao W. Road. *Next to Taipei Central Station* ☎ (02) 2311-8258
Conveniently location and very busy.

■ **Han Men's Sauna** (b DU G SA SB YC) 24hrs
2F 120 Xi-Ning South Road *MRT Ban-chiao line, Xi-men stop, on 2nd floor* ☎ (02) 2311-8681
Busy at WE. Older facility but very friendly.

■ **Huang Szu (King's Pool)** (DU g MC PI SB SNU)
1-42, Alley 402, Singyi Rd, Pektow Hot Springs *MRT Bus 508, 535, 536 at Shipai Station* ☎ (02) 2862-3688
Lockers for your clothes. Guys walk around naked or with small wash towels. Outdoor showers and various pools. Two steam rooms. Not gay, but the gays are easy to spot. This place is popular with mature guys and bears and those who like them. Bring your own towels.

■ **HX** (AC B DU G m SA SB WO)
5/F, N0. 8 Min Tsu East Rd *MRT Dan-shui Line, Yuan-shan station* ☎ (02) 2598-8856
A gay-owned and operated gym and sauna.

■ **Office Club** (B DR DU G LAB M MSG PI SB) 24hrs
265 Chang An West Road ☎ (02) 2550-7766
Very old, smelly and filthy place. Needs urgent refurbishment.

■ **Rainbow** (AC B DR DU I m MA MSG RR SA SB VS WH) 24hrs
2F, 142 Kunming Street *Corner of Chengdu Road, Wanhua District, near Red Playhouse in the Xi Mending area* ☎ (02) 2370 2899
One of the most popular gay saunas, even though its an aging facility. Lots of private cabins on the upstairs floors. Busy, big, and well-worn working-class type of place.

■ **Royal Palace (Huang-Gong)** (b DU G MSG OC SA SB VS) 24hrs
20 Xi-Ning South Road *near Paradise Hotel, MRT-Xi-men* ☎ (02) 2381-5900

MASSAGE

■ **In Touch Spa** (cc G MA MSG OS) 11-24h
50, Lane 147, Sec. 1, Keelung Road, Xinyi District ☎ (093) 037-8666 💻 www.in-touch-spa.com.tw

■ **So Young Men Spa** (cc G MA MSG SA SB WH) 13-1h
2F, No. 4, Lane 91, Sec. 2, Wuchang Street (Cinema Street) *Wanhua District, 2nd floor* ☎ (02) 2381-7676 💻 www.soyoungmenspa.com.tw
Men's spa with many cute, muscular masseurs offering good services. VIP spa rooms with private bathroom. Wellness and beauty treatment as well as hairdresser.

BOOK SHOPS

■ **GinGin's** (AC CC GLM I MA) 11-22h
1/F No. 8, Lane 210, Sec. 3, Roosevelt Road *1st floor* ☎ (02) 2364-2006 💻 www.ginginbooks.com
LGBT books, magazines, DVDs, toys, gifts, clothes & ornaments.

HOTELS

■ **Hondo** (H I MA) All year
55-1 Nanjing E. Road ☎ (02) 8712-1988 💻 www.hondohotel.com.tw

■ **Qstay Hotel** (GLM I m MA)
No. 42, Sec. 2, Changsha St, Wanhua District *Near exit 1 MRT Ximen Station* ☎ (02) 2331 4506 💻 www.qstay.com.tw
The first gay hotel in Taipei and it is right in the heart of Taipei's gay scene with more than a dozen venues within a few blocks.All rooms are connected by MSN chat and cams in case you want to meet the other guests. Breakfast included in room rate.

GUEST HOUSES

Eddies Homestay Hostel (GLM MA)
9/F No. 88, Emei St, Wanhua Dist *Well-located not far from the gay scene in Ximen* ☏ 095 383 1721
Gay homestay hostel. Private room in the apartment of a local gay and his friendly dog, with information about the gay scene.

GENERAL GROUPS

Taiwan Tongzhi Hotline Association (GLM MA)
Thu-Mon 19-22h
12/F #70 Roosevelt Rd, Sec 2 *near Guting MRT* ☏ (02) 2392 1969
www.hotline.org.tw
Founded in 1998, TTHA became the first nationally registered LGBT association in the country.

SWIMMING

-Sha Lun Beach: Dan-hai, Tam-shui, MRT Tam-shui Line, Tam-shui station. Then take a red bus 26 to Hung-shu-lin station
-Youth Park swimming pool (Shui-yuan Road. Open May-Sep, closed Mon)
-Yu-chen Park swimming pool (55 Zhong-po Sough Road, 2726-7381. Open May-Sep).

CRUISING

-228 Park/formerly New Park
-4th Floor Bookshop and WC in the new Asia World Department Store in the new Mitsukoshi Tower (highest building in Taipei)
-Little park in New Peitou (suburb af Taipei)
-Yuan Huan Movie House (near Yuanhuan Road Circus, Chungking North Road)
-Kuang Hua Shang Chang (Basement of Kuang Hua Market on Hsinsheng South Road)
-Chang-te St (Black Street) near old Taidai Hospital next to 228 Peace/ Memorial Park (Xin Gong Yuan). Afternoon until late
-City garden. Large park
-Han No Wa Street, near entrance of old Taidai Hospital
-Han Shin Department Store (Han Lai Hotel), bookshop in basement (level 3). Best 15-18h during working days
-Plaza in front and surrounding food stalls, also starting the basement and up. Many guys hang out there before going to the saunas
-Small park behind Taipei Railway Station and Hilton Hotel, attracts youngster and student types from dark until dawn, especially after Park closes

Taitung ☏ 08

BARS

G-night (B g)
279 Luo-yang Street ☏ (08) 935-9255

GUEST HOUSES

Life Villa (bf H MA)
www.dateline-lifevilla.com.tw

CRUISING

-Beach Park, at the end of Da-tong Road turn right and continue to the end of the beach.

Taoyuan ☏ 03

BARS

Base. The (B G M MA)
3F 197 Min-Chuan Road *Near Lu-zhu, bus stop at temple, 3rd floor* ☏ (03) 331-7225

Boss Men's Club (B G MA VS)
2/F, No.224, Chángshēng Rd ☏ (03) 337-1870

Chuan Ken (B G)
4 Min-zhu Road *2nd floor* ☏ (03) 335-4148

Foxy (B glm m MA)
No. 33, Nánhuá St ☏ (03) 339-5798
Popular with GLM on Fri nights.

Funky (B GLM m MA)
197 Min-Chuan Road *Basement* ☏ (03) 338-3478 www.funky.club.tw

SAUNAS/BATHS

Tai Shi (B DU G m MA SA SB VS WO)
137 Chung Hua Road *Corner Nan Hua Street* ☏ (03) 3355-1123

Xin Tao-yuan (B DU G M MA SA VS WO) 24hrs
182 Min-zhu Road, 5th Lane *About 1.5 km from train station, 3rd floor* ☏ (03) 3353-1757

CRUISING

-Zhong Zheng Park near train station (Yuan-Hua Road). Museum and parking area.

Tanzania

Name: Tansania, Tanzanie
Location: East Africa
Initials: TAN
Time: GMT + 3
International Country Code: ☏ 255 (omit 0 from area code)
Language: Swahili, English
Area: 945,087 km² / 364,899 sq miles
Currency: 1 Tanzanian Shilling (TSh) = 100 Cents
Population: 38,329,000
Capital: Dodoma (official); Dar es Salaam (administrative)
Religions: 40% Christian, 40% Muslim, 15% indigenous beliefs
Climate: The rainy season is from Mar-May. The best time to visit is from Jun-Sep.

In Tanzania, sex acts between men are illegal, and carry a penalty of life imprisonment. Sex acts between women is not mentioned in Tanzanian law, though the autonomous region of Zanzibar outlaws same-sex sexual acts for both men and women.
In the penal code § 157 states Any male person who commits any act of gross indecency with another male, or who procures another male person to commit any act of gross indecency with him, or who attempts to procure a male to commit an indecent act to him, is

guilty of an offence and may be sentenced to five years of imprisonment."

In Zanzibar, an autonomous island which is part of Tanzania, the law changed in 2004 regarding acts of homosexuality. Sodomy and „unnatural acts" were already illegal and now under the new law a penalty of 25 years in prison for sex acts involving two males applies. A homosexual sex act with a minor is punished with life imprisonment.

In Tansania werden sexuelle Handlungen zwischen Männern als Straftaten betrachtet, die mit lebenslanger Haft geahndet werden können. Sexuelle Handlungen zwischen Frauen finden in den Gesetzen des Landes zwar keine Erwähnung, doch im halbautonomen Teilstaat Sansibar sind beiden Geschlechtern alle gleichgeschlechtlichen Handlungen verboten.

Artikel 157 des Strafgesetzbuches besagt: „Männliche Personen, die grob unsittliche Handlungen mit anderen Männern begehen oder andere männliche Personen dazu auffordern, grob unsittliche Handlungen mit ihnen zu begehen oder versuchen, einen anderen Mann zur Begehung grob unsittlicher Handlungen mit ihnen aufzufordern, machen sich einer Straftat schuldig und können mit fünf Jahren Haft bestraft werden. "

In Sansibar, einer autonomen Insel, die einen Teilstaat von Tansania darstellt, sind die gesetzlichen Regelungen im Hinblick auf gleichgeschlechtliche Handlungen im Jahr 2004 verschärft worden. Analverkehr und „widernatürliche Handlungen" waren schon vorher illegal, doch das neue Gesetz verhängt nun eine 25-jährige Haftstrafe für alle sexuellen Handlungen unter Männern. Homosexuelle Handlungen mit Minderjährigen werden mit lebenslanger Haft bestraft.

TEXT KOMMT NOCH...

In Tanzania, sex acts between men are illegal, and carry a penalty of life imprisonment. Sex acts between women is not mentioned in Tanzanian law, though the autonomous region of Zanzibar outlaws same-sex sexual acts for both men and women.

In the penal code § 157 states Any male person who commits any act of gross indecency with another male, or who procures another male person to commit any act of gross indecency with him, or who attempts to procure a male to commit an indecent act to him, is guilty of an offence and may be sentenced to five years of imprisonment."

In Zanzibar, an autonomous island which is part of Tanzania, the law changed in 2004 regarding acts of homosexuality. Sodomy and „unnatural acts" were already illegal and now under the new law a penalty of 25 years in prison for sex acts involving two males applies. A homosexual sex act with a minor is punished with life imprisonment.

TEXT KOMMT NOCH...

En Tanzania, el acto sexual entre hombres es considerado ilegal y conlleva una pena de cadena perpetua. El acto sexual entre mujeres no es mencionado en la ley tanzana, aunque la región autónoma de Zanzíbar declara como ilegal los actos sexuales del mismo sexo, tanto para hombres como para mujeres.

En la Sección 157 del Código Penal tanzano se establece que cualquier persona de sexo masculino que cometa un acto de grave de indecencia con otro varón, que incite a otro varón a cometer cualquier acto de grave de indecencia con él o que intente incitar a un hombre a cometer un acto de indecencia con él, será culpable de un delito y podrá ser condenado a cinco años de prisión.

En Zanzíbar, una isla autónoma que forma parte de Tanzania, la ley con respecto a los actos de homosexualidad fue enmendada en 2004. La sodomía y los "actos antinaturales" ya eran ilegales por aquel entonces y, bajo la nueva ley actual, se aplica una pena de 25 años de prisión por actos relacionados con el sexo entre dos hombres. Un acto sexual homosexual con un menor de edad se castiga con cadena perpetua.

In Tanzania i rapporti sessuali tra uomini sono vietati e possono essere puniti con l'ergastolo. I rapporti sessuali tra donne non sono contemplati dalla legge, sebbene la regione autonoma di Zanzibar vieta espressamente i rapporti sessuali sia tra uomo ed uomo che tra donna e donna. Secondo l'articolo 157 del codice penale qualsiasi uomo trovato a commettere „atti indecenti" con un altro uomo commette un reato e può essere punito con una pena detentiva di 5 anni. A Zanzibar, un'isola autonoma della Tanzania, la legge sull'omosesssualità è cambiata nel 2004: la „sodomia" e gli „atti contronatura" erano già illegali, ma adesso, con la nuova legge due uomini trovati coinvolti in „atti contronatura" rischiano una pena di 25 anni, mentre per i rapporti sessuali con un minore è previsto l'ergastolo.

Zanzibar ☏ 0777

HOTELS

236 Hurumzi (AC B BF CC H M OS RWS) 1st June to 30th April
236 Hurumzi Street *Overlooks the Peace of Love Square*
☏ (024) 2232784 ☏ 742 32 66 www.236hurumzi.com
24 very romantic guest rooms and a Tower Top Restaurant with a magnificent view over the city and Indian Ocean. Atmosphere & antiques. Gay friendly.

Mtoni Marine (AC CC H M OS PI RES WH) All year
PO Box 992 ☏ (24) 2250140 www.mtoni.com
Features 8 palm court rooms,33 Club Rooms,4 family apartments and 1 family house.

GUEST HOUSES

Anna of Zanzibar (AC B BF H M MA MSG PI) Closed in May
South East Coast Dongwe ☏ (0777) 773 999 387
www.annaofzanzibar.com
Offering privacy and exclusivity on a secluded beach with a relaxed atmosphere.

Domokuchu Beach Bungalows (H OS RWB RWS)
Closed in May (due to rainy season)
P.O.Box: 3439 *Near Paje beach, buses 9 & 25 to Paje, 5 mins drive south along the Jambiani Rd from the Paje roundabout* ☏ 776 217 263
www.domokuchu.com
Small friendly hotel at the beginning of the beautiful stretch of beach on the island. Ten guestrooms (6 double, 2 twin, 1 triple and one quad room)

Thailand

Name: Prathet Thai · Thaïlande · Tailandia
Location: Southeast Asia
Initials: THA
Time: GMT +7
International Country Code: ☏ 66
International Access Code: ☏ 001
Language: Thai, English
Area: 513,115 km² / 198,114 sq mi.
Currency: 1 Baht (B) = 100 Stangs
Population: 64,233,000
Capital: Bangkok (Krung Thep)
Religions: 95% Buddhists
Climate: Tropical climate. The rainy, warm and cloudy southwest monsoon lasts from mid-May to September, the dry and cool northeast monsoon lasts from November to mid-March.
Important gay cities: Bangkok, Chiang Mai, Koh Samui, Pattaya, Phuket

The age of consent is set at 18 years. Prostitution with children is severely punished.
The streets of Bangkok are as colourful and lively as ever. Nevertheless pollution is high and can make a longer stay rather tiring. Elections were held in December 2007 ending the military rule. On June 29, 2007, the constitutional assembly decided to include a clause prohibiting discrimination on the grounds of sexual orientation in the constitution, and 57.8 % of the Thai people accepted the passage in a referendum in August. This is another step forward on the way to legal recognition of same-sex couples. Thailand never had any laws against homosexuality in the first place, mainly because sexuality is very much considered to be a private matter. Then the Buddhists believe that homosexuality or a transsexual life is fate and nobody can change it anyway, at least not in this life.
For travellers Thailand is one of the most pleasant places to be because people are very friendly, open and curious about their guests. „Sanuk" – fun – is one of the most important words and the worst you can say about somebody is that they are boring. Many things are not what they seem to be so keep an open mind, e.g. walkways are not for walking but for selling and buying all sorts of things, for eating and drinking and to have a chat with an old friend or one you just met. Don't be surprised if you find names of places or venues spelled in many different ways, there is no official transliteration of Thai language into English. Best advice of all: never ever be in a hurry.

Das Schutzalter liegt bei 18 Jahren. Kinderprostitution wird in Thailand streng geahndet. Das Leben auf den Straßen in Bangkok ist bunt und sprüht vor Lebensenergie, jedoch ist die Luftverschmutzung so hoch, dass ein längerer Aufenthalt in der Stadt anstrengend wird.
Im Dezember 2007 wurde die Militärregierung abgewählt. Schon im Juni 2007 beschloss die verfassungsgebende Versammlung ein Diskriminierungsverbot aufgrund der sexuellen Orientierung in die Verfassung aufzunehmen. Das thailändische Volk hat den Passus im August in einem Referendum mit 57,8 % angenommen. Das könnte der erste Schritt zur Anerkennung gleichgeschlechtlicher Paare sein. In Thailand existierten nie Gesetze, die Homosexualität verbieten, was zum einen daran liegt, dass Sexualität als Privatangelegenheit angesehen wird, andererseits am buddhistischen Glauben, der Homo- oder Transsexualität als Schicksal wahrnimmt, dessen Änderung in Niemandes Macht stehe. Zumindest nicht in diesem Leben.
Thailand ist für Reisende ein sehr angenehmes Urlaubsland, denn die Menschen dort sind ausgesprochen freundlich, tolerant und neugierig. „Sanuk" – Spaß ist eine der wertvollsten Empfindungen in Thailand und demzufolge „langweilig" zu sein eine schwere Beleidigung.
Vieles ist anders, als es zu sein scheint oder wie wir es aus anderen Ländern kennen. So sind Bürgersteige mehr für den Handel, für den Verzehr von Speisen und Getränken gedacht, oder auch einfach, um Unterhaltungen mit alten Bekannten oder neuen Freunden zu führen. Der beste Rat: niemals hetzen, nie in Eile sein.

La majorité sexuelle est fixée à 18 ans. La prostitution infantile est durement réprimée en Thaïlande. Les rues de Bangkok sont très animée et débordent d'énergie mais la pollution est très importante, ce qui rend un séjour prolongé dans la ville assez épuisant. Le gouvernement militaire a démissionné en décembre 2007. L'Assemblée constituante avait décidé en juin 2007 d'adopter l'interdiction de toute discrimination en raison de l'orientation sexuelle, et lors d'un référendum en août le peuple thaïlandais a voté pour la Constitution avec 57,8% de oui. Cela pourrait être le premier pas pour la reconnaissance de l'union homosexuelle. Il n'a jamais existé en Thaïlande de lois interdisant l'homosexualité, ce qui est dû d'une part au fait que la sexualité est considérée comme une affaire privée, et d'autre part à la croyance bouddhiste qui voit l'homo et la transsexualité comme une affaire de destin sur laquelle personne n'a d'influence. Au moins, pas dans cette vie.
La Thaïlande est un pays très agréable pour le voyageur, les gens y sont vraiment sympathiques, tolérants et curieux. „Sanuk" veut dire plaisir et est considéré une des sensations les plus précieuses tandis que son contraire, „ être ennuyeux „, est une grave injure.
Beaucoup de choses ne sont pas ce qu'elles paraissent ou telles qu'on les connaît dans d'autres pays. Ainsi, les trottoirs sont plus pensés pour le commerce, la consommation de repas et de boissons, ou tout simplement la conversation entre personnes qui se connaissent ou pour lier de nouvelles amitiés. Le meilleur conseil : ne jamais se dépêcher, ne pas être pressé.

La edad de consentimiento está en los 18 años. En Tailandia se persigue muy duramente la prostitución infantil. La vida en las calles de Bangkok está llena de color e irradia energía, aunque la contaminación del aire sea tan alta que hace agotadora una larga estancia en la ciudad. En diciembre de 2007 se escogió un gobierno militar. Ya en junio de 2007 la Asamblea constituyente acordó la inclusión en la Constitución de una prohibición de la discriminación por razón de la orientación sexual; y el pueblo tailandés dio su aprobación en el referéndum celebrado en agosto de 2007 con un 57,8%. Esto podría ser el primer paso para el reconocimiento de las parejas del mismo sexo. En Tailandia nunca existieron leyes que prohibieran la homosexualidad

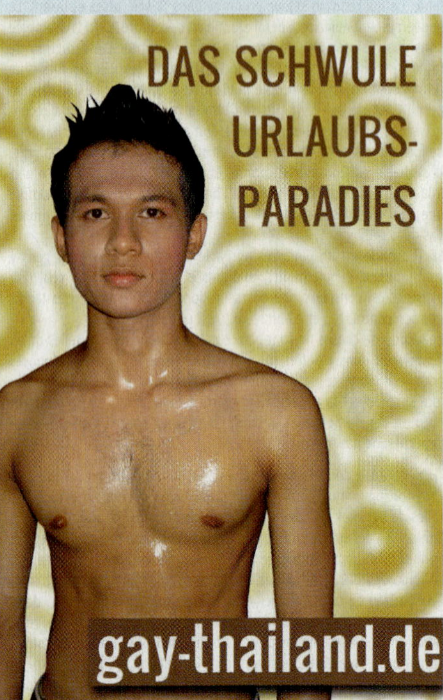

debido a que, por un lado, ésta es vista como un asunto privado y por otro lado, según la fe budista, se percibe la homosexualidad o la transexualidad como un hecho del destino y nadie tiene el poder para cambiar esta identidad, por lo menos, no en esta vida.
Tailandia es un país de vacaciones muy agradable para los turistas, pues sus gentes son muy simpáticas, tolerantes y curiosas. "Sanuk" – diversión es una de las invenciones más valuosas en Tailandia y por lo tanto estar "aburrido" es una de las peores ofensas.
Mucho no es lo que parece, o tal como nosotros conocemos de otros países. Las aceras están pensadas más bien para el comercio, el consumo de comida y bebida, o simplemente para charlar con viejos conocidos o nuevos amigos. El mejor consejo: no atosigue, nunca tenga prisa.

L'età del consenso è di 18 anni. La prostituzione minorile è punita severamente in Tailandia. La vita sulle strade a Bangkok è molto colorata e molto vibrante. Tuttavia l'aria è così inquinata che un lungo soggiorno in città può diventare davvero faticoso. Nel dicembre del 2007 è stato destituito il governo militare. Già nel giugno del 2007 la corte costituzionale decise di inserire nella costituzione il reato per discriminazione sulla base dell'orientamento sessuale. La popolazione tailandese ha accolto il provvedimento positivamente per mezzo di un referendum tenutosi ad agosto tramite il quale il 57% della popolazione si è espresso, appunto, in favore. Questo potrebbe essere il primo passo verso il riconoscimento delle unioni civili tra persone dello stesso sesso. In Tailandia non sono mai esistite leggi contro l'omosessualità ,e questo, da un lato, è dovuto al fatto che la sessualità viene considerata una questione privata, dal'altro è dovuto alla dottrina buddista che percepisce l'omosessualità o la transessualità come destino che nessuno ha il potere di cambiare. Almeno nell'arco di questa vita. La Tailandia è una meta turistica davvero piacevole: le persone del luogo sono molto gentili, cordiali, tolleranti e curiose. In Tailandia il divertimento (sanuk) è una preziosissima qualità, quindi dare del ‚noioso' ad una persona viene considerato come una grave offesa.
Molte cose non sono così come sembrano o come noi le conosciamo in altri paesi. Così, per sempio, i marciapiedi in Tailandia sono luoghi per il commercio, per il consumo di cibo e bevande o semplicemente luoghi per la conversazione con vecchi e nuovi amici. Vi consigliamo, quindi, di non andare mai di fretta.

NATIONAL GAY INFO

Thai Tour Guide
1026/240 Lumpini Park View, Rama 4 Rd, Sathorn ✉ 10120 Bangkok
☎ 818 60 91 59 (international) 💻 www.thaitourguide.com
Private tours in Thailand. Personal tour guide and business assistant.

NATIONAL PUBLICATIONS

Out In Thailand
💻 www.out-in-thailand.com
New printed gay magazine with guides to Bangkok, Chiang Mai, Koh Samui, Pattaya & Phuket. Also online-edition.

Sticky Rice
c/o OPQRS Co, 189/14 Moo 11, Thepprasit Road ✉ 10120 Pattaya
☎ 038 30 01 74 💻 www.stickyrice.ws
Only available as a web magazine.

Thai Puan
29/330 Soi Tonsai, Bangkho, Jomthong ✉ 10150 Bangkok
☎ 086 034 35 34 💻 www.thaipuan.com
Free gay magazine with maps, reviews and actual information about the gay scene covering the whole of Thailand.

NATIONAL COMPANIES

A & F Tour
Kasemkij Bldg groundfloor, Silom Road 120 ✉ 10500 Bangkok *Between Patong and Soi 4, close to train station Sala Daeng*
☎ 022 66 51 05 💻 www.aandftour.com
Thai and regional air tickets, hotels, and tours.

■ **Lost Horizons**
723 Supakarn Bld 4th floor, Room 4B09 ✉ 10600 Bangkok
☎ 018 50 36 32 (mobile) 🖳 www.losthorizonsasia.com
Gay-friendly adventure holidays, trekking and nature resorts in Thailand, promising romantic getaways or exploring Thailand off the beaten track.

Bangkok/Krung Thep

Those who have never experienced a large tropical city might feel overwhelmed by this metropolis of over 6 million inhabitants. High temperatures and humidity, enormous crowds in the streets, noise and traffic jams can be unnerving. But relax; Bangkok has so much more to offer. The city has a large number of palaces and temples, colourful busy markets and shopping malls, great hotels and a seemingly endless number of bars, clubs and restaurants, ranging from seedy to top notch and highly sophisticated. Bangkok surpasses other Asian cities for its vibrant and diverse life by far. Shop till you drop, there are a wide selection of clothes, silk, jewellery and art available.
In Bangkok there are mainly four gay areas. Firstly, Patpong is regarded as the night life address for heteros and gays, but gay life mainly happens in small lanes (called soi) off of Silom Road and Suriwong Road. Gay bars, clubs and restaurants are around Silom Soi 2, 4 and 6. Go-go bars are located in a small Soi off Suriwong Road. It is suggested to avoid touts at the entrance to the gay soi. The second most important area is Sukhumwit Road. In contrast to Patpong this area has a large number of hotels and international restaurants. The third area is Sapan Kwai, which is north of the centre towards the old airport. And last but not least there is Ramkamhaeng north east of the centre. Not many tourists go here but if you are curious about how the locals enjoy themselves in their neighbourhood you will discover that here too there is a lot of fun to have.

Wem tropische Millionenstädte neu sind, wird sich im Moment der Ankunft überwältigt fühlen: vom tropischen Klima und dem Menschengewirr in der Innenstadt, dem enormen Verkehr der überlasteten Hauptstraßen in einer sich rasant motorisierenden und schnell wachsenden Sechs-Milionen-Metropole. Die Stadt bietet zahlreiche Paläste und Tempel, Galerien, Märkte, riesige Einkaufszentren und Unterhaltungszonen. Die schwimmenden Märkte und der „Chao Phraya" (Fluss der Könige), die traditionelle Transportader der Stadt, sind an turbulenter Buntheit nicht zu übertreffen.
In Bangkok gibt es im wesentlichen vier schwule Zentren. »Silom und Suriwong Road« bilden ganz allgemein eine zentrale, kommerziell/touristisch orientierte Nightlifeadresse. Benannt ist die Gegend nach den beiden Verbindungsstraßen (Patong 1 und 2) zwischen der »Silom Road« und der »Suriwong Road«. Dabei konzentrieren sich die schwulen Lokalitäten auf die Silom Soi 2, 4 und 6. Die meisen Gogo Bars liegen in einer kleinen Soi an der Suriwong Road. („Soi" bezeichnet eine kleine Nebenstraße oder Gasse.) Das zweite wichtige schwule Areal ist die Gegend um die »Sukhumvit Road«. Im Gegensatz zum Patong ist dies eher ein Viertel mit großen Hotels und internationalen Restaurants sowie Wohnvierteln für Ausländer. Die schwulen Läden liegen eher verstreut. Ein weiteres Gebiet ist »Sapan Kwai« im nördlichen Stadtzentrum, und ein letztes »Ramkhamhaeng« unweit der gleichnamigen Universität. Diese beiden Viertel werden von Touristen weniger besucht. Wer aber Lust hat, original thailändisches Nachtleben ohne viel Kommerz zu erleben, kann sich auch hier prächtig amüsieren.

Ceux qui ne connaissent pas les villes tropicales de plusieurs millions d'habitants seront très impressionnés en arrivant à Bangkok. Impressionnés par le climat, par la foule dans les rues étroites, par la circulation massive, marquée par la quasi inexistance de transports en commun et par des rues principales surchargées dans lesquelles les 6 millions d'habitants motorisés doivent circuler. Tout ce qui reste à faire est de se détendre, d'observer, et d'en profiter. La ville offre une grande quantité de palaces et de temples. Les marchés flottants et le Chao Pyra (fleuve des rois, l'artère du transport traditionnel de la ville), ne pourraient être plus colorés. Et le shopping est un must! On y trouve d'innombrables vêtements, de la soie, des bijoux, des objets d'arts.
Il y a principalement quatre centres gays à Bangkok. »Silom et Suriwong Road« forment un secteur central avec une vie nocturne plutôt commerciale et touristique. Il tient son nom des deux voies de jonction („ Patpong 1 et 2 „) entre la »Silom Road« et la »Suriwong Road«. C'est là que se concentrent les commerces gays sur la Silom Soi 2, 4 et 6, la plupart des gogo bars se trouvant dans un petit Soi sur la Suriwong Road. (Un „Soi" est une rue secondaire ou une ruelle). Le second secteur gay important est le secteur autour de la »Sukhumvit Road«. Au contraire de Patpong il s'agit ici d'un quartier avec de grands hôtels et des restaurants internationaux ainsi que des quartiers d'habitation pour étrangers, les commerces gays y étant plutôt dispersés. Un autre secteur est celui de »Sapan Kwai« dans le nord du centre-ville, et le dernier est celui de Ramkhamhaeng non loin de l'universtité du même nom. Ces deux quartiers sont plutôt moins fréquentés par les touristes, mais celui qui a envie de connaître une vie nocturne thaï plus authentique et sans trop de mercantilisme pourra aussi très bien s'y amuser.

Quien no conozca ciudades tropicales con millones de habitantes, se sentirá en el momento de su llegada abrumado por el clima tropical, las masas de gente en las callejuelas del centro de la ciudad, el enorme tránsito vial que casi no posee red de servicio público y también por las abarrotadas calles principales de una metrópoli motorizada que cuenta con 6 millones de habitantes. Lo único que puede ayudar es relajarse, tratar de encontrarle diversión al asunto y gozarlo. La ciudad ofrece gran cantidad de palacios y templos para visitar. Los mercados flotantes de Chao Pyra („Río de los Reyes", vía de transporte tradicional de esta ciudad) son de un colorido turbulento que en ningún lugar del mundo encuentran comparación. Puedes ir de compras, adquirir prendas de vestir, seda, joyas y artículos de arte para hacer que una visita a esta ciudad se justifique.
En Bangkok hay básicamente cuatro centros gays »Silom y Suriwong Road« es en general una dirección céntrica, orientada a la vida nocturna comercial y turística. La zona también es conocida por ambas calles que la atraviesan (Patpong 1 y 2), entre la Silom Road y la Suriwong Road. Los locales gays se concentran en la Silom Soi 2, 4 y 6, la mayoría de gogo bars están en un pequeño Soi en la Suriwong Road ("Soi" significa pequeña bocacalle o callejuela). La segunda área gay importante es la zona alrededor de »Sukhumvit Road«. Al contrario que Patpong, esta zona es más bien un barrio de grandes hoteles y restaurantes internacionales así como de barrios residenciales para extranjeros, los locales gays están bastante dispersos. Otra zona es »Sapan Kwai«, al norte del centro, y la última es Ramkhamhaeng, cerca de la universidad del mismo nombre. Los turistas visitan muy poco estas dos zonas pero quien tenga ganas de pasar una "noche thai original", sin mucho comercio, puede pasarlo muy bien aquí.

Per chi non conosce ancora metropoli tropicali, verrà sopraffatto al momento dell'arrivo: dal clima tropicale, dalle affollatissime strade del centro, dall'enorme traffico stradale, carente di mezzi pubblici adeguati e dalle sovraccariche strade principali in una sempre più motorizzata città di oltre 6 milioni di abitanti. In questo caso è consigliabile prendere tutto con calma, guardarsi attorno e godersi l'atmosfera eccezionale. La città offre tantissimi palazzi e templi. I mercati sull'acqua e il Chao Pyra („il fiume dei re", la tradizionale arteria principale di trasporto della città) sono insuperabili per la loro vivace turbolenza. E lo shopping! C'é una vasta offerta di abbigliamento, seta, gioielli e oggetti d'arte.
A Bangkok ci sono 4 zone gay. La Silom Road e la Suriwong Road costituiscono il centro di una scena notturna molto commerciale e turistica. La zona prende il nome dalle 2 strasse che collegano la Silom Road con la Suriwong Road e cioè Patpong 1 e 2. Qui la maggior parte dei locali si concentrano sulla Silom Soi 2, 4 e 6. La maggior parte dei gogo bars si trovano su una piccola Soi sulla Suriwong Road (con Soi si indica un vicolo o una piccola traversina). La seconda principale zona gay è la zona sulla Sukhumvit Road. Al contrario che a Patpong, in questo quartiere (con grandi alberghi e ristoranti internazionali e con quartieri residenziali per stranieri) i locali gay sono piuttosto sparpagliati. Un'altra zona gay è Sapan Kwai, che si trova al nord del centrocittà e per finire la zona Ramkhamhaeng, che è molto vicina dall'omonima università. Questi ultimi 2 quartieri non sono molto visi-

tati dai turisti, tuttavia sono dei quartieri ideali per coloro che abbiano voglia di assaporare l' „original Thai nightlife" senza molto commercio: il divertimento è assicurato.

GAY INFO

Pride Festival (GLM)
www.pridefestival.org
Information about the next Pride Festival in Bangkok and other events.

TOURIST INFO

Tourist Assistance Center (glm)
4 Ratchadamnoen Nok Av., Pom Prap Sattru Phai, Praprachai
☎ 022 82 11 43
Not only gay information.

ESCORTS & STUDIOS

Rainbow Men (G)
☎ 890 00 96 32 www.rainbowmen.com
Specializing in both Caucasian and Asian travel companions and escorts worldwide. Also in Europe at www.gaytailoredtours.com and for handicapped men at www.gayenabledtours.com.

FASHION SHOPS

Prince International Tailor (GLM MA) Mon-Sat 9-22, Sun 14-18h
6/33 Sukhumvit Road Soi 3 *Opp. Ibis Hotel Salathorn*
☎ 022 661 836 5749 www.princetailors.com
Choose from a large selection of materials. Qualities and styles, also mail orders.

TRAVEL AND TRANSPORT

Purple Dragon Tours (CC GLM W) Mon-Fri 10-18h
119/5-10 Surawong Road *Lobby of Tarntawan Place Hotel*
☎ 02 238 32 27 www.purpledrag.com
Main office of this famous Bangkok tour operator. Asia's gay travel pioneers. They provide all-inclusive tours in Thailand and other countries near by.

HOTELS

Beach Residence (AC B G M MA PI SA SB WO) All year
159 Ratchadapisek Road *Near M° Ratchadapisek* ☎ 026 91 57 69
www.thebeach-g-thailand.com

Bangkok/Krung Thep – Sapan Kwai

BARS

Be High Bar (AC B G S) 20-2, show at 24h
11/1 Soi Laleewan, Phahon Yothin Rd, Sapan Kwai *Soi between Phahon Yothin Soi 13 and Pradiphat Rd* ☎ 022 79 63 82
Small gogo bar.

Belami (AC B G S) 19-2.30h
971/29 Phahon Yothin Road, Samsennai, Phaya Thai ☎ 022 79 14 34
Elegant bar with hosts, mainly for a neighbourhood crowd.

Charming (AC B G)
2 Pradiphat Soi 17 (Soi Thawan Sak), Sapan Kwai ☎ 022 79 14 37

Eagle Pub (AC B m MA MSG) 20-1h
172/3-4 Pradaphat Road Soi 10, Sapan Kwai *Next to Mido Hotel*
☎ 081 482 78 64
Comfortable and welcoming place. Karaoke bar with attractive staff.

Hippodrome (AC B CC G MA) 19-3h
18 Pradiphat Soi 12 (Soi Santi Sewi), Sapan Kwai *Behind Mido Hotel*
☎ 022 78 04 13
Karaoke, pub and hosts.

Icy (AC B d G M MA) 21-2h
Kamphaengphet Road, Chatuchak ☎ 022 72 47 75
Popular pub with dance floor. Very busy WE.

Mogue (B D GLM MA S) 20-1h
362 Kamphangphet Road, Chatuchak ☎ 026 18 66 81
Upmarket Thai disco-bar with funky pop design. Popular.

Oasis (AC B G M MA OS)
11/19 Pradipat Soi 20 (Soi Kaw Toey), Sapan Kwai ☎ 022 78 50 58
Bar and restaurant with karaoke.

Stax (AC B G MA)
9 Pradiphat Soi 20, Pradiphat Road, Sapan Kwai *Opp. Street Boy*
☎ 022 78 40 18
Karaoke with hosts.

Street Boy (AC B G MA)
6/1 Soi Pradiphat 20, Sapan Kwai ☎ 022 78 47 39
Small quiet bar.

Talent Pub (AC B glm MA)
36/5-9 Phaholyothin Soi 11 *Corner of Pradiphat Soi 10* ☎ 022 79 15 18

Waterloo (AC B G MA MSG) 18-2h
6/5-6 Pradipat Soi 20 (Soi Kaw Toey), Sapan Kwai ☎ 026 18 73 25

SAUNAS/BATHS

39 Underground Sauna (AC b DR DU G MC OS S SA SB) 12-24, Fri & Sat -2h
1511/39 Phahon Yothin Road *At the end of the soi* ☎ 022 79 15 11
Located in small soi near Saphan Khwai BTS Station. Four floors and a open-air area upstairs. Popular with Thai and Asian gays. Tue, Sat & Sun NU.

Chakran (AC B CC DR DU FC G M MA MSG NU OS PI RR SA SB SH VS WH WO) 15-24, WE & before public holidays 14-24h
32 Soi Ari 4, Phaholyothin 7 *5 mins walk from Sky Train station Ari*
☎ 022 79 13 59 www.chakransauna.net
Large and very clean sauna on four floors.

Cruising Sauna (AC b DR DU FH G m MA SA SB SOL WO) 17-24, Sat & Sun 15-24h
1448/6-7 Phahonyothin Road, Ladyao, Chatuchak *Opp. Major Cineplex, Ratchayothin* ☎ 029 30 35 389
In a popular area with many students.

Farose (AC B cc d DR DU FC G M MA OS SA SB VS WH WO) 14-24h
108/3 Pradiphat Soi 19, Saphan Kwai *Difficult to find, hidden in small complex off main road* ☎ 026 18 45 05
Karaoke, small dancing area. Mostly locals.

CRUISING

-JJ Park
-Central Plaza, Lad Phrao. (Cruisy toilet)
-Chatuchak Park near BTS station Mo Chit Phaholyothin Road at Viphavadee Rangsit Highway.

Bangkok/Krung Thep – Siam Square/Pattunam

SHOWS

Calypso Cabaret (B glm S ST) Shows 20.15 & 21.45h
Asia Hotel, 296 Phaya Thai Road, Pathumwan
☎ 026 53 39 60 www.calypsocabaret.com
Good transvestite shows.

CRUISING

-National Stadium P (Rama 1 Road, Pathumwan)
-Siam Discovery Center (2nd and 3rd floor, also toilets. Best after 15h or WE)

Bangkok/Krung Thep – Silom Road/Surawong Road

All roads lead to Patong, but the taxis alone create a traffic chaos. This fun centre is named after the two streets Patong 1 and Patong 2, which connect the Silom Road with the parallel Surawong road. The night market is renowned for its bargains, bartering is compulsory, watches are cheap and fake, silver often reasonably priced and the real thing.
The gay scene comes to life in the evening in Silom Soi 4, going through the many bars and shows in the Silom Soi 6, Than Thawan or Duangthwee Plaza and ends in the discos in the Silom Road from Soi 2 to Soi 10.

Alle Wege führen nach Patong, schon die Taxis alleine verursachen hier allabendlich ein hoffnungsloses Verkehrschaos: Dieses Vergnügungszentrum ist benannt nach den beiden Straßen Patong 1 und Patong 2, die die Silom Road mit der parallelen Surawong Road verbinden. Der Nachtmarkt ist berühmt für seine günstigen Angebote: Handeln

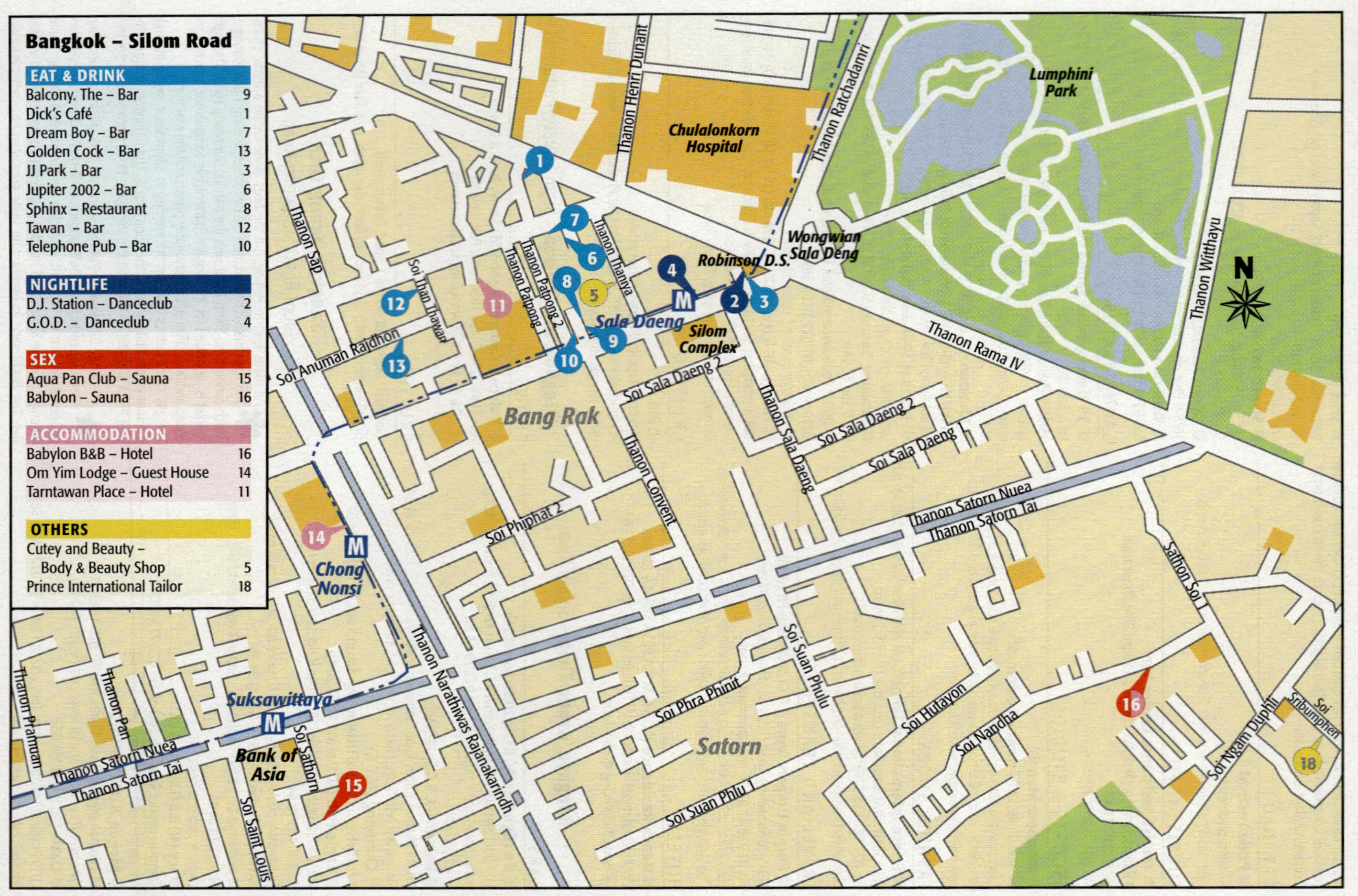
Bangkok – Silom Road
EAT & DRINK
Balcony. The – Bar 9
Dick's Café 1
Dream Boy – Bar 7
Golden Cock – Bar 13
JJ Park – Bar 3
Jupiter 2002 – Bar 6
Sphinx – Restaurant 8
Tawan – Bar 12
Telephone Pub – Bar 10
NIGHTLIFE
D.J. Station – Danceclub 2
G.O.D. – Danceclub 4
SEX
Aqua Pan Club – Sauna 15
Babylon – Sauna 16
ACCOMMODATION
Babylon B&B – Hotel 16
Om Yim Lodge – Guest House 14
Tarntawan Place – Hotel 11
OTHERS
Cutey and Beauty – Body & Beauty Shop 5
Prince International Tailor 18
N
Lumphini Park
Thanon Witthayu
Thanon Ratchadamri
Thanon Henri Dunant
Chulalonkorn Hospital
Wongwian Sala Deng
Robinson D.S.
Silom Complex
Sala Daeng
Thanon Thaniya
Thanon Patpong 2
Thanon Patpong 1
Soi Than Thawan
Soi Anuman Rajdhon
Thanon Sap
Chong Nonsi
Bang Rak
Thanon Rama IV
Soi Sala Daeng 1
Soi Sala Daeng 2
Thanon Sala Daeng
Thanon Convent
Soi Phiphat 2
Thanon Satorn Nuea
Thanon Satorn Tai
Sathon Soi 1
Soi Suan Phulu
Soi Phra Phinit
Satorn
Soi Suan Phlu 1
Soi Hutayon
Soi Nandha
Soi Ngam Duphli
Soi Sribumphen
Thanon Narathiwas Rajanakarindh
Suksawittaya
Soi Sathorn
Bank of Asia
Soi Saint Louis
Thanon Pan
Thanon Pramuan

ist Pflicht, die Uhren sind billig und alle falsch, Silber meistens preiswert und echt. Das schwule Leben beginnt am frühen Abend in Silom Soi 4, streift dann durch die Bars und Shows in Silom Soi 6, Soi Than Thawan oder Duangthawee Plaza und endet nachts in den Diskotheken der Silom Road von Soi 2 bis Soi 10.

A Bangkok, toutes les routes mènent à Patong et rien que les taxis créent chaque soir des embouteillages monstres. Ce centre de divertissement a été nommé d'après les rues Patong 1 et Patong 2, qui connectent la Li Lom Road avec la rue parallèle, la Surawong Road. Le marché de nuit est connu pour ses occasions uniques, le marchandage y est de mise, les montres sont bon marché, l'argent est souvent vrai et offert à des prix raisonnables.
La scène gaie s'éveille le soir dans la Si Lom Soi 4, se déplace ensuite dans les nombreux bars et spectacles de la Si Lom Soi 6, Than Thawan et Duangthwee Plaza, pour finir la nuit dans les clubs de la Si Lom Road, du Soi 2 au Soi 10.

Todos los caminos llevan a Patpong, donde todas las noches ya sólo los taxis causan un increíble caos de tráfico. Esta zona de recreación debe su nombre a las dos calles Patpong 1 und Patpong 2, que unen la Li Lom Road con la calle paralela Surawong Road. El mercado nocturno es famoso por las ofertas económicas; hay que regatear. Los relojes son baratos (y siempre falsificados), la plata suele tener precios atractivos (y ser plata de verdad).
La vida gay empieza por la tarde en Si Lom Soi 4, después se desplaza a los bares y espectáculos de Si Lom Soi 6, Soi Than Thawan o Duangthawee Plaza y termina en la noche en las discotecas de Si Lom Road entre Soi 2 y Soi 10.

Tutte le strade portano a Patpong. Qui bastano già i taxi da soli a provocare tutte le sere ingorghi di traffico. Questo centro di divertimenti prende il nome dalle due strade Patpong 1 e Patpong 2, che collegano la Li Lom Road con la parallela Surawong Road. Il mercato notturno è famoso per le sue favorevoli occasioni d'acquisto, contrattare è d'obbligo, gli orologi si vendono a basso prezzo e sono tutti falsi, l'argento è quasi sempre a buon mercato ed è vero.
La vita gay comincia in prima serata in Si Lom Soi 4, poi passa per i night-club e gli show in Si Lom Soi 6, Soi Than Thawan o Duangthawee Plaza e finisce in nottata nelle discoteche della Si Lom Road da Soi 2 a Soi 10.

BARS

■ **Balcony. The** (! AC B G I M MA OS) 19-2h
86-88 Silom Soi 4, Bang Rak *Soi Jaruwan* ☎ 022 35 58 91
🖳 www.balconypub.com
Very popular and moderately priced night spot. Internet corner. Staff can be a bit pushy.

■ **Balls the Sports Bar** (B GLM M MA OS) 17-2h
894 Soi Pratoochai, Surawong Road, Duangthawee Plaza *At the Rama 4, end of Soi Pratoochai* ☎ 026 37 00 78
Bar with large TV screens to watch sports events. Located at the quiet end of Bangkok's busiest gay street.

■ **Bar Bar** (AC B D GLM MA S WE) 21-1h
Silom Soi 4, Silom Road, Surawongse *Located on the left hand side almost to the end of the Soi* ☎ 086 798 96 82
Special events from time to time.

■ **Boy Zone** (B G MA MSG) 20-2h
11/1 Silom Soi 3 (Pipat), Bangrak *Approx. 500m into Soi off Silom Road left of Bangkok Bank* ☎ 026 36 85 70 (ext. 0-1)
Small beer bar with handsome gogos and massage. Rooms upstairs.

■ **4 Sports** (AC B glm MA)
114/10 Silom Soi 4 ☎ 026 32 80 13
Small bar with friendly staff.

■ **Classic 2nd** (AC B G MSG S)
Duangthawee Plaza, 38/7 Soi Pratoochai, at 38 Surawong Road
☎ 026 37 00 69
Good bar with spectacular Water Ballet Show.

■ **Club Café** (AC B G m MA) 15-3h
8/5 Silom Road, Soi 2, Bang Rak *Next to D. J. Station* ☎ 069 78 52 21

■ **Dream Boy** (AC B CC G OC S) 20-2, shows 22.15 & 0.15h
Boy Plaza – 38/6 Duangthawee Plaza *At 38 Surawong Road*
☎ 022 33 21 21 💻 dreamboy.thaiboy.net

■ **Eve House** (AC B G MA)
18-18/1 Surawong Road, Bang Rak *Opp. Soi Thaniya* ☎ 022 33 65 06
Karaoke for Thais and their friends.

■ **Expresso** (B G MA WE) Daily 21-2h
8/10-11 Silom Road, Soi 2, Bang Rak
💻 www.dj-station.com/expresso.html
Bar with dance music by D. J. Station; many Thai visitors.

■ **Future Boys** (AC B G MA MSG S) 19-2, shows 22+24h
Duangthawee Plaza, 894/5-6 Soi Pratoochai, at 38 Surawong Road, Bang Rak ☎ 026 37 05 07
Very large gogo bar with shows.

■ **Golden Cock** (AC B G m MSG S) 13-1h
39/27 Soi Rajanakarindra 1 (Soi Anuman Rajadhon) Surawong Road, Bang Rak *Off Si Lom Soi 6, off Soi Than Thawan* ☎ 022 36 38 59
Run down gogo bar.

■ **Hot Male** (AC B G MA OS S) 20-2h
38/40 Suriwong Road ☎ 022 35 38 76
Ex „Twilight", gogo bar.

■ **JJ Park** (AC B g m MA S) 21-3h
8/3 Silom Road, Soi 2, Bang Rak *Very small Soi next to Burger King and Robinson Silom. Sky train-station: Sala Daeang* ☎ 022 35 12 27

■ **Jupiter 2002** (AC B G MA MSG S) 20-2, show 22.30h
31/1-33 Surawong Road (Soi Thaniya 2), Bang Rak *Next to Suriwong Hotel*
☎ 022 37 40 50
Big gogo bar, very popular shows. Part of Suriwong Hotel.

■ **Paradiso Karaoke Club** (AC B G M MA) 19-2h
96/16-17 Luang Suan, Balcony, Lumpini *At Lang Suan Balcony Plaza, 2nd floor* ☎ 022 52 12 29
Trendy place, karaoke and club.

■ **Pharao's Music Bar** (AC B cc d GLM M MA) 19-2h
104 Silom Soi 4, Bangrak *Above Sphinx Restaurant* ☎ 022 34 72 49
💻 www.pharaohsmusicbar.com
One of the best bars in Bangkok!

■ **Solid** (AC B G MA R S T) 20-2h
39/2 Soi Anuman Ratchathon, Suriwong ☎ 026 34 26 64
💻 www.solidbangkok.com
Gogo dancing downstairs, friendly staff.

■ **Tawan Bar** (AC B f G MSG S VS WO) 20-1h
2/2 Soi Tawan, Silom Soi 6, Surawong Road, Bang Rak *Near corner of Surawong Road, Si Lom Soi 6* ☎ 026 34 58 33
Gogo bar specialising in muscle men.

■ **Telephone Pub, Restaurant & Karaoke** (! AC B DR FC GLM I M MA NR OS S ST T VEG VR VS WI WL) 18-2h
114/11-13 Silom Soi 4, Silom Rd, Bangrak *3 mins walk from Saladaeng BTS /Skytrain* ☎ 22 34 32 79 💻 www.telephonepub.com
This pub has been connecting guys for 25 years. Great restaurant & Karaoke lounge with private Karaoke rooms. Many SKYPE video phones throughout the pub's 3 floors.

■ **X Boys** (AC B G MA S) 20-1h
Duangthawee Plaza, Soi Pratoochai, Suriwong Road ☎ 091 62 76 52
Shows 22-24h.

■ **X Size** (AC B G MA S)
38/8 Duangthawee Plaza, Soi Pratoochai ☎ 087 99 44 875

CAFES

■ **Babylon Coffee Shop** (B CC GLM H I M MA OS) 11.30-24h
34 Soi Nandha, South Sathorn Rd (Soi 1) *Same location as Babylon Sauna and Bed & Breakfast* ☎ 026 79 79 84 💻 www.babylonbangkok.com
Also gifts, souvenirs and high speed internet access.

■ **Bug & Bee** (AC b DM glm M MA VEG WI) open 24 hours
18 Silom Road, Bangrak ☎ 026 32 88 83 💻 www.bugandbee.com

■ **Dick's Café Bangkok** (AC B BF CC G M MA OS T) 11-2h
Duangthawee Plaza, 894/7-8 Soi Pratoochai, Surawong Road, Bang Rak
Hua Lampong Subway Station
Sala Daeng Skytrain Station ☎ 026 37 00 78 💻 www.dickscafe.com
The pleasant coffee oasis in the heart of the gay scene. Excellent cappuccino, Thai and international food, sandwiches and cakes. Moderately priced. Refreshing contrast to the hawking and noisy gogo bars.

DANCECLUBS

■ **D. J. Station** (AC B D G MA r S VS) 22-2h
8/6-8 Silom Road, Soi 2, Bang Rak *Very small Soi next to Burger King and Robinson Silom. Sky Train station Sala Daeang* ☎ 022 66 40 29
💻 www.dj-station.com
Probably the best and most popular gay disco in southeast Asia. The three floors are packed every night. Show starts around 23h. Very cruisy.

■ **Disco Disco** (B D G MA) 21-2h
8/12-13 Silom Road, Soi 2, Bang Rak *Very small Soi next to Burger King and Robinson Silom. Sky Train station Sala Daeang* ☎ 022 34 61 51
💻 www.dj-station.com/discodisco.html
Bar and disco. The ideal place to chill and observe all the action.

■ **G. O. D.** (AC B D G MA) Daily 21-?h
60/18-21 Soi 2/1 Silom Road *The small alley between Soi 2 and Soi 4, next to Noodi restaurant*
Popular after hour danceclub.

■ **X Boom** (AC B D G MA r S t) Daily from 20-?h
Soi Anuman Ratchathon, Surawong Road
A popular 'after-hours' place for the post-DJ Station crowd. The bar features dancing boys and a show at 23h. The venue turns into a club from midnight.

RESTAURANTS

■ **Babylon's Fine Dining** (AC B BF CC G LM M MA OS VEG)
Daily 12-24h
34 Soi Nandha, South Sathorn Road (Soi 1) *Same building as Babylon Sauna and Bed & Breakfast*
☎ 026 79 79 84 💻 www.babylonbangkok.com
A complete & creative international cuisine and wonderful desserts, along with Thai food specialties. Live Jazz & other music entertainment.

■ **Bug & Bee** (AC b DM glm M MA VEG WI) open 24 hours
18 Silom Road, Bangrak ☎ 026 32 88 83 💻 www.bugandbee.com

■ **Coyote On Convent** (AC g M)
1/2 Convent Road ☎ 026 62 37 73 💻 www.coyotebangkok.com
Gay owned mexican restaurant, mixed crowd, great food, open for lunch and dinner.

■ **Indigo** (AC g M OS) Mon-Sat 12-1h
6 Convent Road (off Silom Rd) *in a small soi off Soi Convent just opposite Shenanigan's* ☎ 022 35 32 68
A place for a romantic night, great french food, beautiful lounge and patio/ garden. Not gay but very gay friendly.

■ **Mali** (AC B g M) 8-23h
43 Sathorn Soi 1 ☎ 026 79 86 93
Lovely little place, very relaxed and friendly, thai and international food. Mixed crowd

■ **Maxis** (AC B CC DM G M MA OS S ST VEG WL) Daily 11-2h
38/1-2 Soi Pratuchai Surawong Road ☎ 022 66 42 25
💻 www.maxisbar.com

■ **Sphinx** (AC B CC GLM M MA OS) 18-2h
100 Silom Soi 4 (Soi Jaruwan), Bang Rak *Within walking distance from Saladaeng BTS and Silom MRT* ☎ 022 34 72 49
💻 www.sphinxbangkok.com
Award winning Thai restaurant.

SAUNAS/BATHS

■ **Aqua Spa Club** (AC b DU G m MA MSG OS SB WH WO) 14-24h
11/5 Soi Sathorn 9, South Sathorn Road *Near Asia Bank, off South Sathon Road, small and winding Soi. Between Sky Train stations Chong Nonsi and Surasak* ☎ 022 86 45 35 💻 www.aquaspaclub.com
Luxury sauna.

■ **The Babylon Bangkok** (! AC B CC DR DU G I LAB M MA MSG OS PI RR S SA SB SH VS WH WO) 10.30-22.30h
34 Soi Nandha, South Sathorn Road (Soi 1) *Same building as Babylon B&B* ☎ 026 79 79 84 💻 www.babylonbangkok.com

A world-class sauna, great Thai massage and spa treatments. A large outdoor area with swimming pool. A second outdoor area which is open at night only. A wonderful restaurant with excellent meals on offer too. Probably Asia's best sauna. Excellent on-site accommodation.

■ **Heaven** (B DU FH G I M MA MSG OS RR SA SB VS WH WO)
15-24, Fri & Sat -1h
Warner Tower, 119 Soi Mahesak, Silom *4th floor, near Surasak Station*
☎ 022 66 90 92
Also interesting for „westerners".

■ **Sauna Mania** (AC B DR DU G MA OS RR SA SB VS WH WO)
17-24, Fri & Sat -3h
35/2 Soi Pipat 2, Convent Road ☎ 081 817 40 73
Popular with locals, only few western visitors.

MASSAGE

■ **Adonis Massage** (G MA MSG) 14-23.30
44/11 Convent Road ☎ 022 36 77 89 💻 www.thaiadonismassage.com
Upmarket massage place located just off Silom in Convent Road – a small sub soi.

■ **Arena** (G MSG) 12-24h
2nd Floor, Silom Plaza, 491/19-21 Silom Road *Five mins from Silom Soi 4, next to Thai Airways Office* ☎ 026 35 36 45
Experienced handsome masseurs.

■ **Senso Spa** (G MA MSG) 14-23.30h
5/8 Sala Daeng Soi *Just off Silom Road* ☎ 026 36 35 35
💻 www.sensomenclub.com
Premier massage place located in Soi Saladaeng.

BODY & BEAUTY SHOPS

■ **Cutey and Beauty** (AC CC g MA MSG) 10.30-20, Sun 12-18h
Thaniya Plaza, 3rd floor, Soi Thaniya at 52 Silom Road *BTS Saladaeng Station* ☎ 02 213 2315 💻 www.cuteyandbeauty.com
Bangkok's premier hair stylists and beauty salon. Internationally trained staff. Cut and colour specialists. Speciality: facials, manicures, pedicure, eyelash & eyebrow coloring, body waxing, foot treatment & foot massage. Gay owned and operated.

HOTELS

■ **Babylon Bed & Breakfast** (! AC B BF CC G I M MA MSG PI RWS RWT SA SB VA WH WO) All year, 24hrs
34 Soi Nandha, South Sathorn Road (Soi 1) *Near to the Austrian Embassy*
☎ 026 79 79 84 💻 www.babylonbangkok.com

■ **Om Yim Lodge** (AC B BF CC GLM I M MA NR OS PK RES RWS RWT VA WI) 24hrs
72-74 Naratiwat Road, Silom, Bangrak *30m from Chong Nonsi Sky Train BTS station; exit no.3* ☎ 026 35 01 69 💻 www.omyimgroup.com
All rooms with safe, fridge, tea making facilities, cable TV. 24hr reception. Just 5 minutes away from Bangkok's most lively area for gays with bars and clubs.

■ **Plaza** (AC B BF cc H m MA PI)
178 Suriwong Road, Bangrak ☎ 022 35 17 60
Cheap hotel, the clean but simple rooms are large, some have a kitchenette.

■ **Swiss Lodge** (AC B BF cc glm M MA OS PI)
3 Convent Road, Silom Road ☎ 022 33 53 45 💻 www.swisslodge.com
Rooms with cable and sat-TV, 24h security service, safe, mini-bar.

■ **Tarntawan Place** (AC B bf CC GLM I M MA MSG PK RWS RWT VA) All year
119/5-10 Surawong Road, Bangrak *In a quiet courtyard off Surawong Road*
☎ 022 38 26 20 💻 www.tarntawan.com
Special discount for SPARTACUS readers!

GUEST HOUSES

■ **Baan Saladaeng** (AC b BF DM DU G M MA NR OS PK RES RWB RWS RWT VEG WI) open: All year, Check in 13, check out 11h
69/2 Soi Saladaeng *Dead-end soi opposite MK Gold restaurant*
☎ 026 36 30 38 💻 www.baansaladaeng.com
The guesthouse is located in a quit and cozy street. Each room have a unique style.

■ **BBB Inn** (b bf G I m MA RWS RWT VA)
918 Rama 4 Road, Bang Rak 💻 bbbinn.thaiboy.net
Gay guesthouse with 23 rooms.

■ **Vincent's Restaurant & The 7 Rooms**
(AC b BF glm H I m MA MSG RWS VA) All year
12/1 Soi Ngam Duphli, Rama 4 Rd., Thungmahamek, Sathorn *Near Lumpini Park and the Night Bazar. 300m from Lumpini Underground Station*
☎ 022 86 33 48 💻 vincentsbangkok.com

SWIMMING

-Outdoor swimming pool at Clark Hatch Fitness, Soi Thaniya, 9/f Thaniya Plaza Building, near Silom Road.

CRUISING

-Lumpini Park (6-22h inside the Park, all day. Especially after dark around Rama VI monument at corner of Rama IV/Silom Road. The most popular Bangkok cruising)
-Car park between Rajadamri Sky-train and Lumpini Park entrance along Lumpini Park (evenings)
-Robinson Department Store (Cruising around all entrances and toilets
-Silom Complex, all floors, toilets
-Robinson Silom outside McDonald's along to 7-Eleven store, especially around Grand Pacific Hotel.

Bangkok/Krung Thep – Sukhumvit Road

SHOWS

■ **Mambo** (B glm MA S) Shows 20.30 & 22h
22-24 Sukhumvit Road *Washington Theatre* ☎ 022 59 51 28
Shows every night at 8:30 PM and 10 PM. Hardly innovative, but professional and well liked by tourists.

BARS

■ **Inter Mustache's House** (B G H m MA) 18-3h
23/12 Sukhumvit Soi 10, Klong Toey *Off Sukhumvit Plaza, near Bangkok Mansion* ☎ 022 50 17 21 💻 www.aboutg.net/intermustache
First floor is a cocktail lounge, 2nd floor is a bar and 3rd floor is a Karaoke bar.

■ **Jet Set** (AC B GLM m MA)
32/19 Sukumvit Soi 21 (Soi Wirot), Khlong Toey ☎ 022 58 43 11
A good karaoke place, popular with locals.

■ **Relax** (AC B cc GLM M MA)
32/20 Sukhumvit Soi 21 *Soi Wirot, next to JetSet Bar*
Karaoke bar and restaurant.

■ **Room Mate** (AC B G M MA PI)
Sukhumvit Soi 40, Soi Saphan Sukjai ☎ 023 91 33 86
Lots of friendly and handsome hosts.

■ **Studio 982** (AC B cc G M MA) 19-2h
161/2-3 Soi 9, Sukhumvit Soi 55, Thong Lo Soi 9 *BTS Station Thong Lo*
☎ 023 91 65 45

■ **Turning Point** (AC B CC d G m MA MSG S ST) 20-2.30h
120/19-20 Sukumvit Soi 23 (Soi Prasan Mit), Khlong Toey *Sub Soi left off Soi 23* ☎ 026 62 19 96
Karaoke bar and cocktail lounge.

DANCECLUBS

■ **Bed Supperclub** (! AC B D G MA WE) Sun 19.30-1h
26 Soi Sukhumvit 11 ☎ 026 51 35 37 💻 www.bedsupperclub.com
The club hosts a ‚think pink' gay night every Sunday. Admission fee applies. Its also the most avantgarde club and restaurant in Bangkok.

■ **Think Pink @ Bed Supper Club** (AC B CC d GLM m MA) Sun 22-1h
26 Sukhumvit Soi 11 ☎ 026 51 35 37 💻 www.bedsupperclub.com
If you are looking for a chic, sylish and trendy night out in Bangkok then this is the place to go. Sundays is gay night.

SAUNAS/BATHS

■ **Beach Resort Sauna. The** (B DU G M MA PI SA SB VS WH) 15-6h
316 Soi Preedeepanomyong 42 (Panich-anan), Sukhumvit 71 R.d, Klongton ☎ 023 92 47 83 💻 www.thebeach-g-thailand.com
Mostly Thai crowd.

■ **Mind Sauna** (B DU G MA MSG SA SB) 14-24h
Sukhumvit Soi 48, Prakanong ☎ 023 91 93 17
Almost entirely Thai.

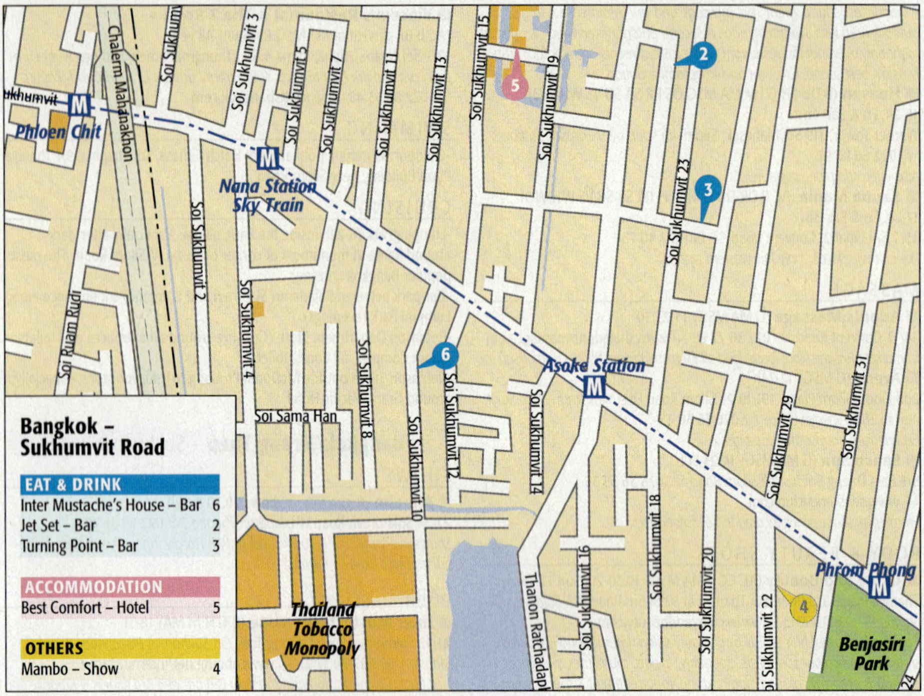

Bangkok – Sukhumvit Road

EAT & DRINK
Inter Mustache's House – Bar 6
Jet Set – Bar 2
Turning Point – Bar 3

ACCOMMODATION
Best Comfort – Hotel 5

OTHERS
Mambo – Show 4

FITNESS STUDIOS

■ **Banana Men's Fitness Club** (B CC FH G M MA MSG SB WH WO) 15-24h
49/9 Sukhumvit 11, Klong Toey *Near Ambassador Hotel* ☎ 026 51 00 02
Oil and cream massage available. Popular with Singaporean clientele.

MASSAGE

■ **Albury Men's Club** (B G MSG SB) 13-2h
71/1 Sukhumvit Soi 11, Sukhumvit Road, Wattnana ☎ 081 91 09 721
💻 www.alburymenclubs.com

■ **Body Club** (G MSG) 12-22h
4/24-25 Sukhumvit Soi 8 *Inside a small sub-soi next to the 7-11 on the right in soi 8* ☎ 026 53 39 42

■ **Hero** (B G M MSG SB) 15-24h
65 Sukhumvit Soi 11 ☎ 022 51 10 33
Very popular up-market venue.

BODY & BEAUTY SHOPS

■ **Thonglor Clinic** (g)
158/1 Anekvanich Building, Sukhum Vit Rd 55 ☎ 02392 3590
💻 www.thonglorclinic.com
Beauty, anti-aging and plastic surgery centre in the heart of Bangkok and Pattaya-Jomtien –Thailand, offering the highest quality of aesthetic treatment and plastic surgeries to improve your appearance and slow down the signs of ageing.

HOTELS

■ **Best Comfort Hotel** (AC bf CC glm H I M MA MSG PI PK RWS RWT SA VA WO) All year
49 Soi Sukhumvit 19, Wattana *Sukumvit Business District*
☎ 026 51 13 10 💻 www.bestcomfortbangkok.com
Luxury hotel and very friendly cute staff. An apartment-hotel, ten stories high, with 60 beautifully decorated rooms.

CRUISING

-Ploenchit Mall next to Marriott Hotel (Sky Train Ploen Chit). Toilet on second floor and bowling alley
-Time Square and adjoing Building (third floor toilets)
-Amarin Plaza, on Ploenchit Road. (Toilets on the second, third, and fourth floor).

Bangkok/Krung Thep – Other Areas

BARS

■ **BearbieBar** (AC B D G M MA S)
2nd Floor, 82 Silom Soi 4, Bangrak

■ **G-Star** (AC B D G MA) 20-1h
Rachada Road, Soi 8, Din Daeng ☎ 026 438 792
💻 www.g-starpub.com

■ **Golden Dome** (AC B d g M S ST) 15-?, shows 17, 19, 21h
252/5 Soi 18, Ratchadapisek Road, (Soi Yocharern), Huai Khwang
☎ 026 92 82 02
Cabaret shows.

■ **Kudos** (AC B G M MA)
The Mall 2, Ramkhamhaeng Road *Soi enterance car park Mall 2*
☎ 023 18 38 88
Small and friendly karaoke bar with Thai food, popular with locals & students.

DANCECLUBS

■ **Fake Club** (AC B D G MA S) 21-2h
Thanon Kamphaeng Phet Road ☎ 089 479 92 62
Live music at 23.30h.

■ **Ick** (AC B D G M MA S) 20-2h
Ramkhamheng Soi 89/2 (Lumsalee) *Near Lumsalee intersection*
☎ 089 113 29 29
Large disco/pub. Mainly Thai music; cabaret shows every night. Best after 21.30h.

■ **Maa See Kaa II** (AC B D G S) 22-1h
2 Ramkamhaeng Soi 18 *Near Ramkamhaeng University*
☎ 023 19 82 48
Popular with young gay Thais.

■ **MTV Remix** (AC B D GLM m)
Ramhamhaeng Soi 24 ☎ 023 19 83 40
Well mixed, popular with many gay students.

■ **T. G. Street** (AC B D G M MA) 22-2h
Tanao Road (Kok Wau Intersection), Rachadamneon Road *Next to Sa-Ke Pub* ☎ 097 48 02 12
Long gallery on 2nd floor with great overview.

ESCORTS & STUDIOS

■ **Rainbowmen** (G MSG)
City centre ☎ 089 00 09 632 (within Thailand)
🖳 www.gaytailoredtours.com
Outstanding world-wide escort and companion service.
See: www.rainbowmen.com. Also in Europe at www.gaytailoredtours.com and for handicapped men at www.gayenabledtours.com.

SAUNAS/BATHS

■ **Beach Resort. The** (b DU G MA NU PI SA SB VS WO) 15-6h
316 Soi Panit Anant, Sukhumvit 71, Klongton ☎ 027 130 007
🖳 thebeach-g-thailand.com
Well equipped sauna with additional karaoke room and a large naked zone.

■ **Edok** (AC b DR G MA MSG SA SB)
Soi LG (near Soi Taksin 14), Taksin Road , Thonburi ☎ 024 66 07 07

■ **Hercules** (B DU G MSG OS SA SB WO) 16-24h
91/194 Siam Park City, Sukhapiban 2 Road, Siam Park Av. ☎ 029 19 96 09

■ **Male Box** (AC b DU G MA SA SB WO)
Rama II Soi 52, Rama II Road (opposite Big C and HomePro)
☎ 028 48 11 90
Small local-style sauna.

■ **Nevada Meeting Sport Club** (AC B DU G MA MSG SA WO) 16-24h
Soi 81/4, Ramkhamhaeng Rd *Between Soi 81 and Soi 83* ☎ 027 32 06 13
Small sauna, mostly local crowd.

■ **Orion** (b G MA MSG SA SB WO) 16-1, Sat & Sun 14-1h
210-212, Soi behind Merry King Department, Pinklao ☎ 028 84 60 90

FITNESS STUDIOS

■ **Hercules Health Club** (AC B G M SA SB WO)
16-23, Fri-Sun 12-24h
91/194 Siam Park City, Sukhapiban 2 Road, Siam Park Av., Bangkapi *Near Fashion Island, Grand Inn Hotel at Siam Park* ☎ 029 19 96 09

CRUISING

-Sanam Luang (large open field between Wat Phra Keow, the Royal Palace and Banglamphu, AYOR)
-Small park next to Ministry of Defence, expecially at night time (AYOR).

Changwat Suratthani

GUEST HOUSES

■ **Our Jungle House** (AC B BF GLM I M MA MSG OS PA PK RWB RWS VA) All year
Khao Sok National Park *Khao Sok* ☎ 089 90 96 814
🖳 www.losthorizonsasia.com
A wonderful location adjoining the Khao Sok National Park. A place for true nature lovers.

Chiang Mai

BARS

■ **Bacchus** (AC B GLM M MA OS)
Nimman 9, Su Thep *On a Soi near new Dusit Thani Hotel, near Night Market*
Features a mixed crowd, with the many attractive waiters drawing in European ex-pats.

■ **Circle Pub** (AC B G MA R S T)
Daily 20-1, cabaret show 22 & 23.30h
161/7-8 Soi Erawan, Changphuek Road, T. Sriphoom A. Muang
☎ 053 21 49 96 🖳 www.circlepubchiangmai.com
Popular modern bar with many gogos. Nightly show.

■ **Glass Onion Bar and Lounge. The** (AC B cc G m MA) 20-1h
61/2 Nimanhaemin Road *Next to Chiang Mai University*
☎ 053 21 84 79
Sophisticated little place.

■ **Lang Matong. Le** (B GLM M MA OS) 12-24h
Jaremsrad Road, Amphur Muang *East side of the Ping River, just south of town* ☎ 053 30 22 60
Gay-owned and managed riverside night spot with live music, young local crowd.

■ **New My Way** (AC B G MA R S) 20-1, show at 22h
3/5-6 Hatsadee Sewee Road, Chang Peuak ☎ 053 40 43 61
🖳 www.newmywaybar.com
Long established bar with gogos and special shows.

■ **Pornping Coffee Shop** (AC B D glm MA)
46-48 Charoenprathet Road, Chang Klan *At Porn Ping Hotel, near the river and the Night Bazaar* ☎ 053 27 00 99
🖳 www.pornpinghotelchiangmai.com

■ **Sandy Bar** (B GLM M MA S ST)
18-2, cabaret show 22.15, Thai boxing show 23.15h
Baar Bar Center, Moon Muang Road *Near Thapae Gate* ☎ 095 58 50 52
Loud and amusing entertainment. Cruisy. Inexpensive. Thai boxing ring and cabaret shows.

■ **Yokka Dok** (b G H MA NR WI)
11, Ratchamankha Road ☎ 053 44 95 29 🖳 www.yokkadok.webs.com
Yokka Dok has a friendly, relaxed atmosphere on a quiet road. It is a gay owned bar with a restaurant and a guesthouse. Rooms from 350-500 Baht.

DANCECLUBS

■ **Adam's Apple** (AC B G MA PK R S ST T)
open daily from 20.30-0.30h, showtime at 22h
1/21-22 Tanon Viengbua, A Muang Chiang Mai *Located above the METRO BAR* ☎ 05 322 03 81 🖳 www.adamsappleclub.com
This bar is totally revamped to a luxury club. Open til late with karaoke after the go-go show.

■ **Bubble Disco** (AC B CC D glm MA) 21-2h
46-48 Charoen Prathet Road, Chang Klan *Basement of Pornping Hotel*
☎ 053 27 00 99 🖳 www.pornpinghotelchiangmai.com
Popular disco.

■ **Spicy** (AC B D GLM m MA)
82 Chaiyapoon Road *Opp. Sompet Market* ☎ 053 23 48 60
Disco plus two live bands. Very popular, many gays. Late night hang out.

RESTAURANTS

■ **House & Ginger Restaurant, The** (AC GLM)
open daily from 10-22h
199 Moonmuang Road ☎ (053) 41 82 63 🖳 www.thehousethailand.com
A trendy and hip all-in-one shop with unique furniture, clothes and a well furnished restaurant.

■ **Tha-Nam** (B GLM H M MA OS) 8-22h
43/3 Thanon Changklan, River Front, Amphur Muang *Centre south, at bank of the Ping River* ☎ 053 27 51 25
Northern Thai cuisine. Popular. Local Lanna style design with lots of wood. Friendly service.

■ **West Restaurant** (NG) open daily from 11.30-2.30, 17.30-22.30h
Fah Tani Square, Nimmanhaemin Soi 5 ☎ 08 01 22 71 36
🖳 www.west-restaurant.com
Wonderful food and incredible desserts. No Thai Food.

■ **Wildflowers** (B bf GLM M MA NR OS PA VEG) 7-21h
Souvenir Guest House, 118 Charoen Prathet Road, Amphur Muang *Near Night Bazaar & Chedi Hotel* ☎ 053 81 87 86
🖳 www.souvenir-guesthouse.com
Thai, American, and European cuisine. Very reasonably priced. Part of Souvenir guest house.

SAUNAS/BATHS

House of Male (B DR DU FH G M MA MSG OS PI r RR SB SH VS WE WO) 12-24h
19 Sirimangklajarn Rd, Soi 3, Tambol Suthep, Amphur Muang *Last house in the soi* ☎ 053 89 41 33 🖳 www.houseofmale.com
Friendly and relaxed sauna set in a traditional Thai house. Popular with both locals and tourists, especially buddy nights on Tue and Thu. Free admission on your birthday.

MASSAGE

Blue's Club. The (AC CC DU FC FH G MA MSG OS PK RR WI) 14-24h
422/18 Chiangmai Land, Changkarn Road, Muang *Between Soi 5 and 7* ☎ 053 20 49 68 🖳 www.blueclub-spa.com
10 % discount for Spartacus readers.

Classic House Massage (AC b CC G M MA MSG) 12-24h
27/2 Thapae Road Soi 4 ☎ 053 90 45 82
Traditional Thai massages, body treatments, aromatherapy, performed by young handsome staff.

Free Guy (B G M MA MSG R S SA T)
Bar: 19-1h, massage & sauna: 17-1h
Chang Phuk Road *Near Thanin Market, Soi Yentafour Sriping* 🖳 www.freeguy-club.com
Beer bar with rustic ambiance, mini pub and karaoke with light music, massage in house or outside service. Special show 22-24h.

Gemini (b G MA MSG) 10-1h
48/1 Hatsadisawee Road *Opp. Soet School* ☎ 053 40 41 46

His Club (CC G MSG) 13-1h
21/43 Soi Wat Pa Phrao nok, Chanklan Road ☎ 053 20 41 48 🖳 www.hisclub-chiangmai.com
Traditional Thai massage, aromatherapy, lovely boys, entertainment & massage services in and outdoor.

One-2-Come (AC b G m MA MSG OS) 13-23h
360/1 Changklan Road *Near Sheraton Hotel* ☎ 053 20 43 85 🖳 www.kadlanna.com/one2come
Gay owned spa with massage, bar and beer garden.

DECORATION

House & Ginger Restaurant, The (AC GLM)
open daily from 10-22h
199 Moonmuang Road ☎ (053) 41 82 63 🖳 www.thehousethailand.com
A trendy and hip all-in-one shop with unique furniture, clothes and a well furnished restaurant.

HOTELS

Lotus (AC B BF CC G I M MA MSG OS PK RWB RWS RWT VA)
All year, garden bar open 19-1h
2/25 Tanon Viengbua, Chang Pheuak Road *Close to most gay bars* ☎ 053 21 53 76 🖳 www.lotus-hotel.com
Part of the largest gay complex in the city and located near the bars in the north. All rooms have bathroom, TV, fridge and mini-bar. Popular garden bar and restaurant.

GUEST HOUSES

Baan Sammi (AC GLM I MA OS PI PK RWB RWS RWT VA) All year
79M6, T. Pa Lan, A. Doi Saket *About 15 km north east of Chiang Mai – between Chiang Mai and Doi Saket* ☎ (053) 868815 🖳 www.baansammi.com
Simple but convenient rooms with room and laundry service and internet (WLAN).

Club One Seven Guesthouse (AC B BF CC DM GLM M MA PI RWB SA SB VEG WI WO) open: All year, Check in 15, check out 12.30h
385/2 Charoen Prathet Rd. Changklan, Muang 🖳 www.clubonseven.net

Lana Thai Villa (AC glm OS RWB RWS RWT) All year
3 Old Maerim Samoeng Road ☎ 053 86 10 75 🖳 www.lana-thai-villa.com

PJ's Place (AC bf cc G I MA MSG OS PK RWB RWS RWT VA) All year
19 Plubplueng Soi, Huay Kaew Road, T. Changphuak, A. Muang ☎ 053 40 48 94 🖳 pjs-place.com
Guesthouse with four deluxe rooms.

Seven Suns (AC B BF CC GLM M MA OS RWB RWS RWT S SA VA)
All year, restaurant 17-24, pub 16-2h
155 Ratchamanka Road, T. Prasingh, Amphur Muang ☎ 053 81 43 25 🖳 www.sevensuns.net
Reopening in 2012.

Soho (AC B G H MA OS) Mon-Sat 12:-24, Sun -18h
20/3 Huay Kaew Road *Opp.Chiang Mai Orchid Hotel and Kad Suan Kaew Shopping Mall* ☎ 053 40 41 75 🖳 www.sohochiangmai.com
Pleasant relaxed atmosphere, very nicely decorated inside. One of the rare gay venues where visitors and gay Thai meet without commercial undertones.

Souvenir (AC B glm M MA OS VS WO) 7-21h
118 Charoen Prathet Road 8 *Near Night Bayaar and Ping Porn Hotel* ☎ 053 81 87 86 🖳 www.souvenir-guesthouse.com
Very friendly staff and gay owner.

CRUISING

-Taepae Gate (after 21h)
-Narawat Bridge (evenings)
-Park opposite market (called locally Moon station) near Post office (after dark)
-Nong Buak Hat Park
-Huay Kaew Waterfall (daytime)
-Huay Kaew recreational park (Arboretum near zoo, Huay Kaew road opposite police station, evenings)
-Fitness Park Chamgmai University International Centre (Nimmanhemmin Road, evenings).

Chiang Rai

BARS

Lobo Boys Boys Boys (AC B G m MA MSG S) 20-1h
869/127 Thai Viwat Road, off Chetyot Road, Amphur Muang ☎ 053 75 25 16
Small and friendly bar with handsome men.

Regency Bar (AC B G MA MSG) 20-1h
869/127 Pemawibhata Road, A. Muang *Opp. Wangcome Hotel* ☎ 053 75 23 29
Do not expect too much English!

Hat Yai

BARS

Buddy Pub (B G m MSG S) 19-1h
37/2 Sriphuvanart Road, Song Khla ☎ 074 42 09 44
Friendly and welcoming place. Busy around 23h. Nice show. At WE popular with Malaysians.

G Men Club (B G m MA MSG OS S) 20-1, show 22.30h
10 Thai Arkan, Songkla *100m south of Thanon Siphunawat* ☎ 074 22 01 49

Studio 54 (B G m MA MSG OS) 19-1h
10-12 Channivate Road, Soi 2, Song Khla *South of Sri Phinawat Road near SK Hotel* ☎ 074 23 05 73

T. Tong (B G MA) 19-1h
38 Thanon Thai Arkan, Song Khla ☎ 081 54 02 410
Karaoke bar.

Top Man Bar (B G MA SNU)
38 Thai-Arkan Road ☎ 081-540 2410
Popular agogo bar in town.

SAUNAS/BATHS

GL Sauna (AC B cc d DR DU FC G M MA OS SA SB VS WH WO)
37/73 Sinbenjapon Centre Building, Soi P. Nattapon 2 Sripoovanart Road ☎ 089-976 7268

Khon Kaen

SAUNAS/BATHS

■ **Beach. The** (b DU G m MA MSG RR SA SB VS WO) 15-6h
Sritaduprasun Road ☎ 043 23 51 71 🖳 www.thebeach-g-thailand.com

■ **Dolphin. The** (B DU G MA MSG SA SB WO) 18-2h
33/6-7 Soi Suphateera, Srichan Road, A. Muang ☎ 043 33 34 68

CRUISING

-Park behind Governors Residence at Lake (best 19-? MC)
-Park around Bung Kaen Nakhon Lake (best 19-21h, cruisy until very late. Many students).

Koh Samui

BARS

■ **Boy Zone Koh Samui** (AC B D G MA MSG S) Daily 21-2h, Show 23.30h
35/16 Moo 3, Bophut ☎ 087 88 14 277 🖳 www.boyzonesamui.com
Stylish gay/mixed bar with two shows every night, also massages.

■ **Moulin Rouge** (B glm MA R S ST) Show 20, 21:30 + 23h
Chaweng Beach Road, Surat Thani *On Soi next to Burger King*
One of Samui's most popular and longest running lady boy cabaret shows. Free entry. The bar has been recently renovated

■ **K Club** (G MA MSG OS R)
166/22 Soi Solo, Chaweng Beach Road, North Chaweng *Behind Starbucks, at north end of Chaweng Beach Road*
This is a rent boy bar. Free entry. Not the cleanest place in town.

■ **Starz Club Cabaret** (AC B D g MA MSG R S ST t) 15-2h
Khun Chaweng Shopping Centre, Chaweng Beach Road, North Chaweng *Located at the back of the Khun Chaweng Shopping Centre*
☎ 084 744 90 74
Samui's largest and most glitzy cabaret. Show times: 20 & 22h. Free entry. Separate, air-conditioned bar opens at 12h. Show changes daily. Mixed crowd.

DANCECLUBS

■ **Green Mango** (B D glm MA)
Chaweng Beach Road, North Chaweng *At the end of the Green Mango Soi*
🖳 www.thegreenmangoclub.com
An institution. One of the original clubs. Big, loud, far from elegant but definitely an experience. Mixed, but many local gay Thai go there at midnight.

MASSAGE

■ **Emerald Green Men's Club** (AC CC G MA MSG OS) 12-22h
9/64 Moo 2 Chaweng Beach Road, North Chaweng *Opp. Nora Beach Resort, north end of Chaweng Beach Road* ☎ (0) 77 601 372
🖳 www.emeraldgreensamui.com
Home of quality massage and body treatments for men by men. English spoken. Open daily. Your holiday really starts there!

■ **Mekkala Men Spa Koh Samui** (AC CC G MA MSG) Daily 10-24h
128/68 Moo 1 Taweeratpakdee Road *Near Big C Center, the entrance is opp. Family Mart, 200m along the road to Chaweng Printing; 10 mins to the beach* ☎ (66) 833948650 🖳 www.mekkalamenspa.com
Private property with exclusive spa treatments available. Handsome & friendly staff.

TRAVEL AND TRANSPORT

■ **Rainbow Scuba & Tour** (G MA) All year
☎ (086) 27 20 980 🖳 www.rainbow-scuba.com
Gay adventure tour operator; offers island road and snorkelling tours, scuba diving, kayak, sailing and cycling trips. Bookings by email contact; meetings by appointment only.

HOTELS

■ **Papillon Resort** (AC B BF CC DU GLM H I M MA MSG NR OS PA PI PK RWB RWS RWT SH VA WH WL WO) 6-24h
1 & 2 Chaweng Beach Road, North Chaweng *At the very north end of Chaweng Beach* ☎ 077 231169 🖳 www.papillonkohsamui.com
Gay / Gay friendly managed bungalow resort with 23 bungalows with AC, mini-bar, sat-TV, video channel, shower/WC and phone.

GUEST HOUSES

■ **Baan Shadis** (AC B cc GLM m MA OS PI PK RWB RWS RWT VA) All year
45/3 Moo 3, Maenam, Surat Thani *2 km from the beach* ☎ 077 24 76 47
🖳 www.sawadee.com/hotel/samui/shadis
Five luxury bungalows with private facilities, cooking place and garden. Gay-owned/operated resort.

■ **Little Palace** (AC BF G I m MA NU OS PI)
64/20 Moo 3, Chaweng South *300m from Chaweng Beach*
☎ 089 58 78 774 🖳 www.littlepalace.org
Owners speak Thai, English, German and French. Three guestrooms and one suite all furnished in teak, each with king-sized bed, private bath, mini-bar, safe and TV/video. There is also a lobby bar and lounge with TV. Nude bathing in the swimming pool is possible.

■ **Mana's Home** (AC b bf GLM m MA OS PA PI PK RWT VA WH)
All year
Chaweng Tropical Sea View Residence 42/26, Moo 6, T. Bophut, Ban Chaweng Yai *On the hills of Chaweng Village, 10 minutes by car or motorbike from Chaweng Beach, 15 minutes from the airport* ☎ 081 89 91 767
🖳 www.premiumwanadoo.com/atmanasamui
Beautiful house on the hills of Chaweng with a great view, offering two guestrooms to gays (b & b). Personalized and private atmosphere.

■ **Villa Oniria** (AC CC G MSG NU PI RWS SA SB SOL WH WO) All year
Bankao Tropical Residence, 69/6 Moo 4 T. Namuang, Suratthani *South of Koh Samui Island* ☎ (+34) 937 21 42 47 (Spain)
Private luxury house with accommodation for six persons. Full room service everyday.

■ **Wonderworld Samui B & B** (AC B BF G H I MA OS PA PK RWB RWS RWT VA) All year
130/24 Moo 1, Tamboon Bophut, Soi Kaophra *Nearby Makro and Big C* ☎ 077 43 05 59 ☎ 086 5533802 (mobile)
🖳 www.wonderworldsamui.com
Small Bed and Breakfast House with tropical garden.The House offer one Apartment and one Double Room in a quiet area close to Chaweng.Also organize private tours around the island.

Krabi

BARS

■ **69** (B D G MA S ST T WE) 20-1h
Ao Nang Centerpoint, 2nd Row ☎ 081 20 55 630
Friendly atmosphere, occasionally shows.

■ **Rainbow Bar** (B G m MA OS) 20-2h
362 Ao Nang Soi 7, Ao Nang *At Ao Nang Pearl* ☎ 048 43 12 90
Small but very friendly Thai style bar.

RESTAURANTS

■ **Lemongrass** (AC B GLM I M MA OS)
1 Thanon Maharaj *Next to Central Inn* ☎ 075 63 04 43
Gay friendly open-air restaurant with internet cafe (DSL). Fine Thai and European cuisine.

HOTELS

■ **Ao Nang Pearl Gay Resort**
(AC B BF G OS PI PK RWB RWS VA) 8-23h
362 Ao Nang Soi 7, Ao Nang *2km to beach, off main road from Krabi to Ao Nang* ☎ 087 26 45 014 🖳 www.aonangpearl.com
Small boutique gay resort with ten rooms set in lush, tropical garden.

PRIVATE ACCOMMODATION

■ **Passe-Temps. Le**
(AC B bf GLM I M MA MSG OS PI PK RWB RWS SOL) 8-20h
73 Moo 3, Ao Thalen, Khao Thong *Next to Sea Kayak, 30 mins from airport, Krabi town, Ao Nang* ☎ 084 65 59 457
🖳 www.lepassetemps-krabi.com
A hidden eco-resort by the sea, in one of the most beautiful bays of Thailand. Wooden bungalows, beach, private swimming pool, restaurant. Far from the crowds. Gay owned and ideal to relax.

Loei

GUEST HOUSES

■ **Chiangkhan** (AC B cc glm I M MA MSG OS)
282 Thanon Chaikhong, Soi 19 *About 50km north of Loei on the Mekhong River* ☏ 042 82 16 91
Fourteen rooms. Laundry service. Restaurant serving Thai and Asian food. Bikes and motorbike for rent.

Nong Khai

BARS

■ **Café Thasadej** (B BF GLM m MA OS) 19.30-1h
387/3 Soi Thepbunterng, Amphur Muang *Opp. Vietnamese restaurant, near Bazaar* ☏ 042 41 20 75 💻 www.gothasadej.com

■ **Chon Beer Bar** (B glm M MA OS) 18-?h
615 Thanon Meechai *Opp. small entrance of Wat Lumduong*
☏ 081 32 00 945
Nice bar with local food on two floors set in a traditional old Thai style house.

Pattaya

Two hours from Bangkok is the former fishing village, which became a rest and relaxation destination for US troops during the Vietnam War. The local government, hotels and restaurants are trying hard, with increasing success, to improve the run-down reputation of this town.
Concerted action against child prostitution and drug abuse go hand in hand with improvements in water quality, and the beach has become good for bathing again, making Pattaya an attractive international resort, with considerable attractions for the gay visitor. Many local and foreign bar owners are taking great care to raise the standards of the accommodation and entertainment.
The gay centre is located in a small but lively part of south Pattaya. But the small number of gay bars in the north of the town shouldn't be ignored. Pattaya is known for its drag bars, which are particularly loved by straight tourists.
Particularly interesting is the neighbouring Jomtien with its large gay beach. Less frantic is the small gay theatre which has just opened.
The centre of Pattaya is less worthwhile, built with US participation while there were regular regional marine manoeuvres here.

Zwei Stunden von Bangkok entfernt befindet sich dieses ehemalige Fischerdorf, das sich während des Vietnam-Kriegs überraschend in ein Erholungszentrum der US-Amerikaner verwandelt sah. Die Vergangenheit hat den Ruf dieser Stadt etwas ramponiert. Gegen Kinderprostitution und Drogenmissbrauch wird nun entschieden vorgegangen und auch die Wasserqualität hat sich deutlich verbessert. Am Strand kann man wieder schwimmen; inzwischen ist Pattaya ein internationaler Urlaubsort von beträchtlichem Charme, besonders für Schwule. Die ausländischen und heimatlichen Barbesitzer geben sich große Mühe, den Standard schwuler Unterhaltung und Unterbringung anzuheben.
In einem kleinem, aber lebhaftem Gebiet Süd-Pattayas findet sich das Zentrum schwulen Lebens. Aber auch eine kleinere Zahl von guten Bars im Norden der Stadt sollte nicht ausgelassen werden. Pattaya wurde durch seine Travestieshows bekannt. Sie sind besonders bei Heterotouristen sehr beliebt.

À deux heures de route de Bangkok est situé l'ancien village de pêcheurs qui devint un lieu de repos pour les troupes étasuniennes pendant la guerre du Viêt-nam. Le gouvernement local, les hôtels et les restaurants s'efforcent avec un succès grandissant d'améliorer la réputation peu reluisante de cette ville.
Une action commune contre la prostitution infantile et la drogue vont de pair avec une amélioration de la qualité de l'eau. La plage étant à nouveau baignable, Pattaya est redevenue un attrait international qui a beaucoup à offrir au visiteur gai. Plusieurs propriétaires de bars prennent grand soin de hausser leurs standards en hébergement et en divertissement.
Le milieu gai est situé dans une petite mais bien vivante partie de Pattaya. On ne devrait tout de même pas négliger les établissements du nord de la ville. Pattaya est reconnue pour ses spectacles de travestis qui sont très appréciés des touristes hétéros.
Le village voisin de Jomtien est tout particulièrement intéressant à cause de sa grande plage gaie. Pour le calme, un petit théâtre gai vient d'ouvrir.

A dos horas de Bangkok se encuentra este antiguo pueblo de pescadores que, durante la guerra de Vietnam, se convirtió por sorpresa en un lugar de descanso para los soldados norteamericanos. La administración municipal, los hoteles y restaurantes intentan con éxito ir mejorando la deteriorada reputación de la ciudad.
Así se realizan campañas conjuntas contra la prostitución infantil o el consumo de drogas, así como la mejora de la calidad del agua para que la playa vuelva a ser apta para los bañistas. Pattaya es un sitio atractivo e internacional para las vacaciones, con una oferta considerable para los gays.
La mayoría de los propietarios, extranjeros o nacionales, de los bares se están esforzando para subir el nivel de calidad del entretenimiento y el alojamiento.
En una pequeña pero animada zona del sur de Pattaya se encuentra el centro del ambiente gay. Sin embargo, hay también algunos buenos bares al norte de la ciudad que tampoco deberían olvidarse. Pattaya es conocido por sus actuaciones de travestis, que gustan especialmente a los turistas heterosexuales.
Resulta cada vez más interesante el vecino Jomtien, con su enorme playa gay. Allí se abrió una pequeña zona gay menos ajetreada. Menos recomendable es el centro de Pattaya en las épocas en las que se realizan regularmente maniobras marinas por la región, bajo participación norteamericana.

A due ore di distanza da Bangkok si trova questo ex-villaggio di pescatori, che, durante la guerra del Vietnam, si era trasformato in un centro di riposo per i soldati americani. L'amministrazione cittadina, gli alberghi e i ristoranti si impegnano con successo nel milgiorare giorno dopo giorno l'immagine di questa città.
Azioni contro la prostituzione di bambini e l'abuso di droghe fanno parte dei loro programmi, tanto quanto il miglioramento della qualità dell'acqua, affinchè le spiagge ridiventino interessanti anche per i bagnanti. Pattaya è un luogo di vacanza internazionale molto interessante con una considerevole offerta per gay.
Molti proprietari di bar, stranieri e nativi, si impegnano molto per poter migliorare il livello di intrattenimento e delle possibilità di pernottamento. In una piccola, ma molto vivace, zona a sud di Pattaya si trova il centro della vita gay.
Ma vale sicuramente la pena frequentare anche i pochi bar nel nord della città. Pattaya si è resa nota grazie ai suoi shows di travestiti, particolarmente amati dai turisti etero. Sempre più interessante è anche il vicino Jomtiem con la sua grande presenza gay. In meno caos è nato un piccolo scenario gay. Meno consigliabile è invece il centro di Pattaya nei periodi di manovre della marina con la partecipazione di americani.

GAY INFO

■ **Pattaya Gay Festival** (GLM)
💻 www.pattayagayfestival.com
Check event calendar at www.pattayagayfestival.com and www.pattaya-pride.com.

BARS

■ **Cartier Club** (B G MA R SNU)
Soi Leng Kee 1 *Between Soi Buakhao + Pattaya 3 rd.*
Showtimes: Sexyboy 22.30 + 23.30, Cabaret 0.15h

RESTAURANTS

■ **Alois** (AC b DM G M MA NR OS VEG WL)
open daily from 12-14:30, 18-0h
Thappraya road *across from the Residence Garden Hotel* ☏ 038 267 19 12
💻 www.aloispattaya.com
Serving gourmet Western and Thai cuisine.

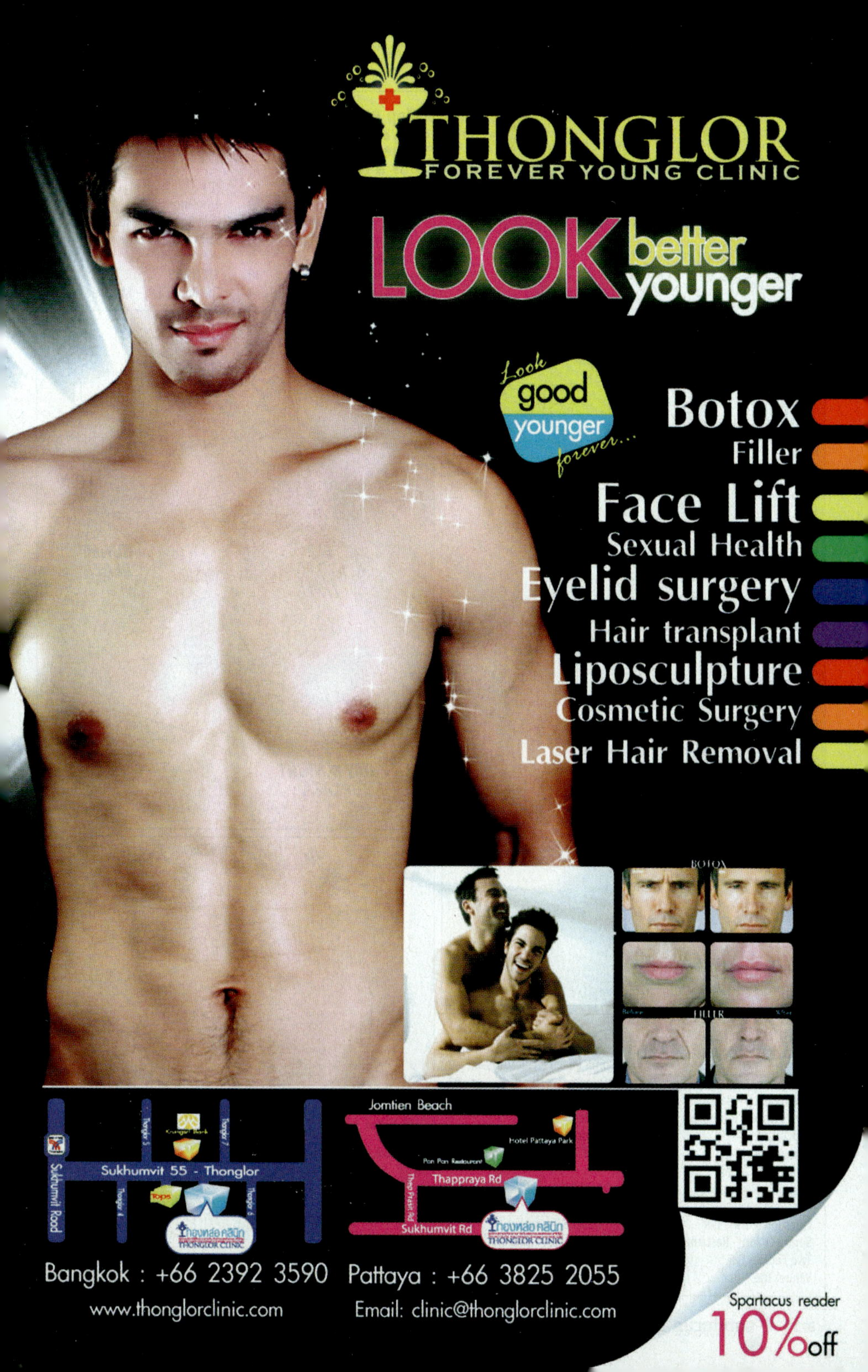

THONGLOR
FOREVER YOUNG CLINIC

LOOK better younger

Look good younger forever...

Botox
Filler
Face Lift
Sexual Health
Eyelid surgery
Hair transplant
Liposculpture
Cosmetic Surgery
Laser Hair Removal

BOTOX

FILLER

Sukhumvit 55 - Thonglor
Sukhumvit Road

Bangkok : +66 2392 3590 Pattaya : +66 3825 2055

www.thonglorclinic.com Email: clinic@thonglorclinic.com

Spartacus reader
10%off

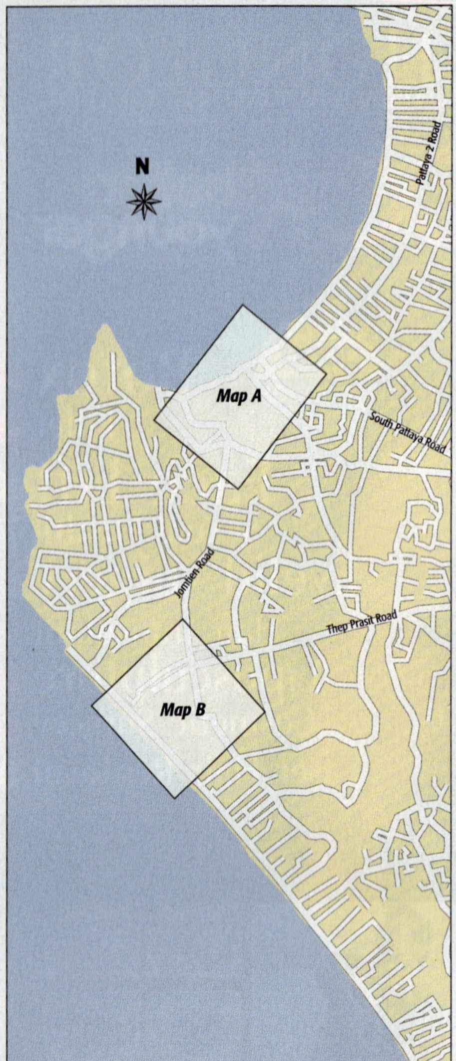

Map A: Pattaya – Boyz Town, Sunee Plaza, Day & Night Plaza

EAT & DRINK

Boyz Boyz Boyz – Bar	3
Café Royale. Le – Bar	6
Copa Showbar	5
Toy Boys – Bar	10
Wild West Boys – Bar	4

SEX

Boyz Sauna & Gym	1
Sansuk Sauna	11

ACCOMMODATION

Ambiance Hotel	2
Café Royal. Le – Hotel	6
Sansuk Guesthouse	11

OTHERS

The Body Club – Massage	7

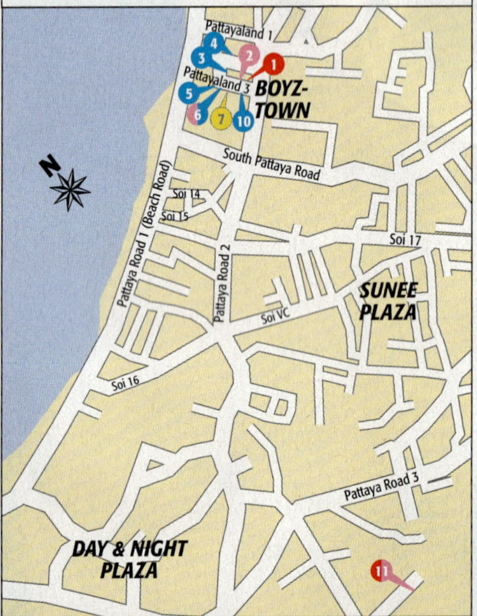

Map B. Pattaya – Jomtien Beach

EAT & DRINK

Bondi Beach – Bar	2
Casa Pascal – Restaurant	14
Dick's Café	6
Ganymede – Bar	8
Lubov Boys – Bar	18
Mignon – Restaurant	7
Poseidon – Restaurant	16
Question Mark – Bar	12
Spring Onion – Restaurant	20
Two Faces – Bar	13
Venue. The – Bar	11

ACCOMMODATION

Bondi Beach – Guesthouse	2
DD Inn – Guesthouse	3
Ganymede Residence – Hotel	8
Poseidon – Guesthouse	16
Venue. The – Hotel	11

OTHERS

Image Limo – Travel & Transport	4
Liam's Gallery – Decoration	1
Vinegar Swimwear – Fashion Shop	10

Phra Tamnak Road
Soi 4
Jomtien Complex
Dong Tan Gay Beach
Thappraya Road
Jomtien Beach Road
Soi 1
Jomtien Plaza

■ **Casa Pascal** (B CC G M MC OS S) Daily 8-23h
485/4 Moo 10, Second Road *Opp. Marriott Hotel & Royal Garden Plaza, 1st Soi after Mini Mart in front of Ruen Thai restaurant* ☎ 038 723 660
🖳 www.restaurant-in-pattaya.com
Daily breakfast & lunch Buffet from 8-14h. Elegant dining from 18-23h.

HOTELS

■ **Amari Orchid Resort & Tower**
(AC B BF CC H I OS PI SA SB WH WO)
240 Moo 5, Pattaya-Naklua Rd, Banglamung ☎ 038 41 84 18
🖳 www.Amari.com/Orchid
A five star, gay-friendly hotel.

GUEST HOUSES

■ **Lonops Gay Paradise** (AC BF G MA NU PI RWS RWT)
All year, 24 hrs
Soi Siam Country Club, Areeya Villa ☎ 895 433 355
🖳 www.lonops-paradise.de
Four rooms, all with AC, TV, DVD, safe, own bathroom.

Pattaya – Boyz Town

BARS

■ **A-Bomb** (AC B G MA MSG S) 20-2h
325/75-76 Pattayaland Soi 2, (Soi 13/4) South Pattaya ☎ 038 42 90 43
Loud gogo bar.

■ **Boyz Boyz Boyz** (! AC B CC D G MA MSG OS S ST t VS WE) 20-2h
325/87 Pattayaland Soi 3, South Pattaya, Chonburi *At the heart of Boyz Town, next to Ambiance Hotel* ☎ 038 42 40 99
🖳 www.boyzboyzboyz.info
Number one gay night club for over 20 years! A multi-level party place. Cabaret show nightly at 0.15h performed by very own Divas and Dudes and a stunning group of host dancers.

■ **Café Royale. Le** (AC B BF CC d G H I M MSG OS S) All year. Reception, coffee shop, terrace bar 24hrs; piano bar, restaurant 19.30-2h
325/102-9 Pattayaland Soi 3, South Pattaya ☎ 038 42 35 15
🖳 www.caferoyale-pattaya.com
All 43 spacious rooms and suites with en-suite facilities, sat TV and DVD player, mini bar, in-room safe, full 24hr reception and room service. Restaurant and Piano Bar (live performers nightly) popular with late night cruisers.

■ **Copa Showbar** (AC B CC D G H MA MSG OS S ST) Terrace bar 12-2, main bar 20-2h
325/106-109 Pattayaland Soi 3, South Pattaya *In the centre of Boyz Town* ☎ 038 42 35 15 🖳 www.copapattaya.com
The most elegant showbar in Pattaya, now featuring „What Lies Beneath", the only erotic underwater show of it's kind on the planet, nightly at 22.30h. Also featuring The Copa Showboys, one of the best cabaret shows in Pattaya, 23 & 0.45h. Friendly staff.

■ **Cupidol** (B G MA R) open daily from 20-1h
325/34-35 Pattayaland Soi 1 🖳 www.cupidolboys.com

■ **David Show Bar** (B G MA S)
Pattayaland Soi 1

■ **Funny Boys 2** (AC B G MA) 20.30-1h
324/98 Pattayaland Soi 3, Chonburi *In easy walking distance from all the downtown nightlife* ☎ 038 71 00 33 🖳 www.panoramapub.com
Gogo bar with no entrance or minimum charge. Around 50-60 young men of all types and ages. Moderate music, realistic drink prices and very comfortable.

■ **Handy Boy** (B G MA R) 20-1h
325/44-45 Soi 13/3 (Pattayaland 1), Banglamung, Chonburi
☎ 086 14 66 856
Friendly and comfortable night club near Boyz Town.

■ **Happy Place** (B G MA S SNU)
Pattayaland Soi 2 🖳 www.happyplacebar.com
Gay Go-go bar in Pattaya. Former Bubbles Boys Club.

■ **Kawaii Boys** (B G MA SNU)
Pattayaland Soi 1

■ **Lucky 777** (B G MA SNU)
Pattayaland Soi 1

■ **Panorama Pub** (AC B G MA OS) 15-2h
244/10-11 Pattayaland Soi 3, South Pattaya *Boys Town, downtown Pattaya*
☎ 038 71 05 97 🖳 www.panoramapub.com
Great views. Snooker and games room with lounge on 2nd floor with a giant TV-screen. Happy hour from 15-19h. Lucky draw every Sat at midnight.

■ **Sawadee Boys** (B G MA S SNU) 20.30-1h
Pattayaland Soi 1 🖳 www.sawadeeboys.com
Cabaret shows Fri-Sun at 23.40h.

■ **Serene Pub** (B G H MA OS) 18-2h
325/110 Pattayaland Soi 3, South Pattaya *Boyz Town* ☎ 038 42 29 52
Open pub with hosts. Part of Serene Hotel.

■ **Star Boys Boys** (AC B G MA S SNU)
194/23-24 Soi Welcome Plaza, Second Road (Soi Toyota Karaoke), South Pattaya *Opp. Pattayaland Soi 2* ☎ 038 24 98 52
Erotic Special Sexy Show: Mon, Wed & Fri 23.30h.

■ **Toy Boys** (AC B G MA) 20-2h
325/100 Pattayaland Soi 3, South Pattaya ☎ 038 42 33 04

■ **Wild West Boys Night Club** (AC B CC G MA S) 20h-late
325/19 M. 10 Pattayaland Soi 2, Nongprue, Banglamung, Chonburi
Between Pattayaland Soi 1 and Soi 3 across from the Penthouse Hotel
☎ 018 65 35 02
Shows 22.30 & 24h.

■ **X Boys** (B G MA SNU)
Pattayaland Soi 1
Shows at 22, 23.30, 0.45h.

DANCECLUBS

■ **Dave Man Club** (AC B D G MA S SNU) busy after 1h
Moo 10 Soi 6, Beach Road *2nd Road north to Central Road and Tops Supermarket, left direction beach, first street at Paddys Bar left, then watch out for chinese lanterns* ☎ 087 13 12 709 🖳 www.thedavemanclub.com
Large gay-disco with coyote-style shows on big stage.

SAUNAS/BATHS

Boyz Sauna & Gym (AC B CC DU FC FH G m MA MSG SA WO) 10-22h
325/89-91 Pattayaland Soi 3, South Pattaya, Chonburi *Adjacent to the Ambiance* ☎ 038 42 40 99 🖳 www.boyzgym.com
The best massage spa for men by men in the heart of Pattaya. Fully equipped gym and sauna. Body and foot massage by trained masseurs avaible. It is a must to try. Chill out area.

MASSAGE

Body Club. The (AC CC G MSG) 12-2h
325/106-109, Pattayaland Soi 3, South Pattaya *Boyz Town*
☎ 038 42 35 15 🖳 www.copapattaya.com/bodyclub.php
Part of Copa Showbar / Café Royale Hotel, featuring qualified masseurs and luxury air conditioned rooms with full private en-suite facilities.

HOTELS

Ambiance (! AC B BF CC D G M MA RWS RWT SA VA WO) All year
325/89 Pattayaland Soi 3, South Pattaya, Chonburi ☎ 038 42 40 99
🖳 www.ambiance-pattaya.com
Luxury accommodation in the heart of Pattaya's gay nightlife. 45 suites and rooms with elevator. Mini bar, sat-TV, private facilities and in house gym. Excellent value for money.

Café Royale. Le (AC B BF CC d G H I M MSG OS S) All year. Reception, coffee shop, terrace bar 24hrs; piano bar, restaurant 19.30-2h
325/102-9 Pattayaland Soi 3, South Pattaya ☎ 038 42 35 15
🖳 www.caferoyale-pattaya.com
All 43 spacious rooms and suites with en-suite facilities, sat TV and DVD player, mini bar, in-room safe, full 24hr reception and room service. Restaurant and Piano Bar (live performers nightly) popular with late night cruisers.

Copa Hotel (AC B D G I MA MSG OS RWB RWS RWT S VA) All year
325/106-109 Pattayaland Soi 3, Pattaya, Chonburi ☎ 038 488 694
🖳 www.copapattaya.com

Orpheus House (AC B BF CC G M MC OS RWS RWT VEG WI) All year
146/8-9, 146/45-46 Moo 10, Thappraya Soi 1, Nongprue, Chonburi *Located on Thappraya Road, Soi 1* ☎ (038) 2505-30 / -60
☎ 085-2542527 (mobile) 🖳 www.orpheus-pattaya.com
Orpheus House is serving the broad leisure and gay segment with spacious facilities and romantic as the friendly class hospitality facilities and services.

Penthouse (AC B CC glm I M MA MSG OS PI PK RWB RWS RWT VA WH WO) All year, 24hrs
325/61 Moo 10 Pattayaland Soi 2, Chon Buri *Near beach, opp. Boyz Town*
☎ 038 42 96 39 🖳 www.penthousehotel.com

Prive. Le (AC B bf G PI) 24hrs
Thapraya Road Soi 1 *Chonbury* ☎ 038 25 01 89 🖳 www.le-prive-pattaya.com
Located in a quiet and luxury neighbourhood, with five bungalows around a swiming pool in a tropical garden. Close to night life and beaches.

Pattaya – Jomtien Beach (South Pattaya)

BARS

Dolce Vita (B G MA OS)
413/40 Jomtien Complex, Moo 12 ☎ 087 148 03 28

Festival Sate Pub (B G MC OS SNU) 15-?h
413/128 Jomtien Complex, Thappraya Rd *Near to Dick's Cafe*
☎ 0879 72 79 37 (mobile)

Ganymede (B DU G H MC s SA) 16-24h
413/85,86 Moo 12 *Jomtien Complex* ☎ 038 304 037
🖳 www.ganymede-jomtien.com
New bar with sauna, karaoke and hotel. Happy hour 16-20h.

Lubov Boys Cocktails (B G MA)
Jomtien Complex

Question Mark (B G MC MSG OS) 14-1h
Jomtien Complex, Thappraya Rd ☎ 084 867 19 37
Host bar with great guys.

Two Faces (B G H M MA MSG r) 9-1h
Jomtien Complex, 413/12 Thappraya Road, Nongprue, Banglamung
☎ 038 25 26 59 🖳 www.twofacesthailand.com
Thai-Bali style bar with lounge for quiet relax. Massage available.

CAFES

Dick's Café Jomtien (B bf G M MA OS) 10-1h
413/129 Thappraya Road *Jomtien Complex, next to Derby's Men, opp. Exxit Bar* ☎ 038 25 24 17 🖳 www.dickscafe.com
Little sister of Dick's Café, Bangkok, with all its ambiance in a seaside setting. Fine Thai and Western food for breakfast, brunch, lunch, dinner or a late night snack. A wide range of foreign and local beers, wines, spirits and cocktails. Lovely garden.

P2 (AC B G MA) 12-1h
Jomtien Complex, Chonburi ☎ 038 252 452
Up-market coffee lounge, decoration art and fashion store.

DANCECLUBS

Marine Disco (AC B D glm)
Beach Road, Chon Buri ☎ 038 42 85 83
Very mixed disco where everybody meets when the bars close.

RESTAURANTS

Bruno's Restaurant & Wine Bar (! AC CC glm M MA)
12-14.30, 18-24h, closed Mon.
306/63 Chateau Dale Plaza, Thappraya Rd, Jomtien ☎ 038 36 46 00
🖳 www.brunos-pattaya.com
Superb international and Thai cuisine, and extensive wine list. Reservation recommended.

Mignon (AC CC GLM M MC OS) 14-23.30h
406/353 Tappraya Road, Jomtien Complex ☎ 038 23 37 63
🖳 www.lemignon.in.th/EN/home.html
French specialties (Caesar Salad, Lobster Bisque) and steaks that are tender and come with a variety of sauces. Moderate prices.

Poseidon (AC B BF cc DM DU FH G M MA MSG NR OS PI PK PP RR RWB RWS RWT SA SH VEG WH WI WL WO)
413/3-5 Moo 12 Nongprue/Banglamung, South Pattaya *At entrance to Jomtien Complex* ☎ 038 303 698 🖳 www.poseidon-pattaya.com
Outstanding boutique guest house with 18 rooms and suites, all with private facilities, mini-bar, sat-TV etc. Many amenities. Regular trips with own yacht to remote islands. Excellent in-house restaurant.

Spring Onion (B G M MA OS)
Jomtien Complex
Thai food for little money (THB 60).

SAUNAS/BATHS

Derby Men's Club (AC B DR G m MA MSG OS SA SB VS WH WO)
13-23h
413/131-132 Thappaya Road, Banglamung, South Pattaya *Jomtien Complex. Next to Dick's Café* ☎ 038 30 34 39

Duo House (AC B G MA MSG OS r SA SB)
open daily from 13-24h
Jomtien Complex, 413/127 Thappraya Road, Chonburi
☎ 081 692 33 09 🖳 www.duohouse.com
Sauna, steam bath and health massage.

MASSAGE

TBMI Thai Blind Massage Institute
(AC B glm m MA MSG OS) 10-22h
413/89 Thappraya Road, Banglamung, South Pattaya *Jomtien Condotel Complex* ☎ 038 25 18 51
22 blind but excellently skilled male (70 %) and female masseurs perform traditional, foot, oil, aroma, herb massage. Also steam herb-sauna available. Clean and friendly place. Highly recommended and strictly no sex!

BODY & BEAUTY SHOPS

Thonglor Clinic (CC g) All year
306/92-13 Thappraya Road ☎ 038 252 055
🖳 www.thonglorclinic.com
Beauty, anti-aging and plastic surgery centre in the heart of Bangkok and Pattaya-Jomtien –Thailand, offering the highest quality of aesthetic treatment and plastic surgeries to improve your appearance and slow down the signs of ageing.

BAAN
souy
A New Luxury Gay Resort
by the Founders of Pattaya Boyztown
www.baansouy.com

DECORATION

Liam's Gallery (b cc G I) Tue-Sun 10-19h
352/107 Soi 4 Pratamnak Rd, Moo 12 Nong Prue, ☎ 038 25 18 08
The only high class gallery of Pattaya, gay owned and managed. Also library, Internet café and wine bar.

FASHION SHOPS

Vinegar Swimwear (cc g) Daily 12.30-22.30h
Jomtien Complex, Thappraya Rd ☎ 038 30 36 70
🖳 www.swimwearthailand.com
Trendy swimwear.

TRAVEL AND TRANSPORT

Image Limousine (CC)
Unit 406/20 Jomtien Plaza Condotel, Thappraya Rd *Chonburi*
☎ 038 75 66 58 🖳 www.imagelimo.com

HOTELS

Baan Souy Resort (AC BF CC G M MA OS PI RWB RWS RWT VA WH WI) All year
308/3 Moo 10, Soi 15 Thappraya Rd. *5 Mins To Town or Jomtien beach*
☎ 38364580/1 🖳 www.baansouy.com
At Baan Souy all of our 37 studios and suites have been equipped to provide the ultimate in luxury, comfort and convenience.

Rabbit Resort (AC B CC glm M MA OS PI RWS RWT WH) 7-22h
318/84 Moo 12 Soi Dongtan, Jomtien *At Dongtan/Pattaya gay beach*
☎ 038 30 33 03 🖳 www.rabbitresort.com
Popular resort with fabulous luxurious accommodation. Each house has private garden.

Room-Club (AC B G I M MA MSG OS PK RWB RWS RWT VA)
All year, bar 12-22h
318/79 Grand Condotel, Trappraya Road, Nongprue Banglamung, Chonburi *Direct on Dongtan Beach* ☎ 038 25 14 61
🖳 www.room-club.com
Small boutique hotel located right on the gay beach at Jomtien.

Venue. The (AC B CC g H I MC OS PI S SOL WH) All year
413/24-28 Jomtien Complex, Thappraya Road *250 metres from the gay beach* ☎ 038 30 37 87 🖳 www.thevenuejomtien.com
Luxury accommodation. Cabaret in the Showbar. Showtimes 21.30, 22.15 and 23h.

GUEST HOUSES

Bondi Beach Bar and Guest House
(AC B D G H M MA MSG S) All year
410/ 51-52 Dongtan Beach Road, Jomtien, Nongprue ☎ 08 063 07 314
🖳 www.bondipattaya.com
Minutes from the Gay nightlife of Jomtien. Directly overlooking the Gulf of Thailand.

Casabella Pattaya (AC G I MA OS PA PK RWB RWS RWT VA)
All year
389/13-14 Pratumnak Road, Soi 4 *Near Buddha Hill* ☎ 038 30 60 65
🖳 www.casabellapattaya.com
All rooms with cable TV, hot showers, big beds and refrigerator.

DD Inn (AC BF G M OS) All year
410/48-50 Moo 12 Jomtien Beach, Nongprue, Banglamung, Choburi
☎ 038 23 29 95 🖳 ddinn.wordpress.com
Guest house with clean, comfortable rooms, air conditioning, cable TV, refrigerator and, of course, hot water showers.

Home Beach (AC b G M MA OS SB WO) 15-22h
334/96-97 Moo 12, Soi Wellcome Hotel ☎ 038 75 68 17
Ten guest rooms with TV, refrigerator. Hairdressing and massage possible. Free access to sauna.

Iluka (AC G RWB RWS RWT WI)
413/6 Thappraya Road *In Jomtien Complex Plaza* ☎ 882156866
🖳 www.iluka-residence.com
ILUKA offers stylish fully serviced rooms and suites.

Poseidon (AC B BF cc DM DU FH G M MA MSG NR OS PI PK PP RR RWB RWS RWT SA SH VEG WH WI WL WO)
413/3-5 Moo 12 Nongprue/Banglamung, South Pattaya *At entrance to Jomtien Complex* ☎ 038 303 698 🖳 www.poseidon-pattaya.com
Outstanding boutique guest house with 18 rooms and suites, all with private facilities, mini-bar, sat-TV etc. Many amenities. Regular trips with own yacht to remote islands. Excellent in-house restaurant.

Tui's Place (AC b BF G M MA OS PI RWB RWS RWT VA WI) 8-18h
316/77 & 78 Moo 12, Tambon Nongprue, Banglamung, Chonburi *Jomtien Beach* ☎ 038 25 14 32 🖳 tuisplace.blogspot.com
The only gay guest house, bar & restaurant on Jomtien beach.

APARTMENTS

Haus Mewie (AC B BF G PI RWB RWS RWT S VA) All year
413/40-42 Moo 12 Thappraya Road, Nongprue, South Pattaya
☎ 038 30 34 37

Pattaya – North & Central

SHOWS

Alcazar (! AC B glm S ST) 18.30, 20, 21.30, Sat also 23h
78/14 Second Road, South Pattaya *Opp. Soi 5* ☎ 038 41 05 05
One of the most famous shows in Thailand. The Miss Alcazar Thailand contest every year in April always selects a man as the most beautiful woman.

FASHION SHOPS

Jim International (AC glm)
213/2 Soi 7, Pattaya Beach Road, Chonburi *In the Flipper House Hotel*
☎ 081 98 38 629 🖳 www.tailorsthailand.com
Hand tailored garments.

Pattaya – South Pattaya

SAUNAS/BATHS

Sansuk Sauna and Guesthouse (AC B BF CC D DR DU FC FH G I M MA MSG OS PI RR RWB RWS RWT SA SB VA VS WH WO)
Guest house 24hrs; sauna 14-23h
391/49 Moo 10, Soi 11, Thapprata Road, Jomtien *Halfway between Pattaya and Jomtien* ☎ 038 364 356 (sauna) 🖳 www.sansukpattaya.com
Three storied sauna complex with up-market guest house.

GUEST HOUSES

Sansuk Sauna and Guesthouse (AC B BF CC D DR DU FC FH G I M MA MSG OS PI RR RWB RWS RWT SA SB VA VS WH WO)
Guest house 24hrs; sauna 14-23h
391/49 Moo 10, Soi 11, Thapprata Road, Jomtien *Halfway between Pattaya and Jomtien* ☎ 038 364 356 (sauna) 🖳 www.sansukpattaya.com
Three storied sauna complex with up-market guest house.

Pattaya – Sunee Plaza/Day & Night Plaza

BARS

All of Me (B G MA OS)
Soi Sunee Plaza 🖳 www.suneeplaza.info/allofme

Corner Bar. The (B G m MA)
60-61/273 Sunee Plaza, Soi VC 🖳 www.thecornerbar-suneeplaza.com

Crazy Pub (B G MA)
Sunee Plaza

Duc's Bar (AC B G M MA OS)
273/49 Soi VC Hotel, Sunee Plaza, Chonburi ☎ 086 15 74 035

Eden Bar (B G m MA OS S) 16.30-1h
273/36 Soi VC Hotel, Sunee Plaza ☎ 087 02 94 061
🖳 www.eden.suneeplaza.info
Former Wan's Place.

Eros (B G MA SNU)
Sunee Plaza, corner Soi Yensabai 🖳 www.erosboybar.com

Forest House (AC B G MA OS) 18-2h
273/94 Moo 10, Soi VC Hotel, Sunee Plaza, South Pattaya

Good Boys (B G MA SNU)
Sunee Plaza

■ **Happy Boys** (B DR G MA)
Sunee Plaza ☏ 089 543 41 61
Bar on two floors with backroom upstairs.

■ **New Queens** (B G MA)
Sunee Plaza

■ **Nice Boys** (B G MA SNU)
Sunee Plaza

■ **Office Boy, The** (B G MA)
Day Night Plaza
Former Fanny's Grove.

■ **Rainbow Bar** (AC B G MA)
273/21 Soi Yensabai, Sunee Plaza ☏ 038 25 17 89

■ **Redgy's Place Boys Club** (B G MA SNU)
Sunee Plaza

■ **Three Zone** (B G MA)
Sunee Plaza

■ **Treetz** (B G MA)
Sunee Plaza

■ **Up2u** (B G I M MA)
Sunee Plaza 273/83 ☏ 895 427 703 💻 www.up2u-boybar-pattaya.com
German onwer, free w-lan.

■ **What Else? Beer Bar** (B G MA OS)
Sunee Plaza

■ **Zub Zib Boy Boy Beer Bar** (B G MA SNU)
Soi VC/17 *Sunee Plaza*

CAFES

■ **YaYa Cafe & Bar** (B G MA)
Sunee Plaza 💻 www.yaya-sunee.com

RESTAURANTS

■ **Dolphin** (AC B CC G M MA OS) 9-23.30h
Day Night Plaza ☏ 522-7318.
Affordable menus for dinner and ten different European breakfasts.

■ **Eldorado** (AC B BF G H I M MA OS PI RES RWB RWS RWT VA WL)
Restaurant 11-1, bar 16-1h, closed Sat
273/84-85 Moo 10, Sunee Plaza, South Pattaya *Between Soi VC Hotel and Soi Yensabai* ☏ 038 71 32 59 💻 www.eldorado-pattaya.com
Also a guest house.

■ **Little Mango** (G M MA OS VEG) Daily 18-23h
Soi V.C. Chon Buri
Thai meals. Good quality.

■ **Mushroom Restaurant** (G M MA OS)
Soi Day Night

■ **Non Café** (B G M MA)
Soi 17 / VC

HOTELS

■ **Don Plaza** (B BF CC D G I M)
273/73-76 Moo 10, Soi Sunee Plaza, Banglamung
💻 www.don-plaza-pattaya.com

GUEST HOUSES

■ **Baan Dok Mai** (H)
20/248-249 Soi Day Night 3, South Pattaya 💻 www.baandm.com

■ **Two Guys Guesthouse Pattaya** (AC b BF G H m MA MSG)
All year
504/497, Moo 10, Soi Yensabai, Chonburi *Close to Yensabai Condotel*
☏ 038 713 652 💻 www.twoguysguesthouse.info

Phuket

The largest island in Thailand, around the size of Singapore, is linked by two bridges to the mainland and lies to the south of Myanmar on the isthmus, which runs westward towards Malaysia. Phuket has around 250,000 inhabitants, who mostly live in Phuket Town, which it is an important business centre and the provincial capital.
The large, hilly island offers wonderful beaches, and is surrounded by numerous tiny islands just offshore. As a result, Phuket is an ideal starting point to visit the beautiful islands of Surin and Similan, which are both national parks. The main centre for gay tourists is Patong Beach, around 13km from Phuket Town.
Phuket's multifaceted and charming gay scene is firmly established in Patong Beach. The beautiful setting and numerous leisure activities, go to make it a perfect year round destination for gay travellers. It's not just the many outdoor beer bars and restaurants so typical of Patong, or the developing Phuket style of nightlife, which makes the place so interesting. The hard sell of Bangkok and Pattaya makes the friendliness of Thais on Phuket come as a relief and will make a holiday here unforgettable.

Die größte Insel Thailands (in etwa der Größe Singapurs) ist über zwei Brücken mit dem Festland verbunden und liegt südlich von Myanmar auf der westlich in Richtung Malaysia verlaufenden Landenge.
Phuket hat etwa 250.000 Einwohner, von denen die meisten in der kommerziell wichtigen Provinzhauptstadt Phuket Town leben.
Die weitläufige, hügelige Insel verfügt über wunderschöne, teilweise noch einsame Strände und ist umsäumt von zahlreichen kleineren Inseln. Phuket ist zudem eine ideale Ausgangsbasis für Besuche auf den schönen Inseln der Nationalparks Surin und Similan.
Das Zentrum für schwule Touristen ist Patong Beach, ca. 13 km von Phuket Town entfernt.
Phukets vielfältige und liebenswerte schwule Szene ist in Patong Beach fest etabliert. Die exzellente Lage und vielfältigen Freizeitangebote machen Phuket zu einem ganzjährig perfekten Ziel für schwule Reisende. Es sind nicht nur die vielen Patong-typischen „Outdoor beer bars & Restaurants" oder die Entwicklung eines eigenen Kabarettstils, die Phuket interessant machen. Die vom knallharten Kommerz in Bangkok oder Pattaya abweichende herzliche gelassene Freundlichkeit der Thais auf Phuket lässt einen Urlaub unvergesslich werden.

La plus grande île de Thaïlande, presque de la taille de Singapour, est située au sud-ouest du pays. Phuket compte 250 000 habitants qui vivent principalement dans la ville du même nom. Celle-ci est moins intéressante pour les touristes mais constitue un important centre d'affaires et aussi la capitale provinciale.
Cette grande île offre de merveilleuses plages est en entourée de nombreuses petites îles. Phuket est aussi un bon point de départ pour la visite de Surin et Similan qui sont deux parcs nationaux.
Le centre principal pour les touristes gais est la plage de Patong, située à treize kilomètres de la ville de Phuket. Une scène gaie charmante et polyvalente y est solidement installée. Le paysage pittoresque et la gamme d'activités offertes en font une destination parfaite pour le touriste gai tout au long de l'année. Les restaurants et les terrasses typiques de Patong, le style émergeant de vie nocturne de Phuket et la gentillesse des gens du coin, contrairement à la dureté relative de Bangkok et de Pattaya, permettent de vraiment relaxer et de passer des vacances inoubliables.

La mayor isla de Tailandia (casi el tamaño de Singapur) está unida a la península por un dique y está situada al sur de Myanmar, en el istmo occidental que lleva hacia Malasia.
Phuket tiene unos 250.000 habitantes, de los cuales la mayoría vive en la capital, Phuket Town, importante comercialmente pero poco atractiva para el turismo.
Esta extensa y montañosa isla posee maravillosas playas en parte solitarias y está rodeada de múltiples islas pequeñas. Phuket es el lugar ideal para poder visitar las hermosas islas de los parques nacionales de Surin y Similan. El centro del ambiente gay está en Patong Beach, a casi 13km. de la Phuket Town.
El agradable y variado ambiente homosexual de Phuket está ya muy asentado en Patong Beach. Su diversidad, excelente situación y variada oferta de entretenimiento hacen de Phuket un destino perfecto para los turistas homosexuales. No son sólo las muchas cervecerías y restaurantes al aire libre típicos en Patong, o el desarrollo de un estilo propio de teatro que hacen a Phuket interesante, sino que es también la amabilidad de los tailandeses de Phuket, alejados del agresivo comercio de Bangkok y Pattaya, lo que hace que unas vacaciones sean inolvidables.

La più grande isola della Tailandia (più o meno grande come Singapore) è unita alla terraferma da una lingua di terra ed è a sud di Myamar sulla fascia di terra occidentale, in direzione Malaysia.
Phuket ha circa 250.000 abitanti, la maggior parte dei quali vive nel capoluogo di provincia Phuket Town, la cui economia si basa non tanto sul turismo quanto sul commercio.
Quest'isola, dal paesaggio collinare, è dotata di meravigliose ed, in parte, davvero solitarie spiagge ed è circondata da numerose piccole isole. Phuket è un'ideale punto di partenza per visitare le belle isole Surin e Similan che sono anche parchi nazionali.
Il centro per turisti gay è Patong Beach, a circa 13 Km dall'estrema conservatrice Phuket Town.
La comunità gay, varia e piacevole, è ben radicata in Paton Beach. L'eccellente posizione e le molte offerte per il tempo libero fanno di Phuket una tra le mete turistiche perfette per gay, durante tutto l'anno. Questa non è resa interessante solo dai tipici e molti „Outdoor beer bars & Restaurants" o dallo sviluppo di un proprio stile cabarettistico; lo spirito differente dai centri del commercio Bangkok e Pattaya e l'estrema ospitalità dei tailandesi di Phuket rendono le vacanze su quest'isola un'esperienza indimenticabile.

SHOWS

My Way (! AC B G MA S ST T) 20-2h
125/15-17 Rath-U-Thit Road, Paradise Complex, Patong Beach *1st soi, way in* ☎ 076 34 21 63
One of the best gogo bars and shows in town. Many beautiful hosts and special shows every night.

Phuket Simon Cabaret (ST) Shows at 19.30 & 21.30h
8 Sirirat Road ☎ 076 34 20 115 www.phuket-simoncabaret.com
Glamorous performers in an exclusive, luxurious and intimate theatre with hi-tech sound and light equipment.

BARS

Backstage (B G MA S)
9/6 Soi Sawatdeelak, Patong Kathu
www.backstagethailand.blogspot.com
With live music, playback-shows, karaoke, cabaret, stand-up-comedy.

Dempsey's (AC B cc d G MA S SNU)
Paradise Complex
Performing Go-Go boys.

Flying Handbag. The (AC B GLM I M MA OS t WE) 17-2h
127/8-9 Rath-U-Thit Road, Paradise Complex, Patong Beach *Behind Connect Bar* ☎ 076 41 94 89
Funniest place in town. Dress code – bring your handbag!

Heaven (B G m MA OS)
125 Rath-U-Thit Road, Paradise Complex, Patong Beach *In the inner section of Paradise Complex*

James Dean Bar and Guesthouse (B G I m MA OS RWS RWT)
188/22 Likit Plaza Phang Muang Sai Gor ☎ 86-942-0957
www.jamesdeanbar.com
Just moved into their fourth venue in the new Likit Plaza. Long running business since 1992.

Kai Boy Bar (B G MA OS) 17-2h
141/15 Rath-U-Thit Road, Paradise Complex, Patong Beach *5th Soi, way out* ☎ 089 54 26 904
Very nice music and friendly gay owner. Former J&B bar.

Kar–Door Host Club (B G MA s) 21-2h
Paradise Complex *opp. Dempsey's GoGo-club*
Kar–Door means 'penis' in Thai. Basically a karaoke bar.

Knud's Bar – Thai's Best Boys (AC B D G M MA OS) 17-2h
123/4 Paradise Complex, Rat-U-Thit Road, Patong Beach, Kathu *In the main street of Paradise Complex* ☎ 076 34 52 91 www.knudsbar.com
Also nice rooms for rent in Patong Beach Gay Centre on offer. Small comfortable garden behind the bar.

Mama San (B G MA S SNU)
70/197-198 Soi Paradise, Patong, Kathu ☎ 089 59 30 612
Intimate bar with billard table on 2nd floor and garden. Features boy A Go-Go and cabaret show twice nightly.

Maprang (AC B G MA) 17-2h
125/2 Rath-U-Thit Road, Paradise Complex, Patong Beach *1st Soi, way in* ☎ 076 34 08 15
For the last drink of the night. Very nice music, very friendly lady-owner.

My Way (! AC B G MA S ST T) 20-2h
125/15-17 Rath-U-Thit Road, Paradise Complex, Patong Beach *1st soi, way in* ☎ 076 34 21 63
One of the best gogo bars and shows in town. Many beautiful hosts and special shows every night.

OK Club (B G MA S) 19-2h
Rath-U-Thit Road Paradise Complex, Patong Beach *Near Tangmo Club Karaoke Club.*

Spartacus (AC B G MA MSG S) 14-2h
123/5 Rath-U-Thit Road, Paradise Complex, Patong Beach *1st Soi, way in* ☎ 076 34 55 17

Sundowners Bar (AC B CC G H M MA OS RWB RWS RWT VA WI) 13-2h
125/10-11 Rat-U-Thit Road, Paradise Complex, Patong Beach *In Royal Paradise Complex, 10 mins walk to the beach* ☎ 076 344 215
www.sundownersinparadise.com
Ground floor terrace bar with pool table. Also guesthouse.

Super Boys (AC B G m OS S) 20-1h
99/1-2 Sawatdirak Road, Patong Beach *Near 7-11, walking distance to Paradise Complex* ☎ 076 34 09 46
Small somewhat rundown gogo bar. Karaoke 2-?h. Mixed reports.

Tangmo Club (AC B G MA S) 20-2h
123/6-7 Rath-U-Thit Road, Paradise Complex, Patong Beach *1st soi, way in, near OK Club* ☎ (07629) 41 15 www.tangmogroup.com/web/tmoclub.htm
Showtimes: 22.30, 23.30 and 1h, every show lasts 40 mins.

Timber Hut (B g MC)
118/1 Yaowarat Road, Phuket Town

Time Bar (AC B G m MA OS) Daily 12-2h
125/12 Rath-U-Thit Road, Paradise Complex, Patong Beach *Soi 5, Paradise Complex* ☎ 097 24 84 97

Twilight (B G MA) 17-2h
135/6-7 Rath-U-Thit Road, Paradise Complex, Patong Beach *3rd Soi* ☎ 016 77 96 15

CAFES

Connect Bistro & Bar (! AC B CC GLM H I M MA OS) 8-2h
125/8-9 Rath-U-Thit Rd, Paradise Complex, Patong Beach *1st Soi, way out* ☎ 076 29 41 95 www.beachpatong.com/connect
Friendly owners and staff. Also information on the gay scene.

DANCECLUBS

Boat Bar. The (AC B d GLM MA OS R S ST T) 21-2h
125/19-20 Rath-U-Thit Rd, Paradise Complex, Patong Beach *Opp. Royal Paradise Hotel, at the street corner* ☎ 076 34 12 37 www.boatbar.com
Very popular gay disco in Patong, with great dance shows. Cruisy night spot, dancing starts after 23h.

Kiss Club (B D G MA S) 18-?h
123/809 Paradise Complex, Patong ☎ 086 94 42 423
DJs play disco, house and electro; cabaret-shows 23.45 & 1.45h. Free entry, gets busy around 23h.

RESTAURANTS

Home Dining Café by Club One Seven (AC B BF CC GLM I M MA OS) 8-22h
Level 1, 9/10 Prachnanukroh Road, Patong Beach *Level 1 of Club One Seven, at the southern part of Patong* ☎ 076 34 19 17
Home cooked style Thai and Vegetarian food, reasonable prices. Cozy indoor and outdoor seating; great service.

Newspaper (g M MA) 20-1h
125/4-5, Rat-U-Thit Road, Paradise Complex, Patong Beach ☎ 076 34 62 76
Nice gay restaurant in Paradise Complex. Thai food for western tongues – not too spicy!

Red Onion (b glm M MA OS VEG) Daily 16.30-23h
486 Patak Road *Karon Beach, between round about and temple*
☎ 076 39 68 27 🖳 siam.de/redonion
Great Thai food, reasonable price.

Sea Hag (! AC B CC glm M MA RES VEG WL) 11-24h
78/5 Permpong Soi 3 (Soi Wattana Clinic), Thaweewong Road (Beach Road), Patong Beach *50m inside the Soi, also called Soi Kebsub*
☎ 076 34 11 11 🖳 www.kenyaphuket.com
One of the best restaurants in town with daily fresh seafood. Gay owned on two floors with splendid hospitality. Selected wines and champagne. Moderately priced. Reservation recommended.

SAUNAS/BATHS

Aquarius Guesthouse & Sauna (AC B bf CC DR DU FH G I LAB M MA MSG OS PA PI PK r RR RWB RWS RWT SA SB SOL VA VS WH WO)
Reception 24hrs, sauna 15.30-21h
127/10-17 Rat-U-Thit Rd, Paradise Complex, Patong Beach *Middle of Royal Paradise Complex gay area, 5 mins walk to the beach & shopping center*
☎ 076 341 668 🖳 www.aquarius-guesthouse.com
Discreet luxury suites or budget rooms and a sundeck with jacuzzi overlooking Patong and the sea. The only strictly men-only accommodation in Phuket. Gay sauna, spa and gym. Bar serving breakfast every morning. Best sauna in southern Thailand. Many „westerners". Restaurant known as „ATM" serving Thai and international food.

Tara (AC B DR DU G m MA OS RR SA SB VR WO) daily 11-1h
Sakdidet Rd *Phuket Modern Life Project Building* ☎ (076) 22 01 72
🖳 www.phuketsauna.com
Sauna with fitness and steam rooms, showers, dark room, private room, DVD room, bar and massage also available.

MASSAGE

Hiranyikara, a spa with men in mind (g MSG PI SA SB WH) 10-21h
133 Moo 7 Vichidsongkram Road, Kathu *15 mins from Patong Beach and ten mins from Phuket town* ☎ 081 37 00 202 🖳 www.hiranyikara.com
Luxurios spa for men in Phuket, providing several spa treatments by well-trained male masseurs.

TRAVEL AND TRANSPORT

SBY Leisure Travel and Tour (AC CC GLM)
Bang Tao Place, Cheng Talay ☎ 084 85 28 142
🖳 www.sbyphuket.com
TAT licensed travel agent, gay owned.

HOTELS

Aleenta Resort & Spa (AC B BF CC glm I M MA MSG OS PI PK RWB RWS RWT SA SB WH WO) All year
33 Moo 5, T. Khokkloy, A. Takuathung *25km from Phuket Intl. Airport*
☎ (076) 580 333 🖳 www.aleenta.com
Luxury Hotel with rooms and suites near the famous Phang Nga Bay.

Baan Yin Dee Boutique Resort Phuket (AC B BF CC glm M MA MSG OS PI ST WH WO) All year
7/5 Muean Ngen Road, Patong Beach *Hillside south of Patong overlooking Patong Bay and Beach* ☎ 076 29 41 04 🖳 www.baanyindee.com
Gay-owned luxury boutique resort. Shuttle service to Patong beach.

CC Bloom's (AC BF cc glm H I M MA OS PA PI RWB RWS RWT VA)
All year
84/21 Patak Soi 10 ☎ 076 33 32 22 🖳 www.ccbloomshotel.com
In the hills above Kata Beach. 20 large rooms, each with small kitchen and a view of the sea or the pool. 20 mins from Patong. Transportation to the beaches and to Patong provided.

Club Bamboo Resort (AC B BF CC glm M MSG OS PA PI PK RWB RWS RWT SA VA WH WO) All year, reception 24hrs
247/1-8 Nanai Road, Patong Beach *On hillside overlooking Patong and the beach* ☎ 076 34 53 45 🖳 www.clubbamboo.com
Gay owned and managed boutique resort. All rooms with cable TV, refrigerator & phone.

Club One Seven Phuket (AC B BF CC GLM I M MA OS PA PI PK RWB RWS RWT VA WH WO) 24hrs
9/9-10 Prachnanukroh Road, Patong Beach *5 mins walking distance to the infamous Patong Beach* ☎ 076 366360
🖳 www.cluboneseven.net
A boutique hip, yet valued-added GLBT oriented accommodation and restaurant.

Katathani Phuket Beach Resort (AC B BF CC glm M MA PI)
All year
14 Kata Noi Road, Karon, Muang ☎ 076 33 01 24
🖳 www.katathani.com
This resort has everything you need for a complete holiday getaway: five swimming pools, six restaurants and more.

Siam Palm (AC B bf cc glm H I M MA MSG OS PK RWS RWT VA)
All year
5/13 Had Patong Road, Aroonsom Square, Rat-U-Thit Road, Patong Beach
Near Club Andaman ☎ 076 34 56 80 🖳 www.siampalmresidence.com

GUEST HOUSES

Adonis (AC GLM I MA RWS RWT) All year, 24hrs
143 / 34-35 Rat-Uthit 200 Road, Patong ☎ (76) 345 800-1
🖳 www.adonis-phuket.com

Amethyst Residence.The (AC B BF glm I RWS RWT)
198/3-4 Phung Muang Sai Gor Rd, Patong, Kathu *Near Ban Zhan Market* ☎ (0)76 366 122 ☎ 087 810 8505 (mobile)
🖳 www.amethystresidence.com
Located only minutes walking distance to many of Patong Beach's most popular attractions. See their website for special offers.

Aquarius Guesthouse & Sauna (AC B bf CC DR DU FH G I LAB M MA MSG OS PA PI PK r RR RWB RWS RWT SA SB SOL VA VS WH WO)
Reception 24hrs, sauna 15.30-21h
127/10-17 Rat-U-Thit Rd, Paradise Complex, Patong Beach *Middle of Royal Paradise Complex gay area, 5 mins walk to the beach & shopping center*
☎ 076 341 668 🖳 www.aquarius-guesthouse.com
Discreet luxury suites or budget rooms and a sundeck with jacuzzi overlooking Patong and the sea. The only strictly men-only accommodation in Phuket. Gay sauna, spa and gym. Bar serving breakfast every morning. Best sauna in southern Thailand. Many „westerners". Restaurant known as „ATM" serving Thai and international food.

Baan Phil Guesthouse (AC B bf CC DM G M MA MSG OS RWS RWT VEG WI) All year
35/22-23 Rat-U-Thit 200 Pee Road *Patong Beach Kathu* ☎ 076 34 06 95
🖳 www.baan-phil.com
The management is French with an efficient, dedicated and friendly Thai staff, onsite 24/24.

Blue Dolphin Guest House & Massage (AC B DR GLM m MA MSG OS PI PK RWB RWS RWT SA SB VA WH WI) All year
135/12-13 Rath-U-Thit, 200 Pee Road, Patong Beach *In the middle of Paradise Complex* ☎ 076 34 16 11 🖳 www.bluedolphinphuket.com
Luxurious spa for men providing several spa treatments by well-trained male masseurs.

Connect (AC B BF CC GLM I M MA OS RWB RWS RWT VA) All year, 24hrs
125/8-9 Rath-U-Thit Road, Paradise Complex, Patong Beach *1st Soi, way out* ☎ 076 29 41 95 🖳 www.connectguesthouse.com
Friendly guest house in the heart of the gay scene. Motorbike rental, laundry.

Fongkaew (AC GLM I MA MSG OS RWB RWS RWT ST t VA VS)
24hrs

Paradise Complex, Rat-U-thit Road, 123/27-30 *Gay centre Phuket – Patong* ☎ 084 84 04 709 💻 www.fongkaew.be
In the middle of tha gay scene and only 300m from the sea. Clean and cheap rooms and apartments.

■ **Hostal Puerta del Sol Phuket** (AC cc G MC RWB RWS RWT VA) All year
105/9 Rachauthid Road, Patong Beach *Near Paradise Complex, street name often spelled Rat-U-Thit* ☎ 087 88 81 158 💻 www.hostalpuertadelsolphuket.com
The same owners and the same service as the famous Hostal Puerta del Sol, Madrid, Spain. Check website for info and map.

■ **James Dean Bar and Guesthouse** (B G I m MA OS RWS RWT)
188/22 Likit Plaza Phang Muang Sai Gor ☎ 86-942-0957 💻 www.jamesdeanbar.com
Just moved into their fourth venue in the new Likit Plaza. Long running business since 1992.

■ **Jochen's Residence** (AC GLM I MA MSG OS PA PK RWB RWS RWT VA) All year
241/9 Rat-U-Thit Road 2, Patong Beach, Kathu *Five mins to beach and 15 mins walk to gay area* ☎ 085 78 13 814 💻 www.siam.de/jochen
Small hotel, higher standard, German owned. Thai classic styled rooms, superior rooms, studio apartments. All rooms with cable-TV, electronic safe, private bathroom.

■ **Rendez-vous** (AC B G MA RWS RWT) All year
143/14-15 Rath-U-Thit Road, Paradise Complex, Patong Beach *5th Soi* ☎ 076 34 24 33 💻 www.boontarika.com
Well managed gay guesthouse.

■ **Sundowners Guesthouse** (AC B G RWB RWS RWT VA WI) All year
125/10 Rat-U-Thit Road, Patong Beach ☎ 076 34 42 15 💻 www.sundownersinparadise.com

■ **The Inn @ Club One Seven** (AC B BF CC G I PI WO) 24hrs
Level 4, 9/9-10 Prachnanukroh Road, Patong Beach *Top floor of Club One Seven Phuket, close to the beach* ☎ 076 366 359 💻 www.cluboneseven.net
The INN @ Club One Seven features unique Japanese hostel with 6 separate beds, communal shower rooms and toilets, all located on the top floor of Club One Seven Bed & Breakfast Phuket.

SWIMMING

-Gay Beach of Patong Beach, near police station and Tsunami Alarm Center, a lot of boys (Beware of hustlers)
-Laem Sing Beach, 10 km north of Patong just past Kamala.

CRUISING

-Phuket Town in Suang Luang Park (King Rama Park)
-Gay Beach of Patong Beach, right from Tsunami Alarm Center, at night.

Trang

GUEST HOUSES

■ **Chai's House** (BF G M MC NU OS) All year
184/37, Suksant Housing Estate, Watsarikaram-Airport Road, Moo 9, T. Khok-Loh, A. Muang ☎ 075 57 25 43
Countryside location 20 mins from Trang. Beautiful garden and delicious fish cuisine.

Udon Thani

BARS

■ **Boy Zone. The** (AC B G MA MSG t) 19-2h
30/3 Si Suttha Road *Off Prajak Road, between the Clock Tower and Thungsi Muang in central Udon Thani* ☎ 084 424 30 16 💻 www.theboyzone-udon.com

■ **Yellow Bar** (AC B GLM m MA OS) 17-2h
Charoensri Road, Amphur Muang *In front of Charoensri Complex shopping mall* ☎ 042 34 45 56

DANCECLUBS

■ **Yellow Bird** (AC B CC D g WE)
Charoen Hotel, 549 Phosri Road, Amphur Muang *Next to Charoen Hotel, opp. Aek Hospital* ☏ 042 24 81 55

GUEST HOUSES

■ **Erwin's Bungalows** (AC B glm M MA OS PI VS) 8-22h
25/15-22 Wattphortivararam Lane, Wat Phore Road *Near Wat Phore, AEK Hospital* ☏ 042 24 78 27
Big comfortable rooms with hot and cold water and TV. Motorcycle and car rental, also restaurant.

CRUISING

-Robinson Shopping Centre
-Nong Prajak Park, after 21h around Rescue Station outside
-Bars along the Nong Prajak Park.

Tunisia

Name: Tunis · Tunesien · Tunisie · Túnez
Location: North Africa
Initials: TN
Time: GMT +1
International Country Code: ☏ 216 (omit 0 from area code)
International Access Code: ☏ 00
Language: Arabic, French
Area: 163,610 km / 63,170 sq mi.
Currency: 1 Tunesian Dinar (tD) = 1,000 Millimes
Population: 10,029,000
Capital: Tunis
Religions: 99% Muslim
Climate: In the north the climate is Mediterranean with hot, dry summers and rain in winter. In the south the weather is influenced by the Sahara desert.

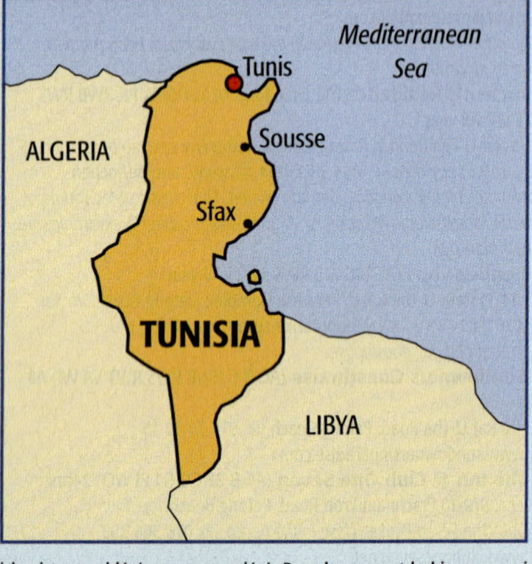

According to article 230, homosexuality is illegal in Tunisia and may lead up to 3 years imprisonment. But convictions of homosexuals are nonetheless relatively rare in comparison with other Islamic countries. The winter of 2010/2011 saw fierce conflicts and protests the regime was ultimately unable to quell. The political leadership was overthrown unexpectedly after President Ben Ali had fled the country in mid-January. Tunisia's first democratic elections were then held the following October, with an Islamic party that is considered moderate the clear winner. The situation of gays and lesbians does not appear likely to improve in the near future.

Nach Artikel 230 ist Homosexualität in Tunesien illegal und kann mit bis zu drei Jahren Gefängnis bestraft werden. Dennoch kommt es, verglichen mit anderen islamischen Ländern, relativ selten zu Verurteilungen Homosexueller.
Im Winter 2010/2011 gab es heftige Auseinandersetzungen und Proteste, die das Regime nicht mehr aufhalten konnte. Der Sturz der politischen Führung kam überraschend, nachdem Machthaber Ben Ali Mitte Januar aus seinem Land floh. Im darauffolgenden Oktober kam es zu den ersten demokratischen Wahlen in Tunesien, in der eine islamistische Partei, die als gemäßigt gilt, als eindeutiger Sieger hervorging. Für Schwule und Lesben dürfte sich in naher Zukunft die Situation nicht verändern.

Selon l'article 230, l'homosexualité est illégale et est passible de peines d'emprisonnement allant jusqu'à 3 ans. Cependant les condamnations d'homosexuels sont relativement rares, comparées à d'autres pays musulmans.
Pendant l'hiver 2010/2011, des affrontements et des contestations ont eu lieu et le régime n'a pu les arrêter. La chute du gouvernement est arrivée avec surprise après la fuite du dirigeant Ben Ali mi-janvier. Au mois d'octobre suivant, les premières élections démocratiques se sont tenues en Tunisie et le vainqueur incontesté s'est révélé être un parti islamiste considéré comme modéré. Pour les gays et lesbiennes, ceci ne devrait pas changer la situation dans un futur proche.

Según el artículo 230 la homosexualidad es ilegal y puede ser castigada con condenas de prisión de hasta tres años. Sin embargo, en comparación con otros países islámicos, hay aquí muchos menos prejuicios contra los homosexuales.
En el inverno de 2010/2011 se produjeron graves altercados y protestas que el régimen no pudo seguir conteniendo. Este golpe a la cúpula política fue algo inesperado después de que su dirigente Ben Ali abandonara el país a mediados de enero. Al octubre siguiente se celebraron las primeras elecciones democráticas en Túnez, en las cuales un partido islamista, el cual se consideraba como moderado, se alzó como ganador indiscutible. Para gays y lesbianas no se espera que la situación vaya a cambiar en un futuro próximo.

Secondo l'articolo 230, l'omosessualità è illegale. La trasgressione di questa legge può essere punita con un massimo di tre anni di pena carceraria. Tuttavia, in confronto agli altri paesi islamici, le condanne per omosessualità sono relativamente rare.
Nell'inverno del 2010/2011 si sono levate molte proteste che hanno, a loro volta, portato a violenti scontri. Il regime, non essendo più capace di sedare le proteste, è sorprendentemente caduto subito dopo la fuga di Ben Ali a metà gennaio. L'ottobre seguente si sono svolte le prime elezioni democratiche del paese, dalle quali è uscito vincitore un partito islamico considerato, dai più, moderato. Non ci sono segni che lascino presagire, a breve, miglioramenti sul fronte omosessuale.

Hammamet ☏ 072

BARS

■ **Euro Bar** (AYOR B D MA NG OS) busy after 1h
Hammamet Sud *Around the corner of Latino*
Open Air bar/club. Not gay, but many gay tourists go here to meet with the locals. Be discreet!

DANCECLUBS

■ **Hotel Kacem Night Club** (AYOR D NG) 23-4h
Av. Habib Bourguiba ☎ 279 580
Not gay but a place to meet local men.

■ **Tatoo** (AYOR B D M MA NG OS) 22-4h
Ave Moncef Bey *ext to club Calypso* 💻 www.calypsotunisia.com
Funky nightclub to be seen. Not gay!

CRUISING

-Medina Centre Ville, Center Square (AYOR at night, be careful, don't carry valueables, mobile phones and much money)
-Hotel Garsaa, Centre de Loisirs
-Beach Zone (AYOR at night)
-Yasmine Hammamet Beach Promenade
-Hammamet train station (AYOR at night)
-Manhattan District (night life district where all the discos and night bars are situated). Cruising at night inside and outside, mostly the relations involve payment.

Nabeul

CRUISING

-In the cafe at La Gare de Nabeul
-Marche de Nabeul at night (AYOR).

Port El Kantaoui

CRUISING

-Fleurs Brassiere, many rent boys by the fountains
-Marina (R, AYOR).

Soliman ☎ 072

HOTELS

■ **Hotel Solymar** (AC B BF H NG OS PI) All year
Soliman – Plage *Five km from Soliman, 30km from Tunis* ☎ (072) 366 605 💻 www.solymar-hotel.com
Not a gay hotel but a possible holiday destination for gay couples. Gay-friendly management.

Sousse ☎ 073

CAFES

■ **Sirene. La** (AYOR MA NG OS)
c/o Hotel Abou Nawas Boujaffar, Av. Habib Bourguiba / Corniche
Hotel cafe. The place to be seen and to watch the passers-by. Popular with gay tourists.

DANCECLUBS

■ **Living Samara** (AC AYOR B D MA NG OS)
Bd. du 7 Novembre ☎ (073) 22 02 00 20
Cool danceclub with international DJs. Not gay, but some gays go there.

■ **Privilége** (AC AYOR B D MA NG OS) 22-4h
Route Touristique – Hotel Soviva *5km from Elkantaoui Port, located in the Soviva Hotel* ☎ 21 377 444
with a capacity of 1200 people. Not a gay bar, but gays can be found.

CRUISING

-Main cruising area starts at the main entrance to the medina or old town (Place des Martyrs) and extends across the busy Place Farhat Hached and then along Av. Habib Bourguiba to the corniche past the Sousse Palace and Abou Nawas hotels and then extends along the sea front at least as far as Dreams discotheque (very busy during the summer months, AYOR: never go on the beach at night with locals. The police in civil clothing is everywhere)
-Around the Jinene hotel after 23h, when the dune motor bike police clocks off duty, many rent boys come out (AYOR, R)
-Cafes along Avenue Habib Bourguiba which are popular with hustlers (AYOR, R), especially below Palace and Abou Nawas hotels.

Tunis ☎ 01

CAFES

■ **Café de Paris** (AYOR B g m MA OS R) 7-23h
Meeting point for hustlers at midday. Busy except during Ramadan.

■ **Café-Terrace in Hotel Africa** (B g m MA OS R)
Av. Habib Bourguiba
Well known and busy café in a 5-star hotel.

■ **Panorama** (B glm MA OS)
Avenue Bourguiba
More gay guests after dark who watch the cruising on the avenue.

DANCECLUBS

■ **Jamaica Club** (B D MA NG)
49 Avenue Habib Boutguiba *10th floor, Hotel El Hana International*

■ **Le Boeuf sur le Toit** (B D MA NG)
3 avenue Fatouma Bourguiba *Suburb of La Soukra*
Lively bar-restaurant attracting a trendy crowd, with a dance floor, good DJs, live music at weekends and Sunday jazz evenings.

■ **Odeon** (B D MA NG OS)
Rte Tourist 1057 💻 www.tunisiaclubbing.com
Very trendy nightclub in the tourist zone of Tunis-Gammarth, international house and electro DJs perform here.

RESTAURANTS

■ **Villa Didon** (B M MA NG OS)
Rue Mendes France, Carthage
Italian cuisine, upscale dining.

SAUNAS/BATHS

■ **Hammam Zriba** (MSG NG PI SB WH)
In Zaghouan
Thermal water Hammam. Not gay, but interesting for having sexual encounters. Take the bus Nabeul – Zaghouan, ask the driver to let you get off at Hammam Zriba.

CRUISING

-Av. Habib Bourguiba between Hotels Africa and El Hana, also on the central strip of pavement of the avenue between the trees (the locals will want to talk. Try to find a streetside café where you will not be disturbed)
-Cinema Afra at Rue Lieutenant Mohamed el Aziz Taj (r)
-Love Park in front of the Abou Nawas Hotel on Mohamed V Av. (r)
-Steps of the municipal theatre opp. Hotel el Hana (YC, evenings).

Turkey

Name: Türkiye · Türkei · Turquie · Turquía · Turchia
Location: Southeastern Europe
Initials: TR
Time: GMT +2
International Country Code: ☏ 90 (omit 0 from area code)
International Access Code: ☏ 00
Language: Turkish
Area: 779,452 km² / 300,946 sq mi.
Currency: 1 Turkish Pound/ Lira (TL) = 100 Kurus
Population: 72,065,000
Capital: Ankara
Religions: 99% Moslems
Climate: The Black Sea coast is best between Apr-Sep. With the exception of Istanbul, Turkey doesn't have a winter tourism season. Spring and autumn are the best times to visit.
Important gay cities: Istanbul

Homosexuality is not illegal in Turkey as words like „homosexual, transgender, and bisexual" do not exist in Turkish law.
The revisions of criminal codes in 2005 retained provisions barring „indecency," „exhibitionism," and „offenses against public morality,"historically often used to restrict LGBT people's rights. Furthermore, recent amendments to a 1934 law on the powers and duties of the police have given the police almost unlimited power to patrol and control public spaces (cruising areas).
Violence has gained visibility: Gangs go to cruising areas and visit internet websites where gay men meet – looking for chances to inflict violence or robbery. Police rarely respond adequately; sometimes even blaming or harassing the victims of violence.
In Turkey, the Penal Code criminalizes encouraging or facilitating sex work; however, prostitution in licensed brothels is legal for women only. Identity cards in Turkey are colour coded: pink for women and blue for men. Sex change operations can only be undertaken with a court decision – thereafter the ID card is changed. Transgender who do not have an operation have a problem. There are also no laws regarding the sex workers working on the streets. The policemen decide arbitrarily which sex workers should be working in which area. In Turkey, military service is mandatory for every man older than 20 years old. Turkey does not recognise conscientious objection to military service. Objectors must identify themselves as „sick" and are forced to undergo humiliating and degrading examinations to „prove" their homosexuality, sometimes even with photos of them having anal sex with the same sex.
Both Lambdaistanbul and KAOS-GL have faced state attempts, using national laws protecting „morality" or „decency," to censor them or close them down. On April 7, 2008, police raided the offices of Lambda Istanbul. The police justified the incursion by claiming the organization „encourages" and „facilitates" prostitution and is a threat to „Turkish family values". Despite the legal expert's report which clearly stated that there was no substant ial reason to close down the association, the local court issued a verdict against Lambdaistanbul on May 29th, 2008 ordering its dissolution. On June 24, 2008 the case was appealed to the Supreme Court. The petition to ban Lambda Istanbul then finally failed in December 2008. Another attempt to bring about a ban in the following year was also unsuccessful.
Turkey is nevertheless a very interesting country, rich in culture, friendly people and fantastic cuisine. A visit to Istanbul is a must!

Da die Begriffe homosexuell, transgender oder bisexuell in der türkischen Gesetzgebung nirgends vorkommen, ist Homosexualität per se auch nicht illegal. Doch trotz der im Jahr 2005 eingeführten Gesetzesänderungen bleiben die traditionell gegen die LGBT-Gemeinde eingesetzten Verbote von „Unsittlichkeit", „Exhibitionismus" und „Erregung öffentlichen Ärgernisses" weiterhin bestehen. Die jüngsten Änderungen im Polizeigesetz räumen Polizeistreifen darüber hinaus an öffentlichen Plätzen (Cruising-Gegenden) praktisch unbegrenzte Vollmachten ein.
Die Gewalt hat merklich zugenommen: Banden suchen in schwulen Cruising-Gegenden und Internetangeboten gezielt nach Opfern. Die Polizei reagiert selten angemessen, gibt den Opfern manchmal selbst die Schuld oder schikaniert sie sogar.
Prostitution ist offiziell nur für Frauen in zugelassenen Bordellen legal, beim Straßenstrich entscheidet die Polizei willkürlich, wer wo seinem Gewerbe nachgehen darf.
Alle Männer ab 20 Jahren sind zum Militärdienst verpflichtet, Kriegsdienstverweigerung ist unmöglich. Wer auf Untauglichkeit plädiert, muss zum Nachweis seiner Homosexualität erniedrigende Untersuchungen über sich ergehen lassen.
Die Regierung versucht ständig, die beiden Schwulenorganisationen Lambda Istanbul und KAOS-GL zu zensieren oder aufzulösen, da sie angeblich gegen die Moral verstoßen. Am 7. April 2008 durchsuchte die Polizei die Büros von Lambda Istanbul, da die Organisation angeblich die Prostitution fördere bzw. erleichtere und eine Bedrohung für türkische Familienwerte darstelle. Trotz der eindeutigen Schlussfolgerung eines Rechtsgutachtens, dass keine erheblichen Gründe für ein Verbot vorliegen, entschied die Justiz am 29. Mai 2008 gegen Lambda Istanbul. Am 24. Juni 2008 ging der Fall dann vor dem obersten Gerichtshof in Berufung. Im Dezember 2008 scheiterte der Verbotsantrag von Lambda Istanbul endgültig. Auch im Folgejahr war ein Verbotsversuch erfolglos.
Trotz alledem ist die Türkei ein äußerst interessantes Land voller kultureller Reichtümer, freundlicher Menschen und kulinarischer Erlebnisse.

La législation turque ne connait pas les notions de bisexualité, transgenre ou homosexualité et l'homosexualité n'est pas de fait illégale. Cependant malgré les changements législatifs de 2005, les interdictions d'"immoralité", „exhibitionnisme", „outrage publique à la pudeur" perdurent et visent traditionnellement la communauté LGBT. Les lois modifiées donnent en pratique aux patrouilles de police les pleins-pouvoirs sur les lieux publics (lieux de drague). La violence a sensiblement augmenté: des bandes cherchent leurs victimes sur les lieux de drague et internet. La police réagit rarement en conséquence, donnant parfois les tords à la victime ou en la chicanant même. La prostitution est officielle uniquement pour les femmes dans des maisons closes agréées, la police est arbitraire en matière de prostitution sur la voie publique. Le service militaire est obligatoire pour les hom-

mes dès 20 ans, l'objection de conscience impossible. L'inaptitude pour homosexualité est étudiée de façon dégradante. Le gouvernement essaie constamment de censurer ou dissoudre les deux associations gays Lambda Istanbul et KAOS-GL pour infraction à la morale. Le 7 avril 2008, la police perquisitionna les bureaux de Lambda Istanbul car, selon elle, l'association favoriserait et faciliterait la prostitution et serait une menace pour les valeurs familiales turques. Malgré les conclusions d'une expertise que des causes considérables n'existent pas, la justice trancha le 29 mai 2008 contre Lambda Istanbul. Le 24 juin 2008, le cas fut renvoyé en appel devant la plus haute cour de justice. En décembre 2008 la demande d'interdiction de Lambda Istanbul a échoué définitivement, et même l'année suivante une tentative d'interdiction est restée sans succès.
Malgré tout, la Turquie reste un pays hautement intéressant, riche en culture à la population accueillante et à la cuisine fantastique.

Puesto que los conceptos „homosexual", „transgénero" o „bisexual" no aparecen en ninguna parte de la legislación turca, la homosexualidad en si no es ilegal.
Sin embargo, a pesar de las modificaciones legislativas introducidas en el año 2005, todavía persisten las sanciones aplicadas tradicionalmente contra la comunidad LGBT de „inmoralidad", „exhibicionismo" y „escándalo público". Las recientes reformas en la ley de la policía, además, otorgan a las patrullas de policía plenos poderes para actuar a la práctica en zonas públicas (zonas de ligue).
La violencia ha aumentado de forma significativa: las bandas buscan víctimas a próposito en zonas de ligue gay y en ofertas por Internet. La policía raramente actúa de manera proporcional, incluso echa la culpa a las víctimas o incluso llega a chantajearlas. La prostitución es legal oficialmente sólo para las mujeres en ciertos burdeles permitidos, en los casos de prostitución callejera la policía decide arbitrariamente quién y dónde se puede ejercer. Todos los hombres están obligados a prestar el servicio militar a partir de los 20 años, no es posible negarse a su prestación. Quien alegase „inaptitud", debería someterse como „prueba" de su homosexualidad a investigaciones humillantes sobre uno mismo.
El gobierno intenta permanentemente censurar o disolver las dos organizaciones homosexuales Lambda Istanbul y KAOS-GL, ya que supuestamente actuarían contra la „moral". El 7 de abril de 2008 la policía registró las oficinas de Lambda Istanbul porque supuestamente esta organización „fomentaba" o „facilitaba" la prostitución y representaba una amenaza para los „valores familiares turcos". A pesar de las inequívocas conclusiones de un dictamen judicial que declaraba que no existía ningún motivo aparente para una sanción, la justicia condenó el 29 de mayo de 2008 a Lambda Istanbul. El 24 de junio de 2008 el caso fue llevado en casación ante el tribunal supremo. En diciembre de 2008, fracasó finalmente la prohibición de Lambda Estambul. También al año siguiente, un nuevo intento de prohibición no tuvo éxito.
A pesar de todo Turquía es un país sumamente interesante, lleno de riquezas culturales, gente simpática y experiencias culinarias fantásticas.

Poiché i termini ‚omosessuale', ‚transgender' o ‚bisessuale' non appaiono neanche nella legislazione turca, l'omosessualità in sé non può quindi definirsi illegale. Tuttavia, nonostante le modifiche legislative introdotte nel 2005, i divieti di ‚immoralità', ‚esibizionismo', e ‚reati contro la morale pubblica e il buon costume' usati tradizionalmente contro la comunità LGBT, continuano a persistere. Le recenti modifiche alla legge sulla pubblica sicurezza danno, in pratica, alla polizia ampia discrezionalità sulle piazze pubbliche e quindi anche sulle zone di cruising. La violenza è drammaticamente aumentata: alcune bande cercano le proprie vittime nelle zone di cruising e adesso anche tramite internet. Solo raramente la polizia reagisce a queste violenze in maniera consona: a volte la polizia incolpa addirittura le vittime stesse ed esercita sulle vittime vessazioni di vario tipo. Ufficialmente la prostituzione è legale solo per le donne e solo all'interno dei bordelli, mentre per quello che riguarda la prostituzione in strada, a decidere chi e dove può esercitare la sua professione è la polizia in tutta la sua arbitrarietà. Tutti i ragazzi che hanno compiuto il 20° anno di età sono obbligati al servizio di leva e non è possibile optare per l'obiezione di coscienza. Chi fa la richiesta per essere riformato, per dimostrare la propria omosessualità, bisogna sottoporsi ad umilianti esami. Il governo prova sempre a censurare se non addirittura a far chiudere le due organizzazioni ‚Lambda Istambul' e ‚KAOS-GL', accusate di andare contro la morale. Il 7 aprile del 2008 la polizia ha perquisito le sedi dell'associazione ‚Lambda Istambul' accusando l'organizzazione di favorire la prostituzione e di rappresentare una minaccia per i „valori familiari turchi". Nonostante una chiaro un parere giuridico, secondo il quale non sussistono motivi per un divieto dell'organizzazione, il 29 maggio 2008 un tribunale di Istambul ha ordinato la chiusura di ‚Lambda Istambul'. Il 24 giugno 2008 è stato presentato un ricorso presso la corte suprema. Nel dicembre del 2008 la richiesta di messa a bando di Lambda Istambul è definitivamente fallita. Un altro tentativo di divieto dell'associazione è ulteriormente fallito l'anno successivo.
Nonostante tutto, la Turchia rimane una Paese interessantissimo, pieno di ricchezze culturali, pieno di persone cordiali e di fantastiche specialità culinarie.

NATIONAL COMPANIES

Sensation Tours @ Istanbul
Karadut Sokak karahan, Merkezi No :28/5 ✉ Istanbul *in the Altiyol Center* ☎ (216) 348 43 81
Travel company in Istanbul.

Sublime Gay Travel Agency Turkey
Gumussuyu Man.Hariciye Konagisk 3/6, *M° Taksim* ☎ (212) 293 6602

NATIONAL GROUPS

Kaos GL Associaiton Office hours 14-18, Sat & Sun 14-18h
GMK Bulvari 29/12 Demirtepe Ankara ✉ Ankara ☎ (0312) 230 03 58
🖳 www.kaosgl.org
One of the first GLBT organizations in Turkey, founded in Sep 1994 and registered since Dec 2005. Publishes the first gay and lesbian magazine „Kaos Kultur Merkezi".

Lambda Istanbul Sundays, 16-18h, mainly in Turkish, other times answering machine
Istiklâl Caddesi, Katip Celebi Mah. ✉ Beyoglu-Istanbul
☎ (0212) 245 70 68 🖳 www.lambdaistanbul.org
A liberation group for gay, lesbian, bisexual, and transgender people in Turkey. See website for the range of activities they organize.

Adana

CRUISING

-Atatürk Park (especially in the evening)
-Mado Ice cream shop area (discreet cruising).

Alanya ☎ 0242

BARS

Amalia (B glm MA) Daily 18-3h
Çarsi mahallesi, Izzat Azakoglu caddesi Isman Ishani No. 20 *Below Robin Hood disco* ☎ (0537) 796 92 89
Owned by two gay dutch men.

CRUISING

All cruising areas in the evenings
-Kleopatra Park (AYOR)
-Port, at the 100 yil Atatürk-Monument
-Street to the castle (R)

Ankara ☎ 0312

BARS

Tribal (B D G MA WE) Wed-Sat
Tunus Caddesi 53/A *In the parallel street of the Ataturk Blvd*

CRUISING

-Bulvar/Blvd (between Kizilaya and Bakanliklar).

Antalya ☎ 0242

CINEMA

Kent (g VS)
Saman Pazari Sokak. Kazim özalp caddesi ☎ (0242) 248 90 85

BARS

DJack Bar (AC B d MA NG)
Old Habour No. 4 *Harbour* ☎ (0535) 298 20 00
Former BarBar. Majority of costumers are straight but it's a gay-friendly place.

Marji Club (B g MA)
Iskele Caddesi No. 22 Yat Limani

CAFES

Cafe Gül (B g M MA OS)
Barbaros Mah. Kocatepe Sok. No 1 *Old town* ☎ (0242) 247 51 26
Restaurant & cafe. Very good European and Turkish food.

Insaat (b M MC OS)
Kilicarslan Mah. Hesapci Sok, No. 66 *Old city* ☎ (0242) 248 65 46
Gay-friendly bar with German/Turkish owner.

RESTAURANTS

Kabanas (B g M OS)
Kilicarslan Mah. Hesapci Sok No.78 *Old town* ☎ (0242) 248 59 61
Cafe-bar & restaurant.

CONDOM SHOPS

Ero Shop (g)
K. Özalp Cd. 404 Sk, Sarilar ish. K2/D/10 ☎ (0242) 244 62 40
🖳 www.trustcondom.net

HOTELS

Berkay (AC B BF H M NG OS PI PK RWB RWS) Mid May – mid Oct
Yenimahalle Atatürk Bulvari, Kemer *45 km from Antalya, 55 km from airport, 200 m from the beach* ☎ (0242) 814 75 12
🖳 www.berkayhotel.com
Fourty double rooms with shower/WC, balconies, tel, radio. TV room. Private beach and hamam.

Paloma. La (AC B glm OS PI RWS RWT) All year
Kilincaslan Mah., Tabakhane Sokak 3 *In the centre of the old city*
☎ (0242) 244 84 97 🖳 www.lapalomapansion.com
Gay owned hotel in old historical city centre.

GUEST HOUSES

Pension Sabah (AC b bf CC H M MA NG OS RWS VA) All year
Kaleici Kilicarsian mh. Hesapci sk. 60 *Kaleici – old town*
☎ (0242) 247 53 45 🖳 www.sabahpansiyon.8m.com
Family run guest house; clean rooms with own bath. Airport transfer and tour organisation upon request. AC/heating costs extra.

CRUISING

-Atatürk monument (R) by day and in winter-times if there are not too many tourists
-Atatürk Caddesi from the Monument to the harbour (r)
-Harbour and Atatürk Park towards the cliff (AYOR R, beware of pick-pockets)
-Konyaalti beach (r)
-In the front of Cafe Kabanas (in the park).

Bodrum ☎ 0252

BARS

Varil (B g)
Barlar Sokagi

HOTELS

Aegean Gate (AC b BF H m PI) Apr-Oct
Akçabuk Mevki, Kumbahçe Mah, Güvercin Sok. no 2 ☎ (0252) 316 78 53
🖳 www.aegeangate.com
Gay-friendly small boutique hotel, in unique setting overlooking Aegean sea. Irish owners.

Marmara Bodrum. The (AC B BF CC H M MA PI SB WE WH WO)
Yokusbasi Mahallesi Suluhasan Caddesi ☎ (0252) 313 81 30
🖳 www.themarmarahotels.com/The-Marmara-Bodrum

PRIVATE ACCOMMODATION

Villa Muranco (bf CC glm OS PI) All year
Bodrum Peninsular ☎ (0252) 373 63 51 🖳 www.villamuranco.com
Villa Muranco is a four-bedroom stone villa which is available for hire. It is not run as a guest house. The gay owners live on site in a private bungalow and provide a catering service to the guests if requested.

CRUISING

-Harbour area behind the castle (Kale) at night. Go up the steps to the toilets. On the harbour wall near the water
-Belediye Park (Townhall-Park) in city centre, afternoons (R)

-Cumhuriyet Caddesi, at night. On the street around the loud discos, at night
-Gay beach in Gümbet, the next town from Bodrum, back side of the small peninsula with the windmills that separate Bodrum and Gümbet harbors(NU R)
-The mandrake and pedestrian walk along the marina (all day, also R).

Cesme

SWIMMING

-Altinkum Plaji beach (g, NU) busy at weekends with gay men from Izmir. Take the minibus from Cesme harbour.

Gaziantep ☎ 0342

SEX CINEMAS

- **Burç** (AYOR NG)
- **Fistas** (AYOR NG)

CRUISING

-Along the river Alleben, in the new park.

Istanbul/Estambul ☎ 0212

Istanbul is, without a doubt, the leading metropolis in Turkey as well as being the gateway to the Orient. An active gay scene can be found in this city, which one could call „advanced" from a Western viewpoint. Istanbul is however, as is the entire country, strongly influenced by Islam. Emancipated homosexuals, from the viewpoint of the west, do exist as does a silent tolerance. But generally the traditional Islamic values dominate life here, meaning one should be very discreet in public places.

Istanbul ist die unumstritten führende Metropole der Türkei und das Tor zum Orient. Es gibt ein ausgeprägtes Szeneleben in dieser Stadt, das den emanzipatorischen Fortschritt im Sinne des Westens widerspiegelt. Istanbul ist jedoch weiterhin, wie die gesamte Türkei, stark islamisch geprägt. Es gibt zwar emanzipierte Schwule im westlichen Sinne und eine gewisse stillschweigende Toleranz, aber größtenteils gelten weiterhin die islamischen und traditionellen Normen, so dass man sich in der Öffentlichkeit unbedingt diskret verhalten sollte.

Istanbul est la capitale économique et culturelle incontestée de la Turquie et une porte s'ouvrant sur l'orient. Le milieu gay y est animé et reflète le „ progrès „ émancipatoire au sens occidental du terme. Istanbul est néanmoins restée, comme le reste du pays d'ailleurs, très musulman, et bien que certains gays et lesbiennes ne se distinguent plus vraiment de leurs confrères et consœurs européens, les règles et traditions héritées de l'islâm exigent toujours une grande retenue en public et la discrétion.

Istambul es indiscutiblemente la metrópolis absoluta de Turquía y la puerta a Oriente. Existe un ambiente gay muy establecido en esta ciudad, que refleja su avance y emancipación en el sentido más occidental. Istambul, sin embargo, sigue marcada por el islamismo, al igual que toda Turquía. Hay en efecto gays emancipados en el sentido occidental y una cierta tolerancia pero mayoritariamente todavía siguen imperando las normas y tradiciones islámicas, por lo que uno deberá comportarse con discreción en público.

Istanbul è l'indiscussa metropoli principale della Turchia ed è considerata la porta sull'oriente. Ad Istanbul c'è una scena molto attiva che rispecchia l'emancipazione occidentale. Tuttavia non bisogna dimenticare che comunque questa città, come tutto il resto della Turchia, è profondamente influenzata dall'Islam. Qui ci sono gay piuttosto emancipati (in senso occidentale) ed una silenziosa tolleranza nei confronti dell'omosessualità, tuttavia a prevalere sono qui le norme tradizionali islamiche e quindi la discrezione in pubblico è una regola essenziale.

BARS

Chillout Hostel Cafe (B g H MA)
Istiklal Cad./Balyoz Sok. 17-19, Ciya Sofrasi, Güneslibahce Nr. 43
☎ (0212) 249 47 84 🖳 www.chillouthc.com
Also guest house.

Club 17 (MA R T) 21-4h
Zambak Sokak No 17. Taksim ☎ 537 481 39 46 (mobile)
Preferred mostly by rentboys, travestites and transsexuals who offer to have sex for money.

Club Privé (B G r) 23.30-4h
Tarlabasi Bulvari, 28/A Taksim ☎ (0212) 235 79 99
One of the oldest surviving gay bars of Istanbul.

Durak (B G) 18-2, Fri & Sat -4h
Muratpaşa Sokak 9 *Near Tram Yusufpasa*
For bear and bear lovers.

Ekoo Bar (AC B CC D g H MA r S WE) 21-3h
Tarlabasi Av. No 248/1, Taksim *Tram Galatasaray, near English Palace*
☎ (0212) 297 25 56 ☎ 537 508 66 26 (mobile)
Bears and young crowd.

Pinokyo (B d GLM MA S ST) 11-3h
Istiklal Caddesi Büyükparmakkap no. 305; sokak no. 26 taksim beyo no. 287 *Near Taksim Square* ☎ (0212) 293 9433
🖳 www.pinokyocafebar.com

Sahra (AYOR B g T)
Istiklal Caddesi 40 *near Club 17* ☎ (0212) 244 33 06

Tek Yön Bar (B g MC s WE) 23-4h
Siraselviler Caddesi no. 63/1 *M° Taksim* ☎ 533 377 23 93
Very trendy local bar where almost everyone knows each other. Nice crowd. Busy on Tue (ST).

CAFES

Mor Kedi (b cc GLM m MA) 10-24h
Istiklal caddesi/Imam Adnan soakak no.9 *Beyoglu, little street opp. Vakko building, 3rd floor* ☎ (0212) 244 25 92
Difficult to find. Somewhat nostalgic, pleasant cafe. Warm snacks, friendly service.

Rocinante Café (B g m MA) 10-2h
Sakizagaci 305; Caddesi Ogut, Sokak no. 6 K. 3 ☎ (0212) 244 82 19

Sugar Club Café (B G M OS YC) 11-1h
Istiklal Caddesi, Saka Salim sokak, No. 7, Beyoglu *Near Odakule Building*
☎ (0212) 245 00 96 🖳 www.sugar-cafe.com
Great, modern cafe bar. Specialized in variety of coffees, home made food and desserts. Lounge upstairs. Terrace in summer.

DANCECLUBS

Love Dancepoint (AC B CC D DR GLM M S SNU VS WE YC) Wed, Fri & Sat 23.30-5h
Cumhuriyet Cd. 349/1, Harbiye *Opp. military museum, Metro Osmanbey* ☎ (0212) 232 25 90
An up-market gay & lesbian place. Stylish and popular.

Other Side (! AC B CC D G MA OS S t WE) Wed-Sun 23-5h
Istiklal Cad. Zambak Sk. 2/5 *M° Taksim* ☎ (0212) 293 88 52

Tek Yön Club (AC B D G m MA R ST) 22-5h
Siraselviler Caddesi No. 63/1 *M° Taksim*
🖳 www.tekyonclub.com

Xlarge Chico's (AC B CC D G MA P S SNU) 22-6h
Mahallesi Küçük Bayram Sokak no. 1 ☎ (0212) 245 68 98

RESTAURANTS

Frappé (AC B BF cc DM GLM LM M MA NR OS PA PK RES S t VEG WE WL) Daily 9-2h. Food served 11-23h
Istiklal Caddesi Zambak Sokak 10A, Beyoglu *M° Taksim. Off Istikal Street*
☎ (0212) 292 38 34
🖳 www.frappeistanbul.com
Istanbul's first and only gay cafe-bar-restaurant.

SAUNAS/BATHS

Aquarius (DU g MA MSG PI R SA SB WH WO) 24hrs
Istiklal Cad./Sadri Aliski No. 29/11, Beyoglu ☎ (0212) 251 89 25
www.aquariussauna.com
Not European sauna standard. Action possible in private rooms only with rent boys. Agree on price prior to massage.

Çesme Hamami (DU g MC MSG SB) 7.30-19.30h
Voyvoda Cad. / Persembe Pazari, Yeni Çesme Sok. *Karaköy*
Not for trendy gay men, rather a down-to-earth crowd. Strong masseur for a good massage.

Yesildirek Hamami (DU g MA MSG SB) 11-21h
Tersane Caddesi 74 *Across the Azapkapi Mosque at the Taksim base of the Ataturk Bridge, Cnr Eflatun Ck.*

TRAVEL AND TRANSPORT

Pride Travel Istanbul (CC GLM) 9-18h, closed Sun
Incili Cavus Sk. No: 33 Kat 2 *Near Hagia Sophia, behind Sultanahmet tram station* ☎ (0212) 527 06 71
www.istanbulgay.com
Gay and gay-friendly tours in Istanbul and all over Turkey since 2002.

HOTELS

Hot Suites Taksim (AC BF CC G MA OS PA RWB RWS RWT)
All year, 24hrs
Feridlye Cad. Taksim Firini Sokak N° 7 *M° Taksim Square*
☎ (0212) 254 36 69 www.hot-suites.com
Gay hotel in the heart of Istanbul and gay life.

SWIMMING

-Florya Plajlari beach (three popular beaches within reasonable distances from the city; all cruisy, especially Günes plaji)
-Küçük Cekmeçe Plaj/beach (NU) (Take subway from European railway station called Galata to Kanarya)

-Kilyos (beach at European part of the city, extending 3km along Black Sea)
-Sile (beach at European part of city, extending 8km along the Black Sea, hidden bays in evening)

CRUISING

-Istiklal Cad., well hidden but as this road coming from the Taksim square leads to many gay bars, it is popular with many gays and hustlers
-Kadiköy Park, from early evening
-Park opp. the Blue Mosque, evenings in summer after the light show taking place at the Blue Mosque (AYOR)
-Taksim Park, day and night (AYOR, R). This is the most active cruising area in the city. Making contact is quite easy. For your own safety, you should not try to do anything outdoor or in a dark corner, but rather in a small hotel nearby
-Fatih Park (near aquaduct), in park near ruins of old Roman prison (AYOR g MC r).

Izmir ☎ 0232

BARS

K Bar (B d g) 22-4h
1471 Sokak 45/A, Alsancak *First right from the Bornova street which is opp. railway station. Brightly lit pink building*
Entrance fee includes one drink. Former Yüzbinyüz Bar.

TRAVEL AND TRANSPORT

Gay Tours Turkey (GLM MA)
1717 Sokak No. 128 Daire. 202 ☎ (0232) 364 45 05
Tours, hotel accommodation and much more.

SWIMMING

-Karaburun (bus from Altay Meydane)
-Sigacek
-Pamucak
-Sifne.

CRUISING

-Fuar (Kultur Park) Kültürparki faregrounds. Minimal entrance fee for the small park. Interesting from 22h
-Waterfront Blvd Kordon 1 – Atatürk Caddesi (Blvd by the waterfront in Alsancak), late evenings
-The traffic circle near the entrance to the faregrounds Fuar, at night
-Konak, town hall park at the clock, day and night (R).

Kusadasi ☎ 0256

BARS

Tattoo Bar (AC D G MA S SNU ST VS WE) 22-4h
12 Camikebir Mahallesi Sakarya Sok.
☎ (0256) 612 53 06
A gay bar since 1992.

CRUISING

-Tea garden.

Mersin ☎ 0392

SEX CINEMAS

Sidali Sinemasi (g)
4728 Sokak Cankaya Mah. *Off Istiklal Caddesi, a bit hidden; there's also an internet café in the street*

CRUISING

-Atatürk Park, towards sports centre, opp. post office, NOT at main entrance near the police office
-Flamingo Yolu (Flamingo Road, in the summer, evenings)
-Along the river, under the bridge at the stadium (on the way from town to the Hilton Hotel).

Ukraine

Name: Ukraïna · Ucraina
Location: East Europe
Initials: UA
Time: GMT +2
International Country Code: ☏ 380 (omit 0 from area code)
International Access Code: ☏ 810
Language: Ukrainian, Russian
Area: 603,700 km² / 233,089 sq mi.
Currency: 1 Hryvna (UAH) = 100 Kopeks
Population: 47,075,000
Capital: Kyiv (Kiev)
Religions: Mostly Ukrainian Orthodox (Moscow Patriarchate) and Ukrainian Orthodox (Kiev Patriarchate), also Ukrainian Greek Catholic, Roman Catholic, Judaism
Climate: Moderate continental climate. Mediterranean only on the southern Crimean coast. The west and north are areas with the highest precipitation. Winters vary from cool along the Black Sea to cold further inland. Summers are warm across the greater part of the country, hot in the south.
Important gay cities: Kyiv (Kiev)

Ukraine is the second largest Eastern European state after Russia. It was the first former Soviet republic to decriminalise sex between adult men. The age of consent is 16 years for both homo and heterosexuals. Ukrainian legislation doesn't provide a sufficient legal mechanism in combating discrimination and preventing hate crimes. The law does not recognise same sex couple.

The results of a national poll showed that only 42% of Ukrainians think that homosexuals should have equal rights. Homophobia and prejudice towards gays and lesbians are still widespread among the society. Last years brought even more radical anti-gay meetings and statements by church leaders.

According to monitoring of Ukrainian LGBT people face discriminated on the basis of their sexual orientation or other violations of their human rights. The most common cases of discrimination and human rights violations are in the spheres of interpersonal communication, interaction with the police, labour relations, privacy, information rights, services and education. Intolerant attitudes, moral pressure and even physical violence and sexual harassment are also common from family members and other people.

The people in the Ukraine are suffering from the catastrophic AIDS epidemic. Especially the harbour city Odessa is completed overwhelmed with this problem – not enough staff or resources. According to data from official statistics, about 3 thousand children live in the streets of Odessa. According to researches of OCF „The Way Home", two thirds of street children are HIV positive. They die with AIDS diagnosis in crude cellars, there are no hospital facilities available for them. The problems faced by the authorities are enormous. If you would like to help these children, see the website of the NGO organisation „The Way Home" where you can make a donation. (http://wayhome.org.ua)

Ukraine is a country with great hospitality and friendly, welcoming people. With patience and some discretion, gay travellers will find Ukraine an interesting, unique and beautiful destination. The cities with the strongest gay presence are Kyiv (the capital), Lviv, Odessa, Dnipropetrovs'k, Donets'k, Kharkiv.

Die Ukraine ist nach Russland der flächenmäßig zweitgrößte osteuropäische Staat und war die erste ehemalige Sowjetrepublik, in der Sex zwischen erwachsenen Männern legalisiert wurde. Das Mindestalter für Hetero- und Homosexuelle liegt gleichermaßen bei 16 Jahren. Die ukrainische Gesetzgebung verfügt noch über keine ausreichenden Rechtsmechanismen zur Bekämpfung von Diskriminierung und Hassdelikten. Gleichgeschlechtliche Partnerschaften genießen keinerlei rechtliche Anerkennung.

Eine landesweite Umfrage hat ergeben, dass nur 42 % der ukrainischen Bevölkerung die rechtliche Gleichstellung von Schwulen und Lesben befürworten. In der Gesellschaft sind Schwulenfeindlichkeit und Vorurteile immer noch weit verbreitet. In den letzten Jahren hat die Zahl der radikal antischwulen Veranstaltungen und Äusserungen kirchlicher Führungspersönlichkeiten eher zugenommen.

Statistiken zeigen, dass die LGBT-Gemeinde der Ukraine aufgrund ihrer sexuellen Orientierung Diskriminierung und anderen Menschenrechtsverletzungen ausgesetzt ist. Am häufigsten treten diese diskriminierenden Vorfälle und Missachtungen der Menschenrechte in zwischenmenschlichen Beziehungen, beim Umgang mit der Polizei sowie in arbeitsrechtlichen Fragen auf, und sie betreffen die Privatsphäre, das Recht auf Information, Dienstleistungen und das Bildungswesen. Intoleranz, moralischer Druck und sogar physische Gewalt oder sexuelle Belästigung sind weit verbreitet, auch innerhalb von Familien.

Außerdem leidet die Bevölkerung der Ukraine unter der katastrophalen AIDS-Epidemie. Besonders die Hafenstadt Odessa wird von diesem Problem überrollt – es stehen nicht genug Personal oder Medikamente zur Verfügung. Laut offiziellen Statistiken leben ungefähr dreitausend Kinder auf den Straßen Odessas. Gemäß Untersuchungen von OCF „Der Weg Nach Hause", sind zwei Drittel von den Straßenkindern HIV-positiv. Sie sterben mit der AIDS-Diagnose in dunklen Kellern, es gibt keine verfügbaren Krankenhausplätze für sie.

Die Probleme für die Behörden sind enorm. Wenn Sie diesen Kindern helfen möchten, besuchen Sie die Website der NGO Organisation „Der Weg Nach Hause", wo Sie auch spenden können. (http://wayhome.org.ua)

Die Ukraine ist nichtsdestotrotz ein äußerst gastfreundliches Land mit freundlichen, warmherzigen Menschen. Solange sie Geduld und eine gewisse Diskretion aufbringen, werden auch schwullesbische Touristen in der Ukraine ein interessantes, einzigartiges und wunderschönes Reiseziel entdecken. Die größten Schwulenszenen finden sich in den Städten Kiew (Hauptstadt), Lwiw (Lemberg), Odessa, Dnipropetrovsk, Donezk und Charkiw.

L'Ukraine est, mise à part la Russie, le plus grand pays d'Europe de l'est et la première république de l'ancienne Union Soviétique à avoir dépénalisé l'homosexualité entre adultes consentants. La majorité sexuelle y est fixée à 16 ans pour tous. Néanmoins, les pouvoirs publics ukrainiens ignorent toujours sciemment les homosexuels et ne mentionnent l'homosexualité pratiquement pas dans la législation. La plus ancienne organisation gay et lesbienne du pays est

le Centre Gay et Lesbien „Nash Mir“ qui existe depuis neuf ans et se bat pour la reconnaissance et l'égalité des droits de la communauté gay/lesbienne/bisexuelle/transgenre. Pour ce faire, elle s'efforce de la rendre plus visible et d'augmenter la tolérance de ses concitoyens. Malgré tout, „Nash Mir“ rapporte que 53 % des homosexuel(le)s du pays ont déjà fait l'expérience de la discrimination.
C'est la raison pour laquelle de nombreux gays et lesbiennes préfèrent ne pas faire leur coming out, surtout s'ils ne vivent pas dans une grande ville. Un autre sondage a montré que seuls 42 % des Ukrainiens jugeaient utile de donner aux homos les mêmes droits civils qu'aux hétéros.
L'Ukraine est un pays aux habitants très ouverts et hospitaliers. Avec un peu de patience et de discrétion, l'Ukraine peut aussi pour les voyageurs homosexuels s'avérer une remarquable destination intéressante et unique en son genre.
De plus la population en Ukraine souffre de l'épidémie catastrophique du SIDA. La ville portuaire d'Odessa est particulièrement concernée, avec un manque important en personnel et médicaments. Selon des statistiques officielles, 3000 enfants vivent dans les rues de la ville. D'après des recherches d'OCF „ The Way Home „, deux tiers des enfants des rues sont séropositifs. Ils meurent avec le diagnostic du SIDA dans de sombres caves, il n'existe pas de places disponibles dans les hôpitaux.
Les problèmes pour les autorités sont énormes. Si vous souhaitez aider ces enfants, visitez la page web de l'ONG „ The Way Home „ où vous pouvez aussi faire un don. (http://wayhome.org.ua)
Les milieux gays les mieux établis se trouvent à Kyiv, Odessa, Dnipropetrovsk, Donetsk et Kharkov.

Ucrania es un país con unos habitantes abiertos y muy hospitalarios. Con un poco de paciencia y discreción, Ucrania es también un destino turístico interesante, único y bonito para los homosexuales. Ucrania es el segundo país más grande de Europa Oriental después de Rusia y fue la primera de las antiguas repúblicas soviéticas que derogó la penalización de los actos homosexuales voluntarios entre mayores de edad. La edad de consentimiento, tanto para homosexuales como para heterosexuales, está fijada en los 16 años. Sin embargo, las autoridades ucranianas actúan todavía como si no existiera la homosexualidad ni los homosexuales y apenas se hace referencia al tema en la legislación.
La organización gay-lésbica más antigua y conocida de Ucrania es el centro para gays y lesbianas Nash Mir (véase en Nash Mir), que desde hace 9 años lucha por la equiparación total y el reconocimiento social de la comunidad homosexual en Ucrania fomentando la visibilidad y la tolerancia hacia la homosexualidad. No obstante, según datos de Nash Mir, un 53% de los homosexuales ha sufrido alguna discriminación social.
Por este motivo, muchos gays y lesbianas prefieren no salir del armario ante su familia ni en su ámbito social, especialmente fuera de las grandes ciudades. Otra encuesta reflejó que sólo el 42% de los ucranianos considera necesaria la equiparación de derechos civiles para los homosexuales. En adición, la población de Ucrania sufre la devastadora epidemia del SIDA, siendo la ciudad portuaria de Odessa una de las más afectadas por este problema; no hay personal suficiente ni medicamentos disponibles. Según las estadísticas oficiales, cerca de tres mil niños viven en las calles de Odessa y, conforme a estudios realizados por la OCF „The Way Home“, dos tercios de estos son VIH-positivos. Los diagnosticados con SIDA mueren en sótanos oscuros, dada la falta de camas de hospital disponibles para ellos.
Los problemas para las autoridades son enormes. Si desea ayudar a estos niños, visite el sitio Web de la ONG „The Way Home“, donde podrá realizar también donativos. (http://wayhome.org.ua)
El ambiente gay se encuentra en las ciudades de Kyiv (la capital), Odessa, Dnipropetrovsk, Donetsk y Kharkov.

Dopo la Russia, l'Ucraina è il secondo Paese esteuropeo più grande per estensione. L'Ucraina è stato il primo Paese ex sovietico ad abolire la persecuzione penale di rapporti omosessuali volontari e consenzienti. L'età del consenso è di 16 anni per omosessuali come per eterosessuali. Tuttavia le autorità del Paese cercano di ignorare gli omosessuali e l'omosessualità in genere evitando di trattare il tema dal punto di vista legislativo. L'organizzazione gay e lesbica più antica e più famosa del Paese è il centro gay-lesbico Nash Mir, fondato nove anni fa; il Nash Mir si impegna per la parificazione e il riconoscimento sociale di gay, lesbiche, bisessuali e transessuali, dando loro la dovuta visibilità e propagando un rapporto più tollerante nei confronti dell'omosessualità. Secondo alcuni dati del Mash Mir, il 53% degli omosessuali ucraini ha dovuto fare i conti con discriminazioni sociali, queste discriminazioni sociali sono addirittura degenerate in veri e propri attacchi e violenze fisiche. Per questi motivi, molti gay e molte lesbiche, specialmente al di fuori delle grandi città, evitano di fare il coming out in famiglia o in un altro contesto sociale. Un'altra statistica rivela che solo il 42% degli ucraini ritiene necessaria una parità omosessuale.
In Ucraina l'AIDS ha raggiunto livelli epidemici molto preoccupanti. Odessa è una città che è particolarmente toccata da questo problema; inoltre nella città manca il personale e i medicinali a disposizione non sono tanti. Secondo statistiche attuali per le strade di Odessa vivono circa 3000 bambini. Secondo le statistiche dell'OFC „la strada per casa“ i due terzi dei bambini di strada hanno l'HIV. Muoiono di AIDS in cantine buie e in ospedale non c'è posto per loro. I problemi per le istituzioni sono enormi. Se volete aiutare questi bambini visitate il sito della ONG e da lì potrete anche fare una donazione (http://wayhome.org.ua).
L'Ucraina è un Paese con una popolazione molto aperta ed ospitale. L'Ucraina può essere una meta turistica bella, interessante e particolare anche per omosessuali. Bisogna solo avere un po' più di discrezione del solito. Le scene gay più organizzate sono nella capitale Kyiv, a Odessa, Dnepropetrosk, Donetsk e a Kharkov.

NATIONAL GAY INFO

Nash Mir (Our World) Gay and Lesbian Center (GLM MA)
PO Box 173, Kyiv ✉ 02100 Kyiv ☎ (044) 296 34 24 🖳 www.gay.org.ua
Official Ukrainian gay and lesbian organization. Conferences, events, monitoring and advocacy, legal advice and information.

NATIONAL PUBLICATIONS

Gay.ua Newspaper (GLM)
PO Box 173, Kyiv ✉ 02100 Kyiv ☎ (044) 573 54 24 🖳 www.gay.org.ua
Information about gay life in Ukraine, with personals.

Odyn z Nas (One of Us)
PO Box 280 ✉ 01001 Kyiv ☎ (044) 284 28 45 🖳 www.gayua.com/on
Gay and lesbian magazine.

NATIONAL GROUPS

Gay Alliance, NGO (G p S WE) 10-22h
PO Box V-466 ✉ 01001 Kyiv ☎ (044) 332 00 63 🖳 www.ga.net.ua

Gay Forum of Ukraine (G)
✉ Lviv ☎ (066) 289 48 89
Lviv regional branch of the Gay Forum of Ukraine. Organisers of city tours and parties. Also tourist information.

HEALTH GROUPS

Chas Zhittya+ (Time of Life+)
✉ Kyiv ☎ (044) 254 58 40
Group for HIV+ gay men.

Cherkassy ☎ (047-2)

BARS

Erik's (B NG)
Possible meeting point for gay men.

Stadion (B NG)
A possible meeting place.

GENERAL GROUPS

Gay group (GLM)
PO Box 1356 ☏ (097) 492 40 14
Gay-Alliance-Cherkassy (GLM)
PO Box 225 ☏ (067) 402 18 78

CRUISING

-Festyvalnyy park, Dolyna Troyand beach, central stadium.

Chernigiv ☏ (046-2)

BARS

Safari (B NG)
Prospekt Myru *In the same building as Hradetsky Hotel, separate entrance from Prospect Myru*
Possible meeting place for gay men.

GENERAL GROUPS

Gay Group (GLM)
c/o Olexiy, PO Box 1221

CRUISING

-Central alley in the direction of the riverboat station on town's banks
-WC near Katerynburgska church at the start of the Blvd (across the entrance)
-Beach at the lake behind the walking bridge over Desna river (summer only)
-Area around the railway station near the pedestrians' bridge.

Chernivtsi ☏ (037-2)

CAFES

Bomond (B MC)
Miteteina (B GLM M MA)
2, Ruska Street *Near Central Square*

GENERAL GROUPS

Parallel Gay Group (GLM)
PO Box 534 ☏ (050) 374 59 70 (Yuriy)

CRUISING

-In the so-called Hydropark, park area along the Prut river
-Yunik internet club, Stashuka Street
-Railway station and the neighbourhood.

Dnipropetrovsk

CRUISING

-Park Shevchenko at the fountain
-Territory at the fountain at Karl Marx Av., near the central store Chkalovsky park
-Vorontsovsky beach.

Donetsk ☏ (062-2)

CAFES

Oleksandr Khanzhenkov Cinema (B NG)
Universytetska *In the building of Zvezdochka cinema*
A possible meeting place.

DANCECLUBS

NLO (B D g YC)
89 Ilyicha Street *At the crossroads with Mariya Ulyanova Street* ☏ 859 944
Virus Night Club (B D g MA)
20 Polotska Street ☏ 231 550

GENERAL GROUPS

Initiative Gay Group (GLM)
☏ (097) 929 14 54

CRUISING

-White Nights beach in Scherbakov park
-Square near Krupskaya library
-Area near/around the opera
-Around the Saint Michael's statue, Soborna Square.

Ivano-Frankivsk ☏ (034-2)

BARS

Dio (B MC NG)
8-a, Mickiewicza
A possible meeting place for gay men.

CRUISING

-Central alley near Adam Mickiewicz monument
-Railway station
-Central alley of the Internationalist soldiers Park.

Kharkiv ☏ (057-2)

BARS

Versal (Verssay) (B g MC)
Svobody Square *M° University, in front of Kharkiv hotel*
Zolotoye Runo (B g MC) 12-22h
37, Sumska Street

DANCECLUBS

Barsaban (B D GLM M MC) Café and restaurant Mon-Fri 11-23, danceclub Thu-Sun 22-6h
19, Rymarska *In the centre of the city* ☏ (057-2) 750 94 13
🖳 www.barbazan.com.ua
Club for GL people with dance hall and three VIP areas, a café and a restaurant.
Bolero (B D G MC)
56, Prospekt 50-Letiya VLKSM ☏ (057-2) 714 07 38

SAUNAS/BATHS

City Bath House No. 2, „Kholodnogorskaya" (g SB WE) 8-21h
140-a, Poltavsky Shliakh *M° Kholodna Gora* ☏ (057-2) 247 65 65
Frequented by gays at the weekend.
Zdorovya (g MC SB) 9-21h
7, Lermontovska Street *M° Pushkinska* ☏ (057-2) 704 13 74

CRUISING

-Gorky Park, Sumska Street, (benches on the central alley and public faciltities near the tennis court)
-Unofficial gay beach in the Hydropark
-Shevchenko Park, near Lenin monument and the internet club, mostly 18-21h.

Kherson ☏ (055-2)

BARS

Bomons (B g MC)
Ushakova Street *In front of Lenin park*

CRUISING

-Park Leninskogo Komsomolu, benches near the fountain
-Embankment of the Dnipro River, at the starting point of Ushakova Av.
-Benches at the crossroads of Suvorova Street near Lenin Park.

Khmelnytsky

CRUISING

-Beach on the Bug river
-Benches near the regional philharmonics
-Ivan Franko Park
-Railway station.

Kirovograd

CRUISING

-Benches on Kirov Square
-Kovalivsky Park
-Embankment from the side of UTO supermarket
-Park near Kirovograd National Technical University
-Park near Taras Shevchenko monument.

Kremenchug ☏ (053-6)

DANCECLUBS

■ **Blakytna Hvilya (Blue Wave)** (B D GLM MA)
☏ (050) 566 77 42 (Yuriy)
Secret gay party. Call for location and further details.

CRUISING

-Park at the central city beach close to Kruchkovsky Bridge.

Kryvyi Rig ☏ (056-4)

MEN'S CLUBS

■ **Nash Klub (Our Club)** (B G MA)
PO Box 110 ☏ (056-4) 91 51 23 (Yuriy)
Call for details!

DANCECLUBS

■ **GL Club** (B D GLM MA)
☏ (066) 285 40 65
Secret club for gays and lesbians. Call for further information!

CRUISING

-Shevchenko Park.

Kyiv ☏ 044

Kiev (Kyiv) is the capital of Ukraine. Today it is a modern city with a population of around 3 million people. Kiev has beautiful architecture in the historic centre and a thriving cultural and cafe scene. The gay community is not particularly strong, but it is developing rapidly. A lot of young men move from the province to Kyiv for jobs and a more tolerant lifestyle.

Kiew (Kyiv) ist die Hauptstadt der Ukraine und heute eine moderne Stadt mit rund drei Millionen Einwohnern. Kiew besticht durch wunderschöne Architektur im historischen Zentrum sowie durch eine blühende Kultur- und Cafészene. Das schwule Leben ist nicht besonders sichtbar, aber es entwickelt sich schnell. Viele junge Männer ziehen vom Land nach Kiew, nicht nur wegen der Arbeit, sondern auch des toleranteren Lebensstils wegen.

Kiev est la capitale de l'Ukraine et est aujourd'hui une ville moderne avec près de 3 millions d'habitants. Kiev éblouit par l'architecture éblouissante de son centre historique de même que par sa vie culturelle et ses nombreux cafés.
La vie gay n'est pas particulièrement visible mais se développe rapidement. Beaucoup d'hommes jeunes déménagent de leur village pour habiter à Kiev.

Kiev (Kyiv) es la capital de Ucrania y hoy en día es una ciudad moderna con cerca de 3 millones de habitantes. Kíev gusta tanto por su maravillosa arquitectura en su centro histórico así como por su floreciente vida cultural y sus cafés.
La comunidad gay no es particularmente fuerte, pero se desarrolla rápidamente. Mucha gente joven se muda de la provincia hacia Kiev.

Kiev è la capitale dell'Ucraina e conta circa 3 milioni di abitanti. Kiev affascina molti turisti per la sua splendida architettura nel centro storico, ma anche per la sua fiorente vita culturale e per i suoi bar e caffè. La scena gay non è molto grossa, ma si sta sviluppando. Molti giovani si trasferiscono dalla campagna a Kiev.

GAY INFO

■ **Gay Alliance** (G)
☏ (044) 332 00 63
■ **Nash Mir (Our World) Gay and Lesbian Centre** (GLM)
PO Box 173 ☏ (044) 573 54 24 🖳 www.gay.org.ua
Non-governmental organisation.

PUBLICATIONS

■ **Odyn z Nas (One of us)** (GLM) 24hrs
PO Box 280 ☏ (044) 228 28 45 🖳 www.gayua.com/on
Gay and lesbian magazine. Information about gay life in the Ukraine with personals.

BARS

■ **Kiber (Cyber)** (B GLM MA) Mon-Sun 22-6h
21, Prorizna Street *In the centre* ☏ (044) 278 05 48

CAFES

■ **Kofta** (B D glm M MA) 24hrs
6-a, Luteranska *Near Khreshatyk Street* ☏ (044) 537 09 02
Frequented by gays, especially in the summer time.

DANCECLUBS

■ **Androgin** (! AC B D DR GLM ST YC) Thu-Sun 22-6h
26/2 Garmatna Street *M° Shulyavska – Rostok Culture Centre*
☏ (044) 496 19 83 🖳 www.gay-club.com.ua
One of Kievs most popular clubs. Two dance halls (with Russian/ Ukrainian and international music), VIP area, darkrooms. Shows on weekends at 2h.
■ **Pomada** (B D GLM M MC) Daily 18-6h
6, Zankovetskoy Street ☏ (044) 279 55 52
🖳 www.pomada-club.com.ua
The most popular gay place to go in the city. It is located in very center of Kyiv, five mins walk from the main street Khreshyatik. There are three different areas in Pomada: disco, lounge and a restaurant offering European and Ukrainian cuisine.

ESCORTS & STUDIOS

■ **Top Escorts**
PO Box 192 ☏ (044) 063 474 0380 (mobile)
Also possible via SMS.

SAUNAS/BATHS

■ **911** (B DR DU GLM PI SA SB VS WE) Tue-Sun 20-6h
Artema Street, 10 *Near Lvivska Square, Lvivska Plotsha area*
☏ (044) 272 15 81
Not like a typical European sauna. Small and somewhat basic.

APARTMENTS

■ **Heaven 7 Apartments** (AC glm I MA MSG PK RWB RWS RWT VA) Daily 9-23.30h local time
Kovpaka Street 17 *City centre* ☏ (044) 093 201 5161
There are 2 apartments in new houses with parking and security in the centre of Kiev. The first one-room apartment is 52 m² with kitchen, bathroom and balcony. It has a king size bed, LCD-TV, unlimited internet. The second apartment is120 m² has 2 rooms, a big hall with studio kitchen, 2 toilets, a big bathroom and 2 balconies. It has 50" plasma TV, unlimited internet WiFi. Both apartments are only 4 minutes walking to metro station. The owner is also a guide (in English or German) as well as translator or driver. He also has information and recommendations about gay life in Kiev.

GENERAL GROUPS

■ **Ukrainian LGBT Center Initiative Group** (GLM)
☏ (067) 503 64 99

HEALTH GROUPS

■ **Help-line on HIV/AIDS** (glm)
☏ (044) 8 (800) 500 45 10

■ **Self-help group for HIV-positive gay men, counselling** (glm)
Hetman Mazepa ☎ (044) 254 58 40

SWIMMING

-Gidropark (towards the Venetsianska Strait) – M° Gidropark
-Nudist beach on Truhanovy island (cross the river by the boat from Hydropark).

CRUISING

-Khreshchatyk Street from M° Khreshchatyk towards Bessarabsky market place
-Hydropark (the bridge to the Venetian strait, near WC)
-Shevchenko Park (alley near WC)
-Internet-clubs: in Orbita cinema on Khreshchatyk Street, Bunker club in basement of Kyiv cinema near M° Lva Tolstogo.

Lugansk ☎ (064-2)

BARS

■ **Halena** (B g MC)
Frunze Street *Near Luganks Machine Building College*
☎ (050) 167 38 49 (Sergey)

GENERAL GROUPS

■ **Gay Forum of Ukraine** (G)
☎ (066) 319 69 30
Lugansk regional branch of the Gay Forum of Ukraine. Good contact for gay info on Lugansk. Ask for Andriy.
■ **Resource Centre for Gay Men** (GLM)
PO Box 62 ☎ (064(2)) 47 12 22 🖳 www.gay.org.ua
HIV/AIDS counselling.

CRUISING

-Okolitsa Case (Sat), take a taxi-bus to Yubileiny settlement, stop Oblastnoe Gai
-Park at Krasnaya Square near Dom Techniky
-Benches near Laval supermarket.

Lutsk

CRUISING

-Railway station and neighbourhood
-Lesya Ukrainka central park
-Area around the embankment in the Park of 900 years of Lutsk.

Lviv ☎ (032-2)

DANCECLUBS

■ **André Gay Parties** (D GLM m YC)
17 Krushelnytskoyi Street ☎ (067) 672 03 42 🖳 www.boys-lvov.at.ua
Call for details. Further party events and information on parties from Gay Parties of Andriy Kosmo, ☎ (066) 289 48 89 or and-lv@mail.ru

CRUISING

-Badyorist public bathhouse (35 Turgenev Street)
-Alley from the opera to Shevchenko monument
-Tsisarska Kava Café near Ivan Podkova monument.
-Videnska Kava Café, Prospect Svobody, opp. Taras Shevchenko monument.

Mariupol

CRUISING

-Primorsky Blvd at the shore
-Square near the Drama Theatre
-Molodezhny Beach in Peschanoe settlement. Nudist beach at the end
-Alley in front of the Central Post Office.

Mykolayiv ☎ (051-2)

GENERAL GROUPS

■ **Liga** 10-19h
110, Potyomkinska ☎ (051-2) 59 49 00 🖳 www.gay.nikolaev.ua
Gay and lesbian community center, self-help group, discussion club.

CRUISING

-Old WC in Pobeda Park near the stadium.

Odessa ☎ (048-2)

DANCECLUBS

■ **Gay Club 69** (B D G YC) Fri-Sat 23-?h
5, Pushkinska *Corner of Deribasovska Street, opp. Tema*
☎ (048-2) 724 23 03
■ **Tema (Theme)** (B D GLM YC) Tue-Sun 22-6h
6, Pushkinska *Corner of Deribasovska Street, opp. Chornomorets*
☎ (048-2) 33 88 24

SWIMMING

-Beach of Chkalov sanatorium, also at adjacent stony beach (NU)
-Frantsuzsky Blvd, beach of Chkalov Sanatorium (take tram 5 to get there).

CRUISING

-From Pushkin monument to Duke Richelier monument along Lanzheronovskaya Street
-City garden along Deribassovskaya Street
-Above Chkalov sanatorium, next to the old elevator (day & night)
-Park next to the railway station, last stop of tram 18 (Kanatnaya Street, AYOR).
-Pobedy Park across from the Sports Palace
-WC on Kalantai Street near railway station.

Poltava

CRUISING

-Slavy Park (near the monument to Poltavskaya bytva)
-Petrovsky Park (between Lenina and Oktyabrskaya Street) in the center of the park.

Sevastopol ☎ (069-2)

BARS

■ **Qbar** (B G MA) Daily 11-24h
8-a, Lenin *100m from Nakhimova square* ☎ (093) 679 31 30 (mobile)
🖳 www.qbar.com.ua
Bar with live music and parties for gays.

CRUISING

-Admirala Ushakova Square
-WC and alleys adjacent to the Matrossky Club (the Chornomorsky Flot Theatre).

Simeiz ☎ (065-4)

BARS

■ **Yozhyki** (B g)
Traditional meeting place for gay men. Very popular in summer among ex-USSR gay community.

SWIMMING

-Wild beach under the Koshka mountain (30 km from Yalta by bus 26 or 43, then direction Lenin Sanatorium, 50 m ahead and down the sea, right after the rock overlooking the sea (Simeiz is a well-known gay resort in summer).

Simferopol ☏ (065-2)

GENERAL GROUPS

■ **Gay Forum of Ukraine** (G)
☏ (050) 163 27 47 (Sergiy)
Crimea Republican branch of the Gay Forum of Ukraine.

■ **LIGS Inintiative Group** (GLM)
☏ (050) 380 86 64 (Ivan)

CRUISING

-Central city baths
-Park between the Central Post Office and Crimean Parliament
-Park near the Gorky Drama Theatre
-Gagarin park.

Vinnytsya ☏ (043-2)

BARS

■ **Na dyvanah (On the Sofas)** (B g MA)
3, Kyivska *In the hall of Zhovtnevy Hotel*

HELP WITH PROBLEMS

■ **Chance** (glm)
PO Box 4266 ☏ (043-2) 57 80 84
Psychological counselling on sexual orientation.

CRUISING

-Central Gorky park
-Railway station
-Central city baths, in the Pershotravneva Street.

Yalta

CRUISING

-Embankment, in particular in the „breach" section, steps to the sea, across from the Bilyy Lev (White Lion) restaurant
-Toilet opp. the marine passenger terminal and the cafe above this WC.

Zaporizhzhia ☏ (061-2)

BARS

■ **Antrakt** (B G)
1, Shevchenko Blvd

DANCECLUBS

■ **Gay Parties** (D GLM MA)
☏ (061 2) 34 66 50 (Fedir)

GENERAL GROUPS

■ **Drugoe Izmerenie (The Other Dimension)** (GLM)
54, Mikoyana, apt. 4a ☏ (061-2) 68 46 20

■ **Zaporizhzhia Center of Sexual Minorities** (GLM)
PO Box 3857 ☏ (061 2) 96 72 49

CRUISING

-Velikoy Otechestvennoy Voiny ploschad (opp. city hall)

United Arab Emirates

Name: Vereinigte Arabische Emirate · Emiratos Árabes Unidos · Emirati Arabi
Location: Middle East
Initials: UAE
Time: GMT +4
International Country Code: ☏ 971
International Access Code: ☏ 00
Language: Arabic
Area: 77,700km² / 29,729 sq. mi
Currency: 1 Dirham (Dh) = 100 Fils
Population: 4,533,000
Capital: Abu Zaby (Abu Dhabi)
Religions: 96% Muslims
Climate: Between November and April the climate is at its best and not too hot.

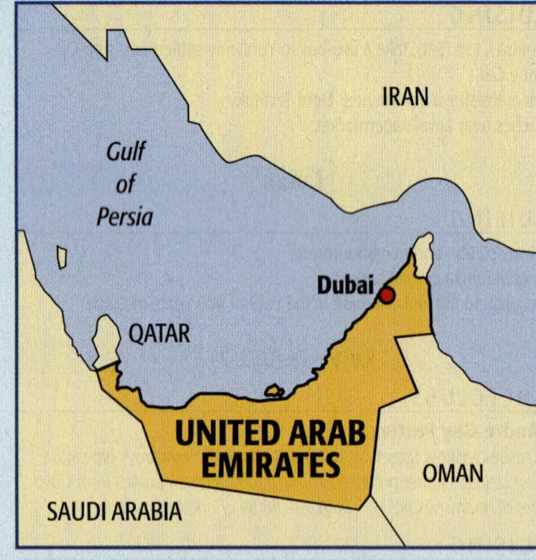

The United Arab Emirates has some sodomy laws, the Abu Dhabi Penal Code makes sodomy punishable with imprisonment of up to 14 years, the Penal Code of Dubai imposes imprisonment of up to 10 years on consensual sodomy, although punishment can be more severe if defendants are charged under Islamic law, rather than under the secular penal code.

After the closure in Dubai of a nightclub on the orders of Dubai's Crown Prince, General Sheikh Mohammed al-Maktoum for hosting a gay night featuring a transvesite from Birmingham, the gay scene came to the surface. The Diamond Club was shut, but for the hundreds who attended its gay night, a taboo was broken in Dubai.

Dubai has a flourishing nightclub scene, and drugs like Ecstasy are readily available, although strictly illegal. The drug scene applies however mainly to the international tourists and not the local inhabitants. As the commercial capital of the Gulf and a major international port, Dubai is home to thousands of expatriate workers from Britain, Russia, South Asia and all the Arab countries.

The local population in certain Arab states like UAE and Qatar, although deeply religious, tend to be more liberal than expected, in respect to homosexuality. They would never admit this to be the case but even the police tend to close an eye to the gay scene and Internet controls, common in many Arab states do not take place here. Nevertheless we strongly advise that you adhere to local customs and avoid any displays of affection in public.

Dubai is a fantastic city with unique architecture and a very high standard of living. The newly opened metro system takes you directly from the airport to the city centre and out to the amazing seaside hotels. Take a cruise on the creek by Abra and just stroll through the gold Souk and the neighbouring Dhow station you will get a feel for the old Dubai.

In den Vereinigten Arabischen Emiraten gibt es verschiedene Gesetze gegen Homosexualität. Das Strafgesetzbuch von Abu Dhabi bestraft homosexuelle Aktivitäten mit bis zu 14 Jahren Gefängnis, nach dem Strafgesetz von Dubai wird einvernehmlicher schwuler Sex mit bis zu 10 Jahren Haft geahndet. Das Strafmaß kann noch höher ausfallen, wenn die Beschuldigten nach islamischem Recht und nicht nach dem weltlichen Strafrecht angeklagt werden.

Auf Geheiß des Kronprinzen von Dubai, General Scheich Mohammed al-Maktoum, wurde der Diamond Nachtclub in Dubai geschlossen, der eine schwule Party mit einem Transvestiten aus Birmingham veranstaltet hatte. Bei diesem Anlass wurde die schwule Szene sichtbar: Für die mehreren hundert Gäste der Gay Night war ein Tabu gebrochen. Im Land gibt es ein blühendes Nachtleben; Drogen, wie das streng verbotene Extasy, sind leicht erhältlich. Die Drogenszene richtet sich allerdings eher auf internationale Touristen und nicht auf die Einheimischen aus. Als Handelszentrum am Golf und große internationale Hafenstadt ist Dubai die Heimat tausender ausländischer Arbeitskräfte- unter anderem aus Großbritannien, Russland und Südasien.

Obwohl die einheimische Bevölkerung in bestimmten arabischen Staaten wie UAE und Qatar tief religiös ist, hat sie liberalere Ansichten hinsichtlich der Homosexualität als allgemein erwartet. Sogar die Polizei tendiert dazu, beide Augen für die homosexuelle Szene zuzudrücken. Die Internetüberwachung, allgemeine Praxis in vielen arabischen Staaten, findet hier nicht statt. Dennoch empfehlen wir, dass Sie die einheimischen Gebräuche respektieren und jede Provokation in der Öffentlichkeit vermeiden.

Dubai ist eine fantastische Stadt mit einzigartiger Architektur und einem sehr hohen Lebensstandard. Das im September 2009 eröffnete U-Bahn-System befördert Sie direkt vom Flughafen bis zum Stadtzentrum und zu den bewundernswerten Strandhotels.

Unternehmen Sie eine Schiffstour auf dem Fluß von Abra, schlendern Sie durch den Gold-Souk und die benachbarte Dhow Station. Hier werden sie ein Gefühl vom alten Dubai erhalten.

Les Émirats Arabes Unis disposent de lois contre la sodomie. Le code pénal d'Abu Dhabi punit la sodomie par des peines pouvant aller jusqu'à quatorze ans de prison. Le code pénal de Dubai impose des peines d'emprisonnement pouvant aller jusqu'à dix ans pour sodomie avec consentement, bien que la punition puisse être beaucoup plus sévère si le coupable est jugé en vertu de la loi islamique plutôt que de la loi civile.

Depuis que le prince de Dubai, le Cheikh Général Mohammed Al-Maktoum, ait fermé un club de nuit pour avoir présenté une soirée gaie mettant en vedette une travestie de Birmingham, la scène gaie a émergé. Le Diamond Club a été fermé, mais pour les centaines de participants à la dite soirée, un tabou a été rompu à Dubai.

Dubai jouit d'une scène nocturne florissante et les drogues telles que l'extasy sont facilement disponibles, bien qu'elles soient strictement illégales. Le commerce de la drogue s'applique plutôt aux touristes qu'aux habitants du pays. En tant que ville portuaire internationale et capitale commerciale du Golfe Persique, Dubai est également le domicile de milliers d'ouvriers expatriés venant de Grande-Bretagne, de Russie, du sud-est asiatique et d'autre régions du globe.

Bien que la population autochtone dans certains pays arabes tels que les E.A.U. et le Qatar soit profondément religieuse, elle a des vues assez libérales quant à l'homosexualité en général. Même la police tend à fermer les yeux devant la scène homosexuelle. La surveillance sur internet, pratique généralisée dans beaucoup de pays arabes, n'a pas lieu ici. Cependant nous vous recommandons de respecter les usages locaux et d'éviter toute provocation en public.

Dubaï est une ville fantastique avec une architecture unique et un niveau de vie très élevé. Le réseau du métro ouvert en septembre 2009 vous transporte directement de l'aéroport au centre-ville et aux magnifiques hôtels en bord de plage.

Faites une ballade en bateau Abra ou Dhow, promenez-vous dans le Gold-Souk et ça vous donnera une idée du vieux Dubaï.

En los Emiratos Árabes Unidos hay diferentes leyes en contra de la homosexualidad. El Código Penal de Abu Dhabi castiga los actos homosexuales con pena de hasta 14 años de cárcel; según la ley penal de Dubai, el sexo homosexual de mutuo acuerdo está penalizado con hasta 10 años de arresto. El grado de la pena puede ser incluso más alto, si los inculpados son acusados según el derecho islámico y no según el derecho penal universal.
Después de que por orden del príncipe heredero de Dubai, el jeque general Mohammed al-Maktoum, fuera clausurado un club nocturno en el que se estaba celebrando una noche gay con un trasvesti de Birmingham, el ambiente homosexual se hizo más visible. El Diamond Club en efecto se clausuró pero así se rompió en Dubai un tabú entre los más de cien invitados a la noche gay. En el país existe una vida nocturna floreciente; las drogas, así como el estrictamente prohibido extasy, están al alcance fácilmente. El mundo de la droga se dirige más bien a los turistas internacionales que a los nacionales. Como importante centro de comercio en el Golfo y gran ciudad portuaria internacional, Dubai es el hogar de miles de trabajadores extranjeros procedentes, entre otros, de Gran Bretaña, Rusia y del sur de Asia.
Aunque la población local en algunos países árabes como Emiratos Árabes Unidos y Qatar es profundamente religiosa, cabría esperar en general una visión más liberal sobre la homosexualidad. Incluso la policía tiende a cerrar los ojos ante el ambiente homosexual. La vigilancia de Internet, una práctica común en muchos estados árabes, no tiene lugar aquí. Sin embargo, le recomendamos respetar las costumbres locales, y evitar la provocación en público.
Dubai es una ciudad maravillosa con una arquitectura única y un estándar de vida muy alto. Inaugurado en septiembre de 2009, el sistema de Metro, le transportará directamente desde el aeropuerto hasta el centro de la ciudad y a hoteles con playas de ensueño.
Haga un tour por el río en un Abra, pasee por los „Gold-Souk" (callejones donde se vende oro) y por la estación de Dhow, aquí se va a poder hacer una idea de cómo era la antigua Dubai.

Negli Emirati Arabi ci sono diverse leggi contro l'omosessualità. Il Codice Penale di Abu Dhabi punisce attività omosessuali con una pena fino a 14 anni di reclusione; secondo la legge penale di Dubai il sesso gay consenziente viene giudicato con una pena fino a 10 anni di prigionia. Il grado di pena può però essere anche aggravato qualora gli imputati vengano giudicati secondo il diritto islamico e non il diritto penale occidentale. Da quando, su ordine del Principe ereditario di Dubai, lo sceicco Mohammed al-Maktoum, è stato chiuso un Nightclub, che aveva organizzato una serata gay con lo show di un travestito di Birmingham, la scena gay è al centro dell'attenzione. Il Diamond Club è stato chiuso, ma per le centinaia di omosessuali della Gay Night ciò ha significato, a Dubai, la rottura di un tabù. Nel paese si avverte la presenza di una sempre maggiore vita notturna; le droghe, come la vietatissima Ecstasy, sono facilmente recuperabili, soprattutto per i turisti internazionali. Essendo centro commerciale sul golfo e una grande città portuale internazionale, Dubai è patria di migliaia di lavoratori stranieri, tra i quali inglesi, russi e sud-asiatici.
Sebbene la popolazione locale di alcuni Stati arabi, come per esempio quella degli Emirati Arabi e del Qatar, sia profondamente religiosa, nei confronti dell'omosessualità hanno un approccio più aperto di quanto ci si possa aspettare. Persino la polizia tende a chiudere un occhio nei confronti della scena gay. La vigilanza su internet, prassi normalissima in tutti i Paesi arabi, non viene praticata negli Emirati Arabi. Tuttavia vi consigliamo di rispettare le usanze locali e di evitare in pubblico ogni tipo di comportamento che possa essere ritenuto provocatorio. Dubai è una città fantastica dall'architettura particolarissima e con uno standard di vita molto alto. La nuova rete della metropolitana, inaugurata a settembre del 2009, collega l'aeroporto con il centro città e con gli spettacolari alberghi lungo la spiaggia. Vi consigliamo di fare un tour in traghetto lungo il fiume Abra, di visitare il mercato dell'oro (Gold-Souk) e di vedere la vicina Dhow Station. In questi luoghi respirerete l'aria della vecchia Dubai.

Abu Dhabi ☎ 2

BARS

AM/PM (AC B CC MA NG)
Seaside Cornish *In Intercontinental Hotel*
Nice place. Busy at the weekends and Thu & Fri.

Eight Restaurant & Bar (! AC B CC DM M MC NG) Open daily 22-3h.
Souk Qaryat Al *At Shangri La* ☎ 558 1988
Best on Sundays. Probably the best club in Abu Dhabi. The DJ's they have are the best in U.A.E. The cocktails here are excellent.

DANCECLUBS

Colosseum (AC B D MC NG PK s) Sun-Fri 22h-late. Closed Sat
Tourist Club Area *Situated very close to Le Meridian Hotel*
The largest nightclub of Abu Dhabi. Monday is Airline Crew Night where 50% discount is given on total bill for all Airline staff and crew when they produce their crew card. A good night to visit.

CRUISING

-The Corniche (Abu Dhabi's coastal road and sidewalk, close to centre of town) 24-2h. From the clocktower roundabout to the Volcano roundabout, cruising is frequent on the Cornish, take care of the escorts & thieves and police controls.
-Hmaidan Mall (Abu Dhabi – Hamdan Street) mostly gay crowds cruise using mobiles Bluetooth while sitting in the numerous cafés in the mall.

Dubai ☎ 4

CAFES

Green Café (AYOR cc MA NG) 24hrs
Deira, Itisalat side *Green Center, near Maktum Bridge*
Be discreet!

DANCECLUBS

Babylon Thu & Fri
Khalid Bin Waleed Road *At Park Regis Hotel*
New club. Close to Submarine Club. It is on Thu and Fri (Friday is a ladies policy so the guys all have to bring a girl to get in).

N-Dulge (AYOR CC MA NG) Fri
Palm of Jumeirah Street *At the Atlantis Palm Jumeirah Hotel*
Former Sanctuary. Not so many gay men here anymore.

Submarine (AC AYOR B CC MA NG)
Mankhoul Street *At Dhow Palace Hotel*
This bar is known to be the hanging out place for the gay cabine crews.

SWIMMING

-Jumeirah open beach (AYOR, g, MA) Seaside Cornish – Jumeirah – opp. Jumeirah Mosque. Especially in summer on Thu nights, late evenings, you have to be aware of the CID (undercover police), as a few people have been caught flirting. Jumeirah is the right place to pick up someone and take him to your hotel room.

CRUISING

-Nasser Square (AYOR, MA, NG), Deira area. Popular & crowded area in the old part of Dubai, beware of escorts and thieves as well as police controls.
-Fitness First Gym at Ibn Battouta Mall. Please be discreet!
-Fitness First Gym at DIFC (Dubai International Financial center)
-Dubai Mall (Sheikh Zayed Road) mostly gay crowds cruise using mobiles Bluetooth while sitting in the numerous cafés in the mall.

Sharjah

CRUISING

-Buhaira (lake) Cornish (AYOR, NG) in Buhaira. Buhaira's Cornish not far from the Buhaira's mosque. Especially in summer on Thu nights, late evenings, you have to be aware of the CID (secret police), thieves and escorts

United Kingdom

Name: Great Britain · Großbritannien · Grande Bretagne · Gran Bretaña
Location: North-western Europe
Initials: GB
Time: GMT
International Country Code: ☏ 44 (omit 0 from area code)
International Access Code: ☏ 00
Language: English
Area: 242,100 km² / 93,451 sq mi.
Currency: 1 Pound Sterling (£) = 100 Pence
Population: 59,867,000
Capital: London
Religions: 57% Anglicans, 15% Protestants, 13% Catholics
Climate: The climate is mild and the rainfall is not spectacular. The least hospitable months for visitors are Nov-Feb.
Important gay cities: London, Brighton, Blackpool, Edinburgh, Manchester

In England, Scotland and Wales the age of consent is 16 years old, equal to that of the heterosexual age of consent. In Northern Ireland the age of consent is currently 17, this was changed to 16 years old in 2009.
Lesbian gay and bisexual people in England, Scotland and Wales are protected by a number of laws. They are protected from discrimination at work, and from discrimination when accessing goods and services, for example, when staying in hotels or when accessing healthcare.
Same-sex couples in England, Scotland, Wales and Northern Ireland can form legally recognised partnerships, called civil partnerships. These give same-sex couples rights akin to those of heterosexual married couples.
Stonewall's research has shown that heterosexual British people are largely in favour of lesbian and gay equality. In our Living Together research in 2007, more than a third of people said they have a high opinion of lesbians and gay men. Nine out of ten people said they want anti-gay bulling to be tackled, and nine out of ten support anti-discrimination law in the workplace.
Civil partnerships have allowed same-sex couples to have the same rights as heterosexual married couples, giving same-sex relationships real credibility and stability in the eyes of the general population. David Cameron, prime minister of the current Conservative/Liberal Democrat government, has voiced his support of same-sex marriage on October 2011.

In England, Schottland und Wales liegt das allgemeine Schutzalter bei 16 Jahren. Nur in Nordirland lag es noch bei 17, wurde aber Anfang 2009 auf ebenfalls 16 Jahre gesenkt.
In England, Schottland und Wales werden Schwule, Lesben und Bisexuelle durch eine ganze Reihe von Regelungen im Berufsleben und bei der Inanspruchnahme von Waren oder Dienstleistungen, zum Beispiel bei Hotelübernachtungen oder in der Gesundheitsversorgung, vor Diskriminierung geschützt. In England, Schottland, Wales sowie Nordirland können gleichgeschlechtliche Paare ihre Partnerschaften eintragen lassen, was ihnen einen ähnlichen Rechtsstatus verleiht wie heterosexuellen Ehen.
Von der Schwulenorganisation Stonewall durchgeführte Umfragen haben ergeben, dass ein Großteil der britischen Heterosexuellen die Gleichstellung von Lesben und Schwulen befürwortet. In der im Jahr 2007 durchgeführten Umfrage "Living Together" verliehen über ein Drittel der Befragten ihrer guten Meinung von Lesben und Schwulen Ausdruck. Neun von zehn Befragten befürworten aktive Maßnahmen gegen die Viktimisierung von Lesben und Schwulen, besonders in Schulen, und ebenfalls neun von zehn Befragten unterstützen arbeitsrechtliche Antidiskriminierungsregeln.
Die eingetragenen Partnerschaften haben schwule und lesbische Paare heterosexuellen Ehepaaren so gut wie gleichgestellt, was den gleichgeschlechtlichen Beziehungen in den Augen der Öffentlichkeit erst wirkliche Glaubwürdigkeit und Stabilität verliehen hat. David Cameron, Premier der derzeitig geführten konservativ-liberalen Regierung plädierte im Oktober 2011 dafür, die Ehe für Homosexuelle zu öffnen.

En Angleterre, Ecosse et au Pays de Galles la majorité sexuelle est fixée à 16 ans. Celle-ci est fixée actuellement à 17 ans seulement en Irlande du Nord mais a été réduite à 16 ans au depart de 2009.
En Angleterre, Ecossse et au Pays de Galles, les gays, lesbiennes et bisexuels sont protégés contre les discriminations par toute une série de réglementations dans la vie professionnelle et également lors de l'accession aux biens et services, par exemple les nuitées à l'hôtel ou les services de santé.
Les couples de même sexe peuvent se faire enregistrer que ce soit en Angleterre, Ecosse, au Pays de Galles ou en Irlande du Nord, ce qui leur accorde des droits semblables aux mariages hétérosexuels
L'enquête menée par l'association gay Stonewall a révélé qu'une grande partie des Britanniques hétérosexuels approuvent l'égalité des droits pour les lesbiennes et les gays. Dans cette enquête „Living Together" réalisée en 2007, plus d'un tiers des interviewés accordent une bonne opinion envers les gays et lesbiennes. Neuf interviewés sur 10 approuvent des mesures actives contre la victimisation des lesbiennes et gays, en particulier à l'école et de même 9 personnes sur 10 soutiennent des réglementations anti-discriminatoires en droit du travail.
L'enregistrement des couples gays et lesbiens les a mis sur un pied d'égalité avec les couples mariés hétérosexuels ce qui leur a donné dès lors une crédibilité et une stabilité aux yeux de l'opinion publique. David Cameron, le Premier Ministre du gouvernement libéral-conservateur actuel plaidait en octobre 2011 pour l'ouverture du mariage aux homosexuels.

La edad de consentimiento sexual en Inglaterra, Escocia y Gales se sitúa en los 16 años de edad. Tan sólo en Irlanda del norte se encuentra el límite de edad en los 17. A principios de 2009, ese fue reducio a los 16.
En Inglaterra, Escocia y Gales se protege de la discriminación a gays, lesbianas y bisexuales mediante una serie de normativas en el ámbito laboral y en la utilización de artículos y servicios, como por ejemplo en la estancia en hoteles o en los servicios de asistencia sanitaria.
En Inglaterra, Escocia y Gales, así como en Irlanda del norte, las parejas del mismo sexo pueden registrarse como parejas de hecho con los mismos derechos que las parejas heterosexuales.
La encuesta organizada por la organización Stonewall muestra que la gran mayoría de los heterosexuales británicos está a favor de la

igualdad de derechos de gays y lesbianas. La encuesta realizada en el año 2007, „Living Together", revela la buena impresión que gays y lesbianas generan en un tercio de los encuestados. A su vez nueve de cada diez encuestados apoya activamente las medidas en contra de la victimización de gays y lesbianas, especialmente en colegios. Igualmente nueve de cada diez encuestados apoya la implementación de normativas antidiscriminación. La reglamentación de las parejas de hecho ha equiparado a las parejas de gays y lesbianas con las parejas heterosexuales, lo cual aporta credibilidad y estabilidad a las parejas del mismo sexo en lo que a visibilidad se refiere. David Cameron, el Primer Ministro de la corriente conservadora-liberal del gobierno, abogó en octubre de 2011 por que se abra el matrimonio a los homosexuales.

In Inghilterra, in Scozia e in Galles, l'età del consenso è di 16 anni. Solo nell'Irlanda del Nord è ancora di 17 anni. Alla inizio 2009, é stato abbassata anche qui a 16 anni. In Inghilterra, in Scozia e in Galles i gay, le lesbiche e i bisessuali vengono tutelati dalle discriminazioni attraverso tutta una serie di regolamenti nella vita lavorativa, ma anche per quello che riguarda l'acquisto di beni e l'usufruizione di certi servizi, come per esempio per i pernottamenti alberghieri o l'assistenza sanitaria.In Inghilterra, in Scozia, in Galles e nell'Irlanda del Nord, le coppie di persone dello stesso sesso possono far registrare ufficialmente la loro unione, potendo così godere di quasi gli stessi diritti delle coppie eterosessuali.
Secondo dei sondaggi fatti dalla associazione ‚Stonewall', una consistente parte degli eterosessuali britannici è a favore della parificazione dei diritti di lesbiche ed omosessuali. Nel sondaggio del 2007, chiamato ‚Living Together', più di un terzo degli intervistati esprimeva un giudizio positivo nei confronti di lesbiche ed omosessuali. Nove intervistati su dieci si sono dichiarati a favore di misure contro il bullismo nei confronti di omosessuali e lesbiche in particolare nelle scuole. Sempre nove su dieci degli interpellati hanno dichiarato di sostenere le regole antidiscriminatorie per quello che concerne il diritto di lavoro.
Le unioni civili hanno equiparato le coppie omosessuali e lesbiche alle coppie eterosessuali, contribuendo così a dare, agli occhi dell'opinione pubblica, più credibilità e più stabilità alle coppie dello stesso sesso. Ad ottobre del 2011 David Cameron, Premier dell'attuale governo liberal-conservatore, invitava ad aprire l'istituto del matrimonio alle coppie omosessuali.

NATIONAL PUBLICATIONS

BENT
c/o APN House, Temple Crescent ✉ LS11 8BP Leeds ☎ 8701 255 555
www.bent.com
Monthly gay magazine.

Diva Magazine
☎ 8448560643 www.divamag.co.uk

Fyne Times (GLM)
c/o Fyne Associates Ltd., Linde Buildings, 7 Nuffield Way ✉ OX14 1RJ Abingdon ☎ (01235) 468 428 www.fynetimes.co.uk
Monthly free gay magazine with a focus on venues in the south and south east.

GT (Gay Times) (GLM MA) Office hours Mon-Fri 10-18h
c/o Millivres Prowler Ltd., Unit M, 32-34 Gordon House Rd
✉ NW5 1LP London ☎ 0179 5414896
www.gaytimes.co.uk
Probably Europe's best selling information, entertainment and lifestyle magazine for gay men.

Hot Magazine
1st Floor, 50 Charles Street ✉ CF10 2GF Cardiff ☎ 845 257 4291
www.hot-magazine.co.uk
Distributed nationally, a sexy and free monthly magazine. For male adults, covering fetish, bear, leather, skinhead and sexual interests.

The UK's award winning gay radio station

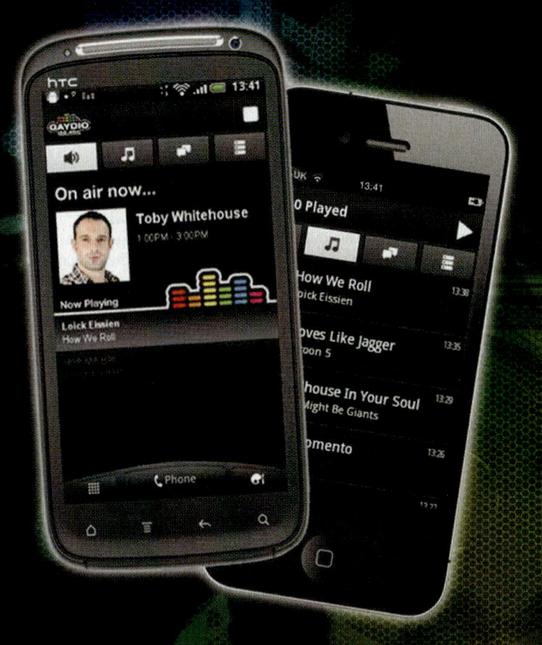

Now available worldwide
in the iPhone App Store and Android Market

Pink Paper. The
Unit M Spectrum House, 32-34 Gordon House Road ✉ NW5 1LP London ☎ (020) 7424 7400 💻 www.pinkpaper.com
Britain's only gay and lesbian newspaper available across UK with news and lifestyle information.

Positive Nation
64 Orchard Place ✉ E14 0JW London ☎ (020) 7001 0754
💻 www.positivenation.co.uk
UK's free monthly HIV magazine, published by the UK Coalition of People Living with HIV and AIDS.

Pride Publishing
1st Floor, 50 Charles Street ✉ CF10 2GF Cardiff ☎ (029) 2066 7234
💻 www.pridepublishing.co.uk
Producing national guides to promote Pride events in the UK. Producers of UK Pride Guide, Blackpool Pride Brochure, GAYBrighton, BAGs Accommodation Guide.

Puffta
c/o Millivres Prowler Ltd., Unit M, 32-34 Gordon House Road ✉ NW5 1LP London ☎ (020) 7424 7400 💻 www.puffta.co.uk
UK's leading website for gay teens.

Refresh
c/o Wild Publishing Limited, 22A Iliffe Yard ✉ SEI7 3QA London
☎ (020) 7277 4517 💻 refreshmagazine.typepad.com
Monthly glossy for gay men.

ScotsGay (GLM)
c/o Pageprint Ltd., PO Box 666 ✉ EH7 5YW Edinburgh ☎ 539 0666
💻 www.scotsgay.co.uk
Monthly magazine covering all aspects of gay life in Scotland. Available at gay venues or by calling (0906) 110 0256.

NATIONAL COMPANIES

Devote Clothing Ltd. (CC F)
Unit 106, Cremer Business Centre, 37 Cremer Street ✉ E2 8HD London Shoreditch ☎ (020) 7729 7595 💻 www.dvote.com
Design, manufacture and retail of exclusive clothing and innovative accessories.

Eurocreme
💻 www.eurocreme.com
Gay porn production company.

Fit and Twisted
✉ London ☎ 871 900 2112 (Order hotline UK)
💻 www.fitandtwisted.com
Online retail company since 1999.

Freedom Health (AC CC GLM MA) Mon-Fri 8-19h
60 Harley Street ✉ W1G 7HA London ☎ 7637 1600
💻 www.freedomhealth.co.uk
The UK's first general health clinic for gay men and lesbians. Staffed by gay doctors.

Gaydar (G)
1 The Green, Richmond, Surrey ✉ TW9 1PL Surrey 💻 gaydar.co.uk
Cruise, chat and search. With over 5,5 million members from over 140 countries worldwide.

Throb Holidays
Atlas House, Mulberry Court ✉ BA11 2UF Frome – Somerset
☎ (01373) 453 550 💻 www.throb.co.uk

Turnaround 9-17h
Unit 3, Olympia Trading Estate, Coburg Road ✉ N22 6TZ London
☎ (020) 8829 3000 💻 www.turnaround-uk.com
Trade distribution for Spartacus and other Bruno Gmünder publications and a wide range of gay & lesbian interest titles.

Yellow Brick Road Tours (G)
Communication Hse, 26 York Street ✉ W1U 6PZ London
☎ (0) 207 5026 587 💻 www.yellowbrickroadtours.com
Provides contemporary, fun and adventurous gay and lesbian holidays.

NATIONAL GROUPS

Consortium of LGBT Voluntary and Community Organisations
Unit J111, Tower Bridge Business Complex, 100 Clements Road, Southwark ✉ SE16 4DG London ☎ (020) 7064 8383
💻 www.lgbconsortium.org.uk
A national umbrella organisation which supports and promotes the work of over 500 LGBT community and voluntary groups.

Food Chain. The (GLM MA)
New North House, 202-208 New North Road ✉ N1 7BJ London
☎ (020) 7354 0333 💻 www.foodchain.org.uk
The mission of the Food Chain is to improve the health and well being of London's population living with HIV by alleviating hunger and malnutrition.

Gay Business Association (GLM MA S)
BCM GBA ✉ WC1N 3XX London ☎ 844 562 4005 💻 www.gba.org.uk
Monthly meetings for gay and lesbian professionals, plus gay exhibitions and travel fairs.

Stonewall Lobby Group (GLM) Mon-Fri 9.30-17h
Tower Building, York Road ✉ SE1 7NX London ☎ (020) 7593 1850
💻 www.stonewall.org.uk
National lobby group working for legal equality & social justice for lesbians and gays in the UK.

COUNTRY CRUISING

-A1 north →, just after Chester Street, turn off and southbound, just after Angel of the North. Woods on southbound, behind garage and travel lodge
-A134 from Thetford → Downham market, it is about 3 miles from Thetford
-A166 Bidlington Road P (5 miles out of the city centre of York)
-A17 from Sleaford, Lincolnshire. Approx. 1 mile → Newark, past the public weighbridge on the right hand side; located on the right hand side of road, hidden behind trees
-A2, follow signs for ‚Waste Reception Area'; P either side before recycling banks (best 14-18h)
-A27→ Littlington Village, before Polegate junction P
-A303 → between Minster & Chester. P Cartgate picnic area
-A33 southbound carriageway, Basingstoke →Winchester. Junction 7 P Popham Layby. AYOR, police
-A40⇆ Oxford, rest area on the left (best 16-18h)
-A41 south, from Chester → Broxton. At roundabout, turn right P also heteros and women at top end, not near toilets
-A4260 → Adderbury. Drive through Adderbury as you approach Deddington turn right at the top of the hill P
-A428 from Northampton → Castle Ashby P just before Yardley Hastings
-A43 P between Northampton & Kettering
-A435, → Studley/Evesham; you will see it signposted Alderhanger lane, it's a truck P
-A452→ Stonebridge, junction 4 of the M6, and before you get to the roundabout with the A45, AYOR, police
-A51 P between Rugeley and Lichfield this lay-by is on the left hand side, after the village of Longdon (ayor – police action!)
-A533 → Chester. Go over the blue bridge and pull into the signposted picnic area
-A580 near Haydock
-A59 → York, past petrol station P on right
-A666 ⇆ Darwen. P is on a sharp curve. Enter the woods via the first path at the Darwen end and then turn right along first path there. Beware of police
-M62, Junction 30, → Wakefield and first left towards Methley, follow road for 1/2 mile until it passes underneath M62 motorway. Immediately on exiting bridge, take immediate left turn.
-B4100 ⇆ Banbury P
-B653 between Welwyn Garden City and Wheathampstead → Welwyn Garden City, pass Lemsford turn off (right) and pass entrance to Brockett Hall P on the right
-E15 at South Shields P Soutar lighthouse
-H7 → Westcroft/Tattenhoe, after Westcroft roundabout, P opp. the district centre
-M1 junction 30 → southbound Woodhall Services only
-M1 junction 30, leaving from south, turn right (left if coming from the north) P Rother Valley

-M20 Exit Junction 8 → A20 turn north. Turn left at big layby P
-M25 Junction 10 (Guildford) 20-1h P (AYOR, police)
-M25, exit at A1081, turn right over roundabout, follow St Albans signs at next roundabout P on both sides
-M6 junction 23 on East Lancs intersection ⇆ Manchester P (AYOR)
-M53 by junction 11 P Ellesmere Port
-M58 exit St. Helens junction,→ St. Helens P best after 20h

Aberdeen - Grampian ☎ 01224

BARS

Cheerz (B d G MC S) 19-2, Fri & Sat -3h
11 Hadden Street ☎ (01224) 594511
Bar with shows and more. Very quiet early in the evening.

Market Arms (B GLM MA) Mon-Sat 11-23, Sun 13-23h
13 Hadden Street
Quizes and karaoke.

DANCECLUBS

Chaplins (B D GLM MA) Sun & Thu 21-2, Fri & Sat -3h
20 Adelphi Street *Near the corner with Market St* ☎ (01224) 592928
Former My Club.

SAUNAS/BATHS

Wellman's Health Studio (b DR DU G GH m MA MSG RR SA SB SOL VS WH) Mon-Fri 12-22, Sat -21, Sun 14-21h
218 Holborn Street *Across from the Talisman Building* ☎ (01224) 211 441
www.wellmans-health-studio.co.uk

CRUISING

-Victoria Park toilets, Watson Street. Police action possible
- P Parkhill Forest, small back road between Dyce & the Bridge Of Don (WE).

Aviemore - Inverness-shire ☎ 01479

GUEST HOUSES

Auchendean Lodge (B BF GLM I M MA OS PA PK RWS RWT)
Open from Easter to end of October
Dulnain Bridge *On A95, 14 km from Aviemore* ☎ (01479) 851 347
www.auchendean.com
Three guest bedrooms, all sharing our sensational views of river, forest and mountains. All rooms with en-suite toilets and bath or shower.

Bangor - Gwynedd ☎ 01248

BARS

3 Crowns (B D G MA s) Wed 19-24, Thu -1, Fri & Sat -2h
Well Street *Off the High Street* ☎ (01248) 351 138
www.thinkpinkuk.com
Entertainment ranges from boozy bingo to karaoke, plus music played by a choice of drag queens, plus many other resident and guest DJs, monthly charity nights in aid of local gay groups.

Bath - Somerset ☎ 01225

BARS

Bath Tap. The (B CC D GLM M MA SNU ST)
19 St. James Parade ☎ (01225) 404 344
Reopened in December 2011.

Mandalyns (B D GLM M MA S)
Tue & Wed 18-23, Thu - Sat -2, Sun 18h - midnight
13 Fountain Buildings *Bottom of Lansdown* ☎ (01225) 425 403
Bath's premiere gay pub.

SAUNAS/BATHS

BathHouse, The (! AC AK B BF DR DU FC FH G I m MA PI RR SA SB SL SOL VS) Sun-Thu 12-23, Fri-Sat -21h
4 Pierrepont Street *Close to the railway station, straight ahead. Below Bath Labour Party Buildings* ☎ (01225) 465 725 www.thebathhouse.org.uk
Probably the best in the southwest. Clean and busy. The way a good sauna should be.

GUEST HOUSES

Guesthouse (G M MA NU p PK) All year
10 Hawarden Terrace, Larkhall *20 mins walk from city centre*
☎ (01225) 310 118
Private house for gay men only - naturists welcome.

Belfast - Antrim ☎ 028

BARS

Dubarry's (B G MC)
10-14 Gresham Street ☎ (028) 9032 3590
www.dubarrysbar.co.uk

John Hewitt (B g M MC S) Mon-Sat 11.30-1h
51 Donegall Street *The Cathedral quarter, Belfast City Center*
☎ (028) 9023 3768 www.thejohnhewitt.com
Traditional pub, superb lunches, live music nightly.

Kremlin (! AC B CC D GLM S VS YC) Tue, Thu 22-2.30, Fri -3, Sat 21-3, Sun 22-3h; Mon, Wed closed
96 Donegall Street *City centre* ☎ (028) 9031 6060
www.kremlin-belfast.com
Two large clubs and a coctail bar. For information on the many special events see the website.

Mynt (B GLM) Mon-Fri 11.30-1, Sat -3, Sun 13-3h
2-16 Dunbar Street ☎ (028) 9023 4520
www.myntbelfast.com

Queens (B BF CC g M MA WE) Mon-Sat 11.30-23, Sun 12-19h
2 Queens Arcade *M° Great Victoria Street* ☎ (028) 9024 9105
www.queenscafebar.co.uk

Slide (B d GLM MA)

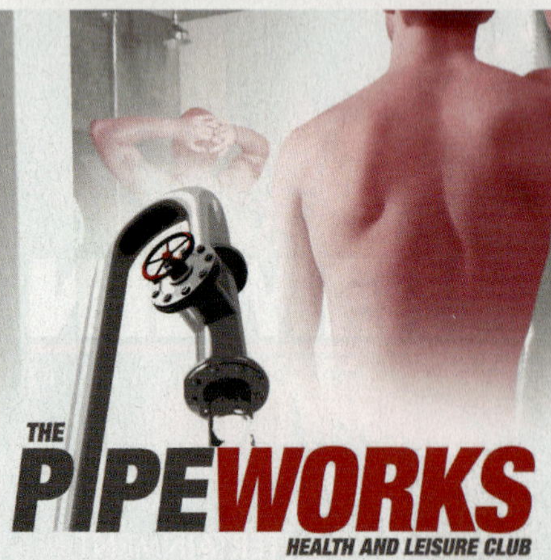

10 Ann Street ☏ (028) 9024 7222
Persian styled venue.

■ **Union Street** (AC B G M MA S ST) 11-1h
8-14 Union Street *Corner of Union and Little Donegall Street*
☏ (028) 9031 6060 💻 www.unionstreetpub.com
This Pub is ideal for lunchtime or evening dining with the ambient music and open fires creating the perfect setting for a unique gastronomic experience. Karaoke.

DANCECLUBS

■ **Thompsons Garage** (B D glm MA) Mon 22-3h
3 Pattersons Place *Beside the City Hall* ☏ (028) 9032 3762
💻 www.clubthompsons.com

SEX SHOPS/BLUE MOVIES

■ **Misstique** (glm) Mon-Thu 9-21, Fri-Sat -18h
27 Gresham Street *Castle Court shopping centre* ☏ (028) 9031 2043
Videos, toys, cards and magazines.

SAUNAS/BATHS

■ **Pipeworks. The** (! b cc DR DU FC FH G I m P RR SA SB SL SOL VR VS WH) Mon-Wed 12-1, Thu -4, Fri 12-Mon 4h (non-stop)
2-6 Union Street *Off Donegall St. City centre* ☏ (028) 9023 3441
💻 www.thepipeworks.com
An exclusive health and leisure club for gay men. There is a second club in Glasgow.

Birmingham – West Midlands ☏ 0121

BARS

■ **Chic** (AC B CC D GLM MA OS) Tue-Fri 17-1, Sat 16-9, Sun 18-1h
28 Horse Fair ☏ (0121) 666 6806
„Bitch" party 1st Mon/month 17-4h. Breakfast club every Sunday.

■ **Equator** (B G MC) Mon-Sat 12-23, Sun -22.30h
125 Hurst Street ☏ (0121) 622 5077 💻 www.equatorbar.co.uk

■ **Fountain Inn. The** (AC B BF CC DR f G H I MA OS s) 16-4.30 , Sat & Sun 14-4.30h
102 Wrentham Street *New Street station* ☏ (0121) 622 1452
💻 www.thefountaininn.com
One of Birmingham's oldest and busiest gay bars, for skins, bears, leather and denim guys. Happy hour Mon-Thu 17-21h. With hotel accommodation too!

■ **Fox. The** (B gLm MA OS)
19-23, Fri & Sat -2, Sun 15-23h, closed Mon & Tue
17 Lower Essex Street ☏ (0121) 622 1210 💻 www.foxbar.co.uk

■ **Loft Lounge. The** (B g M MA) 11-2h
143 Bromsgrove Street ☏ (0121) 622 2444
💻 www.theloftlounge.co.uk

■ **Missing** (B G MC) 12-2, Fri & Sat -4h
48 Bromsgrove Stteet ☏ (0121) 622 4256 💻 www.missingbar.co.uk
Popular, trendy bar.

■ **Subway City Club** (B D g MC)
27 Water Street, Old Snow Hill ☏ (0121) 233 0310

■ **Village Inn. The** (B CC GLM H MA OS)
Mon-Thu 12-2, Fri -4, Sat -5.30, Sun 13-2h
152 Hurst Street ☏ (0121) 622 4742
💻 www.villagebirmingham.co.uk
Traditional gay pub.

■ **Wellington. The** (B CC GLM H M MA) 12-23h
72 Bristol Street ☏ (0121) 622 2592
Also karaoke evenings. M. G. M. (Mature Gay Men) meet on 1st Wed & 3rd Fri/month.

MEN'S CLUBS

■ **Boltz** (B DR G P VS) Sun-Thu 15-24, Fri -3, Sat -?h
40 Lower Essex Street ☏ (0121) 666 6888 💻 www.boltz-club.com
Cruise bar with cabins and sling rooms. Condoms & lube available.

CAFES

■ **Green Room. The** (b glm M MA OS)

11-23, Fri & Sat -1, Sun 10-22.30h
Arcadian Centre, Hurst Street ☏ (0121) 605 4343
🖳 www.greenroomcafebar.co.uk

DANCECLUBS

■ **Nightingale Club. The** (! AC B CC D GLM M MA OS S SNU WE) 19-2, Thu -3, Fri -4, Sat -6h, closed Mon
Essex House, Kent Street *City centre, in the gay village* ☏ (0121) 622 1718
🖳 www.nightingaleclub.co.uk
Three floors with two dance areas. Birmingham's multi-award winning night club. The city's number 1 gay venue – especially busy Thu, Fri & Sat.

SEX SHOPS/BLUE MOVIES

■ **Clone Zone** (AC CC F GLM MA) Mon-Sat 11-21, Sun 12-19h
84 Hurst Street ☏ (0121) 666 6640 🖳 www.clonezonedirect.co.uk
4 stores throughout the UK sell an extensive range of XXX DVDs and videos, leather, rubber, fashion, toys, magazines, music, books, gifts and more.

■ **Prowler/Expectations Birmingham** (AC CC F G) Mon-Wed 10-18, Thu & Fri -19, Sat -18h
29-30 Stephenson Street ☏ (0121) 665 6379 🖳 www.prowler.co.uk
Offers a range of mainly erotica, hardcore videos/DVD's, gifts, books and magazines in similar stylish surroundings. Huge range of Rig and Expectations fetishwear.

ESCORTS & STUDIOS

■ **Escort Guys** (CC G MSG) 24hrs
☏ 07722 062 077 🖳 www.escortguys.co.uk
Gay escort agency with escorts in London, UK and across Europe.

SAUNAS/BATHS

■ **Greenhouse Health Club** (b CC DR DU FC FH G I m OS RR SA SB SOL VS WH) Sun-Thu 10-1, Fri -4, Sat -6h
Willenhall Road, Darlaston *Junction 9/10, M6* ☏ (0121) 568 6126
🖳 www.gay-sauna.com
Big sauna with a roof top garden play-maze, two secure car parks, two TV rooms – one for smokers and one for non-smokers. Recently refurbished.

■ **Spartan Health Club** (AC B DU G I m MA RR SA SB SOL VS) Mon-Fri 11-22, Sat -18.30, Sun 12-20.30h
127 George Road, Erdington *5 mins from Gravelly Hill Station, next door to the Wendy House Nursery* ☏ (0121) 382 3345
🖳 spartanhealthclub.co.uk
A small clean and extremely friendly place. The staff are helpful and the clientele mixed.

■ **Unit 2** (b DR DU G m MA RR SA SB VS WH) Sun-Thu 12-23, Fri & Sat 12-24h
78 Lower Essex Street ☏ (0121) 622 7070 🖳 www.unit2sauna.info

Blackpool – Lancashire ☏ 01253

GAY INFO

■ **BAG's Blackpool** (GLM)
56 High Street 🖳 www.bagsblackpool.com
BAG's is the largest independently owned gay holiday accommodation association in Europe. Established primarily to ensure reputable accommodation for the gay visitor to Blackpool.

BARS

■ **Flying Handbag. The** (AC B D GLM M MSG OS SNU ST T VS WE YC) 11-2h
44 Queen Street *Next to Flamingo* ☏ (01253) 625 522
🖳 www.flyinghandbagonline.co.uk

■ **Funny Girls / FG2** (B glm MA ST) 11-23, Thu -4, Fri -2, Sat -3h
Odeon building, 5 Dickson Road ☏ (0844) 247 38 66
🖳 www.funnygirlsonline.co.uk

■ **Kaos** (AC B D GLM S YC) 20-3, Sat & Sun 11-4h
38-42 Queen Street ☏ (01253) 318 798 🖳 www.kaosbar.co.uk

■ **Mardi Gras** (B CC D GLM MC OS ST T) 12-2, Thu-Sun -3h
114 Talbot Road ☏ (01253) 296 262
🖳 www.themardigrasblackpool.com

■ **Roxy's** (B GLM MA)
23 Queen Street ☏ (01253) 622 573 🖳 www.roxysonline.co.uk

DANCECLUBS

■ **Flamingo** (! AC B CC D GLM I M MA S) Mon, Wed, Fri, Sun 23-4, Sat 22.30-6h, Tue & Thu closed
44 Queen Street ☏ (01253) 649 151 🖳 www.flamingoonline.co.uk
Club on four levels, including two discos and five bars.

SAUNAS/BATHS

■ **Acqua** (! AC b CC DR DU FC FH G GH I m MA P RR SA SB SH SL SOL VS WH) Mon-Thu 11-23, Fri 11-Sun 22h (non-stop)
25-27 Springfield Road *Opp. Metropole Hotel* ☏ (01253) 294 610
🖳 www.acquasaunas.com
Modern bathhouse with lots of pine, bright colours, subdued lighting. Regular theme nights.

■ **Honeycombe Leisure Centre** (b DR DU F FC FH G I M MA P RR SA SB SH SL SOL VS WH) Daily 11-10h
97-107 Egerton Road *Blackpool North* ☏ (01253) 752 211
🖳 www.honeycombe.net
Happy Hour daily from 11-12h

■ **Wetwetwet Sauna Complex** (b DU G I m P RR SA SB SOL VS) Mon-Fri 12-24, Sat 12-Sun 24h (non-stop)
1-3 Charles Street *Entrance is on King Street* ☏ (01253) 751 199
🖳 www.wetwetwetsauna.co.uk
Sauna complex for gay & bi sexual men.

HOTELS

■ **Chaps Hotel** (B BF CC H M MA RWT)
9-11 Cocker Street *10mins walk to railway station and the Coach station* ☏ (01253) 620541 🖳 www.chapshotel.co.uk
Situated near the sea front and close to the gay scene and most the attractions.

■ **Guyz** (B BF cc G I m MA RWS RWT VA) All year
16 Lord Street *Close to train station* ☏ (01253) 622 488
🖳 www.guyzhotel.com

■ **Hotel 365** (B BF CC glm I M MA PK RWS RWT) All year
10 Lonsdale Road ☏ (01253) 400 365 🖳 www.hotel365.co.uk
Gay run and operated hotel with 14 luxury en-suite rooms.

■ **Legends** (B BF cc GLM M MA OS PK RWS RWT) All year
45 Lord Street *Near main station* ☏ (01253) 620 300
🖳 www.legendshotel.co.uk

■ **Mardi Gras** (B BF CC D GLM m MA OS RWS RWT T) All year
41-43 Lord Street *Near gay area* ☏ (01253) 751 087
🖳 www.mardigrashotel.co.uk
Twenty bedrooms with TV, tea & coffee making facilities. Also bar with live entertainment.

■ **Mardi Gras 2** (AC B bf CC GLM MA NR p PA PK RWS RWT VA WI) All year
9-11 Lord Street *North railway station* ☏ (01253) 628 073
🖳 www.mardigras2.co.uk
Situated in the heart of Blackpool's gay village, with many show bars, night clubs and gay bars. For gay people only. Residents receive concessions for Flamingo Club and Acqua sauna.

■ **McHall's Hotel** (B BF GLM M MA t WE) All year
7 Lord Street ☏ (01253) 625 661 🖳 www.mchallshotel.co.uk
In the heart of blackpool gay saunas, bars and night clubs.

■ **Nevada** (B BF cc GLM MA RWS RWT VA) All year
23 Lord Street ☏ (01253) 290 700 🖳 www.hotelnevada.co.uk
All rooms with TV. Some en-suite rooms available. BAG's members.

■ **New Hertford Hotel. The** (B BF CC glm m MA OS PA PK RWS RWT) All year
18 Lord Street *Near town centre* ☏ (01253) 292 931
Small, gay-owned hotel with ten bedrooms (six en-suite).

■ **Rubens** (AC B BF CC GLM MA RWS RWT VA) All year
39 Lord Street *North Station* ☏ (01253) 622 920
🖳 www.rubenshotel.co.uk
Close to gay bars. Discount given for local saunas.

■ **Trades** (B BF CC DR G I m MA OS p RWT SA SOL VA VS) All year

51-55 Lord Street *Near Blackpool North train station* ☎ (01253) 626 401
🖳 www.tradeshotelblackpool.co.uk
The only „men only" hotel in Blackpool, just few mins from all gay night life.

■ **Vidella. The** (B BF CC GLM I M MA PA PK RWS RWT VA) All year
78-82 Dickson Road *Near railway station* ☎ (01253) 621 201
🖳 www.videllahotel.com
All 29 rooms are en suite. A three-diamond property, rated by the English Tourism Council.

■ **Village. The** (BF glm MA)
14 Springfield Road ☎ (01253) 290 840
🖳 www.thevillagehotel.biz

GUEST HOUSES

■ **Grampian House** (BF CC glm I MA RWS RWT VA) All year, front desk 9-23h
4 Pleasant Street *Close to North Train Station* ☎ (01253) 291 648
🖳 www.grampianhouse.com
Situated in Blackpool's gay quarter, 50 m from the Promenade. Ten bedrooms (all en-suite).

■ **Pride Lodge** (BF CC FC FH GLM H M MA NR NU OS RES RWS RWT VA VEG WH WI) All year
12 High Street *Centre of gay scene Blackpool* ☎ (01253) 314 752
🖳 www.pridelodge.com
Quality 4 star accommodation specifically for the LGBT guest and their friends in the centre of the Blackpool gay scene. See website for special offers and free nights.

■ **Seacroft** (BF cc GLM RWT) All year
27 Lord Street ☎ (01253) 628 304
🖳 www.seacroft.me.uk
Spacious suites with fridge, TV and tea/coffee making facilities.

■ **Willowfield** (BF CC glm I MA OS PA RWT) All year
51 Banks Street ☎ (01253) 623 406
🖳 www.willowfield-guesthouse.co.uk

CRUISING

-Bond Street (back of the Pleasure beach)
-North and Central Piers
-Silcocks amusement arcade (top of the building)
-Bus station Talbot Road
-Revoe Park (summer only)
-Starr gate (tram terminus)
-Middle walk (AYOR) (busy, rough types).

Bolton – Greater Manchester ☎ 01204

BARS

■ **Star. The** (B d GLM I m MA T)
Mon-Thu 17-23, Fri & Sat 13-2, Sun 14-23h
11 Bow Street *Town centre* ☎ (01204) 361 113

Bournemouth – Dorset ☎ 01202

BARS

■ **Bakers Arms** (AC B GLM m MA S) 11-23, Sun -22.30h
77 Commercial Road *Back to back with Rubyz 2 Club*
☎ (01202) 555 506

■ **Branksome. The** (B D GLM I MA OS S T) 12-1h
152-154 Commercial Road ☎ (01202) 292 254
🖳 www.branksomepub.co.uk
Popular bar and huge garden terrace. Entertainment most nights.

■ **DYMK-Bar** (B G MC S) Daily 12-1h
31 Poole Hill, Soho Quarter 🖳 www.dymk-bar.com
Regular entertainment including cabaret on Wednesdays and Viva La Diva acts on Thursdays. DJ Luke and guests on Fridays and more to come.

■ **Ventana @ The Cumberland** (B CC MC NG)
East Overcliff Drive ☎ (01202) 202 290722
🖳 www.cumberlandbournemouth.co.uk/hotel/bar-dining/bar

■ **Xchange. The** (AC B CC D GLM MA S SNU)
10-2, Wed & Thu 7.30-3, Fri & Sat -4, Sun -3h
4 The Triangle ☎ (01202) 294 321
Busy bar/disco with mixed crowd. Busy after 22h at the WE.

RESTAURANTS

■ **Rubyz Cabaret Restaurant**
(AC B CC d GLM LM M MA RES S VEG) Wed-Sat 19.30-24h
47 Gervais Road *Hotel Celebrity* ☎ (01202) 552 553
🖳 www.rubyz.co.uk
New and larger location at Hotel Celebrity! Cabaret and restaurant bar.

SEX SHOPS/BLUE MOVIES

■ **White Tiger** (CC GLM) Mon-Sat 10-18, Sun 12-16h
27 The Triangle *In the Heart of the Gay Village*
🖳 www.whitetigerstore.com
DVDs, books, magazines, designer underwear, swimwear and clothing.

SAUNAS/BATHS

■ **Bournemouth Saunabar** (B DR DU FC FH G I m MSG RR SA SB SL VS WH) 11-23, Fri 11-Sun 23h (non-stop)
4 Avenue Lane *Opposite multi-storey carpark and Habitat*
☎ (01202) 552 654 🖳 www.gaysaunabar.com

■ **Spa. The** (AK b DU FH G GH I LAB m OS RR SA SB VS)
Mon-Sat 11-18, Sun 12-18h
121 Poole Road *Behind Marks and Spencer Food Hall in Westbourne*
☎ (01202) 757 591

HOTELS

■ **Claremont** (B BF cc glm H I m PA PK RWS RWT)
89 St. Michael's Road, West Cliff *Town centre* ☎ (01202) 290 875
🖳 www.claremonthotelbournemouth.co.uk
Friendly comfortable hotel close to the gay village with parking. Pets welcome.

■ **Hamilton Hall**
(BF CC D G MA MSG NU OS PA PK RWS S VA VS WE) All year
1 Carysfort Road *Five minutes drive from city centre* ☎ (01202) 399 227
🖳 www.hamiltonhall.info

GUEST HOUSES

■ **Bondi** (BF CC GLM MA p RWB RWS RWT WE) All year
43 St. Michael's Road *Close to Bournemouth International Center*
☎ (01202) 554 893 🖳 www.thebondi.co.uk
Six guestooms with TV and private bathroom or en-suite. Close to gay nightlife.

GENERAL GROUPS

■ **Bourne Free Pride Festival** (GLM)
27 St. Michael's Road 🖳 www.bournefree.co.uk
Organiser of the annual Gay Pride event held on the second weekend in July.

CRUISING

-Alum Chine (at night)
-Sea front (busiest at night, during the day 200m either side of the pier)
-Park in centre of Bournemouth (crusiest at night, go to the quieter side of the square walking with the pier behind you in the direction of Westbourne until you reach the tennis courts)
-Boscombe Gardens (drive to Eastcliffe and walk down through the woody area to the gardens)

Bowness on Windermere
Cumbria ☎ 015394

HOTELS

■ **Lonsdale** (B BF cc glm MA)
Lake Road ☎ (015394) 43 348 🖳 www.lonsdale-hotel.co.uk
Gay owned & operated. Located in the national park. Luxury & friendly accommodation.

Bradford – West Yorkshire ☎ 01274

BARS

Sun Hotel. The (B CC D GLM MA OS ST WE)
12-23, Fri & Sat -24, Sun -22.30h
124 Sunbridge Road
☎ (01274) 737 722
Accommodation available. All rooms with tea & coffee making facilities and TV.

DANCECLUBS

Clublife (AC B D GLM MA) Fri & Sat 21-?h
158 Westgate ☎ (01274) 725 899
Gay night club, straight-friendly.

SAUNAS/BATHS

Lindum (B DR DU FC FH G GH M MA NR p RR SA VS W WO)
12.30-21h, Mon closed
307 Manningham Lane *Opp. Lister Park. Discreet entrance, no sauna sign; just look for house number* ☎ (01274) 546 622
www.lindumsauna.com
Very clean. Owners are friendly and welcoming.

GUEST HOUSES

Ivy Guest House (BF glm I MA PK RWT) All year
3 Melbourne Place *Central Bradford*
☎ (01274) 727 060 www.ivyguesthousebradford.com

CRUISING

-Manningham Park (by Lister Statue)
-Sunbridge Road
-Peel Park.

Bradford-On-Avon – Wiltshire ☎ 01225

GUEST HOUSES

Burghope Manor (BF GLM M MA OS PA PK RWS RWT VA)
All year
Winsley *Near Bath in Wiltshire*
☎ (01225) 720 216
www.burghopemanor.com
All rooms with bath/WC, own key. Full English breakfast and evening meals available. A true dining experience – the menu is chosen by the chef and changes daily and includes wine. One of the few properties in the UK which caters exclusively to gay men. Recommended.

Brighton & Hove – East Sussex ☎ 01273

Sometimes referred to as „London by the sea", Brighton is literally forty five minutes by train from the capital – a train journey that is well worth taking. With an estimated gay population of over 40,000, it seems that the whole city revolves around ensuring that we are welcomed and have a great time. The community is centralised around the city centre and seafront, with a wide selection of bars, cafes and hotels, everything is in walking distance from your door – including the spectacular ocean views, Brighton Pier and the Brighton Pavilion – an Indian-style palace built in 1823. Brighton Pride is the premier gay festival that should not be missed, and is free to attend, with substantial contributions made to UK charities. Most venues are gay/straight mixed, although two late night, male only venues are thriving.

Brighton, manchmal auch „London am Meer" genannt, ist tatsächlich nur eine dreiviertel Stunde mit dem Zug von der Hauptstadt entfernt – eine Fahrt, die sich wirklich lohnt! Mit einem geschätzten schwulen Bevölkerungsteil von 40.000 scheint es, als sei die ganze Stadt bemüht, uns Schwulen und Lesben einen möglichst schönen Aufenthalt zu bieten. Die schwule Szene mit ihren unzähligen Bars, Cafés und Hotels konzentriert sich auf das Stadtzentrum und die Strandpromenade. Auch Aussichtspunkte mit beeindruckendem Meeresblick, der Brighton Pier und der 1823 im indischen Stil erbaute Brighton Pavilion sind bequem zu Fuß zu erreichen. Nicht versäumen sollte man Brighton Pride, das wichtigste schwule Festival. Der Eintritt ist kostenlos; ein großer Teil der Einnahmen wird an britische Wohltätigkeitsorganisationen gespendet. Fast alle Lokale sind schwul/hetero gemischt. Es gibt allerdings zwei Nachtclubs, exklusiv für Männer, die gut laufen.

Connu aussi comme „Londres au bord de la mer", Brighton est à quarante-cinq minutes de train de la capitale, un trajet qui en vaut la peine. Avec une population gaie estimée à 40 000 âmes, on dirait que toute la ville s'affaire à nous souhaiter la bienvenue et à nous assurer le plus merveilleux des séjours. La communauté est concentrée au centre de la ville et au bord de la mer avec une panoplie de bars, cafés et hôtels. L'océan vous offre des points de vue spectaculaires, Brighton Pier et le Brighton Pavilion, un palais à l'indienne construit en 1823, peuvent tous être facilement rejoints à pied. Brighton Pride est le festival gai à ne pas manquer, l'entrée est gratuite et de larges contributions sont fait auprès d'organismes de charités anglais. Presque tous les bars et clubs sont mixtes homos/hétéros. Il existe néanmoins deux boites de nuit exlusivement pour les hommes, qui marchent bien.

Brighton, a veces también llamada el „Londres del Mar", está en efecto situada a sólo ¾ de hora en tren desde la capital, un recorrido que merece realmente la pena. Con una población homosexual aproximada de 40.000 personas, parece que toda la ciudad se esfuerza en hacer agradable la estancia de gays y lesbianas. El ambiente gay, con sus numerosos bares, cafés y hoteles, se concentra en el centro de la ciudad y en el paseo de la playa. También puede irse cómodamente a pie a conocidos lugares con una impresionante vista al mar, como el Brighton Pier y el Brighton Pavilion, construido en 1823 en estilo indio. Tampoco debe faltarse al Brighton Pride, el festival homosexual más importante. La entrada es gratuita y la mayor parte de los ingresos va destinada a organizaciones británicas de beneficencia. Casi todos los locales son mixtos gay/hétero. De cualquier forma hay dos clubs exclusivos para hombres que funcionan bien.

Brighton, definita anche „Londra sul mare", è a soli 45 minuti di distanza dalla capitale, un viaggio che vale la pena intraprendere. Con circa 40.000 gay, sembra che tutta la città si impegni a rendere a noi gay e lesbiche il soggiorno il più piacevole possibile. La comunità gay coi suoi innumerevoli bar, caffè, alberghi, si concentra nel centro della città e sul lungo mare. Anche i punti panoramici con affascinante vista sul mare, il Brighton Pier e il Brighton Pavilio, costruito nel 1823 in stile indiano, sono facilmente raggiungibili a piedi. Non bisognerebbe perdere il Brighton Pride, il festival gay più importante. L'entrata è gratis; una grossa parte del ricavato viene devoluta a organizzazioni assistenziali britanniche. Quasi tutti i locali sono misti. Ci sono comunque 2 locali esclusivamente per uomini e sono molto frequentati.

GAY INFO

■ **Brighton & Hove LGBT Switchboard** (GLM MA T) Help-line: 17-21 Mon-Fri,17-19, Sat & Sun, counselling service by appointment
6 Bartholmews ☏ (01273) 204 050 💻 www.switchboard.org.uk/brighton
Information and support for the LGBT community. Offers a help-line, e-mail enquiry service, counselling service for the LGBT community by counsellors who identify as LGBT. Pages in German, Danish, Spanish, French, Italian, Dutch and Portuguese available.

BARS

■ **Bulldog** (AC B D G MA S ST VS) Mon-Thu 11-2, Fri-Sun non-stop 63 hrs
31 St. James's Street *In the heart of the gay village* ☏ (01273) 696 996
💻 www.bulldogbrighton.com
Brighton's premier gay venue for more than 28 years. Brighton's only 24 hour venue with a 63 hour weekend.

■ **Charles Street** (B D GLM M MA s) 11-23h
8 Marine Parade ☏ (01273) 624 091 💻 www.charles-street.com
Very trendy, self conscious, young and mixed crowd. Food served until 19h.

Brighton

EAT & DRINK
Amsterdam – Restaurant 11
Bulldog – Bar 5
Charles Street – Bar 10
Legends – Bar 15
Marine Tavern. The – Bar 12
Queen's Arms – Bar 3
R-Bar – Bar 21
Vavoom – Bar 16
White Horse. The – Bar 6
Zone. The – Bar 4

NIGHTLIFE
Basement – Danceclub 15
Club Revenge – Danceclub 7
The Club @ Charles St. – Danceclub 9

SEX
Brighton Sauna. The – Sauna 1
Prowler Brighton – Sex Shop/Blue Movies 8

ACCOMMODATION
Amsterdam. The – Hotel 11
Griffin. The – Guest House 14
Home Hotel Brighton – Guest House 20
Hudsons – Guest House 18
Kemp Townhouse – Hotel 17
Kipps Brighton – Hotel 2
Legends Hotel 15
Nineteen – Hotel 13

OTHERS
Cardome – Gift & Pride Shop 19

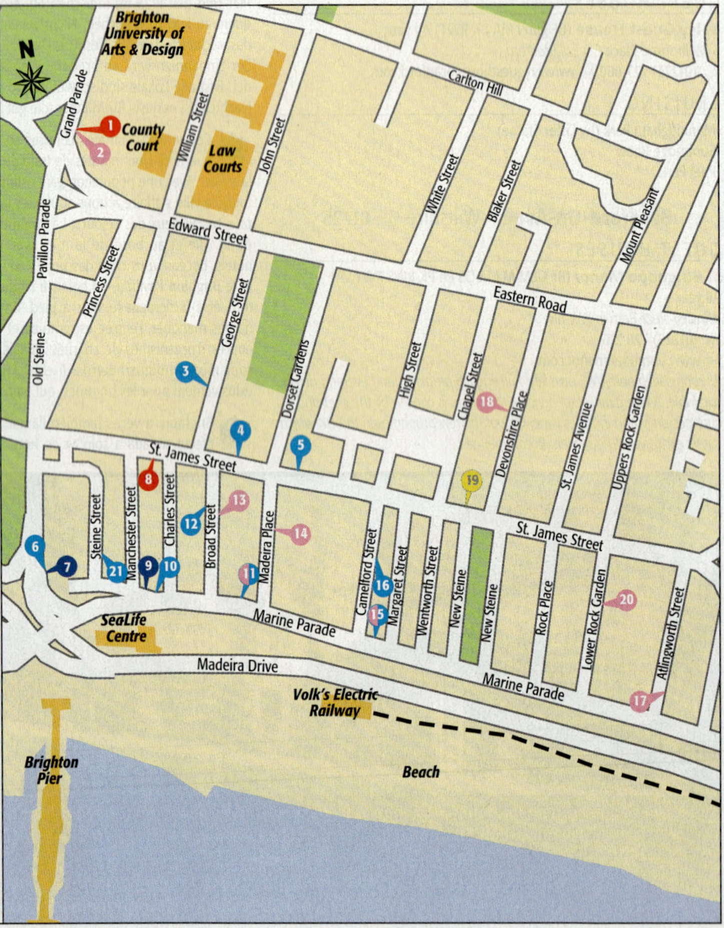

■ **Grosvenor. The** (B CC GLM MA)
Mon-Thu 17-1, Fri -2.30, Sat 14-2.30, Sun -24h
16 Western Street ☎ (01273) 770 712 🖳 www.thegrosvenorbar.com

■ **Legends** (AC B D f GLM m MA OS p S ST VS WE) Daily 11-5h
31-34 Marine Parade ☎ (01273) 624 462
🖳 www.legendsbrighton.co.uk
Brighton's multi-award wining large seafront bar is the best placed gay bar in Brighton offering stunning sea views from both the bar and huge sun terrace. With lunch time food and entertainment throughout the week.

■ **Lounge. The** (B GLM MA) 11-23h
7 Albion Street ☎ 7879 834 835

■ **Marine Tavern. The** (AC B CC GLM MA) 12-0.30h
13 Broad Street ☎ (01273) 681 284 🖳 www.marinetavern.co.uk
Small friendly gay bar.

■ **Marlborough. The** (B gLm m MA s) 11-23, Sun 12-22.30h
4 Princess Street *Opp. Royal Pavilion* ☎ (01273) 570 028
🖳 www.drinkinbrighton.co.uk/marlborough
Mainly a lesbian venue.

■ **Queen's Arms** (AC B CC GLM I MA S ST) 14-24h
7 George Street *Off St. James Street* ☎ (01273) 696 873
🖳 www.queensarmsbrighton.com
Top cabaret acts, drag & karaoke.

■ **R-Bar** (B GLM MA s) 12-2h
5-7 Marine Parade ☎ (01273) 608 133 🖳 www.revenge.co.uk

■ **Vavoom** (B G H MC OS) 16-5, Fri & Sat -6h
31 Old Steine ☎ (01273) 603 010 🖳 www.vavoom.co.uk

■ **White Horse. The** (B CC GLM m MA) 12-23h
30-31 Camelford Street *Off seafront up from Legends*
☎ (01273) 603 726
Pleasant mixed bar.

■ **Zone. The** (B G I m MC)
33 St. James's Street ☎ (01273) 682 249
🖳 www.realbrighton.com/zone

DANCECLUBS

■ **Basement Club** (B D G MC p) Sun-Fri 23-4, Sat -5h
31-34 Marine Parade *Below Legends Bar*
🖳 www.legendsbrighton.com
The club is sumptuously designed to create a space that is both dazzling and intimate and is without doubt the sexiest gay club this side of London. Gay door policy.

■ **Club Revenge** (AC B D GLM MA SNU ST)
Mon-Thu 22.30-3, Fri 22-5, Sat 22-6, Sun 22-3h
32-34 Old Steine Street *Opposite Palace Pier* ☎ (01273) 606 064
🖳 www.revenge.co.uk
Open seven nights a week but busiest on Fri/Sat nights.

■ **The Club @ Charles Street** (B D G m MA) 12-24, Fri & Sat -3h
8 Marine Parade *Next door to Kruze and Audio* ☎ (01273) 624 091
🖳 www.charles-street.com

■ **Wild Fruit** (B D GLM MA S T)
West Street *Central seafront location* ☎ (01273) 327 083
🖳 www.wildfruit.co.uk
Usual drag, camp bar. Brighton's biggest disco.

RESTAURANTS

■ **Amsterdam** (AC B BF CC DM GLM M MA OS RES s VEG WL)
Mon-Sat 11-20, Sun 12-17h
11-12 Marine Parade *In Amsterdam Hotel* ☎ (01273) 688 825
🖳 www.amsterdam.uk.com
Enjoy freshly cooked food ranging from light bites to three course meals, including a range of vegetarian dishes. Plus Special Sunday Roasts .

SEX SHOPS/BLUE MOVIES

■ **Prowler Brighton** (AC CC G) Mon-Sat 11-19, Sun 12-18h
112-113 St. James's Street ☎ (01273) 683 680 🖳 www.prowler.co.uk
The first Prowler store outside London, selling fashion, books, cards, gifts, magazines and accessories. In the rear is the Blue Room with sex toys and porn videos/DVDs.

SAUNAS/BATHS

■ **Bright'n Beautiful**
(b DR DU FC FH G m MA RR SA SB SOL VS) 12-22, Sun -20h
9 St. Margaret's Place *Opp. Sussex Height's* ☎ (01273) 328 330
Attitude-free, this sauna is recommended for men who rate horny action and value for money above sleekness and sophisticated ambience. Cosy and friendly. Reduced entry fee if you arrive after 17.30h every day except Sunday.

■ **Brighton Sauna. The** (AC CC DR f FC FH G m MA MSG PI RR SA SB SOL VS WH) Sun-Thu 10-1, Fri 10 to Mon 1h (non-stop)
75 Grand Parade *10 mins from Brighton train station Opp. Royal Pavillon*
☎ (01273) 689 966 🖳 www.thebrightonsauna.com
Large comfy cinema.

■ **TBS2 Sauna** (b cc DR DU FC FH G I m MA MSG RR SA SB SH SL SOL VS WH WO) Daily 10-1h
84-86 Denmark Villas, Hove *Near Hove railway station*
☎ (01273) 723 733 🖳 www.tbs2.com
Regular party nights and occassional theme nights. Large comfy cinema.

GIFT & PRIDE SHOPS

■ **Cardome** (CC GLM MA SOL) Mon-Sat 10.30-18h
47a St. James's Street *In the heart of the gay village* ☎ (01273) 692 916
🖳 www.cardome.co.uk
Long established and reliable gift shop.

TRAVEL AND TRANSPORT

■ **Galeria Travel** (GLM) Mon-Fri 11-17.30, Sat -14h
2 George Street ☎ 870 220 1705 🖳 www.galeriatravel.com

HOTELS

■ **Amsterdam. The** (AC B BF CC GLM I M MA OS RWB RWS RWT SA SB VA WO) All year
11-12 Marine Parade *In the gay village opp. pier* ☎ (01273) 688 825
🖳 www.amsterdam.uk.com
Large modern rooms. All Double en-suite rooms with walk in showers or wet rooms, all with king size beds, TV and tea and coffee making facilities. All front rooms have stunning views over Brighton's famous Pier, beach and seafront and are fitted with multi-channel digital LCD flat screen TV's. Hotel Bar open Sun-Thu 11-2, Fri & Sat -?h. Quote SPARTACUS for special rates!

■ **Cowards Guest House** (BF CC glm MA OS) All year
12 Upper Rock Gardens *Bus 7 or taxi from station; near gay district*
☎ (01273) 692 677 🖳 www.cowardsbrighton.co.uk
Most rooms are en-suite (only two have shower). All rooms with a fridge, tea/coffee making facilities and TV.

■ **Granville** (B BF CC glm H I M OS PA RWS RWT VA WH) All year
124 Kings Road *Opposite Brighton's historic West Pier* ☎ (01273) 326 302
🖳 granvillehotel.co.uk
24 individual decorated rooms.

■ **Kemp Townhouse** (b BF cc glm MC MSG PA RWS RWT VA WO) All year
21 Atlingworth Street *Kemp Town* ☎ (01273) 681 400
🖳 www.kemptownhousebrighton.com
Boutique accommodation in the heart of Kemp Town. Nine luxurious en-suite bedrooms some with features such as bay windows with sea views, free standing baths or indulgent four-poster beds.

■ **Kipps Brighton** (B BF CC glm MA PA PI RWS RWT SA VA) All year
76 Grand Parade *Opp. Royal Pavilion, close to railway station*
☎ (01273) 604 182 🖳 www.kipps-brighton.com
Located above the Oasis Sauna, offering discounted entry. Nine double rooms and one single room. Within walking distance from many of the gay locations.

■ **Legends Hotel** (B BF CC D GLM I M MA RWS RWT T VA WE) All year
31-34 Marine Parade *Seafront, 3 blocks east of Brighton Pier*
☎ (01273) 624 462 🖳 www.legendsbrighton.com
The UK's largest gay hotel and part of the multi-million pound Legends complex which includes the stylish Legends Bar & The Basement Club. Right opposite Brighton beach, Legends Hotel offers 40 standard and luxury seafront rooms, many with stunning sea views. All rooms are en-suite with flat screen

TV's and offer tea and coffee making facilities. Luxury rooms have been carefully designed to provide a sumptuous, contemporary style with larger bathrooms (many with baths), king size beds and panoramic sea views. Full English breakfast, (with vegetarian & vegan option) is served until 10.30h.

■ **Nineteen** (bf CC glm I MA PK RWS RWT VA WH) All year
19 Broad Street, Kemp Town *Central location* ☎ (01273) 675 529
💻 www.hotelnineteen.co.uk
Gay owned & operated small fashionable hotel with eight double rooms, all en-suite (one has a private 4-man outdoor jacuzzi). Very mixed but friendly guests.

GUEST HOUSES

■ **Avalon** (BF CC glm MA RWS RWT) All year
7 Upper Rock Gardens ☎ (01273) 692 344 💻 www.avalonbrighton.co.uk
All rooms with bath/shower, WC, radio, CD, TV.

■ **Blanch House** (B BF CC GLM MA RWT S VA WE) All year
17 Atlingworth Street *Only a short walk from the centre of Brighton*
☎ (01273) 603 504 💻 www.blanchhouse.co.uk
Twelve individually designed rooms (all en-suite).

■ **Brighton Pavilions** (BF cc glm PA RWS RWT) All year
7 Charlotte Street *Kemp Town* ☎ (01273) 621 750
💻 www.brightonpavilions.com
Ten theme rooms. Near gay scene.

■ **Griffin. The** (BF cc glm I OS PK RWS RWT VA) All year, 24hrs
14 Madeira Place *In the gay village, ten mins walk from the station*
☎ (01273) 691 257 💻 www.griffinbrighton.co.uk
All nine guestrooms are ensuite with either a shower or Jacuzzi, some with four-poster bed. Many rooms have slings available. All room have TV.

■ **Home Hotel Brighton** (bf CC g H MA WE)
18 Lower Rock Gardens ☎ (01273) 674 681 💻 www.comestraighthome.com
Friendly gay owned guest house. Centrally located. One min. from gay village, shopping, pubs and restaurants. Some rooms with sea view.

■ **Hudsons** (BF CC GLM I MA OS PK RWS RWT VA)
Open all year/check in 8-17h
22 Devonshire Place ☎ (01273) 683642 💻 www.hudsonshotel.com
Friendly quality guesthouse. All rooms with showers & toilet, tv, radio, mini-bar, wi-fi and tea and coffee. Full English or vegetarian BF included.

HEALTH GROUPS

■ **Brighton Body Positive** (glm) Mon-Fri 9.30-17.30h
113 Queens Road ☎ (01273) 234 034
Drop-In centre, alternative therapies, information, support for people with HIV.

SWIMMING

-Telscombe Cliffs (G) (Take a bus to Saltdean. This is a very cruisy picnic venue at the weekends)
-Shoream Beach (g nu) (This is an unofficial nudist beach located opposite the old power station chimney)
-Angle Beach (G) (Located on the border of Brighton & Hove, this is the place to tan on a hot summer's day. It can also get quite cruisy when the clubs are closed)

CRUISING

-Goldstone Villas toilets – Hove (Blatchington Road, take a right at Woolworth's. On the right). Very busy at all times.
-Old Shoreham Road/Hove Park Villas – Hove (toilet has two cubicles and is next to the rugby club)
-Toilets at Portland Road, Hove
-Shoreham Harbour Beach, located in Portslade (AYOR, police patrols).

Bristol – Somerset ☎ 0117

BARS

■ **Bristol Bear Bar** (B CC G MC VS WE)
Mon-Thu 19-22.30, Fri & Sat -2, Sun 15-23h
2-3 West Street, Old Market *Cnr. Midland Rd* ☎ (0117) 955 1967
💻 www.bristolbearbar.co.uk
Home of the local bears and their admirers.

■ **Lounge** (B G MA) Mon-Sun 12-1h
53 Old Market Street ☎ (0117) 922 5224

■ **Old Castle Green. The** (B g H MA)
Wed & Thu 17-24, Fri -4, Sat 14-4, Sun -24h
43 Gloucester Lane ☎ (0117) 930 9140

■ **Old Market Tavern. The** (B CC GLM M MA)
11.30-23, Fri -2, Sat 19-2, Sun 12-16h
29-30 Old Market Street ☎ (0117) 922 6123 💻 www.omtbristol.co.uk
Homely pub, serving good home cooked food. Popular place with Bear/Cub/Biker/Leather scene.

■ **Pineapple. The** (B D GLM I MA S) Daily 18-1h
37 St. George's Road *Behind Anchor Rd. Close to the city centre*
☎ (0117) 316 99 38
The home of great entertainment. Friendly bar with events every night of the week including karaoke and cabaret.

■ **Queen's Shilling. The** (AC B CC D GLM MA)
Wed 10-2, Thu-Sat 9-3, Sun 10-2h
9 Frogmore Street *Central Bristol, close to Ice Rink* ☎ (0117) 926 4342
💻 www.queenshilling.com
One of Bristol's favourite gay bar/clubs.

MEN'S CLUBS

■ **Club O Bristol** (B G MA P) Fri 21-5, Sat 14-5h
7 Lawrence Hill

DANCECLUBS

■ **Flamingos Nightclub** (B D GLM MC S WE)
Wed, Thu & Sun 22-3, Fri -4, Sat -5h
23-25 West Street, Old Market ☎ (0117) 955 9269
💻 www.flamingosbristol.co.uk
A new multi-level club in Old Market area of Bristol. Many theme nights and many more fun nights to come. Thu is mainly girls' night.

■ **Wonky @ The Warehouse** (B D G MA) Last Fri/month 22.30-3h
55 Prince Street ☎ (0117) 927 9279

SAUNAS/BATHS

■ **Village Sauna, The**
(AK b CC DR DU FC FH G GH I m MA OS P RR SA SB SH SL SOL VS WH)
Mon & Tue 13-24, Wed & Thu 11-24, Fri 11-Sun 24h (non-stop)
19 West Street *Old Market* ☎ (0117) 330 7719 💻 villagesauna.com
Annual and day membership available. Friendly and welcoming atmosphere: cinema lounge, prison cell, communal and private darkrooms, private rooms for rent, two slings.

BOOK SHOPS

■ **Starbooks** (b g) Mon-Sat 7.30-18, Sun 12-18h
45 West Street, Old Market ☎ (0117) 955 5334
Bristol's only gay-owned and run coffee shop and second-hand bookstore.

CRUISING

-The Promenade – Observation Hill (Clifton; bushes and woodland, twilight)
-Sea Walls/Circular Road (AYOR) (Clifton; walk along Circular Road towards Sneyd Park; very busy at all times, police)
-Berrow Sands (AYOR) (coast north of Burnham-on-Sea 20km from Bristol)
-Ashton Park (opp. Bristol City football ground)

Cambridge – Cambridgeshire ☎ 01223

BARS

■ **Bird in Hand** (B G M)
73 Newmarket Road ☎ (01223) 464845
Also DJs, karaoke, cabaret. The only gay bar in Cambridge.

Canterbury – Kent ☎ 01227

DANCECLUBS

■ **Girls and Boys @ Chill** (! B D GLM S YC) 22h-late (last entry 1h)
41 St. George's Place *Near Odeon Cinema* ☎ (01227) 761276
💻 www.chill-nightclub.com
Kent's most popular monthly L&G event. Check website for dates and details. Now at new location.

Cardiff – South Glamorgan ☎ 02920

SHOWS

■ **Minsky's Showbar** (B GLM M MA ST) Mon-Sat 12-?h
53 Cathedral Walk, St. David's Centre ☎ (02920) 233 128
💻 www.minskys-showbar.com
Food till 15h, shows start at 21.30h.

BARS

■ **Club X** (B D GLM MC OS) Fri & Sat
35-37 Charles Street ☎ (02920) 400 876
💻 www.clubxcardiff.com

■ **Eagle** (AC B f G m MA S SNU) Sun-Thu 17-24, Fri & Sat 17-2h
39 Charles Street *Basement, near Cardiff Central and Queens Street stations* ☎ (02920) 232 859 💻 www.eaglecardiff.com
Regular monthly theme nights like construction, fetish, army gear, sportswear. Near Club X and Locker Room sauna.

■ **Golden Cross** (B D GLM M MA OS S t) Mon-Wed 11-23, Thu-Sat -1, Sun -22.30h
283 Hayes Bridge Road ☎ (02920) 343 129
Popular with gay, lesbians & TV's. They have local and national entertainment and do food at lunch time.

■ **Icon** (B GLM m MA OS WI)
60 Charles Street ☎ (02920) 666 505 💻 www.bariconcardiff.co.uk

■ **Pulse** (B D glm M MC OS S) Mon-Thu 16-23.30,Fri & Sat -0.30h
3 Churchill Way ☎ (02920) 647 380 💻 www.pulsecardiff.com
Bar/club offering food and downstairs dance club.

■ **Wow** (B GLM m MA OS S)
4a Churchill Way ☎ (02920) 666 247 💻 www.wowbarcardiff.com
Cabaret every night.

SAUNAS/BATHS

■ **Locker Room** (DR DU FC FH G GH I LAB M MA OS RR SA SB VS WH) 12-23, Sat 12-Sun 22h (non-stop)
50 Charles Street *Central Cardiff* ☎ (02920) 22 0388
💻 www.lockerroomcardiff.co.uk
Award winning busy city centre sauna.

MASSAGE

■ **Massage4Men & WaxforMen** (CC G MSG) Daily 10-20h
Wenallt Mansions, Thornhill *North of Cadiff* ☎ 7974 328437
💻 www.waxformen.co.uk
Qualified in sports, Swedish, Aroma and Tantric massage and reflexology. We also do male body waxing

GUEST HOUSES

■ **Ty Rosa Boutique Gay B&B**
(BF CC GLM I MA OS PK RWS RWT VA) All year
118 Clive Street ☎ 0845 643 99 62 💻 www.tyrosa.com
Eight luxury guest rooms, some with shared bathrooms.

Carlisle – Cumbria ☎ 01228

SAUNAS/BATHS

■ **Sweat Sauna**
(DR FC FH G I LAB m MSG RR SA SB SH SL SOL VS WH) 11-22h
Atlas Works, Nelson Street *10 mins from railway station* ☎ 0792 642 2178
💻 carlislegaysauna.comule.com

Cheltenham – Gloucestershire ☎ 01242

BARS

■ **EXS** (B D GLM MA OS S) Thu-Sat 21-?h
20 High Street *Top end of High Street* ☎ (01242) 260 706
Large venue with regular changes in entertainment.

HOTELS

■ **Butlers** (BF CC glm H I MA OS PK RWS RWT) All year
Western Road ☎ (01242) 570 771 💻 www.butlers-hotel.co.uk
Award winning and gay owned private/mixed B&B hotel with nine guestrooms in the heart of Cheltenham.

Chester – Cheshire ☎ 0780

CAFES

■ **Blue Moon** (b CC g H M MA) 10-17, Sat & Sun 9.30-17h
23 The Groves ☎ (01244) 322 481 💻 www.bluemooncafe.eu

Chippenham – Wiltshire ☎ 01249

BARS

■ **Little George. The** (B g MC)
29 New Road ☎ (01249) 447 543

Conwy – North Wales ☎ 01492

HOTELS

■ **Pennant Hall** (B CC DR DU FC FH G H I M MA OS P SA SB VS WE WH) 11.30-20; Wed, Fri & Sat -21.30h; closed Sun
Pennant Hall, Beach Road, Penmaenmawr *Three mins from railway station* ☎ (01492) 622 878 💻 www.gaypennanthall.co.uk
Friendly sauna/hotel with sun terrace; food and beverages served all day. Eleven bedrooms.

Derby – Derbyshire ☎ 01332

BARS

■ **Crown Inn** (B D GLM H m OS) Mon-Sat 11-23, Sun 12-22.30h
40 Curzon Street ☎ (01332) 381 742
Pub with beer garden. B&B available.

■ **Freddie's** (AC B d GLM m MA ST VS) Mon-Sat 19-23, Sun -22.30h
101 Curzon Street ☎ (01332) 204 290

SAUNAS/BATHS

■ **City Steam Sauna** (B DU FC G M p SA SB SL VS WH) Daily 12-19h
8-9 St. Mary's Gate *In Cathedral Quarter* ☎ 08712 885 173
💻 www.citysteam.co.uk
Purpose built modern sauna complex.

Dumfries – Dumfriesshire ☎ 01387

DANCECLUBS

■ **Sticky @ The Venue** (B D GLM MA) Last Sat/month
6/7 Church Place 💻 www.clubsticky.co.uk

Dundee – Tayside ☎ 01382

BARS

■ **Abode** (B glm M MA) 11-24, Sun 12.30-24h
22 St. Andrew's Street ☎ (01382) 223 923 💻 www.bebo.com/theabodebar

■ **Brooks** (B GLM MA) 19-24, Fri-Sun 15-24h, closed Mon & Tue
2 St. Andrew's Lane *Next to Out* ☎ (01382) 200 660

■ **Salty Dog. The** (B GLM MA) 12-?h
9 Crichton Street

DANCECLUBS

■ **Out** (B D GLM SNU VS YC) Wed-Sun 23-2.30h
124 Seagate ☎ (01382) 200 660
Commercial & house dance music.

SAUNAS/BATHS

■ **Jocks** (B DR DU FC G GH I M MA NR P RR SA SB T VR VS)
Sun-Sat 12-22h
11 Princes Street ☎ (01382) 451 986 💻 www.jockssauna.co.uk
Dundee's only men-only sauna. Relaxed and friendly atmosphere. Helpful staff. Gay owned & managed.

GENERAL GROUPS

■ **Diversitay LGBT Group** (GLM) Mon 19-21h (helpline)
PO Box 53 ☏ (01382) 202 620 💻 www.diversitay.org.uk

CRUISING

-Templeton Woods P parking spaces in the woods. Best after dark
-Law Hill toilets.

Eastbourne – East Sussex ☏ 01323

BARS

■ **Hart. The** (AC B D GLM I m MA OS S SNU ST)
Mon-Thu 16-24, Fri -2, Sat 12-2, Sun -23.30h
89 Cavendish Place *500 m from Eastbourne Pier* ☏ (01323) 643 151
💻 www.thehart.co.uk
Various theme nights.

Edinburgh – Lothian ☏ 0131

Edinburgh is the capital city of Scotland. As well as being one of the most beautifully situated cities in the world it also has a relatively relaxed and tolerant atmosphere for LGBT life. The gay scene is mostly located in the Georgian New Town, on Broughton Street and at the top of Leith Walk near the Playhouse Theatre. One of the best months for sightseeing (the Castle, the Old Town, museums, galleries etc) is in August when the annual arts festival takes place.

Edinburgh ist die Hauptstadt von Schottland und eine der am schönsten gelegenen Weltmetropolen, in der Schwule, Lesben, Bisexuelle und Transgender in recht entspannter und toleranter Atmosphäre leben können.
Die Szene konzentriert sich überwiegend auf das georgianische New Town, auf die Broughton Street und auf das Ende des Leith Walk unweit des Playhouse Theaters.
Jedes Jahr im August findet das Festival der Künste statt. Ein Besuch der Sehenswürdigkeiten wie der Burg, der Altstadt, der Museen und Galerien lohnt sich in dieser Zeit am meisten.

Edimbourg est la capitale de l'Écosse et une des métroples les plus joliment situées au monde, dans laquelle homos, lesbiennes et trans peuvent vivre dans une atmosphère véritablement détendue et tolérante.
La scène se concentre essentiellement dans la New Town géorgienne, sur la Broughton Street et au bout de la Leith Walk non loin du Playhouse Theatre. Tous les ans en août se déroule le Festival des Arts. Une visite des attractions touristiques comme le château, la vieille-ville, les musées et galeries est particulièrement conseillée pendant cette période.

Edimburgo es la capital de Escocia y a la vez una metrópoli con una de las ubicaciones más bellas en el mundo, en la cual los gays, las lesbianas, los bisexuales y los transsexuales pueden vivir en una atmósfera relajada y tolerante.
La escena gay se concentra principalmente en la zona georgiana de New Town, en la calle Broughton y al final de Leith Walk, no muy lejos de los Playhouse Theatre. Cada año en agosto tiene lugar el Festival del Arte. Una visita a los monumentos como el Castillo, la ciudad vieja, los museos y las galerías bien vale la pena durante esta misma temporada.

Edinburgo è la capitale della Scozia e una delle città, a livello mondiale, con il più bel paesaggio; qui gay, lesbiche, bisessuali e transgender possono vivere armoniosamente in un'atmosfera di relax e di tolleranza.
La scena si concentra soprattutto nella New Town e precisamente nella Broughton Street e alla fine del Leith Walk, non molto lontano dal Teatro Playhouse. Ogni anno in agosto ha luogo il festival artistico. Tra le attrazioni turistiche, di particolare interesse sono il Castello, la città antica, i musei e le gallerie.

GAY INFO

■ **Edinburgh LGBT Centre** (GLM I)
9 Howe Street ☏ (0131) 523 1100 💻 www.lgbthealth.org.uk

BARS

■ **Auld Hoose. The** (B GLM M MC) Mon-Sat 11.30-1, Sun 12.30-1h
23-25 Leonards Street ☏ (0131) 668 2934
💻 www.theauldhoose.co.uk

■ **Deep Blue** (B GLM MC) 16-23h
1 Barony Street / 36 Broughton Street *In the basement of the Blue Moon Cafe* ☏ (0131) 556 2788

■ **Frenchies** (B GLM MA T WE) 13-1h
89 Rose Street Lane North *Off Princess Street* ☏ (0131) 225 7651
💻 www.frenchies-bar.com
Reopened after tasteful refurbishment. A small, cosy bar, the ideal place for a quiet drink with friends. Happy hour 18-20h.

■ **GHQ** (B D GLM MA) Tue, Thu & Sun 23-3, Wed, Fri & Sat 22-3h
4 Picardy Place ☏ (0131) 550 1780 💻 www.ghqedinburgh.co.uk

■ **Habana** (B GLM MA S) 13-1h
22 Greenside Place *Located between the Playhouse Theatre and CC Bloom's* ☏ (0131) 558 1270 💻 www.cafehabanaeh1.com
Popular with loud music and mixed crowd. Pre-club venue.

■ **New Town Bar** (AC B CC D DR GLM I M MA)
12-1, Fri & Sat -2, Sun 12.30-1h
26b Dublin Street *Near Broughton Street* ☏ (0131) 538 7775
💻 www.newtownbar.co.uk
Bright and airy during the day and warm and intimate after dark. Downstairs @ NTB open Fri & Sat 22-2h.

■ **Planet** (AC B CC GLM S WE YC) Mon-Fri 17-1, Sat & Sun 12.30-1h
6 Baxter's Place *Down the road from CC's* ☏ (0131) 524 0061
Discounted bar prices on Mondays.

■ **Priscilla's** (B GLM MA S ST WI) 12-1, Sat 5-12 & 16-1, Sun 14-1h
17 Albert Place ☏ (0131) 554 8962
💻 www.priscillasedinburgh.co.uk
Cabaret on Thu, Fri & Sat.

■ **Regent. The** (B CC F GLM I M MA T) 11-1h
2 Montrose Terrace *Junction of Regent and Easter Roads*
☏ (0131) 661 8198
Warm, friendly, pub atmosphere. Real ales and no loud music.

■ **Street. The** (B gLm M MC WI) 12-1, Sun 12.30-1h
2 Picardy Place ☏ (0131) 556 4272
Small bar. Food served until 19.30h.

CAFES

■ **Blue Moon** (AC B BF CC GLM M MA) 11-23, Sat & Sun 10-23h
1 Barony Street / 36 Broughton Street ☏ (0131) 556 2788
💻 www.bluemooncafe.co.uk
Very popular, licensed cafe with relaxed, laid-back atmosphere. Food served until 22h.

■ **Nom de Plume** (B CC GLM M MA) 11-23, Fri & Sat -1h
60 Broughton Street *Five mins walk from Waverley railway station*
☏ (0131) 478 1372
Located above the LGBT centre. Sala is a Spanish tapas bar with a traditional, healthy tapas menu. They serve Cruz Campo and other Spanish beers.

DANCECLUBS

■ **CC Blooms** (! AC B D GLM MA s) 20-3, Fri & Sat 18-3, Sun 21-3h
23 Greenside Place *Next to Edinburgh Playhouse Theatre*
☏ (0131) 556 9331 💻 www.bebo.com/ccbloomsnightclub
Two dancefloors. Every night from 23h. Thu-Sun Karaoke. Popular club particular on Fri & Sat. Very mixed crowd.

RESTAURANTS

■ **Elbow** (B CC GLM M MA VEG) 11-1h
133-135 East Claremont Street *Close to city centre* ☏ (0131) 556 5662
💻 www.elbowedinburgh.co.uk
Great food. Different groups and events take place here.

ESCORTS & STUDIOS

■ **Escort Guys** (CC G MSG) 24hrs
☏ 07722 062 077 💻 www.escortguys.co.uk
Gay escort agency with escorts in London, UK and across Europe.

SAUNAS/BATHS

Number 18 Sauna (AC B DU FC FH G M MA p RR SA SB VS)
12-22, Fri-Sun -23h
18 Albert Place *Entrance off Leith Walk* ☎ (0131) 553 3222
www.number18sauna.com
Probably Edinburgh's busiest men-only sauna. Offers a relaxed atmosphere with friendly service.

Steamworks
(b CC DR DU FH G H I LAB M MA MSG SA SB SOL VS WE WH) 11-23h
5 Broughton Market *Between Barony & Dublin Streets* ☎ (0131) 477 3567
www.steamworks-sauna.co.uk
Stylish sauna in the middle of the gay quarter. Hotel & sauna complex. No membership required. Gay owned & managed.

BOOK SHOPS

Bobbies Bookshop (g) Mon-Sat 10-17.30h
220 Morrison Street *Near Haymarket* ☎ (0131) 538 7069
UK and imported gay magazines.

Q Store (GLM) 11-19, Sat -18, Sun 13-17h
5 Barony Street ☎ (0131) 477 4756

LEATHER & FETISH SHOPS

Leather & Lace (F G MA) 10-21, Sun 12-21h
8b Drummond Street ☎ (0131) 557 9413
Vast range of leather and rubber wear. Also cards, mags and toys.

GUEST HOUSES

Alva House (BF CC G MA NR PK RWS RWT VA VS) All year
45 Alva Place *Close to gay area* ☎ (0131) 558 1382
www.alvahouse.com
Edinburgh's only all-male guesthouse. Stylish and comfortable accommodation at affordable prices. The guestrooms and public areas were designed by an interior architect and have either an en-suite bathroom or shared facilities.

Amaryllis Guest House (BF CC glm MA RWS RWT) All year
21 Upper Gilmore Place ☎ (0131) 229 3293
www.amaryllisguesthouse.com
Comfortable guest house. All five rooms have TV and tea & coffee making facilities.

Ardmor House (BF CC GLM I MA PA PK RWS RWT) All year, 24hrs
74 Pilrig Street *Seven mins walk to gay area* ☎ (0131) 554 4944
www.ardmorhouse.com
All rooms en suite & with TV, tea/coffee making facilities. Gay owned, non-smoking.

Garlands (BF CC glm I MA RWS RWT VA) All year
48 Pilrig Street *Near town centre* ☎ (0131) 554 4205
www.garlands.demon.co.uk
All rooms ensuite.

APARTMENTS

Village Apartments (BF CC G MA PK RWS RWT VA VS) All year
5 Broughton Market *In the heart of the gay area* ☎ (0131) 556 5094
www.villageapartments.co.uk
Stylish modern living in the heart of Edinburgh's gay village. Each room or suite features private bathroom, TV, DVD player, CD player, radio, fridge, microwave, tea/coffee making facilities and alarm clock, as well as iron and ironing board. Serviced daily.

FETISH GROUPS

MSC Scotland
PO Box 28
They meet on the 3rd Saturday night of each month in the downstairs bar of the Newtown Bar. The dress code is encouraged. A cloakroom is available for guys who wish to change into gear on arrival.

CRUISING

-Calton Hill (at night, AYOR)

-Regent Road (day and night, AYOR. In cemetery on right hand side going away from centre of town)
-Warriston cemetery (day and night, AYOR)
-Dalry cemetary, after dark
-Old Craighall, by Musselburgh at the roundabout A1 and A 720. In truckers wash room
-Corstorphine toilets, Corstorphine Road, all day
-Bristo Square toilets, many students
-Juniper Green toilets, next to post office at 529 Lanark Road.

Exeter – Devon ☎ 01392

BARS

Northbridge Inn. The (B GLM m MA) 12-23h
11 St. David's Hill ☎ (01392) 252 535

Queen's Vaults. The (! AC B D GLM m MA)
Mon-Thu 16-0.30, Fri 16-3.30, Sat 12 -3.30, Sun 19-2.30h
8 Gandy Street *City centre* ☎ (01392) 203 939 💻 www.vaultsexeter.co.uk
Regular events. Karaoke on Tue & Sun. Live cabaret 1st Thu/month.

Glasgow – Strathclyde ☎ 0141

BARS

Court Bar. The (AC B BF glm MA WE) 9-24, Sun 12.30-24h
69 Hutcheson Street *Close to Bennets* ☎ (0141) 552 2463
Gay later on in the evening. BF and snacks Mon-Sat 8-11h.

Delmonica's (AC B CC D GLM MA S) 12-24h
68 Virginia Street ☎ (0141) 552 4803
💻 www.socialanimal.co.uk/GlasgowCityCentre/Delmonicas
Big and busy.

Merchant Pride (B G MC S) Mon-Fri 16-, Sat 12-,Sun 12.30-24h
20 Candleriggs, Merchant City ☎ (0141) 564 1285
Upmarket bar with karaoke, cabaret and disco.

Milk (B G MA) 12-24h
17 John Street 💻 moojuice.co
Former Scene bar.

Moda (B GLM M MA) 17-1, Fri & Sat -3h
58 Virginia Street *Cnr. Wilson Street* ☎ (0141) 553 2553
💻 www.socialanimal.co.uk/GlasgowCityCentre/Moda
Stylish cocktail lounge.

Speakeasy (B G M MA) 16-2, Fri -3, Sat 12-3, Sun 12.30-2h
10 John Street ☎ (0141) 553 5851
💻 www.socialanimal.co.uk/glasgowcitycentre/speakeasy
Food until 21h.

Tron Theatre Bar (B glm m MA) Mon-Sat 10-?, Sun 11-?h
Chishlom Street ☎ (0141) 552 857 💻 www.tron.co.uk

Underground (B G I MA WI) 12-24, Sat & Sun 13-24h
6a John Street ☎ (0141) 553 2456
Formerly Revolver Bar. A refreshing antidote to the current gay scene.

Waterloo. The (B GLM M MA ST) 12-24, Sun 12.30-24h
306 Argyle Street *Central Station* ☎ (0141) 229 5891
💻 www.waterloobar.co.uk *Scotland's oldest gay bar. Busy.*

DANCECLUBS

Allure @ The Tunnel (B D GLM MA) Wed 23.30-3h
84 Mitchell Street ☎ (0141) 204 1000 💻 www.tunnelglasgow.co.uk
Chart, pop, R'n'B.

Bennets (B D GLM MA) 23.30-3h, closed Mon & Tue
80 Glassford Street, Merchant City *Near Ingram Street* ☎ (0141) 552 5761
💻 www.bebo.com/bennetsniteclub
Scotland's oldest gay disco.

Club X (B D GLM MA) 21-3h
68 Virginia Street ☎ (0845) 659 5905 💻 www.clubxglasgow.co.uk

Plush @ Orbis (B D GLM MA) Tue 23-3h
10 Bell Street, Merchant City ☎ (0141) 552 1212 💻 www.orbisglasgow.com

Polo Lounge. The (AC B D GLM MA S) 17-1, Fri & Sat -3h
84 Wilson Street, Merchant City ☎ (0141) 553 1221
Busy night club – long established with regular entertainment at weekends.

ESCORTS & STUDIOS

Escort Guys (CC G MSG) 24hrs
☎ 07722 062 077 💻 www.escortguys.co.uk
Gay escort agency with escorts in London, UK and across Europe.

SAUNAS/BATHS

Ambassadors Rainbow (B DR G I MA MSG SA) 12-24, Fri-Sun -2h
41b York Street ☎ (0141) 237 3011 💻 www.ambassadorsrainbow.com

Babylon (bf DR f G MA S SA SB SOL VS WE) 11-2, Fri & Sat -24h
28 Bath Street ☎ (0141) 332 1377

Pipeworks. The (! B CC DR DU G I M MA SA SB SL VR WH) Mon-Thu 11.30-23, Fri -6, Sat 12 – Sun 23h non-stop
5 Metropole Lane *Close to the main gay pubs and clubs in the centre*
☎ (0141) 552 5502 441 💻 www.thepipeworks.com
The biggest gay men's health & leisure club in Scotland, with state-of-the-art facilities. A second Pipeworks club is in Belfast.

Relax Central (B DR DU FC FH G M PP RR SA SB SOL VS WH)
11.30-22, Sat & Sun 12-20h
3rd Floor, 27 Union Street ☎ (0141) 221 0415 💻 www.relaxcentral.co.uk

GUEST HOUSES

Glasgow Guest House (BF CC glm I MA PA PK RWS RWT SA)
All year
56 Dumbreck Road *Near Burrell Collection, 500 m to Dumbreck Stn., 4 km to city centre* ☎ (0141) 427 0129 💻 www.glasgow-guest-house.co.uk
Three double, three twin, one single room, one apartment. All rooms ensuite. 4 km to the city centre. Relaxed and friendly atmosphere.

HEALTH GROUPS

Terrence Higgins Trust Scotland (glm) Mon-Fri 9-17h
Top Floor, Rothesay House, 134 Douglas Street *Corner of Sauchiehall Street* ☎ (0141) 332 3838 💻 www.tht.org.uk
HIV charity offering services and information; free condoms and lubricant.

CRUISING

-Queens Park (at night AYOR; the most interesting area is the section closest to Victoria Road)
-Kelvin Grove Park (near University especially around the lake, but watch out for police)
-Toilets at Savoy Centre, late afternoon.

Gower – Swansea ☎ 01792

HOTELS

■ **Fairyhill Hotel & Restaurant** (B BF CC GLM M MA OS PK RWS RWT) All year
Reynoldston *Gower Peninsular* ☎ (01792) 390 139
🖳 www.fairyhill.net

Great Yarmouth – Norfolk ☎ 01493

BARS

■ **Kings Wine Bar** (AC B CC d GLM I M MA S) 11-24, Fri & Sat -1, Sun 12-24h
42 King Street ☎ (01493) 855 374 🖳 www.kingswinebar.co.uk
Friendly local crowd. Regular live entertainment. DJ Fri & Sat. Extensive wine list, huge range of drinks. Reservations essential for evening meals.

Harrogate – North Yorkshire ☎ 01423

BARS

■ **Hales Bar** (B CC GLM M MA S) Mon-Sat 10.30-0.30, Sun 12-23.30h
1-3 Crescent Road *Five mins walk from the town centre*
☎ (01423) 725 570 🖳 www.halesbar.co.uk
Monthly party nights.

Harrow – Middlesex ☎ 020

HOTELS

■ **Grim's Dyke** (B BF glm I M MA PA PK RWS RWT) All year
Old Redding, Harrow Weald *Stanmore or Harrow Stations*
☎ (020) 8385 3100 🖳 www.grimsdyke.com
A country house hotel with 46 guest rooms and restaurant, set in forty acres of gardens and woodland.

Helston – Cornwall ☎ 07813

CAMPING

■ **Out in the Open** (GLM MA) May-Sept
Lower Dacum Farm *Halfway between Falmouth & Helston*
☎ (07813) 984 661 🖳 www.outintheopen.co.uk
Probably the only exclusively lesbian & gay campsite in the UK. These days, all are welcome, but we remain predominantly gay. Both camping & beautifully furnished shepherd's huts & tipi for hire.

Hull – Humberside ☎ 01482

BARS

■ **Polar Bear** (B CC d GLM m MA OS) 11-23, Sun 12-22.30h
229 Spring Bank ☎ (01482) 323 959 🖳 www.polarbear-hull.co.uk
■ **Propaganda** (B D g M MA t) Mon-Fri 11-late, Sat & Sun 12h-late
107 Ferensway *Two mins walk from train station* ☎ (01482) 222 700
🖳 www.fuelclubsuk.com
Food served 12-18h.
■ **Vauxhall Tavern. The** (B D GLM S) Mon-Sat 11-23h
1 Hessle Road *Near Alexander Hotel* ☎ (01482) 320 340
■ **Yorkshireman. The** (B d G H m MA S ST t)
Mon-Thu 17-late, Fri & Sat 12-2, Sun 14-24h
2-5 Lombard Street *One min. walk from train station*
🖳 www.fuel-hull.co.uk/Yorkshireman.html
Drag shows, games and karaoke all weekend.

DANCECLUBS

■ **Fuel** (B D GLM m MA S t) Fri & Sat 23-3, Sun -2h
6 Baker Street *Near train station* ☎ (01482) 228 436
🖳 www.fuelclubsuk.com
Fuel is the stylish home of Hull's gay scene.

Ipswich – Suffolk ☎ 01473

BARS

■ **Betty's** (B D GLM MA) Thu-Sat 21-2h
10, Cornhill ☎ (01473) 288 406 🖳 www.bettysbar.plus.com
■ **Dove. The** (B g m MA) 12-23h
76 St. Helen's Street ☎ (01473) 211 270 🖳 www.dovestreetinn.co.uk

SAUNAS/BATHS

■ **Helsinki Health Spa** (b DU g MSG SA SB WH)
Tue-Fri & Sat 10-22, Sun 14-20h (during winter)
115 Penshurst Road ☎ (01473) 724 196
🖳 www.helsinkihealthspa.co.uk

Isleworth – Middlesex ☎ 0208

BARS

■ **George. The** (B d GLM MA OS s)
Mon-Fri 17-23, Sat 12-23, Sun -22.30h
114 Twickenham Road *Opposite War Memorial/buses 37 & 267*
☎ (0208) 8560 1456 🖳 www.georgemusicbar.co.uk
West London's premiere gay cabaret bar. Cabaret Fri & Sat.

Jedburgh – Scottish Borders ☎ 01835

GUEST HOUSES

■ **Willow Court** (glm H I M MA PK RWS RWT) All year
The Friars ☎ (01835) 863 702 🖳 www.willowcourtjedburgh.co.uk

King's Lynn – Norfolk ☎ 01553

BARS

■ **Hob-in-the-Well. The** (B glm WE)
Thu 21-1, Fri & Sat 21-2, Sun 21-1h
Littleport Street *Near town centre* ☎ (01553) 538 431
🖳 www.hobinthewell.co.uk

Leeds – West Yorkshire ☎ 0113

BARS

■ **Base. The** (AC B CC D GLM MA OS S SNU ST)
12-24, Fri-Sat -2, Sun 16-24h
24-32 Bridge End ☎ (0113) 368 4648
Regular shows and cabaret. Fri: Camp Classics, Sat: House & Trance.
■ **Blayds** (B GLM MA)
Blayds Yard 3 ☎ (0113) 244 5590
■ **Bridge. The** (B GLM M MA s ST WE)
Mon-Wed 12-late, Thu-Sat 12-2, Sun 13-?h
1-5 Bridge End ☎ (0113) 244 4734
■ **Fibre** (! B GLM M) 11-24, Thu -1, Fri & Sat -2, Sun -22.30h
Queen's Court, 168 Lower Briggate ☎ 8701 200 888 (mobile)
🖳 www.barFibre.com
One of the most popular bars in Leeds. Upstairs VIP bar.
■ **New Penny. The** (B G MA s ST)
Mon-Thu 12-23, Fri & Sat -4, Sun 13-2.30h
57 Call Lane ☎ (0113) 2438 055
Door charge after 1h.
■ **Viaduct. The** (B GLM M MA ST)
11 Briggate ☎ (0113) 245 4863
■ **Xibit** (B GLM M MA)
24-32 Bridge End

DANCECLUBS

Queen's Court (AC B CC D GLM M MA SNU ST) Mon-Sun 11-23 (Cafe-Bar), Mon-Sat 22-2h (Nightclub)
167-168 Lower Briggate ☎ (0113) 245 9449
www.queenscourtleeds.com
The largest gay bar and club in Leeds.

ESCORTS & STUDIOS

Escort Guys (CC G MSG) 24hrs
☎ 07722 062 077 www.escortguys.co.uk
Gay escort agency with escorts in London, UK and across Europe.

SAUNAS/BATHS

Basement Sauna Complex Leeds (B DR DU G I m MA P PI PP RR SA SB SOL VS WH WO) Daily, 24hrs
Unit 7, Heatons Court *Located in one of the railway arches*
☎ (0113) 242 7730 www.basementcomplex.co.uk

Plastic Ivy Sauna (B DR DU FC FH G I M MA RR SA SB SH VS WH) 12-22h, closed Tue
33 Leeds Road, Dewsbury *South of Leeds City Centre, next to junction 28 of M62 & junction 40 of M1* ☎ (01924) 455 600 www.plasticivy.co.uk
Just outside of Leeds, discreet sauna with a relaxed and friendly atmosphere in beautiful surroundings.

Steam Complex (B DR DU G I m MA SA SB SOL VS WH) 11-23, Fri 11-Sun 23h (non-stop)
Eyres Ave., Armley *Bus 16-Armly Town Street* ☎ (0113) 279 8885
gaybisexualsauna.com
Great atmosphere and everything you will need.

Leicester – Leicestershire ☎ 0116

GAY INFO

Leicester Lesbian, Gay, Bisexual & Transgender Centre
15 Wellington Street ☎ (0116) 254 7412 www.llgbc.com

BARS

Amber (B G MA)
1 Newport Place, Northampton Street *Around the corner from the Rainbow & Dove* ☎ (0116) 255 9986
A small and stylish bar with nice friendly staff.

DDC Dover Castle (AC B CC D GLM MA OS ST T VS) 12-24, Fri & Sat -2h
34 Dover Street *Off Granby Street* ☎ (0116) 255 8510
One of the oldest gay bars in the UK. Gay disco with cabaret.

Quebec (AC B GLM m MA) Mon-Sat 12-2, Sun -0.30h
96 Belgrave Gate ☎ (0116) 251 3811 qbnetwork.ning.com

Rainbow & Dove (B GLM m MA) 12-23h
185 Charles Street ☎ (0116) 254 7568 www.rainbowanddove.co.uk
Popular city centre gay pub near the train station with various theme evenings.

SAUNAS/BATHS

Celts (B DR DU G GH SA SB SL VS WH) 11-22h
38 Narborough Road *Just off the M1/M69* ☎ (0116) 285 6000
www.celts-sauna.co.uk

Liverpool – Merseyside ☎ 0151

BARS

Curzon Club (B D GLM m MA SNU ST T VS) 12-2h, Sun closed
8 Temple Lane *Off Victoria Street* ☎ (0151) 236 5160

Destination (B D G MA S WE)
21 Temple Street

G-Bar (B GLM YC) Thu-Sat
1-7 Eberle Street *Off Dale Street, opp. Garlands* ☎ (0151) 236 4416
www.g-bar.com
Popular before and after Garlands.

Lisbon. The (B glm MA) 11-23h, best Sun
36 Victoria Street ☎ (0151) 286 5466

Masquerade. The (AC B CC GLM M MA s) 12-23, Fri & Sat -1, Sun -24h
10 Cumberland Street ☎ (0151) 236 7786
www.masqueradeliverpool.com

Pink (B G ST YC)
4-6 Victoria Street www.pinkliverpool.co.uk

Poste House. The (B G MA)
23 Cumberland Street ☎ (0151) 236 4130

DANCECLUBS

Garlands (B D GLM PI SNU T YC) Thu-Sat 21-2h
8-10 Eberle Street ☎ (0151) 236 3307 www.garlandsonline.com

Navy Bar (B D G YC) Thu-Sat 22-4h
27-29 Stanley Street

Superstar Boudoir (B D GLM m MA) Daily 21-3h
22-24 Stanley Street
Various themed days.

SAUNAS/BATHS

Dolphin. The (AC DR DU FC FH G GH I m MA RR SA SB SL VS WH) 11-22h
129 Mount Road, Wallasey *Liverpool underground, five mins from New Brighton railway station* ☎ (0151) 630 1516
www.dolphinsauna.co.uk
Friendly sauna.

Llandysul – Ceredigion

GUEST HOUSES

Under the Thatch (B glm M OS PA PI PK RWB RWS RWT SA VA WO) All year
Felin Brithdir, Rhydlewis ☎ (0844) 5005 101
www.underthethatch.co.uk
Self-catering holiday cottages and a Romany caravan.

London ☎ 020

London is a city with a population of around 12 million people, divided into boroughs, operating almost as towns in their own right. The centre is divided into 3 specific cities: the City of London to the east is the financial and business district; Westminster is the seat of the Government with the Houses of Parliament and Buckingham Palace and the West End, with department stores, boutiques, hotels, restaurants, clubs and bars.

In the last fifteen years, a busy gay scene has been overlaid onto the once-seedy area of Soho, bordered by Oxford Street, London's main shopping street, and Shaftesbury Avenue, the theatre district. Old Compton Street is where you will find gay bars, restaurants and pubs, also clothes shops and gay stores for magazines and toys. You'll also find flyers for party nights elsewhere in the city. It's an open, confident, young scene, and is safe. Mardi Gras is held each year in July, a huge gay party in a London park, preceded by a Pride march through the centre of the city.

Vauxhall is the city's second gay centre as well as the clubbing area for gay London. One of the most popular saunas as well as several very popular bars are also found here. The gay summer event in Vauxhall is a must.

London mit seinen rund zwölf Millionen Einwohnern ist in Bezirke unterteilt. Diese wiederum funktionieren fast wie eigenständige Städte. Das Zentrum besteht aus drei Unterbezirken: In der City of London befindet sich das Finanz- und Wirtschaftszentrum der Stadt, in Westminster ist der Regierungssitz mit dem Parlamentsgebäude und dem Buckingham-Palast und im West End findet man die großen Kaufhäuser, Boutiquen, Hotels, Restaurants, Clubs und Bars.

Während der letzten 15 Jahre hat sich im einst heruntergekommenen Bezirk Soho eine geschäftige schwule Szene ausgebreitet, die sich bis zur wichtigsten Shopping-Meile, der Oxford Street und dem Theaterviertel um die Shaftesbury Avenue erstreckt. In der Old Compton Street gibt es schwule Bars, Restaurants und Pubs sowie Bekleidungsgeschäfte und

schwule Läden, die Pornomagazine und Toys verkaufen. Hier werden auch Flyer für Partys in der ganzen Stadt verteilt. Die Szene ist aufgeschlossen, selbstbewusst, jung und sicher vor Übergriffen.
Nach der CSD-Parade durch die Innenstadt findet Anfang Juli der jährliche Mardi Gras als große Party in einem Londoner Park statt.
Neben Soho ist Vauxhall der zweite schwule Szenebezirk, der zum Clubbing einlädt. Auch eine der populärsten Saunen und die vielen beliebten Bars sowie der „Gay Sports Day" machen Vauxhall zu einem Muss für den schwulen Reisenden.

Londres est une ville d'environ 12 millions d'habitants divisée en arrondissements quasi autonomes. On retrouve au centre la ville la City, le centre financier et des affaires, Westminster, le siège du gouvernement avec les Maisons du Parlement et la Palais de Buckingham et le West End et ses grands magasins, boutiques, hôtels, restaurants, clubs et bars.
Au cours des dernières quinze années, une scène gaie bouillonnante s'est installée dans le quartier de Soho, jadis peu réputé, délimité par Oxford Street, la principale artère commerciale de Londres, et Shaftesbury Avenue, le quartier du théâtre. C'est sur Old Compton Street que l'on trouve les bars, restaurants, pubs et boutiques gais. C'est un milieu ouvert, jeune, confiant et sécuritaire.
Le Mardi Gras a lieu au début de juillet. C'est une énorme fête gaie dans un parc de Londres qui est précédée d'une parade à travers le centre de la ville. Vauxhall est un deuxième centre de la scène gay londonienne. Celui-ci comporte non seulement plusieurs discothèques mais aussi un des saunas les plus populaires de toute la ville ainsi qu'un bon nombre de bars particulièrement en vogue. La manifestation estivale „Gay Sports Day" de Vauxhall est un must.

Londres, con unos 12 millones de habitantes, es una ciudad dividida en distritos que funcionan como ciudades independientes. El centro está repartido en tres subdistritos especiales: en la City of London y el este se encuentra el centro financiero y económico de la ciudad; en Westminster está la sede del gobierno con el Parlamento y el palacio de Buckingham; en el West End están los grandes almacenes, tiendas de moda, hoteles, restaurantes, clubes y bares.
Durante los últimos quince años, se ha instaurado en el entonces marginado distrito del Soho un ambiente gay que abarca desde las conocidas calles comerciales de Oxford Street y el barrio de los teatros alrededor de Shaftesbury Avenue.
En la Old Compton Street están los bares, restaurantes y pubs gays así como tiendas de ropa y otras tiendas que venden revistas y artículos porno. Aquí se reparten también las entradas para las fiestas de toda la ciudad. El ambiente es abierto, consciente de sí mismo, joven y seguro ante los ataques.
A principios de julio, después de la Marcha del Orgullo Gay por el centro de la ciudad, se celebra la gran fiesta anual del Mardi Gras en un parque londinense.
Vauxhall es el segundo centro neurálgico del ambiente gay londinense, aquí se pueden encontrar no sólo un gran número de discotecas, sino también algunas de las saunas más populares de la ciudad y toda una serie de bares de moda. El „Gay Sport Day" en Vauxhall es uno de los eventos del verano que no se deben pasar por alto.

Londra, coi suoi circa 12 milioni di abitanti, è una città che è divisa in quartieri, funzionanti ognuno quasi come città a sè stanti.
Il centro è suddiviso in tre speciali sottoquartieri: nella City di Londra e ad est di questa si trova il centro finanziario ed economico della città, a Westminster c'è la sede del governo col palazzo del Parlamento e Buckingham-Palace, al West End ci sono i grandi centri commerciali, le boutiques, alberghi, ristoranti, clubs e bar. Durante gli ultimi quindici anni si è venuto costituendo nel quartiere di Soho il centro della vita gay di Londra, che si estende sino alla più importante strada commerciale, la Oxford-Street, ed al quartiere dei teatri intorno alla Shaftesbury Avenue. Nella Old Compton Street ci sono bar gay, ristoranti e pubs così come negozi di moda e negozi gay che vendono giornali porno e altri articoli per il divertimento sessuale. Qui vengono distribuiti anche inviti per i

London – Soho

EAT & DRINK

79CXR – Bar	9
Admiral Duncan. The – Bar	15
Balans – Restaurant	17
Barcode – Bar	30
Canela Café	4
Comptons of Soho – Bar	18
Duke of Wellington. The – Bar	28
Edge. The – Bar	3
Escape Dance Bar – Bar	23
Freedom – Café	20
Friendly Society – Bar	27
G-A-Y Bar – Bar	10
Halfway to Heaven – Bar	7
Kings Arms – Bar	2
Ku Bar – Bar	8
Ku Bar – Bar	13
Profile – Bar	33
Rupert Street – Bar	31
Village Soho – Bar	32
Yard. The – Bar	25

NIGHTLIFE

Heaven – Danceclub	12
Shadow Lounge – Danceclub	26

SEX

Blue Room – Sex Shop/ Blue Movies	21
Clone Zone – Sex Shop/ Blue Movies	19
SaunaBar. The – Sauna	6
SweatBox – Sauna	34

ACCOMMODATION

Accommodation Outlet – Apartments	11
London Checkin Apartments	37

OTHERS

Kingly Street Fitness First – Fitness Studio	36
Paradiso Bodyworks – Leather & Fetish Shop	14
Prowler – Gift & Pride Shop	21
Rio Beach – Fashion Shop	35
RoB London – Leather & Fetish Shop	1

partys in tutta la città. La comunità gay è aperta, consapevole, giovane e sicura da eventuali attacchi. Dopo il CSD nel centro di Londra, ha luogo a inizio luglio l'annuale Mardi Gras, un gigantesco party in uno dei parchi londinesi.
Vauxhall è il secondo centro della scena gay di Londra. Infatti qui non vi sono solo tantissime discoteche, bensì anche tanti bei bar e una delle saune più frequentate della città. In estate non perdetevi la manifestazione sportiva „Gay Sports Day" di Vauxhall.

GAY INFO

London Lesbian & Gay Switchboard (GLM MA) 10-23h
☏ 0300 3300 630 💻 www.llgs.org.uk
LLGS provides an information, support and referral service for LGBT people and anyone who needs to consider issues around sexuality. Email and Instant Messaging via website.

PUBLICATIONS

Boyz (G)
18 Brewer Street ☏ (020) 7025 6120 💻 www.boyz.co.uk
Free weekly scene guide, with a focus on London and the South/South East.

Out Magazine (G)
37 Ivor Place ☏ (020) 7258 1943 💻 www.outmag.co.uk
London gay monthly magazine.

QX (GLM)
c/o Firststar, 23 Denmark Street ☏ (020) 7379 7887
💻 www.QXmagazine.com
Club news, classifieds, music, lifestyle, contacts which mainly serve London and the South/South East.

BARS

79CXR (AC B G MA) Mon-Sat 13-3, Sun 13-23h
79 Charing Cross Road, Soho *U-Leicester Square, Cambridge Circus intersection* ☏ (020) 7434 2567 💻 www.79cxr.net
Popular late bar. Daily happy hour 20-22h. Regular DJs. A good -pick-up location.

Admiral Duncan. The (AC B CC GLM MA T) 12-23, Sun 12-22.30h
54 Old Compton Street, Soho *U-Piccadilly* ☏ (020) 7437 5300
Very busy bar especially evenings.

Bar 286 (B G LM) Sun-Thu 19-2, Fri & Sat 21-4h
286 Lewisham High Street ☏ (020) 8690 7648 💻 www.two8six.com
Very smart place, DJ at the WE. Free entry before 22h.

Barcode Vauxhall (AC B CC D GLM I MA)
Sun-Thu 16-1, Fri & Sat -4h
69 Goding Street, Albert Embankment *2 mins from U-Vauxhall*
☏ (020) 7582 4180 💻 www.bar-code.co.uk
Happy hours daily from 16-19h.

Black Cap, The (AC B BF CC D GLM M MA OS ST T VS WI)
12-2, Fri & Sat -3, Sun -1h
171 Camden High Street *U-Camden Town* ☏ (020) 7485 0538
💻 www.faucetinn.com/blackcap
Drag/cabaret pub. Popular disco at weekend. Great fund-raising venue.

Castle. The
64 Camberwell Church Street ☏ (020) 7277-2601
💻 www.gaycamberwell.com

Circa (B G WI) 16-1h
62 Frith Street *Tottenham Court Road tube* 💻 www.circasoho.com
Soho gay bar, offering pop and r'n'b tunes, drag hosts and cute bar staff.

Comptons of Soho (! AC B CC F G MA) 12-23, Sun 12-22.30h
53 Old Compton Street *U-Piccadilly* ☏ (020) 7479 7961

Cosmo Lounge (AC B CC d GLM MA) 13-1h
43 Essex Road, Islington ☏ (020) 7688 2882
Stylish lesbian and gay music bar.

Duke of Wellington. The (AC B CC D GLM M MA s)
12-23, Sun -22.30h
77 Wardour Street, Soho *U-Piccadilly Circus* ☏ (020) 7439 1274

Eagle London (B d F G MA S)
Mon-Tue 20-1, Wed-Sat 21-2, Sun 14-22.30h
349 Kennington Lane, Vauxhall ☏ (020) 7793 0903

www.eaglelondon.com
Popular and friendly pub, especially for bears. Regular Eagle 349 event. Beware of pick-pockets in the darkroom.

Edge. The (! AC B CC D G LM M MA NR OS S WE WI WL) Sun 16-23.30h
11 Soho Square *U-Tottenham Court Rd* (020) 7439 1313
A fashionable destination bar with four fabulously different designer style floors. DJs at the weekend.

Escape Dance Bar (AC B CC D GLM MA T WE) Tue-Sat 16-3, Sun -23h, closed Mon
8-10 Brewer Street, Soho *Five mins walk from U-Piccadilly Circus / Tottenham Court Road* (020) 7734 2626 www.escapesoho.com
Great for a pre-club warm up. Video DJ throughout the week and club DJ's from midnight Fri & Sat. Daily happy hour.

Freedom (AC B CC D GLM M MA P S)
Mon-Thu 17-3, Fri & Sat 14-3, Sun 14-23.30h
60-66 Wardour Street, Soho *U-Piccadilly Circus* (020) 7734 0071
www.freedombarsoho.com
Entrance for those over 21 years only.

Friendly Society (AC B CC d g YC) 16-23, Sat 14-23, Sun 14-22.30h
79 Wardour Street *U-Piccadilly Circus* (020) 7434 3805

G-A-Y Bar (AC B CC D GLM M) 12-24, Sun -22.30h
30 Old Compton Street (020) 7494 2756 www.g-a-y.co.uk
Stylish restaurant/bar on three floors.

G-A-Y Late (B G) 23-3h
5 Goslett Yard *Tube Tottenham Court Road* www.g-a-y.co.uk
Entrance +18. G-A-Y Late is the late night „sister" to G-A-Y Bar.

George Music Bar (B G MA OS s) Mon-Fri 17-24, Sat 12-2, Sun -24h
114 Twickenham Road, Old Isleworth (020) 8560 1456
www.georgemusicbar.co.uk
Traditional pub with shows at WE.

Green Carnation. The (B D GLM MA) Mon-Sat 16-2.30, Sun 16-0.30h
5 Greek Street (020) 8123 4267 greencarnationsoho.co.uk
Stylish, inspired by life and times of Oscar Wilde. Sometimes visited by celebrities.

Green. The (AC B CC D G M MA S VS) 17-24, Sat 14-24, Sun 14-23h
74 Upper Street *U-Angel* (020) 7226 8895
Stylish welcoming bar & restaurant for gay people and their friends.

Halfway to Heaven (B CC GLM MA S ST WE) 12-24, Sun -23h
7 Duncannon Street *U-Charing Cross* (020) 7484 0736
www.halfway2heaven.net

Kazbar (AC B CC GLM MA OS VS)
Mon-Thu 16-24, Fri -1, Sat 13-1, Sun -24h
50 Clapham High Street *U-Clapham North* (020) 7622 0070

King Edward VI (AC B CC G M MA OS WE) 12-24, Thu-Sat -1h
25 Bromfield Street, Islington *U-Angel, corner of Parkfield St*
(020) 7704 0745

King William IV (B CC F GLM M MA ST)
11-23, Fri & Sat -24, Sun 12-24h
77 Hampstead High Street *U-Hampstead* (020) 7435 5747
www.kingwilliamhampstead.co.uk
Not far from cruising area Hampstead Heath.

Kings Arms (AC B CC G M MA s)
Mon-Tue 12-23, Wed-Sat -0.30, Sun 13-24h
23 Poland Street *U-Oxford Circus / Tottenham Court Road*
(020) 7734 5907
A bar for beary, hairy, bigger men.

Ku Bar (AC B CC D GLM YC) 12-3, Sun 12-22.30h
30 Lisle Street *U-Leicester Square* (020) 7437 4303
www.ku-bar.co.uk
3 Floors with a new Champagne bar, 2 lounge areas and a dance floor. Cocktails and DJs each night. Ku Klub downstairs – open til 3h (Mon-Sat):

Ku Bar (AC B CC GLM m YC) 12-23, Fri & Sat -24, Sun -22.30h
25 Frith Street, Soho *Cnr. Old Compton Street* (020) 7287 7986
www.ku-bar.co.uk
Second Ku Bar in the city.

Little Apple. The (AC B CC D GLM M MA OS) 12-24, Sun -22.30h
98 Kennington Lane *U-Kennington* (020) 7735 2039

Old Ship. The (AC B GLM M MA ST)
19-0.30, Sun 18-0.30, Mon 16-23h, closed Tue
17 Barnes Street, Limehouse *Limehouse station, DLR* (020) 7790 4082
www.oldship.net
Friendly staff, good atmosphere regular caberet at weekends.

Profile (AC B CC GLM M MA) Mon-Sat 11-23.30, Sun -22.30h
84-86 Wardour Street, Soho *U-Picadilly Circus* (020) 7734 3444
www.profilesoho.com

Quebec. The (AC B D G m MA S ST) 12-2, Fri & Sat -3, Sun -1h
12 Old Quebec Street, Marble Arch *Close to U-Marble Arch, Oxford Street and Hyde Park* (020) 7629 6159 www.thequebec.co.uk
Very busy bar, something for everyone.

Queen's Head (AC B GLM M MA OS)
Mon-Wed 12-23, Thu-Sat -24, Sun -22.30h
25 Tryon Street *U-Sloane Square, just off King's Road* (020) 7589 0262

Retro Bar (B G MA) Mon-Fri 12-23, Sat 14-23, Sun 14-22.30h
2 George Court, Charing Cross (0207) 839 8760
Every Tue very popular pop quiz. Gay scene's indie, alternative and students.

Royal Vauxhall Tavern (! AC B D F GLM M MA S SNU ST VS)
19-24, Fri & Sat -2h
372 Kennington Lane, Vauxhall *U-Vauxhall, near river and Vauxhall Viaduct*
(020) 7820 1222 www.theroyalvauxhalltavern.co.uk
A great place to get a few beers and laugh with your friends. Theme nights include comedy and alternative cabaret, most famously Saturday-regular Duckie.

Rupert Street (AC B CC G M MA) 12-23, Sun -22.30h
50 Rupert Street *U-Piccadilly Circus* (020) 7292 7141
Stylish bar. Very popular in the evenings.

Stag. The (AC B d G I S) 11-23h
15 Bressenden Place *U-Victoria* (020) 35 822 938
Theatre „Above The Stag" also located here.

Two Brewers. The (AC B CC D GLM MA S ST VS WE)
Tue-Thu 16-2, Fri & Sat -3, Sun 14-0.30h
114 Clapham High Street *U-Clapham Common* (020) 7498 4971
www.the2Brewers.com
Cabaret bar and separate night club.

Village Soho (AC B CC G M YC) 16-1, Sun -23.30h
81 Wardour Street *U-Piccadilly Circus, at the top of Old Compton Street*
(020) 7478 0530 www.village-soho.co.uk
Happy hour 12-20h.

Way Out Club. The (B D G MA ST T) Sat 21-4h
9 Crosswall (off Minories) (07778) 157290
www.thewayoutclub.com
An alternative club for transexuals, transgendered, Drag Queens and their friends.

BJ's White Swan (B D G MA S) Tue & Thu 21-2, Wed -3, Fri & Sat -4, Sun 18-24h, closed Mon
556 Commercial Road *U-Limehouse* (020) 7780 9870
www.bjswhiteswan.com
Regular cabaret acts. Free entrance before 22h. Somewhat rough area. Take a cab home.

Windsor Castle (B G MC S) 11-23h
152 Bath Road, Hounslow (020) 8577 6590 www.thewinz.co.uk
Regular drag acts.

Yard. The (! AC B CC G M MA OS)
16-23.30, Fri 16-24, Sat 14 -24h, Sun -22.30h
57 Rupert Street *U-Piccadilly Circus / Tottenham Court Road*
(020) 7437 2652 www.yardbar.co.uk
Unique venue, boasting a huge courtyard space and balcony.

MEN'S CLUBS

Backstreet. The (B DR F G MA P) Thu 22-2, Fri & Sat -3, Sun -1h
Wentworth Mews, Mile End *U-Mile End, off Burdett Road, look for light above entrance* (020) 8980 8557 www.thebackstreet.com
The UK's longest established gay fetish venue, with a strict leather/rubber dress code.

Central Station (AC B CC D DR f G m MA OS SNU VS WI)
Sun-Wed 12-1, Thu -2, Fri & Sat -3h
37 Wharfdale Road, King's Cross *U-King's Cross* ☏ (020) 7278 3294
www.centralstation.co.uk
Three floors including Sports Bar, Cabaret Bar and The Underground hosting diverse club nights like Shoot!, Remix and others.

Hoist. The (AC B F G MA P) Thu 20.30-24, Fri & Sat 22-3, Sun -2h
Arches 47B and 47C, South Lambeth Rd *Opp. U-Vauxhall, Exit One, in arches* ☏ (020) 7735 9972 www.thehoist.co.uk
„Dirty Dance" every Sat. With a Leather & Rubber shop in the building. Entrance fee applies.

Nudity @ Union2 (B D DR G MA NU P S)
Every 2 & 4th Fri/month, 22-4h
65 Albert Embankment; Vauxhall *Entrance: 65 Goding Street*
www.nudityclub.co.uk
NUDITY The Naked nightclub (nudity is compulsory) with large dancefloor and backroom and bar. Usually very busy. Regular events are every 2nd and 4th Fri/month. Big naked foam party held on every UK Bank Holiday.

Play Pit. The (b DR F G MA P VS WE) Thu & Sun 20-?, Fri & Sat 21-?h
357 Caledonian Road *Near Kings Cross Station* ☏ 0333 700 1231
www.playpitcruise.me.uk

Ted's Place (B DR F G MA P T VS) Mon-Wed & Fri 19-24, Thu 20-3, Sun 19-2h, closed Sat
305a Northend Road *Crossing Northend Road & Lillie Road, U-West Kensington / West Brompton* ☏ (020) 7385 9359
www.tedsplaceuk.co.uk
Mon & Tue, Fri 19-24h men-only cruise session; Wed 19-24h strictly underwear party, men-only cruise session; Thu & Sun transsexual and transvestites.

Vault 139 (AC B DR G M MA P VS) Mon-Sun 13-1h
139b-143 Whitfield Street *U-Warren Street* ☏ (020) 7388 5500
www.vault-London.com
Mon and Thur stripped, Wed and Sun underwear/naked party. First drink, cloak,wifi FREE

CAFES

Balans West (AC B BF CC glm M MA OS)
Sun-Thu 8-24, Fri & Sat -1h
239 Old Brompton Road *U-Earl's Court* ☏ (020) 7244 8838
www.balans.co.uk

Canela Café (b bf CC glm M) 9-22.30, Thu & Fri -23.30, Sat 10.30-23.30, Sun -20h
33 Earlham Street, Covent Garden *U-Covent Garden/ Leicester Square*
☏ (020) 7240 6926 www.canelacafe.com
Stylish café, bar & restaurant serving Portuguese and Brazilian specialities. One of the trendiest places in Covent Garden.

DANCECLUBS

Area (! B D GLM MC) Fri 24-6, Sat 23-12h
67-68 Albert Embankment, Vauxhall ☏ (020) 3242 0040
www.areaclublondon.com
Three large dance floors, great bars and staff. Chariots sauna right next door.

Caribana @ Union (B D glm MA)
66 Albert Embankment *U-Vauxhall* ☏ (07931) 395 395 (mobile)
www.caribanaclub.com
See website for details.

Club Colosseum (B D G MC) Thu 21-3, Fri 22-5, Sat 21-6h
1 Nine Elms Lane, Vauxhall *Near corner with Parry Street*
☏ (020) 7627 1283 www.clubcolosseum.com
Regular gay events.

Club Kali (AC B D GLM MA) 3rd Fri/month 22-3h
178 Junction Road, Tufnell Park *U-Tufnell Park, entrance is at 1 Dartmouth Park Hill* ☏ (020) 7272 8153 www.clubkali.com
Large, lesbian and gay club, Bhangra, Hindi, Arabic house party.

Exilio @ Guy's Bar (AC B D GLM MA S ST T VS) Sat 21.30-2.30h
Boland House, St. Thomas Street, London Bridge *U-London Bridge*
☏ 079 56 983 230 (mobile) www.exilio.co.uk
Probably the hottest Latin gay, lesbian, bisexual club in London.

Fire Club (B D G YC)
South Lambeth Road, Vauxhall *U-Vauxhall* ☏ 087 1971 4220 (mobile)
☏ 242 0040 www.fireclub.co.uk
Eight different club nights. See website for opening hours.

Gutterslut (B D GLM MA WE) Last Sat/month
217 City Road *At East Bloc* ☏ 07762 134266
www.myspace.com/gutterslutuk
Monthly extravagant House & Techno party with a sexy up-for-it crowd at East Bloc.

Hard On @ Hidden (! AC B D DR F G MA P S SNU)
4th Sat/month 22-6h
100 Tinworth Street, Vauxhall *U-Vauxhall* ☏ (020) 7636 7630
www.hardonclub.co.uk
Popular fetish night. Membership required, apply online. Also the home of Megawoof! on 1st Fri/month 22-6h.

Heaven (AC B CC D GLM m MA S ST) Thu-Sat 22.30-5h
Under the Arches, Villiers Street *U-Charing Cross/Embankment*
☏ (020) 7930 2020 www.heaven-london.com
Famous club, running for the last 28 years.

LYC Club Night @ The Edge (B CC D G m MA S t) Sun 19.30-24h
11 Soho Square, Soho *U-Tottenham Court Road* www.lyclondon.com
The world's largest gay sports and social club, since 1983, offering a safe space for guys and girls from the East and West to meet and make lasting friendships.

Room Service @ DIU London (G) Thu 22-3h
12-13 Greek Street, Soho www.clubroomservice.com
London's Thursday hotspot

Salvation @ Troxy (B D GLM m MA) 1st Sun/month
490 Commercial Road, Lime House ☏ 0871 474 6002 (ticket sales)
www.salvation-london.com
See website for more information about the Salvation parties in over 40 different countries around the world (14 of them in Europe each month).

Shadow Lounge. The (AC B CC D GLM MA WI) Mon-Sat 10-3; Sun 19h-midnight
5 Brewer Street, Soho ☏ (020) 7317 9270 www.theshadowlounge.co.uk
Late night members cocktail lounge bar / nightclub. Full cocktail menu, table service, parking available nearby. Non-members welcome on a guest list basis.

Union Dance Club (B D DR G MA)
66 Albert Embankment *U-Vauxhall* www.clubunion.co.uk
The only purpose built cruise and dance club in London.

XXL (AC B CC D DR F G MA OS P S VS) Wed 22-3, Sat -6h
The Arches, 53-55 Southwark Street *U-London Bridge*
☏ (020) 740 34 001 www.xxl-london.com
No dress code, attitude free dance club. Inexpensive drink and door entry prices. Always draws a large and diverse crowd of predominantly bears, chubs, otters, muscle bears and chunky hunky men.

RESTAURANTS

Balans (B BF CC GLM M MA WE) 8-5, Fri & Sat -6, Sun -2h
60 Old Compton Street *U-Leicester Square/Piccadilly Circus*
☏ (020) 7439 2183 www.balans.co.uk
Large bar and restaurant.

SEX SHOPS/BLUE MOVIES

Blue Room (CC G) 11-22, Sat 10-22, Sun 13-20h
5-7 Brewer Street, Soho *U-Leicester Square* ☏ (020) 7734 4031
www.prowlerstores.co.uk
Licensed sex shop with R-18 hardcore videos, DVDs, sex toys and accessories.

Clone Zone (CC F GLM MA) Mon-Sat 11.30-20, Sun 12-18h
266 Old Brompton Road, Earls Court *U-Earls Court* ☏ (020) 7373 0598
www.clonezonedirect.co.uk
4 stores throughout the UK sell an extensive range of XXX DVDs and videos, leather, rubber, fashion, toys, magazines, music, books, gifts and more.

Clone Zone (AC CC F GLM MA) Mon-Sat 11-21, Sun 12-20h
64 Old Compton Street, Soho *U-Leicester Square/Piccadilly Circus*
☏ (020) 7287 1619 www.clonezonedirect.co.uk
4 stores throughout the UK sell an extensive range of XXX DVDs and videos, leather, rubber, fashion, toys, magazines, music, books, gifts and more.

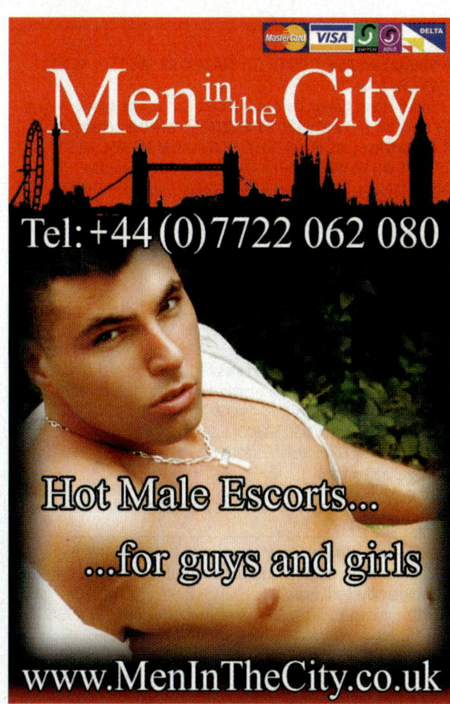

MasterCard VISA SWITCH SOLO DELTA
Men in the City
Tel: +44 (0)7722 062 080
Hot Male Escorts...
...for guys and girls
www.MenInTheCity.co.uk

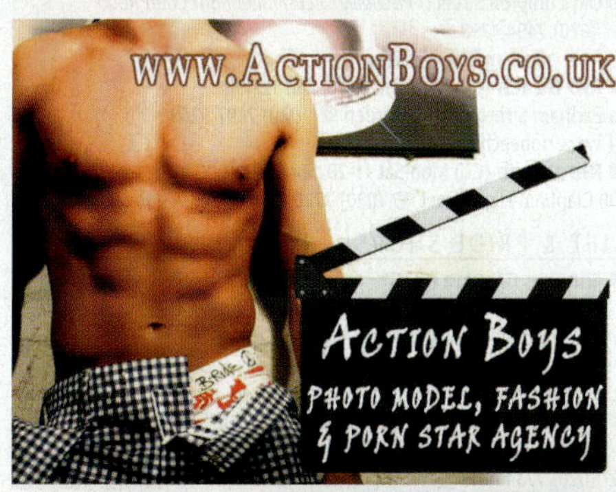

www.ActionBoys.co.uk
Action Boys
Photo Model, Fashion
& Porn Star Agency

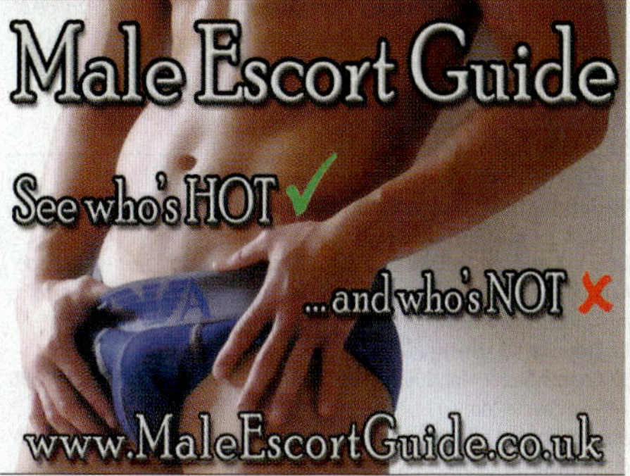

Male Escort Guide
See who's HOT
...and who's NOT
www.MaleEscortGuide.co.uk

DELTA VISA MasterCard
Escort Guys
Escort Guys - The Premier
UK Male Escort Agency
WWW.ESCORTGUYS.CO.UK +44 (0)7722 062 077
GAY ESCORTS, BI ESCORTS, TV/TS ESCORTS, LATINO ESCORTS,
EAST EUROPEANS, MODELS & PORNSTARS, STRAIGHT ESCORTS
INDEPENDENT ESCORTS - IN LONDON AND THROUGHOUT UK & EUROPE

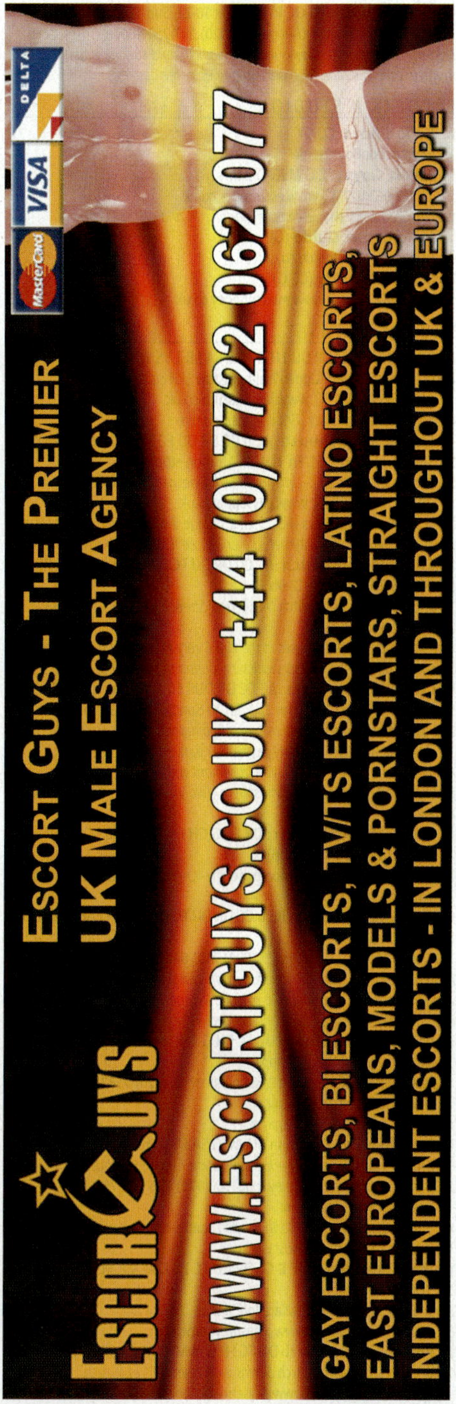

■ **Fantasy Video** (G OC P) Mon-Sat 10-22, Sun 12-21h
279 City Road, Islington *U-Angel* ☎ (020) 207 250 4007
Non-smoking cinema. Always loads of wanking and sucking and quite often more, in both cinemas. Membership and entry fee applies.

ESCORTS & STUDIOS

■ **Action Boys** (CC G)
💻 www.ActionBoys.co.uk
■ **Escort Guys** (CC G MSG T) 24hrs
☎ 07722 062 077 💻 www.escortguys.co.uk
Gay escort agency with escorts in London, UK and across Europe.
■ **Male Escort Guide** (G)
💻 www.maleescortguide.co.uk
■ **Men in the City** (CC G)
☎ 7722 062 080 💻 www.meninthecity.co.uk

SAUNAS/BATHS

■ **800 Club** (B D DR DU FH G P RR SA SB T VS WH) 12-3h
800 Lea Bridge Road, Upper Walthamstow *U-Walthamstow*
☎ (020) 8558 1331 💻 www.legs800club.co.uk
Cruisy sauna complex for TV's and their admirers.
■ **Chariots Limehouse** (AC b CC DR DU FC FH G GH I m MA OS RR SA SB SOL VS WH) 11-1, Fri 11-Mon 1h (non-stop)
574 Commercial Road *U-Limehouse DLR-Line, near the White Swan*
☎ (020) 7791 2808 💻 www.gaysauna.co.uk
A big sauna on four floors with cinema lounge, twelve man dry heat sauna, very large steam room, Internet cafe and three floors of cubicals.
■ **Chariots Shoreditch** (AC CC DR DU FC FH G I MA MSG PI RR SA SB SOL VS WE WH WO) 12-9h
1 Fairchild Street, Shoreditch *U-Liverpool Street* ☎ (020) 7247 5333
💻 www.gaysauna.co.uk
One of the largest bathhouses in the UK. A very mixed crowd can be found there with many tourists. Especially busy during the weekend.
■ **Chariots Streatham** (AC CC DR DU f FC FH G LAB m MA RR SA SB SOL VS WE WH) Mon-Thu 12-1, Fri 12-Sun 24h (non-stop)
292 Streatham High Road *Entrance in Babington Road*
☎ (020) 8696 0929 💻 www.gaysauna.co.uk
A large sauna with a maze in the basement with 25 private rooms. Friendly staff and pleasant atmosphere. Two video rooms. Complimentary refreshments.
■ **Chariots Vauxhall** (B cc DR FC G GH I m RR SA SB SOL VS WH) 12-9, Fri 12-Mon 9h (non-stop)
Rail Arches 63-64, Albert Embankment *U-Vauxhall* ☎ (020) 7735 6709
💻 www.gaysauna.co.uk
■ **Chariots Waterloo** (AC b CC DR DU FC FH G GH I LAB m MA RR SA SB SOL VS) 24hrs
101 Lower Marsh *U-Waterloo* ☎ (020) 7401 8484 💻 www.gaysauna.co.uk
A great sauna to relax and have fun in UK's largest sauna cabin. Fully air conditioned with a huge maze and video lounge. Internet café with complimentary refreshmants. Also a unique idea is the luggage safe room.
■ **Locker Room. The** (b DU FC FH G GH I m MA SA SB SL SOL VS) 10-24, Fri 10-Sun 24h (non-stop)
8 Cleaver Street, Kennington *U-Kennington* ☎ (020) 7582 6288
💻 www.the-lockerroom.co.uk
Clean and extremely friendly place.
■ **Paradise Spa** (DR f G m MA MSG SA SB WH) 13-23h
17 Crouch Hill *U Finsbury Park, train station Crouch Hill, bus 210, W7, W3 Dairy pub/Hanley road* ☎ (020) 726 396 75
💻 www.paradise-spa.co.uk
A clean, busy and friendly North London sauna, come relax and have fun. Worldwide tourists made most welcome.
■ **Pleasuredrome** (AC B CC DR DU FC FH G M MA MSG PP RR SA SB SOL VS WH) 24hrs
Arch 124, Cornwall Road, Waterloo Station *U-Waterloo*
☎ (020) 7633 9194 💻 www.pleasuredrome.com
■ **Portsea Saunabar** (b DU FC FH G m MSG RR SA SB VS WH) 12-23h
2 Portsea Place, Marble Arch *5 mins walk from U-Marble Arch*
☎ (020) 7402 3385 💻 www.gaysaunabar.com
Sauna on four floors with cinema lounge, twelve man dry heat sauna, very large steam room.
■ **Saunabar. The** (B DU FH G m MA MSG RR SA SB SOL VS WH) 11.30-1, Fri & Sat -7h
29 Endell Street, Covent Garden *U-Covent Garden, five mins walk from Old Compton Street* ☎ (020) 7836 2236 💻 www.thesaunabar.co.uk
■ **SweatBox** (! AC CC DR DU FC FH G I LAB M MA MSG RR S SA SB SL VS WE WH WI WO) Mon-Thu 12-2, Fri-Sun 0-24h non-stop
Ramillies House, 1-2 Ramillies Street *U-Oxford Circus* ☎ (020) 3214 6014
💻 www.sweatboxsoho.com
Gym, spa and sauna on 3 floors. The only gay sauna located in Soho, the heart of gay London. Foam parties every Sat & Wed. Under 25s get in for FREE every Monday.

FITNESS STUDIOS

■ **Kingly Street Fitness First** (AC g MC SA SB WO) 24hrs
59 Kingly Street *U-Oxford Circus*
☎ (020) 0844 5712888 💻 www.fitnessfirst.co.uk
The only 24 hour gym in Central London, frequented by fit men straight and gay. Best during peak hours (12-14 and 17-22h).
■ **Paris Gym** (G MA MSG SA WO) 6.30-23, Sat 9-22, Sun -20h
73 Goding Street *U-Vauxhall* ☎ (020) 7735 8989
💻 www.parisgym.com
Men only gym.

BOOK SHOPS

■ **Gay's the Word** (CC GLM) Mon-Sat 10-18.30, Sun 14-18h
66 Marchmont Street *U-Russell Square* ☎ (020) 7278 7654
💻 www.gaystheword.co.uk
The UK's comprehensive gay & lesbian community bookshop, Est 1979. Friendly & knowledgeable staff and regular book events.

FASHION SHOPS

■ **50** (cc G) Daily 11-23h
50 Old Compton Street *U-Piccadilly Circus/Tottenham Court Road*
☎ (020) 7494 4798
Fashion, books, gadgets, accessories.
■ **Rio Beach** (CC) Mon-Sat 11-20, Sun 12-19h
1a Earlham Street, Covent Garden ☎ (020) 7497 5259
💻 www.riobeach.co.uk
■ **Rio Beach** (CC) Mon-Sat 11-20, Sun 12-19h
100 Clapham High Street ☎ (020) 7720 6915 💻 www.riobeach.co.uk

GIFT & PRIDE SHOPS

■ **Gimme Gimme** (CC G)
4 Tisbury Court, Soho *Nearest tube Piccadilly Circus, located in the heart of gay Soho behind The Village Bar* ☎ (020) 7287 4526
A gift & card Shop for the LGBT Community. Sells Pride & Rainbow products:- Jewellery, T-Shirts, Flags, Key-rings, Stickers, Badges.
■ **Prowler Soho** (AC CC GLM) Mon-Fri 11-22, Sat 10-22, Sun 12-20h
5-7 Brewer Street, Soho *Behind the bar Village and opp. The Yard*
☎ (020) 7734 4031 💻 www.prowler.co.uk
Probably London's most popular gay lifestyle shop offering a wide range of cutting, edge contemporary and classic fashion items, gifts, books, videos, DVDs and magazines. Licensed sex shop also inside called the BlueRoom offering R-18 hardcore videos, DVDs, sex toys and accessories.

LEATHER & FETISH SHOPS

■ **Cage X-Press Industries** (F G) Mon-Sat 11-17h
66 Holloway Road *Opp. main church on Holloway Road. U-Highbury / Islington* 💻 www.cxi69.com
London's only fully licensed Dungeon. All goods either off the peg or made to order at no extra cost. Also selling DVDs, full range of Triga and Cazzo plus magazines and sex toys.
■ **Devote Clothing** (CC F G)
37 Cremer Street, Unit 106, Cremer Business Centre ☎ (020) 7729 7595
💻 www.dvote.com
Unique range of rubber gear and accessories. All products hand made with the attention to details.

■ **Expectations** (CC F G) Mon-Fri 11-19, Sat 11-20, Sun 12-17h
75 Great Eastern Street *U-Old Street, Exit 3* ☎ (020) 7739 0292
💻 www.expectations.co.uk
Leather and rubber gear, sex toys and accessories. Mr B depot. A made to measure service is also available.

■ **Fetish Freak** (CC F G) Thu-Sat 13.30-18.30, Sun 14-18.30, add. Fri 22-1.30, Sat -3, Sun -1.30h
Railway Arch 47B, South Lambeth Road, Vauxhall *Next to the Hoist fetish sex club* ☎ 07956 089 748 (Mon-Sat 10-19h) 💻 www.fetishfreak.co.uk
Also online shopping.

■ **Master U London** (F G) 11.30-19h, closed Sun & Mon
330 Kennington Lane, Vauxhall *Near Camberwell Green*
☎ (020) 7582 9406 💻 www.masteru.com
Also online shop/manufacturer.

■ **Paradiso Bodyworks** (CC glm MA T) 11-21h, closed Sun
41 Old Compton Street *U-Piccadilly Circus/Tottenham Court Road*
☎ (020) 7287 2487
With a wide selection of fetish clothing, S/M-equipment, toys, lingerie, kinky boots (large sizes) and body jewellery.

■ **Regulation** (CC F G) Mon-Sat 10.30-18.30, Sun 12-17h
17a St. Albans Place, Islington Green *U-Angel* ☎ (020) 7226 0665
💻 www.regulation-london.co.uk
Large collection of rubber and leather wear plus toys and accessories to suit every taste.

■ **RoB London** (CC F G MA) Mon-Sat 11-19, Sun 12-17h
24 Wells Street *U-Oxford Circus* ☎ (020) 7735 7893 💻 www.rob.eu
Excellent selection of leather, rubber, toys and bondage gear for the serious fetish lover.

HOTELS

■ **Accommodation Outlet** (CC GLM MA)
Mon-Fri 10-19,Sat 12-17h
Head Quarters, 32 Old Compton Street, Soho ☎ (020) 7287 4244
💻 www.outlet4holidays.com
More than 20 clean and well furnished apartments available. Book online with the UK's largest and most popular gay company.

■ **Castleton Hotel. The** (AC BF cc glm H I MC RWS RWT) All year
164-166 Sussex Gardens, Paddington *3 mins walk from Paddington Station*
☎ (020) 7706 4666 💻 www.castletonhotel.co.uk
The Hotel offers 46 comfortable bedrooms, all with en-suite bathroom, air-conditioning, central heating, satellite television and telephone.

■ **Edward Lear** (BF CC glm M RWS RWT VA) All year
28/30 Seymour Street *U-Marble Arch* ☎ (020) 7402 5401
💻 www.edlear.com
Only 30 m from Oxford Street, London's main shopping street.

■ **Lincoln House** (AC BF glm I RWS RWT VA) All year
33 Gloucester Place, Marble Arch *between Marble Arch & Baker St.*
☎ (020) 7486 7630 💻 www.lincoln-house-hotel.co.uk
A delightfully hospitable B&B hotel in the heart of London. Rooms have modern comforts and en-suite facilities. Close to Oxford Street shopping, theatres, nightlife and airport bus routes.

■ **Lynton Hotel** (CC GLM MA RWT VA WI) All year
113 Ebury Street, Belgravia *U-Victoria Station* ☎ (020) 7730 4032
💻 www.lyntonhotel.co.uk

GUEST HOUSES

■ **Gay Hostel Victoria** (AC DU G I) All year
164 Victoria Street *U-Victoria, 5 minute walk from Victoria coach station*
☎ (020) 7834 2007 💻 www.gayhostel.co.uk
A clean, modern hostel catering just for gay men and conveniently located right in the heart of London.

APARTMENTS

■ **Griffin House** (GLM I MA PA PK RWS RWT VA)
22 Stockwell Green *Five mins walk from U-Stockwell* ☎ (020) 7096 3332
💻 www.griffinhouse.info
Quality holiday apartments. One tube stop from Vauxhall Gay Village. TV, DVD and CD, shower, two bedrooms, kitchen, lounge.

■ **London Checkin Apartments** (AC G H MA RWS RWT VA) 24hrs
20 Trentishoe Mansions, 90 Charing Cross Road *U-Leicester Square*
☎ 7808 774 847 💻 www.checkin.se/london
Stylish apartment/rooms in the heart of Soho / Covent Garden. Large rooms, great views, amazing central London location.

PRIVATE ACCOMMODATION

■ **London Gay Accommodation** (G)
Close to Baker Street ☎ (020) 7486 0855 💻 www.londongay.co.uk
Small room/apartment in central location.

FETISH GROUPS

■ **Buff Naked Cruise Party** (! AC B CC DR F FC G LAB MA NU OS PK VR VS) Sun 18-22 (Except 1st Sun/month), Wed 19-23, Sat 18-22h
The Backstreet, Wentworth Mews, Mile End *Minutes from Mile End tube station* 💻 www.ma1.co.uk
One of London's oldest established naked cruise clubs. Large darkrooms, Heated smokers terrace, full bar, climate controlled, Free coatcheck.

HEALTH GROUPS

■ **GMFA – The Gay Men's Health Charity** (G) 10.30-16.30h
Unit 43 Eurolink Centre, 49 Effra Road ☎ (020) 7738 6872
💻 www.gmfa.org.uk
GMFA's mission is to improve gay men's health by increasing the control they have over their lives. All GMFA'S campaigns are designed, planned and executed by positive, negative and untested volunteers. Contact GMFA if you are interested in volunteering.

■ **Terrence Higgins Trust** (G) 9.30-18h
314-320 Grays Inn Road ☎ (020) 955 1000 💻 www.tht.org.uk
Information on HIV/Aids/sexual health and safer sex. Free condoms and lube. Info on gay scene and gay-friendly services available. Drop-in session Tue & Fri 12-14h

SWIMMING

-York Hall Baths, Bethnal Green. Action in the showers
-Highgate Men's Pond (U-Hampstead Heath)
-Highbury Pool (U-Highbury and Islington)
-Oasis Pool (32 Endell St. WC2, ☎ 7831 1804; one indoor and one outdoor pool)
-Tooting Bec Lido (U-Tooting Bec)
-University of London Pool Malet St.WC1 ☎ 7664 2000; host to „Out to Swim".

CRUISING

-Hampstead Heath (activities 24h, but most popular at WE and in the evening)
-Marble Arch, facilities in Oxford Street underpass (very cruisy even during the day)
-Beaulah Heights Park, South Norwood Hill (SE25), in the woods. Best before/at dusk-
-Blackheath, between Vanbrugh Park, Maze Hill & Charlton Way
-Clapham Common, (NW) corner between A3 Clapham Common North Side & A205 The Av. (AYOR)
-Dartford Heath near junction A2/A2018 along Denton Road & Rochester Way, mostly evenings in cars. In woods by side of A2
-Hyde Park, southeast corner in/around Rose Garden / War Memorial. Evenings. (AYOR)
-Streatham Common, top of hill start of Crown Lane SW16. (AYOR)
-Brompton Cemetery (busy in the daytime (esp. lunchtime), near the back of cemetery near the crematorium)
-Holland Park Walk (AYOR) (Busy after 23h (esp. at WE). Start your walk the Holland Park Road junction, walk to the middle of the walk near the school, and jump the fence on the park side)
-Soho Square (summer) more social than cruising
-Liverpool Street Station toilets (downstairs) (AYOR police)
-Toilets at Croydon Clocktower Library in Katharine Street.
-Toilets at Harrow on the Hill underground station. Beware of the CCTV!
-Keston Woods at Fishponds Road (14-20h)
-Toilets at Selfridges Car Park, 3rd Floor (best between 13-15h)
-Walthamstow Marshes, at the triangle between three railway tracks, park at Copper Mill Lane. some hot action under the arches!

Londonderry – Derry ☏ 028

DANCECLUBS

■ **Pepes** (B D GLM MA OS S SNU ST) 21-2h, closed Sun
64 Strand Road *Two mins walk from town centre, opp. police station*
☏ (028) 7137 4002

Luton – Bedfordshire ☏ 01582

BARS

■ **California Inn** (B D G VS) 17-1, Fri & Sat -3h
82 Chapel Street ☏ (01582) 488 098 🖳 www.california-inn.co.uk
Popular bar, the newest addition to Lutons growing gay scene. Lots of fun and themed nights.

■ **Flame Bar & Nightclub** (B D G MA) 16-?h
58 Wellington Street *Five mins walk from the train station*
☏ 0800 093 8442 (info line) 🖳 www.flame-nightclub.co.uk
Popular.

SAUNAS/BATHS

■ **Greenhouse Health Club** (AK b CC DR DU FC FH G I m MA RR SA SB SL SOL VS WH) Mon-Thu 10-24, Fri -4, Sat -6, Sun 11-24h
23 Crawley Road *Junction 10/11 on M1* ☏ (01582) 487 701 🖳 www.gay-sauna.com
Special events for bears and bears' lovers. Opened in 1996, only 30 mins from London, this site is one of the newer and larger Greenhouses. On three floors and with a discreet entrance. One of the only saunas outside London offering accommodation. Sling room available. Clean and modern sauna. Hotel rooms also available.

GUEST HOUSES

■ **Retreat. The** (CC G MC RWS RWT SA VA) All year
23 Crawley Road *Five mins from Luton airport* ☏ (01582) 487 701
🖳 www.gay-sauna.com

Manchester ☏ 0161

GAY INFO

■ **Gaydio** 24hrs
Portland Tower 🖳 www.gaydio.co.uk
Gay and Lesbian radio station on 88.4 FM.

BARS

■ **AXM** (AC B BF CC D GLM M MA S)
12-1, Fri & Sat -2, Sun -0.30h, closed Mon
100 Bloom Street ☏ (0161) 228 7474 🖳 www.axmgroup.co.uk
2 floors.

■ **Baa Bar** (B D GLM YC) 17-2, Fri & Sat -3h
27 Sackville Street *Cnr. Bloom Street* 🖳 www.baabar.co.uk
2 floors, DJs every night.

■ **Company** (AC B G MA) 17-2, Fri & Sat -6h
28 Richmond Street *Behind Rembrandt* ☏ (0161) 237 9329
🖳 www.companybarmanchester.co.uk
Cruisy basement bar. Busy every night.

■ **Coyotes** (B D gLm MA)
14 Chorlton Street ☏ (0161) 237 9329 🖳 www.coyotesbar.co.uk
Lesbian bar.

■ **Crunch** (B D GLM I M MA)
10 Canal Street 🖳 www.crunchbar.co.uk
Dance bar. American themed diner on the 1st floor.

■ **Manto** (! B CC D GLM M YC) Mon-Fri 11-2, Sat -8, Sun 12-0.30h
46 Canal Street ☏ (0161) 236 2667 🖳 www.mantobar.com

■ **Napoleons** (B D G MA T) Closed Tue
35 Bloom Street / Sackville Street ☏ (0161) 236 8800
🖳 www.napoleons.co.uk
One of the oldest clubs in the Gay Village. Video DJ ground floor, DJ first floor and a quiet area in the basement bar.

■ **New Union** (B d GLM MA ST t)
Mon12-22, Tue-Thu 12-2, Fri 12-2.30, Sat 12-3h
111 Princess Street ☏ (0161) 228 1492
🖳 www.newunionhotel.com/bar.html

New York, New York (AC B D GLM m MA ST T) 14-4h
98 Bloom Street ☎ (0161) 236 6556
www.newyorknewyorkbar.co.uk
Very popular on Sat & Sun afternoons (stage show).

Outpost. The (B D F G MA WE)
Mon-Thu 11-23, Fri -2, Sat 12-2, Sun 13-23h
4-6 Whitworth Street *On the edge of the village, adjacent to Picadilly rail/metro station, Same location as Legends* ☎ (0161) 236 5400
www.legendsmanchester.com

Paddy's Goose (B glm MC)
Mon-Tue 12-23, Wed-Fri&Sun -24, Sat -0.30h
29 Bloom Street *Behind coach station* ☎ (0161) 236 1246

Queer (AC B D G M YC) 11-2, Sun 12-0.30h
4 Canal Street ☎ (0161) 228 1360 www.queer-manchester.com

Taurus Bar & Restaurant (B G M MA)
Mon-Thu 12-23, Fri & Sat -1, Sun -22.30h
1 Canal Street ☎ (0161) 236 4593 www.taurus-bar.co.uk
A high standard of food, service and atmosphere. Situated on two levels there is a small intimate bar on the lower floor with the restaurant above.

Thompson Arms. The (B CC GLM m MA) 12-2, Fri & Sat -4h
23 Sackville Street *Next to Chorlton Street bus station* ☎ (0161) 237 5919
Women only 1st & 3rd Sat/month.

Tribeca (B G M MA)
50 Sackville Street ☎ (0161) 236 8300 www.tribeca-bar.co.uk
Café bar & restaurant lounge.

Via (AC B BF CC d GLM M MA S) 11-2, Sun 12-2h
28-30 Canal Street ☎ (0161) 236 6523 www.viamanchester.co.uk

View (AC B CC D GLM M WE YC) 11-24h
Canal Street *Corner of Canal/Chorlton St.* ☎ (0161) 236 9033

DANCECLUBS

Cruz 101 (! AC B CC D GLM MA P s VS) 22-2h, closed Tue
101 Princess Street *Piccadilly train station* ☎ (0161) 950 0101
www.cruz101.com
Manchester's biggest, busiest and longest running club in the gay village. Membership available via website.

Legends (AC B D G MA) Fri 22-3, Sat 22-5, Sun 22-3h
4-6 Whitworth *Same location as The Outpost* ☎ (0161) 236 5400
www.legendsmanchester.com
Lower level men only. Variety of music in two upstairs main areas, plus spacious chill-out area and piano bar.

Poptastic Manchester @ Club Alter Ego (B D GLM MA)
Tue & Sat 23-4h
105 Princess Street *5 mins from Piccadilly train station* ☎ 7974 248 247
www.poptastic.co.uk
Reduction for members. Two rooms of music: the Kittsch Bitch Lounge with 80's, retro, chart, pop and the Indie Playground with Indie, Britpop & Alternative. Features Mr. Poptastic himself – John Hamilton & Comedy.

RESTAURANTS

Eden Bar & Grill (AC B BF CC GLM M MA OS)
10-23, Fri & Sat -2, Sun 11-23h
3 Brazil Street *Off Amazon House Canal Street* ☎ (0161) 237 9852
www.edenbar.co.uk
Also a café.

SEX SHOPS/BLUE MOVIES

Clone Zone (AC CC F GLM MA)
Mon-Thu 11-20, Fri & Sat -21,Sun 11-19h
36-38 Sackville Street *Situated in Manchesters Gay Village*
☎ (0161) 236 1398 www.clonezonedirect.co.uk
Established for over 23 years. 4 stores throughout the UK sell an extensive range of XXX DVDs and videos, leather, rubber, fashion, toys, magazines, music, books, gifts and more.

ESCORTS & STUDIOS

Escort Guys (CC G MSG) 24hrs
☎ 07722 062 077 www.escortguys.co.uk
Gay escort agency with escorts in London, UK and across Europe.

SAUNAS/BATHS

Basement Sauna Complex. The (B DR DU FC FH G I m MA MSG P RR SA SB SL SOL VS WH) Daily, 24hrs
18 Tariff Street *Near Picadilly train station* ☎ (0161) 236 8131
www.basementcomplex.co.uk

H20 Zone (CC DR DU FC G GH m MA P RR SA SB SH SL VS WH)
11-23, Fri 11-Sun 21h (non-stop)
36-38 Sackville Street *Next door to Clone Zone* ☎ (0161) 236 3876
www.h2osauna.co.uk
Large jacuzzi and quite a large steam room. Great cruising area, pleasant areas for sex games.

Inferno Manchester (CC DR DU FC FH G I m MA MSG P RR SA SB SOL VS WH WO) 13-22, Fri 13-Sun 22h (non-stop)
496a Wilbraham Road, Chorlton *Entrance is from car park at rear, behind Chorlton Tandooris* ☎ (0161) 860 6666 www.infernosauna.com

LEATHER & FETISH SHOPS

RoB Manchester (CC F G MA) Mon-Sat 12-19, Sun 13-18h
17 China Lane *Next to Basement Sauna* ☎ (0161) 236 6222 www.rob.eu
Wide selection of leather, rubber, toys and bondage gear for the serious fetish lover. Also in London, Amsterdam and Berlin.

HOTELS

Ascott (BF CC GLM I MA PK RWS RWT) All year except Christmas
6 Half Edge Lane, Ellesmere Park, Eccles ☎ (0161) 950 2453
www.ascotthotelmanchester.co.uk

Hotel International. The (B BF CC H M MA) 24hrs
34 London Road ☎ (0161) 236 1010 www.thehotelinternational.co.uk
Situated in the heart of Manchester, within 2 minute walk from Piccadilly train station and right next to the famous Canal street the hotel provides an ideal venue for the business traveler and tourist alike. Set on four floors, the hotel offers guests all modern comforts. There are 40+ bedrooms to suit every pocket.

New Union. The (b BF CC GLM m MA RWS RWT VA) All year
111 Princess Street *Corner Canal Street* ☎ (0161) 228 1492
www.newunionhotel.com
This hotel with its popular bar provides quality accommodation at a reasonable price. Noisy downstairs bar.

Rembrandt (B GLM M MA RWS RWT VA) All year
33 Sackville Street *City centre* ☎ (0161) 236 1311
www.rembrandtmanchester.com
Hotel and bar.

Velvet (B CC H M MA) All year
2 Canal Street ☎ (0161) 236 9003 www.velvetmanchester.com
A sumptuous bar, restaurant & hotel in the heart of Manchester city centre on bustling Canal Street, a stones throw from Piccadilly train station, amidst lively & vibrant bars & close to the main shopping area. The bespoke 19 bedroom hotel, occupies the four floors above the bar & restaurant, offering individually designed Velvet King Rooms, 3 Balcony King Rooms overlooking Canal Street, and 3 luxurious Duplex Suites. Experience & enjoy a warm, welcome from our friendly & experienced staff, whether visiting us for business or pleasure.

CRUISING

-Piccadilly Gardens (Market Street side)
-Victoria station (concourse facilities, beware of police checks)
-Piccadilly Lock (at night AYOR. Go under the bridge at Rochdale Canal, entrance via Dale Street, a small stone doorway leading to a stairway)
-Rhodes Lodges (A 567 at Middleton)
Near Wilmslow:
-Styal Country Park (AYOR) (bushes left and right of the river near the small bridge. Be discreet)
-Readsmear Lake (between Congleton and Alderney, after 350m picnic area to the left, on the paths. Be discreet)
Near Handforth:
-Alderley Edge (Take a road off A34, turn right, Wizard Restaurant, woods on the right)
-V. I. P. cinema (Oxford Road) straight porno cinema with very interesting possibilities in back row seats.

Mansfield – Nottinghamshire ☎ 01623

DANCECLUBS

■ **Late Lounge. The** (B D GLM m MA) Wed 22-2.30h
62 Leeming Street ☎ (01623) 633 330 🖳 www.andwhynot.co.uk

SAUNAS/BATHS

■ **Manzfield's** (b DR DU FC FH G m MA OS SA SB SH WH)
Daily 12-21, last admissions 20h
71 Ratcliffe Gate *Ten mins from train station, near police station, 40 mins from East Midlands Airport* ☎ (01623) 422 257
🖳 www.gay-mansfield.com
In a converted coach inn dating back to 1677, which has kept a lot of old surprising features that make the place interesting.

Middlesbrough – Cleveland ☎ 01642

BARS

■ **Bar Delano** (B GLM MA) Tue 20-2h
41-43 Albert Road ☎ (01642) 226 009

■ **The Crown Pub** (B glm)
143 Linthorpe Road *Easily accessive from town centre*
☎ (01642) 255 311
Tue Poptarts (unofficial weekly gay night), Wed Bulldozer (less popular gay night).

GENERAL GROUPS

■ **Mesmac** (G MA) 9-17h
4th Floor, Prudential House, 31-33 Albert Road *Central Middlesbrough*
☎ (01642) 804 400 🖳 www.mesmacnortheast.com
Information and advice for gay and bisexual men. HIV rapid test service. free condoms & lube.Tue 19-21h Young Men's Group; Thu 19-21h T-Side Out.

Milton Keynes – Buckinghamshire ☎ 01908

BARS

■ **Pink Punters** (B D GLM M MA ST) Thu-Sun 20-5h
2 Watling Street ☎ (01908) 377 444 🖳 www.pinkpunters.com

Newcastle-upon-Tyne – Tyne & Wear ☎ 0191

BARS

■ **At One Bar (@ne Bar)** (B d GLM I MA s) 11-1h
1 Marlborough Crescent ☎ (0191) 260 3841 🖳 www.atonebar.co.uk
Chilled atmosphere & funky music.

■ **Bank Bar. The** (B d GLM MA S ST T)
12 Scotswood Road ☎ (0191) 230 3863 🖳 www.bankbar.co.uk
Entertainments bar, lots of fun and plenty of laughs.

■ **Eagle. The** (AC B DR F G MA SNU) 17-1, Fri -2, Sat -3h
42 Scotswood Road ☎ (0191) 230 4416
Caters for the leather, denim and uniform crowd.

■ **Eazy Street** (B GLM MA)
8-10 Westmorland Street ☎ (0191) 222 0646

■ **Gossip Bar** (B d GLM MA) Thu-Sun 17-1h
15-19 Westmorland Road ☎ (0191) 261 6824 🖳 www.gossipbar.co.uk
Dance music by night, sports theme during the day.

■ **Secrets Bar** (B GLM MA)
78 Scotswood Road

■ **Switch Bar** (B glm MA S) Daily 11-1h
4-10 Scotswood Road ☎ (0191) 230 3863
Cafe, bar diner, food served until 19h.

■ **Yard. The** (B GLM MA S ST T) 13-2, Fri & Sat 12-2h
2 Scotswood Road *Central Station, near Jurys Hotel* ☎ (0191) 232 2037

DANCECLUBS

■ **Loft. The** (B D GLM S) 23-3 Fri & Sat -4h
7-11 Scotswood Road ☎ (0191) 261 5348 🖳 www.loftluxeclub.co.uk
Located above Switch bar, open seven nights a week.

■ **Powerhouse. The** (B D GLM S) 23-?h
7-19 Westmorland Road ☎ (0191) 261 6824
🖳 www.powerhouseclub.co.uk
A super club in the heart of Newcastle, part of a large group with other bars.

SAUNAS/BATHS

■ **Number 52** (B DU g LAB m RR SA SB SL VS WH)
Mon-Thu 11-22, Fri 11-Sun 22h
50-52 Scotswood Road *4 doors down from the Eagle pub*
☎ (0191) 221 21 89 🖳 www.number52sauna.co.uk
Also with sling room and glory holes, a private courtyard and a full premises licence.

■ **REM Sauna** (B DR G LAB MA MSG SA SB VS WH) 10-23, Fri 10-Sun 23h
85-89 Blandford Street ☎ (0191) 232 9772

HOTELS

■ **Hedgefield House**
(BF CC glm m MA MSG OS PK RWS RWT SA VS WO) All year
Stella Road, Blaydon-upon-Tyne *Newcastle City* ☎ (0191) 413 7373
🖳 www.hedgefieldhouse.co.uk
Beautiful country hotel in an old Georgian Residence. Raffles sauna on ground and basement level.

GENERAL GROUPS

■ **MESMAC North East** (G) Mon-Thu 12-17h
11 Nelson Street *3rd floor* ☎ (0191) 2331333 🖳 www.mesmacnortheast.com
Information and advice for gay and bisexual men. HIV 1 hour test service. Free condoms & lube. Young Men's Group. HIV+ Men's Group. Free counselling service.

CRUISING

-Copthorne Gardens (g OC) Close to Central Station; the cruisiest area is near the entrance on the same side as the Copthorne Hotel.

Newport – Gwent ☎ 01633

SAUNAS/BATHS

■ **Greenhouse Health Club** (b CC DR DU FH G m MA SA SB SOL VS WE WH WO) 10-23, Fri & Sat -7, Sun 11-23h
24 Church Street *Junction 27 on M4* ☎ (01633) 221 172
🖳 www.gay-sauna.com
Upstairs is a large sauna, group shower area and TV lounges. Downstairs has a large cafe as well as showers and the cruise area is complete with cubicles and large empty rooms.

Northwich – Cheshire ☎ 01606

SAUNAS/BATHS

■ **Northwich Sauna**
(b CC DR DU FC FH G GH I M MA OS RR SA SB SL SOL T VS WH) 11-22h
Winnington Lane *2 miles / 3km from Hartford & Northwich train stations*
☎ (01606) 77 144 🖳 www.northwichsauna.co.uk
Sauna on two floors. L-shaped steam room for 50 people.

Norwich – Norfolk ☎ 01603

BARS

■ **Castle. The** (AC B CC D glm H I MA OS S)
Sun-Wed 12-24, Thu-2, Fri -3, Sat-4h
1 Spittalfields *Off Ketts Hill* ☎ (01603) 768 886 🖳 www.thecastle-pub.com
Also accommodation on B&B basis available.

Nottingham – Nottinghamshire ☎ 0115

BARS

■ **Forresters Inn** (AC B d GLM m MA OS)
11-15.30, 17.30-23, Sun 11-23h
183 Huntingdon Street ☎ (0115) 941 9679

■ **Lord Roberts** (B g MA) 11.45-23h
24 Broad Street ☎ (0115) 941 4886
Gay friendly theatre bar.
■ **New Foresters** (B GLM m MA) Sun-Wed 13-24, Thu -1, Fri -4, Sat 12-4h
18 St. Ann's Street ☎ (0115) 958 0432 🖳 www.newforesters.com

DANCECLUBS

■ **Hell Bent @ Stealth** (B D G MC) 22-?h
Masonic Place, Goldsmith Street
■ **NG1** (AC B D GLM OS S YC) Wed & Sun 23-4, Fri 22-5, Sat 22-6h
76-80 Lower Parliament Street *City centre* ☎ (0115) 958 8440
🖳 www.ng1club.co.uk
Two dancefloors, four bars, three separate sound systems and an up-scale atmosphere. Outside smoking terrace.

SAUNAS/BATHS

■ **Reflections Health Club** (DR DU F FC G m MA RR S SA SB SL VS WH WO) Mon-Sat 12-21, Sun 12-20h (last entry 90 mins before closing)
1a Station House, Crocus Street *Close to Nottingham train station*
☎ (0115) 955 3103 🖳 www.reflectionshealthclub.co.uk
Free membership available. 1st Sun/month bears' day, for other party events email to reflectionsnottm@yahoo.co.uk

Oxford – Oxfordshire ☎ 01865

DANCECLUBS

■ **Loveshack** (B D GLM m MA) Fri & Sat
Coven II, Oxpens Road *Next to the Ice Rink* ☎ (01865) 242 770
Looks like a deserted garage from the outside, is a large club with two floors.
■ **Old Fire Station. The** (AC B D GLM OS YC) Mon 22-2h
40 George Street ☎ (01865) 297 190

HELP WITH PROBLEMS

■ **Oxford Friend** (GLM) Hotline Tue, Wed & Fri 19-21h
PO Box 137, East Oxford DO ☎ (01865) 726 893
🖳 www.oxfordfriend.co.uk

Penzance – Cornwall ☎ 01736

BARS

■ **Penzance Arts Club** (B G MA) Sun 17-late
Chapel Street ☎ (01736) 363 761 🖳 www.penzanceartsclub.co.uk
Gay on Sun only.

Peterborough – Cambridgeshire ☎ 01733

BARS

■ **HG's** (B g MA)
10 Queens Street

Plymouth – Devon ☎ 01752

BARS

■ **Clarence. The** (B G MA S)
31 Clarence Place, Stonehouse ☎ (01752) 603 827
■ **Swallow. The** (B GLM m MA) 11-23, Sun 12-22.30h
59 Breton Side *Town centre* ☎ (01752) 251 760
🖳 www.theswallow.co.uk
■ **Wyndham Arms** (B d G m MA S) 11-23h
Wyndham Square, 17 Stoke Road *Close to the Clarence and the Cathedral*
☎ (01756) 565 022
Plymouth's possibly largest gay bar with live music and other events, two large bars, chillout lounge, games room, beer garden, close to The Clarence in Plymouth's newly emerging artists quarter and gay village Stonehouse/Millbridge.

DANCECLUBS

■ **Zeros Nightclub** (B D GLM m MA) 21-2, Sat -4h, closed Tue
24 Lockyer Street ☎ (01752) 662 346

Portsmouth – Hampshire ☎ 023

BARS

■ **Hampshire Boulevard** (B G MA S)
Mon-Thu 11-1, Fri & Sat -3, Sun 12-0.30h
1 Hampshire Terrace, Southsea *Opp. language school*
☎ (023) 9229 7509 🖳 thehampshireboulevard.co.uk
The largest gay owned pub/club in Portsmouth, with DJs and cabaret.
■ **Martha's** (AC B CC D GLM M MA SNU ST) Bar 12-23.30, Sun -22.30; Disco Mon-Sat 22-2h, ex. Wed
227 Commercial Road *Town centre* ☎ (023) 9285 2951
■ **Old Vic** (B CC D GLM I M MA OS S T) Mon-Sat 12-?h, Sun 12.30-?h
104 St. Paul's Road, Southsea *Close to train station* ☎ (023) 92 297 013
🖳 www.oldvicportsmouth.co.uk

Reading – Berkshire ☎ 0118

BARS

■ **Wynford Arms. The** (AC B CC D GLM M MA S t)
Sun-Thu 17.30-24, Fri & Sat -2.30h
110 Kings Road *Town centre* ☎ (0118) 958 9814 🖳 www.wynfordarms.com

Redcar – Cleveland ☎ 01642

BOOK SHOPS

■ **Books & Magazines** (glm) Mon-Sat 9.30-17h
5 Station Road ☎ (01642) 474 144
Good selection of gay mags and Books, Adult DVDs, Toys.

CRUISING

-Promenade from Granville Terrace towards Marske
-Sand dunes opposite blast furnace at British Steel

Rochester – Kent ☎ 01634

BARS

■ **Ship Inn. The** (AC B BF CC D f GLM M MA ST)
Mon-Sat 12-2.30, Sun 12-0.30h
347 High Street *Close to Chatham & Rochester railway station*
☎ (01634) 844 264 🖳 www.theshiprochester.com
Sun open for lunch, disco from Sat-Sun, Karaoke Mon, Tue & Fri nights.

Scarborough – North Yorkshire ☎ 01723

HOTELS

■ **Interludes** (B BF CC glm I M RWS RWT) All year
32 Princess Street *Old town, above harbour but below castle*
☎ (01723) 360 513 🖳 www.interludeshotel.co.uk
Georgian building in the old town. All five rooms non-smoking with hair-dryer, TV, radio, most en suite and with seaview.

Sheffield – South Yorkshire ☎ 0114

BARS

■ **Dempsey's** (AC B CC d glm M MA)
Mon-Wed 12-3, Thu & Sun -4, Fri & Sat -6h
1 Hereford Street *City centre* ☎ (0114) 275 4616
🖳 www.dempseys-sheffield.com

SAUNAS/BATHS

■ **Bronx** (B DR DU G GH I LAB m NU SA SB SL SOL VS WH)
Mon-Sat 11.30-21, Sun 12.30-21, closed Tue (last entry 20h)
208 Saville Street East *On corner with Princess St* ☎ (0114) 278 6440
🖳 www.bronxsauna-sheffield.co.uk

GUEST HOUSES

■ **Brockett House** (BF GLM I MA RWS RWT VS) All year
1 Montgomery Road *Bus 22 from city centre* ☎ (0114) 258 8952
Non-smoking B&B with comfortable & elegant guest rooms with tea/coffee making facilities, TV, DVD, hairdryer and fan.

Skipton ☎ 01756

HOTELS

■ **Boutique 25** (B cc glm I OS RWS RWT VA) All year, 24hrs
25 Newmarket Street ☎ (01756) 793 676 🖳 www.boutique25.co.uk
Gay owned and gay-friendly boutique hotel.

Southampton – Hampshire ☎ 023

BARS

■ **London Hotel. The** (AC b cc D GLM H M MA S t WE)
Mon-Wed 12-23, Thu & Sun -23.30, Fri & Sat -0.30h
2 Terminus Terrace *Ocean village area* ☎ (023) 80 710 652
🖳 www.the-london.co.uk
Southampton's premier cabaret venue.

SAUNAS/BATHS

■ **Pink Broadway** (AC BF CC DR DU f FC FH G GH I LAB m MA MSG RR S SA SB SL SOL VS WH) Sun-Thu 12-22, Fri & Sat -2h
79/80 East Street *Near East Street Shopping Centre, opp. Debenhams*
☎ (023) 80 238 804 🖳 www.pink-broadway.com
Turkish bath large enough for twelve men and two saunas for twelve men. Ten private cubicles and sling. TV lounge and food throughout the day. Playroom and maze.

Southend-on-Sea – Essex ☎ 01702

HELP WITH PROBLEMS

■ **South Essex Switchboard** Helpline: Mon & Thu 19-22h
29-31 Alexandra Street ☎ (01702) 344 355 (helpline)
Helpline for gays, lesbians and bisexual people.

St. Albans/Hatfield – Hertfordshire ☎ 01727

BARS

■ **Fudge/Metro** (B CC D GLM m MA OS SNU ST)
19-2, Fri & Sat -4, Sun -24h
Redbourn Road, Redburn ☎ (01582) 794 053
Free entry before 23h.

St. Austell – Cornwall ☎ 01726

GUEST HOUSES

■ **Harmony Homestay** (bf H MA) All year
7 Trevear Close ☎ (01726) 632 75 🖳 www.harmonyhomestay.org.uk

Stoke-on-Trent – Staffordshire ☎ 01782

BARS

■ **Pink Lounge Bar & Club** (AC B CC D GLM MA S ST)
Mon & Thu 21-3, Fri & Sat 20-4, Sun 21-3h
62-64 Piccadilly, Hanley *Opp. the Regent Theatre in the cultural quarter*
☎ (01782) 272 772 🖳 www.pinkloungebarandclub.com
Busy gay venue situated over two floors. The ground floor is a relaxing luxury lounge bar, whilst the second is a very popular club with drag DJs and regular weekly entertainment.

SAUNAS/BATHS

■ **Inferno Stoke-on-Trent** (CC DR DU FH G I m MA SA SB SOL T VS WH) Mon-Thu 13-22, Fri 13-Sun 22h (non-stop)
14 Garth Street, Hanley *Near corner of Hillcrest Street and junction of A50 & A5008* ☎ (01782) 213 341 🖳 www.infernosauna.com

Stourbridge – West Midlands ☎ 01384

SAUNAS/BATHS

■ **Heroes Health Club** (B DR DU G GH I m MA SA SB SH SL VS WH) Daily 12-23h
4 Lower High Street ☎ (01384) 442 030 🖳 www.heroeshealthclub.co.uk

Stratford-upon-Avon – Warwickshire ☎ 01789

HOTELS

■ **Eastnor** (B BF CC glm H I m MA OS PK RWS RWT) All year
33 Shipston Road *Central town* ☎ (01789) 268 115
🖳 www.eastnorhouse.com
A gay-friendly hotel with extensive array of local attractions, including the world famous Royal Shakespeare Theatre, only five mins walk away!

Swansea – West Glamorgan ☎ 01792

BARS

■ **Bar Creation Club Eden** (! B G MA S) Bar Creation Mon & Tue 12-24, Wed-Sun 12 -23; Club Eden Tue & Wed 10-2.30, Thu 12-3.30, Fri & Sat 10-4.30, Sun 9-1.30h
233 High Street ☎ (01792) 410 964
The biggest gay venue in Wales.

■ **Kings Arms. The** (B d GLM ST T) Sun-Thu 15-24, Fri & Sat -1h
26 High Street ☎ (01792) 642 216

DANCECLUBS

■ **Waterside. The / H20** (B D GLM m MA)
Bar daily 12-23, Club Sun-Thu 22.30-2, Fri & Sat -4h
18 Anchor Court, Victoria Quay ☎ (01792) 648 555
Very large gay venue on three floors.

Swindon – Wiltshire ☎ 01793

BARS

■ **Cricketer's. The** (B G M MA) Mon-Thu 12-23, Fri & Sat -24h, closed Sun
14 Emlyn Square *Near BR station* ☎ (01793) 523 780
Swindon's original gay venue, which has been open for over 15 years. With a traditional bar area. Food served Tue-Fri 15-20, Sat 12-18h.

DANCECLUBS

■ **Pink Rooms. The** (B D GLM MA SNU ST) Fri & Sat 21-5h
3-4 Victoria Road *Opp. old college* ☎ (01793) 488 662
🖳 www.thepinkrooms.co.uk
Thu is girls' night.

Torquay – Devon ☎ 01803

BARS

■ **Hole in the Wall. The** (B g MA) Mon-Thu 12-15 & 17-23, Fri & Sat 12-23, Sun 12-15 & 18-23h. Open Mar-Oct.
8 King Street, Brixham ☎ (01803) 883 408
Quaint harbourside English pub. Gay run.

■ **Ibiza** (B d glm MA) 21-1, Sun 20-22.30h
3-4 Victoria Parade *Under Queens Hotel* ☎ (01803) 214 334

■ **Meadfoot Inn. The** (AC B CC GLM I m MA S t) Mon-Tue 19-24, Wed 18-24, Thu 16-24, Fri-Sun 12-24h
31-33 Meadfoot Lane *Five mins from harbour/clock tower*
☎ (01803) 297 112 🖳 www.meadfoot-inn.co.uk
Gay owned. A small intimate bar with themed nights; karaoke on Thu.

■ **Candyfloss Club** (B D DR GLM m MA OS P VS)
Fri 22.30-2, Sat -3, Sun 20.30-2h
Rock Cottage, Rock Road *Town centre, off Abbey Road* ☎ (01803) 292 279
🖳 www.candyfloss-club-torquay.co.uk

RESTAURANTS

■ **Orange Tree. The** (B CC GLM M MA NR OS PK RES VEG WL)
19h- late, Sun closed
14-16 Parkhill Road *Near Marina and City centre* ☎ (01803) 213 936
🖳 www.orangetreerestaurant.com
Award winning English and European cuisine at affordable prices.

SAUNAS/BATHS

■ **Steamer Quay** (B DR DU G I m NU SA SB VS) Bar: Thu-Sun 21-24, Spa: Wed-Sun 12-22h
Rock Road *Off Abbey Rd* ☎ (01803) 201 401 🖳 www.steamerquay.com

HOTELS

Cliff House (B BF CC G M MA MSG OS PA PI PK RWS RWT SA SB SOL WH WI WO) All year
St. Mark's Road, Meadfoot Beach *Near the harbour* ☎ (01803) 294 656
🖳 www.cliffhousehotel.co.uk
Exclusively gay hotel, established 1973.

Hotel Hudson (B BF CC GLM I MA RWS RWT WI) All year
545 Babbacombe Road ☎ (01803) 203 407 🖳 www.hotelhudson.co.uk

Key West Resort (B CC D G I M MA PI PK RWS RWT SA SB VA WH WO) All year. Bar: 12-24h
Meadfoot Sea Road *Near harbour and town centre* ☎ (01803) 200 063
🖳 www.keywesttorquay.co.uk
UK's first and only exclusively gay resort. 22 bedrooms & 5 self-catering apartments.

GUEST HOUSES

Barangay Richville (BF cc GLM I MA PK RWS RWT VA) All year
80 Avenue Road *On main road from Exeter* ☎ (01803) 296 933
🖳 www.barangayrichville.co.uk
Intimate gay B&B near to town centre.

Manderville (AC B GLM I MA NU OS PK RWT VA WH WO) All year
18 Thurlow Road ☎ (01803) 313 336 🖳 www.eclipse.co.uk/manderville

Truro – Cornwall ☎ 01872

BARS

Qdos (B G MC) Tue-Thu & Sun 18-24, Fri -?, Sat -2h
13 New Bridge Street ☎ (01726) 222 888

Uxbridge – Middlesex ☎ 01895

BARS

Culvert. The (B GLM MC S) Sun-Fri 12-24, Sat-1h
54 Cowley Mill Road ☎ (01895) 256 690

Wakefield – West Yorkshire ☎ 01924

BARS

Club Odyssey (B D GLM MA SNU ST T) Mon-Wed 21-1, Thu-Sat -4h
46 Upper Kirkgate *City centre* ☎ (01924) 201 705

Zeus (B d GLM M MA OS S SNU T)
Tue 11-23, Wed -24 Thu-Fri -1, Sat -2, Sun 15-1h
6 Lower Warrengate *Near Cathedral* ☎ (01924) 201 705
Thu-Sat shows/cabaret.

Walsall – West Midlands ☎ 01922

BARS

Lion Bar & Nightclub. The (AC B CC D DR GLM MA OS P S VS)
Tue 20-2, Thu & Fri -3, Sat -3.30, Sun 14-24h, Mon & Wed closed
41 Birchills Street *Ten mins walk from bus/train station* ☎ (01922) 610 977
🖳 www.lionbarandclub.com
Disco on Sundays.

Waltham Abbey – Essex ☎ 01992

GUEST HOUSES

Woodlands. The (BF G MA)
72 Honey Lane, Waltham Abbey *45 mins from central London*
☎ (01992) 787 413

Watford – Hertfordshire ☎ 01923

BARS

Load of Hay. The (B CC GLM M MA OS SNU ST WI)
Mon-Thu 11-23, Fri & Sat -24, Sun -22.30h
207 Pinner Road ☎ (01923) 441 113 🖳 www.loadofhay.co.uk

Wells-Next-The-Sea – Norfolk ☎ 01328

BARS

Three Horseshoes. The (B BF glm H M MA) 11.30-15, 18-23h
Bridge Street, Warham *Near Wells* ☎ (01328) 710 547
Hotel with bar, located in rural area next to sea and gay beach.

Weston-Super-Mare – Somerset ☎ 01934

BARS

Alexandra Bar. The (B GLM MA)
Mon-Thu 14-23, Fri & Sat 13-24, Sun 12-22.30h
27-28 Alexandra Parade ☎ (01934) 644 244

Britannia (B G MC)
118 High Street ☎ (01934) 632 629

Winchester – Hampshire ☎ 01962

BARS

King's Arms (B glm H M MA)
Fri-Sat 17-1, Thu 17-24, Sun-Wed 17-23h
88 Chesil Street ☎ (01962) 844 465
Also B&B accommodation available.

GUEST HOUSES

Crowded House (AC bf GLM I M MA OS PK RWS RWT SA WH WO) All year
126a Springvale Road, Kingsworthy ☎ (01962) 885 370
🖳 www.crowded-house.co.uk
Three doubles and one single room. 10 % discount for SPARTACUS readers.

Wolverhampton – West Midlands ☎ 01902

BARS

Tomb. The (B glm MA) 7.30-23h
77 Darlington Street *Lower ground floor, between white gates*
☎ (01902) 771 222
Friendly Egyptian theme bar with disco & monthly live shows.

DANCECLUBS

Sky Club (B D GLM m ST YC) Fri & Sat 22-2h
Whitmore Street ☎ (01902) 421 701 🖳 www.skyclub.co.uk

York – North Yorkshire ☎ 01904

HOTELS

Astley House (AC BF CC glm MA RWT WI)
123 Clifton *Near centre* ☎ (01904) 634 745 🖳 www.yorkastleyhouse.co.uk
Small and friendly hotel. All rooms are en-suite with sat-TV, radio alarm, tea/coffee making facilities, hair dryers and phones. Free car park.

GUEST HOUSES

Bloomsbury. The (BF CC glm I MA PK RWS RWT) All year
127 Clifton *Near city centre* ☎ (01904) 634 031
🖳 www.bloomsburyhotel.co.uk

Bull Lodge (BF cc glm H MA PA PK RWS RWT WI) Closed mid Dec – end Jan
37 Bull Lane, Lawrence Street *1km from the centre on Bull Lane, a quiet, tree-lined, side-street off Lawrence Street, the A1079* ☎ (01904) 415 522
🖳 www.bulllodge.co.uk
Gay owned. Visa & Mastercard only.

CRUISING

-Wiggington Road (across from hospital)
-Parking at Haxby Road (Gillygate Road)
-Museum Gardens (daytime)
-Toft Green (daytime)
-Riverbank adjacent to Museums Gardens to Clifton

United States of America

Name: Vereinigte Staaten · Etats-Unis · Estados Unidos · Stati Uniti
Location: North America
Initials: USA
Time: See each state
International Country Code: ☏ 1
International Access Code: ☏ 011
Language: English, (Spanish)
Area: 9,809,155 km² / 3,615,102 sq mi.
Currency: 1 US Dollar (US$) = 100 Cents
Population: 308,000,000
Capital: Washington D.C.
Religions: 26% Catholic, 16% Baptists, 6% Methodists
Climate: Most of the country east of the Rockies is hot and humid during summer, especially the south. The deserts between the Rockies and the Sierra Nevada are very hot and dry during the summer, especially in the southwest. California's southern coast is comfortable year-round.
Important gay cities: Boston, Chicago, Fort Lauderdale, Key West, Los Angeles, New York City, New Orleans, Palm Springs, Provincetown, San Diego, San Francisco.

Sexual acts between persons of the same sex have been legal nationwide in the USA since 2003.
The United States same-sex marriage laws are governed by the fifty U.S. states and the District of Columbia. Consequently, recognition of same-sex marriages differs from state to state. The five U.S. states where same-sex marriages are recognized include: Connecticut, Iowa, Massachusetts, New Hampshire, New York, Vermont and District of Columbia. The current situation in California is complicated. Please refer to the following website for actual information: www.ncsl.org
Things are slowly changing in the United States: The Obama administration removed the entry restrictions to the USA based on HIV status. The removal of HIV-related travel restrictions in the US overturns a policy that had been in place since 1987. President Obama has furthermore championed a reform of the healthcare system – a truly gigantic task which, owing to the massive opposition of the Tea Party, a by now politically influential group within the Republican Party, only took the political hurdles in a highly diluted form. In December 2011, a historic vote in the senate abolished the "Don't ask, don't tell" doctrine originally introduced by Bill Clinton, enabling gays and lesbians to serve their country openly, as Obama emphasized.
Attention: In many states in the USA it is necessary to show ID when entering a club or bar, even if everyone can see you are over 18 /21 years of age. This is a non-discriminatory policy as everyone is asked to show ID. If you have no ID card take your passport with you. A driver's licence is often not accepted.
In our events calendar at the back of this guide you will find an extensive list of the Pride Events for the entire North American gay scene.
From the 12th January, 2009 new entry rules for USA tourists apply. A visa for the entry in the USA must be applied for before the flight via Internet – and no longer during the flight on board. This form must be completed at the latest 72 hours before the flight. The ESTA form (Electronic System for Travel Authorization) is available online at https://esta.cbp.dhs.gov

Seit 2003 ist gleichgeschlechtlicher Sex in allen Bundesstaaten der USA legal.
Da die Regelungen für gleichgeschlechtliche Partnerschaften jedoch den 50 amerikanischen Bundesstaaten bzw. dem Bundesdistrikt Columbia selbst überlassen bleiben, unterscheiden sie sich von einem Staat zum nächsten. Anerkannt wird die Homo-Ehe in den sechs US-Bundesstaaten Connecticut, Iowa, Massachusetts, New Hampshire, New York, Vermont und im District of Columbia. In Kalifornien ist die Lage momentan etwas kompliziert, der jeweils aktuelle Stand kann aber im Internet unter www.ncsl.org abgerufen werden.
In den USA findet gerade ein tiefgreifender Wandel statt: Die Obama-Regierung hat die Einreisebeschränkungen aufgehoben, die seit 1987 für HIV-positive Menschen gegolten hatten. Darüber hinaus hat sich Präsident Obama die Reform des Gesundheitswesens auf die Fahnen geschrieben – eine wirklich gigantische Aufgabe, die auf Grund des massiven Widerstands der mittlerweile politisch einflussreichen Tea Party-Bewegung, einer Gruppierung innerhalb der republikanischen Partei, nur sehr stark abgeschwächt die politischen Hürden überwand. Im Dezember 2010 beschloss der Senat in einer historischen Abstimmung die Aufhebung der „Don't ask, don't tell-Doktrin", die von Bill Clinton eingeführt wurde, so dass schwule und lesbische Amerikaner offen ihrem Land dienen können, wie Obama betonte.
Wichtig: In vielen amerikanischen Bundesstaaten ist beim Betreten von Klubs oder Bars ein Ausweis vorzuzeigen, selbst wenn man offensichtlich über 18 oder 21 Jahre alt ist. Nehmen Sie also ihren Personalausweis oder Reisepass mit, da ein Führerschein oft nicht ausreicht.
In unserem Eventkalender auf den letzten Seiten dieses Buchs können Interessierte Einträge für Gay-Pride-Veranstaltungen in ganz Nordamerika finden.
Seit dem 12. Januar 2009 gelten neue Einreise-Regeln für USA-Touristen. Ein Visum für die Einreise in die USA muss bereits vor dem Flug im Internet beantragt werden – und nicht erst an Bord der Maschine. Dieses Formular muss bis spätestens 72 Stunden vor dem Flug abgeschickt werden. Unter dem Namen ESTA (Electronic System for Travel Authorization) ist das Formular im Internet verfügbar unter https://esta.cbp.dhs.gov

Depuis 2003, le sexe entre personnes de même sexe est autorisé dans tous les Etats. Les partenariats civils étant l'affaire des 50 Etats fédérés ou du District de Columbia, ceux-ci sont différents d'un Etat à l'autre. Le mariage gay est autorisé dans 6 Etats : Connecticut, Iowa, Massachusetts, New Hampshire, New York, Vermont et District of Columbia. La situation est compliquée actuellement en Californie, l'état actuel des choses est consultables sur internet : www.ncsl.org .
Les USA sont phase de grande mutation : Le gouvernement Obama a levé les restrictions d'accès au pays appliquées depuis 1987 pour les personnes séropositives. De plus le président Obama s'est fixé comme objectif la réforme du système de santé – une tâche considérable qui a surmonté les obstacles politiques dans une forme très réduite en raison d'une résistance massive du mouvement Tea Party, un groupe interne au Parti Républicain qui a pris une forte influence politique. Dans un vote historique, le Sénat a décidé en décembre 2011 d'abroger la doctrine „Don't ask, don't tell", instituée par Bill Clinton, pour permettre aux Américains gays et lesbiens de servir leur pays, comme Obama l'a affirmé.
Important: dans beaucoup d'Etats il faut montrer une pièce d'identité à l'entrée des bars et boites, même lorsque l'on a visiblement plus de 18 ou 21 ans. Emportez votre carte d'identité ou votre passeport avec vous car le permis de conduire n'est souvent pas suffisant.
Dans notre calendrier figurant en fin de guide, on trouvera les dates des Gay Pride de toute l'Amérique du nord.
Depuis le 12 janvier 2009, de nouvelles règles sont applicables pour l'entrée des touristes aux USA. Une autorisation d'entrée pour les visiteurs du Visa-Waiver-Programm doit être demandée sur internet avant le vol et non plus à bord de l'avion. Ce formulaire doit être envoyé au plus tard 72 heures avant le vol. Le formulaire nommé ESTA (Electronic System for Travel Authorization) est disponible sur internet à l'adresse https://esta.cbp.dhs.gov

Desde el año 2003 las relaciones sexuales del mismo sexo son legales en todos los estados de los EE.UU.
Dado que las normativas que rigen las asociaciones del mismo sexo en los 50 estados y el Distrito de Columbia en EE.UU. no son las mismas, se puede encontrar diferencias de un estado a otro. En EE.UU. se reconoce el matrimonio homosexual en los 6 estados de Connecticut, Iowa,

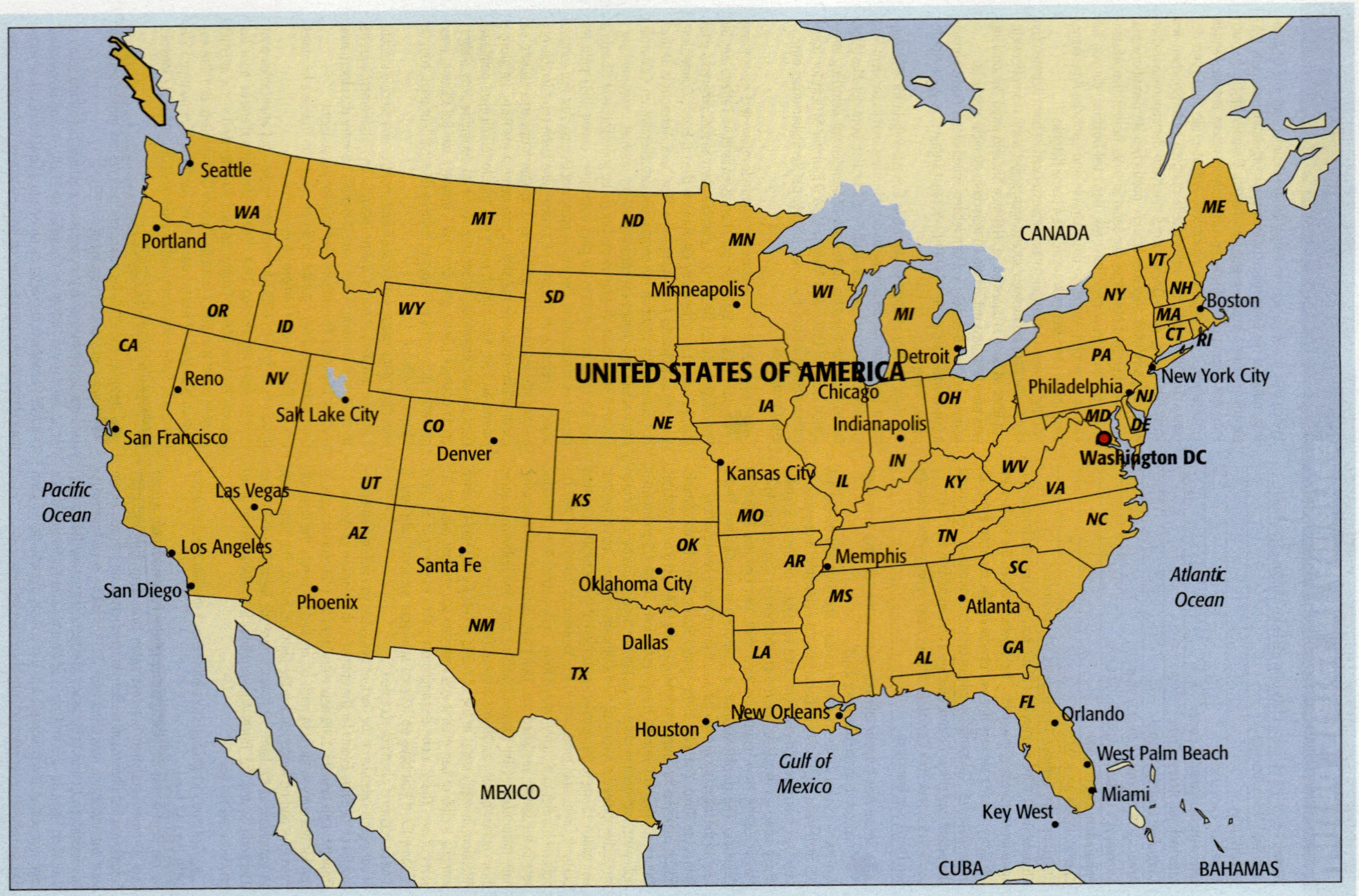
UNITED STATES OF AMERICA
CANADA
MEXICO
CUBA
BAHAMAS
Pacific Ocean
Atlantic Ocean
Gulf of Mexico
WA
OR
CA
ID
NV
MT
WY
UT
AZ
CO
NM
ND
SD
NE
KS
OK
TX
MN
IA
MO
AR
LA
WI
IL
MI
IN
OH
KY
TN
MS
AL
GA
FL
SC
NC
VA
WV
PA
NY
VT
NH
ME
MA
CT
RI
NJ
MD
DE
Seattle
Portland
San Francisco
Reno
Salt Lake City
Las Vegas
Los Angeles
San Diego
Phoenix
Denver
Santa Fe
Minneapolis
Kansas City
Oklahoma City
Dallas
Houston
New Orleans
Memphis
Chicago
Indianapolis
Detroit
Atlanta
Orlando
West Palm Beach
Miami
Key West
Philadelphia
Washington DC
New York City
Boston

Massachusetts, New Hampshire, New York, Vermont y District of Columbia. En California, la situación actual es algo complicada por el momento, pero podrá mantenerse informado accediendo a www.ncsl.org. En EE.UU. está teniendo lugar un profundo cambio: El gobierno de Obama ha levantado las restricciones de visado que se habían aplicado desde 1987 a personas VIH-positivas. Por otra parte, el Presidente de EE.UU., Barack Obama, ha hecho suya la causa de la reforma sanitaria, una tarea verdaderamente titánica que se ha debilitado, en gran medida, debido a los obstáculos políticos y a la masiva resistencia del movimiento Tea Party, un grupo dentro del Partido Republicano que cuenta en la actualidad con influencia política. En diciembre de 2010, el Senado de EE.UU. llevo a cabo, en una votación histórica, la derogación de la doctrina militar conocida como "Don't ask, don't tell" (No preguntes, no digas), que fue introducida por Bill Clinton para que los estadounidenses homosexuales puedan servir abiertamente a su país, aclaró Obama.
Importante: En estados unidos, el carnet de identidad es indispensable en muchos de sus estados a la hora entrar en clubs o bares, aún cuando la mayoría de edad sea obvia. La mayoría de edad legal son los 21 años. Lleve consigo un carnet de identidad o pasaporte, ya que el carnet de conducir por lo general no es suficiente.
En el calendario de eventos que aparece al final de esta guía pueden encontrarse los actos del Orgullo Gay de toda Norteamérica.

✖ Dal 2003 il sesso tra persone dello stesso sesso è legale in tutti gli stati federali. Essendo materia dei singoli Stati federali, le regolamentazioni per le unioni civili omosessuali variano da Stato in Stato. Il matrimonio omosessuale viene riconosciuto dagli Stati federali Connecticut, Iowa, Massachusetts, New Hampshire e Vermont. In California, al momento, la situazione è un po' complicata. La situazione attuale nei diversi Stati può essere consultata tramite internet al seguente indirizzo www.ncsl.org
Al momento gli USA stanno vivendo un profondo cambiamento: il governo di Obama ha rimosso le limitazioni di ingresso per i sieropositivi che vigevano già dal 1987. Inoltre, il presidente Obama ha fatto della riforma sanitaria il suo cavallo di battaglia; una riforma molto ambiziosa che, a causa della forte resistenza dell'ormai influentissimo movimento del Tea Party all'interno del Partito Repubblicano, è riuscita, sì, a superare gli ostacoli politici, ma uscendone fuori in forma molto annacquata. Nel dicembre del 2010, il Senato ha approvato, con un voto storico, l'abrogazione della dottrina del "don't ask, don't tell" introdotta da Bill Clinton; adesso, come ha sottolineato Obama, gli americani e le americane omosessuali possono apertamente servire il loro Paese.
Importante: in molti Stati federali statunitensi, per entrare nei club o nei bar, bisogna mostrare un documento di riconoscimento, anche nei casi nei quali la maggior età risulti evidente. Portate con voi, quindi, la carta dìidentità o il passaporto; la patente spesso non basta.
Nel nostro calendario degli appuntamenti, nelle ultime pagine di questa guida, troverete gli appuntamenti inerenti al Gay Pride in tutto il Nord America. Per i turisti stranieri che hanno intenzione di recarsi negli Stati Uniti, dal 12 gennaio 2009 valgono delle nuove disposizioni di ingresso. I visitatori stranieri nell'ambito del Programma Viaggio senza Visto (Visa Waiver Program) devono presentare la domanda tramite internet prima del viaggio. Questo formulario deve essere spedito al più tardi 72 ore prima del volo. Sul sito https://esta.cbp.dhs.gov troverete il suddetto formulario sotto il nome ESTA (Electronic System for Travel Authorization).

NATIONAL PUBLICATIONS

■ 100 Percent Beef
PO Box 1344 ✉ CA 92263 Palm Springs ☎ (800) 672-3287 (toll free)

💻 www.beefmag.com
100% BEEF is a bi-monthly publication, so it comes out every other month; 6 issues per year.

■ a&u Mon-Fri 9-17h
25 Monroe Street, Suite 205 ✉ NY 12210-2729 Albany *Between Chapel St and Theatre Mow St* ☎ (888) 245-4333 💻 www.aumag.org
Monthly Aids magazine.

■ Advocate. The
PO Box 4371 ✉ CA 90078 Los Angeles ☎ (323) 852-7200
💻 www.advocate.com
The national gay-lesbian news magazine. Featuring national and international news coverage from all areas that are of interest to the gay and lesbian community.

■ Curve Magazine
1550 Bryant Street, Suite 510 ✉ CA 94102 San Francisco
☎ (415) 863-6538 💻 www.curvemag.com
Lesbian magazine.

■ Cybersocket
c/o Cybersocket L.L.C., 964 1/2 North Vermont Avenue ✉ CA 90029 Los Angeles ☎ (323) 650-9906 💻 www.cybersocket.com
Bimonthly gay web magazine.

■ Damron Men's Travel Guide
Damron Co., PO Box 42 24 58 ✉ CA 94142 San Francisco
☎ (415) 255-0404 💻 www.damron.com
Guides covering mainly USA, Canada, Caribbean, Mexico, parts of Europe and Asia too. Also publisher of Accommodations Guide and Women's Travel Guide.

■ Gay & Lesbian Yellow Pages
1712 Montrose Boulevard ✉ TX 77006 Houston ☎ (713) 942-0084
💻 www.glyp.com
Publisher of annual telephone directories for the gay, lesbian, bisexual and transgender community.

■ Gayellow Pages 12-17.30h
PO Box 533-SPART, Village Station ✉ NY 10014 New York
☎ (646) 213-0263 💻 gayellowpages.com
LGBT guide for USA, printed annually, updated monthly online, download at no charge. Canada updated monthly online, download at no charge.

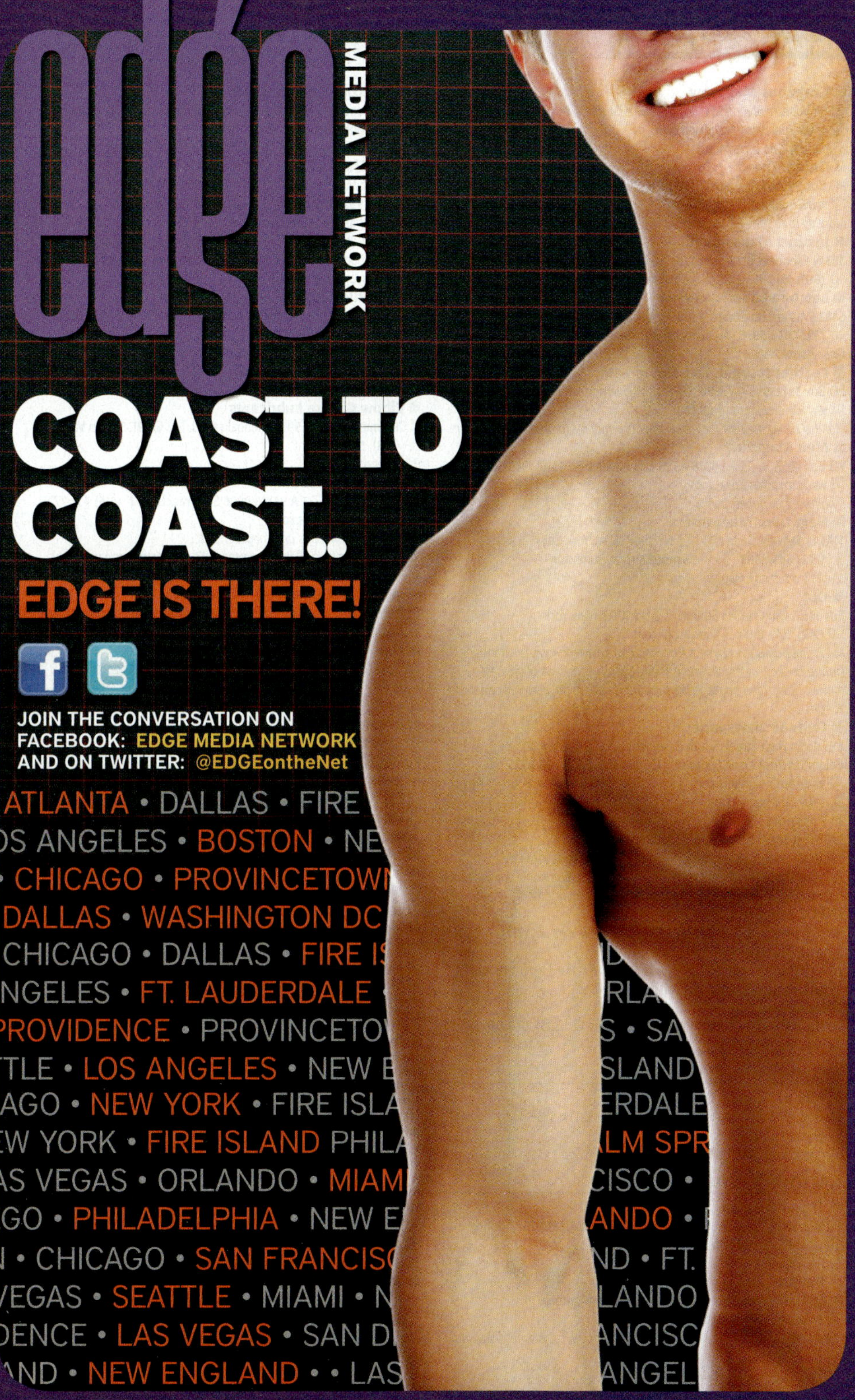
edge
MEDIA NETWORK
COAST TO COAST..
EDGE IS THERE!
JOIN THE CONVERSATION ON
FACEBOOK: EDGE MEDIA NETWORK
AND ON TWITTER: @EDGEontheNet
ATLANTA • DALLAS • FIRE
BOSTON
CHICAGO • PROVINCETOWN
DALLAS • WASHINGTON DC
CHICAGO • DALLAS
FT. LAUDERDALE
PROVIDENCE
LOS ANGELES
NEW YORK
FIRE ISLAND
ORLANDO • MIAMI
PHILADELPHIA
CHICAGO • SAN FRANCISC
SEATTLE • MIAMI
LAS VEGAS
NEW ENGLAND

Gorgeous Magazine
11684 Ventura Blvd, #531 ✉ CA 91604 Studio City ☎ (323) 436-7546
🖳 www.boulevard-magazine.com
Bi-monthly G&L magazine.

Guide. The
PO Box 990593 ✉ MA 02199-0593 Boston ☎ (617) 266-8557
🖳 www.guidemag.com
Monthly magazine featuring gay travel, entertainment, politics etc.

Instinct Magazine (G)
303 N Glenoaks Blvd, Ste L120 ✉ CA 91502 Burbank
☎ (818) 843-1536 x107 🖳 instinctmagazine.com

Lambda Literary Review
5482 Wilshire Boulevard #1595 ✉ CA 90036 Los Angeles
☎ (323) 936-5876 🖳 www.lambdaliterary.org
Online book reviews.

Leather Journal. The Mon-Fri 9-18h
PO Box 381239 ✉ CA 90038-1239 Hollywood ☎ (323) 469-5922
🖳 www.theleatherjournal.com
Monthly newspaper for the gay leather community, for free at leather bars.

Men Magazine
PO Box 4356 ✉ CA 90078-4356 Los Angeles ☎ (310) 943-5859
🖳 www.menmagazine.com
Monthly erotic publication.

Next Door Magazine
1133 Broadway, Suite 503 ✉ NY 10010 New York City
☎ (212) 645-8868 🖳 www.nextdoormagazine.com
Monthly adult gay men's magazine.

Out
Box 1253, Old Chelsea Station ✉ NY 10113 New York
☎ (212) 242-8100 🖳 www.out.com
Magazine published 12x/year featuring real advice on jobs, relationships, staying healthy, getting fit and fashion. On-target reviews of the best movies, music, and books. Articles on travel, grooming, personal finance, the arts.

Outlook Newspaper
815 North High Street, South Basement Suite ✉ OH 43215 Columbus *Rush Creek Commerce Centre* ☎ (614) 268-8525
🖳 www.outlookmedia.com
Biweekly GLB newspaper.

Passport
243 West 30th Street ✉ NY 10001 New York
☎ (800) 999-9718 (toll free) 🖳 www.passportmagazine.net
Published by Q Communications. One of the best international gay travel magazines with many travel articles and recommendations for the gay traveller.

POZ Magazine
500 5th Ave, Suite 320 ✉ NY 10110-0303 New York ☎ (212) 242-2163
🖳 www.poz.com
Monthly publication providing information to HIV positive persons for whom it could extend or improve the quality of their lives.

Unzipped
PO Box 4356 ✉ CA 90078-4356 Los Angeles ☎ (323) 960-5400
🖳 www.unzipped.net

NATIONAL PUBLISHERS

Tom of Finland Company
PO Box 26716 ✉ CA 90026 Los Angeles ☎ (213) 975-9432
🖳 www.tomoffinland.com
Merchandise of Tom of Finland.

NATIONAL COMPANIES

10percent.com
PO Box 38010 ✉ CA 90038 Hollywood ☎ (888) 910-7372 (toll-free)
🖳 www.10percent.com
Gay porn producer and mailorder.

Bel Ami
448 B Washington Street, 342 ✉ CA 93940 Monterey
🖳 www.belamionline.com
Videos, DVDs, photo books, calendars, cards, novelties; internet shopping.

Bookazine Company, Inc.
75 Hook Road ✉ NJ 07002 Bayonne ☎ (800) 221-8112 (toll free)
🖳 www.bookazine.com
Stocks and distributes SPARTACUS and other Bruno Gmünder publications.

Club Channel 1
8721 Santa Monica Blvd #525 ✉ CA 90069 West Hollywood
☎ (800) 997-9071 (toll free) 🖳 www.chichilarue.com
The Club Channel 1 Video Series features Rascal Video stars in hot and sexy non x-rated scenes, images and clips from Chi Chi's Rascal videos, music and video from some of today's hottest artists, and of course footage from hotspots around the world!

Colt Studio Group Mon-Fri 8.30-18.30h
PO Box 1550 ✉ CA 94188-3694 San Francisco ☎ (415) 437-9800
🖳 www.coltstudiogroup.com
DVD, magazines, books, calendars, clothing and more.

Edge Media Network (G)
🖳 www.edgeonthenet.com

Elbow Grease Lubricants
B. Cumming Co., Inc. 9990 Glenoaks Blvd ✉ CA 91352 Sun Valley
☎ (818) 504-2571
Producer of lubricants.

Falcon Studios
PO Box 880906 ✉ CA 94188-0906 San Francisco ☎ (415) 431-7722
🖳 www.falconstudios.com
Producers of porn films and magazines etc.

Frivole.com Toll free between 8-17h (Eastern Standard Time)
14700 NW 7th Avenue ✉ FL 33168 Miami
☎ (888) 374-8653 (toll free) 🖳 frivole.com
Fashion clothing that is exceptionally sophisticated and unique yet a little frivolous and always sexy.

Gay Journey (G MA)
PO Box 573 ✉ TX 75070 McKinney 🖳 gayjourney.com
More than 6,900 listings, world's largest free on-line directory of gay & lesbian owned/operated & gay & lesbian friendly hotels, inns, B&B's, guesthouses, home-stays & resorts.

Gaymagix
PO Box 2457 ✉ CA 91393 North Hills ☎ (818) 947-3779
🖳 www.gaymagix.com
Online shopping: DVDs and videos.

Hot House Entertainment Mon-Fri 9-17.30h
1433 17th Street ✉ CA 94107 San Francisco ☎ 437-9500
🖳 www.HotHouse.com
Producers of high quality porn films and more.

Koalaswim.com (CC G)
P.O. Box 5519 ✉ CA 91380 Sherman Oaks ☎ (818) 904-3301
🖳 www.koalaswim.com
A vast selection of extreme men's swimwear.

Kristen Bjorn Productions
2520 South West 22nd Street #213, Suite 2 ✉ FL 33145 Miami
☎ (305) 860-0992 🖳 www.kristenbjorn.com
High quality gay movie productions, also online catalogue.

Manhunt.net (G)
✉ MA 02142 Cambridge ☎ (617) 225-2727
🖳 www.manhunt.net
Manhunt.net serves as the premier resource for men to meet other men online, for dating, fun, relationships and friendships.

Nakedsword.com
🖳 www.nakedsword.com
Stream or download scenes and full length gay adult videos. Membership necessary.

Pacific Sun
9008 Haskell Avenue ✉ CA 91323 North Hills ☎ (818) 357-5440
🖳 www.pacificsun.tv
Producer of gay porn films. Access top quality gay videos instantly.

Prerogatives
85 Bluxome Street # 201 ✉ CA 94107 San Francisco ☎ (415) 551-1016
🖳 www.pridecatalog.com
Wholesale distributor of GLBT lifestyle gifts and adult items.

■ **Purple Roofs**
PO Box 4666, El Dorado Hills ✉ CA 95762 El Dorado Hills
☎ 916-933-8514 🖳 www.purpleroofs.com
Directory of accommodations in worldwide locations.

■ **Raging Stallion**
1155 Mission Street ✉ CA 94103 San Francisco ☎ (415) 503-1969
🖳 www.ragingstallion.com
Internet sales, wholesale, international distribution.

■ **RSVP Vacations**
2535 25th Avenue South ✉ MN 55406 Minneapolis ☎ (612) 729-1113
🖳 www.rsvpvacations.com
All gay and lesbian vacations. Large and small cruise ships.

■ **Studio 2000** Mon-Fri 9.30-17h (Pacific time)
PO Box 411546 ✉ CA 94141-1546 San Francisco
☎ (800) 935-5771 (toll free) 🖳 www.studio2000video.com
Producers of the famous Studio 2000 porn flims. See their website for online shopping and more.

■ **Titan Media** 9-17h
PO Box 411345 ✉ CA 94141-1345 San Francisco
☎ (800) 360-7204 (orders, toll-free) 🖳 www.titanmen.com
Titan Videos, DVDs, CD-roms and extensive website.

■ **Vista Video International Inc.**
PO Box 370706 ✉ FL 33137 Miami ☎ (305) 754-5717
🖳 www.vistavideo.com

■ **Wet**
Trigg Laboratories, Inc., 28650 Braxton Avenue ✉ CA 91355 Valencia
☎ (661) 775-3100 ext 221 🖳 www.stayswetlonger.com
Producers of Wet lubricants.

NATIONAL GROUPS

■ **Immigration Equality**
40 Exchange Place, 17th Floor ✉ NY 10005 New York
☎ (212) 714-2904 🖳 www.immigrationequality.org
Provides assistance to lesbian & gay immigrants including those seeking asylum through a national campaign of advocacy, support, education and outreach.

■ **International Gay Rodeo Association (IGRA)**
PO Box 460504 ✉ CO 80046-0504 Aurora ☎ (303) 595-4472
🖳 www.igra.com

NATIONAL HELPLINES

■ **Gay, Lesbian, Bisexual and Transgender (GLBT) National Hotline** Mon-Fri 16-24, Sat 12-17h (Eastern Standard times)
✉ San Francisco ☎ (888) 843-4564 (toll free)
🖳 www.GLBTNationalHelpCenter.org
Nationwide information, resources and counselling for the gay, lesbian, bisexual and transgender community. A non-profit organization. Also operate a second national hotline called the Gay, Lesbian, Bisexual and Transgender (GLBT) National Youth Talkline. The toll-free number for that hotline is (800) 246-PRIDE (246-7743). The hours are Mon-Fri 20-24 (eastern standard time).

Alabama

Location: Southeast USA
Initials: AL
Time: GMT -6
Area: 135.775 km² / 55,532 sq mi.
Population: 4,447,000
Capital: Montgomery

Birmingham ☎ 205

BARS

■ **Our Place** (B G MA VS) 16-24, Fri & Sat -2h
2115 7th Ave South *Cnr. 22nd St* ☎ (205) 276-3823

■ **Quest** (B CC D GLM MA OS P ST T) 24hrs
416 24th Street South *At 5th Ave S* ☎ (205) 251-4313
🖳 www.quest-club.com

DANCECLUBS

■ **Pulse** (AC B D GLM MA ST)
2824 5th Ave South *At 29th Street*

Dothan ☎ 334

BARS

■ **Club Imagination** (B D GLM MA P ST) Wed-Sat 18-4h
4129 Ross Clark Circle NW *Off Hwy 431 North* ☎ (334) 792-6555
🖳 www.myspace.com/clubimagination

Geneva ☎ 334

CAMPING

■ **Spring Creek Campground & Resort** (GLM NU)
Office hours 10-18h
163 Campground Road ☎ (334) 684-3891
🖳 www.springcreekcampground.net
Clothing-optional resort.

Huntsville ☎ 256

BARS

■ **Club Ozz** (B D GLM MA S ST) Thu-Sun 18-2h
1204 Posey Street ☎ (256) 534-5970 🖳 www.myspace.com/clubozz

■ **Partners** (B D GLM M MA S) 17-24, Fri & Sat -2, Sun 14-22h, closed Mon & Tue
627 Meridan Street ☎ (256) 539-0975 🖳 www.partnershsv.com

Mobile ☎ 251

GAY INFO

■ **Bay Area Inclusion**
100 South Florida Street ☎ (251) 450-1060
🖳 www.bayareainclusion.org
LGBT community center.

BARS

■ **B-Bob's Downtown** (AC B CC D FC GLM MA S ST VS WI)
18-?, Sat 19-?h
213 Conti Street ☎ (251) 433-2262 🖳 www.b-bobs.com

■ **Bacchus** (AC B GLM MA) Wed-Sat 20-?h
54 South Conception Street ☎ (251) 445-4099
🖳 www.myspace.com/bacchusmobile

■ **Gabriel's Downtown** (AC B CC d GLM MA OS)
Mon-Sat 19.30-?, Sun 14-?h
55 South Joachim Street *Walking distance from all downtown hotels*
☎ (251) 432-4900 🖳 www.gabrielsdowntown.com
One of Alabama's oldest alternative bars and Mobile's favorite neighborhood pubs. Karaoke Wed & Fri.

■ **Midtown Pub** (AC B D GLM M MA S) 12-?h
153 South Florida Street *Cnr. Emogene Street* ☎ (251) 450-1555
🖳 www.themidtownpub.com

■ **Saga** (B D GLM MA) Wed-Sun 16-21h
266 Dauphin St *At Conti St* ☎ (251) 431-9002

Montgomery ☎ 334

BARS

■ **Club 322** (B D GLM MA S) Fri & Sat 21-?, Sun 19-2h
322 North Lawrence Street ☎ (334) 263-4322 🖳 www.club322.com

GUEST HOUSES

■ **Lattice Inn. The** (AC BF GLM I MA OS PI PK RWS RWT WH)
All year
1414 South Hull Street *Historic Garden District in the heart of Montgomery*
☎ (334) 262-3388 🖳 www.thelatticeinn.com

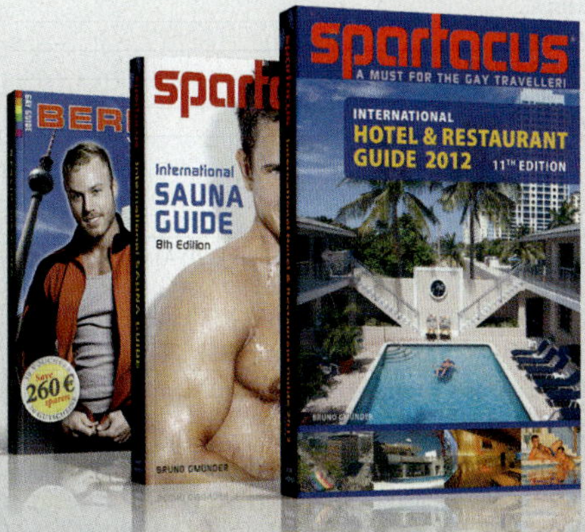

Steele ☎ 256

CAMPING

■ **Bluff Creek Falls** (bf G M MA NU PI VS WO) All year, office 7-17h
1125 Loop Road *50 mins from Birmingham* ☎ (256) 538-0678
www.bluffcreekfalls.com
Clothing optional gay camp resort.

Waverly ☎ 334

GUEST HOUSES

■ **Black Bear Camp** (AC F G I MA NU PI PK RWT VA VS WE WH) All year
10565 US Highway 280 West ☎ (334) 887-5152
www.blackbearcamp.net
Clothing-optional men's retreat.

Alaska

Location: Northern America
Initials: AK
Time: GMT -9
Area: 1,700,138 km² / 695,356 sq mi.
Population: 626,932
Capital: Juneau

Anchorage ☎ 907

NATIONAL COMPANIES

■ **Out in Alaska** (CC GLM MA) All year
no store front ☎ (907) 339-0101 www.outinalaska.com
Explore the wilds of Alaska with local guides at Out in Alaska on a cruise, scenic land tour, or active adventure. See wildlife , kayak to a glacier, raft a wild river and more.

GAY INFO

■ **Gay and Lesbian Community Center of Anchorage** (GLM MA) Helpline 18-23h, tel. 258-4777
336 East Fifth Avenue ☎ (907) 929-4528 www.identityinc.org

BARS

■ **Mad Myrna's** (B GLM M MA S) 16-2.30, Fri & Sat -3h
530 East 5th Avenue *At Fairbanks St* ☎ (907) 276-9762
www.alaska.net/~madmyrna
■ **Raven** (B G m MA) 13-2.30h
708 East 4th Avenue ☎ (907) 276-9672

HOTELS

■ **Copper Whale Inn** (BF GLM I MA PK RWT VA) All year
440 L Street *Downtown* ☎ (907) 258-7999 ☎ 258-7999 (toll-free)
www.copperwhale.com
Small, gay-operated hotel with 14 rooms. Great views.

GUEST HOUSES

■ **Arctic Fox Inn** (BF glm)
327 East 2nd Court *Off Cordova St* ☎ (907) 272-4818
www.arcticfoxinn.com
Centrally located, gay owned inn. Guest rooms and multi-room apartments.
■ **City Garden B&B** (BF GLM I MA PK RWT)
1352 West 10th Avenue *Eight blocks from downtown, on Park Strip*
☎ (907) 276-8686 www.citygarden.biz
Gay owned and operated. Three rooms available. Two share a bath one with a private bath. Complete cooked breakfast. All rooms on second floor. Plus secure WiFi www.citygarden.biz
■ **Jewel Lake Bed & Breakfast** (BF glm I MA RWB RWS RWT) All year
8125 Jewel Lake Road ☎ (907) 245-7321
www.jewellakebandb.com
■ **Wildflower Inn B&B. A** (BF GLM MA RWS RWT) All year
1239 I Street ☎ (907) 274-1239 www.alaska-wildflower-inn.com
Small guesthouse with three guest rooms, run by a fun gay couple.

Fairbanks ☎ 907

GUEST HOUSES

■ **All Seasons B&B Inn** (bf H I) All year
763 7th Avenue ☎ (907) 451-6649 www.allseasonsinn.com

Haines ☎ 907

GUEST HOUSES

■ **Guardhouse Boarding House. The** (bf gLm I MA) All year
15 Seward Drive ☎ (907) 766-2566 www.alaskaguardhouse.com

McCarthy ☎ 907

GUEST HOUSES

■ **McCarthy Lodge** (CC GLM I MA) May-Sep
Ma Johnson's Hotel, PO Box MXY *Downtown* ☎ (907) 554-4402
www.mccarthylodge.com
Historic hotel, bar and restaurant in the middle of Wrangell – St. Elias National Park.

Palmer ☎ 907

TRAVEL AND TRANSPORT

■ **Hunter Creek Adventures** (g MA) May-Sep
Knik River Road ☎ (907) 745-1577 www.knikglacier.com
Gay owned airboat tours of Knik Glacier.

GUEST HOUSES

■ **Alaska Garden Gate B&B** (BF glm MA) All year
950 S. Trunk Road *Between Palmer and Wasilla* ☎ (907) 746-2333
www.gardengatebnb.com
Lesbian run B&B with five bedrooms and five private cottages.

Valdez ☎ 907

TRAVEL AND TRANSPORT

■ **Wild Iris Charters** (CC GLM)
Small Boat Harbour ☎ (907) 460-6447 www.wildirisfishing.com
Lesbian owned and captained charter boat for Halibut fishing, sightseeing, or kayak drop offs.

Arizona

Location: Southwest USA
Initials: AZ
Time: GMT -7
Area: 295,276 km² / 120,768 sq mi.
Population: 4,555,000
Capital: Phoenix

Bisbee ☎ 520

GUEST HOUSES

■ **Doublejack Guesthouse** (AC G I RWS RWT) All year
☎ (520) 559 6708 www.DoublejackBisbee.com
Gay owned and operated. Located in the heart of historic Bisbee.

CAMPING

■ **David's Oasis Camping Resort** (b cc GLM I MA NU P PA PI PK S SA VA WH WO) Office 10-22h
5311 West Double Adobe Road *Mile 3.1 on Double Adobe Road*
☎ (520) 979-6650 www.azgaycamping.com
A private membership gay and lesbian camping resort with gay bar on a Arizona desert oasis.

Bullhead City ☎ 928

BARS

■ **Lariat Saloon** (B GLM I MA OS) 10-2h
1161 Hancock Road ☎ (928) 704-1969 💻 www.lariatsaloon.com

Flagstaff ☎ 520

BARS

■ **Charly's Pub & Grill** (B glm M MA S) 8-2h
23 North Leroux Street *At corner of Aspen and Leroux St*
☎ (520) 779-1919 💻 www.weatherfordhotel.com
In more than 100 years old Weatherford Hotel.

GUEST HOUSES

■ **Inn at 410 B&B** (AC BF GLM I MA PK RWS VA) All year
410 North Leroux Street *Historic downtown* ☎ (928) 774-0088
💻 www.inn410.com
An award-winning, nine-room guesthouse.

■ **Starlight Pines B&B** (BF CC DM GLM I PK RWB RWS VEG WI) All year
3380 East Lockett Road ☎ (928) 527-1912
💻 www.starlightpinesbb.com
Gay owned & operated. Four guest rooms with private baths. Free parking, WIFI and hot breakfast. Grand Canyon, Sedona very close to our B&B

Phoenix ☎ 602

PUBLICATIONS

■ **'N Touch**
PO Box 17674 ☎ (602) 373-9490 💻 www.ntouchaz.com
Free monthly LGBT news magazine.

■ **Desert Knight News**
PO Box 7031 ☎ (602) 327-9931 💻 www.desertknightnews.com
Free monthly magazine for the bear, leather, fetish community.

■ **Echo Magazine**
PO Box 16630 ☎ (602) 266-0550 💻 www.echomag.com
General GLBT interests magazine published fortnightly.

■ **Ion Arizona**
3819 North 3rd Street, Suite 26 ☎ (602) 308-4662
💻 www.ionaz.com
Gay and lesbian entertainment monthly.

SHOWS

■ **Dick's Cabaret** (G MA SNU) 19-2, Fri & Sat -3h
3432 East Illini Street *At 37th St* ☎ (602) 274-3425
💻 www.dickscabaret.com
All nude male strippers. No alcohol served.

BARS

■ **Amsterdam** (B cc D glm M MA OS S) 16-2, Fri & Sat 16-4h
718 North Central Avenue *Between Roosevelt and Fillmore*
☎ (602) 258-6122
💻 www.facebook.com/amsterdam.phoenix
Upscale martini bar with adjoining dance Club Miami and back patio bar Malibu Beach. Popular Mon, Thu, Fri & Sat after 22h. Happy hour 16-19h.

■ **Apollo's Lounge** (AC B CC d G MA S) 12-1, Fri & Sat -2h
5749 North 7th Street ☎ (602) 277-9373 💻 www.apollos.com
Valley gay bar veteran, nice neighbourhood feel.

■ **Babylon Show Club** (AC B G MA SNU) 20-2h
3613 E Van Buren ☎ (602) 306-1000
💻 www.babylonshowclub.com

■ **Bar 1** (B G MA OS) 10-2h
3702 North 16th Street ☎ (602) 266-9001 💻 www.bar1bar.com

■ **BS West** (B D GLM MA s VS) 14-2h
7125 East 5th Ave, Scottsdale ☎ (480) 945-9028 💻 www.bswest.com
Video bar, pool tables, small dance floor, cute bartenders. Popular Wed & WE after 22h.

■ **Bunkhouse** (B G m MA OS) 8-2, Sun 10-2h
4428 North 7th Avenue ☎ (602) 200-9154
💻 www.bunkhousesaloon.com
Darts, pool tables, cruising patio.

■ **Cash Inn Country** (B gLm MA) Tue-Fri 14-2, Sat & Sun 12-?h
2140 East McDowell Road ☎ (602) 244-9943
💻 www.cashinncountry.net
Primarily lesbian Country/Western dance bar.

■ **Charlie's** (B d G MA OS) 14-2, Fri & Sat -4h
727 West Camelback Road *Cnr. 7th Ave* ☎ (602) 265-0224
💻 www.charliesphoenix.com
Country/Western dance bar with patio and volleyball.

■ **Cherry** (B f G M MA) 11-2, Sun 10-2h
1028 East Indian School Road *At 10th St* ☎ (602) 277-7729
💻 www.cherryaz.com
Neighbourhood bar.

■ **Cruisin' 7th** (AYOR B G R SNU) 6-2, Sun 10-2h
3702 North 7th Street ☎ (602) 212-9888
Downtown neighbourhood pub.

■ **Ice Pics** (B GLM MA s VS) 16-2, Sun 14-2h
3108 East McDowell Road ☎ (602) 267-8707
💻 www.icepicsvideobar.com

■ **Kobalt** (B glm MC s) 12-2h
3110 N Central Ave, Ste 125 *In the Shopping Mall* ☎ (602) 264-5307
💻 www.kobaltbarphoenix.com
Sunday evenings are for the boys. Karaoke.

■ **Nutowne Saloon** (B D f G m MA) 12-2h
5002 East Van Buren Street *At 48th St* ☎ (602) 267-9959
💻 www.nutowne.com
Sunday brunch available.

■ **Oz** (B GLM MA) 12-2h
1804 West Bethany Home Road *Cnr. 19th St* ☎ (602) 242-5114
💻 www.ozphx.com
Neighbourhood bar.

■ **Plazma** (B GLM MA s) 15-2h
1560 East Osborn Road ☎ (602) 266-0477
💻 www.myspace.com/phxplazma

■ **Pumphouse II** (B GLM MA s SNU) 12-2h
4132 East McDowell Road ☎ (602) 275-3509
💻 www.pumphouseII.com
Neighborhood bar with strip shows on Tue & Thu.

■ **Rainbow Cactus** (B glm MA)
15615 N. Cave Creek Rd. ☎ (602) 971-1086
💻 www.facebook.com/pages/rainbow-cactus-saloon/164347099748

■ **Rock. The** (B d G MA SNU t WE) 12-2h
4129 North 7th Avenue *At W Indian School Rd* ☎ (602) 248-8559
💻 www.therockdmphoenix.com

■ **Roscoe's on 7th** (B G m MA) 11-15, 16-22; Sat & Sun 11-19h
4531 North 7th Street *At Minnezona* ☎ (602) 285-0833
💻 www.roscoeson7.com
Sports bar, big screen TV, pool tables and darts, nice selection of cute guys. Dining Mon-Fri 11-22, Sat & Sun 12-19. Happy hour Mon-Sat 15-19h.

■ **Velocity** (B D f G MA) 12-1h
2303 E. Indian School Road ☎ (602) 956-2885
💻 www.velocity2303.com

DANCECLUBS

■ **Forbidden** (B D G MA) Thu-Sun 20-2h
6820 East 5th Ave, Scottsdale ☎ (602) 994-5176
💻 www.forbiddenaz.com

■ **Karamba** (B D GLM M MA ST t) 16-?h
1724 East McDowell Road *One block east of 16th St* ☎ (602) 254-0231
💻 www.karambanightclub.com

SEX SHOPS/BLUE MOVIES

■ **Adult Shoppe. The** (g VS) 24hrs
2345 West Holly Street ☎ (602) 253-7126 💻 www.theadultshoppe.com
Toys, DVDs, novelties, magazines, rentals. Two further shops in Phoenix.

■ **Castle Megastore** (g VS) 24hrs
300 East Camelback Road ☎ (602) 266-3348
Leather, lingerie, magazines, books, DVDs, toys and more. Five further shops in Phoenix.

SAUNAS/BATHS

■ **Chute** (AC B DR DU G M NU P SB SH VS WO) 24hrs
1440 East Indian School Road *16th Street and Indian School Rd*
☎ (602) 234-1654 🖳 www.chuteaz.com
For those over 18 only. Private sauna club for bears and leathermen with a cruisy atmosphere.

■ **Flex** (! AC B BF CC DR DU FC FH G GH LAB m MA MSG OS P PI RR S SA SB SH SNU SOL VS WH WO) 24hrs
1517 South Black Canyon Highway ☎ (602) 271-9011
🖳 www.flexbaths.com
Free condoms. Member specials. Mon Levi & leather night, Wed 1/2 price room day, Fri student ID-day.

FASHION SHOPS

■ **Off Chute Too** (CC GLM) Mon-Fri 8-18h MST
4115 North 7th Ave ☎ (602) 274-1429 🖳 www.offchutestore.com
Also pride items, leather, toys, DVDs, books.

GIFT & PRIDE SHOPS

■ **Root Seller Gallery** (AC CC F GLM MA) Mon-Sat 10-7
4015 North 16th Street, Ste H *SE corner of 16th St & Indian School Rd*
☎ (602) 265-7668
Largest GLBT bookstore in Phoenix.
Art, Books, Cards, Gifts, Incense, Music, & More...

LEATHER & FETISH SHOPS

■ **Tuff Stuff Leather** (CC F G MA) 10-18, Sat -16h, closed Sun & Mon
1716 East McDowell Road *Near 17th Street* ☎ (602) 254-9561
🖳 www.tuffstuffleather.com

HOTELS

■ **Arizona Royal Villa Resort**
(AC CC G I MA NU OS P PI PK RWS RWT WH) All year, office: 9-18h
4312 North 12th Street *10 mins from airport* ☎ (602) 266-6883
🖳 www.royalvilla.com
Fifteen units with bath/shower, telephone, TV, minibar, kitchenette, heating and own key.

GUEST HOUSES

■ **Arizona Sunburst Inn** (AC BF CC DU FH G MA MSG NR NU OS PA PI PK RWB RWS RWT VA WH WI) All year
6245 North 12th Place *At Rose Lane* ☎ (602) 274-1474
☎ (800) 974-1474 (toll free) 🖳 www.azsunburst.com
Bask in luxury at the Valley of the Sun's Gay Oasis. Male-only, poolside Bed & Breakfast in the heart of the GLBT district of Phoenix.

■ **Orange Blossom Hacienda** (AC CC glm m MA NU PI) All year
3914 E Sunnydale Drive, Queen Creek ☎ (480) 250-1223
🖳 www.orangeblossomhacienda.com
Gay owned bed and breakfast.

■ **ZenYard** (AC B BF CC DU FH GLM MA MSG NR OS PI PK RWS VA WH WI)
830 East Maryland Avenue *Uptown Phoenix, centrally located, close to bars*
☎ (602) 845-0830 🖳 www.zenyard.com
You will find a lot of space here including the solar heated salt water pool and a couple of jacuzzi tubs. Located centrally in uptown Phoenix's central corridor.

CRUISING

All are AYOR:
-Papago Park
-Dreamy Draw Park, Squaw Peak Parkway
-Thunderbird Park, Glendale
-Washington Park, 21st Ave at night.

Tucson ☏ 520

GAY INFO

Wingspan – Southern Arizona's LGBT Community Center (GLM) Mon-Thu 11-21, Fri -19, Sat & Sun 10-16.30h
425 East 7th Street ☏ (520) 624-1779 www.wingspan.org

PUBLICATIONS

Tucson Observer. The Mon-Fri 9-16h
PO Box 50733 ☏ (520) 622-7176 www.tucsonobserver.com
Gay and lesbian weekly newspaper for Tucson and Greater Arizona.

BARS

Coyote Moon Pub (AC B D f GLM M MA S) 15-1, Sat 11-1, Sun 10-1h
915 West Prince Road *At Fairview Ave* ☏ (520) 293-7339
www.facebook.com/pages/Coyote-Moon-Pub/41858153837

It's Bout Time (IBT's) (B D GLM OS S) 12-2h
616 North 4th Avenue *At University* ☏ (520) 882-3053
www.myspace.com/ibtstucson
Happy hour 12-20h.

Venture-N (B f G m OS) Mon-Fri 12-2, Sat & Sun 11-2h
1239 North 6th Avenue ☏ (520) 882-8224 www.venture-n.com

Woody's (AC B G S VS WE YC) 12-2, Sat & Sun 11-2h
3710 North Oracle Road ☏ (520) 292-6702
www.mywoodysaz.com

DANCECLUBS

Biz. The (B D GLM I MA OS SNU ST VS) Tue-Sat 17-2h
2900 E. Broadway Blvd. #118 ☏ (520) 318-4838
www.thebiztuc.com
Hot gay & lesbian nightclub with specials and happy hour.

RESTAURANTS

Colors (AC B BF CC f GLM M MA S WE)
16-22, Fri & Sat -24, Sun 10-22h
5305 East Speedway Blvd ☏ (520) 323-1840
www.colorstucson.com

GUEST HOUSES

Catalina Park Inn B&B (BF glm I PI RWS RWT) All year
309 East First Street ☏ (520) 792-4541 www.catalinaparkinn.com

Royal Elizabeth B&B Inn (AC BF glm I MA PI PK RWS RWT)
All year
204 South Scott Avenue *Downtown* ☏ (520) 670-9022
www.royalelizabeth.com
An historic inn in an urban, walkable location.

Arkansas

Location: Southern USA
Initials: AR
Time: GMT -6
Area: 137,742 km² / 56,337 sq mi.
Population: 2,673,400
Capital: Little Rock

Fayetteville ☏ (0479)

BARS

Tangerine (B D GLM MA S ST) 21-2h, closed Sun-Tue
21 North Block Ave ☏ (479) 443-4600
www.myspace.com/clubtangerine

Fort Smith ☏ 479

BARS

Kinkead's (B D GLM MA ST t) 12-1, Sun 18-24h, closed Mon-Wed
1004 Garrison Ave ☏ (479) 494-7477 www.clubkinkeads.com

California

Location: Southwest USA
Initials: CA
Time: GMT -8
Area: 424,002 km² / 173,417 sq mi.
Population: 33,871,648
Capital: Sacramento
Important gay cities: Long Beach, Los Angeles, Palm Springs, Russian River, San Diego, San Francisco

Calistoga ☏ 707

GUEST HOUSES

Meadowlark Country House (bf glm MA NU SA WH) All year
601 Petrified Forest Rd ☏ (707) 942-5651 www.meadowlarkinn.com
Meadowlark's atmosphere is hetero, gay and naturist friendly.

Castroville ☏ 408

DANCECLUBS

Franco's Club (B D GLM m MA S ST) Sat 22-2h
10639 Merritt Street ☏ (408) 633-2090

Clearlake ☏ 707

CRUISING

-Austin Beach Park (Clear Lake Highlands)
-Kneeling Park
-Library Park (Lakeport)

Costa Mesa ☏ 714

BARS

Tin Lizzie Saloon (B G MA) 11.30-2h
752 St. Clair Street ☏ (714) 966-2029 www.tinlizziesaloon.com

DANCECLUBS

Lions Den (B D GLM MA ST) Fri 21-2h
719 West 19th Street ☏ (949) 642-2243

Eureka ☏ 707

BARS

Lost Coast Brewery & Café (AC B CC glm M MA) 11-1h
617 4th Street *Downtown Eureka on Highway 101 between G&H St*
☏ (707) 445-4480 www.lostcoast.com
Gay-friendly brewery pub.

Fresno ☏ 559

BARS

Den. The (AC B CC DR f G MA OS S ST t VS) 17-2h
4538 East Belmont Avenue *West of Maple, south side* ☏ (559) 255-3213
www.denfresno.com
Bear and leather bar. Pool table, patio with shows.

DANCECLUBS

Express (AC B D G MA ST) 21-2h, closed Mon & Tue
708 North Blackstone *Between Olive & Belmont* ☏ (559) 445-0878
www.thefresnoexpress.com

Red Lantern. The (B D G MA OS) 14-2h
4618 East Belmont ☏ (559) 251-5898 redlantern.info
A favourite of the Latin and leather crowds.

CRUISING

-Rodeo Park (1st Street & Clinton Street)
-Roeding Park

-Tower District (Olive Street/Wishon Street)
-Woodward Park

Garden Grove ☎ 714

BARS

■ **Frat House. The** (AC B CC D GLM m MA S SNU ST VS) 15-2h
8112 Garden Grove Boulevard *Off the 22 freeway at Beach Blvd*
☎ (714) 373-3728 www.frathouseonline.com
Happy hour Mon-Fri 16-20h, Sun BeerBust 16-20h. Daily Live Video DJ's at 21h.

Hayward ☎ 510

BARS

■ **Rainbow Room** (AC B D GLM MA OS S ST T) 14-2h
21859 Mission Boulevard *Between Sunset & Grove St* ☎ (510) 582-8078
www.rainbow-room.com
Two pool tables, darts, live bands. Fri & Sat DJ dancing.

■ **Turf Club** (B CC D GLM MA OS S WI) 14-2h
22519 Main Street *2 Blocks from BART* ☎ (510) 881-9877
www.wfturfclub.com
With a large outdoor patio and many special events. DJs on weekends.

Huntington Beach ☎ 714

BARS

■ **Metro Q Bar & Grill** (AC B GLM M MA)
15.30-?, Sat 11.30-?, Sun 10-?h, closed Mon
19092 Beach Blvd ☎ (714) 968-6677 www.themetroq.com
Sunday brunch.

Indio ☎ 760

DANCECLUBS

■ **Destino. El** (B D GLM MA S) Fri & Sat 21-2h
83-085 Indio Blvd ☎ (760) 775-0686 www.eldestinonightclub.com

Irvine ☎ 949

DANCECLUBS

■ **Club Lucky @ Tia Juana's** (B D G MA ST) Sun 21-2h
14988 Sand Canyon Avenue *Right off Santa Ana Fwy* ☎ (949) 551-2998
www.luckysundays.com

Laguna Beach ☎ 949

BARS

■ **Club Bounce** (B GLM MA S) 14-2h
1460 South Coast Hwy ☎ (949) 494-0056 bounceatthebeach.com

Lake Tahoe ☎ 619

GUEST HOUSES

■ **Black Bear Inn** (AC BF CC glm H I MA PK RWB RWS RWT) All year
1202 Ski Run Boulevard ☎ (619) 544-4411
www.tahoeblackbear.com
Luxury lodge with five guest rooms and three cabins. All rooms with private bath, fireplace, kingsize beds, TV/DVD.

Long Beach ☎ 562

GAY INFO

■ **The Center Long Beach** (CC GLM MA S) Mon-Fri 11-21h
2017 East 4th Street *At Cherry* ☎ (562) 434-4455 www.centerlb.org

BARS

■ **Brit** (B D G MA OS) 10-2h
1744 East Broadway Avenue *At Cherry* ☎ (562) 432-9742
Happy hour 16-19h

■ **Broadway. The** (AC B GLM MA S) 10-2h
1100 East Broadway ☎ (562) 432-3646

■ **Club Broadway** (B D gLm MA) 11-2h
3348 East Broadway Avenue ☎ (562) 438-7700

■ **Crest. The** (B F G MA OS) 14-2h
5935 Cherry Avenue *At South* ☎ (562) 423-6650
www.thecrestlongbeach.com

■ **Falcon. The** (AC B CC G MA) 7-2h
1435 East Broadway *At Falcon* ☎ (562) 432-4146
www.thefalcon.us
Friendly and cool cruise bar.

■ **Flux** (AC B CC GLM I MA OS VS WE) 12-2h
17817 South Lakewood Blvd ☎ (562) 633-6394
www.fluxgaybar.com
Happy hour Mon-Sat 12-19h.

■ **Liquid Lounge** (B GLM M MA OS s) 11-1, Fri & Sat -2h
3522 East Anaheim St ☎ (562) 494-7564
www.liquidloungelongbeach.com

■ **Mineshaft. The** (B F G MA) 10-2h
1720 East Broadway ☎ (562) 436-2433
www.mineshaftlb.com
Happy Hour 10-19h. Popular and very cruisy.

■ **Paradise** (B GLM M MA S) Bar 15-1.30, restaurant Mon-Fri 15-22h
1800 East Broadway *1 block west of Cherry* ☎ (562) 590-8773
www.paradisepianobar.com
Piano bar; happy hour 15-19, dinner Thu-Sat -24h.

■ **Pistons** (B F G MA) 18-2, Fri & Sat -3, Sun 15-2h
2020 East Artesia Bvd. *At Cherry* ☎ (562) 422-1928
www.pistonsbar.com
Leather and Bear bar.

■ **Que Será** (AC B D glm MA) Tue-Fri 17-2, Sat & Sun 15-2h
1923 East 7th Street ☎ (562) 599-6170 www.thequesera.com

■ **Silver Fox** (AC B G MA VS) 16-2, Sat & Sun 12-2h
411 Redondo Avenue ☎ (562) 439-6343
www.silverfoxlongbeach.com
Happy hour on Tue is very popular. Open since 1981.

■ **Sweetwater Saloon** (B G MA) 10-2h
1201 East Broadway Avenue *At Orange* ☎ (562) 432-7044
Cruisy atmosphere.

CAFES

■ **iCandy Coffee** (b G m MA) 7-22, Fri -24, Sat -1h
2101 East Broadway ☎ (562) 437-3785 www.icandycoffee.com

DANCECLUBS

■ **Boy's Room @ Executive Suite Nightclub** (B D G MA S)
Fri 21-2h
3428 East Pacific Coast Hwy ☎ (562) 597-3884
www.clubboysroom.com
Long Beach's most popular Friday gay hotspot.

■ **Club Ripples** (! AC B CC D G MA S VS) 12-2h
5101 East Ocean Boulevard *Across street from beach* ☎ (562) 433-0357
www.clubripples.com
Two levels, two bars, two dance floors, upstairs bar has a panoramic view of the Pacific Ocean, smoking patio in club. Check www.clubripples.com for theme parties.

■ **Executive Suite** (B D GLM MA) Thu-Sat 20-?h
3428 East Pacific Coast Hwy *Cnr. Redondo Ave* ☎ (562) 572-4810
www.executivesuitenightclub.com

RESTAURANTS

■ **Hamburger Mary's** (B CC D GLM M MA S ST t)
17-2, Fri & Sat 11-2h
740 East Broadway ☎ (562) 291-1368
www.hamburgermaryslb.com
Various events, see www.hamburgermaryslb.com for details.

■ **Raven's Nest. The** (B GLM M MA)
2941 East Broadway *Between Temple & Redondo* ☎ (562) 439-3672

SAUNAS/BATHS

1350 Club
(CC DR DU FC FH G GH I LAB M MA OS P RR SA SB VS WO) 24hrs
510 West Anaheim Street, Wilmington *North of Long Beach, 3 miles west of 710 Freeway* ☎ (310) 830-4784 www.midtowne.com
Large sauna with outside patio and redwood deck, water fountain and a maze. Secured parking lot across the street.

Los Angeles ☎ 213

Nowhere in the US does the dream of stardom, wealth and luxury come more true than in Los Angeles.
Speaking of gay L.A. means in reality speaking of the autonomous city of »West Hollywood«, one of the gayest centers of north America. Santa Monica Boulevard could also be called Rainbow Boulevard. The gay center of Los Angeles is in »Silverlake« to the north of »Downtown«. Smaller centers of gay life are in the Valley to the north of Los Angeles conurbation, on the beaches to the west and in Long Beach to the south. A car is indispensible. With it you can reach the gay resort »Laguna Beach« in 90 minutes. A lot, which seems to be gay, is only a façade, but what can one expect in the city, where façades are produced for films. And looking behind the façade of Hollywood is nearly impossible; production halls are not that impressive. Small glimpses of the myth can be gotten on the »Walk of Fame« on Hollywood Boulevard or in the »Universal Studios« on Hollywood Freeway.
But one product of Los Angeles is not just façade: the charity for AIDS-victims. Events like the »California AIDS Ride« (on bycicle) or the »AIDS Walk LA« bring large amounts of money for the AIDS-stricken, plus the opportunity to exhibit yourself and keep fit. An activity, which can also be done beautifully in »Venice« on the coast. More reasons for visiting L.A. are the pride-events or the gay days at »Disneyland«.

Nirgendwo sonst kommen die USA dem Traum von Starruhm, Reichtum und Luxus näher.
Spricht man in schwuler Hinsicht von L. A., dann meint man am ehesten die eigenständige Stadt »West Hollywood«, eine der schwulsten städtischen Gegenden Nordamerikas. Der Santa Monica Boulevard könnte ebensogut Rainbow Boulevard heißen. Los Angeles' schwules Zentrum findet sich in »Silverlake«, nördlich der »Downtown«.
Kleinere Ballungen schwuler Adressen finden sich auch im Valley (im Norden des Ballungsraums), an den Beaches (im Westen) und in Long Beach (im Süden). Bei diesen Entfernungen ist ein Auto unerlässlich, mit dem man den recht schwulen Badeort »Laguna Beach« im Süden in etwa 90 Minuten erreicht.
Natürlich ist vieles, was so schwul erscheint, nur Fassade. Doch wie sollte es anders sein in der Stadt, in der sich die Fassade »Hollywood« befindet. Zu sehen ist von der allerdings nicht viel, Produktionshallen machen eben keinen Eindruck. Kleine Einblicke in den Mythos erlangt man dennoch am »Walk of Fame« am Hollywood Boulevard oder in den »Universal Studios« am Hollywood Freeway. Ein Besuch des neuen Paul-Getty-Museums ist nicht nur für Kunstfreunde ein Muss.
Eines jedoch ist ganz sicherlich nicht aufgesetzt: Charity, Wohltätigkeit für die Opfer von AIDS. Veranstaltungen wie der »California AIDS Ride« (per Rad) oder der »AIDS Walk LA« (per pedes) generieren große Summen für die Betroffenen. Und damit ideale Gelegenheiten, sich sowohl zu zeigen, als auch fit zu halten. Eine Tätigkeit, die sich übrigens auch in »Venice« am Ozean vorzüglich betrachten lässt.
Weitere Gelegenheiten für einen Besuch LAs sind die Pride-Veranstaltungen oder die schwulen Thementage im »Disneyland« in Anaheim.

Nulle part ailleurs aux Etats-Unis, vous ne verrez ce que peut être le rêve américain: gloire, célébrité, luxe.
Quand on parle du Los Angeles gai, on pense plutôt à West Hollywood, un des bastions gais d'Amérique du Nord. Le Santa Monica Boulevard est aux mains des gais. Le centre gai de Los Angeles se trouve à Silverlake au nord de Downtown.
Les quartiers nord (Valley), ouest (Beaches) et sud (Long Beach) valent également le détour. Vu les distances, une voiture est nécessaire. Pour

aller à Laguna Beach, par exemple, il faut environ une heure et demie. Attention: tout ce qui a l'air gai ne l'est pas forcément! Comme beaucoup d'autres choses, tout est façade ici. Hollywood en premier lieu. De Hollywood, on ne voit pas grand chose, si ce n'est que le „Walk of Fame" sur le Hollywood Boulevard ou les „Universal Studios" sur le Hollywood Freeway.
Une chose au moins n'est pas du cinéma: la „Charity" pour les victimes du sida. Le „California AIDS Ride" (course de bicyclette) et le „AIDS Walk LA" (course à pied) sont des manifestations qui rapportent d'importantes sommes d'argent que l'on distribue aux malades. Deux bonnes occasions de se montrer et de se maintenir en bonne santé. Les amateurs de culturisme se donnent rendez-vous à Venice Beach.
Profitez de la „Gay Pride" ou des journées gaies de Disney Land (Anaheim) pour découvrir Los Angeles.

En ningún otro lugar de los E.E.U.U. se deja palpar tanto el sueño de éxito, riqueza y lujo.
Si se quiere hablar del ambiente gay de L.A. se debe hacer mención inmediata de la ciudad autónoma »West Hollywood«. El Santa Mónica Boulevard podría también llevar el nombre de Rainbow Boulevard. El centro gay de L.A. se encuentra en »Silverlake« al norte de »Downtown«. Pequeñas agrupaciones de direcciones gay se encuentran en Valley (al norte de la aglomeración urbana), en las playas (en el oeste) y en Long Beach (en el sur). Un coche es de vital importancia, debido a las grandes distancias que se deben recorrer. A »Laguna Beach« en el sur, se llega en cuestión de 90 min.. Muchos sitios que parecen a primera vista ser gays, lo son solamente de fachada. Pero qué se puede esperar de una ciudad que se dedica a la producción de ilusiones. Un vistazo detrás de las fachadas es practicamente imposible, por demás los centros de producción tampoco son muy impresionantes. Se puede dar una pequeña ojeada al mito que envuelve a esta ciudad en el »Walk of Fame« en el Hollywood Boulevard o en el »Universal Studios« en Hollywood Freeway.
Las obras de caridad para los afectados de SIDA son de especial mención. La organización de eventos como »California AIDS Ride« (en bicicleta) o la »AIDS Walk L.A.« (a pie) generan grandes cantidades de dinero para los afectados así como la oportunidad ideal para mostrarse y mantenerse en forma. Otras oportunidades ideales para visitar L.A. son las fiestas de Pride Gay (orgullo gay) o los días de tematización de la cuestión homosexual en »Disneyland« en Anaheim.

In nessun luogo gli Stati Uniti si avvicinano tanto al sogno di gloria, ricchezza e lusso come in questa città.
Chi parla della vita gay di Los Angeles intende »West Hollywood«, la zona urbana più gay del Nordamerica. Il boulevard Santa Monica potrebbe chiamarsi bouleverd dell'arcobaleno. Il centro gay di Los Angeles si trova a »Silverlake« a nord di »Downtown«.
Concentrazioni più piccole di indirizzi gay si trovano anche a Valley (a nord della zona densamente abitata), alle Beaches (ad ovest) e a Long Beach (a sud). Considerate le grandi distanze è indispensabile un'automobile: potrete raggiungere così in 90 minuti la stazione balneare di »Laguna Beach«. La vita gay è molto influenzata dalle apparenze, ma come potrebbe essere altrimenti ad Hollywood. Qui non vi è molto da vedere, considerato che i capannoni di produzione non sono un grande spettacolo. Potrete avere un'idea del mito di Hollywood al »Walk of fame«, sull'Hollywood Boulevard o negli »Universal Studios« sull'Hollywood Freeway.
Una cosa però non è artificiale: charity, la beneficenza per le vittime dell'AIDS. Manifestazioni come »California AIDS ride« (in bicicletta) o »AIDS Walk LA« (a piedi) raccolgono ingenti somme e creano occasioni per mostrarsi e per mantenersi in forma; è possibile fare sport anche a »Venice« sull'oceano. Altre occasioni per visitare L.A. sono le manifestazioni Pride e i giorni dei temi gay a »Disneyland« ad Anaheim.

NATIONAL PUBLICATIONS

Out Traveler
10990 Wilshire Boulevard, Penthouse ☎ (323) 871-1225
www.outtraveler.com
The Out Traveler is a gay-themed, online-magazine that features exotic travel stories, service items, and ratings of destinationsí gay-friendliness.

GAY INFO

LA Gay and Lesbian Center (GLM)
9-21, Sat -13h, closed Sun
1625 North Schrader Boulevard ☎ (323) 993-7400
www.lagaycenter.org
The L. A. Gay & Lesbian Center operates five locations, please check their website for further info.

PUBLICATIONS

Frontiers Newsmagazine Mon-Fri 9-18h
5657 Wilshire Blvd, Suite 470 ☎ (213) 930-3220
www.frontiersweb.com
Biweekly magazine. Features gay related news, political reports, community events, reviews, guide to Southern California, and classified ads.

Frontiers yellow pages
2305 Canyon Drive ☎ (213) 469-4454
www.frontiersyellowpages.com
Complete gay & lesbian guide to L. A. Annual.

Odyssey Magazine
7985 Santa Monica Boulevard #447 ☎ (323) 874-8788
www.odysseymagazine.net
News about the gay scene in LA. Appears bi-weekly.

CULTURE

Tom of Finland Foundation Mon-Fri 10-17h
1421 Laveta Terrace, Echo Park *Off Sunset Blvd* ☎ (213) 250-1685
www.TomofFinlandFoundation.org
Non-profit archives established to collect, preserve, exhibit and publish Tom's drawings. Museum of erotic art. Visit Tom's studio, where he lived and worked. Check the website for current exhibitions and links to other erotic art shows.

SPORT GROUPS

Great Outdoors Los Angeles
P.O. Box 811753 www.greatoutdoorsla.org
Non-profit LBGT organization dedicated to the enjoyment of outdoor recreation. Weekly hikes throughout the Los Angeles area.

CRUISING

Lewd conduct entrapment by undercover police officers occurs frequently – be careful.
-Griffith Park (AYOR) (by golf course and Ferndale loop parking lot)
-Elysian Park off Broadway near China Town
-Sunset Drive (near Vista Theater)
-Encino Park (AYOR)
-Sepulveda Dam Recreation Area (West end of parking lot).

Los Angeles – Downtown ☎ 213

BARS

Jalisco Inn (AC B G MA)
245 South Main Street *Between 2nd & 3rd St* ☎ (213) 680-0658

DANCECLUBS

Jewel's Catch One (B D glm MA S)
19.30-2, Fri & Sat 22-4, Thu-Sat from 20h dancing
4067 West Pico Boulevard ☎ (323) 734-8849
www.jewelscatchone.com
Popular club which attracts a diverse crowd. Special theme nights.

SAUNAS/BATHS

K-lyt (G MA SA SB) 24hrs
132 East 4th St ☎ (213) 972-9145
Latino bathhouse.

Midtowne Spa (AC CC DR DU FC FH G GH I M MA OS PI RR S SA SB SNU VS WH) 24hrs
615 South Kohler Street *Near 6th and Central Street, bus 16,18,53,720*
☎ (213) 680-1838 www.midtowne.com

Popular sauna, Sundays @ 4pm and Mondays @ 8pm they have Strip parties and on Thursdays @ 8PM a J/O party. International tourists: don't forget your passport (18 +)!

Los Angeles – East L.A.

BARS

Chico (B D G SNU) 18-2h
2915 West Beverly Boulevard, Montebello ☎ (323) 721-3403
www.clubchico.com
Latino gay club, Hip Hop, Musica Latina & Old School.

Los Angeles – Hollywood ☎ 323

BARS

Faultline. The (AC B F G MA OS S VS)
Wed-Fri 17-2, Sat & Sun 14-2h
4216 Melrose Avenue ☎ (323) 660-0889
www.faultlinebar.com
Popular leather and jeans bar. Hosts many LGBT community events.

Spotlight Bar (AC B CC D GLM MA r S SNU T) 18-2h
1601 North Cahuenga Boulevard *Cnr. Selma Ave* ☎ (323) 467-2425
www.spotlightbar.com
Oldest gay bar in Los Angeles. Established in 1963.

MEN'S CLUBS

Zone. The (B DR G MA P VS) 20-6, Sun 14-6h
1037 North Sycamore Avenue *At Santa Monica* ☎ (323) 464-8881
www.thezonela.com
Popular club in West Hollywood. One-day membership available.

DANCECLUBS

Arena (B D GLM MA) Tue-Sat 21-?h
6655 Santa Monica Blvd ☎ (323) 462-1291
www.arenanightclub.com
Big club, very popular with a young gay crowd. Sat is Boys Night, for other parties, concerts etc check www.arenanightclub.com.

Circus (B D G MA S VS) Tue, Fri & Sat 21-2h
6655 Santa Monica Boulevard ☎ (323) 462-1291
www.circusdisco.com
Mainly Latino and African-American crowd. Many themed parties, see www.circusdisco.com for details.

Miss Kitty's @ Dragonfly Nightclub (B D GLM MA)
Fri 21-2h
6510 Santa Monica Blvd www.misskittysparlour.com
Disco and cabaret, it is fun.

Tempo (B D G MA s) 21-2, Fri & Sat -4h
5520 Santa Monica Boulevard ☎ (323) 466-1094
www.clubtempo.com
Inexpensive and very friendly. Gay Latin Men's Night Club. Check www.clubtempo.com for agenda.

SEX SHOPS/BLUE MOVIES

X Spot (g VS) 24hrs
6775 Santa Monica Boulevard ☎ (323) 463-0295

SAUNAS/BATHS

Flex (AC CC DR DU FC FH G m MA OS P PI RR SA SB SH SOL VS WH WO) 24hrs
4424 Melrose Avenue *Rear entrance off parking lot* ☎ (323) 663-7786
www.flexbaths.com
Outdoor heated swimming pool and whirlpool, full gym equipment, tropical foliage on the deck, maze and many private areas. Free condoms.

Hollywood Spa. The (AC B DU G M MA P RR SA SB VS WH WO)
24hrs
1650 Ivar Avenue *Near cnr. Hollywood Blvd* ☎ (323) 464-0445
www.hollywoodspa.com
ID required. Popular.

HOTELS

Coral Sands Motel (AC bf glm I OS PI PK RWS RWT VA WH)
All year
1730 North Western Avenue ☎ (323) 467-5141
www.coralsands-la.com
Located in the heart of Hollywood, centrally located with access to all major freeways. All 60 rooms with fridge, bath/WC, TV, telephone, safe, hair-dryer and room service.

Los Angeles – San Fernando Valley ☎ 818

BARS

Bullet. The (B F G MA OS) 12-2h
10522 Burbank Boulevard, North Hollywood ☎ (818) 762-8890
www.bulletbarla.com
Bear/jeans/leather bar.

Cobra (B D G m MA S SNU ST) 16-2h
10937 Burbank Blvd *Cnr. Vineland Ave* ☎ (818) 760-9798
www.clubcobrala.com
Latino bar and nightclub.

Silver Rail (B G MA) 16-2h
11518 Burbank Blvd, North Hollywood *Near Colfax* ☎ (818) 980-8310
www.silverrail.net
The Silver Rail hosts many special events, check www.silverrail.net for details.

DANCECLUBS

C. Frenz (B D GLM MA OS SNU) 15-2, Sat -3h
7026 Reseda Blvd, Reseda ☎ (818) 996-2976 www.cfrenz.com
Special events.

Oil Can Harry's (B D f G MA OS) 19.30-2, Fri 21-2, Sat 20-2h, closed Mon
11502 Ventura Blvd ☎ (818) 760-9749 www.oilcanharrysla.com
Country-western bar and dance club.

SAUNAS/BATHS

North Hollywood Spa
(b CC DU FC FH G M p S SA SB SOL VS WH WO) 24hrs
5636 Vineland Avenue, North Hollywood *At Burbank*
☎ (818) 760-6969 www.hollywoodspa.com
Upscale bath house with many parties.

Los Angeles – Santa Monica & West L.A. ☎ 310

BARS

Dolphin. The (B GLM MA) 19-2h
1995 Artesia Blvd *Redondo Beach, nearest major cross street is Aviation Boulevard* ☎ (310) 318-3339 www.thedolphinbar.com
Small but fun bar, Tue and Thu karaoke.

Roosterfish (B G MA OS) 11-2h
1302 Abbot Kinney Boulevard *Venice* ☎ (310) 392-2123
www.RoosterfishBar.com
Very popular with a diverse crowd.

RESTAURANTS

Golden Bull Restaurant & Bar (AC B CC glm M MA OS)
16-24, Sun brunch 11-15h
170 West Channel Road, Santa Monica ☎ (310) 230-0402
www.goldenbull.us
Popular steak and seafood restaurant. Prices are moderate, food is great, and the atmosphere is friendly with great service.

SAUNAS/BATHS

Roman Holiday Health Club (DU FH G m MSG RR SA SB WH) 24hrs
12814 Venice Boulevard, Mar Vista ☎ (310) 391-0200

SWIMMING

-Santa Monica Will Rogers State Beach (Entrada Drive/Pacific Coast Highway)
-Venice beach (Near Westminster Avenue/Ocean Front Walk).

Los Angeles – Silver Lake ☎ 323

BARS

Akbar (AC B CC D GLM MA NR PK S W) 19-2h
4356 West Sunset Boulevard *Corner Sunset Blvd & Fountain Ave*
☎ (323) 665-6810 💻 akbarsilverlake.com
Happy Hour 4-8pm Tu-Sun. Dancing on Thu, Fri, Sat. Rotating clubs on Sundays.

Eagle LA (AC B F G MA OS) 16-2h, Sat & Sun 14-2h
4219 Santa Monica Boulevard *At Hoover* ☎ (323) 669-9472
💻 www.EagleLA.com
Leather bar that welcomes a variety of gay men.

Little Joy (B glm MA) 16-2, Sat & Sun 13-2h
1477 Sunset Boulevard West ☎ (213) 250-3417
Neighbourhood bar with pool tables and jukebox. Popular with Latinos.

MJ's (! AC B cc D f G MA OS S VS) 16-2, Sun 14-2h
2810 Hyperion Avenue *At Rowena* ☎ (323) 660-1503
💻 www.mjsbar.com
Dance and cruising bar. MJ's features state of the art lights and sound, two smoking patios, friendly bar with great attitude. Club Nur on Thu. S.

Other Side. The (B CC f G MA) 12-2h
2538 Hyperion Avenue *At Griffith Park* ☎ (323) 661-0618
💻 www.flyingleapcafe.com/tos/tos/tos.html
Piano bar.

Silverlake Lounge (B d g m MA S) 15-2h
2906 West Sunset Boulevard *At Silver Lake Blvd* ☎ (323) 663-9636
Mainly gay Fri-Mon, Latino crowd and drags .

DANCECLUBS

Barcito. Le (AC B G MA ST) 18-2, Sun 15-2h
3909 West Sunset Blvd *Cnr. Hyperion* ☎ (323) 644-3515
💻 www.lebarcito.com
Latino crowd.

RESTAURANTS

Flying Leap Cafe. The (b GLM M MA)
18-22, Fri & Sat -23, Sun brunch 9-14h
2538 Hyperion Ave ☎ (323) 661-0618 💻 www.flyingleapcafe.com

FITNESS STUDIOS

Body Builders Gym (g MA WO)
Mon-Fri 5-23, Sat 7-21, Sun 8-20h
2516 Hyperion Avenue *Griffith Park Blvd* ☎ (323) 668-0802
💻 www.bodybuildersgym.com

BOOK SHOPS

Circus of Books (CC GLM MA) 8-1h
4001 Sunset Blvd ☎ (323) 666-1304
💻 www.circusofbooks.com
Retail Bookstore with large selection of gay DVDs, magazines, books, lubes, toys and more.

GUEST HOUSES

Sanborn Guest House (AC CC glm I OS PK RWB RWS RWT)
All year
1005 1/2 Sanborn Avenue ☎ (323) 666-3947
💻 www.sanbornhouse.com

Los Angeles – South Bay ☎ 310

GUEST HOUSES

Sea View Inn at the Beach (AC CC glm OS PI RWB RWS RWT WO) Office 7-23h
3400 Highland Avenue, Manhattan Beach *10 mins to LA International Airport* ☎ (310) 545-1504 💻 www.seaview-inn.com
Located two blocks from the ocean with ocean view. 29 guestrooms. Complimentary bicycles, beach chairs, beach towels & boogie boards.

Los Angeles – West Hollywood ☏ 323

BARS

■ **Revolver** (AC B CC GLM I m MA OS) 16.30-2, Sat & Sun 15.30-2h
8851 Santa Monica Blvd *Centre of Boys Town* ☏ (310) 694-0430
www.revolverweho.com
The famous West Hollywood video bar of the ,80s and ,90s reopened in 2011.

■ **Fiesta Cantina** (B G M MC) Mo-Thu 16-2, Fri-Sun 12-2h
8865 Santa Monica Boulevard ☏ (310) 652-8865
Popular mexican bar.

■ **Fubar** (B d GLM MA S) Daily 16-2h
7994 Santa Monica Boulevard ☏ (323) 654-0396 www.fubarla.com
Very popular place, many special events, check their website for details.

■ **Gold Coast** (AC B G MA VS) 11-2, Sat & Sun 10-2h
8228 Santa Monica Boulevard *At La Jolla* ☏ (323) 656-4879
www.goldcoastweho.com
Popular video bar with cocktail hours. Cruisy atmosphere. Live DJs spin every night, from retro to house. Mon oldies – 60ies,70ies & 80ies. Attracts a more mature crowd.

■ **Gym Sportsbar** (AC B G MA) Mon-Fri 16-2, Sat+Sun 12-2h
8737 Santa Monica Boulevard ☏ (310) 659-2004
www.gymsportsbar.com

■ **Here Lounge** (B glm MA) Mon-Sat 20-2, Sun 16-2h
696 North Robertson Boulevard *At Santa Monica Blvd*
☏ (310) 360-8455 www.herelounge.com
A stylish and interesting bar/lounge with a mixed crowd. Busy on WE; parties like „Size" on Sun & „Garage" on Wed,.

■ **Mother Lode** (! B f G MA VS) 15-2h
8944 Santa Monica Boulevard ☏ (310) 659-9700
Beer bust on Sun.

■ **Plaza. La** (B D G MA ST) 21-2, Fri & Sat 20-2h, closed Tue
739 North La Brea Avenue *At Melrose Ave* ☏ (323) 939-0703
Latin clientele.

■ **Trunks** (B G MA VS) 13-2h
8809 Santa Monica Boulevard ☏ (310) 652-1015
Frienly poolbar, good place to calm down for a while.

MEN'S CLUBS

■ **Slammer Club** (DR F G MA NU OS P VS) 20-4, Sat & Sun 14-4h
3688 Beverly Boulevard *Two blocks east of Vermont* ☏ (213) 388-8040
www.slammerclub.com

CAFES

■ **Eat Well** (b CC glm M OS) 7-21.30, Sat & Sun 8-15h
8252 Santa Monica Boulevard *At La Jolla* ☏ (323) 656-1383
Popular place, good affordable food, handsome waiters.

DANCECLUBS

■ **Cherry Pop @ Ultra Suede** (AC B D G MA) Sat 21-?h
661 North Robertson Blvd www.tomwhitmanpresents.com

■ **Factory. The** (! AC B CC D GLM SNU VS YC) Fri & Sat 21-2h
652 North La Peer Drive *Corner of Santa Monica* ☏ (310) 659-4551
www.factorynightclub.com
Largest GLM-danceclub in West Hollywood, very popular on Sat.

■ **Micky's** (! AC B D GLM M OS SNU VS YC) 12-2h
8857 Santa Monica Boulevard *At San Vincente* ☏ (310) 657-1176
www.mickys.com
Popular. Various theme nights. Gogo boys at WE. Very gay and a few women..

■ **Rage** (AC B CC D G S VS WE YC) 13-2h
8911 Santa Monica Boulevard ☏ (310) 652-7055
Plenty of younger peeps here.

RESTAURANTS

■ **Abbey. The** (! AC B BF CC D DM GLM M MA NR OS PA PK S) 8-2h
692 North Robertson Boulevard ☏ (310) 289-8410
www.abbeyfoodandbar.com
Everybody loves this place: beautiful architecture, very popular and cruisy, reservation advisable. Famous for Martinis and desserts. Busy at WE.

■ **Bossa Nova** (AC CC glm M) Sun-Wed 11-24, Thu-Sat 11-1h
685 North Robertson Blvd ☏ (323) 657-5070 www.bossafood.com
Great Latin/Brazilian food.

■ **Eleven** (AC B BF CC D glm I M MA NR OS PK S SNU VS WL) Dinner Tue-Sun 18-22, bar open until late night, brunch Sat & Sun 11-15h
8811 Santa Monica Blvd ☏ (310) 855-0800 www.eleven.la
Fine dining and clubbing in a great location, exceptional interior design.

■ **French Quarter** (b BF CC glm M OS WE) 7-24, Fri & Sat -3h
7985 Santa Monica Boulevard ☏ (323) 654-0898
www.frenchquarterwest.com
Good food at reasonable prices. Popular Sun for brunch.

■ **Hamburger Mary's Bar & Grille** (B CC d GLM I M MA OS S) 11-24, Fri-Sun 10-1h
8288 Santa Monica Blvd *Next to City Hall* ☏ (323) 654-3800
www.hamburgermarysweho.com

■ **Tango Grill** (B GLM M MA) 11.30-23.30h
8807 Santa Monica Blvd *At San Vicente* ☏ (310) 659-3663
Argentinian cuisine.

SEX SHOPS/BLUE MOVIES

■ **ChiChi La Rue's** (AC CC GLM MA) 10-2h
8932 Santa Monica Boulevard *One block west of San Vicente Blvd*
☏ (310) 289-8932 ChiChiLaRue.com
Videos for sale or rent. Condoms, lube, magazines, guides and more. Former Drake's West Hollywood.

■ **Pleasure Chest. The** (CC F GLM MA) 10-24h
7733 Santa Monica Boulevard *In the heart of West Hollywood*
☏ (323) 650-1022 www.thepleasurechest.com
Erotic department store. Certainly one of the largest selections of leather goods and novelties. Mail order.

■ **Unicorn Bookstore** (G) 9-2h
8940 Santa Monica Boulevard ☏ (310) 652-6253

SAUNAS/BATHS

■ **Melrose Spa** (CC DR DU FC FH G GH I m MA OS P RR SA VS WH) 24hrs
7269 Melrose Avenue *Three blocks West of La Brea* ☏ (323) 937-2122
www.midtowne.com
Lockers, TV Lounge, Cedar Sauna, Indoor Whirlpool, Showers, Sundeck, Private Rooms with 3 video channels and 2 Dark Rooms

BOOK SHOPS

■ **Book Soup** (glm)
8818 Sunset Boulevard ☏ (323) 659-3110 www.booksoup.com
Lesbian & gay books.

■ **Circus of Books** (CC GLM MA) 6-2h
8230 Santa Monica Boulevard *Cnr. Santa Monica and La Jolla*
☏ (323) 656-6533 www.circusofbooks.com
Retail bookstore with large selection of gay DVDs, magazines, books, lubes, toys and more.

FASHION SHOPS

■ **Andrew Christian Flagship Boutique** (CC G)
Mon-Thu 12-22, Fri-Sat 11-24, Sun 11-22h
8943 Santa Monica Boulevard ☏ (310) 734-8590
www.andrewchristian.com/retail-weho1.htm
Underwear, beachwear and accessories.

■ **Showtime Clothing** (AC CC glm MA)
8861 Santa Monica Blvd ☏ (310) 659-1067

LEATHER & FETISH SHOPS

■ **665** (F G MA) Sun-Thu 12-20, Fri & Sat 12-22h
8722 Santa Monica Blvd ☏ (310) 854-7276 www.665leather.com

HOTELS

■ **Andaz West Hollywood** (AC B BF CC DM H I M MA OS PI PK RES RWB RWS RWT VEG WL WO)
8401 Sunset Boulevard ☏ (323) 656-1234
www.westhollywood.andaz.com
A cool and hip Designhotel with pool terrace, belonging to the Hyatt group.

N Doheny Dr
Santa Monica Blvd.
Keith Av
Sunset Blvd.
Melrose
West Hollywood Park
San Vicente Blvd
Palm Ave
Sherwood Dr
La Cienega Blvd.
Alfred St
Orlando Ave
Croft Ave
Kings Road
Beverly Blvd.
N
Waring Ave
Sweetzer Ave
Harper Ave
La Jolla Ave
Melrose Ave.
Santa Monica Blvd.
Havenhurst Dr
Crescent Hts Blvd
Willoughby Ave
Laurel Ave
Edinburgh Ave
Hayworth Ave
Fairfax Ave
Orange Grove Ave
Ogden Dr
Genesee Ave
Spaulding Ave
Stanley Ave
Curson Ave
Sierra Bonita
Gardner St
Vista St
Rosewood Ave.
Martel Ave
Plummer Park
Fuller Ave
Poinsettia Place
Altavista Blvd
Formosa Ave
Detroit St
La Brea Ave
Sycamore Ave
Fountain Ave.
Sunset Blvd.
Hollywood Blvd.
Los Angeles West-Hollywood
EAT & DRINK
Abbey. The – Restaurant 2
Eat Well – Café 17
French Quarter – Restaurant 16
Fubar – Bar 19
Fiesta Cantina – Bar 6
Hamburger Mary's – Restaurant 16
Gold Coast – Bar 14
Here Lounge – Bar 3
Mother Lode – Bar 4
Plaza. La – Bar 22
Revolver – Bar 13
Tango Grill – Restaurant 10
Trunks – Bar 10
NIGHTLIFE
Cherry Pop @ Ultra Suede – Danceclub 23
Factory. The – Danceclub 1
Micky's – Danceclub 9
Rage – Danceclub 11
SEX
ChiChi La Rue's – Sex Shop/Blue Movies 5
Melrose Spa – Sauna 21
Unicorn Bookstore – Sex Shop/BlueMovies 4
ACCOMMODATION
San Vicente Inn-Resort – Guest House 7
OTHERS
665 – Leather & Fetish Shop 12
Andrew Christian Flagship Boutique – Fashion Shop 8
Circus of Books – Bookshop 15

■ **Montrose Suite. Le** (AC BF CC glm m PI RWS RWT SA WH WO) All year
900 Hammond Street *just two blocks from the West Hollywood bars*
☏ (310) 855-1115 ▭ www.lemontrose.com
All rooms are suites, each has its own fireplace, living room and balcony.

■ **Ramada Plaza** (AC CC H I PI RWS RWT) All year
8585 Santa Monica Boulevard ☏ (310) 652-6400
▭ www.ramadaweho.com
Centrally located and right next to the gay bars on Santa Monica Boulevard

GUEST HOUSES

■ **Grove Guesthouse. The**
(AC B BF GLM I MA OS PI PK RWB RWS RWT VA) All year
1325 North Orange Grove Ave *Near Sunset & Fairfax* ☏ (323) 876-7778
▭ www.airbnb.com/rooms/169230
One-bedroom villa with every amenity. Quiet and private.

■ **San Vicente Inn** (AC bf CC G I m MA MSG NU PI PK RWB RWS RWT SA SB SOL VA WH WO) All year
845 North San Vincente Boulevard *Short walk from dozens of bars, restaurants & clubs* ☏ (310) 854-6915 ▭ www.thesanvicenteinn.com
Probably the only clothing-optional gay resort in the center of West Hollywood, steps away from the shops, restaurants, theaters, bars & nightclubs.

■ **Secret Garden B&B** (AC BF G I RWS RWT) All year
8039 Selma Avenue *Hollywood Hills* ☏ (323) 656-3888
▭ www.secretgardenbnb.com
Gay owned & operated. Six guest rooms, within walking distance to Sunset Strip and the heart of West Hollywood.

Modesto ☏ 209

BARS

■ **Brave Bull** (B D GLM MA S) 19-2h, closed Mon
701 South 9th Street ☏ (209) 529-6712

■ **Tiki Lounge** (B GLM MA) 14-2h
932 McHenry Avenue *Cnr. Roseberg Ave* ☏ (209) 577-9969

Monterey

SWIMMING

-Garrapata Beach, Carmel (g NU WE)
-Carmel Park Beach (from dunes to North end)

Mountain View ☏ 650

BARS

■ **King of Clubs** (B D GLM MA s) 18-2h
893 Leong Drive *At Moffett Blvd* ☏ (650) 968-6366
▭ www.koclubs.com
Dive bar or Karaoke club? Anyway, people seem to have fun there. Check www.koclubs.com for events.

Oakland ☏ 510

BARS

■ **Alley. The** (B g M MA OS) 16-2h
3325 Grand Ave ☏ (510) 444-8505

■ **Bench and Bar** (AC B CC D GLM MA S ST) Daily 16-2h
510 17th Street *Centre* ☏ (510) 444-2266 ▭ www.bench-and-bar.com
Each Bay's largest dance club.

■ **White Horse Inn** (B D GLM MA OS ST WE) 15-2, Wed-Sun 13-2h
6551 Telegraph Avenue ☏ (510) 652-3820 ▭ www.whitehorsebar.com
Neighbourhood bar and dance club.

DANCECLUBS

■ **Club 21** (B CC D GLM I MA S ST) 21-2h
2111 Franklin Street *Downtown* ☏ (510) 268-9425
▭ www.club21oakland.com
Great danceclub in the former location of „Bench & Bar".

Palm Springs ☏ 760

This is a desert oasis which offers something for everyone. Palm Springs is only two hours drive from Los Angeles and has long been a popular getaway for Californians as well as gay men from all over the US. Activities, apart from the gay ones, include desert hiking, golf and the laid back atmosphere attracts visitors from around the world. There is a very large gay population here. You will find every possible type of guy here. There are many gay bars and even more gay resorts ranging from clothing optional resorts where you can enjoy the sun at the poolside or something a little more sedate.

Diese Wüstenoase bietet für jeden Geschmack etwas. Palm Springs, nur zwei Autostunden von Los Angeles entfernt, ist seit langem ein beliebtes Ausflugsziel von Schwulen sowohl aus Kalifornien als auch der ganzen USA. Neben den schwulen Aktivitäten ziehen u.a. Wüstenwanderungen, Golfplätze sowie die entspannte Atmosphäre Besucher aus aller Welt an. Hier leben auch sehr viele Schwule, sodass man alle möglichen Typen antrifft. Es gibt viele Schwulenbars und noch mehr Gay Resorts, bis hin zu „Clothing optional Resorts", wo man die Sonne am Pool oder die Ruhe wahlweise mit oder ohne Kleidung genießen kann.

Cette oasis dans le désert comble tous les goûts. A seulement deux heures de route de Los Angeles, Palm Springs est depuis longtemps une destination appréciée des gays de Californie et de tout le pays. Outre les activités gays, les balades dans le désert, les terrains de golf et l'ambiance décontractée attirent les visiteurs du monde entier. Beaucoup de gays aussi vivent ici et on trouve donc tous les types. Il existe beaucoup de bars gays et encore plus de resorts (villégiatures) gays, dont naturistes où l'on peut profiter du soleil et de la piscine au choix avec ou sans maillot.

Este oasis en el desierto tiene algo que ofrecer para todos los gustos. Palm Springs, a sólo dos horas en coche de Los Angeles, es desde hace tiempo un destino popular para gays tanto de California como de otras zonas de Estados Unidos. Además de por las actividades gays este destino le atraerá, entre otras muchas cosas, por sus caminatas por el desierto, sus campos de golf y el ambiente relajado e internacional de sus visitantes. Muchos gays residen aquí permanentemente, por lo que no le faltará gente interesante para conocer. Hay muchos bares de ambiente y aún muchos más complejos turísticos gays, podrá encontrar incluso complejos turísticos naturistas, donde poder disfrutar del sol en la piscina o simplemente descansar con o sin ropa.

Su questa oasi sul deserto si trova davvero un po' di tutto. Palm Springs è a solo due ore da Los Angeles ed è già da molto tempo meta di escursioni per gay che vengono dalla California, ma anche da tutto il resto degli USA. A parte la vita gay, ad attirare visitatori da tutto il mondo sono anche le passeggiate nel deserto, i campi di golf e l'atmosfera rilassante di questa città. Qui ci vivono tantissimi gay, quindi non sarà difficile incontrare il tipo giusto per voi. Ci sono anche molti locali gay, molti villaggi turistici gay e alcuni di essi sono anche „clothing optional resorts", ovvero villaggi per nudisti nei quali si può scegliere di rilassarsi e prendere il sole con o senza costume.

GAY INFO

■ **Desert Gay Tourism Guild**
PO Box 2881 ▭ www.palmspringsgayinfo.com

PUBLICATIONS

■ **Bottom Line Magazine**
312 North Palm Canyon ☏ (760) 323-0552 ▭ www.psbottomline.com
The free Bottom Line is published bi-weekly.

■ **Desert Daily Guide**
c/o P. S. Partner Pairing, 541 East Industrial Place ☏ (760) 320-3237
▭ www.desertdailyguide.com
Weekly GLM entertainment magazine.

■ **Pulp**
312 North Palm Canyon ☏ (760) 323-0552
▭ www.psbottomline.com/pulp

Talk
318 North Palm Canyon Drive ☏ (760) 832-8099
🖳 www.talkpublications.com

CULTURE

The Fabulous Palm Springs Follies (AC MA NG)
Nov-May 13:30 & 19h
128 South Palm Canyon Drive ☏ (760) 327-0225 🖳 www.psfollies.com
Famous for it's showgirls aged from 60 to 80.

BARS

Barracks. The (AC B cc D F G MA OS S VS) 14-2h
67-625 East Palm Canyon Drive, Cathedral City ☏ (760) 321-9688
🖳 www.thebarracksbarps.com
The deserts largest leather/levi/fetish bar. Large outdoor smoking & cruise patio..

Club Elevation (AC B D G MA PK ST WE)
67-555 East Palm Canyon Drive ☏ (760) 324-5717
Piano bar with drag shows on the weekend.

Digs (AC B CC D GLM I MA OS S VS) Mon-Sat 12-2, Sun 10-2h
36-737 Cathedral Canyon Drive, Cathedral City *On crossing of Palm Springs and Cath. City Drives* ☏ (760) 321-0031 🖳 www.digsbar.com
Karaoke and other shows. Former Club Whatever.

Georgie's Alibi (AC B G M MA OS VS) 11-?, Sun 10-?h
369 North Palm Canyon Drive *Above „Azul"* ☏ (760) 325-5533
🖳 www.georgiesalibi.com

Hunter's Video Bar (B D G MA S VS) 10-2h
302 East Arenas Road ☏ (760) 323-0700 🖳 www.huntersnightclubs.com
Popular video and dance bar in the heart of Gay Palm Springs.

Score (B G MA) 6-2h
301 East Arenas Road ☏ (760) 327-0753

Spurline (B G MA VS) 11-2h
200 South Indian Canyon Drive *At Arenas* ☏ (760) 778-4326

Streetbar (AC B GLM MA OS s) 10-2h
224 East Arenas Road ☏ (760) 320-1266
Great place to meet friends and make new ones as well as older locals.

Studio One Eleven (AC B G MA) 15-?h
67-555 East Palm Canyon Drive, Cathedral City *Across the street from „Trader Joe's"* ☏ (760) 324-5717 🖳 www.psstudioone11.com

Tool Shed. The (B F G MA) 10-2, Sat & Sun 8-2h
600 East Sunny Dunes Road ☏ (760) 320-3299 🖳 www.toolshed-ps.com
Friendly Palm Springs Leather and Levi Cruise Bar.

CAFES

Cafe Palette (AC CC GLM M) Sun-Thu 10-10, Fr & Sat 10-11h
315 East Arenas Road ☏ (760) 322-9264 🖳 www.cafepalette.com
Pizza, salad and sandwiches.

DANCECLUBS

Toucans Tiki Lounge (B d GLM MA S SNU ST) 12-2h
2100 North Palm Canyon Drive ☏ (760) 416-7584
🖳 www.toucanstikilounge.com
Go-go dancers on WE, drag shows on Mon.

RESTAURANTS

Azul (B GLM M MA OS VS) 11-15 & 16-2h
369 North Palm Canyon Drive ☏ (760) 325-5533
🖳 www.azultapaslounge.com
Tapas inspired lounge & patio.

Blame it on Midnight (B GLM M MA OS S) 17-22, Fri & Sat -23h
777 East Tahquitz Canyon Way *Between S. Calle El Segundo and S. Calle Alvarado in The Courtyard Center, where the Regal movie theatres are*
☏ (760) 323-1200 🖳 www.blameitonmidnight.com
Happy hour Wed-Sun 17-19h. Live entertainment Thu-Sat.

Dink's (AC B CC glm MA PK RES VEG W) Tue-Sun 16-22, Sun 11-15h
2080 North Palm Canyon Drive ☏ (760) 327-7676
🖳 www.dinksrestaurant.com
Popular restaurant named after „Double Income No Kids" (Dinks)

Hamburger Mary's (B GLM M MA OS S) 11-?h
415 North Palm Canyon Drive *South of Alejo Rd* ☏ (760) 778-6279
🖳 www.hamburgermarysps.com

Look (B glm M MA OS VS) Daily 11-22h
139 East Andreas Road *Between Palm Canyon and Indian Canyon Dr*
☏ (760) 778-3520 🖳 www.lookpalmsprings.com
Patio restaurant & video bar.

Rainbow Bar & Grill (AC B CC DM GLM m) Mo-Sun 10-3h
216 S Indian Canyon Drive ☏ (760) 325-3989
🖳 www.rainbowbarngrill.com

Trio (AC B CC DM GLM NR PK) Sun-Thu 4-10h, Fr&Sat 4-11h
707 N. Palm Canyon Drive ☏ (760) 864-8746
🖳 www.triopalmsprings.com
Ultra-chic dining in this gay owned and operated place to be.

Wang's in the Desert (B GLM M MA OS)
17.30-21.30, Fri & Sat -22.30h
424 S Indian Canyon Dr ☏ (760) 325-9264
🖳 www.wangsinthedesert.com
Asian cuisine.

FITNESS STUDIOS

Gold's Gym (AC GLM MA WO) 24hrs
4070 Airport Center Drive *Near Airport* ☏ (760) 322-4653
🖳 www.goldsgym.com

World Gym (AC CC DU GLM MA PK SA SB SH SOL W WI WO) 5-22, Sat & Sun 6-20h
1751 North Sunrise Way *Cnr. of Sunrise & Vista Chino* ☏ (760) 327-7100
🖳 www.worldgympalmsprings.com
Big gym, lots of equipment and gay men. Great music.

BOOK SHOPS

Q Trading Company (CC GLM MA) 10-18h
606 East Sunny Dunes Rd ☏ (760) 416-7150 🖳 www.qtrading.com
Featuring a large selection of unique gay and lesbian merchandise, books, clothing, cards, music and more. Full line of adult products.

FASHION SHOPS

Bear Wear (G) 10-18, Thu-Sat -22, Sun 12-17h
319 East Arenas Road ☏ (760) 323-8940 🖳 www.bear-wear.com
The name says it all.

GIFT & PRIDE SHOPS

Gaymart (AC CC GLM) 10-24h
305 East Arenas Road ☏ (760) 416-6436

Mischief Cards & Gifts (CC GLM)
210 East Arenas Road ☏ (760) 322-8555

LEATHER & FETISH SHOPS

Gear (CC F G) 12-19, Fri & Sat -24h
650 East Sunny Dunes Road *Near cnr. Palo Fierro* ☏ (760) 322-3363
🖳 www.gearleather.com

Tuff Stuff Leatherware (F G) 10-18, Sat -18h, Sun & Mon closed
407 S Industrial Place *Near Tool Shed Bar* ☏ (760) 864-8539
🖳 www.tuffstuffleather.com
Custom leather, alterations, repairs and BDSM gear.

TATTOO/PIERCING

Palm Springs Piercing Company (CC G) 11-7h
210 East Arenas Road ☏ (760) 327-1656 🖳 www.pspiercing.com
Clothes and other accessories.

HOTELS

Ace Hotel (AC B CC DU H I MC OS PA PI PK RWB RWS RWT VEG)
All year
701 East Palm Canyon Drive ☏ (760) 325-9900 🖳 www.acehotel.com
The trendy Hotel & Swim Club belongs to the gay owned hotel brand Ace.

Canyon Club (AC bf CC G I m MA MSG NU PI RWS RWT S SA SB VA WE WH WO) Lobby open 24hrs, office 9-23h
960 North Palm Canyon Drive *1,6 km from International Airport*
☏ (760) 778-8042 🖳 www.canyonclubhotel.com
All 32 rooms with refrigerator, eight with full kitchen. 16-man spa, clothing optional, four adult channels. Steam, gym & sauna.

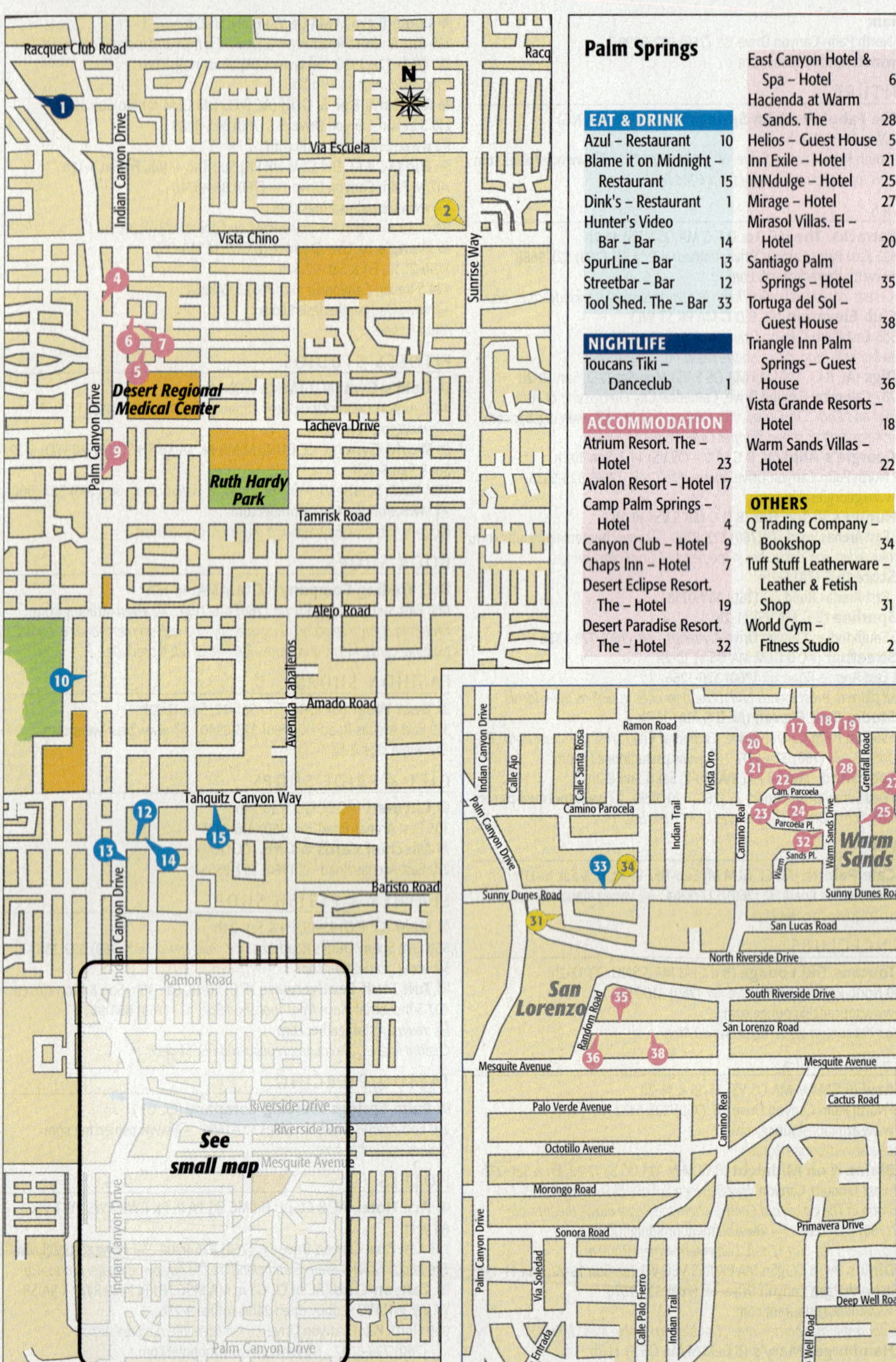
Palm Springs
EAT & DRINK
Azul – Restaurant 10
Blame it on Midnight – Restaurant 15
Dink's – Restaurant 1
Hunter's Video Bar – Bar 14
SpurLine – Bar 13
Streetbar – Bar 12
Tool Shed. The – Bar 33
NIGHTLIFE
Toucans Tiki – Danceclub 1
ACCOMMODATION
Atrium Resort. The – Hotel 23
Avalon Resort – Hotel 17
Camp Palm Springs – Hotel 4
Canyon Club – Hotel 9
Chaps Inn – Hotel 7
Desert Eclipse Resort. The – Hotel 19
Desert Paradise Resort. The – Hotel 32
East Canyon Hotel & Spa – Hotel 6
Hacienda at Warm Sands. The 28
Helios – Guest House 5
Inn Exile – Hotel 21
INNdulge – Hotel 25
Mirage – Hotel 27
Mirasol Villas. El – Hotel 20
Santiago Palm Springs – Hotel 35
Tortuga del Sol – Guest House 38
Triangle Inn Palm Springs – Guest House 36
Vista Grande Resorts – Hotel 18
Warm Sands Villas – Hotel 22
OTHERS
Q Trading Company – Bookshop 34
Tuff Stuff Leatherware – Leather & Fetish Shop 31
World Gym – Fitness Studio 2
N
Racquet Club Road
Via Escuela
Indian Canyon Drive
Vista Chino
Sunrise Way
Desert Regional Medical Center
Palm Canyon Drive
Tacheva Drive
Ruth Hardy Park
Tamrisk Road
Alejo Road
Avenida Caballeros
Amado Road
Tahquitz Canyon Way
Baristo Road
Ramon Road
Riverside Drive
See small map
Mesquite Avenue
Calle Ajo
Calle Santa Rosa
Vista Oro
Camino Parocela
Indian Trail
Camino Real
Cam. Parocela
Parocela Pl.
Sands Pl.
Warm Sands Drive
Grenfall Road
Warm Sands
Sunny Dunes Road
San Lucas Road
North Riverside Drive
South Riverside Drive
San Lorenzo
Random Road
San Lorenzo Road
Palo Verde Avenue
Cactus Road
Octotillo Avenue
Morongo Road
Primavera Drive
Sonora Road
Manzanita Avenue
Via Soledad
Calle Palo Fierro
Deep Well Road
Via Entrada

■ **Desert Paradise Resort Hotel** (AC BF CC FC FH G H I M MA NR NU OS PI PK RES RWS RWT SA SB VA VS WH WI) All year, 24hrs
615 Warm Sands Drive *Centrally located in gay Warm Sands area*
☎ (760) 320-5650 💻 www.desertparadise.com
Rooms and suites with own bath/shower, sat-TV, phone, safe, king beds, non-smoking. 15 free adult video channels. Saltwater pool, steam/dry sauna,Lush Gardens,Continental Breakfast

■ **Pura Vida Palm Springs** (AC B BF CC DU FH G I M MA MSG NR OS PI PK RWS RWT W WH WI) All year
589 S. Grenfall Road ☎ (760) 832-6438 💻 www.puravidaps.com
A new resort catering to adult men seeking an intimate, private, secluded, and sophisticated retreat that offers a new level of comfort and service.

GUEST HOUSES

■ **All World's Resort**
(! AC BF G MA NU OS PI PK RWS RWT SA SB VA WH) All year
526 Warm Sands Drive ☎ (760) 323-7505
💻 www.allworldsresorts.com
Men-only resort with 22 guestrooms and seven secuded villas. four pools, large sauna and steam room.

■ **Avalon Resort** (AC CC G I MA NU OS P PI PK RWS RWT SA SB VA WH) All year
568 Warm Sands Drive ☎ (760) 322-2404
💻 www.mirage4men.com
Part of Vista Grande Resort. 31 guest rooms.

■ **Camp Palm Springs** (AC bf CC G I MA MSG OS PI SB VS WH WO) Sun-Thu 8-23, Fri & Sat -4h
1466 North Palm Canyon Drive ☎ (760) 322-2267
💻 www.camp-palm-springs.com

■ **Casa Ocotillo** (AC BF CC G I MA NU PA PI PK RWS RWT VA WH) All year
240 East Ocotillo Ave ☎ (760) 327-6110 💻 www.casaocotillo.com
Five guestrooms.

WORLD'S FOREMOST GAY & LESBIAN HOTELS
MEMBER
the hacienda
at warm sands
www.thehacienda.com
800.359.2007
Palm Springs
California, USA

CCBC Resort (AC BF CC G I MA NU OS PA PI PK RWB RWS RWT SA SB VA VS WH) All year
68-369 Sunair Rd, Cathedral City *Downtown* ☏ (760) 324-1350 ☏ (800) 472-0836 (toll free) www.ccbcps.com
The largest clothing-optional resort in the desert with 3.5 acres of lush grounds. You will find waterfalls, Danny's dungeon, a love grotto, the compound and more.

Century Palm Springs (AC BF CC G I MA PI) All year
598 Grenfall Road ☏ (760) 323-9966 www.centurypalmsprings.com

Chaps Inn (AC bf CC F G I MA NU OS PA PI PK RWB RWS RWT SA SB VA WH) All year, office 7-20h
312 Camino Monte Vista *Six mins from downtown* ☏ (760) 327-8222 ☏ (800) 445-8916 (toll free) www.chapsinn.com
Don't stay where the boys are; stay where the men are! The ONLY leather/bear hotel in Palm Springs. A 10 room clothing optional hotel. Slings, ceiling hooks, St Andrews Cross, glory holes. Kitchens, private patios, off street parking. Discounts for stays of 7 nights.

Desert Eclipse Resort. The (AC BF CC G I MA NU OS PA PI PK RWS RWT SA WH) Office 8-22h
537 S. Grenfall Road, Warm Sands ☏ (760) 325-0655 www.deserteclipseresort.com
A tropical paradise in Warm Sands.

Dolce Vita Resort & Spa. La (AC BF CC G I MA MSG NU OS PA PI PK RWB RWS RWT SA SB VA WH WI WO) All year
1491 South Via Soledad *Central Palm Springs* ☏ (760) 325-2686 www.LaDolceVitaResort.com
A casually elegant, clothing-optional, European-style 20-room resort hotel and spa. Two pools and two spas. Mountain views, gardens and walkways with fountains and statues.

East Canyon Hotel & Spa (AC BF CC G I MA MSG PI PK RWS RWT VA WH WI) All year
288 East Camino Monte Vista ☏ (760) 320-1928 www.eastcanyonps.com
The hotel has 15 rooms. Heated pool and jacuzzi.

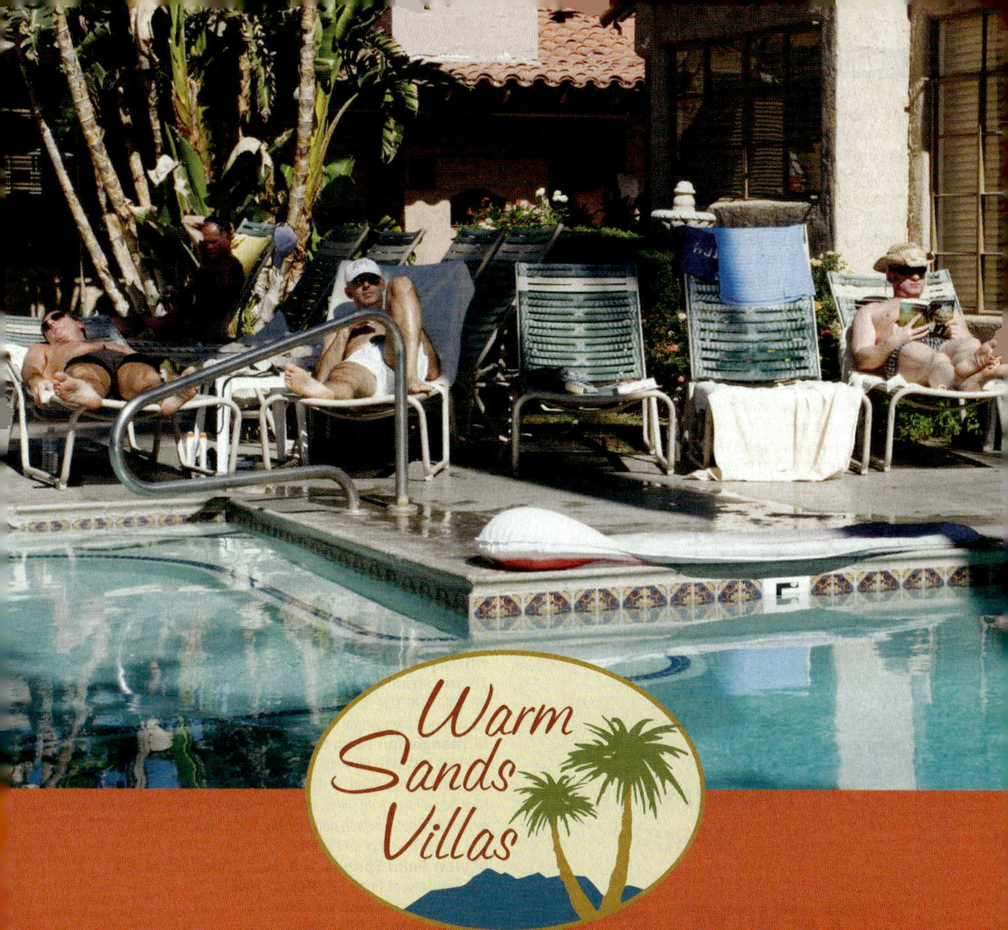

Escape Palm Springs (AC BF CC G I MA MSG NU OS PI PK RWB RWS RWT SA VA VS WH) All year, office hours: 7-19h
641 San Lorenzo Road ☎ (760) 325-5269
www.EscapePalmSprings.com
Clothing optional gay men's resort in San Lorenzo area. Close walk to Downtown Palm Springs & Gay Nightlife. Airport pickup available.

Hacienda at Warm Sands. The (! AC BF CC DU FH G H I M MA MSG NR NU OS PI PK RWB RWS RWT VA W WH WI) All year
586 Warm Sands Drive *Centre of Warm Sands* ☎ (760) 327-8111
☎ (800) 359-2007 (toll free) www.thehacienda.com
One of the top gay hotel resorts in the USA and one of the world's most romantic resorts. 9 suites, 1 room. 2 pools – nude optional. Breakfast & Lunch. 1 to 1 staff/guest ratio.

Helios (AC bf G I NU OS PA PI PK RWB RWS RWT VA) 24hrs
280 East Mel Avenue *North of downtown* ☎ (760) 323-2868
www.yourgayresort.com
Owner claims: „The Playground of the Porn Stars!"

Inn Exile (AC BF CC G I NU PI RWS RWT SB VA WH WO) All year
545 Warm Sands Drive *Warm Sands* ☎ (760) 327-6413
☎ 962-0186 (toll free) www.innexile.com
Large resort with 31 rooms and four pools.

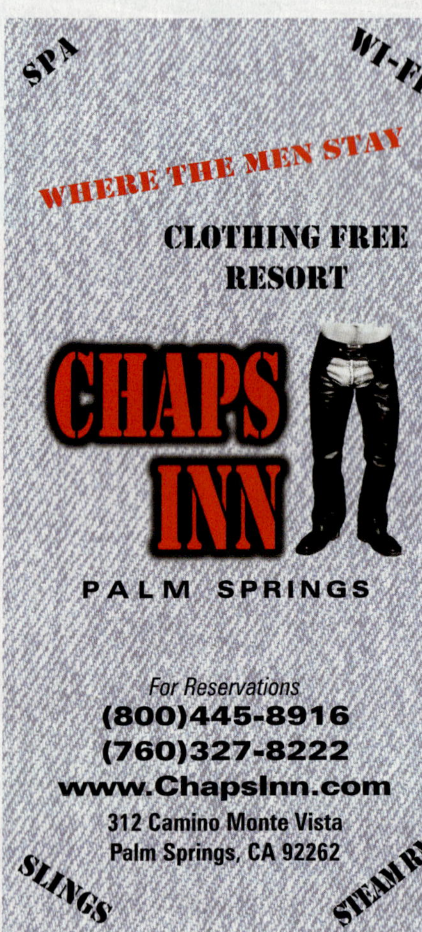

INNdulge (! AC bf CC G I MSG NU PI PK RWS RWT VA VS WH WO) All year
601 Grenfall Road *At Parocela & Warm Sands* ☎ (760) 327-1408
☎ (800) 833 5675 www.inndulge.com
Come to INNdulge Palm Springs, a supreme resort hotel for gay men offering clothing-optional sunbathing and an extensive video library. Pool and jacuzzi, which have been the site of several porn films, are in use 24 hours. Ask about their special offers. 24 guestrooms.

Mirage (AC CC G I MA NU OS P PI PK RWB RWS RWT SA SB VA VS WH) All year
555 Grenfall Road ☎ (760) 322-2404 www.mirage4men.com
Gay man's oasis with three pools and three spas. 18-man jacuzzi, lively steam rooms and multi-level garden with waterfalls. Part of Vista Grande.

Mirasol Villas. El (AC BF CC G I M NU PI PK RWB RWS RWT SA SB VA WH) All year
525 Warm Sands Drive *Warmsands area* ☎ (760) 327-5913
www.elmirasol.com
All 15 rooms with phone, kitchenette, private bath/WC.

Santiago Palm Springs (AC BF G M NU OS PI RWS RWT SA WH WO) All year
650 San Lorenzo Road ☎ (760) 322-1300 ☎ (800) 710-7729 (toll free)
www.santiagoresort.com
This luxurious gay Santiago resort is lushly decorated, the grounds meticulously crafted. Probably one of the most attractive resorts of its kind with 23 individually designed studios and suites, an extensive gay video gallery and stunning mountain views from the terrace. A great place to relax.

Tortuga del Sol (AC bf G I MA MSG NU OS PI PK RWS RWT VA WH) All year
715 San Lorenzo Road *Walking distance to downtown Palm Springs*
☎ (760) 416-3111 ☎ (888) 541-3777 www.tortugadelsol.com
A warm and friendly gay hotel that is conveniently located to all attractions.

Triangle Inn Palm Springs (AC BF CC G I MA MSG NU OS PI PK RWS RWT VA WH) All year
555 San Lorenzo Road ☎ (760) 322-7993 www.triangle-inn.com
Nine beautiful private suites, plus a four bedroom house. Rated four Palms by Out & About. Clothing-optional gay resort. Mid-century Modern Architecture. Caters to European clientele.

View Palm Springs. The (AC bf G MA NU PI) All year
354 East Stevens Road ☎ (760) 327-3866
www.theviewpalmsprings.com

Vista Grande Resorts
(AC CC G I MA NU OS P PI PK RWS RWT SA SB VA VS WH) All year
574 Warm Sands Drive ☎ (760) 322-2404 ☎ (800) 669-1069
www.mirage4men.com
Spectacular tropical gardens with waterfalls and naked men: 3 pools, 3 spas, steam room, koi pond, dry sauna, 33 guest rooms from reasonably priced pool side cabanas to the luxurious Mirage Waterfalls Suites, the Vista Grande remains one of the most amazing gay resorts in the world. Beautiful, enlightened and loads of fun the Vista Grande is unsurpassed and clearly the winner!

Warm Sands Villas (AC BF CC G I MA MSG NU OS PI PK RWS RWT VA VS WH) All year; office 7-21, Fri -23h
555 Warm Sands Drive *Two miles from airport* ☎ (760) 323-3005
www.warmsandsvillas.com
Bilingual (English/German) staff, free parking. All rooms have marble floors, new furniture and the complex is under new management. Nude area around the pool. Some rooms have kitchens.

APARTMENTS

Atrium Garden Apartments (AC CC G I MA NU OS P PI PK RWS RWT SA SB VA VS WH) All year
981 Camino Parocela, Warm Sands ☎ (760) 322-2404
www.mirage4men.com
Reasonably priced well appointed studio, one and two bedroom apartments by the week or month, boasting fireplaces, beamed ceilings, private patios, and kitchens. Relax naked and invigorate yourself in the sparkling pool and soothing spa, enjoy spectacular mountain views and the glorious desert sun. 24 hour access to the legendary clothing optional Vista Grande which is right across the street.

■ **Warm Sands Vacation Rentals** (AC CC GLM I MA OS PI PK RWS RWT VA WH) All year
975 E. Camino Parocela, Suite One ☏ (760) 808-2112
🖳 www.warmsandsps.com
Ideal for a short weekend getaway (2 or 3 night minimum required), or longterm, these apartments are fully capable of providing for all of your vacation needs. All units include full kitchens, large living rooms with flat screen televisions and DVD/VCR/CD player. Some units have private patios. Pool, Spa, Laundry facilities and free wireless Internet access are also available.

Pasadena ☏ 626

BARS

■ **Boulevard. The** (B D G VS) 16-2, Fri-Sun 15-2h
3199 East Foothill Boulevard ☏ (626) 356-9304 🖳 www.blvdbar.com
Little neighborhood bar with karaoke, smoking patio.

Pomona ☏ 909

BARS

■ **Alibi East & Back Alley** (B D G MA OS) 10-2, Fri & Sat -4h
225 South San Antonio Avenue ☏ (909) 623-9422
■ **Hookup. The** (AC B BF CC GLM M MA) 12-2h
1047 East Second Street ☏ (909) 620-2844 🖳 www.hook-up.net
Bar & restaurant.

DANCECLUBS

■ **Brick Nightclub. The** (B d GLM MA) 21-4h, closed Mon & Tue
340 South Thomas ☏ (909) 629-6333
🖳 www.thebricknightclub.com

Redding

CRUISING

-Clear Creek Road (4 miles East of old 99, nude beach, summer)
-Lake Redding Park (near boad ramp, AYOR)

Reseda ☏ 818

DANCECLUBS

■ **Coco Bongo** (AC B CC D GLM MA) 21-2h, closed Mon-Wed
19655 Sherman Way *Between Corbin and Tampa* ☏ (818) 998-8464
🖳 www.cocobongola.com
Latin dance club, check www.cocobongola.com for hours and events.

Riverside ☏ 951

DANCECLUBS

■ **Menagerie** (B D GLM MA OS ST) 16-2h
3581 University Ave *At Orange* ☏ (951) 788-8000
Lounge with dancefloor.
■ **V.I.P. Nightclub** (B D GLM M) 15-2h
3673 Merril Avenue ☏ (951) 784-2370 🖳 www.vip-nightclub.com
Check www.vip-nightclub.com for events.

Russian River ☏ 707

BARS

■ **Rainbow Cattle Co.** (B d GLM m MA) 6-2h
16220 Main Street, Guerneville ☏ (707) 869-0206
🖳 www.queersteer.com
Established in 1979, it is the must-see bar stop in any visit to Russian River.

HOTELS

■ **Ferngrove Cottages** (b glm m)
16650 Hwy 116 ☏ (707) 869-8105 🖳 www.ferngrove.com
Comfortable cottages, swimming pool, B&B.

■ **Highlands Resort**
(BF CC GLM MA MSG NU OS PI PK RWB RWS WH WI) All year
14000 Woodland Drive, Guerneville *Guerneville, 20 mins to the airport*
☏ (707) 869-0333 🖳 www.HighlandsResort.com
Cabins, rooms & camping. TV lounge.
■ **R3 Hotel** (B BF CC f G I M MA MSG NU OS PI PK RWS RWT S VA VS WE WH) Bar 9-2h, restaurant 9-21h
16390 4th Street, Guerneville ☏ (707) 869-8399
🖳 www.ther3hotel.com
Great resort with three bars in high season: indoor, poolside and piano. Special rates: see website.
■ **Village Inn** (B CC glm M MA OS RWB) All year
20822 River Boulevard, Monte Rio *On the Russian River*
☏ (707) 865-2304 🖳 www.villageinn-ca.com
Gay-owned country inn with ten guest rooms, most with private balconies or decks overlooking the Russian River.
■ **Wildwood Retreat** (b BF CC glm NU PI SA WH)
20111 Old Cazadero Road *About 5.5 miles out of town*
☏ (707) 632-5200 🖳 www.wildwoodretreat.com
200 acres of redwoods, very quiet. Stars, views, spiritual renewal, peace, hiking, biking, privacy, nature and European-style accommodations and camp sites, clothing optional. Groups 20 to 65 people only, no individuals.
■ **Woods Resort. The**
(CC GLM I MA MSG NU OS PI PK RWB RWS RWT VA) 7.30-23h
16484 4th Street, Guerneville ☏ (707) 869-0600
🖳 www.rrwoods.com
The Woods Resort offers cottages, free-standing guest cabins and multi-room suites with full kitchens, gas fireplaces, private balconies and stunning views of lush redwood forests.

PRIVATE ACCOMMODATION

■ **HearthSide Cabin** (glm I MC PA PK RWB RWS VA) All year
2320 Cazadero Highway ☏ (707) 255-1099
🖳 www.hearthsidecabin.com
Fifteen minutes to Guerneville.

CAMPING

■ **Faerie Ring Campground** (GLM)
16747 Armstrong Woods Rd ☏ (707) 869-2746

Sacramento ☏ 916

GAY INFO

■ **Sacramento Gay & Lesbian Center** (AC GLM I MA OS)
Mon-Sat 12-18h
1927 L Street *In the heart of midtown and Lavender Heights*
☏ (916) 442-0185 🖳 www.saccenter.org
Various events for youths.

PUBLICATIONS

■ **Outword Magazine**
1722 J Street, Ste 6 ☏ (916) 329-9280 🖳 www.outwordmagazine.com
Bi-weekly LGBT news magazine.

BARS

■ **Bolt. The** (B F G MA) Mon-Fri 17-2h, Sat-Sun 14-2h
2560 Boxwood Street ☏ (916) 649-8420 🖳 www.sacbolt.com
Leather/cowboy/bear bar.
■ **Club Bojangles** (AC B D G MA) Wed & Sat 21-2h
1119 21st Street ☏ (916) 443-1537 🖳 www.clubbojangles.net
■ **Depot, The** (B GLM OS VS) Mon-Thu 16-2, Fri -4, Sat 14-4, Sun -2h
2001 K Street ☏ (916) 441-6823 🖳 www.thedepot.net
■ **Faces** (AC B CC D GLM MA OS S VS) 16-2h
2000 K Street ☏ (916) 448-0706 🖳 www.faces.net
Bar & disco, check www.faces.net for special events.
■ **Head Hunters Video Lounge** (B GLM M MA VS)
17-2, Sun 10-2h, closed Mon
1930 K Street ☏ (916) 492-2922 🖳 www.headhuntersonk.com

■ **Mercantile Saloon** (B G MA) 10-2h
1928 L Street ☎ (916) 447-0792

DANCECLUBS

■ **Badlands** (AC B glm MA OS) Mon-Sat 18-2, Sun 14-2h
2003 K Street ☎ (916) 448-8790 💻 www.sacbadlands.com
Check thedepot.net/sb/index.html for events.

■ **Club 21** (B D glm YC) Wed & Sun 21-2h
1119 21st Street ☎ (916) 443-1537
Mixed danceparty for 18+.

SAUNAS/BATHS

■ **Sacs4men** (DU FC G GH MA MSG OS P RR SA SB SL WH)
Wed-Sat 12-1h
4931 Jackson Road *Cnr. Madison* 💻 powerinnmensclub.zocku.com

San Bernardino ☎ 909

BARS

■ **Lark. The** (B D GLM MA) 12-2h, closed Mon
917 Inland Center Drive ☎ (909) 884-8770 💻 www.the-lark.com

SAUNAS/BATHS

■ **Total Body Therapy Spa** (b DU G m MA P RR SA SB SOL VS WH WO) Daily, 24hrs
808 North Arrowhead Ave ☎ (909) 888-7242
💻 www.totalbodytherapyspa.com

San Diego ☎ 619

GAY INFO

■ **San Diego LGBT Community Center** Mon-Thu 9-21, Fri 9-17h
3909 Centre Street ☎ (619) 260-6380 💻 www.thecentersd.org

PUBLICATIONS

■ **Bottomline. The**
3314 4th Ave ☎ (619) 291-6690 💻 www.psbottomline.com
Fortnightly gay magazine with news and entertainment.

■ **Flesh4Men**
3470 Adams Ave ☎ (619) 299-8041 💻 www.flesh4men.com
Quarterly gay adult entertainment magazine.

■ **Gay & Lesbian Times** (GLM)
1730 Monroe Ave, Suite A ☎ (619) 299-6397
💻 www.gaylesbiantimes.com
Weekly news magazine.

CULTURE

■ **Diversionary Theatre** (GLM)
4545 Park Blvd ☎ (619) 220-0097 💻 www.diversionary.org
The 3rd oldest LGBT theatre in the US.

BARS

■ **Bourbon Street Bar and Grill** (AC B CC GLM MA OS S VS)
Monday-Saturday 16-?, Sunday 10-?h
4612 Park Boulevard *University Heights, bus stop in front*
☎ (619) 291-4043 💻 www.bourbonstreetsd.com
Happy Hour Daily 16-19h. Popular.

■ **Brass Rail. The** (B D G MA s ST VS) 19-2, Fri-Sun 14-2h, closed Tue
3796 5th Avenue *Hillcrest* ☎ (619) 298-2233 💻 www.brassrailsd.com
One of the oldest gay bars in town, still popular. Live music on Thu, Sat Latin night.

■ **Caliph. The** (B G MA S) 11-2h
3100 5th Avenue ☎ (619) 298-9495
Piano bar.

■ **Cheers** (B G MA OS) 11-2h
1839 Adams Avenue *University Heights* ☎ (619) 298-3269

■ **Eagle** (AK B DR F G MA) Mon-Thu 16-2, Fri-Sun 14-2h
3040 North Park Way ☎ (619) 295-8072 💻 www.sandiegoeagle.com
See www.sandiegoeagle.com for events calender.

■ **Fiesta Cantina** (AC B CC GLM M MA NR WE) 10:30-12:30h
142 University Avenue ☎ (619) 298-2500 💻 www.fiestacantina.net
Popular Mexican style gay bar with cheap drinks. Happy hour from 4-8pm

■ **Flicks** (B G VS YC) 14-2h
1017 University Avenue ☎ (619) 297-2056 💻 www.sdflicks.com
Popular on Sun afternoons.

■ **Gossip Grill** (AC B CC gLm M MA WE) 2-1:30
1440 University Avenue ☎ (619) 260-8023 💻 www.thegossipgrill.com
Lesbian hot spot to drink and eat.

■ **Hole. The** (B D F G OS SNU WI) 16-2h
2820 Lytton Street ☎ (619) 226-9019 💻 www.thehole.com

■ **Loft. The** (AC B CC G MA) 11-2h
3610 5th Avenue ☎ (619) 296-6407

■ **Martinis Above Fourth** (AC B CC GLM MA S) 17-23, Fri & Sat 16-24h, closed Sun & Mon
3940 Fourth Avenue, 2nd Floor ☎ (619) 400-4500
💻 www.martinisabovefourth.com
Cabaret lounge in the heart of Hillcrest; live piano entertainment on Fri & Sat.

■ **Number 1 Fifth Avenue** (AC B G OS VS) 12-2h
3845 5th Avenue *Between Robinson and University Avenue*
☎ (619) 299-1911
Smoke friendly patio.

■ **Pecs** (B F G MA OS) 12-2h, Sun 10-2h
2046 University Avenue *North Park* ☎ (619) 296-0889
💻 www.pecsbar.com
Popular & cruisy bear/leather bar.

■ **Redwing Bar & Grill** (B GLM M MA OS)
11-1, Fri & Sat 10-2, Sun 10-1h
4012 30th Street ☎ (619) 281-8700 💻 www.redwingbar.com

■ **SRO** (B CC GLM MA t) 10-2h
1807 5th Avenue *Uptown* ☎ (619) 232-1886

CAFES

■ **Babycakes** (b GLM m MA OS) 9-23, Fri & Sat -24h
3766 Fifth Avenue *At Robinson Street* ☎ (619) 296-4173
💻 www.babycakessandiego.com
Friendly place.

DANCECLUBS

■ **Bacchus House** (AC B CC D GLM m MA S VS) Wed-Sun 20-2h
3054 University Avenue *Cnr. Ohio St* ☎ (619) 299-2032
💻 www.bacchushouse.com
Different theme nights, check www.bacchushouse.com for details.

■ **Eden** (AC B CC D GLM M NR WE YC) Tue-Sun 11 -2h
1202 University Ave. CA 92103 ☎ (619) 269-3336
💻 www.edensandiego.com
Stylish danceclub with restaurant and bar.

■ **Numbers** (AC B D GLM m MA OS P S VS)
16-2, Sat & Sun 13-2h, closed Tue & Wed
3811 Park Boulevard *Hillcrest* ☎ (619) 294-9005
💻 www.numberssd.com
Popular club. ID required. It's possible the doorman refuses to let you in if you are not an US citizen.

■ **Rich's – San Diego** (B D G MA VS) Wed-Sun 22-2h
1051 University Avenue, Hillcrest *Opposite shopping-mall*
☎ (619) 295-2195 💻 www.richssandiego.com
Popular. See www.richssandiego.com for special events.

■ **Spin** (AC B D G MA)
2028 Hancock Street *Cnr. Noell Street* ☎ (619) 294-9590
💻 www.spinnightclub.com

RESTAURANTS

■ **Baja Betty's** (B GLM M MA OS) 11-24, Fri & Sat -1h
1421 University Avenue ☎ (619) 269-8510 💻 www.bajabettyssd.com
Happy hour Mon-Fri. Extensive Tequila menu is the highlight.

■ **Lips** (b GLM M MA ST T) Tue-Sun 17-?h
3036 El Cajon Blvd ☎ (619) 295-7900 💻 www.lipssd.com
Dinner restaurant with drag shows.

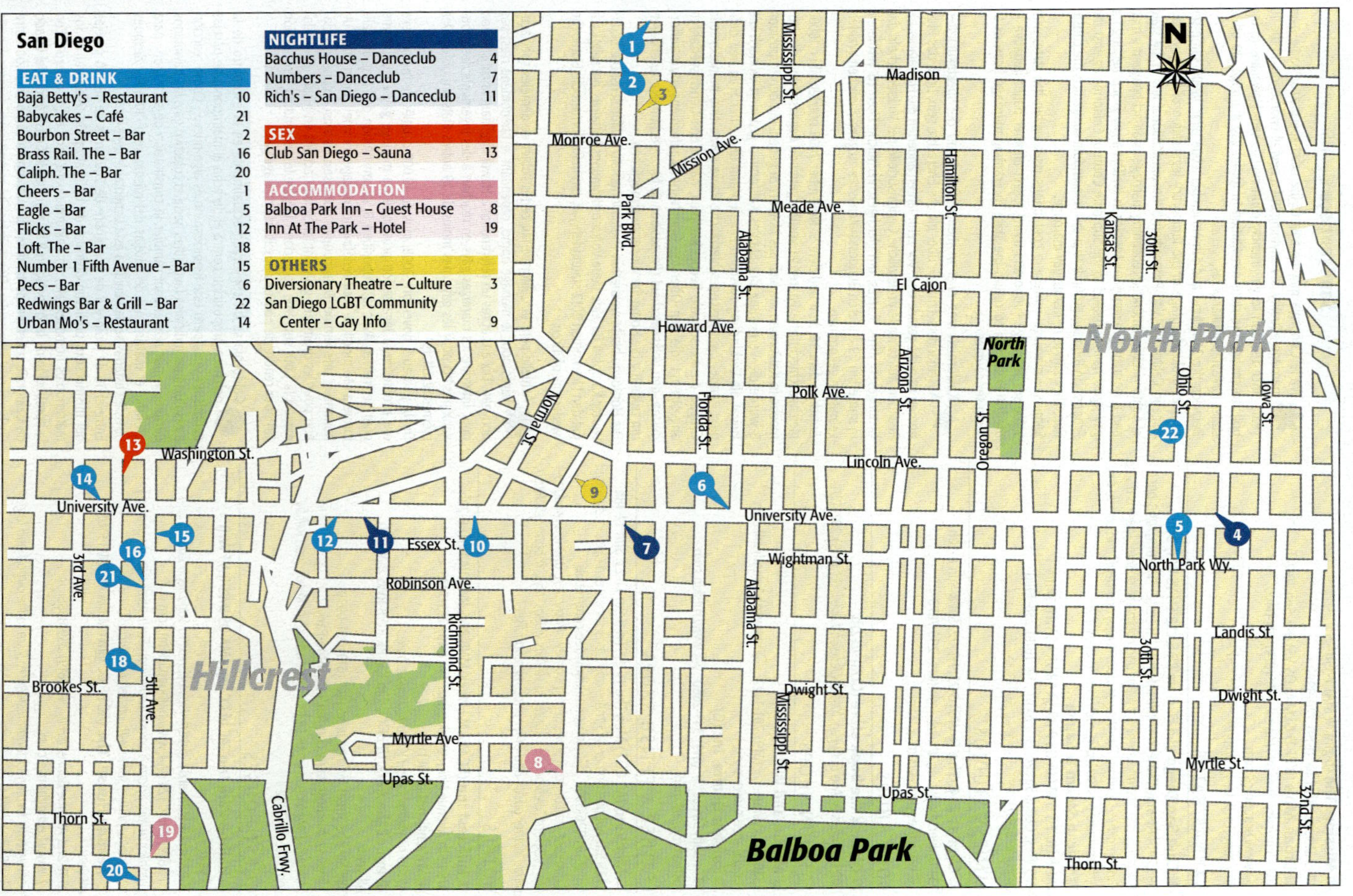
San Diego
EAT & DRINK
Baja Betty's – Restaurant 10
Babycakes – Café 21
Bourbon Street – Bar 2
Brass Rail. The – Bar 16
Caliph. The – Bar 20
Cheers – Bar 1
Eagle – Bar 5
Flicks – Bar 12
Loft. The – Bar 18
Number 1 Fifth Avenue – Bar 15
Pecs – Bar 6
Redwings Bar & Grill – Bar 22
Urban Mo's – Restaurant 14
NIGHTLIFE
Bacchus House – Danceclub 4
Numbers – Danceclub 7
Rich's – San Diego – Danceclub 11
SEX
Club San Diego – Sauna 13
ACCOMMODATION
Balboa Park Inn – Guest House 8
Inn At The Park – Hotel 19
OTHERS
Diversionary Theatre – Culture 3
San Diego LGBT Community Center – Gay Info 9
N
North Park
Hillcrest
Balboa Park
Madison
Mississippi St.
Monroe Ave.
Mission Ave.
Park Blvd.
Meade Ave.
Hamilton St.
Kansas St.
30th St.
El Cajon
Howard Ave.
Alabama St.
Polk Ave.
Arizona St.
Ohio St.
Iowa St.
Oregon St.
Florida St.
Normal St.
Washington St.
Lincoln Ave.
University Ave.
Essex St.
Wightman St.
North Park Wy.
Robinson Ave.
Richmond St.
3rd Ave.
Landis St.
Dwight St.
Brookes St.
5th Ave.
Myrtle Ave.
Myrtle St.
Upas St.
Cabrillo Frwy.
Thorn St.
32nd St.

■ **Mission. The** (b glm M MA) 7-15h
3795 Mission Blvd ☎ (619) 220-8992

■ **Urban Mo's** (B BF D GLM M OS VS) 9-2, Sun 10-24h
308 University Avenue *Hillcrest* ☎ (619) 491-0400
www.urbanmos.com
Also danceclub. Very popular.

SAUNAS/BATHS

■ **Club San Diego** (B d FC G I m RR SA SB SH VS WH) 24hrs
3955 4th Avenue *Between Washington & University* ☎ (619) 295-0850
Condoms are free and there are lubes and cockrings for sale. There is also a snack machine lounge. The shower room is new and clean and can be fun. A three-hours pass to leave and return is available.

■ **Vulcan Steam & Sauna**
(AC B DU FC G M MA OS P RR SA SB VR VS WH) 24hrs
805 West Cedar Street *Downtown* ☎ (619) 238-1980
24 hours open

FITNESS STUDIOS

■ **Gym at 734. The** (g WO) 5-23, Fri -22, Sat & Sun 8-20h
734 University Ave *At 7th Ave* ☎ (619) 296-7878
www.thegym734.com

BOOK SHOPS

■ **Obelisk the book store** (GLM) 10-21h
1029 University Ave *Between 10th & Cleveland Ave* ☎ (619) 297-4171

FASHION SHOPS

■ **Martin and Wall** (CC G)
3828 5th Avenue ☎ (619) 291-1422 www.martinandwall.com
Popular men's wear shop.

■ **Rufskin Denim, Inc** (G)
3944 30th Street ☎ (619) 341-2660 www.rufskin.com
Fashion for gay men.

LEATHER & FETISH SHOPS

■ **Mankind** (AC CC F) Mon-Thu 11-22, Fri & Sat 11-23, Sun 12-18h
3425 5th Avenue *Corner of 5th Ave and Upas St between Upas and Walnut*
☎ (619) 226-3000 www.mankindvideo.com/retail
A different kind of adult store, selling homey atmosphere and knowledgeable „sexperts" behind the counter as well as videos, toys, magazines, fetish wear, leather goods and other pride merchandise.

HOTELS

■ **Hillcrest Inn** (CC f GLM I PA PK RWB RWS RWT VA WH) 8-22h
3754 5th Avenue *Hillcrest gay area* ☎ (619) 293-7078
www.hillcrestinn.net
45 rooms with phone, TV, fridge, private bath.

■ **Inn at the Park** (B BF CC glm I M PK RWB RWS RWT VA)
All year
525 Spruce Street *Hillcrest area* ☎ (619) 291-0999
www.shellhospitality.com/en/Inn-at-the-Park
Formerly Park Manor Suites Hotel. New ownership. Renovation will be completed in 2012

GUEST HOUSES

■ **Balboa Park Inn** (AC bf CC glm I MA OS RWS RWT WH)
All year
3402 Park Boulevard *Centrally located, next to San Diego Zoo*
☎ (619) 298-0823 www.balboaparkinn.com
Complex of four Spanish colonial buildings. Each suite with queen-sized bed, fridge, phone, some with kitchen and Jacuzzi.

■ **Keating House. The** (AC BF CC glm I M MA PK RWB RWS)
All year
2331 2nd Avenue *Banker's Hill* ☎ (619) 239-8585
www.keatinghouse.com
Conveniently located Victorian residence. 3 km to the airport and to gay bars. Shared baths.

San Francisco ☎ 415

While California may be host to the most spectacular battle over marriage equality, it's anything but a new phenomenon. In the 10 years since reaction to gay-friendly court rulings sent Hawaiians to the polls to change the state constitution to forbid gay marriage, 29 other states have had similar votes.

Between the 16th June and 5th November 2008 over 18000 same-sex couples took advantage of the temporary legalisation of the gay marriage in California. With Proposition 8 the constitutional law in the state of California was amended redefining marriage as an act between a man and a woman. Two same-sex couples as well as a gay group fighting for gay rights have appealed to the Supreme Court of California against the Proposition 8 on the grounds that this referendum contradicts the constitution. They aim to re-instate gay marriage.

Same-sex marriage remains a contentious issue within the state, with same-sex marriage supporters trying to get another ballot initiative in the 2012 election to return the state to granting marriage licenses to same-sex couples.

Kalifornien mag zwar momentan Schauplatz der spektakulärsten Auseinandersetzungen über gleiche Eherechte sein, doch das Phänomen ist nicht gerade neu. Vor zehn Jahren änderten die Hawaianer als Reaktion auf schwulenfreundliche Gerichtsurteile per Volksentscheid das Grundgesetz ihres Staates, um gleichgeschlechtliche Ehen zu verbieten. In immerhin 29 anderen Bundesstaaten ist es zu ganz ähnlichen Wahlergebnissen gekommen.

Zwischen dem 16. Juni und dem 5. November 2008 nutzten über 18000 gleichgeschlechtliche Paare die vorübergehende Legalisierung der Homoehe in Kalifornien um sich das JA-Wort zu geben. Mit der Proposition 8 wurde die Verfassung des Staates Kalifornien geändert wonach die Heirat als Verbindung zwischen einem Mann und einer Frau neu definiert wurde. Zwei gleichgeschlechtliche Paare sowie eine homosexuelle Gruppe die für schwule Rechte kämpfen, haben drei Gerichtsverfahren angestrengt, die den Obersten Gerichtshof Kaliforniens dazu aufforderten, den Volksentscheid (Proposition 8) für unrechtmäßig zu erklären um zukünftig die Homoehe wieder zu ermöglichen.

Die Homoehe bleibt weitherhin Thema innerhalb Kaliforniens: Die Befürworter kämpfen für eine neue Volksabstimmungs-Initiative, die zeitgleich mit den Neuwahlen 2012 stattfinden soll, um in Kalifornien die Homoehe wieder einzuführen.

Actuellement la Californie fait certes l'objet de démêlés spectaculaires pour le mariage homo, cependant le phénomène n'est pas nouveau. Dix ans après un référendum à Hawai modifiant la constitution pour interdire les mariages gays en réaction à des jugements des tribunaux positifs pour les gays, pas moins de 29 autres Etats ont obtenu les mêmes résultats.

Du 16 juin au 5 novembre 2008, plus de 18.000 couples de même sexe ont profité de la légalisation provisoire du mariage gay en Californie pour se marier. Avec la Proposition 8, la constitution de l'Etat de Californie a été modifiée pour redéfinir le mariage comme l'union entre un homme et une femme. Deux couples homosexuels ainsi qu'une association pour les droits des gays ont lancé trois actions en justice qui réclament à la Cour suprême de déclarer illégale le référendum (Proposition 18) pour rendre de nouveau possible le mariage gay.

California se ha convertido actualmente en el escenario de la polémica proposición contra el derecho al matrimonio de parejas del mismo sexo; pero este fenómeno no es algo nuevo. Como reacción a resoluciones judiciales favorables hacia el colectivo gay, los hawaianos decidieron por referéndum cambiar la constitución de su estado para prohibir el matrimonio de parejas del mismo sexo. 10 años después otros 29 estados se han unido a esta lamentable decisión.

Entre el 16 de junio y 5 de noviembre de 2008 más de 18.000 parejas del mismo sexo pudieron disfrutar de la legalización temporal de los matrimonios homosexuales en California para decir el „Si quiero". Con la aprobación de la Proposición 8 se modificó la Constitución del Estado de California redefiniendo también el matrimonio como la unión entre un hombre y una mujer. Dos parejas del mismo sexo y agrupaciones

homosexuales que luchan por los derechos LGBT han emprendido tres procesos judiciales exigiendo al Tribunal Supremo de California que se declare ilegal el referéndum de la Proposición 8 y que se restituya la legalidad del matrimonio entre parejas del mismo sexo.
El matrimonio gay continua siendo un tema importante en California: los partidarios a favor luchan por la iniciativa de un nuevo referéndum, que coincidiría con las elecciones en 2012, para volver a establecer el matrimonio gay en California.

Anche se la California è, per adesso, teatro di accese discussioni sui pari diritti matrimoniali, bisogna anche dire che il fenomeno non è poi del tutto nuovo. Dieci anni fa il referendum tenutosi nelle Hawaii, come reazione alle numerose sentenze a favore della causa omosessuale, tramite modifica costituzionale, ha vietato le unioni tra persone dello stesso sesso. Dopo dieci anni da quel referendum 29 altri Stati federali hanno raggiunto risultati simili.
Tra il 16 giugno e il 5 novembre del 2008 più di 18000 coppie dello stesso sesso hanno fatto uso della legalizzazione temporanea del matrimonio omosessuale in California per scambiarsi il fatidico sì. Con la proposition 8 è stata cambiata la costituzione dello stato federale della California ridefinendo il matrimonio non più come unione tra un uomo e una donna. Due coppie dello stesso sesso e un gruppo omosessuale impegnato nei diritti degli omosessuali hanno fatto tre ricorsi presso la corte suprema della California contro il referendum (Proposition 8) affinchè anche in futuro gli omosessuali possano continuare a sposarsi.
Il matrimonio omosessuale rimane un tema molto discusso in California: i favorevoli stanno lottando per indire un nuovo referendum che cada con le nuove elezioni. Con il suddetto referendum gli attivisti mirano alla reintroduzione dei matrimoni omosessuali.

GAY INFO

Castro Country Club. The (b GLM I m MA OS VS)
7-23, Fri & Sat -24, Sun 9-22h
4058 18th Street *Cnr. Hartford St* ☎ (415) 552-6102
www.castrocountryclub.org
Provides a „clean and sober" safe social alternative to bars. No drugs, alcohol, or persons under the influence of drugs and alcohol are allowed.

San Francisco LGBT Community Center. The (GLM OS S t)
1800 Market Street *At Octavia Street* ☎ (415) 865-5555
www.sfcenter.org
Houses a wide range of organizations and groups of the SF community. Call or see website for details.

PUBLICATIONS

BAR – Bay Area Reporter
395 9th Street ☎ (415) 861-5019 www.ebar.com
Weekly newspaper for the greater San Francisco area, free at delivery points in Bay Area. News, sports & entertainment of interest to the gay community.

Bartab (G)
395 Ninth Street ☎ (415) 861-5019 www.bartabsf.com
Very popular San Francisco event guide.

Gay Pocket San Francisco
c/o Gay Pocket Guides, 2215-R Market Street ☎ (415) 864-8869
www.gaypocketusa.com
Free gay guide, available at gay venues.

Gloss Magazine
584 Castro Street, Suite 329 ☎ (510) 451-2090
www.glossmagazine.net
San Franciscos glossy magazine for the Gay Community.

San Francisco Bay Times Mon-Fri 9-18h
3410 19th Street ☎ (415) 626-0260 www.sfbaytimes.com
Weekly magazine covering the Bay Area scene.

SHOWS

New Concervatory Theatre Center (AC CC glm S)
25 Van Ness Avenue, Lower Lobby *At Market Street* ☎ (415) 861-8972
www.nctcsf.org
GLBT theatre for plays, musicals and performance art. Many of the productions are world premieres.

Theatre Rhinoceros (GLM S) Performances Wed-Sun
1360 Mission St, Suite #200 *Mission District* ☎ (415) 552-4100
www.therhino.org
America's oldest and foremost theatre devoted to gay and lesbian issues only.

CULTURE

GLBT History Museum (GLM)
Wed-Sat 11-19, Sun-Mon 12-17h, Tue closed
4127 18th Street *Between Castro and Collingwood St* ☎ (415) 621-1107
www.glbthistory.org/museum
The GLBT History Museum showcases the stories of gay, lesbian, bisexual and transgender people and their communities through dynamic exhibitions and public programs.

TOURIST INFO

San Francisco Convention & Visitors Bureau Mon-Fri 8.30-17h
900 Market Street *Corner Powel & Market St* ☎ (415) 391-2000
www.onlyinsanfrancisco.com

BARS

440 Castro (B F G MA s) 12-2h
440 Castro Street *Between Market & 18th St* ☎ (415) 621-8732
www.the440.com
Come as you are. Levi/leather bar with a mixed crowd.

Aunt Charlie's Lounge (B G MA ST t) 12-2, Sat 10-2, Sun -24h
133 Turk Street *Between Taylor and Jones Streets* ☎ (415) 441-2922
www.auntcharlieslounge.com
Thu „Tubesteak" disco & dance classics, YC, 21-2h (gets busy 23h).

Badlands (! AC B D G MA VS) 14-2h
4121 18th Street *Between Castro and Collingwood* ☎ (415) 626-9320
www.sfbadlands.com
Popular dance bar in the heart of the Castro. Must be 21 with ID. Happy Hour Mon-Sat -20h. Attracts a younger crowd.

Blackbird (B g MC)
2124 Market Street ☎ (415) 503-0630 blackbirdbar.com
The decor is rustic chic, making this probably the best decor of any Castro gay bar. Nice place to meet friends and visit.

blush! (AC B BF G M MA WL)
Mon-Thu 16-0.30, Fri -1.30, Sat 12-1.30, Sun -0h
476 Castro Street ☎ ((415)) 558-0893 www.blushwinebar.com

Café du Nord (B glm m MA S) 20-2h
2170 Market Street ☎ (415) 861-5016 www.cafedunord.com

Café. The (B D GLM OS YC) 17-2, Sat & Sun 16-2h
2367 Market Street *Between 16th & 17th Street* ☎ (415) 861-3846
www.cafesf.com
Following a multi-million dollar remodel, this Castro dance staple is bigger and better than ever. Featuring three bars, a massive dance floor, and new state-of-the-art sound system, Popular dance bar with a younger crowd. Small patio, balcony overlooks Market Street & Castro. Mon Hip-Hop, R&B 21-2h. Thu Pan Dulce latin night with gogo dancers and performances, 21-2h.

Churchill (B D G MA) 16-2, Sat & Sun 14-2h
198 Church Street *At 14th/Market* www.churchillsf.com

Cinch Saloon. The (B G I MA OS ST VS) 6-2h
1723 Polk Street *Between Washington and Clay Streets*
☎ (415) 776-4162
Classical bar with a mixed and open-mided crowd and some whacky events. DJ's Thu & Fri, Pool League on Tue. Smoking patio. Note: All bars with billard have league play Tue evening. Free Wi-Fi available.

Deco Lounge (B d G MA) 10-2h
510 Larkin Street *At Turk Street* ☎ (415) 346-2025
Piano Bar.

Divas (AC B D g MA r S ST T) 18-2h
1081 Post Street ☎ (415) 928-6006 www.divassf.com
The place for transgenders. Dancefloor Wed-Sat 22-2h.

Edge. The (B F G MA s) 12-2h
4149 18th Street *One block from M° Castro-Muni* ☎ (415) 863-4027
www.edgesf.com
A classic in the Castro scene, with a leather/levi crowd. Special events & entertainment.

Esta Noche (B D G MA S ST T VS) 14-2h
3079 16th Street *At Valencia St* ☎ (415) 861-5757
Great gay latino club. Rough neighbourhood, so go with a friend or take a cab after you leave.

Gangway. The (B G MA) 8-2h
841 Larkin Street *Between O'Farrell and Geary Streets* ☎ (415) 776-6828
One of the oldest gay bars in town.

Harvey's (B BF GLM M MA S) 11-23, Sat & Sun 9-2h
500 Castro Street *At 18th St* ☎ (415) 431-4278 www.harveyssf.com
Meals from opening to 23h and various events.

Hole in the Wall Saloon (B F G MA) 12-2h
1369 Folsom Street *Between 9th and 10th St* ☎ (415) 431-4695
www.holeinthewallsaloon.com
Biker and leather bar. Rock music throughout the week, DJ's on Wed and WE. Pool table & billards.

Kimo's (AC B CC d glm MA S) 11-2h
1351 Polk Street *At Pine Street* ☎ (415) 885-4535
www.kimosbarsf.com
Live bands upstairs. Small neighboorhood bar downstairs is queer, the live bands uptairs attract a mixed clientel.

Kok (B F G MA) 18-2, Fri-Sun 16-2h
1225 Folsom Street *Between 8th & 9th St* ☎ (415) 255-2427
www.kokbarsf.com
Different theme nights.

Last Call (AC B GLM MA) 12-2h
3988 18th Street *Cnr. Noe Street* ☎ (415) 861-1310
www.thelastcallbar.com

Lime (AC B GLM M MA) 14-2h, Sat & Sun 11-2h
2247 Market Street *Between 16th & Sanchez* ☎ (415) 621-5256
www.lime-sf.com
Also restaurant.

Lone Star Saloon (! B F G MA OS) 12-2, Sat & Sun 6-2h
1354 Harrison Street *Between 9th and 10th St.* ☎ (415) 863-9999
www.lonestarsf.com
One of the most famous bear bars worldwide! Smoking patio and bear store upstairs.

Lookout. The (B d GLM M MA) 15.30-2, Sat & Sun 12.30-2h
3600 16th Street ☎ (415) 431-0306 www.lookoutsf.com
Popular on Sun for Jock Sundays.

Lush Lounge. The (B g MA S) 16-2h
1092 Post Street *At Polk Street* ☎ (415) 771-2022
www.lushloungesf.com
Piano bar.

Marlena's (B GLM MA S ST) 15-2, Sat & Sun 12-2h
488 Hayes Street, Hayes Valley *Between Octavia and Gough Streets*
☎ (415) 864-6672 www.marlenasbarsf.com
Neighbourhood bar with drag show Fri at 24h. Pool table / billards.

Martuni's (AC B CC glm MA S) 16-2h
4 Valencia Street *At Market* ☎ (415) 241-0205
Piano bar. Full bar specializing in Martinis of all flavours.

Midnight Sun. The (! B G MA VS) Mon-Fri 14-2, Sat & Sun 13-2h
4067 18th Street *Between Castro and Noe Streets* ☎ (415) 861-4186
www.midnightsunsf.com
The well established video bar in town. Also shows regular sitcoms during the week. Cruisy atmosphere.

Mint Karaoke Bar. The (AC B GLM M MA S) 13-2h
1942 Market Street *Between Duboce Street and Van Ness Avenue*
☎ (415) 626-4726 www.themint.net
Karaoke hours 15-2h.

Mix (B GLM m MA OS VS) Daily 6-2h
4086 18th Street *Between Castro and Noe Streets* ☎ (415) 431-8616
sfmixbar.com
Gay sports bar with a heated patio (BBQ on WE) and pool tables.

Moby Dick (B GLM MA VS) 14-2, Sat & Sun 12-2h
4049 18th Street www.mobydicksf.com
Popular neighbourhood bar with a saltwater fish tank. Regular drink specials. Pool table / billards, pinball machines.

Phone Booth (B GLM MA) 12-2h
1398 South Van Ness Avenue *At 25th St* ☎ (415) 648-4683
Pool table, small neighbourhood dive, friendly. ID required.

Pilsner Inn (B GLM MA OS) 10-2h
225 Church Street ☎ (415) 621-7058 www.pilsnerinn.com
Sportsbar with a large patio and a pool table.

San Francisco – Nob Hill/Tenderloin

EAT & DRINK
- Aunt Charlie's Lounge – Bar 13
- Cinch Saloon. The – Bar 1
- Deco Lounge – Bar 11
- Divas – Bar 7
- Dottie's True Blue Café – Café 14
- Gangway. The – Bar 9
- Grubstake – Restaurant 3
- Kimo's – Bar 4
- Lush Lounge. The – Bar 6
- Quetzal – Café 5

NIGHTLIFE
- Fresh @ Ruby Skye – Danceclub 16
- Nob Hill Adult Theatre – Men's Club 18

ACCOMMODATION
- Fitzgerald – Hotel 15
- Renoir – Hotel 12

SEX
- Gulch. The – Sex Shop/Blue Movies 8

■ **Powerhouse** (! B F G MA OS) 16-2, Sat & Sun 12-2h
1347 Folsom Street/Dore Alley *Between 9th and 10th Streets*
☎ (415) 552-8689 💻 www.powerhouse-sf.com
Definitely a must for all leather men. Monthly theme nights. Home of the Bare Chest Calendar. Lots of tattooed and pierced guys enjoy the relaxed atmosphere. Cruisy outdoor patio.

■ **Q Bar** (AC B D G MA) 16-2, Sat & Sun 14-2h
456 Castro Street *Across from Castro Theatre* ☎ (415) 864-2877
💻 www.qbarsf.com

■ **Rio. El** (B D f GLM MA OS S t)
Mar-Nov: 17-2, Fri-Sun 15-2; Dec-Feb: 17-2, Fri 15-2h
3158 Mission Street *Cnr. Cesar Chavez St* ☎ (415) 282-3325
💻 www.elriosf.com
Live DJs or entertainment every night. Nice backyard with lots of plants. Popular with a mixed crowd.

■ **Toad Hall** (AC B G MA) 16-2h
4146 18th Street *Across from „Badlands"* ☎ (415) 621-2811

■ **Trax** (B GLM MA) 12-2h
1437 Height Street *Between Ashbury St & Masonic Ave* ☎ (415) 864-4213
💻 www.sftrax.com

■ **Trigger** (B G MC S) 20-2, Sun 14-2h
2344 Market Street *Near cnr. Castro Street* ☎ (415) 551-2582
💻 www.clubtrigger.com
This sleek, new club is unique with bottle service, unisex bathrooms, caged go-go dancers, and a coveted smoking patio.

■ **Truck** (B GLM M MA) 16-2h
1900 Folsom Street *At 15th St* ☎ (415) 252-0306 💻 www.trucksf.com

■ **Twin Peaks** (B G MA) 12-2, WE 8-2h
401 Castro Street *Gateway to the Castro* ☎ (415) 864-9470
💻 www.twinpeakstavern.com
Classy cocktail bar with an antique interior. No bottled beer available. Always busy, nice interior terrace. Attracts a more mature crowd.

MEN'S CLUBS

■ **Blow Buddies** (! AK DR F FC G GH LAB MA NU OS p SL VR VS)
Wed 20-24; Thu 19.30-3, Fri 15-4, Sat 18-4, Sun 18-2
933 Harrison Street *Between 5th & 6th St* ☎ (415) 777-4323
💻 www.blowbuddies.com
Other events (Wednesdays) at the same location: Naked Buddies, Golden Shower Buddies, Underwear Buddies, Leather Buddies & Bear Buddies.

■ **Eros** (CC DR DU f FC G GH MA MSG NU SA SB SL SOL VS)
12-24, Fri & Sat -3h
2051 Market Street *At Church Street, opp. Safeway* ☎ (415) 864-3767
💻 www.erossf.com
Softly lit playrooms with video pits, bunk beds, cages, glory holes and sling.

■ **Mack Folsom Prison** (DR F G I MA NU P SA VS) 18-6h
1285 Folsom Street *At 9th Street* ☎ (415) 252-1221
💻 www.mackfolsomprison.com
Private club with cells, lockers, slings, mazes, showers and more. Soldiers get in for free. Free internet access.

■ **Nob Hill Adult Theatre** (! AC B CC G MA SNU VS) 9-2.30h
729 Bush Street *At Powell, near Union Square* ☎ (415) 781-9468 (Info)
💻 www.nobhilltheatre.com
One of the best run, state-of-the-art video arcades in the city of San Francisco. Nude stage and shower shows beginning at 12h. Glory holes and more. Video cabins and Cruising Area in the basement.

CAFES

■ **Dottie's True Blue Cafe** (b BF glm m) 7.30-15h, Tue closed
522 Jones Street *Between Geary and O'Farrell Streets* ☎ (415) 885-2767
The perfect place to enjoy a delicious breakfast. Very popular on weekends for brunch.

■ **Flore** (b BF CC GLM I M OS) 7-1, Fri & Sat -2h
2298 Market Street/Noe Street ☎ (415) 621-8579 💻 www.cafeflore.com
A popular place to hang out or just to see and be seen. Free Wi-Fi available.

■ **Jumpin' Java** (b glm I m YC) 7-20h
139 Noe St/14th St ☎ (415) 431-5282
Free Wi-Fi available.

■ **Quetzal** (AC b BF glm I M MA OS s VS) 6.30-22h
1234 Polk Street ☎ (415) 673-4181 💻 www.quetzal.org
Free Wi-Fi available.

■ **Starbucks Coffee** (b GLM m MA) Mon-Thu 5-22.30, Fri -23.30, Sat 5.30-23.30, Sun -22.30h
4094 18th Street *At Castro St* ☎ (415) 626-6263
Popular bear hangout.

■ **Wicked Grounds** (b GLM m) Mon-Thu 10-22, Fri-2, Sat 11-2, Sun -22h
289 8th Street ☎ (415) 503-0405 💻 www.wickedgrounds.com
Kink cafe and boutique.

DANCECLUBS

■ **Cockfight @ Underground SF** (B D G MA)
1st & 3rd Sat/month 21-2h
424 Haight Street *Cnr. Webster* ☎ (415) 864-7386
💻 www.cockfightsf.com

■ **Crib. The** (B D GLM YC) Thu 21.30-3h
715 Harrison Street *At 3rd St* 💻 www.thecribsf.com
Only weekly dance for ages 18+. Multi-room club.

■ **Eight** (B D GLM MA OS) Thu 22-2, Fri 21-2, Sat 22-2, Sun 18-12h
1151 Folsom Street *Between 7th and 8th* ☎ (415) 431-1151
💻 www.eightsf.com
Chic cocktail nightclub with two full bars and levels. Fri Club Dragon (Asian dance). Sun 23-3h Thick (afterparty with House music & Funk).

■ **EndUp** (! B D GLM m MA OS s ST t) Changes daily, WE 24hrs
401 6th Street *Cnr. Harrison St* ☎ (415) 646-0999
💻 www.theendup.com
A San Francisco institution with 35 years history of providing great music. Home of two very popular queer nights: Fri Ghettodisco start at 23h. Sun T-Dance 6-20h, then Sunday Sessions from 20-4h. For all non-stop party-goers this is the place to be.

■ **Fresh @ Ruby Skye** (B D G MA S) Every 3rd Sun/month 18-24h
420 Mason Street 💻 www.freshsf.com
Two levels.

■ **Industry @ Mighty** (B D GLM MA S)
119 Utah Street ☎ (415) 626-7001 💻 www.industrysf.com
House music. Check www.industrysf.com for details.

■ **Ruby Skye** (B D G)
420 Mason Street ☎ (415) 693-0777 💻 www.rubyskye.com
One of the hottest night clubs.

■ **Stud. The** (! B D GLM MA ST) 17-2h
399 9th Street/Harrison Street ☎ (415) 252-7883 💻 www.studsf.com
Various club nights throughout the week.

RESTAURANTS

■ **2223 Restaurant** (B CC GLM M MA) 17-22,
Fri & Sat -23, Sun 10-14.30 & 17-22h
2223 Market Street ☎ (415) 431-0692 💻 www.2223restaurant.com

■ **Asia SF** (B D glm M MA S ST) 17-22h
201 9th Street @ Howard *Two blocks south of Market-Civic Center*
☎ (415) 255-2742 💻 www.asiasf.com
The serving staff are gender illusionists that also perform hourly. Restaurant and bar with Californian-Asian cuisine. Reservation required. Also danceclub.

■ **Catch** (AC B CC GLM M MA)
11.30-15, 17.30-22; Sat & Sun 11-15.30, 17.30-23h
2362 Market Street ☎ (415) 431-5000 💻 www.catchsf.com
International cuisine, specialises in seafood.

■ **Cove on Castro. The** (CC GLM M MA) 8-21, Fri & Sat -22h
434 Castro Street ☎ (415) 626-0462
Well known for its burgers and sandwiches.

■ **Criolla Kitchen** (BF GLM M MA OS) 24hrs
2295 Market Street *Cnr. 16th Street* ☎ (415) 552-5811
💻 www.criollakitchen.com
Former Bagdad Café.

■ **Fuzio** (b GLM M MA)
469 Castro Street *Near 18th Street* ☎ (415) 863-1400
💻 www.fuzio.com
Italian cuisine.

San Francisco – South of Market

EAT & DRINK

Asia SF – Restaurant	4
Hole in the Wall Saloon – Bar	7
Lone Star Saloon – Bar	13
Powerhouse – Bar	14

NIGHTLIFE

Blow Buddies – Men's Club	1
Eight – Danceclub	8
EndUp – Danceclub	3
Mack Folsom Prison – Men's Club	11
Mighty – Danceclub	17
Stud. The – Danceclub	12

SEX

Chaps – Sex Shop/Blue Movies	18
Gulch. The – Sex Shop/Blue Movies	2

OTHERS

Gold's Gym – Fitness Studio	16
Leather Etc – Leather & Fetish Shop	9
Mr. S. Leather – Leather & Fetish Shop	10
Stormy Leather – Leather & Fetish Shop	5

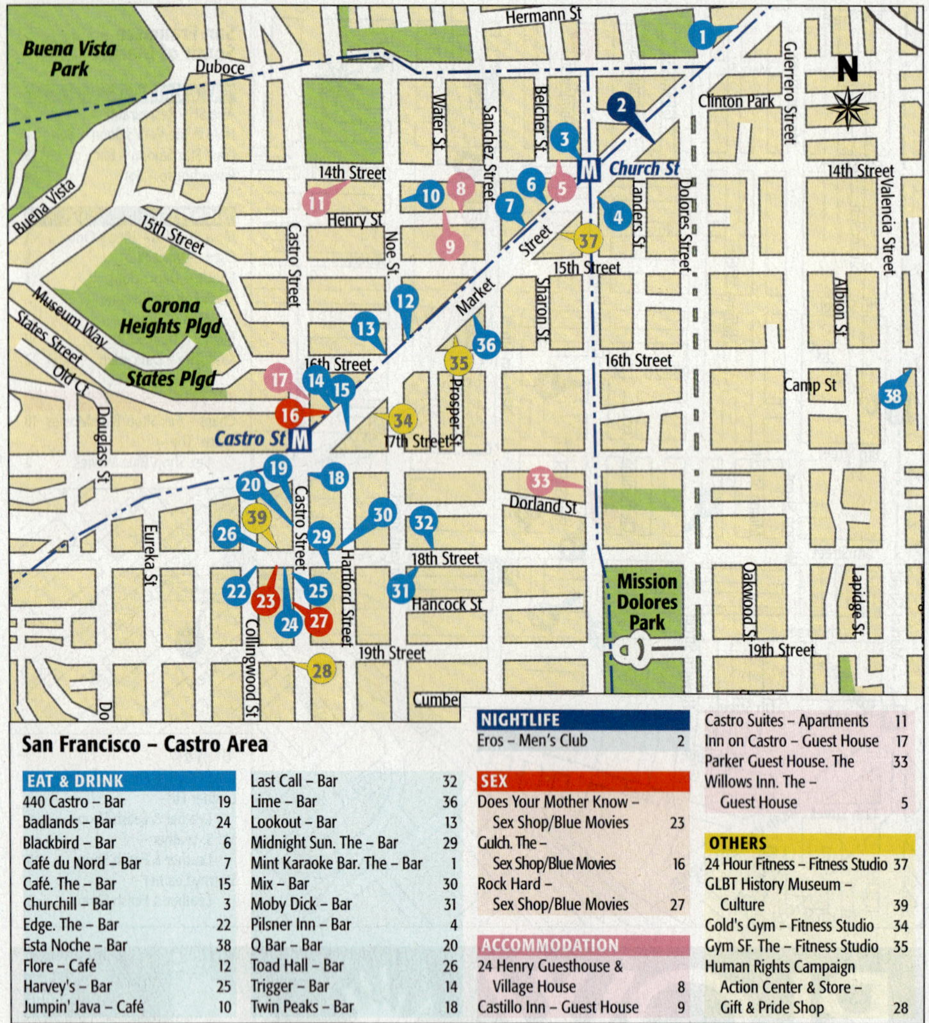

■ **Grubstake** (BF DM glm M MA NR OS VEG) Mon-Fri 17-4, Sat & Sun 10-4h
1525 Pine Street *Between Polk and Van Ness Avenue* ☎ (415) 673-8268
🖳 www.sfgrubstake.com
Hamburgers, chili, steaks and breakfast and Portuguese specialities. Friendly service. Meeting place after the bars are closed.

■ **Orphan Andy's** (CC GLM M MA NR NU) 24hrs
3991A 17th street *Cnr. Castro and Market St* ☎ (415) 864-9795
A fun American diner serving breakfast,lunch and dinner. Open 24/7. Excellent food at reasonable prices. An institution in the Castro for over 35 years. Gay owned and operated.

SEX SHOPS/BLUE MOVIES

■ **Auto Erotica** (CC F GLM MA)
Mon-Thu 10-22, Fri & Sat 10-23, Sun 12-20h
4077-A 18th Street *Just off Castro St, 2nd floor* ☎ (415) 861-5787
🖳 www.mercurymailorder.com
Sex novelty shop with large selection of out-of-print porn magazines and films.

■ **Chaps** (AC CC F G MA) Sun-Thu 10-23, Fri & Sat -24h
4057 18th Street ☎ (415) 863-4777 🖳 www.chapssf.com
Also Leather/Military/Uniform wear.

■ **Does Your Mother Know** (CC GLM MA) Daily 10-22h
4141 18th Street *At Castro St* ☎ (415) 864-3160

■ **Good Vibrations** (glm) 11-19, Thu-Sat -20h
603 Valencia Street *At 17th Street* ☎ (415) 522-5460 🖳 www.goodvibes.com
Popular, well-equipped sex toy store, also mail-order. See website for details on further stores.

■ **Gulch. The** (cc G)
1038 Polk Street *Between Geary & Post* ☎ (415) 775-9076 🖳 sfgulch.com

■ **Gulch. The** (AC CC G MA) 10-24, Fri & Sat -2h
2352 Market Street *At Castro* ☎ (415) 934-8524 🖳 www.sfgulch.com

■ **Gulch. The** (AC CC DR G MA VS) 10-2, Fri & Sat 24hrs, Sun 10-24h
947 Folsom Street *Between 5th & 6th Streets* ☎ (415) 495-6402
🖳 www.sfgulch.com
Video cabins and cruising area.

Phantom (CC G)
516 Castro Street ☎ (415) 864-7529
Rock Hard (CC F G MA) Sun-Thu 9.30-22, Fri & Sat 9.30-24h
518 Castro Street ☎ (415) 437-2430
Cards, gifts, original male erotic art, sex toys, DVDs/films.

SAUNAS/BATHS

Eros (CC DR DU f FC G GH MA MSG NU SA SB SL SOL VS)
12-24, Fri & Sat -3h
2051 Market Street *At Church Street, opp. Safeway* ☎ (415) 864-3767
www.erossf.com
Softly lit playrooms with video pits, bunk beds, cages, glory holes and sling.
Steamworks (! AC DR DU FC FH G GH I LAB MA MSG P RR SA SB SL VS WE WH WO) 24hrs
2107 4th Street, Addison, Berkeley *From the City-Bay Bridge to I-80 N to University Ave exit; Frontage Road ramp; right on 2nd; left on Addison and right onto 4th* ☎ (510) 845-8992 www.steamworksonline.com
This sauna belongs to a group which has properties in Chicago, Seattle and Berkeley, USA as well as Toronto and Vancouver in Canada. Membership applies to all 5 bath houses. A clean and attractive sauna with all the modern facilities.

FITNESS STUDIOS

24 Hour Fitness (cc GLM MA WO)
Mon 5-Fri 24, Sat & Sun 5-22h
2145 Market Street ☎ (415) 864-0822 www.24hourfitness.com
Daily membership available.
Gold's Gym (CC GLM MA SB WO)
Mon-Thu 5-24, Fri 5-23, Sat 7-21, Sun 7-20h
2301 Market Street ☎ (415) 626-4488
www.goldsgym.com/sanfranciscocastroca
Daily membership available.
Gold's Gym (CC GLM MA MSG SA SB SOL WO)
5-24, Fri -23, Sat 7-21, Sun 8-20h

1001 Brannan Street ☎ (415) 552-4653
www.goldsgym.com/gyms/california/san-francisco/408
Gym SF. The (cc G MA SA WO) Mon-Fri 5-23, Sat 7-22, Sun 8-20h
2275 Market Street ☎ (415) 863-4700 www.thegymsf.com
Daily and weekly membership pass available. Tanning, free weights, cardio.
Pacific Heights Health Club (glm WO)
Mon-Fri 5.30-22, Sat & Sun 6-20h
2358 Pine Street *Pacific Heights* ☎ (415) 563-6694
www.phhcsf.com

FASHION SHOPS

Sui Generis Ille (CC G PA) Mon – Fri 12-19, Sat 11-19, Sun 11 -17h
2231 Market Street *Between 16th Street and Sanchez* ☎ (415) 437-2231
www.suiGenerisConsignment.com
New 1600 square store of menswear in the heart of the Castro.

GIFT & PRIDE SHOPS

Human Rights Campaign Action Center & Store (CC GLM MA) 10-19, Sun 11-18h
575 Castro Street ☎ (415) 431-2200 www.hrc.org
Under One Roof (CC GLM MA) 10-20, Sun 11-19h
549 Castro Street ☎ (415) 503-2300 www.underoneroof.org
A non-profit gift store that raises funds for the fight against AIDS.
Wild Card (G SH)
3989 17th Street ☎ (415) 626-4449

LEATHER & FETISH SHOPS

Leather Etc (F G) 10.30-19, Sat 11-18, Sun 12-17h
1201 Folsom Street *At 8th St* ☎ (415) 864-7558
www.leatheretc.com
Mr S Leather (CC F G) 11-19h
385 8th Street ☎ (415) 863-7764 www.mr-s-leather.com
Very large selection of leather clothing, bondage and fetish gear.
Stompers Boots (CC F G MA) 11-18h, Sun 12-16h, Mon closed
323 10th Street *Near Folsom Street* ☎ (415) 255-6422
www.stompersboots.com
The ultimate boot shop (motorcycle, patrol, work).
Stormy Leather (CC F GLM) Tue-Sun 12-18, Fri 12-19h
1158 Howard Street *Between 7th & 8th* ☎ (415) 626-1672
www.stormyleather.com

TRAVEL AND TRANSPORT

Now, Voyager Travel (GLM) Mon-Fri 10-18, Sat 11-17h
4406 18th Street *Castro* ☎ (415) 626-1169 www.nowvoyager.com

DVD SHOPS

Captain Video (AC CC GLM MA)
2358 Market Street ☎ (415) 552-0501
Home delivery service for videos.
Superstar (CC G MA) 10-22, Fri & Sat -23h
474 Castro Street ☎ (415) 863-3333 www.castromoviestore.com
Full range of videos & DVDs. Gay soft and hardcore. Specialize in unsensored mail order versions of adult gay films for rent and purchase. The largest collection of gay soft and hardcore in the Castro.

TATTOO/PIERCING

Cold Steel America (cc g MA) 12-20h
1783 Haight Street *Between Cole and Shrader Streets*
www.coldsteelpiercing.com
Gay owned, mention Spartacus and get 10% off jewelry.

HOTELS

Beck's Motor Lodge (AC glm I MA OS RWS RWT) All year, 24hrs
2222 Market Street ☎ (415) 621-8212 www.becksmotorlodge.com
Motel with basic facilities but very cruisy.
Fitzgerald (bf cc g I MA VS WH) All year, 24hrs
620 Post Street *Located in Union Square shopping and theatre district*
☎ (415) 775-8100 www.fitzgeraldhotel.com
Member of Queer Asian Assoc., IGLTA.

■ **Renoir Hotel** (B BF CC GLM I M MA NR PK RWS RWT VA VEG W) All year
45 McAllister Street *Central downtown location on Market St, between Powell St Cablecars and City Hall* ☎ (415) 626-5200 ☎ 1-800 576-3388 (toll free) 💻 www.renoirhotel.com
A unique triangle-shaped historic hotel in the heart of San Francisco, only minutes from Union Square. 10 mins by tram, subway or night bus to/from the gay scene in the Castro and 10 minutes walk to/from the leather scene around Folsom Street (SoMa). All 130 guestrooms have a private bathroom, telephone, cable TV, hair dryer, safe, iron/ironing board.The new Italian family restaurant „Little Joe's" is now open daily for breakfast lunch, and dinner.

GUEST HOUSES

■ **24 Henry Guesthouse & Village House** (CC GLM I MA MSG RWS RWT VA) All year
24 Henry Street ☎ (415) 864-5686 💻 www.24Henry.com
The Village House is located at 4080 18th Street.

■ **Belvedere House B&B** (BF CC GLM MA OS PA PK RWS RWT VA WI) All year
598 Belvedere Street *At 17th Street, right above the Castro district* ☎ (415) 731-6654 💻 www.GayBedAndBreakfast.net

A place to be and let be. Located right above the Castro. Spectacular views. The plush rooms are spotless and with modern amenities.

■ **Castillo Inn** (BF CC GLM I MA) All year
48 Henry Street *Close to Castro and public transport* ☎ (415) 864-5111 ☎ 1-800-865-5112 (toll free)
Just 7 minutes from the heart of the Castro, this charming guesthouse provides a safe, quiet environment.

■ **Inn On Castro** (BF CC GLM I MA OS RWS RWT) Office: 7.30-22.30h
321 Castro Street *Corner Castro/Market* ☎ (415) 861-0321 💻 www.innoncastro.com
No smoking indoors. Reasonable rates which include full breakfast and evening brandy. The Inn has 8 guest rooms and 6 self catering apartments through out the Castro.

■ **Parker Guest House** (! AC BF CC G I MA OS PK RWS RWT SA SB) All year
520 Church Street *Castro District* ☎ (415) 621-3222 💻 www.parkerguesthouse.com
Parker Guest House is a 21-room hotel located in San Francisco's Castro District. The property enjoys high ratings from many gay guides.

■ **Rose Garden Inn** (BF glm H I PK RWB RWS RWT VA) All year
2740 Telegraph Avenue, Berkeley *Ashby Bart Station* ☎ (415) 549-2145 💻 www.rosegardeninn.com
Fourty guest rooms.

■ **Willows Inn. The** (BF CC GLM I MA RWT T VA) All year
710 14th Street *Castro district, 25 mins to the airport* ☎ (415) 431-4770 ☎ (800) 431-0277 💻 www.WillowsSF.com
With 12 rooms, an attentive staff and a great location just steps away from 4 mass transit lines, The Willows Inn is your Haven in the Castro. Expanded Continental breakfast, evening social hour and a well informed staff on duty 12 hours per day.

APARTMENTS

■ **Castro Suites** (CC G I MA OS RWB RWS RWT VA) 8-22h
927 14th Street *Castro* ☎ (415) 437-1783 💻 www.castrosuites.com
One 1-bedroom / one bath, one 2 bedroom / two bath apartments, each fully furnished, each with a full kitchen, laundry, etc.

FETISH GROUPS

■ **Bears of San Francisco** (G)
584 Castro Street, #266 ☎ (415) 541-5000 💻 www.bosf.org
A non-profit organisation serving the San Francisco Bay Area Bear community. Organiser of the annual International Bear Rendevous.

SWIMMING

-Seal Rock Beach (Enter El Camino del Mar at the west end of Geary street and go from P downhills)
-Black Sand Beach (Other side of the Golden Gate Bridge, go left under freeway, right on Outlook Rd, downhills, NU)
-San Gregorio beach 40 miles south of San Francisco, just north of San Gregorio „state beach". Hidden entrance. Access via dirt road.

CRUISING

-Around Collingwood Park (between 18th & 19th and Collingwood & Diamond, one block west of Castro St). Cruisy year round after bars closed at 2h.
-Ocean beach (between Dutch windmill on Fulton street and Murphy windmill on Lincoln Way)
-Lafayette Park (nights, around the tennis courts)
-Buena Vista Park
-Mission Dolores Park (Church Street at 20th) sunbathing, in Summer only.

San Jose ☎ 408

BARS

■ **Mac's Club** (B d GLM MA OS) 12-2h
39 Post Street *Between 1st & Market* ☎ (408) 288-8221 💻 www.macsclub.com
Friendly neighborhood gay bar.

■ **Renegades** (B F G MA OS) 12-2h
501 West Taylor Street *Cnr. Coleman Ave* ☏ (408) 275-9902
💻 www.renegadesbar.com
Leather/jeans cruise bar.

DANCECLUBS

■ **Brix** (B D G MA) Mon 21-2, Tue-Sat 18-2, Sun 16-2h
349 S. First St ☏ (408) 947-1975 💻 www.brixnightclub.com

■ **Splash** (B D G MA OS ST VS) Wed-Sat 21-2h, closed Sun & Mon
65 Post Street *At 1st* ☏ (916) 441-6823 💻 www.splashsj.com
Reopened in Spring 2010 under new ownership. Check www.splashsj.com for details.

SAUNAS/BATHS

■ **Watergarden** (AC CC DU FC FH G I m MA OS P PI RR SA SB SOL VS WH WO) Daily, 24hrs
1010 The Alameda/Atlas Street ☏ (408) 275-1215
💻 www.thewatergarden.com
Relaxed atmosphere. Membership and current photo I. D. required; one-time-membership available.

LEATHER & FETISH SHOPS

■ **Leather Masters** (CC F G) Tue-Sat 12-20h
969 Park Avenue *Just outside of downtown San Jose* ☏ (408) 293-7660
💻 www.leathermasters.com
One of the leading leather stores, in business for 20 year now. Manufactures its own line as well as wholesale. Second location: 3000 Main Sreet Dallas (Deep Ellum), TX 75226, Tel (214) 528-3865, Fax (214) 528-7881, opening times Tue-Sat 12-22h.

Santa Barbara ☏ 805

BARS

■ **Flavor @ The Wildcat Lounge** (AC B D GLM MA) Sun 21-2h
15 West Ortega Street ☏ (805) 962-7970 💻 www.wildcatlounge.com
Local DJs. Gogo dancers. Special events. No Cover. Hours and schedule vary. Call for info.

SWIMMING

-Cabrillo Beach (East of wharf)
-East Beach (NU)
-Padero Lane Beach (Summers AYOR)

Santa Cruz

CRUISING

-Beer Can Beach (AYOR)
-Bonney Doon Beach (8 miles North on Highway 1)

Sonoma ☏ 707

GUEST HOUSES

■ **Sonoma Chalet Bed & Breakfast**
(AC BF CC glm MA OS PK RWB RWS) All year
18935 Fifth Street West ☏ (707) 938-3129 💻 www.sonomachalet.com
Swiss-style farmhouse and country cottages in the wine country north of San Fransisco.

■ **Thistle Dew Inn** (AC BF glm MA PK RWB RWS RWT) All year
171 West Spain Street ☏ (707) 938-2909 💻 www.thistledew.com

Stockton ☏ 559

BARS

■ **Paradise** (AC B CC D GLM MA WE) 18-2, Sun 15-2h
10100 North Lower Sacramento Road ☏ (559) 477-4724
💻 paradisenightclub.net
Bar/lounge with dancefloor.

Upland ☏ 909

BARS

■ **Oasis** (B D G MA S SNU ST) 19-2, Sun 20-2h
1386 East Foothill Boulevard ☏ (909) 920-9590
💻 www.oasis-nightclub.com
Many special events take place here.

Vallejo ☏ 707

BARS

■ **Townhouse Cocktail Lounge** (B d glm MA ST VS)
401A Georgia Street ☏ (707) 553-9109
Long time running mixed bar with pool tables, sometimes dragshows. Happy Hour.

Ventura ☏ 805

BARS

■ **Paddy's** (B d GLM SNU) 14-2h
2 West Main Street ☏ (805) 652-1071
💻 www.paddysventura.com
Check www.paddysventura.com for events and specials.

CRUISING

-Bates Beach (between Ventura & Santa Barbara, AYOR)
-Emma Wood Street Beach

Victorville ☏ 619

BARS

■ **West Side 15** (B GLM MA) 16-2, Sun 14-2h
16868 Stoddard Wells Road *West side of Interstate 15*
☏ (619) 243-9600 💻 www.westside15.com

DANCECLUBS

■ **Ricky's** (AC B CC D GLM MA s) 12-24, Fri & Sat -2h
13728 Hesperia Rd ☏ (909) 996-4440
💻 www.rickysvictorville.com

Walnut Creek ☏ 925

BARS

■ **Club 1220** (B d GLM MA ST) 16-2h
1220 Pine Street ☏ (925) 938-4550
💻 www.club1220.com
Check www.club1220.com for events.

Colorado

Location: Western USA
Initials: CO
Time: GMT -7
Area: 269,618 km² / 110,274 sq mi.
Population: 4,301,261
Capital: Denver

Aspen ☏ 970

HOTELS

■ **Hotel Aspen** (B bf glm H PI RWS RWT) All year
110 West Main Street ☏ (970) 925-3441
💻 www.hotelaspen.com

■ **St. Moritz Lodge & Condominiums**
(AC cc glm H I MA OS PI PK RWB RWS RWT SA SB VA WH) All year
334 West Hyman Avenue *Near center* ☏ (970) 925-3220
💻 www.stmoritzlodge.com

Colorado Springs ☏ 719

BARS

Bijou Bar and Grill (B d GLM M MC)
Wed-Sat 15-2, Sun & Tue -24h
2510 East Bijou *Between Union and Circle* ☏ (719) 473-5718

Club Q (B CC D f G M MA OS S SNU) 18-2, Sat -4h, closed Mon
3430 North Academy Blvd ☏ (719) 570-1429
www.clubqonline.com
5 bars & restaurant.

Underground (B D G M MA) 16-2, Sun 14-2h
110 North Nevada Avenue *Cnr. Kiowa St* ☏ (719) 578-7771

MEN'S CLUBS

Buddies (B cc DR F G MA MSG P SNU VS)
15-4, Sun -2h, Mon & Tue private parties only
3430 Suite B North Academy Blvd ☏ (719) 591-7660
www.clubbuddies.com
Private men's club. Membership required.

CAFES

Dale Street (b glm M MA) 11-21h
115 East Dale Street ☏ (719) 578-9898
www.mydalestreetcafe.com

Denver ☏ 303

GAY INFO

Gay, Lesbian, Bisexual and Transgender Community Center of Colorado Mon-Fri 10-18h
1050 Broadway *Five blocks south of downtownls major intersection of Colfax and Broadway.* ☏ (303) 733-7743 www.glbtcolorado.org

PUBLICATIONS

Gayzette
☏ (720) 435-8914 www.gayzette.com
Denver's Favorite GLBT Publication!

Out Front Colorado (GLM MA)
827 Grant Street ☏ (303) 778-7900 www.outfrontcolorado.com
Published every other Wednesday. Colorado's No.1 gay publication.

BARS

Atrium. The (B d glm MA SNU) 7-2h
554 South Broadway ☏ (303) 744-1923

Barker Lounge (B G MA OS) 12-2h
225 South Broadway *At Byers* ☏ (303) 778-0545
www.barkerlounge.net

BJ's Carousel (AC B CC G M MC S SNU ST) 16-2, Sat-Mon 10-2h
1380 South Broadway Street *Arkansas & South Broadway*
☏ (303) 777-9880 www.bjsdenver.com
Brunch on Sun, SNU Tue, karaoke Wed, ST Fri & Sat.

Boyztown (B G I MA SNU) 15-2, Fri-Sun 12-2h
117 Broadway *Between 1st and 2nd Ave* ☏ (303) 777-9378

Broadways (B G MA) 14-2, Sat & Sun 12-2h
1027 Broadway ☏ (303) 623-0700
www.broadwaysdenver.com

Charlie's (B CC d G M MA OS S) 11-2h
900 East Colfax Avenue *On the hill at Colfax and Emerson*
☏ (303) 839-8890 www.charliesdenver.com
Two dancefloors: country/western and R'n'B/techno. Gay country-western and pop dance club.

Compound. The (AC B D G I MA OS VS) 7-2, dancing 21-2h
145 Broadway ☏ (303) 722-7977
www.compounddenver.com
One of the most favourite bars in Denver.

Denver Wrangler. The (B F G MA) 11-2h
1700 Logan Street ☏ (303) 837-1075 www.denverwrangler.com
Cruising bar for bears. Beer bust on Sun.

Eagle (B cc F G MA) 11-2h
3600 Blake Street *At Blake* ☏ (303) 291-0250
www.denvereagle.com
Levi, leather, cruise bar.

JR's (B GLM M MA S ST) 15-2h
777 East 17th Ave *At Clarkson* ☏ (303) 831-0459 www.myjrs.com

R&R Denver (AC B GLM m MA s WE)
Mon-Fri 15-2, Sat & Sun 11-2h
4958 East Colfax Avenue *At Elm St* ☏ (303) 320-9337

Swallows (AC B GLM M MA) 16-23h
3090 Downing Street *Cnr. 31st Street* ☏ (303) 832-5482
www.denverswallows.com

DANCECLUBS

Mo's (AC B D GLM YC) 15-2h
1037 Broadway ☏ (303) 235-8593
Daily Happy Hour from 15-20h.

Rumba. La (AC B D glm MA s) 21-2h
99 West 9th Ave *Near Broadway* ☏ (303) 572-8006
More gay on Fri.

Tracks (B D GLM MA SNU ST) Thu-Sat 21-2h
3500 Walnut Street *Between 35th and 36th* ☏ (303) 863-7326
www.tracksdenver.com
Ultramodern light and sound system, two dancefloors.

RESTAURANTS

Hamburger Mary's (AC B GLM M MA) 11-2, Sun 10-2h
700 East 17th Avenue ☏ (303) 832-1333
www.hamburgermarysdenver.com

SAUNAS/BATHS

CCC (Community Country Club) (AC CC DR DU FC FH G LAB m MA NU OS P S SA SB VS WH WO) 24hrs
2151 Lawrence Street *Between 21st and 22nd St* ☏ (303) 297-2601
www.thetriplec.com

Denver Swim Club
(AC cc DR DU FC FH G GH m MA NU OS P PI RR SB SL VS WH) 24hrs
6923 East Colfax Avenue *At Olive* ☏ (303) 322-4023
www.denverswimclub.com
Many special rooms. Free condoms and lube.

Midtowne Spa (AC AK CC DR DU FC FH G GH M MA NR NU OS P PK RR RWT S SA SB SL SNU VR VS WH) 24hrs
2935 Zuni Street ☏ (303) 458-8902 www.midtowne.com
Bath house with a sundeck, a dungeon RM, sling and more. Free condoms. 1st Tues of the month leather night, 2nd & 3rd Tues are Big Boys and Bears Nights. Wed 1/2 price regular Rms.

GIFT & PRIDE SHOPS

Heaven Sent Me (AC CC GLM MA WE)
Mon-Fri 11-21, Sat 10-20, Sun 11-18h
116 South Broadway ☏ (303) 733-9000 www.heavensentme.com
Gay gift items and rainbow merchandise.

LEATHER & FETISH SHOPS

CJ's Leather (CC F G) 11-17.30, Sat -17h, Sun closed
212 South Broadway ☏ (303) 733-6212 www.cjsleather.com

Fort Collins ☏ 970

BARS

Choice City Shots (B d GLM MA S) 17-24, Fri & Sat -2h
124 North LaPorte Ave *At College* ☏ (970) 221-4333
Happy hour 17-19h. Sun men's, Fri women's night.

Pueblo ☏ 719

BARS

Pirate's Cove (B d GLM MA) 14-2h, closed Mon
105 Central Plaza ☏ (719) 542-9624

Connecticut

Location: Northeast USA
Initials: CT
Time: GMT -5
Area: 14,358 km² / 5,872 sq mi.
Population: 3,405,565
Capital: Hartford

Danbury ☎ 203

BARS

■ **Triangles Café** (AC B CC D GLM MA OS S VS) 17-1, Fri & Sat -2h
66 Sugar Hollow Road *Route 7 south* ☎ (203) 798-6996
🖳 www.trianglescafe.com
Check www.trianglescafe.com for events!

Hartford ☎ 860

PUBLICATIONS

■ **Metroline** (GLM)
493 Farmington Avenue ☎ (203) 485-6045 🖳 www.metroline-online.com
Community biweekly news magazine.

BARS

■ **Chez Est Cafe** (AC D GLM MA OS S) Sun-Thu 15-1, Fri & Sat -2h
458 Wethersfield Avenue *At Main St* ☎ (860) 525-3243
🖳 www.chezest.com
Popular.

■ **Polo Club. The** (B d GLM MA S ST)
678 Maple Avenue ☎ (860) 278-3333 🖳 www.hartfordpoloclub.com
Dragshows, check www.hartfordpoloclub.com for calendar and events.

■ **Tisane** (AC B d glm MA) 7-1, Sat & Sun 8-1.30h
537 Farmington Avenue ☎ (860) 523-5417 🖳 mytisane.com
Coffee house and bar, gay on tuesday nights.

Manchester ☎ 860

GUEST HOUSES

■ **Mansion Inn. The** (AC BF CC glm H RWS RWT) All year
139 Hartford Road ☎ (860) 646-0453 🖳 www.themansioninnct.com

New Haven ☎ 203

GAY INFO

■ **The New Haven Pride Center** (GLM)
14 Gilbert Street ☎ (203) 387-2252 🖳 www.newhavenpridecenter.org

BARS

■ **Bar. The** (B d glm MA) 17-1h
254 Crown Street ☎ (203) 495-8924 🖳 www.barnightclub.com
More gay on Tue.

■ **Partners** (AC B CC D f GLM MC s VS) 17-1, Fri & Sat -2h
365 Crown Street *At Park St* ☎ (203) 776-1014 🖳 www.partnerscafe.com

DANCECLUBS

■ **Fucked up Fridays @ Center Street Lounge** (AC B CC D GLM MA S) Fri 22-1h
84 Orange Street *Entrance on Center Street* ☎ (203) 777-7264
🖳 www.myspace.com/cslnewhaven

■ **Gotham Citi Café** (B D G MA s) Sat 20-?h
130 Crown Street ☎ (203) 498-2484 🖳 www.gothamciticafe.com
Gay only on Sat, great dance floor, younger crowd.

RESTAURANTS

■ **168 York Street Café** (! B GLM M MA OS) 15-1h
168 York Street ☎ (203) 789-1915 🖳 www.168yorkstreetcafe.com
In the heart of Yale University, one of the oldest gay bars/restaurants in CT.

New London ☎ 860

BARS

■ **OíNeillís Brass Rail** (AC B CC G MA S) 11-1, Fri & Sat -2h
52 Bank Street ☎ (860) 443-6203 🖳 www.oneillsbrassrail.com
Restaurant/Cafe/Coffee-shop by day, Bar/Lounge/Club by night.

Waterbury ☎ 203

DANCECLUBS

■ **Twisted Wednesdays @ Kriola** (B D G MA) Wed
52 East Main Street ☎ (203) 597-7313

Delaware

Location: Northeast USA
Initials: DE
Time: GMT -5
Area: 6,448 km² / 2,637 sq mi.
Population: 783,600
Capital: Dover

Rehoboth Beach ☎ 302

GAY INFO

■ **Camp Rehoboth** (CC GLM MA OS) 9-17.30, Sat & Sun 10-16h
39 Baltimore Avenue ☎ (302) 227-5620
🖳 www.camprehoboth.com
Community center publishing a bi-weekly magazine.

BARS

■ **Double L** (B F G H MA OS) 16-2h
622 Rehoboth Avenue ☎ (302) 227-0818
🖳 www.doublelbar.net
Leather bar.

■ **Frogg Pond** (B glm M MA S) 11-1h
3 South First Street *Near Rehoboth Avenue* ☎ (302) 227-2234
🖳 www.thefroggpond.com

RESTAURANTS

■ **Back Porch Cafe** (B glm M MA) Seasonal
59 Rehoboth Avenue ☎ (302) 227-3674 🖳 www.backporchcafe.com
Lunch, dinner and Sun brunch.

■ **Blue Moon** (B glm M MA) 18-2, Sun brunch 10.30-14h
35 Baltimore Avenue ☎ (302) 227-6515
🖳 www.bluemoonrehoboth.com
Popular.

■ **Cloud 9** (B D GLM M MA) Thu-Sun 16-2h
234 Rehoboth Avenue ☎ (302) 226-1999
A fusion bistro with a creative menu. Also danceclub on WE 22h.

■ **Dos Locos** (AC B CC GLM M MA NR OS RES S VEG) 11.30-22, Fri & Sat -23h
208 Rehoboth Avenue *Between Baltimore & Rehoboth, across from Fire Company* ☎ (302) 227-3353 🖳 www.doslocos.com
Brings award winning Mexican, Seafood & Stonegrill dining to Rehoboth.

■ **La La Land** (B glm M MA OS) 18-1h, seasonal
22 Wilmington Avenue 302 ☎ (302) 227-3887
🖳 www.lalalandrestaurant.com
Great seafood.

■ **Purple Parrot Grille** (AC B glm m MA S ST)
247 Rehoboth Ave ☎ (302) 226-1139
Downstairs, The Purple Parrot restaurant offers seafood, upstairs, karaoke lovers sing away in The Birdcage. Tropical drinks, DJs and live music. Sunday night drag show.

LEATHER & FETISH SHOPS

■ **Leather Central** (F G MA) 10-22, Sun -19h
4284A Highway One ☎ (302) 227-0700 🖳 www.leathercentral.net

HOTELS

Rams Head Inn. The (AC BF CC G I M MA MSG NU PI PK RWB RWS RWT SA VA WH WO) All year
35006 Warrington Road *3 miles from Rehoboth Beach* ☎ (302) 226-9171
🖳 www.theramshead.com
Ten guestrooms. Men only.

GUEST HOUSES

Rehoboth Guest House (AC BF CC glm I MA OS PK RWS VA) All year
40 Maryland Avenue *Near the beach* ☎ (302) 227-4117
🖳 www.rehobothguesthouse.com
Ten double rooms, three kings and one queensroom, in 100-year-old renovated Victorian beach house.

Shore Inn at Rehoboth Beach (AC CC G MA MSG NU OS PI PK RWS RWT WH) Closed in Jan
703 Rehoboth Avenue *Opposite the Double L Bar* ☎ (302) 227-8487
🖳 www.shoreinn.com
All 15 rooms with private bath, refrigerator, tea/coffee making facilities, TV and phone. Also a separate cottage. Central location.

Silver Lake Guest House (
AC BF CC DU FH GLM I MA NR OS PK RES RWB RWS RWT WI) All year
20388 Silver Lake Drive *Near gay Poodle Beach* ☎ (302) 226-2115
🖳 www.silverlakeguesthouse.com
Thirteen double rooms, 2 apartments with kitchen, shower/bath/WC. All rooms with private bath, king or queen beds, cable LCD TV with DVD, AC, most with balcony.

SWIMMING

-Poodle Beach (at the end of Queen Street
-Cape Henlopen State Park (North Shores)

Wilmington ☎ 302

BARS

Crimson Moon Tavern (AC B CC D GLM S VS)
Tue-Fri 18-2, Sat 19-2h, closed Sun & Mon
1909 West 6th Street ☎ (302) 654-9099
🖳 www.crimsonmoonde.com
Video bar on 1st floor, dancing on 2nd floor.

District of Columbia

Location: East USA
Initials: DC
Time: GMT -5
Area: 177 km² / 72 sq mi.
Population: 529,000

Washington D.C. ☎ 202

PUBLICATIONS

Metro Weekly
1012 14th Street NW, Suite 209 ☎ (202) 638-6830
🖳 www.metroweekly.com
Gay and lesbian weekly distributed free every Thu throughout the DC Metropolitan area.

Washington Blade
☎ (202) 747-2077 🖳 www.washingtonblade.com
Gay and lesbian weekly distributed free every Friday throughout the DC Metropolitan area.

BARS

1409 Playbill Cafe (B GLM M MA S)
16-2, Fri & Sat -3, Sun 11-2h
1409 14th Street NW ☎ (202) 265-3055

Back Door (B d G MA) 17-2, Fri & Sat -3h
1104 8th Street SE, 2nd Floor. Capitol Hill ☎ (202) 546-5979

Black Fox (B CC GLM M MA) Sun-Wed 16-22, Thu-Sat 17-24h
1723 Connecticut Avenue NW *Dupont Circle* ☎ (202) 265-0030
🖳 www.blackfoxlounge.com

D. I. K. Bar (B GLM M MA) 16-2h
1633 17th Street, NW *Upstairs* ☎ (202) 328-0100
The bar at the Dupont Italian Kitchen. Ask the bartender for the daily drink special.

DC Eagle (! B F G MA) 16-2, Fri & Sat -3, Sun 14-2h
639 New York Avenue NW *Two blocks north of Gallery Place metro station*
☎ (202) 347-6025 🖳 www.dceagle.com
Huge and popular bar.

Fab Lounge (B d gLm MA) 17-?h
1805 Connecticut Ave ☎ (202) 797-1122 🖳 www.thefablounge.com

Fireplace. The (B G MA VS) 13-2, Fri & Sat -3h
2161 P Street NW ☎ (202) 293-1293 🖳 www.fireplacedc.com
Affordable drinks and loud music. Mainly Afro-American men.

Green Lantern (B d G MA VS) 16-2, Fri & Sat -3, Sun 13-2h
1335 Green Court NW *Downtown, at the end of an alley at 1335 L Street*
☎ (202) 347-4533 🖳 greenlanterndc.com
Video bar on 2 floors, regular theme nights.

J. R.'s Bar & Grill (! AC B CC f G M MA VS)
Mon-Thu 14-2, Fri 14-3, Sat 12-3, Sun 12-2h
1519 17th Street NW *In the heart of gay district* ☎ (202) 328-0090
Very popular gay bar. Mixed crowd, but tends to young & hunky. Friendly staff.

Larry's Lounge (B glm M MA) 16-1, Fri & Sat -2h
1840 18th Street NW *At T Street* ☎ (202) 483-1483
🖳 www.straitsofmalaya.com

Mova (AC B GLM MA) 17-?h
1435 P Street NW ☎ (202) 797-9730 🖳 www.movalounge.com

Nellie's Sports Bar (B GLM MA OS)
Mon-Thu 17-24, Fri -2, Sat 11-2, Sun -24h
900 U Street NW *M° Green Line U St/ Shaw* ☎ (202) 332-6355
🖳 www.nelliessportsbar.com

Omega DC (AC B G MA S SL SNU ST VR VS WI)
Mon-Thur16-2, Fri 16-3, Sat 20-3, Sun 19-2h
2122 P Street NW *At the rear* ☎ (202) 223-4917 🖳 www.omegadc.com
In the heart of Washington's Dupont Circle. Shirtless men drink free on Wed from 10-11 pm. Pool tournaments Wed and Sat. Men of Omega perform Tues, Wed, Fri and Sat.

Remington's (AC B CC d F GLM I MA S VS) 16-2, Fri & Sat -3h
639 Pennsylvania Avenue South East *M° Eastern Market*
☎ (202) 543-3113 🖳 www.remingtonswdc.com
Regular events, country & western style. Also dance lessons Mon & Wed.

Ziegfeld's / Secrets (AC B d G MA r S SNU ST t WE)
Wed, Thu & Sun 21-2; Fri & Sat -3h; closed Mon & Tue
1824 Half Street SW *No nearby public transport. Take a taxi*
☎ (202) 863-0670 🖳 www.secretsdc.com
The only bar in DC with completely nude male dancers! This place is hot, the guys are multi-national and gorgeous. Hot stripper amateur contests last Wed/month with cash prizes.

DANCECLUBS

Bachelor's Mill (B D G MA s) 17-2, Fri & Sat -3h
1104 8th Street South East *Capitol Hill* ☎ (202) 544-1931
🖳 www.thebachelorsmill.com
Afro-American clientele. Upstairs is a smaller bar with pool tables and video games.

Club Fuego (B D GLM MA S SNU ST) Fri 22.30-3h
1818 New York Ave 🖳 www.clubfuegodc.com
Latin pop.

Cobalt (! AC B D GLM MA S) 17-2, Fri & Sat -3h
1639 R Street NW *Cnr. 17th St* ☎ (202) 462-6569
🖳 www.cobaltdc.com
Very popular, lounge bar & danceclub on 2 levels, located in the heart of Dupont Circle. Exciting place!

Delta Elite (B D G WE) Fri & Sat 23-?h
3734 10th Street NE, Brookland ☎ (202) 529-0626
🖳 www.thedeltaelite.com

■ **Town Danceboutique** (AC B cc D G MA OS ST VS)
21-4, admission -2.30, alcohol service -2.45h
2009 8th Street NM *At the corner of 8th and U Streets NW*
☎ (202) 234-8696 🖳 www.towndc.com
Combination of cabaret performance place, plush lounge and high energy dance club on two floors. Top DJs, fair prices, a must at weekends. Credit cards accepted only for admission.

RESTAURANTS

■ **Annie's** (AC B GLM MA) Extended weekend hours
1609 17th Street NW *In the heart of gay district* ☎ (020) 232-0395
Enclosed patio for people watching.

■ **Café Berlin** (AC B CC DM glm M MA OS)
11.30-22, Fri & Sat -23, Sun 16-22h
322 Massachusetts Avenue, North East *Capitol Hill, three blocks east of Union Station* ☎ (202) 543-7656 🖳 www.CafeBerlinDC.com
German and continental cuisine. Patio dining in season.

■ **Café Luna** (b GLM M MA) 10-23, Fri & Sat -24h
1633 P Street NW ☎ (202) 387-4005 🖳 www.skewers-cafeluna.com

SEX SHOPS/BLUE MOVIES

■ **Pleasure Place** (AC GLM MA) 10-22, Wed-Sat -24, Sun 12-19h
1063 Wisconsin Avenue NW ☎ (202) 333-8570
🖳 pleasureplace.com
Erotic boutique, leather, fetish wear, toys, condoms, etc.

SAUNAS/BATHS

■ **Crew Club. The** (CC DU FC G m P RR SA SB SOL WO) 24hrs
1321 14th Street NW *Metro-rail Red Line -Dupont Circle/Blue or Orange Line -McPherson Square* ☎ (202) 319-1333 🖳 www.crewclub.net
Alcohol and drug free. ID required. Popular on Tue.

■ **Glorious Health Club** (DR DU G GH MC OS SA SB VS WO) 24hrs
2120 West Virginia Ave NE *Just off New York Ave, next to Shell gas station*
☎ (202) 269-0226

FITNESS STUDIOS

■ **VIDA Fitness** (AC glm MA) Mon-Fri 5-23, Sat & Sun 7-21h
1517 15th Street NW ☎ (202) 588-5559 🖳 www.vidafitness.com
Day and week passes available.

BOOK SHOPS

■ **G Books** (CC G) 16-22, Fri & Sat -23h
1520 U Street NW, lower level *Near M° Dupont Circle*
☎ (202) 986-9697
Used and new gay men's books, magazines, movies, gear, gifts & pride.

LEATHER & FETISH SHOPS

■ **Leather Rack. The** (F G) 11-23, Fri & Sat -24, Sun -20h
1723 Connecticut Avenue NW *M° Dupont Circle* ☎ (202) 797-7401
🖳 www.leatherrack.com
Leather accessories, cards, and T-shirts designed exclusively for gay men.

HOTELS

Carlyle Suites Hotel (AC B BF CC glm)
1731 New Hampshire Avenue NW *Dupont Circle* ☎ (202) 234-3200
www.carlylesuites.com
Each studio custom designed, combining art-deco finishes with modern amenities.

GUEST HOUSES

B&B at The William Lewis House (AC BF CC G PK WH)
All year
1309 R Street NW *Close to 17th Street & Dupont Circle* ☎ (202) 462-7574
☎ (800) 465-7574 www.wlewishous.com
This friendly gay guesthouse is conveniently located close to the gay scene and touristic venues. Ten beautifully Edwardian-style furnished rooms with shared bath.

Dupont at the Circle (BF glm I M MA OS)
1604 19th Street NW *At Dupont Circle* ☎ (202) 332-5251
www.dupontatthecircle.com

FETISH GROUPS

DC Bear Club (F G) Meetings 2nd Sun/month 16h, at Green Lantern
PO Box 75273 ☎ (301) 277-0664 www.dcbearclub.org

DC Boys of Leather (F G)
c/o The DC Eagle, 639 New York Avenue NW
www.dcboysofleather.org
Check out www.dcboysofleather.org for special events.

HEALTH GROUPS

Whitman-Walker Clinic
1701 14th Street NW ☎ (202) 745-7000 www.wwc.org
Non-profit community-based health organization for GLBT, with an emphasis on HIV/AIDS.

Florida

Location: Southeast USA
Initials: FL
Time: GMT -5
Area: 170.314 km² / 69.658 sq mi.
Population: 15,982,378
Capital: Tallahassee
Important gay cities: Fort Lauderdale, Key West, Miami, Miami Beach, Orlando, St. Petersburg, Tampa

Clearwater ☎ 727

BARS

Pro Shop Pub (AC B CC G MA OS) 13-2h
840 Cleveland Street ☎ (727) 447-4259 www.proshoppub.us

Dade City ☎ 352

CAMPING

Sawmill Camping Resort (AC B cc d GLM I m MA MSG NU P PA PI s VA VS WE) All year
21710 US Highway 98 *45 mins north of Tampa, 1h west of Orlando*
☎ (352) 583-0664 www.flsawmill.com
Gay camping resort on 100 acres with nature trails, large wooded RV, cabins and tent sites.

Daytona Beach ☎ 386

GUEST HOUSES

Villa. The (AC CC glm I MA MSG NU OS PI PK RWB RWS RWT WH)
All year, 9-21h
801 North Peninsula Drive *1h drive to St. Augustine, Orlando, Space Coast*
☎ (386) 248-2020 www.thevillabb.com
All rooms with TV, tub/shower. Historical Spanish mansion. Continental breakfast, newspaper, TV-Lounge, complimentary coffee & soft drinks, non-smoking.

Fort Lauderdale ☎ 954

Ft. Lauderdale has become a gay-vacation Mecca. It is home to a large gay community, the local government is gay-friendly and a growing number of businesses cater to gay tourists. There is also a good selection of tourist attractions. Fort Lauderdale is one of the most popular departure ports for the many cruise ships, popular with gay couples. Ft. Lauderdale is a less-intimidating kind of gay destination, more popular with mature gay men. With over 37 km of wide, sandy beaches it is the perfect beach holiday location for sunbathing, swimming, fishing and snorkelling.

Each year Fort Lauderdale is home to the largest gay Pride Festival in Florida, that side of The Atlantic. The Stonewall Street Festival is a smaller Pride event occurring each summer, just to mention two of the many events taking place here. See our extensive list of gay events at the back of this guide.

Ft. Lauderdale ist zu so etwas wie einem schwulen Urlaubsmekka geworden. Die hier ansässige Schwulengemeinde ist umfangreich, die Lokalverwaltung schwulenfreundlich und eine wachsende Anzahl von Unternehmen vermarktet spezielle Angebote an schwule Touristen. Aber die Stadt hat auch eine gute Auswahl an Sehenswürdigkeiten zu bieten. Fort Lauderdale ist einer der populärsten Abreisehäfen für die unzähligen, auch bei schwulen Paaren sehr beliebten Kreuzfahrten, gleichzeitig aber nicht so einschüchternd wie viele andere schwule Reiseziele, weshalb es auch eher reifere schwule Männer hierher zieht. Mit seinen breiten Sandstränden, die sich insgesamt über mehr als 37 km erstrecken, bietet Ft. Lauderdale einen idealen Ort zum Sonnenbaden, Schwimmen, Fischen oder Schnorcheln.

In Ft. Lauderdale findet nicht nur alljährlich Floridas größtes CSD-Festival an dieser Seite der Atlantikküste statt, sondern auch noch jeden Sommer eine kleinere CSD-Veranstaltung namens Stonewall Street Festival, um nur zwei der vielen lokalen Events zu erwähnen. Siehe auch unsere ausgiebige Liste schwuler Veranstaltungen am Ende dieses Reiseführers.

Ft. Lauderdale est quasiment devenue une Mecque gay. La communauté locale est forte, l'administration locale positive envers les gays et un nombre croissant d'entreprises proposent des offres dédiées aux touristes gays. Mais la ville offre bien d'autres curiosités touristiques. Fort Lauderdale est un des plus grands ports de départ de nombreuses croisières, très appréciées par les couples gays aussi, et en même temps elle est moins intimidante que d'autres destinations gays, ce qui attire une clientèle d'hommes plus mûrs. Avec ses larges plages de sable qui s'étalent sur 37km, Ft. Lauderdale est un lieu idéal pour les bains de soleil, la natation, pêche et plongée.
A Ft. Lauderdale se déroule tous les ans non seulement la plus grande gay pride de la côte atlantique mais aussi chaque été une plus petite manifestation, le Stonewall Street Festival, pour ne nommer que deux. Jetez un oeil à la longue liste des manifestations gays en fin de guide.

Ft. Lauderdale se ha convertido en la meca del turismo gay, con un gran número de asociaciones, eventos locales y una creciente oferta destinada exclusivamente al turismo gay. Pero la ciudad ofrece también numerosos lugares de interés turístico. Fort Lauderdale es uno de los puertos de escala más populares para innumerables cruceros, una de las ofertas de viaje preferidas por parejas gays, pero a su vez no tan intimidante y/o palpitante como otras ciudades. Es por esto que es uno de los destinos favoritos entre hombres de más edad. Ft. Lauderdale ofrece, con sus increíbles playas de arena de más de 37 km de extensión, un lugar ideal para la nadar, tomar el sol, pescar o bucear en sus cristalinas aguas.
En Ft. Lauderdale tiene lugar cada año no sólo el festival del día del orgullo gay más grande de Florida, sino también un pequeño evento del orgullo gay cada verano llamado Stonewall Street Festival, por nombrar algunos de los eventos locales. No deje de consultar nuestra amplia lista de eventos gays al final de esta guía de viajes.

Fort Lauderdale è diventata una specie di mecca turistica gay. La comunità gay locale è molto grande, l'amministrazione locale è molto gay-friendly e una quantità sempre più crescente di imprese mette sul mercato offerte mirate ai turisti gay. La città ha anche molto da offrire dal punto di vista delle attrazioni turistiche. Fort Lauderdale è uno dei porti più popolari per varie crociere, amate molto anche da coppie gay di una certa età.
Con le sue larghe spiagge che si estendono su più di 37 km di costa, Fort Lauderdale si presta a luogo ideale per prendere il sole, per nuotare, per pescare e per ammirare i fondali con maschera e pinne. A Fort Lauderdale non si svolge solo il più grande Christopher Street Day di questa parte della costa atlantica, bensì anche il ‚Stonewall Street Festival', una manifestazione un po' più piccola nell'ambito del Christopher Street Day, che si svolge ogni estate. Per ulteriori informazioni circa altri eventi locali, vi preghiamo di consultare la lista degli appuntamenti gay sulle ultime pagine di questa guida.

INTERNATIONAL ORGANISATIONS

IGLTA
1201 NE 26th Street, Ste. 103 ☎ +1 (954) 630-1637 www.lgbt.travel
International Gay and Lesbian Travel Association is an international network of travel industry business and professionals dedicated to the support of its members who have joined together to encourage gay travel throughout the world. IGLTA is committed to the welfare of gay and lesbian travelers, and to »shrinking the gay globe«. Spartacus is a proud member of IGLTA.

GAY INFO

Gay Lesbian Community Center of South Florida (AC GLM MA) Mon-Fri 10-22, Sat & Sun 12-17h
2040 North Dixie Hwy, Wilton Manors ☎ (954) 463-9005
www.glccsf.org

Greater Fort Lauderdale Convention & Visitors Bureau
100 East Broward Boulevard, Suite 200 ☎ (954) 765-4466
www.sunny.org
A great website with local information in English, German, Spanish, French and Italian.

South Florida Fun
www.southFLORIDAfun.com
Information on places to stay and things to do in South Florida.

PUBLICATIONS

David
1650 NE 26th Street #206, Wilton Manors ☎ (954) 251-0016
www.davidmagazineflorida.com
Free monthly magazine.

South Florida Gay News
2520 North Dixie Highway, Wilton Manors ☎ (954) 530-4970
www.southfloridagaynews.com
All the news for your life and your style. Published every Friday.

BARS

Bill's Filling Station (AC B G MA) 14-2h
2209 Wilton Drive *Across the Street from Alibi* ☎ (954) 567-5978
www.billsfillingstation.com
Gay Bar/Nightclub, Bears, Burgers, Tacos & More, Drink Specials, Friendly Staff, Piano Lounge, Special Events Stage, Drag Shows. No Cover Charge, Extremely Popular Fridays.

Boardwalk (AC B CC G M MA OS S SNU) 15-2, Fri & Sat -3h
1721 North Andrews Avenue *Four blocks from wilton drive*
☎ (954) 463-6969 www.boardwalkbarxxx.com
Male strippers' bar and full latenight restaurant, ID required, only for 18+ years.

Corner Pub (AC B GLM I M MA) 11-2, Fri & Sat -3h
1915 North Andrews Avenue, Wilton Manors ☎ (954) 564-7335
www.cornerpubbar.com

Cozmos (AC B D G MA S) 15-2h
2674 East Oakland Park Boulevard ☎ (954) 235-0000
www.cozmoslounge.com

Cubby Hole (AC B CC F G I M MA) 11-2, Fri & Sat -3h
823 North Federal Highway ☎ (954) 728-9001
www.thecubbyhole.com
Bar for bears and butch men.

Depot Cabana Bar and Grill. The (B d G I M MA PI VS) 14-2, Fri & Sat -3h
2935 North Federal Hwy ☎ (954) 537-7076 www.thedepotbar.com

Georgie's Alibi (! AC B GLM MA OS) 11-2, Fri & Sat -3h
2266 Wilton Drive, Wilton Manors *At NE 4th Ave* ☎ (954) 565-2526
www.georgiesalibi.com
A friendly bar with pretty whacky events.

Hombre (AC B f G MA) 16-2, Fri & Sat -3h
2500 Oakland Park Boulevard, Oakland Park ☎ (954) 380-4140
www.hombrebar.com
Happy hour 17-20h.

J's (AC B D GLM MA) 21-2, Fri & Sat -3, Sun 12-2h
2780 Davie Boulevard ☎ (954) 581-8400
www.myspace.com/jsbar

Johnny's (AC B CC D G m MA SNU) 15-2, Fri & Sat -3h
1116 West Broward Boulevard *Downtown* ☎ (954) 522-5931
www.johnnysbarfl.com
Stripper bar, no cover charge on weekdays.

Matty's on the Drive (B G MA VS) 11-2, Fri & Sat -3h
2426 Wilton Drive, Wilton Manors ☎ (954) 564-1799
www.mattysonthedrive.com

Monas (AC B G MA) 12-2, Fri & Sat -3h
525 East Sunrise Boulevard ☎ (954) 525-6662 www.monasbar.com

Monkey Business (AC B GLM MA S) 8-2h
2740 N Andrews Ave, Wilton Manors ☎ (954) 514‑7819
monkeybusinessbar.com
Cabaret and karaoke.

Naked Grape Wine Bar. The (AC b GLM MA)
2039 Wilton Drive, Wilton Manors ☎ (954) 563-5631
www.nakedgrapewinebar.com

Oakland Park Blvd.
NE 26th St.
Wilton Dr.
Mills Pond Park
N Andrews Av.
NE 15th St.
Federal Way
Bayview Dr.
NE 13 Str.
NE 4th Av.
Sunrise Blvd.
Holiday Park
NE 3rd Ave
NE 6th Ave
Broward Blvd.
Las Olas Blvd.
See map B
SE 3rd Ave
Davie Blvd
SW 12th St.
Andrews Av.
SE 17th St.
15th Ave
Seabreeze Blvd.
SW 24th St.
Secret Woods Nature Center
A
Terramar St.
Granada St.
S Ocean Blvd.
VALENCIA ST
B
N
Fort Lauderdale – Map B
ACCOMMODATION
Alcazar Resort – Guest House 7
Coconut Cove – Guest House 13
Flamingo Inn Amongst the Flowers. The – Hotel 1
Grand Resort. The – Hotel 11
Palm Plaza Resort – Hotel 10
Villa Venice Resort – Hotel 6
Windamar Beach Resort – Guest House 8
Worthington. The – Guest House 9
Fort Lauderdale – Map A
EAT & DRINK
Bill's Filling Station – Bar 6
Boardwalk – Bar 9
Cubby Hole – Bar 15
Johnny's – Bar 20
Ramrod – Bar 11
Scandals – Bar 5
Smarty Pants – Bar 2
Stable – Bar 7
Tropics – Restaurant 8
NIGHTLIFE
Babylon T Dance @ The Voodoo Lounge – Danceclub 19
Manor. The – Danceclub 16
Slammer Club – Men's Club 22
SEX
Club. The – Sauna 21
Clubhouse II. The – Sauna 1
Tropixxx Video – Sex Shop/Blue Movies 12
ACCOMMODATION
Cabanas. The – Guest House 4
Coral Reef – Guest House 13
Inn Leather – Guest House 18
Pineapple Point – Guest House 17
Schubert Resort – Guest House 23
OTHERS
Gay Lesbian Community Center of South Florida – Gay Info 10

■ **Ramrod** (AC B d F G MC OS SNU VS) 15-2h
1508 North East 4th Avenue ☎ (954) 763-8219
🖳 www.ramrodbar.com
Dress code (levis, leather and uniform) after dark. Happy hour daily 15-21h. Very popular.
■ **Scandals** (B D f G MC OS) 12-2, Fri & Sat -3h
3073 NE 6th Ave, Wilton Manors *One block south of Oakland Park Blvd*
☎ (954) 567-2432 🖳 www.scandalsfla.com
Country Western bar.
■ **Sidelines Sportsbar** (B G MC) 14-2, Sat & Sun 12-2h
2031 Wilton Drive, Wilton Manors ☎ (954) 563-8001
🖳 www.sidelinessports.com
■ **Smarty Pants** (AC B CC G m MA S t VS) 9-2, Sat -3, Sun 12-2h
3038 North Federal Highway *SE cnr. of Oakland Park Blvd & Federal Hwy*
☎ (954) 629-5892 🖳 smartypantsbar.com
Small intimite neighbourhood gay bar, one of the oldest bars in Fort Lauderdale.
■ **Stable Bar. The** (B F G MA) 14-2h
205 East Oakland Boulevard *Cnr. Andrews Avenue* ☎ (954) 565-4506
🖳 www.scandalsfla.com
Leather/Levi.
■ **Torpedo** (B CC D G MA SNU) 0-4h
2829 West Broward Blvd ☎ (954) 587-2500 🖳 www.torpedobar.com

MEN'S CLUBS

■ **Fort Lauderdale Eagle** (AC AK B DR F G MA MSG OS P SL) 21-5, Sun 19-5h, closed Mon & Tue
1208 NE 4th Avenue ☎ (954) 427-2443 🖳 www.ftleagle.com
■ **Slammer Club** (! AC B DR F G MA NU OS P VS)
Mon-Fri 20-?, Sat & Sun 18-?h
321 W Sunrise Blvd ☎ (954) 524-2625 🖳 www.slammerclub.com
Dark, Sleazy, and HOT! Dress code: Leather, uniforms, jockstraps. BYOB bar. Also sales of accessoires. See www.slammerclub.com for more information.

CAFES

■ **Java Boys** (B CC GLM I M MA) 8-24h
2230 Wilton Drive, Wilton Manors ☎ (954) 564-8828

DANCECLUBS

■ **Babylon T Dance @ The Voodoo Lounge** (B D G MA t)
Sun 17-23h
111 SW 2nd Ave 🖳 www.garysantis.com
Gay T-Dance. 3 dancefloors and lounge. Free drinks 18-20h.
■ **Boom** (! B cc D GLM MC S VS) Sun-Thu 16-2, Fri & Sat -3h
2232 Wilton Drive, Wilton Manors ☎ (954) 630 3556
Popular danceclub on two floors with two bars, billard and music-videos. Daily happy hour 2-4-1 Mon-Sat 16-21, Sun 16-18h.
■ **Living Room** (AC B G MC)
300 SW 1st Avenue *On second level of Las Olas Riverfront Complex*
☎ (888) 992-7555 🖳 www.livingroomnightclub.com
Gay night on Friday.
■ **The Manor** (AC B CC D G MC PK S WE)
2345 Wilton Drive, Wilton Manors ☎ (954) 626-0082
🖳 www.themanorcomplex.com
A new gay entertainment complex with danceclub, bar and restaurant.

RESTAURANTS

■ **Courtyard Cafe** (AC GLM M MA OS) 7-23, Thu 7-Sun 3h
2211 Wilton Drive, Wilton Manors *NE 4th Avenue* ☎ (954) 563-2499
🖳 www.wiltonmanorscourtyardcafe.com
■ **Galanga** (B glm M MA)
2389 Wilton Drive, Wilton Manors ☎ (954) 202-0000
🖳 www.galangarestaurant.com
Thai cuisine at its best!
■ **Hi-Life Cafe** (AC glm MA NR PK RES VEG WL)
17.30-23h, closed Mon
3000 N Federal Hwy, #12 *In Plaza 3000* ☎ (954) 563-1395
🖳 www.hilifecafe.com
Romantic, affordable, fine dining.
■ **Humpy's** (GLM M MA) 11.30-22, Thu-Sat -2h
2244 Wilton Drive, Wilton Manors ☎ (954) 566-2722
🖳 www.humpyspizza.com
Pizza & panini.
■ **Lips** (AC B CC GLM M MA PK ST) Tue-Sun 18-?h, Sun 11-?h
1421 East Oak Park Boulevard, Oakland Park ☎ (954) 567-0987
🖳 www.floridalips.com
Dining with drag performances every hour, bitchy bingo on Wednesday, brunch on Sunday.
■ **Rosies Bar & Grill** (B d GLM M MA) 11-23, Fri & Sat -24h
2449 Wilton Drive, Wilton Manors ☎ (954) 567-1320
🖳 www.rosiesbarandgrill.com
■ **Sage Café** (b g M MC) Mon-Sat 11-23, Sun 11-22h
2378 N Federal Hwy ☎ (954) 565-2299 🖳 www.sagecafe.net
Superb country French cuisine at reasonable prices in a casual French bistro ambiance.
■ **Tropics** (B GLM M OS S) 17.30-22.30, Fri & Sat -23h
2004 Wilton Drive, Wilton Manors *NE 4th Avenue* ☎ (954) 537-6000
🖳 www.tropicsftl.com
Restaurant, piano bar & cabaret.

SEX SHOPS/BLUE MOVIES

■ **Tropixxx Video** (G VS)
1514 NE 4th Avenue ☎ (954) 522-5988 🖳 www.tvxusa.com

SAUNAS/BATHS

■ **Club. The** (! AC b CC DU FC FH G m MA OS p PI SA SB SOL VS WH WO) 24hrs
110 NW 5th Avenue ☎ (954) 525-3344 🖳 www.the-clubs.com
THE CLUBS is a national chain of private membership clubs and for that reason you must purchase a membership card in order to use the facilities.
■ **Clubhouse II. The** (B DR DU f FC FH G MC P SA SB VS WH WO) 24hrs
2650 East Oakland Park Blvd ☎ (954) 566-6750
🖳 www.clubhouse2.com
Tue night is leather night. Super friendly staff. Very little attitude. Even in the morning/afternoon it is busy. Might even be a waiting list for rooms at night.

FITNESS STUDIOS

■ **Island City Health & Fitness** (AC g MA WO) 5-23, Sat & Sun 8-20h
2270 Wilton Drive, Wilton Manors ☎ (954) 318-3900
🖳 www.islandcityfitness.com
Guest membership available.

FASHION SHOPS

■ **M4M Outlet** (cc f G) 12-19, Fri & Sat -20h
1212 NE 4th Avenue ☎ (954) 522-1362

GIFT & PRIDE SHOPS

■ **Gaymart** (G) 10-23h
2240 Wilton Drive ☎ (954) 630-0360
■ **Pride Factory** (AC CC GLM MA PK SH W) 10-21, Sun 11-19h
850 NE 13th Street ☎ (954) 463-6600 🖳 www.pridefactory.com
Pride Factory brings you clothing, swim and underwear, novelty gifts, rainbow gear, gay/lesbian interest films, music, jewelry and greeting cards as well as adult toys and DVDs.

LEATHER & FETISH SHOPS

■ **Leather Werks** (AC CC F G) Mon-Sat 11-20, Sun 12-18h
1226 NE 4th Avenue ☎ (954) 761-1236 🖳 www.leatherwerks.com
The South East's largest leather shop. In house tailor. Huge selection of Wesco and other boots.

TRAVEL AND TRANSPORT

■ **Rainbow Alliance** (G) Mon-Fri 10-16h
1628 North Federal Highway, Ste 200 ☎ (954) 258-9915
🖳 www.southfloridafun.com

GUEST HOUSES

Alcazar Resort (AC BF G I NU PI PK RWB RWS RWT VA WH) All year
543-555 North Birch Road *Fort Lauderdale beach* ☎ (954) 563-6819
alcazarresort.com
All male resort, clothing optional, just steps to beach, 2 pools and one hot tub. Guests of the Alcazar & Worthington share the same outdoor amenities, including two clothing optional heated pools and hot tub, which are open 24 hours for your enjoyment.

Cabanas. The (AC bf G I MA OS PI RWS RWT VA) All year
2209 NE 26th Street, Wilton Manors ☎ (954) 564-7764
www.TheCabanasGuesthouse.com

Cheston House (AC BF CC G I MA NU OS PA PI PK RWS RWT VA) All year
520 North Birch Road *On the beach* ☎ (954) 566-7950
www.ChestonHouse.com
An all male resort offering a sun drenched clothing optional heated pool, spacious rooms, suites and apartments, fine amenities and the friendliest staff on Ft. Lauderdale Beach.

Coconut Cove (AC bf CC G I MA OS PI PK RWS RWT VA WH) All year
3012 Granada Street ☎ (954) 523-3226
www.coconutcoveguesthouse.com

Coral Reef (AC BF CC G I NU PI PK RWS RWT VA WH WO)
All year, office 8-20h
2609 North East 13th Court *Coral Ridge* ☎ (954) 568-0292
☎ (888) 354-6948 (toll free) www.coralreefguesthouse.com

Flamingo Resort. The (AC bf CC G MA MSG NU OS PI PK RWS RWT VA WI) All year
2727 Terramar Street ☎ (954) 561-4658 ☎ 286-8218 (toll free)
www.TheFlamingoResort.com
The romatic hotel is proud of its reputation as one of the leading luxury gay hotels, completely renovated. The Flamingo is a European-style intimate boutique hotel.

Granada Inn (AC BF glm MC OS PI) All year
3011 Granada Street *Next door to La Casa Del Mar* ☎ (954) 463-2032
www.granadainn.net
A charming B&B with access to La Casa Del Mar next door (same owners). Ask about the New Owners Specials!

Grand Resort and Spa. The (AC bf CC G I MA MSG NU OS PI PK RWS RWT WH WO) All year
539 North Birch Road *On Ft. Lauderdale Beach, two blocks from the ocean*
☎ (954) 630-3000 ☎ (800) 818-1211 www.grandresort.net
Fort Lauderdale's largest men's hotel, just steps to the beach with oversized pool, clothing-optional jacuzzi, ocean view sundeck and fitness center. Spacious accommodation with king sized beds, full entertainment high speed T-1 access and more.

Inn Leather (AC CC F G I MA NU P PA PI PK RWS RWT SA VA WE WH) All year
610 South East 19th Street *Near airport & downtown* ☎ (954) 467-1444
www.InnLeather.com
Designed by leathermen for leathermen. Have hosted the International Leather & Levi Community since 1999. Clothing-optional, all male compound. Also apartments. Visitors may purchase a day pass to use the pool/hot tub and grounds between 10-18h.

Lambton Court Apartment Motel
(AC bf CC g MA OS PI PK RWS RWT VA) 24hrs
840 NE 17th Terrace ☎ (954) 462-3977

Manor Inn (AC B BF CC G I MC PI PK RWS RWT VA WH) All year
2408 NE 6th Avenue, Wilton Manors ☎ (954) 566-8223
www.wiltonmanorsinn.com

Mary's Resort (AC CC GLM I MA OS PA PI PK RWB RWS RWT VA WH) All year
1115 Tequesta Street *Downtown, close to everything* ☎ (954) 523-3500
www.marysresort.com
Now allowing women guests and are hetero-friendly. No longer clothing optional.

Palm Plaza Resort (AC bf CC G I m MA PI PK RWB RWS RWT VA WO) All year
2801 Rio Mar Street *Near gay beach* ☎ (954) 260-6568
www.palmplazaresort.com

■ **Pineapple Point**
(AC BF G I MA MSG NU OS PI PK RWB RWS RWT VA WH WO) All year
315 North East 16th Terrace ☎ (954) 527-0094
🖳 www.pineapplepoint.com
With 26 rooms and suites, the property has been restored to maintain the original splendour of the 1930's architecture. Lush gardens. A men-only resort.

■ **Royal Palms Resort** (AC B CC G I MA MSG NU OS PI PK RWB RWS RWT VA WH) All year
717 Breakers Avenue *On the beach* ☎ (954) 564-6444
🖳 www.royalpalms.com
New opened gay resort in 2011 next to the old Royal Palms. New management.

■ **Schubert Resort**
(AC bf CC G I MA NU OS PI PK RWS RWT VA WH) All year
855 NE 20th Avenue *Victoria Park* ☎ (954) 763-7434
☎ (866) 763-7435 🖳 www.schubertresort.com
31 deluxe suites designed for the sophisticated traveler who demands space and comfort. All non-smoking. Wet bar with refrigerator, microwave, sink and coffee maker.

■ **Sea Grape House Inn & Cabanas** (AC CC G I NU OS PI PK RWT SA VS WH) All year
1109 NE 16th Place *Four blocks from Wilton Drive, 20 mins to airport*
☎ (954) 525-6586 🖳 www.seagrape.com
Male only inn with 6 rooms.

■ **Soberano Resort La Casa Del Mar**
(AC bf CC GLM I M MA OS PI PK RWS RWT VA) All year
3003 Granada Street *Fort Lauderdale Beach* ☎ (954) 467-2037
🖳 www.lacasadelmar.com
A charming two-storey Mediterranean villa. Guest accommodations include an Internet café and high-speed wireless connections. 16 theme rooms, all with private bathrooms.

■ **Villa Venice Men's Resort & Spa** (AC BF CC G I MA MSG NU OS p PI PK RWB RWS RWT VA WH WO) All year, 8.30-17.30 h
2900 Terramar Street *Just 2 Blocks from the beach* ☎ (954) 564-7855
☎ (877) 591-5127 (toll free) 🖳 www.VillaVenice.com
Fine gay resort with 22 rooms/suites. Experience the intimacy of a bed and breakfast, the friendship in this guesthouse and the service you expect. New gym for guests available.

■ **Windamar Beach Resort**
(AC BF CC G I NU OS PA PI PK RWS RWT VA WH) All year
543 Breakers Avenue *One block from the beach* ☎ (954) 561-0039
🖳 www.windamar.com
Windamar Beach Resort has 18 guestrooms and is a clean, quiet, congenial

and relaxed gay motel located just one short block from the ocean. A tropical sun-drenched patio setting providing you with a full day to soak up the sun by the heated, clothing-optional pool.

■ **Worthington. The**
(AC B bf G I MC NU OS PA PI PK RWS RWT VA WH WO) All year
543-555 North Birch Road ☎ (954) 563-6819
🖳 www.theworthington.com
All 15 guest rooms, including studios & suites with AC, bath, fridge, TV, VCR. Tastefully decorated; a fine assortment of amenities to ensure total comfort included.

APARTMENTS

■ **Liberty Suites** (AC CC G I MA OS PA PI PK RWS RWT VA) 8-20h
1500 SW Second Avenue, Dania Beach *Close to gay beach, within nightlife area* ☎ (954) 927-0090 🖳 www.libertysuites.com
Liberty has 18 intimate, beautifully furnished, fully equipped studios and one/two bedroom apartments with a heated pool and laundry service. Extras include movie cable TV/VCR, CD stereo and voice mail.

SWIMMING

-Fort Lauderdale beach (g) (In front of Sebastian street, and in front of Terramar Street)
-Beach opposite of North-East 18th Street (One mile north of Sunrise Boulevard) – cruisy at night.
-Lloyd Beach State Recreation Area (Take U.S. 1 to Dania Beach Boulevard, east to A1A. Follow signs to park entrance. First parking lot on right. Admission charge. Caution: Undercover police in T-rooms)
-Gay beach – Terramar street and AIA (Ocean).

CRUISING

-Holiday Park (South side of Sunrise Boulevard at North-East 12th Avenue. Check out parking area)
-Beach at Sebastian St (AYOR)
-Fort Lauderdale Beach, opposite 18th St NE (between Oakland Park & Sunrise Blvds) dune area cruisy all night and gay beach during the day
-North Lauderdale Beach
-Pompano Beach 16th St & A1A (N of Atlantic).

Fort Myers ☎ 941

BARS

■ **Mardi Gras Nouveau** (AC B D GLM M MA S) 14-24, Fri & Sat -2h
1341 Southeast 47th Terrace, Cape Coral ☎ (941) 541-8818
🖳 www.mardigrasnouveau.com

■ **Office Pub. The** (B G MA) 12-2h
3704 Cleveland Avenue *Between Grove and Hill Ave* ☎ (941) 936-3212
🖳 www.officepub.com
Neighbourhood leather bar.

■ **Tubby's** (AC B D GLM I S VS) 14-2h
4350 Fowler Street *Off Colonial Blvd* ☎ (239) 274-5001
🖳 tubbysbarfortmyers.com
Video sports show bar.

DANCECLUBS

■ **Bottom Line. The** (AC B D GLM I MA OS S SNU ST VS) 14-2h
3090 Evans Avenue ☎ (941) 337-7292

Gainesville ☎ 352

GAY INFO

■ **Pride Community Center** (GLM) Mon-Fri 15-19, Sat 12-16h, Sun closed
3131 NW 13th St ☎ (352) 377-8915 🖳 www.pridecommunitycenter.org

BARS

■ **Spikes** (! B D GLM OS SNU ST) 17-2, Sun -23h
4130 North-West 6th Street ☎ (352) 376-3772

■ **University Club** (B GLM ST t) 17-2, Sun -23h
18 East University Avenue ☎ (352) 378-6814 🖳 www.ucclub.com

CRUISING

-Newman's Lake (AYOR)
-Park at North East 16th Avenue/Main Street (days)
-Bivens Arm Park
-Lake Alice (at the University)

Holiday ☎ 727

BARS

Frank and Tony's (B f G MA) 15-2, Fri-Sun 13-2h
2419 Grand Boulevard ☎ (727) 942-9734
Featuring a Karaoke Night, an Underwear Night, a Levi/Leather Night.

Hollywood ☎ 323

BARS

Castle Lounge (AC B GLM MA ST t) 19-2h
1322 North Dixie Hwy ☎ (954) 840-9683

HOTELS

California Dream Inn (AC glm I MA OS PK RWS RWT) All year
300-315 Walnut Street ☎ (323) 923-2100
www.californiadreaminn.com
All rooms include equipped kitchens.

Inverness ☎ 352

CAMPING

Camp David (G I MA NU P PI WH)
2000 South Bishop's Point Road ☎ (352) 344-3445
www.campdavidflorida.com

Jacksonville ☎ 904

BARS

616 (AC B CC d f GLM m MA OS S SNU) 16-2h
616 Park Street ☎ (904) 358-6969 www.616parkstreetbar.com

AJ's Bar & Grill (B glm M MC OS) 16-2h
10244 Atlantic Blvd. ☎ (904) 805-9060 www.ajsbarjax.com
Gay owned bar with daily happy hour from 16-18h. Reasonable prices.

Bo's Coral Reef (B d GLM MA OS VS)
201 Fifth Avenue North ☎ (904) 246-9874 www.bosclub.com
Beach bar with patio and dancefloor. Mixed GLM crowd. Open 7 days/week.

In Cahoots (AC B CC D f GLM MA SNU ST T VS) 20-2, Sun 16-2h, Mon & Tue closed
711 Edison Avenue *Between Riverside & Park* ☎ (904) 353-6316

Metro (! AC B CC D f GLM MA S SNU ST WE) 16-2, Fri & Sat 18-4h
2929 Plum Street ☎ (904) 388-8719 www.metrojax.com
Very popular bar/club with regular events, a game room, a patio and a loft. Very mixed GLM crowd.

New Boot Rack Saloon (B f G MA OS) 15-2h
4751 Lenox Avenue ☎ (904) 384-7090 www.bootrack.com
Jacksonville's cruising bar with a patio and a toy store.

Park Place Lounge (AC B CC D GLM MC) 12-2h
931 King Street *At Post* ☎ (904) 389-6616
Happy hour 12-20, 24-2h.

SAUNAS/BATHS

Club Jacksonville (DU FC FH G M MA PI PK RR SB WH WO) 24hrs
1939 Hendricks Avenue *12 blocks from downtown in the San Marco Area*
☎ (904) 398-7451 www.clubjax.com
Picnic every Sunday afternoon from 15-17.00h.

GIFT & PRIDE SHOPS

Rainbows & Stars (GLM)
1046 Park Street ☎ (904) 356-7702 rainbowsandstars.com

Key West ☎ 305

Key West is at the most southern point of the U.S.A. The best way to get there is by a hired car from Miami or to take the shuttle bus from Miami International Airport. The scenic trip across the US 1 to Key West takes roughly three hours and offers the best impression of the island. For those who are not able to wait – take a direct flight from Miami. In Key West you will find a very open minded crowd. Gays are so integrated in the community that they are almost not noticeable in every day life. Duval Street, known as the „longest street of the world" connecting the Atlantic with the Gulf of Mexico, is the main shopping district. But watch out for the shops bearing the rainbow flag, many of these are tourist traps. The „Fantasy Fest" takes place every year in October, which is the largest attraction of Key West. At this time of year this small island seems to almost burst with gays and lesbians gathering here from all corners of the globe. After indulging in a sight seeing trip, including the Ernest Hemingway Home, one of the best things to do is to relax by the pool at your guest house. The early evening starts with a cocktail (normally complimentary in all good guest houses). Most action takes place in the early hours of the morning in the hot tub ! The best time to travel to Key West is in the winter when there are still tropical temperatures.

Key West ist der südlichste Punkt der Vereinigten Staaten. Die letzte Insel der Florida Keys besucht man am besten, indem man sich auf dem Festland einen Wagen mietet oder am Miami International Airport den Bus-Shuttle nimmt. Über die US 1 gelangt man innerhalb von drei Stunden nach Key West. Somit erhält man gleich die besten Eindrücke dieser Insel. Diejenigen, die es kaum erwarten können, nach Key West zu gelangen, sollten direkt von Miami ein Flugzeug nehmen. In Key West erwartet einen das aufgeschlossenste Völkchen, das man sich vorstellen kann. Homosexuelle werden so offenherzig in die Gemeinde aufgenommen, dass sie im Alltag kaum auffallen. »Duval Street«, die liebevoll »die längste Straße der Welt« genannt wird, da sie den Atlantik mit dem Golf von Mexico verbindet, stellt die Einkaufsmeile Key Wests dar. Man hüte sich aber vor den Geschäften, die zwar mit der Regenbogen-Flagge getarnt sind, sich jedoch als reine Schwulen-Fallen herausstellen. Im Oktober findet jährlich die größte Attraktion Key Wests statt: das »Fantasy Fest«. Zu diesem Zeitpunkt scheint die kleine Insel aus allen Nähten zu platzen, pilgern doch aus aller Welt Schwule und Lesben dorthin. Da es neben Attraktionen wie dem »Ernest Hemingway Home« kein wirkliches touristisches Muss gibt, kann man in seinem Guest House gnadenlos am Swimmingpool entspannen. Abends beginnt das alles mit einem Cocktail (in guten Pensionen normalerweise im Preis inbegriffen). Das Interessante findet früh morgens im Hot Tub statt! Ideale Reisezeit für Key West ist der Winter, denn dann herrschen hier noch tropische Temperaturen.

Key West est le point situé le plus au sud des États-Unis. La meilleure façon de visiter cette île, la dernière des keys de Floride, est de louer une voiture ou de prendre une navette de l'aéroport. En environ trois heures, en passant par la US 1, vous arriverez à Key West avec en prime une vue imprenable d'ensemble. Les plus impatients d'entre vous peuvent cependant s'y rendre en avion depuis Miami. A Key West, vous trouverez la population la plus ouverte qui soit. Les homosexuels sont si bien intégrés à la communauté que l'on ne les remarque presque pas. La »Duval Street«, surnommée „la plus longue rue du monde", car elle relie l'Atlantique au Golf du Mexique, est la rue marchande de la ville. Mais méfiez-vous des magasins qui arborent les couleurs de l'arc-en-ciel! Ce sont des véritables attrape-nigauds. Chaque année, en octobre, a lieu à Key West le plus grand événement de l'année : la »Fantasy Fest«. Pendant cette période, l'île est véritablement surpeuplée de gais et lesbiennes venus en pèlerinage des quatre coins du globe. A l'exception de cet événement, l'île n'offre pas beaucoup d'activités, hormis peut-être la visite de la maison d'»Ernest Hemingway«. Il vous restera donc à vous prélasser au bord de la piscine de votre maison d'hôtes. Le début de soirée commence avec un cocktail (normalement gracieusement offert par tout »guest house« de ce nom). Le moment le plus palpitant de la journée se situera aux premières heures du matin lorsque que vous vous plongerez dans votre jacuzzi. L'hiver est la saison idéale pour se rendre à Key West, car les températures y sont encore tropicales.

Gulf of Mexico
N
Mallory Square
Aquarium
Treasure Exhibit
Truman Annex
Front St
Greeno St.
Caroline St.
Eaton St
Fleming St
Whitehead St.
Thomas St.
Simonton St.
Elizabeth St.
William St.
Margaret St.
Grinnell St.
Frances St.
White St.
Trumbo Road
Palm Ave
Southard St
Angela St
Angela St
Petronia St
Petronia St
Newton St
Olivia St
Windsor St
Truman Ave
Georgia St.
Florida St
Emma St.
Lighthouse Military Museum
Hemingway Home
Duval St.
Duval Square
Virginia St.
Amelia St.
Catherine St.
United St.
United St.
South St.
Grinnell St.
Reynolds St.
Flagler Ave
Johnson St.
Southernmost Point
Atlantic Ocean
Key West
EAT & DRINK
Antonia's – Restaurant 10
Bobby's Monkey Bar 15
Bourbon Street Pub – Bar 13
Key West Piano Bar 17
Kwest Men – Bar 11
La-Te-Da – Bar 16
Saloon 1 – Bar 14
NIGHTLIFE
Aqua – Danceclub 12
ACCOMMODATION
Alexander's Guesthouse 2
Big Ruby's Guesthouse 8
Coconut Grove – Guest House 6
Coral Tree Inn – Guest House 3
Equator Resort – Guest House 4
Harbor Inn – Hotel 7
Island House for Men – Guest House 1
La-Te-Da – Hotel 16
New Orleans House – Guest House 13
Oasis Guesthouse 5
OTHERS
Leather Master Key West – Leather & Fetish Shop 9

Key West está situado en el extremo sur de los Estados Unidos. La mejor manera de visitar la última isla de los Florida Keys es alquilando un coche o tomando el autobús que parte del aeropuerto de Miami. Por la autopista US 1 se llega en tres horas a Key West. De esta manera se puede apreciar la belleza natural de esta isla. Si se tiene prisa, se debe coger el avión directamente en Miami. Los habitantes de Key West son abiertos y afables. Los homosexuales están tan integrados a la comunidad, que en la vida cotidiana pasan casi desapercibidos. La »Duval Street«, que se llama también cariñosamente la „calle más larga del mundo", ya que une el Atlantico con el Golfo de México, es la calle comercial de Key West. Un consejo: cuidado con las tiendas que intentan atraer clientela con la bandera de arcoiris, ¡no son más que trampas para homosexuales! En Octubre se celebra anualmente la mayor atración de Key West: El „Fantasy Festival". En estas fechas la isla se llena de gays y lesbianas, que vienen de todas las partes del mundo para participar en estas festividades. Aparte del »Hemingway Home«, no hay muchos sitios para visitar y por ello uno puede dedicar sus vacaciones completamente al descanso en los »guest houses«. Invierno es la temporada óptima para visitar Key West, ya que se pueden disfrutar todavía temperaturas tropicales.

Key West è il punto più al sud degli USA. L'ultima isola del Florida Keys è da visitare alla meglio con una macchina a noleggio che ci si può procurare sulla terraferma o con il servizio navetta dell'aeroporto di Miami (International Airport Bus Shuttle). Dalla US 1 si arriva senza sbagliarsi nel giro di tre ore a Key West. Così si raggolgono già le prime impressioni di quest'isola. Per coloro che non vedono l'ora di arrivare a Key West è consigliabile prendere un volo diretto da Miami. A Key West ci aspetta la popolazione più aperta che si possa immaginare. Gli omosessuali vengono accolti così apertamente nella società del posto che non danno più nell'occhio nella vita quotidiana. La »Duval Street« viene chiamata amorevolmente la strada più lunga del mondo, perché congiunge l'Atlantico con il Golfo del Messico e rappresenta anche la zona shopping di Key West. Si avverte però di fare attenzione ai quei negozi che mettono in mostra la bandiera dell'arcobaleno, ma che poi risultano una truffa per la clientela gay. Ogni anno in ottobre ha luogo l'avvenimento più importante per Key West: il »Fantasy Fest«. In questo periodo la piccola isola sembra scoppiare dalla moltitudine di „pellegrini" gay e lesbiche provenienti da tutto il mondo. Siccome oltre a certi punti d'attrazione come la »Ernest Hemmingway Home« non esistono mete propriamente turistiche è possibile oziare perennemente nel suo »guest house«. Il periodo ideale per un viaggio a Key West è l'inverno, perché si ha un clima tropico.

GAY INFO

Gay & Lesbian Community Center of Key West (GLM)
513 Truman Ave ☏ (305) 292-3223 🖳 www.glcckeywest.org

Gay/Lesbian Key West
☏ (305) 294-4603 (toll-free) 🖳 www.fla-keys.com/gay
Website providing information about gay life and accommodation in Key West.

Key West Business Guild & Visitor Center
513 Truman Avenue ☏ (305) 294-4603 🖳 www.gaykeywestfl.com
Website providing information about gay and gay friendly businesses and accommodations in Key West. Weekly Historic Trolley Tour, Visitor Center open daily.

BARS

801 Bourbon Bar. The (B GLM OS ST T) 11-4h
801 Duval Street *At Petronia* ☏ (305) 296-1992 🖳 www.801bourbon.com
Drag shows every day at 9 and 11 p.m.

Bobby's Monkey Bar (AC B G MA s) 12-4h
900 Simonton Street ☏ (305) 294-2655
🖳 www.bobbysmonkeybar.com
Karaoke, pool table, jukebox, video games.

Bourbon Street Pub (! AC B CC D f GLM H M MA MSG NU OS S SNU ST VS WH) 11-4, Sun 12-4h
724 Duval Street ☏ (305) 296-1992 🖳 www.bourbonstpub.com
Complex/resort: four bars, two restaurants, a cabaret and a 13-rooms guesthouse. Regular Foam Parties. Saturday afternoon pool parties with 2 for 1 drinks.

Key West Piano Bar (AC B glm MA S)
1114 Duval Street ☏ (305) 294-8859 🖳 www.akeywestpianobar.com

■ **Kwest Men** (B CC G MA SNU VS) 16-4h
705 Duval Street ☏ (305) 292-8500 ▭ www.KWESTMEN.com
Shows beginning 22h. Daily Happy Hour from 3-8pm, and a piano sing-a-long every Wednesday night.

■ **La Te Da** (B glm H M MA ST)
1125 Duval Street ☏ (305) 296-6706 ▭ www.lateda.com
Hotel, bar, restaurant and cabaret.

■ **Saloon 1** (AC B F G MA)
801 Duvall Street *Cnr. Petronia* ☏ (305) 294-4737
▭ www.801bourbon.com
Leather bar behind 801 Bourbon.

DANCECLUBS

■ **Aqua** (B D GLM MA OS ST) 15-2, Thu-Sat -4h
711 Duval Street ☏ (305) 292-8500 ▭ www.aquakeywest.com
Key West's largest gay dance club.

RESTAURANTS

■ **Antonia's** (AC B CC DM glm M MA NR PK RES S VEG WL) 18-23h
615 Duval Street *Old town* ☏ (305) 294-6565
▭ www.antoniaskeywest.com
Regional Italian cuisine.

■ **Azur Restaurant** (AC BF CC glm MA OS)
8-14, 18-22; Sat 9-14, 18-22; Sun 10-14h
425 Grinnell Street *Oldtown Key West* ☏ (305) 292-2987
▭ www.azurkeywest.com
Serving breakfast, lunch, and dinner.

LEATHER & FETISH SHOPS

■ **Leather Master Key West** (CC F GLM) 11-23, Sun 12-18h
418 Appelrouth Lane ☏ (305) 292-5051
▭ leathermasterkeywest@gmail.com

TRAVEL AND TRANSPORT

■ **Alyson Adventures** (GLM) All year
626 Josephine Parker Dr. Suite 206, *Above the Wyland Gallery on Duval St. entrance in the rear* ☏ (305) 294-8174 ▭ www.alysonadventures.com
Bike, hike, dive, and cruise with a small gay group.

HOTELS

■ **La Te Da** (AC B BF CC d GLM M MA OS PI RWB RWS RWT S ST VA)
Hotel: 8-22, bar: 12-2h
1125 Duval Street ☏ (305) 296-6706 ▭ www.lateda.com
Blending seamlessly with the tropical paradise of historic centre of Key West, La-Te-Da offers you luxury accommodations that include all amenities plus the Crystal Room cabaret lounge, George bar and the Terrace Garden bar with live entertainment. Tea Dance Sundays 4 p.m.

GUEST HOUSES

■ **Alexander's Guesthouse**
(AC BF CC GLM I OS p PI PK RWB RWS RWT WH) All year
1118 Fleming Street *Central* ☏ (305) 294-9919
▭ www.alexanderskeywest.com
All rooms with bath/WC, fridge, some with balcony. Each room and suite is uniquely decorated in a tasteful Key West casual style. Select rooms have private verandas or decks.

■ **Big Ruby's Guesthouse** (AC BF CC G MA NU OS PI RWS RWT WH WO) All year
409 Appelrouth Lane *1/2 block off Duval Street* ☏ (305) 296-2323
▭ www.bigrubys.com
All 17 rooms with shower/WC, wash-basin and TV. A spacious chaise lounge lined sun deck, treetop walkways overlooking an exotic garden. Fitness center, full breakfast daily.

■ **Coconut Grove** (AC BF CC G NU OS PI RWB RWS RWT WH WO) All year
822-823 Fleming Street ☏ (305) 296-2131 ▭ www.keywest-allmale.com
All 16 rooms with bath/WC, and balcony. Friendly staff and interesting guests blend together perfectly within the casual charm of the guesthouse and tropical gardens. Belongs to the Oasis and Coral Tree guest houses.

■ **Coral Tree Inn** (AC B CC G MA NU OS PI RWS RWT VA WH)
All year, office 8-22h
822 Fleming Street ☎ (305) 296-2131 🖳 www.keywest-allmale.com
Eleven rooms with bath, AC, coffee makers, fridge, TV and phone. Located just a few blocks from the excitements of Duval Street, the gay Coral Tree Inn is an ideal base for both adventure and relaxation. Belongs to the Oasis and Coconut Grove guest houses.

■ **Cypress House** (AC CC glm I OS PI PK RWS RWT VA) 8-20h
601 Caroline Street *Old town* ☎ (305) 294-6969
🖳 www.cypresshousekw.com
Guest house with 22 rooms, some ensuite and with kitchenette.

■ **Equator Resort** (AC BF CC G MA NU OS PI RWB RWS RWT WH)
All year
818 Fleming Street ☎ (305) 294-7775 🖳 www.equatorresort.com
A comfortable, welcoming gay resort. Elegant and spacious Italian tiled guestrooms all equipped with video, fridge, telephone and voicemail surrounded by lavish gardens.

■ **Harbor Inn** (AC BF g OS)
219 Elizabeth Street ☎ (305) 296-2978 🖳 www.keywestharborinn.com

■ **Island House for Men** (AC B BF CC DR FC G I M MA MSG NU OS P PA PI PK RWS RWT SA SB VA VEG VR VS WH WO) All year, 24hrs
1129 Fleming Street *Old town, near Duval Street* ☎ (305) 294-6284
🖳 www.islandhousekeywest.com
Award-winning Island House with its 34 guestrooms is one of the best men-only properties in the entire United States. Private, enclosed clothing optional.

■ **New Orleans House** (AC B CC G I M MA MSG NU OS PI PK RWB RWS RWT S VA WH WO) All year
724 Duval Street *Above Bourbon St. Pub* ☎ (305) 293-9800
🖳 www.neworleanshousekw.com
All male clothing-optional guest house centrally located in the heart of Old Town Key West. Part of the world renowned Bourbon St. Pub Complex with a variety of rooms, private rear sun deck, pool, hot tub, gym and garden bar area, which is open to the public from noon on and clothing optional men only at all times.

■ **Oasis Guesthouse** (AC B BF CC G NU PI RWT WH)
Reservations 8-22h
822-823 Fleming Street ☎ (305) 296-2131 🖳 www.keywest-allmale.com
All 20 rooms with fridge, bath/WC, balcony, TV.

CRUISING

-Higgs Beach, on White Street (AYOR)
-Little Hamaca Park, on Government Road from downtown, go east on Flagler Road, turn right on Government, and follow past airport to park at end of road (AYOR).
-Boca Chica Beach, drive away from Key West on US 1 to the Circle K store, Mile Market 9.5, turn right on Boca Chica Road and drive until dead end. Walk along the road and follow other men to nude beach and cruising area. Usually safe (AYOR)

Lake Worth ☎ 561

GAY INFO

■ **Compass LGBT Community Center** (GLM)
23 South H Street ☎ (561) 533-9699 🖳 www.compassglcc.com

BARS

■ **Bar. The** (AC B GLM MA) 14-2, Sun 12-2h
2211 North Dixie Highway ☎ (561) 370-3954
🖳 www.thebarlakeworth.com

■ **Mad Hatter Lounge. The** (AC B CC G m MC) 13-2, Sun 12-24h
1532 North Dixie Highway ☎ (561) 547-8860
🖳 www.madhatterlounge.com

Lakeland ☎ 863

BARS

■ **Pulse** (AC B D G m OS S SNU) 16-2, Sun -24h
1030 East Main Street ☎ (863) 683-6021 🖳 www.outinlakeland.com

Melbourne ☎ 321

BARS

■ **Cold Keg** (B D GLM MA S ST) 14-2h
4060 West New Haven Avenue ☎ (321) 724-1510
🖳 www.coldkegnightclub.com
Amateur strip contest on Thu, more women 2nd Fri.

SWIMMING

-Beach at the end of the Eau Gallie Causeway
-Canova Beach (AYOR) (at night)
-Melbourne Harbor Marina (AYOR).

Miami ☎ 305

PUBLICATIONS

■ **GMaps**
🖳 www.gmaps360.com
One of the most complete gay guides and maps of Miami. See also www.gcard360.com

TOURIST INFO

■ **Greater Miami Convention & Visitors Bureau**
701 Brickell Avenue, Suite 2700 ☎ (888) 766-4264
🖳 www.MiamiLGBT.com

BARS

■ **Eros Lounge** (B G) 15-3h
8201 Biscayne Blvd ☎ (305) 754-3444 🖳 eroslongemiami.com
Happy Hours 15-21h.

■ **Jamboree** (AC B G MA OS ST VS)
7005 Biscayne Blvd *Cnr. NE 70th Street* ☎ (305) 759-3413

■ **Johnny's** (AC B CC D G m MA SNU) 17-5h
62 NE 14th Street ☎ (305) 640-8749 🖳 www.johnnysbarfl.com

■ **Magnum** (B g M MA S) Bar 17-2, restaurant 18-24h
709 NE 79th Street ☎ (305) 757-3368

■ **Rocks on the Mile** (B D GLM m MA s) 17-2h, closed Sun
96 Miracle Mile ☎ (305) 444-7933

■ **Vlada** (AC B CC D GLM MA S ST t) 16-4h
3215 NE 2nd Avenue *Midtown* ☎ (305) 381-5015
🖳 www.vladabar.com

MEN'S CLUBS

■ **Swinging Richards** (G SNU) Tue-Thu 18-4, Fri-Sat 18-6, Sun 18-3h
17450 Biscayne Blvd ☎ (954) 357 2532 (mobile)
🖳 florida.swingingrichards.com
Gay male strip club.

DANCECLUBS

■ **Club Boi** (B D G MC) Fri & Sat 23-?h
726 NW 79 th Street ☎ (305) 836-8995 🖳 www.clubboi.com
R&B, Hip Hop, House & Reggae, popular with black gay men.

■ **Club Sugar** (AC B D GLM MA ST) Thu-Sat 22.30-5, Sun 20-3h
2301 SW 32nd Avenue *Cnr. Coral Way* ☎ (305) 443-7657
🖳 www.clubsugarmiami.com

■ **Discotekka** (! AC CC D G MA) Fri 5-11, Sat 5-11 & 23-20, Mon 5-11h
950 NE 2nd Avenue ☎ (305) 371-3773 🖳 www.discotekka.com

■ **Sandal Club** (B D G MA SNU ST) 22-5h
1060 NE 79th Street ☎ (305) 758-3556

RESTAURANTS

■ **Mai Tardi** (G M)
163 ne 39th Street ☎ (305) 572-1400 🖳 www.maitardimiami.com

SEX SHOPS/BLUE MOVIES

■ **Curiotica** (g VS) 24hrs
6833 SW 40th Street ☎ (305) 669-9515 🖳 www.curiotica.com
Also with a gay section and cabins.

SAUNAS/BATHS

Club Aqua (AC AK CC DR DU FC FH G m MA NU P PI RR S SB SH SOL VS WH WO) 24hrs
2991 Coral Way *Coral Gables* ☎ (305) 448-2214
www.clubaquamiami.com
Full gym with private rooms, lockers, Jacuzzi and a play area.

BOOK SHOPS

Lambda Passages (CC G) Mon-Sat 11-21, Sun 12-18h
7545 Biscayne Boulevard ☎ (305) 754-6900
Gay DVD rental and sales and bookstore.

FASHION SHOPS

Creative Male (SH) Mon-Fri 12-20, Sat 11-20, Sun 12-18h
222 NE 25th Street *Suite 106; enter the store on NE Second Avenue*
☎ (305) 573-3080 www.creativemale.com
Mens underwear/bathing suits store.

TRAVEL AND TRANSPORT

My Gay Miami Beach (CC GLM)
5445 Collins Ave, Miami Beach ☎ (305) 432-2508
www.mygaymiamibeach.com
They have the best deals in hotels, cars, gay tours, cruise ships, Disney admissions, and all you need to have fun and enjoy the best of Gay Miami Beach.

HOTELS

Miami River Inn (AC CC glm I OS PA PI PK RWS RWT VA WH)
All year, front desk 8-22h
118 South West South River Drive *Corner of SW 2nd Street & SW 4th Ave*
☎ (305) 325-0045 www.miamiriverinn.com

GUEST HOUSES

Grove Inn Country Guesthouse (BF cc glm MA PA RWS RWT VA) All year
22540 Southwest Krome Avenue ☎ (305) 247-6572
www.groveinn.com

APARTMENTS

Boutique Rentals (AC CC glm I MC RWS RWT VA) All year
☎ (305) 5365-4544 www.boutiquerentals.net
The apartments are situated between two international airports, a few blocks from the beach and minutes from South Beach and Bal Harbour. All the apartments are equipped with mobile telephones with free local calls, LCD TV with cable, CD Player, WiFi Internet, alarm clock, DVD player,a fridge, microwave and coffeemaker.

Enjoy Miami (H)
at South Beach ☎ +39 349 64 40 888 (Italy) info@enjoyromebb.com
Large 900 square meters apartment in the middle of South Beach.

CRUISING

-Bayside Market (lots of Latin and Brazilian tourists)
-Matheson Hammock Beach on Old Cutler Road (south of Kendall Dr) (AYOR)
-Indian Hammocks Park on 117 Ave in Kendall, between 107th and 117th Avenues and Sunset and Kendall Dr (AYOR).

Miami Beach ☎ 305

Miami Beach (or »SoBe«, South Beach) is a very trendy place. It's interesting to take a look at the reasons for this. The most obvious reason is the »National Historic District«, consisting of 800 renovated Art-Deco-houses, apartment buildings and small hotels. A kitsch dream in pastel shades. Another reason is the clever way that the city government has used the media and dreamlike beach and palm scenery, to promote the city. The »Ocean Drive« is the boulevard next to the beach, where the beautiful and the wanna-be-beautiful saunter along. Parallel to it run Collins and Washington Avenue, which form one side of the gay right angle. The other side is the »Lincoln Road Mall«, a real pedestrian zone in the US (!). Along one of these axes you'll find all gay establishments of the town in walking distance. It is best to find accommodation in this area and save yourself renting a car. The best time to visit is between October and April, peak season around Christmas to Easter. Important events are the parties, which begin with »Thanksgiving« (last Thu in November). The climax of this party season is the Winter Party in March. SoBe is situated right next to a major city, Miami. And this city has many things to offer: Little Havanna (SW 8th Street/SW 11th Avenue), where the Cuban immigrants have settled, Showtime in Seaquarium, or shopping and strolling around Bayside Marketplace, Coral Gables or Coconut Grove.

Miami Beach (oder modisch »SoBe« für South Beach) ist trendy. Es lohnt sich, den Gründen dafür nachzuspüren. Der offensichtlichste ist der »National Historic District«, 800 renovierte Art-Deco-Häuser. Ein Kitschtraum in Pastell. Ein weiterer Grund sind die Medien: die Stadtverwaltung hat – auch mit Hilfe der Strand-und-Palmen-Traumkulisse – in den letzten Jahren für verstärkte Medienpräsenz der Stadt gesorgt und sie damit noch bekannter gemacht. Der »Ocean Drive« ist die Flaniermeile der Schönen und Schön-Sein-Wollenden direkt am Strand, parallel dazu verlaufen Collins und Washington Avenue und bilden damit die eine Seite des schwulen rechten Winkels. Die andere Seite bildet die »Lincoln Road Mall«, eine richtige Fußgängerzone (!), und das in Amerika. Entlang dieser beiden Achsen finden sich alle schwulen Etablissements des Ortes innerhalb überschaubarer Distanzen. In dieser Gegend sollte man auch übernachten, so dass man kein Auto benötigt. Die beste Zeit liegt zwischen Oktober und April, die Hochsaison um Weihnachten bis in den Januar. Wichtige Events sind die Parties, mit denen es nach »Thanksgiving« (letzter Do im Nov) los geht. Höhepunkt ist die Winter Party im März. SoBe liegt in direkter Nachbarschaft zu einer Großstadt, Miami nämlich. Und diese Stadt hat einiges zu bieten: Little Havanna (SW 8th Street/SW 11th Avenue), in dem sich die kubanischen Einwanderer niedergelassen haben, Showtime im Seaquarium und Shoppen und Bummeln im Bayside Marketplace, Coral Gables oder Coconut Grove.

Miami Beach (ou „SoBe" pour South Beach, comme disent les initiés) est l'endroit „in" de Floride. Voyons donc pourquoi! C'est d'abord grâce à ses 800 maisons art-déco soigneusement rénovées qui forment ce qu'on appelle le „National Historic District". Un vrai rêve dans les couleurs pastel! Les médias y sont également pour beaucoup. La municipalité a joué la carte de la presse et du cinéma et les investisseurs n'ont eu aucun mal à s'installer dans ce décor de rêve, sous les palmiers de Floride. SoBe y a gagné sur tous les plans: toujours plus célèbre, elle a attiré encore plus d'investisseurs et d'entreprises. Ocean Drive, immédiatement au bord de la plage, est la promenade où l'on vient pour voir et être vu. Les dieux et les déesses du littoral s'y bousculent. Les simples mortels aussi. Les artères parallèles sont Collins et Washington Avenue. Elles délimitent le quartier gai avec, de l'autre côté, Lincoln Road Mall, une vraie zone piétonne, chose assez rare en Amérique. C'est le long de ces deux axes que l'on trouve tous les lieux gais de la ville. On peut tout faire à pied, donc pas besoin de voiture, si vous habitez dans le quartier. Le meilleur moment pour visiter Miami Beach, c'est entre octobre et avril. La fête bat son plein entre mi-décembre et mi-janvier. Les fêtes commencent après „Thanksgiving", le dernier jeudi de novembre. On atteint le summum en mars avec la „Winter Party". Une des curiosités de SoBe, c'est sa proximité de Miami qui, elle-même, n'est pas inintéressante: Little Havanna (SW 8th Street/SW 11th Avenue), son aquarium maritime (Seaquarium), ses boutiques et ses boulevards commerçants de Bayside Market, Coral Gables ou Coconut Grove.

Miami Beach (o como se suele decir hoy en día »SoBe« South Beach) está de moda. Una de las razones es el »National Historic District« que cuenta con 800 edificaciones recientemente reformadas en estilo Art-Deco, un cursi sueño en color pastel. Otra razón son los medios de comunicación que con ayuda de la municipalidad y la belleza de las playas y palmeras se han encargado de dar a conocer más la ciudad. El »Ocean Drive«, la pasarela de la gente guapa y de aquellos que desean serlo, se encuentra directamente junto a la playa, paralela a ella se localizan también las avenidas Collins y Washington. Estas forman uno de los centros gay de la ciudad. La »Lincoln Road Mall« es una zona

"Just Expressing Myself."
© Greater Miami Convention & Visitors Bureau – The Official Destination Marketing Organization for Greater Miami and the Beaches.

peatonal (¡Y esto en Estados Unidos!) que también se distingue por su afluencia gay. A lo largo de estas calles y avenidas se encuentran los establecimientos gay del lugar. Es aconsejable pernoctar en esta zona, asi no se necesitará un automóvil. La mejor época es entre Octubre y Abril, el tiempo de mayor apogeo es la navidad. Los eventos más importantes son las fiestas que inician después del »Thanksgiving« (día de gracias) (último jueves de Noviembre). El punto culminante es la fiesta de invierno, que se celebra en marzo. SoBe se localiza directamente en la vecindad de una gran ciudad: Miami, y esta ciudad tiene muchas cosas que ofrecer: Little Havanna (SW 8th. Street/SW 11th Avenue) en la que los emigrantes cubanos se han asentado. Recomendamos la visita al Seaquarium, asi como ir de compras en Bayside Marketplace, Coral Gables o Coconut Grove.

Miami Beach (o »SoBe«, South Beach) è molto alla moda per diversi motivi. Uno è il »National Historic District«, composto da 800 case ristrutturate, in stile art decò: un sogno kitsch dai colori pastello. Un altro motivo è dato dai mass media: l'amministrazione comunale, aiutata dagli scenari favolosi della spiaggia e delle palme, ha incentivato la presenza della città nei film e nelle riprese televisive rendendo Miami ancora più famosa e sempre più interessante come scenario cinetelevi-

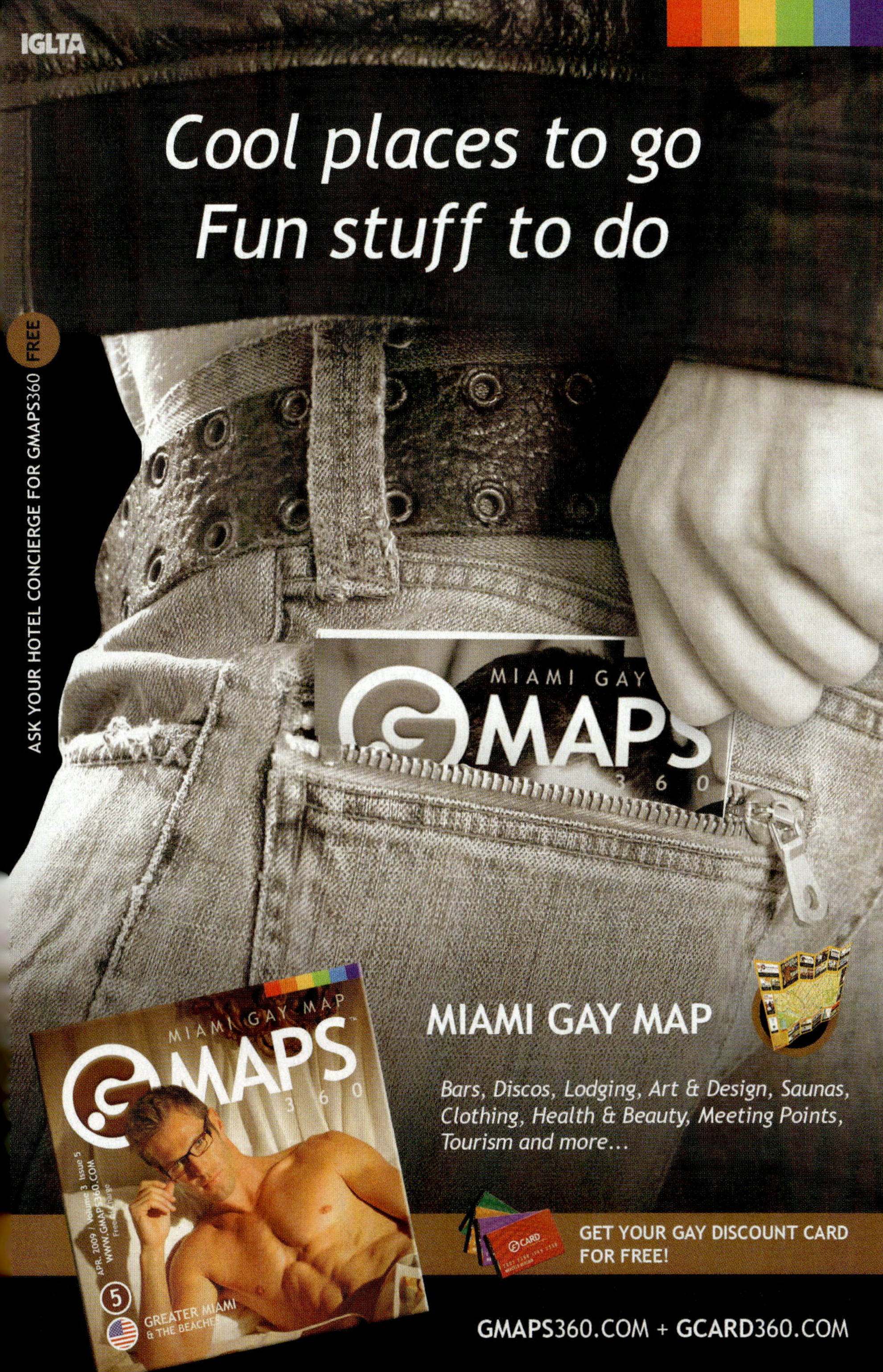

IGLTA
Cool places to go
Fun stuff to do
ASK YOUR HOTEL CONCIERGE FOR GMAPS360
FREE
MIAMI GAY
GMAPS
360
MIAMI GAY MAP
GMAPS
360
APR. 2009 / Volume 3 Issue 5
WWW.GMAPS360.COM
5
GREATER MIAMI
& THE BEACHES
MIAMI GAY MAP
Bars, Discos, Lodging, Art & Design, Saunas, Clothing, Health & Beauty, Meeting Points, Tourism and more...
GET YOUR GAY DISCOUNT CARD
FOR FREE!
GMAPS360.COM + GCARD360.COM

sivo. Direttamente sulla spiaggia, l'Ocean Drive è il passeggio dei belli e di coloro che desiderano esserlo; parallelamente corrono la Collins e la Washington Avenue che insieme formano una parte della zona gay. L'altra parte è costituita dalla »Lincoln Road Mall«, una zona pedonale (molto rara in America). Lungo queste due vie, a piccola distanza, si trovano tutti i locali gay del luogo. Conviene alloggiare in questa zona per fare a meno dell'auto. Il periodo migliore per una visita è tra ottobre ed aprile mentre l'alta stagione va da Natale a gennaio. I »parties« sono eventi molto importanti: il primo è il »Thanksgiving« (l'ultimo giovedì di novembre) ed il culmine il »Winter Party« in marzo. SoBe si trova in prossimità di Miami che offre a sua volta molti svaghi: Little Havanna (SW 8th Street/SW 11th Av.) dove giungevano gli immigrati cubani, Showtime nel Seaquarium o una passeggiata in Bayside Marketplace, Coral Gables e Coconut grove.

MUSEAMS

World Erotic Art Museum Mon-Thu 11-22, Fri-Sun 11-24h
1205 Washington Ave ☎ (305) 532-9336 www.weam.com

TOURIST INFO

Miami-Dade Gay & Lesbian Visitor Center
1130 Washingon Avenue ☎ (305) 673-4440
www.gogaymiami.com

BARS

721 Bar (B G MC) 17-5h
721 North Lincoln Lane ☎ (305) 532-1342 www.bar721.com

Boy Bar (AC B CC DR G MA OS VS) 17-5h
1220 Normandy Drive ☎ (305) 864-2697
Neighbourhood cruise bar. Full liquor, videos, pool table. Back room for men only. Plenty of free parking. The only gay bar in Miami Beach's Normandy Isle neighbourhood.

Creme Lounge (B d GLM MA) Tue & Thu-Sat
725 Lincoln Lane ☎ (305) 535-1163 www.cremelounge.net

Mova (AC B d GLM MA) 15-3, Sun 12-3h
1625 Michigan Avenue ☎ (305) 534-8181 www.movalounge.com
Stylish gay bar and cocktail lounge.

SoBe Social Club (B d G MA)
☎ (305) 604-9050 www.sobesocialclub.com
The SoBe Social Club organizes parties every week at different locations. Classics are „Martini Tuesdays", „ Piano Man Wednesdays" and „Simple Life Thursdays". Check www.sobesocialclub.com to see where and when the action takes place.

DANCECLUBS

Score (! AC B CC D GLM MA OS S SNU VS)
Lounge 15-?, dance club 22-5h
727 Lincoln Road *South Beach, East of Meridian Ave* ☎ (305) 535-1111
www.scorebar.net
A large and busy dance club with Dance music and a big screen video bar. Popular. See www.scorebar.net for details.

Twist (! AC B CC D f G MA OS s SNU ST VS) 13-5h
1057 Washington Avenue *Two blocks from the Atlantic Ocean and the 12th street „gay" Beach* ☎ (305) 538-9478 www.twistsobe.com
A classic in the SoBe scene. Large and popular club with three dance floors, a patio and a bar downstairs. Regular strip acts and drag shows and all without cover charge! On going, better than ever!

RESTAURANTS

Balans (AC B BF CC glm M MA OS WE) Sun-Thu 8-24, Fri & Sat -1h
1022 Lincoln Road ☎ (305) 534-9191 www.balans.co.uk/miami.html

Blue Door Restaurant & Brasserie (B BF CC g M MC) Mon-Sat 7-23.30h
1685 Collins Avenue *At Delano Hotel* ☎ (305) 672-2000
www.delano-hotel.com/delano_hotel_blue_door.asp

Cha Cha Rooster at the Lords South Beach Restaurant (B BF GLM M)
Daily 8-24h; Dinner and Sunday brunch: Mon-Sat 18-24, Sun 11-16h
1120 Collins Ave ☎ (305) 455-2231 (Restaurant) ☎ 455-2232 (Lounge)
chacharooster.com

Da Leo Trattoria (AC B CC DM GLM M MA NR OS PA VEG WL) 17-23.30h
819 Lincoln Road ☎ (305) 674-0350 www.daleotrattoria.com
Italian Tuscan specialities with fantastic outdoor seating. Gay owned and operated.

De Rodriguez Cuba on Ocean (! M) Mon-Thu 12-23, Fri & Sat 12-24, Sun 11-22h
101 Ocean Drive ☎ (305) 672-6624 www.drodriguezcuba.com

Palace. The (B GLM M MA ST) 10-23h
1200 Ocean Drive *Next to gay beach* ☎ (305) 531-7234
www.palacesouthbeach.com
Bar and restaurant. Motto: to see and be seen. So take your shirt off. Drag shows on WE.

Van Dyke Cafe (AC B BF CC glm I M MC)
846 Lincoln Road ☎ (305) 534-3600 www.thevandykecafe.com

HOTELS

Hotel Impala (B BF CC glm I MA) 24hrs
1228 Collins Avenue ☎ (305) 673-2021
www.hotelimpalamiamibeach.com
Luxury, non smoking hotel near beach. Rooms with cable TV and VCR, stereo systems with CD, computer data ports, pet friendly, oversized bathtubs & showers and wheelchair access. Also Italian restaurant.

Hotel Ocean (BF glm M OS) 24hrs
1230-38 Ocean Drive ☎ (305) 672-2579 www.hotelocean.com

Indian Creek Hotel. The (AC BF CC glm MA OS PI RWS RWT) All year
2727 Indian Creek Drive *1 block from Ocean Dr & 10 blocks from South Beach* ☎ (305) 531-2727 www.indiancreekhotel.com

Lords South Beach (AC B CC DU GLM I MA PI RWS RWT) All year
1120 Collins Avenue ☎ ((305)) 674-7800 ☎ 877-448-4754 (toll free)
www.lordssouthbeach.com

Centrally located, this gay-friendly boutique hotel features 3 plunge pools, lively restaurants and bars, and a digital concierge app.

■ **National** (B BF CC g I PI WO) All year
1677 Collins Avenue ☏ (305) 532-2311 🖳 www.nationalhotel.com

■ **Raleigh. The** (AC B CC glm MA PI)
1775 Collins Avenue ☏ (305) 534-6300 🖳 www.raleighhotel.com

■ **Shelborne Beach Resort – South Beach** (AC B CC H I M MA NG OS PI PK RWB RWS RWT SA VA WH WO) All year, 24hrs
1801 Collins Avenue *Trendy North end of South Beach 3 blocks from Lincoln Rd* ☏ (305) 531-1271 🖳 www.shelborne.com

■ **Sole on the Ocean** (AC B BF CC H M MA MSG PI S SA SB WO) All year, 24hrs
17315 Collins Avenue *Sunny Isles Beach, 20 minutes from South Beach* ☏ (786) 923-9300 🖳 www.soleontheocean.com
New very friendly hotel between Miami and Ft. Lauderdale, close to clothing optional Haulover Beach.

■ **Villa Paradiso** (AC CC glm MA OS PA RWB RWS RWT VA) All year
1415 Collins Avenue *Art Deco district, close to Lincoln Rd* ☏ (305) 532-0616 🖳 www.villaparadisohotel.com
Close to South Beach (gay beach).

GUEST HOUSES

■ **European Guesthouse** (AC BF CC glm I MA NU OS p PA PI RWS RWT VA WH) 8-24h
721 Michigan Avenue *Art deco district in South Beach* ☏ (305) 673-6665 🖳 www.europeanguesthouse.com
Walking distance to the beach and gay bars. 12 double rooms. All rooms with bath or shower and WC, telephone, sat-TV.

■ **Island House South Beach** (AC BF CC glm MA MSG RWS RWT VA) 9-23h
1428 Collins Avenue ☏ (305) 864-2422 ☏ (800) 382-2422 (toll free) 🖳 www.islandhousesouthbeach.com
Friendly guesthouse with 20 guestrooms. Walking distance from all major gay venues. Rooms, studios with kitchenettes and suites, complimentary BF.

■ **So Be You** (AC B BF CC glm MA OS PI RWS RWT) All year
1018 Jefferson Avenue *South Beach, near Flamingo Park*
☎ (305) 534-5247 💻 www.sobeyou.us
All rooms with private entrance bath, TV and telephone.

APARTMENTS

■ **Carlyle Miami Beach #1**
(AC H I MA NG NR PK RES RWS RWT WI) All year
1250 Ocean Drive, Miami Beach ☎ +33 663277213 (France)
Luxury furnished apartment for 3 to 4 for rent. Kitchen equipped. Full bathroom. Full-size bed + sofabed. Rate from EUR 850/week(all included). Special price for longer stay. Contact: luc.fayet@noos.fr

■ **Carlyle Miami Beach #2**
(AC H I MA NG NR PK RES RWS RWT WI) All year
1250 Ocean Drive, Miami Beach ☎ +33 674087747 (France)
A gorgeous Art Déco building. Luxury furnished appartment for rent. Large appt 67m2 for up to 4 people. Partial ocean view. Stylish decoration. Contact: jpcharles@noos.fr

PRIVATE ACCOMMODATION

■ **Villa Santa Barbara** (H MA RWS RWT WI) All year
829 Espanola Way *Near to beach and Flamingo park, shuttle available to airports* ☎ (786) 458-1945 💻 www.villasantbarbara.webs.com
Recently renovated villa with 5 bedrooms located in the heart of South Beach. Next to beach, gay bars and clubs. Near to many locations for leisure and sports activities.

SWIMMING

-12th Street beach (off Ocean Drive)
-Haulover Beach (Collins Ave. (A1A), north of Bal Harbour, through underpass) (g NU).

CRUISING

-Ocean Drive (particulary at 12th Street)
-Around the Flamingo Park (particulary at Meridian Ave at 13th St, the park closes from 24-5h, also in the park from 5h)
-Beach between 18th and 21 St (from sunset).

Milton ☎ 850

CAMPING

■ **Compound Campground. The** (GLM I NU PI WH) WE only
7962 Hickory Hammock ☎ (850) 983-8017
💻 www.thecompoundcampground.com

Naples ☎ 239

CRUISING

-Toilet at Golden Gate Community Park (ayor police action)
-Roadside Park (ayor police raids).

Orlando ☎ 407

PUBLICATIONS

■ **Watermark**
PO Box 533655 ☎ (407) 481-2243 💻 www.watermarkonline.com
Florida's biweekly „distinctive gay & lesbian publication".

BARS

■ **Bar Codes** (B f G MA) 12-2h
4453 Edgewater Drive ☎ (407) 532-3627
Former „Bear Bar Orlando" and still a place for bears & otters.

■ **Hank's** (AC B d f G MA) 12-2h
5026 Edgewater Drive ☎ (407) 291-2399 💻 www.hanksorlando.com

■ **Mr Sisters** (AC B D GLM M MA S ST) 11-?h
5310 East Colonial Drive ☎ (407) 545-2467 💻 www.mrsisters.com
New restaurant, sports bar, nightclub complex.

■ **New Phoenix** (B GLM MA ST) 12-2h
7124 Aloma Ave, Winter Park ☎ (407) 678-9070
💻 www.thenewphoenix.com

■ **Paradise Orlando** (B f G MA s) 16-2h
1300 North Mills Ave ☎ (407) 898-0090

■ **Parliament House. The** (AC AYOR B BF CC D G M MA OS PI S SNU ST T VS) 10.30-2h, Motel nonstop
410 North Orange Blossom Trail *South of downtown* ☎ (407) 425-5771
🖳 www.parliamenthouse.com
Six bars, restaurant, gay events with funny drag shows and large motel under one roof! Check www.parliamenthouse.com for details. Dangerous neighborhood – watch out!

■ **Savoy** (B CC GLM I MA OS) 17-2h, closed Mon
1913 North Orange Avenue ☎ (407) 898-6766
🖳 www.SavoyOrlando.com

■ **Stonewall** (AC B GLM MA) 17-2h
741 W Church St ☎ (407) 373-0888 🖳 www.stonewallorlando.com

■ **Wylde's** (B d G MA S) 17-2h
3557 South Orange Avenue ☎ (407) 852-0612 🖳 www.wyldesbar.com
Pool, darts, dancers.

DANCECLUBS

■ **Club @ Firestone** (B D glm MA) Thu-Sun 22-?h
578 N Orange Avenue ☎ (407) 426-0005 🖳 www.firestonelive.net

■ **Pulse Orlando** (B D G MA) Mon-Sat 21-2h
1912 South Orange Avenue ☎ (407) 649-3888
🖳 www.pulseorlando.com

■ **Revolution** (B D GLM MA S ST) 16-2h
375 South Bumby Avenue ☎ (407) 228-9900
🖳 www.RevolutionOrlando.com

RESTAURANTS

■ **Hamburger Mary's Bar & Grille** (AC B CC GLM H M MA S)
Sun-Wed 11-23, Thu-Sat -24h
110 West Church Street Unit H *At Church Street Station, on the corner of Church St and Garland Ave* ☎ (321) 319-0600
🖳 www.hamburgermarys-orlando.com
Restaurant with full bar, live shows, music videos.

■ **Rainbow Café** (AC B BF CC D GLM M MA OS PI S ST) 7-23, Fri-Sun -3h
410 North Orange Blossom Trail *At Parliament House Resort*
☎ (407) 425-7571 🖳 www.parliamenthouse.com

SAUNAS/BATHS

■ **Club Orlando** (! b DU FC G m MA OS P PI SA SB VS WH WO) 24hrs
450 East Compton Street *Downtown Orlando* ☎ (407) 425-5005
🖳 www.theclubs.com
Part of THE CLUB. Membership gives access to other clubs in the chain. Fully equipped gym, certified trainer Mon-Fri 11-19h. All-weather outdoor patio.

HOTELS

■ **Parliament House Resort** (AC AYOR B BF CC D G I M MA PI PK RWS RWT S SNU ST T VA VS) 24hrs
410 North Orange Blossom Trail *Downtown* ☎ (407) 425-7571
🖳 www.parliamenthouse.com
With 112 rooms probably the largest gay resort in Florida. Restaurant, pool, beach, disco, show theater, video bar and more. Dangerous neighborhood – watch out!

■ **Veranda Bed & Breakfast. The** (AC BF CC glm MSG OS PI WH WO) 7-19, WE 8-16h
115 North Summerlin Avenue *In the historic Thornton Park District*
☎ (407) 849-0321 🖳 www.theverandabandb.com
Historic building. Cable-TV, telephone, kitchen, fridge, coffee/tea facilities.

PRIVATE ACCOMMODATION

■ **Rick's B&B** (AC BF G I MA MSG NU OS P PI PK RWT VA VS WO)
All year
PO Box 22318 *Near Walt Disney World* ☎ (407) 396-7751
🖳 www.ricksbedandbreakfast.com
Rick's is an upscale, clothing-optional guesthouse for men only located in the Central Florida area since 1988 and currently serves Orlando's resort communities surrounding Walt Disney World, Universal Studios, Sea World and the Orlando Convention Center. Two night minimum stay applies.

Panama City Beach ☏ 904

BARS

■ **Splash** (B G SNU VS) 18-2, Thu-Sat -4h
6520 Thomas Drive ☏ (904) 236-3450 🖳 www.splashbarflorida.com

GUEST HOUSES

■ **Casa de Playa** (AC glm I MA NU OS PI)
20304 Front Beach Road ☏ (850) 236-8436 🖳 www.vrbo.com/10766

SWIMMING

-Seagrove Beach (NU) (west of Panama City Beach)
-Phillip's Inlet County Beach (½ mile West of Ramsgate Harbor)

Pensacola ☏ 850

BARS

■ **Emerald City** (! AC B D GLM MA OS P s ST WE) Wed-Mon 21-3h
406 East Wright Street *Downtown, behind Crowne Plaza*
☏ (850) 433-9491 🖳 www.emeraldcitypensacola.com
■ **Roundup** (B f G MA VS) 14-3h
706 East Gregory Street ☏ (850) 438-8482 🖳 www.theroundup.net
Very popular with bears, leather and levi-friendly.

SWIMMING

-Beach on Santa Rosa Island (Fort Picken's „BA" Beach)
-Gay Dunes Beach (Dunes and Trails 7 miles West of Navarre Beach)
-Pensacola Beach

Port Richey ☏ 727

BARS

■ **O'Nessa's** (AC B CC D GLM I MA S T VS WE) 16-2, Sun 18-2h
7737 Grand Blvd ☏ (727) 841-7900

Saint Petersburg ☏ 727

BARS

■ **Christopher Street Bar** (B D G MA SNU ST) 14-2h
13344 66th Street North, Largo *At Ulmerton Rd* ☏ (727) 538-0660
🖳 www.christopherstreetbar.com
■ **Detour** (AC B CC D GLM MA S ST) 14-2h
2612 Central Avenue *Cnr. 26th St* ☏ (727) 327-8204 🖳 www.detourfl.com
■ **Haymarket Pub** (B G MA) 17-2h
8308 4th Street North ☏ (727) 577-9621
■ **Lucky Star Lounge** (B G MA) Daily 14-2h
2760 Central Ave.
Small cozy gay bar with friendly staff and very low prices, happy hours.
■ **Oar House / Liquor Store** (B G m MA S) 14-2, Sun 13-2h
4807 South 22nd Avenue ☏ (727) 327-1691
Smoke-friendly gay neighbourhood bar with regular events. Karaoke Wed, Fri & Sun.
■ **Pepperz** (B D GLM m MA s) 14-2h
4918 Gulfport Boulevard, Gulfport *At 49th Street* ☏ (727) 327-4897
Also a liquor store.
■ **Sporters** (AC B f G MA) 14-2h
187 Dr Martin Luther King Street North ☏ (727) 821-1920

DANCECLUBS

■ **Georgie's Alibi** (B D GLM I M MA VS) 11-2h
3100 3rd Avenue North ☏ (727) 321-2112 🖳 www.georgiesalibi.com
■ **Nautico** (AC B D GLM MA ST) Daily 14-2h
4900 66th Street North ☏ (727) 546-7274 🖳 www.nauticostpete.com

HOTELS

■ **Flamingo Resort. The** (AC B bf CC D DR DU f GLM M MA PI RWS RWT S SNU ST VS) All year, 24hrs
4601 34th Street South ☏ (727) 321-5000 🖳 www.flamingofla.com
120 fully equipped rooms, 7 full service bars, a full service restaurant.
■ **Pier Hotel. The** (B bf glm I M MA RWS RWT) All year
253 2nd Avenue North ☏ (727) 822-7500 🖳 www.thepierhotel.com
Within walking distance of antique stores, museums, restaurants and the waterfront parks. A gay-friendly hotel.

GUEST HOUSES

■ **Dickens House B&B** (AC BF GLM I PK RWS RWT) All year
335 8th Avenue N.E *City* ☏ (727) 822-8622 🖳 www.dickenshouse.com
Gay owned. 5 guestrooms.
■ **GayStPete House** (AC bf CC G I MA MSG NU PI RWS RWT WH WO) All year, 24hrs
4505 Fifth Avenue North *Near Central Plaza transfer station*
☏ (727) 365-0544 🖳 www.gaystpetehouse.com
Bed & Breakfast in Central Oak Park Neighborhood of St Petersburg. Private and tropical pool area with hot tub is clothing optional, includes beer/wine/soda happy hour. Located just minuted to beaches, bars and shopping, and GLBT friendly Grand Central District.

CRUISING

-Bayshore Drive (from 2nd Street to Vinoy Park)
-Maximo Park
-Pass-a-Grille Beach (below 8th Street)
-Skyway Bridge Park
-4th Street North at Howard Franklin Bridge (AYOR be aware of undercover police)
-Gandy Blvd at Gandy Bridge (AYOR be aware of undercover police)

Sarasota ☏ 941

CRUISING

-Gulfstream Avenue 🅿 (Ringling Boulevard and Gulfstream)
-North Lido Beach
-Palm Avenue (AYOR R)

Tallahassee

CRUISING

-Rest Area US 319 North
-Florida State University (library)
-Lost Lake (southwest on Route 373)
-Park by post office (opposite Club Park Avenue)

Tampa ☏ 813

PUBLICATIONS

■ **OMG**
701 S. Howard Avenue, Suite 201 🖳 www.omgmag.com
OMG serves the Tampa, St. Petersburg and Orlando areas, as well as Key West, Miami and Ft. Lauderdale.

BARS

■ **2606 Club** (AC B f G MA) 20-3h
2606 North Armenia Avenue ☏ (813) 875-6993 🖳 www.2606.com
Home of the Tampa Leather Club.
■ **Baxter's** (AC B CC D G MA S SNU) 12-3h
1519 South Dale Mabry Highway ☏ (813) 258-8830
🖳 www.baxterslounge.com
Gogo bar with events every night.
■ **Body Shop** (AC B G MA SNU) 15-3h
14905 North Nebraska ☏ (813) 971-3576
Strippers on Fri.
■ **City Side** (B G MA) 12-3h
3703 Henderson Boulevard ☏ (813) 350-0600
🖳 www.clubcityside.com
■ **G Bar** (AC B D GLM) 18-3h
1401 East 7th Ave ☏ (813) 247-1016 🖳 www.yborclubs.com
■ **Metro** (B d G MA S ST) 18-?h
2606 N Armenia Avenue ☏ (813) 876-4650 🖳 www.metrotampa.com

Riverside Lounge (AC B D GLM MA ST) 14-3h
1807 North Tampa Street ☎ 374-0196
www.myspace.com/riverside.lounge

Spurs (B D GLM MA) 20-24, Fri & Sat -2, Sun 16-24h, closed Mon-Wed
1701 E 8th Avenue ☎ (813) 247-7877

Streetcar Charlie's (AC B GLM M MA S) 11-3h
1811 N 15th Street ☎ 248-1444 www.streetcarcharlies.com

CAFES

Sacred Grounds (B GLM MA s) 15-1, Fri & Sat 19-2h
4819 East Busch Boulevard ☎ (813) 983-0837 www.coffeeunchained.com

DANCECLUBS

Castle. The (B D f glm MA)
2004 N 16th St *Ybor City* ☎ (813) 247-7547 www.castleybor.com
Goth themed club.

Chelsea (B D GLM MA SNU ST) 15-3h
1502 N. Florida Ave. ☎ (813) 228-0139 www.chelseanightclub.com
Nightclub with gogo contests and happy hours.

Steam Fridays @ The Honey Pot (B D G SNU ST YC) Fri 22-?h
1507 E 7th Avenue *Ybor City* ☎ (813) 247-4663

Valentine's (B D GLM MA S) 15-3h
7522 North Armenia Avenue *Between Waters & Sligh Ave*
☎ (813) 936-1999 www.valentinesnightclub.com
Danceclub and showbar.

Ybor City Social Club (B D GLM VS YC) 14-3h
1909 N 15th Street
Dance bar and lounge with a young gay-lesbian mixed crowd.

RESTAURANTS

Hamburger Mary's (AC B GLM M MA S) 11-23, Fri & Sat -3h
1600 East 7th Avenue, Ybor City www.hamburgermarystampa.com
Theme nights.

SEX SHOPS/BLUE MOVIES

Buddies Video (GLM VS) 24hrs
4322 West Crest Avenue *Drew Park* ☎ (813) 876-8083
With 24 private booths.

XTC (cc g) 24hrs
4829 North Lois Avenue *Cnr. South Avenue* ☎ (813) 871-6900
www.xtcsupercenter.com
Second shop at 330 East Fowler Avenue.

SAUNAS/BATHS

Club Tampa (B DU FC FH G m P RR SA WH) 24hrs
215 North 11th Street ☎ (813) 223-5181
A medium sized sauna with friendly staff. Not that many facilities.

Rainbow Cabaret (b DU FH G I m MA RR SA VS WH) 24hrs
4421 North Hubert Avenue *Two blocks west from Tampa Bay Bucaneers Stadium* ☎ (813) 877-7585 www.rainbowcabaret.com
A not too flashy sauna with limited amenities.

Tampa Men's Club (AC DR G MA MSG P SB VS WH WO) 24hrs
4061 West Crest Avenue ☎ (813) 876-6367
New all-male fitness center and baths. Full state-of-the-art gym, steamroom, hot-tub, maze, Wi-Fi, TV in each room, mirrored gang showers, plenty of secure private parking.

GIFT & PRIDE SHOPS

MC Film (CC GLM) 10-19, Sat & Sun -24h
1901 North 15th Street ☎ (813) 247-6233 www.mcfilmfest.com

HOTELS

Ybor Resort & Spa (bf CC DR G MA NU P SA SB WH) All year
1512 E. 8th Avenue *Entrance is on 15th St. next the the Social/Eagle Club*
☎ (813) 242-0900 www.yborresortandspa.com
Tampa's largest all gay private club and resort.

CRUISING

-Picnic Island Park
-Ben T. Davis Beach (AYOR) (Campbell Causeway)

Venus ☎ 863

CAMPING

Camp Mars (GLM MA) Office: Mon-Thu 9-19, Fri & Sat -21, Sun -17h
326 Goff Road ☎ (863) 699-6277 www.campmars.com

West Palm Beach ☎ 561

BARS

Fort Dix (B GLM MA) 12-3, Fri & Sat -4h
6205 Georgia Avenue ☎ (561) 533-5355

H. G. Rooster's (AC B G MA OS s SNU VS) 15-3, Fri & Sat -4h
823 Belvedere Road ☎ (561) 832-9119 www.hgroosters.com

Karma Nightclub (AC B d GLM MA ST)
3097 Forest Hills Blvd

Lounge. The (AC B GLM MA OS s)
517 Clematis Street

DANCECLUBS

Respectable Street (B D g MA) 21-3, Fri & Sat -4h, Sun-Tue closed
518 Clematis Street ☎ (561) 832-9999 www.respectablestreet.com

Tabu Nightclub (AC B D GLM MA S) Sat
2677 Forest Hill Blvd

HOTELS

Hibiscus House
(AC B BF CC glm MA OS PA PI PK RWB RWS RWT) 24hrs
501 30th Street *City centre* ☎ (561) 863-5633
www.hibiscushouse.com

CRUISING

-Curry Park (AYOR)
-Dixie Highway (from Belvedere Boulevard to Forrest Hill)
-MacArthur Park Beach
-Seawall (summers)

Georgia

Location: Southeast USA
Initials: GA
Time: GMT -5
Area: 153.952 km² / 62,966 sq mi.
Population: 8,186,453
Capital: Atlanta

Atlanta ☎ 404

BARS

3 Legged Cowboy (B f GLM MA s) Tue-Sat 18-2.30h
931 Monroe Drive *In Midtown Promenade shopping center across from Piedmont Park* ☎ (404) 876-0001 www.3leggedcowboy.net
Country Western bar.

Amsterdam (AC B CC D G MA VS) 11.30-?h
502 Amsterdam Ave NE ☎ (404) 892-2227
Popular video/sports bar and dance club.

Atlanta Eagle (B D F G MA) 19-3, Sat 17-3h, closed Sun
306 Ponce De Leon Avenue *At Argonne* ☎ (404) 873-2453
www.atlantaeagle.com
Leather/Levi/Bear bar.

BJ Roosters (B G MA ST) 14.30-3h
2345 Cheshire Bridge Rd *At La Vista* ☎ (404) 634-5895
Mix of young and older. Strippers for entertainment.

Blake's (B GLM M MA OS ST VS) 11-3, Sun 12.30-24h
227 10th Street North East ☎ (404) 892-5786
www.blakesontheparkatlanta.com

Bulldogs (B F G MA OS) Mon-Fri 14-4, Sat -3h
893 Peachtree Street NE *Near 8th Street NE* ☎ (404) 872-3025
Cruisy.

■ **Burkhart's Pub** (AC B CC GLM M MA OS ST) 16-2, Sat 14-2, Sun 14-24h
1492-F Piedmont Road *Near Ansley Square* ☎ (404) 872-4403
💻 www.burkharts.com
Dragshows and Karaoke, check www.burkharts.com for calendar.

■ **Buzz. Le** (B D GLM M MA OS S ST) 19-3h, closed Sun
585 Franklin Rd A-10, Marietta ☎ (770) 424-1337
💻 www.thenewlebuzz.com
Cabaret show bar just outside of Atlanta in Marietta.

■ **Chaparral** (B D G MA) Fri 22-4h
2715 Buford Highway ☎ (404) 634-3737 💻 www.chaparralatlanta.com
Only Fri is gay, latin music and latin boys.

■ **Felix's on the Square** (B G M MA) 14-2.30, Sun -24h
1510-G Piedmont Avenue NE *In Ansley Square* ☎ (404) 249-7899
Small fun neighborhood bar.

■ **Friends on Ponce** (B GLM MA OS VS) 14-2.30, Sat 12-2.30, Sun -24h
736 Ponce de Leon NE *At Ponce de Leon Pl* ☎ (404) 817-3820
💻 www.friendsonponce-atl.com
Friendly neighbourhood bar.

■ **Heretic. The** (AC B D F G M MA OS s VS) 10-3h, Sun closed
2069 Cheshire Bridge Road, Cheshire Bridge ☎ (404) 325-3061
💻 www.hereticatlanta.com
Shows 1st/3rd Sun at 18h. Wed & Sun parties with strict dress code for access to certain parts of the bar! Leather shop located inside the bar.

■ **Mary's** (! B G MC VS) 17-3h, closed Sun
1287 Glenwood Avenue *East Atlanta at the corner of Flat Shoals & Glenwood* ☎ (404) 624-4411 💻 www.marysatlanta.com
For those over 21 years of age only. Recently voted as one of the best gay bars in the USA. Karaoke and music videos. New bar upstairs called The Boozy Cougar.

■ **Model T** (B G M MA ST) 9-3, Sun 12.30-24h
699 Ponce De Leon Avenue, Suite 11 ☎ (404) 872-2209
💻 www.modeltsatlanta.com

■ **New Order** (AC B G MC) 14-2, Fri & Sat -3h
1544 Piedmont Avenue *On back side of Ansley Mall Shopping Centre*
☎ (404) 874-8247
Here you find a more mature crowd.

■ **Opus 1** (AC B G MA) 11-3, Sat 9-3, Sun 12.30-24h
1086 Alco Street NE ☎ (404) 634-6478

■ **Swinging Richards** (B G MA SNU) Tue-Sat 18.30-3h
1715 Northside Drive ☎ (404) 355-6787 💻 www.swingingrichards.com
Fully nude male strippers, porn stars etc., .

■ **Woofs** (B f G M MC VS) 11.30-2, Sun 12.30-24, kitchen till 22h
2425 Piedmont Road ☎ (404) 869-9422 💻 www.woofsatlanta.com
Gay sports bar, a great place to watch a game or meet friends. Good food daily and lots of TVs, visitors will enjoy the friendly, casual atmosphere and masculine environment.

MEN'S CLUBS

■ **Club Eros** (B DR F G MA NU P VS) Tue-Sun 20-6h
2219 Faulkner Road *Off Cheshire Bridge, look for Rainbow tree*
☎ (404) 287 4482 💻 www.cluberosatlanta.com
This sex-club features bathrooms and plenty of room for hot, safer sex. Theme rooms and erotic video lounge. Entry fee comes with free soft drinks. A very busy club to visit, especially on the weekends. No alcohol is permitted. Free parking. See www.cluberosatlanta.com for more information.

■ **Den. The** (B DR G MA P)
2135 Liddell Drive ☎ (404) 292-7746 💻 www.thedeninc.com
Members only club for men of color, see www.thedeninc.com for details.

■ **Manifest** (B DR F G MA NU P VS) Thu, Fri & Sat 22-5h
2103 Faulkner Rd. ☎ (404) 549-2815 💻 www.manifest4u.org
Gay sex-club. Membership fee applies. Also nude yoga sessions offered.

DANCECLUBS

■ **Club 708** (B D G MA S) Wed 13-?h
708 Spring Street ☎ (404) 874-8125 💻 www.legendaryclub708.com
Popular, mostly African-American crowd, check www.wassupnatl.com for other parties and events.

■ **Grown & Sexy @ Django** (B D G MA) Sun 19-24h
495 Peachtree Street ☎ (404) 246-9000 💻 www.wassupnatl.com
Afro-american crowd.

■ **Jungle** (B D GLM MA ST) 21-?h, closed Sun
2115 Faulkner Road NE ☎ (404) 844-8800
💻 www.jungleclubatlanta.com

■ **Mixx** (B D GLM MA OS) Bar open Mon-Thu 16-1, Fri -3, Sat 13-3h; club open Sat 22-3h
1492 Piedmont Avenue *Near Burkhardt's and Felix's* ☎ (404) 228 4372
💻 www.mixxatlanta.com
Smoke-free gay bar in Atlanta (smoking allowed on the patio). Good lighting and sound systems.

■ **Rain** (B D glm MA OS)
448 Ralph David Abernathy Blvd *M° Westend Marta* ☎ (404) 577 2620
💻 www.rainnightclubatl.com
Club with two dancefloors. Most popular on Fridays.

■ **Traxx** (B D G MA S) Sat 22-?h
1287 Columbia Drive, Decatur 💻 www.traxxatlanta.com
Afro-american crowd, check www.traxxatlanta.com for specials.

■ **Who's Who @ Mark Ultralounge** (B D GLM MA) Wed 22-3h
79 Poplar Street ☎ (404) 904-0050 💻 www.themarkatlanta.com

SAUNAS/BATHS

■ **Flex** (AC CC DU FC FH G m MA P PI SA SB SOL VS WO) 24hrs
76 4th Street North West *At Spring St* ☎ (404) 815-0456
💻 www.flexbaths.com
Only gay bath house in Atlanta.

BOOK SHOPS

■ **Outwrite Bookstore & Coffeehouse**
(! AC b CC GLM m MA OS) 10-23h
991 Piedmont Avenue *At 10th St* ☎ (404) 607-0082
💻 www.outwritebooks.com
Books, music, videos, cards, gifts and refreshments.

GIFT & PRIDE SHOPS

■ **Brushstrokes** (CC GLM) 10-22, Fri & Sat-23h
1510-J Piedmont Avenue NE *Ansley Square* ☎ (404) 876-6567
💻 www.brushstrokesatlanta.com
Gifts, cards, videos and music.

LEATHER & FETISH SHOPS

■ **Leather Company** (F G) 11-20, Sun 13-18h
2111 Faulkner Rd NE ☎ (404) 320-8989

GUEST HOUSES

■ **Gaslight Inn B&B** (BF CC glm MA OS RWS RWT SA SB WH) All year
1001 Saint Charles Ave NE ☎ (404) 875-1001 💻 www.gaslightinn.com

■ **Hello B&B** (AC B BF CC GLM H MSG OS PK RWB RWS RWT SL VA VS WI) All year
1865 Windemere Drive *Midtown-Buckhead* ☎ (404) 892-8111
💻 www.hellobnb.com
Private guest house in the heart of Atlanta. Near Midtown & Buckhead.

CAMPING

■ **In the Woods Campground & Resort** (G MA NU)
142 Casey Court, Canon *At Hwy 327 & Hwy 51* ☎ (706) 246-0152
💻 www.inthewoodscampground.com
Gay, clothing-optional camping site.

CRUISING

-Cabbage Town (AYOR) (Grant Park)
-Chattahoochee Park (AYOR) (nature trails)
-Cypress Street/»The Strip« (AYOR) (alley between Peachtree & West Peachtree from 6th to 8th Streets)
-Lenox Square Mall
-Peachtree Center Shopping Gallery (800 Peachtree N.E.)
-Piedmont Park (AYOR) (nature trails & botanical gardens).

david
Atlanta's only weekly Gay magazine
nightlife • entertainment • music
health • fashion • tv • movies
dining • travel • the Southeast
www.davidatlanta.com

Augusta ☏ 706

BARS

Club Argos (B D glm MA S ST) 17-3, Sat 21-3h, closed Sun
1923 Walton Way ☏ (706) 481-8829
Dance bar downstairs. Levis/leather bar upstairs.

HOTELS

Parliament Resort (AC B CC DR G I M MA NU P PA PI PK RWS RWT SB VS WE WH) All year
1250 Gordon Highway *Historic Augusta* ☏ (706) 722-1155
www.p-house.com
Popular gay resort, cruisy, 70 rooms, heating, A/C, cable TV. Pride Shop, café, wireless internet and video lounge. 10 acres of secure grounds and RV Park. Bar is next door.

Dewy Rose ☏ 706

CAMPING

River's Edge Camping (CC G NU PI WH WO)
2311 Pulliam Mill Road ☏ (706) 213-8081
www.camptheriversedge.com

Savannah ☏ 912

BARS

Blaine's Back Door Bar (B F G M MA)
14-3, Sun 12.30-2h
13 E Perry Lane ☏ (912) 233-6765
www.blainesbar.com

Chuck's Bar (B g YC) Mon-Sat 18-3h
305 West River Street ☏ (912) 232-1005

Venus Di Milo (AC B glm MA) 17-3h, closed Sun
38 MLK Jr. Boulevard ☏ (912) 447-0901

DANCECLUBS

Club One (B D GLM MA S ST) 17-3, Sun -2h
1 Jefferson Street *At W Bay Street* ☏ (912) 232-0200
www.clubone-online.com

PRIVATE ACCOMMODATION

912 Barnard B&B (AC GLM m MA OS PA RWB RWT VS) All year
912 Barnard Street *Historic district* ☏ (912) 234-9121
www.912barnard.com
Two rooms with shared bath, shower and WC. Balcony, TV, VCR, own key and room service.

Unadilla ☏ 478

CAMPING

Lumberjack's Camping Resort (b CC d GLM m PI)
Mon-Thu 9-19, Fri & Sat -23, Sun -18h
50 Hwy 230 *Two hours south of Atlanta off I-75, exit #122.*
☏ (877) 888-1688
www.lumberjackscampground.com
One of Georgia's premier gay resorts and campgrounds.

Hawaii

Location: Pacific region USA
Initials: HI
Time: GMT -10
Area: 28.313 km² / 11,580 sq mi.
Population: 1,211,537
Capital: Honolulu
Important gay cities: Honolulu and Waikiki

Big Island – Kailua Kona ☏ 808

BARS

Mask-Querade. The (B D GLM M MA) 10-2h
75-5660 Kopiko Street, Ste C5 *At Kopiko Plaza* ☏ (808) 329-8558
www.themask-queradebar.com

GUEST HOUSES

Pu'ukala Lodge (bf glm MA)
72-3998 E Mamalahoa Hwy ☏ (808) 325-1729
www.purpleroofs.com/puukala-hi.html

Big Island – Pahoa ☏ 808

HOTELS

Kalani (BF CC D GLM I M MA MSG NU OS PI PK RWB RWS S SA VA WH WO) 8-22h
12-6860 Kalapana-Kapoho Beach Road *Southeast coast of Big Island*
☏ (808) 965-7828 www.kalani.com
Oceanside getaway on a lush tropical coast. 62 guestrooms. Clothing optional olympic size pool. Dance parties, yoga, spa.

GUEST HOUSES

Absolute Paradise B&B
(BF CC DU FH G I MSG NU OS PI PK RES RWB RWS WH WI) All year
Kehena Beach Road *Near „Black Sand Beach"* ☏ (808) 965-1828
www.absoluteparadise.tv
This gay, clothing-optional B&B is a 5 minute walk to the black sand nudist beach.

Isle of You Farm & Retreat (G MA NU)
13-790 Kamaili Rd *Puna District* ☏ (808) 965-1639
www.isleofyounaturally.com
The Isle of You, Naturally on The Big Island of Hawaii surrounds you with 70 acres of beautiful old Hawaii, the one that you've always dreamed of visiting. Gay owned & operated.

Pamalu (bf GLM I MA MSG NU OS PI PK RWS) All year
14-4820 Pua O Kapoho Road, Box 4023 *13 km from Pahoa at Puna Coast*
☏ (808) 965-0830 www.apeacefulenclosure.net
Private 5 acre guest house with bath/shower/WC, terrace, pool and TV/video room, 1h to the Volcano National Park. Work-out in nearby facilities.

Big Island – South Kona

GUEST HOUSES

Aloha Guest House (BF CC glm I MA MSG NU OS PK RWB RWS RWT VA WH) All year, 8-20h
84-4780 Mamalahoa Highway ☏ (808) 328-8955

www.alohaguesthouse.com
Five guest rooms with private bath and shared kitchen.

Kaua'i – Kapaa ☎ 808

GUEST HOUSES

Mahina Kai B&B (AC bf GLM MA NU OS PI)
4933 Aliomanu Road *North of Kapaa in Anahola* ☎ (808) 822-9451
www.mahinakai.com
Beautiful beach location, japanese style, gay owned, mixed clientele, clothing-optional pool.

Maui – Hana ☎ 808

APARTMENTS

Hana Accommodations (CC g MSG NU OS WH WO)
PO Box 248 ☎ (808) 248-7868 www.hana-maui.com
Vacation cottages on the beautiful Hana-Maui coast.

Maui – Kihei ☎ 808

DANCECLUBS

Oceans Bar & Grill (B D GLM MA) Sun 22-2h
1819 South Kihei Road ☎ (808) 891-2414

RESTAURANTS

Ultra Fab @ Gian Don's (B d glm M MA OS) Wed & Sat nights only
1445 S. Kihei Rd. ☎ (808) 874-4041 www.giandons.com
Wed and Sat nights attract an alternative crowd at this otherwise straight italian restaurant. Busier around 23h with a mixed gay/straight crowd.

HOTELS

Maui Sunseeker LGBT Resort (AC CC GLM I MSG PK RWB RWS RWT WH) Office hours 8-17h
551 South Kihei Road *About 9 miles from Kahului airport*
☎ (808) 879-1261 www.mauisunseeker.com
Maui Sunseeker is a 23-room gay-owned and operated hotel. Enjoy the best of Hawaii such as seasonal whale watches, snorkelling, kayaking and biking down the volcano.

GUEST HOUSES

Two Mermaids B&B (AC bf GLM PI)
2840 Umalu Place ☎ (808) 874-8687 www.twomermaids.com
Private, lesbian-owned guesthouse, it has two bright suites with tropical fish and floral decorations, a private Jacuzzi, lanai and access to a swimming pool.

APARTMENTS

Luana Kai (AC cc glm H I PI PK RWB RWS RWT SA VA WH) All year
940 South Kihei Road *30 mins from airport, 2 mins from the beach*
☎ (808) 879-1268 www.luanakai.com
All condominiums with bath, phone, kitchen, TV, radio. Sport facilities and beautiful garden.

Maui – Paia ☎ 808

GUEST HOUSES

Huelo Point Flower Farm (cc glm H I PI PK RWS RWT VA WH WO) All year
PO Box 791808 *Off Hana Highway* ☎ (808) 572-1850
www.mauiflowerfarm.com
Private hideaway with vacation rental homes & cottages.

Oahu – Honolulu ☎ 808

TOURIST INFO

Hawaii Visitors & Convention Bureau
2270 Kalakaua Avenue, Suite 801 ☎ (808) 923-1811
www.gohawaii.com

BARS

Bar 7 (AC B D GLM SNU ST VS YC) 21-4h
1344 Kona St. ☎ (808) 955-2640
Dance club with live performances. Best on Sat night. Strip shows from 22-23h, followed by a Dragshow.

Hula's Bar & Lei Stand (! AC B CC D f GLM I M MA S t VS) 10-2h
134 Kapahulu Ave, Waikiki *At Waikiki Grand Hotel, 2nd floor*
☎ (808) 923-0669 www.hulas.com
Beach bar and disco, weekly events, gay cruise on Sat, also Internet café, check hulas.com for updates.

In-Between (B G MA S) 16-2h
2155 Lau'ula Street, Waikiki *Behind Moose's*
☎ (808) 926-7060 www.inbetweenonline.com
Small & intimate gay bar for tourists and locals.

Lo Jax (AC B cc GLM I M MA) 12-2, Sun 6-2h
2256 Kuhio Avenue, 2nd floor ☎ (808) 922-1422
www.lojaxwaikiki.com
Sports bar.

DANCECLUBS

Fusion (AC B D G MA SNU ST) 22-4, Fri & Sat 20-4h
2260 Kuhio Avenue, Waikiki *2nd floor* ☎ (808) 924-2422
www.fusionwaikiki.com
Popular.

RESTAURANTS

Tapa's Restaurant & Lanai Bar
(AC B CC g LM M MA NR OS WL) 12-24h
407 Seaside Avenue *2nd floor, near Kuhio Avenue* ☎ (808) 921-2288
www.tapaswaikiki.com

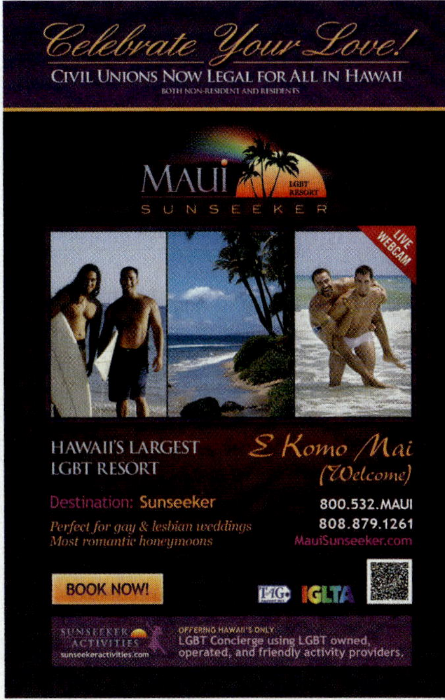

SAUNAS/BATHS

Max's Gym (AC CC DR DU G GH LAB m MA OS P SA SB SL VS WO) 24hrs
438 Hobron Lane, Eaton Square, PH1 *Waikiki beach, in the shopping mall, 4th floor* ☏ (808) 951-8232 www.maxsgym.net
A private club for men, featuring a full gym with sports trainer equipment, free weights, steam room, sauna, showers, lockers, private video rooms and a dark maze area. 18+ with photo ID needed to become member.

HEALTH GROUPS

Life Foundation (GLM) Mon-Fri 9-17h
677 Ala Moana Blvd Suite 226 *easily accessible by bus*
☏ (808) 521-2437 www.lifefoundation.org
Provides free confidential services with HIV/AIDS, and HIV prevention program for the community. Services include: case management, counselling and support groups, benefits and food assistance, weekly meals program, legal clinic, volunteer support, massage therapy, outreach programs, HIV testing.

SWIMMING

-Queen's Surf (G) (To get there, go towards Diamond Head on Kalakaua Avenue into Kapiolani Park and look for the pavilion on the right side. The grassy area between the pavilion and the snack bar: voilà! THE gay beach !)
-Diamond Head Beach (within walking distance of Waikiki. Gay area is just below the lighthouse)
-Ala Moana Beach Park (Across from shopping center of the same name. The area where the beach start to curve at the Diamond Head end usually has a small gay crowd on weekdays)
-Waikiki Beach (extremely long beach. The gay section is on the oceanside of the park, almost adjacent to Queen's Surf, approximately ½ of a mile east of the middle of the straight scene).

Oahu – Kailua

CRUISING

-Kailua Beach Park (AYOR)
-Kona Market Place

Idaho

Location: Northwest USA
Initials: ID
Time: GMT -7
Area: 216.456 km² / 88,530 sq mi.
Population: 1,293,953
Capital: Boise City

Boise ☏ 208

BARS

Lucky Dog Tavern. The (B f G MA OS) 14-2, Sat & Sun 12-2h
2223 Fairview Avenue *Corner 23rd/Fairview* ☏ (208) 333-0074
www.luckydogtavern.com
Bear and leather bar.

DANCECLUBS

Balcony Club. The (B D GLM MA t) 14-2h
150 North 8th Street #224 ☏ (208) 336-1313 thebalconyclub.com

GENERAL GROUPS

TCC – The Community Center
305 East 37th Street ☏ (208) 336-3870 www.tccidaho.org
GLBT Community Center.

CRUISING

-Ann Morrison Park (near archery range)
-Front Street

Coeur d'Alene ☏ 208

BARS

Mik-n-Mac's (AC B D glm MA S) 16-2h
406 North 4th Street ☏ (208) 667-4858

Pocatello ☏ 208

BARS

Charley's (B D GLM S) 17-2, Sun 19-2h
331 East Center Street ☏ (208) 232-9606 www.clubcharleys.com

Illinois

Location: Great Lakes region USA
Initials: IL
Time: GMT -6
Area: 150.007 km² / 61,352 sq mi.
Population: 12,419,293
Capital: Springfield

Alton ☏ 618

BARS

Bubby & Sissy's (B GLM MA S) 15-2, Fri & Sat -3h
602 Belle Street *At 6th St* ☏ (618) 465-4773
www.bubbyandsissys.com

Bloomington ☏ 309

BARS

Bistro (B D GLM MA) 20-1, Fri & Sat -2h
316 North Main Street ☏ (309) 829-2278

Champaign ☏ 217

BARS

Chester Street (B D GLM MA) 17-2h
63 Chester Street ☏ (217) 356-5607 www.chesterstreetbar.com

Chicago ☏ 773

✱ Chicago, called the „City Of Big Shoulder" by Carl Sandburg is a sophisticated, big-hearted city. Chicago is a veritable museum of modern architecture. Although renowned for its skyscrapers, Chicago is a „green" city with more than 500 parks, 46 kilometres of beaches and bike trails. The city relishes public art, unique theatre, cultural festivals and music concerts of every genre. Chicago is the birth place of Blues and House music, which can be found nightly in small and large clubs, along with jazz, rock, techno and country.
Chicago is a city of neighbourhoods, each with their own vibe, look and feel. Most of the gay bars and businesses are situated in „Boys Town," along North Halsted Street between Belmont Avenue and Grace Street and in Andersonville along Clark Street, between Lawrence and just North of Foster Avenue. International Mr. Leather is held in Chicago each year on the Memorial Day weekend and Chicago's pride festival takes place every year the last weekend in June. Another highlight of the summer festival season is North Halsted Market Days, a street festival held in late July or early August.
The gay scene is quite diverse with less attitude and snobbery than in some other cities. People in the Midwest tend to be friendly and more outgoing. The easiest way to get around town is on the rapid transit trains.

★ Chicago, von Carl Sandburg als „Stadt der großen Schulter" bezeichnet, könnte fast als Museum für moderne Architektur durchgehen. Ungeachtet ihrer berühmten Wolkenkratzer ist Chicago jedoch eine ausgesprochen grüne Stadt mit über 500 Parks und insgesamt 46 Kilometern an Stränden und Fahrradwegen. Es gibt unzählige Kunstaus-

stellungen, eine einzigartige Theaterszene, Kulturfestivals und Konzerte für jeden Geschmack. Chicago ist vor allem eine Wiege der Blues- und Housemusik, die neben Jazz, Rock, Techno und Country Nacht für Nacht die kleinen und größeren Clubs beschallt.
Chicago besteht aus vielen Bezirken mit jeweils ganz eigenem Charakter. Die meisten schwulen Bars und Geschäfte befinden sich in der Boys Town, in der North Halsted Street zwischen Belmont Avenue und Grace Street sowie in Andersonville, in der Clark Street zwischen Lawrence und dem Nordende der Foster Avenue. Am Memorial Day-Wochenende findet jährlich das Ledertreffen International Mr. Leather statt, Gay Pride wird im letzten Juni-Wochenende gefeiert. Ein weiterer Höhepunkt der sommerlichen Festivalsaison sind die North Halsted Market Days, ein Straßenfestival, das Ende Juni oder Anfang August stattfindet.
Die Schwulenszene ist ziemlich breit gefächert und weniger versnobt oder unnahbar als in vielen anderen Städten. Die Menschen im mittleren Westen der USA sind allgemein freundlicher und aufgeschlossener. Am schnellsten lässt sich die Stadt mit den Rapid Transit-Bahnen erschließen.

Chicago, que Carl Sandburg appelle „la ville de la grande épaule" pourrait pratiquement passer pour un musée d'architecture moderne. Malgré ses célèbres gratte-ciel, Chicago est une ville „verte" où l'on trouve 500 parcs et un total de 46 kilomètres de plages et de pistes cyclables. On trouvera également d'innombrables exposition d'art, un milieu théâtral unique, des festivals et des concerts pour tous les goûts. Chicago est essentiellement le berceau du blues et de la house, que l'on peut écouter dans les nombreux clubs de toute taille mais ceux-ci se partagent la vie musicale nocturne avec les clubs de jazz, techno, ou de country.
Chicago est constituée de nombreux quartiers disposant chacun de leur caractère propre. La plupart des bars et autres lieux gays se trouvent dans la „Boys Town", dans North Halsted Street, entre Belmont Avenue et Grace Street de même qu'à Andersonville, dans Clark Street entre Lawrence et le nord de Foster Avenue. Le week-end du „Memorial Day" a lieu la rencontre annuelle „International Mr. Leather", tandis que la Gay Pride est fêtée le dernier week-end de juin. Un autre grand moment de la saison des festivals en été sont les North Halsted Market Days, un festival de rue qui se déroule fin juillet ou début août.
Le milieu gay est très diversifié et moins snob ou distant que dans de nombreuses autres villes. Les gens du Middle-West américain sont généralement plus sympathiques et ouverts d'esprit. La façon la plus rapide de se déplacer est d'emprunter les lignes du Rapid Transit.

Chicago fue definida por Carl Sandburg como la „ciudad de los grandes hombros" podría ser considerada como un museo de arquitectura moderna. A pesar de sus famosos rascacielos, Chicago es una ciudad „verde" ya que cuenta con más de 500 parques y un total de 46 kilómetros de playas y carriles para las bicicletas. Se celebran muchas exposiciones de arte, tiene una escena teatral única, festivales de cultura y conciertos para todos los gustos. Chicago es, sobre todo, un referente de la música blues y house, junto con el jazz, el rock, techno y la música country que animan noche tras noche tanto los clubes grandes como los pequeños.
Chicago consta de muchos barrios con sus respectivas características. La mayoría de bares y negocios se encuentran en el llamado „Boys Town", en la calle North Halsted, entre la avenida Belmont y la calle Grace, así como en Andersonville, en la calle Clark, entre la avenida Lawrence y la parte norte de la avenida Foster. Durante el fin de semana del „Memorial Day", tiene lugar anualmente el encuentro internacional de cuero Mr. Leather, la Marcha del Orgullo Gay se celebra el último fin de semana de junio. Otro hito importante de la temporada de festivales de verano son los días de mercado en North Halsted, que es como un festival en la calle que se celebra a finales de junio o a principios de agosto.
El ambiente gay está repartido de manera bastante amplia y es menos arrogante que el de otras muchas ciudades. Los hombres del Medio Oeste americano son en general más simpáticos y abiertos. Lo más rápido para recorrer la ciudad son los trenes llamados Rapid Transit.

Chicago, chiamata „città dalle grosse spalle" da Carl Sandburg, sembra un museo di architettura moderna. Nonostante i suoi grattacieli, Chicago è una città piuttosto verde con più di 500 parchi circa 46 chilometri di spiagge e vie ciclabili. Ci sono tantissime mostre d'arte, una scena teatrale unica, festival culturali e concerti per tutti i gusti. Chicago è soprattutto la culla del blues e dell'house music che insieme al jazz, al rock, alla techno e al country rintronano notte per notte in tutte le discoteche della città.
Chicago incorpora diversi quartieri ognuno dei quali ha il suo proprio specifico carattere. La maggior parte dei bar gay e dei negozi si trovano nella „Boys Town" nella North Halsted Street tra la Belmont Avenue e Grace Street ma anche ad Andersonville nella Clark Street tra Lawrence e la fine della Forster Avenue. Durante il fine settimana del Memorial Day ha luogo annualmente il raduno leather „International Mr. Leather". Il gay pride, invece, si svolge l'ultimo fine settimana di giugno. Un altro highlight della stagione estiva sono i North Halsted Market Days, una specie di festival di strada che ha luogo alla fine di giugno o all'inizio di agosto.
La scena gay è abbastanza variopinta e meno snob meno fredda che in molte altre città. Nella parte centro-occidentale degli Stati Uniti la gente è in genere piuttosto gentile e aperta.

PUBLICATIONS

Boi Magazine
3708 North Halsted Street ☎ (773) 975-0264 💻 www.boimagazine.com
Free magazine with bar listings, articles, photos.

Foster Avenue
Glenwood Avenue
Argyle
Argyle Street
Argyle Street
Lincoln Park
N
St. Bonifacius Cemetery
Hermitage Avenue
Ravenswood
Lawrence Avenue
Lawrence
Chase Park
Damen
Wilson Avenue
Wilson
Clarendon Park
Sunnyside Avenue
Montrose Drive
Montrose
Montrose Avenue
Graceland Cemetery
Ashland Avenue
Paulina Street
Berteau Avenue
Kenmore Avenue
Buena Avenue
N Broadway Street
N Clarendon Avenue
Irving Park Road
Sheridan
Irving P.
Lake Shore Drive
Wunder's Cemetery
Byron Street
Byron Street
Hebrew Cemetery
Grace Street
Kenmore Av.
Sheffield Avenue
Birds Sanctuary
Waveland Avenue
Addison Street
Addison
N Clark Street
Racine Avenue
Boys-town
Roscoe Street
N Halsted St.
Kenmore Avenue
Belmont Avenue
Belmont
Wellington
Diversey
Diversey Parkway
EAT & DRINK
3160 – Bar 28
Big Chicks – Bar 4
Bobby Love's – Bar 9
Buck's Saloon – Bar 18
Cell Block – Bar 8
Charlie's Chicago – Bar 10
Closet, The – Bar 30
Cocktail – Bar 21
Cornelia's – Restaurant 14
Crew – Bar 5
Hydrate – Bar 15
Little Jim's – Bar 13
Lucky Horseshoe Lounge – Bar 26
Minibar – Bar 20
North End – Bar 7
Roscoe's – Bar 19
Scarlet – Bar 23
Scot's – Bar 33
Sidetrack Videobar – Bar 22
Smart – Bar 32
Sofo – Bar 3
Spin – Bar 27
T's – Bar 1
Wilde Plug – Bar 6
Chicago
NIGHTLIFE
Berlin – Danceclub 31
Circuit – Danceclub 11
SEX
Banana Video – Sex Shop 3
Man's Country – Sauna 2
RAM Bookstore – Sex Shop 12
Steamworks – Sauna 29
ACCOMMODATION
Villa Toscana – Guest House 17
OTHERS
Gaymart – Gift & Pride Shop 16
Unabridged Bookstore – Book Shop 24
Universal Gear – Fashion Shop 25

■ **Gay Chicago Magazine**
3115 North Broadway ☎ (773) 327-7271
Entertainment guide for the gay community, containing calendar of events, photos, columns and personal ads. Published weekly, 80-96 pages. Subscriptions available.

■ **Pink Magazine**
5412 N. Clark Street, Suite 220 ☎ (773) 769-6328 🖳 pinkmag.com
LGBT business directory and lifestyle magazine.

■ **Windy City Times**
5315 N. Clark Street #192 ☎ (773) 871-7610
🖳 www.windycitymediagroup.com
The voice of the LGBT community, with other publications and radio: Nightspots, Windy City Radio, Identity. See website for details.

SHOWS

■ **Baton Show Lounge** (AC B GLM ST)
436 North Clark Street ☎ (773) 644-5269
🖳 www.thebatonshowlounge.com
Showtimes at 20.30h, 22.30h, 0.30h.

BARS

■ **3160** (AC B CC GLM MC S ST T) 15-2, Sat -3h
3160 North Clark Street ☎ (773) 327-5969
🖳 www.chicago3160.com/index.html
A great neighbourhood bar.

■ **@mosphere** (AC B D GLM MA) 18-2, Sat 15-3, Sun -2h, Mon closed
5355 North Clark Street ☎ (773) 784-1100
🖳 www.atmospherebar.com
With an intimate dancefloor. No cover charge. Mixed crowd.

■ **Anvil** (B G MA) 9-2h
1137 West Granville *East of Broadway* ☎ (773) 973-0006

■ **Big Chicks** (B glm I M MA OS t) Mon-Fri 16-2, Sat 15-3, Sun 10-2h
5024 North Sheridan Road ☎ (773) 728-5511 🖳 www.bigchicks.com
DJ and no cover charge Fri & Sat. Upscale bar with free BBQ on Sun at 16h. Food 7 nights a week. Brunch at Tweet, the sister restaurant at 5020 N Sheridan Road, same building, same owner. Gay friendly.

■ **Bobby Love's** (B GLM m MA S) 15-2, Sat & Sun 12-2h
3729 North Halsted Street ☎ (773) 525-1200 🖳 www.bobbyloves.com

■ **Boom Boom Boom @ Green Dolphin Street Bar**
(AC B CC D glm YC) Mon 23-4h
2200 North Ashland ☎ (773) 278-5138 🖳 www.music-101.com

■ **Buck's Saloon** (B CC GLM OS) 12-2, Sat -3, Sun 11-2h
3439 North Halsted Street ☎ (773) 525-1125
🖳 www.bucksaloonchicago.com
Featuring a beer garden.

■ **Call. The** (AC B D GLM MA ST) 16-2, Sat -3h
1547 West Bryn Mawr Avenue ☎ (773) 334-2525
🖳 www.cattlecallchicago.com

■ **Cell Block** (B CC d F G MA VS) 16-2, Sat 14-3, Sun -2h
3702 North Halsted Street ☎ (773) 665-8064 🖳 www.cellblock-chicago.com
Beer Bust every Sun.

■ **Charlie's Chicago** (B D G MA) 15-4, Sat -5h
3726 North Broadway ☎ (773) 871-8887 🖳 www.charlieschicago.com
For those who like men in tight wranglers and cowboy boots. Danceclub on Sat with large dancefloor.

■ **Closet. The** (B GLM MA VS) 14-4, Sat 12-5, Sun -4h
3325 N Broadway Street *Cnr. Buckingham* ☎ (773) 477-8533
Video bar.

■ **Club Escape** (B D GLM M MA) 16-2, Sat -3h
1530 East 75th Street *At Stoney Island* ☎ (773) 667-6454

■ **Club Krave** (B D GLM MA s) 20-2, Fri & Sat -3, Sun 18-2h
13126 South Western, Blue Island *In the suburbs* ☎ (708) 597-8379
🖳 www.myspace.com/clubkraveblueisland

■ **Cocktail** (AC B GLM MA VS) 16-2, WE 14-2h
3359 North Halsted Street ☎ (773) 871-8123
Popular.

■ **Crew** (B GLM M MA VS) 11.30-24, Fri -2, Sat 11-2, Sun -24h
4804 N. Broadway *Lawrence and Broadway* ☎ (773) 784 2739
🖳 www.worldsgreatestbar.com
Gay sports bar.

■ **Davenport's** (AC B CC glm MA) 19-24h, closed Tue
1383 North Milwaukee Avenue ☎ (773) 278-1830
🖳 www.davenportspianobar.com

■ **Downtown** (AC B G MA VS) 15-2, Sat & Sun12-2h
440 North State Street ☎ (312) 464-1400
🖳 www.downtownbarandlounge.com

■ **Glenwood. The** (AC B GLM MA) 15-2, Sun 12-2h
6962 North Glenwood Avenue ☎ 764-7363
🖳 www.theglenwoodbar.com

■ **Hydrate** (B CC D GLM MA S ST VS) 20-4, Sat -5h
3458 North Halsted Street ☎ (773) 975-9244 🖳 www.hydratechicago.com
Front bar, at the back bar and disco.

■ **InnExile** (AC B D G I MA S VS) Sun-Fri 20-2, Sat -3h
5758 West 65th Street *Near Midway Airport, 1 mile west of Midway Hotel Center* ☎ (773) 582-3510 🖳 innexilechicago.com
Video bar with male dancers on Fri nights, karaoke on Sun and drag show on Sat once a month, see www.innexilechicago.com for updates.

■ **Jackhammer** (B D F G OS S SNU VS) 16-4, Sat -5h
6406 North Clark Street *At Devon* ☎ (773) 743-5772
🖳 www.jackhammer-chicago.com

Jeffery Pub (AC B D GLM MA VS) 17-4h, closed Mon
7041 South Jeffrey Boulevard *Jackson Park in Chicago's south shore neighbourhood* ☎ (773) 363-8555
Afro-American crowd.

John L's Place (AC B CC GLM MA) 16-2h
335 154th Pl, Calumet City *Calumet City is a suburb of Chicago*
☎ (708) 862-2386

Little Jim's (AC B f G MA VS) 12-4, Sat -5h
3501 North Halsted Street *At Cornelia Street* ☎ (773) 871-6116
Very popular neighbourhood bar. Large afternoon crowds daily.

Lucky Horseshoe Lounge (AC B G MA OS SNU)
16-2, Sat 14-3, Sun -2h
3169 North Halsted Street ☎ (773) 404-3169
Nightly dancers.

Maneuvers (B GLM MA ST t) 20-2, Fri & Sat -3h
118 East Jefferson Street, Joliet ☎ (815) 727-7069
www.jolietmaneuvers.com
Best on Fri & Sat, regular events and shows.

Manhandler (AC B G MA OS) 12-4, Sat -5h
1948 North Halsted Street *At Armitage Street* ☎ (312) 871-3339
Friendly staff. Warm atmosphere.

Minibar (B GLM M MA) Mon-Fri 19-2, Sat 17-3, Sun -2h
3341 North Halsted Street ☎ (773) 871-6227
www.minibarchicago.com

North End (AC B G MA S VS WE) Mon-Fri 15-2, Sat & Sun 14-3h
3733 North Halsted Street *Near Bradley Place & Sports Bar* ☎ (773) 477-7999
Pool tables. Male dancers occasionally.

Roscoe's (AC B D GLM M OS S VS YC) 15-2, Fri 14-2 Sat 13-3, Sun -2h
3358 North Halsted Street ☎ (773) 281-3355 www.roscoes.com
Popular bar and dance club in Chicago for twinks.

Scarlet (B G MA S) 16-2, Sat -3h
3320 North Halsted Street *At Roscoe Street* ☎ (773) 348-1053
www.scarletbarchicago.com
Piano bar.

Scot's (B G MA) 15-2, Sat 12-3, Sun -2h
1829 West Montrose *At Damen* ☎ (773) 528-3253
www.chicagoscotsbar.com
Friendly neighbourhood bar.

Second Story Bar (B G MA) 12-2, Sat -3h
157 East Ohio Street *At Michigan Ave* ☎ (312) 923-9536
Still running strong.

Sidetrack Videobar (! AC B CC GLM OS S VS WE YC) 15-2, Sat -3h
3349 North Halsted Street ☎ (773) 477-9189
www.sidetrackchicago.com
Most popular bar with comedy and show time nights, great frozen drinks.

Smart Bar (B D glm MA s) 22-4, Sat -5h
3730 N Clark Street ☎ (773) 549-0203 www.smartbarchicago.com
See www.smartbarchicago.com for events.

Sofo (B G MA OS VS) 17-2, Sat 15-3, Sun -2h
4923 North Clark Street *Between Ainslie & Argyle Streets* ☎ (773) 784-7636

Sound-Bar (AC D GLM VS) 21-4h, closed Sun-Wed
226 West Ontario Street *Cnr. of Franklin Street* ☎ (312) 787-4480
www.sound-bar.com

Spin (B D GLM MA VS) 16-2, Sat -3h
800 West Halsted *Cnr. Belmont* ☎ (773) 327-7711
www.spin-nightclub.com
Shower contest every Fri.

T's (AC B CC GLM M S) 17-2, Sat 11-3, Sun -2h
5025 North Clark Street *At Winnemac Avenue* ☎ (773) 784-6000
www.tsbarchicago.com

Touché (B CC F G MA) 17-4, Sat 15-4, Sun 12-4h
6412 North Clark Street *At West Devon* ☎ (773) 465-7400
www.touchechicago.com
One of the oldest leather bars in town.

Wilde Pug (B D GLM M MA) Sun-Fri 16-2, Sat -3h
4810 N. Broadway (Andersonville) ☎ (773) 784-4811
www.worldsgreatestbar.com/pug/index.htm
Dancing at WE, Pub with meals, theme nights. Fireplace in winter.

DANCECLUBS

Berlin (AC B D GLM VS WI YC) Sun & Mon 20-4, Tue-Fri 17-4, Sat -5h
954 West Belmont Avenue *In Boystown* ☎ (773) 348-4975
Busy Tue-Sat late.

Chances Dances @ The Subterranean (B D GLM MA t)
3rd Mon/month 21-?h
2011 West North Avenue, 2nd floor ☎ (773) 278-6600
www.chancesdances.org

Circuit (AC B CC D GLM MA S SNU) 21-4, Sat -5h
3641 North Halsted Street ☎ (773) 325-2233 www.circuitclub.com
Also karaoke nights.

Crobar Nightclub (B D glm MA) Fri-Sun 22-4h
1543 North Kingsbury ☎ (312) 243-4800
www.crobarnightclub.com
Occasional gay nights Sun.

Escapades (B D GLM MA) 22-4h
6301 South Harlem Avenue ☎ (773) 229-0886

Hunters (B D GLM MC OS S SNU) 16-2, Thu-Sat -4h
1932 E. Higgins Road, Elk Grove Village ☎ (773) 439-8840
www.huntersnightclubs.com

Rails @ The Prop House (B D G MA SNU) Fri 23-4h
1675 N Elston Ave ☎ (708) 802-1705 www.railschi.net
Latino and Afro-American crowd.

RESTAURANTS

Cornelia's (AC B CC GLM M MA OS S) 17.30-?h, closed Mon
748 Cornelia Avenue ☎ (773) 248-8333 www.corneliaschicago.com
Italian-American cuisine. Live music every day.

Hamburger Mary's & Mary's Attic (AC B CC GLM M MA S)
11-23, nightclub: Tue-Sun 20-2, Sat -3h
5400 North Clark Street *Cnr. West Balmoral Ave* ☎ (773) 784-6969
www.hamburgermaryschicago.com
Nightclub upstairs (Mary's Attic) featuring karaoke, DJs, cabaret and drag shows.

SEX SHOPS/BLUE MOVIES

Banana Video (G MA VS) 16-2, Fri & Sat -4, Sun 12-24h
4923 N Clark Street *Cnr. Argyle St* ☎ (773) 561-8322
Private viewing booths.

Bijou Theatre (AC DR G OC SNU VS) 24hrs
1349 North Wells Street *At Schiller St* ☎ (312) 337-3404
www.bijouworld.com

RAM Bookstore (AC CC DR G MA VS) 9.30-18h
3511 North Halsted Street *At Cornelia* ☎ (773) 525-9528
www.facebook.com/pages/Ram-Bookstore/381955631678?sk=info
Famous for its backroom.

SAUNAS/BATHS

Man's Country (AC DU f FC FH G I m MA P S SB SL SNU VS) 24hrs
5017 North Clark Street *Next to Chicago Eagle, bus Clark/Winnemac St*
☎ (773) 878-2069 www.manscountrychicago.com
Bath house and entertainment complex. Nude strip shows on Fri & Sat.

Steamworks (AC CC DR DU FC G GH I M MA MSG P PI RWT S SA SB SL VS WH WI WO) 24hrs
3246 North Halsted Street *North of Belmont Street* ☎ (773) 929-6080
www.steamworksonline.com
3 floors of stylish and innovative public and private play spaces-!

BOOK SHOPS

Unabridged Bookstore (glm) Mon-Fri 10-21, Sat & Sun -19h
3251 North Broadway Street *In the heart of Boystown* ☎ (773) 883-9119
www.unabridgedbookstore.com
Mixed bookstore with large gay/lesbian section.

FASHION SHOPS

Universal Gear (G YC) 10-21, Fri & Sat -22h
3153 North Broadway ☎ (773) 296-1090 www.universalgear.com
Further stores in New York and Washington.

GIFT & PRIDE SHOPS

Gaymart (CC GLM MA) 11-19, Fri & Sat -19.30, Sun 12-19h
3457 N Halsted Street *Cnr. Cornelius St* ☎ (773) 929-4272
www.gaymart.com

LEATHER & FETISH SHOPS

Leather 6410 (CC F G MA) 12-24h
6410 North Clarke Street ☎ (773) 549-0900

Cupid's Leather Sport (CC F GLM) 11-24, Fri & Sat -1h
3505 North Halsted *Cnr. Cornelia* ☎ (773) 868-0914

DVD SHOPS

Specialty Video Films & DVD (GLM VS) 10-22, Fri & Sat -23h
3221 North Broadway ☎ (773) 248-3434
Also at 5307 North Clark Street.

GUEST HOUSES

Ashland Arms (AC BF CC F GLM I MA MSG RWT WH) 24hrs
6408 North Clark Street *Located in the Jackhammer complex*
☎ (312) 498-9979 www.ashlandarms.com
Five fetish theme rooms: Leather, Sports, Rubber, Dreams and Bunk.

Villa Toscana (! AC bf CC G I MA OS RWS RWT VA) All year
3447 North Halsted Street ☎ (773) 404-2643 www.villa-toscana.com
Eight boutique style rooms with TV, telephone, some with shared bath. Continental bf. Ideal location in the middle of the gay scene.

GENERAL GROUPS

Chicago Area Gay and Lesbian Chamber of Commerce. The (GLM)
3656 North Halsted Street ☎ (773) 303-0167 www.glchamber.org

FETISH GROUPS

International Mr. Leather, Inc.
5015 North Clark Street ☎ (773) 907-9700 ☎ (800) 545 6753 (toll free)
www.IMRL.com
The world's hottest leathermen will once again come together to compete for the title of International Mr. Leather this year.

HEALTH GROUPS

Test Positive Aware Network Mon-Thu 9-21, Fri -16h
5537 North Broadway *Edgewater neighbourhood* ☎ (773) 989-9400
www.tpan.com
HIV/AIDS support and information; medical clinic; publishers of Positively Aware magazine and Illinois HIV Services Directory.

CRUISING

-Halsted and Broadway Streets (between Belmont and Addison. Many gay shops and restaurants)
-Hollywood Beach – Hollywood exit at north end of Lakeshore Drive.

Decatur ☎ 217

BARS

Flashback (B D GLM MA S) 9-2h
2239 East Wood Street *At 22nd St* ☎ (217) 422-3530

East Saint Louis ☎ 618

MEN'S CLUBS

Boxers ,n Briefs (B f G SNU ST VS YC) Tue-Sun 19-?h, closed Mon
55 Four Corners Lane, Centreville Il ☎ (618) 332-6141
www.boxersnbriefs.com
Large, exclusively gay strip club with complete nudity.

Galesburg ☎ 309

SAUNAS/BATHS

Hole in the Wall (b DU FC G m MA NU OS RR SA SB WH WO) 11-23, Thu-Sun 24hrs, closed Mon & Tue
1438 Knox Highway *5 km east of Galesburg* ☎ (309) 289-2375
www.holeinthewallmensclub.org

Iuka ☎ 618

CAMPING

Priapus Pines Campground (G MA NU P PI VS WH) May-Oct., office 10-22h
1372 Treefarm Road *South-central Illinois* ☎ (618) 822-2559
Clothing-optional campground for men.

Peoria ☎ 309

BARS

Buddies On Adams (AC B CC GLM MA NR WI) Tue & Wed, Sun 18-1, Thu 18-2, Fri & Sat 18-4; closed Mon
807 SW Adams St *At Oak St* ☎ (309) 676-7438
www.buddiespeoria.com

CRUISING

-Bradley Park
-Detweiller Park (days)
-West Main Street (on foot or by car).

Quincy ☎ 217

SHOWS

Irene's Cabaret (B d GLM MA S ST) 21-2.30, Fri 19-2.30, Sat -3.30h, Sun-Tue closed
124 N 5th Street ☎ (217) 222-6292 www.irenescabaret.com
See www.irenescabaret.com for details.

Rockford ☎ 815

BARS

Office (AC B D GLM MA OS S SNU ST VS) 17-2, Sun 12-24h
513 East State Street ☎ (815) 965-0344 www.officeniteclub.com

Springfield ☎ 217

BARS

Scandals (B D G MA ST) 14-1, Sun 12-24h
126 East Jefferson Street ☎ (217) 381-9581
www.myspace.com/scandalsspringfield

CRUISING

-Douglas Park (on I-94 North near Zion)
-Riverside Park.

Indiana

Location: Central Northeast USA
Initials: IN
Time: GMT -5
Area: 94.328 km² / 38,580 sq mi.
Population: 6,080,485
Capital: Indianapolis

Bloomington ☎ 309

BARS

Uncle Elizabeth's (B D GLM MA OS SNU ST) 16-3, Sun 17-24h
1614 West Third Street ☎ (309) 331-0060 uncle-elizabeths.com

Chesterton ☎ 219

GUEST HOUSES

Gray Goose Inn (BF CC glm I PA PK RWS RWT) All year
350 Indian Boundary Road ☎ (219) 926-5781
www.graygooseinn.com
Gay owned. 8 en-suite guestrooms overlooking Lake Palomara.

Evansville ☏ 812

BARS

■ **Someplace Else** (B D GLM MA ST) 16-3, Sun -24h
930 Main Street ☏ (812) 424-3202

Fort Wayne ☏ 260

BARS

■ **After Dark** (B D G MA S ST) 12-3, Sun 18-1h
1601 South Harrison Street *At Grand St* ☏ (260) 456-6235

■ **Babylon** (AC B GLM MA)
112 E Masterson Ave ☏ (260) 456-7005

Hammond ☏ 219

BARS

■ **Dick's R U Crazee** (AC CC D GLM M MA S SNU T)
19-3, Mon 21-3, Sun 21-3h
1221 East 150th Street *Cnr. Columbus Ave* ☏ (219) 852-0222
🖳 www.dicksrucrazee.com

Indianapolis ☏ 317

PUBLICATIONS

■ **Word. The**
c/o Word Publications, 110 East Washington St, Ste 1402
☏ (317) 632-8840 🖳 www.the-word-online.com
Monthly gay newspaper for Indiana, Ohio, Kentucky Southern Michigan & Illinois.

BARS

■ **501 Eagle** (B F G MA) 17.30-3, Sat 19.30-3, Sun 12.30-0.30h
501 North College ☏ (317) 632-2100 🖳 www.501eagle.com
Leather and bear bar.

■ **Downtown Olly's** (B G MA VS) 11-1h
822 North Illinois Street *Near Clair Street* ☏ (317) 636-5597
🖳 www.downtownollys.com
Sports bar.

■ **Greg's** (! B D G MA OS s) 16-3h, Sun 18-0.30h
231 East 16th Street ☏ (317) 638-8138 🖳 www.gregsindiana.com
Indianapolis' most famous bar and danceclub.

■ **Metro** (B D GLM M MA OS S) 15-3, Sun 11-0.30h
707 Massachusetts Avenue *At College* ☏ (317) 639-6022
🖳 www.metro-indy.com
Nightclub and restaurant, check www.metro-indy.com for special events.

■ **Talbott Street** (B D g MA ST) 21-4h
2145 North Talbott Street ☏ (317) 931-1343 🖳 www.talbottstreet.com
Bar, lounge and danceclub.

■ **Ten. The** (B D gLm MA S ST) 18-3, Sun -24h
1218 North Pennsylvania ☏ (317) 638-5802 🖳 www.the-ten.com
Popular lesbian dance club.

■ **Varsity Lounge** (B G MA)
1517 N. Pennsylvania ☏ (317) 635-9998

DANCECLUBS

■ **Unicorn Club. The** (! AC B D G MA P SNU ST)
Mon-Sat 20-3, Sun 21-0.30h
122 West 13th Street *At Illinois* ☏ (317) 262-9195 🖳 www.unicornclub.com
Male dancers daily.

SAUNAS/BATHS

■ **Club. The**
(! AC cc DR DU FC FH G I MA OS P PI SA SB SH VS WH WO) 24hrs
620 North Capitol Avenue *Downtown* ☏ (317) 635-5796
🖳 www.theclubs.com
Part of THE CLUB group of private men's clubs. Club Indianapolis is very clean, professionally run, and an all-round, top-rate bath house. Free condoms can be found in all the rooms and throughout the establishment. They also offer free, anonymous HIV testing.

■ **Works. The** (AC b CC DU FC G H MA OS P SA SB SL VS WO) 24hrs
4120 North Keystone Avenue ☏ (317) 547-9210 🖳 theworksindy.com

HEALTH GROUPS

■ **Damien Center**
1350 North Pennsylvania Street ☏ (317) 632-0123
🖳 www.damien.org
HIV/AIDS prevention and service centre.

Kokomo ☏ 765

DANCECLUBS

■ **Bar Blue** (B D GLM MA OS S) Sat only
1400 West Markland Ave ☏ (765) 456-1400 🖳 www.barblue.com
Dance and entertainment night club, check www.barblue.com for calendar.

Lafayette ☏ 765

BARS

■ **Zoolegers** (B D GLM MA S) 20-1, Fri & Sat -3h, Sun closed
644 Main St ☏ (765) 742-6321 🖳 www.zoolegers.com

Lake Station ☏ 219

BARS

■ **Encompass Nightclub & Lounge**
(AC B CC D GLM m MA s SNU ST VS WE) Mon-Sat 20-3h, Sun 19-1h
2415 Rush Street *Next to Fire Dept.* ☏ (219) 962-4640
Piano Lounge open Thu, Fri, Sat 22-1h. Men's night on Mon. Popular on Fri.

South Bend ☏ 574

BARS

■ **Starz Bar** (B D G MA SNU) 21-3, Sat -5, Sun 19-24h, closed Mon
1505 Kendall Street ☏ (574) 288-7827 🖳 www.starzbar.com
Stripshows.

■ **Truman's Entertainment Complex** (AC CC D GLM I m MA OS S ST) Wed-Sat 20-3, Sun -0.30h
100 Center, Mishawaka *Right off Lincoln Way near Downtown Mishawaka*
☏ (574) 259-2282 🖳 www.trumans.com
Complex of bars, nightclub, giftshop. See www.trumans.com for details.

■ **Vickies Bar and Grill** (B glm M MA) Mon-Sat 14-3h
112 West Monroe Street ☏ (574) 232-4090

Terre Haute ☏ 812

BARS

■ **Zim Marss** (B D GLM M MA ST) 18-3h, closed Sun & Mon
1500 Locust St *At 15th St* ☏ (812) 232-3026 🖳 www.zimmarss.com
Wed, Fri and Sat they have drag shows.

Iowa

Location: Middlewest USA
Initials: IA
Time: GMT -6
Area: 145.754 km² / 59,613 sq mi.
Population: 2,926,324
Capital: Des Moines

Cedar Rapids ☏ 319

DANCECLUBS

■ **Club Basix** (AC B D GLM MA S ST WE) 17-2, Sat & Sun 12-2h
3916 1st Ave NE ☏ (319) 363-3194 🖳 www.clubbasix.com

RESTAURANTS

■ **Hamburger Mary's** (b glm M MA ST) 11-24, Thu-Sat -2, Sun -22h
222 Glenbrook Drive SE ☎ (319) 378-4627
🖳 www.hamburgermaryscr.com

CRUISING

-Ellis Park (AYOR)
-Shaver Park

Davenport ☎ 563

BARS

■ **Club Fusion** (B D GLM MA S ST) 16-2h
813 West 2nd Street ☎ (563) 884-8014
■ **Mary's on 2nd** (B D GLM MA) 16-2, Sun 14-2h
832 West 2nd Street ☎ (563) 884-8014

Des Moines ☎ 515

BARS

■ **Blazing Saddle. The** (B d f G MA ST) 14-2, Sat & Sun 12-2h
416 East 5th Street ☎ (515) 246-1299 🖳 www.theblazingsaddle.com
Popular, check www.theblazingsaddle.com for events.
■ **Buddy's Corral** (B glm MA)
418 E. 5th St. *Next door Blazing Saddle* ☎ (515) 244-7140

DANCECLUBS

■ **Garden. The** (B D GLM OS ST VS YC) 20-2h, closed Mon & Tue
112 East 4th Street ☎ (515) 243-3965 🖳 www.grdn.com

Iowa City ☎ 319

BARS

■ **Studio 13** (B D GLM MA S ST) 19-2h
13 S Linn St ☎ (319) 338-7145 🖳 www.sthirteen.com

Sioux City ☎ 712

DANCECLUBS

■ **Jones Street Station** (B D GLM MA ST)
19-2h, closed Sun & Mon
412 Jones Street ☎ (712) 258-6338
🖳 www.facebook.com/pages/Jones-Street-Station-Night-Club/100864689958007

Kansas

Location: Middlewest USA
Initials: KS
Time: GMT -6
Area: 213.111 km² / 87,162 sq mi.
Population: 2,688,418
Capital: Topeka

Junction City ☎ 785

DANCECLUBS

■ **Xcalibur Club** (AC B cc D GLM m MA r S ST t VS WE)
Sun-Thu 18-2, Fri & Sat 20-2h, closed Mon & Tue
384 Grant Avenue ☎ (785) 762-2050 🖳 www.xcaliburclub.com
Check www.xcaliburclub.com for shows and special events.

Overland Park ☎ 913

BARS

■ **Fox. The** (B G MA) 13-2, Fri-Mon 18-2h
7520 Shawnee Mission Parkway ☎ (913) 384-0369

Topeka ☎ 785

BARS

■ **Tool Shed Tap. The** (B d F G MA) 15-2h
921 S Kansas Ave *Near 10th St* ☎ (785) 234-0482

CRUISING

-Gage Park (AYOR)
-Kansas Avenue (downtown by car)
-Shunga Park.

Wichita ☎ 316

PUBLICATIONS

■ **Liberty Press**
PO Box 16315 ☎ (316) 652-7737
🖳 www.libertypress.net
Monthly LGBT publication.

BARS

■ **Fantasy Complex** (B D GLM MA SNU ST) Tue-Sun 15-2h
3201 South Hillside Street ☎ (316) 682-5494
🖳 www.wichitagayclubs.com
Country and dance bar.
■ **J's Lounge** (B GLM MA S) Mon-Sat 16-2, Sun -24h
513 East Central ☎ (316) 262-1363
🖳 www.jsloungewichita.com
Wichita's only gay cabaret featuring piano, local artists, darts, pool and the best karaoke in town.
■ **Side Street Retro-Lounge** (AC B CC D GLM I MA OS) 14-2h
1106 South Pattie Street *Between Hydraulic & Washington Streets, 1 block South off Lincoln Street* ☎ (316) 267-0324
🖳 www.sidestreetretrolounge.com
Pool, darts and dancing.
■ **Store. The** (B gLm MA) 15-2h
3210 East Osie Street ☎ (316) 693-9781

Kentucky

Location: Central East USA
Initials: KY
Time: GMT -5
Area: 104.665 km² / 42,807 sq mi.
Population: 4,041,769
Capital: Frankfort

Covington ☎ 606

BARS

■ **Monet** (AC B D GLM M S) 16-1h
837 Willard Street ☎ (606) 491-2403
■ **Yadda Club** (B GLM M MA ST) Wed-Fri 17-2.30, Sat 19-2.30h
404 Pike St ☎ (606) 491-5600

Lexington ☎ 859

BARS

■ **Bar Complex. The** (AC B CC D f GLM MA S ST t VS) Mon-Fri 16-2.30h
224 East Main Street *On Main St in front of Esplanade* ☎ (859) 255-1551
🖳 www.thebarcomplex.com
„One of the worlds 50 greatest gay bar" according to Out Magazine.
■ **Crossings** (B f G MA) 16-h, closed Sun
117 North Limestone Street ☎ (859) 255-1551
🖳 www.crossingslexington.com
■ **Mia's** (AC B GLM M MA S) 16-2.30h
127 North Limestone ☎ (859) 455-9903

GUEST HOUSES

■ **Bear & Boar B&B Resort. The** (bf G PI)
Wood Creek Lake, London ☎ (606) 862-6557
🖳 www.BearandBoar.com
Also camping.

CRUISING

-Jacobson Park (AYOR)
-University of Kentucky (Fine Arts Building)
-Woodland Park.

Louisville ☎ 502

PUBLICATIONS

■ **Community Letter. The**
PO Box 7842 ☎ (502) 835-2068
🖳 www.theletteronline.com
Monthly gay & lesbian newspaper service Kentucky, Indiana, Ohio, Tennessee, Illinois and Missouri.

BARS

■ **Boots** (AC B F G) 21-2, Fri & Sat -4h
130 South Floyd Street ☎ (502) 585-5752
🖳 www.theconnection.net/boots.htm
■ **Starbase Q** (AC B D G MA VS) 20-4h, closed Mon
921 W Main Street 🖳 www.starbaseq.com
Video/Gogo bar, for special events check www.starbaseq.com.
■ **Teddy Bear's** (B F G MA) 11-4, Sun 13-4h
1148 Garvin Place ☎ (502) 589-2619
Friendly older gay male crowd.
■ **Tink's Pub** (B GLM MA ST) 16-?, Sat 12-?, Sun 13-?h
2235 S Preston Street ☎ (502) 634-8180
🖳 www.tinkspub.talkspot.com
Great drinks, karaoke, pool, games, live drag shows.
■ **Tryangles** (B f G MA S SNU) 16-4, Sun 13-4h
209 S Preston Street *At Market St* ☎ (502) 583-6395
Neighborhood bar, pool, games, karaoke.

CAFES

■ **Lynn's Paradise** (b GLM I m MA) 7-22, Sat & Sun 8-22h
984 Barret Avenue ☎ (502) 583-3447
🖳 www.lynnsparadisecafe.com

DANCECLUBS

■ **Connection Complex** (B D G MA S) 20-4, Mon & Tue -2h
120 South Floyd Street *At Market* ☎ (502) 585-5752
🖳 www.theconnection.net
Four bars in one, dance club with drag shows and more, check www.theconnection.net for special events.

RESTAURANTS

■ **Rudyard Kipling. The** (B glm M MA S) Wed-Sat 18.30-24h
422 W Oak Street ☎ (502) 636-1311
🖳 www.therudyardkipling.com
Restaurant/bar with shows/plays, check www.therudyardkipling.com for calendar.

BOOK SHOPS

■ **Carmichael's** (glm) 8-20h
1295 Bardstown Road ☎ (502) 456-6950
🖳 www.carmichaelsbookstore.com

CRUISING

-The Falls (across Ohio River in Jeffersonville, Indiana)
-Central Park (4th and Magnolia)
-Fourth Street (between St. Catherine and Hill)
-Iroquois Park
-Cherokee Park (at the fountain)

Louisiana

Location: South USA
Initials: LA
Time: GMT -6
Area: 134.275 km² / 54,918 sq mi.
Population: 4,468,976
Capital: Baton Rouge

Alexandria ☎ 318

BARS

■ **Olympus** (AC B GLM MA ST) Tue-Sat 18-3h
4003 MacArthur Drive ☎ (318) 442-6735 🖳 www.olympusbar.com
■ **Unique Bar & Lounge** (B D GLM MA S ST) Wed-Sat 21-3h
3217 Industrial Street *Near Alexandria Mall* ☎ (318) 448-0555

Baton Rouge ☎ 225

BARS

■ **Hound Dog** (B GLM MA) 15-2, Thu-Sat 14-2h, closed Sun
668 Main Street ☎ (225) 344-0807

DANCECLUBS

■ **George's Place** (AC B CC D GLM MA S VS)
15-2, Sat 17-2h, closed Sun
860 Saint Louis St *Cnr. South Blvd, almost under the Mississippi River Bridge*
☎ (225) 387-9798 🖳 www.georgesplacebr.com
■ **Splash** (B D GLM MA) Thu-Sat 21-2h
2183 Highland Road *Near cnr. E Polk St* ☎ (225) 242-9491
🖳 www.splashbr.com
Check www.splashbr.com for special events.

CRUISING

-Capitol Lakes (AYOR) (and adjacent area)
-Manchac Park (AYOR) (Highway 73, north of Bayou Manchac).

Lafayette ☎ 337

CRUISING

-Acadina Park (AYOR)
-Northeast Louisiana University (library)
-U.S.L. Library and Wharton Hall (2nd and 3rd floor)

Lake Charles ☎ 337

BARS

■ **Crystal's** (B d GLM M MA S) 20-2h, Fri 21-4, Sat -2h
112 West Broad Street ☎ (337) 433-5457

Monroe ☎ 318

BARS

■ **Corner Bar. The** (B D GLM MA S)
20-2h, closed Mon & Wed
512 N 3rd St ☎ (318) 329-0046

New Orleans ☎ 504

✱ As most gay/lesbian businesses are located in the historic part of New Orleans (French Quarter, Marigny and Bywater, Garden District etc.) hardly any of them flooded; some experienced wind damage that has been largely repaired. The historic part of New Orleans was founded by the French on the highest ground in the city (twelve feet above sea level). The parts of the city that flooded were generally the newer parts of town. New Orleans is as gay as ever, and has more political clout now as the gay community forms a larger part of the residential and business population than it did previously.

Da die schwul-lesbischen Läden im historischen Teil von New Orleans gelegen sind (French Quarter, Marigny and Bywater, Garden District usw.) sind sie kaum überschwemmt worden und nur einige von ihnen haben Sturmschäden erlitten, die aber mittlerweile weitestgehend repariert sind. Der historische Teil wurde von den Franzosen auf den höchstgelegenen Arealen gegründet (3,65m über dem Meeresspiegel). Die überfluteten Teile sind dagegen eher die jüngeren Stadtteile. New Orleans ist so schwul wie immer und der Einfluss der schwulen Gemeinde hat sich erhöht, da ihr Anteil an der Wohn- und Geschäftsbevölkerung nun größer ist als zuvor.

Comme les lieux gays et lesbiens sont situés dans le quartier historique de la Nouvelle-Orléans (Quartier Français, Marigny, Bywater, Garden Disctrict, etc.), ils ont à peine subi les inondations, le quartier historique ayant été fondé par les Français sur les cites les plus élevés des environs (3,65m au dessus du niveau de la mer). Seuls quelques uns d'entre eux ont été détruits par la tempête, mais ils ont été en grande partie reconstruits depuis. Les régions inondées sont par contre les quartiers plus récents. La Nouvelle-Orléans est toujours aussi gay qu'avant et l'influence de la communauté gay a même augmenté puisque leur nombre est plus élevé que jamais dans les habitations privées et les établissements commerciaux.

Puesto que los locales para gays y lesbianas se encuentran en la parte histórica de Nueva Orleans (Barrio Francés, Marigny, Bywater, Garden District, etc.), la mayoría apenas se inundaron y sólo algunos sufrieron daños a causa de la tormenta, que quedaron reparados enseguida. La parte histórica fue fundada por los franceses en unas zonas más altas (a 3,65 m sobre el nivel del mar). Las zonas que quedaron inundadas son precisamente las partes más nuevas de la ciudad. Nueva Orleans sigue tan gay como siempre e incluso la influencia de la comunidad gay se ha incrementado, ya que su participación en la sociedad y en los negocios es más grande que antes.

I locali gay e lesbici sono situati nel centro storico di New Orleans (French Quarter, Marigny, Bywater, Garden District, ecc.), quindi l'inondazione non li ha poi colpiti più di tanto. Solo pochi di essi hanno subito dei danni, tuttavia adesso sono stati completamente rimessi a nuovo. Il centro storico è stato fondato dai francesi nelle zone più alte dell'area (3,65 m sopra il livello del mare). I quartieri inondati sono invece quelli più nuovi. New Orleans è e rimane gay come lo è del resto sempre stata, anzi la capacità di affermazione della comunità gay è addirittura accresciuta.

GAY INFO

Lesbian & Gay Community Center (GLM)
14-20, Fri & Sat 12-18h, closed Sun
2114 Decatur Street *Right outside the French Quarter, in the heart of Gay Faubourg Marigny* ☎ (504) 945-1103
www.lgbtccneworleans.org
Promotes the vitality and well-being of the lesbian, gay, bisexual, transgender, and queer community of the Greater New Orleans area.

New Orleans

EAT & DRINK

700 Club – Bar	11
Acme Oyster House – Restaurant	22
Brennan's – Restaurant	18
Café Laffite – Bar	6
Corner Pocket – Bar	21
Double Play – Bar	20
Good Friends – Bar	13
John Paul's – Bar	23
Meauxbar – Bistro	24
Napoleon's Itch – Bar	15
Orlando's Society Page Lounge – Bar	3
Phoenix Bar – Bar	23
Rawhide 2010 – Bar	12
Roundup. The – Bar	19

NIGHTLIFE

Bourbon Pub & Parade Disco – Danceclub	8
Oz – Danceclub	7
Starlight by the Park – Danceclub	9

SEX

Club. The – Sauna	16
Flex – Sauna	17

ACCOMMODATION

Dauphine. La – Guest House	4
Royal Barracks – Guest House	2

OTHERS

Hit Parade – Gift & Pride Shop	14
Lesbian & Gay Community Center – Gay Info	1
Second Skin Leather Company – Leather & Fetish Shop	5

PUBLICATIONS

Ambush Magazine
828-A Bourbon Street ☏ (504) 522-8049 www.ambushmag.com
Biweekly magazine.

BARS

4-Seasons (B G MA OS S) 15-4h
3229 North Causeway Boulevard, Metairie ☏ (504) 832-0659
www.4seasonsno.com

700 Club (AC B cc G m MA ST VS) 24hrs
700 Burgundy Street ☏ (504) 561-1095 700clubneworleans.com
Comfortable bar with lounge sofas. Perfect place to chill with friends, go on a date, or relax after work. Now with tapas-style dishes during late hours.

AllWays Lounge (B G MC S) 18-3h, closed Mon
2240 St. Claude Avenue, Marigny *Part of Marigny Theater*
☏ (504) 947-0505 www.theallwayslounge.com

Big Daddy's (B GLM MA s) 24hrs
2513 Royal Street ☏ (504) 948-6288

Cafe Lafitte (AC B f G MA SNU VS) 24hrs
901 Bourbon Street *Dumaine Street* ☏ (504) 522-8397
www.lafittes.com
Karaoke Wed 21-24h, SNU Thu-Sun 20-?h. Popular on Fri.

Corner Pocket (B G SNU ST YC) 12-3, WE 24hrs
940 St. Louis Street *Cnr. Burgundy Street* ☏ (504) 568-9829
www.cornerpocket.net
SNU every day 22h.

Country Club. The (B G MA PI WO) 11-1h
634 Louisa Street *Between Chartres and Royal St* ☏ (504) 945-0742
Poolside bar.

Cutter's (B GLM MA) 11-3h
706 Franklin Ave *Cnr. Royal* ☏ (504) 948-4200
www.cuttersbar.biz
Small piano bar displaying local artwork.

Double Play (B G MA T) 24hrs
439 Dauphine Street *Cnr. St Louis* ☏ (504) 523-4517
www.facebook.com/pages/Double-Play/112631215467659
Cruise bar.

Friendly Bar. The (B GLM m MA) 11-3h
2301 Chartres Street ☏ (504) 943-8929
Pool table and a juke box.

Good Friends (AC B GLM MA VS) 24hrs
740 Dauphine Street ☏ (504) 566-7191 www.goodfriendsbar.com
Perfect meeting place.

John Paul's (B d f G MA S ST) 12-?h
940 Elysian Fields Avenue *Cnr. North Rampart* ☏ (504) 948-1888
www.johnpaulsbar.com

Napoleon's Itch (B GLM MA S) Mon-Thu 16-?, Fri & Sat 12-?h
734 Bourbon Street *At St Ann, in Bourbon Orleans Hotel*
☏ (504) 371-5450 www.napoleonsitch.com

Society Page Lounge (B GLM M MA) 18-2, Sat & Sun 15-2h
542 North Rampart ☏ (504) 299-0156

Phoenix (! B F G M MA) 24hrs
941 Elysian Fields Avenue *At Rampart Street* ☏ (504) 945-9264
Posters from gay bars around the world cover the walls downstairs. Upstairs, you'll find some dark corners, restraints hanging from the ceiling and a cage. Popular gathering for the town's leather crowd.

Rawhide 2010 (AC B F G MA s) Daily 13-5h
740 Burgundy Street *Saint Ann Street, two blocks off Bourbon Street*
☏ (504) 525-8106 www.rawhide2010.com
Happy hour 16-21h daily. Rated one of the top-ten leather bars in the country.

Roundup. The (B G OS ST T) 24hrs
819 Saint Louis Street ☏ (504) 561-8340
Bar with a mixed crowd. Pocket pool, juke box, occasional shows, and a patio (open during the summer).

Sanctuary (B gLm MA s ST) 17-?h
2301 North Causeway Blvd, Metairie *At 34th St* ☏ (504) 834-7979
Lesbian bar.

Tubby's Golden Lantern (B G I MA S SNU ST VS) 12-4h
1239 Royal Street ☏ (504) 529-2860 www.tubbysbarneworleans.com
Happy hour daily 14-20h.

CAFES

Meauxbar Bistro (AC B CC G M MA) 18-22h, closed Sun & Mon
942 North Rampart Street *French Quarter, cnr. St. Philip*
☏ (504) 569-9979 www.meauxbar.com
Great food, fabulous ambience.

DANCECLUBS

Bourbon Pub & Parade (AC B D GLM I s VS YC) 24hrs
801 Bourbon Street ☏ (504) 529-2107
www.bourbonpub-parade.com
Part of the gay scene of New Orleans for more than 30 yeras. Popular tea dance on Sun.

Oz (! B D GLM OS SNU ST YC) 24hrs
800 Bourbon Street ☏ (504) 593-9491 www.ozneworleans.com
Drag show on Wed.

Starlight by the Park (B D GLM MA ST)
12-4, Fri 12-Sun 4h (non stop)
834 North Rampart St ☏ (504) 561-8939
www.starlightbythepark.com

RESTAURANTS

Acme Oyster House (B CC g M MC) Sun-Thu 11-22, Fri & Sat -23h
724 Iberville Street *French Quarter* ☏ (504) 522-5973
www.acmeoyster.com
Delicious seafood, good value for money in a casual atmosphere.

Brennan's (AC B CC glm M MA NR OS VEG WL)
Mon-Fri 9-13 & 18-21, Sat-Sun 9-14 & 18-21h
417 Royal Street ☏ (504) 525-9713 www.brennansrestaurant.com
Brennan's 50,000-bottle wine cellar has repeatedly received the Wine Spectator Grand Award for having one of the most outstanding wine lists in the world.

Bywater (b glm M MA) 11-22, Sat & Sun 9-22h, closed Wed
3162 Dauphine Street *Cnr. Louisa* ☏ (504) 944-4445

SAUNAS/BATHS

Club. The
(! b CC DU FC FH G MA OS P RR SA SB SH SL SOL VS WH WO) 24hrs
515 Toulouse Street ☏ (504) 581-2402 www.the-clubs.com
THE CLUB New Orleans is 5 unique floors of fun, fitness and fantasy! Located in the center of the famous French Quarter. Membership can be used in all THE CLUB locations. See: www.the-clubs.com for more information.

Flex (AC CC DR DU FC FH G m MA P RR SA SB VS WH WO) 24hrs
700 Baronne Street ☏ (504) 598-3539 www.flexbaths.com
Beautiful spa next to the famous French Quarter in a historic building. All spa facilities.

GIFT & PRIDE SHOPS

Hit Parade (GLM) 12-24, Fri & Sat 11-2h
741 Bourbon St ☏ (504) 524-7700 www.hitparadeonline.com
Gay gift & clothing store.

LEATHER & FETISH SHOPS

Panda Bear. The (CC F GLM)
415 Bourbon Street ☏ (504) 529-8064
Leather and toys.

Second Skin Leather (F G) 12-20, Fri & Sat -22h
521 St Philip Street ☏ (504) 561-8167

HOTELS

Frenchmen Hotel. The (AC BF cc glm M PI) All year
417 Frenchmen Street ☏ (504) 948-2166 www.frenchmenhotel.com
Rooms with bath, phone and TV.

Harrah's New Orleans Casino & Hotel
(AC B BF CC DM glm I M NR PK RWS RWT S SH VEG WL) All year
8 Canal Street ☏ (504) 533-6000 www.harrahsneworleans.com

GUEST HOUSES

1870 Banana Courtyard
(AC bf glm I MA OS PK RWB RWS RWT) All year
1422 N. Rampart Street *French Quarter/ Faubourg Marigny*
☎ (504) 947-4475 www.bananacourtyard.com
At the main B&B, there are 8 rooms. Nearby are 4 townhouses, a pool house and a cottage.

5 Continents B&B
(AC BF CC GLM I OS PA PK RWB RWS RWT WI) All year
1731 Esplanade Ave *6 blocks from French Quarter* ☎ (504) 234-2092
www.fivecontinentsbnb.com
XIX century renewed mansion. 4 guestrooms.

Bon Maison Guest House (AC cc GLM I MA OS RWS RWT VA) All year
835 Bourbon Street *Street car 3 blocks away* ☎ (504) 561-8498
www.bonmaison.com
All rooms with private shower baths, kitchenette (refrigerator, microwave, toaster, coffee maker and TV.

Bourgoyne Guest House (AC bf CC H OS) All year
839 Bourbon Street *Cnr. Dumaine Street* ☎ (504) 525-3983
www.bourgoynehouse.com
Old world charm in the heart of the French Quarter.

Burgundy B&B for Gays, Lesbians & Friends
(AC BF CC GLM I MA OS PK RWS RWT WH) All year
2513 Burgundy Street *In Marigny, adjacent to French Quarter*
☎ (504) 942-1463 www.theburgundy.com
A small and cosy gay owned and operated B&B with 4 guestrooms in the Faubourg Marigny, just a few blocks from the French Quarter. Four rooms, all with private bath.

Chez Palmiers B&B (AC bf cc glm H I MA PI PK RWS RWT) All year
1744 N Rampart Street *2 blocks from the French Quarter*
☎ (504) 208-7044 www.chezpalmiers.com
Gay owned and operated.

Dauphine. La (AC CC glm I MA OS RWS RWT) All year
2316 rue Dauphine *Four blocks walk to French Quarter*
☎ (504) 948-2217 www.ladauphine.com
The 3 suites feature queen-size, four-poster beds, cable TV/DVD/VCR, phone and ceiling fans. Free internet access. Advanced reservations required.

Elysian Guest House
(AC CC GLM MA MSG OS PA RWS RWT VA VS WH)
All year, check in 8-16h
1008 Elysian Fields Avenue ☎ (504) 324-4311
www.elysianguesthouse.com
All rooms have cable TV, kitchens, baths with showers, toiletries and own keys. Visa and Mastercard only.

Garden District. The (AC BF CC GLM I OS RWB RWS RWT) All year
2418 Magazine Street *Two miles from Bourbon St* ☎ (504) 895-4302
www.gardendistrictbedandbreakfast.com
Victorian town house. Four rooms with private bath, balconies, ceiling fans, open fire places and cable TV.

Green House Inn. The (AC BF CC GLM I MA MSG PA PI PK RWB RWS RWT T VA WE WH WO) Reception: Mon-Sat 9-14h
1212 Magazine Street *Downtown/Garden District, 12 blocks from French Quarter* ☎ (504) 525-1333 www.thegreenhouseinn.com
All 9 rooms with private bath/WC, colour TV, video, minifridge and phone.

Lions Inn B&B (AC bf CC GLM I m MA MSG OS PA PI PK RWS RWT VA WH) All year
2517 Chartres Street *Faubourg Marigny* ☎ (504) 945-2339
www.lionsinn.com
All 10 rooms with cable TV, radio and hair-dryer. Pool & hot tub in use 24hrs.

New Orleans Guest House (AC b BF CC glm H I MA OS PK RWS RWT VA) 24hrs
1118 Ursulines Street *French Quarter, 3 blocks to Bourbon St*
☎ (504) 566-1177 www.neworleans.com/nogh
Built in 1848. The Slave Quarters have been renovated into guest units. All 14 rooms with private bath, TV, radio and phone.

Olde Town Inn (AC bf CC glm MA OS PA PK RWB RWS RWT VA) All year
1001 Marigny Street *6 blocks to French Quarter* ☎ (504) 949-5815
www.oldetowninn.com
With 21 guest rooms with private or shared bath, tel/fax, TV and hair-dryer. Beautiful courtyard.

Royal Barracks
(AC B CC glm I MA MSG NU OS p RWS RWT VA VS WH) All year
717 Barracks Street *Between Royal & Bourbon St* ☎ (504) 529-7269
www.rbgh.com
All 6 rooms with cable TV, radio, ceiling fan, private bath.

Royal Street Courtyard (AC BF CC DU GLM I MA OS RWB RWS RWT WH WI) All year, office hours 8-17h
2438 Royal Street *Cnr. of Royal and Spain, 6 blocks east of the French Quarter* ☎ (504) 943-6818 www.royalstcourtyard.com
Easy walk into the French Quarter, very gay neighbourhood.

HEALTH GROUPS

Community Awareness Network (CAN) Office (GLM MA)
507 Frenchmen Street ☎ 945.4000 www.noaidstaskforce.com

New Orleans AIDS Task Force
2601 Tulane Avenue, Suite 500 ☎ (504) 821-2601
www.noaidstaskforce.org

CRUISING

-Audubon Park (AYOR)
-Belle Promenade (West Bank)
-City Park (AYOR)
-Oakwood Shopping Center (AYOR)
-Riverwalk
-Tulane University (AYOR) (cafeteria, library & student union)
-U.N.O. (business administration building & library)
-Vieux Carre (especially Bourbon Street between Toulouse & Ursulines Streets)
-Woldenberg Park.

Shreveport ☎ 318

BARS

■ **Central Station** (B D GLM MA S) 15-2, Fri & Sat -6h
1025 Marshall St *Between Fairfield & Creswell* ☎ (318) 222-2216

■ **Korner Lounge. The** (AC B CC GLM I MA VS) 15-2h
800 Louisiana Avenue *Downtown, cnr. of Louisiana & Cotton*
☎ (318) 222-9796 ⌨ www.thekornerlounge.com
Small friendly bar.

Slidell ☎ 504

BARS

■ **Billy's** (B glm MA OS ST) 18-1h
2600 Highway 190 West ☎ (504) 847-1921 ⌨ www.4seasonsno.com

Maine

Location: Northeast USA
Initials: ME
Time: GMT -5
Area: 91.653 km² / 37,486 sq mi.
Population: 1,247,923
Capital: Augusta

Albion ☎ 207

CAMPING

■ **Twin Ponds Lodge and Campground** (CC G I MA MSG NU P SA WH WO) Thu-Sun 10-23h
96 Yorktown Road ☎ (207) 462-7701 ⌨ www.twinpondslodge.com
This is a private club for men only and a simple membership is required. Clothing optional throughout the facility and property.

Bath ☎ 207

GUEST HOUSES

■ **Galen C. Moses House** (AC BF glm I PA PK RWS) All year
1009 Washington Street ☎ (207) 442-8771 ⌨ www.galenmoses.com
Excellent hospitality in this gay owned property with five guestrooms.

Carthage ☎ 207

CAMPING

■ **Blue Moose Campground** (GLM)
405 Carthage Road (Route 142) *At the banks of the Webb River*
☎ (207) 562-4658 ⌨ www.bluemoosecampground.com
Campground, about six miles from Mt. Blue State Park.

Naples ☎ 207

GUEST HOUSES

■ **Lamb's Mill Inn** (AC BF CC glm m OS RWS RWT SB WH) All year
131 Lamb's Mill Road ☎ (207) 693-6253 ⌨ www.lambsmillinn.com
Six rooms with private baths, TV, refrigerator.

Ogunquit ☎ 207

BARS

■ **Front Porch Piano Bar & Restaurant** (B CC glm M S)
9 Shore Road Ogunquit Square ☎ (207) 646-3976
⌨ www.thefrontporch.net
Popular restaurant and bar, check www.thefrontporch.net for hours and special events.

■ **Maine Street Video Bar** (B D GLM MA VS) 17-?h
195 Main Street ☎ (207) 646-5101 ⌨ www.mainestreetogunquit.com
DJ & dancing Fri & Sat at 21h, karaoke Sundays and pool tournaments Sun & Tue at 18h.

RESTAURANTS

■ **Five-O Shore Road Lounge** (AC B CC g M MA) 17-?h
50 Shore Road *Near Downtown* ☎ (207) 646-5001
⌨ www.five-oshoreroad.com
Casual fine dining restaurant serving traditional New England cuisine with Mediterranean influences.

HOTELS

■ **Admiral's Inn**
(AC B bf CC glm I MSG PA PI PK RWB RWS RWT VA WH) All year, 11-23h
87-95 Main Street *Close to beach and downtown* ☎ (207) 646-7093
⌨ www.theadmiralsinn.com
The Admiral's Inn is a resort in the center of the village. Stroll to the beach, Marginal Way, Perkins Cove, Ogunquit Playhouse and all of the village pleasures. Hot tub, heated pool, fire pit, and lounge on premises.

GUEST HOUSES

■ **Beauport Inn**
(AC BF CC glm I m MA OS PI PK RWB RWS RWT SA SB VA WE WH)
339 Clay Hill ☎ (207) 361-2400 ⌨ www.beauportinn.com
4 rooms with private baths. No pets, no kids.

■ **Black Boar Inn** (BF glm MA)
277 Main Street ☎ (207) 646-2112 ⌨ www.blackboarinn.com

■ **Leisure Inn** (AC BF g OS PA RWS RWT) 15 May-15 Oct
73 School Street ☎ (207) 646-2737 ⌨ www.theleisureinn.com
All rooms with TV, most with AC. On-site parking. No kids, no pets.

■ **Moon over Maine** (AC BF CC GLM I OS PK RWB RWS RWT WH) All year
22 Berwick Road ☎ (207) 646-6666 ⌨ www.moonovermaine.com
All rooms with private bath, balcony, radio and sat-TV. Kids welcome, no pets.

■ **Ogunquit Beach Inn** (AC B BF CC G I M MA OS PK RWB RWS RWT VA VS) Open Apr-Oct
67 School Street *Village centre, walk to the beach, close to nightlife*
☎ (207) 646-1112 ⌨ www.ogunquitbeachinn.com
Gay B&B in village centre, walk to beach and all nightlife. All private baths, reasonable rates.

■ **Rockmere Lodge B&B** (AC BF CC GLM I MA MSG NR OS PK RWS RWT WI) All year
150 Stearns Road *On Marginal Way* ☎ (207) 646-2985
⌨ www.rockmere.com
Eight rooms ocean side B&B with private bath and TV.

■ **Two Village Square** (AC BF CC GLM I MA PA PI PK RWS RWT SOL VA WH WO) Mid May-late Oct
14 Village Square Lane, PO Box 864 ☎ (207) 646-5779 (May-Oct)
⌨ www.2vsquare.com
Large decks, heated pool and hot tub. TV room, fire-place. All rooms with TV.

Portland ☎ 207

BARS

■ **Blackstones** (B GLM MA) Mon-Fri 16-1, Sat & Sun 13-1h
6 Pine Street ☎ (207) 775-2885 ⌨ www.blackstones.com
Video games, active pooltable. One of Portland's oldest gay bars!

DANCECLUBS

■ **Styxx Video Club** (B D GLM MA ST VS)
19-1h, Sun 15-1, closed Tue & Wed
3 Spring Street ☎ (207) 828-0822 ⌨ www.styxxportland.com
Eight screen video lounge, a small and a big dance floor and game room with pool table. Portlandis premier entertainment complex with two dance floors

GUEST HOUSES

■ **Inn at St. John. The** (bf cc glm MA) All year
939 Congress Street ☎ (207) 773-6481 ⌨ www.innatstjohn.com
The Inn at St. John is a most unique 100 year old Inn with European charm.

CRUISING

-Deering Oaks Park (AYOR) off Park Avenue)
-Maine Mall (occasional action).

Maryland

Location: East USA
Initials: MD
Time: GMT -5
Area: 32.134 km² / 13,142 sq mi.
Population: 5,296,486
Capital: Annapolis

Baltimore ☎ 410

PUBLICATIONS

Baltimore Out Loud
PO Box 3640 ☎ (410) 244-6780 www.baltimoreoutloud.com
Bi-weekly newspaper with information on the gay scene in Baltimore.

Gay Life
241 W. Chase Street ☎ (410) 837-7748 www.baltimoregaylife.com
Bi-weekly newspaper for the LGBT community in Maryland.

BARS

Baltimore Eagle (B F G MA) 16-2h
2022 N Charles St ☎ (443) 524-5926 www.baltimore-eagle.com
Cruise bar. Also leather/video shop.

Blue Parrot (B GLM M MA) 16-2h
5860 Belair Rd ☎ (410) 254-3785

Club Bunns (B GLM MA SNU) 15-2h
608 West Lexington Street ☎ (410) 234-2866

Club Gypsies (B GLM MA s) 18-2h
4020 East Lombard Street ☎ (410) 522-1602

Club Phoenix (B D GLM M MA ST VS) 16-2, Sun 12-2h
1 W Biddle St ☎ (410) 837-3906

Drinkery, The (B G MA) 11-2h
203 W Read St *At Park* ☎ (410) 225-3100

Gallery, The (B GLM M MA) 14-1h
1735 Maryland Ave *At Lafayette Ave* ☎ (410) 539-6965

Grand Central (AC B CC D GLM MA S SNU ST WE)
16-2, Sun 15-2, dance club: Wed-Sun 21-2h
1001 North Charles Street *Charles and Eager St* ☎ (410) 752-7133
www.centralstationpub.com
Very popular bar. See www.centralstationpub.com for details.

Hippo (B D GLM MA s T) 16-2h
1 West Eager Street ☎ (410) 576-0018 www.clubhippo.com
Very informative website www.clubhippo.com

Jay's on Read (B G MA) 16-1h, closed Sun
225 West Read Street *Near cnr. Park Ave* ☎ (410) 225-0188

Leon's (B G M MA) 11-2, lunch available 11-15h
870 Park Avenue ☎ (410) 539-4993 leonsbaltimore.tripod.com

Mixers (B D GLM MA)
6037 Belair Road ☎ (410) 599-1952
Small gay-lesbian mixed neighbourhood bar, good sound, sometimes karaoke nights.

PW's Sports Bar & Grill (B GLM M MA S)
9855 Washington Blvd N, Laurel ☎ (410) 498-4840 www.pwsplace.com
Daily Happy Hour 14-20h, specials throughout the week.

Quest, The (B G MA) 16-2h
3607 Fleet Street *At Conkling* ☎ (410) 563-2617

Rowan Tree (AC B CC GLM M MA)
1633 S. Charles Street ☎ (410) 468-0550 www.therowantree.net
Karaoke and food bar, also pool table. Welcoming atmosphere and friendly staff.

Walt's Inn (B glm MA) daily 10-2h
3201 O'Donnell Street ☎ (410) 327-1886 www.waltsinn.com
The city's best karaoke bar. Wed Karaoke contest 20-24h. Daily Happy Hour 15-19h.

DANCECLUBS

Club 1722 (B D glm MA) Fri & Sat 1.45h-open end
1722 North Charles St. ☎ (410) 547-8423 www.club1722.com
The city's only after-hour club. More gay on Sat nights with techno & house, Fri nights hip-hop style.

Paradox (B D GLM SNU VS YC) Sat only
1310 Russell St ☎ (410) 837-9110 www.thedox.com
Huge warehouse venue, with two dancefloors and bars. Every Saturday gay night and also home to Gay Black Pride events. Sometimes many lesbians.

GENERAL GROUPS

Gay and Lesbian Community Center (GLM)
241 W Chase Street ☎ (410) 837-5445 www.glccb.org

Massachusetts

Location: Northeast USA
Initials: MA
Time: GMT -5
Area: 27.337 km² / 11.180 sq mi.
Population: 6,349,097
Capital: Boston
Important gay cities: Boston and Provincetown

Barre ☎ 978

GUEST HOUSES

Jenkins Inn & Restaurant (B BF GLM I MA PA RWS RWT) All year
7 West Street *Route 122 Barre Center* ☎ (978) 355-6444
www.jenkinsinn.com
Lovely extras such as fine dining and the full bar and lounge with fireplace make this guesthouse unique.

Boston ☎ 617

PUBLICATIONS

Bay Windows
28 Damrell Street, Suite 204 ☎ (617) 266-6670
www.baywindows.com
Weekly publication. Features news, arts & entertainment, interviews, media watch column.

BARS

47 Central (B D f g M MA S) 14-2h
47 Central Avenue, Lynn ☎ (617) 586-0551

Alley, The (B d f G MA) 10.30-2, Sun 12-2h
14 Pi Alley *At 275 Washington St* ☎ (617) 263-1449
www.TheAlleyBar.com
Bear/leather/levi bar. Cruisy.

Club Café Lounge & Video Bar (! AC B CC D DM GLM LM M MA NR OS S VEG VS W WL) 11.00-02:00 Fri, Sat, Sunday
209 Columbus Avenue *At Berkeley St* ☎ (617) 536-0966
www.clubcafe.com
Features some of Boston's best jazz musicians and excellent American and continental cuisine. Restaurant is part of this complex. ALL NEW DANCE CLUB (Thurs – Sat 21:00 – 02:00)

Dbar (B D GLM M MA) Tue 21-2, Thu 22-24, Fri & Sat 22-2h
1236 Dorchester Avenue, Dorchester ☎ (617) 265-4490
www.dbarboston.com
Great drinks and chic atmosphere. A full service restaurant with an interesting and classy seasonal menu 7 nights a week, seamlessly transforms into a nightclub & lounge after 22h. Check www.dbarboston.com for weekly events.

Eagle (! B f G MA) 15-2, Sun 12-2h
520 Tremont Street *Near cnr. Berkeley St* ☎ (617) 542-4494
Cruise bar with extremely friendly staff. Sadly not that much leather.

Fritz (B GLM M) 12-2h
26 Chandler Street *At Berkeley St* ☎ (617) 482-4428
www.fritzboston.com
Gay sports bar. Brunch Sat & Sun 11-15.30h.

Jacques (B D GLM MA ST) 11-24, Sun 12-24h
79 Broadway Street *At Piedmont Street, behind Howard Johnson's*
☎ (617) 426-8902 www.jacquescabaret.com
Drag cabaret.

■ **Lola's Lounge** (AC B GLM MA)
352 Newbury Street ☎ (617) 277-9979
■ **Paradise** (B d G MA SNU VS) 21-1, Thu -2, Fri & Sat 19-2h
180 Massachusetts Avenue, Cambridge *Near M.I.T. ca. 6 blocks south of Central Square* ☎ (617) 868-3000 💻 www.paradisecambridge.com
Stripper club. Gay adult films after 22h.
■ **Ramrod** (AC B F G MA OS) 12-2h
1254 Boylston Street *At Ipswich* ☎ (617) 266-2986
💻 www.ramrod-boston.com
Leather bar. Still going strong! Also coffeebar and pool-lounge downstairs.

CAFES

■ **Francesca's** (b GLM m MA) 8-23h
564 Tremont Street *Cnr. Clarendon St* ☎ (617) 482-9026

DANCECLUBS

■ **Epic Saturdays @ House of Blues** (AC B D g MA)
Sat 22h-open end
15 Lansdowne Street *In the Fenway* ☎ (617) 262-2424
Gay Parties on Sat (Epic Saturdays). Former Avalon Club. Check www.chrisharrispresents.com for details.
■ **Estate** (B D GLM MA) Thu 22h-open end
1 Boylston Place 💻 www.chrisharrispresents.com
Check www.chrisharrispresents.com for more info.
■ **Machine** (AC B D G I M MA OS S ST WE) 22-2h
1254 Boylston Street *Below Ramrod in Ipswich* ☎ (617) 536-1950
💻 www.machine-boston.com
■ **Rise** (AC B D glm MA) Fri & Sat 1.30-6h
306 Stuart St. ☎ (617) 423-7473 💻 www.riseclub.us
Afterhours club. Sat gaynight. Gay owned, starts to attract a wider audience.
■ **Hot Mess Sundays @ Underbar** (B D GLM MA VS)
Sun 22h-open end
275 Tremont Street ☎ (617) 292-0080
💻 www.underbarsuperlounge.com
Sunday T-Dance parties (Hot Mess Sunday, gay) and Caprice Saturdays (mixed). Music videos from the 80s, 90s and today.

RESTAURANTS

■ **Erbaluce** (cc g M MA) 17-22, Fri & Sat -23h, closed Mon
69 Church Street ☎ (617) 426-6969 💻 www.erbaluce-boston.com
Italian restaurant.

BOOK SHOPS

■ **Calamus Bookstore** (GLM) Mon-Sat 9-19, Sun 12-18h
92B South Street *1 block from South Station Train Terminal*
☎ (617) 338-1931 💻 www.calamusbooks.com

HOTELS

■ **Chandler Inn** (AC B CC glm I MA RWS RWT) All year
26 Chandler Street *At Berkeley, near Back Bay train station*
☎ (617) 482-3450 💻 www.chandlerinn.com
European style hotel.

GUEST HOUSES

■ **Adams B&B** (AC BF CC glm I OS PK RWS RWT VA) 8-22h
14 Edgerly Road *Green Line -Convention Center, Back Bay*
☎ (617) 267-2262 💻 www.adamsboston.com
Fifteen minutes from the airport. Located close to the gay scene. 14 guest rooms with phone, colour TV, some with private bath and balcony.
■ **Encore Bed & Breakfast** (AC BF GLM I MA RWT) All year
116 West Newton Street ☎ (617) 247-3425
💻 www.encorebandb.com
Located in gay neighbourhood, 4 guestrooms.
■ **Oasis Guest House** (AC bf CC glm I OS)
22 Edgerly Road *Green Line-Convention Center, Back Bay*
☎ (617) 267-2262 💻 www.oasisgh.com
Fifteen minutes from the airport. Located close to the gay scene. 16 guest rooms with phone, colour TV, some with private bath and balcony.

CRUISING

-Charles River Esplanade
-The Fens at Victoria Gardens (in the high reeds along the river, near Boylston Street)

Edgartown ☎ 508

GUEST HOUSES

■ **Shiverick Inn** (BF glm I RWS RWT) All year
Five Pease's Point Way ☎ (508) 627-3797 💻 www.shiverickinn.com
Gay owned. 11 guestrooms.

Lenox ☎ 413

GUEST HOUSES

■ **Harrison House** (BF glm H MA RWS RWT) All year
174 Main Street ☎ (413) 637-1746 💻 www.harrison-house.com

Lynn ☎ 781

BARS

■ **Fran's Place** (AC B D GLM MA S) 15-1h
776 Washington Street ☎ (781) 598-5618 💻 www.gofrans.com
■ **Pub at 47 Central. The** (B D GLM MA ST) 14-2h
47 Central Avenue ☎ (781) 586-0551

New Bedford ☎ 508

BARS

■ **Place. La** (B d GLM MA) 14-2h
20 Kenyon Street ☎ (508) 990-1248

Northampton ☎ 413

BARS

■ **Diva's** (B D GLM MA ST) 21-2h, closed Sun+Mon
492 Pleasant Street ☎ (413) 586-8161 💻 www.divasofnoho.com
Huge dancefloor, jam-packed at weekend.
■ **Pearl Street Café** (B D glm MA) 19.30-1h
10 Pearl Street ☎ (413) 584-7771 💻 www.iheg.com

CRUISING

-Route I-91 Springfield →Northampton, P behind Exit 17B
-Route I-91 Northampton →Springfield, P behind Exit 18 (near Easthampton and Holyoke)

Provincetown ☎ 508

✱ Provincetown, also known as „P-Town" is a popular summer vacation and weekend destination for gays and lesbians from New York, Montreal and Boston. Provincetown is located at the very end of Cape Cod. Provincetown has become more commercial and its streets are crowded with tourists. But this town still feels very gay during the summer months with gay people who come here to enjoy the accepting community, the sun, sand and numerous bars and clubs. From Boston it is easy to get to P-Town with the 90 minute „fast ferry". The flight with Cape Air takes around 25 minutes and is a great experience.

★ Provincetown, oft kurz „P'Town" genannt, ist ein beliebtes Urlaubs- und Ausflugsziel von Schwulen und Lesben aus New York, Montreal und Boston. Provincetown liegt an der Spitze von Cape Cod. Die Stadt ist zwar von Kommerz und Touristenströmen geprägt, doch gerade in den Sommermonaten ist die Stadt von schwulem Leben erfüllt, wenn viele Schwule und Lesben hierher kommen, um in dieser offenen und akzeptierenden Gemeinschaft Sonne, Sand und all die zahlreichen Bars und Clubs zu genießen. Von Boston aus gelangt man mit der „Fast Ferry" in nur 90 Minuten nach P'Town. Ein Flug mit Cape Air dauert etwa 25 Minuten und ist ein echtes Erlebnis.

Provincetown, aussi appelée „ P'Town „ est un lieu apprécié par les gays et lesbiennes de New York, Montréal et Boston pour les vacances ou une excursion. Provincetown est située à la pointe de Cape Cod. La ville est certes très commerciale et touristique mais c'est justement en été que la ville se remplit de gays et lesbiennes pour profiter du soleil, du sable et des nombreux bars et clubs de cette communauté tolérante. On accède à P'Town en seulement 90 minutes au départ de Boston avec le „ Fast Ferry „. Le vol avec Cape Air ne dure que 25 minutes mais est une vraie expérience.

Provincetown, a menudo abreviado „P'Town", es un popular destino de vacaciones para gays y lesbianas de Nueva York, Montreal y Boston. Provincetown se encuentra en la punta de Cape Cod. La ciudad se caracteriza por el comercio y los turistas, pero es especialmente en los meses de verano cuando en la ciudad se siente la vida gay; es entonces cuando gays y lesbianas vienen aquí a disfrutar del sol, la arena y de los numerosos bares y clubes en esta comunidad abierta y tolerante . Con el „Fast Ferry" se puede llegar desde Boston a P'Town en tan sólo 90 minutos, con vuelo de Cape Air se tardan unos 25 minutos y es una verdadera experiencia.

Provincetown, chiamata spesso anche „P'Town" è una meta di viaggio e di escursioni molto amata da gay e lesbiche. Provincetown è situata sulla punta di Cape Cod. La città è piena di turisti e specialmente nei mesi estivi si riempe anche di vita gay: infatti proprio in questi mesi i gay e le lesbiche vengono a godersi il sole, le spiagge e i tantissimi bar e discoteche di questa aperta città. Da Boston, in soli 90 minuti è possibile raggiungere per mezzo del „fast ferry" P'Town. Un volo con la Cape Air dura solo 25 minuti ed è davvero un'avventura.

GAY INFO

Provincetown Business Guild Mon-Fri 9-14h
3 Freemen Street, Unit 2 ☎ (508) 487-2313 www.ptown.org
Promotion of gay & lesbian tourism in Provincetown. Publisher of a free gay guide.

CULTURE

Lyman-Eyer Gallery (CC)
11-17 by appointment. Extended hrs in summer
432 Commercial Street *East End* ☎ (508) 487-3937
www.lymaneyerart.com
This wonderful gallery specializes in comtemporary fine art by 30 artisans offering seasonal and beginning collectors an eclectic mix , especially of the gay male nude/Figurative art by 13 gay artists including the internationally renowned gay artist Steve Walker (originals and reproductions available). Official publisher for Steve Walker's canvas reproductions (dealer's welcome). Seer the website www.lymaneyerart.com to view and purchase iteams, including works from Steve Walker.

Post Office Cabaret (AC GLM)
303 Commercial Street ☎ (508) 487-0006
Various shows with singers, drag queens, comedians.

BARS

Atlantic House (B D F G MA OS S)
Little bar 12-1, macho bar & dance club 22-1h
4-6 Masonic Place, West End ☎ (508) 487-3169 www.ahouse.com
Bars and a dance club, including Macho Bar for the fetish crowd. Weekly theme parties. A place to be seen.

Boatslip Resort (B G MC) Daily 16-19h, seasonal
161 Commercial Street, West End ☎ (508) 487-1669
www.boatslipresort.com
Great bar but an admission charge applies.

Club Purgatory (B CC G MA OS S SNU) 17-1h, seasonal
9-11 Carver Street *At Gifford House Inn* ☎ (508) 487-0688
www.giffordhouse.com
Start here before going to the other places.

Paramount (B gLm MA OS) 18-1h
247 Commercial Street *In the Crown & Anchor* ☎ (508) 487-1430
www.onlyatthecrown.com/paramount
Opening from noon in season, T-dance Sun from 18h.

PiedBar (B D GLM m MA OS S) 12-1h
193A Commercial Street ☎ (508) 487-1527 www.piedbar.com
Seasonal May-Oct. After T-Dance popular with gays from 18h.

Porchside Lounge (B G M MA) 17-1h
11 Carver Street *In the Gifford House* ☎ (508) 487-0688
www.giffordhouse.com
Lobby bar from 10h, also restaurant.

Shipwreck Lounge (B G MC) 17-1h
67 Bradford Street *Cnr. Carver* ☎ (508) 487-9005 www.ptownlounge.com
The bar is in the lobby area of the Brass Key Inn – in the courtyard out back.

Vixen (B D gLm H m MA s) 18-1h
336 Commercial Street ☎ (508) 487-6424 www.ptownvixen.com
Late night food, also hotel.

MEN'S CLUBS

Vault. The (B F G MA VS) Thu-Sun 21-1h
247 Commercial Street, West End *Downstairs at Crown & Anchor*
☎ (508) 487-1430 www.onlyatthecrown.com/vault
A real cruise bar with lots of dark corners.

RESTAURANTS

Bayside Betsy's (AC B CC GLM M MA)
Mon-Sun 11-16 & 17-22, Sat & Sun 9-11:30h
177 Commercial Street ☎ (508) 487-6566 www.baysidebetsys.com
Breakfast, lunch, dinner with a great waterfront view.

Ross' Grill (B g M MC)
237 Commercial Street *Whaler's Wharf* ☎ (508) 407-8878
www.rossgrillptown.com
Great wine selection. Quality food prepared by the owner.

FITNESS STUDIOS

Mussel Beach Health Club (AC CC GLM MA SA SOL WO) 6-21h
35 Bradford Street ☎ (508) 487-0001 www.musselbeach.net
Provincetown's premiere health club with daily and 10 visit passes.

Provincetown Gym (AC CC GLM MA SA SOL WO) 6-21h
82 Shank Painter Road ☎ (508) 487-2776 www.ptowngym.com
Day pass available.

FASHION SHOPS

MG Leather Inc (F G MA)
338 Commercial Street *At Standish Street* ☎ (508) 487-4036
www.mgleather.com
Leather, fetish, toys and gifts.

HOTELS

Boatslip Resort (B CC D GLM M MA OS PI s) Apr 14th-Oct 31st
161 Commercial Street *Between Central Street and Atlantic*
☎ (508) 487-1669 www.boatslipresort.com
Also a club with popular T-dance from 16h, special events, outdoor/waterfront grill.

Crowne Pointe Historic Inn and Spa (AC B BF CC GLM I M MA MSG OS PA PI PK RWB RWS RWT SA SB SOL VA WH) All year
82 Bradford Street, Cape Cod *Centre of town* ☎ (508) 487-6767
www.crownepointe.com
Crowne Pointe's 40 beautifully restored guest rooms are designed and furnished to accommodate travellers of all types.

Gifford House Inn (B BF CC D GLM I M MA OS PK RWS VA) 9-23h
9 Carver Street *1 block off Commerical Street* ☎ (508) 487-0688
www.giffordhouse.com
Also danceclub, bar and restaurant.

GUEST HOUSES

Admiral's Landing B&B (AC CC GLM I MA OS PK RWS RWT VA WH) All year, 8-22h
158 Bradford Street *Between Conwell & Pearl* ☎ (508) 487-9665
www.admiralslanding.com
All 8 rooms with bath, TV, VCR, WIFI Internet access, phone, fridge and some with fireplaces and a hot tub. Non-smoking property. Private beach, harbor view.

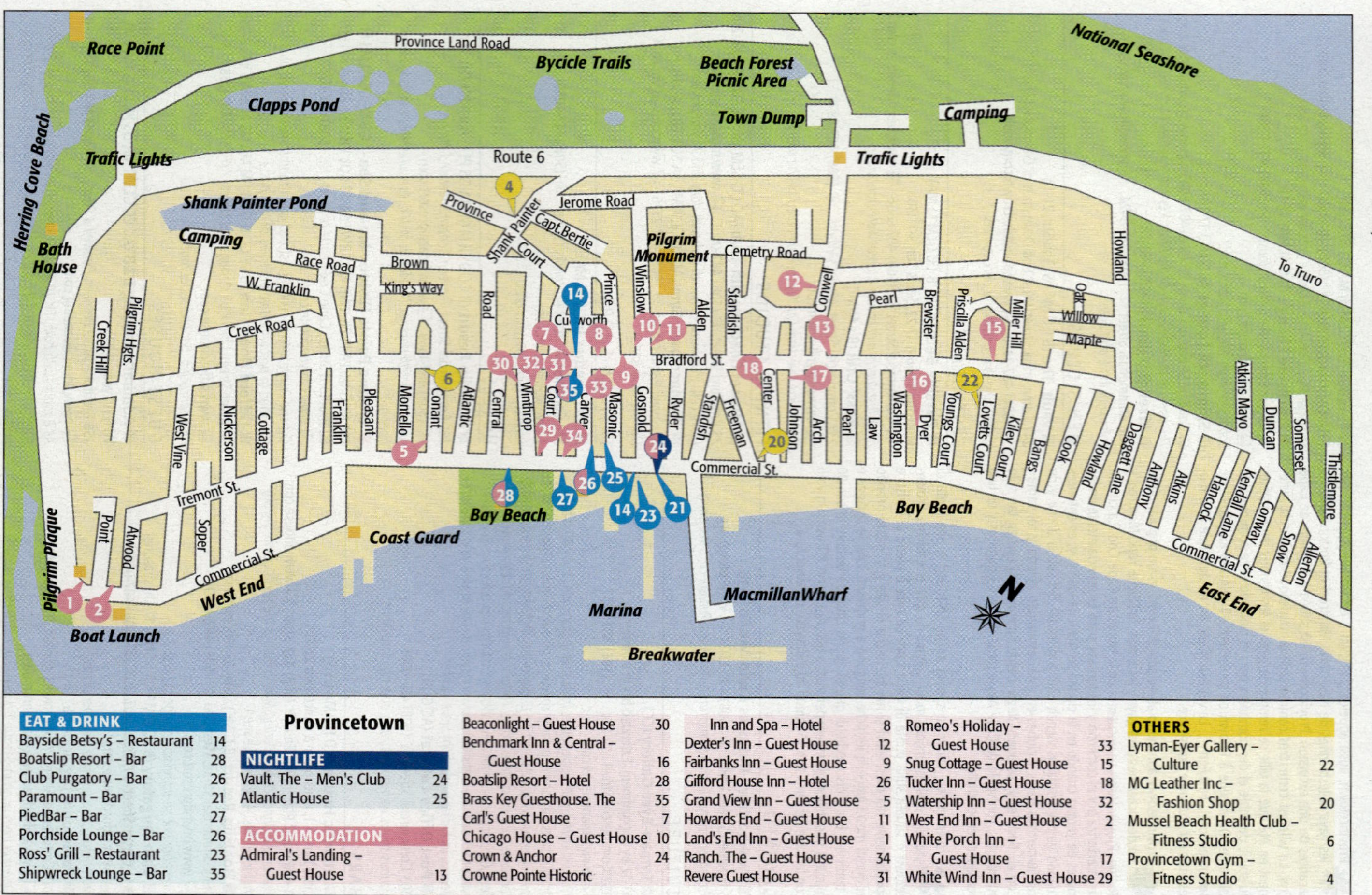
National Seashore
Race Point
Herring Cove Beach
Bath House
Trafic Lights
Province Land Road
Bycicle Trails
Clapps Pond
Beach Forest Picnic Area
Town Dump
Camping
Shank Painter Pond
Route 6
To Truro
Pilgrim Monument
Howland
Oak
Willow
Maple
Miller Hill
Priscilla Alden
Brewster
Pearl
Conwell
Cemetery Road
Standish
Alden
Winslow
Prince
Jerome Road
Capt.Bertie
Shank Painter Court
Province
Road
Brown
King's Way
Race Road
W. Franklin
Creek Road
Pilgrim Hgts.
Creek Hill
Bradford St.
Culworth
Thistlemore
Somerset
Duncan
Atkins Mayo
Allerton
Snow
Conway
Kendall Lane
Hancock
Atkins
Anthony
Daggett Lane
Howland
Cook
Bangs
Kiley Court
Lovetts Court
Youngs Court
Dyer
Washington
Law
Pearl
Arch
Johnson
Center
Freeman
Standish
Ryder
Gosnold
Masonic
Carver
Court
Winthrop
Central
Atlantic
Conant
Montello
Pleasant
Franklin
Cottage
Nickerson
West Vine
Soper
Atwood
Point
Tremont St.
Commercial St.
East End
West End
Bay Beach
MacmillanWharf
Breakwater
Marina
Coast Guard
Boat Launch
Pilgrim Plaque
N
Provincetown
EAT & DRINK
Bayside Betsy's – Restaurant 14
Boatslip Resort – Bar 28
Club Purgatory – Bar 26
Paramount – Bar 21
PiedBar – Bar 27
Porchside Lounge – Bar 26
Ross' Grill – Restaurant 23
Shipwreck Lounge – Bar 35
NIGHTLIFE
Vault. The – Men's Club 24
Atlantic House 25
ACCOMMODATION
Admiral's Landing – Guest House 13
Beaconlight – Guest House 30
Benchmark Inn & Central – Guest House 16
Boatslip Resort – Hotel 28
Brass Key Guesthouse. The 35
Carl's Guest House 7
Chicago House – Guest House 10
Crown & Anchor 24
Crowne Pointe Historic Inn and Spa – Hotel 8
Dexter's Inn – Guest House 12
Fairbanks Inn – Guest House 9
Gifford House Inn – Hotel 26
Grand View Inn – Guest House 5
Howards End – Guest House 11
Land's End Inn – Guest House 1
Ranch. The – Guest House 34
Revere Guest House 31
Romeo's Holiday – Guest House 33
Snug Cottage – Guest House 15
Tucker Inn – Guest House 18
Watership Inn – Guest House 32
West End Inn – Guest House 2
White Porch Inn – Guest House 17
White Wind Inn – Guest House 29
OTHERS
Lyman-Eyer Gallery – Culture 22
MG Leather Inc – Fashion Shop 20
Mussel Beach Health Club – Fitness Studio 6
Provincetown Gym – Fitness Studio 4

■ **Aerie House and Beach Club** (AC BF CC FH GLM MA MSG NR OS PA PK RWB RWS RWT VA WH WI) All year
184 Bradford Street ☎ (508) 487-1197 🖳 www.aeriehouse.com
Sweeping bay views from both our hilltop Guesthouse and waterfront Beach Club. 11 accommodations from economical rooms to deluxe suites and beachfront apartments.

■ **Ampersand** (AC CC GLM I OS PK RWB RWS RWT VA) All year
6 Cottage Street ☎ (508) 487-0959 🖳 ampersandguesthouse.com

■ **Anchor Inn Beach House** (AC BF CC GLM MA OS RWB RWS RWT VA) All year, 9-21h
175 Commercial Street ☎ (508) 487-0432
🖳 www.anchorinnbeachhouse.com
All rooms with private bath, balcony.

■ **Beaconlight** (AC BF CC GLM I MA OS PK RWS RWT VA WH WI) All year
12 Winthrop Street *Town centre* ☎ (508) 487-9603
🖳 www.beaconlightguesthouse.com
Sophisticated meets eclectic- funky, chic clean and beautiful accommodations just off Commercial Street 14 rooms with private bath centrally located. Easy walk to TDance.

■ **Benchmark Inn**
(AC CC glm MA MSG OS PI RWB RWS RWT SA SOL WH) All year
6-8 Dyer Street *Central* ☎ (508) 487-7440
🖳 www.benchmarkinn.com
Rooms with telephone, TV, video, radio, minibar, safe, hair-dryer, some with balcony and kitchenette.

■ **Black Pearl Inn. The**
(AC CC GLM I MA PA PK RWS RWT WE WH) All year
11 Pearl Street *Centre of town* ☎ (508) 487-0302
🖳 www.theblackpearlinn.com
7 rooms decorated by local artists. Private bath, fireplace, TV, hot tub, parking, A/C, Continental breakfast.

Bradford-Carver House. The
(AC BF CC GLM I MA PK RWS RWT VA) 9-21h
70 Bradford Street *Corner Bradford & Carver St* ☏ (508) 487-0728
www.bradfordcarver.com
Rooms with king or queen beds, private baths,TV,A/C,CD clock radio,fridge & phone. Some rooms have gas fireplaces, crystal chandelier & electrified wall sconces & 2 entrance.

Brass Key Guesthouse. The (AC B BF CC DM DU FH GLM I M MA MSG NR NU OS PA PI PK RWB RWS RWT W WH WI WL) All year
67 Bradford Street *Centre of town* ☏ (508) 487-9005
www.brasskey.com
All rooms with private bath, TV, DVD, phone, free Wi-Fi, fridge, hot tub. Luxury and popular. Daily happy hour with free wine and cheese. On site popular bar/lounge and large pool.

Carl's Guest House
(AC CC G I MA OS RWB RWS RWT SOL VA WH) All year
68 Bradford Street *Corner Court Street* ☏ (508) 487-1650
www.carlsguesthouse.com
Excellent location, clean, comfortable, friendly and reasonably priced. Clothing optional sundeck and TV room. 14 differently styled guest rooms to meet everyone's comfort.

Carpe Diem Guesthouse & Namaste Spa
(AC BF CC GLM I MSG OS PK RWB RWS RWT SA SB VA WH) All year
12-14 Johnson Street *Centre of town, half a block from Harbor Beach*
☏ (508) 487-4242 www.carpediemguesthouse.com
18 rooms with private bath, some with whirlpool tubs & fireplaces. Secluded patios and hot tub, gourmet breakfast, afternoon wine & cheese hour. German owned.

Chicago House (BF CC G MA OS PA RWS) All year
6 Winslow Street *2 mins from the centre* ☏ (508) 487-0537
www.chicagohse.com
Some rooms with TV. Free wireless internet throughout the house.

Christopher's by the Bay
(AC BF CC GLM I MA NR OS PA PK RWS RWT VA WI) All year
8 Johnson Street *Located in the centre of town* ☏ (508) 487-9263
www.christophersbythebay.com
Award winning B&B located on a quiet street in the heart of town. Escape and relax.

Crown & Anchor Inn (AC B D f GLM M MA PI RWB RWS RWT) All year
247 Commercial Street ☏ (508) 487-1430
www.onlyatthecrown.com
Accommodation plus 3 clubs: Paramount (danceclub), Wave (video lounge) and The Vault (leather bar).

Dexter's Inn (AC BF GLM OS PK RWS RWT VA) May-Nov.
6 Conwell Street *Central Provincetown* ☏ (508) 487-1911
www.dextersinn.com

Fairbanks Inn (AC BF CC glm I OS PK RWS RWT) All year
90 Bradford Street ☏ (508) 487-0386 www.fairbanksinn.com

Grand View Inn (BF CC GLM I MA OS PA)
4 Conant Street *Between Boatslip Tea Dance and Mussel Beach Health Club* ☏ (508) 487-9193 www.grandviewinn.com
Located in picturesque West End of town with outside decks with a view on the bay.

Howards End (BF GLM I MA OS PK RWT) All year
5 Winslow Street *Town centre* ☏ (508) 487-0169
www.howardsendguesthouse.com

John Randall House (AC BF CC GLM PK RWT VA) 9-21h
140 Bradford Street *Town Center* ☏ (508) 487-3533
www.JohnRandallHouse.com
Free parking, private bath, cable TV & VCR.

Land's End Inn (AC bf CC GLM OS PK RWB WH) Closed Nov-Apr
22 Commercial Street ☏ (508) 487-0706 www.landsendinn.com
Rooms and fully equipped apartments. Suites with balcony and Jacuzzi available.

Prince Albert Guest House
(AC BF CC GLM I MA MSG PA PK RWS RWT SA VA WH) All year
164-166 Commercial Street *West end of Provincetown, Cape Cod*
☏ (508) 487-1850 www.PrinceAlbertGuestHouse.com
No smoking, 18 rooms. All rooms have flat panel TVs, internet access, air conditioning and mini fridge with private baths.

Ranch. The (B BF f G MA OS PK VS) All year
198 Commercial Street *Central* ☏ (508) 487-1542
www.TheRanch.ws
Sundeck and street side patio. TV room and private bar. All rooms with shared bath. Sport activities nearby.

Revere Guest House (AC BF CC GLM I OS PK RWS RWT) 8.30-21h
14 Court Street *Center of town and half block from the bay*
☏ (508) 487-2292 www.reverehouse.com
The charm and ambience of the nineteenth century still prevails throughout the eight rooms of this historic home, which include a two bedroom suite and a one bedroom apartment.

Romeo's Holiday & Spa (AC BF CC G I NU OS PI PK RWS RWT WH) All year
97 Bradford Street ☏ (508) 487-6636 www.romeosholiday.com
With 8 double rooms with shower/WC, CABLE TV radio, clothing optional back deck.

Seasons (AC BF CC GLM I OS PK RWS RWT) All year
160 Bradford Street *Central Provincetown* ☏ (508) 487-2283
www.provincetownseasons.com
Five double rooms with bath, cable TV, DVD, CD/radio. Car park and own key. Wifi

Secret Garden Inn (AC bf cc GLM MA OS WH) All year
300A Commercial Street *Behind Mayflower Restaurant*
☏ (508) 487-9027 www.secretgardenptown.com
Tranquil gardens, hot tub, beach towels, refrigerators, VCRs.

Snug Cottage (AC BF CC glm I MC PK RWS RWT) All year
178 Bradford Street *East end of P'Town* ☏ (508) 487-1616
www.snugcottage.com
Non-smoking guest house with 8 rooms and all the regular amenities.

Somerset House (AC BF GLM I MA PK RWS RWT VA) All year
378 Commercial Street *At Pearl* ☏ (508) 487-0383
www.somersethouseinn.com
Conveniently located on Commercial Street, Somerset House offers boldly painted rooms with plush bedding, a fireplace for cool nights, a/c in the summer months and a complimentary breakfast. Gay-owned and operated, open year round. Shuttle service from the airport or ferry upon request.

Sunset Inn (AC BF CC GLM I OS PK RWS RWT) 15 Apr-31 Oct
142 Bradford Street *Downtown* ☏ (508) 487-9810
www.sunsetinnptown.com
Rooms with shower/WC, TV. radio, minibar, own key. Non-smoking throughout house & sundecks. Continental breakfast.

Tucker Inn (AC BF cc GLM I MA PA PK RWS RWT) All year
12 Center Street ☏ (508) 487-0381 www.TheTuckerInn.com
Eight double rooms & 1 apartment.

Watership Inn (AC BF CC GLM I MA OS PK RWB RWS RWT VA) All year, 9-21h
7 Winthrop Street *5 mins from downtown* ☏ (508) 487-0094
www.watershipinn.com
Built around 1820. Sixteen rooms all with private bath, refrigerator and cable TV. Sun decks and yard.

West End Inn (BF CC GLM MA RWB RWS RWT) All year
44 Commercial Street ☏ (508) 487-9555 www.westendinn.com
All rooms with private bath/WC, TV, video, fax, radio, minibar, kitchenette, hair-dryer, own key,WiFi,direct beach access. Own car park.

White Porch Inn (AC BF glm I MC RWS RWT) All year, 9-18h
7 Johnson Street *Located in the centre of town* ☏ (508) 364-2549
www.whiteporchinn.com
Tastefully decorated rooms with private baths, free WiFi and great views.

White Wind Inn (AC BF CC GLM OS PA PK RWB RWS RWT) All year
174 Commercial Street ☏ (508) 487-1526 www.whitewindinn.com
Double/single rooms with bath/shower/WC, balcony, TV, video, radio, refrigerator.

APARTMENTS

■ **Gallery Inn. The** (AC BF glm MA PA PK RWB RWS RWT)
3 Johnson Street ☎ (508) 487-3010 🖳 www.galleryinnptown.com

CRUISING

-Boatyard behind Boatslip Beach Club, late (AYOR, MA)
-Herring Cove & Beach Forest (AYOR, MA)
-At Spiritus once the bars close as well as other locations along Commercial Street.

Randolph ☎ 781

BARS

■ **Randolph Country Club** (B D GLM M MA OS PI)
17-2, Fri 14-2, Sat & Sun 12-2h
44 Mazzeo Drive, Route 139 ☎ (781) 961-2414
🖳 www.randolphcountryclub.com

Salisbury ☎ 978

BARS

■ **Hobo's Cafe & Lounge** (B GLM MA)
5 Broadway ☎ (978) 465-4626
🖳 www.chefhowieshobocafe.com

Springfield ☎ 413

BARS

■ **Oz** (AC B D G MA S) 19-2h
397 Dwight Street ☎ (413) 732-4562
🖳 www.ozspringfield.com
■ **Pure** (B G MA) 12-2h
234 Chestnut Street ☎ (413) 205-1483

DANCECLUBS

■ **Xstatic** (B D G MA SNU) 19-2h, closed Mon & Tue
240 Chestnut Street ☎ (413) 736-2618
🖳 www.clubxstatic.com

CRUISING

-Downtown Mall
-Forest Park (picnic area near Recreation Department)
-Liberty Street (AYOR)
-Springfield Bus Terminal (AYOR).

Taunton ☎ 508

BARS

■ **Bobby's Place** (B D GLM MA s) 17-1, Fri & Sat -2h
62 Weir Street *Cnr. Route 44* ☎ (508) 824-9997
🖳 www.bobbysplacema.com

Worcester ☎ 508

BARS

■ **MB. The** (B GLM MA) 15-2h
40 Grafton Street *At Franklin St* ☎ (508) 799-4521
🖳 www.mblounge.com
Piano entertainment every Sun night.

DANCECLUBS

■ **Blu** (B D G MA) Tue-Fri 19.30-2, Sat & Sun 21-2h, closed Mon
105 Water St ☎ (508) 756-2227
🖳 www.blu-nightclub.com

CRUISING

-Rest Stop (on 140, Upton)
-Block around Portland & Salem Streets.

Michigan

Location: Great Lakes region USA
Initials: MI
Time: GMT -5
Area: 250.465 km² / 102,440 sq mi.
Population: 9,938,444
Capital: Lansing
Important gay cities: Detroit and Saugatuck

Ann Arbor ☎ 734

BARS

■ **,aút Bar** (AC B BF CC GLM M MA OS)
16-2, Sun 12-2, kitchen hours: 16-23, Fri & Sat -1, Sun 10-15h, 16-23h
315 Braun Court ☎ (734) 994-3677 🖳 www.autbar.com
Also known as Out Bar.

DANCECLUBS

■ **Necto. The** (B CC D GLM OS VS YC) Gay on Fri & Tue only, 21-2h
516 East Liberty Street *Downtown, one block off Campus*
☎ (734) 994-5436 🖳 www.necto.com
Best dance club in Ann Arbor.

BOOK SHOPS

■ **Common Language** (GLM) 11-22, Fri & Sat -24, Sun -19h
317 Braun Court ☎ (734) 663-0036 🖳 www.glbtbooks.com

CRUISING

-Rest Stop (AYOR) (north on US 23 at 31 mile marker)
-Dexter Rest Stop (south side of I-94 West).

Battle Creek ☎ 269

BARS

■ **Partners** (B D GLM I MA S ST) 19-2h
910 North Avenue ☎ (269) 964-7276 🖳 www.partnersbar.com

Detroit ☎ 313

PUBLICATIONS

■ **Between the Lines Newspaper**
c/o Pride Source Corp., 11920 Farmington Road, Livonia
☎ (734) 293-7200 🖳 www.pridesource.com
Michigan's statewide weekly newspaper for the LGBT community. Pride Source Corp. publishes also „Michigan Pride Source", Michigan's gay & lesbian yellow pages. New editions are uploaded every Wed to the website.

BARS

■ **Adam's Apple** (AC B G m MA) Mon-Fri 15-2, Sat & Sun 12-2h
18931 West Warren Avenue ☎ (313) 240-8482
Clean, friendly atmosphere.
■ **Detroit Eagle** (B F G MA OS) 20-2, Fri 17-2h, closed Mon-Tue
1501 Holden Street ☎ (313) 873-6969 🖳 www.detroiteagle.com
Leather & jeans bar.
■ **Diamond Jim's Saloon** (B F G M MA VS) 12-2
19650 W. Warren *At Evergreen* ☎ (313) 336-8680
Cowboy, bear, leather, video saloon.
■ **Gigi's** (AC B CC D GLM m MA p r S SNU ST T)
Mon-Fri 12-2, Sat & Sun 14-2h
16920 West Warren Avenue *Near South Field freeway* ☎ (313) 584-6525
🖳 www.gigisbar.com
Two bars on different levels, dancing every night, shows on Mon, Thu, Fri and Sat.
■ **Gold Coast Club** (B d G MC SNU) Mon-Fri 16-2, Sat & Sun 19-2h
2971 East Seven Mile Road/Mitchell Street ☎ (313) 366-6135
🖳 www.detroitsclubgoldcoast.com
Male dancers Mon-Sat 21h, Sun 20h.

■ **Hayloft Saloon** (B F G MA) 15-2h
8070 Greenfield Rd *Near Tireman* ☏ (313) 581-8913
🖳 www.hayloftsaloon.com
Levi/leather bar.

■ **Male Box** (B d G MA) 14-2.30h
3537 East 7 Mile Road ☏ (313) 893-7696
🖳 www.myspace.com/maleboxbar

■ **Menjo's** (B D G OS S) Mon-Wed 13-22, Sun-Thu 13-2h
928 West McNichols Road/Hamilton Street ☏ (313) 863-3934
🖳 www.menjoscomplex.com

■ **Pronto Video Bar** (B GLM M MA OS)
Bar hours: 11-2, restaurant hours: Mon-Thu & Sun 9-22, Fri & Sat -24h
608 Washington, Royal Oak ☏ (248) 544-7900
🖳 www.prontorestaurant.com

■ **R&R Saloon** (B D F G MA) 14-2h
7330 Michigan Avenue ☏ (313) 849-2751

■ **Rainbow Room** (B CC D GLM MA S ST VS)
Wed-Sun 19-2, shows at 22.30 and 24h
6640 East 8 Mile Road *Westside* ☏ (313) 891-1020
🖳 www.clubrainbowroom.com

■ **Soho** (B G MA) 16-?h
205 West 9 Mile Road, Ferndale *Cnr. Woodward St* ☏ (248) 542-7646
🖳 www.sohoferndale.com

■ **Stingers** (B D GLM M VS) Mon Fri 18-2, Sat & Sun 20-2h
19404 Sherwood Street *Side entrance* ☏ (313) 892-1765

■ **Temple** (B D g WE) 11-2h
2906 Cass Avenue ☏ (313) 832-2822

■ **Woodward** (B d G M MA) 14-2, grill hours: 14-1, Fri & Sat -12.30h
6426 Woodward Avenue *Near Milwaukee* ☏ (313) 872-0166
🖳 www.woodwardbar.com

DANCECLUBS

■ **Backstreet** (B D G MA) Wed & Sat 21-2h
15606 Joy Rd *Near cnr. Greenfield Rd* ☏ (313) 838-6699

■ **Inuendo** (B D GLM MA SNU ST)
744 E Savannah St, Highland Park *At Oakland St* ☏ (313) 891-5798

■ **Nine** (B D GLM MA) Tue-Sat
141 West 9 Mile Road, Ferndale *Cnr. Woodward* ☏ (313) 582-7227
🖳 www.9ferndale.com

■ **Works. The** (B D glm MA S VS) Thu 22-3, Fri -5, Sat -6h
1846 Michigan Avenue ☏ (313) 961-1742
Electronic DJs spin the latest clubsounds, some special events. Also after-hours held.

RESTAURANTS

■ **Dolce Vita. La** (B d GLM M MA)
17546 Woodward Ave *Ferndale* ☏ (313) 856-0331
Very good Italian food, light jazz.

SAUNAS/BATHS

■ **Body Zone**
(AC CC DR DU F FC FH G LAB m MA P RR SA SB SL VS WH WO) 24hrs
1617 East McNichols Road *Interstate 75 at McNichols Road Exit*
☏ (313) 366-9663 🖳 www.bodyzonedetroit.com
75 private changing rooms, 2 TV lounges, steam sauna and more.

■ **TNT Health Club** (AC CC DM DU FC G MA NU OS P PI RR SA SB VS WH WO) 24hrs
13333 West Eight Mile Road *8 Mile road and Schafer between I-75 and US-10*
☏ (313) 341-5322 🖳 www.tnthealthclub.org

GENERAL GROUPS

■ **Affirmations Gay & Lesbian Community Center** (CC GLM T)
290 West Nine Mile Road, Ferndale ☏ (248) 398-7105
🖳 www.goaffirmations.org

■ **Triangle Foundation** (GLM T) 9-17h
19641 West Seven Mile Road ☏ (313) 537-7000 🖳 www.tri.org
Michigan's statewide civil rights, advocacy and anti-violence organization for gay, lesbian, bisexual and transgender people.

Flint ☏ 810

BARS

■ **mi** (B G MA) 15-2h
2406 N Franklin Ave ☏ (810) 234-9481

■ **Pachyderm Pub** (AC B CC D GLM MA SNU VS) 15-2h
G-1408 E Hemphill Rd, Burton ☏ (810) 744-4960 🖳 pachydermpub.com

■ **State Bar** (B D GLM MA) 14-2h
2512 South Dort Highway ☏ (810) 767-7050

■ **Zoo. The** (B D GLM M MA) 14-2h, closed Mon
4511 S Saginaw St ☏ (810) 249-0267

DANCECLUBS

■ **Club Triangle** (B D G MA S)
2101 S Dort Highway ☏ (810) 767-7550

Grand Rapids ☏ 616

BARS

■ **Apartment. The** (B G MA) 12-2, Sun 14-2h
33 Sheldon Boulevard ☏ (616) 451-0815 🖳 www.apartmentlounge.net

■ **Pub 43** (AC B CC GLM M MC) 15-2h
43 S Division Ave *Division South of Fulton St* ☏ (616) 458-2205
🖳 www.pub43gr.com
Casual gay pub. Friendly atmosphere. Best after 23h.

■ **Rumors** (B D f GLM S SNU) 16-2h
69 South Division Avenue *At Oakes St* ☏ (616) 454-8720
🖳 rumorsnightclub.net
Tue Karaoke, Wed Male Strippers. See rumorsnightclub.net for more details.

DANCECLUBS

■ **Diversions** (AC B CC D GLM M MA VS) 20-2h
10 Fountain Street NW *Near cnr. Division* ☏ (616) 451-3800
🖳 www.diversionsnightclub.com
Big complex with dance bar, video bar, quiet solarium area, karaoke bar, check www.diversionsnightclub.com for hours and events.

SAUNAS/BATHS

■ **Diplomat Health Club** (AC CC DR DU FH G MA P SA SL VS) 24hrs
2324 S Division Avenue *2 blocks north of 28th St* ☏ (616) 452-3754
🖳 www.diplomathealthclubs.com

Lansing ☏ 517

BARS

■ **Spiral** (B D GLM s) 20-2h, Mon & Tue closed
1247 Center Street ☏ (517) 371-3221 🖳 www.spiraldancebar.com
See www.spiraldancebar.com for details.

CRUISING

-Rest stop (AYOR) (on I-96, Okemos)
-Rest stop (AYOR) (on Highway 27, 1 mile north of 127).

Port Huron ☏ 810

BARS

■ **Seekers** (B D GLM SNU) Mon-Thu 19-2, Fri & Sat 16-2, Sun 14-2h
3301 24th Street ☏ (810) 985-9349

Saginaw ☏ 989

DANCECLUBS

■ **Mixx Nightclub & Metro Grille. The**
(AC B cc D GLM m MA S SNU ST VS)
Wed-Sun 18-2, food: Wed-Sun 18-22, dance bar: Fri & Sat 22-2h
115 North Hamilton Street *Old town Saginaw near Court Street*
☏ (989) 498-4022 🖳 www.DiversionsCollection.Com
Dance club and video bar in old town Saginaw. Karaoke Thu, Fri & Sat.

Saugatuck ☎ 269

BARS

■ **Bars @ Dunes Resort** (B D G MA OS) 9-2h
333 Blue Star Hwy, Douglas ☎ (269) 857-1401
www.dunesresort.com
Gay venues inside a gay resort. Disco, Bars, Cabaret, gameroom and poolside chilling and the „Tea Deck" patio.

HOTELS

■ **Dunes Resort. The**
(! AC B CC D GLM M MA OS PI PK RWB RWS RWT S VA) All year
333 Blue Star Hwy, Douglas ☎ (269) 857-1401
www.dunesresort.com
Hotel & disco. One of the largest gay and lesbian resorts in the Midwest. Cabaret, games room & bistro. Heavy cruising in the woods.

■ **Pines Motorlodge. The** (AC bf CC G I MA OS RWB RWS RWT)
April 1st to Nov 30th
56 Blue Star Highway *At intersection of Center St and Blue Star Highway*
☎ (269) 857-5211 www.thepinesmotorlodge.com

GUEST HOUSES

■ **Kirby House. The** (AC BF CC glm I MA OS PI PK RWS WH)
Closed for Christmas
294 West Center Street ☎ (269) 857-2904
www.kirbyhouse.com
Eight double rooms with shower/WC, heating, own key. Free bikes, off-street parking.

CAMPING

■ **Camp It** (GLM PI)
Route 6635, 118th Avenue, Fennville ☎ (269) 543-4335
www.campitresort.com
Big camp site under gay management. TV lounge. Laundry facilities. Store and supermarket nearby. No kids.

Traverse City ☎ 616

DANCECLUBS

■ **Side Traxx** (B D GLM MA) 17-2h
520 Franklin St ☎ (231) 935-1666 www.sidetraxxtc.com

Minnesota

Location: Great Lakes region USA
Initials: MN
Time: GMT -6
Area: 225.182 km² / 92,099 sq mi.
Population: 4,919,479
Capital: Saint Paul
Important gay cities: Minneapolis/Saint Paul

Minneapolis/St. Paul ☎ 612

PUBLICATIONS

■ **Lavender Magazine** Mon-Fri 8.30-17h
3715 Chicago Avenue South ☎ (612) 436-4660
www.lavendermagazine.com
Minnesota's GLBT magazine.

CULTURE

■ **Tretter Collection in GLBT Studies** (AC GLM I MA T)
Mon-Fri 8.30-16.30h and by appointment
c/o University of Minnesota Libraries, 111 Elmer L. Andersen Library, 222-21 Avenue South *On West Bank, University of Minnesota*
☎ (612) 624-7526 special.lib.umn.edu/rare/tretter.phtml
One of the largest gay archives in the US. Library, museum and more. Tours available by appointment.

BARS

■ **19 Bar** (AC B G m MA OS) 15-2h
19 West 15th Street, Minneapolis ☎ (612) 871-5553 19bar.itgo.com
Low prices. With pool tables, darts and Pizzas.

■ **Brass Rail** (AC B G S VS) 12-2h
422 Hennepin Avenue, Minneapolis ☎ (612) 333-3016
www.brassraillounge.com
Regular events.

■ **Camp Bar** (B d G M MA s) 16-2, Sat 14-2, Sun 11-2h
490 North Robert Street, St. Paul ☎ (612) 292-1844 camp-bar.net

■ **eagleBOLTbar** (B D G MA OS S VS)
Mon-Fri 16-2:30, Sat-Sun 10-2:30
515 Washington Avenue S, Minneapolis *At Portland* ☎ (612) 338-4214
www.eagleboltbar.com
Large complex with leather bar; video bar and dance club. Outside patio for smokers.

■ **Gay 90's** (! AC B CC D f GLM M MA S SNU ST VS) Mon-Sat 8-2, Sun 10-2h
408 Hennepin Avenue, Minneapolis ☎ (612) 333-7755
www.gay90s.com
Upper Midwest's largest gay entertainment complex: 6 bars, 3 dancefloors, dinner, drag., check www.gay90s.com for events.

■ **Gladius Bar** (B G MA) 17-2h
1111 Hennepin Avenue S, Minneapolis ☎ (612) 332-9963
www.gladiusbar.com
Chic gay bar.

■ **Jet Set** (B glm MA) 17-?, Sat 18-?, closed Sun & Mon
115 North 1st Street, Minneapolis *Warehouse District* ☎ (612) 339-3933
www.jetsetbar.com
Smoke-free, intimate cocktail lounge. Popular before the clubs open.

■ **Lush Food Bar** (B GLM M MA OS VS) Wed-Fri 16-2, Sat & Sun 11-2h
990 Central Avenue NE, Minneapolis www.lushfoodbar.com
Stylish gay lounge offering daily specials. Happy Hour Wed-Sat 16-20h, all day Sunday.

■ **Minneapolis Eagle** (AC B CC D F G M MA S VS)
16-2.30, Fri -3, Sat 10-3, Sun -2.30h
515 Washington Avenue South, Minneapolis ☎ (612) 338-4214
www.minneapoliseagle.com
Friendly and cruisy. Happy hour Fri 14-19h, beer bust Sun 16-20h. Dress code leather/military/jeans enforced after 21h Fri & Sat, check www.minneapoliseagle.com for events.

■ **Rumours & Innuendo** (B D GLM MA) 16-3, danceclub: Fri & Sat 21-3h
213 East 4th Street, St. Paul ☎ (612) 225-4528 www.rumours-stpaul.com

■ **Saloon** (! B D G M MA) 12-2h
830 Hennepin Avenue, Minneapolis *At 9th Street* ☎ (612) 332-0835
www.saloonmn.com
High energy dance music.

■ **Tickles** (B GLM M MC)
420 S 4th St., Minneapolis ☎ (612) 354-3846 www.ticklesbar.com
Bar with live piano on Friday & Saturday.

■ **Town House. The** (B d GLM MA ST) 15-1, Sat & Sun 12-1h
1415 University Avenue West, St. Paul *Near cnr. Pascal Street N*
☎ (612) 646-7087 www.townhousebar.com
Fun neighbourhood bar with a piano lounge.

CAFES

■ **Wilde Roast Cafe** (B GLM M MA) 7-22h
65 Main Street SE suite 143 *Located on Main Street along the Mississippi River* ☎ (612) 331-4544 www.wilderoastcafe.com
European-styled coffee, dessert, wine bar.

DANCECLUBS

■ **Ground Zero** (B D f glm MA) Thu-Sat 22-2h
15 Northeast 4th Street, Minneapolis ☎ (612) 378-5115
Bondage a go-go is the best Thu or Sat nights. Music is mostly Industrial/Gothic.

RESTAURANTS

■ **Cafe Barbette** (b GLM M MA) 8-1, Fri & Sat -2h
1600 West Lake Street ☎ (612) 827-5710 www.barbette.com

GIFT & PRIDE SHOPS

Rainbow Road (GLM) 10-22h
109 West Grant Street, Minneapolis ☎ (612) 872-8448

LEATHER & FETISH SHOPS

Cockpit Minneapolis (cc F G MA) 11-20, Sun 12-17h
2321 Hennepin Avenue, Minneapolis *Near cnr. Dupont Ave*
☎ (612) 824-1377 www.cockpitmn.com

FETISH GROUPS

Knights of Leather (F G)
3403 Nicollet Avenue #5 ☎ (612) 870-7473 www.knightsofleather.org

HEALTH GROUPS

Minnesota AIDS Project Mon-Fri 8.30-17.30h
1400 Park Avenue S ☎ (612) 341-2060 www.mnaidsproject.org

CRUISING

-Hennepin Avenue (AYOR) (downtown)
-IDS Tower (indoor mall, „Crystal Court")
-Loring Park & Oak Grove (AYOR)
-Mississippi River Flats (AYOR) (East River Road, opposite Shriners Hospital)
-University of Minnesota (Minneapolis Campus, Gay Community Center, Coffman Memorial Union at 2nd floor, Northrop Auditorium at 3rd floor)

Mississippi

Location: South USA
Initials: MS
Time: GMT -6
Area: 125.443 km² / 51,306 sq mi.
Population: 2,844,658
Capital: Jackson

Biloxi ☎ 228

BARS

Just Us (B GLM MA SNU ST) 24hrs
906 Division Street ☎ (228) 374-1007 www.justuslounge.net

CRUISING

-Beach Highway (between Biloxi and Gulfport)
-Edgewater Shopping Center (AYOR)
-Gulf Coast Beach (between Holiday Inn and Coliseum)

Jackson ☎ 601

BARS

Dick's & Jane (B D GLM MA ST) Thu-Sun 21-3h
206 East Capitol Street

Jack's Construction Site (AC B d f GLM m MA OS S) 17-?h
425 North Mart Plaza *Off N. State Street* ☎ (601) 362-3108
Beer only bar. Bring your own bottle possible.

Missouri

Location: Middlewest USA
Initials: MO
Time: GMT -6
Area: 180.546 km² / 73,843 sq mi.
Population: 5,595,211
Capital: Jefferson City
Important gay cities: Kansas City and St. Louis

Ava ☎ 417

CAMPING

Cactus Canyon Campground (G MA NU PI SA WH)
East of Ava on Hwy 14 ☎ (417) 683-9199
www.cactuscanyoncampground.com

Boonville ☎ 660

SAUNAS/BATHS

Megaplex Health Club & Spa
(DU G m MA OS RR SA SH SOL VS WH WO) 24hrs
11674 Old Highway 40 ☎ (660) 882 0008 www.megaplexspa.com

Cape Girardeau ☎ 573

DANCECLUBS

Independence Place (B D GLM MA ST) 19-1.30h, closed Sun
5 S Henderson St ☎ (573) 334-2939
www.myspace.com/theplacefornewbeginings

Columbia ☎ 573

BARS

Arch and Column Pub. The (AC B CC G m MA OS) Mon-Sat 17-1.30h
1301 Business Loop 70 East *At College Avenue* ☎ (573) 441-8088
www.archandcolumnpub.com
Home of the Columbia ColumBears.

SoCo Club (B D GLM M MA OS ST VS) 20-1.30h, closed Sun & Mon
128 E Nifong Blvd ☎ (573) 499-9483 www.sococlub.com
Gay cabaret, dance club, video, and karaoke bar.

Kansas City ☎ 816

GAY INFO

Lesbian & Gay Community Center. The (GLM)
Mon-Fri 16-21h
207 Westport Road, Suite 210-218 ☎ (816) 931-4420 www.lgcc-kc.org

BARS

Bistro 303 (B GLM M MA OS) Mon-Sat 11.30-1.30
303 Westport Rd. ☎ (816) 753-2303 www.bistro303kc.com
Very fancy and upscale gay bar/restaurant with upscale prices, cool brick decor, gay owned. Happy hours!

Buddies (B G MA) 11-3, Fri & Sat 18-3h
3715 Main Street *Between W 37th and W 38th* ☎ (816) 561-2600
Popular.

Danny's on Broadway (B CC d GLM I MA S) Mon-Sat 10-1.30h
3611 Broadway ☎ (816) 569-1878 www.dannysonbroadway.com
Fun and new bar with nightly events. Dancing on Fri & Sat.

Missy B's and Bootlegger's Club (B d G MA ST) 12-3h
805 West 39th Street ☎ (816) 561-0625 www.missiebs.com
Most popular bar in town, always busy. Drag shows, live music & vocals, leather parties. Check www.missiebs.com for calendar.

Outa Bounds (AC B GLM M MA VS) 11-1.30, Sun -24h
3601 Broadway Street ☎ (816) 756-2577
Gay sports bar/restaurant.

Sidekicks Saloon Country (AC B CC d G MA ST VS) Mon-Sat 14-3h, closed Sun
3707 Main Street *Near W 36th* ☎ (816) 931-1430
Country western, busy weekends.

Sidestreet (B G MA) 10-1.30, Fri & Sat 18-1.30h, closed Sun
413 East 33rd Street ☎ (816) 531-1775

View. The (B G MA) 16-2, Sun 12-2h, closed Mon
204 Orchard Street ☎ (816) 281-0833

RESTAURANTS

Hamburger Mary's (AC B GLM M MA S) 11-22, Fri-Sun -21h
101 Southwest Boulevard ☎ (816) 842-1919
www.hamburgermaryskc.com

SEX SHOPS/BLUE MOVIES

Erotic City (glm) 24hrs
8401 East Truman Road ☎ (816) 252-3370
Dirty place away from the center but always people looking for sex.

GUEST HOUSES

■ **Hydes KC Guesthouse & Men's Gym** (AC bf G MA WO)
☎ (816) 561-1010 💻 www.hydeskc.com

■ **Ken's Place** (AC CC GLM I OS PI PK RWB RWS RWT VA WH)
All year
18 West 38th Street ☎ (816) 753-0533
💻 www.purpleroofs.com/kensplace-mo.html
Six guestrooms, some with private bathroom. Close to local gay scene.

Springfield ☎ 417

BARS

■ **Edge. The** (AC B D GLM MA OS S) Mon-Sat 16-1.30h
424 North Boonville Avenue *1 block south of Chestnut Expressway*
☎ (417) 831-4700 💻 theedgebar.net

■ **Martha's Vineyard** (AC B CC D GLM MA OS S) Tue-Sat 16-1.30h, Sun & Mon closed
219 West Olive Street *1 block north of Park Central Square in Springfield's dining & entertainment district* ☎ (417) 864-4572

St. Louis ☎ 314

PUBLICATIONS

■ **Vital Voice. The**
4337 Manchester ☎ (314) 289-9666 💻 www.thevitalvoice.com
Bi-weekly LGBT newspaper.

BARS

■ **Absolutli Goosed Martini Bar** (B glm MA OS)
16-24, Fri -1.30, Sat 17-1.30h, closed Sun
3196 S Grand Street ☎ (314) 772-0400 💻 www.absolutligoosed.com
Mixed Gay/Straight, famous for their martinis, what else.

■ **Attitudes** (B d gLm MA) Tue-Sat 19-3h, closed Sun & Mon
4100 Manchester Avenue ☎ (314) 534-3858
Neighborhood bar and dance club, karaoke and country line dancing.

■ **Bad Dog Bar** (AC B CC D F GLM I M MA)
3960 Chouteau Ave ☎ (314) 652-0011 💻 www.baddogstl.com
Leather, bikers, bears.

■ **Clementine's** (AC B CC f G M MA OS) 10-1.30, Sun 11-24h
2001 Menard Avenue *At Allen Avenue* ☎ (314) 664-7869
Popular. Regular events.

■ **Club Escapades** (B D GLM MA s) 18-2h
133 West Main Street, Belleville ☎ (618) 222-9597
💻 www.clubescapade.org

■ **Grey Fox Pub** (B GLM MA OS ST) 14-1.30, Sun 12-24h
3503 South Spring ☎ (314) 772-2150 💻 www.greyfoxstl.com

■ **JJ's Clubhouse and Bar** (B d F G MA)
15-3, clubhouse opens Fri & Sat 21-?h
3858 Market Street *Cnr. Vandeventer* ☎ (314) 535-4100
💻 www.jjsclubhouse.com
Bear/leather/jeans bar.

■ **Just John** (B d GLM m MA OS) 15-1.30, Sun 12-24h
4114 Manchester Avenue ☎ (314) 371-1333
💻 www.justjohnsclub.com

■ **Korner's** (B d GLM MA ST) 16-1.30h, closed Sun & Mon
7101 S Broadway *At Blow* ☎ (314) 352-3088 💻 korners-stl.com

■ **Loading Zone** (AC B GLM ST) 14.30-1.30h
16 South Euclid Avenue ☎ (314) 361-4119

■ **Magnolia's** (B D f G M S) 18-3h
9 South Vandeventer ☎ (314) 652-6500
Very popular restaurant, café, bar and disco.

■ **Novak's Bar & Grill** (B gLm M MA OS S) 16-3, Sun 12-3h
4121 Manchester Ave ☎ (314) 531-3699 💻 www.novaksbar.com
Lesbian/mixed crowd, relaxed and fun place.

■ **Soulard Bastille** (B d f G m MC OS) 11-1.30h
1027 Russell Boulevard ☎ (314) 664-4408
💻 www.soulardbastille.com
In the historic „French Quarter", hosts the Leather Club.

DANCECLUBS

■ **Complex Nightclub. The** (AC B CC D GLM MA OS ST VS)
21-3h, closed Mon
3515 Chouteau Avenue ☎ (314) 772-2645
Newest in dance music & videos, Martini lounge, video bar, drag shows.

RESTAURANTS

■ **Bad Dog Bar & Grill** (! AC AK B CC D DM F FC G I LM M MA NR OS PK S SH VEG W WI) 16-1.30, Sun 14-2h
3960 Chouteau Avenue ☎ (314) 652-0011 💻 www.baddogstl.com
Saint Louis's welcoming fetish/leather bar for bikers and bears with fetish nights, bondage.

SAUNAS/BATHS

■ **Club. The**
(! b CC DU FC FH G I m MA OS P PI SA SB SOL VS WH WO) 24hrs
2625 Samuel Shepard Drive *Near Jefferson* ☎ (314) 533-3666
💻 www.the-clubs.com
Dry sauna, shower area and indoor sunken whirlpool, gym, outside heated pool deck.

BOOK SHOPS

■ **Left Bank Books** (AC glm) 10-22, Sun 11-18h
399 N. Euclid Avenue *At McPherson* ☎ (314) 367-6731
💻 www.left-bank.com
General bookstore with large gay section.

GUEST HOUSES

■ **Brewer's House Bed & Breakfast**
(AC BF CC GLM I MA PA PK RWS RWT WH) Reception 7-24h
1829 Lami Street *South of downtown near brewery* ☎ (314) 771-1542
💻 www.brewershouse.com
Small B&B in historic home.

■ **Napoleon's Retreat Bed & Breakfast**
(AC BF CC glm m MA OS) Reception 7-22h
1815 Lafayette Avenue *1 mile from downtown in historical district*
☎ (314) 772-6979 💻 www.napoleonsretreat.com
Four rooms and 1 apartment in 1880s townhouse. Bath or shower, WC, telephone, TV, own key and room service.

■ **St. Louis Guesthouse**
(AC CC G I NU OS PK RWB RWS RWT VS WH) All year
1032 Allen Avenue *In historic Soulard* ☎ (314) 773-1016
💻 www.stlouisguesthouse.com
Five suites with private bath, cable TV, VCR, fridge, small kitchen and phone.

Montana

Location: North USA
Initials: MT
Time: GMT -7
Area: 380.850 km² / 155,767 sq mi.
Population: 902,195
Capital: Helena

Billings ☎ 406

DANCECLUBS

■ **Loft. The** (B D GLM m MA) 14-2h
1123 1st Ave N ☎ (406) 259-9074
💻 www.theloftbillings.com
Check www.theloftbillings.com for special events.

Missoula ☎ 406

CAFES

■ **Catalyst Espresso** (glm M MA) Daily 7-3h
111 N. Higgins Avenue *Downtown* ☎ (406) 542-1337

Nebraska

Location: Middlewest USA
Initials: NE
Time: GMT -6
Area: 200.358 km² / 81,946 sq mi.
Population: 1,711,263
Capital: Lincoln

Lincoln ☏ 402

BARS

■ **Panic** (B GLM MA) 16-1, Sat & Sun 13-1h
200 South 18th Street *Cnr. North Street* ☏ (402) 435-8764
🖳 www.myspace.com/thepanic2008

DANCECLUBS

■ **Q** (AC B D f GLM MA SNU ST) Tue-Sun 20-1h
226 South 9th Street ☏ (402) 475-2269

CRUISING

-Antelope, Pioneer, Wilderness and Van Dorn Parks (AYOR/police)
-I-80 Westbound (west of 56th Street exit AYOR)
-15th Street (between D & H, „Fruit Loop", very popular).

Omaha ☏ 402

BARS

■ **Connections** (B D gLm MA) 18-1.30h, closed Mon
1901 Leavenworth St *At 19th St* ☏ (402) 933-3033
A place rather for lesbians.

■ **DC's Saloon** (B D GLM SNU) 16-1, Sat & Sun 14-1h
610 South 14th Street ☏ (402) 344-3103 🖳 www.dcssaloonomaha.com
Check www.dcssaloonomaha.com for special events (leather night, karaoke..).

■ **Flixx** (B G MA VS) 17-1h
1019 S 10th St ☏ (402) 408-1020 🖳 flixxomaha.com

DANCECLUBS

■ **Max. The** (B D GLM MA NR OS S SNU ST VS W) 16-2h
1417 Jackson Street ☏ (402) 346-4110 🖳 www.themaxomaha.com
Popular.

■ **Omaha Mining Company** (B D f G MA)
Sun-Thu 14-1, Fri & Sat -4h
1715 Leavenworth Street *Near 18th* ☏ (402) 449-8703
Cruise & Dance!

BOOK SHOPS

■ **New Realities** (GLM)
1026 Howard Street, Old Market Passageway ☏ (402) 342-1863

CRUISING

-Milks Run (R) (Howard & Jackson Streets between 16th and 18th, nights)
-Benson Park
-Carter Lake
-Hanscom Park
-Towl Park (AYOR) (wooded area & jogging path).

Nevada

Location: West USA
Initials: NV
Time: GMT -8
Area: 286.367 km² / 117,124 sq mi.
Population: 1,998,257
Capital: Carson City
Important gay cities: Las Vegas and Reno

Las Vegas ☏ 702

Las Vegas is like no other city in the world. You say you don't like to gamble? No problem. Vegas is not just about gambling anymore. Nowhere else in the world can you enjoy hundreds of world class restaurants, millions of square feet of shopping in some of the worlds most fantastic settings such as Caesar's Palace Forum Shops, Desert Passage at the Aladdin and The Fashion Show Mall, all within a 10 minute drive! There are over 50 spectacular shows to choose from. Ranging from the totally camp impersonator shows to the wildly fantastic, multi-million dollar production shows, as well as concerts, performances and sporting events throughout the strip. Another highlight is the cities water park and the two roller-coasters. Take a helicopter sight-seeing trip to the Grand Canyon or Bryce Canyon.

Keine andere Stadt auf der Welt ist wie Las Vegas. Sie sind kein Spieler, sagen Sie? Kein Problem. Denn in Vegas geht es nicht mehr nur um Glücksspiel. Nirgendwo sonst auf der Welt kann man hunderte weltklasse Restaurants genießen, findet man Millionen von Quadratmetern phantastischster Einkaufszentren in atemberaubender Umgebung, wie zum Beispiel die Caesars Palace Forum Shops, die Desert Passage im Aladdin oder die Fashion Show Mall, alle innerhalb einer Fahrtzeit von 10 Minuten! Unter 50 spektakulären Shows kann man wählen, die von total abgedrehten Imitatorenshows bis zu hochklassigen, Multi-Millionen-Dollar-Produktionen mit Weltstars reichen, außerdem Konzerte, Aufführungen und Sportveranstaltungen am laufenden Band. Weitere Highlights sind der städtische Wasserpark, und zwei riesige Achterbahnen. Oder nehmen Sie an einem Helikopterausflug zum Grand- oder Bryce Canyon teil.

Las Vegas est une ville incomparable qui a bien plus que des casinos à vous offrir. Des centaines de restaurants vous y attendent, de même que des millions de mètres carrés d'espace de shopping dans des décors fantastiques tels que Caesars Palace Forum Shops, Desert Passage à l'Aladdin et aussi The Fashion Show Mall. Il y a plus de cinquante spectaculaires présentations à voir, méga-productions, concerts, événements sportifs et autres spectacles. D'autres attractions sont le parc aquatique et les deux montagnes russes. Faites aussi un tour d'hélicoptère et allez visiter le Grand Canyon ou le Bryce Canyon.

Ninguna otra ciudad en el mundo es como Las Vegas. Si no eres jugador, ningún problema pues en Las Vegas no todo es jugar. En ninguna otra parte del mundo se puede disfrutar de cientos de restaurantes de primer orden, ni existen tantos millones de metros cuadrados de fantásticos centros comerciales como, por ejemplo, el Caesars Palace Forum Shops, el Desert Passage en Aladdin o el Fashion Show Mall, itodo a una distancia de 10 minutos! Se puede elegir entre 50 espectáculos, que van desde los locos shows de imitadores hasta producciones millonarias de primera clase con estrellas mundialmente conocidas, además de conciertos, representaciones y otros espectáculos deportivos sin parar. Otros atractivos son el parque acuático y dos enormes montañas rusas. O bien, una excursión en helicóptero al Grand Canyon o Bryce Canyon.

Nessun'altra città al mondo è come Las Vegas. Non siete dei giocatori? Non c'è problema! Infatti a Las Vegas non c'è solo da giocare. In nessun altro luogo del mondo è possibile scegliere tra centinaia di ristoranti di prima qualità, trovare milioni di metri quadrati di fantastici centri commerciali in un ambiente mozzafiato, come per esempio i Caesars Palace Forum Shops, i Desert Passage in Aladdin o Fashion Show Mall, il tutto raggiungibile nell'arco di 10 minuti! Si può scegliere tra 50 spettacoli d'eccezione, da quelli di imitatori sino alle produzioni di milioni di dollari; oltre a ciò concerti, visite guidate e avvenimenti sportivi. Altre attrazioni sono il parco acquatico cittadino, e due montagne russe gigantesche. Oppure potete partecipare ad un volo a bordo di un elicottero sul Grand o Bryce Canyon.

GAY INFO

■ **Gay & Lesbian Community Center of Southern Nevada. The** (GLM) 11-19, Sat 10-15h, closed Sun
953 East Sahara Avenue, Suite B-31 *Commercial Center*
☏ (702) 733-9800 🖳 www.thecenterlv.com

PUBLICATIONS

■ **QVEGAS Magazine**
Stonewall Publishing Inc, 2408 Pardee Place ☎ (702) 650-0636
💻 www.qvegas.com
Bi-weekly magazine covering regional and national news, culture, ads.

BARS

■ **8 1/2 Ultralounge** (B D GLM S YC) 22-?h
4633 Paradise Road ☎ (702) 791-0100 💻 www.8-1-2ultralounge.com
In the same building: Piranha Nightclub.

■ **Backdoor Lounge** (B D G MA S) 24hrs
1415 East Charleston Avenue *Downtown* ☎ (702) 385-2018
Bar with slot machines and pool tables. Latino on Thu & Fri. Drag show on Sat. Gets busy around 12h.

■ **Badlands** (B d G MA) 24hrs
953 East Sahara Avenue N° 22 *In Commercial Center* ☎ (702) 792-9262
Country music with slot machines and pool tables. Mon-Thu 2-4-1 from 16-19h.

■ **Buffalo. The** (B F G MA VS) 24hrs
4640 Paradise Road ☎ (702) 733-8355
Popular. Home of the Satyricon Motorcycle Club. Beer busts on Fri 21h and Sun 16h.

■ **Charlie's** (AC B D G I MA S WE) 24hrs
5012 S Arville St #4 ☎ (702) 876-1844 💻 www.charlieslasvegas.com
Vegas' Country & Western nightclub for gay men.

■ **Crews'n** (B CC D G S WI)
1000 E. Sahara Ave ☎ (702) 731-0951 💻 crewsnlv.com
Cocktail bar. Happy hours 14-19h.

■ **Escape Lounge** (AC B CC GLM M MA OS) 24hrs
4213 West Sahara Ave *Next to Statue of Liberty* ☎ (702) 394-1167
💻 www.escapeloungelv.com
Local bar with food and games.

■ **Flex** (B d GLM MA S SNU) 24hrs
4347 West Charleston Ave ☎ (702) 385-3539 💻 flexlasvegas.com
Sun Karaoke, Tue amateur strip show, Wed male strippers, Fri drag show. Happy hour Mon-Fri 6-18h.

■ **Fun Hog Ranch** (B D F G MA) 24hrs
495 East Twain Avenue ☎ (702) 791-7001 💻 www.funhogranchlv.com
Bear bar.

■ **Garage. The** (B G)
1487 E. Flamingo Road ☎ (702) 440-6333 💻 www.thegaragelv.com
Close to The Strip, just east of Maryland Pkwy in the Skechers Outlet. Happy hour 11-14h & 16-19h every day, where ANY drink is 2-For-1. Daily drink specials, pool, shuffleboard, darts, gambling machines and more!

■ **Gipsy** (B D GLM MA S ST) 22-?h
4633 Paradise Road ☎ (702) 791-0100 💻 www.gipsylasvegas.com
Show and dance bar, Fri & Sat „Party Marathon".

■ **Goodtimes Bar & Nightclub** (AC B D GLM I m MA OS s) 24hrs
1775 East Tropicana Avenue *At Liberace Plaza* ☎ (702) 736-9494
💻 www.goodtimeslv.com
Popular on Mon 23-4h, Fri & Sat 24-5h.

■ **Las Vegas Eagle** (AC B CC d f G MA s) 24hrs
3430 East Tropicana Avenue *At Pecos* ☎ (702) 458-8662
Leather, bear scene. Strip down to your boxers or briefs every Wed & Fri and get free well drinks and beer; Sat „Shirtless" for a free well or draft.

■ **Las Vegas Lounge** (B glm MA S SNU T) 24hrs
900 East Karen Avenue *Behind Cobalt* ☎ (702) 737-9350
Mon-Sat transgender go-go dancers, Fri & Sat cabaret.

■ **Snick's Place** (B D G MA) 24hrs
1402 South Third Street *Off Las Vegas Blvd* ☎ (702) 385-9298
💻 snicksplace.com
Sat „beer bust" from 21-24h.

■ **Spotlight Lounge** (B D f G m MA) 24hrs
957 East Sahara Avenue *At entrance to Commercial Center*
☎ (702) 696-0202 💻 www.spotlightlv.com
Mon 2-4-1 21-12h, Fri „leather night", Sat „jock night".

DANCECLUBS

■ **Freezone** (B D GLM M S SNU T VS) 24hrs
610 East Naples Ave *Across from the Buffalo* ☎ (702) 794-2300
🖳 www.freezonelv.com
Great all around bar. Karaoke and drag shows. Open 24hours. Play pool & video games. There's always something going @ the Freezone.

■ **Krave** (AC B CC D GLM YC) 22.30-5h
3663 Las Vegas Blvd S ☎ (702) 677-2869 🖳 www.kravelasvegas.com
Check www.kravelasvegas.com for special events.

■ **Piranha** (B D GLM S YC) 21-?h
4633 Paradise Road *One block south of Hard Rock* ☎ (702) 791-0100
🖳 www.piranhalasvegas.com
One of the coolest gay clubs of Las Vegas. In the same building: 8 1/2 Ultra Lounge.

SAUNAS/BATHS

■ **Entourage**
(AC cc DR DU FC FH G m MA p PI RR SA SB SH VS WH WO) 24hrs
953 East Sahara Avenue, Suite A-19 *In Commercial Center, 4 blocks east of Las Vegas Boulevard* ☎ (702) 650-9191 🖳 www.entouragevegas.com
Entourage is the rebranded Apollo Spa, ID required. Daily events.

■ **Hawks Gym**
(! AC DR DU F FC FH G M MA P RR SA SB SH SL VS WH WO) 24hrs
953-35B East Sahara Ave, Suite 102 *SE corner of Commercial Center*
☎ (702) 731-4295 🖳 www.hawksGymLV.com
Gym and mens club. The only gay-owned and operated saunaclub in Las Vegas. Many Latinos.

BOOK SHOPS

■ **Get Booked** (CC GLM MA) Mon-Thu 10-24, Fri-Sun -2h
4640 Paradise Road #15 *Opposite Gipsy* ☎ (702) 737-7780
🖳 www.getbooked.com
Books, videos and gifts.

LEATHER & FETISH SHOPS

■ **Rack. The** (F GLM)
953 East Sahara Ave, Bldg. 16 ☎ (702) 732-7225 🖳 www.theracklv.com

DVD SHOPS

■ **Pride Video** (CC G) 10-22h
700 East Naples Drive ☎ (702) 734-1342
Videos rentals.

HOTELS

■ **Blue Moon Hotel & Spa for Men** (! AC BF CC G I M MA MSG NU OS PA PI PK RWS RWT S SA SB VA VS WH WO) All year
2651 Westwood Drive *3 blocks from the Las Vegas Strip* ☎ (702) 784-4500
☎ (866) 798-9194 (toll free) 🖳 www.bluemoonlasvegas.com
The Blue Moon hotel is a popular all-male resort with 45 guest rooms & suites. A 10 man-Jacuzzi, clothing optional pool compound, steam room, Commando Wax Spa,free breakfast & Wifi

Reno ☎ 775

BARS

■ **1099 Club** (B d glm m MA OS S t VS) Sun-Thu 10-2, Fri & Sat 24hrs
1099 South Virginia *Corner of Caliente and S. Virgina* ☎ (775) 329-1099
🖳 www.ten99club.com
Popular western style bar.

■ **5 Star Saloon** (AC B CC d GLM I MA s WE) 24hrs
132 West Street ☎ (775) 329-2878 🖳 www.5starsaloon.net
A chill-out place for a friendly drink on weekdays, a good place to get your bearings in Reno. Packed dance floor with a mixed crowd of all ages (over 21) on the weekends. Staff is devoted to HIV/STD prevention and can provide condoms or schedule free confidential HIV tests by appointment. Major events tend to support local non-profit agencies. What's better than drinking for a good cause?

■ **Cadillac Lounge** (B GLM MA) 12-2h
1114 East 4th Street ☎ (775) 324-7827

■ **Carl's Pub** (B f G MA s) 14-2h
3310 South Virginia Street ☎ (775) 829-8886 www.renodean.com/carlspub
Popular with the leather, jeans and bear crowd.

■ **Patio. The** (B GLM MA) 11-2h
600 West 5th Street ☎ (775) 323-6565 🖳 www.thepatiobar.com
Mixed crowd. Mostly women on Fri. Pool table etc.

DANCECLUBS

■ **Tronix** (B D GLM MA SNU ST) 10-3h
303 Kietzke Ln ☎ (775) 333-9696 🖳 www.tronixreno.com

SAUNAS/BATHS

■ **Steve's Bathhouse** (DR DU FH G m MA OS RR SA SB SL VS) 24hrs
1030 W 2nd St ☎ (775) 323-8770

New Hampshire

Location: Northeast USA
Initials: NH
Time: GMT -5
Area: 24.219 km² / 9,905 sq mi.
Population: 1,173,000
Capital: Concord

Bethlehem ☎ 603

GUEST HOUSES

■ **Highlands Inn. The** (AC BF cc gLm I m MA MSG OS PA PI PK RWB RWS S VA WH) All year
PO Box 118, Valley View Lane *White Mountains, NH* ☎ (603) 869-3978
🖳 www.highlandsinn-nh.com
A lesbian-only guest house.

Chocorua ☎ 603

GUEST HOUSES

■ **Riverbend Inn B&B**
(AC BF CC GLM I MA OS PK RWB RWS RWT WI) All year
273 Chocorua Mountain Highway (Route 16) *Near North Conway, on Route 16*

and near Lake Chocorua ☎ (603) 323-7440 🖳 www.riverbendinn.com
Award winning B&B with 10 guest rooms in a forest setting along the river.

Eaton ☎ 603

GUEST HOUSES

■ **Inn at Crystal Lake** (AC B BF glm I M PK RWB RWT) All year
Route 153 / 2356 Eaton Road ☎ (603) 447-2120
🖳 www.innatcrystallake.com
A beautiful non-smoking, 11 room guest house and restaurant.

Manchester ☎ 603

BARS

■ **Breezeway. The** (B D GLM MA) 16-1h
14 Pearl Street ☎ (603) 621-9111 🖳 www.thebreezeway.net
■ **Club 313** (B D GLM M MA S)
Tue & Wed 18-1, Thu-Sat 16-1, Sun 19-1, danceclub Tue-Sun 21-1h,
93 South Maple Street *Near Oakdale Ave* ☎ (603) 628-6813
🖳 www.club313.net
Sports bar, danceclub, karaoke & show lounge.
■ **The Element Lounge** (B d GLM m ST VS)
Mon 18-1.30, Tue-Sun 15-1.30h
1055 Elm Street ☎ (603) 627-2922 🖳 www.elementlounge.net
Friendly bar/night club, Wednesday is movie night on their 96 inch screen.

New Jersey

Location: Northeast USA
Initials: NJ
Time: GMT -5
Area: 22.590 km² / 9,239 sq mi.
Population: 8,414,350
Capital: Trenton

Asbury Park ☎ 732

BARS

■ **Georgie's** (B GLM MA) 16-2h
812 5th Avenue ☎ (732) 988-1220 🖳 www.georgiesbar.com
■ **Paradise** (AC B CC D GLM H m MA PI S)
16-2h, closed Mon & Tue through winter until May
101 Asbury Avenue *Asbury Park train station* ☎ (732) 988-6663
🖳 www.paradisenj.com
Heated pool, frozen drinks, 2 dance floors, shows and more. Inside Empress Hotel.

HOTELS

■ **Empress** (AC B bf CC d glm m MA PI S) All year
101 Asbury Ave *Asbury Park train station* ☎ (732) 774-0100
🖳 www.asburyempress.com

Atlantic City ☎ 609

BARS

■ **Westside Bar & Lounge** (B D GLM MA) 16-4, Sat & Sun 12-4h
511 North Arkansas Avenue ☎ (609) 344-0883 🖳 www.WestsideAC.com
Atlantic City's only gay & lesbian venue.

GUEST HOUSES

■ **Ocean House** (AC CC G NU PK) All year
127 South Ocean Avenue *Near beach* ☎ (609) 345-8203
🖳 www.oceanhouseatlanticcity.com

Boonton ☎ 973

BARS

■ **Switch** (B d G M MA s) 18-2, Sat & Sun 16-2h
202 Myrtle Avenue *Near Route 287* ☎ (973) 263-4000 🖳 www.switchbar.com
Dance on Fri & Sat from 22h.

Hoboken ☎ 201

BARS

■ **Cage. The** (AC B D GLM MA) 17-2, Fri & Sat -3h
32 Newark Street *Between Hudson and River Streets* ☎ (201) 216-1766
🖳 www.thecagehoboken.com

Jersey City ☎ 201

BARS

■ **Star Bar** (AC B GLM I MA) 16-2h
34 Wayne Street ☎ 367-1222 🖳 www.gostarbar.com

Plainfield ☎ 908

PRIVATE ACCOMMODATION

■ **Pillars of Plainfield Bed & Breakfast Inn. The**
(AC BF CC glm MA MSG OS PA PK RWS RWT VA) All year
922 Central Avenue *Close to Newark, NY, Sandy Hook*
☎ (908) 753-0922 🖳 www.pillars2.com
Cable modem, digital cable TV, WiFi and evening sherry.

River Edge ☎ 201

BARS

■ **Feathers** (B d GLM MA S) 21-2, Sat -3h
77 Kinderkamack Road *North Jersey* ☎ (201) 342-6410
🖳 www.clubfeathers.com

Somerset ☎ 908

BARS

■ **Den. The** (AC B CC f GLM m MA s VS) 19-2h, Sun & Mon closed
700 Hamilton Street ☎ (908) 545-7329 🖳 www.dennightclub.com

Trenton ☎ 609

CAFES

■ **Café Ole** (b BF glm m MA s) Mon-Thu 7-16, Fri -21.30, Sat 9.30-14h
126 S.Warren Street ☎ (609) 396-2233 🖳 www.cafeolecoffee.com

New Mexico

Location: Southwest USA
Initials: NM
Time: GMT -7
Area: 314.939 km² / 128,810 sq mi.
Population: 1,819,046
Capital: Santa Fé

Albuquerque ☎ 505

BARS

■ **Albuquerque Social Club** (B D GLM MA)
15-24, Fri & Sat -2, Sun 12-24h
4021 Central Ave NE ☎ (505) 255-0887
■ **Sidewinders Ranch** (B D f G MA) 12-2, Sun -24h
8900 Central South East *At East of Wyoming* ☎ (505) 275-1616
Cowboy and leather bar.

GUEST HOUSES

■ **Brittania & W.E. Mauger Estate** (AC BF CC glm m MA PA)
All year
701 Roma Avenue N.W. *Downtown* ☎ (505) 242-8755 🖳 maugerbb.com
Each room has private bath, phone, TV, refrigerator.
■ **Golden Guesthouses** (GLM) All year
2645 Decker Ave NW ☎ (505) 344-9205
🖳 www.goldenguesthouses.com

Santa Fe ☎ 505

BARS

■ **Pink Adobe Dragon Room** (B g MC) 16.30-23h
406 Old Santa Fe Trail ☎ (505) 983-7712
www.thepinkadobe.com/dragonroom.php
Wonderful bar with a great atmosphere and a cute bar tender.

■ **Silver Starlight Lounge & Cabaret** (B GLM MA S)
500 Rodeo Road *On Route 66* ☎ (505) 428-7777
www.rainbowvisionprop.com/santafecalendar.html
Cute barmen. Some of the best shows in town from drag to discos to jazz. Very friendly and mixed crowd.

RESTAURANTS

■ **315 Restaurant & Wine Bar** (B g M MC) 17.30-19h
315 Old Santa Fe Trail *The Plaza* ☎ (505) 986-9190 www.315santafe.com

■ **Cowgirl Hall of Fame** (B g M MC) Daily 11-2h
319 S Guadalupe Street *Guadalupe District* ☎ (505) 982-2565
www.cowgirlsantafe.com

■ **Geronimo's** (AC B CC DM glm M MA NR OS PK VEG WL)
11.30-14.30, 18-22h
724 Canyon Road *Corner Canyon Rd-Camino del Monte Sol*
☎ (505) 982-1500 www.geronimorestaurant.com
Very good Mediterranean cuisine. Gay owned.

■ **Vanessie of Santa Fe** (B glm M MA) 17.30-21, bar -24h
434 West San Francisco Street ☎ (505) 982-9966
www.vanessiesantafe.com
A steakhouse and a piano bar which is rather gay. Gay owned.

GUEST HOUSES

■ **Inn of the Turquoise Bear** (BF CC GLM H M MA MSG NR OS PA PK RES RWB RWS RWT VA VEG W WI) All year, office 7-21h
342 East Buena Vista Street *Downtown, 6 blocks to plaza*
☎ (505) 983-0798 www.turquoisebear.com
Historical ambience within walking distance from downtown attractions. Most of the 10 rooms with private baths.

■ **Inn on the Alameda** (BF g MC) All year
303 East Alameda *Canyon Road* ☎ (888) 984-2121 (toll free)
www.innonthealameda.com
Located in an arty area within walking distance to all the best restaurants in Santa Fe. Genuinely friendly and warm staff.

■ **Triangle Inn – Santa Fe. The** (AC BF CC DU GLM I MA OS PA PK RES RWS RWT W WH WI) All year
14 Arroyo Cuyamungue *12 miles north of Santa Fee* ☎ (505) 455-3375
☎ 877-733-7689 (toll free) www.triangleinn.com
Suites with shower/WC, TV/video, telephone, radio, kitchenette/kitchen and hair-dryer. Run by a lesbian couple.

CRUISING

-Rest Stop (on I-25 15 miles south of Santa Fe)
- P at Villa Linda Mall, off Rodeo Rd (car cruising).

New York

Location: Northeast USA
Initials: NY
Time: GMT -5
Area: 141.080 km² / 57,701 sq mi.
Population: 18,976,457
Capital: Albany
Important gay cities: Fire Island and New York City

Albany ☎ 518

BARS

■ **Fuze Box. The** (AC B D glm MA S) 14-4, Thu-Sat 20-4
348 Central Avenue ☎ (518) 432-4472 www.myspace.com/fuzebox

■ **Oh-Bar** (AC B GLM MA VS) 14-4h
304 Lark Street ☎ (518) 463-9004

■ **Rocks** (AC B CC G I MA OS S) 14-4h
77 Central Avenue *Near cnr. Henry Johnson Blvd* ☎ (518) 472-3588
www.rocks77.com

■ **Water Works** (B D G M MA S) 13-4h
76 Central Avenue *Between Lexington & Northern* ☎ (518) 465-9079
www.waterworkspub.com

CRUISING

-Toilets on 2nd floor at Macy's, 131 Colonie Center
-Toilets at SUNY Albany Performing Arts Center – 2nd floor.

Angelica ☎ 716

CAMPING

■ **Jones Pond Campground & RV Park**
(d G I MC NU P PA PI PK s WE) Seasonal
9835 Old State Rd *1.25 hrs south of Buffalo and Rochester*
☎ (716) 567-8100 www.jonespond.com
Clothing-optional, gay camping facility with Cabins.

Binghamton ☎ 607

BARS

■ **Merlins** (B D GLM MA OS S ST t)
Wed 12-1; Tue, Thu & Sun 20-1; Fri & Sat -3h; closed Mon
201 State Street *In the heart of downtown Binghamton, along „Artists Row"*
☎ (607) 772-1022 www.201merlins.com
Probably Binghamton's largest LGBTQ dance club.

■ **Squiggy's** (B D GLM MA ST) 18-1, Fri -3, Sat 20-3h, closed Sun
34 Chenango Street ☎ (607) 722-2299

■ **Zippers** (AC B D GLM MA ST) Tue-Sat 20-?h
165 Conklin Avenue ☎ (607) 437-9264
www.myspace.com/binghamtonzippers

RESTAURANTS

■ **Whole in the Wall** (b g M MA) Tue-Sat 11.30-21h
43 South Washington Street ☎ (607) 722-5138 www.wholeinthewall.com

Buffalo ☎ 716

GAY INFO

■ **Pride Center of Western New York** (GLM)
206 South Elmwood Ave ☎ (716) 852-7743

PUBLICATIONS

■ **abOUT Magazine**
452 Franklin St ☎ (713) 396-2688 www.about-online.com
Free monthly gay magazine covering Western New York and Southern Ontario.

■ **Outcome Buffalo**
506 Linwood Ave, Suite 6 ☎ (716) 883-2756 www.outcomebuffalo.com

BARS

■ **Adonia's** (B D GLM MA) 15-2, Fri & Sat -4, Sun 12-2h
20 Allen Street *Near Main* ☎ (716) 332-1205

■ **Cathode Ray** (B G MA VS) 13-4, Sun 7-4h
26 Allen Street ☎ (716) 884-3615 www.cathoderaybuffalo.com

■ **Fugazi** (B GLM M VS) 17-2, Fri & Sat 20-2h
503 Franklin Street *Near Allen St* ☎ (716) 881-3588
Martini & video bar.

■ **Q** (B G MA) 15-4, Sat & Sun 12-4h
44 Allen St ☎ (716) 332-2223 www.qbuffalo.com

DANCECLUBS

■ **Club Marcella** (AC B CC D GLM M MA OS PK S SNU ST T W WE)
Wed-Sun 22-4, closed Mon & Tue
622 Main Street *Near the Sheas Theatre* ☎ ((716)) 847-6850
www.clubmarcella.com
Largest gay bar in Buffalo.

■ **Underground. The** (B D G MA) 12-4h
174 Delaware Ave *At Johnson* ☎ (716) 853-0092

BOOK SHOPS

Talking Leaves (glm) Mon-Sat 10-18h
3158 Main Street ☎ (716) 837-8554 www.tleavesbooks.com

CRUISING

-Tillman Road Wildlife Park, in Clarence
-Toilets at University of Buffalo North Campus Student Union, 2nd floor
-Buffalo State College E.H, Butler Library, 3rd floor
-Erie Community College South Campus (building 2).

Elmira ☎ 607

BARS

Chill (B GLM M MA S) 17-1, Fri & Sat -3h
501 Erie St ☎ (607) 732-1414 www.chillwitme.com

Fire Island ☎ 631

BARS

Blue Whale (B D GLM M MA) Seasonal
Harbor Walk, Fire Island Pines ☎ (631) 597-6131
www.thepinesfireisland.com

Cherry's (B GLM M MA S ST) 12-4h, seasonal
Bayview Walk, Cherry Grove ☎ (631) 597-6820
www.cherrysonthebay.com

Ice Palace. The (B D GLM MA ST) from May to September
Bayview Walk, Cherry Grove ☎ (631) 597-6600 www.grovehotel.com
Dance ,till dawn with New York's top DJs. Free drag shows, guest entertainers, theme parties and more. Checkout the lineup of entertainment events for the summer season on www.grovehotel.com.

Jumping Jacks (B G M MA) Seasonal
Ocean Walk, Cherry Grove ☎ (631) 597-4174

Sip n' Twirl (B D G MA OS) Seasonal, 12-4h
36 Fire Island Boulevard, The Pines ☎ (631) 597-3599 www.sipntwirl.com

DANCECLUBS

Pavillon. The (B D G MA) Fri & Sat, seasonal
Fire Island Blvd, Fire Island Pines ☎ (631) 597-6500
www.thepinesfireisland.com

HOTELS

Grove Hotel (AC B CC D GLM MA OS PI RWS RWT S VA WO) All year
PO Box 537, Sayville ☎ (631) 597-6600 www.grovehotel.com
The exciting Grove Hotel, Fire Island's largest hotel and home of the world-famous Miss Fire Island contest. Located in the very heart of Cherry Grove, the hotel is central to the best that Fire Island has to offer. Only a few steps away are the beach, restaurants, shops, dance clubs, and bars.

GUEST HOUSES

Belvedere Guest House for Men (BF CC G I MA NU OS PI RWB RWS RWT VA WH WO) May-Oct
Box 4026, Cherry Grove *Sayville ferry service to Cherry Grove, on the bay*
☎ (631) 597-6448 www.belvederefireisland.com
BF at WE only. 38 en-suite rooms with balcony/terrace, TV, VCR, radio, own key.

Madison Fire Island Pines. The
(AC BF CC G I MSG OS PI WH) All year
22 Atlantic Walk ☎ (631) 597-6061 www.themadisonfi.com
Chic ambience and high-end amenities, including flat-screen televisions, iPod docking stations and more. Huge pool deck, hot tub and roof deck with panoramic views of the island. Online reservations encouraged.

Greene ☎ 607

GUEST HOUSES

Inn at Serenity Farms. The
(AC BF CC glm I M MA NU PA PI PK RWS VA WE) All year
386 Pollard Road *Between Binghamton & Syracuse* ☎ (607) 656-4659
www.geocities.com/WestHollywood/6173/SERENITY/index
100 acres with heated pool, hot tub. Pet friendly. Open year round.

Ithaca ☎ 607

DANCECLUBS

■ **Oasis** (B D GLM MA OS S WE) Tue-Sun 17-1h
1230 Danby Road (Route 96B) *Across American Legion*
☎ (607) 273-1505 www.ithacaoasis.com
Nightclub.

Jamestown ☎ 716

BARS

■ **Sneakers** (B D GLM MA) 14-2, Tue 17-2h
100 Harrison Street ☎ (716) 484-8816

Long Island – Nassau County ☎ 516

BARS

■ **Blanche** (AC B GLM OS S) 17-?h
47-2 Boundary Avenue, South Farmingdale ☎ (516) 694-6906
www.blanchebar.com
Male dancers every Fri, karaoke on Sat nights.

■ **Kelli's** (AC B D GLM m MA) 17-4, Sun 12-4h
2955 Merrick Road, Bellmore ☎ (516) 765-3892 www.kellisbar.net

DANCECLUBS

■ **Shy Lounge** (AC B D GLM MA) Wed & Sat 22-4h
2686 Hempstead Tpke, Levittown ☎ (516) 520-1332
www.clubpureny.com

Long Island – Suffolk County ☎ 631

BARS

■ **Long Island Eagle** (AC B F G MA OS) Mon-Sat 21-4, Sun 16-4h
94 N. Clinton Avenue, Bay Shore *At Union Blvd* ☎ (631) 968-2250
Home of LI Ravens M.C.

New York ☎ 212

New York (also known as the Big Apple) offers an amazing choice, whether it be gay bars, dance clubs or simply shopping. The city, with the history of Stonewall, has a lively LGBT community and it is not without reason that New York is known as the city that never sleeps. Seven days a week you can find what, and also possibly who, you're after – no matter which part of the city you may be staying in. Gay culture has spread its wings throughout New York and the well-known gay areas such as Chelsea and The Village are no longer your only option. Venture over to the Upper West Side or Queens or Park Slope, Brooklyn and expand your options even further.
Tourist areas in Manhattan are generally safe, and the city has experienced a dramatic drop in its crime rate in recent years. The legal age for purchase and consumption of alcoholic beverages in New York is 21 years of age! If you want to purchase alcohol, expect to be required to show proof of age at bars, nightclubs, restaurants and stores. Further, please be aware that carrying an open container with alcohol in public places is illegal!

New York (auch „Big Apple" genannt) hat erstaunlich viel zu bieten, von vielfältigen Schwulenbars und Tanzclubs bin hin zum Shoppen. Die Stadt, in der die Stonewall-Aufstände stattfanden, hat eine lebendige LGBT-Gemeinschaft und ist nicht ohne Grund auch als „Stadt, die niemals schläft" bekannt. Sieben Tage in der Woche findet man hier was – und möglicherweise auch wen – man immer möchte, egal in welchem Teil der Stadt man sich aufhält. Die schwule Kultur hat ihre Flügel über ganz New York ausgebreitet und ist nicht mehr nur in den bekannten Gay Areas wie Chelsea und The Village zu finden. Man kann sich auch zur Upper West Side, nach Queens oder Park Slope, Brooklyn wagen und seine Auswahl stark erweitern!
Die Touristengegenden von Manhattan sind generell sicher, denn in den letzten Jahren ist die Verbrechensrate drastisch gesunken. In New York darf man erst ab 21 Alkohol kaufen oder konsumieren! Aus diesem Grund wird auch in Bars, Nachtklubs, Restaurants und Geschäften häufig ein entsprechender Altersnachweis verlangt. Außerdem ist es verboten, in der Öffentlichkeit offene Alkoholbehälter mit sich zu führen!

New York (surnommée aussi „ Big Apple „) a énormément à offrir avec de multiples bars gays, boites sans parler du shopping. La ville qui a vu les soulèvements de Stonewall compte une communauté LGBT vivante et ne s'appelle pas sans raison „ la ville qui ne dort jamais „. Sept jours sur sept, on trouve tout ce que l'on veut, qu'importe le quartier de la ville où l'on se trouve. La culture gay a étalé ses ailes sur tout New York et non plus seulement dans les quartiers gays connus de Chelsea et du Village. Upper West Side, Queens et Park Slope ou Brooklyn ont aussi beaucoup à offrir.
Les lieux touristiques de Manhattan sont généralement sûrs car la criminalité s'est effondrée ces dernières années. A New York, la consommation et l'achat d'alcool sont réservés aux plus de 21 ans ! Pour cette raison, les bars, boîtes, restaurants et commerces exigent souvent une pièce d'identité. De plus il est interdit d'avoir une bouteille d'alcool ouverte sur soi en public !

Nueva York (también conocida como „La Gran Manzana") tiene muchísimo que ofrecer, desde bares y discotecas gays de todo tipo hasta exclusivas zonas para ir de compras. La ciudad en la que tuvieron lugar los famosos disturbios de Stonewall cuenta con una vibrante comunidad LGBT y, no sin razón, se la conoce como la „ciudad que nunca duerme". Los siete días de la semana podrá encontrar aquí lo que (y, posiblemente, también a quienes) siempre quiso encontrar. No importa en qué parte de la ciudad se encuentre, la cultura gay ha exten-

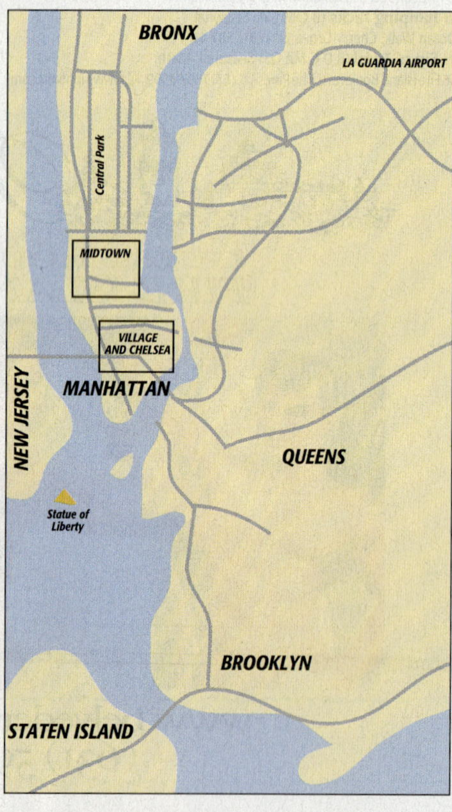

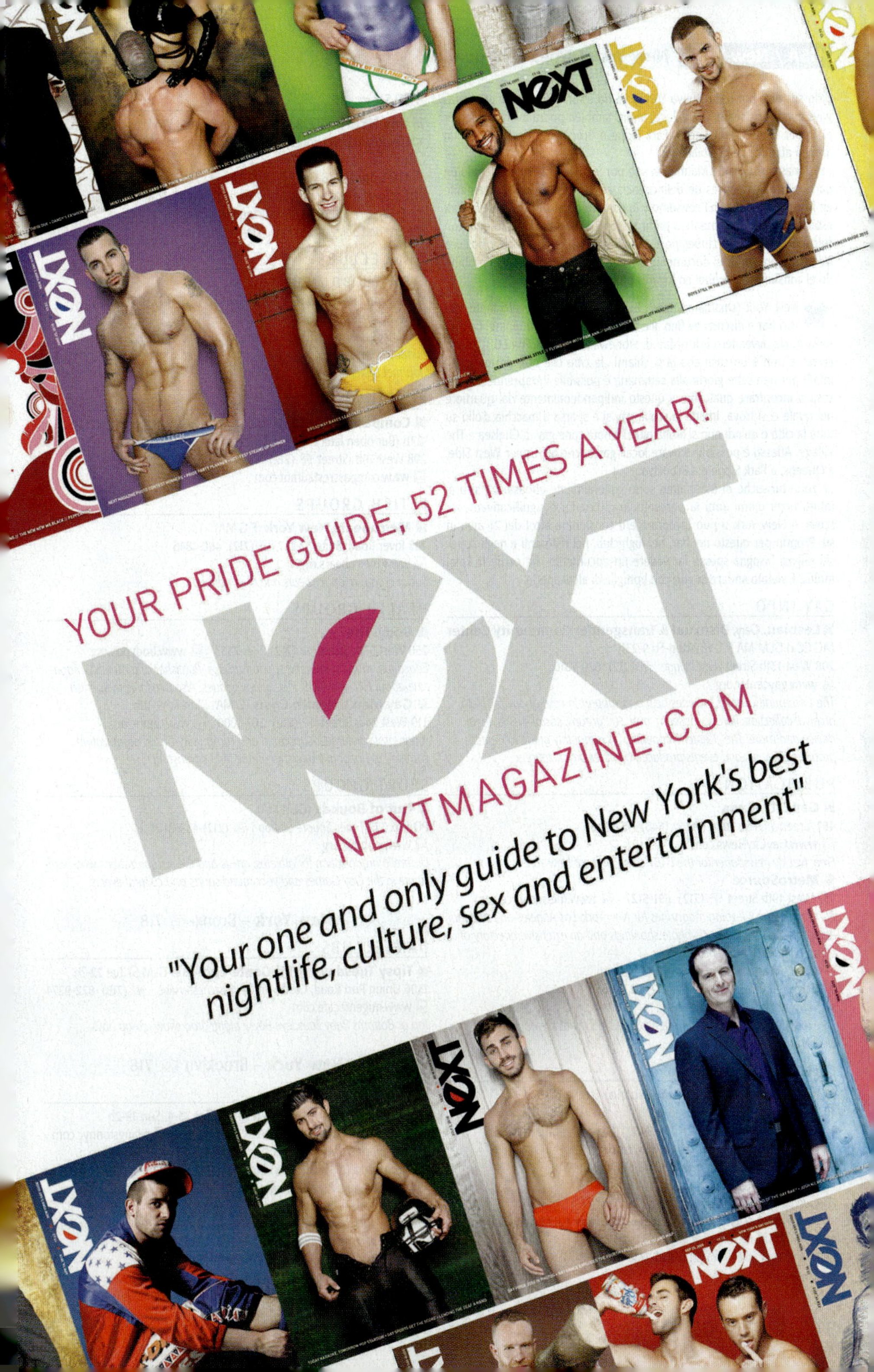

YOUR PRIDE GUIDE, 52 TIMES A YEAR!
NEXT
NEXTMAGAZINE.COM
"Your one and only guide to New York's best nightlife, culture, sex and entertainment"

dido sus alas por toda Nueva York y ya no están sólo las míticas zonas gays como Chelsea o The Village, ahora también podrá aventurarse por el Upper West Side, Queens, Park Slope o Brooklyn y descubrir así un amplio abanico de posibilidades.
Las zonas turísticas de Manhattan son por lo general seguras, debido en parte a que los niveles de delincuencia se han reducido drásticamente en los últimos años. ¡El consumo y la compra de alcohol en Nueva York están permitidos solamente a partir de los 21 años! Es por esto que, con frecuencia, en bares, clubes nocturnos, restaurante y otros negocios sea necesario presentar el documento de identidad. ¡También está prohibido el consumo de alcohol en lugares públicos!

New York (chiamata anche „Big Apple") offre davvero tanto, dai vari bar e discoteche fino alle tante possibilità di shopping. La città nella quale avvennero i disordini di Stonewall ha una scena LGBT molto vivace e non è un caso che la si chiami „la città che non dorme mai". Infatti per ben sette giorni alla settimana è possibile intraprendere qualcosa o incontrare qualcuno, e questo indipendentemente dal quartiere nel quale ci si trova. Infatti, la scena gay si è sparsa a macchia d'olio su tutta la città e quindi non si limita più alle note zone gay di Chelsea e The Village. Adesso è possibile trovare locali gay anche all' Upper West Side, a Queens, a Park Slope e a Brooklyn.
Le zone turistiche di Manhattan sono generalmente abbastanza sicure, infatti negli ultimi anni la percentuale di crimini è significativamente scesa. A New York si può comprare e/o consumare alcol dai 21 anni in su. Proprio per questo nei bar, nei nightclub, nei ristoranti e negli appositi negozi bisogna spesso far vedere un documento che certifichi l'età. Inoltre è vietato andare in giro con bottiglie di alcol aperte.

GAY INFO

Lesbian, Gay, Bisexual & Transgender Community Center (AC CC d GLM MA S T VS) Mon-Fri 9-23h
208 West 13th Street *West Village* ☎ (212) 620-7310
www.gaycenter.org
The Community Center provides help and support in case of any problem, archival collection, library, museum, over 300 groups, social events, legal advice and more. The „Center Happening" is a monthly guide to Center programs, events, and events produced by other organizations.

PUBLICATIONS

Gay City News
487 Greenwich St, Suite 6A ☎ (646) 452-2500
www.GayCityNews.com
Free, weekly newspaper for the LGBT community of New York.

MetroSource
137 West 19th Street ☎ (212) 691-5127 www.metrosource.com
Bi-monthly gay & lesbian magazines for New York, Los Angeles and national editions. Articles on lifestyle, photo shootings and an extensive directory of community-related businesses.

Next Magazine
121 Varick Street *3rd floor* ☎ (212) 627-0165
www.nextmagazine.com
Free weekly magazine with an extensive address list of the gay scene in New York.

CULTURE

Museum of Modern Art (MoMa)
10.30-17.30, Fri -20h, Tue closed
11 West 53rd Street ☎ (212) 708-9400 www.moma.com

National Museum of GLBT History
208 West 13th Street *West Village* ☎ (212) 620-7310
www.gaycenter.org
Founded in 1989. Including library and archives.

Pat Parker/Vito Russo Center Library (GLM MA) Mon-Thu 18-21, Fri & Sat 13-16h
208 West 13th Street ☎ (212) 620-7310 ext. 279
www.gaycenter.org
Over 20.000 books, 1.500 videos and 20 periodicals.

BARS

Boy NYC. Le (AC B CC D G M MA S SNU t VS) Wed-Sun 18-4h
104 Dyckman Street *Uppermost section of Manhattan* www.leboynyc.com
Latino club.

UC Lounge (B G MA OS) 16-2, Fri -4, Sat 13-4, Sun -2h
87 Ludlow Street *Between Delancey and Broome, Lower East Side*
☎ (212) 677-1100 www.ucloungenyc.com
The first and only gay bar in the Lower East Side.

DANCECLUBS

Sea Tea (B D G M MA S)
W Houston Street *South 2 blocks to Pier 40* ☎ (0212) 675 2971
www.seatea.com
New York's only gay sailing tea dance. The Queen of Hearts sails every Sunday from Jun-Sept. Boards 18, sails 19.30, return 22h. Includes a free gourmet buffet dinner and live show, see www.seatea.com for details.

RESTAURANTS

Compass (B CC g M MA WE) Mon-Sat 17-23 (Bar open later), Sun -22h (Bar open later)
208 West 70th Street ☎ (212) 875-8600
www.compassrestaurant.com

FETISH GROUPS

MetroBears New York (F G MA)
725 River Road, Suite 32-137 ☎ (212) 460-1845
www.metrobears.org
Social organisation for bears and their admirers.

HEALTH GROUPS

Body. The
250 West 57th Street ☎ (212) 566-7333 www.bodypos.org
Education, medical info and support groups. Publisher of a monthly magazine about HIV and AIDS. Free at gay venues. Also available in Spanish.

Gay Men's Health Crisis (G MA) Mon-Fri 9-18h
119 West 24th Street ☎ (212) 367-1000 www.gmhc.org
A non-profit, volunteer-supported and community-based organization comitted to national leadership on the fight against AIDS.

SPORT GROUPS

Out of Bounds (GLM MA)
PO Box 372 *Times Square Station* ☎ (212) 439-8179
www.oobnyc.org
Umbrella organization for athletes, artists and their organizations who participate in the Gay Games and year round sports and cultural events.

New York – Bronx ☎ 718

DANCECLUBS

Tipsy Tuesdays @ Mi Gente Cafe (B D GLM S) Tue 22-?h
1306 Union Port Road, Castle Hill *At Westchester Ave* ☎ (718) 822-9274
www.migentecafe.com
Top or Bottoms Ruby Tuesdays Boysz night, drag show, go-go boys.

New York – Brooklyn ☎ 718

BARS

Club Langston (B D GLM MA) Thu-Sat 23-4, Sun 19-2h
1073 Atlantic Avenue ☎ (718) 622-5183 www.clublangstonnyc.com
Afro-american crowd.

Excelsior (AC B GLM OS) Mon-Fri 18-4, Sat & Sun 14-4h
390 Fifth Avenue, Park Slope *At 6th Street* ☎ (718) 832-1599
www.excelsiorbrooklyn.com
Mixed gay cocktail bar with a porch and outdoor garden. Happy hour: Mon-Fri 18-21, Sat & Sun 14-19h.

Ginger's (B gLm MA OS s) 17-4, Sat & Sun 14-4h
363 5th Avenue, Park Slope *At 5th Street* ☎ (718) 788-0924
Lesbian and gay bar, local crowd. Pool table, video games, jukebox.

■ **Metropolitan** (B GLM I MA OS S) 15-4h
559 Lorimer Street, Williamsburg *Metropolitan Ave* ☎ (718) 599-4444
🖳 www.myspace.com/metropolitan11211
Two floors. Video games, pool table, outside patio and free internet. Happy hour: Mon-Fri 15-20h.

■ **Sugarland** (B D GLM MA) Fri & Sat 20-?h
221 North Ninth Street ☎ (718) 599-4044
This hip bar dazzles with awesome performances and dirty dancing.

DANCECLUBS

■ **Gumbo @ Galapagos Art Space** (B D GLM MA)
1st Fri & 3rd Thu/month 20-1h
16 Main Street ☎ (718) 222-8500 🖳 www.gumbonyc.com

■ **Last Monday @ Floyd** (B D GLM MA) Last Mon/month 21h-?h
131 Atlantic Ave *Near Henry Street* ☎ (718) 858-5810
🖳 www.lastmonday.info

RESTAURANTS

■ **Bogota** (B G M MA) Mon-Thu 17-23, Fri -1, Sat 11-1, Sun -23h
141 Fifth Avenue *Park Slope between St. John's and Lincoln Place*
☎ (718) 230-3805 🖳 www.bogotabistro.com
New York's popular latin american / Colombian restaurant and bar.

PRIVATE ACCOMMODATION

■ **Loralei B&B** (AC CC GLM RWS RWT) All year
667 Argyle Road ☎ (646) 228-4656 🖳 loraleinyc.com

New York – Manhattan/Chelsea ☎ 212

BARS

■ **Barracuda** (AC B G MA S ST VS) 16-4h
275 West 22nd Street *Between 7th and 8th Avenue* ☎ (212) 645-8613
Happy hour 16-21h, Mon-Fri 2-4-1, DJs and drag shows, occasional celebrity appearances. No cover charge.

■ **Boxers** (AC B CC G M MA) 12-2h
37 West 20th Street *Between 5th and 6th Ave* ☎ (212) 255-5082
🖳 www.boxersnyc.com
Sports bar with two levels, pool tables, brick oven pizza, beer on tap, full bar, and plasma screens. Happy hour Mon-Fri 16-21.30h.

■ **Eagle. The** (B F G MA OS) 22-4, Sun 17-4h
554 West 28th Street *Between 10th and 11th Ave* ☎ (646) 473-1866
🖳 www.eaglenyc.com
Leather/levi classic on 2 levels, very popular, happy hour 2-4-1 on Fri 17-22h. Beer Blast on Sun 17-22h.

■ **g Lounge** (AC B G MA) 16-4h
225 West 19th Street *Between 7th & 8th Avenue* ☎ (212) 929-1085
🖳 www.glounge.com
The original Chelsea lounge, happy hour 18-21h.

■ **Gym Sportsbar** (AC B CC G MA) 16-2, Fri -4, Sat 13-4, Sun -2h
167 8th Avenue, Chelsea *A, C or E Train to 14th Street, between 18th & 19th Streets* ☎ (212) 337 2439
🖳 www.gymsportsbar.com
New York City's first gay sports bar.

■ **Rawhide** (AC B F G MA S) Daily 10-4h
212 8th Avenue *At 21st Street*
☎ (212) 242-9332
Leather/levi bar, very popular. Go-gos nightly.

■ **Secret** (AC B d G MA) Fri & Sat 20-4h
525 West 29th Street ☎ (212) 268-5580
DJs, drink specials, dancing.

■ **XES Lounge** (! AC B CC G MA OS ST) 16-4h
157 West 24th Street *Between 6th & 7th Ave* ☎ (212) 604-0212
🖳 www.XESnyc.com
A friendly, cruisy bar with great music, great entertainment and generous drinks. Great staff and a smoking patio. Happy hour Mon-Fri 16-21h. Every night different events. See: www.xesnyc.com for more information.

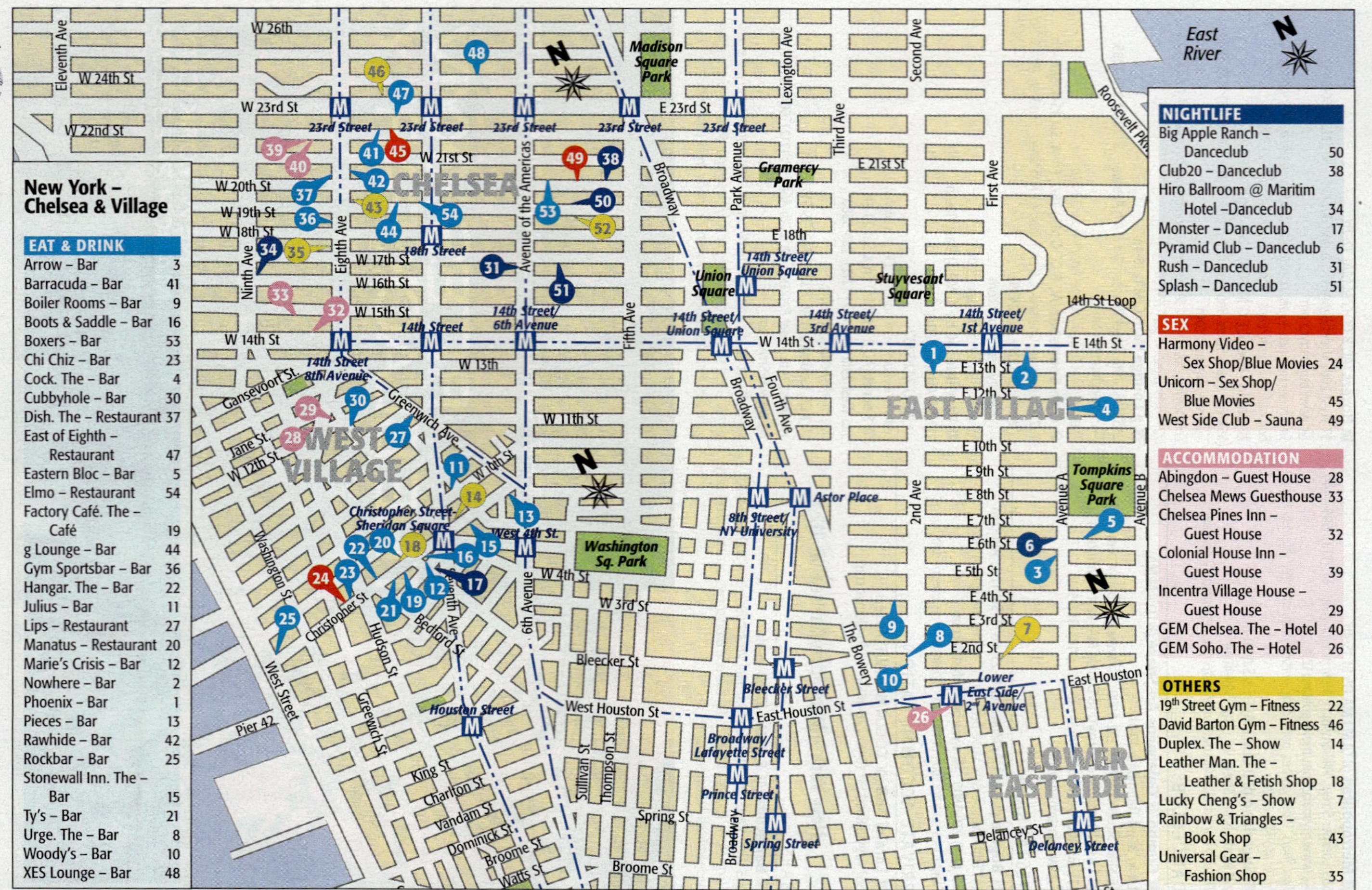
New York – Chelsea & Village
EAT & DRINK
Arrow – Bar 3
Barracuda – Bar 41
Boiler Rooms – Bar 9
Boots & Saddle – Bar 16
Boxers – Bar 53
Chi Chiz – Bar 23
Cock. The – Bar 4
Cubbyhole – Bar 30
Dish. The – Restaurant 37
East of Eighth – Restaurant 47
Eastern Bloc – Bar 5
Elmo – Restaurant 54
Factory Café. The – Café 19
g Lounge – Bar 44
Gym Sportsbar – Bar 36
Hangar. The – Bar 22
Julius – Bar 11
Lips – Restaurant 27
Manatus – Restaurant 20
Marie's Crisis – Bar 12
Nowhere – Bar 2
Phoenix – Bar 1
Pieces – Bar 13
Rawhide – Bar 42
Rockbar – Bar 25
Stonewall Inn. The – Bar 15
Ty's – Bar 21
Urge. The – Bar 8
Woody's – Bar 10
XES Lounge – Bar 48
NIGHTLIFE
Big Apple Ranch – Danceclub 50
Club20 – Danceclub 38
Hiro Ballroom @ Maritim Hotel –Danceclub 34
Monster – Danceclub 17
Pyramid Club – Danceclub 6
Rush – Danceclub 31
Splash – Danceclub 51
SEX
Harmony Video – Sex Shop/Blue Movies 24
Unicorn – Sex Shop/ Blue Movies 45
West Side Club – Sauna 49
ACCOMMODATION
Abingdon – Guest House 28
Chelsea Mews Guesthouse 33
Chelsea Pines Inn – Guest House 32
Colonial House Inn – Guest House 39
Incentra Village House – Guest House 29
GEM Chelsea. The – Hotel 40
GEM Soho. The – Hotel 26
OTHERS
19th Street Gym – Fitness 22
David Barton Gym – Fitness 46
Duplex. The – Show 14
Leather Man. The – Leather & Fetish Shop 18
Lucky Cheng's – Show 7
Rainbow & Triangles – Book Shop 43
Universal Gear – Fashion Shop 35
East River
CHELSEA
WEST VILLAGE
EAST VILLAGE
LOWER EAST SIDE
Madison Square Park
Gramercy Park
Union Square
Stuyvesant Square
Tompkins Square Park
Washington Sq. Park
23rd Street
18th Street
14th Street
14th Street/ 8th Avenue
14th Street/ 6th Avenue
14th Street/ Union Square
14th Street/ 3rd Avenue
14th Street/ 1st Avenue
Christopher Street-Sheridan Square
West 4th St.
8th Street/ NY University
Astor Place
Bleecker Street
Broadway/ Lafayette Street
Prince Street
Spring Street
Houston Street
Lower East Side/ 2nd Avenue
Delancey Street

DANCECLUBS

Big Apple Ranch (B D GLM MA) Sat 20-1h
39 West 19th Street, 5th Floor *5th Floor* ☎ (212) 358-5752
www.bigappleranch.com
New York's gay & lesbian Country Western Dance. Two-Step lessons at 20h.

Club20 (B D G MA S) Sun 17-?h
20 West 20th Street ☎ (212) 633-0934 www.dlist.com/Club20
Only on Sunday nights. Table-dancing.

Hiro Ballroom @ Maritime Hotel (AC B D G MA SNU)
Sun 22.30-?h
363 W 16th St *Cnr. 9th Ave* ☎ (212) 242-4300 www.hiroballroom.com
Popular gay party.

Rebel (AC B D GLM MA S) Fri 22-?h
251 West 30th Street ☎ (212) 695-2747 www.rebelnyc.com
Go-gos on two floors.

Rush (AC B D G MA) Fri & Sat 22-4h
579 6th Avenue *Between 16th and 17th St* ☎ (212) 243-6100
www.boiparty.com
Former „Heaven".

Splash (! AC B D f G S SNU VS YC) 16-5h
50 West 17th Street *6th Avenue* ☎ (212) 691-0073 www.splashbar.com
Probably New York's most popular dance bar. Happy hour 2-4-1 Mon-Thu 16-21, Fri-Sun 16-20h.

RESTAURANTS

Dish. The (B BF CC GLM M MA) Mon-Fri 19-1, Sat & Sun 20-1h
201 8th Avenue *Between 20th & 21st St* ☎ (212) 352-9800
thedishchelsea.com
Gay two level diner.

East of Eighth (B GLM M OS) 12-24, Sat 11-0.30, Sun -22.30h
254 W 23rd Street *Between 7th and 8th Ave* ☎ (212) 352-0075
www.eastofeighthny.com
American cuisine, 2 floors & garden.

■ **Elmo** (AC B CC glm MA NR W) Mon-Sun 11-late
156 7th Avenue *Between 20th and 19th Street* ☎ (212) 337-8000
🖳 www.elmorestaurant.com
Restaurant and lounge, „Best restaurant of the year" by Instinct magazine.

SEX SHOPS/BLUE MOVIES

■ **Blue Store** (CC G VS)
206 8th Avenue *Between 20th St & 21st St*
One of largest gay sex shop of New York City.

■ **Pleasure Chest. The** (AC CC glm) 10-24h
156 7th Ave South *Greenwich Village* ☎ (212) 242-2158
🖳 www.adulttoyexpress.com
Sex toys.

■ **Rainbow Station** (CC G)
207 8th Avenue ☎ (212) 924-0591

■ **Unicorn** (AC CC G MA VS) Sun-Thu 12-4, Fri & Sat -6h
277c West 22nd Street *Between 7th and 8th Ave* ☎ (212) 924-2921
Chelsea hot-spot. Seven video cabins, magazines, DVDs and novelties. One of the hottest places in NYC.

ESCORTS & STUDIOS

■ **Chelsea Guys** (CC G) 24hrs
☎ (212) 586-5200 🖳 www.chelseaguys.com
From college men to porn stars.

SAUNAS/BATHS

■ **West Side Club** (B DU G M P RR SA SB VS WO) 24hrs
27 West 20th Street *2nd floor* ☎ (212) 691-2700
🖳 www.westsideclubnyc.com

FITNESS STUDIOS

■ **19th Street Gym** (GLM MA SA WO) 5.30-23.30, Sat & Sun 8-20h
22 West 19th Street *Between 5th and 6th Ave* ☎ (212) 414-5800
🖳 www.19thstreetgym.com
Day passes available.

■ **David Barton Gym** (b GLM MA SA SB WO)
Mon-Fri 5.30-24, Sat 8-21, Sun -23h
215 West 23rd St *Between 7th and 8th Ave* ☎ (212) 414-2022
🖳 www.davidbartongym.com
Huge gym on 3 floors, very cruisy.

BOOK SHOPS

■ **Rainbows and Triangles** (GLM) 11-22, Sun 12-21h
192 8th Avenue *Between 20th and 21st St* ☎ (212) 627-2166
🖳 www.rainbowsandtriangles.com
Books, magazines, greeting cards as well as DVDs, CDs, under/swimwear and rainbow articles.

FASHION SHOPS

■ **Universal Gear** (cc G YC) 11-22, Fri & Sat -24h
140 8th Avenue ☎ (212) 206-9119 🖳 www.universalgear.com
Further stores in Chicago and Washington.

HOTELS

■ **GEM Hotel Chelsea. The** (AC CC glm H I MA OS WO) All year, 24hrs
300 West 22nd Street *Subway lines C and E one block from hotel*
☎ (212) 675-1911 🖳 www.theGEMhotel.com

■ **Wolcott Hotel New York**
(AC B BF CC glm I M MC PK RWS RWT WO) All year
4 West 31st Street *Between 5th Avenue & Broadway* ☎ (212) 268-2900
🖳 www.wolcott.com

GUEST HOUSES

■ **Chelsea Mews Guesthouse** (AC CC G MA NU OS RWS) All year
344 West 15th Street ☎ (212) 255-9174
🖳 www.chelseamewsguesthouse.com
Chelsea Mews is a clean non-smoking guesthouse for men. A Victorian house with 3 double and 5 single rooms as well as a huge garden. Some bathrooms are shared. Friendly, private and convenient to shopping, transportation and attractions. Local telephone calls are for free.

Chelsea Pines Inn (AC BF CC GLM I OS RWS RWT VA) All year
317 West 14th Street *Border Chelsea/Meatpacking District/Greenwich Village* ☎ (212) 929-1023 ☎ (888) 546-2700 (US Reservations)
www.chelseapinesinn.com
In the Greenwich Village/Chelsea area, 30-45 minutes to airports. Nicely appointed upscale rooms with private bath and on the upper floors have economy rooms (still a nice size).

Colonial House Inn
(AC bf cc GLM I MA MSG OS RWB RWS RWT SOL VA WO) 24hrs
318 West 22nd Street *Between 8th & 9th Ave* ☎ (212) 243-9669
☎ 1-800-689-3779 www.colonialhouseinn.com
Twenty rooms, partly with private bath. Visa or MC accepted. The Inn has been the winner of the Out and About Editor's Choice Award for gay specific accommodations, setting new standards for quality, amenities and service. Continental breakfast included in room rate.

APARTMENTS

Rainbows and Triangles (AC G RWT WI) All year
192 8th Avenue *Walking distance to Greenwich Village* ☎ (212) 6272166
www.rainbowsandtriangles.com
Above the gay book store „Rainbows and triangles".

New York – Manhattan/East Village ☎ 212

SHOWS

Lucky Cheng's (AC B CC G M S ST T) 15-4h
24 1st Avenue *At 2nd Street* ☎ (212) 995-5500
www.luckychengsnyc.com
Original New York/ Pan-Asian drag themed restaurant. Drag shows in the downstairs lounge. Drag hosted karaoke shows.

BARS

Arrow (AC B G MA S) Sundays only
85 Avenue A ☎ (212) 673-1775 www.arrownyc.com
Go-go boys.

Boiler Room (AC B CC G S YC) 16-4h
86 East 4th Street *2nd Ave* ☎ (212) 254-7536
www.boilerroomnyc.com
Big East Village bar, college boys on the weekend. Pool table jukebox. Happy hour 16-20h, drink specials 22-4h.

Cock. The (B G MA S ST) 23-4h
29 Second Avenue *One block above Houston* ☎ (212) 777-6254
www.thecockbar.com
Cover charge applies. Late night location & crowd.

Eastern Bloc (AC B GLM MA S) 19-4h
505 East 6th Street *Between Avenues A & B* ☎ (212) 777-2555
www.easternblocnyc.com
Coolest bar on the East Side. Best on Fri from 22h.

Nowhere (B GLM MC) 15-4h
322 East 14th Street *Between 1st and 2nd Ave* ☎ (212) 477-4744
Mixed gay-lesbian crowd. Cosy, comfortable vibe. Happy hour daily 15-21h.

Phoenix (B G MA OS) 16-4h
447 East 13th Street *At Avenue A* ☎ (212) 477-9979
Very popular, pool table, jukebox, happy hour 16-20h (local beers).

Urge. The (B G MA SNU ST VS) 16-4h
33 2nd Avenue *At 2nd St* ☎ (212) 777-0774
www.theurgenyc.com
Two-tier central bar, go-go boys and cute barmen, gay videos and events, happy hour (2-4-1) 16-22h.

Woody's (AC B G MA s) 20-4h
31 2nd Avenue *Near cnr. 2nd Street* ☎ (212) 777-0774
Underwear night on Fri.

DANCECLUBS

Pyramid (B D GLM MA S) G: Fri 22-4h
101 Avenue A *At 7th St* ☎ (212) 462-9077
www.spincyclenyc.com
Gay on Friday only.

RESTAURANTS

B-Bar (B glm M OS) 11.30-1, Sat & Sun 10.30-1h
40 E 4th Street ☎ (212) 475-2220 www.bbarandgrill.com
American cuisine and trendsetters. Big patio, lounge and open dining room.

New York – Manhattan/Hell's Kitchen, Midtown & East Side ☎ 212

Young, affluent professionals and a sizable gay community have joined the blue collars and largely Latino old-timers calling Hell's Kitchen home. Here you will find chichi boutiques, trendy bars and restaurants. Roughly 59th to 34th Streets, and bounded by the Hudson River and Eighth Avenue demarcates the Hell's Kitchen neighbourhood.

Junge, wohlhabende, hochqualifizierte Fachleute und eine ansehnliche Schwulengemeinde haben sich unter die proletarischeren Alteinsässigen mit ihren vorwiegend lateinamerikanischen Wurzeln gemischt. So findet man hier todschicke Boutiquen, angesagte Bars und Restaurants. Das als Hell's Kitchen bezeichnete Viertel erstreckt sich von der 59. bis zur 34. Straße zwischen den Ufern des Hudson und der Eighth Avenue.

Des personnes qualifiées, jeunes, aisées, hautement qualifiées et une communauté gay considérable s'est mélangée à la population historique prolétaire avec des racines principalement latino-américaines. On trouve ainsi des boutiques de dernier cri, des bars et restaurants à la mode. Ce quartier appelé „ Hell's Kitchen „ s'étend de la 59ème à la 34ème rue, entre la rive de l'Hudson et la 8ème avenue.

Jóvenes, gente acomodada, profesionales altamente cualificados y una imponente comunidad gay se han mezclado con los antiguos habitantes, predominantemente de origen latinoamericano. Es por esto que aquí podrá encontrar boutiques con lo último en moda o los bares y restaurantes del momento más conocidos. El barrio conocido como Hell's Kitchen se extiende desde la calle 59 hasta la calle 34 entre la orilla del río Hudson y la Octava Avenida.

Giovani benestanti altamente qualificati, ma anche molti gay si sono immischiati alla popolazione locale originaria di provenienza proletaria e prevalentemente di radici latinoamericane. Qui è possibile trovare negozi molto chic e bar e ristoranti molto in voga. Il quartiere chiamato Hell's Kitchen si estende dalla 59esima alla 34esima strada tra la rive dell'Hudson e l'Eighth Avenue.

SHOWS

Don't tell Mama (B glm MA S) 16-4h
343 West 46th Street *Between 8th & 9th* ☎ (212) 757-0788
www.donttellmamanyc.com
Piano bar & cabaret. 2 cabaret rooms.

BARS

9th Ave Saloon (B G m MA) Mon-Sat 11-4, Sun 12-4h
656 9th Avenue *Between 45th & 46th St* ☎ (212) 307-1503
Pub for gay theatregoers and locals.

Bar-Tini (B G MC)
642 10th Avenue *At 45 St* ☎ (917) 388-2897
This fun bar has the hottest bartenders and best selection of martinis that a gay bar has to offer. Style, sophistication and great beats.

Barrage (AC B G MA) 17-2, Fri & Sat -4h
401 West 47th Street *At 9th Ave* ☎ (212) 586-9390
Cute guys and loud music. Happy hour 17-20 and 23-24h.

Evolve (AC B GLM MA) 16-4h
221 East 58th Street *Between 2nd & 3rd Avenues* ☎ (212) 355-3395
www.evolvebarandloungenyc.com
Happy hour daily 16-20h.

Industry Bar (AC B G MC S) Mon-Sun 16-4h
355 West 52nd Street *Between 8th and 9th Avenue* ☎ (646) 476-2747
www.industry-bar.com
New stylish bar run by the owners of Barracuda and Elmo. Happy hour from 16-21h.

■ **Posh** (AC B CC G m MA S) 16-4h
405 West 51st Street *At 9th Ave* ☎ (212) 957-2222
🖳 www.poshbarnyc.com
Hot Midtown's gay spot „where the boys are...".

■ **Ritz. The** (B G MA OS) 16-4h
369 W 46th Street *Between 8th & 9th Ave* ☎ (212) 333-2554
3 floors.

■ **Therapy** (B CC G M S YC) 17-4, Sun 12-4h
348 West 52nd Street *Between 8th and 9th Avenue* ☎ (212) 397-1700
🖳 www.therapy-nyc.com
Very trendy. 2 floors of bars. Happy hour daily 17-20h.

■ **Townhouse. The** (AC B GLM MA) 16-3, Thu-Sat -4h
236 East 58th Street *Between 2nd and 3rd Av* ☎ (212) 754-4649
🖳 www.townhouseny.com
A great place for the more mature, upscale professionals, 3 bars on 2 floors. A wonderful piano bar and clubroom with a gentlemen's club feel. Happy hour 16-20h.

■ **Uncle Charlie's** (B G MA OS) Daily 16-4h
139 East 45th Street, 2nd floor *Between 3rd and Lexington Ave*
☎ (212) 661-9097 🖳 www.unclecharliesnyc.com
Sleek piano bar. Happy hour Mon-Fri 16-20h.

■ **Vlada** (AC B CC G M OS S ST T WE) 16-4h
331 West 51st Street *Between 8th & 9th Ave, Hell's Kitchen*
☎ (212) 974-8030 🖳 www.vladabar.com
Two level lounge in the heart of the Broadway theater district. You just might find Cyndi Lauper dropping by for a drink, or Liza or Chaka Khan for a turn at the piano...

DANCECLUBS

■ **Club 57 at Providence** (AC B D GLM MA) Every Sat
311 West 57th Street *Between 8th & 9th Ave* ☎ (212) 307.0062
🖳 www.fvevents.com
One of New York's largest gay dance party with superstar DJs and celebrity performances. Three level mega-club.

■ **Escuelita** (B D G MA ST) Thu-Sat 22-5h
301 West 39th Street *Corner of 8th Ave* ☎ (212) 631-0588
🖳 www.escuelita.com
Very popular bar/club with a Latin flair. Not what it used to be. Cover charge applies.

■ **Pacha** (B D GLM MC)
618 West 46 Street ☎ (212) 209-7500 🖳 www.pacha.com

■ **Web. The** (AC B CC D f G MA S SNU ST VS) 16-4h
40 East 58th Street *At Madison Ave* ☎ (212) 308-1546
🖳 www.thewebnewyork.com
Wild drag shows and go-go boys in a 2-floor dance club popular with Asians and those who love them; popular after-work happy hour.

■ **XL** (! AC B D G MA S) Mon-Sun 16-?h
512 West 42nd Street ☎ (212) 239-2999
🖳 www.xlnightclub.com
Nightclub, cabaret and lounge on 14000m². Opening in January 2012.

RESTAURANTS

■ **44 & X Hell's Kitchen** (AC b CC glm M MA OS VEG WL)
Mon-Fri 11.30-14.30, Sat & Sun -15, Mon-Sun 17.30-24h
622 10th Avenue *At 44th Street* ☎ (212) 977-1170
🖳 www.44andx.com
Reinvented American classics. Brunch on Sat & Sun. Hip, trendy restaurant with sexy staff.

■ **H.K. Restaurant** (AC B glm M MA NR OS) Mon-Sun 7-1h
523 9th Avenue *At the corner of 39th Street & 9th Avenue*
☎ (800) 781-0466
🖳 www.hkhellskitchen.com

■ **Vynl** (AC B glm M MA)
Mon 11-23, Tue&Wed 11-23, Thu&Fri 11-6, Sat&Sun 9:30-6h
754 9th Avenue *At corner of 51st Street* ☎ (212) 974-2003
🖳 www.vynl-nyc.com
Popular restaurant with campy „hall of fame" in the bathrooms.

New York – Manhattan/Hell's Kitchen, Midtown & East Side

SEX SHOPS/BLUE MOVIES

■ **DVD Explosion** (G VS)
412 8th Avenue *Between 30th and 31st St* ☎ (212) 629-6977
Upstairs video area. Some booths show gay and straight films. Some booths are connected by a gloryhole.

■ **Vihan's DVD Palace** (G VS) 24hrs
61 West 37th Street *Between 38th and 39th St* ☎ (212) 397-8680
dvdspalace.com/home.php
Private video booths.

■ **Vishara Video** (G VS) 24hrs
797 8th Avenue *North of 48th St* ☎ (212) 582-2262
Upstairs is a video booth area. They have buddy booths and the booths on the left have large gloryholes.

SAUNAS/BATHS

■ **East Side Club** (G I MA P SB) 24hrs
227 East 56th Street *Between 2nd & 3rd* ☎ (212) 753-2222
www.eastsideclubnyc.com
No smoking of any kind allowed, a labyrinth on 2 floors and lots of private rooms. Membership is required. Gets busy after the bars close. The club consists of three floors.

HOTELS

■ **1291 Cityhomes** (AC B BF CC GLM) Check-in: 8-24h
337 West 55th Street *Between Central Park & Time Square*
☎ (212) 376-9686 www.1291.com
Budget accommodation.

■ **Bryant Park. The** (AC B CC glm M MA PK RWS RWT VA WO) All year
40 West 40th Street, Midtown *Near 5th Avenue* ☎ (212) 869-0100
www.bryantparkhotel.com
Upmarket gay-friendly hotel with 128 rooms.

■ **GEM Hotel Midtown West. The**
(AC CC GLM I MA NR RWB RWS RWT W WI) All year, 24hrs
449 West 36th Street *2 blocks to Javits Center* ☎ (212) 967-7206
www.theGEMhotel.com/lgbt
The GEM Hotel Midtown West is conveniently located in Manhattan Midtown West, between the hottest gay and lesbian neighborhoods in NYC, Chelsea & Hell's Kitchen.

■ **Holiday Inn Midtown** (AC B BF CC glm M PI PK RWS RWT VA WO) All year
440 West 57th Street ☎ (212) 581-8100 www.hi57.com

■ **Parker Meridien New York. Le** (AC B CC glm M MA WO) All year
119 West 56th Street ☎ (212) 245-5000
www.parkermeridien.com
Style and function, great views of Central Park and the Manhattan skyline, Penthouse pool, extremely large gym and fitness centre.

New York – Manhattan/Soho ☎ 212

HOTELS

■ **GEM Hotel SoHo. The** (AC CC glm H I MA) All year, 24hrs
135 East Houston Street *2 blocks from the F and M subway lines*
☎ (212) 358-8844 www.theGEMhotel.com

New York – Manhattan/Upper East Side ☎ 212

BARS

■ **Brandy's Piano Bar** (AC B GLM MA S) 16-4h
235 East 84th Street *Between 2nd & 3rd Ave* ☎ 744-4949
www.brandyspianobar.com
Live music at 21.30h

■ **Tool Box. The** (B G MA S SNU VS) 20-4h
1742 2nd Avenue *Between 90th & 91st Streets* ☎ (212) 348-1288
www.thetoolboxnyc.com
Video/cruise bar.

RESTAURANTS

■ **Lips** (B GLM LM M NR S ST VEG) 17.30-1, Fri & Sat -1.30h
227 East 56th Street ☎ (212) 675-7710 www.lipsnyc.com
Drag restaurant with nightly performances at 19h.

GUEST HOUSES

■ **Bubba and Bean Lodges** (AC glm m MA RWS RWT)
All year, office hours 11-18h
1598 Lexington Ave *Between 101st & 102nd St* ☎ (917) 345-7914
www.bblodges.com
Gay owned budget hotel. Studios are fully furnished with private kitchens and baths.

New York – Manhattan/Upper West Side ☎ 212

BARS

■ **Candle Bar** (B f G MA) 16-4, Sat & Sun 15-4h
309 Amsterdam Avenue *At 74th St* ☎ (212) 874-9155
Cute bartenders at this cruisy local bar.

■ **No Parking** (AC B d GLM MA S SNU ST WE)
18-3, Fri -4, Sat 19-4, Sun -3h, closed Mon
4168 Broadway *At 117th Street* ☎ (212) 923-8700
www.noparkingbar.com
Very mixed clientele from latino, black, european, men, women, young and older. Exotice dancers and internationally known dj's. Gets busy after 22h.

■ **Suite** (B G MC ST) 17-4h
992 Amsterdam Avenue *At 109th St* ☎ (212) 222-4600 suitenyc.com
Happy hour daily 17-20h.

SEX SHOPS/BLUE MOVIES

■ **Hommes. Les** (AC CC G MA VS) Sun-Thu 10-2, Fri & Sat -4h
217-B West 80th Street *2nd floor, between Broadway and Amsterdam Ave*
☎ (212) 580-2445
Extensive DVD and video rental library. No mail order.

New York – Manhattan/West Village ☎ 212

SHOWS

■ **Duplex. The** (B D glm MA S ST) 16-4h
61 Christopher Street *At 7th Ave* ☎ (212) 255-5438 www.theduplex.com
Three floor cabaret and piano bar. Diverse but very gay local crowd. See: www.theduplex.com for more information.

BARS

■ **Boots & Saddle** (B f G MC S) 12-4h
76 Christopher Street *7th Ave S* ☎ (212) 929-9684
www.bootsandsaddlenyc.com
Boots & Saddle attracts regulars and international tourists alike. Happy hour Mon-Fri: 16-20h.

■ **Chi Chiz** (B GLM m MA) 18-4h
135 Christopher Street *Hudson St* ☎ (212) 462-0027
Popular, mainly Afro-Americans. Happy hour (2-4-1) 17-24h Mon-Sat, and all night on Sun.

■ **Cubbyhole** (AC B GLM MA) 16-4, Sat & Sun 14-4h
281 W 12th Street *At W 4th St* ☎ (212) 243-9041
www.cubbyholebar.com
Happy hour Mon-Sat: 16-20h.

■ **Hangar. The** (! AC B f G MA SNU ST) 15-4, Sun 13-4h
115 Christopher Street *Between Bleecker and Hudson St*
☎ (212) 627-2044 www.myspace.com/hangarnyc
Very popular, happy hour 15-21h on Mon-Fri. Beer blast on Sat & Sun. Go go dancers on Sat 23-1h.

■ **Julius** (B G m MA) 11-4h
159 W 10th Street *Between S 7th Ave & Waverly Place* ☎ (212) 929-9672

■ **Marie's Crisis** (AC B GLM MA S) 16-4h
59 Grove Street *At 7th Avenue* ☎ (212) 243-9323
Cheapest happy hour in town, 16-21h. Movies upstairs at weekends.

■ **Pieces** (AC B G MA S ST VS) 14-4, Sun -2h
8 Christopher Street *Heart of historic West Village* ☎ (212) 929-9291
www.piecesbar.com
Attractive local and borough boys, happy hour Mon-Fri 14-20h. Wed 20h „Will Clark's Porno Bingo".

■ **Rockbar** (AC B f G MA) 14-2h
185 Christopher Street *Weehawken Street* ☎ (212) 242-9113
www.rockbarnyc.com
Bear and daddy crowd.

■ **Stonewall Inn. The** (! B G MA S SNU ST) 14-4h
53 Christopher Street *Sheridan Square* ☎ (212) 488-2705
A landmark. Happy hour Mon-Fri 14-20h.

■ **Ty's** (AC B F G MA) Daily 14-4h
114 Christopher Street ☎ (212) 741-9641 www.tysbarnyc.com
Friendly, no attitude atmosphere for bears, daddies and friends.

CAFES

■ **Factory Café. The** (b G m MA) Mon-Thu 8-24, Sat 9-2, Sun 9-24h
104 Christopher Street *Between Bleecker and Bedford St* ☎ (212) 807-6900
European coffee, light meals.

DANCECLUBS

■ **Monster** (! B D G MA S ST) 16-4, Sat & Sun 14-4h
80 Grove Street, Sheridan Square ☎ (212) 924-3558
www.manhattan-monster.com
A great piano bar with fantastic Frozen Margaritas. Downstairs drag shows and a dance floor. Happy hour Mon-Sat 16-21h. Sun T-Dance.

RESTAURANTS

■ **Manatus** (AC B BF CC GLM M MA OS) 24hrs
340 Bleecker Street ☎ (212) 989-7042 www.manatusnyc.com
Breakfast specials before 11h.

SEX SHOPS/BLUE MOVIES

■ **Harmony Video** (G VS) 24hrs
139 Christopher Street ☎ (212) 366-9059
Videos, magazines and cabins.

LEATHER & FETISH SHOPS

■ **Leather Man. The** (CC F GLM MA) 12-21, Sun -20h
111 Christopher Street ☎ (212) 243-5339
www.theleatherman.com
Sales and tailoring on premises.

HOTELS

■ **Washington Square** (AC b CC glm M MA) All year
103 Waverly Place ☎ (212) 777-9515
www.washingtonsquarehotel.com
In the heart of Greenwich Village. The Lobby Cafe serves afternoon tea and cocktails. Request a room with a view of Washington Square.

GUEST HOUSES

■ **Abingdon Guest House** (AC CC glm H I M MA RWS RWT VA) All year
21 Eighth Avenue ☎ (212) 243-5384 www.abingdonguesthouse.com

■ **Incentra Village House** (AC CC GLM I MA RWS RWT) Calls only 9-23h
32 8th Avenue *Between West 12th & Jane St* ☎ (212) 206-0007
www.incentravillage.com
Historic Inn in Greenwich Village. All 11 rooms with private bath and WC, kitchenette, TV, phone, most with a fireplace. It's like living in your own Greenwich Village apartment.

New York – Queens ☎ 718

BARS

■ **Albatross** (B D GLM MA S) 17-4h
36-19 24th Avenue, Astoria *Astoria Blvd* ☎ (718) 204-9045
albatrossbar.com
Cosy gay & lesbian bar with pool table, dartboard and jukebox. Happy hour 16-21h.

■ **Bum Bum Bar** (AC B D GLM MA) Fri & Sat 20-?h
63-14 Roosevelt Avenue ☎ (718) 651-4145
Latino crowd.

■ **Friends Tavern** (AC B GLM MA S ST) 16-4h
78-11 Roosevelt Avenue, Jackson Heights *Between 78th & 79th St*
☎ (718) 397-7256 www.facebook.com/friendstavern
Latin dance bar close to Club Atlantis.

■ **Mix** (AC B glm MA) 18-2, Sat Sun 12-4h
40-17 30th Avenue *Cnr. of 41st Street* ☎ (718) 642-4840
Eastern touches with South American flavors at night.

■ **Music Box** (AC B D GLM MA S ST) 16-4h
40-08 74th Street, Jackson Heights *Cnr. Roosevelt Ave*
☎ (718) 457-5306
Latin dance bar close to Club Atlantis.

■ **Recuerdos. Los** (AC B G MA) 16-4h
79-15 Roosevelt Avenue ☎ (718) 672-7505
Laid-back gay hang with Latin crowd.

DANCECLUBS

■ **Club Atlantis** (AC B CC D GLM MA S SNU ST) Mon-Sun 16-4h
76-19 Roosevelt Avenue, Jackson Heights *At 77th St* ☎ (718) 457-3939
atlantisnyc.com
Hot Latin megaclub. Close to Friends Tavern.

SAUNAS/BATHS

■ **Northern Men's Sauna** (AC FC FH G m MA SA SB VS WO) 12-24h
3365 Farrington Street, Flushing *1 block from Main St & Northern Blvd*
☎ (718) 445-9775
Not a sauna anymore, more a crusing location with condoms for free.

CRUISING

-Forest Park (the footpath parallel to Park Lane South beginning at Metropolitan Avenue, best at night)
-Roosevelt Avenue (woodside, between 69th and 79th Street).

Nyack ☎ 845

BARS

■ **Barz** (B D GLM MA S) 20-4, Sun 15-4h, closed Mon
327 Route 9W North *Near Fairview Ave* ☎ (845) 353-4444
www.barz1.com

Poughkeepsie ☎ 845

BARS

■ **Congress** (AC B GLM MA) Mon-Sat 15-4, Sun 19.30-4h
411 Main Street ☎ (845) 486-9068

Rochester ☎ 585

BARS

■ **Avenue Pub** (B G MA OS) 16-2h
522 Monroe Avenue *At Goodman* ☎ (585) 244-4960
■ **Bachelor Forum** (B F G MA) 14-2h
670 University Avenue *At Atlantic Ave* ☎ (585) 271-6930
www.bachelor4m.com

CAFES

■ **Equal=Grounds / The Pride Connection** (AC b GLM I M MA OS S T) Mon-Fri 7-24, Sat & Sun 10-24h
750 South Avenue ☎ (585) 242-7840 www.equalgrounds.com
Gay owned and operated. A GLBT coffee house and gift shop.

DANCECLUBS

■ **Tilt** (B D GLM MA ST) Thu-Sat
444 Central Avenue ☎ (585) 232-8440

SAUNAS/BATHS

■ **Rochester Spa and Body Club. The** (b DU FC FH G m MA OS SA SB SOL VS WH WO) 24hrs
109 Liberty Pole Way ☎ (585) 454-1074 www.rochesterspa.com

DVD SHOPS

■ **Outlandish** (GLM MA) 11-23, Sun 12-17h
274 North Goodman Street ☎ (585) 760-8383 www.outlandish1.com

Schenectady ☎ 518

BARS

■ **Clinton Street Pub** (B d GLM MA S) 11-4h
159 Clinton Street *Downtown Schenectady* ☎ (518) 377-8555

Schroon Lake ☎ 518

CAMPING

■ **Rainbow Woods Campground** (G MA) May-Sep
PO Box 853 *I-87 Exit 28 Route 74 East* ☎ (518) 532-9728
www.rainbowwoodscampgrounds.com

Syracuse ☎ 315

BARS

■ **Rain Lounge** (B G MA VS) 16-2h
218 North Franklin Street ☎ (315) 473-9759
■ **Trexx** (B D GLM MA OS SNU ST) Thu 20-2, Fri & Sat -4h
319 N. Clinton Street ☎ (315) 474-6408 www.trexxonline.com
■ **X Bar** (B D GLM MA S) 15-2, Mon & Tue 17-1h
205 North West Street ☎ (315) 471-9279

DANCECLUBS

■ **Mystic** (AC B GLM ST) 19-2h, closed Mon & Tue
1203 Milton Avenue ☎ (315) 218-5897
www.myspace.com/themysticlounge

SEX SHOPS/BLUE MOVIES

■ **Boulevard Books** (g VS) 24hrs
2576 Erie Boulevard ☎ (315) 446-1595

SAUNAS/BATHS

■ **Clinton Street Spa** (B DU G I MA MSG SA SB SOL VS WH WO)
Mon-Thu 10-24, Fri-Sun 24hrs
321 North Clinton St, 2nd Fl. ☎ (315) 466-5401
www.clintonstreetspa.com

Troy ☎ 518

SAUNAS/BATHS

■ **River Street Club** (AC B DR DU FC FH G GH I MA NR OS p PK RR S SA SB SH SL VR VS W WH WI WO)
Sun 12- 22, Mon-Thu -7- 22 & Fri -23, Sat 12 -23
540 River Street *15 mins from downtown Albany, cnr. Hoosick Street*
☎ (518) 272-0340 www.riverstreetclub.com
A private membership club for men in the area.

Utica ☎ 315

BARS

■ **That Place** (B D G MA OS P s) 20-2h, closed Sun & Mon
216 Bleecker Street ☎ (315) 724-1446 www.thatplace.us

North Carolina

Location: East USA
Initials: NCA
Time: GMT -5
Area: 139.397 km² / 57.013 sq mi.
Population: 8,049,313
Capital: Raleigh

Asheville ☎ 828

PUBLICATIONS

■ **Stereotypd**
70 Da ☎ (828) 505-2870 www.stereotypd.com

BARS

■ **Hairspray** (AC B CC D GLM MA OS S) 20-2.30h
38 North French Broad Avenue *At Patton Avenue* ☎ (828) 258-2027
www.clubhairspray.com
Karaoke Tuesday and Thursday, College Night Wednesday, Drag on Friday and Saturday.
■ **LaRue's Backdoor** (AC B CC GLM MA P S) 20-2h, closed Sun-Tue
237 Haywood Street ☎ (828) 252-1014
■ **Smokey's** (B G MA) 16-2h
18 Broadway Street *Cnr. College St* ☎ (828) 253-2155

DANCECLUBS

■ **Scandals** (B CC D GLM m MA P S ST VS WE) Fri-Sun 22-3h
11 Grove Street ☎ (828) 252-2838 www.scandalsnightclub.net

GUEST HOUSES

■ **Biltmore Village Inn** (BF glm I MA RWS RWT WH) All year
119 Dodge Street ☎ (828) 274-8707 www.biltmorevillageinn.com
6 unique guest rooms, each with private bath, cable television and telephone.

Charlotte ☎ 704

GAY INFO

■ **Lesbian & Gay Community Center. The** (GLM)
Tue-Thu 17-20, Sat 10-14h
820 Hamilton Street, Suite B11 ☎ (704) 333-0144 www.gaycharlotte.com
Info source for the LGBT community.

PUBLICATIONS

■ **Q-Notes** Mon-Fri 9-18h
PO Box 221841 ☎ (704) 531-9988 ▭ www.q-notes.com
Bi-weekly GLB newspaper for North & South Carolina.

BARS

■ **Bar at 316** (! AC B CC GLM m OS VS) 17-2h
316 Rensselaer Avenue *Located in Historic Dilworth* ☎ (704) 910-1478
▭ www.thebarat316.com
The 130 year old pink house is one of the oldest most established gay/ alternative bars in Charlotte NC, for conversation, refreshing cocktails, and fun times.

■ **Chasers** (B D G MA SNU) 17-2h
3217 The Plaza Charlotte ☎ (704) 339-0500
▭ www.scorpios.com
Exotic dance bar.

■ **Hartigan's Irish Pub** (B d GLM I M MA OS ST) Tue 11-22, Wed & Thu 11-23, Mon & Fri 11-2.30, Sat 17-2.30h, Sun special events
601 S. Cedar St. *Near Football Stadium* ☎ (704) 347-1841
▭ www.hartigans.com
Mixed Irish Pub with more gay folks than straight.

■ **Nickelbar. The** (B D GLM m MA) Thu-Sat 21-2, Sun 17-12h
2817 Rozzelles Ferry Rd. ▭ www.thenickelbar.com
Great music, all races welcome! Ladies night on Thursdays,!

■ **Petra's Piano Bar & Cabaret** (AC B GLM MA S)
1919 Commonwealth Avenue ☎ (704) 332-6609
▭ www.petraspianobar.com
Gay owned piano bar.

■ **Sidelines Bar** (B GLM m VS YC) Mon-Fri 16-2, Sat & Sun 12-2h
4544 South Blvd. *Next to Charlotte Eagle* ☎ (704) 525-2608
▭ www.thesidelinesbar.com
Charlotte's first and only Gay Sports Bar.

■ **Woodshed. The** (B F G M MA OS P) Mon-Sat 17-2, Sun 15-2h
4000 South I-85 Service Road *At Little Rock Rd* ☎ (704) 394-1712
▭ www.woodshedlounge.com
Men's bar with special events.

DANCECLUBS

■ **Closet. The** (B D GLM YC)
1202 Elizabeth Ave ☎ (704) 375-1777

■ **Marigny** (! B D G MA P S) From 22-?h
1440 South Tryon Street *Near Bland St. trolly station* ☎ (704) 910-4444
▭ www.marignycharlotte.com
New club, great staff and fantastic gogo dancers. 18 years and up with no dress code. Charlotte's ONLY upscale gay dance club.

■ **Scorpios** (B D GLM S VS) Wed & Sun 21-2h
2301 Freedom Drive ☎ (704) 373-9124
▭ www.scorpios.com

BOOK SHOPS

■ **White Rabbit** (GLM) Mon-Sat 10-21, Sun 12-18h
920 Central Avenue ☎ (704) 377-4125 ▭ www.whiterabbitbooks.com
Good selection of magazines, videos and guides.

Fayetteville ☎ 910

BARS

■ **Alias** (B GLM MA P SNU VS) Fri & Sat 21-2.30h
984 Old McPherson Church Road ☎ (910) 484-7994
▭ www.clubalias.com

Gastonia ☎ 704

BARS

■ **Night Owl** (B GLM MA ST) Thu-Sun 18-2.30h
420 West Main Ave ☎ (704) 866-7333
▭ www.nightowlsofgastonia.com

Greensboro ☎ 336

BARS

■ **Q Lounge. The** (B D GLM MA OS) 16-?, Sat 21-?, Sun 17-?h
708 West Market Street ☎ (336) 272-2587 ▭ www.theqlounge.com

DANCECLUBS

■ **Warehouse 29** (AC B D G OS P S SNU VS WE) Fri & Sat 21.30-3.30, Sun 15-24h, closed Mon-Thu
1011 Arnold Street ☎ (336) 333-9333 ▭ www.w29.com

Greenville ☎ 252

DANCECLUBS

■ **Great American Mining Co.** (B D GLM MA P SNU ST VS) Thu-Sat 22-3h
1008 Dickinson Avenue ☎ (252) 353-2623 ▭ www.clubbarcode.com

SEX SHOPS/BLUE MOVIES

■ **Late Show Video** (AC cc g MA) 12-2, Fri & Sat -3, Sun -24h
1101 Charles Blvd *At 10th St* ☎ (252) 758-5883
Largest selection of gay videos in the area. Gay owned/operated.

Hickory ☎ 828

DANCECLUBS

■ **Club Cabaret** (B D GLM MA s) 22-2, Sun 20-24h, closed Mon-Wed
101 North Center Street *Cnr. 1st Ave* ☎ (828) 322-8103
▭ www.clubcabaret.net

Raleigh ☎ 919

BARS

■ **Capital Corral** (B D GLM I MA P s) 20-?h, Sun 18-?h
313 West Hargett Street *Near Dawson Street* ☎ (919) 755-9599

■ **Flex** (B D F G MA P) Mon-Sat 17-?, Sun 14-?h
2 South West Street ☎ (919) 832-8855 ▭ www.flex-club.com
Special theme nights.

■ **Legends** (B D GLM MA P ST) 21-?h
330 West Hargett Street *Cnr. Harrigton Street* ☎ (919) 831-8888
▭ www.legends-club.com

CAFES

■ **The Borough** (B glm I M MA) 16-2h
317 W. Morgan Street ☎ (919) 832-8433
▭ www.theboroughraleigh.com
Very gayfriendly bar.

DANCECLUBS

■ **Chemistry** (B D GLM MA VS)
330 West Davie Street ☎ (919) 336-2961 ▭ www.chemistryraleigh.com
Brandnew downtown club and video-bar.

SEX SHOPS/BLUE MOVIES

■ **Our Place** (AC CC g MA VS) 24hrs
327 West Hargett Street *Near Dawson Street* ☎ (919) 833-8968
Video booths, DVDs sales and rentals.

BOOK SHOPS

■ **White Rabbit** (GLM) 11-21, Sun 13-19h
309 West Martin Street *Between Harrington and Dawson*
☎ (919) 856-1429 ▭ www.whiterabbitbooks.com
Wide selection of magazines, books, travel guides, CDs, DVDs.

CRUISING

-West Hargett Street (around gay bars and bookstore)
-Unstead State Park (Glenwood Avenue, near Brownleigh Drive. In cars and around Lake Area. Take steps down to Lake-follow path to the left. Daytime only. Be discreet).

Rocky Mount ☏ 252

BARS

■ **Liquid** (B D G MA s SNU) Sat 22-3.30h
313 Falls Road ☏ (252) 266-6464 🖳 www.geocities.com/liquidrmt
Mainly Afro-American crowd.

Wilmington ☏ 910

BARS

■ **Toolbox** (AC B D f G I S ST) 17-1, Fri & Sat -2h
2325 Burnett Boulevard ☏ (910) 343-6988 🖳 www.toolboxnc.com

CAFES

■ **Cafe Phoenix** (b g M MA) 11.30-22, Fri & Sat -23, Sun 17.30-22h
9 South Frount Street ☏ (910) 343-1395
Coffee shop.

DANCECLUBS

■ **Ibiza** (AC B D G OS P ST YC) Thu-Sun 20-3h
118 Market Street ☏ (910) 251-1301 🖳 www.ibizawilmington.com

CRUISING

-Wrightsville Beach (north end)
-Hugh Macrae Park (Orange & 2nd Street, car cruising 20-24h).

Ohio

Location: Great Lakes region USA
Initials: OH
Time: GMT -5
Area: 116.103 km² / 47,486 sq mi.
Population: 11,353,140
Capital: Columbus
Important gay cities: Cincinnati, Cleveland and Columbus

Akron ☏ 330

BARS

■ **Adams Street Bar** (AC B D f G m MA SNU ST t)
16.30-2.30, Sun 21-2.30h
77 North Adams Street ☏ (330) 434-9794 🖳 www.adamsstreetbar.com
First Sun/month „shower boys", Wed: piano bar night, Thu: Show night with male dancers, Fri: show at midnight, Sat: Dance party/ country western night.

■ **Cocktails & Daddy's Akron** (! B D F G MA ST VS)
11-2.30h, closed Sun
1009 South Main Street ☏ (330) 376-2625 🖳 www.cocktails-daddys.com
Dress code on Fri & Sat.

■ **Tear-ez** (AC B CC f GLM MA S SNU) 11-2.30, Sun 12-2.30h
360 South Main Street ☏ (330) 376-0011 🖳 www.tear-ez.com
Popular. Happy hour until 21h.

DANCECLUBS

■ **Interbelt Nite Club** (B D GLM MA OS s SNU VS WE)
22-2.30, Fri & Sat 21-2.30h
70 North Howard Street ☏ (330) 253-5700 🖳 www.interbelt.net
The only all-gay disco in Akron. Patio bar in summer. Very popular.

■ **Square** (AC B D GLM MA S) 17-2.30, Sat 20-2.30h
820 West Market Street *Akron Highland Square area* ☏ (330) 374-9661
🖳 www.squareatsquare.com

SAUNAS/BATHS

■ **Akron Steam & Sauna** (b CC DU FC G MA SA SB WH) 12-24h
41 South Case Avenue *At Arlington St* ☏ (330) 784-0777
🖳 www.akronsteamandsauna.com
Cubicals cost extra as do extra towels. Best time Fri & Sat after 22h.

CRUISING

-Main Street/Mill Street (in front of public library)
-Metropolitan Park in Goodyear Heights on Eastwood Avenue (in the parking lot by the baseball field)
-Railroad tracks under Talmadge Avenue/Glenwood Avenue.

Cincinnati ☏ 513

GAY INFO

■ **Gay & Lesbian Community Center of Greater Cincinnati** (GLM) 18-21, Fri -23, Sat 12-16h, closed Sun
4119 Hamilton Avenue ☏ (513) 591-0200 🖳 www.cincyglbt.com

BARS

■ **Below Zero Lounge** (AC B CC D G I M MA NR PK S WI)
Wed-Sun 18-2.30h
1122 Walnut Street *In walking distance of central downtown*
☏ (513) 421 9376 🖳 www.belowzerolounge.com
Ultra plush Martini lounge. Cabaret showbar upstairs. DJs Saturdays VJ Fridays and Showtunes Sundays, Karaoke Thursdays.

■ **Golden Lion** (B d G MC S) 11-2.30, Sun 13-2.30h
340 Ludlow Avenue ☏ (513) 281-4179

■ **Home Base Tavern** (B D gLm MA S) Wed-Sat 19-2.30h
2401 Vine Street ☏ (513) 721-8484 🖳 www.freewebs.com/littlebitbar

■ **On Broadway** (B f G MA ST) 16-2.30h
817 Broadway ☏ (513) 421-2555

■ **Serpent. The** (! B F G MA VS) 21-2.30h
4042 Hamilton Avenue ☏ (513) 681-6969 🖳 www.serpentbar.com
Leather dress code is encouraged but optional Sun-Thu, enforced Fri & Sat. Please check their website for do's and don'ts before leaving home (www.serpentbar.com)

■ **Shooters** (B d f G MA SNU) 16-2.30h
927 Race Street ☏ (513) 381-9900
„Cowboy" bar.

■ **Simon Says** (B G MA) 11-2.30, Sun 13-2.30h
428 Walnut Street ☏ (513) 381-7577 🖳 www.simonsdtcincy.com
Small place but great „Happy Hour" prices.

■ **Subway** (B D G M MA SNU) 17.30-2.30h
609 Walnut Street ☏ (513) 421-1294

DANCECLUBS

■ **Adonis** (B D GLM MA ST) Sat 21-2.30h
4601 Kellogg Avenue ☏ (513) 871-1542 🖳 www.adonisthenightclub.com

■ **Bronz** (B D GLM MA S VS) 20-2.30h
4029 Hamilton Ave ☏ (513) 591-2100

■ **Dock. The** (B D GLM OS S SNU ST VS)
21-2.30, Fri & Sat 20-4h, closed Mon-Wed
603 West Pete Rose Way ☏ (513) 241-5623 🖳 www.thedockcomplex.com

CRUISING

-Burnett Woods (AYOR)
-Mt. Airy Forest (AYOR)
-Mc Farland Street (between 3rd and 4th Street, after the bars close).

Cleveland ☏ 216

PUBLICATIONS

■ **Gay People's Chronicle**
PO Box 5426 ☏ (216) 631-8646 🖳 www.gaypeopleschronicle.com
Weekly gay newspaper.

BARS

■ **A Man's World** (AC B D G m MC OS) 7-2.30, Sun & Mon 12-2.30h
2909 Detroit Avenue ☏ (216) 574-2203
This place is connected via a pass through to The Shed.

■ **Bottom's Up** (B D GLM MA SNU ST VS)
1572 W. 117th St. ☏ (216) 521-4386
Bottom's Up has reopened as a gay rock club.

■ **Club Argos** (B D f G MA S) 15-2.30, Sat & Sun 12-2.30h
2032 W 25th St *At 24th St* ☏ (216) 781-9191 🖳 www.club-argos.com
Sports bar. Many black guys.

■ **Cocktails Cleveland** (B D G MA OS S VS) 15-2.30h
9208 Detroit Ave *At W 93rd St* ☏ (216) 961-3115
🖳 www.cocktails-cleveland.com
Sun T-Dance.

■ **Hawk. The** (B GLM m MA s) 10-2.30, Sun 13-2.30h
11217 Detroit Avenue *Near 112th Street* ☏ (216) 521-5443

■ **Hush** (B GLM MA S ST) Mon-Fri 17-2.30, Sat 19-2.30, Sun 12-2.30h
11633 Lorain Ave ☏ (216) 476-1970 🖳 www.hushcleveland.com

■ **Leather Stallion Saloon** (AC B F G MA OS s) 15-2.30h
2205 St. Clair Avenue *Downtown, neat E 21st St* ☏ (216) 589-8588
🖳 www.leatherstallion.com
Oldest gay bar in Cleveland, since 1970. Very popular Sun afternoon.

■ **Paradise Inn** (AC B G MA) 11-2.30h
4488 State Road ☏ (216) 741-9819

DANCECLUBS

■ **Bounce** (AC B GLM M MA) 17-2.30h
2814 Detroit Avenue ☏ (216) 357-2997 🖳 www.clevelandcocktails.com

■ **Mean Bull** (B D G MA) 16-2h
1313 E. 26th Street ☏ (216) 812-3304 🖳 www.meanbull.com
Belongs to Flex Bath/Hotel compound. Features live piano music and plugged beats.

RESTAURANTS

■ **Union Station Video Café** (AC B CC GLM I M VS YC)
Mon-Sat 17-2.30, Sun 11-2.30h
2814 Detroit Avenue *@ Bounce Nightclub* ☏ (216) 357-2997
🖳 www.clevelandcocktails.com
Restaurant, video & internet bar.

SEX SHOPS/BLUE MOVIES

■ **Body Language** (cc F GLM MA) 11-22, Sun 12-17h
11424 Lorain Avenue / West 115th Street *The red door*
☏ (216) 251-3330 🖳 www.body-language.com
Toys, leather, magazines, DVDs and more.

SAUNAS/BATHS

■ **Club. The**
(! b CC DU FC FH G m MA OS PI PP RR SA SB SH SOL VS WH WO) 24hrs
3219 Detroit Avenue ☏ (216) 961-2727 🖳 www.the-clubs.com
THE CLUBS is a national chain of private membership clubs and for that reason you must purchase a membership card in order to use the facilities. Bath house with sun deck and view over Lake Erie. See: www.the-clubs.com for more information.

■ **Flex Hotel & Spa Cleveland** (! AC B BF CC DR DU FC FH G I LAB m MA MSG NU OS P PI PK PP RR RWS RWT S SA SB SH SNU SOL VA VS WH WO) 24hrs
2600 Hamilton Avenue ☏ (216) 812-3304 🖳 www.flexcleveland.com
Resort with hotel, bath, restaurant, bar, entertainment and store. Flex Cleveland is apparently one of the biggest bathhouses in the world! Also have own club called Mean Bull.

HOTELS

■ **Flex Hotel & Spa Cleveland** (! AC B BF CC DR DU FC FH G I LAB m MA MSG NU OS P PI PK PP RR RWS RWT S SA SB SH SNU SOL VA VS WH WO) 24hrs
2600 Hamilton Avenue ☏ (216) 812-3304 🖳 www.flexcleveland.com
Resort with hotel, bath, restaurant, bar, entertainment and store. Flex Cleveland is apparently one of the biggest bathhouses in the world! Also have own club called Mean Bull.

GUEST HOUSES

■ **Clifford House B&B** (BF glm I MC RWS RWT) All year
1810 West 28th Street ☏ (216) 589-0121 🖳 www.cliffordhouse.com
4 guestrooms, all en-suite.

GENERAL GROUPS

■ **Lesbian-Gay Community Center of Greater Cleveland** (GLM) 13-23h
6600 Detroit Avenue ☏ (216) 651-5428 🖳 www.lgcsc.org

CRUISING

-Edgewater Park (AYOR)
-Metropolitan Park (AYOR) (Memphis & Tiedman Street)
-Sauna at Stella Walsh Recreation Center
-North Chagrin Reservation Metropark.

Columbus ☏ 614

GAY INFO

■ **Stonewall Columbus** (AC GLM MA) 9-17h, Sat & Sun closed
1160 North High Street ☏ (614) 299-7764
🖳 www.stonewallcolumbus.org
Organization fighting for gay and lesbian rights in Ohio.

BARS

■ **Awol** (B G MA) 12-2.30, Sun 13-2.30h
49 Parsons Ave ☏ (614) 621-8779 🖳 awolbar.com

■ **Blazer's Pub** (AC CC gLm M MA S) Mon-Fri 16-?, Sun 15-24h
1205 North High Street *Corner of 5th Ave & N. High St.*
☏ (614) 299-1800 🖳 www.blazerspub.biz

■ **Club 20** (B G MA OS) 12-2.30, Sun 13-2.30h
20 E Duncan *At N High St* ☏ (614) 261-9111
🖳 www.myspace.com/club20bar

■ **Club Diversity** (AC B CC GLM MA s) 16-24, Sat 18.30-2.30, Sun 12-24h
863 South High Street *Downtown Colombus* ☏ (614) 224 40 50
🖳 www.clubdiversity.com

■ **Exile** (B G MA) 21-2.30h
893 North 4th Street *Cnr. 2nd Ave* ☏ (614) 299-0069
🖳 www.exilebar.com

■ **Havana Video Lounge** (AC B CC GLM M MA S VS) 17-2h
862 North High Street *At First Ave* ☏ (614) 461-9697
🖳 www.columbusnightlife.com
Martini bar with videos and cigar lounge.

■ **Score** (B GLM MA) 16-2.30h
145 North 5th Street ☏ (614) 849-0099

■ **Slammers** (AC B CC gLm I M MA OS T) 11-0.30, Sun 14-0.30h, closed Mon
202 East Long Street ☏ (614) 221-8880 🖳 www.slammersbar.net

■ **South Bend Tavern. The** (B GLM MA ST) 12-2.30h
126 East Moler Street *At 4th Street* ☏ (614) 444-3386

■ **Tremont II** (B G MC) 13-2.30h
708 South High Street ☏ (614) 445-9365

■ **Union Bar** (B GLM M MA s) 11-2.30, Sun 10-2.30h
782 North High Street ☏ (614) 421-2233 🖳 www.unioncafe.com

DANCECLUBS

■ **Axis** (AC B CC D G MA SNU) Fri & Sat 22-2.30h
775 North High Street *Near Lundy St* ☏ (614) 291-4008
🖳 www.columbusnightlife.com

■ **Wall Street** (B D gLm MA s ST VS)
Wed-Sun 21-2.30h, closed Mon & Tue
144 North Wall Street ☏ (614) 464-2800
🖳 www.wallstreetnightclub.com

SAUNAS/BATHS

■ **Club. The** (! AC CC DR DU FC FH G GH I M MA OS P PI SA SB SH SL VS WH WO) 24hrs
795 West 5th Avenue *Close to Ohio State University* ☏ (614) 291-0049
🖳 www.theclubs.com
Member of THE CLUBS, the largest and very popular chain of gay men's health clubs in the country. Located within walking distance of the OSU campus. Occasional college studs, and some oldsters. See: www.the-clubs.com for more information.

■ **Flex** (AC AK CC DR DU FC FH G GH I LAB m MA P RR SA SB SL VS WH WO) 24hrs
1567 E. Livingston Avenue *Corner of Geers & Livingstone Ave*
☏ (614) 252-0730 🖳 www.flexbaths.com
Clean facility with great staff, lively guests and ample play space.

BOOK SHOPS

Open Book. An (GLM) 12-21, Sat 11-21, Sun 12-18h
685 N High St ☎ (614) 221-6339

LEATHER & FETISH SHOPS

Leather Company (F G)
642 North High Street, Suite B ☎ (614) 224-8989
www.leathercompanyonline.com

GUEST HOUSES

Brewmaster's House. The (AC BF GLM I PK RWT) All year
1083 South High Street *Exit US Route 71-S at Greenlawn to High, located next to BP service station at corner of High and Greenlawn*
☎ (614) 449-8298 brewmastershouseB&B.com

CRUISING

-O.S.U. Botany and Zoology Building
-Larkins Hall (gymnasium, 4th floor, 7-22h)
-Ohio Union (AYOR) (basement)
-The Beach, Whittier Street, west of High and Front Streets
-Big Walnut Park on Livingston Avenue east of Hamilton Street
-Park of Roses on North High, just north of Clintonville, next to public library
-Bull Run Park (AYOR OC) on Clime Road, west of Georgesville Road, before 23h
-Lou Berliner Park (AYOR) on Greenlawn Avenue before 23h, busy all year.

Dayton ☎ 937

PUBLICATIONS

GayDayton
PO Box 4436 ☎ (937) 623-1590 www.gaydayton.org
Monthly.

BARS

Argos (B F G MA) Mon-Sun 18-23h
301 Mabel Ave *Next to I-35 and Linden Ave* ☎ (937) 252-2976
www.argosbardayton.com

Masque (B D GLM MA S) 19-2.30, Fri & Sat -5h
34 North Jefferson Street ☎ (937) 228-2582
www.clubmasque.com

MJ's Cafe and Dance (AC B CC D F GLM M MA NR OS PK S SNU VS W WI) 15-2.30h
119 East 3rd Street *Enter from St Clair St. across form the library. Parking and Entrance in the rear* ☎ (937) 223-3259
www.mjscafedayton.com
Cheap drinks,great shows. Freindly neighbourhood bar.

Stage Door (B f G m MA) 12-2.30h
44 North Jefferson Street ☎ (937) 223-7418
www.stagedoordayton.com

DANCECLUBS

Aquarius (B D GLM MA ST) 20-2.30h
135 East 2nd Street ☎ (937) 223-1723
www.aquariusnightclub.com

CRUISING

-DeWeese Park
-Wright State University (Library, Millet Hall on 2nd floor)
Toilets at Wright State-Fawcett Hall.

Lima ☎ 419

BARS

Somewhere in Time (AC B D GLM m MA s SNU ST)
Sun-Thu 19-2.30, Fri & Sat 20-2.30h
804 West North Street ☎ (419) 227-7288

Lorain ☎ 440

BARS

Tim's Place (B D G m OS p S WE) 20-2.30h, closed Mon
2223 Broadway Avenue *Between 22nd & 23rd St* ☎ (440) 246-9002
www.freewebs.com/timsinlorain/index.htm

Monroe ☎ 513

BARS

Old Street Saloon (B D GLM MA ST)
20-2h, closed Sun-Tue
13 Old St ☎ (513) 539-9183 www.oldstreetbar.com

Sandusky ☎ 419

BARS

Crowbar (B d G MA SNU) 16-2.30h
206 West Market Street ☎ (419) 624-0109
www.sandusky-crowbar.com

Xcentricities (B D GLM MA S ST)
18-2.30, Sat & Sun 14-2.30h
306 West Water Street ☎ (419) 624-8118
www.clubxcentricities.com

Springfield ☎ 937

BARS

Why Not III (B GLM H MA P S WE) 21.30-1, Wed-Sat -2.30h
5 North Murray Street ☎ (937) 324-9758
www.why-not-3.com

Steubenville ☎ 740

BARS

Pj's (B D GLM M MA) 11-2.30h
169 North 4th Street ☎ (740) 283-2747

Toledo ☎ 419

BARS

Bretz (AC B CC D GLM I MA OS SNU WE)
Mon-Thu 14-2.30, Fri & Sat 14-4h
2012 Adams Street ☎ (419) 243-1900
www.myspace.com/bretzthebar

R House (! B D G MA OS P) 16-2.30h
5534 Secor Road ☎ (419) 474-2929
Thu: party night with dancers. Fri: wet underwear competition.

Rip Cord (B GLM MA SNU) 21-2.30h
115 N Erie Street *City Centre* ☎ (419) 243-3412 theripcord.net
A bit seedy but great bartenders.

SAUNAS/BATHS

Diplomat Health Club
(AC CC DU FC G GH MA MSG P SA SB VS WO) 24hrs
1313 N. Summit Street *Between Magnolia & Mulberry Streets*
☎ (419) 255-3700 www.diplomathealthclubs.com
Membership available. Private lockers & rooms cost extra.

Youngstown ☎ 330

BARS

Split Level (AC B D GLM MA S ST)
169 South Four Mile Run Road ☎ (330) 318-9830
www.splitlevelniteclub.com

Utopia Video Nightclub (B d GLM MA ST)
17-?h, closed Mon
876 East Midlothian Boulevard ☎ (330) 781-9000

Oklahoma

Location: Middlewest USA
Initials: OK
Time: GMT -6
Area: 181.048 km² / 74,048 sq mi.
Population: 3,450,654
Capital: Oklahoma City

Oklahoma City ☎ 405

BARS

Bearz 3020 (B glm MA s) 14-2h
3020 N Pennsylvania Avenue *Near cnr. NW 29th St* ☎ (405) 524-9306

Boom. The (B CC D F G MA) 16-2, Fri & Sat 14-2h
2218 NW 36th St ☎ (405) 601-7200 www.theboomokc.com

Copa. The (B D GLM MA SNU ST) 21-2h, closed Mon
2200 North West 39th Expressway *At the Habana Inn*
☎ (405) 528-2221 www.habanainn.com

Finishline. The (B D f GLM MA PI) 12-2h
2200 North West 39th Expressway *At the Habana Inn*
☎ (405) 525-2900 www.habanainn.com
Large dance floor, big screen TV, darts, and two pool tables. On special events weekends, such as Rodeo Weekend, the entire hotel is crammed with cowboys.

Hi-Lo Club (B D GLM S ST) 12-2h
1221 NW 50th Street ☎ (405) 843-1722 www.hiloclub.net

Ledo. The (AC B d f G m MA OS ST) 16-22.30, Fri & Sat -2h
2200 North West 39th Street ☎ (405) 525-0730
www.habanainn.com

Park. The (B D G OS SNU VS) 17-2, Sun 15-2h
2125 North West 39th Street ☎ (405) 528-4690
www.anglesclub.com
Local popular neighbourhood club. Free supper on Sun 5.30h.

Phoenix Rising (B D f G MA OS) 16-2h
2120 NW 39th Street *Cnr. Pennsylvania Ave* ☎ (405) 601-3711

Tramps (B D G MA SNU) 12-2, Sat & Sun 10-2h
2201 NW 39th St *At Barnes Ave* ☎ (405) 521-9888

DANCECLUBS

Angles (B D GLM MA S VS) Fri & Sat
2117 North West 39th Street ☎ (405) 528-0050
www.anglesclub.com

Wreck Room. The (b D GLM MA ST) Fri & Sat 22-7h
2127 North West 39th Street ☎ (405) 525-7610
www.anglesclub.com
Non-alcoholic drinks only.

HOTELS

Habana Inn (AC B BF CC D GLM M MA PI ST) All year
2200 North West 39th Expressway *At Youngs* ☎ (405) 528-2221
www.habanainn.com
All rooms with shower/bath & WC, phone, satellite TV. This huge gay complex has 2 swimming pools, 3 gay clubs, a restaurant and a shop.

Tulsa ☎ 918

BARS

Bamboo Lounge (B D G MA OS SNU ST) 12-2h
7204 E Pine ☎ (918) 836-8700
www.facebook.com/pages/The-Bamboo-Lounge/111891205515118
Dancers on Sun.

End Up (AC B G MA S) 16-2h
5336 East Admiral Place ☎ (918) 836-0915
www.myspace.com/enduptulsa

New Age Renegade (AC B GLM m MA OS ST) 16-2h
1649 South Main Street *Cnr. 17th* ☎ (918) 585-3405
www.club-renegade.com

Tulsa Eagle (B d F G MA OS) 16-2h
1338 E 3rd St *At Peoria* ☎ (918) 592-1188

Yellow Brick Road. The (B GLM MA) 16-2h
2630 E 15th Street *Cnr. Harvard* ☎ (918) 293-0304
www.ybrpub.com

DANCECLUBS

Club Majestic (B D GLM MA ST) Thu-Sun 21-2h
124 N Boston Ave ☎ (918) 584-9494 www.clubmajestictulsa.com

Club Maverick (B D F G MA s) 16-2h
822 S Sheridan Rd *At 9th* ☎ (918) 835-3301
www.tulsamaverick.com
Country-Western.

CRUISING

-Boulder and Boston (between 5th and 10th Streets)
-River Parks (at 21st Street)
-Turkey Mountain Park (61st and South Elwood Streets)
-Woodward Park.

Oregon

Location: Northwest USA
Initials: OR
Time: GMT -8
Area: 254.819 km² / 104,221 sq mi.
Population: 3,421,400
Capital: Salem
Important gay cities: Portland

Medford ☎ 541

SEX SHOPS/BLUE MOVIES

Castle Megastore (CC g MA) Sun-Thu 9-1, Fri-Sat -2h
1113 Progress Drive ☎ (541) 608-9540 www.castlemegastore.com
Videos, leather, magazines, toys, novelties, books, DVDs.

Portland ☎ 503

GAY INFO

Q Center (GLM) Tue-Thu 13-21, Sat & Sun 13-17h
4115 North Mississippi Avenue ☎ (503) 234-7837
www.pdxqcenter.org
Non-profit organization to increase the visibility of and foster connection within metropolitan LGBTQ community. The center builds public awareness and support, and celebrates diversity through art, culture, and community programming.

PUBLICATIONS

Just Out
PO Box 14400 ☎ (503) 236-1252 www.justout.com
Oregon's bi-weekly GL publication.

SHOWS

Darcelle XV (B CC glm M MA SNU ST) Wed-Thu 18-23, Fri & Sat 2.30h
208 NW Third Avenue *Located in Chinatown* ☎ (503) 222-5338
www.darcellexv.com
Showtimes 20.30h, Fri & Sat also 22.30h, male strippers Fri & Sat 24h.

BARS

Boxxes (B d G MA OS SNU) 12-2.30h
1035 SW Stark St. ☎ (503) 226-4171 www.boxxes.com
Connected to „red Cap Bar" by a hallway.

Casey's (B D G MA SNU) 19-2.30h
610 North West Couch Street ☎ (503) 224-9062
www.myspace.com/caseyspdx

Crush (B D GLM M MA)
Mon & Tue 16.30-23, Wed & Thu -24, Fri -1, Sat 17-1h
1412 SE Morrison ☎ (503) 235-8150 www.crushbar.com

■ **Eagle Portland** (B f G MA) daily 11h-open end
835 N Lombard ☎ (503) 283-9734 🖳 www.eagleportland.com
Leather and bear bar.

■ **Embers** (B D GLM m MA ST WE) 11-2.30h
110 North West Broadway *At Couch* ☎ (503) 222-3082
🖳 www.emberspdx.net
Very popular bar/disco, good nightly drag shows.

■ **Fox & Hound** (B G M MA) 11-2h
217 NW 2nd Avenue ☎ (503) 243-5530

■ **Holocene** (B D g MA) Wed-Fri 17-2.30, Sat 20-2.30h
1001 South East Morrison ☎ (503) 239-7639 🖳 www.holocene.org

■ **JOQ's Tavern** (B G M MA) 13-2.30h
2512 North East Broadway ☎ (503) 287-4210

■ **Maricon @ Matador** (AC B D GLM MA ST) 1sr, 2nd & 3rd Sat/ month 22-2.15h
1967 West Burnside Street ☎ (503) 222-5822
🖳 www.thematadorbar.com

■ **Red Cap Garage** (B D GLM I M MA OS S) Mon 15-22, Tue-Sun -2.30h
1035 SW Stark Street ☎ (503) 226-4171 🖳 redcapgarage.com
Bar, restaurant and dance club, connected to Boxxes dance club. Serving lunch now, too.

■ **Scandals** (! AC B G M MA) 12-2.30h
1125 SW Stark Street ☎ (503) 227-5887 🖳 www.scandalspdx.com
The oldest gay bar in Portland.

■ **Silverado** (B d G M MA SNU) 9-2.30h
318 SW Third Avenue ☎ (503) 224-4493 🖳 www.silveradopdx.com
Wed-Sun 20-2h male strippers. Cruisy atmosphere. Very popular.

CAFES

■ **Voodoo Doughnut** (B glm M MA) 6-3h
22 SW Third Avenue ☎ (503) 241-5704
🖳 www.voodoodoughnut.com

DANCECLUBS

■ **CC Slaughter's** (B D GLM MA S) 15-2.30h
219 North West Davis Street ☎ (503) 248-9135
🖳 www.ccslaughterspdx.com
The disco of choice for the younger set.

■ **Escape** (B D GLM MA) Fri & Sat 22.30-?h
333 SW Park Ave ☎ (503) 227-0830

■ **Invasion** (B D GLM m MA S SNU ST) Tue, Thu, Fri & Sat 16h-open end
412 SW 4th St. ☎ (503) 226-7777 🖳 www.invasionpdx.com
New mixed Danceclub with themed parties. Gay specials are „BOYZ-NITE" on Thu.

RESTAURANTS

■ **Hobo's** (B GLM M MA S) 16-2h
120 North West 3rd Avenue *In the heart of Old-Town between Davis & Couch* ☎ (503) 224-3285 🖳 www.hobospdx.com
Popular for drinks and dinner after work. Casual upscale atmosphere. Wed-Sun Piano lounge.

■ **Saucebox** (B glm M) 17-22h
214 SW Broadway ☎ (503) 241-3393 🖳 www.saucebox.com

■ **Starky's** (AC B CC GLM M MA NR OS PK VEG) 11-2.30, Sun 9.30-2.30h
2913 SE Stark Street ☎ (503) 230-7980 🖳 www.starkys.com

SAUNAS/BATHS

■ **Steam Portland** (AC AK CC DR DU FC FH G GH I M MA NR OS P PK RR S SB SL SNU SOL VR VS WH WI) 24hrs
2885 NE Sandy Boulevard *Bus 12 from Downtown* ☎ (503) 736-9999
🖳 www.steamportland.com

LEATHER & FETISH SHOPS

■ **Spartacus Enterprises** (CC F g)
Mon-Wed 10-23, Thu-Sat -24, Sun 12-21h
300 South West 12th Avenue *Downtown Portland* ☎ (503) 224-2604
🖳 spartacusleathers.com
Since 1987, SPARTACUS ENTERPRISES of Oregon has been producing the highest quality of leather bondage toys and nipple clamps. Also mail order.

SPECIAL INTEREST GROUPS

■ **Sexual Minority Youth Recreation Center – SMYRC**
Wed 16-21, Fri -23h
2100 SE Belmont ☎ (503) 872-9664 🖳 www.smyrc.org
A non-profit agency that provides a drop-in center for LGBT youths and their friends 23 years old and under.

CRUISING

-Rest Stop (I-5, both sides)
-Columbia Park (AYOR)
-East Delta Park (showers)
-Rooster Rock State Park (East end of beach, 30 miles East of Portland)
-Sauvie's Island (West end of beach near parking lot)
-Washington Park (by Lewis and Clark Mounument, Burnside & 25th).

Pennsylvania

Location: Northeast USA
Initials: PA
Time: GMT -5
Area: 119.291 km² / 48,790 sq mi.
Population: 12,281,054
Capital: Harrisburg
Important gay cities: Philadelphia, Pittsburgh

Allentown ☎ 610

BARS

■ **Candida** (B GLM m MA) 14-2h
247 North 12th Street *At Chew* ☎ (610) 434-3071
🖳 www.Candidasbar.com

■ **Stonewall / Mooselounge** (B D GLM M S SNU VS)
19-2h, closed Mon
28 North 10th Street ☎ (610) 432-0706
🖳 www.thestonewall.com
Dance floor on the ground floor and a separate bar called the Moose Lounge on the 2nd floor, where food is served.

CAMPING

■ **Woods Campground. The** (f GLM MA NU OS PI)
845 Vaughn Acres Lane, Lehighton *In Lehighton, ca 10 miles north of Allentown* ☎ (610) 217-0342 🖳 www.thewoodscampground.com
Clothing-optional camping site. Membership fee applies.

Bethlehem ☎ 610

BARS

■ **Diamonz** (AC B CC GLM M MA OS WE) 16-2h
1913 West Broad Street ☎ (610) 865-1028
Four bars, restaurant, sports bar, 2 level dance club.

Boyers ☎ 724

CAMPING

■ **Camp Davis** (d G MA NU)
311 Redbrush Road ☎ (724) 637-2402
🖳 www.campdaviscampground.com

East Stroudsburg ☎ 570

GUEST HOUSES

■ **Rainbow Mountain Resort**
(AC B BF CC D FH GLM I M MA PA PI PK RWS RWT S SA SNU VA VEG WO)
All year
210 Mount Nebo Road ☎ (570) 223-8484
🖳 www.rainbowmountain.com
Gay resort with 45 guest rooms in the woods with several cabins, a hot tub, a restaurant, a karaoke lounge and a separate dance club.

Erie ☏ 814

PUBLICATIONS

■ **Erie Gay News**
1115 West 7th St ☏ (814) 456-9833 🖳 www.eriegaynews.com

BARS

■ **Zone. The** (AC B D GLM m MA s) 20-2h
133 West 18th Street ☏ (814) 459-1711 🖳 www.thezonedanceclub.com
Also a piano bar.

Gibson ☏ 570

CAMPING

■ **Hillside Campground** (G MA NU PI) All year
1 Creek Road ☏ (570) 756-2007 🖳 www.hillsidecampgrounds.com

Greensburg ☏ 724

BARS

■ **Longbada Lounge** (AC B CC D GLM I MA P S SNU ST VS WE)
Tue-Sat 21-2h, closed Sun & Mon
106 West Pittsburgh Street *Downtown Greensburg* ☏ (724) 837-6614
🖳 www.myspace.com/longbadalounge
Happy hour 21-23h. Gay owned.

Harrisburg ☏ 717

BARS

■ **704 Strawberry** (B G MC VS) 14-2h
704 N. 3rd Street ☏ (717) 234-4228
■ **Brownstone Lounge** (B f GLM M MA) Mon-Fri 11-2, Sat & Sun 15-2h
412 Forster Street ☏ (717) 234-7009
Country-western/neighbourhood bar, some Levis/Leather scene, pool table.
■ **Liquid 891. The** (B D GLM MA S ST) 19-2h
891 Eisenhower Boulevard ☏ (717) 939-1123 🖳 www.liquid891.com
■ **Neptune's Lounge** (B d GLM MA s WE) 16-2, Sun 14-2h
268 North Street ☏ (717) 233-3078

DANCECLUBS

■ **Stallions** (B D G MA SNU ST) 19-2h
706 N 3rd St ☏ (717) 232-3060 🖳 www.stallionsclub.com

Johnstown ☏ 814

BARS

■ **Lucille's** (AC B D GLM MA OS S SNU) 18-2h, closed Sun & Mon
520 Washington Street *Downtown, 60 miles East of Pittsbourgh*
☏ (814) 539-4448 🖳 www.lucillesjohnstown.com
Night club with karaoke shows on Thu and DJ on Fri & Sat.

Lancaster ☏ 717

BARS

■ **Tally Ho** (B D GLM MA ST) 20-2h
201 W. Orange Street *Ground floor* ☏ (717) 299-0661

New Hope ☏ 215

BARS

■ **Raven Resort** (AC B CC glm H M MA OS PI) 11-2h
385 West Bridge Street ☏ (215) 862-2081 🖳 www.theravenresort.com
Also motel, restaurant, swim club & regular entertainment.

New Milford ☏ 570

CAMPING

■ **Oneida Camp and Lodge** (d G MA PI) All year
2580 East Lake Road ☏ (570) 465-7011 🖳 www.oneidaresort.com

Philadelphia ☏ 215

GAY INFO

■ **William Way Community Center. The** (AC GLM I)
9-22, Sat 10-19, Sun 10.30-19h
1315 Spruce Street ☏ (215) 732-2220 🖳 www.waygay.org

PUBLICATIONS

■ **Philadelphia Gay News** (GLM)
505 South 4th Street ☏ (215) 625-8501 🖳 www.epgn.com
Appears weekly and features reports and articles on Philadelphia's gay and Lesbian community, as well as on cultural events and lots of classified ads.

BARS

■ **Bike Stop** (! AC B d F G m MA VS) 16-2, Sat & Sun 14-2h
204-206 South Quince Street *Near Locust Street* ☏ (215) 627-1662
🖳 www.thebikestop.com
The ultimate leather & bear bar in Philadelphia. Bar on the ground floor, sports bar on the 2nd, dance club on the 3rd and cruising area „Pit Stop" in the basement. No cover charge
■ **Bob and Barbara's Lounge** (B d glm MA ST) 15-2h
1509 South Street ☏ (215) 545-4511
Life Jazz. Bingo on Wed. Drag Shows on Thu.
■ **JR's Lounge** (AC B G M)
1305 Locust Street *Cnr. 13th Street*
■ **Q Lounge** (B GLM M MC OS S) 17-2h
1234 Locust Street ☏ (215) 732-1800 🖳 www.qphilly.com
Former „Bump". Lounge with events.
■ **Stir** (B D GLM MA s) 16-2h
1705 Chancellor Street ☏ (215) 732-2700 🖳 www.stirphilly.com
■ **Tavern on Camac** (AC B D GLM M MA) 16-2h
243 South Camac Street ☏ (215) 545-0900 🖳 www.tavernoncamac.com
Restaurant, piano and dance bar.
■ **Uncle's** (AC B G H OC) 11-2h
1220 Locust Street *Between 12th & 13th Street* ☏ (215) 546-6660
Also rooms for rent upstairs.
■ **Venture Inn** (B GLM M MA) 12-2, dinner 17.30-23, Sun brunch 12-16h
255 South Camac Street *Near Spruce Street* ☏ (215) 545-8731
🖳 www.viphilly.com
■ **Westbury** (B GLM M MA) 11-2h
261 South 13th Street ☏ (215) 546-5170
■ **Woody's** (! B D GLM m MA S VS) 11-2h
202 South 13th Street *At Walnut* ☏ (215) 545-1893
🖳 www.woodysbar.com
A big and popular club with a video bar, internet room and dance floor upstairs. Happy hour daily 17-19h. 18+ on Wed. Some nights cover charge applies.

CAFES

■ **Brew Ha Ha** (B cc glm I M MA OS)
212 South 12th Street ☏ (215) 893-5680 🖳 www.brewhaha.com
Nice café right in the gay district.

DANCECLUBS

■ **12th Air Command** (! B D f G m MA OS SNU ST VS)
17-2h, closed Mon
254 South 12th Street ☏ (215) 545-8088 🖳 www.12thair.com
Multi-level club with an outdoor upper deck and several bars and dance floors. Regular strip and drag shows throughout the week.
■ **Shampoo** (AC B D f glm MA) Wed, Fri-Sun 21-2h
417 North 8th Street *Between 7th and 8th streets.* ☏ (215) 922-7500
🖳 www.shampooonline.com
Every Fri „Shaft Night" (GLM) with two dance floors and regular strip and drag shows. Other nights are mixed.
■ **Voyeur Nightclub** (! B D G MA P ST) Wed-Sun 21-3.30h
1221 Saint James Street *Between Walnut & Locust* ☏ (215) 735-5772
🖳 www.voyeurnightclub.com
Multi-level retro-futuristic club with large dance floors, several bars, VIP-area and a mezzanine with showering gogo boys. After hours.

RESTAURANTS

Knock Bar and Restaurant (AC B GLM M MA) dailiy 11-2h
225 South 12th Street ☎ (215) 925-1166 💻 www.knockphilly.com
Great restaurant with upscale Bar and good food!

SEX SHOPS/BLUE MOVIES

Adonis Cinema Complex (G MA VS) 24hrs
2026 Sansom Street *Near 20th Street* ☎ (215) 557-9319

Danny's (AC CC G MA VS) 24hrs
133 South 13th Street *Between Walnut & Sansom* ☎ (215) 925-5041
💻 www.shopdannys.com
Magazines, videos and all-male cinema upstairs.

SAUNAS/BATHS

Club Body Center (AC b CC DU FC FH G m MA OS P SA SB SOL VS WH WO) 24hrs
1220 Chancellor Street *At 12th Street, 2nd floor* ☎ (215) 735-7671
💻 www.clubbodycenter.com
In the summer there's a sundeck for nude sunbathing. Large sauna on 5 floors.

Sansom Street Gym (AC b DU G LAB MA P SA SL VS WO) 24hrs
2020 Sansom Street ☎ (267) 335-0151 💻 www.sansomstreetgym.com
Clean sauna.

BOOK SHOPS

Giovanni's Room (AC CC GLM MA) Mon-Sat 11.30-19, Sun 13-19h
345 South 12th Street *Downtown* ☎ (215) 923-2960
💻 www.giovannisroom.com
The biggest, best, and most beautiful gay bookstore in the country – says its owner.

HOTELS

Alexander Inn (AC BF CC glm MA PK RWS RWT VA WO) All year
Spruce at 12th Street *Central* ☎ (215) 923-3535
💻 www.alexanderinn.com
Rooms with bath, phone, TV.

Pittsburgh ☎ 412

GAY INFO

GLCC – Gay & Lesbain Community Center (GLM)
Tue-Thu 18-21, Sat 12-21, Sun -18h
210 Grant Street ☎ (412) 422-0114 💻 www.glccpgh.org

PUBLICATIONS

Out Mon-Fri 10-18h
801 Bingham St, Suite 100 ☎ (412) 381-3350 💻 www.outonline.com
Monthly publication serving Pennsylvania, Ohio, West Virginia. News, entertainment, calendar of events, classified ads. The regionís largest LGBT publication and website since 1973!

BARS

5801 Video Lounge (B GLM M MA VS) 16-2, Sun 11-2h
5801 Ellsworth Ave ☎ (412) 661-5600 💻 www.5801videolounge.com
Video lounge and cafe.

941 Saloon (B GLM) 14-2h
941 Liberty Avenue ☎ (412) 281-5222
💻 www.myspace.com/941saloon

Blue Moon (B GLM MA T)
Mon 16-midnight, Tue-Sun 17-2h
5115 Butler Street ☎ (412) 781-1119
This friendly and casual tavern offers a full selection of beers and well drinks. Also special events like barbecues and live entertainers.

Cattivo (B GLM M MA) Tue-Sun 16-2h
146 44th Street ☎ (412) 687-2157

Images (AC B CC D G m MA S SNU VS) 14-2, Sat & Sun 18-2h
965 Liberty Avenue *In the heart of the gay district, next to the convention cente* ☎ (412) 391-9990 💻 www.imagespittsburgh.com

Jitters Club (AC B D GLM MA P) Fri-Sun 14-6h
1615 Penn Avenue *Strip district, in the rear*

Leather Central (B D F G MA VS) Fri & Sat 21-2h
1226 Herron Ave *At Liberty Ave* ☎ (412) 682-9869

P-Town (B D G MA SNU) 17-2h
4740 Baum Blvd ☎ (412) 621-0111 💻 www.ptownpgh.com

Real Luck Cafe (AC B D GLM M MA OS s SNU) Mon-Sat 16-2h
1519 Penn Avenue *Strip District* ☎ (412) 471-7832
💻 www.myspace.com/realluckcafe
2 floors. Kitchen 17-24h. Also known as „Luckie's Tavern".

SPIN (AC B glm MA VS) Daily 16-2h
5744 Ellsworth Ave ☎ (412) 362-7746 💻 www.spinbartini.com
Trendy lounge-bar, friendly staff, happy hour 18-20h.

There Video Lounge (B GLM MA) 17.30-2, Sat & Sun 19.30-2h
931 Liberty Avenue ☎ (412) 642-4435

DANCECLUBS

Pegasus (! AC B D GLM SNU YC) 21-2h, closed Sun, Mon & Wed
1740 Eckert St. *In the first 2 floors of Pittsburgh Eagle* ☎ (412) 281-2151
💻 www.pittpegasus.com
Probably the most popular gay disco in town.

Pittsburgh Eagle (AC B D F G m MA ST VS) Fri & Sat 22-2h
1740 Eckert Street *North Side, 3rd floor* ☎ (412) 766-7222
💻 www.pitteagle.com
Popular bar/dance complex.

SAUNAS/BATHS

Club Pittsburgh (! AC CC DR DU F FC FH G GH I LAB m MA OS P RR S SA SB SH SL SNU VS WH WO) 24hrs
1139 Penn Avenue *In city* ☎ (412) 471-6790 💻 www.clubpittsburgh.com
One of the best gay saunas in the USA.

HEALTH GROUPS

Pittsburgh AIDS Task Force Mon-Fri 9-17h
5913 Penn Avenue, 2nd Floor ☎ (412) 345-7456 💻 www.patf.org

Reading ☎ 610

BARS

Red Star (B D F G MA ST) 21-2h, closed Sun & Mon
11 South 10th Street ☎ (610) 375-4116

Scranton ☎ 570

BARS

Twelve Penny Saloon (B D GLM M MA ST) 18-2h
3501 Birney Ave, Moosic ☎ (570) 941-0444
💻 www.12pennysaloon.com

Spring Grove ☎ 717

DANCECLUBS

Atlands Ranch (B D GLM MA) Fri & Sat 20-2h
8505 Orchard Road ☎ (717) 225-4479 💻 www.altlandsranch.com

State College ☎ 814

BARS

Chumley's (B G MA) 17-2, Sun 18-2h
108 West College Avenue ☎ (814) 238-4446 💻 www.hotelstatecollege.com

CRUISING

-The Wall (100 block of College Avenue)
-Penn State (Hertzel Union Building, Recreation Hall and men's locker rooms).

Sunbury ☎ 570

BARS

CC's (B D GLM ST) Thu-Sat 20-2, Sun 15-21h
555 Klinger Road ☎ (570) 286-6022 💻 www.ccsbar.com

Uniontown ☏ 724

DANCECLUBS

■ **Club 231** (AC B D GLM) 17-?h, closed Sun
231 Pittsburgh Street ☏ (724) 430-1477
www.myspace.com/illusionsnightclub

Williamsport ☏ 570

DANCECLUBS

■ **Z Club** (B D GLM MA s) 17-2.30h
321 Pine Street ☏ (570) 322-6900 www.clubzbar.com

Rhode Island

Location: Northeast USA
Initials: RI
Time: GMT -5
Area: 4.002 km² / 1,636 sq mi.
Population: 1,048,319
Capital: Providence

Newport ☏ 401

GUEST HOUSES

■ **Hydrangea House Inn. The** (AC BF CC glm MA MSG PK RWB RWT VA) All year
16 Bellevue Avenue *In the centre of historic district* ☏ (401) 846-4435
www.hydrangeahouse.com
Nine elegant non-smoking rooms with bath.

CRUISING

-First Beach(Eastons Beach)(in front of the concession stands)
-Purgatory Chasm-Tuckerman Avenue(Middletown)

Providence ☏ 401

BARS

■ **Alleycat. The** (B GLM MA) 15-1, Fri & Sat -2h
17 Snow Street ☏ (401) 273-0951
■ **Club Gallery** (B D GLM MA ST) 12-1, Fri & Sat -2h
148 Point Street ☏ (401) 751-7166 www.clubgalleryri.com
Lesbian events on Sat, karaoke and dragshows on Sun.
■ **Mirabar** (B D G S) 15-1, Fri & Sat -2h
35 Richmond Street ☏ (401) 331-6761 www.mirabar.com
Best on a Saturday night.
■ **Providence Eagle** (AC B F G m MA) 15-1, Fri & Sat -2h
200 Union Street ☏ (401) 421-1447 www.providenceeagle.com
Levi & leather bar.
■ **Sunset Bar & Grille** (B D GLM M MA S) Fri & Sat 18-1h
888 Charles Street ☏ (401) 726-8889
■ **Touch Providence** (B G MC SNU) 21-1, Fri & Sat -2h, closed Mon
257 Allens Avenue ☏ (401) 461-9522 www.touchprovidence.com
■ **Union** (B GLM MA) 17-1, Fri-Sun -2h
200 Union Street *Next to the Providence Eagle* ☏ (401) 421-1447
www.providenceeagle.com

DANCECLUBS

■ **Dark Lady** (B D GLM MA ST) 21-1, Fri-Sat -2h
124 Snow Street ☏ (401) 831-4297
■ **Lot 401** (B D GLM MA) Sun 21-1h
44 Hospital St ☏ (401) 490-3980

SAUNAS/BATHS

■ **Club Body Center** (DU G MA SA SB VS WO) 24hrs
257 Weybossett Street *2nd floor above „Subway"* ☏ (401) 274-0298
www.cbcresorts.com
Door at street level says „Club Providence" – Walk up the stairs!

■ **Gay Mega Plex.The** (! FC FH G MA SA SB VS WH WO) 24hrs
257 Allens Avenue ☏ (401) 780-8769
http://members.cox.net/megaplex
Tue: „Buddy night", Wed: „Pig night" with blackout from 19h. When you don't have any luck here you can always try: Flixx (same building), and AVN (Adult Video News) across the alley.

HELP WITH PROBLEMS

■ **GLBT Helpline of Rhode Island** (GLM MA)
PO Box 41247 www.glbthelpline.org

South Carolina

Location: Southeast USA
Initials: SC
Time: GMT -5
Area: 82.902 km² / 33.906 sq mi.
Population: 4,012,012
Capital: Columbia

Aiken ☏ 803

BARS

■ **Marlboro Station** (B D GLM S) Fri-Sun 22-?h
141 Marlboro Street ☏ (803) 644-6485
www.marlboro.4mg.com

Charleston ☏ 843

BARS

■ **Dudley's on Ann** (B GLM MA) 16-2h
42 Ann Street ☏ (843) 577-6779
■ **Patrick's Pub** (AC B D GLM MA OS S T VS) 18-2h
1377 Ashley River Road ☏ (843) 571-3435
www.myspace.com/patrickspub1
Large dance floor.

DANCECLUBS

■ **Club Pantheon** (B D GLM MA S ST T) Fri-Sun 22-2h
28 Ann Street ☏ (843) 577-6779 www.clubpantheon.net

Columbia ☏ 803

BARS

■ **Capital Club** (B GLM MA P) 17-2h
1002 Gervais Street ☏ (803) 256-6464
Private club.
■ **P&T's 1109** (B D GLM P SNU T) 17-3, Fri -6, Sat & Sun -2h
1109 Assembly Street ☏ (803) 253-8900 www.pts1109.com
Strippers on Wed till Sat.

CRUISING

-Rest Stop (on I-26 South)
-Lake Murray Dam
-Univ of South Carolina (Russel House, Blatte PE Center lockers, pool and Thomas Cooper Library)
-Senate Street from Capitol to Gregg Street (ayor. Very busy at night)
-Main Street

Greenville ☏ 803

BARS

■ **Castle. The** (B D GLM P S ST VS) 21.30-4h, Mon-Thu closed
8-B Legrand Boulevard ☏ (803) 235-9949
www.castlesc.com
■ **Sugar Shack** (B D GLM MA ST) 18-?h, closed Tue & Wed
424 Laurens Road ☏ (803) 242-0294
www.sugarshackclub.com

Myrtle Beach ☎ 843

BARS

Time Out (AC B CC D GLM MA OS P S SNU ST) 17-?h
520 8th Avenue *Cnr. Oak St* ☎ (843) 448-1180 💻 www.timeoutmbsc.com

DANCECLUBS

Rainbow House. The (B D G MA) 15-5, Fri-Sun -2h
815 North Kings Highway ☎ (843) 626-7298
💻 www.rainbowhousemyrtlebeach.com

South Dakota

Location: North USA
Initials: SD
Time: GMT -6
Area: 199.744 km² / 81,695 sq mi.
Population: 754,844
Capital: Pierre

Sioux Falls ☎ 605

BARS

Toppers (AC B D GLM S) 15-2h, Sun closed
1213 North Cliff Avenue ☎ (605) 339-7686 💻 www.sdtoppers.com

Tennessee

Location: Central East
Initials: TN
Time: GMT -6
Area: 109.158 km² / 44,645 sq mi.
Population: 5,689,283
Capital: Nashville
Important gay cities: Memphis, Nashville

Chattanooga ☎ 423

BARS

Alan Gold's (B D GLM M MA SNU ST) 16.30-3h
1100 McCallie Ave ☎ (423) 629-8080
Chuck's II (B D GLM MA) 18-1, Fri & Sat -3h
27 West Main Street ☎ (423) 265-5405
Images (AC B CC D GLM M MA OS S) 17-3h
6005 Lee Highway ☎ (423) 855-8210 💻 imagesbar.com
Very large dance/ show bar.

Greeneville ☎ 423

GUEST HOUSES

Timberfell Lodge (AC B BF F G M MSG NU PI PK RWT SA WH) All year
PO Box 2010 *Exit 36, off 1-81* ☎ (423) 234-0833
💻 www.timberfell.com
Located in the Smokey Mountains. All rooms with TV and phone. Rooms with shared or private bath. Also ideal for camping.

Johnson City ☎ 423

BARS

New Beginnings (B D G M MA ST)
21-2, Fri & Sat 20-3h, closed Sun & Mon
2910 North Bristol Highway ☎ (423) 282-4446 💻 www.newb.com

Knoxville ☎ 865

BARS

Club XYZ (B D GLM MA) Wed-Sun 21-3h
1215 North Central ☎ (865) 637-4999 💻 www.clubxyz-knoxville.com
Kurt's (B D G M MA OS S) 18-3, Mon-Tue 21-3h
4928 Homberg Dr ☎ (865) 558-5720 💻 www.kurtsbar.com
New Rainbow Club West (B D GLM M MA ST) 17-3h
7211 Kingston Pike ☎ (865) 588-8030
💻 www.rainbowclubwest.com

CRUISING

-Fort Dickerson, off Chapman Highway (ayor)
-Downtown between post office and public library
-IC King Park (AYOR).

Memphis ☎ 901

GAY INFO

MGLCC – Memphis Gay & Lesbian Community Center
(GLM) Mon-Fri 14-21h
892 South Cooper ☎ (901) 278-6422 💻 www.mglcc.org

BARS

Backstreet Memphis / The Coliseum (B D GLM MA S)
2018 Court Street *Midtown, near Overton Square* ☎ (901) 722-3077
💻 www.backstreetmemphis.com
Bar with regular Cabaret and Karaoke shows. One of the largest dance bars in the city. Consists of two bars and one dance club (The Coliseum).
Crossroads (AC B GLM MA S ST) 16-24, Fri & Sat 15-3h
1278 Jefferson Avenue ☎ (901) 272-8801
Dru's Place (b CC D gLm M MA OS S)
Mon-Thu 11-24, Fri & Sat -3, Sun 12-24h
1474 Madison Avenue *Midtown, corner of Madison Ave and McNeil.*
☎ (901) 275-8082 💻 www.drusplace.com
Lorenz / Aftershock (B d GLM m MA OS) 11-3h
1528 Madison Avenue *At Avalon* ☎ (901) 274-8272
Metro Memphis (B D GLM m MA OS S) 18-3h
1349 Autumn Avenue *At Cleveland* ☎ (901) 274-8010
💻 www.backstreetmemphis.com
Karaoke Mon-Tue night, T-dance Sun from 16h.
Pumping Station. The (B CC D G M MA OS) 16-3, Fri-Sun 15-3h
1382 Poplar Avenue *1/2 block from Poplar & Cleveland*
☎ (901) 272-7600 💻 www.pumpingstationmemphis.com
Home of Tsarus, Memphis' oldest leather club. Cruise bar but women are welcome.

DANCECLUBS

901 Complex (B D GLM MA) Fri & Sat 22-?h
136 Webster Avenue ☎ (901) 522-8459
💻 www.myspace.com/nine01complex
Afro-american crowd.
Liquid Lounge (B D GLM MA) Wed only
557 S. Highland St.
Gay and Lesbian dance party every Wednesday night.

BOOK SHOPS

Davis Kidd Booksellers (b CC g m) 9-22, Sun 10-20h
387 Perkins Road Extended at Poplar Avenue in Laurelwood Shopping Center ☎ (901) 683-2032 💻 www.daviskidd.com
Also cafe.

Nashville ☎ 615

PUBLICATIONS

Out & About Newspaper Mon-Fri 9-18h
PO Box 330818 ☎ (615) 596-6210
💻 www.outandaboutnewspaper.com
Monthly gay newspaper and daily updated web site covering Tennessee and surrounding areas.

BARS

Blue Genes (B G MA) 15-3, Sun 11-3h, closed Mon
1715 Church Street ☎ (615) 329-3508 💻 www.bluegenes37203.com

■ **Lipstick Lounge. The** (B gLm M MA S)
16-3, Sat & Sun 18-3h, closed Mon
1400 Woodland Street ☎ (615) 226-6343
www.thelipsticklounge.com
Lesbian owned bar.

■ **Purple Heys** (B GLM M MA) 11-3h
1401 4th Avenue South ☎ (615) 242-8131

■ **Stirrup** (AC B CC G MA t) 12-3h
1529 4th Avenue ☎ (615) 782-0043 www.stirrupnashville.com

■ **Trax** (B G I MA) 12-3h
1501 2nd Avenue South *At Carney* ☎ (615) 742-8856
www.traxnashville.com

■ **Tribe** (B GLM M MA S VS) 16-24, Fri & Sat -2h
1517A Church Street ☎ (615) 329-2912 www.tribenashville.com
Bar-restaurant.

DANCECLUBS

■ **Play** (B D G MA S ST T) Wed-Sun 21-3h
1519 Church Street ☎ (615) 322-9627 www.playdancebar.com
Nashvilles Largest Gay Dance Club with DJs & drag shows nightly.

■ **Vibe** (B D G M MA OS ST) Sat 21-?h
1713 Church Street ☎ (615) 329-3838 www.vibenashville.com
After hours club, former Blu Bar, many latinos.

RESTAURANTS

■ **Mad Donna's** (B glm M MA ST)
Tue-Thu 11-22, Fri 11-24, Sat 10-24, Sun 10-22h
1313 Woodland Street ☎ (615) 226-1617 www.maddonnas.com
Restaurant with lounge and entertainment every night.

■ **Suzy Wong's House of Yum** (AC B CC GLM MA PK) Mon-Fri 11-2:30, Sun & Tue-Thu17-23, Fri & Sat 17-4h
1515 Church Street ☎ (615) 329-2913
www.suzywongsnashville.com
Asian fusion tapas, straight friendly.Late dining until 4 am on Friday & Saturday.

HEALTH GROUPS

■ **Nashville Cares** Mon-Fri 8.30-17h
501 Brick Church Park Drive ☎ (800) 845-4266 (toll free)
www.nashvillecares.org
AIDS information and support.

CRUISING

-Toilets at 100 Oaks Mall, Thompson Lane
-Hamilton Creek Park (ayor, police patrols).

Texas

Location: South USA
Initials: TX
Time: GMT -6
Area: 695.676 km² / 284,531 sq mi.
Population: 20,851,820
Capital: Austin
Important gay cities: Austin, Dallas, Houston, San Antonio

Amarillo ☎ 806

BARS

■ **Kick Back** (AC B GLM MA) 15-2h, closed Sun
521 East 10th Street ☎ (806) 371-3535

■ **Sassy's** (B GLM MA) 17-2, Fri-Sun 15-2h
309 West 6th Street ☎ (806) 374-3029

DANCECLUBS

■ **212 Club** (B D GLM MA ST) 14-2h
212 West 6th Avenue, PO Box 2903 ☎ (806) 372-7997
the212club.com
Fri and Sat live DJ from 22h, Wed leather & uniform night.

Arlington ☎ 817

BARS

■ **1851 Club** (B D GLM MA S ST) 15-2h
1851 Division Street ☎ (817) 801-9303 www.1851club.com

Austin ☎ 512

BARS

■ **Bout Time** (! B CC GLM MA) 14-2h
9601 IH-35 North *At Rundberg* ☎ (512) 832-5339
www.bouttimeaustin.com
Western-style bar with pool tables, video games, volleyball court.

■ **Chain Drive** (B CC f G MA) 16-2, Sun 16-2h, closed Mon
504 Willow Street ☎ (512) 480-9017 www.chain-drive.com

■ **Rain** (B d GLM OS YC) 16-2h
217 W 4th Street ☎ (512) 494-1150 www.rainon4th.com
Upscale lounge-bar, sometimes dancing.

■ **Rusty Spurs** (B D G MA ST) 16-2h, Mon closed
405 E. 7th Street ☎ (512) 482-9002 www.therustyspurs.com
Saloon-inspired bar featuring a variety of country western dancing several times a week. Dance lessons available.

DANCECLUBS

■ **Kiss and Fly Austin** (AC B D GLM SNU ST YC)
Wed, Thu & Sun 21-2; Fri & Sat 21-3.30h
404 Colorado St. ☎ (512) 476-7799 www.kissandflyaustin.com
With six bars, three levels and large dancefloor. Daily drink-specials and special events.

■ **Oilcan Harry's** (AC B CC D G MA OS S VS) 14-?, Fri-Sat -4h
211 West 4th Street *Between Lavaca & Colorado Street*
☎ (512) 320-8823 www.oilcanharrys.com
Dance bar, patio, multiple bar areas, pool tables. Popular especially after 23h.

SEX SHOPS/BLUE MOVIES

■ **New Video II** (g VS) 24hrs
7901 South I-35 ☎ (512) 280-1142

SAUNAS/BATHS

■ **Midtowne Spa** (b CC DU FC FH G MA OS SA SB VS WH WO) 24hrs
5815 Airport Boulevard *At Koenig* ☎ (512) 302-9696
www.midtowne.com
Bath house with an outdoor hot tub and many special rooms.

GUEST HOUSES

■ **Park Lane Guest House** (AC BF CC GLM I PA PI PK RWB RWS RWT VA) All year
221 Park Lane *Travis Hights/Soco district* ☎ (512) 447-7460
www.parklaneguesthouse.com
Lesbian run guesthouse with 3 guest cottages and 1 guest room.

CRUISING

-Pease Park (along Lamar Boulevard near West 15th from 22h)
-Mary Moore Searight Park (ayor)
-Toilets at Dobie Mall in Guadalupe Street (2nd floor)
- P Bull Creek Green Belt, Spicewood Springs Road
-Toilets at the university of Texas.

Bryan ☎ 979

DANCECLUBS

■ **Halo Bar** (AC B CC D GLM MA S VS) Thu-Sat 21.30-2h
121 North Main Street ☎ (979) 823-6174
Only GLBT nightclub in Bryan. Two levels with over 6,500 squarefeet with a 1st level video lounge and a second level dance bar. Live DJs every night with drink specials and bi-weekly drag shows.

Corpus Christi ☎ 361

BARS

Get Happy (B GLM MA) 12-2h
526 S Staples ☎ (361) 881-8910

Hidden Door (B d f G MA OS) 15-2, Fri-Sun 12-2h
802 South Staples Street ☎ (361) 882-5002

DANCECLUBS

Sixx (B D GLM MA S ST) Wed & Sun 21-1, Fri & Sat -4h
1212 Leopard Street ☎ (361) 888-7499 www.thesixx.com

GUEST HOUSES

Anthony's by the Sea (BF glm MA WH)
732 South Pearl Street, Rockport ☎ (361) 729-6100
www.anthonysbythesea.com

Dallas ☎ 214

GAY INFO

Dallas Tavern Guild
www.dallastavernguild.org
Info about GLBT Dallas, Pride events, Tavern Guild annual events, bar map and directory.

Gay & Lesbian Community Center (GLM MA)
Mon-Fri 9-21, Sat 10-17, Sun 12-17h
2701 Reagan Street *Community Center, community group meeting space*
☎ (214) 528-0144 www.rcdallas.org
GLBT programs and HIV services.

PUBLICATIONS

Dallas Voice. The
4145 Travis, 3rd Floor ☎ (214) 754-8710 www.dallasvoice.com

Rumba
4350 Maple Avenue ☎ (214) 556-1395 www.rumba.am
Gay Latino magazine.

BARS

Alexandre's (B D glm MA s) 14-2h
4026 Cedar Springs Road ☎ (214) 559-0720 www.alexandres.com

Barbara's Pavillion (B GLM OS) 16-2, Sat 18-2h
325 Centre Street ☎ (214) 941-2145 www.myspace.com/oakcliffpav

BJ's NXS (B G MA SNU) 12-2h
3215 N Fitzhugh ☎ (214) 526-9510 www.bjsnxs.com
Former Cruise-Inn.

Club Cherries (AC B D GLM MA SNU) Daily 12-2h
2506 Knight Street ☎ (214) 520-8251
Gay-lesbian strip bar with gogo-girls and boys.

Cross Bar (B D G MA OS S) 12-2h
5334 Lemmon Avenue ☎ (214) 443-8336

Dallas Eagle (B f G MA) Sun-Thu 16-2, Fri & Sat -4h
5740 Maple Avenue *Behind the strip mall* ☎ (214) 357-4375
www.dallaseagle.com
Levi/Leather bar

Drama Room, The (B D G) 12-2, Sun 13-2h
3851 Cedar Springs ☎ (214) 443-6020
www.facebook.com/pages/Drama-Room/117077128326420
Bar with male dancers.

Havana (B glm M MA ST) Wed-Sun 17-2h
4006 Cedar Springs Road ☎ (214) 526-9494
Latino crowd.

Hidden Door. The (B f G MA) Mon-Sat 7-2, Sun 12-2h
5025 Bowser Avenue ☎ (214) 526-0620
www.hiddendoor-dallas.com
Bar for butch men.

JR's Bar and Grill (AC B GLM M MA s) 11-2, Sun 12-2, Mon 13-2h
3923 Cedar Springs Road *At Throckmorton* ☎ (214) 528-1004
www.jrsdallas.com

Kaliente (B D G MA S ST) 21-2h, Mon-Tue closed
4350 Maple Avenue *Cnr. Hondo Ave* ☎ (214) 520-6676
www.kaliente.cc

Mining Company. The (AC B D F G MA) Wed-Sun 17-3h
3903 Cedar Springs Road ☎ (214) 559-0650 www.caven.com
A dance/cruise club for men.

Pekers (B GLM MA S) 10-2h
2615 Oaklawn Avenue ☎ (214) 528-3333 www.pekersbar.com

Pub Pegasus (B GLM MA) 10-2, Sun 13-1h
3326 N Fitzhugh Ave ☎ (214) 559-4663 www.pubpegasus.com

Rose Room. The (B GLM MA ST)
3911 Cedar Springs Road *Upstairs at Station 4* ☎ (214) 559-0650
www.caven.com
Showtimes Wed-Sun 23h & 0.30h.

Rush (B G MA SNU ST) 16-2, Sat 14-2, Sun 12-2h
3903 Lemmon Avenue ☎ (214) 780-0955 www.clubrushdallas.com

Sue Ellen's (B gLm MA s) 16-2, Fri & Sat 14-2h
3014 Throckmorton ☎ (214) 559-0650 www.caven.com

Tin Room (B G MA SNU) 10-2, Sun 12-2h
2514 Hudnall Street *Cnr. Maple Ave* ☎ (214) 526-6365
www.tinroom.net

Woody's (! B CC D G OS SNU ST) 14-2h
4011 Cedar Springs Road ☎ (214) 520-6629
www.dallaswoodys.com
Three bar areas, pool tables. Gorgeous men.

Zippers (B G MA S) 12-2h
3333 N Fitzhugh Avenue ☎ (214) 526-9519

MEN'S CLUBS

Club Babylon (B D G MA SNU)
Thu 20-2, Fri & Sat 23-6, Sun 20-2h
11311 Harry Hines Blvd. #203 ☎ (214) 247-0073
www.clubbabylondallas.com
All male gay club with strip shows and events, dark and naughty! See www.clubbabylondallas.com for details.

DANCECLUBS

Between Us @ Bacy's (AC B D GLM MA) 1st Sat/month 22-?h
2208 Main Street www.dallasfamily.org

Brick/Joe's. The (B D G MA S SNU) Daily 21-2h (unil 4h at WE)
2525 Wycliff *between Maple Ave. and the Tollway* ☎ (214) 521-3154
www.brickdallas.com
See:www.brickdallas.com for special events.

Elm & Pearl (B D GLM SNU ST YC)
2204 Elm St ☎ (214) 741-0000
Events as Frisky Fridays, Soulful Saturdays and Super Sunday Drag.

Klub Exklusive (AC B D G MA S VS) Thu-Sun 21-?h
4207 Maple Avenue ☎ (214) 520-3900 www.exklusive.tv
Very chic club, friendly bartenders and cool music. Hot latino boys.

Rieles, Los (B D G S)
600 S. Industrial Blvd. ☎ (214) 741-2125
www.myspace.com/losrielesdallas
Large Latino dance club with drag shows and entertainment.

Round-Up Saloon (! B D F G MA) 13-2h
3912 Cedar Springs Road ☎ (214) 522-9611
www.roundupsaloon.com
Western style bar and danceclub.

Station 4 (B CC D f G MA OS SNU ST VS) Wed-Sun 21-4h
3911 Cedar Springs Road ☎ (214) 526-7171 www.caven.com

SEX SHOPS/BLUE MOVIES

Amazing Superstores (g VS)
11327 Reeder Road *At Royal* www.amazing.net

New Fine Arts (G VS) 24hrs
1720 West Mockingbird Lane ☎ (214) 638-0765
www.sexysite.com

Paris Adult Bookstore & Theater (g VS) 24hrs
11118 Harry Hines Blvd

SAUNAS/BATHS

■ **Club. The** (! AC cc DU FC FH G m MA NU OS P PI PP RR SA SB SH SOL VS WH WO) 24hrs
2616 Swiss Avenue *East side of downtown, near Deep Ellum Arts district*
☎ (214) 821-1990 💻 www.the-clubs.com
THE CLUBS is a national chain of bath houses for gay men. Membership is required but can be used in any of the other locations. A huge gym with state of the art equipment. A re-modeled sundeck and a heated pool with breathtaking views of the downtown skyline. Totally remodeled facility. See: www.the-clubs.com for more information.

■ **Midtowne Spa**
(AC CC DR DU FC FH G M MA OS P SA SB VS WH WO) 24hrs
2509 Pacific Avenue ☎ (214) 821-8989 💻 www.midtowne.com

CONDOM SHOPS

■ **Condom Sense** (cc G MC)
4038 Cedar Springs Rd, Oaklawn ☎ ((214)) 522-3141
💻 www.condomsenseusa.com
Offering unique adult products for lovers such as vibrators, novelties, lubricants, and massage oils.

LEATHER & FETISH SHOPS

■ **Leather Masters** (CC F G MA) Tue-Sat 12-22h, Sun & Mon closed
3000 Main Street ☎ (214) 528-3865 💻 www.leathermasters.com

DVD SHOPS

■ **TapeLenders Video** (CC GLM VS) 9-24h
3926 Cedar Springs Road ☎ (214) 528-6344 💻 www.tapelenders.com
A very complete gay and lesbian video store. Unusual gifts for gay and lesbian taste.

GUEST HOUSES

■ **Daisy Polk Inn** (AC BF CC MA RWS RWT)
2917 Reagan Street ☎ (214) 522-4692 💻 www.daisypolkinn.com
Gay owned historic Inn next to the gay scene on Cedar Springs Road.

CRUISING

-Bachman Lake
-Cedar Springs Road (between Oaklawn & Dallas North Toll Road)
-Eastfield College (at night)
-Film World & Kit Kat Book Store (Industrial Boulevard)
-Greyhound Bus Depot
-"Homo Heights" (Oakland and Lemmon Avenues)
-Kiest Park (best on Sun)
-Lee Park (AYOR)
-Mid Continent Truck Stop (on Big Town Boulevard off I-20,east of I-30)
-News Stand Adult Book Store on Cedar Springs Road
-Paris Book I & II (AYOR) (Harry Hines Boulevard)
-Red Letter News (AYOR) (Harry Hines Boulevard)
-Reverchon Park (AYOR) (trails and trees)
-S.M.U. Main Library (1st & 2nd floor)
-Tower Bay Park (Lake Lewisville)
-Town East Mall (Sears)
-White Rock Lake (AYOR)
-Cedar Springs Road (AYOR) (south of to Maple Street, between Regan and Knight Streets).

Denison ☎ 903

BARS

■ **Good Time Lounge** (B GLM MA s) Wed-Sun 19-2h, closed Mon & Tues
2520 Highway 91N ☎ (903) 463-6086 💻 www.goodtimelounge.com

El Paso ☎ 915

BARS

■ **Briar Patch** (B G MA) 12-2h
508 Stanton Street ☎ (915) 577-9555 💻 www.briarpatch-ep.biz

■ **Chiquita's** (B GLM MA) 14-2h
310 Missouri Street ☎ (915) 351-0095

■ **San Antonio Mining Co** (B D G MA) 15-2h
800 East San Antonio Avenue *At Ochoa* ☎ (915) 533-9516

■ **Whatever Lounge. The** (B G MA) 14-2h
701 E. Paisano Drive ☎ (915) 533-0215

DANCECLUBS

■ **New Old Plantation** (B D GLM MA S VS)
21-2, Fri & Sat 21-4h, Mon-Wed closed
301 South Ochoa Street ☎ (915) 533-6055 💻 www.theoldplantation.com
Generation Q II pride store upstairs.

SEX SHOPS/BLUE MOVIES

■ **Tres Equis Exótica** (g MA)
2230 Texas Avenue *At Palm* ☎ (915) 532-6171
Videos, DVD, magazines, books, movie arcade, and more.

CRUISING

-Rest stop-20 miles on I-10 (AYOR) (tourists and truckers)
-Dyer Street (AYOR R) (after dark, weekends)
-McKelligon Canyon (off Alabama, near Beaumont Hospital).

Fort Worth ☎ 817

BARS

■ **Best Friends** (B GLM MA) 15-2h
2620 E Lancaster Avenue ☎ (817) 534-2280 💻 www.bestfriendsclub.net

■ **Crossroads** (B D G MA) 11-2h
515 South Jennings Avenue ☎ (817) 332-0071

■ **Rainbow Lounge. The** (B D GLM MA OS SNU ST)
651 South Jennings Street
Sat drag shows, Mon talent-night.

DANCECLUBS

■ **Copa Cabana** (AC B D glm S YC)
1002 S Main Street ☎ (817) 882-9504
Mixed hot and loud danceclub with many latinos.

CRUISING

-Rest Stop (on I-35 South)
-Benbrook Lake (AYOR) (off US 377, southwest of town)
-Forest Park (picnic area)
-Rockwood Park (days)
-T.C.U. (Burnett Library).

Galveston ☎ 409

BARS

■ **Pink Dolphin** (B G MA ST) 12-2h
1828 Strand ☎ (409) 621-1808

■ **Robert's Lafitte** (AC B CC d GLM m MA OS r s ST) 7-2, Sun 12-2h
2501 Avenue Q *1 block to the beach* ☎ (409) 765-9092
Oldest gay bar on the island, no cover charge, drag shows on WE. Patio.

■ **Third Coast** (B GLM MA) 12-2h
2416 Post Office Street ☎ (409) 765-6911

Groesbeck ☎ 254

CAMPING

■ **Rainbow Ranch** (GLM MA) All year
1662 LCR 800 ☎ (254) 729-8484 💻 www.rainbowranch.net

Gun Barrel City ☎ 903

BARS

■ **Friends** (AC B CC d GLM m MA OS P ST)
Mon-Fri 16-24, Sat 15-1, Sun -24h
410 South Gun Barrel Lane *Highway 198, next to the Wagon Wheel Restaurant* ☎ (903) 887-2061 💻 www.friendsnightclub.net

Houston ☏ 713

PUBLICATIONS

■ OutSmart Magazine
3406 Audubon Place ☏ (713) 520-7237
www.outsmartmagazine.com
Monthly magazine covering community news for Texas, also with a directory for Houston.

BARS

■ 611 Hyde Park Club (AC B CC f G m MA OS r)
Mon-Sat 7-2, Sun 12-2h
611 Hyde Park Boulevard / Stanford Street *Montrose district*
☏ (713) 526-7070
Busy happy hour and DJs. Buffet dinner on weekends. Some hustlers.

■ Bayou City Bar & Grill (B D glm M MA OS) 16-2h, closed Mon
2409 Grant St. ☏ (713) 522-2867 www.bayoucitybar.com
Check website for events. Centrally located in houstons gay district.

■ Blur (B D GLM MA) 20-2, Sun 18-2h
710 Pacific Street ☏ (713) 529-3447 www.blurbar.com

■ Brazos River Bottom Club (B D G MC) 12-2h
2400 Brazos Street *Between Hadley & McIlhenny* ☏ (713) 528-9192
www.brbhouston.com
Popular. Country / Western music. Three bars, a packed dance floor, friendly barmen.

■ Club 2020 (AC B D GLM MA)
2020 Leeland ☏ (713) 227-9667 www.club2020houston.com
Mostly African American crowd.

■ Crocker (B GLM MA) 11-2h
2312 Crocker Street ☏ (713) 529-3355
Gay owned neighbourhood bar.

■ Decades (B GLM MA) 11-2, Sun 12-2h
1205 Richmond Avenue ☏ (713) 521-2224

■ E.J.'s (AC B d f GLM m MA OS SNU ST) 7-2h
2517 Ralph Street *Off Westheimer* ☏ (713) 527-9071

■ George (B G MA OS) 19-2, Sun 12-2h
617 Fairview Street *Cnr. Stanford St* ☏ (713) 528-8102
georgescountrysportsbar.com

■ Guava Lamp (B CC GLM I MA S VS) 14-2h
570 Waugh Drive *Montrose* ☏ (713) 524-3359
www.guavalamphouston.com
Upscale martini lounge / video bar.

■ In & Out (B GLM MA) 16-2h
1537 North Shepherd Road ☏ (713) 589-9780

■ JR's Bar & Grill (AC B CC GLM MA S SNU VS) 12-2h
804/808 Pacific Street *Downtown, Montrose area* ☏ (713) 521-2519
www.JRsBarandGrill.com
Very popular and cruisy.

■ Meteor (AC B CC GLM MA S SNU VS WE) 16-2, Sat 18-2, Sun 15-24h
2306 Genesee Street *At Fairview* ☏ (713) 521-0123
www.meteorhouston.com

■ Mike's Outpost (B G MC S ST) 15-2, Fri-Sun 12-2h
1419 Richmond ☏ (713) 520-8446

■ Montrose Mining Company (AC B CC F G MA OS S SNU) Mon-Fri 16-2, Sat & Sun 13-2h
805 Pacific Street *Downtown, Montrose area* ☏ (713) 529-7488
Very popular cruise bar.

■ Ripcord (B F G MC OS) Sun-Thu 13-2, Fri & Sat -4h
715 Fairview Avenue ☏ (713) 521-2792 www.theripcord.com

■ T.C.'s (B G MA ST) 11-2, Sun 12-2h
817 Fairview Street ☏ (713) 528-9204
Famous for its drag shows. Former „Cousins".

■ Tony's Corner Pocket (B D GLM MA S) 12-2h
817 West Dallas Street *Between Arthur & Crosby St* ☏ (713) 571-7870
www.tonycornerpocketbar.com

■ Viviana's (B cc d G MA SNU ST) 17-2h, closed Mon
4624 Dacoma Street ☏ (713) 681-4101 www.vivianasniteclub.com
Latino club.

■ Whispers (AC B D GLM MA S) 16-2, Wed & Sun -24h, closed Mon
226 First Street East Humble ☏ (713) 359-2900
www.whispersbar.com

DANCECLUBS

■ Club Adam & Eve (B D GLM MA SNU) 19-2h
522 Nasa Parkway, Webster ☏ (281) 557-0434
www.myspace.com/club_adams
Features two clubs: one for the boys (Adam) and one for the girls (Eve).

■ Crystal (AC B D GLM MA)
6680 Southwest Freeway ☏ (713) 278-2582
www.crystaltheclub.com
Many hot Latinos.

■ F Bar (! AC B D G MA OS S SNU ST) daily -2h
202 Tuam St ☏ (713) 522 3227 www.fbarhouston.com
Stylish bar and dancing, hot boys, hot music, hot everything! Sunday brunch party on the patio from 15-2h. Strictly 21 and over.

■ Ranch Hill Saloon (B D GLM MA) 13-2h
24704 I-45, Suite 103, Spring *North of Houston* ☏ (281) 298-9035
www.ranchhill.com

■ South Beach (AC B CC D GLM S SNU ST VS YC)
Wed-Sat 21-4, Sun 17-4h
810 Pacific Avenue *Downtown, Montrose area* ☏ (713) 529-7623
www.southbeachthenightclub.com
Most popular disco in town and after hours.

SAUNAS/BATHS

■ Club. The
(! b CC DU FC FH G m MA OS P PI RR SA SB SH SOL VS WH WO) 24hrs
2205 Fannin Street ☏ (713) 659-4998 www.the-clubs.com
THE CLUBS is a national chain of private membership clubs and for that reason you must purchase a membership card in order to use the facilities. Complete entertainment and physical fitness complex with outdoor pool parties at the WE. See: www.the-clubs.com for more information.

■ Midtowne Spa
(b DU FC FH G MA OS PI SA SB SL SOL VS WH WO) 24hrs
3100 Fannin Street ☏ (713) 522-2379
www.midtowne.com
Bath house with outdoor garden for sun tanning and a steam room modelled after a dark cave with numerous caverns to explore. Many special rooms available.

LEATHER & FETISH SHOPS

■ Black Hawk Leather (F G) 12-20h
711 Fairview Ave www.blackhawkleather.com

GENERAL GROUPS

■ Houston GLBT Community Center (GLM)
Mo-Fri 18-21, Sat & Sun 13-17h
1901 Kane Street *Historic Dow School* ☏ (713) 524-3818
www.houstonglbtcommunitycenter.org
Provides activities including arts & culture, collaborations with other groups, education & public policy, information resources and support groups/ leadership development.

CRUISING

-Bayland Park (on Bissonet)
-Corner of Michigan and Yupon „Club Luscene"
-Galleria Mall/Skating Rink (AYOR)
-Golden Star Theatre (r) (912 Prairie Street, 24h)
-Kasmiersky Park toilets
-Memorial Park and adjacent pathway (AYOR)
-Rest Stop (15 E. on I-10)
-Rest Stop (on I-10 / Columbia)
-Rice U (Memorial Center & Library)
-University of Houston (library, 2nd floor & all A.A. Hall)
-Vicinity of both bus depots
-Westheimer (Montrose)
-YMCA.

Lubbock ☎ 806

DANCECLUBS

Club Luxor (B D glm MA) Thu-Sun 21-2h
2211 4th Street ☎ (806) 744-3744 www.clubluxor.com
Live DJs.

McAllen ☎ 956

BARS

PBDs (B D G MA SNU ST) 20-2h, Mon closed
2908 North Wate Road ☎ (956) 682-8019
www.pbds-mcallentx.com

Trade (AC B D GLM S) Thu-Sat 22-3h
2010 Nolana Avenue ☎ (956) 630-6304

San Antonio ☎ 210

BARS

2015 Place (B D G MA SNU) 16-2h
2015 San Pedro Avenue ☎ (210) 733-3365

Annex (AC B F G MA s) 14-2h
330 San Pedro Avenue ☎ (210) 223-6957
www.theannex-satx.com

Club Unity (AC B GLM MA) 12-2h
1210 East Elmira Street ☎ (210) 320-3787
www.myspace.com/clubunitysa

Cobalt Club (B GLM MA SNU) 7-2, Sun 12-2h
2022 McCullough Avenue ☎ (210) 734-2244

Electric Company (B GLM MA SNU) Tue-Sun 21-3h
820 San Pedro Avenue ☎ (210) 212-6635

Essence (B G MA) 14-2h
1010 North Main Avenue ☎ (210) 223-5418

One-O-Six (B G M MC) 12-2h
106 Pershing Avenue ☎ (210) 820-0906

Pegasus (B CC F GLM MA OS S) 14-2h
1402 North Main Avenue ☎ (210) 299-4222
www.pegasussanantonio.com
Main bar with DJ, Country bar with DJ (WE), leather bar with leather store, patio bar with karaoke.

Saint. The (B D G MA S ST) 16-2h
1430 North Main Street ☎ (210) 225-7330

Silver Dollar Saloon (B GLM MA SNU) 14-2h
1418 N Main Avenue ☎ (210) 227-2623

Sparky's Pub (AC B CC d G MA SNU VS) 14-2h
1416 North Main Avenue ☎ (210) 894-3617 www.sparkyspub.com

MEN'S CLUBS

Alternative Club Inc (B G MA P PI) 12-21h
827 E Elmira Street ☎ (210) 223-2177

DANCECLUBS

Bermuda Triangle (B CC D gLm MA S ST) Tue-Sun
119 El Mio Drive ☎ (210) 342-2276 www.bermudatrianglesa.com

Bonham Exchange (AC B CC D glm MA S SNU VS) Mon-Tue closed, Wed-Fri 16-3, Sat 20-4, Sun 19.30-2h
411 Bonham Street *Behind the Alamo* ☎ (210) 271-3811
www.bonhamexchange.com
Multi-level dance club in a 110 year old historical building hosting up to 2000 people.

Heat (B D GLM MA OS ST) 21-2h, closed Mon
1500 North Main Avenue *At Evergreen* ☎ (210) 227-2600
www.heatsa.com

RESTAURANTS

Luther's Cafe (AC B CC GLM I MA OS S) 11-3h
1425 North Main Avenue *On the Main Ave Strip* ☎ (210) 894-3617
www.lutherssa.com

SEX SHOPS/BLUE MOVIES

Encore-Video.com (AC CC glm MA)
Mon & Tue 9-22, Wed-Sat 9-24, Sun 10-22h
1031 North East Loop 410 *Next to airport* ☎ (210) 821-5345
www.encore-video.com
Video rental and sales.

SAUNAS/BATHS

ACI, Alternative Club (B DR G m MA OS PI SA SB SOL VS WH WO) Mon-Thu 12-9h, Fri-Sun non-stop
827 E. Elmira Street ☎ (210) 223-2177
Older but clean sauna.

Executive Health Club
(b DU FC FH G m MA RR SA SOL VS WH WO) 24hrs
402 Austin Street *Near cnr. Lamar St* ☎ (210) 732-4433
www.bartalksa.com
Gay health club with many latinos.

GIFT & PRIDE SHOPS

Zebraz.com (AC CC GLM MA) 10-22h
1608 North Main Avenue *Next to San Antonio College* ☎ (210) 472-2800
www.zebraz.com
One of the largest gay and lesbian department stores.

GUEST HOUSES

Arbor House Suites B&B (AC cc glm RWB RWS RWT WH) Office 8-22h
109 Arciniega Street *Downtown San Antonio, 1 1/2 blocks from the Riverwalk* ☎ (210) 472-2005 www.arborhouse.com
Four 2 story cottages, each with refrigerator & microwave. Some suites have private balcony. Continental breakfast served at room. Gay owned & operated.

Waco ☏ 254

BARS

■ **Trix** (B GLM MA ST) Thu 22-2, Fri-Sat 20-2h
110 South 6th Street ☏ (254) 714-0767 www.trixclub.com

Wichita Falls ☏ 940

BARS

■ **Odds** (B GLM MA) 16.30-2, Thu & Sun from 15h
1205 Lamar Street ☏ (940) 322-2996

Utah

Location: West USA
Initials: UT
Time: GMT -7
Area: 219.902 km² / 89,940 sq mi.
Population: 2,233,170
Capital: Salt Lake City

Salt Lake City ☏ 801

GAY INFO

■ **Utah Pride Center** (AC GLM MA T) Mon-Fri 10-18h
355 North 300 West, 1st floor ☏ (801) 539-8800
www.utahpridecenter.org
Includes library with over 3,000 circulating items. Many different organizations meet here. Also includes a coffee-shop. Excellent list of links for gay associations and groups in Utah.

PUBLICATIONS

■ **Q Salt Lake** (GLM)
PO Box 511247 ☏ (801) 323-9500 www.qsaltlake.com

BARS

■ **Club Try-Angles** (B D G MA) 14-2h
251 West 900 South ☏ (801) 364-3203
www.clubtry-angles.com
Special offer on beer on Tue, Fri & Sun nights.

■ **JAM** (B D GLM MA OS) Tue-Sat 17h-open end
751 N. 300 West ☏ (801) 891-1162 www.jamslc.com
Gay eco Club and Bar with bamboo floor, natural stone bar and non-hazardous paint.

■ **Trapp. The** (AC B CC D f GLM m MC OS P s VS) 11-2h
102 South 600 West ☏ (801) 531-8727
www.thetrappslc.com/The_Trapp/Home.html
Country/Western music & dancing.

DANCECLUBS

■ **Pachanga @ Karamba** (AC B D G MA) Sun 21-?h
1051 East 2100 South ☏ (801) 637-9197
www.myspace.com/manuel_arano

GUEST HOUSES

■ **Under the Lindens** (AC BF GLM I MA PK RWS RWT VA WH) 8-20h
128 South 1000 East *Downtown* ☏ (801) 355-9808
www.underthelindens.com
4 suites. Kitchen, bath and living space. Gay-owned and operated.

HEALTH GROUPS

■ **People With AIDS Coalition of Utah**
358 South 300 East ☏ (801) 484-2205 www.pwacu.org
Also computers with internet access available.

■ **Utah AIDS Foundation** Mon-Fri 9-18h
1408 South 1100 East *Cream building behind parking building*
☏ (801) 487-2323 www.utahaids.org

CRUISING

-Harmony Park (car cruising)
-Liberty Park
-Memory Grove Park
-South Main (and surrounding area, evenings)
-Vicinity of Greyhound Bus Depot.

Vermont

Location: Northeast USA
Initials: VT
Time: GMT -5
Area: 24.903 km² / 10,185 sq mi.
Population: 608,827
Capital: Montpelier

Brattleboro ☏ 802

GUEST HOUSES

■ **Frog Meadow Farm** (BF G I MA MSG WH WO) All year
34 Upper Spring Hill Road ☏ (802) 365-7242
www.frogmeadow.com
Situated on 63 beautiful and private acres in Southeastern Vermont with mountain views, extensive perennial gardens, and a wood fired hot tub.

Burlington ☏ 802

HOTELS

■ **Black Bear Inn. The**
(AC b BF CC glm H M OS PA PI PK RWB RWS RWT VA WH) All year
4010 Bolton Access Road, Bolton Valley *30 mins from Burlington, in Vermont's Green Mountains* ☏ (802) 434-2126
blackbearinn.travel
For nature and sport lovers.

CRUISING

-Battery Park (North Public Beach)
-Main Square (opposite Bus Terminal)
-Univ of Vermont (Baily Howe Library, 3rd and 4th floor).

Chester ☏ 802

GUEST HOUSES

■ **Williams River House** (BF glm I MA PA PK RWS) All year
397 Peck Road ☏ (802) 875-1790 www.williamsriverhouse.com
All 4 suites have their own bathrooms and are supplied with handmade soaps.

Killington ☏ 802

HOTELS

■ **Cortina Inn & Resort** (AC B BF CC glm H M MA MSG OS PA PI RWB RWS RWT SA WH WO) All year
103 US Route 4 ☏ (802) 773-3333 www.cortinainn.com
96 guestrooms. Gay-friendly resort with tons of facilities.

Websterville ☏ 802

GUEST HOUSES

■ **Millstone Hill** (AC BF glm H MA PA PI PK RWS WO)
59 Little John Road ☏ (802) 479-1000 millstonehill.com

Wells River ☏ 802

GUEST HOUSES

■ **Gargole House. The** (AC bf cc G I m MA MSG NU PA PK RWB RWS SA VA VS WH WO) All year
3351 Wallace Hill Road ☏ (802) 429-2341 www.gargoylehouse.com

Windham ☏ 802

GUEST HOUSES

■ **Stone Wall Inn. A** (CC G PI PK RWB RWS SA SB WH) All year
578 Hitchcock Hill Road ☏ (802) 875-4238 🖳 www.astonewallinn.com
A Stonewall Inn with its ten guestrooms was designed by an award-winning architect. It is solar heated and uses local and recycled materials.

Virginia

Location: East USA
Initials: VA
Time: GMT -5
Area: 110.792 km² / 45,313 sq mi.
Population: 7,078,515
Capital: Richmond

Cape Charles ☏ 757

GUEST HOUSES

■ **Sea Gate B&B** (AC BF GLM I MA PK RWB RWS RWT) All year
9 Tazewell Avenue *Small town located on the shore of the Chesapeake Bay*
☏ (757) 331-2206 🖳 www.seagatebb.com
Four rooms with bath, balcony, phone, TV and radio.

Charlottesville ☏ 804

DANCECLUBS

■ **Club 216** (B D GLM MA P s t) Fri & Sat 22-5h
216 West Water Street, Suite F ☏ (804) 296-8783 🖳 www.club216.com
Occasional shows on Sat. Check www.club216.com for info.

CRUISING

-Rest Stop (Route 64, west of Ivy)
-Lee Park (AYOR).

Norfolk ☏ 757

BARS

■ **Garage. The** (B f G M MA S) Mon-Sat 20-2, Sun 13-2h
731 Granby Street ☏ (757) 623-0303
■ **Nutty Buddys** (B GLM m MA S ST) Sun-Wed 16-2h
143 East Little Creek Road ☏ (757) 588-6474
■ **Wave. The** (B D GLM MA S) 16-2, Sat 17-2h, Sun closed
4107 Colley Avenue *At 41st Street* ☏ (757) 440-5911
Dancers on Wed.

CRUISING

-Ghent Gay Ghetto (around Colley and Princess Anne Road)
-Ocean View Public Park (AYOR)
-Watside Park (South Military Highway, days).

Richmond ☏ 804

BARS

■ **Barcode** (B G MA) 11-2, Fri-Sun 15-2h
6 East Grace Street ☏ (804) 648-2040 🖳 www.barcodeva.com
■ **Godfrey's** (AC B CC D GLM M MA S ST)
Tue 11-14, Wed -2, Thu, Fri, Sun -?, Sat 17-?h, Mon closed
308 East Grace Street *Between 3rd and 4th Street* ☏ (804) 648-3957
🖳 www.godfreysva.com
Sundays Drag Brunch voted best in Richmond.
Check www.godfreysva.com for details.

DANCECLUBS

■ **Club Colors** (B D GLM MA) Sat 21-3h
536 North Harrison Street ☏ (804) 353-9776
More women until 23.30, men from 23.30h.

CRUISING

-The Block (Grace and Franklin between Adams and 3rd)
-The Rocks (James River Park, North Bank near South end of Meadow St)
-Belle Isle (James River Park)
-Bryant Park (summer)
-Byrd Park (AYOR)
-Monroe Park
-Pumphouse Drive (summer)
-The Battle Abby (behind the VA museum).

Roanoke ☏ 540

BARS

■ **Backstreet Café** (B GLM M MA) 19-2, Sun -24h
356 Salem Avenue ☏ (540) 345-1542
■ **Park. The** (B D GLM SNU VS YC) Fri-Sun 21-?h
615 Salem Avenue ☏ (540) 342-0946
🖳 www.facebook.com/pages/The-Park-Roanoke/227633170747

Virginia Beach ☏ 757

BARS

■ **Ambush** (B GLM M MA SNU ST) 17-2h
475 South Lynnhaven Road ☏ (757) 498-4301 🖳 www.klubambush.com
■ **In-Between** (B BF GLM M SNU) 16-2, Sat 17-2h
5266 Princess Anne Road ☏ (757) 490-9498 🖳 www.theinbetweenbar.com
Also restaurant, brunch on Sun.
■ **Rainbow Cactus. The** (B d GLM M MA ST) Wed-Sun 19-2h
3472 Holland Road ☏ (757) 368-0441 🖳 www.therainbowcactus.com

Washington

Location: Northwest USA
Initials: WA
Time: GMT -8
Area: 184.672 km² / 75,530 sq mi.
Population: 5,894,121
Capital: Olympia
Important gay cities: Seattle

Bellingham ☏ 360

BARS

■ **Rumors Cabaret** (AC B D GLM M MA) 16-2h
1119 Railroad Avenue ☏ (360) 671-1849 🖳 www.rumorsCabaret.com

Bremerton ☏ 360

BARS

■ **Brewski's** (B g m MA) 11-2h
2810 Kitsap Way ☏ (360) 479-9100

Kent ☏ 253

BARS

■ **Swank** (B D GLM MA) 15-2, Sat & Sun 12-2h
24437 Russell Road ☏ (253) 854-2110 🖳 www.swankkent.com
■ **Vibe** (B D GLM MA) 12-2, Sun & Mon -24h
226 1st Ave S *Between Gowe & Meeker St* ☏ (253) 852-0815
🖳 www.myspace.com/vibekent

Long Beach ☏ 360

GUEST HOUSES

■ **Anthony's Home Court** (AC CC glm I OS PA PK RWS RWT) All year
1310 Pacific Highway North ☏ (360) 642-2802
🖳 www.anthonyshomecourt.com

Olympia ☎ 360

BARS

■ **Jakes on 4th Ave** (B d G SNU ST) 16-2h
311 East 4th Avenue ☎ (360) 956-3247 🖳 www.jakeson4th.com

Pasco ☎ 509

BARS

■ **Out and About** (AC B CC D GLM I M MA S ST WE)
18-2h, closed Sun & Mon
327 West Lewis ☎ (509) 543-3796 🖳 www.cluboutandabout.com
Fri open to 18+. All other days 21 year old and over only. Cover charge on Fri & Sat. Tue is karaoke night. Restaurant and lounge. Drag shows on Wed and Thu.

Seattle ☎ 206

GAY INFO

■ **Seattle LGBT Community Center. The** (GLM)
10-21, Sun 11-20h
1122 East Pike Street ☎ (206) 323-5428 🖳 www.seattlelgbt.org

PUBLICATIONS

■ **SGN – Seattle Gay News** (GLM)
1605 12th Avenue #31 ☎ (206) 324-4297 🖳 www.sgn.org
Local weekly news & entertainment newspaper. Published every Fri.

BARS

■ **C.C. Attle's** (B G M MA OS VS) 20-2h
1501 East Madison *At 15th Ave* ☎ (206) 726-0565
🖳 www.ccattles.net

■ **Changes** (B G M MA VS) 12-2h
2103 North 45th Street, Wallingford *At Meridian* ☎ (206) 545-8363
🖳 www.changesinwallingford.com

■ **Crescent Lounge. The** (B g MA) 12-2h
1413 East Olive Way, Capitol Hill *At Bellevue* ☎ (206) 720-8188

■ **Cuff. The** (! AC B CC D f G I MA OS VS) 14-2h
1533 13th Avenue *On Capitol Hill* ☎ (206) 323-1525
🖳 www.cuffcomplex.com
One of the most popular men's bars in Seattle.

■ **Double Header** (B g MA) 10-24, Fri & Sat -2h
407 2nd Avenue South, Downtown *At Washington* ☎ (206) 464-9918

■ **Elite. The** (B GLM MA) 12-2h
1520 E. Olive Way ☎ (206) 860-0999 🖳 www.theeliteseattle.com

■ **Lobby Bar** (B GLM m MA) 15-24, Thu-Sat -2h
918 East Pike Street ☎ (206) 328-6707
🖳 www.thelobbyseattle.com
Gay bar on two levels.

■ **Madison Pub** (AC B CC GLM I M MA) 12-2h
1315 East Madison Street *On Madison St. between 13 & 14 Ave*
☎ (206) 325-6537 🖳 www.madisonpub.com
Friendly locals bar with pool, darts, pinball games and an always on national trivia game. Multiple TV's for sports events. Pool & Dart Tourneys. Happy Hours Mon-Sat 18-20h.

■ **Pony** (AC B CC G I MA OS) Mon-Thu 17-2, Fri-Sun 16-2h
1221 E Madison St *Near cnr. E Union Street* ☎ (206) 324-2854
🖳 www.ponyseattle.com
Cruise bar.

■ **Purr** (B G M MA) 15-2, Sun 14-24h
1518 11th Avenue *At E Pike St* ☎ (206) 325-3112
🖳 www.purrseattle.com
Happy hour (special drinks and dishes) Mon-Sat 15-19, Sun 14-19h. Mon & Tue Karaoke.

■ **R Place** (B f GLM m MA SNU VS) 16-2, Sat & Sun 14-2h
619 East Pine Street, Capitol Hill *Near Boylston* ☎ (206) 322-8828
🖳 www.rplaceseattle.com
A video-sport bar on three floors.

■ **Re-bar** (B D glm MA S) 22-2h, closed Mon
1114 Howell Street ☎ (206) 233-9873 🖳 www.rebarseattle.com

■ **Seattle Eagle** (B F G MA OS) 14-2h
314 East Pike Street *At Bellevue* ☎ (206) 621-7591
🖳 www.SeattleEagle.com
Many theme nights.

■ **Sonya's Bar & Grill** (B G M MC) 13.30-2h
1919 1st Avenue, Downtown *Between Virginia & Stewart*
☎ (206) 624-5377

MEN'S CLUBS

■ **Tribe** (B DR f G MA VS) 24hrs
1505 10th Avenue ☎ (206) 323-2799 🖳 tribeseattle.com
Not a gay sauna, but showers and lockers available. Cruise bar.

DANCECLUBS

■ **Neighbours** (B D GLM YC)
Tue-Thu, Sun 21-2; Fri & Sat 21-4h
1509 Broadway East/Pike Street *Entrance rear alley* ☎ (206) 324-5358
🖳 www.neighboursnightclub.com
The longest continually operating dance club in Seattle.

SAUNAS/BATHS

■ **Club Z** (CC DR DU F FC FH G GH I LAB M MA P RR SA SB SL VR VS)
24hrs
1117 Pike Street *Near Boren Avenue, two blocks East of the Washington State Convention and Trade Centre on Pike* ☎ (206) 622-9958
🖳 www.thezclub.com
Three floors sauna, labyrinth, large SM rooms, frequented by leather fans, but has a very diverse crowd of visitors.

■ **Steamworks Seattle** (AC DR DU FC G I MA P RR SB VS WE)
Daily, 24hrs
1520 Summit Avenue *Located in the Capital Hill Neighborhood off of Pike St.* ☎ (206) 388-4818 🖳 www.steamworksonline.com
Steamworks is a private men's bathhouse for men 18 years and older. This sauna belongs to a group which has properties in Chicago, Seattle and Berkeley, USA as well as Toronto and Vancouver in Canada. Membership applies to all 5 bath houses.

HOTELS

■ **Ace Hotel. The** (B bf CC glm I M MA) 7-24h
2423 First Avenue ☎ (206) 448-4721 🖳 www.acehotel.com
Gay owned design hotel.

GUEST HOUSES

■ **Bacon Mansion** (BF CC GLM I MA NR PK RWS RWT WI) All year
959 Broadway East *Capitol Hill* ☎ (206) 329-1864 ☎ 240-1864
🖳 www.baconmansion.com
9 rooms with private bath, 2 with shared bath. Library, living room with grand piano, patio with fountain between main house and carriage house, children allowed in some rooms.

■ **Gaslight Inn** (bf CC glm I MA OS PI RWS RWT VA) All year
1727 15th Avenue ☎ (206) 325-3654 🖳 www.gaslight-inn.com

Spokane ☎ 509

GAY INFO

■ **Inland Northwest LGBT Center** (GLM MA)
508 West 2nd Avenue ☎ (509) 489-1914 🖳 thelgbtcenter.org

BARS

■ **Dempseys Brass Rail** (AC B CC GLM M MA S)
15-2, Fri & Sat -4h
909 W 1st Avenue *Between Lincoln & Monroe* ☎ (509) 747-5362
🖳 www.dempseysbrassrail.net

CRUISING

-High Bridge (NU) (People's Park)
-Manito Park and Mission Park (AYOR).

Tacoma ☎ 253

BARS

Airport Tavern (B GLM MA) 14-2h
5406 South Tacoma Way ☎ (253) 475-9730

Club Silverstone (B D GLM M MA) 11-2h
739 St Helens Avenue ☎ (253) 404-0273

SEX SHOPS/BLUE MOVIES

Castle Superstore Adult Retail (g) 24hrs
6015 Tacoma Mall Boulevard ☎ (253) 471-0391
www.castlemegastore.com
Videos, leather, lingerie, magazines, toys, novelties, books, DVDs.

CRUISING

-Nude beach (follow railroad track 1 mile north of Chambers Creek)
-Wright Park (between 6th & G St).

West Virginia

Location: East USA
Initials: WV
Time: GMT -5
Area: 62.759 km² / 25,668 sq mi.
Population: 1,808,344
Capital: Charleston

Charleston ☎ 304

BARS

Broadway (B D GLM MA OS ST) 16-3, Fri-Sun 13-3h
210 Leon Sullivan Way ☎ (304) 343-2162 www.broadwaywv.com

Huntington ☎ 304

BARS

Jackhammer (AC B D F G MA S) 17-2h
2127 Manchester Avenue ☎ (304) 781-2520
www.myspace.com/thejackhammerclub

Polo Club (B d GLM MA P ST) 17-1, Fri-Sun 14-1h
1037 7th Avenue ☎ (304) 522-3146

Stonewall Club. The (AC B CC D GLM MA OS P S SNU ST) 20-3h, Mon-Tue closed
820 7th Avenue *Entrance in alley* ☎ (304) 523-2242
www.stonewallclub.com
Incredible light show, super-friendly bartenders. Themed nights. West Virginias hottest dance and show bar.

Morgantown ☎ 304

BARS

Vice Versa (B D GLM MA S ST) Thu-Sun 20-3h
335 High Street ☎ (304) 292-2010 www.viceversaclub.com

Weezie's Pub & Club (B GLM) 20-?h, closed Sun
3438 University Avenue ☎ (304) 598-0088
www.myspace.com/weeziespubandclub

Parkersburg ☎ 304

BARS

Woodstarr (B D GLM MA ST) Wed-Sun 18-3h
322 5th Street ☎ (304) 422-3711 www.woodstarr.com

Wheeling ☎ 304

CAMPING

Roseland Resort (B D G MA NU P PI)
RD. 1, Box 185B, Proctor ☎ (304) 455-3838 www.RoselandWV.com

Wisconsin

Location: Great Lakes region USA
Initials: WI
Time: GMT -6
Area: 169.643 km² / 69,383 sq mi.
Population: 5,363,675
Capital: Madison
Important gay cities: Milwaukee

Appleton ☎ 920

BARS

Rascals Bar & Grill (B GLM M MA OS)
Mon-Thu 17-2, Fri-Sat -2.30, Sun 12-2h
702 East Wisconsin Ave ☎ (920) 954-9262 www.rascalsbar.com

Ravens (AC B D G MA ST) 20-2h, closed Sun & Mon
215 East College Avenue ☎ (920) 364-9559 www.ravensnightclub.com

CRUISING

-Sunset Park, in Kimberly at the boat landing parking lot (at night only)
-Lutz Park.

Beloit ☎ 608

BARS

Club Impulse (B D GLM MA)
18-2, Fri 17-2.30, Sat 19-2.30h, closed Mon
132 West Grand Avenue ☎ (608) 361-0000
www.clubimpulsebeloit.com

Eau Claire ☎ 715

BARS

Scooters (B D GLM MA ST) 15-2, Fri & Sat -2.30h
411 Galloway Street ☎ (715) 835-9959 www.scooters-bar.com

Green Bay ☎ 920

BARS

Napalese Lounge (B G M MA ST) 11-?h
1351 Cedar Street ☎ (920) 432-9646

Sass (AC B d GLM MA S)
18-2h, closed Sun-Wed in summer (Mon-Wed in winter)
840 South Broadway ☎ (920) 437-7277

DANCECLUBS

Shelter. The (B D GLM MA S ST T) 16-2h
730 N Quincy Street ☎ (920) 432-2662

CRUISING

-Rest Stop (AYOR) (on US 41, South of DePere)
-Rest Stop (Wisconsin 141, eastside near city limits).

Kenosha ☎ 262

DANCECLUBS

Club Icon (B D GLM MA)
Tue-Thu 19-2, Fri & Sat -2.30, Sun 15-2h, Mon closed
6305 120th Avenue ☎ (262) 857-3240 www.club-icon.com

La Crosse ☎ 608

BARS

Chances Are (AC B GLM MA) 15-?, Sat & Sun 12-?h
417 Jay Street ☎ (608) 782-5105

My Place (B GLM MA) 15-?h
3201 South Avenue ☎ (608) 788-9073

■ **Players** (AC B CC D GLM MA t) 19-2, Fri & Sat 17-2.30, Sun 17-2h
300 Fourth Street South ☎ (608) 784-4200 🖳 www.PlayersBarLaCrosse.com
Popular.

Madison ☎ 608

GAY INFO

■ **OutReach--Madison & south-central Wisconsin's LGBT Community Center** (AC CC GLM I T) Mon-Fri 10-19, Sat 12-16h. Closed on Sun
Gateway Mall, 600 Williamson St, Suite P-1 *Near East Side Madison* ☎ (608) 255-8582 🖳 www.lgbtoutreach.org www.lgbtdirectory.org
Lesbian, gay, bisexual, and/or transgender community center.

BARS

■ **Greenbush** (B glm M MA) 16-24h, Sun closed
914 Regent Street ☎ (608) 257-2874
■ **Shamrock Tavern** (B BF D GLM M MA) 11-2, Fri & Sat 10-2.30, Sun 10-2h
117 West Main Street ☎ (608) 255-5029
🖳 www.facebook.com/pages/Shamrock-Bar/75892898518
Brunch Sat & Sun.
■ **Woof's** (AC B D GLM MA) 16-2, Sun 12-2h
114 King Street ☎ (608) 204-6222 🖳 www.woofsmadison.com

DANCECLUBS

■ **Club 5** (B GLM m MA S ST) 16-2h
5 Applegate Court ☎ (608) 277-9700 🖳 www.club-5.com
■ **Plan B** (B D GLM MA S) 16-2h, closed Mon
924 Williamson Street ☎ (608) 257-5262 🖳 www.planbmadison.com

CRUISING

-Burrows Park
-Fairchild Street (opposite library near square)
-James Madison Park.

Milwaukee ☎ 414

BARS

■ **Ballgame. The** (B D G M S VS) 14-2, Fri & Sun 11-2h
196 South 2nd Street ☎ (414) 273-7474
■ **Boom/ The Room** (B GLM M MA) 17-2, Sun 11-2h
625 South 2nd Street ☎ (414) 277-5040 🖳 www.boommke.com
■ **City Lights Chill** (AC B DR f G m MA S) 16-?, Sat & Sun 12-?h
111 West Howard Avenue *1.6km north of Airport* ☎ (414) 481-1441
■ **Fluid** (AC B CC G MA) 17-2, Fri -2.30, Sat 14-2.30, Sun 14-2h
819 South 2nd Street ☎ (414) 643-5843 🖳 fluid.gaymke.com
Martini cocktail lounge. Warm atmosphere with no attitude and friendly staff. Crowded at WE.
■ **Harbor Room** (AC B CC f G m MA OS) 7-2h
117 East Greenfield Avenue ☎ (414) 672-7988
🖳 www.harbor-room.com
Levi & leather bar. Happy hour 16-18h.
■ **Hybrid Lounge** (AC B G MA) 16-?, Sat & Sun 10-?h
707 East Brady Street ☎ (414) 810-1809 🖳 www.hybridlounge.net
■ **Kruz** (B G MA) 17-1h
354 East National Ave ☎ (414) 272-5789
■ **This is it** (AC B G MC) 15-3h
418 East Wells Street *Milwaukee's East Side* ☎ (414) 278-9192
🖳 www.thisisitbar.com
Very diverse crowd. Friendly atmosphere. The oldest gay bar in Milwaukee.
■ **Triangle** (B G MA) 12-2, Fri & Sat 6-2.30, Sun 6-2h
135 East National Avenue ☎ (414) 383-9412 🖳 triangle.gaymke.com
■ **Woody's** (B G MA) 16-?h
1579 South 2nd Street ☎ (414) 672-0806 🖳 www.woodys-mke.com

DANCECLUBS

■ **Cage. La** (B GLM M S VS WE YC) 17-?h
801 South 2nd Street ☎ (414) 383-8330 🖳 www.lacagemke.com
■ **Mona's** (B D GLM M MA) 16-2, Fri & Sat -2.30h, Sun & Mon closed
1407 South 1st Street ☎ (414) 643-0377 🖳 www.m-o-n-a-s.com
Also restaurant.
■ **Tropical** (B D GLM MA)
626 South 5th Street ☎ (414) 460-6277
Gay Latino danceclub with events.

SAUNAS/BATHS

■ **Midtowne Spa** (AC DU FC G OS P RR SA SB VS WH WO) 24hrs
315 South Water Street *South of the historic third ward at 315 South Water St.* ☎ (414) 278-8989 🖳 www.midtowne.com
Big bath house with a redwood sauna and private sundeck. Free condoms.

BOOK SHOPS

■ **Outwords Books, Gifts & Coffee** (b CC GLM)
Mon & Tue 11-19, Wed-Sat 11-21, Sun 11-18h
2710 North Murray Avenue *Located in Milwaukee's gay-friendly east-side* ☎ (414) 963-9089 🖳 www.outwordsbooks.com
Outwords Books & Coffee is a full service LGBT bookstore offering a diverse range of greeting cards and gifts including music CDs and DVDs plus a coffee bar serving a veriety of light refreshments.

GENERAL GROUPS

■ **Milwaukee LGBT Community Center** (GLM MA)
10-22, Sat 18-22h, Sun closed
315 West Court Street, Suite 101 ☎ (414) 271-2656 🖳 www.mkelgbt.org

CRUISING

-Astor Street (between Juneau and Kilbourn)
-Wisconsin Avenue (between 10th and 17th)
-Toilets at University of Wisconsin Bolton Hall
-Gym at the YMCA Milwaukee (161 W. Wisconsin Ave).

Racine ☎ 262

DANCECLUBS

■ **JoDee's International** (B D GLM MA S ST) 19-?h
2139 Racine Street ☎ (262) 634-9804

Superior ☎ 715

BARS

■ **Flame** (AC B CC D GLM I MA S) 15-2.30h
1612 Tower Avenue ☎ (715) 395-0101 🖳 www.superiorflame.com
■ **JT's Bar & Grill** (AC B GLM M MA S SNU ST)
15-2, Fri 15-2.30, Sat 13-2.30, Sun 13-2h
1506 North 3rd Street ☎ (715) 394-2580 🖳 www.jtsbarandgrill.net
■ **Main Club. The** (B D GLM I MA) 15-2, Fri & Sat -2.30h
1217 Tower Ave ☎ (715) 392-1756 🖳 www.mainclubsuperior.com

SAUNAS/BATHS

■ **Duluth Family Sauna** (cc DU FC G RR SA SB VS) 12-22.30h
18 North 1st Avenue East, Duluth *Duluth is a suburb of Superior on the Minnesota side of the Bay* ☎ (218) 726-1388 🖳 duluthsauna.com
Men-only downstairs.

Wyoming

Location: West USA
Initials: WY
Time: GMT -7
Area: 253.349 km² / 103,620 sq mi.
Population: 480,000
Capital: Cheyenne

Cheyenne ☎ 307

SEX SHOPS/BLUE MOVIES

■ **Cupid's Adult Bookstore** (CC g VS) 12-24h
511 West 17th Street ☎ (307) 635-3837
Also booths for viewing porn films. Some booths with glory holes.

Uruguay

Location: South America
Initials: ROU
Time: GMT -3
International Country Code: ☏ 598
International Access Code: ☏ 00
Language: Spanish
Area: 176,215 km² / 68,037 sq mi.
Currency: 1 Uruguayan Peso (urug$) = 100 Centésimos
Population: 3,463,000
Capital: Montevideo
Religions: 61% Roman Catholic 2% Protestant, 1% Jewish
Climate: Winters are cold and wet with frequent rainfall. Summers are very hot. Best time for a visit is from Apr-Oct.
Important gay cities: Montevideo

Homosexuality is not illegal in Uruguay. There are no specific laws against homosexuality. The age of consent is 18. In August 2003 a new law came in force protecting members of sexual minorities from „physical and printed homophobic abuse". A prison sentence can be enforced against perpetrators. On the other hand, there are some laws put into effect by the authorities „to protect the society from acts against decency". Practice of any sexual act in public can be punished with up to 24 hours detention.

Congress passed a law permitting registered partnerships in November 2007. It is a prerequisite that the couples in question have been together for at least five years. The law covers old age pension rights, inheritance law and the rearing of children. . Montevideo has an old architectural heritage, with beautiful squares and green areas. The city has a very dynamic cultural life throughout the year, particularly in February during the Carnival that includes many other activities.

In addition, a law permitting homosexuals adoption rights was passed in September 2009, making Uruguay a real inspiration for the entire South American continent.

Gay life in Montevideo is exciting and offers a vast variety of places of amusement exclusively for gay men. The best season to visit Uruguay is summer (October to April). Especially attractive for the visitor is the bathing resort Punta del Este, known as the „Star of the Golden Coast". Tourists from all over the world come to enjoy the sea sport facilities, as well as the night life in casinos and discos. Close to Punta del Este is the nudist beach „Chihuahua", with large stretches of white sand and dense green forests.

In Uruguay ist Homosexualität legal und wird durch keinerlei Bestimmungen verboten. Das Schutzalter liegt bei 18 Jahren. Im August 2003 trat ein neues Gesetz in Kraft, das sexuelle Minderheiten vor körperlichen und verleumderischen Angriffen schützen soll. Bei Verstößen drohen Gefängnisstrafen. Gleichzeitig haben die Behörden jedoch einige Verordnungen in Kraft gesetzt, „um die Gesellschaft vor Sittenwidrigkeiten zu schützen". Öffentliche sexuelle Handlungen können mit bis zu 24 Stunden Haft bestraft werden.

Im November 2007 hat der Kongress ein Gesetz beschlossen, welches die Eingetragene Partnerschaft ermöglicht. Voraussetzung ist, dass das Paar seit mindestens fünf Jahren zusammen ist. Das Gesetz beinhaltet das Renten- und Erbrecht sowie Kindererziehung. Zudem wurde im September 2009 die Gleichstellung von Homo-Paaren in Bezug auf das Adoptionsrecht beschlossen. Uruguay gilt schon länger als Vorbild in Sachen Gleichstellung für den gesamten Kontinent.

Montevideo hat ein altes architektonisches Kulturerbe mit schönen Plätzen und viel Grün. Das ganze Jahr über sprüht die Stadt vor Leben, vor allem im Februar während des Karnevals, der mit vielen Überraschungen lockt.

Das schwule Leben in Montevideo ist aufregend und bietet viele interessante Treffs nur für Gays. Uruguay ist besonders schön im Sommer, der besten Urlaubssaison. Vor allem der Badeort Punta del Este, bekannt als „Stern der Goldenen Küste", lockt viele Besucher an. Touristen aus aller Welt nutzen dort die Möglichkeiten zum Wassersport und das Nachtleben in den Casinos und Discos. In der Nähe von Punta del Este liegt der FKK-Strand Chihuahua mit seinem weißen feinen Sand und gesäumt von dichten grünen Wäldern.

En Uruguay, l'homosexualité níest pas un délit et níest régi par aucune réglementation spéciale. La majorité sexuelle est fixée à 18 ans. En septembre 2003, une nouvelle loi protégeant les minorités sexuelles díattaques physiques ou écrites est entrée en vigueur et menace de prison les contrevenants.

Dans le même temps, cependant, une nouvelle législation a été mise en place « pour protéger la société des attaques aux bonnes moeurs ». Les contacts homosexuels en public sont passibles de peines de prison pouvant aller jusquiá 24 heures.

Le Congrès a promulgué en novembre 2007 une loi rendant possible un partenariat enregistré. La condition est que le couple soit ensemble depuis au moins cinq ans. La loi inclut le droit à la retraite, le droit successoral, de même que l'éducation des enfants. En outre l'égalité en matière d'adoption par les couples homosexuels a été adoptée en septembre 2009. L'Uruguay fait figure d'exemple en matière d'égalité pour tout le continent.

Montevideo a un patrimoine culturel architectural ancien avec de beaux palais et beaucoup díespaces verts. La ville est animée toute líannée et à l'époque du carnaval, en février, elle réserve nombre de surprises aux visiteurs.

La vie gay à Montevideo est grisante et offre de nombreux lieux de rencontre pour les gays. La meilleure saison pour se rendre en Uruguay est l'été. Sur la côte, Punta del Este, connue sous le nom « d'étoile de la côte dorée » attire des visiteurs du monde entier qui viennent y faire des sports nautiques et goûter la vie nocturne dans les casinos et les boîtes. Dans les environs de Punta del Este se trouve la plage naturiste de « Chihuahua », paradis de sable fin jouxtant d'épaisses forêts.

En Uruguay, la homosexualidad es legal y no está prohibida por ninguna disposición. La edad de consentimiento es de 18 años. En agosto de 2003 entró en vigor una nueva legislación que debe proteger a las minorías sexuales de ataques corporales y escritos. En caso de infracción, se prevén penas de cárcel. A su vez, las autoridades han aprobado sin embargo algunos reglamentos para „proteger a la

sociedad de actos indecentes". Los actos sexuales en público pueden ser castigados con una pena de arresto de hasta 24 horas.
En noviembre de 2007 el Congreso aprobó una ley que hace posible el registro de parejas de hecho. La condición es que la pareja esté junta desde hace como mínimo cinco años. La ley contiene el derecho a pensión, derecho de sucesión así como la educación de los niños. Por otra parte, se decidió en septiembre de 2009 sobre la igualdad de las parejas homosexuales en cuanto al derecho de adopción. Uruguay es ya más que un modelo en términos de igualdad de género para todo el continente.
Montevideo tiene un patrimonio cultural y arquitectónico antiguo con bonitas plazas y mucho verde. Durante todo el año la ciudad desprende vitalidad, sobre todo en febrero durante el Carnaval, que está lleno de sorpresas.La vida homosexual en Montevideo es emocionante y ofrece muchos puntos interesantes, sólo para gays. Uruguay es especialmente bonito en verano, la mejor época para las vacaciones. Sobre todo la localidad de Punta del Este, conocida como la „Estrella de la Costa Dorada", atrae a muchos visitantes. Turistas de todo el mundo aprovechan la ocasión para practicar deportes acuáticos y disfrutar de la vida nocturna en los casinos y discotecas. Cerca de Punta del Este está la playa nudista „Chihuahua", con su fina y blanca arena y sus verdes y frondosos bosques.

✖ In Uruguay l'omosessualità è legale e non viene vietata da alcuna legge. L'età legale minima per i rapporti sessuali è di 18 anni. In agosto del 2003 è entrata in vigore una nuova legge che tutela le minoranze sessuali da attacchi scritti e fisici. Chi contravviene a questa legge rischia il carcere. Ma nello stesso tempo le autorità hanno varato un ordinamento che mira a „tutelare la società da immoralità". Pratiche sessuali in pubblico possono essere punite con 24 ore di carcere.
A novembre del 2007, il Congresso ha approvato una legge che introduce il riconoscimento delle unioni civili. Il presupposto è che la coppia stia insieme da almeno più di cinque anni. La legge prevede il diritto alla reversibilità della pensione, il diritto all'eredità del compagno, ma anche il diritto alla maternità.
Inoltre a settembre del 2009 il diritto adottivo delle coppie omosessuali è stato equiparato a quello delle coppie omosessuali. Per quello che riguarda i diritti LGBT, l'Uruguay è già da tempo il Paese sudamericano più all'avanguardia. Montevideo ha un patrimonio architettonico ricco di bellissime piazze e di verde. La città è piena di vita tutto l'anno ma in particolar modo in febbraio durante il carnevale, che attira i turisti con le sue numerose sorprese.
La vita gay a Montevideo è interessante ed offre molti locali. L'Uruguay è particolarmente bello durante l'estate, che è sicuramente la stagione migliore per visitare questo paese. Ad attirare particolarmente i turisti è soprattutto la località balneare di Punta del Este, conosciuta anche come „stella della costa dorata". Turisti da tutto il mondo vengono qui a sfruttare le infinite possibilità per gli sport acquatici e la vita notturna con le sue numerose discoteche e casino.Nei pressi di Punte del Este si trova la „Chihuahua", che è una spiaggia per nudisti con sabbia bianca e fine e con boschi verdissimi.

HEALTH GROUPS

■ **Asociación de Meretrices Profesionales de Uruguay (AMEPU)** 15-19h
Av. Daniel Fernández Crespo 1914bis ✉ Montevideo *At corner of La Paz* ☎ 924-5275
Information and counselling about AIDS.

Colonia del Sacramento ☎ 4

HOTELS

■ **Posada del Angel** (AC BF CC glm H I OS PI PK RWS RWT SA WO) All year
C/. Washington Barbot 59 *At the entrance of the historical quarter*
☎ (4) 522-4602 🖳 www.posadadelangel.net
A tastefully decorated and cosy hotel in a colonial style house with a fantastic location and extremely friendly staff. All rooms are en-suite with TV. Also a small garden with a swimming pool.

Montevideo ☎ 2

BARS

■ **@Cafe** (B glm M MA WE) Mon-Fri 9-2, Sat & Sun 12-2h)
Bartolome Mitre 1322 *Old town, one block north of Solis theatre*
☎ (2) 915-0341
■ **Abel** (B f G s YC) Thu-Sun 21-? h
Cerro Largo 1833 ☎ (2) 924-3891
■ **Bacacay** (! B glm M MC) Mon-Sat 9-?h
Bacacay 1310 *At Buenos Aires Street, one block from Independencia square*
☎ (2) 916-6074
■ **Bar 62** (B glm M MC WE)
Barreiro 3301 *Pocitos – two blocks from the seaside* ☎ (2) 707-3022
■ **Don Trigo** (B glm M MC WE) 10-3h
Garcia Cortina y Sarmiento *Parque Rodo two blocks of the seaside*
☎ (2) 711-5952
■ **Fun Fun** (! B glm m MC WE) Mon-Sat 16-4h
Ciudadela 1229 *At old Mercado de la Abundancia* ☎ (2) 915-8005
■ **Jockey Club** (B glm M MC WE) Fri-Sun 9-4h
Bartolome Mitre 1396 *2 blocks north of Sarandi Street* ☎ (2) 916-3287
■ **Lobizón. El** (B g m YC) 20.30-?h
Zelmar Michelini # 1264 ☎ (2) 901-1334
■ **Mitre. El** (B glm MA WE)
Bartolome Mitre 1410 ☎ (2) 915-4425
■ **Queens** (B d DR G r YC) Fri-Sat 23-?h
Plaza Cagancha s/n
■ **Ronda. La** (B glm MA WE)
Ciudadela 1182 *Old town, three blocks south Independencia square, at corner of Canelones* ☎ (2) 903-1353

DANCECLUBS

■ **Caín** (! AC B D DR GLM MA r SNU) Fri-Sat 0-7h
Cerro Largo 1833 *Cordon, between Arenal Grande St. and Fernandez Crespo Av.* ☎ (2) 099 669 369 🖳 www.caindance.com
■ **Ibiza** (ac AYOR b D G MA r S SNU ST T) Thu-Sun 1-7h
Av. Rondeau 1493 *At corner of Uruguay* ☎ (2) 901-6728
■ **Kalu Dance** (AC B D glm MA P) Thu-Sat 23-?h
Juan Carlos Gomez 1323 *Old town, half a block south of Matriz Square*
☎ (2) 915-2916
■ **Lotus** (AC B D glm MA P) Thu 19-?, Fri-Sat 23-?h
Luis Alberto de Herrera 1248 *Pocitos, street level of the Montevideo World Trade Center* ☎ (2) 628-1379
■ **Sonic** (AC B D glm MA) Thu-Sat 23-5h
Buenos Aires 584 *three blocks west from the Independencia Square*
☎ (2) 094 444 225
■ **Velvet** (AC B D glm M MA P) Thu 19-3, Fri-Sat 21-5h
Rincón 613 *Half a block east of the Matriz Square* ☎ (2) 916-4122
■ **W Lounge** (B D glm M MA OS) Fri-Sat 21-?h
Rambla Wilson y Sarmiento *Parque Rodo seaside front* ☎ (2) 712-5287

RESTAURANTS

■ **Arcadia** (AC B CC glm M S)
Radisson Victoria Plaza Hotel 25th Floor *Downtown, Independence Square*
☎ (2) 902-0337
■ **Malaka** (AC CC glm M S)
Rincon 510 ☎ (2) 916-7341

SEX SHOPS/BLUE MOVIES

■ **Erotic Sex Shop** (g MA VS) Mon-Fri 10-19, Sat 10-14 h
Av. 18 de Julio 1953, apto. 204 ☎ (2) 409-8772
Some gay videos/DVDs.
■ **Gourmet Video** (g MA) Mon-Fri 10-19, Sat -13h
Ejido 1431 *At corner of Mercedes, esc. 3* ☎ (2) 902-5333
Section with gay movies for rent/sale.

Private Video (g MA) Mon-Sat 12-0h
Convencion 1290 /San Jose Street ☎ (2) 902-5333
Section with gay movies for rent/sale.

SEX CINEMAS

Cine Multisex (G MA VS) 24hrs
Dr. Salvador Ferrer Serra 2340 ☎ (2) 400-0627

Cine Multisex II (G MA VS) 24hrs
Paraguay 1379

Cine Private (DR G MA VS) 12.30-23h
Convención 1290 *At corner of San José* ☎ (2) 901-9779
One gay cinema in this complex.

Cine TripleSex (G MA VS) 24hrs
Acevedo Díaz 1765 ☎ (2) 402-5131

SAUNAS/BATHS

Korpus (B DR DU FC G GH LAB m MSG RR SA SB SOL VS WH WO)
Sun-Thu 15-24, Fri & Sat -8h
Julio Herrera y Obes 1240 *Downtown, at corner of Soriano*
www.korpussauna.com
Nice sauna in a traditional house in Montevideo's city centre.

BOOK SHOPS

Lupa Libros. La (g) Mon-Fri 10-22, Sat 10-16 & 20-23 h
Peatonal Bacacay 1318bis *Old city, near Teatro Solis* ☎ (2) 916-8574
Exhibitions possible.

TRAVEL AND TRANSPORT

Sunlight VIP Travel
Wilson Ferreira Aldunate 1304, # 502 ☎ (2) 901-2396
www.viajessunlight.com

HOTELS

Lafayette (AC B bf CC H NG PI SB WH WO)
Soriano 1172 ☎ (2) 902-4646 www.lafayette.com.uy
Rooms with private bath, minibar, phone, radio, TV and safe. Parking available.

GUEST HOUSES

Diagonal (g MA)
Colonia 1168 *At corner of Av. Gral. Rondeau* ☎ (2) 901-0390
Rooms by the hour.

Goes (g MA)
Goes 2272 ☎ (2) 408-2597
Rooms by the hour.

Our House (AC BF CC GLM MA PI t)
Stella Maris M 336 S 1 – Parque Solymar *Ciudad de la Costa, 25 km from Montevideo* ☎ (2) 696-6556 www.ourhouse.supersitio.net
Hostel which is designed specifically for the LGBT community around the world, without any discrimination.

SWIMMING

-Playa Miramar (g MA r) (Rambla Tomás Berreta esq. Rafael Barradas, desde la Escuela Naval hasta el Parque Gral. Lavalleja, Bus 104/105 from centre, 14-?h. Action in dunes and bushes)
-Playa Turisferia (g MA r) (Av. Costanera esq. Av. de la Playa, near park F.D.Roosevelt. Take bus from Av. Italia direction Lagomar or Solymar until bus-stop Av. Ing. Luis Giannattasio / Av. de la Playa, 14-?h)
-Playa La Estacada (g MA) (Rambla Mahatma Gandhi, between Punta del Canario & Punta Trouville)
-Playa Pocitos (g MA) (Rambla República del Perú, entre Plaza Daniel Munoz y Plaza W. Churchill)

CRUISING

-Av. 18 de Julio (MA, between Between Ejido & the Obelisco)
-Av. General Flores (YC, 21-?h, between Bulevar Jose Batlle and Ordoñez y Camino Corrales)
-Camino Castro (AYOR, between Av. Agraciada and Av. Dr. Carlos María de Pena (Paso Molino). Cruising in the park is AYOR!)
-Plaza de los 33 (MA, 21-?h, Av. 18 de Julio, between Minas & Magallanes)
-Plaza del Ejército (AYOR, MA, Bulevar José Batlle y Ordoñez, at the corner of Av. General Flores)
-Parque Batlle (AYOR MA, 21-?h, from the Obelisco direction Av. Dr. Luis Morquio until sports park of the Club Nacional de Atletismo)
-Rambla Presidente Wilson (AYOR MA, from the Holocaust Monument until golf-club Punta Brava)
-Rambla República del Perú (MA, between Plaza Daniel Muñoz and Plaza W. Churchill)
-Rambla Gran Bretaña (G MA r, evenings, between Ciudadela & Misiones St. in front of Templo Inglés)
-Parque de Los Aliados (cruisy park near the Obelisk)

Paysandú ☎ 72

BARS

Bahía Pub (B g MA R) 23-5h
Proyectada Segunda, esq. Enrique Chaplin

Can-Cán (B g MA)
Carlos Gardel *Near Av. Brasil*

Intimidades (B g MA)
Por Ruta 3, zona del Trébol *At the north side of Paysandú, near disco Cachabacha*

Leyendas Pub (B glm m MA YC) 20-5h, Mon closed
Uruguay 699 *At corner of Dr. J. Silvan Fernández*

Placeres (B g MA)
Av. Uruguay, esq. Joaquín Suárez

Sexy Pub (B g MA)
Charrúas, esq. Setembrino Pereda

Trampa. La (B G MA)
Av. 18 de Julio esq. Libertad

CAFES

Florencio (B glm MA YC) 18-2h, closed Mon
19 de Abril 932 ☎ (72) 25-722
Café with a long tradition.

DANCECLUBS

Brujas Internacional (AC AYOR b D g P R S T VS YC) 23-5h
Luis Batlle Berres, esq. 25 de Mayo

Cachabacha (B D glm MA) Thu-Sun
Por ruta 3, zona del Trébol *At the north side of Paysandú*

SWIMMING

-Arroyo Las Piedras (g MA) (Beach at the basin of Uruguay River, 6km south of Paysandú)

CRUISING

-Plaza Artigas (g) (in the afternoon)
-Av.18 de Julio (between Baltasar Brum and Cerrito)
-Playa Maya (g) (near the harbour)
-Av. España (between Bulevar Artigas and Cerrito)
-Zona de la Rambla (g) (at the end of Av. Brasil).

Punta del Este ☏ 42

BARS

■ **Moby Dick Pub** (B g MA) Daily
Rambla General Artigas 650 *At the habour*

CAFES

■ **Carnaby** (b g m)
Av. Gorlero 860 ☏ (42) 445-725
■ **Munich** (B G M)
Av. Gorlero esq. Los Muergos
■ **Strada. La** (B G M)
Av. Gorlero, esq. Las Gaviotas

DANCECLUBS

■ **Mercury** (B D G MA S) Open Dec-Feb
Av. Gorlero, esq. C/. 32
Small venue with nice atmosphere.
■ **Morocha. La** (B D glm S YC) Open Dec-Feb
La Barra de Maldonado *Near junction of Puente & ruta 10*

HOTELS

■ **Conrad Resort & Casino** (AC B BF H I NG OS S SA SB WO) All year
Parada 4, Playa Mansa ☏ (42) 491-111 💻 www.conrad.com.uy
A truely gay-friendly hotel, centrally located with 296 rooms and 30 suites. Hotel and casino complex with all the modern comforts.
■ **Paradise Resort** (AC B BF D G M MA MSG NU P PI PK S SB SNU ST WH WO) All year
115 Ruta Interbalnearia *150 m from Chihuahua's nudist beach and 15 km from Punta del Este* ☏ 240 911 44 ☏ 42 – 577 591
💻 www.paradisenudismhotel.com
New 5 level star hotel with 36 rooms, heated outdoor pool, bar, poolside restaurant, buffet restaurant, gym, spa, nightclub, beach club and private parking.
■ **The Chic Collection – Galería Golden Beach** (AC B BF CC glm M MA OS PI PK RWS RWT SA WH WO) All year
Calle 24 N° 34 ☏ (42) 441 314 💻 www.chichotelesresorts.com
There are three hotels in this group: Barradas Parque Hotel, Golden Beach Resort & Spa and Hotel Del Lago. See their website for more information on the Chic Collection with their high level of service, excellent facilities and ideal location in Punta del Este.

GUEST HOUSES

■ **Posada Aldilá** (AC B BF CC GLM H I MC MSG OS PI PK RWB RWS RWT SA VA WO) All year
Km 120, Punta Ballena *15 mins by car from Punte del Este*
☏ (42) 579-202 💻 www.posadaaldila.com
This fantastic guesthouse is halfway between Punte del Este and the only nudist beach in Uruguay called Playa Chihuahua.
■ **Sitges House Pousada Boutique** (bf CC GLM MA PI SOL WH) All year, 24hrs
Viña del Mar y Brighton, Parada 12 – Playa Brava San Rafael *Located 2 blocks from the beach.* ☏ 424 927 75 💻 www.sitges.com.uy
Gay only. 7 comfortable suites. Rental bicycles, horses, cycles available.

Salto ☏ 73

BARS

■ **Mister Jones** (B glm MA)
Av. Brasil, esq. Rambla Costanera

DANCECLUBS

■ **Planeta X** (B D glm MA)
Rambla Costanera Norte, esq. Uruguay

RESTAURANTS

■ **Caldera. La** (CC glm M MA)
Uruguay 221 ☏ (73) 24-648
Seafood cuisine.

CRUISING

-Plaza de los 33 Orientales (g MA r) (Av. Uruguay, corner Rambla Costanera)

Vanuatu

Location: Oceania
Initials: VU
Time: GMT +11
International Country Code: ☏ 678 (no area codes)
International Access Code: ☏ 00
Language: English and French; Bichelamar
Area: 12,190 km² / 4,706 sq mi.
Currency: 1 Vatu (VT)
Population: 207,000
Capital: Port-Vila (on Efate)
Religions: 80% Christian
Climate: Tropical climate that is effected by southeast trade winds.

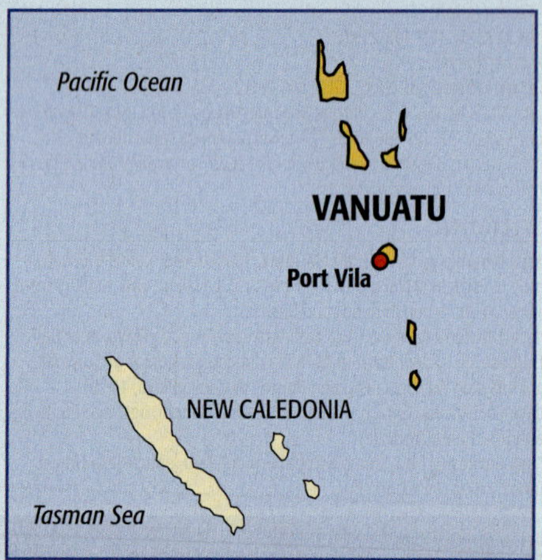

Vanuatu, »the land that rises from the ocean«, has seen the development of a small gay scene. The capital, Port-Vila, is a small town of 34,000 inhabitants, mostly Melanesians, but also Polynesians, Europeans, Vietnamese and Chinese. Melanesians traditionally have little difficulty dealing with homosexuality. We have no exact information on the legal situation here, but it is supposedly more liberal on Vanuatu than on neighbouring islands. This is the perfect place for spending beautiful, quiet and relaxed holidays.

In dem „Land, das sich aus dem Meer erhebt", hat sich eine eher zurückhaltende schwule Szene entwickelt. Die Hauptstadt, Port-Vila, ist eine Kleinstadt mit knapp 34.000 Einwohnern, meist Melanesier, daneben Polynesier, Europäer, Vietnamesen und Chinesen. Den Melanesiern bereitet schwule Lust traditionell wenig Bauchschmerzen. Die zur Zeit gültigen Gesetze – sie liegen uns leider nicht im Einzelnen vor – sollen im Vergleich zu denen benachbarter Inseln im südlichen Pazifik eher liberal sein. Hier kann man einen schönen, ruhigen, entspannten Urlaub verbringen.

Le «pays qui sort de la mer» est un archipel de plus de 70 îles. La vie gay est encore limitée, mais elle se developpe. Port-Vila, la capitale de l'archipel, est une petite ville de 34.000 habitants, en majorité des Mélanésiens. Pour le reste, ce sont des Polynésiens, des Européens, des Vietnamiens et des Chinois. L'homosexualité ne semble pas être un sujet tabou. La législation actuelle (nous ne disposons, hélas, d'aucune information concrète) semble être plutôt tolérante, si on compare avec les autres pays du Pacifique Sud. Calme et détente assurés à Vanuatu !

«El país que emerge del mar». Aqui se ha desarrollado un ambiente gay más bien discreto. La capital Port-Vila es una pequeña ciudad con apenas 34,000 habitantes, la mayoría melanesios, aparte de polinesios, europeos, vietnamitas y chinos. Tradicionalmente el deseo gay no ha sido cosa que les haya dado dolores de cabeza a los melanesios. Las leyes actualmente vigentes – desgraciadamente no las conocemos en detalle – parecen ser, en comparación con las de los demás vecinos de Pacífico Sur, más bien liberales. Aquí se pueden disfrutar unas vacaciones preciosas, tranquilas y relajadas.

"La terra che sorge dall'oceano" è costituita da più di 70 isole. Si è sviluppata una vita gay di dimensioni alquanto modeste. La capitale, Port-Vila, è una piccola cittadina di 34,000 abitanti, in gran parte Melanesiani ma anche Polinesiani, Europei, Vietnamiti e Cinesi. Tradizionalmente, ai Melanesiani l'omosessualità non crea soverchi problemi. Non lo sappiamo con assoluta sicurezza, ma le notizie che ci sono giunte parlano di una situazione legale senz'altro più liberale che nelle isole vicine. Una vacanza bella, quieta e rilassante, quindi, che aspetta soltanto di essere assaporata fino in fondo.

Port-Vila

BARS

■ **Cascade** (B g M)
Late night cabaret.

■ **Elektro Rock** (B D m NG) Thu-Sat 21-6h
Shefa ☎ 25151
Where the tourists meet. Maybe one or other gay guy too.

■ **Hemisphere Lounge Bar** (AC B D M NG) Fri & Sat 20-?h
Lini Highway *Located on the top floor of Grand Hotel and Casino*
☎ 28 882 www.grandvanuatu.com
There is no gay scene in Port-Vila, nor in the whole Vanuatu, however gay men usually go out in bars and clubs such as this one.

■ **Houstalet. L'** (B D g M) 18-3h
French atmosphere restaurant.

Vatican

Name: Status Civitatis Vaticanae Vatikanstadt · Cité du Vatican · Vaticano
Location: Southern Europe
Initials: V
Time: GMT -1
Language: Latin, Italian
Area: 0,44km² / 0.17sq mi.
Currency: 1 Euro (€) = 100 Cents
Population: 500
Religions: 100 % Catholic
Climate: Hostile, especially towards homosexuals.
Important gay cities: (Rome)

Pope Benedict XVI has agreed to allow sex tests for Catholic priests to be carried out, aiming to eliminate applicants with devious sexual urges, especially those with „deep-seated homosexual tendencies".
The tests, compiled by the Vatican's Congregation for Catholic Education, are apparently voluntary, but applicants would be refused entry to the priesthood if it is „evident the candidate has difficulty living in celibacy."
The Vatican confirmed that a priest must have a „positive and stable sense of one's masculine identity, and that the test will aim to identify those who are ‚immature. Areas of immaturity include strong affective dependencies; notable lack of freedom in relations; excessive rigidity of character; lack of loyalty; uncertain sexual identity and deep-seated homosexual tendencies. If this should be the case, the path of formation will have to be interrupted."
Psychological tests have been used in some seminaries for fifty years. A 2005 Vatican document allowed men to become priests if they had suppressed homosexual urges for three years. However, after spending vast sums on law suits in recent years, the Roman Catholic Church has seen the need for less tolerant measures. Figures on how many gay priests have been forced out of seminaries do not exist.
More information regarding the Vatican City includes the fact that most of this city is not freely accessible for the general public. The Vatican City with its famous Swiss Guards is a must on your places to visit when in Rome.

Papst Benedikt XVI hat der Überprüfung des Sexualverhaltens angehender katholischer Priester zugestimmt. Diese Prüfungen sollen Anwärter mit verborgenen sexuellen Wünschen eliminieren, besonders wenn es sich dabei um „tief verwurzelte homosexuelle Tendenzen" handeln sollte.
Die Teilnahme an diesen von der Vatikan-Kongregation für das katholische Bildungswesen zusammengestellten Tests ist anscheinend freiwillig, allerdings würde der Eintritt in das Priesteramt verweigert, wenn „der Kandidat es offensichtlich schwierig findet, im Zölibat zu leben".
Der Vatikan hat bestätigt, dass Priester über ein „positives und stabiles Gefühl der eigenen männlichen Identität" verfügen müssen, „und dass die Prüfung auf die Identifizierung unreifer Anwärter abzielen wird. Merkmale dieser Unreife sind starke affektive Abhängigkeiten, bemerkenswerter Freiheitsmangel in Beziehungen, übermäßige Unbeugsamkeit des Charakters, mangelnde Loyalität, ungefestigte Ge-

schlechtsidentität und tief verwurzelte homosexuelle Tendenzen. In diesen Fällen ist der Weg in die Priesterweihe abzubrechen."
In einigen Seminaren werden bereits seit 50 Jahren psychologische Tests eingesetzt. Ein Vatikanpapier aus dem Jahr 2005 hatte schwule Anwärter noch für das Priesteramt zugelassen, sofern sie ihre Homosexualität drei Jahre lang unterdrückt hatten. Aber seit die katholische Kirche in den letzten Jahren massive Geldsummen für Gerichtsverfahren aufbringen musste, sieht sie jetzt anscheinend einen Bedarf an weniger toleranten Maßnahmen.
Es liegen leider keine Zahlen darüber vor, wie viele schwule Priester bisher aus den Seminaren ausgeschlossen worden sind.
Der größte Teil der Stadt ist für die allgemeine Öffentlichkeit nicht zugänglich. Trotz allem ist die Vatikanstadt mit ihrer berühmten Schweizer Garde ein absolutes Muss bei Rombesuchen.

Le pape Benoît XVI a approuvé la vérification du comportement sexuel des futurs prêtres catholiques. Ces vérifications ont pour but d'éliminer les candidats aux pulsions sexuelles dissimulées, en particulier lorsqu'il s'agit de „tendances homosexuelles profondément ancrées".
La participation à ces tests compilés par la congrégation du Vatican pour l'enseignement catholique est apparemment facultative, cependant l'entrée dans le sacerdoce serait refusée si „le candidat éprouve visiblement des difficultés à vivre dans le célibat „.
Le Vatican a confirmé que les prêtres doivent disposer d'un „sentiment stable et positif de leur propre identité masculine" et que „la vérification a pour but d'identifier les candidats peu mûrs. Les caractéristiques de ce manque de maturité sont de fortes dépendances affectives, un manque caractérisé de liberté dans les relations, une intransigeance du caractère excessive, un manque de loyauté, une identité sexuelle instable et des tendances homosexuelles profondément ancrées. Dans ces cas la voie du sacerdoce doit être interrompue."
Dans quelques séminaires, des tests psychologiques sont déjà employés depuis 50 ans. Un document du Vatican daté de 2005 autorisait encore les candidats homosexuels au sacerdoce pourvu qu'ils aient réprimé leur homosexualité pendant trois ans. Mais depuis que l'Eglise catholique doit apporter des sommes considérables dans des actions judiciaires ces dernières années, elle semble devoir prendre désormais des mesures moins tolérantes. Malheureusement nous ne détenons pas de chiffres sur les prêtres homos exclus des séminaires jusqu'à présent.

El Papa Benedicto XVI aprobó la revisión de la conducta sexual de los futuros párrocos católicos. Estos exámenes deben eliminar cualquier indicio de deseo sexual escondido, especialmente cuando se trate de „tendencias homosexuales profundamente arraigadas".
La participación en estos tests confeccionados por la Congregación del Vaticano para la formación católica parece que es voluntaria; sin embargo, se denegaría la entrada al servicio sacerdotal, cuando „el candidato viera realmente difícil el hecho de vivir en celibato".
El Vaticano confirmó que el cura debe disponer de un „sentimiento positivo y estable de su propia identidad masculina" y que „el examen se centra en la identificación de indicios de inmadurez. Rasgos de esta inmadurez son una fuerte dependencia afectiva, marcada falta de libertad en las relaciones, exagerada testarudez en el carácter, falta de fidelidad, identidad sexual poco definida y tendencias homosexuales profundamente arraigadas. En estos casos se debe interrumpir la carrera sacerdotal".
En algunos seminarios se realizan desde hace 50 años tests psicológicos. Un documento del Vaticano del año 2005 admitió todavía a candidatos homosexuales para el sacerdocio, siempre que mantuvieran sometida su homosexualidad durante tres años. No obstante, desde que la Iglesia católica ha tenido que invertir grandes sumas de dinero en costes procesales, cree supuestamente que es más necesario adoptar medidas menos tolerantes.
Desgraciadamente no existen números fiables sobre cuántos curas homosexuales han quedado excluídos de los seminarios hasta ahora.

Papa Benedetto XVI si è dichiarato favorevole all'esame del comportamento sessuale di aspiranti preti. Questo esame mira ad escludere dal sacerdozio gente che ha desideri sessuali nascosti e specialmente se si tratta „tendenze omosessuali fortemente radicate".
Sottoporsi a questi test psicologici redatti dalla Congregazione per l'Educazione Cattolica è, a quanto pare, facoltativo. Tuttavia l'accesso al sacerdozio verrebbe negato qualora per il candidato „risultasse evidente la difficoltà a vivere nel celibato, vissuto come un obbligo così pesante da compromettere l'equilibrio affettivo e relazionale".
Il Vaticano ha così confermato che i sacerdoti devono disporre di un „senso positivo e stabile della propria identità virile" e che la idoneità del candidato verrà posta sotto esame. Vengono considerati segni di immaturità: „forti dipendenze affettive, notevole mancanza di libertà nelle relazioni, eccessiva rigidità di carattere, mancanza di lealtà, identità sessuale incerta, tendenze omosessuali fortemente radicate". In questi casi „il cammino formativo dovrà essere interrotto". Presso alcuni seminari vengono usati i test psicologici già da 50 ani. Un documento vaticano del 2005 permetteva a candidati omosessuali di accedere al sacerdozio purchè avessero represso la loro omosessualità almeno negli ultimi tre anni. Da quando però negli ultimi anni la chiesa cattolica ha dovuto sborsare ingenti somme di denaro per alcuni processi, le gerarchie ecclesiastiche si vedono adesso costrette ad essere meno tolleranti. Al momento non esistono dei numeri precisi che attestano quanti sacerdoti sono stati esclusi dai seminari.

Vatican City

GAY INFO

Vatican City Official Homepage
www.vatican.va
Here you can find out exactly what the views of the Vatican towards homosexuality are.

Venezuela

Location: South America
Initials: YV
Time: GMT -4
International Country Code: ☏ 58
International Access Code: ☏ 00
Language: Spanish, in some areas Indian languages
Area: 912,050 km² / 353,841 sq mi.
Currency: 1 Bolívar (vB) = 100 Céntimos
Population: 26,577,000
Capital: Caracas
Religions: 86% Roman Catholic, 5% Protestant
Climate: Hot and humid tropical climate which is more moderate in the highlands.
Important gay cities: Caracas

Homosexuality is not illegal in Venezuela, but there are no specific laws offering protection. Different organizations are working together to obtain the proper recognition of the gay community rights. As there is not a specific law regarding homosexuality, there is no specification about the age of consent for same-sex relations, but the age of adulthood is 18. The Supreme Court dealt LGBT activists a severe setback in 2008 with its august decision that neither gay marriage nor registered partnerships are constitutional.
Caracas, Valencia and Porlamar are the most tolerant cities with regard to homosexuality and the country as a whole is becoming more tolerant. Although discrimination exists, Venezuela is not a dangerous place for gays and lesbians. Venezuelans are kind and have a special sense of humour that favours tolerance and comprehension.
Venezuela offers a lot of interesting places to visit: jungles, plains, beaches, mountains and cities. Some guest houses and hotels openly welcome gay couples and there are even some accommodation venues which are exclusively gay. Night life is quite open and it is possible to find exclusive places for the LGBT public in all large cities. Because of the current political and economical situation in Venezuela, it is not unusual to come in contact with local demonstrations and protest marches.

Homosexualität ist in Venezuela nicht verboten. Die Verfassung schützt die Rechte von Schwulen und Lesben im Rahmen eines allgemeinen Antidiskriminierungsgesetzes. Verschiedene Organisationen sind aktiv im Kampf um die gesellschaftliche Anerkennung von Schwulen und Lesben, insbesondere die Alianza Lambda de Venezuela. Das Schutzalter liegt bei 18 Jahren. Der Oberste Gerichtshof hat 2008 LGBT-Aktivisten einen herben Rückschlag bereitet, indem es höchstrichterlich entschied, dass die Ehe sowie eingetragene Partnerschaften nicht mit der Verfassung vereinbar sind.
Caracas, Merida, Maracaíbo, Valencia, Maturín und Barquisimeto sind die tolerantesten Städte, obschon im gesamten Land Homosexuelle respektiert werden. Es kann zu vereinzelten Fällen von Diskriminierung kommen, aber im Allgemeinen können sich die venezolanischen Schwulen und Lesben sicher fühlen. Die Venezolaner sind generell freundlich, tolerant, verständnisvoll und haben Humor.
Venezuela ist landschaftlich sehr vielfältig. Es heißt, alle Kontinente seien im Land vertreten: Man kann morgens an einem der paradiesischen Strände liegen und am Abend im Schnee in den Bergen sein. Das Land hat viele sehenswerte Facetten: Dschungel, Berge, Savannen, Traumstrände, Seen, wilde Flüsse, große Städte und kleine Dörfer. Es gibt Bars, die schwulenfreundlich oder gar exklusiv für Gays sind. In allen großen Städten gibt es Treffpunkte für Schwule und Lesben, wie Bars, Discos, Saunen, Parks, Einkaufszentren etc. Die Veranstaltungen, die für und von Homosexuellen zu bestimmten Anlässen wie dem „Carnaval" organisiert werden, erfreuen sich großer Beliebtheit.

L'homosexualité n'est pas un délit au Venezuela. La constitution garantit les droits des gays et des lesbiennes dans le cadre d'une loi anti-discriminatoire. Différentes organisations, telle l'" Alianza Lambda de Venezuela „ se battent pour obtenir une reconnaissance sociale. La majorité sexuelle est fixée à 18 ans pour tous. Les activistes LGBT ont essuyé un revers, la Cour Suprême ayant jugé le mariage et le partenariat enregistré homosexuels inconstitutionnels.
Caracas, Merida, Maracaíbo, Valencia, Maturín et Barquisimeto sont les villes les plus tolérantes bien que le pays dans son ensemble respecte les homosexuels. Quelques cas isolés de discrimination sont certes observés mais les homos vénézuéliens se sentent plutôt en sécurité. Les Vénézuéliens sont généralement sympathiques, tolérants, compréhensifs et ont le sens de l'humour.
Le Venezuela dispose de paysages diversifiés et on dit que tous les continents y sont représentés, c'est-à-dire que l'on peut se dorer sur une plage paradisiaque le matin et se retrouver, le soir, dans la neige des montagnes. Le pays a ainsi de nombreuses facettes : la jungle, les montagnes, les savanes, des plages de rêve, des lacs et des torrents sauvages, de grandes villes et des villages pittoresques. Il y a des hôtels et des pensions gay friendly ou même complètement gays. On trouve dans toutes les grandes villes des lieux de rencontre pour gays et lesbiennes comme des bars, des boîtes, des saunas, des parcs, des centres commerciaux, etc. En outre, de nombreuses festivités sont organisées pour et par des homos en diverses occasions et, tel le carnaval, jouissent d'une grande popularité.

La homosexualidad en Venezuela no está prohibida pero no existe ninguna ley especial que proteja a gays y lesbianas. Diversas organizaciones trabajan para poder conseguir el reconocimiento necesario para la comunidad gay. Puesto que no existe ninguna base legal sobre la homosexualidad, la edad de consentimiento para relaciones gay-lésbicas tampoco está establecida, pero se acepta como válida la práctica sexual de cualquier tipo, después de la mayoría de edad, la cual se alcanza a los 18 años. En 2008, los activistas LGBT sufrieron un duro golpe por parte de la Corte Suprema. El Tribunal Supremo decidió que el matrimonio y las uniones civiles homosexuales no son compatibles con la Constitución.
Caracas, Valencia y Porlamar son las ciudades más tolerantes. Todo el país es cada vez más tolerante, respetuoso y liberal. Aunque siempre aparece la discriminación, los gays y lesbianas en Venezuela pueden sentirse seguros. Sus habitantes son amables, tolerantes, comprensivos y tienen un buen sentido del humor.
El país dispone de lugares muy atractivos: selvas, montañas, sabanas,

playas, lagos, caudalosos ríos, grandes ciudades y pequeños pueblos de gran belleza. Algunas pensiones y hoteles admiten a parejas homosexuales y hay incluso alojamientos para gays.
En todas las grandes ciudades hay puntos de encuentro para gays y lesbianas. Como la situación política y económica de Venezuela por el momento es bastante tensa, se debe contar siempre con posibles manifestaciones y marchas de protesta, por lo que debe ser un poco cauteloso.

L'omosessualità in Venezuela non è vietata. La costituzione tutela i diritti di omosessuali e lesbiche e li difende con una serie di leggi generali contro la discriminazione. Ci sono diverse organizzazioni in Venezuela che si battono per il riconoscimento di gay e lesbiche. Una di queste organizzazioni è l'Alianza Lambda de Venezuela. L'età del consenso è di 18 anni. Nel 2008 la Corte Suprema ha inferto un grave colpo a spese degli attivisti LGBT, decidendo che il matrimonio omosessuale e le unioni civili tra persone dello stesso sesso non sono compatibili con la Costituzione.
Caracas, Merida, Maracaibo, Valencia, Maturin e Barquisimeto sono le città più tolleranti anche se in generale si può dire che l'omosessualità è piuttosto rispettata un pò dappertutto. Questo non esclude il fatto che ci siano casi singoli di discriminazione ma in generale, comunque, da omosessuale in Venezuela, ci si può sentire piuttosto sicuri. I venezuelani sono in genere cordiali, tolleranti, comprensivi ed hanno il senso dell'humor.
Dal punto di vista paesaggistico il Venezuela è piuttosto variegato. Qui c'è davvero di tutto: di mattina ci si può prendere il sole in una paradisiaca spiaggia e la sera la si può trascorrere sulle nevose montagne. Il paese ha molte ricchezze naturali che vale assolutamente la pena conoscere: la giungla, le montagne, la savana, spiagge, laghi, fiumi, villaggi e grandi città. Ci sono alberghi e pensioni che sono gayfriendly e alcune che sono esclusivamente gay. In tutte le grosse città ci sono punti di incontro per gay e lesbiche come per esempio bar, discoteche, saune, parchi, centri commerciali, ecc.. Gli eventi che vengono organizzati per e da omosessuali, come per esempio il carnevale, godono di particolare popolarità.

NATIONAL COMPANIES

naTOURa (glm MA) Mon-Fri 8.30-18h
Calle 31 entre Avenida Don Tulio y prolongación Avenida 6 # 5-27, Merida ✉ 5101 Merida ☎ 274 252 4216 💻 www.natoura.com
Specializing in adventure tours all around the country and tailor made trips.

Barquisimeto – Estado Lara ☎ 251

BARS

Liberty (B D G MA)
Av. 20 entre C/. 15 y 16 *No house number, black bars. Next to the Iguana Cafe Best on Sunday from 23-3h.*

Seres (B D g P YC) Sun 23-7h
Carrera 16 entre C/. 45 y 46 *No house number, metal door, ring the bell*

CRUISING

-Museo de Barquisimeto
-Ateneo de Barquisimeto
-Entire Av 20 (22-24h).

Caracas – Distrito Capital ☎ 0212

GAY INFO

Caracas Guide
☎ (0212) 794 01 43
Jaime is a tourist guide, working in Caracas. He can help you find your way around the city and arrange your holiday plans. Highly recommended.

BARS

Azul Tequila (B D G H S)
Prolongación Av. Sur Las Acacias, Sabana Grande *Extension of Av. Sur las Acacias, at Plaza Venezuela* ☎ (0212) 782 92 10
Also accommodation available.

B 52 Yayo (B G MA)
Av. Urdaneta. Frente a la Fiscalía General de la República *After the bridge Puente de la Av. Fuerzas Armadas direction east*
All-male location.

Chalana. La (B D glm MA) Daily 18-5h
C/. de Bello Monte, entre Av. Casanova y Blvd de Sabana Grande *Between Av. Casanova & Blvd de Sabana Grande* ☎ (0212) 761 31 77
Very crowded at the weekend.

Cotorra. La (AC B CC G M MA P S) 19.30-3.30h
C. C. Paseo Las Mercedes, Nivel Estacionamiento *Near Tamanaco Hotel Intercontinental* ☎ (0212) 992 06 08

Fortaleza. La (B g MA ST) 20-6h
Av. Solano López, Sabana Grande *Near Tasca Pullman*

Fragata. La (B g MA) Daily 18-5h
C/. Villaflor, Sabana Grande *Next door to Ovejita* ☎ (0212) 762 68 57

Rincón del Gabán. El (! B G YC) 17-2, Fri-Sat -5h
C/. San Antonio, Shopping Centro del Este. loc. 38 *Between Av. Abraham Lincoln/Casanova, Pl. Venezuela Metro* ☎ (0212) 762 78 07

Tasca Don Sol (! B G M MA)
Pasaje Asunción, between Av. Abraham Lincoln (Blvd de Sabana Grande) / Casanova *Near Plaza Venezuela Metro* ☎ (0212) 729 40 6

Tasca Pullman (B d G MA S VS) Daily 19-5h
Av. Francisco Solano López, Edif. Ovidio, Planta Baja, Local G, Sabana Grande *1st floor of Ovidio building* ☎ (0212) 761 11 12
Very popular men-only bar. Shows at WE.

Same Side. The (B gLm MA SNU)
Av. Casanova / C/. El Colegio, Sabana Grande ☎ (0212) 766 05 4
Lesbian bar.

Vía Libre (B g MA)
C/. San Antonio, Edif. Inés, Local B ☎ (0212) 762 08 59

CAFES

Cool Café (g m MA)
C/. Mohedano, Edif. Banco de Lara P. B. ☎ (0212) 265 57 84

Terraza del Ateneo. La (GLM)
Ateneo de Caracas *Near M° de Bellas Artes*
Popular with a young crowd. Alternative music.

DANCECLUBS

Revolution (AC B CC D DR G MA S SNU VS WE)
Thu-Sat 23.30-?h
Av. Principal de Los Cortijos de Lourdes. Edf. Los Hermanos
☎ (0212) 237 62 31

Triskel (AC B CC D DR G MA S SNU ST T VS WE) Fri & Sat 23-7h
Av. San Juan Bosco c/c 3ra., La Placette *Transversal de Altamira, C. C. La Placette, 2nd floor* ☎ (0212) 265 90 36
Three different rooms: Electronic, Latin and Pop and Chill Out/Lounge.

SEX SHOPS/BLUE MOVIES

Sexymnias
C. C. Chacaito. NIvel Sótano *Basement* ☎ (0212) 952 03 8
Videos, vibrators, lubricants and condoms on sale. Friendly staff.

SEX CINEMAS

Cine Metropolitano
City centre *In front of the Congreso Nacional*
Commercial cinema showing conventional films. However you can often find gay men awaiting action especially in the back rows and in the toilets.

SAUNAS/BATHS

Baños Turcos Suecos (! DR DU G LAB MA MSG SA SB) 9-21h
Urb. San Antonio, C/. El Mango, Qta. Rosalia *M° Pl. Venezuela, near cnr. Av. Las Acacias, Sabana Grande Area, near Gran Hotel Meliá Caracas & El Recreo Commercial Mall, no entrance sign* ☎ (0212) 793 77 66

Brick building alongside the funeral parlor San Pedro is a bit shabby but the steam room is great: more than ten rooms linked with corridors, all with different degrees of steam and lighting. Inexpensive and very popular. The area can be unsafe after dark.

■ **Thermal Star** (B DR DU G MA MSG p RR SA SB) 14-21h
C/. Borges, Quinta Ana Julia. Sabana Grande-El Recreo *M° Sabana Grande, down by Negrin Street to C. C. El Recreo, at corner of Av. Casanova turn to the left, Chacaito, walk one block, turn to the left, at the end to the right, 2nd house on the left side* ☎ (0212) 763 06 90
Fri & Sat free beer!

■ **Zeus Steam's House** (! AC B CC DR DU FH G I M MA MSG PI PP RR SA SB VS WE WH WO) 11-22.30, Sat & Sun 9.30-22.30h
C/. Villafor, Edif. Centro Professional del este Sotano 2 *Near Hotel Melia, Caracas. 2 blocks from C. C. El Recreo, M° Sabana Grande*
☎ (0212) 761.42.40 💻 www.saunazeus.com.ve
Excellent sauna. Free towels, sandals and lockers. Attracts a very mixed gay crowd.

DVD SHOPS

■ **Boboy Video**
Av. Quito con Panamá, Edificio: Homero, Piso 1, Apto 3, Los Caobos
☎ (0212) 794 01 43

APARTMENTS

■ **Corpobienes**
Av. la Estancia, Centro Banaven

HEALTH GROUPS

■ **Acción Solidaria**
Av. Orinoco, Qta. Los Olivos, Bello Monte *Between C/. Coromoto & 2a*
☎ (0212) 952 95 54 💻 www.acsol.org
National information centre on HIV and AIDS.

■ **ACCSI – Acción Ciudadana Contra el SIDA**
Av. Romulo Gallegos. Edf. Maracay, # 21, El Marqués
☎ (0212) 232 79 38 💻 www.accsi.org.ve
Organisation fighting AIDS. Website in Spanish only.

SWIMMING

-Playa Culito (Catia La Mar) very gay
-Playa Camuri Chico (La Guaira & Pantaleta, G)
-Playa Camuri Grande (Naiguata)
-Playa Chuspa (La Sabana)
-Playa de Los Angeles (AYOR)
-Playa Macuto Sheraton (next to the Hotel, popular)
-Playa Marina Grande – Catia La Mar
-Playa Bahía de Cata (Maracay, about 3h from Caracas)
-Mochima Nacional Park – fantastic isolated beaches, nature pure. Boat trips available. From Puerto La Cruz to Cumaná
-Parque Nacional Morrocoy. 6 hours from Caracas by bus.
-Choroni. 3 hours from Caracas. Many multiracial locals.

CRUISING

All cruising areas are AYOR, beware of police:
-Centro Comercial Santa Fe, Sambil (toilets) and Paseo Las Mercedes, Urb. Las Mercedes
All the following are in the Estación Rosa:
-C/. Real de Sabana Grande
-Plaza Francia (in front of Four Seasons Hotel, evenings)
-Plaza Candelaria (after 18h)
-Av. Francisco Solano (R)
-Cafés along Blvd de Sabana Grande
-Ateneo de Caracas (WE) (Plaza Morelos)
-Parque Los Caobos (WE) (near Teresa Careños Theatre)
-Parque Central (WE) (near Hilton Hotel and Contemporary Museum)
-Centro de Caracas (Plaza Bolívar y Centro Simón Bolívar)
-C. C. Metrocenter
-C. C. El Recreo, near to the Gran Melia Caracas, in the Francisco Solano Ave.

Cumaná – Estado Sucre ☎ 294

BARS

■ **Café Tabaco y Ron** (B D glm MA)
Av. Universidad

■ **Zagúan** (B D G MA)
C/. Sucre, Zona Centro *Historic centre of Cumaná*

SWIMMING

-Playa San Luis (Along the beach, near the Vivero and Hotel Los Bordones. Let people ask for a cigarette. Sometimes R but not dangerous or expensive).

Isla de Margarita – Estado Nueva Esparta ☎ 295

DANCECLUBS

■ **Mikonos** (B D glm MA) Thu-Sat 22-?h
Av. 4 de mayo, C. C. Galerías Fente, Nivel Sótano, Local 10, Porlamar

■ **Mosquito Coast** (B D GLM MA WE) Thu-Sat 22-5h
Paseo Guaraguuao *At the end of Av. Santiago Marino Por Lamar*
☎ (295) 263 37 20

CRUISING

All are AYOR:
-Av. 4 de Mayo
-Av. Santiago Mariño
-Playa Bella Vista (behind Mosquito Coast, best in the afternoon)
-Playa el Morro (in front of Sol y Mar, best in the afternoon)
-Beach between Playa Moreno and Playa Caracola (from the Hilton hotel 500m past the new harbour)
-Playa El Agua.

Maracaibo – Estado Zulia ☎ 261

BARS

■ **Barra B** (B g MA)
Av. La Limpia *Opp. Delipan bakery*

CAFES

■ **Bambi** (b g m MA)
C/. 77 con Av. 14 *Close to Clínica Damper*

■ **Kabuki** (B G m MA) 9-22h
Blvd 5 de Julio *C/. 77 between Avs. 12 & 13*

■ **Mediterráneo** (b g m MA)
Av. 8 Santa Rita con C/. 75 *Close to Centro Médico de Occidente*

DANCECLUBS

■ **Boodoo Lounge** (AC B CC D DR G MA S SNU VS WE)
Thu-Sat 23.30-?h
C. C. Costa Verde Estado Zulia

■ **Friend** (B D GLM YC)
Av. Las Delicias con C/. 74 y 75 *Near Pollos Krispis*
Best on Sunday.

■ **G-Side** (B D glm MA s) Thu-Sat
Final Av. 20, sector Mara, Maracaibo Estado Zulia
☎ 414 304 71 79 (mobile)

■ **Paparazzi** (B D g MA)
C/. 72 con Av. Baralt

■ **Sodoma Disco** (B D GLM MA)
Av. San Martín con C/. 79 *In front of Salto Angel Commercial Centre*

■ **Unión. La** (B D glm MA)
Av. Bella Vista *Opp. Yonekura*

CRUISING

-Centro Sambil Maracaibo (new shopping centre)
-C. C. Costa Verde
-Av. Bella Vista (off Av. Cecilio Acosta)
-Blvd 5 de Julio (C/. 77)
-Paseo Ciencias (AYOR) (afternoons and nights)
-C. C. Lago Mall.

Mérida – Cord de Mérida ☏ 274

BARS

■ **Friends** (B D GLM MA)
Av. principal de los Chorros de Milla

■ **Rossy Bar/Disco** (B D GLM MA) Fri & Sat 23-5h
C. C. Mamayeya
Many students.

CRUISING

All areas are AYOR:
-Plaza Bolívar
-Parque Los Chorros de Milla
-Av. 4 zona Centro
-Near the library Bolivariana.

Puerto La Cruz – Estado Anzoátegui ☏ 281

BARS

■ **Art Club Tasca** (b g MA ST) Fri & Sat 22-4h
Av. Paseo Colón, C. C. Colón Plaza *Close to Gran Hotel Hesperia*
ST on Sat.

SWIMMING

-Doral Beach
-Cangrejo Beach
-El Morro
-Silver Island
-Guanta Harbor
-Caracas Islands (within the Mochima National Park)
-Arapito Beach
-Colorada Beach
-Beach called Playa Isla de Plata (take a boat to Guanta).

CRUISING

-Paseo Colón
-Plaza Bolívar
-Centro Comercial Plaza Mayor
-Centro Comercial Caribbean Mall.

Valencia – Estado Carabobo ☏ 241

DANCECLUBS

■ **Babylon** (! B D glm MA) Thu-Sun 22-6h
C. C. Camoruco nivel Estacionamiento, Av. Bolívar Norte *Above Quinta Leonor, opp. Banesco*
Very popular.

■ **Choza. La** (B D g MA) Thu-Sun 22-5h
Av. Salvador de la Cruz, Mañongo

CRUISING

-Plaza Bolívar (in and around Hotel Intercontinental)
-Centro Comercial Sambil Valencia
-Centro Comercial Metrópoli
-Riveras del Rio Cabriales
-Parque Francisco Peñalver.

Vietnam

Name: Viêt Nam
Location: South East Asia
Initials: VN
Time: GMT +7
International Country Code: ☏ 84 (omit 0 from area code)
International Access Code: ☏ 00
Language: Vietnamese, English
Area: 331,114 km² / 128,065 sq mi.
Currency: 1 Dong (VND) = 100 Xu
Population: 82,162,000
Capital: Hanoi (Ha Noi)
Religions: 55% Buddhist, 5% Catholic
Climate: Tropical climate in the south, monsoon climate in the north with a hot, rainy season that lasts from mid-May to mid-September and warm, dry season between mid-October and mid-March.

✱ Similar to other south-east Asian countries, Vietnam is relatively tolerant with regards to homosexuality, which was never explicitly forbidden and is not even mentioned in the Penal Code. Prostitution is however forbidden in all forms and is heavily punished. The national parliament clearly stated its rejection of same-sex marriage and the press generally sees homosexuality as a „social evil". Topics such as these and sexually transmitted diseases are avoided in conservative Vietnam and displays of open gay relationships are not gladly seen in public. In the last 10 years however life for gay men has become more relaxed. In Ho Chi Minh City (Saigon) and to some extent in Hanoi there is a small gay scene developing.
The entire country is becoming more accessible for international tourists and for Asian fans a further recommendation. Above all the friendly Vietnamese make a trip well worth while.

★ Wie auch in den anderen südostasiatischen Ländern ist Vietnam einigermaßen tolerant im Umgang mit Homosexualität und sie war niemals explizit illegal – im Strafgesetz wird sie nicht einmal erwähnt. Prostitution dagegen ist in jeder Form verboten und wird streng bestraft. Die Nationalversammlung hat sich eindeutig gegen gleichgeschlechtliche Ehen ausgesprochen und die Diskussion in den Medien sieht in Schwulen verbreitet ein soziales Übel. Zu heiklen Themen wie diesen oder sexuell übertragbaren Krankheiten äußert man sich im eher konservativen Vietnam lieber nicht und überdeutlich offen schwule Verhaltensweisen werden nicht gern gesehen.
In den letzten zehn Jahren ist das Leben für Schwule jedoch sehr viel entspannter geworden und in Ho Chi Minh City (Saigon) und – in geringerem Ausmaß – auch in Hanoi öffnen die ersten Gay-Bars, sodass allmählich eine schwule Szene entsteht.

Das Land wird touristisch allmählich immer mehr erschlossen und ist für den Asien-Fan äußerst empfehlenswert. Nicht zuletzt die freundlichen Vietnamesen machen das Reisen hier zu einem überaus angenehmen Erlebnis.

Comme les autres pays sud-est asiatiques, le Viêt Nam est relativement tolérant en ce qui concerne l'homosexualité qui n'a ainsi jamais été un délit et n'est même pas mentionné dans le code pénal. La prostitution est par contre interdite sous toutes ses formes et elle est sévèrement punie. L'Assemblée nationale s'est unanimement prononcée contre l'instauration d'un mariage homosexuel et la presse considère les gays généralement comme „un fléau social". De tels sujets sensibles comme également les maladies sexuellement transmissibles sont plutôt passés sous silence dans ce pays assez conservateur et les comportements gays étalés au grand jour ne sont pas bien vus.
Ces dix dernières années, la vie s'est néanmoins largement améliorée pour les gays et à Hô Chi Minh-Ville (Saïgon) tout comme, dans une moindre mesure, à Hanoï, des bars gays ont ouvert, et un petit milieu gay commence ainsi à s'installer.
Le pays est une destination de plus en plus choisie par les touristes et tout spécialement par les amateurs de pays asiatiques. La population vietnamienne est particulièrement sympathique et rend le voyage extrêmement agréable.

Como en los otros países del sudeste asiático, Vietnam se muestra bastante tolerante con la homosexualidad y nunca ha estado prohibida de manera explícita: en el código penal ni se menciona la homosexualidad. Al contrario, la prostitución está prohibida en todas sus formas y está penalizada severamente. La Asamblea nacional se ha pronunciado en contra de los matrimonios homosexuales y el debate en los medios de comunicación se centra en los homosexuales como un „mal social" que va en aumento. En el Vietnam más conservador no se habla de estos temas ni tampoco de las enfermedades de transmisión sexual y las relaciones homosexuales abiertas no son bien vistas.
En los últimos 10 años, no obstante, la vida para los homosexuales es mucho más fácil y en Ho Chi Minh (Saigon) y en menor medida también en Hanoi, han abierto ya los primeros bares gays, de tal modo que está apareciendo un cierto ambiente homosexual.
El país se está abriendo poco a poco cada vez más al turismo y es muy recomendable para cualquier enamorado de Asia. Además, los simpáticos vietnamitas hacen el viaje mucho más agradable.

Come altri Paesi sud-est asiatici, il Vietnam è piuttosto tollerante nei confronti dell'omosessualità. L'omosessualità, infatti, non è mai stata illegale e non viene neanche citata dal codice penale. Di contro, la prostituzione in ogni sua forma è vietata e punita severamente. L'Assemblea Nazionale si è espressamente dichiarata contro le unioni tra coppie dello stesso sesso e le discussioni nei mass media tendono a identificare i gay come un „malessere sociale". In questo Paese piuttosto conservatore, temi scottanti come appunto l'omosessualità o le malattie trasmesse sessualmente, vengono intenzionalmente evitate, e un comportamento esplicitamente gay viene considerato molto negativamente.
Negli ultimi dieci anni, tuttavia, la vita per i gay è diventata più facile e a Ho Chi Minh City (Saigon) e in minor misura anche ad Hanoi vengono aperti i primi bar gay e quindi si può parlare di una scena gay che sta nascendo.
Il turismo in Vietnam si va affermando sempre di più, apportando un ulteriore miglioramento alle infrastrutture turistiche. Per chi ama l'Asia, il Vietnam è una meta da visitare assolutamente. I vietnamiti, che si contraddistinguono per la loro gentilezza e la loro cordialità, renderanno il vostro viaggio ancora più piacevole.

NATIONAL COMPANIES

Rainbow Tourism Vietnam
147 Nguyen Van Cu Street ✉ Hanoi *Long Bien District*
☎ 903 286 504
🖳 www.rainbowtourismvietnam.com

Ha Noi ☎ 04

BARS

Aqua Club (B g MA)
333 Kim Ma, Ngoc Khanh, Ba Dinh District *Cnr. Kim Ma Street*
☎ 417 05 69
New bar.

Cay Xoai (B glm MA OS)
Truc Bach lake
Gay-owned mixed bar.

GC (Golden Cock) (B glm MA)
5 Bao Khanh St *West of Hoan Kiem Lake*
Upscale, western music, pool table. Tends to be packed on Sat between 22-23h as it closes early.

Solace Bar (B d glm MA)
Chuong Duong Do St *Across Hong Ha St, on Red River*
After GC bar closes, gays move here. It has a very good crowd from midnight-2h, with hiphop beats.

CAFES

Connect Café (b glm m MA)
8 Road 2, Living Quarter F361, An Duong, Tay Ho District
Near Hanoi's west lake
☎ (04) 717 12 27

SAUNAS/BATHS

Adam (AC b DU G m MA MSG RR SA SB WH WO) 15-23h
92 Ngo Tho Quan, Pho Kham Thien *Quan Dong Da District*
☎ (04) 241 35 41
🖳 www.adamspa.com.vn
Friendly and clean sauna.

GoGoClub (B DU G I M MSG RR S SA SB WH)
Daily 10-23h
55 Phao Dai Lang St, Dong Da Dist *15 mins from Downtown, near Dae-Woo Hotel* ☎ (04) 6296 4865
🖳 www.gogoclub.com.vn

Men Spa (AC b DR DU G m MA OS SA SB) 10.30-22h
17 Tuc Mac Alley *Tran Hung Dao St, near the Train Station* ☎ (04) 3942 2490
Located in a 3-story townhouse, very clean premises. Free drinks and fresh fruit.

CRUISING

-Hoan Kiem Lake. All day (Some r, beware of rip-off criminals pretending to be gay, AYOR)
-Thien Quang Lake (R) (opp. Lenin Park, after dark)
-Lenin Park (also rip-off criminals pretending to be gay, AYOR)
-Lao Dong swiming pool
-Ho Tay lake
-Bao Khanh St (just west of Hoan Kiem Lake), near the outdoor coffee shops where the road bends
-Hang Khong swimming pool
-outside the walls of the French Embassy.

Haiphong ☎ 031

HOTELS

Harbour View (AC B BF CC H M MA PI)
4 Tran Phu Street *Near the main gate of Haiphong port*
☎ (031) 382 78 27
🖳 www.harbourviewvietnam.com
Nice hotel (the only international one in town!) in good central but quiet location overlooking the harbour. Very handsome and friendly staff.

Hô Chi Minh City (Saigon) ☏ 08

BARS

■ **Eden** (B glm H M MA) 6-1h
236 De Tham, District 1 *Pham Ngu Lao area* ☏ (08) 836 81 54
www.elephantguide.com/edenbar
Safe place for gays and lesbians.

■ **Nang Xanh Cafe Bar** (B D g MA) 21-24h
Phan Xich Long Street, Binh Thanh District
Karaoke and cafe.

■ **Paris Dong Phuong** (B G MA) 18-?h
22 Ba Huyen Thank Quan P6, District 3 ☏ (08) 930 27 96
Karaoke bar. Crowded with cute gays who come to sing.

■ **Thoi Gian (Time Café)** (B glm MA) 20-24h
28 Tan Xuan Street, Tan Binh District *Near Thing Nhat Hospital*
Karaoke bar. Popular with local gays from 20h-midnight.

CAFES

■ **343** (b BF g m MA) 7-23.30h
343 Nguyen Trai Street, District 1 ☏ (08) 920 09 88
www.cafe343.com
Coffees, ice creams, fresh juices and shakes, some food. AC inside areas on two levels. TVs showing music videos. Popular with gays.

■ **Café Terrace** (B glm m MA OS)
Corner Le Loi St/Pasteur St, Dist. 1 *1st floor Saigon Center*
Popular with local gays looking for foreigners.

■ **Lang Café** (b g M MA OS) Daily 7-23h
573/12 Su Van Hanh Street, Ward 13, District 10 ☏ (08) 3868 09 99
www.langcoffee.com
Great Asian hospitality, friendly environment which is a great social spot to all the men.

■ **Papa coffee shop** (B glm m MA OS)
Dist. 1 *Near Reunification Palace*
Nice gay meeting place, cute waiters, best time Mon evening and on weekends.

■ **Phuong Cac** (glm m MA OS VS) Sun 8-12h (glm)
Bis Nam Ky Khoi Nghia 213, District 3 ☏ (08) 932 74 84 (mobile)
Best on Sun morning at this coffee shop / garden cafe. Make sure to come between 9 & 10h. Everyone leaves around 12h.

DANCECLUBS

■ **Apocalypse Now** (B D g MA r WE) 20-?h
2B-2C Thi Sach Street, District 1 ☏ (08) 825 61 24

■ **Villa** (AC B G MA)
131 Dong Khoi St *across from Gucci and Sheraton Hotel, on 2nd floor, above Gloria Jeans*

SEX CINEMAS

■ **Vuon Lai** (AYOR glm MA VS)
Corner of Tran Nhan Ton St and Vinh Vien St, Dist 10
Very cruisy and busy on weekends. Beware of pickpockets.

SAUNAS/BATHS

■ **Adam Spa** (AC B DU G I MA MSG RR SA SB VS WH) 10-23h
573/12 Su Van Hanh St., Ward 13, Dist. 10 ☏ (08) 3868 0999
www.adamspa.com
Many cute local guys.

■ **An Thien** (B DU G m MA MSG SA SB)
District 8 *Go past the old International Club at 285B Cach Mang Thang 8 Street and turn right and Thien An is on your right, next to a billiard club*
Very small sauna.

■ **Golden Smile Club** (B DU g I MA MSG SA SB VS WH WO)
Daily 10-23h
656 Su Van Hanh, District 10 ☏ (08) 862 61 19
Lot of cute guys, but no action.

■ **Ho Chi Minh Blind Association** (b DU g MC MSG OS SA)
185 Cong Quynh Street, District 1
Not exclusivly gay. Some action in the sauna room.

■ **Nadam Spa** (AC B DU G MA MSG SA SB WH)
12/29/1 QL13, Hiep Binh Chanh Ward, Thu Duc Dist *near Binh Trieu Bridge* ☏ (08) 083 726 8028 www.adamspa.com.vn
Very clean and good service. Recommendable body scrub.

■ **Phi Thuyen Spa** (AC b G MSG SA SB)
13 Cuu Long, Phuong 2, Tan Bing Dist. *Near the Superbowl*
Relocated spa (former near airport) with nice masseurs and spa.

■ **Quyet Thang 2** (G MSG SA SB WH) Daily 9-23h
212 Thong Nhat Phuong 16 Quan, Go Vap

■ **Toan Thang Sauna** (b DU g m MSG PI SA SB WH) 9-21h
126 Thanh Thai, P12, District 10 ☏ (08) 863 20 96
Small but cruisy sauna. A little dirty.

■ **Vat Ly Tri Lieu** (b g MA MSG PI SB) 12-23h
70 Ba Huyen Thanh Quan, District 1 ☏ (08) 932 58 84
No sex possible on the premises, but a good place to get to know someone that you meet elsewhere later.

MASSAGE

■ **Spa Bi Bo** (AC G MSG OS SB)
21 Hong Ha, P2 Tan Binh Dist. *Close to airport*
Nice garden and masseurs, not cheap!

HOTELS

■ **Hong Kong** (AC bf H MA)
22 Bui Vien, District 1 ☏ (08) 836 49 04

■ **Spring** (AC B BF H M MA)
44-46 Le Thanh Ton, Q 1 *Near Peoples Committee HQ in District 1*
☏ (08) 829 73 62 www.vietnamonline.com/spring/spring2.html
Hotel with economic rooms and suites.

SWIMMING

-Water World at Dist. 5, many gay visitors, best time 18h, closes at 21h
-Nguyen Tri Phuong swimming pool, Dist. 10, also cruising in the changing rooms, best time 16-18h

Nha Trang ☏ 058

RESTAURANTS

■ **Pho King Good** (glm M OS) All year
17A Biet Thu Street
Gay-friendly restaurant.

TRAVEL AND TRANSPORT

■ **3K Tourist Service Office** (glm MA)
3k Hung Vuong St ☏ (058) 058 527 008
Ask for Khan, good tours around the city and helpful with local gay scene.

Vung Tau

BARS

■ **Blue Moon** (B glm MA OS)
Ha Long Street *Behind the Grand Hotel*
Regular hangout for gays and lesbians. Loud music and good light-show.

DANCECLUBS

■ **Club 7** (B D glm MA)
Quang Trung Street *At the end of the street, near former post office, on the way from Front Beach to Back Beach*
No entry fee, but minimum consumption is compulsory.

CRUISING

-Dolphin swimming pool facing the sea on the one side and the Sammy Hotel on the other side (shower cabins in the basement)
-Beach O Quan, small, secluded beach located between Back Beach (Bai Sau) and Strawberry Beach (Bai Dau), right underneath the Jesus statue. At low tide between the rocks, also some nude sunbathing
-Promenade on Quang Trung Street, after 23h.

Zambia

Name: Sambia · Zambie
Location: Southern central Africa
Initials: Z
Time: GMT +2
International Country Code: ☎ 260 (omit 0 from area code)
International Access Code: ☎ 00
Language: English (official)
Area: 752,614 km² / 290,586 sq mi.
Currency: 1 Kwacha (K) = 100 Ngwee
Population: 11,668,000
Capital: Lusaka
Religions: 87% Christian
Climate: Tropical climate that is modified by altitude. The rainy season lasts from October to April.

In Zambia homosexual acts are illegal between men of any age under Sec. 155-158 of the Penal Code. The maximum sentence applicable is fourteen years imprisonment. In Zambian society, even among the more „liberal" urban population, homosexuality is a taboo and homosexuals are stigmatized.
At the beginning of 2009 the Vice President of Zambia called upon fellow citizens to denounce all homosexuals in the country, and thereby bringing about their imprisonment.
Zambia is one of the poorest countries in the world, where many people must survive on less than one US Dollar per day. The average life expectancy (also affected by the local AIDS epidemic) has dropped in the last fifteen years from 60 to 38 years.

Homosexuelle Beziehungen zwischen Männern jeden Alters sind gemäß den Artikeln 155-158 des Strafgesetzbuches illegal. Die Höchststrafe liegt bei 14 Jahren Gefängnis. Jedoch vertreten die Behörden des Landes gelegentlich die Meinung, in ihrem Staat gebe es gar keine Homosexuellen und somit sei auch nichts zu bestrafen. Über die Einstellung der Bevölkerung gegenüber Schwulen ist uns nichts bekannt.
Anfang 2009 hat der Vizepräsident seine Landsleute aufgerufen, Homosexuelle zu denunzieren und sie damit ins Gefängnis zu bringen.
Sambia ist eines der ärmsten Länder der Welt. Viele Leute müssen mit weniger als 1 US Dollar pro Tag auskommen. In den vergangenen 15 Jahren hat sich die durchschnittliche Lebenserwartung (auch wegen der AIDS-Epidemie) von 60 auf 38 Jahre abgesenkt.

En Zambie, l'homosexualité masculine est un délit, même entre adultes consentants (articles 155 à 158 du code pénal). On risque un maximum de 14 ans de prison, même si, bizarrement, les autorités du pays affirment que l'homosexualité n'existe pas dans le pays. Nous ne sommes pas en mesure de dire si la population est plutôt homophobe ou homophile.
Début 2009 le vice-président a appelé ses compatriotes à dénoncer les homosexuels pour les mettre en prison.
La Zambie est un des pays les plus pauvres au monde. Beaucoup de gens vivent de moins de 1 dollar US par jour. Ces 15 dernières années l'espérance de vie est passée en moyenne de 60 à 38 ans, aussi du fait de l'épidémie du SIDA.

Las relaciones homosexuales entre hombres, sean de la edad que sean, son ilegales de acuerdo a los párrafos 155-158 del Código Penal. La pena máxima comprende 14 años de cárcel. Así y todo, las autoridades de este país sostienen a veces la opinión de que en Zambia no existen homosexuales y por ende tampoco hay nada que castigar. Sobre la actitud de la población hacia los gays no sabemos casi nada.
A principios de 2009, el Vicepresidente del gobierno animó a sus compatriotas a denunciar a homosexuales para poder así encarcelarlos.
Zambia es uno de los países más pobres del mundo, muchas personas viven aquí con menos de 1 dólar al día y en los últimos 15 años, la esperanza media de vida (también a causa de la epidemia del SIDA) se ha reducido de los 60 a los 38 años.

I paragrafi 155-158 del codice penale considerano illegali le relazioni omosessuali fra maschi di qualsiasi età. Quattordici anni di prigione rappresentano il massimo della pena comminabile. Nonostante tutto, però, il governo s'è dato gran pena per sottolineare che in Zambia il problema non esista. Non abbiamo informazioni sull'atteggiamento generale nei confronti dei gay.
All'inizio del 2009 il vicepresidente ha esortato i suoi concittadini a denunciare gli omosessuali per sbatterli in prigione. Lo Zambia è uno dei Paesi più poveri del mondo. Molte persone sono costrette a vivere con meno di un dollaro al giorno. Negli ultimi 15 anni l'età media della popolazione si è abbassata (anche a causa dell'AIDS) da 60 a 38 anni.

Livingstone ☎ 021

HOTELS

Livingstone Safari Lodge (B BF cc H M MA MSG PI WH WO) All year
Victoria Falls Road ☎ 955 832 169 www.livingstonebushlodge.com
Luxury large chalets in natural setting near the Victoria Falls, safe and discreet, some local gay clientele.

Royal Livingstone (AC B BF CC M MC NG OS PI) All year
Mosi-oa-Tunya Road *In Mosi-oa-Tunya National Park* ☎ (21) 332 11 22
royal-livingstone-hotel.com
Not a gay hotel but a fantastic choice when planning a trip to the Victoria Falls, only five mins walk from the hotel.

Lusaka ☎ 01

BARS

Alpha (B d MC NG)
Landa Road *In Northmead Shopping Centre*
This place has a great atmosphere and is packed every night. Anything goes. Local gay guys meet here.

Eureka (B MC NG)
Kafue Road *About 15 mins south of Lusaka* ☎ (01) 272 351
Popular meeting place, pool table, dart board and a legendary barman.

Safari Bar (B H NG)
c/o Hotel Intercontinental, Haile Selassie Av. *Top floor* ☎ (01) 250 600

DANCECLUBS

■ **Mr. Pete's** (B D NG) 22-5h
Panganani Road
Although not gay, it is possible to meet gays in this huge disco. Best on Fri nights. Rave and house music.

■ **Room 101** (! B MC NG p PK) Wed, Fri & Sat 21-?h
Great East Road *Arcades Shopping Centre* ☎ 977 800 029
This is probably the most distinctive, select and sophisticated night club in Lusaka.

Zimbabwe

Name: Simbabwe
Location: Southern Africa
Initials: ZW
Time: GMT +1
International Country Code: ☎ 263 (omit 0 from area code)
International Access Code: ☎ 00
Language: English
Area: 390 757 km² = 150,800 sq mi.
Currency: 1 Zimbabwe Dollar (Z$) = 100 Cents
Population: 13,010,000
Capital: Harare
Religions: 65% Christian
Climate: The summer rainy season from October to March is hot; winters are mild and dry. Temperatures in the low lands are more extreme with widespread Malaria during the summer months. The highlands in the east are wet and cool.

Sodomy between two men in Zimbabwe is illegal. In addition, there are clauses relating to public morality and „unnatural offences". No distinction is made between consensual and enforced sodomy. Stay away from Zimbabwe. Your safety cannot be guaranteed and the situation will not change as long as the contry suffers under this dictator!

Sexuelle Handlungen unter Männern sind in Simbabwe illegal. Außerdem gibt es Bestimmungen, die sich auf die öffentliche Moral und deren „widernatürliche Verletzungen" beziehen. Als Reiseziel ist Simbabwe nicht zu empfehlen. Die Sicherheit von Touristen kann nicht garantiert werden, was sich wohl auch nicht ändern wird, solange das Land unter diesem Diktator zu leiden hat!

Les relations sexuelles entre hommes sont interdites au Zimbabwe, qu'elles soient forcées ou entre adultes consentants. Il existe en outre des lois concernant les „délit contre-nature" et le respect de l'ordre moral. Le Zimbabwe est une destination déconseillée aux voyageurs. La sécurité des touristes ne peut pas être garantie, ce qui ne changera pas tant que le pays sera sous le joug de ce dictateur !

Los actos sexuales entre hombres están penalizados en Zimbawe. Además existen leyes sobre „delitos contra natura" y la protección de la moral pública. Con ello no se diferencia entre actos voluntarios y forzosos. Como destino turístico, Zimbawe no es recomendable. No se puede garantizar la seguridad de los turistas, hecho que probablemente tampoco cambiará mientras el país siga viviendo bajo este dictador!

In Zimbabwe, i rapporti omosessuali tra uomini sono penalmente perseguibili. Inoltre ci sono leggi sui „delitti contronatura" e sulla tutela della decenza pubblica. In questo non viene fatta alcuna distinzione tra rapporti volontari e imposti. Lo Zimbabwe non è un Paese che ci sentiamo di consigliare come meta turistica: la sicurezza dei turisti non è garantita, e questo non cambierà fin tanto che il Paese sarà costretto a soffrire sotto il governo di questo dittatore.

NATIONAL GAY INFO

■ **GALZ – Gays and Lesbians of Zimbabwe** (GLM MA S WE)
Mon-Fri 9-17h (Fri & Sat evenings social events)
35 Colenbrander Road, Milton Park ✉ Harare ☎ (04) 741 736
Contact GALZ for any information about visiting Zimbabwe. Counselling information available from: counselling@galz.co.zw The GALZ Resource centre provides a safe space for the LGBT community to meet and socialise, we have a book and DVD/video library on-site which you can enjoy. Various activities are organised for the community and take place at the Resource Centre. Please contact the GALZ Director (director@galz.co.zw) for more details on our projects

■ **Zimbabwe Lawyers for Human Rights**
6th Floor Beverley Court, 100 Nelson Mandela Av. ✉ Harare
☎ (04) 251 468 🖳 www.zlhr.org.zw
HIV/AIDS Legal Unit, which offers free legal advice and instituting litigation on HIV/AIDS-related matters.

Harare ☎ 04

DANCECLUBS

■ **Cyberia** (B D MA NG) Fri
Sam Levy's Village, Borrowdale
Basically a straight teeny-bopper scene.

■ **Origins Night Club** (B g M MA)
Sam Levy's Village, Borrowdale
Often frequented by many gay people. It is quite mixed racially and music ranges from Raggae to Hiphop or Techno.

XLSIOR
MYKONOS
22-26 AUGUST 2012
www.xlsiorfestival.com
XL

Countries not listed

Here is a list of the countries not specifically listed in this edition of Spartacus. There are several reasons for this: either there is no evident gay scene or there is an overwhelming hostility towards homosexuals (see map on page 1098) or upon specific request from organisations and locals who fear reprisals when listed in our guide.

Hier folgt eine Liste von Ländern, die nicht in dieser Ausgabe SPARTACUS gelistet sind, da in diesen Ländern entweder keine schwule Szene existiert, die rechtliche Situation extrem schwulenfeindlich ist (siehe Karte auf Seite 1098) oder wir einem speziellen Wunsch von einigen Einrichtungen, nicht in unserem Guide gelistet zu werden, nachgekommen sind.

Les pays ci-dessous n'ont pas été inclus dans cette édition du SPARTACUS pour plusieurs raisons: soit parce qu'il n'existe pas de milieu gay dans ces pays, soit parce que la situation légale de ces pays est extrêmement homophobe (voir carte à la page 1098), soit parce que certains établissements nous ont explicitement demandé à ne pas être recensé dans notre guide.

A continuación enumeramos una serie de países que no aparecen en la lista de esta edición de la SPARTACUS, bien porque en estos países no existe ningún ambiente homosexual, la situación jurídica es totalmente contraria hacia los homosexuales (véase mapa en la página 1098) o bien porque hemos querido respetar el deseo específico de algunos negocios de no aparecer en nuestra guía.

Qui a seguito una lista di paesi che non sono stati inclusi in questa edizione SPARTACUS per l'assenza di una scena gay, a causa di una situazione giuridica estremamente antiomosessuale (vedi piantina a pagina 1098) o per rispettare il particolare desiderio di alcuni di non apparire nella ns. guida.

Afghanistan

No specific laws regarding homosexuality exist. Article 427 stipulates detention for adultery and pedophilia of between 5 to 15 years. According to article 130, the Shari'a laws can be applied, which forbids homosexual acts. As of 2008, it appears that the regime change has not had much impact on the legal status of homosexuals in Afghanistan.

Algeria

According to Article 388 of the penal code from 1996, sodomy may be punished with imprisonment from two months to two years and a fine of o500 to 2000Dinar. According to Article 333 an "outrage to public decency" increases the penalties in the case of "acts against nature with a member of the same sex" with a prison sentence of between 6 months to 3 years and a fine of between 1,000 to 10,000 Dinar.

Andorra

Homosexual acts are legal. The age of consent is 16 for all. In 2005, they have legalized civil unions. A small gay scene does exist, but is difficult to find.

Angola

Homosexuality is according to the law "an offence against the public moral" Articles 70 and 71 and therefore prohibited. We have no information regarding possible penalties for "offenders".

Antigua & Barbuda

According to Act No. 9 of the Sexual Offences Act, buggery (anal sexual intercourse) is illegal and for life imprisonment applies, if committed by an adult on a minor. Homophobia is wide spread.

Azerbaijan

2000 saw the abolishment of the law forbidding homosexual interactions (gay sex). Article 150, bans forcible sexual acts.The age of consent is 16 for both homosexuals and heterosexuals. Freedom of expression continues to be heavily restricted.

Bangladesh

According to article 377 homosexual acts are illegal and will be punished with deportation, fines and/or up to 10 years, sometimes life imprisonment. The number of prosecutions under this law are low. However militant Islamic fundamentalism is gaining ground in Bangladesh. And there is a real danger that Bangladesh may follow Pakistan down the road of fundamentalist intolerance, in which case there will be many more Bangladeshi gay men seeking asylum in other countries.

Benin

Same-sex sexual acts for both men and women are legal in Benin. We have no information on any possible gay scene in Benin.

Bhutan

Male homosexuality is forbidden by law (Art. 213 & 214) and is punishable with a prison sentence from between one month to one year.

Botswana

According to chapter 8.01, section 164 to 167, homosexuality is an "unnatural tendency" and can be punished with up to 7 years of imprisonment. Acts of gross indecency are also punishable according to this article.

Brunei

In this Islamic country homosexual acts are forbidden according to chapter 22, section 377 of the penal code and can be punished with up to 10 years imprisonment or a fine of 30,000 Brunei Dollar.

Burkina Faso

Homosexual acts are not directly forbidden. Article 410 of the penal code makes any act which leads to a public offence punishable with a fine of between 50,000 to 600,000 Franc. Article 411 prohibits any sexual act which is deemed to be unnatural or against the public morals. Articles 412-415 stipulate the punishment of acts against the public "sense of shame" of under-aged persons to be a prison sentence of between 2 months to 10 years. According to Article 416 anyone who offends the public "sense of shame" together with a second person (either by force, surprise or constraint) can be imprisoned for a period of between 1 to 3 years. Underage sexual practices are punishable with up to 5 years imprisonment.

Burundi

The lower house in the East African country of Burundi passed legislation in 2009 making homosexuality a federal crime. Under the new law (article 567), anyone convicted of homosexuality can be sentenced to a two-year prison sentence.

Cameroon

Homosexuality is punishable according to Article 347 of the penal code with a prison sentence of 6 months to 5 years and/ or a fine of 200,000 CFA. More severe sentencing is likely when one of the "offenders" is under 21 years of age.

Central African Republic

According to our information, homosexuality is illegal although it is not mentioned in the local criminal law.

Chad

According to our information, homosexuality is illegal although it is not mentioned in the local criminal law.

Comoros Islands

So-called "impudent acts against the nature" are illegal in Comoros according to article 318 of the Penal Code. Such acts were punished with up to five years imprisonment as well as a fine.

Cook Islands

Sodomy is punishable with up to 7 years imprisonment and up to 5 years for "indecent acts with males". Further reference to homosexuality and the law does not exist in the penal code of the Cook Islands.

Democratic Rep. of Congo

Homosexuality is not illegal but article 168-170 and 172 punish so-called "crimes against family life". These articles are used to punish homosexuals. A prison sentence for those punished under these articles can be from 5 to 20 years.

Djibouti

Homosexuality is illegal and sodomy laws do exist in the penal code of Djibouti. We do not however have further information regarding these laws.

Dominica

According to Article 14 of the Sexual Offences Act from 1998, anyone caught perpetrating an act of gross indecency can be punished with imprisonment of up to 5 years. Article 15 punishes anal sex (regardless of whether with men or women) with a prison sentence of up to 10 years, or in some cases can lead to internment in a mental asylum. Article 16 states the punishment for attempted anal sex is imprisonment of up to 4 years.

Equatorial Guinea

We have no information available as to whether homosexuality is illegal in Equatorial Guinea. Nor do we have any information regarding sodomy laws or the age of consent.

Eritrea

According to section II of the penal code from 1960, Article 600 "unnatural carnal offences" can be punished with internment for between 10 days to 3 years. Article 601 (grievous contraventions) in which the perpetrator can be imprisoned for between 3 months to 5 years, especially in the case of violence and acts of force.

Ethiopia

Article 629 prohibits homosexual acts. Article 630 punishes such acts with a maximum prison sentence of 10 years – applied when the victim is subjected to acts of cruelty or sadism; when the offender knowingly transmits a sexually transmitted disease (STD) or when the offender commits homosexual acts with a person under the age of 15 years. Article 631 punishes pedophilia.

Gambia

According to the criminal code from 1965, § 15, Offences against Morality Act, Article 144: homosexuality is an "unnatural offence" and is illegal. According to Article 145 a prison sentence for perpetrators can be for up to 7 years. Article 146 states those who commit "unnatural acts" with anyone under the age of 14 years can also be imprisoned for up to 7 years. Article 147 states homosexual acts, even in privacy are considered acts of gross indecency and can be punished with imprisonment for up to 5 years. In 2009 hotel owners were prohibited from renting rooms to homosexuals. Housing rights were also effected in this ruling.

Gabon

Homosexuality is legal in Gabon, and the age of consent is 18 for both same-sex and opposite-sex sexual activity. In December 2008, Gabon (one of only six African countries) signed the UN declaration on sexual orientation and gender identity aimed at decriminalizing homosexuality worldwide.

Ghana

According to the Criminal Code from 1960-Chapter 6, Sexual Offences Article 105 sets to punish "unnatural sexual intercourse" with a) anyone over the age of 16 and without his consent – punishable with imprisonment of between 5 and 25 years. A gay scene in Ghana does not exist.

Guam

Although no juridical information is available, it is mentioned in Internet that the age of consent is generally 16 years of age.

Guinea

Article 325 prohibits same-sex acts with a maximum penalty of 3 years imprisonment and a fine of up to 1 million Guinea-Francs. This maximum penalty is enforced if one of the offenders are under 21 years of age. Article 362/327 can punish offenders who publicly commit an "act of indecency".

Guinea-Bissau

Homosexual acts are legal. Here a military code of law applies. No mention to homosexuality is made and no sodomy laws exist.

Guyana

According to the penal code of Guyana (§ 8.01, point 25, section 352)"indecent behavior" committed by men, either in a public or private sphere, will be punished with imprisonment for up to 2 years. For attempted anal sex the punishment is 10 years and for anal sex life imprisonment is possible.

Haiti

Homosexuality is legal. After the devastating earthquake from the 12 January 2010 Haiti needs help more than ever. Two organisations SEROvie and ACCV (Civic Action Against HIV) are providing people with essentials such as food and clothes. You can help too. Contact SERvie at: serovielife@yahoo.com

Iraq

According to paragraph 394 of the penal code anyone caught engaging in "unnatural fornication" where the person/s involved is/are over 15 and under 18 years of age can be sentenced to a maximum of 7 years imprisonment. When the person has not yet reached 15 years of age the maximum sentence is 10 years imprisonment. This has become one of the most dangerous countries in the world! Police violence against minorities is not uncommon.

Ivory Coast

Due to the political turmoil and the change of government in Ivory Coast, extreme caution is recommended to gay visitors. Outbreaks of violence are still being reported and the civil war is still going on. At present we have no up-to-date information regarding the legal situation of homosexuals. Get in touch with your ministry of foreign affairs before travelling to Ivory Coast.

Korea, North

Homosexuality is not forbidden but "violating the rules of collective socialistic life" can be punished with up to 2 years imprisonment. It is unclear as to whether this code of conduct is implemented to punish homosexuals.

Kuwait

The Shari'a is part of the Kuwaiti judicial system. According to the local penal code, Article 193 states that sexual acts between men over the age of 21 can be beguilement with anyone under 21 years of age is punishable with life imprisonment.

Lesotho

Homosexuality is legal but not mentioned in the criminal law. There is also no mention of legislation against sodomy. The age of consent is also unknown.

Liberia

According to Article 14.74 homosexuality is "voluntary sodomy" and is punishable. The exact extent of punishment is unknown to us.

Libya

Homosexuality is illegal and can be punished according to article 407/4 with up to 5 years imprisonment, or 10 years when committed in an act of violence. Article 408 (amended by Article VIII/2) punishes both parties for "indecent acts".

Macao

No information about homosexuality and the law is available. Macao is part of the People's Republic of China, were homosexuality is not recognized or mentioned in the penal code.

Malawi

Homosexual acts are illegal in Malawi. Section 153 prohibits "unnatural offences". Section 156 concerning "public decency" is used to punish homosexual acts. Europeans who commit acts of homosexuality with locals can be prosecuted under article 156 and expelled as "undesirable aliens". On December 28, 2009 two LGBT and HIV/AIDS activists were arrested and prosecutors subjected them to internal medical examinations without their consent. They were charged according to Sections 153 and 156 of the Malawi Penal Code.

Maldives

The Indian penal code applies on all the Island of the Maldives and according to this code, homosexuality is illegal. For gay couples visiting the islands we recommend you act discreetly.

Mali

Homosexuality is legal in Mali but "offending people in public" can be punished according to article 179 with imprisonment of up to 2 years and a fine.

Mauritania

The Shari'a law applies in Mauritania. According to the penal code from 1983, part II chapter 1, section 4, Article 308 states" any adult Muslim caught engaging in an "unnatural act" with a member of the same sex is punishable with the death sentence by public stoning.

Micronesia

There are seven island groups making up Micronesia. The laws regarding homosexuality are very diverse, ranging from Guam which bans anti-gay discrimination to criminal penalties for homosexual activity in e.g. Kiribati and Nauru. We have no information regarding the legal situation in Northern Mariana Islands and Palau.

Monaco

Homosexuality is legal under the Monegasque Penal Code. Criminal penalties for homosexual acts were eliminated in 1793 due to the adoption of French laws. Monaco does not recognise same-sex partnerships. The age of consent is set at 16 years. There are no official gay places in Monaco.

Nigeria

Homosexuality in Nigeria is illegal according to paragraph 214 as well as 217 of the Nigerian penal code and can be punished by imprisonment of up to 14 years. The north of Nigeria is Islamic and extremely conservative. As with most large, developing countries, it is not advisable to walk around at night, but rather to take a taxi to and from your destination. This warning should be taken very seriously, indeed, because politicians have been trying to pass harsher punishments for homosexuals for several years already. At this moment in time (11/2011) the Nigerian senate is hence considering a further intensification of the discrimination against homosexuals.

Niger

Homosexuality is not forbidden in Niger but a punishment is possible should you "offend the public moral" according to Articles 275-279 or engage in sexual intercourse with minors under the age of consent, which is set at 21 years of age (Article 282). An imprisonment of 6 months to 3 years and a fine of between 10,000 and 100,000 CFA-Franc is possible for offenders.

Oman

Homosexuality in the Sultanate of Oman is illegal according to § 32 of the penal code and can be punished with a jail sentence of up to 3 years. In Oman it is said that cases only get to court if "public scandal" is involved. We have no further information regarding homosexuality in Oman.

Palestinian Territories

In the Gaza Strip according to Section 152 of the penal code, sexual intercourse with another person is against the order of nature, which is punishable by imprisonment for a term of ten years.

Pakistan

Homosexual activity is illegal, punishable according to Islamic Laws which were re-introduced in 1990 and according to paragraph 377 with life in prison, corporal punishment of 100 lashes or even death by stoning. Despite the strict laws of Islam regarding moral standards, gay men, transvestites and transsexuals live relatively undisturbed from the police. On the other hand they cannot expect much protection from the authorities.

Papua New Guinea

Homosexuality is prohibited according to section 210 of the penal code. Those caught engaging in anal sex can get punished with up to 7 years imprisonment. This also applies to heterosexual "offenders". Other homosexual sex acts (acts of indecency) can be punished with up to 3 years imprisonment.

Qatar

The judicial system in Qatar is based on the Shari'a, homosexual acts are punished with up to 5 years imprisonment.

Rwanda

Homosexuality is legal although no specific laws regarding homosexuality exist. The age of consent is 18. Section 362 of the penal code prohibits sexual relations with persons under the age of 18. In December 2009 Rwanda's Minister of Justice overturned a proposed law criminalizing homosexuality.

San Marino

Homosexuality has been legal in San Marino since 1964. The age of consent for both homosexuals and heterosexuals is 14 years of age.

Saudi Arabia

The judicial system is based on the Shari'a. It is however unclear whether lashes apply to unmarried men and capital punishment applies to married men who engage in homosexual acts, as is the case in many countries where Shari'a Law applies. Gay Saudi prince Saud faces the death penalty if he ever returns to Saudi Arabia - not because he beat and strangled his servant to death, but because being gay is a capital offence there and may have to apply for asylum when he is eventually released after serving his 20-year sentence in the UK.

Senegal

Senegal is one of the few Francophone African countries that penalize homosexuality. There has been an alarming increase in the number of arrests for alleged sexual acts "against nature". Homosexuality is said to be an "immoral and unnatural act" and is illegal according to article 319, paragraph 3 of the Penal Code in Senegal. It is punishable with imprisonment of up to five years and fines. If the act was committed with a person under the age of 21, the maximum penalty is always applied. Islam condemns homosexuality and forbids believers from becoming involved, but the Senegal society tolerates homosexuals.

Seychelles

Homosexuality is Illegal in the Seychelles. No reliable information regarding the legal situation is available.

Sierra Leone

According to the law homosexuality is an "unnatural act" and is forbidden. Information regarding possible punishments is not available.

Somalia

Article 409 prohibits homosexual acts. Punishment can be up to 3 years imprisonment. According to article 410, a security measure may be added to a sentence for homosexual acts, to prevent re-occurrence.

Solomon Islands

According to the penal code, chapter 26, section 160: anyone who engages in anal sex acts with another person or with an animal are punishable with up to 14 years imprisonment. Attempted anal intercourse can be punished with up to 7 years imprisonment. Acts of gross indecency (even in private) can be punished with 5 years imprisonment.

Sudan

The judicial system is based on the Shari'a and according to Article 148, capital punishment applies should the offence be repeated for the third time. Before this 100 lashes apply to unmarried men who engage in homosexual acts. Lashes apply to "cross dressers" too.

Suriname

Section 302 of the penal code criminalizes homosexual acts with anyone under the age of 18 with a penalty of up to 4 years imprisonment.

Swaziland

Homosexuality is illegal. According to the Prime Minister homosexuality is an "abnormality and sickness". According to Swazi tradition however, two women can lawfully marry.

Tajikistan

Homosexuality is legal. The age of consent is 17 for all.

Tanzania

The penal code from 2002, chapter 1, § 154 prohibits "unnatural" sex acts. The punishment for offenders is up to life imprisonment, but more common is a sentence of no less than 30 years. Life imprisonment applies when the act was carried out with a child under the age of 10 years. Chapter 1.b § 157 states that sexual acts between men (seen as acts of "gross indecency") can receive a prison sentence of up to 5 years.

Togo

According to Article 88 of the penal code of Togo, homosexuality is illegal and can be punished with up to 3 years imprisonment as well as a fine of between 100,000 to 500,000 Francs.

Tonga

Homosexual relationships are illegal. Possible punishment up to 10 years imprisonment.

Trinidad & Tobago

Article 13 of the Sexual Offences Act punishes anal sex with 5 to 10 years imprisonment (also for heterosexuals) and up to 25 years for those caught engaging in homosexual sex acts.

Turkmenistan

Article 135 of the criminal code of Turkmenistan punishes homosexual men with up to 2 years of imprisonment. Acts where violence or where misuse of those in need of protection can lead to a penalty of 3 to 6 years imprisonment. The sentence is especially applicable in cases of repeated offences; where three or more people are involved, without previous arrangement; in cases where under-aged "participants" are involved or where a sexually transmitted disease resulted from the act – here a prison sentence from 5 to 10 years is possible. When the act leads to the death of the other "participant" including the infection with the AIDS virus, a sentence from 10 to 20 years is common. Foreigners who "out" themselves can be deported.

Uganda

According to section 145 of the penal code "carnal knowledge against the order of nature" can be punished with lifetime imprisonment. According to Article 145 attempts of carnal knowledge can be punished with up to 7 years of imprisonment. In 2009 a new law was proposed in Uganda that would make homosexuality punishable by death and would impose prison terms of up to three years for any person who fails to report (within 24 hours) the identities of everyone they know who is lesbian' gay' bisexual or transgender. This anti-homosexuality bill has lost support due to local and international opposition.

Uzbekistan

Homosexuality is unlawful according to Art. 120 of the Uzbek penal code, but which applies only to masculine homosexuality, there is no provision on women in this matter. In reality, homosexuals are rather rarely taken to court. The penal code provides for prison sentences of up to three years. Sexual contact with minors under the age of 16 is forbidden.

Yemen

The Shari'a law applies here. According to the local penal code from 1994, § 264: homosexuality amongst men is defined as "the insertion in the anus". Unmarried men are punishable with 100 lashes or one year imprisonment. Married men are sentenced to death by stoning. Homosexuality amongst women (stimulation through attrition) can be punished with between 3 to 7 years imprisonment.

The legal situation worldwide for male homosexuality

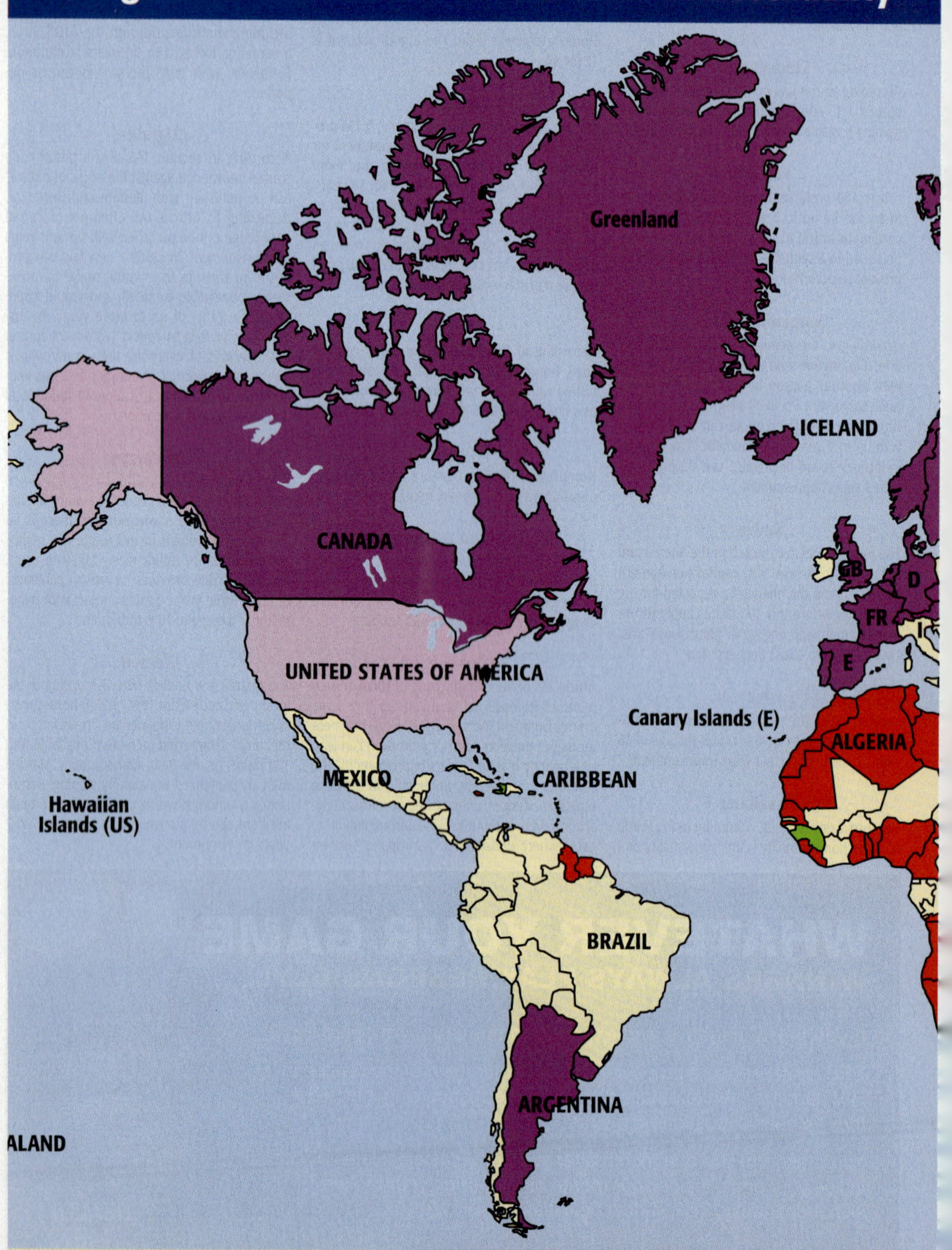

legal / legal / légale / legal / legale

Gay marriage or similar / Homoehe oder Vergleichbares / mariage gai ou similaire / Matrimonio gay o similar / Matrimonio gay o simile

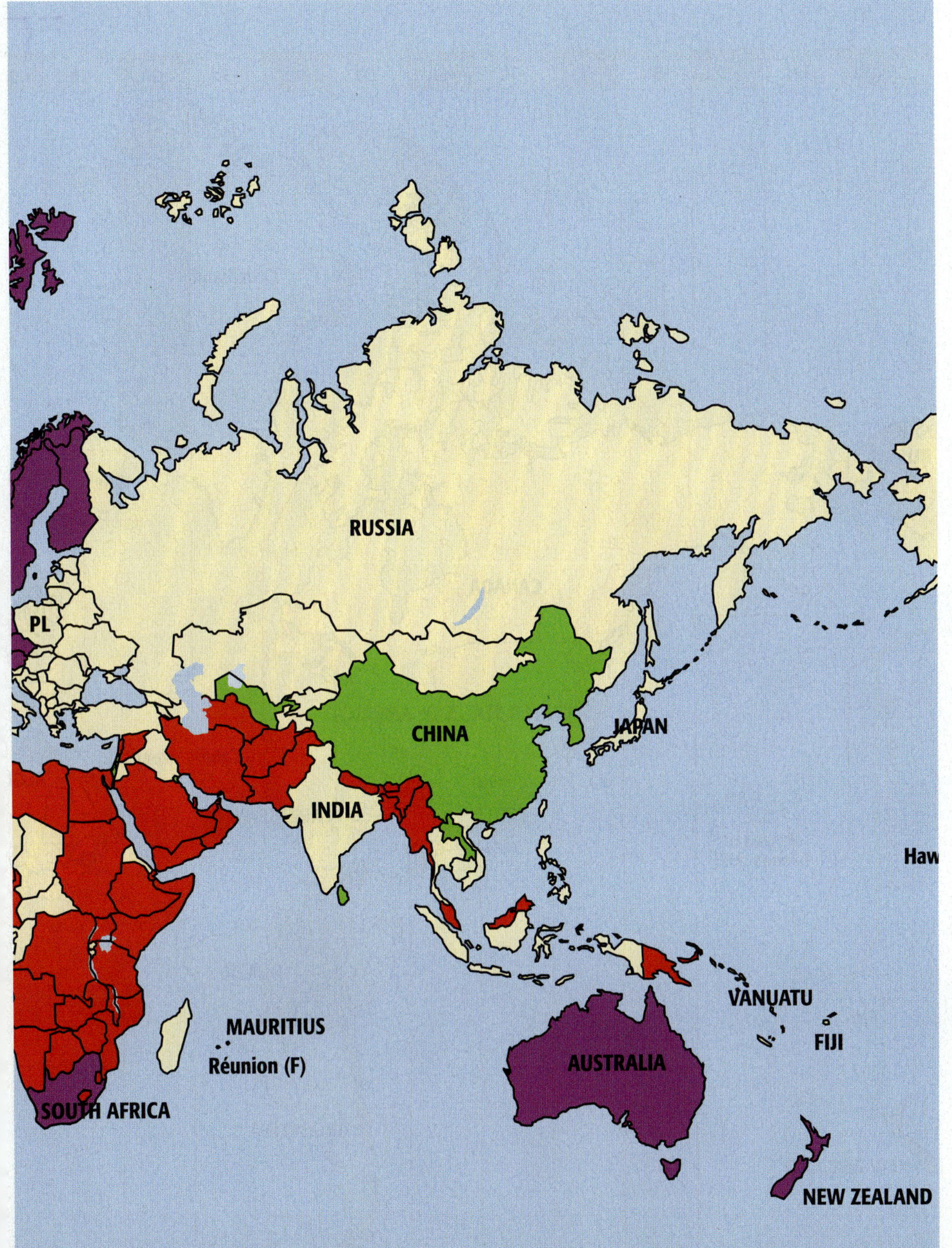

illegal / illegal / illégale / ilegal / illegale

not mentioned / nicht erwähnt / n'est pas mentionnée / non mencionado / non menzionato

+12h-
-11h
-10h
-9h
-8h
-7h
-6h
-5h
-4h
-3h
-2h
-1h
Greenland
RUSSIA
ICELAN
CANADA
GB
UNITED STATES OF AMERICA
E
International Date Line
Canary Islands (E)
ALG
MEXICO
CARIBBEAN
Hawaiian Islands (US)
BRAZIL
FIJI
-13h
ARGENTINA
NEW ZEALAND
-12h
Midnight
1AM
2AM
3AM
4AM
5AM
6AM
7AM
8AM
9AM
10AM
11AM
Noo

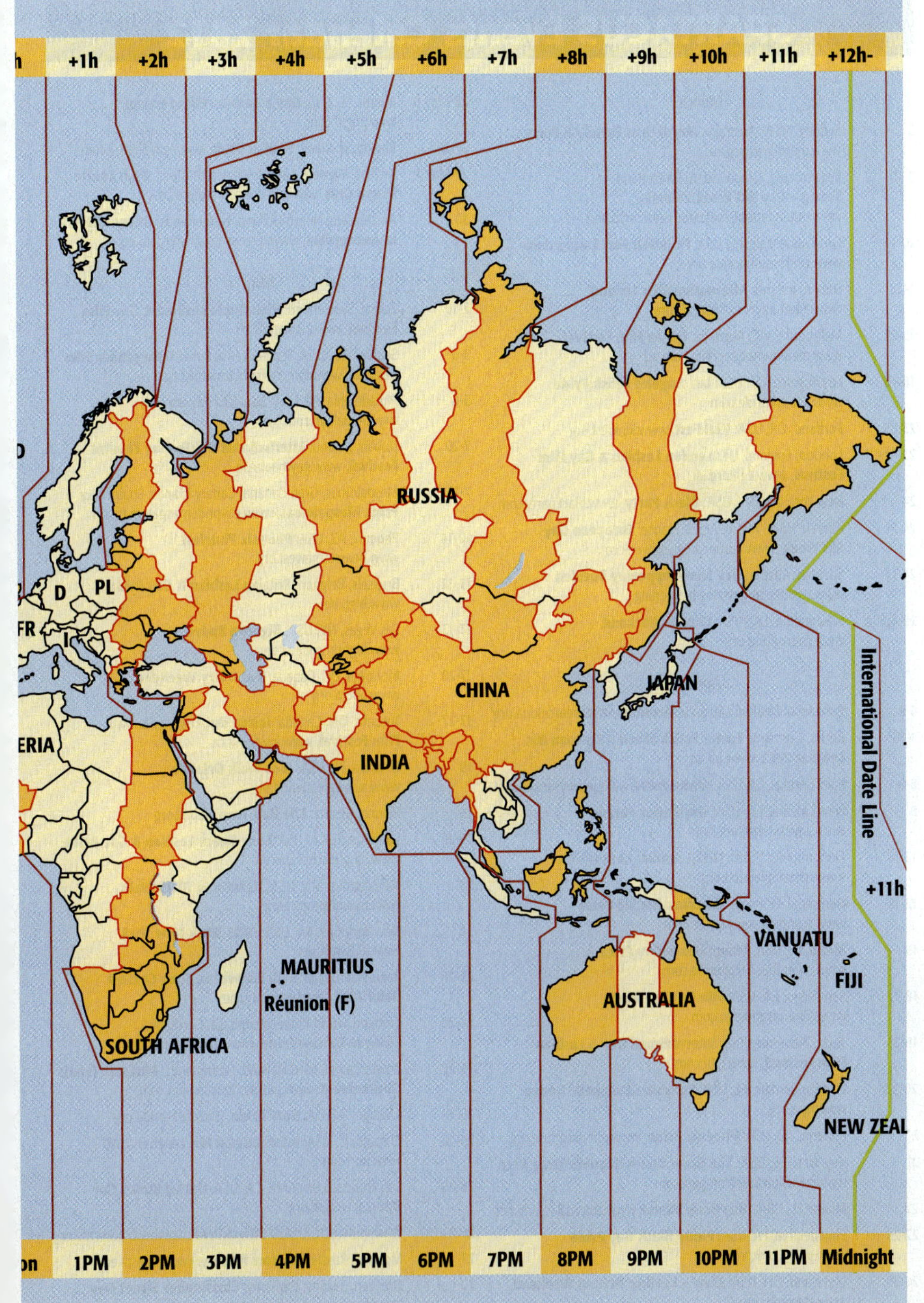
h
+1h
+2h
+3h
+4h
+5h
+6h
+7h
+8h
+9h
+10h
+11h
+12h-
D
PL
FR
I
RUSSIA
CHINA
JAPAN
INDIA
ERIA
International Date Line
+11h
VANUATU
FIJI
MAURITIUS
Réunion (F)
AUSTRALIA
SOUTH AFRICA
NEW ZEAL
on
1PM
2PM
3PM
4PM
5PM
6PM
7PM
8PM
9PM
10PM
11PM
Midnight

SPARTACUS Events Calendar 2012

March

3 Sydney, NSW, Australia: **Mardi Gras Parade & Party** www.mardigras.org.au

3-10 Lenzerheide, Graubünden, Switzerland: **Swing – Gay Ski Week Valbella** www.outandaboutravel.com/gayskitrips.htm

10-11 Fort Lauderdale, FL, USA: **Pridefest Fort Lauderdale** www.pridesouthflorida.org

14 Dublin, Ireland: **Alternative Miss Ireland** www.alternativemissireland.com

15-25 Melbourne, VIC, Australia: **Queer Film Festival** www.melbournequeerfilm.com.au

16-25 Los Angeles, CA, USA: **Los Angeles Fetish Pride** www.lafetishpride.com

23-25 Portland, OR, USA: **KinkFest**, www.kinkfest.org

23-Apr. 1 London, England, UK: **London Lesbian & Gay Film Festival**, www.llgff.org.uk

24 New York City, NY, USA: **Black Party**, www.blackparty.com

24-31 Alpe de'Huez, Rhône-Alpes, France: **European Gay Ski Week**, www.europeangayskiweek.com

24-31 Soelden, Austria: **Gay Snowhappening Soelden** www.soelden.at/gaysnowhappening

29-Apr. 1 Washington, DC, USA: **Cherry Weekend** www.cherryfund.org

April

4-9 Barcelona,Catalonia,Spain:**Bearcelona**,www.bearcelona.org

4-10 Berlin, Germany: **Easter Fetish Week & German Mr. Leather 2012**, www.blf.de

6-9 Palm Springs, CA, USA: **White Party**, www.jeffreysanker.com

8 New Orleans, LA, USA: **Gay Easter Parade** www.gayeasterparade.com

12-14 Florianopolis, Brazil: **IGLTA Annual Convention** www.igltaconvention.org

12-15 Hemsedal, Norway: **Skandinavian Ski Pride** www.scandinavianskipride.com

15 Miami, FL, USA: **Miami Beach Gay Pride** www.miamibeachgaypride.com

18-22 San Diego, CA, USA: **FilmOut San Diego** www.filmoutsandiego.com

19-25 Turin, Piemonte, Italy: **International Gay & Lesbian Film Festival**, www.tglff.com

20-22 Fort Lauderdale, FL, USA: **Sunshine Stampede Rodeo** www.fgra.org

21 Phoenix, AZ, USA: **Phoenix Pride**, www.phoenixpride.org

21 Key West, FL, USA: **The Great Conch Republic Drag Race** www.bourbonstreetcomplex.com

22 Miami, FL, USA: **Aids Walk Miami**, www.aidswalkmiami.net

22-29 Philadelphia, PA, USA: **Philly Black Gay Pride** www.phillyblackpride.org

26-29 Cleveland, OH, USA: **Claw – Leather Annual Weekend** www.clawinfo.org

26-May 6 Miami, FL, USA: **Gay & Lesbian Film Festival** www.mglff.com

27-28 Phuket, Thailand: **Phuket Pride**, www.gaypatong.com

27-May 1 Knysna, Western Cape Town, South Africa: **Pink Loerie Mardi Gras**, www.pinkloeriemardigras.co.za

30 Amsterdam, Noord-Holland, Netherlands: **Queen's Day in Amsterdam**, www.queensdayamsterdam.eu

May

2-10 Zurich, Switzerland: **Pink Apple Lesbian & Gay Film Festival**, www.pinkapple.ch

3-6 Seattle, WA, USA: Seattle Translations: **Transgender Film Festival**, www.threedollarbillcinema.org

3-6 Philadelphia, PA, USA: **Equality Forum** www.equalityforum.com

7-20 Dublin, Ireland: **International Dublin Gay Theatre Festival**, www.gaytheatre.ie

7-13 Maspalomas, Gran Canaria, Canary Islands, Spain: **Gay Pride Maspalomas**, www.gaypridemaspalomas.com

10-14 Phoenix, AZ, USA: **Phoenix Phurfest** www.bearsofthewest.org

11-12 Brussels, Belgium: **Belgian Lesbian & Gay Pride** www.blgp.be

11-13 Las Vegas, NV, USA: **Bighorn Rodeo** www.bighornrodeo.com

17-20 Montreal, QC, Canada: **Hot & Dry Weekend** www.bbcm.org

17-27 Toronto, ON, Canada: **Inside Out Lesbian & Gay Film Festival**, www.insideout.ca

19 Orlando, FL, USA: **Aids Walk Orlando** www.aidswalkorlando.org

19 Vienna, Austria: **Life Ball**, www.lifeball.org

19-20 Long Beach, CA, USA: **Long Beach Lesbian & Gay Pride**, www.longbeachpride.com

20 Minneapolis, MN, USA: **Minnesota AIDS Walk**, www.mnaidsproject.org

20 New York City, NY, USA: **AIDS Walk New York** www.aidswalk.net

22-26 Baku, Azerbaijan: **57th Eurovision Song Contest Baku 2012,** www.esctoday.com

24-28 Cologne, North Rhine-Westphalia, Germany: **Cologne LeatherPride,** www.rheinfetisch.com

25-28 Amsterdam, Noord-Holland, Netherlands: **Pinkster Tennis Tournament**, www.pinkstertournament.com

25-28 Chicago, IL, USA: **Bear Pride**, www.bearpride.org

25-28 Chicago, IL, USA: **International Mr. Leather 2010** www.imrl.com

25-28 San Francisco Bay Area, CA, USA: **United States Gay Open**, www.gltf.org

26-27 Washington,DC,USA: **DC Black Pride,** www.dcblackpride.org

27 Moscow, Russia: **Moscow Pride**, www.gayrussia.eu

27-Jun. 3 Dresden, Saxony, Germany: **Christopher Street Day Dresden**, www.csd-dresden.de

SPARTACUS Events Calendar 2012

29-Jun. 4 Orlando, FL, USA: **Gay Days**, www.gaydays.com

30-Jun. 2 Riga, Latvia: **Baltic Pride**, www.balticpride.eu

30-Jun. 10 Washington, DC, USA: **Capital Pride**, www.capitalpride.org

3 -Jun. 3 Honolulu, Oahu, HI, USA: **Honolulu Rainbow Film Festival,** www.hglcf.org

June

1-3 Salt Lake City, UT, USA: **Utah Pride** www.utahpridefestival.org

1-9 Hartford, CT, USA: **Connecticut Gay & Lesbian Film Festival**, www.ctglff.org

1-10 Boston, MA, USA: **Boston Pride**, www.bostonpride.org

1-10 Pittsburgh, PA, USA: **Pittsburgh Pride** www.pittsburghpride.org

2 Warsaw, Poland: **Parada Równosci** paradarownosci.eu

2 Lille, Nord-Pas-de-Calais, France: **Lille Pride** www.lillepride.com

2 Mexico City, Federal District, Mexico: **Mexico City Pride** www.mexcity.8m.com

2 Birmingham, England, UK: **Birmingham Pride** www.thepridehub.com

6-10 Key West, FL, USA: **PrideFest Key West** www.pridefestkeywest.com

7-10 Atlanta, GA, USA: **Southeast LeatherFest** www.seleatherfest.com

7-10 Athens, Greece: **Haircules**, www.haircules.gr

7-11 São Paulo, Brazil: **Gay Pride São Paulo** www.gaypridebrazil.org

8 Tel Aviv, Israel: **Tel Aviv Pride**, www.gaytlvguide.com

8-10 Los Angeles, CA, USA: **LA Pride**, www.lapride.org

8-10 Milwaukee, WI, USA: **Pridefest**, www.pridefest.com

8-17 Oxford, England, UK: **Oxford Pride** www.oxfordpride.org.uk

9 Athens, Greece: **Athens Pride**, www.athenspride.eu/v2

10 Philadelphia, PA, USA: **Philly Pride Parade & Festival** www.phillypride.org

10-17 Melbourne, VIC, Australia: **Southern HiBearnation** www.southernhibearnation.com

14-24 San Francisco, CA, USA: **Frameline – International LGBT Film Festival**, www.frameline.org

15-16 Columbus, OH, USA: **Stonewall Columbus Pride** www.columbuspride.org

15-17 Portland, OR, USA: **Portland Pride**, www.pridenw.org

15-17 Zurich, Switzerland: **Christopher Street Day Zürich** www.csdzurich.ch

15-24 Utrecht, Netherlands: **The MidZomerGracht Festival** www.midzomergracht.nl

16 Vienna, Austria: **Vienna Rainbow Parade** www.hosiwien.at/regenbogenparade/?lang=en

16-17 Berlin, Germany: **Lesbian & Gay City Festival Berlin** www.gay-stadtfest.de

16-17 Denver, CO, USA: **Denver PrideFest** www.denverpridefest.org

17 New York City, NY, USA: **Folsom Street East** www.folsomstreeteast.org

22-24 Paris, Ile-de-France, France: **Solidays**, www.solidays.org

22-Jul. 1 Toronto, ON, Canada: **Pride Toronto** www.torontopride.com

22-Jul. 1 Dublin, Ireland: **Dublin Pride Festival** www.dublinpride.org (Parade Day 30)

22-Jul. 1 Oslo, Norway: **Oslo Lesbian and Gay Pride Week** www.skeivedager.no

23 Cleveland, OH, USA: **Cleveland Pride** www.clevelandpride.org

23 Lisbon, Estremadura, Portugal: **Lisbon Pride** www.portugalpride.org

23 Berlin, Germany: **Christopher Street Day Berlin** www.csd-berlin.de

23 Houston, TX, USA: **Houston Pride**, www.pridehouston.org

23-24 Minneapolis, MN, USA: **GLBT Pride Twin Cities** www.tcpride.com

23-24 San Francisco, CA, USA: **San Francisco Pride** www.sfpride.org

23-24 St. Louis, MO, USA: **Pride St. Louis**, www.pridestl.org

24 Chicago, IL, USA: **Chicago Pride Parade** www.chicagopridecalendar.org

24 Seattle, WA, USA: **Seattle Pride,** www.seattlepride.org

24 New York City, NY, USA: **New York City Pride** www.hopinc.org

25-Jul. 1 Helsinki, Finland: **Helsinki Pride**, www.helsinkipride.fi

27-Jul. 1 Budapest, Hungary: **EuroGames**, www.eurogames.info

28 Las Palmas, Gran Canaria, **Canary Islands, Spain**: Gay Pride Las Palmas

29-Jul. 1 Barcelona, Catalonia, Spain: **Pride Barcelona** www.pridebarcelona.org

29-Jul. 1 Calgary, AB, Canada: **Canadian Rockies International Rodeo**, www.argra.org

30 Madrid, Spain: **Gay Pride Madrid** www.madridgaypride.com

30 Valencia, Spain: **Gay Pride Parade Valencia** www.lambdavalencia.org

30 St. Petersburg, FL, USA: **St. Pete Pride**, www.stpetepride.com

30 Paris, Ile-de-France, France: **Paris Gay Pride** www.marche.inter-lgbt.org

July

4-8 Loa Angeles, CA, USA: **Los Angeles Black Pride** www.atbla.com

5-9 Sitges, Catalonia, Spain: **Gay Pride Sitges** www.gaypridesitges.com

6-8 Cologne, North Rhine-Westphalia, Germany: **Christopher Street Day Cologne**, www.csd-cologne.de

6-9 New York City, NY, USA: **Liberty Open** www.metrotennisgroup.com

SPARTACUS Events Calendar 2012

6-9 Atlanta, GA, USA: **Atlanta Bear Fest** www.atlantabearfest.com

7 London, England, UK: **World Pride London** www.pridelondon.org

7-15 Provincetown, MA, USA: **Bear Week Provincetown** www.ptownbears.org

12-22 Los Angeles, CA, USA: **Outfest – LA Gay & Lesbian Film Festival**, www.outfest.org

12-23 Philadelphia, PA, USA: **QFest**, www.qfest.com

13-15 Frankfurt/Main, Hessen, Germany: **Christopher Street Day Frankfurt**, www.csd-frankfurt.de

14-15 Munich, Bavaria, Germany: **Christopher Street Day Munich**, www.csd-munich.de

15 San Francisco, CA, USA: **AIDS Walk San Francisco** www.aidswalk.net

19-22 Key West, FL, USA: **Bone Island Bare it All I** www.nakedkeywest.com

19-26 New York, NY, USA: **NewFest – NY LGBT Film Festival** www.newfest.org

20-29 Stuttgart, Baden-Württemberg, Germany: **Christopher Street Day**, www.csd-stuttgart.de

21 San Diego, CA, USA: **San Diego Pride**, www.sdpride.org

23 Tilburg, Noord-Brabant, Netherlands: **Pink Monday on Tilburgse Kermis**, www.rozemaandag-tilburg.nl

27-29 Helsinki, Finland: **Finlandization**, www.mscfin.fi

27-29 Bournemouth, England, UK: **Bourne Free Pride Festival** www.bournefree.co.uk

29 San Francisco, CA, USA: **Up Your Alley Fair** www.folsomstreetfair.com

30-Aug. 5 Stockholm, Sweden: **Stockholm Pride** www.stockholmpride.org

August

1-5 Sydney, NSW, Australia: **Bear Pride** www.bearpride.com.au

2-12 Barcelona, Catalonia, Spain: **Circuit Festival** www.circuitfestival.net

3-5 Amsterdam, Noord-Holland, Netherlands: **Amsterdam Gay Pride**, www.amsterdamgaypride.nl

4 Hamburg, Germany: **Christopher Street Day Hamburg** www.hamburg-pride.de

5 Vancouver, BC, Canada: **Vancouver Pride** www.vancouverpride.ca

6-12 Antwerp, Belgium: **Antwerp Pride**, www.antwerppride.com

9-12 Reykjavík, Iceland: **Reykjavík Gay Pride** www.visitreykjavik.is

10-12 Toronto, ON, Canada: **Leather Pride** (Leather Ball, Mr. Rubber Toronto, Bootblack, Mr. Leatherman), www.torontoleatherpride.ca

11 Tokyo, Japan: **Tokyo Pride Parade**, www.tlgp.org

11 Mannheim, Baden-Wurttemberg, Germany: **Christopher Street Day Rhein-Neckar**, www.csd-rhein-neckar.de

12-18 Provincetown, MA, USA: **Provincetown Carnival** www.ptown.org/carnival.asp

13-19 Prague, Czech Republic: **Prague Pride** www.praguepride.com

14-19 Montreal, QC, Canada: **Montreal Pride** www.facebook.com/fiertemontrealpride

14-19 Copenhagen, Denmark: **Copenhagen Pride** www.copenhagenpride.dk

16-19 Key West, FL, USA: **Tropical Heat** www.tropicalheatkw.org

16-20 Hamburg, Germany: **Leatherparty** www.spike-hamburg.com

16-26 Vancouver, BC, Canada: **Vancouver Queer Film Festival** www.queerfilmfestival.ca

17-19 Chicago, IL, USA: **Windy City Rodeo**, www.ilgra.com

17-26 Ottawa, ON, Canada: **Capital Pride**, www.capitalpride.ca

17-27 Manchester, England, UK: **Manchester Pride** www.manchesterpride.com

18 Cambrigde, England, UK: **Pink Festival** www.pinkfestival.com

18 Munich, Bavaria, Germany: **Gay Street Festival** www.schwules-strassenfest.de

25–Sep.. 1 Queenstown, New Zealand: **Gay Ski Week** www.gayskiweekqt.com

29-Sep. 3 New Orleans, LA, USA: **Southern Decadence** www.southerndecadence.com

September

1 Cardiff, Wales, UK: **Cardiff – Wales Lesbian & Gay Mardi Gras**, www.cardiffmardigras.com

1-2 Brighton, England, UK: **Pride in Brighton & Hove** www.brightonpride.org

7-8 Las Vegas, NV, USA: **Las Vegas Pride** www.lasvegaspride.org

7-9 San Diego, CA, USA: **Greater San Diego Rodeo** www.sandiegorodeo.com

8 Berlin, Germany: **Folsom Europe Street Fair** www.folsom-europe.info

9 Frankfurt/Main, Hessen, Germany: **Run For More Time** www.lauf-fuer-mehr-zeit.de

16-21 Oslo, Norway: **International Gay and Lesbian Filmfestival,** www.oglff.org

21-23 San Francisco La Honda, CA, USA: **Gay Rodeo @ Driscoll Ranches**, www.bestbuckinthebay.com

21-29 Lisbon, Estremadura, Portugal: **Lisbon Gay & Lesbian Film Festival,** www.queerlisboa.pt

22 Ottawa, ON, Canada: **AIDS Walk for Life** www.aidswalkottawa.ca

23 San Francisco, CA, USA: **Folsom Street Fair** www.folsomstreetfair.com

23 Munich, Bavaria, Germany: **Gay Oktoberfest** www.mlc-muenchen.de

27-30 Provincetown, MA, USA: **Mates Leather Weekend** www.matesleatherweekend.com

SPARTACUS Events Calendar 2012/ 2013

October

4-7 Key West, FL, USA: **Key West Bear Fest** www.keywestbearfest.com

4-14 Tampa, FL, USA: **Tampa International Gay & Lesbian Film Festival**, www.tiglff.com

5-7 Anaheim, CA, USA: **Gay Days at Disneyland** www.gaydaysanaheim.com

6 Johannesburg, Gauteng, South Africa: **Johannesburg Pride** www.joburgpride.org

6 Orlando, FL, USA: **Come out with Pride Orlando** www.comeoutwithpride.org

7 San Francisco, CA, USA: **Castro Street Fair** www.castrostreetfair.org

7 Philadelphia, PA, USA: **OutFest**, www.phillypride.org

7-9 Berlin, Germany: **Gay Rubber & Fetish Weekend**, www.blf.de

10-16 Montreal, QC, Canada: **Black & Blue Festival** www.bbcm.org

11-21 Seattle, WA, USA: **Seattle Lesbian & Gay Film Festival** www.threedollarbillcinema.org

12-14 Fort Worth, TX, USA: **World Gay Rodeo Finals** www.igra.com

12-21 Pittsburgh, PA, USA: **International Lesbian & Gay Film Festival** , www.pilgff.org

13-14 Atlanta, GA, USA: **Atlanta Pride Festival**, atlantapride.org

14 Los Angeles, CA, USA: **AIDS Walk Los Angeles** www.aidswalk.net

14 Rio de Janeiro, Brazil: **Rio de Janeiro Gay Pride** www.gaypridebrazil.org

14-21 Provincetown, MA, USA: **Fantasia Fair** www.fantasiafair.org

16-21 Hamburg, Germany: **Hamburg International Lesbian & Gay Filmfestival**, www.lsf-hamburg.de

19 Berlin, Germany: **HustlaBall**, www.hustlaball.de

19-28 Copenhagen, Denmark: **Mix Copenhagen Film Festival** www.mixcopenhagen.dk

19-28 Key West, FL, USA: **Fantasy Fest**, www.fantasyfest.net

19-28 Barcelona, Catalonia, Spain: **Gay & Lesbian Film Festival** www.barcelonafilmfestival.org

25-28+31 New Orleans, LA, USA: **Halloween New Orleans** www.halloweenneworleans.com

26-Nov. 5 Montreal, QC, Canada: **image+nation Montreal LGBT Film Festival**, www.image-nation.org

27-Nov. 3 Bologna, Toscana, Italy: **Gender Bender**, www.genderbender.it

27-Nov. 11 Melbourne, VIC, Australia: **Leather Pride Festival 2012**

November

1-4 Berlin, Germany: **Gay Skinhead Weekend,** www.blf.de

2-4 Amsterdam, Noord-Holland, Netherlands: **Leather Pride** www.get-ruff.com

2-4 Chicago, IL, USA: **Mr. International Rubber** www.MIRubber.com

3-4 Palm Springs, CA, USA: **Greater Palm Springs Pride** www.pspride.org

9-11 Ottawa, ON, Canada: **Mr. Leather Ottawa** www.mrleatherottawa.ca

10-15 Adelaide, SA, Australia: **Feast Festival**, www.feast.org.au

21-26 Miami, FL, USA: **White Party Week**, www.whiteparty.org

23-25 Toronto, ON, Canada: **Toronto Bound** www.torontoleatherpride.ca

27- Dec. 2 Cologne, North Rhine-Westphalia, Germany: **International German Bear Pride Week**, www.bearscologne.de

December

1 Manila, Philipines: **Manila Pride March** taskforcepride.blogspot.com

1 Diverse Cities: **World AIDS Day**, www.worldaidsday.org

1 New York City, NY, USA: **World AIDS Day** www.housingworks.org

6-9 Key West, FL, USA: **Bone Island Bare it All II** www.nakedkeywest.com

7-9 Provincetown, MA, USA: **Holly Folly** www.ptown.org/happenings/hollyfolly

January 2013

6-13 Arosa, Graubünden, Switzerland: **Arosa Gay Skiweek** www.arosa-gayskiweek.com

17-21 Antwerp, Belgium: Leather Pride Antwerp www.leatherpride.be

19-20 Antwerp, Belgium: **1st International Gayrotica Fair & Fetish Fair**, www.gayroticafair.com

February 2013

3 Melbourne, VIC, Australia: **Pride March Victoria** www.midsumma.org.au

3-10 Whistler, BC, Canada: **Winter Pride** www.gaywhistler.com

7-16 Brussels, Belgium: **Gay & Lesbian Film Festival** www.fglb.org

8-13 Rio de Janeiro, Brazil: **Carnival Rio de Janeiro** www.rio-carnival.net

9-12 Salvador da Bahia, Brazil: **Carnival Salvador da Bahia** www.carnaval.salvador.ba.gov.br

15-17 San Francisco, CA, USA: **SF Bear Weekend**

15-17 Phoenix, AZ, USA: **Road Runner Regional Rodeo** www.igra.com

15-17 Montreal, QC, Canada: **Red Weekend**, www.bbcm.org

March 2013

1-3 Brighton, UK: **National Student Pride** www.studentpride.co.uk

22 New York City, NY, USA: **Rites XXXIV – The Black Party** www.blackparty.com

Index

C

D

E

F

IT'S COMING

BIGGER THAN THE BIG 5
MR GAY
WORLD
2012

M

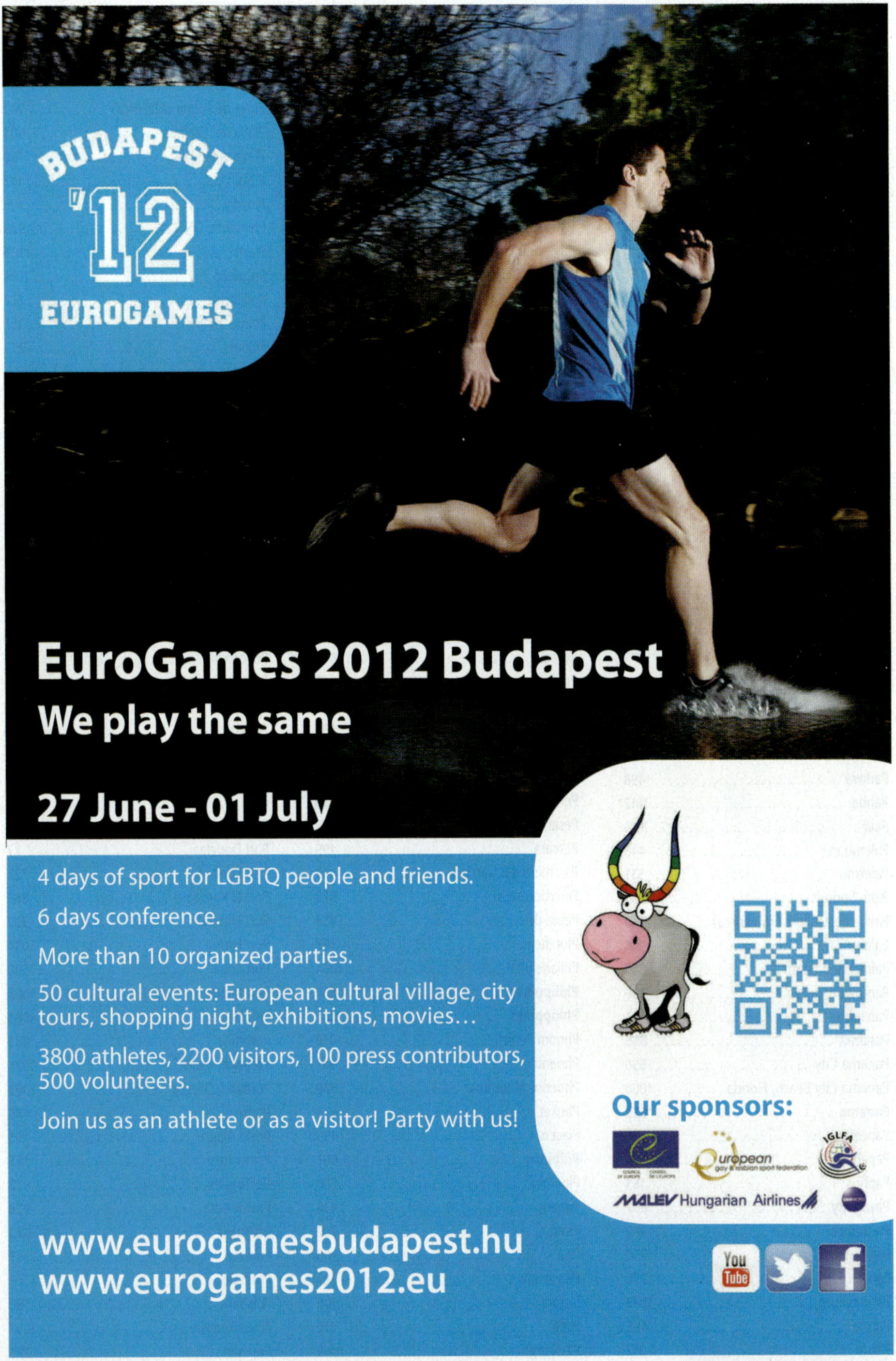

BUDAPEST '12 EUROGAMES

EuroGames 2012 Budapest

We play the same

27 June - 01 July

4 days of sport for LGBTQ people and friends.

6 days conference.

More than 10 organized parties.

50 cultural events: European cultural village, city tours, shopping night, exhibitions, movies…

3800 athletes, 2200 visitors, 100 press contributors, 500 volunteers.

Join us as an athlete or as a visitor! Party with us!

Our sponsors:

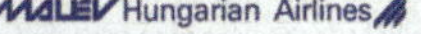

www.eurogamesbudapest.hu
www.eurogames2012.eu

P

T

U

V

ENGLISH

!	A must
AC	Air conditioning
AK	St. Andrew's Cross
AYOR	At your own risk. Danger of personal attack or police activity
B	Bar with full range of alcoholic beverages
BF	Full breakfast
CC	All major credit cards accepted
D	Dancing / Discotheque
DM	Daily menu
DR	Darkroom
DU	Showers
F	Fetish (leather, latex or uniform)
FC	Free condoms
FH	Free extra towels
G	Gay. Exclusively or almost exclusively gay men
GH	Glory holes
GLM	Gay and lesbian mixed crowd
H	Hotel or other accommodation welcoming gay men
I	Internet access
LAB	Maze / Labyrinth
LM	Live music
M	Meals. Extensive menu available
MA	Mixed ages
MC	Middle-aged crowd (30 - 50 years old)
MSG	Massage on offer
NG	Not gay, but possibly of interest to gay men
NR	Non-smoking area
NU	Nudist area
OC	Mostly older gay men (50 or older)
OS	Outdoor seating, terrace or garden
P	Private club or strict door control
p	You must ring to enter
PA	Pets allowed
PI	Swimming pool
PK	Parking available
PP	Plunge pool
R	Frequented by hustlers
RES	Reservation advisable
RR	Relax room
RWB	Guestrooms with Balcony
RWS	Guestrooms with private bath/shower
RWT	Guestrooms with television
S	Shows or other events
SA	Dry sauna
SB	Steam bath
SH	Shop
SL	Sling
SNU	Strip shows
SOL	Solarium
ST	Drag shows
T	Transvestites and/or transsexual clientele
VA	Overnight guests allowed
VEG	Vegetarian meals on the menu
VR	Video room
VS	Video shows
W	Barrier-free for wheelchairs
WE	More popular at the weekend
WH	Whirlpool / Jacuzzi / Hot tub
WI	Free WiFi
WL	Extensive wine list
WO	Work-out equipment available
YC	Younger crowd (18-28 years old)

DEUTSCH

!	Besonders empfehlenswert, ein Muss
AC	Klimaanlage
AK	Andreaskreuz
AYOR	Auf eigenes Risiko, möglicherweise gefährlich oder häufige Polizeikontrollen
B	Bar mit breitem Angebot alkoholischer Getränke
BF	umfangreiches Frühstück
CC	Alle gängigen Kreditkarten akzeptiert
D	Tanzmöglichkeit/Diskothek
DM	Täglich wechselnde Menüs
DR	Darkroom
DU	Dusche
F	Fetisch (Leder, Latex oder Uniform)
FC	Kondome gratis
FH	Extra Handtuch gratis
G	ausschließlich oder überwiegend schwules Publikum
GH	Glory Holes
GLM	Ausschließlich oder überwiegend schwul-lesbisches Publikum
H	schwulenfreundliche Unterkunft
I	Internetzugang
LAB	Labyrinth
LM	Live Musik
M	umfangreiches Speisenangebot
MA	gemischte Altersklassen
MC	Gäste mittleren Alters (30-50 Jahre)
MSG	Massage möglich
NG	Nicht schwul, aber interessant
NR	Nicht-Raucher Bereich
NU	FKK/Nacktbademöglichkeit
OC	Eher ältere Gäste (ab 50 Jahre)
OS	Terrasse oder Garten
P	Privatclub oder strenge Einlasskontrolle
p	Sie müssen klingeln
PA	Haustiere akzeptiert
PI	Swimmingpool
PK	Parkplätze vorhanden
PP	Tauchbecken
R	Regelmäßig Stricher
RES	Reservierung notwendig
RR	Ruheraum
RWB	Gästezimmer mit Balkon
RWS	Gästezimmer mit eigenem Bad/eigener Dusche
RWT	Gästezimmer mit Fernseher
S	Shows/Veranstaltungen
SA	Trockensauna
SB	Dampfsauna
SH	Shop
SL	Sling/s
SNU	Stripshows
SOL	Solarium
ST	Travestieshows
T	Transvestiten und/oder transsexuelles Publikum
VA	Übernachtungsgäste erlaubt
VEG	Vegetarische Gerichte auf der Karte
VR	Videoraum
VS	Videoshows
W	Barrierefrei
WE	Betrieb vor allem am Wochenende
WH	Whirlpool
WI	kostenloses WiFi
WL	Ausführliche Weinkarte
WO	Bodybuilding möglich
YC	Junge Schwule (18 - 28)

FRANÇAIS

!	Un must
AC	Climatisation
AK	Croix de saint andré
AYOR	À vos risques et périls dangereux ou contrôles fréquents de la police
B	Bar avec boissons alcoolisées
BF	Petit déjeuner complet
CC	Principales cartes de crédit acceptées
D	Discothèque
DM	Plats du jour
DR	Darkroom
DU	Douche
F	Fétichiste (cuir, latex ou uniformes)
FC	Preservatifs gratuits
FH	2ieme serviette gratuite
G	Clientèle majoritairement gaie
GH	Glory holes
GLM	Clientèle majoritairement gaie et lesbienne
H	Hôtel / lieu d'hébergement où les gais sont bienvenus
I	Internet
LAB	Labyrinthe
LM	Musique live
M	Restauration / repas servis
MA	Tous âges
MC	Gais d'âge moyen (30 – 50 ans)
MSG	Massage possible
NG	Pas forcément gai mais intéressant
NR	Coin non-fumer
NU	Nudisme possible
OC	Gais plutôt âgés (+ 50 ans)
OS	Plein air, terrasse ou jardin
P	Club privé ou contrôle strict à l'entrée
p	Il faut sonner
PA	Animaux domestiques bienvenus
PI	Piscine
PK	Parking
PP	Bassin refroidissement
R	Fréquenté aussi par des gigolos
RES	Réservation nécessaire
RR	Salle repos
RWB	Tout les chambres ont balcon
RWS	Tout les chambres avec salle de bain/douche
RWT	Tout les chambres ont télévision
S	Spectacle ou autre manifestation
SA	Sauna finlandais
SB	Bain turc, hammam
SH	Boutique
SL	Sling
SNU	Strip-tease
SOL	Solarium
ST	Spectacle de transformisme
T	Fréquenté aussi par des travestis/transsexuels
VA	Visites autorisées
VEG	Plats végétariens aussi proposés
VR	Salle video
VS	Projection de vidéos
W	Accès handicapés
WE	fréquenté plutôt le week-end
WH	jacuzzi / bain à tourbillons
WI	WiFi gratuite
WL	carte des vins
WO	musculation possible
YC	clientèle jeune (18-28 ans)

ESPAÑOL

!	Especialmente recomendable
AC	Aire acondicionado
AK	Cruz San Andrés
AYOR	A su propio riesgo. Peligro de ser atacado o de actividades de la policía
B	Bar con oferta amplia de bedibas
BF	Desayuno tipo buffet
CC	Se acepta la mayoria de las tarjetas de crédito
D	Bailar / discoteca
DM	Menú de día
DR	Cuarto oscuro / sala oscura
DU	Ducha
F	Fetichismo (cuero, látex, uniformes)
FC	Preservativos gratuitos
FH	2a toalla gratis
G	Exclusivamente o casi exclusivamente público gay
GH	Glory Holes
GLM	Público gay y lesbiano mezclado
H	Hotel o tipo parecido de alojamiento donde se recibe bien a los gays
I	Internet
LAB	Labirinto
LM	Música en directo
M	Comida. Disponibilidad de menús completos
MA	Edades mixtas
MC	Clientes de edades medias (de 30 a 50 años)
MSG	Masajes
NG	No es gay pero posiblemente de interés para gays
NR	Zona para no fumadores
NU	Nudismo
OC	Clientes más bien mayores (+ 50 años)
OS	Terraza o jardín
P	Club privado o control estricto de acceso
p	Hay que tocar el timbre para entrar
PA	Se aceptan animales
PI	Piscina
PK	Plazas de parking
PP	Piscina para sumergirse
R	Bastante frecuentado por personas que ejercen la prostitución
RES	Se necesita reserva
RR	Sala de descanso
RWB	Habitación con balcón
RWS	Baño / ducha en la habitación
RWT	Habitación con televisión
S	Espectáculo / programa
SA	Sauna finlandesa
SB	Baño de vapor
SH	Tienda
SL	Sling
SNU	Espectáculos de striptease
SOL	Solarium
ST	Espectáculo de travestis
T	También frecuentado por travestis / transsexuales
VA	Se aceptan visitas
VEG	También comida vegetariana
VR	Sala de video
VS	Proyección de video
W	Sin barreras para sillas de ruedas
WE	Más animado los fines de semana
WH	Whirlpool / jacuzzi
WI	WiFi gratis
WL	Extensa carta de vinos
WO	Fisioculturismo / gimnasio
YC	Clientes jóvenes (18 a 29 años)

TRAVEL / GAY

spartacus®
INTERNATIONAL GAY GUIDE

A must for the gay traveller: yearly revised with all the current addresses worldwide!

Bars, clubs, discos • baths, beaches • cruising areas • hotels, apartments • cafés, restaurants • bookshops, gay stores

Bars, Clubs, Diskotheken • Hotels, Apartments • Restaurants, Cafés • Saunen, Strände • Läden, Buchhandlungen • Treffpunkte

Bars, clubs, discothèques • hôtels, appartements • restaurants saunas, plages • magasins et librairies • lieux de rencontre

Bares, pubs, discotecas • saunas, playas • hoteles, apartamentos • cafés, restaurantes • tiendas y librerías • lugares de encuentro

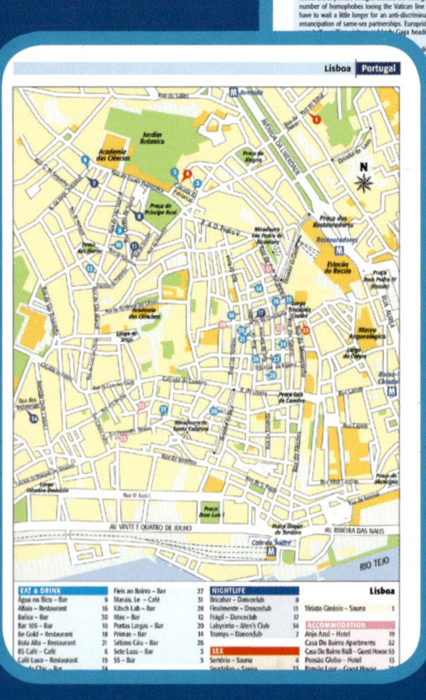

Bar, circoli, discoteche • saune, spiagge • luoghi di incontro • alberghi, appartamenti • caffé, ristoranti • negozi e librerie

ISBN 978-3-86787-360-4
9 783867 873604

Australia	A$ 56,00	Europe	€ 25,95	Schweiz	Sfr 38,90
Denmark	Dkr 255,00	GB	£ 19,99	USA	$ 32,99

BRUNO GMÜNDER VERLAG
Kleiststraße 23-26 · 10787 Berlin · Germany · 49-30-61 50 03 0